PLATOON

POWER

SOMEThiNG Wild

desert bloom

MALCOLM

Under the CHERRY MOON

The Boy Who Could Fly

BY ME

THE MOTION PICTURE GUIDE

★ ★ ★ ★ ★ ★ ★ ★ ★ ★ ★ ★ ★ ★ ★

1987 ANNUAL

THE MOTION PICTURE GUIDE

★ ★ ★ ★ ★ ★ ★ ★ ★ ★ ★ ★ ★ ★ ★

1987 ANNUAL
(THE FILMS OF 1986)

Jay Robert Nash
Stanley Ralph Ross

Senior Staff Writer
James J. Mulay

Staff Writers
Arnie Bernstein
Daniel Curran
Phil Pantone
Michael Theobald

CineBooks, Inc.
Chicago, 1987
Publishers of The Complete Film Resource Center

Publishers: Jay Robert Nash, Stanley Ralph Ross; **Editor in Chief:** Jay Robert Nash; **Executive Editor:** Stanley Ralph Ross; **Associate Publisher:** Kenneth H. Petchenik; **Editorial Director:** William Leahy; **Senior Editor:** David Tardy; **Associate Editors:** Oksana Lydia Creighton, Jeffrey H. Wallenfeldt, Jeannette Hori, Michaela Tuohy; **Senior Staff Writer:** James J. Mulay; **Staff Writers:** Daniel Curran, Michael Theobald, Arnie Bernstein, Phil Pantone; **Research Staff:** William C. Clogston, Shelby Payne; **Contributing Editors:** Andrew S. Ross, Dan Harrison, James Gibson, Marshall Hyman, Marla Brooks, Brian Brock; **Business Staff:** Manager, Jack Medor; Assistant, Bernie Gregoryk.

Editorial and Sales Offices
CINEBOOKS
990 Grove
Evanston, Illinois 60201

Library of Congress Catalog Number: 85-71145

ISBN: 0-933997-00-0 THE MOTION PICTURE GUIDE
           (10 Vols.)
      0-933997-11-6 THE MOTION PICTURE GUIDE
           INDEX (2 Vols.)
      0-933997-15-9 THE MOTION PICTURE GUIDE
           1987 ANNUAL (THE FILMS OF 1986)

Printed in the United States
First Edition

1   2   3   4   5   6   7   8   9   10

Table of Contents

HOW TO USE THE INFORMATION IN THIS GUIDE

ALPHABETICAL ORDER

All entries have been arranged alphabetically throughout this and all subsequent volumes. In establishing alphabetical order, all articles (A, AN, THE) appear after the main title (AFFAIR TO REMEMBER, AN). In the case of foreign films the article precedes the main title (LES MISERABLES appears in the letter L) which makes, we feel, for easier access and uniformity. Abbreviations are treated as if spelled out (i.e., "DR." is alphabetized as "DOCTOR"). Apostrophes are ignored (L'ATALANTE follows LAST YEAR AT MARIENBAD). Numerals and characters such as dollar signs are alphabetized as if spelled out. B.F.'s DAUGHTER is at the beginning of the letter B, not under BF.

TITLES

It is important to know the *complete* title of the film you seek. ADVENTURES OF ROBIN HOOD, THE cannot be found under merely ROBIN HOOD. Many films are known under different titles and we have taken great pains to cross reference these (SEE:) by their alternate titles (AKA:) as well as by titles used in Great Britain (GB:). In addition to the cross-references, AKAs and Great Britain titles can be found in the lead line for each entry.

TRANSLATION OF FOREIGN TITLES

Foreign-language films reviewed in the country of origin before their U.S. release often have English-language translations of their titles provided by the distributor (FIGLIO MIO INFIN-ITAMENTE CARO = My Infinitely Dear Son). These English titles are often literal translations of the foreign titles and are not an actual reflection of the eventual English-language release title. We provide the English-language translation so the reader may, at least, have an estimation of the meaning of a foreign film's title. The translated title can be found in the title line and appears thusly: (Trans: My Infinitely Dear Son).

RATINGS

Films seen by our reviewers have been rated at critical levels that include acting, directing, script, and technical achievement. We have a *five*-star rating to signify a film superbly made on every level—in short, a masterpiece. At the lowest end of the scale is *zero*. The ratings are as follows: *zero* (not worth a glance), *(poor), **(fair), ***(good), ****(excellent), *****(masterpiece, and these are few and far between). Half-marks mean almost there but not quite. Films unseen by our reviewers have, naturally, not been critically appraised, and have no star rating. These films are identified with †.

YEAR OF RELEASE

We have used in all applicable instances the year of United States release. This sometimes means that a film released abroad may have a different date elsewhere than in these volumes but this is generally the date released in foreign countries, not in the U.S. Where possible, we have included this information in the synopsis.

FOREIGN COUNTRY PRODUCTION

When possible, we have listed abbreviated names of the foreign countries originating the production of a film. This information will be found within the parentheses containing the year of release. If no country is listed in this space, it is a U.S. production.

RUNNING TIME

A hotly debated category, we have opted to list the running time a film ran at the time of its initial U.S. release but we will usually mention in the text if the film was drastically cut.

PRODUCING AND DISTRIBUTING COMPANIES

The producing and/or distributing company of every film is listed in abbreviated entries next to the running time in the title line (see abbreviations; for all those firms not abbreviated, the entire firm's name will be used).

COLOR OR BLACK-AND-WHITE

The use of color or black-and-white availability appears as c or bw following the producing/releasing company entry.

CASTS

Whenever possible we give *the complete cast and the roles played* for each film. The names of actors and actresses are in Roman lettering, the names of the roles each played in Italic within parentheses.

REMAKES, SEQUELS, AND SERIES

Information regarding films that have sequels, are sequels themselves, or are remakes of films can be found at the very end of each synopsis.

DUBBING AND SUBTITLES

We will generally point out in the synopsis when a foreign film is dubbed in English, mostly when the dubbing is poor. When voices are dubbed, particularly when singers render vocals on songs mimed by stars, we generally point out these facts either in the cast/role listing or inside the synopsis. If a film is in a foreign language and subtitled, we signify this fact in a paren-thetical statement at the end of each entry (In Italian; English subtitles.).

CREDITS

The credits for the creative and technical personnel of a film are extensive and they include: p (producer, often executive producer); d (director); w (screenwriter, followed by adaptation, if any, and creator of original story, if any, and other sources such as authors for plays, articles, short stories, novels, and non-fiction books); ph (cinematographer, followed by camera system and color process when applicable; m (composer of musical score); ed (film editor); md (music director); art d (art director); set d (set decoration); cos (costumes); spec eff (special effects); ch (choreography); m/l (music and lyrics); makeup; stunts, and other credits when merited. When someone receives two or more credits in a single film the credits may be combined (p&d, John Ford) or the name repeated in subsequent credits shared with another (d, John Ford; w, John Ford, Dudley Nichols).

GENRES/SUBJECT

Each film is categorized for easy identification as to genre and/or subject and themes at the left-hand bottom of each entry. (Drama, Western, Prison, Spy, Romance, Musical, Comedy, War, Horror, Science Fiction, Adventure, Biography, Historical, Children's, Animation, etc.)

PR AND MPAA RATINGS

The Parental Recommendation provides parents having no knowledge of the style and content of each film with a guide; if a film has excessive violence, sex, strong language, it is so indicated. The Parental Recommendation (PR) is to be found at the right-hand bottom of each entry, followed, when applicable, by the MPAA rating. The PR ratings are as follows: AAA (must for children); AA (good for children); A (acceptable for children); C (cautionary, some objectionable scenes); O (objectionable for children). PR ratings for films unseen by our reviewers are based upon available information concerning the film.

KEY TO ABBREVIATIONS

Foreign Countries:

Arg.	Argentina
Aus.	Australia
Aust.	Austria
Bel.	Belgium
Braz.	Brazil
Brit.	Great Britain (GB when used for alternate title)
Can.	Canada
Chi.	China
Czech.	Czechoslovakia
Den.	Denmark
E. Ger.	East Germany
Fin.	Finland
Fr.	France
Ger.	Germany (includes W. Germany)
Gr.	Greece
Hung.	Hungary
It.	Italy
Jap.	Japan
Mex.	Mexico
Neth.	Netherlands
Phil.	Philippines
Pol.	Poland
Rum.	Rumania
S.K.	South Korea
Span.	Spain
Swed.	Sweden
Switz.	Switzerland
Thai.	Thailand
USSR	Union of Soviet Socialist Republics
Yugo.	Yugoslavia

Production Companies,
Studios and Distributors (U.S. and British)

AA	Allied Artists
ABF	Associated British Films
AE	Avco Embassy
AEX	Associated Exhibitors
AIP	American International Films
AM	American
ANCH	Anchor Film Distributors
ANE	American National Enterprises
AP	Associated Producers
AP&D	Associated Producers & Distributors
ARC	Associated Releasing Corp.
Argosy	Argosy Productions
Arrow	Arrow Films
ART	Artcraft
Astra	Astra Films
AY	Aywon
BA	British Actors
BAN	Banner Films
BI	British Instructional
BIFD	B.I.F.D. Films
BIP	British International Pictures
BJP	Buck Jones Productions
BL	British Lion
Blackpool	Blackpool Productions
BLUE	Bluebird
BN	British National
BNF	British and Foreign Film
Boulting	Boulting Brothers (Brit.)
BP	British Photoplay Production
BPP	B.P. Productions
BRIT	Britannia Films
BRO	Broadwest
Bryznston	Bryantston Films (Brit.)
BS	Blue Streak
BUS	Bushey (Brit.)
But	Butchers Film Service
BV	Buena Vista (Walt Disney)
CAP	Capital Films
CC	Christie Comedy
CD	Continental Distributing
CHAD	Chadwick Pictures Corporation
CHES	Chesterfield
Cineguild	Cineguild
CL	Clarendon
CLIN	Clinton

COL	Columbia
Colony	Colony Pictures
COM	Commonwealth
COMM	Commodore Pictures
COS	Cosmopolitan (Hearst)
DGP	Dorothy Gish Productions
Disney	Walt Disney Productions
DIST	Distinctive
DM	DeMille Productions
DOUB	Doubleday
EAL	Ealing Studios (Brit.)
ECF	East Coast Films
ECL	Eclectic
ED	Eldorado
EF	Eagle Films
EFF & EFF	E.F.F. & E.F.F. Comedy
EFI	English Films Inc.
EIFC	Export and Import Film Corp.
EL	Eagle-Lion
EM	Embassy Pictures Corp.
EMI	EMI Productions
EP	Enterprise Pictures
EPC	Equity Pictures Corp.
EQ	Equitable
EXCEL	Excellent
FA	Fine Arts
FC	Film Classics
FD	First Division
FN	First National
FOX	20th Century Fox (and Fox Productions)
FP	Famous Players (and Famous Players Lasky)
FRP	Frontroom Productions
GAU	Gaumont (Brit.)
GEN	General
GFD	General Films Distributors
Goldwyn	Samuel Goldwyn Productions
GN	Grand National
GOTH	Gotham
Grafton	Grafton Films (Brit.)
H	Harma
HAE	Harma Associated Distributors
Hammer	Hammer Films (Brit.)
HD	Hagen and Double
HM	Hi Mark
HR	Hal Roach
IA	International Artists
ID	Ideal
IF	Independent Film Distributors (Brit.)
Imperator	Imperator Films (Brit.)
IP	Independent Pictures Corp.
IN	Invincible Films
INSP	Inspirational Pictures (Richard Barthlemess)
IV	Ivan Film
Javelin	Javelin Film Productions (Brit.)
JUR	Jury
KC	Kinema Club
KCB	Kay C. Booking
Korda	Alexander Korda Productions (Brit.)
Ladd	Ladd Company Productions
LAS	Lasky Productions (Jesse L. Lasky)
LFP	London Films
LIP	London Independent Producers
Lorimar	Lorimar Productions
LUM	Lumis
Majestic	Majestic Films
Mascot	Mascot Films
Mayflowers	Mayflowers Productions (Brit.)
Metro	Metro
MFC	Mission Film Corporation
MG	Metro-Goldwyn
MGM	Metro-Goldwyn-Mayer
MON	Monogram
MOR	Morante
MS	Mack Sennett
MUT	Mutual
N	National
NG	National General
NGP	National General Pictures
NW	New World
Orion	Orion Productions
Ortus	Ortus Productions

PAR	Paramount
Pascal	Garbiel Pascal Productions (Brit.)
PDC	Producers Distributors Corp.
PEER	Peerless
PWN	Peninsula Studios
PFC	Pacific Film Company
PG	Playgoers
PI	Pacific International
PIO	Pioneer Film Corp.
PM	Pall Mall
PP	Pro Patria
PRC	Producers Releasing Corporation
PRE	Preferred
QDC	Quality Distributing Corp.
RAY	Rayart
RAD	Radio Pictures
RANK	J. Arthur Rank (Brit.)
RBP	Rex Beach Pictures
REA	Real Art
REG	Regional Films
REN	Renown
REP	Republic
RF	Regal Films
RFD	R.F.D. Productions (Brit.)
RKO	RKO Radio Pictures
Rogell	Rogell
Romulus	Romulus Films (Brit.)
SB	Samuel Bronston
SCHUL	B.P. Schulberg Productions
SEL	Select
SELZ	Selznick International (David O. Selznick)
SF	Selznick Films
SL	Sol Lesser
SONO	Sonofilms
SP	Seven Pines Productions (Brit.)
SRP	St. Regis Pictures
STER	Sterling
STOLL	Stoll
SUN	Sunset
SYN	Syndicate Releasing Co.
SZ	Sam Zimbalist
TC	Two Cities (Brit.)
T/C	Trem-Carr
THI	Thomas H. Ince
TIF	Tiffany
TRA	Transatlantic Pictures
TRU	Truart
TS	Tiffany/Stahl
UA	United Artists
UNIV	Universal (and Universal International)
Venture	Venture Distributors
VIT	Vitagraph
WAL	Waldorf
WB	Warner Bros. (and Warner Bros.-Seven Arts)
WEST	Westminster
WF	Woodfall Productions (Brit.)
WI	Wisteria
WORLD	World
WSHP	William S. Hart Productions
ZUKOR	Adolph Zukor Productions

Foreign

ABSF	AB Svensk Film Industries (Swed.)
Action	Action Films (Fr.)
ADP	Agnes Delahaie Productions (Fr.)
Agata	Agata Films (Span.)
Alter	Alter Films (Fr.)
Arch	Archway Film Distributors
Argos	Argos Films (Fr.)
Argui	Argui Films (Fr.)
Ariane	Les Films Ariane (Fr.)
Athos	Athos Films (Fr.)
Belga	Belga Films (Bel.)
Beta	Beta Films (Ger.)
CA	Cine-Alliance (Fr.)
Caddy	Caddy Films (Fr.)
CCFC	Compagnie Commerciale Francais Einematographique (Fr.)
CDD	Cino Del Duca (Ital.)
CEN	Les Films de Centaur (Fr.)
CFD	Czecheslovak Film Productions

CHAM	Champion (Ital.)
Cinegay	Cinegay Films (Ital.)
Cines	Cines Films (Ital.)
Cineriz	Cinerez Films (Ital.)
Citel	Citel Films (Switz.)
Como	Como Films (Fr.)
CON	Concordia (Fr.)
Corona	Corona Films (Fr.)
D	Documento Films (Ital.)
DD	Dino De Laurentiis (Ital.)
Dear	Dear Films (Ital.)
DIF	Discina International Films (Fr.)
DPR	Films du Palais-Royal (Fr.)
EX	Excelsa Films (Ital.)
FDP	Films du Pantheon (Fr.)
Fono	Fono Roma (Ital.)
FS	Filmsonor Productions (Fr.)
Fala	Fala Films (Ital.)
Galatea	Galatea Productions (Ital.)
Gamma	Gamma Films (Fr.)
Gemma	Gemma Cinematografica (Ital.)
GFD	General Film Distributors, Ltd. (Can.)
GP	General Productions (Fr.)
Gray	Gray Films (Fr.)
IFD	Intercontinental Film Distributors
Janus	Janus Films (Ger.)
JMR	Macques Mage Releasing (Fr.)
LF	Les Louvre Films (Fr.)
LFM	Les Films Moliere (Fr.)
Lux	Lux Productions (Ital.)
Melville	Melville Productions (Fr.)
Midega	Midega Films (Span.)
NEF	N.E.F. La Nouvelle Edition Francaise (Fr.)
NFD	N.F.D. Productions (Ger.)
Ortus	Ortus Films (Can.)
PAC	Production Artistique Cinematographique (Fr.)
Pagnol	Marcel Pagnol Productions (Fr.)
Parc	Parc Films (Fr.)
Paris	Paris Films (Fr.)
Pathe	Pathe Films (Fr.)
PECF	Productions et Editions Cinematographique Francais (Fr.)
PF	Parafrench Releasing Co. (Fr.)
PIC	Produzione International Cinematografica (Ital.)
Ponti	Carlo Ponti Productions (Ital.)
RAC	Realisation d'Art Cinematographique (Fr.)
Regina	Regina Films (Fr.)
Renn	Renn Productions (Fr.)
SDFS	Societe des Films Sonores Tobis (Fr.)
SEDIF	Societe d'Exploitation ed de Distribution de Films (Fr.)
SFP	Societe Francais de Production (Fr.)
Sigma	Sigma Productions (Fr.)
SNE	Societe Nouvelle des Establishments (Fr.)
Titanus	Titanus Productions (Ital.)
TRC	Transcontinental Films (Fr.)
UDIF	U.D.I.F. Productions (Fr.)
UFA	Deutsche Universum-Film AG (Ger.)
UGC	Union Generale Cinematographique (Fr.)
Union	Union Films (Ger.)
Vera	Vera Productions (Fr.)

Film Reviews

FILM REVIEWS

A BALADA DA PRAIA DOS CAES†   (1986, Port.) Luso-Spanish

Raul Solnado, Assumpta Serna, Patrick Bauchau.

d&w, Jose Fonseca E Costa (based on the novel by Jose Cardoso Pires).

A FLOR DO MAR†   (1986, Port.) 145m c

Laura Morante, Philip Spinelli, Manuela de Freitas.

Morante stars as a Portuguese woman who can no longer find happiness in her homeland. With her children in tow, she takes off for Rome, but after just a year finds that she must return to her family and her Portuguese roots.

d&w, Joao Cesar Monteiro; ph, Acacio de Almeida; m, Johann Sebastian Bach.

Drama   **(PR:NR MPAA:NR)**

A HORA DA ESTRELA   (SEE: HOUR OF THE STAR, THE, 1986, Braz.)

A LA PALIDA LUZ DE LA LUNA†   (1986, Spain) Agata (Trans: By the Pale Light of the Moon)

Jose Sacristan, Fiorella Faltoyano, Emilio Guterrez Caba, Maria Luisa San Jose, Luis Escobar, Esperanza Roy, Rafael Alonso.

d, Jose Maria Gonzalez Sinde; w, Jose Luis Dibildos, Jose Maria Gonzalez Sinde; ph, Hans Burmann.

A LA SALIDA NOS VEMOS†   (1986, Colombia/Venezuela) 85m Focine-Cinematographicas Macuto-Hangar Films-Producciones Solsticio c (Trans: See You After School)

Santiago Madrinan, Alejandro Madrinan, John Klonis, Johnny Price, Jose Luis Botero, July Pedraza, Bacheba Aguia, Krisnaiza Castro, Angela Maria Ortegon, Abril Mendez, Luis Miguel Gonzalez.

A gentle look at the school days of a group of teenagers who are trying to survive amidst the strict ways of the Catholic nuns and priests who teach them. Set in the 1960s.

p, Esperanza Palau, Maria Teresa Bonilla; d, Carlos Palau; w, Carlos Palau, Sandro Romero; ph, Jose Medeiros; m, Alejandro Blanco Uribe; ed, Armando Valero; art d, Pedro Alcantara.

Drama   **(PR:NR MPAA:NR)**

A NAGY GENERACIO   (SEE: GREAT GENERATION, THE, 1986, Hung.)

AAH . . . BELINDA†   (1986, Turk.)

Odak Mujde Ar, Macit Koper, Yilmaz Zafer, Guzin Ozipek, Azmi Orses.

d, Atif Yilmaz; w, Barris Pirhasan; ph, Orhan Oguz.

AB HEUTE ERWACHSEN†   (1986, E. Ger.) 86m DEFA-"Berlin" Group/ DEFA c (Trans: Grown Up Today)

David C. Bunners *(Stefan)*, Jutta Wachowiak *(His Mother)*, Kurt Bowe *(Herr Grunbaum)*, Katrin Sass *(Christel)*.

An 18-year-old construction worker, Bunners, is torn between his desire to be "grown up" and have a life of his own and the dependence he still has on his accommodating mother, Wachowiak. The relationship grows tense when Bunners takes it upon himself to rent an apartment, sending Wachowiak into a rage. By the finale, however, the teenager and his mother come to an understanding.

d, Gunther Scholz; w, Helga Schubert, Gunther Scholz; ph, Micheal Gothe; m, Jurgen Balitzki.

Drama   **(PR:C MPAA:NR)**

ABDUCTED†   (1986, Can.) 91m Erin/Modern Cinema Marketing-InterPictures c

Dan Haggerty *(Joe)*, Roberta Weiss *(Renee)*, Lawrence King-Phillips *(Vern)*, John Welsh, Jim Brown, Rae Ford, Jarold J. McCullough, Skip Borland, Rob Morton, Nelson Camire, Earl Jergens, Roy Waggoner, William Nunn, Steven E. Miller.

Set in the wilderness of Canada's Pacific Northwest, ABDUCTED stars Weiss as a pretty student who spends her free time up in the hills. One fateful day she is abducted by a bearded wild man, King-Phillips, who knocks her around and attempts rape. Life is brutal for the girl, but things look up when her abductor's father, mountain man Haggerty, arrives on the scene. He explains that his boy has had some problems and has had difficulty adjusting to the fact that his mother slept around. Haggerty hoped that by raising his son in the wilderness he would learn to appreciate beauty and nature. No such luck, however. King-

Phillips is determined to keep Weiss as his pet and knocks his father cold when ordered to free her. Haggerty eventually regains consciousness, and hunts them down, and is forced to kill his son by the film's finale, as Weiss hitches a ride on a passing train. While an excess of violence and brutality is aimed at Weiss, director Collins avoids the expected sex scenes and nudity.

p, Harold J. Cole; d, Boon Collins; w, Boon Collins (based on a story by Lindsay Bourne, Boon Collins); ph, Robert McLachlan (Medallion Color); m, Michel Rubini; ed, Bruce Lange; art d, Kim Steer; set d, Alan Wilson; spec eff, J.J. Makaro; makeup, Kathy Kuzyk, Todd McIntosh; stunts, Dawn Stofer, Jacob Rupp, J.J. Makaro.

Crime Drama   Cas.   **(PR:O MPAA:PG)**

ABOUT LAST NIGHT**   (1986) 113m Tri-Star c

Demi Moore *(Debbie)*, Rob Lowe *(Danny)*, James Belushi *(Bernie Litko)*, Elizabeth Perkins *(Joan)*, George DiCenzo *(Mr. Favio)*, Michael Alldredge *(Mother Malone)*, Robin Thomas *(Steve Carlton)*, Donna Gibbons *(Alex)*, Megan Mullally *(Pam)*, Patricia Duff *(Lesslie)*, Rosanna DeSoto *(Mrs. Lyons)*, Sachi Parker *(Carri)*, Robert Neiches *(Gary)*, Joe Greco *(Gus)*, Ada Marks *(Carmen)*, Rebecca Arthur *(Crystal)*, Tim Kazurinsky *(Colin)*, Kevin Bourland *(Ira)*, Dean Bastounes *(Man in Joan's Apartment)*, Marjorie Bransfields *(Gloria)*, Charlotte Mauer *(Madge)*, Kimberly Pistone *(Girl at Bar)*, Lindy Huddleson *(Lisa)*, Raffi Diblasio, Sheenika Smith, Heath Wagerman, Brie O'Banion *(Kids)*, Dawn Arnemann *(Ruthie)*, Catherine Keener *(Cocktail Waitress)*, Steven Kckholdt *(Man in Bar)*, Robert B. Durkin, Ray Wohl *(Friends of Danny and Bernie)*.

David Mamet's 1976 play "Sexual Perversity in Chicago" was an honest and cynical look at the battle-scarred veterans of sexual revolution, written as a series of blackout scenes between two male buddies and their female counterparts. This dark-humored one-act play was quickly snapped up by Hollywood, but what emerged on the screen ten years later was a simplistic, almost completely visceral account of relationships between men and women. Lowe is a pleasant young man in his early twenties who pals around with Belushi, an older and foulmouthed coworker. At a softball game in Chicago's Grant Park, Lowe is attracted to

Moore, a husky-voiced designer who has eyes for her boss at an ad agency. He runs into her again at a post-game affair held at a popular singles bar, and before you can say "what about VD, herpes, or AIDS?" Moore adjourns to Lowe's apartment for an evening's dalliance. The next day both find themselves more than a little embarrassed about the whole thing, but the two soon become romantically involved. Moore's roommate Perkins, a kindergarten teacher, has taken her share of lumps from men, which has left her scornful towards the opposite sex. She works hard on her friend to break off with Lowe, but to no avail. Despite Perkins' strong objections, Moore moves in with Lowe, though the two are still unsure of their feelings towards one another. Their relationship is based largely on sex and once the physical excitement burns out, Lowe and Moore find they really don't have that much in common. Their tensions build during the holiday season, and they finally agree that the romance is over after a disastrous New Year's Eve. Moore moves back with Perkins, and tries dating other people. So does Lowe, but the poor boy just can't cope without Moore in his life. He follows her around, then finally throws in the towel, which naturally doesn't make for much of a happy ending. The story ends on a more fortuitous (and contrived) note as Lowe and Moore begin a tentative reconciliation after another chance meeting in the park.

The biggest problem here is the shallow approach taken towards the central relationship. Lowe and Moore's courtship consists of a few musical interludes as they proceed down the merry road of romance. Love is built on museum visits, baseball games, lakeside walks (complete with a balloon in Moore's hand), and, of course, artistically photographed sex. In a few cliched strokes, former television director Zwick shows he's mastered the basic fundamentals of his previous medium and can successfully transfer them to the big screen. Zwick never probes beyond surface issues, opting for a calculated plot development that offers no challenge to the viewer. Kazurinsky and DeClue's adaptation of Mamet's play expands the story beyond the four-person, 34 vignette structure, but this is a case of more being less. The rough language of the original has been toned down—and the characters filled out—in a cheery, if unrealistic, manner. By the film's end Lowe has fulfilled a personal dream by opening his own trendy little diner,

though how he is able to fund it is never explained. Never mind that he had earlier complained to Moore he was a college dropout and unable to get a bank loan; in this sanitized world, anything is possible. Genuine concerns of modern dating, including the increasingly haunting specter of sexually transmitted diseases, are conveniently and glibly ignored. Essentially, ABOUT LAST NIGHT is an update of the old "boy meets girl, boy loses girl, boy gets girl" formula, revamped and fitted to satisfy 1980s expectations. Instead of looking beyond the exterior, the film is all appearance, catering to the wants of its obviously intended Yuppie audience. As the leads, Lowe and Moore are passable, fulfilling what little is required for their stock characterizations. Under director Zwick's guidance, they are perfect for their roles: young, amiable, and too good-looking for words. The saving grace of ABOUT LAST NIGHT is the driving force of Belushi. Essaying a role he also played on stage, Belushi brings a brash, hearty presence that the film desperately needs. His boorish manner recalls the slob comedy pioneered by his late brother John, but James is clearly a strong enough actor to make the obnoxious behavior something beyond a few simple belly-laughs. (Ironically, "Sexual Perversity in Chicago" was once considered as a possible movie project for John Belushi and Dan Aykroyd, with Belushi to play the role that eventually went to his younger brother.) Belushi's opening scene with Lowe—describing an incredible night of sexual adventure—is the film's best and, by no accident, is the only portion of Mamet's play to survive intact. The title was changed from its original, as many newspapers and broadcast media refused to accept advertisements with the moniker SEXUAL PERVERSITY IN CHICAGO. The catalog of cream-cheese rock songs includes: "(She's the) Shape of Things to Come" (John Oates, performed by Oates), "Words Into Action" (Mike Leeson, Peter Vale, performed by Jermaine Jackson), "So Far, So Good," "Natural Love" (Tom Snow, Cynthia Weil, performed by Sheena Easton), "Living Inside My Heart" (Bob Seger, performed by Seger), "Step by Step" (J.D. Souther, Karla Bonoff, performed by Souther), "If We Can Get Through the Night" (Brock Walsh, performed by Paul Davis), "True Love" (Scott Kempner, performed by The Del Lords), "Trials of the Heart" (Thom Bishop, Michael Day, Rocky Maffit, performed by Nancy Shanks), "If You Love Somebody" (Bob Marlette, Sue Shifrin, performed by Michael Henderson), "If Anybody Had a Heart" (Souther, Danny Kortchmar, performed by John White).

p, Jason Brett, Stuart Oken; d, Edward Zwick; w, Tim Kazurinsky, Denise DeClue (based on the play "Sexual Perversity in Chicago" by David Mamet); ph, Andrew Dintenfass (MGM Labs Color); m, Miles Goodman; ed, Harry Keramidas; prod d, Ida Random; art d, William Elliott; set d, Chris Butler, Beverli Eagan; cos, Deborah L. Scott; m/l, John Oates, Mike Leeson, Peter Vale, Tom Snow, Cynthia Weil, Bob Seger, J.D. Souther, Karla Bonoff, Brock Walsh, Scott Kempner, Thom Bishop.

Romance/Comedy   Cas.   (PR:O MPAA:R)

ABSOLUTE BEGINNERS***
(1986, Brit.) 107m
Palace-Virgin-Goldcrest/Orion c

Eddie O'Connell (Colin), Patsy Kensit (Crepe Suzette), David Bowie (Vendice Partners), James Fox (Henley of Mayfair), Ray Davies (Arthur), Mandy Rice-Davies (Mum), Eve Ferret (Big Jill), Tony Hippolyte, (Mr. Cool), Graham Fletcher-Cook (Wizard), Joe McKenna (Fabulous Hoplite), Steven Berkoff (The Fanatic), Sade [Adu] (Athene Duncannon), Tenpole Tudor (Ed the Ted), Bruce Payne (Flikker), Alan Freeman (Call-Me-Cobber), Anita Morris (Dido Lament), Paul Rhys (Dean Swift), Julian Firth (The Misery Kid), Chris Pitt (Baby Boom), Lionel Blair (Harry Charms), Gary Beadle (Johnny Wonder), Robbie Coltrane (Mario), Jess Conrad (Cappuccino Man), Smiley Culture (D.J. Entertainer), Ronald Fraser (Amberly Drove), Slim Gaillard (Party Singer), Irene Handl (Mrs. Larkin), Peter Hugo-Daly (Vern), Amanda Jane Powell (Dorita), Johnny Shannon (Saltzman), Sylvia Syms (Cynthia Eve), Ekow Abban (Santa Lucia Club Owner), Robert Austin (Slim Brother), Gerry Alexander (Ton-Up Vicar), Jim Dunk (Slim Brother), Johnny Edge (Trader Horn), Carmen Ejogo (Carmen), Paul Fairminer (Eddie Sex), Hugo First (Maltese Lodger), Pat Hartley (Ms. Cool, Sr.), Astley Harvey (Mr. Cool, Sr.), Colin Jeavons (Pamphleteer), Alfred Maron (Bert the Tailor), G.B. [Zoot] Money (Chez Nobody Barman), Sandie Shaw (Baby Boom's Mum), Bruno Tonioli (Maltese Lodger), Roland Alexander, Shalin Alexander, Ayo Antaeus, John Aron, Hoyle Baker, Chris Baldock, Andree Bernard, Warren Bird, Richard Bodkin, Timothy Brennan, Ho Bright, Roland

Brine, Kelvin Carter, Imogen Clare, Clive Clark, Kristy Davide, Vince Debono, Dennis Elcock, Sylvia Ellis, King Masher Fontaine, Wayne Fowkes, David Foreman, Lucille Gaye, Elliot Gilbert, John Gordon, Lorna Gray, John Greaves, Robert Grimsey, Robert Grose, Michael Ho, Isobel Hurill, Johnny Hotch, Kim St. James, Peter Jessup, Clive Johnson, Chua-Kaa-Joo, Val Joseph, Trevor Kelly, Tony Kemp, Chrissie Kendal, Olivia Komlosy, Viv Law, Madeleine Lawrence, Paul Leonard, Kenny Linden, Tom Lock, Tricia Lockhart, Jerry Manley, Peyton Martin, Robin Martyne, Jack Migdalek, Bob Newent, Albin Pahernik, Neil Patterson, William Perrie, Shanti Ruchpaul, Corrinne Russell, Les Saxon, Gary Sellars, Alan Spencer, Chris Sullivan, Paul Telford, Michelle Thorne, Christina Thornton, Carl Trevors, Oke Wambu, Anthony Wellington, Elizabeth Wendon, John Willet, Sabra Williams, Barrie J. Wilkinson, Glen Wilkinson, Barrie Young, David Morgan Young (Dancers).

Colin MacInnes predicted in his 1959 cult novel of British youth that "they'll make musicals one day about the glamour-studded 1950s." Surely the most visually inventive and energetic film to come out of England since Richard Lester's 1964 classic A HARD DAY'S NIGHT and the liveliest musical since the MGM reign, ABSOLUTE BEGINNERS is that picture. The film is directed by rock video ace Temple (his "Jazzin' For Blue Jean" for David Bowie and "Undercover" for The Rolling Stones are among the best music videos to date), who burst onto the scene in 1980 with THE GREAT ROCK AND ROLL SWIN-

DLE which starred the ultimate punk rock band, The Sex Pistols. He followed up in 1981 with a feature documentary, THE SECRET POLICEMAN'S OTHER BALL, and then two years later with a BBC television film, "It's All True." While his 1986 feature video RUNNING OUT OF LUCK (a showcase for Mick Jagger) proved to be an unwatchable disaster, Temple more than made up for it with ABSOLUTE BEGINNERS.

After a subdued opening credit sequence, this tale of two teens shows us a colorful, neon-lit London of 1958, as O'Connell, the film's star and narrator, sets the stage: "I remember that hot, wonderful summer when the teenager miracle reached full bloom and everyone in England stopped what they were doing to stare at what had happened . . . for the first time ever, kids were teenagers." Inside O'Connell's tiny bedroom, our stylish 18-year-old hero is deciding what to wear for the evening. Helping him decide is Crepe Suzette, played by Kensit, whose photograph on the wall comes to life with a nod of approval when he picks out the perfect shirt. With a blast of energy, O'Connell, still camera in hand, slides down a bannister and lands in the middle of a glossy, wet street. What follows is a three-minute plus shot (which has the appearance of being a single take) that rivals Orson Welles' bravura opening to TOUCH OF EVIL. Following O'Connell through crowded London, the camera glides along, crossing streets, dodging traffic, snaking through alleyways, swirling with dazzling intensity through a Soho overrun with the flashing lights of sex shops and the flashing skin of streetwalkers. Over the pounding jazz beat of "Boogie Stop Shuffle," O'Connell introduces the "same old young faces" that turn up every night on these streets. We meet Fletcher-Cook's Wizard, "baby-faced like a mask over his 2,000-year-old soul;" Hippolyte's trumpet-blowing Cool, "a colored cat . . . so cool, for reasons too obvious to mention;" McKenna's Fabulous Hoplite, "our own low-rent Oscar Wilde;" Rhys' dapper Swift, "a sharp modern jazz creation;" and Ferret's leopard-skinned Big Jill, who likes "chicks only" but is still a "boy's best friend." After this dynamic introductory explosion, O'Connell enters the Chez Nobody nightclub to meet his beloved Kensit, a spirited blonde who lives and loves with passion and speaks in a breathy whisper. Underneath the celebration of dancers and jazz bands is the unrest that will later lead to the bloody Notting Hill riots. Choreographed fights break out between "Mods" and "Trads" (two factions of British youth, divided by their tastes in music), recalling the stylized rumbles of WEST SIDE STORY. Meanwhile, O'Connell tries to charm Kensit, who loves her idealistic fellow teenager but wants fame and money as well. When O'Connell tells her that money isn't everything, she answers,

"Well, it'll do until everything comes along." Later, while thinking about the night before with Kensit, O'Connell says, "It's not that I've got anything against money, it's just what you have to do to get it." While O'Connell, who lives in the racially integrated slums of Napoli, makes a few dollars taking pornographic pictures, Kensit is trying to get noticed in the fashion business. Hoping to get enough money to keep Kensit content, O'Connell takes a job with pop music star maker Blair. Meanwhile, Kensit has made a splash at a fashion show organized by the effete *haute couture* designer Fox, who is so impressed with her style that he offers her a chance at designing his new Paris collection. Later, at a colorfully lit nightclub, Kensit bids farewell to O'Connell, singing a torchy ballad promising, "No one's gonna stop me from having it all." Feeling blue, O'Connell pays a visit to Pimlico, where his parents live in a rundown flat. His mum, Rice-Davies, is less than thrilled by his presence (she refers to him as her "blitz baby"), as is his mutant half-brother, Daly. The only one slightly interested in him is his friendly dad Davies, who stays around in order to keep the place looking respectable, while Rice-Davies sleeps with the borders. Returning to Napoli to visit Hippolyte, O'Connell learns that some wealthy neighborhood developers have begun buying buildings and evicting black tenants. In addition, there's a group of young racists who are making life tough for the blacks. No longer able to stand his separation from Kensit he goes to a party thrown by trashy gossip columnist Morris. Disgusted by the phoniness of Kensit, Fox, and his manufactured friends, O'Connell gets blind drunk, torn between his youthful idealism and his desire to do whatever is necessary to lure Kensit back. To add to his disgust, O'Connell is told that Kensit has become engaged to Fox. Watching all this is Bowie, an icy ad executive and slogan-maker who prides himself on marketing excellence and who offers O'Connell a future with his company. Bowie promises O'Connell that he'll get anything he wants by working for him. "We don't sell *things*," Bowie assures him. "We sell . . . *dreams*." In a remarkably inventive fantasy sequence, Bowie sings "That's Motivation" as he dances on the keys of a gigantic typewriter (not unlike the one upon which Ruby Keeler danced in 1937's READY, WILLING AND ABLE), climbs an imaginary Mount Everest to "the peak of perfection," tap dances in the clouds, performs a Frank Sinatra routine on a spinning globe, and finally promises O'Connell that he "can commit horrible sins and get away with it." Persuaded by his energetic hard sell, O'Connell emphatically informs Bowie, "I'm your boy, Vendice!"

While Kensit climbs to the top of the fashion world, O'Connell reaches the peak of professional photography. His success hasn't brought him happiness, however, and he still pines for Kensit. When he appears on a television show, O'Connell becomes outraged by the phonies he encounters, and proceeds to tell them off while the show is on the air. Among the viewers is Kensit, dressed in her wedding gown and watching from her bedroom at Fox's home, tears streaming down her face. O'Connell becomes a hero to his friends, the ultimate teenage rebel. Later, at the Chez Nobody, O'Connell arrives to listen to the sultry, silky voiced Sade perform. During the performance, O'Connell is devastated when he sees a newspaper headline that reads "Fashion Couturier Marries Teenage Bride" under a photo of Fox and Kensit.

In the meantime, the slums of Napoli are falling victim to the racists of the White Defense League, led by the evil Payne and the destructive Tudor. Tenements burn, windows break, and black tenants stand defenseless against the rioters. Rather than join the racists, O'Connell stands by his friend Hippolyte. O'Connell then learns that Bowie and Fox are behind the redevelopment project and have paid Payne and Tudor to intimidate the blacks into leaving. The violence escalates in Napoli when a Hitler-styled fascist speaks at a neo-Nazi rally, inciting a group of angry teenagers, including O'Connell's former friend Fletcher-Cook, to take to the streets and trash the homes of black families. Caught in the crossfire, O'Connell is hunted by the fascists who view him as a "nigger lover," and blacks who see him as the white enemy. In a final showdown outside an integrated jazz club, Hippolyte and Payne get in a brutal fight. Hippolyte has the chance to kill Payne, but instead backs off and lets him live. With the teenagers having defeated the oppressors, a shower of cleansing rain pours from the sky. The riots bring O'Connell and Kensit together for their long-awaited night of love. As Kensit tosses her wedding ring into the streets, all is well for the absolute beginners.

One of the most talked-about films of the decade in Britain, ABSOLUTE BEGINNERS is a marvel of color, movement, music, and youthful enthusiasm. It had been envisioned as a film project for years, and optioned numerous times since the novel's publication in 1958. Renewed interest came in 1981 when the MacInnes-influenced Paul Weller, the lead singer and songwriter for a British punk band called The Jam, wrote a U.K. hit single titled "Absolute Beginners." At about the same time, Temple was approached with the idea of making a modern musical based on MacInnes' novel (the second in a London trilogy begun with *City of Spades* in 1957 and completed with *Mr. Love and Justice* in 1960). When funding from British television's Channel Four failed, Temple went to Palace Productions, a new film company which chose instead to back Neil Jordan's COMPANY OF WOLVES. Eventually, in early 1984, Virgin Films took an interest in the project. By the time the production began, Palace, Virgin, and Goldcrest had combined to provide a budget which was upwards of $10 million (an average Hollywood budget, but ultra-expensive for England). After an endless amount of media hype, the film flopped in England. It received even worse treatment in the U.S., opening and closing in a blink in New York and Los Angeles and not even opening in most other major markets.

Coming from a background in rock video, Temple was perfectly suited for an extravagant musical and ABSOLUTE BEGINNERS is just that. Unfortunately, it seems the younger generation, raised on MTV and rock videos, were not ready for a musical. Avoiding the temptation of stretching a three-minute rock video into a feature-length rock video, Temple has instead successfully constructed a narrative picture with its stylistic roots set deeply in the MGM musical tradition. The choreography by Toguri (THE ROCKY HORROR PICTURE SHOW) is brilliant, Stapleton's photography and his Vincente Minnelli-like use of color is amazing (he also worked wonders with MY BEAUTIFUL LAUNDRETTE, 1986), and the music (a blend of jazz and pop that runs the gamut from the great arranger Evans to popular stars Bowie, Davies, and Sade) brims with energy. Like the great musicals of the past, ABSOLUTE BEGINNERS has a handful of marvelous musical numbers. Besides the opening sequence, there's Kensit's tantalizing cafe number "Having It All," Sade's smooth "Killer Blow," Davies' delightful delivery of "Quiet Life" in his cross-sectioned house, the fever-dream schizophrenia of O'Connell in Gaillard's "Selling Out," and the phenomenally inventive Bowie-O'Connell routine to "That's Motivation"—one of the greatest film scenes of the decade, and surely in the history of musicals. As for relevant content, ABSOLUTE BEGINNERS has more than SINGING IN THE RAIN, THE BAND WAGON, and AN AMERICAN IN PARIS combined, dealing as it does with racism, fascism, greed, and materialism. Temple has combined entertainment, genre elements, and social politics all in one ball, which rolls non-stop and gathers speed in the process. It's almost as if Temple feared he would never make another feature and wanted to make sure he got everything in this one. The film was criticized for its use of stock, one-dimensional characters which serve more as representations of concepts (innocence, greed, racism) than actual people. This, however, is in keeping with MacInnes' intent. "The figures in *Absolute Beginners*," he writes, "are all emblematic—real, I hope, as created essences, but never to be found intact in real life." The film does have its faults, however. The brutalities of the end seem forced rather than a logical progression of previous action. O'Connell's parents—Rice-Davies (who first gained attention in the 1950s as a result of her involvement in a government sex scandal) and Davies (lead singer of the rock band The Kinks)—are introduced early on and then completely forgotten. In contrast, MacInnes' novel probes far deeper into his protagonist's relationship with his parents, including a brilliant passage on the death of his father. Unfortunately (probably for budgetary reasons), Temple's vision and scope fall short of MacInnes'. While Temple's finale has his teenage characters winding up in each other's arms, MacInnes has the relationship ending somewhat ambiguously with Colin falling out of love with England and making an attempt to leave it all behind. Still, Temple holds true to the rebellious, invigorating spirit of the novel, delivering what someday may be seen as one of the most important films of the decade.

Two soundtracks were released in conjunction with the film, a single album in the U.S., and a double album in Britain. The songs recorded especially for the film are: "Absolute Beginners," "That's Motivation" (David Bowie, performed by Bowie), "Volare (Nel Blu Dipinto Di Blu)" (Domenico Modungno, Franco Migliacci, performed by Bowie), "Killer Blow" (Sade Adu, Booth, Stabbins, performed by Sade), "Have You Ever Been Blue?" (Paul Weller, performed by The Style Council), "Quiet Life" (Ray Davies, performed by Davies), "Having It All" (Patsy Kensit, Godson, Beauchamp, performed by Eighth Wonder, Kensit), "Selling Out" (Slim Gaillard, Julien Temple, Taylor, performed by Gaillard), "Va Va Voom," "The Naked and the Dead" (Gil Evans, performed by Evans), "Absolute Beginners" (Bowie, performed by Evans), "Better Git It In Your Soul (the Hot and the Cool)," "Boogie Stop Shuffle (the Rough and the Smooth)" (Charles Mingus, performed by Evans), "Rodrigo Bay" (Booth, Stabbins, Roberts, performed by Working Week), "Riot City" (Jerry Dammers, performed by Dammers), "Ted Ain't Dead" (Edward Tudorpole, Temple, performed by Tenpole Tudor), "Napoli" (Clive Langer, Temple, performed by Langer, The Perils of Plastic, Tom Morley, Gary Barnicle), "Cool Napoli" (Langer, Temple, performed by Gil Evans), "Little Cat" (Nick Lowe, performed by Jonas [Hurst]), "Landlords and Tenants" (Laurel Aitkin, performed by Aitkin), "Santa Lucia" (Ekow Abban, performed by Abban), "So What?" (Miles Davis, Smiley Culture, performed by Smiley Culture, Evans). The following incidental songs are also heard in the film: "Hey Little Schoolgirl" (R. Palmer, performed by The Paragons), "Rock Baby Rock" (Bertice Reading, perform by Reading), "Scorpio" (Edward Barber, performed by The Scorpions), "Switching It Off" (MacManus), "Hancock's Half Hour (from the BBC radio series)" (Angela Morley), "Here Comes The Bride" (arranged by Luis Jardim), "My Mammy" (W. Donaldson, S. Lewis, J. Young), "Rock A Bye Baby" (arranged by Clive Langer, Steve Allen), "Sleep Lagoon" (Eric Coates), "Teddy Bears Picnic" (J. Bruton, J. Kennedy), "Rocking At The 21's" (performed by Wee Willie Harris), "Bongo Rock" (Preston Epps, Arthur Egnoian, performed by The Jet Streams), "Great Balls of Fire" (Jack Hammer, Otis Blackwell), "Heat Doesn't Bother Me" (Animal Nightlife, performed by Animal Nightlife).

p, Stephen Woolley, Chris Brown; d, Julien Temple; w, Christopher Wicking, Richard Burridge, Don MacPherson (based on the novel by Colin MacInnes); ph, Oliver Stapleton (Super Techniscope, Rank Color); m, Gil Evans; ed, Michael Bradsell, Gerry Hambling, Richard Bedford, Russell Lloyd; prod d, John Beard; md, Gil Evans; art d, Stuart Rose, Ken Wheatley; set d, Joanne Woollard; cos, Sue Blane, David Perry; ch, David Toguri; m/l, David Bowie, Ray Davies, Sade Adu, Nick Lowe, Paul Weller, Clive Langer, Julien Temple, R. Palmer, Beatrice Reading, Edward Barber, Miles Davis, Smiley Culture, Edward Tudorpole, Angela Morley, W. Donaldson, S. Lewis, J. Young, Eric Coates, J. Bruton, J. Kennedy, Ekow Abban, Laurie Aitken, Domenico Modungno, Franco Migliacci, Jerry Dammers, Patsy Kensit, Slim Gaillard, Charles Mingus; makeup, Peter Frampton.

Musical **Cas.** **(PR:C MPAA:PG-13)**

ACES GO PLACES IV† (1986, Hong Kong) 98m Cinema City/Golden Princess c (AKA: MAD MISSION IV)

Sam Hui, Karl Maka, Sally Yeh, Sylvia Cheng, Ronald Lacey, Peter Macaully, Onno Boulee, Sin Lam Yuk, Sandi Dexter, Gayle Anne Jones.

An action picture shot with a cast from Hong Kong and photographed, in part, in New Zealand. The plot has a few police from Hong Kong—Hui, Maka, and Cheng—heading down under on the trail of a scientific rainmaking secret.

p, Raymond Wong, Dean Shek; d, Ringo Lam; w, Karl Maka, Ringo Lam; ph, Sander Lee; ed, Tony Chow; art d, Vincent Wai; spec eff, Kevin Chisnall; stunts, Joe Chi, Peter Bell.

Action (PR:NR MPAA:NR)

ACHALGAZRDA KOMPOZITORIS MOGZAUROBA (SEE: YOUNG COMPOSER'S ODYSSEY, A, 1986, USSR)

ADA† (1986, Yugo.) Bosna

Zoja Odak, Alaksandar Bercek, Adi Karalic.

d&w, Milutin Kosovac; ph, Mustafa Mustafic; m, Esad Arnautalic; set d, Maglajlija Mehmedalija.

ADI VASFIYE† (1986, Turkey) 88m Estet c (Trans: Her Name Is Vasfiye)

Mujde Ar *(Vasfiye)*, Aytac Arman *(Emin)*, Macit Koper *(Rustem)*, Yilmaz Zafer *(Fuat)*, Levent Yilmaz *(Hamza)*, Erol Durak *(The Writer)*.

An interesting fantasy picture about a young writer in the Turkish coastal town of Izmir who becomes fascinated with a poster of a singer billed as Sevim Suna. While looking at the poster, he is approached by a man who informs him that he once knew the singer, whose real name is Vasfiye. The man had, years before, eloped with the then-young singer, but his story ends there. The writer meets others who knew the singer, but their stories are just as incomplete as the first man's. Finally, the writer gets an opportunity to meet the singer backstage at a nightclub, but their meeting also includes characters from the stories he has been told. The now-thoroughly confused writer is stabbed and returned to the streets, though he wonders if everything that occurred may have taken place inside his head. Named Best Picture at International Istanbul Filmdays—the Turkish film fest—an honor which director Yilmaz also won in 1985 with his film BIR UDUM SEVGI.

d, Atif Yilmaz; w, Baris Pirhasan (based on stories by Necati Cumali); ph, Orhan Oguz; m, Atilla Ozdemiroglu; art d, Sahin Kaygun.

Comedy/Drama (PR:C-O MPAA:NR)

ADIOS PEQUENA† (1986, Span.) (Trans: Goodbye My Lovely)

Ana Belen, Antonio Valero, Juan Echanove, Jose Manuel Cervino, Marcel Bozufi.

p, Javier Inchaustegui; w, Imanol Uribe, Ricardo Franco (based on a novel by Andreu Martin); ph, Angel Luis Fernandez.

ADJO SOLIDARITET (SEE: FAREWELL, ILLUSION, 1986)

ADVENTURE OF FAUSTUS BIDGOOD, THE† (1986, Can.) 110m Faustus Bidgood-National Film Board of Canada-Atlantic Region Production Studio bw-c

Andy Jones *(Faustus Bidgood)*, Greg Malone *(Vasily Bogdanovich Shagoff)*, Robert Joy *(Eddy Peddle)*, Brian Downey *(Fred Bonia-Coombs)*, Maisie Rillie *(Phyllis Meaney)*, Mary Walsh *(Heady Nolan)*, Beni Malone *(Henry Harry)*, Tommy Sexton *(Frank Dollar)*, Nelson Porter *(Premier Jonathan Moon)*.

A bizarre comedy from Newfoundland which tells the satirical story of a meek Department of Education clerk, Jones, who imagines himself as the leader of a revolutionary group that secedes from Canada. His real life, however, is just as strange, involving him in a scheme to denounce the Minister of Education, Joy, as having previously worked as a flamenco dancer. Eventually, he loses touch with the boundaries of real life and fantasy and rapidly loses his grip on the world. Reportedly, the film was ten years in the making, employing members of the Newfoundland Comedy Collective. Photographed on 16mm film and alternating between black-and-white (for the fantasy sequences) and color (for reality).

p,d&w, Michael Jones, Andy Jones; ph, Michael Jones; m, Paul Steffer, Robert Joy, Pamela Morgan; ed, Michael Jones; set d, Michael Kearney, Bawnie Oulton, Susan Hickey.

Comedy (PR:C MPAA:NR)

ADVENTURES OF THE AMERICAN RABBIT, THE** (1986) 85m Toei Animation/Atlantic Releasing Clubhouse Pictures c

Voices: Bob Arbogast *(Theo)*, Pat Freley *(Tini Meeny)*, Barry Gordon *(Rob/American Rabbit)*, Bob Holt *(Rodney)*, Lew Horn *(Dip/Various Characters)*, Norm Lenzer *(Bruno)*, Ken Mars *(Vultor/Buzzard)*, John Mayer *(Too Loose)*, Maitzi Morgan *(Lady Pig)*, Lorenzo Music *(Ping Pong)*, Lauri O'Brien *(Bunny O'Hare)*, Hal Smith *(Mentor)*, Russi Taylor *(Mother)*, Fred Wolf *(Fred Red)*.

This animated feature involves the adventures of a plucky lapin who becomes a super bunny after a strange encounter with a mystical rabbit wizard. In his travels, Rob Rabbit (voiced by Barry Gordon) gets a job playing piano in a nightclub, meets up with a nasty group of bikers, and helps out a rock 'n' roll band. The story peters out towards the end, and running at nearly an hour and a half, may not hold the attention of its intended younger audience.

p, Masaharu Etoh, Masahisa Saeki, John G. Marshall; d, Fred Wolf, Nobutaka Nishizawa; w, Norm Lenzer (based on characters created by Stewart Moskowitz); m/l, Mark Volman, Howard Kaylan, John Hoier.

Animated Feature Cas. (PR:AAA MPAA:G)

AFZIEN† (1986, Neth.) 77m Rolf Orthel Filmproducties c (Trans: Second Wind)

Ger Thijs, Mies de Heer, Pierre Bokma, Cathrien ten Bruggecate, Jentien de Boer, Gerardjan Rijnders, Annet Nieuwenhuizen.

A sort of BIG CHILL from Holland, this film explores a group of friends in their late 30s who have known each other since their college days. All have experienced success in their chosen artistic disciplines but there is uniform unhappiness in their lives. As students during the 1960s the group had thrived on idealism. This has been replaced by the harsher views reality has shown them, a sad fact of life they must now deal with. (In Dutch; English subtitles.)

p, Rolf Orthel; d, Gerrard Verhage; w, Gerrard Verhage, Jose Alders, Gerrit van Elst; ph, Goert Giliay; m, Bernard Hunnekink; ed, Jan Wouter van Reijen; art d, Hadassah Kahn.

Drama (PR:O MPAA:NR)

AGENT ON ICE* (1986) 96m Louis & Clark Expedition/Shapiro c

Tom Ormeny *(John Pope)*, Clifford David *(Kirkpatrick)*, Louis Pastore *(Frank Matera)*, Matt Craven *(Joey)*, Debra Mooney *(Secretary)*, Donna Forbes *(Jane)*, Jennifer Leak *(Helen Pope)*.

In a prolog set in Hungary (though actually filmed in New Jersey, an unlikely substitute to say the least) CIA boss David cuts a deal with Mafia man Pastore. In return for laundering mob money, Pastore agrees to kill selected political figures on a CIA hit list. As a cover, a fake killing of Pastore is rigged while the mobster hightails it to Italy. Ormeny, an innocent agent assigned to "assassinate" Pastore gets fired as part of a cover-up, then sinks into unending self-pity.

Years later Pastore decides he wants to return to the US. He bumps off the men behind his fake death, then goes after Ormeny. Ormeny's personal life may be a

mess, but he manages to evade Pastore's bloodthirsty goons. Meanwhile David learns of Pastore's doings and tries to have both the mobster and his former agent knocked off. As the bodies pile up, David is added to their numbers, but Ormeny continues to elude death time and again. In the end he faces off with Pastore in the obligatory climactic gun battle, and who comes out on top is certainly no surprise. For his efforts, Ormeny is offered David's former job and given a medal, two honors the hardened man angrily rejects.

There's not much to this cliched thriller, other than a compendium of stock situations and uniformly bad acting. Pastore was also the film's producer as well as cowriter (with director Worswick).

p, Louis Pastore; d, Clark Worswick; w, Clark Worswick, Louis Pastore; ph, Erich Kollmar (DuArt Color); m, Ian Carpenter; ed, Bill Freda.

Thriller (PR:O MPAA:R)

AGHAAT† (1986, India) 148m Neo Films c (Trans: Blood of Brothers)

Om Puri *(Madhav Verma)*, Gopi *(Krishnan Raju)*, Pankaj Kapoor *(Chotelal)*, Naseeruddin Shah *(Rustom Patel)*, Deepa Sahi, Amrish Puri, Sadashiv Amrapurkar, Rohini Hattangadi, K.K. Raina, M.K. Raina, Harish Payel.

In an Indian factory, two widely disparate trade union groups attempt to gain power in employee-management relations. Puri is a Communist leader who takes a peaceful approach with his supervisors, while Shah, head of an opposing union, prefers direct and violent action. He uses a small army of musclemen to gain headway with the factory owners, a situation that forces Puri to reconsider his own positions. Another social-relevance film from award-winning director Nihalani, whose ARDH SATYA gained him the Best Director prize at the 1983 Indian Film Directors' Association ceremonies. Star Puri won the Best Actor prize for his role in that same film at the Karlovy Vary Festival.

p, Manmohan Shetty, Pradeep Uppoor; d, Govind Nihalani; w, Nijay Tendulkar; ph, Govind Nihalani; m, Ajit Varman; ed, Sutanu Gupta; art d, Nitish Roy.

Drama (PR:C MPAA:NR)

AIQING QUIANGFENG XUNHAO (SEE: JUST LIKE THE WEATHER, 1986, Hong Kong)

AKLI MIKLOS† (1986, Hung.)

Istvan Hirtling.

d, Gyorgy Revesz; w, Gyorgy Revesz (based on the novel by Kalman Mikszath); ph, Ferenc Szecsenyi.

AL ASHEKE† (1986, Iraq) 110m Babel c (Trans: The Lover)

Jawad Al Choukrgi *(Abdullah)*, Layla Mohamed *(Nerjis)*, Khalil Chawki *(Mullah)*.

Set during the period of British colonialism in Iraq, AL ASHEKE features Choukrgi as a man on the run after he castrates the cruel overseer who raped and murdered Mohamed, the girl for whom Choukrgi longed. He escapes from Iraq, and, after many years in exile, returns to his village where, in a contemporary setting, he helps his people in the war against Iran.

d, Mohamed Mournir Fanari; w, Tamer Mahdi (based on a novel by Abdulkhalek Al Rakabi); ph, William Daniel; m, Helmi Al Wadi; ed, Tarek Abdulkarim; art d, Najem.

Drama (PR:O MPAA:NR)

AL BEDAYA† (1986, Egypt) 123m Al Alamiya c (Trans: The Beginning; AKA: SATAN'S EMPIRE)

Ahmed Zaki *(Painter)*, Yousra *(Hostess)*, Safiya El Omari *(Journalist)*, Gamil Ratib *(Businessman)*, Hamdi Ahmed *(Peasant)*, Soad Nasr *(Belly Dancer)*, Sabri Abdel Moneim *(Boxer)*, Medhat Morsi *(Pilot)*, Nagat Ali *(Metallurgist)*, Hussain El Hakim *(Steward)*, Samir Wahid *(Copilot)*, Wissam Hamdi *(Boy)*.

When an airplane carrying the classic slice-of-life group crash-lands on a desert oasis, the survivors set up their own colony. Ratib, a wealthy businessman, immediately takes charge and forces the others to do his bidding. The group builds Ratib a house and puts up with his rule until Zaki, a painter (and popular Egyptian actor) starts a rebellion against this oppressive reign. The political allegory ends as the frazzled people are ultimately rescued.

p, Hussein Kalla; d, Salah Abou Seif; w, Salah Abou Seif, Lenine El Ramli; ph, Mohsen Ahmed (Hungarofilm Color); m, Ammar El Cherii, Sayed Hegab; ed, Hussein Afifi; art d, Mahmoud Mohsen.

Comedy (PR:O MPAA:NR)

AL DAHIYA† (1986, Egypt) 117m Mohamed Muktar Pictures c (Trans: The Victim)

Nadia El Gindi *(Zinip)*.

Gindi is a homemaker whose life takes an abrupt turn when the apartment building in which she lives unexpectedly collapses. She and her family move into a hastily constructed tent city, then she leaves to take a good-paying job in an out-of-town hospital. Though she works hard as a nurse for eighteen months, Gindi is fired from her job after a coworker accuses her of stealing morphine. Her troubles are compounded when she learns that her spouse has remarried during her absence. Gindi takes her ex-husband to court hoping to gain custody of their children but loses the case after the morphine scandal comes to light. Her life ruined by these tragic events, Gindi ultimately takes to using the drug, numbing herself to the horrors fate has dealt her.

d, Atif Salim; w, Bashir El Deek (based on a story by Hosam Shah); ph, Mohesen Nasr; m, Gamal Salama.

Drama (PR:O MPAA:R)

AL KETTAR† (1986, Egypt) 95m Ahab El Leassy c (Trans: The Train)

Nour El Sherif *(Khalid)*, Marvat Amin *(Farida)*, Fouad Ahmed *(Train Engineer)*, Abou Bak Ezzat *(Assistant Engineer)*, Amin El Henidi *(Drunk)*, Nabila El Sayed *(Drunk's Wife)*.

Though made a few years before RUNAWAY TRAIN (1985), this Egyptian variation on that film's premise was not released until 1986. A railroad engineer murders his wife after learning his assistant has been having an affair with her. Later the two men battle on board the train as it begins a nonstop run with no one in control. Though they are on a collision course with another train, plucky Nour El Sherif manages to put on the brakes after boarding the engine via a helicopter.

p, Hussein Yahout, El Leassy; d, Ahmed Fouad; w, Sayed Mohamed Marzuk, Ahmed Fouad; ph, Ramses Marzuk; m, Tarak Sarara; ed&art d, Ahmed Fouad.

Action (PR:C-O MPAA:NR)

ALCESTES† (1986, Gr.) 94m Lycouressis/Greek Film Center c

Antonis Theodoracopoulos *(G.Z. the Author)*, Olia Lazaridou (Anna), Maria Zafiraki, Alexandros Mylonas.

Theodoracopoulos is a middle-aged writer who returns to his boyhood home on a Greek isle after experiencing professional disappointment. Upon learning that an old love is also on the island, he begins a futile search for this link to his past. Instead he meets Lazaridou, a younger woman, who helps the writer come to terms with the troubles in his life.

p&d, Tony Lycouressis; w, Tony Lycouressis, Demetris Nollas; ph, Andreas Bellis; ed, Giorgos Triantafillou; set d&cos, Julia Stavridou.

Drama (PR:O MPAA:NR)

ALEM DA PAIXAO (SEE: HAPPILY EVER AFTER, 1986, Braz.)

ALEX KHOLE AHAVA† (1986, Israel) 94m Berkey-Pathe-Humphries/ Noah c (Trans: Lovesick Alex)

Yosef Shiloach, Hana Roth, Avraham Mor, Sharon Hacohen, Eitan Anshel, Avi Kushnir, Uri Cabiri, Shmuel Rodensky, Yael Wasserman, Gad Keinar.

When a woman visits some relatives, her 13-year-old nephew falls hopelessly in love with her. As their story develops, we learn that the woman is searching for a lover from her past.

p, Itzhak Shani, Yosef Diamant; d, Boaz Davidson; w, Boaz Davidson, Eli Tavor; ph, Amnon Salomon; ed, Bruria Davidson; cos, Ron Salomon.

Drama (PR:C-O MPAA:NR)

ALIEN WARRIOR (SEE: KING OF THE STREETS, 1986)

ALIENS**** (1986) 137m Brandywine/FOX c

Sigourney Weaver *(Ripley)*, Carrie Henn *(Newt)*, Michael Biehn *(Cpl. Hicks)*, Paul Reiser *(Burke)*, Lance Henriksen *(Bishop)*, Bill Paxton *(Pvt. Hudson)*, William Hope *(Lt. Gorman)*, Jenette Goldstein *(Pvt. Vasquez)*, Al Matthews *(Sgt. Apone)*, Mark Rolston *(Pvt. Drake)*, Ricco Ross *(Pvt. Frost)*, Colette Hiller *(Cpl. Ferro)*, Daniel Kash *(Pvt. Spunkmeyer)*, Cynthia Scott *(Cpl. Dietrich)*, Tip Tipping *(Pvt. Crowe)*, Trevor Steedman *(Pvt. Wierzbowski)*, Paul Maxwell *(Van Leuwen)*, Valerie Colgan *(ECA Rep)*, Alan Polonsky *(Insurance Man)*, Alibe Parsons *(Med Tech)*, Blain Fairman *(Doctor)*, Barbara Coles *(Cocooned Woman)*, Carl Toop *(Alien Warrior)*, John Lees *(Power Loader Operator)*, Louise Head, Kiran Shah *(Doubles for Newt)*.

The long-awaited (and rather unexpected) sequel to the successful ALIEN (1979) is a nonstop, high tech, souped-up war movie, with gung-ho Marines blasting special-effects creatures and the most convincing, exciting female action heroines anywhere in cinema. The film opens just where the last ended, with Weaver asleep in suspended animation in the life pod out of which she blew the creature at the conclusion of the former. In deep space she is found by a salvage ship and brought back to a space station. A young representative of The Company, Reiser,

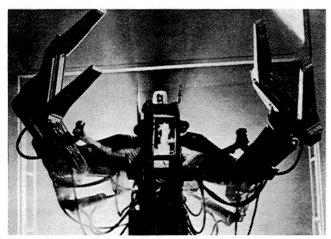

tells her that she has been unconscious for 57 years. (A deleted scene informs Weaver that the daughter she left behind has died an old woman.) She tells representatives of The Company about the creature that destroyed the *Nostromo*, but they are skeptical, and she is horrified when she hears that the planet on which they found the creature has been colonized. She tries to adapt to her new environment, but she is plagued by nightmares. One day she is approached by Reiser and a Marine who tell her that contact has been lost with the colony and ask her to accompany a platoon of Colonial Marines to the planet as an adviser. Her nightmares persuade her to agree, and soon she finds herself with a squad of hardbitten, foul-mouthed grunts who could just have come back from the invasion of Grenada except for the fact that some of them are women, including the toughest, Goldstein, playing a Latino with a wicked-looking weapon and a macho attitude more powerful than that of the men. Landing on the planet, they find the installation abandoned, but ample evidence of a desperate last stand in one wing. Then they find the sole survivor, a little girl (Henn) who has remained alive by hiding in the air ducts. Somewhere between catatonic and feral, the girl soon provokes Weaver's maternal instincts. Henn asks Weaver to return with her to her hiding place, but Weaver tells her, "These men are soldiers, they're here to protect you." The Marines go to investigate signals from under the atmosphere processor, but because the position could blow up if a stray bullet should hit some parts, everyone has his ammunition taken away. "What are we supposed to use, man, harsh language?" asks the crusty, cigar-chomping sergeant. They find the larder of the creatures, with colonists stuck to the walls, hosting embryos like that which burst so memorably from John Hurt's chest in the first film. In a flash the creatures attack, seeming to emerge from the very walls to destroy half the force before the green lieutenant, watching the carnage through monitors back in a command vehicle with Weaver and Reiser, can make a decision. Finally Weaver takes over and rescues the survivors. They decide to call for their landing ship to take them off, planning to nuke the site from orbit, but creatures kill the flight crew, and the group is stranded. As they barricade themselves in the installation, android Henriksen ("I prefer the term 'artificial person'") volunteers to climb through a shaft to remote-pilot a rescue ship down from the orbiting mother craft, though he's not enthused ("I may be synthetic, but I'm not stupid."). Meanwhile, while Weaver and Henn sleep, Reiser lets some of the creatures in so that they will infest the pair and he can slip a creature back through quarantine to The Company's Bioweapons Division. They are rescued, and Reiser soon meets his comeuppance in the glistening jaws of a creature. As the group tries to make its way to the landing bay to meet the rescue ship, three more Marines are killed. Now only Weaver, Henn, Biehn (severely wounded by acid from an exploding creature), and Henriksen remain. Henn falls down a shaft and is carried off by a creature, and Weaver arms herself to go back for a rescue. Weaver tracks Henn down into the bowels of the station and saves her, but soon runs face-to-face into

the queen creature, the biggest and nastiest-looking of them all, with a huge egg sack and tube for laying eggs. The two mother figures eye each other for a moment, then Weaver incinerates the nest. The humans reach the surface, the queen in pursuit, and are lifted off in the nick of time by Henriksen. Back at the orbiter, they have no sooner gotten off the rescue craft than Henriksen is torn in two by the queen, which has hung onto the bottom of the ship. While the monster goes after Henn, Weaver suits herself up in a massive robot power loader. She emerges to fight the monster head-to-head, yelling "Get away from her, you bitch!" as she advances, hydraulic pincers snapping. As they fight, both fall down an airlock and Weaver manages to get it open and flush the creature away. The last scene is maternal, Weaver tucking Henn into her suspended animation pod for the flight back before retiring herself.

Weaver is superb, and she carefully studied her part for every nuance (her script was reportedly marked up in 17 colors of ink), although she later expressed some dissatisfaction over the film's preoccupation with weaponry. She is tough, smart, and the best fighter, male or female, in the movie. (Interestingly, the role of Ripley in the original film was intended for a man, and this role could have also been played by a man, with only minor changes in the script.) The rest of the

small cast also does well, and director Cameron proves that he may be the best action director working today. The two big alien attack scenes are nailbiters, especially the first, witnessed largely through TV monitors and cameras attached to each soldier's helmet, with the monitors going dead as the monsters decimate the unit. The cutting is quick, the suspense unrelenting, and the monsters thoroughly frightening. The action is almost entirely interior, and not a glimpse of daylight is seen at any time throughout. Whenever Cameron can get away with it, the ceiling is dripping, be it from alien secretions, ruptured pipes, or the sprinkler system. The main theme throughout is maternity, Weaver versus the queen, with some side shots at corporate immorality in the person of Reiser and military incompetence in the person of inexperienced officer Hope. The film was made on a surpisingly small budget of $18 million (it looks like twice that) and under schedule, thanks to the matrimonial harmony of Cameron and producer Hurd, who kept the budget under control. The film made extensive use of the latest in military hardware—in fact the technology on display is more likely to be available in 20 years rather than 200—and the credits thank Ferranti Defense Systems and other high-tech firms. One of the biggest hits of the summer of 1986, ALIENS made better than $42 million in rentals (making it the 60th biggest hit of all time, according to trade publications) and earning a Best Actress Oscar nomination for Weaver in addition to nominations for Original Score, Editing, Art Direction, Sound Effects, and Visual Effects.

p, Gale Anne Hurd; d, James Cameron; w, James Cameron (based on a story by James Cameron, David Giler, Walter Hill based on characters created by Dan O'Bannon, Ronald Shusett); ph, Adrian Biddle (Eastmancolor); m, James Horner; ed, Ray Lovejoy; prod d, Peter Lamont; art d, Bert Davey, Fred Hole, Michael Lamont, Ken Court; set d, Crispian Sallis; cos, Emma Porteous; spec eff, Stan Winston, The L.A. Effects Group, John Richardson, Norman Baillie; makeup, Peter Robb-King; stunts, Paul Weston.

Science Fiction   **Cas.**   **(PR:O MPAA:R)**

AL-KAS†   (1986, Tunisia) 76m SATPEC c (Trans: The Cup)

Slim Mahfoudh *(Mustapha)*, Fatma Larbi *(Mustapha's Wife)*, Kamel Touati *(Rached)*, Hassen Hermes *(Hedi)*, Nabil Kaaniche *(Hassan)*, Jamila Ourabi *(Lamine)*, Fathi Haddoi *(Malabar)*, Mohamed Lassoued.

This anecdotal comedy follows a group of rabid soccer fans whose lives revolve around the game. Mahfoudh shows undying support for his favorite team, though he secretly wagers money on an opposing squad. His wife, in the meantime, is having an affair with Mahfoudh's cousin. At the all-important match the battle is fought not only on the field, but amidst the delirious soccer enthusiasts in the stands as well. Though the favored team loses, Mahfoudh is comforted by the money he has won on his bets.

d, Mohamed Damak; w, Mohamed Mahfoudh; ph, Belgacem Jelliti; ed, Sabiha El Haj Slimane.

Comedy   **(PR:C MPAA:NR)**

ALLA VI BARN I BULLERBY†   (1986, Swed.) 90m Svensk Filmindustri c (Trans: The Children of Bullerby Village)

Linda Bergstrom *(Lisa)*, Crispin Dickson Wendenius *(Lasse)*, Henrik Larsson *(Bosse)*, Ellen Demerus *(Britta)*, Anna Sahlin *(Anna)*, Harald Lonnbro *(Olle)*, Tove Edfeldt *(Kerstin)*, Soren Pettersson *(Norrgards-Erik)* Ann-Sofie Knape *(Norrgards-Greta)*, Ingwar Svensson *(Mellangards-Anders)*, Elisabeth Nordkvist *(Mellangards-Maja)*, Bill Jonsson *(Sorgards-Nisse)*, Catti Edfeldt *(Sorgards-Elin)*, Louise Raeder *(Agda)*, Peter Dywik *(Oskar)*, Olof Sjogren *(The Shoemaker)*, Lasse Stahl *(Country Store Owner)*, Sigfred Eriksson *(Granddad)*, Ewa Carsson, Britt Sterneland, Nina Englund.

This film, based on a novel by popular children's writer Astrid Lindgren (author of the *Pippi Longstocking* series), follows a group of Swedish schoolchildren in the 1920s as they enjoy their summer vacation. The three boys and three girls while away their time by searching for hidden riches and making friends with a seemingly ill-tempered pooch. Reportedly, an English-dubbed version of this was to be prepared for American audiences in 1987. Filmed at the same time and scheduled for a 1987 Christmas release is the sequel, MORE ABOUT THE CHILDREN OF BULLERBY VILLAGE.

p, Waldemar Bergendahl; d, Lasse Hallstrom; w, Astrid Lindgren (based on her novel); ph, Jens Fischer, Rolf Lindstrom, Mats Ardstrom (Fujicolor); m, Georg Riedel; ed, Susanne Linnman; prod d, Lasse Westfelt; cos, Inger Pehrsson, Susanne Falck, Carina Dalunde; makeup, Helena Olofsson-Carmback, Eva Bagge.

Children's Adventure   **(PR:AA MPAA:NR)**

ALLIGORIA†   (1986, Gr.) 120m Anna Sfika/Greek Film Center c (Trans: Allegory)

K. Papazois, G. Lambros, Marina Moschopoulou, Panos Chalkos, Mich. Galnakis, Vana Minou, D. Indares, Themis Parlaventzas, Iraklis Pnevmatikakis, G. Stamatiou, Th. Marselos, Thomas Bontinas.

As the title states, this Greek picture is an allegory which addresses the end of paganism and the rise of mythology.

p, Anna Sfika; d&w, Costas Sfikas; ph, Giorgos Kavayias; ed, Vangelis Gousias; set d&cos, Dora Lelouda Papailiopoulou.

Historical   **(PR:NR MPAA:NR)**

ALMACITA DI DESOLATO†   (1986, Neth.) 110m Stiching Cosmic
Illusion/Hungry Eye c

Marian Rolle *(Solem)*, Gwendomar Roosje *(Lucio)*, Nydia Ecury *(Mama Grandi)*, Yubi Kirindongo *(Alma Sola Yon)*, Imelda Valerianus *(Papia Un Papia Dos)*, Ana Muskus *(Palomba)*, Irene van Grieken *(Marga)*, Rina Penso, Eligio Melfor.

A fantasy in which Rolle is a mute priestess in an isolated village who must remain a virgin to retain her powers and ensure the fertility of the crops. Seduced by an evil spirit disguised as a wounded man, she bears a child, is driven away from her village, and goes with her infant daughter to look for a mystical place where all the spirits of deceased ancestors live in happiness. She is accosted constantly by the evil spirit, who appears in various guises. Shot on the Dutch commonwealth island of Curacao, the film takes traditional folktale themes, uses nonprofessional native actors and actresses, and is entirely performed in the Papiamentu language. (In Papiamentu; English subtitles.)

p, Norman de Palm; d, Felix de Rooy; w, Norman de Palm; ph, Ernest Dickerson; m, Grupo Issoco; ed, Ton de Graaff; art d, Felix de Rooy.

Fantasy   **(PR:C   MPAA:NR)**

ALSKA MIG   (SEE: LOVE ME!, 1986, Swed.)

AM NACHESTEN MORGEN KEHRTE DER MINISTER NICHT AN SEINEN ARBEITSPLATZ ZURUCK†   (1986, Ger.) 70m Monika Funke-Stern c (Trans: On the Next Morning the Minister Didn't Return to His Post)

Udo Kier *(The Minister)*, Magitta Haberland, Ciliane Dahlen, Ric Schachtebeck, Frieder Butzmann, Peter Althoff, Walter Sprungalla, Christian Golusda, Gunther Nolden.

This erotic science-fiction film is the first feature-film work of Monika Funke-Stern, a West German film and video artist. The largely visual story follows the adventures of the Minister for LUST, who takes a rather unearthly journey through a land of high tech and lusty imaginings.

p,d&w, Monika Funke-Stern; ph, Nicolas Joray; m, Frieder Butzmann.

Fantasy   **(PR:O   MPAA:NR)**

AMANSIZ YOL†   (1986, Turkey) 94m Sineray c (Trans: The Desperate Road)

Kadir Inanir *(Hasan)*, Zuhal Olcay *(Sabahat)*, Yavurer Cetinkaya *(Yavuz)*.

Ianir is a truck driver who returns to his native land after doing time in a German jail. There he finds an old friend who is now a cripple engaged in some criminal activity. The friend soon vanishes after entrusting Ianir with his wife and daughter and a bundle of cash. Off they go in Ianir's rig, villains in pursuit, and the picture turns into a routine chase for the duration of its running time.

d, Omer Kavur; w, Omer Kavur, Baris Pirhasan; ph, Orhan Oguz; m, Ugur Dikmen.

Action   **(PR:A-C   MPAA:NR)**

AMAZONIA—THE CATHERINE MILES STORY   (SEE: WHITE SLAVE, 1986, It.)

AMERICA†   (1986) 83m Moonbeam/ASA c

Zack Norman *(Terrence Hackley)*, Tammy Grimes *(Joy Hackley)*, Michael J. Pollard *(Bob Jolly)*, Richard Belzer *(Gypsy Beam)*, Monroe Arnold *(Floyd Praeger)*, Liz Torres *(Dolores Frantico)*, Pablo Ferro *(Hector Frantico)*, David

Kerman *(Mr. Management)*, Howard Thomashefsky *(Earl Justice)*, Michael Bahr *(Martin Lang)*, Laura Ashton *(Tina Lyle)*, Robert Downey, Jr., Corinne Alphen, Minnie Gentry, Chuck Griffin, Ron Nealy, Forrest Murray, Melvin Van Peebles, Michael Rubenstein, Rudy Wurlitzer.

Robert Downey, "the legendary director of PUTNEY SWOPE" (that's what the ads for this film call him), turns up again to trade on his once-good name with this feeble satire. Norman, a newscaster for an underground cable TV station in New York, gets into various predicaments with his sidekick, Michael J. Pollard, the station's weatherman. In the end, the station is bought out by a homosexual lottery winner. Originally shot in 1982, this film remained on the shelf since, and one can only wonder what motivated anyone to release it now. One song, "America" (Leon Pendarvis, sung by Janice Pendarvis).

p, Paul A. Leeman; d, Robert Downey; w, Robert Downey, Sidney Davis; ph, Richard Price (Movielab, Guffanti color); m, Leon Pendarvis; ed, C. Vaughn Hazell; art d, C.J. Strawn; m/l, Leon Pendarvis.

Comedy   **(PR:O   MPAA:R)**

AMERICA 3000*   (1986) 92m Cannon c

Chuck Wagner *(Korvis)*, Laurene Landon *(Vena)*, William Wallace *(Gruss)*, Sue Giosa *(Morha)*, Victoria Barrett *(Lakella)*, Galyn Gorg *(Lynka)*, Shai K. Ophir *(Lelz)*, Camilla Sparv *(Reya)*, Karen Lee Sheperd *(Keva)*, Ari Sorko-Ram *(Relk)*, Ezra Dagan *(Amie)*, Joanna Reis *(Freyha)*, Steve Malovic *(Aargh the Awful)*, Anat Zachor *(Bowa)*, Pierre Henry *(Troke)*, Zipora Peled *(Gramma)*, Steve Stroppiana *(Young Korvis)*, Eli Pilo *(Young Gruss)*, Marvin Friedman *(Gen. Greer)*, Silvian Imberg *(The Seeder)*, Elki Jacobs *(Redcross)*, Dada Rubin *(Yuke)*, Barak Negby *(Tuke)*, Helen Eleazari *(Paradise Elder)*, Dodik Samdar *(Dob)*, Mafi Salah *(Oul)*, Zazy Shavit *(Mela)*.

More low-rent science fiction from Israeli *schlockmeisters* Golan and Globus. In the title year and place, some 900 years after nuclear Armageddon, tribes of amazons dominate, enslaving men for various duties ranging from manual labor through procreation. As the film opens, one boy about to be branded into servitude escapes with a companion into a contaminated area where they are not pursued. The two (Wagner and Wallace) grow up to become warriors, staging raids to free other slaves to add to their army. Meanwhile, in the camp of the Thunder Women, Landon is about to assume leadership of the tribe. Her sister, Barrett, is upset about the title going to her sister, and her dissatisfaction is noted by Giosa, the evil head of a rival tribe. Fleeing the camp after a raid, Wagner stumbles across an old bunker that turns out to have been constructed for a long-dead president of the United States. Inside he finds a laser gun and a portable cassette player (read ghetto blaster). Now blessed with superior weaponry, Wagner's first thought, unlikely as it seems, is to make peace once and for all (sure). He kidnaps a close friend of Landon's to draw Landon into the bunker, and there they almost instantly discover love. Their plans for a reconciliation of the men and the women are endangered when Landon learns that Barrett, with Giosa's backing, has taken control of the tribe. Before Landon can reassert her leadership, Barrett launches an attack against the men's camp. Wagner believes that Landon has broken her word and prepares to attack, but Landon manages to open the camp gates and avoid bloodshed. Everyone vows to be nicer from now on and civilization gears up to make a comeback. The script for this trenchant piece of social criticism was written in the mid-1970s and then mercifully forgotten until writer Engelbach finally got an opportunity to direct a feature and pulled this dusty relic from the back of his drawer. "So I read it and thought it was still a chuckle," the director said. "Currently, films set in a post-nuclear-war world look familiar due to the rash of MAD MAX sequels and spin-offs. But 11 years ago, AMERICA 3000 was way ahead of its time." Engelbach must be talking about some other film, because instead of chuckles, the only thing this film is likely to elicit is howls of derision from the audience. The film is more like MESA OF LOST WOMEN than MAD MAX, and is hardly a candidate for way-ahead-of-its-time status. The film was shot in some particularly bleak region of Israel in reported 125-degree heat. Another daunting problem was finding 40 horses in Israel and an equal number of Israeli women who could ride them. None of the effects is especially convincing, the pace is creakingly slow, and the performances are all of the somnambulistic variety. The only saving graces are a relatively exciting climax and a funny monster named Aargh the Awful (Malovic) who gets all the best lines.

p, Menahem Golan, Yoram Globus; d&w, David Engelbach; ph, David Gurfinkel (Rank Color); ed, Alain Jakubowicz; art d, Kuli Sander, Stephen Dane; set d, Pat Tagliaferro; cos, Debbie Leon; spec eff, Carlo De Marchis; ch, Ernie Reyes; makeup, Rinat Aloni; stunts, Mario De Barros.

Science Fiction   **(PR:C   MPAA:PG-13)**

AMERICAN ANTHEM*½   (1986) 100m Fields–Doug Chapin–Lorimar/COL c-bw

Mitch Gaylord *(Steve Tevere)*, Tiny Wells *(Jake)*, Janet Jones *(Julie Lloyd)*, Michael Pataki *(Coach Soranhoff)*, Patrice Donnelly *(Danielle)*, R.J. Williams *(Mikey Tevere)*, John Aprea *(Mr. Tevere)*, Michelle Phillips *(Linda Tevere)*, Katherine Gosney *(Landlady)*, Stacy Maloney *(Kirk Baker)*, Peter Tramm *(Ron Denver)*, Maria Anz *(Becky Cameron)*, Jenny Ester *(Tracey Prescott)*, Andrew M. White *(Arthur)*, Dick McGarvin *(Announcer Prelim Meet)*, Mark Oates *(Danny Squire)*, Jan Claire *(Announcer Final Meet)*, Megan Marsden *(Jo-Ellen Carter)*, Li Yuejiu *(Ling Xiang)*, Bruce Burns, Lisa Marie Campos, Bob Gauthier, Lisa Green, Chris Riser, Lyn Schmitt, Kent Weaver, Steve Elliott, Tim Darling *(Tops Club Members)*, Matt Arnot, Scott Barclay, Mike Bowers, Phillippe Chartrand, Glen Cooper, John Eccelston, Mark Ewers, Brett Finch, Doug Foerch, Steve Friedman, Rick Hall, Paul Hartman, Celeste Kelty, Tom Kennedy,

Jeff Knepper, John Levy, Wes Lewis *(Competition Gymnasts)*, Popeye *(Mikey's Dog)*.

There's nothing like becoming a publicly recognized hero to guarantee getting a crack at the movies. Mitch Gaylord had been one of the stars of the 1984 Los Angeles Olympics, taking home one gold, one silver, and two bronze medals in gymnastic events. No mean feat, and with the resulting media attention and national exposure Gaylord subsequently received on a promotional tour, his place in Hollywood was just about assured. "I never had any ambition to be an actor," Gaylord stated, "but when I read the script for AMERICAN ANTHEM I knew I

could do it." No kidding, Mitch. AMERICAN ANTHEM gives the athletic champ a chance to stretch his acting range about as far as a gym mat in what is simply an extended rock video with a smattering of silly dialog. Gaylord plays a former athlete whose glory days of high school are two years gone. His troubles are compounded by a brutal father (Aprea) who once broke Gaylord's arm during a family squabble (shown in a black-and-white flashback). Equally distressed is Jones, a noted gymnast in her own right, who comes to Gaylord's Arizona home town in hopes of winning a spot on a national gymnastic team. Gaylord notices her one night and romance quickly blooms. Now Gaylord has some inspiration to make a comeback, while Jones must fight against the rigid directives of Pataki, the team coach with a Slavic accent of indeterminate origin. He wants her to perform a floor routine to semi-classical music, but Jones *knows* that Pataki's choice just isn't for her (none of the instruments plugs in and there's no pulsating drum beat). After much trial, tribulation, and fancy backlighting, Gaylord conquers his familial problems to score a resounding success at the qualification meet. Jones, at the last minute, substitutes Pataki's stodgy music with an electronic score composed by her disabled cousin (White) and she too wins a spot on the team. The film closes with Gaylord and Jones standing jubilant on the winner's podium, though surprisingly there is no semi-obligatory triumphant freeze-frame.

This was director Magnoli's follow-up to his 1984 success PURPLE RAIN, which should come as no surprise. AMERICAN ANTHEM is virtually a remake of the earlier film, with gymnastic competition substituting for rock music as the road to personal salvation. The elements of familial troubles, talented though tortured hero, beautiful girl friend, and flashy visual style are all firmly in place. The only thing missing is Morris Day. Other than the sketchy backgrounds offered on Gaylord and Jones, the characters here are right out of Screenwriting 101, easily identifiable stereotypes without much depth. The performances largely match the unchallenging script, but these elements are secondary to the real star of the show: exciting visuals. Magnoli may not have the best storytelling skills, but he knows how to put an attractive picture on the screen. The rock video aesthetic is firmly in place here with strict adherence to its ever-dull guidelines. Flashy lighting, flashy editing, and that driving rock beat, along with beautiful, occasionally sweaty bodies, are the dominant attractions, with periodic interruptions of banal dialog. It seems just a little more than coincidental that AMERICAN ANTHEM's costume designer has the same chore on the television hit "Miami Vice," another offspring of the MTV era where appearance is everything. Despite the predominant rock soundtrack, some of the gymnastic sequences are accompanied by a semi-religious background chorus, causing more unintended hilarity than dramatic appeal. Yet, for all its problems, AMERICAN ANTHEM's final scene is an entertaining one. Magnoli's techniques are perfect for the gymnastic competition, injecting a sense of excitement into the proceedings that is lacking in the visceral story. It's here that Gaylord gets to show his real talents, and Jones, a professional dancer (she was featured in 1985's A CHORUS LINE) struts her stuff with finesse. Plenty of songs here by popular artists, including: "Two Hearts" (John Parr, performed by Parr), "Same Direction" (Andrew Farriss, Michael Hutchence, performed by INXS), "Battle of the Dragon" (Stevie Nicks, Gary Nicholson, John Jarvis, performed by Nicks), "Take It Easy" (Andy Taylor, Steve Jones, performed by Taylor), "Run to Her" (Richard Page, Steve George, Pat Mastelotto, Steve Farris, performed by Mr. Mister), "Angel Eyes" (Taylor, Jones, performed by Taylor), "Wings to Fly" (Giorgio Moroder, Tom Whitlock, performed by Graham Nash), "Love and Loneliness" (Nick Garvey, Gordon Hann, performed by Chris Thompson), "Wings of Love" (Taylor, Jones, performed by Taylor).

p, Robert Schaffel, Doug Chapin; d, Albert Magnoli; w, Evan Archerd, Jeff Benjamin (based on a story by Evan Archerd, Jeff Benjamin, Susan Williams);

ph, Donald E. Thorin (Panavision, MGM Color); m, Alan Silvestri; ed, James Oliver; prod d, Ward Preston; set d, Chris Westlund, Jo-Ann Chorney; cos, Jodie Tillen; spec eff, Don Elliott; ch, Kathy Johnson, Lisa Green; makeup, Cheri Minns, Steve PaPorte; stunts, Chuck Waters.

Sports Drama (PR:C MPAA:PG-13)

AMERICAN COMMANDOS* (1986) 88m Panorama–Ader–Spiegelman c (AKA: HITMAN)

Christopher Mitchum *(Dean Mitchell)*, John Phillip Law *(Kelly)*, Franco Guerrero *(Somsak)*, Willie Williams *(Creeper)*, Robert Marius *(Brutus)*, Ken Metcalfe *(Brady)*, Kristine Berlandson *(Lisa)*, Karen Lopez *(Mitchell's Wife)*.

An unintentionally hilarious action picture that was shot entirely on location in the Philippines, although much of the action takes place in Los Angeles, Vietnam, and Thailand. Mitchum (son of Robert) plays a Vietnam vet who now owns and operates a gas station in Los Angeles. One day his filling station is besieged by a youth gang seeking cash. Mitchum successfully repels the would-be thieves, but the loathsome youths have their revenge by invading Mitchum's home, killing his son and raping his wife, Lopez, who commits suicide shortly thereafter. With nothing left to live for and his bloodlust boiling, Mitchum hooks up with CIA-type Metcalfe who enlists the angry vet to help clean up a nefarious drug ring in Southeast Asia. Mitchum rounds up a bunch of his old Vietnam buddies and together they launch an invasion of Thailand (in an armored van!) to stop the drug traffic. Before it's over we've sat through too many Vietnam flashbacks, and even more scenes of carnage. AMERICAN COMMANDOS is an incredibly cheap production that brings back fond (in a perverse sort of way) memories of such "classic" 1960s U.S.-Filipino coproductions as MORO WITCH DOCTOR and THE MAD DOCTOR OF BLOOD ISLAND. Although the use of Philippine locations to simulate Vietnam and Thailand is acceptable, trying to pass off Manila (or the like) for downtown L.A. is downright laughable. The versatile Filipino extras double for every non-white race from Vietnamese to Chicano and serve mostly as cannon-fodder for Mitchum and his group of trigger-happy goons. Only for the desperate.

p, Just Betzer; d, Bobby A. Suarez; w, Ken Metcalfe, Bobby A. Suarez (based on a story by Bobby A. Suarez); ph, Jun Pereira (Technicolor); m, Ole Hoyer; ed, Suarez, Sing Yim; prod d, Butch Santos.

Action (PR:O MPAA:R)

AMERICAN JUSTICE** (1986) 92m Hunter–MFG/Movie Store c (AKA: JACKALS)

Jack Lucarelli *(Joe Case)*, Jameson Parker *(Dave Buchanon)*, Gerald McRaney *(Jake Wheeler)*, Wilford Brimley *(Sheriff Mitchell)*, Jeannie Wilson *(Jess Buchanon)*, Dennis A. Pratt *(Connie)*, Warner Glenn *(Warner)*, David Steen *(Hobie)*, Rick Hurst *(Harley)*, Danelle Hand *(Angelina)*, Sharon Hughes *(Valerie)*, Rosana DeSoto *(Manuela)*, Sherry Adamo *(Little)*, Roman Cisneros *(Raul)*, Robert Covarrubias *(Ramon)*, Randy Hall *(Raybo)*, Billy Chandler *(Deputy)*, Frank Soto *(Sanchez)*, Jared Snyder *(Yaney)*, Mary Francis Glenn *(Mabel)*, Greg Finley *(Chuck)*, Michael Bandoni *(Greg)*, Martin F. Goldman *(Tour Guide)*, Daria Jo Spurling *(Woman Hostage)*, Jack Dunlap *(Supervisor)*, Terry Seago *(Jud)*, Senator Bill Richardson *(Plummer)*, John Kinerk *(Angel Face)*, Danny O'Haco *(Frazer)*, John Tatum *(Badass)*, Lawrence Blaine Manthey *(Zach)*, Sal Acquisto *(Peter)*, George Roland *(Greasyman)*, Christopher Law *(Jake's Man)*, Brian Beach *(Border Patrolman)*, Frank Armenta *(Coyote)*, Dirk Kancilia *(Joe's Partner)*, Inez Perez *(Mexican Woman)*, Deanna Hinojos *(Girl)*, Peter Murray *(Pilot)*, Spenser Lucarelli, Jamie Parker *(Little Boys)*, Sam Goldman, Charles Goldman, Michelle Weaver, Christy Starr *(Bus Passengers)*, Michael Murray *(Boy at Border)*, Linda Murray *(Girl at Border)*, Patty Murray *(Woman at Border)*, Derra Shelley *(Ethereal Voice)*.

Uninspired action film set on the Arizona-Mexico border stars Lucarelli as an ex-Los Angeles cop who comes to visit former partner Parker, now a sheriff's deputy. While on an outing with Parker, his wife Wilson, and their guide Glenn, Lucarelli is forced to turn back when his steed begins acting up in dangerous-mountain-lion territory. Riding back alone, Lucarelli is thrown from his horse and forced to walk. As he wanders through the desert he witnesses the murder of a young Mexican girl by McRaney, a white slaver who kidnaps female illegals and sells them. The killer instructs the two men with him to bury the girl. The next

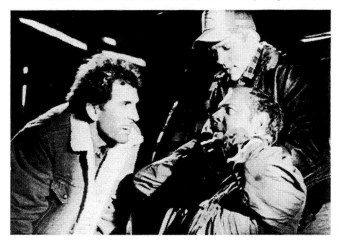

morning Parker brings Lucarelli to the police station to report the crime to sheriff Brimley. Lucarelli is stunned to see that the killer, McRaney, is one of the sheriff's key deputies. Without revealing the identity of the killer, Lucarelli shows the sheriff and his men the murder site, but the body is gone (McRaney phoned his cronies to have the body moved), and a desperate Lucarelli accuses McRaney of the murder. No one, including Parker, believes him and for all intents and purposes the case is dropped. Later, Lucarelli persuades Parker that it was McRaney he had seen, and together with veteran guide Glenn they find where the body had been moved. Meanwhile, McRaney makes moves to cover his tracks. He hides in the brush and shoots one of his weakling partners with an M-16 just as Parker and Lucarelli arrest the man. Brimley still refuses to believe that McRaney is a killer and does nothing. More investigating by Lucarelli and Parker reveals the white slavery headquarters, and the men set out to close it down. A bloody gunfight ensues in which many of the white slavers are killed, Lucarelli is badly wounded and left for dead, and Parker is cold-bloodedly shotgunned by McRaney. Just before pulling the trigger, McRaney informs the naive Parker that Brimley was in on the white-slave trade from the very beginning (the audience learns this several scenes before—if they hadn't guessed already). When the smoke clears, Lucarelli forces Brimley to tell him where McRaney is hiding and then arms himself for a final confrontation. He finds McRaney near the border with the rest of his gang. All dressed in Border Patrol uniforms, the men waylay illegals trying to cross the border and kidnap the women. Lucarelli intercepts the Mexicans and sends them back. With a laser-lock sighting system on his shotgun, Lucarelli faces the five Border Patrol impostors. He scares three of them off with his high-tech weapon (when they see the red dot on their chests—they flee in fear), but the fourth tries to draw and is killed, leaving only McRaney. The ever-confident McRaney attempts to pull his gun, but Lucarelli shoots him down.

Half THE BORDER and half ROLLING THUNDER, AMERICAN JUSTICE never transcends the action genre by bringing any significant meaning to its situation or characters. The film is basically a good guys versus bad guys shoot 'em-up with some innocent, exploited Mexicans thrown in for a vain stab at social relevance. The entire project appears to be a "buddy" film. Stars Lucarelli and Parker produced the film and found bit parts for their young sons; supporting player Pratt wrote it; and Parker's "Simon and Simon" television partner McRaney plays the villain. There hasn't been this much Hollywood nepotism since the last Burt Reynolds-Hal Needham epic. The film betrays the television experience of most of its creators through its workmanlike visuals, standard plot, and sketchy, cliched characters. To its credit, McRaney does manage to get some impressive mileage out of his cold-blooded white slaver. Sporting an ultra-close crew-cut, a low growl, and a mean set of eyes, his character is coiled so tight that he might explode at any moment. Unfortunately, the same cannot be said for Lucarelli and Parker. These guys come off looking pretty stupid as they flounder around trying to nail McRaney, and it nearly ruins the film because McRaney's character proves to be so ruthless that he should have wiped them out 15 minutes into the film. AMERICAN JUSTICE was filmed entirely on location in Tucson, Arizona. Songs include: "Red River Valley" (anonymous, performed by The Dean Armstrong Trio); "Tryin' to Say Goodbye" (Paul Chihara, Candy Chase, Gary Chase, performed by Jeannie Wilson); "Body Builder Blues" (Craig Huxley); "The Price You Pay" (Paul Chihara, Candy Chase, Craig Huxley, performed by David Goss).

p, Jack Lucarelli, Jameson Parker; d, Gary Grillo; w, Dennis A. Pratt; ph, Steve Yaconelli (Panavision, DeLuxe Color); m, Paul Chihara; ed, Steve Mirkovich; art d, Bruce Crone; set d, Bruce Gibeson; spec eff, Richard Helmer, Grant McCune; m/l, Paul Chihara, Candy Chase, Gary Chase, Craig Huxley; stunts, Bill Burton.

Action/Crime   **Cas.**   **(PR:O   MPAA:R)**

AMERICAN TAIL, AN**   (1986) 80m Amblin Entertainment/UNIV c

Voices: Erica Yohn *(Mama Mousekewitz)*, Nehemiah Persoff *(Papa Mousekewitz)*, Amy Green *(Tanya Mousekewitz)*, Phillip Glasser *(Fievel Mousekewitz)*, Christopher Plummer *(Henri)*, John Finnegan *(Warren T. Rat)*, Will Ryan *(Digit)*, Hal Smith *(Moe)*, Pat Musick *(Tony Toponi)*, Cathianne Blore *(Bridget)*, Neil Ross *(Honest John)*, Madeline Kahn *(Gussie Mausheimer)*, Dom DeLuise *(Tiger)*.

Steven Spielberg has long been an admirer of Disney animation, and many considered him the heir to Uncle Walt's family market empire. However, Spielberg's work in recent years has been consistently pockmarked by his commercial zeal and a rather generic quality to his films. Such is the case with AN AMERICAN TAIL, a beautifully animated feature which suffers from executive producer Spielberg's overbearing hand. Bluth himself was a former Disney animator who left the studio in a much publicized 1979 walkout over the declining artistic values he felt permeated the animation department. Bluth went on to

create THE SECRET OF NIMH (1982), a much praised feature-length animation that caught Spielberg's attention. Bluth later developed animation for the video games "Dragon's Lair," and "Space Ace," before finally hooking up with Spielberg to create AN AMERICAN TAIL. The collaboration unfortunately brought out the worst in Spielberg while maintaining Bluth's high standards for animation.

The story opens in turn-of-the century Russia where the Mousekewitz family, a clan of Jewish mice, are forced to emigrate after suffering through the pogroms of Czarist cats. Little Fievel Mousekewitz becomes separated from his family en route to New York, and washes up on the shores of the New Land inside a bottle. Once in the big city, Fievel encounters a variety of mice both friendly and vicious, as well as discovers to his horror that America also has its share of cats. Eventually Fievel, through pluck and cunning, schemes with his new found friends an ingenuous way to ship all cats off to the Orient. Their plan is a success and the film ends happily as Fievel is reunited with his family.

The elements would all seem right for a marvelous work of animation. Bluth's artistry is magnificent, employing close to one million animation cells to create some powerful images. His recreations of the Russian Jewish shtetls and the ghettos of New York's Lower East Side are certainly impressive, inhabiting these locations with some remarkably lively figures. Yet in order for the film to work, a strong faith in story and character is essential, and that key element is missing. Though voiced by some talented actors (Dom DeLuise, Madeline Kahn, Nehemiah Persoff, Christopher Plummer, and 8-year-old Phillip Glasser as Fievel), there is no conviction to the story. Even though the Mousekowitzes are clearly portrayed as Jews, their ethnicity is veiled shortly after the family is introduced, as if their religious background would alienate filmgoers. Rather than become an interesting allegory for children and adults, AN AMERICAN TAIL takes a much easier route, creating commonplace characters that would supposedly appeal to a broader audience. Released for the 1986 holiday season, the Fievel character was used by one large department store chain for their Christmas campaign, further emphasizing the film's intended generic qualities. Other moments, such as the funeral of one mouse friend and the frightening images of the pogrom, make this rather questionable entertainment for the youngest family members. By avoiding a solid background, and coupling this with some truly disturbing images, AN AMERICAN TAIL falls into an uncomfortable position of being too bland for adults, yet not quite appropriate for its intended audience.

The Spielberg stamp of marketablity is firmly planted on this feature, and that alone fated the film's quality from the start. Fievel, as it was so heavily publicized, was named after Spielberg's grandfather, himself a Russian Jewish immigrant. This is the sort of "personal touch" that undoubtedly looks great in press material, but really adds nothing to the overall product. Bluth got it right in THE SECRET OF NIMH, and if he can shake off the Spielbergian influences, he'll get it right again. The original songs by Cynthia Weil, James Horner, and Barry Mann include: "There Are No Cats in America" (performed by Nehemia Persoff, John Guarnieri, Warren Hays), "Never Say Never" (performed by Christopher Plummer, Phillip Glasser), "Somewhere Out There" (performed by Phillip Glasser, Betsy Cathcart), "A Duo" (performed by Dom DeLuise, Phillip Glasser), "Somewhere Out There (End Title Version)" (Linda Ronstadt, James Ingram). Also included was "Stars and Stripes Forever" (John Philip Sousa, performed by H.M. Royal Marines).

p, Don Bluth, John Pomeroy, Gary Goldman; d, Don Bluth; w, Judy Freudberg, Tony Geiss (based on a story by David Kirschner, Judy Freudberg, Tony Geiss); m, James Horner; ed, Dan Molina; m/l, Cynthia Weil, James Horner, Barry Mann; design & storyboard, Don Bluth; layout art, Mark Swan, Mark Swanson; animation d, John Pomeroy, Dan Kuenster, Linda Miller.

Animated Children's   (PR:AA MPAA:G)

AMIGOS*   (1986) 108m Manicato c

Ruben Rabasa *(Ramon)*, Reynaldo Medina *(Pablo)*, Lucy Pereda *(Magaly)*, Juan Granda *(Olmedo)* Armando Naser *(Gavilan)*, Blanca de abril *(Cecilia)* Lillian Hurst *(Mirta)*, Luisa Gil *(Consuelo)* Juan Troya *(Pellon)*, Dania Victor, Uva Clavijo, George Prince, Mercedes Enriquez, Celia De Munio, Manuel Estanillo, Ellen Cody, Carlos Bermudez, Tony Calbino.

An ambitious and admirable independent film which presents a more human and realistic view of the plight of the Mariel boat people—prisoners allowed to leave Castro's Cuba in 1980—than the one portrayed in Brian DePalma's bloody gangster epic SCARFACE (1983).

The story follows the hapless Rabasa, a Cuban who wound up in Castro's jail through a quirk of fate. After spending nearly two decades in prison, Rabasa suddenly finds himself released and on a boat headed for Miami. Suffering from culture shock, Rabasa is taken in by an old friend, Medina, whose family fled Cuba in 1958. A fervent anti-communist, Medina has worked his way into Miami's comfortable Cuban middle class by setting up a truck dealership and is about to marry his pretty fiance, Pereda. Though given support by Medina, Rabasa finds himself discriminated against by longtime Cuban-Americans because of the stigma surrounding the Mariel boat people (dangerous criminals, the mentally ill, and many retarded people were among the actual refugees) and he has difficulty finding work. To add to his troubles, Rabasa's ex-wife Gil (who had left him to rot in prison), turns out to have emigrated to Miami years ago and now seeks a reconciliation. The now-obese Gil is determined to recapture Rabasa's love, even if she has to use witchcraft to do so. After a series of frustrating setbacks while trying to land a steady job, the naive Rabasa is hoodwinked into driving a cache of contraband from Miami to Union City, New Jersey, for a sleazy Cuban crook (Troya). Rabasa's friends learn of Troya's plan and quickly take off after the gullible Cuban. Rabasa winds up in New York City, but luckily his friends find him before he can get into trouble. Reunited with his amigos, Rabasa uses the opportunity to go sightseeing in the Big Apple.

Written and directed by playwright Acosta, whose off-off Broadway play "El Super" garnered raves and was made into a movie by Leon Ichaso and Orlando Jimenez-Leal, AMIGOS is an insightful examination of the Cuban-American experience that pulls no punches and harbors no illusions. Acosta points a spotlight on the smug Cuban-American middle class who would rather spend their time fantasizing about another Bay Of Pigs-style attack on Castro than helping the refugees seeking employment. In addition to the biting social observations, Acosta also brings a great sense of warmth, humor, and compassion to his film and presents us with a well-balanced view of the characters that is as entertaining as it is enlightening. (In Spanish; English subtitles.)

p, Camilo Vila; d&w, Ivan Acosta; ph, Henry Vargas; m, Sergio Garcia-Marruz; ed, Gloria Pineyro; art d, Siro Del Castillo.

Drama   (PR:C MPAA:NR)

AMMA ARIYAN†   (1986, India) Odessa-People's Collective for Good Films
                                              (Trans: Report To Mother)

A film about the relationship between a mother and her son in which the son reports on the sufferings of humanity that he has encountered along his journeys.

d&w, John Abraham; ph, Venu.

Drama   (PR:NR MPAA:NR)

AMOR A LA VUELTA DE LA ESQUINA†   (1986, Mex.) 95m
                  Producciones Emyil/Azteca c (Trans: Love Around the Corner)

Gabriela Roel *(Maria)*, Alonso Echanove *(Julian)*.

The life of a Mexico City streetwalker, Roel, is presented in an episodic and dispassionate manner by Mexican filmmaker Calderon. Based on the novel *El Astralago [The Anklebone]* by Albertine Sarrazin, the film begins as Roel escapes from an unnamed institution by climbing over a wall (breaking her ankle in the process). She travels to Mexico City in search of a friend, and eventually drifts into prostitution, supplementing her income by stealing from her customers. As much of an enigma to her cliental as she is to the viewer, Roel maintains an odd relationship with two of her regular customers, showing slight affection for one, and degrading another. Sarrazin's novel was filmed previously in France as L'ASTRAGALE (1968). AMOR A LA VUELTA DE LA ESQUINA, Calderon's first feature length film, was shown in New York City as part of the 10th Latino Festival, and won first prize in the III Competition of experimental cinema.

p, Miguel Camacho; d&w, Alberto Cortes Calderon (based on the novel *El Astralago* by Albertine Sarrazin); ph, Guillermo Navarro; m, Jose Elorza; ed, Juan Manuel Vargas.

Drama   (PR:O MPAA:NR)

AMORE INQUIETO DI MARIA†   (1986, Ital.) Cooperativa il Mezzogiorno
                    Nuovo D'Italia/Casual Film c (Trans: Maria's Restless Love)

Jeannette Len, Giorgio Ardisson, Adriano Gallina, Simonetta Gallese, Italo Riccardi, Mike Jurla, Gianni Dei, Linda Christian.

A famous actress who had emigrated to Italy from Czechoslovakia tells a journalist her life story. Shown in flashback, she decides to leave her homeland and find fortune—just as her father, a noted violinist, had done many years before. In Rome, she meets with a renowned actress who was a friend of her father. Aided by the actress, the young Czech girl enters into a successful performing career of her own. After a failed love affair with a prominent Italian writer, the Czech actress becomes obsessed with finding her father and devotes her life to the search.

d&w, Sergio Pastore; ph, Domenico Paolercio (Agustus Color); m, Manna Di Napoli; ed, Gianfranco Amicucci.

Drama   (PR:C-O MPAA:NR)

AMOROSA†   (1986, Swed.) 117m Sandrew Film and Teater-Swedish Film
          Institute-Swedish Television SVT1/Sandrew Film and Teater c

Stina Ekblad *(Agnes von Krusenstjerna)*, Erland Josephson *(David Sprengel)*, Philip Zanden *(Adolf von Krusenstjerna)*, Peter Schildt *(Gerhard Odencrantz)*, Olof Thunberg *(Ernst von Krusenstjerna)*, Catherine de Seynes *(Eva von Krusenstjerna)*, Lauritz Falk *(Hugo Hamilton)*, Gunnel Brostrom *(Evelina Hamilton)*, Karin Forslind *(Eva Hamilton)*, Helene Friberg *(Viveka Hamilton)*, Efva Lilja *(Aimee Hamilton)*, Johan Rabeus *(Jan Guy Hamilton)*, Mimi Pollak *(Baroness Rosenhjelm)*, Borje Ahlstedt *(Joachim Rosenhjelm)*, Gosta Krantz *(Mr. Tollen)*, Inga Gill *(Mrs. Tollen)*, Aina Landgree *(Magnhild Tollen (Hanna Wanngard (Gota Tollen)*, Inga Landgree *(Klara)*, Margreth Weivers *(Beda Odencrantz)*, Henrik Schildt *(Frey Odencrantz)*, Johan Schildt *(Knut Odencrantz)*, Annelie Martini, Nils Eklund, Anita Bjork, Eva von Hanno, Heinz Hopf, John Zackarias, Sten Lonnert.

Agnes von Krusenstjarna was a Swedish writer whose private life was almost as notorious as her erotically charged novels. Born to a prominent family, Agnes (Ekblad) rejects it all to marry David Sprengel (Josephson), a hedonist who opens new vistas of sensuality to his young wife. The film is told in flashback from an opening that sees Ekblad suffering a nervous breakdown in Venice, then moving back to tell her whole story and her descent into madness. Director Zetterling has imbued her film with stunning production values, fine acting, and a marvelous amount of insight into the motivations and insanity of her subject.

p, Brita Werkmuster; d&w, Mai Zetterling; ph, Rune Ericson, Mischa Gavrjusjov (Fujicolor); m, Roger Wallis; ed, Darek Hodor, Mai Zetterling; art d, Jan Oqvist, Cecilia Iversen; cos, Gertie Lindgren, Kerstin Lokrantz; makeup, Johan Kindahl, Athanasios Vovolis.

Biography   (PR:O MPAA:NR)

ANAADI ANANT†   (1986, India) National Film Development Corporation
                                              (Trans: End Without End)

Surekha Sikri, Vasant Jasaljar, Suman Kumar.

A tale of a landowner and how he changes when, after 30 years of marriage, he is finally given an heir to his fortune.

p,d&w, Prakash Jha; ph, Rajan Kothari.

Drama   (PR:NR MPAA:NR)

ANANTARAM†   (1986, India) Ravi-General Pictures (Trans: The Rest of
                                                              the Story)

Mamootty, Sobbhana, Asokan, Adoor Bhasi, B.K. Nair, Vembayam Thampi.

A storyteller and stories he tells make up this entry dealing with human relationships on a mystical level.

d&w, Adoor Gopalakrishnan; ph, Ravi Varma.

Fantasy   (PR:C MPAA:NR)

ANCHE LEI FUMAVA IL SIGARO†   (1986, Ital.) Matthex's Coop./I.M.C.
                             c (Trans: She Too Smoked Cigars)

Maurizio Donadoni, Marietta Mehas, Haruko Yamanouchi, Alessandro Haber, Jole Silvani, Giovanni Rubens, Victor Poletti.

A disaffected urban youth meets up with a fascinating girl and becomes obsessed with her. In order to give the girl a gift, the youth tries to rob a local boutique but is caught by police. In a brutal battle the youth kills four policemen and is forced to take it on the lam. A determined policeman goes after the youth, but his efforts are constantly thwarted by the girl and her partner, a blind bar owner who has done several questionable favors for the cop in the past. The girl goes so far as to become the policeman's lover. While the youth plays this cat-and-mouse game with the cop, he is inspired to resurrect his passion for rock 'n' roll music. An ambitious music publisher signs the youth to a contract and is determined to make a star of him. On the night of his debut performance, the girl shows up to announce that the cop committed suicide and that he is now free from persecution. Opting for the girl over rock 'n' roll stardom, the youth abandons his budding musical career and leaves with the girl for parts unknown.

d, Alessandro di Robiland; w, Julio Salinas, Alessandro di Robiland; ph, David Scott; m, Tony Carnevale; ed, Ruggero Mastroianni.

Drama   (PR:O MPAA:NR)

ANEMIA†   (1986, Ital.) Rai Radiotelevisione c

Hanns Zischler, Gioia Maria Scola, Gerard Landry.

An aging Italian Communist Party leader is plagued by a morbid malaise that becomes an obsession with death and decay. In an effort to break this spell he takes time off to visit the home of his dead grandfather. There he finds his grandfather's diary and is shocked to discover that his elder was also possessed by the same morbid thoughts and nightmares. The house seems alive with fear and anxiety and the man begins to relive his grandfather's past.

d, Alberto Abruzzese, Achille Pisanti; w, Alberto Abruzzese, Achille Pisanti (based on the novel by Alberto Abruzzese); ph, Angelo Sciarra; m, Lorenzo Ferrero.

Drama **(PR:O MPAA:NR)**

ANGEL RIVER** (1986, U.S./Mex.) 92m Robert Renfield–Dasa c

Lynn-Holly Johnson *(Jensie)*, Salvador Sanchez *(Toral)*, Janet Sunderland *(Hannah)*, Peter Matthey *(Zach)*, Joey Shea *(Dee)*.

An old-fashioned tale with roots in the "Beauty and the Beast" legend, ANGEL RIVER is set on the Arizona frontier in the 1870s. Johnson, best known for her role as the skating star in ICE CASTLES, here plays a virginal young woman who lives with her parents on a remote ranch. One sunny day, while bathing in a nearby river, Johnson is spied upon by a leering Mexican bandido, Sanchez. Intent on capturing her beauty for himself, Sanchez abducts the girl, carries her off, and proceeds to beat and rape her. The following morning, Johnson wakens weakened from the previous evening's battle. Sanchez realizes that he has been a beast and nurses the battered girl back to health. They hole up in his cave hideout, where he devotes all his time and energy to serving the debilitated Johnson. When she does regain her strength, she plans her escape, only to be confronted by Sanchez, who refuses to let her go. Determined to flee, Johnson shoots Sanchez. Lying on the ground, bleeding profusely, Sanchez begs Johnson not to let him die there. Torn between her desire to escape and her obligation to nurse him as he did her, Johnson stays behind. She now tends to his wounds, bathing him and bringing him his dinner. Her curiosity also unearths a chest full of clothes, jewelry, and gems—a bandit's booty which he acquired over years of robbing. Sanchez showers Johnson with his riches as a sign of his love for her. The two grow to respect each other, and expose their true selves to each other, until they realize they are in love. Johnson, however, longs to return to her parents' ranch, fearful that they might think her dead. She becomes convinced that she can bring Sanchez home to meet her parents, pretending that he is the man who saved her from her abductor. When the pair reach the river near the ranch, however, they realize that they must separate. Johnson returns to her parents, while Sanchez heads back to the hills.

ANGEL RIVER is a thoroughly well-intentioned film that attempts to return to a long-lost idea of fairy tale-style romance. Johnson and Sanchez do what they can with their characters but neither of them is able to carry it off, more a criticism of the weak direction and dialog, which is too naive to prove effective. The filmmakers seem to understand the innocence of the "Beauty and the Beast" fairy tale, but there just isn't enough depth here to make it worthwhile for thinking audiences. On the other hand, there's far too much violence (the overly graphic and brutal rape scene oversteps the bounds of good taste and seems more exploitative than purposeful) to make this otherwise good-hearted love story presentable to youngsters.

p, Robert Renfield; d, Sergio Olhovich Greene; w, Robert Renfield (based on the novel *Rockspring* by Vilet); ph, Rosalio Solano; m, El Garcia Campos; ed, Victor Petrashevich, Suzanne Fenn; art d, Teresa Pecanins.

Romance/Drama **(PR:O MPAA:NR)**

ANGKOR-CAMBODIA EXPRESS* (1986, Thai./It.) 92m Network-Spectacular Trading/Monarex c

Robert Walker *(Andy Cameron)*, Christopher George *(MacArthur)*, Woody Strode *(Woody)*, Nancy Kwan *(Sue)*, Lui Leung Wai *(Mitr Saren)*, Sorapong Chatri *(Porn Pen)*, Nit Alisa *(Mieng)*, Suchao Pongwilai *(Montiri)*.

Filmed in 1981, but not seen in the U.S. until 1986 when it was released on videocassette, ANGKOR-CAMBODIA EXPRESS would have been better left unseen. Set in Thailand and Cambodia two years after the U.S. pulled out of Vietnam, the film follows American magazine journalist Walker as he returns to Cambodia to cover a press conference held by vicious Khmer Rouge warlord Wai. Feigning a stomach ache, Walker leaves the press conference and creeps off into the dark to meet with Alisa, his Cambodian girl friend who refused to flee her home country with him two years before. Now a member of the Khmer Rouge, and Wai's lover (both against her will), Alisa regrets not having fled with Walker. In an effort to reassure his love, Walker lovingly tells Alisa, "I could never throw away the memories of what we had in Pnompenh." Vowing to find a way to get her out of Cambodia, Walker leaves his love only to bump into another old friend, Pongwilai. A photographer, Pongwilai has negatives of a Khmer Rouge slaughter of civilians. He gives the film to Walker and begs him to tell the world of the atrocity. Unfortunately, both men are soon captured by Wai's Khmer Rouge. The pictures are confiscated, Pongwilai is killed, and Walker is tortured and released. Undeterred, Walker slogs through the jungles of Thailand to meet with renegade American general George who is now fighting the war on his own terms (shades of Colonel Kurtz in APOCALYPSE NOW). Known as Mad Mac because he calls himself MacArthur, George laughs off Walker's request for assistance in getting his girl friend out of Cambodia. George's trusted sergeant Strode, however, takes pity on Walker and quits the outfit to help him. Eventually there is a pitched battle among George's army, the Khmer Rouge, and even some Vietnamese. During the battle Strode is killed, Walker finds Alisa (who is suffering severe shrapnel wounds), and they try to make it to the Thailand-Cambodia border. At the river they encounter Wai blocking their path. After some intense hand-to-hand combat Walker and Alisa kill Wai, but then she soon dies from her wounds, leaving Walker to sit and yell "Why her?" to no one in particular.

Tedious, poorly filmed, and badly scripted, ANGKOR-CAMBODIA EXPRESS manages to drag out nearly every war-movie cliche in the book. The dialog is frequently laughable with such classically hackneyed lines as "There are many ways to make you talk" during the torture scene, and the old standby "So we meet again," uttered by Wai just before the climactic hand-to-hand contest. If the English dialog wasn't bad enough, there are several key scenes between the Thai actors that are spoken entirely in Thai (or Mon-Khmer if they are staying in character as Cambodians) without benefit of subtitles, leaving the audience totally in the dark as to what has occurred. Boasting a cast of down-and-out American actors, the film is a symphony of thespian mediocrity with Walker making a tiresome hero and George (complete with eye-patch and cigar) doing what looks like a parody of Robert Duval from APOCAYLPSE NOW. Although the 67-year-old Strode looks to be in incredible physical shape, he is just too old to be taken seriously in this enviornment and his appearance here makes one wonder if he really needs money that badly.

p, Lek Kitiparaporn, Richard Randall; d, Lek Kitiparaporn; w, Roger Crutchley, Kailan; ph, Roberto Forges Davanzati (Technicolor); m, Stelvio Cipriani; ed, Morris Goodyear; art d, U-Rai Sirisombat; set d, Anuchart Poomala, Kusarin Thamwong; spec eff, Eduardo Torrente, Bung Sarasuk; makeup, Renato Frankola, Cristeta Sanchez.

War/Drama **Cas.** **(PR:O MPAA:NR)**

ANGRY HARVEST† (1986, Ger.) 102m CCC Filmkunst–Admiral/European Classics c (BITTERE ERNTE)

Armin Mueller-Stahl *(Leon)*, Elisabeth Trissenaar *(Rosa)*, Kathe Jaenicke *(Anna)*, Hans Beerhenke *(Kaspar)*, Isa Haller *(Magda)*, Margit Carstensen *(Eugenia)*, Wojciech Pszioniak *(Cybolowski)*, Gerd Baltus *(Cleric)*, Anita Hofer *(Pauline)*, Kurt Raab *(Maslanko)*, Gunter Berger *(Walden)*, Wolf Donner *(Dan)*.

Mueller-Stahl is a Polish farmer who has found conditions under the German WWII occupation not so bad. He has taken over the house and lands of a wealthy Jew who fled, and does a profitable business selling off property similarly abandoned. His conscience bothers him slightly, but his priest tells him there's no sin in making money. While he is working in his fields one day, a woman (Trissenaar) emerges from the woods and tries to steal a loaf of bread. Mueller-Stahl catches her and discovers her to be a Jew who has escaped a deportation train along with her husband, from whom she has become separated. She is starving and feverish and Mueller-Stahl takes her back to her home, hides her in his basement, and nurses her back to health. His intentions are not entirely altruistic, though, and he is soon forcing himself upon her sexually. She is so dependent on him for her very survival that she accepts these embraces, and in time she comes to feel something akin to love for her captor/protector. Outside events doom her, though. When an old woman for whom Mueller-Stahl once worked dies, her middleaged daughter is sent to live with him. Mueller-Stahl tells Trissenaar that she will have to be moved somewhere else, but she takes this as a rejection by her lover and kills herself. Before he can hide the body, fighters from the local resistance group show up at his door, Trissenaar's husband among them. They ask if he has seen her and he tells them he hasn't. We last see him after the war, settled down with a buxom young wife and only moderately troubled by his conscience. Polish filmmaker Agnieszka Holland's first film since the imposition of martial law in Poland (while she was in Sweden) made her an exile. Nominated for an Academy Award for Best Foreign Language Film in 1985.

p, Peter Hahne; d, Agnieszka Holland; w, Agnieszka Holland, Paul Hengge (based on material by Hermann Field); ph, Josef Ort-Snep; m, Jorg Strassburger; ed, Barbara Kunze; set d, Werner Schwenke; cos, Hanne-Lore Wessel.

Drama **(PR:C MPAA:NR)**

ANNE TRISTER*** (1986, Can.) 115m National Canadian Film Office–Les Films Vision 4/Cine 360 c

Albane Guilhe *(Anne Trister)*, Louise Marleau *(Alix)*, Lucie Laurier *(Sarah)*, Guy Thauvette *(Thomas)*, Hugues Quester *(Pierre)*, Nuvit Ozdogru *(Simon)*.

One of the two best films to emerge from the Quebecois cinema in 1986 (the other is DECLINE OF THE AMERICAN EMPIRE), ANNE TRISTER is a slow-moving but often insightful portrait of a woman artist (Guilhe). The film opens with the funeral of her father in Israel. Soon thereafter Guilhe leaves her home in Switzerland to come to Montreal, where her father had long lived. There she meets an old friend of her father's, Ozdogru, who finds a studio in which she can work. She also renews a friendship with Marleau, a child psychologist who insists that Guilhe move out of her hotel and into her spacious apartment, despite the objections of Marleau's boy friend. Guilhe becomes obsessed with her work, turning the huge, crumbling studio into a massive work of art. Meanwhile, she grows further apart from her lover back in Switzerland and finds herself increasingly attracted to Marleau, who rejects her advances. Her project is almost completed when she falls off her scaffold and is seriously injured. While she is in the hospital, the entire building in which she had her studio is demolished, her months of work gone with it. Recovering back at Marleau's apartment, Guilhe is crushed to learn of the destruction, but she and Marleau do finally become lovers. They remain so only for a short time before Guilhe leaves Canada to return to Israel to visit the grave of her father. The film ends with Marleau receiving a letter from Guilhe containing a handful of sand and a film of herself at the gravesite, looking for the first time like someone at peace with herself.

The film is very carefully paced, and a great deal of the plot seems extraneous except to provide spaces between the important revelations of character. The performances of Guilhe and Marleau are superb, and a fascinating portrayal is also given by Laurier, a disturbed child patient of Marleau's (although the parallels the film attempts to draw between Laurier and Guilhe are muddy at best). Cinematographically the film is superb, full of muted colors and a marvelous sense of composition (cinematographer Mignot has recently been associated with Robert Altman on several films). A great success on the international film festival circuit, ANNE TRISTER is technically proficient, intelligent, sensitive, and ultimately rather uninvolving. (In French; English subtitles.)

p, Roger Frappier, Claude Bonin; d, Lea Pool; w, Lea Pool, Marcel Beaulieu; ph, Pierre Mignot; m, Rene Dupere; ed, Michel Arcand; art d, Vianney Gauthier.

Drama (PR:O MPAA:NR)

ANOTHER LOVE STORY**½   (1986, Arg.) 90m Instituto Nacional de Cinematografia Argentina/Juan Muruzeta c (OTRA HISTORIA DE AMOR)

Arturo Bonin, Mario Passik, Nelly Prono, Daniel Gelarza, Alicia Aller, Carlos Munoz, Roxana Berco, Maria Jose Demare, Hector Bidonde, Susana Cart.

Major breakthroughs in the treatment of homosexuals on-screen were seen in 1986 with the films MY BEAUTIFUL LAUNDRETTE and PARTING GLANCES. In light of these two successful ventures, ANOTHER LOVE STORY is a disappointment, presenting a simpleminded, cliched romance of star-crossed lovers who happen to be gay rather than straight. Bonin is a successful businessman in his early forties, trapped in a loveless marriage but with no real desire to leave the situation. Passik is a new man with Bonin's company who asks Bonin if they might speak in private. Once in Bonin's office, Passik admits an attraction for the older man and tells his shocked colleague that an affair would not be out of the question. At first Bonin doesn't know what to think, but he eventually agrees to meet Passik for coffee. Though initially hesitant, the older man finally has a liaison with Passik. This first encounter gradually builds into a genuine love affair, though both men realize it must be kept secret. One night, while the lovers are attending the movies, a secretary from their office spies the couple touching. She reports this to her superior and all hell breaks loose. The ensuing scandal turns the workplace upside down. Bonin is transferred to Madrid out of respect for his many years with the company. Passik is fired, however, and he angrily storms into the office, screaming that he has a right to love whomever he wants. With his marriage a shambles, Bonin seemingly has no choice but to accept the overseas transfer. Passik drives him to the airport and bids his lover a tearful adieu. The plane takes off but Passik is overjoyed to see Bonin waiting for him at the car, unable to leave the one person he truly loves.

If it weren't for the naked bodies, this could easily pass as an American "Problem of the Week" made-for-television movie. De Zarate's treatment of the subject is trite and unimaginative, parading a few stock characterizations through a prosaic series of events. When Bonin is first shown making love with his wife, the act is mechanical, with a look of bored detachment on the actor's face. This quickly establishes that he needs something to rejuvenate his life, be it male or female. In many ways, ANOTHER LOVE STORY is exactly what the title states, merely substituting a homosexual couple as the misunderstood lovers, rather than heterosexuals. De Zarate includes a particularly annoying character of an earthy, fun-loving aunt who tells nephew Bonin, "Love is a miracle, kiddo. Don't turn your back on it." It's exactly the sort of thing one would expect a character like this to say, and the line (albeit a true one) reeks of pretentious significance. To the film's credit, Bonin and Passik give intelligent performances, infusing their relationship with empathy and humor. Bonin's confusion about the situation and the sudden, unexpected changes in his life is bona fide, an honest performance that overcomes the slight script's limitations. Passik is a likeable rogue who also goes beyond de Zarate's simplistic ideas. The two actors—both popular Argentinian television stars and both heterosexual—worked together for two months in creating their characters before shooting commenced. Made just a few years after the fall of Argentina's military dictatorship, this film received 30 percent of its financing from the new national government.

d, Americo Ortiz de Zarate; w, Americo Ortiz de Zarate, Juan Carlos Brow; ph, Hector Morini; prod d, Aldo Guglielmone; set d, Juan Carlos Brown, Aldo Guglielmone.

Drama (PR:O MPAA:NR)

ANTICASANOVA†   (1986, Yugo.) Jadran–Master

David Bluestone, Ljubisa Samardzic, Elisa Tebith, Brigid O'Hara, Milena Dravic, Claudia Lyster, Semka Sokolovic-Bertok, Cintija Asperger.

d&w, Vladimir Tadej; ph, Goran Trbuljak; m, Arsen Dedic; set d, Vladimir Tadej.

APRIL FOOL'S DAY**   (1986) 88m Hometown/PAR c

Jay Baker (Harvey), Pat Barlow (Clara), Lloyd Berry (Ferryman), Deborah Foreman (Muffy/Buffy), Deborah Goodrich (Nikki), Tom Heaton (Potter/Uncle Frank), Mike Nomad (Buck), Ken Olandt (Rob), Griffin O'Neal (Skip), Leah King Pinsent (Nan), Clayton Rohner (Chaz), Amy Steel (Kit), Thomas F. Wilson (Arch).

Not content to simply disgust audiences with his ultra-violent, ultra-mindless FRIDAY THE 13TH series of slasher movies, producer Mancuso decided to put a spin on the tired formula by making a comedy out of it with the help of screen writer Bach (BEVERLY HILLS COP). Eight college friends—Baker, Goodrich, Olandt, O'Neal, Pinsent, Rohner, Steel, and Wilson—are invited for an April Fool's weekend party at the exclusive island mansion of heiress Foreman—a fellow classmate. On the ferryboat ride over, two of the boys play a practical joke that makes it appear that one of them, O'Neal (son of Ryan), is accidentally

stabbed. O'Neal falls into the water and several of the boys jump in to rescue him, only to discover it was all a put-on.

Real tragedy soon strikes, however, when one of the boys is seriously injured while trying to dock the boat. The victim is rushed off to the hospital by a local constable, Heaton, while the shaken friends walk to Foreman's mansion. Foreman greets her friends with a sly smile on her face which betrays the fact that they will soon be subjected to a seemingly endless series of April Fool's day jokes, including collapsing chairs, whoopee cushions, dribble glasses, squirting faucets, and the like. Suddenly things turn serious when O'Neal winds up missing, and soon several others appear to have been murdered. The guests are whittled away like Agatha Christie's "Ten Little Indians," each dispatched in a bloody manner by an unseen assassin. Soon Foreman begins acting strangely, and from clues left around the mansion the two survivors conclude that Foreman, who is named "Muffy," has an insane twin sister named "Buffy." Cornered by Foreman, the terrified couple dash into the dining room, only to find all their friends alive and well. It is revealed by Foreman that the whole thing was a big prank designed by her to test the feasibility of turning her mansion into a "murder-mystery weekend" resort where guests try and figure out a staged whodunit.

Mostly played for laughs, APRIL FOOL'S DAY is clever enough, but as is the case with all stalk-and-slash films, it becomes repetitive and boring very quickly. The gross-out effects are kept to a minimum, and the standard sexual scenes are handled fairly discreetly and are obviously meant to parody those in other slasher films. Foreman leads a cast of fairly likable youths, though none of them registers strongly. Shot on location in Victoria, British Columbia, there were actually two houses on the same property used during the six-week shoot. The exterior and the main floor interior were used in one house, and the crew shot in the upper-floor bedrooms from another house (this house also appeared in FIVE EASY PIECES). APRIL FOOL'S DAY did poorly at the box office, which, if we're lucky, means audiences won't be subjected to the incredible number of sequels that Mancuso's gratuitous and moronic spawn Jason has inspired. Songs include: "Too Bad You're Crazy" (Charles Bernstein, performed by Jerry Whitman, Linda Harmon, Angie Jane, Donna Davidson), "Mama Told Me Not to Come" (Randy Newman, performed by Three Dog Night).

p, Frank Mancuso, Jr.; d, Fred Walton; w, Danilo Bach; ph, Charles Minsky (Panavision, Metrocolor); m, Charles Bernstein; ed, Bruce Green; art d, Stewart Campbell; set d, Della Johnston; spec eff, Martin Becker, Reel SFX, Christopher Swift, Jim Gill, Bettie Kauffmann; m/l, Charles Bernstein, Randy Newman; stunts, John Wardlow.

Horror/Comedy Cas. (PR:O MPAA:R)

ARCTIC HEAT   (SEE: BORN AMERICAN, 1986, U.S./Fin.)

ARMED AND DANGEROUS*½   (1986) 88m Frostbacks/COL c

John Candy (Frank Dooley), Eugene Levy (Norman Kane), Robert Loggia (Michael Carlino), Kenneth McMillan (Clarence O'Connell), Meg Ryan (Maggie Cavanaugh), Brion James (Anthony Lazarus), Jonathan Banks (Clyde Klepper), Don Stroud (Sgt. Rizzo), Larry Hankin (Kokolovitch), Steve Railsback (The Cowboy), Robert Burgos (Mel Nedler), Tony Burton (Cappy), Robert Gray (Butcher), Larry Flash Jenkins (Raisin), Stacy Keach, Sr. (Judge), Bruce Kirby (Police Captain), Savely Kramarov (Olaf), Judy Landers (Noreen), Tom "Tiny" Lester, Jr. (Bruno), James Tolkan (Brackman), K.C. Winkler (Vicki), Glenn Withrow (Larry Lupik), David Wohl (Prosecutor), Melanie Gaffin (Little Girl), Ira Miler, Royce O. Applegate (Toxic Guards), John Solari (Dolan), David Hess (Gunman), Sharon Wyatt (BMW Woman), Joe Seely (Kid), Christine Dupree (Peep Show Girl), Richard Blum, Randolph L. Pitkin (Loaders), Nicholas Worth (Transvestite), Seth Kaufman (Gay Biker), Mark Carlton (Court Clerk), Sylvia Kauders (Older Woman at Party), Wilson Camp (Older Man at Party), Murray Lebowitz (Party Gent), Edith Fields (Party Guest), Lisa Figus (Woman at Party), J. Jay Saunders (Mayor), Lynn Vandegrift (Party Woman), Richard Walsh (Aerobics Instructor), Teagan Clive (Staff Member), Tina Plackinger, Susie Jaso (Health Club Women), Tito Puente (Band Leader), Nils Nichols (Senator), Martin Charles Warner (Porno Clerk), Rick Avery (Cobb), Christopher Mankiewicz (Plainclothes Detective).

We are always amazed when several first-rate talents combine to make a third-rate picture. On paper, a cast including John Candy, Eugene Levy, Robert

Loggia, and Steve Railsback, and a script by another pair of SCTV alumni should have been a rollicking success. However, movies are made on film, not on paper, and the resultant picture falls apart as director Lester failed to take advantage of the talents of his cast. Candy is a former police officer who lost his job when he was framed. Levy is a one-time attorney who has been disbarred for incompe-

tence. Faced with no employment, both men take jobs as security guards at a bare minimum wage. (Levy had already done this role as a dopey guard at the SCTV station). The security company is owned by McMillan, who is frightened by the power of Loggia, the union mob boss who seems to have everyone under his control. Ryan, who plays McMillan's daughter, (she was outstanding in TOP GUN) is one of the bright spots in the generally forced proceedings. The movie is flat, often pushy, and has none of the bubbling joy of the SCTV sketches that Candy and Levy illuminated with their presence. Set pieces are tossed in every few minutes in a vain reach for laughter but, under Lester's sloppy hand (his previous credits include such "comedies" as COMMANDO, STEEL ARENA, TRUCK STOP WOMEN, and ROLLER BOOGIE), there is very little to laugh at. These scenes include the protagonists being placed in a toxic dump, getting trapped in a warehouse guarded by vicious dogs (Candy gets out of this by kicking and biting the dogs), finding themselves in a steam room, a pornography store, a Mexican restaurant, a health club, a Bel-Air mansion, and more and more. Candy spends most of his time dressing up in one outrageous costume after another, including one get-up where he resembles Johnny Madden in a "Divine" (LUST IN THE DUST) outfit. Levy also revels in the costumery by wearing a gay leather get-up. But costumes alone do not a comedy make, nor do car chases. The final chase sequence has autos piling up with wanton abandon. Candy gets to pilot an oil rig and a huge motorcycle while dressed in a WW I German pilot's uniform. The plot is inconsequential and will be easily spotted by anyone who watched Mack Sennett comedies. ARMED AND DANGEROUS owes a great deal to the early Keystone shorts as well as more than just a passing nod to POLICE ACADEMY, BEVERLY HILLS COP, and any number of similar lightweight spoofs. Note Larry Hankin as a doltish guard. Hankin spent many years in an improvisation troupe in San Francisco but will best be recalled for a serious role in ESCAPE FROM ALCATRAZ. Railsback does a small bit as "Cowboy" and his talents are wasted. A large bringdown for the actor who was THE STUNT MAN as well as Charles Manson in TV's "Helter Skelter." This could have been a funny film, and it does begin well as Candy and Levy are inducted into the security guard business and given all of two hours' training before they assume their jobs. The number of Canadians in the cast makes us wonder if the picture wasn't done under the "Canadian Content" rule that used to apply in order to qualify for aid from the government. It was that rule that caused SCTV's Rick Moranis and Dave Thomas to do their "Great White North" sketches featuring the boorish "McKenzie Brothers" who later starred in their own film, STRANGE BREW. The house seen in the movie is the famed Kirkeby Estate which was, in 1987, valued at more than $25 million. TV fans will recognize it as the home where "The Beverly Hillbillies" lived. But when the sets are more intriguing than the characters and the story, you know a movie is in trouble. And so it was here. Now, filmmakers will have to wait a few more years before tackling another comedy about the multi-billion dollar private security business. Lots of music from several sources to brighten up the sound track by Bill Meyers (additional music by James Di Pasquale). They include: "Armed and Dangerous" (Maurice White, Garry Glenn, Martin Page, performed by Maurice White), "Candy's Theme" (Bill Meyers, Maurice White, performed by Bill Meyers), "Steppin' Into the Night" (Garry Glenn, Dianne Quander, performed by Cheryl Lynn), "The Walls Came Down" (Martin Page, performed by Eve), "She's My Man" (Martin Degville, Tony James, Neal Whitmore, performed by Sigue Sigue Sputnik), "That's The Way It Is" (Michael Henderson, performed by Michael Henderson), "Respect, Respect, Respect!" (Dan Serafini, performed by United Streets of America), "I Need You" (Priscilla J. Coolidge, William Smith, Mary Unobsky,

performed by Maurice White), "Some Kind of Day" (Glen Burtnick, Bill Meyers, performed by Glen Burtnick), "Oye Como Va" (written and performed by Tito Puente and his Latin Ensemble), plus four tunes written by Michael Melvoin, "Our Thing," "You're The V.I.P.," "Shake it Up," "We're Dancing." The album from this picture is more fun than the picture.

p, Brian Grazer, James Keach; d, Mark L. Lester; w, Harold Ramis, Peter Torokvei (based on a story by Brian Grazer, Harold Ramis, James Keach); ph, Fred Schuler (DeLuxe Color); m, Bill Meyers, James DiPasquale; ed, Michael Hill, Daniel Hanley, Gregory Prange; prod d, David L. Snyder; set d, Tom Pedigo; cos, Deborah L. Scott; spec eff, Mike Wood; makeup, Ben Nye, Jr.; stunts, Alan Gibbs.

Comedy   (PR:C   MPAA:PG-13)

ARMED RESPONSE*½   (1986) 86m CineTel c

David Carradine *(Jim Roth)*, Lee Van Cleef *(Burt Roth)*, Mako *(Akira Tanaka)*, Lois Hamilton *(Sara Roth)*, Ross Hagen *(Cory Thorton)*, Brent Huff *(Tommy Roth)*, Laurene Landon *(Deborah Silverstein)*, Dick Miller *(Steve)*, Michael Berryman *(F.C.)*, David Goss *(Clay Roth)*, Sam Hione *(Jackie Hong)*, Dah've Seigler *(Lauren Roth)*, Conan Lee *(Kon Ozu)*, Burr DeBenning *(Lt. Sanderson)*, Susan Stokey *(Judy)*, Bob Hevilon *(Nate)*, Kai Baker *(Pam)*, Bobbie Bresee *(Anna)*, Michelle Bauer *(Dancer)*, Dawn Wildsmith, Dave O'Hara *(Thugs)*, Fred Olen Ray, Jimmy Williams *(Soldiers)*, Pat Culliton *(Patrolman)*, Richard Lee Sung *(Kenji)*, Cary Tagawa *(Toshi)*, Brad Arrington *(Dealer)*, Jerry Fox *(Club Owner)*, Lisa Hayward *(Mother)*, Lauren Hertzberg *(Young Girl)*, Jordan Hertzberg *(Young Boy)*, Hisako Mura *(Vietnamese Girl)*, Mayann Zvoleff *(Prostitute)*.

With Carradine, Van Cleef, and Mako in the cast, this had the potential to be a better-than-average low-budget action film. Too bad little attention was paid to the poor quality of the script and the downright bad performances from certain members of the supporting cast. Set in Los Angeles' Chinatown, the film begins as a Japanese *Yakuza* (gangster) hacks off his little finger to atone for the theft of a valuable jade statue. The patriarch of the clan, Mako, accepts the apology and sends the thief off. As the thief expresses relief to his girl friend for having gotten

off so easily, the two are blown up in their car. Mako desperately needs the statue, for it is a gift that he has promised the leader of the Chinese tong as an atonement for encroaching on Chinese-mob territory. Mako orders his men to find out to whom the dead thief sold the statue.

The film cuts to a Chinatown bar owned by Vietnam vet Carradine, the eldest son in a tightly knit family led by retired cop Van Cleef. Carradine's brother, Huff, is a Vietnam vet as well, and their younger brother, Goss, works as a private detective. These men take no guff from anyone, and prove that they are very adept at tossing loudmouthed toughs out of the bar. Mako discovers that his statue is now in the hands of crook Miller and his Amazonian partner Landon. The Japanese mobster hires Goss and his sleazy partner Hagen to meet the crooks and deliver $500,000 for the jade statue. At a meeting in the desert, the wily Hagen double-crosses Miller and Landon and tricks Goss into shooting them both. When Hagen's men suddenly arrive on the scene, Goss assumes they are associates of Miller and Landon, and he kills them as well. Realizing that he now has the perfect chance to collect all the money, Hagen shoots Goss in the stomach. Goss manages to make his way home with the jade statue, but he falls dead before providing a clue to the identity of his killer.

Meanwhile, Hagen calls Mako and tells him that it was Goss who engineered the double-cross and made off with both the statue and the money. Mako sends his men to Carradine's house to recover the statue. Soon all-out war erupts between Mako and Carradine's clan. Younger brother Huff is caught while trying to uncover evidence at Mako's headquarters, and he is tortured and killed. In the meantime, Carradine discovers that Hagen was his brother Goss' killer, but the unscrupulous private eye manages to escape, only to be caught by the now-crazed, Landon who has survived her wounds and now demands the money. Desperate to reclaim the statue, Mako has Carradine's wife and child kidnaped and tells Carradine he will release one for the statue and the other for the money. Carradine protests that he doesn't have the money, but Mako doesn't believe him and responds by saying that it is up to Carradine to chose which of his loved ones will live.

Carradine arranges the exchange with Mako, while Van Cleef waits in the wings in case of trouble. Mako, too, has a small army posted nearby, and after mother and daughter are safe, a massive gunfight ensues. When the smoke clears only Mako, Van Cleef (who has returned to the bar with the women), Carradine, and Mako's grotesque henchman Berryman survive. Mako tries to make off with the jade statue, but Carradine rigged it with explosives and it blows the *Yakuza* to smithereens. Carradine rejoins his family at the bar, but Berryman crashes his car into the building and tries to kill him. Berryman wounds Carradine, but the bar owner's pacifist wife grabs her husband's gun and finishes the creepy gangster off. The family is reunited, and we see that the sleazy Hagen has wound up dead in the bottom of a river.

Dull and utterly predictable, ARMED RESPONSE is nearly saved by a self-deprecating sense of humor which employs some funny dialog and a sense of film history. References are made to those stereotypical movie portrayals of Orientals found in the films of the past. The opening scene is a direct reference to the best of the Hollywood East-meets-West films, THE YAKUZA. In the torture scene Mako remarks how absurd it is that in this day and age we have the " . . . evil yellow man torturing the heroic white hero," and just before the climactic battle, a MR. WONG film is seen playing on television. There are subtle references to THE MALTESE FALCON as well, but all of this is just an interesting subtext to a film that doesn't do much to break the stereotypes. What could have been an interesting look at the rivalry between the Japanese and Chinese underworlds is only talked about, and the film becomes simply a family revenge tale. You've seen it all before. Carradine's character is poorly developed and, of course, being a Vietnam vet he is plagued by badly staged flashbacks of his war experiences (an animal park in Riverside, California doubled for the tropical jungles of Vietnam—and it's painfully obvious). Carradine can be an effective actor when given a good role, but his heart wasn't in this one. Van Cleef manages to inject some life into his scenes, but he vanishes for practically half the film. Huff and Goss are such anonymous talents that it is apparent to anyone who's ever seen a movie before that they'll soon wind up dead, and the women in the film, with the exception of the little girl (Seigler), are awful. Hagen makes memorable villain; Miller, as usual, does wonders with nothing in a small role; and Berryman is always a strong visual presence; but only Mako generates any real interest, for he brings some personality to his character that obviously wasn't in the script. Even if one doesn't expect much of ARMED RESPONSE, it is still a disappointment. Background songs include: "Over Night Sensation" (Rick Phillips, performed by Abandon Shame), "Emily" (Jace Smith, performed by "Jace"), "Kicks" (Rick Philips, Tane Cain, performed by Tane Cain), "Mad Hateress" (Tomas Chase, Steve Rucker, performed by Tomas Chase, Steve Rucker), "Love is Just a Heartbeat" (James Saad, Jeannie Cunningham, performed by Jeannie Cunningham), "Bag Man" (Gary Wallis, performed by Gary Wallis), "Feel Me" (Barry Trop, Barry Levinson, performed by The Flix).

p, Paul Hertzberg; d, Fred Olen Ray; w, T.L. Lankford (based on a story by Paul Hertzberg, Fred Olen Ray, T.L. Lankford); ph, Paul Elliott (United Color); m, Tom Chase, Steve Rucker; ed, Miriam L. Preissel; art d, Maxine Shepard; spec effects, Douglas J. White, John R. Fifer, Allan A. Apone; m/l, Rick Phillips, Jace Smith, Tane Cain, Tomas Chase, Steve Rucker, James Saad, Jeannie Cunningham, Gary Wallis, Barry Trop, Barry Levinson.

Crime   Cas.   (PR:O MPAA:R)

ARMOUR OF GOD, THE†   (1986, Hong Kong) 98m Golden Harvest/Toho-
                                                                    Towa c

Jackie Chan *(Jackie, Hawk of Asia)*, Alan Tam *(Alan)*, Rosamund Kwan *(Loralie)*, Lola Forner *(May)*, Bosidale Sumiljanik *(Count)*, Ken Boyle *(Conjurer)*, Mars, Brackie Fong, Alicia Shawnte, Marcia Chizam, Vivian Wickliff, Linda Denly.

Chan (the biggest movie star in the Orient) directs himself here as a superspy who is working to gather the pieces of a fantastic suit of armor dating from the crusades. Working against him are two factions, one led by Forner (Miss Spain of 1980), the other by a bunch of pseudo-monks fond of staging orgies in their monastery. Chan fights swarms of villains in his usual impressive manner, but most of the film is a waste, rife with bad writing, worse dubbing, and lackluster direction. Shot largely in Yugoslavia, this film is probably most noted (in Hong Kong, at least) for nearly costing Chan his life in a stunt gone awry. As the credits roll at the end, the audience is treated to scenes of Chan, bloody, being carried off on a stretcher.

p, Chua Lum; d, Jackie Chan; w, Edward Tang (based on a story by Barry Wong from an idea by Eric Tsang); ph, Bob Tompson, Peter Nakaguro Ngor (Technicolor); m, Michael Rai; ed, Cheung Yiu Chung; art d, William Cheung.

Martial Arts   (PR:O MPAA:NR)

AROUND THE WORLD IN EIGHTY WAYS†   (1986, Aus.) 91m Palm
                                                                    Beach Entertainment c

Philip Quast *(Wally Davis)*, Allan Penney *(Roly Davis)*, Gosia Dobrowolska *(Nurse Ophelia Cox)*, Diana Davidson *(Mavis Davis)*, Kelly Dingwall *(Eddie Davis)*, Rob Steele *(Alec Moffat)*, Judith Fisher *(Lotte Boyle)*, Jane Markey *(Miserable Midge)*, John Howard *(Dr. Proctor)*, Frank Lloyd *(Mr. Tinkle)*, Cathren Michalak *(Mrs. Tinkle)*, Ric Carter *(Financier)*, Jack Allan *(Mailman)*,

Nell Schofield *(Scottish Scrooge)*, Kaarin Fairfax *(Checkout Chick)*, Micki Gardner, Helen Simon, Elizabeth Burton *(Geisha Girls)*.

An original comedy from beyond the Equator, AROUND THE WORLD IN EIGHTY WAYS tells the story of a senile, crippled, and nearly blind old man, Penney, who decides to follow his younger wife on a round-the-world junket when he discovers that she will be accompanied by his hated neighbor and business rival, Steele. His two sons, Quast and Dingwall, concoct a scheme to convince their father that he is traveling around the world when he actually remains in his own backyard, while the two sons pocket the money he was going to spend. To this end Quast assumes a variety of disguises, ranging from a geisha girl to Elvis Presley, while Dingwall, a sound effects expert, works to make the auditory illusion perfect. They further enlist the help of nurse Dobrowolska. The whole illusion works almost perfectly: so well, in fact, that Penney begins to recover some of his old vigor. His mind clears. He begins to walk and dance. Even his vision returns. While the old man has the time of his life, his wife and rival encounter nothing but misery throughout their trip. The trip ends with Penney fully recovered and wreaking vengeance on Steele's home. An unusual film to come from down under, where broad comedies like CROCODILE DUNDEE or the BARRY MACKENZIE films are the norm, although films like this and BLISS are starting to show a loopier, more cerebral side of the Australian humor.

p, David Elfick, Steve Knapman; d, Stephen Maclean; w, Stephen Maclean, Paul Leadon; ph, Louis Irving (Colorfilm); m, Chris Neal; ed, Marc von Buuren; prod d, Lissa Coote; cos, Clarrissa Patterson.

Comedy   (PR:C-O MPAA:NR)

ARRIVING TUESDAY†   (1986, New Zealand) 90m Cinepro-New Zealand
                                                    Film Commission-Walker c

Judy McIntosh *(Monica)*, Peter Hayden *(Nick)*, Rawiri Paratene *(Riki)*, Heather Bolton, Lee Grant, Te Paki Cherrington, Sarah Peirse.

McIntosh returns home to New Zealand after spending nearly a year living in Europe. She attempts to renew her affair with artist Hayden, but in the months she has been gone they have drifted apart. She talks him into accompanying her on a vacation to the North Island. There they meet Paratene, a Maori poet who tells them about the permanent damage to the islands wreaked by the European settlers. Tired of this implicit criticism and noting the increasing attraction between McIntosh and Paratene, Hayden decides to cancel the trip and return home, and forcing McIntosh to make up her mind. She decides to continue on alone and eventually reaches some kind of conclusion about her home, her love, and her identity. Rife with themes common to New Zealand cinema (the dislocation of being a European country in the south Pacific; guilt over treatment of Maoris), the film does manage to avoid the single greatest cliche of New Zealand films, the omnipresent Bruno Lawrence.

p, Don Reynolds, Chris Hampson; d, Richard Riddiford; w, Richard Riddiford, David Copeland; ph, Murray Milne; m, Scott Calhoun; ed, John McWilliams; prod d, Roger Guise.

Drama   (PR:O MPAA:NR)

ARTHUR'S HALLOWED GROUND½**   (1986, Brit.) 84m
                                    Enigma-Goldcrest-Techno Sunley Leisure/Cinecom c

Jimmy Jewel *(Arthur)*, Jean Boht *(Betty)*, David Swift *(Lionel)*, Michael Elphick *(Len)*, Derek Benfield *(Eric)*, Va Blackwood *(Henry)*, John Flanagan *(Norman)*, Bernard Gallagher *(George)*, Sam Kelly *(Sales Representative)*, Al Ashton *(Billy)*, Mark Drewry *(Kev)*.

An old man's obstinate refusal to change his standards runs up against modern pragmatism in this entry in the "First Love" series of British executive producer David Puttnam. Jewel is a groundskeeper who has been tending the same small cricket field for almost 50 years, refusing to cant the field to favor the home team (as his detractors insist every other team does) and refusing to retire so that team owner Elphick can spend less on maintenance and more on players and comforts for the fans. A government program forces him to take on a black youth as an assistant, and he goes out of his way to make the lad, Blackwood, uncomfortable. Predictably, by the end of the film, Jewel has seen the light and turned into a lovable codger.

p, Chris Griffin; d, Freddie Young; w, Peter Gibbs; ph, Chic Anstiss (Kay Color); ed, Chris Risdale; cos, Tudor George.

Drama   (PR:C MPAA:NR)

ARUNATA PERA†   (1986, Sri Lanka) 80m New Wave bw (Trans: Before
                                                                    the Dawn)

Wijertna Warakagoda *(Banda)*, Chandi Rasika *(Menika)*, D.M. Denawaka Hamine *(Banda's Mother)*, Joe Dambulugala *(Landlord)*, Ranjeewa Amarajit Jayatilaka *(Eldest Child)*, Sundeep Sanjaya Jayatilaka *(Youngest Child)*, Madhuri Anjana Jayatilaka *(Daughter)*.

The big winner at the film awards sponsored by the government of Sri Lanka and, as such, arguably that nation's finest cinematic achievement in 1986, ARUNATA PERA tells, in a complicated structure, the story of a man who has his crops confiscated for nonpayment of debts, gets thrown into jail, then returns to find that his wife has died in chilbirth. It is intended as the first installment of a trilogy on Sri Lankan peasants.

p, Ananda Gunasekara; d, Amarnath Jayatilaka; w, Amarnath Jayatilaka, Kumara Karunaratna (based on a story by Kumara Karunaratna); ph, Suminda

Weerasingha; m, W.B. Makuloluwa; ed, Elmo Holliday; prod d, Joe Dambulugala.

Drama (PR:A-C MPAA:NR)

AS SETE VAMPIRAS† (1986, Braz.) 100m Embrafilme-Superoito/ Embrafilme c (Trans: The Seven Female Vampires)

Alvamar Tadei, Andrea Beltrao, Ariel Coelho, Bene Nunes, Cole, Carlo Mossi, Danielle Daumerri, Dedina Bernadelli, Felipe Falcao, Ivon Curi, John Herbert, Leo Jaime, Lucelia Santos, Nicole Puzzi, Nuno Leal Maia, Pedro Cardoso, Simone Carvalho, Suzana Matos, Tania Boscoli, Wilson Grey, Zeze Macedo.

Ivan Cardoso, once one of the most experimental of Brazilian filmmakers, pays homage to his favorite stars and horror films of the 1950s in this picture. Bene Nunes, Zeze Macedo, and a few others were all major Brazilian celebrities when the director was a youngster, and he troops them out for his cameras here, along with a thin plot about a man-eating plant, a mad scientist who turns into a vampire, and a gaggle of show girls. Cardoso has tapped this vein before, with O SEGREDO DA MUMIA.

p, Ivan Cardoso, Mauro Taubman, Claudio Klabin, Antonio Avilez, Flavio Holanda, Skylight; d, Ivan Cardoso; w, R.F. Lucchetti; ph, Carlos Egberto Silveira (Eastmancolor); m, Julio Medaglia; ed, Gilberto Santeiro; art d, Oscar Ramos; spec eff, Antonio Pacheco; ch, Carlos Wilson; m/l, Leo Jaime; makeup, Antonio Pacheco.

Horror/Comedy (PR:O MPAA:NR)

ASESINATO EN EL SENADO DE LA NACION (SEE: MURDER IN THE SENATE, 1986, Arg.)

ASILACK KADIN† (1986, Turkey) (Trans: A Woman to be Hanged)

Mujde Ar, Yalcin Dumer, Guler Okten, Can Kolukisa, Haldun Erguvenc.

d&w, Basar Sabuncu (based on the novel by Pinar Kur); ph, Ertunc Senkay.

ASILO DI POLIZIA (SEE: DETECTIVE SCHOOL DROPOUTS, 1986, U.S./Ital.)

ASSAULT, THE**** (1986, Netherlands) 155m Cannon c

Derek de Lint *(Anton Steenwijk)*, Marc van Uchelen *(Anton as a Boy)*, Monique van de Ven *(Truus Coster/Saskia de Graaff)*, John Kraaykamp *(Cor Takes)*, Huub van der Lubbe *(Fake Ploeg/His Father)*, Elly Weller *(Mrs. Beumer)*, Ina van der Molen *(Karin Korteweg)*, Frans Vorstman *(Father Steenwijk)*, Edda Barends *(Mother Steenwijk)*, Caspar De Boer *(Peter Steenwijk)*, Wim de Haas *(Mr. Korteweg)*, Hiske van der Linden *(Karin as a Young Girl)*, Piet de Wijn *(Mr. Beumer)*, Akkemay *(Sandra)*, Kees Coolen *(Gerrit-Jan)*, Eric van Heijst *(Mr. DeGraaff)*, Mies de Heer *(Elisabeth)*, Olliver Domnick *(SD Officer)*, Amadeus August *(Haupsturmfuhrer)*, Matthias Hell *(Sergeant)*, Horst Reichel *(Officer)*, Ludwig Haas *(General)*, Mike Bendig *(Fake Ploeg as a Boy)*, Michel van Rooij *(Cor Takes as a Young Man)*, Guus Hermus *(Mr. van Lennep)*, Manon Alving *(Mrs. de Graaff)*, Tabe Bas *(Jaap)*, Cas Baas *(Henk)*, Okke Jager *(Vicar)*, Eric van der Ronk *(Simon)*, Ab Abspoel *(Man in Cafe)*, Pierre Bokma, Fillip Bolluyt, Willem van de Sande Bakhuijzen, Jan Pieter Koch, Gijs de Lange, Kees Hulst *(Students)*, Kenneth Oakley *(Westminster Abbey Guide)*, Eric van der Hoff *(Bastiaan)*, Krijn ter Braak *(Uncle Peter)*, Nico Jansen *(Police Sergeant)*, Willem van Ransum *(Prison Guard)*, Lex Wiertz *(Herring Dealer)*, Karl Golusda, Harold Bendig *(Officers)*, Monique Spijker *(Servant Girl)*, Paula Petri *(Woman in Window)*, Norman Longdon *(English General)*, Lisa Takacs *(Sandra as a Young Girl)*.

A powerful motion picture that asks more questions than it answers, THE ASSAULT will haunt the memory of anyone who lived through WW II. It takes place over a 40-year period and begins in Holland (where it was shot in its entirety, except for one brief scene at Westminster Abbey in London) as the war is waning, and the Nazis realize they will be beaten. Uchelen is a young lad living at home with his family, de Boer, Barends, and Vorstman. They are dining by candlelight one night (curfew is in effect) when they see a local collaborator, der

Lubbe, riding his bike. He is shot by a sniper and dies in front of their neighbor's home. Der Lubbe's son is Bendig, a pal of Uchelen's despite the fact that the father works with the Nazis. Fearing that they will be blamed, the family watches in horror as their neighbors pull the dead body in front of their home. De Boer runs outside to drag the body away but, by that time, the Nazis are everywhere. The family is arrested and shot, the house is burned, and the little boy is taken to a prison cell where he meets a jailed saboteur, van de Ven. She is very kind to the frightened boy but then she is taken away and executed. Uchelen grows up with relatives and becomes de Lint.

The picture then marches across several decades as he becomes a physician, meets and marries van de Ven (who plays two roles), sires a child, etc. The memory of that bleak night haunts the anesthesiologist, and he keeps trying to understand why it happened as the movie records the years 1952, 1956, 1966, and 1984, through the use of historical touchstones, such as Korea, Hungary, Vietnam, and, at the conclusion, the protest march against the implacement of missiles in Europe. (This was the first scene shot, and it was lensed during the actual demonstrations). It is here that de Lint learns the truth about what happened. The neighbors, de Has and van der Linden, had been, like so many brave Dutch people, harboring a Jewish family in their home and feared that the Nazis might come into the house, find the Jews, and kill them all. At the missile demonstration, de Lint meets the now-aged van der Molen (van der Linden as an adult), who never married, and she admits the truth, thus ending de Lint's four-decade search for the truth. In the course of the film, we've watched a boy grow into a man who finally finds the reason for his family's deaths.

THE ASSAULT was winner of the Academy Award for Best Foreign Film and also won the Best Film and Best Direction awards at the 1986 Seattle International Film Festival. It's a powerful indictment of the Nazi horror although it seldom editorializes. Rather, it resembles more a documentary piece than one that has been scripted and acted. The use of voice-over narration is tasteful, and there is just enough newsreel footage to lend authenticity without the appearance of padding. Based on a best-selling book by a man whose Jewish mother was killed

in a concentration camp and whose father was a collaborator with the Nazis, the film is faithful to the author's story, with the location shooting adding greatly to its credibility. Interiors were shot in Almere, a small town near Amsterdam, and exteriors in Haarlem. De Lint's career took off after this film with leading roles in three other films following in quick succession. Miss de Ven will be remembered as the star of TURKISH DELIGHT and KAATJE TIPPEL. She is married to cinematographer Jan De Bont (CLAN OF THE CAVE BEAR, RUTHLESS PEOPLE). Although THE ASSAULT begins as a picture about the war, it is more an exploration of the people whose lives were torn apart by the Nazi occupation. A serious movie that will provoke thoughts. Music performed by the Rotterdam Philharmonic. One song, "Tombe La Neige" (performed by Adamo). (In Dutch; English subtitles.)

p&d, Fons Rademakers; w, Gerard Soeteman (based on the novel by Harry Mulisch); ph, Theo van de Sande (Fujicolor); m, Jurriaan Andriessen; ed, Kees Linthorst; md, Rogier van Oterloo; art d, Dorus van der Linden; set d, Allard Bekker; cos, Anne-Marie van Beverwijk; spec eff, Harry Wiesenhaan; makeup, Ulli Ullrich.

Drama (PR:C MPAA:PG)

ASTERIX CHEZ LES BRETONS† (1986, Fr./Den.) 78m Gaumont-Dargaud-Gutenberghus c (Trans: Asterix in Britain)

Voices: Roger Carel *(Asterix)*, Pierre Tornade *(Obelix)*, Pierre Mondy *(Cetinlapsus)*, Serge Sauvion *(Caesar)*, Nicolas Silberg *(Motus)*, Graham Bushnell *(Jolitorax)*.

This followup to 1985's ASTERIX VS. CESAR is another animated adventure involving the little hero Asterix, his slow but amiable partner Obelix, and their lovable pooch Idefix. This time the trio is off to merry old England where that old nemesis Cesar is trying to invade the hometown of Asterix's British cousin. Like the original, this was adapted from the popular cartoon books by Goscinny and Uderzo.

p, Yannick Piel; d, Pino Van Lamsweerde; w, Pierre Tchernia (based on the cartoon album by Rene Goscinny, Alberto Uderzo); ph, Philippe Laine

(Eastmancolor); ed, Robert Insnardon, Monique Isnardon; art d, Michel Guerin; anim d, Keith Ingham; m/l, Vladimir Cosma, Jeff Jordan.

Animation   **(PR:AA   MPAA:NR)**

AT CLOSE RANGE****½   (1986) 111m Hemdale/Orion c

Sean Penn *(Brad Whitewood, Jr.)*, Christopher Walken *(Brad Whitewood, Sr.)* Mary Stuart Masterson *(Terry)*, Christopher Penn *(Tommy Whitewood)*, Millie Perkins *(Julie Whitewood)*, Eileen Ryan *(Grandmother)*, Alan Autry *(Ernie)*, Candy Clark *(Mary Sue)*, R.D. Call *(Dickie Whitewood)*, Tracey Walter *(Patch)*, J.C. Quinn *(Boyd)*, David Strathairn *(Tony Pine)*, Jake Dengel *(Lester)* Crispin Glover *(Lucas)*, Kiefer Sutherland *(Tim)*, Noelle Parker *(Jill)*, Stephen Geoffreys *(Aggie)*, Paul Herman *(Salesman)*, Gary Gober *(District Attorney)*, Marshall Fallwell, Jr. *(Bartender)*, Doug Anderson *(Marshall)*, Nancy Sherburne *(Waitress)*, Terry Baker *(Customer)*, Michael Edwards, Myke R. Mueller *(Car Salesmen)*, Bob McDivitt *(Farmer with Shotgun)*, Bonita Hall *(Buxom Woman)*, Terri Coulter, Anna Levine *(Barroom Dancers)*, Janie Draper *(Stripper)*, Charles "Tatoo" Jensen *(Older Guy)*, E.R. Davies *(Detective Mosker)*, James Foley *(Assistant District Attorney)*.

One of the most chilling and realistic crime films to hit the screen in recent years, AT CLOSE RANGE is a deeply disturbing experience that features unforgettable performances by Walken and Sean Penn. Based on actual events that took place in Pennsylvania in 1978 (though the film was shot in Tennessee), the film follows the fresh-out-of-high-school Penn as he struggles against the boredom of his rural existence. Living in a run-down house with his half-brother Christopher Penn (Sean's real-life brother), his grandmother, Ryan (the Penn boys' real mother), and his mother, Perkins, Sean fills his time tinkering with his pick-up truck, watching television, and getting drunk or stoned. He has little interest in finding a job, having quit his last one when he earned enough money to finish paying off his truck.

Suddenly, two events collide that will change his life forever: he falls in love with a local girl, Masterson; and his wayward father, Walken, wanders through the front door. Fascinated by this handsome man with a pocket full of $100 bills and a flashy sports car, Sean is choses to ignore the fact that his father is a criminal. His grandmother's warning, "Don't even think about it," goes unheeded. After being thrown out of the house by one of his mother's lovers, Sean

calls his father and arranges a meeting. During a ride in one of his fancy cars, Walken tells his son, "According to some folks, I'm just the devil in blue suede shoes," then adds, "Don't believe it, okay?" But Sean should believe it, for Walken is one of the most heinous beings ever seen on the screen. Hiding his evilness in a shroud of charm, Walken seems friendly, at times even likable, but his wicked smile betrays his true nature. Sean, however, finds his father's life much more exciting than his own and is happy to meet his father's gang of professional thieves, among whose members are Walken's two brothers Call (who may be even more evil than Walken himself) and Walter (a dimwit). Also around for decoration is Walken's live-in, Clark.

Father and son are strangely affected by each other. Penn revels in the new attention, while Walken seems delighted at his son's interest and fascination. Soon brother Christopher is brought into the circle and Walken decides to break the boys in on his million dollar empire. No petty thief, Walken steals everything from safes to tractors and has a network of people throughout the country looking out for his interests. He even has an agent in the police department who warns him when the heat is going to be turned up. Walken gives his sons a couple of easy tasks to do, and Sean recruits several of the local boys (Geoffreys, Glover, and Sutherland) to help. Like a good son, Sean introduces his girl friend to his father. Unfortunately, the meeting goes sour when Masterson appears a bit too eager to assert herself among the "family." Walken warns his son that the girl has a big mouth that should be held in check.

Things get worse when Walken makes the mistake of taking Sean along when the gang kills a suspected informant. The murder shocks Sean back to reality and he decides to quit the gang and run off to start a new life with Masterson. In order to finance the trip, Sean organizes one last big score—stealing tractors from a dealership. Unfortunately, the plan goes awry and the entire gang is caught and thrown in jail. While all the others are bailed out, Sean is forced to stay behind because the district attorney believes that the boy holds the keys to cracking Walken's operation. When Walken learns of this, he coldly orders the executions

of the entire teenage gang, including Chris Penn (whose parentage has always been in question—he may also be Walken's son), and then rapes Masterson as a warning to Sean. Desperate to skip town with Masterson, Sean demands to be let out on bail and alludes to knowing all about the murder of the informant—a subject he will spill his guts about if allowed to leave jail. The D.A. reluctantly agrees.

Hours after his release Sean and Masterson pack their bags and get into his car. While Walken sits at a strip joint enjoying the show, his brothers ambush Sean and Masterson, riddling the car with bullets. Masterson is killed instantly, but somehow Sean survives. Pale and weak from loss of blood, Sean shows up at his father's door. Walken is barely able to hide his shock when he sees his son alive. Feigning the need to go to the bathroom, Sean finds the gun his father keeps there and then corners Walken in the kitchen. His face a grimace of anger, pain, and tears, Sean blurts out, "Is this the family gun, Dad?" Scared and panicky, Walken begins weaving a tapestry of lies in an effort to diffuse the situation. Sean answers by taking shot after shot at Walken, all just missing. The tension building, Sean pushes the barrel into Walken's face and stares him right in the eye. Suddenly calm, Walken's evil eyes stare right back. The truth suddenly dawns on Sean and he pulls back. He's not like his father—he's better, and he won't kill. Practically collapsing from the loss of blood, Sean holds his father at bay until the police arrive. The film ends as Sean, trying desperately to hold back the tears of anguish, identifies his father for the jury.

An relentlessly grim film, AT CLOSE RANGE offers a frightening glimpse at the dark side of American life and poses some disturbing questions about family ties. Kazan (son of director Elia) based his script on the Johnston family murders in Brandywine River Valley, Pennsylvania, in 1978. Bruce Johnston, Sr., the patriarch of a large crime family, ordered the murder of his son Bruce, Jr., and put a $15,000 bounty on the boy's head. Two of Bruce, Jr.'s uncles ambushed the boy and his 14-year-old girl friend, Robin Miller, killing her with one bullet and filling Bruce, Jr. with eight slugs. Incredibly, the boy survived and testified against his father.

Though Kazan's original screenplay focused more on the relationship between the Sean Penn and Mary Stuart Masterson characters, director Foley and Penn felt that the chemistry between father and son was the more relevant and valuable aspect of the story and they adjusted accordingly. Needless to say, this move did not endear the screenwriter to the director and star, but it was definitely the right choice to make. Instead of dramatizing a tragic romance, AT CLOSE RANGE examines the natural empathy between father and son, and how destructive family ties can be if they are perverted. Penn, a normally decent young man who knows the difference between right and wrong, is drawn into a life of crime because his father—traditionally the approved archetype of the family—condones and supports it. Though the boy's common sense (represented by his grandmother) tells him not to "even think about it," the ceaseless boredom of his existence draws him to Walken like a moth to a flame. How can anything bad happen? After all, my father will look out for me. What Penn's character doesn't realize is that his father is an animal driven only by survival instincts. The most frightening aspect of Walken's character is that he can coldly order the murder of his own flesh and blood without hesitation or regret. Walken is not concerned with preserving the sanctity of the gang—there is every indication that they are in constant fear of their lives as well—it's purely a matter of his own survival.

Walken is superb is this difficult role. While it would be easy to turn the part into a swaggering, obviously psychotic individual, Walken takes the opposite approach and quietly creates a vividly realistic character that is much more frightening because most viewers will feel that at some point in their lives they have actually met a man such as this. It is the actor's finest performance to date, and, tragically, his efforts were not given the kind of recognition they deserved. Penn is magnificent as well. The young actor built up his body for the role and spent time living in the kind of hopeless environment that spawns men like Bruce Johnston, Sr. Penn manages to convey the complex emotional forces that pull at the boy without ever calling attention to his "acting." Also excellent are Sean's brother Christopher, Tracey Walter, R.D. Call (who barely says a word), and especially Masterson, who is rapidly proving herself to be the finest actress of her generation.

Peter Jamison's production design is superb, perfectly capturing the look and feel of 1978 low-income existence, and rural *nouveau riche* (the above-ground swimming pool at Walken's house is brilliant). The major flaw in AT CLOSE RANGE is Foley's overly flashy direction. While he handles the performances with skill (one can't help but think that was mostly up to the actors themselves), Foley indulges in some annoyingly stylized visuals such as the brilliant lavender night sky during Walken's execution of Penn's friends, and the slow-motion, extreme close-ups of Penn ritualistically washing the blood from his wounds with a garden hose. In what is basically an incredibly realistic film that demands a matter-of-fact presentation, these (and other) concessions to the "pretty-picture" school of directing are distracting and frustrating, and mar an otherwise excellent film. The popular songs picked to play in the background were well chosen and include: "Miss You" (Mick Jagger, Keith Richards, performed by The Rolling Stones), "Boogie Oogie Oogie" (Janis Johnson, Perry L. Kibble, performed by Taste of Honey), Mrs. Sean Penn's minor hit "Live to Tell" (Patrick Leonard, Madonna, performed by Madonna), "It Started with a Touch" (Leon Medica, performed by Leroux), "High Time" (Leon Medica, Hoyt Garrick, Jr., performed by Leroux), "October" (Tom Elliott), "In Between Rainbows" (John Townsend, Charles John Quarto, performed by Townsend), "Technique" (Bill LaBounty, Craig Brickhardt, performed by LaBounty).

p, Elliott Lewitt, Don Guest; d, James Foley; w, Nicholas Kazan (based on a story by Elliott Lewitt, Nicholas Kazan); ph, Juan Ruiz Anchia (Panavision, CFI Color); m, Patrick Leonard; ed, Howard Smith; prod d, Peter Jamison; set d, R. Chris Westlund, Mark Ragland; cos, Hilary Rosenfeld; spec eff, Burt Dalton, Adams Calvert; m/l, Patrick Leonard, Madonna, Mick Jagger, Keith Richards, Leon Medica, Hoyt Garrick, Jr., Janis Johnson, Perry L. Kibble, Tom Elliott, John Townsend, Charles John Quarto, Bill LaBounty, Craig Brickhardt; makeup, Richard Arrington; stunts, Chuck Waters.

Crime   **Cas.**   **(PR:O MPAA:R)**

ATOMOVA KATEDRALA† (1986, Czech.) Barrandov (Trans: An Atomic Cathedral)

Jiri Krampol, Jan Vlasak, Ota Sklencka, Josef Vinklar, Jan Teply, Libuse Stedra, Ida Rapaicova.

d, Jaroslav Balik; w, Stanislav Rudolf, Jarolsav Balik; ph, Viktor Ruzicka; m, Karel Mares.

AUF IMMER UND EWIG† (1986, Ger.) 91m Rocco–ZDF/Oko c (Trans: Forever and Always)

Eva Mattes, Werner Stocker, Teo Gostischa, Silke Wolfing, August Zirner, Hans Kremer, Ulrich Wildgruber, Hans Wyprachtiger, Eva Zlotnitzky, Barbara Ossenkopp.

Mattes is a woman who goes to find an old lover (and father of her nine-year-old son) after she learns that she is dying from an inoperable brain tumor. The former lover, Stocker, is surprised to see her and she never tells him why she has come, even after a steamy lovemaking session. Later she dies, leaving Stocker's name and address for her son, who has never known his father.

p,d&w, Christel Buschmann; ph, Frank Bruhne; m, Chris Rea; ed, Jane Seitz; art d, Georg von Kieseritsky, Heidrum Brandt; m/l, Chris Rea.

Drama   **(PR:O MPAA:NR)**

AURELIA† (1986, Ital.) Telecentauro c

Maddalena Crippa, Fabio Sartor, Carlo Manni, Nicola Pistoia.

A young man sets out on foot to reach the church where he is to be married, some 600 kilometers away. He meets a young woman who joins him on his travels and together they have several adventures, make new discoveries about life, then separate as he marries his fiancee. More about travel itself than about any personal growth among the characters.

p, Giovanni Morina; d&w, Giorgio Molteni; ph, Raffaele Mertes.

Drama   **(PR:O MPAA:NR)**

AUSTRALIAN DREAM† (1986, Aus.) Filmside c

Noni Hazlehurst, Graeme Blundell, John Jarratt.

Suburban life in Brisbane is satirized in this debut feature from McKimmie, which stars Hazlehurst as a housewife married to a local butcher. Underneath the seemingly well-respected facade of surburbia lie the sexual and social vices of its inhabitants.

p, Jackie McKimmie, Susan Wild; d&w, Jackie McKimmie; ph, Andrew Lesnie.

Comedy   **(PR:O MPAA:NR)**

AVAETE, A SEMENTE DA VINGANCA† (1986, Braz.) c (Trans: Avaete, A Seed of Vengeance)

Hugo Carvana, Renata Sorrah, Macsuara Kadiweu, Milton Rodrigues, Jones Bloch, Jose Dumont, Claudio Mamberti, Claudio Marzo.

A young Indian boy's life is saved during the massacre of his tribe, building a strong friendship between him and the man who saved him, which lasts through his adolescence.

d, Zelito Viana; w, Zelito Viana, Jose Joffily; ph, Edgard Moura; m, Egberto Gismonti; ed, Gilberto Santeiro; art d, Carlos Liuzzi.

Drama   **(PR:C MPAA:NR)**

AVANTI POPOLO† (1986, Israel) 84m Kastel c

Suheil Hadad, Salim Daou, Danny Roth, Danny Segev, Tuvia Gelber, Michael Koresh, Shalom Shmuelov, Barry Langford, Dan Turgeman, Mukhammad Manadre.

In the aftermath of the Six Day War in 1967, two Egyptian soldiers find themselves stranded in the middle of the Sinai Desert, miles behind the Israeli lines. As they try to make their way homeward, they encounter a series of obstacles, most of them comical. At one point they run into an Israeli patrol and only persuade the patrol to let them go after one of the Egyptians, an actor, does the entire "Hath not a Jew eyes?" speech from Shakespeare's "Merchant of Venice". Begun as a student film, director/writer/producer Raphi Bukaee scraped together the money to expand it into a feature, then found himself with the film completely shot but no money for postproduction. The film was saved at the last minute by Kastel films, which financed the completion and saw the film become the hit of the Jerusalem film festival. Filmed in 16mm.

p,d&w, Raphi Bukaee; ph, Yoav Kosh (Agfacolor); m, Uri Ofir; ed, Zohar Sela; art d, Ariel Glazer; makeup, Irith Elazar.

Drama/Comedy   **(PR:C-O MPAA:NR)**

AVENGING FORCE**½ (1986) 103m Cannon c

Michael Dudikoff *(Matt Hunter)*, Steve James *(Larry Richards)*, James Booth *(Adm. Brown)*, John P. Ryan *(Glastebury)*, Bill Wallace *(Delaney)*, Karl Johnson *(Wallace)*, Mark Alaimo *(Lavall)*, Allison Gereighty *(Sarah Hunter)*, Loren Farmer *(Parker)*, Richard Boyle *(Grandpa Jimmy)*, Robert Taylor *(Larry Richards, Jr.)*, Bruce Johnson *(Jeff Richards)*, Sylvia Joseph *(Daisy Richards)*, Robert Cronin *(T.C. Cooper)*, John Wilmot *(Gen. Wyatt)*, James Bonders *(Charles Kray)*, Nelson Camp *(Fifi)*, Lyla Kay Owen *(Becki Davis)* *(Doctors)*, Claudia Vasilovik *(Military Clerk)*, Ramon Olavanetta *(CIA Agent)*, John Barber *(Butler)*, Paul Staples *(Jack Cain)*, B.J. Davis *(Joe Perris)*, Kane Hodder, Steve Hulin, Alan Marcus, Charlie Skeen, Gary Alexander.

A martial arts-trained ex-Secret Service operative smashes a neo-fascist organization in this better-than-average action offering. Dudikoff (AMERICAN NINJA) is the hero, a retired Secret Service agent who has been taking care of his sister since the murder of their parents. His old comrade, James, is a black man running for the Senate in Louisiana, an action opposed by the Pentangle, a group made up of wealthy, right-wing creeps and survivalists who have been seen in the film's opening indulging in their favorite pastime, hunting men down through the bayous. The group is composed of Johnson, who shaves his head hulk, is "the current holder of the World Ironman Championship," and likes to hunt in a leather bondage mask with a spear or crossbow; Alaimo, "who made a couple of million dollars before age 21" and who hunts in a white rubber mask with a

samurai sword; Wallace, a Heisman Trophy winner at Harvard and "the South's youngest senator" who looks about 23 (despite the Heisman, he is the worst sportsman of the group, hunting men with a shotgun); and Ryan, the leader of the Pentangle, a professor, "a philosopher, a thinker, a soldier, and founder of the giant Hadley Corporation." His gig on the hunting parties is to hide underwater and kill the prey with his garotte when it tries to swim to safety.

They make an early attempt to kill James at a Mardi Gras parade but fail thanks to Dudikoff. He dispatches all the hired killers, though James' son is killed in the attack. Soon they are invited to what looks like an ambush. It is, but, even though they are unamred, James and Dudikoff eliminate another dozen henchmen handily before returning to Dudikoff's ranch to hide out with their respective families. The Pentangle leaders, much impressed with Dudikoff's fighting abilities, decide to take matters into their own hands and dispatch James once and for all in a grenade-and-machine-gun attack on the ranch. They wipe out a contingent of Secret Service agents, Dudikoff's grandfather, and all of James' family for good measure. They kidnap Dudikoff's sister, Gereighty, and use her as hostage to guarantee Dudikoff shows up at their next hunt, to be held in two weeks at a town in the bayous.

Dudikoff turns up on schedule and wanders through a Cajun celebration where dangerous-looking men block his way with shotguns. Eventually he is directed to the local brothel where he finds his sister being made up in preparation for being auctioned off. He takes her and heads for the swamps, with the Pentangle members in pursuit. He evades them that night and the next day he kills Alaimo, Johnson, and Wallace in hand-to-hand matches. When he and Gereighty try to swim the last stretch to safety, Ryan appears from underwater with his garotte and attempts to strangle him, but Dudikoff manages to plunge a knife into his assailant's leg, sending him off howling in pain. He takes his sister to Secret Service headquarters and leaves her there, with a warning that if she dies (she was injured in one of the fights) he will kill those responsible. Then he goes to Ryan's house, where the villain tells him that the Pentangle is just getting started and refuses to disclose who the fifth member of the group is. They fight and Dudikoff kills him. When he goes back to headquarters he confronts his superior, Booth, telling him that if the Pentangle is just getting started, so is he. It has been obvious for some time that Booth is the fifth member and it is eqully obvious as the film concludes that there will be a sequel.

Director Firstenberg has directed several action films for Cannon (REVENGE OF THE NINJA, AMERICAN NINJA, NINJA III: THE DOMINATION, and others) and he brings to this project a skilled hand at action scenes. Dudikoff (AMERICAN NINJA, BLOODY BIRTHDAY, and a few others) is also good, and Cannon has shown enough faith in his talent to sign him to a long-term contract. The villains steal the show, though, with Ryan—so memorable as the warden in RUNAWAY TRAIN—taking top honors as he creates an old-fashioned villain who only lacks a moustache to twirl. He also gets the best lines. "It is our constitutional right to bear arms, it is out sacred duty to do so as efficiently as possible," he declares while raving on to an appreciative audience in tuxedos about "dope pushers, niggah rapists, and Communists" about to cross the Rio Grande in force.

Only the silliness of the hunt, the umpteenth variation of THE MOST DANGEROUS GAME, detracts from the film. After all, just how much hunting can you do in a swamp with a garotte? The scene in the Cajun town continues the current Hollywood trend of using Cajuns as the stylish ethnic minority of the day, a trend that started with SOUTHERN COMFORT, and has included BELIZAIRE THE CAJUN, ANGEL HEART, and NO MERCY. Hardly one of the best films of the year, but a film that delivers what it promises, good action without too much stupidity.

p, Menahem Golan, Yoram Globus; d, Sam Firstenberg; w, James Booth; ph, Gideon Porath (TVC Color); m, George S. Clinton; ed, Michael J. Duthie; prod d, Marcia Hinds; art d, Bo Johnson; set d, Michele Starbuck; cos, Audrey Bansmer; spec eff, William O. Purcell; makeup, Gabor Kerny Aiszky; stunts, B.J. Davis.

Action/Drama   **Cas.**   **(PR:O   MPAA:R)**

AWAITING THE PALLBEARERS†   (1986, Arg.) 94m Instituto Nacional de Cinematografia c (ESPERANDO LA CARROZA)

Antonio Gasalla, Julio de Grazia, China Zorilla, Monica Villa, Betiana Blum, Luis Brandoni.

Four grown siblings are forced to care for their aging and senile mother, a task none of them relishes. She goes to live with one son and his wife, and there becomes an even greater burden through her insistence on helping out, because she botches nearly everything she tries. Finally, the son's wife loses her temper and her mind, and suffers a nervous breakdown. Fleeing to the home of one of the other children, she tries to get them to take the old woman, but no one wants her. When they finally go back to the house, they can find her nowhere (she's gone for a walk). A frantic search takes them to the morgue, where they are shown the mangled corpse of an old woman who jumped under a train. They identify the body as that of their mother, then return home, only to have the old woman return. They begin to celebrate, though they don't dare let her know why.

p, Diana Frey; d, Alejandro Doria; ph, Juan Carlos Lenardi; ed, Silvia Ripoll.

Comedy   **(PR:C-O   MPAA:NR)**

AWDAT MOWATIN†   (1986, Egypt) 116m Actor/Misr c (Trans: Return of a Citizen)

Yehia El Fakharani *(Chaker)*, Marvet Amin *(Fawzia)*, Magda Zakhi *(Younger Sister)*, Sherif Mounir *(Ibrahim)*.

Fakharani, a young Egyptian who has made his fortune abroad, returns home to find that Western ideas and influences have eaten away at traditional Arab family unity. At his parents' home, he discovers that although his brothers and sisters still live under the same roof, they have little interest in each other. His younger sister, Zakhi, is about to be wed, but the rest of the family shows little interest. His older sister, Amin, welcomes her brother home only to ask for a loan so she can open a European-style sweet shop. Fakharani finds one of his brothers has become an unemployed drug addict, and his other brother ends up in jail because of his involvement with a radical political group. Fakharani is so dismayed by the state of his family that he is forced to decide whether to abandon them to their fate, or stay and make the best of it.

p, Yehia El Fakharani; d, Mohamed Khan; w, Assem Tawfik; ph, Ali El Ghazuli; m, Kamal Bakir; ed, Nadia Chukri.

Drama   **(PR:C   MPAA:NR)**

AZ DO KONCE†   (1986, Czech.) Barrandov Studios (Trans: Till the Very End)

Eduard Cupak, Vitezslav Jandak, Jan Kohut, Eva Matejckova.

d, Antonin Kopriva; w, Antonin Kopriva, Otakar Chaloupka; ph, Martin Benoni.

AZ UTOLSO KEZIRAT†   (1986, Hung.) Dialog Studio (Trans: The Last Manuscript)

Jozef Kroner, Alexander Bardini, Eszter Nagykalozy, Iren Psota, Hedi Varady, Bela Both.

d, Karoly Makk; w, Karoly Makk, Zoltan Kamondy; ph, Janos Toth.

B

BABEL OPERA, OU LA REPETITION DE DON JUAN † (1986, Bel.)
95m National Lottery of Belgium-National Opera-Niews Imago c

Francois Beukelaers, Stephane Excoffier, Alexandra Vandernoot, Ben Van Ostade, Jacques Sojcher, Bernard Yerles, Jose Van Dam, Pierre Thau, Ashley
Putnam, Stuart Burrows, Christiane Eda-Pierre.

A complex picture which takes place entirely in the Royal Brussels Opera House
during the rehearsal of Mozart's opera, "Don Giovanni." What appears as
documentary soon turns fictional as the characters of the opera and its director,
Beukelaers, become absorbed in the lives of Mozart's characters. At the same
time, Beukelaers has hopes of staging his own version of the myth of Don Juan.
While the film combines aspects of an opera documentary with cultural information and a fictional treatment, underneath it all is a comment on Belgian life in
general.

d, Andre Delvaux; w, Andre Delvaux, Denise Debaut, Jacques Sojcher; ph,
Charlie van Damme, Walter van den Ende; m, Wolfgang Amadeus Mozart; ed,
Albert Jurgenson.

Drama (PR:C MPAA:NR)

BACK TO SCHOOL***½ (1986) 96m Paper Clip/ORION c

Rodney Dangerfield (*Thornton Melon*), Sally Kellerman (*Diane*), Burt Young
(*Lou*), Keith Gordon (*Jason Melon*), Robert Downey, Jr. (*Derek*), Paxton White-
head (*Philip Barbay*), Terry Farrell (*Valerie*), M. Emmet Walsh (*Coach
Turnbull*), Adrienne Barbeau (*Vanessa*), William Zabka (*Chas*), Ned Beatty
(*Dean Martin*), Severn Darden (*Dr. Barazini*), Sam Kinison (*Prof. Terguson*),
Robert Picardo (*Giorgio*), Kurt Vonnegut, Jr. (*Himself*), Edie McClurg (*Marge*),
Sarah Abrell (*Sorority Girl*), Dana Allison (*Young Woman*), Boris Aplon (*Tony
Meloni*), Nora Boland (*Agnes*), Kimberlin Brown (*Girl in Dorm Hallway*), Lisa
Denton (*Lisa*), Bob Drew (*Contractor*), Holly Hayes (*Girl in the Crowd*), Jason
Hervey (*Young Thornton*), Leslie Huntly (*Coed*), James Ingersoll (*Judge*),
Michael McGrady (*Player*), Santos Morales (*Bartender*), Beth Peters (*Mrs. Stuy-
vesant*), Phil Rubenstein, John Young (*Executives*), Timothy Stack (*Trendy
Man*), Steve Sweeney (*Security Guard*), Stacey Toten, Beck LeBeau (*Hot Tub
Girls*), Brad Zutaut (*Petey*), Josh Saylor (*Student in Diane's Class*), William
Grauer (*Drunken Student*), Kristen Aldrich (*Student in Diane's Class*), Tricia Hill
(*Lisa's Friend*), Jill D. Merin (*Girl at Dorm Party*), John James (*Man in Stands*),
Eric Alver (*Student at Fraternity Party*), Theresa Lyons (*Cashier*), Dallas Win-
kler, Lisa Le Cover, Kimberlee Carlson (*Rodettes*), Curtis Stone, Michael Reid,
Cactus Moser, Brian O'Dougherty, Davey Faragher, Cliffie Stone (*"Twist &
Shout" Band*), Danny Elfman, Steven Bartek, John Hernandez, Sam Phipps,
Leon Schneiderman, Dale Turner, John Avila, Mike Bacich (*Oingo Boingo Band
Members*).

With this smash-hit summer comedy, Rodney Dangerfield has finally achieved
what he's always wanted: respect. Rodney—born Jacob Cohen and later known
as Jack Roy—was 64 when he made this. His first film was a bit role in THE
PROJECTIONIST (with Chuck McCann in the title role), and then it was many
years until he was tapped to appear in CADDYSHACK and EASY MONEY.
This movie puts him in the forefront of film comedians, though not necessarily of
film actors. Essentially, he is still Rodney, the same vulgar, bug-eyed one-liner

rattler who made countless appearances on the "Ed Sullivan Show" as well as
"The Tonight Show." If you like Rodney, you'll love this movie. If you don't
like him, then you'll still enjoy this. It's like a comedy of the 1940s in that it has a
traditional structure with three acts, which means a beginning, a solid center, and
the right kind of denouement to send audiences out with a good feeling. Dangerfield plays the immensely wealthy owner of a chain of "Tall and Fat" men's
clothing stores. He's married, for the second time, to predatory Barbeau, a shrew
and an adulteress who is more interested in scaling the social ladder than in
pleasing her husband. Rodney's son by his first marriage is Gordon, who is now

attending Grand Lakes University. Gordon has lied and told his father that he is a
big man on the campus and that he is a champion diver. The truth is that the boy
is only a nerdy towel attendant for the diving team and has only one friend,
Downey, a revolutionary. Dangerfield made all of his money without benefit of
education, and when he learns that his son is ill-equipped to face life in the real
world, he decides to enroll in the school and kill two birds with one stone; he will
get his degree and he will also be able to be closer to his son and help him through
his current problems. Dangerfield has problems getting the school to accept him
until he begins tossing money around, going so far as to endow a business school.
The dean of the University is Beatty (his character name, "Martin," gives rise to
a running gag calling him "Dean Martin"), a man who will do anything for the
school. Dangerfield has his dormitory room and his son's room rebuilt into
sumptuous quarters, has his chauffeur Young (who is also a bodyguard) squire
him around the large campus, and then gets down to business. After not having
been in school for decades, Dangerfield finds it's not as easy as he'd thought, but
money goes a long way, and he uses some of it to engage a few huge corporations
to help him with his homework; he even hires Kurt Vonnegut, Jr. to write his
thesis on Kurt Vonnegut, Jr. Dangerfield and Gordon take an English class
taught by sexy, sultry (though somewhat hammy) Kellerman and Dangerfield
falls hard for her. She is dating stuffy Whitehead, who teaches business and is the
height of pomposity. Whitehead is appalled by Kellerman's interest in Dangerfield and thus becomes the villain, seeking at every turn to thwart Dangerfield's
college career. Dangerfield and Gordon become closer and the boy is beginning to
emerge from his wimp shell, going so far as to court Farrell, a comely coed. Then
Gordon realizes that Dangerfield's way of going to school is not the right way.
Dangerfield is challenged by the vengeful Whitehead and he is made to submit to
an arduous oral examination by the school's administration. Gordon helps him
cram for it and, after a grueling test, he passes. To top it off, the school is in the
midst of a diving match, which they are losing until Dangerfield comes out of the
audience, dons his trunks, and executes a perfect "Triple Lindy" to win the
match. (Don't bother to look the dive up in Greg Louganis' records. It's uniquely
Dangerfield's.)

The plot is a deceptively simple straight-line development. The fun arises from
the barrage of verbal jokes that come trippingly off Dangerfield's tongue. Ramis
and Torokvei, two of the seven writers it took to concoct this, also were involved
with ARMED AND DANGEROUS, a not-nearly-as-funny (or successful) movie
also released in 1986. BACK TO SCHOOL is not sophisticated, it will not raise
the level of satire one degree, it does not alter or illuminate our time. What it does
is make you laugh, often. And how much more does one want from a comedy?
Dangerfield functions very much the way Groucho did in the Marx Brothers
movies, sending out zingers that the people on screen don't react to at all (as
witness Margaret Dumont, for instance). Sam Kinison does a funny turn as a
hysterical Vietnam vet who teaches history the way he recalls it. The direction, by
Metter (GIRLS JUST WANT TO HAVE FUN as well as Dangerfield's music

video "Rappin' Rodney"), is functional and, thank heaven, not overly artsy.
When you have a good script and good performers, why get in the way? Although Dangerfield is already at an age when most show-business people begin to
think of retiring, his energy seems boundless, and therefore he is thought of as a
"young" comedian, a peer of Robin Williams or Eddie Murphy, rather than Bob
Hope, George Burns, or even Don Rickles (who, though younger than Dangerfield, has been in the limelight far longer).

p, Chuck Russell; d, Alan Metter; w, Steven Kampmann, Will Porter, Peter
Torokvei, Harold Ramis (based on a story by Rodney Dangerfield, Greg Fields,
Dennis Snee); ph, Thomas E. Ackerman (Panavision, DeLuxe Color); m, Danny
Elfman; ed, David Rawlins; prod d, David L. Snyder; set d, Edmund Silkaitis;
cos, Durinda Wood; spec eff, Michael Lantieri; makeup, Hallie D'Amore;
stunts, Dick Ziker.

Comedy (PR:C MPAA:PG-13)

BACKLASH*** (1986, Aus.) 90m Mermaid Beach-Multifilms/J.C.
Williamson c

David Argue (*Trevor Darling*), Gia Carides (*Nikki Iceton*), Lydia Miller (*Kath*),
Brian Syron (*The Executioner*), Anne Smith (*Mrs. Smith*), Don Smith (*Mr.
Smith*), Jennifer Cluff (*Waitress*).

Argue is a marijuana-smoking, racist, sexist cop assigned as punishment to escort a female aboriginal prisoner back to an isolated outback community where she is accused of murdering a man by slicing off his penis. Accompanying them is Carides, an idealistic young policewoman and law student. Along the way their car breaks down and they are forced to take shelter against the heat in an abandoned sheep-shearing station. Gradually the two policemen come to understand their prisoner and decide that she is innocent. In the end they manage to force the dead man's widow to confess to the crime.

Largely improvised, with varying success, though when it works it is startlingly good. Only an embarrassing performance by Anne Smith as the widow and some technical gaffes (including the reflection of the camera crew in a windshield) keep this from looking like a much more expensive production than it actually is. Shot in 16mm on a shoestring budget (raised from small private investors including a pub owner who gave director Bennett $250,000 [Australian] before he could even finish his pitch), the film garnered favorable reviews on the international festival circuit.

p,d&w, Bill Bennett; ph, Tony Wilson (Atlab color); m, Michael Atkinson, Michael Spicer; ed, Denise Hunter.

Crime Drama   **(PR:O   MPAA:NR)**

BACKSTAGE†   (1986, Aus.) Backstage c

Laura Brannigan.

A popular American singer decides she wants to become a dramatic actress and ventures to Australia to make her dream come true. To some extent life is imitating art here, since the film's star, Brannigan, was a popular singer who, in the early 1980s had a few forgettable hit singles. She gained her greatest notoriety when THE FRENCH CONNECTION director William Friedkin directed her in an overtly sexual and extremely bad rock video for her song "Self Control."

p, Geoff Burrowes; d, Jonathan Hardy; w, Jonathan Hardy, Frank Howson; ph, Keith Wagstaff.

Comedy/Drama   **(PR:O   MPAA:NR)**

BAD COMPANY*   (1986, Arg.) 90m Instituto Nacional De
                                Cinematografia Argentina c (MALAYUNTA)

Federico Luppi (Bernardo), Barbara Mujica (Amalia), Miguel Angel Sola (Nestor), Silvia Millet (Angelita), Jorge Petraglia, Edgardo Moreira, Florencia Firpo, Ernesto Michel, Jorge Caponbianco.

BAD COMPANY is a disturbing, surrealistic black comedy, which—like most recent Argentine films—criticizes the hypocritical nature of the overthrown military regime. Luppi and Mujica are a seemingly innocent and well-mannered middle-aged couple whose desperate need for lodgings leads them to take a room in the flat of a narcissistic young sculptor Sola. The older people are more-or-less kept prisoners in their small, barren room which contains a bed with a worn-out mattress. Sola's eccentric nature requires a lot of space. He insists that when he entertains guests, his two boarders never leave their room—not even to go to the restroom. When Mujica attempts to clean the moldy, garbage-filled kitchen so that she can cook, Sola throws a violent fit, demanding the kitchen remain as is. Trapped inside their little room, the elderly couple patiently contend with their repressed situation until the tables take a swift turn. Jointly they attack Sola, tie him to his bed, and make the apartment a model of their own perspective. In addition, Luppi and Mujica attempt to rid Sola of what they consider his sexual deviation and his improper manners through periodic beatings and the forced feeding of healthful foods. Sola is able to withstand the punishment until his strength is almost completely depleted. By attempting to seduce Mujica, he almost escapes, but Luppi catches him and delivers the worst beating yet. As these incidents unfold, the girl who lives below silently gazes from the corners and shadows.

BAD COMPANY is a film rich in complex and symbolically significant charcters. Sola, for all his selfishness, is charming and charismatic. His strong individuality upsets Luppi's and Mujica's righteousness; instead of reassessing their own values, they resort to violence. Luppi's character represents a member of the fallen regime which incarcerated and tortured those individuals who threatened its order. Sola's artistic nature, which looks for fulfillment completely outside the moralistic order, is seen as the greatest threat to repression. (In Spanish; English subtitles.)

d, Jose Santiso; w, Jose Santiso, Jacobo Langsner; ph, Eduardo Legaria; m, Litto Nebbia; ed, Valencia-Blanco; art d, Ponchi Morpurgo.

Comedy/Drama   **(PR:O   MPAA:NR)**

BAD GUYS zero   (1986) 88m Tomorrow Entertainment/InterPictures c

Adam Baldwin (Skip Jackson), Mike Jolly (Dave Atkins), Michelle Nicastro (Janice Edwards), Ruth Buzzi (Petal McGurk), James Booth (Lord Percy), Gene LeBell (Turk McGurk), Norman Burton (Capt. Watkins), Dutch Mann (Murphy Green), Harvey Jason (Prof. Gimble), Helena Carroll (Elsie), Micole Mercurio (Vicki), Prof. Toru Tanaka (Lord Percy's Bodyguard), Pepper Martin (Ringside Commentator), Frank Birney (Comedian), Jack Eisman (Reporter), Hank Garrett (Bud Schultz), Joan Lemmo (Lady at Nellie's), Susan Luck (Desk Sergeant), Tommy Madden (Tommy), Roxanne Rolle (Mary Lou), Johnny Silver (Tiny), Count Billy Varga (Referee), Paula Victor (Little Old Lady), Arthur Abelson, Didi Alan, Don Richey (Spectators), Robert Axelrod (Prof. Gimble's Assistant), Red Bastin (TV Announcer), Terry Brodt (Ring Announcer), David DeLange (Maitre d'), Eric Fleeks (Cop), Peter Griffin (Police Sergeant), Mando Guerrero, William Kulzer (Referees), Jesse Hernandez Lizarraga (Referee No. 2), Jerry Melton (Ring Manager), Leila Hee Olsen (Pop), Charles Picerni (Referee No. 1),

Mike Rauseo (TV Announcer), Mike Reynolds (Repo Man), Jeff Walton (Ring Announcer); Wrestlers: Alexia Smirnoff, Jay York (Kremlin Krushers), Steve Olsonoski, Brad Rheigans (Freedom Fighters), Jack Armstrong, Chief Jay Strongbow (Sod Busters), Buddha Kahn, Pete Marquez (Side Winders), Salvadore Lothario, Victor Rivera (Padres), Ray Gedeon, Jack Jacobs (Old Guys), Bengali (Alfonso the Magnificent), Goliath (The Crimson Bulldozer), Curt Henning (Wrestler), Sergeant Slaughter.

Some films are just so plain awful that they simply defy adjectival assault. Such is the case with BAD GUYS, an inconsequential saga of two cops who turn to the world of pro wrestling after being suspended from the force. Baldwin (the troubled youth of MY BODYGUARD, now crowned with painfully dyed blond tresses) and Jolly are the heroes in question, who begin looking for new employment after a scandalous altercation in a biker bar. After trying their hands at construction and as male strippers, the two contact Nicastro, a wide-eyed journalist who wants to help the pair make it in the wrestling game. She hooks them up with LeBell, a grizzled old-timer who trains men for the ring (a chore he also took on off-screen for the film's preparation). His wife is the hyperkinetic "Laugh-In" TV refugee Buzzi. LeBell, Buzzi, and Nicastro soon have the boys ready for the ring, transforming them from a couple of good-looking kids into "The Boston Bad Guys," a mean and ruthless team that fans will love to hate. Baldwin and Jolly prepare for a big match against "The Kremlin Krushers," a pair of Soviet brawlers managed by LeBell's old rival Booth. On their way to the event, however, they are intercepted by Mann, the head biker back at the bar Baldwin and Booth had busted up. The two wrestlers are soundly beaten by thugs, but fortunately the cops arrive in time to save the day. Baldwin and Jolly are rushed to the arena (which looks more like a refurbished warehouse with about a hundred or so extras doubling for thousands of fans) to do battle with the Kremlin Krushers. The Krushers, being Russians, are sneering, evil villains who would think nothing of defiling Old Glory during what turns into a battle for American honor. Cheating left and right, the Krushers seem to have licked the Bad Guys when fortunately famed wrestler Sergeant Slaughter steps out of his cameo appearance and into the ring. He helps out Our Heroes, who fight back to defend everything this country stands for, and ultimately pin the dirty Russkies down to the mat.

Slamming this film for its myriad ineptitudes (script, direction, acting, subsophomoric humor, inane jingoism, et al) is simply too easy a task, sort of like not missing the hole when you hit a golf ball into the Grand Canyon. Rather, let BAD GUYS gather some well deserved dust as it patiently sits on the shelf of your local video store, waiting until eternity for some hapless soul to rent it. Songs include: "Don't Hang My Pictures" (John Gary Smith, performed by Smith), "Respect Yourself" (Luther Ingram, Mack Rice, performed by Kane Gang), "Courting Disaster" (Paul Chiten, Susan Sheridan, performed by Chiten), Medley: "You Don't Know What You Mean to Me" (Eddie Floyd, Steve Cropper), "Soul Man," "Hold On, I'm Coming," "Soul Sister (You're Sugar Brown)," "I Thank You" (Issac Hayes, David Porter, performed by Stars on 45), "Don't Blame Me" (Matthew Ender, performed by Ender), "Mean Streak" (Robert John, Bobby Mancari, performed by John), "Snap Dance" (Chiten, Sheridan, performed by Hand Tools), "The Bad Guys" (Leslie Knauer-Waffer, Benny Knauer, performed by Precious Metal), "Mean Machine" (George-Michael Ilian, Dwight David, Barbara Rothstein, performed by Spyder Turner), "My Heart's Desire" (Jeff Tyzik), "Theme from BAD GUYS" (William Goldstein). Ex-professional wrestler Verne Gagne served as a consultant on the film.

p, John D. Backe, Myron A. Hyman; d, Joel Silberg; w, Brady W. Setwater, Joe Gillis; ph, Hanania Baer (Cinema Color); m, William Goldstein; ed, Peter Parasheles, Christopher Holmes; art d, Ivo Cristante; set d, Julie Kay Towery; spec eff, Rick H. Josephsen; makeup, Jefferson Dawn; stunts, Eddy Donno.

Comedy   **Cas.**   **(PR:C-O   MPAA:PG)**

BAIROLETTO†   (1986, Arg.)

Arturo Bonin, Luisina Brando.

d, Atilio Polverini.

BAL NA VODI†   (1986, Yugo.) 112m Avala-Inex/Smart Egg c (Trans:
                                                        Dancing on Water)

Gala Videnovic (Esther), Milan Strljic (Rile), Dragan Bjelogrlic (Sasha), Goran Radakovic, Nebojsa Bakocevic, Srdan Todorovic, Relja Basio, Marko Todorovic.

Four male Yugoslavian emigres who have settled in different parts of the world reunite for the funeral of a woman they all knew and loved back in their home country. In flashback to the 1950s we see the characters as middle-class teenagers in Belgrade trying to adjust to their new social status after Tito's assumption of power. Their group is invaded by a young party member, Strljic, a boy from the country who sets his sights on Videnovic, the young woman whom they have all known since childhood. Nicknamed Esther after her movie idol Esther Williams, Videnovic succumbs to Strljic's charms but winds up pregnant. When Strljic hears the news he abandons Videnovic. Knowing that Videnovic wishes to join her father who has escaped to Italy, the boys hide her in a boat and cross the Adriatic. Once they arrive the group is arrested, but it is a fortunate run-in with the law for it is their ticket to freedom in the West. The film returns to the funeral and the men, now middle-aged, are shocked to see Strljic arrive to pay his respects. Having abandoned the party to become a businessman, Strljic complains about party interference in free enterprise.

p, George Zecevic; d&w, Jovan Acin; ph, Tomislav Pinter; m, Zoran Simjanovic; ed, Snezana Ivanovic; art d, Sava Acin.

Drama   **(PR:C   MPAA:NR)**

BALBOA* (1986) 91m Production Associates/Entertainment Artists-Vestron Video c

Tony Curtis *(Ernie Stoddard)*, Carol Lynley *(Erin Blakely)*, Jennifer Chase *(Kathy Love)*, Chuck Connors *(Alabama Dern)*, Lupita Ferrer *(Rita Carlo)*, Sonny Bono *(Terry Carlo)*, Catherine Campbell *(Cindy Dern)*, Cassandra Peterson *(Angie Stoddard)*, David Young *(Lance Armstrong)*, Martine Beswicke [Beswick] *(Narrator)*, Russell Nype *(Sen. Highsmith)*, Henry Jones *(Jeffry Duncan)*, Joy Brent *(Joy Eastland)*, Shirley Rothman *(Shirley Sanders)*, Steve Kanaly *(Sam Cole)*, Jaime Allison *(Robin Woodbury)*, Michael Polakof *(Benjie)*, Linda Kenton *(Candy)*, Kay Parker *(Apple)*, Jennifer Smith *(Kathleen Blakely)*.

Filmed in 1982, BALBOA was originally conceived as a possible series for cable television which would take the machinations of network shows such as "Dallas" and "Dynasty" a step further by including foul language and nudity. There were no takers in cable-land so the producers pared the film down to feature length, and the now-defunct distributor Jensen Farley bought the rights and added footage with British B-picture star Martine Beswicke [Beswick] as narrator. Unfortunately, Jensen Farley went bankrupt before the film could be released and it sat on the shelf for years until a 1984 British video release. BALBOA finally premiered in the U.S. in 1986 on videotape, and it would have been better off lying forgotten on a shelf. Filled with so many muddled characters and plot twists that one needs a scorecard to keep things straight (the confusion is obviously due to the unenviable task of editing down a multi-episode series into a 90-minute feature). Curtis stars as an unscrupulous wheeler-dealer in the chic Balboa district of California. The plot sees Curtis attempt to build a legalized gambling empire on nearby Goat Island. Out to get Curtis, however, are Campbell, the granddaughter of a man Curtis had financially ruined, and Peterson, Curtis' ex-wife. The women blackmail Curtis' secretary into handing over key documents detailing Curtis' bribes to prominent officials. Campbell and Peterson turn the documents over to Kanaly, a trusted local politician. But Curtis is prepared for such attacks and uses his political influence to have the case thrown out by discrediting his own secretary. This move sends Kanaly into a rage and he attacks Curtis physically. Seizing the opportunity to strike another blow, Curtis has the politician arrested and presses charges. Although Curtis has survived this assault on his empire, others wait in the wings for their chance.

If the above plot line sounds straightforward, it is only because the dozens of subplots weren't mentioned. BALBOA is like watching an entire season of "Dallas" flash by in a matter of seconds. Characters jump in and out of bed, double-cross, plot, scheme, and vow revenge every few minutes. By the end of the film narrator Beswicke informs us that there is plenty more to come—luckily, that doesn't seem likely. The bizarre cast is made up of such has-beens and hopefuls as Curtis, Lynley, Connors, Bono, Peterson (aka Elvira—star of a syndicated "creature-feature" show), and even hard-core porno star Parker. "Dallas" star Kanaly puts in a "guest appearance" as the noble politician. Everyone looks embarrassed to be involved in this mess and they probably hoped it would stay unreleased.

p&d, James Polakof; w, James Polakof, Gail Willumsen, Nicki Lewis; ph, Christopher Lynch (DeLuxe Color); m, Richard Hieronymus; ed, Millie Paul; prod d, Charles D. Tomlinson; cos, Nicki Lewis.

Drama   Cas.   (PR:O MPAA:NR)

BALLERUP BOULEVARD† (1986, Den.) 83m Metronome–Danish Film Institute/Metronome c (AKA: PINKY'S GANG)

Stine Bierlich *(Pinky)*, Anja Kempinski *(Janni)*, Anja Toft *(Eva)*, Morton Grunwald *(Pinky's Father)*, Helle Hertz *(Pinky's Mother)*, Pelle Koppel *(Pinky's Brother)*, Allen Olsen, Otto Brandenburg, Edward Fleming, Ole Ernst, Mika Heilmann.

After her mother is jailed for a minor bookkeeping theft (committed in an effort to help her husband), 13-year-old Bierlich is shunned by her schoolmates, but finds solace in the rock combo she is a member of, as well as in her close-knit family. Told in an anecdotal manner, this children's film was funded in part by the Danish government.

p, Tivi Mahnusson; d, Linda Wendel; w, Linda Wendel, Kirsten Thorup, Synne Rifbjerg; ph, Anja Dalhoff (Eastmancolor); m, Elizabeth Gjerluff Nielsen; ed, Stefan Henszelman; prod d, Poul Dubienko.

Children's Adventure   (PR:AA MPAA:NR)

BANANHEJKERINGO† (1986, Hung.) Hunnis Studio (Trans: The Banana Skin Waltz)

Mihaly Dea, Dorottya Udvaros, Juli Basti, Gyorgyi Kari, Gyula Benko, Dezso Garas, Gyorgy Melis, Teri Torday, Tibor Bitskev.

d&w, Peter Bacso; ph, Tamas Andor; m, Gyorgy Vukan.

BAND OF THE HAND** (1986) 109m Tri-Star–Delphi IV & V/Tri-Star c

Stephen Lang *(Joe)*, Michael Carmine *(Ruben)*, Lauren Holly *(Nikki)*, John Cameron Mitchell *(J.L.)*, Daniele Quinn *(Carlos)*, Leon Robinson *(Moss)*, Al Shannon *(Dorcey)*, Danton Stone *(Aldo)*, Paul Calderon *(Tito)*, Larry Fishburne *(Cream)*, James Remar *(Nestor)*, Tony Bolano *(Felix)*, Frank Gilbert *(Antoine)*, Erla Julmiste *(Celeste)*, Deborah King *(Yvette)*, Jimi Ruccolo *(Diablo)*, Bill Smitrovitch *(Chavez)*, Luis Valderrama *(Chooch)*, Roy Datz *(Rene)*, James Eros *(Hakim)*, Ken Colman *(Helicopter Pilot)*, Carl Cofield *(27th Avenue Player)*, T.R. Durphy *(Drug Dealer)*, Eddie Edenfield *(Counselor #1)*, Matt Buther, Dan Fitzgerald *(Cops)*, Christopher Berry *(Moss' Clipboard Guard)*, Peter Fournier *(Ruben's Clipboard Guard)*, Julian Byrd *(J.L.'s Father)*, Joan Murphy *(J.L.'s Mother)*, Allyson Garret *(J.L.'s Sister)*, Michael Gregory *(Van Guard)*, Sandy Mielke *(Reception Guard)*, D.L. Blakely *(Guard)*, Jim Zubiena, Nelson Oramas *(Officers)*, Antonio Corone, Joe Petrullo *(Narcs)*.

South Florida, neon-lit streets, flashy clothes, expensive cars, rock music, drugs, and violence—all the staples of producer Michael Mann's television hit "Miami Vice," make the transition to the big screen here. Five tough teenage criminals from divergent economic, racial, and social backgrounds (Carmine, Mitchell, Quinn, Robinson, and Shannon) are taken out of their juvenile-detention facility and unceremoniously dumped in the middle of the Everglades without explana-

tion. They spend their first few hours in the wild arguing among themselves in a general panic until a man dressed in black, Lang, steps out of the brush to inform them that they have been paroled to his custody. They will learn to work as a team to survive, or they will die. Possessing the intimidating combination of Vietnam vet and Miccosukee Indian, Lang teaches the boys how to survive in the wild by hunting their own food, building their own huts, and pitching together for the benefit of the group. The formerly unruly, selfish, and individualistic lads do learn to depend on one another, and when Lang senses it is time, he gives them their final exam. Armed only with a map and a compass, Lang deserts the teenagers and tells them to make it back to civilization on their own. With their mentor gone, the boys once again begin to fight among themselves, but they soon realize that they will perish unless they work together.

Eventually the boys find their way out of the Everglades, to the surprise of Lang, who fully expected to have to rescue them. They are the first group to have made it out on their own. Phase two of their rehabilitation takes them to Miami—their old stomping ground. Having learned to survive in the wild, the teenagers now must apply the same principles to urban life. Lang and the teens move into a decrepit house in a bad neighborhood that serves as a shooting gallery for the local junkies. Sharing the house with the junkies is a family of homeless Haitians. Lang and his boys kick the junkies out and let the Haitians stay. Soon Lang has his charges improving and redecorating the house. None of this sits well with flamboyant drug dealer Fishburne, whose heroin sales have dropped off since the arrival of the do-gooders. Fishburne must answer to Miami drug kingpin Remar, who demands that Lang and his boys be wiped out without further ado. As it happens, one of the boys, Carmine, used to work for Remar, and subsequently learns that his 16-year-old girl friend, Holly, has become the unwilling concubine of the drug lord. Breaking with the group to save his girl, Carmine finds her and flees Miami. But when he learns from her that Fishburne plans to attack the house that very evening, he turns around to join his friends. In a lengthy and unbelievable fire-fight between Fishburne's and Lang's forces (not a cop to be seen during ten minutes of automatic weapons fire and explosions), Lang is killed. After taking his body back to his tribe for burial, the boys decide to go their separate ways. But the gutted house they shared draws them back and they decide to get revenge on Remar by destroying his drug trade. Arming themselves to the teeth, the teenagers execute an elaborate plan that wipes out Remar's new distribution headquarters. During the fight, Holly comes face-to-face with Remar and kills him. Their mission accomplished, it seems as if the boys intend to remain a team.

While the first hour of BAND OF THE HAND is fairly engrossing as we watch the rowdy, explosive teens slowly discover self-worth, respect for others, and teamwork under the stern guidance of Lang, the rest of the film dissolves into a teenage DIRTY DOZEN which seems to condone and encourage vigilantism. If Lang's Outward-bound-style rehabilitation program is meant to teach these boys that it is acceptable to take the law into your own hands if you possess the proper moral stance and several automatic weapons, are we, as a society, better off than if these kids stayed in jail? The final implications of this film are far more disturbing than they are hopeful. Major conceptual problems aside, BAND OF THE HAND does feature a solid performance from Lang, a Michael Mann favorite who went on to have a featured role as a crusading attorney in Mann's other TV series "Crime Story" (righteous indignation seems to be Lang's forte). Remar does his usual fine job as a totally reprehensible villain, and Fishburne is memorable as the flashy pusher. Unfortunately, the five teenagers are basically a colorless lot, none of whom generates much interest—a combination of a weak script and mediocre players. The nicest thing to be said about Glaser's direction is that it betrays his TV roots. Producer Mann's forays on the big screen are better when he directs the films himself, such as THIEF (1981) and MANHUNTER

(1986). Music includes a pretty good title tune produced by Tom Petty: "Band of the Hand" (Bob Dylan; performed by Dylan and The Heartbreakers: Mike Campbell, Stan Lynch, Howie Epstein, Benmont Tench); "Carry Me Back Home" (Andy Summers; performed by Summers); "Let's Go Crazy" (Prince; performed by Prince and the Revolution); "Faded Flowers" (written and performed by Shriekback); "All Come Together Again" (written and performed by Stephen Tiger); "Waiting For You," "Hold On," "Mission" (Rick Shaffer; performed by The Reds); "Turn It On" (Shaffer, Bruce Cohen, performed by The Reds); additional music created and performed by The Reds.

p, Michael Rauch; d, Paul Michael Glaser; w, Leo Garen, Jack Baran; ph, Reynaldo Villalobos (Metrocolor); m, Michael Rubini; ed, Jack Hofstra; prod d, Gregory Bolton; art d, Mark Harrington; set d, Don K. Ivey; cos, Robert DeMora; spec eff, Ken Pepiot; m/l, Andy Summers, Prince, Shriekback, Stephen Tiger, Rich Shaffer, Bruce Cohen, The Reds, Bob Dylan; makeup, Marie Del Russo.

Crime   **Cas.**   **(PR:O MPAA:R)**

BANDERA NEGRA†   (1986, Span.) 88m Altube-ETB c (Trans: Black Flag)

Alfredo Landa (Patxi), Imanol Arias (Esteban), Virginia Mataix (Begona), Carlos Lucena (Don Javier), Luis Ostalot, Juan Jesus Valverde, Alito Rodgers, Jr.

An unemployed Spanish sea captain, Landa, and his friend Arias, a machinist, become entangled in an illegal arms-peddling operation run by an evil shipping magnate. The pair winds up sailing to Africa to deliver a shipment of weapons to a corrupt government. Both are caught and thrown into an African prison, and the captain's daughter, Mataix, comes from Spain in an attempt to rescue them. Soon after her arrival, however, Landa is killed. The tragedy draws Mataix and Arias together, and the two become lovers. Returning to Spain, they learn that the shipping tycoon was behind the entire affair and enact revenge on him.

d, Pedro Olea; w, Pedro Olea, Rafael Castellano; ph, Carlos Suarez (Fujicolor); m, Carmelo Bernaola; ed, Jose Salcedo; set d, Ramiro Gomez; makeup, Manuel Martin.

Action-Adventure   **(PR:O MPAA:NR)**

BAR 51—SISTER OF LOVE*½   (1986, Israel) 95m Sadar/Shapira c (AKA: SISTER OF LOVE)

Giuliano Mer (Thomas), Semadar Kilchinsky (Mariana), Irith Shelag (Zara), David Patrick Wilson (Nicholas), Ada Valeria Tal (Appolonia), Alon Aboutboul (Aranjuez), Moscu Alkalay (Karl).

The second feature from Israeli director Guttman is a tedious and sordid affair about Mer, a morose 22-year-old man who is sexually obsessed with his 16-year-old sister, Kilchinsky. The opening is torturously slow as the siblings' mother finally succumbs to the cancer that has ravaged her body and spirit. Now that they are orphans, the authorities want to ship Kilchinsky off to boarding school, but Mer cannot stand the thought of being separated from his obsession, so he takes his sister and they run away to Tel Aviv. Mer and Kilchinsky both find work in a big downtown hotel, but when Mer suspects that his boss has less than honorable intentions anent Kilchinsky, he becomes jealous and forces her to quit with him. Living in an abandoned building, Mer wanders the city's seedier districts and eventually becomes the gigolo of Tal, an obese, aging nightclub singer. Mer and Kilchinsky move in with the woman (her elderly manager lives there as well) and she begins to suspect something peculiar when Mer leaves her bed every night to sleep next to his sister.

Tal gets Mer a job working in a sleazy nightclub where he catches the eye of Shelag, an exotic dancer who has grown tired of her American boy friend, Wilson. Also working at the nightclub is Shelag's brother, Aboutboul, a flamboyant, likable young homosexual who befriends Kilchinsky. Kilchinsky harbors the desire to become a dancer and wants permission from Mer to take dance classes and acting lessons. Sensing that this would eventually lead to her independence from him, Mer refuses to consider it. As the weeks drag on, Kilchinsky begins to defy her brother and gets Wilson, who is an actor, to take her to classes. When Mer learns that his sister has been dating Wilson he goes wild. This leads Kilchinsky to break from her brother and go off on her own with Wilson. Brother and sister are kept informed of each other's activities by Aboutboul, who shuttles

back and forth between them (Mer has gone back to living in the abandoned building) trying to make peace. One night Mer finally snaps and he tricks Kilchinsky into coming to visit him at the abandoned building alone. There he indulges in some pathetic babbling before trying to rape her. Before he gets too far, the crying Kilchinsky grabs a piece of broken glass and stabs Mer in the stomach, killing him.

Seedy, distasteful, and exploitative, BAR 51—SISTER OF LOVE is a hard film to sit through. Since the film offers no insight into, compassion for, or understanding of these characters, Guttman milks the incest premise throughout the entire movie in a perverse effort to titillate audiences into staying in their seats. If the weak script wasn't bad enough, we are asked to watch the unsympathetic and hopelessly dreary Mer plod through his scenes, never offering a shred of evidence that he is indeed playing a living human being. Kilchinsky's character doesn't fare any better. Though she does seem to hold some promise as an actress, the script shows Kilchinsky to be pathetically naive until the last 30 minutes. It is painfully obvious to every other character in the film that Mer is sexually obsessed with his sister, and she seems totally oblivious of his true intentions until he tries to rape her. Just how stupid is this girl? Director/writer Guttman (a man seemingly obsessed with deviate sex—his first film, DRIFTING (1984), was about a film director struggling with his homosexuality) seems to delight in showing the seamier side of Tel Aviv life, but he makes absolutely no effort to justify the trip. Only Aboutboul manages to wrest some life and relevance out of his character, and in this film that is an accomplishment worthy of respect. Shown at film festivals in the U.S. in 1986. (In Hebrew; English subtitles.)

p, David Lipkind; d, Amos Guttman; w, Amos Guttman, Edna Mazia; ph, Yossi Wein; m, Erich Rudich; ed, Tova Asher; art d, Ariel Roshko.

Drama   **(PR:O MPAA:NR)**

BARNDOMMENS GADE†   (1986, Den.) 90m Metronome-Danish Film Institute-Danmark's Radio-TV/Metronome c (Trans: Street of My Childhood)

Sofie Grabol (Esther), Vigga Bro (Her Mother), Torben Jensen (Her Father), Carl Quist Moller (Her Brother), Louise Fribo (Lisa), Claus Nissen, Kirsten Lehfeldt, Daimi Gentle, Lene Vasegard, Benny Poulsen, John Hahn-Peterson, Litten Hansen, Peter Schroder, Margrethe Koytu, Eva Madsen.

Danish period picture—circa 1935—based on the autobiographical poetry and prose of writer Tove Ditlevsen. Grabol stars as a young girl who escapes the blight of a Copenhagen slum by writing about her most secret dreams and fantasies.

p, Tivi Magnusson; d, Astrid Henning-Jensen; w, Astrid Henning-Jensen, Erik Thygesen (based on the novel Street of My Childhood and the autobiography The Early Spring by Tove Ditlevsen); ph, Mikael Salomon; m, Ann Linnet; ed, Ghita Beckendorff; prod d, Soren Krag Sorensen; cos, Manon Rasmussen.

Drama   **(PR:C MPAA:NR)**

BBONG†   (1986, S. Korea) 107m Tae Hung c (AKA: PONG) (Trans: The Mulberry Tree)

Lee Mee-sook, Lee Tae-gun, Lee Moo-jung, Han Tai-il Kim Jung-Ha.

In an unusual subject for a comedy, this South Korean motion picture focuses on a woman who is forced to sleep around with the men in her village in order to support herself. Her husband is often out of town on business, and thus her dalliances occur with increasing regularity. Naturally this angers the women of the village, who would prefer that their rival left town. When the lady in question rejects the advances of the village idiot, the scorned man gets his revenge by causing him trouble. Eventually a village elder tries to convince the woman to leave town. After she shows him the results of a beating inflicted by the jealous women of the village, the old man succumbs to this vixen's charms as well.

p, Lee Tae-won; d, Lee Doo-yong; w, Yoon Sam-yook; ph, Son Hyunchae; m, Choi Chang-kwon.

Comedy   **(PR:O MPAA:NR)**

BEAU TEMPS, MAIS ORAGEUX EN FIN DE JOURNEE†   (1986, Fr.) 83m Diagonale-JM-Films A2/Gerick c (Trans: Fine Weather, But Storms Due Towards Evening)

Micheline Presle, Claude Pieplu, Xavier Deluc, Tonie Marshall.

A domestic drama about an older couple—Presle and Pieplu—who are visited by a son whom they rarely see. The young man, Deluc, has come home to introduce his parents to his fiancee, Marshall (Presle's real-life daughter), and announce their forthcoming marriage. The meeting is not without ripples, and the stark realism of this uneasy situation takes an unexpected sorrowful turn when Pieplu dies suddenly. The debut feature from director Frot-Coutaz.

d, Gerard Frot-Coutaz; w, Gerard Frot-Coutaz, Jacques Davila; ph, Jean-Jacques Bouhon (Agfa color); m, Roland Vincent; ed, Paul Vecchiali, Frank Mathieu.

Drama   **(PR:C MPAA:NR)**

BEE-EATER, THE   (SEE: PLACE AT THE COAST, THE, 1986, Aus.)

BEER*½   (1986) 82m Orion c

Loretta Swit (B.D. Tucker), Rip Torn (Buzz Beckerman), Kenneth Mars (A.J. Norbecker), David Alan Grier (Elliot Morrison), William Russ (Merle Draggett), Saul Stein (Frankie Falcone), Peter Michael Goetz (Harley Feemar), David Wohl

(Stanley Dickler), Dick Shawn *(Talk Show Host)*, Ren Woods *(Mary Morrison)*, Alar Aedma *(Thief)*, William Mooney *(Newscaster)*, Robert Wolberg *(Smythe)*, Gerald Vichi *(Bartender Freddie)*, Maurice Shrog *(Bartender Eddie)*, Ray O'Connor *(Martin)*, David Lipman *(Ernie)*, Donald Agree *(Michael Morrison)*, Amy Wright *(Stacy)*, Charlie Barnett *(Himself)*, John Bennes *(Lawrence Talbot)*, Elena Kudaba *(Frankie's Mom)*, Gino Marrocco *(Francie's Pop)*, Ralph Manza *(Frankie's Grandfather)*, Donald Ewer *(Priest)*, Deena Levy *(Makeup Girl)*, Matthew Kimbrough *(Joel)*, Jade D. Bari *(Feminist at Rally)*, Steve Mittleman *(Reemer)*, Richard Litt, *(Brimley)*, Tracy Berg *(Grace)*, Robert Blumenfeld, Willy Nikels, Jonathan Slaff, Roy K. Stevens, W.M. Supernaw *(Board Room Executives)*, Gene Mack *("Mack Truck" MacKenzie)*, Sharon Dyer, Terry Elik, Caitlin Hicks *(Talk Show Audience)*, Jan Saint *(Drunk)*, Charles Bolender *(Little Man at Door)*, Doug Anderson *(Policeman)*, Jeff Scott *(Mail Boy)*, John Meanes *(CLIO Announcer)*, Cassandra Danz *(Sheila)*, Rosalyn Braverman *(Woman with Pasta)*, Jean Bruno *(Woman in Church)*, Joseph Battle, Drew Geraci, Jesse Holmes *(Men in Steambath)*.

BEER first saw the light of a projection bulb in late summer 1985, when Orion nervously gave the film a few test screenings in Colorado movie theaters. A general release was held back, and the film ultimately became available on videocassette in 1986. Such is the fate of many bad films, and while BEER isn't an average inane teen-sex comedy, it's certainly no shining example of the art of comic film.

The story opens as Swit, a zealous ad executive, sets out to revive her company's sagging account with Mars' old family brewery. Beer sales have been down, and unless she can come up with an astounding campaign, Mars will take his business elsewhere. In the meantime, Russ, a good ol' boy from Texas, Stein, a handsome Italian, and Grier, a well-dressed black lawyer, all end up drinking in the same bar. When a psychotic hoodlum tries to rob the place, this unlikely trio inadvertently saves the day, becoming instant heroes. Swit sees them on the news and immediately hires them as the regular kind of guys she hopes will appeal to American consumers. She engages her old pal Torn, a reformed alcoholic, to direct the commercials and the result is an unmitigated success. Russ, Stein, and Grier are a hit and Mars' Norbecker Beer becomes a popular item at taverns and liquor stores. Swit then decides to change the advertising campaign from the macho sounding "Are you tough enough for Norbecker?" to something with more sexual appeal. The result is "Whip out your Norbecker," which pushes beer sales even higher.

Russ, Stein, and Grier are sent with Torn to film a commercial out West, but their light plane crashes in the desert. They now must find their way back to civilization, while Swit plots ways to capitalize on their disappearance. Eventually the media stars and their injured director are found and commercials based on their desert experiences are planned. However, Torn has once again gone back on the bottle, so Swit fires him. Russ and Stein decide to quit, then go looking for Grier, who has vanished. They find him drinking with his new friends, who, unbeknownst to the much-inebriated Grier, are the patrons of a gay bar. The three finally return to their quiet lives, while Swit wins a CLIO award for her success with the account. Mars, realizing there is a whole new market for his product, appears in a commercial aimed at the gay community, asking potential consumers, "Are you sensitive enough?" [for Norbecker Lite].

This is a largely predictable comedy that depends on stereotypes to carry much of the film's witless humor. Blacks, Italians, and homosexuals will probably be the most offended, though the jokes aren't vicious, merely stupid. Swit, like many a "M*A*S*H" costar, shows her television success was based more on luck than talent. Her performance here shows little ability for anything beyond a guest starring role on "The Love Boat." Russ, Stein, and Grier fare better, considering they don't have to do much beyond look handsome. Though the script and Kelly's direction are simplistic, there are sporadic hints that BEER was intended to be a much more pointed satire. There is an occasional black-humor swipe at the influence of television on the public consciousness ("There's 220 million Americans out there waiting to have their minds twisted and bent . . . " Torn declares at one point), and Shawn provides an amusing cameo as a Phil Donahue sort. With the help of his female audience, Shawn attempts to probe beneath the surface of Norbecker's advertising, putting the company's three stars under grueling scrutiny. Swit replaced the film's original lead, Sandra Bernhard, further suggesting this movie's original concept was something beyond its ultimate result.

p, Robert Chartoff; d, Patrick Kelly; w, Allan Weisbecker; ph, Bill Butler (Panavision, Deluxe Color); m, Bill Conti; ed, Alan Heim; prod d, Bill Bordie; art d, Tony Hall, Bill McAllister; set d, Steve Shewchuk, Michele Guiol; cos, Olga Dimitrov; spec eff, David Reid; m/l, Jerry Connolly; makeup, Patricia Green.

Comedy **(PR:O MPAA:R)**

BEGINNER'S LUCK** (1986) 83m Hot Talk/NW c

Sam Rush *(Hunter)*, Riley Steiner *(Tech)*, Charles Humet *(Aris)*, Kate Talbot *(Bethany)*, Mickey Coburn *(Babs)*, Bobbie Steinbach *(Courtney)*, Rima Miller *(Judith)*, Phil Kilbourne *(Willem)*, John Adair *(Reverend/Gas Attendant)*, Cynthia Weagle *(Stella/Bonnie)*, Stephen Weagle *(Don/Ronnie)*, John Eisner *(Nathan)*.

Frank and Caroline Mouris, the husband-and-wife team best known for their wonderful experimental short, FRANK FILM, turned to feature filmmaking with this independent production. It's a strange conglomerate of ideas that alternates between fresh and original stylizations and predictable, boring slapstick. When it's neither of these, it's often downright weird. Steiner, an alluring redhead, is stood up at the altar by her fiance Humet, a poet who writes limericks for greeting cards. Humet is a little marriage shy, so Steiner moves in with her intended, hoping he will eventually come around. Their downstairs neighbor, Rush, is a shy law student inexperienced in worldly ways. Steiner and Humet befriend him and agree to help him expand his horizons. Rush takes out an ad in the personal column of the local newspaper seeking adventurous couples. This leads to a few strange experiences, then the three friends decide to go off for a weekend together. Rush tries to help solidify the consistently shifting romance between Steiner and Humet, which inadvertently leads to a *menage a trois*. The band tries to keep their love triangle a secret, but are nearly undone when Rush's unattractive but wealthy fiancee arrives unexpectedly. Steiner considers marrying a young man her mother was involved with, but manages to reunite with her two loves as the story comes to its happy conclusion.

The Mourises certainly display a talent for filmmaking, yet the nature of that talent is often difficult to discern. The opening ten minutes of the film are almost completely silent, accompanied by a few of Humet's limericks as subtitled narration. Some imaginative montage sequences show week-by-week development of the three-way relationship, and double casting is cleverly used. Cynthia and Stephen Weagle play both couples who answer Rush's advertisement and this leads to some inspired moments. Despite these strengths, and the affable performance of the three leads, BEGINNER'S LUCK never gels. It plays like a sort of spin on JULES AND JIM, but the spin often goes out of control, leaving the viewer perplexed about the film's intentions. When they stick to the story, offering their own novel conceptions, the film is a real treat. Unfortunately, they can't keep in step with their own ideas and the results are disappointing. Shot on location in 1983 along the coast of Maine, BEGINNER'S LUCK was copyrighted the next year but remained unreleased until 1986.

p, Caroline Ahfors Mouris; d, Frank Mouris; w, Caroline Ahfors Mouris, Frank Mouris; ph, Anne S. Coffey (Fujicolor); m, Richard Lavsky; ed, Ray Anne School.

Comedy **Cas.** **(PR:O MPAA:NR)**

BEI AIQING YIWANGDE JIAOLUO† (1986, Chi.) 95m E Mei/China Film c (Trans: A Love-Forsaken Corner)

Shen Danping, He Xiaoshu, Yang Hailian, Zhang Shihui.

The lives of three peasant women are brought to the screen in this politically frank story that follows the rise of communism in China in the 1940s through the downfall of the Gang of Four. One of the women decides to make drastic changes in her life, renouncing her arranged marriage and taking up with a Communist farmer. The logic of their new political party is drawn into question, however, when the Communist leaders take action that destroys the village orange groves on which the farmer has been dependent. Based on a best-selling novel, this film was completed in 1981. It received some attention in China for its political openness and its treatment of sexual roles, before being banned, then resurfacing at the Hong Kong Film Festival to a less-than-enthusiastic audience who viewed it more as a relic than anything relevant to today's Chinese film industry.

d, Zhang Qi, Li Yalin; w, Zhang Xian (based on his novel); ph, Mai Shuhuan; m, Wang Ming; ed, Li Ling; art d, Chen Desheng, Wu Zujing.

Drama **(PR:A-C MPAA:NR)**

BELIZAIRE THE CAJUN*** (1986) 103m Cote Blanche/Skouras-Norstar c

Armand Assante *(Belizaire Breaux)*, Gail Youngs *(Alida Thibodaux)*, Michael Schoeffling *(Hypolite Leger)*, Stephen McHattie *(James Willoughby)*, Will Patton *(Matthew Perry)*, Nancy Barrett *(Rebecca)*, Loulan Pitre *(Sheriff)*, Andre DeLaunay *(Dolsin)*, Jim Levert *(Amadee Meaux)*, Ernie Vincent *(Old Perry)*, Paul Landry *(Sosthene)*, Allan Durand *(Priest)*, Robert Duvall *(Preacher)*, Bob Edmundson *(Head Vigilante)*, Robin Wood, Charlie Goulas, Robert Earl Willis *(Vigilantes)*, Harold Broussard *(Parrain)*, Merlyn Foret *(Parrain's Wife)*, Marcus Delahoussaye *(Theodule)*, Ken Meaux, Craig Soileau *(Card Players)*, Mike Doucet *(Fiddler)*, Lauren Greene *(Dancing Girl)*, Dennis LeBlanc *(Father of Dancing Girl)*, Bertrand DeBlanc *(Man on Porch)*, Steve Broussard *(Man at Gallows)*.

A period melodrama set in Louisiana's Cajun country in the mid-1800s which stars Assante as a healer who becomes the central figure in a battle between his fellow French-Canadian settlers and the racist local good ol' boys. Assante, the most intelligent and most admired of the Cajuns, gets himself in trouble when he protects his childish cousin, Schoeffling, from a posse which is hunting him down for cattle rustling. The posse is also intent on running a number of problem Cajuns out of town. What makes matters worse for Assante is that his Cajun former sweetheart, Youngs, is now the common-law wife of posse leader Patton, a semi-sympathetic local who is caught between the world of the Cajuns and his powerful landowner father to whom he is the heir to the family fortune. Next in line for the fortune is McHattie, a malevolent vigilante who is tormented by his jealousy of Patton. Schoeffling is soon corralled by the posse and whipped by Patton, who takes his anger against McHattie out on the Cajun. The following morning Patton is found belly-up in a nearby swamp and Schoeffling, who was in the medical care of Assante, is accused of the murder. After regaining his strength, Schoeffling flees on horseback, hounded by the posse. Assante then becomes a pawn in a scheme engineered by McHattie to pin the murder on Assante. Assante is hauled in by the sheriff (played by director Pitre's father) and confesses to the murder, thinking that by doing so he can save Schoeffling and put an end to the posse's reign of terror. His plan goes awry when Schoeffling is murdered anyway. In order to save face, the sheriff then arrests two of the vigilantes and sends them to the gallows, along with Assante. In the meantime, Youngs has been completely shut out of the family fortune by McHattie, who selfishly leaves her and her three children without even a morsel of food to live on. In the town square, hundreds of locals turn out for the hanging. As Assante is pulled from the jailhouse, the crowds cheer, hoping that their hero's life will be spared. Standing with a noose around his neck, awaiting his death, Assante has a

priest declare that Youngs was legally married in the eyes of God, and then proceeds to hand out his few possessions to the crowd. He produces a magical root that will kill any murderer who touches it and, by throwing it to the fearful McHattie, proves who the real murderer was. Youngs and her children are accepted back into the family and Assante, who has been spared the noose, proposes to his former Cajun sweetheart.

A labor of love for 30-year-old first-time feature director Pitre (pronounced "Peet"), BELIZAIRE THE CAJUN is one of the few films in the history of cinema that has examined the life styles and customs of the Cajun people. The Cajuns, a community of French settlers in Louisiana, came to the U.S. from settlements in Acadia, Nova Scotia. In 1775, after the British conquered the region during the French and Indian War, the Acadians, or "Cajuns" as they soon came to be known, headed for the French port of New Orleans and soon spread throughout Louisiana. Almost completely ignored on the big screen, the most famous Cajun film was the 1929 picture EVANGELINE, which starred Dolores Del Rio as an Acadian who travels to the New World in search of her lost love. While pictures like Anthony Mann's THUNDER BAY (1953) and Walter Hill's SOUTHERN COMFORT (1981) have been set in Cajun regions, the people have never been thoughtfully portrayed on the screen (a situation similar to the image of the Mennonite and Amish communities in 1985's WITNESS). Pitre, a Harvard graduate and a native of Cut Off, Louisiana, brings his experience with the Cajun people to BELIZAIRE, having directed a number of 16mm Cajun-language (a unique amalgam of French and English) docu-dramas. Once Pitre's proposal was accepted by Robert Redford's Sundance Institute, the project fell into gear. Robert Duvall came aboard as a creative consultant, as did Redford, and Duvall's wife Youngs was cast in a lead role. After an enthusiastic showing at the Cannes Film Festival, BELIZAIRE found a U.S. distributor and soon turned a profit on its $900,000 investment.

Filmed with great regard to period detail and authenticity—mostly in a tourist spot, Acadian Village, and Longfellow Evangeline State Park in St. Martinsville (EVANGELINE was also filmed there)—BELIZAIRE must be commended for bringing a unique aspect of the American heritage to a wide audience. Unfortunately, its well-intentioned depiction of the Cajun community cannot erase its multitude of flaws. While the film succeeds overall as an exciting and energetic piece of melodrama, it never digs past the surface and as a result offers nothing more than shallow underdeveloped characters in patented situations. Why, for example, has it taken so long for this feud to erupt? The Cajuns have been there for years (Patton and Youngs have a child of about 10) and it seems as if only now they are being persecuted. More than for any one specific reason, BELIZAIRE seems to falter, somewhat, on every facade. The dizzying handheld camerawork is a strain on the eyes, the sound (not its foreign dialog) is technically murky, and too much of the plot and character motivations are left in the dark. Aside from its problems, however, BELIZAIRE still manages to work at involving the audience, especially in its dynamic gallows finale, which serves as a tour-de-force for Assante. The superb soundtrack is by Cajun musician Doucet and his band Beausoleil who perform their own original music—"Contradanse de Doucet," "Petit Jean Pas Danser," "Belizaire Overture," "Mon Mari Est Parti" (Michael Doucet; performed by Beausoleil)—and a number of traditional Cajun tunes—"Madame Etienne," Grand Mallet," "Madame Sosthene," "Mardi Gras," "Hip Et Tailleau," "Reel Cadjin," "Contradanse," and "Mc-Gee's Danse Carre."

p, Allan L. Durand, Glen Pitre; d&w, Pitre; ph, Richard Bowen; m, Michael Doucet; ed, Paul Trejo; prod d, Randall LaBry; art d, Deborah Schildt; cos, Sara Fox; ch, Miriam Lafleur Fontenot.

Historical Drama   Cas.   (PR:C MPAA:PG)

BEST MAN, THE†   (1986, Brit.) 85m Northlands c

Seamus Ball (Billy Maguire), Denis McGowan (Jamsie McDaid), Mairead Mullan (Maureen McDaid), Jean Flagherty (Mrs. Maguire), Mickey McGowan (Joe McLaughlin), Aiden Heaney (Pat McIntyre), Hugh McIntyre (Professor).

A comedy set in Northern Ireland about a hard-drinker, Ball, who can barely stay sober enough to play the role of best man at his best mate's wedding. Ball lives with his mother, but that doesn't stop him from going through life in a stupor, spending most of his time at the local pub. When not gambling or being the drunken know-it-all, Ball directs his energies towards trying to inebriate Mc-

Gowan, a married friend who has sworn off the bottle. There's not much plot, thereby requiring the film to stand on the strength of its characterizations. Ironically, THE BEST MAN practically ignores the tense political situation so prevalent in most other films set in this troubled locale.

p, Denis Bradley; d&w, Joe Mahon; ph, Terry McDonald; m, Eamon Friel; ed, Terry McDonald; prod d, Denis Bradley.

Comedy   (PR:A-C MPAA:NR)

BEST OF TIMES, THE*½   (1986) 104m Kings Road Entertainment/UNIV c

Robin Williams (Jack Dundee), Kurt Russell (Reno Hightower), Pamela Reed (Gigi Hightower), Holly Palance (Elly Dundee), Donald Moffat (The Colonel), Margaret Whitton (Darla), M. Emmet Walsh (Charlie), Donovan Scott (Eddie), R.G. Armstrong (Schutte), Dub Taylor (Mac), Carl Ballantine (Arturo), Kathleen Freeman (Rosie), Tony Plana (Chico), Kirk Cameron (Teddy), Robyn Lively (Jaki), Eloy Casados (Carlos), Jeff Doucette (Olin), Anne Haney (Marcy), Bill Overton (Luther Jackson), William Schilling, Hugh Gillin, Jake Dengel (Caribous), Peter Van Norden (Mando), Patrick Brennan (Ronny), Linda Hart, Marie Cain, Peggy Moyer (Blenders), Jeff Severson (Johnny "O"), Hap Lawrence (Dickie Larue), Nick Shields (Bam Bam), Hugh Stanger (Old Man Lester), Wayne Montanio (Felipe), "Iron Jaws" Wilson ("Iron Jaws"), Brenda Huggins (Mrs. Jackson), Hilary Davis (Michelle), Michael Rich (Blade), Norm Schachter (Referee), Christopher Mankiewicz (Safari Room Security Guard), J.P. Bumstead (Cop), Robert Dickman (Taft Business Man), Jim Giovanni, Steve Shargo (Taft Football Players), Darryl B. Smith, Wayne Adderson, Raymond W. Clanton, Fred A. Nelson (Bakersfield Coaches), Vister Hayes (Dr. Death), Michelle Guastello, Cathy Cheryl Davis, Susan Signorelli (Taft Women), Philipe Gerard (Disgruntled Fan), Christopher Cory (Assistant Football Trainer), Kim Romano, Steve Riley, Kelly Thomas, Mike Douglas, Herman Edwards, Chuck Ramsey, Buck the Dog.

Everyone has something in his past that will remain forever haunting, but few people would allow such ghosts to grow to the obsessive levels that this film deals with. Williams is a banker in a small town, married to Palance (the real-life daughter of Jack Palance). His whole life is mired in failure, a condition he traces back to his dropping of a crucial pass during a high-school football game some 13 years before. Russell, the star quarterback of that fateful contest, has also been plagued by unhappiness in the years that followed. He now owns a garage, and is

vainly trying to keep together the tattered shreds of his marriage with Reed. After another in a series of clandestine meetings with masseuse-cum-hired-paramour Whitton, Williams is struck by inspiration. His old team will stage a rematch against their 13-year-old nemesis, thus restoring Williams' confidence. Most dismiss this plan as foolhardy, but Williams—disguised as the rival high school's tiger mascot—goes on a one-man vandalizing spree that unites the townspeople with a sense of community pride. The game is agreed to, which temporarily reconciles Williams and Russell with their long-suffering wives. Palance's father, Moffat, happens to be a strong supporter of the opposition, which doesn't help Williams' feelings of self-worth. But as he pushes his former teammates towards the big day, Williams' confidence soars. Russell, on the other hand, is terrified of the game's outcome. Because he is such a legendary figure in the town, this single competition could wipe out all of the myths that have been built around his former skills.

In the big game Williams' team takes a sound beating during the first two quarters. At halftime Russell learns of Williams' chicanery with the tiger suit, and justifiably angered, the quarterback hangs Williams up on a hook. With renewed zeal Russell goes back to the game determined to win. The team rallies back and, with just seconds to go, is only a few points behind. Williams, who has managed to get off the hook, is put into the game and at last relives that crucial moment. This time the pass is completed and Williams is vindicated.

Williams' unique improvisational talents are tightly restricted by the script, and as a result his performance is too lethargic. It's hard to believe this little man could care about the day-to-day events of his life, let alone a 13-year-old football game. There are a few moments during the training sequences whereong Williams is allowed to break loose, giving only a hint of what this could have been if he had been allowed more control of his character. Russell is good considering the material, and he does develop a nice rapport with his costar. As the long-

suffering wives, Reed and Palance are fine, though their roles consistently take a background to the comedy.

In emphasizing the slapstick, director Spottiswoode runs roughshod over some of the intriguing qualities of the film. He captures well the atmosphere and residents of a small, isolated American town, but rather than sympathize with their situation, Spottiswoode plays it for big laughs. Williams' obsession promptly becomes ludicrous and it's really hard to care about him or this film. The more interesting relationships between characters and their surroundings are consistently ignored, ultimately generating an unfunny waste of time and talent. Songs include: "Don't Say Nothin' Bad (About My Baby)" (Gerry Goffin, Carole King, performed by Gigi and the Blenders), "He's Sure the Boy I Love" (Barry Mann, Cynthia Weil, performed by Gigi and the Blenders), "(They Long to Be) Close to You" (Burt Bacharach, Hal David), "Remember Then" (Stan Vincent, performed by The Earls), "The First Time Ever I Saw Your Face" (Ewin Mac Coll, performed by Roberta Flack), "Land of Hope and Glory" ("Pomp and Circumstance No. 1") (Sir Edward Elgar, Arthur Benson).

p, Gordon Carroll; d, Roger Spottiswoode; w, Ron Shelton; ph, Charles F. Wheeler (Panavision, Technicolor); m, Arthur B. Rubinstein; ed, Garth Craven; art d, Anthony Brockliss; set d, Marc E. Meyer, Jr.; cos, Patricia Norris; spec eff, Garry J. Elmendorf; m/l, Gerry Goffin, Carole King, Barry Mann, Cynthia Weil, Hal David, Burt Bacharach, Stan Vincent, Ewin Mac Coll, Sir Edward Elgar, Arthur Benson; makeup, Bradley Wilder.

Comedy/Drama   (PR:O   MPAA:PG-13)

BETTER TOMORROW, A†   (1985, Hong Kong) 98m Cinema City/Golden
                                                         Princess c

Chow Yun Fat, Ti Lung, Leslie Cheung, Young Pao I.

Heavy on action, violence, and bloodletting, this familiar story tells of two brothers, Cheung, a hard-working cop, and Ti, his mob-connected older brother. They have long gone their separate ways, though Ti has now turned over a new leaf. Ti soon finds that it is not easy to survive in Hong Kong when you have the type of past he has. (In Cantonese; English subtitles.)

p, Tsui Hark; d&w, John Woo; ph, Wong Wing Hang; m, Joseph Koo; ed, Kam Ma; art d, Bernie Liu.

Action   (PR:O   MPAA:NR)

BETTY BLUE**   (1986, Fr.) 120m Constellation-Cargo/Alive c (37.2 LE
                                                         MATIN)

Beatrice Dalle (Betty), Jean-Hugues Anglade (Zorg), Consuelo de Haviland (Lisa), Gerard Darmon (Eddy), Clementine Celarie (Annie), Jacques Mathou (Bob), Claude Confortes (Owner), Philippe Laudenbach (Gyneco Publisher), Vincent Lindon (Policeman Richard), Raoul Billeray (Old Policeman), Claude Aufaure (Doctor), Andre Julien (Old Georges), Nathalie Dalyan (Maria), Louis Bellanti (Mario), Bernard Robin (Renter No. 2), Nicolas Jalowyj (Little Nicolas), Dominique Besnehard.

By combining the energetic high-gloss finish of his debut feature DIVA with the raw poetic intensity of MOON IN THE GUTTER, Beineix has created in BETTY BLUE a brilliant, charming, and compelling tale of amour fou, or crazy, obsessive love. In a no-holds-barred opening, the camera zooms in on two naked lovers, Anglade and Dalle, ecstatically making love. While this first shot (which seems to last an eternity) produces an alarmingly uneasy reaction in the viewer, it simultaneously makes the audience as intimate with the characters as they are with themselves. Anglade and Dalle hide nothing from the viewer—not their bodies, not their emotions, and not their love for each other. After the couple finishes making love, the film's narrator (Anglade's character, Zorg) puts the audience at ease with his deliberately humorous comment, "I had known Betty for a week." Anglade—small, handsome, and unshaven—knows as little about Dalle as we do. Dalle, a curvaceous object of desire with perpetually pouty lips that could battle Brigitte Bardot to a standoff, is as unpredictable as she is beautiful—a fact that Anglade and the audience soon discover.

Barely existing in a surrealistic beachside shantytown, Anglade (who has invited Dalle to move in with him) earns his keep by doing handiwork. His piggish boss gives Anglade the impossible task of painting all 500 of the beach bungalows

by himself. Equipped with only a couple of rollers and an endless supply of pink and blue paint, Anglade goes to work. Dressed in a revealing pair of bib overalls sans undershirt, Dalle is determined to help the man she loves, grabbing a brush and working beside him. Before long, Dalle (who, along with Anglade, seems to have a predilection for traipsing around in the nude, indifferent to the presence of strangers) has thrown a bucket of paint on Anglade's boss' car, tossed all of Anglade's possessions out the window in a peculiar housecleaning effort, and set the bungalow ablaze with devastating finality. In the process, however, she has found the manuscript to a novel that Anglade has written. Having read it, Dalle stubbornly insists that Anglade is a genius and determines to win him the attention he deserves.

Dalle and Anglade leave the burning bungalow behind and head for Paris where they meet up with Dalle's widowed friend, de Haviland, and her boy friend, Darmon, the owner of an Italian restaurant. The four become fast friends. Having found herself a typewriter, Dalle, a two-finger typist who makes more mistakes than progress, spends her days banging out Anglade's novel. Once finished, she sends it off to every publisher in Paris. Life goes on for the foursome—Anglade (or, more correctly, Dalle) has no luck with the novel; they all work together at the restaurant; and eventually Darmon's mother dies. As life

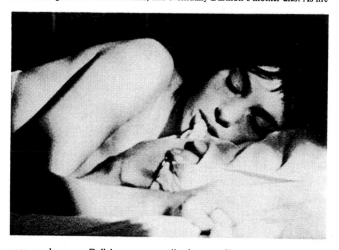

goes on, however, Dalle's grasp on reality loosens. She slashes the face of a publisher who cannot appreciate Anglade's genius, stabs an indignant restaurant customer with a fork, and in an argument with Anglade, shoves her hand through a window. Anglade and Dalle accept an offer from Darmon to manage his deceased mother's piano shop and live in her vacated apartment. Having nowhere else to go, the two agree.

As much as Anglade loves Dalle, he cannot keep her from slipping further over the edge. Growing increasingly depressed, she persuades herself that she will be better off if she has a child. Anglade is thrilled at the prospect, but when Dalle loses the baby she completely snaps. She complains of hearing voices, and, one afternoon while Anglade is out, she pokes out one of her eyes. Not surprisingly she is committed to an asylum—completely mentally incapacitated. Unable to see Dalle live that way, Anglade steals into her room and smothers her with a pillow. Later he sits alone in his dark kitchen, pecking at a typewriter, unable to forget her.

With BETTY BLUE, Beineix has discovered the depth that was missing from DIVA and the cohesion that was lacking in MOON IN THE GUTTER, creating a wonderful synthesis of the two. Taking the advice of the "Try Another World" billboard in MOON IN THE GUTTER, Beineix has created an imaginary place that knows no limits and exists within the boundaries that he himself has created. Although it has a facade of normalcy, the world of BETTY BLUE is one painted by the rules of poetic license: houses are pink and blue; carnivals appear then disappear; saxophone players come and go; birthday candles stay lit inexplicably; and policemen in the street burst into song. With this kind of imaginary existence, Beineix manages to lure his audience into the world of Betty Blue and Zorg, bridging any distance that may exist between the audience and his characters—a technique which is the polar opposite of the Brechtian/Godardian "distancing." Rather, Beineix practices a "cinema of identification," making the audience fall in love with the characters and their world. Like Zorg, the viewer falls in love with Dalle; and, like Dalle, the viewer wants to expose Anglade's genius. From the opening shot of this *film intime*, the viewer is propelled right into Betty and Zorg's bed, as if being a third (though unseen) partner in their passion. Once lured into their world, one doesn't want to leave. By doing this, Beineix has successfully enabled the viewer "try another world"—that seems to continue to exist long after the end credits have gone. The feeling of identification with the characters is intense, chiefly due to their charisma and the resulting *esprit de corps*. Because of Beineix's handling, the viewer experiences the same feelings that the director, himself, has stated: "This movie perturbed our whole lives. It overflew into our nights, stepped into our dreams . . . After constantly following this character (Zorg) in his strong quest for happiness and his passionate drift, I felt a distress that, oddly, stimulated me . . . I identified myself completely with him, to the point of assimilating his pain to my own suffering."

This feeling of identification would never have been possible had Beineix found any less-suited actors than Anglade and Dalle. Anglade, best known in the U.S. as the "roller" in SUBWAY (he also appeared as a prisoner in L'ADDITION and as the lead in L'HOMME BLESSE), is perfect cast as Zorg. (His character in the Djian novel didn't have a name, "Zorg" being chosen because Beineix liked the uniqueness of beginning someone's name with the letter *Z*.) The magical element of the film, however, is the 21-year-old Dalle, a phenomenon who has subsequently taken Paris by storm with a fervor no less than that of Bardot some 30 years earlier. A young punk who frequented Paris' Les Halles/Place de la Republique area, Dalle was spotted by a photographer who persuaded her to pose. Her face soon made it to a magazine cover that caught the attention of BETTY BLUE's casting agent, Dominique Besnehard. Although Dalle has complained that "my skull is too flat, my ears stick out, my mouth is too big, my belly too round and my buttocks too heavy," Beineix's opinion differs. "She wasn't an actress," says Beineix, "She had no job. When I saw her picture I thought she was very strange. Such eyes. Such a mouth. She was some kind of challenge to the rules of beauty. Then we tested her and discovered she was a natural. She had something which is a gift of God. The camera loves her. Only a few women in France have this—Catherine Deneuve, Isabelle Adjani." Besides being the eighth highest grossing film of 1986 in France, BETTY BLUE managed to receive eight Cesar nominations: Best Director; Best Picture; Best Actor; Best Actress; Best Supporting Actor (Darman); Best Supporting Actress (Celarie); Best Score; Best Editing; and Best Poster Design, winning only the latter. While not a box-office smash on this side of the Atlantic, BETTY BLUE did garner an Oscar nomination as Best Foreign Language Film. (In French; English subtitles.)

p, Claudie Ossard, Jean-Jacques Beineix; d&w, Jean-Jacques Beineix (based on the novel *37.2 Le Matin* by Philippe Djian); ph, Jean-Francois Robin (Fujicolor); m, Gabriel Yared; ed, Monique Prim; art d, Carlos Conti; set d, Jacques Leguillon; cos, Elisabeth Tavernier; spec eff, Jean-Francois Cousson, George Demetreau; makeup, Judith Gayo.

Drama (PR:O MPAA:R)

BEYOND THE MIST† (1986, Iran) Farabi c

Ali Reza Shoja Noori, Iraj Tahmasb.

When a new governor is appointed, a band of assassins is determined to do him in. Also figuring in the story is a recent veteran of Iran's war with Iraq. Before the would-be killers can reach their target, they end up dead themselves. The governor, however, is seriously injured when his car accidentally falls in a river. Lingering precariously between life and death, he contemplates the meaning of it all. Throughout the film, his pragmatic nature and the war veteran's spiritual existence are contrasted, but by the end, the governor, too, has an appreciation for life lived on a higher plane.

d, Manoochehr Asgari-Nasab; w, Seyed Mohammad Beheshti; ph, Tooraj Mansoori; m, Fereydoon Naseri; ed, Davood Yoosefian.

Drama (PR:O MPAA:NR)

BI CHAMD KHAYRTAY† (1986, Mongolia) 91m Mongolkino c (Trans: I Adore You)

D. Erdenbayer *(Delger)*, D. Purevmaa *(Urlei)*, Z. Jarantau *(Sambuu)*, N. Badral *(Bayaras)*.

A teen romance picture starring Erdenbayer and Badral as a pair of young men who, upon graduation from school, must decide whether to apply for college or join the work force. While trying to come to a decision, both boys find themselves in love with the same girl, Purevmaa, a schoolmate who talks of having babies. Filled with the usual dose of teen parties and rock 'n' roll.

p&d, B. Baljinnyam; w, B. Baljinnyam, N. Nyamgawaa; ph, B. Baljinnyam, G. Tseren.

Drama (PR:A MPAA:NR)

BIBBI, ELIN AND CHRISTINA† (1986, Norway) A/S Filmgruppe 84

Marit Ostbye, Gro Solemdal, Janne Kokkin, Trude Birkelund.

d, Egil Kolsto; w, Anne Gullbjorg Digranes; ph, Rolv Haan.

BIG BET, THE† (1986) 98m Golden Communications–Golden Harvest c

Lance Sloane, Kim Evenson, Sylvia Kristel, Ron Thomas.

Bert I. Gordon, a director whose initials are B.I.G. and who has brought you such

gargantuan gems as THE AMAZING COLOSSAL MAN (1957), WAR OF THE COLOSSAL BEAST (1958), and VILLAGE OF THE GIANTS (1965), tries his hand at a teenage-sex comedy. This time a sex-starved young man, Sloane, is trying to make it with a minister's daughter, but has only a week to do so. Luckily he gets some helpful hints from soft-porn star Kristel, who is more than eager to be of aid.

p,d&w, Bert I. Gordon; ph, Tom DeNove.

Comedy (PR:O MPAA:NR)

BIG HURT, THE† (1986, Aus.) 93m Big Hurt/Ultimate Show c

David Bradshaw *(Price)*, Lian Lunson *(Lisa)*, Simon Chilvers *(Algerson)*, John Ewart *(Harry)*, Nick Waters *(McBride)*, Alan Cassell *(Blake)*, Alethea McGrath *(Mrs. Trent)*, Joanne Canning *(Ballerina)*, Syd Conabere *(O'Neal)*, Tommy Dysart *(Schwartz)*, Dorothy Cutts *(Rachel)*, Gary Adams *(Fletch)*, Abbe Holmes *(Jenny)*, Robin Cuming *(Monk)*, Julie Jones *(Wendy)*, Paul Young *(Smudge)*, Julie Du Rieu *(Street Whore)*, Paul Russell *(David Myles)*, Mira Babic *(Temptress)*, Yvonne Braumann *(Human Ashtray)*, John Allan *(Jogger)*, James McRae *(News Editor)*, Ronnie Burns, Norman Hancock, Elwin Bradshaw *(Journalists)*, Finn Keane *(Jane)*, John Raaen, Billy Smith *(Thugs)*, Kurt Schneider *(Guard)*, Niki Lane, Anna Knappe, Elizabeth Archer, Yvonne Braumann *(Tank Girls)*, David Bickerstaff *(Doctor)*, Lyn Heggarty *(Receptionist)*, Dorothy Lawrence *(Mrs. Sartore)*, Geoff Parry *(Mr. Gregg)*, Lawrence Mah *(Shopkeeper)*.

A traditionally structured crime story about a private eye, Bradshaw, who gets involved with *femme fatale* Lunson, who drags him through the criminal underground in search of her scientist father. Though her father reportedly committed suicide 15 years earlier, Lunson is convinced that he is still alive as part of a government coverup.

p, Chris Kiely; d, Barry Peak; w, Barry Peak, Sylvia Bradshaw; ph, Malcolm Richards (Eastmancolor); m, Allan Zavod; ed, Ralph Strasser; art d, Paddy Reardon; cos, Anna Jakab; makeup, Karla O'Keefe.

Mystery (PR:C MPAA:NR)

BIG TROUBLE**½ (1986) 93m COL–Delphi III/COL c

Peter Falk *(Steve Rickey)*, Alan Arkin *(Leonard Hoffman)*, Beverly D'Angelo *(Blanche Rickey)*, Charles Durning *(O'Mara)*, Paul Dooley *(Noozel)*, Robert Stack *(Winslow)*, Valerie Curtin *(Arlene Hoffman)*, Richard Libertini *(Dr. Lopez)*, Steve Alterman *(Peter Hoffman)*, Jerry Pavlon *(Michael Hoffman)*, Paul La Greca *(Joshua Hoffman)*, John Finnegan *(Detective Murphy)*, Karl Lukas *(Police Captain)*, Maryedith Burrell *(Gail)*, Edith Fields *(Doris)*, Warren Munson *(Jack)*, Rosemarie Stack *(Mrs. Winslow)*, Barbara Tarbuck *(Helen)*, Al White *(Mr. Williams)*, Theodore Wilson *(Porter)*, Gloria Gifford *(Wanda)*, Herb Armstrong *(Night Security Guard)*, Jaime Sanchez *(Chief Terrorist)*, Gaetano Lisi *(Gaetano Lopez)*, Chester Grimes *(Flavio Lopez)*, Irene Olga Lopez *(Lopez' Receptionist)*, Daphne Eckler *(Receptionist)*, Carol Reinhard *(Winslow's Secretary)*, Conroy Gedeon *(Reporter)*, Lenny Geer *(Whitlow Keppler)*, Melvin Jones, Luis Contreras, John M. Kochian, Jr., Domingo Ambriz, John Bianchini, Nafa Rasho, Roger Ito, Perry Fluker, Lynn Ready, Steven Lambert, Yukio G. Collins *(Terrorists)*, Howard Clapp, Jeff Howard *(Executives)*, Leland Sun, Albert Leong, Danny Lew, Michaelani, Dennis Phung, Walter Soo Hoo *(Chinese Laborers)*, Richard Walter *(Hog Dog Eater)*, Joseph G. Medalis *(Salesman)*.

The director of the probing social dramas A WOMAN UNDER THE INFLUENCE and LOVE STREAMS, Cassavetes here applies his remarkable talent for social observation in a light comedy context and creates one of the strangest, and in many ways most frustrating, screen comedies in recent years. Originally screenwriter Andrew Bergman (using the pseudonym Warren Bogle) had been slated to direct, but last-minute troubles resulted in his replacement by Cassavetes. Berg-

man had been the screenwriter for the previous Arkin/Falk teaming, the immensely successful THE IN-LAWS (1979), which served as the conceptual basis for BIG TROUBLE (Falk and Arkin essentially reprise the same characters). As in the earlier film, Arkin plays the straight man to crazed Falk, a confidence artist with an unlimited supply of schemes designed to rake in loads of cash.

The film opens with Arkin searching for a means to send his musical-genius triplets to Yale. No other school will do for wife Curtin, who insists that the boys will succeed only if they attend that school. Appealing for help to his boss at the insurance company, Stack—also a Yale man—Arkin is given no more than a pat on the back and sent on his way. Here the plot becomes a satirical reworking of Billy Wilder's *film noir* classic DOUBLE INDEMNITY (1944), which starred Fred MacMurray and Barbara Stanwyck as lovers who scheme to murder Stanwyck's husband for his insurance money. The teasingly beautiful D'Angelo comes to Arkin for an insurance policy for her "husband," Falk, whom she claims is a kind-hearted big game hunter. She then informs Arkin that in actuality Falk is a very sick man with a heart condition, and that he will probably be dead within a week. Unfortunately, as D'Angelo tells Arkin, Falk has been far too generous with his money, and she will be penniless if he dies. Recognizing an

opportunity when presented with one, Arkin agrees to help D'Angelo kill Falk and split the insurance money with her. Just as in DOUBLE INDEMNITY, the two plot to disguise the murder by having it appear that Falk accidentally fell from a train. This will double the payoff on the policy because of a special clause concerning train accidents. The plan is carried out with minimum difficulty and Arkin and D'Angelo prepare for the big meeting with the insurance company executives to collect the money. At the meeting, however, Arkin discovers that Falk, wearing a bald wig and posing as D'Angelo's lawyer, is not dead at all, but has been conning Arkin with a scheme that doesn't even end here. Using his charm to string the malleable Arkin along even further, Falk formulates a plan to make millions. Through a series of whirlwind events—that follow no logical pattern—the film reaches its climax as Arkin and Falk attempt to rob Stack of the contents of the ultra-high-security safe located on the top floor of the insurance company building. While the burglary is in procees, a gang of Latino terrorists attacks the building, giving Arkin the the opportunity to become a hero and earn the money he so desperately needs.

There are moments of absolute comic brilliance in this film, but as a whole BIG TROUBLE seems unsatisfactory. In part, this results from the manner in which Cassavetes approaches plot developments, which, for him, always assume secondary importance in favor of an analysis of character interaction. Unfortunately, here the approach just doesn't work. The characters are mainly cartoon sketches lacking the humanity required for the Cassavetes method to be effective. By the film's end Falk and Arkin appear hopelessly in need of one another as essential elements of their respective personalities. As a whole, performances are up to the caliber Cassavetes elicits from his actors. Stack is a particular standout as the owner of the insurance company, so secure in his own power that he is completely without feeling. The chemistry between Arkin and Falk that made THE IN-LAWS such a success is again present in BIG TROUBLE, with Arkin's stoical seriousness the perfect foil for Falk's unpredictable absurdity. After completion, BIG TROUBLE remained on the shelf for an entire year, finally having a limited theatrical release to prepare for its videocassette release.

p, Michael Lobell (uncredited); d, John Cassavetes; w, Warren Bogle [Andrew Bergman]; ph, Bill Butler (Panavision, Metrocolor); m, Bill Conti; ed, Donn Cambern, Ralph Winters; prod d, Gene Callahan; art d, Pete Smith; set d, Joseph Hubbard; cos, Joe I. Tompkins; m/l, Mildred J. Hill, Patty S. Hill, Giacomo Puccini, Wolfgang Amadeus Mozart, Franz Josef Haydn; makeup, Monty Westmore; stunts, Gray Johnson.

Comedy   Cas.   (PR:C MPAA:R)

BIG TROUBLE IN LITTLE CHINA***   (1986) 99m FOX c

Kurt Russell *(Jack Burton)*, Kim Cattrall *(Gracie Law)*, Dennis Dun *(Wang Chi)*, James Hong *(Lo Pan)*, Victor Wong *(Egg Shen)*, Kate Burton *(Margo)*, Donald Li *(Eddie Lee)*, Carter Wong *(Thunder)*, Peter Kwong *(Rain)*, James Pax *(Lightning)*, Suzee Pai *(Miao Yin)*, Chao Li Chi *(Uncle Chu)*, Jeff Imada *(Needles)*, Rummel Mor *(Joe Lucky)*, Craig Ng *(One Ear)*, June Kim *(White Tiger)*, Noel Toy *(Mrs. O'Toole)*, Jade Go *(Chinese Girl in White Tiger)*, Jerry Hardin *(Pinstripe Lawyer)*, James Lew, Jim Lau, Ken Endoso, Stuart Quan, Gary Toy, George Cheung *(Chang Sings)*, Jimmy Jue *(Wounded Chang Sing)*, Noble Craig *(Sewer Monster)*, Danny Kwan *(Chinese Guard)*, Min Luong *(Tara)*, Paul Lee *(Chinese Gambler)*, Al Leong, Gerald Okamura, Willie Wong, Eric Lee, Yukio G. Collins, Bill M. Ryusaki, Brian Imada, Nathan Jung, Daniel Inosanto, Vernon Rieta *(Wing Kong Hatchet Men)*, Daniel Wong, Daniel Eric Lee *(Wing*

Kong Security Guards), Lia Chang, Dian Tanaka, Donna L. Noguschi, Shinko Isobe *(Female Wing Kong Guards)*.

Did the entire critical community get up on the wrong side of the bed on the morning that BIG TROUBLE IN LITTLE CHINA was screened? This hilarious, action-packed, extremely *fun* movie was viciously maligned at the time of its release and the film subsequently sank like a stone at the box office. What is not to like here? Written and directed in a campy tongue-in-cheek manner, this film is a loving homage to those wild imports from Hong Kong—kung-fu movies. Russell stars as a swaggering truck driver who would like to think he's as tough as John Wayne, but who in reality is more than a little clumsy. He may be a braggart, but he's got a good heart. During a stop in San Francisco, Russell accompanies his Chinese-American friend Dun to the airport where they are to meet the beautiful Pai, Dun's fiancee who has just flown in from China. Pai is a rare beauty, for she has green eyes, an unusual occurrence in China. At the airport, another woman with green eyes, Cattrall, catches the attention of the ever-amorous Russell. Dun informs Russell that Cattrall is a local attorney who helps newly arrived immigrants from China adjust to life in the U.S. Just as Dun is about to greet Pai, young thugs from a Chinese street gang appear and kidnap the girl. Russell and Dun give chase, and they wind up back in Chinatown where they find themselves stuck in the midst of a massive street brawl fought by rival Chinese gangs. Suddenly, a 7-foot-tall Chinese man dressed in full imperial regalia, Hong, appears in front of the truck. Russell can't stop in time and runs Hong over. The truck driver immediately leaps out of his vehicle to see what happened, only to find Hong intact and standing behind the truck. Bright white light emits from the grotesque-looking Hong's eyes and mouth. Dun pulls Russell away and the pair abandon the truck and head for shelter. Later Dun explains that Hong is the most powerful sorcerer in Chinatown and legend has it that he is a 2,258-year-old ghost who was doomed to face a "fleshless" existence after being cursed by the very first Chinese emperor. Hong's normal form is that of an ancient businessman confined to a wheelchair, but he is able to transform himself into the 7-foot-tall warlord at will. Eventually it is learned that in order to make himself flesh again, Hong must marry a woman with green eyes and then sacrifice her to the emperor. Aided by friends Cattrall, Li, ditzy reporter Burton, and wily old wizard Victor Wong (who has a small army of his own), Russell and Dun enter the netherworld of Chinatown to rescue Pai. Unfortunately, Hong is protected by a wide variety of strange beasts, including a sewer monster, an ape-like wild man, a floating head of many eyes which serves as his spy, and an army of martial-artists led by three warriors with supernatural powers, Thunder (Carter Wong), Rain (Kwong), and Lightning (Pax). While the rescuers fight their way through a maze of such obstacles, Cattrall is captured. When Hong learns that she has green eyes, he happily cackles that he will marry both girls, sacrifice Cattrall, and spend the rest of his life in matrimonial bliss with Pai. Just as the wedding ceremony gets underway, our heroes burst in. Much to Dun's dismay, Victor Wong recommends that they allow the ceremony to be completed before the rescue attempt is made for Hong will then be flesh, thus mortal. The gang follows the wizard's suggestion, and when Hong is flesh, they attack. A huge, hilarious kung-fu free-for-all ensues with characters running in every direction and some even flying through the air sword-fighting. The ineffectual Russell gets caught up in the excitement and fires his gun into the air while letting loose a war yell. Unfortunately, the ceiling is only inches above his head and the bullets send a pile of bricks crashing down on his noggin. Eventually all the villains are defeated with the exception of Hong and Carter Wong. When Hong throws a knife at Russell, Russell immediately throws it back and gets the former ghost right in the head. When Carter Wong discovers the death of his leader, the angry warrior is so upset that his body balloons to monstrous proportions and explodes. The evildoers defeated, peace comes back to Chinatown and Russell drives his truck off to new adventures.

This movie is just plain fun. Screenwriters Richter, Goldman, and Weinstein and director Carpenter go for laughs at every opportunity and have managed to create a parody that is at the same time a celebration of what is being made light of—the Chinese kung-fu movie. This film is filled with so many likable characters that even the villains (especially Hong) are sympathetic. Russell is, once again, terrific. His false bravado is so paper-thin as to make him endearing. It is obvious to the other characters (and the viewer) that Russell is just a storyteller who has never fired a weapon in his life (Wong gives him a huge .44 magnum pistol and

laughs, saying, " . . . make you feel like 'Dirty Harry'."). During the climactic battle scene, Cattrall gives Russell a passionate kiss and our unknowing hero plays his big confrontation scene with a huge smear of red lipstick on his lips. Also excellent are Cattrall, Dun (the real hero), and the delightful Victor Wong who adds loads of charm as the impish good sorcerer. Taking top honors, however, is Hong as the villainous Lo Pan. His 2,258-year-old ghost is a wonderfully cranky character whose long-standing frustrations have driven him a bit mad. Hong mumbles to himself throughout the film and, though thousands of years old, he has a good grasp of modern American slang and uses it frequently. Hong turns in such a splendid performance that he becomes the most captivating character in the film. Also notable is the man who played "Thunder," Carter Wong. Wong, an acknowledged master of the martial arts, is a big star in his native Hong Kong and has appeared in more than 40 films. BIG TROUBLE IN LITTLE CHINA was his U.S. debut. In addition to the incredible amount of physical action, the film is filled with complicated special effects, most of which were handled by Richard Endlund's company Boss Film. Everything from Hong's old-man makeup to the comical floating head-with-many-eyes (which was a puppet controlled by as many as 20 people) was designed, constructed, and executed by Boss Film and they did a superb job. Dean Cundey's cinematography is excellent as well, making the film one of the best-looking of the year. Designer John Lloyd re-created the streets and alleys of San Francisco's Chinatown in a huge indoor sound stage (Stage 6) on the Fox lot. A silk the size of two square blocks was stretched over the entire stage so that cinematographer Cundey could simulate the overcast, foggy quality of light common in San Francisco. Why then, did all these excellent elements fail to score with the critics and the public? Perhaps because BIG TROUBLE IN LITTLE CHINA is not the kind of cookie-cutter product usually churned out by Hollywood. The wild combination of quirky humor, kung-fu action, adventure, and special effects threw everyone, including the studio, for a loop. No one knew what to make of this film. That is unfortunate, for BIG TROUBLE IN LITTLE CHINA is a wholly enjoyable romp that deserved to be a hit. Perhaps this original and very funny film will gain a cult following on videotape, although much of its visual detail will be lost in the transition.

p, Larry J. Franco; d, John Carpenter; w, Garry Goldman, David Z. Weinstein, W.D. Richter; ph, Dean Cundey (Panavision, DeLuxe Color); m, John Carpenter, Alan Howarth; ed, Mark Warner, Steve Mirkovich, Edward A. Warschilka; prod d, John J. Lloyd; art d, Les Gobruegge; set d, George R. "Bob" Nelson; cos, April Ferry; spec eff, Richard Edlund; ch, James Lew; makeup, Ken Chase; stunts, Kenny Endoso; m/l, John Carpenter.

Adventure/Comedy   Cas.   (PR:C-O MPAA:PG-13)

BIGGLES†   (1986, Brit.) 108m Compact Yellowbill-Tambarle/NVC c

Neil Dickson *(Biggles)*, Alex Hyde-White *(Jim Ferguson)*, Fiona Hutchison *(Debbie)*, Peter Cushing *(Col. Raymond)*, Marcus Gilbert *(Von Stalhein)*, William Hootkins *(Chuck)*, Michael Siberry *(Algy)*, Daniel Flynn *(Ginger)*, James Saxon *(Bertie)*, Francesca Gonshaw *(Marie)*, Alan Polonsky *(Bill)*.

Hyde-White is a fast-food magnate of sorts who, through some freakish occurrences, time travels from his home in 1986 New York City to the thick of battle in WW I-ravaged Europe. Once there he links up with British flyboy *extraordinaire* Dickson. Poor Hyde-White bounces back and forth through time, and his girl friend Hutchison ultimately joins him. The film climaxes with Hyde-White bringing a modern-day helicopter across the time barrier to help his British comrade defeat the enemy. This science-fiction adventure is based on a series of books popular with the British.

p, Pom Oliver, Ken Walwin; d, John Hough; w, John Groves, Ken Walwin (based on characters created by Capt. W.E. Johns); ph, Ernest Vincze (Techni-

color); m, Stanislas; ed, Richard Trevor; prod d, Terry Pritchard; cos, Jim Acheson; stunts, Gerry Crampton.

Science Fiction   (PR:C MPAA:NR)

BILLY GALVIN†   (1986) 94m American Playhouse–Cinema Ventures I–Indian Neck–Mark Jett/Vestron c

Karl Malden *(Jack Galvin)*, Lenny Von Dohlen *(Billy Galvin)*, Joyce Van Patten *(Mae)*, Toni Kalem *(Nora)*, Keith Szarabajka *(Donny)*, Alan North *(Georgie)*, Paul Guilfoyle *(Nolan)*, Barton Heyman *(Kennedy)*, Lynne Charnay *(Margaret the Bingo Queen)*, Steve Sweeney, Mary Ann Stackpole.

Malden is an ironworker who wants his son to fulfill his own dream of becoming an architect. Von Dohlen is the son, who has little ability and less inclination for college, and who actually hopes to follow in his father's footsteps as a construction worker. Malden, needless to say, is dead set against this, and tries to see that Von Dohlen is unable to get in the union or find a construction job. Produced in conjunction with public television, the film failed to receive a national theatrical release.

p, Sue Jett, Tony Mark; d&w, John Gray; ph, Eugene Shlugleit; m, Joel Rosenbaum; ed, Lou Kleinman; prod d, Shay Austin; art d, Cecilia Rodarte; cos, Oleska.

Drama   (PR:A-C MPAA:PG)

BIR AVUO CENNET†   (1986, Turkey) 99m Mine c (Trans: A Handful of Paradise)

Tarik Akan, Hale Soygazi.

In hopes of finding greater wealth in the city, a poor Turkish family leaves its village home to join a friend in Istanbul. Unfortunately, the friend has been killed in an accident, leaving the clan without prospects or a place to stay. They end up living in an abandoned bus, while the father secures employment with the railroad. Eventually the authorities force them to leave their ramshackle home, but the family continues its struggle, taking up residence under a tarpaulin.

p,d,w&ed, Muammer Ozer; ph, Huseyin Ozsahin; m, Tarik Ocal; set d, Yurdaer Hrsan.

Drama   (PR:C-O MPAA:NR)

BIRDSVILLE   (SEE: BULLSEYE, 1986, Aus.)

BITTERNE ARNTE   (SEE: ANGRY HARVEST, 1986, Ger.)

BLACK AND WHITE*   (1986, Fr.) 80m Films du Volcan–Ministry of Culture/Forum bw (NOIR ET BLANC)

Francis Frappat *(Antoine)*, Jacques Martial *(Dominique)*, Josephine Fresson, Marc Berman, Benoit Regent, Christophe Galland, The Rhapsodes Choir.

An unsettling picture which presents a stark view of a sado-masochistic relationship that is simultaneously frightening and oddly romantic. Frappat is a quiet, cautious, married accountant who is hired to balance the books of a local health club. He attracts the attention of the office flirt, but ignores her not-so-subtle advances in favor of his ledger and calculator. When the owner suggests that he make use of the club facilities, Frappat agrees to a massage from Martial, a hefty black man with huge hands. After sheepishly undressing, Frappat lies down on the table as Martial squeezes, slaps, and twists Frappat's white skin and knotted muscles with invigorating energy. Frappat returns each night for (non-sexual) massages which gradually become more and more violent; the more Frappat moans, the more intense the massage. This nightly ritual can no longer be hidden, however, as Frappat is covered with bruises. One evening, Martial breaks Frappat's arm and is fired by his disgusted employer. Later, Martial helps Frappat escape from the hospital. They take refuge in a seedy hotel where they continue their painful escapades. All of this is in preparation for an inevitable conclusion which takes their sado-masochistic relationship to the extreme, resulting in death by ritualistic torture of Frappat.

Perfectly synthesizing style (black-and-white photography and the film's title) with the content of the film (a black man and white man, opposites but each unable to exist without the other), BLACK AND WHITE is a shocking and aggressive feature film debut from Claire Devers. With a minimum of dialog, the film is pared down to its barest, most raw essentials. Unfortunately, however, the film falls short of developing its characters, as if Devers was too enthralled with the visual contrasts of black skin and white skin to bother giving any motivations for the principals' enslavement to each other. The first half of the film (the realization that they are partners in this relationship) holds the most interest, but by the time Frappat's arm is broken, the film begins to deteriorate and interest wanes. The result is that the audience is reduced to being merely observers without receiving any substantial emotional or psychological explanation for the characters' actions. They are involved in a sado-masochistic relationship and that's that. One can't help but leave the theater frustrated, and with a multitude of unanswered questions. There is clearly talent and inspiration in Devers' filmmaking, though in BLACK AND WHITE it never reaches a consistently interesting plateau. The Cannes Film Festival awarded BLACK AND WHITE the Camera d'Or (its award for best first feature), and it gained a Cesar nomination as Best First Feature.

d&w, Claire Devers; ph, Daniel Desbois, Christophe Doyle, Alain Lasfargues, Jean Paul Da Costa; ed, Fabienne Alvarez, Yves Sarda; art d, Anne Isabelle Estrada.

Drama   (PR:O MPAA:NR)

BLACK JOY**½   (1986, Brit.) 97m Oakwood c

Norman Beaton *(Dave)*, Trevor Thomas *(Ben)*, Dawn Hope *(Saffra)*, Floella Benjamin *(Miriam)*, Oscar James *(Jomo)*, Paul Medford *(Devon)*.

This film, based on a British play, is one of the few films from that country to feature a predominantly black cast. Set in the Brixton sector of London, the story follows the adventures of Thomas, a newly arrived emigre from Guyana. Having been raised in a small village, Thomas is overwhelmed by the sights and sounds that this strange but wonderful city has to offer. Reality soon catches up with him, however, when he finds himself being conned and hustled out of his hard-earned wages. Thomas works as a garbage man and slowly, as he meets new and different people, assimilates to these very different surroundings. With the influence of Beaton, a street-smart con man, Thomas evolves from the naive young man who arrived from Guyana to a regular member of the community. The story is told with energy and a good feeling for the atmosphere of Brixton, though the film follows a none-too-surprising line of development.

p, Elliott Kastner, Martin Campbell; d, Anthony Simmons; w, Anthony Simmons, Jamal Ali; m, Lou Reizner; ed, Tom Noble.

Comedy/Drama   **(PR:O   MPAA:R)**

BLACK MIC-MAC†   (1986, Fr.) 92m Chrysalide-Films Christian Fechner-FR3/Fechner-Gaumont c (Trans: Black Hanky Panky)

Jacques Villeret *(Michel Le Gorgues)*, Isaach de Bankole *(Lemmy)*, Felicite Wouassi *(Anisette)*, Khoudia Seye *(Amina)*, Cheik Doukoure *(Mamadou)*, Mohamed Camara *(Samba)*, Sidy Lamine Diarra *(Ali)*, Lydia Ewande *(Aida)*, Daniel Russo *(Rabuteau)*.

When some Africans are faced with eviction from their Parisian flat, they send for a witch doctor from their native land, hoping he can help them out. En route, the witch doctor encounters a con artist who sees a chance to make some money. Knowing there will be plenty of money handed over in return for voodoo services, the sly individual poses as a follower of the witch doctor. This, of course, leads to all sorts of predicaments which manage to work themselves out by the film's end. This unusual comedy proved to be one of the highest-grossing films of the year in France.

p, Monique Annaud; d, Thomas Gilou; w, Monique Annaud, Patrick Braoude, Cheik Doukoure, Thomas Gilou, Francois Favre; ph, Claude Agostini (Fujicolor); m, Ray Lema; ed, Jacqueline Thiedot; art d, Dan Weil; cos, Corinne Jorry.

Comedy   **(PR:C MPAA:NR)**

BLACK MOON RISING**½   (1986) 100m New World c

Tommy Lee Jones *(Quint)*, Linda Hamilton *(Nina)*, Robert Vaughn *(Ryland)*, Richard Jaeckel *(Earl Windom)*, Lee Ving *(Ringer)*, Bubba Smith *(Johnson)*, Dan Shor *(Billy Lyons)*, William Sanderson *(Tyke Thayden)*, Keenan Wynn *(Iron John)*, Nick Cassavetes *(Luis)*, Don Opper *(Frenchie)*, William Marquez *(Reynoso)*.

Based on a story written by John Carpenter (director of HALLOWEEN), BLACK MOON RISING has all the marks of a project that he would have directed himself had he so desired. The imperturbable hero normally played in Carpenter's films by Kurt Russell (ESCAPE FROM NEW YORK, THE THING, BIG TROUBLE IN LITTLE CHINA) is played here by the always-impressive Tommy Lee Jones. Jones is a professional thief hired by the FBI to steal some top-secret computer tapes from a powerful corporation being prosecuted by the justice department. Jones succeeds in breaking in and boosting the tapes, but

corporation security forces led by Ving (former leader of the L.A. punk band Fear) are hot on his trail. At a gas station, Jones hides the tapes in the back of a fancy new jet-powered sports car called the "Black Moon" which is being transported to Los Angeles by its designer, former NASA engineer Jaeckel. Under pressure from both Ving and the FBI (represented by Smith) to cough up the tapes, Jones quickly tracks down Jaeckel and the car in Los Angeles. Unfortunately, just as Jones is about to reclaim the tapes, a pretty professional auto thief, Hamilton, steals the car. Hamilton delivers the car to Vaughn, the leader of a

multi-million dollar theft ring whose headquarters are located in a high-tech security twin-tower skyscraper that is as impregnable as a fortress. Hamilton is the apple of Vaughn's evil eye, he having recruited her to the operation when she was just a teenage runaway. Hamilton, however, has grown tired of Vaughn and his operation, and looks for a way out. She finds it in Jones and together they team up with Jaeckel to get back the car and the computer tapes. Unfortunately, Vaughn learns of the plan and kidnaps Hamilton. He then plays a cat-and-mouse game with Jones, who has managed to sneak into the building. Eventually, Jones finds Hamilton, and together they get to the Black Moon and drive it to the top floor of the headquarters building. Blocked by Vaughn and surrounded by his gun-wielding goons, Jones has no choice but to throw the car into jet-power. Running over Vaughn, the car crashes through the upper-floor windows of one office tower and goes flying over to the other, making a rough, but safe, landing.

Yes, it's all very silly, but it makes a decent-enough action film that should satisfy anyone looking for some mindless thrills. Jones makes a fine rugged hero (he has lent excellent support in such films as ROLLING THUNDER and COAL MINER'S DAUGHTER, and starred as killer Gary Gilmore in television's "The Executioner's Song"), and he deserves to be given the lead more often. Hamilton, fresh from her success in THE TERMINATOR, does well as the sexy car thief, and Jaeckel lends his usual solid support as the determined car designer. Vaughn, unfortunately, isn't given a whole lot to work with by the script, and the always reliable Ving is only around to beat up Jones every 20 minutes or so. Harley Cokliss directs in a workmanlike manner (Carpenter surely would have milked the visual potential inherent in the script), but his action scenes are unimaginatively handled and lack pizzazz—luckily, his cast is almost strong enough to make up for it.

p, Joel B. Michaels, Douglas Curtis; d, Harley Cokliss; w, John Carpenter, Desmond Nakano, William Gray (based on a story by John Carpenter); ph, Misha Suslov (CFI Color); m, Lalo Schifrin; ed, Todd Ramsay; prod d, Bryan Ryman; spec eff, Max W. Anderson; stunts, Bud Davis.

Action   **Cas.**   **(PR:O   MPAA:R)**

BLACK TUNNEL†   (1986, Ital.) Future World c

Flaminia Cirani, Carl Heimo, Gianni Garko, Spiros Focas, John Francis.

When a man with connections to both the Mob and the Secret Service is arrested, authorities hope he will reveal his consorts when he comes to trial. On the outside a group of underworld types concoct a plan to rescue their colleague. After learning the route along which the arrested man will be transported, the band attempts a rescue in a mountain tunnel.

d,w&ph, Federico Bruno; m, Paolo Rustichelli.

Crime   **(PR:O MPAA:NR)**

BLACKOUT†   (1986, Norway) 88m Norsk-Esselte Video-Kodak/KF c

Henrik Scheele *(Werner)*, Juni Dahr *(Stella Hvidtsteen)*, Elizabeth Sand *(Lill)*, Tommy Korberg *(Max)*, Per Bronken *(Police Chief)*, Peter Lindbeck, Ella Hval, Hans-Jacob Sand, Kalle Oeby, Terje Stromdal, Espen Dekko, Pal Skjonberg, Ramon Gimenz.

This Norwegian homage to *film noir* features Scheele as a private eye in the Sam Spade tradition, working the seamier streets of an anonymous big city. The metropolis is rife with corruption within the police department, while underworld figures are muscling their way into city government. In between plucking corpses from the estuaries and evading obstacles set up by the law and underworld alike, Scheele manages to make some time with the gorgeous females who drop in with dangerous assignments for him to tackle. The set design and *mise-en-scene* were created with care as a loving tribute to American films of the 1930s. Both the film's cinematographer and production designer won the Norwegian equivalent to an Academy Award.

p, Anders Enger; d, Erik Gustavson; w, Erik Gustavson, Eirik Ildahl; ph, Kjell Vassdal (Eastmancolor); m, Oistein Boassen; ed, Torleif Hauge; art d & set d, Frode Krohg; cos, Inger Derlick.

Crime   **(PR:O MPAA:NR)**

BLADE IN THE DARK, A*½   (1986, Ital.) 96m National Cinematografica-Nuovo Dania Cinematografica/Lightning Video c (LA CASA CON LA SCALA NEL BUIO; AKA: HOUSE OF THE DARK STAIRWAY)

Andrea Occhipinti *(Bruno)*, Anny Papa, Fabiola Toledo, Michele Soavi, Valeria Cavalli, Stanko Molnar, Lara Naszinski.

Produced in 1983 (at 110 minutes) but unreleased in the U.S. until Lightning Video debuted it on cassette, A BLADE IN THE DARK is an early film by Lamberto Bava, son of Italian horror-film king Mario Bava, and protege of Italian slasher-movie king Dario Argento. The younger Bava has since been heralded as some sort of cinematic genius among horror cultists because of last year's grievous DEMONS. A BLADE IN THE DARK, while no masterpiece of horror, is a bit more palatable than DEMONS and owes much to Argento's style of suspense.

Occhipinti is a young composer who has been hired by a female movie director to score her latest horror epic. Alone in a rented villa, Occhipinti begins to notice some strange goings-on which all seem to relate to the previous tenant, a woman named Linda. Occhipinti learns that Linda was harboring some sort of deep dark secret, and it appears that she has returned to make sure it is kept. After two local girls who knew Linda disappear, Occhipinti finds enough evidence to be convinced that they have been murdered by the mysterious Linda. In another twist, it turns out that the film director Occhipinti works for knows this Linda personally and has based much of her psychological horror film on Linda's personality. Linda learns of this and manages to destroy the last reel of film (the part that reveals the deep dark secret). Meanwhile, Occhipinti's groundskeeper is murdered by Linda seconds after he finds the hidden bodies of the first two victims. Then the movie director happens by and the crazed Linda strangles her with 35mm footage from the destroyed film. Of course at this point, Occhipinti's girl friend happens to wander in and she too is attacked by Linda. Occhipinti attempts to rescue his girl friend, but he is too late and she is killed. The distraught composer attacks Linda and hits her in the head with a brick. Linda falls to the ground, revealing herself to be a man named Tony (actually the owner of the villa). He/ She soon gets up and lunges at Occhipinti with a knife, but the composer counters and the knife winds up in Linda/Tony's gut. Back at the movie studio, Occhipinti watches the restored final reel of the film and explains Tony's motivations to an assistant: "His ego as a child was too fragile, which caused his masculinity to regress. But he couldn't kill his alter ego, so he projected his anger onto other girls, wishing to kill the girl in himself." Yeah, sure.

Yet another boring Italian retread of Hitchcock's PSYCHO (the killer's name is Tony. Get it? Tony Perkins from PSYCHO?), most of the film's running time is devoted to solitary characters walking down dark, shadowy hallways and staircases, intercut with shots of the blade of a knife held by the unseen killer who waits nearby. Bava never diverges from the standard formula here, and he is not yet (and probably never will be) the accomplished visual stylist that his mentor Argento is. Some may find the self-reflexive, film-within-a-film angle intriguing, but it's all been done before and Bava later beat it to death in DEMONS. The performances are serviceable, with Occhipinti making for a fairly appealing hero (he's best known to American audiences as the impotent bullfighter in Bo Derek's disastrous BOLERO), and Lara Naszinski, cousin of Nastassja Kinski, making her debut as one of the many victims. In its favor, the film does boast a mildly interesting musical score, and whoever handled the English dubbing on Occhipinti's dialog did a surprisingly good job.

d, Lamberto Bava; w, Dardano Sacchetti, Elisa Briganti; ph, Gianlorenzo Battaglia (Luciano Vittori Color); m, Guido De Angelis, Maurizio De Angelis; ed, Lamberto Bava; set d & cos, Stefano Paltrinieri; makeup, Giovanni Amadei; spec eff, Giovanni Corridori.

Horror   Cas.   (PR:O MPAA:NR)

BLEU COMME L'ENFER†   (1986, Fr.) 100m
Garance-Transcontinentale-FR3/UGC c (Trans: Blue Like Hell)

Lambert Wilson (Ned), Myriem Roussel (Lilly), Tcheky Karyo (Franck), Agnes Soral (Carol), Sandra Montaigu [Sandra Majerowicz] (Sara), Benoit Regent (Henri).

An energetic thriller which pits a vicious cop, Karyo, against carefree criminal Wilson, who has skipped town with the cop's wife, Roussel. Roussel, however, is a willing participant, escaping from her abusive husband with the help of her sister, Soral. Karyo has no intention of letting Wilson or Roussel get away and sets off to catch them before they reach the safety of the border. The film stars Roussel, who made history last year as the star of Jean-Luc Godard's HAIL, MARY. BLEU COMME L'ENFER is based on a novel by Philippe Djian, an author whose work also served as the basis for Jean-Jacques Beineix's BETTY BLUE (1986).

p, Dominique Vignet; d, Yves Boisset; w, Yves Boisset, Jean Herman, Sandra Majerowicz (based on the novel by Philippe Djian); ph, Dominique Brenguier; m, Pierre Porte; ed, Jacques Witta; art d, Patrice Mercier; cos, Rosalie Varda.

Crime/Thriller   (PR:O MPAA:NR)

BLIND DIRECTOR, THE*½   (1986, Ger.) 113m Kairos-ZDF-Stadtisch
Buhne-Main Opera/Spectrafilm c

Jutta Hoffmann (Gertrud Meinecke), Armin Mueller-Stahl (Blind Director), Michael Rehberg (Herr von Gerlach), Peter Roggisch (Big Boss), Rosel Zech (Superfluous Person), Maria Slatinaru (Tosca), Gunther Reich (Scarpia), Piero Visconti (Cavaradossi).

This multi-storied film weaves a common thread through each tale: the effect of sudden, overwhelming crises on the lives of common folk. The first vignette takes place in WW II Poland. Hoping to save the archives of a film studio, the caretaker humbly hands over his daughter to a Nazi soldier. In another story of unexpected change, a little girl survives after her parents are tragically killed in a car wreck. Next, there is a businessman for whom the business of traveling becomes an all-consuming matter. The last two stories involve first, a family overtaken by their devotion to a home computer, and, finally, the title character. In the concluding vignette, madness reigns supreme, as a nearly sightless filmmaker drives those around him crazy with his current project.

Kluge is notable for his contributions to the rise of the New German Cinema movement, yet this work is largely disappointing. It is an often self-indulgent piece that never really connects its theme from story to story. The use of an intrusive narrator—who pops in randomly to explain things when it all gets a little—is more annoying than effective. (In German; English subtitles.)

d&w, Alexander Kluge; ph, Thomas Mauch, Werner Luring, Hermann Fahr, Judith Kaufmann; ed, Jane Seitz.

Comedy   (PR:O MPAA:NR)

BLOOD RED ROSES†   (1986, Scotland) 150m Freeway-Lorimar-Channel
Four/Other Cinema c

Elizabeth MacLennan (Bessie), James Grant (Sandy), Gregor Fisher (Alex), Louise Beattie (Young Bessie), Dawn Archibald (Catriona).

A literal telling of the life of a woman from her teenage years when her mother deserted her, to her adult years as a militant trade unionist. The film takes place in the Scottish Highlands and is shown in flashback as the woman's family life and her relationship with her father intertwine with her work.

p, Steve Clark-Hall; d&w, John McGrath; m, Eddie McGuire; ed, Jane Wood; prod d, Shirley Russell.

Drama   (PR:A-C MPAA:NR)

BLOODY BIRTHDAY*   (1986) 85m Judica c (AKA: CREEPS)

Susan Strasberg (Mrs. Davis), Jose Ferrer (Doctor), Lori Lethin (Joyce Russel), Melinda Cordell (Mrs. Brody), Julie Brown (Beverly Brody), Joe Penny (Mr. Harding), Billy Jacoby (Curtis), Andy Freeman (Steven Seaton), Elizabeth Hoy (Debbie Brody), K.C. Martel (Timmy Russel), Ben Marley (Duke), Erica Hope (Annie), Cyril O'Reilly, Shane Butterworth, Michael Dudikoff, Daniel Currie, Norman Rice, Georgie Paul, Bill Boyett, Ellen Geer, Ward Costello, Ruth Silveira, Bert Kramer, Sylvia Wright, John Avery, Nathan Robert.

An unredeemed waste of everyone's time, BLOODY BIRTHDAY gets off to a dull start with Jose Ferrer delivering three infants almost simultaneously during a total eclipse of the sun. Ten years later, the terrible trio (Jacoby, Freeman, and Hoy), apparently now possessed of the strength to hold up a gun, go on an inexplicable murder binge. As usual, the wages of sin is death, and the first to go are a couple making love in the cemetery. Hoy's father, the sheriff, is investigating the case, so they dispatch him with a baseball bat. The boy next door (Martel) sees them moving the body, so he becomes the next target, barely escaping with his life when they lock him in a refrigerator at the junkyard. Their teacher (Susan Strasberg in a brief and meaningless role) is killed next, while her assistant, Lethin, a high schooler with an interest in the Zodiac (and, coincidentally, Martel's sister), manages to escape. Lethin theorizes that because Saturn was blocked by both the sun and the moon when the three young killers were born, none of them has a conscience. Unfortunately, Lethin is lacking in common sense, and when Hoy (who has just shot her sister in the eye with an arrow) asks for her to babysit, she foolishly agrees. In the house, all three children stalk her, Hoy being especially fond of hiding in closets then jumping out to strangle victims with her jump rope. Lethin manages to subdue the two boys when they run out of bullets, but Hoy runs to her mother as she drives up and convinces her that she was not to blame. In the last scene, mother and daughter are at a gas station, and Hoy is drilled on her new identity. She promises to be good from now on, but as they drive away the camera reveals a mechanic smashed under a truck after she has apparently released the jack on him.

A real bore, with the director seemingly incapable of creating suspense. Killings simply occur with no build-up and no rationale, and the children never generate any menace (though Hoy does have a disconcerting gleam in her eye). Originally shot in 1980, the film has had only sporadic regional releases. Songs include: "My Woman," "My Darling Don't You Cry," and "Music" (John O. Jones).

p, Gerald T. Olson; d, Ed Hunt; w, Ed Hunt, Barry Pearson; ph, Stephen Posey (Panavision); m, Arlon Ober; ed, Ann E. Mills; art d, Lynda Burbank, J. Rae Fox; cos, Michelle Logan; spec eff, Roger George; m/l, John O. Jones; makeup, Michelle Logan.

Horror   Cas.   (PR:O MPAA:R)

BLOUDENI ORIENTACNIHO BEZCE†   (1986, Czech.) Barrandov (Trans:
Going Astray in an Orientation Course)

Filip Tousek, Juraj Matula, Vladimira Nejepsova, Alena Knotkova.

d, Julius Matula; w, Miroslav Sovjak; ph, Juraj Sajmovic.

BLUE CITY*½   (1986) 83m Par c

Judd Nelson (Billy Turner), Ally Sheedy (Annie Rayford), David Caruso (Joey Rayford), Paul Winfield (Luther Reynolds), Scott Wilson (Perry Kerch), Anita Morris (Malvina Kerch), Luis Contreras (Lt. Ortiz), Julie Carmen (Debbie Torez), Allan Graf (Graf), Hank Woessner (Hank), Tommy Lister, Jr. (Tiny), Rex Ryon (Rex), Felix Nelson (Caretaker), Willard E. Pugh (Leroy), Sam Whipple (Jailer), David Crowley (Bartender), Paddi Edwards (Kate), John H. Evans (Young Cop), Rick Hurst (Redneck), Lincoln Simonds (Johnny Perks), Ken Lloyd (Young Bartender), Vaughn Tyree Jelks (Boy at Cafe), Roxanne Tunis (Cashier), Roberto Contreras (Hot Dog Vendor's Voice), Carla Olsen, Tom Junior Morgan, Phil Seymour, Joe Read, George Collins (The Textones).

This one is about as brainless as they come. Based on an old Ross MacDonald novel, BLUE CITY begins as young drifter Nelson returns to his home town in South Florida after having traveled the country aimlessly for five years. Smug Nelson gets himself thrown in the clink soon after his arrival and boasts how one phone call to his father the mayor will have him out in no time. Nelson has a bit of a surprise, however, when police chief Winfield informs him that his father was murdered nine months before. Hinting that local crime boss Wilson may have been the culprit, Winfield releases Nelson with the understanding that the angry young man will do all the investigating, as Winfield can't trust his own corrupt police force. Learning that his voluptuous stepmother Morris and Wilson have become something of an item, Nelson tries to harass the dim-witted redhead into admitting complicity in the murder. When this fails he confronts Wilson himself and is beaten by a pack of muscle-bound goons. Turning to his old highschool chum Nelson for help, Nelson finds his pal less than enthusiastic, because in his activities as a small-time hood, he had run afoul of Wilson and the crime boss had the kid's kneecap rearranged. Not one to take no for an answer, Nelson engages in a brief fist-fight with Caruso, a maneuver that apparently reignites their male bonding. Caruso forgets about his painful encounter with Wilson's

thugs and joins in the battle. Caruso's sister Sheedy thinks the whole thing is stupid and worries that her brother will get killed, but a quick trip on Nelson's old Triumph motorcycle soon has her signing on as well. While Sheedy—who just happens to work as a clerk at the police station—gathers incriminating evidence against Wilson and Morris from the files, Nelson and Caruso launch a two-man war against Wilson's businesses, which includes torching his car, robbing his skim of the dog-track take, and shooting up his casino. Nelson goes too far, however, when he and Caruso kill a few of Wilson's henchmen while trying to defend themselves against an ambush, and Winfield throws him out of town. As Nelson rides his motorcycle to points North, Caruso is killed by an unseen assassin. When Nelson learns of his friend's murder, he returns to Blue City and wages a one-man war against Wilson by attacking his house. After killing several of Wilson's goons, Nelson finds that one of the henchmen has the drop on him. Bang! The man suddenly lies dead and out from the bushes steps Winfield with his smoking .357 magnum. Nelson and Winfield make short order of the remaining crooks, but then Winfield reveals that he is the real killer. While trying to hunt Nelson down in a greenhouse, Winfield prattles on about how Nelson's father was a crook who sliced up the local graft pie among all the corrupt officals and businessmen. Winfield got greedy, however, and knocked off Nelson's old man and then goaded Nelson into eliminating the only other competition— namely Wilson. Taking advantage of the villain-who-talks-too-much-before-killing-the-hero rule, Nelson turns the tables and kills Winfield. Having preserved his dubious family honor, Nelson and Sheedy visit his pop's grave and then jump on the motorcycle, leaving Blue City behind them.

First-time director Manning proves that women are perfectly capable of making the same sort of mindless, vulgar, violent films that male directors have specialized in for years. Her direction is lackluster, although pity must be taken on anyone who has to provoke anything resembling a performance from the stoical Nelson who wanders through this film like a zombie. Sheedy, an actress who can manage an occasional burst of talent, is simply bad here. Winfield seems to be taking any role offered him these days. Here he struggles to bring a little life in this vapid mess and fares well until his last scene. The script, cowritten with Heller by the usually reliable Hill (who also coproduced) doesn't help matters either. Nelson's character proves to be fairly clever in the early going, demonstrating an awareness of tricks and double-crosses. Then, in the last half-hour, he makes so many stupid mistakes that viewers may wonder if they missed a scene where Nelson's body was taken over by a space alien ignorant of the preceding 60 minutes. It's that way with most of the characters—their behavior is so erratic, unmotivated, and unrealistic that it is pointless to pay any attention between gun battles. The film's only saving grace is a listenable musical score by Hill favorite Ry Cooder. Songs include: "Blue City Down" (Ry Cooder, Jim Dickinson,

performed by Cooder, Bobby Knight, Terry Evans), "Tell Me Something Slick and Make It Quick" (Cooder, performed by Knight, Evans), "Marianne" (Javier Escovedo, performed by True Believers), "You Can Run (But You Can't Hide)"

(George Callins, Tom Junior Morgan, Joe Read, performed by Textones), "Don't Take Your Guns to Town" (Johnny Cash, performed by Ry Cooder), "Latin" (Charles Bernstein), "Love Theme from THE GODFATHER" (Nino Rota).

p, William Hayward, Walter Hill; d, Michelle Manning; w, Lukas Heller, Walter Hill (based on the novel by Ross MacDonald); ph, Steven Poster (Technicolor); m, Ry Cooder; ed, Ross Albert; art d, Richard Lawrence; set d, Richard C. Goddard; spec eff, Joseph P. Mercurio, John R. Elliott; m/l, Ry Cooden, Bobby Knight, Terry Evans, Javier Escovedo, George Callins, Tom Junior Morgan, Joe Read, Johnny Cash, Charles Bernstein, Nino Rota; makeup, Edouard F. Henriques III.

Crime　　　　　　　　　　Cas.　　　　　　　　　(PR:O MPAA:R)

BLUE MAN, THE†　　　　　　　　　(1986, Can.) 87m New Century c

Winston Rekert *(Paul Sharpe)*, Karen Black *(Janus)*, John Novak *(Kauffman)*.

Astral travel is the idea behind this heavily atmospheric thriller that stars Rekert as a television producer who has picked up a little trick from drug addict/dancer Black—how to free your soul and travel around in your sleep. Rekert's astral body gets carried a bit too far away however, and before long his doctor and his father-in-law have both died in a grisly manner. Police detective Novak has his suspicions, and he snoops into Rekert's past, where he learns that the producer once made a documentary about astral travel. It takes him a while, but he finally figures out what's going on, though not before the astral bodies and physical bodies have a climactic showdown. Directed by Mihalka, the man who brought us such class acts as MY BLOODY VALENTINE (1981) and PICKUP SUMMER (1981).

p, Pieter Kroonenburg; d, George Mihalka; ph, Paul Van der Linden; ed, Nick Rotundo; art d, John Meighen; set d, Skip Hobbs; cos, Paul-Andre Guerin; spec eff, Jacques Godbout; makeup, Charles Carter, Edward French.

Drama/Horror　　　　　　　　　　　　　　　　(PR:O MPAA:NR)

BLUE VELVET****　　　　　(1986) 120m DiLaurentiis Entertainment Group c

Kyle MacLachlan *(Jeffrey Beaumont)*, Isabella Rossellini *(Dorothy Vallens)*, Dennis Hopper *(Frank Booth)*, Laura Dern *(Sandy Williams)*, Hope Lange *(Mrs. Williams)*, Dean Stockwell *(Ben)*, George Dickerson *(Detective Williams)*, Priscilla Pointer *(Mrs. Beaumont)*, Frances Bay *(Aunt Barbara)*, Jack Harvey *(Mr. Beaumont)*, Ken Stovitz *(Mike)*, Brad Dourif *(Raymond)*, Jack Nance *(Paul)*, J. Michael Hunter *(Hunter)*, Dick Green *(Don Vallens)*, Fred Pickler *(Yellow Man/ Detective T.R. Gordon)*, Philip Markert *(Dr. Gynde)*, Leonard Watkins *(Double Ed)*, Moses Gibson *(Double Ed)*, Selden Smith *(Nurse Cindy)*, Peter Carew *(Coroner)*, Jon Jon Snipes *(Little Donny)*, Andy Badale *(Piano Player)*, Jean Pierre Viale *(Master of Ceremonies)*, Donald Moore *(Desk Sergeant)*, A. Michelle Depland, Michelle Sasser, Katie Reid *(Party Girls)*.

One of the most original films in years, BLUE VELVET has not only split critical and public opinion down the center, it has, in the process, become a strange cultural phenomenon. A deeply personal film from David Lynch, it is less similar to his films DUNE and THE ELEPHANT MAN (neither of which was based on his own ideas) than it is to ERASERHEAD, his "dream of dark and troubling things." With BLUE VELVET he has taken the dream out of the industrial bleakness of a factory location and transferred it to the blue skies, red roses, and white picket fences of Lumberton, North Carolina. Strains of Bobby Vinton's "Blue Velvet" fill the air, firemen wave a friendly hello, and school guards help the kiddies across the street, but something is wrong beneath this superficial tranquility. Dad (Harvey) calmly waters his healthy green lawn, but the water

spigot begins to malfunction. It emits a loud, thundering rumble, there is a kink in the hose, Harvey is suddenly victimized by a stroke, and drops squirming to the ground. As the water sprays from his hose, the family dog excitedly drinks from it, blissfully unaware of his master's condition. The camera burrows underneath the lawn, to find that the soil is overrun by insects. Lynch has just lured his audience into a dark, mysterious, and troubling world.

Arriving home to visit his dad in the hospital is MacLachlan, a handsome, square-jawed college kid, who is an archetype of the perfect young man. While wandering through a deserted field, MacLachlan finds a severed human ear, decaying and crawling with ants. He picks it up, plops it in a brown paper bag, and takes it to police detective Dickerson. With the detached manner of an investigative professional, Dickerson declares that it is indeed a human ear. The coroner's office report indicates the ear was cut off with scissors. Later that night, MacLachlan stops at Dickerson's house, finding him strangely elusive about the ear. As he leaves MacLachlan is approached by Dickerson's daughter, Dern, a vision of innocence who appears out of the shadows, hoping that her father won't catch her with MacLachlan. After engaging in some small talk, MacLachlan presses Dern to see if she knows some of the details he believes Dickerson is hiding from him. Dern admits she has overheard her father discussing the case and she tells MacLachlan that Rossellini, a singer who lives in the eerie Deep River apartment complex near the vacant field, seems to be a suspect in the investigation. "It's a strange world," MacLachlan naively replies. Dern shows him the apartment building, further sparking his curiosity. The next day MacLachlan stops by the high school to pick up Dern. He takes her to a local snack shop and asks her to help him sneak inside Rossellini's apartment. Pretending to be an exterminator MacLachlan climbs the stairs to the seventh floor (the elevator, which played so prominent a part in ERASERHEAD, is out of order) and is admitted to Rossellini's apartment. When a visitor, the "yellow man" (Pickler), momentarily distracts Rossellini, MacLachlan gets the chance to steal a spare apartment key. Digging deeper into the mystery, MacLachlan, with Dern's help, decides to sneak into the apartment later that evening while Rossellini is doing her nightclub act. They visit The Slow Club and while awaiting Rossellini's performance, discuss the quality of Heineken beer and share a toast to "an interesting experience." When Rossellini is on stage, performing as "The Blue Lady," she wears a blue velvet dress, a curly black wig, blue eye shadow, and bright red lipstick. MacLachlan and Dern leave before the show's end and drive to Rossellini's apartment. While Dern waits in the car to signal Rossellini's arrival, MacLachlan goes inside to find clues. He is surprised by Rossellini's sudden return and hides in a closet, peeking through wooden slats as she undresses. He is confused by a telephone call she receives which reveals that her husband and child have been kidnaped. Rossellini discovers her visitor and, at knifepoint, begins to seduce him, before a knock at the door interrupts her. Frightened and now thoroughly confused, MacLachlan heads back into the closet. The arrival of Hopper, an inherently evil monster, sends MacLachlan (and every audience member) into a state of immobilizing fear. Hopper, dressed in a leather jacket, demands that Rossellini have everything just right for his arrival. He wants his bourbon poured and the lights turned down low, he doesn't want to be looked at, and, most of all, he wants her to be wearing blue velvet. After inhaling a nondescript drug from a gas mask, he proceeds to rape her—a scene that is as difficult for MacLachlan to watch as it is for the audience. Before Hopper leaves he warns Rossellini, "You stay alive, baby . . . do it for Van Gogh." Trying to console Rossellini, MacLachlan emerges from the closet to find she has retreated into another world. Having turned completely submissive, she surrenders herself to MacLachlan, begging that he hit her. He refuses and readies to leave, but before doing so finds a treasured photo of Rossellini's husband and child.

The next evening MacLachlan tells Dern what happened—that Hopper has kidnaped Rossellini's husband and child in order to force her to have sex with him. He wonders aloud, "Why do there have to be people like Frank [Hopper]?" Rather than tell the police, MacLachlan decides to get additional, more solid, evidence. He stakes out Hopper's hideout and takes photos of his secret meetings with the "yellow man" and the "well-dressed man," as they watch the aftermath of a drug dealer's murder. MacLachlan later returns to the Deep River Apartments because, as he tells Dern, "he is seeing something that was always hidden." Rossellini admits that she genuinely likes him. They make love, but when she again asks him to hit her, he is torn between his conscience and his desire to please her, until he finally gives vent to a heretofore contained violence and brutalizes her. As MacLachlan prepares to leave Rossellini's apartment he is met in the hallway by Hopper and his gang of degenerates, who invite him to come along for a "joyride," which ends up at a bizarre bar called This Is It. Run by the ridiculously "suave" Stockwell, the bar is peopled with grade-A weirdos. It also is the place where Rossellini's son is being held and, while she visits him behind closed doors, Hopper guzzles down some Pabst Blue Ribbon beer and delights in Stockwell's lipsynched rendition of Roy Orbison's mellow tune "In Dreams." After a short stay, the gang takes to the road again. The joyride turns ugly when MacLachlan, upset by Hopper's treatment of Rossellini, denounces Hopper and punches him in the face. Hopper tells MacLachlan: "You're like me," before dragging him out of the car for some abuse. With "In Dreams" again playing in the background, Hopper has his pals restrain MacLachlan while he threatens to send him a "love letter straight from [his] heart" and then explains that one of his love letters is a bullet from a gun. Promising to "send him straight to hell," Hopper rubs MacLachlan's face with lipstick and blue velvet, then brutally beats him while a helpless Rossellini stands by screaming.

When he comes to on the following morning, MacLachlan visits the police station to meet with Dickerson. Passing through the halls, he notices the "yellow man" sitting behind a desk—a police lieutenant. Later, at Dickerson's house, MacLachlan reveals everything he knows. MacLachlan and Dern admit they are in love with each other and while out together, find a naked, bruised and catatonic Rossellini wandering across MacLachlan's front lawn. They take her home to Dern's house and call an ambulance. Frightened and emotionally distraught, she clings to MacLachlan while Dern looks on in horror. When Rossellini begs for MacLachlan to love her and cries out that Hopper has "put his disease in me," Dern breaks down. MacLachlan tries to explain, but Dern slaps him and makes him leave.

Still obsessed with the mystery, MacLachlan heads back to Rossellini's apartment, arriving just shortly before Hopper, in disguise as "the well-dressed man." MacLachlan flees to Rossellini's apartment where he finds the corpses of the "yellow man" and Stockwell. MacLachlan takes a gun from the "yellow man" and once again hides in Rossellini's closet, which is no longer a location for passive voyeurism but one for the active destruction of evil. When Hopper finally locates him he is met with a "love letter" from MacLachlan's gun. Dickerson and Dern arrive to find Hopper dead. The trouble passed, Lumberton returns to normal. MacLachlan's dad has been released from the hospital; MacLachlan and Dern watch from their kitchen window as a robin munches on an insect; and Rossellini sits on a park bench hugging her young son.

Every so often in the history of film a picture comes along and knocks the critics and public into a state of shock with its originality and its demand to be recognized. Luis Bunuel split the opinion of audience and critics alike in 1928 with his short UN CHIEN ANDALOU, Michelangelo Antonioni did it in 1959 with L'AVVENTURA, Alfred Hitchcock did it in 1960 with PSYCHO. More recently, with the widening acceptance of personal expression and sexual freedom, the film community has been thrown into an uproar by Bernardo Bertolucci's LAST TANGO IN PARIS, Martin Scorsese's TAXI DRIVER, and Jean-Luc Godard's HAIL, MARY. This year, David Lynch has brought his "disease" of dark mysteries before the public, exploring the connections between sex and violence, light and darkness, and good and evil. As expected, BLUE VELVET has drawn scathing criticism from those who view Lynch and his film as nothing more than sick.

Drawing on many dream images of ERASERHEAD, Lynch has fashioned in BLUE VELVET a perfect artistic and poetic vision which may or may not be sexually perverse and morally depraved. Lynch's world is one in which disturbing truths exist underneath the surface. Rather than ignore them, he probes deeper in order to reveal them. In BLUE VELVET Lynch is digging under the lawn at the Lumberton home, to see what insects infect the wholesomeness of the neighborhood, and inside the human ear, to see what infects the mind. What Lynch finds is a disturbing evil that not only cannot be ignored, it must be destroyed before it destroys that which is good in the world. In order to illustrate the conflict, Lynch makes his characters (with the possible exception of MacLachlan) one-dimensional. They are archetypes created in small-town U.S.A. and turned to myth by the Hollywood dreammakers. MacLachlan is the handsome hero, Dern is his innocent blonde-haired love, Rossellini is the dark prisoner of evil, and Hopper is the embodiment of that evil. The more complex MacLachlan finds himself caught in a battle of mythic proportions between good and evil (represented by his love for both Dern and Rossellini). He begins on the side of the good, only to be lured into the darkness of the underworld. It is through contact with Hopper that he is contaminated by evil. Only when he can destroy the evil within himself can he destroy the evil in Lumberton. To do so he must journey into this underworld of perversion and violence, come face-to-face with his nemesis and alter-ego, Hopper, and defeat him before being allowed to emerge the victor. Buoyed by Dern's innocence, MacLachlan does so and assures that the world will be bathed in the "light of love." Rossellini, who has been held in the grip of evil, has now been set free by MacLachlan.

In demonstration of belief that people would rather avoid confronting the dark side of life—the sadism, the perversions, the fetishism, the drug addiction, the violence—many critics complained that BLUE VELVET was "dangerous" in its exploration of these traits. They contended these taboos were better left in the closet. Lynch has addressed that belief in the film, since Hopper, the voice of evil, demands that people not look at him, while MacLachlan, the voice of good, not only looks but fights back. What makes BLUE VELVET even more impressive, is that it was made within the rules established by the Hollywood system. By following a basic narrative structure (from which he occasionally departs), guidelines defined by the mystery genre (which he occasionally bends), and casting big name stars, Lynch has created a guise of respectability (Lynch's "well-dressed filmmaker" disguise?) for his film which enables him to deal with subjects mainstream Hollywood normally avoids. Lynch's strategy also gained bookings for the film in hundreds of theaters across the country. BLUE VELVET played not only in art houses (as did ERASERHEAD), but in suburban shopping malls, where the moviegoer could be exposed to the same "disease" Lynch sees in the world. While many people no doubt left the movie puzzled and disturbed, it still marks a major cultural leap for both Hollywood and independent filmmaking. This leap is not unprecedented, however, as Alfred Hitchcock had many times forced his audiences to confront "dark and troubling things." His SHADOW OF A DOUBT covered (or dug under) much of the same ground as BLUE VELVET in exploring the mind of a killer (Joseph Cotten) who resides in the quiet town of Santa Rosa, California. As in Lumberton, Santa Rosa's inhabitants are oblivious to the murderer in their midst and they ignorantly go about their daily business. Like MacLachlan, Theresa Wright must face her alter ego (Hitchcock makes it obvious by giving both Wright and Cotten the same name—Charlie) and destroy him in order to release the town from evil's grip. One does not have to stretch the imagination too far to think that Hitchcock, were he making films today, would be capable of creating a BLUE VELVET. He had already made the connection between sex and violence in VERTIGO, PSYCHO, and MARNIE, before becoming explicit with the brutal rape scene in 1972's FRENZY. In that film, Barry Foster's malicious character Robert Rusk, with his repetitive "lovely, lovely" during the rape/murder scene (*Lynch* doesn't even carry the connection as far as death), clearly serves as the cinematic father to Hopper's Frank Booth, with his disturbing repetitions of "mommy, mommy" during the attack on Rossellini.

In addition to Lynch's brilliant and totally controlled vision, the film boasts the gorgeous photography of Elmes (ERASERHEAD) and the multi-textured sound design of Alan Splet (who worked on all three previous Lynch pictures). The performances are excellent, each one giving to his role exactly what Lynch intended. While Dern and MacLachlan provide that corny, 1950s America, Hardy Boys-Nancy Drew innocence, Rossellini and Hopper draw on raw emotion and intensity. A tour de force for Hopper, this performance marks a solid return to Hollywood, after several years' absence. BLUE VELVET marks the fourth decade of filmmaking for Hopper, who has (perhaps not coincidentally) appeared

in some of the most talked-about films of the last four decades—REBEL WITH-OUT A CAUSE in the 1950s, EASY RIDER is the 1960s, APOCALYPSE NOW in the 1970s, and BLUE VELVET in the 1980s. Surprisingly, for a picture as steeped in controversy as it was, BLUE VELVET *did* earn an Oscar nomination for Lynch as Best Director, a category he was nominated in six years earlier with THE ELEPHANT MAN. Hopper did receive a 1986 nomination as Best Supporting Actor, not for his role as Frank Booth, however, but for his performance in HOOSIERS, which, although excellent, is hardly the better of the two. Songs include "Blue Velvet" (Lee Morris, Bernie Wayne, performed by Bobby Vinton, reprised by Isabella Rossellini), "Blue Star" (Angelo Badalamenti, David Lynch, performed by Rossellini), "In Dreams" (Roy Orbison, performed by Orbison), "Love Letters" (Victor Yound, Edward Heyman, performed by Ketty Lester), "Mysteries of Love" (Badalamenti, Lynch; performed by Julee Cruise), "Honky Tonk (Part I)" (Shep Shepherd, Clifford Scott, Bill Doggett, Billy Butler, performed by Doggett), "Livin' For You Lover," and "Gone Ridin'" (Chris Isaak).

p, Fred Caruso; d&w, David Lynch; ph, Frederick Elmes (Joe Dunton Camera Widescreen); m, Angelo Badalamenti; ed, Duwayne Dunham; prod d, Patricia Norris; md, Angelo Badalamenti; cos, Gloria Laughride; spec eff, Greg Hull, George Hill; m/l, David Lynch, Angelo Badalamenti, Lee Morris, Bernie Wayne, Victor Yound, Edward Heyman, Roy Orbison, Shep Shepherd, Clifford Scott, Bill Doggett, Billy Butler; makeup, Jeff Goodwin; stunts, Richard Langdon.

Mystery   Cas.   (PR:O MPAA:R)

BORIS GODUNOV†   (1986, USSR/Czech.) 164m Mosfilm-Studio Barrandov/Sovexport c

Sergei Bondarchuk *(Boris Godunov)*, Alexander Soloviev *(Grigorij Otrepev)*, Anatoli Romachine *(Petr Bosmanov)*, Anatoli Vassiliev *(Vasilij Sujskij)*, Adriana Bierdjinskay *(Marina Mnisek)*, Elena Bondarchuk *(Ksenija)*, Roman Flippov *(Patriarch)*, Jevgenij Samoljiov *(Pimen)*, Vjaceslav Butenko *(Ivan Vorotynskij)*, Fjodr Bondarchuk *(Fedor)*, Gennadij Mitrofanov *(Blazen)*, Valerij Storozik *(Kurbskij)*, Jurij Lazarov *(Gavrila Pushkin)*, Gregorij Burkov *(Varlaam)*, Vadim Alexandrov *(Misail)*, Irina Skobcevova *(Majitel'ka Krcmy)*.

An adaptation of Alexander Pushkin's epic poem, this film retells the story of the man who took control of Russia after Ivan the Terrible killed his son. Bondarchuk, in the title role, begins a reign of violent terror that ends after six years when he succumbs to illness. (In Russian.)

d&w, Sergei Bondarchuk (based on the epic poem by Alexander Pushkin); ph, Vadim Yusov; m, Vyacheslav Ovchinnikov; art d, Vladimir Aronin; prod d, Vladimir Arenin, Oldrich Okac, Milan Nejedly; cos, Eliska Nova.

Historical/Drama   (PR:O MPAA:NR)

BORN AMERICAN*   (1986, U.S./Finland) 95m Cinema Group-Larmark/Concorde c (AKA: ARCTIC HEAT)

Mike Norris *(Savoy)*, Steve Durham *(Mitch)*, David Coburn *(K.C.)*, Thalmus Rasulala *(The Admiral)*, Albert Salmi *(Drane)*, Piita Vuosalmi *(Nadja)*, Vesa Vierikko *(Kapsky)*, Ismo Kallio *(Zarkov)*, Laura Heimo *(Irina)*, Antti Horko *(Cossack)*, Pauli Virtanen *(Sergei)*, Jouni Takamaki *(Interrogator)*, Inkeri Luoma-Aho *(Female Guard)*, Markku Blomqvist *(Irina's Father)*, Casper Anttila *(Chess Player)*, Sari Havas *(Girl at Party)*, Marjo Vuollo *(Tamara)*, Orava Family *(Russian Family)*, Aapo Autola *(Car Salesman)*.

One of the silliest action movies of the year, BORN AMERICAN offers audiences three of the dumbest, least sympathetic all-American jerks (Norris, Durham, and Coburn) as protagonists whose idea of a good time is to get blasted on beer, then sneak across the border from Finland into Russia. Surprised when, the next morning, the whole area is swarming with Russian soldiers, they catch a ride on a truck to a village, where they become separated. Norris and Durham are

captured by the locals and blamed for the murder of a girl. Kallio is the sister of the murdered girl, and she knows that it was actually the local Orthodox priest who raped and killed her sister, so when she finds the lost Coburn, she leads him back to the church where the funeral service is being conducted and where his two friends are being held. Naturally he puts an arrow through the priest, then flees with his friends and the girl, blowing up half the village and wiping out a platoon of Soviet regulars in making good their escape. They soon arrive back at the border and are preparing to swim through the ice floes when Norris reaches down to pick something up. "Hey, what's this?" Before his friends can stop him, he has pulled on a wire and set off every alarm for miles. A spotlight hits the group and they are captured and marched off to prison. There Durham—the most hostile and obnoxious member of the group—is subjected to electric shocks at his nipples and a Pepsi bottle upside the head, while Norris agrees to sign anything, including a confession that he is a terrorist sent by the U.S. Next the prisoners are chucked into a cell, stripped, beaten, and given rags to wear. Coburn—injured in the earlier gun battle—lies slowly dying while Durham and Norris learn the ways of prison life, that consist of stoking coal in a foundry in return for washers which can be traded for a peek at the women's showers.

Durham starts a fight and gets tossed in the special section, beyond the control of the guards, where a giant, demented game of chess is played, with players killing each other as a slobbering crowd looks on. Friendly prisoner Vierikko smothers Coburn to put him out of his misery, then leads Norris to Rasulala, who is apparently some kind of mercenary allowed special privileges in the prison while he writes a book exposing the KGB and the CIA. He offers to help Norris escape with Vuosalmi, a friend of Heimo (who can't go herself because she has committed suicide). Next comes the obligatory workout set to music as Norris practices his kick boxing for the escape. He and Rasulala rescue the now-crazed Durham from the chess room, where he has risen to be Black Queen, and Norris and Durham flee through a sewer. Durham is shot and killed and Norris meets with Rasulala, Vuosalmi, and a truck that takes them back toward the border. After trashing another unit of the Red Army, Rasulala gives Norris his manuscript and tells him to get it to certain people who will see that it is published and will allow Rasulala to return to his North Carolina home.

The strange thing about this film is that there are some interesting—albeit half-baked—ideas floating around in the script, and the direction shows some skill

and style, but the plot is so ludicrous from start to finish, the characters so one-dimensional, and the world-view so simplistic, it is astounding that anyone would finance such a production. On the other hand, what could be more natural, in this period of Reagan-style patriotic chest beating? While Sylvester Stallone, Chuck Norris (Mike's dad), and others are taking on Arab terrorists, Vietnamese, and other Soviet surrogates and lackeys, isn't the ultimate extension the sight of a couple of good ol' boys in an old Mercury gunning down Commies while whipping empty beer cans out the window? The biggest surprise is that the film was made by a Finn (of all people) and that it shows as much restraint as it does.

Much more entertaining than the film itself was the controversy around it. The Finnish government invoked a seldom-used 1948 law to ban the film on the grounds that it might harm relations between Finland and another nation. The same law had also been invoked to stop ROCKY IV from playing in Helsinki, though it was dropped on appeal. After several cuts and resubmissions, the ban on BORN AMERICAN was dropped on appeal as well. Alas, Finland.

p, Markus Selin; d, Renny Harlin; w, Renny Harlin, Markus Selin; ph, Henrik Paerchs (Fujicolor); m, Richard Mitchell; ed, Paul Martin Smith; set d, Torsti Nyholm; cos, Anja Pekkala; spec eff, Osmo Savolainen, Karl Von Kugelgen; makeup, Suzanne Sanders; stunts, Eddie Braun.

| Drama | Cas. | (PR:O MPAA:R) |

BOSS' WIFE, THE* (1986) 83m Tri-Star c

Daniel Stern *(Joel Keefer)*, Arielle Dombasle *(Louise Roalvang)*, Fisher Stevens *(Carlos Delgado)*, Melanie Mayron *(Janet Keefer)*, Lou Jacobi *(Harry Taphorn)*, Martin Mull *(Tony Dugdale)*, Christopher Plummer *(Mr. Roalvang)*, Diane Stilwell *(Suzy Dugdale)*, Robert Costanzo *(Eddie)*, Thalmus Rasulala *(Barney)*, Stanley Ralph Ross *(Stationmaster)*.

A lame comedy from the author of PORKY'S REVENGE, this movie has nothing to offer other than a few adequate performances. Stern (who was so good in DINER and even scored in his brief bit as the rock star in HANNAH AND HER SISTERS) is little more than a reactor as he plays a young stockbroker working for Plummer. Stern is married to Mayron who is trying to get pregnant (the opening sequence is a much-too-long set piece about Stern having to deliver a sperm sample to a doctor while a fuming messenger waits). He and co-worker Mull are both in line for a higher position in the brokerage firm, the winner of the job to be determined after a weekend in the country with Plummer observing. Plummer's wife is the pneumatic Dombasle, who rather fancies Stern. The question then is: should Stern sleep with his boss' wife in order to gain a better job at the company? Mull, looking very beefy, is the smarmy antagonist and does the best with the few jokes he gets to speak. Mayron is a book editor who is, at present, putting together a portfolio of photographs by Stevens, a Puerto Rican lenser who specializes in snapping shots of people when they are angry. In order to do this, Stevens berates everyone with whom he comes in contact so he can capture their faces in rage. That's good for one or two laughs but it continues on and on until all vestiges of humor have dissipated. Nothing much happens in the movie, which seems to keep vamping until ready, but never does. Writer/director Steinberg was making his first appearance behind the camera and may have some better things in his future, but it would be hard to tell from this mishmash. In the end, as can be anticipated, Stern stays true to Mayron and bids adieu to his boss and his boss' wife. Plenty of money was spent on the production, including a couple of all-night shoots at Los Angeles' Union Station where the cast is supposedly boarding a private railroad car. Lou Jacobi, a most able *farceur*, is not used to good advantage as Stern's pal at the office. The producer was former production executive Tom Brodek, who also had a hand in THE AVIATOR, a film that crashed to earth as quickly as this one. Lots of dubious language and aborted sexual situations make this a poor bet for children of any age.

p, Thomas H. Brodek; d&w, Ziggy Steinberg; ph, Gary P. Thieltges (Metrocolor); m, Bill Conti; ed, John A. Martinelli; prod d, Brenton Swift; art d, Albert J. Locatelli.

| Comedy | | (PR:C-O MPAA:R) |

BOY IN BLUE, THE*½ (1986, Can.) 98m ICC–Denis Heroux–John Kemeny/FOX c

Nicolas Cage *(Ned)*, Cynthia Dale *(Margaret)*, Christopher Plummer *(Knox)*, David Naughton *(Bill)*, Sean Sullivan *(Walter)*, Melody Anderson *(Dulcie)*, James B. Douglas *(Collins)*, Walter Massey *(Mayor)*, Austin Willis *(Bainbridge)*, Philip Craig *(Kinnear)*, Robert McCormick *(Trickett)*, Tim Weber *(Cooney)*, George E. Zeeman *(Cop)*, Geordie Johnson *(Bothwell)*, Brian Thorne *(Plaisted)*, Don Mac-Quarrie *(Temp Leader)*, James Edmond *(Chairman)*, Greg Swanson *(Oscar Hale)*, Gerald Isles *(Butler)*, J. Gordon Masten *(Toad)*, Bruce McFee *(Ship Steward)*, Doris Malcolm *(Aunt Gert)*, Ian D. Clark *(Aussie No.1)*, Dan Hennessey *(American Reporter)*, Jeff Wincott *(Riley)*, Aiden Devine *(Junior Cop)*, Lee-Max Walton *(Urchin)*, Roger A. McKeen *(McCoy Man No.1)*, Kim Coates *(McCoy Man No.2)*, Ted Dykstra *(Hanlan Man No.1)*, Michel Perron *(Hanlan Man No.2)*, Bob Bainborough *(Boston Betting Clerk)*, John Dunn-Hill *(Riley Tout)*, Germain Beauchamp *(Photographer)*, Philip Neilson *(2nd Brahmin)*, Eric Fink *(Hawker for Dr. Morse)*, Patrick Sinclair *(Philly Referee)*, Elizabeth Rukavina *(Philly Barmaid)*, Ian Heath *(Boy on Steamer)*, Jain Dickson *(Suffragette)*, Claude Rae *(Boston Bettor)*, Peter Peer *(Prison Turnkey)*, Doug Lennox *(Knox's Pug)*, Dave De Sanctis, Ken Rogers, Barry Edward Blake *(Philly Thugs)*, Anne Farquhar *(High Class Girl)*, Art Grosser *(Bookie)*, Paul Craig *(English Judge)*, Teddy Donville *(Betting Runner)*, Gorman Miller *(Hanlan Fan)*, Robert Buck *(English Thug)*, Diane Hollingsworth *(Alley Tart)*, Graham MacCready, Graham Haley, John Cain *(Aussies)*.

In the late 1800s, sculling was as popular a sport as baseball or football is today, with fierce competition coupled with high stakes spectator gambling. Ned Hanlan was a Canadian rowing champion who honed his skills by running illegal liquor in his skiff. During his life, Hanlan survived unscrupulous competitors, crooked gamblers, and alcoholism to become an international star in the sport. He set many records that have stood for more than 100 years. In his later years, he achieved success in Canadian politics. Unfortunately, his film biography is nothing more than a perfunctory sports drama that is flat and predictable.

Cage stars as Hanlan, a roguish young man who runs illegal moonshine along Lake Ontario. He soon encounters Naughton, a gambler who has had his eye on

Cage for some time. Naughton is convinced that with proper management Cage will be an outstanding competitive rower and takes it upon himself to guide Cage's career. After some slightly underhanded doings by Naughton, the two form a partnership and Cage is soon attracting attention as a top-line sculler. Plummer, a wealthy businessman, decides to take over as Cage's manager, realizing there is much earning potential in the talented athlete. Cage agrees, and is immediately taken with Plummer's niece Dale. He tries wooing her, but Dale continues her romance with a more socially acceptable Harvard man. Later, Cage discovers just how conniving and ruthless Plummer is when he is disqualified from competition for an altercation during a Boston meet and learns that Plummer was behind it. Down but not out, Cage is taken in by Sullivan, a shrewd old man who has invented a movable rowing seat. He previously had only let Cage use it, but now bets Plummer the patent on his invention that Cage will beat Plummer's new boy in a race on the Thames River. At the big London race, Naughton, who has been paid well by Plummer, sabotages Cage's boat. However, Naughton has a change of heart after the race begins, and valiantly leaps into the water to repair the damage he has inflicted. Cage handily defeats his adversary and is reunited with his old friend. He also manages to capture the heart of socialite Dale, who becomes his bride.

The production design is immaculate, from the painstakingly recreated sets to the 1,400 period costumes employed throughout the story. So much for the film's attributes. Other than its impeccable look, THE BOY IN BLUE has little to offer even the most understanding of audiences. The story is all cliche and stereotype, going from one stock genre element to another in a wholly expected development. Jarrott's direction is flat and anonymous, adding nothing to his material in the least. Worst of all is the ensemble, a surprisingly uniform group of wooden actors. Naughton and Dale try to pump a little life into their characters without much success, while Plummer practically sleepwalks through his part. The real disappointment though is Cage. Undoubtedly one of the most intense actors of his generation (witness his performances in such varied films as THE COTTON CLUB, BIRDY, and PEGGY SUE GOT MARRIED), Cage brings none of his usual energy to the part. Instead he merely goes through the motions, reading off lines with little enthusiasm or conviction. Cage did do his own rowing, which adds a nice touch of realism, but that appears to be the extent of his character involvement.

In many ways THE BOY IN BLUE resembles those boring educational films grade schoolers are forced to watch when it's raining during their recess period. There is one notable exception here from those grammar school tortures, however. Despite the noticeable absence of profanity in its stilted dialog, the film contains a few moments of gratuitous sexual encounters, the only reason for its "R" rating. This alone makes THE BOY IN BLUE questionable entertainment for the audience it's most likely to be appreciated by.

p, John Kemeny; d, Charles Jarrott; w, Douglas Bowie (based on an original idea by John Trent); ph, Pierre Mignot (Panavision, Deluxe Color); m, Roger Webb; ed, Rit Wallis; prod d, William Beeton; set d, Jean-Baptiste Tard; cos, John Hay; makeup, Brigitte McCaughry.

| Sports/Biography | Cas. | (PR:C-O MPAA:R) |

BOY WHO COULD FLY, THE**** (1986) 114m Gary Adelson-FOX c

Lucy Deakins *(Milly)*, Jay Underwood *(Eric)*, Bonnie Bedelia *(Charlene)*, Fred Savage *(Louis)*, Colleen Dewhurst *(Mrs. Sherman)*, Fred Gwynne *(Uncle Hugo)*, Mindy Cohn *(Geneva)*, Janet MacLachlan *(Mrs. D'Gregario)*, Jennifer Michas *(Mona)*, Michelle Bardeaux *(Erin)*, Aura Pithart *(Colette)*, Cam Bancroft *(Joe)*, Jason Priestly *(Gary)*, Chris Arnold *(Sonny)*, Sean Kelso *(Bad Boy)*, Meredith B. Woodward *(Female Administrator)*, Raimund Stamm, Dan Zale *(Attendants)*, Dwight Koss *(Dad)*, James McLarty *(Tour Guide)*, Betty Phillips *(Institute Receptionist)*, Terry D. Mulligan *(Mr. Brandt)*, Tannis Rae *(Ms. O'Neil)*, Tom Heaton *(Dr. Nelson)*, Angela Gann *(Mrs. Betuel)*, Scott Irvine *(Officer)*, Karen Siegel *(Dr. Karen Siegel)*, John Carpenter, Nick Castle, Tommy Wallace *(The Coupe de Villes)*, Warren Carr *(Guest Coupe)*, Jake *(Max)*.

The subject of human flight is one that has been explored by filmmakers in several imaginative pictures, including Robert Altman's BREWSTER McCLOUD (1970) and Alan Parker's BIRDY (1984). THE BOY WHO COULD

FLY is another variation on this idea, presented as a gentle and often touching evocation of adolescent pains and joys.

The film opens as Bedelia, a recent widow, moves into a new home with her 15-year-old daughter Deakins and 8-year-old son Savage. The family has some trouble adjusting to the new surroundings, but gradually begin to settle in. Deakins soon notices her neighbor, Underwood, a boy her own age who lives with his alcoholic uncle, Gwynne. Underwood is a handsome boy, but has been autistic ever since his parents died in a plane crash when he was five. Never speaking a word, Underwood is convinced he can fly and spends much of his time perched on the roof, silently flapping his arms. He is allowed to attend the local

high school where Dewhurst, a sympathetic teacher, notices a tentative rapport between the boy and her new student. She takes Deakins aside and asks her to encourage Underwood, hoping the sensitive girl will be able to do for the boy what psychiatrists have been unable to accomplish. Deakins agrees and begins keeping a progress journal of her activities. At first the work is frustrating, but gradually she is able to coax some reaction out of Underwood. While on a school field trip, Deakins precariously stands on a high bridge, hoping to pluck a beautiful rose. She slips and hits her head, knocking herself unconscious. Rushed to the hospital, Deakins dreams that Underwood comes to her room and takes her on a magical flight. Upon awakening, she insists to psychiatrist Fletcher that Underwood must have been able to fly and catch her before she fell, for there is no logical explanation as to why she survived the plunge. Deakins also admits, to both Fletcher and herself, that her father committed suicide rather than subject the family to his slow death through cancer.

When Underwood is unexpectedly taken away to a mental institution, Bedelia takes her children to visit him. They are denied access to him, however, though Underwood hears the family and vainly pounds on a window to gain their attention. During a terrible thunderstorm, Underwood mysteriously reappears and Deakins is convinced he is able to fly. The next day she takes Underwood to a school carnival, and there the two are forced to run in an effort to escape the authorities looking for the boy. Trapped on the school rooftop, Underwood takes Deakins' hand and the two go off on a magical flight through the neighborhood. The astonished carnival-goers follow as Underwood brings Deakins home, then takes off into the clouds. Though he never returns, Underwood's presence has had a benevolent effect on the people who loved him.

Rich in many elements, THE BOY WHO COULD FLY is that rare sort of film that appeals to both adults and children without taking any feelings or perceptions for granted. Castle, directing from his own script, delicately weaves together the story's dark and light elements, letting things develop in a natural manner. He builds his story on small, everyday experiences, wisely keeping many of his respective characters' major life crises off-screen. The moments of fantasy are slowly worked into the story, carefully blended with the realistic elements and thus all the more believable. Special effects, though necessary, are kept to a minimum. This is a story about human feelings, yet Castle never allows it to become a Steven Spielberg light show.

Clearly, the film's casting is another strong point. Everyone, from the leads to supporting roles, and even Savage's beloved pooch (whom film fans will recognize as "Mike the Dog" from DOWN AND OUT IN BEVERLY HILLS), gives a performance that resonate with honest feelings. Gwynne (former star of TV's "The Munsters"), Dewhurst, and Fletcher have small roles, but they are key in relation to Underwood and Deakins, and they take their assignments seriously, creating memorable portraits that belie their screen time. Bedelia, unlike so many screen mothers, is a real parent with problems of her own that she must balance with the responsibilities of raising her children. Her troubles with her new job, coping with her husband's death, and the realities of being a single parent require much of the actress, and she delivers with sincerity that is never saccharine. Savage provides some marvelous comic relief as the predicament-plagued little brother, as does Cohn (from television's "The Facts of Life") as a nagging neighbor who immediately latches onto Deakins. The true heart of this film, of course, is the relationship that builds between Deakins and Underwood. As the autistic boy, Underwood gives a touching, heartfelt performance in a role that requires him to react only with his face and eyes. He remains silent throughout the film until the end, a difficult task that Underwood accomplishes with the skill of a seasoned actor twice his age. Deakins is another revelation. She carries the majority of the film with her complex character, experiencing a gamut of emotional highs and lows. Deakins plays the girl for what she is, a real teenager faced

with extraordinary problems. There is the pain of her father's suicide, the difficulties of being the new kid in school, and her unspoken affection for Underwood, all carried by the young actress with a beautiful sense of dignity. THE BOY WHO COULD FLY, with all its subtleties and honest sentiments, is a work of striking originality, a film that retains its freshness with every subsequent viewing.

Castle, son of film choreographer Nick Castle, Sr., grew up in the movie industry and his love for film is evident here. Deakins' dream sequence has a visual quote from Alfred Hitchcock's TO CATCH A THIEF, a film Deakins and Cohn watch on television earlier in the story. More obvious are the references from Vincente Minnelli's MEET ME IN ST. LOUIS, a musical Castle openly admits influenced his film. Bedelia's house bears the same address as the Smith family, and Savage, like Margaret O'Brien, has created a graveyard for his dead toys. Songs include: "Walkin' on Air" (written and performed by Stephen Bishop), "Back of the Bus" (Bruce Broughton, Nick Castle).

p, Gary Adelson; d&w, Nick Castle; ph, Steven Poster, Adam Holender (Panavision, DeLuxe Color); m, Bruce Broughton; ed, Patrick Kennedy; prod d, Jim Bissell; art d, Graeme Murray; set d, Jim Teegarden, Kimberley Richardson; cos, Trish Keaton; spec eff, John Thomas; m/l, Stephen Bishop, Bruce Broughton, Nick Castle; makeup, Maurice Parkhurst; stunts, John Scott.

Drama/Fantasy   Cas.   (PR:A MPAA:PG)

BOYCOTT†   (1986, Iran) 120m c

Majid Majidi, Mohammad Kasebi, Zohreh Sarmadi.

d&w, Mohsen Makhmal Baaf; ph, Faraj Haydari, Ebrahim Ghazi Zadeh; ed, Roobik Mansoori.

BRAS CUBAS†   (1986, Braz.) 100m Embrafilme–Julio Bressane/Embrafilme
                                                                                    c

Luiz Fernando Guimaraes (Bras Cubas), Bia Nunes (Virgilia), Ankito (Bento Cubas), Regina Case (Marcela), Renato Borghi (Quincas Borba), Cole (Tio Joao), Paschoal Vilaboim (Lobo Neves), Guara (Cotrim), Cristina Pereira (Sabina), Helio Ari, Maria Gladys, Wilson Grey, Telma Reston, Breno Moroni, Marcia Rodrigues, Ariel Coelho, Dede Veloso, Sonia Dias, Jorge Cherques, Sandro Siqueira, Marise Farias, Martim Francisco.

Brazilian experimental director—one of that country's Cinema Novo group—Bressane brings to the screen an adaptation of Machado de Assis' 19th-Century iconoclastic novel. Through a dead man's tale of his life on earth, Bressane comments on the social conditions of Brazil, combining the flavor of the novel with his own personality.

p&d, Julio Bressane; w, Julio Bressane, Antonio Medina (based on the novel by Machado de Assis); ph, Jose Tadeu (Eastmancolor); ed, Dominique Paris; art d, Luciano Figueiredo; cos, Vera Barreto Leite, Kika Lopes.

Fantasy   (PR:A-C MPAA:NR)

BREEDERS zero   (1986) 77m Tycin/Empire (Wizard Video) c

Teresa Farley (Dr. Gamble Pace), Lance Lewman (Detective Dale Andriotti), Frances Raines (Karinsa Marshall), Natalie O'Connell (Donna), Amy Brentano (Gail), Leeanne Baker (Kathleen), Ed French (Dr. Ira Markum), Matt Mitler (Ted), Adriane Lee (Alec), Owen Flynn (Monster), Mae Cerar (Mrs. Moore), Mark Legan (Brett), Don Geffen (Gentleman), Pat Rizzolino (Intruder), Derek Dupont (Jeoffrey), Raheim Grier (Deformed Creature), Rose Geffen (Bag Lady), Doug Devos (Security Guard), Michael Zezima (Basement Guard), Brian Barnes (Dave), Norris Culf (Waiter), Louis Spudeas (Donna's Date), Kent Perkins (Taxi Driver), Roxie (Rudolph).

New York City-based Tycin Films struck a deal with West Coast schlock-king Empire Pictures to produce a series of low-budget exploitation pictures that Empire would release either theatrically or directly to video through their home-entertainment division, Wizard Video. BREEDERS has the dubious distinction of being the Empire/Tycin team's first direct-to-video release, and it is a stinker. The time-honored, aliens-from-outer-space-breeding-with-Earth-women concept (I MARRIED A MONSTER FROM OUTER SPACE in 1958 is probably the best example) is bludgeoned to death here, spiced with heavy doses of nudity unthinkable 30 years ago. Farley stars as a pretty young Manhattan doctor who is disturbed by a series of violent rapes perpetrated on virginal women. A strange black substance is found on each of the victims, and their bodies have been scarred with acid. Detective Lewman (who looks to be about 21 years old—only one of the many unintentionally hilarious aspects of this film), who is convinced that he has a serial rapist on his hands, attempts to question the zombie-like victims, but each gives a different description of her assailant. While Lewman and Farley stand around looking puzzled for most of the movie, the viewer is treated to seemingly endless scenes of nubile young virgins (presumably a rare breed in Manhattan) disrobing at the drop of a hat who are subsequently raped by male humans who have suddenly burst open to reveal themselves as bug-eyed aliens. As the victims stack up in Farley's hospital, Lewman discovers clues that lead him to the labyrinth of tunnels beneath Manhattan. The connection is soon made explicit, for the rape victims, their faces magically healed, wander naked out of the hospital to an underground chamber that serves as a nest for the aliens. When Lewman and Farley discover the nest (basically a gooey pool of gelatin and flour where the five naked girls writhe about smearing the gook on each other), they are confronted by another doctor, French, who stands there explaining the whole movie to them before turning into an alien himself (which is just as well since French also created the special make-up effects). Farley manages to impale the creature before it can rape her (yes, she's a virgin too), and then she and Lewman toss an electrified cable into the nest and fry the girls who are just about to hatch more aliens.

Although BREEDERS is really bad, it has enough unintentional laughs to satisfy any fan of truly bad cinema. The performances are incompetent, with Farley and Lewman being two of the most catatonic heroes in recent memory. These two can't even do something as simple as register shock or horror in a reaction shot. They look so bored and disinterested that their closeups during French's transformation scene appear to be culled from footage the cameraman ran off before the director yelled "action!" The stupefyingly banal dialog doesn't help much. In an emotional scene where Lewman questions Brentano—the female boss of one of the rape victims—about the possibility of another coworker having been the culprit, the following exchange occurs: "There just isn't any way it could have been Ted," insists Brentano. "Listen," asserts Lewman, "I know teachers, businessmen, politicians, and priests who were all rapists. No one is beyond suspicion!" Brentano becomes adamant "Detective, I guess I'm not making myself clear. Ted is GAY!" "Maybe," Lewman grimly intones, "but maybe just real clever!" This is priceless stuff for fans of bad movies, and BREEDERS is chock-full of such inane dialog. The effects by French are charmingly sub-par; considering that the whole film was shot in eight days, one shouldn't expect much.

p, Cynthia DePaula; d&w, Tim Kincaid; ph, Thomas Murphy, Arthur D. Marks (Precision Color); m, Tom Milano, Don Great; art d, Marina Zurkow; set d, Ruth Lounsbury; cos, Joni George; makeup, Erin Pollitt; spec eff, Ed French, Matt Vogel.

Science Fiction   Cas.   **(PR:O   MPAA:NR)**

BRENNENDE BLOMSTER†   (1986, Nor.) Norsk Film (Trans: Burning Flowers)

Lise Fjeldstad, Torstein Holmebakk.

d, Eva Dahr, Eva Isaksen; w, Lars Saabye Christensen; ph, Rolv Haan.

BRIDGE TO NOWHERE†   (1986, New Zealand) 90m Mirage–New Zealand Film Commission/Challenge c

Matthew Hunter *(Carl)*, Margaret Umbers *(Tanya)*, Shelly Luxford *(Julia)*, Stephen Judd *(Gray)*, Philip Gordon *(Leon)*, Bruno Lawrence *(Mac)*, Alison Routledge *(Lise)*.

That stalwart of the fledgling New Zealand cinema, Bruno Lawrence, is on hand for another one in this Kiwi variation on DELIVERANCE (1972) and THE MOST DANGEROUS GAME (1932). Five city youths tote their ghetto blaster and some naive ideas into the woods with them on a search for a semi-legendary site known as the Bridge to Nowhere (actually a fairly amazing structure abandoned after the 1920s). Unfortunately they stumble into the self-proclaimed domain of Lawrence, a rugged mountain-man type who lives with Routledge (his costar from THE QUIET EARTH). A girl from the group spots the pair in their camp and is shot for her trouble by Lawrence, who then decides he has to hunt down and kill the rest of the group, as well. What follows is a routine—though well-crafted—pursuit through the beautiful countryside of New Zealand's north island, with the teenagers barely able to outwit Lawrence and stay alive.

p, Larry Parr; d, Ian Mune; w, Bill Baer, Ian Mune (based on a story by Larry Parr); ph, Kevin Hayward (Kodakcolor); m, Stephen McCurdy; ed, Finola Dwyer; art d, Mike Becroft; spec eff, Selwyn Anderson; stunts, Peter Dall.

Action Drama   **(PR:O   MPAA:NR)**

BRIGHTON BEACH MEMOIRS*½   (1986) 108m Rastar/UNIV c

Blythe Danner *(Kate)*, Bob Dishy *(Jack)*, Brian Drillinger *(Stanley)*, Stacey Glick *(Laurie)*, Judith Ivey *(Blanche)*, Jonathan Silverman *(Eugene)*, Lisa Waltz

(Nora), Fyvush Finkel *(Mr. Greenblatt)*, Kathleen Doyle *(Mrs. Laski)*, Alan Weeks *(Andrew)*, Marilyn Cooper *(Woman in Street)*, Jason Alexander, Christian Baskous *(Pool Players)*, Brian Evers, Ed Deacy *(Policemen)*, Wanda Bimson *(Dance Teacher)*, Edgard Mourino *(Stunt Driver)*, Richard Bright *(Recruiting Sergeant)*, James Handy *(Frank Murphy)*, Bette Henritze *(Mrs. Murphy)*, Steven Hill *(Mr. Stroheim)*, David Margulies *(Mr. Farber)*.

Neil Simon is at his best when writing about his and/or his brother Danny's life. (Simon's older sibling reckons that he's been in six of Neil's plays—COME BLOW YOUR HORN, THE ODD COUPLE—Danny is the neat one—and others.) This film is adapted from the first of Simon's B trilogy of plays, which also includes "Biloxi Blues" and "Broadway Bound." Although Simon was born in the Washington Heights section of Manhattan, he chose the Coney Island area of Brighton Beach as the setting for his story.

Silverman is the protagonist, a teenager living in Brighton Beach with parents Danner and Dishy (who was actually reared about two miles from Brighton), older brother Drillinger (who played the role on Broadway as well as on the national tour), widowed aunt Ivey and her two daughters, Waltz and Glick. (In real life, it was Simon, brother Danny, and his mother who moved in with relatives, but he uses his family as the original occupants of the house). The septet raises endless possibilities for interplay that are all plumbed. Danner (who could never convince anyone that she's a Jewish mother) sends Silverman to the local

grocery several times daily, sometimes for real items, sometimes to get him out of the house. Drillinger is always in trouble, has recently lost all of his cash wagering the wrong way, and is now thinking about joining the army to get away from the area (The time is 1937, and the army is still a safe bet). The focus throughout is on Silverman and his twin passions: baseball and women. Drillinger fills Silverman full of misinformation about women and the youngster believes him. He is aroused by looking through every teenage boy's dream magazine (in 1937), the *National Geographic*, which often contained photos of bare-topped native tribeswomen, the censors having justified their inclusion as anthropologically significant. Dishy works 18 hours a day to keep the family afloat and Drillinger supplements the family income with his paycheck as a clerk in a haberdashery. Waltz, at 16, is already a woman and desires nothing more than a Broadway career as a dancer, but she, and everyone else, takes second place to Glick, the younger sister, who is supposedly frail and wan and uses that to rule the combined household. Silverman's greatest desires in life are to be a baseball star and to see a nude woman, if only for an instant. Danner is not the mother portrayed in "Broadway Bound." Instead, she is tough, lacking in humor, and is long-suffering. We cannot be sure which of Simon's stage mothers is closer to the real one; perhaps, she embodied a bit of both.

Unfortunately, there is no real thrust to this story, just a series of incidents, a lot of arguing, and many fewer laughs than we have come to expect from Simon. However, it was with this play and screenplay that Simon crossed into new territory where he was able to forgo the easy one-liner (and nobody writes one-liners as well as he does), instead combining pathos and heart with his jokes. Gene Saks won a Tony for his stage direction and repeats his chores here, even managing to put some "air" into a stagebound work, but much of the spontaneity of the theater version seems to have fled in favor of the mechanics of moviemaking. The play also won a Tony for Best Featured Actor as well as the Drama Critics Circle Award for Best Play of 1983. Stage-goers will recognize Fyvush Finkel as the man who played "Muchnick" in "Little Shop of Horrors". Making his debut as executive producer was long-time studio development veteran David Chasman, and a good debut it was as the movie did well, though not a smash-hit. More of a nostalgic piece than anything else, much of the story will be lost on people of a different era or cultural background. Much of the same territory is covered by Woody Allen in his 1987 release RADIO DAYS, which also suffers from the lack of any main theme, but is somewhat more successful overall. Tunes included to set the scene are "Good Morning Glory" (Harry Revel, Mack Gordon, performed by the George Hall Orchestra), "Jungle Drums" (Charles O'Flynn, Ernesto Lecuona, Carmen Lombardo, performed by Guy Lombardo and the Royal Canadians), "Infatuation" (Leonard Whitcup, Walter G. Samuels, performed by the George Hall Orchestra), and the Yiddish tune "A Doinele A Volechl Geit" (Ray Musicker, performed by the New York Klezmer Ensemble). The play opened in Los Angeles to fair reviews in December, 1982, then went on to be a huge hit on Broadway. (Los Angeles critics never seem to like anything unless it's first been a hit in New York, as witnessed by the lukewarm reviews given "Evita" when it opened in The Big Orange. After it went east and won a fistful of Tonys, the L.A. critics embraced it.) One of the problems with the settings of the film is that several different areas were used to represent Brighton Beach, including Ridgewood, Queens. The whole place looked sanitized and more like a setting for a musical version of STREET SCENE than an authentic period piece. Silverman's career has been meteoric since he was found performing at Beverly Hills High School and thrust into this role as Broderick's replacement. He has since gone on to a number of TV and film roles. Texan Ivey will be best recalled for her Broadway debut in the play "Steaming," a British import in which she appeared totally nude for a great deal of the play. Her performance won her both the 1982 Tony and the Drama Desk Award. Her second Tony was for "HurlyBurly" in 1985. Anyone who lived in Brighton Beach will feel that this picture doesn't come close to the excitement of the place and the time depicted. Perhaps the filmmakers felt that it could never be recaptured.

p, Ray Stark; d, Gene Saks; w, Neil Simon (based on his play); ph, John Bailey (Panavision); m, Michael Small; ed, Carol Littleton; prod d, Stuart Wurtzel; art d, Paul Eads; set d, George DeTitta, Jr., Gary Jones; cos, Joseph G. Aulisi; makeup, Allen Weisinger, Mickey Scott.

Comedy   **(PR:C MPAA:PG-13)**

BRODERNA MOZART†   (1986, Swed.) 98m Crescendo-Swedish Film
Institute-SRTV2/Sandrews c (Trans: The Mozart Brothers)

Etienne Glaser (Walter), Philip Zanden (Flemming), Henry Bronett (Fritz), Iwar Wiklander (The Technical Director), Loa Falkman (Giovanni/Eskil), Agneta Ekmanner (Donna Elvira/Marian), Lena T. Hansson (Donna Anna/Ia), Helge Skoog (Don Ottavio/Olof), Grith Fjeldmose (Zerlina/Therese), Rune Zetterstrom (Leporello/Lennart), Niklas Ek (The Stone Guest), Krister St. Hill (Mazetto), Malin Ek ((Switchboard Operator), Anders Clason, Gudrun Henricsson, Amanda Ooms, Bjorn Kjellman, Lars Hansson, Lars Wiik, Saara Salminen, N.A. Numminen, Pedro Hietanen, Ann Petren Okko Kamu, Yrsa Falenius, Henric Holmberg, Bjorn Gedda, Nils Gredeby, Inga Sarri, Bo Samuelsson, Marian Grans, Iwa Boman, Vladimir Puhony, Lottie Ejebrant, Kristof Kovacs, Inga Landgre, Gerd Andersson, Lars Bethke, Jenny Tillstrom, Frida Hassellvall, Gerd Hegnell, Berit Bohm, Elisabeth Eriksson, Doris Fallquist, Gunilla Soderstrom, Iwa Sorenson, Roger Andersson, Lars-Gunnar Axelsson, David Matscheck, Anders Wallgren.

Walter is a young opera director who comes to a Swedish company with strange ideas for a new production of Mozart's "Don Giovanni". He demands that all cut their hair and dispense with lavish costumes in favor of colored rags, arousing the ire of the company members. He even tries to make the orchestra members take on some of the roles, but they stand firm and quote union rules to him. Meanwhile the ghost of the composer is showing up at odd intervals to talk with Walter. In the end, the staging looks idiotic, but the opera survives solely on its own strength. A rare thing, a good comedy from the suicide capital of the free world, directed by the daughter of a noted Swedish critic.

p, Goran Lindstrom; d, Suzanne Osten; w, Etienne Glaser, Suzanne Osten, Niklas Radstrom; ph, Hans Welin, Solveig Warner (Fujicolor); m, Wolfgang Amadeus Mozart, Bjorn Jison Lindh; ed, Lars Hagstrom; prod d, Roland Soderberg; cos, Eva Fenger; makeup, Eva Fange, Eva Rizell.

Comedy   **(PR:C MPAA:NR)**

BULLIES*   (1986, Can.) 96m Simcom/UNIV c

Jonathan Crombie (Matt Morris), Janet Laine Green (Jenny Morris), Stephen B. Hunter (Clay Morris), Dehl Berti (Will Crow), Olivia D'Abo (Becky Cullen), Bill Croft (Ben Cullen), Bernie Coulson (Jimmy Cullen), Adrien Dorval (Judd Cullen), William Nunn (Jonah Cullen), Thick Wilson (Sam Hogan), Shay Garner (Maggie Sullivan), Wayne Robson (Vern), Ed Milaney (Frank Furlong), Brock Simpson (Arnie Furlong), LeRoy Shultz (Murray Sullivan), Ernie Prentice (Fred Hobbs), Beth Amos (Martha Hobbs), Christianne Hirt (Girl Dancing in Bar).

This year was one of the better ones for the Canadian film industry, which found international success with such productions as THE DECLINE OF THE AMERICAN EMPIRE, ANNE TRISTER, and DANCING IN THE DARK. BULLIES, however, falls far short, foolishly trying to emulate Hollywood's low standards. It's the trite tale of a peaceful, hardworking family that becomes terrorized by a group of demented locals who have everyone in the town wrapped around their sadistic fingers. The film opens with an elderly couple driving home from their 50th wedding anniversary celebration. An ominous vehicle—driver unseen, of course—plays bumper-cars with the old folks for a while before forcing them over a cliff. Enter the Morris clan—wimpy dad Hunter, pretty mom Green, and their teenage son from her first marriage, Crombie—who have just arrived from the city to run the grocery store vacated by the murdered old folks. It's a small town where everyone knows each other, so the Morris clan soon hears stories of the nasty Cullens, led by the bearish, voracious Nunn. (The control that the Cullens have is not unlike that of Robert Ryan and his bullies in BAD DAY AT BLACK ROCK, 1954.) Everyone in the town has a bruised face, so one can assume that something has gone awry. The Cullens are the town's wealthiest family, threatening everyone in the area, including sheriff Wilson and thus having everything in their control. When Hunter refuses to let them have food on credit, Nunn gives him a fierce warning.

Unable to stand up against the Cullen bullies, Hunter loses the respect of Crombie, who comments that his real father would fight back. The Morrises soon become the target of the Cullens' wrath. Hunter is browbeaten by Nunn and his

burly redneck boys, Green is molested by one of them, and Crombie is used as a punching bag when he talks to D'Abo, the only girl in the Cullen family. The pouty, amply endowed D'Abo (who manages to appear in a revealing wet T-shirt for no purpose other than to titillate) is attracted to Crombie. She dreams of getting away from her loony family and living in New York City, wearing pretty dresses and makeup. When their relationship is discovered, however, she is brutally beaten by her family, who then accuse Crombie of raping her.

In the meantime, Crombie has made friends with Berti, an old Chief Dan George-style Indian who teaches the youngster "the old ways." The tension between the Morrises and the Cullens hits its peak when Green is raped (a brutally effective scene which takes place offscreen, behind a shuttered door) and Crombie, held at knife point, is forced to watch. Driven to action, Hunter gets the sheriff (who has also had enough of the Cullens' ways) and heads out to get Nunn. The Cullens quickly open fire, killing the sheriff and wounding Hunter. Crombie comes along to rescue dad and, in a variety of novel ways, picks off all the Cullens, except for Nunn, who receives a shotgun blast from Hunter. Hunter and Crombie have now learned to respect each other—and all it took was killing off a few rednecks.

Everything here is predictable and has been seen in countless other films of this sort. From the first five minutes of BULLIES any moderately intelligent viewer knows exactly *what* is going to happen. It's just a waiting game to see *how* it will happen. Fortunately, the acting saves BULLIES from being a complete waste. Crombie, in his first feature appearance (he was seen in the PBS presentation of the Canadian TV miniseries "Anne of Green Gables") avoids the usual trappings of this sort of role and manages to make his character believable. Hunter brings some substance to his character and keeps from playing the stereotyped wimp, while Green does a fine job with an underwritten role. Although her character is neglected, the 19-year-old D'Abo, previously seen in CONAN THE DESTROYER and BOLERO, has a compelling presence (she's something of a Canadian Pia Zadora) that shows promise. D'Abo and Crombie build a likable rapport in the Romeo-and-Juliet-style romance as two youngsters in love who must contend with their feuding families. Rather than developing this angle, however, the director choses to play to the audience's presumed desire for action and violence.

p, Peter Simpson; d, Paul Lynch; w, John Sheppard, Bryan McCann; ph, Rene Verzier; m, Paul Zaza; ed, Nick Rotundo; prod d, Jack McAdam; set d, Linda Allen; cos, Maya Mani; spec eff, Bob Shelley; m/l, Peter Simpson, Paul Zaza; makeup, Nancy Howe; stunts, Larry McLean.

Action   **Cas.**   **(PR:O MPAA:R)**

BULLSEYE† (1986, Aus.) 95m PBL-Dumbarton/Cinema Group c

Paul Goddard *(Harry Walford)*, Kathryn Walker *(Lily Boyd)*, John Wood *(Bluey McGurk)*, Paul Chubb *(Don McKenzie)*, Lynette Curran *(Dora McKenzie)*, Bruce Spence *(Purdy)*, David Slingsby *(Spence)*, John Meillon *(Merritt)*, Kerry Walker *(Mrs. Gootch)*, Rhys McConnochie *(Judge)*.

In 1860s Australia, Goddard is an unhappy laborer working on a ranch owned by Chubb. The only thing that perks up his lowly spirits is Walker, who works as the housemaid for Chubb's wife Curran. This little happiness comes to a sudden end when Walker inherits some money from a recently-deceased aunt. She leaves, and to console himself Goddard decides to rustle some of Chubb's cattle. With his buddy Wood, Goddard takes more than 1000 hoofed beasts and heads out for the range. Along the way they pick up Slingsby and Spence (the latter best known to American audiences for his appearances in THE ROAD WARRIOR and MAD MAX BEYOND THUNDERDOME). Despite overwhelming odds the four survive rugged terrain (the same ground first traversed by Australian heroes Burke and Wills in 1860) and sell the cattle for an enormous sum. To celebrate, Goddard heads for the local bordello where, to his shock and dismay, he finds that his old sweetie Walker is now working. It seems her inheritance was less than the vast sum she had imagined, and in desperation she had been forced to take employment as the brothel's maid. She just decided to make the switch to "working girl," and as luck would have it, Goddard is her very first client. He rescues her from the establishment, and after a comical climactic trial, the film comes to a happy ending. Amazingly enough, this large-scale Australian comedy is based on a true incident!

p, Brian Rosen; d, Carl Schultz; w, Robert Wales, Bob Ellis; ph, Dean Semler (System 35 Widescreen, Eastmancolor); m, Chris Neal; ed, Richard Francis-Bruce.

Comedy/Western (PR:C-O MPAA:NR)

BURYS (SEE: OTRYAD, MPG 1986 Annual)

BUS, THE† (1986, Iran) 120m Ayat c

Hadi Eslami, Morteza Ahmadi, Saeid Abbasie, Asghar Zamani, Yoosef Samad Zaldeh.

A small village is thrown into a state of chaos when a group of people save enough money to buy a bus, endangering the livelihood of the local cart drivers.

d, Yadollah Samadi; w, Daryoosh Farhang; ph, Morteza Rastegar; m, Babak Bayat; ed, Hassan Zand Baaf.

Drama/Comedy (PR:A MPAA:NR)

BUSTED UP* (1986, Can.) 90m Busted Up–Rose & Ruby/Shapiro c

Paul Coufos *(Earl Bird)*, Irene Cara *(Simone)*, Stan Shaw *(Angie)*, Tony Rosato *(Irving Drayton)*, Frank Pellegrino *(Nick Sevins)*, Gordon Judges *(Tony Tenera)*, Nika Kaufhold *(Sara)*, Mike D'Aguilar *(Granite Foster)*, George Buza *(Capt. Hook)*, John Dee *(Daddy Ray)*, Nick Nichols *(Mr. Greene)*, John Ritchie *(Phil)*, Rick Orman *(Teddy)*, Garfield Andrews *(Bobby)*, Al Bernardo *(Al)*, Lawrence King-Phillips *(Kenny)*, David Mitchell *(Greg Bird)*, Sonja Lee *(Darlene)*, Tony Morelli *(Jackson)*, Louis Di Bianco *(Frankie)*, Marshall Perlmuter *(Superintendent)*, Zack Nesis *(Spence)*, Raymond Marlowe *(Jake)*, Dan Dunlop *(Man in Restaurant)*, Teddy McWharters *(Johnny)*, Pat Patterson *(Neil)*, Dennis Strong *(Fight Promoter)*, Damian Lee, John Lapadula, Helder Goncalves *(Gangsters)*, Gordon Masten *(Justice of the Peace)*, Reg Dreger *(Jail Cop)*, Conrad Palmisano *(Monty)*, Frank Ruffo, Errol Slue, Robert Welsh *(Fight Referees)*, Richard Todd, Jerome Tiberghien, John Scott, Paul MacCullum *(Drayton's Thugs)*, Ken Hamilton, Dale Tourangeau *(Tenera's Cornermen)*, Dale Hirtle *(Foster's Cornerman)*, Kevin Godding, Dennis Salovic *(Corsican Brothers)*, Robert O'Ree *(Corsican's Manager)*, Janet Good *(Fat Rosie)*, Wendy Lands *(Drayton's Date)*, George Hevenor *(Croupier)*, Annie McCauley *(Cigarette Girl)*, Richard Guenette, Claude Salvas, Ole Thinius, Real Andrews, Branko Racki *(Auditioning Fighters)*, Marco Bianco, T.J. Scott, Clark Johnson *(Stunt Fighters)*, George Apostolou, Ray Beaulieau, *(Nick's Fighters)*, John Lenard, Billy Calahelo, *(Nick's Gamblers)*, William Paris, Ken Stern *(Prison Inmates)*, Nimrod King, Steve Mousseau, Tex Konig, Malcolm McCuaig, Braun McAsh *(Bouncers)*, Brent Moss, Wayne McPherson *(Kids in Gym)*, Brian Bell, Gowan, Gary O'Connor, Gary Boigon, Gary McCraken *(Musicians)*, Joanne Garfinkle, Kim Caruso, Nancy Wilson *(Girls in Restaurant)*, Daryl Sarkisian *(Guy in Restaurant)*, John Dario *(Man in Gym)*.

What hath Sylvester Stallone wrought? Ten years (and three sequels) after his smashing success with ROCKY, low-level producers are still pirating his boxing film formula, which, if anyone really noticed, is merely a good rehash of every fight-film cliche known to man. In this ragged twist of the old plot devices Coufos is a pug who, with his friend Shaw, owns a neighborhood gym. Some nasty real estate men want to close the place down, then kick the local residents out of their homes so the area can be redeveloped. Rosato is the head bad guy who bets the feisty club owners to send Coufos up against another fighter. If Coufos loses, the club goes down along with the rest of the neighborhood. The outcome of this bout is already predestined, but to give Coufos just a little more to fight for, his ex-girl friend Cara enters the scene. She wants the daughter she had with Coufos six years before and won't take no for an answer. Threatened with the loss of both club and offspring, Coufos enters the ring determined to come out on top. Several bloodsoaked punches later . . .

The predictable plot development and cliched characters make this a monotonous reworking of these tired elements. BUSTED UP never amounts to much, showing meager glimmers of life only during the all-too-familiar climactic bout. Cara manages to belt out four tunes including the popular "She Works Hard For

the Money" (Donna Summer, Michael Omartian). The other three are: "Dying For Your Love" (Gordon Groddy, Carlota McKee), "I Can't Help Feeling Empty" (Cara), and "Busted Up" (Cara, Groddy).

p, Damian Lee, David Mitchell; d, Conrad E. Palmisano; w, Damian Lee; ph, Ludvik Bogner; m, Charles Barnett; ed, Gary Zubeck; art d, Stephen Surjik; set d, William Fleming; cos, Nancy Kaye; m/l, Gordon Groddy, Carlota McKee, Irene Cara, Donna Summer, Michael Omartian; makeup, Kathleen Graham; stunts; Ted Hanlan, The Stunt Team; fight coordinator, Tony Morelli.

Sports Drama Cas. (PR:O MPAA:NR)

BUTNSKALA† (1986, Yugo.) Viba (Trans: Bumpstone)

Emil Filipcic, Marko Derganc, Janez Hocevar-Rifle, Majolka Sukle, Mila Kacic.

d, Franci Slak; w, Emil Filipcic; ph, Vilko Filac; m, Bojan Adamic; set d, Zdravko Papic.

C

CABARET† (1986, Jap.) 104m Toho c

Takeshi Kaga, Hironobu Nomura, Mitsuko Baisho, Junko Mihara, Tetsuro Tamba.

Nomura is an adolescent saxophone player who dreams of the glory he associates with professional jazz musicians. He gets hired by a band working in a mob-owned nightclub. One gangster, Kaga, takes a particular liking to Nomura, especially when the teenager plays the tune "Left Alone," a song which reminds the killer of a murder he once committed. Kaga introduces Nomura to the dangerous underworld, with tragic results as the girl friend of the boy is raped by another mobster and Kaga is killed.

p&d, Haruki Kadokawa; w, Yozo Tanaka (based on a book by Kaoru Kurimoto); ph, Seizo Senmoto; art d, Chikara Imamura.

Crime (PR:O MPAA:NR)

CACTUS½** (1986, Aus.) 93m Dofine/International Spectrafilm c

Isabelle Huppert *(Colo)*, Robert Menzies *(Robert)*, Norman Kaye *(Tom)*, Monica Maughan *(Bea)*, Banduk Marika *(Banduk)*, Sheila Florance *(Martha)*, Peter Aanensen *(George)*, Julia Blake *(Club Speaker)*, Lionel Kowal *(Eye Specialist)*, Jean-Pierre Mignon *(Jean-Francois)*, Elsa Davis *(Elsa)*, Ray Marshall *(Kevin)*, Maurie Fields *(Maurie)*, Sean Scully *(Doctor)*, Dawn Klingberg *(Pedestrian)*, Curtis Easton *(Young Robert)*, Kyra Cox *(Sister)*, Tarni James *(Mother)*, Tony Llewellyn-Jones *(Father)*.

Having already dented the American market with his previous films—LONELY HEARTS, MAN OF FLOWERS, and MY FIRST WIFE—Australian director Paul Cox has delivered CACTUS, an unconventional story about love and seeing. Huppert is a French woman who leaves her husband and travels to Australia to find herself. While driving through a dirt road in the forest, Huppert loses control of the car and crashes. Her friend, Kaye, emerges unharmed, but Huppert gets a sliver of glass in her left eye. As a result of a sympathetic reaction, she is gradually becoming blind in the other eye. Unless the injured eye is removed, Huppert will completely lose her sight. Her friends, Kaye and Maughan, introduce her to a blind neighbor, Menzies, a thirtyish virgin who takes refuge in caring for a greenhouse full of plants. His favorites are cacti—plants which, he

explains to Huppert, are generally believed to thrive on neglect, but actually need much care. The two inevitably fall in love, with Huppert exposing Menzies to a newfound sexuality, and Menzies helping her cope with a life in the dark. The sudden arrival from Paris of her businessman husband, Mignon, throws Huppert into an even more confused state. Jealous of Mignon, Menzies withdraws from his relationship with Huppert, who still wants to see him. Huppert forces Mignon to return home without her, gets the needed operation for her eye, and returns to Menzies. The pair embrace in the greenhouse as Menzies passionately tells her, "I wanted to see you"—a final piece of dialog which sums up his love and frustration in one simple line.

Beautifully photographed by Yuri Sokol, CACTUS is not about blindness as much as it is about seeing. The film opens with a slow, all-encompassing panoramic shot which takes in a full view of the trees and hills that surround Huppert's house. From this first shot it is clear that Cox is interested in what is to be seen, as opposed to telling an action-packed story. Images such as the opening shot, however, are in danger of disappearing forever from Huppert's sight, as they already have from Menzies'. In addition to the picturesque Australian landscape, Cox uses haunting flashbacks from Huppert's and Menzies' pasts, employing super-8mm footage and a visual style borrowed from avant-garde filmmakers. Huppert's footage is shown in the seconds during her accident—shots of a young Huppert (from actual home movies of Huppert) and the Arc d'Triomphe in Paris. Menzies' childhood is recalled when he explains to Huppert that, although he has been blind from birth, he did see momentarily when, as a young boy, he fell to the ground and bumped his head. We see the blind young

Menzies (played by Easton) walking through the woods with his family when he tumbles to the ground. For a split second a blurred shot of the ground is seen—an uninformative and obscure view of the world which is the only view Menzies has ever had.

The chief fault of CACTUS lies in its sloppy and predictable script. Most of the dialog scenes resort to archaic convention, while the film's end comprises a trap in which the audience is supposed to wonder which man Huppert will choose. Huppert's husband, Mignon, is painted so blackly and is so underdeveloped that it is impossible to sympathize with him, even though he has traveled halfway around the world to regain Huppert's love. Besides paying great attention to the visuals, Cox also took time with his soundtrack. The sounds of the Australian outback have rarely played such a major role (PICNIC AT HANGING ROCK and WALKABOUT are exceptions). Unfortunately, the sounds become so obtrusive (chiefly, the cry of the whip bird, which sounds like a synthesized science-fiction effect) that they stand in the film's forefront rather than becoming part of the whole atmosphere. Huppert, as always, is superb and is photographed with a keen, respectful eye by Sokol. Menzies, who has only a minimum of film experience, is also excellent, playing wonderfully off Huppert and portraying a thoroughly convincingly blind man. Although Cox's last three films have received much praise from the critics, CACTUS (the only one of these films with an internationally known star) came and went in American theaters with barely a notice—opening in the U.S. at the New York Film Festival, playing in Los Angeles for one dismal week in 1986, and then showing up in a small arthouse in Chicago in 1987. Songs include "Stabat Mater" (Giovanni Pergolese, performed by Hartley Newnham, Jane Edwards), "Chansons der Trouvere" (Traditional), "To Kariofili Mana Mou" (Yannis Markopolous), and "Colo's Song" (Elsa Davis).

p, Jane Ballantyne, Paul Cox; d, Paul Cox; w, Paul Cox, Norman Kaye, Bob Ellis; ph, Yuri Sokol (Fujicolor); m, Giovanni Pergolese, Yannis Markopolous, Elsa Davis; ed, Tim Lewis; md, Spiros Rantos; prod d, Asher Bilu; art d, Lirit Bilu; cos, Missoni; makeup, Pietra Robins.

Romance (PR:C MPAA:NR)

CAGED GLASS† (1986, Span.) 112m TEM c (TRAS EL CRISTAL)

Gunter Meisner *(Klaus)*, David Sust *(Angelo)*, Marisa Paredes *(Griselda)*, Gisela Echevarria *(Rena)*, Imma Colomer *(Maid)*, Josue Gausch, Alberto Manzano, Ricart Carcelero, David Cuspinet.

Meisner is a fugitive Nazi war criminal, a concentration-camp doctor whose officially sanctioned horrors aroused a sexual lust not to be quieted once the war ended. The film opens with a powerfully disturbing scene of a naked boy, hanging by his wrists, receiving a brutal beating from Meisner, who kisses him before delivering the *coup de grace*. Later, Meisner is confined to an iron lung in the aftermath of an accident. He lives in a large house with his wife and daughter. A young man, Su⸱, arrives to take a job as caretaker, but it is soon clear that the scars he bears were suffered at the hands of Meisner, and that he has assumed his tormentor's demented pleasures himself. He begins regaling Meisner with readings from Meisner's own diary, murders his mentor's wife, seduces his daughter, and begins abducting young boys from the village to torture and kill in front of him. An extremely troubling picture, but a truer one than most will care to admit. Likely to be widely banned.

p, Teresa Enrich; d&w, Agustin Villaronga; ph, Jaume Peracaula; m, Javier Navaretto; ed, Raul Roman; art d, Case Candini.

Drama (PR:O MPAA:NR)

CALACAN† (1986, Mex.) 80m Emulsion y Gelatina-Dasa/Pelic Mexicanas c

David Gonzalez *(Ernesto)*, Humberto Leon *(Felipe)*, Silvia Guevara, Mauro Mendoza, Emilio Ebergenyi, Members of La Trouppe Theater Group.

A Mexican children's film starring Gonzalez as a youngster who is afraid that the traditional "Day of the Dead" celebration is going to be taken over by the devil and his henchmen. Gonzalez learns that the devil plans to replace the traditional sugar skulls made in Calacan with plastic jack-o-lanterns made in the U.S. With the help of Leon, a skeleton boy, Gonzalez is able to foil the devil's plan and preserve the true spirit of the "Day of the Dead." Shown as part of New York's 10th Latino Festival.

p, Luis Kelly Ramirez, Mauro Mendoza, Fernando Fuentes; d&w, Luis Kelly Ramirez; ph, Fernando Fuentes; m, Luis Guzman; ed&art d, Luis Kelly Ramirez.

Children's (PR:A MPAA:NR)

CAMORRA½** (1986, Ital.) 93m Cannon Tuschinski–Italian International/Cannon c (UN COMPLICATO INTRIGO DI DONNE, VICOLI E DELITTI; Trans: A Complicated Intrigue of Women, Alleyways and Crimes)

Angela Molina, *(Annunziata)*, Francisco Rabal *(Guaglione)*, Harvey Keitel *(Frankie Acquasanta)*, Daniel Ezralow *(Antonio)*, Paolo Bonacelli *(Tango)*, Isa Danieli *(Carmela)*, Tommaso Bianco, Vittorio Squillante, Raffaele Verita, Elvio Porta, Muzzi Loffredo, Sebastiano Nardone, Mario Scarpetta, Anni Papa, Franco Angrisano.

When Molina, a former child prostitute—a hustler turned hosteler—is raped in her own *pensione* and her attacker is killed by an unseen vigilante, a rash of unexplained murders plagues the Camorra—the Naples crime syndicate. All the murders bear a common trait—each person is killed by hypodermic injection to the testicles. Molina is questioned by local authorities and underground mob figures, but it is apparent that she did not see the vigilante. Each of Molina's friends has an idea as to the murderer's identity and they follow their own clues. Rabal is a blind, elderly leader of the Camorra who begins to feel shame for his criminal associations even though he has two sons who have been murdered. Ezralow, a homosexual childhood friend of Molina who is now a dance teacher, also offers assistance in solving the crime. The chief suspect is Keitel, Molina's former lover, who has a violent streak and is still possessive of Molina. Contrary to everyone's belief, the string of murders has been committed by an angry group of Neapolitan housewives who are upset by the Camorra's use of their pre-teen children as drug-runners. The mothers are brought to trial, but everyone in the courtroom is in full support of their retaliatory actions.

Lacking the broad humor of the better-known Wertmuller films (SEVEN BEAUTIES and SWEPT AWAY), CAMORRA pays more attention to elements of the melodrama and the crime thriller. There is the usual Wertmuller lush photography and artistic composition, as well as the anti-male message, making this film far closer to her previous SOTTO, SOTTO (1985) than to her works of the 1970s. Released in Italy in 1985, CAMORRA, with its title shortened from the traditionally lengthy original, didn't reach U.S. screens until this year in a rather carelessly dubbed version. Wertmuller's following film, NOTTE D'ESTATE CON PROFILO GRECO, OCCHI A MANDORLA E ODORE DI BASILICO (Summer Night with Greek Profile, Almond Eyes, and the Scent Of Basil) was released this year in Italy.

p, Menahem Golan, Yoram Globus; d, Lina Wertmuller, w, Lina Wertmuller, Elvio Porta; ph, Giuseppe Lanci (Cinecitta Color); m, Tony Esposito; ed, Luigi Zita; prod d, Enrico Job; cos, Benito Persico; ch, Daniel Ezralow.

Crime Drama (PR:O MPAA:R)

CAN YUE† (1986, China) 90m Pearl River Film Studio c (Trans: Broken Moon)

Zheng Zhenyao, Zhao Erkang, Hong Rong, Huo Xiu.

The survival of old-fashioned, big-studio, Hollywood-model productions in Communist Mainland China is truly remarkable. Impressive features continue to be released, although the most interesting and domestically successful are generally banned for export. Less interesting is this melodrama, an account of the sufferings of Zheng as she sacrifices her own happiness (personified by her true love) for the benefit of her five daughters. After struggling through the Revolution as well as its aftermath, the Great Leap Forward and other periods of strife, her daughters grow and become complacent, and when as an old woman their mother wants at last to marry the man of her dreams, they oppose her.

p, Tao Yi; d, Cao Zheng; w, He Jiesheng (based on the novel *Sacrifice of the Heart* by Wen Bin); ph, Wei Duo, Pang Lei; m, Du Jiang.

Drama (PR:A MPAA:NR)

CAPABLANCA† (1986, Cuba/USSR) 95m Instituto Cubano de Artes y Industrias Cinematograficas c

Cesar Evora *(Jose Raul Capablanca)*, Galina Belyayeva *(Sacha Mozhaeva)*, Beatriz Valdes *(Amelia)*, Marina Yakovlieva *(Vera)*, Adolfo Llaurado *(Jose Maria Picon)*, Ramon Veloz *(Gonzalo)*, Boris Nevsorov *(Eremaev)*, Alejandro Lugo *(Barraque)*, Javier Avila, Rogelio Meneses, Igor Tarasov, Grigori Liampe, Dimitri Orlovki.

This biography of Jose Raul Capablanca, a Cuban world-class chess master of the 1920s, is a joint venture between Cuban and Soviet filmmakers. With the action beginning in 1925, Evora decides to depart for Moscow to compete in the international competitions, though Cuban friends strongly urge him not to go. Upon arriving in the Soviet Union he meets Valdes, a former girl friend and also engages in a new romance with Belyayeva, a well-known Russian dancer. As a competitor Evora proves to be inconsistent. At times he will take on several players simultaneously; other games he deliberately loses in order to spend some time with Belyayeva. Though he wins the International, Evora is destined to lose the championship in two years to Alexander Allojin during a competition in Buenos Aires.

p, Santiago Llapur, Nicolai Velmiski; d, Manuel Herrera; w, Manuel Herrera, Eliseo Alberto Diego, Dal Orlov; ph, Igor Klebanov; m, Sergio Vitier; ed, Justo Vega.

Biography (PR:O MPAA:NR)

CAPTIVE† (1986, Brit.) 95m Virgin–World Audio Visual Entertainment–Les Productions Belles Rives–UGC/Virgin–CineTel c

Irina Brook *(Rowena Le Vay)*, Oliver Reed *(Gregory Le Vay)*, Xavier Deluc *('D')*, Corinne Dacla *(Bryony)*, Hiro Arai *(Hiro)*, Nic Reding *(Leo)*, Annie Leon *(Pine)*.

The first directorial effort from the screenwriter of THE MAN WHO FELL TO EARTH, EUREKA, and MERRY CHRISTMAS, MR. LAWRENCE is an exploration of kidnaping, brainwashing, and personal freedom as seen through the eyes of Brook. She plays a rich young woman, unhappily living in a castle provided by her father, Reed. Brook's mother died while giving birth to her, and Reed now dominates his daughter, treating her more as an object than a person. The spoiled girl's life takes a dramatic twist when three fellow rich kids—Deluc, Dacla, and Arai—kidnap her and begin turning her against Reed's oppressive control. She is blindfolded, gagged, and hung upside down, all in an effort to wear down her resistance. Gradually the methods take hold, and when Brook is freed, she finds life with Reed intolerable. She returns to her captors, then leads her comrades in defacing a work of art Reed has donated to a gallery. Reed closes in on his daughter's whereabouts through the use of a psychic. When the band

tries to escape, Deluc and Dacla are killed. Arai manages to get away, but Brook is caught and sent to jail for her crimes. After two years behind bars, she returns to her former dwellings. She is surprised to find Arai waiting there for her, and she hides him on the premises. When Reed offers Brook a new life in New York, she stubbornly refuses. The events of the past few years have toughened her, and Brook will not allow any man to run her life, not even her father. Overhearing this convinces Arai he will never fit into Brook's life, and he kills himself according to Japanese tradition. Brook is the daughter of famed theatrical director Peter Brook and actress Natasha Perry. This is her first starring role in a feature film. Arai also makes his feature film debut here. For French players Deluc and Dacla, this is their first English-language feature appearance.

p, Don Boyd; d&w, Paul Mayerberg; ph, Mike Southern (Fujicolor); m, The Edge, Michael Berkeley; ed, Marie-Therese Boiche; art d, George Djurkovic; m, The Edge, Michael Berkeley.

Drama (PR:O MPAA:NR)

CAR TROUBLE† (1986, Brit.) 93m GTO–Double Helix–Goldfarb/ COL–EMI–WB c

Julie Walters *(Jacqueline Spong)*, Ian Charleson *(Gerald Spong)*, Stratford Johns *(Reg Sampson)*, Vincenzo Ricotta *(Kevin O'Connor)*, Hazel O'Connor *(Kevin's Wife)*.

In 1984, Julie Walters (EDUCATING RITA) and Ian Charleson (CHARIOTS OF FIRE) played the explosive, tortured lovers in the National Theatre's production of Sam Shepard's "Fool for Love." In the British film comedy CAR TROUBLE they play a very different kind of couple. Charleson is a boring air traffic controller and Walters his sexy ex-flight attendant wife of eight years. Their home and their values are distinctly suburban: she is preoccupied with an upcoming Mexican vacation, and he thinks about cars, in particular about a glossy, red, mint-condition E-type Jaguar for sale at Sampson's Garage. But when her thoughts turn to sex, his never stray from the car. Determined to make the Jag his, Charleson enlists the help of salesman Ricotta to help persuade Walters to approve the purchase, which includes the trade-in of their tiny Citroen 2CV. While Charleson is firming up the deal with the garage's proprietor, Johns, sparks are flying between Walters and Ricotta. An angry Charleson returns to interrupt their flirtation. Johns has apprised him of recent repair work done to the Citroen, the result of an accident that Walters has kept secret, but that now means considerably less trade-in value for the 2CV. Still, the deal goes through and they return home with Charleson's dream car; however, he forbids her to drive it and she retaliates by refusing him sex. This ugliness between them lasts the weekend.

When Monday rolls around and Charleson is back at his radar screen, Walters finds the hidden car keys and takes off in the off-limits auto. Before her day of shopping is over, she stops by a pub, where she runs into Ricotta. A few drinks later, out of the pub, a sudden downpour forces them to take refuge in the sports car. Before long Walters and Ricotta are revving each other's engines, but because the E-type only offers a limited amount of legroom, Walters tries to create a little extra space by releasing the parking brake, providing the necessary spark for their internal combustion, but sending the car rolling down a hill on a collision course with a tree. To make matters worse, they are not only locked in the car, but the shock of the crash has left them frozen in the most compromising of positions. Soon their predicament is witnessed by neighbors, Ricotta's pregnant wife (O'Connor), police, firemen, and ultimately by a national TV audience that includes Charleson, who watches from a pub as his dream car is cut open to reveal his wife in flagrante delicto. Out of his mind, he embarks on a vengeful tirade, first attacking Walters with an axe, then attempting to burn down their house with her in it, and lastly trying to merge a couple of blips on his radar screen, one of which happens to be the jet in which Walters is attempting to escape to Brazil.

The inspiration for CAR TROUBLE came from a newspaper account of an embarrassing auto-bound coupling like the one in the film. It was first conceived as a sitcom, then seemed like a better idea as a stage review, and finally reached fruition as director Green's first feature film. Charleson received a script from a friend of screenwriter Whaley, and suggested to Walters that she join him in the project. In addition to costarring in "Fool for Love" at the time, Walters and Charleson were also romantically linked.

p, Howard Malin, Gregory J. De Santis; d, David Green; w, James Whaley, A.J. Tipping; ph, Michael Garfath; ed, Barry Reynolds; prod d, Hugo Luczyc; cos, Vanessa Clarke; m/l, Meatloaf.

Comedy (PR:C-O MPAA:NR)

CARAVAGGIO**½** (1986, Brit.) 93m British Film Institute–Channel 4/ BFI–Cinevista c

Nigel Terry *(Caravaggio)*, Sean Bean *(Rannuccio Thomasoni)*, Garry Cooper *(Davide)*, Spencer Leigh *(Jerusaleme)*, Tilda Swinton *(Lena)*, Michael Gough *(Cardinal Del Monte)*, Nigel Davenport *(Marchese Giustiniani)*, Robbie Coltrane *(Cardinal Borghese)*, Jonathon Hyde *(Baglione)*, Dexter Fletcher *(Young Caravaggio)*, Noam Almaz *(Boy Caravaggio)*, Jack Birkett *(The Pope)*.

Derek Jarman has never been known for catering to the tastes of the filmgoing public. His four releases to date, SEBASTIANE, JUBILEE, THE TEMPEST, and THE ANGELIC CONVERSATION (a Super-8mm film blown up to 35mm), all obsessive and excessive works with limited distribution and appeal, have established Jarman as the so-called *enfant terrible* of the British Cinema. Easily his most accessible film, CARAVAGGIO is a sketchy biography of the Late-Italian-Renaissance painter Michelangelo Merisi da Caravaggio. Having very little documented material as reference, Jarman deduced that Caravaggio's paintings were essentially autobiographical: that the subject matter, the models, and the style had some relation to Caravaggio's life. Combining discoveries from his diligent canvas research with the few known facts, Jarman wrote the script for his version of the painter's life. That was in 1978. Twenty rewrites later, with the budget of $715,000 funded by the British Film Institute, he made the movie.

The known facts about Caravaggio's life are: as a youth he sold his paintings on the streets of Rome; he bought a deaf-mute as a child to act as a slave and caretaker; his models were usually prostitutes and street toughs; he fled from Rome to Naples to escape arrest for killing a man; and, like all great painters whose genius is never fully appreciated during their lifetime, he died a pauper. Ascertaining that the painter was probably bisexual, Jarman constructed a personal depiction of his life based on what he construed to be Caravaggio's passionate temperament. As could be expected from such an approach, reality becomes less significant than fantasy as Jarman builds events based on his *own* personal history.

The film opens with Terry, as the painter, lying in a desperate fever on his deathbed in a small, barren room; his faithful mute servant selflessly attends to him. It then flashes back to the young painter, played by Fletcher (looking like a young version of the rock singer Mick Jagger), as a street thug selling paintings and robbing people. Gough, a wealthy cardinal, recognizes talent in the boy—though equally motivated by sexual attraction—and agrees to commission a work by him. When the time comes to receive his payment, Fletcher only asks for the long dagger that Gough had confiscated. Gough complies, offering to become the painter's sponsor, to give him a place to paint and live in, and to take care of his material needs. Several years into the future, Fletcher becomes Terry, still painting under the sponsorship of the cardinal. Between etching religious incidents onto large canvases in his chiaroscuro style, Terry drinks heavily, gambles, and associates with the low-life types who reflect his own origins. One gambler in particular sparks Terry's passionate interest: the handsome, blond Bean. Terry persuades Bean to become his model by passing gold coins from mouth to mouth. Accompanied by his prostitute girl friend Swinton, Bean models for a series of paintings, becoming Caravaggio's constant companion. Though passionately in love with the thug, the painter is never shown to consummate the relationship. Swinton also notices Terry's affection for Bean. At first she expresses her jealousy, but as she, also, models for Terry, her attitude changes. After one wealthy and prominent citizen buys a painting, he invites Terry to a celebration. Terry insists on bringing his models with him, an occasion for which he prepares them by adorning them in elegant finery. Swinton is transformed from a street tramp into a divine lady. Terry's affection to his new creation becomes as great as that he feels for Bean. The man who sponsors the ball also falls in love with Swinton. Attracted to the new wealth at her disposal, Swinton leaves Bean. When her dead body is found floating in the river, Bean is charged with her murder. Terry believes in his model's innocence and emphatically pleads his case with officials powerful enough to grant Bean freedom. This accomplished, Bean admits to Terry that he did in fact kill Swinton, "So" as he tells the painter "that we can now be together." Enraged, Terry slits the street urchin's throat with the dagger he carried in his youth.

Jarman couldn't tell this tale without adding peculiar eccentricities to interrupt the dramatic flow. This comes in the form of typewriters, calculators, motorbikes, an automobile, a few modern-day outfits, and the noises of airplanes. These are all introduced in a matter-of-fact manner, without the slightest attention being drawn to them. The point being made is not clear. Perhaps they are Jarman's way of poking fun at the medium of film and the manipulative techniques that are its basis. These modern-day items constitute an eyesore on otherwise beautiful and inventive, though minimal, sets. Because the budget did not allow location filming in Italy, abandoned warehouses along the London docks were transformed into sets. These work well, especially when photographed in the chiaroscuro style (Caravaggio's innovation) of Gabriel Beristain, for which the cinematographer received a Silver Bear for Outstanding Single Achievement at the Berlin Film Festival. Undoubtedly Jarman had a lot of passion for his subject; unfortunately, he does not transmit this to the screen. Beyond the beautiful photography, statuesque characters, and realistic renditions of the painter's work lies an aloof and mocking film, one that Caravaggio might have actually liked.

p, Sarah Radclyffe; d&w, Derek Jarman; ph, Gabriel Beristain (Technicolor); m, Simon Fisher Turner, Mary Phillips; ed, George Akers; prod d, Christopher Hobbs; cos, Sandy Powell.

Biography **(PR:O MPAA:NR)**

CARAVAN SARAI† (1986, Gr.) 115m Greek Film Center–Tassos Psarras c

Thimos Karakatsanis, Dimitra Hatoupi, Mirka Kalotzopoulou, Vassilis Kolovos, Lazaros Andreou, Tassos Palaizidis, Zafiris Katramadas, Melina Botelli, Costas Itsios, Alex. Revidis.

A 45-year-old Greek villager finds his entire life changed when civil war suddenly forces him to evacuate his home. He and his two children are relocated to an urban area, settling in a building where they remain until the war's end.

d&w, Tassos Psarras; ph, Stavros Chassapis; m, Giorgos Tsangaris; ed, Panos Papakyriakopoulos; set d, Antonis Chalkias; cos, Anastasia Arseni.

Drama **(PR:C-O MPAA:NR)**

CARE BEARS MOVIE II: A NEW GENERATION** (1986) 77m Nelvana/COL c

Voices of: Maxine Miller *(True Heart Bear)*, Pam Hyatt *(Noble Heart Horse)*, Hadley Kay *(Dark Heart/The Boy)*, Cree Summer Francks *(Christy)*, Alyson Court *(Dawn)*, Michael Fantini *(John)*.

This followup to 1985's THE CARE BEARS MOVIE is, like its predecessor, perfect viewing for the preschool set in terms of character and story, though its blatant intent as a 77-minute toy commercial should make parents wary. The simple narrative follows the adventures of True Heart Bear and his friend Noble Heart Horse. Their nemesis Dark Heart is working his sinister tricks on a group of summer campers, turning the normally likable tykes into a gang of irritating whelps. The two ethereal good guys, aided by some of the Care Bear kin, manage to put an end to Dark Heart's scheme as the story comes to its inevitable happy conclusion.

The animation isn't bad, considering the lower standards of the current era of cost control. With its unpretentious moral tale of good and evil, CARE BEARS MOVIE II treats the needs and expectations of its target audience with the utmost consideration. Unfortunately, the same can also be said of its manipulation of the child consumer. The children's toy market is a lucrative one, and CARE BEARS MOVIE II parades the new lovable stuffed animals with unashamed zeal. The subtitle A NEW GENERATION refers to the new featured characters, who, more than coincidentally, have ended up on the toy shelves of stores everywhere. Though certainly past children's films have inspired toy lines of their own, when the toys themselves serve as inspiration the objective behind the work takes on a whole new meaning. The songs by the Parks team are rendered by Stephen Bishop and Debbie Allen.

p, Michael Hirsh, Patrick Loubert, Clive A. Smith; d, Dale Schott; w, Peter Sauder; m, Patricia Cullen; ed, Evan Landis; anim d, Charles Bonifacio; m/l, Dean Parks, Carol Parks.

Animated Feature **Cas.** **(PR:AAA MPAA:G)**

CARNAGE zero (1986) 91m Jaylo International/Media Home Entertainment c

Leslie Den Dooven *(Carol)*, Michael Chiodo *(Jonathan)*, John Garitt *(Walter)*, Deeann Veeder *(Susan)*, Chris Baker *(Ann)*, Jack Poggi *(Minister)*, Albert Alfano *(Tony)*, Che Moody *(Mother-in-Law)*, Rosemary Egan *(Margaret)*, Ellen Orchid *(Judy)*, Chris Georges *(Mark)*, Bill Grant *(Dad)*, Judith Mayes *(Martha)*, Lola Ross *(Rose Novak)*, Lon Freeman *(Nathan Frye)*, Joseph Vitagliano *(Plumber)*, Victor Logan *(Dr. Marcus)*, Willis Karp *(Ray Trail)*, Susan Ortiz *(Secretary)*, William Cooner, David Marks *(Burglars)*.

Written, photographed, and directed in 1983 as "Hell House" by Staten Island's favorite low-budget exploitation king, Andy Milligan, this haunted-house/gore film is so bad it never saw a theatrical release and went straight to video.

The film, shot in Milligan's usual home-movie style, opens as a bride and groom, Veeder and Georges, bid each other a passionate goodbye before he shoots her in the head and then commits suicide himself. Three years later another newlywed couple, Den Dooven and Chiodo, move into the house, which still contains all the furnishings of the previous couple. In a matter of minutes inanimate objects begin to move around on their own, and while Chiodo is oblivious to the strange goings-on, Den Dooven begins to think she's going mad. That night the stove turns its gas on by itself and the two are nearly poisoned. Things soon get worse when Den Dooven's new housekeeper, Ross, is attacked by the ghost of Veeder (still wearing her wedding gown) in the cellar. Thinking the woman mad, Den Dooven and Chiodo take the housekeeper home and call a doctor. When everyone leaves, the catatonic woman walks zombie-like to her medicine cabinet, grabs a straight razor, and cuts her throat. Den Dooven and Chiodo are shaken by the news, and shortly thereafter, two burglars are attacked by flying garden tools and killed, but for some reason Den Dooven and Chiodo never find the bloody bodies.

Despite the strange happenings, the couple decide to go ahead with the housewarming party they had planned. That weekend two couples arrive to help the new homeowners celebrate. The party is ruined when a rug zooms out from under a pregnant guest and she falls into some broken glass. The husband of the other couple is electrocuted when invisible hands push a radio into the bathtub in which he is relaxing. Determined to learn why such horrible things are happening, Den Dooven goes to the hall of records and talks with the man who sold the house to the previous couple. He tells her that the previous tenants loved the house very much and refurbished it with care. Things turned sour when the woman had a miscarriage and then discovered she had terminal breast cancer. Distraught, the two dressed up in their wedding clothes and committed suicide.

Now convinced that the house is haunted, Den Dooven turns to a minister, Poggi, to investigate. The ghosts don't take kindly to this and promptly send a meat cleaver flying into the minister's head. Fed up, the couple decide to move. As Chiodo loads up the car, Den Dooven is confronted by the ghosts, who beg her not to leave. Possessed by spirits, Den Dooven and Chiodo commit suicide in the exact same manner as the previous tenants, as the ghosts look on approvingly.

Tedious, talky, and incredibly inept, CARNAGE is laughably amateurish. Incredibly, writer-director-photographer Milligan has made a mind-boggling 23 movies (among them THE GHASTLY ONES, BLOODTHIRSTY BUTCHERS, and the classically awful THE RATS ARE COMING! THE WEREWOLVES ARE HERE!) and brags that he has not spent more than $10,000 on any of them. It shows. Most scenes appear to be lit by one—very bright—light source, which illuminates the actors, but leaves the rest of the set in darkness. Everything is done in one take with very little editing, so when Den Dooven goes to make some tea, we watch her make tea in real time. The only way to pad out a cheap feature with a concept this lame is to have the characters talk and talk and talk without saying anything. There are several long, pointless conversations between Den Dooven and Chiodo, and then Den Dooven and her father (on the phone), and then Den Dooven and the minister, and even a subplot from hell involving the collapsing marriage of Den Dooven's best friend Baker, where we watch Baker talk with *her* mother, Moody, for what seems like an eternity. These long passages of boredom are punctuated by unintentionally hilarious "special-effects" sequences where objects are supposed to be moving by themselves, but which are obviously being propelled by strings or even hands just out of frame. (There is a scene involving a long-handled axe which is uproarious.)

The gore effects look as if they were done by grade schoolers who had raided the refrigerator, and the appearances of the ghosts were done by simply telling the actors to stand still while Milligan turned off the camera and sent one of the ghosts to go stand in the shot. Then he turned the camera back on, making the ghost suddenly appear. Unfortunately, there is a flash-frame every time this happens. (A flash-frame is one frame of film which is over-exposed just as the camera starts running—you're supposed to edit them out, Andy.) One could make a case that all these ineptitudes combine to form a perversely charming film, sort of like the short Super-8 films that ambitious teenagers make at home. Maybe so, but just try to imagine yourself sitting through a *90 minute* home-movie made by the neighborhood kids. If you can take that, then you'll almost be ready to suffer through CARNAGE.

p, Lew Mishkin; d,w&ph, Andy Milligan; ed, Gerald Bronson.

Horror   (PR:C MPAA:NR)

CARNE CHE CRESCE†   (1986, Ital.) Istituto "Fermi"–Assessorato
Pubblica Istruzione e Cultura della Provincia di Roma/Marco Perrone c
(Trans: Growing Flesh)

Fulvio Capitanio, Andrea Benedetti, Federico De Angelis, Sara Chievari, Claudio Cameli.

Frustrated and upset with how adults perceive their generation, a group of adolescents decides to lodge a protest by locking themselves in the school restroom until they get some respect from their elders. Parents, teachers, and priests try to persuade the teens to come out, first by using such bribes as fast-food and trendy clothes, then resorting to more harsh measures such as harassment and starvation. Finally the students decide to storm the adults, but when they emerge from the restroom, they find a field of flowers and chirping birds and realize that youth will always have the advantage over age. The film is structured in a comic-surreal manner with characters talking to the audience.

d&w, Students of Istituto "Fermi"; ph, Giulio Cavallone; m, Erwin Helfer.

Comedy   (PR:C MPAA:NR)

CASTAWAY†   (1986, Brit.) 118m Cannon Screen Entertainment–United
British Artists/Cannon c

Oliver Reed *(Gerald Kingsland)*, Amanda Donohoe *(Lucy Irvine)*, Georgina Hale *(Nun)*, Frances Barber *(Young Nun)*, Tony Richards *(Jason)*, Todd Rippon *(Rod)*, Len Peihopa *(Ronald)*, Virginia Hey *(Janice)*, Sarah Harper *(Schoolteacher)*, Stephen Jenn *(Shop Manager)*, Sorrel Johnson *(Lara)*, John Sessions *(Man in Pub)*, Paul Reynolds *(Mike Kingsland)*, Sean Hamilton *(Geoffrey Kingsland)*, Arthur Cox *(Manager)*.

Roeg's film, which premiered in late 1986 at the London Film Festival, is a straightforward narrative (as opposed to Roeg's previous reconstructive editing) telling of a man and a woman who spend a full year together on a desert island. Reed stars as a middle-aged man who runs an ad in a London publication for a woman to join him for a year's stay on an island. Donohoe, tired of her dreary, repetitious London life, answers and before long both are dropped off on the island of Tuin near Australia. There is an initial sexual tension which carries through the film as the characters grow to dislike one another but still must depend on each other for survival. Based on an actual incident involving Gerald Kingsland and Lucy Irvine, both of whom wrote books detailing their experiences.

p, Rick McCallum; d, Nicolas Roeg; w, Allan Scott (based on the books *Castaway* by Lucy Irvine and *The Islander* by Gerald Kingsland); ph, Harvey Harrison (Fujicolor); m, Stanley Myers; ed, Tony Lawson; prod d, Andrew Sanders; cos, Nic Ede.

Adventure/Drama   (PR:O MPAA:NR)

CASTIGHI†   (1986, Ital.) Atalante Coop/Europa Cine TV c (Trans:
Punishment)

Giorgio Losego, Lidia Montanari, Stefano Amicarelli, Andrea Crudo.

One night a newly engaged businessman writes a letter to a friend who is in Russia on a visit, hoping his pal will be able to attend the wedding. He wants to read the letter to his father, but finds the sick and elderly man has already fallen asleep. After drifting off himself, the young man has a terrible dream in which he is put on trial by friends and relatives for betraying someone close to him as well as showing familial disloyalty. For this he is condemned to die. Upon waking, the terrified young man carries out the sentence himself by committing suicide.

p, Maurizio Spinelli; d, Giorgio Losego, Lidia Montanari; w&ph, Lidia Montanari; m, Edizioni Musicali Cometa.

Drama   (PR:NR MPAA:NR)

CATTIVI PIERROT†   (1986, Ital.) Freeway/Image International c (Trans:
Black Nightmare)

Pierfrancesco Campanella, Milly D'Abbraccio, Angelo Cannavacciolo, Claudia Cavalcanti, Rosanna Banfi, Giorgio Ardisson, Didi Perego, Paolo Gozlino.

This unusual story of obsessive and senseless violence begins when a shy college student meets a wealthy young woman who is mentally unstable. A twisted affair develops as the two plot against what they perceive to be the distorted values of society. The couple then go on a wild murder spree and reality becomes interwoven with fantasy in the disturbing series of events that follow.

d, Fabrizio Rampelli; w, Pierfrancesco Campanella; ph, Carlo Poletti (Fotocinema); m, Gianni Marchetti.

Drama   (PR:O MPAA:NR)

CHAMS†   (1986, Morocco) 81m Camera 3 c

Aicha Sefrioui *(Chams)*, Khadija Bouderba *(Aicha)*, Bousalem Guennoun *(El Haj)*, Abdou Sefrioui *(Salim)*.

When wealthy businessman Guennoun's son Abdou Sefrioui returns home to Morocco after attending school in Switzerland, the scion announces plans to run against his father in an upcoming election. This causes untold confusion amidst the voting public, and Guennoun finds relief in alcohol. Also coming to his aid is the title character Aicha Sefrioui, who is the beautiful daughter of one of Guennoun's former mistresses.

d&w, Najib Sefrioui; ph, Mohamed Affane, Thierry Lebigre; ed, Najib Sefrioui, Anne Leconidec, Maria Lebbar.

Drama   (PR:O MPAA:NR)

CHARLEY†   (1986, Neth.) 90m Wanker Bros./Kriterion bw

Maria Kooiman *(Charley)*, Rosita Steenbeek *(Berte)*, Eric Schreurs.

Shot on 16mm black-and-white stock, the third feature of director Theo van Gogh attempts to shock by portraying such taboo subjects as incest, cannibalism, murder, and necrophilia in a comedic manner. Kooiman stars as a beautiful mute woman (her father sexually abused her as a child) who lures men to her apartment where she and her roommate Steenbeek poison them and then feed off their sex organs.

p,d&w, Theo van Gogh; m, Trea Dobs, Willy Alberti; ph, Willem Hoogenboom; ed, Willem Hoogenboom, Theo van Gogh.

Comedy/Drama   (PR:O MPAA:NR)

CHARLOTTE AND LULU   (SEE: L'EFFRONTE, Fr., MPG 1986 Annual)

CHARLOTTE FOR EVER†   (1986, Fr.) 94m GPFI–Constellation/AMLF c

Serge Gainsbourg *(Stan)*, Charlotte Gainsbourg *(Charlotte)*, Roland Bertin *(Leon)*, Roland Dubillard *(Herman)*, Anne Zamberlan *(Lola)*, Anne Le Guernec *(Adelaide)*, Sabeline Campo *(Therese)*.

Writer-director-composer Gainsbourg's daughter Charlotte has followed her successful 1985 film L'EFFRONTEE (released in the U.S. this year as CHARLOTTE AND LULU), for which she won a Cesar (the gallic equivalent of an Oscar), in this semi-incestuous father-daughter story in which she stars opposite her dad. He's an unshaven, hungover, sex-obsessed former screenwriter who cavorts with a vile prostitute, an offensive film producer, and a despondent homosexual—and then wonders why his daughter can't stand to be near him. By the finale, Serge and Charlotte are reconciled, and the audience is let in on a secret—it wasn't really a story, but a drama played on a studio set.

p, Jean-Claude Fleury, Claudie Ossard; d&w, Serge Gainsbourg; ph, Willy Kurant (Fujicolor); m, Serge Gainsbourg; ed, Babeth Si Ramdane; art d, Raoul Albert.

Drama   (PR:O MPAA:NR)

CHECK IS IN THE MAIL, THE   (1986) 91m Robert Kaufman–Ted
Kotcheff/Ascot Entertainment Group c

Brian Dennehy *(Richard Jackson)*, Anne Archer *(Peggy Jackson)*, Hallie Todd *(Robin Jackson)*, Chris Hebert *(Danny Jackson)*, Michael Bowen *(Gary Jackson)*, Nita Talbot *(Mrs. Rappaport)*, Dick Shawn *(Donald Rappaport)*, Kathy Maisnik *(Sally Jackson)*, Thomas Rollerson *(Sally's Boy Friend)*, Greg Mullavey *(Harry Danvers)*, Ronnie Schell *(Dr. Brannigan)*, Beau Starr *(Rocco)*, Emily Banks *(Travel Agent)*, Fred Pinkard *(Skycap)*, Nanci Christopher *(Airline Representative)*, Richard Minchenberg *(Paul Silver)*, Chris Rydell *(Drunken Sailor)*, Robert Clotworthy *(Moonie)*, Benjamin Lum *(Janitor)*, Haunani Minn *(Desk Clerk)*, Yjui Okumoto *(Bell Boy)*, Michael Horse *(Pool Attendant)*, Lewis Arquette *(Man at Pool)*, Marilyn Wolf *(Harriet)*, Guy Remsen *(Man at Danvers Motors)*, Christina Hart *(Janet)*, Robin Kaufman *(Kathy Stivers)*, Richard Foronjy *(Tony the Brake Man)*, Bruce Grey *(Robert Howe)*, Larry Gellman *(Byron Turtlelaub)*, Herb Kerns *(TV Announcer)*, Leonard Hirschfeld *(TV Reporter)*, Harry Townes *(Fred Steinkrause)*, Ken Olfson *(Assessor)*, Walter Mathews, Eric Fleeks *(Water and Power Men)*, Leonard Lightfoot, Russell Curry *(Burglars)*, Milt Kogan *(Mr. Fanning)*, Howard Storm *(Dr. Korngold)*, Renny Temple *(Bob Schick)*.

In recent years, Brian Dennehy has become one of the most popular supporting players in Hollywood, appearing in COCOON, GORKY PARK, NEVER CRY WOLF, and SILVERADO. Here, he gets his first shot at playing the lead. In this occasionally funny domestic comedy, he portrays a pharmacist who leads his family on a lonely crusade against the system. His troubles begin when his new car turns out to be a lemon. The brakes repeatedly fail after allegedly having been fixed, and the resulting accidents lead to the cancellation of his insurance. He takes his wife (Archer) and two youngest children on a Hawaiian vacation that turns into an ordeal of cancelled flights, overbooked hotels, and deck chairs that have to be occupied all night in order to be used the next day. To top it all off, Dennehy ran up a huge gambling debt playing blackjack in Las Vegas and a goon named Rocco wants to collect it. Finally, Dennehy snaps. Determined to live outside the system, he pulls out every phone and unscrews every lightbulb in his house. He tears up the front lawn to plant a vegetable garden and digs a well in the back yard but ends up hitting a water main. He buys goats and chickens to raise, and he begins riding to work on a bicycle, or on a skateboard when the bike has a flat. While the kids enjoy their pioneer-like life style, it begins to wear on Archer, and the neighbors are up in arms. Finally, Dennehy concedes when the guy who sold him the car (which sits in the driveway with lemons taped to it) offers to lend him the money necessary to get him out of debt. Soon everything is back to normal.

The familiar plot is not especially well done, but Dennehy and Archer manage to save it somewhat, thanks to their sheer likability and what seems to be genuine affection between them. The film barely got a theatrical release before going to video. Includes the song "White Lies" (Darrel Brown, Adryan Russ, Syreeta Wright).

p, Robert Kaufman, Robert Krause; d, Joan Darling; w, Robert Kaufman; ph, Jan Kiesser; m, David Frank; art d, Linda Pearl; set d, Dena Roth; cos, Marilyn Pusich; m/l, Darrel Brown, Adryan Russ, Syreeta Wright; makeup, James Gillespie.

Comedy   **Cas.**   **(PR:C-O　MPAA:R)**

CHICHERIN†

(1986, USSR) 148m Mosfilm c

Leonid Filatov *(Georgi V. Chicherin)*, Rolan Bykov *(Gabriele D'Annunzio)*, Leonid Bronievoy, Oleg Golubitski, Ruben Simonov, Vera Venczel, Valeri Zolotukhin, Algimantas Masyulis, Natalia Saiko.

The career of Georgi V. Chicherin, a nobleman whose sympathies lay with the Bolsheviks—and who became the statesman who established the first links between Lenin's government and the rest of the world—is heralded in this lavish, officially sanctioned biography. Given a massive release in the Soviet Union, the film is likely to be of little interest to any but scholars of 20th-Century history and Soviet cinema. Veteran director Zarkhi—who codirected his first feature in 1930—lived through the events depicted. Actor Bykov is also a director of Soviet cinema.

d, Alexander Zarkhi; w, Alexander Zarkhi, Vladen Loginov; ph, Anatoli Moukassei; m, Irakly Gabeli; art d, David Vinitzki.

Biography   **(PR:A　MPAA:NR)**

CHICO REI†

(1986, Braz.) 112m Embrafilme c (Trans: King Chico)

Severo D'Acelino, Othon Bastos, Cosme dos Santos, Carlos Kroeber, Antonio Pitanga, Alexander Allerson, Rainer Rudolf, Mario Gusmao.

Set in the 18th Century, this picture explores the atrocities to which black slaves in Brazil were subjected. One of the slaves eventually earns his freedom after finding a mother lode of gold in his master's mine. He then goes on to become the country's first black mine owner and, later, a national folk hero.

d&w, Walter Lima, Jr.; ph, Jose Antonio Ventura, Mario Carneiro; ed, Walter Lima, Jr., Mario Carneiro.

Historical Drama   **(PR:O　MPAA:NR)**

CHIDAMBARAM**

(1986, India) 103m Suryakanthi Filmmakers c

Gopi *(Shankaran)*, Smita Patil *(Sivakami)*, Sreenivasan *(Muniyandi)*, Mohan Das *(Jacob)*, Nedumudi Venu.

India has the largest film production output of any country in the world, with more than 700 pictures made in 1986. Despite this fact, very few of these films will ever be seen by Western audiences, but if CHIDAMBARAM is representative of India's cinematic output, it is easy to understand why. Basically, the film is an overly melodramatic love story, similar in many respects to a Harlequin romance. Lacking in technical proficiency and a finer knowledge of filmmaking, it is brought to the screen in a boring manner that will have the average American yearning for the manipulative wonders of Steven Spielberg and George Lucas. The setting is an animal farm in Southern India, a very beautiful area that the film fails to use to advantage. Gopi plays the tolerant, intellectual supervisor who is obviously out of place in this pastoral land. Despite the beauty of the natural wonders that surround him, there just isn't enough to keep his mind occupied. The only other supervisor, Das, is little more than a brute, who rides around on his motorcycle all day in a display of power, terrorizing the workers. The laborers are mainly uneducated men who hold Gopi in too high an esteem to approach him as an equal. When one of the workers brings his beautiful young bride to the farm, Gopi's thoughts quite naturally turn to her, and he falls in love. The husband, Sreenivasan, has been highly respectful of Gopi, looking to him for advice and as a safeguard against the maliciousness of Das. When Gopi offers Sreenivasan a friendly toast in response to his marriage, the elated worker bows in gratitude before Gopi, thinking that this man must surely be the kindest and wisest person alive. Likewise, Gopi has developed a form of brotherly appreciation of Sreenivasan as the only worker who has appealed to him on a humanistic level. But this is not enough to discourage Gopi's lust for Sreenivasan's wife, Patil. After hours of turmoil pondering the subject, Gopi finds an opportunity to seduce the woman, who quite willingly becomes his lover. There is some justification here in that Patil is far too beautiful and divine a creature for Sreenivasan, a nice guy but basically an oaf. The cheated husband soon discovers the secret liaison, and unable to approach his superior, he beats his wife, leaving her gorgeous face permanently disfigured. He then hangs himself in the cowshed. The guilt-ridden Gopi goes into a state of shock, somnambulistically wandering the countryside in search of alcohol to drown his sorrows. The film ends with Gopi placing a few pennies in the outstretched hand of a veiled woman. On closer inspection, he recognizes the haggard and pitiful face of his once-cherished Patil.

Though not a very good movie overall, CHIDAMBARAM does have some

extraordinary moments, particularly a scene where Patil fondles a gigantic rose while a ballad in praise of Shiva plays over the soundtrack. But moments like this are far too few to captivate an audience. As the story monotonously unravels, long, listless shots of the supposedly pastoral landscape account for most of the screen time. Gopi has the face and gestural dignity of a very fine actor, but—forced to sit and ponder heavy existential questions with a camera focused on him—he hardly has the opportunity to use his skill. Buried beneath its inept exterior is a simple love story that explores the dichotomy between passion and place, touching upon the inequities of India's class system without preaching. But poor scripting and incapable direction have rendered its themes as little more than a trite soap opera. (In Malayalam; English subtitles.)

d&w, G. Aravindan; ph, Shaji; m, Devarajan.

Drama   **(PR:O　MPAA:A)**

CHILDREN OF A LESSER GOD****

(1986) 119m PAR c

William Hurt *(James Leeds)*, Marlee Matlin *(Sarah Norman)*, Piper Laurie *(Mrs. Norman)*, Philip Bosco *(Dr. Curtis Franklin)*, Allison Gompf *(Lydia)*, John F. Cleary *(Johnny)*, Philip Holmes *(Glen)*, Georgia Ann Cline *(Cheryl)*, William D. Byrd *(Danny)*, Frank Carter, Jr. *(Tony)*, John Limnidis *(William)*, Bob Hiltermann *(Orin)*, E. Katherine Kerr *(Mary Lee Ochs)*, John Basinger *(Alan Jones)*.

All the cliches have already been written about this poignant love story between a speech teacher, Hurt, and a deaf beauty, Matlin. We could regale you with lines like "Silence is Golden" and "Falling on Deaf Ears" and "Hearing is Believing." But none of those do this movie justice. The last important film about deafness had been shot 25 years before with THE MIRACLE WORKER, although love stories where one of the protagonists is somehow impaired have been going on forever. Pictures like the schmaltzy LOVE STORY or THE OTHER SIDE OF THE MOUNTAIN all pale when placed next to this decided improvement over the Medoff stage play that won the 1980 Tony, the same year Hurt was making his film debut in ALTERED STATES. The major problem with the play (which was yawnable) and the movie is that the audience is never left to its own devices. Because Matlin is severely hearing-impaired in real life (the result of a

childhood bout with roseola), Hurt translates everything she says for the benefit of motion picture viewers. Some of it would have been necessary, but Matlin's silent acting is so expressive, we know exactly what is going through her mind as the emotions flicker across her face. The translation routine (Hurt often says things like "You say you're angry? Okay, why?"—which could have been condensed into "Why are you so angry?") interrupts the flow of the story time and again and is infuriating. Further, many deaf people in the audience will be frustrated unless they see a subtitled version of the picture; Hurt's signing is just adequate and Matlin's is so rapid—especially in the scenes where her emotions are raging—that they go by too fast to be read, even by good sign language readers. The signing and the translation take far too long, and the picture could have lost 15 minutes of its running time had the filmmakers had some faith in their audience. All that aside, however, this is a crackling good drama with lots of leavening humor and magnificent performances by Oscar winner Hurt (KISS OF THE SPIDER WOMAN) and newcomer Matlin, whose only previous experience had been a few stage appearances which included the minor role she took in a Chicago revival of the play. It was that job that led to her audition and subsequent casting in the lead role, a part originated by deaf actress Phyllis Frelich, who won a Tony for her performance.

Hurt is a maverick speech teacher who arrives at a facility for the deaf known as the Governor Kittridge school supposedly on the coast of Maine (shooting actually took place in the small town of Rothesay in New Brunswick, Canada). Hurt is quickly established as an oddball when he admits that he used to work as a bartender and a disk jockey (not that either of those jobs is unique, just that Hurt is seen to be a man who has his own ideas about how to teach, and he would rather not teach if he has to knuckle under to rules he doesn't support). School administrator Bosco sets Hurt straight from the start. Just do what has to be done and don't try altering the system. Well, if that were the case, the movie would end right there! Naturally, Hurt has his own plans for his students, and immediately begins using heavy metal rock 'n' roll in order to get his deaf charges to *feel* music. He plays the music loudly so they have the sense of vibrations rather than the sound. Next, he forms a vocal group called "The No-Tones," and when these kids mime singing to rock music at a school show, it's a glorious

moment. Hurt meets Matlin, a graduate of the school who has chosen to stay and work in a menial job (cleaning up the garbage, etc.) rather than attempt to go out into the world that the school has supposedly taught her to face. Matlin is extremely bright, though quite bitter, and Hurt begins to gain her confidence after several misfires. He falls in love with her almost instantly, but she stays away at first and steadfastly refuses to lip-read or attempt to talk, both of which other students can do. She insists on signing (and, as noted, she does it so expertly and quickly that the spoken equivalent would be that of listening to a tobacco auctioneer). In an attempt to learn why Matlin will not venture out into the world, Hurt visits her mother, Laurie, who explains why she hasn't seen much of her daughter and how Matlin was abused sexually as a teenager. Laurie has apparently been unable to accept the fact that she has a deaf daughter, and Hurt does his best to get the truth through to the woman. It's a brief sequence but quite moving, and Laurie shows once again that she is one of the most underappreciated actresses in the business. Maintaining any love relationship is never easy, and when one of the lovers is deaf, problems are compounded. Several incidents take place in and around the school and in and around the Hurt/Matlin affair, none of which is particularly memorable. What *is* memorable is the electricity generated when Hurt and Matlin occupy center screen. That amperage spilled over into real life, and the two lived together later, despite the 15-year difference in their ages. Hurt—who was formerly married to actress Mary Beth Hurt and who has a young son by dancer Sandra Jennings—is this generation's Gene Hackman, in that he always convinces when he acts. Just as Hackman has the ability to become the role, so does Hurt, and had he not won the Oscar the year before, he might have won it for this performance. Illinois-born Matlin actually has 20 percent hearing in her left ear (with an aid), can read lips, and can also speak. Her acceptance of the Golden Globe Award for her role in the picture was done with her "signer" and will remain a highlight in that sometimes-tawdry awards evening. She did so well that she was used as a signer for the later Academy Awards ceremony, signing the names of the Best Sound nominees as an interpreter intoned them. This was an apparent apology to the non-hearing community from the Academy to make up for an incident in the 1977 ceremony, when a youthful group—who were *not* hearing-impaired—were revealed to have been employed to sign the lyrics to Debbie Boone's rendition of "You Light Up My Life"). Later Matlin signed "I Love You" when she won the Best Actress award. The picture was nominated in several other Oscar categories, including Best Picture, Best Actor (Hurt), Best Screenplay Adaptation (Anderson and Medoff), and Best Supporting Actress (Laurie). Evidently, Matlin is very much like her character in the film: she can be vulgar and is fiercely independent. The picture is rated R because of the rough language, both verbal and signed, and there is a bit of nudity. The title is drawn from the Tennyson poem, "Idylls of the King," which reads, in part, "For why is all around us here/As if some lesser god had made the world/But had not force to shape it as he would?" Debuting feature director Haines, who will also be recalled for her excellent TV movie "Something About Amelia", which dealt with the shattering topic of incest, was overlooked by the Academy when it came to directorial nominations, an undeserved slight, as her work was exemplary. It took several years for the film to be realized and, for a time, there was talk of Robert Redford playing the role with first Sydney Pollack, then Mark Rydell to direct. Fortunately, none of that came to pass. This is a wonderful romantic film that seldom looks like the play that spawned it. And that's a compliment. Matlin's auditory problems have classified her as "profoundly deaf." She is also profoundly gifted.

p, Burt Sugarman, Patrick Palmer; d, Randa Haines; w, Hesper Anderson, Mark Medoff (based on the stage play by Mark Medoff); ph, John Seale (Medallion Film Lab Color); m, Michael Convertino; ed, Lisa Fruchtman; prod d, Gene Callahan; art d, Barbara Matis; set d, Rose Marie McSherry; cos, Renee April.

Drama/Love Story   (PR:C-O MPAA:R)

CHOKE CANYON★★   (1986) 94m UFDC c

Stephen Collins *(David Lowell)*, Janet Julian *(Vanessa Pilgrim)*, Lance Henriksen *(Brook Alistair)*, Bo Svenson *(Captain)*, Victoria Racimo *(Rachel)*, Nicholas Pryor *(John Pilgrim)*, Robert Hoy *(Buck)*, Mark Baer *(Orrin)*, Michael Flynn *(Governor)*, Frank Kanig, Robert Conder *(Reporters)*, Jill Freeman *(Woman in Crowd)*, Emmet Larimer *(Uncle Charles)*, Gloria Fioramonti *(Passenger)*, Walter Robles *(Jim)*, Ted Petersen, Michael Gates, Marc De Nunzio *(Security Guards)*,

Kurt Woodruff *(Crane)*, Sherry Sailer *(Mrs. Pilgrim)*, Alan Gregory Greenwood *(Pilgrim's Secretary)*, John Fountain *(Man in Crowd)*, Mitchell Scott Thompson *(Technician)*, Denver Mattson *(Truck Driver)*.

A mildly entertaining action film which combines the dangers of nuclear energy with the scientific logic of a 1940s serial. Collins plays his Harvard-graduate

physicist role as if he's a devoted student at the Indiana Jones School of Charm in the Face of Death. Collins has set up a high-tech lab in a Utah canyon where he hopes to harness a "safe" energy that will replace nuclear power. This energy is to be drawn from high-frequency sound waves that will be at full potential when

Halley's Comet passes directly over the canyon, thereby increasing the gravitational pull on the sound waves. Although it all sounds like Buck Rogers-style mumbo-jumbo, Collins thinks it can work. Naturally there are bad guys who plan on throwing a wrench—or more correctly nuclear waste—into Collins' system. He has leased a section of the canyon from the Pilgrim Oil Company and they've decided that he must clear out in 24 hours. They offer a buy-back, but Collins is determined to remain for the next nine days, at which time Halley's Comet will have arrived. Pilgrim Oil sends out its top tough guy, Svenson, to change his mind. What follows is a series of scenes in which Collins, dressed in his cowboy duster and riding a horse, tries to outwit Svenson, an aerial expert who flies a World War I biplane. Eventually all of Collins' equipment is destroyed and, in retaliation, he has set a number of explosive charges through the canyon which detonate every five hours. His trump card is Julian, the pretty daughter of the president of Pilgrim Oil, whom he kidnaps and holds prisoner to force her father to comply with Collins' demands. Luckily for Collins, Julian is a nuclear activist who has been protesting Pilgrim Oil's policies. She not only helps Collins fight his battle, but she also falls in love with him. By the finish, Collins has rebuilt his equipment and Halley's Comet passes overhead. His experiment works, but for just a minute. His theories were correct, but his life work is not yet complete.

CHOKE CANYON is a pretty ridiculous film which still manages to be fun, mainly becomes it doesn't take itself too seriously. The dialog is filled with moderately witty one-liners, the relationship between Collins and Julian is cute, and the bad guys are notoriously bad. Collins, who is well-suited for this kind of role, is basically a comic-strip hero. He's a brilliant physicist who can not only ride a horse with grace, but can also fly a helicopter. Julian is a delicate debutante who—surprise!—also knows how to fly a helicopter. Their relationship is more reminiscent of old Hollywood films than it is of real life. One pleasant dialog exchange occurs just after Julian escapes from the pit where she was imprisoned. She balks, "How could you put me in a pit?" "It wasn't that bad," he answers. "How would you like it?" "I like pits," he answers with charming smugness. Svenson also fits the bill, overplaying his heavy with just the right amount of evil. All he's missing is a handlebar mustache to curl. The film's best moments are the aerial-chase scenes between Collins' helicopter and Svenson's biplane. Director and former stunt coordinator Bail (who, in the mid-1970s directed CLEOPATRA JONES AND THE CASINO OF GOLD, which only *sounds* like a precursor to INDIANA JONES AND THE TEMPLE OF DOOM) proves that directing stunts and action scenes are his forte. One of the best moments comes as Collins' helicopter (which is towing a "black ball" full of nuclear waste) begins to overheat. Rather than stop completely, he sets down on the back of an empty car transporter which is traveling down the highway. Svenson's biplane follows suit and rests on the top of a bus which is behind the transporter. The result is a rather unique "chase" scene reminiscent of the oddball quality of Bail's previous film THE GUMBALL RALLY (1976). CHOKE CANYON is not an example of great, or even good, filmmaking, but then again the same criticism can be leveled at those Saturday morning serials. CHOKE CANYON's only worth is, quite simply, that it is fun.

p, Ovidio G. Assonitis; d, Chuck Bail; w, Sheila Goldberg, Ovidio G. Assonitis, Alfonso Brescia, Steve Luotto, Victor Beard; ph, Dante Spinotti; m, Sylvester Levay; ed, Robert Silvi; prod d, Frank Vanorio; cos, Michele Gisotti; stunts, Phil Adams.

Action/Adventure   **Cas.**   **(PR:A MPAA:PG)**

CHOPPER†   (1986, India) 105m Zoom Enterprises c

Joy Bannerjee *(Rajat Ray)*, Sreela Mazumder *(Reena)*, Pradip Mukherjee *(Shubhra Ray)*, Karunakanta Bhattacharya *(Father)*, Sova Sen *(Mother)*, Niranjan Roy, Goutam Chakraborty, Santana Basu, Mrinal Basu, Chowdhury, Bidyut Chatterjee, Ajoy Bhattacharya, Bidyut Nag.

A dark look at family life in modern Calcutta which examines the struggles of one family. When Mukherjee, the family's eldest brother and chief financial supporter, is killed in a trade-union dispute, his younger brother, Bannerjee, steps into the role. His family, however, takes offense at his strict ways and grows to dislike him. He rules the family with an iron fist, especially when his young sister turns towards prostitution. Eventually the family sees that his highly moral way is the only reasonable one.

d&w, Nabyendu Chatterjee (based on a story by Ajoy Bhattacharya); ph, Pantu Nag; m, Nikhil Chattopadhyay; ed, Bulu Ghosh; art d, Prasad Mitra.

Drama   **(PR:NR MPAA:NR)**

CHOPPING MALL**   (1986) 76m Concorde–Trinity/Concorde c (AKA: KILLBOTS; R.O.B.O.T.)

Kelli Maroney *(Allison Parks)*, Tony O'Dell *(Ferdy Meisel)*, John Terlesky *(Mike Brennan)*, Russell Todd *(Rick Stanton)*, Karrie Emerson *(Linda Stanton)*, Barbara Crampton *(Suzie Lynn)*, Nick Segal *(Greg Williams)*, Suzee Slater *(Leslee Todd)*, Mary Woronov *(Mary Bland)*, Paul Bartel *(Paul Bland)*, Dick Miller *(Walter Paisley)*, Gerrit Graham *(Technician Nessler)*, Mel Welles *(Cook)*, Angela Aames *(Miss Vanders)*, Paul Coufos *(Dr. Simon)*, Arthur Roberts *(Mr. Todd)*, Ace Mask, Will Gill, Jr. *(Janitors)*, Lenny Juliano *(Burglar)*, Lawrence Guy *(Dr. Carrington)*, Morgan Douglas *(Technician Marty)*, Toni Naples *(Bathing Beauty)*, Robert Greenberg *(Big Eater)*, Maurie Gallagher *(Girl in Restaurant)*.

The Park Plaza Mall has just installed the latest in security systems, three robots that cruise the corridors at night, armed with a variety of ways of subduing malefactors, including electric stun darts, lasers (technically just for cutting away debris, but we know better), and nasty-looking steel pincers. Needless to say, something goes wrong when lightning strikes the control center on the roof, and the robots kill their supervising technicians, then go out to patrol the mall. Meanwhile, four young couples are having a party in the furniture store where three of the boys work. One girl (Slater) asks her boy friend (Terlesky) to go out in the mall to get her a pack of cigarettes from a machine. A robot cruises up and snips Terlesky's jugular vein, and when Slater goes out to look for him, she is chased until she is right in front of the furniture store, where a laser burst splatters her head all over the glass while the other six watch horrified. The mechanical monsters crash into the store after the others, who flee to a storeroom.
   The girls are put into an air shaft to head for the safety of the parking levels, while the boys make their way to a sporting goods store and arm themselves to the teeth (the obligatory arming-up scene). In the air shaft, Crampton has a fit of claustrophobia and exits into an auto parts store (when was the last time you saw a mall with an auto parts store?). The girls arm themselves with firebombs and find the boys, but Crampton is injured by a laser bolt, then set afire when another bolt hits the can of gasoline near her. Her boy friend, Segal, is the next to go, tossed off a balcony by one of the robots. Next dead is Emerson, struck with a laser blast, followed quickly by husband Todd in a fit of stupidity. A fire extinguisher thrown at his stomach puts O'Dell out of action and now only Maroney is left. She leads the one remaining robot (the other two have been destroyed by various means) into a paint store, then tosses in a road flare that blows up the whole place. She turns around and sees that her boy friend, O'Dell, is not dead, so there is something of a happy ending.
   There is nothing original or especially interesting about this film, and the victims die off in totally predictable order, according to their likableness and

sexual habits, the most obnoxious couple first, then the almost-as-obnoxious couple, then the married couple, leaving only the two who don't have sex to survive. Crampton gives the best performance here, maintaining her reputation as the best screamer in the business (a crown once held by Fay Wray) she previously established in RE-ANIMATOR. The best things about the film, though, are the robots themselves, which take on an almost comical personality as they kill off promiscuous teens, stopping over each body to give a cheery "Have a nice day" to the corpse. In-jokes abound throughout the film, ranging from appearances by Paul Bartel and Mary Woronov, repeating their EATING RAOUL parts, Dick Miller in his Walter Paisley role from BUCKET OF BLOOD (now reduced to a janitor), and Mel Welles of LITTLE SHOP OF HORRORS as a none-too-sanitary pizza cook, to a visit by the boys to Peckinpah's Sporting Goods store from which they emerge looking like something out of THE WILD BUNCH. The potential was there for the film to be more than it turned out to be, and at times the film comes close to capturing something of the capitalism-gone-amok theme of the similarly located DAWN OF THE DEAD, but it drops these overtones for another wages-of-sin dead-teenager movie almost indisinguishable from a FRIDAY THE 13TH sequel. The robots are pretty neat, though.

p, Julie Corman; d, Jim Wynorski; w, Jim Wynorski, Steve Mitchell; ph, Tom Richmond (DeLuxe Color); m, Chuck Cirino; ed, Leslie Rosenthal; art d, Carol Clements; set d, Corey Kaplan; spec eff, Roger George, Anthony Showe; makeup, Blake Shepard; stunts, Paul Shaver.

Horror   **Cas.**   **(PR:O MPAA:R)**

CHRZESNISAK†   (1986, Pol.) 96m Zespoly Filmowe–Iluziion/Film Polski c (Trans: The Godson)

Maciej Goraj *(Gregori Purowski)*, Franciszek Pieczka *(Strzykalski)*, Leon Nieczyk *(Wacek, the Minister)*, Gustaw Lutkiewicz *(Blicharski)*, Jerzy Michotek *(Chaladaj)*, Emilia Krakowska *(Gregori's Lover)*.

The ramifications of events in Poland today are brought to the screen in this story of a state farm director, Goraj, whose personal and political lives are equally problematic. His wife has run away to Canada, his son wants to follow, and he has gotten himself into trouble with the state by refusing some Austrian businessmen who are interested in the farm he manages. Goraj pleads with his godfather, a government official, to come to his defense, but finds that having a relative in high places is not sufficient.

d, Henryk Bielski; w, Jerzy Janicki; ph, Boguslaw Lambach; m, Waldemar Kazanecki; ed, Ewa Smal; set d, Jerzy Karol Zielinski, Edward Papierski.

Drama   **(PR:A-C MPAA:NR)**

CHRISTOPHORUS†   (1986, Yugo.) 100m Jugoslavija c

Milena Zupancic, Radko Polic, Boris Juh.

This parable reworks the biblical story of St. Christopher for modern times, setting the action in postwar Yugoslavia. The story follows two men, one the murderer of the other's father, as they are forced to confront each other in their small rural village.

d, Andrej Miakar; w, Zeljko Kozinc; ph, Rado Likon.

Drama   **(PR:O MPAA:NR)**

CHTO U SENJKI BYLO†   (1986, USSR) 79m Filmstudio Odessa/Goskino c (Trans: The Unjust Stork)

Alyshoa Vesselov *(Senka)*, Yulia Kosmacheva *(Matruska)*, Vladimir Nossik, Yekaterina Vassilyeva, Nadeshda Butyrzewa.

A children's tale about a preschool-age lad, Vesselov, who is curious about the birth of a new sister. He's heard stories about "where babies come from," but isn't satisfied with any of the explanations. When his baby sister finally arrives, he decides that a local bride-to-be should have her instead. Believing that babies are picked from a nearby cabbage patch, he and his companion Kosmacheva leave his bundled newborn sister out in the field, sending everyone into a panic. All works out by the end, however, as the little one is found and returned. Recipient of a UNICEF Children's Film Festival special mention at the 1986 Berlin Film Festival.

d, Radomir Vassilevsky; w, Radi Pogodin; ph, Vadim Yefrimov.

Children's Adventure   **(PR:AAA MPAA:NR)**

CHUZHAJA, BELAJA I RJABOJ†   (1986, USSR) 98m Kazach bw-c (Trans: The White Dove)

Slava Iliutschenko, Sergei Garmache, Soultan Banov, Vladimi Steklov, Ludmila Savelieva.

A humanistic parable set in Kazakhstan in 1946, which revolves around a young war veteran's return to his small village. He encounters a morose, defeatist atmosphere in which some of the villagers engage in the trading and sale of pigeons. The young man catches a prized white dove, but it is quickly stolen by a gang of delinquents. The film, which employs a great deal of impressive camera technique, is strangely framed at its opening and close by newsreel footage of a manned space flight.

d&w, Sergei Soloviev; ph, Youri Klimenko; m, Isaak Schvartz; art d, Marxen Gaukman-Sverdlov.

Drama   **(PR:A MPAA:NR)**

CINEMA FALADO† (1986, Braz.) 110m Caetano Veloso–Guilherme Araujo/Embrafilme c (Trans: Talking Pictures)

Caetano Veloso, Regina Case, Antonio Cicero, Paula Lavigne, Elza Soares, Chico Diaz, Hamilton Vaz Pereira, Rogerio Duarte, Felipe Murray, Dede Veloso, Dadi, Dorival Caymmi, Mauricio Mattar, Julio Bressane, Dona Cano Veloso.

A non-narrative film essay from popular singer/composer Veloso in which he expounds on a variety of subjects from Fidel Castro to the state of Brazilian cinema to his own impressions of Wim Wenders' 1984 film PARIS, TEXAS. There are also readings from Thomas Mann's "Death in Venice," Guimaraes Rosa's "Grande Sertao Veredas," and as the writings of Jean-Paul Sartre and Martin Heidegger.

p, Caetano Veloso, Guilherme Araujo; d&w, Caetano Veloso; ph, Pedro Farkas (Eastmancolor); ed, Mair Tavares; md, Caetano Veloso.

Film Essay (PR:A MPAA:NR)

CIPLAK VATANDAS† (1986, Turkey) Uzman (Trans: The Naked Citizen)

Sener Sen, Nilgun Akcaoglu, Kamuran Usluer, Pekcan Kosar, Candan Sabuncu, Zihni Mucumen.

d&w, Basar Sabuncu; ph, Ertunc Senkay.

CITY OF MICE† (1986, Iran) c

[No cast available.]

p, Abbas Ahmadi Morlagh; d, M. Boroomand, A. Talebi; w, Ahmad Behbahani; ph, Mohammad Zarfam; m, M. Aligholi; ed, Hassan Hassandost.

CLAN OF THE CAVE BEAR, THE*½ (1986) 98m Jozak/Decade–Jonesfilm–Producers Sales Organization–Guber-Peters/WB c

Daryl Hannah *(Ayla)*, Pamela Reed *(Iza)*, James Remar *(Creb)*, Thomas G. Waites *(Broud)*, John Doolittle *(Brun)*, Curtis Armstrong *(Goov)*, Martin Doyle *(Grod)*, Adel C. Hammoud *(Vorn)*, Tony Montanaro *(Zoug)*, Mike Muscat *(Dorv)*, John Wardlow *(Droog)*, Keith Wardlow *(Crug)*, Karen Austin *(Aba)*, Barbara Duncan *(Uka)*, Gloria Lee *(Oga)*, Janne Mortil *(Ovra)*, Lycia Naff *(Uba)*, Linda Quibell *(Aga)*, Bernadette Sabath *(Ebra)*, Penny Smith *(Ika)*, Joey Cramer *(Young Broud)*, Rory L. Crowley *(Durc)*, Nicole Eggert *(Middle Ayla)*, Emma Floria *(Young Ayla)*, Pierre Lamielle *(Brac)*, Mary Reid *(Ayla's Mother)*, Samantha Ostry *(Young Uba)*, Shane Punt *(Young Vorn)*, Christiane Boyce, Catherine Flather *(Baby Durc)*, Guila Chiesa, Shauna Fanara, Amy Cyr *(Young Girls)*, Colin Doyle *(Young Boy)*, Natino Bellantoni *(Gorn)*, Rick Valiquette *(Voord)*, Alan Waltman *(Norg)*, Paul Carafotes *(Brug)*.

Jean M. Auel's well-received novel *The Clan of the Cave Bear* (as well as its two sequels *The Valley of Horses* and *The Mammoth Hunters*) was considered by both readers and experts alike to be an exciting and accurate account of prehistoric man. The cinematic adaptation of the novel, however, is so laughably

awful that Auel later sued the producers for creating such an inaccurate work. The film opens as a blonde-haired Cro-Magnon child (Floria) is separated from her mother during a sudden earthquake. Forced to wander in the wilderness, Floria gets trapped in a small crevice by a lion, who takes a nasty swipe at the poor girl's thigh. After escaping from the beast (never mind how, it's never explained), Floria is found by a passing tribe of Neanderthals. With their hairy bodies and protruding foreheads, the group finds this blonde child something of a wonder. Reed, the clan's medicine woman, adopts the girl as her own despite objections by her peers. Remar, a one-eyed, bum-legged "Mog-ur" (a sort of Neanderthal wise man) also looks after the girl, who proves to be a few steps higher in the evolutionary chain. Eggert briefly plays the girl as a teenager, then Daryl Hannah takes over the adult incarnation. Hannah's presence causes a good deal of unrest since she's smarter, stronger, and prettier than anyone else in the tribe. Waites, a rather egotistical Neanderthal, decides not to put up with Hannah's apparent superiority and shows her who's boss by having his way with her. By now Hannah has mastered weaponry better than any man in the tribe. When a child is threatened by wolves, Hannah whips out the old slingshot and saves the kid. The Neanderthals don't exactly cotton to a woman using weapons,

even if it was to rescue a youngster, and Hannah is temporarily kicked out into the wilderness. Hannah manages to survive and even has a baby (the result of Waites' rape) while out in the cold, wintry forest. After returning home, Hannah ventures with the rest of her clan to a gathering of various tribes. There new mates are to be chosen, new tribal leaders picked, and new Mog-urs selected. One Neanderthal finds this blonde-haired, blue-eyed cave *shiksa* extremely attractive, but he ends up with his head bitten off by a bear before the romance can begin. Later, Hannah and Remar share a vision in which the girl symbolically learns that her future lies outside her Neanderthal family. Upon returning home Waites takes over as the clan's new leader, and promptly orders Remar to leave. Hannah will hear nothing of this and takes on the bully in a fight. She wins, but following the course of her vision, Hannah leaves the tribe, heading toward the unknown as she walks into the sunset.

Auel had every right to be angry with this often silly adaptation of her thoughtful work. Hannah isn't an intelligent Cro-Magnon: she's a cave girl for the eighties. Her body is lean, her teeth perfectly straight, and her hair always looks freshly shampooed. Hannah apparently knows the address of a good prehistoric leg-waxer to boot. She plays the part as a feisty, self-reliant woman who does

everything except grunt "Go for it!" John Sayles did the script adaptation, and this alone could do in his reputation as a major creative force of independent cinema. The "dialog" consists of grunts and hand gestures, which look authentic, but their intent is sabotaged by accompanying subtitles. "The Mog-urs say you are of the Others. You will anger the spirits," is a typical example of the well-spoken translations. Even the Flintstones weren't that articulate, and they had the wheel. A voice-over narration is equally inflated, read in a hopelessly solemn tone that becomes increasingly pretentious as the film drags on. Director Chapman has no handle on the material, presenting the story in a predictable manner and with so little humanity that at times, it all resembles a glass-enclosed museum exhibit. As a result, THE CLAN OF THE CAVE BEAR is largely dull, but when the group arrives at the cave-man gathering, the film gets downright silly. It's never established how the various tribes contact one another, and the scene plays more like a prehistoric convention then a setting for tribal rites. All that's missing is a big sign saying "Welcome Neanderthals!" In what is supposed to be a frightening sequence pitting men against a bear, a fake, hairy double can be clearly observed in some shots. The film's one minor plus is the often beautiful photography of the scenic Canadian woodlands used for location. Warner Bros. knew the film was going to be a problem and delayed its release for as long as possible. It had a deservedly quick box-office death, and probably knocked off any chance for a VALLEY OF HORSES or MAMMOTH HUNTERS movie. Universal originally considered adapting Auel's book as a television miniseries, a format that would have better suited the material. Reportedly Chapman shot over four hours of footage, then pared it down to a scant 98 minutes. Similar subject matter fared a lot better just a few years earlier in the 1982 film QUEST FOR FIRE.

p, Gerald I. Isenberg; d, Michael Chapman; w, John Sayles (based on the novel *The Clan Of The Cave Bear* by Jean M. Auel); ph, Jan De Bont (Technovision, Technicolor); m, Alan Silvestri; ed, Wendy Greene Bricmont; prod d, Anthony Masters; art d, Guy Comtois, Richard Wilcox; set d, Kimberley Richardson; cos, Kelly Kimball; spec eff, Gene Grigg, Michael Clifford; makeup, Michael G. Westmore, Michele Burke; stunts, John Wardlow.

Drama Cas. (PR:O MPAA:NR)

CLASS OF NUKE 'EM HIGH* (1986) 92m TNT–Troma/Troma c

Janelle Brady *(Chrissy)*, Gilbert Brenton *(Warren)*, Robert Prichard *(Spike)*, R.L. Ryan *(Mr. Paley)*, James Nugent Vernon *(Eddie)*, Brad Dunker *(Gonzo)*, Gary Schneider *(Pete)*, Theo Cohan *(Muffey)*, Gary Rosenblatt *(Greg)*, Mary Taylor *(Judy)*, Rick Howard *(Spud)*, Heather McMahan *(Taru)*, Chris McNamee *(Joe)*, Anthony Ventola *(George)*, Arthur Lorenz *(Dewy)*, Donald O'Toole *(Mr. Westly)*, Seth Oliver Hawkins *(Lumpy)*, Larae Dean *(Cathy)*, Reuben Guss *(Mr. Hyde)*, Diana DeVries *(Miss Stein)*, Lauraine Austin *(Ms. Austin)*, Dianna-Jean Flaherty *(Denise)*, Sloane Herz, Lily Hayes Kaufman *(Tromaville Kiddies)*, Don Costello *(Nuclear Worker)*, Frank Cole *(Mr. Flint)*, Sam Scardino *(Mr. Hanson)*, Barbara Ann Missbach *(Barbi)*, Andy Newton *(Beetovan)*, Skip Hamra *(Nuclear Worker in Basement)*, Donnie Reynolds *(Tom)*, Joe Severino *(Jimmy)*, Jeffrey Grossi *(Bill)*, Maezie Murphy *(Mrs. Crabtree)*, Rick Collins *(Ron Simms)*, Bob Schenck *(Harry)*, Belle Maria Wheat *(Mrs. Murphy)*, Libby Miller *(Mugged*

Woman), Ron Giles *(Dr. Herz)*, Donna Nardo *(Girl On Party Steps)*, Ann Mc-Cabe *(Westly's Secretary)*, Kitty Alson *(Gym Teacher)*, Thomas Feeney *(Orderly)*, Richard W. Haines *(Dr. Howard)*, Leonard Tepper *(Bald Teacher)*, Nicky Baker, Seth Kadish, Louise Edwards, Ava Kelly, Elizabeth [Locky] Lambert, Gerald Willaidom, Gersa Arias, Glaurys Arias *(Bake Sale People)*, Brian Quinn *(Monster)*, Erika Zatt, Michael Popowitz *(Group at Party)*, Jon Kurtis *(Muscle Man)*, Virginia Kurtis *(Muscle Man's Chick)*.

When last we visited Tromaville, site of 1985's THE TOXIC AVENGER, the town was rocked by strange happenings after a harassed young man fell into a vat of hazardous chemical waste and became a super-strong monster. Now Tromaville, "The Toxic Waste Capital of the World" as it likes to call itself,

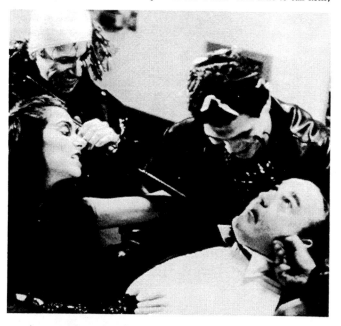

experiences another series of catastrophes after a leak at the nearby nuclear power plant infects the water supply.

A student drinks from a water fountain, starts spewing green gunk, and later in class begins foaming at the mouth and ears, attacking another student before diving out a window and dissolving into a steaming pile of noxious jello. The porcine manager of the power plant denies that this incident has anything to do with his utility, and tells the press that the fact that the young man had *two* microwave ovens was probably to blame. Meanwhile, the halls of Tromaville High are being terrorized by the Cretins, a vicious gang all done up in Heavy Metal leather and lingerie drag, all of them former members of the honor society who underwent a mysterious and simultaneous overnight transformation. They force students to buy marijuana that they harvest from the grounds of the power plant. A joint of this contaminated reefer finds its way into the hands of "good" kids Brady and Brenton, who are peer-pressured into smoking it. Brady is turned into a lust-crazed wanton and attacks Brenton, who is none too unwilling himself. Later both have terrible nightmares and physical reactions. Brenton occasionally glows green as his head bulges, and he attacks some of the Cretins, though he can't remember doing so. Brady is overcome with a wave of nausea during cheerleader practice and in the bathroom throws up a nasty little creature that swims around in the toilet before another girl flushes it down. It makes its way through the pipes to the basement fallout shelter, where it falls into a nurturing barrel of toxic waste. Meanwhile the Cretins are expelled when Brenton comes to the rescue of a student they're shaking down, so they decide to avenge themselves on him and the school. First they force Brady down into the fallout shelter and tie her up, then they pull the nuclear evacuation alarm to empty the school. Brenton is lured back in to rescue Brady, but when the confrontation comes in the basement, the monster, now man-size, attacks, and the two escape. The Cretins are roaming the halls, smashing and spray painting, and the two lovers narrowly escape them time and again, with a little help from the monster. Eventually they make it out of the school, which blows up behind them.

Hardly an example of cinematic art, CLASS OF NUKE 'EM HIGH does have a kind of loopy charm and ingenuousness that keeps its aggressive stupidity from being too offensive. The violence is explicit to the point of silliness (one memorable moment of gore coming when the monster punches his fist right through a girl's head, then wags his fingers to show us they came out the back of her head). There are a number of good lines, including the nuclear plant manager solemnly telling reporters, "This plant will be here long after most of you are gone." The technical credits and production values are up to Troma's usual low standards, and the acting is laughably wooden, but it's all harmless enough, and guaranteed to make money for Troma. Songs include: "Rock 'n' Paradise" (Stormbringer, performed by Stormbringer), "Run for Your Life" (Stratus, performed by Stratus), "Emotional Refugee" (David Behennah, performed by Behennah), "Angel" (GMT, performed by GMT), "Nuke 'em High" (Ethan, Paul Nowak, performed by Ethan and the Coup), "You're the One," "Take Me Away," "Now Society," "Whisper" (Michael Lattanzi, performed by Lattanzi), "Much Too Much" (The Smithereens, performed by The Smithereens), "B.J.'s Mes-

sage" (Bernard Jones, performed by Jones), "Nightmare Music" (Biohazard, performed by Biohazard).

p, Lloyd Kaufman, Michael Herz; d, Richard W. Haines, Samuel Weil [Lloyd Kaufman]; w, Richard W. Haines, Mark Rudnitsky, Lloyd Kaufman, Stuart Strutin (based on a story by Richard W. Haines); ph, Michael Mayers (TVC color); m, Michael Lattanzi, Biohazard; ed, Richard W. Haines; art d, Art Skopinsky, Arthur Lorenz; cos, Ivy Rosovsky; spec eff, Kay Gelfman; m/l, Stormbringer, Stratus, David Behennah, GMT, Ethan Nowak, Paul Nowak, Michael Lattanzi, The Smithereens, Biohazard, Bernard Jones [The Messenger]; makeup, Scott Coulter, Brian Quinn; stunts, Jeff Gibson.

Horror   **Cas.**   **(PR:O MPAA:R)**

CLASS RELATIONS**½   (1986, Ger.) New Yorker Films bw

Christian Heinisch *(Karl Rossmann)*, Mario Adorf *(Uncle)*, Reinald Schnell *(Heizer)*, Harun Farocki *(Delamarche)*, Manfred Blank *(Robinson)*.

Applying their keen visual sense and excessively cerebral style to Franz Kafka's classic unfinished novel *Amerika*, structuralists Straub and Huillet have created a frighteningly cold and distancing film that is as emotionally taxing as it is intellectually rewarding. Kafka wrote the posthumously published novel about America without ever having been there, relying upon his insight to draw a portrait of an individual traveling to a land of symbolic freedom only to discover illusory dreams in a place of strange people, manners, and landscapes.

Heinisch plays a member of the German middle class forced to flee his country after a damaging scandal. He travels to America hoping to appeal to his wealthy uncle for assistance. But Heinisch is unable to shake his Old World ways—where his class did not perform menial labor—and adapt to the working-class ethic of America. Wandering from one place to another, from position to position, sterile hotel room to sterile hotel room, the German fails to find the riches—or to find anything for that matter—that he believed would be waiting at his feet. Heinisch's problem is his inability to change, to adapt his attitudes to his place in society, rather than the other way around. The picture ends with several uninterrupted minutes of a river filmed from a moving train.

Filming in high-contrast black-and-white, Straub and Huillet make America a land of claustrophobic buildings, mechanized people, and unrealized dreams. They use extraneously long takes to study this environment, making it even more distancing, while their characters speak an unemotional rhetoric vaguely imitating human speech. (In German; English subtitles.)

d&w, Jean-Marie Straub, Danielle Huillet (based on the unfinished novel *Amerika* by Franz Kafka); ph, William Lubtchansky.

Drama   **(PR:A-C MPAA:NR)**

CLOCKWISE***   (1986, Brit.) 96m Moment/Universal-Cannon c

John Cleese *(Brian Stimpson)*, Alison Steadman *(Gwenda Stimpson)*, Penelope Wilton *(Pat Garden)*, Stephen Moore *(Mr. Jolly)*, Joan Hickson *(Mrs. Trellis)*, Sharon Maiden *(Laura)*, Penny Leatherbarrow *(Woman Teacher)*, Howard Lloyd Lewis *(Ted)*, Jonathan Bowater *(Clint)*, Mark Bunting *(Studious Boy)*, Robert Wilkinson *(Streaker)*, John Bardon *(Ticket Collector)*, Mark Burdis *(Glen Scully)*, Nadia Carina *(Mandy Kostakis)*, Dickie Arnold *(Man at Station)*, Angus Mackay *(Man on Train)*, Peter Needham *(Porter)*, Peter Lorenzelli *(Taxi Driver)*, Chip Sweeney *(Paul Stimpson)*, Constance Chapman *(Mrs. Wheel)*, Ann Way *(Mrs. Way)*, Ann-Marie Gwatkin *(Petrol Station Cashier)*, Mohammed Ashiq *(Manager of Petrol Station)*, Pat Keen *(Mrs. Wisely)*, Geoffrey Hutchings *(Mr. Wisely)*, Geoffrey Greenhill *(Policeman with Mrs. Wheel)*, Richard Ridings, Geoffrey Davion *(Policeman at Crash)*, Charles Bartholomew *(Man in Telephone Box)*, Sheila Keith *(Mrs. Garden)*, Christian Regan *(Pat's Son)*, Alan Parnaby *(Policeman at Telephone Box)*, Tony Haygarth *(Ivan with the Tractor)*, Michael Aldridge *(Prior)*, Ronald Sowton, Alan Granton *(Monks)*, Susan Field *(Woman at Low Church Appearance)*, Leslie Scofied *(Policeman Arresting Pat)*, Mike Glynn *(Policeman with Black Eye)*, Benjamin Whitrow, Geoffrey Palmer, Nicholas LePrevost *(Headmasters)*, Peter Cellier, David Conville, Patrick Godfrey, Rupert Massey, John Rowe, Philip Voss, Jeffry Wickham.

Punctuality is next to spirituality for John Cleese in this clever comedy written by Michael Frayn, whose play "Noises Off" has played London for four years running.

Cleese is the headmaster of a non-fee-paying comprehensive school (public high school principal in American) who has been elected chairman of the Conference of Headmasters. This august body, which includes administrative headmasters of schools such as Eton and Harrow, has never before "in all of history" elected a master of a state-subsidized school as their head. Cleese wins this accolade by running the tightest school in the land, and he lords over the courtyard with a pair of binoculars and a loudspeaker from his office window, summoning malefactors to his office at 9:20 precisely. After his morning duties on the day he is to attend the conference, his wife (Steadman) picks him up and drives him to the station to catch the 10:25 to Norwich. At the station, though, he is so preoccupied with yelling at a hooky-playing student that he confuses the stationmaster's instructions and boards the Plymouth train, then watches in horror as the Norwich train leaves without him. When he runs off the Plymouth train, leaving his speech on the seat, it too pulls out. He then tries to catch his wife in the parking lot, but she is off to the hospital to take some old ladies for a drive in the country. While racing down the street he runs into (is run into, more correctly) a female student, Maiden, and he persuades her to drive him to the conference. One delay builds on another as he is plagued by faulty pay phones, discovers a girl friend from 20 years ago (Wilton) whom he quickly reduces to tears, and finally gets the car stuck in the middle of a farmer's field. Looking for a tractor to pull the car out, Cleese stumbles into a monastery where he finally resigns himself to the likelihood of missing the conference. But he doesn't give

up. Wearing a monk's cassock, Cleese—with Maiden—tries to catch up with the car, in which the flustered Wilton drives off. While Cleese lies in a roadside ditch musing to himself "It's not the despair. I can stand the despair. It's the *hope!*," Maiden flags down a Porsche. The driver is easily tricked out of his suit and his

car keys and Cleese and Maiden take off at high speed for Norwich, arriving at exactly 5:00, just in time for his speech. Waiting for Cleese, though, are at least a half-dozen policemen, Maiden's parents, Steadman, the three old ladies she was driving (including the delightful Hickson), and Moore, one of Cleese's teachers who has been having an affair with Maiden. While Cleese tries to give his vaguely recalled speech, they wander in one by one, only to be chastised and ordered to find a seat in best headmaster fashion. In the end he orders the gathered headmasters to sing a hymn as he marches out to face his accusers.

Cleese has built his career on "Monty Python's Flying Circus" and "Fawlty Towers" portraying just such characters as he plays here, men gone 'round the bend of hysteria whose fragile world is falling apart in front of their eyes. In this film, however, he seems comparatively laid-back, and the expected explosion never comes. This seems mostly the fault of Morahan's direction, which fails to build up any momentum as misery heaps on misery. The film is Cleese's all the way, and had anyone else essayed the role, the result probably would have been a total bore. Though the explosion of frustrated fury doesn't come, Cleese manages to show it seething just below the surface, ready to erupt at any moment.

Although blessed with generally good reviews, CLOCKWISE did only disappointing business in the U.S. and didn't even receive national release.

p, Michael Codron; d, Christopher Morahan; w, Michael Frayn; ph, John Coquillon (Technicolor); m, George Fenton; ed, Peter Boyle; prod d, Roger Murray-Leach; art d, Diana Charnley; cos, Judy Moorcroft; makeup, Kezia De Winne, Michael Morris.

Comedy Cas. (PR:A MPAA:PG)

CLOSE TO HOME† (1986, Can.) 95m Hy Perspectives–Telefilm Canada c

Daniel Allman *(Flynn)*, Jillian Fargey *(Michelle Fontaine)*, Anne Petrie *(Donna Pedlar)*.

In the setting of a TV documentary being filmed on the same subject, CLOSE TO HOME is a look at juvenile prostitution in Vancouver and the abused runaways who work the streets. The film focuses on Fargey, a girl who drifts in and out of prostitution, and Allman, a hardened professional boy who is stabbed by one of his tricks. This subject has been handled much more compellingly as a documentary (STREETWISE). A first feature film from director Beairsto.

p, Harvey Crossland; d, Ric Beairsto; w, Ric Beairsto, Harvey Crossland; ph, Tobias Schliessler; m, Ken Hemmerick, Richard Baker; ed, Harvey Crossland; art d, Anne O'Donoghue.

Drama (PR:O MPAA:NR)

CLOSED CIRCUIT† (1986, Iran) 95m Taavon c

Habib Esmaeili, Jafar Valley, Manijeh Mohammadi, Nemat Gorji, Fariba Shams, Mahmood Bahrami.

After making the last payment on his house, an aging Iranian reflects on his past.

d&w, Rahman Rezaie; ph, Ali Reza Zarin Dast; m, Mohammad Reza Aligholi.

Drama (PR:A MPAA:NR)

CLUB PARADISE** (1986) 104m WB c

Robin Williams *(Jack Moniker)*, Peter O'Toole *(Gov. Anthony Croyden Hayes)*, Rick Moranis *(Barry Nye)*, Jimmy Cliff *(Ernest Reed)*, Twiggy [Leslie Hornby] *(Phillipa Lloyd)*, Adolph Caesar *(Prime Minister Solomon Gundy)*, Eugene Levy *(Barry Steinberg)*, Joanna Cassidy *(Terry Hamlin)*, Brian Doyle-Murray *(Voit Zerbe)*, Steven Kampmann *(Randy White)*, Joe Flaherty *(Pilot)*, Mary Gross *(Jackie)*, Robin Duke, Bill Curry.

We can just hear the conversation at the studio chief's office. "This is the greatest idea you've ever heard, boss. Robin Williams is a Chicago fireman who gets burnt out after one too many greater alarm fires, has an accident, collects big from the Windy City insurance company, takes his money, and moves to a Caribbean Island called St. Nicholas." "So what's so great about that?" says the

boss. "Well . . . now that he's on this British island, he falls in love with Twiggy, she gained a little weight but she still looks good, and the governor of the island is Peter O'Toole. Williams next gets involved with Jimmy Cliff, the reggae singer, and he's promised to write and perform seven songs. Cliff owns this little place that needs some money to fix up and Williams gives him all the insurance settlement cash and becomes his partner. Then they turn it into a tacky version of Club Med. But here's the catch. Adolph Caesar is the prime minister, and he's in cahoots with Doyle-Murray, a real estate tycoon, and they want the property so they can sell it to Arab types. How do you like it so far?" "I don't know . . ." "Wait! Here's where the fun comes in. We hire some Second City TV people like Eugene Levy and Rick Moranis to play nerds, both named Barry, who are trying to find marijuana and women. Then we get more SCTV people like Joe Flaherty to play the nutty pilot who ferries people to the island, Mary Gross and Robin Duke to play data processors looking for husbands, plus Andrea Martin and Steve Kampmann as the ultimate kvetchy couple. And then, to top it all off, we'll bring in Joanna Cassidy, put her in the same outfit she wore in UNDER FIRE, and then we'll toss in an island revolution and lots of people running around. So! What do you think?" The chief lights up another cigar, takes a reflective puff, and replies "Sounds good when you tell it. But will it be funny on film?" "Sweety-baby, would I lie to you? This will be the one that makes Robin Williams the star he should have been after making all those turkeys like POPEYE, THE SURVIVORS, and THE BEST OF TIMES." Well, that may have been how the conversation went, but the picture sounded better than it turned out. Bill Murray was supposedly set to play the lead, a role that Williams handles simply as a reactor with none of his manic energy captured onscreen. Filmed in Jamaica with help of the island's Jamaica national investment program, CLUB PARADISE does have its moments, but they are not enough to sustain the 104-minute running time. Director Ramis, himself a one-time SCTV actor and head writer, has had enormous success due to his work on GHOSTBUSTERS. He also directed CADDYSHACK and NATIONAL LAMPOON'S SUMMER VACATION, and contributed heavily to a number of other films, including ARMED AND DANGEROUS and BACK TO SCHOOL. Here, he is one of six writers who worked on the story and screenplay. The movie is a succession of shticks, which, when they succeed, are very funny. Unfortunately, not all of them succeed. The entire revolution sequence seems to have been added to give the plot

some weight. The whole production is only slightly more successful than another movie which dealt with some similar themes, WATER, starring Michael Caine. The funniest parts of this movie come when Moranis (who went on to star in THE LITTLE SHOP OF HORRORS) and Levy are out hunting women and pot. As the ultimate boors named Barry, they deserve their own movie. Some good lines, a few sparkling moments from the SCTV folks, and the authentic reggae from Cliff are the only reasons to pay the freight.

p, Michael Shamberg; d, Harold Ramis; w, Harold Ramis, Brian Doyle-Murray (based on a story by Ed Roboto, Tom Leopold, Chris Miller, David Standish); ph, Peter Hannan (Technicolor); m, David Mansfield, Van Dyke Parks; ed, Marion Rothman; prod d, John Graysmark; art d, Tony Reading; set d, Peter Young; m/l, Jimmy Cliff.

Comedy   Cas.   (PR:C MPAA:PG-13)

COBRA zero   (1986) 87m Cannon/WB c

Sylvester Stallone *(Marion Cobretti)*, Brigitte Nielsen *(Ingrid)*, Reni Santoni *(Gonzales)*, Andrew Robinson *(Detective Monte)*, Lee Garlington *(Nancy Stalk)*, John Herzfeld *(Cho)*, Art La Fleur *(Capt. Sears)*, Val Avery *(Chief Halliwell)*, Brian Thompson *(Night Slasher)*, David Rasche *(Dan)*, Christine Craft *(TV Reporter)*, David Rasche *(Dan)*, Bert Williams *(Comdr. Reddesdale)*.

Obviously sensitive to detractors who insist he is only capable of playing two characters, Rocky and Rambo, "America's hero" Sylvester Stallone took a chance here and played a trigger-happy hero with a difference—this guy Cobra can shoot villains by the score and never drop the wooden match perched languidly on his lower lip (. . . and the winner is!). Inspired by the most mindless and narrow interpretation of DIRTY HARRY, i.e., shoot first and never ask questions, Stallone plays a cop by the name of Marion Cobretti—his enemies call him Cobra. Stallone is the goon the cops keep in a cage until some psycho almost as crazy as he is needs to be eliminated. The opening scene sees a mad gunman armed with a shotgun and a load of explosives holding the patrons of a supermarket hostage. After director Cosmatos instructs his villain to shoot every food item on the shelves that will splatter in an nice cinematic manner, he has the nut hole-up in the back of the store and surround himself with innocent bystanders. Enter Stallone, who roars in driving a vintage 1950 Mercury. Dressed in black, with mirror sunglasses, wooden match, and automatic weapons in place, Stallone confronts the gunman. The psycho screams that he'll blow the place to smithereens, and in a brilliant bit of reverse psychology, Stallone tells him, "Go ahead. I don't shop here." Stallone takes advantage of the nut's momentary confusion to dispatch him to his maker. An officer-of-the-law's work is never done, however, and Stallone must put up with the pathetic whining of bill-of-rights cheerleader Robinson (the memorable psycho-killer in DIRTY HARRY), a fellow detective who's fed up with Stallone's fascist instincts. Stallone's junk-food eating partner Santoni (hey, he was in DIRTY HARRY too, could this be an homage?) puts everything in proper perspective when he declares that his partner " . . . sure is good at catching psychos." There's only one problem with that statement, however. Stallone doesn't *catch* criminals, he *kills* them. With that cheerful opening behind us, COBRA settles down to the real story: how does Stallone nab a crazed cult of serial killers while protecting a pretty fashion model who is the only witness against them? It's easy when you have the most stupid group of villains ever to grace the screen and an endless supply of ammo. Stallone takes the girl, Nielsen (Mrs. Stallone), to a remote town for safekeeping, but one of the cultists, Garlington, works for the police department, and she sends her minions off to get them. A small army of anonymous goons roars into town on motorcycles, giving Stallone ample opportunity to indulge in some shoot-the-heavily-padded-stuntman-off-the-motorcycle-in-slow-motion fun. Eventually there is a showdown between Stallone and the chief psycho, Thompson, where our hero gets to

utter the immortal words, "You're the disease, and I'm the cure." If that line doesn't turn your stomach, how about Stallone lighting a match and drawing it toward the gasoline-soaked villain while sarcastically murmuring, "You have the right to remain silent . . . ." Perhaps most disappointing of all is that fate intervenes and kills the villain before Stallone can make the decision to commit such a heinous violation of the law. Thus, the audience is spared the troubling notion that maybe our hero went a bit too far. Robbed of this death, Stallone releases his pent-up aggressions by punching that annoying knee-jerk liberal Robinson in the nose before riding off into the sunset with the vapid Nielsen.

Every aspect of this film is reprehensible. After suckering the public to join him in his humiliation of all thinking Vietnam veterans in the moronic RAMBO, Stallone and his favorite director (other than himself) Cosmatos ventured forth to embarrass the fraternity of police. Stallone's character is an empty hulk, so much

so that virtually no attempt is made to give him anything resembling a personality. However, Cosmatos and his set designers do attempt to provide us with little insights into Stallone's character, and they are downright laughable. We are supposed to believe this goon lives in a chic Venice Beach apartment replete with all the latest decor. In addition, he has set himself up with a super-sophisticated computer system where he maintains his own crime files that are much more useful than those of the police. Are we supposed to assume he wrote the program for such a system? Of course, when you have a hero as single-mindedly dim as the one in COBRA, your supporting characters and villains have to be even dumber. Nielsen, Santoni, and Robinson simply serve as devices with which to show different aspects of Stallone's character (Nielsen—the tender side, Santoni—humor and loyalty, Robinson—frustration with the justice system), and screenwriter Stallone gives them no personalities of their own. Even worse are the villains. Who are these people and what do they want? The scenes where they get together to perform the sledgehammer dance and prattle on about creating a "new order" are unintentionally hilarious. Villains in comic books are better developed than these lackluster miscreants. But really, what does one expect from an action film other than action? Well, there is plenty of action in COBRA, but as was the case with RAMBO, director Cosmatos proves he has no flair for it. The film is so ineptly staged and unimaginatively directed that scene follows scene in a dull, predictable, and repetitive manner. Cosmatos is no Sam Peckinpah or Walter Hill, and if he isn't capable of injecting some purely visceral excitement into a badly written cop film, then he has no business being behind the camera. Does Stallone work with this guy because he's an "actor's director?"

Hoping to ride the RAMBO wave, Warner Bros. invested heavily to make COBRA a blockbuster. The studio launched a huge advertising campaign and then released a mind-boggling 2131 prints to theaters nationwide (an industry record). To avoid negative press (an anti-Stallone backlash was brewing, the studio refused to show advance screenings to critics so bad reviews wouldn't hit the papers until Saturday or Sunday. This would ensure a strong opening weekend gross and get the film off to a good start before professional opinion and word-of-mouth could do much damage. The trick worked to some extent. COBRA was a hit (domestic rentals of $28 million), but nowhere near as big a one as the studio had anticipated. All these factors seem to indicate one of two things: either the public refuses to support Stallone unless he plays Rocky or Rambo; or that the mindless "might makes right" mentality embodied by Stallone has finally started to fall from favor.

p, Menahem Golan, Yoram Globus; d, George P. Cosmatos; w, Sylvester Stallone (based on the novel "Fair Game" by Paula Gosling); ph, Ric Waite (Technicolor); m, Sylvester Levay; ed, Don Zimmerman, James Symons; prod d, Bill Kenney; art d, William Skinner, Adrian H. Gorton; set d, David Klassen; cos, Tom Bronson; stunts, Terry Leonard.

Crime   Cas.   (PR:O MPAA:R)

COBRA MISSION† (1986, Ital.) Fulvia International–Ascot/Vip–Delta
(AKA: THE RAINBOW PROFESSIONAL; MISSION COBRA) c

Oliver Tobias, Christopher Connelly, Manfred Lehman, John Steiner, Ethan Wayne, Donald Pleasence.

Four U.S. Vietnam vets go back to look for any POWs missed by Sylvester Stallone, Gene Hackman, or Chuck Norris on their respective cinematic forays into the jungle (RAMBO: FIRST BLOOD PART 2, UNCOMMON VALOR, and MISSING IN ACTION). They locate a few, but all save one die on the way back, and he decides to remain behind at the last minute. Yet another example of Italy's plundering of American film genres for idiotic action movies.

d, Larry Ludman; w, Gianfranco Clerici, Vincenzo Mannino, Fabrizio De Angelis, Erwin C. Dietrich (based on a story by Vincenzo Mannino, Gianfranco Clerici); ph, Sergio D'Offizi; m, Francesco De Masi; ed, Alberto Moriani.

War Drama (PR:O MPAA:NR)

COCAINE WARS*½ (1986) 83m Aries–Roger Corman/Concorde

John Schneider (Cliff), Kathryn Witt (Janet), Royal Dano (Bailey), Federico Luppi (Gonzalo Reyes), Rodolfo Ranni (Gen. Lwan), Ivan Grey (Klausman), Richar Hamlin (Wilhelm), Edgar Moore (Rikki), Armando Capo (Oswaldo), Martin Korey (Gomez), Tom Cundom (Balley's Driver), Ken Edgar (Kenny), Joe Capanga (Miguel), Mark Woinski (Pugg), Jacques Arndt (Franco), Willy Marcos (Hernando), John Vitaly (Marcelo Villalba), Patricia Davis (Rosita), Heidi Paddle (Lola), Helen Grant (Pia), Ted McNabney, Patricia Schener (TV Reporters).

In some parallel universe, there may really exist the kind of generic Latin American country so often seen in scores of bad action films, where drug czars live on huge estates guarded by inept gunmen while generals plot to seize the government, where American expatriates play piano in brothels, beautiful lady journal-

ists are constantly being kidnaped and tortured, and where John Schneider can pass for a top Drug Enforcement Agency man working undercover as a cocaine-running pilot. That is the imaginary setting for this below-average action film, with Luppi the drug czar, Ranni his pet general, Dano the bordello pianist, and Witt the beautiful lady journalist.

As the film opens, Luppi has Schneider's partner killed for allegedly stealing from him. Later he approaches Schneider with an offer: $200,000 if he assassinates Vitaly, a rising liberal newspaper editor and political candidate whose platform calls for the elimination of the drug trade. Schneider refuses and between dodging inept attempts on his life he sets the wheels in motion that will destroy Luppi's empire. From a dossier of incriminating information he has compiled, Schneider gives Vitaly a photograph of Luppi and Ranni together, then starts taking bids from the two men to buy the rest of the information. Ranni has him arrested and taken in for a session of torture with an electric prod applied to his tongue and other sensitive spots. Witt finds the torture chamber and gives Schneider a chance to escape and kill Ranni. Next he goes after Luppi, and after a hand-to-hand battle he shoves the drug kingpin's face into a pile of cocaine and drives off, leaving a bomb behind that blows up the whole compound.

There's nothing especially offensive here—the technical credits are passable, the production values adequate, and Schneider is a little better than he absolutely needs to be—but the whole thing is just boring from beginning to end, never generating any particular interest in its hero, or what he's up to, or anything. Semi-comic killers come after him all the time, and he has an amazingly difficult time getting rid of them, though all he usually has to do is jump off their cars before they drive over a cliff or into a building or similarly kill themselves when he appears unable to do it. How Luppi could have become a major drug dealer in spite of the kind of help he hires is a mystery. The only audiences for this kind of minor exploitation item are those easily duped by a lurid title and a picture of a guy with an assault rifle in one hand and a sexy girl on the other.

p, Roger Corman, Alex Sessa; d, Hector Olivera; w, Steven M. Krauzer (based on a story by Hector Olivera, David Vinas); ph, Victor Kaulen; m, George Brock; ed, Edward Lowe; art d, Julie Bertotto; set d, Al Guggenheim; spec eff, Willy Smith; makeup, Laura Lowe; stunts, Arthur Chestnut.

Action/Crime Cas. (PR:O MPAA:R)

COLOR OF MONEY, THE***½ (1986) 119m Touchstone/BV c

Paul Newman (Eddie), Tom Cruise (Vincent), Mary Elizabeth Mastrantonio (Carmen), Helen Shaver (Janelle), John Turturro (Julian), Bill Cobbs (Orvis), Robert Agins (Earl at Chalkies), Keith McCready (Grady Seasons), Carol Messing (Casino Bar Band Singer/Julian's Flirt), Steve Mizerak (Duke, Eddie's 1st Opponent), Bruce A. Young (Moselle), Alvin Anastasia (Kennedy), Randall Arney (1st Child World Customer), Elizabeth Bracco (Diane at Bar), Vito D'Ambrosio (Lou in Child World), Ron Dean (Guy in Crowd), Lisa Dodson (2nd Child World Customer), Donald A. Feeney (1st Referee), Paul Geier ("Two Brothers/Stranger" Player), Carey Goldenberg, Lawrence Linn, Rick Mohr, Rodrick Selby (Congratulating Spectators), Joe Guastaferro (Chuck the Bartender), Paul Herman (Player in Casino Bar), Mark Jarvis (Guy at Janelle's), Jimmy Mataya (Julian's Friend in Green Room), Grady Mathews (Dud), Lloyd Moss (Narrator—Resorts International), Michael Nash (Moselle's Opponent), Mario Nieves (3rd Latin Guy), Miguel A. Nino (1st Latin Guy), Andy Nolfo (2nd Referee), Ernest Perry, Jr. (Eye Doctor), Jerry Piller (Tom), Iggy Pop (Skinny Player on the Road), Richard Price (Guy Who Calls Dud), Juan Ramirez (2nd Latin Guy), Alex Ross (Bartender Who Bets), Peter Saxe (Casino Bar Band Member), Charles Scorsese (1st High Roller), Christina Sigel (Waitress), Harold L. Simonsen (Tournament Chief Justice), Fred Squillo (2nd High Roller), Brian Sunina (Casino Bar Band Member), Wandachristine (Casino Clerk), Forest Whitaker (Amos), Jim Widlowski (Casino Bar Band Member), Zoe (Dog Walkby).

Twenty-five years after being banned from ever again setting foot in a big-time pool room in THE HUSTLER, Paul Newman's "Fast Eddie" Felsen resurfaces older, wiser, and much more cynical in THE COLOR OF MONEY. Newman hasn't touched a cue since, but his passion for pool has turned into a jaded lust for money.

He has become what he hated 25 years ago, a "stakehorse"—a man who fronts money to young pool hustlers for upwards of 60 percent of the take. Now Newman is the man in the expensive suit sitting on the sidelines waiting to reap the reward of a younger man's talent. Newman's legitimate job is as a liquor salesman who specializes in selling cheap hooch packaged in name-brand bottles. While visiting a small midwestern bar owned by his sometime girl friend Shaver, Newman notices the hyperactive, cocky, and very talented Cruise playing pool. Newman sees the opportunity to make some big money off of Cruise's natural goofiness (he calls the kid a "flake"), so he works on Cruise's savvy, tough girl friend, Mastrantonio, who shares Newman's passion for cold cash. The two manipulate the naive Cruise into quitting his job so that Newman can shape him into a pool hustler. "Money won is twice as sweet as money earned," he tells the kid.

Newman takes the couple on a six-week road trip where he will teach Cruise all the secrets, including getting the kid to use his "flaky" behavior to purposely distract opponents. The training period is designed to culminate in a national pool tournament held in Atlantic City where there is big money to be made. Though Cruise's passion for the game is such that he is willing to play just for the thrill of it, Newman attempts to teach the youth that it's not about winning at pool, it's about making money: "Sometimes if you lose, you win." It's called "dumping," losing on purpose in order to raise the odds so that later, when the money is really big, you can clean up. Losing on purpose is a concept totally alien to Cruise and he resists Newman's advice, frequently succumbing to his natural urge to totally devastate his opponents in the most flashy manner possible (he wields his cue stick like a samurai sword and emits grunts and howls with an evil grin on his face). This proves doubly frustrating for Newman, for while he is in jealous awe of Cruise's talents, he becomes increasingly angry with the boy's inability to see the bigger picture.

Eventually Newman can no longer stand living vicariously through Cruise and he returns to the tables with cue in hand. After carefully hustling a few easy opponents, Newman gets a bit too cocky and begins drinking heavily while playing (a major flaw in his character from 25 years before). He enters into a long series of games with a fat black youth, Whitaker. Whitaker seems pretty stupid and chatters endlessly during the match. The youth makes several lucky shots and manages to win quite a few games. With Cruise and Mastrantonio watching, Newman moves in for the kill and suggests raising the stakes. Whitaker shrugs his shoulders as if to say "what the hell" and takes the plunge. Although Newman turns on the heat, Whitaker keeps on winning, and also keeps up his dim-witted facade. Newman becomes certain that the kid is a hustler, but he can't get Whitaker to reveal his hand. Without ever admitting to being anything but lucky, Whitaker wins every game, takes Newman's money, and leaves. For the first time in his life Newman has been hustled by a pro and the humiliation proves too much. Angrily he tells Cruise and Mastrantonio that he's got nothing left to teach them ("I showed you my ass in there, what else do you want?") and that they should go on to Atlantic City without him. He gives Cruise $2,000 and tells him to get lost. Feeling abandoned and used, Cruise refuses the money and storms out. The more pragmatic Mastrantonio picks up the money and follows Cruise out.

Newman decides to rehabilitate his talents—not at hustling, but at shooting pool—and go on to Atlantic City by himself. He gets a pair of eyeglasses he has long needed, practices the fundamentals of the game, and hits the circuit rediscovering his passion for winning. By the time he gets to Atlantic City he has recovered enough of his talents to make it to the semi-finals where his opponent is Cruise. Newman and Cruise play an intense match and Newman winds up the victor. Elated and feeling vital again, Newman is quickly crushed when Cruise shows up in his hotel room with $8,000—Newman's share of a lucrative side bet the kid made on the match. Cruise dumped the game for the big money—just like Newman taught him—and Newman didn't even notice. For the first time in 25 years, Newman angrily refuses to take the money. The next day at the finals, Newman suddenly forfeits the match to his opponent because he doesn't deserve to be there. Mastrantonio once again tries to give Newman his share of the previous day's winnings, and he again refuses, saying, "Tell him I want his best game." Cruise saunters into the practice room and gloats a bit ("Stings like a bitch, don't it?" he tells Newman) before agreeing to play Newman again. The kid taunts his mentor and tells him that he's going to lose again, but Newman is unfazed and replies that if he loses today, he'll get him tomorrow or the next day: "I'm back," he confidently declares before breaking.

For what had first appeared to be an alarming commercial sell-out of his highly individualistic talents, director Scorsese managed to put forth a very entertaining and successful film—$50 million at the box office as of this writing—without totally relinquishing his unique style or vision. The project was originally instigated by Newman himself—a man who normally disdains sequels—because he felt that the character of "Fast Eddie" Felsen needed new exploration. An admirer of Scorsese's gritty, street-smart work, Newman called the director and set up a meeting. Scorsese and novelist Richard Price (The Wanderers) met with Newman and together discussed where they thought "Fast Eddie" would be at this point in his life. Although there were a few screenplay drafts derived from novelist Walter Tevis' follow-up to The Hustler entitled The Color of Money, they were rejected as too literal and only the title and Felsen's character were retained. After casting Cruise and Mastrantonio, Scorsese entered into pre-production rehearsals where all the motivations and fine-tuning of the characters were brought out. Novelist-turned-screenwriter Price then assimilated the ideas brought up at the rehearsals into his screenplay and shooting began.

Scorsese left his usual New York City turf to shoot the film in Chicago because the "Windy City" had a larger variety of visually interesting pool halls than did the "Big Apple." Although the big city seen in the film is never mentioned by name, Scorsese, cinematographer Ballhaus, and veteran production designer Leven (who died soon after the release of the film) used Chicago to supreme advantage and created a unique urban backdrop that feels as authentic as the New York City of MEAN STREETS, TAXI DRIVER, or AFTER HOURS. Once again Scorsese proves himself to be one of the American cinema's most brilliant visual stylists—a man in complete control of his medium. Scorsese knows where to put the camera and when to move it for maximum impact. Although very mobile, his camera movement is never as pointless, flashy, or gratuitous as that of the vastly overrated Coen brothers (BLOOD SIMPLE) whose visuals create *false* excitement, suspense, and power. Scorsese's unique visual sense, combined with Thelma Schoonmaker's keen editing, is designed to enhance the emotional impact on an audience and to serve the narrative—never to overpower it. As the superb performances in THE COLOR OF MONEY prove, Scorsese's actors are not merely fodder for his technique.

Newman was finally awarded a long overdue Best Actor Oscar for his performance in THE COLOR OF MONEY (he was nominated for THE HUSTLER in 1961). The veteran actor brought his usual skill, subtlety, and grace to the role, but there is also an inner fire burning deeply within the tortured Felsen. Although cool, suave, and confident on the outside, Newman is a man in turmoil who has perverted his talents for mere money. As with most of Scorsese's heroes, Felsen is a desperate blind man who eventually sees the light of self-awareness and attains a state of grace, or as the director himself has stated: "The movie is about a deception and then a clarity, a perversion and then a purity." It is Newman's quiet authority and passion that carries this film and it is his introspective journey through the darkness that makes THE COLOR OF MONEY so compelling.

Cruise is superb as well. In what may be an underrated performance overshadowed by Newman, Cruise has finally taken some chances with a role and created the most vivid, challenging, and artistically successful character of his career. In most of his previous films Cruise has appeared as a smooth, confident, and bright character who totally dominates those around him. In THE COLOR OF MONEY he is a ragged, raw talent and supremely confident at the pool table, but away from his game he's a somewhat dim, naive, and almost helpless little boy who looks to others for help and support (ironically he works at a toy store called Child World). He is totally dominated by his girl friend, Mastrantonio, and is very insecure about their relationship—a fact she knows and uses to her advantage. His skill at the pool table—his ability to win—fuels his confidence and allows him to function among adults. When he finally capitulates to Newman's demands and plays the patsy, dumping game after game, he feels impotent and frustrated. Ironically, just as he

learns the perverted logic of losing to win, Newman rediscovers the pure joy of honest play-your-best-game winning. Cruise's comment to Newman, "Stings like a bitch, don't it?" proves that he has learned in six weeks what it took Newman 25 years to realize—that mere money isn't worth compromising your pride and self-esteem (he was a good student after all).

Also nominated for an Oscar (Best Supporting Actress) was Mastrantonio for her excellent performance as Cruise's streetwise girl friend. Tough, intelligent, and uncompromising, Mastrantonio is a gifted manipulator who definitely has Cruise's number, and, at times, seems to have Newman's as well. Although she gets in over her head at one point by clumsily trying to seduce Newman, she does demonstrate a keen sense of character (a student of "human moves," as Newman calls it) and proves to be just as clever and able as her teacher. The complex interplay between these three characters is a joy to watch, for the viewer never knows just who is hustling whom. Shaver, although she disappears in the middle of the film, is wonderful as well, portraying a sexy, confident, and independent woman who takes abuse from no one. Her relationship with Newman is refreshingly mature and honest. As usual Scorsese stocks his film with dozens of vividly etched bit parts, and Whitaker, as the pool shark who hustles Newman, packs a stunning amount of subtlety and detail into his brief performance. He manages to create a vivid, fascinating, and memorable human being in a scant amount of screen time—no mean feat in a film starring Paul Newman and Tom Cruise. While not as visionary, unique, or passionate as most of his past work, Scorsese proves in THE COLOR OF MONEY that he can collaborate with a strong personality from another generation (Newman) and help create a quality mainstream film that is a worthy addition to both his and Newman's filmographies.

p, Irving Axelrad, Barbara De Fina; d, Martin Scorsese; w, Richard Price (based on the novel by Walter Tevis); ph, Michael Ballhaus (DuArt color); m, Robbie Robertson; ed, Thelma Schoonmaker; prod d, Boris Leven; set d, Karen A. O'Hara; cos, Richard Bruno; spec eff, Curt Smith; makeup, Monty Westmore; stunts, Rick LeFevour; tech adv, Michael Sigel.

Drama   Cas.   **(PR:C-O MPAA:R)**

COM LICENCA, EU VOU A LUTA†   (1986, Braz.) 84m Embrafilme-R.F. Farias Producoes-Time de Cinema/Embrafilme c (Trans: Sorry, I'll Make it My Way)

Fernanda Torres *(Eliane)*, Marieta Severo *(Mother)*, Carlos Augusto Strazzer *(Otavio)*, Reginaldo Farias *(Father)*, Yolanda Cardoso *(Grandmother)*, Tania Boscoli *(Aunt)*, Duse Nacaracci *(Neighbor)*, Ilva Pino *(Otavio's Mother)*, Analu Prestes *(Lawyer)*, Carlos Wilson *(Inspector Braulio)*, Marise Farias *(Janina)*, Caio Torres *(Daniel)*, Paulo Porto *(Judge)*.

Torres is a fifteen-year-old girl who lives with her family in a suburb outside Rio de Janeiro. Life in the household is tense, with the family constantly pressuring Torres to conform. She experiences severe mental strain and ends up pregnant. This is the directorial debut of Farias, whose father Roberto Farias had previously headed Brazil's Embrafilme.

d, Lui Farias; w, Lui Farias, Alice de Andrade, Marcos Magalhaes, Fernanda Torres, Marieta Severo, Roberto Farias (based on the novel by Eliane Maciel); ph, Walter Carvalho (Eastmancolor); prod d, Marcos Magalhaes; set d, Mauricio Sette; cos, Tete Amarante; m/l, Marina Lima, Antonio Cicero.

Drama   **(PR:O MPAA:NR)**

COMBAT SHOCK zero   (1986) 96m 2000 A.D./Troma c (AKA: AMERICAN NIGHTMARES)

Ricky Giovinazzo *(Frankie Dunlan)*, Veronica Stork *(Cathy Dunlan)*, Mitch Maglio *(Paco the Gang Leader)*, Aspah Livni *(Labo the Gang Leader)*, Nick Nasta *(Morbe the Gang Leader)*, Mike Tierno *(Mike the Junkie)*, Mary Cristadoro

(Mary the Mugging Victim), Ginny Cattano *(Vietnamese Woman),* Doo Kim *(Vietnamese Man),* Leo Lunney *(Frankie's Father),* Bob Mireau *(Security Guard),* Nancy Zawada *(Girl on Motorcycle),* Ed Pepitone *(Strung Out Junkie in Station),* Brendan Tesoriero *(Weird Guy in Unemployment Line),* Ray Pinero *(Welfare Worker),* Jim Cooney *(Interrogating GI),* Yon Lai *(Viet Soldier with Rifle),* Shinri Saito *(Viet With Pliers),* Martin Blank *(Doctor),* Clare Harnedy *(Nurse),* Carmine Giovinazzo *(Medical Attendant),* Melissa Tait, Stacy Tait *(Young Prostitutes),* Arthur Saunders *(Pimp),* Lori Labar, Janet Ramage, Col-

lette Geraci *(Prostitutes),* Dean Mercil *(Passerby),* Vinnie Petrizzo *(Bum in Garbage),* Judy Tait, Pete Marino, Cathy Labarbera, Sue Parker, Betty Ann Walstrom, Phil Ciulo, Marylyn Marcinek, Tony Noe, Tom Devito, Leif Vetland, Tom Desantis, Robert Pillorella, Keith McIsaac, Ken Mezzacappa, Jimmy May, Lou Rinaldi, Bernadette Golden, Eddie Panelli, Jeffrey Mathes, Howie Murphy, Barry McBride, Joe Loach, George Perry.

Ricky Giovinazzo is a Vietnam veteran plagued with nightmares about his role in a My Lai-style massacre and his subsequent years of imprisonment and torture at the hands of the North Vietnamese. When he returns home, conditions are even worse. He is unable to find a job, his wife turns into a grossly overweight, nagging virago, and his son is horribly deformed, the result of Giovinazzo's exposure to Agent Orange. On the streets around his Staten Island home, he sees nothing but teenage prostitution, drug dealing, and misery. Finally he snaps, gets a pistol, and blows away a gang of drug dealers, then going home and killing his wife and child and then putting himself out of his misery. An intensely downbeat film, though one with some obviously serious (though unsuccessfully realized) pretensions.

p,d&w, Buddy Giovinazzo; ph, Stella Varveris; m, Ricky Giovinazzo; ed, Buddy Giovinazzo; spec eff, Ed Varuolo, Jeff Matthes; makeup, Jeff Matthes, Ralph Cordero, Jr.

Crime Drama   **(PR:O MPAA:NR)**

COME AND SEE*½   (1986, USSR) 142m Byelarusfilm-Mosfilm/
                                Sovexportfilm c (IDI I SMOTRI; AKA: GO AND SEE)

Aleksei Kravchenko *(Florya Gaishun),* Olga Mironova, Lyubomiras Lautsiavitchus, Vladas Bagdonas, Victor Lorentz.

A highly charged, emotionally exhausting indictment of war and the inhumanity of the Nazis, set in Byelorussia during the 1943 Nazi invasion. COME AND SEE focuses on the experiences of an adolescent transformed, in a matter of days, from a naive boy to a worn man. Before the credits begin, Kravchenko is shown digging through mounds of sand—the graves of recently killed Russian soldiers—to uncover a rifle, the only requirement for membership in the local freedom fighters' outfit. He finds a rifle and immediately joins, despite the desperate and hysterical pleas of his mother who doesn't want her son to be a soldier or to lose the only source of protection for her and her two young daughters. At the camp of the high-spirited, though ill-equipped, partisans, Kravchenko is treated as a comrade, even though he is relegated to the most menial jobs. When the makeshift army prepares to meet Hitler's forces, Kravchenko—referred to as "the newcomer"—is left behind so that his boots can be used by an older soldier who wouldn't be able to make the trek without them. The humiliated boy immediately goes crying back to his mother, happening upon a hysterical teenage girl along the way. While the two playfully taunt one another, the Germans launch an air raid, which is followed by an invasion of paratroopers. The boy and girl hide in the rain-drenched forest before heading toward Kravchenko's home. By the time the two arrive in the village, the Germans have already struck, slaughtering every man, woman, and child. Kravchenko refuses to notice the dead bodies sprawled out behind a shed; instead, he desperately runs to "the island," deluding himself into thinking his family fled there for refuge. The girl follows, pleading with him to accept the truth. The two wade through a virtual wall of mud in order to reach "the island," where a number of the local peasants, mainly elderly, wailing women, have come to escape the invaders. After being told that his mother and sisters were slaughtered, along with the rest of the villagers, Kravchenko goes into a state of shock. The girl nurses him back to health and he assists the other able-bodied men in the search for food. Two of these men are killed while crossing a mine field, and another while he and Kravchenko attempt a night crossing of a guarded field with a stolen cow. The cow is also killed, providing the boy with a

shield against a hail of German bullets. The next morning Kravchenko finds a horse and cart to transport the cow back to "the island," but a regiment of enemy soldiers surrounds the area so he must pretend he is a resident of the nearby village, Perekhody. Seizing the tiny village, the Nazis require that every person in Perekhody gather inside a barn. The building is set on fire and riddled with bullets, assuring that all its inhabitants are killed. The final Nazi atrocity inflicted on Kravchenko is to have a gun pointed at his head while he is photographed (an allusion to the experiments in terror the Nazis were known to perform). As the Germans leave to commit genocide in another innocent village, an attack by the partisan army kills all but a handful of officers. These men are given a mock trial before every one of the partisans empties his rifle into their bodies. The film ends as Kravchenko, with wrinkles on his face more fitting for a man of 50, fires a series of bullets into a portrait of Hitler that is lying in a puddle while newsreel footage unwinds in reverse, undoing all that Hitler has accomplished. The footage ends with a picture of Hitler as a baby in his mother's arms; Kravchenko stops firing to join the marching soldiers.

Only cold-hearted people could sit through COME AND SEE without being emotionally devastated. From its opening scene, COME AND SEE descends into a virtual hell-on-earth that becomes increasingly more frightening as the film advances to the final horror, the burning of Perekhody—an event which the final credits indicate occurred at some 620 Russian villages during the 1943 Nazi invasion. Perhaps the film's most moving image is the change in Kravchenko's face as he goes from being a naive, happy boy filled with noble illusions to one deeply involved in the arduous struggle to survive. Amidst all this death, the life of one individual able to escape the doom becomes that much more valuable. As part of the 40th anniversary of Hitler's defeat, COME AND SEE looks back at these events as a reminder of the inhumanity of war. This film won the Grand Prix at the Moscow film festival; its director, Elem Klimov, was recently named the head of the Soviet Filmmakers Union. (In Russian; English subtitles.)

d, Elem Klimov; w, Ales Adamovich, Elem Klimov (based on *The Story of Khatyn and Others* by Ales Adamovich); ph, Alexi Rodionov.

War   **(PR:O MPAA:NR)**

COME LA VIDA MISMA†   (1986, Cuba) 100m ICAIC c (Trans: Like Life
                                                                      Itself)

Fernando Echevarria *(Fernando),* Beatriz Valdez *(Madeleine),* Pedro Renteria, Sergio Corrieri, Flora Lauten, The Theater Group of Escambray.

Adequate comedy from Cuba concerns the adventures of a young actor who leaves his Havana home to join a theater group that performs in the remote mountains, as well as working side-by-side with the peasants. One member of the group cheats on an exam and the rest decide the best way to rehabilitate him would be to put his crime on the stage. Too heavy-handed in the way it wrings socialist messages out of what could have been a likable comedy.

p, Jose R. Perez; d, Victor Casaus; w, Victor Casaus, Luis Rogelio Nogueras (based on works by Rafael Gonzalez); ph, Raul Rodriguez (ICAIC Color); m, Silvio Rodriguez; ed, Roberto Bravo.

Comedy/Drama   **(PR:C MPAA:NR)**

COMIC MAGAZINE*½   (1986, Jap.) 120m New Century c (KOMIKKU
                                                          ZASSHI NANKA IRANI)

Yuya Uchida *(Kinameri),* Yumi Asou, Beat Takeshi, Hiromi Go, Yoshio Harada, Taiji Tonoyama, Masahiro Kuwana, Rikiya Yasuoka, Tsurutaro Kataoka, Daisuke Shima, Kazuyoshi Miura.

The world of Japanese journalism is scarcely to be believed by westerners. Objectivity and accuracy are of little importance, and it is the sensational stories that attract the readers and viewers. The extent to which the Japanese press had lost contact with the real world was shown in 1985 in the wake of the collapse of a fraudulent investment scheme. While literally dozens of reporters besieged the home of one of the principals, two thuggish gentlemen approached and announced to the cameras that they had been hired by some disgruntled investors to kill the man inside. Then, with no one lifting a finger to stop them, they broke through a window, pulled out a bayonet, and climbed in. The reporters heard screams, and a minute later out came the two assassins, covered with blood. "We are murderers. Call the police," they said. Then, with the press still watching and filming, they left unhindered (though they were caught later). The incident was news throughout the world, not because of the murder, but because of the way the Japanese media simply stood by and watched, no doubt thinking about the terrific ratings achievement the event would capture. Uchida, once known as "Japan's Mick Jagger," portrays one of these journalists, a showbiz reporter for a TV station, who is constantly badgered by his bosses to get the big stories even if it means poking his nose where it's least welcome. He tries to get celebrities to talk about their romances, Yakuzas to talk about their latest wars, and murder suspects to talk about their cases. Despite the abuse he receives at every turn, his ratings soar, and his editors keep pushing him to further debase himself in the search for the big story. He comes across a gold-buying scheme that seems dubious and asks to investigate, but his superiors keep him interviewing schoolgirl pop singers, illegal Korean workers, and sex club habitues, though he works on the story in his spare time. Eventually the scandal breaks. While the boss of the gold scam is locked in his house, awaiting a subpoena or some similar action, two thugs show up, announce their intentions, and break in and kill the man. Uchida, though, has had enough, and he goes in after them. They stab him and leave through the crowd. A few moments later, Uchida rises bloody from the floor and walks out, where reporters besiege him with questions. He snubs them, saying in English that he doesn't speak Japanese. Perhaps the most remarkable thing about this very enjoyable film is the fact that most of the interviews are the real thing. The Yakuzas interviewed are real gangsters, the murder suspect was finally arrested just a few days after filming, and the celebrity wedding was authentic. The film crew even earned the enmity of the real journalists by competing with them for stories. Well crafted, and with an impressive performance by Uchida at its core, the film garnered good reviews and got a minor release in the U.S. For a look at the nearly equally daffy journalistic practices of the U.S., see Haskell Wexler's fascinating film about media detachment MEDIUM COOL (1969).

p, Yutaka Okada; d, Yojiro Takita; w, Yuya Uchida, Isao Takagi; ph, Yoichi Shiga; m, Katsuo Ono; ed, Masatsugi Kanazawa.

Comedy (PR:O MPAA:NR)

COMING UP ROSES***½   (1986, Brit.) 93m Red Rooster-S4C/Skouras c
(RHOSYN A RHITH)

Dafydd Hywel *(Trevor Jones)*, Iola Gregory *(Mona)*, Olive Michael *(Gwen)*, Mari Emlyn *(June)*, W.J. Phillips *(Eli Davies)*, Glan Davies *(Dino)*, Gillian Elisa Thomas *(Sian)*, Ifan Huw Dafydd *(Dave)*, Rowan Griffiths *(Pete)*, Bill Paterson *(Mr. Valentine)*, Clyde Pollitt *(Councillor)*.

Reminiscent of Bill Forsyth's human comedies, this charming Welsh-language film presents a humorous, touching, and ultimately uplifting look at the closing of the last movie house in a depressed town in South Wales. When the Rex is shuttered, no one is more shaken than the projectionist, Hywel, who looks upon his job as a profession and only grudgingly takes on the duties of caretaker when it becomes an economic necessity. Hywel is divorced and has three sons who live with his ex-wife and her new husband. Because this new husband is unemployed, Hywel is still the family's de facto provider, as well as a friend to the man who has replaced him in his family.

Like Phillips, the former manager of the Rex who reluctantly accepts an early retirement, Hywel holds onto the slim hope that the Rex will reopen, but it seems far more likely that a wrecking ball is in its future. When some outside money people are scheduled to inspect the theater, Hywel works frantically to clean up the moviehouse, aided by Gregory, the Rex's ice-cream lady in better times. The facelift notwithstanding, the visitors (including COMFORT AND JOY star Paterson) are interested not in reopening the Rex but in converting it into a parking lot. Though disappointed by this prospect, Hywel has been luckier in other ways. While he and Gregory don't exactly fall for each other, they certainly gravitate in each other's direction, despite her lack of culinary skills (one bad meal is particularly amusing).

Meanwhile, Hywel's ex-wife's husband, who is about to lose his motorcycle— and his self-respect with it—asks Hywel for a loan of 700 pounds sterling. With nowhere near those sorts of resources, Hywel turns to ex-manager Phillips for the loan. The old man obliges, lending him the money he has set aside for a "proper funeral," and securing Hywel's promise that should anything happen to him he would see to it that Phillips gets his desired funeral. Not long after that, Phillips falls ill and a desperate Hywel racks his brain for a way to come up with the money for the imminent funeral.

Hywel and Gregory hit upon a scheme to use the dark, dank theater to grow mushrooms. With the help of Gregory's daughter (a scatterbrained unwed mother who proves to be quite a salesman), several senior citizens, and the dirge-playing rock band that practices in the Rex, Hywel and Gregory don miners' helmets and set to scientific mushroom farming. All of this transpires in an air of secrecy—no one can know the Rex is being put to this use—and is set against the backdrop of the deteriorating health of Phillips, whom Hywel exhorts to hang on just a little bit longer. After some initial success, they decide to plow their profits back into the operation in hope of producing an even larger harvest. Big, beautiful mushrooms begin sprouting, new orders come in as fast as old ones are filled, and it looks as if everything is going to work out according to plan. But without warning, the town council decides to take over the Rex. Accompanying this report is the news that the councillors are on their way to have a look at the place. A scene follows in which the mushrooms are transferred to an abandoned mine— an evacuation that makes Dunkirk look like a fire drill. The mushrooms are out before the council honchos arrive; however, the mine is not nearly so salubrious an environment for the mushrooms as is the climate-controlled Rex. The overheated mushrooms begin to die, but just when all hope seems exhausted, the ever-resourceful Hywel comes up with the idea of selling the failed crop as compost. Needless to say, Phillips gets his funeral and a fancy headstone to boot.

Even if everything doesn't strictly come up roses, the ending remains upbeat, a celebration of perseverance, innovation, and the human spirit in the face of hard times and bad luck. This is also a film about a community coming together to triumph, or at least to survive. Director Bayly—an American-born British resident trained at the British national film school—and writer Carter have created characters who are colorful and comical yet wholly believable, demanding both empathy and admiration. The performances are uniformly understated and excellent (no small feat considering the limited pool of Welsh-speaking actors), particularly Hywel and Gregory.

If the audience must willingly suspend disbelief at moments to allow the film to work its magic, the essential reality of the situation is never compromised. Though the town's closed coal mine plays only a minor role in the story, it doesn't take much of a leap of imagination to see the parallel between the shuttered theater and the 1984 pit closures by the National Coal Board that dramatically altered the fabric of life in the erstwhile mining region of South Wales. However, the political message of the film is ambiguous: arguably it can be interpreted as either a condemnation of Tory balance-sheet economics—that pay short shrift to the human consequences of industrial realignment—or as an endorsement of the plucky entrepreneurial spirit championed by Prime Minister Margaret Thatcher. Whichever the case, COMING UP ROSES has the unmistakable ring of truth.

The story behind the making of the film is itself somewhat magical. The inspiration for the Phillips character, a moviehouse impresario in Aberdare, South Wales, where COMING UP ROSES was shot, was to have appeared as an extra, but on the day they were shooting Phillips' funeral scene, he died. The line between life and art blurred further when the real-life Rex was threatened with closure and filmmaker Bayly and others associated with the movie attempted to purchase it to turn it into a revival house. Made under the auspices of 4-year-old Welsh TV, the film was shot in four weeks on a budget of approximately 250,000 pounds sterling. (In Welsh; English subtitles.)

p, Linda James; d, Stephen Bayly; w, Ruth Carter; ph, Dick Pope (Kay Color); m, Michael Storey; ed, Scott Thomas; prod d, Hildegard Bechtler; cos, Maria Price.

Comedy (PR:A MPAA:NR)

COMRADES†   (1986, Brit.) 160m Skreba Curzon-National Film
Finance-Film Four International/Film Four International c

Robin Soans, William Gaminara, Stephen Bateman, Philip Davis, Jeremy Flynn, Keith Allen, Alex Norton, Michael Clark, Arthur Dignam, James Fox, John Hargreaves, Michael Hordern, Freddie Jones, Vanessa Redgrave, Robert Stephens, Imelda Staunton.

In 1830s England, with the Industrial Revolution heating up, a group of rural craftsmen seeking higher wages form a trade union, but end up paying a heavy price themselves. The July Revolution in Paris and the spirit of reform afoot in England have put the powers-that-be on the defensive. The "Tolpuddle Martyrs," as the union members come to be known, incur the wrath of the authorities and are exiled to Australia. But the times are changing: literacy is on the rise among the toiling masses, who have come to sense that there is power in organizing; Parliamentary reforms are being enacted. Finally, the hue and cry for the return of the Martyrs becomes so great that they are repatriated. COMRADES, the first feature film in color for Scottish director Douglas, was shot in southwestern England and Australia and boasts cameo performances by James Fox and Vanessa Redgrave. The first opulent epic from the writer/director of the small-budget, black-and-white trilogy MY CHILDHOOD (1972), MY AIN FOLK (1974), MY WAY HOME (1978).

p, Simon Relph; d&w, Bill Douglas; ph, Gale Tattersall; m, Hans Werner Henze, David Graham; ed, Mick Audsley; prod d, Michael Pickwoad; art d, Derrick Chetwyn; set d, Clive Winter; cos, Doreen Watkinson, Bruce Finlayson.

Historical/Drama (PR:C MPAA:NR)

CONFIDENTIAL†   (1986, Can.) 95m Brightstar/Cineplex Odeon c

Neil Munro *(Hugh Jameson)*, August Schellenberg *(Charles Ripley)*, Chapelle Jaffe *(Amelia)*, Tom Butler *(Edmund Eislin)*, Antony Parr *(Rufus)*, Doris Petrie *(Mrs. McAlister)*, Kay Hawtrey *(Doris)*.

Unfathomable *film noir* of the worst kind, CONFIDENTIAL tells the story of a reporter in the late 1940s who becomes fascinated by a decades-old axe murder. He sets about trying to find the wife of the victim, finds the house of her son, then disappears. His wife hires a detective, but he soon vanishes too. Shot on a tiny budget in a couple of weeks and unlikely to be heard from again.

p, Anthony Kramreither; d&w, Bruce Pittman; ph, John Herzog; m, Bruce Ley; ed, Bruce Pittman.

Crime (PR:C-O MPAA:NR)

CONGO EXPRESS†   (1986, Bel.) 85m Cinete c

Francoise Beuckelaers *(Jean the Mercenary)*, Caroline Rottier *(Nadia)*, Mark Verstraete *(Jean)*, Mark Peeters *(Roger)*, Christine Bosmans *(Lucienna)*, Chris Cauwenberghs *(Gilberte)*, Mark van Eeghem *(Louis)*, Veronique Waumans *(Louisette)*, Filip van Luchene *(Theo)*, Dries Wieme, Elie Aerts.

The bleakness of contemporary Belgian life is held up for analysis in this independent feature by a duo who have been making short subjects for a decade. Set largely in the title bar, run by an old mercenary from the Belgian Congo, the story focuses on three couples and is told through flashbacks, eventually relating them all into a picture of the decline and fall of Belgium as a world power. Good camerawork and a cynical sense of humor get this film through some lapses of script and direction.

p, Willem Tijssen; d, Armand de Hesselle, Luk Gubbles; w, Bob Goossens (based on his script "Everything Remains, Nothing Changes"); ph, Willy Stassen; m, Kreuners Group; ed, Chris Verbiest; art d, Hubert Pouille; cos, Frieda Dauphin.

Drama (PR:C-O MPAA:NR)

CONSEIL DE FAMILLE†   (1986, Fr.) 123m K.G. Productions-GAU-Films
A2/GAU c (Trans: Family Council)

Johnny Hallyday *(The Father)*, Fanny Ardant *(The Mother)*, Guy Marchand *(Faucon)*, Laurent Romor *(Francois as a Teen)*, Remi Martin *(Francois as an Adult)*, Juliette Rennes *(Martine as a Child)*, Caroline Pochon *(Martine as a Teen)*, Anne Gisel Glass, Fabrice Luchini, Patrick Bauchau, Françoise Bette, Francoise Michaud, Laurent Peters, Rosine Cadoret, Vincent Martin, Julien Bertheau, Philippe de Brugada, Robert Deslandes, Michel Cremades, Anne Macina, Gerard Dubois, Charly Chemouny, Mouss, Alexandra Vidal, Stephanie Vidal, Emmanuelle Collomb, Florence Collomb, Anne Loisel, Emmanuelle Loisel.

It had been three years since Costa-Gavras' last film, the less-than-successful HANNA K., and with CONSEIL DE FAMILLE the director has found a satirical, comic tone that has never before been present in his work. Hallyday (the pop-singer star of last year's DETECTIVE directed by Jean-Luc Godard) stars as a safecracker who has recently been freed from prison. He goes back to his wife, Ardant, and their children, planning to start over in a more conservative manner. With his former partner Marchand, Hallyday plans a series of robberies which, he hopes, will not interfere with his family life. His son (played by both Romor and Martin), however, wants to follow in dad's footsteps and go along on their heists. As time goes on Hallyday and Marchand rise to the top of the crime world, living a comfortably wealthy life style. When the son decides that he wants to lead a normal life as a cabinet maker, tension rises and a family council is called to deal with the problem. In order to gain his freedom, the son informs on his father, who is then apprehended, leaving the rest of the family finally free to lead a normal life. CONSEIL DE FAMILLE opened in France in mid-March and played for just a few weeks before disappearing. Remi Martin, who plays the son as an adult, was nominated for a Cesar in the category of Best Young Male Hopeful.

p, Michele Ray; d&w, Constantin Costa-Gavras (based on the novel by Francois Ryck); ph, Robert Alazraki (Eastmancolor); m, Georges Delerue; ed, Marie-Sophie Dubus; art d, Eric Simon.

Crime/Comedy   (PR:NR MPAA:NR)

CONTACTO CHICANO zero   (1986, Mex.) 98m Producciones de Rey/
                                      Peliculas Mexicanas c (Trans: The Chicano Connection)

Gerardo Reyes *(Tony Andrade)*, Rosa Gloria Chagoyan *(Linda Lince)*, Armando Silvestre *(Gino Valetti)*, Livia Michel *(Ivonne)*, Alvaro Zermeno, Carlos Leon, Lilian Gonzales, Olivia Roival, Los Diablos, Federico Villa, Rosenda Bernal, Victor Manuel Sosa.

A ridiculously inept crime-action film about an Italian mobster, Silvestre, who uses frogmen to smuggle diamonds from Mexico into the U.S. Although the U.S. government wants to stop the smuggling, it does not want to strain relations with Mexico, so two Mexican detectives, Reyes and Chagoyan, are given the case. Apparently emulating the current stateside vogue for including popular music interludes into the action, the story is frequently interrupted so that various singers can warble their latest tunes. The result is inadvertently hilarious, as is the rest of the film.

p, Arnufo Delgado; d, Luis Quintanilla; w, Augusto Novaro, Laura H. de Marchetti; ph, Antonio Ruiz; m, Rafael Elizondo; ed, Angel Camacho.

Crime   (PR:O MPAA:NR)

CONTAR HASTA TEN**   (1986, Arg.) 105m Instituto Nacional de
                                      Cinematografia c (Trans: Count To Ten)

Oscar Martinez, Hector Alterio, Arturo Maly, Julia von Grolman, Arturo Bonin, Selva Aleman, China Zorrilla, Olga Zubarry.

With the advent of renewed political freedom in Argentina came a number of socially conscious films which criticized the atrocities and social injustices accompanying the recently ousted regime. CONTAR HASTA TEN is one such film, centering upon a young man's search for the brother who has mysteriously disappeared. After several years' absence, Martinez returns to his familial home to discover his elder brother, the favored child of a one-time political father, to have severed contact with all family and friends. Martinez attempts to unravel this mystery, and along the way uncovers aspects concerning his own past, particularly the relationship to his father and brother, long dormant in the back of his mind. He finds his brother in a mental hospital, his mental state a mere shadow of its former self.

p&d, Oscar Barney Finn; ph, Carlos Lonardi; m, Luis Maria Serra; ed, Julio Di Risio.

Drama   (PR:O MPAA:NR)

COOL CHANGE†   (1986, Aus.) 90m Delatite/Hoyts c

Jon Blake *(Steve)*, Lisa Armytage *(Joanna)*, Deborra-Lee Furness *(Lee)*, David Bradshaw *(James Hardwicke)*, Alec Wilson *(Bull Raddick)*, James Wright *(Senior Ranger)*, Mark Albiston *(Frank Mitchell)*, Marie Redshaw *(Rob Mitchell)*, Clive Hearne *(Ray Reagan)*, Christopher Stevenson *(Jim Regan)*, Jennifer Hearne *(Jennifer Regan)*, Robert Bruning *(Minister)*, Wilbur Wilde *(Wally West)*, Alistair Neely *(Joanna's Child)*, Chris Waters *(Agent)*, Ray Pattison *(Curly)*.

Until the advent of CROCODILE DUNDEE this year, the most successful Australian film (at home) was THE MAN FROM SNOWY RIVER, directed by George Miller, who is generally confused with the other Australian director George Miller, who directed MAD MAX. This film is by the former Miller, and it is a return for him to the outback highlands, long the domain of the rugged cattlemen. Lately, though, this area has begun to attract nature enthusiasts, who use their political muscle to have the region designated a conservation area where cattle grazing would be forbidden. Miller's sympathies are evident; his "greenies" (conservationists) are shown as a greedy, opportunistic, shifty lot, while his cattlemen are good-natured types who don't understand why they can't share the range. At the center of the conflict is forest ranger Blake who is simultaneously plagued by his family's opposition to the woman he loves.

p, Dennis Wright; d, George Miller; w, Patrick Edgeworth; ph, John Haddy (Eastmancolor); m, Bruce Rowland; ed, Philip Reid; prod d, Leslie Binns; art d, Barry Kennedy; stunts, Bill Stacey, Chris Peters.

Comedy/Drama   (PR:C MPAA:NR)

CORPS ET BIENS†   (1986, Fr.) 100m Lyric International-FR3-Ministry of
                                      Culture/Films du Semaphore c (Trans: Lost with All Hands)

Dominique Sanda *(Helene)*, Lambert Wilson *(Michel Sauvage)*, Danielle Darrieux *(Mme. Krantz)*, Jean-Pierre Leaud *(Marcel)*, Sabine Haudepin *(Paule Krantz)*, Laura Betti *(Laurie)*, Ingrid Held *(Ariane)*, Roland Bertin *(Dr. Loscure)*, Jerome Zucca *(Filasse)*, Siener *(Francois)*, Marie Wiart *(Simone)*.

The plot workings of a complex pulp novel by American writer James Gunn are tackled by flashy director Jacquot, employing the talents of a number of box-office names in the process. Wilson is a gigolo who murders one client, Betti, and then marries another, wealthy Parisian Held. Held's half-sister, Sanda, grows suspicious but is attracted to Wilson, while the dead woman's neighbor, Darrieux—an alcoholic amateur private eye—begins to snoop about. Leaud, Wilson's demented accomplice, is supposed to keep Darrieux in line, but when trouble arises Wilson kills him. Photographed by Renato Berta, who shot Wilson's previous film, RENDEZVOUS (1985), an equally expert work of camera styling.

d&w, Benoit Jacquot (based on the novel *Deadlier than the Male* by James Gunn); ph, Renato Berta (Eastmancolor); m, Eric Lelann; ed, Dominique Auvray; art d, Dominique Dalmasso; cos, Christian Gasc; makeup, Jacques Clemente.

Crime   (PR:C MPAA:NR)

COSMIC EYE, THE***   (1986) 72m Hubley/Upfront c

Voices of: Dizzy Gillespie, Linda Atkinson, Sam Hubley, Maureen Stapleton.

With her husband John, Faith Hubley created some imaginative and award-winning works of animation. Though John Hubley died in 1977, Faith has continued working in the field and in 1986 released her first solo feature (she had previously worked on her husband's feature of OF STARS AND MEN in 1961). Essentially, THE COSMIC EYE is a free-form narrative loosely telling the story of three musicians (jazz great Gillespie, Atkinson, and Sam Hubley) as they take a voyage through the outer reaches of space. Looking in on Mother Earth (voiced by Stapleton), the three observe the planet's evolution from the dawn of time through the current jumble of modern society. Footage from the Hubley shorts MOONBIRD, WINDY DAY (1967), and COCKABOODY (1973) are gracefully incorporated into new material, while Gillespie himself, with others, provides the film's score. Hubley chooses not to inject a heavy theme into the film, instead allowing images to speak for themselves and letting her audience consider the possibilities.

p,d&w, Faith Hubley; m, Benny Carter, Elizabeth Swados, Dizzy Gillespie, Conrad Cummings, William Russo; animation, Fred Burns, William Littlejohn, Emily Hubley.

Animated Feature   Cas.   (PR:AA MPAA:NR)

COUNT TO TEN   (SEE: CONTAR HASTA 10, 1986, Arg.)

COURS PRIVE†   (1986, Fr.) 95m Sara-La Cinq/Sara-CDF c (Trans: Private
                                      Classes)

Elizabeth Bourgine *(Jeanne Kern)*, Michael Aumont *(Bruno Ketti)*, Xavier Deluc *(Laurent)*, Sylvia Zerbib *(Patricia)*, Emmanuelle Seigner *(Zanon)*, Lucienne Hamon *(Mme. Ketti)*.

Director Granier-Deferre collaborated with screenwriter-novelist Roberts (after their successful pairing in 1982's UN ETRANGE AFFAIR) and fellow director Frank on this psychological drama about a schoolteacher, Bourgine, who becomes the subject of a denunciation involving damaging photos of her private sex life. It turns out that frustrated school head Aumont, who has been after the lovely Bourgine, is the one responsible, jealous of the teacher's past lesbian affair with a student. Includes the song "The Ballad of Lucy Jordan" (performed by Marianne Faithful), which is played to death by Bourgine.

p, Louis Grau; d, Pierre Granier-Deferre; w, Jean-Marc Roberts, Pierre Granier-Deferre, Christopher Frank (based on the novel *Portait Crache* by Jean-Marc Roberts); ph, Robert Fraisse; m, Philippe Sarde; ed, Jean Ravel; art d, Dominique Andre.

Drama   (PR:O MPAA:NR)

CRAWLSPACE*   (1986) 77m Charles Band/Empire c

Klaus Kinski *(Dr. Karl Gunther)*, Talia Balsam *(Lori Bancroft)*, Barbara Whinnery *(Harriet)*, Sally Brown *(Martha)*, Carol Francis *(Jess)*, Tane *(Sophie)*, Jack Heller *(Alfred)*, Kenneth Robert Shippy *(Joseph Steiner)*.

Klaus Kinski has made a career of playing homicidal nutcases on the big screen whether it be in such exploitative cheapies as SCHIZOID or in such brilliant pictures as AGUIRRE, THE WRATH OF GOD and FITZCARRALDO. This time out he has topped even himself in his caricature as the demented son of a Nazi war criminal. A physician, expert in euthanasia, Kinski runs a safe-looking boarding house for nubile young starlets. Behind the walls, however, lie a maze of crawl spaces through which Kinski slinks on his belly. For cheap thrills he peeks through the heating vents to watch the girls undressing. To give them a little scare, he bangs on the vents, and later blames the racket on rats. Kinski's main drawback to being a likable fellow is that he is perversely addicted to murder—not your everyday style of murder, but violent, sadistic, torturous murder. When an unsuspecting young lady, Balsam, arrives on the scene, things get tough for Kinski, since she's not as easy to kill as the rest. The pressures of dementia are getting a bit too much for him, especially when a Nazi hunter starts snooping around. Balsam eventually discovers that Kinski has a secret attic where a de-tongued female prisoner lives in a small cage. There are also some rats, body parts in formaldehyde, and torture devices, not to mention old 16mm Nazi war footage and an SS uniform. Of course, the evil Kinski is offed by the finale, but not before giving Balsam and the audience a few genuinely creepy moments.

CRAWLSPACE is a depraved and vile film that preys on the very real fear of Naziism and memories of concentration-camp atrocities. There is, however, some strange fascination that the movie holds in its portrayal of a truly sick killer. Kinski's "Dr. Gunther" is not the kind of glorified and idealized bogeyman that appears in the FRIDAY THE 13TH series or the NIGHTMARE ON ELM STREET series. Amidst all the sleaze on CRAWLSPACE's film frames, there is some fascinating probing into the mind of the killer. Kinski, as vile as he is, has convinced himself that he is meant to kill. After each murder, he ritualistically puts a bullet into the chamber of a revolver, spins the barrel, and puts the gun to his head. He pulls the trigger and, hearing only a click, his life is spared again. Reading this as a sign to continue his killing, Kinski utters the words "So be it." Not as gory as most slasher entries, CRAWLSPACE is instead ugly and disturbing, but underneath it all there may be a frightening truth.

p, Roberto Bessi; d&w, David Schmoeller; ph, Sergio Salvati; m, Pino Donaggio; ed, Bert Glastein; prod d, Giovanni Natalucci; art d, Gianni Cozzo.

Horror   **Cas.**   **(PR:O MPAA:R)**

CRAZY BUNCH, THE†   (1986, Phil.) F. Puzon/Cinex Films c

[No cast or credits available]

A comedy about a gang of mercenaries who possess a variety of skills (pilot, sharpshooter, martial-arts expert, etc.) led by a diminutive explosives expert. The warriors blunder their way into a revolution and end up winning it for the good guys.

Comedy/Action   **(PR:C MPAA:NR)**

CRAZY FAMILY, THE***   (1986, Jap.) 106m New Yorker c

Katsuya Kobayashi (Father), Mitsuko Baisho (Mother), Yoshiki Arizono (Son), Yuki Kudo (Daughter), Hitoshi Ueki (Grandfather).

The manic energy of modern Japanese life is transferred to film in this wildly bizarre black comedy from 29-year-old director Ishii. After years of scrimping and saving, Kobayashi's family finally manages to leave the crowded city and move into a nice suburban home. His children are thrilled with the new living quarters. Sixteen-year-old Arizono finally has a place where he can study uninterrupted for his all-important college entrance exams. His 12-year-old sister Kudo delights in the fact that she now has a room where she can ply her twin obsessions: singing pop music, and rehearsing to be a professional wrestler. Kobayashi's wife, Baisho, is so ecstatic that she presents herself to her husband gift-wrapped (literally). Kobayashi's eyes widen in anticipation of the carnal pleasures that await him. Later that night he writes in his diary that at long last his family may be "cured" of their "sickness."

Of course, living in the suburbs means commuting to work, and the next morning Kobayashi crams onto the subway with thousands of others to be shuttled off to their nondescript desk jobs at huge corporations. Kobayashi's optimism is short-lived, however, because two things conspire against him: the arrival of his father, Ueki, for an extended visit, and the discovery of a termite living on the family dog—the first tangible sign of decay from within. Kobayashi is horrified to discover that the sickness has returned when he comes home from work to find his wife performing a sexy strip-tease for Ueki and his drunken senior-citizen friends. Checking in on his son, Kobayashi finds the boy huddled in the blue-green glow given off by a maze of electronic equipment. The boy is so obsessed with his studies that he eats a disgusting combination of foods while sitting in a plastic pyramid to maintain his energy level and then periodically stabs himself in the leg to stay awake. The next day Baisho and Kudo demand that Kobayashi tell his father to leave—there's no room for him. Feeling guilty, Kobayashi decides to dig a basement in the house and construct a room for Ueki in it. The work annoys Arizono, who leaves his humming electronic dungeon to complain about the distraction. While digging, Kobayashi finds dozens of termites, and he goes insane trying to kill them. In his excitement he does more damage to the house than the termites would have.

Now very paranoid, Kobayashi becomes convinced that his family has had a relapse of the disease, and there is nothing left but to put them out of their misery. He boards up the house from the inside and tries to get them to drink poisoned coffee, but the group catches on and the family members arm themselves and splinter into individual warring clans. Baisho camps out in the kitchen and wears a cooking pot on her head with a variety of cooking utensils at her disposal. Arizono constructs some vicious-looking weapons out of an aluminum baseball bat, a coat hanger, and some rubber bands, and dresses himself up to look like a demented samurai. Kudo dons her spiffiest wrestling outfit, while grandpa digs out his 40-year-old WW II military uniform and imagines that he's back in Manchuria.

All hell breaks loose, with family members attacking each other, holding hostages, etc., until they all band together and destroy the house with chain-saws. The film ends as the family sets up new living quarters, outdoors, under an expressway.

Cowritten by star Kobayashi, THE CRAZY FAMILY is a crude allegory for the effect Western culture has had on everyday Japanese life. But the West is not entirely to blame. The writers and director Ishii also point the finger at the Japanese obsession with discipline, order, and perfection. The pressure they put on themselves and their children to succeed is the "sickness." The film is both funny and terrifying. One of the most profoundly shocking moments of the film occurs when the grandfather first appears decked out in his Imperial Japanese

uniform, cackling madly about the rape and pillage of the enemy—an image that recalls the propaganda films churned out by the U.S. during WW II, and one that has become taboo to Americans and Japanese alike.

The problem with THE CRAZY FAMILY is that the film is so manic and goofy from the very beginning that by the time the climax unfolds, the viewer is just too exhausted to endure it (director Ishii makes rock videos and has his own heavy-metal band—that itself may explain a lot). The film maintains a state of hysteria for more than 100 minutes, and unfortunately, some of its relevance gets bulldozed along the way. But at least THE CRAZY FAMILY takes some chances and is a welcome addition to the flood of wildly creative comedies that have come from Japan in the last few years. (In Japanese; English subtitles.)

p, Kazuhiko Hasegawa, Toyoji Yaname, Shiro Sasaki; d, Sogo Ishii; w, Yoshinori Kobayashi, Fumio Kohnami, Sogo Ishii; ph, Masaki Tamura; m, 1984; ed, Junichi Kikuchi; art d, Terumi Hosoishi.

Comedy   **(PR:O MPAA:NR)**

CRAZY MOON†   (1986, Can.) 87m National Film Board–Allegro/Cinegem
Canada c

Kiefer Sutherland (Brooks), Peter Spence (Cleveland), Vanessa Vaughan (Anne), Ken Pogue (Alec), Eve Napier (Mimi), Harry Hill (Dr. Bruno), Sean McCann (Anne's Father), Bronwen Mantel (Anne's Mother), Terry Hawkes, Harry Hill, Barbara Jones, Eddie Roy, Sheena Larkin, Chantal Condor, Carla Napier, Tara O'Donnell, Andrea Robinson, Joanne Meath, Michael Duguay, Rodney Gorchinsky, Rational Youth, Tracy Howe, Kevin Breit, Jim MacDonald, Owen Tennyson, Rick Joudrey.

Sutherland is a goofy kid with a 1930s fetish who falls in love with a deaf girl, Vaughan. He teaches her to dance and she teaches him to swim. Nothing impressive throughout, and the result is sort of a lesser CHILDREN OF A LESSER GOD.

p, Tom Berry, Stefan Wodoslawsky; d, Allan Eastman; w, Tom Berry, Stefan Wodoslawsky; ph, Savas Kalogeras; m, Lou Forestieri; ed, Franco Battista; art d, Guy Lalande; makeup, Tom Booth.

Comedy/Drama   **(PR:C MPAA:NR)**

CRIMES OF THE HEART*½   (1986) 105m Fields–Sugarman/DD
Entertainment c

Diane Keaton (Lenny Magrath), Jessica Lange (Meg Magrath), Sissy Spacek (Babe Magrath), Sam Shepard (Doc Porter), Tess Harper (Chick Boyle), David Carpenter (Barnette Lloyd), Hurd Hatfield (Old Grandaddy), Beeson Carroll (Zackery Botrelle), Jean Willard (Lucille Botrelle), Tom Mason (Uncle Watson), Gregory Travis (Willie Jay), Annie McKnight (Annie May Jenkins).

Three Oscar-winning actresses playing a trio of oddball Southern sisters immediately casts CRIMES OF THE HEART in a special light. Even before its release, critics and studio personnel were talking about more Academy Award nominations for Diane Keaton, Jessica Lange, and Sissy Spacek. Spacek ultimately was the only one of the three to get a Best Actress nomination in what conceivably could have been the Academy's consolation prize to the film. For despite the name value of Keaton, Lange, and Spacek, along with a script based on a Pulitzer Prize winning play (which also saw an Oscar nomination), CRIMES OF THE HEART is a dismal affair that reeks of pretentious self-importance.

Keaton is the eldest sibling who, at the film's opening, is packing the belongings of the youngest sister, Spacek. Spacek is currently in a local jail, where she is being held after shooting her husband Carroll, a state senator. After returning home Keaton tries to hold a small celebration for herself, seeing that no one seems to remember this is her birthday. Harper, a shrewish cousin, (whose performance earned her an Oscar nomination) gives Keaton a box of candy left

over from Christmas, which is the only present Keaton receives all day. Arriving in town on a bus from Hollywood is the middle sister, Lange. She is a singer who just can't get a break and has been working in a dog food factory in order to get by. Spacek is released on bond, and at last the three sisters are reunited. They return to their grandfather Hatfield's home, where the girls had all grown up after their mother committed suicide in a bizarre manner. Hatfield is in the hospital now, and the girls try to cheer him up with bedside visits. Gradually old hurts and jealousies arise as Keaton, Lange, and Spacek get used to living with one another. Keaton's inability to meet a good man is contrasted by Lange's all-too-many flings and one-night stands. Lange also has a moonlight reunion with Shepard, a mild-mannered veterinarian with whom she had an affair years before. Spacek, in the meantime, has just had an affair with Travis, a local teenager. Because the boy is black, the affair has raised numerous complications within the straitlaced Southern society ("I didn't even know you were liberal!" Lange exclaims to her sister after hearing about the affair). Spacek's dalliance had led to the shooting but Carpenter, Spacek's lawyer, plans to get his client off by claiming she was the victim of physical abuse. This defense falls to pieces when Carroll produces graphic photos of Spacek and Travis in compromising positions, but the wounded senator agrees to let his wife off with a simple divorce if Travis is sent out of town. After returning from her all-night reunion with Shepard, Lange lazily walks into the house. While Keaton tries to tell her of a sudden change in Hatfield's condition, Lange wishes the old man would go into a coma. The joke is on her, for that is exactly what Keaton was trying to explain, and the three girls erupt into a fit of helpless, nervous laughter. Spacek grows despondent over Travis and tries to commit suicide, first by hanging, then by sticking her head in the oven. Lange finds her in time and stops Spacek from killing herself. Neither tells Keaton about the incident, as juxtaposed upon this near-death is Keaton's first real victory. She telephones a man she had once seen but had subsequently parted from. With this tentative victory for their sister, Spacek and Lange surprise Keaton with a belated birthday cake, which the three gobble down in sheer delight.

This is a story that quickly develops into unabashed excess. CRIMES OF THE HEART doesn't really take place in the South: this is the land of forced eccentricities. Everybody has some sort of strange quirk, be it Lange combing her bangs with a razor, Keaton's problems with "a deformed ovary," or Spacek's penchant for playing a saxophone while wearing a bizarre headdress. The film boils over with such things, subordinating any real character development to the idiosyncracies that comprise much of the humor. Screenwriter Henley covered the same territory in her other 1986 films, NOBODY'S FOOL and David Byrne's TRUE STORIES, pillaging outlandish concepts for every laugh she can squeeze out—the girls' mother hanged the family cat before similarly killing herself; Spacek makes lemonade, then offers a glass to her husband while he lies bleeding on the floor. The incidents sound as if they've been culled from supermarket tabloids and no attempt is made to make them seem real. Instead, the film's elements of black comedy flail about madly, without any central theme to anchor them. Certainly the sisters learn something about themselves and their intertwining relationship, but this is only treated viscerally and with no real concern for who these people are. Perhaps the biggest problem was in casting such powerhouse names in the first place. These aren't so much characters we are watching, but an ensemble of talented women playing their parts. Keaton is the worst of the lot, coming off as

little more than Annie Hall with a Southern accent. She has every mannerism firmly locked into place, right down to the crinkle of her nose. The jealous tirades aimed at Lange are Keaton's set-pieces and she revels in these histrionic moments (interestingly, Keaton first expressed interest in the role after the play's 1980 debut). Lange also gives a studied performance from the moment she arrives on the scene. Only her moments with Shepard have any feeling of honesty, a reflection, no doubt, of their well-known off screen relationship (for his part, Shepard doesn't have much to do in his virtual walkthrough role). Only Spacek, as the scatterbrained baby of the family, gives any naturalism to the proceedings. Her brief moments with Travis have a sweet air to them, a nice escape from the frantic, overbearing humor that otherwise comprises the film. Still, Spacek has been better, and her appearance here isn't Oscar material. The scenes in which all three women come together are often painful to watch. While there's no fighting for control of a scene, each actress does her best to give a dynamic performance.

The result is hammy exchanges and occasional shrill screaming. Director Beresford more or less gives Lange, Keaton, and Spacek freedom to do as they please, and thus loses control of his material. His cast becomes more important than the story and consequently nothing ever gels. The film doesn't really have a denouement: it just sort of comes to a halt. Beresford also exhibits some of the most amateurish camera style ever to be seen in a major motion picture. One sequence views a personal discussion between Lange and Spacek from behind a preponderance of trees and bushes, allowing leaves and branches to practically brush against the camera lens. This distracts from the intimate nature of the conversation and only frustrates the viewer. Another shot looks at Hatfield's house at a cockeyed angle, an easy symbol that only calls attention to itself. Made for only $9 million (Lange, Keaton, and Spacek each earned about 75 percent less than they normally would get), CRIMES OF THE HEART was shot in Southport, North Carolina, the same location site used for David Lynch's far superior look at the underside of small-town life, BLUE VELVET.

p, Freddie Fields; d, Bruce Beresford; w, Beth Henley (based on her play); ph, Dante Spinotti (Technicolor); m, Georges Delerue; ed, Anne Goursaud; prod d, Ken Adam; art d, Ferdinando Giovannoni; set d, Garrett Lewis; cos, Albert Wolsky.

Drama/Comedy   Cas.   (PR:C-O   MPAA:PG-13)

CRITTERS**½   (1986) 86m Sho/New Line–Smart Egg c

Dee Wallace Stone *(Helen Brown)*, M. Emmet Walsh *(Harv)*, Billy Green Bush *(Jay Brown)*, Scott Grimes *(Brad Brown)*, Nadine Van Der Velde *(April Brown)*, Terrence Mann *(Bounty Hunter/Johnny Steele)*, Don Opper *(Charlie McFadden)*, Billy Zane *(Steve Elliot)*, Ethan Phillips *(Jeff Barnes)*, Jeremy Lawrence *(Preacher)*, Lin Shaye *(Sally)*, Michael Lee Gogin *(Warden Zanti)*, Art Frenkel *(Ed)* Corey Burton *(Critter Voices)*.

One of the most enjoyable films of the summer, CRITTERS harkens back to the low-budget science fiction films of the 1950s and balances the thrills with heavy doses of humor. It turned out to be a surprise hit, earning $4.7 million in rentals,

an excellent return on a low-budget film. The story begins as a group of nasty outer-space creatures known as "Krites" escape from a maximum-security penal colony located on an asteroid. The Krites are furry little creatures that resemble a demented porcupine with rows of sharp teeth and evil-looking red eyes. They zoom toward Earth and crash-land in a remote Kansas farming community. The hungry varmints immediately descend on a cow and devour it. Meanwhile, the intergalactic police force in charge of the prison dispatches two bumbling bounty hunters, Mann and Opper, to recapture the Krites if possible, or kill them if necessary. The bounty hunters have no facial features and possess the ability to change like chameleons in order to adapt to any environment. While scanning the Earth's media via satellite to learn more about the planet, Mann's eye is caught by an MTV rock video and he decides to change his face into that of a famous rock star. Opper, in the meantime, is indecisive and changes his face every time he sees one he likes better. The Krites launch an attack on the quiet farm of Bush and his family (Stone, Van Der Velde, and Grimes). The first victim is daughter Van Der Velde's boy friend, who is devoured after enjoying a roll in the hay with her. Together the family tries to fend off the "critters" (as Bush calls them) as they wreak their havoc.

While all this has been going on, Opper and Mann have invaded the nearby town in search of the critters, and being no-nonsense aliens, they begin blasting their way through buildings in an effort to flush the creatures out. Eventually the bounty hunters team up with the local police led by sheriff Walsh and converge on the farmhouse, blasting it to the ground until the last critter is destroyed. Though relieved that the menace is over, the family members are dismayed to find themselves homeless, so before departing, the bounty hunters magically restore the property.

Produced on a budget of $2 million with only $100,000 going to special effects, CRITTERS works surprisingly well as escapist entertainment. The quirky sense of humor is what makes the difference here, and clever jokes abound. Opper's constant facial transformations are consistently amusing, as is the bounty hunters' difficult adjustment to Earth life (they drive cars in reverse until they figure out they're doing it wrong). Most amusing, however, are the critters themselves. Though deadly, the critters are imbued with plenty of personality as they jabber away in their own language, which we read via subtitles. One joke has a critter trying to communicate with an E.T. doll sitting on Grimes' nightstand. When the mute E.T. refuses to answer, the critter angrily bites the doll's head off.

The critters were created by three brothers, Charlie, Steve, and Ed Chiodo, who run a small special-effects company in Los Angeles. The Chiodo brothers produced a variety of critters in all shapes and sizes, many of which perform distinct functions such as biting, rolling, shooting quills, etc. Four of the critters

were articulated puppets that could move their eyes through radio controls and move their limbs via cables. On short notice the Chiodos created one four-foot-tall critter suit (to be worn by a midget) for a scene where one of the monsters grows much larger than his comrades.

CRITTERS was originally released with two different endings. The first left the farmhouse totally destroyed, but test-market audiences reacted badly to the negative conclusion. New Line Cinema decided to film a new ending (at a cost of $60,000) in which the alien bounty hunters restore the house. The special-effects crew constructed a scaled-down version of the house out of balsa wood and then filmed it being destroyed. The footage was then printed in reverse so that the house appeared to be re-forming itself. Prints of both endings circulated during the film's original release, but now the second ending is considered definitive. CRITTERS is a lot of fun and fairly tame for this type of film, though at times the violence does get too intense, and one of the Critters utters a profanity that is relayed in English via subtitles. In the final scene, a Critter egg is seen to survive, which suggests a sequel.

p, Rupert Harvey; d, Stephen Herek; w, Stephen Herek, Domonic Muir; ph, Tim Suhrstedt (DeLuxe Color); m, David Newman; ed, Larry Bock; prod d, Gregg Fonseca; art d, Philip Foreman; set d, Anne Huntley; spec eff, Chiodo Brothers, Quicksilver FX; makeup, Chris Biggs; stunts, Mike Cassidy.

Science Fiction/Comedy   Cas.   (PR:C-O   MPAA:PG-13)

"CROCODILE" DUNDEE*½   (1986, Aus.) 102m Rimfire/PAR c

Paul Hogan (Michael J. "Crocodile" Dundee), Linda Kozlowski (Sue Charlton), John Meillon (Wally Reilly), Mark Blum (Richard Mason), Michael Lombard (Sam Charlton), David Gulpilil (Neville Bell), Irving Metzman (Doorman), Graham Walker (Bellhop), Maggie Blinco (Ida), Steve Rackman (Donk).

Paul Hogan is an Australian phenomenon and now his fame has spread world-wide with the release of this amiable, good-natured, and often very funny movie. Hogan, known affectionately as "our Hoges" in Australia, spent the first 30 years of his life in obscurity and was, in fact, working as a rigger with a Sydney bridge when he applied to appear on the Down-Under version of "The Gong Show" as a fraudulent tap-dancing blindfolded knife-thrower from the Outback (that area so far from civilization). His stint was so successful and hilarious that he got the chance to be a commentator on a TV show, then went on to have his own enormously successful comedy program which was syndicated in the United States some years ago. Within about 10 years, Hogan went from nonentity to international celebrity due to his TV shows and due to his gratis work on behalf of the Australian tourist industry, a business he promoted with a series of commercials that nearly doubled the number of visitors coming from the United States.

Attempting to analyze the incredible business this movie did is not easy. On the surface it's the standard fish-out-of-water comedy done so many times before on film, the most recent version being BROTHER FROM ANOTHER PLANET, and even overdone on TV on shows like "Mork and Mindy" and the 1986 "Perfect Strangers". Even the specific Aussie-abroad theme is nothing new; the films based on Barry Humphries' famed adult comic-strip character, ADVENTURES OF BARRY MCKENZIE (1972) and BARRY MCKENZIE HOLDS HIS OWN (1975), were hilarious looks at the oddness of urban culture through the eyes of an Australian innocent.

Hogan is a crocodile hunter (his friends refer to him more as a poacher) in the bleak Northern Territories area of Australia. He has a run-in with a snarly crocodile and the result is a gnarled leg. But legend speaks louder than truth, and by the time the word gets out around the world, the story goes that he lost his leg in the encounter and managed to heroically crawl back to safety. Eager to find a human-interest story, reporter Kozlowski (the daughter of Lombard, the man

who owns the newspaper for which she works) treks down to meet Hogan. The two meet, fall into heavy like, and he takes her out into his world where this urban princess seems to have brought more clothes than could have fit into 12 suitcases. They trudge through the back country, he shows her how he can tell time by looking at the sun, regales her with lies that rival Paul Bunyan and Baron Munchhausen at their best, and manages to show her that he is a man of the land, something impressive for a woman from New York who has probably only seen trees in Central Park. Along the way, they meet the only well-known aboriginal actor in the world, David Gulpilil (WALKABOUT, THE LAST WAVE), so that Hogan can show that Aussies and their black brothers have no problems. (It's a bit simplistic and there's a tad too much Zen wisdom in the scene, but it's brief, and that's a blessing.) Hogan and Kozlowski go on canoe trip, he puts the Indian sign on some wild-eyed oxen, he chases off some redneck kangaroo hunters, and gets Kozlowski away from a croc before the animal can take a chunk out of her comely rear. Up until now, the picture moves along at a leisurely pace with a few mild funnies. It takes off when Kozlowski brings Hogan back to New York and he has to face a city jungle far more dangerous than anything he's ever seen before. Hogan is ensconced in a suite at the Plaza Hotel; has the predictable trouble identifying a bidet ("It's for washin' yer backside, right?"); runs into a transvestite; gets propositioned by a pair of streetwalkers; meets winos, muggers, waiters, and snobs; is saved when his black chauffeur twists the aerial off a limousine and makes it into a boomerang; and, in the end, triumphs over the city and what little story there is.

What makes the picture work so well (it is the highest-grossing film in Australian history, far outstripping both RAMBO and E.T., the previous box-office winners) is Hogan's appeal. He is a weatherbeaten, crinklyfaced man with a glint in his eye and sort of the Aussie version of Chuck Norris with a generous sampling of every likable comedian who ever strutted and fretted across a stage. Hogan put up a great deal of his own money for this feature (a bit less than $6 million), 12 weeks in the making, and his faith has been rewarded. The director is his longtime TV helmer Peter Faiman and the producer is his handshake partner John Cornell. Hogan has been married long enough to be a grandfather and is still under 50. The movie had to be titled with quotation marks around the word "Crocodile" so people would realize that was a name and that this wasn't a jungle epic which took place in a small Scottish city. (Dundee, in Scotland, is the traditional home of jute, jam, and journalism.) Hogan's emergence as a full-fledged star makes him the third male super-talent to come out of the area. Errol Flynn was born on the island of Tasmania; Mel Gibson (born in the U.S.) made his mark in Australian films. There will surely be a sequel to this film, and it might be fun to see the character take on the Parisians or the Londoners or even the Los Angelenos next time. The biggest flaw in the film was the casting of Kozlowski (seen in "Death of a Salesman" on the Broadway stage and in the TV version with Dustin Hoffman) who didn't have charisma to match Hogan's. Good work from Mark Blum as the weakling editor affianced to Kozlowski. If Hogan can keep his health intact (he suffered a cerebral hemorrhage a while ago while attempting to lift 250 pounds at a local gymnasium), he will have a long and fruitful career in movies.

p, John Cornell; d, Peter Faiman; w, Paul Hogan, Ken Shadie, John Cornell (based on a story by Paul Hogan); ph, Russell Boyd (Kodakcolor); m, Peter Best; ed, David Stiven; prod d, Graham Walker.

Comedy   (PR:A-C   MPAA:PG-13)

CRONICA DE FAMILIA†   (1986, Mex.) Compania Productora
        Imaginaria-Mexican Film Institute c (Trans: A Family Chronicle)

Ernesto Gomez Cruz, Martha Verduzco, Fernando Balzaretti, Ana Silveti, Alfonso Andre, Claudia Ramirez.

This film is an examination of family values and class relations as seen through the world of two powerful Mexican families. One clan is important in business, the other involved with government and politics. The two households come together over a land and construction deal, but fate dictates that their collaboration end with tragic results. The families both try to gloss over the seamy eruption, revealing the cruel nature of their enormous collective power. The story is told largely through the eyes of their children. The businessman's daughter is a design student who despises her native Mexico, while the politician's son is a cocaine-addicted musician.

p&d, Diego Lopez; w, Diego Lopez, Juan Tovar, Juan Mora; ph, Arturo de la Rosa; m, Humberto Alvarez; ed, Juan Mora.

Drama (PR:O MPAA:NR)

CROSSROADS*** (1986) 96m Columbia-Delphi IV/COL c

Ralph Macchio *(Eugene Martone)*, Joe Seneca *(Willie Brown)*, Jami Gertz *(Frances)*, Joe Morton *(Scratch's Assistant)*, Robert Judd *(Scratch)*, Steve Vai *(Jack Butler)*, Dennis Lipscomb *(Lloyd)*, Harry Carey, Jr. *(Bartender)*, John Hancock *(Sheriff Tilford)*, Allan Arbus *(Dr. Santis)*, Gretchen Palmer *(Beautiful Girl/ Dancer)*, Al Fann *(Pawnbroker)*, Wally Taylor *(O.Z.)*, Tim Russ *(Robert Johnson)*, Tex Donaldson *(John McGraw)*, Guy Killum *(Willie at 17)*, Akosua Busia *(Woman at Boardinghouse)*, Edward Walsh *(Harley Terhune)*, Allan Graf *(Alvin)*, Royce Wallace *(Hotel Proprietress)*, J.W. Smith *(Man at Auto Wrecking Yard)*, Diana Bellamy *(Hospital Supervisor)*, Johnny M. Reyes *(Orderly)*, Karen Huie, Robin Townsend, Jeanne Kiely, Winifred Freedman, Dolores Aguanno, Debra Laws, Diane Robin *(Nurses)*, Leslie Morris *(Bus Station Clerk)*, Gloria

Delaney, JoMarie Payton-France , Angela Robinson, Deborra Hampton *(Jookhouse Women)*, Le Van Hawkins, Jason Ross *(Jookhouse Men)*, Natasha Peacock *(Young Girl at Crossroads)*, Agnes Narciso *(Miss Narciso)*; Jookhouse Musicians: Frank Frost *(Harmonica/Vocalist)*, John Price *(Drums)*, Otis Taylor *(Lead Guitar)*, Richard "Shubby" Holmes *(Bass Guitar)*, Terry L. Evans *(Keyboard)*, Bobby A. King, Sam King, Arnold McCuller, Willie J. Greene, Jr. *(Guitar Duel Sequence Singers)*.

After the twin disappointments of the frustrating STREETS OF FIRE (1984) and the disastrously unfunny BREWSTER'S MILLIONS (1985), director Walter Hill bounced back a bit with this heartfelt tribute to the Mississippi Delta blues.

The film opens in 1936 on a historical moment for American music. The mysterious young Mississippi blues singer known as Robert Johnson sits down in a small hotel room to record his songs. Nearly 50 years later, Macchio, a teenage musical prodigy studying at Julliard, sits in his dorm room immersed in blues lore. Though studied in the classics, Macchio's true love is the Mississippi blues, and his god is Robert Johnson. Johnson recorded 29 songs during those sessions, and he was murdered two years later at the age of 28. Mystery surrounds Johnson and the nature of his murder. It has been said he was poisoned by a jealous woman or stabbed by a jealous husband. A more incredible Johnson legend relates how the singer sold his soul to the Devil at a lonely delta crossroads in exchange for the talent to play the blues. Many of Johnson's songs tell of mighty confrontations with the dark side, including "Hell Hound on My Trail," "Me and the Devil Blues," and the terrifying "Stones in My Passway." The most beguiling Johnson legend, as far as Macchio is concerned, is that Johnson recorded a 30th song but it has been lost.

Macchio becomes determined to uncover the lost song. He starts by trying to

contact an old blues singer who knew Johnson, Willie Brown, aka "Blind Dog" Fulton (Seneca), who is locked up in a Harlem nursing home. To get close to the man, Macchio takes a job as a janitor in the home. At first Seneca denies his identity and mocks the white teenager from Long Island for his desire to be a blues man. Seeing that the boy is determined, Seneca finally reveals the truth and makes a deal with Macchio: if the kid can get him out of the nursing home and back to the Mississippi delta, Seneca will teach him Robert Johnson's lost song.

With little money, the odd couple leave New York and hobo their way down South. En route Seneca teaches Macchio about the hardships one must experience in order to play the blues. Seneca has had his share of woe, for he too sold his soul to the Devil at the crossroads and has been paying for it ever since. After his brief moment in the limelight, Seneca murdered a man and spent the rest of his life in prison. He now wants to go back to the crossroads and try to break his contract with the devil. Seeking shelter from a rainstorm, Seneca and Macchio encounter a young girl runaway, Gertz, who is on her way to Los Angeles to become a dancer. Tough and independent, Gertz doesn't need help from Seneca and Macchio, but they need her because women get rides faster than men. Though antagonists at first, Macchio and Gertz fall in love, and she teaches the naive boy the ways of the flesh.

After a successful gig at a rural black nightspot, Macchio thinks he is a fullfledged blues man, but he still has an essential lesson to learn—heartbreak. Although she feels strongly for both Macchio and Seneca, Gertz's dream is dancing and she won't realize that with them, so early in the morning she heads off on her own. Macchio is crushed, but Seneca teaches the boy to channel his anguish into the music. At this point Seneca confesses to Macchio that there is no 30th Robert Johnson song, and that he used him to get back to Mississippi. Macchio seems to understand, and he accompanies Seneca when they finally make it back to the crossroads.

Seneca instructs Macchio to stand under the gnarled dead tree—the only marker for miles around—and play the blues. From out of nowhere arrives a black man dressed in the clothes of a preacher, Judd. Seneca demands he be given his soul back while the bemused Macchio, who thinks the whole thing hogwash, stands nearby. Judd refuses, but seeing an opportunity to gain a new soul, offers to release Seneca from his contract if Macchio can win a guitar duel against one of the devil's own. Seneca does not want to involve the boy, but Macchio cockily accepts the challenge, despite the fact that if he loses, the devil has his soul. That night, in front of a large congregation, Macchio matches up against a demoniclooking long-haired heavy metal rock 'n' roll guitar player (Vai). Macchio matches Vai screeching chord for screeching chord, and the contest appears to be a draw until Macchio throws in some of his amazingly fast, precise classic guitar playing with a helping of blues for good measure (rock guitarist Vai actually plucked both parts, so he was really dueling himself). Vai gives up in frustration and Macchio wins back Seneca's soul. Macchio and Seneca hit the road again, this time heading for Chicago.

Based on a screenplay that won NYU film student John Fusco his second consecutive Nissan FOCUS award for student screenwriting, CROSSROADS is a loving, detailed tribute to a purely American art form—the blues. Steeped in blues folklore, even the most bizarre elements of the story have their roots in historical fact, music, and legend (in Robert Johnson's song "Crossroads," he mentions a friend named Willie Brown—the name of Seneca's character). Fusco's screenplay reflects his own experience as a young white blues singer who toured the South singing for his supper. After nearly ruining his throat, Fusco was forced to retire at the age of 22 and return to Connecticut. Shortly thereafter he learned of an old black man carrying a harmonica who had recently been admitted to the nursing home where his girl friend worked. This incident, combined with events in his own life—and spiced up with heavy doses of blues folklore—formed the basis for the CROSSROADS screenplay. The perfect director for the project was Walter Hill, who, in many of his previous films, had demonstrated an affinity for both American folk music and the rural South (HARD TIMES, THE LONG RIDERS, SOUTHERN COMFORT). Hill and cinematographer Bailey perfectly capture the look and feel of the Mississippi delta, which has been little seen on film. Hill brings out the best in his actors as well. Although cries of a KARATE KID rip-off sounded as soon as Macchio was cast as the young guitarist, such criticisms are unfounded, for the project, and Macchio, had the skill and integrity to ensure that the two films remained quite different. Macchio had music coaches who taught him how to look as if he were actually playing the instrument (Ry Cooder did most of the actual playing), and he does a superb job. Also notable is Gertz as the tough young runaway who has the strength to make it on her own and realize her dream. But it is the elderly Seneca who dominates CROSSROADS. Having lived, as he says, "like a gypsy" most of his life as a singer and songwriter, Seneca came to acting quite late in life. Hill spotted him on Broadway when the actor starred in the Tony-nominated "Ma Rainey's Black Bottom." Before CROSSROADS Seneca had memorable supporting roles in THE VERDICT and SILVERADO. Seneca is superb in CROSSROADS and brings a sense of warmth, emotion, and realism to the film that a recognizable star couldn't have. Perhaps the most important aspect of the film is the music itself, however, and it is skillfully handled by the always excellent Cooder. Songs include: "Crossroads" (Robert Johnson, performed by Terry Evans, Ry Cooder), "Turkish March" (Wolfgang Amadeus Mozart, performed by William Kanengiser), "He Made a Woman Out of Me" (Fred Burch, Donald Hill, performed by Amy Madigan), "If I Lose" (Ralph Stanley, performed by Amy Madigan), "Cotton Needs Pickin" (Richard Holmes, Otis Taylor, John Price, Frank Frost, performed by The Wonders), "Maintenance Man" (John Price, Frank Frost, performed by The Wonders), "Willie Brown Blues" (Joe Seneca, Ry Cooder, performed by Joe Seneca, John "Juke" Logan), "Feelin' Bad Blues" (Ry Cooder, performed by Ry Cooder), "Butler's Bag," "Head Cuttin' Duel" (Steve Vai, Ry Cooder, performed by Steve Vai, Ry Cooder), "Eugene's Trick Bag" (reprise of "Turkish March" arranged by William Kanengiser, performed by Steve Vai), "Walkin' Blues" (Sonny Terry, Ry Cooder, performed by Sonny Terry, Ry Cooder). The main-title harmonica was played by Sonny Terry. Viewers lacking an appreciation for delta blues may find the film nothing more than a typical rites-of-passage road movie (as apparently did the general public; the film grossed only $2.7 million in rentals—a certifiable flop), but for those who know where to look, there are many fine moments here. CROSSROADS was given a surprisingly harsh rating by the MPAA considering there is no violence or nudity, only some rough language.

p, Mark Carliner; d, Walter Hill; w, John Fusco; ph, John Bailey (Panavision, Technicolor); m, Ry Cooder; ed, Freeman Davies; prod d, Jack T. Collis; art d, Albert Heschong; set d, James Tocci, Nancy Patton; cos, Dan Moore, Barbara Siebert-Bolticoff; spec eff, Larry Cavanaugh; makeup, Michael Germain.

Drama   Cas.   (PR:C-O MPAA:R)

CRVENI I CRNI†   (1986, Yugo.) Jadran (Trans: Red and Black)

Bekim Fehmiu, Milan Strljic, Olivera Jezina, Miodrag Krstovic, Radko Polic, Fabijan Sovagovic, Boris Kralj.

d, Miroslav Mukiljan; w, Marija Peakic-Mikuljan; ph, Andrija Pivcevic; m, Neven Franges; set d, Tihomir Piletic.

CRY FROM THE MOUNTAIN†   (1986) 90m Billy Graham Film Ministry/
                                              World Wide c

Wes Parker (Larry Sanders), Rita Walter (Carolyn Sanders), Chris Kidd (Cal Sanders), James Cavan (Jonathan), Coleen Gray (Marian Rissman), Jerry Ballew (Dr. Carney), Allison Argo (Laurie Matthews), Glen Alsworth (The Pilot), Myrna Kidd (Dr. Blake).

Parker (a former first baseman with the Los Angeles Dodgers) is an executive conducting an affair with his secretary, Argo. His wife, Walter, has just found out about it and is threatening to divorce him and abort the fetus she is carrying. Before they separate, Parker takes son Kidd on a camping trip to Alaska. While kayaking through some rapids they capsize and Parker suffers a concussion. Kidd finds help in the person of crusty old-timer Cavan, who works a small mine and broods about his disobedient son. They nurse Parker until a helicopter comes to carry him off to Anchorage for surgery. Kidd and Cavan come along, and Walter shows up. The miner convinces Walter that she should go with him to the Billy Graham crusade. There she accepts Jesus as her personal savior and reconciles with Parker.

The production company reveals the origin of this mildly inspirational saga, and it is to the credit of the filmmakers that this actually got shown in theaters and not just church basements. The failings are obvious; if ever a film could be called "preachy" this is it, though some of the Alaska footage is pretty. The rather surprising PG rating is because of frank discussion of divorce and abortion.

p, William F. Brown; d, James F. Collier; w, David L. Quick; ph, Gary D. Baker; m, J.A.C. Redford; ed, J. Michael Hooser; prod d, J. Michael Hooser; set d, James Sewell; cos, M. Butler.

Drama   (PR:A MPAA:PG)

CUODIAN YUANYANG†   (1986, Hong Kong) Shaw Bros. (Trans: Love
                                         with the Perfect Stranger)

Er Dongsheng, Wang Xiaofeng [Pauline Wong].

A sex comedy from first-time director Lu Jianming in which a whirlwind marriage leads to numerous misunderstandings and a mass breakdown of communication. Wang Xiaofeng won Best Actress at the Hong Kong Film Awards for her performance, while the Best Screenplay award went to Lu Jianming and Deng Ronglu.

d, Lu Jianming; w, Lu Jianming, Deng Ronglu.

Comedy   (PR:C MPAA:NR)

CUT AND RUN**   (1986, Ital.) 87m Racing/New World c (INFERNO IN
                                                        DIRETTA)

Lisa Blount (Fran Hudson), Leonard Mann (Mark), Willie Aames (Tommy), Richard Lynch (Col. Brian Horne), Richard Bright (Bob), Karen Black (Karin), Valentina Forte (Ana), Michael Berryman (Quecho), John Steiner (Vlado), Gabriele Tinti (Manuel), Luca Barbareschi, Barbara Magnolfi, Penny Brown, Carlos De Carvalho, Edward Farelly, Ottaviano Dell'Acqua, Roffredo Gaetani.

Inspired by RAIDERS OF THE LOST ARK and APOCALYPSE NOW, Italian filmmakers have been endlessly reworking the basic elements, jungles full of booby traps and dangerous natives, journeys up rivers to meet long-lost white men, and great dollops of violent, sudden death.

The plot of this one has Blount as a TV journalist whose investigation of a cocaine ring turns up a photograph showing Lynch alongside an airplane being loaded with cocaine. Research leads her to discover that Lynch was a former Green Beret who became the right-hand man of the Reverend Jim Jones and the engineer of the Guyana Massacre, in which he too was believed to have died. With this proof that he is still alive, Blount takes off for South America with cameraman Mann. They persuade a pilot to fly them to a cocaine processing camp, but when they arrive the camp is under attack by indians led by Berryman (from THE HILLS HAVE EYES 1 and 2, and apparently the Rondo Hatton of the 1980s). The pilot is killed, but Blount and Mann hide in the jungle until morning, when they search the camp and find everyone dead. In the radio hut they find Forte hiding in a locker, and she leads them through the jungle to another camp. Along the way she is killed, and Blount and Mann find the other camp the scene of another massacre, though they do find Aames, who escaped the earlier holocaust and who just happens to be the son of Blount's boss, Bright. The three head downriver on a motorboat, but they are captured by Indians and taken to Lynch's camp. Tied to a tree, they are to be killed in the morning, but already they are the subject of a search by Bright and South American drug agents. The searchers spot Lynch's camp but are unable to do anything until the next day. For the present all they can do is fire few shots before flying off. One of the bullets hits Lynch, who retires to his home aboard a seaplane to bleed. Calling for Blount, he mumbles some incoherent Oriental-style philosophy, then tells her that in the morning he will grant her an interview on live TV. The next day he babbles that because society made fun of Jim Jones, he is going to get even by cornering the market on cocaine (you figure it out). He then takes his hand from the hole in his stomach, kneels on the ground, and is decapitated by the machete of one of his lieutenants. The army comes swooping in, Blount and Mann flee to Lynch's seaplane, and within moments the whole area is secured. Aames is reunited with his father, and Blount and Mann fly away laughing (after dispatching Berryman).

The film wears its influences on its sleeve, and Lynch is so similar to Marlon Brando's Col. Kurtz in APOCALYPSE NOW that one expects him to lapse into a bad Brando impression at any moment. Blount comes through the film with her dignity relatively unscathed, though not the same can be said for the others, who at least die quietly for the most part. Worst of all, though, is Karen Black, who plays her minor role on the edge of hysteria, though all she does is watch monitors back in the control room. Shot in Miami and Venezuela, the film has little of the explicit gore for which director Deodato is known. Released in Italy in 1985 with more gore as INFERNO IN DIRETTA (see the 1986 MPG Annual volume).

Although hardly on a par with the films it was inspired by, CUT AND RUN isn't all bad. The jungle settings are convincing, and the swarms of blowgun-toting Amazonian Indians appear to be the real item. If one is prepared to accept this film on its own merits as an import action item, one could find worse ways to drop their video-store bucks.

p, Alessandro Fracassi; d, Ruggero Deodato; w, Cesare Frugoni, Dardane Sacchetti; ph, Alberto Spagnoli (Telecolor); m, Claudio Simonetti; ed, Mario Morra; art d, Claudio Cinini; set d&cos, Francesca Panicali; makeup, Maurizio Trani, Alberto Blasi.

Action/Adventure   Cas.   (PR:O MPAA:R)

CYOEI NO MURE†   (1986, Jap.) 140m Shochiku c (Trans: The Catch)

Ken Ogata (Fusajiro Kohama), Masako Natsume (Tokiko), Koichi Sato (Shunichi), Yukiyo Toake (Aya).

Ogata is an old tuna fisherman who lives with his daughter after his wife leaves him. The daughter falls in love with Sato, a good-natured young shopkeeper who wants to learn to be a fisherman. After much nagging from his daughter, Ogata agrees to take Sato out, but on the first voyage the younger man becomes deathly seasick, and on the second he somehow manages to get a line with a fish on it wrapped around his head. Ogata seems most concerned about the fish getting away, but eventually Sato manages to escape his predicament. The daughter and Sato marry and move away, leaving the old man alone. He locates his ex-wife and goes to visit her, but they are beyond reconciliation. Overlong, and with not nearly enough dramatic incident to fill its daunting running time. Director Somai came to some prominence last year with his film TYPHOON CLUB.

p, Akira Oda; d, Shinji Somai; w, Yozo Tanaka (based on the novel by Akira Yoshimura); ph, Mitsuo Naganuma; m, S. Saegusa.

Drama   (PR:C MPAA:NR)

D

DA EBICHASH NA INAT† (1986, Bulg.) 87m Bulgariafilm c (Trans: All For Love)

Velko Kunev *(Rado)*, Maria Statoulova *(Rado's Wife)*, Ivan Velko *(Plamen, Rado's Son)*, Leda Tasseva *(Stefka the Controller)*, Yordan Spirov *(Headmaster)*, Yulia Kozhinkova *(Teacher)*.

Velko is an adolescent who gets into trouble at school when he corrects a teacher's off-key singing. Ordered to apologize, he refuses, and is brought up before the administration. His father Kunev is called in, but takes his son's side when it becomes obvious that the boy was right. The lad learns that dad is a black marketeer, and he refuses to hear anything more his parent has to say. Eventually this treatment makes the father feel so guilty that he cleans up his life and gets out of the rackets.

d, Nikolai Volev; w, Nikolai Volev (based on a short story by Chavdar Shinov); ph, Krassimir Kostov; art d, Konstantin Roussakov.

Drama (PR:C MPAA:NR)

DAHALO DAHALO† (1986, Madagascar) 93m Sorex International Engineering c (AKA: ONCE UPON A TIME IN THE MIDWEST)

Masy Fonteno, Eugene Randrianarison, Thomas Rakotoyao.

Dahalos are Madagascar's version of rustlers, and Zebus (a hump-backed member of the bovine family) are their quarry in this oddity. As the film opens a pair of Dahalos kill some hunters, which brings the law down on them. The problems of the police in catching a criminal in this terrain are detailed, as is the hatred of the farmers, always the victims, for the rustlers. Unlikely to be widely seen outside its island home.

d, Benoit Ramampy; ph, Justin Limby Maharavo.

Crime Drama (PR:C MPAA:NR)

DAHAN† (1986, Bangladesh) 120m Snap/Nasco bw (Trans: Affliction)

Humayun Faridee *(Munir)*, Babita *(Ivy)*, Buibul Ahmed *(Mustaq)*, Dolly Anwar *(Lina)*.

Faridee is a young journalist disillusioned by the lack of public interest in societal conditions in favor of lurid headlines about sex and crime. He tutors a rich girl, his aging uncle just wanders off one day never to be seen again, his sister goes crazy in the wake of a romance gone bad, and he loses all of a friend's money in a doomed venture. Maybe the best film to emerge from Bangladesh this year, though that's faint praise if ever there was.

d&w, Sheikh Niamat Ali; ph, Anwar Hossain; m, Amanul Haque; ed, Saidul Anam; art d, Moshooq Helal.

Drama (PR:A-C MPAA:NR)

DANCING IN THE DARK** (1986, Can.) 98m Brightstar–Film Arts–Film House–CBC/NW–Simcom c

Martha Henry *(Edna Cormick)*, Neil Munro *(Harry Cormick)*, Rosemary Dunsmore *(The Nurse)*, Richard Monette *(The Doctor)*, Elena Kudaba *(Edna's Roommate)*, Brenda Bazinet *(Susan)*, Anne Butler *(Beautician)*, Vince Metcalfe *("Accountant" Party Guest)*, Janet Bailey *(Night Nurse)*, Carole Galloway *(Dottie Franklin)*, Marshall Margolis *(Lawyer)*, Florence Catalano-Carenza *(Cleaning Lady)*, Barbara McMullen, Bob Shaw, John Shepherd, Amanda Smith *(Neighbors)*, Olwyn Chipman *(Policewoman)*, Alan Rose *(Policeman)*.

"If one does the same thing over and over again," says Henry, the film's obsessive housewife-turned-murderess, "each time properly, each time to the best of one's ability, still what one has is a handful of endless, identical tasks." DANCING IN THE DARK is filled with such endless tasks, which identify Henry—a 40-year-old middle-class woman—as the ultimate housewife, one who strives for the perfect home and marriage, the sort she reads about in women's magazines. Henry is compulsive: she spends every minute of every waking day doing chores. When housecleaning, she is obsessed with the fear that she may have missed a spot. She vacuums, she bakes, she tends to plants, she dusts, she polishes, and she dusts some more. Meanwhile, her husband, Munro, is trying to climb the corporate ladder, hoping to get that big promotion—the one with the corner office and the six-week vacation. They've been married 20 years and things seem just fine between them. They seem to like each other, they have quiet candlelight dinners, they dance romantically in the living room, and they even have a great sex life. There's a catch, however—Henry is a full-blown loony. When she learns from a friend that Munro is having an affair with his secretary, she comes unglued and stabs him to death. At the start of the film, the near-catatonic Henry is shown sitting in her hospital bed at the local asylum. The ward nurses tend to her. She is fed, bathed, dressed, and made-up. It's all very neatly contrasted to her earlier days, when she could do all these things herself. Before she killed her husband she took care of everything; now she can't even comb her own hair. All she can do is scribble her diary entries in a spiral notebook. These pages and pages of thoughts that she writes are heard in an excessively literary voice-over which runs through nearly the entire film. "On this day," Henry remembers the day she killed her husband, "the vision slipped, instead of larger purpose, I saw the tiny tasks."

Unfortunately, the film's "larger purpose" is made clear in the first minutes, leaving nothing but "tiny tasks" to fill the remainder of the film. DANCING IN THE DARK is not a case study in psychology, but a feminist fable which shows a woman's role in the most extreme manner. Henry is not just *a* housewife, but *the* housewife—the one deified by the magazines. Apparently as a result of this attempt to have the perfect house and serve her husband faithfully, she is driven off the edge. She seems, however, to have been emotionally unfit to start with.

The expectations society has placed upon the housewife are supposed to be so great the only way she can free herself of the emotional shackles that bind her to the vacuum cleaner is to kill her husband. But later, in the asylum, she becomes aware of the paradox of the situation. She has lived her entire life for her husband, has now freed herself from him, and as a result has no will to live.

Marr directs with a style which is as meticulous as the compulsive cleaning of his main character, but this style is so cold and calculated that identification with Henry is impossible. Viewing her from a distance, it is clear that she is a madwoman. One can't help but wonder why her husband spent 20 years with her without realizing this. The foundation of the film is shaky because Henry seems less like a housewife gone mad than an emotional cripple who has retreated into a life of housework. There's something else at work on Henry's mental state that Marr (or his source material) chooses to ignore, instead laying the blame at the door of society and on men specifically. The result is that the film, like Henry's life, seems like "a handful of endless, identical tasks." Because of repetition, everything she does becomes too predictable and too carefully planned—exercises in banality. That's probably the point, but it doesn't make for a compelling picture—unlike Henry, the audience doesn't share the vision of "larger purpose," a vision that only a mad mind can see. Visually rich, though repetitious, DANCING IN THE DARK benefits from a very carefully composed soundtrack. In this case, it is the sounds excluded rather than included that arouse interest. During the exceptionally staged murder scene, the sound completely drops out as Henry, with her intense expression, plunges a kitchen knife into her husband, who is just slightly off-screen. After the murder has been committed, the sound returns, almost unnoticed. Henry is superb (relying on expressions and gestures over dialog), but her zombie state doesn't allow for much variation. Half the time she is expected to act like a real, flesh-and-blood housewife, while the remainder of the time she is a plastic representation of the housewife. Marr's extreme use of narration grows awkward and tiresome after just a few minutes. DANCING IN THE DARK opens with the song "Only You" (Buck Ram, Ande Rand, performed by The Platters) and ends with the misused Erik Satie piece "Trois Gnossiennes." Chantal Akerman, in her critically praised 1975 Belgian film JEANNE DIELMAN, 23 QUAI DE COMMERCE, 1080 BRUXELLES, more successfully covered much of the same territory as DANCING IN THE DARK.

p, Anthony Kramreither; d, Leon Marr; w, Leon Marr (based on the novel by Joan Barfoot); ph, Vic Sarin; m, Erik Satie; ed, Tom Berner; art d, Lillian Sarafinchan; m/l, Buck Ram, Ande Rand; makeup, Julian Chojnacki.

Drama Cas. (PR:C MPAA:PG-13)

DANDELION (SEE: TAMPOPO, 1986, Jap.)

DANGEROUS ORPHANS† (1986, New Zealand) 90m New Zealand Film Commission–Cinepro c

Peter Stephens *(O'Malley)*, Jennifer Ward-Lealand *(Costello)*, Michael Hurst *(Moir)*, Ross Girven *(Rossi)*, Peter Bland *(Jacobs)*, Ian Mune *(Hanna)*, Zac Wallace *(Scanlan)*, Grant Tilly *(Beck)*, Ann Pacey *(Mooney)*, Peter Vere-Jones *(Handesman)*, Michael Haigh *(Dutchman)*, Des Kelly *(O'Malley, Sr.)*, Tim Lee *(Krebs)*, Michala Hanas *(Anna Hanna)*, Toby Laing *(Young O'Malley)*, Alexis Banas *(Young Rossi)*, Edin Cox *(Young Moir)*, Miles Tilly *(Pope)*, Kevin Wilson *(Inspector Lucas)*.

Stephens is a young man who has waited years to avenge the murder of his father at the hands of a large, well-organized drug-running operation. He teams up with two other orphans and begins picking apart the operation with selective killings and robberies, while simultaneously infiltrating the organization to get close to the real bosses. Fast-moving, suspenseful, and featuring an acting turn by director Ian Mune (CAME A HOT FRIDAY, BRIDGE TO NOWHERE).

p, Don Reynolds; d, John Laing; w, Kevin Smith; ph, Warrick Attewell

(Colorfilm N.Z.); m, Jonathan Crayford; ed, Michael Horton; prod d, Ralph Davies.

Crime Drama (PR:O MPAA:NR)

DANGEROUSLY CLOSE**½ (1986) 95m Golan-Globus/Cannon c

John Stockwell *(Randy McDevitt)*, J. Eddie Peck *(Donny Lennox)*, Carey Lowell *(Julie)*, Bradford Bancroft *(Krooger Raines)*, Don Michael Paul *(Ripper)*, Thom Mathews *(Brian Rigletti)*, Jerry Dinome *(Lang Bridges)*, Madison Mason *(Corrigan)*, Anthony DeLongis *(Smith Raddock)*, Carmen Argenziano *(Matty)*, Miguel Nunez *(Leon Biggs)*, Dedee Pfeiffer *(Nikki)*, Karen Witter *(Betsy)*, Greg Finley *(Morelli)*, Debra Berger *(Ms. Hoffman)*, Angel Tompkins *(Ms. Waters)*.

A high school in a Southern California suburb is plagued by drugs, graffiti artists, and bad attitude until a group of WASPish, affluent students organize themselves into "The Sentinels," who don hoods to conduct kangaroo courts and torture sessions against the undesirable elements. Everything is all in good fun until some of the victims are murdered after the group lets them go. Suspicion falls obviously on Stockwell, the leader of the group, and his support by the student body begins to fall away. He decides that the best thing to do is get the press on his side, so he befriends Peck, editor of the school paper. Later, though, when a punk-rocker friend of Peck's (Krooger, in the film's best performance) disappears after standing up and speaking out about The Sentinels' fascist ways, Peck teams up with Stockwell's ex-girl friend to smash the gang. After a few fistfights, Peck discovers that the murders were actually committed by the group's Vietnam-veteran faculty advisor, Mason. But wait! Another plot twist reveals that it actually was Stockwell. It is always a fascinating experience to watch a film disintegrate before your eyes, and here we have another opportunity to observe this phenomenon. What starts out as a novel premise (although there was a made-for-TV film on a similar theme) turns into a routine action picture, with the most unlikely people turning into fierce fighters. The direction is slick (occasionally too slick) and the acting adequate, though none of this can save the film once it begins to go astray.

p, Harold Sobel; d, Albert Pyun; w, Scott Fields, John Stockwell, Marty Ross (based on a story by Marty Ross); ph, Walt Lloyd (TVC Color); m, Michael McCarty; ed, Dennis O'Connor; prod d, Marcia Hinds; art d, Bo Johnson; set d, Piers Plowden.

Crime Drama (PR:O MPAA:R)

DANILO TRELES, O FIMISMENOS ANDALOUSIANOS MOUSIKOS†
(1986, Gr.) 80m Greek Film Center-Stavros Tornes c (Trans: DANILO TRELES, THE FAMOUS ANDALUSIAN MUSICIAN)

Sotiria Leonardou *(Sotiria)*, Stelios Anastassiades *(The Fox Man)*, Aren Bee *(British Musician)*, Deedee Mafdul *(African Man)*, Roberto de Angelis, Francesco Calimera, Yannis Eliopoulos, Francois Stephanou, Elias Kanellis, Helen Staphanou, Danayota Lattas, Christos Marcopoulos, Yannis Kostoglou.

The title character Danilo Treles is an Andalusian musician who disappeared into the Greek mountains years before. Now a horde of characters, ranging from a blues player to a biologist, are searching for Treles, each guided by his/her own strange motivation.

p&d, Stavros Tornes; w, Charlotte Van Gelder, Stavros Tornes; ph, Yannis Daskalothanassis; m, Pepe de la Matrona, Aren Bee, Deedee Mafdul; ed, Spyros Provis; cos, Anastassia Arseni.

Comedy (PR:C MPAA:NR)

DANS UN MIROIR† (1986, Fr.) 65m Maison de la Culture de Grenoble bw-c (Trans: In a Mirror)

Anne Alvara *(Louise)*, Jean-Claude Wino *(Leonard)*, Melvil Popaud.

The 16mm DANS UN MIROIR is one of a handful of government-sponsored films that Raul Ruiz directed during the year, most of which were produced for French television. Following the same line of surrealistic logic as his other pictures (the best known being THREE CROWNS OF A SAILOR and THE CITY OF PIRATES), Ruiz has two people—Alvara and Wino—living in a Gothic house discussing a prospective assault on an acquaintance who is perhaps Alvara's brother. An unnaturally gifted youngster, Popaud, who is deeply interested in literature, shares the house with the pair. After the adults discuss a multitude of obscurities, their characters are blown away by a gust of wind. They appear to have been the cerebral creations of Popaud. As with all Ruiz films, a plot description is futile and ends up looking ridiculous. The art of Ruiz lies in his eclectic command of his own unique visual language, which, if not always comprehensible, is consistently exciting. Unfortunately, most of Ruiz's films never make it even as far as U.S. art-houses, only surfacing at film festivals with less-than-satisfying frequency.

d, Raul Ruiz; w, ([uncredited] based on the novel by Louis Rene Des Forets); ph, Acacio de Almeida; ed, Rodolpho Wedeles; prod d, Alain Hecquard.

Fantasy/Drama (PR:O MPAA:NR)

DARK AGE† (1986, Aus.) F.G. Film Productions c

John Jarratt, Nikki Coghill, Max Phipps, Ray Meagher, David Gulpilil.

Darwin, a city of Northern Australia, is sent into chaos when a wild crocodile threatens the town's inhabitants. As a result, tensions between the white and aboriginal locals explode.

d, Arch Nicholson; w, Tony Morphett, Sonia Borg, Stephen Cross; ph, Andrew Lesnie.

Thriller (PR:O MPAA:NR)

DARK NIGHT† (1986, Taiwan/Hong Kong) 115m Goodyear c

Sue Ming-Ming *(Li Ling)*, Hsu Ming *(Yeh Yuen)*, Chang Kuo-Chu *(Hwong Cheng-teh)*, Emily Y. Chang *(Mrs. Niu)*.

A Taiwanese housewife, bored with her constantly absent husband, finds herself drawn to her spouse's closest pal. Though she realizes that an affair will bring nothing but troubles, the woman enters into a new romance after a period of hesitance. Based on a popular, steamy Taiwanese novel, this marked writer/director Tan's film debut. He had previously worked as a film critic in Los Angeles, and DARK NIGHT saw its American debut at his alma mater, UCLA. (In Chinese; English subtitles.)

p, Hsu Li-Hwa; d, Fred Tan (based on the novel by Sue Li-Eng); ph, Yang Wei-Han; m, Peter Chang; ed, Chen Po-Wen; art d, Yu Wei-Yen; cos, Yu Wei-Yen.

Drama (PR:O MPAA:NR)

DAS HAUS AM FLUSS**½ (1986, E. Ger.) 88m DEFA c (Trans: House on the Riverside; House by the River; The House on the River)

Katrin Sass *(Agnes Eckert)*, Manfred Gorr *(Jupp Eckert)*, Jutta Wachowiak *(Mother Voss)*, Rolf Hoppe *(Director Husgen)*, Corinna Harfouch *(Emmi Voss)*, Johanna Schall *(Lena Brinken)*, Sylvester Groth *(Heinz Husgen)*, Peter Zimmerman *(W. Tiedemann)*, Werner Codemann *(Schimmelpfennig)*, Mathis Schrader *(Ferdinand Belz)*, Arianne Borbach *(Lisbeth Voss)*, Hermann Beyer *(Piter Dressen)*, Eckhard Becker *(Gestapo Man)*.

Based on the story "The Russian Pelt" written by renowned East German author Friedrich Wolf in 1942, DAS HAUS AM FLUSS concentrates on the moral decay and guilt that destroy a small family of fisherfolk who live near a river just outside wartime Berlin. The film begins as Harfouch, one of matriarch Wachowiak's daughters, receives a package containing a Ukrainian peasant blouse sent by her fiance, who is fighting on the Eastern front. Harfouch is elated by the gift and dances happily for having heard from her beloved. Her older sister, Sass, works at a nearby factory, as does her husband, Gorr, who has been given a deferment from service because the factory produces goods essential to the war effort. Tension at the factory is both conspicuous and personal, with several sabotage attacks having recently taken place. In addition, the owner's decadent son, Groth, has become more explicit about his sexual desire for Sass. Although somewhat intrigued, Sass resists Groth's advances, but the junior tycoon persists. Capitalizing on the fact that the local Gestapo chief covets his own fiancee, Groth strikes a depraved deal in which Gorr's deferment is revoked in return for an evening of carnal pleasure between the Gestapo chief and Groth's fiancee.

Once Gorr is sent to the front, Sass can no longer resist Groth's advances. She engages in a guilt-filled affair with the sleazy heir and even accepts the gift of a beautiful Russian fur piece. Meanwhile, Harfouch learns that her beloved has been killed in action. Nearly catatonic with despair, she hangs herself. Soon after, Gorr returns from the front, having lost a leg in battle. Although insecure and embarrassed over his amputated leg, he proudly presents his wife with a fur pelt he brought back from Russia. Although wracked with guilt and despair over her tryst with Groth, Sass becomes determined to salvage her marriage. But Groth does not give up so easily, and in a confrontation with Gorr and Sass, he declares he will turn Gorr in to the Gestapo for committing treasonable activities while a soldier at the front, and for complicity in the sabotage of the factory (Sass' young brother, a Communist, is the saboteur). Finally at her breaking point, Sass kills the arrogant and manipulative Groth, but the Gestapo chief and his men have surrounded the house and wait patiently outside the door (a chilling and unforgettable image).

Although nicely acted and well-produced, DAS HAUS AM FLUSS is an unremarkable addition to the plethora of metaphorical act-of-contrition films produced by Germans (especially those in East Germany) since the end of the war (the late 1970s gave us the most internationally recognized output with Rainer Werner Fassbinder's THE MARRIAGE OF MARIA BRAUN, Volker Schlondorff's THE TIN DRUM, and Hans-Jurgen Syberberg's OUR HITLER among the most notable). Oddly, the film that bears the most resemblance to DAS HAUS AM FLUSS is the Italian-West German co-production of THE DAMNED, directed by Luchino Visconti, which follows an ultra-decadent family of industrialists as they are slowly destroyed by collusion with the treacherous Nazis. These films do have important statements to make and are sociologically fascinating, but by 1986, German filmmakers, both East and West, have begun repeating themselves and are in desperate need of exploring new territory. DAS HAUS AM FLUSS was shown at film festivals in the U.S.

d&w, Roland Graf (based on the story "The Russian Pelt" by Friedrich Wolf); ph, Roland Dressel; m, Gunther Fischer; ed, Monika Schindler; set d, Alfred Hirschmeier.

Drama (PR:O MPAA:NR)

DAS SCHWEIGEN DES DICHTERS† (1986, Ger.) 98m Edgar Reitz–Westdeutscher Rundfunk/Filmverlag der Autoren c (Trans: The Poet's Silence)

Jakov Lind *(Jacob)*, Len Ramras *(Gideon)*, Daniel Kedem *(Gideon as a Child)*, Towje Kleiner, Vladimir Weigl, Barbara Lass, Gudrun Weichenhahn, Roberto Polac, Jacob Ben-Sira, Peter Freistadt, Mischa Natan.

Poet-writer Jakov Lind stars as a famous Israeli poet who, in the twilight of his life, has given up his art without ever revealing why. Although he remains at his job as a newspaper editor, he tells those who ask that he must focus his energies on raising his 17-year-old "borderline" retarded son, Ramras, who was born to Lind's wife late in life. Lind's wife never quite recovered from the pregnancy and died after a long illness. Despite this explanation, there are indications that other factors conspire against Lind's inspiration as well. Lind's brother was recently blinded in the Sinai War, and his daughter, newly married to a college-educated man who can't find a job, is seriously considering moving to Canada with her husband. All these troubling events have crippled his will to create. Things begin to change, however, when the retarded Ramras learns that his father was once a famous poet. The boy assumes that he is responsible for Lind's lack of inspiration and takes to leaving sharpened pencils and paper for his father. Ramras then leaves the house for the day so as not to be a bother. As the days go by Ramras becomes more and more confident and self-sufficient. This gives Lind the freedom he needs to retire from his editing job, sell the house, and spend the rest of his days traveling, free of any guilt or sorrow. The film ends as Lind is inspired to write poetry again. DAS SCHWEIGEN DES DICHTERS was Germany's official entry at the Venice Film Festival and was shot in Israel.

p, Edgar Reitz; d&w, Peter Lilienthal (based on a story by Abraham B. Yohoshua); ph, Justus Pankau; m, Claus Bantzer; ed, Siegrun Jager; art d, Charlie Leon, Franz Bauer; cos, Rina Doron.

Drama   **(PR:C MPAA:NR)**

DAYS OF HELL†   (1986, Ital.) 88m Mary/Gel International c (I GIORNI
                                                              DELL'INFERNO)

Conrad Nichols *(Capt. Williams)*, Kiwako Harada *(Samantha)*, Werner Pochath *(Prof. Sanders)*, Richard Raymond *(Russ)*, Steve Eliot [Stelio Candelli] *(Gen. Smith)*, Lawrence Richmond *(Amin)*, Howard Ross *(Grayson)*.

Four soldiers-of-fortune are enlisted by the U.S. government to rescue a father-and-daughter team of journalists who have uncovered evidence of Russian use of nerve gas in the Afghanistan War. What these intrepid mercenaries don't know is that the U.S. is in cahoots with the Soviets to hush up the whole thing, and that they will be betrayed once they locate the journalists. Nichols is the commander of the group, and he leads his men into Afghan territory via Iran, assuring safe passage by bringing in spare parts for fighter planes (an amazing coincidence, considering the scandal that broke right around the time of this film's video release). Things go so well that Nichols figures out that they're being set up, but they press on, locate Harada, the daughter of the journalist (who has already died from nerve gas exposure), and start back toward Pakistan and asylum. Harada dies on the way out, but the four commandos and Harada's sidekick (Larry Richmond, presumably the director's equally pseudonymous son) escape in a stolen Russian helicopter to tell the world. This new wrinkle in Italian action film—the Afghan setting—may be an attempt to preempt the proposed RAMBO III, supposedly taking Sylvester Stallone to the same area. DAYS OF HELL sidetracked being lumped with all the other Christmastime U.S. releases by avoiding the theaters altogether and going straight to video.

p, Eugenio Startari; d, Anthony Richmond [Tonino Ricci]; w, Tito Carpi, Tonino Ricci; ph, Giacomo Testa (Luciano Vittori Color); m, Francesco De Masi; ed, Vincenzo Tomassi; spec eff, Paolo Ricci; stunts, Neno Zamperla.

War Drama   **Cas.**   **(PR:O MPAA:NR)**

DE AANSLAG   (SEE: ASSAULT, 1986, Neth.)

DE L'ARGENTINE†   (1986, Fr./Brit.) 90m FR3-Out One c (Trans: About
                                                                 Argentina)

This non-traditional narrative chronicles the effect of the recently felled Argentinian military dictatorship on the innocent victims of that oppressive regime. The film mixes the honest confessions of torture victims with fictional stories: Galileo (as played by a woman) trying to defend his theories before the Inquisition, and a movie star in discussion with Eva Peron's real-life dress designer. Also included are sequences involving a child of the *desaparecidos*, the people kidnaped and murdered by the dictatorship, whose orphaned children were subsequently given in for adoption to complying Argentinian families.

p,d&w, Werner Schroeter; ph, Werner Schroeter, Carlos Bernando Wajsman; m, Gustav Mahler; ed, Catherine Brasier, Claudio Martinez.

Drama   **(PR:O MPAA:NR)**

DE MISLUKKING   (SEE: FAILURE, THE, 1986, Neth.)

DE VAL VAN PATRICIA HAGGERSMITH†   (1986, Neth.) 90m Frans van
                               de Staak c (Trans: The Fall of Patricia Haggersmith)

Helene Kampvereen, Gerald Stadwijk, Peter Zegveld, Maureen Birney.

Not having made a film for several years, 1960s experimental filmmaker Mattijn Seip broke a long silence with his first feature-length production, a psychological study of a woman struggling to obtain some control over her life. The film premiered at the Rotterdam Film Festival.

p, Frans van de Staak; d&w, Mattijn Seip; ph, Frans Bromet; m, Herman de Wit, Eva Bouman; ed, Marcus Nijssen.

Drama   **(PR:C-O MPAA:NR)**

DE WISSELWACHTER†   (1986, Neth.) 95m Jos Stelling Filmprodukties/
                                         Concorde c (Trans: The Pointsman)

Jim Van Der Woude *(Pointsman)*, Stephane Excoffier *(Woman)*, John

Kraaykamp *(Engineer)*, Josse De Pauw *(Postman)*, Tom Van Dort *(Assistant Engineer)*.

Van Der Woude is an unassuming railroad switchman who lives and works near a small, isolated country town. Despite the infrequency of rail traffic in his area, and the consequent boredom of the job, Van Der Woude remains steadfast. His monotonous life undergoes an unexpected change, however, when Excoffier, a well-dressed woman, inadvertently gets off at Van Der Woude's stop and decides to remain. The railman is soon in love, but De Pauw, a local postal official, is also attracted to Excoffier and he will stop at nothing to get her. His zealous pursuit ultimately results in Van Der Woude's demise.

p, Stanley Hillebrandt; d, Jos Stelling; w, George Brugmans, Hans De Wolf (based on the novel by Jean-Paul Franssens); ph, Frans Bromet, Theo Van de Sande, Paul Van Den Bos, Goert Giltaij; m, Michel Mulders; ed, Rimko Haanstra; art d, Gert Brinkers.

Drama   **(PR:O MPAA:NR)**

DEAD-END DRIVE-IN*½   (1986, Aus.) 92m Springvale–New South
                                                              Wales/NW c

Ned Manning *(Crabs)*, Natalie McCurry *(Carmen)*, Peter Whitford *(Thompson)*, Wilbur Wide *(Hazza)*, Brett Climo *(Don)*, Ollie Hall *(Frank)*, Sandie Lillingston *(Beth)*, Lyn Collingwood *(Fay)*, Nikki McWatters *(Shirl)*, Melissa Davies *(Narelle)*, Dave Gibson *(Dave)*, Margi Di Ferranti *(Jill)*, Desiree Smith *(Tracey)*, Murray Fahey *(Mickey)*, Jeremy Shadlow *(Jeff)*, John Patterson *(1st Punk)*, Ken Snodgrass *(1st Cop at Accident)*, Alan McQueen *(2nd Cop at Accident)*, Garry Weston, Bill Lyal *(Cops at Drive-In)*, Bernadette Foster *(Momma)*, Ron Sinclair *(News Reporter)*, Ghandi McIntyre *(Indian)*, David Jones *(TV Newsreader)*.

In the near future (only 1990) the world economy has collapsed and Australia has been racked by massive unemployment, crime, and rioting. Cars are the ultimate status symbol and gangs of Karboys roam the streets destroying cars and strip-

ping them for parts. In this mean world Manning is a young man doing his best to survive, avoiding the Karboys and worshipping his older brother, Hall, who works one of the most dangerous jobs in this brave new world, tow truck driver. Manning wants to follow in his footsteps, despite his brother's warnings about the dangers of the job. One night he borrows Hall's '56 Chevy and takes girl friend McCurry to see a movie at the Star Drive-In, but while they have sex in the car, the rear wheels are stolen, stranding them. Manning follows the thieves and discovers they are policemen, but when he tries to report this to manager Whitford, he is told to come back in the morning.

The next day dawns and Manning and McCurry look around the bleak drive-in and see acres of cars occupied by hundreds of punkish teenagers. They again try to complain to Whitford, but he tells them he can do nothing until the government comes for them. Then he gives them meal tickets they can exchange for cheeseburgers and the like at the drive-in snack shop. Slowly it dawns on Manning exactly what is happening. The government, invoking "emergency powers" has established a series of these facilities, designed to lure in unemployed youths and keep them pacified with junk food, drugs, birth control pills, and nightly exploitation films. McCurry readily falls in with this carefree life style and is content to gossip with friends and have her hair done, but Manning refuses to accept his confinement, and he remains aloof from most of his fellow inmates. Constantly he plots his escape, but his initial plans are dashed when Whitford has his engine stripped. Another influx of prisoners, all of them Asian immigrants, arrives in the camp and the white inmates begin organizing a racist committee to keep them in their place. Manning also refuses to join in this and uses their meeting as a cover to steal a truck and make a dash for freedom. A chase ensues all through the drive-in lot, destroying the truck Manning is driving, but after forcing Whitford to erase his name from the computer, Manning grabs a police truck and jumps it right over the manager's office, through a neon sign, and onto the highway back home.

One of the most interesting *(and least unlikely)* post-civilization films of the last couple of years, DEAD-END DRIVE-IN is reminiscent of the original MAD MAX, and like that film it is a testament to the availability of cheap junker used cars and completely insane Australian stuntmen. Manning is a refreshing hero, a runtish fellow who has his own ideas about what he wants out of life and who simply refuses to accept the mindless existence the government offers him for free. He is a sharp contrast to McCurry, for whom these installations are custom-made, and who refuses to leave when Manning makes his big break.

Over 300 wrecked cars were used to create the setting, and the production design is a triumph of post-modern decay. Production values are high and the performances are all good. The film does lag in some parts, and Manning seems awfully slow about figuring out the sinister purpose of the drive-in, but the film works well and the final breakout, climaxed by one of the most spectacular stunts ever pulled, is satisfyingly cathartic. Since MAD MAX first turned up in 1979 and pointed the way, the screens of the world have been flooded with post-civilization car-chase fantasies from the U.S., Italy, and others, but here it is the Australians who prove again that they can do it better than anyone.

p, Andrew Williams; d, Brian Trenchard-Smith; w, Peter Smalley (based on the short story "Crabs" by Peter Carey); ph, Paul Murphy (Eastmancolor); m, Frank Strangio; ed, Alan Lake, Lee Smith; prod d, Larry Eastwood; art d, Nick McCallum; cos, Anthony James; makeup, Lloyd James; stunts, Guy Norris.

Science Fiction/Action   Cas.   (PR:O MPAA:R)

DEAD END KIDS**½   (1986) 90m Ikon–Mabou Mines c

Ellen McElduff *(Television Host/Army Stenographer/Schoolteacher)*, Ruth Maleczech *(Madame Curie)*, George Bartenieff *(Faust/Gen. Groves)*, David Brisbin *(Nightclub Comic/Gen. Farrell)*, B-St. John Scofield *(Lecturer in Lab Coat/Devil)*, Frederick Neumann *(Alchemist/Academician)*, Terry O'Reilly *(Magician/Devil)*, Greg Mehrten *(Television Technician/Devil)*.

Cinema adaptations of works that are inherently theatrical present a challenge to any director, particularly one closely associated with the original presentation. "Dead End Kids" was an unusual production, staged in 1980 by New York's Mabou Mines theatrical company. It combined blackout sketches, found film footage, and cuttings from Johann Wolfgang von Goethe's classic play "Faust" to create an avant-garde examination of the effect of the atomic bomb on American culture. The filmed version is a less successful work, an obvious statement rather than subtle satire. Essentially, the play's collage structure is retained, along with many of the same sequences and actors. Among the highlights are a cinematic juxtaposition of the real Madame Curie (via still photos) with an actress portraying the scientist. Another sequence, in homage to the B musicals of the 1940s, features Ellen McElduff singing about exploding atom bombs.

With its incorporation of found material, DEAD END KIDS often resembles the 1982 compilation documentary THE ATOMIC CAFE. Unlike this earlier counterpart, however, DEAD END KIDS lacks unity within its structure. Other than the basic theme addressing the dangers of nuclear armaments, the film is too disjointed. Akalaitis originally had no intention of transmuting this production to film, and for good reason. The material was originally staged in a small Off-Broadway theater, and by bringing it to a larger format, immediacy and intimacy were lost. DEAD END KIDS was three years in the making, though the actual shooting period was three weeks. Akalaitis was given $150,000 by the National Endowment for the Arts, then set out to raise additional funds to finance the work. Backers included the Public Broadcasting System, and private donations from antinuclear activists and supporters of the Mabou Mines company were secured. One supporter, in a generous effort to help defray expenses, allowed the filmmakers free run of her home for a day of shooting.

p, Marian Godfrey, Monty Diamond; d&w, JoAnne Akalaitis; ph, Judy Irola; m, David Byrne, Philip Glass; ed, Darren Kloomok; prod d, John Arnone; cos, Kristi Zea.

Drama/Comedy   (PR:C-O MPAA:NR)

DEADLY FRIEND**   (1986) 92m Pan Arts–Layton/WB c

Matthew Laborteaux *(Paul)*, Kristy Swanson *(Samantha)*, Anne Twomey *(Jeannie Conway)*, Michael Sharrett *(Tom)*, Richard Marcus *(Harry)*, Anne Ramsey *(Elvira Williams)*, Lee Paul *(Police Sgt. Volchek)*, Russ Martin *(Dr. Johanson)*, Andrew Roperto *(Carl Denton)*, Charles Fleischer *(Voice of Bee Bee)*, Robin Nuyen *(Thief)*, Frank Cavestani *(Angry Resident)*, Merritt Olsen *(CAT Scan Technician)*, William H. Faeth, M.D. *(Doctor in Sam's Room)*, Joel Hile *(Deputy)*, Tom Spratley *(Neighbor)*, Jim Ishida *(Coroner)*.

Horror director Wes Craven's first film since his 1984 triumph A NIGHTMARE ON ELM STREET is a big disappointment. Something of an uneasy cross between the classic FRANKENSTEIN and the 1986 cute-robot hit SHORT CIRCUIT, the film begins as a brilliant young teenager, Laborteaux, and his mother, Twomey, move into a new community near the university that has given the boy a grant to continue his research on artificial intelligence. Laborteaux's crowning achievement is a robot he has named Bee Bee, which, while obeying verbal commands from the boy, also can learn and think for itself. Laborteaux quickly makes friends with local paper boy Sharrett and the pretty next-door-neighbor girl Swanson. Unfortunately, Swanson's alcoholic father abuses her and her turmoil is a constant source of frustration for Laborteaux and his mother. One afternoon the friends accidentally lose their basketball in the yard of paranoid old lady Ramsey, who has erected a cyclone fence around her property. When the shotgun-toting woman refuses to give the ball back, Bee Bee the robot wants revenge, but Laborteaux stops his creation from causing trouble. By Halloween night, however, Laborteaux allows himself and the robot to become involved in a prank against Ramsey that ends in disaster when the woman destroys the robot with two blasts of her shotgun. Shortly thereafter, on Thanksgiving night, Swanson's father pushes her down the stairs and the doctors declare the girl brain dead. The distraught Laborteaux enlists the aid of the wary Sharrett, and they steal Swanson's body just after life-support systems are turned off. Laborteaux implants Bee Bee's computer chips into Swanson's brain, and the girl comes back to life. Although alive, Swanson is mute and behaves like the robot, right down

to Bee Bee's incredible strength (she walks with her arms stretched out in front of her and her fingers shaped like the robot's claws). Not only does Swanson move like Bee Bee, she has the same revenge impulses as Bee Bee and she soon embarks on a murder spree, killing her father and Ramsey, with Laborteaux frantically trying to keep the cops from closing in on her. Eventually the girl-robot is cornered and police are forced to shoot her.

Just what Craven was trying to do with this material is anybody's guess. The first half of the film feels like a standard teenager film with the robot thrown in as a twist, and then it turns into a rather dull teenage mad-scientist romp.

Craven's direction is nothing more than workmanlike, and it appears that he threw two gratuitous nightmare sequences into the mix out of sheer boredom. Both sequences work well (they are the most frightening parts of the film) but they are poorly integrated into the narrative and this makes them all the more annoying, for it seems as if Craven is desperately trying to generate some excitement and has fallen back on former glory by echoing A NIGHTMARE ON ELM STREET. What strengths the film does have come from the likable performances of Laborteaux, Swanson, Sharrett, and Twomey (Ramsey makes a memorable grouch as well), and Craven's usual detailed depiction of suburban life. There are scant amounts of gore here, but one big splash when Swanson decapitates Ramsey with a basketball (the effect is so cartoonish that it is unintentionally funny). Which leads us to the one puzzling point of the film: Why does a normal teenage girl inherit the incredible strength of a mechanical machine if all she received from the latter was its computer-chip brain? Maybe Laborteaux can explore that scientific phenomenon in graduate school.

p, Robert M. Sherman; d, Wes Craven; w, Bruce Joel Rubin (based on the novel *Friend* by Diana Henstell); ph, Philip Lathrop (Panavision); m, Charles Bernstein; ed, Michael Eliot; prod d, Daniel Lomino; set d, Roy Barnes; spec eff, Peter Albiez; makeup, Mike Hancock; stunts, Terry Leonard, Tony Cecere.

Horror   Cas.   (PR:O MPAA:R)

DEATH OF A SOLDIER***½   (1986, Aus.) 93m Suatu/Scotti Brothers c

James Coburn *(Maj. Patrick Danneberg)*, Reb Brown *(Edward J. Leonski)*, Bill Hunter *(Detective Sgt. Adams)*, Maurie Fields *(Detective Sgt. Martin)*, Belinda Davey *(Margot Saunders)*, Max Fairchild *(Maj. William Fricks)*, Jon Sidney *(Gen. MacArthur)*, Michael Pate *(Maj. Gen. Sutherland)*, Randall Berger *(Gallo)*, Nell Johnson *(Maisie)*, Mary Charleston *(Pauline Thompson)*, John Cottone, Jeanette Leigh, Rowena Mohr, Duke Bannister, John Murphy, Brian Adams, Arthur Sherman, Terry Donovan, Ken Wayne, Ron Pinnell.

In 1942, Australia was hard on the defense against the Japanese in New Guinea, and Japanese bombers were hitting the northern coast of the country. The U.S. was still reeling after its Philippine debacle, and the American troops pouring into Australia were green recruits whose cocky attitudes did not sit well with the war-weary locals. The inherent tension in this situation was heightened when a series of women were strangled by an American GI. While Australian police and American MPs raced to find the murderer, General Douglas MacArthur saw to it that, when caught, the culprit would be tried under an Army court martial and then hanged, a measure that was designed to restore American credibility with the Australian public. When finally caught, the killer, Eddie Leonski, of New York, was clearly insane, but the Army would hear none of it, and a court martial condemned and hanged him right on schedule. Such is the factual base for this occasionally annoying, but generally fascinating, Australian production by French-born, Australian-raised Philippe Mora, a U.S. resident for some years at the time of the film's release.

Most of the film details the murders, with Brown a chilling, childlike killer who pleads with women to "sing for me. I want your voice" as he tightens his grip on their throats. Coburn is an Army major in the Military Police. At first he works to catch the killer, while trying to keep a lid on the murders until the culprit is apprehended. With tensions at a peak, a trainload of American soldiers encounters some battle-weary Australians on a station platform. Insults are traded, a shot is fired, and soon a full-fledged gun battle is going, leaving dozens dead. This too is hushed up, with the injured sent to special quarantine wards under tight security. Finally, after three women are murdered, Brown's tentmate turns him in. Coburn is chosen to assist in Brown's defense, although MacArthur has already determined he is to hang. Psychiatrists examine Brown, who tells them

that he just wanted the girls' voices, then proceeds to sing in a broken falsetto to show why. This little display convinces Coburn of his client's insanity, but the Army doctors find what they are told to find, and Brown faces the court proven sane. The defense counsel is shipped off somewhere and Coburn has to take over. He continually tries to prove that Brown was not responsible for his actions, but the court ignores him, and as Coburn tries to appeal to the Supreme Court, Brown is hanged. A crawl at the end of the film tells that the postwar examination of the case led to the creation of the Uniform Code of Military Justice to protect American servicemen from having their rights denied.

Coburn is quite good in his first decent part in recent memory, and Brown is more than effective as the gentle but psychotic Leonski, who asks Coburn to hold his hand when the verdict is read, and who goes cheerfully to the noose. The direction is occasionally too flashy, with exotic lighting and slow motion for no real reason. The picture of wartime Australia is fascinating (and certainly more realistic than in the atrocious REBEL), and the subject, the corruption of justice for political ends, is one that has eternal importance.

p, David Hannay, William Nagle; d, Philippe Mora; w, William Nagle; ph, Louis Irving (Panavision); m, Alan Zavod; ed, John Scott; art d, Geoff Richardson; cos, Alexandra Tynan.

Crime Drama   Cas.   (PR:O MPAA:NR)

DEATH OF THE HEART, THE†   (1986, Brit.) 109m Granada c

Jojo Cole *(Portia Quayne)*, Patricia Hodge *(Anna Quayne)*, Nigel Havers *(Thomas Quayne)*, Wendy Hiller *(Matchett)*, Miranda Richardson *(Daphne)*, Daniel Chatto *(Eddie)*, Robert Hardy *(Maj. Brutt)*, Jonathan Hyde *(St. Quentin Miller)*, Phyllis Calvert *(Mrs. Hecomb)*, Samantha Gates *(Lilian)*, Damaris Hayman *(Miss Paullie)*, Meryl Hampton *(Phyllis)*, Sophie Thompson *(Doris)*.

In 1937 England, Cole is a 16-year-old orphaned girl forced to live with her uncle Havers and aunt Hodge. Hodge is not entirely faithful to her husband and is carrying on with (among others) Chatto. Ignorant of her aunt's philandering, Cole falls for Chatto, a roguish young man who likes to insult her in front of her peers. Finally Cole leaves this environment, seeking assistance from the somewhat impoverished Hardy. In an effort to settle the situation, Hodge and Havers invite Hyde over to dinner, hoping this urbane idiot will be able to help them.

p, June Wyndham-Davies; d, Peter Hammond; w, Derek Mahon (based on the novel by Elizabeth Bowen); ph, Ray Goode; m, Geoffrey Burgon; ed, David Reece; art d, Peter Phillips; cos, Anne Salisbury.

Comedy/Drama   (PR:C-O MPAA:NR)

DEATH SENTENCE½**   (1986, Pol.) 104m Film Polski–Silesia/Sphinx c
                                                    (WYROK SMIERCI)

Doris Kunstmann *(Christine)*, Wojciech Wysocki *(Smukly)*, Jerzy Bonczak *(Nurek)*, Stanislaw Igar *(Von Dehl)*, Stawromira Lozinska *(Zyta)*, Erich Thiede *(Heinrich Himmler)*, Holger Mahlich *(Hans Frank)*.

In wartorn Poland of 1943, a few villagers of a Nazi-occupied area form an underground league to fight their oppressors. Wysocki is a member of this hit squad, knocking off Nazis and villagers who inform to German authorities. He falls in love with Kunstmann, a cabaret singer who is the mistress of a German officer. She is next on his list of victims, and despite his emotional feelings, Wysocki dispatches her. The film suffers from stock portraits of evil Nazis and too-good-to-be-true freedom fighters, but director Orzechowski manages to give his story enough surprising twists to make it work. DEATH SENTENCE was shot in Poland in 1981, shortly before the government imposition of martial law. It took five years for it to hit a U.S. screen and this is the first of Orzechowski's films to be shown here. (In Polish; English subtitles.)

d&w, Witold Orzechowski; ph, Kazimierz Konrad; m, Andrzej Korzynski.

War Drama   (PR:O MPAA:NR)

DEATHMASK†   (1986) 103m Art Theater Guild/Prism Entertainment c
                                                    (AKA: UNKNOWN)

Farley Granger *(Doug Andrews)*, Lee Bryant *(Jane Andrews)*, John McCurry *(Jim O'Brien)*, Arch Johnson *(Dr. Riordan)*, Barbara Bingham *(Suzy Andrews)*,

Ruth Warrick *(Beatrice Van den Berg)*, Danny Aiello *(Capt. Mike Gress)*, Veronica Hart *(Victoria Howe)*, John Calonius, Erika Katz, Kelly Nichols, R. Bolla.

An interesting film that probably deserved better distribution, DEATHMASK opens in 1970 as coroner's investigator Granger is assigned to look into the case of an unidentified 4-year-old boy found dead in a cardboard box in a forest. Because the case touches him personally (recalling the drowning death of his own daughter), his efforts to learn who the dead boy was become an obsessive quest. Ten years later he is still on the case, carrying around a death mask made from the boy's corpse as his tangible link to him, and disregarding the disintegration of his own family around him. Finally he is led to Hart, who confesses that she accidentally killed her son in a fit of jealousy over the affairs of her husband. In the end, freed of his obsession, Granger tosses the mask into the ocean. Surprisingly good performances by Granger and one-time porn queen Hart, who appears in a flashback sequence with two other skinflick stalwarts, Kelly Nichols and R. Bolla. Shot in 1983, the film briefly played Phoenix in 1984 before finally emerging on video this year.

p, Louis K. Sher; d, Richard Friedman; w, Jeffrey Goldenberg, Richard Friedman; ph, Yuri Denysenko (Movielab Color); m, Robert Ruggieri; ed, Ian Maitland; art d, James Sherman.

Crime Drama   Cas.   (PR:O MPAA:NR)

DEBAJO DEL MUNDO†   (1986, Arg./Czech.) (Trans: Under the World)

The first film produced jointly by Czechoslovakia and Argentina deals with an immigrant family in Argentina.

d, Beda Ocampo Feijoo, Juan Bautista Stagnaro.

DEBELI I MRSAVI†   (1986, Yugo.) Union (Trans: Fat and Thin)

Milan Gutovic, Radmila Zivkovic, Velimir Bata Zivojinovic, Tatjana Stepanovic, Dragan Zario.

d, Svetislav Bata Prelic; w, Leon Kovke; ph, Zoran Hochstratter; m, Vojislav Voki Kostic; set d, Nemanja Petrovic.

DEBSHISHU†   (1986, India) 100m National Film Development Corp. of India bw-c (Trans: The Child God)

Smita Patil, Sadhu Meher, Rohini Hattangady, Om Puri, Sushanta Sanyal, Shyamalal Jalan.

A poor couple, their home and possessions washed away by a killer flood, arrive in a new town where they find their long-abandoned child, who was born with three heads. The child is now a local deity being exploited by a confidence artist who bilks the locals of their money. Wanting a piece of the action, the father tries to get his child back, and when that fails, he demands that his wife bear him another. A parable of political corruption, the tragic consequences of superstition, and the exploitation of the poor, DEBSHISHU is shot in color with flashbacks to the flood scenes photographed in black-and-white.

d&w, Uptlendu Chakraborty; ph, Soumendu Roy; m, Uptlendu Chakraborty.

Drama   (PR:C MPAA:NR)

DECLARATIE DE DRAGOSTE†   (1986, Rumania) 99m Studio 3-Romaniafilm c (Trans: Declaration of Love)

Teodora Mares *(Ioana Popa)*, Adrian Paduraru *(Alexander Birsan)*, Tamara Buciuceanu *(Mihaela)*, Ion Caramitru, Cristina Deleanu, Carmen Enea, Dorel Visan, Florin Chiriac, Adela Marculescu, Constantin Diplan.

Adolescent angst in Rumania as two teen lovers find it difficult to spend time together. Paduraru doesn't help the situation with his girl friend Mares any when he has a brief dalliance with Buciuceanu. After a fracas at school, Paduraru is punished by not being allowed to take a college entrance test. Next he's off to the mines for gainful employment, but finally ends up in Mares' arms in a blissful seaside ending.

d, Nicolae Corjos; w, George Sovu; ph, Doru Mitran (Orwocolor); ed, Elena Pantazica; art d, Ion Nedelcu

Drama   (PR:C MPAA:NR)

DECLINE OF THE AMERICAN EMPIRE, THE*½**   (1986, Can.) 101m Malo Film Group-National Film Board of Canada–Telefilm Canada–La Societe Generale Du Cinema Du Quebec-/Cineplex Odeon c (LE DECLIN DE L'EMPIRE AMERICAIN)

Pierre Curzi *(Pierre)*, Remy Girard *(Remy)*, Yves Jacques *(Claude)*, Daniel Briere *(Alain)*, Dominique Michel *(Dominique)*, Louise Portal *(Diane)*, Dorothee Berryman *(Louise)*, Genevieve Rioux *(Danielle)*, Gabriel Arcand *(Mario)*.

Four men swap stories of their sexual escapades while preparing an elaborate dinner, four women do the same while working out in a gym, and when the two groups come together mutual betrayals come to light and shatter some illusions. On the surface that is all that happens in this fine film, on its way to becoming the most successful Canadian export ever, but it is the sparkling wit of the dialog and the acutely observed jabs at our contemporary preoccupation with sex (the title refers to the trend of which this is symptomatic) that distinguish this film. The men are Girard and Curzi, professors of history at a Montreal university, and veteran philanderers; Jacques, their homosexual counterpart from the art history department (his favorite painter is Caravaggio, naturally); and Briere, a graduate assistant who acts as wide-eyed receptor to the bragging of his superiors. The women are Michel, head of the history department and no sexual slouch herself; Portal,

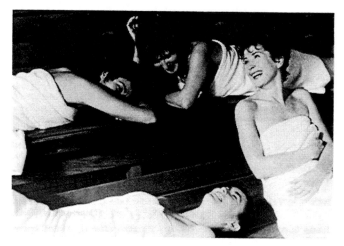

an associate professor and veteran of the Sexual Revolution who has now drifted into sadomasochism; Berryman, Girard's wife, blind to his infidelities; and Rioux, a young student who is Curzi's latest conquest. At one point the men are joined by a dangerous-looking character, Arcand (the director's brother) who is looking for Portal. He listens to the men's sex talk then leaves, bored. Michel and Portal take turns shocking Berryman with tales of one-night stands and lesbian experiences. Over their dinner of *coulibiac* they are again joined by Arcand, who is disappointed that nothing more interesting is going on: "They talked about sex all afternoon as if they were getting ready for an orgy. Instead the big deal is a fish pie," he says. Eventually Michel reveals that she has slept with Girard and Curzi, news that crushes Berryman. Later she overhears Michel telling Briere that Girard has slept with hundreds of women, including Berryman's own sister. She asks Jacques to hold her that night. Arcand and Portal make violent love, and Michel takes Briere to bed with her. In the morning they all separate after hugs while Girard tries to salvage his marriage.

The philosophy of the film is best summed up by a line uttered by Curzi: "Love—the kind that makes your heart race—lasts two years at best, then the compromises begin." Arcand was himself a history major and the characters in the film are composites of many of his friends and acquaintances. Arcand collected over 400 sexual anecdotes that he sorted out to stock his film. Perhaps the most valid criticism of the film is that its questions are too easy, its answers too pat, and its characters too similar. On the other hand, the ensemble performance is impeccable, the technical credits flawless, and the whole thing quite enjoyable. Nominated for 13 Genies (Canada's equivalent of the Oscar), it won eight,

including Best Picture, Best Director, Best Supporting Actor and Actress (Arcand and Portal, respectively). It was also nominated for an Academy Award for Best Foreign-Language Film. (In French; English subtitles.)

p, Rene Malo, Roger Frappier; d&w, Denys Arcand; ph, Guy Dufaux; m, Francois Dompierre (from themes by George Frederick Handel); ed, Monique Fortier; art d, Gaudeline Sauriol; cos, Denis Sperdouklis; makeup, Micheline Trepanier.

Drama   **(PR:O   MPAA:R)**

DELITTI†   (1986, Ital.) Cooperativa Mezzogiorno Nuovo d'Italia c (Trans: Crimes)

Saverio Vallone, Michela Miti, Gianfranco Gallo, Debora Ergas, Solvi Stubing, Alessandra Izzo, Lara Orfei.

When a philandering wife finds her lover growing insanely jealous, she decides to leave him. The lover's obsession with her has gone too far, and he has taken to mistreating her. After a few dalliances with other men, she decides to return to her old paramour despite their troubles. The woman's unsuspecting husband is glad to see the man back in his family's life, not realizing this friend is sleeping with his wife. The unknowing spouse is convinced that by showing faith in his wife, she will remain forever loyal to him.

d, Sergio Pastore; w, Giovanni Lenzi; ph, Domenico Paolercio; m, Maurizio De Angelis, Gianfranco De Angelis.

Drama   **(PR:O   MPAA:NR)**

DELTA FORCE, THE**   (1986) 129m Golan-Globus/Cannon c

Chuck Norris *(Maj. Scott McKay)*, Lee Marvin *(Col. Nick Alexander)*, Martin Balsam *(Ben Kaplan)*, Joey Bishop *(Harry Goldman)*, Robert Forster *(Abdul)*, Lainie Kazan *(Sylvia Goldman)*, George Kennedy *(Father O'Malley)*, Hanna Schygulla *(Ingrid)*, Susan Strasberg *(Debra Levine)*, Bo Svenson *(Capt. Campbell)*, Robert Vaughn *(Gen. Woolbridge)*, Shelley Winters *(Edie Kaplan)*, William Wallace *(Pete Peterson)*, Kim Delaney *(Sister Mary)*, David Menahem *(Mustafa)*, Assaf Dayan *(Raffi Amir)*.

This is an old-time action film which employs all the war cliches without a real war being present, except for the one invented by producers Golan and Globus. Norris, backed up by Marvin, is a one-man army who dispatches bloodthirsty terrorists with the same calm precision he brought to his martial-arts films. Golan, who directs without much imagination, manipulates contemporary head-

lines to get the public into the theaters for another "fantasy through firepower," RAMBO-style. In this case, a TWA airliner was hijacked by terrorists in Athens, then flown to Beirut, after which followed several trips back and forth to Algiers until the terror ended back in Beirut. The terrorists killed a U.S. Marine and had several passengers removed and held hostage in Beirut.

In the film, the terrorist operation is headed by Forster, who, once he instructs the plane to head for Beirut, separates the Jewish males from the rest of the passengers. Also picked out of the crowd are three young U.S. Navy recruits whom the terrorists insist on labeling Marines. While the plane is in the air, Marvin and Norris join their exclusive anti-terrorist military team—the "Delta Force"—which has been ordered to Lebanon by the president to free the passengers. Meanwhile, the terrorists release the women and children, but they split the Jewish men and the American men into two groups and stash them in terrorist hideouts in Beirut. More terrorists board the plane to hold the rest of the men and the flight crew on the tarmac. Norris and company go to Israel and are about to launch their assault on the plane when they learn that some of the passengers have been taken off and will be killed if they attack. Now the operation switches to the city of Beirut, where, with the help of spies, the Delta Force launches an attack on the terrorist strongholds. The commandos manage to rescue the hostages, kill a mess of terrorists, and then head for the airport where they make quick work of the terrorists on the plane. Meanwhile, Norris races after chief terrorist Forster, who has fled to a remote house. After a bit of hand-to-hand combat, Forster manages to flee in a car. Not to worry, for Norris simply blows him up with a rocket shot from his military motorcycle. Meanwhile, back at the plane, the Delta Force members can't afford to wait for Norris any longer because they are besieged by angry terrorists. Norris heads for the airport at full throttle and just barely manages to haul himself into the moving plane via a rope thrown to him by comrades. In Israel, the hostages are reunited with their loved ones and Marvin, Norris, and the other members of the Delta Force board a military transport bound for home.

THE DELTA FORCE is yet another action film that seeks to satisfy the frustrations of the public by creating a fictitious situation where it is possible to win a decisive victory against an elusive foe. While producers Golan and Globus tell us that this film makes for a healthy release of tension, one must wonder. Is it really better to oversimplify a complex situation to the point of absurdity and then offer false solutions than it is to deal with reality? The film forgets any semblance of logic as it shows the Pentagon and an unseen president brashly order troops to full-scale combat, risking a wide-open war in Lebanon. Golan barely touches on the fundamental conflicts that have created the entire situation and simply offers up a pack of wild-eyed, swarthy Arabs preying on a pack of passive middle-aged Jews represented by the likes of Winters, Balsam, Bishop, and Kazan. Of course such things happen, but they do not have to be presented as a cartoon. If one can ignore the lack of characterization and the rather repugnant pandering to a frustrated public and just consider DELTA FORCE in pure action film terms, it still fails. The same contempt for logic found in the other weak

areas of the film applies to the action sequences as well. The battle scenes are confusing and repetitive with a seemingly endless number of explosions which send Arabs flying through the air in all directions. If the operation enacted here was actually attempted by a military unit it would be slaughtered instantly. The basic problem with THE DELTA FORCE is that we are asked to arrive as slobbering, frustrated jingoists and leave our good sense at the door.

p, Menahem Golan, Yoram Globus; d, Menahem Golan; w, James Bruner, Menahem Golan; ph, David Gurfinkel; m, Alan Silvestri; ed, Alain Jakubowicz; prod d, Lucisano Spadoni; set d, Leonardo Coen Cagli; cos, Tami Mor; spec eff, Don Gant; stunts, Don Pike.

Action   **Cas.**   **(PR:O MPAA:R)**

DEMONER†   (1986, Swed.) 125m Viking Film-Swedish Film Institute c

Ewa Froling *(Katarina)*, Lars Green *(Frank)*, Bjorn Granath *(Thomas)*, Pia Oscarsson *(Jenna)*.

Froling and Green are a married couple always at each other's throats. The night before Green's mother is to be buried the tension is particularly high, so they invite their neighbors, Granath and Oscarsson, over. Soon, largely at Green's instigation, everyone is attacking everyone else's dignity and sexuality in a sort of Nordic "Who's Afraid of Virginia Woolf."

p, Bo Jonsson; d, Carsten Brandt; w, Carsten Brandt (based on a play by Lars Noren); ph, Goran Nilsson (Fujicolor); m, Federico Mompou, Giuseppe Verdi, Giacomo Puccini, Gianna Nannini; ed, Kasper Schyberg, Lars Hagstrom; art d, Mona Theresia Forsen; makeup, Suzanne Bergmark; stunts, Jan Kreigsman.

Drama   **(PR:O MPAA:NR)**

DEMONI 2—L'INCUBO RITORNA†   (1986, Ital.) 94m DAC/Titanus c
(Trans: Demons 2—The Nightmare is Back)

David Knight, Nancy Brilli, Coralina Cataldi Tassoni, Bobby Rhodes, Asia Argento, Virginia Bryant, Marco Vivo.

Sequel to the inexplicably successful (both financially and critically) Argento/Bava disgust-o-rama DEMONS, this film sees the slime-drooling zombies loose in a high-rise apartment building. Whereas DEMONS linked the zombie attack with an evening at the cinema (the film took place in a movie theater), DEMONS 2 has the first zombie emerge from a television set showing a late-night horror movie. The grisly zombie promptly attacks a teenager's birthday party, and soon the victims rise to become zombies themselves, wreaking havoc on the rest of the tenants in the building—including a dog, which comes back as a canine zombie. Curiously, black actor Bobby Rhodes appeared in DEMONS as a pimp (who was killed), and now he shows up in DEMONS 2 as a body builder. His very presence seems to be in homage to the take-charge black characters in the films of American horror king George Romero.

p, Dario Argento; d, Lamberto Bava; w, Dario Argento, Lamberto Bava, Franco Ferrini, Dardano Sacchetti; ph, Lorenzo Battaglia (Luciano Vittori Color); m, Simon Boswell; ed, Pietro Bozza; art d, David Bassan; spec eff, Sergio Stivaleti; makeup, Rosario Prestopino.

Horror   **(PR:O MPAA:NR)**

DEN FRUSNA LEOPARDEN†   (1986, Swed.) 97m Viking-Swedish Film Institute-Svensk Filmindustri-Sonet/Svensk Filmindustri c (Trans: The Frozen Leopard)

Joakim Thastrom *(Kiljan)*, Peter Stormare *(Jerry)*, Christian "Crillan" Falk *(Morris)*, Maria Granlund *(Rita)*, Jacqueline Ramel *(Stella)*, Agneta Ekmanner *(Bess)*, Keve Hjelm *(The Father)*, Bjorn Granath *(Todd)*, Gosta Bredefeldt *(Ot-*

tosson), Tuncel Kurtiz *(David)*, Hjalti Rognvaldsson *(Rip)*, Tord Pettersson *(Bill)*, Fanny Hulten-Aulin *(Julia)*, Mikaela Steen *(Hanna)*.

Thastrom is a rootless young man who, with an old friend, goes to visit his father and brother. The pair travel in Thastrom's refurbished American-made auto but things don't turn out as planned. Unexpected occurrences force Thastrom to make some harsh decisions as he finds both love and danger over the next three days. The symbolic title refers to an old legend about the carcass of a leopard, mysteriously found frozen atop Mt. Kilimanjaro. Its presence is inexplicable, much like the chain of events Thastrom confronts within the film's plot. Thastrom, a member of the rock 'n' roll band Imperiet, made his acting debut with this film.

p, Peter Hald, Bo Jonsson; d, Larus Oskarsson; w, Lars Lundholm; ph, Goran Nilsson, Jan Pehrson, Nils Wallin (Eastmancolor); m, Leifur Thorarinsson; ed, Larus Oskarsson; art d, Mona Theresia Forsen; makeup, Suzanne Bergmark.

Drama   **(PR:O MPAA:NR)**

DEN' GNEVA†   (1986, USSR) 85m Studio Yalta Central-Gorki Studios c
(Trans: Day of Wrath)

Juosas Budrajtis *(Donald Batley)*, Alexei Petrenko *(Meller)*, Anatoli Ivanov *(Fiedler)*, Grazyan Bajkschtite *(Batley's Wife)*.

Don't think the Sylvester Stallone Rocky-Rambo-Cobra machine has the corner on the market for patriotic action films. Stallone's number-one nemesis, those rascally Russkies, have taken a shot at the genre themselves. Though Soviet-made, this endeavor takes place in the U.S., where a TV reporter learns of a mad scientist's experiments in mind control. After working his way into a hidden mountain laboratory, the plucky newsman discovers a colony where farmers are despondent and children have extraordinary mental abilities. Next is a hidden lair where Our Heroski is attacked by a strange beast before he finally gets to the bottom of the madman's fiendish plans. The film winds up with a moral about the evil things that can happen when decadent capitalists dip their filthy hands into modern science. This sort of fare is, to say the least, a rare excursion for Soviet filmmakers.

d, Sulambek Mamilov; w, Alexander Lapshin (based on a story by Sever Gonsovski); ph, Alexander Rybin (Sovcolor); m, Gija Kantscheli; art d, Boris Dulenkov.

Horror/Adventure   **(PR:C MPAA:NR)**

DEPARTURE†   (1986, Aus.) 93m Rychmond/Cineaust c

Patricia Kennedy *(Sylvia Swift)*, Michael Duffield *(Presley Swift)*, June Jago *(Frances)*, Serge Lazareff *(Simon Swift)*, Sean Scully *(Alex Rowen)*, Jon Sidney *(Joseph)*.

Duffield is a retired diplomat who is growing bored with the sedate life in his Australian home. He and wife Kennedy decide to return to his former post city of Rome, first spending a weekend with their son Lazareff, an aspiring politician with a good future. The plans for a happy farewell are shattered, however, when a scandal from Duffield's past is unearthed by the press. In his younger days the ambassador had been part of a well-covered incident which led to the death of a young lady. Lazareff is convinced his budding career will be destroyed by his father's past indiscretion, while Jago, a family friend, feels betrayed by this shattering news.

p, Christine Suli, Brian Kavanagh; d, Brian Kavanagh; w, Michael Gurr (based on his play "A Pair of Claws"); ph, Bob Kohler (Eastmancolor); m, Bruce Smeaton; ed, Ken Sallows; art d, Paddy Reardon.

Drama   **(PR:C MPAA:NR)**

DER PENDLER†   (1986, Switz.) 100m Limbo/Metropolis bw (Trans: The Informer)

Andreas Loeffel *(Tom)*, Elisabeth Seiler *(Su)*, Anne-Marie Blanc *(Aunt Martha)*, Bruno Ganz *(Steiner)*, Tiziana Jelmini *(Elsbeth)*, Beat Sieber *(Sander)*.

Loeffel plays a police informant trapped between two worlds—those of the drug-trafficker and the law enforcer. The pressures of this life are not self-imposed, but are forced upon him by a hard-edged police inspector played by the exceptional Ganz.

p, Theres Scherer, d, Bernhard Giger; w, Bernhard Giger, Martin Hennig; ph, Pio Corradi; m, Benedikt Jeger; ed, Daniela Roderer; art d, Marianne Milani; m/l, Markus Kuhne, Polo Hofer.

Crime Drama   **(PR:O MPAA:NR)**

DER POLENWEIHER†   (1986, Ger.) 104m Sudwestfunk Baden-Baden c
(Trans: The Polish War Worker)

Ursula Cantieni, Gerhard Olschewski, Wolf-Dietrich Sprenger, Eberhard Feik, Britta Pohland, Manfred Epting.

A grim adaptation of a grim play, this film concerns a Polish girl sent to live with a German farm family as a slave laborer. She is adopted into the family, even eating at their table, but later she is found dead at the bottom of a lake. The local police chief investigates, but what he is really looking for is a place to hide until the front passes them and he can surrender to the approaching American forces. When it is revealed that the dead girl was pregnant by the farmer, who killed her, the farmer goes off to the front to be killed, and the policeman insinuates himself into the good graces of the wife. The film ends after the war, with the former police chief looking over his farm and talking with a neighbor about the new Germany. Shot on 16mm and unlikely to see a wide release.

p, Susan Schulte; d, Nico Hoffmann, Thomas Strittmater; w, Thomas Strittmater; ph, Ernst Kubitza; m, Thomas Timmler, Dieter Gutfried.

Drama (PR:O MPAA:NR)

DER ROSENKONIG*** (1986, Ger.) 103m Udo Heiland Filmproduktion–Werner Schroeter/Film International c (Trans: The Rose King)

Magdelena Montezuma *(Anna)*, Antonio Orlando *(Arnold)*, Mostea Djayam *(Albert)*.

Despite his profound influence upon his colleagues of the "New German Cinema," Werner Schroeter has remained virtually unknown in the U.S. This can be blamed partly on limited 16mm availability for the majority of his work, and partly on the 1960s American Underground "camp" evocations in his work. DER ROSENKONIG is a lushly photographed combination of sound and imagery, set on a pastoral Portuguese estate. Montezuma plays an aging German beauty who lives with her handsome young son. A local laborer enters their lives, generating an excessive and obsessive tale of passion involving all three characters.

Shortly after production of this film was complete, its star, Montezuma, passed away from cancer. Appearing in almost all of Schroeter's films, she was recognized for her exquisite classical beauty. Despite her illness, Montezuma put all her energies into DER ROSENKONIG, even collaborating on the script. This film is definitely not for all audiences, mainly due to its eroticism. But those drawn toward the surreal and the absurd will find this a real treat. (In German; English subtitles.)

p, Werner Schroeter, Paolo Branco; d, Werner Schroeter; w, Werner Schroeter, Magdalena Montezuma; ph, Elfi Mikesch; ed, Juliane Lorenz; art d, Caritas de Witt.

Fantasy/Drama (PR:O MPAA:NR)

DER SCHWARZE TANNER† (1986, Switz./Ger./Aust.) 106m Catpics–SRG–ZDF–ORG–Egli Film & Video–Glass Family Trust/Columbus c (Trans: The Black Tanner)

Otto Machtlinger, Renate Steiger, Dietmar Schonherr, Liliana Heimberg, Susanne Betschart, Elisabeth Seiler, Ernst Sigrist, Albert Freuler, Dieter Moor, Ingold Wildenauer, Heinz Buhlmann, Giovanni Fruh, Nikola Weisse, Johannes Peyer, Volker Prechtel, Herbert Leiser, Wolf Kaiser, Eva Rieck, Ilja Smudla, Martin Steiner, Jurgen Cziesla, Othmar Betschart, Michael Gempart, Vera Schweiger, Beat Fah.

In early 1940s Switzerland, the government decrees that all available land shall be used for growing food lest the country grow too dependent on unreliable foreign sources. Machtlinger (who died shortly after this film's completion) is a mountain farmer who disobeys the order, claiming some land must be left alone. Good grazing areas should not be sacrificed for harvest space, Machtlinger argues, and his fellow villagers agree to stand with the rebel. Gradually Machtlinger and his family are abandoned by their friends, but they take this development in stride. Refusing to accept wartime rationing, Machtlinger uses his animals to make his own dairy goods. When accused of dealing in the black market, the unwavering Machtlinger openly defies the authorities, forcing them to jail him. But even this drastic measure will not wear him down. He goes on a hunger strike, remaining steadfast to the things he believes in until ultimately he is freed.

p, Peter Spoerri; d, Xavier Koller; w, Xavier Koller, Walter Deuber (based on a story by Meinrad Inglin); ph, Elemer Ragalyi; m, Hardy Hepp; ed, Fee Liechti; art d, Rolf Engler; cos, Sylvia de Stoutz; makeup, Anna Wyrsch, Anne-Rose Schwab.

Drama (PR:C-O MPAA:NR)

DER SEXTE SINN† (1986, Ger.) 85m Hoizont c (Trans: The Sexth Sense)

Albert Heinz *(Alfred)*, Ingolf Gorges *(Hans)* Ulrike Schirm, Ela Behrends, Barbara Morawiecz, Jutta Kloppel, Susanne Stahl.

A young man, after many years of being psychologically bound to his dominating mother, finds himself free to pursue erotic adventures beyond his wildest imaginings. To this end, he enlists the help of his older brother, a man of depth and knowledge in such matters. Together the brothers explore the physical pleasures to be found in Berlin, soon encountering a most interesting young lass. She has her own set of libidinous quandaries, which are fortuitously attended to by the story's end.

d&w, Dagmar Beiersdorf, Lothar Lambert; ph, Hans Guter Bucking; m, Albert Kittler; ed, Verena Neumann.

Comedy (PR:O MPAA:NR)

DER SOMMER DES SAMURAI† (1986, Ger.) 105m Radiant–Cinenova–ZDF/Cine International c (Trans: Summer of the Samurai)

Cornelia Froboess *(Christiane Land)*, Hans Peter Hallwachs *(Wilcke)*, Wojciech Pzoniak *(Gerhard Krall)*, Nadja Tiller *(Dr. Feuillade)*, Peter Krauss *(Schirmer)*, Hannelore Hoger *(Doris)*, Anton Diffring *(Weinrich)*, Matthias Fuchs *(Dr. Herbst)*, Karl-Heinz von Hassel *(Heideman)*, Miko *(Marianne)*.

A thriller set in Hamburg and directed in the style of early silent series a la France's Louis Feuillade and Germany's Fritz Lang. When a rash of attacks on German businessmen terrorizes Hamburg, journalist Froboess sets out to expose the criminal mastermind behind it all. What she finds is a German raised in Japan who is searching for the man who stole a rare samurai sword. The trail leads to a remote ninja-guarded castle that houses the wealthy Pzoniak, the culprit whom the samurai is trying to locate. What follows is a generous offering of old-fashioned confrontation scenes, executed in a style long-forgotten by most filmmakers. The homage seems completely conscious, as director Blumenberg goes so far as to name one of his characters after Feuillade. This is Blumenberg's second picture, his first being titled THE THOUSAND EYES, a clear homage to Lang's last picture, THE THOUSAND EYES OF DR. MABUSE (1960).

p, Michael Bittins; d, Hans Christof Blumenberg; w, Hans Christof Blumenberg, Carol H. Stern, Frederick Spindale; ph, Wolfgang Dickmann; m, K. Bartholome; ed, M. Barius.

Crime (PR:C MPAA:NR)

DER WILDE CLOWN† (1986, Ger.) 107m Bavaria Filmverleih-Joseph Roedl Filmproduktion-ZDF c (Trans: The Wild Clown)

Sigi Zimmerschied *(Jacob)*, Sunnyi Melles *(Janis)*, Peter Kern *(The Boss)*, Ivo Vrzal-Wiegand, Ursula Straetz, Jack Luceno, Elisabeth Bertram, Renate Muhri, Erich Kleiber, Otto E. Fuhrmann.

In this West German comedy, Zimmerschied takes a job as chauffeur to local businessman Kern who hires him in hopes of getting his grubby hands on an estate owned by Zimmerschied's aunt, presently locked up in an asylum. The estate encompasses land Kern wants to develop in order to cash in on the lucrative market created by a nearby U.S. military base. Zimmerschied won't play the game, though, so Kern sets the beautiful Melles after his driver, hoping her persuasive manner will help the cause. Once Zimmerschied finds out what Melles is up to, he leaves Kern's employ and holes up in an outbuilding on the military base's firing range. He shaves his head, and, with a few confederates, stages assaults on Kern's home. Melles rejoins him, and the aunt is freed from the asylum. Eventually Melles' missing husband, an American military man, shows up, and she returns to him.

p, Helmut Krapp, Tilman Taube; d&w, Josef Roedl; ph, Karlheinz Gschwind; m, Eberhard Schoener; ed, Juliane Lorenz; prod d, Gert B. Venzky; cos, Barbara Grupp; spec eff, Heinz Ludwig.

Comedy (PR:O MPAA:NR)

DERNIER CRI† (1986, Fr.) 87m Harvert c (Trans: The Last Word)

Hubert Lucot *(Henri)*, Christine Laurent, Catherine Bonin, Julien Dubois, Eric Mitchell, Anne Gautier, Jean-Claude Vannier.

Sex and violence abound in this French action picture set in the world of terrorism as Lucot, a veteran member of an anti-American group, is ordered to track down and kill a woman who could turn informer. Lucot, however, has had enough of the misguided bloodshed and breaks from the group, which leads to an excess of chasing and gunplay. The film wallows in a plethora of nude women and bloodshed.

p, Marc Andre Grynbaum; d, Bernard Dubois; w, Bernard Dubois, Baynac Biegalski; ph, Marc Andre Batigne; m, Frederic Chopin, Ludwig van Beethoven; ed, Bernard Dubois; art d, Berthelemy Fougea.

Action (PR:O MPAA:NR)

DESCENDANT OF THE SNOW LEOPARD, THE**** (1986, USSR) 134m Kirghizfilm/Sovexportfilm c (POTOMOK BELONGO BARSSA)

Dokdurbek Kydralijev *(Koshoshash)*, Aliman Shankorosova *(Saikal)*, Doskhan Sholshakssynov *(Mundusbai)*, Guinara Alimbajeva *(Aike)*, A. Chokubajev *(Kassen)*, M. Shantelijev *(Sajak)*, Sh. Seidakmatova *(Begaim)*, G. Kadyralijeva *(Sulaika)*, K. Akmatova *(Batma)*, Aibek Kydryralijev *(Kalygul)*, A. Kulanbajev *(Karypbai)*, S. Chebodejeva-Chaptykova *(Sonun)*, S. Kababajev *(Bijaly)*, M. Machmadov *(Sultanbek)*, R. Seitov *(Bakass)*, D. Achimov, A. Arashtajev *(Merchants)*.

This cinematic adaptation of a Kirghizian folktale is an invigorating and breathtakingly beautiful experience. Like all good legends it mythically relates important historical events in the evolution of a culture, citing violations of sacred rules as the ultimate source of change. The Snow Leopards are a tribe of hunters who inhabit the rugged terrain of the Kirghizian mountains. During one particularly violent winter, the entire tribe faces extinction unless help from the closest lowland tribe can be solicited. The tribe's most virile and capable hunter, Koshoshash (Kydralijev), volunteers to make the dangerous journey across the snow-covered path to the lowlands. Accompanied by Chokubajev, Kydralijev barely manages to reach the other tribe, which graciously gives him the needed horses, but in return for a future favor. Come spring, the lowland tribe requires that the Snow Leopards uphold their end of the bargain. The daughter of the tribe's leader is to marry a prince, and trader, from the south in a grand celebration that could make an easy target for attacking enemies. The Snow Leopards are asked to act as guards against possible invasion. During the games that are part of the celebration, Kydralijev displays his superior skill and prowess by beating all competitors. He loses in only one event, jousting, to a woman, disguised as a man, fighting for the freedom of her enslaved husband. During the games, the young and beautiful wife of the leader becomes increasingly infatuated with Kydralijev, and he with her. Their love affair—which is eventually discovered by the husband—creates tension between the two tribes that will have future detrimental effects on the Snow Leopards. The backward mountain tribe is also introduced to easy-loading rifles by an Arab trader. In exchange for furs, the Snow Leopards attain the technological means to kill a greater and greater number of animals, upsetting their ecological balance. As the next winter approaches, the Snow Leopard tribe is once again facing possible starvation. This time, the love affair between Kydralijev and the lowland wife prevents the possibility of appealing to the lowlanders for help. Armed with their new rifles—

despite a warning from the shaman woman who acts as their spiritual leader—the hunters heedlessly slaughter dozens of animals. In the reckless bloodbath, a sacred goat is also killed, an infraction against nature and a symbol of the impending doom of the Snow Leopards. Also accidentally killed is the son of Kydralijev, who represents the descendants of the Snow Leopard; his death is the figurative end of the entire tribe.

Director Okeyev received a Silver Bear for Outstanding Single Achievement at the 1985 Berlin Film Festival, a result of his subtle combination of intriguing characters and a multidimensional story against the stunning background of the mountainous terrain. THE DESCENDANT OF THE SNOW LEOPARD has its basis in an actual Kirghizian folk legend, explaining the occasional lapses into heavy melodramatics, specifically in the love scenes. Otherwise, all the events are rendered in an engrossing, realistic fashion. Before movies and books existed to retell history, people depended on folk legends passed via word of mouth from village elders to captivated children. Viewing THE DESCENDANT OF THE SNOW LEOPARD has much the same effect; it takes us to a time when the natural order battled civilization, presenting a hero—with qualities realizable only in the imagination—in conflict with both. It also has a subtle message: the delicate balance between nature and civilization exists via a set of unspoken rules, and an imbalance in either direction can be devastating. (In Kirghizian; English subtitles.)

d, Tolomush Okeyev; w, Mar Baydjiev, Tolomush Okeyev (based on folk legends); ph, Nurtoy Borbijev; m, M. Begalijev; ed, R. Shershneva; cos, M. Abdijev.

Adventure/Drama   (PR:AA MPAA:NR)

DESCENTE AUX ENFERS†   (1986, Fr.) 90m Partner's–La Cinq/AAA c
                                         (Trans: Descent Into Hell)

Claude Brasseur (*Alan Kolber*), Sophie Marceau (*Lola Kolber*), Sidiki Bakaba (*Theophile Bijou*), Hyppolyte Girardot (*Philippe Devignat*), Gerard Rinaldi (*Elvis*), Marie Dubois (*Lucette Beulemans*), Betsy Blair (*Mrs. Burns*), Umban U'kset (*Commissioner Redoux*).

Another in a long string of adaptations of the American pulp novels of David Goodis (who is practically unheard of in his native country, but a cult figure in France), which began as early as the 1947 Humphrey Bogart-Lauren Bacall vehicle DARK PASSAGE, progressed to Francois Truffaut's SHOOT THE PIANO PLAYER in 1962, and then to Jean-Jacques Beineix's THE MOON IN THE GUTTER (1983), the most notable of recent entrants. This time out the hard-drinking Brasseur and the frigid Marceau are the tormented couple of Goodis' design. They vacation in Haiti in the hope that their rocky marriage will find new passion. Instead Brasseur finds himself entangled in a blackmail scheme that evolves from his self-defense killing of a nighttime attacker. Oddly, this expression of violence brings Brasseur close to Marceau, who, in the past, similarly defended herself against a would-be rapist. DESCENTE AUX ENFERS did well at the French box office and earned a Best Supporting Actress nomination in the French Cesars contest for Marie Dubois, who also had appeared in SHOOT THE PIANO PLAYER. Fans of the popular 1983 film LA BOUM will remember in that picture Brasseur and Marceau appeared as father and daughter, adding a strange incestuous tinge to this film.

p, Ariel Zeitoun; d, Francis Girod; w, Francis Girod, Jean-Loup Dabadie (based on the novel *The Wounded And The Slain* by David Goodis); ph, Charlie van Damme (Eastmancolor); m, Georges Delerue; ed, Genevieve Winding; art d, Jacques Bufnoir.

Crime   (PR:O MPAA:NR)

DESERT BLOOM**½   (1986) 104m Carson–Sundance Institute/COL c

Jon Voight (*Jack*), JoBeth Williams (*Lily*), Ellen Barkin (*Starr*), Allen Garfield (*Mr. Mosol*), Annabeth Gish (*Rose*), Jay D. Underwood (*Robin*), Desiree Joseph (*Dee Ann*), Dusty Balcerzak (*Barbara Jo*), Tressi Loria (*Shelly*), Laura Rasmussen (*Meryl*), William Lang (*Colonel*), Jim McCarthy (*Driver*), Ann Risley (*Mrs. Muratore*), Rick Scheiffer (*Mr. Brandal*), Irene Goodnight (*R.C. Volunteer*), Eugenia Moran (*R.C. Nurse*), Danica Remy (*Nurse*), Bruce Wineinger (*Texan*), Armen Dirtadian (*Publicist*), Molly Fontaine (*Ava*), Al Petito (*Radio Clerk*), Randy Harris (*Photographer*), Chris Corr (*Delivery Boy*), Fred C. Smith (*Tour Guide*), Steven Mastroieni (*Nick*), Bob Gish (*Superintendent*), Onna Young, Jesse Sloan, Kiysha Doty, Todd Barish, Sherry Allen (*Spelling Bee Contestants*), Doris Berman (*Woman at Spelling Bee*), Reynaldo Villalobos, Jr. (*Boy Finalist*), Judith Gish (*Spelling Bee Moderator*), Mike Stein, Ray LeFre, Tamara Cooley, Patty Harbor (*Adult Party Goers*), Johnny L. Watkins (*Cab Driver*), Mark Jenkins (*AEC Officer*).

A troubled family living near atomic test sites in Nevada is the subject of this flawed but well-acted production. The story is told as a reminiscence of an unseen narrator, the adult voice of 13-year-old Gish. It is shortly before Christmas, 1950, and Gish has just received new glasses, something she feels gives her sophistication. She lives on the outskirts of Las Vegas with her two younger sisters, their mother Williams, and their stepfather, Voight, who is haunted by his memories of WW II combat, and as a result is struggling with an alcohol problem. Williams, who insists her children call their stepfather "Dad," is fully aware of her husband's troubles and his occasionally violent temper, but copes as best she can. The family enlarges by one when Williams' sister, the flirtatious Barkin, arrives for a temporary stay. She is in the process of ending her marriage and needs to live in Nevada for 42 days (the period covered by the picture) in order to fulfill the residency requirement for a quickie divorce. Gish adores her aunt and the two develop a close, affectionate relationship. The story develops in an anecdotal manner as Gish learns some hard lessons in growing up.

Voight's alcoholism lands him in the hospital, and he vows to quit, though this

is a promise he cannot keep. His obsession with war memories is coupled with Voight's growing interest in the rumored atom-bomb test to be held soon outside of Reno. Williams is a proud woman, trying to hold her family together while turning a blind eye toward the overt tensions. Gish will not follow her mother's example, though she tries to create family harmony. When Voight drunkenly knocks over the shortwave radio on which he monitors military reports, Gish replaces the broken vacuum tubes as a Christmas gift. Still, a flaring anger exists between the two, and shortly before a special party, Voight slaps his stepdaughter and forbids her to attend. But with Barkin's help Gish is able to cover her bruises and sneak out of the house. At the party, Garfield—a concerned parent whose daughter is hosting the affair—takes Gish aside and tells her she is welcome to confide in him if she ever has any troubles at home. Garfield later beseeches Williams for the actual day of the nuclear test. Despite government reassurances, he is worried about the effects of radioactive fallout and wants to send his wife and children to Los Angeles before the test. Though Williams has taken an oath of secrecy, she gives Garfield a clear indication of when the test will be.

Returning home one day, Gish is shocked to find Barkin and Voight in an embrace. Gish runs out of the house, then goes to the county spelling bee in which she is competing. Despite overwhelming emotional feelings, Gish wins, then returns home for her aunt's divorce party. The family tensions erupt into physical violence when Williams learns of Voight and Barkin's indiscretion. Garfield and other party guests arrive in the midst of the confrontation, effectively breaking up the fight. Gish, who has had enough of this turbulent home life, sneaks out in the middle of the night, taking her friend Underwood with her. The two adolescents hitchhike to Reno, where they end up at the bomb test site. The military finds them and Voight is asked to take the girl home. During the return drive, he admits his shortcomings to Gish, and the two arrive at a tentative reconciliation. The next morning the family gathers on the front porch to watch the mushroom cloud of the atomic test.

DESERT BLOOM is a drama of character, and the adult roles are perfectly cast. Voight, Williams, and Barkin play familiar stereotypes, yet their collective performances have enough rough edges to make these people unique, not cliches. Though Garfield's role is small, he brings great heart to the character, producing a memorable performance that belies his screen time. Less successful is Gish, making her film debut with DESERT BLOOM. At times lethargic and uninteresting, only occasionally able to elicit our sympathy, she is simply too inexperienced to carry the weight of the story. Writer/director Corr was also making his feature-film debut and, like his young star, is not fully up to the task. Although his screenplay captures the feelings of these people and their circumstances, Corr's direction puts some situations at an uncomfortable distance. A more intimate style would have helped bring out the delicate emotions inherent within his film. This was a unique time and place, which Corr understands well. Such everyday details as air-raid drills and identification tags worn by children in case of nuclear attack are presented matter-of-factly, a simple part of the life of people who have learned to accept. One unsettling sequence with Gish and her sisters in sailor suits posing for a Christmas picture has a strange resemblance to a Diane Arbus photograph. In another disturbing, though aesthetically beautiful shot, a group of children fall to their knees and cover their heads at the sound of an air raid siren. Corr shows them on the playground, framed against a background of mountains and the stunning Western skyline, creating an image of eerie power. More moments such as these would have benefitted the film tremendously. DESERT BLOOM was produced through Robert Redford's Sundance Institute, the first venture under their Co-Production Program. Oscar-winning screenwriter Waldo Salt also lent a hand, helping with the script as its development progressed. Though set in Las Vegas, Nevada, the film was actually shot in a Tucson, Arizona neighborhood which more closely resembled a Western town of 1950. Songs include "Mockin' Bird Hill" (Vaughn Horton, performed by Patti Page), and a Chesterfield cigarette jingle of the period.

p, Michael Hausman; d&w, Eugene Corr (based on a story by Linda Remy, Eugene Corr); ph, Reynaldo Villalobos (Panavision, Metrocolor); m, Brad Fiedel; ed, David Garfield, John Currin, Cari Coughlin; art d, Lawrence Miller; set d, Bob Zilliox; cos, Hilary Rosenfeld; spec eff, Boss Film Corp.; m/l, Vaughn Horton; makeup, Ben Nye, Jr.

Drama   Cas.   (PR:A-C MPAA:PG)

DESIDERANDO GIULIA† (1986, Ital.) Medusa-National-Dania-Filmes International/Medusa c (Trans: Desiring Giulia)

Serena Grandi, Johan Leysen, Valeria D'Obici.

A lonely and bored young writer meets a beautiful girl one night at a theater. They have a brief, passionate affair that the man quickly tries to end and forget. Forgetting is not so easy, though, and he returns to her, pulling away from a strange relationship with his own sister. However, his new love proves to be a promiscuous, duplicitous doxy whom he eventually dumps, though only after his sister kills herself. Just what the world needs, another erotic drama from Italy.

d, Andrea Barzini; w, Gianfranco Clerici, Andrea Barzini, Domenico, Matteucci (based on a story by Gianfranco Clerici, Andrea Barzini); ph, Mario Vulpiani (Telecolor); m, Antonio Sechi.

Drama (PR:O MPAA:NR)

DESORDRE† (1986, Fr.) 90m Forum c (Trans: Disorder)

Wadeck Stanczak (Yvan), Ann-Gisel Glass (Anne), Lucas Belvaux (Henri), Simon de la Brosse, Remi Martin, Corinne Dacla, Etienne Chicot, Juliette Mailhe, Philippe Demarle, Etienne Daho.

A stylish look at a group of youths in a rock 'n' roll band who have as much difficulty getting their band together as they do their own lives. Their troubles begin when, during a music store robbery, one of the members kills the watchman. Although they are not caught, their guilt chisels away at their sanity. When their music begins to fail them, some find that they can no longer survive (one hangs himself) while the others struggle to carry on. First-time director Assayas previously received credit as the co-scriptwriter on Andre Techine's last two pictures, 1985's RENDEZVOUS and this year's SCENE OF THE CRIME. Produced in connection with Virgin Records, a top force in the music scene in London, where part of the film was photographed. (In French; English subtitles.)

p, Claude-Eric Poiroux; d&w, Olivier Assayas; ph, Denis Lenoir; m, Gabriel Yared; ed, Luc Barnier; art d, Francois-Renaud Labarthe.

Drama (PR:O MPAA:NR)

DESPERATE MOVES* (1986, Ital.) 98m Chesham c

Steve Tracy (Andy Steigler), Dana Handler (Olivia), Eddie Deezen (Red), Isabel Sanford (Dottie Butz), Paul Benedict (Cosmo), Christopher Lee (Dr. Boxer), Dan Leggant (Earnie Steigler), Michael Phenicle (Earl), Donald McLean (Beefy), Linda Hoy (Mrs. Evinson), Sallee Young (Hooker).

This silly story was shot at the height of the roller skating fad of the late 1970s-early 1980s. After sitting on the shelf for six years the film finally saw a release thanks to the availability of the videocassette market, a far less discriminating venue then theatrical distribution. Tracy is a roller skatin' fool who heads off to San Francisco, where wheeled shoes are king. He ends up working at a skating rink and tries his hand at wooing Handler, a real tease who makes his efforts at romance rather difficult. Tracy gets some help from Benedict and Sanford (both from the television sitcom "The Jeffersons") via cash and sage advice. Eventually Benedict sends the lad to a psychiatrist to help work out his troubles, but the shrink proves to be none other than the sinister Lee. All this fluffy nonsense leads to an inevitable happy ending in a film even more forgettable than ROLLER BOOGIE or SKATETOWN U.S.A. Surprisingly, this minor feature is an Italian production made by the same people who gave us BEYOND THE DOOR.

p, Ovidio G. Assonitis; d, Oliver Hellman [Avidio G. Assonitis]; w, Allan Berger, Kathy Gori (based on a story by Robert J. Gandus); ph, Roberto D'Ettore Piazzoli (DeLuxe Color); m, Steve Power; ed, Robert Curi; prod d, Roger Salvadori; set d, Frank Vetrano; ch, Fred Curt.

Comedy/Romance Cas. (PR:C-O MPAA:NR)

DETECTIVE SCHOOL DROPOUTS* (1986) 90m Cannon c (AKA: DUMB DICKS)

David Landsberg (Donald Wilson), Lorin Dreyfuss (Paul Miller), Christian De Sica (Carlo Lombardi), Valeria Golino (Caterina), Rick Battaglia, Francesco Cinieri.

DETECTIVE SCHOOL DROPOUTS is a good example of bad marketing. This funny film came and went with the speed of lightning and merited a far better fate than it received. Dreyfuss (brother of Richard) and Landsberg wrote the screenplay and costar in the crime comedy set primarily in Italy. Landsberg—a tiny man about 5 feet 3 inches tall—is seen as a klutz who keeps getting into trouble at his various jobs and can't hold steady employment. His hobby is reading detective stories and he thinks he might have a career in that field so he contacts Dreyfuss, a bust-out detective who is in danger of being evicted for nonpayment of his rent and who has several other debts. Dreyfuss signs Landsberg on as a "student" with the idea of milking the tiny guy of all his money. In the twinkling of a private eye, the duo is in the midst of a battle between a pair of Italian families and a kidnaping, with a possibility of a murder rap over their heads. They must get a message to a guy who is about to fly to Italy so they pilfer a pair of boarding passes from some Japanese and hop aboard the airliner. (The fact that they are obviously caucasian doesn't dawn on the dim-witted flight attendant.) Once in Italy, they are stranded with no money, no passports, no nothing. The rest of the picture is a breakneck chase filled with some excellent sight gags, some old jokes, and two winning performances from Dreyfuss and Landsberg, who could very well be the next comedy team to make a mark, if their next pictures are handled better by the distributor. Good cinematography, nice production values, and, rarest of all, a comedy that you can take the children to

see because it has none of the smarmy gags which have dominated the screen for the last few seasons.

p, Menahem Golan, Yoram Globus; d, Filippo Ottoni; w, David Landsberg, Lorin Dreyfuss; ph, Giancarlo Fernando (Telecolor); m, G. DeVangelis, M. DeVangelis; ed, Cesare d'Amico; prod d, Antonello Geleng.

Comedy Cas. (PR:A-C MPAA:PG)

DEVASTATOR, THE† (1986, U.S./Phil.) 78m Rodeo/Concorde c (AKA: KINGS RANSOM; THE DESTROYERS)

Richard Hill (Deke Porter), Katt Shea (Audrey King), Crofton Hardester (Carey), Kaz Garas (Sheriff), Terrence O'Hara (Spencer), Bill McLaughlin (Bartlett), Jack S. Daniels (Ox), Steve Rogers (Reese), Debbie Brooks (Elaine).

Vietnam veteran Hill, on a visit to the widow of an old comrade, finds the whole area controlled by marijuana growers. They take a dislike to Hill and burn down the house where he is staying, so he gets some of his old Army buddies and wipes out the whole gang. Shot in the Philippines, this film received limited regional release before emerging on videocassette.

p&d, Cirio H. Santiago; w, Joseph Sugarman; ph, Richard Remington (Metrocolor); m, Matthew Ender, Mark Governor; ed, George Saint, Margaret Carlton; prod d, Joe Mari Avallon; art d, Ronnie Cross.

Crime Drama Cas. (PR:O MPAA:NR)

DEVIL IN THE FLESH† (1986, Aus.) 103m Collins Murray/J.C. Williamson Film Management-World Film Alliance c

Katia Caballero (Marthe), Keith Smith (Paul Hansen), John Morris (John Hansen), Jill Forster (Jill Hansen), Colin Duckworth (Pierre Fournier), Reine Lavoie (Madeleine Fournier), Luciano Marcucci (Ermanno), Louise Elvin (Blonde Model), Jeremy Johnson (Simon Greene), Odile Le Clezio (Simone), John Murphy (Brother Murphy), Peter Cummins (Disciplinarian Brother).

Based on the novel by French author Raymond Radiguet, which influenced the 1947 Claude Autant-Lara film LE DIABLE AU CORPS, this picture transfers the action from WW I France to WW II Australia but still retains that decidedly European flavor. Caballero is a Frenchwoman interned in Australia until the war's end, effectively keeping her away from her Italian husband. She becomes the lover of a schoolboy, Smith. They manage to hide their secret from townspeople, but word eventually leaks out and they become the subject of controversy and reproach. Faithful to the novel, the film has an air of eroticism that includes a great deal of nudity, both male and female. This version's sex scenes, however, didn't cause nearly as much controversy as Marco Bellocchio's Italian version, which was also released this year.

p, John B. Murray; d&w, Scott Murray (based on the novel Le Diable Au Corps by Raymond Radiguet); ph, Andrew de Groot (Eastmancolor); m, Philippe Sarde; ed, Tim Lewis; art d, Paddy Reardon; cos, Frankie Hogan.

Drama (PR:C MPAA:NR)

DIAPASON† (1986, Arg.) 94m P.K.H. c

Harry Havilio (Ignacio), Marta Frydman (Boncha), Margot Moreyra (Margarita), Carlos Kaufman (Franz).

A political exercise that embodies the problems of bourgeois society and sexual repression in the lives of two lovers. Havilio is a man of about 50 who meets the unkempt Frydman and tries to transform her into the lady of his dreams. No good comes of his manipulation, however, and the relationship is ultimately destroyed. A debut feature from Polaco.

p, Pedro Passarini; d&w, Jorge Polaco; ph, Carlos Torlaschi; m, Lito Vitale; ed, Jose del Peon; art d, Rodolfo Hermida; set d&cos, Norma Romano.

Drama (PR:O MPAA:NR)

DIE LIEBESWUSTE† (1986, Ger.) 85m Lothar Lambert bw (Trans: The Desert of Love)

Ulrike S., Dieter Schidor, Dorothea Moritz, Jessica Lanee, Doreen Heins, Abbas Kepekli, Semra Uysallar, Stefan Menche, Friederike Menche, Hans Marquardt, Michael Hulsmann, Lothar Lambert, Dagmar Beiersdorf, Albert Heins, Erika Rabau.

Filmmaker Lothar Lambert salvages what is left of a film after a disaster in the lab destroys much of its footage. The story begins with Lambert sitting in the cutting room desperately trying to make some sense of the surviving footage. The story concerns a woman, Ulrike S., who escapes from a mental institution wearing nothing but a raincoat. As she wanders the streets she is subjected to lecherous advances made by a variety of characters. She has no choice but to reject their offers and continue on her way if she is to keep a modicum of self-respect. Beiersdorf, a friend of the filmmaker in the Berlin Underground, arrives and asks Lambert whether the film made any sense when it was intact. They then discuss their different viewpoints regarding Lambert's oft-explored subject: sexual and social alienation. Producer Heins arrives and offers his support, but there is little one can do when there isn't enough footage to make an understandable film. They are joined by Ulrike S., who offers her insights into the craziness of Lambert's career since his recent recognition and success.

p,d,w,ph,&ed, Lothar Lambert.

Docu-Drama (PR:O MPAA:NR)

DIE MITLAUFER (SEE: FOLLOWING THE FUHRER, 1986, Ger.)

DIE NACHTMEERFAHRT† (1986, Aust.) 80m Thalia–ORF c (Trans: The Nocturnal Voyage; Voyage By Night)

Anita Kolbert *(Lilly)*, Wilfried Scheutz *(Richard)*, Christine Jirku *(Margret)*, Beatrix Wipperlich *(Sue)*, Anne Mertin *(Lady Caretaker)*, Lotte Loebenstein *(Lady Caretaker's Daughter)*, Joesi Prokopetz *(Pepo)*.

Kolbert plays a photographer's model who has become frustrated with the direction her life has taken. Annoyed with her job, which requires nothing of her except looking beautiful, she yearns for something more challenging and rewarding. She has also grown tired of her married boy friend, Scheutz, who treats her as if she were his property. Although angry and resentful about her situation, Kolbert does not have the will to change it. Suddenly, life takes a bizarre twist when she awakens one morning to find that a beard is beginning to form on her face. At first she tries desperately to hide the hair, but eventually she decides to let it grow and pass herself off as her brother. Now experiencing the world through a man's eyes, Kolbert finds herself to be more confident than ever before. In her masculine guise, she is able to lose her inhibitions more easily and to take charge of her life. Just as she makes the decision to break off her stagnant relationship with Scheutz, the whiskers vanish, leaving her a new woman with new-found confidence.

d&w, Kitty Kino; ph, Hanus Polak, Frederic G. Kacek; m, Polio Brezina; ed, Charlotte Mullner, Brigitte Frischler; set d, Elisabeth Klobassa; cos, Cera Graf.

Comedy   **(PR:C-O MPAA:NR)**

DIE REISE   (SEE: JOURNEY, THE, 1986, Ger.)

DIE WALSCHE†   (1986, Ger./Aust./Switz.) 95m Peter Voiss/ ZDF–ORF–SRG c (Trans: The False One)

Marie Colbin *(Olga)*, Lino Capolicchio *(Silvano)*, Johannes Thanheiser *(The Father)*, Martin Abram *(Florian)*, Michele Remo Remotti, Anni Pircher, Siegelinde Muller, Otto Donner, Raimund Marini.

The tension between the German-speaking minority of Northern Italy and the rest of the people of the country is embodied by Colbin, a woman dubbed "Die Walsche" ("The False One" or "The Tramp") by her fellow villagers for her fraternization with the Italians to the south. She had left her northern village to live with a southern Italian in Bolzano, but when she returns to attend her father's funeral, she finds herself treated as an enemy. Back in Bolzano, she does not quite fit in either, because of her insistence on speaking only German. The southern Italians accept her decision and treat her warmly, although they do think she is a bit strange. Although made by Germans exploring a German-minority problem, the filmmakers find the Italians to be more sympathetic than the stubborn, backward villagers of the German-speaking north.

p, Peter Voiss; d, Werner Masten; w, Werner Masten, Joseph Zoderer (based on the novel by Joseph Zoderer); ph, Klaus Eichhamer; m, Muzzi Loffredo; ed, Michael Breining; art d, Peter Kaser; cos, Karin Gulberlet.

Drama   **(PR:C MPAA:NR)**

DIE ZWEI GESICHTER DES JANUAR†   (1986, Ger.) 100m Monaco–Suddeutscher Rundfunk c (Trans: Two Faces of January)

Yolande Gilot *(Colette MacFarland)*, Charles Brauer *(Chester MacFarland)*, Thomas Schucke *(Rydal Keener)*.

This is the 16th film to be based on mystery writer Patricia Highsmith's novels (the best of which was Wim Wenders' THE AMERICAN FRIEND). Set in Greece, the film follows Brauer and his wife Gilot as they escape a bank fraud charge in the United States. After a stop in Switzerland where they deposit their take, the two travel to Athens under assumed names. Enter Schucke, a young archaeology student who spots Brauer and follows him because of his close resemblance to the boy's recently deceased father. Schucke sees Brauer kill a hotel detective and then joins the couple on their getaway to Crete. The situation soon leads to a *menage a trois*, but the relationship ends in tragedy when the jealous Brauer accidentally kills his wife.

p, Georg Althammer; d, Wolfgang Storch; w, Karl Heinz Willschrei, Wolfgang Storch (based on the novel by Patricia Highsmith); ph, Wolfgang Treu; m, Eberhard Schoener; ed, Inez Regnier; set d, Mike Karapiperis.

Crime   **(PR:O MPAA:NR)**

DIRT BIKE KID, THE   (1986) 90m Trinity/Concorde–Cinema Group c

Peter Billingsley *(Jack Simmons)*, Stuart Pankin *(Mr. Hodgkins)*, Anne Bloom *(Janet Simmons)*, Patrick Collins *(Mike)*, Sage Parker *(Miss Clavell)*, Chad Sheets *(Bo)*, Gavin Allen *(Max)*, Danny Breen *(Flaherty)*, "Weasel" Forshaw *(Big Slime)*, John William Galt *(Chief)*, Rocky, the Dog *(Himself)*, Courtney Kraus *(Beth)*, Holly Schenck *(Sue)*, Al Evans *(Mr. Zak)*, Angie Bolling *(Pretty Woman)*, Gena Sleete *(Widow White)*, Betty R. King *(Secretary)*, Bill Shaw *(Ben)*, Barnett Shprize *(Little Man)*, Brian Sadler *(Jimmy)*, Harvey Christiansen *(Security Guard)*, Gary Carter *(Biker No. 1)*, Dale Kassel *(Umpire)*, Beth Larsen *(Clerk)*, Elaine Williams *(Teenage Girl)*, Tyress Allen *(Sergeant)*, Emily Rose Kelley *(Waitress)*.

Trade in a Steven Spielberg space alien for a Yamaha motor bike, keep the special effects on the inexpensive side, then assume filmgoers under age twelve are morons, and what you get is THE DIRT BIKE KID, an innocuous and wholly forgettable effort aimed at the pre-teen set. Billingsley (the young hero of 1983's A CHRISTMAS STORY) is an independent youngster who lives with his presumably widowed mother Bloom (it's never explained why there is no father around, but never mind). In a modern twist on the old "Jack and the Beanstalk" story,

Billingsley spends $50 of what was supposed to have been grocery money and throws in his bicycle for a mudcaked dirt bike. Bloom is understandably angered with her son, though it turns out Billingsley has gotten quite a deal for his money. This dirt bike is magical, gunning its engine to speak and flashing its big eye-like headlights. Bloom takes the bike to a dealer and gets back her 50 but the bike makes its own way back to the wide-eyed Billingsley. The spunky kid arranges a deal to earn the bike, a beneficial arrangement considering what happens next.

Pankin, the local oily banker, is eager to get his hands on a hot-dog stand owned by Collins, a bumbling nice-guy the neighborhood kids all adore. It's Pankin's plan to put a new branch of his bank on the hot-dog stand site, but naturally, Billingsley and his bike won't allow this. The boy declares war, yet quickly learns one doesn't mess with the infinite when the powerful Pankin retaliates. He lies to Billingsley about looking for alternate sites, then sets out to destroy Collins' place anyway. By using a school computer to tap into the bank, Billingsley discovers Pankin intends to make substantial profits by building on the hot-dog stand site, since he is also involved in real estate. Billingsley and the bike are chased by some motorcycle thugs but manage to stop the destruction in the nick of time. One silly chase sequence later, Pankin agrees not to tear down Collins' place and the bike, having done its job, goes on to a new owner.

Viewers might want to watch this with a checklist to keep track of numerous lifts from E.T. They're hard to miss, particularly when the bike takes Billingsley on an aerial night ride complete with John Williams-like music blaring on the soundtrack. Bloom, in "The-Mom-With-A-Heart-Of-Gold" role, bears more than a passing resemblance to Dee Wallace (aka: Dee Wallace Stone), and the list goes on and on. The film's other big problem is that it's just plain stupid. The adult characters seem to have a collective IQ that rivals the bike's, and when the going gets tough they're generally reduced to yelling and arm flaying. Pankin is a notable exception, giving some depth to the slimy banker, though that's really not saying much. The not-so-special effects consist of conspicuous rear-screen projections and poorly cut shots of the bike going through motions. There's some occasional salty language tossed in to satisfy a "PG" rating, though it's nothing that hasn't hit the playgrounds of American grammar schools. What may bother some parents, however, is the sexual harassment Pankin inflicts on would-be employees, which gets played for laughs here. It's not funny in real life, it's not funny in adult comedies, and it's most certainly not funny in films specifically aimed at youngsters.

p, Julie Corman; d, Hoite C. Caston; w, David Brandes, Lewis Colick (based on a story by J. Halloran [Corman]); ph, Daniel Lacambre; m, Bill Bowersock, Phil Shenale); ed, Jeff Freeman; art d, Becky Block; set d, J. Grey Smith; cos, Sawnie R. Baldridge; makeup, Jean A. Black.

Comedy   **Cas.**   **(PR:A MPAA:PG)**

DIRTY GAMES†   (1986, Phil.) Cinex-F.Puzon

[No cast or credits available.]

A gang of backstabbing, crooked individuals become enmeshed in a kidnaping plot when a businessman fakes the abduction of his son in order to ruin his wife's extramarital affair. Thinking the child has been fathered by her lover, the businessman has a henchman kidnap the boy. The henchman in turn frames the wife's lover, a small-time crook, but he manages to get away with the crime and the ransom money, only to go face to face with the businessman in their climactic "dirty game."

Action   **(PR:O MPAA:NR)**

DO YOU REMEMBER DOLLY BELL?*   (1986, Yugo.) 106m Sutjeska Film Sarajevo-TV Sarajevo/International Home Cinema c (SJECAS LI SE DOLLY BELL?)

Slavko Stimac *(Dino)*, Slobodan Aligrudic *(Father)*, Ljiljana Blagojevic *(Dolly Bell)*, Mira Banjac *(Mother)*, Pavle Vujisic *(Uncle)*, Nada Pani *(Aunt)*, Boro Stjepanovic *(Pog)*.

As a result of the international acclaim accorded Emir Kusturica's WHEN FATHER WAS AWAY ON BUSINESS, his 1981 debut film, DO YOU REMEMBER DOLLY BELL?, was given its initial American release on the small art-house circuit. Covering terrain similar to his later film, Kusturica uses the events in the life of one family—specifically the experiences of the teenage son, Stimac—as an allegory for the political climate in Yugoslavia at the time. This is a particularly effective form of political analysis in that the people shown are those actually affected by abstract theoretical decisions, and not the privileged policy makers.

It is the early 1960s, and there is a strong push by the Tito regime for a cultural revolution to keep Yugoslav youth up to date with Western influences, particularly rock 'n' roll and movies. Stimac and his family live in an impoverished Moslem section on the outskirts of Sarajevo (looking nothing like the glamorous Olympic city it was to become 20 years later). The teenagers spend much of their time at the local youth center, watching movies from the West and listening to rock music. The director is a soft-spoken intellectual given the arduous task of interesting the kids in something beyond pursuing petty thrills. One of his specific goals is the formation of a rock band to play at the center and to represent the area to the entire city. He hears Stimac sing, and immediately makes the boy and his closely knit band of friends the focus of his pet project. The director slowly works on gaining Stimac's confidence, playing chess with him and introducing him to things beyond his small world.

A setback occurs when the director is confronted by the teenagers' hero, an older bully who rides around on a motorcycle and has money and girls. The brute taunts the director by defiantly breaking the rules of the center. By reacting to the challenge passively, the director loses the confidence of the kids, who cheer on the bully. To further impress Stimac and friends, the brute drops off a girl for Stimac to shelter until the biker is ready to take her to the city to be a prostitute. Stimac keeps the girl concealed from his family in a pigeon coop, establishing a quick friendship with her, unaware of her future with the brute. She is called "Dolly Bell," the name of a British stripper who appeared in one of the films the kids saw at the center. By caring for Dolly Bell, while sharing intimate secrets with her, Stimac soon falls in love. But the brute who brought her soon destroys Stimac's bliss by bringing the boy's closest friends to have sex with the reluctant and crying girl. She is then taken to the city, where she dons a blonde wig and performs a striptease in a sleazy nightclub, additionally acting as a prostitute with the brute as her pimp. Later, Stimac decides to pursue the girl with whom he has fallen in love. Scratching together a few dollars, he travels to the city and the nightclub where Dolly Bell dances. She introduces him to intimate sex before her pimp barges in on them. With Stimac hiding in the corner, the brute beats Dolly Bell, demanding she give him more money. Stimac attempts to retaliate, but is easily beaten. He returns home to face the death of his father, a man who fervently believed in Marxist ideology over his Moslem religion and freely expressed this while hiding behind a bottle. Treating her husband's expressed beliefs as so much hot air, Stimac's mother takes her dead husband's body and points it toward Mecca. An uplifting ending, symbolizing a bright future for Stimac, and for the youth of Yugoslavia, has Stimac and his band playing in front of a large, frantically cheering audience.

Winner of the Golden Lion for Best First Film at the 1981 Venice Film Festival, DO YOU REMEMBER DOLLY BELL? first revealed director Kusturica's ability to effectively weave insightful drama, interesting characters, and colorful backgrounds into a meaningful whole. The messages he hopes to transmit lurk subtly beneath the action, and are introduced without sermon or force. Basically, DO YOU REMEMBER DOLLY BELL? presents a positive solution to the Yugoslavian youth—it is not rhetoric or political theory that controls a person's life, but the willingness to learn and grow. Stimac's continual repetition of "Every day in every way, I'm a little better" expresses this perfectly. By the end of the film he has learned that what will become of him will be the result of his own efforts, in contrast with his father who continually blamed the inefficiency of the political system for his troubles. Ultimately it is Stimac's tender initiation into sexual relations by Dolly Bell that pushes him into manhood and responsibility. Through this relationship he learns to respect and care for a woman instead of regarding her as nothing but a sex object. (In Serbian; English subtitles.)

d, Emir Kusturica; w, Abdulah Sidran; ph, Vilko Filac; m, Zoran Simjanovic; art d, Kemal Hrustanovic.

Drama   **(PR:O   MPAA:NR)**

DOBRE SVETIO†   (1986, Czech.) Barrandov (Trans: Amateur
                                                              Photographer)

Karel Hermanek, Jana Sulcova, Anna Tomsova, Ivana Chytilova.

d, Karel Kachyna; w, Karel Cabranek; ph, Vladimir Smutny; m, Angelo Michajlov; set d, Boris Moravec.

DOBROVOLJCI†   (1986, Yugo.) 96m Zeta–Dunav–Televizija c (Trans:
                                                              Volunteers)

Velimir Bata Zivojinovic, Ljubisa Samardzic, Boro Begovic, Mustafa Nadarevic, Bogdan Kiklic, Radko Polic, Ljuba Tadic, Zarko Lausevic, Biljana Ristic.

Seven bungling Slavs are stranded on a desert island where their comic misadventures include a visit by a platoon of parachuting dancing girls. Eventually the group captures an enemy submarine, keeping its crew as their prisoners and supplying the groundwork for more fun and games. Basically the film is a series of sketches strung together with little logic except to entertain. Sort of an Eastern Bloc STRIPES (1981), but lacking the charm of the latter's star, Bill Murray.

d, Predrag Golubovic; w, Predrag Golubovic, Vlatko Gilic, Ratko Durovic; ph, Milivoje Milivojevic; m, Kornelije Kovac; art d, Milenko Jeremic.

Comedy   **(PR:C   MPAA:NR)**

DR. OTTO AND THE RIDDLE OF THE GLOOM BEAM**   (1986) 88m
                                                              Sweat Equities

Jim Varney *(Dr. Otto/Rudd Hardtact/Laughin' Jack/Guy Dandy/Auntie Nelda)*, Glenn Petech *(Otto's Head Hand)*, Myke Mueller *(Lance)*, Jackie Welch *(Doris)*, Daniel Butler *(Slave Willie)*, Esther Huston *(Tina)*, Tina Goetze *(Rhonda Sue)*, Jennifer Wood *(Monique)*, David Landon *(Bank President Rutherford)*, Mack Bennett *(V.P.)*, Winslow Stillman *(Lance's Dad)*, Irv Kane *(Herr Vonschnck)*, Leslie Potter *(Mme. Vonschnck)*, Bill Middleton *(Man at Autoteller)*, Nancy Alderson *(Woman at Autoteller)*, Bonnie Keen *(Checkout Girl)*, Shauree Crooks *(Shopper)* Bill Byrge *(Gas Station Attendant)*, Tom Nix *(Gas Station Customer)*, Royce Clark *(Suburbanite)*, Mac Pirkle *(Drunk)*, Terri Merryman *(Newswoman)*, Joey Anderson *(Miss Apple)*, John B. Murrey *(Science Fair Judge)*, Jimmy Jacobs *(The Dump)*, Carl Graves *(President of the U.S.A.)*, Daniel Butler *(Aide No. 1 Kegler)*, Robert Wynne *(Aide No. 2 Feldon)*, Jorn Hall *(Man at Street with Newspaper)*, Chris Reguli, B.J. Rogers *(Nurses)*, Beverlee Ogles *(Girl at the Bait Stake)*, Henry Arnold *(Bank Officer)*, Charles Hughes *(News Director)*, Michael Cisneros *(Student [Weenie])*, Steven Leasure, Warren Meigs, Dick Frankhauser, Larry Frankenbauch, Donald Fahey, Jim Tolley, Van W. Liggett *(Pirates)*, George Frasier *(Bartender)*, Mindy Briggs *(Barfly)*, Katie Ingelson *(Girl in Arcade)*, Christian Bell *(Boy in Arcade)*, Rick Stewart, Scott Jones *(POWs)*, Raymond S. Childs, J.R. Cherry, Jr., Charles Baker, W.S. Cooke, Jr., D.M. Maillie, Al Behel, Charles Norton, Tom Sparks, John R. Cherry, Sr. *(Bank V.P.s)*, Boy Scout Troop 217: Jim Neville, John Eubank, Chris Dunham, Joseph Muse, John Garth, Ben Lawhon, Carter Baker, John

Feger, David Dixon, Michael Cisneros, Chad Chadwick, William Key, Josh Cherry, Matt Mather, Gabe Jacobs, Art Holscher, Brian Bradley, Lee Teal, Brock Flynn, Robert Hendrickson, Jeff Dillon, Trey Harwell, Chris Harwell, Steven Shaffer, Brad Mangrum, Chris Tapia, Mike Oliver, Eddie Childers, Steve Warden, Jory Gregory *(Rudd Hardtacts' Boys)*, Tim Wright, Russell Johnston, Cecilia Johnson, Robbie Douglas, Demitri Stokes, Laura Petach, Kim Collins, Amy Ingleson, Veronica Lawson, Chris Chamberlain, Whit Martin, Kris Brodersen, Mike Brown, Tom Bailey, Mike Buhl, Karen Jordan, Chip Chilton, Maddie Kahane *(High School Students)*.

Jim Varney, a rubber-faced comedian from Down South, achieved national prominence in a series of television advertisements with an annoying character named Ernest. Addressing his silent buddy "Vern" (played by the camera), Varney's elbow-in-the-ribs style—and the phrase "know whut I mean, Vern?"— brought him instant success and made Varney a sort of icon in American pop culture. Undoubtedly his film debut in DR. OTTO AND THE RIDDLE OF THE GLOOM BEAM will come as a surprise to anyone who has deliberately avoided buying a product Varney endorsed. While by no means an exercise in sparkling wit, there are a few moments within the film that might get a rise from comedy fans. Among other characters, Varney plays Dr. Otto, a mad scientist who plots to take over the world by destroying the global economy. He uses a giant degausser to erase bank computer records, sending dollar values skyrocketing to incredible heights. Mueller, an old schoolmate of Varney's, sets out with his long-suffering assistant Welch to find out just who is behind these evil goings-on. Back in his laboratory, Varney sets out to stop his foe. Using a machine which can alter his appearance, Varney alternately adopts the guises of an Australian mercenary and a pirate in an effort to trap the handsome hero. Mueller and Welch manage to escape, but when Varney adopts the guise of a kindly (though slightly sinister) old woman, they fall into his trap. With the help of Varney's sympathetic assistant Huston, the plucky duo are once again freed but they still must deal with another of Varney's incarnations. This time he's a dapper song-and-dance man who lures them into an elevator. The door closes, then cables snap, sending Mueller and Welch plummeting towards certain death. Instead they end up in Varney's secret laboratory, where Mueller rescues Huston before routing the mad scientist's evil plans. Welch and Huston are left to push Mueller's gas-empty car in search of fuel, and end up at a service station run by—who else?—Varney, this time in his renowned "Ernest" persona.

Had DR. OTTO been a non-stop 90 minutes of Varney mugging into the camera saying "know whut I mean?", this would have been an excruciating exercise in pure cinematic torture. But the format of a science-fiction parody actually suits Varney, who shows some good comic ability within his multiple characterizations. The film is marked by clever touches, such as a smiley-faced robot whose expression changes to fit his mood, a game-show spoof in the midst of a jungle, and a day-care center which teaches young boys the art of mercenary warfare. Varney's Dr. Otto has a mysterious hand on top of his head, with fingers that wiggle whenever the scientist goes mad with evil glee (the actor playing the crown palm is never seen, but amazingly received screen credit for his unusual role). The production design is imaginative and the special effects look good, belying the film's obvious low budget. Still, this is a far-from-perfect comedy. While the lampooning clearly has some thought behind it, some ideas are never developed beyond their initial gag value. The wishy-washy nature of Mueller's character is another detriment. Initially introduced as an honest and true-blue hero in the Biff Baxter mold (Jeff Daniels' role in THE PURPLE ROSE OF CAIRO, a character to whom Mueller bears more than a passing resemblance), Mueller degenerates into a simple-minded fool. This is hardly a worthy adversary for Varney's diabolic fiend, and damages a good deal of the story's comic conflict. Such problems are genuine disappointments for, amazing as it sounds, DR. OTTO AND THE RIDDLE OF THE GLOOM BEAM shows an inventive flair that is often missing from big-budget, "name star" comedies. Songs include: "If I Were a Carpenter" (Tim Hardin), "Our Love Festers" (Bruce Arntson, performed by Lisa Silver), "Meet Me at the Rainbow Grill" (Craig Roads, performed by Turley Richards), "Attack and Coffin Themes" (Aaron Keister), "The Riddle" (Shane Keister, John Cherry, Coke Sams).

p, Coke Sams; d, John Cherry; w, John Cherry, Coke Sams, Daniel Butler, Glenn Petach, Steve Leasure, Jim Varney; ph, Jim May; m, Shane Keister; ed, Pamela Scott Arnold; prod d, Glenn Petach; cos, Kathy Cherry; spec eff, Frank Cappello; m/l, Tim Hardin, Bruce Arntson, Craig Roads, Aaron Keister, Shane Keister, John Cherry, Coke Sams; stunts, Roger Fleming.

Comedy/Science Fiction   **Cas.**   **(PR:A   MPAA:PG)**

DOEA TANDA MATA†   (1986, Indonesia) 93m Citra Jaya/Indonesian Film
                                                 Council c (Trans: Mementos)

Alex Komang, Jenny Rachman, Hermin Chentini, Sylvia Wdiantono, Corbi, Eka Gandara, Bambang.

Extremely successful in its native Indonesia, DOEA TANDA MATA is an overtly political picture set in the 1930's in what was then the Dutch East Indies. The film's protagonist is a young violinist, Komang, who is shaken by the death of a close friend at the hands of a police commissioner. Komang vows to get vengeance and spends his time plotting and preparing an assassination attempt. In the meantime he becomes involved with the dead friend's sister, Rachman, the star of a traveling theater troupe. His relationship with Rachman and his failure to act immediately against the commissioner anger his militantly anti-Dutch cohorts, who lash out against him. The work of Indonesia's most popular director, DOEA TANDA MATA received awards for Best Actor, Best Cinematography, Best Art Direction, and Best Sound in that country's Citra Awards ceremony.

p, Haryoko Punarwan; d, Teguh Karya; w, Teguh Karya, Alex Komang; ph, George Kamarullah; m, Idris Sardi; ed, Rizal Asmar.

Drama   **(PR:C MPAA:NR)**

DOGS IN SPACE†   (1986, Aus.) 105m Central Park/Entertainment
                                    Media-Burrowes-Dennis Wright c

Michael Hutchence *(Sam)*, Saskia Post *(Anna)*, Nique Needles *(Tim)*, Deanna Bond *(The Girl)*, Tony Helou *(Luchio)*, Chris Haywood *(Chainsaw Man)*, Peter Walsh *(Anthony)*, Laura Swanson *(Clare)*, Adam Briscomb *(Grant)*, Sharon Jessop *(Leanne)*, Edward Clayton-Jones *(Nick)*, Martii Coles *(Mark)*, Chuck Meo *(Charles)*, Caroline Lee *(Jenny)*, Fiona Latham *(Barbara)*, Stephanie Johnson *(Erica)*, Gary Foley *(Barry)*, Glenys Osborne *(Lisa)*, Helen Phillips *(Stacey)*, Barbara Jungwirth *(Sam's Mother)*, Joe Camilleri *(Terry Toweling Man)*.

Though the title implies a film with characters like Scottie and Mr. Spock, the anecdotal narrative involves a group of eight young adults who all share the same house. Located in Richmond, an inner-city suburb of Melbourne, Australia, the house seems to be in the throes of a never-ending party, with bottle-strewn decor and a constant state of hangover among the residents. Hutchence and Post are a couple living at the house. Though Post has some ambition, her boy friend's attitudes shoot down whatever potential she envisions. Bond is a drifter who has come to the lodging, while Helou, a student, seems to be the only one who gets anything done. The youthful band causes trouble in the neighborhood, but local cops put up with the shenanigans that ultimately lead to a tragic end.

p, Glenys Rowe; d&w, Richard Lowenstein; ph, Andrew de Groot; ed, Jill Bilcock; md, Ollie Olsen; art d, Jody Borland.

Drama   **(PR:C-O MPAA:NR)**

DOKTOR†   (1986, Yugo.) 95m Viba c (Trans: The Doctor)

Slavko Cerjak *(Dr. Vladimir Kantet)*, Tea Glazar, Zvone Hribar, Ivan Rupnik, Demeter Bitenc, Dare Valio, Andrej Kurent.

Based on fact, the film tells the story of a highly respected doctor in the Nazi-occupied Ljubljana region of Yugoslavia who secretly works with the underground resistance movement. Because he is a "citizen above suspicion," it takes the authorities some time to begin their investigation. They eventually do, however, and he is tortured and killed, though not before he has done considerable damage to the occupying forces.

d&w, Vojko Duletic; ph, Karpo Godina; ed, Toni Ziherle; art d, Mirko Lipuzic; cos, Milena Kumar.

War/Biography   **(PR:O MPAA:NR)**

DONA HERLINDA AND HER SON**   (1986, Mex.) 90m Cinevista c
                                    (DONA HERLINDA Y SU HIJO)

Guadalupe Del Toro *(Dona Herlinda)*, Arturo Meza *(Ramon)*, Marco Antonio Trevino *(Rodolfo)*, Leticia Lupersio *(Olga)*, Guillermina Alba.

A sex comedy usually succeeds when it gives a fresh twist to old expectations, something DONA HERLINDA AND HER SON does with unrelenting zest and novel ideas. Del Toro is the wealthy mother of Trevino, a doctor involved in a homosexual relationship with Meza, a younger music student. The two men are in desperate need of some privacy to carry on their affair, so Del Toro invites Meza to move into her home. This is more than an act of charity, though, for Del Toro has an intricate plan to keep her son happy. She next brings in Lupersio to become Trevino's heterosexual wife, which sets off the green-eyed monster in Meza. He goes out for a romp, hoping to forget the traitorous Trevino, but it just doesn't work. Instead Meza returns to Del Toro's home, where he is named godfather to Trevino and Lupersio's baby. Since Lupersio wants to return to her job with Amnesty International, Meza takes over the mothering chores. Trevino has the best of both worlds, Lupersio has her career, Meza has what he wants, and, thanks to Del Toro's careful maneuverings, everyone lives happily ever after.
   Marvelously funny, DONA HERLINDA AND HER SON develops its unusual plot line in a simple, matter-of-fact style. Each new turn seems perfectly logical, belying the complications involved in Del Toro's orchestration of personality and situation. The characters are mindfully etched, with performances that make the viewer honestly care about these people. Sexual situations, be they homosexual or heterosexual, are wisely presented without comment, simply becoming a part of the comic tableau. Director Hermosillo's goal is to entertain while making an unpretentious statement about human nature. Overall, an engaging and charming work. (In Spanish; English subtitles.)

p, Manuel Barbachano Ponce; d&w, Jaime Humberto Hermosillo (based on a novel by Jorge Lopez Paez); ph, Miguel Ehrenberg; ed, Luis Kelly.

Comedy   **(PR:O MPAA:O)**

DONNA ROSEBUD†   (1986) 90m Somersaulter c

Elizabeth Miller, Kathleen Sykora.

The first live-action film from animator J.P. Somersaulter (usually paired with Lillian Somersaulter Moast), which places a real-life character in a cartoon-like fantasy world. This world is one which knows no real logic, allowing its inhabitants to change their ages and professions at will. As a result, the title character is sometimes a doctor, or a marathon runner, or a lawyer, or a musician. When she starts to have nightmares, her fantasy world gets even stranger. An independent feature from the Chicago area, DONNA ROSEBUD emerges as an interesting

synthesis of the Tex Avery/Chuck Jones style of craziness in the confines of a real-life setting.

d, J.P. Somersaulter.

Fantasy   **(PR:C MPAA:NR)**

DOT AND KEETO†   (1986, Aus.) 80m Yoram Gross c

Voices: Keith Scott, Robyn Moore.

In this entry of the popular part-animation children's series, the ever-plucky heroine Dot explores the world of insects. After eating a red root, Dot finds herself reduced to the size of an average bug. She is befriended by Keeto, a mosquito, and Butterwalk, a caterpillar, who rescue the poor girl after she is taken hostage by a group of ants. Other six-legged confrontations involve some hungry cockroaches, a religious praying mantis, a dragonfly, and a nasty wasp. Eventually Dot munches on an antidotal green root, which restores her to normal size as she bids adieu to her insect friends.

p&d, Yoram Gross; w, John Palmer (based on a character created by Ethel Pedley); ph, Graham Sharpe; m, Guy Gross, John Levine, John Zulaikha, John Palmer; ed, Rod Hay, Andrew Plain; anim, Ray Nowland, Andrew Szemenyei, Ariel Ferrari, Nicholas Harding, Rowen Avon, Paul McAdam, Stan Walker, John Berge, Wal Louge.

Animated Feature   **(PR:AAA MPAA:NR)**

DOT AND THE WHALE†   (1986, Aus.) 75m Yoram Gross c

Voices: Keith Scott, Robyn Moore.

This time out the popular Australian cartoon character Dot joins her friend Nelson, a dolphin, in a humanitarian effort to save a whale. The seagoing mammal is stuck on an Australian beach and whale-hunters and a greedy shop-keeper want the poor beast for their own purposes. Leave it to the ever-resourceful Dot to rescue her new friend with a plan that puts the nefarious nogoodniks in their place.

p&d, Yoram Gross; w, John Palmer; ph, Graham Sharpe; m, Guy Gross; ed, Rod Hay; animation, Ray Nowland.

Animated Feature   **(PR:AAA MPAA:NR)**

DOUBLE MESSIEURS†   (1986, Fr.) 90m Sagamore Cinema/BAC c (Trans:
                                    Double Gentlemen)

Jean Francois Stevenin *(Francois)*, Yves Alonso *(Leo)*, Carole Bouquet *(Helene)*.

Stevenin produced, wrote, directed, and costars with Alonso in this story of two lifelong, fun-loving friends who have trouble accepting the fact that they are growing older. When they decide to look up a former friend they find his wife instead, and she fills them in on her less-than-happy existence. Mixed in with the characters' revelations is a swipe at France's perpetually adolescent box-office star, Jean-Paul Belmondo. Alonso's character is a Belmondo-ish looking fellow who claims to be the star's stunt double.

p,d&w, Jean Francois Stevenin; ph, Pascal Marti; ed, Yann Dodet.

Comedy   **(PR:C MPAA:NR)**

DOUCE FRANCE†   (1986, Fr./Ger.) 90m Les Films 2001 c (Trans: Gentle
                                    France)

Barbara Rudnik *(Lise)*, Andrea Ferreol *(Mme. Maurin)*, Hito Jaulmes *(Frederic)*, Hanns Zischler *(Karl)*, Patrick Bouchitey *(Roland)*, Jacques Nolot *(Jeannot)*, Bernadette Le Sache *(Frederic's Mother)*, Paul Le Person *(Frederic's Grandfather)*.

It is the early 1940's and Rudnik, a German cabaret singer, is forced to leave her native land because of her Jewish heritage. She takes refuge in France, but when the Nazis occupy that land, she must go into hiding. With the help of her manager Zischler, she assumes a new identity and settles in a mountain village. The locals are uncertain about this new well-dressed resident, and many suspect she is really a German agent. Community ire is further aroused when it's learned that Rudnik has been sleeping with a local youth. When the area is freed from German control in 1944, Rudnik is shot by a French Resistance fighter whose sexual advances she had previously spurned. This unusual story is based on a true incident of the era.

p&d, Francois Chardeaux; w, Francois Chardeaux, Serge Schoukine, Michel del Castillo (based on a story by Michel del Castillo); ph, Jean-Claude Larrieu (Fujicolor); m, Nicolas Skorsky; ed, Anna Ruiz; m/l, Nicholas Skorsky, Vera Baudey.

Drama   **(PR:O MPAA:NR)**

DOWN AND OUT IN BEVERLY HILLS**   (1986) 103m Touchstone/
                                    BV c

Nick Nolte *(Jerry Baskin)*, Richard Dreyfuss *(Dave Whiteman)*, Bette Midler *(Barbara Whiteman)*, Little Richard *(Orvis Goodnight)*, Tracy Nelson *(Jenny Whiteman)*, Elizabeth Pena *(Carmen)*, Evan Richards *(Max Whiteman)*, Mike the Dog *(Matisse)*, Donald F. Muhich *(Dr. Von Zimmer)*, Paul Mazursky *(Sidney Waxman)*, Valerie Curtin *(Pearl Waxman)*, Jack Bruskoff *(Mel Whiteman)*, Geraldine Dreyfuss *(Sadie Whiteman)*, Barry Primus *(Lou Waltzberg)*, Irene Tsu *(Sheila Waltzberg)*, Michael Yama *(Nagamichi)*, Ranbir Bahi *(Ranbir)*, Eloy Casados *(Tom Tom)*, Felton Perry *(Al)*, Michael Greene *(Ed)*, Ken Koch *(Patrick)*, Dorothy Tristan *(Dorothy)*, Raymond Lee *(Yamato)*, Carolyn Allport *(Girl*

Feeding Kerouac), Sue Kiel (Roxanne), Reza Bashar (Iranian Neighbor), Joseph Makkar (Iranian Boy), Jason Williams (Lance), Darryl Henriques (Geraldo), Nick Ullett (Nigel), Michael Blue (Cop), Allan Malamud (Caterer), Salvatore Espinoza (Caterer's Assistant), Michael Voletti (Maurice), Betsy Mazursky (Stylish Jogger), Donald V. Allen, Neil Cunningham (Security Guards), Bobby Good (Security Alarm Dispatcher), Sandy Ignon (Barry), Margrit Ramme (Sandra Goodnight), Pearl Huang (Translator), Yung Sun (Minister Chan), Eugene Choy, Mae Koh-Ruden, George Sasaki, Leland Sun (Chinese Delegation), Andre Philippe (Party Guest), Lew Hopson (Paramedic), Carlton Cuse (Water Man), Bill Cross (Helicopter Pilot), Alexis Arquette (Band Member), Dr. Toni Grant (Herself).

This is the very first R-rated picture ever to come out of that bastion of squeaky cleanliness, the Walt Disney Studios. True, it was made under the aegis of their subsidiary Touchstone, which has since been responsible for several more of this genre. Walt would have liked it anyhow. This is a howl from start to finish. Paul

Mazursky, the one-time actor (THE BLACKBOARD JUNGLE) and TV writer (The pilot for "The Monkees" with his former partner, Larry Tucker) and sketch writer (The Danny Kaye Show) is at his best when he writes what he knows. In the case of his hits like I LOVE YOU, ALICE B. TOKLAS and BOB & CAROL & TED & ALICE it was clear that he was on familiar ground. His flops, including THE TEMPEST, WILLIE AND PHIL, and ALEX IN WONDERLAND, may have been too fanciful. Once again, Mazursky deals with things he knows as he and cowriter Capetanos rework the Renoir classic BOUDU SAUVE DES EAUX (BOUDU SAVED FROM DROWNING) to wonderful advantage.

Dreyfuss is a grown-up version of "Duddy Kravitz" who has made it big in the coat hanger business. He and wife Midler live with their children, Nelson and Richards, in a huge house on the right side of the tracks in Beverly Hills. (There really are railroad tracks in Beverly Hills that run parallel with Santa Monica Boulevard. The homes north of the tracks are in an area known as "the flats," and those are the million-dollar houses that sit no more than 10 feet from each other, creating the most expensive and densest slum one could ever find. South of the tracks is where all of the commercial streets are, like famed Rodeo Drive, Bedford Drive—where the psychiatrists sit and listen to neurotic moguls—Beverly Drive, and a few others. South of those is where the "poor people" of Beverly Hills live—south of Wilshire and Olympic Boulevards—and where Mazursky himself keeps an office.) Midler is the ultimate yenta who spends her days having her hair and nails done, going to classes, and living the Beverly Hills credo: "Shop 'till you drop." Dreyfuss drives a Rolls convertible to his downtown manufacturing plant, where he is a benevolent exploiter of the wetback laborers who toil in his factory. Nelson is the anorectic daughter who attends school in the east, something that galls Dreyfuss, who is paying lots of money for her education and can't understand why she has to attend a college so far away (and so expensive) when kids from the east are clamoring to come to places like UCLA, USC, and the other schools in the area. Son Richards is a budding filmmaker and walks around the house with his state-of-the-art video camera shooting everything that happens. He is also an androgynous child and can't make up his mind if he wants to be number one son or number two daughter to the family. Also living in the house are Pena, a succulent Latino maid with whom Dreyfuss is having it off, and Matisse (Mike), the family dog, a border collie who has taken a cue from Nelson and is refusing to eat, despite regular visits to a doggie psychiatrist, Muhich. Dreyfuss is doing big business with the Chinese and his life seems to be without worry.

Nolte is a tramp, walking the streets of Beverly Hills looking for a place to rest his head. When his dog runs away, Nolte is distraught to the point of suicide. He leaps the fence of the Dreyfuss home and attempts to drown himself in their swimming pool. (There really are some people who have been down and out in Beverly Hills and who sleep in the parks and use the public bathroom on the corner of Santa Monica Boulevard and Beverly Drive to freshen up.) Next door to the house lives Little Richard, a famous rock 'n' roller who bristles because when the Dreyfuss security system goes off, cops and overhead copters arrive within seconds, and Richard feels that he doesn't get that kind of service because he is black. Nolte's life is saved and he is taken into the family, against his wishes. He immediately proves his worth by opening all of the dog food cans and making up a mixture for Matisse. He explains to Midler that since Matisse lives in the house with no dog pals, the dog thinks he's human and wants to eat what humans

eat. He fixes the dog a bowl of the food, then eats some himself in front of the animal, thus convincing Matisse that it's good enough for canine consumption. Midler is fascinated by Nolte. (She sings "You Belong to Me" after they make love.) She does work for the homeless, but never dreamed she'd actually have one living in her home.

Dreyfuss invites Nolte to become part of the family and it is this decision that serves as the core of the story. In the course of events, Nolte sleeps with Midler *and* Nelson *and* Pena, and when Dreyfuss learns about this he wants to kill Nolte.

He learns the flaming facts at a large party tossed for the Chinese delegation and all of the guests wind up in the inevitable "everyone into the pool" sequence. The picture ends as Nolte is about to move off on the road again, but the entire family stands in the alley behind the mansion. Nolte turns around and sees that they still love him and want him to stay (no word is spoken, but it's evident), and he turns to come back to them, an alteration from the Renoir ending.

Lots of very funny moments throughout the film, and the dog steals whatever scene he is in. His real name is Mike, and he was trained by Clint Rowe, who was also responsible for the excellent animal, Jed, who costarred in THE JOURNEY OF NATTY GANN. Mike is so funny that he reminds one of the famous cartoon that showed a dog wearing sunglasses as he was being interviewed by some panting Hollywood reporters. His comment was "What I really want to do is direct." Congratulations to everyone for this depiction of how the other half loves and lives. Anyone who has ever spent any time in Beverly Hills will agree that this is far more accurate than BEVERLY HILLS COP or any other film set in the famed city within a city. (Beverly Hills, population about 35,000, is surrounded on all four sides by Los Angeles. It has its own school system, police force, library system, and fire department, and has a considerably lower real estate tax base than the rest of Los Angeles.) The prices along Rodeo Drive are so outrageous that most residents prefer to do their shopping elsewhere in less crowded and less expensive stores. It's a great place to live but, because of the money it might cost, you wouldn't want to visit it. Songs include "Once in a Lifetime" (David Byrne, Brian Eno).

p&d, Paul Mazursky; w, Paul Mazursky, Leon Capetanos (based on the play "Boudu Sauve Des Eaux" by Rene Fauchois); ph, Donald McAlpine (Technicolor), m, Andy Summers; ed, Richard Halsey; prod d, Pato Guzman; art d, Todd Hallowell; set d, Jane Bogart; cos, Albert Wolsky; spec eff, Ken Speed; makeup, Bob Mills.

Comedy   Cas.   (PR:C-O MPAA:R)

DOWN BY LAW**½ (1986) 106m Black Snake-Grokenberger/Island bw

Tom Waits *(Zack)*, John Lurie *(Jack)*, Roberto Benigni *(Roberto)*, Nicoletta Braschi *(Nicoletta)*, Ellen Barkin *(Laurette)*, Billie Neal *(Bobbie)*, Rockets Redglare *(Gig)*, Vernel Bagneris *(Preston)*, Timothea *(Julie)*, L.C. Drane *(L.C.)*, Joy Houck, Jr. *(Detective Mandino)*, Carrie Lindsoe *(Young Girl)*, Ralph Joseph, Richard Boes *(Detectives)*, Dave Petitjean *(Cajun Detective)*, Adam Cohen *(Uniformed Cop)*, Alan Kleinberg *(Corpse)*, Archie Sampier *(Prisoner)*, David Dahlgren, Alex Miller, Elliott Keener, Jay Hilliard *(Guards)*.

"It's a sad and beautiful world," says Italian actor Roberto Benigni in DOWN BY LAW, describing not only the film's New Orleans locale but also the theme which runs through all three of Jim Jarmusch's films—PERMANENT VACATION, STRANGER THAN PARADISE, and this latest entry. After the success of the independently made STRANGER THAN PARADISE, the Camera d'Or winner at 1984's Cannes Film festival, the 33-year-old Jarmusch refused to defer to Hollywood's siren song and chose to make another low-budget, black-and-white picture. With a $1 million budget (far more than the $120,000 cost of his previous film), Jarmusch hired STRANGER star John Lurie, gravel-voiced singer-songwriter Tom Waits, Italian comedian Benigni, and cinematographer

Robby Muller, whose work with Wim Wenders has made him one of the world's most respected cameramen.

Set in the New Orleans that Tennessee Williams made famous, DOWN BY LAW begins by introducing, separately, two of its main characters—disc jockey Waits and pimp Lurie. Waits, after having a fight with his girl friend Barkin, ends up out on the street. A small-time neighborhood criminal, Redglare, gives Waits a chance to make some quick bucks by driving a stolen car across town. Waits reluctantly takes the job. He gets pulled over by the police and is thrown into jail when a body is found stuffed in the car's trunk. Lurie, in the meantime, is striking a deal with former enemy and fellow pimp Bagneris. While Lurie thinks he is being befriended by Bagneris, he is actually being set up with a 10-year-old girl in a hotel room. He too is carted off by police and thrown into Orleans Parish Prison, where his cellmate is Waits. Both prisoners have too much of an attitude to be civil to each other. They rarely speak and when they do, they exchange insults.

Into the confines of their small cell comes Benigni, a confused and likable Italian who knows only a few phrases of English, which he keeps written in a pocket notebook. He introduces himself to the unreceptive Waits and Lurie and comments on the close quarters that they must share—"Not enough room to swing a cat." Quickly driven to boredom, Benigni draws a window on the bare

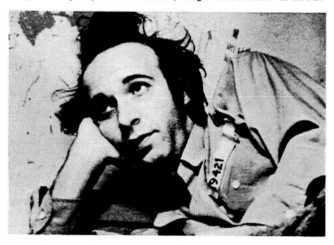

stone walls, while Lurie looks at him strangely. He then asks Lurie, "Do you say in English 'I look *at* the window' or 'I look *out* the window.' " Lurie responds, "Well, in this case, Bob, I'm afraid you gotta say 'I look *out* the window.' " Lurie and Waits slowly come around to Benigni, who seems completely lost in his environment. When they learn that Benigni is in prison for an accidental murder (he threw a billiard ball—the eight ball—at a man, fatally striking him in the forehead), they feel for him even more. "I am a good egg," Benigni insists.

Eventually the three escape through an underground tunnel of the sort you see only in prison escape films. They are chased through a bayou by unseen police and bloodhounds which bay insufferably. They find a boat which knifes through the mucky swamp water and leads them to a dilapidated shack. Once inside, they find the small room to be an exact duplicate of their prison cell, as if fate has played a cruel joke on them. Hungry, tired, lost, and having run out of patience with one another, the three split up. In the black of night, Lurie goes one way, Waits travels the opposite way, and Benigni stays in the middle. Lurie and Waits soon are not only hungry, lost, and tired, but also completely alone in the dark. They eventually reunite and stumble upon a road which leads them to a remote, rundown diner called "Luigi's Tin Top." Still dressed in prison clothes, Benigni goes inside while the other two nervously wait in the bushes. Hours later, Benigni has still not emerged. Lurie and Waits finally get the nerve to go inside, where they find Benigni sitting with a beautiful Italian woman, Braschi, at a candlelight dinner. Benigni declares that he is in love with Braschi and plans to stay with her to help run the Italian diner. The following morning Lurie and Waits, now dressed in new clothes, bid farewell to their Italian friends and walk off down a quiet road. They come to a fork and go their separate ways.

As in STRANGER THAN PARADISE, Jarmusch has created a world which lies somewhere between the poetic atmosphere that often characterizes European films and the narrative construction common to American films. His characters are insignificant antiheroes adrift in an America which is both "sad and beautiful." This is not the usual America—the beautifully picturesque landscapes of John Ford's classic westerns or the simulated, plastic suburbia of Steven Spielberg's fantasies—but a desolate and barren one. Instead of the crowded New Orleans streets one associates with Mardi Gras, Jarmusch gives us starkly lit streets with garbage blowing across the screen. To Jarmusch, America is not Mardi Gras, but a seedy hotel room lit by an unshaded light bulb, or the undisturbed algal scum that lies atop the bayou (or as in STRANGER THAN PARADISE, a frozen Lake Erie). Jarmusch continues to prove that he has one of the keenest compositional eyes in American film, rating beside—though completely different from—DAYS OF HEAVEN director Terrence Malick and the consistently underrated Clint Eastwood. While Jarmusch has a powerful visual sense, he weakens in the realm of content. Like the characters in STRANGER THAN PARADISE—Lurie again, Richard Edson (who is unfortunately absent from DOWN BY LAW), and the Hungarian Eszter Balint—Waits and Lurie are acting what the dirge is to music. This is not a matter of talent and technique (which they clearly have, however unorthodox it may be), but of a style of listlessness which drags through the film like a fugitive's ball-and-chain. The

jazzy relationship between Lurie and Waits never quite clicks—like an improvisational scene which never reaches its full potential. As a result, DOWN BY LAW merely reiterates the ideas about people and American life that Jarmusch has already stated in STRANGER THAN PARADISE.

The only sign of life in the film is Benigni, the scrawny comedian who was previously a well-kept Italian secret but now has won the heart of everyone who has seen DOWN BY LAW. Having appeared in a half-dozen Italian films (including Bernardo Bertolucci's LUNA) and directed one of his own, Benigni works wonders for DOWN BY LAW. Like the Balint character in STRANGER THAN PARADISE, Benigni is a lost soul in an unfamiliar place who massacres the English language in a humorous way. Constantly referring to his notebook of phrases and repeating whatever words he hears, Benigni delivers some wonderful bits, including an exchange with Waits on their first meeting. After he bothers Waits, the gruff disc-jockey tells him to "buzz off." Parroting Waits and combining a number of other phrases, Benigni answers with his thick accent—"Good ev-a-ning, buzz-a off-a ev-ery-body. Oh, thank you, buzz-a off-a to you too. Oh, oh. Eets a pleasure. Thank you." Later, in the prison cell, Benigni nearly starts a riot when he begins to chant "I scream-a, you scream-a, we all scream-a for ice cream-a!" Lurie and Waits join in, screaming at the top of their lungs, inciting their fellow prisoners to do the same. It's a scene worthy of the Marx Brothers. The supporting roles—played by Barkin, Neal, Redglare, and Bagneris—are also impressive, but serve mainly to provide motivations and a backdrop for the leads. Appearing in the last portion of the film is Braschi, an Italian actress and the real-life girl friend of Benigni, who is marvelous as the young Italian restaurant owner who is stuck in the middle of American nowhere. The film features the music of Tom Waits (he also performed on the soundtrack of Francis Coppola's ONE FROM THE HEART). Songs include "Jockey Full of Bourbon," "Tango Till They're Sore" (Tom Waits, performed by Tom Waits), and "It's Raining" (Naomi Neville, performed by Irma Thomas). The perceptive people at Island Films reportedly put up 90 percent of the minimal funds required to produce the picture, while allowing Jarmusch to exercise total control and to retain ownership of the finished product. The releasing company's judgment in such matters has proved to be pretty good; either alone or in conjunction with Alive Films, it recently gave the public such sleepers-turned-blockbusters as KISS OF THE SPIDER WOMAN, MONA LISA, and TRIP TO BOUNTIFUL. The film is dedicated, in part, to Pascale Ogier, the vibrant 24-year-old star of Eric Rohmer's 1984 film FULL MOON IN PARIS, who died suddenly of a heart attack later that year.

p, Alan Kleinberg; d&w, Jim Jarmusch; ph, Robby Muller; m, John Lurie; ed, Melody London; cos, Carol Wood; m/l, Tom Waits, Naomi Neville; makeup, Donita Miller.

| Comedy | Cas. | (PR:O MPAA:R) |

DRAGON RAPIDE†   (1986, Span./Ital.) 105m Television
Espanola-Tibidabo-Rete 1 c

Juan Diego *(General Franco)*, Victoria Pena *(Carmen Polo de Franco)*, Manuel de Blas *(General Mola)*, Saturno Cerra *(General Kindelan)*, Eduardo McGregor, Francisco Casares, Pedro D. del Corral, Santiago Ramos, Laura Garcia Lorca, Miguel Molina, Jose L. Pellicena, Pedro del Rio.

Events leading up to the outbreak of the Spanish Civil War in 1936 are detailed in this film. Much international maneuvering was required to find the financial and political backing for the Franco-led military coup. It was only after these were in place that the title airplane brought Franco (Diego) to Spanish Morocco, where the revolt had already started, and ferried the Generalissimo and the first of the feared Moorish troops to Spain. Diego is an impressive Franco in this low-budget, left-leaning effort.

p&d, Jaime Camino; w, Roman Gubern, Jaime Camino; ph, Juan Amoros (Eastmancolor); m, Xavier Montsalvatje; ed, Teresa Alcocer; set d, Felix Murcia.

| Historical Drama | | (PR:C MPAA:NR) |

DREAM LOVER*   (1986) 104m MGM/UA c

Kristy McNichol *(Kathy Gardner)*, Ben Masters *(Michael Hansen)*, Paul Shenar *(Ben Gardner)*, Justin Deas *(Kevin McCann)*, John McMartin *(Martin)*, Gayle

Hunnicutt *(Claire)*, Joseph Culp *(Danny)*, Matthew Penn *(Billy)*, Paul West *(Shep)*, Matthew Long *(Vaughn Capisi)*.

An insufferable exercise of sleep-inducing monotony that probes the "exciting" world of dream research and has about as much liveliness to it as the snoring theater patrons who paid their hard-earned dollars to see it. McNichol is an aspiring jazz flutist who has recently moved into a New York apartment and joined a respected ensemble. Her overbearing father, Shenar, frowns on her independence and her career choice and pressures her into reconsidering. The weight of her father's wishes and the rocky relationship with her boy friend Deas begin to take their toll. Late one night, McNichol awakens to make herself some hot milk. Wandering through her apartment, McNichol hears a sound and is attacked by an intruder who tries to rape her before she fatally stabs him in the back. In order to avoid any problems with the law, Shenar persuades his daughter to lie about the entire incident, a clear example of "character stupidity," as the murder is obviously one of self-defense.

These are only the beginnings of McNichol's problems. She is tormented nightly by a recurring dream of the incident, which director Pakula, pointlessly, shows us over and over and over again. When McNichol meets Masters, a dream researcher, she hopes that her nightmarish evenings will subside, but they only get worse. She has been turned into his guinea pig (she has electrodes attached to her head for most of her scenes) for untested methods, none of which works to any lasting effect. Not surprisingly, she falls in love with this pseudo-scientific cretin. When one experiment goes completely haywire, McNichol bolts out of the lab and takes off for London to tour with her ensemble. The dreams get worse and

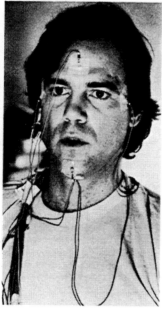

McNichol begins to flip out, totally immersed in a gothic netherworld. While visiting her father in a high-rise hotel, she loses her hold on reality, stabs her father, and attempts to flee via the window. This "climactic" finale takes place in a dream world in which the hotel has been transformed into the stone tower of a castle. Masters arrives at the hotel/castle in the nick of time to save McNichol from a deadly fall to the ground.

Astonishing in its ineptitude and laughable in its supposedly scientific approach (great pains are taken to credit the numerous dream researchers who added their expertise to the film's making), DREAM LOVER gives one the impression that there are perhaps *two* Alan J. Pakulas directing films in Hollywood: the one who has given us such gems as KLUTE, ALL THE PRESIDENT'S MEN, THE PARALLAX VIEW, and SOPHIE'S CHOICE, and the one who has given us this piece of drivel. Rather than use his imagination in presenting McNichol's dreams in a cinematic manner, Pakula chooses to give his audience irrelevant mumbo-jumbo about the nature of dream research, as if he is more concerned with completing a college thesis than with making a film. While the facts behind dream research may be of the utmost validity and importance, Pakula uses them to no effect other than as a crutch to support his crippled script. As a result of his misguided direction, nothing happens in the film. When the scientific explanations aren't padding the length, the inexorable repetition of the dream scene is. McNichol, who has proven that she can act if directed well (as she did under Sam Fuller's lead in WHITE DOG), is given nothing to do. When not on screen in her recurring dream (which must take up half her screen time), she is handicapped by having to play her dramatic scenes with electrodes all over her face (taking up the other half of her screen time). The only worthwhile aspect of the entire project is the photography of Sven Nykvist, whose visual style is rooted in the mysterious dream atmosphere of his Swedish background and his association with Ingmar Bergman.

p, Alan J. Pakula, Jon Boorstin; d, Alan J. Pakula; w, Jon Boorstin; ph, Sven Nykvist (Technicolor); m, Michael Small; ed, Trudy Ship; prod d, George Jenkins; art d, John J. Moore.

Drama   **Cas.**   **(PR:C MPAA:R)**

DREAM LOVERS†   (1986, Hong Kong) 98m D&B Films–Pearl City c

Chow Yun Fat, Lin Ching Hsia, Cher Yeung, Mandred Wong.

Popular Hong Kong actor Chow Yun Fat stars in this bizarre romance that stretches across 2,000 years. Chow Yun Fat, a successful orchestra conductor, arrives in his home town to preside over a special homecoming concert. While conducting the orchestra, he is suddenly struck by a vision of an ancient stone statue, bearing a stunning resemblance to him and rising out of a lake. When the vision fades, the conductor collapses on stage. Days later, he is seized by another vision. This time he sees a beautiful woman in period dress dancing and singing. While on a visit to a museum to view the precisely detailed statues of the ancient terracotta army that were buried with the Qin Emperor, Chow Yun Fat finds himself powerfully drawn to Lin Ching Hsia, the daughter of an antique collector. She too has visions, and the two soon realize they are the reincarnated spirits of lovers who shared a tragic romance 2,000 years before. Together they investigate what had happened in their former lives, and after some frightening flashbacks, they decide to tempt fate and go their separate ways. (In Cantonese; English subtitles.)

p, Dickson Poon; d, Tony Au; w, Chui Dai An Pin; ph, Bill Wong; m, Law Wing Fai; art d, William Chang.

Romance   **(PR:C MPAA:NR)**

DREAM OF NORTHERN LIGHTS†   (1986, Norway) 87m Marcusfilm/
                                                         Norsk Film (HAVLANDET)

Stein Bjorn, Arja Saijonmaa, Bjorn Sundquist, Sven Wollter, Anitta Suikkari.

Photographed in the snowy wilderness of Norway, this entry tells the story of an adventurous young boy in the 1860s who journeys deep into the northern hemisphere in search of one of nature's great phenomena—the aurora borealis. Along the way, the boy, accompanied by his horse and a sled full of supplies, makes a journey into adulthood as well. Shown at film festivals in the U.S. in 1986.

p, Bente Erichsen; d, Lasse Glomm; w, Lasse Glomm, Andrew Szepesy (based on the novel by Idar Kristiansen); ph, Erling Thurmann-Andersen.

Drama   **(PR:NR MPAA:NR)**

DREPTATE IN LANTURI†   (1986, Rumania) 116m Bucharest Film Studios-
                                       Group 1/Artexim bw (Trans: Chained Justice)

Ovidiu Iuliu Moldovan, Victor Rebengiuc, Claudiu Bleont, Nicolae Petrica, Sebastian Comanici, Ana-Maria Calinescu, Maia Istodor, Patricia Grigoriu.

Set in Rumania at the turn of the century, Moldovan stars as a real-life Robin Hood who steals from the rich and gives to the poor. Although he is finally captured by the authorities, the government does not want to prosecute him, fearing that his popularity with the peasants may cause trouble. Instead the police are told to release him, and a two-part plan is put into place. In an effort to ruin the folk-hero's reputation, the police rob stagecoaches *and* steal from the poor while claiming that they are agents of the beloved Moldovan. The second part of the plan calls for the police to kill Moldovan rather than capture him. An entry at the Berlin Film Festival's Black Sea Panorama, DREPTATE IN LANTURI was produced in 1983.

d, Dan Pita; w, Dan Pita, Mihai Stoian; ph, Vlad Paunescu; m, Adrian Enescu; ed, Cristina Enescu; set d, Calin Papura; cos, Daniela Codareco.

Historical Drama   **(PR:C MPAA:NR)**

DROMMESLOTTER†   (1986, Norway) 92m Norsk Film/Kommunernes
                                       Filmcentral c (Trans: The Dream Castle)

Oyvin Berven *(Thomas)*, Brigitte Victoria Svendsen *(Trine Lise)*, Lasse Lindtner *(Anders)*, Mari Maurstad *(Kjersti)*, Petter Vennerod *(Arild)*, Hilde Grythe *(Mona)*, Torstein Holmebak *(Lars)*, Jorunn Kjelsby *(Else)*, Nikolai Kolstad, Runa Grandlund, Yvonne Fosso, Hans Krovel, Dag Richard Badendyck, Richard Egede Nissen, Anders Hatlo, Mette Wesenlund.

The final installment of a trilogy of films about idealist radicals of 1968, DROMMESLOTTER is actually second in terms of chronological order. This film's predecessor, FAREWELL, ILLUSION, takes place in the 1980s and shows the final destruction of ideals, while DROMMESLOTTER depicts the transition period in the 1970s. Using a different cast, the directing team of Wam and Vennerod (this is their 11th film) set this film in a house—"the dream castle"— which is shared by three couples and their children. Their intention is to live as in a commune, but they cannot escape the fact that they are rapidly becoming financially independent urban professionals. There is nothing communal about their living arrangements as each resident takes responsibility for his own financial situation. Finding the reality of their lives to be at odds with their professed political sensibilities, the characters begin to self-destruct, culminating with the suicide of one of them. With FAREWELL ILLUSION's U.S. release, there's a fair chance DROMMESLOTTER will make its way to these shores in the future.

p,d&w, Svend Wam, Petter Vennerod; ph, Philip Oegard (Eastmancolor); m, Svein Gundersen; ed, Inge Lise Langfeldt; prod d, Tone Skjelfjord; cos, Eirin Olsen.

Drama   **(PR:O MPAA:NR)**

DRZANJE ZA VAZDUH†   (1986, Yugo.) Union (Trans: Hanging on to
                                                               Thin Air)

Velimir Bata Zivojinovic, Marko Vojnovic, Slavko Stimac, Danilo Stojkovic, Dragomir Bojanic Gidra.

d, Zdravko Sotra; w, Slobodan Stojanovic; ph, Bozidar Nikolic; m, Dusan Karunovic; set d, Stevo Skoric.

DUET FOR ONE***   (1986) 101m Golan-Globus/Cannon c

Julie Andrews *(Stephanie Anderson)*, Alan Bates *(David Cornwallis)*, Max von Sydow *(Dr. Louis Feldman)*, Rupert Everett *(Constantine Kassanis)*, Margaret Courtenay *(Sonia Randvich)*, Cathryn Harrison *(Penny Smallwood)*, Sigfrit Steiner *(Leonid Lefimov)*, Liam Neeson *(Totter)*, Macha Meril *(Anya)*.

The story is pure soap opera, the dialog a bit overwritten, but Julie Andrews' performance in DUET FOR ONE is a strong one that turns what could have been an insufferable property into a thoughtful drama. Andrews plays a world-famous

violinist married to Bates, an equally acclaimed orchestra conductor. Other characters in Andrews' active life include Steiner, a long time friend as well as frequent accompanist, and Everett, Andrews' prize student. When Andrews experiences temporary paralysis, a doctor diagnoses her problem as multiple sclerosis, a degenerative disease which will eventually kill her. Forced to contemplate

the inevitable, Andrews must face not only her physical condition, but the changes that rapidly develop within her various relationships. Steiner dies, the alcoholic Bates runs off with his considerably younger secretary (Harrison), and Everett decides to take up a lucrative offer from the unlikely area of Las Vegas. With no one to turn to, Andrews begins seeing a psychiatrist (von Sydow) and enters into an affair with Neeson, a working-class junk dealer. As her life continues to spiral out of control, Andrews attempts suicide, but eventually she is able to come to terms with the tumultuous events. In the film's epilog, Andrews stands outside her home where all her friends have gathered for a party, and looks through the glass at what has been her life.

This was Andrews' second opportunity to play a dying woman in 1986, following THAT'S LIFE, and her performance in this film is much better (the part originally was intended for Faye Dunaway). In DUET FOR ONE she must contend with her inner demons, not with Jack Lemmon's self-pity, and that alone makes for a considerable difference. As the assertive woman who finds her life falling apart in almost every conceivable manner, Andrews accurately captures the frustration, the rage, and the ultimate acceptance of what fate has dealt her. Though Nigel Kennedy dubbed the violin music for the actress' concert scenes,

Andrews went through six weeks of training, practicing three to four hours daily, so her on-screen aptitude with the instrument would appear convincing (a double was also used in long shots during concert sequences). Konchalovsky, after his 1985 films MARIA'S LOVERS and RUNAWAY TRAIN, turned away from his usual directorial style, instead shooting DUET FOR ONE in the more classical Hollywood tradition. In the process something was lost, and as a result his work is a little uneven. Another problem lies with the script, penned by Konchalovsky, Lipp, and Kempinski, the latter the author of the play on which the film is based. Kempinski's original work, loosely based on the troubles suffered by cellist Jacqueline Du Pre, had been a two-character study between the violinist and her psychiatrist. In opening up the play, the plethora of characters tends to swamp some of the ideas, despite good ensemble playing by the majority of the cast. Bates looks awful, with a performance that simply grows aggravating. Although his character is intentionally unsympathetic, that doesn't excuse the histrionic excesses to which Bates subjects the audience. Steiner, as Andrews' old comrade, is a standout among the supporting players, giving his character some real charm and depth. His post-mortem appearance as a ghostly apparition is one Steiner's best moments, effective and delicately played. DUET FOR ONE also suffers from some wordy dialog that grows a little tedious and that probably worked better on stage. Despite these caveats, the film is still an effective drama of troubling emotions. Thanks largely to the wisdom Andrews brings to her difficult role, the maudlin elements become something genuinely human, as she explores a painful gamut of deeply felt emotions.

p, Menahem Golan, Yoram Globus; d, Andrei Konchalovsky; w, Tom Kempinski, Jeremy Lipp, Andrei Konchalovsky (based on the play by Tom Kempinski); ph, Alex Thomson (Rank Color); ed, Henry Richardson; prod d, John Graysmark; art d, Reg Bream, Steve Cooper; set d, Peter Young; cos, Evangeline Harrison.

Drama   (PR:O MPAA:R)

DUMB DICKS   (SEE: DETECTIVE SCHOOL DROPOUTS, 1986)

DUNKI-SCHOTT†   (1986, Switz./Ger.) 90m Bernard Lang-Zurich-Maran-SDR-Alfred Richterich-Walter Schoch/Rex Film Zollikon c

Franz Hohler *(Dunki-Schott)*, Rene Quellet *(Santschi)*, Dodo Hug *(Doltschi Bea)*, Elisabeth Muller-Hirsch *(Frau Ruegg)*, Christel Forstsch *(Pia)*, Jodoc Seidel *(Dr. Indermuhle)*, Herbert Leiser *(Lt. Witschi)*, Walter Hess *(Herr Schnyder)*.

Hohler stars in this comedy as an eccentric professor of history who takes a sabbatical to write a book about the influence of the crusaders on the history of Switzerland. Hohler becomes obsessed by the idea that he cannot properly explore the subject unless he experiences the life of a crusader himself. Taking inspiration from Cervantes' "Don Quixote" (his character name echoes the German pronunciation of the fictional crusader's name), Hohler gets himself a horse, finds a Sancho Panza in a local scrap dealer (Quellet), installs the sponsor of his book, Hug, as his Dulcinea, and rides off to do battle with the evils of modern civilization, including pollution, automobiles, and nuclear power plants. In the process, he becomes something of a folk hero.

d, Tobias Wyss, Hans Liechti; w, Franz Hohler, Tobias Wyss; ph, Hans Liechti (Eastmancolor); m, Ruedi Haeusermann; ed, Fee Liechti; art d, Fritz Huser, Chrigi Seiler; cos, Monika Schmid.

Comedy   (PR:C MPAA:NR)

E

EAST OF THE WALL** (1986, Ger.) 94m c (WESTLER)

Sigurd Rachman, Rainer Strecker, Andi Lucas, Sascha Hammer, Frank Redies.

This inexpensive feature explores the simple love affair between two young men separated by the Berlin Wall. While sightseeing with an American friend in the Eastern sector, the man from the Western side becomes attracted to a blond-haired man he spots on the street. The two develop a quick friendship that blossoms into a love affair based on weekly visits and occasional telephone conversations. Despite the stresses of separation and bureaucratic red tape, their relationship flourishes. This is partially due to the immense attraction each has for the other's significantly different life style. Eventually the Easterner's yearnings for the freedom of the West and for his lover's companionship force him to defect.

As a debut film, EAST OF THE WALL exhibits a number of promising attributes for its young director, Speck. The relationships, specifically the tenderness between the two boys, are realistically and insightfully developed. Speck thoughtfully questions the complexities of separated love, while posing questions about the nature of love as a whole. However, the cinematic problems of EAST OF THE WALL—stilted dialog, actors uncomfortable in their roles, and an uneven rhythm—signify the need for added maturity in Speck's directorial style. A number of scenes were actually filmed on the streets of East Berlin. These were filmed in Super-8mm without any dialog, and artfully included with the other footage. (In English and German; English subtitles.)

d, Wieland Speck; w, Wieland Speck, Egbert Hormann; ph, Klemens Becker.

Romance (PR:C MPAA:NR)

EAT AND RUN* (1986) 90m BFD/NW c

Ron Silver (Mickey McSorely), Sharon Schlarth (Judge Cheryl Cohen), R.L. Ryan (Murray Creature), John F. Fleming (Police Captain), Derek Murcott (Sorely McSorely), Robert Silver (Pusher), Mimi Cecchini (Grandmother), Tony Moundroukas (Zepoli Kid), Frank Nastasi (Pick-up Driver), Peter Waldren (Dinkleman), Gabriel Barre (Mime), Ruth Jaroslow (Crossing Guard), George Peter Ryan (Narcotics Cop), Lou Criscuolo (Italian Ices Vendor), Tim Mardirosian (Scarpetti), Louis Turenne (Dr. Gretel), Matt Fischel (District Attorney), Joe Barrett (Bartender), Brian Evers (Man on Phone), Malachi Throne (Opera Announcer), Anthony Bishop (Old Man).

A potentially funny premise is driven into the ground by repetition in this tedious send-up of science-fiction and horror films which was filmed in 1984 and given a very limited release in 1986 before going to video. Ryan plays a bald, 500-pound, human-looking alien dressed in a loud plaid suit who becomes addicted to "Italian food" after he eats the first Earthling he meets, an old Italian sausage-maker. Ryan makes his way to Manhattan's Little Italy where he makes a quick meal of 35 Italians and spits out their buttons after belching. The police treat the disappearances as a missing persons case and assign Silver, a dim-witted Irish cop who talks as if he were writing a 1940s detective novel, to investigate (after NIGHT OF THE CREEPS and RADIOACTIVE DREAMS these homages to 1940s detectives are getting very tiresome). Eventually, Silver realizes that all the victims were Italian, and while phoning his commander from a pizza joint, he witnesses Ryan eat the waiter. Of course, no one believes him. In an effort to apprehend the alien, Silver persuades his girl friend, a bleeding-heart liberal judge (Schlarth), to release an infamous drug dealer into his custody. Thinking Silver a humanitarian, Schlarth agrees. Silver then acquires a fortune in heroin from the police evidence lock-up and straps it to the annoyed drug dealer. Disguising the criminal as an organ grinder, Silver waits nearby in the hopes that Ryan will soon be along and eat the "world's largest sleeping pill." Sure enough, Ryan devours the drug dealer and collapses on the sidewalk.

In court, with Schlarth presiding, Ryan's lawyer reveals that the alien is a juvenile (he's only 12 years old) and dresses him up in a huge cub scout uniform. Since Ryan's lawyer has taught him to understand English only the day before, it is determined that the alien didn't understand Silver when he read him his rights. The alien gets off scott-free and the outraged Silver is shocked to learn that Schlarth has taken up with the huge beast. Silver is jealous, but he doesn't worry about Schlarth's life because she is Jewish. Drunk and lonely, Silver calls Schlarth at her grandmother's house. It turns out that her grandmother is Italian, and that Schlarth's ex-husband was Jewish. Terrified that the alien will learn that Schlarth is Italian and eat her, Silver launches into a plan to kill the monster once and for all. To divert the alien's attention, Silver tells him that the annual San Gennaro Festival is taking place in Little Italy—thousands of Italians just waiting to be eaten. While Ryan runs off to pig out, Silver prepares his trap. Because the festival isn't for another month, Ryan returns angrier than ever and is intent on eating Schlarth. Silver arrives just in time to save her by giving the alien a doll that looks like a baby alien. Ryan coos and cuddles the doll until he sees the "Made in Italy" tag and bites the head off it. Silver had filled the head of the doll with poison and the alien dies ("Twas baby killed the beast," Silver solemnly intones). Realizing that Silver had been right all along about the law and criminals, Schlarth quits her judgeship and becomes a district attorney. Unfortunately, her first case is to try Silver for murder.

The few genuinely funny moments in EAT AND RUN are buried under an avalanche of stupid bits, silly dialog, and a distracting amount of gratuitous swearing. Silver and Schlarth are an ineffective screen couple and their scenes together seem to last forever. Ryan, as the huge alien, is funny-looking and

manages to garner a few laughs here and there, but he basically just glowers and grunts before showing his sharp teeth and eating people. Most of the humor is scattershot and the film contains several annoying running gags that never let up. Silver's constant talking as a first-person novelist (" 'Trust your instincts,' I said, trying to be kind to the old-timer."), his boss Fleming's stuffing of his face with cake in every scene, and Schlarth's sexual dissatisfaction (until she meets Ryan) are used again and again in an attempt to be "zany." First-time director Hart, who coscripted with his father, never expands his ideas past the original joke and simply repeats the same gags over and over ad nauseam. Hart's biggest concern visually is getting as much mileage as he can out of the master shot. Most of the action in the film takes place off screen, including Ryan's consumption of the Italians and a laborious scene in which Silver talks with an elderly crossing guard as we hear unattended children being hit by cars. Although rated "R" for language, the film contains no on-screen violence and no nudity.

p, Jack Briggs; d, Christopher Hart; w, Stan Hart, Christopher Hart; ph, Dyanna Taylor (DuArt Color); m, Donald Pippin; ed, Pamela S. Arnold; art d, Mark Selemon.

Comedy/Science Fiction Cas. (PR:O MPAA:R)

EAT THE PEACH† (1986, Ireland) 95m Strongbow/Film Four–IFEX c

Eamon Morrissey (Arthur), Stephen Brennan (Vinnie), Catherine Byrne (Nora), Niall Toibin (Boots), Joe Lynch (Boss Murtagh), Tony Doyle (Sean Murtagh), Takashi Kawahara (Bunzo).

Promoted as "an Irish BUTCH CASSIDY AND THE SUNDANCE KID," EAT THE PEACH tells the story of a pair of ordinary men—Morrissey and Brennan—who decide to make something of their lives. After watching the film ROUSTABOUT, in which Elvis Presley rides his motorcycle in a fairground Wall Of Death, Morrissey decides he wants to do the same. So, with his brother-in-law Brennan's assistance, Morrissey goes about raising funds to build his Wall. Choosing his wife's vegetable plot as his location, the dream begins, but before long, financiers back out on the pair, leaving them to find other resources. They resort to running illegal goods (booze, videos, and livestock) to the Irish Republic across the Northern Ireland border, involving themselves in another, less glamorous, Wall of Death.

p, John Kelleher; d, Peter Ormrod; w, Peter Ormrod, John Kelleher; ph, Arthur Wooster; m, Donal Lunny; ed, J. Patrick Duffner; prod d, David Wilson.

Drama/Comedy (PR:C MPAA:NR)

ECHO PARK* (1986, Aust.) 92m Sasha-Wein/Atlantic c

Susan Dey (May Greer), Thomas Hulce (Jonathan), Michael Bowen (August), Christopher Walker (Henry Greer), Shirley Jo Finney (Gloria), Heinrich Schweiger (August's Father), John Paragon (Hugo), Richard Marin (Sid), Cassandra Peterson (Sheri), Timothy Carey (Vinnie), Martin Suppan (Austrian Consul), Robert R. Shafer (Commercial Director), Dorothy Dells (Consulate Secretary), Yana Nirvana (Woman in Bar), Paul Anselmo, Jesse Aragon, Robert Cabral (Policemen), Peter Drain, Top Jimmy, John Pochna (Bar Customers), Dee Cooper (Man in Park), Douglas M. Ford (Biker), Stephen Gaines (Desk Sergeant), Fred Leaf (Burt Reynolds' Look-Alike), Mary Thompson, Anne Marie Bates, Jason Mayall, Renee LeBallister (Prospective Roommates), Michael Marloe, Jim Smith (Party-Goers), Skip O'Brien (Prisoner), Biff Yeager (Jailer), Jacki Easton Toelle (Girl in Commercial), Bob Moss (Birthday Boy), Doug Knott (Birthday Man), James Helppi (Guest in Elevator), George W. Scott (Man with Tip), De Schneider (Real Estate Secretary), Patricia Tippo, Max Trumpower, Penny Harris, Merrill Ward, Dana Collins (Telegram Strippers).

Austrian director Dornhelm, who in 1977 received an Oscar nomination for his documentary THE CHILDREN OF THEATER STREET, here tries to capture the desperation and hope of the aspiring young talents who live in Echo Park, a

rundown section of Los Angeles. The film centers on Dey, a single mother and would-be actress who advertises in the local paper, "Leading Lady, Available Immediately." Working in a sleazy bar and struggling to make ends meet, Dey runs an ad to take in a roommate. The chipper Hulce, a pizza delivery man who shows a smidgen of talent as a songwriter, responds. He is immediately attracted to Dey and becomes a father figure for her 8-year-old son, Walker, dubbing him "Hank" instead of calling him by the name the boy hates—"Henry." Dey, however, is interested in her neighbor, Bowen, an Austrian "body sculptor" who aspires to take over Arnold Schwarzenegger's role in society. Bowen has invented a muscle developer he calls Viking Spray ("For work or play . . . use Viking Spray") that employs some crackpot theory that relates bodybuilding to orgasms. When Dey gets a response to her newspaper ad, she thinks she has finally gotten her big break. It turns out, however, to be an audition for a strip-o-gram company headed by Paragon, a sleazy but personable greaseball. Dey decides to give stripping a try because, after all, "it's show biz." Hulce objects, citing that it could harm Walker.

As things progress Bowen's Viking Spray goes nowhere (even with the promotional help of a Burt Reynolds look-alike and an extremely bad viking commercial), Dey's stripping career is cut short when Walker accidentally sees her performing, and Hulce is left supporting both of them. Disgusted with the way of life in Los Angeles, Hulce tries to yell some sense into Dey: "I am so sick of the people in this town who are poets or screenwriters or actresses when we're all really just delivering pizzas, every last one of us." By the finale, Dey has been called for an audition for a commercial (stripping for a lingerie ad), Bowen has been reunited with his father, who has flown in from Austria (apparently just to slap his son in the face—a freeze frame which closes the film), and Hulce is . . . well, the same place he was when the film started.

Funded by Austrian backers and photographed in Los Angeles, ECHO PARK (which premiered at the 1985 Venice Film Festival) has its heart in the right place. Dornhelm manages to capture the hopelessness of those countless aspiring young-sters who are willing to sacrifice everything in order to get the smallest break. As Dey proudly states when she finally gets an audition, "It's not just *a* break, it's *my* break." The film's open ending leaves its characters without much of a future, just a faint glimmer of hope. As hard as Dey's character tries, she, like most others in Los Angeles, probably will never "make it" as an actress. Bowen will never be the body-sculptor superstar of his dreams. Hulce is the only one with his feet on the ground, but he'll probably do nothing more than own a pizza parlor someday. It's a brutal outlook, but one based in fact. Unfortunately Dornhelm's good intentions aren't enough to overcome the insipid dialog (it's second-rate Neil Simon, at best) that flows out of the characters' mouths as if one can see the ink flowing out of the screenwriter's pen. Nothing here rings true except the basic premise. These characters act as if they're in a movie, instead of trying to land a part in one. Sight gags and stupid dialog are more distracting than humorous. Worst of all is the ridiculous subplot of Bowen and his Viking Spray. Topping all this off is some sophomoric locker-room humor, most of it involving Bowen's attempt to harness his sexual energy. Dey, once of TV's "Partridge Family," and Hulce, of AMADEUS fame, are okay in their roles, but seem more concerned in expressing acting-school techniques than in creating honest characters. Bowen (another brother of David Carradine) manages quite well with his convincing Austrian accent, even though his role is rather embarrassing. The most impressive, however, is Paragon, who makes a promising showing after appearing, just barely, in EATING RAOUL and PEE-WEE'S BIG ADVENTURE. Also in the cast are Richard "Cheech" Marin of Cheech and Chong fame and Cassandra Peterson showing off a head of red hair—a far cry from her sleek black hair as TV's Elvira. The music consultant was Bill Wyman, bass player for the Rolling Stones. The collection of background songs includes: "Strip-O-Gram" (Bo Harwood, Bobbi Permanent), "She's About a Mover" (Doug Sahn, performed by Jimmy Woods and the Immortals), "Immortal Strut" (Jimmy Woods and the Immortals, performed by Jimmy Woods and the Immortals), "The Need" (Dean Chamberlain, performed by Chamberlain), "Twice As Hard" (Steve Richardson, Chris Shaw, performed by the Sights), "Wild Roses" (Mark Walton, Shandi, Tom Boles, performed by Shandi), "Tomorrow's Gonna Be a Better Day" (Mark Walton, Tom Boles, performed by Johnette), "My Eyes Have Seen" (Black Patti, performed by Black Patti), "Imagination" (David Boerwald, performed by Boerwald), and "Give and Take" (Bill Wyman, John Wilson, performed by Julie Christensen, Mike Sherwood).

p, Walter Shenson; d, Robert Dornhelm; w, Michael Ventura; ph, Karl Kofler; m, David Rickets; ed, Ingrid Koller; cos, Patti Callicot; m/l, Bo Harwood, Bobbi Permanent, Doug Sahn, Jimmy Woods, Dean Chamberlain, Steve Richardson, Chris Shaw, Mark Walton, Shandi, Tom Boles, Black Patti, Bill Wyman, John Wilson, David Boerwald.

Drama/Comedy   **Cas.**   **(PR:O MPAA:R)**

EHRENGARD†   (1986, Ital.) Antea Cinematografica-RAI TV Rete Uno/
New Cinema c

Jean Pierre Cassel, Audrey Matson, Lea Padovani, Alessandro Haber, Christian Borromeo, Catherine Jarret, Caterina Boratto, Patrizia de Clara, Odino Artioli, Anita Laurenzi.

Based on the novel by Karen Blixen (aka Isak Dinesen), which was published in 1963, EHRENGARD takes place in a fantasy world of the past where a distraught Archduchess worries because her only son has no desire to marry and carry on the bloodline. Eventually the son capitulates and marries, but it is learned that the baby to be born to the couple will arrive a few months too soon. Rumors and innuendo regarding the mother's chastity soon follow, and it is suggested by the Archduchess' trusted advisor that the girl be taken to the remote location until the rumors die down. Accompanying the girl is a lady-in-waiting whose virginal beauty obsesses the royal advisor. Determined to seduce the chaste handmaiden, the advisor follows the caravan on their journey. The advisor tries many methods of seduction, but the beautiful virgin proves to be more clever than he as she humiliates and disgraces the lecherous counsel.

d, Emidio Greco; w, Emidio Greco and Enrico Filippini (based on a novel by

Karen Blixen [Isak Dinesen]); ph, Giuseppe Lanci (Technicolor); m, Wolfgang Amadeus Mozart; ed, Gino Bartolini.

Drama   **(PR:C MPAA:NR)**

8 MILLION WAYS TO DIE*   (1986) 115m Producers Sales Organization/
Tri-Star c

Jeff Bridges *(Matthew Scudder)*, Rosanna Arquette *(Sarah)*, Alexandra Paul *(Sunny)*, Randy Brooks *(Chance)*, Andy Garcia *(Angel Maldonado)*, Lisa Sloan *(Linda Scudder)*, Christa Denton *(Laurie)*, Vance Valencia *(Quintero)*, Wilfredo Hernandez *(Hector Lopez)*, Luisa Leschin *(Hector's Wife)*, Vyto Rugins *(Durkin)*, Chip Arnold *(Homicide Detective)*, James Avery *(Deputy D.A.)*, Jack Younger *(Drunk)*, Zoaunne LeRoy *(Nurse)*, Abigail Shelton *(AA Member)*, Don Edmonds *(Elderly Man)*, Phil Peters *(Rugged Man)*, Elva Garcia *(Daughter)*, Michael Galindo, Pete Galindo *(Sons)*, Miriam E. Schubach, Lois Gerace *(AA Speakers)*, Jay Ingram *(AA Member)*, Sue Rihr *(Young Woman)*, Gene Ross *(Slim)*, Tom "Tiny" Lister, Jr. *(Nose Guard)*, William Marquez *(Tip)*, Fred Asparagus *(Mundo)*, Robb Madrid *(Victor Podillo)*, Raegan Newman *(Girl)*, Richard A. Michels *(Player)*, Arie Gedis *(Gambler)*, Rosalind Ingledew *(Tote Lady)*, Arthur Ervin *(Waiter)*, Frank Dent *(Boot Salesman)*, Henry Lewis *(Po' Boy's Market Manager)*, Roberto Jimenez *(Jamie Rodriquez)*, Victor Rivers, Danny De La Paz *(Angel Heavies)*, Oliver "Ollie" Farley *(Ollie)*, Gilbert O. Parra *(Gil)*, Loyd Catlett *(Buster)*, Art Fransen *(Cop)*.

Considering the major talents involved here (Stone, Ashby, Bridges, and Arquette), one would expect to find something more than a run-of-the-mill crime thriller. And in a sense one does, for 8 MILLION WAYS TO DIE is such a paralyzingly inept film one can safely state that nothing quite like it has ever been done before.

Bridges stars as a Los Angeles sheriff's detective with a severe drinking problem that causes him to lose his job, wife, and child. Divorced and unemployed, he tries to clean up his life by attending Alcoholics Anonymous meetings and staying dry for six months. At the invitation of a woman in his AA group, Bridges meets a pretty young girl, Paul, at a party held at the home of one of his ex-vice busts,

Brooks. Paul cuddles and coos with Bridges as if they have been lovers for years. She introduces him to her friend Arquette, who seems to be Brooks' girl. Brooks is none-too-happy to see Bridges, and Arquette takes an immediate dislike to him as well. Also at the party is a weasel-like drug dealer, Garcia, who seems very fond of both Arquette and Paul. Well, Bridges may be a drunk but he's not stupid, and he soon surmises that both these young ladies are hookers and Brooks is their pimp. Paul drags Bridges away from the party and back to his place where she reveals her occupation and begs Bridges to tell Brooks she wants to quit the business as she's afraid to tell him herself. Reluctantly Bridges agrees and goes back to Brooks who is outraged at the thought and declares that he is not a pimp and would do nothing to harm anyone. Bridges smells a rat and confronts Paul, but she begs him to escort her to the airport so she can leave town. En route, however, Paul is kidnaped and whisked off in a van where she is killed, and her body dumped in a nearby ditch.

Paul's murder sends Bridges back to the bottle, and he wakes up days later in a hospital after drinking himself into a stupor. For some reason never explained, Bridges becomes obsessed with finding the girl's killer (after all she was just some hooker he had met only the night before) and acts like a lunatic while doing so. Realizing that Brooks was set up to take the fall, Bridges eventually discovers that Paul was dealing cocaine for Garcia, and that he is the murderer. With help from Arquette and Brooks, Bridges sets up a meeting with Garcia on the premise that he would like to start dealing as well. In a tortuously long and pointless scene, Bridges and Garcia play dueling profanities while eating tropical fruit-flavored snow cones made by one of Garcia's henchmen. Garcia finally agrees to the deal, but only if Bridges brings in Brooks as his partner. In yet another strange move, Bridges allows Garcia virtually to kidnap Arquette. Garcia inexplicably has been trying to muscle in on Brooks' apparently legitimate business and has his cache of cocaine secretly stored in fireplace logs stocked in one of Brooks' grocery stores. When Brooks learns of this he goes wild and agrees to go all the way to help Bridges bring down Garcia.

Bridges gathers Garcia's cocaine in an empty warehouse and informs the drug dealer that if he doesn't hand over Arquette, his coke will be destroyed. Garcia arrives with his goons, one of whom has a shotgun wired around the blindfolded

Arquette's neck. Well prepared himself, Bridges has the cocaine-filled logs drenched in gasoline, with Brooks and his huge enforcer, Lister, in plain view and a couple of SWAT team guys in the rafters. Yet another agonizingly long scene drags on as all the principals scream profanities at each other in this huge, echoing warehouse. It must take Garcia 10 minutes to walk from one end of the warehouse to the other, where Bridges sits frantically destroying the cocaine a kilo at a time to prove he means business. Then, at the point where most sensible audiences would head for the exits, all hell breaks loose and ends with the cocaine totally destroyed, Brooks lying dead, and several gunmen wounded or dying. Although Garcia escapes, Bridges and Arquette decide it is safe to return to her house. Of course Garcia and one of his goons await them, and after another long, bloody, profanity-filled scene, both the bad guys wind up dead. Bridges returns to his AA meetings (finally at peace with the fact that he exists in a world he never made ?!) and starts a new life with Arquette.

This totally incompetent $18 million mess (it grossed less than a million) has the dubious honor of being one of the three big-budget turkeys that destroyed Producers Sales Organization, a successful foreign sales company that keeled over after these disasters (the others were CLAN OF THE CAVE BEAR, cost: $18 million, gross: $1.2 million; and 9 ½ WEEKS, cost: $17 million, gross: $2.7 million). Jeff Bridges is one of America's finest actors and has managed to salvage many a film in the past, but Stone, who should stick to directing (see SALVADOR and PLATOON), and Henry's script, coupled with Ashby's direction, never gives him a chance. To its detriment, the film has a totally improvised

feeling where the actors are left standing still, glancing in every direction and swapping inane dialog whenever they get stuck for something to say. This happens in nearly every scene. None of the characters has a shred of motivation, development, or purpose. We don't buy any of these people for a minute, so they simply become an annoyance. Who are these people and what do they want? The "plot" hinges on some kind of rivalry between Garcia and Brooks that even Brooks doesn't seem to understand.

Arquette is so unappealing here—spending much of her time snorting cocaine and mumbling incoherently—that one wonders why Bridges would risk his life to get her back. Garcia is laughable as a villain—he looks as if he's about to cry in every scene—and Brooks is downright hyperactive with his constant shouting of popular profanities and flailing of arms. Perhaps director Ashby was trying to make one of those destroy-the-genre-in-order-to-recreate-it films like Boorman's POINT BLANK or Altman's THE LONG GOODBYE. Or maybe he was poking fun at the genre as Arthur Penn did with gangster films in BONNIE AND CLYDE, or *film noir* in NIGHT MOVES, or westerns in THE MISSOURI BREAKS, or spy thrillers in TARGET. If so, Ashby forgot one key ingredient: the resulting experiment has to be watchable, and 8 MILLION WAYS TO DIE just isn't. Songs include: "Cachumbambe" (Miguel Cruz), "If You Have to Know" (Will Jennings, Lonnie Mack, Tim Drummond, sung by Lonnie Mack), "Last Mistake" (Barry Coffing, sung by New Toys), "On the Edge of Love" (Cynthia Weil, Scott Cutler, sung by Tollok), "Thanks But No Thanks" (Emery Williams, Jr., sung by Koko Taylor).

p, Steve Roth, Charles Mulvehill; d, Hal Ashby; w, Oliver Stone, David Lee Henry (based on books by Lawrence Block); ph, Stephen H. Burum (Panavision, Technicolor); m, James Newton Howard; ed, Robert Lawrence, Stuart Pappe; prod d, Michael Haller; art d, Mark W. Mansbridge; set d, Barbara Krieger, John Thomas Walker; cos, Tony Scarano, Cheryl Beasley Blackwell; spec eff, Phil Corey; m/l, Miguel Cruz, Will Jennings, Lonnie Mack, Tim Drummond, Barry Coffing, Cynthia Weil, Scott Cutler, Emery Williams, Jr.; makeup, Nedia, Pete Altobelli.

Crime   Cas.   (PR:O MPAA:R)

EIN BLICK—UND DIE LIEBE BRICHT AUS†   (1986, Ger.) 91m c (Trans: One Look—And Love Begins)

Elida Araoz, Rosario Blefari, Regina Lamm, Margarita Munoz, Maria Elena Rivera, Norberto Serra, Daniela Trojanovsky.

An abstract, poetic dissertation on female views of love from Jutta Brueckner, one of Germany's prominent feminist filmmakers. Brueckner approaches women's relations with men by analyzing seven different scenarios, from a devoted wife to a hardcore feminist. In each case the woman has been forced into a

submissive role. Though mainly an analytical work, EIN BLICK combines a variety of poetry, music, and distorted sounds with both abstract and narrative images.

p, Joachim von Vietinghoff; d&w, Jutta Brueckner; ph, Marcelo Camorino; m, Brynmore Jones; ed, Ursula Hof, Jutta Brueckner; art d, Guillermo Kuitka; cos, Marion Vollmer, Britta Vollmer.

Drama   (PR:O MPAA:NR)

EIN FLIEHENDES PFERD†   (1986, Ger.) 105m Artus-Westdeutscher Rundfunk c (Trans: A Runaway Horse)

Vadim Glowna (Helmut Halm), Rosel Zech (Sabine, His Wife), Dietmar Mues (Klaus Buch), Marita Marschall (Helene, His Wife).

Set in a middle-class resort town near the Swiss border, this entry tells the story of two friends who, like the title horse, find themselves running away from their lives. Glowna is a schoolteacher whose life is no longer inspired, while his friend, Mues, boasts of his sexual conquests. Yet neither man is what he seems. Costarring as Glowna's wife is Rosel Zech, best known for her work in the R.W. Fassbinder films LOLA and VERONIKA VOSS. Based on the popular 1978 novella by Martin Walser, which was initially published in serial form before becoming a radio show and a theater production.

p, Hartwig Schmidt; d, Peter Beauvais; w, Ulrich Plenzdorf, Peter Beauvais, Martin Walser (based on the novella by Martin Walser); ph, Gernot Roll; ed, Liesgret Schmitt-Klink; set d, Peter Scharff; cos, Anastasia Kurz.

Drama   (PR:O MPAA:NR)

EIN VIRUS KENNT KEINE MORAL   (SEE: VIRUS HAS NO MORALS, A, 1986, Ger.)

EINS OG SKEPNAN DEYR†   (1986, Iceland) 97m Bio-Finnish Film Foundation/Bio c (Trans: As the Beast Dieth)

Trostur Gunnarsson (Helgi), Edda Heidrun Backmann (Lara), Johann Sigurdarson (Baldur), Torgeir Gunnarsson, Sigurdur Palsson, Hallgrimur Helgasson, Torarinn Gudnason, Fridgeir Olgeirsson, Hilmar Oddsson.

This debut feature from Oddsson received a great deal of attention on its home turf, with some hoping that it would provide the sagging Icelandic film industry with a shot in the arm. Trostur Gunnarsson and Backmann star as a young couple who leave the city for the solitude of the country. He is an aspiring novelist and she a flute player, both hoping they will be able to devote all their energies to achieving their goals. The countryside, however, holds more mystery than calm. Soon Trostur Gunnarsson is driven off the brink of sanity by his dreams of herds of reindeer meant to represent his relationship with a mother who deserted him as a child. The film's title is taken from the Biblical quote: "as the beast dieth, so doth man."

p, Jon Olafsson; d&w, Hilmar Oddsson; ph, Sigudur Sverrir Palsson (Agfacolor); m, Hrodmar Sigurdbjornsson, Hilmar Oddsson, Wolfgang Amadeus Mozart; ed, Hilmar Oddsson, Kristin Palsdottir, Valdis Oskarsdottir; art d, Togeir Gunnarsson; cos, Hulda Magnusdottir.

Drama/Thriller   (PR:O MPAA:NR)

EL AMOR BRUJO*   (1986, Span.) 100m Emiliano Piedra-Orion Classics c (Trans: A Love Bewitched)

Antonio Gades (Carmelo), Cristina Hoyos (Candela), Laura del Sol (Lucia), Juan Antonio Jimenez (Jose), Emma Penella (Aunt Rosario), La Polaca (Pastora), Gomez de Jerez (El Lobo), Enrique Ortega (Jose's Father), Diego Pantoja (Candela's Father), Giovana (Rocio), Candy Roman (Chulo), Manolo Sevilla (Singer), Antonio Solera, Manuel Rodriguez, Juan Manuel Roldan (Guitarists), The Antonio Gades Dance Troup.

The third entry in Spanish director Saura's flamenco dance trilogy, which was preceded in 1981 by BLOOD WEDDING and in 1983 by CARMEN. This time Saura and his choreographer Gades have turned to the Manuel de Falla opera for their source of inspiration. Using much of the same cast from CARMEN—del Sol has here been relegated to a supporting role while Hoyos has been given the lead—Saura has set the film on an exotically colored and stylishly designed studio set of a Madrid shantytown. Jimenez and Hoyos are two gypsies who have been betrothed since childhood, when their fathers, having drunk too much wine, decided such. Early in the film a splendid wedding takes place, but we learn that each mate has another love interest. Gades admires Hoyos from a distance, while Jimenez is carrying on an affair with the gorgeous del Sol. After the betrothed are wed, a dance takes place, during which a gang fight breaks out. In the ensuing ruckus, Jimenez is fatally knifed. Because of his adoration for the bride, Gades is assumed guilty, arrested, and jailed for four years. When he is released he returns to Hoyos, only to find that she is visited nightly by her dead husband's ghost, still dressed in the bloodied shirt that he was wearing when he died. The only way to win Hoyos love, Gades is told, is to confront the ghost with his former lover, del Sol. After this is done, Hoyos is released from her ties to the past and free to marry Gades.

Following the critical and commercial success of CARMEN, which became one of Spain's highest-grossing pictures and received an Academy Award nomination as Best Foreign Film, EL AMOR BRUJO has been considerably less appreciated by critics and audiences alike. Perhaps this is because the general audience is more familiar with Bizet's "Carmen" than with de Falla's "El Amor Brujo" (also known here as "Love, The Magician"). EL AMOR BRUJO is somewhat more stylized that its two predecessors, but otherwise it is just as accomplished. The dancing is at least equally as astounding and, according to some dance enthusiasts, better with Hoyos having taken over the lead from del Sol. Seemingly aware that Hoyos is a superior dancer, while del Sol is more pleasing to the eye, Saura has del Sol comment to Hoyos while learning a dance step, "Isn't my body more beautiful?" Visually, EL AMOR BRUJO is a celebration of sensational camera fluidity that marks a third successful collaboration between Saura and Escamilla. From the opening shot's camera moves—as it surveys the elaborate studio set and then travels into the shantytown—the photography does not quit. Equally lively is the fiery, erotic flamenco music, played by the National Orchestra of Spain, conducted by Jesus Lopez Cobos, and sung by Rocio Jurado. (In Spanish; English subtitles.)

p, Emiliano Piedra; d, Carlos Saura; w, Carlos Saura, Antonio Gades (based on the ballet by Manuel de Falla); ph, Teo Escamilla (Eastmancolor); m, Manuel de Falla; ed, Pedro del Rey; md, Jesus Lopez Cobos; set d&cos, Garardo Vera; spec eff, Basilio Cortijo; ch, Carlos Saura, Antonio Gades.

Dance   **(PR:A   MPAA:PG)**

EL ANO DE LAS LUCES†   (1986, Span.) 120m Iberoamericana de TV c (Trans: The Year of Awakening)

Jorge Sanz *(Manolo)*, Maribel Verdu *(Maria Jesus)*, Manuel Alexandre *(Emilio)*, Rafaela Aparicio *(Rafaela)*, Lucas Martin *(Jesus)*, Veronica Forque *(Irene)*, Santiago Ramos, Chus Lampreave, Jose Sazatornil, Pedro Reyes, Violeta Cela, Miguel Angel Rellan.

Another story of kindling adolescent sexuality features Sanz as a 16-year-old boy sent to recuperate at a tuberculosis sanatorium. Since the hospital is primarily for children, Sanz feels out of place and turns his attentions to staff nurses. His first attempt yields nothing but reprimands, but Sanz's second bid for romance is more successful. He takes up with a staff helper, who at first rebuffs Sanz's suggestions of an interlude. Eventually she acquiesces, though their affair is short-lived. Once the romance is in the open, Sanz is taken home to Madrid while his love is castigated by her father.

p, Andres Vicente Gomez; d, Fernando Trueba; w, Rafael Azcona, Fernando Trueba; ph, Juan Amoros (Eastmancolor); m, Francisco Guerrero; ed, Carmen Frias; set d, Josep Rosell.

Comedy   **(PR:O   MPAA:NR)**

EL BRONCO†   (1986, Mex.) 92m Producciones Egan/Peliculas Mexicanas c

Valentin Trujillo *(Ulises Vargas)*, Maribel Guardia *(Gabriela Meneses)*, Alberto Rojas [El Caballo] *(Burro)*, Tony Bravo *(Ernesto)*, Ana Luisa Peluffo *(Beatriz)*, Jorge Patino, Armando Silvestre.

The "Romeo and Juliet" theme of star-crossed lovers is reworked in this unlikely Mexican romance. Guardia (a former Miss Costa Rica in real life) plays an apparently wealthy young lady set to marry Bravo, a fellow plutocrat. The union will benefit Guardia's family, as they are in financial difficulties. Intruding on this happy scene is Trujillo, an uneducated boxer from the lower classes, who falls hopelessly in love with Guardia. When Trujillo gives Guardia mouth-to-mouth resuscitation after a waterskiing accident, the potential romance comes to fruition. Though the inevitable troubles ensue, love ultimately triumphs.

p&d, Edgardo Gazcon; w, Edgardo Gazcon, Rene Retes; ph, Agustin Lara; m, Ernesto Cortazar; ed, Sergio Soto.

Romance   **(PR:C-O   MPAA:NR)**

EL CABALLERO DEL DRAGON†   (1986, Span.) 90m Salamandra/Cinetel c (Trans: The Knight of the Dragon)

Klaus Kinski *(Boetius)*, Harvey Keitel *(Clever)*, Fernando Rey *(Fray Lupo)*, Maria Lamor *(Alba)*, Jose Vivo *(Count of Ruc)*, Miguel Bose *(Ix)*, Julieta Serrano, Jose Maria Pou, Carlos Tristancho, Santiago Alvarez.

Some names well known to American audiences pop up in this odd Spanish blend of science fiction, history, and comedy. Vivo is a count whose beautiful daughter is being wooed by Keitel, a klutzy knight. Kinski, the local alchemist and all-around sorcerer, is trying to get into Vivo's good graces, something Rey, a priest who feuds with Kinski, is also trying to do. The world of these eccentric characters is turned upside down when a stranger enters their midst. The stranger, Bose, is a helmeted, mute visitor from another planet who ends up winning the heart of the count's daughter. This leads to Keitel and Rey leaving the region via the alien's spaceship. Because the local population believes Bose is a dragon, the ill-fated wayfarer is slain, but Kinski is able to revive him. Eventually, Bose is knighted and he marries Vivo's daughter, giving the tale an offbeat happy ending. This film is available in both English and Spanish.

p&d, Fernando Colomo; w, Andreu Martin, Miguel Angel Nieto, Fernando Colomo; ph, Jose Luis Alcaine (Eastmancolor); m, Jose Nieto; ed, M.A. Santamaria; prod d, Enric Ventura; art d, Felix Murcia; cos, Javier Artinano; spec eff, Reyes Abades.

Comedy   **(PR:O   MPAA:NR)**

EL CORAZON SOBRE LA TIERRA†   (1986, Cuba) 95m ICAIC c (Trans: The Heart on the Land)

Reinaldo Miravalles, Nelson Villagra, Annia Linares, Tito Junco, Argelio Sosa.

Unadulterated Castro propaganda that urges the stubborn farmers in the hinterlands to get with it and join the glorious revolution. An old farmer and his young adult son yearn to start a farming cooperative in the Sierra Maestra mountains, but they meet with tough resistance from the wary peasants. When the son is killed fighting in Ethiopia, the father becomes obsessed with realizing their dream. The old man works tirelessly to convert the locals to the cause by using his son's sacrifice as a rallying cry. Eventually the stubborn farmers see the light and the co-op is a reality. EL CORAZON SOBRE LA TIERRA is director Constante Diego's feature debut.

p, Miguel Mendoza; d, Constante Diego; w, Eliseo Alberto Diego, Constante Diego; ph, Livio Delgado (ICAIC color); m, Jose Marie Vitier; ed, Roberto Bravo.

Drama   **(PR:C   MPAA:NR)**

EL DIA DE LOS ALBANILES II†   (1986, Mex.) 89m Frontera/Peliculas Mexicanas c (Trans: Bricklayer's Day, Part II)

Alfonso Zayas *(Roberto)*, Angelica Chain *(Beatriz/Julieta)*, Hugo Stiglitz *(Fernando)*, Luis de Alba *(Juan)*, Rene Ruiz [Tun Tun] *(Compadre [El Enano])*, Lupita Sandoval *(Lupita)*, Arlette Pacheco *(Letitia)*, Gerardo Zepeda [Chiquilin] *(Reynardo [Chiquilin])*, "Pelon Solares", Yhira Aparicio.

This sequel to the successful Mexican sex comedy DIA DE LOS ALBANILES sees the comedic marital woes of long-suffering wife Chain, and philandering husband Zayas, combined with a low-rent horror story about a Jack-the-Ripper type who murders prostitutes. Thrown into the mix is a dual role for Chain, playing both the wife and her redheaded twin sister who has a penchant for disrobing at the most inopportune times. Zayas and Chain are a popular Mexican comedy team who have made several films together.

p, Gilberto Martinez Solares, Adolfo Martinez Solares, Alejandro Seberon, Santos Seberon; d, Gilberto Martinez Solares; w, Gilberto Martinez Solares, Adolfo Martinez Solares; ph, Fernando Colin; m, Ernesto Cortazo; ed, Jose J. Manguia.

Comedy   **(PR:O   MPAA:NR)**

EL DIA QUE ME QUIERAS†   (1986, Col.) FOCINE c (Trans: The Day You Love Me)

Claudio Verge, Juan Leyrado, Fausto Verdial, Graciela Dufau.

d&w, Sergio Dow; ph, Ed Lachman.

EL DISPUTADO VOTO DEL SR. CAYO†   (1986, Span.) 98m Prods. Cinematograficas Penelope c (Trans: The Disputed Vote of Mr. Cayo)

Francisco Rabal *(Cayo)*, Juan Luis Galiardo *(Victor)*, Inaki Miramon *(Rafael)*, Lydia Bosch *(Laly)*, Eusebio Lazaro, Mari Paz Molinero, Abel Viton, Gabriel Renom, Paco Casares, Juan Jesus Valverde.

Told as a flashback shared by Bosch, the widow of a recently deceased former-socialist politician, and his congressman friend, Miramon, during lunch, EL DISPUTADO VOTO DEL SR. CAYO is a rumination on the superiority of the natural life over intellect. Reminiscing about a campaign trip to the country that she, Miramon, and her late husband, Galiardo, took in 1977, Bosch recalls the profound effect a peasant man named Cayo (Rabal) had on her husband. Rabal's simple approach to life and his indifference to politics challenged the socialist Galiardo and made him sell his views to the old man even harder. But eventually Rabal's earthy outlook affected Galiardo more than socialism affected Rabal. Soon after returning to the city, Galiardo withdraws from the race and leaves politics. Back in the present, Bosch urges Miramon to return to the village and see if Rabal still lives there. Miramon finds the old man and learns that his wife has died since their last visit. In ill health and with only a dog for company, Rabal is taken away in an ambulance, forced to leave his beloved pueblo.

p, Jose G. Blanco Sola; d, Antonio Gimenez-Rico; w, Manuel Matji, Antonio Gimenez-Rico (based on a novel by Miguel Delibes); ph, Alejandro Ulloa; ed, Miguel Gonzalez Sinde; set d, Rafael Palmero.

Drama   **(PR:C   MPAA:NR)**

EL ESTRANGER—OH! DE LA CALLE CRUZ DEL SUR†   (1986, Sp.) Campoy/Lauren c (Trans: The Stranger from Cruz del Sur Street)

Jose Sacristan, Serena Vergano, Emma Cohen, Teresa Gimpera.

d&w, Jordi Grau; ph, Domingo Solano, Tote Trenas.

EL EXTRANO HIJO DEL SHERIFF†   (1986, Mex.) 90m ATA-Conacite Dos-Estudios America/Peliculas Mexicanas c (Trans: The Sheriff's Strange Son)

Eric del Castillo *(Sheriff Frederick Jackson)*, Mario Almada *(Dr. Jack Miller)*, Rosa Gloria Chagoyan *(Rosa)*, Luis Mario Quiroz *(Fred/Erick)*, Ramon Menedez *(Sam)*, Alfredo Gutierrez *(Judge)*, Wally Baron *(Jeremias Santos)*, Mario Delmar, Guillermo Inclan, Edmundo Barahona, Antonio Aguilar, Julian Abitia, David Montenegro, Blanca Lidia Munoz.

A strange chiller in which Siamese twins are born to a small-town sheriff. Ashamed and afraid, the sheriff, Castillo, keeps the boys hidden until years later, when he forces the local doctor to separate them. During the haphazard operation, one of the twins dies, but he transfers his spirit into the surviving boy's body. Both personalities fight for domination of the body, but the consciousness of the dead boy becomes dominant and it demands revenge on the father.

p, Armando Duarte; d, Fernando Duran; w, Eric del Castillo, Barbara Gil; ph, Agustin Lara; m, Rafael Carrion; ed, Angel Camacho.

Horror   **(PR:O   MPAA:NR)**

EL HERMANO BASTARDO DE DIOS† (1986, Span.) 110m
Almadraba–Television Espanola–Ministry of Culture c (Trans: The Bastard
Brother of God)

Lucas Martin *(Pepe Luis [7-8 years])*, Paco Rabal Cerezales *(Pepe Luis [10-11 years])*, Francisco Rabal *(Grandfather)*, Asuncion Balaguer *(Grandmother)*, Maria Luisa Ponte *(Alejandra)*, Mario Pardo *(Uncle Julio)*, Agustun Gonzales *(Don Enrique)*, Terele Pavez *(Ramona)*, Miguel Angel Rellan *(Commissario)*, Manolo Zarzo *(Doctor)*, Juan Diego *(Omar Hazim)*, Jose Luis Coll *(Narrator [Pepe Luis as an Old Man])*.

An old man looks back at his childhood 50 years before, in the opening days of the Spanish Civil War, recalling how his leftist parents fled the country, how his uncle lost his leg, and how Republican forces searched his uncle's house for a secret radio only to come up with an old movie projector. An official entry in the Venice Film Festival, where it was largely ignored.

p, Ricardo Garcia Arrojo; d, Benito Rabal; w, Benito Rabal, Agustin Cerezales Laforet (based on the novel by Jose Luis Coll); ph, Paco Femenia; m, Juan Pablo Munoz Zielinski; ed, Jose Maria Biurrun; art d, Felix Murcia; cos, Javier Artinano.

Drama **(PR:C MPAA:NR)**

EL HOMBRE QUE GANO LA RAZON† (1986, Arg./Neth.) 68m
Movimiento Falso–Haags Filmhuis/Film International bw (Trans: The Man
Who Gained Reason)

Elio Marchi *(Ricardo)*, Marina Skell *(Leticia)*, Sergio Poves Campos *(Sergio)*.

Marchi is a struggling author who also wants to try his hand at filmmaking. He's assisted in this venture by Skell and Campos, as well as a host of offbeat personalities. One woman he encounters is convinced that Argentina would be better off if Japan bought the South American country as an investment. Marchi also runs into his new husband of his ex-wife, who warns the budding director of the dangers artists face under the Argentine military government. Marchi realizes what he must do with his art, and ultimately takes a strong stand for the things in which he believes.

This film has one of the more interesting behind-the-scenes stories in quite some time. Director Agresti began working in motion pictures at age fifteen, became a cameraman three years later, then began directing this feature when he was twenty years old (he also managed to get a novel published during this period). The film took four years to complete because of Argentina's political climate. Agresti used leftover film stock pirated from television studios and began shooting without benefit of a script. With no money for sets or expensive technical effects, Agresti was forced to make do with location shooting and natural light sources. The military dictatorship's police force dogged the filmmaker's trail, but with that government's fall Agresti was allowed to work as he pleased. A lack of funds nearly ended the project, forcing Agresti to relocate to the Netherlands where the living was less expensive. Once abroad, Agresti was generously provided post-production assistance by the Hague Film House, where EL HOMBRE QUE GANO LA RAZON was finally completed.

p,d&w, Alejandro Agresti; ph, Alejandro Agresti, Nestor Sanz; m, Alejandro Agresti, Igor Stravinsky; ed, Rene Wiegmans.

Drama/Comedy **(PR:O MPAA:NR)**

EL IMPERIO DE LA FORTUNA† (1986, Mex.) 155m Instituto Mexicano
de Cinematografia/Direccion General de Cinematografia c (Trans: The Realm
of Fortune)

Ernesto Gomez Cruz *(Dionisio Pinzo)*, Blanca Guerra *(La Caponera)*, Alejandro Parodi *(Benavides)*, Zaide Silvia Gutierrez *(La Pinzona)*, Margarita Sanz *(Canary Face)*, Ernesto Yanez *(Patilludo)*.

Gomez Cruz is an impoverished Mexican peasant further handicapped by a shriveled hand. To support himself, he gets involved with cock-fighting and the high gambling stakes of that world. He takes a bird that might otherwise be ready for the frying pan and trains it to be a winner. As he finds success in this new milieu, Cruz's self-confidence rises. He then meets Guerra, a cabaret singer who becomes a sort of human good luck charm for him. When she vanishes from his life, Cruz becomes a broken man, and his new-found prosperity disintegrates.

d, Arturo Ripstein; w, Paz Alicia Garaciadiego (based on an original story by Juan Rulfo); ph, Angel Goded; m, Lucia Alvarez; ed, Carlos Savage; art d, Anna Sanchez.

Drama **(PR:O MPAA:NR)**

EL JUEGO DE LA MUERTE† (1986, Mex.) 93m Cinematografica
Rodriguez/Peliculas Mexicanas c (Trans: The Death Game)

Blanca Guerra *(Yolanda)*, Valentin Trujillo *(Lorenzo Rojas)*, Victor Junco *(Don Rafael)*.

In this new version of an old theme, Guerra plays a wealthy young woman who has grown bored with the life of the *chi-chi*. She can't talk to either of her parents as they're both engaged in marital infidelities. Angered by the enormous disparities between the wealthy and the poor, Guerra's consciousness is raised after she and a boy friend are mugged by a gang of motorcycle-riding thugs. She later hooks up with Trujillo, the gang's leader, and soon becomes an outlaw fighting society. When Guerra's father has Trujillo knocked off, the feisty lass forms her own pack of bandits.

d, Alfredo Gurrola; w, Roberto Rodriguez, Jorge Patino; ph, Javier Cruz Osorio; m, Suzy Rodriguez; ed, Federico Laneros.

Action/Crime **(PR:O MPAA:NR)**

EL MALEFICIO II† (1986, Mex.) 105m Televicine/Videocine c (Trans: The
Spell II)

Ernesto Alonso *(Enrique de Martino)*, Lucia Mendez *(Marcela)*, Antonio Monsell *(Gabriel)*, Alejandro Camacho *(David)*, Juan Carlos Ruiz *(Guillermo)*, Eduardo Yanez *(Prof. Andres)*, Manuel Ojeda *(Abel Romo)*, Maria Teresa Rivas *(Aunt)*.

In 1983 the television soap opera "El Maleficio" proved to be an overwhelming success with Mexican viewers. Thanks to this triumph, "El Maleficio's" sequel was created with the big screen in mind, rather than the orthicon tube. Araiza, who directed the original work, was brought back for the film, as was Alonso, the television movie's star. Though Alonso had been killed in the telefilm, he was brought back for the sequel, based on the fact that his character's body had never been found. The story opens with Alonso searching for a child who had been immortalized in a painting. The boy has quiescent psychic powers and ultimately is to succeed Alonso in satanic rituals. The youngster has learned about these powers and is now using his telekinetic abilities to frightening ends. When Alonso falls for Mendez, the boy's sister, the jealous lad retaliates, which leads to a deadly encounter.

p, Gabriel Figueroa; d&w, Raul Araiza (based on characters from the Televisa TV play "El Maleficio"); ph, Jose Ortiz Ramos; m, Guillermo Mendez; ed, Jesus Paredes; spec eff, Juan Carlos Munoz.

Horror **(PR:O MPAA:NR)**

EL MERCADO DE HUMILDES† (1986, Mex.) 87m Televicine/Videocine c
(Trans: Market of the Humble)

Rafael Inclan *(El Multiple)*, Maribel [La Pelongocha] Fernandez *(Lupe)*, Leticia Perdigon *(Rita)*, Lilia Prado *(Concepcion[Conchita])*, Pedro Weber [Chatanooga] *(Don Proculo)*, Manuel [El Flaco] Ibanez *(Piston)*, Lupita Sandoval *(Maid)*, Edith Gonzalez *(Mariela)*, Mario Cid, Carlos East, Lyn May.

The lives of some rascally characters who float around an open-air market are chronicled in this Mexican comedy. While everyone wants to make it big, no one is willing to put in an honest day's work. No one, that is, except Weber, the owner of an antique shop. He strives toward his goal of financial success, but his efforts are for naught: while on a vacation his shop is pillaged by thieves, and he loses everything. In the meantime, idler Inclan decides to make his fortune by smuggling his family into the U.S. Once there Inclan and his brood earn a living selling hot goods. With their earnings Inclan is able to open his own restaurant, ironically in the same location where Weber formerly hawked antiques. Director Cardona is best known to U.S. audiences for his two sleazoid exploitation features SURVIVE! (1977) and GUYANA: CULT OF THE DAMNED (1980).

d, Rene Cardona, Jr.; w, Alfonso Torres Portillo, Fernando Galiana; ph, Raul Dominguez; m, H. Baltazar; ed, Sergio Soto.

Comedy **(PR:C-O MPAA:NR)**

EL NARCO—DUELO ROJO† (1986, Mex.) 94m Corporativa
Cinematografica Astro-S.A. de C.V./Peliculas Mexicanas c (Trans: The
Narc—Red Duel)

Leonel Gonzalez *(Leonel [El Narco] Rojas)*, Victor Junco *(Frank)*, Arturo Martinez *(Ramon Solis)*, Antonio Zunbiaga *(Octavio Loyo)*, Jorge Fegan, Mario Cid, Armando Duarte, Douglas Sandoval, Braulio Zertuche, Tammy Gonzalez, Lisa Willer, Oscar Trevino.

When a U.S. political candidate promises to bear down hard on drug trafficking, he is mysteriously assassinated by a crossbow-wielding killer. Detective Martinez begins an investigation, but his efforts are futile. He realizes that only one man can solve this case: his retired partner Gonzalez, known to many as "El Narco." Martinez finds Gonzalez in a drunken state, psychologically battered by his daughter's accidental drowning and his wife's subsequent hospitalization for mental instability. Gonzalez at first objects, but gradually Martinez gets through to his friend. Gonzalez leaves his tenement apartment, gets off the sauce and goes into training, and then goes on to solve the murder.

p, Leonel Gonzalez; d&w, Alfonso de Alva; ph, Xavier Cruz; m, Hector Sanchez; ed, Enrique Murillo.

Crime/Action **(PR:O MPAA:NR)**

EL OMBLIGO DE LA LUNA† (1986, Mex.) Producciones
Volcan–Universidad Autonoma Metropolitana–Mexican Film Institute c
(Trans: The Naval of the Moon)

Angeles Marin, Darinka Ezeta, Ignacio Guadalupe, Antonio del Rivero, Ernesto Schwarts.

d, Jorge Prior; w, Jorge Prior, Juan Mora; ph, Marco Antonio Ruiz; m, Jorge Reyes; ed, Juan Mora.

EL PUENTE† (1986, Mex.) Plag c (Trans: The Bridge)

Rafael Inclan, Sergio Goyri, Carmen Cardenal, Leonel Gonzalez, Raul Herrera, Monica Mesones, Yolanda Noguera.

p, Leonel Gonzalez; d, Jose Luis Urquieta; w, Jose Luis Urquieta, Leonel Gonzalez; ph, Alberto Arellanos; m, Susana Rodriguez; ed, Enrique Murillo.

EL RIGOR DEL DESTINO†   (1986, Arg.) 100m Vallejo c (Trans: Hardships of Destiny; Cruel Fate)

Carlos Carella, Alejandro Copley, Lenor Manso, Ana Maria Picchio, Victor Laplace, Alberto Benegas.

When a young boy and his mother return to Argentina after ten years in exile, they are taken in by the lad's grandfather. The old man's son (the young boy's father) had been a lawyer, killed by the recently deposed Argentine military dictatorship. A special relationship builds between grandfather and grandson as they share ideas and memories, then begin a search for their dead kin's papers and effects. Sadly they discover that their late relative was not the hero he was believed to be, but a drunken philanderer.

p,d&w, Gerardo Vallejo; ph, Yito Blanc; ed, Luis Mutti; set d, Abel Facello; cos, Beatriz di Benedetto.

Drama   (PR:C-O MPAA:NR)

EL RIO DE ORO†   (1986, Span./Switz.) Tesauro-Marea-INCINE/Federal c (Trans: The Golden River)

Angela Molina *(Laura)*, Bruno Ganz *(Peter)*, Francesca Annis *(Dubarry)*, Stefan Gubser *(Juan)*, Nacho Rodriguez, Juan Diego Botto, Carolina Norris.

Ganz plays an unhappy middle-aged man who brings his wife to a country home where he had spent one glorious summer. They are visiting a writer friend and his wife, for whom Ganz has always yearned. Ganz gets to know his friends' children, and the youngsters take a real liking to him. When it appears that he is finally experiencing some happiness, Ganz takes a raft he has built for the children and mysteriously vanishes down a nearby river. Available in both English and Spanish versions.

p, Herve Haohuol; d&w, Jaime Chavarri; ph, Carlos Suares (Eastmancolor); ed, Pablo del Amo; art d, Adi Gisler; cos, Yolanda Alimbau.

Drama   (PR:C-O MPAA:NR)

EL SECUESTRO DE CAMARENA†   (1986, Mex.) 90m A.D. Agrasanchez-Filmadora Dal/Peliculas Mexicanas c (Trans: Camarena Taken Hostage)

Armando Silvestre *(George Camarena)*, Fernando Casanova *(Criston Caro Quintero)*, Sasha Montenegro *(Alejandra)*, Rebeca Silva, Jorge Vargas, Arlette Pachéco, Estela Inda, Los Invaciones de Nuevo Leon.

Silvestre, a U.S. agent investigating Mexican drug dealing, is kidnaped, tortured, and ultimately killed. This quickie Mexican exploitation film is a thinly veiled telling of what reportedly happened to real-life narcotics agent Enrique Camarena Salizar after his 1984 disappearance.

p, J. David Agrasanchez; d, Alfredo B. Crevenna; w, Jose Loza; ph, Antonio Ruis; m, Marco Flores; ed, Fernando Landero.

Crime/Drama   (PR:O MPAA:NR)

EL SECUESTRO DE LOLA-LOLA LA TRAILERA 2†   (1986, Mex.) 103m Scope/Peliculas Mexicanas c (Trans: Lola's Kidnaping-Lola the Trucker 2)

Rosa Gloria Chagoyan *(Lola Cuevas)*, Rolando Fernandez Lopez *(Jorge)*, Isela Vega *(Federal Police Captain)*, Emilio [Indio] Fernandez *(Police Chief)*, Wolf Rubinskys *(Comandante)*, Frank Moro *(Maestro)*, Maria Cardinal, Isaura Espinoza, Edna Bolkan, Borolas Rizzo, Xavier Rizzo.

In 1985, Mexican audiences were delighted by the film LOLA LA TRAILERA, an inconsequential but flesh-filled work that was one of the country's biggest box-office successes of the year. Naturally, a sequel followed. In this outing, plucky lady trucker Chagoyan is shot in the chest by machine-gun fire. Fortunately she is able to recover in record time (must have been a flesh wound) and is soon on the trail of some nefarious drug traffickers and gun runners. The women are women in this racy feature, and many of the men are rather effeminate as well (macho Mexicans have discovered homosexuality and find it screamingly funny in many contemporary films). Producer/actor Fernandez Lopez's wife Laura handles the camera capably.

p, Rolando Fernandez Lopez; d, Raul Fernandez; w, Carlos Valdemar, Rolando Fernandez; ph, Laura Ferlo [Laura Fernandez Lopez]; m, Tino Geisar, Los Joao, Conjunto Michoacan, Grupo Audaz; ed, Jorge Rivera.

Action/Adventure   (PR:O MPAA:NR)

EL SOL EN BOTELLITAS†   (1986, Arg.) c (Trans: Bottled Sun)

Ana Maria Picchio, Cipe Lincovsky, Edgardo Suarez.

An entry from the blossoming Argentine industry that tells the story of a provincial group who travel to Buenos Aires in the hope of escaping poverty.

d, Edmund Valladares.

Drama   (PR:NR MPAA:NR)

EL SUIZO—UN AMOUR EN ESPAGNE†   (1986, Switz.) 90m Dindo-Boner-SAGA c (Trans: The Swiss—A Love in Spain)

Jurg Low *(Hans)*, Aurore Clement *(Anne)*, Silvia Munt *(Margareta)*, Alfredo Mayo, Luis Barbero, Juan Folguera, Carmen Liano, Jesus Munt, Walter Ruch, Jose Solans, Maria Soley Marti.

In this story, told in flashback, Low is a Swiss writer who travels to Spain, seemingly to cover the repercussions of Generalissimo Francisco Franco's death.

But Low has another purpose as well: to relive events his late father experienced while fighting in the Spanish Civil War. He becomes involved with two women who hold links to the past. The first is a Frenchwoman, whose own father was most likely a soldier in the conflict. The second is the daughter of an old love of Low's father. By living out the past, Low hopes to experience the relevance of life missing in his own generation.

d, Richard Dindo; w, Richard Dindo, Georg Janett; ph, Ranier Trinkler, Jurg Hassler; ed, Ranier Trinkler.

Drama   (PR:O MPAA:NR)

EL TREN DE LOS PIONEROS†   (1986, Colombia) 72m Maya TV-Institute for the Development of Antioquia c (Trans: The Train of the Pioneers)

Manuel Restrepo, Ana Maria Ochoa, Fabio Rios, Alvaro Guerrero, Pablo Agudel, Raul Emilio Correa, Donald Esguerra, Ernesto Aguilar, Ruben Dario Trejos.

In 19th-Century Colombia, a railway is built from the town of Medellin to the Magdalena River. The train's path must cut through forbidding swamp and jungle terrain. Construction is further hindered by the problems of civil war and changing governments, all of which add up to a carload of difficulties before the work can finally be completed.

p, Focine; d&w, Leonel Gallego; ph, Carlos Sanchez; m, Mauricio Mejia; ed, Patricia Bruggisser; set d, Yolanda Botero; cos, Ana Maria Gallon.

Drama   (PR:C-O MPAA:NR)

EL VECINDARIO—LOS MEXICANOS CALIENTES†   (1986, Mex.) 92m Frontera/Peliculas Mexicanas c (Trans: The Neighborhood—Oh Those Hot Mexicans)

Alfonso Zayas *(Roberto)*, Angelica Aragon *(Irma)*, Rafael Inclan *(Ruben)*, Angelica Chain *(Julieta)*, Ana Luisa Peluffo *(Hilda)*, Rossy Mendoza *(Sofia)*, Gilberto Trujillo *(Edmundo)*, Anais de Melo *(Anita)*, Rene Ruiz *(El Compadre)*.

The notorious Solares brothers, who in the past have given us such gems as FACE OF THE SCREAMING WEREWOLF and ATTACK OF THE MAYAN MUMMY, combine their "talents" here to deliver a comedy with a rather dubious premise. A trio of philandering Mexicans—Zayas, Inclan, and Trujillo—loose their sexual appetites on their neighbors, gleefully raping women who refuse to press charges because of their attackers' knack at satisfying them. It doesn't sound very funny to us either.

p, Alfonso Martinez Solares; d, Gilberto Martinez Solares; w, Alfonso Martinez Solares, Gilberto Martinez Solares; ph, Armando Castillon; m, Ernesto Cortazar; ed, Jose Monguia.

Comedy   (PR:O MPAA:NR)

EL YOM EL SADES†   (1986, Egypt) 110m MISR-Lyric c (Trans: The Sixth Day)

Dalida Moshen *(Saddika)*, Moheidine Chouikar *(Okka)*, Hamdy Ahmad, Salal Saadani, Sanaa Younes, Mohamad Mounir, Youssef El Ani.

It is 1947 and Egypt is suffering from the effects of a deadly cholera epidemic. As in Manuel Puig's novel *Betrayed By Rita Hayworth*, many of the characters here have formed their ideas about life through watching movies. Moshen supports her disabled spouse by doing menial work for an important actress who ignores the struggling woman's fantasies. Chouikar is an organ grinder who dreams of being Gene Kelly, a notion he later fulfills in a fantasy song and dance routine. The starry-eyed lad also hopes to meet a blonde, blue-eyed European gentlewoman. Hearing of a mysterious female who is snatching British soldiers for sexual pleasures, Chouikar dyes his hair and dons a military uniform. He ends up getting bashed by a gang of toughs, and is taken to Moshen's house to recover. Though she is twice his age, Chouikar falls for Moshen, but he is kicked out of her house. Later Moshen's husband, a cholera victim, kills himself, which brings the unusual couple back together. But the romance is not to be, and Moshen tells her would-be suitor to find a girl in his own age bracket.

d&w, Youssef Chahine (based on the book by Andree Chedid); ph, Moshen Nasr; m, Omar Khairat; cos, Yvonne Sassinot, Nahed Nasrallah.

Drama/Comedy   (PR:O MPAA:NR)

EL-GOOA†   (1986, Egypt) 121m Egypt Video Cassette c (Trans: Hunger)

Souad Hosni *(Zebeda)*, Mahmoud Abdelaziz *(Farag)*, Yosra *(Malak)*, Abdul-Aziz Makoun *(Gaber)*.

Abdelaziz and Makoun are two brothers living in a ghetto in 19th Century Cairo. Both want to escape this life, while dreaming of the day when they will see social equality. Eventually Abdelaziz achieves a position of power as the local "foutua," a job that walks a fine line between legal authority and influential mob boss. Corrupted by the job, Abdelaziz forgets about his ghetto roots and leaves his wife for another, more affluent woman. In the meantime Makoun decides on a nobler route. Despite the trouble it will cause, he marries Hosni, who has shamed herself by getting impregnated by another man. Makoun grows to be as powerful as his brother by working with the commonfolk, and he prepares them for an eventual revolt.

p, Mamdo Youssef; d, Ali Badrakhan; w, Mustapha Moharram, Ali Badrakhan; ph, Mahmoud Abdessamieh; m, George Kaza Zayani; ed, Adel Mounir; art d, Salah Mari.

Drama   Cas.   (PR:O MPAA:NR)

ELIMINATORS**
(1986) 96m Empire c

Andrew Prine *(Harry Fontana)*, Denise Crosby *(Nora Hunter)*, Patrick Reynolds *(Mandroid)*, Conan Lee *(Kuji)*, Roy Dotrice *(Abbott Reeves)*, Peter Schrum *(Ray)*, Peggy Mannix *(Bayou Betty)*, Fausto Bara *(Luis)*, Tad Horino *(Takada)*, Luis Lorenzo *(Maurice)*.

Following the rescue of the leading players by the ninja and the half-man/half-robot who also get rid of the Neanderthal tribe, the crusty riverboat captain says to the beautiful lady scientist, "What is this, a comic book?" That sums up this serviceable science-fiction item from Empire, the American International Pictures of the 1980s. Reynolds is the Mandroid, built of android parts grafted onto the shattered body of a pilot whose plane crashed in a remote Mexican jungle. His creator is mad scientist Dotrice, who also has a time machine and a bizarre plot to rule ancient Rome. When Dotrice's use for the Mandroid—whose will and memory have been erased—is over, he orders him dismantled. Dotrice's Japanese assistant, Horino, refuses to go through with this—helping Reynolds escape at the cost of his own life—after telling Reynolds to look for a Colonel Hunter. He makes his way out of the jungle and back to the U.S. with a poncho thrown over his mechanical parts and tracks down Hunter, who turns out to be a woman cybernetic scientist (Crosby). She recognizes some of the technology used to build Reynolds as her own and she is upset at this "bastardization" of her work. She is also surprised to learn that Dotrice is alive, because the institute for which she works is sponsored by Dotrice's estate. She decides to go along with Reynolds as he seeks revenge. They hire riverboat captain Prine and head upriver, fighting off a very butch female riverboat captain and assorted goons along the way. Crosby and Prine are captured by Neanderthals (apparently resulting from one of Dotrice's time-machine experiments) but are rescued by Reynolds and Lee, a ninja whose father just happens to have been Horino. The four reach Dotrice's compound and wipe out his forces, though at the cost of Reynold's life (that's okay, though, because he said earlier he wanted to be dismantled after this was all

over). Dotrice, who has his own android suit so he can rule Rome, manages to escape in his time machine, but Prine punches the computer and sends him back to 3,000,000 B.C. Hardly a distinguished credit in anyone's book, the worst acting offenses are committed by Crosby, who walks through the whole thing with such gravity of bearing that she seems to have wandered in from some other movie. The direction is listless and many scenes seem to be missing or cut short. So what have we got here? We got robots, we got ninjas, we got a mad scientist, we got a beautiful lady scientist, we got cavemen, we got a cute little R2-D2 ripoff, we got bumbling henchmen . . . the list goes on and on, and if this innocuous hodgepodge sounds like your cup of tea (don't be ashamed), you could do worse than ELIMINATORS.

p, Charles Band; d, Peter Manoogian; w, Danny Bilson, Paul DeMeo; ph, Mac Ahlberg (Fotofilm Color); m, Richard Band; ed, Andy Horvitch; prod d, Phillip Foreman; art d, Gumersindo Andres Lopez; cos, Jill Ohanneson; spec eff, Juan Ramon Molina; makeup, John Buechler; stunts, Jose Luis Chinchilla.

Science Fiction/Adventure   Cas.   **(PR:A-C MPAA:PG)**

ELOGIO DELLA PAZZIA†
(1986, Ital.) Cinestudio 12/IMC c (Trans: In Praise of Folly)

Marcel Marceau, Don Hodson, Fernando Grillo, Franco Piacentini, Riccardo Pagni, Gionni Voltan, Marco Paoli, Emanuela Rigacci, Elisabeth Lindauer, Luciano Crovato, Marco Scala, Gaia Gastreghi, Renato Condeleo.

The internationally acclaimed mime Marcel Marceau is featured in this portmanteau film exploring the mystical aspects of man's nature. The first story involves an industrialist who uses wizardry to advance his career, then tries to kill the man who helped him. Next is a father who, through self-deception, manages to oversee his family. The third tale looks at a general who learns how power corrupts

and destroys; and, lastly, a young fellow discovers his own importance after a disturbing journey.

d&w, Roberto Aguerre; ph, Giuseppa Ganci (Technicolor); m, Alessandro Sbordoni, Wolfgang Amadeus Mozart; ed, Amedeo Salfa.

Comedy/Drama   **(PR:C-O MPAA:NR)**

EL-SADA EL-RIGAL†
(1986, Egypt) 113m Studio 13 c (Trans: The Gentleman)

Mali Zayed *(Fawzia/Fawzi)*, Mahmoud Abdelaziz, Hala Foad, Ibrahim Yousri.

The world of transsexuals has seen a few cinematic examinations including Ed Wood's cult favorite GLEN OR GLENDA? (1953) and the 1979 exploitation schlockumentary LET ME DIE A WOMAN. This Egyptian study is another look at the unique subject and begins when Zayed, a chubby bank worker, grows tired of the way she's been treated by men. In order to get out of this grind, Zayed pays a little visit to the hospital and becomes a he. Zayed's male coworkers have no problem with this radical change, but Abdelaziz, Zayed's spouse, has a few problems with his mate's new status. Zayed ends up flipping Abdelaziz around with a few fancy karate moves, causing the much befuddled man to wonder if perhaps he too should consider such an operation. With a new gender, Zayed soon grows intolerant of women, though a pretty young bank clerk and an ailing babe soon bring about a change in attitude.

p,d&w, Rafaat El Mihi; ph, Samir Farag; m, Mohamed Hellal; ed, Sayed El Sheikh.

Comedy/Drama   **(PR:O MPAA:NR)**

EL-TOUK WA EL-ESSWERA†
(1986, Egypt) 116m El Alamia c (Trans: Fetters)

Ezzat El Alaily *(Behet/Mustapha)*, Sherihan *(Fahima/Farhana)*, Fardos Abdelhamid *(Hazina)*, Mohamed Mounir.

Sherihan is a young Egyptian girl of the 1930s who marries a local blacksmith after her father El Alaily dies. Tragedy shrouds this union when it's learned that Sherihan's new spouse is unable to father children. Sherihan's mother Abdelhamid suggests the unhappy girl follow an old tradition by letting a stranger get her pregnant. Once he learns the truth, Sherihan's husband kicks her out of the house. After giving birth, she becomes ill and dies. The actress now plays the fated woman's daughter some twenty years later, at a time when Abdelhamid's long-gone son (also played by El Alaily) has returned home. When Sherihan becomes pregnant while still unmarried her enraged uncle has her buried in the ground up to her neck. Fortunately, Sherihan is rescued from this horrifying fate by a young man who is in love with her.

p, Hussein Kalla; d, Khairy Bishara; w, Yahia Azmi, Khairy Bishara; ph, Tarek El Telmissany; m, Intisar Abdul-Fatah; ed, Adel Moneir.

Drama   **(PR:O MPAA:NR)**

ELVIS GRATTON, LE KING DES KINGS†
(1986, Can.) 90m Provifilms c (Trans: Elvis Gratton, The King Of Kings)

Julien Poulin, Denise Mercier.

Based on a Canadian short made in 1985 under the same title, this outlandish comedy tells the story of a man who is obsessed with Elvis Presley. He so admires the "king of rock 'n' roll" that he pursues a career in music in order to fill the void left by his dead idol.

p, Bernadette Payeur; d, Pierre Falardeau.

Comedy   **(PR:NR MPAA:NR)**

ELYSIUM†
(1986, Hung.) 118m Hungarian Television-Daniel-Mafilm/ Daniel c

Ferenc Bacs *(Zsamboki)*, Zoltan Nagy *(Gyuri)*, Klaus Abramowsky *(Doctor Helmer)*, Tibor Szilagyi *(Father)*, Anna Rackevei *(Mother)*, Erzsebet Kutualgyi *(Aunt)*, Risarda Hanin *(Grandmother)*.

During WW II a family of Hungarian Jews manages to evade deportation to a concentration camp, and are allowed to remain in their home, though they must wear the yellow Star of David to signify their status. When the clan's 10-year-old boy goes out to visit friends, he is arrested and sent to Elysium, a camp specifically for children. Though Elysium is a beautiful place to live, beneath its tranquil appearance lurk unmitigated horrors, for the camp's real purpose is to serve as a holding pen for potential victims of fiendish Nazi medical experiments. The child's parents, sick with worry after his sudden disappearance, enlist the help of a Gentile friend in hopes of finding their son. This film is based on a popular Hungarian novel, which itself was based on a true story.

p, Akos Ravasz; d, Erika Szanto; w, Eva Schulze, Erika Szanto (based on the novel by Imre Keszi); ph, Ferenc Zadori; m, Wolfgang Amadeus Mozart; ed, Vera Hertzka; art d, Tamas Vayer; cos, Fanny Kemenes.

Drama   **(PR:O MPAA:NR)**

EMMA'S WAR†
(1986, Aus.) 95m Belinon/Curzon c

Lee Remick *(Anne Grange)*, Miranda Otto *(Emma Grange)*, Bridey Lee *(Laurel Grange)*, Terence Donovan *(Frank Grange)*, Mark Lee *(John Davidson)*, Pat Evison *(Miss Arnott)*, Donal Gibson *(Hank)*.

Otto is a young girl who comes of age during WW II as her mother (Remick) turns into an alcoholic and her father is badly injured while serving as an official war artist.

p, Clytie Jessop, Andrena Finlay; d, Clytie Jessop; w, Peter Smalley, Clytie Jessop; ph, Tom Cowan (Kodak color); m, John Williams; ed, Sonia Hoffman; art d, Jane Norris.

Drama (PR:C MPAA:NR)

EN PENUMBRA† (1986, Span.) 89m Jose Miguel Juarez c (Trans: Among the Shadows)

Antonio Canto *(Daniel)*, Amparo Munoz *(Helena)*, Miguel Bose *(Maniqui)*, Lola Herrera *(Mother)*, Antonio Garisa *(Father)*, Miguel Molina *(Rosario)*, Emilio Lain *(Reyes)*, Miguel Ortiz *(Braulio)*.

Canto is a young man who falls in love with an older woman. He follows her through a decadent underworld of drugs, sex, and boring parties until he finally rejects the whole thing. (In Spanish.)

p, Jose Miguel Juarez; d, Jose Luis Lozano; w, Luis Arino Torre, Jose Luis Lozano; ph, Tote Trenas (Eastmancolor); m, Fernando Civil, Mariano Diaz; ed, Luis Manuel de Valle; set d, Victor Alarcon; cos, Jose Maria Garcia; spec eff, Reyes Abades.

Drama (PR:O MPAA:NR)

ENAS ISICHOS THANATOS† (1986, Gr.) 88m Greek Film Centre-Negative Ltd. c (Trans: A Quiet Death)

Eleonora Stathopoulou, Pemy Zouni, Takis Moschos, Giorgos Moschos, Electra Alexandropoulou, Christos Nikitaidis, Rasme Soukouli.

A female novelist suffers writer's block, and wanders the rain-slick streets at night to overcome her problems.

d, Frieda Liappa; w, Frieda Liappa, Kyriakos Angelakos, Christos Angelakos, Giorgos Bramos; ph, Nikos Smaragdis; ed, Takis Yannopoulos; set d&cos, Panos Papadopoulos.

Drama (PR:O MPAA:NR)

END, THE† (1986, Iran) IFA Cinematic Group c

Iraj Tahmasb, Parviz Poor Hosseini, Hamid Jebeli.

d, Ali Talebi; w, Ali Talebi, G. Moosavi; ph, Daryoush Ayari; m, M. Aligholi; ed, Rouhollah Emami.

EQUINOXE† (1986, Can.) 83m Ateliers Audio-Visuel du Quebec c

Jacques Godin *(Guillaume)*, Ariane Frederique *(Nathalie)*, Marthe Mercure *(Rita)*, Michel Sabourin *(Rosario)*, Andre Melancon *(Bert)*, Luc Proulx *(Arthur)*, Jerry Snell *(Joe)*.

Godin is an aging man who has returned home after years abroad following a prison sentence. Convicted on the basis of the perjured testimony of a former friend, he is back, his 12-year-old granddaughter in tow, looking for the man in order to avenge himself. Along the way he drives so recklessly that three young toughs chase him. One of Canada's official entries in the World Filmfest in Montreal, where it didn't even place.

p, Nicole Lamothe; d, Arthur Lamothe; w, Arthur Lamothe, Gilles Carle, Pierre-Yves Pepin; ph, Guy Dufaux; m, Jean Sauvageau; ed, Francois Gill.

Drama (PR:C MPAA:NR)

ER WOO DONG† (1986, S. Korea) 115m Tae Hung c (Trans: The Entertainer)

Ahn Sung-ghi *(Er Yoon Chang/Hyanjgi)*, Lee Bo-hee *(Assassin)*.

Ahn Sung-ghi is a a 14th Century courtesan and entertainer who retires to an isolated valley where she is protected by her deaf-mute bodyguard. Her father, a powerful official ashamed of his daughter's career, hires an assassin to kill her. Lots of nudity and violence in this exploitation item.

p, Lee Tae-won; d, Lee Jang-ho; w, Lee Hyon-hwa (based on a story by Bang Gi-hwan); ph, Park Sung-bae; m, Lee Chong-ku; ed, Hyung Dong-choon; prod d, Yun Geong-hwan; cos, Lee Hon-gung.

Historical (PR:O MPAA:NR)

ERDSEGEN† (1986, Ger./Aust.) 110m MR-ORF-ZDF c (Trans: Blessings of the Earth)

Dietrich Siegl *(Hans Trautendorffer)*, Alexander Wagner *(Herr Adamshauser)*, Barbara Petritsch *(Frau Adamshauser)*, Cilli Wang *(Micheline)*, Gudrun Trummer *(Barbel)*, Sepp Trummer *(Michel)*, Karl Pongratz *(Rocherl)*, Christian Spatzek *(Guido Winter)*, Heinrich Schweiger *(Dr. von Stein)*.

Based on a novel by Peter Rosegger, an author widely read by Austrian students, ERDSEGEN is set in 1910 and stars Siegl as a Viennese journalist who leaves the city and takes work as a farm laborer. Hired by a family in the Styria region, Siegl is initially faced with a variety of unfamiliar customs. He is befriended by farm girl Gudrun Trummer, who is as interested in Siegl's city ways as he is in Styrian tradition. Eventually, Siegl is accepted by the others who no longer view him as an outsider but as a capable worker. Directed by Karin Brandauer, the wife of the superb actor Klaus-Maria Brandauer (MEPHISTO, OUT OF AFRICA).

p&d, Karin Brandauer; w, Felix Mitterer (based on the novel by Peter Rosegger); ph, Hans Liechti, Helmut Pirnat; ed, Marie Homolka.

Drama (PR:NR MPAA:NR)

ERZEKENY BUCSU A FEJEDELEMTOL† (1986, Hung.) 102m Mafilm-Dialog Studio c (Trans: A Fond Farewell to the Prince)

Ferenc Bessenyei *(Gabor Bethlen)*, Krzysztof Wakulinski *(Don Diego di Estrada)*, Hanna Mikuc *(Catherine of Brandenburg)*, Vera Papp, Istvan Avar, Peter Andorai, Laszlo Vajda.

Set in the principality of Transylvania in the early 1600s, this historical drama examines the reign of aging prince Gabor Bethlen (Bessenyei). Life under Bessenyei flourishes both economically and culturally. Determined to document his successes, Bessenyei invites a Spanish knight, Wakulinski, to visit his court and write the history of the province. Wakulinski not only unearths some well-kept secrets, but romances Mikuc, Bessenyei's pretty and much younger wife. Although Bessenyei and Wakulinski have a falling out, they eventually renew their friendship while the prince is on his deathbed.

d, Laszlo Vitezy; w, Agnes Hankiss; ph, Peter Jankura (Eastmancolor); m, Istvan Martha; ed, Terez Losonci; prod d, Tamas Banovich; cos, Erzsebet Mialkovsky.

Historical/Biography (PR:NR MPAA:NR)

ES MI VIDA—EL NOA NOA 2† (1986, Mex.) 106m Producciones del Ray-Producciones Alarca-Pelinez Mexicanas c (Trans: It's My Life—El Noa Noa 2)

Alberto Aguilera [Juan Gabriel] *(Himself)*, Narciso Busquets *(Daniel)*, Guillermo Murray *(Don Alfredo Moras)*, Fernando Balzaretti, Marcela Rubiales, Leonor Llausas, Cesar Bono, Edgar Wald, Lilian Gonzalez, Meche Carreno, Federico Villa, Dacia Gonzalez, Tito Junco, La Prieta Linda, Bruno Rey.

A sequel to the 1979 Mexican production, EL NOA NOA, which told the tale of the early years of popular national balladeer Juan Gabriel. This entry follows him (he plays himself) as he is wrongly imprisoned in Mexico City. His time behind bars serves as musical inspiration and, in a series of dream sequences, he imagines himself performing and recording his songs. When he is finally released, success and fame soon follow.

p, Arnulfo Delgado, Alberto Aguilera [Juan Gabriel]; d&w, Gonzalo Martinez Ortega; ph, Feberon Tepoztle; m, Gabriel Malallemo, Eduardo Malallemo; ed, Angel Camacho.

Biography (PR:NR MPAA:NR)

ESCORT GIRL (SEE: HALF MOON STREET, 1986, Brit.)

ESE LOCO LOCO HOSPITAL† (1986, Mex.) 90m Esme-Seneca-Alianza Cinematografica Mexicana/Peliculas Nacionales c (Trans: That Mad Mad Hospital)

Susana Dosamantes *(Doctor Matilda)*, Fernando Lujan *(Doctor Chivago)*, Guillermo Rivas *(Gino Beruggi)*, Lucila Mariscal *(Nurse Bigotes)*, Sergio Ramos *(Edipo Peres)*, Rebeca Silva *(Lucy)*, Jose Magana *(Dr. Luis Rubio)*, Charly Valentino, Polo Ortin, Raul Padilla, Gina Leal, Yiran Aparicio, Jose Natera, Juan Palaez, Paco Sanudo, Alejandra Peniche, Julio Ruiz Llaneza.

One of the oldest scenarios in film comedy is the hospital story, allowing for all kinds of slapstick, double entendre wordplay, and nurses in skimpy uniforms. The British CARRY ON series set several of its films in hospitals, and Dirk Bogarde launched his career with the DOCTOR films. This time the material is approached by a Mexican director, Julio Ruiz Llaneza, who had worked in dramas until he got fed up with their lack of financial success, a problem he sought to rectify with this film.

p, Carlos Vasallo; d, Julio Ruiz Llaneza; w, Ramon Obon; ph, Xavier Cruz; m, Carlos Torres; ed, Jorge Pena.

Comedy (PR:O MPAA:NR)

ESPERANDO LA CARROZA   (SEE: AWAITING THE PALLBEARERS, 1986, Arg.)

ESCUADRON DE LA MUERTE†   (1986, Mex.) Metropolitana c (Trans: Death Squad)

Mario Almada, Miguel Angel Rodriguez, Rojo Grau, Gerardo Vigil, Sergio Goyri, Rubi Re, Hugo Stiglitz, Jorge Luke, Dalia Casanova, Norma Lazareno, Carlos Cardan, Alejandro Parodi, Eduardo Lopez Rojas.

d, Alfredo Gurrola; w, Vicente Armendariz, R.L. Arego; ph, Agustin Lara; ed, Francisco Chiu.

ESTHER†   (1986, Fr./Israel/Brit.) 93m Agav-Channel 4-ORF-IKON-United/Agav c

Mouhammad Bakri *(Mordechai)*, Simona Binyamini *(Esther)*, Shmuel Wolf *(narrator)*, Giuliano Mer *(Haman)*, Zare Vartenian *(Ahashverosh)*, David Cohen *(Hatak)*.

This film recounts the biblical tale of Esther with connections to the current political situation in Israel woven into the story. Binyamini is featured as the heroine who marries an emperor in an effort to save her fellow Jews from mass slaughter. Director Gitai, a former documentary filmmaker who specialized in left-wing subjects, shot the story on location in Haifa, freely incorporating such modern-day facts-of-life as traffic noises and current styles of dress in order to give the work a contemporary feel. The cast is a deliberate mixture of Jews and Arabs, indicating that Esther's story has more than one interpretation in 1986 Israel.

p&d, Amos Gitai; w, Amos Gitai, Stephen Levine (based on the Biblical story); ph, Henri Alekan (Fujicolor); m, Sikumar Tumar, Isi Yashi, Rin Banah, Sarah Cohen; ed, Sheherezade Saadi; prod d, Richard Ingersoll; cos, Thierry Fortan.

Drama   (PR:O MPAA:NR)

ET SKUD FRA HJERTET†   (1986, Den.) 80m Gronlykke-Levring-Magnusson/Metronome c (Trans: A Shot From the Heart)

Claus Flygare *(Captive Gangleader)*, Lars Oluf Larsen *(Rookie Soldier)*, Niels Skousen *(Brok, Older Soldier)*, Susanne Voldmester *(Roaming Girl)*, Frank Schaufuss *(Army Captain)*, Steen Birger Jorgensen *(Yellow, Rival Gangleader)*, Lizzie Corfixen, Pouel Kern, Lars Sidenius, Ejner Jensen, Claus Lembeck, Morten Suurballe, Henrik Birk.

The Danes take a stab at current science fiction with this low-budget epic. Larsen is a young soldier in some post-apocalyptic army assigned to escort the leader of a rebel band to a fort where he will be tortured and executed. Along the way the two men come to one of those understandings that prisoners and warders always do in these films (3:10 TO YUMA, ASSAULT ON PRECINCT 13, UNCERTAIN GLORY, and scores of others), and the prisoner even helps fight off an attack by another band of brigands. At film's end, Larsen shoots his prisoner dead himself rather than let him be tortured.

p, Tivi Magnusson; d, Kristian Levring; w, Leif Magnusson (based on an idea by Kristian Levring); ph, Steen Veileborg (Eastmancolor); m, Lars Hug; ed, Leif Magnusson; prod d, Claus Bjerre; cos, Stine Marott.

Science Fiction   (PR:O MPAA:NR)

ETATS D'AME†   (1986, Fr.) 100m Films 7-FR3/AMLF c (Trans: Moods)

Robin Renucci *(Maurice)*, Jean-Pierre Bacri *(Romain)*, Francois Cluzet *(Pierrot)*, Tcheky Karyo *(Bertrand)*, Xavier Delluc *(Michel)*, Sandrine Dumas *(Marie)*, Nathalie Nell *(Martine)*, Zabou *(Helene)*, Pascal Bardet, Martine Sarcey, Guillaume Le Guellec, Jean-Paul Roussilon, Evelyne Didi.

A quintet of friends who have been together since the French student riots of 1968 are overjoyed with the victory of socialism in the 1981 May elections. During the celebration they meet a pregnant girl who goes into labor that very night. Over the years the five men—each of whom is growing disillusioned with France's political situation—attempt in their own separate ways to find and become involved with the enticing girl. To them she represents youthful exuberance and is a reminder of times that are forever lost.

p, Marie-Dominique Girodet; d&w, Jacques Fansten; ph, Dominique Chapuis (Fujicolor); m, Jean-Marie Senia; ed, Nicole Saulnier; art d, Jean-Louis Poveda;

Drama   (PR:O MPAA:NR)

EU SEI QUE VOU TE AMAR†   (1986, Braz.) 104m Sagitario c (Trans: Love Me For Ever or Never)

Fernanda Torres, Thales Pan Chacon.

Torres and Chacon are a divorced couple who meet accidentally a few months after their two-year marriage has officially ended. Though each bears hostilities and resentments towards the other, they manage to discuss their mutual past. By bringing shared pain to the surface, they are able to exorcise old psychological demons that have long been deeply embedded in them.

p, Arnaldo Jabor, Helio Paula Ferraz; d&w, Arnaldo Jabor; ph, Lauro Escorel; m, Maurice Ravel, Giuseppe Verdi, Christoph Gluck; ed, Mair Taveres; art d, Sergio Silveira, Maria Helena Salles; set d, Oscar Niemeyer, Sergio Silveira.

Drama   (PR:O MPAA:NR)

EVENING DRESS   (SEE: MENAGE, 1986, Fr.)

EVERY TIME WE SAY GOODBYE**½   (1986) 95m Tri-Star c

Tom Hanks *(David)*, Cristina Marsillach *(Sarah)*, Benedict Taylor *(Peter)*, Anat Atzmon *(Victoria)*, Gila Almagor *(Lea)*, Moni Moshanov *(Nessin)*, Avner Hizkiyahu *(Raphael)*, Caroline Goodall *(Sally)*, Esther Parnass *(Rosa)*, Daphne Armony *(Clara)*, Orit Weisman *(Mathilda)*.

It is 1942 and Hanks, an American flier serving with the British Royal Air Force, is in Jerusalem where he is recuperating from an injury. His squadron leader is about to marry, and Hanks falls in love with Marsillach, best friend of the bride-to-be. Though Marsillach is initially hesitant, the romance blossoms, much to the dismay of her family. They are Sephardic Jews and strongly disapprove of Hanks, whose father is a Christian minister. Finally, in an outlandish attempt at extracting obedience from their daughter, Marsillach's parents hold her captive in her room. Marsillach's clothing is taken away so that should she escape she won't go far. She gets out anyway, but gradually her parents' tactics wear down Marsillach's will. Marsillach prepares to marry a Jewish man she does not love, but she still cannot forget Hanks. When Hanks returns to Jerusalem, Marsillach realizes how much she cares for him and the two are happily reunited.

Hanks, as usual, is extremely likable in this real change-of-pace role for the comic actor. Hanks' performance gives an extra spark to the routine romance, which is merely a reworking of the old Romeo and Juliet star-crossed lovers theme, conventionally told without much embellishment. Director Mizrahi (best known for his 1977 Oscar-winning feature MADAME ROSA) doesn't really capitalize on the film's time and place, other than a few token statements about British colonial rule. Marsillach makes a nice counterpart to Hanks; their pairing does give EVERY TIME WE SAY GOODBYE a few moments of sweetness.

p, Jacob Kotzky, Sharon Harel; d, Moshe Mizrahi; w, Moshe Mizrahi, Rachel Fabien, Leah Appet (based on a story by Moshe Mizrahi); ph, Giuseppe Lanci; m, Philippe Sarde; ed, Mark Burns; art d, Micky Zahar.

Romance   **Cas.**   (PR:C MPAA:PG-13)

EVIXION†   (1986, Can.) 78m Chbib c

Roland Smith, Claire Nadon, Kennon Raines, Pierre Curzi, Piotr Lysak, Jean-Claude Gingras, Suzanne Stark.

This experimental narrative deals in an anecdotal fashion with the inhabitants of a decrepit apartment building somewhere in Montreal. The stock bunch consists of (among others) a Jayne Mansfield-worshiping drag queen, a peddler of narcotics, a homosexual couple, and a revolutionary feminist. Producer, director, editor, and cowriter Chbib—whose first feature film was MEMOIRS (1984)—is a Syrian who was funded in part by a Canadian government grant.

p&d, Bachar Chbib; w, Bachar Chbib, Claire Nadon, Dafna Kastner, Stephen Reizes; ph, David Wellington, Sylvain Gingras; ed, Bachar Chbib.

Drama   (PR:O MPAA:NR)

EXIT-EXIL†   (1986, Fr./Bel.) 110m MBC-Cinete c (Trans: Exit-Exile)

Philippe Leotard *(Dutch)*, Frederique Hender *(Olivia)*, Magali Noel *(Solange)*, Georges Geret, Jean-Pierre Sentier, Fabrice Eberhard, Jean Lescot, Jean De Coninck, Brigitte Audrey.

Hender is a nightclub stripper whose down-and-out parents live in a garbage dump with other homeless people. Her oft-drunken boy friend Leotard tries his best to help change her life, which leads to a number of slam-bang scream fests. Amazingly, this portrait of humanity at its lowest point was produced in association with both the French and Belgian Ministries of Culture.

p, Willum Thijssen; d&w, Luc Monheim; ph, Mario Barroso, Frederic Variot (Fujicolor); ed, Yves Deschamps; art d, Pierre Cadiou.

Drama   (PR:O MPAA:NR)

EXTREMITIES***   (1986) 90m Atlantic c

Farrah Fawcett *(Marjorie)*, James Russo *(Joe)*, Diana Scarwid *(Terry)*, Alfre Woodard *(Patricia)*, Sandy Martin *(Officer Sudow)*, Eddie Velez *(1st Officer)*, Tom Everett *(2nd Officer)*, Donna Lynn Leavy *(Woman on Phone)*, Enid Kent *(Mother at Police Station)*, Michael C. Hennessy *(Pizza Man)*, Danika Hendrickson *(Joe's Daughter)*, Clare Wren *(Racquetball Player)*, James Avery *(Security Guard)*.

How does one make a film about rape, showing the full horror of the situation, yet without exploiting the on-screen victim? In an age when the FRIDAY THE THIRTEENTH series and countless other women-in-danger films proliferate, this seems a difficult task for any serious commercial filmmaker. In EXTREMITIES Robert M. Young—director of such varied films as the prison drama SHORT EYES (1979), singer Paul Simon's feature ONE TRICK PONY, and the oft-praised BALLAD OF GREGORIO CORTEZ (1982)—seeks to answer this question, though the results are not entirely successful.

Fawcett is a museum worker who stops for an ice cream cone on her way home one night. An unknown man wearing a ski mask is prowling the shop's parking lot, looking for a potential victim. When she gets back in her car, she is assaulted by him, and forced to drive to an isolated location. She manages to escape, but when she goes to the police she is shocked to learn that because she would be unable to identify her masked attacker, and because there were no witnesses, little can be done. The unknown assailant has her wallet, however, and Fawcett is terrified by the thought that he will come to her home. Her housemates Scarwid and Woodard try to downplay her fears, but to no avail. A week after the attack her worst nightmare comes true when the assailant, Russo, barges into her home, claiming to be looking for a friend. His real intentions become clear when he forces his terrified victim to put on a sexy outfit and, in a demented mockery of

domesticity, has Fawcett make him something to eat. Next Russo takes her to the floor and demands that his victim say, "I love you. I want to make love."

As Russo kisses her, Fawcett grabs a can of insect repellent lying nearby and blasts it into his face, temporarily blinding him. Fawcett makes the most of her advantage, tying Russo up with a phone cord and then knocking him unconscious. She pushes Russo into a fireplace, and holds him captive behind an old brass bedframe secured to the mantel. Fawcett then begins digging a grave in the back yard, intending to bury Russo alive, but she is interrupted when Scarwid returns home. Scarwid is terrified, and when Woodard arrives, this bizarre scene takes on a new dimension. Woodard is a social worker, and she attempts to see the situation from both sides. She realizes that there is no proof that Russo tried to rape Fawcett, and furthermore, unless he sees a doctor, the insect repellent will kill him. Fawcett, driven over the edge, takes Russo's knife and forces a confession from her victim, threatening him with castration unless he tells the truth. Russo breaks down, and Fawcett's roommates go to get the police.

Fawcett and Russo deliver incredible performances as they give and receive intense physical and mental abuse with uncompromising realism. Young's direction of the attempted rape makes frighteningly effective use of the subjective camera, often showing action through the eyes of both victim and attacker. His uncomfortable long takes and closeups, along with disorienting camera angles, put the viewer in an unyielding position of witness to this harsh, traumatic

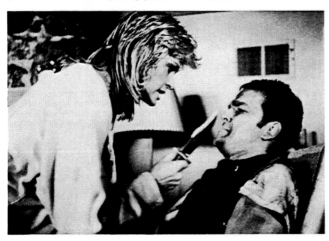

violence. When Russo controls the situation, he is a brash, macho individual, working with the precision of a skilled prizefighter going after his opponent. He never lets Fawcett get the edge on him, anticipating her every move, until she hits him with the bug spray. Fawcett takes an extraordinary amount of abuse as she is slapped, beaten, and psychologically humiliated. When she is able to turn the situation around, her approach is cool and assured, always in control. Yet as victim, Russo is also able to fight, using words to gain sympathy, knowing full well what he is doing.

EXTREMITIES was originally an off-Broadway play, performed with the same amount of physical and mental fervor as the film version. Fawcett, the third actress to take the role (after Susan Sarandon and Karen Allen), broke her wrist during the play's run, while Russo ended up with two cracked ribs. Although the costars got along during their stage run, animosity developed between them during the intense film shooting, and this led to a falling out. "I don't know if it's the best thing I've ever done," Fawcett later said of her film performance. "I do know it's the hardest. And even when it was over, none of us let up. I think we were all delighted that we wouldn't have to see each other again."

Though the powerful rancor of the play comes through, the film also retains some deadening theatricality that doesn't work onscreen. Both Woodard and Scarwid are simplistic characters with too-obvious functions when the women try to figure out what to do with Russo. Scarwid is reduced to the crying hysteric and Woodard to the equivocating liberal, both going through the motions without much character depth. When Scarwid reveals that she was raped years before, it

comes across more as a character trait grafted on by a writer than anything genuine. The finale, with the roommates going for help while Fawcett sits quietly near the imprisoned Russo, also smacks of staginess. All that's missing from the scene is a closing curtain. Another hindrance is the undeniable fact that even as she is being attacked, Fawcett is still the beautiful movie star. Though her performance is excellent, she brings with her a certain glamour image that is only heightened by the lingerie in which Russo attires her. This predetermined element is one that EXTREMITIES simply cannot avoid.

Because the film was written and directed by men, some critics averred that EXTREMITIES was a male fantasy about women, power, and revenge. Nothing could be further from the truth. Mastrosimone wrote his original play as a reaction to rapes experienced by a friend and by his girl friend; Young originally turned down the project, then reconsidered after discussing it with his daughter, herself a rape victim at age sixteen. She read the script some fourteen years after her attack and felt it to be a liberating experience. Though the revenge aspects of the story are fictional, the outrage Fawcett expresses is painfully realistic. EXTREMITIES represents a personal and professional triumph for the actress. After her appearance on the cheesecake television detective show "Charlie's Angels," and her posing for some popular swimsuit posters, Fawcett made four inconsequential movies that capitalized on her sudden fame (SOMEBODY KILLED HER HUSBAND in 1978, SUNBURN in 1979, SATURN 3 in 1980, and CANNONBALL RUN in 1981). Her career took a better turn after good performances in the TV features "Murder in Texas" (1981) and "The Burning Bed" (1984), and Fawcett was given a chance to reestablish herself in theatrical film after her gutsy work in the stage version of EXTREMITIES.

p, Burt Sugarman; d, Robert M. Young; w, William Mastrosimone, Edwin Cook, Wendy Cutler, Andy Goldberg, Roger Steffens (based on the play by William Mastrosimone); ph, Curtis Clark; m, J.A.C. Redford; ed, Arthur Coburn; prod d, Chester Kaczenski; set d, Rosemary Brandenburg; cos, Linda Bass; makeup, Richard Arrington; stunts, Jeannie Epper.

Drama   Cas.   (PR:O   MPAA:R)

EYE OF THE TIGER*½   (1986) 90m Scotti Bros.-International Video
                                                        Entertainment c

Gary Busey (*Buck Mathews*), Yaphet Kotto (*J.B. Deveraux*), Seymour Cassel (*Sheriff*), Bert Remsen (*Father Healey*), William Smith (*Blade*), Kimberlin Ann Brown (*Dawn*), Denise Galik (*Christie*), Judith Barsi (*Jennifer*), Eric Bolles (*Doctor*), Joe Brooks (*Jake*), Douglas Dirkson (*Jimmy*), Kathryn Fuller (*Bingo Lady*), Jorge Gil (*Jamie*), Amelia Haas (*Melody*), Ray Habercorn (*Police Officer*), Cooper Huckabee (*Roger*), Ted Markland (*Floyd*), Brigitte Muller (*Kidnaped Girl*), Tom Rosales (*Jamie's Relative*), Jim Staskel (*Raider-Napper*), Timothy Scott (*Deputy*), Nicholas Testa (*Rolls Royce Driver*), Mike Walter (*Ray*).

Considering the quality of the personnel involved (Busey, Kotto, Cassel, Smith, and VANISHING POINT director Sarafian), EYE OF THE TIGER should have been a solid action film boasting some good acting. Unfortunately, the script by

Montgomery is an endless barrage of stale revenge-film cliches, and director Sarafian blithely ignores its faults by concentrating entirely on the action scenes and ignoring the actors. The new lean-mean Busey (he recently lost over 60 pounds) stars as a convict recently paroled after serving time for manslaughter. Much to the chagrin of Cassel, the local sheriff who set Busey up (this is all very vague), the ex-con returns home to his wife and daughter. Cassel would prefer Busey to leave town and vows to go out of his way to catch him on a parole violation. During Busey's absence a nearby motorcycle gang led by Smith (with his head shaved save for half a mohawk running down the back) has taken over the town, raping and pillaging whomever, wherever, and whenever they wish. Cassel is on the take and ignores the bikers' escapades. One night Busey hears the screams of a woman and the roar of motorcycles near his home. He jumps into his pickup truck to investigate and finds that Smith and his bikers are about to rape a nurse. Busey fends off the rapists, but Smith is bent on revenge. Busey's heroism makes the local TV news and the gang learns where he lives. That night, before Busey and his family can flee, dozens of bikers crash into the house. Busey's wife is murdered, he is beaten severely, and his daughter becomes catatonic. Vowing revenge, Busey looks to his friend Kotto for help. The only black man on the police force, Kotto is bitter because he had to leave the big city and come to this hick town just to make sergeant. Now, only a few days away from his pension, he simply wants to collect his due and leave forever. Kotto offers Busey nothing but good advice. With nowhere else to turn, Busey contacts a Latino drug kingpin whose life he saved in prison. Eager to repay his debt, the drug lord sends Busey a super-pickup truck armed with an array of death-dealing gadgets not seen since the last James Bond movie. Busey's first strike against Smith is to string a wire cable across the road in the middle of the night, which decapitates Smith's brother and another biker as they roar through. Smith retaliates and Busey counterstrikes until the bikers kidnap Busey's daughter. Busey's HIGH NOON-style plea for help from the townsfolk draws a blank, and it looks like he'll have to face the bikers alone. Kotto finally breaks down, however, and decides to help Busey by tossing grenades on the biker encampment from his biplane while Busey drives his super-pickup into the midst of the stronghold. Eventually, the battle boils down to a hand-to-hand combat between Smith and Busey, and our hero triumphs. Without a leader, the remaining bikers pack their bags and roar off to terrorize some other town.

EYE OF THE TIGER is the first feature film produced and released by Scotti Brothers Entertainment Industries. Before branching out into movies, the Scotti brothers ran a successful record-promotion business and released albums on their own label. Not surprisingly, the rock band Survivor was one of the Scotti discoveries. It is their insipid hit tune which serves as the title of this film, and—most annoyingly—drones on throughout the action scenes (for those of you with short memories, the song was used by Sylvester Stallone as the theme, more or less, of ROCKY III). The problem with EYE OF THE TIGER is that Montgomery's script is so vague in the essential areas of background story and characterization that one can never be certain what motivates any of these characters. If that isn't bad enough, there are plot holes big enough for Busey to drive his super-pickup through. If sheriff Cassel is so bent on catching Busey in a parole violation, why doesn't he haul him in for carrying a shotgun or simply for driving his pickup since parolees cannot drive vehicles without written permission in California (Busey should know that—he co-starred with Dustin Hoffman in STRAIGHT TIME, the most detailed and realistic film ever made about the parole system)?

Why doesn't anyone call the state police, the FBI, the national guard? These questions and many others are ignored by Sarafian's direction which steamrolls over such minor matters. Regrettably, the action scenes are not exciting enough for an audience to ignore these nagging details. Busey, Kotto, and Cassel are wasted in their underdeveloped roles (although Kotto scores a laugh as he bops to a James Brown tune blaring away in his biplane as he drops grenades on the bikers) and Smith is given little to do other than remove his motorcycle helmet and glower menacingly in every scene (which he does quite well). Filmed in and around Valencia, California, in July and August of 1986, EYE OF THE TIGER was rushed into post-production and released in late November. The incredibly quick production met an equally quick fate at the box office and wound up on videocassette shortly thereafter. Songs are "Eye of the Tiger" (Jim Peterick, Freddie Sullivan, performed by Survivor), "Gravity" (Dan Hartman, Charlie Midnight, performed by James Brown).

p, Tony Scotti; d, Richard Sarafian; w, Michael Montgomery; ph, Peter Collister (United color); ed, Greg Prange; art d, Wayne Springfield; set d, Kurt Gauger; cos, Lori McClellan, Barbara Inglehart; spec eff, John G. Belyeu, Richard Helmer, James Schwalm, John Coles, Michael Barrett, Jr., David Peterson, Gunther Jennings, Louis Siegfried, Tom Thelen; m/l, Jim Peterick, Freddie Sullivan, Dan Hartman, Charlie Midnight; makeup, Kathy Logan.

Action   **Cas.**   (PR:O   MPAA:R)

F

F/X* ½** (1986) 107m Orion c

Bryan Brown *(Rollie Tyler)*, Brian Dennehy *(Leo McCarthy)*, Diane Venora *(Ellen)*, Cliff De Young *(Lipton)*, Mason Adams *(Col. Mason)*, Jerry Orbach *(Nicholas DeFranco)*, Joe Grifasi *(Mickey)*, Martha Gehman *(Andy)*, Roscoe Orman *(Capt. Wallenger)*, Trey Wilson *(Lt. Murdoch)*, Tom Noonan *(Varrick)*, Paul D'Amato *(Gallagher)*, Jossie deGuzman *(Marisa Velez)*, Jean De Baer *(Whitemore)*, M'eL Dowd *(Miss Joyce Lehman)*, Tim Gallin *(Adams)*, Patrick Stack *(Sgt. Littauer)*, John Doumanian *(The Director)*, Ray Iannicelli *(Charlie)*, Edward Crowley *(Ballistics Expert)*, Gibby Brand *(1st Reporter)*, Jim Elliott *(Car Pound Attendant)*, Christopher Curry *(Mitchell)*, James Lovelett *(McCoy)*, George Kodisch *(Capt. Tolosa)*, Jim Cordes *(Capt. Watts)*, Richard Hayes, Christopher McHale, Jim Babchak *(State Troopers)*, James Pickens, Jr. *(Ambulance Driver)*, Michael Fischetti *(State Police Chief)*, Angela Bassett *(TV Reporter)*, Yolanda Lloyd *(Receptionist)*, Marvin Beck *(Medical Examiner)*, John McLoughlin *(Hospital State Trooper)*, Bernie Friedman *(Bum)*, Drummond Erskine *(Boat House Guard)*, Joseph Petangelo *(Police Officer)*, Gerald Campbell *(Doctor)*.

The title was a turnoff, but the picture is a turn-on. Unless you knew that F/X was the way movie people refer to special effects, you might think that this was a Catholic film about Francis Xavier. It's not that at all. It's a crackling good thriller with lots of style, too much plot, and more than a few laughs. Brown is an ace special-effects man for hire in various New York movies. His fame is widespread; he specializes in such memorable pictures as "I Dismember Mama" and the like. The movie begins at what appears to be an assassination in a seafood restaurant as a mysterious man walks in and begins shooting up the place, sending scores of live lobsters out of their glass tanks and slithering madly across the floor. Soon we realize that it's just a movie and that the explosions were caused by tiny detonators simulating bullets. (According to the publicity, not one lobster was lost in the "gag"—which is what they call the stunts—although many of them did pay the ultimate price by winding up as dinner for the cast and crew.)

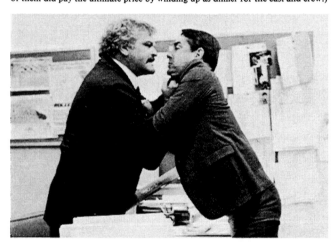

Brown is approached by smiling De Young, who identifies himself as a government agent working for the Justice Department. De Young wants to hire Brown for a most interesting task. The Department is about to get Mafia kingpin Orbach to testify against the others of his family, but they fear that the mobster may be knocked off before he has the chance to squeal in court. To that end, De Young asks if Brown can arrange to fake Orbach's death, thus temporarily taking the heat off the honcho. When the time is ripe, Orbach will surface and spill his guts. Brown listens to the proposition but turns it down; he's a movie man, not a spy. De Young and his boss, Adams, say that they understand and so they'll hire a Brown competitor to do the job. The thought that anyone around even comes close to him in expertise sticks in Brown's throat, so his pride goes before his brains and he accepts the assignment. Brown meets Orbach, makes a face mask of the man, and rigs him with all sorts of squibs and electronic gear so it will appear he is being shot as the assassin fires the blank bullets. At a fashionable restaurant where the world can see everything, Brown enters wearing a disguise. Orbach is seated alone at a prominent table. Brown fires and it appears that Orbach is dead.

Later, Brown phones in the news at a pay phone and is told to stay right where he is. It's raining and another man wants to use the phone so Brown steps out and stands in a doorway to keep out of the deluge. The innocent man is making a call when a police car pulls up and machine-guns him. Brown realizes those lead pellets were meant for him and that he is in big trouble. He can't go back to his apartment (a very funny place, with much of his movie gear) so he goes to girl friend Venora, an actress, and doesn't realize that they are being watched until she is shot dead through the window by a high-powered rifle. Brown doesn't know where to go now; he contacts his female assistant Gehman and tries to stay out of the limelight, which is not easy because he is living in his large van. While Brown is using his talent for disguise to get to the bottom of things, tough Irish cop Dennehy is also investigating. It was Dennehy who brought Orbach in, and

he doesn't believe the dead body is Orbach's (another corpse was switched but the face was shot away). Dennehy won't tolerate the way the case is being handled by a fellow cop, and his rough tactics get him tossed off the force. He goes after Brown on his own and the denouement, which takes place at Adams' palatial home, is the capper to a fast-moving picture. Orbach is alive and in cahoots with Adams and De Young. There is a great deal of money at stake and the plan is to have Orbach, De Young, and Adams leave the country, get to the loot in Switzerland, and live high on the hog forever.

Brown arrives at the Adams mansion and uses his guile and special effects to cause the various hoodlums in the employ of Adams to kill each other, placing trip wires and phony mirrors down long hallways, etc. Brown triumphs when Orbach, who wears a pacemaker, has a heart attack. Then Brown leaves a machine gun lying around for Adams to pick up. Adams does that, and then is shocked to find that it has been coated with glue that can't be pulled apart. By this time, cops are outside the house. When Adams is pushed out the door with machine gun in hand, he is shot down. Next, Brown fakes his own death by using latex rubber around his wrists and neck so it appears that he has no heartbeat. He is tossed into a body bag and taken to the coroner's office. He manages to slip away, only to be found by Dennehy, who has been on to him from the start. The

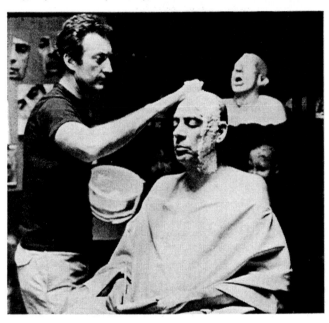

final scene takes place in Switzerland where Brown, wearing a latex face mask of Orbach, goes to the bank and withdraws about $15 million in ill-gotten gains. The two men drive off laughing.

One of the major problems in the picture is over-plotting and another is the fact that Brown and Dennehy, the two leads, are seldom together in any scenes. They have such magic on screen together that the producers should think of a sequel with the two. The movie cost about $11 million and may eventually recoup the 2½ times the budget to put it in the black. With another title, it might have gone right through the roof. Naturally, the special effects are sensational. They were devised by Oscar-winner (for THUNDERBALL and STAR WARS) John Stears, who also holds the patent on the latter film's R2D2. His assistant on these chores was Conrad Brink, and the two must be congratulated for their work. Although most of the blood and gore is "staged" rather than depicted as real, the movie merits the R rating given by the MPAA for that as well as for the rough language. Australian Brown went on to make the awful TAI-PAN (actually, it was probably shot before this, because it was a mammoth film). Longtime radio actor and commercial spokesman Adams ("With a Name Like Smuckers, It Has to Be Good") has only come to the screen in the last few years, first becoming familiar to TV audiences on "Lou Grant." Keep an eye out for Diane Venora. With the right role, she could be a major star. The same goes for director Mandel (INDEPENDENCE DAY) who knows how to tell a complex story and still manages to get some fine characterizations out of the actors. An excellent screenplay debut for actor Fleemand and documentary filmmaker Megginson.

p, Dodi Fayed, Jack Wiener; d, Robert Mandel; w, Robert T. Megginson, Gregory Fleeman; ph, Miroslav Ondricek (Technicolor); m, Bill Conti; ed, Terry Rawlings; prod d, Mel Bourne; md, Harry Rabinowitz; art d, Speed Hopkins; set d, Steven Jordan; cos, Julie Weiss; spec eff, John Stears; makeup, Carl Fullerton.

Thriller (PR:C-O MPAA:R)

FAILURE, THE** (1986, Neth.) 78m Hans de Ridder c (DE MISLUKKING)

Peter Kolpa *(Erik)*, Pie Slot *(Paul)*, Theun Huisman *(Leo)*, Ruud Mes *(Martin)*, Jan Cudde *(Old Man)*, Puck van Loon *(Mother)*.

This slow-moving drama from first-time director de Ridder painstakingly details the uneventful life of a young homosexual contending with the loneliness and despair which dominate his life. Kolpa plays the young gay man in an extremely low-key manner, wearing the same masklike expression, consisting of a slight frown and sorrowful glance, throughout the entire film. Recently jilted by his lover, Kolpa mechanically attends to his everyday tasks. He wakes in his small, sparsely furnished apartment, prepares for his boring job as an office clerk, and then returns home to his empty flat. Some evenings he visits his parents for dinner, where only the barest form of conversation takes place; other evenings he goes out to the local nightspot with his friend, the buffoonish Huisman. Across from Kolpa's apartment building lives an old man who continuously moves empty crates to the front of his building, purposefully ignoring the trivial nature of his pursuit.

While out with Huisman one night, Kolpa spots the Apollonian Pie Slot dancing and immediately becomes infatuated with him. Pie Slot has curly long blond hair, a sensuously moving body, and a face that freely expresses the emotions missing from Kolpa's life. The two start a brief and tender affair that momentarily relieves Kolpa of his existential misery. Pie Slot doesn't work for a living and has no qualms about living off his lover. When he becomes attracted to a younger boy, he leaves Kolpa, only to return when money becomes too tight. Soon the lovers split. Kolpa remains obsessed with memories of the brief happiness he shared with Pie Slot, but realizes the two have no chance of rekindling their affair when he spots his old lover dancing with someone else at a nightclub. Meanwhile, Huisman has been badly beaten by a gang of gay-hating punks and is recuperating in the hospital. Kolpa visits his friend, only to become that much more depressed by his own situation. For companionship, Kolpa buys a puppy. While petting the dog, he looks out the window and notices the old man across the street stacking his crates. Kolpa confronts the man for the first time and is greeted with "So there you are at last"—a statement affirming Kolpa's resignation to a life of mindless and meaningless toil, from which he unsuccessfully tried to escape.

Though dealing specifically with a gay situation, THE FAILURE addresses important issues that are universal for a generation forced to question the paths of its forefathers. However, de Ridder's handling of the themes of loneliness, loss of love, and finding one's place in society lessens their universality. His characters are extremely one-dimensional, especially Kolpa, who is so stuck in his own self-pity it is almost impossible to empathize with him. In only one instance, his cutting snub of a promotion-seeking coworker, does he display qualities that demand respect and only then does his plight become interesting. De Ridder should, however, be credited with his subtle handling of the love scenes between Kolpa and Pie Slot, which shy away from explicitness to concentrate on the tenderness the two share. Other actor interactions are far too rigid to appear as if any communication is actually occurring (which may be de Ridder's point). THE FAILURE was made for a meager $18,000 and took more than a year to complete. (In Dutch; English subtitles.)

p,d,w,ph&ed, Hans de Ridder; m, Lelijke Mannen; art d, Hans de Ridder.

Drama **(PR:O MPAA:NR)**

FAIR GAME** (1986, Aus.) 85m Southern Films International/C.E.L. c

Cassandra Delaney *(Jessica)*, Peter Ford *(Sunny)*, David Sandford *(Ringo)*, Garry Who *(Sparks)*, Don Barker *(Frank)*, Carmel Young *(Moire)*, Adrian Shirley *(Victor)*, Wayne Anthony *(Derek)*.

Nice cinematography and slick direction do not an intelligent action film make. FAIR GAME looks nice, and director Andreacchio proves that he can handle suspense and action sequences. Unfortunately, the script by George provides no characterizations whatsoever, so the film basically boils down to a live-action "Roadrunner" cartoon. Delaney stars as a pretty young woman who runs a wildlife sanctuary in the South Australian outback. One morning she finds a baby kangaroo wandering amidst the spent shells fired by the poachers who killed its mother. She takes the little roo in and then, with her faithful dog, drives into town to pick up some supplies and report the poaching to the local sheriff. On the way to town, her car is boxed in between a huge refrigeration truck driven by Who and a modified four-wheel-drive pickup truck complete with sunroof, roo-bars (to which to lash dead kangaroos), rifle racks, and plenty of shiny chrome. Nicknamed "The Beast," the off-road pickup is driven by Ford. The passenger of The Beast, Sandford, climbs onto its hood, leaps to Delaney's car, and then jumps to the back of the truck in front of her. After playing some dangerous road games with the woman, the hunters let her go. Delaney's subsequent expression of outrage falls on the unhearing ears of the unsympathetic sheriff. To make matters worse, she runs into the same bunch of deadbeats while picking up her supplies. As she puts her groceries into the car, she hears the whirring sound of a Polaroid camera. She looks down to see Sandford underneath her car—he'd aimed his camera up her skirt. After dumping a bag of flour on the photographer's face, she makes some vague threats to the bunch and goes home. She talks with her out-of-town husband (or boy friend; it's never made clear) on the phone, but in the middle of their conversation the line goes dead. Later, she takes a nap in the nude. Awakening, she is shocked to see a picture of herself sleeping taped inside her refrigerator. From this point on, the film becomes a seemingly endless game of cat-and-mouse between Delaney and the poachers, culminating in the men lashing her to the roo-bars and practically stripping her naked (the "games" take at least two days). They drive in circles for what seems like hours (this scene is particularly hard to take) and finally dump her back at her house. Delaney doesn't get mad, she gets even (after changing her clothes, of course). Mounting her horse, she gallops into the outback with the poachers in hot pursuit. She eventually lures them into a cave (she's not in it) and then causes a small avalanche, sealing them inside. As she gallops off, Sandford pokes a high-powered rifle through the rubble and shoots her horse. This outrage, for some reason, is really the last straw for Delaney. She goes home, sets up a dozen booby traps on her property, and dispatches the villains one-by-one (Sandford is electrocuted, Who impales himself on an anvil, Ford is blown up in his beloved truck). With her home destroyed and three men dead on the property, Delaney comforts her wounded dog, which comes limping up to her (the dog virtually vanishes about 10 minutes into the movie).

As exploitation films go, FAIR GAME is a competent enough effort. The action scenes are good, the performances serviceable, and the photography very professional, but the script is a one-note job where the only thing that develops is the amount of brutality. Delaney is convincing as a tough, independent, brave woman, but there are no other aspects to her character. What is it that compels her to risk the destruction of her beloved wildlife sanctuary to play tit-for-tat games with these sadists rather than going back to town and having them arrested? Don't these guys have anything better to do than to torment this woman for several days? If George's screenplay had explored other aspects of Delaney's character (she seems very stubborn; she cares more for animals than for humans) it might have made for a more interesting film. As it is, the games between the woman and her tormentors become tedious about halfway into the movie, and nothing changes from that point until the end except the escalating severity of the violence. Songs are "Seeing Things" (Ashley Irwin, Terry McCarthy, performed by The Black Crow), "I Can Fly" (Terry McCarthy, Ashley Irwin, performed by Keren Corby).

p, Ron Saunders, Harley Manners; d, Mario Andreacchio; w, Rob George; ph, Andrew Lesnie (Eastmancolor); m, Ashley Irwin; ed, A.J. Prowse; art d, Kimble Hilder; m/l, Ashley Irwin, Terry McCarthy.

Action **Cas.** **(PR:O MPAA:NR)**

FALOSNY PRINC† (1986, Czech.) Koliba Studios-Omnia Film (Trans: A False Prince)

Svietislav Goncic, Dusko Vojnovic, Kamila Magalova, Jana Holenova.

d, Dusan Rapos; w, Jaroslav Dietl; ph, Stanislav Szomolanyi.

FAMILY, THE† (1986, Hong Kong) 95m D&B c

Richard Ng, Fung Bo Bo, Lui Fong, May Law, Pauline Kwan, Danny Chan, Lee Lai Chun.

A nuclear family serves as the backdrop for a number of jokes and light comic situations. (In Cantonese; English subtitles.)

p, Dickson Poon; d, Raymond Fung; w, Ko Chi Sum; ph, Chan Hou Ming; m, Lam Mun Yee; ed, Chan Fung; art d, Li Yiu Kwong.

Comedy **(PR:A MPAA:NR)**

FAREWELL ILLUSION† (1986, Norway) 100m Mefistofilm c (ADJO SOLIDARITET)

Svein Sturla Hungnes, Nhut Husebo, Jorunn Kjellsby, Wenche Foss, Thomas Robsahm, Bjorn Skagestad, Per Frisch, Ellen Horn, Per Sunderland.

Two successful Norwegian men, one a doctor, the other a burned-out stage director, go on a night's carousing, becoming more and more depressed about the collapse of the dreams they had built during the turbulent 1960s. Now they see their marriages failed, their children turned either conservative or punk. Norway has never been known as a hotbed of radical reform, and one wonders why it took these men so long to figure out that the 1960s were just a passing phase. The film garnered generally favorable reviews and managed a fairly successful international release. Originally released in 1984, this is the second part of a trilogy which was completed in 1986 with DROMMESLOTTER.

p,d&w, Svend Wam, Petter Vennerod; ph, Philip Ogaard; m, Svein Gundersen; ed, Inge-Lise Langfeldt.

Drama **(PR:O MPAA:NR)**

FAT GUY GOES NUTZOID!!* (1986) 88m Troma c

Tibor Feldman *(Roger Morloche)*, Douglas Stone *(Doogle Morloche)*, Max Alexander *(Harold Morloche)*, John McEvily *(Oscar Henderson)*, John Mackay *(Ronald Whitesox)*, Lynne Marie Brown *(Hooker)*, Mark Alfred *(Milton)*, Joan Allen *(Lala)*, Josh Blake *(Older Boy)*, Anthony Ettari, Thomas Ettari *(Younger Boy)*, Annette Mauer *(Aunt Marietta)*, Joniruth White *(Woman Screamer)*, Libby Miller *(Mrs. Morloche)*, Maize Murphy Klein, Emanuel Ferrante *(Corpses)*, Jay Natelli *(Guard)*, Joyce Sozen *(Judge Baker)*, Max Jacobs *(Mr. Gruber)*, Chris Liano *(Morey)*, Peter Linari *(The Mouka)*, Jerold Goldstein *(Freddie Fisher)*, Chris Burke, David Stern, Gerard Gilch, Hektor Munoz, Clement Roberson, Loren Bass *(Camp Croton Retarded)*, George Ross *(Gas Station Attendant)*, Danny Shea *(Himself)*, Rick Schneider, Ted Bardi, Hilly Michaels, Rich Oppenheim *(Bank Members)*, Eve Van Sickle *(Waitress)*, Willard Morgan *(Cab Driver)*, Karla White *(Slap-Woman)*, Mic Muldoon *(Desk Sergeant)*, James Sullivan *(Policeman at Station)*, Phillip Dachille, Michael Carrafa, Jack Du-Vall, T.G. Welles, Peter A. Levine *(Policemen at Phone Booth)*, Sam Goldrich *(Mr. Marshack)*, Beverly Vail *(Nurse at Hollowbrook)*, Anthony Di Pietro *(Bender)*, Craig Barnett, Crawford Young *(Orderlies)*, Stephen Salter, David Sheridan, Howard Spiegel, Marc Duncan, Mark Deikman *(Hollowbrook Inmates)*.

This is hardly a sophisticated comedy, though it's exactly what you'd expect from the same company that gave us THE TOXIC AVENGER and THE CLASS OF NUKE 'EM HIGH. The ridiculous story revolves around Fat Guy, a fun loving resident of an insane asylum who does exactly what the title says once he sees the outside. Accompanied by a former hospital employee and his brother, the newly liberated corpulent hero finds love, adventure, and plenty to eat before ending up back in custody. Though sent to another hospital, intrepid friends Feldman and Stone use a helicopter to rescue their plump pal as the film comes to its happy conclusion. It's not much of a movie, but hey, you just can't beat that title.

p, Emily Dillon; d, John Golden; w, John Golden, Roger Golden; ph, John Drake; m, Leo Kottke; ed, Jeffrey Wolf; prod d, Martin De Maat; set d, Philip Rossiello; cos, Lindsay W. Davis; makeup, Susan Giammusso; stunts, Jery Hewitt.

Comedy   Cas.   (PR:O MPAA:NR)

FATHERLAND†   (1986, Brit./Ger.) 110m Kestrel II–Clasart–MK2/Film Four International c

Gerulf Pannach (Klaus Drittemann), Fabienne Babe (Emma de Baen), Cristine Rose (Lucy Bernstein), Sigfrit Steiner (James Dryden), Robert Dietl (Lawyer), Heike Schrotter (Marita), Stephan Samuel (Max), Thomas Oehlke (Young Drittemamm), Patrick Gillert (Thomas), Heinz Diesing (Jurgen Kirsch), Eva Krutina (Rosa), Hans Peter Hallwachs (Schiff), Ronald Simoneit (Uwe), Marlowe Shute (American Official), Jim Raketa (Braun), Bernard Bloch (Journalist), Winfried Tromp (Herr Hennig).

Loach, whose POOR COW (1967) was the first of a number of thoughtful, individualistic films, returned to features here after four years during which he concentrated on documentaries. Political exploitation in the arts on both sides of the Berlin Wall is the theme of the film. Folk singer Pannach is forced to depart from East Germany—as his father and sister did 30 years previously—because the political content of his ballads has offended the authorities. He arrives in West Berlin bearing a key to a safe-deposit box that his father had left behind. Record company representative Rose offers Pannach a lucrative contract and all the perquisites that go with stardom on the condition that his songs and his public pronouncements criticize the left. Reluctant to compromise either his art or his beliefs, Pannach is unresponsive to her overtures. He opens the safe-deposit box, which holds memorabilia of his father. Consumed with the desire to find his father, Pannach joins forces with French journalist Babe (who has hidden motives for helping him) and travels with her to Cambridge, England. His quest proves successful because he finds his father, but he learns to his dismay some painful facts that he would rather not have known.

Screenwriter Griffiths' story closely parallels the real-life story of this picture's protagonist. Pannach—like the character he plays—was forced to leave East Germany after his songs led him to be labeled a "hostile agitator." Oscarwinning cinematographer Menges (THE KILLING FIELDS) had worked with director Loach on his first feature, and on five others, in their long and fruitful association.

p, Raymond Day; d, Ken Loach; w, Trevor Griffiths; ph, Chris Menges; m, Christian Kunert, Gerulf Pannach; ed, Jonathan Morris; prod d, Martin Johnson; cos, Antje Petersen.

Drama   (PR:C MPAA:NR)

FAUBOURG SAINT-MARTIN†   (1986, Fr.) 87m Films du Passage/Gerick c

Francoise Fabian (Marquessa), Marie Christine Rousseau (Marie), Patachou (Madam Coppercage), Stephane Jobert (Paul), Ingrid Bourgoin (Suzanne), Emmanuel Lemoine (Francois), Patrick Couet, Chantal Delsaux, Valerie Jeanet, Renaud Victor, Vincent Ducastel, Howard Vernon, Greg Germain.

Romantic Parisian streetwalkers are the subject of this film, exhibited in the Critics Week at Cannes. Rousseau is a young newcomer whose lover is murdered by her pimp. Fabian is an experienced pro trying to raise a ten-year-old son. Patachou (a noted French variety star) is the hotel concierge, providing a center to it all.

p, Paolo Branco; d&w, Jean-Claude Guiguet; ph, Alain Levent; m, Serge Tomassi, Giuseppe Verdi; ed, Kadicha Baraha; makeup, Pascale Tisseraud.

Drama   (PR:O MPAA:NR)

FEAR†   (1986, It./Fr.) 90m Dionysio Cinematografica–Societe Nouvelle Cinevox/Enzo Boetani–Giuseppe Collura–Simon Mizrahi c (AKA: UNCONSCIOUS; MURDER SYNDROME)

Stefano Patrizi (Michael Stanford), Martine Brochard (Shirley), Henri Garcin (Hans), Laura Gemser (Beryl), John Richardson (Oliver), Anita Strindberg (Glenda), Silvia Dionisio (Deborah).

Patrizi is an actor plagued with nightmares about the murder of his father when he was a child. When he goes with a film crew to scout locations, they stop at the home of his mother and more killings occur. A little bit of everything from incest to the Kirlian effect is tossed into this shocker, shot in 1980 and only now reaching the U.S. on videocassette.

d, Riccardo Freda; w, Antonio Cesare Corti, Fabio Piccioni, Riccardo Freda; ph, Cristiano Pogany (Telecolor); m, Franco Mannino; set d, Georgio Desideri; cos, Giorgio Desideri.

Crime   Cas.   (PR:O MPAA:NR)

FEIFA YIMIN†   (1986, Hong Kong) Shaw Bros. (Trans: The Illegal Immigrant)

Jing Yongzhuo, Wu Fuxing.

Yongzhuo plays a refugee from mainland China living in New York City, where he struggles both to make ends meet and to please the woman he married to gain entry into the U.S. This first feature for director Wanting was shot completely on location in New York.

d, Zhang Wanting; w, Luo Quiro.

Drama   (PR:A MPAA:NR)

FEMMES DE PERSONNE½**   (1986, Fr.) 106m T. Films–F.R.3/European Classics c (Trans: Nobody's Women)

Marthe Keller (Cecile), Jean-Louis Trintignant (Gilquin), Caroline Cellier (Isabelle), Fanny Cottencon (Adeline), Philippe Leotard (Antoine), Patrick Chesnais (Marc), Elisabeth Etienne (Julie), Pierre Arditi (Patric), Marcel Bozonnet (Philippe Dubly), Yvette Delaune (Monica Gilquin), Karol Zuber (Arnaud).

Love and sex and their effect on four female friends in a radiology lab are the basis for this intelligent but rather predictable drama. The film revolves around two strong-willed, independent women, Keller and Cellier, each of whom is missing something in her life. Keller, while raising a young son, is searching for someone to fill the romantic void in her life. Driven by loneliness to a series of one-night stands, Keller only finds herself getting increasingly desperate. When she finally meets the gentle Trintignant she remembers the happiness and fulfillment that she is missing. Cellier is also a mother and has a husband, but there is just as much of a void in her life as in Keller's. In order to shake up her colorless husband, Chesnais, and provide the necessary spark, she persuades an alluring fellow worker, Etienne, to seduce him. Each of the women is involved in her own little drama, though their friendship is tightened when a fourth friend, the promiscuous Cottencon, attempts to kill herself after a reunion with a former lover.

This sort of tragedy and desperation is nothing new to films and is a common trait of even the least accomplished soap operas. Much of FEMMES DE PERSONNE concerns itself with the emotions of the "modern woman" and her need to keep her feelings inside, hidden by a cold, controlled exterior—an emotional restriction apparently placed upon her by the independence that has come from the sexual revolution. Nothing is immoral here. Everyone has sex with everyone, teenagers have sex, and preteens watch pornography on television, while the four women of the film never express much shock or negativity, as if they have been desensitized to it all. Director Frank manages to keep the familiar script from falling apart by his excellent choice of actresses, especially the strong and sensual Keller. Another plus is the usual strong score from Delerue, who composed the music for another, radically different film this year—PLATOON. FEMMES DE PERSONNE was released in France in 1984 but did not receive a U.S. theatrical release until 1986. (In French; English subtitles.)

p, Alain Terzian; d&w, Christopher Frank; ph, Jean Tournier (Eastmancolor); m, Georges Delerue; ed, Nathalie Lafaurie; art d, Dominique Andre; cos, Yvette Frank; makeup, Jackie Raynal.

Drama   (PR:O MPAA:NR)

FERRIS BUELLER'S DAY OFF**   (1986) 103m PAR c

Matthew Broderick (Ferris Bueller), Alan Ruck (Cameron Frye), Mia Sara (Sloane Peterson), Jeffry Jones (Ed Rooney), Jennifer Grey (Jeanie Bueller), Cindy Pickett (Katie Bueller), Lyman Ward (Tom Bueller), Edie McClurg (School Secretary), Charlie Sheen (Boy in Police Station), Ben Stein (Economics Teacher), Del Close (History Teacher), Virginia Capers (Florence Sparrow), Richard Edson (Garage Attendant), Larry "Flash" Jenkins (Attendant's Sidekick), Jonathan Schmock (Chez Quis Maitre 'd), Tom Spratley (Men's Room Attendant), Dave Silvestri (Businessman), Debra Montague (Girl in Pizza Joint), Joey Viera (Pizza Man), Louis Anderson (Flower Deliveryman), Stephanie Blake (Singing Nurse), Robert McKibbon (Balloon Man), Paul Manzanero (Pumpkin Head), Miranda Whittle (Girl on Trampoline), Robert Kim (Police Officer), Dick Sollenberger (Politician at Parade), Bob Parkinson, Richard Rohrbough (Ministers at Parade), Edward Le Beau (Gym Teacher), Polly Noonan (Girl on Bus), Dee Dee Rescher (Bus Driver), Kristy Swanson, Lisa Bellard, Max Perlich, T. Scott Coffee (Economics Students), Eric Saiet, Jason Alderman, Jay Garfield, Kristin Graziano, Bridget McCarthy, Anne Ryan, Eric Edidin, Brendan Babar, Tiffany Chance (Shermerites), Heidi Meyer, Lee Ann Marie, Annette Thurman,

Gail Tangeros, Tricia Fastabend, Sue Cronin, Vlasta Krsek *(Parade Partici-pants)*, South Shore Drill Team, Lockport High School Band.

"Life moves pretty fast. If you don't stop and look around once in awhile you might miss it." This is the philosophy of Broderick, a popular high-school student living in one of the well-to-do suburbs north of Chicago. What Broderick really needs, he confides to the audience, is a day off. After convincing his parents that he truly is sick, Broderick calls on his friend Ruck to join him. Ruck, the sort of kid who is always taking allergy pills and nasal decongestants, is less than willing to join Broderick, particularly when it means taking a classic 1961 red Ferrari 250 GT convertible that is the prized possession of Ruck's father.

Eventually Ruck concedes, and Broderick picks up his girl friend, Sara, who also has been procured from the classroom. By now Broderick's nemesis, Jones, the high school's dean of students, has caught on to the popular lad's scheme. Having had enough of Broderick's elaborate hoaxes in the past, Jones is determined this time to catch the boy in the act. Also in the conspiracy against this handsome and charming young man is Broderick's sister Grey. She has grown weary of seeing her popular sibling continue to get away with his machinations while becoming something of a hero to their classmates. Meanwhile, Broderick and his two comrades have hit downtown Chicago and park the car in a garage. They begin a whirlwind tour of the city's sights which begins with the lofty view

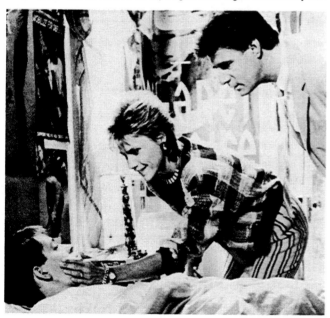

from the Sears Tower skydeck. The three next visit the stock exchange, then head to a fancy restaurant where Broderick cons his way past a huffy maitre d'. After dining, the group nearly runs into Broderick's father, but they are able to evade him and head out to a baseball game. From there it's off to the Art Institute, then Broderick manages to take over a parade with a rousing lip-synch of the Beatles' hit "Twist and Shout" (Bert Russell, Philip Medley). While Broderick has been enjoying his day, Jones has been going through absolute misery trying to catch up with his prey. He's mangled by a vicious dog at Broderick's house, but manages to get inside. When Grey comes home, hoping to catch her brother, she finds Jones and kicks him in the head before calling the cops. Broderick, Ruck, and Sara begin their drive home, and looking at the odometer realize that the parking attendants had used the vehicle for a joyride. Ruck goes catatonic so Broderick and Sara take him to a backyard swimming pool hoping to snap their friend out of it. Eventually Ruck reveals that he had been faking and the kids decide to fix

the odometer by elevating the car on a jack and running the auto in reverse. This doesn't work though, and Ruck, in a furious lash at his father, kicks the front fender until the car ends up crashing in a ditch behind the garage. Grey is picked up by her mother at the police station (after an encounter with a hysterically deadpan Charlie Sheen, in a wonderful comic cameo). While driving home she sees her brother fleeing pell-mell through the streets, hoping to return to his sickbed before his parents arrive at the house. Broderick manages to make it in time, but he's met at the door by a seemingly victorious Jones. However, Grey, realizing that Jones was the intruder she earlier encountered, allows Broderick to slip by. Her brother nimbly makes it back up the stairs, and into the safety of his bed where his parents find him, convinced that Broderick has spent the whole day there. Considering that the story and pacing of this offbeat comedy wear thin after the first twenty minutes, FERRIS BUELLER'S DAY OFF has more funny moments than most bad teenage comedies. This is due almost completely to Broderick, who brings some real charm and chutzpah to the part, along with a genuine sense of innocence. As the best friend, Ruck gives a good performance. Sara is wasted in a part that only requires her to look beautiful and smile. The film starts off strong as Broderick speaks directly to the camera, making the audience an immediate, all-knowing confidante. Broderick even gives a lesson on "Faking Out Parents," complete with an on-screen guide of do's and don'ts with which anyone who ever skipped a class will instantly identify. "It's a little childish and stupid," Broderick explains in summation, "but then so's high school." Unfortunately, the wonderfully clever promise of the film's opening is never fulfilled. Hughes, directing from his own script, starts off well, but pushes his premise too far and ultimately kills the joke. By the time Broderick takes over the parade, the antics have grown wearisome. Hughes' error comes in not developing the rapport Broderick has with the audience beyond the opening sequences. Apart from an occasional knowing glance, or a parenthetical comment on the action, viewers are left out as Hughes allows his now-familiar cliches to take hold. Like 1985's THE BREAKFAST CLUB, Hughes presents a group of privileged adolescents whose worldly goods have made them cynical and unhappy. Ruck's despondency stems from his parents showing him no love (another carryover from THE BREAKFAST CLUB). The destruction of his father's beloved auto is presented as a victorious moment of liberation. It's an all-too-handy psychology lesson that Hughes utilizes time and again. The on-screen adults don't fare any better. Pickett and Ward, as Broderick's parents, are a pair of simpletons who fall easy victim to their son's manipulations. It's a real crime to see Jones, who was so good as the king in AMADEUS, reduced to playing a comic buffoon suffering at the hands of Hughes' post-adolescent fantasies. Where Hughes really succeeds is in his wonderful and obviously affectionate depiction of Chicago. "A lot of FERRIS BUELLER is sort of my love letter to the city," he told one interviewer. Though Broderick's whirlwind trip through the city sites defies Einstein's time-and-space theories, Hughes creates a beautiful tableau out of the downtown locations. His best sequence (indeed, probably the best scene from any of his work) comes when the kids hit the Art Institute. He photographs the precious works of art with care, and nicely captures his trio's reactions. Ruck's fascination with Georges Seurat's famed masterpiece "Sunday Afternoon on the Island of La Grande Jatte," as the boy stares utterly transfixed by the painting's beauty, is a tender moment. It sticks out as a special fragment in a film marked by overindulgence. The film's other songs: "Bad" (Mick Jones, Don Letts, performed by Big Audio Dynamite), "Beat City" (Ben Watkins, Adam Peters, performed by Ben Watkins, Adam Peters), "Danke Shoen" (Bert Kaempiert, Kurt Schwabach, Milt Gabler, performed by Wayne Newton), "The Edge of Forever" (Nick Laird-Clowes, Gilbert Gabriel, performed by The Dream Academy), "I'm Afraid" (David Joyner, Paul Mansfield, performed by Blue Room), "Jeanie (theme from 'I Dream of Jeannie')" (Hugo Montenegro), "Love Missile F1-11" (Tony James, Neil Whitmore, Martin Degville, performed by Sigue Sigue Sputnik), "March of the Swivelheads" (The [English] Beat), "Oh Yeah" (Boris Blank, Dieter Meier, performed by Yello), "Please Please Please Let Me Get What I Want" (Steven Morrissey, Johnny Marr), "Radio People" (Larry Troutman, Zapp Troutman), "STAR WARS [main title]" (John Williams), "Taking the Day Off" (David Wakeling, performed by General Public).

p, John Hughes, Tom Jacobson; d&w, John Hughes; ph, Tak Fujimoto (Panavision, Metrocolor); m, Ira Newborn, Arthur Baker, John Robie; ed, Paul Hirsch; prod d, John W. Corso; set d, Louis Mann; cos, Marilyn Vance; ch, Kenny Ortega; m/l, Mick Jones, Don Letts, Ben Watkins, Adam Peters, Bert Kampiert, Kurt Schwabach, Milt Gabler, Nick Laird-Clowes, Gilbert Gabriel, David Joyner, Paul Mansfield, Hugo Montenegro, Tony James, Neil Whitmore, Martin Degville, The [English] Beat, Boris Blank, Dieter Meier, Steven Morrissey, Johnny Marr, Larry Troutman, Zapp Troutman, John Williams, David Wakeling; makeup, Michael Germain; stunts, Bennie Dobbins.

Comedy   Cas.   (PR:C PG-13)

FIELD OF HONOR†   (1986, Neth.) 95m Orianda/Cannon c

Everett McGill *(Sire)*, Ron Brandsteder, Jun-Kyung Lee, Frank Schaafsma, Hey Young Lee, Min Yoo, Guus Van Der Made, Marc Van Eegham, Dong Hyun Kim.

A real oddity, a Dutch film, shot in English, about the Korean War. McGill is a tough sergeant given a platoon of Dutch volunteers. Most of the unit is wiped out when they are ambushed while raping a Korean woman and her daughter, so McGill goes out and kills all the Chinese responsible. Produced by Golan and Globus, so it seems only a matter of time until it turns up on U.S. video shelves.

p, Menahem Golan, Yoram Globus; d, Hans Scheepsmaker; w, Henk Bos; ph, Hein Groot (Fujicolor); m, Roy Budd; ed, Victorine Habets.

War   (PR:O MPAA:NR)

50/50†

(1986, Ger.) 105m New Line bw

Hans Peter Hallwachs *(Bert Maschkara)*, Bernd Tauber *(Thomas Berger)*, Agnes Duenneisen *(Katrin Adams)*, Masch Gonska *(Eva Hauff)*, Kai Fischer *(Heidi Brunner)*, Ivan Desny *(Baron Wurlitzer)*, Gerhard Olschewski *(Walter Brunner)*.

Two men, one a 40-ish architect suddenly out of a job, the other a 30-year-old air traffic controller embittered because he must now go to school to learn the skills he has practiced in the army for the last seven years, come together in their mutual disillusionment and become friends. Convoluted construction doesn't make this tale of apathy any more intelligible.

d&w, Uwe Brandner; ph, Juergen Juerges; m, Peer Rabin, J.J. Cale, Munich Factory; ed, Helga Beyer.

Drama (PR:O MPAA:NR)

52 PICK-UP**½

(1986) 114m Cannon c

Roy Scheider *(Harry Mitchell)*, Ann-Margret *(Barbara Mitchell)*, Vanity *(Doreen)*, John Glover *(Alan Raimy)*, Robert Trebor *(Leo Franks)*, Lonny Chapman *(Jim O'Boyle)*, Kelly Preston *(Cini)*, Clarence Williams III *(Bobby Shy)*, Doug McClure *(Averson)*, Alex Henteloff.

While much better than last year's Elmore Leonard film adaptation, STICK, 52 PICK-UP suffers from much the same problem: villains who are much more intriguing than the hero. Scheider stars as an independent, tough Korean War veteran who, in his middle years, enjoys the best things life can offer. He has made himself rich with his own metallurgy company and has recently landed a contract with NASA; he owns a fancy house with a swimming pool and a Jaguar

XKE; he has a beautiful and politically ambitious wife who is running for a seat on the Los Angeles city council (Ann-Margret); and he is having an illicit affair with a topless dancer in her early 20s. Scheider's world is shattered, however, when he goes to visit his mistress but finds instead three blackmailers (Glover,

Williams, and Trebor) who show him a videotape of his last tryst. Glover demands a realistic—based on Scheider's net worth—payment of $105,000 or the tape goes public. A stubborn man, Scheider decides to defy the blackmailers by telling Ann-Margret about the affair and refusing to pay. Ann-Margret has suspected something all along, but really didn't want to know ("How old is she?" is upmost on her mind). Upset that the revelations will destroy her political future, she nonetheless stands by her husband's decision. When the blackmailers learn of Scheider's defiance, they up the stakes. Scheider is waylaid and brought to an abandoned warehouse, where he is tied to a chair and shown yet another videotape. This one depicts the brutal murder of his mistress, with a gun that was stolen from his house, in the very chair in which he's sitting (Glover, in one of the most brilliantly seedy performances of recent years, comments wryly on his

camera technique while the video plays out its horrid scene). Now the terms are: pay the money, or go to jail for murder. Scheider protests that he doesn't have that kind of money at his disposal, so the educated Glover agrees to meet the businessman at his offices to look over the company books. "Well, sir," Glover concludes perusing the bottom line, "like a lot of people who make a lot of money, you don't seem to have any." $52,000 is all that Scheider can afford and that is what he will pay. Only Scheider has no intention of paying—he fights back. Working from the few clues he has, Scheider learns that Glover and the feeble Trebor are involved in the Los Angeles porno scene, the former a sometime director, the latter a dealer. Williams, who is harder to find, is a coked-out killer in dreadlocks who runs some ladies on the side. Scheider begins to play one blackmailer against another until both Trebor and Williams wind up dead. His operation crumbling at his feet, Glover kidnaps Ann-Margret, drugging and raping her. Scheider finally agrees to pay, and throws his fancy car in on the deal. But, unbeknownst to Glover (until, the very last second, that is), Scheider has wired his car with explosives and he blows the blackmailer to kingdom come once Ann-Margret is safe.

One of the most downright *sleazy* major films in recent memory, 52 PICK-UP works mainly because of its vivid villains. Glover is superb as the college-educated, totally amoral blackmailer who uses his superior intelligence to keep his dimmer comrades in check. Although intelligent, Glover seems perversely fascinated with the porno underworld and prefers to work as a projectionist and even a director (with aspirations toward legitimate films, of course), while reaping the carnal benefits of the porno meat-market. Trebor is a trembling simp of little nerve who never thought things would get so complicated and violent, and Williams is chilling as the drugged-up assassin who doesn't flirt with violence like Glover, but actually performs it. Director Frankenheimer, who hasn't had material even this average to work with in quite some time, vividly captures the milieu in all its vulgar glory almost too well. The porno underworld is so slimy and depressing that it nearly overwhelms the viewer (the novel was set in Detroit, not Los Angeles, and one wonders if Detroit's porno underworld is as self-consciously decadent). Less successful are the Scheider and Ann-Margret characters. When we meet them their 23-year-marriage seems to have died from lack of interest. They seem self-absorbed, arrogant, and complacent. Scheider's actions seem more motivated by mild annoyance than by any sense of justice (it is very hard to feel sorry for a rich man who drives a Jaguar, is married to the beautiful Ann-Margret, and who maintains a mistress in her early 20s). Both characters as written and played are pretty unsympathetic, and the fact that this criminal outfit brings them closer together does not ring true at all. Also the ridiculous conclusion raises more questions than it answers: How is Scheider going to explain murdering this man? Doesn't all the evidence still show that it was he who murdered his mistress? And how do a middle-aged, upper-class couple simply walk away from this carnage and go on to business as usual? In terms of character insight, both Leonard's novel and Frankenheimer's film ignore the more interesting questions they raise.

p, Menahem Golan, Yoram Globus; d, John Frankenheimer; w, Elmore Leonard, John Steppling (based on the novel by Elmore Leonard); ph, Jost Vacano (TVC Color); m, Gary Chang; ed, Robert F. Shugrue; prod d, Philip Harrison; art d, Russell Christian; set d, Max Whitehouse; cos, Ray Summers.

Crime/Thriller Cas. (PR:O MPAA:R)

FILME DEMENCIA†

(1986, Braz.) 90m E.M. Cinematografica–Cinearte–Beethoven Street–Embrafilme c (Trans: The Last Faust)

Enio Goncalves, Emilio di Biasi, Imara Reis, Fernando Benini, Rosa Maria Pestana, Benjamin Cattan, Orlando Parolin.

This Brazilian film freely mixes fantasy and reality, exploring the world of a man whose life has gone sour. After his family's cigarette business goes belly up, the man's marriage falls apart. His mind snaps and he goes off on a shooting spree, sniping at people who are truly bad. His story is told in three ways: what is actually happening, what the protagonist perceives is going on, and the things he would like to come to fruition. Scantily clad women abound in this dark comedy, which has frequent asides to the audience, and characters represented as "E.V. Stroheim" and "C.Th. Dreyer" to round out an occasional homage.

d&w, Carlos Reichenbach; ph, Jose Roberto Eliezer; m, Manoel Paiva, Luiz Chagas; ed, Eder Mazini.

Comedy (PR:O MPAA:NR)

FINAL EXECUTIONER, THE*

(1986, It.) 94m Immagine/Cannon c (AKA: THE LAST WARRIOR)

William Mang *(Alan)*, Marina Costa *(Edra)*, Harrison Muller *(Erasmus)*, Woody Strode *(Sam)*, Margi Newton, Stefano Davanzati, Renato Miracco, Maria Romano, Luca Giordana, Karl Zinny.

It's another post-nuclear-holocaust action film from Italy, with nothing special to distinguish it from dozens of others almost like it. In this particular survivor society, those uncontaminated by radiation have set themselves up as "privileged," living in protected cities, while the contaminated are declared "target material" and hunted down for sport. Eighty million are killed until the supply runs out. By now, though, the very privileged enjoy the hunt too much to let this stop them, so they use the judicial system to declare new citizens "target material" and ship them out to game preserves to be hunted down. Mang is a cybernetics engineer who discovers the truth about the hunt. When he tries to go to the authorities with what he has discovered, they strip him of his privileges and put him on a subway train for the game preserve. There, some idle rich types lounge around Costa's chateau before going out to massacre the latest shipment of quarry. Mang and a young woman escape the general massacre, but are soon captured. Mang is tied to a jeep while the woman is raped and murdered. Then Mang is set free to be hunted by Costa and Muller, who has wagered a valuable white rifle that he can kill Mang before she can. Costa spots him climbing up a tree and shoots him, but he falls in the river and is swept away. He wakes up in Strode's house, and after he proves his mettle in a raid on a food supply, Strode begins training him to go back to the chateau to get "justice." It turns out that Strode is also into justice, being a former cop who turned in his badge in disgust. After some period of training (like crawling through pipes filled with broken glass and barbed wire and running through racks of swinging sandbags), Strode pronounces Mang ready, and gives him his pistol and his last bullet. Mang heads back to the chateau and begins dispatching minor characters with little difficulty until finally just Costa and Muller are left alive. Mang uses the bullet on Muller, but Costa gets the drop on him and is about to kill him. She takes too long and Strode turns up to shoot her dead. The two men decide to team up to fight for justice, setting up a sequel that appears unlikely.

Very little of interest here except to diehard fans of Italian science fiction and those who marvel that Woody Strode is still playing tough guys in films even though the man is well into his 70s. On nearly every count the film is a waste of time and money. There is never any suspense, and the audience never gets to know any of the characters, neither sympathizing with Mang nor disliking his victims. There are no special effects, the film has no particular style, and the script doesn't have even one good line. This film also falls into that class of films in which the people a century into the future drive amazingly well-preserved Detroit muscle cars from the 1960s, unless they ride 1980s Moto Guzzi motorcycles. Only Strode redeems the film, impressively trouncing thugs a good half-century younger than himself. Shot in 1983, the film is not as relentlessly, aggressively stupid as others of the genre, but there is nothing to make this straight-to-video release anything more than just a way to kill an hour and a half.

p, Luciano Appignani; d, Romolo Guerrieri; w, Roberto Leoni; ph, Guglielmo Mancori (Luciano Vittori Color); m, Carlo De Nonno; ed, Alessandro Lucidi; set d, Eugenio Liverani; spec eff, Roberto Ricci.

Science Fiction   **Cas.**   **(PR:O MPAA:NR)**

FINAL MISSION†   (1986, U.S./Phil.) 84m Santiago–Maharaj/ Westbrook-M.P. Film-D.S. Pictures-Thorn EMI-HBO c

Richard Young (*Vince Deacon*), John Ericson (*Col. Joshua Cain*), Christine L. Tudor, Jason Ross, John Dresden, Karen Ericson, Kaz Garas, E. Danny Murphy, Jack Daniels.

More made-in-the-Philippines action fodder, once again bypassing the theaters to debut at the video store. This time Young is a Vietnam vet whose family gets blown up by villains hired by an old nemesis from his fighting days in Laos. Predictably, Young then goes out for revenge, leaving a trail of dead bad guys in his wake.

p&d, Cirio H. Santiago; w, Joseph Zucchero, J.M. Avelcana; ph, Ricardo Remias (Technicolor); m, George Garvarentz; ed, Bass Santos; art d, Fiel Zabat.

Action   **Cas.**   **(PR:O MPAA:NR)**

FINE MESS, A*½   (1986) 88m B.E.E.–COL-Delphi V/COL c

Ted Danson (*Spence Holden*), Howie Mandel (*Dennis Powell*), Richard Mulligan (*Wayne "Turnip" Farragalla*), Stuart Margolin (*Maurice "Binky" Dzundza*), Maria Conchita Alonso (*Claudia Pazzo*), Jennifer Edwards (*Ellen Frankenthaler*), Paul Sorvino (*Tony Pazzo*), Rick Ducommun (*Wardell*), Keye Luke (*Ishimine*), Ed Herlihy (*TV Reporter*), Walter Charles (*Auctioneer*), Tawny Moyer (*Leading Lady*), Emma Walton, Carrie Leigh (*Extras*), Sharan Lea (*Young Girl*), Rick Overton (*Companion*), John Short (*Assistant Director*), Theodore Wilson (*Covington*), Valerie Wildman (*Anchorwoman*), Larry Storch (*Leopold Klop*), C. James Lewis (*Detective Albert*), Robert Hoy (*Detective Levine*), John Davey (*Detective Horn*), Frederick Coffin (*Traffic Cop*), Darryl Henriques (*Landlord*), Sharon Hughes (*Tina*), Garth Wilton (*Houseman*), Castulo Guerra (*Italian Director*), Sharon Barr (*Director's Wife*), Jack O'Leary, Doug Cox (*Piano Movers*), Elaine Wilkes (*Carhop*), Jeffrey Lampert (*Car Salesman*), Jim Byers (*Track Announcer*), Shep Tanney (*Dr. Henry Garfurg*), Vic Polizos (*Detective Hunker*), James Cromwell (*Detective Blist*), Dennis Franz (*Phil*), Brooke Alderson (*Aileen*).

Resisting doing a play on the picture's title for a lead line was difficult. When a respected filmmaker (this is the 43rd movie with which Blake Edwards has been associated) chooses to make a trite, old-fashioned comedy and then has the chutzpah to name it A FINE MESS, that is a difficult bit of bait to withstand. Based very, very loosely on the Laurel and Hardy classic short "The Music Box," but any similarity between the characters in this one and that one is hard to find. Oliver Hardy used to look at the scrunched-up face of the tearful Stan Laurel and say "Well! This is another fine mess you've gotten us into." In the case of the classic duo, for all their shenanigans, we had to love them. In this film, we are given almost nobody to care about, and all of the klutzy comedy is given not to the two heros, Danson and Mandel, but to their gangland pursuers Margolin and Mulligan.

Danson is a Hollywood hanger-on, a movie extra scraping to make ends meet. He is also a lothario, close to the character he's played to four Emmy nominations on TV's "Cheers." He's working on location at a racetrack and overhears a plot to dope a horse. The men doing the doping (via a horse-type suppository) are Mulligan and Margolin. Danson contacts Mandel, a roller-skating carhop who works at one of those drive-ins that no longer exist in Hollywood. (They had to build one on an empty lot.) Mandel has a few bucks put away for a rainy day and Danson persuades him to bet it all on the horse, a sure thing. When the crooks'

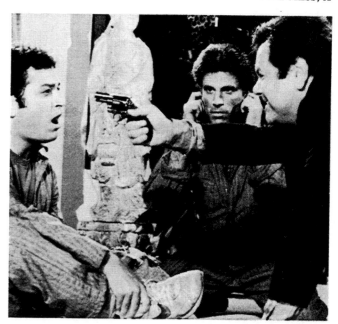

boss, Sorvino, learns that someone else knows of the bet, he sics his hoods on Mandel and Danson as they are collecting ten grand at the track. The rest of the movie is almost totally a chase. Danson and Mandel wind up at an auction house and Mandel makes the mistake of raising his hand at the wrong time, thus becoming the owner of a prized antique piano sold by auctioneer Jennifer Edwards (Blake's daughter). Auction bidder Alonzo is married to Sorvino, who fancies himself as "The Singing Godfather," and he wants that piano. She contacts Danson and Mandel in order to get the piano from them. In the course of events, she falls for Danson. Meanwhile, the horse has run and won again and dies in the process, thus alerting the cops to the fact that the animal had been doped to win. The picture winds up at the Sorvino residence for a bit of "lover under the bed" and a final frantic chase.

Mulligan and Margolin are a large part of what little joy can be found in this movie. Mandel has had success beyond his potential and this role is a setback for his amazingly burgeoning career. Alonzo has a few nice moments as the pneumatic wife of Sorvino, who also impresses at times. The picture was made at what used to be Selznick Studios, then was renamed Laird, and is now part of the huge Gannett Entertainment company. Locations at a racetrack, Santa Monica, Westwood, Venice, and Brentwood, where the phony drive-in was built. Jennifer Edwards has appeared in many of her father's films, including another 1986 release, THAT'S LIFE. Some of the other familiar faces in the film (an obvious attempt to pepper the picture with well-known cameos to supplement the weak leads) were Keye Luke (Charlie Chan's Number One Son), Ed Herlihy (The voice of "Kraft TV Theater's" cheese commercials as well as the beloved host for the "Horn & Hardart Children's Hour" radio show in the 1940s), comic Larry Storch, who spent so many years on TV's "F-Troop," and stage star Walter Charles, who played the queen in Broadway's "La Cage Aux Folles" as well as on the road. In small roles, note two of the better comedians on the nightclub circuit, Ric Ducommun and Rick Overton, and Blake Edwards' doctor, Shep Tanney, who sometimes puts in an appearance in his patient's films. Edwards confused humor with speed and so the pace is 150 mph but there is no time to laugh, and little reason to, either. Mancini phoned in the score and the 11 musical numbers used to punctuate the action don't help much. They include: "Don't Slow Down" (Richard Page, John Lan, Steven George, Steve Farris, performed by Mr. Mister), "A Fine Mess" (Henry Mancini, Dennis Lambert, performed by The Temptations), "Walk Like a Man" (Bob Gaudio, Bob Crewe, performed by The Mary Jane Girls), "Love's Closin' In" (Nick Jameson, performed by Nick Jameson), "Easier Said Than Done" (William Linton, Larry Huff, performed by Chico DeBarge), "Now I'm Talking About Now" (Anne Boston, John F. Calder, William Burton, Robert Elsey, John E. Garnett, performed by The Swimming Pool Q's), "Can't Help Falling In Love" (George Weiss, Huge Peretti, Luigi Creatore, performed by Christine McVie), "Movin' So Close" (Eric Douglas, Darryl Littlejohn, Keith Burston, performed by Second Generation), "I'm Gonna Be a Wheel Someday" (Roy Hayes, Dave Bartholomew, Antoine "Fats" Domino, performed by Los Lobos), "Wishful Thinking" (David Bryant, Bobby Sandstrom, Michael Price, performed by Smokey Robinson), and "Slow Down" (Larry Williams, performed by Billy Vera and The Beaters).

p, Tony Adams; d, Blake Edwards; ph, Harry Stradling (Panavision, DeLuxe Color); m, Henry Mancini; ed, John F. Burnett, Robert Pergament; prod d, Rodger Maus; set d, Stuart A. Reiss; cos, Patricia Norris; spec eff, Roy L. Downey; ch, Phil Gerard; m/l, Richard Page, John Lan, Steven George, Steve Farris, Henry Mancini, Dennis Lambert, Bob Gaudio, Bob Crewe, Nick Jameson, William Linton, Larry Huff, Anne Boston, John F. Calder, William Burton, Robert Elsey, John E. Garnett, George Weiss, Huge Peretti, Luigi Creatore, Eric Douglas, Darryl Littlejohn, Keith Burston, Roy Hayes, Dave Bartholomew, Antoine "Fats" Domino, David Bryant, Bobby Sandstrom, Michael Price, Larry Williams; makeup, Rick Sharp; stunts, Joe Dunne.

Comedy   **(PR:A-C MPAA:PG)**

FIRE IN THE NIGHT zero (1986) 89m Medallion/Shapiro c

John Martin *(Jason Williams)*, Graciela Casillas *(Terry Collins)*, Patrick St. Esprit *(Mike Swanson)*, Muni Zano *(Manolo Catalba)*, Burt Ward *(Paul)*, E.J. Peaker *(Mary Swanson)*, Peter Henry Schroeder *(Hubert Swanson)*, Robin Evans *(Kathy)*, Ron Leath *(Bill Collins)*, Jacquelyn Masche *(Elaine Collins)*, Mark Stuart Lane *(Fred)*, Susan Schroder *(Blonde)*, Terry Ballard *(Sheriff)*.

Good-versus-bad via martial arts is the point behind this insipid bit of nonsense. Casillas is a college coed living in a small California town where St. Esprit, a big rich brat, causes her nothing but trouble. St. Esprit's folks practically own the town, so there's not much anyone can do other than tolerate his Neanderthal mentality. The big lug tries to have his way with Casillas, though her pal Martin manages to put a stop to this. Unable to fulfill his sexual urges, St. Esprit does the next best thing and tries to have his father foreclose a mortgage on Casillas' father's business. Although she knows nothing about martial arts, Casillas challenges St. Esprit to a fight. If she wins, the mortgage is lifted; if he wins, she goes to bed with him. Since Casillas was the martial-arts advisor for this film, the outcome is more or less predestined, but in keeping with the plot's logic the resolute girl hooks up with a mentor, Zano. Zano is a cement contractor, dance instructor, and Filipino martial-arts expert whose unlikely resume is exactly the sort of thing Casillas is looking for. She helps him out with the cement business in exchange for lessons in fight techniques, and to no one's great surprise, she proves to be an apt pupil. After handily disposing of St. Esprit, Casillas becomes Zano's colleague in the cement business for an inevitable happy conclusion.

This is nothing more than a grade-Z ripoff of THE KARATE KID, with the muscular Casillas subbing for the considerably scrawnier Ralph Macchio. Apart from her flips and kicks, Casillas isn't much of an actress, but at least she's a good match for the film's other amateurish qualities. This might have been tolerable had there been a sense of humor to it; instead, it's a boring waste of celluloid.

p, Norbert Buddy Reyes, Simeon Muni Zano; d&w, John Steven Soet; ph, Eugene W. Jackson III; m, Toti Fuentes; ed, Gani Pastor; art d, Norbert Buddy Reyes; ch, Ted White.

Action/Drama   Cas.   (PR:O MPAA:NR)

FIRE WITH FIRE* (1986) 103m PAR c

Craig Sheffer *(Joe Fisk)*, Virginia Madsen *(Lisa Taylor)*, Jon Polito *(Boss)*, Jeffrey Jay Cohen *(Mapmaker)*, Kate Reid *(Sister Victoria)*, Jean Smart *(Sister Marie)*, Tim Russ *(Jerry)*, David Harris *(Ben)*, D.B. Sweeney *(Baxter)*, Dorrie Joiner *(Sandy)*, Evan Mirand *(Manuel)*, Ann Savage *(Sister Harriet)*, William Schilling *(Watley)*, Penelope Sudrow *(Stephanie)*, Star-Sheemah Bobatoon *(Margo)*, Kari Wuhrer *(Gloria)*, Smitty Smith *(Keyes)*, Franklin Johnson *(Old Man)*, Enid Saunders *(Old Woman)*, Birde M. Hale *(Arlene)*, Dwight McGee, David Longworth, Gary Chalk *(Deputies)*, Howard Storey *(Police Driver)*, Steve J. Wright *(Helicopter Pilot)*, Ian Tracey, Andy Gray *(Panthers)*, Lesley Ewen, Janine Mortil, Robyn Stevan *(School Gang)*, Ken Douglas *(Davis)*.

Technically, this film should be classified as a fantasy: the folks behind it ask the viewer to swallow so many unlikely premises it boggles the mind. Sheffer is the resident of a reform camp for handsome and muscular juvenile delinquents. While out on an athletic event in the Oregon (actually British Columbia) woods where the camp is located, Sheffer sees a mysterious and beautiful woman floating in a pond. This lady of the lake is Madsen, a student at a nearby Catholic girls school who is working on a photography project. Of course it's young love at first sight, but there remains the problem of getting these kids together. On an in-town trip to the movies where the boys are treated to FRIDAY THE 13TH: A NEW BEGINNING (great way to punish those juvenile delinquents, eh?), Sheffer spots Madsen, but they still can't connect. Madsen is just as eager to get together with the lad, and to that end concocts a grand scheme. When the nuns at school call for ideas on charitable projects, Madsen suggests the selfless girls should forgo the annual benefit for starving Africans. Instead, she argues, the school should help local organizations, particularly those suffering boys at the nearby work camp. The nuns, though taken aback, agree to hold a dance for the boys, apparently forgetting that they're the ones in charge.

Sheffer and Madsen finally get together and the romance blossoms. They manage to consummate their unbounded lust in a crypt located in a cemetary where Sheffer works. This brief moment of graveyard groping is interrupted when Polito, a camp guard who acts like he's really in COOL HAND LUKE, bursts in, shotgun in hand. The kids are separated, but it doesn't take Sheffer long to steal a car and grab his girl. The two hole up 100 miles north in a cabin formerly owned by Sheffer's late father. All seems blissful (never mind that other than a bit of passion and a few brief conversations these two hardly know each other), but of course that doesn't last long. Polito, with flaring gun and nostrils, brings along a helicopter and armed deputies to take in these no-good rebels. The cabin is burned to the ground, but Sheffer and Madsen manage to escape, leaping off a high cliff with no fear whatsoever. The river below breaks their fall (you expected they would be smashed to death on the rocks?), and the film ends with the happy lovers running off into the mountains, blissfully unconcerned with what the future may hold.

Director Gibbons makes his feature debut here after cutting his eye teeth in the artistically challenging field of rock videos. The aesthetics of his former medium are evident throughout, including artfully lit shots, beautiful actors, and plenty of pop tunes. Missing are characters of any reasonable intelligence or believability. Let's face it, there's just no way a nun would start off a boy-girl dance with a Prince song. It's strange little character details like that which make this so laughably awful. There's no real point to the film other than to watch Sheffer and Madsen make out. Their brief and boring lip locks aren't enough to base a film on despite the promised passion of a poorly chosen title. Songs include:

"Fire With Fire" (Chris Sanford, performed by Wild Blue), "Computer Blue" (Prince, Wendy Melvoin, Lisa Coleman, John J. Nelson, performed by Prince), "Bit by Bit (Theme from FLETCH)" (Harold Faltmeier, Franie Gold, performed by Stephanie Mills), "Heart of Rock and Roll" (Johnny Colls, Huey Lewis, performed by Huey Lewis and the News), "Slave to Love" (Bryan Ferry, performed by Bryan Ferry), "If Anybody Had a Heart" (Danny Kortchmar, J.D. Souther, performed by John Waite), "I'm In it for Love" (Patrick Henderson, Andy Goldmark, performed by James House), "From Nags to Witches" (Winston Sharpies).

p, Gary Nardino; d, Duncan Gibbins; w, Bill Phillips, Warren Skaaren, Paul Boorstin, Sharon Boorstin; ph, Hiro Narita (Metrocolor); m, Howard Shore; ed, Peter Berger; prod d, Norman Newberry; art d, Michael Bolton; set d, Rondi Johnson; cos, Enid Harris; spec eff, John Thomas, Stewart Bradley; ch, Sarah Elgart; m/l, Chris Sanford, Prince, Wendy Melvoin, Lisa Coleman, John J. Nelson, Harold Faltmeier, Franie Gold, Johnny Colls, Huey Lewis, Bryan Ferry, Danny Kortchmar, J.D. Souther, Patrick Henderson, Andy Goldmark, Winston Sharpies.

Drama/Romance   Cas.   (PR:O MPAA:PG-13)

FIREWALKER*½ (1986) 104m Golan-Globus/Cannon c

Chuck Norris *(Max Donigan)*, Lou Gossett *(Leo Porter)*, Melody Anderson *(Patricia Goodwyn)*, Will Sampson *(Tall Eagle)*, Sonny Landham *(El Coyote)*, John Rhys-Davies *(Corky Taylor)*, Ian Abercrombie *(Boggs)*, Richard Lee-Sung *(Chinese Man)*, Zaide S. Gutierrez *(Indian Girl)*, Alvaro Carcano *(Willie)*, John Hazelwood.

Chuck Norris again fails to find a niche for his limited talent in this cross between RAIDERS OF THE LOST ARK and a buddy picture. His buddy is Gossett, and they are hired in an Arizona saloon by Anderson, who wants them to help her locate a fabulous treasure-filled Aztec temple an old map shows to be nearby. Their early explorations uncover old Indian Sampson, who sends them further south in their quest, to that misnamed Latin American country so familiar to lousy action-movie fans. The trio travels disguised as a pair of priests and a nun, leading to some tired gags (Norris, with his mustache and longish hair, is an unlikely clergyman). Penetrating into the jungle, they are captured by hostile Indians and are about to be sacrificed when suddenly a large fellow in a paramilitary uniform steps up and kills the native who was about to lop off Norris' head. He turns out to be Rhys-Davies, an old friend of Norris' who just happens to be in the same place at the same time pursuing some scheme for world domination of his own. Gossett disappears, apparently eaten by a crocodile, and now the expedition is threatened by an enormous Aztec warrior who defends the treasure (Landham). Gossett reappears, and the reunited pair manage to vanquish all the assorted bad guys and get for themselves all the treasure, a huge room full of plastic items which have been spray-painted gold. The conclusion finds them in the middle of the desert, presumably waiting for the unlikely sequel.

There was some potential in this film, and Gossett could have been just the actor to offset Norris' usual wooden delivery, but instead of the witty, intelligent script needed to pull off an interracial buddy story, the scenario for this film is an

obvious lift from RAIDERS and a flat, uninteresting piece of writing, occasionally interspersed with embarrassingly sappy affirmations of friendship. Gossett seems almost reluctant to be on screen beside Norris, but he still manages to be the best thing here. Norris shows all his usual faults and few of his talents, squirming uncomfortably during love scenes, failing to ever convey any emotion, and only busting one saloon full of roughnecks. Production values are generally slick, though the temple set is appallingly bad.

p, Menahem Golan, Yoram Globus; d, J. Lee Thompson; w, Robert Gosnell (based on a story by Robert Gosnell, Jeffrey M. Rosenbaum, Norman Aladjem); ph, Alex Phillips (TVC Color); m, Gary Chang; ed, Richard Marx; prod d, Jose Rodriguez Granada; set d, Poppy Cannon; cos, Poppy Cannon.

Action/Adventure   Cas.   (PR:A MPAA:PG)

FLAGRANT DESIR† (1986, Fr.) 95m Martel Media-Sofracima Films A2-Third Eye-Odessa/Hemdale c (Trans: A Certain Desire)

Sam Waterston *(Gerry Morrison)*, Marisa Berenson *(Jeanne Barnac)*, Bernard-

Pierre Donnadieu *(Robert Barnac)*, Lauren Hutton *(Marlene Bell-Ferguson)*, Arielle Dombasle *(Marguerite Barnac)*, Anne Roussel *(Eveline Barnac)*, Francois Dunoyer *(Vittorio)*, Francois Dyrek *(Georges Barnac)*.

A "Lifestyles of the Rich and Famous"-style murder mystery which places its palette of wealthy, high-bred family members against a canvas of deception and intrigue. Waterston heads the international cast as an Interpol agent investigating the murder of Dombasle, a beautiful heiress of a Bordeaux wine dynasty. Things aren't what they seem, and Waterston's investigation manages to shake many skeletons out of the closet. Donnadieu, the head of the estate, turns out to be malicious, Berenson and Hutton are lesbian lovers, and Roussel is a virgin who falls in love with her mother's gigolo, Dunoyer. The film boasts some appropriately gorgeous photography by Willy Kurant, who began his career in the 1960s with such great films as Jean-Luc Godard's MASCULINE-FEMININE, Alain-Robbe Grillet's TRANS-EUROP-EXPRESS, and Orson Welles' THE IMMORTAL STORY, but has recently been reduced to such drivel as HARPER VALLEY P.T.A, MAMMA DRACULA, and 1985's TUFF TURF.

p, Catherine Winter; d&w, Claude Faraldo; ph, Willy Kurant; m, Gabriel Yared; ed, Chris Holmes, Marie Castro; art d&cos, Francoise Deleu.

Crime/Drama   **(PR:O MPAA:NR)**

FLAMBEREDE HJERTER†   (1986, Den.) 112m Per Holst–Danish Film Institute/Karne Film c (Trans: Flaming Hearts)

Kirsten Lehfeldt *(Henriette)*, Torben Jensen *(Loewe)*, Peter Hesse Overgaard *(Ole)*, Anders Hove *(Finn)*, Ingolf David *(Mr. Holm)*, Lillian Tillegren *(Mrs. Holm)*, Kirsten Peuliche *(Lisbeth Castillo)*, Aage Haugland *(Woodroof)*, Yrsa Gullaksen, Arne Siemsen, Else Petersen, Pernille Hojmark, Margrethe Koytu, Knud Dietmer, Morten Suurballe.

Lehfeldt is a daffy nurse who ditches her boring boy friend for doctor Jensen. When he doesn't return her affections, she trashes his life, ruining a dinner Jensen hosts for a famous foreign surgeon (opera star Aage Haugland).

p, Per Holst; d&w, Helle Ryslinge; ph, Dirk Bruel (Eastmancolor); m, Peer Raben; ed, Birger Moller-Jensen; cos, Malin Birch-Jensen.

Comedy/Drama   **(PR:C MPAA:NR)**

FLAMING BORDERS†   (1986, Iraq) 93m General Establishment for Film and Theater/Iraqi Cinema c

Hind Kamel *(Sana)*, Saadia Ezzidi *(Mother)*, Hamded *(Soldier Faycel)*, Sami Khaftan *(Mansour Majiid)*.

The war between Iran and Iraq is celebrated in a government-sponsored film. Like all modern combatants, both sides keep theaters stocked with war movies that glorify their own cause and vilify the enemy's. This example has extensive, realistic battle scenes, a young hero with a girl friend back in Baghdad, human wave assaults, bottom-of-the-barrel Iranian youths awaiting decimation, and even an appearance by President Saddem Hussein exhorting the masses to defend the borders against any encroachment.

d, Sahib Haddad; w, Kacem Mohamed; ph, Nihad Ali; m, Solhi El Wadi.

War   **(PR:C MPAA:NR)**

FLASH†   (1986, Israel) 90m YNYL c

Nitza Shaul, Amos Lavi, Zeev Shimshoni.

The happy married life of a young couple is thrown into disarray when the wife's first husband returns to the scene. An aggressive, gun-toting pyschopath, he fights for his former mate, challenging her more reasonable husband to a duel.

p, Yeud Lavanon; d, Doron Eran; w, Razi Levinas; ph, Gad Danzig; ed, Lina Kadish.

Drama   **(PR:C MPAA:NR)**

FLIGHT NORTH†   (1986, Finland./Ger.) 130m Theuring-Engstrom–Jorn Donner/Cine-International c (FLUCHT IN DEN NORDEN)

Katharina Thalbach *(Johanna)*, Jukka-Pekka Palo *(Ragnar)*, Lena Olin *(Karin)*, Tom Poysti *(Jens)*, Kabi Laretei *(Mother)*, Britta Pohland *(Maid)*.

Based on a 1934 novel by Klaus Mann, FLIGHT NORTH is an account of a German woman, Thalbach, who flees increasing repression in Berlin (where she was active in the anti-Nazi movement) for Finland. There she stays with her lesbian lover's family, falling in love with one of the brothers, Palo. They travel north, making love frequently but with increasing sadness and hopelessness. In the end she decides to go to Paris to continue the fight against Hitler.

d&w, Ingemo Engstrom (based on the novel *Entkommen zum Leben* by Klaus Mann); ph, Axel Block (Eastmancolor); m, Johann Sebastian Bach, Jean Sibelius; ed, Thomas Balkenhol; prod d, Kristiina Tuura, Jukka Vikberg, Ben Gyllenberg; cos, Heidi Wujek, Marja-Liisa Tielinen, Leila Oksanen.

Drama   **(PR:O MPAA:NR)**

FLIGHT OF RAINBIRDS, A†   (1986, Neth.) 94m World Artists c

Jeroen Krabbe *(Maarten)*, Marijke Merckens *(Mother)*, Willeke Van Ammelrooy, Henriette Tol, Simone Kleinsma.

A 34-year-old Dutch biologist may be the last virgin in the country, so God comes to him in a dream and gives him a week to do something about it or he'll die. The problem is the deep attachment he feels for his aging mother.

p, Mattijs Van Heyningen; d&w, Ate De Jong (based on the novel by Maarten't Hart); ph, Paul van den Bos; ed, Edgar Burcksen.

Comedy/Drama   **(PR:O MPAA:NR)**

FLIGHT OF THE NAVIGATOR***   (1986) 90m PSO/Disney–BV c

Joey Cramer *(David Freeman)*, Veronica Cartwright *(Helen Freeman)*, Cliff De Young *(Bill Freeman)*, Sarah Jessica Parker *(Carolyn McAdams)*, Matt Adler *(Jeff at Age 16)*, Howard Hesseman *(Dr. Faraday)*, Paul Mall *(Max)*, Robert Small *(Troy)*, Albie Whitaker *(Jeff at Age 8)*, Jonathan Sanger *(Dr. Carr)*, Iris Acker *(Mrs. Howard)*, Richard Liberty *(Mr. Howard)*, Raymond Forchion *(Detective Banks)*, Cynthia Caquelin *(Woman Officer)*, Ted Bartsch *(Night Guard Brayton)*, Gizelle Elliot *(Female Technician)*, Brigid Cleary, Michael Strano *(Technicians)*, Parris Buckner, Robyn Peterson *(Scientists)*, Tony Tracy *(Observation Guard)*, Philip Hoelcher *(NASA Officer)*, Julio Mechoso, Butch Raymond *(Hangar Guards)*, Bob Strickland, Michael Brockman *(Control Room Guards)*, Louis Cutolo, Debbie Casperson *(Radar Technicians)*, Chase Randolph *(Lt. King)*, John Archie, Tony Calvino *(Agents)*, Rusty Pouch *(Gas Station Attendant)*, Robert Goodman *(Tourist Man)*, Ryan Murray *(Tourist Child)*, Keri Rogers *(Jennifer Bradley)*, Peter Lundquist, Jill Beach *(Newscasters)*, Kenny Davis *(Kid in Mustang)*, Bruce Laks *(Bixby)*, Arnie Ross, Fritz Braumer *(NASA Technicians)*.

A charming little picture that came along a bit too late in the Steven Spielberg cycle and dropped from sight quickly. It opened with no fanfare and closed the same way, despite being one of those rare fantasy pictures that both parents and children could enjoy. Cramer is a 12-year-old boy who is out in the woods one day when he falls into a ravine and is knocked unconscious. It's 1978, the year of John Travolta and the BeeGees, and Cramer is an average young kid with average parents, De Young and Cartwright, as well as the typical kid brother, Whitaker, whom he'd like to strangle. When Cramer wakes up, he goes straight back to his house only to find that there are people living there he doesn't know! The cops arrive and the boy is understandably confused. Things really get muddled in the

boy's mind when he learns that he supposedly disappeared eight years ago. This is now 1986. He's taken to meet his parents, who have since moved, and is shocked to find that 8-year-old Whitaker is now 16-year-old Adler. At the same time, NASA has discovered the existence of a spaceship in a field and the scientists wonder what that has to do with the young lad who vanished eight years ago and is still the same age. Eventually, in a story leap of logic, it's reckoned that this boy had something to do with that craft.

When NASA specialists study young Cramer, they plumb his mind with space-age technology and see that his brain contains heretofore unseen star charts of unexplored territory in the heavens. Cramer has no idea of all of this in his mind; he'd just like to go home, eat some ice cream, and be a son again. But the NASA people won't let him. The group is headed by Hesseman (an unusual choice for a role usually played by types like Hume Cronyn) and he is determined to get to the bottom of this. The boy is now a virtual captive until NASA aide Parker begins to feel sorry for him and helps him escape. Cramer is being psychically called by the spaceship (which is now inside a NASA hangar). He gets to the ship, makes his way inside (where nobody else has been able to visit), and takes off with himself as the navigator. The ship is run by the alien equivalent of HAL (2001, 2010), except this one's name is MAX and it has a sense of humor. It turns out that Cramer had been taken by the alien to a planet far away, where the young boy's mind was tapped. They were to return him to earth right away but there were miscalculation problems (never fully explained) and so eight years passed before he was deposited back in the ravine.

MAX is in trouble because there's been a short in the on-board computer and the spaceship can't return to its home planet. The only way the ship can make it safely back is by tapping all the star charts which now reside in Cramer's tousled head. The boy's brain is examined and all of the star charts are pulled out, but so are the lad's memory banks; the computer begins sounding a great deal like Pee Wee Herman. (Pee Wee, or Paul Reubens, actually did the voice, but was not credited on the screen.) All the while, Hesseman's people are trying to catch the spaceship and it drops Cramer off at his parents' home.

Meanwhile, Cramer is not so sure he likes what 1986 has to offer a 12-year-old. Gone are his favorite TV shows and many of the things that made growing up as a pre-teen in 1978 so much fun. He also knows that NASA will never stop

wanting to examine him so he takes a big chance and goes back in time to 1978 and emerges to return to a younger De Young, Cartwright, and, again, Whitaker.

Good but sparse special effects from Peter Donen, whose work will be recalled on SUPERMAN I, II, III, OUTLAND, and BLUE THUNDER. Coproducer on the film was Australian David Joseph, who was responsible for THE PRIVATE MOVIE, a not-so-successful film. Although listed with that credit, he was never present while the movie was shot. Baker wrote the story financed by Joseph, who then took it to PSO (now since defunct), who took it to Disney. And that's how movies are made. Most of the time, they are a bollix. This time it worked, and the movie will probably have a longer life on pay TV, airplanes, and videocassettes than it did in the theater. Kleiser, who made THE BLUE LAGOON and GREASE (which gets a prominent mention in this film) again shows that he can handle youngsters well. While they were shooting this in Florida, the shuttle disaster took place, thus throwing a pall over the make-believe as reality impinged. The MPAA PG rating is due to some mild language and a few scenes that might scare very impressionable children who've not seen STAR WARS.

p, Robby Wald, Dimitri Villard; d, Randal Kleiser; w, Michael Burton, Matt MacManus (based on a story by Mark H. Baker); ph, James Glennon (Technicolor); m, Alan Silvestri; ed, Jeff Gourson; prod d, William J. Creber; art d, Michael Novotny; set d, Scott Jacobson; spec eff, Peter Donen, Petter Borgli; makeup, Philip Goldblatt.

Fantasy (PR:A MPAA:PG)

FLIGHT OF THE SPRUCE GOOSE† (1986) 97m Michael Hausman/ Filmhaus c

Dan O'Shea (Adam), Jennifer Runyon (Terry), Karen Black (Mother), Dennis Christopher (Friend).

Howard Hughes' famed aircraft "The Spruce Goose" takes on symbolic overtones in this love story which stars O'Shea as a Pittsburgh coal miner who falls in love with Runyon, a beautiful model. Black, as the model's mother, disapproves of O'Shea and makes their possible romance difficult. The desperate O'Shea kidnaps Runyon and they travel cross-country to California to see the "Spruce Goose"—a symbol that their love, like Hughes' craft, can get off the ground. The original Hughes craft—part boat, part plane—was the largest ever built and it quickly became a laughing stock among those critics who predicted it would never fly. Hughes, however, proved them wrong. On November 2, 1947, in Long Beach Harbor, he flew the craft at an altitude of 70 feet for a distance of one mile. The Spruce Goose never flew again and is now on exhibition in Long Beach with a wax figure of a young and dashing Howard Hughes in the cockpit.

p, Michael Hausman; d, Lech Majewski; w, Lech Majewski, Chris Burdza; ph, Jerzy Zielinski; m, Henri Seroka; ed, Corky O'Hara.

Drama (PR:C MPAA:NR)

FLODDER† (1986, Neth.) 111m First Floor Features/Concorde c

Nelly Frijda, Huub Stapel, Tatjana Simico, Rene van't Hof, Lou Landre, Herbert Flack, Nano Lehnhausen, Jan Willem Hees, Appolonia van Ravenstein.

The seven members of a poor family are evicted from their home when it is discovered that it sits atop a toxic-waste dump. The government decides to place the family in an upper-class area where they promptly go about destroying the place and arousing the ire of the snobby neighbors.

p, Laurens Geels, Dick Maas; d&w, Dick Maas; ph, Marc Felperlan (Fujicolor); m, Dick Maas; ed, Hans van Dongen; art d, Hubert Pouille; set d, Hans Voors; stunts, Marc Boyle.

Comedy (PR:C MPAA:NR)

FLOODSTAGE† (1986) 80m Spring Films c

Deborah Barham (Faye), Diane Brown (Mona), David Dawkins (Lenny), Gregory Frank (Cookie), David Jaffe (Red), Patience Pierce (Pinky), Lenard Petit (Merrit), Marty Rossip (Marty), Joanne Zonis (Maggie), Roger Rabb (Narrator), Leslie Winston (Percussion), David Winston (Bass).

An odd, low-budget independent film that treads the line between documentary and fiction. Every summer for ten years a theater group traveled down the Mississippi River on a raft, performing a strange, modern form of street theater for residents of river towns along the way. This already interesting premise would have made a fascinating documentary, but instead of playing it straight, director Dawkins (who also directs the theater group and plays himself in that role) chooses to add a fictional overlay about a newcomer to the group who becomes romantically involved with Pierce, Dawkins' longstanding girl friend. Shot on a microbudget of $33,000, the film has yet to see a wide release.

p,d&w, David Dawkins; ph, Wade Hanks; ed, David Dawkins; art d, Gregory Frank; cos, Lois Simbach.

Drama (PR:C-O MPAA:NR)

FLUCHT IN DEN NORDEN (SEE: FLIGHT NORTH, 1986, Fin./Ger.)

FLY, THE**** (1986) 100m Brooksfilm/FOX c

Jeff Goldblum (Seth Brundle), Geena Davis (Veronica Quaife), John Getz (Stathis Borans), Joy Boushel (Tawny), Les Carlson (Dr. Cheevers), George Chuvalo (Marky), Michael Copeman (2nd Man in Bar), David Cronenberg (Gynecologist), Carol Lazare (Nurse), Shawn Hewitt (Clerk).

Obsessive Canadian director David Cronenberg's American mainstream breakthrough film is also his most controlled, mature, and insightful work to date. A filmmaker obsessed with the horrifying implications of science and technology when combined with the powerful potentials of the human mind, body, and sexuality, Cronenberg has created several highly personal films over the last 15

years. While the concepts of these films are interesting and unique, the films themselves have been sloppy, undisciplined, and sometimes incoherent, with little or no attention paid to the development of his characters as complex, emotional human beings (in his early films it seems as if he has nothing but fear, loathing, and contempt for his protagonists). With his decision to remake the 1958 science-fiction classic THE FLY, Cronenberg found the perfect outlet for his obsessions, while at the same time finally demonstrating great compassion for both the strengths and weaknesses of the human race. Updated and improved by a more complex personal relationship between the protagonists and a more realistic examination of the science and technology involved, the new version of THE FLY begins as a young female science-magazine reporter, Davis, meets a somewhat shy, awkward scientist, Goldblum, at a cocktail party. Although brilliant intellectually, Goldblum lacks adult social skills and clumsily tries to seduce the pretty Davis like a nerdy high schooler trying to impress the prom queen with his science project. He hints that he is working on an incredible experiment that will change "life as we know it," but instead of telling her about it where other eager scientists will overhear, he invites her to his warehouse loft/lab for a demonstration. There he reveals three man-sized "telepods" (one is a prototype for the others) which can disintegrate matter in one and then reintegrate it in the other—thus transporting an item across space. Goldblum transports one of Davis' stockings, but explains that so far only inanimate objects can be safely transported. Davis is amazed and excited by the invention, but Goldblum begs her not to report on his discovery just yet, and later offers to give her exclusive book rights when he figures out how to transport human beings. She agrees, but her editor (and former lover), Getz, thinks that the whole thing is a magician's trick. During the next few weeks, Davis and Goldblum fall deeply in love as he works on the problem of transporting living beings. He attempts to transport a baboon, but the poor animal is literally turned inside out during the experiment. The setback is a crushing blow to Goldblum, but Davis is drawn to the scientist at this vulnerable moment and they make love. After Davis makes an offhanded comment stating that " . . . it's the flesh that makes you crazy," Goldblum suddenly realizes what has been wrong with his experiments. The computer disintegrates an item and then offers its interpretation of that item in the reintegration. Goldblum must program the computer to understand what he calls "the poetry of the flesh." Soon after, he successfully transports another baboon. Later that night Davis' jealous former boy friend begins to cause trouble and she leaves Goldblum to go and settle things with Getz once and for all. Goldblum misinterprets her departure and his jealousy leads him to drink. Drunk and upset, the scientist impulsively decides to teleport himself. Unbeknownst to Goldblum, a common housefly has entered the telepod with him. The teleportation is successful, but the computer, not knowing what to make of the second item in the telepod, fuses it genetically with Goldblum. The scientist knows none of this, however, and is amazed and delighted when he finds a shocking increase in his physical prowess, reflexes, and sexual stamina. Goldblum assumes that teleportation acts as a purification filter for the human body. Davis is more than a little concerned by the physical changes in Goldblum, for his personality has changed as well. The normally thoughtful, relaxed Goldblum is now a hyper, insensitive live wire who constantly craves sweets. She also notices thick, dark hairs growing out of his back. Like a born-again zealot, Goldblum insists that Davis take a trip through the teleporter so she too can be purified. Afraid, she refuses and Goldblum angrily seeks sexual gratification elsewhere. Distraught, Davis has some of Goldblum's new hairs analyzed and learns that they are not human, but possibly insect. Meanwhile, Goldblum is undergoing a more drastic metamorphosis. His fingernails and teeth begin to fall out. Four weeks later he has become a hideous, hunched-over monster whose human appendages molt and fall off. He begs to see Davis and she is horrified by the sight of him, although he retains a rather resigned-but-sarcastic wit (he keeps his useless human appendages in the medicine cabinet, which he calls "The Brundle Museum of Natural History"). By now he has figured out what happened to him, and he refuses to turn to other scientists for fear of becoming a lab specimen. With nowhere else to go, Davis consults her ex-lover, Getz, and after she shows him a videotape of Goldblum—who, among other things, now walks on walls and ceilings, and eats like a fly (i.e., vomiting a corrosive acid on his food and then re-ingesting the goo)—Getz agrees to help. Then Davis learns she is pregnant and becomes desperate to abort for fear that

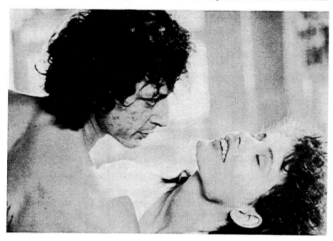

the baby she carries will be something hideous (she has a gruesome nightmare wherein she gives birth to a huge maggot). She goes to tell Goldblum her decision, but finds him in even worse shape. His mind is slowly being taken over by that of the fly. In a lucid moment he tells her that he'd like to become the first insect politician, for insects are cruel, brutal, and uncompromising. "I'm an insect who dreamt he was a man, and loved it. But now the dream is over and the insect is awake." Davis is confused by all of this and Goldblum puts it more simply: "I'll hurt you if you stay." Hysterical, Davis leaves with Getz and is determined to have an abortion immediately. Goldblum overhears this. He follows them to the abortionist and kidnaps Davis before the operation begins. He begs her to have the baby because it is the only part of his former self left (she could have conceived before the disastrous teleportation). Half crazed, he takes her back to his lab where he intends to perform a three-way genetic splice that would meld him, her, and their baby together in the third pod. Getz arrives with a shotgun and is attacked by Goldblum, who spews acid on the man's arm and leg. At this point Goldblum's metamorphosis becomes complete and he is now a huge, 185-pound fly. Getz manages to sever the cable to Davis' telepod just as the teleportation begins, leaving the fly to fuse with the remaining telepod. A horrible twisted fusion of fly and metal falls out of the telepod and it crawls to Davis. The fly grabs the barrel of the shotgun and guides it to its wretched head. More out of love than loathing, Davis pulls the trigger and ends Goldblum's suffering.

THE FLY succeeds on every level. As a remake, it does what remakes rarely do and improves upon the original, taking it in new directions and exploring the unused potential of the source material. Whereas the original film deteriorated into a hunt for the tiny fly that possessed scientist Al [David] Hedison's head and arm (which was necessary if any attempt was to be made to correct the horrible accident), the remake opts for a slow metamorphosis from man to fly—developing as a disease would. This gives Cronenberg time to examine the implications of

such an event and the film explores our fear of disease, death, and change. Most audiences scream with revulsion when Davis impulsively hugs the wretched-looking Goldblum after his ear molts and falls off. This moment—and viewer reaction to it—is crucial, for it points up most people's reaction to the suffering of diseased patients. "How could she possibly touch him?" viewers ask. The answer is simple. She loves him and would do anything to ease his pain. Anyone loving a diseased or dying person would do the same. This kind of love and devotion is rare in modern films, especially science-fiction/horror films. What Cronenberg has found in THE FLY that was missing from most of his previous films (save THE BROOD and THE DEAD ZONE) is that the capacity for human beings to love and care for one another is just as powerful as any wayward scientific-technological discovery that spins beyond our control to cause anguish, pain, and death. Human emotions, not simply intellect, seem to motivate everything that happens in THE FLY. Goldblum's loneliness compels him to bring Davis into his life. His jealousy causes him to carelessly test his invention. Her love for him runs deep and we share her pain as she begins to collapse from the strain of losing him, finally finding enough strength in her love to end his suffering. The reason this film is so nerve-wracking and draining an experience has little to do with the frequently nauseating special effects. Rather, during the first 60 minutes of this film, we have come to know and care for the people on the screen and it hurts us to watch Goldblum's horrible transformation as much as it does Davis. The orgy of gross effects during the last part of the film may be excessive, but Cronenberg isn't interested in sparing the viewer from the disturbing realities of the situation—just as the loved one of a terminal patient must endure the day-to-day horrors of that reality. This is not an easy film to watch, and it shouldn't be. Much of the success of the film must go to Goldblum and Davis (real-life lovers when the film was shot), who turn in two of the best performances to be found in any science fiction-horror film, or, for that matter, any recent film. Goldblum is superb as he changes from an insecure, shy scientist into a sensitive, caring, devoted lover; then into a cruel, arrogant bastard; then into a witty, sarcastic Brundlefly (as he calls himself) desperately trying to find some meaning in his existence; and finally into a schizophrenic, dangerous creature only interested in its own survival. The Motion Picture Academy continued its long-standing prejudice against genre films by not awarding Goldblum even a nomination for what surely ranks as one of the best performances of the year (the one and only Best Actor award in a horror film went to Fredric March for DR. JEKYLL AND MR. HYDE in 1932). Davis, in her first starring film role, does a fine job as the self-confident journalist who chooses to join Goldblum on his search into the unknown. Her performance also runs the range of emotions, right down to the ability to see a glimmer of her lover's humanity in the eyes of the hideous fly. For once in a science-fiction film, the effects were designed to enhance and complement the narrative, not to overpower it. Spier's production design, the Oscar-winning special-effects makeup by Chris Walas and Stephan Dupuis, Irwin's cinematography, and Shore's musical score are uniformly excellent and mesh together as one powerful force. After years of intellectual rumination, narrative incoherence, and delight in the gross and bizarre, David Cronenberg has finally brought all his highly personal demons under control and created a unique, moving, and thought-provoking examination of the human condition which will echo in the viewer's mind long after it has faded from the screen.

p, Stuart Cornfeld; d, David Cronenberg; w, Charles Edward Pogue, David Cronenberg (based on a story by George Langelaan); ph, Mark Irwin (DeLuxe Color); m, Howard Shore; ed, Ronald Sanders; prod d, Carol Spier; art d, Rolf Harvey; set d, James McAteer; cos, Denise Cronenberg; spec eff, Louis Craig, Ted Ross; makeup, Shonagh Jabour; stunts, Dwayne McLean.

Science Fiction/Horror   Cas.   (PR:O MPAA:R)

FLYING† (1986, Can.) 97m Brightstar-Rawifilm/Golden Communications c

Olivia D'Abo (Robin), Rita Tushingham (Jean), Keanu Reeves (Tommy), Jessica Steen (Cindy), Renee Murphy (Leah), Sean McCann (Jack).

D'Abo is a young girl with most of the problems that plague such adolescents: parents who don't understand her, crushes on boys who don't know she exists, and the like. She also has a recurrent leg injury (the result of an accident that killed her father) that keeps her from fulfilling her biggest dream, to become a gymnast and represent her school at the big competition. Does she win the boy? Does she win the contest? If you don't know, you obviously haven't seen enough of these things yet.

p, Tony Kramreither; d, Paul Lynch; w, John Sheppard; ph, Brian Foley (Filmhouse Color); m, Ollie E. Brown, Joe Curiale; ed, Ernie Rotundo; m/l, Ollie E. Brown.

Drama   (PR:C MPAA:NR)

FOLLOWING THE FUHRER**½ (1986, Ger.) 90m EML-ZDF/Futura bw
(DIE MITLAUFER)

Friedrich W. Bauschulte, Edith Teichmann, Armin Mueller-Stahl, Karin Baal, Lisi Mangold, Felix von Manteuffel, Gottfried John, Regina Lemnitz, Horst Bollman, Therese Lohner.

A worthy effort from director Leiser which artfully combines newsreel footage and scenes from 1930s-era films with newly shot scenes to create an impression of the everyday life of ordinary citizens in Nazi Germany. No specific plot or story line runs through the film; a series of short vignettes describes people living with the sacrifices necessitated by political oppression. This film is similar in many ways to Leiser's 1960 documentary MEIN KAMPF, in which he combined footage from different sources during Nazi times in Germany to create an in-depth portrait of Hitler and the sociopolitical environment that allowed him to exist.

FOLLOWING THE FUHRER was produced in 1984 but did not have its limited theatrical release in the U.S. until 1986. (In German; English subtitles.)

p, Christine Carben-Stotz; d, Erwin Leiser; w, Oliver Storz; ph, Gerard Vandenberg, Jochen Radermacher; ed, Elisabeth Imholte, Margot von Oven, Jutta Niehoff; set d, Peter Scharff; cos, Nikola Hoeltz.

Historical/Drama   **(PR:C   MPAA:NR)**

FOOTROT FLATS†   (1986, New Zealand) 80m Magpie/Endeavour c

Voices: Peter Rowley *(Dog)*, John Clarke *(Wal)*, Rawiri Paratene *(Rangi)*, Fiona Samuel *(Cheeky Hobson/Pongo)*, Peter Hayden *(Cooch/Irish Murphy)*, Dorothy McKegg *(Aunt Dolly)*, Billy T. James *(Pawai)*, Brian Sargent *(Spit Murphy)*, Marshall Napier *(Hank Murphy)*.

"Footrot Flats" is a sophisticated comic strip popular with New Zealand and Australian newspaper readers. Book compilations of the cartoon are consistent bestsellers, and have been successfully marketed to such varied audiences as Scandinavians and the Japanese. This film rendition of the popular characters is of historical note, since it is the first animated feature to come out of the New Zealand film industry. The story revolves around Wal Footrot (voiced by Clarke), who lives on a farm with his pet pooch, Dog (voiced by Rowley). Dog will do anything to protect his master, which nearly upsets Wal's love life in the process. Dog's own amorous adventures take some unusual turns when he is forced to risk his life time and again in order to woo a certain comely canine.

p, John Barnett, Pat Cox; d, Murray Ball; w, Murray Ball, Tom Scott (based on characters created by Murray Ball); m, Dave Dobbyn; ed, Michael Horton, Denis Jones; anim, Robbert Smit; backgrounds, Richard Zaloudek.

Animated Feature   **(PR:A   MPAA:NR)**

FOR LOVE ALONE†   (1986, Aus.) 102m Waranta-UAA/UAA c

Helen Buday *(Teresa Hawkins)*, Sam Neill *(James Quick)*, Hugo Weaving *(Jonathan Crow)*, Huw Williams *(Harry Girton)*, Hugh Keays-Byrne *(Andrew Hawkins)*, Odile Le Clezio *(Kitty Hawkins)*, Linden Wilkinson *(Miss Havilland)*, Judi Farr *(Aunt Bea)*, Anna Phillips *(Ann)*, Regina Gaigalas *(Jean)*, John Polson *(Leo Hawkins)*, Nicholas Opolski *(Lance Hawkins)*, Naomi Watts *(Marion)*, Jill Clayton *(Aunt Di)*, Renee Wray *(Landlady)*, Jennifer Hagan *(Manette)*, Fiona Stewart *(Martha)*, Anna North *(Lucy)*, Mercia Dean-Jones *(Clara)*, Tracey Higginson *(Malfi)*.

Based on a successful (in Australia, at least) novel, this is a romantic drama set in the 1930s. Buday is a young woman who feels increasingly confined by the narrow local ways and by her repressive father (Keays-Byrne). She falls in love with her Latin tutor, Weaving, a popular figure on the university campus, though he only wants to string her along. When he leaves to take a job in England, he encourages her to write and keep her love for him. She takes a job and works for three years to earn her passage to England. On the ship she meets Neill, a banker with progressive ideals. She is attracted to him but retains her love for Weaving until the latter finally tells her that he was never in love with her. She turns to Neill and soon they are living together. When she finds herself attracted to socialist poet Williams, Neill encourages her to sleep with him in order to discover herself. After doing so, she decides that while great sex is nice, love is better, and she marries Neill.

p, Margaret Fink; d&w, Stephen Wallace (based on the novel by Christina Stead); ph, Alun Bollinger (Eastmancolor); m, Nathan Wax; ed, Henry Dangar; prod d, John Stoddart; art d, John Wingrove; cos, Jennie Tate; makeup, Lesley Vanderwalt.

Drama   **(PR:O   MPAA:NR)**

FOREIGN BODY**   (1986, Brit.) 108m Neame-Brewer/Orion c

Victor Banerjee *(Ram Das)*, Warren Mitchell *(I.Q. Patel)*, Geraldine McEwan *(Lady Ammanford)*, Denis Quilley *(Prime Minister)*, Amanda Donohoe *(Susan)*, Eve Ferret *(Norah Plumb)*, Anna Massey *(Miss Furze)*, Stratford Johns *(Mr. Plumb)*, Trevor Howard *(Dr. Stirrup)*, Jane Laurie *(Jo Masters)*, Rashid Karapiet *(Mr. Nahan)*.

Veteran British director Neame takes a playful look at the odyssey of an Indian who loses his job in Calcutta and, in remarkably short order, finds himself acting as a physician for the British prime minister. After being fired from his job as a desk clerk in a fleabag hotel, Banerjee (A PASSAGE TO INDIA, THE HOME AND THE WORLD) steals—from his father—the funds necessary to emigrate to England. Once in London, he looks up Mitchell, a now-not-so-distant cousin who works as a washroom attendant at Heathrow Airport. Following Mitchell's advice, Banerjee gets a job "on the buses," working as a conductor on a double-decker. Besides trying to keep his head above water, Banerjee is dead set on losing his virginity. When he meets lusty, busty Ferret on the bus one night, he thinks he's well on the way to reaching his goal. Unfortunately, Ferret's racist, imperialist father not only puts an end to Banerjee's relationship with his daughter, but also sees to it that the Indian loses his job.

However, Banerjee's life is a roller-coaster ride that never stops. Almost before he knows it he finds himself administering mouth-to-mouth resuscitation to the victim of a bus accident, Donohoe, a model with plenty of friends in high places. Donohoe is so beholden to this fine Indian "doctor" that she says she will recommend him to her many friends. Delighted by the whole turn of events, Mitchell—who has put aside a nice sum from his well-paid dalliance with his landlady—stakes Banerjee to an office on Harley Street, where London's medical elite hang their shingles. Banerjee crams from medical books and picks the brain of Howard, a physician-cum-alcoholic buddy of Mitchell's. Banerjee fills the bill so

well that Donohoe's titled aunt, McEwan, puts in a good word for him with Quilley, whose home address just happens to be No. 10 Downing Street. Along the way, Banerjee also has more than a little luck with Donohoe, developing an effective bedside manner that has nothing to do with medicine and everything to do with playing doctor.

Based on a novel by Roderick Mann, FOREIGN BODY has some amusing moments, but the film is as much of a roller-coaster ride as is Banerjee's life. Banerjee turns in a fine performance, and the supporting cast is a distinguished one—fine character actor Mitchell, award-winning stage actress McEwan, and the well-traveled Howard—but they cannot overcome an unimaginative story line that refuses to catch fire.

p, Colin M. Brewer; d, Ronald Neame; w, Celine La Freniere (based on the novel by Roderick Mann); ph, Ronnie Taylor (DeLuxe Color); m, Ken Howard; ed, Andrew Nelson; prod d, Roy Stannard.

Comedy   **(PR:C-O   MPAA:PG-13)**

FORMULA FOR MURDER†   (1986, It.) 88m Fulvia International c (AKA: FORMULA FOR A MURDER)

Christina Nagy *(Joanna)*, David Warbeck *(Craig)*, Carroll Blumenberg *(Ruth)*, Rossano Brazzi *(Dr. Sernich)*, Andrea Bosic, Loris Loddi, Adriana Giuffre, Daniela De Carolis, Arthur Webber, Jr.

Nagy has been wheelchair-bound since a man disguised as a priest tried to rape her and she fell down a flight of stairs attempting to escape. While training for the Special Olympics she falls in love with her coach, Warbeck, who is actually involved in a complex plot designed by Nagy's roommate to steal her money. Warbeck reenacts the traumatic rape incident before attempting to murder the helpless woman.

d, Martin Herbert [Alberto De Martino]; w, Hank Walker, Martin Herbert [Alberto De Martino]; ph, Lawrence Barkey (Luciano Vittori Color); m, Francesco De Masi; ed, Vincent P. Thomas; art d, Julian Wilson; stunts, Arthur Mulkey.

Thriller   **Cas.**   **(PR:O   MPAA:NR)**

45MO PARALLELO†   (1986, It.) 85m MVM-International Movie Company bw (Trans: 45th Parallel)

Thom Hoffman *(Tom)*, Valeria D'Obici *(Anna)*, Andrea Puglisi *(Andrea)*, Enzo Robutti *(Salati)*.

This atmospheric film—made by a former fashion photographer—details one summer in the Po valley. Hoffman is a foreign photographer shooting local ecological problems is befriended by D'Obici, a waitress, and Puglisi, a 12-year-old visiting aunts in the area.

p, Paolo Pagnoni; d, Attilio Concari; w, Attilio Concari, Davide Ferrario; ph, Renato Tafuri; m, Manuel De Sica; ed, Michael Hesser; art d, Francy Bertagnolli.

Comedy/Drama   **(PR:C-O   MPAA:NR)**

FORTY SQUARE METERS OF GERMANY***   (1986, Ger.) 80m Baser–Studio Hamburg/Filmverlag der Autoren c (40 M DEUTSCHLAND)

Ozay Fecht *(Turna)*, Yaman Okay *(Dursun)*, Deir Gokgol, Mustapha Gupinar.

This emotionally and psychologically exhausting film, set almost completely inside the confines of a one-room apartment measuring approximately 40 square meters (thus the descriptive title), besides being a treatise on claustrophobia and loneliness, is also a revealing social document. Fecht plays a young Turkish newlywed swept away from her small village to the wonders of Europe by a migrant worker who had returned home to buy a wife. As the husband, Okay promises his new bride riches and excitement she could never find in her village. With these dreams in her mind, Fecht is willing to leave her family and friends in Turkey to live in Germany. However, once she is settled in their small apartment, her husband locks her in, never allowing her to leave and explore the things of which she has heard. To keep herself occupied, Fecht continuously scrubs the floor and hand-washes the laundry. A small window her only connection with the outside world, she spends hours gazing out of it in hope of relieving her boredom. She briefly makes contact with a small German girl who lives opposite her. The two communicate with hand signals and facial gestures, but the girl's mother pulls her away and closes the drapes. To further her feelings of isolation, Okay refuses to talk with Fecht beyond the most mundane subjects. He demands that his dinner be ready when he is hungry and that his wife have sex with him when the urge arises, an act in which Fecht takes no pleasure. At one point Okay promises to take his wife to a carnival so that she can finally leave the house, but when the day actually arrives he leaves to buy a paper, not returning until late in the day. Fecht has carefully dressed herself in colorful traditional clothing, only to sit on the edge of the bed waiting, her expression of happiness slowly turning to one of despair. Eventually, Fecht becomes pregnant, something that pleases her husband immensely, but only makes her imprisonment that much more unbearable. The film ends with Okay suffering an epileptic attack and dying when Fecht refuses to help him. His body lying in front of the door that means freedom to Fecht, she desperately struggles to move it. This done, she wanders out into the street, completely alone, and unable to understand a word of German, but feeling free for the first time in two years.

This first effort for Turkish-born director Baser won the Silver Leopard at the Locarno Film Festival and has garnered praise at the festivals where it has been shown. Baser has proven himself to be a competent director and storyteller, taking the flimsiest of material and minimal settings to produce a deeply moving film. Perhaps his biggest problem is not allowing his audience the chance to see Fecht in actual contact with the alien world of Europe, something for which viewers painstakingly wait, without being fulfilled. In a role that would be difficult for the most trained actress to tackle, Fecht—a singer by profession—is surprisingly good. Using the slightest of facial expressions and body movements, she effectively communicates the monumental despairs and few pleasures she experiences, without ever being boring. (In Turkish; English subtitles.)

d&w, Tevfik Baser; ph, Izzet Akay; m, Claus Bantzer; ed, Renate Merck; cos, Marina Heinrich.

Drama   **(PR:A   MPAA:NR)**

FOTOROMANZO†   (1986, It.) Gloria/Intra Film c (Trans: Picture Story)

Nino D'Angelo, Maria Chiara Sasso, Gabriele Villa, Cinzia De Ponti, Bruna Feirri, Pietro Tordi, Nuccia Fumo, Lucio Montanaro.

A meek Neapolitan poet follows the woman he loves to Milan, but still can't make her love him. He does become a success, though, when one of his poems is set to music and becomes a hit single.

d, Mariano Laurenti; w, Francesco Calabrese, Piero Regnoli, Mariano Laurenti (based on a story by Francesco Calabrese, Nino D'Angelo); ph, Federico Lanni; m, Franco Chiaravalle, Nino D'Angelo; ed, Carlo Broglio.

Comedy/Drama   **(PR:C   MPAA:NR)**

FOUETTE***   (1986, USSR) 99m Lenfilm/Sovexportfilm c

Ekaterina Maximova, Vladimir Vasiliev, Natalia Bolshakova, Valentin Graft, Aristarkh Livanov.

Described by some as a Russian version of the 1977 U.S. film THE TURNING POINT, FOUETTE's title comes from a ballet move in which a dancer makes a whipping movement with an upraised leg. Maximova, a prima ballerina in her late forties, is preparing to dance her last role. In a sense, she is also getting ready for a psychological fouette, as her career will soon take a sudden and unfamiliar switch. In learning to cope with the upcoming change in her life's course, Maximova must fight against problems raised by her husband, her choreographer, and her own inner demons. For her final appearance, Maximova wants her company to perform a new experimental ballet based on Goethe's "Faust." Though her decision causes a stir with the ballet company's executive board, Maximova manages to push her choice through. At the film's end, this strong and determined woman has learned several things about life and her place in the world.

Maximova, a lead dancer with the Bolshoi Ballet, makes her screen acting debut here with a competent performance. Though the story's dramatic structure is confusing at some points, Maximova is effective enough to compensate for this weakness. FOUETTE's dance sequences are the real highlights, a neat balance between classical ballet (including highlights from "Swan Lake") and more avant-garde work. Scenes of dream and fantasy are imaginatively staged at seaside locations, employing large tarlatan capes to heighten this mystical imagery. Because of the underlying spiritual nature of FOUETTE, there was some difficulty in getting the project approved by Soviet officials. The real-life fight to get this film made closely paralleled the arguments portrayed in the office of the ballet boardroom and the cinematic re-creation caused something of a scandal in the Soviet motion picture industry. Another problem arose with the choice of "Mephisto" as Maximova's consummating piece. Again the issue of spirituality rankled the approval committee and a replacement was demanded with the logic that any work would easily substitute. The filmmakers refused to accept this "a ballet is a ballet" thinking and fought back until their choice was finally allowed. Despite the troubles, FOUETTE had a smooth production schedule, and completed shooting in a surprisingly short three weeks.

d, Vladimir Vasilyev, Boris Yermolayev; w, Boris Yermolayev, Savra Kulish; ph, Valery Mironov; m, Anatoly Balchev, Oleg Karavaichuk; art d, Mikahail Sheglov, Yelizaveta Urlina.

Drama/Dance   **(PR:O   MPAA:NR)**

FOURTEEN NUMARA†   (1986, Turkey) 86m Hakan c (Trans: Number 14)

Hakan Balamir, Serpil Cakmakli, Keriman Ulusoy, Bulent Bilgic.

An innocent country girl arrives in Istanbul from the countryside and becomes a prostitute. Her pimp is brutal and terrorizes her, and when her family sees her picture in a newspaper after a police raid, her brother sets out for the city with a gun to set things straight. The soiled heroine is seemingly rescued from her life of degradation by a good young man, but her maniacal pimp turns slasher and prevents her happiness. Interesting treatment of vice not usually seen from a Moslem country.

d&w, Sinan Cetin (based on a novel by Irfan Yalcin); ph, Cem Molvan; m, Baris Manco, Kurtalan Ekspres.

Drama   **(PR:O   MPAA:NR)**

FOXTRAP†   (1986, U.S./It.) 88m Realta-Po' Boy/Snizzlefritz c

Fred Williamson *(Thomas Fox)*, Chris Connelly *(John Thomas)*, Arlene Golonka *(Emily)*, Donna Owen *(Susan)*, Beatrice Palme *(Mariana)*, Cleo Sebastian *(Josie)*, Lela Rochon *(Lindy)*.

Fred Williamson's career has been in decline for years, ever since his heyday in early 1970s black exploitation pictures. In the last few years he has trod the path taken by so many slipping stars, to Italy, where having an English name that's your own is a real plus. Here Williamson flexes his directing muscle, in addition

to acting in this action film. Williamson plays a professional bodyguard/courier hired by Connelly to track down his niece, Owen, who disappeared in Rome. Williamson finally runs her down in Monte Carlo and forces her to return to Los Angeles with him. There he discovers that Connelly is not really Owen's father, but her pimp, who wants back information that she stole for blackmail purposes. Naturally, Williamson doesn't allow that to happen without a fight.

p&d, Fred Williamson; w, Aubrey K. Rattan (based on a story by Fred Williamson); ph, John Stephens, Steve Shaw (Luciano Vittori color); m, Patrizio Fariselli; ed, Giorgio Venturoli.

Crime/Action   **(PR:O   MPAA:R)**

FRANCESCA E MIA†   (1986, It.) Komika c (Trans: Francesca is Mine)

Monica Vitti, Pierre Malet, Corrado Pani, Manuela Gatti.

Vitti is a woman who has decided love is compromise, in her case meaning that she shares her husband with another woman. One day she witnesses a hit-and-run accident involving a young man who suffers amnesia. She takes care of him and they fall in love, though not happily. Vitti also cowrote the script for this effort.

p&d, Roberto Russo; w, Vincenzo Cerami, Monica Vitti, Roberto Russo (based on a story by Monica Vitti, Roberto Russo); ph, Franco Di Giacomo (Luciano Vittori Color); m, Tullio De Piscopo; ed, Alberto Gallitti.

Drama   **(PR:C   MPAA:NR)**

FRANZA†   (1986, Aust.) 100m Heinz Scheiderbauer c

Elisabeth Trissenaar *(Franza)*, Gabriel Barilly *(Martin)*, Armin Muller-Stahl *(Dr. Jordan/Dr. Koerner)*, Gottfried John *(British Officer)*, Hilde Krahl, Jan Niklas.

Trissenaar tells her younger brother Barilly about how miserable her life is since she married a mean doctor after a whirlwind affair with a dashing British officer in 1945. Locations are the Austrian Alps and Egypt.

d, Xaver Schwarzenberger; w, Rolf Basedow, Consuleo Garcia (based on the novel *The Franza Case* by Ingeborg Bachmann); ph, Xaver Schwarzenberger; m, Bert Breit; ed, Ulrike Schwarzenberger; art d, Egon.

Drama   **(PR:C   MPAA:NR)**

FREE ENTERPRISE†   (1986, Aus.) B&D Productions

Jon Blake, Mark Hembrow, Nikki Coghill, Terry Donovan.

p, Geoff Burrows; d&w, John Dixon; ph, Keith Wagstaff.

FREE RIDE zero   (1986) 82m Galaxy International c

Gary Hershberger *(Dan Garten)*, Reed Rudy *(Greg)*, Dawn Schneider *(Jill Monroe)*, Peter DeLuise *(Carl)*, Brian MacGregor *(Elmer)*, Warren Berlinger *(Dean Stockwell)*, Mamie Van Doren *(Debby Stockwell)*, Babette Props *(Kathy)*, Anthony Charnota *(Vinnie Garbagio)*, Mario Marcelino *(Vito Garbagio)*, Frank Campanella *(Old Man Garbagio)*, Joe Tornatore *(Murray Garbagio)*, Ken Olfson *(Prof. Lennox)*.

Yet another entry in the seemingly endless series of rancid teenage sex comedies, this sorry excuse for entertainment stars the totally vapid Hershberger as an obnoxious prep-school brat who lies his way into a popular singles bar. In a desperate effort to impress an equally vapid young woman, Hershberger pretends that the flashy red sports car brought to the door by a valet is his. The trick works, and rather than reveal the truth to the woman, Hershberger sits her in the passenger seat and roars off for a joyride. The car really belongs to a trio of mobster brothers (Charnota, Marcelino, Tornatore) who have stashed $250,000 under the seat. The crooks take off after Hershberger, but he eludes them. The following morning, Hershberger discovers the cash and decides to hide both it and the car until things cool down. Action then shifts to life at Monroe Prep School. The usual bullies vs. cool kids conflicts dominate, and of course Hershberger is at odds with the Dean (Berlinger). Berlinger's lusty wife, Van Doren, happens to be the school nurse, and she constantly tries to seduce the student body. Meanwhile, Hershberger has decided to make the most of the fortune he has discovered. He uses the money to win friends, buy better grades, and bribe school officials. He also begins dating Schneider, daughter of the school's namesake. Eventually the mobsters catch up with the arrogant Hershberger, kidnap Schneider, and hold her hostage pending return of the cash. Hershberger meets with Charnota and when the mobster releases Schneider, Hershberger tosses the money toward a nearby fountain. Chaos erupts as $100 bills fly everywhere, and Hershberger makes good his escape.

This is about as bad as it gets. A stupid script combined with a wholly annoying cast makes for one tedious film—even by the supposed standards of this questionable genre. The characters are all the standard stereotypes: uptight administrators, bullies, nerds, blondes who take their clothes off every few minutes, and, of course, the ultra-cool dude who gets away with everything. As tiresome as the characters are, the stock offensive situations that pop up again and again are worse. These include the ultimate humiliation of the uptight administrator, the besting of the bullies, the lascivious leering at the naked blonde girls in the shower, the play-on-names gag (i.e., Dean Stockwell) and, of course, the ultimate trimumph of Mr. Cool. Unfunny, unimaginative, and unbelievably dumb, the only reason for this film's existence is that it can be used as evidence proving that 1950s cult figure Mamie Van Doren is alive and well and continuing to appear in the sort of film she did while in her prime.

p, Tom Boutross, Bassem Abdallah; d, Tom Trbovich; w, Ronald Z. Wang, Lee Fulkerson, Robert Bell (based on a story by Ronald Z. Wang); ph, Paul Lohmann (United Color); ed, Ron Honthaner; art d, Daniel Webster; set d, Joe Mirvis; spec eff, A&A Special Effects.

Comedy (PR:O MPAA:R)

FRENCH LESSON**½   (1986, Brit.) 90m Enigma–Goldcrest/WB c (GB: THE FROG PRINCE)

Jane Snowden (*Jenny*), Alexandre Sterling (*Jean-Philippe*), Jacqueline Doyen (*Mme. Peroche*), Raoul Delfosse (*Mons. Peroche*), Jeanne Herviale (*Mme. Duclos*), Francoise Brion (*Mme. Bourneuf*), Pierre Vernier (*Mons. Bourneuf*), Diana Blackburn (*Ros*), Oystein Wiik (*Niels*), Fabienne Tricottet (*Annie Bourneuf*), Jean-Marc Barr (*James*), Arabella Weir (*Zar*), Lucy Durham-Matthews (*Prissie*), Marc Andre Brunet (*Didier*), Brigitte Chamarande (*Dominique*), Catherine Berraine (*Chantel Peroche*), Andre Dumas (*Prevost*), Martine Ferriere (*Tante Billy*), Olivier Achard (*Claude*), Michele Gleizer (*Lucienne*), Paul Yvon Colpin (*Serge*), Hugette Faget (*Mme. Comte*), Bernard Rosselli (*Man on Train*), Serge Uzan (*Guard on Train*), Gilles Laurent (*Gilles*), Louis Leonet (*Resident*), Laurence Merchet, Manuel Collas (*Students*), Rene Urlreger, Alby Cullaz, Jean-Louis Chautemps, Eric Dervieu (*Dance Band*).

A moderately charming coming-of-age tale about a young British girl, Snowden, who takes classes at Paris' Sorbonne and boards with a conservative family in the French countryside. Somewhat shy and interested more in reading D.H. Lawrence than in dancing, Snowden resists the temptations of casual sex, hoping instead to find the right boy with whom to lose her virginity. Her brassy English friend, Blackburn, is a different case—ready and willing to hop under the covers with any French boy who comes along. In one of her classes, Snowden meets a charming and romantic Norwegian, Wiik, but their relationship never becomes physical. She is more interested in Sterling, a handsome young man who speaks halting English with a heavy French accent. She is charmed, but torn between her desire to sleep with him and her apprehension that he may not be the right one. Meanwhile, he tries his best to talk her into bed. He is angry when she says "No," and ecstatic when she finally says "Yes." She imposes one condition however; before Sterling can make love to her, he must be able to recite, in English, specific passages of "Romeo and Juliet." He refuses this test of love, and their relationship seems to be over. But at the last minute, as Snowden is about to board a Metro train amidst rush-hour crowds, Sterling recites Shakespeare's immortal words, an act that convinces Snowden that Sterling is her man. She then asks her Nordic friend if she may borrow his apartment, and he nobly obliges. The following morning Snowden goes off to class with "that certain glow" about her. Having slept with a French boy, she has now become completely initiated into the French way of life (a notion that has a rather disturbing subtext). As the rousing Edith Piaf song "Les Flons Flons du Bal" plays, Snowden walks down the narrow streets of Paris, radiant in her happiness. All the men she passes, young and old, are enraptured by her presence.

FRENCH LESSON tries hard. The script takes a likable young girl, locates her in Paris, surrounds her with romantic images (the usual shots of the Eiffel Tower, the banks of the Seine, the Louvre), and then introduces her to an equally likable French boy. The story proceeds at this pace for the first two-thirds of its length, with Snowden stuck between her interest in Wiik and her fascination with Sterling. The film takes a downward turn, however, when she makes her decision, and it is difficult to comprehend why she picks the sex-starved and egotistical Sterling rather than the more ideally romantic Wiik. When Snowden has the nerve to borrow Wiik's apartment (kicked out of his own place, he heads for the Cinematheque to see a Josef von Sternberg film) in order to sleep with Sterling, she comes across more as a manipulator than as a friend. One's sentiment is not with Snowden and Sterling, but with the ill-treated Wiik. Perhaps this is director Gilbert's intention, for he seems to sympathize with the character throughout the film (it is Wiik who tells Snowden the story of "The Frog Prince" and his test of love, and he is also a diehard movie devotee who praises von Sternberg and calls Louis Malle's ZAZIE DANS LE METRO a film of genius). For some inexplicable reason, FRENCH LESSON takes place in 1961, though the film has the look and feel of present-day France. No reference is made to the 1960s, and the sexual attitudes seem no different than those of today, leading one to wonder what the point is. The film's executive producer was David Puttnam, the man behind CHARIOTS OF FIRE and THE KILLING FIELDS. He has since emigrated to Hollywood to become the head of Columbia Studios. (Released in Britain in 1985 as THE FROG PRINCE; see the MPG 1986 Annual.)

p, Iain Smith; d, Brian Gilbert; w, Brian Gilbert, Posy Simmonds (based on the story "The Frog Prince" by Posy Simmonds); ph, Clive Tickner (Eastmancolor); m, Enya Ni Bhraonain; ed, Jim Clark; prod d, Anton Furst; cos, Judy Moorcroft; makeup, Tommie Manderson.

Romance Cas. (PR:C MPAA:PG)

FRIDAY THE 13TH PART VI: JASON LIVES*   (1986) 87m Terror, Inc./ PAR c

Thom Mathews (*Tommy Jarvis*), Jennifer Cooke (*Megan*), David Kagen (*Sheriff Garris*), Kerry Noonan (*Paula*), Renee Jones (*Sissy*), Tom Fridley (*Cort*), C.J. Graham (*Jason Voorhees*), Darcy DeMoss (*Nikki*), Vincent Guastaferro (*Deputy Rick Cologne*), Tony Goldwyn (*Darren*), Nancy McLoughlin (*Lizbeth*), Ron Palillo (*Allen Hawes*), Alan Blumenfeld (*Larry*), Matthew Faison (*Stan*), Ann Ryerson (*Katie*), Whitney Rydbeck (*Roy*), Courtney Vickery (*Nancy*), Bob Larkin (*Martin*), Michael Nomad (*Officer Pappas*), Wallace Merck (*Burt*), Roger Rose (*Steven*), Cynthia Kania (*Annette*), Tommy Nowell (*Tyen*), Justin Nowell (*Billy*), Sheri Levinsky (*Bus Monitor*), Temi Epstein (*Little Girl*), Turas O'Har (*Little Boy*).

Just before being dismembered in this, the sixth entry in one of the most revolting film series ever made, an alcoholic grave-digger quips, "Some folks have a

strange idea of entertainment." Hear, hear. FRIDAY THE 13TH PART VI: JASON LIVES maintains the same depressing body-count formula to which the previous films adhered, but this time writer-director McLoughlin, who is new to the series, adds a refreshing (relatively speaking, of course) element—self-parody.

This one begins as Mathews, the troubled teen who dispatched the last two Jasons, goes with his friend Palillo (remember the obnoxious Horshack in TV's "Welcome Back Kotter"? Same guy.) to the killer's grave. Although there seems to be a bit of confusion over which Jason is resurrected in this film (is it the one killed in Part IV, or the "new" Jason killed in Part V?), Mathews intends to dig up Jason's corpse and cremate it, thus ensuring that the unstoppable killer can never return. Once the corpse is uncovered, however, Mathews goes into a rage and skewers it with a metal rod. Guess what? Suddenly lightning strikes not once, but twice, and brings the corpse back to life. The resurrected Jason immediately

kills the annoying Palillo—the only justifiable murder in the entire series—and then goes after Mathews, who manages to escape. This leaves Jason (Graham) to kill a couple of camp counselors (what else?) on their way to his beloved Camp Crystal where they were to greet lots of innocent little grade-schoolers (Jason fodder). Sheriff Kagen thinks Mathews is nuts, of course, and tells him to get lost, but when word of the new murders arrives he assumes the crazy kid is killing people in a warped effort to convince him that Jason is indeed back. While Kagen tracks down and arrests Mathews, Jason kills people right and left, and by the time Kagen's teenage daughter Cooke (who has taken a fancy to Mathews) breaks Mathews out of jail, Jason has wiped out another entire batch of teenage camp counselors, *and* sheriff Kagen himself.

Mathews finally confronts Jason after all the characters over the age of 10 have been murdered (save Cooke). In a fight in the lake, Mathews manages to lasso Jason around the neck with a chain connected to a heavy rock. The hockey-masked killing machine finds himself stuck underwater in the very same lake where he drowned so many years before (consult the original FRIDAY THE 13TH for more details). Cooke herself administers the coup de grace by cutting Jason's throat with the propeller of an outboard motor. But guess what? Jason survives to slaughter another day.

From the parody of the classic James Bond looking-down-the-gun-barrel credits sequence (in an iris effect, Jason strolls in, turns to the camera, and pulls his machete) to the dozens of little self-conscious jokes sprinkled throughout, PART VI: JASON LIVES proves to be a little different. In sharp contrast to PART V, which had the most gratuitous nudity in the series, there are no female teenagers showing off their bosoms in PART VI. The violence is also toned down considerably, and with only a few bloody moments, most of the killing is suggested or done offscreen. The visual style of this film is superior as well. Departing from the cheap, grainy look of the first five films, cinematographer Kranhouse does a beautiful slickly professional job here, with some very accomplished camera moves and some good underwater footage. In addition to the humor and the technical savvy, the biggest difference between this film and the five before it is that the characters are actually allowed to live long enough for the audience to develop some sort of empathy toward them. Some of these teenagers are downright likable, and we don't want to see them get killed. That element, more than any other, is a genuine breakthrough for this series. Be that as it may, however, FRIDAY THE 13TH PART VI: JASON LIVES is still a member of the same heinous family of films kept alive by the greed of Paramount Pictures, which continues to exploit viewers' rankest instincts. The advertising flyers sent to videotape rental stores contain some revolting promotional ideas, including one which urges store owners to "Hold a 'Body Count Contest' to guess how many people Jason kills in all six FRIDAY THE 13TH films," and then, "Put all of the correct entries into a bloody hat and draw a grand prize winner . . ." If that doesn't appeal to you how about, "Dress your sales staff up like Jason's victims. Use bloody T-shirts, horror makeup, and novelty devices like the knife-through-head toy, etc." Unfortunately, these ideas will probably drive away a store's normal customers and attract only the demented goons who have faithfully supported this idiocy through all six installments. This one made over $9.4 million in rentals—less than the others, but still a solid hit—so you can bet there'll be a PART VII. Faded rock idol Alice Cooper was kind enough to supply some totally forgettable songs including: "He's Back (The Man Behind the Mask)" (Alice Cooper, Tom Kelly, Kane Roberts, performed by Cooper), "Teenage Frankenstein," "Hard Rock Summer" (Cooper, Roberts, performed by Cooper), "Animal" (Jefferey Spry, C.J. Spry, performed by Felony).

p, Don Behrns; d&w, Tom McLoughlin; ph, Jon R. Kranhouse (Metrocolor); m, Harry Manfredini; ed, Bruce Green; prod d, Joseph T. Garrity; art d, Pat Tagliaferro; set d, Jerie Kelter; cos, Maria Mancuso; spec eff, Martin Becker; m/l, Alice Cooper, Tom Kelly, Kane Roberts, Jeffery Spry, C.J. Spry; makeup, Chris Swift, Brian Wade.

Horror   Cas.   (PR:O MPAA:R)

FRINGE DWELLERS, THE***   (1986, Aus.) 98m Fringe Dwellers–Ozfilm/
                                                             Atlantic c

Kristina Nehm *(Trilby)*, Justine Saunders *(Mollie)*, Bob Maza *(Joe)*, Kylie Belling *(Noonah)*, Denis Walker *(Bartie)*, Ernie Dingo *(Phil)*, Malcolm Silva *(Charlie)*, Marlene Bell *(Hannah)*, Michelle Torres *(Audrena)*, Michele Miles *(Blanchie)*, Kath Walker *(Eva)*, Bill Sandy *(Skippy)*, Maureen Watson *(Rene)*, Robert Ugle *(Tim)*, Alan Dargin *(Bruce)*, Terry Thompson *(Horrie)*, Annie Saward *(May)*, Dianne Eden *(Matron)*, Wilkie Collins *(Dr. Symons)*, Lisa-Jane Stockwell *(Nurse McCarthy)*, Sandra Lehane *(Nurse Creswell)*, Theresa Stafford *(Schoolgirl)*, Leo Wockner *(Stockman)*, Wilf Campagnoni *(Bert)*, David Clendinning *(Headmaster)*, Noanie Wood *(Miss Simmons)*, Gabrielle Lambrose *(Mrs. Henwood)*.

The plight of the aborigine has long been a preoccupation of Australian filmmakers, though usually they are represented as mystical types whose profound knowledge of the land is in danger of being lost. Here Bruce Beresford takes a different tack, returning to his native land between shooting KING DAVID and CRIMES OF THE HEART to put to film a novel by an aborigine woman. Nehm is the central figure, the beautiful daughter of Saunders and Maza. She and her two siblings live in a corrugated tin shack on the edge of town, part of a shantytown of aborigines who have formed a tight and supportive community despite grinding poverty and racism. Saunders persuades her family to move from their shack to a new house in a middle-class suburb, where they soon realize they don't fit among neighbors who are alternately condescending and cruel. Soon swarms of relatives, distant and close, show up, and aborigine custom demands that they be taken in, again depriving Nehm of her own room. Maza gambles away the rent, then disappears, and Nehm finds herself pregnant by her cattle-drover boy friend, Dingo. She refuses to let the baby condemn her to a life of poverty, and in an ambiguous and confusing scene, the baby conveniently dies. Ultimately, Nehm leaves her family to strike out on her own in the big city. Well

crafted throughout, the film benefits from excellent performances by all concerned, particularly Nehm and Saunders (whom many critics likened to Jane Darwell in THE GRAPES OF WRATH). Beresford's directorial style has always favored actors over sweeping settings, and while this killed KING DAVID, it keeps FRINGE DWELLERS right where it belongs, among the characters.

p, Sue Milliken; d, Bruce Beresford; w, Bruce Beresford, Rhoisin Beresford (based on the novel by Nene Gare); ph, Don McAlpine (Eastmancolor); m, George Dreyfus; ed, Tim Wellburn; prod d, Herbert Pinter; art d, Stewart Way; cos, Kerri Barnett; makeup, Viv Mepham.

Drama   (PR:A-C MPAA:PG)

FROM BEYOND**½   (1986) 85m Empire c

Jeffrey Combs *(Crawford Tillinghast)*, Barbara Crampton *(Dr. Katherine McMichaels)*, Ted Sorel *(Dr. Edward Pretorious)*, Ken Foree *(Bubba Brownlee)*, Carolyn Purdy-Gordon *(Dr. Roberta Bloch)*, Bunny Summers *(Hester Gilman)*, Bruce McGuire *(Jordan Fields)*, Del Russel *(Ambulance Driver)*, Dale Wyatt *(Paramedic)*, Karen Christenfeld *(Nurse)*, Andy Miller *(Patient in Straitjacket)*, John Leamer *(Shock Technician)*, Regina Bleesz *(Bondage Girl)*.

Stuart Gordon, whose debut RE-ANIMATOR was the sleeper horror hit of 1985, returns again to the fever-dreamlike stories of H.P. Lovecraft for his source, and

once again the author's work is done a disservice by the movies. The film opens in the typical big scary house, where strange sounds and lights are seen from the highest window. Inside, Combs is making the final adjustments on a strange machine, the centerpiece of which is a purple glass globe and four long tuning-fork arms that reach into the air. He flips a switch and suddenly the air is alive with jellyfish-like creatures and something like flying eels, one of which bites a chunk out of his cheek. He flips the machine off and they disappear. Combs runs downstairs and fetches his mentor, Sorel, and they return to turn on the machine again. The same creatures appear again, joined by a larger one that bites off

Sorel's head. Combs runs terrified out of the house and is tossed into a mental ward, suspected of murder. He tells his story to psychiatrists Purdy-Gordon and Crampton and to the district attorney, who remands him to Crampton's custody, over Purdy-Gordon's objections. Along with policeman and former football player Foree (known to horror buffs from DAWN OF THE DEAD), she takes Combs back to the house. He gets the machine running again and shows them the creatures, warning his guests not to move or they will attack. The machine is designed to resonate the vestigial "third-eye," the pineal gland, and open the senses to that which lies "beyond"; it also causes sexual excitation as every sense becomes heightened. Combs tells Foree and Crampton, "Five senses just weren't enough for him, he wanted more." Unexpectedly, Sorel appears along with the creatures and attacks, his shape changing at will. Combs manages to turn off the machine again. Combs wants to destroy the machine now that he has proven himself innocent. Foree just wants to leave, but Crampton, excited by the new things she has seen and felt, wants to repeat the experiment in the morning.

As each returns to their rooms, they are troubled by bad dreams, and Crampton wakes up and goes back up to the Resonator. She turns it on again and Sorel reappears, this time an oozing mass. Combs and Foree awake and try to reach the switch, but Sorel has Crampton and threatens to kill her if they go near the switch. The two men run to the basement to cut the power, but an enormous lamprey eel guards the room. The two men fight it, and it starts to devour Combs when Foree reaches the fuse box and pulls out the wires. Instantly Sorel disappears upstairs, and the eel vanishes, dropping Combs naked and hairless on the floor. Foree now demands that they leave, but Crampton insists on staying. While he goes to get the van, she explores Sorel's private bondage room, and she begins putting on some erotic leather gear she finds. When Foree returns, he finds her trying to make love to the unconscious Combs. She tries to seduce Foree as well, but he tells her he is leaving. She plans to try the experiment again, saying she can control it, but she is clearly out of control. Suddenly the machine turns itself on, and when the three (the sound awakens Combs) run upstairs, Sorel is there in yet another form. He seizes Crampton and drags her toward him, while flying creatures attack Foree and reduce him to scraps of meat hanging on bone. Crampton manages to grab a fire extinguisher and use it to short out the Resonator, and once again Sorel vanishes.

The two survivors are taken to the hospital, where a bitter Purdy-Gordon decides that Crampton is insane and orders electroshock. Before they can do it, though, Combs regains consciousness, this time with his pineal gland protruding through the front of his head on a stalk. He kills Purdy-Gordon by sucking her brains out through her eye (he was to spit the eye out, but that had to be cut to get the film an R rating), and escapes. Crampton also escapes and makes it back to the house first. She puts a bomb with a five-minute timer on the resonator and tries to leave, but Combs arrives and chains her up in the bondage room. He is about to suck out her brains when she bites off his pineal gland, which actually helps. She works free of her chains but is again confronted by Sorel in the upstairs lab. He begins to devour her, raving about the pleasure of consuming another mind, but Combs arrives and begins taunting the monster. Sorel twists his head off, then returns to Crampton, but now Combs is in the "beyond" too, and he appears out of Sorel's body, fighting him. Crampton escapes his clutches and dives out a window just as the bomb goes off and destroys everything.

Clearly now, though, she is totally unhinged (in the proper fashion of Lovecraft story survivors).

The concepts are fascinating, and the one line that everyone keeps repeating is "I want to see more," but what a pity that there aren't any characters. Crampton acts so unprofessionally from the first time we see her that she can never be accepted as a well-known psychiatrist. Combs has little to do but issue ignored warnings and start the machine until his pineal gland sprouts, but his background, except that he has a Ph.D in physics, is never mentioned. These reservations aside, FROM BEYOND is a well-constructed, atmospheric drama offering something unique to the horror genre. The creatures that populate the film are totally new, and the notion that they swim around us all the time—as oblivious to us as we are to them—is effectively creepy. One problem inherent in all monster movies is the fact that once shown, a monster is never so scary as when it is all in the imagination. Here the problem is overcome by having the chief creature, Sorel, change his appearance every time he turns up, and even shift his shape while we watch. The effects are good in the heads-splitting-open-with-lots-of-goo style, and they were created by four separate special effects teams, each trying to outdo the others. Producer Yuzna was quoted as saying, "In this film, there is enough stuff for three movies! It never stops. The audience will go crazy for it!" Director Gordon appeared well on his way to becoming the Roger Corman of the decade with this, his third film of the year, shot in Italy on the surprisingly low budget—considering the special effects—of only $4.5 million. Shooting took place over a 40-day period in the old-dark-house set that had been constructed on the old Dino DeLaurentiis soundstages (Empire had purchased them for $20 million) originally used for Gordon's yet-unreleased feature, DOLLS. The film has some of the same sexual perversity that made RE-ANIMATOR so lively, though here it is much more intelligent and integral to the plot—the whole notion of "I want to see more" is directly linked to the jaded sexuality of Sorel, and everyone else falls into the same trap, particularly Crampton. Whatever the merits of the film, though, it still hasn't captured the essential quality of gnawing uneasiness giving way to mind-numbing terror found in so much of Lovecraft's best work, and Gordon has announced that he plans to direct another adaptation of the author's work. Maybe this time he'll get it right.

p, Brian Yuzna; d, Stuart Gordon; w, Dennis Paoli, Brian Yuzna, Stuart Gordon (based on the story "From Beyond" by H.P. Lovecraft); ph, Mac Ahlberg (Technicolor); m, Richard Band; ed, Lee Percy; prod d, Giovanni Natalucci; set d, Robert Burns; cos, Angee Beckett; spec eff, John Buechler, Anthony Doublin, John Naulin, Mark Shostrom; makeup, Giancarlo Del Brocco; stunts, Remo De Angelis.

Horror   **Cas.**   **(PR:O MPAA:R)**

FROSTY ROADS†   (1986, Iran) 87m Cooperative Group c

Ali Nassirian, Hamid Jebeli, Majid Nassiri, Esmail Mohammadi.

A slowly paced vision of the struggle between life and death in a poor peasant village. The film's climactic point comes when a schoolteacher, one of his students, and a local laborer make a dangerous journey to the city for some much-needed medicine.

d, Massood Jafari Jozani; w, Seyamak Taghipoor; m, Kambiz Roshan Ravan; ed, Davood Yosefian.

Drama   **(PR:A MPAA:NR)**

FRUHLINGSSINFONIE   (SEE: SPRING SYMPHONY, 1986, Ger.)

FULANINHA†   (1986, Braz.) 95m Encontro-Ipe Artes-Embrafilme-Skylight Cinema-Nadia/Embrafilme c

Mariana de Moraes *(Fulaninha)*, Claudio Marzo *(Bruno)*, Katia D'Angelo *(Rose)*, Zaira Zambelli *(Sulamita)*, Roberto Bonfim *(Canela)*, Jose de Abreu *(Jardel)*, Flavio Sao Thiago *(Herminio)*, Paulo Vilaca *(Armando)*, Marcos Palmeira *(Rubinho)*, Nelson Dantas *(Doorman)*, Gilson Moura *(Police Inspector)*, Ivan Setta *(Officer)*, Mario Petraglia *(Sabonete)*, Pascoal Vilaboim *(S. Antonio)*, Mario Tupinamba *(Camarao)*.

The second of a proposed trio of autobiographical films from director Neves (the first was MUITO BRAZER in 1979). This comedy stars Marzo as a filmmaker who falls in love with Moraes, the teenage daughter of sexy widow D'Angelo, with whom Marzo has had an affair. Set entirely within one block of Prado Junior Street in Copacabana, the house in which Marzo's character lives is actually the home of director Neves. One song, "Fulaninha" (Paulhino da Viola, performed by Paulhino da Viola).

p, Paulo Thiago, Carlos Moletta; d, David Neves; w, David Neves, Haroldo Marinho Barbosa, Onezio Paiva, Paulo Thiago; ph, Antonio Penido (Eastmancolor); m, Sergio G. Saraceni; ed, Marco Antonio Cury; set d, Paulo Dubois; cos, Isabel Paranhos; m/l, Paulhino da Viola.

Comedy   **(PR:C-O MPAA:NR)**

FUTURE OF EMILY, THE†   (1986, Fr./Ger.) 107m Les Films du Losange-Helma Sanders Filmproduktion-Literarisches Colloquium-ZDF-BMI-FFA-Berliner Film forderung/Mainline c (FLUGEL UND FESSELN; L'AVENIR D'EMILIE)

Brigitte Fossey *(Isabelle)*, Hildegarde Knef [Neff] *(Paula)*, Ivan Desny *(Charles)*, Hermann Treusch *(Frederick)*, Camille Raymond *(Emilie)*, Mathieu Carriere.

Fossey is an actress who leaves her young daughter with her mother (Knef, in her first screen appearance since FEDORA in 1978) while she shoots a film in Berlin. After production is wrapped, she goes off to her parents' home in Normandy, her actor lover following, for a visit. Her mother also had dreams of being an actress,

but had to abandon them when she became pregnant with Fossey. Knef makes no bones about her resentment toward her daughter for now having the things she had prevented Knef from acquiring. They fight, scream, hug, and run the gamut of mother-daughter relationships, all while competing for the affections of Raymond, Fossey's daughter. The film's most interesting moment comes when Fossey, who made her debut at age 5 in FORBIDDEN GAMES (1953) finds Raymond burying a dead seagull on the beach. She tells her daughter that when she was her age, she made a movie about burying things, "and it was my best movie." Originally released in Europe in 1984. (In French; English subtitles [German version also available].)

p, Ursula Ludwig, Nicole Flipo; d, Helma Sanders-Brahms; w, Birgit Kleber; ph, Sacha Vierny (Eastmancolor); m, Jurgen Knieper; ed, Ursula West; art d, Jean-Michel Rugon, Rainer Schaper; cos, Rose Becker, Ulrike Schutte.

Drama   **(PR:C-O MPAA:NR)**

GALOSE STASTIA†   (1986, Czech.) 92m Koliba Studios (Trans: Overshoes of Happiness)

Jana Brejchova, Tereza Pokorna, Jose Luis Lopez Vazquez, Towje Kleiner, Marek Brodsky, Jan Hrusinsky, Vlado Muller, Julius Vasek, Karol Calik, Andrej Hryc, Valeria Kelescenyiova, Vladimir Javorsky.

d, Juraj Herz; w, Alex Koenigsmark, Juraj Herz (based on the story by Hans Christian Andersen); ph, Dodo Simoncic; m, Michal Kocab; ed, Jaromir Janacek; art d, Vladimir Labsky; cos, Jan Ruzicka.

GARDIEN DE LA NUIT†   (1986, Fr.) 104m Films du Passage–Forum–Ministry of Culture/Forum c (Trans: Night Guardian)

Jean-Philippe Ecoffey *(Yves)*, Aurelle Doazan *(Aurore)*, Nicolas Silberg *(Vaillant)*, Vincent Perez *(Armand)*, Olivier Perrier *(Lecoeur)*, Mireille Perrier *(Post Office Clerk)*, Philippe de Brugada *(Achard)*, Jean-Claude Frissung, Serge Giamberardino, Jean-Paul Bonnaire, Guy Pannequin, Anne Gautier, Francois Bourcier.

Ecoffey stars as a likable fellow who works for the police during the evening and steals cars by daylight. But this double life raises difficulties: the girl he loves by day doesn't know that he is a lawman by night, and, if that isn't bad enough, he becomes the subject of a police manhunt. In the lead is the energetic Ecoffey who has also been seen in the U.S. this year in CHARLOTTE AND LULU (released last year as L'EFFRONTEE). Limosin's first solo directorial effort.

p, Renaud Victor; d, Jean Pierre Limosin; w, Jean Pierre Limosin, Pascale Ferran; ph, Thierry Arbogast (Eastmancolor); m, Eric Tabuchi; ed, Claire Simon; art d, Laurence Brenguier.

Crime/Comedy   (PR:O MPAA:NR)

GAVILAN O PALOMA†   (1986, Mex.) 106m Peliculas Mexicanas c (Trans: Hawk or Dove)

Jose Jose [Jose Sosa] *(Himself)*, Gina Romand *(First Wife)*, Cristian Bach *(Anel)*, Jorge Ortiz de Pineda *(Jorge)*, Anel Norena, Manolo Norena, Fernando Hernandez *(Themselves)*.

One of Mexico's top singers, Jose Jose [Jose Sosa] plays himself in this biographical feature. Starting with his childhood of poverty, his romance with Bach, and his rapid rise to fame as a singer, the film goes on to detail the singer's slide into drugs, alcohol, and a poisonous marriage to Romand. Eventually his liver fails and he is placed in a hospital, critically ill. Bach comes to see him, the old spark flares up, and she and her love restore the singer to health. (Anel, the real person upon whom Bach's character is based, makes a cameo appearance.) This is all supposed to be true, but nobody's life could be this faithful to Hollywood cliche.

p, Carlos Amador; d, Alfredo Gurrola; w, Fernando Gaiano; ph, Javier Cruz; ed, Francisco Chiu.

Biography   (PR:C MPAA:NR)

GENESIS†   (1986, India/Fr./Bel./Switz.) 108m Mrinal Sen–Les Films de la Dreve–Cactus–Scarabee–French Ministry of Culture–French Ministry of Foreign Relations–Belgian Ministry of French Communications–Swiss Federal Department of the Interior–Maran Films–Film Four/Cactus c

Shabana Azmi *(The Woman)*, Naseeruddin Shah *(The Farmer)*, Om Puri *(The Weaver)*, M.K. Raina *(The Trader)*.

Another critically acclaimed film from India's "other" director, Mrinal Sen, whose most recent films have gained more favor abroad than those of his fellow countryman Satyajit Ray. Shah and Puri star as a pair of local workers who chose to leave their oppressed village and set up a new life outside established society. Their simple life is complicated, however, by the arrival of a beautiful woman, Azmi, who tempts both the men and causes them to become enemies, and by the trader Raina, who exploits the men for his own gain. For its Cannes Film Festival release this year, director Sen wrote: "Disinheriting the earth, the defiants among the poor build a new world. The new world thus built breeds virtue and vice. The virtue enriches the world and vice weakens its foundation. The exploiter reappears on the scene and what follows is History repeating itself." This international co-production was filmed in Hindi.

p, Marie Pascale Osterrieth; d, Mrinal Sen; w, Mrinal Sen, Mohit Chattopadhya (based on a story by Samaresh Basu); ph, Carlo Varini (Eastmancolor); m, Ravi Shankar; ed, Elizabeth Waelchli; prod d, Nitish Roy.

Drama   (PR:C MPAA:NR)

GENKAI TSUREZURE BUSHI†   (1986, Jap.) Toei (Trans: Ballad of Genkai-Sea)

Sayuri Yoshinaga, Aki Yashiro, Morio Kazama, Mitsuko Kusabue, Ken Iwabuchi, Sentaro Fushimi.

d, Masanobu Deme; w, Kazuo Kasahara, Kikuma Shimoizaka, Takeshi Hyodo; ph, Masahiko Iimura; m, Masaru Hoshi, Mark Goldenberg.

GERONIMA†   (1986, Arg.) 96m Cooperativa de Arte Cinematografico Avellaneda c

Luisa Calcumil *(Geronima)*, Patricio Contreras *(Morales)*, Mario Luciani *(El Turco)*, Ernesto Michel *(El Huinca)*, Rufino Muoz *(Eliseo)*.

A strange hybrid of video and 16mm, documentary and re-created footage blown up to 35mm detailing the death of an Indian woman from the Patagonia region of Argentina. Her flocks are killed in a blizzard, so the government steps in to take care of her. She and her children are placed in a hospital where her four children quickly contract whooping cough, two of them dying. This and other culture shocks drive Geronima around the bend, and she dies shortly thereafter in a mental hospital. The film combines the voice of the real Geronima during taped interviews with her doctor with scenes of Calcumil (herself a member of the same Mapuche tribe) as Geronima.

p, Luis Barberis; d, Raul Tosso; w, Carlos Paola, Raul Tosso (based on the book by Jorge Pellegrini); ph, Carlos Torlaschi; m, Arnaldo di Pace, Aime Paine; ed, Fernando Guariniello, Ulises Francezon, Juan Jose Arhancet.

Docu-drama   (PR:A MPAA:NR)

GETTING EVEN*½   (1986) 89m AGH/American Distribution Group c (AKA: HOSTAGE: DALLAS)

Edward Albert *(Taggar)*, Audrey Landers *(Paige Starsen)*, Joe Don Baker *(King Kenderson)*, Rod Pilloud *(Doc)*, Billy Streater *(Ryder)*, Blue Deckert *(Kurt)*, Don Shackelford *(Roone)*, Caroline Williams *(Molly)*.

Albert is an oil company magnate who stages a raid deep into Afghanistan to steal a secret new nerve gas from the Russians. His company has contracted with the government to come up with an antidote to the gas, which has the unusual property of growing without dissipating and eating the flesh of human beings. Progress on the antidote is slow, so the government sends beautiful lady agent Landers to check on things. She turns out to be an former lover of Albert, and it isn't long before they're at it again. Meanwhile, Albert's chief business rival, Baker, is so desperate for money that he steals the gas and threatens to drop it on Dallas unless Albert personally coughs up $50 million. Needless to say, crime does not pay and Dallas is not obliterated, thanks to some impressive helicopter stunts.

While hardly a well-crafted action film, this effort does manage to create some tension despite the wooden performances of Albert and Landers. Baker is a likable villain, but his character's notion of threatening to destroy Dallas is just colossally stupid. What redeems the picture is the final helicopter chase sequence among the skyscrapers of Dallas. While the film did little business theatrically, it seems bound for a long video life.

p, J. Michael Liddle; d, Dwight H. Little; w, M. Phil Senini, Eddie Desmond; ph, Peter Lyons Collister (CFI Color); m, Christopher Young; ed, Charles Bornstein; prod d, Richard James; set d, Derek Hill; spec eff, Jack Bennett, Jack Bennett, Jr.; makeup, Larry Aeschlimann.

Action   Cas.   (PR:O MPAA:R)

GHAME AFGHAN†   (1986, Switz.) 90m Europa c (Trans: The Tragedy of the Afghan)

Aamir Farid, Jawed Babur, Bushra Ejaz, Hukun Jana Abai, Anita Gul, Zar Khan, Muhamad Asam, Muhamad Yuesuf, Besmilla, Silvia Silva.

The introduction of fictional elements into a documentary is always a dubious proposition because the line between what the filmmaker has created and what is real is given to manipulation and to the passing off of propaganda as truth. The Swiss, paragons of neutrality, are for some reason the greatest practitioners of this class of film. Here they turn their cameras on an Afghan family who find themselves dragged into the war then forced to flee to Pakistan, where the squalid life in the refugee camps destroys what is left of the clan.

p, Mark M. Rissi; d, Zmarai Kasi, Mark M. Rissi; w, Zmarai Kasi; ph, Werner Schneider; m, Malek Salam, Mark M. Rissi; ed, Evelyne von Rabenau.

Docu-drama   (PR:A-C MPAA:NR)

GHOST WARRIOR   (SEE: SWORDKILL, 1984 Films, MPG Vol. IX)

GILSODOM*½   (1986, S. Korea) 97m Hwa Chun Trading c

Kim Ji Mi *(Hwayong)*, Sin Song-Il *(Tongjin)*, Han Ji-Il *(Soktschol)*, Kim Ji-Yong *(Tuknam)*, Lee Sang-A *(Hwayong as a Girl)*, Kim Jong Sok *(Tongjin as a Young Man)*, Kim Ki Ju *(Tongjin's Father)*, Kim Bok Hi *(Tongjin's Mother)*, Jon Moo-Song *(Hwayong's Husband)*.

In 1983, some 30 years after the end of the Korean War, a unique event in television history had consequences well beyond the scope of anyone's imagination. In association with the Red Cross, KBS-TV undertook a campaign to unite relatives separated by the war, broadcasting descriptions of missing people as well as showing the often heart-rending family reunions. This series of highly emotional programs was viewed by close to 90 percent of the country's population, in addition to capturing much international attention. GILSODOM is a fictional account of one of those reunions, an eloquent statement that explains why the past is sometimes best left buried. Kim is a Korean housewife who had lost her illegitimate son during the war. After viewing the program, her understanding husband urges Kim to see if she can locate her now-grown child. In flashback Kim recalls the events leading up to this tragic incident. In flashback Kim recalls the events leading up to this tragic incident. After her real parents die from an illness that is sweeping the country, Lee (playing Kim as a young girl) is adopted by another couple. These benefactors have a boy, Kim Jong Sok, who is Lee's age. Though they risk parental disapproval, the two teenagers fall in love and begin an affair. When Lee becomes pregnant, she is sent to live with an aunt. The war further separates the young lovers, and Lee later gives birth in the town of Gilsodom. Though she and Kim Jong Sok try to connect, their efforts are fruitless. Later, when her music teacher is arrested for illegal activities, Lee is taken in as his accomplice and jailed for seven years. She loses touch with her son, who ends up in an orphanage. In the meantime, Kim Jong Sok becomes a beggar, then marries a blind woman who helps him forget the past.

Flashing to the present day, the adult Kim accidentally runs into her old lover (now played by Sin) at the television station. After exchanging stories the two realize that they have traveled divergent paths over the years. Despite this uncomfortable gap, Kim and Sin agree to work together to find their boy. Having seen a tape of someone who conceivably could be their child, Kim and Sin drive out to meet him. Both are shocked by what they see. The man they encounter is a brutal, drunken oaf who lives with his family in a ramshackle hut. There are indications he might very well be the person Kim and Sin have been searching for, but to make sure, the three take a blood test. The results show strong evidence that he could be their offspring, but Kim demands to know if the test is 100 percent accurate. When the doctor replies no, Kim decides not to accept the man as her son. Putting this painful episode behind her, Kim returns to her husband and children, knowing that they are her one and only family.

Kim Ji Mi is excellent in a role that requires her to experience a gamut of highly charged emotions. Her performance is remarkable, a studied portrait of a woman able to mask deep pain. The supporting cast matches her well, and Lee and Kim Jong Sok do a fine job in the flashback sequences. For the most part, director Im develops his film with sensitivity, gradually building scenes as he lets the audience experience Kim's feelings and, in particular, her disappointment and denial at the story's end, a portrayal that touches the heart without exploiting its inherent anguish. The story drags slightly when Kim and Sin finally meet the man who could be their son, as Im protracts scenes a bit longer than need be. This is, however, just a minor blemish on an otherwise sensitive and often moving work. For its tender dealing with an unusual subject, GILSODOM was awarded the Getz Peace Prize at the 1986 Chicago International Film Festival.

p, Lee Woan-Ho; d, Im Kwon-Taek; w, Song Kil-Han; ph, Jong Il-Song; m, Kim Jong-Kil; ed, Park Soon Dok; set d, Kim Yoo Joon.

Drama   **(PR:O MPAA:NR)**

GINGA-TETSUDO NO YORU†   (1986, Jap.) Asahi Newspaper-TV
Asahi-Nippon Herald (Trans: The Night Train for the Milky Way)

d, Gisaburo Sugii; w, Minoru Betsuyaku (based on the novel by Kenji Miyazawa); ph, Haruomi Hosono; m, Mihoko Mabe.

GINGER & FRED*   (1986, It./Fr./Ger.) 126m
P.E.A.-Revcom-Stella-RAI 1/MGM-UA c

Giulietta Masina *(Amelia Bonetti [Ginger])*, Marcello Mastroianni *(Pippo Botticella [Fred])*, Franco Fabrizi *(Show Host)*, Frederick Von Ledenburg [Ledebur] *(Admiral Aulenti)*, Martin Maria Blau *(Assistant Director)*, Toto Mignone *(Toto)*, Augusto Poderosi *(Transvestite)*, Francesco Casale *(Mafioso)*, Frederick Von Thun [Frederich Thun] *(Kidnaped Industrialist)*, Jacques Henri Lartigue *(Brother Gerdamo)*, Ezio Marano *(Writer)*, Antoine Saint Jean *(Bandaged Man)*, Antonio Iuorio *(Television Inspector)*, Barbar Scoppa *(Pretty Journalist)*, Elisabetta Flumeri *(Journalist)*, Salvatore Billa *(Gable Double)*, Jean Michel Antoine, Antonio Lurio, Nanda Pucci Negri, Laurentina Guidotti, Elena Cantarone.

Produced by an international consortium of companies, GINGER AND FRED is a movie that could have been great, but isn't. It has a little bit of almost every film Fellini ever worked on, from VARIETY LIGHTS to FELLINI'S ROMA to 8½ to LA DOLCE VITA. The movie takes almost an hour in getting started and

only comes to life once the two leads are reunited. Masina (Fellini's wife and star of LA STRADA and THE NIGHTS OF CABIRIA, both Oscar winners as Best Foreign Film) is a widow with a large family. She lives in the north where she runs a small business. Many years ago, she and Mastroianni had been a moderately successful dance team who emulated their idols, Fred Astaire and Ginger Rogers. (Rogers sued for $8 million, claiming that this movie damaged her reputation.) They have not seen each other for many decades, and when a tacky TV show

called "We Are Proud to Present" calls for them both to be brought together on the national airwaves, they accept. The TV show is a satire of such things as "Real People" and "That's Incredible," and this particular segment will have such diverse guests as the aforementioned geriatric dance team, a troupe of midget Iberian dancers, celebrity lookalikes for Ronald Reagan, Telly Savalas, and Clark Gable, a hunger striker, a fallen-away priest who will marry on the stage, an old navy hero, a Mafia chief, a man who has invented edible panties that are laced with vitamins, et al.

Masina arrives at a typically chaotic Italian train station and is whisked to a noisy hotel to await the arrival of her former partner. Mastroianni, an aging roue who has spent some time in an institution after having a breakdown, has also been the owner of a prosperous dance school and, later, a door-to-door book salesman. It feels like forever until Masina finds Mastroianni; she first meets all the bizarre characters who will also be on the show, and must deal with the TV production people. She is eager to see her once-handsome partner and is shocked when she finds him in the next room, snoring so loudly that he vibrates the walls. Masina has taken the job because it might be fun, because she is lonely, and because she'd hoped that some semblance of her partner's charm and good looks may have remained. They haven't. Mastroianni looks, sounds, and dresses in the way the real-life Fellini does, right down to the cape and thin, flowing white hair. As the story develops, we learn that Masina and Mastroianni never really were much of a dance team. Rather, they were the first of the celebrity imitators (like the hundreds of Elvis impressionists who continue to haunt the U.S.), and their

act was hardly more than a direct steal of Astaire and Rogers. They watch as the other "acts" have their moments, and now it's time for them to perform. Just as they are about to begin, there is a power failure, which Mastroianni, unsure of himself, thinks may be an omen. He considers getting away before they (meaning he) make fools of themselves. But they take their cue and step forward, she in a glimmering evening dress and he in sleek formal dress. While dancing, he suffers a leg cramp but, troupers to the end, they manage to get through their version of Irving Berlin's "Cheek to Cheek" to heavy mitting and a beg-off from the crowd (i.e., a big hand and a "thank you very much but that's all we can do"). Thus the picture closes on their triumphant, and what must be their final, performance.

Intellectuals may read more into the story than was intended (as so often has been done with Fellini). If we take it as a simple story of two people who never played because of more than a third-rate nature and who have now been given their place in the sun, that's enough. It's charming, weird, funny, wistful, endearing, and too long for the slight story. Still, even too long Fellini is better than no Fellini at all.

p, Alberto Grimaldi; d, Federico Fellini; w, Federico Fellini, Tonino Guerra, Tullio Pinelli; ph, Tonino Delli Colli, Ennio Guarnieri; m, Nicola Piovani, Ugo De Rossi, Ruggero Mastroianni; ed, Nino Baragli; art d, Dante Ferretti; cos, Danilo Donati.

Drama/Comedy   **(PR:A-C MPAA:PG-13)**

GIOVANNI SENZAPENSIERI†   (1986, It.) 97m ASA-RAI 1-Istituto Luce/
Istituto Luce-Italnoleggio c (Trans: Thoughtless Giovanni)

Sergio Castellitto *(Giovanni)*, Eleonora Giorgi *(Claire)*, Franco Fabrizi *(Gino)*, Aldo Fabrizi *(Armando)*, Anita Durante *(Teresa)*, Luigi De Filippo *(Achille)*, Gastone Pescucci *(Gastone)*, Rodolfo Bigotti *(Mechanic)*, Franca Ballette *(Letizia)*, Valerio Isidori, Claudio Spadaro, Fabrizio Costantini, Tatiana Farnese, Pasquale Zito, Richard McNamara, Allesandro Fersen.

When it's announced that Leonardo Da Vinci has passed away, a duke with artistic interests is so shocked he has a heart attack, then promptly falls from a window. Some 460 or so years later, the unfortunate duke's family has now filtered down to one descendant: the ingenuous Castellitto. He lives in the ancient family home, along with two old ladies, Durante and Ballette. Because of his rather odd demeanor, neighbors have taken to calling Castellitto "Thoughtless Giovanni." The love of Castellitto's life is Giorgi, but this romance is decidedly one-sided. Castellitto loves Giorgi from afar, but she doesn't even realize who he is. The foppish, yet endearing man eventually learns of his ancestor's connection to the great Da Vinci. Through a long-kept secret of his late relative, Castellitto learns what he must do to win Giorgi's affection. A first feature film from director Colli.

p, Gabriella Curiel; d, Marco Colli; w, Gianni Di Gregorio, Marco Colli; ph, Emilio Bestetti (Eastmancolor); m, Lamberto Macchi; ed, Roberto Schiavone; art d, Enrico Colli; cos, Clary Mirolo, Valeria Sponsoli; makeup, Franco Rufini.

Comedy (PR:O MPAA:NR)

GIRL FROM MANI, THE† (1986, Brit./Gr.) 110m M.N.K. c

Angela Gerekou *(Eleni Kaleas)*, Alex Hyde-White *(Alan Cooper)*, Andreas Manoslikakis *(Petros)*, George Katuridis *(Calchas)*, George Foundas, Emilia Della Rocca.

When Hyde-White, a British music teacher, falls in love with his Greek pupil Gerekou, a storm of trouble begins to brew. Though Gerekou has like affection for her instructor, she is bound by a commitment to marry Manoslikakis, a promise which was made in childhood. Manoslikakis, though a mean-spirited young man, comes from a fabulously wealthy family which helped Gerekou and her relatives with tuition and other debts. Having left the milieu of a small Greek village, Gerekou's world has expanded tenfold. Though she loves her newfound life, Gerekou realizes the grief she will cause if she doesn't return home. A head-to-head conflict erupts between Gerekou's rival suitors.

p, Noyes-Kyriazis; d, Paul Annett; w, Nikos Gatsos, Philip Broadley; ph, Takis Zervoulakis (Panavision, Rank color); m, Theodore Antoniou; ed, Bob Dearberg; art d, Kes Karapiperis.

Romance (PR:C-O MPAA:NR)

GIRLS SCHOOL SCREAMERS*½ (1986) 85m Bandit/Troma c

Mollie O'Mara *(Jackie/Jennifer)*, Sharon Christopher *(Elizabeth)*, Mari Butler *(Kate)*, Beth O'Malley *(Karen)*, Karen Krevitz *(Susan)*, Marcia Hinton *(Adelle)*, Monica Antonucci *(Rosemary)*, Peter C. Cosimano *(Paul)*, Vera Gallagher *(Sister Urban)*, Charles Braun *(Tyler Wells)*, Tony Manzo *(Dr. Robert Fisher)*, John Turner *(Bruce)*, James Finegan, Sr. *(Paul's Father)*, Jeff Menapace *(Billy the Coma Boy)*, Colleen Harrity *(Sister Mary)*, Eva Keating McKendrick *(Young Mother Urban)*, John McKeever, Vicki McKeever *(Coma Boy's Parents)*, Daniel J. Keating, Jr. *(Reader of Will)*, Miriam Spiller *(Sister Agnes)*, Ray Spiller *(School Van Driver)*, Katie Keating *(Hospital Nurse)*, Kim Robinson *(Candy Striper)*.

A dull—even by Troma standards—haunted-house epic which employs the done-to-death TEN LITTLE INDIANS formula where a houseful of characters disappear one by one. When it is learned that a recently deceased millionaire has left

his estate to a local Philadelphia girls' college, an instructor and seven of her most trusted students are dispatched to the mansion to catalogue the estate. Filled with valuable old statues and other priceless works of art, the girls spend much of the day taking inventory. That evening their instructor falls ill and the girls take the opportunity to roam the dark hallways of the mansion. Of course, as the evening progresses, the girls disappear one by one and are murdered. As it turns out one of the survivors, O'Mara, is the living reincarnation of the niece of the dead millionaire. The girl was killed in the mansion in 1939 when she spurned the advances of her amorous uncle, and her spirit has come back seeking revenge.

Terribly tedious, GIRLS SCHOOL SCREAMERS offers nothing in the way of chills, and in fact, offers little in the area of basic technical competence. Slapdash direction, production values, and performances are the order of the day here, but even these can be overcome if the script has an inkling of creative energy. Unfortunately, the script is the film's most major flaw and its lameness permeates the rest of the movie.

p, John P. Finegan, Pierce J. Keating, James W. Finegan; d&w, John P. Finegan (based on a story by John P. Finegan, Katie Keating, Pierce Keating); ph, Albert R. Jordan (DuArt color); m, John Hodian; ed, Thomas R. Rondinella; prod d, John P. Finegan; art d, Glenn Bookman; cos, Katie Keating; makeup, John Maffei, Maryanne Ebner.

Horror Cas. (PR:O MPAA:R)

GIURO CHE TI AMO† (1986, It.) Gloria Cinematografica/Titanus c
(Trans: I Swear I Love You)

Nino D'Angelo, Roberta Olivieri, Gabriele Tinti, Tommaso Paladino, Gabriella Di Luzio, Vittorio La Rosa, Silvana Carucci, Stefania Ventura, Olga Gardenia, Rick Battaglia, Bombolo, Marco Vivo.

A fisherman who lives with an orphaned child is given an old boat by a Mafia don. The man loves a local girl, whose father is a union organizer fighting mob control. After a tipster phones the police, the child is taken from the fisherman, but the youngster escapes the authorities and returns home. Later the Mafia don tells the fisherman to clear the harbor so his cronies can use the waters for smuggling purposes. The fisherman refuses and, when his boat is rigged with explosives as punishment, he turns the situation to his advantage. Using the boat as a floating bomb, he rams the don's boat and puts an end to the man's cruel reign. The fisherman receives a new boat as a reward for this brave act and ultimately marries the girl he loves.

d, Nino D'Angelo; w, Francesco Calabrese, Piero Regnoli, Nino D'Angelo (based on a story by Francesco Calabrese, Nino D'Angelo); ph, Giancarlo Ferrando; m, Nino D'Angelo, Franco Chiaravalle; ed, Carlo Broglio.

Crime (PR:O MPAA:NR)

GOBOTS: BATTLE OF THE ROCKLORDS* (1986) 75m Hanna-Barbera-Tonka/Clubhouse-Atlantic c

Voices: Margot Kidder *(Solitaire)*, Roddy McDowall *(Nuggit)*, Michael Nouri *(Boulder)*, Telly Savalas *(Magmar)*, Arthur Bughardt, Ike Eisenmann, Bernard Erhard, Marilyn Lightstone, Morgan Paull, Lou Richards, Leslie Speights, Frank Walker, Dick Gautier, Foster Brooks.

For every film like THE GREAT MOUSE DETECTIVE, which celebrates the art of animation, there unfortunately exists a work of this ilk, mired in the substandard values that have unfortunately become commonplace in cartoons. GOBOTS: BATTLE OF THE ROCKLORDS is merely an extension of the television and subsequent videocassette series, both tie-ins to the line of toys popular with eight-year-olds. GoBots, as anyone who lives with a grammar schooler knows, are robots that can turn themselves into a variety of devices, from rugged-terrain vehicles to spaceships. The philosophical implications of such creatures are astounding, but this theme is ignored in this presentation, which is designed strictly to satisfy the expectations of your average GoBot-hungry tyke.

The Rock People, a group of mutant humans who can alter themselves into rocks when danger is near, suffer from the oppressive regime of the Rock Lords, who are headed by a nasty wizard. Like all good bad wizards, this one wants to rule the Universe. Of course the GoBots just won't stand for this sort of thing and, as a result, become deeply involved with the issue. Sure it's silly, but what did you expect, Brechtian theatrics? As poorly animated features go, this one ranks down there with the worst of them. The characters have no real personalities, and the whole thing is just too somber for its own good. Although the voices were provided by such personalities as Margot Kidder, Telly Savalas, Roddy McDowall, and Foster Brooks, for some strange reason they have all been electronically altered. What's the point? If producers want to hire "name talent" why not get full value for their money? The film was cosponsored, to no one's surprise, by the Tonka Toy corporation. Wonder what they had in mind?

p, Kay Wright; d, Ray Patterson; w, Jeff Segal; ed, Larry C. Cowan; md, Hoyt Curtin; anim, Paul Sabella.

Animated Feature (PR:AAA MPAA:G)

GOING SANE† (1986, Aus.) 90m Sea Change–New South Wales Film c

John Waters *(Martin Brown)*, Judy Morris *(Ainslee Brown)*, Linda Cropper *(Irene Carter)*, Kater Raison *(Nosh)*, Frank Wilson *(Sir Colin Grant)*, Jim Holt *(Irwin Grant)*, Tim Robertson *(Owen Owen)*, Anne Semler *(Marta)*.

When a midlife crisis hits Waters, a mining engineer, he sinks into a self-induced funk. In an effort to climb out of it, he leaves his shrewish wife (Morris) for his secretary (Cropper) and takes off with his new amour for the Australian outback, where they meet Robertson, a mad Welshman, who is married to Semler, a German woman with a passion for new men. All these adventures are to no avail, however, for Waters cannot escape his depression. He goes to the hospital, where he meets Raison, and the two skip off to Raison's country home. But instead of bliss, they find only trouble when Waters' former employer wants to mine the area.

p, Tom Jeffrey; d, Michael Robertson; w, John Sandford; ph, Dean Semler (Eastmancolor); m, Cameron Allan; ed, Brian Kavanagh; prod d, Igor Nay; cos, Jan Hurley.

Comedy (PR:O MPAA:NR)

GOLDEN CHILD, THE* (1986) 93m FM Entertainment–Eddie Murphy Productions/PAR c

Eddie Murphy *(Chandler Jarrell)*, Charles Dance *(Sardo Numspa)*, Charlotte Lewis *(Kee Nang)*, Victor Wong *(The Old Man)*, J.L. Reate *(The Golden Child)*, Randall "Tex" Cobb *(Til)*, James Hong *(Dr. Hong)*, Shakti *(Kala)*, Tau Logo *(Yu)*, Tiger Chung Lee *(Khan)*, Pons Maar *(Fu)*, Peter Kwong *(Tommy Tong)*.

Neil Simon wrote a script for Eddie Murphy, but the young comedian turned it down in favor of this. So much for Murphy's taste. Director Ritchie has had a hit-and-miss career, and this is definitely a miss—a muddle of alleged comedy, Eastern mysticism, and a heavy dose of Indiana Jones-type adventure. It begins promisingly enough with the bold kidnaping of a Tibetan holy youth, Reate (who, we are told, is a girl in boy's clothing), from a temple high in Shangri-La land. The evildoers are led by Dance (costar with Meryl Streep in PLENTY), who knows that this child will bring peace to the earth if allowed to. As Dance is an ambassador of the devil, his task is to make certain that the child can never get

around to bestowing tranquility upon civilization. Murphy is a free-lance child-finder working in Los Angeles where there are, evidently, a great many missing children. (There's a joke going around Hollywood concerning an 8-year-old who saw Paul Newman's face on salad dressing and spaghetti sauce bottles in a supermarket. This caused her to ask her mother if Newman was missing.) Murphy appears on a local cable TV show and, in the best comedy scene in the movie, makes mincemeat out of the fawning host. He is then contacted by Lewis, who works for the Tibetans. She wants Murphy to find this Golden Child and this starts a hegira around Los Angeles that includes Murphy's having to vanquish a bunch of bearded motorcyclists. After vamping till ready in L.A., they go off to Tibet where Murphy meets Wong, a jive-talking holy man. Murphy has to prove he is the right person for the job by walking across a series of pillars carrying a glass of water. The drop, if he falls from the pillars, is bottomless, and nobody has ever negotiated the task successfully before. Naturally, he does it. Then it's back to L.A., but Murphy is now in possession of a magic sword (reeks of CAMELOT, no?) with which he can slay Dance, who has the ability to turn into various creatures, including a fire-breathing dragon-like being. Murphy saves the child, who has been kept in a cage. (The youth can't be killed, but as long as he is penned, the world will continue in its evil orbit.) While this is being accomplished, Lewis is slain, which, as Murphy has fallen in love with her, is a bummer. The Golden Child uses magic to breathe life back into Lewis, Murphy goes after Dance with the magic sword (in a special-effects sequence orchestrated by George Lucas' Industrial Light & Magic organization), and the picture ends.

THE GOLDEN CHILD cost more than $24 million and looks it. A patina of heavy money is everywhere but in the script, which surely must rank as one of the silliest attempts at blending action and laughter ever written. The music by Colombier is mind-numbing and inappropriate. Another score had been written by John Barry, but it was deleted in favor of Colombier's atrocious noise. Lewis' martial-arts moves are as phony looking as those Hong Kong quickies that starred actors who slightly resembled Bruce Lee. The jokes are mostly flat, the action is frenetic, the motivations are murky, and there are some choices that

defy understanding, such as a non-sequitur scene with a dancing soft-drink can that looks like a music video commercial for MTV. Lots of karate fights, a 300-year-old woman with a dragon's tail and a penchant for chain smoking, all of the standard adventure gimmicks seen in movies since well before GUNGA DIN, and a general feeling of cliche make this one strictly missable. The effects will scare little children and cause adult viewers to laugh.

p, Edward S. Feldman, Robert D. Wachs; d, Michael Ritchie; w, Dennis Feldman; ph, Donald E. Thorin (Metrocolor); m, Michel Colombier; ed, Richard A.

Harris; prod d, J. Michael Riva; art d, Lynda Paradise; set d, Virginia Randolph; cos, Wayne Finkelman; spec eff, Industrial Light & Magic; makeup, Ken Chase.

Comedy/Adventure (PR:C MPAA:PG-13)

GOLDEN EIGHTIES*½ (1986, Fr./Bel./Switz.) 92m Paradise-French Ministry of Culture-Limbo-Ministry of the French Community of Belgium/ Pari-Gerick c

Delphine Seyrig *(Jeanne)*, Nicolas Tronc *(Robert)*, John Berry *(Eli)*, Lio *(Mado)*, Fanny Cottencon *(Lili)*, Charles Denner *(Mons. Schwartz)*, Jean-Francois Balmer *(Mons. Jean)*, Myriam Boyer *(Sylvie)*, Pascale Salkin *(Pascale)*, Francois Beukelaers, Eric Chale, Xavier Lukomsky, Estelle Marion, Marie-Rose Roland.

The director of such structurally oriented films as JEANNE DIELMAN, 23 QUAI DU COMMERCE, 1080 BRUXELLES (1975), and LES RENDEZ-VOUS D'ANNA (1978) focuses her dialectical analysis on the most steadfast of American film genres, the musical, to perceptively comment on the state of modern romanticism. GOLDEN EIGHTIES is set completely inside the restricted, claustrophobic environs of a sterile, ultramodern shopping mall. Every day the mall fills up with hurried, fashion-conscious workers, who contend with the dreariness of their working routines by filling their heads with dreams of romantic love. There is the girl, Boyer, who runs the tiny snack bar, anxiously awaiting the next letter from her boy friend who is searching for riches in Canada. The letter arrives; a crowd gathers around the snack bar while Boyer reads it aloud, shifting into song as she becomes dreamily immersed in the letter's contents. There is the American, Berry, just off a plane, who wanders through the mall in search of a new suit. He has not been in Belgium since WW II as a GI, when he had a brief affair with a young woman who has never escaped his thoughts, and, so he says, is the only woman he has ever really loved. Secretly he hopes to meet her again—which he does, as Seyrig, in the store where he buys his suit. Seyrig and her husband Denner, through a marriage of convenience, own the boutique and have been leading a moderately happy life. Berry plans a rendezvous with his long-lost love, begging her to come away with him. Seyrig refuses, claiming that her life with her husband and the store is set, and cannot be changed on the idealistic whims that belong to a younger generation. Her son, Tronc, is involved in his own romantic turmoil. He is head-over-heels in love with the coquettish Cottencon, the owner of the beauty salon—bought for her by her mobster lover Balmer—across from the boutique. Lio, who works for Cottencon, is in love with Tronc, but he—as long as Cottencon is around—won't give her the time of day. But this quickly changes when Tronc has a jealous fit over Cottencon's relationship with Balmer, a buffoonish oaf who literally begs for the slightest bit of affection from Cottencon. After a fatherly talk from Denner about planning for the future and the just route to take, Tronc proposes to Lio. Several months into the future, the beauty salon is now replaced by an expansion of Denner's store, with Lio and Tronc anxiously preparing for their wedding day. A veiled Cottencon mysteriously enters the store, begging Seyrig to allow her to meet with Tronc one last time before the wedding. She contends that if Tronc is no longer in love with her it doesn't matter if they meet, but if he does still love her things will work themselves out. Cottencon and Tronc meet and immediately resume their earlier passion. The dejected Lio, dressed in her wedding gown for a fitting, is comforted by Denner and Seyrig. They walk the girl out into the street (the only shot outside the claustrophobic mall), where they run into Berry parading down the street with his new bride.

Though GOLDEN EIGHTIES can be easily enjoyed, a fuller appreciation of it does require some introduction to Chantal Akerman's earlier works. Her first films were a series of shorts that were heavily influenced by the American structuralist filmmakers of the 1970s, like Michael Snow. Akerman's features revolved around studiously long shots of women involved in their daily routines. Much of this approach is evident in GOLDEN EIGHTIES, except that the long takes have been replaced by a quick editing pace that takes full advantage of the nonstop movement in the shopping mall. Akerman's cinematic style complements the sterility of the mall through geometric placement of the camera and arduously composed shots. Absolutely nothing is allowed to appear out of place, not even the people of the film who mechanically attend to their daily routines ever mindful of the clock that will bring their working day to an end. The musical numbers, occurring randomly throughout the film, blend perfectly with Akerman's theoretical stylistics, implying a parallel between the rhythm inherent in singing and dancing and the daily rituals of the film characters. Oddly, the lyrics in the songs—all composed by Akerman—cynically comment upon, and act as an emotional balance to, the little melodramas that take place. GOLDEN EIGHTIES was developed from an earlier, shorter film sporadically screened in 1983, basically a partial documentary on the making of a musical. Prior to this, Akerman's last theatrical release was the 1978 film LES RENDEZ-VOUS D'ANNA. Collaborating screenwriter Gruault has been a prominent figure in the French film industry, working with such directors as Francois Truffaut (THE STORY OF ADELE H., JULES AND JIM, TWO ENGLISH GIRLS), Jean-Luc Godard (LES CARABINIERS), Jacques Rivette (THE NUN), and Alain Resnais (MON ONCLE D'AMERIQUE, LIFE IS A BED OF ROSES). Actress Delphine Seyrig also appeared in Akerman's earlier film JEANNE DIELMAN, 23 QUAI DU COMMERCE, 1080 BRUXELLE as a struggling mother who helps make ends meet by doubling as a prostitute. In GOLDEN EIGHTIES she transmits a beauty and gracefulness that defies her age, making her as much a pleasure to watch as the younger actresses. Her character, like the less mature, is a product of the commercial world of the shopping mall, making her dreams and romantic ideals as much a commodity as the clothes she sells. (In French; English subtitles.)

p, Martine Marignac; d, Chantal Akerman; w, Pascal Bonitzer, Henry Bean, Chantal Akerman, Jean Gruault, Leora Barish; ph, Gilberto Azevedo, Luc Benhamou (Fujicolor); m, Marc Herouet; ed, Francine Sandberg, Nadine

Keseman; art d, Serge Marzolff; cos, Pierre Albert; m/l, Marc Herouet, Chantal Akerman.

Musical   (PR:A MPAA:NR)

GOOD FATHER, THE*   (1986, Brit.) 90m Greenpoint–Film Four
                                                        International/Skouras c

Anthony Hopkins *(Bill Hooper)*, Jim Broadbent *(Roger Miles)*, Harriet Walter *(Emmy Hooper)*, Fanny Viner *(Cheryl Miles)*, Simon Callow *(Mark Varner)*, Joanne Whalley *(Mary)*, Miriam Margolyes *(Jane Powell)*, Michael Byrne *(Leonard Scruby)*.

Starring the actor some have called Laurence Olivier's heir-apparent and directed by the man responsible for DANCE WITH A STRANGER, this film is much more than merely a role-reversal British version of KRAMER VS. KRAMER. Hopkins is an executive with a publishing company, divorced and distraught, a self-diagnosed victim of the feminism he so ardently supported in the salad days of his idealism. As the film opens Hopkins guides the 6-year-old son he sees only on weekends through Clapham Common in south London. Hopkins carries the boy on his shoulders, but there is a distant cast to his eyes; when he pushes his son on a swing, he pushes a little hard. He is curt with his ex-wife (Walter); when he returns the boy to her, he quickly jumps on his motorcycle and speeds off into the night. As he zooms along, his mind's eye is overtaken by the surreal image of a baby's face smothered by womblike plastic. His bike skids out of control, but Hopkins, unhurt, collects himself, dusts off his black leather jacket, and continues on to a party. There he watches Broadbent break down in tears, devastated by his own divorce and separation from his young son. Hopkins learns that schoolteacher Broadbent's radical-feminist wife, Viner, has left him for a lesbian lover. The two men, sharing a history of 1960s activism, become friends, coming together with their sons on weekends, forming a kind of family.

In the meantime, Hopkins has entered into a relationship with an attractive young coworker. He gives little of himself to her, but she asks almost nothing from him. Upon returning his son to Walter on one occasion, Hopkins learns that she is no longer living with the man she had taken up with after Hopkins *left her*. Yet Hopkins remains haunted, stewing in tenuously repressed anger. Presumably offering a window to Hopkins' thoughts, Newell repeatedly presents an image of Walter from some time in the past, a tear meandering down her cheek. Each time this image recurs the camera pulls back a little farther, revealing more of Walter set against a window, the lushness of spring or summer outside. The image of the smothered child is also repeated several times.

One evening, Hopkins returns to his dingy flat by a motorway to find Broadbent, head in hands, beside himself. Viner has announced her intention to emigrate to Australia, taking their son with her, Broadbent explains. Hopkins encourages him to fight back. He takes Broadbent to a solicitor friend—a woman and a feminist—but she refuses to help, adhering to her inflexible rule of never defending a man in a custody case. Later, they visit another solicitor who outlines a legal course of action, including the enlistment of a high-powered, high-priced barrister (Callow) to plead the case. Hopkins spurs on Broadbent at every turn, vicariously waging the campaign of vengeance he has never carried out against his own ex-wife. Callow's fee is well beyond Broadbent's means, but Hopkins assures his friend that he will make up the difference. Callow sees to it that the case will be heard by a staunchly conservative judge, a man who is likely to react strongly to Viner's militant-feminist past and lesbianism.

As the preparations and proceedings progress, Hopkins becomes increasingly more at ease, even taking a new flat nearer to his wife and son and furnishing it. His undemanding girl friend has fallen in love with him, and though she still asks little of him, she now wants to have his child. Hopkins retreats. He accompanies Broadbent in court, where he watches the self-satisfied, haughty, upper-class Callow go for Viner's jugular. The case turns ugly, more vicious than Broadbent or Hopkins had ever dreamed. Broadbent is furious with Hopkins, whom he blames for pushing him into actions he would never have taken on his own. The judge rules in favor of Broadbent, taking the child from Viner. In the end, though, Viner and Broadbent reach their own amiable understanding: she won't go to Australia and they will split time with their child.

His demon exorcized by proxy, Hopkins approaches Walter, but it is clear that they will never be able to get together again. His son would still require the love, attention, and time that Hopkins and Walter had reserved for each other (and themselves) before his birth. Hopkins is anything but a good father: despite his overtures to the contrary, he left his son and not his wife. As the film closes, the screen is again filled with the familiar tearful image of Walter. This time, however, the camera pulls back to reveal her not only crying, but pregnant.

Though nicely adapted from a novel by Peter Prince, adroitly directed by Newell, and photographed with grainy realism, THE GOOD FATHER is, from start to finish, Hopkins' film. His vindictive, selfish Bill Hooper practically quivers with intensity. Submerged hostility lurks beneath his every action, threatening to burst forth in violence—though it never does. Bill Hooper is a hard man to like, yet, by the film's end, Hopkins has made him a tragic figure. The emptiness that is the final reward for his idealism seems somehow unjust. Ultimately he is a victim, though the majority of his wounds have been self-inflicted.

After a long hiatus in Hollywood, Hopkins made a triumphant return to the London stage in 1985 as the scheming newspaper magnate in "Pravda," a performance to which many pointed as proof that the Welshman was ready to claim the place in the British acting pantheon that was frequently predicted for him at the start of his stormy career. Hopkins' performance here—and as a vastly different character in 84 CHARING CROSS ROAD—only confirms his stature as one of the very finest of Britain's actors.

p, Ann Scott; d, Mike Newell; w, Christopher Hampton (based on the novel by

Peter Prince); ph, Michael Coulter; m, Richard Hartley; ed, Peter Hollywood; prod d, Adrian Smith; art d, Alison Stewart-Richardson.

Drama   (PR:O MPAA:R)

GOOD TO GO†   (1986) 87m Island Alive/Island c

Art Garfunkel *(S.D. Blass)*, Robert DoQui *(Max)*, Harris Yulin *(Harrigan)*, Reginald Daughtry *(Little Beats)*, Robert Brooks *(Chemist)*, Paula Davis *(Evette)*, Richard Bauer *(Editor)*, Michael White *(Gil Colton)*, Hattie Winston *(Mother)*.

Go-go is a style of funk music indigenous to Washington, D.C., in which bands play very long songs (an hour or more, sometimes) complete with call-and-response with the audience, elaborate dance instructions, and an absolutely irresistible beat. The best-known practitioner of go-go is Trouble Funk, with several albums and a hit single ("Drop the Bomb") to their credit. For a period in late 1985 and early 1986, go-go was *the* hot new music style, briefly replacing New York-based Hip Hop. Island Records has been behind some of go-go's recent prominence, so it seemed natural that their film production arm should back a movie about the music and its background. The story opens as a street gang is

turned away from a go-go concert. Wasted on PCP and irate over being shut out of the show, they gang-rape and kill a girl. Police use this as an excuse to clamp down on the whole scene, and they give Garfunkel, a down-on-his-luck political reporter reduced to covering the police beat, a scoop about the supposed crime wave the music is causing. He dutifully writes the story, but later finds the music not so bad as he was led to believe. He figures out that he was used by the police, and he later witnesses the cold-blooded killing of a gang member by detective Yulin. Now turned into a champion of go-go, Garfunkel manages to defuse the tension in the ghetto neighborhood and become a hero. The film provoked a great deal of controversy in Washington, D.C., where it was felt it showed the black community in a bad light. The film never received wide release, and as the brief go-go fad faded, the film quietly disappeared.

p, Doug Dilge, Sean Ferrer; d&w, Blaine Novak; ph, Peter Sinclair (Technicolor); m, Trouble Funk, Redds and the Boys, Chuck Brown and the Soul Searchers; ed, Gib Jaffe, Kimberly Logan, D.C. Stringer; art d, Ron Downing.

Musical/Drama   (PR:O MPAA:R)

GOSPEL ACCORDING TO VIC, THE*   (1986, Brit.) 92m Island–Skreba/
                                                        Skouras c (GB: HEAVENLY PURSUITS)

Tom Conti *(Vic Mathews)*, Helen Mirren *(Ruth Chancellor)*, David Hayman *(Jeff Jeffries)*, Brian Pettifer *(Father Cobb)*, Jennifer Black *(Sister)*, Dave Anderson *(Headmaster)*, Tom Busby *(Brusse)*, Sam Graham *(Doctor)*, Kara Wilson *(McAllister)*, Robert Paterson *(MacKrimmond)*, John Mitchell *(Gibbons)*.

Pettifer is a Glaswegian priest trying to convince the Vatican to canonize Edith Semple, a woman who died in 1917 with not quite enough miracles attributed to her to qualify for sainthood. Back in Glasgow, at Semple's namesake school for slow students, one teacher (Conti) has some strong disagreements about what actually constitutes a miracle. Conti believes that the day-to-day victories of his struggling students are wonderful miracles in themselves, and he has little use for religious dogma. Though others in the school hope desperately for a miracle in Semple's name to be accepted, Conti remains unconvinced. When Conti enters the hospital after a fainting spell and tests show he has an incurable brain tumor, no one wants to tell him about his condition. After he falls from a ladder rescuing a student from the school's roof, his tumor mysteriously vanishes. This is just the first of many strange happenings. Conti finds that his stereo continues playing after he switches it off, and traffic signals change from red to green whenever he drives up to an intersection. The media grab hold of these phenomena, and the Semple school is swept by "miracle fever." Conti refuses to get caught up in this nonsense, instead turning his attentions to Mirren, the school's new music teacher. The romance has its troubles, while Conti's cavalier attitudes draw the wrath of school authorities. But Conti and Mirren are able to overcome all of the obstacles that tumble their way as the amiable story comes to its cheerful conclusion.

Conti is perfectly cast to type in his nonconformist role. The story is unassuming, concentrating on the small moments of life that Conti considers to be the true miracles of the world. Yet a door is left open to the possibilities of things beyond understanding, conveyed without compromising the film's central theme. Writer/director Gormley makes effective comic use of offbeat touches, such as the computers that keep the Vatican running smoothly. Overall, though hardly memorable, THE GOSPEL ACCORDING TO VIC is a quaint and enjoyable little comedy.

p, Michael Relph; d&w, Charles Gormley; ph, Michael Coulter; m, B.A. Robertson; ed, John Gow; prod d, Rita McGurn.

Comedy   (PR:C   MPAA:PG-13)

GRANDEUR ET DECADENCE D'UN PETIT COMMERCE DE CINEMA†
(1986, Fr.) 90m Hamster c (Trans: Grandeur And Decadence Of A Small-time Film Company)

Jean-Pierre Leaud, Jean-Pierre Mocky, Marie Valera, Jean-Luc Godard.

After completing the post-production work on his 1985 films HAIL, MARY and DETECTIVE, Jean-Luc Godard turned once again to a television project. (His work for French television was extensive in the late 1970s, peaking with his video series "France Tour Detour Deux Enfants" in 1978.) Here, Leaud and Mocky star as a film producer and director who are trying desperately to find enough financing to get a film made. While they search for funding, they also attempt to cast the leads, concerned more with bedding beautiful ingenue Valera than testing her acting ability. All the success for which they strive is represented by a Mercedes Benz, a status symbol they eventually attain and in which the producer and a flunky ultimately die. Godard, with his usual unpredictability, includes on the soundtrack a pair of Janis Joplin songs, including "Me and Bobby McGee" (Kris Kristofferson, Fred L. Foster, performed by Janis Joplin). Though intended for television, this film was screened at the Montreal Film Festival and, like most Godard films, will probably receive a limited art-house run in the States.

p, Pierre Grimblat; d&w, Jean-Luc Godard (based on the novel by James Hadley Chase); ph, Caroline Champetier.

Drama/Comedy   (PR:O   MPAA:NR)

GRANDFATHER, THE†   (1986, Iran) c

Jamshid Mashayekhy, J. Almassi, A. Kheradmand.

p, Ahmad Motavassel; d&w, Majid Gharizadeh; ph, H. Jafarian, F. Saba; m, Kambiz Roshan Ravan; ed, Davood Yosefian.

GRANDI MAGAZZINI†   (1986, It.) 100m C.G. Silver/COL Italia c (Trans: Department Store)

Alessandro Haber (Umberto Anzellotti), Laura Antonelli (Elena Anzellotti), Enrico Montesano (Alvise), Paolo Villaggio (Robot), Nino Manfredi (Salvietti), Michele Placido (Store Manager), Renato Pozzetto (Fausto), Massimo Civilotti (Young Kruger), Heather Parisi (Girl with Contacts), Lino Banfi (Street Singer), Ornella Muti (Herself), Christian De Sica (Prize Winner), Massimo Boldi (Guard), Sabrina Salerno, Paolo Panelli, Antonella Vitale, Gianni Bonagura, Rosanna Banfi, Claudio Botosso, Massimo Ciavarro.

An all-star Italian comedy that follows myriad characters during one week's work in a large department store. The daily activities of each worker from the owner to the delivery boys are explored as the film shifts from character to character. Old vaudeville-style gags abound, and much is made of the quirky behavior of the employees. One clerk selects a new dress every night and then goes to the ladies' room wearing only her overcoat so that she can put on the stolen dress and leave unnoticed. Another, Villaggio, dons a plastic wig and attempts to fool store managers into thinking that he's a robot. Antonelli, playing the wife of personnel director Haber, is convinced that the bumbling salesman in bathroom fixtures is the owner's son sent to spy. The couple become obsessed with the idea and, as is to be expected when Laura Antonelli is involved, they stop at nothing short of seduction to wrest the truth from the salesman.

p, Mario Cecchi Gori, Vittorio Cecchi Gori; d&w, Castellano & Pipolo; ph, Nino Celeste; m, Detto Mariano; ed, Antonio Siciliano.

Comedy   (PR:C   MPAA:NR)

GRANNY GENERAL†   (1986, USSR) 72m Uzbek Studio c

Zainob Sadrieva (Granny), Hussan Sharipov (Husband), Noila Tashkenbaira (Wife).

A comedy from young Uzbek director Absalov, which sees Sadrieva, the domineering mother of Sharipov, arrive at his village via helicopter to help her son raise his 10 children. Sharipov is possessed by his love for soccer and has almost produced enough children to field his own team. His ever-pregnant wife, Tashkenbaira, carries the proposed final member of the squad. Sadrieva puts a stop to her son's soccer mania by locking him out of his own house. Fed up, he wanders off into the wilderness muttering that he'll move to Japan where women respect men. In addition to running her roost, Sadrieva imposes her strong will on the local government and tries to force them to build a useless bridge. The elderly Sadrieva falls ill, however, and she makes her peace with her family and the village before walking off into the mountains to die amidst natural surroundings rather than suffering in a hospital.

d, Melo Absalov; w, Resivoi Muhamidjanov; ph, Najmidin Gulyamov (Panavision); m, Mirhalil Makmudov; ed, Rano Hamraeva.

Comedy/Drama   (PR:C   MPAA:NR)

GREAT EXPECTATIONS—THE AUSTRALIAN STORY†   (1986, Aus.)
International Film Management

John Stanton, Sigrid Thornton, Robert Coleby, Noel Ferrier.

Inspired by Dickens' classic novel, this film centers on the criminal Abel Magwitch, Pip's secret benefactor.

p, Ray Alchin, Tom Burstall; d&w, Tim Burstall (based on the novel by Charles Dickens); ph, Peter Hendry.

Drama/Adventure   (PR:NR   MPAA:NR)

GREAT GENERATION, THE*½**   (1986, Hung.) 109m Dialog Studio-Mafilm c (A NAGY GENERACIO)

Gyorgy Cserhalmi (Reb), Karoly Eperjes (Makay), Mari Kiss (Mari, Reb's Ex-wife), Melanie Jane Ventilla (Marylou, Their Daughter), Dorottya Udvaros (Bea, Makay's Wife), Robert Koltai (Nikita), Tamas Major (Makay's Father), Gyorgy Gal (Csaba, Makay's Son), Peter Andorai.

A unique film that manages to be both insightful and entertaining, THE GREAT GENERATION centers on Cserhalmi as he returns from America to Hungary after an 18-year absence. With him is his teenage daughter by Kiss, Ventilla. Kiss had fled to the U.S. with Cserhalmi, but quickly returned home after finding life in the new country too taxing. The first thing Cserhalmi does is contact his best friend, Eperjes, now a popular disc jockey. Eighteen years earlier Eperjes and Cserhalmi, along with Koltai, had agreed to leave their native soil to find wealth in America. Eperjes was the only one of the trio who had a passport. Cserhalmi stole the passport, pasted his own picture on it, and then flew off to America. He has now returned, not so much to see old friends, but to make some quick cash. His scheme is to secure the rights to a valuable agricultural invention developed by a peasant, who happens to be an acquaintance of Eperjes' father. He also wants to get Kiss, now living with Koltai, to take custody of their daughter. Cserhalmi, Eperjes, and Eperjes' father travel across the countryside in search of the elusive peasant inventor, an eccentric genius who has taken to the bottle. Going from jails to detoxification centers, the three are unable to find their man. But when visiting Eperjes' son in a mental hospital—where he is trying to escape induction into the army—Eperjes' father notices the inventor. He refrains from telling Cserhalmi, feeling it best to leave the old man in peace. Kiss agrees to take care of Ventilla, but fearful of remaining with a woman she barely knows, the girl runs to catch her father just before he boards his plane to America. Seeing Cserhalmi off, Eperjes and the others have mixed emotions. They are glad to see him go since he caused such havoc with his wild schemes, yet they also know they will probably never again see this man who so enlivened them even as he took advantage of them.

Winner of the Best Screenplay Award at the Chicago Film Festival and a Special Jury Prize at San Sebastian, THE GREAT GENERATION handles a number of serious subjects with a sense of humor and humanity. All the characters are multi-dimensional and believable. Though Cserhalmi may be one of the most opportunistic people alive, he has qualities that make his friends love him. The people in this film are continuously fighting, loving, breaking up, making up, hating, and, ultimately, cherishing one another. Their actions and stories are told in an unpretentious manner that doesn't pass judgment. If THE GREAT GENERATION has any message to convey, it is praise for those who have remained in Hungary while others have left in search of riches. Cserhalmi is a drifter, while his friends have created successful careers and have stable family lives. (In Hungarian; English subtitles.)

d, Ferenc Andras; w, Geza Beremenyi, Ferenc Andras; ph, Elemer Ragalyi (Eastmancolor); m, Gyorgy Kovacs; ed, Mihaly Morell; set d, Attila Kovacs; cos, Maria Benedek.

Drama   (PR:O   MPAA:NR)

GREAT MOUSE DETECTIVE, THE**   (1986) 73m Disney-Silver Screen Partners II/BV c

Voices: Vincent Price (Professor Ratigan), Barrie Ingham (Basil/Bartholomew), Val Bettin (Dawson), Susanne Pollatschek (Olivia), Candy Candido (Fidget), Diana Chesney (Mrs. Judson), Eve Brenner (The Mouse Queen), Alan Young (Flaversham), Basil Rathbone (Sherlock Holmes), Laurie Main (Watson), Shani Wallis (Lady Mouse), Ellen Fitzhugh (Bar Maid), Walker Edmiston (Citizen/Thug Guard), Wayne Allwine, Val Bettin, Tony Anselmo (Thug Guards).

With the Disney studios concentrating on their Touchstone division—maker of such quality productions as THE COLOR OF MONEY, RUTHLESS PEOPLE and DOWN AND OUT IN BEVERLY HILLS—it appeared that the best-known name in animation had lost interest in creating new animated features. THE GREAT MOUSE DETECTIVE, therefore, surprised and pleased many animation enthusiasts; it combined the sophistication of the new Disney era with the well-loved traditions and standards of the past. Based on the children's novel Basil of Baker Street by Eve Titus, the story is an adaptation of Sherlock Holmes motifs interpreted by a few cartoon mice living in Victorian London. Price provides the voice of Ratigan, a Moriarty-like genius who wants to control the mouse world. To this end, he kidnaps a brilliant mouse toymaker (voiced by Young), intending to have the poor whiskered creature build a terrifying rodent robot. Once he has the metallic creature under his command, Price intends to take over by using it to dethrone the current mouse queen (voiced by Brenner). Young's daughter Pollatschek is found by Dr. Dawson (voiced by Bettin), the Dr. Watson counterpart to the Holmesian mouse, Ingham. Ingham agrees to help the poor child find her father, and the trail leads to all sorts of pitfalls. Eventually the detective confronts his nemesis in the gearworks of Big Ben, and there Ingham

and Price have it out. Of course justice triumphs, as the film comes to its happy conclusion.

This is animation at its finest. The engaging characters play out the action against elegantly designed backgrounds. The story is genuinely exciting, a well-told tale that is entertaining to both children and adults without compromising the expectations of either group. The voices are perfectly cast, particulary Price as the evil Ratigan. He sneers and cackles like a classic villain right out of one of his old horror films. The original idea had been to use a Ronald Colman-type voice for the character, and to that end, a print of the actor's 1950 film CHAMPAGNE FOR CAESAR was screened. The producers were taken with Price's neurotic supporting role, which led to his being cast for this film. Though Price is wonderful, Candido (a Disney voice veteran, having worked in PETER PAN, SLEEPING BEAUTY, and ROBIN HOOD) as Ratigan's peg-legged bat assistant just about steals the film. Consistently annoyed, the character is a lively sidekick who is a never-ending source of amusement. In many ways, THE GREAT MOUSE DETECTIVE could be considered a bridge between the old Disney animated features and the studio's plans for the future. The film's creative consultant, Eric Larson, was the last of Walt Disney's "Nine Old Men" still working with the studio. Larson (on whom the character of Dr. Dawson was loosely modeled) had been with Disney since 1933, and was part of the original animation team that created the classic SNOW WHITE AND THE SEVEN DWARFS. The production crew he worked with here, Disney's new guard, was a vibrant team of young people, a few of whom were still in their early twenties. Though the animators adhered to the old traditional Disney standards of the studio's heyday of the 1940s, a new and revolutionary technique also played an important role in creating THE GREAT MOUSE DETECTIVE. With THE BLACK CAULDRON, inroads had been made in developing computer-animated graphics. In THE GREAT MOUSE DETECTIVE, these techniques were further improved, with astounding results. Although story development took four full years, the actual production work was completed in slightly more than one year, just half the time required for some of the classic Disney animated features. The reduction in time can be attributed to the computer-assisted techniques used. Backgrounds for the Big Ben sequence, with hero and villain racing about the intricate gearworks, were generated entirely by computer. This enabled animators to create breathtaking chase sequences through the machinery without painstakingly drawing the sequence by hand. After creating the individual shots by computer, the drawings were printed and transferred to animation cels. Color and characters were subsequently added by hand. The overall effect was a marvel, and the process reduced time and expenses considerably. The total budget on THE BLACK CAULDRON was $36 million; a year later THE GREAT MOUSE DETECTIVE came in at only $13 million. Released to 1,200 theaters, the picture recovered its cost in three weeks. The three songs are: "The World's Greatest Criminal Mind" (Henry Mancini, Larry Grossman, Ellen Fitzhugh, performed by a chorus of the criminal mastermind's cohorts), "Goodbye, So Soon" (Mancini, Grossman, Fitzhugh, performed by Vincent Price), and "Let Me Be Good to You" (Melissa Manchester, performed by Melissa Manchester).

p, Burny Mattinson; d, John Musker, Ron Clements, Dave Michener, Burny Mattinson; w, Pete Young, Vance Gerry, Steve Hulett, Ron Clements, John Musker, Bruce M. Morris, Matthew O'Callaghan, Burny Mattinson, Dave Michener, Melvin Shaw (based on the book *Basil of Baker Street* by Eve Titus); ph, Ed Austin; m, Henry Mancini; ed, Roy M. Brewer, Jr., James Melton; md, Jay Lawton; art d, Guy Vasilovich; m/l, Henry Mancini, Melissa Manchester, Larry Grossman, Ellen Fitzhugh; anim, Mark Henn, Glen Keane, Robert Minkoff, Hendel Butoy.

Animation/Mystery   (PR:AAA MPAA:G)

GREAT WALL, A**½   (1986) 97m W&S/Orion c (AKA:THE GREAT
                                                      WALL IS A GREAT WALL)

Peter Wang *(Leo Fang)*, Sharon Iwai *(Grace Fang)*, Kelvin Han Yee *(Paul Fang)*, Li Quinqin *(Lili Chao)*, Hu Xiaoguang *(Mr. Chao)*, Shen Guanglan *(Mrs. Chao)*, Wang Xiao *(Liu Yida)*, Xiu Jian *(Yu)*, Ran Zhijuan *(Jan)*, Han Tan *(Old Liu)*, Jeannete Pavini *(Linda)*, Howard Friedberg *(Neil Mahoney)*, Bill Neilson *(Mr. Wilson)*, Teresa Roberts *(Kathy)*.

Reportedly the first American feature lensed in Communist China, A GREAT WALL minimizes story development in favor of exploring the cultural contrasts

between Americans and Chinese. Though graced with rich, likable characters, and a perceptive wit, the film remains an unsatisfactory effort, offering superficial comparisons rather than in-depth enquiry. Wang, an actor in the Chinese-American breakthrough film CHAN IS MISSING, stars as a computer engineer employed in Silicon Valley outside San Francisco. When passed by for a promotion for which he had all the requirements and which he thought rightfully belonged to him, he accuses his superiors of racism. In a fit of anger he spills coffee onto his boss' pants, then quits. Wang arrives home and immediately informs his family that it is time to travel to China to explore their cultural origins and discover what it really means to be Chinese. Wang's wife, Iwai, is a first-generation American with no knowledge of the Chinese language, while their son, Yee, is a typical competitive American teenager, in love with sports and the latest fashions. Wang had left China when he was 10, leaving behind a sister with whom he has retained written contact over the past thirty years. The sister, Guanglan, lives in Peking with her retired-bureaucrat husband and her teenage daughter, who is rigorously preparing for her college entrance exams. The Chinese family members graciously accept their American relatives into their home and allow for the expected cultural confrontations. The majority of the film's time is spent on the young, perhaps because the attitudes of today's teenagers will determine future policies. Quinqin, as the Chinese daughter, has already expressed a respectful curiosity about America, studies English, and likes to drink Coca-Cola. Though barely able to communicate, the two teenagers take an immediate liking to each other, spending excessive amounts of time together. Quinqin starts to wear American clothes and makeup, while almost completely ignoring her boy friend in favor of her cousin. The boy friend comes from a less well-to-do family and is studying for the same exams as Quinqin, the passing of which will assure him a better place in Chinese society. He becomes much more critical of American culture as he sees the strange changes in Quinqin. Feeling rejected, he reacts in a competitive manner that equals the spirit of Yee. The two have their expected confrontation in the form of a heated table tennis match, which the boy friend wins. The boy friend passes his exams—which Quinqin does not do—and wins back her respect just before the Americans return home. Back home, Wang is offered his job back. His rediscovery of his Chinese origins takes the form of the Tai Chi exercises learned from his brother-in-law, which he now practices daily.

Despite a number of flaws—specifically, forced plot situations—A GREAT WALL is almost impossible to dislike, because the characters are portrayed as simple people in the process of questioning their cultural identities. Everyday tasks usually taken for granted are revealed as strange when placed in a foreign context. Wang, who directed as well as acted in this film, approaches these differences with a sense of humor that makes the human animal appear mysteriously complex, and often a bit absurd. Wang also touches upon those things that never change despite cultural differences. One of the film's warmest sequences occurs when the two men, Wang and Xiaoguang, spend an evening drinking in a bar, bragging about their conquests of women, before laughingly stumbling home in complete stupors. But it is the young Chinese who are Wang's prime concern, reacting to artifacts from the West slowly sifting into their country. A GREAT WALL reluctantly reaffirms the vision of America as an imperialistic parasite, continually searching for new regions to exploit for profit. (Partly in Chinese; English subtitles.)

p, Shirley Sun; d, Peter Wang; w, Peter Wang, Shirley Sun; ph, Peter Stein, Robert Primes; m, David Liang, Ge Ganru; ed, Graham Weinbren.

Drama/Comedy   (PR:A MPAA:PG)

GREEN RAY, THE   (SEE: SUMMER, 1986, Fr.)

GRINGO MOJADO   (SEE: IN 'N' OUT, 1986, U.S./Mex.)

GRITTA VOM RATTENSCHLOSS†   (1986, E. Ger.) 91m DEFA-
                  "Johannisthal" Group c (Trans: Gritta of the Rat Castle)

Kadja Klier *(Gritta)*, Hermann Beyer *(Count Julius Ortel)*, Fred Delmare *(Van Muffert, The Servant)*, Suheer Saleb *(Countess Nesselkrautia)*, Mark Lubosch *(Peter)*, Wolf-Dieter Lingk *(Pekavus)*, Peter Sodann *(King)*, Ilja Kriwoluzky *(Prince Bonus)*, Peter Dommisch *(First Guardian)*, Horst Papke *(Second Guardian)*, Heide Kipp *(Abbess)*.

Children's fairytale film starring Klier as the daughter of eccentric widowed inventor Beyer who has let their castle fall into disrepair. The place is overrun with rats, but rather than being a problem, the rodents are the 13-year-old girl's friends. After Beyer marries a pretty countess, Klier's vindictive new stepmother sends her off to a convent. With the girl gone, the stepmother turns her attention to eradicating the friendly rats. While cloistered in the convent, Klier learns that the abbess is evil and plans to lock her charges up and steal their inheritances. But with the help of her rodent friends, Klier manages to escape the convent and reveal the truth about her stepmother and the evil nun.

d, Jurgen Brauer; w, Christa Kozik (based on a novel by Bettina von Arnim and Gisela von Arnim); ph, Jurgen Brauer; m, Stefan Carnow; ed, Evelyn Carow; set d, Alfred Hirschmeier.

Children's/Fantasy   (PR:A-C MPAA:NR)

GRONA GUBBAR FRAN Y.R.†   (1986, Swed.) 85m Sandrew Film &
             Theater AB-Broderna Lindstrom-Terra Film International/Sandrew Film &
                                                      Theater AB c (Trans: Green Men From Outer Space)

Keijo Salmela *(Yr-ving)*, Ricky Danielsson *(Yr-sel)*, Annika Nuora *(Yr-vaken)*, Roland Jansson *(Finkelstein)*, Charlie Elvegard *(Bernhard)*, Carl Billquist *(Pansarsson)*, Curt Broberg *(Frans)*, Daniel du Rietz *(Micke)*, Jennifer Wesslau *(Fia)*,

Asa Dahlenborg *(Marre)*, Thomas Johansson *(Paul)*, Duane Loken, Leif Alderskanz, John Sand, Christer Nordstrom, Roger Nordstrom.

A children's film directed by German expatriate Hatwig, whose previous career encompassed pop-magazine publishing and videotape features. Three little green men crash-land in Sweden and turn to 19-year-old du Rietz for help. Unable to survive in Earth's atmosphere, the aliens have only 24 hours to repair their ship and return home. Unfortunately, rabid UFO-hunters are in hot pursuit of the trio, further complicating the aliens' race against time.

d, Hans Hatwig; w, Hans Hatwig, Christine Lindsjoo, Claes Vogel; ph, Peter Mokrosinsky; m, Patrik Henzel, Peo Thyren, Kjell Lovbom; ed, David Gilbert; cos, Marie Sorman, Madeleine Bruzelius, Nadia Danielsson; makeup, Dick Ljungberg, Rita Rak.

Children's/Science Fiction   **(PR:AA   MPAA:NR)**

GULSUSAN†   (1986, Turkey) Seref

Halil Ergun Okten, Yaprak Ozdemiroglu, Meral Orhonsay.

d&w, Bilge Olgac; ph, Huseyin Ozsahin.

GUN BUS   (SEE: SKY BANDITS, 1986, Brit.)

GUNESE KOPRU†   (1986, Turkey) Topkapi (Trans: Bridge to the Sun)

Kadir Inanir, Guzin Dogan, Gokhan Mete, Halil Ergun.

d&w, Erdogan Tokatli; ph, Aytekin Cakmakci.

GUNG HO**½   (1986) 111m PAR c

Michael Keaton *(Hunt Stevenson)*, Gedde Watanabe *(Kazihiro)*, George Wendt *(Buster)*, Mimi Rogers *(Audrey)*, John Turturro *(Willie)*, Soh Yamamura *(Sakamoto)*, Sab Shimono *(Saito)*, Rick Overton *(Googie)*, Clint Howard *(Paul)*, Jihmi Kennedy *(Junior)*, Michelle Johnson *(Heather)*, Rodney Kageyama *(Ito)*, Rance Howard *(Mayor Zwart)*.

Many movies have been made about the rank-and-file. Warner Bros. celebrated the common man for years and, more recently, films like BLUE COLLAR, NORMA RAE, and THE DEER HUNTER dealt with the factory types whom Chaplin first limned in MODERN TIMES. This Ron Howard comedy tries to plumb the same genre but comes up short. The attempt at whimsy disintegrates into smart-aleckdom and the result is a middling-good picture that might have been superb if someone like Preston Sturges or Frank Capra had been at the reins. Based on an idea by veteran screenwriter Ed Blum, who saw it first on TV's "60 Minutes" (Blum is coproducer Blum's father), it's the story of what happens when a large Japanese automaker decides to build a plant in a down-at-the-heels Pennsylvania town. (The truth is that Nissan opened a factory in Tennessee.) Hadleyville is a pleasant little one-industry burg that has gone straight to hell since its car factory closed. Keaton is a former employee of the company and he is deputized by the jobless to go to Japan to talk some Nipponese auto executives into considering the downsliding town as an automaking site. He meets with them at their offices and almost blows the whole presentation when he mentions the fact that his father was part of the Occupation Forces in 1946. Keaton manages to see how the Japanese instill company loyalty by attending a Tokyo business school where the students are given ribbons of "shame" which are removed, one by one, as they pass the various tests in their executive gauntlet-run. (Recently, life again imitated art as "60 Minutes" did a story on just such a school.) Despite his near screw-up, the Japanese choose Hadleyville as their location and Keaton is acclaimed a conquering hero. The Japanese arrive en masse and their leader is Watanabe, a young exec who is determined to make this plant a success. But the town's American workers, who had featherbedded for years, rankle under the work rules imposed by the Japanese. These include a pay cut and an almost tyrannical reign of terror by the budget-minded Japanese. Keaton appeals to his fellow-workers to cool it and allow the new employers to have their way until East greets West and the twain meet. The local workers can't handle some of the restraints and morale soon breaks down, production schedules fall behind, and problems arise. The Japanese are of the opinion that all the workers must be dealt with in one self-same fashion, but Keaton argues that Americans like to think they are individuals. In the end, a bet is made that the Americans can turn out enough cars to match the high expectations of their Japanese employers, but they have to do it their own way. The men eventually work loads of overtime in order to meet the schedule, and they barely manage it (did anyone at all think they wouldn't?), and the picture ends with the Japanese theory of teamwork being accepted while the American image remains untarnished.

The synopsis promises more than it delivers because almost all of the characters are too familiar. Whereas other union-based pictures have lauded the worker, this one takes pot shots at the men and women in the blue collars, and mean-spirited pot shots at that. The picture swings from reality to farce to even a bit of choreographed assembly-line footage as the cars are being put together. (The car factory scenes were shot in Argentina, according to an interview with Keaton. No U.S. factories would devote any time to making the movie. They must have read the script.) Rogers appears briefly as Keaton's girl friend and then gets lost. They must have snipped some scenes with her, because that relationship goes nowhere. Nothing wrong with the acting that 114 pages of good dialog couldn't cure. Yamamura, at the time the most revered actor in Japan, plays the boss of the automaker, and the other Japanese actors were very impressed. He had to learn his lines by rote, as he doesn't function too well in English. Pittsburgh and Tokyo were also used for locations, and the picture did well enough to inspire a TV series. Keaton is lovable, as usual, but he comes across as a dumb jerk. This was an obvious attempt at a 1930s-type social comedy. Social it may have been, comedic it wasn't. Still, it was pleasant enough for 111 minutes, and in a world

where John Landis gets to make "comedies" like THE BLUES BROTHERS and INTO THE NIGHT, this stands out as being gloriously adequate. The picture was panned by socially conscious critics on its release, many pundits of the press averring that the problems it addressed so shallowly were too sweeping to be treated in such an offhand manner. Well, heck: it's a movie, not a manifesto (although that might be small comfort to the jobless viewer).

p, Tony Ganz, Deborah Blum; d, Ron Howard; w, Lowell Ganz, Babaloo Mandel; ph, Don Peterman (Continental Film Color); m, Thomas Newman; ed, Daniel Hanley, Michael Hill; prod d, James Schoppe; art d, Jack G. Taylor, Jr.

Comedy   **(PR:C   MPAA:PG-13)**

GURU DAKSHINA†   (1986, India) Film Angan (Trans: Disciples' Offerings to the Priest)

Anupam Kher, K.K. Raina, Satish Kaushik, Suhas Palsikar, Pallavi Joshi.

A runaway youth becomes the disciple of a passing stranger, who attempts to instill his own philosophies in the boy. The deified stranger proves to be a criminal, and tragedy results.

p, K.K. Wattal; d&w, Dayal Nihalani; ph, Sanjay Dharankar; m, Ajit Verman.

Drama   **(PR:NR   MPAA:NR)**

H

HADDA† (1986, Morocco) 110m Prodar-Ohra/Ohra c

Zohra Obaha *(Hadda)*, Hamid *(Hamid)*, Mohamed Mechaal *(The Poet)*, Thourayah *(Aouicha)*.

A picturesque allegory about an arid desert village waiting for the arrival of rain. Hamid is a young heir who must fight to gain control of the land that is rightfully his, and Obaha is an outcast who wanders the desert with her sister Thourayah. Moroccan folk traditions and poetry form the basis of the tale.

p, Chkili Farad, Izza Gennini; d, Mohamed Aboulouakar; w, Mohamed Aboulouakar, Tijani Chrigui, Mohamed Mechaal; ph, Mustapha Sitou; ed, Marie Josef Yoyotte, Tijani Chrigui, Mohamed Aboulouakar; art d, Mohamed Aboulouakar, Tijani Chrigui; cos, Mosaique.

Drama **(PR:C-O MPAA:NR)**

HAJNALI HAZTETOK† (1986, Hung.) Budapest Studio–Hungarian Television (Trans: Roofs at Dawn)

Peter Andorai, Gyorgy Cserhalmi, Dorottya Udvaros, Kati Takacs.

d&w, Janos Domolky (based on the novel by Geza Ottlik); ph, Lajos Koltai.

HAKRAV AL HAVA'AD† (1986, Israel) 90m Kayitz/Noah c (AKA: MONDO CONDO; Trans: House Committee Rivalry)

Shayke Levy *(Khalfon)*, Israel Poliakoff *(Dr. Shemesh)*, Gavri Banai *(Jimbo)*, Tamar Gingold, Shyula Khen, Dori Ben-Ze'ev, Moshe Ivgi, Eyal Geffen, Alon Aboutboul.

Levy, Poliakoff, and Banai are a popular Israeli comedy troupe who have yet to translate their stage and TV success to film. This, their third film, doesn't seem to do it for the trio either, though some of their satirical arrows are aimed at the right targets. Two condominium owners come into conflict over a variety of issues, and the situation escalates from there.

p, Avraham Desha [Peshanel]; d, Avi Cohen; w, Assi Dayan; ph, Gad Danzig, Benny Carmeli; ed, Anath Lubarsky; cos, Ruth Dar; m/l, Erich Rudich, Eli Mohar.

Comedy **(PR:C MPAA:NR)**

HALF-DUAN QING† (1986, Hong Kong) 95m Centro Film (Trans: Infatuation)

Ye Tong [Cecilia Yip], Lu Guanting [Lowell Lo], Xu Guanying [Ricky Hui], Angela Wilson, Eric Yeung.

Lu falls in love with Ye while videotaping her marriage to a man who has been carrying on with another woman. Though Ye learns about the affair, through Lu's taping of a rendezvous, she remains devoted, determined to hold onto her man. An impressive film debut for director Chen.

p, Zhu Jiaxin [John Chu]; d, Chen Guoxi [Louis Tan]; w, Ho Kangqiao [Josephine Ho]; ph, Abdul Rumjahn; m, Lu Guanting [Lowell Lo]; art d, Zhang Shuping [William Cheung].

Romance/Comedy **(PR:C MPAA:NR)**

HALF MOON STREET* (1986) 90m RKO–Pressman–Showtime–The Movie Channel/FOX c (AKA: ESCORT GIRL)

Sigourney Weaver *(Lauren Slaughter)*, Michael Caine *(Lord Bulbeck)*, Patrick Kavanagh *(General Sir George Newhouse)*, Faith Kent *(Lady Newhouse)*, Ram John Holder *(Lindsay Walker)*, Keith Buckley *(Hugo Van Arkady)*, Annie Hanson *(Mrs. Van Arkady)*, Patrick Newman *(Julian Shuttle)*, Niall O'Brien *(Captain Twilley)*, Nadim Sawalha *(Karim Hatami)*, Vincent Lindon *(Sonny)*, Muriel Villiers *(Madame Cybele)*, Michael Elwyn *(Tom Haldane)*, Ninka Scott *(Mrs. Haldane)*, Jasper Jacob *(Rex Lanham)*, Donald Pickering *(George Hardcastle)*, Maria Aitken *(The Hon. Maura Hardcastle)*, Hossein Karimbeik *(Colonel Hassan Ali)*, Anita Edwards *(Mrs. Hassan Ali)*, Angus MacInnes *(Bill Rafferty)*, John Sinclair *(French Businessman)*, Eiji Kusuhara *(Japanese Businessman)*, Togo Igawa *(Japanese Waiter)*, Rupert Vansittart *(Alan Platts-Williams)*, Anne Lambton *(Sidney Platts-Williams)*, Judy Liebert *(Dutch)*, Brian Hawksley *(Institute Porter)*, Dulice Liecier *(Jamaican Escort-Girl)*, Judy Maynard *(Cherubic Woman)*, Andy Lucas, Kevork Malikyan *(Diplomats)*, Haluk Bilginer *(Arab)*, Dave Duffy *(Bodyguard)*, Philip Whitchurch *(Plainclothesman)*, Hugo De Vernier *(Wine Waiter)*, Mac MacDonald *(Eddy Pressback)*, Robert Lee *(Chinese Ambassador)*, Andrew Seear *(TV Newsreader)*, Janet McTeer *(Van Arkady's Secretary)*, Carol Cleveland *(American Wife)*, Katharine Schofield *(Overdressed Lady)*, Siobhan Redmond *(Institute Secretary)*, Claude Villers *(Concierge Clerk)*, Robert Guillermet *(French Waiter)*, Joy Lemoine *(Soft-Voiced Woman)*, Timothy Peters *(Barry Gingham)*, Rosemary McHale *(Woman)*.

Fortunately for Sigourney Weaver, the phenomenal success of ALIENS overshadowed the fact that she appeared in two other films this year—HALF MOON STREET and ONE WOMAN OR TWO—both excruciatingly bad and which, were it not for her gutsy science-fiction heroine role, could have severely crippled her reputation as an actress. As it is, most audiences are going to have a hard time forgiving her for HALF MOON STREET—an intended romantic thriller based

on the novel *Dr. Slaughter* by Paul Theroux (this year's other Theroux adaptation, THE MOSQUITO COAST, also flopped at the box office). Bogged down in cinematic sludge, the film stars Weaver as "one of those peculiar Americans who wants to live abroad," as her character describes herself.

A scholar studying at London's Middle East Institute, Weaver has difficulty making ends meet financially. She is overlooked by a fellowship committee because she is a woman; she lives in a fleabag hotel where she regularly exposes herself to the landlord; and, of course, she has a brilliant mind when it comes to international affairs. One day her life changes when she receives a videotape in the mail from a high-class escort service. She decides to supplement her paltry income by becoming a hooker—not the sleazy kind, but an independent-minded one who picks and chooses her customers. Yeah, sure! She bed hops with some of the brightest and the best, eventually arriving at the door of Caine, a renowned diplomat whom she has admired over the years. Not only do they roll around under the covers, but they also exchange intellectually stimulating conversation about international oil exports. In the meantime, Weaver has become a frequent guest at diplomatic affairs, hobnobbing with princes and executives. Not only does she thrill them with her overbearing sexual effervescence, but she also wows them with her worldliness. It is at one of these gatherings that she meets Sawalha, a filthy rich sheik who showers her with love and gifts. He even sets her up in a luxurious apartment. For all her brains, however, she fails to realize she is being set up in an international scheme engineered by Sawalha, which eventually erupts into a violent shoot-'em-up finale.

Director Swaim, an American (hailing from Evanston, Illinois) living abroad, made a heavy impression on the French box office with his overrated 1982 Cesarwinning *policier*, LA BALANCE. Rather than build on LA BALANCE's strong points (a visually exciting style and some fine acting), Swaim has lost himself in an excess of plodding plot points and intrigue. Caine turns in his usual accomplished performance, but Weaver shows a side of her acting self that has rarely been matched for gross incompetence. In fairness to Weaver, she gets not an iota of help from a script which goes to great pains to make everyone thoroughly detestable. The Mid-Eastern characters are painted as swarthy, scheming louses, while almost all the males are sexist, close-minded cretins. With Weaver's character, Swaim has tried to paint a portrait of the proverbial "woman for the eighties," but has failed miserably. Swaim has said, "I wanted to do a woman's picture and I found a vehicle for that in Paul Theroux's book . . . I think there's a strong feminist slant to the story." Instead, he has created a character who, rather than appeal as intelligent and sensual, comes across as a dimwitted, indecisive slut.

p, Geoffrey Reeve; d, Bob Swaim; w, Bob Swaim, Edward Behr (based on the novel *Doctor Slaughter* by Paul Theroux); ph, Peter Hannan (Technicolor); m, Richard Harvey; ed, Richard Marden; prod d, Anthony Curtis; art d, Peter Williams; set d, Peter Young; cos, Louise Frogley; spec eff, Arthur Beavis; makeup, Linda De Vetta; stunts, Joe Powell.

Drama/Crime **Cas.** **(PR:O MPAA:R)**

HAMBURGER zero (1986) 90m FM Entertainment c

Leigh McCloskey *(Russell)*, Dick Butkus *(Drootin)*, Randi Brooks *(Mrs. Vunk)*, Chuck McCann *(Dr. Mole)*, Jack Blessing *(Nacio Herb Zipser)*, Charles Tyner *(Lyman Vunk)*, Debra Blee *(Mia Vunk)*, Sandy Hackett *(Fred)*, John Young *(Prestopopnick)*, Chip McAllister *(Magneto)*, Barbara Whinnery *(Sister Sara)*, Maria Richwine *(Conchita)*, Karen Mayo-Chandler *(Dr. Gotbottom)*.

HAMBURGER is a follow-up to coproducer Feldman's HOT DOG, which had nothing to do with frankfurters (It's a word referring to a certain type of showoff skiing). This, unfortunately, is about hamburgers. We are told that the MacDonalds corporation does have a school where they teach people how to run the most successful fast-food operation in history. Whether or not the makers of this movie had that school in mind is beside the point. What they have done here is satirize something that nobody knows anything about, and since satire insists that the viewer know what's being parodied, this doesn't work. HOT DOG was skewered by critics, but managed to earn a good deal of money, so this follow-up was in order. What's next? Pizzas? Knishes? McCloskey is a womanizer in his early 20s who has been tossed out of several colleges, mostly because coeds find him immensely attractive, and that seems to be forbidden at the schools from which he's been cashiered. His grandfather has left him a quarter of a million dollars, but there's a kicker in the will. He must graduate from a college with a degree in order to get the money. Desperate, McCloskey sees a TV commercial about "Busterburger U." and enrolls. Once at the school—which is run with Nazi-like military precision by former Chicago Bears linebacker Butkus—McCloskey runs afoul of the behemoth when Blee, Butkus' beloved, falls for him. Several other students have come to the school to learn the ins and outs of burgerbiz in a whirlwind 12-week course. These include McCann, Tyner, Brooks, and Mayo-Chandler (the latter two being around so we can see what they look like without tops on). The curriculum of the school is what one might think and there are a few nude bits to go with the comedy, all leading to the final scene where the students are required to actually man—and woman—a fast-food stand to which real customers will be coming. To sabotage McCloskey's graduation exercise, Butkus arranges to have a battalion of grossly obese people arrive. These porkers run through the food like locusts through a wheatfield while making noises like hogs. (Get it?) In order to get rid of the fatties, the students mickey-finn their milkshakes with heavy laxatives, and the rotund ones race for the john, which then explodes. Next, a pack of tough bikers arrive followed by a group of black motorcycle police officers. Finally, some Mexican chicken farmers crash into the fast-food stand. Then, wonder of wonders, a chicken falls into the fryer and when it is retrieved, it's delicious. This is the exact thing that Busterburger U. had been looking for. The students graduate with honors, Butkus is stripped of his rank, and it ends on an upbeat note . . . perhaps a G Flat . . .

because Gee, this is sure a flat picture, barring some topless chests. The jokes are puerile, the acting is universally obvious (with the exception of McCann and a couple of others), the direction has no subtlety, and the movie will probably go on to make a lot of money and prove H.L. Mencken right. (You'll have to look up what the sage of Baltimore said about the taste of the American people). Marvin, the director, coproduced and wrote the earlier HOT DOG. This one was written by Donald Ross, a man who has written some of the best and wittiest TV shows on the air. Whether the final result resembles his script at all is something we'll never know. Nudity and foul language make this off limits to children. Downright stupidity makes it off limits to adults.

p, Edward S. Feldman, Charles R. Meeker; d, Mike Marvin; w, Donald Ross; ph, Karen Grossman (CFI Color); m, Peter Bernstein; ed, Steven Schoenberg, Ann E. Mills; prod d, George Costello; art d, Maria Rebman Caso; cos, Shari Feldman.

Comedy **(PR:O MPAA:R)**

HAME'AHEV† (1986, Israel) 90m G.G./Cannon c (Trans: The Lover)

Michal Bat-Adam *(Assia),* Yehoram Gaon *(Adam),* Avigail Arieli *(Daffi),* Roberto Pollak *(Gavriel),* Awas Khatib *(Naim),* Fanny Lubitsch *(Grandmother).*

One of the most successful Israeli novels of recent years was the source for this film. Directed by star Bat-Adam, the film was much criticized for ignoring many of the novel's ramifications in favor of simply telling the story of Bat-Adam's brief, intense affair with a stranger who ingratiates himself with her family. When the 1973 War breaks out, he disappears. Canny filmgoers reduced their expectations for this film as soon as they saw that Golan and Globus owned the rights.

p, Menahem Golan, Yoram Globus; d, Michal Bat-Adam; w, Michal Bat-Adam, Zwika Kertzner (based on the novel by A.B. Yehoshua); ph, David Gurfinkel; m, Dov Seltzer; ed, Tova Asher; art d, Eytan Levy.

Drama **(PR:C-O MPAA:NR)**

HANA ICHIMOMME† (1986, Jap.) Toei (Trans: Life with Senility)

Yukiyo Toake, Teruhiko Saigo, Yumiko Nogawa, Minoru Chiaki, Haruko Kato.

d, Toshiya Ito; w, Hiroo Matsuda; ph, Isamu Iguchi; m, Shin-ichiro Ikebe.

HANDS OF STEEL* (1986, It.) 94m National Cinematografica–Dania –Medusa/Almi c

Daniel Greene *(Paco Querak),* Janet Agren *(Linda),* John Saxon *(Francis Turner),* George Eastman *(Raoul Fernandez),* Amy Werba *(Dr. Peckinpaugh),* Claudio Cassinelli, Robert Ben, Pat Monti, Andrew Louis Coppola, Donald O'Brien.

The Italians have long been known for their cannibalizing of American film genres and rip-offs of big hits. This film is one of the latter, a knock-off of THE TERMINATOR. Greene is the killer cyborg, 70 percent of his body rebuilt as a fantastically strong, electronically controlled robot assassin after he was injured in some Central American war. Saxon is the heavy, head of the giant conglomerate whose scientists created Greene. Sent to kill a blind, wheelchair-bound ecology leader (whose slogan is a cheery "you have no future"), Greene has a sudden pang of conscience and softens his punch to only rupture his victim's spleen. He runs away to the desert near his birthplace and takes a job with Agren, who runs a sleazy motel with a bar where truckers come to arm wrestle. After beating the local champ, then trouncing everyone in the bar, Greene naturally makes some enemies, and he is later lured out to the desert and badly beaten and left tied up. He escapes, though, and beats the tri-state champion. Meanwhile Saxon has sent some killers after his rogue cyborg, and they eventually track him down. After ripping the head off a female cyborg (her character copied from that of Daryl Hannah in BLADE RUNNER), and killing a pack of others, he eventually comes to Saxon, who is armed with a laser bazooka. Saxon panics and starts to plead for his life, but Greene tells him, "You thought you could own me by controlling my brain, but what you didn't realize was that you don't own a man until you control his heart." Then he rips out Saxon's heart, just to illustrate his point.

No style, no suspense, no acting, no script, and nothing to relieve the boredom of sitting through this turkey. Greene never generates any sympathy for his plight and nothing ever seems to really matter here. The main action of the middle part of the film is the two arm-wrestling matches, and a less cinematically dynamic sport would be hard to find. Since we know that Greene has a robot arm, the results of the matches are never in doubt. In fact, the only thing interesting about the film is trying to keep track of all the films from which it borrows, from the obvious TERMINATOR through BRAZIL (every room has cheap plastic ducts). Unlike most of the Italian science-fiction films that turn up on these shores, this one actually managed to get a theatrical release, briefly playing the southern drive-in circuit.

d, Martin Dolman [Sergio Martino]; w, Martin Dolman [Sergio Martino], Elisabeth Parker, Saul Sasha, John Crowther, Lewis Clanelli (based on a story by Martin Dolman [Sergio Martino]); ph, John McFerrand [Giancarlo Ferrando] (Luciano Vittori Color); m, Claudio Simonetti; ed, Alan Devgen; spec eff, Robert Callmard, Paul Callmard, Elio Terry; spec eff makeup, Sergio Stivaletti.

Science Fiction **Cas.** **(PR:O MPAA:R)**

HANNAH AND HER SISTERS*** (1986) 106m Orion c

Woody Allen *(Mickey),* Michael Caine *(Elliot),* Mia Farrow *(Hannah),* Carrie Fisher *(April),* Barbara Hershey *(Lee),* Lloyd Nolan *(Hannah's Father),* Maureen O'Sullivan *(Hannah's Mother),* Daniel Stern *(Dusty),* Max Von Sydow *(Frederick),* Dianne Wiest *(Holly),* Lewis Black *(Paul),* Julia Louis-Dreyfus *(Mary),*

Christian Clemenson *(Larry),* Julie Kavner *(Gail),* J.T. Walsh *(Ed Smythe),* John Turturro *(Writer),* Rusty Magee *(Ron),* Allen Decheser, Artie Decheser *(Hannah's Twins),* Ira Wheeler *(Dr. Abel),* Richard Jenkins *(Dr. Wilkes),* Tracy Kennedy *(Brunch Guest),* Fred Melamed *(Dr. Grey),* Benno Schmidt *(Dr. Smith),* Joanna Gleason *(Carol),* Maria Chiara *(Manon Lescaut),* Stephen Defluiter *(Dr. Brooks),* The 39 Steps *(Rock Band),* Bobby Short *(Himself),* Rob Scott *(Drummer),* Beverly Peer *(Bass Player),* Daisy Previn, Moses Farrow *(Hannah's Children),* Paul Bates *(Theater Manager),* Carrotte, Mary Pappas *(Theater Executives),* Bernie Leighton *(Audition Pianist),* Ken Costigan *(Father Flynn),* Helen Miller *(Mickey's Mother),* Leo Postrel *(Mickey's Father),* Susan Gordon-Clark *(Hostess),* William Sturgis *(Elliot's Analyst),* Daniel Haber *(Krishna),* Verno O. Hobson *(Mavis),* John Doumanian, Fletcher Previn, Irwin Tenenbaum, Amy Greenhill, Dickson Shaw, Marje Sheridan *(Thanksgiving Guests),* Ivan Kronenfeld *(Lee's Husband).*

At 106 minutes, this is somewhat longer than most of Allen's movies, but he had much more of a story to tell and it never feels slow. Essentially three separate tales which intertwine at times, HANNAH AND HER SISTERS is, by far, Allen's most complex film and the first one where the neurotic shlep is left with a glimmer of happiness. Perhaps all those years on his analyst's couch are now paying off. Many of Allen's pictures had similar scenes. In THE FRONT and MANHATTAN and PLAY IT AGAIN, SAM, he was always after the elusive

shiksa goddess and there was usually a scene where he is running after her at the end. It also happened in BROADWAY DANNY ROSE. Seeing many of his films in a row, one notes the similarities in them. This time, that theme goes out the window in favor of a mural, whereas the others were line drawings or charcoal sketches.

Farrow is married to Caine, a business manager for rock stars. She used to be married to Allen, who produces a TV show like "Saturday Night Live," and they had children together. Farrow's sisters are Hershey, who is living with witty, bitter Von Sydow—a SoHo artist who stays in his loft and communicates with the rest of New York through her—and Wiest, an actress who is a bundle of nerves. Farrow had been a successful actress but gave that up to be Allen's and then

Caine's wife. Whatever talent coursed through the sisters' genes, little of it has been bestowed on Wiest. Their parents are the bickering show business duo of O'Sullivan (Farrow's real-life mother and once "Jane" to Johnny Weismuller's "Tarzan") and Nolan (who died shortly after the film was completed). The picture takes place over a couple of years and is framed by Thanksgiving dinners. This is the first time Allen has shown family life rather than the single existence in his beloved Manhattan.

Caine carries a passion around for Hershey and eventually makes it known to her. She resists his advances for a while, then succumbs, guilt-ridden at doing this to her elder sister. Eventually, Hershey decides to leave Von Sydow (who has a wonderfully funny scene as Caine brings one of his clients, Stern, to buy some art and Von Sydow won't deal with the rock 'n' roll Philistine in favor of Caine, but he can't bear to say farewell to Farrow. Wiest is a former cocaine addict and always on the edge. In order to supplement her meager acting income, she works with Fisher and they run a catering service. Fisher is also an actress and a predatory woman. She first pilfers Wiest's current lover (the uncredited Sam Waterston), and then an acting job Wiest had her heart set upon. This almost sends Wiest over into a mental abyss. Before Allen had married Farrow, he'd dated Wiest, and we get to see that in a flashback that is hysterically funny, as everything that can possibly go wrong on a date does. As the movie cuts from the Caine/Hershey affair and Wiest, it also includes Allen's life. He is a world class hypochondriac and is convinced that he is dying of a brain tumor, even after he is assured he is not. This "brush with death" causes him to change his life, exit his high-paying job, and consider seeking a new religion: Catholicism. To that end, he brings home white bread, mayonnaise, and a picture of Jesus. He even talks to a Hare Krishna monk to see if that sect can offer him anything. He finally realizes that all that matters is to enjoy oneself. This he learns as he laughs happily at a print of the Marx Brothers in DUCK SOUP.

Meanwhile, we see the various plights of Farrow and her sisters, and only one major scene in which they are alone together. This takes place at a Manhattan restaurant where they have lunch. The camera moves around the women in one long, continuous shot, and the take is a marvel of writing and realistic acting. Wiest can no longer contain her envy of Farrow, who is the oldest and the most perfect sister. Farrow has a lovely husband (who is sleeping with Hershey), lovely children, and what appears to be a blissful existence to the nervous Wiest. The scene is brief, but telling, and it is this single sequence that explains the relationship among the trio. At the conclusion, after Allen has dealt with his illnesses (he *knows* he's going deaf but can't reckon which ear), he and Wiest decide that they are two neurotics cut from the same cloth, and they wind up together with her expecting. Once again, Allen is part of the family and the Thanksgiving dinners, and the movie ends on what must be the most uplifting note of his career to date.

Long-time Allen pal Tony Roberts chimes in with an uncredited appearance, as does Joanna Gleason (daughter of Monte and Marilyn Hall of TV's "Let's Make a Deal"). The plot could easily have been an afternoon soap opera, but Allen has infused it with wit, superb casting, and his traditional "the best direction is the least direction," so it never seems as though a camera is turning. His cinematographer was Italian Carlo Di Palma, thus putting an end to a series of films for which Gordon Willis turned the crank. Allen won British Film Academy Awards for Best Screenplay and Best Direction for the movie in March, 1987. The picture also culled three Academy Awards: Best Original Screenplay (Allen), Best Supporting Actress (Wiest), and Best Supporting Actor (Caine).

Allen uses a chapter structure and heads each chapter with a title, something he's done in other films. Much of this was shot in the fecund Farrow's own apartment and seven of her eight children are seen at the dinners. Many would say that director Allen took a lot of chances with this. We think not. After all, he had screenwriter Allen, actor Allen, Allen's girl friend (Farrow), Allen's girl friend's mother (O'Sullivan), and many of the same crew he'd used before. The movie earned more than any other Allen picture ever and appealed to many people who had always felt that his work was too New York-narrow. Allen seldom has to rely on off-color jokes to get laughs. There are a few words in the script which may be unsuitable for children under 13, but they are rare. The

adulterous theme is what might give kids the wrong idea, especially in the late 1980s, when the threat of AIDS was rampant. Barbara Hershey was superb and, after beginning her career in 1968 in WITH SIX YOU GET EGGROLL, she has established herself as a major force in movies, having appeared in such diverse films as THE NATURAL, THE STUNT MAN, THE RIGHT STUFF, and HOOSIERS. Allen followed HANNAH AND HER SISTERS with RADIO DAYS, a totally different kind of movie. Ever on a quest for expansion, let's hope he continues expanding, like a one-man universe, until he has covered every possible type of movie as only he can. Music includes plenty of pop standards, classical chamber music, and a couple of operas.

p, Robert Greenhut; d&w, Woody Allen; ph, Carlo Di Palma (Panavision, Technicolor); ed, Susan E. Morse; prod d, Stuart Wurtzel; set d, Carol Joffe; cos, Jeffrey Kurland; makeup, Fern Buchner.

Comedy/Drama   (PR:C   MPAA:PG-13)

HAPPILY EVER AFTER†   (1986, Braz.) 110m Producoes Cinematograficas/European Classics c (ALEM DA PAIXAO)

Regina Duarte *(Fernanda Sampaio)*, Paulo Castelli *(Miguel)*, Patricio Bisso *(Bom Bom)*, Flavio Galvao *(Roberto)*, Flavio Sao Thiago, Ivan Setta, Felipe Martins.

The bulk of Brazilian film is composed of soft core pornographic features, and occasionally one of them makes it to the U.S., like this 1985 release helmed by the director of the most successful Brazilian film of all time, DONA FLOR AND HER TWO HUSBANDS. Like that film, the central character is a repressed housewife who finds sexual liberation at the hands of a sexy young man (just about the oldest story in smut). Duarte is the woman, upper-class, reasonably happily married, and unable to forget a dream in which she dances with a woman who turns out to be a man. One day she hits a pedestrian with her car, and he turns out to be the man from the dream. He robs her, but leaves behind a book of matches that lead her to a transvestite club where he dances in drag. Soon the two have become lovers, but she is so blinded by passion that she cannot see that her bisexual Romeo is robbing her blind and using the money to finance drug deals. (In Portuguese; English subtitles).

p, Lucy Barreto, Antonio Calmon; d, Bruno Barreto; w, Bruno Barreto, Antonio Calmon; ph, Affonso Beato; ed, Vera Freire; set d, Oscar Ramos.

Drama   (PR:O   MPAA:NR)

HAPPY DIN DON†   (1986, Hong Kong) 98m Golden Harvest-Paragon c (AKA: HUANE DINGDANG)

Michael Hui Cherie Chung, Tung Pui, Michael Lai, Wong Ching, Wong Waan Sze, Ricky Hui, Anita Mui, Winnie Chin, Tin Ching, Shen Wai.

Hui, one of the top film comedians in the Crown Colony, returns to the movies after a two-year hiatus, directing and starring in this variation of SOME LIKE IT HOT. He plays a musician who overhears plans for a drug murder. He goes into hiding in an all-girl band bound for Bangkok, where predictable complications ensue. While Hui's previous two features were huge hits, this one did disappointing business. (In Cantonese; English subtitles.)

d, Michael Hui; ph, Ardy Lam; m, Michael Lai; ed, Chueng Yiu Chung; prod d, David Chan; art d, Carman Wan.

Comedy   (PR:C   MPAA:NR)

HARD ASFALT†   (1986, Nor.) 97m Filmkammeraterne–Norway Film Development/Norsk c (Trans: Hard Asphalt)

Kristin Kajander *(Ida)*, Frank Krog *(Knut)*, Marianne Nilsen *(Ase)*, Tone Schwarzott *(Ida's Mother)*, Tom Tellefsen *(Ida's Father)*.

Based on a best-selling novel, HARD ASFALT recounts the true story of a prostitute hardened by an unhappy childhood, her marriage to an alcoholic husband, and a number of other unfortunate circumstances. Kajander plays the struggling hooker who learns to overcome adverse situations and retain her dignity.

p, John M. Jacobsen; d&w, Solve Skagen (based on the novel by Ida Halvorsen, Liv Finstad, Cecilie Hoigard); ph, Erling Thurmann (Eastmancolor); m, Marius Muller; ed, Malte Wadman; prod d, Anne Siri Bryhni.

Drama   (PR:O   MPAA:NR)

HARDBODIES 2*   (1986) 95m Chroma III–First American–Lee Fry/Cintel c

Brad Zutaut *(Scott)*, Sam Temeles *(Rags)*, Curtis Scott Wilmot *(Sean Kingsley)*, Brenda Bakke *(Morgan)*, Fabiana Udenio *(Cleo)*, Louise Baker *(Cookie)*, James Karen *(Logan)*, Alba Francesca *(Zachery)*, Sorrells Pickard *(Carlton Ashby)*, Roberta Collins *(Lana Logan)*, Julie Rhodes *(Ms. Rollins)*, Alexi Mylones *(Brucie)*, George Tzifos *(Cleo's Father)*, Ula Gavala *(Kidnaper's Wife)*, George Kotandis *(Kidnaper)*, Robert Rhine *(Camera Assistant)*, Brad Zutaut *(Scotty Palmer)*, Nana *(Fantasy Stewardess)*, Ulrika Hellstrom *(Girl at Airport)*, Lefteris Andrikos *(Custom Agent)*, Thanassis Christopoulos *(Hotel Clerk)*, Alexandra Paylides *(Albertine)*, Elizabeth Pericolo, Vicky Kougianos *(Semester-at-Sea Girls)*, Panos Logothetis *(Mr. Pujapipoint)*, Vassili Karamesinis *(Bodyguard of Stunt Coordinator)*, Charles P. Bernuth *(Dancing Thief)*, Maxine Ain *(Cabin Attendant)*.

This followup (of sorts) to 1984's HARDBODIES has little in common with its predecessor other than director, title, and plenty of exposed female flesh. Rest assured, however, the complete switch in story and characters raises little, if any, argument with the film's intended audiences. The story opens as some incredibly handsome surfers go flying off to Greece where they are scheduled to appear in a film. Upon arrival at the airport, the gorgeous lugs are seized by customs for transporting dope, but wait! Its all part of the movie. Gradually it develops that Zutaut, Temeles, and the not-so-nice Wilmot are the stars of the film within a film. What's missing is a comely lass to costar in this extravaganza (entitled FOREIGN AFFAIRS) and auditions turn up nothing. While dining at an outdoor cafe the filmmakers come across Udenio, a beautiful Greek girl with a sweet smile and no acting experience. Of course she's hired on the spot, and Zutaut falls for her for her considerable charms. Problems arise when Zutaut's shopping-mad fiancee Bakke grows jealous, while Udenio makes it clear she's no easy pickings. In the meantime, all sorts of intrigues develop in the fascinating world of exploitation filmmaking. Francesca, the film's director, is an aspiring Lina Wertmuller, chain-smoking thin brown cigarettes as she attempts to bring some semblance of artistic vision to her opus. She's assisted by Baker, a scatterbrained blonde who serves as this film's homage to Chrissy Snow, the character played by Suzanne Sommers on the television series "Three's Company." Other subplots involve marital infidelities, and a Greek extra who misunderstands the producers when they ask him to play a kidnaper. At the film's climax, Zutaut and Udenio manage to overcome their differences and hurriedly board a plane bound for the good ol' U.S., leaving behind an astonished FOREIGN AFFAIRS crew.

Okay, so it's not great art. But then again, it's not meant to be. Mostly, HARDBODIES 2 is bared bosoms and handsome hunks with a little bit of moronic humor tossed in to break up the monotony. The cast is likable enough, albeit there isn't much talent there. Udenio comes off the best, and she doesn't

have to work real hard at that. This wasn't a film aimed at scholars, but at kids driving around in daddy's car on a Saturday night. On the other hand, with the confusing beginning, as the film inexplicably alters between the "reality" of HARDBODIES 2 and the "fiction" of FOREIGN AFFAIRS, we conceivably could be witnessing the birth of a new cinematic hybrid: the first Godardian make-out movie. Songs and musical numbers include: "Adventures in Paradise," "Going Through the Motions," "Keep on Following Your Heart" (Jay Levy, Terry Shaddick, performed by Dave Morgan), "Foreign Relations" (Eddie Arkin, Levy, performed by Linda Lawley), "Rachael" (Sorrels Pickard, performed by Pickard), "Expose Yourself" (Arkin, Larry Cox, performed by Suzanne Wallach), "Children of the Night" (Levy, Shaddick), "Searching for You" (Mary Eckler, performed by Eckler), "Hardbodies" (Richard Marx, Bruce Gaitson, performed by Ress), "Close Your Eyes" (Levy, Arkin, performed by Don Markese).

p, Jeff Begun, Ken Solomon, Dimitri Logothetis, Joseph Medawar; d, Mark Griffiths; w, Mark Griffiths, Curtis Scott Wilmot (based on characters created by Steve Greene, Eric Alter); ph, Tom Richmond; m, Jay Levy, Eddie Arkin; ed, Andy Blumenthal; art d, Theodosis Davlos; spec eff, Yannis Samioths; m/l, Jay Levy, Terry Shaddick, Eddie Arkin, Sorrels Pickard, Larry Cox, Mary Eckler, Richard Marx, Bruce Gaitson; makeup, Stella Votson.

Comedy   Cas.   (PR:O MPAA:R)

HARU NO KANE†   (1986, Jap.) Toho (Trans: Spring Bell)

Kin-ya Kitaoji, Yuko Kotegawa, Yoshiko Mita, Eiji Okada, Kyoko Kishida.

d, Koreyoshi Kurahara; w, Koji Takada (based on the novel by Masaki Tatsuhara); ph, Akira Shiizuka; m, Yuzuru Hisaishi.

HARUKOMA NO UTA†   (1986, Jap.) Kyodo Eiga Sha (Trans: Ballad of
                                                                     Pony)

Takahiro Tamura, Sachiko Hidari, Takashi Tosaka, Kaori Chigira, Kyoko Kagawa.

d, Seijiro Koyama; w, (based on the novel by Hiro Miyagawa); ph, Fuminori Minami; m, Masao Haryu.

HASHIGAON HAGADOL†   (1986, Israel) 105m G.G. Studios/Cannon c
     (AKA: THE WILD, CRAZY, AND THE LUNATICS; Trans: Funny Farm)

Seffi Rivlin, Arik Lavie, Yehuda Efroni, Dina Doron, Anath Waxman, Louis Rosenberg, Shmuel Vilozhni.

Rivlin is a bank manager who finds a counterfeiting operation in the basement of an insane asylum. Despite a big-budget ad campaign emphasizing Rivlin and Israel's first production in Dolby stereo, the film failed at home and seems unlikely to be exported.

p, Menahem Golan, Yoram Globus; d, Naftali Alter; w, Menhem Golan (based on a story by Yossi Savaya); ph, Ilan Rosenberg; m, Naftali Alter; ed, Moshe Avni; cos, Debbie Leon.

Comedy   (PR:C MPAA:NR)

HAUNTED HONEYMOON*½   (1986) 82m Orion c

Gene Wilder *(Larry Abbot)*, Gilda Radner *(Vickie Pearle)*, Dom DeLuise *(Aunt Kate)*, Jonathan Pryce *(Charles)*, Paul L. Smith *(Dr. Paul Abbot)*, Peter Vaughan *(Francis, Sr.)*, Bryan Pringle *(Pfister)*, Roger Ashton-Griffiths *(Francis, Jr.)*, Jim Carter *(Montego)*, Eve Ferret *(Sylvia)*, Julann Griffin *(Nora Abbot)*, Jo Ross *(Susan)*, Ann Way *(Rachael)*, Will Keaton *(Werewolf)*, Don Fellows *(Pro-*

ducer), Lou Hirsch *(Sponsor)*, Christopher Muncke *(Announcer)*, Bill Bailey *(The Host)*, David Healy *(Public Relations Man)*, Howard Swinson *(Eddy, SFX Man)*, Edward Wiley *(Engineer)*, Andrea Browne *(Production Assistant)*, Matt Zimmerman *(1st Radio Actor)*, Francis Drake, Mac McDonald, William Hootkins, Barbara Rosenblat *(Reporters)*, John Bloomfield, Colin Bruce *(Photographers)*, Sally Osborn *(Larry's Mother)*, Alastair Haley *(Little Larry)*, Scampi *(Toby the Dog)*, Andy Ross *(Conductor)*, Claire Deniz, Paul Henessey, Brian Kershaw, Don Morgan, Ernest Mothle, Zorak Okai, Robert Turrell, Justin Ward *(Orchestra)*.

A humorless throwback to the nostalgic days of haunted house comedies made popular by such teams as Abbott and Costello (HOLD THAT GHOST) and Bob Hope and Paulette Goddard (THE CAT AND THE CANARY, GHOST BEAKERS) and on radio with "I Love A Mystery." Directed by Wilder, HAUNTED HONEYMOON begins in a radio studio as a mystery show called "Manhattan Mystery Theater" is being broadcast. The show's stars, Wilder (who, not coincidentally, is named Abbott) and Radner, are set to leave for their honeymoon later that evening. Wilder, however, is victimized by a variety of phobias that are triggered by the spooky special effects created for their show. Certain that he is a werewolf, Wilder loses his concentration and begins to garble his lines, turning the chilling mystery into a comedy. His psychiatrist uncle, the ominous-looking Smith, has a plan to cure his phobias by scaring him. In the meantime, Wilder's aging aunt (DeLuise in drag, which turns him into a caricature of Ethel Barrymore) has made him the sole beneficiary of her new will. If he should die, however, the money will be split among the surviving family members.

Wilder and Radner plan to celebrate their honeymoon at the family mansion—a frightening-looking place that would appeal only to mad scientists and their creations. A number of family members are also in attendance—the stately and forgetful butler Pringle, greedy and penniless cousin Pryce and his sexpot girl friend Ferret, uncle Vaughan and his transvestite son Ashton-Griffiths, and others who are elaborately introduced and then, inexplicably, forgotten (specifi-

cally Carter and Ross). Smith undertakes his campaign to frighten Wilder: he bricks up his bedroom door, sends a disfigured monster to walk up and down the walls, has a hand pop up from a grave, and turns Radner into an apparition in her wedding gown. Meanwhile, as part of Pryce's evil plan, someone disguised as a werewolf actually *is* trying to kill Wilder, disposing of others in the process. What initially seems to be Smith's work becomes a mystery to everyone involved. Wilder eventually uncovers both Smith's and Pryce's schemes, but wait! Surprise. It was all just another episode of "Manhattan Mystery Theater" with Wilder, Radner, Pryce, and DeLuise standing behind studio microphones and holding scripts in their hands. Wilder and Radner then go off on their real honeymoon together. But wait! Surprise. Is it just another episode of "Manhattan Mystery

Theater?'' If it is then why is there a werewolf watching as Wilder and Radner drive off?

An innocuous comedy chiller, HAUNTED HONEYMOON isn't very chilling, and worse yet, isn't very funny. Wilder, in his fourth directorial effort, has an engaging idea with this picture as he tries to re-create a style of filmmaking long forgotten. Unfortunately, although filled with the spirit of nostalgia, this sort of film no longer works. Old Abbott and Costello or Hope and Goddard chillers are only fun to watch today because of those stars. They were vehicles, but, all in all, not very good films. HAUNTED HONEYMOON may be paying homage, but the nostalgia is hollow. Why watch Wilder and Radner doing old routines when you can see the real thing? Audiences today have, for better or worse, become far too sophisticated to accept this film's whimsy. As director, Wilder succeeds most not when he is trying to be funny or chilling, but when he makes certain stylish decisions. There are a number of inventive techniques in the film's structure and production design that, believe it or not, are culled from the genius of Jean Cocteau's BEAUTY AND THE BEAST (1947) and Carl Theodor Dreyer's VAMPYR (1932). The most obvious influence, however, is Mel Brooks' spoof YOUNG FRANKENSTEIN, a film Wilder coscripted and that will forever be the yardstick that measures his talent. HAUNTED HONEYMOON falls far short.

p, Susan Ruskin; d, Gene Wilder; w, Gene Wilder, Terence Marsh; ph, Fred Schuler (DeLuxe Color); m, John Morris; ed, Christopher Greenbury; prod d, Terence Marsh; art d, Alan Tomkins; set d, Michael Seirton; cos, Ruth Myers; spec eff, John Stears; ch, Graciela Daniele; makeup, Stuart Freeborn; stunts, Colin Skeaping.

Comedy/Horror   Cas.   (PR:A MPAA:PG)

HAVLANDET   (SEE: DREAM OF NORTHERN LIGHTS, 1986, Norway)

HEAD OFFICE zero   (1986) 86m HBO–Silver Screen Partners/Tri-Star c

Eddie Albert *(Helmes)*, Merritt Butrick *(John Hudson)*, George Coe *(Sen. Issel)*, Danny DeVito *(Stedman)*, Lori-Nan Engler *(Rachael Helmes)*, Ron Frazier *(Nixon)*, Ron James *(Mark Rabinovich)*, John Kapelos *(Gen. Sepulveda)*, Don King *(Himself)*, Richard Masur *(Max Landsberger)*, Rick Moranis *(Gross)*, Brian Doyle-Murray *(Col. Tolliver)*, Don Novello *(Sal)*, Michael O'Donoghue *(Dantley)*, Judge Reinhold *(Jack Issel)*, Diane Robin *(Gross' Secretary)*, Jane Seymour *(Jane)*, Wallace Shawn *(Hoover)*, Bruce Wagner *(Kennedy)*, Hirant Alianak *(President Sanchez)*, Lee Broker *(Mover)*, Howard Busgang *(Medic)*, Tom Butler, Ralph Small *(Security Monitors)*, Jeremiah Chechik *(Hysterical Man)*, Richard Comar *(TV Reporter)*, Nancy Cser *(Dantley's Secretary)*, Billy Curtis *(Rev. Lynch)*, Dominic Cuzzocrea *(Reporter No.1)*, William Davis *(Dean)*, Louis De Bianco *(Workman)*, Carolyn Dunn *(Yonge's Secretary)*, Denis Forest *(Rich)*, Elizabeth Irwin *(America A.M. Host)*, Wally Kanin *(Security Monitor No.4)*, Marvin Karon *(Art)*, Derek Kuervost *(Fund Raiser)*, Kathy Lasky *(Miss Kline)*, Don McManus *(Albert)*, Mike McManus *(Branch Kipp)*, Robin Menken *(Marge)*, Maxine Miller *(Stedman's Secretary)*, Myron Natwick *(TV Anchorman)*, Laura Press *(V.P. Secretary)*, Elizabeth Shepherd *(Mrs. Issel)*, Barry Thomson *(Security Guard)*, Shawn Thomson *(Trevor Koback)*, Christopher Ward *(Another Executive)*, Gay Claitman, Megan Smith, Myra Fried, Theresa Tova *(Women Protestors)*, Eric Keenleyside, Don Keppy, Tex Konig, Francine Volker *(Whale Protestors)*, Devonne L. Green, Patricia Nember, Eric Young *(Senate Investigation Reporters)*, Annie McAuley, Catherine McClenahan *(Max's Girls)*, General Public *(Rock Band)*.

Unforgivably bad, painfully unfunny, and downright stupid, HEAD OFFICE tries to do to the corporate world what AIRPLANE did to the airlines. Director Finkleman previously failed as a director with AIRPLANE II: THE SEQUEL, which nearly managed to erase the memory of the merit of the original. Here, Finkleman seems to have been out to lunch during the filming. One has a better

chance of finding a needle in a haystack than finding a laugh in HEAD OFFICE, which comes as something of a surprise as the cast includes such names as Danny DeVito, Rick Moranis, Don Novello (better known as Father Guido Sarducci), Brian Doyle-Murray, and Wallace Shawn.

The film begins as Reinhold, a recent business school graduate and son of senator Coe, is hired to work for an international conglomerate called INC, which is headed by the profit-minded Albert. Reinhold begins at the bottom of

the corporate ladder—in the public relations department—where he meets a spunky blonde, Engler, who presents him with a petition to keep INC from closing its operation in a place called Allentown. Engler charges that INC is closing its doors in order to move their business to Central America where the labor comes much cheaper. As a result, most of the citizens of tiny Allentown will lose their jobs.

Reinhold is charmed by Engler and invites her to lunch, but she'll have nothing to do with anyone from INC. Within a week Reinhold is promoted and sent, along with Masur, to Allentown to present INC's side of the story. Rather than feed the press a line of corporate doublespeak, Reinhold tells the truth about INC's motives. An infuriated Albert watches as television newsmen relay the story. Much to everyone's surprise, however, Reinhold is praised for his candidness and made a national hero for being an honest businessman. Instead of firing Reinhold, Albert makes him vice-president, hoping to seal the support of senator Coe. Engler changes her opinion of Reinhold, and the pair soon spend the night together, during which encounter he learns that she is Albert's daughter. Reinhold invites her to a reception between INC shareholders and the leaders of a militaristic Central American country, during which a multi-million dollar deal is to be made. After much gunplay, Reinhold and Engler expose Albert and INC, and even save Allentown in the process.

HEAD OFFICE is one of those ideas that must have been presented to its Hollywood studio executives by an extremely persuasive pitchman. Maybe it sounded good as a ''concept,'' or maybe HBO and the Silver Screen Partners had money to burn, or maybe the editor left all the funny scenes on the cutting room floor. Whatever the reason, HEAD OFFICE fails miserably. Nothing works here, which probably explains why so many big name comedians were included in the project—to add some box office appeal. Fans of DeVito and Moranis will be bitterly disappointed. Not only is it some of the worst work either of them has done, but they are both killed within the first 20 minutes. Reinhold and Engler do the best they can with the script and manage to emerge unblemished from the experience. Novello also manages to survive this fiasco as a likeable chauffeur who is overprotective of his limousine and his Julio Iglesias cassette. The best part of the film, however, is a cameo by real-life boxing promoter Don King (the one with the wild hair) who is, unfortunately, on-screen for no more than a couple of minutes.

For music fans, there is a short sequence featuring the band General Public performing their song ''Don't Cry on Your Own Shoulders.'' Other songs include: ''You're in My Dreams'' (Bruce Witkin, performed by Witkin), ''Sly Times'' (Dunn Pearson, Joe Porrello, performed by Roger Hatfield), ''Music Lovers'' (Pearson, Porrello, performed by Pearson), ''You Need Love'' (Witkin, Jimmy Gambone, performed by Witkin), ''Flyer'' (GEO, performed by GEO), ''Far Side of Crazy'' (Andy Prieboy, performed by Wall of Voodoo), ''Watching You'' (Gary O'Connor, performed by O'Connor), ''Military Madness,'' ''Groove #1'' (Alan Howarth), ''Goin' Down'' (Rich Gibbs).

p, Debra Hill; d&w, Ken Finkleman; ph, Gerald Hirschfeld (Panavision, Metrocolor); m, James Newton Howard; ed, Danford B. Greene, Bob Lederman; prod d, Elayne Barbara Ceder; art d, Gavin Mitchell; cos, Judith R. Gellman; m/l, Bruce Witkin, Dunn Pearson, Joe Porrello, Jimmy Gambone, GEO, Andy Prieboy, Gary O'Connor, Alan Howarth, Rich Gibbs.

Comedy   (PR:C MPAA:PG-13)

HEARTBREAK RIDGE**   (1986) 130m Malpaso–Jay Weston/WB

Clint Eastwood *(Tom Highway)*, Marsha Mason *(Aggie)*, Everett McGill *(Maj. Powers)*, Moses Gunn *(Sgt. Webster)*, Eileen Heckart *(Little Mary)*, Bo Svenson *(Roy Jennings)*, Boyd Gaines *(Lt. Ring)*, Mario Van Peebles *(Stitch)*, Arlen Dean Snyder *(Choozoo)*, Vincent Irizarry *(Fragetti)*, Ramon Franco *(Aponte)*, Tom Villard *(Profile)*, Mike Gomez *(Quinones)*, Rodney Hill *(Collins)*, Peter Koch *(''Swede'' Johanson)*.

Producer-director-star Eastwood proves once again that he knows what most contemporary Hollywood filmmakers have never learned: that it is possible to make financially successful, entertaining, intelligent films quickly and economically. Eastwood also proves that he has a better sense of American film history than many of the directors who graduated from prestigious film schools. More than any movie in recent memory, HEARTBREAK RIDGE echoes the classics of Howard Hawks and the gritty realism of Sam Fuller, without ever blatantly ''stealing'' from either filmmaker. Eastwood understands their spirit, and knows what made their films work.

Further exploring his screen persona, Eastwood stars as a gruff, foul-mouthed anachronism of the old Marine Corps who drinks too much. Nearing retirement age, and having alienated most of his young superior officers, Eastwood asks to end his career where it began. He is given a transfer to perform gunnery sergeant duties in his old outfit. On the bus to his new assignment he encounters Van Peebles, a hip, fast-talking young black man who wants to be a rock 'n' roll star. Peebles is a bit amused by the staunch old Marine (he notices that this supposed tough guy is leafing through issues of *Cosmopolitan*, *MS.*, and *Vogue*—when Eastwood senses this, he tries to hide the magazines) and begins chattering in his ear. Perhaps pining for the days when there was a clear-cut generation gap, Eastwood growls, ''Shut your face, hippie.'' Van Peebles can barely contain his laughter.

Eventually Eastwood makes it to his outfit where he is greeted by one of his oldest friends, Snyder, a fellow veteran of Korea and Vietnam, and one of the last of the old guard. Unfortunately, Eastwood's commanding officer, McGill, is a by-the-book type who really believes in the new, high-tech military and has nothing but contempt for soldiers like Eastwood who give the service a bad image. ''You ought to be sealed in a case labeled 'Break open only in case of war','' he tells Eastwood. When Eastwood finally confronts the small reconnaisance platoon he is to train, he finds a group of lazy malcontents who feel that

they've been duped by all the slick military advertising shown on television. Of course, the lead malcontent is none other than Van Peebles. After earning the admiration of these young hot-shots by besting them physically and mentally at every turn, Eastwood proceeds to whip them into a self-respecting fighting unit that knows how to work as a team. During the training, Eastwood tries to rekindle the love of his ex-wife, Mason, who divorced him because she was tired of his insensitivity and his love for the military. She still lives near the base, working as a cocktail waitress and occasionally sleeping with her boss, Svenson. Eastwood hopes to impress Mason with his newfound awareness ("Did we mutually nurture each other?" he clumsily asks her), which was culled by reading women's magazines on the sly. Just as it seems that he is making progress with Mason, duty intervenes. He and his troops are sent off to a small Caribbean island that none of them have ever heard of to rescue some American medical students from a hostile Marxist government defended by Cuban troops. The island is called Grenada.

Eastwood's platoon finally gets to find out what it is that they have been trained to do. The nervous troops pull together under Eastwood's steady leadership. There are no grandstanding heroics, they work as a team. Real bullets are being fired at them by people who want to kill them. The death of one of their comrades is real. The platoon is horrified when they see Eastwood shoot a Cuban soldier in the back, and they become confused when he takes the time to turn the dead boy over to look at his face. The fighting is quick and the operation is a success. Back home, the soldiers are greeted by cheering crowds, who feel compelled to celebrate this simple victory as if it will erase the pain of the last war. Eastwood does not join in the festivities. He searches the crowd hopefully for Mason. She is there for him. They walk off arm in arm, leaving the cheering crowds behind.

HEARTBREAK RIDGE has drawn some flak from those who think that Eastwood is somehow approving of the Grenada invasion by refusing to blatantly criticize it. In this film Eastwood isn't interested in the political ramifications of the action; what concerns him is how it defines his characters. He and screenwriter Carabatsos have developed a group of vivid individuals who operate on an immediate, realistic level. The 20/20 hindsight provided by journalist Sydney Schanberg and director Joffe in THE KILLING FIELDS is a useful device for a sweeping examination of an entire chapter in history. But the young soldiers in HEARTBREAK RIDGE aren't concerned with the larger geopolitical implications of their action, they only want to survive it. The strengths and foibles of human beings are what this film—and all of Eastwood's other directorial efforts—are all about. His Tom Highway is one of the most vividly etched male characters seen on the screen in years. Eastwood makes no apologies for this man who knows only how to train men to kill, but he does understand him. Highway knows he is an anachronism and sees that he will soon have to leave the only place where he feels confident. Through his youth he has made the Marines his family, and now that family is rejecting him in favor of a much more glamourous image. Only self-pity and loneliness await. But Highway isn't the kind of man who is willing to wallow in the mistakes he has made in his life. In the only way he knows how, however superficial, he makes an attempt to understand the woman he had taken for granted, for that woman will be his salvation. The beautifully played scenes between Eastwood and Mason contain some of the most telling and realistic emotions between a man and a woman to be found in any recent film. Eastwood believes that people can change, that contact with other human beings can enlighten, and that attempting to understand one another is extremely valuable. His characters do not spill their emotions in clever torrents of theatrical dialog. They behave like real people. They are close-mouthed, wary, and afraid of appearing vulnerable, simply because they are vulnerable. Truth is found in their interplay with others. Actions speak louder than words, but that action and the subsequent reaction must be carefully observed. Eastwood understands that people do what they are trained to do, the truth lies in the aftermath. When Highway turns over the Cuban soldier he has just killed to look at his face, he shows a respect and compassion for the man. He wants to have some sense of the "enemy" as a human being—not a faceless horde (this isn't RAMBO).

Eastwood the producer ran into trouble with the American military on this film. The Army rejected the script outright, so the Marines were contacted and asked for their assistance. The Department of Defense gave tentative approval if some script changes were made (they objected to the profanity; "drill instructors are not permitted by regulations to swear at recruits"; and to the scene where Eastwood shoots a wounded enemy in the back). Executive producer Fritz Manes

later stated that he and Eastwood had agreed to tone the script down, but that they made no specific agreement to make additional changes. By the time the film was ready to premiere at a benefit for the San Diego County Armed Forces YMCA, the Department of Defense withdrew its support, citing the profanity as their major objection (the benefit went on without official Marine support, but the Marine-sponsored "Toys For Tots" drive—which was to have featured Eastwood—was adversely affected). Unbiased Marines were shown the film and asked if they thought it realistic, and the response was overwhelmingly in favor of the film. Manes, an ex-Marine who served in Korea, condemned the attitude of the Department of Defense and stated that " . . . they should get out of their chairs in Washington D.C., and get out in the field with the troops. They might have a better idea what's going on in the world." (The DOD also rejected PLATOON, but they did provide massive support for the vapid TOP GUN, a film which embodies the new, slick, high-tech image that the military is anxious to project.) The controversy gave the film loads of free press just before it was released. As a director and as an actor, Eastwood skillfully plays on viewer expectations and delivers a wholly entertaining film while exploring some very serious and complex issues—just as John Ford, Howard Hawks, Alfred Hitchcock, Sam Fuller, Nick Ray, and Anthony Mann did decades earlier. Eastwood proves that it is still possible to infuse an "entertainment" with greater relevance. Those of his fans who choose to simply go and root for the "good guys" will not be disappointed, but neither will those looking for something with a little depth and truth regarding the human condition.

p&d, Clint Eastwood; w, James Carabatsos; ph, Jack N. Green (Technicolor); m, Lennie Niehaus; ed, Joel Cox; prod d, Edward Carfagno; set d, Robert Benton; cos, Glenn Wright.

War/Drama   **Cas.**   **(PR:O   MPAA:R)**

HEARTBURN**   (1986) 108m PAR c

Meryl Streep *(Rachel)*, Jack Nicholson *(Mark)*, Jeff Daniels *(Richard)*, Maureen Stapleton *(Vera)*, Stockard Channing *(Julie)*, Richard Masur *(Arthur)*, Catherine O'Hara *(Betty)*, Steven Hill *(Harry)*, Milos Forman *(Dmitri)*, Natalie Stern *(Annie)*, Karen Akers *(Thelma Rice)*, Aida Linares *(Juanita)*, Anna Maria Horsford *(Della)*, Ron McLarty *(Detective O'Brien)*, Kenneth Welsh *(Dr. Appel)*, Kevin Spacey *(Subway Thief)*, Mercedes Ruehil *(Eve)*, Joanna Gleason *(Diana)*, R.S. Thames *(Dan)*, Jack Gilpin *(Ellis)*, Christian Clemenson *(Sidney)*, John Wood *(British Moderator)*, Sidney Armus *(Jeweler)*, Yakov Smirnoff *(Contractor Laszlo)*, Caroline Aaron *(Judith)*, Lela Ivey *(Hairdresser)*, Tracey Jackson *(Hairdresser's Friend)*, Libby Titus *(Rachel's Sister)*, Angela Pietropinto *(Hospital Receptionist)*, Cynthia O'Neal, Susan Forristal *(Magazine Colleagues)*, Dana Ivey *(Wedding Speaker)*, John Rothman *(Jonathan Rice)*, Elijah Lindsay *(Anesthetist)*, Jack Neam *(Butcher)*, Kimi Parks *(Arthur and Julie's Daughter)*, Salem Ludwig *(Judge)*, Patricia Falkenhain *(Dinner Party Hostess)*, Margaret Thomson *(Irritated Wedding Guest)*, Charles Denney, Gregg Almquist, Garrison Lane, Ryan Hilliard, Dana Streep, Mary Streep, Cyrilla Dorn, May Pang *(Dinner Party Guests)*, Michael Regan *(Father of the Bride)*, Ari M. Roussimoff, Luther Rucker *(Workmen)*.

Two name talents in leading roles don't guarantee success, a point proven all too clearly with HEARTBURN. The film is based on the infamous *roman a clef* by Nora Ephron detailing her marital breakup with journalist Carl Bernstein, one of the two men who broke the Watergate scandal. This best-seller, which contained both the story and recipes of its food critic/narrator, was a bitter response to the Ephron-Bernstein breakup, and critics were sharply divided over the *Heartburn's* merit and intentions. But while the book had a distinctive bite, the film is a colorless adaptation, lacking any of the novel's punch. While attending a friend's wedding, Streep, a divorced magazine writer, is attracted to Nicholson, another wedding guest. She learns Nicholson is an important Washington columnist, then asks if he's single. "He's famous for it," is the ominous reply Streep receives. Nicholson woos Streep almost instantaneously, and within five minutes of film time, the two are preparing to marry. Right before the ceremony Streep gets cold feet, but she overcomes this nervousness and the wedding proceeds. Streep quits her New York job to move to Washington, where Nicholson has purchased a somewhat shabby townhouse. Because the home had been ravaged by fire, Nicholson has gotten a good deal, and now hires a contractor (Smirnoff) to rehab the place. Smirnoff's ineptitude causes some friction between Nicholson and Streep, but when she announces her pregnancy, their rift quickly heals. Nicholson delights in singing every song he can think of that contains the word "baby." But gradually Nicholson feels stifled by the marriage. After the baby's birth, these feelings come to a head and Nicholson complains bitterly about small things like missing socks. Eventually Streep learns her husband has been having an affair with socialite Akers. She takes the baby and flies back to New York, determined that she is through with Nicholson. He eventually joins her, and they reconcile. Streep becomes pregnant again, but Nicholson's philandering days have not ended. Once again Streep suspects extramarital activity and, at a dinner party, expounds on what she believes a marriage should be. As she finishes her speech, Streep picks up a key lime pie she has been preparing, then ceremoniously plops it in Nicholson's face. She packs up her toddler and newborn and heads back for New York, determined never to see Nicholson again.

HEARTBURN features some good individual moments from Streep and Nicholson, but together they don't amount to much. There's no spark between the two, and that missing element is one of HEARTBURN's major flaws. Streep, well known for her acting versatility, is atypically bland. Her character is without much depth, and her attempts at humor are only mildly amusing. Her best moments are opposite her film daughter Stern, who interestingly enough, is Streep's real-life daughter, Willa. There's a warm, loving quality to their scenes, one that surely must be an extension of the offscreen mother/daughter relationship (Streep insisted Willa be billed as "Natalie Stern" and that another child be used for publicity shots). Nicholson is good when he hams it up, particularly during his singing sequence and when he gleefully shows Streep their newborn daughter. But these, too, are rare moments which are lost in an otherwise uninspired performance. Nicholson's role originally was to be played by Mandy Patinkin (the love interest from YENTL), who was replaced after a week of work because he reportedly had no chemistry with Streep, a problem which the casting change did not solve. Nichols' direction is another problem. He never really defines the characters or establishes motivation; we know both Nicholson and Streep are famous writers, yet not once are they ever seen plying their craft. The courtship takes all of three scenes, and Akers' role as mistress is barely noticeable. She and Nicholson don't have a single scene together. Akers is relegated to a cameo role when the story all but demands her greater involvement (a fantasy WIZARD OF OZ sequence—with Streep as Dorothy and Akers as the Witch—was shot, but cut from the final print). Secondary characters, including Stapleton, Masur, O'Hara, Daniels and director Milos Forman, remain background props as well, a real waste of some good talent. In adapting her own novel, Ephron (who also cowrote SILKWOOD) has deemphasized much of the original's acidity. Part of this, no doubt, was a direct result of Carl Bernstein's anger. Having faced public humiliation through his ex-wife's thinly disguised fiction, Bernstein demanded (and received) the right to approve the way he would be portrayed in the film. This deflected any potential lawsuits HEARTBURN could have incurred, yet the resulting work just doesn't live up to the personal turmoil its title implies. Simon's treacly music doesn't help much either; it's a light score that attempts to use the children's song "The Eency Weency Spider" for symbolism in HEARTBURN's closing moments. Ephron is the daughter of screenwriters Phoebe and Henry Ephron, who penned the cinematic version of Rodgers and Hammerstein's wonderful musical CAROUSEL. That film gets an offhand homage when Nicholson delivers a rousing version of "Soliloquy," the song in which Gordon MacRae wondered about his unborn child's future.

p, Mike Nichols, Robert Greenhut; d, Mike Nichols; w, Nora Ephron (based on her novel); ph, Nestor Almendros (Technicolor); m, Carly Simon; ed, Sam O'Steen; prod d, Tony Walton; art d, John Kasarda; set d, Susan Bode; cos, Ann Roth; makeup, J. Roy Helland, Lee Halls.

Drama/Comedy   Cas.   (PR:C-O MPAA:R)

HEATHCLIFF: THE MOVIE**   (1986) 73m DIC Audiovisual-LBS
Communications-McNaught Syndicate/Atlantic Releasing-Clubhouse c

Mel Blanc *(Voice of Heathcliff)*.

George Gately's popular newspaper comic strip "Heathcliff" finally makes it to the big screen, though the film's secondary appellation is a complete misnomer. HEATHCLIFF: THE MOVIE is actually "Heathcliff the Saturday morning cartoon show edited for theatrical release." If Junior has seen every episode of this mediocre series, the film will hold few surprises. Though some new introductory footage has been added, the body consists merely of some rehashed adventures that have been run countless times on the orthicon tube. The opening has the title feline baby-sitting his three nephews, keeping the kits amused by relating some of his past escapades. The unexceptional incidents include Heathcliff's altercations with a nasty but slow witted bulldog, an encounter with a pair of Siamese cats who (of course) are experts in martial arts, and a look at Heathcliff's papa, a prison escapee.

Animation is of the substandard caliber that permeates television, and the gags are predictable. Even the presence of Mel Blanc, providing the star's voice, isn't enough to provide any real degree of enjoyment. Though made for kids, even the younger set will find this boring after the first 30 minutes.

p, Jean Chalopin; d, Bruno Bianchi; w, Alan Swayze (based on the comic strip "Heathcliff" by George Gately).

Children's/Animation   (PR:AAA MPAA:G)

HEAVENLY PURSUITS   (SEE: GOSPEL ACCORDING TO VIC, THE, 1986, Brit.)

HEIDENLOCHER†   (1986, Aust./Ger.) 102m Voissfilm-Marwo-Bayerischer Rundfunk bw (Trans: Hideouts)

Florian Pircher *(Santner)*, Albert Paulus *(Ruap)*, Helmut Vogel *(Jacek)*, Matthias Aichhorn *(Durlinger)*, Rolf Zacher, Gunther Mixdorf *(Guards)*, Claus-Dieter Reents *(1st Gestapo Man)*, Maria Aichhorn *(Frau Durlinger)*, Gerta Rettenwender *(Frau Santner)*, Joanna Hadej *(Agnes)*, Franz Hafner *(Forester)*, Doris Kreer *(Lisabeth)*, Hubsi Aichhorn *(Festl)*, Darius Polanski *(Staschek)*, Piotr Firackiewicz *(Kowal)*, Hans-Jorg Unterkrainer *(Weissbauer)*, Jurgen Bretzinger *(2nd Gestapo Man)*, Walter Oczlon *(Soldier on Furlough)*, Milena Oczion, Barbara Reitter, Marzena Krupinski *(Three Polish Girls)*.

High in the Austrian Alps in the winter of 1942, a deserter from the German army hides in a cave above his village, protected and fed by his wife and the whole village. The tensions this creates between the Austrian villagers and the local Gestapo are heightened when a number of French, Russian, and Polish prisoners of war arrive for slave labor on the farms. These men are well treated by the locals, except for one boy, who is upset that his brother has been sent to the front. When his father beats him for abusing a Polish laborer, he goes to the Gestapo and tells them of the deserter up in the cave. When he leads them up the mountain, he is shot by the deserter, who then kills himself.

d&w, Wolfram Paulus; ph, Wolfgang Simon; ed, Wolfram Paulus; set d, Christoph Kanter.

Drama   (PR:C MPAA:NR)

HEILT HITLER!†   (1986, Ger.) 145m Herbert Achternbusch c (Trans: Heal Hitler)

Gunter Freyse *(Gunter/Traudylein)*, Herbert Achternbusch *(Herbert the Cripple)*, Gabi Geist *(Gaby/ Gabylein)*, Waltraud Galler *(Traudy)*, Annamirl Bierbichler *(Annamirl)*, Anita Geerken *(Annytta/ Anita)*, Judit Achternbusch *(The Girl)*, Luisa Francia *(Luise)*, Josef Bierbichler *(Farmer)*, Franz Baumgartner *(The Man)*, Hias Schaschko *(Hi)*, Helmut Neuayer *(He)*, Hartmut Geerken *(Penisdiener)*, Ruth Drexel, Hans Brenner.

An overlong exercise in super-8mm polemics concerns the survival of the Nazi ethos in some regions of Bavaria. The Berlin Film Festival allows Achternbusch a screening every year, and one can only wonder why.

d&w, Herbert Achternbusch; ph, Herbert Achternbusch, Gunter Freyse, Adam Olech; cos&makeup, Ann Poppel.

Drama   (PR:O MPAA:NR)

HELL SQUAD zero   (1986) 87m Cinevid/Cannon c

Bainbridge Scott *(Jan)*, Glen Hartford *(Jack)*, Tina Lederman *(Tina)*, Maureen Kelly, Penny Prior, Kimberly Baucum, Delynn Gardner, Lisa Nottingham, Kathy Jinnett, Loren Chamberlain *(Members of Squad)*, Jace Damon *(Mark)*, Walter Cox *(Jim)*, Frank Romano *(Drill Sergeant)*, Marvin Miller *(Sheik)*, Sally Swift *(Ann)*, William Bryant *(Nightclub Owner)*, Lee Coy *(Col. Balin)*, Mark Brandon *(Transvestite Spy/Principal Terrorist)*, Robert Searles *(Terrorist Chief)*, Steve Wallace *(1st Scientist)*, Marianne Zvoleff *(2nd Scientist/Showgirl)*, Gary Sebunia *(Chauffeur)*, Dennis MacArthur *(Abductor Driver)*, Larry Lyons *(Dying Man in Dungeon)*, Phillip Rhee, Dean Marsh *(Karate Fighters)*, Dawn Smith, Sheyla Havard, Joyce Rush, Mary Asta, Connie Porter *(Showgirls)*, Hisham Wer, John Diaz, William Meyers, Hugo Limon *(Principal Terrorists)*, Toni Alessandrini, Karey Sinclair *(Night Club Waitresses)*, Anaheed, Narayama *(Belly Dancers)*, Hubert Wells, Julian Sylvester *(Sheikh's Guards)*.

A stupendously stupid example of the kind of film hardly anyone makes anymore. The "Ultra-Neutron" bomb makes people or animals disappear completely, but leaves buildings intact (cue for shots of empty animal cages and horseshoes just sitting on the ground). Following the successful test of the bomb, the young son of an American ambassador is kidnaped by terrorists who demand the fissionable material in the bomb as ransom. The government's hands are tied, so the only obvious option is to pick nine Las Vegas showgirls, give them a couple of weeks of commando training, then send them in after the boy. Scott is the leader of the killer showgirls (and the only one to have seen action). After arriving in an unnamed Middle Eastern country, the girls intersperse their dance routines with forays into the desert, where they destroy numerous military installations without ever finding their objective. After they return from their missions, they all get in a big bathtub. Finally they discover where the boy is being held. He is a captive on an island in the middle of a lake, so the girls have to put on their bathing suits and fight the climactic battle in bikinis. The guards virtually fall over each other in their eagerness to die, so the girls make short work of the garrison. Soon they are back in Vegas, where Scott reveals that the girls were nearly betrayed by a spy disguised as the Ambassador's secretary.

The film is unrelenting in its idiocy. The girls are pretty, but none of them could act their way out of a paper bag, and the notion of their being able to beat up a trained terrorist is too silly to believe. The film is very weak technically, with the bad dubbing especially annoying. It should come as no surprise that this film, shot in 1983, received no theatrical release in the U.S., debuting on videocassette.

p,d&w, Ken Hartford; ph, John McCoy; m, Charles P. Barnett; ed, Robert Ernst; spec eff, Harry Woolman.

Action/Adventure   Cas.   (PR:O MPAA:R)

HELLFIRE†   (1986) 88m Manley c

Kenneth McGregor *(Corby McHale)*, Sharon Mason *(Samantha Kelly)*, Julie Miller *(Caitland Foster)*, Jon Maurice *(Frank Gitto)*, Joseph White *(Nicky Fingers)*, Stephen Caldwell *(Colan Foster)*, Edward Fallon *(Kesselman)*, Mickey Shaughnessy *(Waxman)*.

In the indeterminate future, scientists develop a controversial new energy source, Hellfire. An unfortunate side effect of the substance is that anyone exposed to it, either accidentally (as in careless handling) or intentionally (as in murder) emits blue sparks and bursts into flames. Although released abroad, this film has yet to appear on a U.S. screen and appears likely to go straight to video.

p, Howard Foulkrod; d&w, William Murray; ph, Dennis Peters (Du-Art color); m, Mark Knox; ed, Keith L. Reamer; art d, Robert Zeier; spec eff, David DiPietro.

Science Fiction   (PR:C-O MPAA:NR)

HENRI†   (1986, Can.) 91m Les Vision 4 c

Eric Brisebois *(Henri)*, Jacques Godin *(Joseph)*, Marthe Turgeon *(Jeanne Painchaud)*, Claude Gauthier *(Roch Chabot)*, Yvan Ponton *(Raoul Martineau)*, Lucie Laurier *(Lilianne)*, Julien Poulin *(Begin)*, Kim Yaroshevskaya *(Dr. Lamarre)*.

A family is torn apart after a boating accident which left the father, Godin, to make a horrible choice between saving his wife or his 9-year-old daughter. Godin rescued his daughter (Laurier), but guilt over his decision now haunts him, and the girl has spent the years since the accident in the hospital recovering from the mental anguish of losing her mother. Because of his pain and guilt, Godin has become sullen, spending his time drinking and watching television, paying little attention to his children. Only his 15-year-old son, Brisebois, has found a way to escape the pain—he runs. Brisebois finds a friend in local mechanic Gauthier, a man who shares his passion for running and who acts as a father figure for the boy. Much to Godin's dismay, Brisebois enters the village marathon. The night before the race, Brisebois finally confronts his father and tells him that Laurier has preferred to stay in the hospital all these years because she can't stand the way Godin looks as her—as if she has no right to live. Godin suddenly comes to grips with his emotional turmoil and begins to make amends by appearing at the race with Laurier at his side. Brisebois runs a hard race and wins with his reunited family waiting for him at the finish line.

p, Claude Bonin; d, Francois Labonte; w, Jacques Jacob; ph, Michel Caron; m, Denis Larochelle; ed, Andre Corriveau; md, Marcel Pothier; art d, Jean-Baptiste Tard; set d, Michele Forest; cos, Blanche-Danielle Boileau; makeup, Diane Simard.

Drama   (PR:A MPAA:NR)

HIGH SPEED**   (1986, Fr.) 86m Orca–Avida–Frankfurter Filmwerkstatt c

Mireille Perrier *(Edith)*, Bruce Thurman *(Gordon)*, Reinhardt Koildehoff, Peter Schlesinger.

Referring to light sensitive film known as "high speed," the title of this trilingual thriller also refers to the dangerous and eventful life led by its characters. Thurman is a Pulitzer-Prize-winning American photojournalist who lives in Frankfurt snapping free-lance surveillance shots for private parties and gorgeous ladies for his own pleasure. One day he takes some photographs of the lovely Perrier, a French film editor who has come to Frankfurt to help a friend with her film. Unbeknownst to Thurman or Perrier, the woman Thurman has been hired to get incriminating photos of is Perrier's filmmaker friend. After overcoming some initial obstacles (like Thurman's rather cocky attitude) Thurman and Perrier become involved. However, they are too enmeshed in the mystery and intrigue to emerge from Frankfurt alive together.

There's a good movie in here somewhere that is trying to get out, but HIGH SPEED gets too wrapped up in its own weighty plot twists to prove a success. Much of the plot is confusing to the characters and even more so to the audience, which is barely informed of the ever-changing situations. Perrier is a blessing to look at (as she was in Leo Carax's 1984 film BOY MEETS GIRL) and turns in an accomplished performance. One can't help but wonder, however, how she got a job as an editor after stepping carelessly on so much film on the editing room floor. The unconvincing half of the couple, Thurman, is less successful in his role, appearing too cocky and smug to be likable. The most interesting aspect of the film is its attempt to achieve an international flavor—setting the action in Frankfurt and casting French and American leads—though the result seems more of an emulation of Hollywood standards than German or French. (In French, German, and English; English subtitles.)

p, Jean-Luc Ormieres; d, Monique Dartonne, Michel Kaptur; w, Olivier Douyere, Monique Dartonne, Michel Kaptur; ph, Alain Lasfargues; m, Olivier Hutman; ed, Monique Dartonne.

Crime/Thriller   (PR:O MPAA:NR)

HIGHLANDER**   (1986) 111m Highlander/FOX c

Christopher Lambert *(Connor MacLeod)*, Roxanne Hart *(Brenda Wyatt)*, Clancy Brown *(Kurgan)*, Sean Connery *(Ramirez)*, Beatie Edney *(Heather)*, Alan North *(Lt. Frank Moran)*, Sheila Gish *(Rachel Ellenstein)*, Jon Polito *(Detective Walter Bedsoe)*, Jugh Quarshie *(Sunda Kastagir)*, Christopher Malcolm *(Kirk Matunas)*,

Peter Diamond *(Fasil)*, Billy Hartman *(Dugal MacLeod)*, James Cosmo *(Angus MacLeod)*, Celia Imrie *(Kate)*, Alistair Findley *(Chief Murdoch)*, Edward Wiley *(Garfield)*, James McKenna *(Father Rainey)*, John Cassady *(Kenny)*, Ian Reddington *(Bassett)*, Sion Tudor Owen *(Hotchkiss)*, Damien Leake *(Tony)*, Gordon Sterne *(Dr. Willis Kenderly)*, Ron Berglas *(Erik Powell)*, Louis Guss *(Newsvendor)*, Peter Banks *(Priest)*, Ted Maynard *(Newscaster)*, Nicola Ramsey *(Rachel as a Girl)*, Waldo Roeg *(German Soldier)*, Anthony Mannino *(Boisterous Drunk)*, Helena Stevens *(Old Woman in Car)*, Frank Dux *(Old Man in Car)*, Prince Howell *(Drunk in Hotel)*, Anthony Fusco *(Barman)*, Ian Tyler *(Lab Technician)*, Corrinne Russell *(Candy)*, Buckley Norris *(Derelict)*.

After watching a wrestling match in Madison Square Garden, Lambert (an unlikely looking Manhattan antique dealer) goes to the parking garage, where a man in an overcoat steps in front of him and draws a broadsword. Apparently prepared for this unlikely event, Lambert pulls a samurai sword out from under his own overcoat and the two go at it, sparks flying off their crashing blades. Eventually Lambert disarms his adversary, then lops the stranger's head off with a stroke. Immediately he is transported by lightning (or some similar metaphysi-

cal phenomenon that comes out of the dead man's body) to 1536 Scotland, where he is a warrior of the MacLeod clan riding into his first battle. In the thick of it, all avoid him, except for a stranger among the enemy clan, Brown, a fierce warrior from the steppes of Russia. Brown stabs his broadsword deep into Lambert, but before he can slice off his head, he is swept away by the tide of battle. Terribly wounded, Lambert is carried back to his father's castle, and the last rites are said over him, but the next day he is healed. His own kinsmen turn against him and, accusing him of witchcraft, drive him out.

Lambert then takes up residence in a small castle and marries Edney, but one day Connery arrives and introduces himself as Ramirez, the Spanish royal mineralogist. He tells Lambert that he sought him out after hearing of his remarkable recovery from the wound, and he explains who he is and the rules of his existence. According to his story, warriors will come from different times and places (Con-

nery is actually an ancient Egyptian) to duel until only a few are left. These will then come together for "The Gathering" and fight until there is only a single survivor, who will receive "The Prize," though no one knows what it is (just who figured this out and told it to Connery is never explained either). He also tells Lambert that Brown is the biggest and nastiest immortal warrior of them all, and that it would be disastrous if he won. He teaches Lambert how to fight Brown, and then one day, while Lambert is away, Brown turns up, chops off Connery's head, and rapes Edney.

Meanwhile, back in present day Gotham, the police are baffled by the decapitated body in the parking garage and the Salamanca broadsword found nearby. They suspect Lambert, whom they caught fleeing the scene, and a special interest is taken in his case by Hart, who just happens to be the police sword expert. She shows incredibly poor judgment by falling in love with her suspect, even after seeing him in an alley fighting off Brown, who has arrived for "The Gathering." Eventually Lambert lays it all out for her, forcing her to jab a knife in his stomach to prove his point. In the final battle, he slays Brown and gets "The Prize," which turns out to be the ability to know what everyone is thinking. Hardly seems worth all the trouble.

Adapted from a senior thesis written by UCLA film student Gregory Widen, the story is not nearly the problem that the dialog is. Lambert's embarrassing French accent (when questioned about it by a cop, Lambert sneers, "I'm from lots of places") virtually destroys what little credibility his character has. (This may be the only film to give us a Swiss playing a New Yorker who's actually a 16th Century Scot and a Scot playing a Spaniard who's actually an ancient Egyptian.) Connery, on the other hand, is a welcome sight indeed, and one can readily accept him when he talks about his romance with a Japanese girl centuries before, because one can sense the weight of time on him. Brown is also effective as the Kurgan, decked out in punk leather gear and carrying his disassembled broadsword around in a case like a pool cue. It is director Mulcahy's style that doesn't work here, and his experience with rock video inanities for groups like Duran Duran is relentlessly obvious in flashy cutting, gratuitous effects, and an abysmal, thumping rock 'n' roll score by washed-up glam-rockers Queen. While the film failed to find an audience in the U.S., in France it was the fifth biggest film, largely on the strength of Lambert's name.

p, Peter S. Davis, William N. Panzer; d, Russell Mulcahy; w, Gregory Widen, Peter Bellwood, Larry Ferguson (based on a story by Gregory Widen); ph, Gerry Fisher (Technicolor); m, Michael Kamen, Queen; ed, Peter Honess; prod d, Allan Cameron; art d, Tim Hutchinson, Martin Atkinson; set d, Ian Whittaker; cos, Jim Acheson; spec eff, Martin Gutteridge; m/l, Queen; makeup, Lois Burwell; stunts, Vic Magnotta.

Action/Fantasy   Cas.   (PR:O MPAA:R)

HIJO DEL PALENQUE†   (1986, Mex.) 88m Producciones Chapultepec/ Peliculas Mexicanas c (Trans: Child of the Palenque)

Valentin Trujillo *(Damian Corona)*, Patricia Maria *(Flor Corona)*, Pedro Infante, Jr. *(Anatasio)*, Los Cadetes de Linar.

Trujillo sets out to avenge the murder of his parents, but a pair of the killers has been imprisoned for other crimes, so he gets himself chucked in the slammer. There he fills his time witnessing the wretched conditions until fate throws his parents' murderers his way. He kills them, then escapes to do in the other guilty parties.

d&w, Ruben Galindo; m, Gustavo Carrion.

Crime/Drama   (PR:C MPAA:NR)

HITCHER, THE*   (1986) 97m Silver Screen–HBO/Tri-Star c

Rutger Hauer *(John Ryder)*, C. Thomas Howell *(Jim Halsey)*, Jennifer Jason Leigh *(Nash)*, Jeffrey DeMunn *(Capt. Esteridge)*, John Jackson *(Sgt. Starr)*.

Were it not for the eerie elegance of Rutger Hauer, this film would be a complete washout. One of the more sadistic films in recent memory, THE HITCHER follows the terror-filled trip of young Howell as he drives a Cadillac Seville from Chicago to San Diego to earn some extra money. Somewhere in Texas he picks up a hitchhiker (pretentiously named "John Ryder"), played by the obviously psychotic Hauer. Hauer calmly tells the teenager that he has just massacred the carload of folks who picked him up last time, and holds a knife to Howell's eye to prove his point. Hauer isn't going to kill Howell, he says; rather, he wants Howell to kill him (the "why" of all this is never explained). Howell manages to eject his unwanted passenger, but instead of getting rid of Hauer it only makes the maniac mad. Soon Hauer is playing a game of cat-and-mouse with the frightened Howell by pursuing him in the stolen pickup truck of yet another

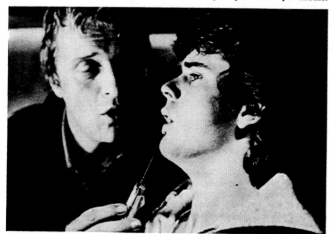

victim. At a roadside cafe, Howell manages to persuade a young waitress, Leigh, that he is being pursued by a madman. Unfortunately, Hauer has framed Howell so that it appears that he is responsible for the score of corpses that Hauer has left in his wake (Howell also makes some incredibly stupid mistakes and implicates himself even further). Now the cops are out looking for Howell rather than

for Hauer. After helping Howell escape from the local sheriff, Leigh accompanies the terrorized teen to a truck stop where they get a room so that he can get some sleep. Howell awakens to find Leigh gone and a huge commotion outside his door. Howell runs out to see what is happening and is horrified to find that Hauer has tied Leigh's feet to the cab of a semi-truck and her arms to the trailer—she's become a living hitch. With cops all around, their guns pointed at Hauer's head, the killer taunts by revving the engine and threatening to lift up on the clutch. The police encourage Howell to enter the cab and try to talk Hauer out of killing the girl. When Howell climbs into the truck, Hauer smiles demonically at him and gives it the gas and eases off the clutch—end of Leigh (luckily, we are left to only *imagine* the girl torn apart, we aren't shown it). Being upstanding officers of the law, the local cops don't kill Hauer, but take him alive. Howell knows better, however, and this time he's prepared when Hauer slaughters all his guards and hits the road again. Howell commandeers a police car and catches up with the mad killer (who has acquired an incredibly intimidating firearm along the way). In a bloody showdown, Hauer finally gets his wish and is killed by Howell.

This is about as mindlessly vicious as they get. Despite the impressive cast, slick direction, and beautiful cinematography (by John Seale, the man who shot WITNESS), the picture is nothing more than a fancy-pants slasher film. First-time director Harmon imbues the movie with a self-important air—as if there is much more going on here than meets the eye (Titanic social allegory? Homoerotic struggle? Supernatural huggabugga?). Unfortunately, there is *nothing* else going on here. No subtext. No characterization. No relevancy. Zip. Only hyper-violence and death on a lonely Texas highway. Howell and Leigh do fine with what little they're given to do, which is basically to cower in fear, and the supporting cast of redneck sheriffs and deputies is convincing as well. But it is Hauer who almost makes this torturous (literally) ordeal worth sitting through. Although he could probably play this role in his sleep, Hauer injects a restrained, very pure evil into his homicidal maniac that is truly chilling (young actor Howell declared later in interviews that he was actually frightened of Hauer throughout the filming and not just acting). Perhaps sensing that his effort to bring some class into the proceedings was in vain, Hauer declared to the press that THE HITCHER was going to be his last villainous role for a while. Screenwriter Eric Red borrowed more than a little from the 1953 Ida Lupino-directed *film noir* THE HITCH-HIKER, starring Edmond O'Brien and Frank Lovejoy as the hapless drivers and William Talman as their unwanted passenger.

p, David Bombyk, Kip Ohman; d, Robert Harmon; w, Eric Red; ph, John Seale (Metrocolor); m, Mark Isham; ed, Frank J. Urioste.

Thriller/Horror   Cas.   (PR:O MPAA:R)

HITOHIRA NO YUKI†   (1986, Jap.) Toei c (Trans: A Snowdrop)

Kumiko Akiyoshi, Naomi Oki, Chiharu Iwamoto, Arisa Fujita, Kazunori Kishibe, Masahiko.

d, Kichitaro Negishi; w, Haruhiko Arai, Jun-ichi Watanabe; ph, Koichi Kawakami.

HIUH HAGDI   (SEE: SMILE OF THE LAMB, 1986, Israel)

HOB FEE BAGHDAD†   (1986, Iraq) 102m General Establishment for Cinema and Theater c (Trans: Love in Baghdad)

Kasim Al Mallak *(Hamadi/Cassam)*, Ikbal Naaim *(Fitna)*, Sanaa Abdul Rahman *(Jemil)*.

A rare treat for Iraqi moviegoers, a purely entertaining film with absolutely no propaganda for the Iran-Iraq war. Mallak plays a dull country peasant married to Naaim. One day he falls out of a palm tree and strikes his head. In flashbacks we learn that he had received a blow to the head years before and lost his memory. While wandering in this state he met Naaim, and despite his mysterious past, they married. Back in present time, Mallak awakes in a hospital and remembers his previous identity. He slips out and returns to Baghdad where he had worked as a successful carpenter. Mallak learns he is rich and decides to marry his childhood sweetheart, but his country wife and her brother are hot on his trail.

d&w, Abdul Hadi Al Rawi; ph, Hatam Hoosein; m, Abdul Amtr Alcarraf; ed, Al Rawi; art d, May Dawood.

Comedy   (PR:A MPAA:NR)

HOLLYWOOD VICE SQUAD**   (1986) 101m Cinema Group/Concorde c

Ronny Cox *(Capt. Jensen)*, Frank Gorshin *(Jim Walsh)*, Leon Isaac Kennedy *(Hawkins)*, Trish Van DeVere *(Pauline Stanton)*, Carrie Fisher *(Betty Melton)*, Ben Frank *(Daley)*, Evan Kim *(Chang)*, Robin Wright *(Lori Stanton)*, H.B. Haggerty *(Tank Romero)*, Joey Travolta *(Stevens)*, Cec Verrell *(Judy)*, Julius W. Harris *(Jesse)*, Robert Miano *(Lucchesi)*, Marvin Kaplan *(Man with Doll)*, Beau Starr *(Farber)*, Ben Frank *(Daley)*, Tom Everett *(Miller)*, Eloy Casados *(Chavez)*, Alonzo Brown *(Overnight Man)*, Nova China *(2nd Transvestite)*, Logan Carter *(Hooker)*, Sandie Crisp *(Charlene)*, George Fauntleroy *(3rd Transvestite)*, Rick Garia *(1st Hood)*, Robin Harlan *(4th Hooker)*, Vaughan Jelks *(Tommy Hawkins)*, Bitten Knudsen *(Lucchesi's Girl Friend)*, Dorrie Krum *(3rd Hooker)*, Amelia Lesniak *(Linda)*, Rico Mancini *(2nd Hood)*, Molly Matthiesen *(2nd Hooker)*, Lisa Maurer *(1st Hooker)*, Dorothy Meyer *(Heavyset Woman)*, Larry Mintz *(Daniello)*, Irvin Mosley *(Male with Jesse)*, David Patch *(Pornographer)*, Fred Pierce *(Hairdresser)*, Loyda Ramos *(Veronica)*, Michele Rogers *(Candy)*, Phil Rubenstein *(Detective)*, Alice Spivak *(Betty's Mother)*, Claudia Templeton *(1st Hooker)*, Howie Weiner *(Night Clerk)*, Richard L. Duran *(Nasty Man)*.

Made from a script written by the real chief of the Hollywood Vice Squad and directed by a woman known best for her punk rock documentary THE DE-

CLINE OF WESTERN CIVILIZATION, you would expect this film to have a hard, clear-eyed edge that would lift it above exploitation films like ANGEL or VICE SQUAD. Instead, Spheeris turns in her flattest movie yet, recycling one cliche after another, interspersed with some of the lowest cop jokes this side of the POLICE ACADEMY films. Three different story lines occupy the running time, coming together only in the person of squad chief Cox (who also worked for the Beverly Hills Police in BEVERLY HILLS COP). One story concerns a

worried mother (Van DeVere) who comes to Hollywood looking for her runaway daughter. Her only lead is a letter in which the daughter (Wright) tells a friend that she is going to get into show business with the help of Gorshin. Actually Gorshin is a pimp who turns his girls into heroin addicts before turning them out onto the streets. Cox assigns two detectives (Kennedy and Verrell) to the case, and they come up with a scheme to pose Kennedy as a pimp from Detroit interested in buying a few girls from Gorshin's stable. They would then arrest him for white slavery. The plan goes ahead, but Gorshin is suspicious, and he forces Kennedy to send another cop (Kim), posing as his bodyguard, to a motel room to have sex with one of the girls for sale. Gorshin and the cops know that if Kim does it, the entire arrest will be thrown out. If he doesn't, a psychopathic hood with a sawed-off shotgun in the closet will kill him and the girl. Fortunately, Kennedy manages to contact Cox, though he gets shot, and Kim is rescued in the nick of time. Gorshin escapes and flees back to his office, but before he can leave there with the money from his safe, Verrell arrives and shoots him dead. Mother and

daughter are reunited. Another plot concerns rookie officer Fisher. While jogging, she discovers an S&M porno film shooting in a backyard in her neighborhood. One boy in the film is clearly underage, so Fisher goes to Cox and asks to investigate the case. He is concerned about her inexperience, so he assigns Casados and Everett, two more experienced officers, to the case with her. They continually warn Fisher that her impetuousness will get the case thrown out of court. But when they hear screams from inside the house while on stakeout, they break down the door and arrest the pornographer after a strange fight between the cops and the leather-clad, whip-toting, sword-wielding porn actors and actresses. The last story thread centers on the investigation of a New York mobster muscling in on bookmaking operations. Cops Haggerty and Frank lean on bookie Harris to make him identify the mobster (Miano). When the gangsters find out Harris has talked, they rough him up. Harris refuses to talk to the police after that, but the gangsters think he has talked again and are about to kill him when the police come crashing in. Miano smugly sits in his chair until the ruckus is over, then calmly asks to go to the station, where no doubt he will be on the street before the cops finish their paperwork. Harris beats Miano with his cane until the police stop him. There is also a running gag about Kim and Travolta on hooker patrol, with Kim acting like a Japanese tourist to bust whores, but always getting beaten up until her partner arrives to claim all the glory.

How were respectable actors like Cox, Fisher, and Van DeVere lassoed into

such a silly film? How did a director known for her unblinking looks at the underside of Los Angeles in films like SUBURBIA, THE BOYS NEXT DOOR, and the above-mentioned DECLINE OF WESTERN CIVILIZATION come up with such a lame, lifeless, cliche-ridden film still so close thematically to her other works? The only thing that comes close to working is the odd character part, particularly the performance by Harris. Among the good guys, everyone is likable enough, but no one is especially interesting. The only cops we learn anything about are Cox, who only tells that his job is his family since his wife died; Haggerty, who has a little daughter named "Pumpkin;" and Fisher, whose mother disapproves of her career. Not much to build characters on, but more than anyone else has. On the plus side, the film boasts an impressive visual style that highlights the lurid side of Hollywood Boulevard. The scene where Kim tries to stall having sex while the killer waits, trigger finger twitching, in the closet, also generates some real tension. The Gorshin plot falls apart because of his horrible overacting (he seems almost unable to speak a single line straight without hamming it up). The S&M pornography story doesn't work because it has no development. The cops just identify the perpetrator, then bust down his door. The mobster story works best thanks to Harris and Haggerty and Frank, but this episode occupies only a small portion of the running time. Best of all, though, are Kim and Travolta, who actually have some chemistry together, though they can't carry the film. Thanks to an aggressive advertising campaign, the film did fair business despite negative reviews.

p, Arnold Orgolini, Sandy Howard; d, Penelope Spheeris; w, James J. Docherty; ph, Joao Fernandes (Foto-Kem Color); m, Keith Levine, Michael Convertino, Chris Spedding; ed, John Bowey; prod d, Michael Corenblith; set d, Donna Stamps; cos, Jill Ohanneson; m/l, Chris Spedding.

Crime/Action   **Cas.**   **(PR:O MPAA:R)**

HOLLYWOOD ZAP!*   (1986) 93m Protovision–Ben/Bar/Troma c

Ben Frank *(Nash)*, Ivan E. Roth *(Tucker "Downer" Downs)*, De Waldron *(Tee Tee)*, Neil Flanagan *(Sister Grace E. Magno)*, Annie Gaybis *(Debbie)*, Claude Earl Jones *(Uncle Lucas)*, Chuck "Porky" Mitchell *(Mr. Prideman)*, Stan Ross *(Derelict)*, Helen Verbit *(Housekeeper)*, Millie Moss *(Customer)*, Shirley Prestia *(Cashier)*, Addington Wise *(Store Manager)*, Sandy Rose *(Waitress)*, Don Carmona *(Cheek)*, Nancye Ferguson *(Cheek's Girl Friend)*, Carmen Filpi *(Magazine Vendor)*, Jason Edwards *(Video Game Attendant)*, Louise Hartley *(Nurse)*, Walter Stocker *(Father Priest)*, Tony Cox *(Kong)*, Wayne Montanio *(Ventriloquist)*, Eric Marvin *(Hospital Patient)*.

Troma was a day late and a dollar short in trying to capitalize on the video game craze which had just about dried up by the time this went into release. Roth stars in this so-called "riotous, action-packed comedy" as a meek young man who quits his nowhere job at a women's clothing store and heads for Hollywood in search of fame, fortune, and his father, who has been missing for 24 years. On the road he meets up with a slovenly drifter, Frank, who is obsessed with video games and spends his life in pursuit of good times. Roth is a bit unnerved by the hyper Frank, and the boy deserts him at a roadside diner. Once in Los Angeles, however, Roth and Frank cross paths again, but this time Frank is accompanied by a young girl, Waldron. Frank makes a living as a video game hustler and he soon establishes himself as the man to beat in Hollywood. Roth learns that Frank used to be a successful stockbroker but collapsed from the pressure and was institutionalized. Frank found salvation in video games and has been pursuing the all-time "Zap!" championship ever since. While in Hollywood, Roth continues to search for his missing father, and after some discouraging false clues, he finally finds him—only he's not a him anymore; *he's* a transsexual nun. Having completed his quest, Roth takes Waldron from Frank and heads back home.

Not much action and not very funny, HOLLYWOOD ZAP! is tedious going. Writer-director Cohen seems as obsessed with video arcades as the character played by Frank, but unless one shares his enthusiasm, one is in for a long 93 minutes. None of the performers is particularly engaging, despite the dubious boasting of PORKY'S veteran Mitchell (who played "Porky" himself) in a supporting role. About the only interesting thing here is New York City-based Troma's view of Hollywood.

p, Bobbi Frank, Ben Frank; d&w, David Cohen; ph, Tom Frisby Fraser (Fotokem color); m, Art Podell, James Ackley, Paul Hertzog; ed, Rick Westover; md, Art Podell, James Ackley, Paul Hertzog; art d, Vicki Auth; makeup, Lou Lazzara.

Comedy   **Cas.**   **(PR:O MPAA:R)**

HOMBRE MIRANDO AL SUDESTE   (SEE: MAN FACING SOUTHEAST, 1986, Arg.)

HOOSIERS***   (1986) 114m Hemdale/Orion c

Gene Hackman *(Coach Norman Dale)*, Barbara Hershey *(Myra Fleener)*, Dennis Hopper *(Shooter)*, Sheb Wooley *(Cletus)*, Fern Persons *(Opal Fleener)*, Brad Boyle *(Whit)*, Steve Hollar *(Rade)*, Brad Long *(Strap)*, David Neidorf *(Everett)*, Kent Poole *(Merle)*, Wade Schenck *(Ollie)*, Scott Summers *(Whit)*, Maris Valainis *(Jimmy)*, Chelcie Ross *(George)*, Robert Swan *(Rollin)*, Michael O'Guinne *(Rooster)*, Wil Dewitt *(Mr. Doty)*, John Robert Thompson *(Sheriff Finley)*, Gloria Dorsen *(Millie)*, Michael Sassone *(Preacher Purl)*, Mike Dalzell *(Carl)*, Eric Gilliom *(J. June)*, Laura Robling *(Loetta)*.

Hemdale, the small British production company formed by David Hemmings and John Daly, was cooking on all burners in 1987. They had three big winners in the movie business: the much-lauded PLATOON, the formerly overlooked SALVADOR (both Oliver Stone projects), and HOOSIERS, which is the best movie ever made about basketball. By the late 1980s, Hemmings was no longer associated with the company, which was making its mark by backing some very American projects, the most American being this story of a most American game. Basketball began in 1891 when Dr. James Naismith put a peach basket on a gym wall so young men could get indoor exercise during the cold New England winters. In

1893, the first basketball game outside of the Commonwealth of Massachusetts was played in Crawfordsville, Indiana, and the sport has been close to a religion in "the Hoosier State" ever since.

This film is loosely based on the true story of the Milan High School team (with 164 students) that went all the way to the 1954 Indiana state championship. It's set during the 1951 season and Hackman takes a job coaching basketball at the tiny high school in Hickory, Indiana. He's been in the Navy for the last 10 years and his past is clouded. From the moment he accepts the position offered by old pal Wooley, the principal of the institution, it's obvious that Hackman is a no-nonsense kind of coach with very definite ideas. It's also evident that he knows what he's doing. So the question in the minds of many is: What's that kind of guy doing in such a hick town? The townsfolk are accustomed to coming to basketball practice and offering their "advice," something that Hackman feels he can easily do without, so he tells them that he'd appreciate their support once the games begin but would rather they stay away from the practices, which are a return to basics. This creates a great deal of unrest in a town that lives only for each high school basketball season. Wooley looks on warily from the periphery, ready to help if need be, until the stress becomes too much for his heart and he ends up in a sickbed. Hackman tries to establish a relationship with Hershey, a teacher and the acting principal in Wooley's absence, but she suspects that he is not who he seems to be. She also looks after Valainis, a player of astonishing talent whose devotion to Hackman's predecessor (who died) prevents him from playing for the new coach. Hershey is determined to keep Hackman from pressuring the boy into playing, but Hackman never forces the issue, telling Valainis

that his talent is his own to do with as he pleases. When one of the boys gets sassy, Hackman tosses him off the team and the first few games are debacles as his boys go down to defeat. They can just about field five good players in the school, which has a population of approximately 65.

One of the few people who offers any sincere help is Hopper, the drunken father of player Niedorf. Hopper is the town alcoholic, lives in a cabin, and spends most of his time getting blasted. He is also the most knowledgeable basketball person in the area. He sees what Hackman is attempting to do and tries to help with his scouting reports on the other teams. Hackman realizes that Hopper, whom he likes, will be a good man to have on his side and he offers him the unpaid job of assistant coach, *if* Hopper will walk away from the bottle. This is a great hardship to a man who begins the day with liquor. With Hopper at Hackman's side, the team begins to get it all together. Hopper remains sober for most of the season and twice has to direct the team when Hackman is ejected from games: the first time he is terrified, the second he more than rises to the

challenge. Eventually, however, he falls off the wagon and must listen to the final games from his bed in a hospital alcoholism ward. When the team's fortunes hit rock bottom, the outraged Hickory residents demand Hackman's ouster. A town meeting is held and the coach's fate hangs in the balance. Hershey holds a trump card—she has discovered the reason for Hackman's dismissal from big-time college coaching—but she never plays it. A vote is taken and Hackman is about to be sacked when Valainis enters and announces to the gathering that he is ready to play again—but only if Hackman is the coach. As you surely know, movies about losers don't inspire, so this one is about winners. With the extraordinary Valainis back in the lineup, the team barely manages to scrape by the sectionals, regionals, and finally plays for the state championship at the Butler University Fieldhouse, and the outcome is as predictable as a ROCKY knockout. But that's just fine because it sends the audience out feeling ecstatic and any movie that can do that will be a hit.

Filmed in New Richmond, Indiana, an hour by car from where Hackman was reared in Danville, Illinois, it features a script by former TV executive Angelo Pizzo (born in Bloomington, Indiana) and a superb feature debut by TV director David Anspaugh ("Hill Street Blues," "St. Elsewhere," "Miami Vice"), born in Decatur, Indiana. With the exception of Neidorf, all of the boys on the team were non-actors when they began. To Pizzo's and Anspaugh's credits, there's never a false moment in the movie and the non-pros just seemed to be acting themselves which is, of course, what countless hungry and aspiring actors spend thousands of dollars to learn in smoke-filled Hollywood acting academies. Steve Hollar (Rade) went on to play college ball and the collegiate governing group reckoned that he should be penalized for having made this movie. They claimed that he was playing basketball for money (against the rules) and made him give back a percentage of the $15,000 he earned for his role. But they figured that he acted more than he played so it was less than 25 percent. Amateur athletic associations have done a number of dumb things. This ranks well up there on that list.

A successful film is an amalgam of many small details. In HOOSIERS, attention is paid to those details and the result is refreshing. When at last we learn what caused Hackman to leave the coaching profession (he'd hit a player at his last school, a la Woody Hayes), it's not much of a revelation but it suffices to explain his presence in the town. As Hershey says, "A man comes to a place like this, either he's running away from something or he has nowhere else to go." Hershey has less to do in this than in her other big movie of the year, HANNAH AND HER SISTERS, and the sort-of love story between she and Hackman is never truly resolved, but that's a nit-pick because the focus is on the game and Hackman and Hopper. The likable hero facing overwhelming odds and triumphing has been a staple in drama and this is no exception. Basketball fans will recognize one flaw in the film. The best players are all jump shot artists and that particular shot was not in great favor in those years. The number one shot, from the outside, was the two-handed set shot. In 1951, the power dunk was illegal and

players seemed to be allowed one step, after terminating the dribble, before shooting. Fans will also note that players are able to take two steps without being called for traveling. If the name of the principal seems familiar, he was also a recording artist, besides being in many films, and his most famous song was "Purple People Eater." Musically, HOOSIERS is also a standout with a dramatic score by Jerry Goldsmith that's perfect for the time and the place. Other basketball movies such as ONE ON ONE and THE FISH THAT SAVED PITTSBURGH don't belong on the same court as this one.

p, Carter DeHaven, Angelo Pizzo; d, David Anspaugh; w, Angelo Pizzo; ph, Fred Murphy (CFI Color); m, Jerry Goldsmith; ed, C. Timothy O'Meara; prod d, David Nichols; art d, David Lubin; set d, Janis Lubin, Brendan Smith; cos, Jane Anderson.

Sports/Drama   (PR:A-C MPAA:PG)

HORVATOV IZBOR† (1986, Yugo.) Zagreb c (Trans: Horvat's Choice)

Rade Serbedzija, Milena Dravic, Fabijan Sovagovic, Mira Furlan.

d, Eduard Galic; w, Ivo Stivicic; ph, Mario Perusina; m, Zivan Cvitkovic; prod d, Stanislav Dobrina.

HOSTAGE: DALLAS (SEE: GETTING EVEN, 1986)

HOT CHILI zero (1986) 91m Cannon c

Charles Schillaci *(Ricky)*, Allan J. Kayser *(Jason)*, Joe Rubbo *(Arney)*, Chuck Hemingway *(Stanley)*, Taaffe O'Connell *(Brigette)*, Victoria Barrett *(Victoria)*, Robert Riesel *(Mr. Lieberman)*, Jerry Lazarus *(Estaban)*, Peter Bromilow *(Herr Fritz)*, Flo Gerrish *(Mrs. Baxter)*, Armando Silvestre *(Pedro)*, Peg Shirley *(Mrs. Lieberman)*, Bea Fiedler *(Music Teacher)*, Ferdinand Mayne *(Mr. Houston)*, Connie Sawyer *(Mrs. Houston)*, Katherine Kriss *(Allison)*, Jill Mallorie *(Sheila)*, Theresa Mesquita *(Kathy Davis)*, Robert Zdar *(Bruno)*, Federico Gonzalez *(Emilo)*, Louisa Moritz *(Chi Chi)*, Lupito Peruyero, Olga Armendariz *(Two Fat Singers)*.

HOT CHILI isn't just bad; it's a film that goes beyond the boundaries of a zero rating into a realm all its own. The only practical use for the film is to pop it in the VCR when you just can't get rid of unwanted company. If that doesn't clear the house in two minutes, it's Armageddon.

The plot involves four teenage California boys—Schillaci, Kayser, Rubbo, and Hemingway (despite his tough guy name, the kid is really a whining four-eyed twerp)—who get jobs working for a fancy Mexican resort. This resort, it seems, is a posh getaway for incredibly beautiful blonde women who lust for sexual encounters with *real* men of 14. O'Connell, a German with a murderous husband, has a passion for kinky encounters; Fiedler is a musician who prefers to play such varied instruments as the cello, tuba, and piccolo wearing nothing but her birthday suit; Barrett is a rich snob; and Moritz is the resort's blonde, blue-eyed Mexican chef, who enjoys an occasional tryst in the meat locker. Oh, there are a few subplots involving a nice girl with a haughty mother and some male bonding between fat guy Rubbo and his sniveling pal Hemingway, but these hold all the substance of a slightly used cheesecloth. This isn't really a movie: it's a 13-year-old boy's puberty-induced fantasy come to life. Unlike other horrors, at least we know who to blame for this mess. At the frenzied climax, as Rubbo is chased through Mexican streets by a crazed bull, fellow cast members in tow, we are treated to shots of the smiling crew, faithfully lugging their equipment with them. It's all too insufferable to be watched. HOT CHILI had some minor screenings in 1985, disappeared into the land of the unwatched, then rematerialized in 1986 for a general release on videocassette.

Songs include: "She Doesn't Know Me," "Mad Enough," "Because We're Young," "A Little Affection," "Help, Help" (Ken Brown, performed by Brown), "All I Want Is Everything" (Stephen Feldman, Ray Jarvis, Kathy Roshay Jarvis, performed by Feldman, Jarvis, Roshay Jarvis), "Get Me to the Show," "Body Shop" (David Powell, performed by Powell), "What Kind of Girl Are You?" (Robert Ragland, performed by George Griffin), "Snapshot" (Ron Wright-Scherr, performed by Wright-Scherr, Air Pocket), "El Amante Triste" (Arlon Ober, Robert Beltran, performed by Bruce Scott), "Jamaica Sun," "Best of Life" (Bruce Scott, performed by Bruce Scott), "Let the Spirit Move Ya" (Wright-Scherr, performed by Wright-Scherr), "Kissing Rocko's Girlfriend" (Steve Feldman, performed by Feldman), "Fat People" (Kathy Carter, Robert Hott, William Sachs), Tango from BREAKIN' (Gary Remal, Michael Boyd), Theme from RAPPIN' (Michael Linn).

p, Menahem Golan, Yoram Globus; d, William Sachs; w, Joseph Goldman, William Sachs; ph, Jorge Senyal (TVC Color); ed, Michael J. Duthie; prod d, Alberto Negron; art d, Ana Maria Vera; cos, Laura Santi; spec eff, Raul Palumir; m/l, Ken Brown, Stephen Feldman, Ray Jarvis, Kathy Roshay Jarvis, David Powell, Robert Ragland, Ron Wright-Scherr, Arlon Ober, Robert Beltran, Bruce Scott, Gary Remal, Michael Boyd, Michael Linn, Kathy Carter, Robert Hott, William Sachs; makeup, Graciela Munoz; stunts, Hernando Name.

Comedy Cas. (PR:O MPAA:R)

HOTEL DU PARADIS† (1986, Brit./Fr.) Umbrella-Portman-London Trust–Film Four International–Films A2 c

Fernando Rey, Fabrice Luchini, Berangere Bonvoisin.

Documentary filmmaker Bokova uses past experiences to create this low-budget look at the guests of a Parisian hotel.

p, Simon Perry; d&w, Jana Bokova; ph, Gerard de Battista.

Drama (PR:NR MPAA:NR)

HOUR OF THE STAR, THE*** (1986, Braz.) 96m Embrafilme/Kino Intl c
(A HORA DA ESTRELA)

Marcelia Cartaxo *(Macabea)*, Jose Dumont *(Olimpico)*, Tamara Taxman *(Gloria)*, Fernanda Montenegro *(Mme. Carlotta)*, Umberto Magnani, Denoy de Oliveira, Claudia Rezende.

Playing a frumpy 19-year-old orphan from northern Brazil, Marcelia Cartaxo reveals herself in beautifully simple terms: "I am a typist, I am a virgin, and I like Coca-Cola." Uneducated, unwashed, and unnoticed by most of the people around her, Cartaxo has no confidence and no desire to be anything but someone's wife. Sharing a broken-down one-room apartment with three other young women, she is unable to adjust to their ways. On weekends her friends meet with their lovers, while Cartaxo indulges in her favorite pastime—riding the subway. At work, where she is an underpaid typist for a small and dreary company, she makes little effort. She can barely type without smudging the paper or filling it with holes and is always on the verge of being fired. Only her immediate supervisor has any sympathy for her, treating her with respect and patience. With her office mate, Taxman, however, it is a different story. A jaded, whorish type and the veteran of five abortions, Taxman is concerned more with bedding her latest boy friend than anything else. She laughs when she learns that Cartaxo is still a virgin, but, unbeknownst to her, acts as something of a role model for Cartaxo.

Seeing Taxman ask for the afternoon off, Cartaxo does likewise the following day, claiming to have a dental appointment. While walking through the park, she spots the swarthy Dumont being photographed. They begin to chat, he asks her to take a walk with him, and they become friends. He tells her of his great plan to become a congressman, though he is too uneducated to explain what one does, knowing only that they get to drive fancy cars. Cartaxo, impressed with the idea that she's found a man who can look after her, now has a reason to improve her appearance. She buys makeup, wears nicer clothes, combs her hair. Hungry for knowledge as well as beauty, Cartaxo faithfully listens to an educational radio station, picking up a variety of insignificant facts (did you know that if a fly flew in a straight line it would take 28 days for it to travel around the earth?). However, when she asks Dumont the definition of culture, which she has difficulty even pronouncing, he angrily responds, "Culture? . . . culture? . . . culture is . . . uh, culture."

Despite such revelatory conversations, their relationship never gets anywhere—both of them being too displaced for any real contact, emotional or physical. Nevertheless, Cartaxo still is attached to Dumont, if only because she can now say she has a boy friend. But her life is about to get worse. Taxman visits a local fortune teller, Montenegro, who advises that she steal the boy friend of a friend. Taxman decides to woo Dumont, who then proceeds to dump Cartaxo, only to have Taxman dump him later. Taxman, who is more unthinking than uncaring, lends Cartaxo the money to visit Montenegro. Although the crystal ball initially paints a grim picture for Cartaxo, things suddenly change with the promise that she will find a rich, handsome "gringo" who will love her, marry her, and take her away from her impoverished existence in Sao Paulo. Giggling and bursting with happiness, Cartaxo buys herself a new dress, lets her hair down, and heads for her destined meeting with the gringo, a meeting which, in a strange twist, finally allows her to abandon her life of poverty.

An impressive showing from first-time director Amaral, who at age 52, after raising nine children, and graduating from the NYU Film School, returned to her native Sao Paulo, Brazil, to begin production. Based on the 1977 novella by the late Clarice Lispector, THE HOUR OF THE STAR approaches the style of neo-realism in both its photography and the plight of its poor heroine. The success of the film rests heavily on the debut performance of the 23-year-old stage actress Cartaxo, whose own beginnings were as humble as those of the character she portrays (her father a farmer, her mother a seamstress)—a heritage she projects through her simple, pure, and unprotected face. Not only has the superb Cartaxo received international critical acclaim, but the Berlin Film Festival awarded her the Best Actress prize. THE HOUR OF THE STAR was Brazil's official entrant in the 1986 Academy Awards, but it failed to receive a nomination. (In Portuguese; English subtitles.)

d, Suzana Amaral; w, Suzana Amaral, Alfredo Oroz (based on the novel by Clarice Lispector); ph, Edgar Moura; m, Marcus Vinicius; ed, Ide Lacreta; art d, Clovis Bueno.

Drama (PR:O MPAA:NR)

HOUSE* (1986) 93m NW c

William Katt *(Roger Cobb)*, George Wendt *(Harold Gorton)*, Richard Moll *(Big Ben)*, Kay Lenz *(Sandy)*, Mary Stavin *(Tanya)*, Michael Ensign *(Chet Parker)*, Erik Silver, Mark Silver *(Jimmy)*, Susan French *(Aunt Elizabeth)*, Alan Autry, Steven Williams, Ronn Carroll *(Cops)*, Jim Calvert *(Grocery Boy)*, Mindy Sterling *(Woman in Bookstore)*, Jayson Kane *(Cheesy Stud)*, Billy Beck *(Priest)*, Bill McLean *(Older Man)*, Steve Susskind *(Frank McGraw)*, John Young *(Would-Be Writer)*, Dwier Brown *(Lieutenant)*, Joey Green *(Fitzsimmons)*, Stephen Nichols *(Scott)*, Donald Willis *(Soldier)*, Robert Joseph *(Robert)*, Curt Wilmot *(Skeleton Big Ben)*, Ronn Wright *(Enthusiastic Patron)*, Renee Lillian *(Zealous Fan)*, Peter Pitofsky *(Witch)* , Elizabeth Barrington, Jerry Marin, Felix Silla *(Little Critters)*.

A surprise hit early in 1986, HOUSE is an ineptly structured horror film that tries to combine both scares and laughs without succeeding at either. Katt stars as a successful Stephen King-like horror novelist who is suffering from writer's block due to a recent divorce from his TV-actress wife, Lenz, and the disappearance of their son, Silver (played by twins Eric and Mark). Although urged by his agent to crank out another horror novel, Katt instead concentrates on writing about his experiences as a soldier during the Vietnam War. After the mysterious suicide of his rather eccentric aunt, Katt decides to move into her huge Victorian home in search of solitude. The house holds many memories for Katt—he grew up there—but most vivid is the day that his son disappeared after jumping into the swimming pool. Despite the fact that Katt saw the boy disappear in the pool, the FBI has treated the case as a kidnaping. Soon after Katt moves in, strange things begin happening. He finds hideous monsters in the closets, hand tools float through the air on their own, he sees his aunt commit suicide again, and a prize-winning marlin mounted on the wall comes to life. Katt at first attributes these strange visions to the tension he is suffering from while reliving his Vietnam experience for his book, but soon he becomes convinced that what he sees is very real. His nosy next-door neighbor, Wendt, thinks that Katt is simply crazy—as crazy as his aunt.

Now in frenzy over the demons and ghosts that haunt him, Katt dons his old Army fatigues and wields a shotgun. Lenz turns up unexpectedly at the house and a nervous, slightly embarrassed Katt tries to think of an excuse for his appearance. When Lenz bends down under a table to pick up a loose shotgun shell, she comes up a hideously bloated monster and moves to attack Katt. Katt immediately shoots the monster and it lands flat on its back on the front porch. When Katt runs outside to examine the body, he is horrified to find Lenz lying dead instead of the monster. Brought to his window by the shotgun blast, Wendt sees Katt wielding the shotgun, but doesn't see the body. He calls the police and tells them that Katt is about to commit suicide. By the time the cops arrive, Katt has stashed the body under the stairs and spends several nervous moments with the

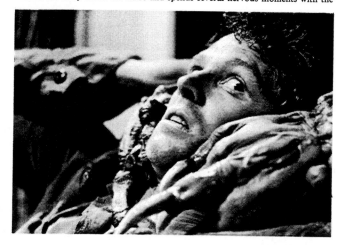

police and Wendt before persuading them he was just cleaning his gun when it went off. Of course, when he returns to the body it has disappeared. Checking upstairs, Katt is ambushed by the bloated monster again. Katt manages to trick the floating tools into decapitating the beast and he then tries to bury the parts in his back yard (for some reason all of this is performed to a bad cover version of "You're No Good"). Unfortunately, the body is still moving and it nearly grabs Katt's other neighbor, Stavin, a gorgeous blond who has been giving him the eye since he moved in. After she leaves, Katt decides to cut the monster's body up into little pieces and digs dozens of holes in the lawn. Later that night a local dog digs up one of the monster's still-writhing hands and Katt chases the hound but can't catch it. Minutes later the sexy Stavin drops by and foists her young son on Katt so that she can go out. The kid has the missing monster hand attached to his back and Katt manages to flush the demonic digits down the toilet before Stavin notices.

Once he puts the kid to bed, Katt sits down at his word processor and relives the night his buddy Moll got badly wounded in Vietnam. Not wanting to be taken alive by the Viet Cong, Moll begged Katt to finish him off, but Katt refused and ran for help. Moll was then dragged off by the Viet Cong, vowing to get revenge on Katt. His writing is interrupted again when two little demons kidnap the neighbor boy and Katt has to rescue the kid in time for his mother to take him home. Eventually Katt discovers that certain doors, including his medicine cabinet, lead to another dimension. Enlisting the aid of Wendt, Katt tries to capture one of the monsters in his closet, but winds up getting sucked into the void. He lands back in Vietnam where he again relives Moll's death. Seeing a light in the forest, Katt runs for it and winds up back in his house where he finds Wendt passed out. Katt finally figures out that his son is somewhere in the other dimension and he goes back to rescue him.

As it turns out, the rotting corpse of Moll has been holding the kid hostage while sending all manner of demons out to torture Katt. Katt manages to escape back to the reality of the house, but Moll's skeletal corpse follows. Finally Katt realizes that Moll is merely a figment of his own (Katt's) tortured conscience and he decides to destroy Moll by blowing him up with one of his own grenades (yeah, but if he's not real, how come the explosion from this supposedly imaginary grenade burns down the house?). As the house is engulfed in flames, father, mother (the bloated monster really wasn't Lenz after all), and son are reunited.

There are about six films going on at once in HOUSE and none of them works. Monsters, a haunted house, comedy, traumatic divorce, a search for a missing child, and Vietnam plot lines are mixed together so haphazardly that little in this film makes any sense. It feels as if screenwriter Wiley and director Miner made this film up as they went along and never went back to check if the preceding footage shot would match the brainstorm they just had. There is no logic to the strange things that happen in the house, not even the warped logic found in horror films. Of course horror films aren't logical when compared with normal life, but they do (and must) maintain a concrete logic within the context of the fantastic storyline. HOUSE doesn't do this and the film suffers because of it. Suspense is lost due to the fact that at any moment all the rules in this film change and it is pointless to try to anticipate what will happen next because anything can happen. Despite the special effects (which are mediocre—all the monsters look like silly, overstuffed rubber toys) and bizarre images—the film becomes dull and dragged out.

The performances don't help much either. Recruiting a cast mainly known for their television work, HOUSE has the look and feel of a TV movie. Katt ("The Greatest American Hero"), Moll ("Night Court"), Wendt ("Cheers"), and Lenz (countless TV movies and series) are all competent, likable actors, but none save Wendt has any real appeal on the big screen. Wendt proves adept at handling his character and he is solely responsible for any laughs in the film. Once again, however, producer Cunningham, the sick mind responsible for spawning the reprehensible FRIDAY THE 13TH series, and director Miner (who directed films

II and III in the aforementioned series) prove they have a knack for pleasing the undiscriminating public. HOUSE was quite a hit in 1986 ($8.6 million in rentals on a very low budget) and a sequel is due out in 1987. For some reason the producers decided to add two extraneous musical interludes: the aforementioned "You're No Good" (Clint Ballard, Jr.) and another bad cover version, "Dedicated to the One I Love" (Lowman Pauling, Ralph Bass). Neither singer was given screen credit and it's just as well. Note: HOUSE is nowhere near as bloody or depraved as the FRIDAY THE 13TH films, and, in fact, is downright tame when compared with the rest of the genre (no nudity, little blood or bad language)—the MPAA "R" seems harsh.

p, Sean S. Cunningham; d, Steve Miner; w, Ethan Wiley (based on a story by Fred Dekker); ph, Mac Ahlberg (Metrocolor); m, Harry Manfredini; ed, Michael N. Knue; prod d, Gregg Fonseca; art d, John Reinhart; set d, Anne Huntley; cos, Bernadette O'Brien; spec eff, Backwood Film; makeup, Ronnie Spector; stunts, Kane Hodder.

Horror/Comedy   Cas.   (PR:C-O MPAA:R)

HOUSE OF THE DARK STAIRWAY   (SEE: BLADE IN THE DARK, 1986, It.)

HOWARD THE DUCK*½   (1986) 111m UNIV c

Lea Thompson (*Beverly Switzler*), Jeffrey Jones (*Dr. Jenning*), Tim Robbins (*Phil Blumburtt*), Ed Gale, Chip Zien, Tim Rose, Steve Sleap, Peter Baird, Mary Wells, Lisa Sturz, Jordan Prentice (*Howard T. Duck*), Paul Guilfoyle (*Lt. Welker*), Liz Sagal (*Ronette*), Dominique Davalos (*Cal*), Holly Robinson (*K.C.*), Tommy Swerdlow (*Ginger Moss*), Richard Edson (*Ritchie*), Miles Chapin (*Carter*), Richard McGonagle (*Cop*), Virginia Capers (*Coramae*), Debbie Carrington (*Additional Ducks*), Jorli McClain (*Waitress*), Michael Sandoval (*Club Owner*), Sheldon Feldner (*Hot Tub Spa Owner*), Lee Anthony (*Grossbach*), Paul Comi (*Dr. Chapin*), Maureen Coyne (*Teacher*), James Lashly (*State Trooper*), Tom Parker (*TV Reporter*), Ed Holmes (*TV Duck Hunter*), David Paymer (*Larry Scientist*), William Hall (*Hanson*), Denny Delk (*Sergeant*), Martin Ganapoler, Tom Rayhall, Gary Littlejohn (*Truckers*), Thomas Dolby (*Bartender in Rock Club*), Kristopher Logan (*Punk*), Reed Kirk Rahlmann (*Bender*), John Fleck (*Pimples*), William McCoy (*Skin Head*), Steve Kravitz (*Lover Boy*), Anne Tofflemire (*Lover Girl*), Marcia Banks (*Mama Biker*), Nancy Fish (*Bag Lady*), Monty Hoffman (*Club Bouncer*), Ted Kurtz (*Kirby*), Wood Moy (*Chef*), Wanda McCaddon (*Hostess*), James Brady (*Tour Guide*), Carol McElheney (*Screaming Woman*), Jeanne Lauren (*Bear*), Margarita Fernandez, Felix Silla (*Stunt Ducks*), Richard Kiley (*Voice of the Cosmos*).

It would be unfair to say that HOWARD THE DUCK is the worst big-budget movie ever made. So let's just designate it as *one* of the worst big-budget movies ever made. And it would be easy to trot out word-plays to describe this duck that turned into a turkey; phrases like "lame duck," "fowl play," "Waddle I do Now?" "duck lays an egg," and the like. We'll heroically attempt to resist all of those especially since we've managed to get them into the entry anyhow. The film is on the cult comic created by Steve Gerber (who is also known for his work as

story editor on TV's "G.I. Joe" as well as for his association with "Thundarr, The Barbarian" and "The Transformers.") If Huyck and his wife Katz had only followed the excellent, witty, irreverent comic-book adventures, they might have produced a movie with some merit. As it is, this husband-and-wife team—responsible for the dull BEST DEFENSE, the duller FRENCH POSTCARDS, and the dullest LUCKY LADY (this, after having done the script for AMERICAN GRAFFITI with their old film school chum, George Lucas, who also functioned as executive producer on this)—have been going steadily downhill, with the exception of their contribution to INDIANA JONES AND THE TEMPLE OF DOOM. The rule of thumb is that show people can usually work for three pictures that bomb if they've had one success. Huyck and Katz may have overstayed their welcome with HOWARD THE DUCK.

We first meet the fowl-mouthed waddler in his life on "Duck World," a planet where he is just an ordinary bird. He's an advertising copywriter, drinks beer, chomps on cigars, utters Groucho Marxian jokes, and likes reading "Playduck" magazine. Due to the work of a laser scientist, Howard is ripped out of this existence and winds up on the streets of Cleveland, Ohio, where he meets Thompson, supposedly a punk-rocker singer with a group called "Cherry Bomb" (the others are Holly Robinson, Dominique Davalos and Liz Sagal, the actress who starred with her twin sister on NBC's "Double Trouble" for about 10 minutes), although Thompson is so sweet and innocent that it's hard to picture her in any metal heavier than aluminum foil. They fall in like with each other and there's a moment when it appears that they might get down in a featherbed together. Most of the Clevelanders respond to seeing the 3-foot creature by thinking that all he is is a midget in duck's clothing. That's *supposed* to be funny, but the outfit is so patently a costume that it's exactly what anyone's response might be. About midway through the film, Jones—a laser scientist—suddenly transforms into an evil being who has been mistakenly brought to earth. Jones (so good in AMADEUS) becomes the "Dark Overlord of the Universe" and the rest of the

movie is a special-effects jamboree from Lucas' Industrial Light & Magic company. Naturally, Howard saves the world from these creatures and everything's ducky at the end. (Please forgive the overuse of puns but when the picture one is writing about is so humorless, one has to make yolks somewhere.) There are a couple of mildly amusing moments, one in particular when Howard comes face to face with an unemployment counselor.

The picture cost between $34 million and $50 million, depending on the source, and the publicity campaign cost about $8 million, thereby making this one of moviedom's biggest losers—big enough to cause Universal's film chief, the respected Frank Price, to resign shortly after the movie escaped. John Barry's score and Tom Dolby's songs couldn't help matters, which got off on the wrong webbed foot right at the start. It began shooting on the traditional Armistice Day (11/11/85) and continued through March 27, 1986, with second unit and stunt shooting going through April. There was a general call for actors to do Howard's voice, and some of the very best were brought in to audition. The readings, however, were unbelievably inept. Actors were given a sample of dialog and sat on a couch as they spoke into a battery-operated Sony Walkman, hardly the kind of electronic equipment to use when auditioning for the lead voice in a multimillion dollar movie. As it was, the voice they chose for Howard goes uncredited and it sounds more like the average AM radio newscaster than a comic voice. The huge size of the production was awesome, and most of the more than 30 exteriors were shot in and around San Francisco to double for Cleveland. (Why didn't they just call it San Francisco so they could use some of the more familiar sites such as Fisherman's Wharf, Chinatown, Coit Tower, and Lombard Street?) They had to build a mammoth Laser Spectroscope (whatever that is) and were forced to spend millions to realize Huyck's and Katz's dreams. There was a scene at a fictional place called "Joe Roma's Cajun/Sushi Cafe" (built on a highway in the Napa Valley) which gave the overuse of puns but an interesting sidelight. A local columnist wrote about the fictional place, apparently thinking it was real, and decried the state's cuisine. Dolby's songs for "Cherry Bomb" were about as interesting as the movie. According to some published reports, Frank Price and Universal big-cheese Sid Sheinberg scuffled physically over this movie, but that may just be hearsay from somebody talking out of the wrong side of his bill. HOWARD THE DUCK is a monumental waste of time and deserves to be mentioned in the pantheon of flops such as HEAVEN'S GATE (which almost brought down United Artists), 1941 (another Universal disaster), ONE FROM THE HEART (which did bring down Francis Coppola's dream of Zoetrope Studios), and any of several movies by Irwin Allen. Everyone concerned with this should have been seated on a ducking stool and drenched. Songs and musical numbers include: "Hunger City" (Thomas Dolby, Allee Willis, performed by Lea Thompson, Dominique Davalos, Liz Sagal, Holly Robinson), "Don't Turn Away" (Thomas Dolby, Allee Willis, performed by Thomas Dolby, and then performed again by Lea Thompson, Dominique Davalos, Liz Sagal, Holly Robinson), "It Don't Come Cheap" (Thomas Dolby, Allee Willis, performed by Lea Thompson, Dominique Davalos, Liz Sagal, Holly Robinson), "Howard the Duck" (Thomas Dolby, Allee Willis,

George Clinton, performed by Lea Thompson, Dominique Davalos, Liz Sagal, Holly Robinson), "I'm On My Way" (Frederick Loewe, Alan Jay Lerner, performed by Tata Vega), "Duckter Dread Dub" (Thomas Dolby, performed by Thomas Dolby), "Two More Bottles of Wine" (Delbert McClinton, performed by Karen Blake.)

p, Gloria Katz; d, Willard Huyck; w, Willard Huyck, Gloria Katz (based on the Marvel Comics character "Howard the Duck" created by Steve Gerber); ph, Richard H. Kline (Panavision, DeLuxe Color); m, John Barry; ed, Michael Chandler, Sidney Wolinsky; prod d, Peter Jamison; art d, Blake Russell, Mark Billerman; set d, Jim Pohl, Pamela Marcotte; cos, Joe Tompkins; spec eff, Bob MacDonald, Jr.; ch, Sarah Elgart; m/l, Thomas Dolby, Allee Willis, George Clinton, Delbert McClinton, Frederick Loewe, Alan Jay Lerner; makeup, Karen Bradley.

Comedy/Fantasy   Cas.   **(PR:A-C MPAA-PG)**

HRY PRO MIRNE POKROCILE†   (1986, Czech.) 84m Barrandov Film Studio c

Lucie Tomkova *(Klarka)*, David Novotny *(Stepan)*, Evelyna Steimarova *(Mother)*, Jirina Steimarova *(Grandmother)*, Ivan Vyskocil *(Professor)*, Magdalena Hamoova *(Kamoska)*, Petr Cepek *(Father)*, Jaroslava Ticha *(Professor Zena)*, Jan Faltynek *(Stepanuv Otec)*.

d, Oto Koval; w, Oto Koval, Daniela Fischerova; ph, Vladimir Smutny; m, Stepan Lucky; ed, Dalibor Lipsky; art d, Jindrich Goetz; cos, Marta Kaplerova.

HUAJIE SHIDAI†   (1986, Hong Kong) 98m Shaw Bros. c (Trans: My Name Ain't Suzie)

Pat Ha, Angela Yu, Anthony Perry, Kuan Yi Nan, Li Shih Ping, Ku Chia Ling, Wang Hei, Deanie Yip, Betty Ting.

The second feature film from female director Angie Chan is set in the Wanchai area of Hong Kong in the late 1950s and early 1960s. Ha stars as an impoverished young woman living on a sampan off Lantau Island. To survive Ha is forced to go to Wanchai and become a bar girl under the employ of local madam Ting (former girl friend of the late Bruce Lee, who died in her apartment in 1973). While working there she falls in love with an Amerasian boy who is searching for his father. Their relationship raises the hackles of jealous bar owner Sui Ling Yuk, and Ha soon finds herself working the street. The Amerasian boy eventually finds his father and deserts Ha to move to the U.S. Determined to make it on her own, she tries to establish her own whorehouse, but several beatings from rival organizations dissuade her. In the end, she tries once again to start a new business. (In Cantonese; English subtitles.)

p, Mona Fong, Wong Ha Hee; d, Angie Chan; w, Chang Koon Chung; ph, Bob Huke; m, Anders Nelsson, Stephen Shing, So Chun Hou; art d, Chen Ching Shen, Teng Kuang Hsien.

Drama   **(PR:O MPAA:NR)**

HUANLE DINGDANG   (SEE: HAPPY DIN DON, 1986, Hong Kong)

HUD†   (1986, Norway) 186m As–Norway Film Development/Synchron c (Trans: Skin)

Vibeke Lokkeberg *(Vilde)*, Keve Hjelm *(Sigurd, Her Stepfather)*, Per Oscarsson *(The Vicar)*, Elizabeth Granneman *(Vilde's Mother)*, Terence Stamp *(Edward, an Artist)*, Patricia Hodge *(Edward's Wife)*, Tonje Kamilla Kristiansen *(Malene)*, Per Janssen, Reine Torleifsson, Tage Svenneby.

Heavy, dark *sturm und drang* drama from Norway set in 1895, with Lokkeberg as a woman who has been sexually abused by her father, Hjelm, since childhood. She has a daughter, Kristiansen, possibly the progeny of an affair with artist Stamp, and has been promised by her father to a rich, boorish tanner. On their wedding night she stabs him to death, then has to watch as her daughter appears bound for the same abuse experienced by Lokkeberg at the hands of Hjelm. Very expensive for a Norwegian film, HUD was a box-office disappointment.

p, Vibeke Lokkeberg, Terje Kristiansen; d, Vibeke Lokkeberg; w, Terje Kristiansen, Vibeke Lokkeberg; ph, Paul Roestad (Technicolor); m, Arne Nordheim; ed, Terje Kristiansen; prod d, Grethe Heier; cos, Tull Engo.

Drama   **(PR:O MPAA:NR)**

HUOMENNA†   (1986, Fin.) 90m Skandia–Finnish Film Foundation/Kinosto c (Trans: Tomorrow)

Jukka Puotila *(Lt. Leimu)*, Katja Kiuru *(Irene)*, Aake Kalliala *(Kott)*, Heikki Luukas *(Luke)*, Bibi Andersson *(The Singer)*, Pertti Sveholm, Mikko Majanlahti, Jukka-Pekka Palo, Markku Maalismaa, Jussi Parviainen.

An odd, visually stylish allegory that concerns Puotila, an interrogator for one side in an unspecified civil war. He is responsible for the executions of scores of prisoners, but when peace is finally declared, he resists demands that they all be finished off and eventually risks his own life to save one man.

p, Kaj Holmberg; d&w, Juha Rosma; ph, Esa Vuorinen (Fujicolor); m, Edward Vesala; ed, Kristina Schulgin; art d, Janusz Sosnowski; cos, Kaija.

War/Drama   **(PR:C MPAA:NR)**

HYIUCH HA'GDI   (SEE: SMILE OF THE LAMB, 1986, Israel)

HYPER SAPIEN: PEOPLE FROM ANOTHER STAR†   (1986) 93m
Taliafilm II/Tri-Star c

Sydney Penny *(Robyn)*, Ricky Paull Goldin *("Dirt" [Robert Edward McAlpin])*, Keenan Wynn *(Jasper McAlpin)*, Rosie Marcel *(Tavy)*, Gail Strickland *(Sen. Myrna King)*, Dennis Holahen *(Uncle Aric)*, Chuck Shamata *(Les)*.

Three aliens escape their mother ship parked on the moon and flee to earth. Hunted by alien Holahen, they are taken in by ranch boy Goldin and his grandfather Wynn (in his 211th and last film). Produced by Talia Shire's company and shot in western Canada.

p, Jack Schwartzman, Ariel Levy; d, Peter Hunt; w, Christopher Adcock, Christopher Blue, Marnie Page (based on a story by Christopher Blue); ph, John Coquillon (Technicolor); m, Arthur B. Rubenstein; ed, Robert Benrich; prod d, Harold Lange; cos, Kathy Marshall; spec eff, David Harris.

Science Fiction
                                              (PR:A   MPAA:PG)

I

I GIORNI DELL'INFERNO

(SEE: DAYS OF HELL, 1986, It.)

I LAGENS NAMN†

(1986, Swed.) 87m Sprice–Swedish Film Institute–Sandrew–Swedish Television–SVT1/Sandrews c (Trans: In the Name of the Law)

Sven Wollter *(Police Capt. Jarnebring)*, Stefan Sauk *(Patrolman Hall)*, Pia Green *(Patrolwoman Pilstam)*, Marvin Yxner *(Patrolman Mikkelsson)*, Sven Holm *(Patrolman Berg)*, Ernst Gunther *(Narcotics Chief)*, Carlo Barsotti *(Djurgevic)*, Micke Klover *(The Greek)*, Gustav Bartfay *(The Yugoslav)*, Rolf Skoglund *(Nabben)*, Jonas Granstrom *(Puma)*, Anita Wall *(Secretary)*, Johan Ulvesson, Asko Kivisto, Sten Johan Hedman, Lennart Hjulstrom, Mathias Henrikson, Margreth Weivers-Norstrom, Niels Dybeck, Anne Petren, Jans-Erick Lindquist.

Four Stockholm police officers, one of them a woman, outraged by the rising tide of drug addiction and crime, go beyond the law, savagely beating malefactors who, not unnaturally, prefer jail to treatment at the hands of the rogue cops. Wollter is the police inspector who investigates the group and discovers its crimes.

p, Hans Iveberg; d, Kjell Sundvall; w, Hans Iveberg, Leif G.W. Persson (based on the novel *Samhallsbararna* [Pillars of Society] by Leif G.W. Persson); ph, Peter Mokrosinski (Panavision, Eastmancolor); m, Ulf Dageby; ed, Ulla Lennman; prod d, Eric Lison Johnson; makeup, Kjell Gustavsson, Agneta Lindqvist.

Crime
(PR:C MPAA:NR)

I LOVE YOU†

(1986, Fr./Ital.) 100m Alliance–Films A2–UGC–23 Guigno–Top 1/UGC c

Christophe [Christopher] Lambert *(Michel)*, Eddy Mitchell *(Yves)*, Agnes Soral *(Helene)*, Anemone *(Barbara)*, Flora Barillaro *(Maria)*, Maro Berman *(Pierre)*, Laura Manszky *(Camelia)*, Jeanne Marine *(Prostitute)*, Jean Reno *(Dentist)*.

Lambert stars as a handsome, motorcycle-riding young man whose love affair with Anemone has failed, leaving him with a romantic void in his life. One evening he finds a key chain shaped like a beautiful woman's head. What makes this key chain so special is that it whispers the words "I Love You" whenever Lambert whistles—adding new meaning to Lauren Bacall's immortal lines from TO HAVE AND HAVE NOT (1944). Although one can't easily curl up in front of the fireplace with a key chain, Lambert carries on his "romance" nevertheless. He becomes jealous, however, when he realizes that the key chain is not faithful and will say "I Love You" to anyone who whistles. In a rage Lambert crashes his motorcycle into a brick wall, knocking out some of his teeth in the process and rendering himself unable to whistle. As a result, he loses his key chain to his friend Mitchell. A rather strange parable of modern love from director Ferreri, which just may be strange enough to find an audience. As with all of Lambert's European films the actor is billed as "Christophe," though you can be sure that once the film hits the States he will, for some feeble reason, again become "Christopher" as has happened with his SUBWAY billing.

p, Maurice Bernart; d, Marco Ferreri; w, Marco Ferreri, Didier Kaminka, Enrico Oldoni; ph, William Lubtchansky (Panavision, Eastmancolor); m, Les Jivaros, 2eme Prix de Beaute and Les Illumines du 8 Decembre; ed, Ruggiero Mastroianni; art d, Jean-Pierre Kohut-Svelko.

Romance
(PR:O MPAA:NR)

I NICHTA ME TI SILENA†

(1986, Gr.) 80m Greek Film Centre c (Trans: The Night with Silena)

Antonis Kafetzopoulos *(Christos)*, Eva Vlahakou *(Silena)*, Loukia Sterguiou, Magda Mavroyanni, Michalis Gounaris, Fotis Mestheneos, Alexis Pezas, Maria Peza, Constantinos Maguioros.

Kafetzopoulos is a lonely young man who becomes obsessed with Vlahakou, a prostitute in the saloon across the street from his home. He believes her to be the woman he sees in his dreams, but he isn't ready for what happens when he tries to make his fantasy real.

p&d, Demetris Panayotatos; w, Demetris Panayotatos, Antonis Kafetzopoulos (based on an idea from the novel *Silena* by Vassilis Vassilicos); ph, Tassos Alexakis; m, Kyriacos Sfetsas; ed, Yannis Tsitsopoulos; set d, Maria Kaltsas; cos, Spyros Karayannis.

Drama
(PR:C-O MPAA:NR)

I PHOTOGRAPHIA†

(1986, Gr.) 102m Ikones–Greek Film Centre c (Trans: The Photograph)

Christos Tsangas *(George)*, Aris Retsos *(Elias)*, Zozo Zarpa, Christos Valavanidis, Despina Tomazani.

A young man fleeing repression under the Colonels in 1971 pockets a photograph he finds in the street before leaving for Paris, where the photograph causes unforeseen problems.

p,d&w, Nikos Papatakis; ph, Aris Stavrou, Arnaud Desplechin; m, Christodoulos Chalaris; ed, Delphine Desfons; set d&cos, Nikos Meletopoulos.

Drama
(PR:C MPAA:NR)

I TO CE PROCI†

(1986, Yugo.) Kinema c (Trans: That Too Will Pass)

Fabijan Sovagovic, Olivera Markovic, Velimir Bata Zivojinovic, Branko Vidakovic, Bogdan Diklic.

A WW II drama about an average Yugoslav citizen who discovers an untapped source of bravery within himself. He joins the resistance movement and ultimately becomes a great war hero.

d, Nenad Dizdarevic; w, Abdulah Sidran; ph, Mustafa Mustafic; m, Zoran Simjanovic; prod d, Milenko Jeremic.

War
(PR:NR MPAA:NR)

IDEAALMAASTIK†

(1986, USSR) 90m Tallinnfilm c (Trans: Ideal Landscape)

Arvo Kukumagi *(Kukumagi)*, Tonu Kark *(Trunike)*.

Kukumagi is a young Komsomol organizer who is sent to Estonia by party officials to speed up the local farmers' harvest. When his superiors learn he has had no effect, he is sent into the fields to work beside the locals. He is befriended by the farmers and ultimately impresses the officials. He is so efficient, in fact, that they give him a promotion and make him stay in Estonia, though he would rather attend a university.

d, Peeter Simm; w, Karl Helemae; ph, Arvo Iho; m, Jaanus Nogisto, Erkki-Sven Tuur; art d, Priit Vaher.

Drama
(PR:A MPAA:NR)

IDI I SMOTRI

(SEE: COME AND SEE, 1986, USSR)

IL BI E IL BA†

(1986, It.) 89m San Francisco–New Team/ Medusa–Filmexport Group c (Trans: The Bi and the Ba)

Nino Frassica *(Antonino)*, Maria Giovanna Elmi *(Herself)*, Leo Gullotta, Marco Messeri, Pietro De Silva, Sergio Cosentino, Alessandra Costanzo, Ana Telio, Clelia Piscitello.

Frassica (a popular TV comic) is considered by his Sicilian neighbors to be the smartest man in the village, so they raise money to send him to Rome to look for a dandruff cure. There he has a number of close calls at the hands of criminals and the like, constantly making himself misunderstood through his Italian malapropisms, oblivious to all the chaos that surrounds him.

p, Giovanni Bertolucci, Nicola Carraro; d, Maurizio Nichetti; w, Maurizio Nichetti, Nino Frassica, Daniela Conti, Silvia Napolitano; ph, Cristiano Pogany (Telecolor); m, Detto Mariano; ed, Fiorenza Muller.

Comedy
(PR:A MPAA:NR)

IL CAMMISSARIO LO GATTO†

(1986, It.) International Dean –Reteitalia–Medusa/Medusa c (Trans: Commissioner Lo Gatto)

Lino Banfi, Maurizio Ferrini, Maurizio Micheli, Isabella Russinova, Galeazzo Benti.

An inept detective for the Vatican police makes the mistake of grilling the Pope about his whereabouts on the night of a murder, and gets exiled to a remote resort island, where he plays cards with the locals most of the time. When a young girl disappears, he assumes foul play and the whole island is in a uproar, but soon she reappears, having been the guest of the prime minister on a navy vessel. Because of all the commotion, the scandalous incident makes the papers and the prime minister and his cabinet are forced to resign. The detective is rewarded with an important post in Milan, and before the film is over he has botched his way into another promotion and been assigned to take on the mafia.

d, Dino Risi; w, Dino Risi, Enrico Vanzina (based on a story by Dino Risi); ph, Sandro D'Eva (Telecolor); m, Manuel De Sica; ed, Alberto Gallitti.

Comedy
(PR:C MPAA:NR)

IL CAMORRISTA†

(1986, It.) 140m Titanus–Reteitalia–Arlac/Intra Film c (AKA: THE PROFESSOR)

Ben Gazzara *(The Professor)*, Laura Del Sol *(Rosaria)*, Leo Gullotta *(Chief Jervolino)*, Lino Troisi.

Gazzara portrays an Neapolitan tough who murders a man who has shown too much interest in his sister (shades of SCARFACE!). He is sentenced to 20 years in prison, where he sets about seizing control of the Camorra through thugs he recruits there and messages he sends out with sister Del Sol. In time he escapes to continue his rise, but when he orders some of his own men killed to atone for the murder of an American mobster, they turn against him and go to the police. He spends his last days in a desolate island prison, his sanity slipping. Based on the life and career of Raffaele Cutolo.

p, Enzo Silvestri; d, Giuseppe Tornatore; w, Massimo De Rita, Giuseppe Tornatore (based on the novel *Il Camorrista* by Giuseppe Marrazzo); ph, Blasco Giurato (Telecolor); m, Nicola Piovani; ed, Mario Morra; art d, Osvaldo Desideri, Antonio Visone; cos, Luciana Marinucci.

Crime/Prison
(PR:O MPAA:NR)

IL CASO MORO†

(1986, It.) 110m Yarno Cinematografica/Columbia c (Trans: The Moro Affair)

Gian Maria Volonte *(Aldo Moro)*, Margarita Lozano *(Eleanora Moro)*, Sergio Rubini, Daniela De Silva, Emanuela Taschini, Ginella Vocca *(Moro Family)*

Mattia Sbragia, Bruno Zanin, Consuelo Ferrara, Enrica Maria Modugno, Enrica Rosso, Maurizio Donadoni, Stefano Abbati, Danilo Mattei, Massimo Tedde, Francesco Capitano *(Red Brigades)*, Daniele Dublino, Piero Vida, Bruno Corazzari, Gabriele Villa, Francesco Carnelutti, Paolo M. Scalondro, Dante Biagioni *(Politicians)*, Umberto Raho, Luciano Bartoli, Silverio Blasi, Franco Trevisi, Pino Ferrara, Nicola Di Pinto *(Secret Service)*.

In early 1978, Aldo Moro, head of Italy's Christian Democratic party, had emerged as the leader of the first coalition government to include the Communists. Then he was kidnaped by the Red Brigades and held in a "people's prison" for two months, during which time he wrote a number of letters to the government asking for negotiations that would free him. The government held firm to its pledge not to negotiate with terrorists, and on May 9 he was murdered by his captors and left in the trunk of a parked car. These are the bare facts of the case, but here the filmmakers probe deeper to find the reasons various factions in the government did not especially want Moro back. Using evidence from various hearings, they ask the still-unanswered questions: What happened to the briefcase full of sensitive documents that the kidnapers left behind? Why did the Italian anti-terrorist police drag their feet so much, and were they actually responsible for acts blamed on the Red Brigades as a way of keeping the official Communist party off balance and looking bad? Based on a book by an American journalist living in Italy, this film provoked major controversy before it opened. It was widely denounced in newspapers of the Christian Democrats, who come across worst in this political drama, and, of course, controversy packed the theaters.

p, Mauro Berardi; d, Giuseppe Ferrara; w, Robert Katz, Armenia Balducci, Giuseppe Ferrara (based on the book *Days Of Wrath* by Robert Katz); ph, Camillo Bazzoni; m, Pino Donaggio; ed, Roberto Perpignani; md, Natale Massara; art d, Francesco Frigeri; cos, Laura Vaccari.

Historical/Drama (PR:C MPAA:NR)

IL DIAVOLO IN CORPO† (1986, It./Fr.) 110m Instituto Luce-Italnoleggio–Film Sextile-L.P. Film/Instituto Luce-Italnoleggio c (Trans: Devil In The Flesh)

Maruschka Detmers *(Giulia)*, Federico Pitzalis *(Andrea)*, Anita Laurenzi *(Mrs. Pulcini)*, Riccardo De Torrebruna *(Giacomo Pulcini)*, Anna Orso *(Mrs. Dozza)*, Alberto Di Stasio *(Prof. Raimondi)*, Catherine Diamant *(Mrs. Raimondi)*, Claudio Botosso *(Don Pisacane)*, Lidia Broccolino, Stefano Abbati *(Terrorists)*.

The second remake this year of Raymond Radiguet's novel which came to the screen in 1947 as LE DIABLE AU CORPS (THE DEVIL IN THE FLESH) under Claude Autant-Lara's direction and caused something of a scandal in its time. A scandal has again erupted with Bellochio's version, starring the ravishing star of Jean-Luc Godard's PRENOM: CARMEN (FIRST NAME: CARMEN), Detmers, in some graphic sex scenes. Only peripherally resembling Radiguet's original, Bellocchio's film has the teenage Pitzalis falling in love with Detmers, the fiancee of an imprisoned terrorist, De Torrebruna. When De Torrebruna is released, Detmers is caught between two lovers, skipping her wedding ceremony with the one-time terrorist in order to be with Pitzalis. The sex scenes raised a few eyebrows in its European release, sparking a feud between Bellocchio and producer Pescarolo. The media attention, if anything, helped the film get a U.S. distribution deal with Orion Classics, which planned to release the film in art houses with an X rating.

p, Leo Pescarolo; d, Marco Bellocchio; w, Marco Bellocchio, Ennio De Concini (based on the novel *Le Diable au Corps* by Raymond Radiguet); ph, Giuseppe Lanci; m, Carlo Crivelli; ed, Mirco Garrone; art d, Andrea Crisanti; cos, Lina Nerli Taviani.

Drama (PR:O MPAA:NR)

IL 45MO PARALLELO (SEE: 45MO PARALLELO, 1986, It.)

IL GIARDINO DEGLI INGANNI† (1986, It.) Ferruccio Casati Studio c (Trans: The Garden of Deception)

Anna Caravaggi, Cesare Benini, Mirella Falco, Gino Lana, Milly Falsini, Gabriella Giordano, Federico Relle, Enrica Ciabatti.

An old man who has led a scholarly life of self-denial finally marries a young girl. But she is unfaithful and he realizes that she doesn't know what love is, so he creates another identity for himself, that of a mysterious knight, and leads her to fall in love with him. Then, in her arms, he kills himself, and she finally knows love and loss.

d&w, Ferruccio Casati (based on a play by Federico Garcia Lorca); ph, Domenico Murdaca; m, Massimiliano Casacci.

Drama (PR:C MPAA:NR)

IL MIELE DEL DIAVOLO† (1986, It.) Selvaggia/Uniexport c (Trans: The Devil's Honey)

Brett Halsey, Corinne Clery, Blanca Marsillach, Stefano Madia, Paola Molina, Bernard Seray.

When her husband dies, a beautiful young girl blames the doctor, so she kidnaps him and subjects him to assorted bondage and domination tableaus. In time they fall in love with each other. The Italians are good at this type of soft-core "erotic drama," but since this is the worst of all genres, that's a dubious distinction.

d, Lucio Fulci; w, Ludovica Marineo, Vincenzo Salviani, Jesus Balcazar; ph,

Alessandro Ulloa (Luciano Vittori Color); m, Claudio Natili; ed, Vincenzo Tomassi.

Drama (PR:O MPAA:NR)

IL MOSTRO DI FIRENZE† (1986, It.) 92m Gruppo Milano/Medusa c (Trans: The Monster of Florence)

Leonard Mann *(Andreas Ackermann)*, Bettina Giovannini *(Julia)*, Lidia Mancinelli *(Mother)*, Gabriele Tinti *(Newsman)*, Francesca Muzio, Federico Pacifici, Alberto Di Stasio, Anna Orso.

In 1968, a man and woman were murdered in their car on a moonless night outside of Florence. Six years later, the same gun was used to kill another couple. Then in 1981 two different couples were killed, and every year since then two more have died, and police still have no idea who the killer might be. The fact that these murders, obviously sexually motivated (the women are mutilated), are still unsolved and presumably still continuing poses but little problem for the filmmakers, who frame their story around a young reporter investigating the killings. Scenes illustrate the type of sexual trauma that could be responsible for the killer's psychosis, and for a while the reporter trails a man whom he feels might be the killer, but he loses him in a crowd. The film, shot on some of the actual murder sites, provoked a controversy in Italy amidst police fears that a copycat killer might take it as inspiration.

p, Mario Giacomini, Bruno Noris; d, Cesare Ferrario; w, Fulvio Ricciardi, Cesare Ferrario (based on the book by Mario Spezi); ph, Claudio Cirillo (Cinecitta, Kodak Color); m, Paolo Rustichelli; art d, Mario Ambrosino.

Crime (PR:O MPAA:NR)

IL RAGAZZO DEL PONY EXPRESS† (1986, It.) 108m Numero Uno-Reteitalia/CIDIF c (Trans: The Pony Express Boy)

Jerry Cala *(The Beast)*, Isabella Ferrari *(Claudia)*, Alessandro Benvenuti *(Accountant)*, Emanuela Taschini, Gabriella Saitta, Germana Dominici, Sergio Di Pinto, Stefano Sabelli, Nerina Montagnani, Tiberio Murgia.

Cala cannot find the entry-level executive position he wants, so he is finally forced to take a job as a messenger, provided he has his own motor scooter. He steals a woman's purse to buy one and starts out on his rounds. Before long he has caught the eye of Ferrari, another messenger from an upscale service. When he gets arrested for the purse-snatch, she manages to get him released and they form their own messenger service.

p, Claudio Bonivento; d, Franco Amurri; w, Franco Amurri, Cesare Frugoni, Jerry Cala, Stefano Sandrie, Marco Cavaliere; ph, Giuseppe Berardini (Fujicolor); m, Umberto Smaila; ed, Raimondo Crociani; art d, Egidio Spagnini.

Comedy (PR:C MPAA:NR)

IL TENENTE DEI CARABINIERI† (1986, It.) C.G. Silver c (Trans: The Lieutenant of the Carabinieri)

Enrico Montesano, Nino Manfredi, Claudio Botosso, Massimo Boldi, Alessandro Partexano, Marisa Laurito.

A false 100,000 lira note passed to a policeman in a gas station leads to a murdered painter and an international counterfeiting ring.

d, Maurizio Ponzi; w, Leo Benvenuti, Piero De Bernardi, Maurizio Ponzi; ph, Carlo Cerchio (Technicolor); m, Bruno Zambrini; ed, Antonio Siciliano.

Crime (PR:C MPAA:NR)

ILLUSION, THE† (1986, Iran) IRIB c

Jalil Farjad, Reza Payam, Malileh Nazari.

d&w, Sa'id Haji-Miri; ph, Kamal Tabizi; m, A.R. Mohseni; ed, Sa'id Haji-Miri.

IMAGEMAKER, THE* (1986) 93m Screenscope/Castle Hill–Manson c

Michael Nouri *(Roger Blackwell)*, Anne Twomey *(Molly Grainger)*, Jerry Orbach *(Byron Caine)*, Jessica Harper *(Cynthia)*, Farley Granger *(Ambassador)*, Richard Bauer *(Morris Brodkin)*, Roger Frazier *(Victor Griffin)*, Maury Povich *(Talk Show Host)*, Patrick Blake *(Martin)*, Jerome Dempsey *(Congressman Lyons)*, Arthur Dailey *(Black Man)*, David Rosenbaum *(Chet)*, Doug Tillet *(Sal)*, Betty Jerome *(Margaret Holye)*, Diana McLellan *(Gossip Columnist)*, Henry Strozier *(Accountant)*, Bruce Godfrey *(Campaign Manager)*, Will Smith *(Pollster)*, James Adams *(Newscaster)*, Noah Berlin *(Timmy Blackwell)*, Billie Jackson *(Ellen Blackwell)*, David Hammond *(1st Aide)*, Joshua Billings *(2nd Aide)*, Rosemary Polen *(Autograph Seeker)*, Arlene Stern *(Roger's Secretary)*, Catherine Flye *(Molly's Secretary)*, Mike Handley *(Video Director)*, Marcia Gay Harden *(Stage Manager)*, Mark Hammer *(President Manning's Voice)*, Sandy Anderson *(Tony LaCorte's Voice)*, Timothy Rice *(Matt Gant's Voice)*, Franchelle Dorn *(Surveillance Voice)*, John Flynn, Scott Sedar *(Commercial Voices)*, Dennis Owens, Bill Thompson *(Radio Voices)*, Gred Spriggs *(Bodyguard)*, Michael Gabel, Michael Fiske, Steve Hayes *(Surveillance Team)*, Danita Manley, Margaret Huffstickler, Patricia Newman *(Nightmare Sequence)*, Mike Barsalou *(Motorcyclist)*, Suellen Estrin *(Woman with Stroller)*.

A fictional expose of corruption within the U.S. government and the role the media plays in manipulating the public. Nouri—whose greatest claim to fame was his role in FLASHDANCE (1983)—plays a former media adviser to the president (voiced by Hammer). Depressed over the suicide of his wife, Nouri falls down on his job and is exposed in a hard-hitting report delivered by Twomey, his one-time lover, an unscrupulous newsperson aiming at a news anchor spot. To help deal with the loss of his wife, Nouri devises a complex video system in his home which projects a video image of his "dead wife" onto video monitors throughout the house. It's not actually his dead wife, but Harper, a friend who agrees to dress up as his wife and talk to him via the tape as he does his morning ablutions. This video fetish is kept secret by Nouri and Harper. Nouri and his partner Orbach are planning a feature film which will, like THE IMAGEMAKER, expose corruption in the U.S. government and the role that the media plays in manipulating the public. The Washington power-structure people want to keep him quiet. The most determined of these is Granger, a mysterious ambassador, who tries to corrupt Orbach with money and power in order to keep Nouri from making the film. Because of a red-herring plot about a tape Nouri possesses which may or may not contain a conversation between the president and a crime-connected union boss, a couple of people are killed, which only hardens Nouri's resolve to make the film. Granger and his goons move in on Twomey and pressure her to denounce Nouri with another of her reports. Hungry for the news anchor-job, she agrees. Through Harper, she uncovers Nouri's video fetish and threatens to ruin him. Nouri, in retaliation, forces her at gunpoint to undress in front of his

video cameras, and promises to blackmail her, as well. Then comes Nouri's big plan. Appearing on a nighttime news show called "Capital Report," Nouri plays an audiotape conversation between the president and the mob boss. The host is outraged at the tape, but Nouri calms everyone's fear by confessing that the tape is a fake. "Hey, look how easy it is to be manipulated by the media," Nouri seems to be saying. Then, to ensure that he gets the $5,000,000 in film financing he needs, Nouri acts out another scene. Promising to give the audience what they want—blood and guts—Nouri puts a gun (full of blanks, as we earlier learned) to his head and pulls the trigger. Chaos follows in the studio. A news show reports that the president's former media adviser has killed himself. But wait, he's still alive, as Twomey discovers while wandering through his house. It was all an elaborate gag, he confesses—a bunch of actors at the studio who went along with his scheme to raise funds for his proposed film. Nouri promises to go hold a press conference later that evening to clear the air. But again, wait, there's more. As Nouri stands with his back to the door, Orbach enters. Orbach's body is partly obscured but it appears that he is about to kill his partner in an even more elaborate conspiracy to silence Nouri. A gunshot rings out. Relax, it was only a champagne bottle popping. Orbach and Nouri are celebrating their success in financing their film. But wasn't that a distinct gunshot we heard?

While filmmakers Marilyn and Hal Weiner may have had good intentions in making THE IMAGEMAKER, they are undone by the unbelievable scenario they've created. This film is filled with one preposterous idea after another. Nouri is not credible as a man who has advised dozens of major politicians on their media campaigns, nor as the widower of a woman who blew her brains out less than five feet away from him. Even if one manages to believe in Nouri's character, plausibility is stretched to the breaking point by his on-air practical joke. The filmmakers are expecting a lot if they think a news-show host would broadcast a scandalous audiotape of the president without a pre-hearing, research back-up, and some skepticism. The host in THE IMAGEMAKER, however, is an utter dolt. Nouri is even worse—traumatizing countless viewers by "killing" himself on the air and then thinking it will be all right the following day when he explains himself. Such a fool would get his fanny kicked out of public life for eternity. (Nor would the deception work; actor Jon-Erik Hexum playfully put a blank-loaded pistol to his head and pulled the trigger the year of this film's release; the blank wadding blasted into his brain and killed him.) To top it off, someone actually gives Nouri money to make his film. Why, he's supposed to be dead, isn't he? THE IMAGEMAKER also has the distinction of having the cheapest, most offensive ending in recent memory, with its champagne-bottle deception. The filmmakers have extensive experience in documentary production and in the Washington political scene, but that just isn't enough. THE IMAGEMAKER was the first independent locally produced film shot in Washington, D.C., and it must be commended for that, but for a more insightful film on the subject of media manipulation, watch Sidney Lumet's POWER, which starred Richard Gere and was also released this year. THE IMAGEMAKER is based, in part, on a real-life 1974 incident in which news anchor Christine Chubbock killed herself during her morning newscast. A similar incident happened in 1986 when politician R. "Bud" Dwyer held a press conference and, in front of reporters and television cameras, killed himself.

p, Marilyn Weiner, Hal Weiner; d, Hal Weiner; w, Dick Goldberg, Hal Weiner; ph, Jacques Haitkin (Fujicolor); m, Fred Karns; ed, Terry Halle; prod d, Edward Pisoni; art d, Russell Metheny; set d, Henry Shaffer; cos, Catherine Adair; spec eff, Frank Rogers; m/l, Fred Karns; makeup, William Whited.

Political Drama   Cas.   **(PR:C-O MPAA:R)**

IMPURE THOUGHTS†   (1986) 83m ASA Communications c

John Putch *(Danny Stubbs)*, Terry Beaver *(William Miller)*, Brad Dourif *(Kevin Harrington)*, Lane Davies *(Steve Barrett)*, Benji Wilhoite *(Young Bill)*, J.J. Sacha *(Young Danny)*, Sam McPhaul *(Young Kevin)*, Jason Jones *(Young Steve)*, Mary McDonough *(Sister Juliet)*, Joe Conley *(Father Minnelli)*, Mary Nell Santacroce *(Sister Gertrude)*, Charlie Hill *(Bill Miller, Sr.)*, Carmen Thomas *(Marie Borkowsky)*, Sandra Dorsey, Randi Layne, Muriel Moore, Carol Haynes, Dennis Harrington, Bob Bost, Shirlene Foss, Dame Judith Anderson *(Narrator)*.

Four schoolmates from a Catholic high school in the 1960s meet each other a lifetime later as all languish in Purgatory (a large gray room) waiting for Judgment Day. As they talk among themselves, there are flashbacks to their school days and their later lives. The film saw only a limited release in a few cities, and seemed bound for the video stores in short order.

p, William VanDerKloot, Michael A. Simpson, Michael J. Malloy; d, Michael A. Simpson; w, Michael J. Malloy, Michael A. Simpson; ph, William VanDerKloot (Eastmancolor); m, James Oliverio; ed, William VanDerKloot, Wade Watkins; prod d, Guy Tuttle.

Drama/Comedy   **(PR:A-C MPAA:PG)**

IN DE SCHADUW VAN DE OVERWINNING   (SEE: SHADOW OF VICTORY, 1986, Neth.)

IN 'N' OUT†   (1986, U.S./Mex.) 95m Instituto Mexicano de Cinematografica-Conacite Dos-Camrose/NW c (GRINGO MOJADO)

Sam Bottoms *(Murray Lewis, Jr.)*, Rafael Inclan *(Nieves Blanco)*, Rebecca Jones *(Lupita Blanco)*, Isela Vega *(Mona Mur)*, Pat Hingle *(Oscar Milstone)*.

Bottoms is a down-on-his-luck musician who receives word from Mexico to come down for his father's funeral. Since he has thought his father dead for the last 30 years, he is naturally interested enough to go. He is befriended there by Inclan, a daffy musician-type who worships Dean Martin, and Inclan's sister, Jones. Bottoms discovers he is to inherit a fortune, but assorted bad guys want to prevent this, and he gets kicked back into the U.S. several times but always comes back. Shot in English in 1984, the film was dubbed into Spanish and released in Mexico, as well as to Spanish-language theaters in the U.S., but has yet to see an English-language release. Chances are it never will, appearing on videocassette instead.

p, Michael James Egan; d, Ricardo Franco; w, Eleen Kesend, Ricardo Franco; ph, Juan Ruiz Anchias; m, T. Bone Burnett.

Comedy   **(PR:C MPAA:NR)**

IN THE RAIN†   (1986, Iran) Yosef Mahdavi c

Hossein Khanibeyk, Nasrin Pakkhoo.

d&w, Seyfollah Dad; ph, Behruz Afkhami; m, K. Roshan Ravan; ed, Mehrzad Minooi.

IN THE SHADOW OF KILIMANJARO✱✱   (1986) 97m Intermedia/Scotti Brothers c

John Rhys-Davies *(Chris Tucker)*, Timothy Bottoms *(Jack Ringtree)*, Irene Miracle *(Lee Ringtree)*, Michele Carey *(Ginny Hansen)*, Leonard Trolley *(Col. Emerson Maitland)*, Patty Foley *(Lucille Gagnon)*, Calvin Jung *(Mitsuki Uto)*, Don Blakely *(Julius X. Odom)*, Jim Boeke *(Claud Gagnon)*, Patrick Gorman *(Eugene Kurtz)*, Mark Watters *(Carlysle Bandy)*, Ka Vundla *(District Officer Tshombe)*.

Supposedly based on a true story which occurred in 1984, IN THE SHADOW OF KILIMANJARO takes place in Kenya in the Amboselli National Park. Bottoms runs a wildlife preserve amongst the native Masai tribe in a region which is suffering from a severe draught. Because there is a shortage of food and water, the animals have become difficult to control—especially the baboons, which are now traveling in packs looking for food. When the dismembered body of a young native boy is found, Bottoms makes an appeal to have the area's 200 residents evacuated. His chief opponent is Rhys-Davies, a rugged mine operator who is determined to keep his men on the job and finish out his government contract. When one of the miners is killed and eaten by a pack of baboons, Rhys-Davies decides to take action. With Bottoms' help, a shooting party locates one of the packs and kills the elder males, assuming that the pack will disperse without its leaders and, simultaneously, be supplied with food (we're told that if hungry enough the baboons will cannibalize each other). This, however, is only a temporary solution. The baboons continue to attack. Bottoms' wife Miracle, who has just arrived from California via Nairobi, is also attacked when the angry primates try to break into her house. Eventually all the locals are gathered under one roof. Boards are nailed to the windows and doors and are well secured. Bottoms and Rhys-Davies arm themselves and their men and prepare for the descent of the baboons. When it looks as if the baboons are going to win, they begin to disperse. As Rhys-Davies looks outside he sees a downpour of rain which has apparently cooled the baboons' frenzy for water.

Amounting to nothing more than THE BIRDS meets BORN FREE, this formula thriller combines Hitchcock's revolt-of-nature theme with a Kenyan game reserve locale. Whether it is possible that baboons would organize and attack innocent people is a moot point (the same argument could be raised against THE BIRDS), but what is questionable is whether or not people in this situation would act as stupidly as those in the film did. Like so many other thrillers of this sort, one wonders how the characters could be so stupid. Haven't they ever seen movies like this one? Bottoms, the game warden who supposedly knows about wildlife, is consistently more foolish than anyone in the picture. When he and Rhys-Davies are confronted with a pack of baboons they scatter them with one gunshot and expect them to stay away. Well, of course, the angry baboons are going to be coming back—and in full force. At another point Bottoms specifically warns his wife to stay in the compound. But that isn't clear enough for the brain-dead blonde from California. She wanders off and is promptly chased down by an angry pack, barely escaping a grizzly death. After this brazen act of stupidity, she deserves to become a baboon's lunch. While the acting leaves much to be desired (Rhys-Davies outperforms the rest, but is only passable at best), first-time director Patel, an Indian-born native of Nairobi, manages to create uncompromising suspense. The use of a Steadicam to simulate the point of view of the baboons' attack is harrowing, especially when coupled with the shrieking of the baboon voices (created in the sound studio by Percy Edwards). There is also some unexpected ethnographic footage of the Masai tribe, the most memorable of which is the opening scene of a young boy in the bush killing a deadly snake with his slingshot. IN THE SHADOW OF KILIMANJARO was reportedly photographed in 1984, which would shed a dubious light on the film's claim that it is based on an actual incident that occurred that same year. Another killer primate movie, LINK, also saw a release this year. Less suspenseful, it suffered a similar fate at the box office. The fine rhythm-based soundtrack by Arlon Ober includes the title song "In the Shadow of Kilimanjaro" (Allan Smallwood, Chieli Minuci).

p, Gautam Das, Jeffrey M. Sneller; d, Raju Patel; w, Jeffrey M. Sneller, T. Michael Harry; ph, Jesus Elizondo (Technicolor); m, Arlon Ober; ed, Pradip Roy Shah; art d, Ron Foreman; m/l, Allan Smallwood, Chieli Minuci; makeup, Jack Petty.

Action/Horror **Cas.** **(PR:O MPAA:R)**

IN THE WILD MOUNTAINS*½** (1986, China) 99m Xi'an Film Studio/ China Films c (YE SHAN)

Du Yuan, Yue Hong, Xin Ming, Xu Shaoli, Tan Xihe, Qiu Yuzhen.

Set in the Shaanxi province of Northern China, IN THE WILD MOUNTAINS is a simple, yet insightful, tale of village life and how economic changes in the country affect even the most remote regions. Hehe and Huihui are brothers of completely opposite disposition. Huihui as the elder is content with a simple lifestyle, while the industrious Hehe is continuously searching for means to better his life. Huihui's greatest desire is to have a child, but his wife Guijan is barren. As the film opens, Hehe has been kicked out of the house by his wife Qiurong because he demands too much independence and refuses to ask for any assistance. He stays at his brother's house where he develops a strong attachment to Guijan, who admires him for his hard-working nature while deriding her own husband for his laziness. This leads to further family strife that forces Hehe to leave the village to search for work in the city. Meanwhile, Huihui watches over Qiurong at his brother's request, and grows increasingly fond of her as the young child he has always wanted. Hehe comes back to the village with tales of all the wondrous things in the city, completely mystifying Guijan. On Hehe's next trip, Guijan follows him. Rumors that the two have eloped spread throughout the village, so that when Guijan comes back she is publicly humiliated and Huihui refuses to allow her back into the house. He eventually marries the more suitable Qiurong, achieving the settled family life he has always desired. Ostracized by the village, Guijan and Hehe resist getting together though harboring a deep affection for one another. Hehe becomes a truckdriver's assistant, making loads of money because of his hardworking nature. When he comes back to the village, he and Guijan marry, working together to harvest their land and better themselves. They eventually bring electricity to the village, becoming its wealthiest citizens.

Essentially IN THE WILD MOUNTAINS is about wife swapping, a subject sporadically dealt with in such American films as BOB & CAROL & TED & ALICE and a few tasteless sex comedies. Unlike these films it is not the changes in sexual consciousness that affects the social order, but an awareness of economic opportunity and the desire to become part of the modern world. Hehe and Guijan are the dreamers and adventurers, ridiculed by peers for their extravagance, but who are ultimately beneficial to everybody's welfare. IN THE WILD MOUNTAINS has an extremely humanistic light quality which studiously captures the eccentricities of the characters without making any crass judgment. At times these pastoral people appear quite funny with their backward customs and ancient rules, yet director Xueshu presents these mannerisms as being equally fascinating. This dichotomy between the old and new leads to the film's most touching moments involving Hehe and Guijan as the explorers stuck between both worlds. In one scene humor is explored: Guijan visits the city for the first time where she behaves like a young child in a toy store around the townspeople who take these goods for granted. Another scene depicts isolation and loneliness, as a frustrated Hehe drinks too much one evening, then lashes out in the middle of the street at the city people he thinks make fun of him. IN THE WILD MOUNTAINS has much to recommend it: superb acting, beautiful photography of the mountainous terrain, and a stimulating soundtrack. Hopefully more Chinese films of such merit will make their way to Western screens.

d, Yan Xueshu; w, Zhu Zi, Yan Xueshu (based on the novel *The People Of Jiwowa* by Jia Ping'ao); ph, Mi Jiaqing; m, Xu Youfu; art d, Li Xingzhen.

Comedy/Drama **(PR:C MPAA:NR)**

INFERNO IN DIRETTA (SEE: CUT AND RUN, 1986, It.)

INNOCENZA† (1986, Switz.) 90m Imago-SSR-RTSI c (Trans: Innocence)

Enrica Maria Modugno *(Schoolteacher)*, Alessandro Haber *(Mayor)*, Patrick Tacchella *(Luca)*, Teco Celio, Sonia Gessner, Marino Campanaro, Franco Serena.

Modugno is a beautiful young schoolteacher hired to teach in a small Swiss village accessible only by ferryboat. Her students are enraptured, and she sets about playing teasing, sexual games with a few of them, playing one against another. Her downfall at the hands of the townsfolk is precipitated by the jealousy of the mayor, Haber.

p&d, Villi Hermann; w, Villi Hermann, Angelo Gregorio (based on a short story by Francesco Chiesa); ph, Hugues Ryffel (Eastmancolor); m, Graziano Mandozzi; ed, Claudio Cormio; art d, Raffaella Leggeri; cos, Sylvia de Stoutz.

Drama **(PR:O MPAA:NR)**

INSIDE OUT** (1986) 87m Beckerman c

Elliott Gould *(Jimmy Morgan)*, Howard Hesseman, Jennifer Tilly, Beah Richards, Nicole Norman, John Bleifer, Dana Elcar.

The film has a potentially absorbing premise, and Gould gives a sensitive performance, but INSIDE OUT is an unsatisfying feature that suffers from underdeveloped ideas and uninteresting direction. Gould is a seemingly successful New York businessman with a few strange eccentricities. He carries the remote controls for his television, stereo, VCR, and telephone answering machine in a bathrobe pocket, conducts all his business over the telephone, and has an escort service send him over a companion for an evening's entertainment. Later, Gould's old pal Hesseman comes over for a visit and invites his friend to come out to California some time. Hesseman grows annoyed at Gould's reluctance, then learns the man hasn't been outside his apartment in years. Shocked, Hesseman tells Gould he is sick and needs help. The cocoon Gould has carefully built for himself suddenly begins to fall apart when he learns that his ex-wife intends to take their daughter out of town when she moves to Chicago. Gould then discovers that his business partner has been slowly cheating him and gaining control of the firm. This, coupled with enormous gambling losses, pushes Gould to financial ruin. He sells all his possessions, finding himself a broken man in an empty apartment, a pathetic victim of his agoraphobia. Finally, realizing what he must do, the frightened Gould ventures through the safety of his door to the imperiling streets of the city. He goes to his daughter's school and there, in a tearful embrace, promises the girl that he will try to make it on the outside.

This study of agoraphobia (an intense, overwhelming fear of leaving one's home) is marked by good performances, particularly Gould's leading role. Confined to one set for nearly the whole of the film, Gould takes a new variation on his familiar schlepp persona by slowly allowing the character's horrible secret to slip through his seemingly cavalier facade. Tilly (the sister of actress Meg Tilly) is sweet and sympathetic as the not-too-bright call girl sent by Gould's service, while Hesseman provides a good probing counterpoint to his friend's secretiveness. The confrontation scene, in which Hesseman learns of Gould's illness, is well-acted and intense in its psychological pain. Unfortunately, despite the competent cast, INSIDE OUT fails to work as a whole. Taicher, making his directorial debut, doesn't seem to have any real sense of how to augment his material. He allows things to develop too slowly, and often relies on cliched secondary characters such as a wisecracking maid and a streetwise coke dealer to fill out undeveloped scenes. Working from his own original screenplay (cowritten with Kevin Bartelme), Taicher seems to have plenty of ideas but no comprehension of how to use or expand on them. One particularly interesting notion has Gould observing a homeless man who camps out nightly on the other side of the apartment door. Gould watches the man through a television monitor and carries on a short dialog with him before the character mysteriously disappears. The man is shown throughout the film, then vanishes without a word. Had Taicher built on this relationship, he could have cultivated some fascinating ideas, but instead he wastes a vast source of possibilities.

p, Sidney Beckerman; d, Robert Taicher; w, Robert Taicher, Kevin Bartelme; ph, Jack Wallner; m, Peer Raben; ed, David Finfer; art d, Jack Wright III; cos, Arlene Ansel.

Drama **(PR:O MPAA:NR)**

INSOMNIACS** (1986, Arg.) 78m Ferlain/Instituto Nacional de Cinematografia c (LOS INSOMNES)

Elsa Berenguer, *(Mayorquina)*, Seva Aleman *(Wife Shopping for Baby)*, Bettiana Blum *(Lota)*, Mirta Bushnelli *(Isabel)*, Roberto Carnaghi *(Carlitos)*, Alberto Fernandez de Rosa *(Garro)*, Marta Gam, Marcos Zucker *(Old Furriers)*, Antonio Grimau *(Man Shopping for Baby)*, Hugo Midon *(Hilarion)*, Boy Olmi *(Kidnaped Boy)*, Edgardo Suarez *(Kid Cachetada)*, Maria Vaner *(Jacinta Rubiales)*, Elvira Vicario *(Interior Wife)*, Juan Leyrado *(Pepe)*, Mario Luciani *(Janitor)*, Ana Maria Pitaluga *(Maria Constelacion)*, Christian Cardoso *(Othus)*, Gabriel Gonzalez *(Mario Jupiter)*, Ana Chevalier *(Pandora)*, Juan Rago *(Mario Atilio)*, Alejandro Resnik *(Chipo)*.

This wild romp is full of nightmarish characters and vivid color but there's no real sense by the director of what to do with these elements. INSOMNIACS follows a bizarre clique of characters as they make their way through darkened city streets. A group of kids leads the way, trying to caution adults about the terrors of the night, though their warnings are of no use. The grownups these children of the night encounter are fitted with grotesque make up and utterly mad personalities. In many ways this resembles a Fellini film with its eccentric characters and largely incomprehensible plot. Presumably allegorical, INSOMNIACS is too crazed for its own good, and ultimately the unorthodoxies send the film spinning out of control. (In Spanish; English subtitles.)

p, Jaime Pinkus, Miguel Weyrauch; d, Carlos Orgambide; w, Beatriz Guido, Bernardo Raitman, Carlos Orgambide (based on a story by Beatriz Guido); ph, Eduardo Legaria; m, Luis Maria Serra; ed, Eduardo Lopez; set d, Leandro Rogucci.

Comedy   (PR:O MPAA:NR)

INSPECTEUR LAVARDIN†   (1986, Fr.) 99m Films A2–Television Suisse
                                         Romande-Cab/MK2 c

Jean Poiret (Jean Lavardin), Bernadette Lafont (Helene Mons), Jean-Claude Brialy (Claude Alvarez), Jacques Dacqmine (Raoul Mons), Hermine Claire (Veronique Manguin), Jean-Luc Bideau (Max Charnet), Pierre-Francois Dumeniaud (Marcel Vigouroux), Florent Gibassier (Francis), Guy Louret (Buci), Jean Depusse (Volga).

In last year's POULET AU VINAIGRE Poiret had a small but significant role as a criminal inspector which proved to be the film's best feature. This time out, director-coscripter Chabrol has expanded Poiret's contribution to the lead performer and built his criminal plot around the actor's character. In the title role, Poiret travels to a coastal town to investigate the murder of a Catholic writer whose nude body is found on the beach. In the process of uncovering the murderer's identity, Poiret probes into the private lives of the disinterested and unaffected local bourgeoise townspeople. While it fared fine at the French box office, INSPECTEUR LAVARDIN has failed to restore Chabrol—the once-compelling New Wave director—to his former seat of prominence, a seat he long ago vacated.

p, Marin Karmitz; d, Claude Chabrol; w, Claude Chabrol, Dominique Roulet; ph, Jean Rabier (Eastmancolor); m, Mathieu Chabrol; ed, Monique Fardoulis; art d, Francoise Benoit-Fresco.

Crime   (PR:O MPAA:NR)

INSTANT JUSTICE zero   (1986) 101m Mulloway Limited–Craig T. Rumar/
                                                    WB c

Michael Pare (Scott Youngblood), Tawny Kitaen (Virginia), Peter Crook (Jake), Charles Napier (Maj. Davis), Eddie Avoth (Silke), G. Scott Del Amo (Dutch), Lynda Bridges (Kim), Lionel A. Ephraim (Ambassador Gordon), Maurice E. Aronow (Shelton), Aldo San Brell (Juan Munoz), Peter Boulter (Clarke), Thomas Abbott (Lt. Hardroy), Anthony Bingham (Sgt. Wilker), Scott Miller (Col. Parker), Steve Haywood (Corp. Atkinson), Marvel De Blas (Ochoa), Angel Mancuso (Tony), Sylvie Coffin (Bar Girl), Barry Zimmerman (Aide), Louis Lorenzo (Dufour), Kunyo Kobayashi (Cook), Tessa Hewitt (Model), Pepe Gallego (Ripal), James Finnerty (Marine Officer), Ruben Tobias, Louis Barboo (Toughs).

Mere words cannot properly convey just how appallingly inept this film is. Pare stars as a Marine guard stationed at the American embassy in Paris. After saving the ambassador's life during an assassination attempt, Pare receives a desperate phone call from his sister Kim (Bridges) in Madrid. Distraught and stoned, the girl babbles incoherently about needing his help. Unbeknownst to Pare, his sister has become a high-class call girl working exclusively for Spanish flesh-peddler/drug dealer Avoth. Immediately after she calls, Bridges is murdered by Avoth's slimy enforcer, Del Amo. Pare takes a week-long leave and goes to Madrid. For reasons never explained, Pare's Marine buddy slips a .45 automatic into his luggage. After Pare leaves for the airport his buddy mutters, "What the hell did I do that for? God! How stupid of me!" Indeed. Pare is soon detained at customs in Madrid and turned over to Napier, the American Marine commander in charge of the embassy. Napier lets the incident slide and Pare goes to his sister's apartment. There he finds an American expatriate photographer and friend of the deceased, Crook, who informs him of Bridges' murder. Pare learns of Avoth's crime empire from Crook, and the Marine vows revenge. He drags the hapless Crook along on his quest and then infiltrates the local Marine base and steals a machine gun. Pare then kidnaps Kitaen, a call girl from Beverly Hills who has come to Madrid on her friend Bridges' advice to make big money working for Avoth. After she warns Pare several times that he'll get in "big trouble," Kitaen reluctantly joins the crusade. Of course, she soon falls in love with the big lug (maybe because he calls her "Babe"), and they share many incredibly insipid moments between shoot-outs. After gathering enough information to hang Avoth, Pare goes off by himself to bring the criminal and his enforcer to justice. In a ludicrous finale, Pare manages to chop Del Amo up in the propeller of a small plane and trap Avoth in the gasoline-soaked wreckage of his Rolls Royce. Kitaen shows up with the Marines, and as she gleefully jumps into Pare's arms she accidentally fires a shot into the Rolls, causing it to burst into flames and cook Avoth. Marine commander Napier, Pare, and Kitaen smile happily at the freeze frame.

INSTANT JUSTICE was the brainchild of "veteran theatrical agent" Rumar, who made his producer-writer debut with this wretched effort. His dialog is unspeakable and his plot line is so poorly conceived that there isn't any plausible motivation for most of the action. The scene where the Marine buddy plants the .45 in Pare's bag for no apparent reason was obviously designed to provide a lame excuse for Pare to meet with sympathetic Marine commander Napier. The casting is as bad as the script. Believe it or not, Michael Pare makes Sylvester Stallone look like Laurence Olivier. His monotonous "dese-dems-and-dose" delivery is unintentionally hilarious and he shouts most of his dialog. Pare must repeat the lines "I need your help and I need it now. If not for me, do it for Kim" at least six times. Even worse than Pare is Kitaen. With a hairdo from Mars and a total inability to utter anything resembling a spontaneous thought, this actress

wears on the nerves very quickly, leaving the viewer hoping that she will soon suffer the same fate as Pare's sister. The build up to the big chase scene is laughable as well. When we see that the supposedly filthy-rich Avoth has a fleet of motor vehicles consisting entirely of an old Rolls Royce, a decrepit early 1960s Cadillac, and a mid-1970s Trans Am, we know all these cheap cars will soon be destroyed in a poorly staged action sequence. The scene takes place in the middle of a desert, which, we are told, is supposed to be an airport (no buildings, runways, skycaps, or any other signs of airport life are in sight). Several fake-looking private planes (probably made out of cardboard) sit nearby so that these crummy old cars can crash into them. The life-sized dummy that doubles for Del Amo during his big death scene is absurdly obvious as it limply slides off the hood of Pare's car and into the barely rotating plane propeller. The entire film smacks of a home movie with its amateurish script, performances, direction, photography, and editing masquerading as a major Hollywood release. We can find no evidence of a U.S. release, but the film was released in Spain as OJO POR OJO, DIENTE POR DIENTE (Eye for an Eye, Tooth for a Tooth). The songs are on par with the rest of the film and they include: "How Does Love Go Wrong" (Brenda Russell, Bobby Caldwell, performed by Brenda Russell), "Victim of Paradise" (Sam Lorber, Dave Innis, performed by Donna Cooper), "Manhunt" (James Wirrick), "Shake Me Up" (Gary Wright, performed by Gary Wright), "Lookin' for Trouble" (Sam Lorber, Dave Innis, performed by T.J. Seals), "One for One" (David Kurtz, Monday, performed by Tony McShear), "Danger in the Streets" (Lee Hart, Ray Callcut, Terry Stevens, Graham Garrett, performed by Lee Hart).

p, Craig T. Rumar; d, Christopher Bentley; w, Craig T. Rumar; ph, Douglas F. O'Neans; m, David Kurtz; ed, Pieter Bergema; art d&set d, Luis Vazquez.

Action   Cas.   (PR:O MPAA:R)

INTIMATE POWER*   (1986, Can.) 87m Les Films Vision 4/Vivafilm c
                                               (POUVOIR INTIME)

Marie Tifo, Pierre Curzi, Jacques Godin, Eric Brisebois, Robert Gravel, Jacques Lussier, Jean-Louis Millette, Yvan Ponton.

A dazzling and energetic twist on the gangster film which keeps its audience tense for the duration and offers nearly nonstop splashes of color and sound. The film begins simply enough with a planned robbery of an armored car by Godin and his amateur gang—his son Brisebois, an ex-con, Curzi, and Curzi's girl friend, Tifo. A wrench is thrown into Godin's carefully laid plan causing Brisebois to panic and gun down two guards. A third injured guard, Gravel, takes refuge in the back of the armored car. The criminals drive off with him lying unconscious in the back. They drive the vehicle to a secluded warehouse where they plan to leisurely divide the money. Gravel, however, is not dead, as the criminals believe. He locks himself in the back of the armored car—with the money. It's a stalemate. He can't get out to escape, while they can't get in to grab the loot. Gravel tries to shoot at them through gunports, injuring Brisebois. Godin spends his time caring for his son, unable to call for a doctor. Godin then telephones a corrupt politician, the one who has hired him to pull the robbery in order to retrieve some incriminating papers. Godin pleads with him to call a doctor, but the politician refuses to risk his own neck for someone else's sake. In the meantime, Curzi is trying to force Gravel out. He first rams heavy poles through the gunports, nearly skewering Gravel in the process and preventing him from doing any more shooting. Curzi also spray-paints the windows and pounds mercilessly on the cavernous vehicle with a sledgehammer, hoping to burst Gravel's eardrums. When none of those techniques ferret Gravel out of his hideout, Curzi begins filling the vehicle with water. Still refusing to unlock the door, Gravel presses his nose to the roof gasping for his last few breaths in preparation to die. Outside, the criminals wait for their catch to submit. Suddenly a rush of water pours from the bottom of the armored car, while inside Gravel is seen opening a locked vent. Having failed to get inside the armored car, things take a turn for the worse for the criminals. Brisebois dies. The politician intervenes, determined to get his photos. Then, in a rather abrupt finale of gunplay, nearly all involved die. Directed with passion and verve by the 25-year-old Simoneau, INTIMATE POWER is a stylish film which uses color and sound to full extent. Simoneau must be commended for his talent at creating a highly charged situation which explodes on the screen. While the story line bears a substantial resemblance to the striking 1962 crime film THE WORLD IN MY POCKET, starring Rod Steiger and Nadja Tiller, Simoneau has done a remarkable job with a very low budget. (In French; English subtitles.)

p, Claude Bonin; d, Yves Simoneau; w, Yves Simoneau, Pierre Curzi; ph, Guy Dufaux; m, Richard Gregoire; ed, Andre Corriveau; art d, Michel Proulx.

Crime   (PR:C-O MPAA:NR)

INTRUDER, THE†   (1986, Indonesia) 90m Punjabi/Shapiro c

Peter O'Brian, Craig Gavin, Dana Christina, Lia Warokka, Jenny Farida.

A Third World RAMBO rip-off shot on a small budget offers a hero named Alex Trambuan, Rambu to his friends, who takes off after local gangsters after they kill his girl friend and beat him.

p, Dhamoo Punjabi, Raam Punjabi; d, Jopi Burnama; w, Debby Armand; ph, Sodikin; m, GSD'Arto.

Action   (PR:C-O MPAA:NR)

INVADERS FROM MARS*½   (1986) 100m Golan-Globus/Cannon c

Karen Black (Linda), Hunter Carson (David Gardner), Timothy Bottoms (George Gardner), Laraine Newman (Ellen Gardner), James Karen (Gen. Wilson), Louise

Fletcher *(Mrs. McKeltch)*, Bud Cort *(Mark Weinstein)*, Jimmy Hunt *(Police Chief)*.

Director Tobe Hooper's remake of William Cameron Menzies' cult-classic 1953 science fiction film INVADERS FROM MARS should serve as a warning to anyone wishing to remake a fondly remembered old film: don't do it unless you can improve on it (see: THE FLY). The Menzies film was sweet simplicity, perfectly combining the elements of script, performance, camera angles, and set design to create a unique and memorable child's view of the world. Hooper's remake—obviously intended as a loving homage—ignores everything that made the original so effective. Although the scripts of the two films nearly match, the new big-budget production is so wrong-headed that it bears little resemblance to

the original. Carson (son of actress Karen Black and screenwriter L.M. Kit Carson) is the happy young son of perfect American couple Bottoms and Newman. His dad, who works at a nearby NASA base, is very attentive and loving, as is his mother. One night Carson is awakened by the light and sound coming from a spaceship that lands just behind the ridge in back of his house and sinks into a sandpit. He tries to persuade his father to go and investigate, but the groggy Bottoms refuses to go until morning. True to his word, Bottoms goes over the ridge before breakfast to placate his son's fears, but when he returns he seems different—he behaves like a zombie. Carson notices that Bottoms has a fresh scar on the back of his neck and the boy's imagination goes wild. Soon he suspects that several of his friends, their parents, his mother, and his teacher, Fletcher (who was scary enough to begin with), have all been taken over by the aliens. The only person who will listen to him is the school nurse, Black, and although she suspects the boy is having problems at home, she soon comes to believe the fantastic tale. The alien visitors are from Mars, and they have come to halt the launch of a new NASA rocket aimed at their planet. The "drones," silly looking creatures with legs like an ostrich, huge heads, even bigger mouths, and beady eyes, are controlled by a large brain with a cute face known as the Supreme Intelligence. After coming face-to-face with the creatures in their spaceship (he was sucked into the sandpit), Carson escapes and persuades gung-ho Marine general Karen to send in the troops. The soldiers invade the spaceship and easily defeat the Martians (these drones were not designed for combat—they can barely walk). Just as in the original film, the whole thing turns out to be a dream—but Carson is again awakened by a landing spacecraft and this time it's for real.

All the tongue-in-cheek humor, film-buff jokes, and special effects in the world can't save this mess. While the performances in the original version weren't going to garner any raves, with few exceptions the cast of the remake is awful. Carson proved to be an exceptional young in actor in PARIS, TEXAS (1984), but his screenwriter father had tailored the role to fit the child like a glove. Here he overacts and seems to think that the whole thing is a bit silly (he's right). His real-life mother, Black, is even worse as she plays one of those Steven Spielberg adults who allows herself to be dragged through an entire film by a child who is infinitely more capable of handling intense situations than she is. Bottoms and Newman are simply insufferable, with Newman even going so far as reverting to her TV "Saturday Night Live" Conehead character voice for a forced laugh—the effect is embarrassing. Fletcher fares a bit better as a child's view of evil incarnate, and in one scene little Carson watches in horror as she swallows a frog whole in the school biology lab. Karen as the ultimate 1950s military man is hilarious as he gleefully slaughters the Martians—all the while concerned with the welfare of innocent women and children. Only Fletcher and Carson look as if they had any fun on this film. The one charming piece of casting is that of Hunt—the little boy from the original film—as one of the policemen who investigate the spaceship crash. As Hunt and his partner walk up the ridge lined by a picket fence (an almost exact duplicate of the original) the former child-actor remarks: "Gee, I haven't been up here since I was a kid." Hunt retired from acting in 1953 after the release of INVADERS FROM MARS and went on to become a successful businessman. Hooper's remake was his first appearance on

screen in more than 33 years. Film buffs may spot another reference to the original film in the scene where Hunt explores the school basement. Sitting atop a pile of junk is the glass globe that housed the Supreme Intelligence in the 1953 film (the prop seen here was used for long shots in the original film; midget actress Luce Potter played the Supreme Intelligence in close-ups). Although the self-conscious references to the original film can be a fun diversion, they shouldn't be the only interesting thing in the movie. Menzies' original film used such simple tricks as forced perspective (to make the adult world seem bigger), low camera angles (everyone looks down at the child), and a brilliant use of colors to bring us into a child's viewpoint. Hooper uses some child's-point-of-view camera angles, but they seem to be an afterthought; his vision is not nearly as well thought out or creative as Menzies'. The creatures designed by Stan Winston are funny, and they're meant to be, but not very effective (the tall men in fuzzy green suits with the seams showing in the 1953 version were scarier).

Veteran visual effects artist John Dykstra turns in some mundane work here, and the Martian ship interior created by concept artist William Stout, art director Craig Stearn, and production designer Leslie Dilley is an unimaginative anatomical structure (inspired by the architecture of Antonio Gaudi) so massive that it had to be constructed in the enormous hangar that once housed Howard Hughes' famed "Spruce Goose." Player Fletcher described the set aptly: "What am I doing inside this colon?" This film was Hooper's second bomb for Cannon ($12 million budget—only $1.9 in rentals—LIFEFORCE in 1985 did even worse), and he would quickly follow with a third—an awful sequel to his own horror classic, THE TEXAS CHAIN SAW MASSACRE.

p, Menahem Golan, Yoram Globus; d, Tobe Hooper; w, Dan O'Bannon, Don Jakoby (based on a screenplay by Richard Blake); ph, Daniel Pearl (J-D-C Widescreen, TVC color); m, Christopher Young; ed, Alain Jakubowicz; prod d, Leslie Dilley; art d, Craig Stearns; cos, Carin Hooper; spec eff, John Dykstra.

Science Fiction   Cas.   **(PR:C   MPAA:PG)**

IRON EAGLE*½   (1986) 116m Tri-Star c

Louis Gossett, Jr. *(Chappy)*, Jason Gedrick *(Doug)*, David Suchet *(Defense Minister)*, Tim Thomerson *(Ted)*, Larry B. Scott *(Reggie)*, Caroline Lagerfelt *(Elizabeth)*, Jerry Levine *(Tony)*, Robbie Rist *(Milo)*, Michael Bowen *(Knotcher)*, Bobby Jacoby *(Matthew)*, Melora Hardin *(Katie)*, David Greenlee *(Kingsley)*.

Take parts of RAMBO, STAR WARS, AN OFFICER AND A GENTLEMAN, add elements from almost every right-wing movie you've ever seen, blend in some John Wayne heroics and what do you have? The very derivative IRON EAGLE, which came out at just the right time because Americans were being shot down all over the world and there was a glimmer of reality to the premise. Gedrick is a teenager about to go to his high school prom when he learns that his father, Thomerson, has been shot down over an unnamed Arab country for venturing too close to its borders. Gedrick, his family, and his friends feel that it will be only a short time until the U.S. government springs his father. But no . . . the bureaucracy bogs down and time is wasting because Thomerson has been tried and convicted and will be hanged in about three days, which puts a time clock on the action, always a good gimmick. Suchet is the head of the Arab country, a man cut from the same cloth as the Japanese villains seen in so many WW II movies, leering, smiling, and, in general, acting like a subhuman. Since Gedrick and pals are Air Force brats, they have more-or-less free rein around the base and the lad spends a great deal of time in the flight simulator when it's not being used by pilots. Gedrick thinks that since the government is sitting by, it's up to him to save his father. To that end, he enlists all of his pals to arrange matters so that the F-16 he steals will be allowed to go across thousands of miles, be refueled, etc. They do this by getting into the top-secret security system. Gedrick contacts Gossett, a retired Air Force colonel, when he realizes that there is no way he will be able to do this himself.

Gossett is at first against the idea, but, due to the possibility that the movie might end right then and there, he finally agrees. He whips the youngsters into order in the same way that he harangued recruits in his Oscar-winning role in AN OFFICER AND A GENTLEMAN and he and Gedrick steal a pair of F-16s and off they go to the Middle East. As the planes fly closer to the target, they are attacked by hostile aircraft. Gossett appears to have been shot down and Gedrick must now pull off the rescue on his own. Thomerson is conveniently on an airstrip as Gedrick lands the fighter, saves his dad, then proceeds to blow up everything and everyone in sight. Suchet is killed (crowds cheered at this because his character was so heinous, almost like making Khadaffy Duck look like Uncle Remus); Gedrick and Thomerson escape and return to the U.S. without sparking a global conflict. Upon touching down, they learn that Gossett has survived (another hooray). Gedrick is rewarded by admittance to the Air Force Academy, which had rebuffed him earlier in the film because his grade point average was marginal.

If there is a cliche missing from IRON EAGLE then we must have overlooked it. Produced by Ron Samuels and Joe Wizan, a man who makes better deals than movies, IRON EAGLE soared at the box office, grossing almost $20 million in the first three weeks of release, before the word got out that this eagle was a turkey. Director Furie, who used to specialize in style over substance, showed that he can direct action with the best of them, but that he has no idea of good

dialog because the words these actors spoke were mostly ludicrous. Watch it on cable TV and turn off the sound and you may enjoy it more. Thomerson, an underrated actor, didn't have enough to do for us to realize why he is underrated. Gedrick's prior experience included a nonspeaking role in BAD BOYS and the same in RISKY BUSINESS, both shot in Chicago, where Gedrick was reared. If you can believe that a young boy, whose only flight experience was in a simulator, could manage this, you'll believe anything.

p, Ron Samuels, Joe Wizan; d, Sidney J. Furie; w, Kevin Elders, Sidney J. Furie; ph, Adam Greenberg (Metrocolor); m, Basil Poledouris; ed, George Grenville; prod d, Robb Wilson King.

Drama   Cas.   (PR:C MPAA:PG-13)

ISLE OF FANTASY†   (1986, Hong Kong) 95m Cinema City/Golden
                                                        Princess c

Raymond Wong, Teresa Carpio, Ann Bridgewater, Fennie Yuen, Loletta Lee, Charine Chan, May Lo, Bonnie Law, Tang Kee Chun.

A plane with a half-dozen Chinese Girl Scouts crashes at sea and the girls make their way to a nearby island paradise, where the only other inhabitant is salesman Wong. The island has one serious drawback, though: it rises and sinks unpredictably.

d, Michael Mak; w, Raymond Wong; ph, Johnny Koo; m, Mahood Rumjahn; ed, Wong Ming.

Comedy   (PR:C MPAA:NR)

ITALIAN FAST FOOD†   (1986, It.) 84m CG Silver–Reteitalia–Video 80/
                                                        Filmexport c

Susanna Messaggio, Sergio Vastano, Carlo Pistarino, I Trettre, Enzo Braschi.

The misadventures of five Italian youths who frequent a Milan hamburger stand make up this youth-oriented product. One lad flunks out of school but tries to make his way up the social ladder by gate-crashing, another sets out to thrash the punks who have insulted his clique, a waitress wants to be Marilyn Monroe, a messenger barely escapes an amorous fashion model with AIDS, and an actor/waiter watches his big chance get rained out. Meanwhile the manager of the stand is having his own staff problems.

p, Mario Cecchi Gori, Vittorio Cecchi Gori; d, Lodovico Gasparini; w, Carlo Vanzina, Enrico Vanzina, Lorenzo Beccati, Ezio Greggio (based on a story by Steno De Caro, Lucio De Caro); ph, Luigi Duveiller (Luciano Vittori Color); m, Detto Mariano; ed, Raimondo Crociani; art d, Ennio Michettoni.

Comedy   (PR:C MPAA:NR)

J

JACKALS (SEE: AMERICAN JUSTICE, 1986)

JAILBREAK . . . 1958† (1986, Phil.) Cinex/F. Puzon c

[No cast and credits available.]

A young man escapes prison to avenge the murder of his sister at the hands of her criminal American husband. After torturing the culprit to death, he is arrested again and sentenced to die in the gas chamber.

Crime (PR:C MPAA:NR)

JAKE SPEED**½ (1986) 100m Crawford-Lane-Force Ten-Balcor/New World c

Wayne Crawford *(Jake Speed)*, Dennis Christopher *(Desmond Floyd)*, Karen Kopins *(Margaret Winston)*, John Hurt *(Sid)*, Leon Ames *(Pop)*, Roy London *(Maurice)*, Donna Pescow *(Wendy)*, Barry Primus *(Lawrence)*, Monte Markham *(Mr. Winston)*, Millie Perkins *(Mrs. Winston)*, Rebecca Ashley *(Maureen)*, Alan Shearman *(Rodrigo)*, Karl Johnson *(Charles)*, Sal Viscuso *(Newsstand Attendant)*, Ken Lerner *(Ken)*, Peter Fox *(Priest)*, Ian Yule *(Bill Smith)*, Ken Gampu *(Joe Smith)*, Joe Ribeiro *(Nigel)*, Jean Marc Morel, Bernard Crombey *(Paris Gunmen)*, Thys Du Plooy *(Creep)*, Jason Ronard, Robert Winley *(Rowdies)*, Lisa Lucas, Wendy Stockle *(Girl Friends)*, Jean Pierre Lorit, Vincent Nemeth, Etienne Le Foulon *(Boy Friends)*, Franz Dubrovsky *(Mustafa)*, Will Bernard *(Turk)*, Sammy Davis *(Sid's Driver)*, Nancy Riach *(Barbara)*, Ivan Joseph *(Servant)*, June Maforimbo *(Hostage)*, Mark Orthwaite *(DC-3 Pilot)*.

Wayne Crawford and Andrew Lane had developed reputations in Hollywood for their work as the writers and producers of VALLEY GIRL and NIGHT OF THE COMET, but here their ambitions exceed their abilities as they take on acting and directing in addition to their usual chores. The plot is original enough: Crawford

is the partner of Christopher, the author of trashy paperback adventure series novels, but with the difference that he actually lives the outlandish written adventures. When an American college girl in Europe is kidnaped by white slavers, no one is able to help her family until her sister, Kopins, is approached by Crawford and Christopher, his personal Boswell. They offer to rescue the sister and chronicle it in their next book, and they give Kopins tickets to Africa and instructions on where to meet them. She is naturally dubious about these two characters, but desperate to find her sister, she agrees. Arriving in some hellish backwater town in the U.S.A. (United States of Africa), she finds the country's two states on the verge of civil war, and she has a number of narrow escapes in the company of Crawford, until finally she has had enough. She abandons the two while they sleep in a barn, finds a ride with some friendly Europeans, and soon finds herself at the British embassy. There she is shown a photo of Crawford and Christopher and told they are really a pair of con men. She leads an armed party back to the barn, where she and Crawford are both seized and tied up (Christopher is out at the moment). The two are taken back to the embassy, which turns out to be a front for the white-slave operation run by Hurt. It turns out that Crawford and Hurt are old enemies, going all the way back to volume two, and Hurt plans to be rid of him once and for all this time, but makes the classic villain mistake of locking his captives in a room and giving them enough time to work free of their restraints and overpower the stooge sent to execute them. They find Kopins' sister and free her, then try to escape from the house, now under attack from some faction of the civil war. Christopher arrives on the scene with HARV, Crawford's Heavily Armed Raiding Vehicle, and kills a swarm of Hurt's private soldiers. Crawford and the two women narrowly escape the hungry lions Hurt keeps in his basement before finally getting away, pursuing Hurt. At the airport, the civil war is closing in and the place is jammed with refugees. Hurt is there and a gun battle breaks out in which Christopher is wounded. Crawford gets the two women on the last plane out then goes back to save his friend. Months later, back home,

Kopins goes to the newsstand and there sees the latest Jake Speed novel, with her picture on the cover and a personal dedication from Crawford.

While the film fails at a number of levels, most acutely in never making us care much about any of the characters or their problems, it possesses a loopy charm that makes it a pleasure to watch. Crawford is a delightfully unlikely hero, not quite as brave or self-assured as his fictional alter ego, and genuinely hurt when Kopins refuses to believe in him. He is constantly speaking in cliches about good triumphing over evil, though it is Hurt who has the best line of this sort, as he tells Crawford, "You see, Jake, I'm a bad guy. I do anything I like. I lie, I cheat, I steal, I kill. Let's see, have I left anything out?" Hurt's villainous white slaver is the best thing here, coolly shooting his servants for disturbing him while he does a hard sell on two girls whom a pair of Arabs are interested in purchasing. Shot on location in Zimbabwe, the production used hundreds of weapons borrowed from the local police, who cleaned out their closets full of arms confiscated from various groups that tried to infiltrate the borders. Shot on a smallish $3 million budget, the film received generally unfavorable reviews and proved a box-office failure. Songs include: "Night After Night" (Mark Holden, Lea Hart, Steve Legassick, performed by Mark Holden), "Small Change" (Chris Farren, performed by Chris Farren), and "After the Lovin'" (A. Bernstein, R. Adams, performed by Leo Krokos).

p, Andrew Lane, Wayne Crawford, William Fay; d, Andrew Lane; w, Wayne Crawford, Andrew Lane; ph, Brian Loftus; m, Mark Snow; ed, Fred Stafford; prod d, Norm Baron; md, Don Perry; set d, Mike Phillips; cos, Dianna Cilliers; spec eff, John Hartigan; m/l, Mark Holden, Lea Hart, Steve Legassick, Chris Farren, A. Bernstein, R. Adams; makeup, Colin Polson; stunts, Grant Page.

Adventure/Comedy Cas. (PR:A-C MPAA:PG)

JAZOL† (1986, Yugo.) Varda c (Trans: The Knot)

Lazar Ristovski, Kostadinka Velkovska, Petar Arsovski, Aco Jovanovski, Mustafa Jasar.

d, Kiril Cenevski; w, Slavko Janevski; ph, Dragan Salkovski; m, Ilija Pejovski; set d, Nikola Lazarevski.

War (PR:NR MPAA:NR)

JE HAIS LES ACTEURS† (1986, Fr.) 95m Septembre-Gaumont-Films A2/GAU c-bw (Trans: I Hate Actors)

Jean Poiret *(Orlando)*, Michel Blanc *(Mr. Albert)*, Bernard Blier *(J.B. Cobb)*, Patrick Floersheim *(Korman)*, Michel Galabru *(Bison)*, Pauline Lafont *(Elvina)*, Dominique Lavanant *(Miss Davis)*, Guy Marchand *(Egelhofer)*, Vojtek Pszoniak *(Potnik)*, Jean-Francois Stevenin *(Devlin)*, Sophie Duez, Patrick Braoude, Jezabel Carpi, Claude Chabrol, Lionel Rocheman, Alexandre Mnouchkine, Yann Epstein, Mike Marshall, Michel Such, Jean-Paul Comart, Allan Wenger.

Since he was one of Hollywood's top screenwriters, Ben Hecht's novels have, surprisingly, not often made it to the big screen. The first Hecht adaptation was THE FLORENTINE DAGGER in 1935, followed by MIRACLE IN THE RAIN 21 years later, and, most successfully, GAILY, GAILY in 1969. With a renewed interest in Hecht's work in France, first-time director Krawczyk decided to bring to the screen Hecht's indictment of Hollywood in the 1940s. Shot in France, the Riviera doubles for Los Angeles, while Cenet's glamorous black-and-white photography adds to the illusion. When a murder occurs on the set of a studio production everyone is suspected, especially actor's agent Poiret. The cast also includes New Wave director Claude Chabrol.

d, Gerard Krawczyk; w, Gerard Krawczyk (based on the novel *I Hate Actors* by Ben Hecht); ph, Michel Cenet (Kodak Color); m, Roland Vincent; ed, Marie-Joseph Yoyotte; prod d&art d, Jacques Dugied; cos, Rosine Lan; makeup, Irene Ottavis.

Mystery (PR:C MPAA:NR)

JEAN DE FLORETTE† (1986, Fr.) 120m Renn-Films A2-RAI 2-DD/AMLF c

Yves Montand *(Cesar Soubeyran "Le Papet")*, Daniel Auteuil *(Ugolin)*, Gerard

Depardieu (*Jean Cadoret*), Elisabeth Depardieu (*Aimee Cadoret*), Ernestine Mazurowna (*Manon Cadoret*), Marcel Champel (*Pique-Bouffique*), Margarita Lozano (*Baptistine*), Bertino Benedetto (*Guiseppe*), Armand Jeffre (*Philoxene*), Andre Dupont (*Pamphile*), Pierre Nougaro (*Casimir*), Marc Betton (*Martial*), Jean Maurel (*Anglade*).

Based on a two-part novel by author and former filmmaker Marcel Pagnol, JEAN DE FLORETTE and its sequel MANON DES SOURCES were the most talked-about French productions of the year as well as the most expensive ever in France, costing about $17,000,000 for the pair. Shot back-to-back with MANON DES SOURCES over a nine-month stretch, JEAN DE FLORETTE takes place in provincial France and stars Montand as a coarse villager who is driven by greed to take over a piece of fertile land that sits over a natural spring. When the landowner dies, Montand thinks he finally has the plot for himself. There is an heir, however—the hunchbacked Gerard Depardieu, who arrives from the city with his wife Elisabeth Depardieu (his wife in real-life) and their young daughter Mazurowna. Hoping to discourage Depardieu and drive him off the land, Montand avoids telling him of the spring. Montand sits back and watches as Depardieu is forced to travel a long and arduous distance to get water—a chore which wears him down physically and emotionally, eventually killing him. With the second part of the story, MANON DES SOURCES, Depardieu's young daughter grows up (played by the gorgeous Emmanuelle Beart) and learns of Montand's deception. JEAN DE FLORETTE was the top-grossing French-made film in France, placing second behind the US-made top-grosser OUT OF AFRICA. MANON DES SOURCES, which was released three months after its predecessor, ranked fourth in the standings. JEAN DE FLORETTE was also showered with eight Cesar nominations, accolades which were also bestowed on MANON DES SOURCES, as the cast and credits are identical with a few exceptions—including the winner of the Best Actress award, MANON DES SOURCES star Emmanuelle Beart, who does not appear in JEAN DE FLORETTE, but is nevertheless nominated for it. Winning for Best Actor was Auteuil (who appears in both films as the cretinous, hypocritical cohort of Montand). Other nominations include Best Film; Berri as Best Director; Berri and Gerard Brach for Best Screenplay; Jean-Claude Petit for Best Score; Bruno Nuytten for Best Cinematography; and Pierre Gamet and Dominique Hennequin for Best Sound. A U.S. release is expected in mid-1987 by Orion Pictures.

p, Pierre Grunstein; d, Claude Berri; w, Claude Berri and Gerard Brach (based on a novel by Marcel Pagnol); ph, Bruno Nuytten (Eastmancolor, Technovision); m, Jean-Claude Petit; ed, Arlette Langmann, Herve de Luze, Noelle Boisson; prod d, Bernard Vezat; cos, Sylvie Gautrelet; makeup, Michel Deruelle, Jean-Pierre Eychenne.

Drama   (PR:C   MPAA:NR)

JEZIORO BODENSKIE†   (1986, Pol.) 90m Zespoli Filmowe, Perspektiwa Unit/Film Polski c (Trans: LAKE CONSTANCE)

Krzysztof Pieczynski, Malgorzata Pieczynska, Joanna Szczepkowska, Maria Pakulnis, Gustaw Holoubek, Andrzej Szczepkowski, Henryk Borowski, Krzysztof Zalewski.

A Polish laborer who spent World War II in an German internment camp near the Swiss border returns years after the war to reminisce about the war and the nature of the Polish mentality through a series of monologs and remembered encounters.

d, Janusz Zaorski; w, Allan Starski; ph, Witold Adamek; m, Jerzy Satanowski; ed, Halina Prugal-Ketling.

Drama   (PR:C   MPAA:NR)

JIBARO†   (1986, Cuba) 84m ICAIC c (Trans: Wild Dog)

Salvador Wood, Rene de la Cruz, Adolfo Llaurado, Flora Lauten, Ana Vina.

Set in Cuba in 1960, shortly after Fidel Castro has assumed control of the island. The film focuses on an old rancher who has proven to be proficient in hunting down and killing the wild dogs that prey on cattle. Though he initially has problems with the new regime, he eventually grows comfortable with it and uses his talents to organize an outfit to battle counter-revolutionaries who are holding out in the hills.

p, Santiago Llapu; d, Daniel Diaz Torres; w, Daniel Diaz Torres, Norberto Fuentes; ph, Pablo Martinez (ICAIC color); ed, Justo Vega.

Drama   (PR:A-C   MPAA:NR)

JO JO DANCER, YOUR LIFE IS CALLING**   (1986) 97m COL c

Richard Pryor (*Jo Dancer/Alter Ego*), Debbie Allen (*Michelle*), Art Evans (*Arturo*), Fay Hauser (*Grace*), Barbara Williams (*Dawn*), Carmen McRae (*Grandmother*), Paula Kelly (*Satin Doll*), Diahnne Abbott (*Mother*), Scoey Mitchlll (*Father*), Billy Eckstine (*Johnny Barnett*), E'lon Cox (*Little Jo Jo*), Tanya Boyd (*Alicia*), Wings Hauser (*Cliff*), Michael Ironside (*Detective Lawrence*), J.J. Barry (*Sal*), Michael Genovese (*Gino*), Marlene Warfield (*Sonja*), Virginia Capers (*Emma Ray*), Dennis Farina (*Freddy*), Frederick Coffin (*Dr. Weissman*), Dr. Richard Grossman (*Dr. Carlyle*), Ken Foree (*Big Jake*), Gloria Charles, Mary Bond Davis, Cheri Wells, Valerie McIntosh (*Ladies at Grandmother's House*), Bebe Drake-Massey (*Angry Prostitute*), Charlie Dell (*1st John*), Teri Hafford (*Olivia*), Edy Roberts (*Madelyn*), Michael Prince (*Screening Room Producer*), Rocco Urbisci (*Screening Room Director*), Rod Gist (*Manager*), Elizabeth Robinson (*Secretary*), Beau Starr (*Vito*), Ludie C. Washington (*Backstage Manager*), Kiblena Peace (*Joy*), Larry Murphy (*Male Attendant*), Linda Hoy (*Emergency Room Nurse*), Dennis Hayden (*1st Policeman*), Sam Hennings (*2nd Policeman*),

Rashon Kahn (*Bodyguard*), Charles Knapp (*Fat Man*), Tracy Morgan (*Female Heckler*), Gary Allen (*Male Heckler*), Jack Andreozzi (*1st Gangster*), Martin Azarow (*2nd Gangster*), Dean Wein (*Stage Hand*), Sig Frohlich (*Ziggy*), Joanna Lipari (*Night Club Patron*), Jo Ann Mann (*Madam*), Richard Daugherty (*2nd John*), Alicia Shonte Harvey (*Waitress*), Robin Torell (*Michelle's Dance Partner*), Laura Rae (*Dawn's Friend*), Erika Marr, Angella Mitchell, Roxanne Rolle, Geraldine Mason (*Showgirls*), Michael Williams (*Raymond*), Deon Pearson (*Charlie*), Dorothy McLennan (*Dorothy*), Erastus Spencer (*Mr. Spencer*), Edwin Hausam (*Desk Clerk*), Howard L.W. Fortune (*Hotel Bouncer*), Dewayne Taylor (*Boy on Bus*), Jimmy Binkley Group (*House Band at Spencer's*).

Richard Pryor, who produced, directed, starred in, and cowrote this movie, insists that it is not a reflection of his life. Hard to believe, because it's the story of a comedian who was born in a brothel (as was Pryor), has several wives (as did Pryor), had problems with drugs (no comment), and wound up in a burn ward at a hospital when a free-basing experiment went awry. Cox is the 7-year-old who is raised in the bagnio under the aegis of his beloved grandmother, McRae (one of the best jazz singers in the business). Cox's parents are Mitchlll (the one-time comic turned TV actor and producer) and Abbott. As the child grows into Pryor, he is aided by Eckstine (a giant in jazz vocals whose unique style influenced many and whose particular high-roll shirts inspired the "Mr. B" collars worn by everyone who was hip in the 1950s), a nightclub singer.

The picture begins with Pryor's "accident" and flashes back as he sees his life unreel before him. Abbott works as a prostitute in the brothel, and as Pryor grows up, he can't get through to Mitchlll, so he leaves the tank town and moves

off to the relatively busy metropolis of Cleveland where he meets Eckstine and stripper Kelly. Both take an interest in Pryor and help him along in his career after a bout of unemployment. His tenure at the club ends when he can't get along with the hoodlums who run the place and he is again out of a job. Pryor meets and marries Williams, a white woman of superior intellect. The decade of the 1960s arrives and Pryor changes his stand-up routine to reflect what's going on in the newspapers. (In real life, Pryor was working at places like the Los Angeles club owned by Doug Weston, the Troubador, where he convulsed audiences with his rowdy talk and his racial references. He was being touted then as a black Lenny Bruce and, no doubt, Lenny's presence had some influence on Pryor when it came to free speech on a stage.) Pryor and Williams briefly enjoy his celebrity status, but booze and controlled substances are abused and their marriage disintegrates. Life goes by quickly as Pryor takes more drugs and more wives (he'd been briefly married to Fay Hauser before Williams), like Tanya Boyd and Debbie Allen, who seems to be a composite of a few women Pryor knew. Pryor's life is truly in the fast lane. He attempts to quit his addiction and can't make it; then comes the accident and a few moments when he is in a coma and is not sure whether he should live or die (it sounds a bit reminiscent of ALL THAT JAZZ, Bob Fosse's equally personal movie that he says is not his life) and finally commits to the hard way: living. In the last sequence, Pryor is seen on stage in a show similar to his two post-drug concert films, RICHARD PRYOR HERE AND NOW and RICHARD PRYOR LIVE ON THE SUNSET STRIP, in which he talks about his demons.

Pryor had a chance to make a very important movie here, something that could have influenced a generation against drugs. He stopped a bit short, but still has to be congratulated for the attempt. Pryor's direction is better than the script and it was nice to see Eckstine and McRae make their dramatic debuts under Pryor's firm hand. Herbie Hancock's music is excellent and is augmented by a few tunes from other sources: "Mannish Boy" (McKinley Morganfield, Ellis McDaniel, Mel London, performed by Muddy Waters), "My Destiny" (Chaka Khan, performed by Chaka Khan), "Hey Lawdy Mama" (Cleve Reed, performed by Count Basie), "Out in the Cold Again" (Ruby Bloom, Ted Koehler, performed by Gene Ammons, Sonny Stitt), "Devil with the Blue Dress On" (Frederick Long, William Stevenson, performed by Mitch Ryder and the Detroit Wheels), "I Do Love You" (Billy Stewart, performed by Billy Stewart), "For the Love of Money" (Kenneth Gamble, Leon Huff, Anthony Jackson, performed by The O'Jays), "Mighty Love" (Joseph Jefferson, Bruce Hawes, Charles Simmons, performed by The Spinners), "Just Squeeze Me" (Duke Ellington, Lee Gaines, performed by the Miles Davis Quintet), "In the Upper Room" (Mahalia Jackson, performed by Mahalia Jackson), "I Heard It Through the Grapevine" (Norman Whitfield, Barrett Strong, performed by Gladys Knight and The Pips), "Shotgun" (Autry DeWalt, performed by Jr. Walker and The All Stars), "Ooh Baby, Baby" (Warren Moore, William Robinson, performed by Smokey Robinson and The Miracles), "What's Going On" (Renaldo Benson, Alfred Cleveland, Marvin Gaye, performed by Marvin Gaye), "Satin Doll" (Billy Strayhorn, Duke Ellington, Johnny Mercer), "Goin' to Chicago Blues" (Count Basie, Jimmy Rushing), "Lonesome Lover Blues" (Spencer Williams, Josephine Baker). Debbie Allen is not used to much advantage, and that's a loss, as she is immensely gifted in so many ways (see RAGTIME). Pryor is an awesome talent, but his choice of movie scripts has been suspect, with such bombs as THE TOY and BREWSTER'S MILLIONS on his resume. Now, with this misfire, he had better be careful in his upcoming selections or he will wear his welcome thin. Foul language and tawdry situations make this something children should avoid.

p&d, Richard Pryor; w, Rocco Urbisci, Paul Mooney, Richard Pryor; ph, John Alonzo (DeLuxe Color); m, Herbie Hancock; ed, Donn Cambern; prod d, John De Cuir; set d, Cloudia; cos, Marilyn Vance; spec eff, Larry Fuentes; ch, Jennifer Stace; m/l, McKinley Morganfield, Ellis McDaniel, Mel London, Chaka Khan, Cleve Reed, Ruby Bloom, Ted Koehler, Frederick Long, William Stevenson, Billy Stewart, Kenneth Gamble, Leon Huff, Anthony Jackson, Joseph Jefferson, Bruce Hawes, Charles Simmons, Duke Ellington, Lee Gaines, Mahalia Jackson, Norman Whitfield, Barrett Strong, Autry DeWalt, Warren Moore, William Robinson, Renaldo Benson, Alfred Cleveland, Marvin Gaye, Billy Strayhorn, Duke Ellington, Johnny Mercer, Count Basie, Jimmy Rushing, Spencer Williams, Josephine Baker; makeup, Tony Lloyd, Terry Miles; stunts, Ron Oliney; tech adv, Marilyn Bradfield.

Drama/Comedy (PR:C-O MPAA:R)

JOGO DURO† (1986, Braz.) 91m Luar c (Trans: Hard Game)

Cininha de Paula, Carlos Augusto Carvalho, Jesse James, Valeria de Andrade, Antonio Fagundes, Cleide Yaconis, Paulo Betti, Eliane Giardini, Luiz Guilherme, Carlos Meceni, Paulo Ivo, Veronica Teijido.

An empty mansion in a wealthy section of Sao Paulo is the setting for this drama, with a woman and her daughter becoming squatters in the house and coming into conflict with the watchman and the real estate agent.

p, Raul Rocha; d&w, Ugo Giorgetti; ph, Pedro Pablo Lazzarini (Eastmancolor); m, Mauro Giorgetti; ed, Paulo Mattos; art d, Maria Isabel Giorgetti.

Drama (PR:C MPAA:NR)

JONAS, DEJME TOMU VE STREDU† (1986, Czech.) 86m Barrandov Studios c (Trans: Jonas, Say, For Instance, on Wednesday)

Jiri Suchy, Jitka Molavcova (Jonas and Char).

The Semafor theater group of Prague was one of the greatest influences on the generation of Czechs who created a brief, brilliant renaissance in the arts before the Russian tanks rolled in to put a stop to it. Jiri Menzel and Milos Forman were both involved with the group, which is still in existence today. This is a tribute to the Semafor, starring Suchy (the group's longtime lyricist) and Molavcova as a pair of entertainers who perform some of the highlights of the Semafor's musical and comedy repertoire. It also includes old footage of the group in its heyday (some of it from COMPETITION [1963] directed by Forman).

d, Vladimir Sis; w, Jiri Suchy (based on a stage play by Magdalena Dietl); ph, Ota Kopriva.

Musical Comedy (PR:C MPAA:NR)

JONSSONLIGAN DYKER UPP IGEN† (1986, Swed.) 90m Svensk Filmindustri–Nordisk/Svensk Filmindustri c (Trans: The Jonsson Gang Turns Up Again)

Gosta Ekman (Sickan Jonsson), Ulf Brunnberg (Ragnar Vanheden), Bjorn Gustafson (Dynamite Harry Krut), Birgitta Andersson (Doris), Per Grunden (Wall-Enberg), Kent Anderson (Inspector Persson), Dan Ekborg (Police Sergeant), Johannes Brost (The Iron Man), Lars Dejert (Biffen), Jarl Borssen, John Harryson, Jan Dolata, Jacob Dahlin, Sten Johan Hedman, Frederich Offrein.

The fourth installment of the Swedish comedy series (based on the Danish "Olsen Gang" films which have now reached 13 in number) continues with the same characters. Ekman is the brains of the gang, which is a good thing because his two cohorts would be hard-pressed to come up with a thought between them. This time they turn their attention to the vault of a furniture company, but become entangled with a scheme by the president of the company to sell smuggled computer chips to the Russian submarine offshore.

p, Waldemar Bergendahl, Ingemar Ejve; d, Mikael Ekman; w, Rolf Borjlind, Gosta Ekman, Mikael Ekman; ph, Gunnar Kallstrom (Eastmancolor); m, Ragnar Grippe; e, Jan Persson; prod d, Bengt Peters; cos, Inger Pehrsson.

Comedy (PR:A MPAA:NR)

JOUR ET NUIT† (1986, Switz./Fr.) 90m Strada–Flach/Metropolis c (Trans: Day and Night)

Peter Bonke (Harry), Mireille Perrier (Anna), Patrick Fierry (John), Lisbeth Koutchoumow (Ingrid).

Bonke plays a Danish diplomat living in Switzerland who is unhappy with his life. He is divorced from his wife and lives with his likable teenage daughter, Koutchoumow, but cannot find a reason to live. When he meets friendly limousine driver Fierry and has an affair with escort girl Perrier, his life takes a positive turn, but not for long. A first feature from Menoud, who was one of two cinematographers on Jean-Luc Godard's HAIL, MARY (1985).

d, Jean-Bernard Menoud; w, Jean-Bernard Menoud, Hubert Selby, Jr.; ph, Patrick Blossier; m, Dmitry Shostakovich; ed, Christine Benoit.

Drama (PR:O MPAA:NR)

JOURNEY, THE*** (1986, Ger./Switz.) 110m Limbo–Westdeutscher Rundfunk–Scweizerische Radio un Fernsehgesellschaft c (DIE REISE)

Markus Boysen (Bertram Voss), Corinna Kirchhoff (Dagmar), Claude Oliver Rudolph (Schroder), Gero Preen (Bertram as a Child), Christa Berndl (Mrs. Voss), Will Quadflieg (Mr. Voss), Alexander Mehner (Florian).

The sources of European terrorism are examined in this fascinating, if ultimately superficial, drama. The film opens with a gang of terrorists preparing to smuggle a bomb from Italy into Germany, where it will be used in an attack on the U.S. embassy. The children of the gang are not far away, and they are about to be shipped off to a PLO training camp for safekeeping and indoctrination. A bearded man turns up and kidnaps one of the children, but he turns out to be Boysen, the boy's father. The boy's mother, Kirchhoff, is outraged to hear that her son has been taken by Boysen, who has split from the gang. From here the film moves back and forth in time, from the terrorists' pursuit of Boysen to Boysen's memories of his childhood as the son of a famous Nazi poet.

His father is a hard man who refuses to compromise his principles even in the postwar period, although he cannot get his work published anymore and has been forced from his mansion by occupying American troops. His son grows more and more distant from him, joining a commune in his student years and beginning a relationship with Kirchhoff. They join protests and participate in other political acts, and as police repression grows, they become radicalized, though Boysen is always a little reluctant. When they firebomb the police stables, Boysen braves the flames to let the horses go free. The time comes to make a decision to go underground and continue the struggle or try to work within the system. Boysen picks the latter, while Kirchhoff opts for the former, taking their son with her. In the end, after eluding the pursuing terrorists, Boysen takes his son back to the mansion where he grew up, now boarded up and abandoned. The police are after him, though, and they finally catch up and arrest him. As the child is taken away in the arms of a policeman, it is clear that this trauma will affect him in some way not to be known for years.

It's all laid out a little too clearly to be believable, with the story conforming to typical movie plotting, but it remains a fascinating examination of the roots of terrorism in Europe. There are some interesting performances, particularly Kirchhoff as a woman who turns into a conscienceless killer while still thinking herself a good mother, and Quadflieg as the unrepentant Nazi poet, who, in one of the film's most poignant moments, begs his son to try to pull some strings to get his works published again, showing him poems he thinks harmless enough, but that are filled with imagery of Aryans working the land in the noblest way. Boysen is less effective, seeming too indecisive and weak-willed to have ever gotten involved in such things to begin with, though to be fair, this aspect of his personality motivates most of the action.

Boysen's character is based on Bernward Vesper, son of Nazi poet Will Vesper. He was married to Gudrun Ensslin, later a member of the notorious Baader-Meinhoff gang. After typing out a 700-page autobiographical novel that served as the source of this film, Vesper committed suicide in a Hamburg hospital in 1971. Ensslin followed suit in 1977 in the mass suicide of the Baader-Meinhoffs in prison.

p, George Reinhart, Regina Ziegler; d, Markus Imhoof; w, Markus Imhoof,

Martin Wiebel (based on the novel by Bernward Vesper); ph, Hans Liechti; m, Franco Ambrosetti; ed, Ursula West; art d, Gotz Heymann.

Drama   (PR:O MPAA:NR)

JOURNEY OF A YOUNG COMPOSER   (SEE: YOUNG COMPOSER'S ODYSSEY, A, 1986, USSR)

JRI FALESNY HRAC†   (1986, Czech.) 77m Gottwaldov c

Roland Samek *(Dusan)*, Filip Moural *(Adam)*, Iva Janzurova *(Teacher)*, Daniela Kolarova *(Dusan's Mother)*, Ladislav Mrkvicka *(Dusan's Father)*, Vaclav Babka *(Bandleader)*, Vlasta Fialova *(Reditelka)*, Evelyna Steimarova *(Adam's Mother)*, Petr Popelka *(Adam's Father)*.

p, Zdenek Stibor; d, Zdenek Zelenka; w, Zdenek Zelenka, Jan Gogola; ph, Jiri Kolin; ed, Peter Sitar; m, Jiri Svoboda; art d, Peter Smola; cos, Jana Kaplerova.

JUBIABA†   (1986, Braz./Fr.) 101m Regina–Societe Francais–Antenne- 2/ Embrafilme c

Charles Balano, Francoise Goussard, Grande Otelo, Raymond Pellegrin, Zeze Motta, Betty Faria, Ruth DeSouza, Alayr Bigori, Ylmara Rodrigues, Tatiana Issa, Catherine Rouvel, Luiz Santana.

A poor boy and a rich girl fall for each other from a distance, but are never able to consummate their love. Years go by, the girl becomes a drug-addicted prostitute, and the boy goes through a variety of jobs ranging from thief to union organizer, but still they never get together. Based on a 1935 novel by Jorge Amado.

d&w, Nelson Pereira dos Santos (based on a novel by Jorge Amado); ph, Jose Medeiros; m, Gilberto Gil.

Drama   (PR:O MPAA:NR)

JUDGEMENT IN STONE, A†   (1986, Can.) 100m Rawifilm–Schulz/ Norstar c

Rita Tushingham *(Eunice Parchman)*, Ross Petty *(George Coverdale)*, Shelley Peterson *(Jackie)*, Jonathan Crombie *(Bobby)*, Jessica Steen *(Melinda)*, Jackie Burroughs *(Joan Smith)*, Tom Kneebone *(Norman Smith)*, Peter MacNeill *(William)*, Donald Ewer *(Mr. Parchman)*, Joyce Gordon *(Aunt)*, Aisha Tushingham *(Young Eunice)*.

Tushingham is a housekeeper who emigrates from Britain to the States and finds a job with a family. Unfortunately she is dyslexic and psychotic, so whenever anyone teases her about her inability to read, she kills them.

p, Harve Sherman; d, Ousama Rawi; w, Elaine Waisglass (based on the novel by Ruth Rendell); ph, David Herrington; m, Patrick Coleman, Robert Murphy; ed, Stan Cole; art d, Reuben Freed; cos, Linda Matheson.

Drama   (PR:C MPAA:NR)

JUE XIANG†   (1986, Chi.) 99m Pearl River/China Film c (Trans: Swan Song)

Kung Zianzhu, Chen Rui, Feng Diqing, Mo Shaoying.

The relationship of a Cantonese father and son is told over a 30-year span as the father, a composer, is berated for his traditional and old-fashioned taste in music. Over time the father's wife leaves him, and his son, after being imprisoned in a labor camp, turns his back on him. The Cultural Revolution of the late 1960s is anything but a blessing for the father, whose style of music and musical instrument (the *zheng*) are banned. While the father, now nearing death, tries to retain his old-fashioned ways, the son grows increasingly rebellious. The film depicts the changes that occur within a family with the passing of time, but on a larger scale it addresses the death over the years of the traditional values and customs of China. A debut feature from Zhang Zeming which earned two prizes in the Sixth Golden Rooster Awards—Best Photography and Best Production Design. (In Mandarin.)

d&w, Zhang Zeming (based on a novel by Kung Jiesheng); ph, Zheng Kangzhen, Zhao Xiaoshi; prod d, Zhang Jingwen, Peng Jun; m, Zhao Xiaoyuan.

Drama   (PR:C MPAA:NR)

JUMPIN' JACK FLASH★★   (1986) 100m FOX c

Whoopi Goldberg *(Terry Doolittle)*, Stephen Collins *(Marty Phillips)*, John Wood *(Jeremy Talbot)*, Carol Kane *(Cynthia)*, Annie Potts *(Liz Carlson)*, Peter Michael Goetz *(Mr. Page)*, Roscoe Lee Browne *(Archer Lincoln)*, Sara Botsford *(Lady Sarah Billings)*, Jeroen Krabbe *(Mark Van Meter)*, Vyto Ruginis *(Carl)*, Jonathan Pryce *(Jack)*, Tony Hendra *(Hunter)*, Jon Lovitz *(Doug)*, Phil E. Hartmann *(Fred)*, Lynne Marie Stewart *(Karen)*, Ren Woods *(Jackie)*, Tracey Reiner *(Page's Secretary)*, Chino Fats Williams *(Larry the Heavyset Guard)*, Jim Belushi *(Sperry Repairman)*, Paxton Whitehead *(Lord Malcolm Billings)*, June Chadwick *(Gillian)*, Tracey Ullman *(Fiona)*, Jeffrey Joseph *(African Embassy Guest)*, Caroline Ducroca *(French Embassy Guest)*, Julie Payne *(Receptionist at Elizabeth Arden)*, Deanna Oliver *(Karen at Elizabeth Arden)*, Carl LaBove *(Earl the Guard)*, Donna Ponterotto *(Pedicurist at Elizabeth Arden)*, Matt Landers *(Night Guard at Bank)*, Jamey Sheridan, Charles Dumas *(New York Officers)*, James Edgcomb, Gerry Connell *(Lincoln's Aides)*, Miguel A. Nunez, Jr., Jose Santana, Bob Ernst *(Street Toughs)*, Benji Gregory *(Harry Carlson, Jr.)*, Kellie Martin *(Kristi Carlson)*, Kim Chan *(Korean Flower Vendor)*, Anthony Hamilton *(Man in Restaurant)*, Heide Lund *(Woman in Restaurant)*, Kenneth Danziger, Eric Harrison *(Embassy Computer Men)*, Edouardo DeSoto *(Superintendent)*,

Garry K. Marshall *(Detective)*, Teagan Clive *(Russian Exercise Woman)*, Tom McDermott *(Minister)*, Mark Rowen *(Blond Cab Driver)*, J. Christopher Ross *(Hairdresser)*, Hilaury Stern *(Customer)*, George Jenesky *(Man with Umbrella)*.

With her notable stage work and Oscar-nominated film debut in the otherwise middling THE COLOR PURPLE, it seemed Whoopi Goldberg was poised at the beginning of a challenging career as one of the modern screen's most unusual and diverse actresses. Unfortunately her follow-up film points her in a completely different direction, as Goldberg takes on a far less daring role as a stock Hollywood individualist caught up in outlandish circumstances. Goldberg is a computer processor at a New York City bank whose vast knowledge allows her to get her work done while using the terminal to contact folks from around the world for fun and amusement. Of course, Goldberg's boss can't stand her or the little plastic dinosaurs she decorates her workplace with, but her fellow employees simply adore this dreadlocked woman's rebellious nature. Goldberg begins receiving computer messages from "Jumpin' Jack Flash," a British agent trapped behind the Iron Curtain. Because Goldberg is a fan of old spy movies, she decides to help out the poor man. This, of course, leads her through some dangerous and wacky moments as she enters the underworld to save her computer pal. In the course of these zany events Goldberg falls in love with this mysterious stranger she's never met. When her unlikely adventure finally comes to an end, Goldberg finds herself in a funk, depressed and broken hearted over her computer amour. Who should show up but Pryce, the very man Goldberg saved and the incarnation of everything she hoped he would be.

The only real surprise in this supposedly plot-twisting comedy is how so many talented people could be put to such waste. The performance of Pryce (the hero of BRAZIL) and those of such fine comic actors as Belushi, Kane, Lovitz, and Ullman are reduced to little more than cameos, as only Goldberg is allowed to hold center stage. Browne, a fine, droll actor, is completely misused. If Goldberg had been allowed to develop something beyond a few stock character traits she might have made this interesting. Instead, she merely runs through a predictable series of destructive slapstick sequences, including impersonating a Supreme to gain entrance to a party at the British consulate, and being dragged along by a tow truck while trapped inside a phone booth. Goldberg is totally generic in a role that could have been played by anyone with enough energy to go through the motions (the story, in fact, was planned with Bruce Willis in mind).

The real fault lies with the substantial problems that marked JUMPIN' JACK FLASH's production. The original director, Howard Zieff, was fired over what studio executives politely called "creative differences." A replacement was quickly needed, so Penny Marshall (formerly Laverne on the inane TV sitcom "Laverne and Shirley") was hired immediately. She was a rather odd choice for a major production considering her inexperience. Marshall had previously directed a TV pilot ("Working Stiffs"), as well as a few episodes of her own television show. Her background in feature film, on the other hand, was a bit shaky. Marshall had been set to helm PEGGY SUE GOT MARRIED (with Debra Winger in the title role) but ultimately left the project over that old standby "creative differences." Her direction here is passable, setting up the comic and suspenseful moments in a workmanlike and anonymous fashion. In addition to the directorial woes, JUMPIN' JACK FLASH had another significant creative dilemma. The film's original screenwriters, Charles Syer and Nancy Meyers, left with Zieff (all three had done PRIVATE BENJAMIN together), and were subsequently replaced by *four* others (Franzoni, Melville, Irving, and Thompson). The script was still being written while shooting was in progress, which probably accounts for the helter skelter nature of the plot and the underdeveloped characterizations. Undoubtedly, this would explain the presence of the numerous obscenities Goldberg mouths, as four-letter words are usually the last bastion for punchline-desperate comedy writers.

Songs include: "Jumpin' Jack Flash" (Mick Jagger, Keith Richards, performed by Aretha Franklin, also performed by The Rolling Stones), "Set Me Free" (Allee Willis, Danny Sembello, Cynthia Weill, performed by Rene and Angela), "You Can't Hurry Love" (Eddie Holland, Lamont Dozier, Brian Holland, performed by The Supremes), "Window to the World" (Lauren Sargent, Angelo, performed by Face to Face), "Trick of the Night" (Steve Jolley, Tony Swain, performed by Bananarama), "Hold On" (Billy Brannigan, performed by Brannigan), "Misled" (Robert Bell, James Taylor, Kool and the Gang, performed by Kool and the Gang), "Rescue Me" (Carl William Smith, Raynard Miner, performed by Fontella Bass).

p, Lawrence Gordon, Joel Silver; d, Penny Marshall; w, David H. Franzoni, J.W. Melville, Patricia Irving, Christopher Thompson (based on a story by David H. Franzoni); ph, Matthew F. Leonetti (DeLuxe Color); m, Thomas Newman; ed, Mark Goldblatt; prod d, Robert Boyle; art d, Frank Richwood; set d, Donald Remacle; cos, Susan Becker; spec eff, Thomas Ryba; m/l, Mick Jagger, Keith Richards, Allee Willis, Danny Sembello, Cynthia Weill, Eddie Holland, Lamont Dozier, Brian Holland, Lauren Sargent, Angelo, Steve Jolley, Tony Swain, Billy Brannigan, Robert Bell, James Taylor, Kool & the Gang, Carl William Smith, Raynard Miner; makeup, Michael Germain; stunts, Bennie E. Dobbins.

Comedy   Cas.   (PR:O MPAA:R)

JUNGLE RAIDERS*   (1986, It.) 102m L'Immagine/Cannon c (LA LEGENDA DEL RUDIO MALESE; AKA: CAPTAIN YANKEE)

Christopher Connelly *(Capt. Yankee)*, Marina Costa *(Yanez)*, Lee Van Cleef *(Inspector Warren)*, Alan Collins *(Gin Fizz)*, Dario Pontonutti, Mike Monty, Rene Abadeza, Cirillo Vitali, Francesco Arcuri.

Once again the Italians copy RAIDERS OF THE LOST ARK and come up with a cheap, gaudy adventure yarn that makes a U.S. debut on videocassette. Connelly, known as "Captain Yankee" to friends, is an adventurer and guide in Malaysia in 1938 (unfortunately, the country was then known as Malaya) who is hired by museum curator Costa to help her find the fabulous Ruby of Gloom, hidden in the back of an enormous system of caverns where all sorts of pitfalls for cliff-hanging wait around every corner. When they aren't leaping across chasms by the skin of their teeth, they're fighting off ugly Asian pirates.

Nothing here to distinguish this effort from a hundred others just like it, even down to the semi-obligatory appearance of Van Cleef, sometimes dressed all in white, sometimes dressed all in black. Production values are low, and the music awful. The film doesn't even have decent action scenes, and with little sexploitation potential, it is unlikely to attract much of a home video audience.

p, Luciano Appignani; d, Anthony M. Dawson [Antonio Margheriti]; w, Giovanni Simonelli; ph, Guglielmo Mancori (Luciano Vittori Color); m, Cal Taormina; ed, Alberto Moriani; set d, Walter Patriarca; spec eff, Cataldo Galiano.

Action/Adventure   Cas.   (PR:A-C MPAA:PG-13)

JUST BETWEEN FRIENDS**   (1986) 110m MTM/Orion c

Mary Tyler Moore *(Holly Davis)*, Ted Danson *(Chip Davis)*, Christine Lahti *(Sandy Dunlap)*, Sam Waterston *(Harry Crandall)*, Susan Rinell *(Kim Davis)*, Timothy Gibbs *(Jeff Davis)*, Diane Stilwell *(Carla)*, James MacKrell *(Bill)*, Julie Payne *(Karen)*, Beverly Sanders *(Judy)*, Read Morgan *(Charlie)*, Chet Collins *(Stage Manager)*, Castulo Guerra *(Sportscaster)*, Mark Blum *(George Margolin)*, Terri Hanauer *(Woman in Shower)*, Helene Winston *(Woman in Ice Cream Shop)*, Gary Riley *(Clerk in Ice Cream Shop)*, Leda Siskind *(Coffee Shop Waitress)*, Joshua Harris *(Boy with Runny Nose)*, Robert Kino *(Mr. Hasegawa)*, Lisle Wilson *(Newswriter)*, John Terry Bell *(Minister)*, Jane Greer *(Ruth Chadwick)*, George D. Wallace *(Bob Chadwick)*, Andra Akers *(Andrea)*, Robert Rothwell *(Bill)*, Darwyn Carson *(Janet)*, Lewis Arquette *(TV Station Guard)*, Brigitte Desper, Tiffany Desper *(Heather)*, Dorothy Francis *(Herself)*, Suzanne Wishner *(Receptionist at Gym)*, Jeannie Elias *(Marci)*, Christina Kokubo *(Nurse)*, Leslie Ann Rieder *(Candy Striper)*.

Take a soap opera story, throw in some ridiculous plot twists, then combine them with sincere, if sappy, performances and you have all the makings for an average

and wholly forgettable made-for-TV film. Though JUST BETWEEN FRIENDS fulfills all these requirements nicely, it amazingly was produced as a theatrical motion picture. Moore is a bored southern California housewife whose only social outlet is attending an aerobics class. When a mild earthquake hits the area, her seismologist husband, Danson, is interviewed on the television news by reporter Lahti. The story is broadcast that evening, but Moore is tied up with a phone call and ends up missing her husband's television appearance. The call, it

seems, was from her aerobics teacher, asking Moore to fill in for an ailing instructor. Moore agrees to substitute and meets Lahti, a student in the class. The two women go out afterwards and develop an immediate rapport, though Moore doesn't realize Lahti had earlier interviewed her husband. Moore invites her new friend over for a Saturday night dinner, an offer Lahti accepts after some initial hesitance. Once home, Lahti turns on her telephone answering machine and listens to a message from her married lover. Of course this man is none other than Danson, though Lahti isn't aware that her paramour is Moore's husband. Likewise, Moore hasn't the faintest idea the man Lahti said she was involved with is Danson, so naturally things get a bit strained at the big dinner party. Danson's colleague, Waterston, is also there, in an attempt by Moore to fix him up with Lahti. The well-meaning woman's intentions are doomed from the start, for Waterston is a reluctant confederate with Danson and knows full well what is going on. Moore, ever the chipper host, is oblivious to the tension between her husband and the guests, though she later fights with Danson over his rather odd mood.

The next day Lahti tells Danson they must end their affair. Danson goes to Washington, D.C., to speak at an anti-nuclear rally, where he is killed in an off-screen traffic accident. Lahti hears about this at her television station and goes to the aerobics studio to break the heartrending news to Moore. After the funeral, Moore is devastated, but Lahti encourages her friend to build a new life for herself. She lends Moore $8,000 to buy the aerobics studio from its current owner and gradually Moore comes out of her mourning. When Moore goes to clean out Danson's office she finds a picture of him and Lahti together. Realizing what this means, she confronts Lahti, who then admits to the affair. Moore pays Lahti back her money, determined to cut all ties to this woman, but a new twist is added to this increasingly tangled emotional knot. Lahti is with child, courtesy of the late Danson, and is fully prepared to go through with her pregnancy. Moore wants nothing more to do with Lahti, but after the baby is born, she decides to sneak a look at the newborn boy. At the hospital Lahti confronts her former friend, and the two have a heart-to-heart talk. All is eventually forgiven, seeing as time and movie denouements are always great healers. After Lahti is discharged from the hospital, the two women watch a video tape of Lahti and her child. Suddenly some old pictures of Danson flash on the television screen. Moore and Lahti hold a moment of shared pain, then realize that, despite all their mixed emotions, they cannot deny their friendship.

If it all weren't so silly, JUST BETWEEN FRIENDS would be impossible to sit through. Moore's character is a hopeless simp who makes Olivia de Havilland in GONE WITH THE WIND seem like a pinnacle of sophistication. She's excessively cheery and bright eyed, in a performance that suggests an older version of Mary Richards from Moore's 1970s television sitcom, "The Mary Tyler Moore Show." Danson creates a man who conceivably could love both wife and mistress for one basic reason: he's too boring to go through any personal turmoil. Danson has justifiably been praised for his television work on the sitcom "Cheers" and the powerful telefeature "Something About Amelia." However, with this, A FINE MESS, and 1985's LITTLE TREASURE on his resume, Danson appears to be dead set on destroying any possibilities for a career in feature films (his bit part in 1981's BODY HEAT is notably excepted). Lahti and Waterston fare better than their costars, providing the only really interesting moments, though that's not saying much.

The real fault lies with writer/director Burns, who had previously worked with Moore on her hit television show. He simply has no idea how to develop a serious drama beyond obvious cliches, moving from one episode to another as if following lines along a map. The dinner party, with its awkward confrontations, unfolds like a bad farce, though Burns doesn't seem to understand the humor in the situation. As the story takes contrived twist after twist, the film develops a strange sense of inadvertent humor. Lahti's revelation of pregnancy is one of the film's biggest laughs, when the moment undoubtedly was intended as one of high drama. In its own way, JUST BETWEEN FRIENDS plays like a mocking self-parody, and when viewed in this sort of light, turns into an almost entertaining waste of time.

p, Edward Teets, Allan Burns; d&w, Allan Burns; ph, Jordan Cronenweth (DeLuxe Color); m, Patrick Williams; ed, Ann Goursaud; prod d, Sydney Z. Litwack; md, Patrick Williams; set d, Bruce Weintraub, Chris Butler; cos,

Cynthia Bales; spec eff, Eric Rylander; makeup, Richard Blair, Hallie Smith-Simmons.

Drama   **Cas.**   **(PR:O MPAA:PG-13)**

JUST LIKE THE WEATHER†   (1986, Hong Kong) 98m Feng Huang/
                                    Sil-Metropole c (AIQING QIANFENG XUNHAO)

Christine Li, Chan Hung-Lin, Allen Fong.

A Hong Kong couple comes to the United States seeking a chance to form a new life and achieve some material gain, but they find their adopted home not so much to their liking. Shot partly in the U.S. on 16mm with the help of Chinese-American filmmaker Wayne Wang. (In Cantonese, Mandarin, and English; English subtitles.)

d, Allen Fong.

Drama   **(PR:C MPAA:NR)**

K

KGB—THE SECRET WAR*½
(1986) 89m Cinema Group c (AKA: LETHAL)

Michael Billington *(Peter Hubbard)*, Denise DuBarry *(Adelle Martin)*, Michael Ansara *(Taylor)*, Walter Gotell *(Viktor/Nickolai)*, Sally Kellerman *(Fran Simpson)*, Christopher Cary *(Alex)*, Philip Levien *(Ryder)*, Julian Barnes *(Ilya)*, Clement St. George *(Yuri)*, Paul Linke *(Frank)*, Richard Pachorek *(Marine)*, Gerrod Miskovsky *(Thedor)*, Kim Joseph *(Shirley Marks)*.

Billington plays a Russian spy who has penetrated the security of a top-secret microchip factory thanks to the unwitting help of his girl friend (DuBarry). Unfortunately, a change of regimes back in Moscow (specifically, Andropov for Chernenko) has made him a target for purging. He realizes his precarious situation and goes to National Security Agency agent Kellerman and asks to be taken in as a defector. She demands that he produce a list of names that is to arrive from Moscow in a sealed diplomatic pouch before she will give him any protection. Meanwhile, the Russians, commanded by Gotell, have surmised that their man is going to defect, so they set about trying to kill him. The Russian killers prove hopelessly incompetent, and he evades them time after time, while trying to persuade the other members of his network to also defect before they are killed. The list finally arrives, carried by Billington's young son, whom he had thought dead. Billington demands that the NSA help him get his son back, and they agree. Gotell contacts Billington and tells him to deliver the pictures of the microchip but NSA men are all over the place, and a bloody shoot-out ensues. Billington manages to chase down Gotell, but his thoroughly brainwashed son demands that he be returned to his embassy. Gotell also claims diplomatic immunity and ends up simply expelled from the U.S., but Billington's son has a last minute change of heart and runs into his father's arms.

If the KGB and the NSA really conducted themselves in this way, the streets would be littered with their victims. Both sides prove themselves idiots time after time, losing people they're supposed to tail and committing murders on the slightest of pretexts. The plot is all but incomprehensible, and the acting merely serviceable, but the greatest sin this film commits is being astoundingly dull. No suspense is generated and no character is the least bit likable. To top it all off, everyone seems to have at least three names—a real name, a cover name, and a code name—and it quickly becomes impossible to figure out who is talking about whom without a scorecard, despite the fact that the filmmakers have been nice enough to put titles over some characters telling who they are like in a documentary. The high point of the film is the very beginning, in which a man with a Russian accent is identified as a real defected KGB agent, who then tells the audience that while this is not his story, it is somewhat similar. Sure it is.

p, Sandy Howard, Keith Rubinstein; d, Dwight Little; w, Sandra K. Bailey (based on a story by Dwight Little, Sandra K. Bailey); ph, Peter Collister (Bellevue Pathe Quebec Color); m, Misha Segal; ed, Stanley Sheff, John Peterson; art d, Phillip Duffin; set d, Farnouche Kamran; cos, Gail Viola; stunts, Dan Bradley.

Spy   **Cas.**   **(PR:C MPAA:PG-13)**

KAHAN KAHAN SE GUZAR GAYA†
(1986, India) M.S. Sathyu c (Trans: The Many Phases of Life)

Anil Kapoor, Sharon Prahakar, Pankaj Kapoor, Nitin Sethi.

A young man leaves the home of his wealthy father to take up residence with a nightclub performer. Disgusted with his father's conduct in business, the upstart gets involved with political activities, accidentally causing the death of the leader of his group. Ironically, it is the young man's father who manages to keep him out of legal trouble.

d, M.S. Sathyu; ph, Irshaan Arya.

Drama   **(PR:O MPAA:NR)**

KAHIR ELZAMAN†
(1986, Egypt) 115m El Rania/Tamido c (Trans: Conquerors of Time)

Nour El Sherif *(Kamal)*, Athar El Hakim *(Zein)*, Gamil Ratap *(Dr. Halim)*, Khalid Zaki *(Cousin)*.

Sherif is a young lad who begins looking into the mysterious disappearances of patients from a hospital. When his cousin joins the ranks of the missing, he redoubles his efforts and eventually finds a mad scientist who is freezing people and then restoring them to life. After Sherif resuscitates his cousin, an earthquake buries the doctor and his lab. Possibly Egypt's first science-fiction film.

d, Kamal El Cheik; w, Ahmed Abdel Wahab (based on a novel by Nihad Sherif); ph, Ramses Marzouk; m, Georges Kazazian; ed, Hassan Helmi; art d, Mokhtar Abdel Gawad.

Science Fiction   **(PR:A MPAA:NR)**

KAK MOLODY MY BYLI†
(1986, USSR) 92m Alexander Dovzhenko Studio c (Trans: How Young We Were Then)

Taras Denisenko *(Sascha)*, Jelena Sehkurpelo *(Julka)*, Nina Sarolapova *(Maria)*, Alexander Paschutin *(Uncle Petja)*, Alexander Sviridovski *(Uncle Valja)*, Anatoli Lukjaneko *(Viktor)*, Tatiana Kravtshenko *(Tosja)*, Mikhail Kokshenkov *(Gavril Michalovich)*.

Romance blossoms in the Ukraine in the 1950s, but the lovers are kept apart, first by their studies, and later by sickness caused by chemical poisoning the girl suffered as a child during the war.

d&w, Mikhail Belikov; ph, Vassili Truschkovski (Sovcolor); m, Yuri Vinnik; art d, Alexi Levtschenko.

Drama   **(PR:A MPAA:NR)**

KALI PATRITHA, SYNTROFE†
(1986, Gr.) 85m Greek Film Centre c (Trans: Happy Homecoming, Comrade)

Athena Papadimitriou, Peter Trokan, The Inhabitants of Beloiannisz, Hungary.

In the wake of WW II, civil war broke out in Greece between the rival partisan

armies of the Communists and Royalists, a war that continued until 1949, when the Greek army, backed by U.S. and British troops, crushed what remained of the leftist insurgency. 1,800 Communist rebels left the country with their families and created a village named Beloiannisz, south of Budapest, Hungary. Now, with a socialist government ruling Greece, these people are beginning to return home. But is it still home? This is the factual base on which director Xanthopoulos creates a slight fiction about the dilemmas involved when exiles return.

p&d, Lefteris Xanthopoulos; w, Lefteris Xanthopoulos, George Bramos, Thanassis Scroumbelos, Fekete Ibolya; ph, Andreas Sinanos; m, Eleni Karaindrou; ed, Antonis Tempos; art d&cos, Panos Papadopoulos.

Docu-drama   **(PR:A MPAA:NR)**

KAM DOSKACE RANNI PTACE†
(1986, Czech.) 85m Barrandov c

Pavel Divis *(Pavel)*, Lubos Divis *(Pavel II/Pavel III)*, Lenka Termerova *(Dr. Musilova)*, Jiri Ornest *(Trcka)*, Blazena Holisova *(Mrazova)*, Josef Somr *(Mraz)*, Dana Hlavacova *(Brabcova)*, Ladislav Zupanic *(Brabec)*, Miloslav Simek *(Reditel)*, Martin Wimmer *(Sedlak)*, Jiri Sanders *(Cunderlik)*, Jiri Petr *(Vrba)*, Karolina Jirikova *(Lenka)*, Roman Bednar *(Mirek)*, Miroslav Lochman *(Semerad)*, Martin Senberger *(Piskacek)*.

d, Drahomira Kralova; w, Jana Knitlova, Milos Cajthami, Vladimir Klapka; ph, Jan Nemecek; m, Jaroslav Uhlir; ed, Dalibor Lipsky; art d, Bohumil Novy; cos, Marta Kaplerova.

KAMIKAZE†
(1986, Fr.) 87m Films du Loup–GAU–ARP/GAU c

Michel Galabru *(Albert)*, Richard Bohringer *(Romain)*, Dominique Lavanant *(Laure)*, Riton Liebman *(Olive)*, Kim Massee *(Lea)*, Harry Cleven *(Patrick)*, Romane Bohringer *(Julie)*, Etienne Chicot *(Samrat)*.

A strange crime film directed by first-timer Grousset from a script he co-authored with Luc Besson, the film's executive producer and the director of 1985's immensely popular and overrated SUBWAY. Galabru is an electronics whiz who spends too many hours in front of the TV screen after losing his job. Proving that idle hands definitely are the devil's tool, Galabru invents a ray gun that can kill anyone that appears on the television screen. Bohringer, a quiet detective, figures out Galabru's game and manages to jam the ray gun, before having a final showdown with the madman. Marshall McLuhan would have had a field day with all this.

p, Louis Duchesne; d, Didier Grousset; w, Michele Halberstadt, Luc Besson, Didier Grousset; ph, Jean-Francois Robin (Eastmancolor); m, Eric Serra; ed, Olivier Mauffroy; art d, Dan Weil; cos, Creation Express; spec eff, Georges Demetreau, Pierre Foury, Jacky Dufour.

Thriller   **(PR:O MPAA:NR)**

KAMIKAZE HEARTS†
(1986) 87m Legler-Bashore c

Tigr Mennett, Sharon Mitchell.

A docu-drama about the San Francisco pornographic-filmmaking scene centers on Mitchell and her lesbian lover, Mennett, and their experiences in the industry. Mitchell is a real porn star, but just how much of this film is fiction and how much documentary is unknown.

p, Heinz Legler; d, Juliet Bashore; w, Juliet Bashore, Tigr Mennett; ph, David Golia; m, Paul M. Young, Walt Fowler; ed, John Knoop; art d&set d, Hans Fuss, Miriam Tinguely.

Docu-drama (PR:O MPAA:NR)

KANGAROO** (1986, Aus.) 108m Dimsey-Naked Country/Enterprise Pictures-Filmways c

Colin Friels *(Richard Somers)*, Judy Davis *(Harriet Somers)*, John Walton *(Jack Calcott)*, Julie Nihill *(Victoria Calcott)*, Hugh Keays-Byrne *(Kangaroo)*, Peter Hehir, *(Jaz)*, Peter Cummins *(Will Struthers)*, Tim Robertson *(O'Neil)*.

Yet another filmed adaptation of a D.H. Lawrence novel that fails to capture the intellectual essence or passionate spirit of the book. The novel was Lawrence's account of the six weeks he and his wife spent in Australia in an attempt to escape the political upheavals in the early 1920s in Europe. The film opens with the seaside home of Friels, a writer of controversial literature, being broken into by British authorities who suspect him of collaborating with the German enemy. Friels is under suspicion because his wife, played by Davis, is German and because he has been openly critical of the British war effort. Momentarily ignoring his conscientious-objector status, Friels volunteers for the army, but is refused because of his tuberculosis. The film then leaps several years into the future; it is 1922, the war is long over, and Friels and his wife arrive in Australia hoping to find a sanctuary away from the reactionary politics so prevalent in Europe. The couple is quickly befriend their next door neighbors, Walton, a manly former army officer, and his sweetly naive wife Nihill. It is through Walton that Friels is introduced to a militaristic group with visions of controlling Australia. The group is headed by Keays-Byrne, referred to as "Kangaroo," an important Australian military figure in WW I. It is Kangaroo's quest to rid Australia of what he claims are foreign entrepreneurs seeking to destroy the country's purity. Specifically, he sees his enemies as the socialist trade unions which threaten the totalitarian form of government Keays-Byrne favors. He quickly takes Friels to his bosom, hoping to use the writer's skills for political purposes. The socialist party, led by Cummins, is also courting Friels, offering him the role of publisher of their newspaper, allowing him complete editorial control and freedom. Friels is attracted to Kangaroo's group because of their manly values, but he remains undecided until his wife enlightens him as to what Keays-Byrne really is: a psychotic fascist. Davis chides her husband for playfully involving himself in a potentially explosive situation. The conflict between the two political groups is brought to its eventual violent clash when Keays-Byrne has his trained soldiers attack a meeting where Cummins is speaking. Mortally wounded in the skirmish, the dying Keays-Byrne beckons Friels to his bedside, requesting that the writer say he loves him. Friels refuses, and Keays-Byrne dies. Friels and Davis leave Australia, concluding that the country is not the haven they thought it to be, and head off in search of another spot in the world to fulfill their ideals.

KANGAROO was nominated for several Australian Film awards, including Best Actress, Best Supporting Actress, Best Adapted Screenplay, and Best Costume Design. It won in the costume design and actress categories, with Davis the recipient of the latter for a performance that is really not very convincing. She looks great, evoking an elegant maturity and gracefulness one would expect of Frieda Lawrence. But her crass German accent makes her appear quite comical at times. Davis' real-life husband, Friels, is equally out of place as the legendary author. Much of Lawrence's work centered on the contradictions between the intellect and an individual's passionate nature. This is quite evident in KANGAROO, but Friels' rendition of the writer has him as a wide-eyed child, gleefully awed by the events in which he is involved. A line by Davis, as she is chastising her husband, is a fair summation of KANGAROO's political commitment and exploration: "A bunch of childish boys, playing deadlier and deadlier games." Which is exactly how all the characters seem, devoid of any conviction or real concern for the actual political outcome. Keays-Byrne is perhaps the most obvious case, a chubby, somewhat effeminate man, he manically spouts off empty ideology like a young boy imitating a war film. KANGAROO does have its points of interest, particularly to fans of Lawrence, but on the whole, the film remains a flat, unrewarding cinematic exercise.

p, Ross Dimsey; d, Tim Burstall; w, Evan Jones (based on the novel by D.H. Lawrence); ph, Dan Burstall (Panavision, Eastmancolor); m, Nathan Waks; ed, Edward McQueen-Mason; prod d, Tracy Wyatt; set d, Jill Eden; cos, Terry Ryan.

Drama (PR:C MPAA:PG)

KAPAX DEL AMAZONAS† (1986, Col.) 92m Maro-Focine/Pel-Mex c (Trans: Kapax of the Amazon)

Alberto Rojas Lesmez *(Kapax)*, Maria Bauza Max *(Woman)*, Aldo Sambrell *(Man)*, Eva Bravo, Rosa Maria Mora, Flor Marina Rodriguez, Elza Cristina Porras, Alfonso Sanahuria Lozano, Pepe Lozano Vargas, Gabriel de los Rios.

A female anthropologist and her husband fly deep into the Amazon rain forest, but due to his drunkenness, the husband crashes the plane and is killed. His wife survives, however, and is pulled from the wreckage by a member of the Yagua tribe. He looks after her and eventually takes her for his wife. When she is finally faced with the option of returning to civilization, she refuses, preferring to remain in the jungle. Based on the true story of anthropologist Linda Smaely, who joined the Yaguas in 1965.

d&w, Miguel Angel [El Indio] Rincon; ph, Tote Trenas; m, Miguel Angel Rincon; ed, Jose Rojo.

Drama (PR:C MPAA:NR)

THE KARATE KID PART II**½ (1986) 113m COL c

Ralph Macchio *(Daniel)*, Noriyuki "Pat" Morita *(Miyagi)*, Nobu McCarthy *(Yukie)*, Danny Kamekona *(Sato)*, Yuji Okumoto *(Chozen)*, Tamlyn Tomita *(Kumiko)*, Pat E. Johnson *(Referee)*, Bruce Malmuth *(Announcer)*, Eddie Smith *(Bystander)*, Martin Kove *(Kreese)*, Garth Johnson, Brett Johnson *(Autograph Fans)*; The Cobras: William Zabka *(Johnny)*, Chad McQueen *(Dutch)*, Tony O'Dell *(Jimmy)*, Ron Thomas *(Bobby)*, Rob Garrison *(Tommy)*; Will Hunt *(Postman)*, Evan Malmuth *(Cab Driver)*, Lee Arnone *(Stewardess)*, Sarah Kendall *(2nd Stewardess)*, Joey Miyashima *(Toshio)*, Danny Kamekona *(Sato)*, Raymond Ma *(Cab Driver in Okinawa)*, George O'Hanlon, Jr. *(Soldier)*, Charlie Tanimoto *(Miyagi's Father)*, Tsuruko Ohye *(Village Woman)*, Arsenio "Sonny" Trinidad *(Ichiro)*, Marc Hayashi *(Taro)*, Robert Fernandez *(Watchman)*, Natalie N. Hashimoto *(Kumiko's Street Friend)*, Diana Mar *(Girl in Video Store)*, Bradd Wong *(Boy on Street)*, Clarence Gilyard, Jr., Michael Morgan, Jack Eiseman, Jeffrey Rogers, Aaron Seville *(GI's)*, Wes Chong *(Sato's Houseman)*, Traci Toguchi *(Girl Bell Ringer)*.

The incredible $100 million box-office gross of THE KARATE KID spawned the inevitable sequel. Director Avildsen won an Oscar for his work on the thematically similar ROCKY, then declined the opportunity to helm the follow-up. This

time he was smarter and the result was another hit with the audience, though not critically. Having won a karate championship in Southern California, where he was transported from New Jersey, Macchio (the Kid) and Morita find new adventures on Morita's home island of Okinawa (although the movie was actually shot in Kahalulu on the island of Ohau, Hawaii, because the real Okinawan landscape was not suitable for the story). This sequel begins about 10 minutes after the original one ended. Macchio and Morita are in the parking lot of the place where Macchio won his big bout and they are set upon by Nazi-like Kove, the coach of the opposition. Morita deftly dispenses with the bigger bully and then the picture gets started. Morita's father is dying on Okinawa and he is now about to return after a self-imposed 40-year exile. (The background for Morita seems to have been somewhat altered to accommodate the new story. In the original, if you recall, Morita had been married in California, volunteered for service during WW II, and been given the Congressional Medal of Honor for his heroism against the Nazis. If we are to believe this new history of the character, he left Okinawa after WW II. Moviemakers have been known to make such alterations, though, as witnessed by the incredible metamorphosis of Adrian [Talia Shire] in the ROCKY series. When she was first encountered, she was hardly more than a slightly retarded employee of a pet shop. Since marrying the boxer she has become infinitely smarter, more deeply emotional, and a whiz at managing his career. Oh well . . .)

Macchio decides to go with his teacher to Okinawa and the two arrive to be plunged into another adventure. It seems that Morita's childhood sweetheart, McCarthy, had been pledged to marry his old pal, Kamekona. Both men loved her but she loved Morita, which caused Kamekona to want to have a fight to the death for the hand of McCarthy. Rather than do that, Morita left and assumed that Kamekona and McCarthy married. That did not happen. She is still single, still beautiful, and Kamekona is still angry. Kamekona channeled his frustrations into becoming a very successful businessman and now owns the land upon which their old village sits. Kamekona wants to have that fight with Morita, and unless the transplanted Japanese-American agrees, Kamekona will toss everyone off the land and turn it into a real estate development. Meanwhile, Macchio has run afoul of Kamekona's Americanized nephew Okumoto (he wears gold chains around his neck) because he has fallen hard for local beauty Tomita. So there are two fights in the offing, the one Kamekona insists upon with Morita and Okumoto's desire to wipe the mat with Macchio. Morita finally acquiesces and it looks as though the two senior citizens will finally settle the score. Suddenly, a typhoon hits the area (for about two minutes on screen, thus making it the

shortest typhoon in modern history) and Kamekona is almost killed. Morita saves his life and the men are again friends, as Kamekona realizes that Morita loves him too much to allow him to die. But the fight between Macchio and Okumoto has to take place and it's a dandy. Unless you've just arrived from another galaxy, you should have no difficulty knowing which of the young men wins that skirmish.

Morita, who was nominated for an Oscar for his work in the original, reprises his role well, although much of the scripter Kamen's humor from the first picture seems to have been replaced with Confucius-like sayings, a mistake, as there aren't too many people around who can deliver comedy lines as well as Morita, who spent many years on countless nightclub stages as a comic. Macchio, who is approaching his middle twenties, has the ability to look like a teenager, something which has stood him in good stead in such projects as CROSSROADS, the TV series "Eight is Enough," and the stage production of "Cuba and His Teddy Bear," in which he starred with Robert De Niro in the New York Public Theater production. Macchio is an obviously intelligent actor with terrific instincts (and what must be some good training) and is the East Coast version of a Hollywood Brat Pack member insofar as he has talent, taste, and charm.

This movie leaves a few things to be desired. Much of it feels recycled in a different locale and there is precious little subtlety in the villains' characterizations. It's about 15 minutes too long and there are just too many conveniences, such as the fact that Tomita wants to leave Okinawa and take dance instruction in the U.S., something with which Macchio will happily help her. Although sequels seldom fare better than the originals, this one made a ton of money, despite not having the power of the first. Avildsen also aided in the editing, and although he is not credited as the cinematographer, you can be sure he never took his eye off of the lens because he has done his own camera work on a few other projects and fancies himself a director of photography par excellence, which, in fact, he is. Screenwriter Kamen is, himself, a karate enthusiast of many years and so is Okumoto. McCarthy is Canadian born and will be recalled for her film debut opposite Jerry Lewis in THE GEISHA BOY plus several other films. She also appeared with Morita in the TV film "Return to Manzanar," which was about the Japanese incarceration in northern California during WW II. Morita actually did spend time in what was euphemistically termed a "relocation" camp as a youth. No doubt KARATE KID III is on the way. Let's hope it has more punch than this one. Songs include: "The Glory of Love (Theme from THE KARATE KID PART II)" (Peter Cetera, David Foster, Diane Nini, Michael Omartian, performed by Cetera), "This Is the Time" (Dennis DeYoung, performed by DeYoung), "Fish for Life" (Ian Stanley, Roland Orzabal, performed by Mancrab), "Let Me at 'Em" (Richard Wolf, Wayne Perkins, performed by Southside Johnny), "Rock and Roll Over You" (John Lodge, performed by the Moody Blues), "Rock Around the Clock" (Jimmy DeKnight, Max Friedman, performed by Paul Rodgers), "Earth Angel" (Curtis Williams, Dootsie Williams, performed by New Addition), "Two Looking at One" (Carly Simon, Bill Conti, Jacob Brackman; performed by Simon).

p, Jerry Weintraub; d, John G. Avildsen; w, Robert Mark Kamen (based on characters created by Robert Mark Kamen); ph, James Crabe (DeLuxe Color); m, Bill Conti; ed, David Garfield, Jane Kurson, John G. Avildsen; prod d, William J. Cassidy; art d, William F. Matthews; set d, Lee Poll; cos, Mary Malin; spec eff, Dennis Dion; ch, Paul De Rolf, Nobuko Miyamoto, Jose De Vega, Pat E. Johnson; m/l, Peter Cetera, David Foster, Diane Nini, Dennis DeYoung, Michael Omartian, Ian Stanley, Roland Orzabal, Richard Wolf, Wayne Perkins, John Lodge, Jimmy DeKnight, Max Friedman, Curtis Williams, Dootsie Williams, Carly Simon, Bill Conti, Jacob Brackman; makeup, Jim Kail, John Elliott; tech adv, Yasukazu Takushi, Zenko Heshiki.

Drama   **(PR:A-C MPAA:PG)**

KARMA*   (1986, Switz.) 103m Ho Quang Minh bw

Tran Quang (Binh), Phuong Dung (Nga), Le Cung Bac (Tri), Ba Nam Sa Dec, Thuy An.

Ho Quang Minh, a Vietnamese who left his homeland in 1962 to study in Switzerland, was the first outside filmmaker allowed to shoot a film in Vietnam since the fall of Saigon in 1975. Based on the short story "The Wounded Beast" by Nguy Ngu, KARMA begins in 1972 as Phuong Dung and a family friend, Le

Cung Bac, await the arrival of a Buddhist monk who is to perform the burial rights of her husband Tran Quang. In flashback, the story shifts to the first time Phuong Dung thought her husband was dead, back in 1968, when he was listed as missing in action. After the South Vietnamese army evacuates her entire village, Phuong Dung finds herself in the city with no place to go. In order to survive, she becomes a bar girl and entertains corrupt officers of the South Vietnamese army. When Tran Quang turns up badly wounded, but very much alive, Phuong Dung is overjoyed. But her joy soon turns to despair when she is rejected by the bitter Tran Quang, who is ashamed that his wife has become a whore. He ignores her repeated attempts to contact him and throws himself back into battle with renewed fervor, commanding an elite band of fighters. Although he shows moments of regret over his wife's situation and his treatment of her, he is incapable of salvaging their marriage. The war has changed him—for all intents and purposes he is emotionally and spiritually dead. Phuong Dung refuses to give up her love for Tran Quang and follows him from base to base in an effort to prove her loyalty, but her efforts are fruitless, for Tran Quang's body is finally killed in battle.

KARMA is fascinating, for it is the first Vietnam War film to be shot in Vietnam, made by a Vietnamese crew, and featuring an all-Vietnamese cast. By the same token, this is what makes the film somewhat disappointing. The material is simple melodrama with the tragedy of that war as a backdrop. Although the characters and situation are interesting enough, the film lacks a larger scope and offers little insight regarding the South Vietnamese perspective of the war. Little is made of the larger conflict—there is no portrayal of the North Vietnamese other than as the faceless enemy—and the film instead concentrates wholly on the emotional conflict between man and wife. Not that KARMA is by any means a bad film. Tran Quang (whose performance seems somewhat influenced by Japanese actor Toshiro Mifune) and the beautiful Phuong Dung are fine actors and carry the viewer throughout the film, and director Ho Quang Minh successfully evokes a past time and place. Unfortunately, one cannot escape the feeling that there was a chance here for something better, more important, and for whatever reasons—quite possibly political—that opportunity was lost. KARMA was shown at film festivals in the U.S. in 1986. (In Vietnamese; French and English subtitles.)

p&d, Ho Quang Minh; w, Nguy Ngu, Ho Quang Minh (based on the short story "The Wounded Beast" by Nguy Ngu); ph, Tran Dinh Muu, Tran Ngoc Huynh; art d, Le Troung Tieu, Ngo Huu Phuoc.

War   **(PR:O MPAA:NR)**

KATAKU NO HITO†   (1986, Jap.) Toei c (Trans: Man in a Hurry)

Ken Ogata, Ayumi Ishida, Mieko Harada, Keiko Matsuzaka, Fumi Dan, Renji Ishibashi.

d, Kinji Fukasaku; w, Kinji Fukasaku, Fumio Kan-nani; ph, Daisaku Kimura.

KATAYOKU DAKE NO TENSHI†   (1986, Jap.) Project A-Herald Ace c
(Trans: An Angel with One Wing)

Hideaki Nitani, Yoko Akino, Tamori, Takahiro Tamura, Keishi Takamine.

d, Toshio Masuda; w, Mitsuru Tamura (based on the novel by Jiro Ikushima); ph, Yukio Yada; m, Naruaki Saigusa.

KDO SE BOJI, UTIKA†   (1986, Czech.) 95m Barrandov c

Pavel Kriz (Schoolmaster Dudek), Josef Somr (Smrcek, The Janitor), Ludek Munzar (Accountant Trabach), Ilja Prachar (Fores), Vladimir Kratina (Bartos), Anna Kazmierczakova (Jitka Beranova), Rudolf Ziga (Jurka), Petr Cepek (Mizikar), Zita Furkova (Mizikarova), Yveta Blanarovicova (Ilona), Karol Polak (Imre), Peter Stanik (Kotlar's Father), Hugo Kaminsky (Kotlar's Grandfather), Otto Lackovic (Bihary), Rene Pribyl (Cureja), Jan Pohan, Jan Vlasak.

d, Dusan Klein; w, Dusan Klein, Ladislav Pechacek, Marcela Pittermannova, Josef Pohl; ph, Jaroslav Brabec; m, Zdenek Marat; ed, Jiri Brozek; art d, Boris Halmi; cos, Marie Frankova.

KESERU IGAZSAG†   (1986, Hung.) 88m Hunnia Studio-Mafilm bw (Trans: The Bitter Truth)

Ferenc Bessenyej (Sztanko), Miklos Gabor (Palocz), Eva Ruttkai (Klari), Vera Szemere (Mrs. Sztanko), Tibor Molnar (Bonis), Imre Sinkovits (Buvesz), Bela Barsj (Barczen), Oszkar Ascher (Old Bela), Gyorgy Kalman (Bonczol), Gabor Madj Szabo (Ornagy), Margit Nesmith.

Just out of prison for leaving the country without permission, Gabor wanders through 1956 Hungary looking for a way to restart his life. He finds an old friend, Bessenyej, now a minor Party official in charge of building an apartment block. He gives Gabor a job, but soon Gabor is criticizing the shoddy, cost-cutting, construction techniques. However, his warnings go unheeded. Eventually a wall collapses, killing a worker, and Bessenyej finds a way to blame Gabor for the "sabotage." Filmed during the brief flowering of freedom in early 1956, the film was shelved when the Russian tanks rolled in to put a stop to such things. Only now, with Mikhail Gorbachev's glasnost policy loosening up the old restrictions throughout the Communist bloc, has this and other banned films seen the light of a projector.

d, Zoltan Varkonyi; w, Endre Kovesi, Laszlo Nadasy, Zoltan Varkonyi (based on a story by Endre Kovesi); ph, Barnabas Hegyi; m, Ferenc Farkas; ed, Zoltan Kerenyi; prod d, Melinda Vasary.

Drama   **(PR:A MPAA:NR)**

KHOZIAIN†   (1986, USSR) 97m Armenfilm c (Trans: The Master)

Khoren Abramyan *(Rostom Sarkisyan)*, A. Gukasyan *(Rostom's Wife)*, O. Galoyan *(Director)*, K. Dzhanibekyan *(Senik)*, A. Martirosyan *(Felix)*.

An old forester is disliked by most of the locals, a sentiment he returns as he communes with nature and works to stop illegal felling of trees by nocturnal woodcutters in this film from the Armenian Republic of the USSR.

d, Bagrat Oganesyan; w, Grant Matevosyan; ph, G. Avakyan; m, T. Mansuryan; ed, N. Oganyan; art d, L. Gevorkyan.

Drama   **(PR:A MPAA:NR)**

KHRANI MENIO, MOI TALISMAN†   (1986, USSR) 70m Dovzhenko Studios c (Trans: Protect Me, My Talisman)

Oleg Yankovski *(Liosha Dmitriev)*, Tatiana Droubitch *(Tania)*, Alexandra Abdoulov *(Klimov)*, Alexandre Zbrouev *(Mitia)*.

A festival devoted to the poetry of Pushkin attracts people from across the Soviet Union, including a couple who run afoul of an evil character who seduces the woman. When her husband finds out, he challenges the interloper to a duel with shotguns.

d, Roman Balajan; w, Roustam Ibragimbekov; ph, Vilene Kaliuta; m, Vadim Khrasatchev; art d, Alexei Levtchenko.

Drama   **(PR:A MPAA:NR)**

KILLBOTS   (SEE: CHOPPING MALL, 1986, US)

KILLER PARTY*½   (1986) 91m Marquis/UA–MGM c

Martin Hewitt *(Blake)*, Ralph Seymour *(Martin)*, Elaine Wilkes *(Phoebe)*, Paul Bartel *(Prof. Zito)*, Sherry Willis-Burch *(Vivia)*, Alicia Fleer *(Veronica)*, Woody Brown *(Harrison)*, Joanna Johnson *(Jennifer)*, Terri Hawkes *(Melanie)*, Deborah Hancock *(Pam)*, Laura Sherman *(Sandy)*, Jeff Pustil *(Virgil)*, Pat Hyatt *(Mrs. Henshaw)*, Howard Buscang, Jason Warren *(Bee Boys)*, Majda Rogerson *(Mom)*, Danielle Kracy *(April)*, Scott Coppala *(Stosh)*, Denise Ferguson *(Dr. Bain)*, Cynthia Gillespie *(Diver)*, Elizabeth Hanna *(Stephanie)*, Derek Keurvorst *(Clerk)*, Camir Andre *(Daniel)*, Dora Danton *(Kosima)*, John Dee *(Mr. Katz)*, Jack Duffy, Don McManus *(Security Guards)*, Sherry Cook, Celine Crimmer *(Hot Tub Girls)*, Branco Racki *(Policeman)*, Eric Bradsma, Bernadette Gale, Malcolm Gale, Candee Jennings, Ken Schnmidt *(Dancers)*.

Ah, collegiate days in splatter films, where every campus has a hushed-up death in its closet (this one even has a guillotine in its warehouse) and a mad slasher

preying on coeds and their careless dates. Johnson, Wilkes, and Willis-Burch are three friends who are pledges at the Sigma Alpha Pi sorority house. When the sorority plans its annual April Fool's Day dance in an old frat house abandoned for 20 years after a pledge was decapitated in a hazing accident, the boy's spirit (he's buried in the back yard) comes back and possesses Johnson. She dispatches hapless victims with the usual bewildering array of techniques, including drowning, decapitation (in the guillotine), a claw hammer to the head, electrocution, a shovel to the face, and an auger from a heating duct, some of the time while dressed in a deep-sea diving helmet and suit. After a long, dull build-up, the violence finally breaks out and within 15 minutes the body count has reached lofty heights, until only the three heroines are left. Wilkes and Willis-Burch try to make their way out of the house-turned-abattoir, but they are confronted by Johnson, who rolls her eyes and growls in best EXORCIST style before unleashing demonic powers that destroy the house. The two girls who are not possessed make their way upstairs with Johnson climbing the walls after them. Willis-Burch falls off the roof and breaks her legs, and while Johnson slavers over her, Wilkes climbs down and clubs her on the head with a board. Johnson's original personality fights its way to the surface and begs Wilkes to kill her, something the coed does with a plank through the heart. Police arrive and begin dragging out the bodies, and the two surviving girls are loaded into an ambulance, but from the way Wilkes is rolling her eyes and growling at the screaming Willis-Burch, it is clear that the latter is doomed.

Not exactly on a par with NOSFERATU or even HALLOWEEN, KILLER

PARTY does have a few moments, most of them with stuffy professor Bartel (who gets an electric line shoved into his neck) or weirdo Seymour (who actually gets to survive the film when he leaves early before the killing gets well underway). The killings are refreshingly bloodless or offscreen and the film even comes close to generating a little tension. The three girls give good performances and form a convincing group of friends, and none of them are the kind of idiots-to-the-slaughter usually found in these films. The production values are respectable enough, as are the supporting performances, but just what an exploitation item like this is doing on MGM's roster of summer releases remains a mystery.

p, Michael Lepiner; d, William Fruet; w, Barney Cohen; ph, John Lindley (Technicolor); m, John Beal; ed, Eric Albertson; prod d, Reuben Freed; set d, Enrico Campana; cos, Gina Keillerman; spec eff, Gordon J. Smith; m/l, Carri Brandon, Dennis Churchill, Richard Wright, Rick Chadock, Harry W. Casey, Deborah Carter, Bruce Roberts, Alan Brackett, Scott Shelly; makeup, Susan Benoit.

Horror   **Cas.**   **(PR:O MPAA:NR)**

KILLING CARS†   (1986, Ger.) 115m Sentana c

Jurgen Prochnow *(Ralph Korda)*, Senta Berger *(Marie)*, Agnes Soral *(Violet)*, Daniel Gelin *(Kellermann)*, Stefan Meinke *(Niki)*, Bernhard Wicki *(von der Muhle)*, Peter Matic *(Dr. Hein)*, Marina Larsen *(Dina)*, William Conrad *(Mahoney)*.

Prochnow is an automotive engineer who invents a car that runs on "cellular energy" instead of gas. Naturally, there are people who don't want to see him succeed. While thugs from OPEC and rival car companies try to kill him, he has to search for the car, which has been stolen by some joy-riding punks. (In English.)

p,d&w, Michael Verhoeven; ph, Jacques Steyn; m, Michael Landau; ed, Fred Srp.

Action   **(PR:O MPAA:NR)**

KILLING MACHINE†   (1986, Span./Mex.) 95m Golden Sun-Esme/ Embassy Home Entertainment c

George "Jorge" Rivero *(Chema)*, Margaux Hemingway *(Jacqueline)*, Lee Van Cleef *(Maitre Julot)*, Willie Aames *(Tony)*, Richard Jaeckel *(Martin)*, Ana Obregon *(Liza)*, Hugo Stiglitz *(Picot)*.

Rivero is driving his truck full of vegetables from Spain to France, his wife at his side, when the truck is stopped by angry French farmers who set it on fire, killing his wife. The farmers are defended in court by shady lawyer Van Cleef and acquitted. Rivero gets his revenge by killing the attackers and their attorney. Shot in 1983, the film, not surprisingly, went to videocassette without benefit of a theatrical release.

p, Carlos Vasallo; d&w, J. Anthony Loma; ph, Alexander Ulloa; m, Guido de Angelis, Maurizio de Angelis; ed, Nicholas Wentworth; stunts, Remy Julienne.

Action/Crime   **Cas.**   **(PR:O MPAA:NR)**

KILLING OF SATAN, THE†   (1986, Phil.) Cinex/F. Puzon c

Ramon Revilla *(Lando San Miguel)*, Elizabeth Oropesa *(Lagring San Miguel)*, George Estregan *(Enchong)*, Paquito Diaz *(Pito)*, Cecile Castillo *(Luisa)*, Charlie Davao *(Satan)*.

Revilla is an ex-convict who becomes embroiled in a battle against Evil begun by his uncle, a battle that eventually leads to a toe-to-toe fight with Satan himself.

p, Pio C. Lee; d, Efren C. Pinon; w, Jose Mari Avellana; ph, Ricardo Herrera; m, Ernani Cuenco.

Fantasy   **(PR:C MPAA:NR)**

KIMI GA KAGAYAKU TOKI†   (1986, Jap.) Kinema Tokyo c (Trans: Glittering You)

Takeshi Nishiyama, Yoshihisa Masuyama, Yoshiko Aoyama, Rentaro Mikuni, Ryuzo Tanaka.

d, Tokihisa Morikawa; w, Zenzo Matsuyama; ph, Shinsaku Himeda.

KIMI WA HADASHI NO KAMI O MITAKA†   (1986, Jap.) Nihon Eiga Gakko–ATG c (Trans: Have You Seen the Barefoot God?)

Tamotsu Ishibashi, Gen Kodama, Yoriko Doguchi, Tomoko Kanazawa, Midori Hagio.

d, Kim Soo-gil; w, Nobuyuki Nishimura; ph, Kim Tok-Tetsu.

KIND OF ENGLISH, A†   (1986, Brit.) 75m Sliver-Film Four International c

Lalita Ahmed *(Mariom, the Mother)*, Andrew Johnson *(Tariq, the Uncle)*, Badsha Haq *(Chan, the Father)*, Afroza Bulbul *(Shahanara, the Grandmother)*, Jamil Ali *(Samir, the Boy)*.

Culture shock and kinship are at the center of this story about an immigrant family from Bangladesh trying to make sense of life in its adopted home of London. Two brothers react very differently to their new surroundings. Having "done the knowledge" (mastered the mental map of London's streets), Tariq is content to drive a cab, happy just to be in England. His brother, Harq, on the other hand, is exasperated by his new existence. Grandmother Bulbul and Haq's 9-year-old son, Ali, spend most of their time constructing a miniature version of their hometown. Haq's wife, Ahmed, tries with a stiff upper lip to hold together a family that is bursting at the seams. Finally, a heated argument between Ahmed and Haq sends a terrified Ali fleeing from their home. The ensuing search for the boy strengthens the family ties that were always there. The subject matter here is less reminiscent of MY BEAUTIFUL LAUNDRETTE than of "The Great Celestial Cow," Sue Townsend's touching play about an Indian immigrant family living in the north of England. Lucy Rahman performs the songs that accompany the film.

p, Richard Taylor; d, Ruhul Amin; w, Paul Hallam (based on an idea by Ruhul Amin); ph, Jonathan Collinson (Technicolor); m, Fire House; art d, Jock Scott; cos, Leslie Gilda.

Drama (PR:A-C MPAA:NR)

KINEMA NO TENCHI† (1986, Jap.) 125m Shochiku c (Trans: Final Take: The Golden Days of Movies)

Narimi Arimori *(Koharu Tanaka)*, Kiyoshi Atsumi *(Kihachi, Her Father)*, Kiichi Nakai *(Kenjiro Shimada)*, Chieko Baisho *(Yuki)*, Koshiro Matsumoto *(Kida, Studio Head)*, Keiko Matsuzaka *(Sumie Kawahima)*, Kei Suma *(Ogura)*, Ittoku Kishibe *(Ogata)*, Chishu Ryu *(Tomo)*.

A celebration of the 50th anniversary of Shochiku's Ofuna Studios, this film explores the early days of the Japanese film industry circa 1933. Focusing on Narimi Arimori, a beautiful young candy seller who is "discovered" and made a star, KINEMA NO TENCHI provides a behind-the-camera glimpse of the Japanese film industry. Kishibe plays a film director obviously patterned after the renowned Yasujiro Ozu, and it is he and his determined pursuit of perfection that begin to wear away at the inexperienced Arimori, who suddenly finds herself elevated from the purely entertaining pictures she makes for the studio, to the star of the oft-filmed classic FLOATING WEEDS. Only after her father, Kiyoshi Atsumi, provides the proper inspiration (he tells her of her mother's sorrowful life) is the actress able to convey the right intensity demanded by director Kishibe in the climactic scene. Chishu Ryu, a favorite actor of Yasujiro Ozu, makes a cameo appearance as a studio janitor.

p, Yoshitaro Nomura, Shigemi Sugisaki, Nobutoshi Masmuoto, Kiyoshi Shimazu; d, Yoji Yamada; w, Hisashi Inoue, Taichi Yamada, Yoshitaka Asama, Yoji Yamada; ph, Tetsuo Takaba; m, Naozumi Yamamoto; art d, Mitsuo Dekawa.

Drama/Comedy (PR:C MPAA:NR)

KING AND HIS MOVIE, A*½** (1986, Arg.) 104m Carlos Sorin Cine/ Progress Communications c (LA PELICULA DEL REY)

Julio Chaves *(David Vass)*, Ulises Dumont *(Arturo)*, Villanueva Cosse *(Desfontaines)*, Ana Maria Giunta *(Madama)*, Miguel Dedovich *(Oso)*, David Llewellyn *(Lachaise)*, Roxana Berco *(Lucia)*, Marilia Paranhos *(Lula)*, Ruben Szuchmacher *(German Translator)*, Cesar Garcia *(Bonnano)*, Eduardo Hernandez *(Rosales)*, Ruben Patagonia *(Quillapan)*, Ricardo Hamlin *(Maxi)*, Alicia Dolinsky, Marcela Luppi.

For his first feature film effort, former cinematographer and documentary filmmaker Carlos Sorin drew from his experiences on the crew for a 1972 moviemaking project by Juan Fresan about a 19th-Century French lawyer who claims himself "King of Patagonia." Before shooting even began on the film, which had the working title "The New France", the financial backers withdrew their money. With a small crew, Fresan attempted to shoot his movie anyway, but was beset by a number of problems which forced the project to a halt. Taking a tongue-in-cheek attitude, Sorin fictionalized the incidents Fresan encountered en route to making his epic. As A KING AND HIS MOVIE opens there is mass hysteria as a giant film production is in its preproduction phase. The director, Chaves, is busy making decisions about casting, costume design, catering, and a number of other things. Even the local media are hounding him for information about his great project. At this point, Chaves' biggest problem is finding the right actor to portray the lead, a crazy Frenchman intent on becoming King of Patagonia. When none of the actors screen-tested appears to fit the bill, the director hits the streets to find the right man. He spots a long-haired hippie selling trinkets at a carnival. Chaves and his producer try to corner this man, but he thinks they're police and shaves his head as camouflage. Eventually this man agrees to take the role, and the crew is set to travel to Southern Argentina to commence shooting. The financial backer withdraws his money at the very last moment and flees to Europe. Instead of postponing the shoot, Chaves insists upon continuing. Unable to pay the actors, he is forced to use people he finds on the streets, cutting the crew to the barest necessities. Traveling by train and then by an old, decrepit bus, the small group eventually reaches its destination. They have no money for hotel accommodations, but an orphanage gives them room and board until one of the actors is accused of indecent behavior by the head priest. Forced to sleep in tents, some of the crew members decide this is too much and leave. Rapidly dwindling funds and problems with the local population cause more dissension and more of Chaves' cast and crew members depart. Eventually only Chaves and his loyal producer, Dumont, remain. Not even at this point does the obsessive Chaves retreat; donning the wardrobe of the king, he plays the part himself, using mannequins in place of real people for the other roles. In a surreal and immensely beautiful scene, Chaves is seen riding past the dummies as smoke rises from the ground. Because of the smoke, the local police accuse Chaves of arson. He is thrown in jail, then bailed out only on condition he never return to that part of the country again. On the train ride home, the depressed Chaves has his spirits lifted when the idea of a new film pops into his head, one as difficult and absurd as the film that recently failed.

Winner of the Silver Lion for First Film at the Venice Film Festival, and the Grand Prix at the Biarritz Festival of Iberian and Latin American Films, A KING

AND HIS MOVIE is one of the finest movies about movies ever made, placing it among the ranks of Fellini's 8 1/2 and Truffaut's DAY FOR NIGHT. Though some of the comic situations appear a bit forced, the general atmosphere is effectively and surprisingly realistic. The viewer is made to feel that he really is in the process of making a movie, experiencing the hopes and failures that accompany any film production. As the film within a film heads toward complete failure, the accompanying hopelessness—with a touch of driving faith and then ultimate barrenness—is also felt. Sorin put his knowledge gained as a cinematographer to good work, framing the landscape in a dynamic fashion, always changing as the mood in the film changes. All in all, A KING AND HIS MOVIE is a superior first effort, proving that Sorin has the knowledge necessary for making good films. (In Spanish; English subtitles.)

p, Axel Harding; d, Carlos Sorin; w, Jorge Goldenberg, Carlos Sorin; ph, Esteban Courtalon (Eastmancolor); m, Carlos Franzetti; ed, Alberto Yaccelini; art d&cos, Margarita Jusid.

Comedy (PR:C MPAA:NR)

KING KONG LIVES* (1986) 105m DEG c

Peter Elliot *(King Kong)*, George Yiasomi *(Lady Kong)*, Brian Kerwin *(Hank Mitchell)*, Linda Hamilton *(Amy Franklin)*, John Ashton *(Col. Nevitt)*, Peter Michael Goetz *(Dr. Ingersoll)*, Frank Maraden *(Dr. Benson Hughes)*, Alan Sader, Lou Criscuolo *(Faculty Doctors)*, Marc Clement *(Crew Chief)*, Richard Rhodes, Larry Souder, Ted Prichard, Jayne Linday-Gray, Debbie McLeod, Elizabeth Hayes *(Reporters)*, Natt Christian, Mac Pirkle *(Surgeons)*, Larry Sprinkle *(Journalist)*, Rod Davis *(TV Reporter)*, David DeVries, Bonnie Cook, J. Michael Hunter *(Technicians)*, Robin Cahall *(Mazlansky)*, Don Law *(Security Chief)*, Jack Maloney *(1st Wrangler)*, Jimmie Ray Weeks *(Major Peete)*, Jeff Benninghofen *(1st Radioman)*, Jim Grimshaw *(Sergeant)*, Bernard Addison, Michael McLendon *(Captains)*, Jimmy Wiggins *(Boy Friend)*, Mary Swafford *(Girl Friend)*, Michael Forest *(Vance)*, Leon Rippy, Wallace Merck, Dean Whitworth, Hershel Sparber *(Hunters)*, Dandy Stevenson, Lydia Smith *(Moms)*, Hope Nunnery *(Lady in Phone Booth)*, Margaret Freeman *(Native Woman)*, Winston Hemingway *(Staff Sergeant)*, Tom Parkhill *(Radioman)*, Buck Ford *(Guard Sergeant)*, Derek Pearson *(Youth)*, Gary Kaikaka *(Boat Skipper)*, Duke Ernsberger, Mike Starr *(Cell Guards)*, Shannon Rowell *(Female in Crowd)*.

Only Dino De Laurentiis would dare to make the same colossal mistake twice. When we last saw Kong in 1976, he had taken a nosedive off New York City's

World Trade Center and gone splat on the pavement below. Well fans, Kong didn't die. You see, he just fell into a deep coma and has been kept in a huge warehouse for the last 10 years until doctors and technicians had time to invent an artificial heart the size of a Volkswagen "Bug." Kong's doctor, the indepen-

dent-minded Hamilton, is thrilled by the arrival of the huge pump, but then it dawns on her that since the operation is likely to be quite long and bloody, the big ape is going to need massive monkey-blood transfusions to survive. Lucky for her, Kerwin, an adventurer who patterns himself after "Indiana Jones," has just discovered a female Kong on the island of Borneo. For the right price, the mercenary Kerwin agrees to ship the big gal to the U.S. so that she can be Kong's blood donor. The operation is a success (it is also one of the goofiest scenes ever committed to film) and Kong's diseased heart is replaced with a brand-spankin'-new steel-and-fiberglass one. Actually, the heart works too well, and when Kong smells a female his size in the warehouse next door, he becomes amorous. Breaking his bonds, the big ape leaves his warehouse hospital room and rescues his newfound love. The apes then make a dash for the mountains with the Army, led by crazed colonel Ashton, in hot pursuit of the lovesick leviathans. Hamilton and Kerwin pursue their charges on their own, and as Kong and his lady fall in love, so do the humans (aw, how cute). These scenes of bliss are soon interrupted by more battles between the Army, the scientists, redneck hunters, and the apes, until eventually Kong and his gal (who is pregnant) are finally cornered. Lady Kong falls into a barn and stays there while Mr. Kong wages yet another bloody stand with the trigger-happy soldiers. Despite his new pumper, Kong succumbs to the Army's superior fire power just as his lady gives birth to a baby Kong (call your local zoo to find out the gestation period of gorillas, we'll bet it isn't just three days). In an act of maudlin melodrama that would embarrass any self-respecting primate, Kong crawls over to his infant and holds it in his hand before dying—maybe this time for real.

This was all a joke, right? One can only imagine the production meeting that took place between studio chief De Laurentiis, producer Schumacher, director Guillermin (who actually came back for more after the first-remake disaster), and writers Shusett and Pressfield. "I know! We'll give him an artificial heart!" "Yeah, and then we'll give him a wife!" "And to-a top-a it off, we geeve Konk a leetle baby Konk! Morea people gonna cry than last time!" To be fair, there is a lot of camp value here. Fans of truly bad cinema couldn't ask for a sillier big-budget production that was envisioned with the utmost seriousness. Another point in De Laurentiis' favor is that he learned a lesson from the last time. In his first travesty he tried to convince the world that a multi-million dollar robot played Kong, when in reality it was the talented makeup artist Rick Baker in a monkey suit. Baker didn't even receive screen credit. This time the studio was more up front about men in monkey suits and the actors, Elliot and Yiasomi, received top billing for cavorting around in designer Carlo Rambaldi's articulated suits. (Rambaldi had received an Oscar for his work on the remake, and the award angered famed stop-motion animator Jim Danforth so greatly that he resigned from the Academy that presented the prize.) A large, very hollow, very inanimate Kong was built for scenes where the big guy just lies around, and the huge heads of Kong and Lady Kong (which look a bit different—her hair is redder) were interchangeable on the full-scale body. Production assistants could climb into the hollow body and manually manipulate the chest, mouth, and nostrils to simulate breathing—not exactly high-tech, but cheap and effective. (Visitors to the studio could hardly avoid viewing the recumbent form of the 1976 remake's full-scale Kong, its foam skin in tatters, lying in a field behind the studio.) The miniature model work supervised by David Jones and Dave Kelsey is fine, but one can't escape the reality that the once-respected King Kong has sunk to the absurd level of Godzilla and his rubbery friends who have spent their careers sauntering through toy buildings, that—though constructed carefully—look like toy buildings. Thankfully, KING KONG LIVES was a resounding flop at the box office and maybe we won't be subjected to De Laurentiis' "Son of Kong." But don't bet on it, the man owns his own studio.

p, Martha Schumacher; d, John Guillermin; w, Ronald Shusett, Steven Pressfield (based on a character created by Merian C. Cooper, Edgar Wallace); ph, Alec Mills (J-D-C Widescreen, Technicolor); m, John Scott; ed, Malcolm Cooke; prod d, Peter Murton; art d, Fred Carter, Tony Reading, John Wood; set d, Hugh Scaife, Tantar LeViseur; cos, Clifford Capone; spec eff, Barry Nolan, Carlo Rambaldi; makeup, Gianetto DeRossi.

Adventure/Fantasy   Cas.   (PR:C   MPAA:PG-13)

KING OF THE STREETS*   (1986) 100m Good Luck/Shapiro c

Brett Clark *(Buddy)*, Pamela Saunders *(Lora)*, Reggie DeMorton *(Mr. One)*, Nelson Anderson, Norman Budd, Elodie McKee, Bill Woods, Jr.

In this strange blend of SUPERFLY, MAN FACING SOUTHEAST, and ENTER THE DRAGON, Clark is a space alien who appears in a big-city ghetto. In addition to having an aptitude for leaving his body at will, Clark is also a martial-arts expert (handy skills for interplanetary travel, no?). He helps out the locals, teaching people the value of their own self-worth, and becomes friendly with Saunders, a teacher, and Budd, one of the neighborhood's many vagrants. Clark's journey takes a dangerous twist when his revitalization of the area draws the wrath of DeMorton, a vicious pimp who wants to put an end to Clark's do-gooding. Clark saves Saunders from being raped and cleans up the neighborhood's gang troubles. Then, in an all-out battle between the just and the diabolic, Clark takes on his nemesis to stop DeMorton's reign once and for all. It's not much, but then what did you expect from a director whose previous credits include BLOODY BIRTHDAY (1980) and PLAGUE (1978)?

p, Yakov Bentsvi, Edward Hunt; d, Edward Hunt; w, Edward Hunt, Ruben Gordon, Steven Shoenberg, Barry Pearson.

Science Fiction/Crime   (PR:O   MPAA:R)

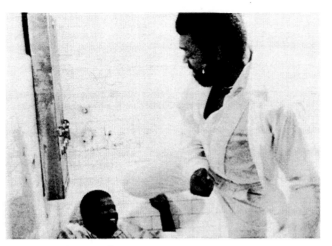

KIRLANGIC FIRTINASI†   (1986, Turkey) 97m Candimir c (Trans: The Swallow Storm)

Halil Ergun, Perihan Savas, Aytan Kavas, Huseyin Kutman, Asuman Arsan, Jale Aylanc.

A young man rejects his father's wishes that he become a cobbler in their village, choosing instead to marry a schoolteacher and move to Istanbul. Their life is not happy, especially when he loses his job and his younger brother comes to live with them. Eventually these and other strains kill the marriage and the two separate. A rare independent feature from Turkey, the title refers to sudden storms that kill whole flocks of young swallows.

p, Tulin Candimir; d, Atilla Candimir; w, Halil Ergun; ph, Selcuk Taylaner; m, Engin Noyan.

Drama   (PR:A   MPAA:NR)

KISMASZAT ES A GEZENGUZOK†   (1986, Hung.) 77m Hungarian Television–Mokep/Hungarofilm c (Trans: Little Smite and the Scamps)

Bence Sagodi *(Little Smite)*, Zsofi Javor, Sandor Palok, Gabor Csore *(Tercsi, Berci, Karcsi, The Scamps)*, Csilla Maronka *(The Mother)*, Andras Schlanger *(The Father)*, Gyula Bodrogi *(Dome)*.

A tourist couple in Budapest accidentally abandon their baby when they split up to do some sightseeing, each thinking the other has the baby. The child is found on the sidewalk by a trio of kids who set about locating the parents, enlisting the help of every taxi driver in the city.

d, Miklos Markos; w, Miklos Markos, Miklos Ronaszegi (based on a novel by Miklos Ronaszegi); ph, Janos Illes (Eastmancolor); m, Ivan Madarasz.

Children's/Comedy   (PR:A   MPAA:NR)

KLASSENVERHALTNISSE   (SEE: CLASS RELATIONS, 1986, Ger.)

KNIGHTS AND EMERALDS†   (1986, Brit.) 94m Enigma/WB c

Christopher Wild *(Kevin Brimble)*, Beverley Hills *(Melissa)*, Warren Mitchell *(Mr. Kirkpatrick)*, Bill Leadbitter *(Enoch)*, Rachel Davies *(Mrs. Fontain)*, Tracie Bennett *(Tina)*, Nadim Sawalha *(Bindu)*, Tony Milner *(Ted)*; The Windyvale Band: Patrick Field *(Terry)*, Maurice Dee *(Gary)*, David Keys *(Arthur)*, Andrew Goodman *(Billy)*, Shelly Willetts *(Dawn)*, Simon Taylor *(Tom)*, Amanda Ellis *(Sonya)*, Marianne Uden *(Charlotte)*, Janice Bishop *(Maureen)*, Carl Jewkes *(Dukes)*, Stephen Page *(Basket)*, Nicola Garbett *(Nessie)*; The Marching Emeralds: Francesca Marino *(Julie)*, Fiona Edwards *(Sophie)*, Helen Daniels *(Donna)*, Debbie Palmer *(Sharon)*, Lynne Shaw *(Denise)*, Vanessa Lee *(Maggie)*, Amanda Huggins *(Sally-Anne)*; The Crusaders: Clive Wedderburn *(Aubrey)*, Robert Knight *(Onion)*, Ruby Hutchinson *(Gabby)*, Dolly Henry *(Jo)*, Terry Beaupierre *(Sunjoy)*, T-Bone Wilson *(George)*, Sarah-Jane Campbell *(Hyacinth)*, David Cann *(Albert Brimble)*, Annette Badland *(Daisy)*, Rodney Litchfield *(Kevin's Dad)*, Mary Ordish *(Kevin's Mum)*, David Neilson *(Ashby)*, Gordon Coulson *(Compere)*, Ingram Hood *(West Indian Doctor)*. James Mahoney, Justin Pickett, Stacey Haynes, Roxanne McDougall, Bunty Mathias, Oke Wambe, Michael Skyers, Ian Laird, Pauline Mayers, Marilyn Bennett, Dennis Allen, Nigel Hanson, Mark Lewis, Merva Smith, Noel Wallace, Lorna Gray, Richard Sweeney, Sabra Williams, Bruce Leader, Estrild Mwendwa, Christopher Grearson, Corinne Bougaard, Simon Smith, Michael Joseph.

The racial tension Britain has been suffering for the last few decades forms the backdrop for this comedy-drama with music. Wild is a working-class white lad who plays drum for a broken-down marching band known as the Knights. Teamed with a majorette troupe called the Emeralds, they enter a competition but are knocked out by a vastly more talented all-black group, the Crusaders. Wild begins hanging out with the black youths and even has a tentative romance with one girl, bringing the wrath of his racist family and friends down on him. The film never received a theatrical release in the U.S. and now appears bound for a video debut here. Songs and musical numbers include: "Stand On the Word" (Joubert Singers), "Wild, Wild Party" (Slade), "Something Special" (Stephen Duffy and Sandii), "I'm the One That Really Loves You" (Austin

Howard), "Tremblin'" (Mel Smith), "Modern Girl" (Rick Astley), "First Love" (Annie Kavanaugh), "Strolling On" (Maxi Priest), "We a Go Bubblin'" (Maxi Priest), "Ready or Not" (Carroll Thompson), "Tell Me Tomorrow" (Princess), "Life of Crime" (Eugenie Arrowsmith), "We Won't Give In" (Slade).

p, Susan Richards, Raymond Day; d&w, Ian Emes; ph, Richard Greatrex (Panavision); m, Colin Towns; ed, John Victor-Smith; art d, Deborah Gillingham; cos, Ann Hollowood; ch, Quinny Sacks; makeup, Nick Forder.

Comedy/Drama   **(PR:C MPAA:NR)**

KNOCK-OUT†   (1986, Gr.) 100m Greek Film Center-Pavlos Tassios c

Giorgos Kimoulis, Costas Arzoglou, Fanis Chinas.

A young man disgusted with his boring life makes a number of unsuccessful suicide attempts, but when a secret society takes pity on him and sets out to kill him as a favor, he begins fighting to stay alive.

d&w, Pavlos Tassios; ph, Philipos Koutsaftis; m, George Hadzinassios; ed, Yannis Tsitsopoulos; set d, Dimitris Kakridas.

Drama   **(PR:C MPAA:NR)**

KOHUT NEZASPIEVA†   (1986, Czech.) 76m Slovenska Filmova Tvorba
                                                                   Bratislava c

Karol Machata (Fischl), Marek Tapak (The Hobo), Leopold Haverl (Uhrik), Milan Knazko (Tomko), Vladimir Durdik (Sustek), Gustav Valach (Terezcak), Zuzana Vackova (Fanka), Boris Slivka (Ondrej), Viera Strniskova (Lekarnikova), Zita Furkova (Babjakova), Zdena Studenkova (Marika), Dusan Jamrich (Maj. von Lucas).

p, Igor Fabry; d, Martin Tapak; w, Dagmar Ditrichova, Igor Rusnak; ph, Vladimir Ondrus; m, Svetozar Stracina; ed, Maximilian Remen; art d, Juraj Cervik; cos, Milan Corba.

Drama   **(PR:NR MPAA:NR)**

KOIBUMI   (SEE: LOVE LETTER, 1986, Jap.)

KOJAK BUDAPESTEN†   (1986, Hung.) 96m Mafilm bw (Trans: Kojak in
                                                                   Budapest)

Laszlo Inke (Kojak), Cecilia Esztergalyos, Gabor Harsanyi, Lajos Oze, Klari Tolnay, Adam Szirtes, Hilda Gobbi, Ildiko Pecsi.

Inke, a Telly Savalas lookalike, portrays the American TV detective whom Savalas made famous in this oddity. Arriving in Budapest for a conference, Inke announces that he is actually Hungarian, and was a member of the Budapest

police before going to New York. Now, back on the familiar streets of Hungary's capital, he takes on the case of a missing scientist while dealing with seductive blondes, nasty taxi drivers, and low-level party officials. Filmed in 1980 and released internationally in 1986.

d, Sandor Szalkai; w, Sandor Szalkai, Istvan Kallai; ph, Ivan Lakatos; ed, Andrea Gellert.

Crime/Comedy   **(PR:A MPAA:NR)**

KOL AHAVO-TAI†   (1986, Israel) 85m YNYL (Trans: All My Loving)

Alon Abutbul, Ri Rosenfeld.

After his wife leaves him, a young man is forced to recall his entire romantic past, gaining a fuller understanding of his relationships in the process. This was the feature film debut for Valler, whose previous work included the direction of a number of commercials and short films.

p, Doron Eran, Yeud Levanon; d&w, Jorge Valler; ph, Gad Danzig; ed, Era Lapid.

Drama   **(PR:O MPAA:NR)**

KOMIKKU ZASSHI NANKA IRANI   (SEE: COMIC MAGAZINE, 1986,
                                                                   Jap.)

KONEKO MONOGATARI†   (1986, Jap.) 90m Fuji Television Network/
                                                 Toho c (Trans: The Adventures of Chatran)

Live-action animal story with a cat (actually played by five cats) that lives on a farm and that has a series of adventures with other animals when it wanders the countryside. Over 400,000 feet of film were shot for this, over a five-year period, without a single human ever showing up onscreen.

p, Masaru Kakutani, Satoru Ogata; d, Masanori Hata; w, Masanori Hata, Shuntaro Tanigawa; ph, Hideo Fujii, Shinji Tomita; m, Ryuichi Sakamoto; ed, Chizuko Osada.

Children's/Adventure   **(PR:AA MPAA:NR)**

KONZERT FUR ALICE†   (1986, Switz./Ger./Aust.) 87m
                                   Condor-SRG-ZDF-ORG/Columbus c (Trans: Concert for Alice)

Beate Jensen (Alice/Margot), Towje Kleiner (Ljova), Anne-Marie Blanc (Frau Keller), Erwin Parker (Conductor), Angelica Arndts, Grete Heger, Heinz Buhlmann, Peter Holliger, Johannes Silberschneider, Yvonne Kupper, Michael Gempart, Patrick Frey, Hermann Guggenheim, Matthias Gunther.

Kleiner is a Russian concert flautist who defects to Switzerland, where he meets Jensen, a street musician who plays the same instrument. He arranges for her to have a concert, but she manipulates things to actually put him on the stage, starting his career in the West in a big way.

d&w, Thomas Koerfer (based on a story by Alexander Schargorodsky, Lev Schargorodsky); ph, Martin Fuhrer; m, Louis Creilier, Antonio Vivaldi; ed, Fee Liechti; art d, Kathrin Brunner; cos, Monika Schmid.

Romance/Comedy   **(PR:C MPAA:NR)**

KORMORAN†   (1986, Yugo.) 88m Viba c (Trans: Cormorant)

Boris Cavazza (Maks Cok), Milena Zupancic (Lenka Cok), Igor Samobor (Zoran), Mila Kacic (Mother).

Cavazza is a bibulous sailor who returns home and immediately finds a lady of easy virtue. She steals his money and makes love to his son when he falls asleep. Before much longer he has drunk himself nearly to death and his family must try to find a new way to support itself.

d, Anton Tomasic; w, Boris Cavazza; ph, Jure Pervanje (Eastmancolor); m, Zoran Predin; ed, Andrija Zafranovic; art d, Janez Kovic; cos, Irena Felicijan.

Drama   **(PR:O MPAA:NR)**

KOUZELNIKUV NAVRAT†   (1986, Czech.) Barrandov c (Trans: Conjurer's
                                                                   Return)

Martin Huba, Julie Juristova, Jan Kanyza, Jiri Klem, Vaclav Kotva.

d, Antonin Kachlik; w, Vladimir Bor; ph, Frantisek Uldrich.

KRAJ RATA†   (1986, Yugo.) Avala-Union c (Trans: The End of the War)

Velimir Bata Zivojinovic, Marko Ratic, Aleksandar Bercek, Neda Arneric, Gorica Popovic.

d, Dragan Kresoja; w, Gordan Mihic; ph, Pedrag Popovic; m, Braca Vranesevic; set d, Vladislav Lasic.

KRAJINA S NABYTKEM†   (1986, Czech.) 93m Barrandov c

Vladimir Javorsky (Zdenek), Yvetta Kornova (Eva), Michal Suchanek (Frantisek), Petr Cepek (Painter), Marcela Martinkova (Mother), Evzen Jegorov (Father), Monika Horakova (Alena), Gabriela Wilhelmova (Bratkova), Dasa Rufusova (Lenka), Simona Stasova (Eliska), Marketa Fiserova (Marketa), Ruzena Rudnicka (Dasa), Frantisek Hammerle (Tomasek).

p, Jan Balzer; d, Karel Smyczek; w, Vaclav Sasek, Milan Lezak; ph, Jiri Macak; m, Emil Viklicky; ed, Jiri Brozek; art d, Jiri Matolin; cos, Kristyna Novotna.

Comedy   **(PR:NR MPAA:NR)**

KRONIKA WYPADKOW MILOSNYCH†   (1986, Pol.) 120m Zespoly–Film
Group Perspektyva c (Trans: A Chronicle of Love Affairs)

Paulina Mlynarska, Piotr Wawzynczak, Bernadetta Machala, Dariusz Bobkowski, Jaroslaw Gruda, Tadcusz Lomnicki, Tadeusz Konwicki.

Politics takes a back seat to romantic nostalgia in the most recent film from
Andrzej Wajda, who has previously delivered such blistering political dramas as
MAN OF IRON (1981, a Cannes Festival grand prize winner) and DANTON
(1983). Set in 1939, the film's hero is a young man, about to enter the university
at Vilna, who falls in love with a military officer's daughter. In a Romeo-Juliet
manner, the lovers contemplate suicide, but the onset of WW II ends their
romantic game and contributes to their loss of innocence. Wajda, after making
two films outside Poland—DANTON and A LOVE IN GERMANY—returned to
his native country and chose to premiere this film at the Gdansk Film Festival,
rather than at the more international Cannes, Venice, or Berlin festivals.

d, Andrzej Wajda; w, Tadeusz Konwicki (based on his novel); ph, Edward
Klosinski; m, Wojciech Kilar; ed, Halina Prugar-Ketling.

Romance/Drama   **(PR:O   MPAA:NR)**

KUEI-MEI, A WOMAN†   (1986, Taiwan) 116m Central Motion Picture c

Loretta Yang *(Kuei-Mei)*, Lap Kwan Li *(Ho)*.

The history of Taiwan since 1959 is seen in microcosm in this big-budget production. Yang is a young woman exiled from the Chinese mainland and forced to
marry Lap, a widower with three children, to which family she soon adds twins of
their own. Later, compulsive gambler Lap loses his job as a waiter, and the two
are forced to move to Japan, where they slave in restaurants and homes, eventually saving enough to return to Taiwan and open their own restaurant. Business
thrives for a while, the children grow to adulthood, and Yang finally dies an old
woman whose sacrifices are unappreciated until she is gone.

p, Lin Dun-Fei; d, Chang Yi; w, Sho Sa, Chang Yi (based on the novel *The
Chavannes House* by Sho Sa); ph, Yang Wei-Han; m, Chang Hung-Yi; art d,
Wang Shai-Chun.

Drama   **(PR:A-C   MPAA:NR)**

KUKACKA V TEMNEM LESE†   (1986, Czech./Pol.) Barrandov–Profil
(Trans: A Cuckoo in a Dark Wood)

Oleg Tabakov, Miroslava Souckova, Alicja Jachiewicz, Vilem Besser.

d, Antonin Maskalyk; w, Vladimir Korner; ph, Josef Samal.

KUNINGAS LAHTEE RANSKAAN†   (1986, Fin.) 85m Reppufilmi/Kinosto
bw (Trans: The King Goes Forth to France)

Paavo Piskonen *(The King)*, Susanna Haavisto *(Caroline the Cheerful)*, Harri
Nikkonen *(The Prime Minister)*, Riitta Havukainen *(Anne the Stripper)*, Kati
Outinen *(Caroline Mare's Mane)*, Lasse Poysti *(The Stablemaster)*, Kalevi Kahra
(King of Bohemia), Heikki Paavilainen, Matti Pellonpaa, Markku Toikka, Pertti
Sveholm, Heikki Ortamo, Timo Toikka, Tupuna Vaissi.

A strange Finnish opera which began life as a radio play now finds its way to the
screen in this oddity. Set during the Hundred Years War, the film follows Piskonen, the King of England, as he tries to make his way through war-torn France
to Paris, his whole entourage on his heels.

d, Anssi Manttari; w, Paavo Haavikko, Anssi Manttari, Heikki Katajisto (based
on Paavo Haavikko's original radio play and on his libretto for the opera "The
King Goes Forth to France"); ph, Heikki Katajisto; m, Aulis Sallinen; ed, Irma
Taina, Marjo Valve; prod d, Pertti Hilkamo, Tuula Hilkamo.

Musical Comedy   **(PR:A   MPAA:NR)**

KURBAGALAR†   (1986, Turkey) 98m Gulsah c (Trans: The Frogs)

Hulya Kocyigit, Talat Buluk, Yavuser Cetinkaya, Yaman Okay, Hikmet Celik,
Metin Cekmez, Cengiy Ekinci, Nesrin Cetinel.

A rice farm along Turkey's swampy border with Greece is the setting for this
melodrama, as a widow goes to work in the fields to support her son while
fending off the advances of the men with whom she labors. The title refers to the
frogs the workers catch and sell as delicacies to supplement their income.

d, Serif Goren; w, Osman Sahin; ph, Erdogan Engin; m, Atilla Ozdemiroglu.

Drama   **(PR:A   MPAA:NR)**

KURSUN ATA ATA BITER†   (1986, Turkey) Ares c (Trans: Hero's Way)

Hakan Balamir, Meral Orhansay, Ahmet Mekin, Zuhal Olcay.

d, Umit Elci; w, Tarik Dursun K., Sener Gezgen, Umit Elci; ph, Orhan Oguz.

KUYUCAKLI YUSUF†   (1986, Turk.) 127m Mine Film c (Trans: Yusuf
From Kuyucak)

Talat Bulut, Derya Arbas, Ahmet Mekin, Engin Inal, Sema Ceyrekbasi, Melih
Cardak, Nilgun Nazli, Ferda Ferdag, Atilla Yigit, Seda Yildiz, Bulent Oran,
Kemal Inci.

Based on a classic Turkish novel written in 1937, this film tells the story of a
young man whose parents are murdered by bandits. Adopted by the local magistrate, he grows up and falls in love with the magistrate's daughter, but after the
magistrate's death, she is coveted by the son of the local rich man, who arranges
to have the hero given a job as tax collector that will take him out of town a lot.

He returns one day to find his love harassed by her suitor's agents, so he kills
them all. The two lovers flee, but she was wounded in the fight and soon dies,
whereupon he buries her beneath her favorite tree.

p, Kadri Yurdatap; d&w, Feyzi Tuna (based on Sabahattin Ali's novel); ph, Cetin
Tunca; m, Timur Selcuk; set d, Gurel Yontan.

Drama   **(PR:A   MPAA:NR)**

L

L.A. STREETFIGHTERS (SEE: NINJA TURF, 1986)

LA ALACRANA† (1986, Mex.) 86m Cinematografica Rodriguez/Peliculas Mexicanas c (Trans: The Scorpion)

Maribel Guardia (*Eugenia/La Alacrana*), Carlos Ancira (*Don Eliseo Mendieta*), Juan Delaez (*Fernando*), Naciso Busquets (*Colonel*), Claudia Guzman (*Raquel*), Susy Rodriguez (*Irene*), Barbara Gil, Gina Morett, Sandra Boyd, Maria Luisa Alcala, Carlos Pouliot, Rojo Grau.

A detective drama which stars Guardia, the former Miss Costa Rica, as a female investigator who calls herself "The Scorpion." She's on the trail of Ancira, a schizophrenic killer who heads a sect of sexually deviate religious fanatics. Of course she finds her man, but in the process is dragged through the seedy underground of the perverse world of the upper crust.

p, Roberto Rodriguez; d, Jose Luis Urquieta; w, Jorge Patino (based on an argument by Roberto Rodriguez); ph, Alberto Arellanos; ed, Rogelio Zuniga.

Crime (PR:O MPAA:NR)

LA BALLATA DI EVA† (1986, It.) 86m Aura/Instituto Luce-Italnoleggio c (Trans: The Ballad Of Eva)

Ida Di Benedetto (*Eva*), Concetta Barra, Nunzia Fumo, Massimo Ghini, Maria Luisa Santella, Lino Troisi, Vanessa Petillo, Mico Galdieri, Gigi Uzzo, Carolynn De Fonseca, Mariano Provenzano, Giula Urso.

Di Benedetto is a factory worker in Northern Italy whose 15-year-old daughter lives in Naples with her grandmother. When Di Benedetto learns that her daughter is working as a prostitute she heads to the South in order to save her from such a life. The tough mother must fight for her daughter, getting harassed and beaten in the process. In the end, however, the girl is saved from prostitution and mother and daughter are reunited.

p, Roberto Cicutto, Vincenzo De Leo; d, Francesco Longo; w, Manlio Santanelli, Francesco Longo (based on a story by Claudio Lazzaro, Francesco Longo); ph, Claudio Meloni (Eastmancolor); m, Tony Esposito; ed, Cleofe Conversi.

Drama (PR:O MPAA:NR)

LA BANDA DE LOS PANCHITOS† (1986, Mex.) 85m Producciones Mexico-Mexican Film Institute c (Trans: The Panchito Gang)

Oscar Velasquez, Mario de Jesus Morales, Oscar Medina, Claudia Sanchez, Los Panchitos, Los Musgos, Los Pitufos, Z.R.

Gang life among Mexican youth is explored in this dramatic film which employs a cinema verite style. Director Velazco cast a number of local street kids in the film, adding an air of authenticity that Luis Bunuel had already mastered in 1950 with his LOS OLVIDADOS.

p, Roberto Leycegui; d, Arturo Velazco; w, Arturo Velazco, Roberto Madrigal; ph, Donald Bryant; m, Federico Alvarez del Toro, El Tri; ed, Carlos Savage.

Drama (PR:O MPAA:NR)

LA BODA DEL ACORDEONISTA† (1986, Columbia) FOCINE c (Trans: The Accordionist's Wedding)

Orangel "Pangue" Maestre, Iris Oyola.

d&w, Luis Fernando [Pacho] Bottia; ph, Fernando Riano.

LA BONNE† (1986, It.) Faso-Producteurs Associes/Filmexport c

Florence Guerin, Katrine Michelsen, Cyrus Elias, Ida Eccher, Lorenzo Lena, Benito Artesi.

A young woman is employed as a domestic servant in a wealthy household and is expected to care for the lady of the house—a severely depressed woman of about her same age. Over time, the women become friends, and then lovers. They learn that they have both become pregnant by a mutual sexual partner. The servant girl must now face the problem of having her child out of wedlock.

d, Salvatore Samperi; w, Salvatore Samperi, Alessandro Capone, Riccardo Ghione, Luca D'Alisera (based on a story by Salvatore Samperi); ph, Camillo Bazzoni (Luciano Vittori Color); m, Riz Ortolani; ed, Sergio Montanari.

Drama (PR:O MPAA:NR)

LA CASA CON LA SCALA NEL BUIO (SEE: BLADE IN THE DARK, A, 1986)

LA CASA DEL BUON RITORNO† (1986, It.) Beppe Cino-Movie Machine/OSCAR c (Trans: The House of the Good Return)

Amanda Sandrelli, Stefano Gabrini, Fiammetta Carena, Lola Ledda, Francesco Costa, Eloisa Cino.

A story of supernatural horror and psychological mystery, this entry tells of a young man who returns to the house of his childhood to find a strange and haunting woman there to remind him of his past. As a young boy, he and a friend were both in love with the same girl—a girl he accidentally killed. Returning to

the scene of the murder, the man is driven by a supernatural force to hurl himself off of the same balcony that claimed the dead girl years earlier.

d&w, Beppe Cino; ph, Antonio Minutolo (Fotocinema Color); m, Carlo Siliotto.

Thriller (PR:O MPAA:NR)

LA CROCE DALLE 7 PIETRE† (1986, It.) G.C. Pictures c (Trans: The Cross of the Seven Stones)

Eddy Endolf, Annie Belle, Gordon Mitchell, Paolo Fiorino, Giorgio Ardisson, Zaira Zoccheddu, Piero Vivaldi.

International intrigue and high-level murder are the backdrop for this story of good versus evil. A young boy "born of the devil" is protected from his evil impulses by a cross he wears around his neck, but when the cross is stolen he is no longer able to ward off evil, resulting in a rash of murders.

d&w, Antonio Andolfi; ph, Carlo Coletti (Augustus Color); m, Paolo Rustichelli.

Thriller (PR:O MPAA:NR)

LA DERNIERE IMAGE (SEE: LAST IMAGE, THE, 1986. Fr.)

LA FEMME DE MA VIE† (1986, Fr.) Odessa-TF-1-Investimage-Regional Council for the I'Ile De France/UGC c (Trans: The Woman of My Life)

Christophe Malavoy (*Simon*), Jane Birkin (*Laura*), Jean-Louis Trintignant (*Pierre*), Beatrice Agenin (*Marion*), Andrzej Seweryn (*Bernard*), Didier Sandre (*Xavier*), Dominique Blanc (*Sylvia*), Jacques Mercier (*Jacques*).

The winner of the Best First Feature prize at this year's Cesar awards, LA FEMME DE MA VIE is the story of an alcoholic violinist, Malavoy, who loses the respect of his fellow musicians as well as his suffocatingly possessive wife, Birkin. He is saved by Trintignant, a former alcoholic who has organized a support group to help drinkers get back on their feet. Malavoy finds some sense of purpose in his life in the form of an alcoholic female group member who is even worse off than he—a situation which only aggravates the unsympathetic and jealous Birkin.

d, Regis Wargnier; w, Regis Wargnier, Alain Le Henry, Catherine Cohen, Alain Wermus; ph, Francois Catonne (Eastmancolor); m, Romano Musumarra; ed, Noelle Boisson; art d, Jean-Jacques Caziet; cos, Corinne Jerry, Cristine Geugan.

Drama (PR:O MPAA:NR)

LA FEMME SECRETE† (1986, Fr.) 95m Flach-FR 3-Selena/AAA c (Trans: The Secret Wife)

Jacques Bonnafe (*Antoine Beraud*), Clementine Celarie (*Camille Alligheri*), Philippe Noiret (*Pierre Franchin*), Francois Berleand (*Zaccharia Pasedeloup*), Wladimir Yordanoff (*Marc Alligheri*), Claire Nebout (*Marie*), Jean-Louis Richard (*Stirner*).

A crime thriller which stars Bonnafe as a young man whose wife of six years has just been dragged out of the Seine—an apparent suicide. Since he's been away working at an oil rig in the North Sea for most of the marriage he doesn't realize that his wife had been leading a secret life. She had a lesbian love affair with Celarie, worked as a model for lunatic painter Noiret, and got mixed up in an embezzlement scheme. Bonnafe follows the clues through the underworld where he learns that his wife's death was murder, not suicide. A first-time directorial effort for Grall.

p, Jean-Francois Lepetit, Pascal Hommais; d, Sebastien Grall; w, Sebastien Grall, Sylvain Saada; ph, Robert Alazraki; m, Bruno Coulais; ed, Jacques Comets; art d, Valerie Grall.

Crime (PR:O MPAA:NR)

LA GALETTE DU ROI† (1986, Fr.) 90m Hachette Premiere-Partners-MG/ AMLF-Hachette Premiere c (Trans: The King's Cake)

Jean Rochefort (*Arnold III*), Roger Hanin (*Victor Harris*), Pauline Lafont (*Maria-Helena*), Jacques Villeret (*Utte of Denmark*), Eddy Mitchell (*Jo Longo*), Jean-Pierre Bacri (*L'Elegant*), Pierre-Loup Rajot (*Leo*), Philippe Khorsand (*Clermont*), Claude Pieplu (*Costerman*), Christophe Bourseiller (*Jeremie*), Jess Hahn (*Morrison*).

Rochefort, the ruler of a Mediterranean island kingdom, arranges to marry his daughter (Lafont) to the hapless son of a business tycoon (Hanin), hoping to replenish his treasury and pay off gambling debts owed gangster Mitchell. Unfortunately, Hanin is also broke, and is planning to use Lafont's dowry—half the kingdom—to restart his business by selling it to an Arab oil sheik.

p, Ariel Zeitoun; d, Jean-Michel Ribes; w, Jean-Michel Ribes, Roland Topor; ph, Francois Catonne (Fujicolor); m, Vladimir Cosma; ed, Genevieve Winding; art d, Pierre Gompertz.

Comedy (PR:C MPAA:NR)

LA GITANE† (1986, Fr.) 92m T. Films-Films A2/AMLF c (Trans: The Gypsy)

Claude Brasseur (*Hubert Durieux*), Valerie Kaprisky (*Mona*), Clementine Celarie (*Elsa*), Stephane Audran (*Brigitte*), Valerie Rojan (*Florence*), Marie-Anne Chazel (*Miss Chaprot*), Rosine Cadoret (*Mme. Chomard*), Martin Lamotte (*Commissioner*), Jacques Legras (*Pilu*), Henri Virlojeux (*Old Gypsy*).

A light comedy from the once-innovative De Broca, LA GITANE stars Kaprisky as the sexual, free-spirited, amoral temptress of staid, uptight businessman Brasseur. Brasseur has a wife (Audran), a mistress (Celarie), a high-paying job, and a nice car, but still Kaprisky manages to lure him away for a dangerous adventure of outlaw romance. Kaprisky, if you remember, was the beautiful French girl for whom Richard Gere lived and died in the 1983 remake of BREATHLESS.

p, Alain Terzian; d&w, Philippe De Broca (based on a screenplay by Jean-Loup Hubert); ph, Robert Fraisse (Eastmancolor); m, Claude Bolling; ed, Francoise Javet; art d, Dominique Andre; makeup, Muriel Baurens.

Comedy (PR:O MPAA:NR)

LA GUEPE† (1986, Can.) 93m Vie Le Monde Francois Floquet c (Trans: The Wasp)

Chloe Sainte-Marie, Warren Peace, Donald Pilon, Ethne Grimes, Claude Gauthier, Gilbert Turp.

Sainte-Marie stars as a beautiful but angry mother who avenges the death of her two young children by launching an all-out attack on their murderer, the voodoo-practicing wife of a wealthy industrialist. Directed by Canadian veteran Carle and photographed by one of the country's finest cinematographers, Guy Dufaux.

d, Gilles Carle; w, Gilles Carle, Camille Coudari, Catherine Hermary-Vielle; ph, Guy Dufaux; m, Osvaldo Montes; ed, Michel Arcand.

Action (PR:O MPAA:NR)

LA LEGENDA DEL RUBINO MALESE (SEE: JUNGLE RAIDERS, 1986 It.)

LA MACHINE A DECOUDRE† (1986, Fr.) 82m M. Films/Jacques Leitienne c (Trans: The Unsewing Machine)

Jean-Pierre Mocky (Ralph Enger), Peter Semler (Steff Muller), Patricia Barzyk (Liliane), Francoise Michaud (Betty), Sophie Moyse (Rubis), Herve Pauchon (Sam), Jean Paul Maçoni (The Mayor), Francois Toumarkine (Thomas Bourne), Isabelle Strawa (Yoyo), Patrick Granier (Henri), Alan Dan (Jack Mironi).

Jean-Pierre Mocky handles a majority of the duties in this black comedy/crime thriller as producer, director, writer, and principal actor. He plays a demented doctor who escapes from an insane asylum, takes two hostages—Semler and Barzyk—and tries to raise money to commission a hospital for infant war victims. He uses a pistol as enhancement to his collection methods among the monied. Mocky goes on a killing spree in the French Riviera and is nearly captured by police until his hostages begin to sympathize with him and plan his escape.

p,d&w, Jean-Pierre Mocky (based on the novel A Killer is Loose by Gil Brewer); ph, Edmond Richard (Eastmancolor); m, Jacky Giordano; ed, Benedicte Teiger; art d, Etienne Mery; makeup, Jose De Luca.

Comedy/Crime (PR:O MPAA:NR)

LA MANSION DE ARAUCAIMA† (1986, Columbia) 86m Focine c (Trans: The Araucaima Mansion)

Adriana Herran (Girl), Vicky Hernandez (Machiche), Antonio Luis Sampaio (Servant), Luis Fernando Montoya (Pilot), Jose Lewgoy (Landowner), Alejandro Buenaventura (Priest), Carlos Mayolo (Guardian), David Guerrero (Boy Friend), Luis Ospina (Director).

When a young girl, Herran, accidentally arrives at a mansion occupied by a strange assortment of characters, her visit shatters the tranquility of the inhabitants and ultimately leads to violence. Based on a story by Alvaro Mutis, this film was one of many uncompleted projects intended for but left undone by the death of the great Luis Bunuel.

d, Carlos Mayolo; w, Julio Olaciregui (based on a story by Alvaro Mutis); ph, Rodrigo Lalinde; m, German Arrieta; ed, Luis Espina, Karen Lamassone; art d, Miguel Gonzalez.

Drama (PR:O MPAA:NR)

LA MITAD DEL CIELO† (1986, Spain) 127m Luis Megino c (Trans: Half Of Heaven)

Angela Molina (Rosa), Fernando Fernan Gomez (Don Pedro), Margarita Lozano (Grandma), Antonio V. Valero (Juan), Nacho Martinez (Delgado), Santiago Ramos (Antonio), Francisco Merino, Monica Molina, Carolina Silva, Enriqueta Carballeira, Julia Martinez, Mercedes Lezcano, Concha Leza.

Molina stars in a real-life story of a woman from Madrid who started at the bottom of the social ladder and ended up becoming a top restaurateur. After scrounging enough money to open a small food stand, Molina—with political connections in the Franco postwar years—climbs to the top, becoming a friend to the most powerful figures in the region.

p, Luis Megino; d, Manuel Gutierrez Aragon; w, Manuel Gutierrez Aragon, Luis Megino; ph, Jose Luis Alcaine; m, Milladoiro; ed, Jose Salcedo; set d, Gerardo Vera; cos, Marina Rodriguez.

Drama (PR:O MPAA:NR)

LA MOITIE DE L'AMOUR† (1986, Bel.) 90m Les Productions de la Phalene c (Trans: Half of Love)

Margit Carstensen, Christophe Donnay, Alexandre Von Sivers, Patrick Bauchau.

Carstensen is a psychiatrist who suffers a bullet wound to the head that results in amnesia. She can't even remember if it was a suicide attempt, an accident, or attempted murder. A young man befriends her in the hospital and eventually she is released in his care, but when he takes her home (to his big spooky villa) he begins terrorizing her psychologically, sexually, and physically.

p, Jacqueline Louis; d&w, Mary Jiminez; ph, Michel Houssiau; m, Johann Sebastian Bach; ed, Jacqueline Lecompte; art d, Mitchelle Noterman.

Drama (PR:O MPAA:NR)

LA MONACA NEL PECCATO† (1986, It.) Filmirage/Medusa (Trans: A Nun in the State of Sin)

Eva Grimaldi, Karin Well, Gilda Germano, Martin Philips, Gabriele Gori.

The scandalous acts that supposedly go on behind the closed doors of convents are once again brought to the screen. This time a young woman escapes the hateful clutches of her abusive father only to be trapped by lesbian nuns who deceive, manipulate, and emotionally torture the new girl. When she shares her story with her male spiritual advisor, he promises to investigate, but she is eventually denounced as a heretic.

d, Dario Donati; w, Antonio Bonifacio, Daniele Stroppa; ph, Aristide Massaccesi; m, Guido Anelli, Stefano Mainetti.

Drama (PR:O MPAA:NR)

LA MUERTE CRUZO EL RIO BRAVO† (1986, Mex.) Esme–Alianza Cinematografica c (Trans: Death Crossed the Rio Bravo)

Eduardo Yanez, Eric del Castillo, Carmen del Valle, Maribel Guardia, Narciso Busquets, Carlos Cardan.

d, Hernando Name; w, Carlos Valdemar; ph, Antonio de Anda; m, Hector Sanchez; ed, Rogelio Zuniga.

LA NOCHE DE LOS LAPICES† (1986, Arg.) 95m Aries c (Trans: The Night of the Pencils)

Alejo Garcia Pintos, Vita Escardo, Pablo Novarro, Adriana Salonia, Pablo Machado, Jose Monje Berbel, Leonardo Sbaraglia, Tina Serrano, Hector Bidonde, Lorenzo Quinteros, Alfonso De Grazia.

This film, based on a true 1976 incident, deals with a group of Argentine students who protest restrictions imposed by the country's military dictatorship. The seven teenagers are arrested in the middle of the night, then tortured as their captors seek information the students do not have. Pablo Diaz, the only surviving member of the group, served as an adviser to the production. LA NOCHE DE LOS LAPICES premiered in Buenos Aires in the fall of 1986, but a more extensive international distribution is reportedly being planned for 1987.

p, Fernando Ayala; d, Hector Olivera; w, Hector Olivera, Daniel Kon (based on a story by Maria Seoane, Hector Ruiz Nunez); ph, Leonardo Rodriguez Solis (Eastmancolor); m, Jose Luis Castineira de Dios; tech adv, Pablo Diaz.

Drama (PR:O MPAA:NR)

LA PELICULA DEL REY (SEE: KING AND HIS MOVIE, A, 1986, Arg.)

LA PURITAINE† (1986, Fr./Bel.) 86m Philippe Dussart-Man's-La Sept-CNC-Belgian Ministry of Francophone Culture-Cinergie-Investimage/ MK2 c (Trans: The Prude)

Michel Piccoli (Pierre), Sandrine Bonnaire (Manon), Sabine Azema (Ariane), Laurent Malet (Francois), Brigitte Coscas, Anne Coesens, Corinne Dacla, Jessica Forde, Vinciane LeMen, Kitty Kortes-Lynch, Nicole Persy, Pascale Salkin, Pascale Tison.

The star of last year's VAGABOND, Bonnaire, plays the runaway daughter of Antwerp theater manager Piccoli, reuniting with her father after a one-year separation. In order to help cope with the problems he has in communicating with Bonnaire, Piccoli has some of his actresses play out the role of his daughter. With the help of go-between Azema, Piccoli's lover, the father and daughter learn to come to terms with each other.

p, Philippe Dussart; d, Jacques Doillon; w, Jacques Doillon, Jean-Francois Goyet; ph, William Lubtchansky; m, Philippe Sarde; ed, Marie Robert; art d, Jean-Claude de Bemels.

Drama (PR:O MPAA:NR)

LA RADIO FOLLA† (1986, Span.) Opal c (Trans: Crazy Radio)

Sergi Mateu, Pep Munne, Silvia Sabate, Carme Conesa, Rosa Maria Sarda, Jose Maria Canete.

d, Francesc Bellmunt; w, Quim Casas, Carlos Benpar, Santiago Lapeira, Francesc Bellmunt; ph, Hans Burmann.

Comedy (PR:NR MPAA:NR)

LA RAGAZZA DEI LILLA† (1986, It.) Haker-Rai Radiotelevisione Haliana/Intra Film (Trans: The Lilac Girl)

Laurent Terzieff, Mimsy Farmer, Mario Adorf, Pascale De Boysson, Meme Perlini, Britt Bergman.

A beautiful and radiant 13-year-old girl becomes involved with an archaeologist who is three times her age. Interconnected with their relationship is the unearthing of the tomb of a beautiful young Etruscan princess who fatefully, and symbolically, disintegrates before the archaeologist's eyes.

d, Flavio Mogherini; w, Massimo De Rita, Flavio Mogherini (based on the novel *Il Grande Tumulo* by Giovanni Nicosia); ph, Carlo Carlini; m, Franco Perini; ed, Adriano Tagliavia.

Drama   **(PR:O MPAA:NR)**

LA ROSSA DEL BAR†   (1986, Span.) Films de la Rambla–Lauren c (Trans: The Blonde at the Bar)

Enric Majo, Nuria Hosta, Carme Sansa, Ramoncin, Pepe Martin.

d, Ventura Pons; w, Raul Nunez; ph, Tomas Pladevall.

LA SECONDA NOTTE†   (1986, It.) 95m BOA Cinematografica/Futura c (Trans: The Second Night)

Maurice Garrel *(Fabris)*, Margherita Buy *(Lea)*, Kara Donati *(Mother)*, Katia Rupe *(Singer)*, Luigi Mezzanotte *(Hotel Guest)*, Mauro Caruso *(Walter)*, Ernesto Massi *(Friend)*.

A story of an old man's obsession with a young girl whom he spots at a luxurious hotel where both are staying. He writes her numerous anonymous letters, sparking her curiosity, but she ultimately falls for the hotel desk clerk, who is her age.

p, Emilio Bolles, Enzo Bruno; d, Nino Bizzarri; w, Nino Bizzarri, Andrea Ferreri, Lucio Gaudino; ph, Franco Lecca (Fujicolor); m, Luigi Cinque; ed, Alberto Benotti; art d, Massimo Corevi; cos, Simonetta Leoncini.

Drama   **(PR:C MPAA:NR)**

LA SIGNORA DELLA NOTTE†   (1986, It.) San Francisco/Filmexport Group (Trans: The Lady Of The Night)

Serena Grandi, Fabio Sartor, Francesca Topi, Alberto Di Stasio, Emanuela Taschini, Stanko Molnar.

An overworked aeronautical engineer cannot find enough time for his wife, who consequently begins to get involved with other men. The pair split up, but find they cannot exist apart and reunite.

d&w, Piero Schivazappa (based on a story by Galliano Juso); ph, Giuseppe Ruzzolini; m, Guido De Angelis, Maurizio De Angelis.

Drama   **(PR:O MPAA:NR)**

LA SPOSA AMERICANA†   (1986, It.) Scena Film/Medusa–Titanus c (Trans: The American Bride)

Stefania Sandrelli, Tommy Berggrreen, Trudie Styler, Harvey Keitel.

An Italian man is about to wed an American woman when he takes notice of his bride-to-be's best friend—another Italian. Although he is happy with his practical and faithful wife, he begins to take interest in her friend's temptations. He returns to the U.S. with his wife and accepts a teaching post at Berkeley, but her best friend, who is also married, is close at hand. Unable to exit the situation, he must learn to juggle his two desires.

p, Augusto Caminito; d, Giovanni Soldati; w, Gino Capone, Giovanni Soldati, Brian Frielino (based on the novel by Mario Soldati); ph, Romano Albani (Telecolor); m, Gino Paoli; ed, Roberto Martini.

Drama   **(PR:O MPAA:NR)**

LA SPOSA ERA BELLISSIMA†   (1986, It./Hung.) A.M.A.–MAFILM/ Intra (Trans: The Bride Was Very Beautiful)

Angela Molina, Massimo Ghini, Marco Leonardi, Stefania Sandrelli.

Molina is a lovely Sicilian woman who is raising her teenage son alone, as her husband took off to Germany without her. The son looks forward to the day that he will meet his father, but when that day is finally scheduled, the father never arrives. The boy is discouraged at his lack of contact with his father, but Molina's relationship with the local doctor, a kind and thoughtful man, eases some of the boy's suffering. Molina dies and the boy blames his father's negligence. Leaving Sicily behind, the boy heads for Germany to kill his father, but has a change of heart when he sees how pathetic his father really is.

p, Gianni Minervini; d, Pal Gabor; w, Enzo Lauretta, Stefano Milioto, Lucio M. Battistrada, Pal Gabor (based on the novel by Enzo Lauretta); ph, Janos Kende; m, Nicola Piovani.

Drama   **(PR:O MPAA:NR)**

LA STORIA†   (1986, It.) 251m RAI 2–Ypsilon–Antenne 2–Maran–TVE/ Sacis c (Trans: The Story)

Claudia Cardinale *(Ida Raimundo)*, Lambert Wilson *(Carlo/Davide)*, Francisco Rabal *(Bartender)*, Andrea Spada *(Useppe)*, Antonio Degli Schiavi *(Nino)*, Fiorenzo Fiorentini *(Cucchiarelli)*.

Luigi Comencini, the 70-year-old veteran of the Italian film industry, has here delivered, on a grand scale, a story of single mother, Cardinale, who is hit hard by the reality of the war-torn years in Rome from 1940-1947. Having already raised a 15-year-old son (Degli Schiavi), Cardinale, a widowed Jewish schoolteacher, again becomes pregnant after being raped by a German soldier. While she raises her newborn (Spada), Degli Schiavi fights with the Partisans. As Italy crumbles, so too does Cardinale's life—Degli Schiavi is killed while driving a truck full of smuggled goods, Cardinale's close friend Wilson, a tortured intellec-

tual, falls to pieces after killing an enemy soldier, and Spada suffers a fatal epileptic seizure. Retreating to her house, Cardinale completely shuts herself off from the world outside.

Of lower-class Italians during the war, Comencini has said: "Today, of course, we are not that aware of poor people around us . . . The poor and the persecuted disappeared from the scene and were substituted by heroes. Television proliferated and filled our eyes with dream worlds, driving out reality and replacing it with 'a world in which one would like to live, peopled by personalities one would like to resemble.'" Filmed as a project for Italian television, LA STORIA has been edited down for a theatrical release. Based on a novel written by Elsa Morante, the late wife of famed Italian writer Alberto Moravia.

p, Paolo Infascelli; d, Luigi Comencini; w, Suso Cecchi D'Amico, Cristina Comencini, Luigi Comencini (based on the novel by Elsa Morante); ph, Franco Di Giacomo; m, Fiorenzo Carpi, ed, Nino Baragli; art d, Paola Comencini; cos, Carolina Ferrara.

Drama   **(PR:C MPAA:NR)**

LA TIERRA PROMETIDA†   (1986, Mex.) 101m Peliculas Mexicanas c (Trans: The Promised Land)

Roberto [Flaco] Guzman *(Serafin)*, Manuel [Flaco] Ibanez *(Pascual)*, Pedro Weber [Chatanooga] *(Con Man)*, Claudia Guzman *(Serviana)*, Alejandro Guce *(Tolin)*, Alejandra Meyer *(Mother)*, Lilia Prado *(The Madame)*.

A propagandistic tale of a farmer, Guzman, who takes his family to the city when he finds there is little hope of making a living otherwise. The city is even worse, however. Disease, crime, prostitution, and corruption plague the members of his family. They return to the land whence they came and find that it is a cornucopia of good fortune. The workers have banded together, a cooperative has been formed, and government loans are now low-interest.

p&d, Roberto G. Rivera; w, Ricardo Gariby; ph, Raul Dominguez; m, Rafael Carrion; ed, Enrique Puente Portillo.

Drama   **(PR:C MPAA:NR)**

LA VENEXIANA†   (1986, It.) 84m Lux International/Titanus c (Trans: The Venetian Woman)

Laura Antonelli *(Angela)*, Monica Guerritore *(Valeria)*, Jason Connery *(Foreigner)*, Claudio Amendola, Clelia Rondinella, Cristina Noci, Annie-Belle, Stefano Davanzati.

Veteran Italian filmmaker Bolognini delivers another erotic period drama, this time set in Venice in the 16th Century. The Black Plague has just been defeated and, apparently, the survivors are ready to get back to the bedroom. Connery (son of Sean) is a foreigner wandering through Venice when he meets the most beautiful woman he has ever laid eyes on, Guerritore. Moments later he meets the equally lovely Antonelli. So what is the poor boy to do but make passionate love to both of them, though not at the same time. This arrangement, however, cannot last for long, and when Guerritore learns that he has been with Antonelli, the game is over. Antonelli, who has made a career of such films, peaking with 1977's WIFEMISTRESS, performs again as no one else can, proving once and for all that she is a genre unto herself.

d, Mauro Bolognini; w, Mauro Bolognini, Massimo Franciosa (based on an anonymous 16th Century play); ph, Beppe Lanci (Luciano Vittori Color); m, Ennio Morricone; ed, Alessandro Lucidi; cos, Aldo Buti.

Drama   **(PR:O MPAA:NR)**

LA VITA DI SCORTA†   (1986, It.) Selvaggia (Trans: The Spare Life)

Jean Boissery, Manuela Torri, Anna Galiena, Bruno Corazzari, Anna Orso, Urbano Barberini, Enrica Maria Scrivano, Piero Vida.

A filmmaker meets and falls in love with a pretty young drug addict who prefers to live on her own in the streets rather than be dependent on someone. Her character provides material for the filmmaker and in return he offers her his patient love and affection, to which she temporarily responds. But when he attempts to put their relationship on more equal footing, she feels vulnerable and decides that he is unable to commit to her because he is still too much in love with his late wife. She turns her back on him and his love and returns to an addiction which eventually kills her.

d&w, Piero Vida; ph, Angelo Bevilacqua (Fotocinema Color); m, Francesco Verdinelli; ed, Graziana Quintall, Angelo Nicolini.

Drama   **(PR:O MPAA:NR)**

LABYRINTH***½   (1986) 101m Tri-Star c

David Bowie *(Jareth)*, Jennifer Connelly *(Sarah)*, Toby Froud *(Toby)*, Shelley Thompson *(Stepmother)*, Christopher Malcolm *(Father)*, Natalie Finland *(Fairy)*, Brian Henson (voice), Shari Weiser *(Hoggle)*, Ron Mueck (voice), Rob Mills *(Ludo)*, David Shaughnessy, David Barclay *(Didymus)*, Timothy Bateson (voice), Karen Prell *(The Worm)*, Michael Hordern (voice) Frank Oz *(The Wiseman)*, David Shaughnessy (voice), Dave Goelz *(The Hat)*, Denise Bryer, Karen Prell *(The Junk Lady)*, Anthony Jackson, Douglas Blackwell, David Shaughnessy, Timothy Bateson (voices), Steve Whitmire, Kevin Clash, Anthony Asbury, Dave Goelz *(The Four Guards)*, David Healy (voice), Anthony Asbury *(Right Door Knocker)*, Robert Beatty, Dave Goelz *(Left Door Knocker)*, Kevin Clash, Charles Augins, Danny John-Jules, Richard Bodkin (voices) Kevin Clash, David Barclay, Karen Prell, Ian Thom, Dave Goelz, Rob Mills, Steve Whitmire, Cheryl Henson, Toby Philpot, Sherry Amott, Kevin Bradshaw, Anthony Asbury, Alistair Fullarton, Rollin Krewson *(Fireys)*, Percy Edwards (voice), Steve Whitmire, Clash *(Ambrosius)*, Elfrida Ashworth, Elizabeth A. Gilbert, Margaret Foyer, Louise Gold, Moira Grant, San Lee, Janis Mackintosh, Penny Marsden, Kim Mendez, Wendy Millward, Leonie Pallete, Caroline Pope, Sharon White, John Aron, Terry Dane, Derek Hartley, Douglas Howes, Christopher Preston, Peter Salmon, Peter Sim, Graeme Sneddon, Graham Tudor-Phillips, David Turner, Barrie J. Wilkinson *(Ballroom Dancers)*, Marc Antona, Kenny Baker, Danny Blackner, Peter Burroughs, Toby Clark, Tessa Crockett, Warwick Davis, Malcolm Dixon, Anthony Georghiou, Paul Grant, John Key, Andrew Herd, Richard Jones, Jack Purvis, Mark Lisle, Peter Mandell, Linda Spriggs, Katie Purvis, Nicholas Read, Albert Wilkinson, Penny Stead, Michael Henbury Ballan *(Goblin Corps)*.

If French filmmaker Georges Melies, the turn-of-the-century creator of film magic and cinematic special effects, were alive today he would be thrilled with the

phantasmagorical LABYRINTH. Muppet creator Jim Henson, who previously directed THE DARK CRYSTAL (1984), here combines his talents with those of special-effects master George Lucas, ex-Monty Python writer Terry Jones, and rock star/actor David Bowie to produce a children's fantasy reminiscent of the writings of L. Frank Baum (on which THE WIZARD OF OZ was based) and Lewis Carroll, the creator of "Alice in Wonderland." Drawing specifically on Maurice Sendak, whose story "Outside Over There" is a direct inspiration, LABYRINTH stars Connelly (the endearing 15-year-old first seen in ONCE UPON A TIME IN AMERICA) as a suburban teenager who lives in a fantasy world dictated by Carroll, Baum, and Sendak. Her bookcases are filled with their books, and she even memorizes favorite passages.

Naturally, she's upset when her parents force her to baby-sit for her little brother, Froud (the son of the film's "conceptual" designer, Brian Froud). Letting her imagination run wild, Connelly takes the baby in her arms and says, "I wish the goblins would take you away right now." Well, lo and behold, the goblins just happened to be listening with bated breath. Froud is taken away and Bowie, the long-haired Goblin King, materializes in Connelly's bedroom. He tells her that he has followed her request and in just a few hours Froud will be transformed into a goblin. Connelly, however, has realized the seriousness of her mistake and wants the baby back. The only way she can save her little brother is by making her way through the labyrinth that snakes its way to Bowie's castle. In front of the gates of the labyrinth, Connelly meets a crusty little gnome called Hoggle who spends his free time killing faeries. A coward at heart, Hoggle shows Connelly the way inside, but offers no more help than that. Along the way the astonished Connelly gets a number of surprises—a worm with a cockney accent that invites her for tea, a wizard with a talking hat, two talking door knockers that argue with one another, and a group of singing creatures that play catch with each other's heads. When she thinks she has finally found the right passageway to the castle, she falls down a tunnel lined with hundreds of talking hands, which group together and make faces as they speak. She is dropped into a dark pit and rescued by Hoggle, who has been sent by Bowie to deceive her and lead her back to the beginning of the maze. When Bowie finds out that Hoggle is helping Connelly instead of hindering her, he threatens to send the gnome to the Bog of Eternal Stench, a place that smells as bad as it sounds. Hoggle continues to help and along the way they meet up with Ludo, a hulking furry creature which looks threatening but is a pussycat at heart.

Meanwhile, back at the goblin castle, Bowie is bouncing little Froud on his knee while watching Connelly's time slowly run out. Connelly, Hoggle, and Ludo end up stuck in the Bog of Eternal Stench and must persuade the bog's tiny guard, Didymus, a brave military-minded puppet who rides on the back of a dog, to let them pass. Didymus not only gives them permission to pass, but decides to travel along with them on their mission to the castle. Along the way, Connelly takes a bite of a poison peach that makes her forget about her brother. She falls asleep and enters a fantasy masquerade ball where she is dressed in a glamourous white dress and dances with the gentle Bowie. She now finds herself attracted to Bowie, whom she previously despised. In the midst of the masquerade, Connelly comes to her senses and escapes through a mirror which leads into the middle of a junkyard. After escaping from a replica of her own bedroom, and battling an army of goblins, Connelly and her friends finally make it to the castle, where she realizes that she has to confront Bowie. She enters a room full of staircases that go nowhere (a set based on a drawing by M.C. Escher). Sitting on one of the

staircases is Froud. Before she can rescue him, Bowie tries to intimidate her into giving up. Connelly's will, however, is stronger than his. Bowie confesses that everything he has done has been done for her, declaring that he will be her slave. Once Connelly discovers that Bowie is a creation of her imagination, and as a result has no power over her, she safely returns to her suburban bedroom. Froud is safely asleep in his crib, mom and dad have come home from their night out, and Connelly has realized that "every now and again in life, for no reason at all," she needs the characters of her imagination.

An overwhelming display of imagination, LABYRINTH is the finest work that the Henson team (THE MUPPET MOVIE, THE MUPPETS TAKE MANHATTAN, DREAMCHILD) has produced thus far. While THE DARK CRYSTAL failed because of the absence of human characters, LABYRINTH has cast the charming Connelly and has employed the talents of screenwriter Jones (who was hired after Henson read a children's book he wrote called *Erik the Viking*) to add humor and realism to the characters' speech. Although there are enough surprises to capture an audience of children, there is also enough wisecracking to keep adults laughing. Thirty years ago this is the type of film Walt Disney Studios would have made; today the genre of children's fantasy is in the care of Jim Henson (along with his collaborator Frank Oz and the others at Jim Henson's Creature Shop). Henson has, in LABYRINTH, created a magical world which recalls the escapades of Dorothy and her friends in the wonderful land of Oz. Like Dorothy, Connelly's character leaves her bedroom for a world of surprises in which she learns something about herself and about her role in the family. By having to fight for the recovery of her brother, Connelly is taught responsibility. She also learns about friendship in her relationships with Hoggle and Ludo. Most interesting is the lesson she learns from Bowie. As Connelly has stated about her character: "She's on the dividing line between childhood and womanhood. So she's trying to grow up and hold onto the past at the same time."

While there are some moments in LABYRINTH that are a little spooky (the brilliant "Helping Hands" sequence, for example, might give a scare, but no more so than the killer monkeys in THE WIZARD OF OZ), the film is highly recommended for youngsters of all ages. In Henson's world, all things are possible, but nothing is harmful. No characters are killed, no blood is spilled, and nothing is exploited—all of which are charges that could be seriously leveled at Steven Spielberg's supposed children's films. Besides acting in the role of the goblin king, Bowie (who was chosen from a group of other rock stars which included Mick Jagger, Sting, and Michael Jackson) also composed and performed a number of songs for the film, including "Underground," "Dance Magic," "Chilly Down," "As the World Falls Down," and "Within You."

p, Eric Rattray; d, Jim Henson; w, Terry Jones (based on a story by Dennis Less, Jim Henson); ph, Alex Thomson; m, Trevor Jones; ed, John Grover; prod d, Elliot Scott; art d, Roger Cain, Peter Howitt, Michael White, Terry Ackland-Snow; cos, Brian Froud, Ellis Flyte; spec eff, George Gibbs; ch, Cheryl McFadden, Charles Augins, Michael Moschen; m/l, David Bowie; makeup, Wally Schneiderman, Nick Dudman.

Children's/Fantasy   Cas.   (PR:AAA MPAA:PG)

LADIES CLUB, THE½   (1986) 90m Media Home Entertainment-Heron/New Line Cinemac

Karen Austin *(Joan Taylor)*, Diana Scarwid *(Lucy Bricker)*, Christine Belford *(Dr. Constance Lewis)*, Bruce Davison *(Richard Harrison)*, Shera Danese *(Eva)*, Beverly Todd *(Georgiane)*, Marilyn Kagan *(Rosalie)*, Kit McDonough *(Carol)*, Arliss Howard *(Ed Bricker)*, Randee Heller *(Harriet)*, Paul Carafotes *(Eddie)*, Nicholas Worth *(Jack Dwyer)*, Scott Lincoln *(Pete Campanella)*.

The idea of castrating convicted rapists is, to say the least, a controversial one. THE LADIES CLUB unsuccessfully attempts to deal with this difficult issue from the victims' point of view. Austin is a policewoman who spends a day on a boat with her cop boy friend Davison and other members of the force. On her way home, she is mercilessly attacked by a gang of vicious rapists. Hospitalized following the attack, she meets Belford, a doctor whose daughter was raped and murdered by a man who had committed rape many times before. Austin's attackers are arrested, but she is outraged when they are tried and found not guilty. This unexpected acquittal reaps massive publicity and Austin hears from numerous rape victims. She and Belford decide to form a discussion group for rape victims. Members of the newly formed group include Danese, Kagan, Todd,

McDonough, and Scarwid (with this and EXTREMITIES on her 1986 resume, Scarwid seems to be making a minor career of rape revenge films). The group, at Danese's suggestion, decides on an ultimate solution to the problem of rape. With Austin's access to police files, they can obtain a list of repeat rapists. The women will seduce these men and ply their targets with drug-spiked liquor, leaving them knocked out so Belford can castrate them. The film reaches its climax when the man who murdered Belford's daughter is snared by "The Ladies Club," and the group members are forced to take a hard look at their methods of dispensing "justice."

Director Allen (a pseudonym for first timer Janet Greek) does a commendable job in expressing the pain and humiliation of a rape victim. She presents the vicious act for what it is, a crime of violence. The questions raised by the film are disturbing, but Allen deals with them in a mixed fashion. The performances are fine, particularly that of Austin. However, Allen reverts to simplistic stereotypes when dealing with the attackers, and fills the story with some incomprehensible gaps in story logic. For example, it's implausible that a judge would take the word of three gang rapists over that of policewoman Austin. These moments mar an otherwise thought-provoking film.

p, Nick J. Mileti, Paul Mason; d, A.K. Allen [Janet Greek]; w, Paul Mason, Fran Lewis Ebeling (based on the novel *Sisterhood* by Betty Black, Casey Bishop); ph, Adam Greenburg; m, Lalo Schifrin; ed, Marion Segal, Randall Torno; prod d, Stephen Myles Berger; md, Lalo Schifrin.

Drama   Cas.   (PR:O MPAA:R)

LADY JANE***½   (1986) 142m PAR c

Helena Bonham Carter (*Lady Jane Grey*), Cary Elwes (*Guilford Dudley*), John Wood (*John Dudley, Duke of Northumberland*), Michael Hordern (*Dr. Feckenham*), Jill Bennett (*Mrs. Ellen*), Jane Lapotaire (*Princess Mary*), Sara Kestelman (*Frances Grey, Duchess of Suffolk*), Patrick Stewart (*Henry Grey, Duke of Suffolk*), Warren Saire (*King Edward VI*), Joss Ackland (*Sir John Bridges*), Ian Hogg (*Sir John Gates*), Lee Montague (*Renard, the Spanish Ambassador*), Richard Vernon (*The Marquess of Winchester*), Pip Torrens (*Thomas*), Matthew Guinness (*Dr. Owen*), Guy Henry (*Robert Dudley*), Andrew Bicknell (*John Dudley*), Clyde Pollitt (*Peasant Leader*), Morgan Sheppard (*Executioner*), Zelah Clarke (*Lady Anne Wharton*), Laura Clipsham (*Katherine Grey*), Janet Henfrey (*Housekeeper*), Brian Poyser (*Under Treasurer*), Phillip Voss (*Herald*), Robert Putt (*Steward*), Stewart Harwood (*Tavern Keeper*), Carole Hayman (*Brothel Keeper*), Richard Moore (*Soldier*), Michael Goldie (*Porter*), Denyse Alexander (*Dressmaker*), Gabor Vernon (*Jeweler*), Robin Martin Oliver (*Singer*), Nicky Croydon (*Singing Maid*), John Abbott (*Manservant*), Jeanette Fox, Alison Woodgate, Philippa Luce, Eliza Kern, Krzysia Bialeska, Cryss Jean Healey (*Wedding Dancers*), Adele Anderson (*Lady Warwick*), Anna Gilbert (*Lady Robert Dudley*).

The superb Bonham Carter stars in this biographical look at the life of Lady Jane Grey, the 15-year-old Queen of England whose reign lasted only a scant nine days, but made her a legendary figure in English history. With the death of King Henry VIII in 1547, the throne has been passed on to his 16-year-old son, Edward VI (Saire), the favorite cousin of the young Lady Jane (Bonham Carter). Because of the imminent death of Saire, a successor has to be chosen, as he has no offspring to assume the throne. Fearing that the Protestant monarchy will fall into the hands of the rival Catholic faction, the Duke of Northumberland, Wood, puts into effect his plan—betrothing Bonham Carter, the daughter of the Duke and Duchess of Suffolk, to his son, Elwes. Bonham Carter, who is most concerned about her studies, has no desire to marry and refuses to accede to her parents' wishes. Elwes, a hard-drinking, irresponsible 17-year-old who spends time in brothels, is no more enthusiastic about the marriage than Bonham Carter. The dying Saire manages to persuade Bonham Carter to heed her parents' wishes. The marriage gets off to a rocky start when Elwes drinks himself into a stupor and passes out. Young, idealistic love soon overtakes the couple. Bonham Carter tells Elwes of her belief in Catholicism, denouncing the "rich-get-richer" stand of the Protestantism of the day. Together they dream of an England in which the beggars are restored to their rightful place as landowners; in which the church opens its riches to the people; and the shilling is again made of silver and worth a shilling.

Unaware of their plans, Wood persuades Saire, now on his deathbed, to rewrite his will and name Bonham Carter as his successor. When the king's death comes, Bonham Carter is, without explanation, whisked to a ceremony and crowned Queen of England. She refuses to wear the crown, but after being consoled by Elwes, she relents. The following morning Bonham Carter and Elwes present the members of the Royal Council with their plan for reform. The shocked Council does not know how to respond. In the meantime, Bonham Carter's cousin, the Catholic Princess Mary (Lapotaire), plans a takeover. After nine days of reform, Bonham Carter is forced out when her troops, led by the hated Wood, are unable to defeat Lapotaire's army. Bonham Carter and Elwes are imprisoned and Lapotaire is crowned queen, promising that she will pardon the lovers. Lapotaire, however, has problems of her own. She hopes to marry the Spaniard whom she loves, though her council is vehemently against the notion of a Spaniard being crowned king of England. In order to be with her love, Lapotaire strikes a deal which will send Bonham Carter and Elwes to the guillotine. Refusing to renounce their beliefs, the lovers are dragged off to the chopping block, with only the hope that they will be together in the eternal afterlife.

Gorgeously photographed and elegantly told, LADY JANE, if not faithful to the letter of history, remains faithful to the spirit of the young lovers. The lovers are presented as two souls who are disgusted at the way their elders have ruled the country, disillusioned by greed, vice, and manipulation. Fired with the burning desire to change the status quo, but unable to act against such a large system of corruption, the lovers can only dream of change. Their rebellious spirit is no different than that of youth in the 1960s. Whether it be England in 1553 or the

Chicago Democratic Convention in 1968, there will always be a faction of disillusioned youth who envision great changes in the way the world is run.

Bonham Carter and Elwes do not exist as stiff historical figures that one cannot relate to, but as real people. Because she is in love, Bonham Carter giggles—an expression of real joy that is rarely attributed to historical characters in films. We are not merely told that they are in love; we see it. They run through the grass,

they laugh, and, in one especially natural scene, the ticklish Bonham Carter squirms as Elwes gently kisses each of her toes. The film's finest scenes are when they are on the screen together, alone. Their first love scene is played with remarkable honesty, as Bonham Carter, who has just lost her virginity, learns that Elwes too was a virgin, having never actually had a prostitute as he had bragged. Another scene that is a joy to behold occurs at the lovers' dinner table as they drunkenly break expensive wine glasses while planning their reform.

The direction by Trevor Nunn, the noted stage director whose only other film credit is HEDDA—the 1975 adaptation of the play "Hedda Gabler" that starred Glenda Jackson—sparkles with sincerity and a clear understanding of his characters' youthful idealism. While the film is long, it is not overlong. Nunn rushes nothing for the sake of fitting a 90-minute time slot; instead he patiently tells the lovers' story. Yet, the film never feels as long as its 142-minute running time. Every frame of the film seems to fit without excess. Only Bonham Carter's execution scene feels unnecessary, not for aesthetic reasons, but for sentimental ones—the viewer already feels bad enough that this marvelous girl has been dethroned and is sentenced to be beheaded, without having to see the nape of her neck rest vulnerably on the chopping block.

The real success of the film belongs to Bonham Carter (also seen in 1986 in A ROOM WITH A VIEW) who, at age 20, effectively captures the air of youthfulness and, at the same time, carries herself as if she truly is a peeress of the realm. She has an unforgettable face that is reminiscent of the religious paintings of Sandro Botticelli and a presence that is seen only in the greatest of actresses—a quality of utmost professionalism that comes across as naturalism in its purest form. Unfortunately, she and this film were overlooked, which is no real surprise judging from the length and its historical subject matter. Lady Jane Grey's life was brought to the screen once before in the 1936 British film TUDOR ROSE (released in the U.S. as LADY JANE GREY) starring Nova Pilbeam and John Mills as the doomed lovers.

p, Peter Snell; d, Trevor Nunn; w, David Edgar (based on a story by Chris

Bryant); ph, Douglas Slocombe (Technicolor); m, Stephen Oliver; ed, Anne V. Coates; prod d, Allan Cameron; art d, Fred Carter, Martyn Hebert; set d, Harry Cordwell; cos, Sue Blane, David Perry; ch, Geraldine Stephenson, Sheila Falconer; makeup, Peter Frampton.

Historical/Drama/Biography   Cas.   (PR:C MPAA:PG-13)

L'AMANT MAGNIFIQUE†   (1986, Fr.) 100m G.P.F.I.–Soprofilms–C.N.C./
AAA Classic c (Trans: The Magnificent Lover)

Isabelle Otero *(Viviane)*, Hippolyte Girardot *(Vincent)*, Robin Renucci *(Antoine)*, Didier Agostini *(Luc)*, Daniel Jegou *(Marc)*, Michel Fortin, Corinne Cosson, Anna Azevedo, Patrick Perez, Renaud Isaac, Marie Guyonnet, Gregory Cosson.

Otero, who is married to wealthy horse-breeder Renucci, decides she is fed up with the union and runs off with Girardot, one of her husband's grooms. The lovers flee to a cottage owned by Otero's brother, but their idyll soon comes to an end. When Girardot's horse incurs an injury, he refuses to part with it. Instead Girardot takes the animal to a horse doctor, while Otero, knowing the affair is over, goes her own separate way. Director Issermann, a former cartoonist, shot this on location in Portugal.

p, Patrick Denauneux, Antonio Cunha Telles; d, Aline Issermann; w, Aline Issermann, Michel Dufresne; ph, Dominique Le Rigoleur (Eastmancolor); ed, Dominique Auvray; art d, Danka Semenovicz.

Drama   (PR:O MPAA:NR)

LAND OF DOOM zero   (1986) 87m Matterhorn Group c

Deborah Rennard *(Harmony)*, Garrick Dowhen *(Anderson)*, Daniel Radell *(Demister/Slater)*, Frank Garret *(Purvis)*, Richard Allen *(Halsey/Alfred)*, Akut Duz *(Orland)*, Bruno Chambon *(Man in Cabin)*, Fatosh Celik, Hulta Palanci, Ellen Caborn, Sondra Farrell *(Village Women)*, Keith Bordie, Robie Stein, Jason Koch, Joseph Costello *(Raiders)*, Sandy Goldman, Barbara Goldberg *(Raider's Girls)*, Richard D. Cade, Kin Jacobson, Rickey Curtis *(Bodyguards)*, Tom Vermig, Thomas Bordie, Carlo Goldsmith *(Village Fighters)*.

The worst sin that an action-adventure film—especially a science-fiction action-adventure—can commit is to be boring, and that's what's wrong with this tedious story of life after the big one goes off. Rennard and Dowhen team up to find the city over the mountains where everyone is nice, aiming to leave behind them the wasteland where the few communities are regularly pillaged by motorcycle-riding raiders commanded by Radell with a leather mask over most of his face. The two narrowly escape some cannibals with French accents, but are eventually captured by Radell's men, who plan to gang-rape her before skinning him alive. Fortunately, their friend Duz arrives in the nick of time with a bunch of little people in robes and cowls who lead the hero and heroine to safety after a few more fights. The end has the pair and Duz still walking across the desert and Radell still alive following them.

A sequel is left open, but appears unlikely, considering that this one never even got a theatrical release after being shot in 1984. Mostly inspired by MAD MAX and THE ROAD WARRIOR, this film has none of the manic energy that those films had. Dowhen and Rennard are unsympathetic leads, and no background on the two is ever given. Plot development is null, so the viewer is left with plenty of time to consider some of the details of life in the post-apocalyptic world such as "Who makes all this elaborate leather gear?" and "Where do they get the gas for their motorcycles?" The most nagging question is, "Why am I still watching the stupid movie?" One song, "Harmony's Land of Doom" (Carl Protho, performed by Jackie Lee).

p, Sunny Vest, Peter Maris; d, Peter Maris; w, Craig Rand (based on a story by Peter Kotis); ph, Orhan Kapai (Getty Color); m, Mark Governor; ed, Richard Casey; set d, Christopher Watson; cos, Oya Vest; m/l, Carl Protho; makeup, Monique Aznar.

Science Fiction/Adventure   Cas.   (PR:C MPAA:NR)

LANDSCAPE SUICIDE*½   (1986) 95m James Benning/Film-Maker's
Co-op c

Rhonda Bell *(Bernadette Protti)*, Elion Sucher *(Ed Gein)*.

An independent avant-garde work from former Midwesterner James Benning which explores the connection between environment and the killers that it sometimes produces. Benning deals specifically with two locales and their corresponding murderous offspring—the wealthy Southern California suburb which produced Bernadette Protti (played by Rhonda Bell), a high-school girl who stabbed a cheerleader to death, and the Wisconsin farm town which produced the infamous murderer Ed Gein (played by Elion Sucher), the man who served as model for the films PSYCHO, THE TEXAS CHAINSAW MASSACRE, and DERANGED.

The film is divided into four sections. The first begins in the wealthy California suburb where, in 1984, the teenage Protti—disturbed by her own unpopularity in high school—murdered a well-liked cheerleader on the front porch of the girl's home. In a series of long, mostly static takes, Benning shows us the neighborhood, the high school, the victim's house, the road that Protti and her victim drove before the murder. The second segment is a mock interview with the killer as she sits against a blank wall. Her interchange with the unseen interviewer is taken wholly from police and courtroom transcriptions. Also included in this section is an overlong, re-created scene of the victim listening to a record of the soundtrack from the play "Cats" while she sits on her bed and talks on the phone.

For the third segment, the scene shifts to the farmlands of Wisconsin—Gein's landscape. Again we see roads, fields, farmhouses (since Gein's farmhouse has been destroyed, this isn't shown), and the general store where he shot to death an older woman employee who, says Gein, resembled his mother. The final part has this simple-looking killer—played by Sucher—placed, again, in front of a blank wall. He demonstrates how he used the shotgun to kill the employee, and answers questions from the unseen interviewer (again taken from police records and court transcripts). Not included in Gein's interview (it doesn't pertain specifically to the murder of the store employee) is a photograph of some actual transcript pages which detail some of the more heinous crimes of the demented farmer—killing a number of women, skinning them, wearing their flesh, and constructing pieces of furniture from their bones. In contrast to the "Cats" sequence earlier, this half of the film has one of Gein's victims listening to Patti Page's version of "The Tennessee Waltz," a remarkable and touching sequence, which succeeds where the "Cats" sequence failed.

More concerned with the film's structure than documenting two murder cases, Benning presents a contention that a landscape produces and influences its inhabitants who, if they are turned into killers, can in turn destroy the landscape itself—in effect the landscape (or community) is killing itself. Unfortunately, these ideas are undeveloped. The lengthy duration of each of the film's shots serves more as a structural technique than an emotional one—the viewer thinks more about the technique than the landscape. This may be Benning's intent, though it seems rather self-defeating. The "interviews" are also problematic. Both Bell and Sucher are amateurish, though others would praise this quality as naturalistic. Only occasionally can viewers become engrossed in the interviews and forget that they are watching actors who are struggling to remember lines. Also frustrating is the Gein interview which is based on published transcripts (the local sheriff wrote an uninvolving book on the murders which includes the actual police interviews), thereby losing the interest of those viewers who have already read Gein's comments. According to Benning, the genesis of this project occurred when his 13-year-old daughter became disturbed by a 1984 article in *Rolling Stone* titled "Death Of A Cheerleader," which chronicled the Protti case. Benning drew a comparison to a murder case from his childhood, the 1957 Gein case, which invoked the same emotions that his daughter was feeling. The result is this very personal, though unsatisfying, picture. Benning, who has received a great deal of praise for such experimental works as 11 X 14 (1976) sparked the interest of New York critics, many of whom viewed the faults of LANDSCAPE SUICIDE and turned them into strengths, accusing detractors of being blinded by the urge for a Hollywood-style narrative. LANDSCAPE SUICIDE fails, not on narrative Hollywood terms, but on the experimental terms that Benning, as director, himself set up.

p,d,w,ph&ed, James Benning.

Crime   (PR:O MPAA:NR)

LAONIANG GOUSAO†   (1986, Hong Kong) c (Trans: Show)

Ye Dexian, Hou Xiaoxian, Ke Yizheng.

d, Ye Jianxing.

L'APACHE BIANCO†   (1986, It./Span.) Beatrice-Multivideo/Filmexport
Group c (Trans: White Apache)

Sebastian Harrison, Lola Forner, Albert Farley, Charlie Bravo, Cinzia De Ponti.

This Italian B-movie version of LITTLE BIG MAN opens as an Apache chief "adopts" a white baby, the child of a woman who died shortly after her wagon train was attacked by a gang of vicious bandits. The child grows up as the chief's son, but when he accidentally kills his adopted father's biological offspring, the boy leaves the tribe for the world of white men. He is repelled by this new life, however, and ultimately decides to return to his Indian home. Later, he finds an enemy from the white world trying to rape the Indian girl he loves. He stops the attack, leaving his nemesis permanently disfigured. The adopted Indian and his love go off together, and after some time, a child is born. When their hardened adversary returns with assorted cutthroats, the devoted couple is mercilessly killed. However, their child, hidden away in some nearby rocks, survives the attack and carries on his parents' legacy.

d, Vincent Dawn; w, Franco Prosperi (based on a story by Roberto Di Girolamo); ph, Julio Burgos, Luigi Ciccarese (Telecolor); m, Luigi Ceccarelli.

Western   (PR:O MPAA:NR)

LAPUTA†   (1986, Ger.) 90m Von Vietinghoff c

Sami Frey *(Paul)*, Krystyna Janda *(Malgortzata)*.

Frey is a Frenchman in West Berlin staying in a small apartment with Janda, his Polish lover. A photographer, Janda is currently developing some pictures she took on an assignment in Africa, all the while planning to return to her native land. A former paramour of hers is now a political prisoner in Poland and Janda longs to return to him. Frey, who has a wife and child in Paris, offers to go with her to Warsaw. He is willing to leave everything he has for a fresh start with Janda. The title comes from the mythical airborne city from Jonathan Swift's *Gulliver's Travels*, a book Frey refers to throughout the film. (In French.)

p, Johakim Von Vietinghoff; d&w, Helma Sanders-Brahms; ph, Eberhard Geick; m, Matthis Meyer; ed, Eva Schlensag.

Drama   (PR:O MPAA:NR)

LAS NOCHES DEL CALIFAS†   (1986, Mex.) 92m Producciones Filmica/
American General c (Trans: Caliph's Nights)

Hector Suarez *(Macho Prieto)*, Sasha Montenegro *(Marda)*, Manuel Capetillo *(Hugo/"El Conde")*, Pedro Weber *(Rengo)*, Sergio Ramos *(Muneca)*.

Suarez owns a Mexican nightspot, Las Noches del Califas. He meets Capetillo and develops a fatherly sort of affection for the younger man. Suarez has Capetillo come down to his club, then makes time with his younger friend's new girl. In the meantime, Montenegro, one of Las Noches' regulars, has some fun toying with Capetillo's feelings. Capetillo and his girl try to break free from this new life but find themselves trapped in a situation they can't control. However, Suarez is ultimately the story's victim, losing mastery over the young couple as well as control of himself. Montenegro is a popular Mexican box-office attraction, while Suarez is known in the country for both his acting skills and as host of a celebrated television program.

p, Morau Montes; d, Jose Luis Garcia Agraz; w, (based on the novel by Armando Ramirez); ph, Enrique Murillo; m, Son de Merengue; ed, Martin Luis.

Drama   **(PR:O MPAA:NR)**

LAST EMPEROR, THE†   (1986, Hong Kong/Chi.) 100m New Kwun
Lun–China International Television Corp./Southern c

Tony Leung *(Emperor Pu Yi)*, Pan Hung *(Li Shu Xian)*, Li Dien Lang *(Empress Wan Rung)*, Li Dien Xing *(Li Yu Qin)*.

The last stage of the life of China's final emperor, Pu Yi, is chronicled in this epic film biography. Leung is the one-time boy emperor who becomes a figurehead when the Japanese occupy China in 1931. At the end of WW II Leung is reduced from a life of wealth and privilege to the status of a peasant as as the country begins to undertake its Cultural Revolution. His world of numerous wives and concubines is forever gone and Leung prepares to marry a nurse at the story's close. THE LAST EMPEROR combines filmed scenes of epic grandeur and daily human existence with sepia-toned footage shot during China's Cultural Revolution. Pu Yi is to be the subject of another epic biography (also titled THE LAST EMPEROR) which director Bernardo Bertolucci began shooting with actor John Lone in 1987. (In Mandarin; English subtitles.)

d&w, Li Han Hsiang (based on "Pu Yi and I," "Pu Yi's Latter Life," and "Pu Yi's My Former Life" by Li Shu Xian).

Historical/Biography   **(PR:O MPAA:NR)**

LAST IMAGE, THE†   (1986, Fr./Algeria) 109m EMA –TF-1–SIA/ENADEC
c (LE DERNIERE IMAGE)

Veronique Jannot *(Claire Boyer)*, Merwan Lakhdar-Hamina *(Mouloud)*, Michel Boujenah *(Simon Attal)*, Hassan El Hassani *(Touhami)*, Jean Francois Balmer *(Miller)*, Malik Lakhdar-Hamina *(Bachir)*, Jean Bouise *(Langlois)*, Mustapha El Anka *(Kabrane)*, Jose Artur *(Forrestier)*, Mustapha Preur *(Boutaleb)*, Genevieve Mnich *(Mme. Lanier)*, Brigitte-Catillon *(Mme. Leguenne)*, Radid Fares *(Omar)*.

Merwan Lakhdar-Hamina is an Algerian adolescent who falls hopelessly in love with the French woman (Jannot) who comes to teach in his hometown during WW II. Other boys are smitten by her charms as well, and so is Boujenah, a Jewish colleague of Jannot. The story unfolds anecdotally but the film gradually develops a darker side. Trouble brews because Algeria is controlled by the French Vichy government and eventually the village is tainted by two murders. Later, Jannot and some friends sneak off to liberate Boujenah when he is scheduled for deportation because of his religion. Merwan Lakhdar-Hamina is the son of the film's writer/director, Mohamed Lakhdar-Hamina.

d&w, Mohamed Lakhdar-Hamina; ph, Youcef Sahraoui (Panavision, GTC Color); m, Phillippe Arthuys, Jean Paul Cara; ed, Youcef Tobni; art d, Mohamed Kessai; cos, Sylviane Combes, Mohamed Bouzit; makeup, Phuong Maittret.

Drama   **(PR:C MPAA:NR)**

LAST OF PHILIP BANTER, THE†   (1986, Span./Switz.) 103m
Tesauro-Banter c

Scott Paulin *(Philip Banter)*, Irene Miracle *(Elizabeth Banter)*, Gregg Henry *(Robert Prescott)*, Kate Vernon *(Brent)*, Tony Curtis *(Charles Foster)*, Jose Luis Gomez *(Dr. Monasterrio)*, Patty Shepard *(Alicia)*, Fernando Telletxea *(Enrique)*, Lola Bayo *(Carmen)*.

Paulin plays a man whose life is falling apart. His marriage with Miracle is on the rocks and his father-in-law-cum-employer Curtis is going to great lengths to agitate further Paulin's existence. One day Paulin finds some writing in his office that chronicles his tumultuous life. The film wavers between reality and what is found in this manuscript as Paulin grows more troubled about his life. Henry, a good friend, and his blonde sidekick, Vernon, also seem to be in on the supposed plot against Paulin as the line between fiction and fact continues to blur. Shot on location in Madrid, this is one of Curtis' sporadic and insignificant European ventures. (In English.)

p&d, Herve Hachuel; w, Alvaro De La Huerta, Herve Hachuel (based on a novel by John Franklin Bardin); ph, Ricardo Chara (Eastmancolor); m, Phil Marshall; ed, Eduardo Biurrun; art d, Jose Maria Tapiador; m/l, Gregg Henry.

Mystery/Thriller   **(PR:O MPAA:NR)**

LAST RESORT, THE zero   (1986) 80m Concorde-Cinema Group-Trinity c

Charles Grodin *(George Lollar)*, Robin Pearson Rose *(Sheila Lollar)*, John Ashton *(Phil Cocoran)*, Ellen Blake *(Dorothy Cocoran)*, Megan Mullally *(Jessica Lollar)*, Christopher Ames *(Brad Lollar)*, Scott Nemes *(Bobby Lollar)*, Jon Lovitz *(Bartender)*, Gerrit Graham *(Curt)*, Mario Van Peebles *(Pino)*, Brenda Bakke *(Veroneeka)*, William Bumiller *(Etienne)*, Phil Hartman *(Jean-Michel)*, Mimi Lieber *(Mimi)*, Steve Levitt *(Pierre)*, Zane Buzby *(Martine)*, Victor Rivers *(Klaus)*, Brett Clark *(Manuello)*, Ian Abercrombie *(Maitre d')*, Jacob Vargas *(Carlos)*, Irina Maleeva *(Maria)*, Eduardo Ricard *(Juan)*, Morgan Douglas *(Pilot)*, Joycee Katz *(Connie)*, David Mirkin *(Walter Ambrose)*, Buck Young *(Mr. Emerson)*, Twinkle Bayoud *(Herself)*, Wally Wharton *(Wanda)*, Patti R. Lee *(Patti)*, Chip Johannessen *(Firebreather)*, Gregory Michaels, Michael Markowitz, Sandy Ignon *(Guerrillas)*.

An unhappy man takes his family to a cheesy resort and consequently has a miserable time. On paper it looks like a bad idea for a comedy, but on film it looks even worse. Grodin is a Chicago furniture salesman who takes his clan

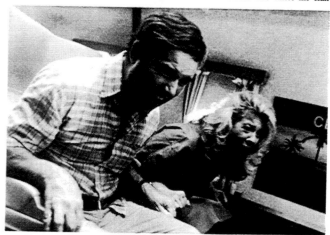

(wife Rose, daughter Mullally, and sons Ames and Nemes) to Club Sand, a sort of bargain-basement Club Med, in hopes of lifting their sagging Christmas spirits. After a turbulent flight to the island resort, the family settles into some less than ideal cottages. The plumbing is awful, the rooms are dirty, and the walls are paper thin. Grodin tries to encourage his family to enjoy Club Sand's many recreational activities and eventually they begin having a little fun. Nemes, his youngest boy, is put in the children's camp, run by the Nazi-like Buzby (who also directed this mess). Mullally gets involved with Bumiller, another of the club's many workers, while Ames takes up with Bakke. Rose also begins having fun, particularly when she indulges in chemical recreation. Grodin, in the meantime, is growing increasingly unhappy as he watches his family disintegrate around him. While foraging through some nearby woods, Grodin accidentally stumbles onto a band of guerrillas, which sends him scurrying back to Club Sand. He now begins questioning why the place is surrounded by barbed wire and soldiers. These inquiries are dismissed, and Grodin tries to enjoy camp activities. After participating in a series of humiliating games, Grodin is ready to up and leave, but

suddenly the guerrillas attack. Bumiller takes Mullally hostage, and this pushes the much-beleaguered Grodin over the edge. He grabs a gun, fires back, and then leads Camp Sand's employees and visitors in a battle against the revolutionaries. Having lived through this rather tumultuous week, Grodin decides the experience has been well worth the problems and begins talking happily about next year's vacation.

It may be alright for Grodin, but the same can't be said for anyone who has the patience to sit through LAST RESORT. This is an excruciatingly unfunny comedy that depends almost entirely on Grodin's humiliation to carry the flimsy premise. Normally a good comic actor (witness his supporting work in such films as HEAVEN CAN WAIT and REAL LIFE), Grodin creates a character that maintains a perpetual state of whining. He's unappealing to begin with and certainly doesn't get any more endearing as the story grinds on. The supporting cast isn't any better, a harmoniously unfunny group throughout. Van Peebles, as a flamboyant island native, is particularly annoying, while Lovitz shows none of the talent he usually displays on TV's "Saturday Night Live." Many of the gags are based on sexual situations, though surprisingly there's not too much naked flesh displayed. As always in films of this level, homosexuals are caricatures, not characters, and meant to be laughed at.

Zacharias and Buhai had previously scripted REVENGE OF THE NERDS, an enjoyable low-budget comedy, but their screenplay here is rudimentary at best. There's no sense of building humorous situations and the one-liners drop from actors' mouths like lead weights. Buzby, making her directorial debut, shows no aptitude for the medium whatsoever. Her work is lackluster, a simplistic job that doesn't go much beyond pointing the camera and shooting. This was 1986's second failed attempt at Caribbean resort comedy, following Robin Williams' tedious CLUB PARADISE. Songs include: "Step by Step" (Evan Archerd, Steve Nelson, performed by David Lasley), and "To Love in the Islands" (David Schwartz, David Lasley, performed by David Lasley).

p, Julie Corman; d, Zane Buzby; w, Steve Zacharias, Jeff Buhai; ph, Stephen Katz, Alex Nepomniaschy; m, Steve Nelson, Thom Sharp; ed, Gregory Scherick; prod d, Curtis A. Schnell; art d, Colin Irwin; set d, Douglas Mowat; cos, Julia Gombert; spec eff, Ronald O. Coe; ch, JoAnn Harris; m/l, Evan Archerd, Steve Nelson, David Lasley, David Schwartz; makeup, Robert Hallowell II; stunts, John "Bud" Cardos.

Comedy   Cas.   (PR:O MPAA:R)

LAST SONG†   (1986, Fr./Switz.) 90m La Cecilia c

Gabrielle Lazure, *(Julie)*, Scott Renderer *(Tommy)*, Anna Karina, Anouk Grinberg, Geoffrey Carey, Remy Kolpa, Michel Didym, Laurent Allaire, Steve Baes, Jimi Dragotta, Peter Smith.

A heavy dose of melodrama fills the screen in this murder mystery about Renderer, a young American from Hoboken, New Jersey, who heads for Paris in order to uncover the details of the death of his brother, a popular Bruce Springsteenesque rock star. Renderer finds that his brother lived life in the fast lane and was most likely murdered, but no one is willing to divulge any information—not chanteuse Karina; not his friends and former band members; and not his former American girl friend, Lazure. Renderer and Lazure eventually become lovers, as she is intrigued by the resemblance between him and her dead mate. Renderer then learns that his brother was carrying on with Lazure's transvestite brother, the son of a U.S. senator. Filmed in English by an American director with a script by Anna Karina, Jean-Luc Godard's former wife and leading lady.

p, Martine Marignac; d, Denis Berry; w, Denis Berry, Anna Karina; ph, Armand Marco; m, Stephane Vilar; ed, Jennifer Auge; prod d, Laurent Allaire; cos, Eve Marie Arnaul.

Crime   (PR:O MPAA:NR)

LAST SONG IN PARIS†   (1986, Hong Kong) 98m Chor Yuen/Golden
                                            Harvest-Gala c

Leslie Chung, Anita Miu, Wong Joe Ying, Cecilia Yip, Chu Kwong, Lam Hung.

Rock star Chung has a one-night stand with Mui, a dancer who performs in his show. The conceited young man cares little for her, though, as he really has his eyes on Ying, the mistress of his widowed father. Later, Chung allows Mui to perform a number in his show. She is an instant success and the narcissistic Chung angrily storms off to Europe to get away from the pressures in his life. He's soon broke and sick, though after meeting Yip, a young Vietnamese girl, his life takes a sudden turn. The two fall madly in love, get married, then go to work in a restaurant. When Yip abruptly passes away, Mui arrives to help the former rock idol (whom she still loves) get through his hard times. (In Cantonese; English subtitles.)

d, Chor Yuen.

Romance   (PR:C MPAA:NR)

L'AUBE†   (1986, Fr./Israel) 92m Swan-VNYL-Odessa c (Trans: The Dawn)

Philippe Leotard *(God)*, Redjep Mitrovitsa *(Elisha)*, Michael York *(Dawson)*, Christine Boisson *(Ilana)*, Serge Avedekion *(Yoav)*, David Burstein *(Dan)*, Paul Blain *(David)*.

It is the era when Britain still controls Israel and a group of resistance fighters captures an English officer. One man is assigned to kill the hostage at dawn. Throughout the night the appointed executioner grapples with moral issues, debating whether the intended victim's life has less importance than the group's overall goals. As he attempts to come to a decision, he reflects on his experience as a Holocaust survivor and on the convictions held by his comrades. The film's story is taken from an incident in a novel by Elie Wiesel.

p, Evelyne July; d, Miklos Jancso; w, Miklos Jancso (based on a novel by Elie Wiesel); ph, Armand Marco; m, Zoltan Simon; ed, Jean-Paul Vauban; set d, Yves Brocer; cos, Pierre Albert.

Drama   (PR:O MPAA:NR)

LE BONHEUR A ENCORE FRAPPE†   (1986, Fr.) 80m
                    Harvert-Chloe-CNC/Visa c (Trans: Happiness Strikes Again)

Jean-Luc Bideau *(Achille Pinglard)*, Michele Brousse *(Ginette Pinglard)*, Jean-

Noel Broute *(Adolf Pinglard)*, Caroline Appere *(Josette Pinglard)*, Denise Peron *(Grandma Pinglard)*, Marie-Christine Orry *(Ingrid Bermouthe)*, Raymond Aquilon *(Charles Delacroix)*, Valerie Schoeller *(Marie-Eve Etrecy)*.

This French black comedy uses an anecdotal style to present the adventures of a rather bizarre family of misfits. Bideau, the clan's head, is the foreman at an arms factory, while his wife, Brousse, works at a pornographic movie theater. To make some extra cash, the couple rent out their son's room while he is in the military, something that naturally upsets the boy after his discharge. In hopes of profiting further from their offspring, Bideau and Brousse get hold of a diary penned by their daughter, Appere. Constrained by a neck brace, and the human dumping ground for her family's troubles, Appere uses the journal as her only confidante. Her highly personal document is ultimately capitalized on by her parents when they publish its contents.

p, Patricia Fauron; d, Jean-Luc Trotignon; w, Jean-Luc Trotignon, Sylvie Chauvet, Gerard Krawczyk; ph, Michel Abramowicz (Eastmancolor); m, Jean-Claude Deblais; ed, Thierry Rouden; art d, Laurence Vendroux.

Comedy   (PR:O MPAA:NR)

LE COMPLEXE DU KANGOUROU†   (1986, Fr.) 84m
    Fildebroc-CAPAC-Investimage/AMLF c (Trans: The Kangaroo Complex)

Roland Giraud *(Loic)*, Clementine Celarie *(Claire)*, Zabou *(Odile)*, Stephane Freiss *(Bob)*, Francois Berleand *(Brother-in-law)*, Maaike Jansen *(Polish Neighbor)*, Maka Kotto *(Arthur)*, Stephane Duchemin *(Eric)*, Caroline Chaniolleau *(Jeanne)*, Robert Rimbaud *(Bank Manager)*, Marc Jolivet *(Fabrice)*.

Giraud, having caught the mumps at age 26, is now sterile and none too happy with his condition. He longs to have a child, a wish that seems to be fulfilled when he runs into Celari, an old girl friend. Celari has a 6-year-old son who bears a strong resemblance to Giraud, and the man believes the child is his. Complications arise when Giraud's current girl friend, Zabou, isn't thrilled at Celari's attempt to use her child to win back Giraud's heart. Giraud previously starred in the similarly themed hit French comedy THREE MEN AND A CRADLE.

p, Michelle de Broca, Paul Claudon; d, Pierre Jolivet; w, Pierre Jolivet, Olivier Schatzky, Henry Behar; ph, Christian Lamarque (Fujicolor); m, Serge Perathoner; ed, Jean-Francois Naudon; art d, Eric Simon.

Comedy   (PR:C-O MPAA:NR)

LE DEBUTANT†   (1986, Fr.) 88m T Films–Films A2/AMLF c (Trans: The
                                            Debutant)

Francis Perrin *(Francois Veber)*, Valerie Michel *(Christiane Jean)*, Julien Guiomar *(Lucien Berger)*, Dominique Lavanant *(Marguerite)*, Jean-Claude Brialy *(Willy)*, Francois Perrot *(Jean Rex)*, Philippe Lelievre, Christian Charmetant, Cecile Magnet, Valerie Rojan, Angela Torossian, Patricia Elig, Philippe Brizard, Henri-Jacques Huet, Xavier Saint-Macary, Maurice Baquet, Roger Dumas, Bertrand Lacy, Pierre-Yves Pruvost, Charlotte Walior.

Francis Perrin, a French funnyman, cowrote and starred in this comedy that reportedly is based on events in his own life. He plays a struggling actor trying to win a place on the stage as well as in actress Michel's heart. In the meantime Perrin plays the part of an amorous rover, bedding down with young ladies at the blink of an eye. Eventually, after several comic episodes, Perrin achieves success both on stage and with the lovely Michel.

p, Alain Terzian; d, Daniel Janneau; w, Daniel Janneau, Francis Perrin (based on a story by Francis Perrin); ph, Robert Fraisse (Agfacolor); m, Yves Gilbert; ed, Ghislaine Desjonqueres; art d, Dominique Andre.

Comedy   (PR:C-O MPAA:NR)

LE DECLIN DE L'EMPIRE AMERICAIN   (SEE: DECLINE OF THE
                                    AMERICAN EMPIRE, THE, 1986, Can.)

LE LIEU DE CRIME   (SEE: SCENE OF THE CRIME, 1986 Fr.)

LE MAL D'AIMER†   (1986, Fr./It.) 88m Sandor-FR3-Selena
    Audiovisuel-AFC-Cinema & Cinema-French Ministry of Culture-RAI-Radio
                Televisione Italiana/AAA c (Trans: The Malady of Love)

Robin Renucci *(Robert Briand)*, Isabelle Pasco *(Marie-Blanche)*, Carole Bouquet *(Eleonore)*, Piera Degli Esposti *(Therese)*, Erland Josephson *(Robert's Father)*, Andrzej Seweryn *(Trader)*.

Renucci is a 15th Century doctor who works as the director of a leper colony. As if this dreaded ailment isn't burden enough, Renucci must also deal with newly admitted patients who suffer from the then-mysterious disease syphilis. Pasco is one of these so afflicted patients, a beautiful young woman brought to the settlement though she displays none of the malady's characteristics. Renucci comes to Pasco's defense and eventually falls in love with her. Though he risks condemnation by his peers, as well as the possibility of falling victim to syphilis himself, Renucci openly resists society's constraints by leaving his position to be with Pasco. Director Treves was a former assistant to Italian filmmakers Vittorio de Sica and Luchino Visconti.

d, Giorgio Treves; w, Vincenzo Cerami, Pierre Dumayet (based on a story by Vincenzo Cerami); ph, Giuseppe Ruzzolini (Eastmancolor); m, Egisto Macchi; ed, Carla Simoncelli; art d, Lorenzo Baraldi; cos, Jost Jakob; makeup, Claudia Reymond-Shone.

Drama   (PR:O MPAA:NR)

LE MATOU†   (1986, Can.) 135m Justine Heroux-Vivafilm c (Trans: The Alley Cat)

Serge Dupire, Jean Carmet, Monique Spaziani.

A man and his wife are restaurant proprietors who employ a temperamental French chef. They hook up with a strange man who harbors mysterious supernatural powers and a street urchin who cares only for his pet cat.

d, Jean Beaudin (based on the novel by Yves Beauchemin).

Drama   **(PR:C-O MPAA:NR)**

LE MINIERE DEL KILIMANGIARO†   (1986, It.) Scena/Filexport Group c (Trans: The Mines of Kilimanjaro)

Cristopher Connelly, Tobias Hoesl, Elena Pompei, Gordon Mitchell, Matteo Corsini, Francesca Ferre.

In 1934, after the Nazis have gained power, an American university professor is murdered. It seems he knows the location of an African diamond mine and has been killed by Nazi sympathizers fearful that he will reveal this secret to U.S. authorities. One of the late professor's students attempts to solve the mystery behind this murder. He goes to Africa, where several people make attempts on his life. The student later joins a team of English astronomers. He learns their expedition is merely a front for British intelligence, which also has an interest in the hidden diamond mine. The inquiring pupil and the daughter of one agent-cum-scientist, are kidnaped by African natives but manage to escape their captors. The couple is then taken hostage by Nazi forces, and the student discovers that one local tribe has been storing explosives with the intent of destroying the mine. After saving the girl, the plucky pupil knocks off a few Nazi guards, then tosses a flaming torch into a dynamite-packed well. Of course it explodes and he barely escapes with his life. After this harrowing adventure, the student and the agent's daughter realize their escapades have created an unexpected romance.

p, Augusto Caminito; d&w, Mino Guerrini; ph, Sandro Mancori; m, Luigi Ceccarelli.

Action/Adventure   **(PR:O MPAA:NR)**

LE MOME†   (1986, Fr.) 100m Orly-Sara/AMLF c (Trans: The Kid)

Richard Anconina (Willie), Ambre (Jo), Michel Duchaussoy (Darmines), Georges Montillier (Rene), Yan Epstein (Michel Charki), Thierry de Carbonnieres (Jean Pierre Charki), Kamel Cherif (The Tunisian).

Anconina is a Paris cop who becomes obsessed with the mulatto prostitute working for a pair of Lebanese gunrunners he is pursuing. He sets out to rescue her, but she runs away several times before he finally breaks through her self-protective shell and she falls for him.

p, Jean-Jose Richer; d, Alain Corneau; w, Alain Corneau, Christian Clavier; ph, Jean-Francis Gondre (Fujicolor); ed, Marie-Josephe Yoyotte; m/l, Otis Redding; stunts, Philippe Guegan.

Crime/Drama   **(PR:O MPAA:NR)**

LE PALTOQUET†   (1986, Fr.) 92m Elefilm-Erato-Soprofilms-TF 1-Sofia-Sofima-Centre National de la Cinematographie/AAA c (Trans: The Nonentity)

Fanny Ardant (Lotte), Daniel Auteuil (The Journalist), Richard Bohringer (The Doctor), Philippe Leotard (The Honorable Tradesman), Jeanne Moreau (The Proprietress), Michel Piccoli (The Nonentity), Claude Pieplu (The Professor), Jean Yanne (The Commissioner), An Luu (The Heiress).

An Agatha Christie-type murder mystery which is photographed stylistically in a single cafe studio set and features some of France's most popular actors. The cafe is run by Piccoli and Moreau and is frequented by Bohringer, Auteuil, Leotard, and Pieplu, four locals who come to play cards, and by a mysterious nymphomaniac, Ardant, who is the object of everyone's desire. When a murder occurs nearby, detective Yanne conducts his investigation with an eye that suspiciously examines all the cafe's customers. Even with the popular appeal of the cast and the name value of Deville (who was awarded the 1985 Cesar for Best Director for PERIL), the quirky LE PALTOQUET made little more than a dent in the French box office. Jeanne Moreau, however, did rate a Cesar nomination for Best Supporting Actress.

p, Rosalinde Damamme; d&w, Michel Deville (based on the novel, On a Tue Pendant L'Escale by Franz-Rudolf Falk); ph, Andre Diot (Cinemascope, Eastmancolor); m, Anton Dvorak, Leos Janacek; ed, Raymonde Guyot; art d, Thierry Leproust; cos, Cecile Balme; makeup, Ronaldo Ribeiro de Abreau.

Mystery/Comedy   **(PR:C MPAA:NR)**

LE PASSAGE†   (1986, Fr.) 79m Adel-LM/UGC c (Trans: The Passage)

Alain Delon (Jean Diaz), Christine Boisson (Catherine Diaz), Alain Musy (David Diaz), Jean-Luc Moreau (Patrick).

Delon makes a bid to change his tough-guy screen image here, playing a filmmaker whose plans to make an antiwar cartoon are abruptly stopped when he is killed in a car crash. Death is not the end, though, and Delon wakes up to find a cowled Death standing over him, demanding that he make a film showing the ultimate destruction Death is planning or he will kill the son who survived the accident but lies comatose.

p, Alain Delon, Francis Lalanne; d&w, Rene Manzor; ph, Andre Diot

(Eastmancolor); m, Jean-Felix Lalanne; ed, Roland Baubeau; art d, Emmanuel de Chauvigny; spec eff (makeup), Christopher Tucker; anim, Rene Manzor.

Fantasy   **(PR:C MPAA:NR)**

LE RAYON VERT   (SEE: SUMMER, 1986, Fr.)

LEFT ALONE   (SEE: CABARET, 1986, Jap.)

LEGAL EAGLES*   (1986) 114m Northern Lights/UNIV c

Robert Redford (Tom Logan), Debra Winger (Laura Kelly), Daryl Hannah (Chelsea Deardon), Brian Dennehy (Cavanaugh), Terence Stamp (Victor Taft), Steven Hill (Bower), David Clennon (Blanchard), John McMartin (Forrester), Roscoe Lee Browne (Judge Dawkins), Jennie Dundas (Jennifer Logan), Christine Baranski (Carol Freeman), Sara Botsford (Barbara), David Hart (Marchek), James Hurdle (Sebastian Deardon), Gary Klar (Hit Man), Christian Clemenson (Clerk), Bart Burns (Judge), Bruce French, Ken Kliban, Debra Stricklin, Ron Foster, Rudy Willrich, Gabrielle DeCuir (Reporters), Lynn Hamilton (Doreen), Paul Jabara (Taxi Driver), Chevi Colton (Short Lady), Annie Abbott, Kristine Sutherland (Secretaries), Everett Quinton (Attorney), Peter Boyden (McHugh), Thomas Barbour (Bored Judge), Mary Alison Griffin (Young Chelsea), Vincent Guastaferro, Burke Byrnes, Kevin Hagan (Cops), Robert Benedetti (Bearded Speaker), Grant Heslov (Usher), Robert Curtis Brown (Roger), Brian Doyle-Murray (Shaw), Shannon Wilcox (Mrs. Williams), Charles Brown (Real Cavanaugh), Jay Thomas (Waiter in Restaurant), Alex Nevil (Messenger), Lou Cutell (Kapstan), Olivia Ward (Nanny), Duitch Helmer (Lady in Gallery), John Marion (Auctioneer), Barbara Pallenberg (Assistant to Auctioneer), Liz Sheridan (Little Old Lady), Michael Anthony (Courtroom Spectator).

Redford, in a long-awaited return to humor, is a hotshot assistant district attorney who has been given the task of prosecuting spaced-out Hannah. She is the daughter of a long-dead artist who has been accused of an attempt to steal a painting done by her father, who perished in a fire when she was only 8 years of age. Hannah is being defended by Winger, a tough, no-nonsense attorney whom the court appointed because Hannah has no money to hire her own legal aid. Winger is reputed to be a woman who will stop at nothing to achieve her goals and supposedly once put a pet dog on the witness stand during a case. Much of

her expertise is only talked about and seldom seen. Redford is fascinated by Hannah and wants to know more about her. In a nonsensical performance-art set piece (devised by Hannah, Lin Hixon, and Arnold Glimcher) she works out her memory of what happened that night when her father burned to death. Her contention is that all of the paintings which supposedly burned that night were not burned. It was an insurance fire and the art survived. (Arsonists and lovers of the flame will enjoy this movie as it has several fires to delight their eyes.)

Winger and Redford are supposed to have the chemistry of dueling lawyers like Katharine Hepburn and Spencer Tracy in ADAM'S RIB but they don't even have biology, much less chemistry. The logic holes in the movie are enough to drive a forklift through—which is exactly what Redford and Winger drive in a later scene. Redford winds up sleeping with Hannah after she seduces him. (He's up late anyhow because he has insomnia and spends many hours tap dancing in his flat to try and get to sleep. We kid you not.) At the same time, one of the art dealers in the case is being murdered and Hannah becomes the suspect. When she is found in the sack with the man who was supposedly prosecuting, he loses his job. Now unemployed, Redford is persuaded by Winger to join forces on the other side of the courtroom and he turns up as her partner to help Hannah's defense. So far, just a few lapses from the script of Jim Cash and Jack Epps, Jr. (the teacher-and-student team who write 2000 miles apart by modem and had great success this same year with TOP GUN after striking out with several other scripts). The movie now launches into a hell-bent thriller in and around the New York art scene. (This was far better plumbed in a Lawrence Sanders novel which had a similar theme.) One of the largest holes in the story is about the charred art. If, in fact, the paintings survived and were paid for by the insurance company, how are they to be sold now without letting the cat out of the bag? Stamp is the villainous art gallery owner (everyone in the Manhattan art business seems to be a cad or worse) and when he smells Redford and Winger on his trail, he goes to the warehouse where he keeps his financial records (they've been subpoenaed) and blows up the place, never mind the fact that he is also destroying some fine art work he has there for safekeeping.

Along the way, we meet a mean-spirited millionaire, McMartin, and 1986's John Lithgow, Brian Dennehy, who has supported more stars than Maidenform bras. Redford is properly slick and the script takes the opportunity to show him as vulnerable, klutzy, and just one of the guys. The movie had been written as a "buddy" piece for Dustin Hoffman and Bill Murray, but when Hoffman accepted another "buddy" piece with Warren Beatty in ISHTAR, Murray lost interest and the script was rewritten to make it a romantic comedy. (What seemed

to be left over from the other script was Redford's dalliance with Hannah. Another man in the role of the opposing attorney would have responded the way Winger does. But Winger, as a woman and as a person who is falling in love with Redford, does not have a real feminine reaction to what's happened.) Redford's first comedic work was on Broadway in "Sunday in New York," then "Barefoot in the Park," and he is excellent at it, provided he gets the right material. But Epps and Cash are not Neil Simon or Norman Krasna and what is meant to be brittle dialog becomes downright breakable. At a cost of around $30 million, this picture needed to make a fortune to break even. There was great attention to detail and Redford and Winger even attended some trials so they would know how to comport themselves in a courtroom. It was made in eight weeks around Manhattan in locations ranging from 57th street (where the art gallery was) to the Supreme Court of New York, with stops at fashionable Sutton Place and Sotheby's and various precinct houses of the N.Y.P.D. There's no mistaking that this movie owes much to CHARADE, ADAM'S RIB, HOW TO STEAL A MILLION, THE 39 STEPS, and any number of other Hitchcock films. But all of the mentioned had good scripts. This doesn't. The lack of "legs" (staying power) on this movie, coupled with the abysmal failure of HOWARD THE DUCK, must have contributed to the resignation of Frank Price as Universal's film chief. The denouement is a cheat but we won't tell you who the real brains is because you might want to rent the tape.

Perhaps the most disappointing moments of the film are those with Hannah. After a smashing performance in SPLASH, she seems to be sleepwalking through this one, the same way she did in CLAN OF THE CAVE BEAR. There was no sensuality, no warmth, and none of the humor she showed she had under Ron Howard's guidance. Hannah is the stepdaughter of Chicago real estate tycoon Jerry Wexler and thus the niece of Oscar-winning cinematographer and director Haskell Wexler as well as actor/producer Yale Wexler (STAKEOUT ON DOPE STREET). She is capable of much more than she showed in this. The most pleasing aspect of the film was the presence of millions of dollars worth of important art. Would that they could have trained their cameras on the artwork rather than on some of the actors. The artists represented included Pablo Picasso, Joan Miro, Alberto Giacometti, Alexander Calder, Jean Dubuffet, Andy Warhol, Saul Steinberg, Kenny Scharf, Jim Dine, Willem De Kooning, Roy Lichtenstein, Robert Motherwell, Louise Nevelson, and many more. The paintings and sculpture were lent by some of the most prestigious galleries and private collectors, some of whom included Cary Grant, Dr. Armand Hammer, and David Wolper. LEGAL EAGLES is a visual treat, cost a great deal of money, and looks it. The problems arise when people speak and that should never happen as this is a talkie. Music included "Magic Carpet Ride" (Moreve Rushton, John Kay, performed by Steppenwolf), "Good Lovin' " (Rudy Clark, Arthur Resnick, performed by the Rascals), "Put Out the Fire," (Daryl Hannah, performed by Daryl Hannah), and "Love Touch" (Mike Chapman, Gene Black, Holly Knight, performed by Rod Stewart).

p&d, Ivan Reitman; w, Jim Cash, Jack Epps, Jr. (based on a story by Ivan Reitman, Jim Cash, Jack Epps, Jr.); ph, Laszlo Kovacs (Panaflex, Technicolor); m, Elmer Bernstein; ed, Sheldon Kahn, Pem Herring, William Gordean; prod d, John DeCuir; art d, Ron Hobbs; set d, Peter S. Kelly, Carlos Cerrada, Steve Sardanis; cos, Albert Wolsky; spec eff, Boss Film Corp.; m/l, Moreve Rushton, John Kay, Rudy Clark, Arthur Resnick, Daryl Hannah, Mike Chapman, Gene Black, Holly Knight; makeup, Gary Liddiard; stunts, Alan R. Gibbs.

Comedy/Thriller (PR:C MPAA:PG)

LEJANIA† (1986, Cuba) 83m ICAIC/MECLA c (AKA: THE PARTING OF THE WAYS; Trans: Distance)

Veronica Lynn *(Susana)*, Jorge Trinchet *(Reinaldo)*, Isabel Santos *(Ana)*, Beatriz

Valdes *(Aleida)*, Monica Guffanti, Mauricio Renterio, Roselia Blain, Polcma Abraham.

Ten years after abandoning her 16-year-old juvenile-delinquent son to leave Havana for Miami, Lynn returns for a visit, weighed down with armloads of hard-to-get gifts. Her son, Trinchet, is now a respectable husband and father, however, and he refuses to be impressed, though it is his wife Valdes who finally has to tell Lynn off. Also along is Santos, a young woman who has fully acclimated to life in New York and who is baffled by the land where she was born. The theme is the contrast between those who opted for the easy life and went north and those who remained behind and built a strong Cuba, and things don't look good for reconciliation, according to writer-director Diaz.

p, Humberto Hernandez; d&w, Jesus Diaz; ph, Mario Garcia Joya (ICAIC Color); ed, Justo Vega; set d&cos, Jose M. Villa.

Drama (PR:A MPAA:NR)

LEL HAB KESSA AKHIRA† (1986, Egypt) 129m El Alamia/TV–Cinema ATV c (Trans: Broken Images)

Yehia El Fakharani *(Rifat)*, Maali Zayed *(Salva)*, Tahia Karioka *(Rifat's Mother)*, Ahmed Rateb, Rohia Khalid, Abdel Aziz Makhiou, Abdel Hafiz El Tatawi, Abla Kamel, Fatma Mahmoud.

The simple lives of the inhabitants of a poor village on an island in the middle of the Nile are the subject of this film, with El Fakharani a sick man who tries to reconcile his dowry-less wife and his traditional, superstitious old mother before he dies.

d&w, Rafaat El Mihi; ph, Mahmoud Abdel Sameii; m, Mohamed Hilal; ed, Said El Sheik; set d, Maher Abdel Mour.

Drama (PR:A MPAA:NR)

LEONSKI INCIDENT, THE (SEE: DEATH OF A SOLDIER, 1986, Aus.)

LEPOTA POROKA† (1986, Yugo.) 113m Centar c (Trans: The Beauty of Vice)

Mira Furlan *(Jaglika)*, Miodrag Karadzic *(Luka)*, Petar Bozovic *(George)*, Mira Banjac, Alain Nouny, Ines Kotman *(Nudists)*.

A straitlaced couple from the Montenegran hinterlands come to live with the woman's godfather, the operator of a seacoast nudist colony for tourists. She is put to work as a maid there, and finds herself carried away with admiration for a golden-looking young British couple. Eventually, she allows herself to be seduced by the pair. When she confesses her transgression to her husband, he kills himself.

d&w, Zivko Nikolic; ph, Radoslav Vladic; m, Zoran Simjanovic; ed, Zoltan Vaghen; art d, Miodrag Miric.

Drama/Comedy (PR:O MPAA:NR)

LES CLOWNS DE DIEU† (1986, Fr.) 100m L'Atelier 8–Gazan c (Trans: The Clowns of God)

Daniel Kenigsberg *(Melies)*, Jean-Paul Roussillon, Jean-Roger Milo, Nathalie Schmidt.

A bizarre portrait of the underside of Paris life that centers on Kenigsberg, a drunken would-be filmmaker who falls in love with an escaped lunatic. Numerous other odd characters dot the scene, including a figure of death who cruises the streets on roller skates with a flowing black cape and a skull on his chest.

p, Dolly Schmidt; d&w, Jean Schmidt; ph, Pierre Boffety; m, Mikis Theodorakis; ed, Noun Serra; art d, Emmanuel Maintifneux.

Fantasy (PR:O MPAA:NR)

LES FRERES PETARD† (1986, Fr.) 90m Films Christian Fechner–Optimistes–A2 J J Fechner–GAU c (Trans: The Joint Brothers)

Gerard Lanvin *(Manu)*, Jacques Villeret *(Momo)*, Michel Galabru *(Mr. Javert)*, Josiane Balasko *(Aline)*, Valerie Mairesse *(Brigitte)*, Daniel Russo, Bruce Johnson, Philippe Khorsand, Raymond Aquilon, Jean-Paul Bonnaire, Dominique Lavanant, Alain Pacadis, Cheik Doukoure.

Lanvin and Villeret are a pair of lowlifes who stumble on a lucrative new profession, dope dealing, then spend their time planning to make the really big score and retire. The film's treatment of drug dealers came under criticism in France, which was then in the midst of a government anti-drug campaign.

d, Herve Palud; w, Herve Palud, Igor Aptekman; ph, Jean-Jacques Tarbes (Eastmancolor); m, Jacques Delaporte; ed, Roland Baubeau; art d, Jean Maussion; cos, Martine Rapin; makeup, Eric Muller; tech adv, Jean-Paul Meurisse.

Comedy (PR:C MPAA:NR)

LES FUGITIFS† (1986, Fr.) 87m Fideline–D.D.–Efve–Orly/GAU c (Trans: The Fugitives)

Gerard Depardieu *(Jean Lucas)*, Pierre Richard *(Francois Pignon)*, Jean Carmet *(Mr. Martin)*, Michel Blanc *(Dr. Bourdarias)*, Maurice Barrier *(Commissioner Duroc)*, Jean Benguigui *(Labib)*, Roland Blanche *(Idriss)*, Anais Bret *(Jeanne)*.

The third comic teaming of Depardieu and Richard under the directorial hand of Veber, who previously scored big at the box office with LA CHEVRE and LES COMPERES. In keeping with the characters of the previous two films,

Depardieu is handsome and sensible, while Richard is wimpy and neurotic. Both men, however, have a sensitive streak which bonds them through whatever trying times they are up against. This time out, Depardieu is a seasoned ex-convict just released from prison who—unfortunately for him—opens a bank account in a bank which the desperate, unemployed Richard is about to rob. When the robbery attempt gets botched, like everything else Richard attempts, Depardieu is taken hostage. The police think that Depardieu is an accomplice, forcing him and Richard to flee. Not content with standard car chases and comic gags, Veber brings his two characters together and forces them to communicate. Depardieu initially plans to dump Richard, but grows attached to him as a friend, as well as to Richard's autistic 6-year-old daughter, who struggles to utter her first words—a plea for Depardieu to stay. Veber, who has proven his directorial skill with his previous two pictures, received a Cesar nomination for Best Screenplay for LES FUGITIFS, while Jean Carmet received one for Best Supporting Actor as a senile veterinarian. LES FUGITIFS, which didn't open in Paris until mid-December, was a smash at the box-office and, in that short amount of time, ranked as the fifth most popular French film of the year.

p, Jean-Jose Richer; d&w, Francis Veber; ph, Luciano Tovoli (Eastmancolor); m, Vladimir Cosma; ed, Marie-Sophie Dubus; art d, Gerard Daoudal.

Comedy/Drama/Crime   **(PR:A MPAA:NR)**

LES LONGS MANTEAUX†   (1986, Fr./Arg.) 106m Les Films de la
Tour–TF1–AKF/Fechner–GAU c (Trans: The Long Coats)

Bernard Giraudeau *(Murat)*, Claudia Ohana *(Julia)*, Robert Charlebois *(Laville)*, Federico Luppi *(Garcia)*, Richard Darin *(Lama)*, Lito Cruz *(Miguel)*, Franklin Caicedo *(Vinchina)*, Victor Laplace *(Cesario)*, Oscar Martinez *(Figueras)*, Raul Rizzo *(Zarate)*, Vincente Buono *(Ruiz)*, Juan Palomino *(Juy)*, Dario Grandinetti *(Gayata)*.

A famous Argentine novelist is freed from a Bolivian prison and put on a train back to Argentina, but a renegade Argentine general has taken an oath to kill him. The general's men take over the town and wait for the train, while geologist Giraudeau tries to rally the townspeople against them.

p, Adolphe Viezzi, Henri Lassa; d, Gilles Behat; w, Jean-Louis Leconte, Gilles Behat (based on the novel by G.J. Arnaud); ph, Ricardo Aronovich (Fujicolor); m, Jean-Francois Leon; ed, Genevieve Vaury; m/l, Daniel Lavoie.

Drama   **(PR:C MPAA:NR)**

L'ETAT DE GRACE†   (1986, Fr.) 89m Mod Film–Selena Audiovisuel/AAA
c (Trans: State of Grace)

Nicole Garcia *(Florence Vannier)*, Sami Frey *(Antoine Lombard)*, Pierre Arditi *(Jean-Marc Vannier Buchet)*, Philippe Leotard *(Pierre-Julien)*, Dominique Labourier *(Angele Lombard)*.

Romance blossoms across ideological lines when a minor cabinet official of the Socialist government (Frey) and a married, conservative businesswoman (Garcia) fall in love.

p, Jacques Kirsner; d, Jacques Rouffio; w, Jacques Kirsner, Jacques Rouffio; ph, Dominique Chapuis (Fujicolor); m, Philippe Sarde; ed, Anna Ruiz; art d, Jean-Jacques Caziot; m/l, Philippe Sarde, Pierre Perret; makeup, Judith Gayo.

Romance/Drama   **(PR:O MPAA:NR)**

LETHAL   (SEE: KGB—THE SECRET WAR, 1986, US)

LET'S HOPE IT'S A GIRL†   (1986, Fr./It.) 121m Clemi/Original c
(SPERIAMO CHE SIA FEMMINA)

Liv Ullmann *(Elena)*, Philippe Noiret *(Count Leonardo)*, Bernard Blier *(Uncle Gughi)*, Catherine Deneuve *(Aunt Claudia)*, Giuliana De Sio *(Francesca)*, Athina Cenci *(Fosca)*, Lucrezia Lante Della Rovere *(Bambina)*, Giuliano Gemma *(Guido Nardoni)*, Stefania Sandrelli *(Gym Owner)*, Paolo Hendel.

An international cast makes up an extended family in this women-talking drama. Ullmann lives on a farm raising her two daughters and the daughter of her actress sister, Deneuve. Although Ullmann is separated from her husband Noiret, he comes around hoping that she will finance a new scheme, and then drives his car off a cliff. After some sibling backbiting, Ullmann decides to sell the farm to pay off a loan Noiret got from his mistress. At the last minute she changes her mind and everyone comes to live together in the country, including the now-pregnant daughter, De Sio, who evokes the gender-discriminating hopes expressed by the title.

p, Giovanni Di Clemente; d, Mario Monicelli; w, Leo Benvenuti, Piero De Bernardi, Suso Cecchi d'Amico, Tullio Pinelli, Jacqueline Lefevre, Mario Monicelli; ph, Camillo Bazzoni; m, Nicola Viovanni; ed, Ruggero Mastroianni; art d, Enrico Fiorentini.

Drama/Comedy   **(PR:O MPAA:NR)**

LETTER TO BREZHNEV***½   (1986, Brit.) 94m Yeardream–Film
Four–Palace/CIRCLE c

Alfred Molina *(Sergei)*, Peter Firth *(Peter)*, Margi Clarke *(Teresa)*, Tracy Lea *(Tracy)*, Alexandra Pigg *(Elaine)*, Susan Dempsey *(Girl in Yellow Pedal Pushers)*, Ted Wood *(Mick)*, Carl Chase *(Taxi Driver)*, Robbie Dee *(Charlie)*, Sharon Power *(Charlie's Girl Friend)*, Syd Newman *(Dimitri)*, Eddie Ross *(Rayner)*, Wendy Votel, Jeanette Votel *(Girls on Bus)*, Mandy Walsh *(Mother)*, Angela Clarke *(Josie)*, Joey Kaye *(Father)*, Frank Clarke *(Vinny)*, Paul Beringer *(Boy at

Party)*, Ken Campbell *(Reporter)*, Neil Cunningham *(Foreign Office Official)*, John Carr *("Sweaty Arse")*.

LETTER TO BREZHNEV is a low-budget gem. The price of making this entire movie was only slightly more than what was paid for flowers on Mike Nichols' HEARTBURN, an alleged comedy that doesn't come within miles of the freshness, audacity, and sheer insouciance of this picture, which took about three weeks to shoot on a budget of $70,000! Frank Clarke wrote a play in a few weeks, put it on for a short run in September, 1983 at Liverpool's Unity Theatre, and that served as the basis for this picture, which is almost an incestuous project insofar as Clarke's sister, Margi, is one of the stars—and their good friend Bernard is it, with their equally good pal Goddard as the coproducer. They all met while working on a TV soap opera called "Brookside" and decided to join forces for an attempt at the big screen.

Clarke and Pigg (that will *have* to be changed if she comes to the U.S.) are best pals. Clarke works in a frozen-chicken factory stuffing innards into the birds after she's pulled them out and wrapped them in cellophane. Pigg is unemployed, as are many thousands in the depressed area of Liverpool. Firth and Molina are two Russian sailors about to land at Liverpool for some R&R and when Molina learns the name of the town, he speaks just about the only words we understand as he says "Leeverpool, Bittles, ahhhh." Work has ended for Clarke and the

women decide to go out on the town for the little time they have before the pubs close. At a local spot, Clarke steals the wallet out of a Cypriot's pocket and the two girls search for someplace to spend their money. They enter an upscale disco, where they meet Firth and Molina. Clarke likes Molina. She doesn't want to talk, just wants to have some sexual dalliance. (This is the story of her life, as she states later, admitting she has no formal education but she has "a degree in men.") With the money she stole, Clarke rents a pair of rooms at a local hotel, drags Molina into hers, and the two have at it. The sweeter, gentler Pigg spends the evening talking to Firth. Both are terminally romantic and in the course of the nonstop conversation, they decide that they are in love and would like to get married.

The next morning, the women see the men off at the docks (in a wonderful scene as Firth tosses his hat back at Pigg so she'll have something of his). Time drags by and Pigg is writing letters to Firth. His letters come back censored. Pigg wonders if Firth is married and Clarke mentions that since she's had her share of married men, she knows better than anyone how they behave, and she assures Pigg that Firth is single. Clarke suggests that Pigg petition the Russian government about her joining her lover, which she does in a letter to the Soviet chief. Amazingly, she receives a one-way ticket to Moscow. The moment this gets out among her family, friends, the newspapers, and the official arm of the government, everyone is opposed to the idea. The local consul says that since she is collecting compensation from the government, doing something like this might cause her to lose her dole, and that she is surely going to lose her "freedom" if she leaves Liverpool in favor of the Soviet Union. Pigg's response is a shrug, it can't be any worse than the way she's living now and the way she will have to live forever unless she leaves. Pigg makes the decision and departs, looking forward to being reunited with Firth and whatever her new life brings.

A simple story on the surface, but the details are many and the individual moments are joyous. It's a mature picture, and there is no stinting on the raunchy and often incomprehensible Liverpudlian dialog. It's unabashedly romantic but not sentimental. When Pigg is told by a nerd in government that Firth is married, her love falters slightly, but she has faith and presses on. Firth (EQUUS) is the only marquee name but we wonder how many people looking at the newspaper will say "Hey look, here's the new Peter Firth movie at the Odeon, let's skip dinner and go see it." Pigg makes an auspicious feature debut here, and if she can ever master speaking English without an accent, she could be a star. Clarke already had lots of TV experience as a punk comedienne named "Margox." The wonder of this movie is not that it was made; many low-budget movies are actually finished. The amazing part is that it's so good. Sure, there are amateurish moments here and there, and one wishes that the production values were better, but they all fade away when one considers the overall impact of the love story. Raw language, sexual situations, and some nudity all contribute to making this merit the R rating it received.

Clarke seems to be the person for whom EDUCATING RITA was written and her own brother admits that her character is really based on her persona, sort of a "tart with a heart." Lots of music in the movie including "Lockets and Stars" (performed by Margi Clarke), "Wild Party" (performed by A Certain Ratio), "Hit That Perfect Beat, Boy" (performed by Bronski Beat), "Heavens Above" (performed by the Communards featuring Jimmy Somerville), "Mercy" (performed by Carmel), "Bring it Down" (performed by The Redskins), "Don't Ask Me to Choose" (performed by the Fine Young Cannibals), "Always Something There to Remind Me" (performed by Sandie Shaw), "You Can Help" (performed by Flesh). LETTERS TO BREZHNEV is dated by its title because the Russian rulers come and go with alarming rapidity, mostly because they are so old when they take over. It's not a left-wing tract at all, rather a celebration of young love and the fact that love can cross any barrier when it is strong enough. A must-see for anyone old enough to appreciate it.

p, Janet Goddard, Caroline Spack; d, Chris Bernard; w, Frank Clarke; ph, Bruce McGowan; m, Alan Gill; ed, Lesley Walker; prod d, Lez Brothrston, Nick Englefield, Jonathan Swain; cos, Mark Reynolds; makeup, Viv Howells.

Romantic Comedy   (PR:C-O MPAA:R)

LEV S BILOU HRIVOU†   (1986, Czech.) 130m Barrandov c

Ludek Munzar (Leos Janacek), Jana Hlavacova (Zdena Janackova), Zlata Admovska (Kamila), Hana Militka (Mara the Housekeeper), Veronika Zillkova (Olga Janackova), Magda Vasaryova (Calma Vesela), Borik Prochazka (Frantisek Vesely), Valerie Zawadska (Gabriela Preissova), Katarina Synkova (Mila Urvalkova), Jiri Bartoska (David), Lubor Tokos (Antonin Dvorak), Jiri Adamira (Karel Kovarovic), Frantisek Rehak (Joza Uprka), Karel Jansky (Mrstik), Tatana Fischerova (Gabriela Preissova), Zbynek Honzik (Hudecek).

This Czechoslovakian effort, directed by a 1960s contemporary of Milos Forman and Ivan Passer, is a cinematic biography of the composer Leo Janacek.

d, Jaromil Jires; w, Jiri Blazek; ph, Jan Curik; m, Leos Janacek, Zdenek Pololanik; ed, Jozef Valusiak, Peter Sitar; art d, Milos Cervinka, Jindrich Goetz; cos, Irena Greifova.

Biography   (PR:NR MPAA:NR)

L'EXECUTRICE†   (1986, Fr.) 87m Tiphany Films-Fil a Film-Zoom 24/ Films Jacques Leitienne c (Trans: The Executor)

Brigitte Lahaie, Pierre Oudry, Michel Godin, Michel Modo, Dominique Erlanger, Jean-Hugues Lime.

When Lahaie's younger sister is kidnaped, the tough-as-nails cop forgets her loyalty to the force and goes looking for the girl herself. Lahaie is best known for her apperance in the 1985 semi-pornographic feature JOY AND JOAN.

p, d&w, Michel Caputo; ph, Gerard Simon (Fujicolor); ed, Annie Lemesles.

Crime   (PR:O MPAA:NR)

L'HOMME DE CENDRES   (SEE: MAN OF ASHES, 1986, Tunisia)

LIANG JIA FUNU†   (1986, China) 102m Beijing Film Studio/China Film c (Trans: A Girl of Good Family)

Cong Shan, Zhang Weixen, Zhang Jian, Ma Lin, Liang Yan.

In 1948, the Communists have finally won the Chinese Civil War, but in one isolated village, life goes on as it has for centuries. An 18-year-old woman's marriage to a six-year-old boy has been arranged by her parents. Her relationship with her child-husband is more maternal than anything, and soon she has commenced an affair with a married man.

d, Huangjian Thong; w, Li Kuanding; ph, Yun Wenyao; m, Shi Wanchun; art d, Shao Ruigang.

Drama   (PR:A MPAA:NR)

LICEENI†   (1986, Rum.) 98m Bucharest Studios c (Trans: The Teenagers)

Stefan Banica, Jr., Mihai Constantin, Oana Sirbu, Cesonia Postelnicu, Tudor Petrut, Tamara Buciuceanu-Botez, Ion Caramitru, Silviu Stanculescu, Dorina Lazar, Sebastian Papaiani, Cristina Deleanu, Iarina Demian, Liviu Craciun.

A humorous look at the mating rituals of high-school students revolves around the efforts of one particularly shy boy to win the affections of a girl who doesn't know he's alive. Director Corjos and screenwriter Sovu previously teamed together to produce CONFESSIONS OF LOVE, the most financially successful film of 1985 in Rumania.

d, Nicolae Corjos; w, George Sovu; ph, Alexandru Groza; m, Florin Bogardo; art d, Ion Nedelcu; cos, Lidia Luludis.

Drama/Comedy   (PR:C MPAA:NR)

LIEN DE PARENTE   (SEE: PARENTAL CLAIM, 1986, Fr.)

LIGHTNING—THE WHITE STALLION**   (1986) 95m Cannon c

Mickey Rooney (Barney Ingram), Isabel Lorca (Stephanie Ward), Susan George (Mme. Rene), Billy Wesley (Lucas Mitchell), Martin Charles Warner (Emmett Fallon), Francoise Pascal (Marie Ward Leeman), Read Morgan (Harry Leeman), Stanley Siegel (Jim Piper), Jay Rasumny (Johnny), Debra Berger (Lili Castle), Murray Langston (Gorman), Rick Lundin (Max), Justin Lundin (Wiley), Charles Pitt (Judge), Sheila Colligan (Registrar), Karen Davis (Melinda), Claudia Stenke (Danielle), Rob Gage (Himself), Jennifer Young (Rob Gage's Girl Friend), Shannon McLeod (Daphne), William A. Levey (Opthalmologist), John Warren James (Mailman), Bradley Golden (Neighbor), Ayanna Dulaney (Nurse).

Disgruntled over not having been paid for two months, horse trainer Warner steals his boss' favorite animal. Rooney is the boss, a breeder whose penchant for gambling has reduced him to penury. He is heartbroken over the loss of his favorite animal and spends his days pouting about it and avoiding his creditors. Warner's truck cracks up and the horse escapes. A school bus happens upon the accident and the driver takes Warner to the hospital. One of the passengers, Lorca, stays at the hospital with Warner, and he asks her to find the horse and take care of it. Along with her friend, Wesley, she finds the horse and takes it back to her home, but her mean stepfather won't let her keep it. She takes it to George's farm, where she arranges to work in the stables in return for the horse's board. Eventually she begins to ride and jump under George's instruction, and then enters a local show-jumping contest which she wins. Meanwhile, Lorca has learned that she is suffering from a degenerative eye disease and unless she has an expensive operation she will be blind within a year. She goes on to win the state championship, finally gaining some measure of approval from her stepfather, who turns out to be a nice guy after all. Some thugs to whom Rooney owes money find out from him about Warner taking the horse, so they find him and

seize the animal themselves. Lorca goes to Rooney, thinking he might have repossessed his horse, but he tells her what has happened and where the horse might be. With Wesley, she manages to rescue Lightning, and goes on to ride in the national championship, which, of course, she wins.

Not a bad film as the performances help keep the cliches of the plot from seeming too familiar. Lorca is quite a good performer, possessed of a beautiful French accent, and no one can touch Rooney when he stops doing "Sugar Babies" on the road and turns on the cutes for a film. He has the curious distinction of having also appeared in the titular opposite of this film, THE BLACK STALLION. Production values are high, and the film moves along well, with a surprising lack of scenes of the horse romping across the countryside while the music wells up. The film scarcely saw a theatrical release, but will probably have a long life on the video shelves, appealing to youngsters and to adolescent girls enamored of horses.

p, Harry Alan Towers; d, William A. Levey; w, Peter Welbeck [Harry Alan Towers]; ph, Steven Shaw (TVC Color); m, Maurizio Abeni, Annakarin Klockar; ed, Ken Bornstein; art d, Hector B. Lopez; set d, William Northcott; cos, Richard Abramson; makeup, Alicia Tripi.

Drama   **Cas.**   (PR:A MPAA:PG)

LIGHTSHIP, THE**   (1986) 89m CBS-Castle Hill c

Robert Duvall (Caspary), Klaus Maria Brandauer (Capt. Miller), Tom Bower (Coop), Robert Costanzo (Stump), Badja Djola (Nate), William Forsythe (Gene), Arliss Howard (Eddie), Michael Lyndon (Alex), Tim Phillips (Thorne).

Released in Europe in 1985, where it won a Special Jury Prize from the 1985 Venice Film Festival, THE LIGHTSHIP did not find a U.S. release until this year—and then not much of a release at all. Produced by the since-defunct theatrical film division of CBS, the picture was originally scheduled to be released by Warner Bros. (see the MPG 1986 Annual). When WB backed out, it was left dead in the water until Castle Hill picked it up for its stateside release—opening it in only New York and Los Angeles where it died quickly at the box-office. Set in 1955, the film takes place, almost exclusively, aboard the U.S. Coast Guard lightship "Hatteras," an anchored vessel which functions in much the same way as a lighthouse, keeping other ships from bashing into the rocky Virginia shore. The lightship is captained by Brandauer, a German-born American citizen who is haunted by his naval past. During WW II, while commanding a destroyer,

Brandauer was faced with a difficult decision: sink an enemy U-boat or pick up some of its victims from the sea. He went after the U-boat, leaving many sailors to drown. As a result, he was court-martialed. Although acquitted, Brandauer is tormented by his conscience. Living on the lightship with his delinquent teenage son Lyndon (director Skolimowski's real-life son) and a small crew, Brandauer spots a stranded speedboat. He brings the boaters aboard—the frightfully effete and evil Duvall, with his pink shirt, bow tie, and walking stick, and two leather-clad brothers, Forsythe and Howard. An odd trio of unnaturally close fugitives, the men demand that Brandauer deliver them to their chosen destination. Brandauer, however, cannot desert the Virginia coast. In a show of strength, Duvall takes over the lightship and, in an offbeat change of pace, engages in lengthy philosophical discussions with Brandauer. In the meantime, Brandauer's relationship with his son is rapidly disintegrating, as he is unable to earn the boy's

respect. The pressure builds and Brandauer is forced to take action against Duvall, leading to a climactic showdown between the two forces. Although Brandauer is killed, he gains the respect and understanding of his son, while Duvall awaits a certain fate at the hands of the law.

Combining the father-and-son relationship of his previous film SUCCESS IS THE BEST REVENGE (1984) and the Conradian allegorical style of his previous films (THE SHOUT, 1979 and MOONLIGHTING, 1982), Skolimowski has fashioned an interesting though flawed picture. The screenplay lacks coherence which necessitated the post-production addition of narration by Lyndon, but the performances more than make up for it. Each of the leading players was originally cast in the other's roles. The leads switched when Duvall complained that his own background (his father was a naval captain in WW II) was too close to the Capt. Miller character. Duvall's flamboyant Caspary, the embodiment of evil, is a near-camp treat. He has since stated that he based many of his quirky mannerisms on William F. Buckley and that he improvised much of his dialog. Brandauer, who is best known for his sinister portrayal in MEPHISTO, turns in a powerful performance as a gentle and distraught father. THE LIGHTSHIP was surrounded with on-location problems ranging from scheduling delays caused by the treacherous North Sea (the film was made off the coast of Germany) to reported tensions between Skolimowski and Brandauer, Duvall and Brandauer, Duvall and Skolimowski, coproducer Borman and Duvall, the German crew and the American crew, and just about every possible combination thereof. In spite of its problems, THE LIGHTSHIP is a compelling picture that left critics with mixed reactions. Perhaps because of these problems, Skolimowski's first American picture and his initial attempt to break into Hollywood's mainstream cinema is marked as a commercial failure.

p, Bill Benenson, Moritz Borman; d, Jerzy Skolimowski; w, William Mai, David Taylor (based on the novel *Das Feuerschiff* by Sigfried Lenz); ph, Charly Steinberger; m, Stanley Myers; ed, Barry Vince; art d, Holger Gross.

Drama   **(PR:C   MPAA:PG-13)**

LIJEPE ZENE PROLAZE KROZ GRAD†   (1986, Yugo.) 95m
Zvezda-Croatia-Forum-Art Film/Art Film '80 c (Trans: Beautiful Women
Walking Around Town)

Ljuba Tadzic, Svetolik Mikacevic, Hahela Ferari, Nikola Milic, Milena Dravic, Rade Markovic, Ljubisa Ristic, Tom Gottowac.

The Yugoslavs get into the post-civilization genre with this political allegory. Journalist Tadzic becomes involved with some schoolgirls who want to reinhabit the ruins of Belgrade, despite the leather-jacketed police who now rule the country. Shot on a stupendously low budget of $9000.

d, Zelmir Zilnik; w, Zelmir Zilnik, Miroslav Mandic; ph, Ljubomir Becejski; m, Koja; art d, Slobodan Djosic; cos, Bjanka Andzic-Ursulov.

Comedy/Science Fiction   **(PR:C   MPAA:NR)**

LIL HOB KESSA AKHIRA   (SEE: LEL HOB KESSA AKHIRA, 1986,
Egypt)

L'INCHIESTA†   (1986, It.) Italian International-Clesi-Rai Uno-Sacis/Sacis
c (Trans: The Inquest)

Keith Carradine, Harvey Keitel, Phyllis Logan, Angelo Infanti, Lina Sastri.

An investigator is sent from Rome to Palestine to look into the strange rumors relating to the execution of one Jesus Christ. He becomes involved in a confusing web of religion, politics, and mystical events.

p, Fulvio Lucisano, Silvio Clementelli, Anna Maria Clementelli; d, Damiano Damiani; w, Vittori Bonicelli, Damiano Damiani (based on a story by Suso Cecchi D'Amico, Ennio Flaiano); ph, Franco Di Giacomo; m, Riz Ortolani.

Religious/Historical   **(PR:A-C   MPAA:NR)**

LINK*   (1986, Brit.) 103m Thorn EMI/Cannon c

Terence Stamp *(Dr. Steven Phillip)*, Elisabeth Shue *(Jane Chase)*, Steven Pinner *(David)*, Richard Garnett *(Dennis)*, David O'Hara *(Tom)*, Kevin Lloyd *(Bailey)*, Locke *(Link)*, Jed *(Imp)*, Carrie *(Voodoo)*.

Coming off the moderate success of PSYCHO II, Australian director Franklin again delves into the thriller genre with borrowings from Hitchcock's REBECCA (1940) and THE BIRDS (1963). The story begins in London as Shue, an innocent

young blonde zoology student, meets Stamp, an eccentric university professor who studies chimpanzees. She is hired to work as his lab assistant at his Victorian mansion, remotely located along England's coast. When she arrives at the front door, she is greeted not by a human servant but by Link, a well-mannered chimpanzee dressed in a tuxedo. Shue becomes familiar with Link and his two companions, Imp and Voodoo, but before long mysterious things begin to happen. One day Stamp disappears without a trace. Then Voodoo is found dead. Link begins to act strangely, disobeying Shue's orders and bullying Imp. Link's actions, however, seem more mischievous than dangerous, especially when he decides to cook a telephone in the microwave. When Lloyd, an acquaintance of Stamp's, arrives to take away Voodoo, the situation begins to intensify. Lloyd tries to kill Link, but is scared off by the raging chimp, who proceeds nearly to overturn his van. As time passes, Shue grows increasingly perturbed at Link, locking him out of the house—an action that infuriates the chimp. Link, by now, has turned bloodthirsty. Shue, however, acts as if nothing strange is going on, wandering through the mansion's grounds unconcerned for her own safety. In the nick of time, Shue's boy friend and his pals arrive on the scene. Two of them are killed by the crazed chimp, but Shue manages to outsmart Link and blow him to smithereens in a finale that looks like KING KONG meets WHITE HEAT. Director Franklin likes to call LINK "an anthropological thriller as opposed to a psychological one"—a distinction that might have been valid had LINK worked as a thriller. Unfortunately, the film fails to provide much thrill, instead coming across as hilariously inept. The blame seems best laid at the feet of the screenwriters who consistently paint Shue as one of those characters in suspense pictures who always do stupid things. She does everything that Stamp has warned her not to do when interacting with the chimps, she wanders around dark cellars, she ignores warnings of vicious wild dogs, she even undresses in front of an overly curious Link. After a point, her stupidity becomes so frustrating that one hopes Link will tear her to shreds. What is even more distressing is that Shue has a wonderfully innocent screen presence (she's been seen before as Ralph Macchio's girl friend in THE KARATE KID) that fights against the inanity of her character. Stamp is likable as always, stepping into a role that is an extension of Peter O'Toole's eccentric-scientist character of CREATOR, but he disappears from the screen far too early in the film. The performances from the three chimps are amazingly expressive, thanks to the expertise of animal trainer Ray Berwick, who also worked for Hitchcock on THE BIRDS. Although the film falters in creating suspense, it impresses with some exceptional technique, chiefly in its use of the Steadicam combined with a wide-angle lens and slow-motion photography to duplicate the chimps' point of view. Leading-chimp Locke is actually an orangutan, a more docile, readily manipulated animal than the chimpanzee. Wearing slip-over ears and dentures, and with his fur trimmed and dyed black, the animal actor simulated the real thing well and stole his every scene.

p&d, Richard Franklin; w, Everett DeRoche (based on a story by Lee Zlotoff, Tom Ackerman); ph, Mike Molloy; m, Jerry Goldsmith; ed, Andrew London; prod d, Norman Garwood; art d, Keith Pain; cos, Terry Smith.

Thriller (PR:O MPAA:R)

LINNA† (1986, Fin.) 99m Skandia/Kinosto-Finnish Film Foundation c (Trans: The Castle)

Carl-Kristian Rundman *(Josef K.)*, Titta Karakorpi *(Frieda)*, Pirkka-Pekka Petellius, Vesa Vierikko, Risto Autio, Sari Mallinen, Anna-Leena Harkonen, Ulla Koivuranta.

Franz Kafka's strange allegory *The Castle* is brought to the screen again (Maximillian Schell produced and starred in a 1969 German version). This time Rundman is the hapless Josef K., a surveyor who finds himself in the shadow of a castle that he is never able to enter.

d&w, Jaakko Pakkasvirta (based on Franz Kafka's unfinished novel); ph, Esa Vuorinen (Cinemascope, Fujicolor); m, Otto Donner; ed, Pipsa Valavaara; prod d, Pentti Valkeasuo.

Fantasy/Drama (PR:O MPAA:NR)

LISI UND DER GENERAL† (1986, Switz.) 118m Europa Film Locarno c (Trans: Lisi and the General)

Walo Luond *(General)*, Silvia Silva *(Lisi)*, Franz Matter *(Commissar)*, Eva Bendig-Luond *(Rosa)*, Peter Schneider *(Max)*, Manfred Liechti *(Edi)*, Sabine Stutzmann *(Katrin)*, Daniel Ludwig *(Soldier)*.

Mid-life crisis (and a bottle of whiskey) lead Luond to leave his home, driving nowhere in particular. He picks up Silva, who turns out to be a robber with a half-million Swiss francs in her suitcase. She calls him "the general" because of an Army overcoat and hat in his back seat, and soon the two become lovers, hiding out in a snowbound mountain cabin until police come to provoke an unexpected happy ending.

p&d, Mark M. Rissi; w, Steve Burckhardt (based on the novel "Lisi" by Alexander Heimann); ph, Edwin Horak; m, Renato Anselmi; ed, Evelyne von Rabenau; m/l, Peter E. Mueller, Pia Emmenegger; stunts, Markus Scharowsky, Verkehrs-Sicherheitszentrum Veltheim, Skischule Lenk.

Comedy (PR:O MPAA:NR)

L'ISOLA† (1986, It.) Regency-RAIZ/Sacis c (Trans: The Island)

Massimo Ghini, Paolo Bonacelli, Ida Di Benedetto, Marina Vlady, Christiane Jean, Stephane Audran.

In the early 1930s, an Italian leftist is forced by fascist repression to flee to Paris, where he meets a French girl. Later he returns to Italy and is arrested, but she eventually manages to rejoin him and marry him. He leads a revolt and is transferred to a prison in Naples, and later he manages to again rejoin her in Paris, though the Germans are poised to invade France and separate the two lovers again.

p, Maurizio Amati; d, Carlo Lizzani; w, Carlo Lizzani, Lucio De Caro, Giuliano Montaldo (based on a book by Giorgio Amendola); ph, Mario Vulpiani (Telecolor); m, Armando Trovaioli.

Drama (PR:O MPAA:NR)

LITTLE SHOP OF HORRORS* (1986) 88m WB c

Rick Moranis *(Seymour Krelborn)*, Ellen Greene *(Audrey)*, Vincent Gardenia *(Mushnik)*, Steve Martin *(Orin Scrivello, D.D.S.)*, Tichina Arnold *(Crystal)*, Tisha Campbell *(Chiffon)*, Michelle Weeks *(Ronette)*, James Belushi *(Patrick Martin)*, John Candy *(Wink Wilkinson)*, Christopher Guest *(lst Customer)*, Bill Murray *(Arthur Denton)*, Stanley Jones *(Narrator)*, Bertice Reading *("Downtown" Old Woman)*, Ed Wiley, Alan Tilvern, John Scott Martin *("Downtown" Bums)*, Vincent Wong *(Chinese Florist)*, Mak Wilson, Danny Cunningham, Danny John-Jules, Gary Palmer, Paul Swaby *(Doo Wop Street Singers)*, Mildred Shay *(2nd Customer)*, Melissa Wiltsie *(3rd Customer)*, Kevin Scott *(4th Cus-*

tomer), Barbara Rosenblat *(5th Customer)*, Adeen Fogle *(Radio Station Assistant)*, Kelly Huntley, Paul Reynolds *(Audrey & Seymour's Kids)*, Miriam Margolyes *(Dental Nurse)*, Abbie Dabner *(Boy Patient)*, Frank Dux *(2nd Patient)*, Peter Whitman *(Patient on Ceiling)*, Heather Henson *(Girl Patient)*, Judith Morse *(Girl's Mother)*, Bob Sherman *(Agent)*, Doreen Hermitage *("Life" Magazine Lady)*, Kerry Shale *(Her Assistant)*, Robert Arden, Stephen Hoye, Bob Sessions *(Network Executives)*, Michael J. Shannon *(Television Reporter)*, Levi Stubbs *(Voice of "AUDREY II")*.

Who'd ever thought that a Roger Corman low-budget quickie would have evolved into a $26 million musical? Corman directed the 2½-day wonder (with some uncredited assistance by the screenwriter, Charles Griffith—who wrote it in less than two weeks) on existing sets that were standing for another movie. The original cast had Jonathan Haze in the male lead and Jackie Joseph (who was married to TV's Ken Berry) as the femme costar, with second-banana work from Dick Miller (one of Corman's favorites and a costar of TV's "Fame"), Mel Welles as the harassed florist, an early appearance by Jack Nicholson as a devout masochist, plus excellent cameos from Leola Wendorff (in a role cut from the musical) and Myrtle Vail as Haze's mother—also cut from this film. That picture was far blacker and far funnier than this one, but there is more than enough music and color to make up for the lack of dark humor.

The action takes place in 1960 down on Skid Row. (The mammoth set was entirely indoors and very stylized. It was shot on the same stage where the "James Bond" pictures are done, at Pinewood in England). We meet Arnold, Campbell, and Weeks, who function as sort of a Supremes-style Greek Chorus (matter of fact, their names in the cast are the same as a trio of famous R&B groups: Chiffon, Crystal, and Ronette). Moranis is a nerd who works in the flower shop owned by Gardenia (who says he got the role because of his name) and lives beneath the store. Business is terrible and Gardenia is thinking about firing Moranis and his coworker Greene (who played the role in the off-Broadway musical and made it her own). Moranis is daffy over Greene but doesn't

think he has a chance with her. He doesn't know that she loves him, too, but she is currently enmeshed in a black-and-blue relationship with Martin, a sadistic dentist who spends his time alternately making love and whipping the tar out of Greene. She dreams of a life with Moranis and pictures them in a suburban house with all the trappings, including watching "I Love Lucy" on TV as their imaginary children, Huntley and Reynolds, join them in a warm scene of domestic bliss. Despite her feelings for Moranis, Greene continues her situation with Martin, who rides a huge motorcycle, wears black leather, talks like Elvis, and takes delight in inflicting horrific pain on his patients. (Martin's character and the Nazi dentist played by Laurence Olivier in MARATHON MAN have done more to set back the dental profession than eating plates full of sugar.)

One day, Moranis meets a wise old Mandarin type, Wong, who sells flowers on a street corner, and buys a weird plant at the exact moment of a solar eclipse, bringing the plant back to his apartment. Since he adores the ditsy Greene (she wears a blonde wig and tight clothes, and talks like Judy Holliday would have in BORN YESTERDAY if Holliday had a harelip), he names the odd plant "Audrey II." Gardenia scoffs at the plant and wishes that Moranis would concentrate on getting some business rather than fooling around with such things. No sooner does Moranis put the plant in the window when Guest (THIS IS SPINAL TAP, THE LONG RIDERS, HEARTBEEPS) enters, comments on how much he likes the plant, and promptly buys some other flowers. Before long, many people are dropping in to see the unusual growth, and Gardenia is thrilled. Then Moranis discovers something eerie. The plant is beginning to wilt, but when Moranis cuts his finger, a few drops of blood cause the plant to perk up. As the plant expands (there were seven versions of it), Moranis is losing blood and his fingers are covered with band-aids. The plant gets larger and larger, but so does its appetite. By this time, it's also developed a voice (wonderfully supplied by Levi Stubbs of The Four Tops) which demands "Feed Me!" Moranis goes to visit Martin to say something about the way the brute has been beating up Greene. Murray arrives at the dentist's office and wants lots of work done on his mouth, with no anesthesia. Since Martin's jollies come from inflicting pain, he becomes increasingly frustrated by Murray's acceptance of it, and finally throws the masochist out. Moranis walks in and, through an accident, kills Martin. Now, the question is . . . what to do with the body?

By now, Audrey II is large, and needs more than just some droplets of blood

from Moranis' anemic fingers. Moranis dumps Martin's body into Audrey's maw and the plant loves it and gets bigger and bigger. Gardenia has witnessed some of this and when he threatens to blow the whistle, he, too, becomes plant food for Audrey. By this time, Moranis has become a celebrity, interviewed on the local Skid-Row radio station by Candy (his old pal from SCTV), profiled in "Life" Magazine by Hermitage, having network executives Arden, Hoye, and Sessions plan a national show for him, and fending off Belushi, as a hustler looking to cash in on the phenomenon that has packed the florist shop. When the plant reveals itself to be from outer space, with plans to conquer the world, Moranis must make a last-ditch stand to save civilization. In a spectacular final sequence, he blows the plant to bits and he and Greene are united.

This was not the original ending shot for the film. In that, they stayed closer to the play, with Greene and Moranis being consumed by the plant. But preview audiences—which had thoroughly enjoyed the film until then—grew angry at what they saw, so the picture was pulled, a new ending and a few other scenes were shot, and the result is an upbeat conclusion. The musical numbers are largely fun and mostly forgettable. A few of the play's numbers were cut and others were added. Those deleted were "Ya Never Know," "Now," "Call Back in the Morning," "Mushnik and Son," and "Closed For Renovations." The new tunes are: "Mean Green Mother From Outer Space," "Some Fun Now," and "Your Day Begins Tonight." The play opened in May, 1982 at the WPA, then moved to larger quarters two months later, winning the Drama Critics Circle, Outer Critic's Circle, and Drama Desk Awards, and played all over the world in road companies from Australia to Israel to Japan to Iceland with many stops in between. Other songs that stick out in memory are "Downtown" (the cast), "Suddenly Seymour" (Moranis, Greene), "Somewhere That's Green" (Greene), and "Suppertime" (Stubbs).

The special-effects accomplishments of Lyle Conway must be acknowledged. He designed the Audrey that went through several generations from a potted plant to a mammoth 12½-foot-tall creature that took over the entire florist shop. It weighed, at the close, more than 2000 pounds and used almost 12 miles of cable to make it look like it lived. The most remarkable part of the device was the lips that were perfectly in sync with the singing and dialog. If they ever give an Oscar for creatures, they should name it the "Audrey" after this amazing achievement. Lyle Conway *did* receive an Oscar nomination, along with Bran Ferren and Martin Gutteridge, but lost to the effects team that handled ALIENS. The song "Mean Green Mother . . ." was similarly nominated, losing to "Take My Breath Away" from TOP GUN. Moranis was already well-known for his work in GHOSTBUSTERS, CLUB PARADISE, and STRANGE BREW, but Greene was making her first starring appearance after some smaller roles in NEXT STOP, GREENWICH VILLAGE and I'M DANCING AS FAST AS I CAN. At 88 minutes, this is a short film when one considers the money spent but "less is more" in movies as in architecture and it's packed with fun from fade-in to The End. Kudos for everyone concerned, as they resisted the opportunity to cast someone like Barbra Streisand in the Greene role and also stayed in the 1960s rather than try to make it look like an MTV video. Some rough language from "Audrey II" and a few frightening moments make it questionable for tots.

p, David Geffen; d, Frank Oz; w, Howard Ashman (based on his musical stage play); ph, Robert Paynter (Panavision, Technicolor); m, Alan Menken, Miles Goodman; ed, John Jympson; prod d, Roy Walker; art d, Stephen Spence; set d, Tessa Davies; cos, Marit Allen; spec eff, Bran Ferren; ch, Pat Garrett; m/l, Alan Menken, Howard Ashman; makeup, Paul Engelen.

Musical   Cas.   (PR:C MPAA:PG-13)

LJUBAVNA PISMA S PREDUMISLJAJEM† (1986, Yugo.)
Marjan-Croatia (Trans: Love Letters with Intent)

Irina Alferova, Zlatko Vitez, Krunoslav Saric, Relja Basic, Mustafa Nadarevic, Sinisa Popovic.

d&w, Zvonimir Berkovic; ph, Goran Trbuljak; m, Wolgang Amadeus Mozart; set d, Zeljjko Senecic.

LJUBEZEN† (1986, Yugo.) Viba (Trans: Love)

Rok Bogataj, Lenka Ferencak, Bernarda Gaspercic, Vesna Jevnikar, Gojmir Lesnjak.

d&w, Rajko Ranfl; ph, Jure Pervanje; m, Urban Koder; set d, Janez Kovic.

LOI RE TRAI TREN DUONG MON† (1986, Vietnam) 96m Ho Chi Minh City Studios/Famin c (Trans: Return to the Right Path)

Lam Toi, Kim Thanh, Kim Thi, Kung Bac.

A minor Communist official is plagued with guilt after a female security guard is made comatose in an industrial accident for which he is responsible. His family is well-off, despite the new "classless" society of which he is allegedly a part, and they are against his admitting his complicity in the accident because they may lose their special place. Only his youngest daughter expects her father to do the right thing, which, of course, he does.

d, Huy Thanh; w, Nguyen Manh Tuan; ph, Le Dinh An; m, Hong Dang.

Drama   (PR:A MPAA:NR)

LOLA† (1986, Span.) 100m Figaro c

Angela Molina (*Lola*), Patrick Bauchau (*Robert*), Feodor Atkine (*Mario*), Assumpta Serna (*Silvia*), Angela Gutierrez, Constantino Romero, Marian Rodes, Pepa Lopez, Maria Gonzalez, Rosa Gabin, Andres Salmon, Patrick Honore, Boris Mastramon.

Molina finally works up the nerve to leave her sadistic lover (Atkine) and move to Paris, where she marries Bauchau and has a daughter. After four years, Atkine turns up and tries to again force Molina into a sexual relationship. Bauchau returns from a trip and finds the two together, and in a subsequent scuffle, Atkine stabs Molina to death.

d, Bigas Luna; w, Luis Herce, Bigas Luna, Enrique Viciano; ph, Jose Maria Civit (Eastmancolor); m, Jose Manuel Pagan; ed, Ernest Blasi; set d, Felipe de Paco; cos, Consol Tura.

Drama   (PR:O MPAA:NR)

LONGSHOT, THE zero (1986) 90m Longshot/Orion c

Brad Trumbull (*Track Cop*), Tim Conway (*Dooley*), Jack Weston (*Elton*), Harvey Korman (*Lou*), Ted Wass (*Stump*), Pat Li (*Ono*), Garry Goodrow (*Josh*), Dave Johnson (*Track Announcer*), Dick Enberg (*Radio Announcer*), Anne Meara (*Madge*), Frank Bonner (*Realtor*), Benny Baker (*Mr. Hooper*), Yvonne Del Walker (*Mrs. Hooper*), Ernie Anderson (*Old Man*), Jinaki (*Toby*), Anzio (*Cashier*), Jorge Cervera (*Santiago*), Stella Stevens (*Nicki Dixon*), Susan Tolsky (*Dee*), Ted Bolczak (*Cab Driver*), Brad Logan (*Doorman*), Stephen Ciotta (*Lizard*), George DiCenzo (*DeFranco*), Edie McClurg (*Donna*), Hank Rolike (*Jelly*), Eddie Deezen (*Parking Attendant*), Gregory Wolf (*Bell Captain*), Don Draper (*Desk Clerk*), Maria Korman (*Assistant Clerk*), Mickey Elliott (*Receptionist*), Joseph Ruskin (*Fusco*), Ollie the Fish (*Himself*), Jonathan Winters (*Tyler*), Kelly Conway (*Program Seller*), Virginia Vincent (*Waitress*), James Bacon (*Track Usher*), Nick Dimitri (*Track Cop*), Buckley Norris (*Man in Stands*), Pat Kehoe (*Man at Jail*), Pat Studstill (*Jail Cop*), Tom Finnegan (*Desk Cop*).

LUST IN THE DUST made fans of cult comedy director Paul Bartel uneasy about where he was going and THE LONGSHOT will confirm their worst fears. Though labeled a comedy, the film would more properly be classified as an excruciating travesty; one that makes Bartel's previous effort look like a delightful exercise in wit. Conway, Korman, Weston, and Wass are four losers whose collective lives revolve around betting on horses. Their home lives are miserable (Wass, the youngest of the quartet, has only his pet fish to talk to) and pennyante gambling is their only saving grace. Cervera, a Mexican track worker, persuades these dumb lugs that he can arrange for a long-shot horse to win a race, reaping big bucks for anyone who bets on the nag. Conway and his pals agree to

the scheme, but now must raise $5000 to place their wager. Conway first goes to Stevens, a rich, beautiful woman who apparently has an eye for the short, balding man. Instead, she proves to be psychotic, convinced that Conway is a former lover who jilted her years before. Conway is barely able to escape from Stevens' hotel room with his life, and the gang must go elsewhere for the dough. They end up borrowing money from DiCenzo, a seedy mobster, who demands the loan be paid back soon with excessive interest. When the big day arrives, the four have some car trouble but are helped out by Winters (in a completely wasted cameo role). After giving their money to Cervera, they learn that the potential long shot is merely a moneymaking scam on the stableman's part. In desperation, Conway leaps onto the track, waving a red dress (ripped unabashedly off Stevens) in hopes of egging on their horse. The horse, we have earlier been told, runs faster when he sees red, and the race ends in a photo finish. Conway is arrested, along with Wass, but they are eventually bailed out by their two cohorts. Korman and Weston bring good news, as well, for their horse won the race and now they are all rich.

THE LONGSHOT isn't just unfunny, it's downright repulsive. If the problems of four pot-bellied losers, gags revolving around broken toilets, and stereotypical henpecking wives don't sound terribly amusing, it's for good reason. These are pathetic people with shallow concerns, which isn't exactly an ideal situation for riotous comedy capers. Conway's script should take a good deal of the blame. It plods from one insufferable sequence to another, while would-be jokes drop leadenly from cast members' mouths. Fans of the old "Carol Burnett Show" will be disappointed by the on-screen teaming of Conway and Korman. While the two worked well together on the popular variety show, here they are merely bumblers who raise nary a laugh. Weston and Wass provide equally loathsome characters, while the few women in the film (Stevens, Conway's screen wife Meara, and Korman's screen wife Tolsky) are treated with no respect. Not even the presence of Winters can inject any humor into this ill-fated project. Bartel's direction is practically nil, merely pointing the camera, recording the action, then probably romping off to the bank to cash his check. Amazingly, this was the first feature film for which Mike Nichols served as executive producer. Not even his presence can help this abysmal feature. Save your money and watch your neighbors bicker over their barbecue. It's probably just as creative an enterprise, and unquestionably more entertaining. Songs include "The Longshot" (Gloria Sklerov, Lenny Macaluso, performed by Irene Cara), "Rappin' on Down the Track" (Charles Fox, Tim Conway, performed by Ice T, Tim Conway).

p, Lang Elliott; d, Paul Bartel; w, Tim Conway; ph, Robby Muller (DeLuxe Color); m, Charles Fox; ed, Alan Toomayan; prod d, Joseph M. Altadonna; set d, Bob Schulenberg; cos, Sandra Culotta; spec eff, A&A Special Effects, Richard Albain, Jr.; m/l, Gloria Sklerov, Lenny Macaluso, Tim Conway, Charles Fox; makeup, Debra Figuly; stunts, Hank Hooker.

Comedy   **Cas.**   **(PR:O   MPAA:PG-13)**

LOS ASES DE CONTRABANDO†   (1986, Mex.) 92m Hermanos Tamez/
                                      Peliculas Mexicanas c (Trans: The Aces of Contraband)

Sergio Goyri (*Ernesto Castro*), Rebeca Silva (*Elizabeth Calvo*), Gregorio Casals (*Commandant Rodolfo Benavitas*), Juan Valentin (*Marcos*), Humberto Herrera (*Jesus Castro*), Diana Ferreti, Carlos East, Manolo Cardenas, Armando Araiza, Nena Delgado.

Despite a national anti-drug campaign (mostly at the urging of the U.S.), drug smugglers still appear as the heroes in a number of low-budget Mexican action films. This is one of them, a virtually plotless excuse to smash a lot of cheap used cars, interspersed with hypocritical diatribes about the dangers of the very life style they're glamorizing.

p, Orlando Tamez; d, Fernando Duran; w, Carlos Valdemar (based on a story by Matilde Rivera, Felipe Morales); ph, Agustin Lara; m, Diego Herrera, Los Liricos de Teran, Hermanos Mier; ed, Enrique Murrillo; spec eff, Jorge Farfen.

Crime/Action   **(PR:O   MPAA:NR)**

LOS HIJOS DE LA GUERRA FRIA†   (1986, Chile/Fr.) 75m Arca-Out
                                      One/Conate c (Trans: Children of the Cold War)

Eugenio Morales, Pachi Torreblanca, Javier Maldonado, Nestor Corona, Sonia Mena, Nene Larrain, Juan Enrique Forch, J.L. Gutty, Ernesto Munoz, Sigfrid Polhammer.

Santiago is the setting for this Chilean-French coproduction that looks at life in the difficult years following the economic prosperity of the early 1970s. The unexpected decline towards poverty is symbolized in the deterioration of a marriage. A man takes over the management of a liquor importation business when its owner leaves the country, only to learn that firm is losing money and in debt. As a result his relationship with his wife suffers. Shown at the Biarritz film festival in 1985, but not released in its native Chile until early this year.

d&w, Gonzalo Justiniano; ph, Jorge Roth; m, Jorge Arriagada; ed, Rodolfo Wedeles, Claudio Martinez.

Drama   **(PR:NR   MPAA:NR)**

LOS INSOMNES   (SEE: INSOMNIACS, 1986, Arg.)

LOS PARAISOS PERDIDOS†   (1986, Span.) La Linterna Magica (Trans:
                                                          The Lost Paradise)

Charo Lopez, Alfredo Landa, Juan Diego, Miguel Narros, Ana Torrent, Francisco Rabal.

Exiled in Germany since her childhood, a young woman returns to Spain hoping to rediscover those things she left behind. By looking at the changes that have occurred in Spain through the eyes of this woman, director Patino (noted for his probing NUEVA CARTAS A BERTA, 1966) attempts a critical analysis of post-Franco life. Two of Spain's most prominent actors, Ana Torrent— the childhood star of CRIA (1975) and THE SPIRIT OF THE BEEHIVE (1976)—and Francisco Rabal (VIRIDIANA, 1962) appear in supporting roles.

d&w, Basilio Martin Patino; ph, Jose Luis Alcaine.

Drama   **(PR:C   MPAA:NR)**

LOST!†   (1986, Can.) 93m Rosebud–Victor Solnicki–CBC–Telefilm Canada/
                                                   Simcom–Norstar c

Kenneth Welsh (*Jim*), Helen Shaver (*Linda*), Michael Hogan (*Bob*), Linda Goranson (*Wilma*), Charles Joliffe (*Nick*).

Welsh is a zealous minister who leaves his home in Canada hoping to do missionary work in Central America. He invites his brother, Hogan, and his sister-in-law, Shaver, to join him aboard a small trimaran for the sailing trip. Along the way they are hit by a storm and the craft capsizes. The three cling to the over-turned boat and manage to hack a hole through the hull to get to the food and water still in the cabin. The food supplies dwindle faster than expected and it turns out that Welsh, mad with religious fervor, is tossing food overboard in the night to put their fate more fully in the hands of God. Based on a true story.

p,d&w, Peter Rowe (based on the novel by Thomas Thompson); ph, Don Wilder; m, Micky Erbe, Maribeth Solomon; ed, Christopher Hutton; art d, Bill Fleming; set d, Lizette St. Germaine.

Docu-drama   **(PR:A-C   MPAA:NR)**

LOST IN THE WILDERNESS   (SEE: UEMURA NAOMI MONOGATARI,
                                                          1986, Jap.)

LOVE LETTER†   (1986, Jap.) 109m Shochiku-Fuji–Kosaido Eizo–Kei/
                                             Shochiku c (KOIBUMI)

Kenichi Hagiwara (*Shoichi*), Mitsuko Baisho (*Kyoko*), Keiko Takahashi (*Etsuko*), Motoyoshi Wada, Kaoru Kobayashi, Noburo Nakaya, Tokie Hidari.

Baisho is a long-suffering wife and mother who suffers a little more when her husband Hagiwara receives a letter telling him that an old flame, Takahashi, is dying. He leaves his wife to go to her, and after he takes up residence near her apartment Baisho visits Takahashi as his cousin. Eventually Hagiwara goes all the way and divorces Baisho to marry his doomed love, who lasts only a little while longer. (In Japanese; English subtitles.)

d, Tatsumi Kumashiro; w, Jun Takada, Tatsumi Kumashiro (based on a novel by Mikihiko Renjo); ph, Yoshihiro Yamazaki; m, Takayuki Inoue.

Drama   **(PR:A-C   MPAA:NR)**

LOVE ME!†   (1986, Swed.) 126m Swedish Film Institute–Swedish
     TV2–Svensk Filmindustri–Esselte Video–FilmStallet/Swedish Film Institute c
                                                      (ALSKA MEJ!)

Anna Linden (*Sussie*), Lena Granhagen (*Martha*), Tomas Laustiola (*Gunnar*), Tomas Fryk (*Son Thomas*), Jenny Kai-Larsen (*Daughter Ann*), Ernst Gunther (*The Social Worker*), Orjan Ramberg (*The Ox*), Stig Torstensson, Hans Straat, Elisabet Palo.

Linden is a 15-year-old girl whose mother has lost her custody rights due to her alcoholism. The girl is placed with a foster family composed of husband Laustiola, wife Granhagen, son Fryk, and daughter Kai-Larsen, where she veers constantly among seduction, friendliness, depression, and violence. Fryk falls in love with her, Laustiola makes a clumsy attempt to seduce her, and Granhagen confides all her problems to her like an old friend. Linden can't handle it all and runs away, but she is soon returned, and in another tantrum, she trashes the whole house, spray-painting the walls and smashing furniture. Well-received critically, the film played the international festival circuit with some success.

p, Staffan Hedqvist, Anders Birkeland, Goran Lindstrom; d, Kay Pollak; w, Kay Pollak, Johanna Hald, Ola Olsson (based on an original idea by Kay Pollak, Binnie Kristal-Andersson); ph, Roland Sterner (Fujicolor); m, Allan Pettersson, Gustav Mahler, Antonin Dvorak, Aston Reymers Rivaler, Jean Frederic Axelsson, Tomas Lindahl, Andreas Arflot; ed, Thomas Holewa; art d, Pelle Johansson, Lotta Melanton; makeup, Eva Rizell, Eva Fange.

Drama   **(PR:O   MPAA:NR)**

LOVE SONGS*½   (1986, Fr./Can.) 107m 7 Films Cinema–CIS–FR 3/
               Spectrafilm c (PAROLES ET MUSIQUES; Trans: Words and Music)

Catherine Deneuve (*Margaux*), Richard Anconina (*Michel*), Christopher Lambert (*Jeremy*), Jacques Perrin (*Yves*), Nick Mancuso (*Peter*), Dayle Haddon (*Corinne*), Charlotte Gainsbourg (*Charlotte*), Frank Ayas (*Elliot*), Dominique Lavanant (*Florence*), Nelly Borgeaud (*Julie*), Lazslo Szabo (*Alain*), Inigo Lezzi (*Jean-Paul*), Julie Ravix (*Claire*), Lionel Rocheman (*Gruber*), Yuni Fujimori (*Switchboard Operator*), Guy Thomas (*Jeremy's Singing Voice*), Terry Lauber (*Michel's Singing Voice*).

The French rock 'n' roll scene (yes, one apparently does exist, at least in this film) serves as the backdrop for this rather bland tale of modern-day relationships. Deneuve is a talent agent whose marriage has hit a dry spot. The tensions between her and her husband, Mancuso, the proverbial writer suffering from a creative block, have grown so high that they have decided to separate. Hoping to find inspiration, Mancuso relocates to Montreal. Deneuve is left to raise her two children while pursuing a career. When she discovers a new pop singing duo— Jeremy (Lambert) and Michel (Anconina)—her life becomes even more hectic. The band is supposed to be a new sensation, singing their songs in English to enthusiastic French audiences. Although she is a number of years his senior, Deneuve falls in love with Lambert. Deneuve begins to neglect her job and family, while Lambert starts ignoring Anconina and his song-writing chores.

Eventually he misses an important audition. Anconina, however, is hired as a solo act, leaving Lambert out in the cold. No longer able to handle her swinging life style, Deneuve packs her bags and runs to her husband in Montreal. Meanwhile, Lambert teams up again with Anconina and the duo churns out a string of love songs.

Released in Paris in 1984, this sugary filler should never have had the privilege of gracing American screens—a distribution mistake that Spectrafilm hopefully won't forget. LOVE SONGS does have the good fortune of boasting the names

of Deneuve, Lambert (THE LEGEND OF GREYSTOKE, SUBWAY), and Anconina (TCHAO PANTIN, POLICE), which momentarily overshadows the banality of the direction and script. Worst of all is the music, which is third-rate fluff that may sound great in France (which is starved for good rock 'n' roll) but is insufferable to most American ears. The songs are also sung in English, for reasons which are unsatisfactorily explained by the director: "I wanted to say that Jeremy and Michel are the 'children' of Simon and Garfunkel, and of Daryl Hall and John Oates, and that they have the ambition of their generation. This is to say that music is now what makes the world go round." Well, maybe Simon and Garfunkel make the world go round, but a couple of bozos like Jeremy and Michel grind this big globe to a halt. Michel Legrand, who, in the 1960s, created

some great soundtracks for Jacques Demy (especially THE UMBRELLAS OF CHERBOURG), is clearly unable to compose a rock 'n' roll song, a fault he also displayed in his 1985 reunion with Demy, PARKING. Songs include "Leave It to Me," "Psychic Flash," "I Am with You Now," "Human Race," "We Can Dance," "One More Moment," "From the Heart" (Michael Legrand, Gene McDaniels, performed by Guy Thomas, Terry Lauber), and "This Must Be Heaven" (S. Staplayet, A. Russell). (In French; English subtitles.)

p, Elie Chouraqui, Robert Baylis; d, Elie Chouraqui; ph, Robert Alazraki; m, Michel Legrand; ed, Noelle Boisson; art d, Gerard Daoudal; cos, Caroline De Vivaise; m/l, Michel Legrand, Gene McDaniels; makeup, Ronaldo Ribeiro.

Musical/Drama (PR:C MPAA:NR)

LOW BLOW* (1986) 85m Action Communications/Crown International c

Leo Fong (*Joe Wong*), Cameron Mitchell (*Yarakunda*), Troy Donahue (*John Templeton*), Diane Stevenett (*Diane*), Akosua Busia (*Karma*), Patti Bowling (*Karen Templeton*), Stack Pierce (*Duke*), Woody Farmer (*Fuzzy*), Elaine Hightower (*Cody*), Manny Dela Pena (*Sticks*), David Cochran (*Chico*), Roger Gundert, Mike York, Lyle Compo, Gary R. Stroupe, Nestor Gandia, Gerry Monti, Sam Baca, Nestor C. Albalos, Jack L. Farley (*Card Players*), Ann Bridges (*Card Room Cashier*), Larry Meredith (*College Professor*), Grady Butler, Joel Hinger (*Bikers*), Steve Tognini, Tony Petrali (*Purse Snatchers*), John Zgraggen (*Boxer*), John Drebinger, Jr. (*Boxing Manager*), Scott Hall (*Boxing Promoter*),

Lisa Chun, Anita Cerqui, Karen Yee, Helen Yee (*At Chinese Restaurant*), Lynda Wong (*Waitress*), Gene Lee (*Cook*), William Hunt (*Chauffeur*), Ella Marie Hunt (*Bag Lady*), Ron Ackerman (*Police Chief*), Harold Strome (*Police Detective*), Al Allen (*Shoe Shine Boy*), Doug Jukich, Randall Witt (*Arm Wrestlers*), Steve Tognini, Tony Petrali, Tim Perez (*Deli Robbery*), Darrin Westbrock (*Waiter*), Elizabeth Wilkinson (*Camp Nurse*), Frank Dianette (*Camp Doctor*), Billy Blanks, Jay Garber, Cory Troxclair, Ray Lewis, Michael Hughes, Ansel Chin, Raul Magadia, Gerald Sakata, Tom Ligenfelter, Wesley Suttles, Marilyn Tanner, Emil Jaurequi, Jr., Doug Parker, Michael Zezima, Curtis Johnson, Scott Cherney, Loyd Garmany, Wilbert Chin, Lim Sisson, Andre Waters, Jeffery Moznett, Charlie Cook, Bernard Bang, Shirley Nelson, Rick Knoernschild, Doug Weeks (*Guards*).

A tedious martial-arts opus that offers audiences Fong as one of those ex-cops-turned-first-rate-private-eyes so common in the movies, but whom you never seem to meet in real life. He is hired by Donahue—one of those many wealthy industrialists whose daughters join cults—to get the daughter, Bowling, back from the insidious brainwashing cult run by blind guru Mitchell, one of those Jim

Jones types. Fong's first step is to walk straight into Mitchell's fortified and heavily guarded commune/temple, where he is promptly exposed by Mitchell's right-hand girl, Busia. She has him bound and tortured, but he doesn't talk. Later she makes the classical villain mistake of not killing your enemy now, and he escapes. Returning home, he is soon accosted by three thugs sent by Busia, who is the real power behind the cult. They prove little problem for a tough guy like Fong, though, and he kills them all. He makes plans for an assault on the commune, and to gather his team he stages a toughest-street-vigilante contest to pick the top half-dozen, including demolition expert Pierce and lady bodybuilder Hightower (every commando assault team needs a lady bodybuilder). Under cover of darkness the attack goes down, and the bodies pile up knee-deep until our heroes (and heroine) free Bowling and destroy the evil cult.

Fong is an unappealing screen hero, and his fight sequences are astoundingly dull affairs. Mitchell proves again that he has no shame, and Busia, impressive in THE COLOR PURPLE, almost foams at the mouth as she plays her part to the hilt and beyond. Production values are pallid, the script is stupid, and the sound is muddy. On the plus side, it is only 85 minutes long.

p, Leo Fong; d, Frank Harris; w, Leo Fong; ph, Frank Harris; m, Steve Amundsen; ed, Frank Harris; art d, Diane [Stevenett] Harris; set d, David Cox; ch, George Chung; stunts, Gene Lefeldt.

Crime/Martial Arts Cas. (PR:O MPAA:R)

LOYALTIES*** (Brit./Can.) 100m Lauron–Dumbarton–Telefilm Canada & Canadian Broadcasting–Alberta Motion Picture Development/Norstar Releasing c

Kenneth Welsh (*David Sutton*), Susan Wooldridge (*Lily Sutton*), Tantoo Cardinal (*Rosanne Ladouceur*), Vera Martin (*Beatrice*), Diane Debassige (*Leona*), Tom Jackson (*Eddy*), Jeffrey Smith (*Nicholas Sutton*), Meredith Rimmer (*Naomi Sutton*), Alexander Tribiger, Jonathan Tribiger (*Jeremy Sutton*), Christopher Barrington-Leigh (*Robert Sutton*), Yolanda Cardinal (*Lisa*), Dale Willier (*Jesse*), Wesley Semenovich (*Wayne*), Janet Wright (*Audrey Sawchuk*), Don Mackay (*Mike Sawchuk*), Paul Whitney (*Joe Pilsudski*), Tom Heaton (*Pilot Henry*), Sam Mottrich (*Manager*), Eric Kramer, Wendell Smith (*Construction Workers*), Joan Hinz (*Waitress*), Jill Dyck (*Paulette*), Colin Vint (*Amir*), Veena Sood (*Sima*), Doris Chilcot (*Mrs. Hatter*), Terri Daniels (*Marlene*), Susan MacNeill (*Woman at Table*), Ben Cardinal (*Man at Table*), Bryan Fustukian (*Lead Singer 1st Band*), Larry Yachimec (*Frank the Mountie*), Larry Musser (*Marvin the Mountie*), Eddy Washington (*Mover*), Emilie Chervigny (*Receptionist*).

As its title may suggest, LOYALTIES is about friendship and devotion, a theme that movies refrain from approaching beyond the most mundane treatments. But director Anne Wheeler and screenwriter Sharon Riis have created a complex and involved story in which the plot is secondary to the delineations of the characters and the changes that occur in their lives. Set in the backwoods Alberta community of Lac La Biche, Welsh and Wooldridge are a well-to-do English couple resettled from their traditional realm of propriety and tradition to a land of hearty settlers and struggling Indians. Though Welsh's new position at the local hospital is the accepted reason for their move, there is obviously some secret reason for their relocation that is not completely revealed until the movie's end. Wooldridge comes from an upper-crust British family that instilled in her the rather snobbish values common to this breed. The importance she places on decorum and proper manners is wholly out of place in a community where the locals speak their minds regardless of the impressions they make. Wooldridge feels completely isolated, unable to find friendship among the catty doctors' wives or with her busy husband. To help maintain their new home, Welsh hires the half-breed Cardinal as a maid for Wooldridge.

Cardinal has just lost her job as a barmaid at a country-and-western bar because of a fight she had with her unruly common-law husband. After this brawl she immediately left her husband, taking her brood of kids to live with her mother. Though skeptical of waiting on a snobbish British woman, Cardinal's desperate need for money forces her to accept the position.

At first Wooldridge and Cardinal are at complete odds with each other, but they soon develop an intimate friendship that has seemingly always been absent from Wooldridge's life. The emotional openness and frankness of Cardinal and her family is a sharp contrast to the coldness of Wooldridge's. But this new friendship is quickly threatened when Welsh's actual reason for hiring Cardinal—his lustful attraction to her teenage daughter—is revealed. His attack on an adolescent girl in England was the real reason for the family's move to this rural region. Wooldridge has painstakingly attempted to hide this dark secret that has almost torn her family apart. Her 11-year-old son has already witnessed Welsh's deviousness and remained in England at a private school, refusing to even acknowledge his father. On one particularly stormy night, Welsh assaults Cardinal's daughter. The girl's screams bring her mother, who threatens to shoot Welsh with a shotgun, but is hit over the head with a brick by Wooldridge before firing a shot. The next morning Wooldridge reports her husband's action to the police, the need to protect the decorum of her marriage having been replaced by her friendship with Cardinal.

The preachy stance that is the curse of most socially conscious films is absent from LOYALTIES as a result of the attention to an honest depiction of the characters and the emotional changes they experience. No one is shown as completely good or evil, but as normal people whose personalities and needs are formed by their environment. Even the husbands, for all their poor treatment of their wives, have their good sides. After losing Cardinal, her husband makes an ardent effort to attract his wife back by bending over backwards to prove his love. Though Cardinal has emphatically denied her desire to ever see him again, her affection for him is stronger than the hurt she nurses, so that by the end of the film she admits to her willingness and unrevealed need to have him back. Welsh also is initially shown as a likable man who will do anything to keep his family happy. His inability to do so stems mainly from Wooldridge's reluctance to face the fact that her marriage and her husband have some very serious problems. It is the insightful handling of the changes that Wooldridge experiences that is the backbone of LOYALTIES' development. In this respect the film becomes a criticism of the limitations inherent in class structures. Wooldridge's ability to overcome her stifling sense of decorum to create an emotional bond with a member of a lower class fulfills her needs for friendship as well as instigates the changes necessary for her family.

LOYALTIES was the first feature for director Wheeler, whose other credits include the popular television drama "A Change of Heart," also scripted by Sharon Riis, and the award-winning documentary A WAR STORY. Screenwriter Riis based much of Wooldridge's character on her own experiences as an isolated newcomer to Lac La Bishe in 1975.

p, William Johnston, Ronald Lillie, Anne Wheeler; d, Anne Wheeler; w, Sharon Riis (based on a story by Anne Wheeler, Sharon Riis); ph, Vic Sarin; ed, Judy Krupanszky; art d, Richard Hudolin; cos, Wendy Partridge; spec eff, Dave Gauthier; makeup, Jan Newman.

Drama   **(PR:O MPAA:NR)**

LUCAS***   (1986) 104m Lawrence Gordon/FOX c

Corey Haim *(Lucas Blye)*, Kerri Green *(Maggie)*, Charlie Sheen *(Cappie Roew)*, Courtney Thorne-Smith *(Alise)*, Winona Ryder *(Rina)*, Thomas E. Hodges *(Bruno)*, Ciro Poppiti *(Ben)*, Guy Boyd *(Coach)*, Jeremy Piven *(Spike)*, Kevin Gerard Wixted *(Tonto)*, Emily Seltzer, Erika Leigh, Anne Ryan *(Cheerleaders Marie, Mary Ellen, Angie)*, Jason Robert Alderman *(Tony)*, Tom Mackie *(Billy)*, Garrett M. Brown *(Mr. Kaiser)*, Donald Harrigan *(Man at Symphony)*, Judy Leavitt-Wells *(Cheer Coach)*, Christina Baglivi *(Spanish Teacher)*, Shirley Madlock, Rosanne E. Krevitt *(Teachers)*, Gregg Potter *(Tough Kid)*, Polly Augusta Noonan *(Punk Girl)*, James Krag *(Usher)*, R.G. Clayton *(Band Teacher)*, Patti Wilkus *(Home Economics Teacher)*, Martha Murphy *(Choir Teacher)*, Lucy Butler *(Maggie's Mom)*, Gary Cole *(Assistant Coach)*, Jerald Edward Cundiff, Jr. *(Karger)*, Carol Haim.

Finally, after years of sophomoric teenage sex comedies written by dirty old men or horny film school graduates, a film has been made that deals with *real* problems of adolescent love. Not since George Roy Hill hit the mark on the subject with his 1979 film A LITTLE ROMANCE has there been such an accurate portrait of first love. The love in LUCAS is not one based on bedding some tall, blonde, bikini-clad airhead, but on true friendship and honesty. Unlike PORKY'S and its clones, LUCAS doesn't have any scenes in which the young virgin boy is wowed by a naked girl in a locker room. Haim plays the title character, a 13-year-old eccentric who likes bugs and classical music and, being a short, four-eyed intellectual, is the victim of all the high-school bullies. He is offended by the social system of rewarding people for their physical prowess, taking specific aim at high-school football players and their cheerleader acolytes. One day Haim spots a lovely 16-year-old girl, Green, on the tennis court. Thoughts of her fill his romantic head as she is seen moving gracefully in slow-motion on the tennis court. They become friends, but nothing more. Haim has

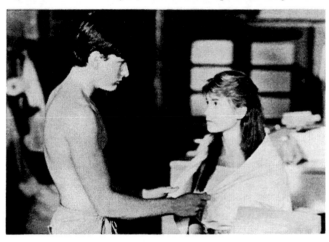

fallen in love with her, but she values his friendship. Haim introduces Green to classical music and talks to her as she has never been spoken to before—like a person and not a sex object. Green is fascinated by Haim and tells that "it's nice to know somebody has real heavy thoughts." Haim's ideal is threatened, however, by Green's attraction to Sheen, a handsome, well-built football player. Green decides to become a cheerleader, alienating Haim in the process. Caught between being a child and a woman, Green is intimidated by—yet attracted to—Sheen. At one point, she and Sheen are alone in the school's laundry room when the gentlemanly Sheen asks if he can kiss Green. Haim eventually learns that Sheen isn't a bullying jock like all the rest, but a decent and thoughtful person. When Sheen's teammates give Haim a hard time, Sheen sticks up for him, earning Haim's respect. Haim still ends up on the short end when he asks Green to go to a school dance. She agrees, but at the last minute backs out in favor of seeing Sheen. To avoid losing Haim as a friend, Sheen suggests that the three of them go out together. Haim declines, preferring to mend his broken heart alone. Convinced that he must somehow win Green's heart, Haim tries out for the football team, selling out all his beliefs in order to get the girl. When the coach, Boyd, tries to block his tryout, Haim threatens legal action on grounds of

discrimination. When the big game comes along and the home team is losing, Haim suits up and demands that the coach let him play. Knowing the game is a loss and hoping to shut Haim up, the coach lets him in for one play. Not surprisingly, Haim gets the stuffing knocked out of him. The coach tries to pull him out of the game, but no time-outs are left and Haim stays in. Haim gets his chance to make a big catch for the touchdown. Reality sets in, however, and he is knocked out. He ends up in a hospital and, upon returning to school, is hailed as something of a hero, presented with a letter jacket by his former jock antagonists.

A first-time directing chore for Seltzer, the screenwriter of THE OMEN, THE OTHER SIDE OF THE MOUNTAIN, SIX WEEKS, and TABLE FOR FIVE, LUCAS has more honest teenage scenes than all of John Hughes' films combined. Seltzer, like Hughes, is from the posh Northern suburbs of Chicago, as are the characters in their films. Where Hughes' characters seem like teenage kids speaking the lines of an adult screenwriter (resulting in pint-sized versions of THE BIG CHILL characters), Seltzer's characters are real. Seltzer, a single father of four, cites his own children as "barometers" for the film's reality. "They would tell me if something struck them as phony," says Seltzer. After such a glut of pathetic, stereotypical teenagers in movies, Haim, Green, and Sheen are a joy to watch. As a result, LUCAS is not just a film for teenagers but for anyone who has ever *been* a teenager. One cannot watch LUCAS without feeling some attachment to at least one of the characters. Even the bullying football player, Hodges, has more than one dimension, proving to be just as insecure about himself as is Haim. The film's greatest fault, and it's a major one, is its reliance on football heroics at the end. This ROCKY-style ending comes out of nowhere and turns the humanism of the film into spectacle. Haim has successfully persuaded everyone that physical power is not the answer, so there is no reason to sympathize with his decision to run onto the field. From all he has said, he doesn't care about proving his virility, nor does Green or Sheen. Why then should anyone else? After such wonderfully developed relationships, it hurts to see LUCAS take such a cheap turn.

Not surprisingly, Twentieth Century-Fox didn't have the foggiest notion of how to advertise LUCAS, concentrating on the Green-Sheen romance, rather than the real story. Making only a meager $1.8 million in its first week of release, through favorable word-of-mouth and the championing of television reviewers, LUCAS did manage to bring in $8 million over the next few weeks. (In Hollywood, it is a rarity—and the sign of a quality film—to do better business in the second and third weeks than in the opening week.) Still, LUCAS fast faded from movie screens in favor of the exploitative and predictable drivel to which audiences have become accustomed. Songs include: "Walk of Life" (Mark Knopfler, performed by Dire Straits), "Follow Your Heart" (Peter Rafelson, performed by Peter Rafelson), "Night Rolls On" (Chris Farren, Curtis Stone, performed by Chris Farren), "King for a Day" (Tom Bailey, Alannah Currie, Joseph Leeway, performed by The Thompson Twins), "Hit Me With Your Best Shot" (Edward Schwartz, performed by Pat Benatar), "Strut" (Charlie Dore, Julian Littman).

p, David Nicksay; d&w, David Seltzer; ph, Reynaldo Villalobos (Panavision, DeLuxe Color); m, Dave Grusin; ed, Priscilla Nedd; art d, James Murakami; set d, Linda Sutton; cos, Molly Maginnis; m/l, Mark Knopfler, Peter Rafelson, Chris Farren, Curtis Stone, Tom Bailey, Alannah Currie, Joseph Leeway, Edward Schwartz, Charlie Dore, Julian Littman; makeup, Jamie Sue Weiss.

Drama/Romance   Cas.   (PR:A MPAA:PG-13)

L'ULTIMA MAZURKA†   (1986, It.) Rai Radiotelevisione Italiana–Rai
Uno–Comune Di Milano–Regione Lombardia/Sacis c (Trans: The Last Mazurka)

Erland Josephson, Senta Berger, Mario Scaccia, Paolo Bonacelli, Marina Berti, Adele Cossi, Giuseppe Fallisi.

The collapse of a small operetta company serves as a metaphor for the end of enlightenment and the rise of Fascism in Italy circa 1921. Arriving in Milan to perform Franz Lehar's "Blue Mazurka," the operetta company inadvertently becomes embroiled in a local conflict between Fascists and Anarchists. On the opening night of the operetta, a bomb explodes in the audience and many patrons are killed. The Fascists blame the Anarchists and use the occasion of the victims' mass funeral to further their cause. The operetta company disbands, Mussolini rises to power, and the stages are filled with Fascist propaganda.

d, Gianfranco Bettettini; w, Gianfranco Bettettini, Luigi Lunari, Alberto Frarassino, Aldo Grasso, Tatti Sanguineti; ph, Giulio Albonico; m, Gino Negri, Franz Lehar.

Drama   (PR:C-O MPAA:NR)

L'ULTIMO GIORNO†   (1986, It.) Libera Cooperativa Cinematografica/Art
Film c (Trans: The Last Day)

Silvano Tranquilli, Susan Doyle, Carlo Giudice, Franca Gonella.

An ailing 60-year-old widower with a chronic heart problem tries to find someone to care for his 20-year-old retarded son who is incapable of doing anything for himself. The father finds himself blocked at every turn until he meets a pretty young woman who willingly takes care of the boy for absolutely no reward. She treats the boy as if he is perfectly normal, and this increases his confidence. One night, while returning from a trip to a circus, father and son are separated. The father spends an anxiety-filled evening trying to locate the retarded boy to no avail. He eventually gives up and returns home, only to find his son sitting on the doorstep awaiting his arrival. The shock is too much for the man and he suffers a fatal heart attack, leaving his son in the care of the young woman.

p, Marcello Berni; d, Amasi Damiani; w, Alberto Damiani (based on a story by Amasi Damiani); ph, Felice De Maria (Luciano Vittori Color); m, Nedo Benvenuti.

Drama   (PR:C MPAA:NR)

LULU DE NOCHE†   (1986, Span.) 95m Kaplan–Fernando Trueba c (Trans:
Lulu By Night)

Imanol Arias (Rufo), Amparo Munoz (Nena), Antonio Resines (Germain), Assumpta Serna (Amelia), Patricia Adriani (Lola), Asuncion Balaguer (Josefina), Fernando Vivanco (Cesar), El Gran Wyoming (Paco).

A bizarre black comedy from Spanish director Martinez-Lazaro follows the bumbling efforts of theater director Resines to cast—and then find backers for—a pretentious play titled "The Wolfman's Politics" which features a psychotic with a mother fixation and an uninhibited vamp named Lulu. Resines must fend off his ex-wife, Serna, who begs for the role of the vamp, while trying to persuade his former girl friend, Munoz, to take the part. Not only does he want Munoz to play the seductress, but he tries to persuade her rich husband, Vivanco (who knows nothing about his wife's affair with the theater director) to help bankroll the production. Munoz refuses to take the part and in desperation Resines turns to a strange woman he met in a taxicab, Adriani. For the role of the psycho, Resines tries to cast Arias, a swarthy professional thief. Soon all the characters begin falling in love with each other. Vivanco becomes infatuated with the wild Adriani; Munoz falls for Arias, but his only concern is his crazy mother who sees visions of the Pope while stoned on drugs; Resines' ex-wife has an affair with a

dimwitted soccer player, while the frustrated Resines still pines for Munoz. LULU DE NOCHE had its world premiere at the Miami Film Festival in 1986.

d&w, Emilio Martinez-Lazaro; ph, Juan Amoros; m, Angel Munoz-Alonso; ed, Nieves Martin; art d, Carlos Ruiz Castillo.

Comedy   (PR:O MPAA:NR)

LUNATICS, THE***   (1986, Hong Kong) 95m D&B Films c

Fung Sui Fan, Deanie Yip, Chow Yun Fat, John Sham, Chun Pui, Lai Huen, Dennis Chan, Leung Chieu Wai.

A cinematic oddity, LUNATICS is a film from Hong Kong that is neither a Kung Fu extravaganza nor a drippy love story. In fact it is a well made, consciousness-raising film that attacks a theme frequently overlooked in the movies: mental illness. Fung plays a social worker whose job it is to check on outpatients spread across the city. As the film opens, one such patient has walked into a small market, creating mass hysteria by wandering about with a meat cleaver. Fung arrives on the scene, gently coaxes the weapon from the man, and brings him back to his home. In covering the incident, reporter Yip charges that the health system encourages such potentially dangerous occurrences. Fung invites Yip to accompany him on his rounds in order to help her gain a better understanding of his job and the people he treats. Traveling across the city, the reporter is introduced to a number of eccentric, harmless people who shy away from unfamiliar people. These include an old woman with an amazing collection of what would be considered trash, and a man living in a garbage dump where he attempts to care for a child. The child is in desperate need of medical care, but the man is afraid of losing her. The persistent social worker sees that the child receives proper attention, and thus saves her life. Another man whom Fung and Yip visit is a seemingly well-adjusted person who suffered a breakdown shortly after being married. He has a son, and when he has a run-in with his former wife while visiting the child, he is threatened with never being allowed to see his child again. This confrontation sends him into a rage, and locks himself inside his apartment, killing chickens. Aware of his condition, his neighbors attempt to restrain him, but he breaks away, wounds several people, and then barricades himself in his son's kindergarten. He kills one teacher before Fung arrives on the scene. Fung's only recourse is to kill the man. Soon after this, the man he aided in the market at the beginning of the film repeats the same ritual. A reporter snaps a picture, frightening the knife-wielding man, who then fatally wounds Fung. The end of the film shows reporter Yip taking up the work of Fung.

Despite its unusual theme, THE LUNATICS has become one of the most commercially successful films of all time in Hong Kong. This can possibly be attributed to the controversy created by the publicity campaign and the subsequent criticism of the film by social workers fearful that people would think Hong Kong was filled with insane, potentially dangerous people. The film had its origins in an actual event perpetrated by a one-time mental patient, an incident similar to the kindergarten scene of the film. Several of the actors portraying mental patients were Hong Kong matinee idols who risked tainting their images through their involvement in the project. As a whole THE LUNATICS is a well-made film; its only drawback is its tendency to sentimentalize events, specifically the relationship between Yip and Fung. Otherwise, the film is devastatingly brutal in its depiction of eccentric individuals, who quickly win audience empathy before the climactic bloodbath occurs. (In Cantonese; English subtitles.)

p, John Sham; d&w, Yee Tung Sing [Derek Erh]; m, Deanie Yip.

Drama   (PR:O MPAA:NR)

L'UNIQUE†   (1986, Fr.) 81m Belles Rives/Revcom c (Trans: The One and
Only)

Julia Migenes Johnson (The Singer), Tcheky Karyo (Michel), Sami Frey (Colewsky), Charles Denner (Vox), Jezabel Carpi (Aline), Fabienne Babe (Sarah), Thierry Rode (Rey), Benjamin de Borda (Tom).

A mixture of science fiction and pop music forms the basis for this French feature. Johnson is a temperamental, yet popular, singer who has been giving her producer (Denner) nothing but headaches. Denner hires Frey, a pioneering scientist, to create a hologram of Johnson to perform in her place. Johnson's unrecognized former amour, Karyo, attempts to film a concert but is tossed out of the hall when it's learned he has a camera. Through the hologram double, Johnson finally learns Karyo's identity, and discovers her own child by Karyo. The computer-engineered figures, created by the French organization Sogitec, were reportedly the first of their type ever used in a European release.

p&d, Jerome Diamant-Berger; w, Jerome Diamant-Berger, Olivier Assayas, Jean-Claude Carriere; ph, Jean-Francois Robin (Panavision, Fujicolor); m, Guy Boulanger; ed, Luc Barnier; art d, Nikos Meletopoulos; cos, Dona Turnier; spec eff, Christian Guillon; makeup, Sophie Landry, Alain Moize.

Science Fiction   (PR:O MPAA:NR)

LUSSURI† (1986, It.) Cinema 80/Continental c (Trans: Lust)

Lilli Carati, Noemie Chelkoff, Al Cliver, Martin Philips, Ursula Foti.

A young man, tormented by the psychological demons of his past, is plagued by a series of sado-sexual nightmares. The female figure in these dreams is usually his mother, his sister, or an aunt. Eventually, after reaching a point of sheer despair, the tortured individual murders his sister and commits suicide.

d, Joe D'Amato; w, Rene Rivet; ph, Aristide Massaccesi (Luciano Vittori Color); m, Guido Anelli, Stefano Mainetti.

Drama (PR:O MPAA:NR)

MACARONI BLUES† (1986, Nor.) 78m A/S Elan-Norsk/Norena b&w

Riccardo de Torrebruna, Anne Marie Ottesen, Patrizio Caracchi, Odd Borretzen, Arild Nyquist, Knut Andersen, Harald Krogtoft, Hot Club of Norway, Eddie Constantine.

De Torrebruna is an Italian restaurateur living in Norway. When the government's unwavering liquor laws prove to be detrimental to his business, de Torrebruna must turn his restaurant into a speakeasy. When this leads to his untimely death, de Torrebruna's brother Caracchi arrives from Italy to retaliate against the Norwegian system. With the help of some of the late de Torrebruna's friends, Caracchi sneaks through a picket line of striking warehouse workers and makes off with a hefty supply of spirits. This pilfered booze is then slipped into the city's milk supply, causing public drunkenness throughout Oslo. Caracchi, having completed what he set out to do, gets in a final verbal jab at the government before finally beginning his journey home to Italy.
   Csepcsanyi, the film's co-director, is a Hungarian-born Italian citizen who has taken to working in Norway. Eddie Constantine makes a brief cameo as a bootlegger working the waterways, and manages to slip in a quick homage to his famed "Lemmy Caution" persona.

p, Kirsten Bryhni; d, Bela Csepcsanyi, Fred Sassebo; w, Odd Borretzen; ed, Fred Sassebo; prod d, Frode Krogh.

Comedy/Crime (PR:C MPAA:NR)

MAHULIENA, ZLATA PANNA† (1986, Czech.) 92m Bratislava c

Vladimir Hajdu *(Jan)*, Heinz Moog *(King)*, Lara Naszinski *(Mahuliena)*, Martin Remy *(Prince)*, Maru Valdivielso *(Diva)*, Jiri Krytinar *(Zlatovlad)*, Jan Kozuch *(Koktavy)*, Miroslav Noga *(Bradaty)*, Vilhelm Perhac, Jan Mildner.

d, Miloslav Luther; w, Martin Porubjak, Miloslav Luther; ph, Jan Malir, Vladimir Hollos; m, Quido De Angelis, Michele De Angelis; ed, Alfred Bencic; art d, Viliam Gruska; cos, Jozef Jelinek.

MAINE-OCEAN† (1986, Fr.) 132m Films du Passage–French Line–FR3/AAA Classic c (Trans: Maine-Ocean Express)

Bernard Menez *(Le Garrec)*, Luis Rego *(Pontoiseau)*, Lydia Feld *(Lawyer)*, Rosa-Maria Gomez *(Dejanina)*, Bernard Dumaine *(The Judge)*, Pedro Armendariz, Jr. *(Impresario)*, Mike Marshall *(A Lawyer)*, Yves Afonso *(The Sailor)*.

The Maine-Ocean Express is a train route that originates in Paris and takes passengers to Brittany. Menez and Rego, two ticket-takers aboard the train, run into a variety of oddball characters over the course of the journey. One woman, Gomez, is a Brazilian dancer, while Feld (who cowrote MAINE-OCEAN's screenplay) is an inept lawyer retained to defend sailor Afonso against assault charges. They all end up on a Brittany island before boarding a plane headed for the United States at the film's end.
   This was the first film in years from director Jacques Rozier, a minor director from the French New Wave era best known for his 1962 work ADIEU, PHILIPPINE.

p, Paolo Branco; d, Jacques Rozier; w, Lydia Feld, Jacques Rozier; ph, Acacio de Almeida (Eastmancolor); m, Chico Buarque, Hubert Dege, Anne Frederic; ed, Jacques Rozier.

Comedy (PR:C MPAA:NR)

MALA NOCHE† (1986) 75m Northern Film bw

Tim Strecter *(Walt Curtis)*, Doug Cooeyate *(Johnny)*, Ray Monge *(Roberto Pepper)*.

Strecter is a homosexual store clerk living in Portland, Oregon with his sister. When Strecter becomes attracted to Cooeyate, an illegal Mexican immigrant, he invites the newcomer over for dinner. Cooeyate immediately falls for the sister, and Strecter is left with his guest's friend Monge. Later Monge is killed by the law, and Strecter's sister leaves town to work in an Alaskan strip joint. The film closes as Strecter once more runs into Cooeyate on the street. This independent American production, based on an autobiographical story, was screened in 1986 at the Berlin Film Festival.

p,d&w, Gus Van Sant (based on the novella by Walt Curtis); ph, John Campbell; m, Creighton Lindsay; ed, Gus Van Sant.

Drama (PR:O MPAA:NR)

MALABRIGO† (1986, Peru/Cuba/Ger./Brit.) 84m Perfo–ICAIC–Channel Four–ZDF c

Charo Verastegui, Luis Alvarez, Ricardo Blume.

When a woman travels to the Peruvian fishing village of Malabrigo to meet her accountant husband, she is shocked to learn that no one has seen him in two days. After various inquiries prove fruitless, it is learned the missing individual had worked at a factory which exploded under mysterious circumstances. An investigator from an insurance firm comes to find out exactly what occurred and his path leads him to unexpected answers.

p, Andres Malatesta, Emilio Salomon; d, Alberto Durant; w, Jorge Guerra, Alberto Durant; ph, Mario Garcia Joya; ed, Justo Vega.

Drama/Mystery (PR:O MPAA:NR)

MALACCA† (1986, Swed.) 90m FilmStallet–Swedish Film Institute–Swedish Television–SVT2/Swedish Film Institute c

Gunilla Olsson, Charlotta Larsson, Kjell Bergqvist, Carl Gustaf Lindstedt, Marc Klein-Essink.

The director of the popular erotic dramas I AM CURIOUS—YELLOW, and I AM CURIOUS—BLUE made this tale of carefree youths traveling through Asia whose encounters with a mysterious man endanger their lives.

p&d, Vilgot Sjoman.

Thriller (PR:O MPAA:NR)

MALANDRO**½ (1986, Braz./Fr.) 105m MK2–Austra–TF-1 –Ministere de la Culture/Samuel Goldwyn c (OPERA DO MALANDRO)

Edson Celulari *(Max)*, Claudia Ohana *(Lu)*, Elba Ramalho *(Margot)*, Ney Latorraca *(Tigrao)*, Fabio Sabag *(Otto Strudell)*, J.C. Violla *(Geni)*, Wilson Grey *(Satiro Bilhar)*, Maria Silvia *(Victoria Strudell)*, Claudia Gimenez *(Fiorella)*, Andreia Dantas *(Fichinha)*, Ilva Nina *(Doris Pelanca)*, Zenaide *(Dorinha Tubao)*, Djenane Machado *(Shirley Paquete)*, Katia Bronstein *(Mimi Bibelo)*, Luthero Luiz *(Porfirio)*.

This Brazilian musical, loosely adapted from "The Threepenny Opera," features Celulari as a pimp working in WW II-era Rio. When Ramalho, the classic hooker with a heart of gold, is fired from the nightclub where she works, Celulari decides to get even with Sabag, the Nazi club owner who fired her. Celulari sets out to seduce Sabag's daughter, Ohana, but this girl requires more work than the smooth-talking sharpie imagined.
   Like so many musicals, the plot and characters are thin, the song and dance numbers taking precedence. These are done in a splashy style that harkens back to the 1940s Hollywood musicals, with few homages to CASABLANCA and a number of gangster films tossed in for good measure. However, despite the well-intended efforts of director Guerra, the film serves only as a reminder of what might have been. The spirit is there, but the talent is not quite up to the mark.

p, Marin Karmitz, Ruy Guerra; d, Ruy Guerra; w, Chico Buarque, Orlando Senna, Ruy Guerra (based on the musical "Opera do Malandro" by Chico Buarque); ph, Antonio Luis Mendes; m, Chico Buarque; ed, Mair Tavares, Ide Lacreta, Kenout Peltier; md, Mauro Monteiro, Irenio Maia; cos, Maria Cecilia Motta; ch, Regina Miranda; m/l, Chico Buarque.

Musical (PR:C MPAA:NR)

MALAYUNTA (SEE: BAD COMPANY, 1986, Arg.)

MALCOLM*** (1986, Aus.) 90m Cascade/Vestron c

Colin Friels *(Malcolm)*, John Hargreaves *(Frank)*, Lindy Davies *(Judith)*, Chris Haywood *(Willy)*, Charles Tingwell *(Tramways Supervisor)*, Beverly Phillips *(Mrs. T.)*, Judith Stratford *(Jenny)*, Heather Mitchell *(Barmaid)*, Katerina Tassopoulos *(Jenny's Mother)*.

A small and endearing film which crams as much sheer delight into its 90 minutes as humanly possible. The title character, played by Friels, is a socially withdrawn man of about 30 who lives alone in the small house that his deceased mother left him. A mechanical genius, Friels has filled his house with electronic gadgets—a miniature gauge train that transports the mail from the post box to Friels' desk, a radio-controlled car which cruises down to a neighboring shop to pick up milk, and a kitchen straight out of a Rube Goldberg drawing. A local shopkeeper, Phillips, keeps a maternal eye on Friels and extends him a never-ending line of credit. Anxious to see Friels support himself, she suggests that he take in a boarder. The first one to respond is Hargreaves, a mean looking ex-con who is looking for a place where he can lay low while planning some upcoming heists. He brings with him his faithful moll Davies, who shows Friels more patience and understanding than does Hargreaves. The two become amazed with Friels' mechanical know-how and love of gadgetry, while he becomes interested in their less-than-discreet romancing. When one of Hargreaves heists nets him a supply of televisions, he gives one to Friels—more as a bribe to keep quiet than as a gift of affection. As he overdoses on crime shows, Friels decides to give a gift to Hargreaves in return—a miniature radio-controlled car equipped with a gun and a video camera that can successfully pull off a bank robbery. Naturally, Hargreaves thinks of ways to use Friels' genius to the fullest extent. Hargreaves, Davies, and Friels work together to pull a major heist at a large bank. By using three radio-controlled trash cans and an ample amount of ingenuity, they manage to get away with the cash.
   The directorial debut for the 30-year-old Nadia Tass, whose husband, David Parker, wrote and photographed the $650,000 film, MALCOLM took the Australian Film Institute Awards by surprise, winning a grand total of eight categories. MALCOLM won as Best Film; Tass as Best Director (a first for a woman in Australia); Friels as Best Actor; Hargreaves and Davies in their respective Best Supporting catagories; Parker for Best Screenplay; as well as taking the prizes for Best Editing and Sound. Not only is the film an engaging comedy, but it is a warm and personal appeal for socially isolated people like Malcolm. The film's success has been especially meaningful to Tass, on whose brother, John Tassopoulos, the film is based. "Basically he had the characteristics you saw in Malcolm," Tass has said. "He was very withdrawn, socially inept. He had a difficult time being accepted into society because of his inability to communicate verbally. However, he was a very clever person." In 1983, John Tassopoulos died after

being hit by a car while suffering an epileptic seizure. MALCOLM, however, is anything but a heavy-handed plea for the socially retarded. Friels is a mischievous character who is equally as responsible for the bank heist as Hargreaves. Their only difference lies in their naivete, or lack of it—Hargreaves is fully aware of the illegality of his actions, while Friels is simply exercising his mechanical creativity. Friels is exceptional in the lead. Relying on facial expressions and using a minimum of dialog, he is able to gain audience sympathy while at the same time creating a character that becomes a hero. Although his actions are rather embarrassing, audiences soon find themselves rooting for Friels and his seemingly harmless criminal exploits. In case there is any doubt as to Friels' talent, one need only watch him in a completely different role as the bearded D.H. Lawrence in 1986's KANGAROO. Hargreaves, previously seen on American screens in CAREFUL, HE MIGHT HEAR YOU (1984), is equally captivating as the tough guy who initially thinks that Friels is a retarded dunce but soon grows to admire him. Rounding out the lead players is Davies who acts as a go-between for Friels, whom she finds likable and tender, and Hargreaves, who is as hard and jaded as she, but who she dearly loves. As important to the film's success as the acting is the gadgetry, which becomes as fascinating to the audience as it is to the characters. Designed by Parker (who proves to be something of a renaissance man on this picture) with the assistance of Tony Mahood and Steve Mills, the gadgets are essentially toys for grown-ups. Aside from the bandit trash cans, the most amazing of Parker's inventions is a little yellow Honda car which splits down the middle into two sections—one half for the driver, the other for the passenger, each with its own steering control. Tass and Parker used three cars for the filming—one they kept intact and two that were cut down the middle with an angle grinder and a hacksaw. "We naturally think of a getaway car as something high-powered and something the police are not likely to pull over because it looks out of the ordinary," Parker has explained. "But Malcolm's a bit bent. He's been watching TV and he feels what you need is something that can disappear down a lane and get away, so he splits the car in half." When the car does split in two it comes as an unbelievable surprise. What shows up on the screen is not trick photography, but two halves of a car weaving through the streets of Melbourne. It is one of the best sight gags ever committed to film and this alone is reason enough to see the film.

p, Nadia Tass, David Parker; d, Nadia Tass; w&ph, David Parker; ed, Ken Sallows; prod d, Rob Perkins; m/l, The Penguin Cafe Orchestra.

Comedy (PR:C MPAA:PG-13)

MALKAT HAKITA† (1986, Israel) 89m Golan-Globus/Cannon c (Trans: Prom Queen)

Alon Aboutboul, Itzhak Ben-Ner, Avital Beer, Ranan Hefetz, Doron Avrahami, Shmuel Shilo, Ronnie Arditi, Rami Baruch, Anath Sanderovitch.

A temperamental student at an Israeli boarding school lashes out at those around him when he's dumped by his girl friend. The fiery lad gets involved in a project to build an airplane, while his ex-flame expresses love for one of the school's instructors. The story comes to a brutal climax when the brother of the school's prom queen arrives and tries to take control of events.

The cast is comprised of both professional and amateur actors in this Israeli release from the men behind Cannon Films, Menahem Golan and Yoram Globus.

p,d&w, Itzhak [Zeppel] Yeshurun; ph, Avi Karpik; m, Alex Kagan; ed, Tova Asher; art d, Zmira Hershkovitz; cos, Anath Messner.

Drama (PR:C MPAA:NR)

MAMA IS BOOS!† (1986, Neth.) 110m Movies Film Productions/Meteor –The Movies c (Trans: Mama Is Mad!)

Peter Faber (John Gisberts), Geert de Jong (Danny Gisberts), Sanne van der Noort (Jan-Julius Gisberts), Alexander Mouissie (Valentijn Gisberts), Rijk de Gooyer (Pete Stewart), Adelheid Roosen (Jane Fongler).

This sequel to the highly successful 1984 Dutch film SCHATJES finds chopper pilot Faber and his wife de Jong celebrating their twentieth wedding anniversary. When de Jong finds out that her husband has been keeping company with another woman, she orders him out of the house. Faber moves in with his lover, and de Jong goes to extraordinary lengths to keep her children from their father. Faber, who is employed at a nearby air base, gets involved with a television extravaganza celebrating the fortieth anniversary of the North Atlantic Treaty Organization. De Jong has friends trash her husband's love nest during rehearsals, then stages her own attack on Faber during the television broadcast.

This wild comedy features much of the same cast as SCHATJES (translation: Darlings), and again was directed by Ruud van Hemert.

p, Chris Brouwer, Haig Balian; d&w, Ruud van Hemert; ph, Theo van de Sande (Eastmancolor); m, Ruud van Hemert; ed, Wim Louwriter; art d, Jan Blokker, Dirk Debou, Dorus van der Linden; spec eff, Harry Wiessenhaan, Leo Cahn.

Comedy (PR:C-O MPAA:NR)

MAMBRU SE FUE A LA GUERRA† (1986, Span.) 100m Altair–Filmograficas c (Trans: Mambru Went to War)

Fernando Fernan-Gomez (Emiliano), Marla Asquerino (Florentine), Agustin Gonzalez (Hilario), Emma Cohen (Encarna), Jorge Sanz, Nuria Gallardo, Carlos Cabezas, Maria Luisa Ponte, Alfonso del Real, Francisco Vidal.

During the 40-year reign of Generalissimo Francisco Franco, one man hides out in a cave rather than face political troubles. His exile comes to an end with Franco's death in 1975, but now his wife—who has claimed to be a widow all these years—may lose her pension money as a result. Several solutions are considered, including the murder of the old man, but the concern proves to be unjustified. It turns out that because the old man has been in exile so long no one recognizes him, and his former friends refuse to believe he is who he claims to be.

p, Miguel A. Perez Campos; d, Fernando Fernan-Gomez; w, Pedro Beltran; ph, Jose Luis Alcaine (Eastmancolor); m, Carmelo Bernaola; ed, Pablo Gonzalez del Amo; set d, Julio Esteban.

Comedy (PR:C MPAA:NR)

MAMMAME† (1986, Fr.) 65m Maison de la Culture du Havre c

Eric Alfieri, Mathilde Altaraz, Muriel Boulay, Christophe Delachau, Jean-Claude Gallota, Pascal Gravat, Priscilla Newell, Viviane Serry, Robert Seyfried.

Yet another entry from the amazingly prolific Ruiz, the Chilean expatriate surrealist who has been commissioned by the French government to make his films. MAMMAME is a short, semi-narrative feature which interconnects modern dance with a tale of the sexual roles of men and women. The nine dancers/actors (five men and four women) are arranged in four pairs with one man vacillating between heterosexuality and homosexuality. Like all of Ruiz's films, MAMMAME is rooted in surrealism and is wonderfully stylized.

p, Jean-Luc Larguier; d&w, Raul Ruiz; ph, Jacques Bouquin; m, Henry Torque, Serge Houppin; ed, Martine Bouquin; prod d, Raul Ruiz; cos, Francoise Chanas, Patricia Goudinoux; ch, Jean-Claude Gallota.

Dance (PR:NR MPAA:NR)

MAN AND A WOMAN: 20 YEARS LATER, A*** (1986, Fr.) 108m Films 13/WB c (UN HOMME ET UNE FEMME: VINGT ANS DEJA)

Anouk Aimee (Anne Gauthier), Jean-Louis Trintignant (Jean-Louis Duroc), Evelyne Bouix (Francoise), Marie-Sophie Pochat (Marie-Sophie), Philippe Leroy-Beaulieu (Prof. Thevenin), Charles Gerard (Charlot), Antoine Sire (Antoine), Andre Engel (Film Director), Richard Berry, Patrick Poivre d'Arvor, Thierry Sabine, Robert Hossein, Tanya Lopert, Nicole Garcia, Jacques Weber (Themselves).

In 1966, a young Claude Lelouch made a picture that won the Oscar as Best Foreign Film, and Best Original Screenplay, and also earned nominations for Lelouch as Best Director and Anouk Aimee as Best Actress. In this, he visits the two protagonists again. It's not quite a sequel because so much time has elapsed and the people have changed so much, but it helps if you have seen the other picture before seeing this. The liberal use of scenes from the earlier movie only heightens the alterations in the faces of Trintignant and Aimee (more so in his). She has become more beautiful and he more craggy and wizened and, perhaps, more interesting.

Aimee, the former script girl, is now a full-fledged movie producer. However, her career is in deep trouble as she most recently has been responsible for France's version of HOWARD THE DUCK or HEAVEN'S GATE, take your pick. In other words, if she doesn't come up with a hit soon, her welcome will have been worn to the ground. Trintignant is no longer a race driver. Instead, he arranges races for younger drivers and is, at present, getting the Paris-to-Dakar rally in order. He has not married again but he is involved with Pochat, a woman half his age whom he met at his son's (Sire, who also played his son in the first movie two decades before) wedding. It's almost a full 40 minutes into the film when Aimee calls Trintignant. She wants to make a musical version of their love story of 20 years before with Richard Berry, playing himself, in the lead. Several stories interweave now. They include the real-life happenings between Aimee and Trintignant, the tale she is telling on screen, and an extraneous subplot about a mad man who has escaped from a mental hospital, plus the aforementioned race. Before Trintignant can give himself fully to his renewed relationship with Aimee, he must first break his engagement to Pochat, and there is a silly sequence in

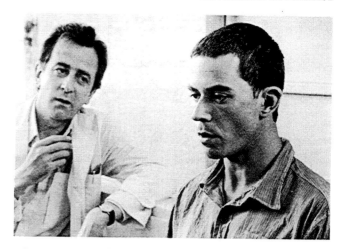

which he and Pochat are stranded in the desert in Niger and almost bake to death before they are rescued.

The movie tries to alight in too many genres. It is, at once, a love story, a musical version of an earlier love story, a racing adventure, a thriller, and a bog of cinematic ploys, most of which are not needed. Lai's music, which the 1960s hummed for years, is again introduced, and romantics will glow upon seeing the man and the woman together again. Lots of laughs and a few platitudes and an oddly unsentimental way of looking at things all add up to making this a mostly pleasing, though far too gimmicky, return. Good acting from all concerned and a nice cameo from Patrick Poivre d'Arvor, the Peter Jennings/Dan Rather of France. He plays Aimee's current amour and his role in the movie is exactly what he is, a media personality. Robert Hossein, Tanya Lopert, Jacques Weber, and Nicole Garcia of the Theatre De L'Atelier, all appear as themselves. A remarkable bit of casting is Evelyn Bouix as Aimee's daughter. She looks enough like Aimee to be her daughter. Approximately eight minutes were cut from the original French version and a new ending was added for the U.S. release (which is really an old ending, the scene from the earlier film in which Trintignant and Aimee embrace) as the camera swirls around them. Despite having so much story packed into the 108-minute running time, it still feels long and could have done with some judicious snipping. However, since most movies in 1986 are about lovers not much older than Molly Ringwald and Tom Cruise, this story of mature love does have many refreshing insights.

p&d, Claude Lelouch; w, Claude Lelouch, Pierre Uytterhoeven, Monique Lange, Jerome Tonnerre; ph, Jean-Yves Le Mener (Eastmancolor); m, Francis Lai; ed, Hugues Darmois; md, Christian Gaubert; art d, Jacques Bufnoir; cos, Emanuel Ungaro, Mic Cheminal; spec eff, Georges Demetrau; m/l, Francis Lai, Pierre Barouh; stunts, Remy Julienne.

Romance   (PR:C MPAA:PG)

MAN FACING SOUTHEAST**   (1986, Arg.) 105m Cinequanon/Film
        Dallas c (HOMBRE MIRANDO AL SUDESTE; AKA: MAN LOOKING
                                                        SOUTHEAST)

Lorenzo Quinteros *(Dr. Dennis)*, Hugo Soto *(Rantes)*, Ines Vernengo *(Beatriz)*, Cristina Scaramuzza *(Nurse)*, Rubens W. Correa *(Dr. Prieto)*, David Edery, Rodolfo Rodas, Jean Pierre Requeraz.

The story of Christ has always intrigued filmmakers and has been examined under a variety of interpretations. There have been the more literal renderings, including Cecil B. DeMille's 1927 silent feature KING OF KINGS (remade in 1961 by Nicholas Ray) and George Stevens' 1965 epic THE GREATEST STORY EVER TOLD. Others, such as Frank Borzage in 1940's STRANGE CARGO, have taken an allegorical approach, a method that is also employed by Argentinian filmmaker Eliseo Subiela in his complex work MAN FACING SOUTHEAST.

Quinteros is a doctor working in a mental asylum. Professionally burned out, Quinteros becomes intrigued when Soto, an intense and solemn man, suddenly appears from nowhere in his ward. Upon questioning, Soto explains he is a holographic being from another planet. Quinteros is convinced this odd man is merely running from legal authorities for some unknown reason, yet a fingerprint check proves otherwise. In fact, Soto's fingerprints are untraceable, lending further credence to his strange story. An intelligence test shows Soto to have a genius level IQ, and Quinteros' curiosity towards this unusual patient grows. Rather than prescribe tranquilizers to wear down Soto's delirium, Quinteros allows him free run of the hospital. Quinteros notices that each day Soto stands in the hospital gardens, facing exactly southeast as he stares unblinkingly towards the sky. Soto later explains that this is how he receives and transmits information from his planet. Other patients are visibly changed by Soto's presence, and they quietly follow him around the hospital grounds. Gradually an unusual friendship builds between Quinteros and Soto, and the doctor even arranges for his patient to work in the hospital morgue as janitor. There, and with Quinteros' complete knowledge, Soto begins dissecting human brains, hoping to find a clue to man's behavior. When Quinteros, a divorced man, takes his estranged children to the circus, he brings Soto along as well. Later the two get into a discussion of what Quinteros insists is Soto's delirium. Soto, in turn, asks deeper philosophical questions of his doctor, implying, perhaps, that Soto's mission is something beyond an intergalactic visit.

Quinteros has some hope of breaking Soto's delusions when Vernengo mysteriously arrives to visit the patient. After chatting with her, the doctor learns that Soto was a recovering alcoholic who had helped Vernengo with her work as an evangelist. Soto admits to knowing her, but explains that she too is an alien visitor, who, unlike himself, has succumbed to earthly temptations. Now, he tells Quinteros, whenever she feels emotional love, a blue liquid seeps from her mouth. The three attend an outdoor concert where Beethoven's Ninth Symphony is being played. Soto happily disrupts the situation by waltzing with Vernengo, and soon other couples join them. Then, and with no objections, Soto walks up to the conductor's stand and takes the baton, leading the orchestra and chorus in the glorious "Ode to Joy." Back at the hospital, Soto's followers awaken mysteriously and react ecstatically when the music at the concert reaches its peak. As a result, Quinteros is severely reprimanded, and he agrees to put Soto on a strong drug to counteract the delirium, knowing full well that ultimately this will kill his patient. Soto goes into a catatonic state, and Vernengo does what she can to comfort him. Later, she visits Quinteros at his apartment where the two make love. Just as Soto had claimed, a mysterious blue liquid trickles from her mouth. She explains that she too is from outer space, and Quinteros angrily throws her out, convinced that he has been toyed with by two crazy people. Going through Vernengo's purse, Quinteros finds a photograph of her and Soto, while the image of a third person has been torn off. Returning from an extended fishing trip with his children, Quinteros learns that Soto died in his absence and that the body was shipped to an anonymous medical school for autopsy, so the mystery behind the man will remain forever intact. The hospital patients gather in the garden where Soto once stood, convinced he will return in a spaceship. Quinteros simply waits in his apartment, contemplating the meaning of the torn photo, and wondering if Vernengo will ever come back.

In this unusual parable, writer/director Subiela incorporates a wide variety of visual and literary influences to create a fascinating, multifaceted work of art. The reworking of the Christ tale is obvious, with Soto as Jesus, Quinteros as a self-admitted Pilate, and Vernengo as Judas who sells out for pleasure rather than money. Yet Subiela does not restrict himself to a literal updating, instead using the Biblical figures as a basis for his own characters. If Christ returned, could it be as an extraterrestrial hologram in a lunatic asylum? Subiela presents an intelligent argument, never quite answering the questions he poses. Instead, he leaves it to the viewer's mind to examine what could be possible. In developing the story, Subiela clearly expresses the influence of the mystical tradition in Latin American literature. Soto has mysterious, unexplained telekinetic powers that he uses not only to rouse his followers during the concert, but to feed the poor as well. Quinteros never witnesses this ability, only the film audience does, and this further enhances the film's enigmatic quality. Subiela has also considered a variety of painting styles in the film's *mise-en-scene*, from familiar European representations of Christ to more disturbing surrealist and Dadaist images. At one point, Vernengo holds the dying Soto in the tender, mothering way of Michelangelo's *Pieta* as Quinteros silently looks on. Another moment, as the drugged Soto cries out "Doctor, why do you forsake me?" Subiela's design resembles a brooding painting of Christ as he lay in death. Throughout the film, Subiela makes consistent visual references to the surrealist Rene Magritte. A patient's hallucinatory image of two hooded figures kissing, strongly resembles Magritte's 1928 work *The Lovers*. Soto's physical appearance, and even the film's title recall another 1928 Magritte work, *Person Meditating on Madness*. Indeed, this appellation could serve as a subtitle for MAN FACING SOUTHEAST.

Soto's performance is remarkable. He maintains an intense presence throughout with a face that paradoxically tells all while revealing nothing. (In addition to his physical parallel to the Magritte painting, Soto at times bears a strange resemblance to Talking Heads singer David Byrne.) Quinteros, as the self-tortured doctor, is an excellent counterpart to Soto, experiencing a gamut of emotions within his complex character. The chemistry that builds between the two is natural and often affectionate, a unique relationship that becomes the film's heart. Subiela truly cares about these characters, creating a profound and highly personal film that will linger in the viewer's mind. Subiela stated that the purpose of MAN FACING SOUTHEAST was to discuss man and love without conveying a political or social message, a task that ultimately proved to be impossible considering the film's nature. This is a film that succeeds on every level, constantly probing the realms of what is possible in the scope of man's imagination. (In Spanish; English subtitles.)

p, Lujan Pflaum; d&w, Eliseo Subiela; ph, Ricardo de Angelis; m, Pedro Aznar; ed, Luis Cesar D'Angiolillo; art d, Abel Facello; set d, Marta Albertinazzi.

Drama   **(PR:O MPAA:R)**

MAN OF ASHES†   (1986, Tunisia) 108m Satpec–Cineteiefilms c (RIH ESSED)

Imad Maalal *(Hachemi)*, Khaled Ksouri *(Farfat)*, Habib Belhadi *(Touil)*, Mohamed Dhrif *(Azaiez)*, Mouna Noureddine *(Neffisa)*, Mahmoud Belhassen *(Mustapha)*, Mustafa Adouani *(Ameur)*, Yacoub Behiri *(Levy)*, Wassila Chawki *(Sejra)*.

Maalal, a young woodcarver, is engaged to be married, but is terrified of women. It turns out that in his younger days Maalal, along with his friend Ksouri, was sexually molested by the man to whom they were both apprenticed. The rigid attitudes of Maalal's family and the society in which he lives prevent him from discussing the assault and from getting help in dealing with the trauma it has caused. After Ksouri and Maalal have sex with prostitutes (their first experiences with women), Ksouri's outrage overwhelms him and he confronts the former master and stabs him. This was the first feature directorial effort for Bouzid who, among other jobs, worked as an assistant director on RAIDERS OF THE LOST ARK.

d&w, Nouri Bouzid; ph, Youssef Ben Youssef (Satpec Gammarth Color); m, Salah Mahdi; ed, Mika Ben Miled; art d, Claud Bennys, Mohsen Rais; cos, Laila B. Mahmoud, Lilia Lakhoua; spec eff, Ahmed Bourguiba, Med Choukou.

Drama   **(PR:O MPAA:NR)**

MANANA DE COBRE†   (1986, Mex.) CCC–CPC (Trans: Bitter Taste in the Morning)

Fernando Balzaretti, Angeles Castro, Eraclio Zepeda, Alvaro Carcano, Armando Martin, Ignacio Guadalupe.

d, Miguel Mora; w, Miguel Mora, Georgina Balzaretti, Julio Ortega (based on the novel by Fernando Macotela); ph, Roberto Menendez.

MANDEN I MAANEN†   (1986, Den.) 90m Film-Cooperativet Denmark 1983–Danish Film Institute–Metronome–C.C. Cosmos/Metronome c (Trans: The Man in the Moon)

Peter Thiel *(Johannes)*, Catherine Poul Jupont *(Maria Bianca)*, Christina Bengtsson *(Christina)*, Kim Jansson *(Her Husband)*, Yavuzer Cetinkaya *(Turkish Guest Worker)*, Roy Richards *(African Guest Worker)*, Berthe Quistgaard *(Johannes' Mother)*, Erik Truxa *(Police Lieutenant)*, Anne Nojgard, Marianne Mortensen *(Hookers)*, Stig Hoffmeyer *(Waiter)*.

After spending 16 years in prison for murdering his wife, Thiel is freed into a Copenhagen with which he is unable to cope. The middle-aged man (who killed his spouse rather than face the possibility of losing her) finds that the city, in its own way, is very much a prison as well. He finds, too, that love does not equate with acquisitiveness.

d&w, Erik Clausen; ph, Morten Bruus (Eastmancolor); m, Robert Broberg; ed, Ghita Beckendorff; prod d, Leif Sylvester Petersen; cos, Gitte Kolvig.

Drama   **(PR:C-O MPAA:NR)**

MANHATTAN BABY zero   (1986, It.) 89m Fulvia c

Christopher Connelly *(Prof. George Hacker)*, Martha Taylor, Birgitta Boccoli, Giovanni Frezza, Cinzia De Ponti, Laurence Welles, Andrea Bosic, Carlo De Mejo, Vincenzo Bellanich, Mario Moretti, Lucio Fulci, Antonio Pulci.

Connelly is a hapless archaeologist in this Italian horror item. He has the misfortune of digging up the wrong amulet while exploring in Egypt. He loses his eyesight as a result, though doctors promise Connelly this is only a temporary condition. In the meantime, Connelly's equally hapless daughter receives a similar rock from a strange woman. This gives her incredible telekinetic abilities, so it's time to call in the parapsychologists. They want to investigate the girl's abilities, but a substitute takes her place at the last minute. A few magic incantations and cheesy gore effects later, this ill-fated individual is history. Back in Egypt the whole thing starts over when another young lady is presented with a similar amulet.

Lacking much in the way of logic, clarity, or anything that even remotely resembles intelligence, MANHATTAN BABY is a sad excuse for a film. Originally shot in 1982, it bounced around through different hands before it finally saw release on videocassette some four years later.

p, Fabrizio De Angelis; d, Lucio Fulci; w, Elisa Livia Briganti, Dardano Sachetti; ph, Guglielmo Mancori (Telecolor); m, Fabio Frizzi; ed, Vincenzo Tomassi; prod d, Massimo Lentini; cos, Massimo Lentini; makeup, Maruizio Trani.

Horror   **Cas.**   **(PR:O MPAA:NR)**

MANHATTAN PROJECT, THE**   (1986) 120m Gladden Entertainment/ FOX c (AKA: MANHATTAN PROJECT: THE DEADLY GAME)

John Lithgow *(John Mathewson)*, Christopher Collet *(Paul Stephens)*, Cynthia Nixon *(Jenny Anderman)*, Jill Eikenberry *(Elizabeth Stephens)*, John Mahoney *(Lt. Col. Conroy)*, Sully Boyar *(Night Guard)*; University Lab: Richard Council *(Government)*, Robert Schenkkan *(Government Aide)*, Paul Austin *(General)*, Adrian Sparks, Curt Dempster *(Scientists)*, Bran Ferren *(Lab Assistant)*; Ithaca: Greg Edelman *(Science Teacher)*, Abe Unger *(Roland)*, Robert Leonard *(Max)*, David Quinn *(Tennis)*, Geoffrey Nauffts *(Craig)*, Katherine Hiler *(Emma)*, Trey Cummins *(Terry)*, Steve Borton, Harlan Cary Poe *(Local FBI)*, Ned Schmidtke,

Sarah Burke *(Jenny's Parents)*, Allan DeCheser, Arthur DeCheser *(Jenny's Brother)*; Science Fair: Fred G. Smith *(Conroy's Lieutenant)*, John David Cullum *(Eccles)*, Manny Jacobs *(Moore)*, Charlie Fields *(Price)*, Eric Hsiao *(Saito)*, Trevor Bolling *(Halley's Comet Kid)*, Richard Cardona *(Laser Efficiency Kid)*, Heather Dominic, Bruce Smolanoff *(Flirting Kids)*, Joan Kendall *(Registrar)*, John Doumanian *(Cabbie)*, Tom Tarpey *(Injection Doctor)*, Alec Massey, Edward D. Murphy, Dee Ann McDavid *(FBI)*, Joan Harris *(TV Reporter Barbara Collins)*, Kerry Donovan *(Himself)*; Nuclear Emergency Search Team: Ken Chapin *(Command)*, Peter McRobbie *(Electronics)*, Warren Keith *(Computer)*, Bruce Jarchow, Stephen Markle *(Interrogators)*, Al Cerullo *(Helicopter Pilot)*; Medatomics Lab: Richard Jenkins *(Radiation Controls Officer)*, Timothy Carhart *(Relief Guard)*, Fred Melamed *(Assay Technician)*, Warren Manzi *(Day Attendant)*, Michael Telesco *(Day Security Receptionist)*, Frank Ferrara, Jimmy Ray Weeks, William Weslow, Dan E. Butler, Steve Zettler, Richard Caselnova *(SWATS)*.

What would happen if a private citizen, through his own research and handiwork, was able to construct a nuclear bomb capable of mass annihilation? It's a fascinating and complex premise that has been explored several times, most notably by Larry Collins and Dominique La Pierre with their intelligent novel *The Fifth Horseman*. In THE MANHATTAN PROJECT writer/director Marshall Brickman looks at this issue through the eyes of a sensitive teenager. Unfortunately, though Brickman clearly is concerned with the questions his story raises, the film is a bland and predictable account that occasionally feels like a remake of 1983's WARGAMES.

Collet is a bright high school student who lives with his mother, Eikenberry, in Ithaca, New York. Eikenberry is separated from her husband, which causes her some heartache, though she is able to cope with her problems. Eikenberry works at a local real estate agency where Lithgow comes one day looking for an apartment. He's a scientist employed by a local research firm, and being new in town, wants a little companionship. He asks Eikenberry to dinner, though she initially refuses his offer. Collet stops by his mother's office and Lithgow notices a science magazine among the boy's schoolbooks. He offers Collet a tour of his plant in return for the privilege of taking both mother and son out for a Sunday dinner. Eikenberry is charmed by this, but Collet is wary of Lithgow's sudden interest in his mother. Nevertheless, he agrees to the tour, with Lithgow promising to show Collet some of "the sexiest lasers" modern technology has to offer. Collet closely observes everything Lithgow shows him on the tour, then asks his guide about some mysterious bottles containing a green liquid. Lithgow dismisses this as an experimental substance for medical purposes, but Collet is convinced the man is lying. On the factory grounds Collet finds several five-leaf clovers, a mutation he realizes could only be induced through radioactivity. This substantiates his hunch that Lithgow's company is merely a government front for developing nuclear weapons.

He takes this news to Nixon, a girl friend from school, and persuades her to help him sneak into the plant so he can steal a bottle of the liquid. They rig up a scheme involving frisbees, a radio-operated toy car, and a bottle of shampoo, then manage to get past a not-too-bright security guard. Using a robot arm and the lasers Lithgow previously showed him, Collet retrieves a bottle of the green liquid, replacing it with a container holding the shampoo. Once outside, Collet confirms his belief that the green substance is liquid plutonium and decides to join the exclusive "nuclear club" by building his own atomic bomb. Using books from the library and parts available from a local hardware store, Collet is able to create a small-scale nuclear device. He also obtains some black market explosives to use as a detonator, then plans to expose the government's facade at a statewide science fair in New York City.

Meanwhile, the authorities have discovered Collet's break-in and are able to trace the missing plutonium to the boy genius. Agents head off to the hotel where Collet and Nixon are staying, but with the help of other science fair participants, the two teenagers are able to escape. They take a bus back to Ithaca, and en route Collet learns he is the subject of a statewide hunt. On the outskirts of town, Collet places a call to the plant, telling them he will be arriving shortly, bomb in hand. Nixon returns home, where she is to round up friends and relations, then bring them to the plant's gates. Inside the plant Lithgow tries to persuade Collet to give up his bomb. Suddenly the bomb's timer goes off and Lithgow realizes if it's not diffused the device could destroy a good section of New York State. They

Graham), Benjamin Hendrickson (Dr. Chilton), Michael Talbott (Geehan), Dan E. Butler (Jimmy Price), Michele Shay (Beverly Katz), Robin Moseley (Sarah), Paul Perri (Dr. Sidney Bloom), Patricia Charbonneau (Mrs. Sherman), Bill Cwikowski (Ralph Dandridge), Alex Neil (Eileen), Norman Snow (Springfield), Jim Zubiena (Spurgen), Frankie Faison (Lt. Fisk), Garcelle Beauvais (Young Woman Housebuyer), Joanne Camp (Mother on Plane), David A. Brooks (Mr. Leeds), Lisa Ryall (Mrs. Leeds), Chris Elliot (Zeller), Gary Chavaras (Guard), Chris Cianciolo (Attendant), Ken Colquitt (Husband Housebuyer), Ron Fitzgerald, Dennis Quick (Storage Guards), David Meeks (Dr. Warfield), Sherman Michaels (Technician), Robin Trapp, Lisa Winters (Secretaries), Daniel T. Snow (State Trooper), Cynthia Chvatal (Airport Waitress), King White (SWAT Man), Mickey Lloyd (Atlanta Detective), Dawn Carmen (Child on Plane), David Fitzsimmons (Bill), Robert A. Burton (Doctor), Steve Hogan (Helicopter Pilot), Mickey Pugh (Lear Jet Technician), Kin Shriner (Mr. Sherman), John Posey (Mr. Jacobi), Kristin Holby (Mrs. Jacobi), Greg Kelly, Brian Kelly, Ryan Langhorne (Jacobi Boys), Hannah Cacciano, Lindsey Fonora (Sherman Children), Jason Frair, Bryant Arrants, Christopher Arrants (Leeds Children), Capt. Melvin Clark, Officer Renee Ayala, Officer Dana Dewey, Officer Stephen Hawkins, Officer Leonard Johnson, Officer Keith Pyles, Officer Michael Russell, Officer Micheal Vitug, Officer Pat Williams, Officer Charles Yarbaugh (SWAT Team Members), Bill Smitrovich (Lloyd Bowman), Peter Maloney (Dr. Dominick Princi), Michael D. Roberts (The Runner).

After a disappointing foray into the supernatural with THE KEEP (1983), TV's "Miami Vice" and "Crime Story" producer Michael Mann has returned to the crime world that fueled his impressive feature directorial debut, THIEF (1981). Based on Thomas Harris' gripping novel *Red Dragon*, MANHUNTER in-

troduces us to the Behavioral Science Unit of the FBI and its best agent, Petersen. Brought out of early retirement by his friend and colleague Farina, Petersen launches an investigation of a serial killer operating on a "lunar cycle"—he kills only when the moon is full. Dubbed the "Tooth Fairy" by investigators—for he leaves horrible bite marks on his victims—the killer has slaughtered two young, affluent Southern families. What is odd about the murders is that both times the killer broke a mirror and placed the pieces over the eyes of the dead—as if he could see them watching him.

In addition to being a superior deductive thinker, Petersen's special talent is the ability to adopt the mind-set of the killers he pursues and to begin thinking like them. If he takes the process far enough, he can begin to predict what the killer's next move will be. Unfortunately, Petersen became so absorbed by his last case— where he caught a brilliant-but-deranged doctor (played superbly by British actor Brian Cox)—that he had great difficulty in shaking Cox's evil thoughts from his mind and had to be hospitalized. Petersen left the bureau soon afterwards and has spent the last few years with his wife, Greist, and son, Seaman. Armed with only the evidence file and a tape recorder, Petersen enters the blood-splattered house of the last victims. He walks through the scene of the crime as if he were the killer. Muttering his possible motivations into the tape recorder, Petersen begins assuming the mind-set of the killer. In a move that worries Farina, Petersen decides he must visit his jailed quarry, Cox, at the prison hospital for the criminally insane—as he puts it—"recover the mind-set." Rather than being a writhing, screaming lunatic, Cox is a very calm, almost charming man who is extremely observant and intelligent ("That's the same atrocious after-shave you wore in court three years ago," is the first thing Cox says to Petersen). Petersen allows the criminal to look at the evidence file in the hope that Cox will deduce how the killer chooses his victims. The meeting soon turns nasty as the adversaries begin trading subtle insults back and forth. Petersen is obviously afraid of Cox, and the criminal plays on the investigator's fear. "Do you know how you caught me, Will? The reason you caught me is that we're just alike." Petersen cannot face this reality and he quickly leaves the room. As the cell door shuts Cox

---

manage to disarm Collet's handiwork in time, while authorities prepare to arrest him. But the presence of numerous civilians outside is Collet's saving grace, and he is allowed to go free. Lithgow, having been forced to consider the moral consequences of his work, decides he has had enough and joins Collet as he leaves the plant.

Brickman deals with several disturbing ideas, including the moral issues raised by nuclear capabilities and the ethics of the people behind the faceless bomb. Yet within the format of a teenage thriller, these problems fall to the side, giving way to genre conventions that keep the story moving. Brickman has the complete package, including evil government goons, a couple of chase sequences, a danger-packed climax, and the inevitable teen romance. In catering to these concerns, Brickman subordinates his own intention of creating a cautionary atomic fable. He also leaves other potential areas of interest unexplored, particularly Collet's Oedipal protectiveness towards Eikenberry when Lithgow shows interest in her. Another problem is the simplistic logic that allows Collet to obtain plutonium in the first place. One would assume that a highly secret government operation would have strict security precautions, something beyond an all-night guard and a few easily fooled electronic gizmos.

To his credit, Brickman avoids politics and sticks with the human values. His best choice by far was casting Lithgow in the scientist's role. Lithgow gives the man warmth and character rather than playing the part as just another single minded government bad guy. He starts off as a person who loves his job solely for the thrill of research, but ultimately faces up to the consequences of that work. Lithgow's confrontation with Collet in the bowels of the laboratory at the story's climax is one of the film's best moments, as various emotions come to a head within the scientist. But Lithgow alone is just not enough to save THE MANHATTAN PROJECT from its altogether routine development. Simply put, the film is merely another addition to an already overworked genre. The production on THE MANHATTAN PROJECT began on July 10, 1985, which ironically was almost 40 years to the day after the first atomic bomb, created through the real Manhattan Project, was exploded at the Alamogordo, New Mexico, test site.

p, Jennifer Ogden, Marshall Brickman; d, Marshall Brickman; w, Marshall Brickman, Thomas Baum; ph, Billy Williams (Technicolor); m, Philippe Sarde; ed, Nina Feinberg; prod d, Philip Rosenberg; art d, Robert Guerra; set d, Philip Smith, Nina Ramsey; cos, Shay Cunliffe; spec eff, Bran Ferren, Connie Brink; makeup, Richard Dean; stunts, Frank Ferrara.

Drama   Cas.   (PR:A   PG-13)

MANHUNT, THE*   (1986, It.) 89m Fulvia Film/Goldwyn c

John Ethan Wayne (Stranger), Raymund Harmstorf (Guard), Henry Silva (Prison Boss), Bo Svenson (Sheriff), Ernest Borgnine (Ben Robeson), Terry Lynch, Don Taylor, Randy Mulkey, Farris Castleberry, Susan Wilson.

Wayne (yes, the Duke's son) buys a couple of horses at a racetrack, but this purchase leads him to unforeseen troubles. He attempts to water the steeds in transit, but makes a terrible mistake by stopping on some land owned by Borgnine, a malevolent rancher. With sneer in place, Borgnine insists the horses are his and kicks Wayne off his land. When the wronged man returns to collect his animals, Borgnine has him arrested and Wayne is tossed in the clink for a three-year sentence. Wayne won't put up with this unfair treatment and plans an escape. He manages to flee the pen, though—not too surprisingly—the authorities are soon on his trail.

This low-budget Italian offering has little that will excite action fans. Basically, it's a rehash of prison-film cliches, treated in a routine manner. Borgnine and Wayne are passable in their unchallenging roles.

p,d&w, Larry Ludman [Fabrizio De Angelis]; ph, Joseph Mercury [Guglielmo Mancori] (Luciano Vittori Color); m, Francesco De Masi; ed, Vincent P. Thomas [Vincenzo Tomassi]; stunts, Alan Petit.

Action/Drama   Cas.   (PR:O   MPAA:NR)

MANHUNTER***   (1986) 119m DEG c

William Petersen (Will Graham), Kim Greist (Molly Graham), Joan Allen (Reba), Brian Cox (Dr. Lektor), Dennis Farina (Jack Crawford), Stephen Lang (Freddie Lounds), Tom Noonan (Francis Dollarhyde), David Seaman (Kevin

shouts, "Smell yourself." Later, Cox gets Petersen's home address by conning Petersen's psychologist's secretary into giving him the information.

After a few more dead-ends and an encounter with an obnoxious reporter, Lang, who works for a *National Enquirer*—type newspaper (called the *Tattler*), there is a breakthrough in the case. Guards find a message from the killer, written on toilet paper, in Cox's cell. Though part of the message is destroyed, FBI forensic specialists discover that Cox and the killer have been communicating through personal ads in the *Tattler*. The feds eventually break the code and discover that Cox has given the killer Petersen's home address. The FBI scrambles quickly and takes Petersen's family to a safe house. Petersen tries to provoke the killer into revealing himself by planting stories in the *Tattler* that portray the killer as a homosexual. The trick fails, but the angry killer, who turns out to be a very tall, gaunt, balding man with a terrifying face (Noonan) kidnaps reporter Lang and kills him. While Petersen spends much of his time poring over the possessions of the murdered families to find some connection, the killer meets and becomes attracted to a beautiful blind woman (Allen) who works at the photo lab where he is employed. Noonan takes Allen to the zoo where a friend of his is about to work on the teeth of a tiger. The zoo employee encourages the blind woman to stroke the drugged tiger and the amazed woman feels the beast's breath and listens to its heartbeat (the scene is highly erotic). Allen is turned on by the experience and later, at Noonan's house, she seduces the somewhat shocked and confused killer (he later cries while she's asleep). This healthy sexual experience appears to bring about a change in the killer, and he seems to be less obsessed. Tragically, his bliss ends when his darker impulses override his sense and he imagines Allen passionately kissing another coworker who had driven her home. Noonan's mind snaps and he kills the man and kidnaps Allen, taking her back to his house.

Meanwhile, Petersen stares at home movies of the previous victims and asks himself (in second person) how the killer knew so much about his victims. Suddenly he realizes that the killer derived all his knowledge about the victims from the films themselves. A check of the processing label on both families' home-movie cans reveals that they were developed by the same lab in St. Louis. Petersen and Farina fly in a Lear jet from Chicago to St. Louis while on the phone with local police to match up employees of the lab with the few pieces of physical evidence the killer left behind. Finally they learn that Noonan is their man. Once in St. Louis, they race to the rural house where the killer lives. At the same time, the crazed Noonan has put heavy-metal rock group Iron Butterfly's semi-classic 20-minute anthem "In-A-Gadda-Da-Vida" on the stereo at full blast in an attempt to scare and confuse the blind Allen. Noonan breaks a mirror and selects a long piece with which to kill the woman. By this time Petersen is on the property and he sees Noonan about to stab the girl. Without waiting for a backup, Petersen crashes into the house through a window and lands right in the arms of Noonan, who slashes his face with the broken mirror. Noonan then grabs a shotgun and kills several police officers before Petersen comes to and kills him. This time, Petersen is able to shake the killer's perverted thought process, and he returns home to his family.

As a director, Michael Mann is his own worst enemy. For MANHUNTER he wrote a superior script and assembled an incredible cast, but his obsession with superficial visual "style" nearly destroys this engrossing film. The set design in much of MANHUNTER borders on the ludicrous. Every character from Petersen to Noonan works and lives in a totally sterile environment with pastel-colored walls, art deco lamps, and ultra-modern furniture. The various FBI buildings are immaculate, bright white with absolutely no sign that anybody human works there—no clutter whatsoever. The prison hospital which houses Cox is a blinding white building which looks like an art museum because it is an art museum—the scene was shot at Atlanta's High Museum of Art. Only Noonan's abode shows a glimmer of personality, but it is a bit too far out to be believable, even if he is psychotic. Giant posters and wallpaper depicting various planets (including the moon, remember, he's on a "lunar cycle") are seen at every turn. A foyer of emerald-green glass blocks lends an eerie glow to the scene, and a spinning lamp that looks like Sputnik hangs overhead. Sure the guy's crazy, but it still looks as if he had an Italian designer come by and decorate his house. The overbearing, unreal set design creeps into the lighting and camera-placement choices as well. The film's opening shot is a much too studied formal composition with Petersen (facing the camera) and Farina (with his back to the camera) sitting on opposite ends of a piece of driftwood. Water at the horizon line, bright white sky above, the shot is so self-consciously composed it looks like a magazine ad. For some

reason all the nighttime scenes in Petersen's seaside house are shot in deep-blue lighting (actually, it was probably a blue camera filter) which makes Petersen, Greist, and their son look hideous.

Most annoying of all, perhaps, is the unrestrained use of rock music throughout. While a few of the choices work remarkably well ("In-A-Gadda-Da-Vida" at the climax and Shriekback's "Coelocanth" during the incredible tiger scene), the rest eat at the effectiveness of otherwise powerful scenes (especially where Noonan imagines Allen kissing another man—there should have been silence as he rips the vinyl off his dashboard in emotional anguish, rather than the Prime Movers' forgettable and much too obvious "Strong As I Am" droning on). The incidental musical score by The Reds and Michel Rubini echoes Tangerine Dream's superior score for Mann's THIEF too often and isn't nearly as effective. All these highly personal choices that Mann makes are very distinctive, and he does create his own movie universe, but it bears little resemblance to life as we know it. Luckily, these seemingly insurmountable problems are outweighed by gripping performances from Petersen, Noonan, and Cox, complemented by strong support from Farina, Allen, Griest (although she's given far too little to do), and Lang. Petersen draws the viewer into the complex minds of irrational murderers—minds he shares. Although there is little onscreen violence in the film, it *feels* violent because we share the thoughts of the killer through Petersen's second-person dialogs.

As he did in THIEF, Mann brings a fascinating amount of procedural detail—both law-enforcement and criminal—to the film. Watching the FBI departments work swiftly as a team is as exciting as it is interesting, as is watching Cox pick apart Petersen's psyche in a matter of seconds. Mann also creates some truly touching and emotional scenes amid all the macho posturing. The aforementioned scene with Allen and the tiger, and a scene between Petersen and his son in a grocery store, are the highlights of the movie. MANHUNTER is a very frustrating film, for Mann is a strong writer and has an incredible sense for casting actors (look at THIEF if you need more proof), but his visual style is too studied, too self-consciously "slick," too distracting, and it gnaws at the excellence of the rest of the film. Songs include: "Graham's Theme" (Michel Rubini, performed by Michael Rubini), "Seiun" (Kitaro, performed by Kitaro), "Freeze" (Klaus Schulze, performed by Klaus Schulze), "Evaporation" (David Allen, Barry Andrews, Carl Marsh, performed by Shriekback), "Coelocanth," "This Big Hush" (David Allen, Barry Andrews, Martyn Barker, Carl Marsh, performed by Shriekback), "Strong As I Am" (Severs Ramsey, Gary Putman, Curt Lichter, Gregory Markel, performed by The Prime Movers), "In-A-Gadda-Da-Vida" (Doug Ingle, performed by Iron Butterfly), "Heartbeat" (Michael Becker, Gene Stashuk, performed by Red 7).

p, Richard Roth; d&w, Michael Mann; (based on the book *Red Dragon* by Thomas Harris); ph, Dante Spinotti (Technicolor); m, The Reds, Michel Rubini; ed, Dov Hoenig; prod d, Mel Bourne; art d, Jack Blackman; cos, Colleen Atwood; spec eff, Joseph DiGaetano II; m/l, Michel Rubini, Kitaro, Klaus Schulze, David Allen, Barry Andrews, Carl Marsh, Martyn Baker, Severs Ramsay, Gary Putnam, Curt Lichter, Gregory Markel, Doug Ingle, Gene Stashuk; makeup, Stefano Fava; stunts, Bud Davis.

Crime/Thriller   **Cas.**   **(PR:O MPAA:R)**

MANON†   (1986, Venezuela) 112m Gente de Cine c

Mayra Alejandra *(Manon)*, Victor Mallarino *(Roberto)*, Miguelangel Landa *(Lescaut)*, Eva Moreno *(Obsidiana)*, Gonzalo J. Camacho *(Diaz Lopez)*.

Abbe Prevost's novel *Manon Lescaut* has been adapted by several filmmakers, including silent versions made in 1914 (U.S) and 1916 (Germany), as well as 1950 and 1968 French renditions. In this contemporary Venezuelan interpretation Alejandra plays the enticing title character who becomes involved with Mallarino, a seminary student. Mallarino forsakes his religious calling for Alejandra's charms, then takes a substantial amount of cash from his wealthy father so he can live with his beloved. The couple takes a hotel room in Caracas, but their bliss is shortlived. Having depleted their money supply, Mallarino is forced to get a sales job, one which barely covers expenses. Alejandra grows bored with this life and leaves Mallarino for an older, wealthier businessman. Alejandra's infidelities eventually catch up with her, and the fiery woman meets with an unhappy end.

d, Roman Chalbaud; w, Emilio Carballido, Roman Chalbaud (based on the novel by the Abbe Antoine-Francois Prevost d'Exiles); ph, Javier Aguirresarobe; m, Federico Ruiz; ed, Jose Alcalde.

Drama   **(PR:O MPAA:NR)**

MANON DES SOURCES†   (1986, Fr.) 113m Renn-Films A2-RAI 2-DD
                                –AMLF c (Trans: Manon Of The Springs; AKA: JEAN DE FLORETTE II)

Yves Montand *(Cesar "Le Papet")*, Daniel Auteuil *(Ugolin)*, Emmanuelle Beart *(Manon Cadoret)*, Hippolyte Girardot *(Bernard Olivier)*.

The follow-up to JEAN DE FLORETTE (also released this year), both remakes of Marcel Pagnol's four-hour 1952 film on which he based his two-part novel, MANON DES SOURCES provides its audience with the same visual splendor displayed in the first of the two films. MANON DES SOURCES picks up ten years after the finish of JEAN DE FLORETTE, which saw the death of Gerard Depardieu's hard-toiling novice-farmer character. The farmer's daughter, Manon, has now grown up and is played by the lovely Beart as a shepherdess who has withdrawn from the other villagers. She is determined to get vengeance on the two men who caused her father's death—Montand and Auteuil, the latter of whom has since fallen in love with her. Having discovered the underground spring that passes through her land, she blocks it up in order to prevent the water from flowing to neighboring farms. She then publicly accuses Montand and Auteuil of engineering their scheme to drive Depardieu off the farm. Unable to gain Beart's love or forgiveness, Auteuil hangs himself. Shortly afterwards, Montand also dies, upon learning that Depardieu was actually his illegitimate son. The JEAN DE FLORETTE – MANON DES SOURCES combination was nominated as a package for eight Cesars, including a win for Beart as Best Supporting Actress. MANON DES SOURCES, along with JEAN DE FLORETTE, is set for U.S. distribution in 1987 by Orion Classics.

p, Pierre Grunstein; d, Claude Berri; w, Claude Berri, Gerard Brach (based on the novel by Marcel Pagnol); ph, Bruno Nuytten (Technovision, Eastmancolor) m, Jean-Claude Petit (theme adapted from "La Forza del Destino" by Giuseppe Verdi; ed, Genevieve Louveau, Herve de Luze; prod d, Bernard Vezat; cos, Sylvie Gautrelet; makeup, Michele Deruelle, Jean-Pierre Eychenne.

Drama   (PR:C   MPAA:NR)

MARE, THE†   (1986, Iran) Cooperative Group

Soosan Taslimi, Firooz Behjat Mohammadi, Hossein Mahjoob, Moji Long Danesh Pooy.

When their family faces intense economic problems after heavy flooding damages their crops, a poor girl is forced into a marriage with her uncle's wealthy friend from the city. Before the wedding ceremony occurs, the girl flees in a desperate attempt to retain her freedom.

d&w, Ali Jekan; ph, Firooz Malek Zadeh; m, Sharif Lotfi; ed, Mehrzad Minooie.

Drama   (PR:A   MPAA:NR)

MARIA†   (1986, Neth.) 90m Kaktus–CNR/Cannon Tuschinski c

Jeanne Marleau (Maria), Liesbeth Sjollema (Young Maria), Peter Jan Rens (Erik), Huub Stapel (Paolo Pietrosanti), Annemieke Hoogendijk (Sister Elisabeth), Kika Keus (Anneke), Rosita Steenbeek (Danielle), Tony Maples (Luca), Joekie Broedelet.

Marleau is an old woman who must spend her last days in a nursing home. There she meets Rens, a young male attendant who reminds Marleau of a past lover. Marleau and Rens develop a warm friendship, and in flashback her past is revealed. As a young girl (played by Sjollema in these sequences), the woman fell in love with Stapel, a member of Italy's fascist movement. Though the two marry, their relationship comes to a tragic end when Stapel's homosexual commander grows envious of this union.

Rens, who also wrote and directed this feature, based his story on his experiences working as a male nurse in a number of Danish nursing homes. The film was funded in part through a radical publicity stunt. Before beginning production, Rens placed advertisements in local newspapers, inviting potential backers to buy tickets for his yet unmade film. These tickets cost ten guilders (about $3.50) and could be turned in for admission when MARIA was finally released. The idea proved fruitful, as pre-sold tickets ultimately provided about twenty percent of the film's $270,000 budget. Though Rens' money-raising methods are certainly unorthodox, they are not without precedent. No less a talent than Jean Renoir attempted a similar tactic in producing his 1938 drama LA MARSEILLAISE. (In Dutch; English subtitles.)

p, Jules Bruessing; d&w, Peter Jan Rens; ph, Frans Bromet; m, Tonny Eyk; ed, Victorine Habets; art d, Hemmo Sportel.

Drama   (PR:O   MPAA:NR)

MARTIAL ARTS OF SHAOLIN†   (1986, Hong Kong/China) 97m Pearl River Film/Sil-Metropole Organization Ltd. c

Jet Lee, Hu Jiang-Qiang, Huang Qui-Yan, Yu Cheng-Hui, Yu Hai, Sun Jian-Kiu, Liu Huai-Liang, Ji Chun-Hua.

A big-budget coproduction of the Crown Colony of Hong Kong and mainland China, which will be reclaiming the city before the end of the century. The story concerns the children of two men wrongfully executed years before who independently seek vengeance on the corrupt nobleman responsible. Spectacular locations within China, including a fight atop the Great Wall, highlight this effort.

p, Ann Tse Kai, Liu Yet Yuen, Lam Ping Kwan, Lu Yin Pei, Wong Ying Cheong; d, Lau Kar-Leung; w, Sze Yeung Ping; m, James J.S. Wong.

Martial Arts   (PR:A-C   MPAA:NR)

MARVADA CARNE†   (1986, Braz.) (Trans: Strong Meat)

Adilson Barros, Fernanda Torres, Dionisio de Azevedo, Lucelia Macchiavelli, Geni Prado, Paco Sanchez.

d&w, Andre Klotzel; ph, Pedro Farkas; m, Rogerio Duprat, Passoca; ed, Alain Fresnot; art d, Adrian Cooper.

MASSEY SAHIB†   (1986, India) National Film Development Corp.

Raghuvir Yadhav, Barry John, Arundhati Roy, Sudhir Kulkarni, Virendhra Saxena, Jaquilline Grewal.

Set in a backward region of India during the final days of the British rule, a man is caught between his allegiance to the colonial system, which has supplied him with decent position and secure life style, and the customs of his native culture. His inability to identify completely with either cultural perspective precipitates his eventual tragic end.

d, Pradip Krishen; ph, Rajkumar Bose; m, Vanraj Bhatia.

Drama   (PR:A   MPAA:NR)

MATADOR†   (1986, Span.) 102m Andres Vicente Gomez c

Assumpta Serna (Maria), Antonio Banderas (Angel), Nacho Martinez (Diego), Eva Cobo (Eva), Julieta Serrano, Chus Lampreave, Carmen Maura, Eusebio Poncela, Bibi Andersson.

A strange pitch-black comedy that concerns a retired matador, Martinez, who runs a bullfighting school and sates his old bloodlust by appearing in snuff films. One of his students is Banderas, who attempts to prove his manhood by raping Martinez's girl friend. He fails, but still goes to the police to confess. The woman refuses to press charges, however, and the police are about to toss him out when he suddenly confesses to four unsolved murders. Two of them were actually committed by Martinez for the movies, and the other two by his defense lawyer, Serna, a woman who has always hero-worshipped Martinez and who satisfies her own bloodlust by killing men on the verge of orgasm. Naturally, Serna and Martinez find each other and launch into a perverse affair of sex and death.

d, Pedro Almodovar; w, Pedro Almodovar, Jesus Ferrere; ph, Angel Luis Fernandez; m, Bernardo Bonezzi; ed, Jose Salcedo.

Comedy/Drama   (PR:O   MPAA:NR)

MATANZA EN MATAMOROS†   (1986, Mex.) 86m Cinematografica Rodriguez/Peliculas Mexicanas c (Trans: Slaughter in Matamoros)

Jorge Luke (Maximino Castro), Sergio Goyri (Silverio Bernal), Patricia Rivera (Estela), Marcela Camacho (Elena), Jorge Fegan, Aaman Mendez, Antonio Zubiaga, Servando Manzetti, Alfredo Mutierrez, Jorge Victoria, Carlos Teran.

Drug dealings along the U.S.-Mexico border lead to violent, bloody, and ultimately deadly encounters when the Mexican mob enters into the fray. According to the film's advertisements, the Italian branch may be better known, but " . . . the Mexican Mafia is most efficient." The story is based on an allegedly true incident, with a generous helping of scenes pirated from Francis Ford Coppola's GODFATHER films.

p, Roberto Rodriguez; d, Jose Luis Urquieta; w, Jorge Patino; ph, Alberto Areltanos; m, Susan Rodriguez, Chola and Yeni, Carlos and Jose, Carmen Cardenal and Rojo Gran; ed, Francisco Chiu.

Crime   (PR:O   MPAA:NR)

MAUVAIS SANG†   (1986, Fr.) 128m Films Plain Chant–Soprofilms–FR3/ AAA Classic c (Trans: Bad Blood)

Denis Lavant (Alex), Juliette Binoche (Anna), Michel Piccoli (Marc), Hans Meyer (Hans), Julie Delpy (Lise), Carroll Brooks (The American), Hugo Pratt (Boris), Serge Reggiani (Charlie), Mireille Perrier (Young Mother), Jerome Zucca, Charles Schmitt, Philippe Fretin, Ralph Brown.

Leos Carax, the 24-year-old French director of 1985's BOY MEETS GIRL, has again forced French audiences to take notice with his latest film, MAUVAIS SANG. Drawing on the influence of Jean-Luc Godard's PIERROT LE FOU, Carax casts an energetic romantic, Lavant (Carax's version of Jean-Paul Belmondo), opposite an alluring female, Binoche (Carax's Anna Karina). Lavant falls in love with Binoche when he gets involved in a gangster plot which involves the shady Brooks, known only as "The American." Lavant's father has been murdered and he is taken under the wing of his father's pals, Piccoli and Pratt. Although Lavant has declared his love for Binoche, she has devoted herself to Piccoli. This pulp-novel-style thriller goes even further when Piccoli and his gang battle Brooks and his men over a secret serum. The serum prevents a new, fatal disease which one contracts by "making love to those you don't love." MAUVAIS SANG is not, however, about gangsters and secret serums, but about ideas. As in the films of Godard (and so many other great filmmakers), plot takes a back seat to the director's beliefs and philosophizing. MAUVAIS SANG is also the first film to deal with the disease AIDS (though it is not called so by name) not in realistic terms, but in a larger, mythical sense. Carax has said, "When I first read about AIDS in American newspapers, I thought, 'My god, this has to be the scenario for a film, this can't be real, that you would catch a disease that will kill you from making love.' " The film includes the David Bowie song "Modern Love." MAUVAIS SANG received three Cesar nominations—Binoche for Best Actress, Delpy for Best Young Female Hopeful, and Escoffer for Best Cinematography.

p, Alain Dahan; d&w, Leos Carax; ph, Jean-Yves Escoffier (Fujicolor); m, Benjamin Britten, Serge Prokofiev, Charlie Chaplin; ed, Nelly Quettier; m/l, David Bowie, Charles Aznavour, Serge Reggiani; makeup, Chantal Houdoy.

Romance   (PR:O   MPAA:NR)

MAX MON AMOUR†   (1986, Fr.) 98m Greenwich–Films A-2/AAA c (Trans: Max My Love)

Charlotte Rampling (Margaret), Anthony Higgins (Peter), Diana Quick (Camille), Christopher Hovik (Nelson), Milena Vukotic (Margaret's Mother), Victoria Abril (Maria), Pierre Etaix (Detective), Claude Jaeger (Zoologist), Sabine Haudepin (Francoise), Bernard-Pierre Donnadieu (Archibald), Nicole Calfan (Helene), Fabrice Luchini (Nicolas), Anne-Marie Besse (Suzanne), Bernard Haller (Robert), Laurent Spielvogel (Dr. Mischler).

It has been three years since the release of Oshima's last film, MERRY CHRISTMAS MR. LAWRENCE, and this time out he has become even more commercial. Like Yugoslavian filmmaker Dusan Makavejev, the Japanese Oshima has become far more accessible and commercial in the 1980s than in the previous two decades. In MAX MON AMOUR, Oshima has found a niche between the screwball primate antics of Howard Hawks' MONKEY BUSINESS and the assault on the bourgeoisie of Luis Bunuel's films. Coscripted with former Bunuel screenwriter Jean-Claude Carriere, MAX MON AMOUR stars Rampling as a rich, fashionable member of the upper class who falls in love with a circus chimp. (This chimpanzee is not a real animal but an actor inside a masterfully crafted ape suit designed by Rick Baker.) Naturally her British ambassador husband Higgins doesn't understand. A black comedy, MAX MON AMOUR probes into the animal nature and repressed primitive desires of the bourgeoisie in a manner which has been unexplored since Bunuel's death in 1983. The film has extremely slick production values which stem from producer Serge Silberman's belief in Oshima (Silberman previously produced Akira Kurosawa's RAN, as well as Bunuel's later films). Budgeted at $5 million (a hefty price tag for a European film), the film boasts the talents of Raoul Coutard, best known for his work with Jean-Luc Godard and Francois Truffaut, and production designer Pierre Guffroy, who has worked for Europe's greatest directors—Godard, Truffaut, Bunuel, Jean Cocteau, Robert Bresson, Costa-Gavras, and Roman Polanski. Released in 1986 at the Cannes Film Festival, the film has had distribution difficulties and gained no support from American distributors. (In French and English; English subtitles.)

p, Serge Silberman; d, Nagisa Oshima; w, Nagisa Oshima, Jean-Claude Carriere (based on an idea by Jean-Claude Carriere); ph, Raoul Coutard (Panavision, Centralcolor); m, Michel Portal; ed, Helen Plemianníkov; prod d, Pierre Guffroy.

Comedy (PR:O MPAA:NR)

MAXIMUM OVERDRIVE zero (1986) 97m DD c

Emilio Estevez *(Bill Robinson)*, Pat Hingle *(Hendershot)*, Laura Harrington *(Brett)*, Yeardley Smith *(Connie)*, John Short *(Curt)*, Ellen McElduff *(Wanda June)*, J.C. Quinn *(Duncan)*, Christopher Murney *(Camp Loman)*, Holter Graham *(Deke)*, Frankie Faison *(Handy)*, Pat Miller *(Joe)*, Jack Canon *(Max)*, Barry Bell *(Steve)*, John Brasington *(Frank)*, J. Don Ferguson *(Andy)*, Leon Rippy *(Brad)*, Bob Gooden *(Barry)*, R. Pickett Bugg *(Rolf)*, Giancarlo Esposito *(Videoplayer)*, Ned Austin *(Bridgemaster)*, Richard Chapman, Jr. *(Helper)*, Bob Gunter *(Coach)*, Bill Huggins *(Umpire)*, Martin Tucker, Marla Maples.

Possibly no contemporary author has ever been so abused by the movies as Stephen King. No less than 11 of his novels and short stories have been turned into films, but with the exception of STAND BY ME, all have been artistic or box-office failures, and usually both. This time, though, King has no one to blame but himself for what may be the worst Stephen King adaptation yet.

The plot has a comet passing near the Earth and mysteriously turning some (but not all) machines into mad killers. At a Little League game a soda machine begins spitting out cans at high velocity, killing most of the players. One boy is on the verge of escaping the flying cans when a steamroller crashes through the fence and flattens him with a splat. Another boy (Graham) does escape and rides through the streets observing myriad corpses and lawnmowers, remote control airplanes, and other appliances dripping with fake-looking blood. Meanwhile, at the Dixie Boy truck stop, several semis have besieged the patrons and staff of this greasy spoon, including peckerwood manager Hingle, former college boy and prison parolee Estevez, tough-but-sweet hitchhiker Harrington, ditzy redneck newlyweds Short and McElduff, and about a dozen others whose only plot function is to act scared then become victims. At first the trucks are content simply to run down anyone who shows his face outside the restaurant, but later they muster up an Army vehicle with a machine gun that riddles the joint with bullets while beeping out a Morse code message on its horn demanding that the people inside fill up the gas tanks of the trucks. This goes on endlessly, and when the gas runs out, another tanker pulls in to refill the storage tanks.

Finally, after much pointless running around, periodic panic attacks, and a foray out to rescue a dead Bible salesman (they bring back Graham instead), Estevez emerges as the leader (he's the only one who seems to have more than half a brain in his head). He takes the survivors out through a sewer and they head for the nearby coast, where they hope to find a sailboat they can sail to an offshore island where there are no cars. When the trucks find they have left, they plow into the Dixie Boy, which blows up. The fleeing group narrowly makes it onto a yacht and escapes, and an end title rolls up to tell the audience that a

Russian satellite destroyed an alien spaceship and immediately everything went back to normal.

Without doubt one of the dumbest movies of the year, MAXIMUM OVERDRIVE doesn't work on any level. As a comedy it's obvious and asinine, as a horror film it's simply not scary, and as an action film it's a bore. The inconsistencies of internal logic are too messy to detail, but one of the most annoying is Hingle's refusal to use more than two of the scores of anti-tank missiles he has in his basement. Does he think some bigger crisis is coming along and he doesn't want to waste them? To be fair to Hingle, though, he does give the most enjoyable performance of the film simply by refusing to take it at all seriously and hamming up his white trash villain to a cartoon. Estevez, on the other hand, seems dead serious throughout, and therefore the biggest idiot of all as he tries to synthesize some rational explanation for events. Everyone else is mercifully easily forgotten. The soundtrack is the most unbearable ingredient of all here, a grinding heavy metal score by Australian headbangers AC/DC, including such touching ballads as "Who Made Who?" "Ride On," "Sink the Pink," "Shake Your Foundations," "For Those About to Rock (We Salute You)," "Hell's Bells," "You Shook Me All Night Long," (Angus Young, Malcolm Young, Brian Johnson), and "Ride On" (A. Young, M. Young, Bon Scott, performed by AC/DC). Also on the soundtrack are "The Ride of the Valkyries" (Richard Wagner) and "King of the Road" (Roger Miller, performed by an ice cream truck that sinisterly cruises the streets while Graham hides from it).

King was at first reluctant to direct, thinking that while he could probably deal with choreographing the vehicles and the violence, his skills with actors were dubious. In the end it turned out that directing actors was less a burden than he thought, but the trucks were breaking down constantly and delaying the production. One accident involved a radio-controlled lawnmower that went out of control, struck a wooden block, and shot out splinters that put out an eye of cinematographer Nannuzzi. Savaged by critics and ignored by audiences, MAXIMUM OVERDRIVE quickly disappeared from the theaters, and almost as quickly from the memories of the few who actually sat through it.

p, Martha Schumacher; d&w, Stephen King; ph, Armando Nannuzzi (Technicolor); m, AC/DC, Richard Wagner; ed, Evan Lottman; md, Todd Kasow; prod d, Giorgio Postiglione; set d, Hilton Rosemarin; cos, Clifford Capone; spec eff, Steven Galich; m/l, Angus Young, Malcolm Young, Brian Johnson, Bon Scott, Roger Miller; makeup, Dean Gates, Marlana May; stunts, Glenn Randall, Jr.

Horror Cas. (PR:O MPAA:R)

MAYBE I'M A LOSER, BUT I LOVE YOU (SEE: SERE CUALQUIER COSA PERO TE QUIERO, 1986, Arg.)

ME HACE FALTA UN BIGOTE† (1986, Span.) 90m M2 Films–Bermudez de Castro c-bw (Trans: I Need a Mustache)

Jacob Echeverria, Paloma San Millan, Gregorio Garcia Morcillo, Manuel Summers, Paco Lara Polop, Pedro Civera.

After viewing a few scenes from director Summers' real-life 1963 film, DEL ROSA AL AMARILLO, a television talk show host asks his guests (one of whom is Summers himself) to discuss the first love in their respective lives. After appearing on the show, Summers receives a letter from his girl friend of three decades earlier. This inspires the director to begin a film chronicling the would-be romance between a young Spanish boy of the post-WW II era and a girl hopelessly in love with a Mexican movie star. The film within a film is contrasted with Summers' attempts to find youngsters suitable for his new project.

d&w, Manuel Summers; ph, Tote Trenas; m, Carlos Vizziello, David Summers; ed, Maria Elena Sainz de Rozas; set d, Gumersindo Andres; makeup, Fernando Perez.

Comedy (PR:A MPAA:NR)

MEGLIO BACIARE UN COBRA† (1986, It.) Scena/Filmexport Group (Trans: Better Kiss a Cobra)

Andy J. Forest, Danilo Mattei, Milly D'Abbraccio, Mohamed Attifi.

In this unlikely adventure story, an American and his girl friend find themselves stranded in North Africa. In order to get some money for a ticket to New York, the man steals a ring from an ancient tomb, hoping to sell it to a local. Unfortunately for the American, the man he approaches prefers to cut off the hands of any tomb robber. A quick game of Russian roulette gets our hero out of this jam, but he's soon arrested and sentenced to a 30-year prison term. The warden of the penitentiary gives the American a unique offer that is simply impossible to turn down. All he has to do is find the hidden treasure of Cleopatra and he will be allowed to go free. The American enlists the help of the scoundrel he tricked in the Russian roulette game. Several dangerous and violent adventures later, the American turns up with Cleopatra's treasure. A paper lying amidst the jeweled goodies, signed by the Egyptian queen thousands of years before, states the finder shall be named ruler of the entire region. The American cares little for the honor, though, preferring to hang onto the loot, as well as the comforting arm of his girl.

p, Augusto Caminito; d, Massimo Pirri; w, Tito Giuliani, Massimo Pirri (based on a story by Morando Morandini, Jr., Massimo Pirri); ph, Luigi Ciccarese, Otello Spila; m, Bixio CEM, Artem Publishing.

Action/Adventure   **(PR:O   MPAA:NR)**

MEIER†   (1986, Ger.) 98m Project Film im Filmverlag der Autoren c

Rainer Grenkowitz, Nadja Engelbrecht, Alexander Hauff, Thomas Bestvater, Jochen Kemmer, Dieter Hildebrandt, Jurgen Klauss.

This comedy, well received in its native West Germany, marks the feature debut for writer/director Peter Timm. Bestvater is a common housepainter living in East Berlin. When he learns of a small inheritance waiting for him on the other side of the Berlin Wall, Bestvater gets himself smuggled across. Once he has his money, Bestvater decides to take a trip to a variety of foreign countries. To this end, he obtains a new passport, which means he now holds such a document for both East and West Germany. He chooses to profit by this quirk, and begins smuggling woodgrain wallpaper through the Berlin Wall. Though the paper is aesthetically unappealing to the Western eye, East Berliners, having grown tired of the same floral wallpaper patterns, just can't get enough of the stuff. Bestvater's scheme is a success, and he is honored by Communist officials for work efficiency. But the celebration causes Bestvater to be late for his daily crossing through the wall, and he inadvertently shows border guards the wrong passport, putting an effective end to his machinations.

d&w, Peter Timm; ph, Klaus Eichhammer; ed, Corinna Doetz; art d, Martin Dostal.

Comedy   **(PR:C   MPAA:NR)**

MELO†   (1986, Fr.) 110m MK2-Films A2-CNC/MK2 c

Sabine Azema (Romaine Belcroix), Pierre Arditi (Pierre Belcroix), Andre Dussollier (Marcel Blanc), Fanny Ardant (Christiane Levesque), Jacques Dacqmine (Dr. Remy), Hubert Gignoux (Priest), Catherine Arditi (Yvonne).

Reassembling the cast of his previous film L'AMOUR A MORT, Resnais has put Azema, Pierre Arditi, Dussollier, and Ardant in the sixth film version of Henri Bernstein's 1929 stage play "Melo" (the best known are a 1937 British version and a 1958 German version—both titled DREAMING LIPS). The story here is the same as before. Dussollier and Arditi are both violinists and friends from their youthful days at the conservatory. Dussollier has gone on to find fame as a soloist, while Arditi leads a simpler life married to Azema. Dussollier, however, is in love with Azema, and she with him. They carry on a secret romance, which initially causes Azema to plan Arditi's murder, but then leads her to jump to her death in the Seine. Her suicide note makes no mention of her affair, instead declaring her love for her husband. Arditi lives with this illusion, but finally confronts Dussollier. Rather than destroy the faith that Arditi has built up in his dead wife's memory, Dussollier insists that no secret romance ever existed. Filmed with attention paid to the actors, who are photographed in a number of long takes, MELO marks a departure for Resnais, who has built his reputation on complex narrative structures that are dependent on editing. MELO also is the first time that Resnais has worked from his own screenplay, having in all his previous films left that chore to established and accomplished literary figures (Marguerite Duras, Alain-Robbe Grillet, Jorge Semprun, David Mercer). MELO was showered with Cesar nominations, winning two—Azema for Best Actress and Arditi for Best Supporting Actor. Besides the nomination the film and director received as Best Picture/Best Director MELO was also nominated for Best Actor (Dussollier), Best Cinematography, Best Production Design, and Best Costumes.

p, Marin Karmitz; d&w, Alain Resnais (based on the play "Melo" by Henry Bernstein); ph, Charlie Van Damme (Agfa-Gevaert Color); m, Johannes Brahms, Johann Sebastian Bach, Philippe Gerard; ed, Albert Jurgenson; prod d, Jacques Saulnier; cos, Catherine Leterrier; makeup, Dominique De Vorges.

Drama   **(PR:C   MPAA:NR)**

MEMOIRES D'UN JUIF TROPICAL†   (1986, Fr.) 75m Boites A Images c
                                         (Trans: Memories of a Tropical Jew)

Narrator: Joseph Morder, Francois Michaud, Vincent Toledano, Nicole Tufelli.

This filmed diary by Joseph Morder traces its creator's memories as the son of Jewish refugees who fled from Poland to safety in Ecuador. The production was shot in Paris, using a Super-8 film stock which was subsequently blown up to 35mm.

p,d&w, Joseph Morder; ed, Yves Abdreys, Arnaud Boland, Sophie Revault d'Allones.

Drama/Biography   **(PR:O   MPAA:NR)**

MENAGE*   (1986, Fr.) 81m Hachette Premiere-DD Productions-Cine Valse-Philippe Dussart/Norstar c (TENUE DE SOIREE)

Gerard Depardieu (Bob), Michel Blanc (Antoine), Miou-Miou (Monique), Bruno Cremer (Art Collector), Jean-Pierre Marielle (Depressed Man), Caroline Sihol (Depressed Woman), Michel Creton (Pedro), Jean-Yves Berteloot (Man in Night Club), Jean-Francois Stevenin, Mylene Demongeot (Burgled Couple).

A bawdy sex comedy from Blier, the director of 1978's Oscar-winning foreign film GET OUT YOUR HANDKERCHIEFS, which takes an unflinching and absurdly hilarious look at sexual power and desire. Blanc is a puny, balding, diminutive man who is unhappily married to Miou-Miou, a rather cruel woman who revels in browbeating her mate. At the film's opening, the two seem prepared to kill each other, arguing about money in a nightclub. Enter Depardieu, a brash bull who storms into their life, flattens Miou-Miou, quiets her with a shower of money, and defends the poor, helpless Blanc. Miou-Miou is attracted to Depardieu's money, while Blanc is attracted to a newly discovered sense of worth. An unredeemable thief, Depardieu sparks the couple's life by teaching them about stealing—an act he views as greatly dependent on a spiritual harmony that the thief must obtain with his surroundings. Attracted to his ruggedness, Miou-Miou soon becomes jealous of Depardieu's advances to Blanc. The heterosexually minded Blanc—who has never before even considered a homosexual encounter—finds himself attracted to Depardieu. For the first time in his life, Blanc feels needed—even if it is by a man. Depardieu ends Miou-Miou's interference by pushing her off on a pimp, thereby liberating Blanc completely from her influence. Gradually, Blanc assumes the most submissive role, stepping closer and closer to becoming a housewife. He dresses in women's clothes (as does Depardieu) and cakes his face with makeup. While Blanc has always been a dominated personality (by both men and women), he discovers that he now has power over the brutish Depardieu. The finale has Depardieu and Blanc walking down the street beside hooker Miou-Miou—all three of them donning their most feminine attire.

Colored with bizarre, almost surreal, humor and paced with manic energy, MENAGE (the real title translation, "Evening Dress," is more pointed) is a love story, not a homosexual or heterosexual love story, just a not-so-simple love story. Like all of Blier's films, there is razor-sharp wit to the dialog and situations, which always manage to offend someone. Blier, who in 1973 directed GOING PLACES, had hopes of reuniting that film's cast—Depardieu, Miou-Miou and Patrick Dewaere—in another film. When Dewaere died in 1982 that thought was forgotten, and it appeared that the script for MENAGE would not get filmed. After nearly casting French actor Bernard Girardeau (BRAS DE FER, LES SPECIALISTES, both 1985), Blier settled on Blanc. It turns out that Blanc was the perfect choice. Acting submissive, dressing as a woman, and wearing makeup, Blanc risked embarrassment and a critical haranguing by taking the role. Unlike Dustin Hoffman's character in TOOTSIE, Blanc is not simply a man wearing women's clothes. Blanc's characterization goes far deeper than gimmickry, exploring the psychological necessity of love. Because Blanc needs Depardieu's affections, he does anything he can to keep him. Blanc's brilliant performance not only carries the entire film, but won him a Best Actor prize—shared with MONA LISA's Bob Hoskins—from the Cannes Film Festival. Depardieu, as expected, turns in a powerful performance and must be commended for his continued desire to take roles which could threaten his popular image. Miou-Miou, in a difficult role as an unappealing third-wheel in the relationship, somehow manages to come through the film retaining the audience's sympathy. MENAGE is not a film for everybody, especially those whose values lean towards the prudish side, but its energy (it zips along at a breakneck 81 minutes) and intelligence must be contended with. (In French; English subtitles.)

p, Rene Cleitman; d&w, Bertrand Blier; ph, Jean Penzer (Panavision, Eastmancolor); m, Serge Gainsbourg; ed, Claudine Merlin; set d, Theobald Meurisse; cos, Michele Cerf; makeup, Michel Deruelle, Joel Lavau.

Comedy   **(PR:O   MPAA:NR)**

MENGZHONG REN   (SEE: DREAM LOVERS, 1986, Hong Kong)

MEN'S CLUB, THE*½   (1986) 100m Atlantic Releasing c

David Dukes (Phillip), Richard Jordan (Kramer), Harvey Keitel (Solly Berliner), Frank Langella (Harold Canterbury), Roy Scheider (Cavanaugh), Craig Wasson (Paul), Treat Williams (Terry), Stockard Channing (Nancy), Gina Gallegos (Felicia), Cindy Pickett (Hannah), Gwen Welles (Redhead), Penny Baker (Lake), Rebeccah Bush (Stella), Claudia Cron (Stacey), Ann Dusenberry (Page), Marilyn Jones (Allison), Manette LaChance (Billy), Jennifer Jason Leigh (Teensy), Ann Wedgeworth (Jo), Alurie Ambert (Waitress), Joan Foley (Nurse), Kelly Haverur (Phoebe).

It would be very hard to find seven brides for the seven "brothers" in this long-winded attempt at masculinism (as opposed to feminism). A septet of men get together, talk forever about women, jobs, women, politics, women, emotions, women, secrets, and women. They meet at the home of Berkeley shrink Jordan, who is probably not crazy enough to be tossed in a mental hospital, but if he were already inside as a patient, he'd have a hard time getting out. The men don't know each other very well but they have no compunctions about baring their souls in short order. They include Scheider, who is supposedly an ex-major league player with a lifetime batting average of .320. Scheider is now an administrator in the athletic department at Cal, but it's hard to believe that he ever did anything more physical than throw darts in a pub. Keitel is a high-powered real estate man

who likes to sleep with women, but he doesn't much like them for any other reason. Dukes is a professor at the college, a stiff prude who takes Scheider to task for the man's philandering. Williams is a physician who lives for pleasure, Langella is a gentle attorney with a bizarre sexual fetish, and Wasson rounds out the group as a man who likes to light up a joint and just listen. They sit around, drink, talk, and have a knife-throwing contest in Jordan's kitchen. When Jordan's wife, Channing, comes home and sees the mess they've made, she bops her husband on the head with a frying pan. His psychiatric response is, of course, "How do you feel about that?" The men are tossed out by Channing and promptly go off to a "house of affection" where six of them have to cough up more than $4,000 for their fun.

Medak's direction is to take this insular novel and make it appear like a stage play, which it really should have been. He will be remembered best for his cult film THE RULING CLASS, rather than for this or THE CHANGELING or even A DAY IN THE LIFE OF JOE EGG. Screenwriter Michaels, who adapted the script from his own book, probably knows the territory since he is a professor of English at Berkeley, but that doesn't necessarily make him a screenwriter. Wedgeworth has little to do as the mistress at the bordello, nor does Leigh as the youthful hooker. They apparently tried to make a film like THE BIG CHILL for mature men but they were left out in the cold. All of the men are so broadly drawn that they become laughable, rather than interesting. Langella seems to be playing DRACULA again and portraying the psychiatrist as a nut case has been done many times before and far better. The least humorous of the actors, Keitel, gets the best joke when a hooker asks him if she reminds him of his wife. He thinks a moment and replies: "Not yet. Complain about something." A few tunes lighten the activities. They include: "A Fool for Love" (Lee Holdridge, John Bettis, performed by Jim Gilstrap), "La Vie En Rose" (Louis Guy, Edith Piaf, performed by Sally Stevens), "Taking a Stand" (Peter Beckett, performed by Jim Gilstrap), "Shake Me Up" (Gary Wright). Almost stealing the movie from these high-powered actors is "Shadow," a cute animal supplied by a group known as Critters of the Cinema.

p, Howard Gottfried; d, Peter Medak; w, Leonard Michaels (based on his novel); ph, John Fleckenstein (CFI Color); m, Lee Holdridge; ed, Cynthia Scheider, David Dresher, Bill Butler; prod d, Ken Davis; art d, Laurence Bennett; set d, Thomas Lee Roysden; cos, Marianna Elliot, Peter Mitchell; spec eff, Frank Inez; ch, Lester Wilson; m/l, Lee Holdridge, John Bettis, Louis Guy, Edith Piaf, Peter Beckett, Gary Wright; makeup, Sheryl Leigh Shulman, Kelcey Weyers, Tonga W. Knight; stunts, Jay Jones.

Drama (PR:C-O MPAA:R)

MERCI MONSIEUR ROBERTSON† (1986, Bel.) 77m SODEP SPRL c
(Trans: Thank You Mr. Robertson)

Suzy Falk, Catherine Ferriere, Pierre Laroche, Jean Marie Petiniot, Robert Roanne, Felix Simtaine, Nicholas Talalaeff, Jean Marc Turine.

Combining narrative historical re-creations and a semi-documentary approach, Belgian director Levie has brought to the screen the life of the 18th Century film pioneer Etienne Gaspard Robert [Robertson]. During the days of the French Revolution when everyone else was worrying about a government overthrow, Robertson was using a "magic lantern" to project shadow images of ghouls and skeletons in his auditorium. Intercut with the narrative of his exploits is a history of film up to the late 1800s, including the early work of Thomas Edison and the brothers Lumiere.

p,d&w, Pierre Levie; ph, Paul Vercheval, Michel Baudour, Raymond Fromont, Desire Berckmans; ed, Rosanne Van Haesbrouck; prod d & cos, Claire Lise Leisegang; spec eff, Etienne De Bruyne, Daniel Schelfthout.

Historical/Docu-drama (PR:NR MPAA:NR)

MES ENLLA DE LA PASSIO† (1986, Span.) 98m Manderley –Cyrk-I.C.C.
c (Trans: Beyond Passion)

Patricia Adriani, Junajo Puigcorbe, Angel Jove, Rosa Novell, Remei Barrio, Arnau Vilardebo.

A vocalist loses her ability to sing shortly before performing in front of a live audience. Her physical troubles are compounded when she suddenly develops the

mysterious condition stigmata. Balanced within these events are the singer's relationships with a writer and small-time filmmaker.

d&w, Jesus Garay; ph, Carles Gusi (Agfacolor); m, Leo Marino; ed, Ernest Blasi.

Drama (PR:NR MPAA:NR)

MESHWAR OMAR† (1986, Egypt) (Trans: Omar's Journey)

Farouk El Feshaoui, Madiha Kamel, Mamdouth Abdel Alim.

Two men named Omar, of opposite social positions, become attached to each other after the poorer Omar saves the wealthier one's life. Accompanied by a prostitute, they spend an enlightening and intense two days traveling together before heading their separate ways.

d, Mohamed Khan; w, Raouf Tawfik, Mohamed Khan.

Drama (PR:C MPAA:NR)

MIAMI GOLEM† (1986, It.) Filmustang/Uniexport c

David Warbeck, John Ireland, Laura Trotter.

No, this is not a cross between the work of Michael Mann and Paul Wegener. Rather, MIAMI GOLEM deals with the scientific investigation of an unknown animal cell which has lain dormant for eons. A spark brings the mysterious speck to life, and the scientist investigating the cell is murdered. A television cameraman, who has filmed the experiments, begins to unravel the twisted enigmas and theorizes that the cell originated on some unknown planet. The cameraman, with the help of a lady scientist, continues to uncover strange facts but runs across an unknown international organization of bad guys who want the cell for their own nefarious purposes. They are the fiends behind the murder of the scientist investigating the cell, and now want to do in the cameraman as well. The beleaguered man doesn't know where to turn, and even suspects the lady scientist may be part of the conspiracy. Finally the cell, which proves to be a potent agent of death from outer space, brings events to a hallucinatory edge before it is ultimately destroyed.

d, Herbert Martin; w, Gianfranco Clerici, Vincenzo Mannino (based on story by Herbert Martin); ph, Lorenzo Battaglia, Paolo D'Ottavi (Fotocinema Color); m, Detto Mariano.

Science Fiction/Action (PR:O MPAA:NR)

MILLIONAIRE'S EXPRESS, THE† (1986, Hong Kong) 98m Bo Ho
–Golden Harvest c

Samo Hung, Olivia Cheng, Yuen Biao, Kenny Bee, Wang Yu, Lydia Sum, Kwan Pak Hing.

This Eastern western features a plethora of Hong Kong celebrities, Three Stooges-styled slapstick, and enough chop socky to satisfy any kung fu fan. The simple story follows a group of characters making their way from snowy Canadian mountains to the outskirts of Shanghai, finding time to throw in nearly every genre cliche in the process.

p,d&w, Samo Hung.

Western (PR:C MPAA:NR)

MILWR BYCHAN† (1986, Brit.) 98m Cine Cymru-S4c c (Trans: Boy
Soldier)

Richard Lynch (Wil Thomas), Dafydd Hywel (Sgt. Crane), Janes Donnelly (Lt. Col. Truscott Jones), Bernard Hill (Officer), Emer Gillespie (Deirdre), Bernard Latham (Roberts).

Lynch is a Welsh soldier stationed in Northern Ireland who is used as a patsy following his involvement in a shooting incident. After being imprisoned and harassed by his guards, Lynch thinks back to the events leading up to this moment. In flashback we learn of Lynch's affair with Gillespie, an Irish woman who is castigated by her peers for the romance. Gillespie is tarred and feathered by an angry mob and Lynch returns to his military duties. Back in present time, Lynch steadfastly refuses to knuckle under to pressure and will not plead guilty to murder charges. Hywel, Lynch's superior officer, manages to get the severity of the charges reduced, and Lynch is ultimately jailed for two years before receiving a dishonorable discharge. The actors speak in both English and Welsh, with subtitles explaining the Welsh-language portions. This is a film debut for Lynch, who is not to be confused with the American actor of the same name.

p, Karl Francis, Hayden Pierce; d&w, Karl Francis; ph, Roger Pugh Evans (Rank Color); m, Graham Williams; ed, Aled Evans; prod d, Hayden Pierce; cos, Katie Pegg.

Drama (PR:O MPAA:NR)

MIN PAPA AR TARZAN† (1986, Swed.) 80m Movie Makers–Swedish Film
Institute–Swedish Television–SVT2/Swedish Film Institute c (Trans: My Dad is
Tarzan)

Majsan Mattsson (Moa), Kim Anderzon (Sonja), Inga Gill (Grandma), Lars Amble (Alfred), Johannes Brost (Curt), Max Winerdal (Erik), Carl Billquist (Larsson), Meg Westergren (Harry the Hamster), Richard Armstrong (Tarzan), Nils Eklund (Alex the Crook), Sonja Hejdeman (Sonja's Boss), Lottie Ejebrant (Lady with Poodle), Bjorn Granath (Scrap Merchant), Gun Jonsson (Hot Dog Lady), Johan Rabaeus (Superannuated Hippie), Karl La Courbiniere (Sailor), Ralph Bengtsson (Gorilla), Thorsten Flinck, Claes Mansson (Motorcycle Police).

Mattsson is a 7-year-old girl who wants to live with her father in Africa when her mother (Anderzon) remarries. The girl is convinced her father is good pals with the legendary Tarzan, and might even be attending the latter's classes in animal languages. Mattsson begins studying animal tongues herself, which causes some trouble with the clients Anderzon serves as a beautician. Gill, Mattsson's motor-cycle-riding grandmother, arrives to take the girl off Anderzon's hands. Mattsson decides she wants her grandmother to join her in the journey to Africa, and Gill is talked into buying a sidecar for her motorcycle. Gill has reservations about leaving for a foreign land, though, preferring instead to enter a road rally. Brost, Mattsson's father, returns to his native Sweden, though the girl has already run away from home. Mattsson and Brost finally meet when, with the skills she learned in studying animal language, the girl rescues her father from a vicious canine.

p, Bert Sundberg, Lasse Lundberg; d&w, Judith Hollander (based on a book by Tove Ellefsen); ph, Roland Lundin, Torbjorn Andersson; m, Georg Riedel; ed, Susanne Linnman; art d, Bo Lindgren; cos, Sven Lunden, Kim Astrom; makeup, Sven Lunden, Kim Astrom.

Children's   **(PR:AA MPAA:NR)**

MIRCH MASALA†   (1986, India) National Film Development Corp. of
                                                    India c (Trans: Chilli Bouquet)

Naseeruddin Shah, Smita Patil, Om Puri, Suresh Oberoi, Deepti Naval, Mohan Cokhale.

This is a chronicle of relations between men and women in a rural Indian village. When a tax collector upsets the sedate lives of local residents, one women slaps his face and this leads to unexpected developments.

d, Ketan Mehta; w, Ketan Mehta, Shaji Hakim; ph, Jenhangir Choudhury; m, Rajat Dholakia.

Drama   **(PR:O MPAA:NR)**

MIRZA NOWROUZ' SHOES†   (1986, Iran) 106m Novin c

Ali Nassirian *(Mirza Nowrouz)*, Mohammad-Ali Kechavarz *(Governor)*, Zahra Boroumand *(Wife)*, Said Amir Soleimani *(Merchant)*.

This fantastic children's story features Nassirian as a wealthy man who simply refuses to replace a worn-out pair of shoes. His wife, shamed by this public embarrassment, eventually leaves Nassirian. Finally, having little choice, Nassirian gets rid of his old footwear and sets out to buy some new shoes. The trouble is that no matter how hard he tries to be rid of it, Nassirian's old footgear faithfully returns to him time and again.

p, Houchang Nourollahi; d, Mohammad Motevasselani; w, Dariouch Farhang; ph, Maziar Parto; m, Freydoun Nasseri; ed, Mehdi Radjaian; art d, Valiollah Khakdan.

Fantasy/Children's   **(PR:AA MPAA:NR)**

MISS MARY†   (1986, Arg.) 102m GEA/NW c

Julie Christie *(Miss Mary Mulligan)*, Sofia Viruboff *(Carolina)*, Donald McIntire *(Johnny)*, Barbara Bunge *(Teresa)*, Nacha Guevara *(Mecha [Mother])*, Eduardo [Tato] Pavlovsky *(Alfredo [Father])*, Guillermo Battaglia *(Uncle Ernesto)*, Iris Marga *(Aunt, Abuela)*, Luisina Brando *(Prostitute)* Nora Zinsky *(Adult Teresa)*, Gerardo Romano *(Ernesto)*.

Christie stars as an English one-time governess for three children of a wealthy Argentinean family who, in 1945, decides to return to her native England. Her relationship with the family, dating back to her arrival in 1938, is seen in flashbacks leading up to her dismissal for sleeping with McIntire, the 15-year-old eldest son of the family. MISS MARY received a Venice Film Festival showing in 1986 and has been scheduled for a 1987 release by New World Pictures in the U.S. Filmed in Argentina in both an English-language version and a Spanish-language version.

p, Lita Stantic; d, Maria Luisa Bemberg; w, Maria Luisa Bemberg, Jorge Goldenberg (based on an idean by Maria Luisa Bemberg, Beda Docampo Feijoo, Juan Batista Stagnaro); ph, Miguel Rodriguez (Eastmancolor); m, Luis Maria Serra; ed, Cesar D'Angiolillo; art d, Esmeralda Almonacid; cos, Garciela Galan.

Drama   **(PR:O MPAA:R)**

MISSION, THE*   (1986, Brit.) 126m Enigma-Goldcrest-Kingsmere/WB c

Robert De Niro *(Mendoza)*, Jeremy Irons *(Gabriel)*, Ray McAnally *(Altamirano)*, Liam Neeson *(Fielding)*, Aidan Quinn *(Felipe)*, Ronald Pickup *(Hontar)*, Charles [Chuck] Low *(Cabeza)*, Cherie Lunghi *(Carlotta)*, Bercelio Moya *(Indian Boy)*, Sigifredo Ismare *(Witch Doctor)*, Asuncion Ontiveros *(Indian Chief)*, Alejandrino Moya *(Chief's Lieutenant)*, Daniel Berrigan *(Sebastian)*, Rolf Gray *(Young Jesuit)*, Alvaro Guerrero *(Jesuit)*, Tony Lawn *(Father Provincial)*, Joe Daly *(Nobleman)*, Carlos Duplat *(Portuguese Commander)*, Rafael Camerano *(Spanish Commander)*, Monirak Sisowath *(Ibaye)*, Silvestre Chiripua *(Indian)*, Luis Carlos Gonzalez *(Boy Singer)*, Maria Teresa Ripoll *(Carlotta's Maid)*.

South America, circa 1750. A Jesuit priest who has been lashed to a large wooden cross is being carried through the South American jungle by Guarani natives. When they reach the banks of a river the natives place the cross in the water and watch it float away. The priest bobs along with the current, picking up speed. The sound of the rushing water becomes a deafening roar as the priest tumbles over the falls and disappears 230 feet below. Undeterred, the church sends another Jesuit, Irons, back to the jungle. Irons must scale the sheer rock face next to the mighty falls, for the Guarani live high above the cascading water. The priest finally makes it to the top of the falls, and then finds a spot in the river. He sits

on a rock and plays his flute until a group of Guarani warriors appear from the jungle, weapons drawn. This time the priest is accepted. Months later, having begun to build a mission for the Guarani, Irons encounters De Niro, a ruthless slave trader. De Niro kills several of the natives and captures many more, taking them back to town as slaves. Soon after, De Niro walks in on his fiancee, Lunghi, in bed with his handsome young brother, Quinn. In a fit of jealous rage, De Niro engages in a duel with Quinn and kills him. Because he is an aristocrat, De Niro is not punished for his crime. But the slave trader has a conscience, for he truly loved his brother, so he cloisters himself in the local monastery and refuses to talk or eat. The priests summon Irons to talk with De Niro, and he learns that the slave trader feels that he must do penance. Irons arranges for De Niro to join him on his journey back to the mission—back to where he had committed so many sins. De Niro makes the trip dragging a huge net full of armor, swords, and other weapons—the baggage of his past life—behind him. De Niro struggles mightily and very nearly loses his life several times because of his burden. One of the young Jesuits takes pity on De Niro and severs the heavy rope tied to the net and watches as it tumbles downward. Silently, De Niro retrieves his burden and ties it back together—he refuses to ease his pain. Eventually the group arrive at the top of the falls where they are met by the Guarani Indians whom De Niro had murdered and sold into slavery. A warrior, with knife in hand, approaches the haggard De Niro. The slave trader has accepted his fate and is prepared to die, but rather than kill him, the Guarani see that he has paid his penance and forgive him by freeing him from his burden. De Niro weeps like a child as the Guarani come up and touch him reassuringly. After working with Irons at the mission for several months, De Niro, who has fallen in love with the Guarani people, asks to be allowed into the Jesuit order. Irons warns him of the vow of obedience, and De Niro assures him that he will obey the will of the church. By 1756 trouble arrives in the form of McAnally, an emissary sent by the pope to settle a dispute between Spain, Portugal, and the church which involves the fate of the seven Jesuit missions in the area. Although Spain has outlawed slavery, Portugal has not, and a new treaty between the countries will turn over some Spanish holdings—land where the missions now sit—to the Portuguese. This, of course, opens up the Guarani Indians to enslavement by the Portuguese. Both Spain and Portugal have assured the pope that if he does not capitulate and dissolve the missions, the fate of the entire Jesuit order in Europe will be in jeopardy. Rather than risk the annihilation of the entire order, it is decided *before* McAnally arrives that the missions in South America will be dissolved. McAnally pretends to listen to arguments from both the settlers and the Jesuits, and deep in his heart sides with the natives. He asks to visit the missions and is awestruck at the beauty and self-sufficiency of the oldest mission. Here the natives grow and market their own food, are experts at hand-crafting and exporting musical instruments (the violins are prized throughout Europe), and can read and write their own language. McAnally realizes that what has been accomplished here in the faraway jungle is truly for the glory of God, but his decision is a foregone conclusion and he coldly informs the Jesuits that they must leave or Portuguese troops will slaughter them. The Guarani tell McAnally that they have done nothing to displease God, and they refuse to leave the missions. Both Irons and De Niro break their vows of obedience, but in very different ways. Irons opts to stay with the Guarani and pray with them, while De Niro and some of the other young Jesuits join forces with the native warriors who plan to wage war against the foreign soldiers. Of course the might of Europe proves too much for the natives and the missions turn into bloody slaughterhouses. Both De Niro and Irons die, the former with sword in hand, the latter clutching a cross.

Ambitious, moving, and visually stunning, THE MISSION falls right in step with other British historical epics, but also fails in some fundamental areas that plague all projects of this nature. The film was originally conceived by Italian producer Ghia in the early 1970s. He had been inspired by a stage play by German dramatist Fritz Hochwalder entitled "The Strong Are Lonely," which was based on the same historical events. Ghia approached veteran screenwriter Robert Bolt (LAWRENCE OF ARABIA, A MAN FOR ALL SEASONS, DR. ZHIVAGO) and the pair traveled to ruins of the great South American Jesuit missions near the Iguassu falls that border Brazil, Paraguay, and Argentina. Bolt agreed to write the screenplay, but Ghia could not find financing for over nine years. In 1984, Ghia and David Puttnam formulated a deal that finally got THE MISSION off the ground. Puttnam brought in KILLING FIELDS director Joffe and shortly after casting the major roles (including a small part for Jesuit priest/social activist Daniel Berrigan, who also worked as a technical advisor on the

production—he published a fascinating collection of the journals he kept during the filming) the crew found themselves in Colombia where most of the film was to be shot, with three weeks scheduled in Argentina for the filming of the Iguassu falls scenes. If heat, mosquitos, and illness were not enough hardship for cast and crew, Joffe soon learned that he had built his massive mission set smack in the middle of a major Colombian drug-smuggling route. Armed Colombian troops wandered the area constantly in search of drug traffickers. To play the Guarani Indians, Joffe chose to cast the Waunana Tribe of Colombia. Rather than subject a truly primitive tribe to the horrors of Hollywood technology, or work with "Westernized" natives too sophisticated to realistically portray a primitive people, Joffe chose the Waunana because they maintained their seclusion while having had some contact with the outside world. With the help of 15 Colombian actors, the Waunana were soon able to fully understand the implications of the screenplay and more or less direct themselves (the Waunana were paid the same scale as other Colombian extras, and the cast and crew set up an investment fund for them to be administered by Survival International in London). Without a doubt, THE MISSION is an impressive production. From the pre-credits sequence at the waterfall, right down to the conclusion, the film contains several awe-inspiring, very spiritual scenes (enhanced greatly by Ennio Morricone's superb, Oscar-nominated score). De Niro's salvation at the hands of the Guarani, McAnally's encounter with the Indians and their beautiful missions, and Irons facing the impending slaughter with prayer as his only defense are all very poignant moments. Unfortunately, THE MISSION tries to do so much, that little is explored fully. A bit of research on one's own helps to more fully understand the historical and political situation rather sketchily portrayed in the film. Irons' character is really more an icon rather than a man, as is De Niro's. De Niro's conversion from arrogant imperialist to holy man, while inspiring and touching, is underdeveloped and rushed so that the main focus of the film—the political and social implications of the Spain-Portugal Treaty—can begin. Also, the Spanish and Portuguese are nothing more than overbearing cardboard villains—especially Low, who shouts his way through his entire performance. Perhaps most distressing is the fact that THE MISSION is yet another (and this includes Werner Herzog's Amazon films) film made by Europeans or Americans which, while sympathetic to the plight of the natives, portrays them as an indistinguishable mass of childlike innocents just waiting to be exploited by white men. The Guarani are given no individual personalities, no inner conflicts, no real identity other than that of the eternal victim. The question of whether the Jesuits should have "converted" the Guarani at all is only raised once and never answered. The problem with films like THE MISSION is that they all too often tend to slip into self-righteousness—a fate also suffered by Joffe's debut film, THE KILLING FIELDS. Only McAnally manages to bring the correct amount of ambiguity and depth to his performance. His character is torn between what he knows in his heart is right, and what his mind tells him is his duty. Although we hear his voice explain this much to us in his narration, the verbal explanation is unnecessary, for we can see it in his face. It is a subtle and detailed performance and this alone makes the film worth seeing. Script and directorial problems aside, THE MISSION comes at a time when the cinema needs more films that attempt to grapple with complex moral and social issues relevant to our current world situation. The conflict felt by the Jesuits in the film is one that occurs every day among holy men and women in places like Central America, South Africa, and Poland. Perhaps there is a case for some optimism here, for THE MISSION broke the box office record set by the wholly offensive and mindless RAMBO at London's Warner West End cinema, was awarded the Golden Palm at Cannes, and was nominated for Best Picture by the Academy. Joffe received a Best Director nomination, Clark was nominated for Best Editing, Craig and Stephens for best art and sets, and Menges was the sole Oscar recipient for his fine cinematography.

p, Fernando Ghia, David Puttnam; d, Roland Joffe; w, Robert Bolt; ph, Chris Menges (J-D-C Widescreen, Rank Color); m, Ennio Morricone; ed, Jim Clark;

prod d, Stuart Craig; art d, George Richardson, John King; set d, Jack Stephens; cos, Enrico Sabbatini; spec eff, Peter Hutchinson; makeup, Tommie Manderson; stunts, Vic Armstrong.

Historical/Drama   Cas.   (PR:C   MPAA:PG)

MR. LOVE½**   (1986, Brit.) 91m Enigma/WB-Goldcrest c

Barry Jackson *(Donald Lovelace)*, Maurice Denham *(Theo)*, Margaret Tyzack *(Pink Lady)*, Linda Marlowe *(Barbara)*, Christina Collier *(Esther)*, Helen Cotterill *(Lucy Nuttall)*, Julia Deakin *(Melanie)*, Donal McCann *(Leo)*, Marcia Warren *(Doris Lovelace)*, Tony Melody *(Ferris)*, Kay Stonham *(Maggie Capstick)*, Patsy Byrne *(Mrs. Lunt)*, Jeremy Swift *(Boy in Projection Room)*, Janine Roberts *(Little Alice)*, John Joyce *(Parson)*, Dave Atkins *(Undertaker)*, George Malpas *(Old Gardener)*, Chris Jury, James Benson *(Apprentice Gardeners)*, Jacki Piper *(Leo's Girl Friend)*, Robert Bridges *(Landau Proprietor)*, Alan Starkey *(Landau Man)*, Lill Roughley *(Nubile Housewife)*, Tina Simmons *(Art Teacher)*

Another charming British film from executive producer David Puttnam, who has managed to provide audiences with consistently pleasant entertainment. A very English variation on Francois Truffaut's THE MAN WHO LOVED WOMEN, MR. LOVE stars Jackson (who bears more than a passing resemblance to Terence Stamp) as a reserved small-town gardener who has captured the fancy of all the women in town, becoming something of a local folk hero. The film begins with his funeral, which is attended almost exclusively by the women who loved him. His last words, we learn, were "she loves me." As his best friend Denham reminisces, the film flashes back to Jackson's days above earth. Jackson comes to the realization one afternoon that he is 50 years old and has never been in love. In addition to his gardening, he takes time to visit his women friends, allowing a specific day throughout the week for each of them. He carries on with a local prostitute, with her charming grown-up daughter, with a pristine, tea-sipping lady, with a spider-collecting divorcee, and with the counter-girl at the local theater. He begins spending more and more time with Marlowe, the daughter of the prostitute, who juggles her schedule to accommodate raising her young daughter and her classical singing lessons. She eventually proclaims her love to Jackson and the pair seem ready to start a romantic life together. Concentrating more on love than on driving, Jackson loses control of a car and is killed in a freak accident. The town then erects a statue in memory of Jackson.

Directed by Battersby with subtlety and a tranquil pace, MR. LOVE exists in a rare world where love is the most important thing to a man. Jackson plays his role with a peaceful quality that recalls Terence Stamp's character in THE HIT (1985) and Peter Sellers' seemingly insightful gardener in BEING THERE. Although there is very little depth or development in the script or the characterization, MR. LOVE does contain a number of exceptional moments. The most memorable scene is a truly magical one in which Jackson, who works part-time as a projectionist at the local movie theater, must calm the audience when the projector fails during a screening of CASABLANCA. Together with his co-worker Deakin, a diehard movie fan and aspiring actress, Jackson acts out a scene from the classical film on stage. It is the scene in which Ingrid Bergman visits Humphrey Bogart in a last-ditch effort to obtain the letters of transit. Deakin, with a near-perfect accent, portrays Bergman, while Jackson, in an affected tough guy voice, is Bogart. They both remember the dialog, word for word, and entertain the audience just as Bogart and Bergman did—though without the assistance of any props (Deakin uses her fingers for a gun) or stage sets. Their rendition is just as powerful as Bogart and Bergman's, but in a different, more human way, which strikes a common chord with every filmgoer who has seen CASABLANCA. All the supporting performances are fine, though it is Deakin who stands out with her enthusiastic performances as Bergman and various other Hollywood stars, including Vivien Leigh from GONE WITH THE WIND. The moviehouse scenes were photographed in the Phoenix, which, as the film credits inform us, is the longest-running cinema in Britain. Songs include the dreamy "Mr. Love" (Ruth Russell, Willy Russell, performed by Rebecca Storm), "Rollin'," and "Naked Man" (Randy Newman), and GONE WITH THE WIND's "Tara Theme" (Max Steiner).

p, Susan Richards, Robin Douet; d, Roy Battersby; w, Kenneth Eastaugh; ph, Clive Tickner; m, Willy Russell; ed, Alan J. Cumner-Price; art d, Adrienne Atkinson; cos, Ann Hollowood.

Comedy   Cas.   (PR:A   MPAA:PG-13)

**MR. VAMPIRE†   (1986, Hong Kong) 95m Bo Ho/Golden Harvest c

Ricky Hui *(Man Chor)*, Moon Lee *(Ting Ting)*, Chin Suit Ho *(Chau)*, Lam Ching Ying *(Master)*, Pauline Wong *(Jade)*, Billy Lau, Anthony Chan, Wu Ma, Wong Ha, Yuen Wah.

A bizarre comedy which combines elements from horror films and kung-fu epics. A small Chinese family is plagued by a group of weird vampires who work under rules quite different from their undead European cousins. In place of a fear of crucifixes, garlic, mirrors, and the like, these Chinese vampires hate things like sticky rice and victims who hold their breath.

p, Samo Hung; d, Lau Kun Wai; w, Wong Ying, Szeto Cheuk Hon; ph, Peter Ngor; m, Anders Nelson; ed, Cheung Yiu Chung; spec eff, Ng Kok Wah; ch, Lam Ching Ying, Yuen Wah; stunts, Pang Yau Cheung.

Comedy/Horror   (PR:C   MPAA:NR)

**MLADE VINO†   (1986, Czech.) 94m Barrandov c (Trans: Young Wine)

Vladimir Mensik *(Michal Janak)*, Josef Abrham *(Petrus)*, Jiri Sovak *(Semerad)*, Ivana Andrlova *(Lenka)*, Iva Janzurova *(Ruzena)*, David Schneider *(Karlik)*, Jiri

Bartoska *(Bartak)*, Vaclav Sloup *(Kuna)*, Frantisek Nemec *(Urban)*, Josef Somr *(Ovecka)*.

d, Vaclav Vorlicek; w, Milos Macourek, Jan Kozak, Svatopluk Novotny, Vaclav Vorlicek; ph, Josef Vanis; m, Karel Svoboda; ed, Miroslav Hajek; art d, Oldrich Bosak; cos, Zuzana Bartova; makeup, Vaclav Frank, Jirina Bisingerova.

MOA†   (1986, Swed.) 96m Filmstallet–SVT2–Swedish Film
Institute–Sandrew/Sandrew–Swedish Film Institute c

Gunilla Nyroos *(Moa)*, Reine Brynolfsson *(Harry)*, Lennart Hjulstrom *(Karl)*, Grethe Ryen *(Ottar)*, Berta Hall *(Moa's Mother)*, Percy Brandt *(Karl Otto Bonnier)*, Roland Hedlund *(The Editor)*, Krister Henriksson *(The Director of Broadcasting)*, Lars Humble *(Karl Gerhard)*, Mats Bergman *(Isidor Knoos)*, Dan Ekborg *(Artur Lundkvist)*, Harald Hamrell *(Erik Asklund)*, Anders Ekborg *(Josef Kjellgren)*, Mikael Segerstrom, Lars Stromstedt, Stig Engstrom, Anita Irene Wall, Margreth Weivers, Susanne Lorenz, Elisabeth Lee, Finn Lennartsson, Mikael Naeslund, Ivan Oljelund, Krister Kalte, Tobias Hardelin, Carl Sjostrom.

Gunilla Nyroos stars in this biography of Moa Martinson, one of Sweden's best-loved writers. The film begins at the turn of the century when the 18-year-old Nyroos marries Hjulstrom, a hulking stone-worker. The union quickly spawns five children and Hjulstrom begins drinking heavily and leaving the family for days at a time. The children live in fear of their father and often hide from him when he is home. Nyroos channels her fears and frustrations into writing and soon she meets Ryen, a lecturer on sexual problems, who works to have her writing published. Nyroos accompanies Ryen to a town meeting where she speaks frankly and passionately about the ill-treatment of women in Sweden. Although her speech is met with disfavor, one young poet, Brynolfsson, is enthralled with the outspoken Nyroos and he falls in love with her. Soon after, two of her youngest children drown after falling though melting ice. Shortly after that, Hjulstrom kills himself with dynamite not far from their cottage. Weeks later, Brynolfsson, who is 13 years her junior, moves in with Nyroos. Eventually the two are married, but the difference in their ages and her burgeoning critical and popular success affects the relationship. Eleven years later Brynolfsson leaves her to forge his own career (he eventually becomes a Nobel Laureate). Nyroos stays in her little cottage and continues writing and working her land until her death in 1964. Writer-director Wahlgren based his film on writings by the Martinsons he had discovered in their cottage attic which had been undisturbed for nearly 40 years.

p, Anders Birkeland; d&w, Anders Wahlgren; ph, Roland Sterner, Mats Ardstrom; m, Gunnar Edander; ed, Solveig Nordlund; art d, Lasse Westfeldt; cos, Ingrid Hjelm, Hedvig Ander, Asa Hjelm; makeup, Agneta Lindqvist, Kjell Gustafsson, Cia Sparrflo.

Biography   **(PR:C MPAA:NR)**

MODERN GIRLS*   (1986) 84m Atlantic c

Daphne Zuniga *(Margo)*, Virginia Madsen *(Kelly)*, Cynthia Gibb *(Cece)*, Clayton Rohner *(Clifford/Bruno X)*, Chris Nash *(Ray)*, Steve Shellen *(Brad)*, Rick Overton *(Marsalis)*, Quin Kessler *(Retro Vamp)*, Pamela Springsteen *(Tanya)*, Charles Zucker *(Guy in Line)*, Carl Weintraub *(Bartender)*, Michael Clarke *(Police Officer)*, Mike Muscat *(Mechanic)*, Sharron Shayne *(Supervisor)*, Troy Evans *(Club Owner)*, Vojo Goric *(Doorman)*, Gary Goetzman *(Undercover Cop)*, Michael Frost *(Music Video A.D.)*, Richard Fullerton *(Redneck)*, Steve Nemith *(Flunky)*, John Dye *(Hunk)*, Cameron Thor, Ron Campbell *(DJs)*, Janet Bowen *(Girl in Line)*, Mark Holton *(Boss)*, Josh Richman *(Milo)*, Martin Ferrero *(Music Video Director)*.

Apparently the rather dubious goal here was to prove to the public that young

women can be just as sexist, obnoxious, and stupid as the young men we've seen in the endless series of youth sex comedies that have plagued movie screens over the last 10 years. Well, if that is what they were trying to accomplish, then the makers of MODERN GIRLS have succeeded admirably. Unfortunately, they have warped a fairly likable cast to fit the basic sleaziness of the story. Three "kooky" L.A. girls share an apartment. Zuniga is the brain of the trio, for she studied literature during a brief fling with college. She works at her boring phone

sales job by day and goes partying with her roomies by night. Madsen is a flirtatious blonde who works at a pet store, more or less seducing men into buying house pets. Gibb has recently lost her job as a department store makeup counter girl, and spends her time daydreaming about her favorite British punk-rock star, Rohner. The girls' club-hopping ritual is interrupted somewhat by Madsen's sudden decision to take off with the car they all share to try to salvage her relationship with insensitive disk-jockey Nash. Since everybody knows that "nobody walks in L.A.," Zuniga and Gibb waylay nerdy driving instructor Rohner (yes, he plays a dual role) who has arrived at their door looking for Madsen (they had a date, she stood him up). The girls persuade Rohner that Madsen will meet them at one of the nightclubs, and the dork agrees to chauffeur them. Madsen's mission fails and she does run into her friends at one of the clubs. She drinks, sulks, and does drugs. Gibb, however, actually meets her idol, rock star Rohner, and the two hit it off. Unfortunately, the club is raided by the fire department and they are split up. In a revolting scene (it's supposed to be funny), Madsen becomes so stoned that she crawls onto a pool table and offers to take on the dozens of drooling rednecks standing around (uncomfortable shades of the famous pool table-top gang rape-case a few years back in Massachusetts). By the end of the film, Madsen has managed to prevent several rape attempts, Zuniga has fallen for the nerdy incarnation of Rohner, and Gibb nobly turns down rock-star Rohner's offer to join him on his world tour (she'd rather stay with her friends).

Considering that the film features three seemingly intelligent young actresses, was written by a woman, filmed by a woman (this, unfortunately, is unusual), and the assistant director was a woman (also unusual), one would think MODERN GIRLS would be a refreshing look at the lives of young women, rather than the exploitative, insensitive, and downright offensive drek that it is (rape and drugs are not funny). After all, it is possible to inject some charm and insight into this genre, as was proved by Martha Coolidge in VALLEY GIRL, and, to a lesser extent, by Lisa Gottlieb in JUST ONE OF THE GUYS. But MODERN GIRLS is disturbingly sleazy. This isn't a comedy; it's a Geraldo Rivera syndicated special on the sordid nightlife of today's youth. What makes the film even more annoying is the insincere "life isn't one long party" message tacked on at the end. After sitting through the horrors these girls put themselves through, presumably on a nightly basis, is anyone really supposed to believe that the characters have learned anything from all this? When this film isn't sleazy it's just plain cliched and stupid. The only redeeming aspect of MODERN GIRLS is the three main actresses, misguided though they might be. Zuniga was very impressive in THE SURE THING, Madsen drew notice in both ELECTRIC DREAMS and CREATOR, and Gibb, who had a brief role in SALVADOR, was one of the original cast members of the television series "Fame." They are all very likable, very capable actresses who will surely go on to better things. A strange note: Pamela Springsteen, the younger sister of rock mega-star Bruce Springsteen, is one of the girls with whom Madsen gets so stoned—the anti-drug "Boss" must be a bit dismayed.

p, Gary Goetzman; d, Jerry Kramer; w, Laurie Craig; ph, Karen Grossman (United Color Labs); m, Jay Levy, Ed Arkin; ed, Mitchell Sinoway; prod d, Laurence Bennett, art d, Joel Lang; set d, Jill Ungar; cos, Beverly Klein; ch, Sarah Elgart; makeup, Julie Purcell.

Comedy   **(PR:O MPAA:PG-13)**

MOI DRUG IVAN LAPSHIN†   (1986, USSR) 92m Lenfilm/Sovexportfilm
bw-c (Trans: My Friend Ivan Lapshin)

Andrei Boltnev *(Ivan Lapshin)*, Nina Rouslsnova *(Natasha Adashova)*, Andrei Mironov *(Khanin)*, Alexei Jarkov *(Friend)*.

Shot several years ago, but only now beginning to see international release, this film tells the story of the head of criminal investigations (Boltnev) in a small Soviet village in the 1930s. He is in love with actress Rouslsnova, but she tells him that she loves his best friend, Mironov. Later, during the pursuit of a murderous black market operator, Mironov is badly wounded in a gunfight. When the quarry is finally captured, Boltnev kills him to gain revenge for the death of his friend.

d, Alexei Guerman; w, Edouard Volodaraki; ph, Valeri Fedossov; m, Arkadi Gagulachvili; ed, L. Semionova; art d, Yuri Pougatch; cos, G. Deyeva.

Drama   **(PR:C MPAA:NR)**

MOMO†   (1986, It./Ger.) Cinecitta–Sacis–Rialto–Iduna/Sacis c

Radost Bokel, Mario Adorf, Armin Muller-Stahl, Leopoldo Trieste, Ninetto Davoli, Bruno Stori, Elide Melli, Isabel Russinova, John Huston.

A fable based on a popular children's story centers on an orphan girl who lives in an abandoned outdoor theater and is cared for by the townsfolk. A group of mysterious gray men arrive smoking gray cigars and concocting a scheme to steal everyone's spare time, which they put into their cigars. The little heroine finds Father Time and together they arrive at a solution: he will fall asleep (stopping everything) while she frees up all the stolen hours.

d, Johannes Schaaf; w, Johannes Schaaf, Rosemarie Fendel, Marcello Coscia (based on the novel by Michael Ende); ph, Xavier Schwarzenberger; m, Angelo Branduardi.

Children's/Fantasy   **(PR:A MPAA:NR)**

MON BEAU-FRERE A TUE MA SOEUR†   (1986, Fr.) 100m
Cineproduction/World Marketing c (Trans: My Brother-In-Law Has Killed My Sister)

Michel Serrault *(Octave)*, Michel Piccoli *(Etienne)*, Juliette Binoche *(Esther)*, Jean Carmet *(Jocelyn)*, Milva Biolcati *(Renata)*.

A gangster film with a French flavor that twists the usual expectations of the genre—something the French have been doing since Jean-Pierre Melville's BOB LE FLAMBEUR (1955), Jean-Luc Godard's BREATHLESS (1959), and Francois Truffaut's SHOOT THE PIANO PLAYER (1960). French film veterans Serrault and Piccoli play a pair of Academie Francaise members who come under the spell of a lovely young veterinarian, Binoche, who insists, as the title clearly states, that her brother-in-law has killed her sister. Not only is there no proof of her claim, there isn't a dead body anywhere is sight. Piccoli and Binoche also appeared together in 1986 in MAUVAIS SANG, another unorthodox gangster film.

p, Giorgio Silvagni; d, Jacques Rouffio; w, Jacques Rouffio, Georges Conchon; ph, Jacques Loiselleux; m, Philippe Sarde; ed, Anne Ruiz; set d, Jean-Jacques Caziot; cos, Michele Cerf.

Crime   **(PR:NR MPAA:NR)**

MON CAS†   (1986, Fr./Portugal) 90m Les Films du Passage-La
                                                      Sept-Filmargen c (Trans: My Case)

Bulle Ogier, Luis Miguel Cintra, Axel Bougousslavsky, Fred Personne, Wladimir Ivanovsky, Heloise Mignot, Gregoire Oestermann.

Portugal's foremost filmmaker, the 79-year-old de Oliveira, has followed his seven-hour 1985 epic THE SATIN SLIPPER with this 90-minute entry that explores the relationship between theater and film. It stars Ogier as a stage actress whose rehearsal is disrupted by a disturbed young man, Cintra, who enters the stage and offers forth the dilemmas of his personal life to an audience which consists of de Oliveira and his technical crew. After a while, de Oliveira looks back at the film they just shot of Cintra, playing it back in various ways with a narration from a text by Samuel Beckett. De Oliveira further stretches the limits of filmed theater by using two opposite devices—long takes and freeze frames—as Cintra tells the Biblical story of Job while arguing with Ogier. A superb actress, Ogier has previously appeared in many of the films of Jacques Rivette (L'AMOUR FOU, CELINE AND JULIE GO BOATING), whose career in film has been devoted to the relationship between theater and film.

p, Paulo Branco; d&w, Manoel de Oliveira (based on the play "O Meu Caso" by Jose Regio, "Pour finir encore et autres foirades" by Samuel Beckett, and *The Book of Job)*; ph, Mario Barroso; m, Joao Pais; art d, Maria Jose Branco, Luis Monteiro; cos, Jasmin.

Drama   **(PR:NR MPAA:NR)**

MONA LISA*½   (1986, Brit.) 104m Palace/Island-Handmade c

Bob Hoskins *(George)*, Cathy Tyson *(Simone)*, Michael Caine *(Mortwell)*, Clarke Peters *(Anderson)*, Kate Hardie *(Cathy)*, Robbie Coltrane *(Thomas)*, Zoe Nathenson *(Jeannie)*, Sammi Davies *(May)*, Rod Bedall *(Terry)*, Joe Brown *(Dudley)*, Pauline Melville *(Dawn)*, David Halliwell *(Devlin)*, G.B. "Zoot" Money *(Carpenter)*, Hossein Karimbeik *(Raschid)*, John Darling *(Roberts)*, Donna Cannon *(Rosie)*, Mandy Winch *(Flower Shop Girl)*, Maggie O'Neill *(Girl in Paradise Club)*, Dawn Archibald *(Girl Prostitute in Joint)*, Geoff Larder *(Hotel Clerk)*, Robert Dorning *(Hotel Punter)*, Helen Martin *(Peep Show Girl)*, Richard Strange *(Porn Shop Man)*, Jeremy Hardy *(Shop Assistant)*, Bryan Coleman *(Stanley)*, Raad Raawi *(Arab Servant)*, Alan Talbot *(Bath Attendant)*, Stephen Persaud *(Black Youth)*, Bill Moore, Kenny Baker *(Buskers)*, Gary Cady *(Waiter)*, Perry Fenwick *(White Pimp)*.

Irish director Neil Jordan (DANNY BOY, THE COMPANY OF WOLVES) continues to breathe new life into the staid British film industry with his remarkable combination of visual style and narrative content. Hoskins stars as a recently released convict who has just served a seven-year sentence because he was a good soldier and took the fall for his mob boss, Caine. In an attempt to gather up the pieces of his shattered life, Hoskins goes to visit his now-teenage daughter,

Nathenson, at the home of his ex-wife. Although the girl is happy to see him, his ex-wife is not, and she slams the door in his face. Hoskins goes to live with his best friend, Coltrane, who lives in a trailer home and makes a living fixing cars

and moving bizarre stolen merchandise like light-up Jesus statues and a fork-in-a-plate-of-spaghetti sculpture made of plastic. Looking to collect his due, Hoskins goes for a meeting with Caine, only to find the mob boss out of town. A lackey informs Hoskins that he's been assigned a job chauffeuring a high-class black call girl, Tyson, who carries herself like royalty. In addition to driving her around, Hoskins must serve as her "beard" and appear to be her date when she visits expensive hotels to service her clients. Hoskins and Tyson take an intense dislike to each other at first. He resents the job and considers her a pretentious "tart," while she thinks he's crude and common. In time they begin to warm up to each other and she buys him an expensive, very classy suit so he won't look so shady while he waits for her in hotel lobbies. Nearly every night, Tyson has Hoskins drive her through the seedy King's Crossing area where the common street whores ply their trade. Tyson came from these streets and is searching for her only friend, a younger white whore—a junkie—who worked for the same pimp, Peters, a cruel man who beat them both up without provocation. Hoskins finds the trips to King's Crossing particularly distasteful, for most of the prostitutes are his daughter's age (whom he's been seeing on the sly). After work, Hoskins returns home to tell Coltrane, an avid detective-thriller fan, of the "tall, thin black tart," and how he could write a book about it. Coltrane shakes his head in disagreement and comments, "Too many 'T's.'"

As the days go by, Hoskins finds himself falling in love with the enigmatic Tyson ("She may be a tart, but she's a lady as well"), and he agrees to spend his daylight hours searching the seedy sex shops of London seeking Tyson's friend. After an encounter with Peters, Hoskins discovers a connection between the pimp

and Caine. The next day, Hoskins follows Peters and finds the girl, Hardie, in a church. Peters appears and takes the girl away and Hoskins follows them to Caine's mansion. Hoskins breaks in and discovers a back room with a two-way mirror and a camera which looks directly at a bedroom where prominent British citizens come to relieve their perverted passions. When Hardie's middle-aged "john" has his back turned, Hoskins opens the secret mirror-door and snatches Hardie. He then meets with Tyson and the three escape to the seaside resort of Brighton. To his shock and disappointment, Hoskins discovers that Tyson and Hardie are not just friends, but lovers as well. Feeling shamed, rejected, and used, Hoskins practically drags Tyson to the boardwalk and forces her into a ridiculous parody of a romantic outing. He buys silly plastic sunglasses for them both (his shaped like stars, hers like hearts) and holds her close to him as he pours out his anger and disappointment. His tirade is interrupted by Peters and two other mob goons who chase after them. Hoskins manages to get the jump on them and give them all a good beating. When he and Tyson return to the hotel room, they are shocked to find Caine. Peters stumbles up to the room as well and Caine is about to order their execution when Tyson produces the pistol Hoskins had given her for protection and shoots both Caine and Peters. Confused, angry, and no longer willing to take the rap for anybody, Hoskins leaves the sobbing Tyson with the bloody bodies and returns home. Working underneath a car with Coltrane, Hoskins finishes his "book" with the line, "Yes, she was in love all right, but not with him. And that's the story."

Hoskins is superb in MONA LISA and it is his sensitive, multifaceted performance that infuses the film with an inner life. Although a member of the underworld, Hoskins' George is a good-hearted man who has gotten involved in a world where there is no room for romance and sentiment. His first perception of Tyson as a cold, snobby whore is essentially correct, but his basic good nature allows her to skillfully manipulate him until he sees her as his queen and himself as a white knight riding to her rescue. When his illusions are shattered, Hoskins once again picks up the pieces and finds solace in his friendship with Coltrane and his relationship with his daughter. His habit of relating his experiences to Coltrane in the form of stories allows Hoskins a new perspective on the events—one that helps him understand and accept what happened. Tyson, however manipulative, is sympathetic as well. Tired of being abused by men, she has transformed herself from a common street whore to a high-class call girl who has some control over her life. Although not in love with Hoskins the way he is with her, she is affected by him and does care about him. Her fierce independence and refusal to ever let anyone abuse her again forces her to manipulate Hoskins unfairly. She, like Hoskins, maintains illusions, for her love for Hardie is not returned. "She likes me," the stoned Hardie tells Hoskins of Tyson, "She likes me a lot." There is no note of compassion in her statement—only a detached amusement. Hardie really couldn't care less where she winds up.

Director Jordan was inspired by a newspaper article he had read while shooting THE COMPANY OF WOLVES. The item told of a man who was charged with grievous bodily harm who claimed he was trying to save two young prostitutes from their vicious pimp. The fact that the man had this "vision of himself as St. George" intrigued Jordan and he asked writer David Leland to begin the script. Anxious to direct a much simpler film (technically) after THE COMPANY OF WOLVES, Jordan made MONA LISA his next project. Jordan immediately saw the short, burly Hoskins in the role, and on the next draft of the script he tailored the part to the actor. For the role of the prostitute, Jordan selected unknown 20-year-old actress Tyson (niece of American actress Cicely Tyson). Tyson is perfect as Simone, bringing an enigmatic quality to the role that captures the essence of the title (Caine is quite creepy as well in his brief appearances). The plot's similarity to Martin Scorsese's TAXI DRIVER is not lost on Jordan, who pays homage to Scorsese frequently by simulating shots from the earlier film (the camera attached very low to the front bumper on the passenger's side of the car; Hoskins' point-of-view as he drives with Tyson's face reflected in the rear-view mirror as we see the blurred neon cityscape out the front windshield; Hoskins' first encounter with pimp Peters in a seedy hotel—very reminiscent of the scene in TAXI DRIVER where Robert De Niro pays Jodie Foster's fat timekeeper Murray Moston for the room where he talks to her). But MONA LISA is a wholly original film and Jordan has his own distinct vision. MONA LISA is a detailed, thoughtful film that explores the emotions surrounding its exploitative milieu. The motivations of the main characters are dictated by love—however deluded or confused—and not viciousness, revenge, hate, or ambition, and therein lies the film's uniqueness. There is one minor point where the film falters, however. When Hoskins launches his search into the London sex club underworld the romantic, lush musical score which echoes Nat "King" Cole's version of "Mona Lisa" suddenly shifts to a rock song by the band Genesis. While not an out-and-out gratuitous rock video, the shift in tone is unnecessarily jarring and one cannot help but assume it was made for commercial reasons, as the song is out of place and adds nothing to the film. Songs include: "Mona Lisa" (Jay Livingston, Ray Evans, performed by Nat "King" Cole), "When I Fall in Love" (Victor Young, Edward Heyman, performed by Nat "King" Cole), "The Very Thought of You" (Ray Noble), "In Too Deep" (Genesis, performed by Genesis).

p, Steve Woolley, Patrick Cassavetti; d, Neil Jordan; w, Neil Jordan, David Leland; ph, Roger Pratt (Technicolor); m, Michael Kamen; ed, Lesley Walker; prod d, Jamie Leonard; art d, Gemma Jackson; cos, Louise Frogley; m/l, Jay Livingston, Ray Evans, Victor Young, Edward Heyman, Ray Noble, Genesis; makeup, Lois Burwell, Nick Dudman; stunts, Terry Forrestal.

Crime/Drama   Cas.   (PR:O MPAA:R)

MONDO CONDO   (SEE: HAKRAV AL HAVA'AD, 1986, Israel)

MONEY PIT, THE✱✱   (1986) 91m Amblin Entertainment/UNIV c

Tom Hanks *(Walter Fielding)*, Shelley Long *(Anna Crowley)*, Alexander Godunov *(Max Beissart)*, Maureen Stapleton *(Estelle)*, Joe Mantegna *(Art Shirk)*, Philip Bosco *(Curly)*, Josh Mostel *(Jack Schnittman)*, Yakov Smirnoff *(Shatov)*, Carmine Caridi *(Brad Shirk)*, Brian Backer *(Ethan)*, Billy Lombardo *(Benny)*, Mia Dillon *(Marika)*, John van Dreelen *(Carlos)*, Douglass Watson *(Walter Fielding, Sr.)*, Lucille Dobrin *(Macumba Lady)*, Tetchie Agbayani *(Florinda)*, Scott Turchin, Radu Gavor, Grisha Dimant *(Movers)*, Lutz Rath *(Geza)*, Joey Balin *(Jimmy)*, Wendell Pierce *(Paramedic)*, Susan Browning *(Samantha)*, Henry Baker *(Oscar)*, Mary Louise Wilson *(Benny's Mom)*, Irving Metzman *(Sid)*, Frank Maraden, Mike Russo *(Mattress Men)*, Joe Ponazecki *(Mr. Shrapp)*, Michael Hyde *(Driver of Eighteen-Wheeler)*, Mike Starr *(Lenny)*, Frankie Faison *(James)*, Jake Steinfeld *(Duke)*, Matthew Cowles *(Marty)*, Nestor Serrano *(Julio)*, Michael Jeter *(Arnie)*, Afemo Omilami *(Bernie)*, Bruno Iannone *(Sol)*, Ron Foster *(Record Producer)*, Alan Altshuld *(Driver of Volkswagen)*, Tzi Ma *(Hwang)*, Cindy Brooks *(Benny's Girl Friend)*, Leslie West *(Lana)*, "The Fabulous Heavyweights": Tom Filiault, Doug Plavin, Chris Tuttle, Ed Vadas *("Cheap Girls")*, "White Lion" *(Rock Group)*, Robey *(Female Vocalist)*, Matthew Cowles, Frankie Faison, Michael Jeter, Frank Maraden, Afemo Omilami, Nestor Serrano, Mike Starr, Jake Steinfeld *("The Construction Crew")*.

The behemoth house, daring its owner to repair its monstrous cracks and crevices, has been looked at in comedy films from Buster Keaton's classic two-reeler ONE WEEK (1920) to the sound features GEORGE WASHINGTON SLEPT HERE (1942) and MR. BLANDINGS BUILDS HIS DREAM HOUSE (1948). THE MONEY PIT is another variation on this idea, and while there is some imagination behind the destruction of the title abode, the film quickly grows into a tired repetition of one long joke.

Hanks and Long are a cohabiting couple who share a bed in the apartment of Long's ex-husband, Godunov. Hanks has had some rather distressing news recently, in that his father has taken a child bride down in South America. When Godunov, an orchestra conductor, returns home after a two-year European tour, the lovers are hard pressed to find some new digs. Hanks, an attorney for rock bands, finds an old house through a friend (Mostel) that is being sold by Stapleton for a phenomenally low figure. Though he and Long are a bit hesitant, they finally decide to take the place. Hanks borrows the money from Lombardo, a bratty child pop star, then he and Long set out to repair the place with their own

hands. Despite the combined efforts of Hanks and Long, the house refuses to cooperate as their investment grows into an increasingly larger disaster. Hanks finally calls Mantegna, a professional carpenter, to help out, but this sleazy character is only interested in working on Long. Mantegna's brother Bosco is brought in next and the house turns into one giant construction area. Any time Bosco is asked how much longer the repairs will take, he slyly tosses off the pat answer, "Two weeks."

Hanks begins to crack, crying to Long that what they've acquired isn't a house: it's a "money pit" that is rapidly eating their every last dime. In the meantime, Long, who plays violin in Godunov's orchestra, is having to fend off amorous overtures from her ex. When Hanks must go out of town on business, Long ends up having dinner with her former spouse. She has too much to drink and wakes up the next morning in Godunov's bed. Terrified about what she will tell Hanks, Long tries to evade the truth, but eventually her secret comes out. Hanks is understandably furious and it appears their relationship is over. While they have

a terrific fight the construction crew takes a break from their work to watch this real-life soap opera. Finally, after much labor, slapstick, and heartache, the rehab work on the house is completed. The relationship between Hanks and Long appears to have taken on the home's former condition, but Godunov reveals he never slept with Long on that fateful night. Before she can tell Hanks this bit of news, he confronts her on their newly rebuilt staircase. Hanks says he doesn't care whether she slept with Godunov and the two finally make up. They are married, while in the film's epilog, Stapleton is selling another grand looking home, this time in South America, to Hanks' unsuspecting father.

If anything, THE MONEY PIT is ingenious in its design. One can't help but be impressed by the elaborate work that went into making the film and creating a house built specifically to fall apart in a variety of cataclysmic ways. One sequence, in which Hanks helplessly watches as his kitchen methodically eats itself up, is a marvel in disaster precision as appliances explode and electrical wiring burns on cue. Some moments, such as when the home's imposing staircase collapses, were so immense in the scope of their demolition that six cameras were simultaneously run so nothing would have to be restaged for alternate takes. Both Hanks and Long give likable performances in what are genuinely physically demanding roles. Godunov, the ballet star who made his acting debut in 1985's WITNESS, is fine as the conceited orchestra conductor, and has a fairly good rapport with Long.

So with all these attributes, why is THE MONEY PIT boring and almost consistently unfunny? The fault clearly lies with the script. Giler simply repeats different variations on the same joke without adding new twists. His gags are merely a laundry list of what can and will go wrong, run down in an increasingly predictable fashion. Director Benjamin showed he knew a thing or two about slapstick with his debut feature MY FAVORITE YEAR (1982), and while he does a few interesting things here with elaborate sight gags, it's just not that funny. One Rube Goldberg-styled disaster, which begins when Long innocently unplugs an electrical cord, shows excellent craftsmanship as this simple act leads to a more and more complex series of accidents. Yet that's all it shows, for, try as they may, this is a case where more is not merrier. The best comedy is almost always based in character, but unfortunately Hanks and Long are consistently forced to take a back seat to the destruction that is this film. Songs and music include: "The Heart Is So Willing," "Sitting on a Dream," "Skin Tight," "Cowboy Paradise" (Michel Colombier, Kathleen Wakefield), "Web of Desire" (White Lion, performed by White Lion), "Gavotte (Sonata VI for Violin, E Major Partita)" (Johann Sebastian Bach, performed by Christopher Parkening), "I Gotta Be Me" (Walter Marks, performed by Sammy Davis, Jr.), "Mi Orquestra" (Julian Bargas, peroformed by Los Tuparmaros), "Rush Rush" (Giorgio Moroder, Deborah Harry, performed by Deborah Harry), "Candy Gal" (Bill Munroe, performed by Bill Munroe), "Wedding Contract" (Gaetano Donizetti, Salvatore Cammanrano), "I Am a Pizza (The Pizza Man)" (Peter Alsop, performed by Peter Alsop), "La Bamba" (performed by Ritchie Valens), "Niene Geiht's So Schon U Lustig."

p, Frank Marshall, Kathleen Kennedy, Art Levinson; d, Richard Benjamin; w, David Giler; ph, Gordon Willis (DeLuxe Color); m, Michel Colombier, Johann Sebastian Bach; ed, Jacqueline Cambas; prod d, Patrizia von Brandenstein; md, Michel Colombier; art d, Steve Graham; set d, George De Titta, Sr.; cos, Ruth Morley; spec eff, Michael Wood; m/l, Michel Colombier, Kathleen Wakefield, White Lion, Johann Sebastian Bach, Walter Marks, Julian Bargas, Giorgio Moroder, Deborah Harry, Bill Munroe, Gaetano Donizetti, Salvatore Cammanrano, Peter Alsop, Ritchie Valens; makeup, Mickey Scott.

Comedy   Cas.   (PR:A-C MPAA:PG)

MONITORS†   (1986, It.) Valadier c

Susanna Javicoli, Piero Panza, Angelo Mandruzzato, Nicola Saponaro, Enzo Spaltro.

A middle-aged businessman experiences a crisis when he cannot accept the changes in personality his friends have gone through. This, coupled with his unreasonable dependence on modern technology, sends him to a clinic for help.

d&w, Piero Panza; ph, Elisa Basconi (Fujicolor); m, Stefano Moni.

Drama   (PR:O MPAA:NR)

MONSTER, THE†   (1986, Iran) 100m Cooperative Group c

Jahangir Almasi, Majid Mozafari, Syroos Gorjestani, Farzaneh Kaboli, Roohollah Mofidi, Mohsen Makari, Mehri Mehrinia, Esmaiel Mohammadi.

A villager wants to restore a nearby well in hopes of solving a local water shortage. According to legend, a monster loves to quench his thirst in wells, drinking them bone dry. This tale continually haunts the protagonist in his endeavors.

d,w&ph, Keyanoosh Ayari; m, Mohammad Reza Aligholi; ed, Keyanoosh Ayari.

Drama   (PR:C-O MPAA:NR)

MONSTER DOG zero   (1986) 84m Continental/Trans World Entertainment c

Alice Cooper (Vincent), Victoria Vera (Sandra), Carlos Sanurio (Frank), Pepita James (Angela), Emilio Linder (Jordan), Jose Sarsa (Marilou), Luis Maluenda (Deputy), Ricardo Palacios (Sheriff Morrison), B. Barta Barri (Old Man), Charley Bravo, Fernando Conde, Fernando Baeza, Nino Bastida (Townsfolk).

There is usually a very good reason why some films are never shown in theaters and released straight onto videocassette—they stink. Shot mostly in Spain in 1984, MONSTER DOG is a truly wretched horror film with laughable special effects. Notable only for the appearance of has-been rocker Alice Cooper, the film begins with a lame rock video set to a new Cooper song entitled "Identity Crisis." Cooper, appropriately enough, plays a rock star named Vincent Raven (a small joke from the filmmakers since Cooper's real name is Vincent Furnier) who decides to shoot his next rock video at his ancestral home—a spooky old mansion. With his girl friend Vera set to direct and his cast, crew, and equipment in tow, Cooper drives through the fog-shrouded countryside. The troupe soon comes upon a roadblock and the sheriff informs them that a pack of wild, rabid dogs has been wreaking havoc in the area. The sheriff, Palacios, remembers Cooper as a child and hints at horrible past events involving the rock star's father. After the rock 'n' rollers drive through, the sheriff and his deputy are killed by a growling beast.

At the mansion Cooper and his guests are harassed by an old man in a bloody white shirt who tells them that they will all die. That night one of the girls has a nightmare that Cooper has turned into a werewolf and killed them. The troupe laughs it off, but Cooper isn't amused. Angrily his girl friend denounces his fears and states: "The year 2000 is just around the corner. I am a recognized expert in electronic videos, and you're the hottest rock 'n' roll star in the world . . . and you're afraid of werewolves!" Cooper informs Vera that his father had a strange "heart ailment" that turned him into a werewolf. The local villagers finally got fed up with dad's midnight wandering and killed him with pitchforks. The next day, while the crew prepares to shoot another rock video featuring Cooper and James (in a wedding dress), the bloody body of the mansion's caretaker crashes through a window and lands on the leading lady. The hysterical actress runs off into the countryside and Cooper grabs a shotgun and goes to fetch her back.

Meanwhile, a swarthy bunch of locals who look as if they have escaped from the set of a Sergio Leone western arrive to kill Cooper. They believe that he is a "monster dog" like his father. The gang holds the crew members hostage and waits for Cooper's return. When the rock star returns, James is shot with the silver bullet by mistake. Cooper hunts the villagers down one by one and kills

them. At the same time in a different part of the mansion, the pack of wild dogs and their leader, the "monster dog," roll in with the dark and fog and attack the poor rock-video crew (viewers will note that the classic Edward Wood, Jr. [PLAN NINE FROM OUTER SPACE] mise-en-scene occurs here: it is daytime when Cooper goes after the villagers, and nighttime when the dogs attack, and, with both scenes intercut, the scene goes from day to night and back again several times).

Eventually only Vera and Sarsa are left to fend off the "monster dog" in the bathroom. Basically just a big mangy-looking papier-mache head that looks like it was stolen off a Mardi Gras float, the beast rams through the pre-cut bathroom wall and growls at the girls. Suddenly the beast disappears and Cooper arrives. Sarsa is convinced that Cooper is the monster dog and tells him so in a frenzied soliloquy: "You are the monster dog! You are the murdering animal! Damn you! Damn you! You are the werewolf! I know you are! I know it! Sob! Sob! Sob!" This prompts most viewers to ask: If Cooper is a monster, is he a "monster dog" or a werewolf? Is there a difference? Ignoring Sarsa's hysterics, Cooper loads her and Vera into a car and then goes back (with Vera) to the mansion to get the keys. While they're gone, the monster dog gets in the car and kills Sarsa. Of course Cooper and Vera don't discover this until they're driving and the car immediately crashes when they do. Cooper is bitten by the monster dog and the ragged Vera encounters the old man in the bloody white shirt again (this guy pops up throughout the entire film like a bad rash). Cooper then turns into the monster dog in one of the most lame transformation scenes in recent memory (his hands cover his face as he writhes around on the ground through most of the scene). Bravely, Vera shoots Cooper/monster dog and puts him out of his misery. The viewer is then treated to a reprise of the "Identity Crisis" (get it?) video from scene No.1, intercut with highlights from the film.

A word to the wise: don't bother watching the whole movie, just fast-forward to the last rock video and watch the condensed version at the end. This is about as inept as it gets. From the stupid script which can't even decide whether its monster is a werewolf or a "monster dog," to some of the worst dubbing (including Cooper's post-dubbing) in recent memory, MONSTER DOG is a boring mess. Writer-director Anderson (which could be a pseudonym for producer Aured) is an amateur talent at best, and his efforts at creating atmosphere, suspense, and shock are laughable. Cooper looks like he belongs in a horror film, but he keeps the same blank expression on his face throughout the entire film and the other performers are simply fodder for the body count. The special effects and gore are just plain silly and the pack of wild dogs that follow the monster dog are a bunch of harmless mutts that don't take direction very well. The film is so dull that it's not even unintentionally funny. Cooper contributes two songs here: "Identity Crisis" and "See Me in the Mirror."

p, Carlos Aured; d&w, Clyde Anderson; ph, Jose Garcia Galisteo (Technicolor); m, Grupo Dichotomy; ed, Antonio Jose Ochoa, Gabrio Astori, Peter Teschner; art d, Gumersindo Andres; cos, Eugenia Escriva; spec eff, Carlo De Marchis; m/l, Alice Cooper.

Horror   Cas.   (PR:O MPAA:NR)

MONSTER SHARK zero   (1986, It./Fr.) 92m Filmes Internationale-Nuovo Dania-National Cinematografica-Les Filmes du Griffon/Cinema Shares c (AKA: RED OCEAN)

Michael Sopkiw (Peter), John [Gianni] Garko (Sheriff Gordon), William Berger (Dr. West), Iris Peynard, Valentine Monnier, Lawrence Morgant, Dagmar Lassander (Sonja).

More dredge from the limited talent of Italian schlock horror director Lamberto Bava (DEMONS), this time hiding behind the pseudonym of "John Old, Jr." The simpleminded story involves a mutant creature that takes to munching swimmers along the shores of Florida. Sopkiw and a crew of scientists learn the hungry monster is an eons-old predecessor of the modern-day shark. The 40-foot beast also has a little bit of octopus in its genes, and has the potential to reproduce itself literally millions of times. Naturally this could spell trouble for global waters, to say nothing of the folks running around on dry land, so Garko, a Florida lawman, wants to destroy the malevolent monster. But no film like this would be complete without a little conflict, which comes in the form of bad scientist Berger. He wants to preserve the creature for study, regardless of the cost in human terms. There are some ugly moments between Berger and Garko, but eventually science loses out, as the creature comes to a rather inglorious end.

This grade-Z remake of JAWS is a lame, wholly amateurish work that might garner a few laughs but certainly won't frighten anyone. The "monster" is barely seen at all, and for good reason: it looks like the cheesy model it is. Bava wasn't the only one who changed his name on this one. Producer Mino Loy took no billing at all, while two of the story writers (Luigi Cozzi and Sergio Martino) and the cameraman (Giancarlo Ferrando) also used the safety of another guise for their screen credits.

p, Mino Loy (uncredited); d, John Old, Jr. [Lamberto Bava]; w, Gianfranco Clerici (based on a story by Lewis Coates [Luigi Cozzi], Don Lewis, Martin Dolman [Sergio Martino]); ph, John McFerrand [Giancarlo Ferrando] (Telecolor); m, Antony Barrymore; ed, Bob Wheeler; prod d, A.M. Geleng; spec eff, Germano Natali; monster shark creator, Ovidio Taito.

Horror/Science Fiction   (PR:O MPAA:NR)

MORD I MORKET†   (1986, Den.) 96m Nordisk-Danish Film Institute/ Nordisk c (Trans: Murder in the Dark)

Michael Falch (Reporter), Ove Sprogoe (Bille), Ole Ernst (Police Lieutenant), Morten Grunwald (Editor-in-Chief), Tommy Kentner (Ole Kok), Kine Knutzon (Hanne), Lise-Lotte Norup (Barbara), Peter Schroder (Bartender), Ahmed Rahmani (Cabbie), John Martinus (Transvestite), Hans Henrik Voetman (Kaspersen), Bent Warburg, Gorm Valentin, Martin Spang Olsen, Benny Bundgaard, Jorn Budolfsen, Arne Hansen, Benny Juhlin, William Kisum, Kit Eichler.

In the dark streets of Copenhagen, a teenage hooker becomes a junkie while her friend, an aspiring jazz musician, is murdered. A reporter becomes a suspect, as does a well-known drug dealer. This homage to *film noir* is based on a popular Danish novel which was a loving tribute to the Dashiell Hammett school of writing.

d, Sune Lund-Sorensen; w, Erik Balling, Henning Bahs, Sune Lund-Sorensen (based on a novel by Dan Turell); ph, Claus Loof (Eastmancolor); m, Michael Falck, Pete Repete; ed, Leif Axel Kjeldsen; prod d, Peter Hoimark; cos, Annelise Hauberg; spec eff, Peter Hoimark.

Crime   **(PR:O MPAA:NR)**

MORE THINGS CHANGE, THE†   (1986, Aus.) 94m Syme
International–New South Wales/Hoyts c

Judy Morris *(Connie)*, Barry Otto *(Lex)*, Victoria Longley *(Geraldine)*, Lewis Fitz-Gerald *(Barry)*, Peter Carroll *(Roley)*, Louise Le Nay *(Lydia)*, Owen Johnson *(Nicholas)*, Brenda Addie *(Angela)*, Joanne Barker, Harriet Spalding *(Bridesmaids)*, Adrienne Barrett *(Karen)*, Bill Bennett *(Eric)*, Paddy Burnet *(Mim)*, John Egan *(Vince)*, Chris Gaffney *(Sponge)*, Joan Harris *(Matron)*, Robert MacGregor *(Baby)*, Margo McLennan *(Barbara)*, Alex Menglet *(Telecom Man)*, Robert Ratti *(Jolian)*, Colwyn Roberts *(Truck Driver)*, Malcolm Robertson *(Sam)*, George Trotman *(Edgar)*, Joy Westmore *(Mrs. Degan)*, Eddy Zlaty *(Michael)*.

Well received in its native Australia, THE MORE THINGS CHANGE follows Otto and Morris, a married pair of city dwellers who decide to relocate in the country. With their 3-year-old son Johnson, Otto and Morris find a small farm near Melbourne where Otto intends to till the soil himself. Because Morris works for a publishing company, the couple is able to make ends meet. However, Otto's newfound dependence on his wife puts increased tension into their already-troubled marriage. Since Otto cannot tend both the farm and Johnson at the same time, he and Morris hire Longley as a nanny. Longley, a pregnant, unwed 19-year-old, is engaged to marry Fitz-Gerald. She wants to conceal her pregnancy from her parents, then give up her child for adoption before proceeding with the already-planned-for wedding. Because they spend so much time together Otto and Longley develop a warm friendship. Eventually, though, this close, platonic relationship comes to an end as the two friends begin drifting apart. Longley returns to her fiance, but not before revealing why she is so insistent about giving up her unborn child.

This film, exploring the shifting roles within relationships, marks the directorial debut for Nevin, best known to American audiences for her performances in such films as THE CHANT OF JIMMIE BLACKSMITH and CAREFUL, HE MIGHT HEAR YOU. Producer Robb, who performed that chore on CAREFUL, HE MIGHT HEAR YOU as well, had formerly worked as a production secretary for British director Michael Powell on his 1966 Australian production THEY'RE A WEIRD MOB.

p, Jill Robb; d, Robyn Nevin; w, Moya Wood; ph, Dan Burstall (Panavision, Eastmancolor); m, Peter Best; ed, Jill Bilcock; prod d, Josephine Ford; md, Peter Best; set d, Steve Jones Evans; makeup, Joan Hills.

Drama   **(PR:C-O MPAA:NR)**

MORENA†   (1986, Fin.) 78m Reppufilmi Oy/Finnish Film Foundation c

Anssi Manttari *(Redbeard)*, Caroline Kruger *(Morena)*, Claes Andersson *(Piano Player)*, Dan van Husen *(Painter)*, Klaus Tonke *(Layabout)*.

Manttari is a wandering musician who drifts through Berlin bars looking for a friend from his native Finland. He discovers that his friend, a piano player, has given up faith in life. After carrying on a brief affair with barmaid Kruger, Manttari eventually leaves Berlin, taking his clarinet to Copenhagen, where he becomes a street musician. Interspersed with this story is flashback footage of an unhappy child growing up in loveless environment. This low-budget production ($140,000) was shot in only 10 days, utilizing the talents of a largely non-professional cast.

d&w, Anssi Manttari; ph, Heikki Katajisto (Agfa Color); m, Jukka Hakokongas, Costas Papanastasiou, Asko Manttari, Claes Andersen; ed, Raija Talvio.

Drama   **(PR:O MPAA:NR)**

MORIRAI A MEZZANOTTE†   (1986, It.) Reteitalia–Dania/VIP c (Trans:
You Will Die at Midnight)

Valeria d'Obici, Leonardo Treviglio, Paolo Malco, Lara Wendel, Lea Martino, Eliana Hoppe, Loredana Romiti, Massimo Baratta, Barbara Scoppa.

A vanished lawman is suspected of killing his spouse, but when another body turns up, one investigator believes the missing cop is not the killer. The man he suspects, now locked up in a mental institution, dies when the place burns to the ground. When there is yet another murder, the investigator sees a photograph of the supposedly dead man that implicates him in this crime. The chief of police's daughter is taken hostage, and the case takes an unusual twist that leads to a surprising solution.

d, John Old, Jr. [Lamberto Bavo]; w, Dardano Sacchetti, John Old, Jr. [Lamberto Bavo]; ph, Gianlorenzo Battaglia (Telecolor); m, Claudio Simonetti; ed, John Old, Jr. [Lamberto Bavo].

Crime/Mystery   **(PR:O MPAA:NR)**

MORNING AFTER, THE**½   (1986) 103m American Filmworks/FOX c

Jane Fonda *(Alex Sternbergen)*, Jeff Bridges *(Turner Kendall)*, Raul Julia *(Joaquin Manero)*, Diane Salinger *(Isabel Harding)*, Richard Foronjy *(Sgt. Greenbaum)*, Geoffrey Scott *(Bobby Korshack)*, James "Gypsy" Haake *(Frankie)*, Kathleen Wilhoite *(Red)*, Don Hood *(Hurley)*, Fran Bennett *(Airline Clerk)*, Michael Flanagan *(Airline Supervisor)*, Bruce Vilanch *(Bartender)*, Michael Prince *(Mr. Harding)*, Frances Bergen *(Mrs. Harding)*, Jose Santana *(Driver)*, Bob Minor *(Man)*, George Fisher *(Cabbie)*, Rick Rossovich *(Detective)*, Laurel Lyle *(Secretary)*, Kathy Bates *(Woman on Mateo Street)*, Anne Betancourt *(Nurse)*, Patti Song *(Hairstylist)*, Betty Lougaris *(Salon Customer)*, Drew Berman, Sam Scarber, Michael Zand *(Detectives)*, Gladys Portugues *(Body Builder)*, Corinna Everson *(Miss Olympia)*, George Howard *(Saxophonist)*.

A promising beginning peters out for this questionable thriller that owes much to Fonda's award-winning KLUTE, as well as 1985's THE JAGGED EDGE, which also starred Bridges. Fonda is a down-at-the-heels actress with a drinking problem. At one point in her career, she had been groomed to be "the next Vera Miles" (the only laugh in the movie) but a succession of bad roles and drinking bouts have reduced her to the point where she is now going on open auditions (cattle calls) for commercials. She wakes up one morning in a large Los Angeles loft with a gargantuan hangover. Next to her in bed is a man with a knife through his heart. At the same time, that man is being shown on the TV in a taped interview in which he talks about the soft-porn movies he makes for a living. Fonda's worst alcoholic fears have been realized. She doesn't remember where

she met the guy and who he is. Further, she is not even sure if she herself dispatched the sleazeball (we learn that she has been given to violence while under the influence). Since her history is that of erraticism (as well as eroticism), she doesn't call the cops. Rather, she carefully wipes her fingerprints from any and all surfaces she might have touched and decides to leave town right away. She drives her classic Mercedes (a remnant of better days) to the airport and wants to get on the very first plane anywhere. But it's Thanksgiving Day and every seat is booked. She gets into a hassle at the curb where she's parked (the white zone is for loading and unloading passengers only) and her car is towed away, an implausible moment because this is a valuable auto and it's hard to believe she'd just let it go like that. With no wheels now, she runs into ex-cop and apparent bigot Bridges, who is repairing his ancient convertible.

Bridges is a retired police officer from Bakersfield who is now living on a pension because he was hurt on the job. He lives in a Quonset hut that he has made into a fairly habitable place and he survives by repairing things. Fonda is fearful that someone saw her with the dead man and she wants to lay low. Bridges is a pleasant hayseed and takes her in, not knowing her problem. He is still married to a fabulously successful hairdresser, Julia, who now wants a divorce because he is in love with a wealthy heiress, Salinger, the daughter of Bergen and Prince.

Twists and turns abound as Bridges helps Fonda unravel the piece. In the meantime, their relationship has gone on an equally convoluted roller coaster ride as she promises to stop drinking, then falls off the wagon hard. The denouement is one of the most ludicrous ever shot and it's hard to believe that Lumet was there when it was made. About 45 minutes into the picture, anyone with any sense will be able to figure out that Fonda was framed and that Julia is the brains behind it. It seems that Salinger, in a weak moment, had posed for some pornography and the dead man was behind it and was threatening to expose her. He had to be killed if Julia and Salinger were to live a happy Bel-Air life together. When, at last, Fonda confronts Julia at his posh hair salon (the place seen is the Beverly Hills salon of Tyler-Lord), he tries to kill her and she is, of course, rescued by Bridges and the cops who have been looking for her.

Fonda is about 12 years older than Bridges but there was no mention of that. Nor was there a mention of the fact that it's hard to believe she'd lead such a dissolute life, especially since the 49-year-old Fonda is in such good condition that the muscles in her back almost ripple. There is no dealing with why she drinks, so any opportunity to make a point in that department is overlooked. This was Lumet's first Los Angeles-based film after a career of more than 30 that has included FAIL SAFE, SERPICO, NETWORK, EQUUS, DOG DAY AFTERNOON, THE VERDICT, THE PAWNBROKER, and 12 ANGRY MEN, in which he directed Fonda's father, Henry. In a career that also numbers several misses, such as POWER, DANIEL, GARBO TALKS, and THE WIZ, this one must be counted also as a miss. The holes in the story are gaping and often so much so that audiences buzzed. Interesting to look at, though, with Lumet and his cinematographer, Bartkowiak, roaming the Los Angeles landscape and offering bold, bizarre colors as the camera eyed the Westside Pavilion Mall, the Pacific Design Center (nicknamed "The Blue Whale" because of its shape and the fact that the color resembles a Milk of Magnesia bottle), and several other landmarks.

The author, whose real name is James Cresson (theatergoers will recall him as the producer or coproducer of such plays as "Chicago," "On the 20th Century," and "The Norman Conquest," as well as having been involved with such films as THE BOSTON STRANGLER, THE SHINING, TRAVELS WITH MY AUNT, and THE PRIME OF MISS JEAN BRODIE), patterned Fonda's character after the life of tragic Gail Russell (THE UNINVITED, OUR HEARTS WERE YOUNG AND GAY, WAKE OF THE RED WITCH, and many others) who died surrounded by liquor bottles at the age of 36. Bridges and Fonda are both from acting families. His brother is Beau and his father is Lloyd, her brother is Peter, and both show their genes are strong as they manage to convince us they are who they say they are. The problem here is the questionable script and the long stretches in the middle of the movie where absolutely nothing of any consequence happens. One source says that longtime Lumet pal Jay Presson Allen had her uncredited hand in writing the script as well. Hard to believe, since she was the force behind PRINCE OF THE CITY, did the adaptation for DEATHTRAP, and has a list of excellent other credits.

Paul Chihara's music adds nothing to heighten the tension, but the score does have a few nice moments with the inclusion of some other tunes: "Save Some (For Me)" (John Martyn, performed by Martyn), "Chief Inspector" (Wally Badarou, performed by Bardarou), "Can't Stop Giving It" (The Earons, performed by the Earons), and the huge hit "Addicted to Gypsy" (Robert Palmer, performed by Palmer). In a small role, note James "Gypsy" Haake, who will be remembered as a rare bright spot in Mel Brooks' remake of TO BE OR NOT TO BE. Haake is the host (hostess?) of the female impersonation show at the successful L.A. nightspot La Cage Aux Folles.

p, Bruce Gilbert; d, Sidney Lumet; w, James Hicks; ph, Andrzej Bartkowiak (DeLuxe Color); m, Paul Chihara; ed, Joel Goodman; prod d, Albert Brenner; art d, Kandy Stern; set d, Lee Poll; cos, Ann Roth; spec eff, Tom Ward; m/l, Robert Palmer, The Earons, Wally Badarou, John Martyn; makeup, Gary Liddiard, Pete Altobelli.

Crime/Drama   (PR:C-O   MPAA:R)

MORRHAR OCH ARTOR†   (1986, Swed.) 101m Cinema Art-Svensk
    Filmindustri-Film Teknik-Deadline/Svensk Filmindustri c (Trans: Peas and
                                                            Whiskers)

Gosta Ekman (Claes-Henrik "Hana" Ahlhagen), Margaretha Krook (His Mother), Lena Nyman (Boel), Kent Andersson (Crille), Sten Ljunggren (Shop Owner), Claes Jansson (Tompa), Sanna Ekman (Linna), Robert Sjoblom (Sergio), Margareta Pettersson (Ullabritt), Iwa Boman (Shop Assistant), Peter Huttner (Adam), Borje Nyberg (Ticket Collector), Carl-Axel Elfving (Pal).

A slapstick comedy directed by and starring Ekman as a hapless everyman who must contend with his overbearing mother, Krook. In an effort to make some extra money, Ekman accepts a large amount of cash from a movie producer for the use of his mother's apartment. Without revealing what he has done, Ekman urges his mother to take a three-day trip. Once she is on her way, Ekman meets Nyman, a woman with a young son. They fall in love and soon Ekman is muttering openly about murdering his mother. A series of misunderstandings soon follows and Ekman winds up the victim.

p, Christer Abrahamsen; d, Gosta Ekman; w, Rolf Borjlind, Gosta Ekman; ph, Lasse Bjorne (Fujicolor); m, Stefan Nilsson; ed, Jan Persson; art d, Gert Wibe.

Comedy   (PR:O   MPAA:NR)

MORT UN DIMANCHE DE PLUIE†   (1986, Fr./Switz.) 109m
    Incite-Soprofilms-FR3 Films-Slotint-Radio Television Suisse Romande-Centre
        National de Cinematographie/AAA Classic c (Trans: Died On A Rainy
                                                            Sunday)

Nicole Garcia (Elaine Briand), Jean-Pierre Bacri (David Briand), Jean-Pierre Bisson ("Cappy" Bronsky), Dominique Lavanant (Hazel Bronsky), Cerise Leclerc (Cric Briand), Etienne Chicot (Christian), Christine Laurent (Diane), Celine Vauge (Betty Bronsky), Marshall Titus (Singer), Jean-Pierre Malo (Alain Miller).

Situated in the rainy countryside at an austere modern home of his own design, Bacri, a successful architect, and his wife Garcia are visited by a destitute crippled man, Bisson, and his family. Taking pity on the man, Bacri hires Bisson as their gardener and the man's wife as a babysitter. Unbeknownst to the successful couple, however, is that Bisson was a former construction worker who lost his arm and had his leg crushed at one of Bacri's building sites. Bisson has vowed revenge on the architect and waits for the right moment to make his move. Eventually the time comes and Bisson drives a knife into Bacri's back. Garcia escapes but the seemingly unstoppable Bisson comes after her. She hacks off his artificial limb with a meat cleaver and then delivers a shotgun blast to the madman's chest, but not until Bisson is buried under the rubble of a collapsing garage does the terror end.

p, Yves Perrot; d, Joel Santoni; w, Joel Santoni, Philippe Setbon (based on the novel Died On A Rainy Sunday by Joan Aiken); ph, Jean Boffety (Eastmancolor); m, Vladimir Cosma; ed, Martine Barraque; art d, Max Berto; spec eff, Coyote; m/l, Vladimir Cosma; makeup, Joel Lavau.

Thriller   (PR:O   MPAA:NR)

MOSQUITO COAST, THE*½   (1986) 117m WB c

Harrison Ford (Allie Fox), Helen Mirren (Mother), River Phoenix (Charlie), Jadrien Steele (Jerry), Hilary Gordon (April), Rebecca Gordon (Clover), Jason Alexander (Clerk), Dick O'Neill (Mr. Polski), Alice Sneed (Mrs. Polski), Tiger Haynes (Mr. Semper), William Newman (Capt. Smalls), Andre Gregory (Rev. Spellgood), Melanie Boland (Mrs. Spellgood), Martha Plimpton (Emily Spellgood), Raymond Clare (1st Convert), Emory King (Man at Bar), Conrad Roberts (Mr. Haddy), Michael Rogers (Francis Lungley), Tony Vega, Sr. (Mr. Maywit), Aurora Clavel (Mrs. Maywit), Butterfly McQueen (Ma Kennywick), Michael Opoku (Bucky), Aldolpho Salguero (Drainy), Rafael Cho (Leon), Sofia Cho (Alice), Margarita Cho (Verny), Wilfred Peters (Dixon), Luis Palacio (Peaselee), Juan Antonio Llanes, Abel Woodrich, Jorge Zepeda (Mercenaries).

The almost mythic attraction of an untamed jungle for civilized man has seen a variety of treatments in the last ten years, including Werner Herzog's AGUIRRE, THE WRATH OF GOD (1977) and Francis Ford's Coppola's APOCALYPSE NOW (1979). Both portrayed the effects that the seemingly endless walls of foliage had on already unbalanced minds, a theme Peter Weir also tries to deal with in THE MOSQUITO COAST. His work is considerably less accomplished in developing the corollary between the enveloping jungle and madness, but results

are well photographed though painfully lethargic. Ford plays an inventor, tired of what he perceives to be a dying America. In an attempt to emulate the pioneer spirit, he decides to relocate and takes his family to an unsettled area near Honduras called the Mosquito Coast. Though his wife Mirren (whom Ford refers to as "Mother") has some qualms, she doesn't openly express her feelings. The family—including 15-year-old Phoenix, his younger brother Steele, and eight-year-old red headed twins Hilary and Rebecca Gordon—reaches the South American shores where they run into Gregory, an eccentric missionary. Ford, an unbeliever who quotes the Bible to refute Gregory's faith, buys the deed to an isolated town, then heads upriver to the new family home. The "town" consists of only a few shacks and a handful of residents (including, film fans will note, Butterfly McQueen), but Ford hides his initial disappointment by throwing himself and the family into building a thriving community, which he dubs "Jeronimo." With the help of the villagers Ford constructs a giant monolith in the midst of the jungle, a towering machine dubbed "Fat Boy" which manufactures ice. "Ice is civilization," declares Ford, and to this end he decides to take a large chunk to the natives dwelling deeper inside the jungle. With the help of his sons and the family friend and guide Roberts, Harrison makes his way to an Indian village. By the time they arrive though, the ice has melted. The group manages to leave safely, but shortly afterward three gun-toting terrorists show up at Jeronimo. In a vain attempt to drive them off, Ford claims the village is ant infested and begins chopping and burning his home. The three are not fooled by this, but Ford has an alternative plan. He builds the intruders a bunk inside of "Fat Boy," intending to freeze them after they are asleep. The trapped men begin firing their guns when they realize what is happening, setting off an enormous explosion that destroys all of Jeronimo. But Ford will not give up. Claiming America has been destroyed in a nuclear holocaust, he resettles the family in a small area near the ocean, building a house that can float in an emergency. Roberts refuses to join them. Since he is a better judge of the area, he knows a good storm will wash Ford's new home out into the ocean. Ford will not accept Roberts' help but Phoenix does, and clandestinely accepts a pair of spark plugs from him. Roberts' prophesy comes true and the family home is nearly washed away. Only the spark plugs, plugged into an old outboard motor, save the clan. Phoenix and Steele, having survived so much turmoil, decide they have had enough. Ford refuses to listen though, and continues moving along the river on what remains of their ramshackle home. Upriver is life Ford insists, and only dead things go downriver. Soon the family hears a choir singing and one of the girls asks if this is the sound of angels. They have come upon Gregory's mission and the sound is of a television monitor broadcasting one of the oily minister's homilies. Phoenix attracts the attention of Gregory's daughter Plimpton, who gives him the keys to her family's jeep. Phoenix and Steele return to their mother, telling her they are leaving, unable to take any more of Ford's insane impositions on their lives. Though at first Mirren agrees, she cannot bear to leave her husband. Suddenly Gregory's church blows up in a ball of flame and the family instantly realizes Ford is behind it. The madman returns to the boat, bearing a can of gasoline for the motor, but he is shot by the enraged Gregory. Phoenix and Mirren quickly evacuate down the river, as Ford quietly lies dying, unable to let go of his dream.

In Paul Theroux's novel the events are recounted through the tortured eyes of Phoenix's character. The film switches its emphasis to Ford and in doing so loses much of the story's fervor. Phoenix gives some voice-over narration, but Weir uses this sparingly and without much care for its relation to the action. The effect of Ford's obsessions on his family is thus shunted off to the side, coming to a

head only at a few key moments toward the inevitable climax. The family is primarily a prop for Ford; he rarely interacts with them. Phoenix shows glimmers of what he could have done had the character been better developed by Weir, but this talented young actor is largely wasted. Ford's descent into madness is unbelievable. The opening establishes him as a quirky individual, but these eccentricities rarely change through the story. At one point Mirren calls him stubborn, which sums up the character perfectly. Ford operates on manic adrenaline, and though his performance is never uninteresting, he goes through no visible changes from beginning to end. His death is inevitable, mostly because there's no place else for the story to go. The portrait of life in the jungle is ridiculously simplistic. Though there are references to insects and other vermin, Ford's settlements are amazingly bug-free. There's no mention of disease, not even heatstroke, and food is always plentiful. The children are hardy and, other than an initial leech upon arrival, suffer nary a scratch throughout the film. (Try saying the same thing about any neighborhood playground during summertime.) Ford's second settlement on the oceanfront is also ludicrous. Considering how much knowledge he has apparently accumulated on survival tactics, it seems unlikely that even a man as obsessed as he would build a permanent residence in such a dangerous spot. The film's greatest problem is its lack of passion. The resources for a dark, intense study of madness and its effects are inherent in Weir's material, yet he never explores beyond the surface. Paul Schrader, who worked with similar themes and ideas in some of his past films, wrote the initial screenplay, then left the project to work on his 1985 release MISHIMA. By his own admission, Weir revised Schrader's script. Somewhere between the first draft and the final cut, THE MOSQUITO COAST lost its bearings. Seale's cinematography is the one saving grace. Working under extraordinary conditions in the Central American jungles, he manages to give the film a sharp and often stunning look. His lighting of "Fat Boy" shortly before it's blown up makes the structure look almost ethereal, creating a surreal image of nature and technology achieving a weird harmony. Unfortunately, his images aren't enough to carry the story, and THE MOSQUITO COAST ultimately becomes lifeless as it lurches from one episode to the next.

p, Jerome Hellman; d, Peter Weir; w, Paul Schrader (based on the novel by Paul Theroux); ph, John Seale (Technicolor); m, Maurice Jarre; ed, Thom Noble;

prod d, John Stoddart; art d, John Wingrove; set d, John Anderson; cos, Gary Jones; spec eff, Larry Cavanaugh; m/l, Gary Johnson, Anthony Carter.

Drama/Adventure   **Cas.**   **(PR:O   MPAA:R)**

MOTTEN IM LICHT†   (1986, Switz.) 90m Xanadu Films–Swiss-German (DRS) TV–George Reinhart/Metropolis Film c (Trans: Flies In The Light)

Patrick Bauchau, Renee Soutendijk, Ivan Desny, Kurt Raab, Sibylle Courvoisier, Therese Affolter, Sven-Erich Bechtoff, Norbert Schwientek.

Yet another European homage to American B pictures of the 1930s and 1940s. Bauchau stars as a suave thief who is hired to steal a priceless painting from an art gallery. Later, he is hired to steal the same painting again, this time from a mysterious religious cult.

d, Urs Egger; w, Urs Egger, Martin Henning, Michael Zochow; ph, Hugues Ryffel; m, Stephane Wittwer; ed, Georg Janett.

Thriller   **(PR:C-O   MPAA:NR)**

MOUNTAINTOP MOTEL MASSACRE zero   (1986) 95m Jim McCullough/ New World Pictures c

Bill Thurman (*Rev. Bill McWilley*), Anna Chappell (*Evelyn*), Will Mitchel (*Al*), Virginia Loridans (*Tanya*), Major Brock (*Crenshaw*), James Bradford (*Sheriff*), Amy Hill (*Prissy*), Marian Jones (*Mary*), Greg Brazzel (*Vernon*), Jill King (*Lorie*), Rhonda Atwood (*Bar Owner*), Foster Litton (*Sheriff Dispatcher*), Linda Blankenship (*Al's Secretary*), Angela Christine (*Singing Voice*).

The title says it all. A recently released middle-aged mental patient, Chappell, returns home to run her mountaintop motel. Her daughter, King, is a little strange herself and worships the Devil in the basement. When Chappell catches her daughter praying at the Satanic shrine, she has a relapse and accidentally severs most of the kid's head with a sickle. She drags the girl's body upstairs and calls the police telling them it was an accident. The stupid sheriff, Bradford, takes that excuse at face value and closes the case. After the girl's funeral Chappell's mind snaps completely and she decides to murder some of her guests. In what must be the biggest night of the year for her out-of-the-way motel, no fewer than seven customers show up looking for rooms during a nasty rainstorm. As the unsuspecting guests go about their business, Chappell wanders through the series of tunnels that run underneath the motel rooms. Entering the rooms via some very obvious trapdoors in the bathrooms, Chappell lets loose poisonous snakes, large rats, and nasty little cockroaches that crawl on the guests and bite them ("They ought to call this place a Roach Motel," declares one annoyed guest). After the infestation of vermin, Chappell becomes a bit more direct and takes to stabbing guests to death with her sickle. Eventually only an elderly black handyman, Brock, a talent scout for Columbia records, Mitchel, and a hopeful young singer, Loridans, are left alive. Brock and Mitchel trap Chappell by nailing all the trapdoors shut. Instead of waiting for the sheriff, they decide to go in after the crazed woman—one from each end of the tunnel. Brock is killed by the sickle-wielding loony before the sheriff arrives. The sheriff engages in a titanic struggle with the big woman. She swings her sickle at him, misses, and gets the weapon stuck in an overhead beam. As she struggles to pull the sickle free, she causes a collapse of the tunnel system and the beam swings down upon her head. The part of the sickle sticking out of the beam hits her in the neck and kills her. The sheriff loads Mitchel and Loridans into his squad car and leaves as the dead daughter of Chappell, now apparently a zombie, watches them go.

Instead of a homicidal Jason running through the woods of a summer camp slaughtering teenagers, MOUNTAINTOP MOTEL MASSACRE gives us an overweight, middle-aged crazy woman with a sickle running through the underground tunnels of a seedy motel butchering adults. All the characters suffer from terminal stupidity and deserve what they get from the slow-moving crazy woman. Except for insanity, no motivation is given for Chappell's crimes, and the throwaway satanic zombie angle at the end comes in from left field. Director McCullough, Sr. and cinematographer Wilcots have some sense of visual style—one scene is lit through a spinning window fan and the effect is creepy (a trick done to death in 1987's ANGEL HEART)—but a slasher film is a slasher film no matter how stylish the look. The gore effects (done by the same guy who did the production design!) are straight from the Herschell Gordon Lewis school of "cheapo" and are only glimpsed briefly to conceal how bad they are. Self-conscious references to Hitchcock's PSYCHO are scattered throughout the film, but they only serve to remind viewers of just how pathetic MOUNTAINTOP MOTEL MASSACRE really is. Even as cheap horror films go, this is a sloppy and incredibly tedious effort.

p, Jim McCullough, Sr., Jim McCullough, Jr.; d, Jim McCullough, Sr.; w, Jim McCullough, Jr.; ph, Joe Wilcots (Eastman Kodak); m, Ron Dilulio; ed, Mindy Daucus; prod d, Drew Edward Hunter; cos, Melinda McKeller; spec eff, Drew Edward Hunter; makeup, Cathy Glover.

Horror   **Cas.**   **(PR:O   MPAA:R)**

MOVIE HOUSE MASSACRE*   (1986) 75m Movie House c

Mary Woronov, Jonathan Blakely, Lynne Darcy, Cynthia Hartline, Lisa Lindsley, Pam McCormack, Joni Barnes, Laurie Tidemanson, Barrie Metz, Terry Taylor, Joe Howard, Alice Raley, Bruce Nangle, Kim Clayton, Sam Bowe, Dee-Dee Hoffman.

Yet another straight-to-videocassette low-budget horror epic. Filmed in 1984, the relatively unique (in the slasher genre) premise sees an old theater as the place that is supposed to be haunted. Years before, when the house presented stage plays, the theater's manager went crazy, stabbed the ticket girl, and started a fire that created a mass panic. Now a greedy 11-theater chain owner has bought the "haunted" theater and intends to add it to his movie exhibition franchise. (This guy would make MPAA president Jack Valenti's hair curl: he makes illegal videotape copies of the films he exhibits.) Eager to collect the $25,000 reward offered by persons unknown who dare anyone to do business there, he dispatches three employees to clean up the dreaded cinema in time for its gala opening night. Of course the bodies soon pile up (one of the workers is a high school cheerleader, so an endless parade of her bouncy teammates drop by long enough to get killed) and the usual stupid twist-ending makes it all seem even more pointless.

Produced, written, and directed by Raley, who apparently knows nothing about making films, MOVIE HOUSE MASSACRE is incredibly inept. Only the presence of veteran low-budget star Woronov, as the manager's assistant, makes this even remotely tolerable. Los Angeles locals may notice that the film was shot in the Beverly Theater in Beverly Hills and the Fairfax Theater in L.A.

p,d&w, Alice Raley; ph, Bill Fishman.

Horror   Cas.   (PR:O MPAA:NR)

MUJ HRISNY MUZ†   (1986, Czech.) 99m Barrandov c

Dagmar Veskrnova *(Marta)*, Oldrich Kaiser *(Zdenek)*, Jan Hartl *(Vasek Hornak)*, Petra Janu *(Irena)*, Radovan Lukavsky *(Hradecky)*, Kveta Fialova *(Hradecka)*, Marie Rosulkova *(Grandmother)*, Josef Somr *(Barta)*, Jana Svandova *(Tana Bartova)*, Michal Nesvadba *(Assistant Petricek)*, Milos Vavra *(Dr. Pavlicek)*, Raduz Chmelik *(Dr. Vanicek)*, Svatopluk Matyas *(Dr. Benak)*, Vera Vlckova *(Dr. Kolska)*, Ivana Chylkova *(Masa)*, Julius Satinsky *(Interpreter)*, Jiri Kodet *(Kadlec)*, Jirina Jiraskova *(Jenikova)*.

d, Vaclav Matejka; w, Halina Pawlovska, Milan Steindler, Vaclav Matejka; ph, Jiri Macak; m, Michael Kocab; ed, Josef Valusiak; art d, Jindrich Goetz; cos, Marta Kaplerova.

MUKHAMUKHAM†   (1986, India) 107m General Pictures c (Trans: Face to Face)

P. Ganga *(Sreedharan)*, B.K. Nair *(Old Farmer)*, Ponnamma *(Savitri)*, Krishna Kumar *(Sreedharan's Son)*, Karamana Thilakan *(Trade Union Leaders)*, Vishwanathan *(Child Sudhakaran)*, Ashokan *(Sudhakaran)*, Lalitha *(Party Worker)*, Vembayan *(Teashop Owner)*.

Ganga is a political agitator whose presence is welcomed in a small village. But 10 years later, when he returns to the same town, Ganga has lost his urge to fight. Rather than become involved in local politics, he seeks refuge in alcohol.

p, Ravi; d&w, Addor Gopalakrishnan; ph, Ravi Varma (Eastmancolor); m, M.B. Srinivasan; ed, M. Mani; prod d, Sivan; art d, Meera.

Drama   (PR:C-O MPAA:NR)

MULLERS BURO†   (1986, Austria) 95m Wega Film c (Trans: Muller's Bureau)

Christian Schmidt *(Max Muller)*, Andreas Vitasek *(Andy)*, Barbara Rudnik *(Bettina Kant)*, Sue Tauber *(Frau Schick)*, Gaby Hift *(Frau Copain)*.

This hybrid of classic Hollywood detective films and pop musicals stars Schmidt as a private eye hired by the sultry Rudnik to trace the whereabouts of her missing fiance. The next day Schmidt learns from the newspaper that Rudnik had supposedly been murdered the day before she hired him. Determined to get to the bottom of the mystery, Schmidt discovers the local Mafia wants his snooping stopped. As is the case with most detective stories, a confusing number of corpses follows in Schmidt's wake, but here the performers break out into song to explain the incongruities in the plot.

d&w, Niki List; ph, Hans Selikovsky; m, Ernie Seubert; ed, Ingrid Koller; set d, Rudolf Czettel; cos, Martina List.

Mystery/Musical   (PR:C-O MPAA:NR)

MURDER SYNDROME   (SEE: FEAR, 1986)

MURPHY'S LAW**   (1986) 97m Golan-Globus/Cannon c

Charles Bronson *(Jack Murphy)*, Kathleen Wilhoite *(Arabella McGee)*, Carrie Snodgress *(Joan Freeman)*, Robert F. Lyons *(Art Penney)*, Richard Romanus *(Frank Vicenzo)*, Angel Tompkins *(Jan)*, Bill Henderson *(Ben Wilcove)*, James Luisi *(Ed Reineke)*, Clifford A. Pellow *(Lt. Nachman)*, Janet MacLachman *(Dr. Lovell)*, Lawrence Tierney *(Cameron)*, Jerome Thor *(Judge Kellerman)*, Mischa Hausserman *(Dave Manzarek)*, Cal Haynes *(Reese)*, Hans Howes *(Santana)*, Joseph Spallina Roman *(Carl)*, Chris De Rose *(Tony Vincenzo)*, Frank Annese *(Kelly)*, Paul McCallum *(Hog)*, Dennis Hayden *(Sonny)*, Tony Montero *(Max)*, David Hayman *(Jack)*, Lisa Vice *(Blonde)*, Janet Rotblatt *(Mrs. Vincenzo)*, Greg Finley *(Booking Sergeant)*, Jerry Lazarus *(Lawyer)*, Robert Axelrod *(Hotel Clerk)*, John Hawker *(Hotel Guest)*, Bert Williams *(Police Capt.)*, Daniel Nalleck *(Lead Cop)*, Randall Carver *(Mechanic)*, Gerald Berns *(Young Cop)*, Don L. Brodie *(Old Man)*, Graham Timbes *(Detective)*, David K. Johnston, Frank Bove *(Guards)*, Paul McCauley *(Bailiff)*, Brooks Wachtel *(Maitre d')*, Richard Hochberg *(Man with Glasses)*, John F. McCarthy *(Patrol Cop)*, Leigh Lombardi *(Stewardess)*, Charlie Brewer *(Security Guard)*, Charles A. Nero *(Liquor Clerk)*, Wheeler Henderson *(Woman in Bathroom)*, Chris Stanley *(Ambulance Attendant)*, Linda Harwood *(Waitress)*, Nancie Clark *(Restaurant Patron)*.

Charles Bronson seems intent on destroying whatever critical favor he once enjoyed, endlessly recycling his avenger role from DEATH WISH through a number of minor variations. And woe to anyone for whom Bronson shows any affection in one of his films, for that person is sure to be killed to trigger Bronson's righteous wrath. In this effort he's a detective who finds himself framed for the murder of his estranged stripper wife and her lover. The real malefactor is Snodgress, a psychopath he sent to an asylum 10 years before and who is now out looking for revenge. She tails Bronson, taking photographs of his activities, then, one night, waits in the backseat of his car. When he gets in, she clubs him on the head, then drives his car to his ex-wife's apartment and guns her and her lover down with Bronson's pistol. She drives away slowly to let witnesses identify the plates, and the next day Bronson is arrested and tossed into jail. He is handcuffed to foul-mouthed punk pixie Wilhoite, whom he had earlier arrested for stealing his car, and when he escapes (remarkably easily), she is along for the ride. They run to the roof and steal a helicopter and get away after a dangerous encounter with some dope farmers. The pair hides out on the farm of Henderson, Bronson's old partner, now and invalid and retired. They stay the night, but as soon as they leave Snodgress turns up and kills Henderson with a shotgun, blood splattering her face.

Meanwhile, some mobsters under Romanus are after Bronson at the behest of the gangster's mother because Bronson killed her other son. At first Bronson had

thought they were behind everything, but after invading Romanus' penthouse and beating him up, he realizes someone else is after him, although Romanus is now very angry. Bronson goes to a police friend and asks him to run a check on anyone Bronson sent away who has recently been released. He turns up three names, including Snodgress, and when Bronson learns that the judge in the case has been found dead in his bathtub, he knows who is behind it all. Bronson and Wilhoite, who by now are developing some real affection for each other, go to the hotel where Snodgress is staying and find her social worker strangled in the closet. They narrowly escape the police and head out to the home of the prosecutor in the case. Bronson finds him dead with a plastic bag over his head, and Wilhoite is knocked out by Snodgress and taken away. Bronson finds a message telling him to meet Snodgress at the building where he arrested her, where she killed her boy friend 10 years before.

Bronson calls the police to tell them he knows who killed his wife, but the only cop he can get on the phone is Luisi, long antagonistic toward Bronson and in the pocket of Romanus. Instead of calling for help, Luisi calls Romanus and joins the mobster and two of his gunmen on an errand to kill Bronson. Romanus sends Luisi in first and he manages to get the drop on Bronson, but before he can shoot him, Snodgress shoots a crossbow bolt into his back. Romanus and his gunmen come in and Bronson kills them all in short order. Snodgress tells him that she is now going to kill Wilhoite and she sends the elevator down. Bronson looks down and sees Wilhoite tied at the bottom of the shaft, about to be crushed. He races down and frees her in the nick of time, but Snodgress shoots her with another bolt from her crossbow. Now Bronson is really mad, and he tears up the stairs after Snodgress, who slashes him across the stomach with an axe. He manages to kick her over a railing, where she hangs tenuously, whining for Bronson to help her. He just stands there holding his guts in until Snodgress, her grip slipping, screams at him, "You go to hell!" "Ladies first," the hero says, and Snodgress falls to her death. In the ambulance, we see that Wilhoite isn't dead after all, and Bronson threatens to wash her mouth out with soap.

There is nothing very original about the film except Snodgress as one of the first female psycho killers in memory. She manages to convey a good deal of her madness in the way she screws up her face, mouth twitching, when she kills. Unfortunately, no one else in the film is nearly as interested in creating a character. Bronson seems bored by the whole thing; even his own plight fails to ruffle his composure. He doesn't even seem interested in defending himself against the murder rap (why doesn't he show them the lump he got when he was knocked out?). Wilhoite makes a good foil for Bronson, and the rapport between the two is the most entertaining thing in the film. Almost universally panned by critics, the film still managed to draw the sizable coterie of Bronson fans who will line up for anything in which their hero appears. Songs include "Murphy's Law" (Paul McCallum, Kathleen Wilhoite, John Bishardt, performed by McCallum, Wilhoite, Bishardt) and "It's Got to Get Better" (Jim Cushinery, Val McCallum, performed by the Wigs).

p, Pancho Kohner; d, J. Lee Thompson; w, Gail Morgan Hickman; ph, Alex Phillips (TVC Color); m, Marc Donahue, Valentine McCallum; ed, Peter Lee Thompson, Charles Simmons; prod d, William Cruise; set d, W. Brooke

Wheeler; cos, Shelley Komarov; m/l, Paul McCallum, Kathleen Wilhoite, John Bishardt, Jim Cushinery, Val McCallum; makeup, Lily Benyar.

Action/Crime   Cas.   (PR:O MPAA:R)

MUTCHAN NO UTA†   (1986, Jap.) Kansai Kyodo Eiga (Trans: Song of
                                                                        Mutsuko)

Akiko Isozaki, Takanobu Yamanoi, Hiroshi Arikawa, Yukiko Takabayashi, Mari Sato.

d, Hiromichi Horikawa; w, Natsu Komori; ph, Jun-ichiro Hayashi.

MUZ NA DRATE†   (1986, Czech.) Barrandov c (Trans: The Man on the
                                                                         Line)

Jiri Bartoska, Stanislava Bartosova, Vladimir Cerny, Jana Drbohlavova.

d, Julius Matula; w, Martin Bezouska; ph, Ivan Slapeta.

MUZSKOE VOSPITANIE†   (1986, U.S.S.R.) 77m Turkmenfilm c (Trans:
                                                                    Manly Education)

Bengene Kurbandurdyev *(Caman)*, Ata Dovletov *(Mergenaka)*, Dyrdymamet Oraev *(Sejli)*, Gulja Kerimova *(Dzeren)*.

A Soviet children's film starring Kurbandurdyev as a timid young boy whose father decides to teach him some manly lessons after seeing that his son is too scared to cross a narrow mountain bridge. Snatching the boy from his overprotective mother, the father makes Kurbandurdyev spend several months in the desert herding the family sheep and lambs to market. The boy slowly begins to adapt to some of the harsh realities of life on the way, but recoils in horror when he learns what fate has in store for the sheep at the end of the trail (skinning them for coats). Kurbandurdyev finally stands up to his father, rescues the lambs from slaughter, and earns his father's respect as well.

d, Usman Saparov, Jazgeldy Siedov; w, Cary Japan, Usman Saparov; ph, Nurjagdy Shamuchammedov; m, Nury Chalmemedov; art d, Aleksandr Mitta.

Children's   (PR:AA MPAA:NR)

MY BEAUTIFUL LAUNDRETTE*½**   (1986, Brit.) 93m Working
                                                     Title-SAF-Channel Four/Orion Classics c

Daniel Day Lewis *(Johnny)*, Saeed Jaffrey *(Nasser)*, Roshan Seth *(Papa)*, Gordon Warnecke *(Omar)*, Shirley Anne Field *(Rachel)*, Rita Wolf *(Tania)*, Richard Graham *(Genghis)*, Winston Graham, Dudley Thomas *(Jamaicans)*, Derrick Branche *(Salim)*, Garry Cooper *(Squatter)*, Charu Bala Choksi *(Bilquis, Nasser's Wife)*, Souad Faress *(Cherry, Salim's Wife)*, Persis Marvala *(Nasser's Elder Daughter)*, Nisha Kapur *(Nasser's Younger Daughter)*, Neil Cunningham *(Englishman)*, Walter Donohue *(Dick O'Donnell)*, Gurdial Sira *(Zaki)*, Stephen Marcus *(Moose)*, Dawn Archibald, Jonathan Moore *(Gang Members)*, Gerard Horan *(Telephone Man)*, Ram John Holder *(Poet)*, Bhasker *(Tariq)*, Ayub Khan Din *(Student)*, Dulice Leicier *(Girl in Disco)*, Badi Uzzaman *(Dealer)*, Chris Pitt, Kerryann White *(Kids)*, Colin Campbell *(Madame Butterfly Man)*, Sheila Chitnis *(Zaki's Wife)*.

Besides constructing one of the most unlikely film plots in recent memory—two homosexuals running a laundromat in a British slum—director Frears and screen-

writer Kureishi have fashioned a wonderfully fresh examination of the political and racial climate in Margaret Thatcher's Britain. Warnecke is a young Pakistani living in London with his father, Seth, a drunk who was previously one of Pakistan's top writers and intellectuals. Upon his arrival in London, interest in his work dried up and his idealism soured to alcoholism. Living on government handouts, Seth asks his brother, Jaffrey, an underworld crime boss, to find temporary work for Warnecke. Jaffrey takes a liking to Warnecke, offers him a menial job as a car-washer, and eventually makes him the manager of a run-down laundrette. Rather than run the operation alone, Warnecke enterprisingly employs Day Lewis, a London street punk and a boyhood friend whom Warnecke has not seen since Day Lewis joined a fascist anti-Pakistani group. The very mention of Day Lewis upsets Seth, whose wife killed herself because of racial tensions. Warnecke and Day Lewis make their laundrette into a brightly colored,

neon-lit environment where the locals can happily clean their soiled clothes. Seth, however, is still rooted in his past and prefers that his son go to college instead of being an "underpants cleaner." In addition to becoming work partners, Warnecke and Day Lewis also become lovers, keeping their secret of homosexuality from Jaffrey and the Pakistani clan. In the meantime, Day Lewis' friends have turned against him, baffled by his devotion to the "Pakis." The racial tensions hit the breaking point when Day Lewis' former friends trash Warnecke's cousin's car. When Day Lewis intervenes he is given the same brutal treatment usually reserved for the hated Pakistanis. The final scene has Day Lewis standing by his friend and lover Warnecke, choosing to fight with, instead of against, him.

An extremely dense film, MY BEAUTIFUL LAUNDRETTE was written by Hanif Kureishi (who received an Oscar nomination for his work), a 29-year-old British playwright born of a Pakistani father and an English mother, placing him on the same racial fence as Warnecke's character. Rather than creating one or two complex characters, Kureishi has come up with at least a half-dozen. Amaz-

ingly, their development does not seem stunted, despite the film's relatively short 93 minutes. Characters this complex are usually reserved for an epic undertaking such as THE GODFATHER, which, not coincidentally, was Kureishi's original intent. Budgetary restrictions prevailed, however, and MY BEAUTIFUL LAUNDRETTE (costing $900,000 and filmed on 16mm) stuck to a commercial running time. Because of the homosexual romance in the film, one would think that MY BEAUTIFUL LAUNDRETTE is about sexual roles. Instead, Kureishi plays the homosexuality like any other story of lovers who must struggle to be together, even against the most impossible odds. Like a romance set against the backdrop of the feuding Capulets and Montagues or the Hatfields and the McCoys, the romance between Warnecke and Day Lewis must (and does) survive the racial battle between native Britons and Pakistani newcomers, the moral battle between liberalism and conservatism, the intellectual battle between idealism and capitalism, and the political battle between Prime Minister Thatcher and the unemployed working class.

While Warnecke and Day Lewis represent the successful union of the two factions, the rest of Kureishi's characters exist on the fringe. Warnecke's father, Seth, who resorts to passive alcoholism, is a failed answer to the problematic question of integrating Pakistani culture into English life. At the opposite end of the spectrum is Jaffrey, who, rather than letting England defeat him, chooses to find financial success in the criminal world. His most-prized possession is not his money and his fancy car, but his mistress Field, a woman he genuinely loves and who serves as his truest example of acceptance by the British. There's also Jaffrey's daughter, Wolf, a dark-skinned girl who denies her Pakistani heritage but cannot accept the ways of the English. She wants to marry both Warnecke and Day Lewis, but in the end packs her bags and leaves everything behind.

Amidst all the conflicts of racism, sexuality, bigotry, violence, and politics, MY BEAUTIFUL LAUNDRETTE still manages to be a humorous and entertaining film because of Frears' skill as a director. It is visually inventive, intelligently constructed, and filled with truly excellent performances, not one of which can be singled out and labeled as "best." Originally planned for British television because of its small and particularly British subject matter, the film achieved a theatrical release, due partly to Frears' critical success with his 1985 film, THE HIT. MY BEAUTIFUL LAUNDRETTE can also boast one of the most vigorous title sequences in some time—its credits spinning onto the screen as if inside a washing machine—which serves as a hint of the energy that constantly churns inside of Frears' frame.

p, Sarah Radclyffe, Tim Bevan; d, Stephen Frears; w, Hanif Kureishi; ph, Oliver Stapleton; m, Ludus Tonalis; ed, Mick Audsley; prod d, Hugo Luczyc Whyhowski; cos, Lindy Hemming; makeup, Elaine Carew; stunts, Rocky Taylor, Jim Dowdall, Bill Weston, Nosher Powell.

Drama   Cas.   (PR:O MPAA:R)

MY CHAUFFEUR**   (1986) 97m Crown International Pictures c

Deborah Foreman *(Casey Meadows)*, Sam J. Jones *(Battle Witherspoon)*, Sean McClory *(O'Brien)*, Howard Hesseman *(McBride)*, E.G. Marshall *(Witherspoon)*, Penn Jillette *(Bone)*, Teller *(Abdul)*, John O'Leary *(Giles)*, Julius Harris *(Johnson)*, Laurie Main *(Jenkins)*, Stanley Brock *(Downs)*, Jack Stryker *(Moses)*, Vance Colvig *(Doolittle)*, Ben Slack *(Dupont)*, Elaine Wilkes *(Colleen)*, Diana Bellamy *(Blue Lady)*, Leland Crooke *(Catfight)*, Robin Antin *(Bimbo)*, Cindy

Beal *(Beebop)*, Sue Jackson *(Boom Boom)*, Darian Mathias *(Dolly)*, Mark Holton *(Doughboy)*, Carlton Miller *(Amy)*, Stan Foster *(LaRue)*, Regina Hooks *(Charmaine)*, John Martin *(Manager)*, Leslee Bremer, Jeannine Bisignano, Sheila Lussier, Vickie Benson *(Party Girls)*, Daria Martel *(Georgia)*, David Donham *(Dobbs)*, Daniel Hirsch *(Fryer)*, Jim Holmes *(Punk)*, Nick De Mauro *(Maitre 'd)*, Carmen Filpi *(Mop Man)*, Robert Q. Lewis *(Businessman)*, Robin Nolan *(Mother With Baby)*, Kevin G. Tracey *(Butler)*, Rick Garia *(Stage Manager)*, Jacqueline Jacobs *(Party Animal)*, Jim Cushinery, Val McCallum, Marty Ross, Bobby J. Tews *(The Wigs)*.

This could have been a sweet, charming little romantic comedy in the same vein as 1983's VALLEY GIRL (which also starred Deborah Foreman), but it is ruined by excessive vulgarity and gratuitous nudity. The always spunky Foreman stars as a fast-talking, goofy, and rebellious young woman who receives a mysterious

note from millionaire Marshall informing her that she's been hired as a chauffeur for his limousine company. She is given a cool reception by her stuffy new boss, Hessman, and is treated with outright hostility by the grouchy male chauffeurs. Only McClory, Marshall's chauffeur, shows an interest in Foreman and treats her kindly (there are hints that Marshall is the girl's father). In an effort to make her quit, Hessman assigns Foreman to their most difficult client, Crooke, a spoiled British rock star who never makes it to his performances on time. Ignoring his demands that she strip off her uniform and join his orgy, Foreman dumps ice water on the rock star and hauls him and his entourage off to the concert hall. For the first time in his career Crooke makes it to a performance on time and Foreman is rewarded handsomely by the singer's agent. Eventually Foreman is assigned to chauffeur Jones, the uptight and overworked son of Marshall. Jones knows only running his father's businesses and has little room in his heart for humor, love, or compassion. When his fiancee announces that she's become pregnant by another man—the man she truly loves—Jones commands Foreman to drive aimlessly while he sulks silently in the back. Fed up with driving in circles, Foreman provokes the reserved Jones to get rip-roaring drunk. Predictably, Jones becomes a wild man when inebriated and runs through a public park naked. When Jones becomes unable to walk by himself, Foreman (who doesn't know the man's name) is forced to take him home to her apartment. When he awakes the next morning, Jones is once again his uptight, businesslike self and he storms out of Foreman's apartment assuming she had seduced him. Sensing his son's distress, Marshall demands he take a vacation and visit the family vineyards upstate. Foreman, of course, is his chauffeur and the two are immediately at each other's throats. He treats her like a brainless female, and she gives abuse back as hard as she gets it. When the car overheats in the mountains the pair is forced to

walk through the desert 20 miles toward the nearest house. During the ordeal Jones loosens up and the couple grow close. By the time they make it to a farmhouse they are ready to become lovers. Foreman tries to keep Jones awake

for fear he will revert to his uptight state, but he assures her that he is a changed man. The next morning he asks her to marry him, but she wants to wait. Back at the limousine service, an excited Foreman tells McClory of her romance. McClory immediately informs Marshall, and the millionaire sets out to end the relationship. In a ridiculous conclusion, Marshall reveals to Jones and Foreman that he is the girl's father (her mother was a former servant). The question of incest is dealt with by an innocent but, "Uh, oh. We've been bad," confession from Foreman. As Marshall's eyes widen, McClory appears with the millionaire's former chauffeur, O'Leary, who admits that it is he who is the girl's father. No longer half-brother and sister, Foreman and Jones are free to marry.

There is so much to like about MY CHAUFFEUR that it makes the film's wrong-headedness that much more annoying. Foreman is terrific as the spunky young chauffeur and she successfully echoes such luminaries of screwball comedy as Carole Lombard (an avowed goal of both Foreman and writer-director Beaird). The handsome-but-uptight Jones is a perfect foil for her and the pair sparkle in several scenes together. Marshall is his usual consummately professional self, and the supporting cast of McClory and grouchy chauffeurs leaves the viewer wanting more. Unfortunately, there are several pointless, gratuitously offensive digressions in the basically sweet plot line. For starters, the incest bugaboo is totally unnecessary and brings a distasteful, uneasy air to the otherwise charming romance. Hesseman is miscast as the sarcastic chauffeur chief and he is given nothing but insipidly foul dialog to spew. The escapade with the rock star is unfunny, offensive, and vulgar, as is most of a torturously long and out-of-place routine by the stage comedy team of Penn and Teller (in their film debut) which seems tacked on at the last minute (Penn is a street hustler and Teller is a shy oil sheik). There is absolutely no need for any of this crudeness and it makes one wonder if such scenes were inserted to insure an "R" rating from the MPAA to draw teenage lechers to the box office. Director Beaird, one of the founders of Chicago's renowned Wisdom Bridge Theater, should have known that these sequences would throw his film totally out of whack. Perhaps such sleaze was inserted at the insistence of producer Tenser who can boast such exploitative dreck as THE POM POM GIRLS, THE VAN, MALIBU BEACH, VAN NUYS BOULEVARD, THE BEACH GIRLS, MY TUTOR, WEEKEND PASS, and TOMBOY on her filmography. Whoever is to blame, MY CHAUFFEUR is a tragically schizophrenic comedy that fails both as an homage to the screwball classics of the 1930s and as a simple juvenile T&A farce.

p, Marilyn J. Tenser; d&w, David Beaird; ph, Harry Mathias (Panavision, DeLuxe Color); m, Paul Hertzog; ed, Richard E. Westover; prod d, C.J. Strawn; md, Matthew D. Causey; set d, A. Rosalind Crew; cos, Camile Schroeder; ch, Damita Joe Freeman; m/l, Michael Galasso, Martin Ross, James Cushinery, Scott Krueger, Peter Zaremba, Keith Streng, Westerberg, Stinson, Stinson, and Mars; makeup, Christa Reusch.

Comedy   Cas.   (PR:O   MPAA:R)

MY LITTLE PONY**   (1986) 87m Sunbow/De Laurentiis Entertainment
                                                            Group c

Voices of: Danny DeVito *(Grundle King)*, Madeline Kahn *(Draggle)*, Cloris Leachman *(Hydia)*, Rhea Perlman *(Reeka)*, Tony Randall *(The Moochick)*, Tammy Amerson *(Megan)*, Jon Bauman *(The Smooze)*, Alice Playten *(Baby Lickety Split/Bushwoolie No.1)*, Charlie Adler *(Spike/Woodland Creature)*, Michael Bell *(Grundle)*, Sheryl Bernstein *(Buttons/Woodland Creature/Bushwoolie)*, Susan Blu *(Lofty/Grundle/Bushwoolie)*, Cathy Cavadini *(North Star)*, Nancy Cartwright *(Gusty/Bushwoolie #4)*, Peter Cullen *(Grundle/Ahgg)*, Laura Dean *(Sundance/Bushwoolie #2)*, Ellen Gerstell *(Magic Star)*, Keri Houlihan *(Molly)*, Katie Leigh *(Fizzy/Baby Sundance)*, Scott Menville *(Danny)*, Laurel Page *(Sweet Stuff)*, Sarah Partridge *(Wind Whistler)*, Russie Taylor *(Morning Glory/Rosedust/Bushwoolie/Skunk)*, Jill Wayne *(Shady/Baby Lofty)*, Frank Welker *(Bushwoolie/Grundle)*.

With the Care Bears and Go-Bots being the subjects of animated films cum feature length commercials, it was only a matter of time before the "My Little Pony" toys also hit the big screen. Aimed at the preschool viewer, the story is a basic good versus evil saga involving the happy residents of Ponyland. These miniature horses are celebrating the coming of spring, but their lighthearted festivities are to be short-lived. At the appropriately named Volcano of Doom an evil witch, along with her two odious daughters (voiced by Leachman, Perlman, and Kahn respectively) is scheming ways to flood out Ponyland. To this end Leachman creates a living substance called Smooze (with a voice provided by Sha-Na-Na singer Bauman). Most of the ponies are able to escape, but one young equine and her dragon pal end up trapped in a cave with some creatures called the Grundles. DeVito, aptly cast as the Grundle King, helps these two escape but Leachman's powers appear to hold the lead. The Smooze covers the pony home, but with the help of Randall (voicing an ancient but sage adviser) the My Little Pony group is able to regain their home by contacting the extremely helpful Flutter Ponies. These winged steeds use their appendages to create a powerful wind, driving back the Smooze and saving Ponyland's Dream Castle. DeVito and his bunch are given the castle as their new home, and everyone learns a lesson about friendship and sharing.

As with THE CARE BEARS MOVIE (both I and II) the story is treacly sweet, told in a simplistic animation style that has lamentably become an industry standard. Kids will enjoy the events, however, and parents might be mildly amused by the cast of famous voices. At close to an hour and a half though, MY LITTLE PONY pushes the limits of a younger child's attention span. Of course MY LITTLE PONY will—as intended—whet a juvenile consumer's appetite for the array of "My Little Pony" toys, games, videos, sleepwear, etc., undoubtedly available in the same mall where you and your tyke see the film.

p, Joe Bacal, Tom Griffin; d, Michael Joens; w, George Arthur Bloom; m, Rob Walsh; m/l, Tommy Goodman, Barry Harman.

Animation/Children's   Cas.   (PR:AAA MPAA:G)

MY MAN ADAM zero   (1986) 84m Tri-Star-Delphi III–Mount Co./Tri-Star Pictures c

Raphael Sbarge *(Adam Swit)*, Page Hannah *(Sabrina)*, Veronica Cartwright *(Elaine Swit)*, Dave Thomas *(Jerry Swit)*, Charlie Barnett *(Leroy)*, Kelly Wolf *(Tina Swit)*, Larry R. Scott *(Donald)*, Austin Pendleton *(Mr. Greenhut)*, John Kapelos *(Mr. Rangle)*, Chris Elliott *(Mr. Spooner)*, Grant Forsberg *(Ty Redbyrn)*, Sam Slovik *(Raymond)*, Winifred Freedman *(Amanda)*, Gary Hershberger *(Stan)*, Eddie Roe Smith *(Eddy)*, Alan Haufrect *(John Walker)*, Danny Goldman *(Dr. Blaustein)*, Joan Pape *(Ms. Fluger)*, Garry Goodrow *(Mr. Drum)*, Sam Scarber *(Emerson Crabbe)*, Jedd Nabonsal *(Nick McKay)*, Denise Gordy *(Willette)*, Jack Yatis *(Blond Man)*, Jeffrey Mylett *(Phillip)*, Linda Finzi *(Sunbather)*.

Sbarge is a privileged high school student who dreams of becoming a television news anchorman. His parents (Thomas and Cartwright) don't understand him and Sbarge's life at school is a mess. Sbarge is working on a friend's campaign for student body president at their high school, but finds himself continually fantasizing about a mysterious redhead whom he is convinced is the girl of his dreams. One day Sbarge sees this vision come to life in the form of Hannah, but has trouble connecting with her. Eventually he and Hannah meet but even then she's still hard to get. The two find Pendleton, a popular teacher, lying in the school parking lot, the victim of a brutal beating. As they try to help the poor man, Pendleton slips a roll of undeveloped film into the unsuspecting Sbarge's coat pocket. Hannah disappears and Sbarge goes out searching for her once more. He finds himself being drawn into an increasingly complex web of conspiracy which leads to an illegal scheme by a group of automobile repossessors. Hannah, it turns out, has been protecting her brother Nabonsal, who was part of the plot. Also involved is the snooty rival for Sbarge's love interest, but this blond Aryan's hopes quickly fade as his evil deeds are ultimately exposed. Sbarge ends up with Hannah, his candidate wins the election, and you wake up when you realize the VCR has rewound itself.

As a teen comedy, this should have been pretty harmless and mildly amusing stuff. However, MY MAN ADAM lacks one sufficient item necessary for success: a plot. The characters run around looking for something to do before the mystery unravels and even then it's hard to figure out what all the fuss is about. It seems as if the film was made up as they went along, hoping against hope they'd actually hit on something. What makes the whole thing really obnoxious is a narration provided by Barnett. He's a peripheral character who provides voice-over commentary on Sbarge's adventures, but because Barnett is portrayed as Hollywood's version idea of a street-wise black kid, he's provided with a plethora of descriptive four-letter words. Sbarge (who played one of Tom Cruise's buddies in the excellent 1983 film RISKY BUSINESS) is passable in the lead, considering he really doesn't seem to know what's going on. He usually looks lost, which is probably more a reflection on the filmmakers than Sbarge's talents. Hannah, the younger sister of actress Daryl Hannah, isn't particularly memorable in her walk-through role, while Thomas and Cartwright should be downright ashamed of themselves. Surely their respective agents could have found them something better than this rambling mess. MY MAN ADAM saw a scant, barely mentionable release in late 1985 but received a general distribution in 1986 through the saving grace of videocassettes. Along with Smokey Robinson and the Miracles' hit tune "I Second That Emotion," the songs (all penned by Sylvester Levay and Kathy Wakefield) include: "I Want To Rock On" (performed by David Lasley), "Tender Breakdown" (performed by Shandi), "Lost in the Dark" (performed by

Amy Holland), "Game of Suspense" (performed by Joe "Bean" Esposito), "Faith in the Hand of Magic" (performed by Gary U.S. Bonds).

p, Renee Missel, Gail Stayden, Paul Aratow; d, Roger L. Simon; w, Roger L. Simon, Renee Missel; ph, Donald McAlpine; m, Sylvester Levay; ed, Don Zimmerman; prod d, Ferdinando Scarfiotti; art d, Ed Richardson; set d, Daniel L. May; cos, Robert Weiner; spec eff, Joe DiGaetano III; stunts, M. James Arnett.

Comedy   Cas.   (PR:O MPAA:R)

MY NAME AIN'T SUZIE   (SEE: HUAJIE SHIDAI, 1986, Hong Kong)

N

NADIA† (1986, Israel) 90m Abba c

Hanna Azoulai-Haspari *(Nadia)*, Yuval Banai *(Ronen)*, Meir Banai *(Dani)*, Meir Suissa *(Udi)*, Yussuf Abu-Warda *(Ali)*, Ossi Hillel *(Nurith)*, Ree Rosenfeld *(Tami)*, Salwa Nakkara-Hadad *(Dr. Najla)*.

The tensions between Israelis and the Arabs who live among them are explored in this feature, more oriented toward youths than to adults. Azoulai-Haspari is the title character, an Arab girl who has to leave the security of her family and community to go to an Israeli boarding school to prepare her to pursue her dream of studying medicine.

p, David Lipkind; d, Amnon Rubinstein; w, Amnon Rubinstein, Eitan Green, Galila Ron-Feder (based on a story by Galila Ron-Feder); ph, Ilan Rosenberg; m, Yoni Rechter; ed, David Tur; m/l, Yoni Rechter, Eli Mohar.

Drama **(PR:A MPAA:NR)**

NAERATA OMETI† (1986, USSR) 90m Tallinnfilm c (Trans: Keep Smiling, Baby!)

Monika Karv *(Mari)*, Hendrik Toompers *(Robi)*, Touri Tallermaa *(Tauri)*.

After being kicked out of his alcoholic father's home, Karv ends up at a Soviet institution where teenagers with similar hard-luck stories live. Unhappy with this new situation, Karv runs off, but is attacked by Toompers and his group of hooligans. She is returned to the institution, and discovers that Toompers is also a resident. Eventually the two become friends, and Toompers grows protective of Karv. Their budding relationship comes to an end when Toompers gets into a brawl and is subsequently sent to another institution.

d, Leida Laius, Arvo Iho; w, Marina Sheptunova (based on the novel *Stepmother* by Silvia Ranama); ph, Arvo Iho; m, Lepo Sumera; art d, Tonu Virve.

Drama **(PR:C MPAA:NR)**

NAKED CAGE, THE*½ (1986) 97m Cannon Group c

Shari Shattuck *(Michelle)*, Angel Tompkins *(Diane)*, Lucinda Crosby *(Rhonda)*, Christina Whitaker *(Rita)*, Faith Minton *(Sheila)*, Stacey Shaffer *(Amy)*, Nick Benedict *(Smiley)*, Lisa London *(Abbey)*, John Terlesky *(Willy)*, Aude Charles *(Brenda)*, Angela Gibbs *(Vonna)*, Leslie Huntly *(Peaches)*, Carole Ita White *(Trouble)*, Seth Kaufman *(Randy)*, Larry Gelman *(Doc)*, Susie London *(Martha)*, Valerie McIntosh *(Ruby)*, Flo Gerrish *(Mother)*, James Ingersoll *(Father)*, William Bassett *(Jordan)*, Nora Niesen *(Bigfoot)*, Jennifer Anne Thomas *(Mock)*, Chris Anders *(Miller)*, Al Jones *(Bartender)*, Sheila Stephenson *(Bank Teller)*, Bob Saurman *(Motorcycle Cop)*, Rick Avery *(Security Officer)*, Christopher Doyle *(Police Officer)*, Gretchen Davis, Beryl Jones, Michael Kerr *(Prison Guards)*.

An innocent girl goes to jail on a bum rap in this minor exploitation effort, which looks like a flashback to the peak of the genre 15 years ago. Whitaker is an escaped convict who is picked up by cocaine addict Terlesky in a Corvette he has just stolen. After she clubs a cop and shoots the counterman in a diner, they decide they have a lot in common so they agree to launch into a life of crime, starting with the bank where Terlesky's ex-wife (Shattuck) works. The robbery goes badly, a guard is killed, and Shattuck ends up arrested. Whitaker lies in court and Shattuck finds herself in the classic exploitation predicament. She is befriended by Shaffer, a former junkie who sets her straight on prison life. The top prisoner is amazonian Minton, who runs the drug concession and smothers anyone who falls behind in her payments under a pile of laundry. Tompkins is the warden, a lesbian who brings certain prisoners into her apartment for fun and games. She takes a liking to Shattuck, but when the good girl spurns her advances, Tompkins has her chucked into solitary and sends bad guard Benedict down to rape her. Instead Shattuck breaks his nose.

Meanwhile, Whitaker has arrived in prison, and after drugging Minton, beats her to a pulp and reclaims her former place as drug dealer. For some reason she has it in for Shattuck, driving a screwdriver through her hand as soon as she gets to prison. Whitaker gets Shaffer hooked on heroin again, then manipulates her into tricking Shattuck into a basement where Whitaker can murder her. At the last minute Shaffer lets Shattuck out, a crime for which Whitaker kills her. Tompkins figures out that guard Crosby is an undercover investigator, so she provokes a riot in which she plans to have Benedict murder her. Things get out of hand, though, and Benedict and Tompkins are both killed. Shattuck runs down into another basement with Whitaker after her. They fight and Shattuck manages to get the drop on her with a gun. Whitaker begs for her life and offers to change her testimony to free Shattuck. Still gullible, Shattuck agrees, but Whitaker gets the gun and is about to kill Shattuck when Crosby shows up. Crosby is shot in the shoulder and Shattuck pushes Whitaker into an electrical panel, where she fries. The last scene shows Shattuck back at her parent's farm, riding her horse, Misty.

Women-in-prison films occupy a special niche in the canon of exploitation films; they have everything their audiences want: women taking showers, women fighting each other, women having sex with guards, women having sex with each other, crime, guns, usually a car chase, and an innocent girl, framed and locked in these never-never land hellholes. The heyday of the sub-genre was the early 1970s, just before the rise of hardcore pornography killed off the softcore market, and the best of the films (like Jonathan Demme's debut, CAGED HEAT) could become political allegories for women's liberation and the corruption of

law enforcement, as long as they showed the requisite number of bare breasts and exploding blood squibs. Now, after years of neglect, women-in-prison films are on the comeback, fueled by the videocassette boom. Not only are many of the old titles coming out on tape, new films are coming out, ranging from the overboard parody of REFORM SCHOOL GIRLS to this minor effort, which touches every exploitation base but has no higher purpose than to entertain.

Whitaker is a memorable bad girl, but Shattuck is too bland as the heroine. Tompkins manages to add new aspects to the warden role, chiefly kinkier sex (one prisoner brandishes a riding crop with her), and some of the prisoners succeed in sticking out of the crowd, especially the massive Minton. These films are always beyond criticism because they revel in what would be attacked in any other film, but the good points here include slightly better-than-average acting, and some well-constructed sequences. Neglected during a brief theatrical release, THE NAKED CAGE promises to have a long life on video. Soundtrack includes: "Tuff Enuf" (Kim Wilson, performed by The Fabulous Thunderbirds), "Mediocre Dreams" (Kristan Hoffman, performed by The Swinging Madisons), "You Lied Your Way" (Sandy Rogers, performed by Rogers).

p, Chris D. Nebe; d&w, Paul Nicholas; ph, Hal Trussell (TVC Color); ed, Anthony DiMarco; art d, Alex Hajdu; set d, Marlene McCormick; cos, Shelly Komarov; makeup, Lily Benyar, Gabor Kernyaiszky; m/l, Kim Wilson, Kristan Hoffman, Sandy Rogers.

Prison **Cas.** **(PR:O MPAA:R)**

NAKED VENGEANCE* (1986, U.S./Phil.) 97m Concorde c (AKA: SATIN VENGEANCE)

Deborah Tranelli *(Carla Harris)*, Kaz Garas *(Fletch)*, Bill McLaughlin *(Sheriff Cates)*, Ed Crick *(Burke)*, Nick Nicholson *(Sparky)*, Don Gordon *(Arnie)*, David Light *(Ray)*, Steve Roderick *(Timmy)*, Carmen Argenziano *(Detective Russo)*, Terence O'Hara *(Mark Harris)*, Joseph Zuccero *(Dr. Fellows)*, Henry Strzalkowski *(Deputy)*, Helen McNeely *(Mrs. Olson)*, Doc McCoy *(Mr. Olson)*, Bill Kipp *(Deputy Reilly)*, Rosemarie Gil *(Jesse)*, Barbara Peers *(Estelle)*.

Tranelli is a married actress living in Los Angeles whose world is shattered when her husband is murdered while trying to prevent a rape. She leaves the city to visit her parents in the small town where she grew up and there attracts the lustful stares of the locals. They make crude advances to her, which she turns aside. One night, the men—five of them, plus teenager Roderick—get drunk and decide to go to her house (her parents are gone for the weekend) and "teach her a lesson," which, of course, ends in gang rape. Roderick regains his sobriety during this episode and is properly horrified, but while another rapist tries to calm him down, Tranelli's parents come home. Her father seizes a shotgun which goes off, killing her mother. One of the men gets the gun away from the father and kills him. Roderick tries to run out the door to call police, but he is shot in the back. Tranelli falls down and hits her head and is thought dead. The men put the gun in her father's dead hands and make it look as though the old man killed Roderick, who will be thought to have raped Tranelli. The sheriff is suspicious from the beginning, but Tranelli is catatonic and a doctor won't let the lawman disturb her. She regains her sanity quickly, and goes out on the revenge trail. Her first victim is a bartender, who is forced to soak himself in alcohol and is set alight. Next is a rapist who comes to check her mental state for himself by driving his boat up to the mental hospital. Tranelli takes off her clothes and starts to make love to the man in the water, then grabs a knife and castrates him. Victim three is a service-station mechanic who gets a car dropped on him. Four works at an ice factory and he ends up in the ice crusher. By now the entire community is up in arms against the madwoman, led by the last survivor, Garas, who is in serious fear for his life. They chase her to her home and set it on fire, but she escapes through a basement window and kills the last assailant, a butcher, with a cleaver in his back. Then she goes off to New York, where she tracks down the man who murdered her husband and wastes him.

As bad as the now-familiar plot sounds, it is actually carried off with a little finesse and a performance by Tranelli that almost keeps the film from the zero pile. Like any exploitation film, this one has the requisite amounts of exposed breasts and spurting blood, but slick direction keeps the story moving ahead at a sufficient pace to keep the exploitation material from getting offensively gratuitous. Prolific Filipino director Santiago's second picture to be released by Roger Corman's Concorde Pictures group (DESERT WARRIOR came first) is a substantial improvement over the girls-and-gore films he made so cheaply in his native islands in earlier years (THE VAMPIRE HOOKERS, THE BLOOD DRINKERS). Released on videocassette in two versions, one R-rated and the other unrated, containing more sex and violence for home consumption.

p, Cirio H. Santiago, Anthony Maharaj; d, Cirio H. Santiago; w, Reilly Askew (based on a story by Anthony Maharaj); ph, Ricardo Remias; m, Ron Jones; ed, Pacifico Sanchez, Noah Blough; art d, Boyel Camaya; cos, Elvira Santos, Gloria Garcia, Remia Mendoza; m/l, Michael Cruz; makeup, Teresa Mercedes, Norma Remias.

Crime/Action **Cas.** **(PR:O MPAA:R)**

NAME OF THE ROSE, THE** (1986) 130m Bernd Eichinger-Bernd Schaefers-Neue Constantin-Cristaldifilm-Films Ariane/FOX c

Sean Connery *(William of Baskerville)*, F. Murray Abraham *(Bernardo Gui)*, Christian Slater *(Adso of Melk)*, Elya Baskin *(Severinus)*, Feodor Chaliapin, Jr. *(Jorge de Burgos)*, William Hickey *(Ubertino de Casale)*, Michael Lonsdale *(The Abbot)*, Ron Perlman *(Salvatore)*, Volker Prechtel *(Malachia)*, Helmut Qualtinger *(Remigio de Varagine)*, Valentina Vargas *(The Girl)*, Michael Habeck *(Berengar)*, Urs Althaus *(Venantius)*, Leopoldo Trieste *(Michele da Censena)*, Franco Valobra *(Jerome of Kaffa)*, Vernon Dobtcheff *(Hugh of Newcastle)*, Donal O'Brian *(Pietro d'Assisi)*, Andrew Birkin *(Cuthbert of Winchester)*, Lucien

Bodard *(Cardinal Bertrand)*, Peter Berling *(Jean d'Anneaux)*, Pete Lancaster *(Bishop of Alborea)*, Franco Adducci, Niko Brucher, Aristide Caporali, Fabio Carfora, Peter Cloes, Mario Diano, Fabrizio Fontana, Rolando Fucili, Valerio Isidori, Luigi Leone, Armando Marra, Maurizio Mauri, Ludger Pistor, Francesco Scali, Maria Tedeschi, Andrea Tilli *(Monks)*, Ennio Lollainni, Emil Feist, Francesco Maselli, Renato Nebolini *(Swineherds)*, Antonio Cetta, Franco Covielleo, Daniele Ferretti, Sabatino Gennardo, Luciano Invidia, Mauro Leoni, Massimiliano Scarpa, Umberto Zuanelli *(Peasants)*, Mark Bellinghaus *(Jorge's Novice)*, David Furtwaengler, Patrick Kreuzer, Kim Rossi Stuart *(Novices)*, Lars Bodin-Jorgensen *(Adelmo)*, Franco Diogene, Giodano Falzoni, Eckehard Koch, Gina Poli, Gianni Rizzo, Lothar Schonbrodt, Vittorio Zarfati *(Papal Envoys)*, Carlo Bianchino *(Papal Guard)*, Eugenio Bonardi, Pietro Ceccarelli, Franco Marino, Hans Schoedel *(Inquisition Guards)*, Peter Welz *(Nero)*, Alberto Capone *(Executioner)*, Dwight Weist *(The Voice of Adso as an Old Man)*.

Anytime a picture has four different production companies and screenwriters, you can be sure of a hodgepodge. So it is with this, what director Annaud called a "palimpsest of Umberto Eco's novel." In case you don't know what palimpsest means (we didn't), it's a Greek designation for a manuscript which has been

erased so a second bit of writing can be entered over it, while some of the original writing still shows through. This is a literary conceit on Annaud's part. However, the book itself (which sold 4 million copies) was also a literary conceit, filled with scholarly inside jokes.

It's the late 1300s and there is to be a conference of some of the Catholic church's hierarchy at a Benedictine monastery. Arriving to be part of the meeting are Connery, an intellectual monk, and his teenage novice, Slater. The Franciscans, who have nothing more than the sackcloth on their backs, are about to do battle with the Dominicans, who enjoy a life of luxury. The nature of the meeting is to wrestle with a theory: did Jesus own the clothes he wore? If the answer is "no," it may spell the end of the church's acquisitions of money, art, and accoutrements. That is the backdrop for an interesting Middle Ages mystery. (We say Middle Ages but the cinematography on this film is so dim, it could have been the Dark Ages.) A series of five murders takes place during the religious conference. The first is thought to be a suicide but when murders keep occurring, Lonsdale, the Abbot, calls upon the brilliant mind of Connery to help unravel the enigma. Connery and Slater visit Hickey, a man possessed with zeal and black predictions. When a second monk dies under questionable circumstances, it's for certain that someone is killing them and that the murderer has been reading the account of The Apocalypse. (Eco's novel was quite scholarly and demanded that the reader have some knowledge of many things. For example, the very name

Connery carries is William of Baskerville, and since he is functioning as a cassocked Sherlock Holmes and the first Holmes' case was THE HOUND OF THE BASKERVILLES, that sets the stage immediately. At one point in the picture,

Connery answers Slater by saying "Elementary"—another Sherlockian trademark.)

The monastery is high on a windy mountain, and the thought that a murderer is loose causes great fear among the remaining inhabitants. When Baskin, an herbalist, and Connery discover a black stain on the second man's index finger, they think they are on to something. Connery and Slater visit a part of the monastery known as "The Scriptorium," where manuscripts are painstakingly copied by several monks under the baleful eye of Prechtel. Also in that sanctuary is Chaliapin (son of the famous opera singer), a blind, frail man who will not allow any laughter in the room believing that it harms the soul and creates doubt. (Chaliapin's character is Jorge de Burgos, an obvious reference to the blind Argentine writer Jorge Luis Borges, who once wrote a story set in a library which contained "every book that was ever written.") Vargas is a sensuous peasant woman who is starving, and has come to the monastery to offer her body in return for food. When she meets the teenage Slater, she goes about luring him to her bed. The poverty-stricken Franciscans enter the monastery and offer their tithes to Qualtinger, who accepts them with a wave of his hand and a by-rote blessing. Connery and Slater continue their investigation as more deaths occur. Connery feels that the answer to the murders may be in a library in a tower that is off-limits to everyone, but he is forbidden entry by Lonsdale. Abraham (making a late appearance in the film when one considers that he was paid $750,000 for his labors) is about to arrive. He is the official Inquisitor and a man who thinks the devil is behind anything evil that happens. He and Connery are old enemies and if Abraham alleges that Connery is in league with Satan, that could mean the end of the monk's life. Connery and Slater make their way into one secret room after another, discovering thousands of rare books that the world no longer believed existed. The two roam the area and become lost, but Slater calls upon his recollection of Greek mythology (the minotaur and the maze) to lead them back to the outside. The Dominicans, along with Abraham, arrive in all their finery. When Vargas and a hunchback monk, Perlman, are caught together by Abraham's private Gestapo, they are quickly convicted of engaging in Beelzebubian activities and sentenced to death by fire. Connery and Slater can do nothing to stop the madness in Abraham's eyes. Now Habeck, the assistant to Prechtel, is found dead and the same stain appears on his finger. Next, Abraham tortures Qualtinger and Perlman until, to save further pain, they confess to crimes they did not commit. Connery is accused of being a heretic and when Prechtel is murdered, the charge of killing him is added to Connery's list of crimes. The flames are being kindled for the burning at the stake of all concerned when Connery and Slater go back to the library and finally uncover the truth. It seems that Chaliapin had put poison ink on the pages of a Greek comedy. Rather than destroy the famous book, he desired to destroy the men who read it and laughed. And so it happened that all of the readers (and laughers) died with a smile on their lips and poison on their fingers (which they must have put to their mouths for page-turning). Chaliapin sets fire to the library and Connery saves the book for humanity as the picture ends. There is never a decision as to whether or not the church should forego the riches it has accumulated (a short visit to the Vatican will show anyone the outcome).

At two hours and 10 minutes, this is slow-going. Delli Colli's cameras seem to have been covered with dark filters because there are times when it is almost impossible to discern what's going on. The monks are the ugliest cusses anyone has ever seen, sort of a cross between players in a Federico Fellini picture and the entire cast of Tod Browning's FREAKS. The monastery for this $18 million production was Kloster Eberbach, near Frankfurt. It was built in 1145 with additions in 1250. Other scenes were shot near Rome, where there was so much noise from traffic, both on land and overhead, that the crew had to spend 10 days looping lines in a studio. Lots of gore and a panoply of accents coming from France, New York, Russia, Scotland, Chile, England, and more and more. The fire at the monastery library was accomplished by special effects and seven cameras shooting simultaneously. Odd that Abraham, who was making his first movie since his Oscar-winning role as Salieri in AMADEUS, would choose this role. It wasn't large but it did pay all that money and since Abraham's other job is teaching at Brooklyn College (he never left the old neighborhood), we might suppose he needs the money. The film is a disappointment when one considers all of the talent involved. Because of the blood and some explicit sexual moments between Vargas and Slater, parents would be well-advised to rent a Disney tape rather than take any children to see this. Birkin, one of the quartet of writers, also appears as a Franciscan. He is no stranger to acting, having portrayed the movie husband of his real-life sister, Jane in LA PIRATE in 1984.

p, Bernd Eichinger; d, Jean-Jacques Annaud; w, Andrew Birkin, Gerard Brach, Howard Franklin, Alain Godard; ph, Tonino Delli Colli (Technicolor); m, James Horner; ed, Jane Seitz; prod d, Dante Ferretti; art d, Giorgio Giovannini, Rainer Schaper; set d, Francesca Lo Schiavo; cos, Gabriella Pescucci; spec eff, Andriano Pischiutta; makeup, Hasso Von Hugo; stunts, Sergio Mioni.

Mystery   **Cas.**   **(PR:C-O MPAA:R)**

NANOU†   (1986, Brit./Fr.) 110m Umbrella/Arion c

Imogen Stubbs *(Nanou)*, Jean-Philippe Ecoffey *(Luc)*, Christophe Lidon *(Jacques)*, Daniel Day Lewis *(Max)*, Valentine Pelca, Roger Ibanez.

A debut feature from Templeman which stars Stubbs as a pretty young Englishwoman who travels around Europe before settling in France with the politically radical Ecoffey. Before long she has become mixed up with Ecoffey's militant friends and their terrorist attempt to derail a train. Eventually she sees Ecoffey for what he really is—a loser caught up in a lost generation—and decides to leave him. In a small role is Daniel Day Lewis, the costar of this year's MY BEAUTIFUL LAUNDRETTE.

p, Simon Perry; d&w, Conny Templeman; ph, Martin Fuhrer (Kay-MGM Color); m, John Kean; ed, Tom Preistley; prod d, Andrew Mollo.

Drama (PR:NR MPAA:NR)

NAS CLOVEK†
(1986, Yugo.) Viba c (Trans: Our Man)

Boris Juh, Ales Valic, Ivo Ban, Miranda Caharija, Boris Kralj, Vesna Jevnikar.

d, Joze Pogacnik; w, Janez Pavse; ph, Janez Verovsek; m, Bojan Adamic; set d, Mirko Lipuzic.

NATIVE SON**½
(1986) 112m Diane Silver-American Playhouse-Cinetudes/Cinecom c

Carroll Baker *(Mrs. Dalton)*, Akosua Busia *(Bessie)*, Matt Dillon *(Jan)*, Art Evans *(Doc)*, John Karlen *(Max)*, Victor Love *(Bigger Thomas)*, Elizabeth McGovern *(Mary Dalton)*, John McMartin *(Mr. Dalton)*, Geraldine Page *(Peggy)*, Willard E. Pugh *(Gus)*, David Rasche *(Buckley)*, Lane Smith *(Britton)*, Oprah Winfrey *(Mrs. Thomas)*.

The second film version of black author Richard Wright's brilliant and important novel *Native Son* is even more frustrating than the first—a 1951 low-budget production featuring Wright himself in the lead—for it misses the mark again. Produced on a shoestring budget ($2.4 million) by independent producer Diane Silver, the film stars Love, in his film debut, as the discouraged, inarticulate, frustrated, and deeply angry young black man Bigger Thomas. Set in Chicago in the 1930s, the film opens as Love, his little brother and sister, and their mother, Winfrey, awaken to the cold reality of South Side slum living. A rat has infested the tiny apartment and Love kills it with an iron skillet. At breakfast, Winfrey pushes Love into following up on a job that was offered him: working as a chauffeur for a rich, white, liberal family in the exclusive Hyde Park area. Love reluctantly promises that he will, but instead goes off to the local pool hall where he plans an armed robbery with his friends. The robbery never materializes and Love finally goes to see about the job. He is greeted in the huge mansion by the owner, McMartin, who immediately hires him. Love meets McMartin's wife (Baker), who is blind, and the cook, Page. Page prattles on about how the family goes out of their way to help "his" people, and she feeds Love the best meal he's had in months. She then shows him to his quarters—a room to himself that is almost as big as the apartment he shares with his family.

His first night on duty, Love is told to drive McMartin's impetuous daughter, McGovern, to her evening class at the University of Chicago. Once in the car, McGovern contradicts her father's instructions and tells Love to drive downtown. He reluctantly obeys and finds himself parked in front of a Communist meeting hall. McGovern returns with her boy friend, Dillon, a young, idealistic Communist who insists that he drive and that all three of them ride in the front seat. Eager to prove how open-minded and liberal they are, Dillon and McGovern ask the uneasy Love all sorts of personal questions and insist on eating where he eats—at a South Side all-black restaurant. Love is ashamed and embarrassed by the experience, and becomes increasingly angry at the couple's patronizing attitudes—although he represses his rage. By the time Love gets McGovern home, the girl is extremely drunk. Not wanting to get in trouble for disobeying McMartin's orders, Love carries the drunk girl to her bedroom. Once in the bedroom, McGovern drunkenly flirts with the black chauffeur. Love allows himself to respond, but at that moment McGovern's blind mother enters the room. Panic stricken at being caught in an white girl's bedroom and guilty for even thinking sexually about McGovern, Love covers the drunken girl's face with a pillow to keep her quiet while Baker stands at the door calling for her. After what seems like an eternity to Love, Baker is satisfied that there is no one in the room and leaves. Love removes the pillow from McGovern's face, and to his horror discovers that she is dead. Knowing that he will surely be hanged for rape and murder, Love attempts to cover up the death by stuffing McGovern's body into her trunk (which he is supposed to deliver to the train station in the morning—McGovern was to go on a trip the next day) and then taking it down to the basement. He crams the corpse into the house's huge furnace and covers it with coal. The next morning he takes the empty trunk to the train station as scheduled and acts as if nothing had happened.

The family worries when there is no sign of McGovern. Finally the police are called in and when Love is questioned, he implicates Dillon, knowing that Dillon's Communist activity would certainly make him a suspect. Love then goes even further by faking a ransom note from Dillon. When word gets out, the mansion is besieged by reporters. Not wanting the house overrun, Baker orders the newspapermen into the basement to wait for her husband's statement. When the furnace begins to malfunction, a reporter notices bones among the ashes. Love panics and flees. Soon a manhunt closes in around Love and he is arrested. In jail, Love finds that Dillon (who has learned the truth about the murder) remains sympathetic to his plight and helps him by arranging for a lawyer to defend him. Although McMartin and Baker also feel for Love's plight (and are subjected to an unbearably hammy scene of Winfrey begging for mercy on her son), they decide to let justice run its course. Predictably, Love is found guilty and sentenced to death. With the end of his life tangibly close, the sullen Love suddenly becomes articulate about his life and fate in a conversation with his lawyer, and faces death with a new perspective.

Although producer Silver worked passionately to get her meager production financed through complicated financial arrangements with Cinecom, American Playhouse, and Vestron Video, she diluted the power of Richard Wright's novel by insisting on changing key elements of the story. In the novel, Bigger is forced to decapitate Mary so that her body will fit in the furnace (the omission of this aspect of the scene is understandable). Later, when he's on the run with his girl friend Bessie, Bigger worries that she might give him away and then murders her in a fit of paranoia. Silver worried, and justifiably so, that if those scenes remained in the film there would be no way an audience could sympathize with

Bigger (director Freedman objected strongly about the latter omission). While this may be true, it totally destroys the power and honesty of Wright's concept. In his foreword "How Bigger Was Born," Wright states that he didn't want the reader to have the "consolation of tears" regarding Bigger. Where readers can forgive the accidental killing of Mary Dalton, they cannot ignore the cruel, calculated murder of Bessie. Bessie's murder illustrates just how much hatred, frustration, and rage there is inside Bigger, and how society's victim can become a victimizer. Wright wasn't interested in sympathy for Bigger; what he wanted was an understanding of the elements that formed such an "animal" (Wright's description). Silver had the perfect opportunity to do Wright's powerful, honest, and frightening vision justice—with the same budget, cast, and crew—but she backed off and instead opted for a safe, middle-of-the-road, sympathetic portrayal that shows Bigger as a victim only. To her credit, Silver and her crew performed miracles on the limited budget. The film has a strong sense of time and place (although Chicago residents will notice a few of the modern Chicago Housing Authority housing projects visible in the background) and the cast is quite good. Love is fine in a complicated role, though one wonders what he would have done if allowed to explore the more distasteful aspects of the character. Page, McMillan, and Baker turn in solid performances, and McGovern and Dillon are surprisingly good (their scenes with Love being the finest in the film). The movie is at its best while setting up the events that lead to the murder (the Daltons' thoughtlessly condescending liberalism, Bigger's uneasiness and anger), but it retreats into sentiment once the murder is committed and disintegrates into a lot of hanky-wringing speeches about racism, mercy, and justice (Winfrey unabashedly chews the scenery for maximum heart-tugging impact). Ultimately, the film fails because of Silver's fears of offending the audience, the same fear that Wright himself faced and overcame, he writes in "How Bigger Was Born": "The more I thought of it the more I became convinced that if I did not write of Bigger as I saw and felt him, if I did not try to make him a living personality and at the same time a symbol of all larger things I felt and saw in him, I'd be reacting as Bigger himself had reacted: that is, I'd be acting out of *fear* if I let what I thought whites would say constrict and paralyze me."

p, Diane Silver; d, Jerrold Freedman; w, Richard Wesley (based on the novel by Richard Wright); ph, Thomas Burstyn; m, James Mtume; ed, Aaron Stell; prod d, Stephen Marsh; m/l, James Mtume, Diane Silver.

Drama Cas. (PR:C MPAA:PG)

NATTSEILERE†
(1986, Nor.) 110m Norsk-NRK-TV/Norsk c (Trans: Night Voyage)

Vera Holte *(Girl from the Sea)*, Helge Jordal *(Borr)*, Frode Rasmussen *(Olai)*, Katja Medboe *(Andrea)*, Per Oscarsson *(Wieth)*, Kalle Oeby *(Jeppe)*, Sigmund Saverud *(Provincial Governor)*.

Following a shipwreck, Holte reaches shore suffering from amnesia. Vagabond Jordal helps her find her own people, even though he's being hunted by the law.

p, Svein H. Toreg; d, Tor M. Torstad; w, Ivar Enoksen; ph, Svein Krovel (Eastmancolor); m, Geir Bohren, Bent Aserud; ed, Edith Toreg.

Comedy/Adventure (PR:NR MPAA:NR)

NAVRAT JANA PETRU†
(1986, Czech.) Koliba c (Trans: Jan Petru's Return)

Milan Knazko, Marek Tapak, Emilia Zimkova.

d, Martin Tapak; w, Igor Rusnak; ph, Vladimir Ondrus.

NEBYVALSHINA†
(1986, USSR) 83m Lenfilm Studios c (Trans: Impossible Things)

Aleksandr Kuznetzov *(Neznam)*, Aleksei Buldakov *(Soldier)*, Sergei Bekhterev *(Bobyl)*.

Using Russian folk tales as its source, this film tells the story of a country bumpkin who, after being rejected by his girl friend, takes to wandering the countryside. The film recounts his misadventures as he pairs up with a crafty soldier, meets an inventor, and visits hell.

d&w, Sergei Ovcharov; ph, Valery Fedosov; m, I. Matzievsky; ed, I. Tarsonova; art d, Victor Amelchekov.

Children's/Fantasy (PR:A MPAA:NR)

NEM TUDO E VERDADE†
(1986, Braz.) 95m Rogerio Sganzerla Cinematograficas c-bw (Trans: Not Everything Is True)

Arrigo Barnabe *(Orson Welles)*, Grande Otelo, Helena Ignez, Nina de Padua, Mariana de Maraes, Vania Magalhaes, Abrao Farc, Otavio Terceiro, Gudra, Jose Marinho, Geraldo Francisco, Mario Cravo, Nonato Freire.

An odd docu-drama that fictionalizes Orson Welles' 1942 visit to Brazil and his attempt to make a film called IT'S ALL TRUE, which was never released. In this picture Brazilian actor Barnabe portrays Welles as he wanders through the South American country meeting with people and making his film. This is intercut with footage from CITIZEN KANE and TOUCH OF EVIL, interviews with people who knew Welles, and radio shows that he broadcast. Perhaps not coincidentally, Paramount Pictures discovered in its vaults 300 reels of Welles' missing footage from IT'S ALL TRUE just after NEM TUDO E VERDADE was completed.

p,d&w, Rogerio Sganzerla; ph, Jose Madeiros, Edson Santos, Edson Batista, Carlos Alberto Ebert, Afonso Viana, Vitor Diniz; m, Joao Gilberto; ed, Severino Dada, Denise Fontoura.

Docu-drama (PR:NR MPAA:NR)

NEMESIO†   (1986, Chile) 80m Cristian Lorca B. Producciones/Compania
Cinematografica Nacional c

Andres del Bosque *(Nemesio)*, Marcela Medel, Hugo Medina, Ana Victoria
Mourgues, Ignacio Aguero, Douglas Hubner, Luz Jimenez, Winzlia Sepulveda,
Javier Maldonado, Faruko Abdalah, Manuel Velasco, M. Eugenia Lorca, Ro-
berto Roth, Joaquin Eyzaguirre.

Del Bosque finds his job gone when the department he heads is phased out, and
he is forced to accept an inferior position in another department. His date stands
him up, and he fails to perform during a visit to a prostitute. In his room,
though, he fantasizes about being Richard Chamberlain in TV's "Shogun".

p, Alberto Celery; d&w, Cristian Lorca; ph, Humberto Castagnola; m, Payo
Grondona; ed, Jorge Valenzuela.

Drama   **(PR:NR   MPAA:NR)**

NENI SIROTEK JAKO SIROTEK†   (1986, Czech.) 79m Barrandov c

Ondrej Havelka *(Spevacek)*, Vlastimil Brodsky *(Klofac)*, Robert Vrchota
(Mosazny), Radoslava Bohacova *(Kamila)*, Jana Nagyova *(Jitka)*, Josef Blaha
(Zalud), Ludmila Roubikova *(Landova)*, Vladimir Hlavaty *(Rajman)*, Karel
Vochoc *(Hores)*, Ladislav Potmesil *(Oves)*, Eva Kudlackova *(Verunka)*, Jiri Kuc-
era *(Vavra)*, Milan Simacek *(Landa)*, David Hlasovi, Daniel Hlasovi *(Twins)*.

d, Stanislav Strnad; w, Karel Cop, Josef Pohl, V.A. Sekyrova; ph, Jiri Tarantik;
m, Ladislav Staidl; ed, Miroslav Hajek; art d, Karel Cerny; cos, Jan Kropacek.

NEON MANIACS*   (1986) 91m Cimmaron/Bedford Entertainment c

Allan Hayes *(Steven)*, Leilani Sarelle *(Nathalie)*, Donna Locke *(Paula)*, Victor
Elliot Brandt *(Devin)*.

A very silly little science fiction/horror film which sees a bunch of cheap-looking
monsters with guns invade San Francisco. Where these monsters come from is
anybody's guess since the filmmakers felt it unnecessary to provide an explanation, but they appear nonetheless and slaughter some San Francisco teenagers.
One girl, Sarelle, survives the attack but, of course, local law-enforcement officers refuse to believe that armed monsters have arrived to wreak havoc. Luckily
her boy friend, Hayes, does believe her fantastic tale and they enlist the aid of
Locke—a talented teen who owns her own video equipment—to help them track
down the monsters. Eventually the teens discover that the monsters are defenseless against plain old water and soon half the citizens are armed with water pistols
to defend themselves. Finally able to convince police that the creatures exist, the
teens lead the law to the monster's hideout where the creatures are hosed down.
    This one is amateur-hour all the way. From the silly costumes to the truly
incompetent acting, NEON MANIACS must have been somebody's idea of a
joke. Director Mangine tries hard to evoke the science fiction and horror films of
the 1950s, but he fails at every turn (none of the films that Mangine is trying to
pay homage to ran 90 minutes!). For the undiscriminating there is a bit of quirky
charm to the whole affair, but aside from a precious few laughs, most of the film
is difficult to sit through.

p, Steven Mackler, Chris Arnold; d, Joseph Mangine; w, Mark Patrick Carducci;
ph, Joseph Mangine, Oliver Wood (Cinema Color); m, Kendall Schmidt; ed,
Timothy Snell; art d, Katherine Vallin; cos, Joseph Porro; spec eff, Image
Engineering; makeup, Allan A. Apone, Douglas J. White.

Science Fiction/Horror   **(PR:O   MPAA:R)**

NEVER TOO YOUNG TO DIE∗∗½   (1986) 92m Paul Entertainment c

John Stamos *(Lance Stargrove)*, Vanity *(Danja Deering)*, Gene Simmons *(Velvet
Von Ragner/Carruthers)*, George Lazenby *(Drew Stargrove)*, Peter Kwong
(Cliff), Ed Brock *(Pyramid)*, John Anderson *(Arliss)*, Robert Englund *(Riley)*,
Tara Buckman *(Sacrificed Punkette)*, Chris Taylor *(Barton)*, Jon Greene *(Coach
Madsen)*, Tim Colceri *(Grady)*, John Miranda *(Mr. Wilder)*, Patrick Wright
(Exploding Biker), Art Payton *(Minister)*, Gary F. Kasper *(Wrestler)*, Ivar
Mireles *(Waitress)*, Randy Hall *(Minkie)*, Branscombe Richmond *(Minkie's
Partner)*.

Imagine an amalgam of THE ROAD WARRIOR, GYMKATA, James Bond
films, and THE ROCKY HORROR PICTURE SHOW and you'll have NEVER
TOO YOUNG TO DIE, an often hysterically funny action film which happily
doesn't take itself very seriously. Simmons (from the rock group Kiss) is a
leather-clad hermaphrodite rock 'n' rolling ruler of a renegade biker throng. They
hope to poison the city's water supply with radiation, but a computer floppy
disc—the vital link in this nefarious scheme—has been stolen. At a nearby boarding school, Stamos sits chatting with his ingenious roommate Kwong. Just for
kicks, Kwong likes to invent little items such as listening devices hidden in bubble
gum and flamethrower laser guns (you just *know* these things are going to pop up
somewhere down the road). Stamos tells Kwong that his father (Lazenby) won't
be arriving for the school's Parents' Day because of his important work for
international oil companies. Little does Stamos realize that Lazenby is actually a
super secret agent for the U.S. government. Lazenby has caught on to Simmons'
plans, but is killed in an attempt to stop the mad fiend. At the instant of
Lazenby's death, Stamos—who is participating in a gymnastics tournament—
takes a bad tumble. Stamos is told Lazenby died in an auto wreck, but the young
man refuses to fall for this ruse. After learning that he has inherited Lazenby's
farm, Stamos goes to look at the property and there meets Vanity, his father's
former assistant. She is evasive about Lazenby's real work, but when some of
Simmons' henchmen arrive to do Vanity in, Stamos finds himself swept up in the
fray. After they successfully fight off the bad guys, Vanity tells Stamos not to get
involved. There wouldn't be much of a movie if that happened, so Stamos tails

Vanity when she leaves the house that evening. They end up in a biker nightclub
(which employs the same sets from the bar in 1984's STREETS OF FIRE) with
even more bizarre patrons than those who surprised Luke Skywalker in STAR
WARS' bar scene. Simmons is the star attraction, and much to the delight of his/
her fans, sings "It Takes a Man Like Me to Be a Woman Like Me." Afterwards
Stamos goes to Simmons' dressing room, pretending to ask for an autograph,
while he secretly plants one of Kwong's chewing-gum bugs. Simmons recognizes
Stamos as Lazenby's son, though Stamos denies the connection. When Stamos
returns to his motorcycle, he is pushed around by a drunken thug. Good thing
too, for the bike has been wired to explode, and Stamos is miraculously spared
when the motorcycle is stolen. The next day, Stamos demands some answers from
Vanity. He still doesn't get much out of her, but Stamos' involvement in these
increasingly strange events grows deeper. Vanity is captured by Simmons' thugs,
but Stamos manages to fight them off time and again, using his well-developed
gymnastic skills. After finding a hidden room in the farmhouse, Stamos learns of
Lazenby's true nature. During this moment of revelation, Stamos is surprised by
Kwong, who has arrived with a new arsenal of homemade gadgets. He also has
the secret floppy disc, which, it turns out, Lazenby had sent to Stamos in an
unassuming box of groceries. The boys rescue Vanity, then retreat to a secret
hideout where they are watched by government agents. The inevitable finally
takes place when Vanity seduces Stamos (one of the film's funniest sequences),
then the two set off to finish this adventure. It turns out that Vanity's superior is
actually Simmons in disguise and the couple is brought to Simmons' fortress.
Stamos repels hordes of biker baddies, then the young adventurer confronts
Simmons near the water reservoir. Having gotten access to the disc, Simmons has
set everything in motion to poison the water supply. "Don't you see the greatness
in me," he sneers at Stamos. "I'm female and male. Man and woman. I'm *better*
than you are!" Stamos, cool as a cucumber, nonchalantly replies: "Yeah, but
don't you understand something? You're only half of each. I'm a whole man, so
if you'll excuse me, I don't have a lot of time here. I've got to save the world." A
struggle ensues, but Stamos tricks Simmons and sends him hurtling to his death.
Next, with only seconds to go, he destroys the computer programmed to dump
the radioactivity into the water, thus saving the city from a horrible fate. He,
Kwong, and Vanity are reunited and, in the best of movie traditions, go riding off
into the sunset.
    There's no point to any of this other than simply having fun. It's like a comic
book come to life, complete with colorful villains, mindless violence, nifty gadgets, sparse logic, and some wonderfully silly dialog. Stamos plays his part well,
never attempting to go beyond the bounds of his deliberately stereotyped character. Vanity is pleasing in her often sensual performance, and Kwong gives enthusiastic support in his role. Lazenby enjoys some self-parody in his cameo part
(he's a better agent here than in his one-shot Bond appearance in ON HER
MAJESTY'S SECRET SERVICE), but Simmons is the real star of the show.
Paul Newman may have won the Oscar in 1986 for Best Actor, but it's unlikely he
had as much fun in THE COLOR OF MONEY as Simmons does in NEVER
TOO YOUNG TO DIE. Looking like a cross between Lainie Kazan and Divine,
Simmons gives new meaning to the word camp, playing up the character's outlandish nature with unashamed zeal. Between the seductive glances and the maniacal laugh, it's hard not to enjoy Simmons' constant scene stealing. The script is
inventive in a ridiculous sort of way (cowriter Semple also worked on the Bond
film NEVER SAY NEVER AGAIN, among other big-budget films) and
Bettman's direction often sparks with an engaging sense of energy. The film is
not without its faults, particularly a few amateurish jump cuts and choppy editing
glitches, along with some slow spots in the plot's development. Still, these
problems are tolerable and well overshadowed by the film's outrageous frolicking. You could see better-made movies that aren't nearly as entertaining as
NEVER TOO YOUNG TO DIE. Songs include: "Stay and Burn" (Jon Voight,
Chip Taylor, Ralph Lane, Iren Koster, performed by Ralph E. Boy, Major
Catastrophe), "Stargrove" (Chip Taylor, Ralph Lane, Michael Kingsley, Iren

Koster, performed by Tommie Lee Bradley), "I'll Find You" (Chip Taylor, Ralph Lane, Michael Kingsley, performed by Minor Messages), "Spotlight" (Chip Taylor, Ralph Lane, Michael Kingsley, performed by Minor Messages), "Fire Up the Night" (Chip Taylor, Ralph Lane, Michael Kingsley, Iren Koster, performed by Deedee Bellson), "Never Too Young to Die" (Iren Koster, performed by Koster).

p, Steven Paul; d, Gil Bettman; w, Lorenzo Semple, Steven Paul, Anton Fritz, Gil Bettman (based on a story by Stuart Paul, Steven Paul); ph, David Worth (Metrocolor); ed, Bill Anderson, Paul Seydor, Ned Humphreys; prod d, Dale Allan Pelton; art d, Dean Tschetter, Michelle Starbuck; set d, Deborah K. Evans, Carol Westcott; cos, Fred Long; spec eff, Roger George; m/l, Jon Voight, Chip Taylor, Ralph Lane, Iren Koster, Michael Kingsley; makeup, Michael Spatola.

Action/Spy   **Cas.**   **(PR:O MPAA:R)**

NEW DELHI TIMES†   (1986, India) 123m P.K. Communication Private c

Shashi Kapoor, Sharmila Tagore, Om Puri, Kulbhushan Kharbanda, Manohar Singh, A.K. Hangal.

The corrupt side of an important political figure is uncovered by hard-working newspaper editor Kapoor, whose investigative efforts connect a top government official to murder, drug trafficking, and a number of other illegal activities. NEW DEHLI TIMES was slated to appear on Indian TV, but was withdrawn at the last minute because of its controversial themes. Director Sharma won the A.M. Brousil Award for Best First Film at the Karlovy Vary Film Festival. Before entering the film industry, Sharma worked as journalist in Montreal.

p, P.K. Tewari; d, Ramesh Sharma; w, Gulzar; ph, Subrata Mitra; m, Louis Banks; ed, Rene Saluja; art d, Nitish Roy, Samir Chandra.

Crime/Drama   **(PR:C MPAA:NR)**

NEW MORNING OF BILLY THE KID, THE†   (1986, Jap.) 109m
                                            Parco–VAP c (AKA: NEW KID 21)

Hiroshi Mikami *(Billy the Kid)*, Kimie Shingyoji *(Sharlotte Rampling)*, Shigeru Muroi *(Nakajima Miyuki)*, Renji Ishibashi *(Master)*.

Another entry from one of a new crop of young Japanese directors (which includes Sogo Ishii, the director of THE CRAZY FAMILY), THE NEW MORN-ING OF BILLY THE KID is an eclectic mish-mash of Japanese and American cultures. The film takes place in a Tokyo bar called Schlachtenhaus (Slaughter-house)—a last holdout for civilization—and stars Mikami as Billy the Kid, who emerges from a painted backdrop of Monument Valley (the Utah location of John Ford's great westerns). He works there as a waiter along with a strange crowd of folks, including a youth named Ryan and his girl friend Tatum (a reference to the acting O'Neals), an all-girl rock band called Zelda, a dishwasher named Marx Engels, a samurai warrior, and a trio of gang members who use the names Sharlotte Rampling, Bluce Springsteen, and Hurry Carahan (the Japanese pronunciation of Clint Eastwood's DIRTY HARRY character). Eventually a shootout erupts in the bar which leaves almost everyone dead. It's all rather chaotic and apocalyptic but there is definitely a cinematic energy in director Yamakawa to be reckoned with. (In Japanese; English subtitles.)

p, Akira Morishige; d, Naoto Yamakawa; w, Naoto Yamakawa, Genichiro Takahashi; ph, Kenji Takama; m, Shuichi Chino; ed, Kan Suzuki.

Comedy   **(PR:NR MPAA:NR)**

NEXT OF KIN   (SEE: PARENTAL CLAIM)

NEXT SUMMER†   (1986, Fr.) 100m Sara/European Classics (L'ETE
                                                            PROCHAIN)

Fanny Ardant *(Dino)*, Jean-Louis Trintignant *(Paul)*, Claudia Cardinale *(Jeanne)*, Philippe Noiret *(Edouard)*, Marie Trintignant *(Sidonie)*, Jerome Ange *(Jude)*.

The lives and loves of three generations of French women are examined in this tale directed by Nadine Trintignant. The film centers on Cardinale, a mother in her late forties, her eldest daughter, Ardant, in her early thirties, and Marie Trintignant (the director's daughter) as the 20-year-old youngest daughter. The three women are brought together after a long separation when Noiret, the family patriarch, falls seriously ill. While each of the women must cope with the pressure of Noiret's illness, they each also have their own personal problems. Cardinale is faced with the fact that her husband, Noiret, has been unfaithful, as does Ardant, who discovers her husband, Trintignant (Jean-Louis, the director's husband), in bed with another woman. In the meantime, the young Trintignant, a budding concert pianist, must constantly battle her crippling stage fright. Released in France in 1984 and not shown here until this year, NEXT SUMMER is Trintignant's eighth film as a director. (In French; English subtitles.)

p, Alain Sarde; d&w, Nadine Trintignant; ph, William Lubtchansky; m, Phillipe Sarde; ed, Marie-Josephe Yoyotte.

Drama   **(PR:O MPAA:NR)**

'NIGHT, MOTHER*½**   (1986) 96m UNIV c

Sissy Spacek *(Jessie Cates)*, Anne Bancroft *(Thelma Cates)*, Ed Berke *(Dawson Cates)*, Carol Robbins *(Loretta Cates)*, Jennifer Roosendahl *(Melodie Cates)*, Michael Kenworthy *(Kenny Cates)*, Sari Walker *(Agnes Fletcher)*.

Deceptively complex, this adaptation of the 1983 Pulitzer Prize winner hews closely to the grim line of the stage play and seldom compromises. It's early evening in a small house in the Midwest. Spacek, a woman in her late 30's, is

going about what seems to be a normal state of affairs, as though she is about to take a trip. She winds the clocks, cleans the refrigerator, cancels the newspaper delivery, packs and labels her clothes for the Salvation Army, and does a few other chores. Then, after only 10 minutes or so have elapsed, she tells her mother,

Bancroft, that she is going to kill herself later that evening. Spacek is an epileptic; she has an ex-husband and a son who is on his way to becoming a criminal. The only person she ever loved, her father, has died and now she is living with her mother. Her life has spun out of control and it appears that she is about to take the only step which she can dictate by ending it. Spacek's epilepsy has caused her to be unable to work, and to exhibit a mild case of agoraphobia, inasmuch as she never leaves the house. (The picture hardly leaves the house, as well.)

As the drama unfolds—in the same amount of time on screen as in the viewer's life—sympathy shifts from Spacek to Bancroft and back again. Although Spacek is matter-of-fact about her decision, Bancroft, at first, doesn't believe it and thinks her leg is being pulled. The drama continues and Bancroft, using a south-ern accent to match Texan Spacek, becomes frightened, then angry, then at-tempts to divert Spacek's mind to another place with aimless conversation. Meanwhile, Spacek is continuing her plans, choosing which gun to use (her dad's or her former husband's; she chooses daddy's), writing up a list of Christmas gifts that her brother might buy Bancroft in the next few years, etc. It appears that Spacek is almost delighted in the way she is manipulating Bancroft, and one has the feeling that her upcoming suicide is little more than an act of vengeance. The dialog covers some background on Spacek's marriage, the son she fears for, and Bancroft's admission that she never loved Spacek's father. Near the end, Spacek instructs Bancroft on what to do after her death. She's very organized in her instructions, but Bancroft still can't believe it's going to happen. When Spacek walks toward the bedroom, Bancroft steps in front of her. Spacek pushes past, locks the bedroom door and, as Bancroft shrieks and cries for Spacek to hold back, the gun goes off.

There is never any doubt that Spacek will do what she talks of early in the movie. It's just a question of when. By making her an epileptic, a frightened woman, a failed wife, and the mother of a dope addict/criminal son, the deck has

been stacked against her from the start. It's no wonder that she takes the cow-ard's way out. Casting Spacek in the role created on stage by Kathy Bates was wrong, but they needed a name like hers (she is, after all, a multi-Oscar nominee and won the statuette for COAL MINER'S DAUGHTER) to make the movie. She is far too healthy, radiant, and tough to make us believe she is who Marsha Norman (who wrote the play and the screenplay) says she is. The fact that Spacek and Bancroft look as much like mother and daughter as, let's say, Lana and Tina Turner, is another mistake, although Bancroft's excellent mimicking of Spacek's twang helps the credibility somewhat. Kathy Bates is not a movie name but she is a wonderful actress and her Broadway performance as the chubby yet frail daughter is etched in the memory of anyone who saw it. The same holds true for

Anne Pitoniak as the mother. Co-executive producer Byck was the stage producer and director Moore was the play's director. He makes a fairly good debut in a difficult task because the play was seen in one room and he opted to keep it simple. This necessitates having to use the camera perhaps a bit too snakingly as it darts quickly around the various rooms of the house. Spacek and Bancroft have the only speaking roles but we get a glimpse of some of the other family members so the picture shouldn't feel totally stagebound, which it is.

Norman's script had many levels, switching sympathies for both actresses at the turn of a phrase. It is to her credit that it works. The play was first seen in Massachusetts at Cambridge in 1982; then it went to Broadway in late March, 1983. A brace of Tony nominations, the Pulitzer, and several other awards soon put Norman on the cover of *Time* magazine with a few other contemporary playwrights. Since the play has only two characters, it is a perfect piece for small theaters. And because it is easily translatable, it has been seen in more than 30 countries. The unlikely producer of the filmed version was Aaron Spelling, television's king of mental chewing gum, and there was some worry that he might alter the play's philosophy to a more commercial stance. Most people don't realize that Spelling began as a writer—and a fairly good writer at that—and is a man who, like Steven Spielberg (his speech at the 1986 Oscar awards stated his views on the importance of writers in the most eloquent fashion), believes in the written word, so the intent of the play (and its power) has not been dulled. It was shot in sequence for 35 days on stage 19 at Universal. Everyone worked for far less than they usually earn. Spacek's price is $1 million, and she took $300,000. Bancroft accepted one-third her customary fee and Moore worked for Directors Guild scale (a bit less than $100,000). Everyone else of importance deferred their fees in the hope of a large profit participation. Chances are against that, as the picture is apparently too intense for the tense times. Even though it's rated PG-13, we'd advise against it even for teenagers, mostly because of the teenage suicide rate which went soaring in early 1987.

p, Aaron Spelling, Alan Greisman; d, Tom Moore; w, Marsha Norman (based on her play); ph, Steven M. Katz (DeLuxe Color); m, David Shire; ed, Suzanne Pettit; prod d, Jack De Govia; art d, John R. Jensen; set d, Bonnie Dermer; cos, Bob Blackman; makeup, Brenda Todd.

Drama **(PR:C MPAA:PG-13)**

NIGHT OF THE CREEPS** (1986) 85m Tri-Star c

Jason Lively *(Chris Romero)*, Jill Whitlow *(Cynthia Cronenberg)*, Tom Atkins *(Ray Cameron)*, Steve Marshall *(J.C. Hooper)*, Wally Taylor *(Detective Landis)*, Bruce Solomon *(Sgt. Raimi)*, Vic Polizos *(Coroner)*, Allan J. Kayser *(Brad)*, Ken Heron *(Johnny)*, Alice Cadogan *(Pam)*, June Harris *(Karen)*, David Paymer *(Young Scientist)*, David Oliver *(Steve)*, Evelyne Smith *(House Mother)*, Ivan E. Roth *(Psycho Zombie)*, Daniel Frishman *(Alien Zombie)*, Kevin Thompson, Joseph S. Griffo *(Alien Pursuers)*; 1959: Katherine Britton *(Sorority Girl on Phone)*, Leslie Ryan *(Sorority Girl with Hairbrush)*, Dave Alan Johnson *(Young Roy Cameron)*; The Kappa Deltas: Suzanne Snyder *(Lisa)*, Jay Wakemann *(Judy)*, Elizabeth Cox *(Kathy)*, Emily Fiola *(Jennifer)*; The Betas: Russell Moss *(Biff)*, Richard DeHaven *(Dick)*, John J. York *(Todd)*, Jim Townsend *(Chett)*; The Police: Tex Donaldson *(Cop Outside Sorority)*, Jay Arlen Jones *(Cop at Police Station)*, Craig Schaefer *(Irksome Cop at Cryogenics Lab)*, Richard Sassin *(Irksome Cop at Murder Scene)*, Robert Kerman *(Policeman with Searchlight)*, Jack Lightsy *(Patrol Car Driver)*, Elizabeth Alda *(Cop in Alley)*; The Beta Zombies: David B. Miller, Earl Ellis, Arick Stillwagon, Robert Kurtzman, Ted Rae, Keith Werle, Howard Berger, Beal Carrotes; Robert Kino *(Mr. Miner)*, Todd Bryant *(Informative Student)*, Dawn Schroder *(Sorority Girl at Squad Car)*, Chris Dekker, Brian MacGregor *(Dormies)*, Dick Miller *(Police Armorer)*.

A clever debut film from young writer/director Fred Dekker that combines science fiction, horror, and comedy into a fairly entertaining package. A tiny hairless alien creature runs through a huge spaceship clutching a metal canister. Two other aliens armed with ray-guns pursue the first in an attempt to prevent their quarry from jettisoning the canister into space. They fail.

Sorority Row, 1959—A young college couple parked on lovers' lane watch as the canister plummets to Earth like a meteor. The boy grabs a flashlight and looks for the spot where the "meteor" has landed. When he finds the canister it has popped open and there are large slimy slugs inside. One of the slugs suddenly zooms out of the canister and into his mouth. Meanwhile, a crazed boy with an ax murders the girl waiting in the car.

Sorority Row, 1986—Two nerdy freshmen, Lively and Marshall (who walks with the aid of crutches), roam the campus during pledge week. Lively sees a beautiful young coed, Whitlow, and falls in love. Unfortunately, she has a boy friend who belongs to the biggest fraternity on campus. To get closer to the girl, the nerds decide to pledge the frat. The fraternity brothers tell them that they cannot be accepted until they steal a cadaver from the medical building and leave it on the steps of a rival fraternity. The boys sneak into the medical building and stumble across the corpse of the boy who swallowed the space-slug in 1959 encased in a cryogenic chamber as part of an experiment. They break the corpse free of the chamber, but chicken out at the last minute and flee. Once thawed out the corpse comes to life and walks across campus to Whitlow's sorority. There its head splits apart and dozens of the slimy space-slugs slither out of the skull, moving as fast as cockroaches. As it turns out these slugs enter humans through the mouth and lay eggs in the brain (transforming the host into a zombie). When the eggs hatch the host's head splits open and the slugs scurry out searching for new hosts.

After a half dozen zombies turn up on campus, a Chandleresque police detective, Atkins, becomes obsessed with the case. Atkins was a young cop in 1959, and the girl who was ax-murdered was his former girl friend. Interested only in revenge, he killed the crazed zombie and secretly buried the body. Eventually the campus is overrun with slugs on the night of a big dance. An entire busload of fraternity brothers is victimized and these tuxedo-clad zombies then wander to the sorority to pick up their dates. Lively discovers that fire kills the slugs, so he, Atkins, and Whitlow (in her evening formal) take turns shooting zombies in the head and then scorching the slugs with a flame-thrower. Later, Atkins discovers thousands of slugs in the basement of the sorority and he douses them with gasoline, killing them and himself. Thinking the terror over, Whitlow takes the time to pet a cute little doggy, but it, too, is a zombie and spits a slug at her.

A pretty goofy combination of chills and laughs, NIGHT OF THE CREEPS is one of those hit-or-miss propositions that throws so many scares and jokes into the mix that there isn't time to ponder those that fall flat. (One of the more successful gags has the angry frat brothers confronting the two nerds after the cadaver has turned up at their girl friends' sorority: "We said the Phi Mega Gamma house, not the Kappa Delta sorority! Do you know the difference?" Lively shrugs and responds with a straight face, "It's all Greek to me.") The performances by the youths are likable enough, and Atkins is frequently amusing in an intentionally overblown performance patterned after the detectives of the 1940s. Writer/director Dekker does a good job of re-creating the sci-fi films of the 1950s during the 1959 sequence, which was filmed in black and white. Dekker deliberately cast actors who looked too old to be teenagers and instructed them to give faltering performances in order to capture the flavor of a cheap 1950s film.

The movie is filled with a variety of special effects, most of them done quite well, with the "creeps" themselves taking top honors as they slither across the ground accompanied by appropriate sound effects. A small complaint: the habit hip young genre filmmakers have of naming their characters after famous directors is getting a bit tiresome. NIGHT OF THE CREEPS has characters named after George Romero (NIGHT OF THE LIVING DEAD), David Cronenberg (THE FLY), Tobe Hooper (THE TEXAS CHAINSAW MASSACRE), Sam Raimi (THE EVIL DEAD), John Landis (AMERICAN WEREWOLF IN LONDON), Steve Miner (several FRIDAY THE 13TH films), James Cameron (THE TERMINATOR), and Wes Craven (THE HILLS HAVE EYES), with veteran Roger Corman bit player Dick Miller as a cop thrown in for good measure. It's like watching a film student's master's thesis. Dekker picked some good tunes to play in the backround and they include: "Smoke Gets in Your Eyes" (performed by The Platters), "The Stroll" (performed by The Diamonds), "Teen Beat" (performed by Sandy Nelson), "Bongo Rock" (performed by Preston Epps), "Put Your Head on My Shoulder" (performed by Paul Anka), "Let Go," "In the Wilderness," "Flame On," "Deliverance" (performed by Intimate Strangers), "Nightmares" (performed by C-Spot Run), "Blue Kiss" (performed by Jane Wiedlin), "The Big Heat," "Drive, She Said" (performed by Stan Ridgway), "Leave This Girl Alone" (performed by Loretta and the Signals), "Caught in the Crossfire" (performed by The Charm Kings), "You Got Me Thinkin' Twice" (performed by Christina Criscione).

p, Charles Gordon; d&w, Fred Dekker; ph, Robert C. New (CFI color); m, Barry DeVorzon; ed, Michael N. Knue; prod d, George Costello; art & set d, Maria Caso; cos, Eileen Kennedy; spec eff, David Stripes Productions, Dimensional Animation Effects, Ted Rae; makeup, David B. Miller.

Science Fiction **Cas.** **(PR:O MPAA:R)**

NIGHTMARE WEEKEND zero (1986, Brit./U.S./Fr.) 85m Vision Communications–English Film–G.I.G.–Les Films des Lions/Troma c

Debbie Laster *(Julie Clingstone)*, Dale Midkiff *(Ken)*, Debra Hunter *(Jessica Brake)*, Lori Lewis *(Annie)*, Preston Maybank *(Bob)*, Wellington Meffert *(Edward Brake)*, Kim Dossin *(Mary-Rose)*, Andrea Thompson *(Linda)*, Kimberly Stahl *(Pamela)*, Bruce Morton *(Tony)*, Karen Mayo *(Sue)*, Nick James *(Gary)*, Robert Burke *(Dave)*, Scott Proctor *(Ralph)*, John Sandford *(Harry)*, Joan Krosche *(Linda's Mother)*, Jason *(Doberman)*, Barbara Lee *(James Winn)*, Lori Strup *(Karl Kunz)*, Marc Pacheco *(Jack Adams)*, Tarantula *(Himself)*, George *(George)*, Dean Gates, Mark Gotlieb *(Gas Pump Attendants)*.

Genius scientist Meffert has invented a device that can—among its other accomplishments—take any personal object and change it into a silver sphere that can attack people and go down their throats, turning them into mindless, computer-controlled zombies. The benign uses he envisions for the machine are perverted when the invention is used by his evil, but beautiful, assistant (Laster), who tests it on a trio of beautiful college coeds invited to the house for the weekend. When some boys they picked up at a bar show up, they get turned into "neuropaths" as well, as does a maid who's afraid of spiders. The scientist has a nubile daughter (Hunter) who has a computer-run hand puppet named George that can talk to her and give her advice. Hunter is out roller skating one day when she rolls into the very same bar where the coeds picked up those guys and falls in love with Midkiff, who is in cahoots with Laster. While Meffert goes off to a veterinarian to find out why his Doberman died, and Hunter loses her virginity to Midkiff, Laster turns practically everyone into a neuropath and sends them after Hunter, whose father gets back just in the nick of time to shut down the computer. The neuropath who was the maid stabs all the other ones, then kills Laster at the airport. Midkiff goes after the maid with an axe, but just then the computer comes back on. Hunter's puppet friend George comes back to life, sees Midkiff with an axe, and fires one of those silver balls at him as Hunter screams.

Watching this sleazy, unscary, pseudo-softcore stab at filmmaking is an experience evenly divided between confusing and excruciating. The characters are indistinguishable, the nudity gratuitous and ample, and the shocks few and feeble. The editing is incomprehensible, and the action limited to just three locations, though they seem like fewer. One could go on bashing this wretched exploitation item, but that would be a waste of time. Perhaps needless to say, this film has seen the dark of theaters thanks to current sleaze kings Lloyd Kaufman and Michael Herz at Troma.

p, Bachoo Sen; d, Henry Sala; w, George Faget-Benard; ph, Denis Gheerbrant, Bob Baldwin (Eastmancolor); m, Martin Kershaw; ed, David Gilbert; art d,

George Faget-Benard; spec eff, Mike de Silva, Dan Gates; makeup, Lydia Kaleidjan; stunts, Gerry Barrett.

Horror   Cas.   (PR:O   MPAA:R)

NIGHTMARE'S PASSENGERS***½   (1986, Arg.) 95m Instituto Nacional De Cinematografia Argentina c (PASAJEROS DE UNA PESADILLA)

Federico Luppi *(Bernardo Fogelman)*, Alicia Bruzzo *(Susana Fogelman)*, Gabriel Lenn *(Younger Son)*, German Palacios *(Elder Son)*, Gabriela Flores *(Daughter)*, Gilda Lousek, Nelly Prono, Dalma Melevos, Esteban Massari.

Based on a true story that filled Argentine headlines in 1981, NIGHTMARE'S PASSENGERS paints a convincing portrait of the disintegration of a family from within. The film opens on an empty car parked on a side street, blood dripping out of the trunk. The bodies of Luppi and his wife, Bruzzo, are inside. Their two sons are arrested, and the youngest, Lenn, tells the story in flashback under interrogation. It seems their father, a Jewish executive in an arms firm with extensive ties to the military junta, has a closet streak of homosexuality. His wife is an alcoholic nymphomaniac who is constantly trying to seduce her own son. Their children, two sons and a daughter, are horrified as their parents stage orgies in their home and they try to straighten them out, but to no avail. NIGHTMARE'S PASSENGERS ends with the parents realizing just how low they've sunk.

The film leaves open the question of who killed the parents, and when it was released, the actual case was still in the courts, though evidence pointed away from the children and to a right-wing paramilitary death squad. Technically, the film is up to the generally high standards of Argentine cinema, and the performances impressively illustrate the weaknesses in the parents, particularly Bruzzo, and the helplessness of their children. Based on the book written by the younger son (with the help of a journalist) that exposed his parents' self-destructive habits and connections to the military junta's "dirty war."

d, Fernando Ayala; w, Jorge Goldenberg (based on a book by Pablo Schoklender); ph, Victor Hugo Caula; m, Oscar Cardozo Ocampo; prod d, Emilio Basaldua.

Drama   (PR:O   MPAA:NR)

NIJE LAKO S MUSKARCIMA†   (1986, Yugo.) Avala Pro c (Trans: Men Only Mean Trouble)

Milena Dravic, Ljubisa Samardzic, Velimir Bata Zivojinovic, Mica Tomic, Ana Simic.

d, Mihailo Vukobratovic; w, Predrag Perisic; ph, Zivko Zalar; m, Dragan Illic; set d, Milenko Jeremic.

9½ WEEKS**   (1986) 113m MGM/UA c

Mickey Rourke *(John)*, Kim Basinger *(Elizabeth)*, Margaret Whitton *(Molly)*, David Margulies *(Harvey)*, Christine Baranski *(Thea)*, Karen Young *(Sue)*, William De Acutis *(Ted)*, Dwight Weist *(Farnsworth)*, Roderick Cook *(Sinclair, the Critic)*.

In an attempt to cash in on the hordes who went to see LAST TANGO IN PARIS, this movie is purported to be a smoldering epic about sadomasochism. If this is Hollywood's idea of S&M, then THE SOUND OF MUSIC has to be reckoned as a prime example of show business back-stabbing. First announced as a Tri-Star project, it was dropped by that studio and picked up by MGM/UA, shot, and then sat gathering dust on a shelf until some discreet cuts were made for the final R-rated release. Based on a steamy novel about pain by Elizabeth McNeill (a *nom de plume* for Swedish/French author Ingebord Day), it hedges almost every bet and what is left is something that, with a few more edits, could play on the Disney Channel. In other words, it's an exploitation film with very little to exploit.

Rourke is a well-paid Wall Street arbitrageur (the same business Ivan Boesky and a few others were in) and Basinger is a freshly divorced art gallery owner in Manhattan's fashionable SoHo district. They meet across some chickens in a Chinese poultry market, their eyes rivet on each other, not a single word is spoken but it's easy to see they have connected. They meet again later at a flea market and he purchases a fur stole for her. Before you can say Drexel Burnham

Lambert, he has whisked her to his houseboat on the Hudson River. It has everything the successful Wall Streeter could want, including a fabulous view of the Big Apple. He changes the sheets, slips a Billie Holiday record on the stereo, and they go to bed. But sex turns into something more than simple frolicking. Rourke enjoys variances, such as blindfolds, whips, and the like. At one point, he buys a riding crop and one expects that he will play some serious "horsey" with Basinger, but it never comes to pass, thus refuting Chekhov's theory. (The great Russian once said something to the effect that if a gun is introduced on a stage, it had better go off before the play ends. Nothing of the sort happens here.) Instead, we are treated to an all-style, no-story series of music videos (remember, this was directed by Adrian Lyne, who gave us the same sort of thing in FLASHDANCE). For almost two hours, Rourke and Basinger make love in all sorts of places, with lots of food props like ice cubes and chocolate syrup. It's mostly foreplay with very little fulfillment for the actors or the audience.

There were many trims in the picture which effectively cut out any meat and any story, including one sequence where Rourke tosses dollar bills at Basinger who is playing the role of a hooker. A more explicit version was to be released in Europe, but it's hard to believe that it would do any better at the box office than the film did in the U.S., which was far below expectations. What was advertised as daring and provocative turned out to be tame and ordinary. Several companies

were involved in the production. (It's listed as "an MGM/UA release of a Producers Sales Organization (now defunct) and Sidney Kimmel (who's he?) presentation of a Keith Barish (who was co-executive producer with ex-agent Frank Koenigsberg) production from Jonesfilm in association with Galactic Films and Triple Ajaxx.") Phew! One of the producers and cowriters was ex-actor Zalman King. So there were at least five producers and three writers, and, it would seem, that adds up to too many cooks—not that this was a delicious broth to begin with. Lots of flash, very little dance.

p, Antony Rufus Isaacs, Zalman King; d, Adrian Lyne; w, Patricia Knop, Zalman King, Sarah Kernochan (based on the novel by Elizabeth McNeill); ph, Peter Biziou (Technicolor); m, Jack Nitzsche, Michael Hoenig, ed, Tom Rolf, Caroline Biggerstaff, Mark Winitsky, Kim Secrist; prod d, Ken Davis; art d, Linda Conaway-Parsloe; set d, Christian Kelly; cos, Bobbie Read.

Drama   Cas.   (PR:O   MPAA:R)

90 DAYS***   (1986, Can.) 99m National Film Board of Canada/Cinecom International c

Stefan Wodoslawsky *(Blue)*, Christine Pak *(Hyang-Sook)*, Sam Grana *(Alex)*, Fernanda Tavares *(Laura)*, Daisy De Bellefeuille *(Mother)*.

This offbeat Canadian comedy features Wodoslawsky as a confused individual frustrated by the continued troubles plaguing his love life. In a desperate move to find the right girl, Wodoslawsky begins looking through a Korean mail-order bride catalog and soon becomes engaged in correspondence with Pak. After several months, Pak arrives in Canada on a 90-day visa. If love blossoms during these three months, the couple will wed; if not, then Pak will return to her home in the Orient. In the meantime, Wodoslawsky's good friend Grana is having romance troubles of his own. Not only has his wife just ended their marriage, but his mistress has walked out on him as well. While drowning his sorrows in a neighborhood bar, Grana meets Tavares, a beautiful lawyer who makes him an unexpected offer. It seems Tavares is in search of a sperm donor for a wealthy client seeking artificial insemination. Grava is taken aback by the proposition, but also feels somewhat flattered. Grava finds himself attracted to Tavares, but he is ultimately rejected again by two women when the attorney explains his ''lazy'' sperm is simply not good enough. At the same time, Wodoslawsky is having difficulties with Pak. Beyond the cultural differences (she can't play catch; he is intimidated by Oriental cuisine), and Pak's steadfast disapproval of premarital sex, problems arise with the unexpected arrival of Wodoslawsky's mother, De Bellefeuille, who attempts to put a damper on the would-be nuptials by suggesting that Pak knows nothing about her son. Resentful of De Bellefeuille's suffocating presence, Wodoslawksy angrily retorts, ''You don't know me either!''

This is a comedy built on the small personal events of everyday life. Consequently the pacing is slow, reflecting the natural cadences of 90 DAYS' cast members. The film is largely improvised by its nonprofessional ensemble, which results in occasional stumbling within scenes, but also lends a bright, refreshing air to the proceedings. These are not just actors mouthing someone else's words, but people developing their own thoughts and feelings. The key to this lies in the working methods of filmmakers Walker and Wilson. Rather than pen a formal script, the two sketched a bare-bones outline of their intentions. Cast members were given the basic elements of a scene shortly before shooting, leaving the unfolding and climax of a situation largely in their hands. Though this could leave itself open to numerous problems, the improvisational style works well here, and the cast's accomplishments in 90 DAYS are often little gems of honesty. Different versions of the film were screened to test audiences until a final cut was decided upon—another typical facet of Walker and Wilson's style. Walker knew his leading men well, for all three hold staff positions on the National Film Board of Canada. When not acting, Wodoslawsky works as a producer, while Grana handles administrative chores. Pak is a former beauty contest winner (Miss Korea of Canada), and ironically got her part when she drove her sister to the film's auditions. 90 DAYS, which is a sequel to the similarly created picture THE MASCULINE MYSTIQUE, was awarded a special prize at the 1985 Chicago Film Festival for its uncommon approach to film comedy. Following this success, the film received a general release in 1986. Plans were also made for a third film, tentatively titled THE LAST STRAW.

p, David Wilson, Giles Walker; d, Giles Walker; w, David Wilson, Giles Walker; ph, Andrew Kitzanuk; m, Richard Gresko; ed, David Wilson.

Romance/Comedy   **(PR:O MPAA:NR)**

NINGUEN NO YAKUSOKU†   (1986, Jap.) 123m Seibu Saison Group–TV Asahi-Kinema Tokyo c (Trans: The Promise)

Rentaro Mikuni *(Grandfather)*, Sachiko Murase *(Grandmother)*, Choichiro Kawarazaki *(Yoshio)*, Orie Sato *(Ritsuko)*, Tetsuta Sugimoto, Kumiko Takeda, Reiko Tazima, Koichi Sato, Tomisaburo Wakayama.

Director Yoshishige Yoshida, after a 13-year hiatus, returns to the screen with this unsentimental drama addressing the question of euthanasia in a day and age in Japan when the traditional preparations for, and acceptance of, death are no longer practiced. The film opens as police question the family of an old women who was murdered. Surprisingly, the victim's husband comes forward to confess. In a lengthy flashback it is revealed that the woman had become very ill, feeble, and unable to control her mind or body. Her entire family suffered with her and each wanted to end her pain.

d, Yoshishige Yoshida; w, Yoshishige Yoshida, Fukiko Miyauchi (based on the novel by Shuichi Sae); ph, Yoshishiro Yamazaki (Fujicolor); m, Haruomi Hosono; ed, Akira Suzuki; art d, Yoshie Kikukawa.

Drama   **(PR:C MPAA:NR)**

NINI TERNO-SECCO†   (1986, It.) C.G. Silver Film c (Trans: Nini The Gambler)

Giancarlo Giannini, Victoria Abril, Lino Troisi.

Giannini works in a small lottery office run by his father-in-law, where he uses numerology to predict winners, with little success. When his father-in-law is murdered, Giannini is wrongfully put in jail, and there he meets a Camorra boss who runs his empire from within his cell using a secret, numerological book similar to the Cabala. Giannini becomes his student and after the old man's death, his successor. Upon his release he uses his knowledge to strike against the Camorra inner circle and anticipate their countermoves. He turns them all against each other, but when they are all dead he learns that his wife was also involved, so he manipulates her to kill her lover, then returns to jail.

d&w, Giancarlo Giannini; ph, Marcello Gatti; m, A. Infantino.

Crime   **(PR:C-O MPAA:NR)**

NINJA TURF zero   (1986) 86m Action Bros./Ascot Entertainment c (AKA: L.A. STREETFIGHTERS)

Jun Chong *(Young)*, Phillip Rhee *(Tony)*, James Lew *(Chan)*, Rosanna King *(Lily)*, Bill Wallace *(Kruger)*, Dorin Mukama *(Dorin)*, Arlene Montano *(Chan's Girl Friend)*, Ken Nagayama *(Yoshida)*, Frank Marmolejo *(Frank)*, Darren Muriel

(Darren), Mark Hicks *(Mark)*, Gina S. Im *(Young's Mother)*, Toma Gjokaj *(Syndicate Boss)*, Hila Popaj *(Young's Mother's Boy Friend)*, Leena Parkvermonsky *(Rich Girl)*, Igor Shektman *(Rich Guy)*, John Rosas *(Blades Gang Leader)*, Danny Gibson *(Spikes Gang Leader)*, Brinke Stevens *(Boss' Girl Friend)*, Theresa Vinegar, Bob Melling *(Schoolteachers)*, Celeste Laing *(Hooker)*, Tena Parido, Lyndsy Maxwell *(Girls on Street)*, Arthur Fuller, Ricky Davis, Ken Daughtrey, Kerwin LeDuff, Tyrone Davis *(Liquor Store Gang)*, Dong Min Lee *(Tony's Father)*, Kathy Kim *(Tony's Mother)*, Vidal Reyna *(Mexican Restaurant Manager)*, Rick Brown, Howard Ng, Richard Ng, Loren Rains Avedon, Mario Casara, Jason Hom, James Warr, Richard Shin, Howard Cohen, Tom Keller, William Mendoza, Steve Rogers, Eugene Brochette, Raul Proano *(Chan's Gang)*, Eric Megason, Tom Wilson, Dean Meschi, Gary Graber, Mitch Carson, Nick King, Ron Sunn, Jeff Allison, Scott Rodgers, George Tony *(Spike's Gang)*, Vacho Assoyan, Bill Darlington *(Drug Buyers)*.

Rhee is the new boy in his Los Angeles high school and he quickly falls afoul of Lew, chief of the local gang. Rhee is saved from a sound beating by the arrival of Chong, who has his own band of followers (not a gang), and from whom Lew backs down, snarling about getting even. Chong and Rhee become friends, and Rhee joins Chong's martial-arts club, members of which soon start to get jobs working as security guards at rich people's parties. Rhee falls even further into Lew's bad graces by dating Lew's sister. The boys get a job guarding a drug dealer's party, and when Chong figures out what's going on he steals the drug money. Of course the gangsters are upset, so they hire the best killers in the world to go after Chong. Lew directs the hit men, a Japanese and an American, to Chong, who manages to kill them both in a huge fight. On the way home, however, just after his party-girl mother tells him she'll clean up her life and take him back to Korea, Lew shows up with his gang and shoves a knife into Chong's belly. He fights bravely for a while, but he eventually weakens and gets stomped until Rhee finds out what's going on and beats up all the bad guys. It's too late, and Chong dies.

Not exactly what you might call the peak of cinematic art, NINJA TURF is good for laughs. The dubbing is uniformly wretched, and the actors who did it seemed to be making up their lines on the spot, tossing in as much bad language as they could muster in order to justify an R rating. What makes this even stranger is the fact that it was shot in the U.S. with an English-speaking cast, and still dubbed badly. Intended mostly for foreign distribution under the title L.A. STREETFIGHTERS. By the way, there are no ninjas in NINJA TURF.

p, Phillip Rhee; d, Richard Park; w, Simon Blake Hong; ph, David D. Kim (DeLuxe Color); m, Charles Pavlosky, Gary Falcone, Chris Stone; ed, Alex Chang; prod d, David Moon Park.

Martial Arts   **Cas.**   **(PR:O MPAA:R)**

NJERIU PREJ DHEU†   (1986, Yugo.) Kosovafilm c (Trans: Man of Earth)

Abdurrahman Shala.

d, Agim Sopi; w, Fadil Hysaj, Agim Sopi; ph, Menduh Nushi; m, Rauf Dhomi; set d, Nuredin Loxha.

NO MERCY**½   (1986) 105m Tri-Star –Delphi IV and V/Tri-Star c

Richard Gere *(Eddie Jillette)*, Kim Basinger *(Michel Duval)*, Jeroen Krabbe *(Losado)*, George Dzundza *(Capt. Stemkowski)*, Gary Basaraba *(Joe Collins)*, William Atherton *(Allan Deveneux)*, Terry Kinney *(Paul Deveneux)*, Bruce McGill *(Lt. Hall)*, Ray Sharkey *(Angles Ryan)*, Marita Geraghty *(Alice Collins)*, Aleta Mitchell *(Cara)*.

While by no means a great detective film, NO MERCY is a fairly entertaining, albeit predictable, story that benefits from a good performance by Gere. He plays an undercover Chicago cop who, with his partner Basaraba, follows up on a tip provided by Sharkey, a regular informant. Sharkey sends them to Kinney, a New

Orleans hood who needs someone to kill his boss, Krabbe. Not realizing Gere and Basaraba are policemen, Kinney appears impressed when Gere smarts off to Kinney's girl friend, Basinger, and slaps her in the face. While Kinney and Gere are driving through the night streets, they notice a car following them. Gere manages to escape in time, but Kinney is killed when his automobile is blown up. The killer is Krabbe, of course, who has been trailing Kinney during the evening.

Basaraba, in the meantime, goes to Krabbe's hotel room, where he is disemboweled when Krabbe cuts him open with a hunting knife. Krabbe takes Basinger (who is really his mistress) and heads back to New Orleans, and Gere misses capturing him by only a few minutes.

Devastated by the brutal death of his partner, Gere ignores the warnings of his superior officer, Dzunda, and flies down to New Orleans to find Krabbe. Gere makes some inquiries, but is repeatedly warned not to go looking for Krabbe, whose murderous temperament is legendary. Gere enters Algiers, a notoriously dangerous area populated by Cajuns, where Krabbe is considered the overlord. There Gere finds Basinger in a ramshackle nightclub, recognizing her by the blue parrot she has tattooed on her shoulder. He handcuffs himself to the woman, then escorts her out of the club. Krabbe is in hot pursuit and threatens to kill the two as they quietly hide in the waters beneath a pier. Gere and Basinger manage

to get into a boat and escape from Krabbe, ending up in the Louisiana bayous. The two struggle through the swamp and find an abandoned shack, where they are able to briefly rest. Basinger reveals that as a child she was sold to Krabbe and has grown up with a loving fear of him. When some Cajuns discover Gere and Basinger, Gere yells, "This is Losado's woman!" The very mention of Krabbe's name is enough to frighten these people, and Gere steals one of their automobiles, taking Basinger to the nearest police station. Gere is blasted by local authorities who demand he leave town immediately, but Dzundza, who has come to fetch his errant man, has other ideas. Before flying back to Chicago, Dzundza slips Gere a gun and tells him to get Krabbe no matter what the cost may be. From there Gere checks into a fleabag hotel, rents all the rooms, and orders the clerk to leave. Basinger meets up with Gere, and with her help he booby traps the place in anticipation of Krabbe's arrival. He and Basinger make love, then, sure enough, Krabbe shows up with henchmen in tow. During the bloody shootout the hotel catches fire, but Gere is able to knock off his foes and escapes with Basinger. The two walk off, arm in arm, planning their future together while the hotel burns behind them.

There's not much beneath this story: NO MERCY is a lean thriller with an uncomplicated linear plot. What hampers its overall impact is an occasional reliance on genre cliches, an unbelievable ending, and the simple fact that Basinger is clearly not much of an actress. This was a real change of pace for director Pearce, whose previous efforts included HEARTLAND, THRESHOLD, and COUNTRY (he also worked as cameraman for such documentaries as WOODSTOCK, MARJOE, and HEARTS AND MINDS). His switch from humanist dramas to action thriller is successful in that he is able to tell an interesting story here in spite of Carabatsos' elementary script. Even worse than the script is the romance between Gere and Basinger. Certainly a sexual tension is inherent in the film, yet the arm in arm finale is simply too silly to be believed. The handcuffed journey by Gere and Basinger, which comprises a good section of the film, never takes on the intensity implied. It's certainly an interesting idea (both THE DEFIANT ONES, 1958, and Alfred Hitchcock's 1935 classic THE THIRTY NINE STEPS made excellent use of the concept) but the urgency just isn't there. Pearce gives an appropriately dark setting to his Chicago and New Orleans locations, though he never really differentiates between his locales. Both cities have the same look and feel, without Pearce capitalizing on their unique, extremely distinct personalities (to Pearce's credit, this is the first of the many recent Chicago-made films that *doesn't* feature an obligatory trip to a Cubs game).

Dzundza's character easily could have come out of any television cop show, and his scenes with Gere feel like rubber stamp situations. Krabbe, a Dutch actor best known to American audiences for his performances in such films as SOLDIER OF ORANGE and THE FOURTH MAN, is appropriately creepy as the evil Losado. With his ponytailed hair and dry delivery, he is the very essence of a maniacal killer, providing some much needed intensity. Basinger, at best, is a pretty face who can go through the motions reasonably well. Too often, though, Basinger is bland and uninteresting, occasionally looking bored by what she has to do. Gere is fine in the physically demanding lead, though it's certainly no challenge to his talent as an actor. Still, with this film and POWER, Gere is taking definite strides towards breaking his pretty boy image. In order to prepare for the role, Gere donned a bulletproof vest and accompanied Chicago cops during drug busts. This proved to be something of a surprise for the arrested suspects who recognized Gere from past movie roles. One hysterical fan exclaimed, "You're the guy in AN OFFICER AND A GENTLEMAN!" while she was being arrested on drug charges. Basinger, on the other hand, hated making

NO MERCY. The physical exhaustion of her role, a good part of which found her handcuffed in a swamp, proved to be a little more than the actress could bear. According to one person involved with the film, once shooting was completed Basinger viewed any unappealing circumstance as tolerable in comparison, exclaiming: "It beats making NO MERCY!"

p, D. Constantine Conte; d, Richard Pearce; w, Jim Carabatsos; ph, Michel Brault (Metrocolor); m, Alan Silvestri; ed, Jerry Greenberg, Bill Yahraus; prod d, Patrizia von Brandenstein; art d, Doug Kraner; cos, Hilary Rosenfeld

Crime   Cas.   (PR:O MPAA:R)

NO RETREAT, NO SURRENDER* (1986) 83m NW–Seasonal–Balcor/NW
c

Kurt McKinney *(Jason Stillwell)*, Jean-Claude Van Damme *(Ivan the Russian)*, J.W. Fails *(R.J. Madison)*, Kathie Sileno *(Kelly Reilly)*, Kim Tai Chong *(Sensei Lee)*, Kent Lipham *(Scott)*, Ron Pohnel *(Ian Reilly)*, Dale Jacoby *(Dean)*, Pete Cunningham *(Frank)*, Tim Baker *(Tom Stillwell)*, Gloria Marziano *(Mrs. Stillwell)*, Joe Vance *(New York Agent)*, Farid Panahi, Tom Harris *(New York Assistants)*, John Andes *(New York Boss)*, Mark Zacharaios, Ty Martinez *(New York Fighters)*, Bob Johnene *(Karate Fight Emcee)*, Dennis Park *(Karate Fight Referee)*, Alex Stelter, Harold Engle, Jerry Cole, Ken Firestone, Wayne Yee *(Karate Fight Judges)*, Charlie Sparks *(Scott's Father)*, Lynetta Welch, Carin Badger, Tina Erickson *(Kelly's Girl Friends)*, Corey Jacoby, Neil Rozbaruch *(Dean's Friends)*, George Mason, Robert Villeaux, Dave Robinson, Keith Strange *(Bar Thugs)*, Ruckings McKinley Roz McKinley *(Disco Dancers)*.

Paying no attention to such archaic notions as logic, motivation, or intelligence, NO RETREAT, NO SURRENDER is a deliciously bad reworking of THE KARATE KID, with just a touch of ROCKY IV tossed in at the story's end. McKinney is a happy-go-lucky Bruce Lee disciple who practices martial arts at a Los Angeles karate school run by his father, Baker. When a group of enigmatic mobsters tries to take over the place by force, Baker packs up the family and

moves to Seattle, where he becomes a bartender. Fortunately for McKinney, Seattle is also where his hero Bruce Lee is buried (what a coincidence!) and, with his newfound pal Fails, the impressionable young man makes a solemn graveside pilgrimage. In another extraordinary twist of fate, McKinney's girl friend Sileno also lives in Seattle. Her brother Pohnel is—surprise, surprise—a national karate champ who owns the local martial arts school. McKinney goes to check out the place but is quickly humiliated by some of the most narrow-minded sadists ever collected in one room. Later, while attending Sileno's birthday party, McKinney once more suffers at the hands of these cretins, and he angrily storms out. Baker, who also has had a taste of degradation at the hands of some local thugs (are Seattle residents really this intolerant of new comers?), decides enough is enough. He throws McKinney's karate equipment out of the garage, then tears down a beloved poster of Bruce Lee (at this point, creative audiences may want to shout in unison: "Not the Bruce Lee poster!"). Fails helps McKinney move his gear to an abandoned house, and there the plucky lad begins training himself.

One evening McKinney is visited by an unexpected supernatural figure. Who should arrive to help him but Chong, a bad Bruce Lee impersonator! (You know Chong is playing Bruce Lee because all of his dialog is poorly dubbed.) After teaching the lad various skills (as well as dabbling in a mystical ceremony using a glass of water and a can of Diet Coke), Chong disappears and McKinney is ready to use his new skills. First he helps Baker when some barroom bullies attempt to ambush him. Baker realizes that sometimes it is necessary to take a stand, and the two are reconciled. Following this moment of beautiful revelation, McKinney makes up with Sileno. He then attends a karate exhibition where Pohnel and some teammates are scheduled to go against some tough New Yorkers! Who should be behind these bad guys from the Big Apple but the very gangsters who menaced Baker in the first place! These slick-haired *gumpas* take over the ring, then pull a surprise on the eager crowd. Instead of the three announced fighters, Van Damme, a one-man killing machine, is going to take on the boys from Seattle. And just to make this sneering hulk extra bad, he's a *Russian* karate expert! Van Damme makes short order of his first opponents by tossing one from the ring and knocking the other unconscious. The really good stuff is being saved for Pohnel. Van Damme flagrantly violates every known rule of fair play, sending the crowd into an uproar. Sileno jumps up to defend her brother, and Van

Damme responds by pulling her hair. Naturally the chivalrous McKinney is infuriated and decides it's time to put Chong's lessons to the test. He jumps into the ring and quickly overpowers the dirty Russkie, winning the fight for his girl, his father, his country and anything else on the top ten cliches list.

NO RETREAT, NO SURRENDER is a wonderfully silly romp, so consistently ridiculous in intent and execution that it's hard not to enjoy. The cast is uniformly awful, though they should be awarded an "A" for effort. Despite their collective inability to act their way out of the proverbial paper bag, the cast valiantly plod on as though they were trained by Stanislavsky himself. Fails, as the best friend, is a particular standout. The kid is so well meaning and earnest you want to pat him on the head and give him a doggie yum yum for doing such a good job. The karate sequences actually aren't too bad and McKinney puts himself through rigorous physical punishment that unquestionably is the real thing. Technically, the film is about average, though some of the editing continuity is pretty amusing. All in all, this is a bad film to savor.

p, Ng See Yuen; d, Corey Yuen; w, Keith W. Strandberg (based on a story by Ng See Yuen, Corey Yuen); ph, John Huneck, David Golia (Technicolor); m, Paul Gilreath; ed, Alan Poon, Mark Pierce, James Melkonian, Dane Davis; spec eff John Ting; ch (martial arts), Harrison Mang; m/l, Joe Torono; makeup, Sher Flowers, June Brickman.

Martial Arts **Cas.** **(PR:C MPAA:PG-13)**

NO SURRENDER*½** (1986, Brit.) 100m Dumbarton-National Film Finance Corporation-Film Four International-William Johnston-Ronald Lillie-Lauron International/Norstar

Michael Angelis *(Mike)*, Avis Bunnage *(Martha Gorman)*, James Ellis *(Paddy Burke)*, Tom Georgeson *(Mr. Ross)*, Bernard Hill *(Bernard)*, Ray McAnally *(Billy McRacken)*, Mark Mulholland *(Norman)*, Joanne Whalley *(Cheryl)*, J.G. Devlin *(George Gorman)*, Vince Earl *(Frank)*, Ken Jones *(Ronny)*, Michael Ripper *(Tony Bonaparte)*, Marjorie Sudell *(Barbara)*, Joan Turner *(Superwoman)*, Richard Alexander *(Smoking Kid)*, Pamela Austin *(Organist)*, Paul Codman *(Member of Rock Group)*, Paul Connor, Lovette Edwards, Ina Clough, Helen Rhodes, Vera Kelly *(The Infirm)*, Elvis Costello *(Rosco de Ville)*, James Culshaw *(Gorman's Cab Driver)*, Gabrielle Daye *(Winnis)*, David Doyle *(Ulster Boy)*, Gerry Fogarty *(Mustached Veteran)*, Harry Goodier *(Cleanshaven Veteran)*, Eric Granville *(Donald Duck)*, Robert Hamilton *(Special Branch Officer)*, Ian Hart *(Uncertain Menace)*, Gerard Hely *(Senior Policeman)*, Joey Kaye *(Driver, Catholic Party)*, Phil Kernot *(Stan Laurel)*, Al Kossy *(Bobby)*, Penny Leatherbarrow *(Mrs. Morgan)*, Mark McGann *(Rock Group Leader)*, Stephen Lloyd, Mike Starke *(Rock Group)*, Johnny Mallon *(French Onion Seller)*, Joe McGann, Frank Vincent *(Policemen)*, Ron Metcalf, Steve O'Connor, Tommy Ryan *(Veterans)*, Bill Moores *(Quasimodo)*, Robert Nield *(Yousee)*, Doc O'Brien *(Driver, Protestant Party)*, Peter Price *(Comedian)*, Christopher Quinn *(Warden)*, Linus Roache *(Ulster Boy)*, Tony Rohr *(McCarthur)*, Andrew Scofield *(Macker)*, Tony Scoggo *(Cold Eyes)*, Mabel Seward *(Older Waitress)*, Georgina Smith *(Oliver Hardy)*, Eileen Walsh *(Waitress)*, Harry Webster *(Priest)*, Gery White *(Driver For Infirm Party)*, Dean Williams *(Real Menace)*, Peter Wilson *(Comedian's Boy Friend)*, Arthur Spreckley *(Matthew)*.

Never in the history of the cinema has the world's bleakness and man's small-mindedness been such a romping good time as in this black comedy from the hand of writer Bleasdale, the man also responsible for the popular British television play "Boys from the Blackstuff." Set on New Year's Eve at a rundown nightclub on the outskirts of Liverpool, NO SURRENDER ruthlessly takes jabs at the religious controversy in Ireland, the gross unemployment of England's industrial cities, and the corrupt businessmen/mobsters who selfishly, and forcefully, take advantage of the less fortunate. Arriving for his first day's work as manager of the Charleston Club, Angelis is faced with a complicated situation stemming from the outgoing manager's plans for revenge against the crooked owner. For the New Year's celebration three vastly different groups have been booked into the club; these include Irish Catholic pensioners prepared for a costume ball, their longtime Protestant adversaries, and a group of helplessly senile inmates of a nursing home. With the assistance of the half-witted bouncer, Hall, an outdated Teddy boy, and the kitchen aide, Whalley, a would-be torch singer, Angelis must maintain order as well as perform the impossible task of offering his guests a good time. Complications increase when an untalented magician (played by rock star Elvis Costello), a struggling, quarreling punk-rock band, and an unfunny, gay comedian, are discovered to be the evening's entertainment, booked as a last laugh from the former manager. The old people, however, prove perfectly capable of entertaining themselves. Their long-dormant, fiery blood reactivated by the presence of longtime enemies and abundant drink, they become obsessed with reliving their violent past. Tensions continuously mount until the Protestant leader, former gunman McAnally, is spurred on to fight the Catholics' prize puncher, the blind boxer Ellis, in the men's restroom. The skeptical McAnally lands a couple of quick punches into Ellis that send him sprawling into a stall where Protestant terrorist Mulholland lies dead. The Catholics make up far-fetched stories of how Mulholland was killed, unaware that McAnally is actually responsible. On the run from the police for his acts of terrorism, Mulholland had appealed to his one-time comrade in arms, McAnally, for assistance. A successful businessman wishing to forget his past, McAnally dismissed Mulholland until the terrorist threatened harm to his daughter, who lives in Belfast with a Catholic man. McAnally took Mulholland to the festivities, where he hid him in the washroom to escape detection. Increasingly incensed by Mulholland's crass threats, McAnally's cool demeanor broke, and he accidentally killed Mulholland. When the evening's events come to end, McAnally has a new perspective that allows him to call the daughter he had formerly denounced for marrying a Catholic.

While all this activity is occurring on the main floor of the nightclub, the former manager is being tortured and beaten by the shady owner in the basement. Angelis journeys into this dungeon to beg relief from his precarious situation, but is only threatened with the same treatment as his predecessor should he quit. The manager retaliates by anonymously tipping off the police on his crooked boss. The police arrive at the scene at the same time as detectives tailing Mulholland, bringing the events of the night to a cataclysmic finale. During the evening, Angelis and Whalley develop adolescent crushes on one another which have their expression during the ceremonious kiss at 12 o'clock. As the night draws to an end, Angelis informs Whalley that unfortunately he is happily married. She responds with: "That'll change soon enough." An apropos light ending to a night where the striving for routine and order have become obsolete formalities in Angelis' life.

NO SURRENDER was the feature film debut for a number of people involved in its production. Producer Hassan had been involved with the British Film Institute for a number of years but was never directly involved in production. Director Smith likewise was initiated into feature-film production after a career spent in television and on documentaries. Writer Bleasdale never wrote directly for the screen prior to this venture. He achieved some popularity with the television production of "Boys from the Blackstuff," a socio-political satire that starred Hill and Angelis, who then received their first major film roles with NO SURRENDER. The majority of the cast, however, consists mainly of veteran actors from the British stage and screen whose faces will appear obscurely familiar to the average viewer. It is the bizarre caricatures presented by these aging performers—combined with the witty dialogue of Bleasdale—that gives NO SURRENDER its air of lighthearted mirth despite the seriousness of its themes. Solemn events like a woman having a heart attack, completely incapacitated mental patients trying to eat, torture, death, and murder are interspersed with a continuous influx of comical situations. The constant mood swings make viewing NO SURRENDER an exhausting emotional exercise. Like any good satire, this film makes us laugh at events that normally make us sad, a credit to the finesse of Bleasdale in highlighting the absurdities of the world in a Liverpudlian microcosm.

p, Mamoun Hassan; d, Peter Smith; w, Alan Bleasdale; ph, Mick Coulter (Panavision); m, Daryl Runswick; ed, Kevin Brownlow, Rodney Holland; prod d, Andrew Mollo; set d, Alison Stewart-Richardson; cos, Emma Porteous; m/l, Andrew Schofield; makeup, Lois Burwell; stunts, George Leech.

Comedy **(PR:O MPAA:R)**

NO TIME TO DIE† (1986, Ger.) 87m Rapid-Lisa-Rapi c

John Phillip Law *(Ted Barner)*, Horst Janson *(Martin Forster)*, Grazyna Dylong *(Judy Staufer)*, Barry Prima *(Pat Lesmany)*, Francis Glutton *(Jan Van Cleef)*, Christopher Mitchum *(Jack Gull)*.

Shot in Indonesia in 1984, this film finally emerges in the U.S., thanks to the miracle of videocassette. Law, a hired gun for the Indonesian branch of the Multi Industrial Corporation, is assigned to protect a new laser cannon as it is taken to a remote mine for testing. Needless to say, there are evil men who would like to take the laser cannon, chiefly Mitchum, and the film is mostly a long chase between the two factions, with Dylong, the obligatory beautiful-lady-journalist, along for the ride.

p, Wolf C. Hartwig, Gope T. Samtani; d, Helmuth Ashley, Has Manan, E.G. Bakker; w, Heinz Werner John, Gunther Heller, Helmuth Ashley; ph, Wolfgang Grasshoff, Asmawi; m, Hans Hammerschmid; ed, Norbert Herzner; spec eff, Nuryadi; stunts, Kerry Rossall.

Action **Cas.** **(PR:O MPAA:NR)**

NOAH UND DER COWBOY† (1986, Switz.) 82m Felix Tissi bw

Frank Demenga *(Bede/Noah)*, Yves Progrin *(Luki/Cowboy)*, Claude Inga Barbey, Marion Widmer, Philipp Engelmann, Felix Rellstab.

Two men friends, after suffering a series of romantic disappointments, decide to take to the road. An old man they meet during their travels involves the two in a cocaine deal. The two argue, split up, and reunite, all the while engaging in witty banter. Debut feature from Tessi, who shot the film on a small budget on 16mm black-and-white. A hit at the Saarbrucken film festival.

p,d&w, Felix Tissi; ph, Hansueli Schenkel; m, Andreas Litmanowitsch.

Comedy **(PR:C MPAA:NR)**

NOBODY'S FOOL** (1986) 107m Katz-Denny/Island c

Rosanne Arquette *(Cassie)*, Eric Roberts *(Riley)*, Mare Winningham *(Pat)*, Jim Youngs *(Billy)*, Louise Fletcher *(Pearl)*, Gwen Welles *(Shirley)*, Stephen Tobolowsky *(Kirk)*, Charlie Barnett *(Nick)*, J.J. Hardy *(Ralphy)*, William Steis *(Frank)*, Belita Moreno *(Jane)*, Lewis Arquette *(Mr. Fry)*, Ronnie Claire Edwards *(Bingo)*, Ann Hearn *(Linda)*, Scott Rosensweig *(Winston)*, Cheli Chew *(Prissy Lee)*, Sheila Paige *(Mrs. Cain)*, Alma Beltran *(Jennieva)*, Budge Threlkeld *(Hank)*, Lisa DeBennedetti *(Tracy)*, Wylie Small *(Barb)*, Natalie Golden *(Miss Francis)*, Kristy Kennedy *(No. 1 Fairy Dancer)*, Arwen Nichols *(No. 2 Fairy Dancer)*, Loraine Wallace *(Madge)*, Rod Hart *(Band Singer)*, Mark Atkinson *(Skinny Kid)*, Derek Barnes *(1st Boy)*, John Hoover *(2nd Boy)*, Mark Sanders *(3rd Boy)*, Brian West *(4th Boy)*, Jay Dusard *(Ranch Hand)*, Christopher Michael Johnson *(Church Soloist)*, Diane Costa *(Bride)*, Marsha Hicks *(Mother of the Bride)*, Walt Zandt *(Father of the Bride)*, Kat, Barbara Brown, Beth Henley *(Bridesmaids)*, Kay Pasa *(Bea Burger)*, Brian Fitzgerald *(Stuart Andrews)*, Bonnie Oda Homsey, Dean Ricca, Joe Clarke, Becky Bell Maxwell, Bruce Wright, Frederick Bailey, Melissa Grier *(Shakespearean Troupe)*, Kerrie Cullen *(Stunt Double/Cassie)*, Paul E. Pinnt *(Stunt Driver)*.

NOBODY'S FOOL is yet another entry in the increasingly popular genre of quirky Americana that can be found in a number of other recent films, including this year's TRUE STORIES, SOMETHING WILD, and CRIMES OF THE HEART. The thread that all of these films have in common (besides a handful of interchanging creative talents—Beth Henley, David Byrne, Jonathan Demme, and his former wife Evelyn Purcell) is a mid-American locale that seems to be populated with characters who have wandered in from a Federico Fellini film. Disguised as small-town tales about normal people, these films are more interested in the bizarre and grotesque than in the everyday drama of the average

person. In NOBODY'S FOOL, Arquette plays a withdrawn young girl who becomes pregnant by a boy friend, Youngs, who reneges on his promise to marry her. She goes a bit crazy, pokes him in the throat with a fork, and as a result is shunned by most of the people in her small town of Buckeye Basin. This jaded past of hers is told in a flashback. Arquette is now a little older and her baby has been put up for adoption. She takes an interest in a traveling theater troupe which has stopped over in Buckeye Basin for some outdoor performances. After watching "The Tempest" with her friend Winningham, Arquette decides to sign up for an acting workshop. She tells the class that "watching that Shakespeare show got me thinking how good it would be to be someone other than me. Even if it was just for an hour or a half hour." She also meets Roberts, a T-shirted lighting director who looks tough but acts sensitive. Her interest in acting grows, despite the criticism of her lazy mother Fletcher and her porcine younger brother Hardy. She receives support from theater director Tobolowsky (the real-life director of most of Beth Henley's plays) who encourages her to find the courage within herself to act like a hero. In the meantime, Youngs, who has since married and has a child on the way, has become bored with his wealthy in-laws and wants to start up again with Arquette. Weakened by the memories of the good times she had with Young (which we see in another flashback), Arquette has to fight the desire to go back to him. Although Roberts has asked her out a few times, Arquette's typical response is to back off from him, waving her arms and mumbling "Ooh, oh, gawd, I don't know." Roberts finally gets her to take a drive with him during which he explains that his past is even worse than hers. Before long these half-crazy misfits realize they love each other. Since the theater troupe is nearing the end of its stay, Roberts asks Arquette if she'll return with him to Los Angeles. In case she says no and wants to change her mind later, he writes his address on his shirt (while he's wearing it) and gives it to her to keep. As part of her workshop, Arquette gets to give a performance for the troupe's closing night. The monologue she picks is from "Romeo and Juliet" and her performance naturally warms the initially unreceptive crowd. Still unsure whether she should leave for L.A. with Roberts, she decides at the last minute to go, leaving her lousy waitress job and her stigmatized small-town past behind. She races to Roberts' apartment and, just as his car is pulling away, gets his attention and hops in, driving off through the night to Los Angeles.

The genesis of NOBODY'S FOOL goes back to 1977 when the 25-year-old Henley, a native of Jackson, Mississippi, wrote her first screenplay. Then titled "The Moonwatcher," the screenplay pre-dated Henley's ventures into playwriting and her 1981 Pulitzer Prize for her play "Crimes of the Heart" (which also hit the screen this year). Optioned in 1981 by Purcell, the script to NOBODY'S FOOL took five years to reach the screen. In the meantime, Henley also co-scripted David Byrne's TRUE STORIES, which, like NOBODY'S FOOL and CRIMES OF THE HEART, probes into the idiosyncracies of Americana. Released the same day as Purcell's former husband Jonathan Demme's SOMETHING WILD, NOBODY'S FOOL, which was budgeted at a slim $3,000,000, never quite lives up to what it promises to be—an honest romance between two odd characters. Perhaps it's the inexperience that comes from a first-time director working with a first script. Although a few scenes gel, most of the film falls flat, chiefly because Roberts, the film's supposed co-star, is barely seen in the first forty-five minutes. Purcell spends so much time setting up Arquette's desperation

and uncertainty, that the relationship between her and Roberts never gets a chance to begin. Every time Roberts enters a scene, he goes within a minute. Meanwhile, Arquette, who is dressed like a ragamuffin from the Annie Hall school of fashion, ponders her dreary life and stares off into space. NOBODY'S FOOL seems to attempt a character drama, though the script bogs Arquette down with endless flashbacks, grotesque characters (Hardy, for example, is a cartoon who is given no dimension until his very last scene), and humorless exchanges with background characters—leaving no room for the audience to develop an emotional attachment to her. Purcell and Henley, for the film's first half, are so concerned with striking a realistic chord, that the characters soon begin to seem like parodies and caricatures. The elaborate stories these characters tell are chock-full of absurdities and exist more to show off the writer's talent than to actually develop the characters. Fortunately, by the film's second half, NOBODY'S FOOL becomes the film it should have been all along—the meeting of two emotionally disturbed people who finally find someone to love. Rarely does a love between such displaced characters as Arquette and Roberts hit the screen. Arquette is a suicidal, hard-drinking, unwed mother who has attempted murder, while Roberts is a disturbed keg of dynamite ready to explode. What they have in common, however, is a need for the love and support of someone else. Arquette's performance, while limited by the script, is as accomplished as always. She is in especially good form during her reading of Shakespeare's Juliet speech, capturing the vitality of a tortured young romantic. Roberts, who can go overboard if not well-directed, is superb in an intense but restrained performance. Winningham and Youngs are both excellent in their roles, especially Youngs who plays an unlikable character but manages to gain sympathy. Fletcher, however, is given absolutely nothing to do and never has the chance to show the talent that earned her an Oscar in 1975 for ONE FLEW OVER THE CUCKOO'S NEST. Dozens of popular rock tunes fill the background soundtrack, including a number of songs by Robert Palmer.

p, James C. Katz, Jon S. Denny; d, Evelyn Purcell; w, Beth Henley; ph, Mikhail Suslov (CFI color, Panavision); m, James Newton Howard; ed, Dennis Virkler; prod d, Jackson DeGovia; art d, John R. Jensen; set d, Laurie Scott; cos, Ellen Mirojnick; spec eff, The EFX Shop; ch, Bonnie Oda Homsey; makeup, Pat Gearhardt; stunts, Michael Adams.

Drama/Romance   **Cas.**   **(PR:C   MPAA:PG-13)**

NOCHE DE JUERGA†   (1986, Mex.) 91m Televicine/Videocine c (Trans: A Night On The Town)

Juan Ferrara (*Ricardo Bermudes*), Helena Rojo (*Dolores Vertiz*), Victor Junco (*Police Lieutenant*), Norma Herrera (*Alicia Bermudes*).

Ferrara meets a beautiful woman (Rojo) at a nightclub, and when she takes him home he finds the dead body of her politico husband on the floor. He flees, but soon finds that he has been framed for the killing, and even his wife and lawyer don't believe his story.

d, Manuel M. Delgado; w, Jose Maria Fernandez Unsain; ph, Miguel Arena; m, Nacho Mendez.

Mystery   **(PR:O   MPAA:NR)**

NOE HEIT ANNET†   (1986, Nor.) 77m Norsk Film–Media Vision/ Kommunernes Filmcentral c (Trans: Something Entirely Different)

Trond Kirkvaag (*Buff*), Knut Lystad (*Judge*), Lars Mjoen (*Vulvatt*), Linn Stokke (*Svalbard*), Minken Fosbeim (*Mrs. Bull*), Geir Borresen (*Valentino*), Dag Vagsas, Sigve Boe, Lars Andreas Larsen, Henrik Scheele, Kine Allebust, Per Christonsen, Sr., Anne Stray, Mari Bjorgan, Ingolf Karinen.

A popular trio of Norwegian TV comedians make their feature debut here, with Kirkvaag a descendant of Dracula who doesn't want to follow in the nocturnal footsteps of his ancestor. His two cohorts (Lystad and Mjoen) play most of the picture's other roles.

p, Odd Wenn; d&w, Morten Kolstad (based on a story by Trond Kirvaag, Knut Lystad, Lars Mjoen); ph, Halvor Nass; m, Hissa Nyberget; ed, Tore Tomter; prod d, Jon Arvesen, Dagfinn Kleppan; cos, Wenche Petersen.

Comedy   **(PR:A-C   MPAA:NR)**

NOI, CEI DIN LINIA INTII†   (1986, Rum.) 160m Bucharest Studio No. 5 c (Trans: The Last Assault)

George Alexandru, Anda Onesa, Valentin Uritescu, Ion Besoiu, Sergiu Nicolaescu, Stefan Iordache, Mircea Albulescu, Emil Hossu, Marian Culineac, Bogdan Stanoevici, Cristian Sofron, Ion Siminie, Traian Costea, Stelian Stancu, Geo Dobre.

In the final days of the Nazi occupation of Rumania, a group of fighters is given the arduous task of destroying the last remnant of the Germans, a heavily armed radio station. Against this war background, the developing love affair between an army lieutenant and a nurse adds a personal balance. Director Nicolaescu, also one of Rumania's leading actors, is featured as a general. NOI CEI DIN LINIA INTII was released on the anniversary of Rumanian independence from the Nazis.

d, Sergiu Nicolaescu; w, Titus Popovici; ph, Nicolae Girardi, Sorin Chivulescu; Mircea Mladin; m, Adrian Enescu; art d, Radu Corciova; cos, Gabriela Nicolaescu.

War   **(PR:C   MPAA:NR)**

NOIR ET BLANC   (SEE: BLACK AND WHITE, 1986, Fr.)

NOTHING IN COMMON*** (1986) 118m Rastar/Tri-Star c

Tom Hanks *(David Basner)*, Jackie Gleason *(Max Basner)*, Eva Marie Saint *(Lorraine Basner)*, Hector Elizondo *(Charlie Gargas)*, Barry Corbin *(Andrew Woolridge)*, Bess Armstrong *(Donna Mildred Martin)*, Sela Ward *(Cheryl Ann Wayne)*, Michael Hagerty *(Eric)*, John Kapelos *(Roger)*, Carol Messing *(David's Secretary)*.

Unfortunately, the title is prophetic. Not only do Hanks and Gleason and Saint have nothing in common, this picture is two halves that also don't have anything

in common. The two halves are both good pictures, but they just don't seem to fit. It's one thing to shift moods and quite another to shift genres. Hanks is the ultimate yuppie, a highly successful advertising man with a great sense of humor. His sort-of girl friend is Armstrong and, like so many ad men, he fears any sort of commitment beyond breakfast. His agency lands a huge airline's account after a hilarious presentation. He also manages to land his client's sexy but icy daughter, Ward, which helps the agency nab the account. At the same time, his family's life is falling apart. Gleason, in an understated role as a modern Willy Loman, is

a garment salesman whose life is shattered when he loses his job (in a scene not unlike that in DEATH OF A SALESMAN). At the same time, his wife, Saint, tells him that she wants out. They've been married for 36 years and she has had it with his bitter attitude, his cantankerous ways, and his frequent retreats into silence. It's at that point the picture turns into a drama as Hanks acts as a mediator between his folks. When Gleason's life is threatened by a diabetic attack, melodrama creeps in.

Gleason is unremittingly tough and we can just barely see any humanity under that lizard exterior. Saint's character is given short shrift, and although we see why she left her husband, there is so much more that could be done. Hanks reportedly was paid about $1 million for this movie and earned every penny, as he had to go through several changes, perhaps too many, in order to satisfy the requirements of the script by Podell and Preminger, both veteran comedians who play The Improvisation and other comedy clubs when they aren't writing movies. Lots of laughs but just as many tears. It was a valiant try at doing something different from the mindless comedies of the 1980s, and for that alone, the picture deserves applause.

Set in Chicago, it captures the City of the Big Shoulders well and was one of several movies shot there in recent years, including ABOUT LAST NIGHT, which was based on David Mamet's play "Sexual Perversity in Chicago." The funny stuff could have come right out of an Abrams, Abrams, and Zucker movie, while the drama smacks of afternoon soaps. The acting ranges from light, as in Neil Simon, to depressing, as in Henrik Ibsen. Good cameo from Hector Elizondo as Hanks' harassed advertising boss and some particular fun with the fact that he is bald and wears an awful toupee. Garry Marshall also directed the excellent FLAMINGO KID as well as a send-up of the medical profession, YOUNG DOCTORS IN LOVE. He has a great picture in him somewhere. This is not it, but it's a good indication of better things to come.

p, Alexandra Rose; d, Garry Marshall; w, Rick Podell, Michael Preminger; ph, John A. Alonzo (Metrocolor); m, Patrick Leonard; ed, Glenn Farr; prod d, Charles Rosen; set d, William L. Skinner, Roland E. Hill, Jr.; cos, Rosanna Norton.

Comedy/Drama   Cas.   (PR:A-C MPAA:PG)

NOTTE D'ESTATE CON PROFILO GRECO, OCCHI A MANDORLA E ODORE DI BASILICO (SEE: SUMMER NIGHT, GREEK PROFILE, ALMOND EYES AND THE SCENT OF BASIL, 1986, It.)

NOVEMBERKATZEN† (1986, Ger.) 100m Quadriga Film c (Trans: November Cats)

Angela Hunger *(Ilse)*, Ursela Monn *(Mother)*, Katharina Brauren *(Grandma)*, Robert Zimmerling *(Grandpa)*, Jurgen Vogel *(Dieter)*, Andreas Kastning *(Horst)*, Katja Engelhard *(Marga)*, Dorothea Carrera *(Frau Schuster)*, Christian Woyda *(Bruno Schuster)*, Jens Schuldt *(Philipp Schuster)*, Claudia Schuldt *(Katrin Schuster)*.

This first film from woman director Sigrun Koeppe is set in a small village immediately following WW II. Hunger plagues a lonely 11-year-old whose after-school activities consist of cleaning the house where she, her mother, and two brothers reside. A spark of joy enters her dismal life when she befriends an abandoned kitten.

p&d, Sigrun Koeppe; w, Vera von Wilcken (based on a novel by Mirjam Prossler); ph, Volker Tittel; m, Gunter Ress; ed, Sabine Schonecker; set d, Dieter Reineke.

Drama   (PR:A MPAA:NR)

NTTURUDU† (1986, Guinea-Bissau/Fr.) 75m Republic of Guinea-Bissau–Wac–SFC c

Mario Acqlino *(Mario)*, Joao Bento *(N'Bedjo)*, Faustino Gomes *(Faustino)*, Adalgiza Vaz *(Giza)*, Bya Gomez *(Mario's Wife)*.

Bento is a 12-year-old living in a small farm community. Rumors of a nearby carnival spark his imagination, inciting the adventurous lad to leave his small world behind and join in the fun. His elder brother, Acqlino, is then beset with the task of retrieving the runaway. This 16mm production was the directorial debut for U'Kset, an actor, who depended upon improvisational techniques to develop much of this story.

d, Umban U'Kset; w, Umban U'Kset, Benjamin Legrand; ph, Jean Michel Humeau; m, Wazis Diop, Ze Manel, Loy Ehrlich; ed, Mireille Abramovici.

Children's/Drama   (PR:AA MPAA:NR)

NUIT D'IVRESSE† (1986, Fr.) 85m Trinacra –ICE-Films Flam-La Cinq/ Fechner– GAU c (Trans: Drunken Night)

Thierry Lhermitte *(Jacques Belin)*, Josiane Balasko *(Frede)*, France Roche, Jean-Michel Dupuis, Marc Dudicourt, Jean-Claude Dauphin.

Adapted from a 1985 stage play penned by Balasko, this comedy comes to the screen with Balasko in the lead (a role she also played on stage) opposite Lhermitte, with both of them acting as screenwriters. Lhermitte is a French television personality who is on his way home after receiving an award as the Most Courteous Frenchman of the Year. He has had a bit too much to drink and is extremely discourteous when he meets Balasko, a pudgy ex-prison inmate. An evening of drunken abandon follows. Lhermitte becomes filthy drunk, makes a fool out of himself, utterly destroys his public image, and then proposes to Balasko. The following morning he wakes up with a terrible hangover and is unable to remember anything that happened the night before. Balasko, however, won't let him forget and carries on with her marriage plans. After some initial obstacles in their relationship, Lhermitte realizes that he does indeed love Balasko and they agree to marry. The stage production of NUIT D'IVRESSE starred Michel Blanc, of this year's MENAGE, opposite Balasko.

p, Josiane Balasko, Thierry Lhermitte; d, Bernard Nauer; w, Thierry Lhermitte, Josiane Balasko (based on a play by Josiane Balasko); ph, Carlo Varini (Eastmancolor); m, Jacques Delaporte; ed, Olivier Morel; art d, Ivan Maussion; m/l, Rita Mitsouko.

Comedy/Romance   (PR:NR MPAA:NR)

NUREN XIN† (1986, Hong Kong) Pearl City-Shaw Brothers c (Trans: Women)

Miao Qianren, Li Linlin, Zhou Runfa, Zhong Chuhong.

d, Guan Jinpeng [Stanley Kwan]; w, Li Jie, Qiu Dai Anping.

NUTCRACKER: THE MOTION PICTURE* (1986) 84m
Hyperion–Kushner-Locke/Atlantic Releasing c

Hugh Bigney *(Herr Drosselmeier)*, Vanessa Sharp *(Young Clara)*, Patricia Barker *(Dream Clara)*, Wade Walthall *(Nutcracker)*; Act I: Party Scene: Maia Rosal *(Frau Stahlbaum)*, Carey Homme *(Dr. Stahlbaum)*, Martha Boyle, Dianne Brace, Elizabeth McCarthy, Laura Schwenk *(Mothers)*, Christian Cederlund, Gerard Ebitz, Benjamin Houk, Sterling Kekoa *(Fathers)*, Benjamin Bassett, Beatrice Bassett *(Grandparents)*, Gregory Draper *(Uncle)*, Jennifer Homans, Ann Renhard *(Maiden Aunts)*, Lisa Stolzy, Jeffery N. Bullock *(Foreign Guests)*, Patricia Barker *(Ballerina Doll)*, Courtland Weaver *(Sword Dancer)*, Alejandra Bronfman, Kevin Kaiser, Reid Olson *(Pas de Trois)*, Russell Burnett *(Fritz)*, Whitney Onishi, Natalie Ryder *(Teenagers)*, Emerald Stacy *(Little Girl)*, Cary Stidham *(Little Boy)*, Elizabeth Parham, Vera Parham, Emily Penhollow, Gloria Riviera *(Girls)*, Joseph Carver, Alex Gardner, Jason Takamaru, Andrew Wilson *(Boys)*; Fight Scene: Jacob Rice *(Nutcracker)*, Banjamin Houk *(Mouse Captain)*, Deborah Inkster *(Mother Mouse)*, Chaundra Bigney, Bridget Alsdorf *(Baby Mice)*, Todd Brown, Erik Cederlund, Margaret Farmer, Robert La Turner, Katrenna Marenych, Jeffrey Plourde, Christopher Smidt, Carolyn Stoklosa, Anne Wescott *(Fighting Mice)*, Marianne Chikos, Elizabeth Christianson, Lindsay Clothier, Sarah Frederick *(Officers)*, Michele Blue, Sarah Coan, Rebecca Dunne, Christa Halby *(Artillery)*, Heather Boe, Tracy Carboneau, Charina Dimaano, Nicole Fiset, Joey-Lynn Mann, Erin Sokol *(Cavalry)*, Hannah Brudge, Laara Estelle, Betsy Fenton, Gabrielle Gardner, Eugenia Georvasilis, Lee Johnson, Christine Lebar, Catherine Mee Moen, Christina Nicolaidis, Rebecca Osmon, Freedom Ozog, Amy Ritter, Noelle Schroeder, Ashley Sherwood, Rana Standal, Nicole Wolgamott *(Infantry)*; Act II: Heather Boe, Tracy Carboneau, Charina Dimaano, Nicole Fiset, Joey-Lynn Mann, Erin Sokol *(Scrim Mice)*, Bridget Alsdorf, Rebecca Brown, Michele Blue, Kippy Clark, Rebecca Dunne, Christine Elias, Christa Halby, Abby Hall, Heather Hollenbeck, Jennifer Kader, Sun Lee, Mandi Lyons-Hansen, Michelle McRae, Sara Pritchard, Jennifer Taylor, Kyoko Terada *(Servant Children)*, Lisa Stolzy, Carey Homme, Dianne Brace, Christian Cederlund, Erica Fischbach, Gerard Ebitz, Elizabeth McCarthy, Kevin Kaiser, Laura Schwenk, Reid Olson *(Moors)*, Maia Rosal *(Peacock)*, Erik Cederlund, Jeffrey Plourde *(Slaves)*, Jeffery N. Bullock *(Chinese Tiger)*, Rachel Harrison, Lee Johnson, Jennifer Owen, Nicole Wolgamott *(Chinese Girls)*, Benjamin Houk, Jacob Rice, Courtland Weaver *(Dervishes)*, Alejandra Bronfman, Sterling Kekoa, Carron Donaldson *(Commedia)*, Kara Chin, Jamie Geier, Christine Lebar, Mari London, Caroline Newman, Christina Nicolaidis, Freedom Ozog, Jenifer Peterson *(Toy Theater)*, Lucinda Hughey, Martha Boyle, Dianne Brace, Irene Damestoy, Carron Donaldson, Susan Gladstone, Amy Greene, Jennifer Homans, Stephanie Irwin, Elizabeth McCarthy, Kay Preston, Ann Renhard, Laura Schwenk, Lisa Stolzy, Julie Tobiason, Heidi Vierthaler, Clara Wilson *(Waltz of the Flowers)*, Todd Brown, Marianne Chikos, Laara Estelle, Margaret Farmer, Betsy Fenton, Sarah Frederick, Gabrielle Gardner, Eugenia Georvasilis, Catherine Mee Moen, Jennifer Porter, Amy Ritter, Ashley Sherwood, Christopher Smidt, Angela Sterling, Carolyn Stoklosa, Anne Wescott, Tryon Woods *(Observers)*; Snow Scene: Carol Anderson, Martha Boyle, Dianne Brace, Irene Damestoy, Carron Donaldson, Susan Gladstone, Amy Greene, Jennifer Homans, Stephanie Irwin, Elizabeth McCarthy, Ann Renhard, Angela Sterling, Laura Schwenk, Lisa Stolzy, Julie Tobiason, Lisl Vaillant, Clara Wilson *(Snowflakes)*.

Transferring ballet to film has always been a difficult task. Part of the art form's beauty comes in witnessing the dance unfold before one's eyes and such elements as close-ups and editing intrude on the dancer's and the choreographer's art. However, there have been successful incorporations of ballet into fiction films, most notably THE RED SHOES (1948), LIMELIGHT (1952), and THE TURNING POINT (1977). The few full-fledged ballet productions which have been committed to film, such as 1967's SWAN LAKE, featuring Rudolf Nureyev and Dame Margot Fonteyn, have generally been created with the idea of capturing important performances. This has been a slowly growing trend with the popularity of videocassettes, yet a full-length ballet shot expressly for the cinema still remains an avenue largely unexplored by filmmakers.

Carroll Ballard's 1986 version of the Christmas classic THE NUTCRACKER attempts to rework a highly praised stage production for screen, and while not entirely successful as a dance film, Ballard does capture the uniqueness of the Pacific Northwest Ballet's revolutionary production. In 1979 Kent Stowell and his wife Francia Russell, codirectors of this Seattle-based company, approached noted children's author/illustrator Maurice Sendak *(Where the Wild Things Are)* about possibly designing the sets for a new staging of "The Nutcracker." Sendak, who had just designed a highly praised set for the Houston Grand Opera's production of Mozart's "The Magic Flute," initially turned down the offer, saying he felt the ballet was too carefree and lacked a really intriguing plot. Stowell had similar feelings about the longtime audience favorite, but after much discussion with Sendak, it was decided they would abstain from a traditional presentation.

The Tchaikovsky ballet, originally staged in 1892 by the Imperial Ballet of Russia, was based on an adaptation that Alexandre Dumas, pere, had done of E.T.A. Hoffman's fairy tale (first published in 1816) emphasizing the story's sweeter elements. Sendak later wrote that he and Stowell found their "Nutcracker" . . . in the grave, often threatening, subterranean child's world that coexists inside the safe and happy house of Clara's parents . . . It is this truthfulness to child life that gives resonance to Hoffmann's tale and makes it an extraordinary work of art. The production of the ballet that [we] conceived of was our effort to embrace Hoffmann—to get back to the gritty, slap-happy German Marchen, or tale that never quite explains itself but is fiercely true to the child's experience." To achieve this spirit, Sendak, whose own work often emphasizes the darker dreams of childhood, felt this "Nutcracker" should be underscored by the newfound maturity and blossoming sexuality of Clara, the story's

young heroine. Clara's attempt to come to terms with things she cannot understand would be the ballet's focus as the girl passed from her parents' home to a world of fantasy during her special Christmas night. Sendak's set design reflected this theme, and what was once a light Christmas entertainment produced by ballet companies around the world suddenly took on a whole new countenance. Critics were almost unanimous in acclaiming the production, and Lincoln Kirstein, founder and director of the prestigious New York City Ballet, stated: "I was filled with a violent greed and envy."

The production, which resulted in a new publication of Hoffman's story accompanied by Sendak's illustrations, was approached by the Arts and Entertainment Network and public television's "Dance in America" series for a possible adaptation. However, both Sendak and Stowell felt their work would lose its impact on a small screen. Instead, they turned their sights towards theatrical film and the project was kicked around for a few years. In December 1985 Carroll Ballard saw the stage production and decided to get involved with the film version. It seemed like an ideal project for the director of THE BLACK STALLION and NEVER CRY WOLF, two films which were praised for their unique visual style. Shooting began in summer of 1986 and proceeded through a rapid 10 day filming schedule.

The story follows Clara, a girl danced first by 12-year-old Sharp. At a family Christmas party Sharp is continually bothered by Drosselmeier (danced by Bigney), a strange old man who offers her toys. Bigney also poses an underlying threat of things of which Sharp is unsure, so to escape this situation, Sharp imagines herself to be whisked away by her dream lover, the Nutcracker (danced by Walthall). In this dream, Clara is now danced by Barker, a woman in her early twenties. Barker travels to a magic kingdom where she learns not even dreams carry a guarantee of safety as she finds herself being wooed by a mysterious pasha (also danced by Bigney). This man wants Barker for himself, and attempts to woo her with an amazing array of entertainment. Yet Barker, for the first time in her life, knows what she wants and takes to the air with her beloved Walthall. Bigney will not give in so easily, and separates the lovers as they soar through the sky. The story ends with Sharp safely asleep, while Bigney (as Drosselmeier) sits bitterly alone in his workshop.

Ballard is faithful to Sendak's intent, creating a film that captures the essence of Hoffman's deeper meanings. Sendak's unusual sets, featuring pop-eyed creations and grandiose architecture, transfer well to film, and the special effects (which were not part of the stage production) are a fine addition to the story. Yet, for all intents and purposes, this is also a ballet and THE NUTCRACKER suffers from an uneasy clash between dance and cinematic style. Much of Stowell's choreography is lost due to Ballard's concentration on the story, which emphasizes the characters more than the dance. Bigney, Barker, and Walthall are strong enough dancers to overcome this, but the corps du ballet does not come off as well as they might have. Undoubtedly this is due in part to the hurried production schedule ("We had to bring the dancers onto the stage and shoot it like a football game," Ballard later remarked) and, to Ballard's credit, THE NUTCRACKER maintains a conscious effort to bring new meaning to a well-known work. Though perhaps not all it should be, THE NUTCRACKER is certainly worth seeing by both dance and film enthusiasts. Despite the deeper meanings to the relationship between Drosselmeier and Clara, the film was rated G by the MPAA and is excellent fare for younger audiences.

p, Willard Carroll, Donald Kushner, Peter Locke, Thomas L. Wilhite; d, Carroll Ballard; w, Kent Stowell, Maurice Sendak (based on the fairy tale "The Nutcracker and the Mouse King" by E.T.A. Hoffman); ph, Stephen H. Burum (MGM Color); m, Peter Ilyich Tchaikovsky; ed, John Nutt, Michael Silvers; prod d, Maurice Sendak; md, Charles Mackerras; art d, Peter Horne; cos, Maurice Sendak; spec eff, Esquire Jauchem, Gregory Meeh; ch, Kent Stowell; makeup, Richard Snell.

Dance (PR:AAA MPAA:G)

NYAMANTON†   (1986, Mali) 90m Centre National de Prod.
                    Cinematographique du Mali c (Trans: The Garbage Boys)

Diarrah Sanogo *(Mother)*, Macire Kante *(Kalifa)*, Ada Thiocary *(Fanta)*, Alikaou Kante *(Karim)*.

Kante plays an impoverished eight-year-old forced to leave school because he doesn't have a desk. The industrious boy collects garbage to fund one, thus gaining readmission into the school. Intertwined with this simple drama are other observations of the poor's struggle to survive in adverse conditions. This inexpensive feature was the directorial debut of Sissoko, a student of *cinema verite* filmmaker and theorist Jean Rouch.

d&w, Cheik Omar Sissoko; ph, Cheik Hamala Keita; m, Sidiki Diabate, Moriba Keita, Mamadou Diallo, Marouna Barry; ed, Vojislav Korijenac.

Drama   (PR:C   MPAA:NR)

O

O HOMEM DA CAPA PRETA†

(1986, Braz.) 119m
Morena-Embrafilme-Therezinha Calil Petrus-Lock All-Montevideo/
Embrafilme c (Trans: The Man with the Black Coat)

Jose Wilker *(Tenorio Cavalcanti)*, Marieta Severo *(Zina)*, Jonas Bloch *(Adolfo)*, Carlos Gregorio *(Silas Goncalves)*, Paulo Vilaca *(Inspector Maragato)*, Tonico Pereira *(Bereco)*, Jackson de Souza *(Cabral)*, Chico Dias *(Manezinho)*, Isolda Cresta *(Tenorio's Mother)*, Jurandir de Oliveira *(Venancio)*, Guilherme Karan *(Flavio Cavalcanti)*.

A biographical feature on Tenorio Cavalcanti, a notorious figure in Brazilian politics in the 1940s and 1950s, known for showing up at meetings of the national legislature wearing a black coat and brandishing a machine gun named Lurdinha. Shot with the cooperation of Cavalcanti's family at the castle he built to protect himself, the film has been criticized for taking too favorable a view of its subject, who, incidentally, is still alive and living in a Rio de Janeiro suburb.

d, Sergio Rezende; w, Sergio Rezende, Tairone Feitosa, Jose Louzeiro (based on *Tenorio, o Homem e o Mito* by Maria do Carmo Cavalcanti Fortes, *Meu Pai, Tenorio* by Sandra Cavalcanti Freitas Lima, and *Capa Prete e Lurdinha* by Israel Beloch); ph, Cesar Charlone (Eastmancolor); m, David Tygel; ed, Rafael Valverde; art d, Rita Murtinho; set d, Alexandre Mayer, Pedro Nanni, Barbara Mandonca; cos, Rita Murtinho, Isabel Paranhos.

Biography   **(PR:C MPAA:NR)**

O JE†

(1986, Czech.) Gottwaldov c (Trans: Oh Dear)

Matin Krb, Jiri Devat, Klara Pollertova, Jakub Spalek, Zdenka Hadrbolcova.

d, Vladimir Drha; w, Petr Bartunek, Vladimir Drha; ph, Juraj Fandli.

O MELISSOKOMOS†

(1986, Gr.) 142m Greek Film Center-Marin Karmitz-ERT-1-Theo Angelopoulos c (Trans: The Bee Keeper)

Marcello Mastroianni *(Spyros)*, Nadia Mourouzi *(The Girl)*, Serge Reggiani *(Sick Man)*, Jenny Roussea *(Anna)*, Dinos Iliopoulos *(Friend)*, Vassia Panagopoulou, Dimitris Poulikakos, Nikos Kouros, Yannis Zavradinos, Chris Nezer.

Mastroianni plays an aging, defeated man who immerses himself in beekeeping to escape his inability to find fulfillment in personal relationships. He travels across the countryside in his truck attending to his various beehives, paying brief visits along the way to members of his family in the hopes of creating meaningful contact. During his journey a young woman hitches a ride with him. Mastroianni is obviously attracted to her, but shrinks from any physical or emotional contact. He becomes hysterically jealous when spotting her with another man, leading to a forced, brief romance between them.

d, Theo Angelopoulos; w, Theo Angelopoulos, Dimitris Nollas, Tonino Guerra; ph, Giorgos Arvanitis; m, Helen Karaindrou; ed, Takis Yannopoulos; art d, Mikes Karapiperis; cos, Giorgos Ziakas.

Drama   **(PR:O MPAA:NR)**

O MEU CASO—REPETICOES†

(1986, Portugal)

Luis Miguel Cintra.

Variations on a one-act play by Jose Regio performed by Cintra and directed by De Oliveira, who had previously worked with the actor on the sprawling epic O SAPATO DE CETIM.

d, Manoel De Oliveira; w, (based on the play "O Meu Caso" by Jose Regio).

Drama   **(PR:A MPAA:NR)**

O SLAVE A TRAVE†

(1986, Czech.) Koliba (Trans: On Glory and Grass)

Milan Knazko, Monika Hilmerova, Jana Plichtova, Zdena Studenkova.

d, Peter Solan; w, Zora Krystufkova; ph, Stanislav Szomolanyi.

O VESTIDO COR DE FOGO†

(1986, Port.) 92m L.A. Producoes Cinematograficas c

Jorge Vale, Acacia Thiele, Mariana Rey Monteiro, Josefina Silva, Rosa Lobato Faria, Guida Maria, Carlos Wallenstein, Adelaide Joao, Luisa Barbosa, Margarida Carpinteiro, Jose Severino, Manuela Carlos.

Love blossoms during the Portuguese political upheavals of 1974, but the lovers are torn apart because the man is so overwhelmed by the woman's love that he abandons her.

p,d&w, Lauro Antonio; ph, Elso Roque; m, Carlos Mendes, Giacomo Puccini.

Drama   **(PR:C MPAA:NR)**

OBDULIA†

(1986, Mex.) Kinam A.C.-Mexican Film Institute c

Veronica Nieba, Ignacio Guadalupe, Fabiola Araiza, Angelica Guerrero.

d, Juan Antonio de la Riva; w, Arturo Villasenor; ph, Leoncio Villarias; m, Antonio Avitia; ed, Luis Kelly.

OBECANA ZEMLJA†

(1986, Yugo.) 117m Jadran/Croatia c (Trans: The Promised Land)

Bata Zivojinovic *(Markan)*, Mirjana Karanovic *(Marta)*, Dara Dzokic *(Stana)*, Vjenceslav Kapural *(Milisa)*, Vanja Drach *(Judge)*, Dragan Nikolic *(Zec)*.

In 1946, the newly established Communist government of Yugoslavia is striving to institute collectivism among the farmers. Zivojinovic is the head of one collective, and he is opposed by crusty old peasant Kapural. Their dispute is personal as well as political, and Zivojinovic ends it by shooting the old man. After his trial, the government announces the failure and cancellation of collectivism.

d, Veljko Bulajic; w, Ivo Bresan; ph, Goran Trbuljak (Eastmancolor); m, Alfi Kabiljo; art d, Milenko Jeremic; cos, Jasna Novak.

Drama   **(PR:A-C MPAA:NR)**

OCEAN DRIVE WEEKEND zero

(1986) 98m L.A. Prods./Troma c

Charles Redmond *(Miller)*, Robert Peacock *(Chuck Watkins)*, P.J. Grethe *(Jeannie)*, Konya Dee *(Linda)*, Jon Kohler *(Kirk)*, Tony Freeman *(Allen)*, John Aschenbrenner *(Mark)*, Sharon Brewer *(Patty)*, Kay McCelland *(Marsha)*, Will Redmond *(Hank)*, Dan Byrd *(Billy)*, Wallace Eastland *(Freddy)*, Grant Elliot *(Danny)*, Dan Moran *(Tommy)*, Hall Gritz *(Gas Attendant)*, Marian Bolton *(Waitress)*, Susan C. Jones *(Teller)*, Bryan Jones *(Cop)*, H.C. Jones *(Cop on Beach)*, Happy Huskey *(Motel Manager)*, Henry Cox *(Manager's Son)*, Danny Grinnell *(Drunk)*, Gordon Oresta, Virgil Hopkins, Jef Bailey, Carol Doherty, Smitty Flynn and The Rivieras.

Filmed on location at Georgetown and Myrtle Beach, South Carolina in 1984, given a limited release in that state in 1985, and finally finding its way to mass distribution on videocassette in 1986, OCEAN DRIVE WEEKEND is simply pathetic. Brainless, boring, and technically incompetent, this alleged "comedy" is supposed to be set in the mid-1960s, but aside from some bouffant hairdos and a couple of old jalopies there is absolutely no sense of time or place conveyed here. Virtually plotless, the film follows several groups of college students from various Southern universities who converge on "Ocean Drive" for a weekend of dancing, beer, and sex. Among the hopelessly stereotyped characters are nice guy Peacock, slob Charles Redmond, nerds Will Redmond (who also worked on the crew as the Best Boy) and Dan Byrd, pot-smoker Kohler, failing-and-soon-to-be-drafted Freeman, overweight-but-brilliant Eastland, suave ladies' man Aschenbrenner, fraternity snob Elliot, nice girl Grethe, "loose" girl McCelland, snobby girl Dee, and uptight intellect Brewer. Of course, by the end of the film the fraternity snob and his buddies get their comeuppance, nice guy Peacock and nice girl Grethe fall in love, the intellects, Eastland and Brewer, discover sex, and the rest of the cast drink, dance, and play a lot of pranks.

OCEAN DRIVE WEEKEND is woefully unfunny and torturously tedious as it attempts to be a cross between ANIMAL HOUSE and PORKY'S. Most of the scenes are done in one-take master shots with a minimum of editing. Long pauses between passages of mundane dialog are common as the amateur actors struggle to remember their lines (like the classic: "Don't be a drip, Patty!"). The ads for the film promise loads of great old rock 'n' roll tunes, but what they don't tell you is that most of them are sung by cast members (usually while driving) or a wretched garage band called Smitty Flynn and the Rivieras. Somehow the producers did secure the rights to use The Drifters' classic "Under the Boardwalk," but the tune is beaten to death on the soundtrack and is heard more than six times. Other fondly remembered 1960s classics mangled beyond recognition by lousy cover versions are: "Showdown" (Gamble & Huff, performed by Smitty Flynn and the Rivieras), "Under the Boardwalk" (Resnick & Young, performed by The Drifters), "Double Shot" (Vetter & Smith, performed by Smitty Flynn and the Rivieras), "It Will Stand" (Norman Johnson, performed by The Showmen), "Peanut Butter" (Barner, Cooper, Smith, Goldsmith, performed by Smitty Flynn and the Rivieras), "Be Young, Be Foolish, Be Happy" (Whitley & Cobb, performed by The Tams), "39-21-46" (Norman Johnson, performed by Smitty Flynn and the Rivieras), "Come Go With Me" (C.E. Quick, performed by Smitty Flynn and the Rivieras), "Girl Watcher/Boy Watcher" (Karen & Ron Killett, performed by Karen & Ron Killett).

p, Marvin Almeas; d, Bryan Jones; w, Bryan Jones (based on a story by Bryan Jones, Charles Redmond); m, Alan Kaufman; ed, John Godwin; cos, Ann Jones.

Comedy   **Cas.**   **(PR:C MPAA:PG-13)**

OD PETKA DO PETKA†

(1986, Yugo.) Dalmacija (Trans: From One Friday to the Next)

Boris Dvornik, Zdravka Krstulovic, Katija Zubcic, Vladimir Rupcic, Lukrica Breskovic-Opalk.

d, Anton Vrdoljak; w, Miljenko Smoje; ph, Tomislav Pinter; m, Arsen Dedic; set d, Zeljko Senecic.

ODA NA RADOST†

(1986, Czech.) Barrandov (Trans: Ode to Happiness)

Magda Wollejo, Hanna Bieluszko, Josef Abrham, Viktor Preiss, Bohumila Dolejsova.

d&w, Jaroslav Balik; ph, Jaroslav Brabec.

ODD JOBS**½

(1986) 89m HBO-Silver Screen Partners/Tri-Star c

Paul Reiser *(Max)*, Robert Townsend *(Dwight)*, Scott McGinnis *(Woody)*, Rick Overton *(Roy)*, Paul Provenza *(Byron)*, Leo Burmester *(Wylie D. Daiken)*, Thomas Quinn *(Frankie)*, Savannah Smith Boucher *(Loretta/Lynette)*, Richard Dean Anderson *(Spud)*, Richard Foronjy *(Manny)*, Ken Olfson *(Mayor Brady)*, Jake Steinfeld *(Nick)*, Eleanor Mondale *(Mandy)*, Charlie Dell *(Earl)*, Starletta

DuPois *(Dwight's Mom)*, Don Imus *(Monty Leader)*, Wayne Grace *(Roy's Father)*, Julianne Phillips *(Sally)*, Leon Askin *(Don Carlutci)*, Andra Akers *(Mrs. Finelli)*, Chuck Pfeifer *(The Don's Body Guard/Dead Meat Warrior)*, Patti Clifton *(Mrs. Brady)*, Martha Jane Urann *(Dalene)*, Tom Dugan *(Lester)*, Jim Holmes *(Jeff)*, Chris Hubbell *(1st Young Executive)*, Jeff Maxwell *(2nd Young Executive)*, Fred Pierce *(Waiter)*, Diana Bellamy *(Woman in Restaurant)*, Janet Clark *(80-Year-Old Woman)*, Zero Hubbard *(Brad)*, Dermott Downs *(Boy)*, John Furlong *(Readmont Owner)*, Eve Smith *(Elderly Woman)*, Harvey Levine *(White Homeowner)*, Vance Colvig *(Chairman)*, Susan Krebs *(Gloria)*, Darlene Chehardy *(Girl with Refrigerator)*, Arleen Sorkin *(Diner Waitress)*, Donald J. Westerdale *(Microwave Man)*, Jill Goodacre *(Co-ed)*, Andre Veluzet *(Tank Driver)*, Michael Ragsdale *(Bartender at Dead Meat)*, Keith Joe Dick *(Himself)*, Diane Willson Dick, Debbie Tilton, Cindy Bernstein *(Dickettes)*, Wesley A. Pfenning *(Interviewer)*, Arlin Miller *(Newscaster)*, Anita Sherman, Denise Routt, Sharon Robinson, Marcia Bullock, Dee Dee Belson, Leslie Smith, Terry Bradford, Lloyd C. Wilkey, Josef Powell, Arno Lucas *(Choir Members)*, Norman Thalheimer *(Organist)*, Cecili Stewart, Lisa Fulton, Debbie Rothstein, Keith Clifton, Mark Nordike, Jim Ruttman *(Dancers in the Lion's Den)*, Heidi Hunter, Kris Molina, Julie Trei, Cammy Trei, Sherene Sedgewick, Becki Weeks, Scott Carrington, Pete Fleury *(College Students)*.

This cheerful little comedy follows five college friends (Reiser, Townsend, McGinnis, Overton, and Provenza) who band together during summer break to form their own moving company. Told in flashback, with the five heroes giving a present-time narration on the soundtrack, ODD JOBS opens as each young man takes on a summer job. Overton, a white youth, is to spend the summer with Townsend, a black friend, and his family. In hopes of ingratiating himself Overton speaks in black street dialect, but this only annoys Townsend's cultured family. The two take jobs as caddies, while Provenza becomes involved with an evangelist who sponsors nuclear-powered vacuum cleaners. Provenza sells the gadgets door-to-door, an occupation that inevitably leads to some strange confrontations. McGinnis becomes a waiter at a fancy restaurant, and there catches the eye of Mondale, the sexy daughter of mayor Olfson. (Is this typecasting? Mondale is the real-life daughter of former Minnesota senator, vice president, and 1984 presidential candidate Walter Mondale.) Reiser gets a job with a shady moving firm ("Caprizzi—rhymes with sleazy"), which compounds his troubles with girl friend Phillips. She is frustrated by Reiser's unstable nature and takes up with Anderson, a wealthy snob whom Phillips doesn't really love. When Reiser is sent out on a week-long road trip by the Caprizzis, he's paired with Burmester, a greasy-haired, fun-loving good ol' boy. Reiser is less than thrilled by this arrangement, but gradually he and Burmester become friends. Inspired by Burmester's example and tired of the Caprizzis' working conditions, Reiser leaves his job and talks his buddies into forming their own moving company. They take out a loan from Askin, a corpulent Mafioso, then get themselves an office. To drum up business, the boys indulge in a little underhanded dealing themselves and the firm is soon thriving. Naturally the Caprizzis aren't thrilled with the competition and begin retaliating. Reiser's office is blown up, yet the gang is determined to be a success. They borrow Burmester's truck for an important job, but must look elsewhere to secure a trailer. It's decided to pilfer one from Reiser's former employer, and, once inside the opposition's warehouse, the boys learn the Caprizzis are behind a series of local car thefts. Reiser calls the cops while the gang tries to fend off Caprizzi goons. Burmester arrives to save the day, along with the law, and Reiser, Townsend, McGinnis, Overton, and Provenza are declared citywide heroes.

Unlike so many low-budget comedies, ODD JOBS doesn't base its humor on a group of guys trying to get a peek at some naked female breasts. Rather, it couples some offbeat notions with good comic performances, and while nothing memorable, the results are fairly enjoyable. Reiser, best known for his roles as Modell in Barry Levinson's DINER and the evil Burke in ALIENS, also works as a stand-up comic. His character here is a good extension of his nightclub persona, a confused but likable young man who just can't quite put his life together. Another enjoyable performance comes from Townsend, a talented individual who would gain wider exposure in 1987 with his directorial debut film, HOLLYWOOD SHUFFLE. Story's direction gives this a nice energetic feeling, adding a sense of fun to individual anecdotes without subordinating the plot development. There are some points in which Story overplays his hand, such as the overlong fight sequence, but these flaws aren't too detrimental. Phillips is better known for her real-life offscreen role as Mrs. Bruce Springsteen. Shot on location in southern California (though the story apparently takes place in Pittsburgh, Pennsylvania, of all places), ODD JOBS was filmed in part at Heritage Square, an open air museum devoted to preserving turn-of-the-century California homes. Songs include "Prime Time" (Robert Folk, Brenda Folk, Keith Landry, performed by Landry), "Heat of the Night" (John Leffier, performed by Leffier), "Cadillac Crusin'" (Keith Joe Dick, performed by Keith Joe Dick and the Dickettes), "I Judge the Funk" (E. Horan, H. Murrell, D.J. Emile), "My Turn" (H. Murrell, J. Mitchell), "Duelin' Banjos" (Arthur Smith), "Next Time You Leave Me" (G. Lupton), "Macho Shuffle Theme" (Rob Walsh), "Turn Your Radio On" (A. Brumley), "No One's Safe at Home" (Jamie Newman), "The Magic of Thinking Big" (David J. Schwartz).

p, Keith Fox Rubinstein; d, Mark Story; w, Robert Conte, Peter Martin Wortmann; ph, Arthur Albert (Metrocolor); m, Robert Folk; ed, Dennis M. Hill; prod d, Robert R. Benton; set d, Sydney Ann Smith-Kee; cos, Betty Pecha Madden; spec eff, R. Beezts Company; ch, Bob Banas; m/l, Robert Folk, Brenda Folk, Keith Landry, John Leffier, Keith Joe Dick, E. Horan, H. Murrell, D.J. Emile, J. Mitchell, Arthur Smith, G. Lupton, Rob Walsh, A. Brumley, Jamie Newman, David J. Schwartz; makeup, Julie Purcell, Toni Trimble; stunts, Buck McDancer; ch, Bob Banas.

Comedy (PR:C-O MPAA:PG-13)

ODINOTCHNOYE PLAVANIYE† (1986, USSR) 93m Mosfilm Studios c
(Trans: The Detached Mission)

Mikhail Nozhkin *(Shatokhin)*, Aleksandr Fatiushin *(Kruglov)*, Sergei Nosibov *(Danilov)*, Nartai Begalin *(Parshin)*, Vitaly Zikora *(Harrison)*, Arnis Litzitis *(Hassolt)*.

Soviet action film sees the CIA attempting to provoke WW III by sending a small nuclear rocket into Soviet battleships while they perform their annual maneuvers in the Pacific. While preparing to launch the nuclear weapon from a tiny atoll that serves as their secret headquarters, the CIA accidentally sends a rocket crashing into a pleasure cruiser. In an effort to cover up the incident, the CIA sends assassins to kill an American couple who survived the disaster. The woman is murdered, but the man escapes and is taken in by the Soviet navy. Outraged at his homeland, the man joins up with the Russians and helps them infiltrate the CIA base and destroy it before the CIA can launch the nuclear rocket.

d, Mikhail Tumanishvili; w, Evgeny Mesiatzev; ph, Boris Bondarenko; m, Victor Babushkin; ed, I. Tzinin; art d, Tatyana Lapshina, Aleksandr Myagkov.

Action (PR:C MPAA:NR)

OFF BEAT*** (1986) 92m Ufland-Roth-Ladd/Touchstone Films–Silver Screen Partners II c

Judge Reinhold *(Joe Gower)*, Meg Tilly *(Rachel Wareham)*, Cleavant Derricks *(Abe Washington)*, Joe Mantegna *(Pete Peterson)*, Jacques D'Amboise *(August)*, Amy Wright *(Mary Ellen Gruenwald)*, John Turturro *(Neil Pepper)*, James Tolkan *(Harry)*, Julie Bovasso *(Mrs. Wareham)*, Anthony Zerbe *(Mr. Wareham)*, Fred Gwynne *(The Commissioner)*, Harvey Keitel *(Mickey)*, Victor Argo *(Leon)*, Austin Pendleton *(Gun Shop Salesman)*, Penn Jillette *(Norman)*, Jack Fletcher *(Alvin)*, Mel Winkler *(Earl)*, Irving Metzman *(DeLuca)*, Mike Starr *(James Bonnell)*, Shawn Elliot *(Hector)*, Stanley Simmonds *(Pud)*, Nancy Giles *(Celestine)*, Paul Butler *(Jordan)*, John Kapelos *(Lou Wareham)*, Bill Sadler *(Dickson)*, Christopher Noth *(Ely Wareham, Jr.)*, Mark Medoff *(Sgt. Tiegher)*, Yvonne Talton Kersey *(Lucinda)*, Fyvush Finkel *(Vendor)*, Ann McDonough *(Bank Teller)*, Mary Duncan *(Saleslady)*, Laura Crimmins *(Teenage Dance Student)*, Carmine Foresta *(E.S. Lieutenant)*, Madeleine Berger *(Bank Customer)*, Helen Hanft *(Waitress)*, Peter Wise *(Car Thief)*, Jhoe Breedlove, Gregory Uel Cole, Aisha Coley, Ed Deacy, Yvonne Erwin, Gia Galeano, Jeffrey Anderson-Gunter, Christine Jacobsen, Michael Lisenco, Marilynn Lyons, Faye Fujisaki Mar, Rome Neal, Frank Patton, Lisa Paulino, Linda Ravin *(Dancing Cops)*.

The talents on both sides of the camera are mildly impressive, but OFF BEAT is a bland, wholly contrived comedy that fails to deliver any solid humor. Derricks (Robin Williams' benefactor from MOSCOW ON THE HUDSON) is a cop on an undercover assignment following a long sought after drug dealer. Just as he and his fellow officers are about to take their man, Derricks' buddy Reinhold rides along on his bicycle. Thinking the drug dealer is also a cop, Reinhold asks

Derricks what sort of undercover case he's working on, effectively blowing a carefully constructed cover. This gets Derricks in big trouble with his superior officers, and as a punishment he is forcibly volunteered to audition for a charity dance show. This benefit, to be choreographed by D'Amboise, will feature a troupe of dancing cops, so Derricks sends Reinhold in his place. Reinhold, figuring he owes his pal one, agrees though he is not thrilled with the idea of impersonating a police officer. At the audition, in an effort ingratiate himself with the other cops, Reinhold makes an offhand remark about the Knapp Commission (the 1970 inquiry into police corruption). Mantegna, a cop who had been investigated during the course of that study, is furious with Reinhold over this comment and takes an instant dislike to the newcomer. During the audition Reinhold becomes attracted to Tilly, another would-be dancer cum cop (in real life, Tilly does have a strong dance background), who had a brief affair with Mantegna. In hopes of impressing her, Reinhold wins a spot in the show, as does Mantegna who wants to keep his eye on his former amour. When Derricks hears the news, he is terrified someone will find out and get him in big trouble. Reinhold tries to reassure his friend and continues with his evening dance rehearsals. After her brief affair with Mantegna, Tilly has decided she wants no more romances with policemen. Reinhold's charm breaks down her will, however, and the two begin a tentative relationship. Now Reinhold must balance his increasingly complex double life between would-be policeman/dancer and his day job as a library clerk. One night, while Reinhold and Tilly are leaving rehearsal, a coworker from the library recognizes Reinhold. Reinhold convinces Tilly this was someone from his days as an undercover officer, but when a former love of Reinhold's turns up naked in his apartment, Tilly refuses to listen. Frustrated by these unwanted turns in his life, Reinhold quits his library job, dons his police uniform, and goes to the bank to cash his last check. Keitel and Argo, a pair of small-time hoods, try to hold up the bank and end up taking all the customers hostage. Thinking Reinhold to be a real cop, Keitel decides to use him as a bargaining chip with police negotiators. Who should be on the negotiating team but Tilly and Mantegna, who must drop their personal differences despite their opposing feelings for Reinhold. Inside the bank Reinhold decides it's time to take some action. He begins a few steps from his role in the dance number, which surprises the robbers and entertains the other hostages. When Keitel turns his head, Reinhold is able to kick the gun out of his captor's hand and subsequently brings an end to the situation. Gwynne, the city's police commissioner, is furious when he learns Reinhold was impersonating an officer and promises to ruin Derricks' career. But Reinhold, knowing how important the dance show is, threatens to drop out unless Derricks is absolved of any wrongdoing. Gwynne reluctantly agrees and Reinhold goes to the Lincoln Center to appear in the presentation. He and Tilly reconcile moments before the curtain rises, then dance up a storm over the end credits.

Reinhold and Tilly are an attractive team but the potential humor within their romance is consistently subordinated to a series of forced and largely unfunny plot developments. Reinhold performs his job of library clerk while wearing roller skates, zipping up and down the aisles with tape recorder headphones dutifully strapped to his head. This is the sort of on-the-job behavior that exists only in a Hollywood movie, and feels like it came out of a manual for creating cute characters. Likewise, the idea of Reinhold's maintaining a phony identity to appear in a police benefit and win Tilly's heart is artificially strained. The few quiet scenes between the two would-be lovers reveal a natural chemistry between Reinhold and Tilly that should have been emphasized rather than the contrived comic setups. A good comedy is based on strong characters, not outlandish premises, and OFF BEAT's gimmicky setups simply don't have that essential factor. What is all the more frustrating is the quality of names associated with the film. The script was penned by Mark Medoff, who also wrote 1986's much praised CHILDREN OF A LESSER GOD. Somewhere between that drama and this comedy, he lost any sense of realistic situations and dialog. Dinner, who directed the bright comedy HEAVEN HELP US, also seems to have relinquished his previous talents when he turned to this project. His direction is rudimentary at best, staging situations without any real attempt to expand the comic possibilities. Di Palma, who photographed (among other things) BLOW-UP, RED DESERT, and HANNAH AND HER SISTERS, does nothing of interest here. Some scenes contain a few diversions in moody lighting, but it's nothing any competent cameraman couldn't create given the same situation. And as for Keitel, he's merely passable in a role that doesn't do a thing for his much beleaguered career. D'Amboise, interestingly enough, not only played the film's choreographer but served in that capacity off-screen as well. He had been the subject of an Oscar winning documentary HE MAKES ME FEEL LIKE DANCING, chronicling his real-life attempts to make dancers out of the most unlikely candidates. His work was the inspiration for OFF BEAT, but somewhere between idea and finished product D'Amboise's spark of imagination was irreparably lost. Songs here include: "Copacabana (At the Copa)" (Barry Manilow, Bruce Sussman, Jack Feldman), "Georgia On My Mind" (Stuart Correll, Hoagy Carmichael, performed by Ray Charles), "Down on the Corner" (John Fogerty, performed by Creedence Clearwater Revival), "Yankee Doodle Boy," "Give My Regards to Broadway" (George M. Cohan), "Embraceable You" (George Gershwin, Ira Gershwin), "Ain't She Sweet" (Milton Ager, Jack Yellen), "The Ballad of Davy Crockett" (Tom Blackburn, George Bruns), "Pleasure & Pain" (Holly Knight, Mike Chapman, performed by Divinyls), "Sonata in F Major for Violin and Piano" (Felix Mendelssohn), "Moon River" (Johnny Mercer, Henry Mancini), "Put On a Happy Face" (Lee Adams, Charles Strouse), "Raindrops Keep Fallin' On My Head" (Burt Bacharach, Hal David), "Take Me Out to the Ball Game" (Albert Von Tilzer, Jack Norworth), "Selections from 'Rigoletto' " (Giuseppe Verdi).

p, Joe Roth, Harry Ufland; d, Michael Dinner; w, Mark Medoff (based on a story by Dezso Magyar); ph, Carlo Di Palma (Panaflex, Technicolor); m, James Horner; ed, Dede Allen, Angelo Corrao; prod d, Woods MacKintosh; set d, Justin Scoppa, Jr.; cos, Joseph G. Aulisi; ch, Jacques D'Amboise; makeup, Kevin Haney; stunts, Cliff Cudney.

Comedy   **Cas.**   **(PR:C MPAA:PG)**

OFFRET   (SEE: SACRIFICE, THE, 1986, Swed.)

OLDRICH A BOZENA†   (1986, Czech.) Barrandov c (Trans: Oldrich and Bozena)

Jiri Bartoska, Ilona Svobodova, Ladislav Frej, Libuse Geprtova, Jaromir Hanzlik.

d, Otakar Vavra; w, Otakar Vavra, Frantisek Hrubin; ph, Jiri Macak.

OLMEZ AGACI†   (1986, Turkey) Maya c (Trans: Eternal Tree)

Necla Nazir, Hakan Balamir, Cetin Oner, Gulsen Tuncer.

d, Yusuf Kurcenli; w, Ayse Sasa, Oya Beygo, Yusuf Kurcenli; ph, Kenan Davutoglu.

ON A VOLE CHARLIE SPENCER!†   (1986, Fr.) 96m Pacific-Selena Audiovisuel-Films A2/AAA c (Trans: Charlie Spencer's Been Robbed!)

Francis Huster (Bank Employee), Beatrice Dalle (Movie Star), Isabelle Nanty (Suzette), Jacques Spiesser, Jean-Pierre Aumont, Anne Lasmezas, Emmanuelle Devos, Antoine Dulery, Elisabeth Rodriguez, Eric Wapler, Christian Zanetti, Monique Melinand.

Huster, who last year starred in Jacques Demy's modernization of the Orpheus legend, stars here as a drab bank employee who escapes from his equally drab real-life existence to lead an exciting fantasy life. Tied into a relationship with Nanty, a pretty blonde whom he refuses to marry even though she is pregnant, Huster imagines a life as a fugitive on the lam with a pretty movie star, Dalle, who has turned bank robber. Directed and written by Huster, ON A VOLE CHARLIE SPENCER! is filled with film allusions, including a title which refers to the full name of Charles Spencer Chaplin. Another reference sees the casting of Jean-Pierre Aumont in a reprise of the role he played in the 1938 French Marcel Carne film HOTEL DU NORD. Rightly cast as the alluring movie star is Dalle, who has since become France's most alluring movie star after appearing as the crazed object of desire in Jean-Jacques Beineix's 1986 film BETTY BLUE.

p, Patricia Novat, Pierre Novat; d&w, Francis Huster; ph, Daniel Vogel (Eastmancolor); ed, Nicole Berckmans; art d, Herve Boutard; cos, Evelyne Correard; makeup, Eric Muller.

Crime/Romance   **(PR:O MPAA:NR)**

ON VALENTINE'S DAY*½**   (1986) 106m Guadelupe-Hudson-Lumiere/ Cinecom International Films c

Hallie Foote (Elizabeth Robedaux), Michael Higgins (Mr. Vaughn), Richard Jenkins (Bobby Pate), William Converse-Roberts (Horace Robedaux), Jeanne McCarthy (Bessie), Steven Hill (George Tyler), Irma Hall (Aunt Charity), Rochelle Oliver (Mrs. Vaughn), Matthew Broderick (Brother Vaughn), Carol Goodheart (Miss Ruth), Horton Foote, Jr. (Steve Tyler), Oskar Kelly (Old Black Man), Bill McGhee (Sam), Tim Green (Sheriff), Peyton Park (Dr. Goodhue), Ed Holmes (Ned), Artist Thornton (Young Black Man), Jack Gould (Baptist Preacher).

The film 1918 (released in 1985) was adapted from one of Horton Foote's nine loosely autobiographical plays that follow the residents of a rural Texas town during the early 20th Century. That film's story, which examined life on the home front during WW I, featured the author's daughter Hallie Foote and William Converse-Roberts as a young married couple. The pair cope with life, death, and the familial problems surrounding their day-to-day activities. ON VALENTINE'S DAY, which was taken from another of Horton Foote's nine-play series, is 1918's prequel, looking at the days following Hallie Foote's and William Converse-Roberts' elopement (the title refers to the day they eloped). The two have married, despite the disapproval of Foote's wealthy parents Higgins and Oliver. The couple now live in a small house with Jenkins, an alcoholic whose wife has left him, and Goodheart, a lonely spinster. Other visitors to this household include Converse-Roberts' cousin Hill, an unhappy man slowly losing his mind over love for a long dead woman; and McCarthy, a nervous young girl who enjoys sitting and talking with Foote. On Christmas Day, Foote is overjoyed when her estranged parents telephone and ask if they might drop over for a visit. Though this meeting is tinged by Higgins' dislike for Converse-Roberts' lower class background, the family is glad to be together after their long silence. But with this gathering comes unhappiness. Broderick, Foote's younger brother, is quickly turning into a gambler and a drunkard. Foote also implores her parents not to ask Converse-Roberts about his own mother and late father, because there has been much sorrow in her husband's background. A few months pass but the troubles surrounding this household remain and fester. Jenkins' alcoholism only gets worse, while Hill's mind completely snaps. He runs wild and Converse-Roberts joins a group who search for Hill in a nearby woods. Eventually Hill commits suicide in the town square by thrusting a knife into his stomach. Later, in hopes of regaining his daughter, Higgins makes Converse-Roberts an offer. Knowing the young man wants to buy a home of his own, Higgins offers to put up the needed funds so Converse-Roberts can donate his money to the war effort. The young man, confused by what he feels, discusses the situation with his spouse, and they reach an agreement. The story ends with a sense of reconciliation.

The story is told in a low-key manner, and this understated style deepens the complex emotions of the characters. Foote and Converse-Roberts are excellent as the struggling couple, bound by a love that overcomes the tragedies that surround their union. In the film's strongest scene, Converse-Roberts bares his soul to Foote, telling his wife all the hopes, fears, and dreams he has, and declaring his undying love for her. The things he expresses are as old as time, but Converse-Roberts' raw and honest feelings, complemented by Foote's devoted support, make this tender moment fresh and very special. Supporting roles are perfectly cast, and, like its predecessor, the period detail is impeccable. Many of the same ensemble, including Higgins, Oliver, Broderick and McCarthy, and director Ken Harrison, had also worked on 1918. It's clear that this ensemble know each others' characters well, giving ON VALENTINE'S DAY an added and very human sense of realism. Harrison's direction matches his previous work, allowing the pacing of Horton Foote's dialogue to set the film's natural development. ON VALENTINE'S DAY moves at a slow, almost lyrical tempo, allowing its characters and themes to develop without affectation. Like 1918, one of the film's most important themes is a reverence held for the dead, and the continuing influence they have on the living. In 1987, ON VALENTINE'S DAY and 1918 were combined with a third unreleased feature (directed by Howard Cummings) based on the Horton Foote plays and broadcast on the public television series

American Playhouse. Retitled "The Story of a Marriage," the new work traced the couple from their courtship in 1916 to the end of WW I two years later.

p, Lillian V. Foote, Calvin Skaggs; d, Ken Harrison; w, Horton Foote (based on his play "Valentine's Day"); ph, George Tirl (DuArt Color); m, Jonathan Sheffer; ed, Nancy Baker; art d, Howard Cummings; set d, DonnaSu Schiller; cos, Van Broughton Ramsey; makeup, Carla Palmer Rulien.

Drama   Cas.   (PR:A-C MPAA:PG)

ONDORT NUMARA   (SEE: FOURTEEN NUMARA, 1986, Turk.)

ONE CRAZY SUMMER**½   (1986) 93m A&M Films/WB c

John Cusack (Hoops McCann), Linda Warren (Mrs. McCann), Joel Murray (George Calamari), Grenville Cuyler (Graduation Orator), Kristen Goelz (Squid Calamari), Sky (Boscoe), Laura Waterbury (Crossing Guard), Jennifer Yahoodik (Andrea), Rachel C. Telegen (Brunhelda), Demi Moore (Cassandra), John Matuszak (Stain), Paul Lane, Don Ruffin, Gary Littlejohn, Pat McGroarty (Bikers), Anthony Viveiros (Man On Ferry Boat), Bobcat Goldthwait (Egg Stork), Tom Villara (Clay Stork), Isidore Mankofsky (Cameraman), Matt Mulhern (Teddy Beckersted), Kimberly Foster (Cookie Cambell), Jeremy Piven (Ty), Billie Bird (Grandma), Bruce Wagner (Uncle Frank), Joe Flaherty (Gen. Raymond), Curtis Armstrong (Ack Ack Raymond), Al Mohrmann (Yuppie Preacher), Mark Metcalf (Aguilla Beckersted), Sharon Hope, Donna Clements, Alberta Glover, Pamela Shadduck (Aguilla's Maids), William Hickey (Old Man Beckersted), Jerry Winsett (Big Man On Beach), Bill Hoversten, Donald Watson (Medics), Lisa Melilli (Ty's Girlfriend), Deborah Bial (Screaming Girl), Taylor Negron (Taylor), Rich Hall (Wilbur), Bob Gage, Bob Duncan, Herb Mingace, Earl Blank (Dew Drop Inn Musicians), Donald Li (Chrong Freen), Barry Doe (Giant), Scott Richards (Victim), Elizabeth Field (Beautiful Girl), Len Lawrence (Producer), Barry Karas (Doctor), John Blood (Patient), Joan Drott (Nurse), Jim Cooke (Regatta Judge), Robert Boardman (Man Overboard), John Fiore (Crewman), Rich Little (Disc Jockey).

Young director Holland's second film is just as quirky and bizarre as his zany debut feature BETTER OFF DEAD (1985). Cusack (the hapless protagonist of BETTER OFF DEAD) stars as a frustrated young animator named "Hoops"

who has disappointed his parents because he has not proven to be the star basketball player they had envisioned (he can't even hit a waste basket with a wad of paper from three feet away—a running gag used throughout the film). After graduating from high school, Cusack joins his friend Murray (younger brother of Bill Murray) on a vacation to Nantucket, where he plans to prepare his art portfolio for entry into the Rhode Island School of Design. Cusack is working on an animated cartoon featuring his alter ego, a hapless rhino looking for love. The rhino is always being tortured by the "cute and fuzzy bunnies" as he searches for true love (the superior animation sequences—done by Bill Kopp, a friend of Holland's—are particularly well integrated into the story line). On the road to Nantucket, Cusack meets Moore, a confident and beautiful young woman who aspires to be a rock 'n' roll star. As it turns out, Moore is also on her way to Nantucket to attend the funeral of her grandfather. Once there, she learns that she must raise $2,000 to prevent the retirement home her grandfather owned from being bought up and turned into a lobster restaurant by nasty real estate developer Metcalf. Metcalf is so mean, that he sticks a stethoscope in a pot of boiling water so he can hear live lobsters scream in agony while they cook. Joined by newfound friends Armstrong (the pacifist son of militaristic boy scout leader Flaherty), and the dissimilar "Stork" twins, played by Villard and manic nightclub comic Goldthwait, Cusack enacts a plan to humiliate Metcalf and his preppy jock-type son Mulhern and save Moore's retirement home. They do this by winning the prestigious Nantucket regatta race—an event won every year by Mulhern—and swapping the trophy for the deed to the house. Mulhern's crotch-

ety old grandfather, Hickey (in a cameo), lets the kids have both the trophy and the deed.

As was the case with BETTER OFF DEAD, director Holland fills this film with so many throwaway gags that it is impossible to communicate the outright zaniness of his movies. Every scene contains dozens of jokes, some that work and some that don't, but they keep coming so fast and furious that the duds are easily forgotten. Strung together on only the flimsiest of plots, Holland's films work as well as they do because he stocks them with several likable characters. Cusack is the perfect "Everyteen" who reacts to the insanity around him with utter calm and a bemused smirk. Murray, in his film debut, is wonderful as Cusack's easygoing best friend, and Moore is likable as Cusack's true love (unfortunately the actress isn't much of a singer and her stage mannerisms during her rock 'n' roll scenes are insufferably calculated). Nightclub comedian Goldthwait—whose persona is something like a confused mental patient given to stuttering and screaming—takes a bit of getting used to for the uninitiated, but he manages to become a perfectly lovable character and has many of the film's best gags (including a romp through real-estate developer Metcalf's model city while wearing a Godzilla suit). While certainly not for all tastes, Holland's films are refreshing teenage fare, for in their cartoonishness is a pleasant innocence and naivete that isn't found in the leering, lecherous, mean-spirited teenage sex comedies or the self-consciously "relevant" and formulated John Hughes films that usually plague movie screens during the summer. Songs include: "Don't Look Back" (Hawk Wolinski, performed by Demi Moore), "Take A Bow" (Patrick Leonard, Keithen Carter, performed by Jaime Segel), "Easy Street" (Dan Hartman, performed by David Lee Roth), "Be Chrool to Your Scuel" (Dee Snider, performed by Twisted Sister), "What Does It Take" (Derry Grehan, performed by Honeymoon Suite), "Dirty Dog" (Billy Gibbons, Dusty Hill, Frank Beard, performed by ZZ Top), "Do It Again," "Fun, Fun, Fun" (Brian Wilson, Mike Love, performed by The Beach Boys), "Wouldn't It Be Nice" (Brian Wilson, Tony Asher, performed by The Beach Boys), "In My Room" (Brian Wilson, Gary Usher, performed by The Beach Boys), "Fandango" (Juan Carlos Calderon, performed by Herb Alpert), "I Go To Rio" (Peter Allen, Adrienne Anderson, performed by Peter Allen), "Outa-Space" (Billy Preston, Joe Greene, performed by Billy Preston), "Dancing in the Street" (William Stevenson, Marvin Gaye, Ivy Jo Hunter, performed by Martha and the Vandellas), "Would I Lie to You" (Annie Lennox, Dave Stewart, performed by Eurythmics), "Born To Be Wild" (Mars Bonfire, performed by Steppenwolf), "Down On the Corner" (John Fogerty, performed by Creedence Clearwater Revival), "Wipe Out" (Surfaris), "Theme From 'Jaws'" (John Williams).

p, Michael Jaffe; d, Savage Steve Holland; w, Savage Steve Holland; ph, Isidore Mankofsky (Panavision, CFI Color); m, Cory Lerios; ed, Alan Balsam; prod d, Herman Zimmerman; md, David Anderle; set d, Gary Moreno; cos, Brad R. Loman; spec eff, Joe Mercurio; m/l, Hawk Wolinski, Patrick Leonard, Keithen Carter, Dan Hartman, Dee Snider, Derry Grehan, Billy Gibbons, Dusty Hill, Frank Beard, Brian Wilson, Mike Love, Tony Asher, Gary Usher, Juan Carlos Calderon, Peter Allen, Adrienne Anderson, Billy Preston, Joe Greene, William Stevenson, Marvin Gaye, Ivy Jo Hunter, Annie Lenox, Dave Stuart, Mars Bonfire, John Fogerty, John Williams; makeup, Dennis Eger; stunts, Everett Creach; anim, Bill Kopp, Savage Steve Holland.

Comedy   Cas.   (PR:C MPAA:PG)

ONE MORE SATURDAY NIGHT*   (1986) 95m AAR-Tova Laiter/COL c

Tom Davis (Larry), Al Franken (Paul), Moira Harris (Peggy), Frank Howard (Eddie), Bess Meyer (Tobi), Dave Reynolds (Russ Cadwell), Chelcie Ross (Dad Lundahl), Eric Saiet (Doug), Jessica Schwartz (Traci), Dianne B. Shaw (Lynn Neal), Nina Siemaszko (Karen Neal), Jonathan Singer (Kevin Lundahl), Meshach Taylor (Bill Neal), Nan Woods (Diane Lundahl), Wynton Harris, Wynetta Harris (Jason Neal), Jon Tiven (John), Sally Tiven (Sally), Del Close (Mr. Schneider/Large Tattooed Man), Patrick Billingsly (Mr. McGrath), Shirley Spiegler-Jacobs (Mrs. McGrath), Nathan Davis (Desk Clerk), Ann Coyle (Night Clerk), Jack Callahan (Mr. Becker), Rondi Reed (Mrs. Becker), Kevin J. O'Connor (Hood), Joey Garfield (Mouse), Tom Tucker (Freddie), Steve Pink (Dogman), Charles Fink (Woody), Amy Benedict (Mouse's Girl), Bridget M. McCarthy (Party Kid), Aviva Brill, John Cameron Mitchell, Julie Busch (Teenagers), Tim Markiewicz (Bouncer), Jonathan Bernstein (Club Manager), Tyler Ann Carroll (Lea), Chad Smith (Matthew), Shawn Simons (Fat Girl), Nancy Baird (Matron), Chris Holloway (Young Cop), Mike Hagerty (Cop), Eric Bernt (Cop in Chase), Ted Levine (Cop in Station), Tom Joyce, Joe Krowka (Detectives), Dean Hill (Bartender), James Willis (Man by Restaurant Phone), Evelyn Kashefska (Mrs. Henzel).

In TV's "Saturday Night Live" glory days of the mid-1970s, writers Al Franken and Tom Davis developed a reputation for wit and sharp-edged political satire. Their occasional solo spots, dubbed simply "The Franken and Davis Show," became audience favorites and the team developed something of a cult following. Franken and Davis made a brief cameo appearance in John Landis's 1983 TRADING PLACES, and released a concert video of material developed on a nationwide college tour. ONE MORE SATURDAY NIGHT marked the duo's first venture into screenwriting and undoubtedly will be a disappointment to Franken and Davis fans. This is not the clever parody one might expect from the brains behind "The Coneheads," but rather a dimwitted teenage comedy that plays like a subpar John Hughes film. In the small Minnesota town of St. Cloud, local residents are preparing for the biggest social night of the week. Taylor and Shaw, parents of a newborn, are going out for the first time since their child's birth. Tensions have built up between the couple and they are eagerly awaiting this long anticipated evening. Siemaszko is their babysitter; before the night is through, her boy friend Howard will have turned Taylor and Shaw's quiet home into a party for a few dozen close, personal friends. Meanwhile Saiet, a 15-year-old whose parents don't seem to notice his existence, starts the evening off by having a friend pierce his ear. Next Saiet heists his father's car and heads over to the house of his girl friend Schwartz. He thrills her with tales of on-the-edge behavior, but Saiet lives to regret this when Schwartz insists they burglarize someone's home. Ross, a middle-aged widower, is preparing for his first date in nearly twenty years. He gets advice from Woods, his pretty teenage daughter, then heads out for his evening on the town. Woods is having problems of her own with her boy friend Reynolds. Though the two have been dating for two years, Woods has resisted Reynolds' pressures for sex. Reynolds has had just about enough of this and has already rented a motel room in anticipation of getting his girl into bed this evening. However, these plans go awry after Reynolds and Woods get into a fight. Woods hooks up with her best friend Meyer, and the two girls head over to a local bar to hear some music by the group Badmouth. Franken and Davis are two members of the band, interested more in adventuresome groupies than in playing music. Out of anger and sexual frustration, Reynolds telephones a bomb threat to the club and the place quickly empties. Woods and Meyer accompany Franken and Davis back to their motel, but not much happens. Try as he may, Franken cannot get Woods to succumb to his wishes and the two end up spending their evening discussing Woods' troubles. Saiet and Schwartz end up returning the items they have pilfered, and Siemaszko manages to clean things up before Taylor and Shaw return home. Ross discovers that he's changed since his teenaged years, though dating hasn't, while Franken and Davis hit the road once more.

Had Franken and Davis focused on one of these stories rather than taking the scattershot approach, this might have made for an average after-school television special. ONE MORE SATURDAY NIGHT suffers from trying to explore a variety of situations, and ultimately gets nothing said at all. The situations are routine, lacking wit or originality. Klein, making his feature film debut behind the camera, doesn't show much flair for the medium. His pacing is slack, and reveals no sense for comedy development, a real surprise considering that Klein's television work included such highly praised shows as "Mary Hartman, Mary Hartman" and "Buffalo Bill." Shot on location in and around Chicago; many of the cast members are area actors making their motion picture debuts with ONE MORE SATURDAY NIGHT. No one is particularly memorable with the exception of Woods, whose good performance somehow manages to rise above the weak script and inept direction. As the two rock stars, Franken and Davis are simply dreadful. They approach the material with all the zest of processed cheese, relying heavily on moldy drug jokes to punch up their comic sequences. There's also something inordinately distasteful in watching two burned-out musicians take excessive measures to commit what amounts to statutory rape. Maybe the project sounded funny in story conference, but it doesn't work on film. Serving as executive producer was another "Saturday Night Live" veteran, a dubious film comedian in his own right, Dan Aykroyd. Franken and Davis' live-music segments were produced by the Grateful Dead's head man, Jerry Garcia. Songs include: "One More Saturday Night" (Bobby Sandstrom, Michael Price, performed by Maureen Steele), "Shop Around" (Berry Gordy, William "Smokey" Robinson, performed by Smokey Robinson and The Miracles), "Brick House" (Milan Williams, Walter Orange, Thomas McClary, performed by the Commodores), "War" (Norman Whitfield, Barrett Strong, performed by Edwin Starr), "If I Could Build My Whole World Around You" (Johnny Bristol, Vernon Bullock, Harvey Fuqua, performed by Tammi Terrell, Marvin Gaye), "Excusez Moi, Mon Cherie" (Lawrence V. Hayes, performed by Badmouth), "Upper Mississippi Shakedown" (Pat Hayes, Bruce McCabe, performed by Badmouth), "Fresh Fruit" (Jon Tiven, Sally Tiven, Peter Aykroyd, performed by Badmouth), "I Wanna Rock You" (Jon Tiven, Sally Tiven, Al Franken, performed by Guy Perry), "Love Nazi" (Jon Tiven, Sally Tiven, Joel Bantzig, Tom Davis, performed by Badmouth), "Don't Lie to Me" (Jon Tiven, Sally Tiven, Tom Davis, performed by Badmouth), "Maajo" (King Sunny Ade, performed by King Sunny Ade and His African Beats), "Loose, Over the Line" (David McHugh, performed by Rick Gallaher), "The Teddy Bear's Picnic" (Jimmy Kennedy, John W. Bratton, performed by Alan O'Day).

p, Tova Laiter, Robert Kosberg, Jonathan Bernstein; d, Dennis Klein; w, Al Franken, Tom Davis; ph, James Glennon (Panavision, DeLuxe Color); m, David McHugh; ed, Gregory Prange; art d, Maher Ahmad; set d, Karen O'Hara; cos, Mickey Antonetti, Jay Hurley; m/l, Bobby Sandstrom, Michael Price, Berry Gordy, William "Smokey" Robinson, Milan Williams, Walter Orange, Thomas McClary, Norman Whitfield, Barrett Strong, Johnny Bristol, Vernon Bullock, Harvey Fuqua, Lawrence V. Hayes, Pat Hayes, Bruce McCabe, Jon Tiven, Sally Tiven, Peter Aykroyd, Al Franken, Joel Bantzig, Tom Davis, King Sunny Ade, David McHugh, Jimmy Kennedy, John W. Bratton.

Comedy   Cas.   (PR:C-O   MPAA:R)

ONE NIGHT ONLY zero   (1986, Can.) 86m RSL Entertainment c

Lenore Zann (Anne), Helene Udy (Suzanne), Taborah Johnson (Louella), Judy Foster (Elizabeth), Hrant Alianak (Winkeau), Ken James (Wes), Jeff Braunstein (Mack), Wendy Lands (Jean), Martin Neufeld (Johnny), Geoffrey MacKay (Jamie).

It's New Year's Eve and a group of sexually aggressive sorority sisters decide they want a celebration to remember. Led by Zann, the group manages to horn their way into a party run by Alianak, a mobster. The girls move the shindig over to a palatial mansion belonging to the parents of sorority member Foster. The girls' ultimate purpose is to sleep with an entire professional hockey team, but because there aren't enough sorority sisters to go around, a few local prostitutes are recruited for the evening. The hookers teach the sorority girls a few lessons they wouldn't normally get in Principles of Accounting, and everyone, male and female, leaves the party wearing a smile.

To no one's surprise, this Canadian film was originally conceived as a project

for the Playboy cable television channel. Consequently, the humor is lowbrow and the sexual situations feature plenty of fantasy images (to say nothing of the abundance of naked female flesh). Incompetently made and acted, ONE NIGHT ONLY is nothing more than an adolescent fantasy committed to celluloid.

p, Robert Lantos, Stephen J. Roth; d, Timothy Bond; w, P.Y. Haines; ph, Rene Verzier (Medallion Color); m, Lawrence Shragge; ed, Michael Karen, Jaki Carmody; prod d, Csaba Kertesz; cos, Laurie Drew.

Comedy   Cas.   (PR:O   MPAA:NR)

OP HOOP VAN ZEGEN†   (1986, Neth.) 102m Sigma-Elsevier-Vendex-TROS/Concorde c (Trans: The Good Hope)

Kitty Courbois (Kniertje), Danny de Munk (Barend), Renee Soutendijk (Jo), Huub Stapel (Geert), Rijk de Gooyer (Clemens Bos), Willeke van Ammelrooy (Mathilde Bos), Ramses Shaffy (Simon), Leen Jongewaard (Kaps), Dorijn Curvers, Luc Lutz, Tamar van den Dop, Lex Goudsmith, Albert Mol.

An adaptation of the popular Dutch writer Herman Heijerman's The Good Hope, a play centering on a small fishing hamlet at the turn of the century. Previously filmed three times, the original story has been restructured to bring more attention to de Munk, the young son of widow Courbois, who has already lost three of the men in her life to the sea. By the film's end, de Munk also becomes the sea's victim.

d, Guido Pieters; w, Karin Loomans (based on the play by Herman Heijermans); ph, Frans Bromet; m, Rogier van Otterloo; ed, Ton Ruys; art d, Dick Schillemans; set d, Peter Jansen; cos, Jany van Hellenberg Hubar; spec eff, Martin Gutteridge.

Drama   (PR:C   MPAA:NR)

OPERA DO MALANDRO   (SEE: MALANDRO, 1986, Braz.)

OPERACE ME DCERY†   (1986, Czech.) 83m Barrandov c

Vlastimil Harapes (Dusan Rocek), Jana Sulcova (Magda Rockova), Klara Pollertova (Milena Rockova), Jiri Kodet (Cholensky), Oldrich Vizner (Bures), Jan Kacer (Krajicek), Vladimir Kudla (Fric), Dagmar Carova (Jarunka), Jana Ditetova (Janitor in Hospital), Kveta Fialova (Bahenska), Jan Preucil (Burian), Svatopluk Benes (Bahensky), Zora Ulla Keslerova (Stejskalova), Vaclav Kotva (Liberce's Husband), Stanislava Bartosova (Eliska), Adolf Kohouth (Frantisek), Pavel Novy (Zdenek Cech), Marcela Martinkova (Head Nurse), Libuse Geprtova.

d, Ivo Novak; w, Stanislav Rudolf, Ivo Novak; ph, Jiri Macak; m, Petr Hapka; ed, Ivana Kacirkova; art d, Jaromir Svarc; cos, Olga Jedlickova.

ORA TOKYO SA YUKUDA†   (1986, Jap.) 93m Shochiku c (Trans: I Go to Tokyo)

Eisaku Shindo, Yoshie Kashiwabara, Hitoshi Ueki, Michiko Hayashi, Ikuzo Yoshi.

Japanese comedy which follows the trials and tribulations of an old farming couple who travel to Tokyo to visit their photographer son. The hustle and bustle of the city nearly overwhelms the couple, and the wife assumes she should make the bed in their motel room. They eventually find their way to their son's apartment, but he is less than thrilled to see them. While the wife sets about cleaning her son's home, the husband wanders the neighborhood and is shocked to find such oddities as breakdancing and transvestites. While the son acts as if he can't be bothered with his parents, a female colleague gladly takes the elderly couple off his hands and makes sure they have a good time during their stay.

p, Yoshihide Konda; d, Tomio Kuriyama; w, Masakuni Takahashi, Toshio Sekine; ph, Kosuke Yasuda; m, Hiroshi Wada; ed, Masuichi Tsuruta; art d, Mamoru Narusawa.

Comedy   (PR:C   MPAA:NR)

ORDOGI KISERTETEK†   (1986, Hung.) 85m Hungarian Television-Mokep c (Trans: Temptations of the Devil)

Andras Kozak (Mr. Gy.), Anna Feher (Anna, his Wife), Gyorgy Dorner (G.), Lajos Oze (The Invalid), Janos Ban (Anna's Younger Brother), Istvan Iglodi (Preacher), Maria Kovacs (Lady's Maid), Vilmos Kun (Her Husband).

An odd tale set in Hungary during the 16th Century, where Kozak is the lord of a castle. His wife is unfaithful and her brother-in-law plots his murder to gain the man's estate. But the brother-in-law has second thoughts and instead warns Kozak to leave if he values his life. Kozak escapes and his wife turns the castle into a pleasure palace that corrupts the whole area. After Kozak meets the devil, who is disguised as an old woman, at an inn, he returns home and kills his cheating bride before fleeing again.

d&w, Gyula Maar; ph, Ivan Mark; m, Gyorgy Orban; ed, Andras Horvath; set d, Tamas Banovich; cos, Judit Schaffer.

Drama   (PR:C   MPAA:NR)

ORIDATH†   (1986, India) Sooryakanthi c (Trans: Once Somewhere)

Venu, Screenivasan, Tilakan, Chandran Nair, Soorya.

When electricity comes to an isolated Indian hamlet during the 1950s, the villagers must overcome a variety of troubles.

d&w, G. Aravindan; ph, Shaji.

Comedy   (PR:C   MPAA:NR)

ORKESTAR JEDNE MLADOSTI† (1986, Yugo.) Avala-Union c (Trans: Orchestra of Youth)

Ljubisa Samardzic, Gordana Bjelica, Marjan Srienc, Miodrag Radovanovic.

d, Sveta Pavlovic; w, Sveta Pavlovic, Jovan Markovic; ph, Branko Ivatovic; m, Darko Kraljic; set d, Miodrag Nikolic.

ORMENS VAG PA HALLEBERGET† (1986, Swed.) 112m Svensk Filmindustri-Swedish Film Institute-Swedish Television-SVT 1-Crescendo Film/Svensk Filmindustri c (Trans: The Serpent's Way Up the Naked Rock)

Stina Ekblad *(Tea)*, Stellan Skarsgard *(Karl Orsa)*, Reine Brynolfsson *(Jani)*, Pernilla W. Ostergren *(Eva)*, Tomas von Bromssen *(Jakob)*, Pernilla Wahlgren *(Johanna)*, Ernst Gunther *(Ol Karlsa)*, Birgitta Ulfsson *(Grandma)*, Nils Brandt *(Grandpa)*, Johan Widerberg *(Jani as a Child)*, Melinda Kinnaman *(Eva as a Child)*, Amelia Glas-Drake *(Tilda)*, Lisa Tonnerfors *(Sara)*, Emma Tonnerfors *(Rakel)*.

Life is tough in a bleak, northerly region of Sweden during the 19th Century. Existence is so difficult that one family must prostitute its own women to keep the creditors from the door. Ekblad must sleep with the local storekeeper to pay off debts. Her husband hangs himself in shame, but she must continue to sleep with the storekeeper. Eventually he dies, and his son takes over the debt collection. When he declares that Ekblad is too old, and that he now wants her oldest daughter, Ekblad tries to convince him that the girl is actually his father's daughter. He refuses to accept the revelation (though it is true), and when the man tries to have sex with the daughter, one of her little brothers attacks him with a knife and castrates him. A grim story about grim people in a grim place.

p, Goran Lindstrom; d&w, Bo Widerberg (based on a novel by Torgny Lindgren); ph, Jorgen Persson, Rolf Lindstrom, Olof Johnsson (Eastmancolor); m, Stefan Nilsson; ed, Bo Widerberg; art d, Pelle Johansson, Kicki Ilander; cos, Inger Pehrsson, Susanne Falck; makeup, Horst Stadlinger, Siw Jarbyn.

Drama **(PR:O MPAA:NR)**

OSOBISTY PAMIETNIK GRZESZNIKA PRZEZ NIEGO SAMEGO SPISANY† (1986, Pol.) 125m Zespoly Filmowe Film Unit-Rondo/Film Polski c (Trans: The Memoirs Of A Sinner)

Piotr Bajor, Maciej Kozlowski, Janusz Michalowski, Hanna Stankowna, Eva Wisniewska, Franciszek Pieczka.

An odd allegory based on an 18th Century novel. This film concerns a young man who ponders all sorts of weighty philosophical matters concerning good and evil before killing his evil alter-ego by committing suicide.

d, Wojciech Has; w, Michal Komar (based on a novel by James Hogg); ph, Grzegorz Kedziersky; m, Jerzy Maksymiuk; ed, Barbara Lewandowska-Cunio; prod d, Andrzej Przedworski.

Drama **(PR:C MPAA:NR)**

OTELLO*½ (1986, It.) 120m Cannon-RAI c

Placido Domingo *(Otello)*, Katia Ricciarelli *(Desdemona)*, Justino Diaz *(Iago)*, Petra Malakova *(Emilia)*, Urbano Barberini *(Cassio)*, Massimo Foschi *(Lodovico)*, Edwin Francis *(Montano)*, Sergio Nicolai *(Roderigo)*, Remo Remotti *(Brabanzio)*, Antonio Pierfederici *(Doge)*.

Serious opera enthusiasts will be appalled by the cuts made in this cinematic version of the opera which Shakespeare inspired. But when Verdi and librettist Boito united to bring the Moor's tale to the musical stage in 1887 (Verdi was, by then, 74 years old and much of his original genius had been replaced with dazzling technique), they had to make many alterations in the Bard's story and Zeffirelli made similar cuts and pastes in order to make it work for the screen ("I

only did to Verdi what Verdi did to Shakespeare," said the director). Verdi fans may hate this, but people who have to be dragged kicking and screaming to an opera will probably love what they see though not necessarily what they hear.

It's near the end of the 15th century on the isle of Cyprus. Domingo, the governor of the island, is returning from a successful campaign against the Turks,

whom he has vanquished. Ricciarelli, looking like a Wagnerian Valkerie, awaits his return and pledges her love upon seeing him. Domingo's "friend," Diaz, is angry because Barberini had been promoted over him, so he begins his treacherous behavior. First, he promotes a duel between Barberini and Nicolai. For that, Domingo demotes Barberini, unaware that Diaz is behind the machinations. Next, Diaz begins his campaign against Domingo by sowing seeds of jealousy and making it seem as though Barberini has been having an affair with Ricciarelli. When she requests that Domingo give Barberini back his former position, the Moor is enraged, as that seems to seal the suspicion that the two are lovers. Diaz enlists the aid of his unaware wife, Malakova, to steal one of Ricciarelli's unique handkerchiefs. Once that's been accomplished, he places the handkerchief in the residence of Barberini. Domingo is maneuvered by Diaz to see the handkerchief in Barberini's possession. As a result, Domingo is plunged into deep depression and soaring anger. The Venetian ambassador, Foschi, arrives to call Domingo back to Venice, but that is not Domingo's main concern now. He stalks into Ricciarelli's bed-chamber, orders her to say her final prayers, which she does, then he strangles her to death. Malakova sees what's happened and tells Domingo what Diaz has done. But it's too late to bring Ricciarelli back to life, so Domingo kills Diaz (unlike the play or Boito's operatic libretto), stabs himself with a knife, and dies as he is kissing the dead body of Ricciarelli.

Zeffirelli is no stranger to Shakespeare, having made ROMEO AND JULIET and THE TAMING OF THE SHREW. He is more than passingly conversant with opera, as witnessed by his versions of LA TRAVIATA and LA BOHEME. He has been quoted as saying that Verdi [actually Boito] had to rewrite "Othello" to make it play as an opera, so he felt that he was just as righteous in rewriting the opera to function as a film. There is no question that he pulled out all stops in order to get the story off a stage and make it feel like a movie. To that end, he shot in a castle in Barletta, southern Italy, as well as in a Venetian fort in

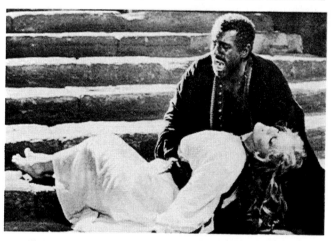

Crete. This $9 million production is fabulous to look at, and the acting is superb, but the picture is weak in the music department, mainly because some of the best music has been excised to make the movie zip along. Since the opera was nearly three hours in length and the movie is just two hours, quite a lot had to be sacrificed on the altar of cinema. These moments included Desdemona's "Willow Song," the chorus known as "Fuoco di Giola," the last moments of Iago's telling of Cassio's dream, fully 50 percent of the "Revenge" duet, and a great slash at act three's *concertato*. Further, Verdi's "storm music" has been softened to accompany the sounds of a real storm, and it is now only a background counterpoint to the blowing of the wind. To accommodate Domingo, the "Esultate" has been transposed to a more facile key, but that diminishes the difficult *tessitura* to a point where almost anyone could sing it. The third-act ensemble has been tossed aside, whereas it might have been possible to use the shorter version Verdi himself penned for the Paris opening.

Zeffirelli was quite familiar with "Otello," having staged the opera several times, including a performance at the Met in 1972 as well as one at La Scala in Milan in 1976 with Domingo as the Moor. The movie is dazzling to behold, but there are a few mistakes, such as the fact that the young "Otello" (seen briefly in his desert youth) is of a decidedly different hue than Domingo's blackface. On balance, it's still a good introduction to the work of Verdi, although it's more a series of highlights than the entire opera. Those inclined to listen to the entire work would be better off buying John Vickers' version of "Otello." Beefcake is supplied by the muscular Barberini (whose singing is done by Ezio di Cesare), a real-life playboy prince who decided to become an actor, and who played his first leading role in the 1985 shocker DEMONS.

Domingo was the person who first suggested that Zeffirelli film the opera. He had met exploitation moguls Golan and Globus (whom the director calls "Gamma Globulin") while working in Israel, and knew that they wanted to sponsor the picture as a prestige venture. Shooting was delayed for a time when a high-Richter-scale earthquake leveled parts of Mexico City. Domingo returned to the Mexican capital to help in rescue operations (the singer lost an uncle, an aunt, and two cousins to the quake). The dust he inhaled while sorting through the rubble may help to explain why his vocal performance for the picture failed to come up to the best of his stage work. The film was further delayed when shooting had to be interrupted while Zeffirelli recovered from bronchial pneumonia.

The acting is so uniformly good that the English subtitles are hardly needed. One murder and one suicide are what give this film a PG rating and a "caution" attached to our "Acceptable" recommendation for children. (In Italian; English subtitles.)

p, Menahem Golan, Yoram Globus; d, Franco Zeffirelli; w, Franco Zeffirelli (based on Arrigo Boito's libretto for Giuseppe Verdi's "Otello"; ph, Ennio Guarnieri (Eastmancolor); prod d, Gianni Quaranta; md, Lorin Maazel; cos, Anna Anni, Maurizio Millenotti.

Opera   (PR:A-C MPAA:PG)

OTOKO WA TSURAIYO, SHIBAMATA YORI AI O KOMETE†   (1986, Jap.) Shochiku c (Trans: Torasan, from Shibamata, with Love)

Kiyoshi Atsumi, Chieko Baisho, Komaki Kurihara, Jun Miho, Ryuzo Tanaka, Takuzo Kawatani, Kiyoshi Shimazu.

d, Yogi Yamada; w, Yogi Yamada, Yoshitaka Asama; ph, Tetsuo Takaba; m, Naozumi Yamamoto.

OTRA HISTORIA DE AMOR   (SEE: ANOTHER LOVE STORY, 1968, Arg.)

OUR EXPLOITS AT WEST POLEY†   (1986, Brit.) Children's Film and TV Foundation c

Charlie Condon, Jonathan Jackson, Anthony Bate, Brenda Fricker.

p, Pamela Lonsdale; d, Diarmid Lawrence; w, James Andrew Hall; ph, Ray Orton.

OUT OF BOUNDS zero   (1986) Fries Entertainment-COL-Delphi V/COL c

Anthony Michael Hall *(Daryl Cage)*, Jenny Wright *(Dizz)*, Jeff Kober *(Roy Gaddis)*, Glynn Turman *(Lt. Delgado)*, Raymond J. Barry *(Hurley)*, Pepe Serna *(Murano)*, Michelle Little *(Crystal)*, Jerry Levine *(Marshall)*, Ji-Tu Cumbuka *(Lemar)*, Kevin McCorkle *(Tommy Cage)*, Linda Shayne *(Chris Cage)*, Maggie Gwinn *(Mrs. Cage)*, Ted Gehring *(Mr. Cage)*, Meatloaf *(Gil)*, Allan Graf *(Biker)*, Dan Lewk *(Cop on Melrose)*, John Vickery, Tony Acierto, David Chung *(Detectives)*, Tony Kayden, John Tarnoff *(Snide Patrons)*, Jennifer Balgobin *(Martha)*, Kevin Breslin *(News Vendor)*, Murray Lebowitz *(Police Captain)*, Peggy Jo Abraham, Bill Press *(Newscasters)*, Scott Edmund Lane *(Duty Sergeant)*, Stephanie Gregg *(Punker Store Clerk)*, Lloyd Nelson *(Mechanic)*, Ollie Lake *(Airport Security Guard)*, James Espinoza *(Olivera Street Vendor)*, Barbara Lee Soltani *(Dirtbox Bartender)*, Jeffery Smith *(Stardust Bartender)*, Bill Lane *(Neighbor)*, Dick Ziker *(Trucker Cowboy)*, Bennie Moore *(Bus Driver)*, Popeye *(Barney the Dog)*, Siouxsie and the Banshees *(Dirtbox Band)*, Tommy Keene *(Stardust Band)*.

An unbelievably stupid crime film which attempts to turn John Hughes' favorite nerd, Hall (THE BREAKFAST CLUB, WEIRD SCIENCE), into a macho action hero. The first five minutes of the film work well enough: Hall is a lonely Iowa farmboy who is sent on a trip to visit his older brother in Los Angeles while his parents—their marriage disintegrating—attempt a trial separation. At the L.A. airport, Hall's brother accidentally picks up the wrong duffel bag from the luggage carousel and unwittingly throws a fortune in heroin into the back of his pickup truck. The drug smuggler, Kober, grabs Hall's bag and immediately realizes the mistake. He manages to spot the license plate of the truck before it speeds off. At the brother's house, Hall is shown his apartment, which is a room

separate from the house with an entrance obscured by vines. Now let us pause a minute and take inventory of the incredibly dumb plot thus far. The drug dealer, Kober, is stupid enough to actually check a carry-on bag full of heroin through luggage and then not be waiting for it when it comes off the carousel. Hall and Kober happen to own the same exact bright-orange duffel bag. Hall is given a

room where it will be impossible for the drug dealer to find him. What does all this lead up to?

The next morning Hall awakens and opens his duffel bag (did he sleep in his clothes?) to find at least 10 kilos of heroin. With duffel bag in hand, he runs to tell his brother, only to find his brother and his sister-in-law murdered with a gun on the floor next to them. Of course, Hall picks up the gun just in time to accidentally shoot a neighbor who has barged in on the scene. Rather than apologizing and calling the police, Hall runs through the streets of L.A. with the bag of heroin and the gun. He eventually decides to call the cops, but as he talks, a squad car pulls up to arrest him (they got a description from the wounded neighbor). Hall puts his hands over his head and then realizes that the gun stuck in his pants is visible. As the cops cock their weapons, Hall suddenly grabs for the gun in the most menacing way possible (just to hand it over) and the cops start shooting. Hall runs off, grabs a bus, and stashes the dope behind a vent panel under one of the seats. He then goes to Barney's Beanery where the only person he knows in L.A., Wright—a ditzy punk whom he met on the plane—works. After a breathless explanation from Hall, she quits her job to help him out. They go to her apartment, an oh-so-chic designer's dream that a waitress couldn't possibly afford, where he plans his revenge. Wright takes him on a shopping spree on Melrose Avenue—land of vintage clothing (where Molly Ringwald does all her shopping)—and buys him a hip L.A. outfit complete with leather jacket and sunglasses (they also dye his blond hair black). With a change of clothes, this Iowa farmboy suddenly transforms into a veteran street punk who swaggers, swears, and isn't afraid to kick recalcitrant informants in the privates to encourage their assistance. At this point, the film becomes an endless series of violent shoot-outs with the police, Kober, and two renegade Drug Enforcement Agency agents all out to get Hall. Bonehead move after bonehead move is made by every cast member until everyone but Hall, Stewart, and police detective Turman winds up dead. Despite the fact that his arrival in L.A. from Iowa has left at least a half-dozen bodies in Hall's wake, Turman allows Hall and Stewart to walk off arm-in-arm without any further questioning.

The scant description above cannot fully convey just how mind-numbingly moronic this film is. If Hall had stopped to catch his breath once in the opening 15 minutes, he might have had a nice little vacation. Instead, the script gives Hall and the other cast members so many foolish things to say and do that the viewer is left wishing that they would all kill each other early on and save us the pain of having to watch the rest of the film. Director Tuggle, who had written the superior Clint Eastwood prison film ESCAPE FROM ALCATRAZ, and directed the interesting Eastwood thriller TIGHTROPE, mishandles every task assigned him here, confirming suspicions that Eastwood needs to be on the set for Tuggle to look good. To be fair, the script by Kayden is atrocious and the cast is less than exemplary, and it appears that Tuggle attempted a "damn-the-torpedos-full-steam-ahead" style that would hopefully bowl over the more asinine plot points. Unfortunately, these blunders are too glaring and too numerous for this directorial approach to work, and that doesn't excuse Tuggle's handling of actors. Hall is remarkably convincing as a shy Iowa farm boy, but from the moment he lands in L.A. any credibility with which he had imbued his character goes right out the window. Sure, the kid is from the heartland, but is everybody from Iowa as stupid as he is when faced with intense situations? Perhaps the most frustrating aspect of OUT OF BOUNDS is that some excellent work by veteran cinematographer Surtees (an Eastwood favorite) and the score by former "Police" drummer Copeland are both buried beneath the rubble. As is now obligatory in films of this ilk, there are a number of totally forgettable songs pounding away on the soundtrack. They include: "Out of Bounds" (Stewart Copeland, Adam Ant, performed by Stewart Copeland, Adam Ant), "Wild and Innocent Youth" (Blades/Keagy, performed by Night Ranger), "Little By Little" (Robert Daigle, performed by Robert Daigle), "Shot in the Dark" (Paula Jean Brown, Jim Whelan, performed by Belinda Carlisle), "So Many Thangz" (Babyface Dee, Daryl Simmons, performed by The Deele), "Move" (Walter "Kandor" Kahn, Ray Monahan, performed by Funk Crew), "Run Away" (Robert Berry, performed by Robert Berry), "American Girl" (Brie Howard, Hillary Shepard, D.B. Tressler, Mieko Wantanabe, performed by The American Girls), "How Soon Is It Now?" (Morrissey and Marr, performed by The Smiths), "Fresh Flesh" (Stiv Bator, Brian James, performed by The Lords of the New Church), "Electric Ocean" (Ian Astbury, William H. Duffy, peformed by The Cult), "Burnin' Down the City" (Sammy Hagar, performed by Sammy Hagar), "Cities in Dust" (Siouxsie and the Banshees, performed by Siouxsie and the Banshees), "Run Now" (Tommy Keene, performed by Tommy Keene), "Raise the Dragon" (Richard Spellman, Sean Lyons, performed by Intimate Strangers), "Wild If I Wanna" (Y&T, performed by Y&T).

p, Charles Fries, Mike Rosenfeld; d, Richard Tuggle; w, Tony Kayden; ph, Bruce Surtees (DeLuxe Color); m, Stewart Copeland; ed, Kent Beyda, Larry Bock; prod d, Norman Newberry; set d, Joseph Pacelli, Jr.; cos, Donna Linson.

Crime/Thriller   **Cas.**   (PR:O MPAA:R)

OUTSIDER†   (1986, Czech.) 76m Gottwaldov c

Robert Panc *(Jozka)*, Milan Sandhaus *(Vit)*, Vladimir Fedorowicz *(Tonik Machuta)*, Jiri Wohanka *(Krystof)*, Miroslav Donutil *(Dr. Bartos)*, Oldrich Vlach *(Jozka's Father)*, Jana Vankova *(Jozka's Mother)*, Alois Svehlik *(Journalist)*, Daniel Sedivak *(Paka)*, Miroslav Cermak *(Hezoun)*, Jiri Devat *(Miki)*, Jiri Schmitzer, Jan Preucii.

d, Zdenek Sirovy; w, Jiri Krizan; ph, Jiri Kolin; m, Ondrej Soukup; ed, Antonin Strojsa; art d, Petr Smola; cos, Zdena Jarosova.

OVER THE SUMMER**½   (1986) 96m Shine Productions/Shapiro Entertainment c

Laura Hunt *(Tina)*, Willard Miller *(Grandpa Roy)*, Johnson West *(Rich)*, Catherine Williams *(Rose)*, David Dickson *(Jimmy)*, David Romero *(Joe)*, Jo Anna Jones *(Loretta)*, Jill Renee Sparks *(Sherrie)*, Robert Hutchens *(Deputy Barnes)*, Phillip Pitman *(Phil)*, Dennis Sutton *(E.K.)*, Geneva Hiergesell *(Grandma Virgie)*, Scott Stevens *(Danny, Rose's Brother)*, Nicole Smathers *(Lily, Rose's Sister)*, Ian Lindsay *(Baby Peanuts)*, Rick Burgsteiner *(Mack, Joe's Friend)*, Gary Carden *(Postmaster Hardin)*, Buffy Queen *(Waitress)*, Rebecca Meadows *(Tina's Mother)*, John Howard *(Tina's Father)*, Betsy Davidson *(Sherrie's Friend)*, Mac McBrayer *(Minister)*, Sam L. Queen *(Man at Bar)*, James Robert Rupe *(Kid at Dimestore)*, George Hyatt *(Policeman)*, Mary Ann Sutton, Michael Money *(Pool Hall Locals)*, Lisa Birchfield, Kelly Birchfield, Rita Birchfield, Kim Bowles, Albie Gilman, Dawn Heatherly, David Messer, Lana Parton, Jeffrey Queen, Charlie Sutton *(Kids at Dairy Bar)*, John Hearndon, Danny Edwards, Gus Morris, Stuart Rhinehart, Steve Becker, Doug James *(Sock Hop Musicians)*, Mark Sturgeon, Robin Trapp *(Tina's Arcade Friends)*; Barn Dance Participants: Robert Howell *(Tina's Partner)*, Ted White, William Cunningham, David Burnette, Everett Whitman *(Musicians)*, Danny Carvalho, Tammy Cogburn, Darren McCracken, Devin McCracken, Kim Warren, Chip Summey, Wayne Norman, Misty Craven, Janene Conrad, Terry Edwards, Joe Edwards, Scottie Edwards, Christy Reece, Tanya Craven *(Square Dancers)*; Kathy Cole, Ritta Cole, Carl Cutshaw, Philip Davis, John Dyer, Robert Dyer, Billy Glass, Bobby Scott, Betty Stamey, William Underwood *(Funeral Goers)*.

This sweet, often painfully honest coming-of-age film stars Hunt as a 16-year-old from Atlanta who is reluctantly spending the summer on a farm with her grandparents Miller and Hiergesell. Hunt is uncomfortable with the situation, for Miller—a rather odd old man—likes to stroke a naked Barbie doll and shows incestual interest in his granddaughter. Williams, Hunt's best friend in the small town of Frog Level, quickly becomes a confidante, though this pretty teenager is plagued with troubles of her own. She lives with Jones, her unmarried mother, along with a half-brother and sister who have turned into Williams' responsibility. Adding to this burden is the constant presence of Jones' loutish boy friend, who has his eyes set on Williams. The girls manage to cope with their troubles,

and Williams fixes Hunt up with West, one of the local boys. Hunt, Williams, and their beaus go skinny-dipping in a secluded pond, then are caught by lawman Hutchens while smoking marijuana. Hunt and Williams are let off with a warning, though Hutchens uses the opportunity to get some jabs in at Miller when he arrives at the police station to fetch his granddaughter. Later Miller spies Hunt and West making love in the local cemetery. This sets off feelings of sexual jealousy in the old man, which are coupled with the humiliation he feels after the incident with Hutchens. In retaliation, Miller (who was blamed for a past arson incident) sets fire to Hutchens' home, an act Hunt secretly witnesses. West is blamed for the incident, though eventually his innocence is proven. Miller, after toying with the idea of suicide for some time, finally kills himself after Hunt's parents arrive to pick her up at summer's end. Following his funeral, Hunt returns to Atlanta and contemplates the difficult experiences of the past few months.

The sexual tensions among characters are well handled, giving OVER THE SUMMER a darker edge that separates this from many films about adolescence. Hunt's newfound self-awareness, along with the uncomfortable feelings she has being around Miller, are well drawn by writer/director Sparks, who clearly empathizes with her characters. She infuses this with honesty, accurately capturing the mood and characters of a small Southern town. Williams, despite a few awkward moments in her performance, is a good counterpart to Hunt. Her anger directed towards Jones is another of OVER THE SUMMER's strong points, a painful relationship tinged with both hostility and sadness. Miller, as the confused old man, brings a quiet presence to the story that well counters the teenagers' vitality. OVER THE SUMMER suffers from the underdeveloped characterizations and relationships of important secondary characters (a local retarded boy is brought in on occasion, then shunted to the side when he's no longer needed), as well as wooden acting from some of the nonprofessional cast members. Surprisingly, Sparks gives Hunt a number of topless scenes, which add nothing to the story. Sparks, whose short films were prizewinners in a few regional film festivals, originally submitted her script for OVER THE SUMMER to the Samuel Goldwyn screenwriting competition. Her work made it to the finals, and eventually won a top award when entered in the Nissan FOCUS competition. Songs include: "Better and Better," "Once and For All," "I Never

Believed in Love," "Here I Am" (Steven Heller, performed by Jill Renee Sparks), "Once and For All," "This Ole House" (Heller, performed by Dan Riser), "Point of No Return" (Heller, Malcolm Holcombe, performed by Jaqui Perry), "Hello Baby" (Heller, performed by Heller), "Stranded in Self Pity" (Larry Rhodes, performed by Larry Rhodes), "I Miss My Cowboy" (Heller, performed by Gaye Johnson), "How Do You Do It?" (Heller, performed by Jaqui Perry).

p, Sara Margaret "Buffy" Queen; d&w, Teresa Sparks; ph, Afshin Chamasmany (Eastmancolor); ed, Afshin Chamasmany, Teresa Sparks; m, Steven Heller; cos, Mary Ellis; m/l, Steven Heller, Malcolm Holcombe, Larry Rhodes; makeup, Mary Ellis.

Drama   **Cas.**   **(PR:O MPAA:R)**

OVERNIGHT†   (1986, Can.) 98m Exile Production c

Victor Ertmanis *(Scott)*, Gail Garnett *(Del)*, Barbara Gordon *(Alison)*, Alan Scarfe *(Vladimir Jezda)*, Duncan Fraser *(Arthur)*, Ian White *(Livingstone)*.

A down-on-his-luck actor finds work in a pornographic film directed by a once-talented Czech emigre filmmaker. Partly a satire of the Canadian motion-picture industry, the film has little hope of being seen outside its own borders.

p, Jack Darcus, John Board; d&w, Jack Darcus; ph, Brian Hebb; m, Glenn Morley, Michael Conway Baker; ed, Sally Paterson; art d, Andrew Deskin.

Drama   **(PR:O MPAA:NR)**

OVNI IN MAMUTI†   (1986, Yugo.) 90m Yugoslavia c (Trans: Rams and Mammoths)

Slavko Stimac, Bozidar Bunjevac, Marko Derganc.

A political drama with allegorical intent that intertwines three stories in the city of Ljubljana as the citizens attempt to keep the illegal aliens of Bosnia from taking over. Directed by Robar-Dorin, a Slav who attended film school in the States before returning home, OVNI IN MAMUTI played the Chicago Film Festival in 1986 and was awarded the top prize at the Mannheim Film Festival. (In Slovenian; English subtitles.)

d&w, Filip Robar-Dorin; ph, Karpo Godina.

Drama   **(PR:O MPAA:NR)**

P

P.O.W. THE ESCAPE**

(1986) 90m Golan-Globus/Cannon c

David Carradine *(Col. Cooper)*, Charles R. Floyd *(Sparks)*, Mako *(Capt. Vinh)*, Steve James *(Johnson)*, Phil Brock *(Adams)*, Daniel Demorest *(Thomas)*, Tony Pierce *(Waite)*, Steve Freedman *(Scott)*, James Acheson *(McCoy)*, Rudy Daniels *(Gen. Morgan)*, Ken Metcalfe *(Gen. Weaver)*, Kenneth Weaver *(Teague)*, Michael Jame *(Veteran Sergeant)*, Irma Alegre *(Bar Girl)*, Spanky Manikin *(North Vietnamese Army Officer)*, Estrella Antonio *(Vietnamese Mother)*, Tony Beso, Jr. *(Young Boy in Sea Village)*, John Falch *(GI with Thomas)*, Chris Aguilar *(Bouncer)*, Crispin Medina, Ray Ventura *(North Vietnamese Army in Empty Camp)*, Lusito Hilario *(Radio Operator)*, Chris Gould, Brian Robillard, Leif Erlandson, Brian Tasker, James Gaines *(POWs)*, Eric Hahn, Mansour Khalili, Tony Realle, Tony Williams, Wally Williams *(GIs)*, Avi Karpick *(Murphy)*, Bill Kipp, Andrew Sommer, Victor Barjo, John Barrett, Zenon Gil, Henry Strazalkowski *(Soldiers at Fuel Dump)*.

Every war develops its own cinema, and the Vietnam movies are showing no sign of slowing up as they come out in every form from the big-budget star-studded spectacular (APOCALYPSE NOW and the long-awaited FULL METAL JACKET) to B-movie fodder (P.O.W. THE ESCAPE). The film opens as Carradine, a fighting colonel whose motto is "Everybody goes home", leads a mission to rescue POWs from a secret camp in the last days of the war. The mission is botched and Carradine ends up a prisoner in the camp. Commanding the camp is Mako, who has a trunk full of gold bullion and another filled with the watches and trinkets he has stolen from prisoners. With the war coming to an end, Mako is eager to get to the U.S. with his loot, and he proposes a deal to Carradine in which they will travel to Saigon, each the respective prisoner of the

other, depending on where they are, until they reach Saigon. Carradine refuses to cooperate unless all the men are included (there are only about a dozen), and eventually Mako agrees. Along the way, though, they run into trouble at a border check, and most of the guard force is killed. Mako is knocked unconscious by a shell and Carradine leads his men toward a helicopter rendezvous. Floyd is a slightly insane soldier who finds the loot and bides his time until he can steal it. Carradine also learns about the gold and he takes it out of the trucks and puts it into a backpack. Later, while Carradine is off stealing some canoes, Mako shows up and demands his money. Floyd escapes in the jeep he thinks still contains the loot and Mako goes after him. Eventually Mako catches up with Floyd in a brothel and Floyd tells him where Carradine is heading. Then he escapes before Mako can kill him. Meanwhile, Carradine and his men find a pair of G.I.s who were sent from an embattled firebase to get help. The rest of the men are reluctant to help, so Carradine rescues the surrounded men almost singlehandedly. At the rendezvous site, a village on the coast, Mako sets up an ambush, but Carradine manages to kill him and all his men. A grenade falls on the ground next to the truck with all the men inside, but Floyd suddenly rides up on a motorcycle and throws himself on the grenade, dying a hero at the last. Everyone who's still alive gets on the helicopters and flies to safety.

Coming in an obscure fourth in the Vietnam-prisoner-rescue mission sweepstakes (after RAMBO: FIRST BLOOD II, the Chuck Norris MISSING IN ACTION films, and the Gene Hackman starrer UNCOMMON VALOR), P.O.W. THE ESCAPE has a few things going for it most of the others don't. First of all, it takes place during the war, so we don't have any of those one-man armies invading sovereign nations in time of peace. Second, it has a fairly interesting performance by Carradine, remote from the variations of his TV "Kung Fu" character he usually does. Carradine has the potential to become an excellent character actor if he picks his roles more carefully. Third, it has a fascinating performance from Floyd—who is almost the main character—with a good chunk of running time devoted to his mental anguish. Although he is painted as the bad guy among the prisoners, he manages to convey an essential sympathy with his expressive, tortured eyes. It is in the classic tradition that he redeems himself at the end by sacrificing his life for the comrades he earlier betrayed. Technically, the film is quite good, making the most of its obviously limited funds to create a

passable Vietnam out of the Philippines using only three helicopters. Songs are "Proud Mary" (John Fogarty), "On the Fenceline" (Fontaine Brown, performed by Brown).

p, Menahem Golan, Yoram Globus; d, Gideon Amir; w, Jeremy Lipp, James Bruner, Malcolm Barbour, John Langley (based on a story by Avi Kleinberger, Gideon Amir); ph, Yechiel Ne'eman (TVC Color); m, David Storrs; ed, Marcus Manton; prod d, Marcia Hinds; art d, Bo Johnson; cos, Audrey Bansmer; m/l, John Fogarty, Fontaine Brown; makeup, Jeanne Van Phue.

War   Cas.   (PR:O MPAA:R)

PA LIV OCH DOD†

(1986, Swed.) 89m Swedish Film Institute–Filmfotograferna AB–Swedish Television/SVT 2-Ariane Filmproduktion c (Trans: A Matter of Life and Death)

Lena Olin *(Nadja)*, Svante Martin *(Stefan)*, Leif Ahrle, Tin-Tin Anderzon, Sten Ardenstam, Margaretha Bystrom, Lena Pia Bernhardsson, Eva Maria Bjorkstrom, Henry Bronett, Bengt CW Carlsson, Dick Eriksson, Ewa Froling, Svante Grundberg, Marian Grans.

The second part of a proposed trilogy by writer-director Ahrne (the first part was NEAR AND FAR in 1976) follows the love of a successful newspaper correspondent, Olin, for a happily married doctor, Martin. Although chosen for a prestigious assignment in Japan, Olin turns it down in favor of a potentially mundane series of articles about a maternity hospital in Stockholm. She disdains pregnancy and infants, but takes the assignment so she can be close to her lover, Martin. He is a man of few words and keeps his emotions secret. Olin is both frustrated and fascinated by this man who continually appears and disappears from her life, and her pursuit of passion leads to emotional encounters she never expected.

p, Stefan Hencz; d, Marianne Ahrne; w, Marianne Ahrne, Bertrand Hurault; ph, Hans Welin, Lisa Hagstrand (Agfa Color); m, Ilja Cmiral; ed, Marianne Ahrne; art d, Anna Brown; cos, Tania Alyhr, Rebecka Wallero; makeup, Lolo Murray.

Drama   (PR:C-O MPAA:NR)

PANTHER SQUAD zero

(1986, Fr./Belg.) 77m Eurocine–Brux Inter Film/Greenwich Intl. c

Sybil Danning *(Ilona)*, Karin Schubert *(Barbara)*, Jack Taylor, J.R. Gossar, Joan Virly, Franca Bocci, Donna Cross, Karin Brussels, Virginia Svenson, Donald O'Brien, Arch Taylor, Roger Darton, John Rounds, Robert Foster, Shirley Knight.

The world has come together, formed the New Organization of Nations (N.O.O.N.), and dedicated itself to space exploration. But during the launch of their new "space jeep," an ecology group known as Clean Space electronically seizes control and demands the entire program be cancelled to keep pollution from spreading any further. A second space jeep is readied to assist the other, but its female astronaut-pilot is waylaid and held hostage by Clean Space. Obviously this is a job for a half-dozen gals in miniskirts, just the sort of team Danning has trained. Danning traces the Clean Space kidnapers to the tiny country of Wazura, where the military dictator has a heavy moustache and plans for world domination. Gathering her forces and teaming with the local drunkard secret agent, Danning makes short work of the guards, who seem trained exclusively in being knocked unconscious, rescues the lady astronaut, and finishes off the final gunfight by pulling a disintegrator gun out of a case and zapping the bad guys and the jeep they are hiding behind.

Shot in Belgium and Spain in 1985, PANTHER SQUAD looks ten years older. The color is washed out and occasionally disappears completely. The sound is wretched and the way the film cuts away from people whenever they speak (to avoid having to match their lips) is hilarious. The editing is on par with the other technical credits. Danning, who has been the best thing in a lot of bad movies, seems utterly uninvolved and almost blank as she beats up thugs who simply stand around and wait for her to hit them again. The surprise of the film is that there is no sex, no nudity, no bad language, and almost no violence, Predictably, the film couldn't find a theatrical distribution and went straight to video.

p, Daniel Lesoeur, Sybil Danning, Ken Johnston; d, Peter Knight; w, George Freedland (based on a story idea by Ilona Koch); ph, Phil Uyuer (GTC color); m, Douglas Cooper Getschal, Jeffrey G. Gusman; ed, Barry Lensky, Peter Marks; cos, Ann Laynn; stunts, Johnny Polck.

Action/Adventure   Cas.   (PR:A MPAA:NR)

PAPILIO†

(1986, Czech.) 99m Barrandov c

Milan Knazko *(Hrabe)*, Filip Renc *(Cepek)*, Lenka Skopalova *(Anna)*, Ivana Chylkova *(Telcova)*, Marcel Vasinka *(Cynda)*, Pavel Novy *(Bobr)*, Stefan Misovic *(Matejka)*, Frantisek Svihlik *(Knobloch)*, Miloslav Stibich *(Cepek's Father)*, Jana Vychodilova *(Cepek's Mother)*, Jiri Kodet.

d, Jiri Svoboda; w, Miroslav Vaic, Jiri Svoboda; ph, Josef Vanis; m, Jozef Revallo; ed, Josef Valusiak; art d, Bohumil Novy; cos, Dmitrij Kadrnozka.

PARADIES†

(1986, Ger.) 100m Delta c (Trans: Paradise)

Heiner Lauterbach *(Victor Ptyza)*, Katharina Thalbach *(Lotte Kovacz)*, Sunnyi Melles *(Angelica Ptyza)*, Hanne Wieder *(Angelica's Mother)*, Ernst-Erich Buder *(Lotte's Customer)*, Ulrike Kriener *(Prostitute)*, Brigitte Janner *(Private Detective)*.

Doris Dorrie's follow-up to last year's immensely successful MEN, PARADIES reverses that film's situation of two men fighting over one woman and replaces it with two women—Melles and Thalbach—battling over a man, Lauterbach. Melles and Lauterbach are husband and wife, though their relationship is threatened by Melles' erroneous belief that Lauterbach is having an affair. She introduces him to her childhood friend, Thalbach, a promiscuous fraulein from the country, in the hope that his sexual fire will become ignited. Melles miscalculates her husband's desires and is thrown off guard when he falls in love with Thalbach and follows her to Hamburg where she has become a prostitute. Announced under the original title "Land Of Milk And Honey" (Schlaraffenland), this film was shown briefly in Germany and will get a wide release in 1987.

p, Chris Sievernich, Richard Claus; d&w, Doris Dorrie; ph, Helge Weindler; m, Claus Bantzer; ed, Raimund Barthelmes; art d, Jorg Neumann; set d, Jurgen Bauer, Gofi Hohn, Dani Handl.

Comedy/Drama   **(PR:O MPAA:NR)**

PARENTAL CLAIM†   (1986, Fr.) 98m Plaisance–Les Films de la Rochelle c
                             (LIEN DE PARENTE; AKA: NEXT OF KIN)

Jean Marais *(Victor Blaise)*, Serge Ubrette *(Clem)*, Anouk Ferjac *(Patricia Guerin)*, Roland Dubillard *(Philippe Guerin)*, Diane Niederman *(Cecile)*, Charles Millot, Michel Amphoux, Bernard Farcy, Ivan Romeuf, Marie Palmieri, Giselle Touret, Jane Watts.

Racial issues reminiscent of the 1960s social consciousness films arise in this odd comedy about an old French farmer, Marais, who is asked to take care of his grandson. Marais' long-estranged son has just died and the farmer has never even met has grandson. Marais is surprised to find that this grandson is a delinquent black Londoner, Ubrette. After the initial shock wears off, Marais grows to like Ubrette, coming to terms with his own racial ignorance in the process. Ubrette also manages to find a place for himself in the old-fashioned community, falling in love with a local girl and standing up to her angry boy friend. Based on an English-language novel by Oliver Lang, PARENTAL CLAIM is the debut feature from West Indian director Rameau, who successfully talked the 72-year-old Marais (a veteran of the French stage and film best known for his lead roles in Jean Cocteau's ORPHEUS and BEAUTY AND THE BEAST) out of retirement for this role. Marais, however, had appeared in a cameo in 1985's ORPHEUS-inspired PARKING. (In French; English subtitles.)

p, Daniel Vaissaire; d, Willy Rameau; w, Willy Rameau, Jean-Pierre Rumeau, Didier Kaminka (based on the novel *Next of Kin* by Oliver Lang); ph, Jimmy Glasberg (Panavision, Fujicolor); m, Bruno Coulais; ed, Delphine Desfons; art d, Benedict Beauge.

Comedy/Drama   **(PR:C MPAA:NR)**

PARIS MINUIT†   (1986, Fr.) 94m Mai Prod. c (Trans: Paris Midnight)

Frederic Andrei *(Serge Cartan)*, Isabelle Texier *(Marie)*, Gabriel Cattand *(Lt. Belland)*, Philippe Malignon *(Rougier)*, Michel Creton *(Leproux)*, Jean-Pierre Malignon *(Carmona)*, Alain Sachs *(Martin)*, Jean-Paul Comart *(Alexis)*, Jerome Nobecourt *(Roubaud)*, Ginette Garcin *(The Tramp)*, Isabelle Willer *(Frederique)*.

The motorscooter-riding star of 1981's DIVA, Frederic Andrei, directed, co-wrote, and acted in this policier which mixes crime and romance on the streets of Paris. Andrei is one of a group of thieves whose robbery of a ritzy jewelry store goes awry. Three of the gang are killed, while Andrei and his girl friend Texier escape. In order to avoid detection they split up, meeting secretly at various Parisian spots in the dark of night. They communicate through coded radio broadcasts and by writing lines from an Appollinaire poem on postcards which they leave for each other at various French sites. Eventually they are discovered by a detective, Cattand, who knows the lovers' methods but can't predict them.

p, Jean-Pierre Malignon; d, Frederic Andrei; w, Philippe Malignon, Frederic Andrei; ph, Bertrand Chatry (Fujicolor); m, Christophe Donnet; ed, Dominique Roy.

Crime/Romance   **(PR:NR MPAA:NR)**

PARTING GLANCES***   (1986) 90m Rondo/Cinecom International c

Richard Ganoung *(Michael)*, John Bolger *(Robert)*, Steve Buscemi *(Nick)*, Adam Nathan *(Peter)*, Kathy Kinney *(Joan)*, Patrick Tull *(Cecil)*, Yolande Bavan *(Betty)*, Richard Wall *(Douglas)*, Jim Selfe *(Douglas' Sidekick)*, Kristin Moneagle *(Sarah)*, John Siemens *(Dave)*, Bob Kohrherr *(Sam)*, Theodore Ganger *(Klaus)*, Nada *(Liselotte)*, Patrick Ragland *(Ex-Seminarian)*, Cam Brainard *(Ricky)*, Daniel Haughey *(Commendatore [Ghost])*, Sylwia Hartowicz *(Chris [Little Girl])*, Hana Hartowicz *(Chris' Mother)*, Nicholas Hill *(Cab Driver)*.

Unlike several major studio productions, in which homosexuality is used either as an issue or as comic relief, PARTING GLANCES takes an inside look at New York's gay community. The pain and joys of love, unspoken cultural rules, as well as the specter of AIDS are all dealt with in an energetic manner that balances the story's varying shades of emotion. Ganoung is a pleasant young man about to end a six-year relationship with his live-in lover Bolger. Bolger is preparing to leave for Africa, ostensibly to accept an employment opportunity, but also to give himself a little breathing room from Ganoung's steady companionship. Before going to a dinner to be hosted by Bolger's boss Tull and wife Bavan, Ganoung stops off at a record store where he attracts the attention of Nathan, a young clerk. From there Ganoung drops by the apartment of Buscemi, a cynical New Wave musician who is dying of AIDS. After arriving at Tull's home, Ganoung engages in a conversation with Bavan while Bolger discusses his new job with his boss. In addition to this subject, Tull tells Bolger about his own escapades with men even though his wife contentedly chats in the next room. Bolger and Ganoung say goodbye, then head to a going-away party being held at the loft space of Kinney, a jolly Soho artist. The place is packed to the rafters with all sorts of artists, including Bolger's ex-girl friend Moneagle as well as Ganger and

Nada. The latter two are a pianist and his extremely tattooed wife, and the couple entertain the party with a rather strange bit of performance art. Buscemi also drops by for an appearance, while Ganoung must fight off the advances of the overeager Nathan. All the while, Ganoung is becoming more despondent as Bolger's departure time rapidly approaches. The next morning Ganoung receives a surprise when Bolger decides not to leave. Another shock arrives when he receives a suicidal telephone call from Buscemi. Ganoung quickly hires a small plane to fly to Fire Island where he encounters his friend on the beach. Buscemi exclaims that the two should run off to Europe, then spins Ganoung around, determined to travel in whichever direction Ganoung's finger points.

The plot is fairly simple but the affection felt within PARTING GLANCES' marvelous ensemble makes these everyday events something more than commonplace. At the center of it all is Ganoung, a confused and often frustrated individual trying to come to terms with the difficult feelings he holds both for his lover and for the unsure directions in which his life seems to be headed. Ganoung handles this key role well, taking on the various circumstances with a good-natured humor. Buscemi's performance as the dying musician is another stand-

out. He injects the character with hyperkinetic drive as well as a caustic sense of self-parody. Rather than feel sorry for himself or allow others to pity him, Buscemi fights back. When Buscemi videotapes his will, he directs pointed jabs at the people in his life, doling out items with a flippant, tongue-in-cheek attitude. It's a terrific moment, as are the majority of Buscemi's scenes. Whether talking with Nathan on the stairs about Ganoung, or taking out frustrations on friends ("Gay men are jerks! Straight men are jerks!" he angrily tells Ganoung at one point), Buscemi gives the story a good punch in the ribs, providing PARTING GLANCES with its most memorable character. Secondary roles are also well cast, particularly the warm and thoughtful Kinney as Ganoung's friend and sympathetic confidant. Writer/director Sherwood shows marvelous talent in his feature debut. He deals with touchy issues in a forthright manner, and, like Buscemi, doesn't allow these events to unfold without a well-aimed sense of humor. Sherwood doesn't pretend to speak for the entire gay community, but the people he shows here have a good sense of self and are unashamed of who they are. One character, who is somewhat overweight, even jokingly exclaims he is violating the gay code of behavior by not being rail-thin. Through Buscemi, Sherwood explores the problems and issues AIDS raises, but he never allows these to dominate the film. There is a united feeling among Buscemi's friends brought on by the implications of his approaching demise, and this is as hard a stance as Sherwood takes. The importance of friendship is PARTING GLANCES' most important theme and Sherwood wisely allows this to take precedence. Music is another prominent factor in PARTING GLANCES. The story is backed by a strong, bouncy mixture of classical music and rock 'n' roll that well complements Sherwood's fast-paced direction. The cinematography is another fine point, well capturing the color and intensity of these characters and their surroundings. Still, this is a far-from-perfect film. Sherwood's fantasy sequences only detract from the fast-moving plot, and Bolger's character is that of a bland individual who doesn't seem terribly involved despite his importance to the plot. Bolger's decision to remain seems just a little too neat to be believed, echoing the finale of PARTING GLANCES' Argentinean counterpart ANOTHER LOVE STORY. Yet unlike that film, PARTING GLANCES is a conscious effort to make more than just a gay romance, and the film has had enormous crossover appeal to straight audiences. Much like the independent American features DESERT HEARTS and SHE'S GOTTA HAVE IT, PARTING GLANCES' success came through the talent and determination of a strong-willed director. Sherwood, along with coproducer Silverman, managed to raise $40,000 to fund the project, then shot the feature in just eight weeks. Both cast and crew worked for deferred salaries, and Sherwood's location sites were cheaply rented—if not outright donated—by generous benefactors. Interestingly, although Ganoung and Bolger's yuppie apartment looks much different from Buscemi's grubby flat, these were actually different rooms within one large Manhattan suite.

p, Yoram Mandel, Arthur Silverman; d&w, Bill Sherwood; ph, Jacek Laskus (DuArt Color); ed, Bill Sherwood; prod d, John Loggia; art d, Daniel Haughey, Mark Sweeney; set d, Anne Mitchell; cos, Sylvia Heisel; makeup, Franco.

Drama   Cas.   (PR:O MPAA:NR)

PASAJEROS DE UNA PESADILLA   (SEE: NIGHTMARE'S PASSENGERS, 1986, Arg.)

PASO DOBLE†   (1986, Rumania) 110m Artexim Bucharest/Romaniafilm c

Claudiu Bleont, Ecaterina Nazare, Petre Nicolae, Anda Onesa, Mircea Constantinescu, Valentin Popescu, Aurora Leonte.

This rare glimpse into everyday Rumanian life explores the relationship between two very different young men, Bleont and Nicolae, who share a room at the factory hostel. Although Bleont is handsome and outgoing and engaged to a sweet girl from a good family, Nicolae is sullen and hopelessly in love with an unwed mother who doesn't return his affection. Eventually Bleont and the unwed mother meet and they fall in love. Bleont finds himself in a difficult situation and tries to juggle both women while maintaining his friendship with Nicolae, who feels betrayed by him. In the end Bleont's maneuvering gets him into deep trouble with all concerned and he winds up alone.

d, Dan Pita; w, George Busecan, Dan Pita; ph, Marin Stanciu; ed, Cristina Ionescu; art d, Calin Papura; cos, Maria Malita.

Drama   (PR:C MPAA:NR)

PASODOBLE PRE TROCH†   (1986, Czech.) 70m Bratislava c

Renata Neudorflova (Iris), Ladislav Jezek (Blazej), Milan Jankovic (Roman), Milan Stiavnicky (Strba), Jarka Calabkova (Kosinarova), Zdenek Polasek (Father Antal), Libusa Kucerova (Danka), Peter Patak (Oskar), Jana Chvojkova (Katarina), Eduard Slimak (Dusan).

d, Vladimir Balco; w, Ivan Stadtrucker, Vladimir Balco; ph, Vincent Rosinec, Zoltan Weigl; m, Angelo Michajlov, Ladislav Jezek; ed, Roman Varga; art d, Jan Svoboda; cos, Anna Cserhalmiova.

PASSION†   (1986, Hong Kong) 98m D&B Films c

Silvia Chang, George Lam, Cora Miao

Two women, longtime friends, get together for an afternoon of tea and gossip. The differences in their lives are apparent—Chang is a traditional Chinese woman who nobly suffers through her life, while Miao is an independent woman who fights for and wins the man they both confess to loving. (In Cantonese; English subtitles.)

p, John Sham; d&w, Silvia Chang; ph, Ma; m, Lowell Lo; ed, Cheong Kwok Kuen; art d, William Chang.

Drama   (PR:A MPAA:NR)

PASSION OF REMEMBRANCE, THE†   (1986, Brit.) 80m Sankofa Film/ Video Collective c

Anni Domingo (Female Speaker), Joseph Charles (Male Speaker), Antonia Thomas (Maggie Baptiste), Carlton Chance (Gary), Jim Findley (Tony Baptiste), Ram John Holder (Benjy Baptiste), Shiela Mitchell (Glory Baptiste), Tania Morgan (Tonia), Gary McDonald (Michael), Janet Palmer (Louise).

The plight of blacks in Britain is shown in this part-documentary, part-fiction film. The first half of the film is simply two actors talking in front of a barren landscape, complaining about the various problems and attitudes that blacks in Britain face, both from the white population and from themselves. The second part concerns a West Indian family and their troubles, not least of which is the homosexuality of one of the sons. Produced on a shoestring budget by a black film collective, the film is interspersed with documentary footage of the Brixton riots of a few years ago and other scenes of racism and intolerance.

p, Martina Attille; d&w, Maureen Blackwood, Issac Julien; ph, Steven Bernstein (Technicolor); m, Tony Remy; ed, Nadine Marsh-Edwards.

Drama   (PR:O MPAA:NR)

PATRIOT, THE*   (1986) 88m Patriot/Crown International c

Gregg Henry (Lt. Matt Ryder), Simone Griffeth (Sean), Michael J. Pollard (Howard), Jeff Conaway (Mitchell), Stack Pierce (Atkins), Leslie Nielsen (Adm.

Frazer), Glenn Withrow (Pink), Larry Mintz (Bite), Diane Stevenett (Maggie), Anthony Calderella (Eight Ball), Mike Gomez (Kenwood), Larry Moss (Devon), Smith Osborne (Rosa), Sally Brown (Girl in Bar), Mike Muscat (Pool Room Bully), Lorin Vail (Howard's Girl), Gene Lehfeldt (Shore Patrol), Gary Kalpakoff (Rig Worker), B.L. Foley (Crane Operator), Andy Lentz (Party Guest), Rick McCallum (Hairy Hand), Peter Griffin (Kregg Guard), Ron Adams (Radio Dispatcher), Ross Borden (Navy Officer), Jacqueline Jacobs (Bar Fly).

With a title like this, one might expect another cinematic victory in the Vietnam war, or perhaps a successful annihilation of some rabid-eyed, brown-skinned terrorists. Instead THE PATRIOT is a confusing and altogether silly exercise in adventure redeemed only by its unintentionally funny climax. At a naval storage base somewhere in the desert (that's not a misprint), a bunch of Ninja-garbed bad guys easily breach security and heist a couple of atomic bombs. Led by Pierce, a

man apparently capable of only one facial expression, the baddies shoot up a storm, then safely make it back to a secret hideout. In a nearby town, Henry (best known as Brian de Palma's nasty-hearted villain in BODY DOUBLE) is a burned-out Vietnam veteran who hangs around barrooms and gets into easily winnable fights. He's summoned by Stevenett, an old girl friend (at least its assumed she's an old girl friend) to help her investigate some strange happenstances at an ocean-based oil rig. The two don scuba gear and Stevenett comes across a mysterious piece of paper. Henry recognizes this as something from an atomic bomb (just how is really never explained), and the mystery deepens. Stevenett is summoned by Nielsen, his old Navy superior. Here we learn that Henry was dishonorably discharged for some rather insignificant reasons, though it does give the leading man a chance to show Nielsen some disrespect. It's also learned that the stolen bombs could theoretically annihilate a good-sized portion of real estate, so Henry's help in recovering these devices is desperately needed. Griffeth, Nielsen's niece and a handy love interest, also turns out to be Henry's old girl friend. Eventually, after a time-padding reunion sequence, the two make love. This makes Griffeth's new beau, Navy man Conaway, pretty jealous. But not only is Conaway bitten by the green-eyed monster, he's also part of the atomic bomb plot. Pierce offs his two goofy henchmen, neither of whom you would want working on your Chevy's engine, let alone guarding an atomic bomb. Henry, Griffeth, Henry's pal Pollard, and Gomez, a Mexican chopper pilot, fly to the oil rig. More underwater adventures follow as goons fire spears at the good guys, who emerge from the drink for a poorly edited and delightfully campy fight sequence aboard the rig. Henry emerges victorious; he disconnects one bomb (what happened to the second one is never mentioned) and rides his motorcycle off into the sunset.

Coherence, as one might imagine, is not exactly the order of the day in THE PATRIOT. The plot twists merrily along with little logic as things grow increasingly confusing. Why are the bombs stolen? Something's mentioned about keeping the balance of power in check, though this is never really elaborated on. The acting is largely bad, though Neilsen (with a role so small you can't even call it a cameo) provides some comic relief with a tongue-in-cheek performance. Bullets fly frequently, though the damage they inflict usually resembles red paint sloppily dabbed onto costumes. The rig-mounted fight sequence is poorly edited, with lots of jump cutting and clumsy looking stunt work. The production company claims that this is the first film to be electronically edited on George Lucas' new EditDroid machine; with THE PATRIOT's jumpy cutting and time padding, it serves as a poor prototype for that system's potential. In addition to being its inept director, Frank Harris also served as THE PATRIOT's cinematographer. Though he is credited with developing an underwater camera, his below-sea-level work is murky, often to the point where characters aren't discernible. This was the first film made in association with the Navy's SEAL division (Sea, Air, Land), though there's nothing remarkable in the achievement. Songs include "You" (Bert Sommer, performed by Sommer), "I Gave Up All I Had" (Theodore Hawkins, Jr., performed by Hawkins, Jr.), "Blankets of Snow" (The Agin Brothers Band, performed by The Agin Brothers Band), "Hully Gully" (Fred Smith, Cliff Goldsmith, performed by The Olympics), "Ese Barrigon No Ese Mio" (Jesus Sanchez, performed by Wilfrido Vargas), "Dance the Night Away" (Randy Jackson, Liz Jackson, performed by Randy Jackson, Liz Jackson), "Attack" (Michael Licari, Kathy Malcolm, performed by On-Line), "Peace and Happiness" (Theodore Hawkins, Jr., performed by Ted Hawkins, Jim Odum).

p, Michael Bennett; d, Frank Harris; w, Andy Ruben, Katt Shea Ruben; ph,

Frank Harris (Fotokem Color); m, Jay Ferguson; ed, Richard E. Westover; art d, Brad Einhorn; set d, Tori Nourafchan; cos, Robin Lewis; spec eff, Fred Cramer; m/l, Bert Sommer, Theodore Hawkins, Jr., The Agin Brothers Band, Fred Smith, Cliff Goldsmith, Jesus Sanchez, Randy Jackson, Liz Jackson, Michael Licari, Kathy Malcolm; makeup, Tena Austin; stunts, John Barrett.

Action   Cas.   **(PR:O MPAA:R)**

PAULETTE†   (1986, Fr.) 91m GPFI–AMLF–CAPAC c

Jean Marine (*Paulette*), Luis Rego (*Georges*), Catherine Leprince (*Joseph, Female*) Charles Schmitt (*Joseph, Male*), Gerard Desarthe (*Guillaume*), Roland Blanche (*Albert-Henri*), Christian Sinniger (*Gilbert*), Eric Metayer (*Prosper*), Georges Beller (*Alphonse*), Roland Dubillard, Mylene Demongeot, Jean-Marie Riviere, Guy Montagne, Michele Bernier, Philippe Avron, Maurice Risch, Jean Francois Perrier, Dominique Besnehard, Jean-Paul Farre, Marie-Chrisine Descouard, Roland Giraud, Cerise, Maurice Baquet, Clause Evrard, Gerard Caillaud, Francois Cavanna, Professor Chron.

Another erotic French comic strip comes to big screen life as Marine portrays the title heroine. Her fabulously rich parents die when she is young, but her social conscience prevents her from enjoying her money. Eventually she hits on a scheme to redistribute the wealth to anyone with a good reason for needing it. Blanche, the administrator of the estate, is appalled and has her committed to an asylum, but she escapes and hooks up with some rivermen who help her to put things right. Cartoonist Wolinski has a brief cameo here, as do many other figures from the French cartoon world.

p, Jean-Claude Fleury; d&w, Claude Confortes (based on the comic strip by Wolinski and Pichard); ph, Claude Agostini (Fujicolor); m, Nicolas Errera; ed, Ghislaine Desjonqueres; art d, Francoise de Leu; cos, Edith Vesperini; makeup, Maryse Felix; spec eff makeup, Reiko Kruk.

Comedy   **(PR:O MPAA:NR)**

PAVUCINA†   (1986, Czech.) 96m Czechoslovak Filmexport/Gottwaldov Film Studios c/bw (Trans: Cobweb)

Eva Kulichova (*Radka*), Jirina Trebicka (*Marie*), Milena Svobodova (*Helena*), Jiri Zahajsky (*Father*), Radka Fiedlerova (*Mother*), Miroslav Machacek (*Psychiatrist*), Jana Kremanova (*Head Doctor*), Frantisek Husak (*Psychologist*), Zdenek Dusek (*Karel*), Yvetta Kornova (*Marcela*).

The netherworld of drug addiction behind the Iron Curtain is shown in this odd film. The central character is Kulichova, whose addiction stems from her unhappy family life (one of mother's boy friends was the first to start her on the spike, after which he seduced her). In a state-run hospital she undergoes therapy, constantly lying about a boy friend who died in Sweden but who is really a fabrication. An unusual film on a subject rarely touched by Communist bloc filmmakers.

d&w, Zdenek Zaoral; ph, Michal Kulic; m, Vaclav Halek.

Drama   **(PR:C MPAA:NR)**

PEAU D'ANGE†   (1986, Fr.) 69m Films de l'Atalante–Zora c (Trans: Angel Skin)

Robin Renucci (*Milo*), Alexandra Stewart (*Helena Werner*), Veronique Delbourg (*Angelina*), Jean-Paul Muel (*Alexandre*), Jeffrey Kime (*The Gigolo*), Agnes Cassandre (*Helena, as a young girl*), Patrice Melennec (*The Lover*).

This psychological drama with a supernatural tone stars Renucci as a young man who gets himself hired as the private secretary to the reclusive Stewart. Stewart thinks Renucci resembles her dead husband, who committed suicide after catching her with a lover. Renucci completely takes over her life, managing her finances, cutting her off from the outside world, and eventually raping her. It is then discovered that Renucci is actually the supposedly dead husband, who has returned with a vengeance. Filmed in 1983, PEAU D'ANGE couldn't find a release until its star, Renucci (who appeared that year in ENTRES NOUS), made a splash on Paris screens in the 1985 film ESCALIER C.

p, Daniele Molko; d, Jean-Louis Daniel; w, Jean-Louis Daniel, Philippe Setbon; ph, Richard Andry (Fujicolor); m, Philippe Servain; ed, Isabelle Rathery; art d, Denise Cohen; makeup, Tania Martin.

Drama/Thriller   **(PR:O MPAA:NR)**

PEESUA LAE DOKMAI†   (1986, Thailand) 125m Five Stars Prod. c (Trans: Butterflies and Flowers)

Suriya Yaovasang (*Huyan*), Vasana Pholyiem (*Mimpi*), Suchow Phongvilai (*Father*), Rome Isra (*Naka*).

After his father is crippled in a railroad accident, a young man becomes involved in smuggling rice across the border into Malaysia to support his family. Released in Thailand in 1985, the film won the Thai Film Awards for Best Film, Best Director, and five others.

p, Chareon Iamphungporn; d, Euthana Mukdasnit; w, Euthana Mukdasnit; ph, Panya Nimchareonpong; m, Butterfly; ed, M.L. Varapa Kasaemsri.

Drama   **(PR:A MPAA:NR)**

PEGGY SUE GOT MARRIED***½**   (1986) 104m Rastar/Tri-Star c

Kathleen Turner (*Peggy Sue*), Nicolas Cage (*Charlie Bodell*), Barry Miller (*Richard Norvik*), Catherine Hicks (*Carol Heath*), Joan Allen (*Maddy Nagle*), Kevin J. O'Connor (*Michael Fitzsimmons*), Barbara Harris (*Evelyn Kelcher*), Don Murray

(*Jack Kelcher*), Maureen O'Sullivan (*Elizabeth Alvorg*), Leon Ames (*Barney Alvorg*), Helen Hunt (*Beth Bodell*), John Carradine (*Leo*), Sofia Coppola (*Nancy Kelcher*), Jim Carrey (*Walter Getz*), Lisa Jane Persky (*Delores Dodge*), Lucinda Jenney (*Rosalie Testa*), Wil Shriner (*Arthur Nagle*).

This movie had a rocky start insofar as Jonathan Demme was originally announced to direct with Debra Winger as the star. Then Penny Marshall was penciled in to handle the helming chores but she was bypassed in favor of Coppola who had a string of bombs to his credit and needed something to take him out of the doldrums. This almost was it. (Marshall went on to make her feature-film direction debut with JUMPING JACK FLASH.) Although PEGGY SUE GOT MARRIED has been compared with BACK TO THE FUTURE, it was in development before that picture came out to cream the box-office receipts. A first-time script by the husband-wife team of Leichtling and Sarner, this is a cross between OUR TOWN and IT'S A WONDERFUL LIFE, and even has touches of Jack Finney's novel *Time and Again*.

Turner, who was 32 when the picture was shot, plays a 43-year-old housewife on the verge of a divorce from Cage (who is actually in his early twenties). Cage is an obnoxious philanderer who is famous in the town as one of those nuts who does wild TV commercials for his retail appliance business. Turner has been

invited to her 25th high school reunion and manages to squeeze into her old prom dress with the help of her daughter, Hunt. Returning to meet all of her old friends from James Buchanan High, she has fun as she talks with now-divorced Hicks, who always was a rakehell and hasn't changed, and Allen, who married right out of school and "missed the sexual revolution entirely." The most successful graduate is school nerd Miller, now a computer millionaire married to a knockout wife who is pregnant. Miller recalls that Turner was the only person who ever treated him with kindness while they were teenagers. Turner is asked about where her husband is and she has to tell them that things have not been going well between them. When Turner is named queen of the reunion, she ascends the podium to accept her crown and then passes out and is tossed into a time warp. (If you can accept this, then you'll buy everything else in the movie.)

She awakens in 1960, a 43-year-old person in a 17-year-old body. (This is the largest problem about the movie. It's easier to accept Turner and the others as 40-year-olds than as high schoolers.) The premise then is . . . if you had the chance to go back and do it again, would you make the same mistakes or would you do anything differently? Turner rises from a cot where she has been resting, sees her old friends, now young, then goes home to visit her parents, Harris and Murray. They are the same way she remembers them back in the 1960s and her obnoxious little sister is still obnoxious. Turner is startled when she gets a phone call from her grandmother, O'Sullivan, and has the chance to talk to her, as well as her long-dead grandfather, Ames. Cage arrives. He was a smarmy adult and he is the same way as a teenager, with dreams of becoming a big rock star. Turner knows that he will wind up in the family business but she doesn't have the heart to tell him that all of his rehearsing with his quartet is for naught. With the knowledge of having lived 25 years more than anyone else in this 1960 setting, Turner's attitude is intriguing. She's always had a curiosity about campus beatnik O'Connor and wondered what would have happened if she had chosen him over Cage. She explores the possibility and learns that he is weird, spouts awful poetry, and dreams of living in a polygamous relationship with her and several other women on a chicken farm in Utah. That turns her off right away and she goes back to Cage, trying all the while to talk him out of his ardor for her as she knows what's going to transpire. But fate has different ideas and she makes love to Cage (which, we assume, leads to a pregnancy like the one that occurred the first time around and sent her to the altar), and then awakens in 1985 with a tearful Cage standing over her and pleading for forgiveness. He'll get rid of his young bimbo and try to make a success of their marriage. Turner doesn't take him back that easily but there is hope for their future when she agrees to have dinner with him as the picture fades.

The movie title is taken from the Buddy Holly tune, one of the many oldies but goodies that inspired several movies in recent years, including "Blue Velvet," "Stand By Me," and "Mona Lisa." Good acting from almost everyone, the one notable exception being Coppola's nephew, Cage, whom he used in COTTON CLUB and RUMBLE FISH, two of his recent flops. When Cage is good, as in BIRDY, RAISING ARIZONA, and even VALLEY GIRL, he can be terrific. But here he isn't. It looks as though he had no direction whatsoever and was allowed to try a strange, constricted voice for his character that was, at times, unintelligible, although that hardly mattered because he didn't have anything interesting to say. Some of the anachronistic jokes are very funny as Turner tells Miller about computers and panty hose, and says that everything in the future has been made smaller, "except for portable radios." When she sees the early Dick Clark on TV she also mentions that fact that "the man never ages." A particularly big laugh comes when Murray shows the family his new car, an Edsel.

The picture came in at about $13 million, which is small compared to what Coppola spent on COTTON CLUB and, more recently, his biggest disaster, ONE FROM THE HEART. A few trick shots, not unlike those in ONE FROM THE HEART, but they are not dwelt upon. Turner was Oscar-nominated for her role and justly so. With virtually no makeup change (other than hair styles), she was able to convey the hyper attitude of a teenager vis-a-vis the more sedate demeanor of middle age. A happy ending was reputedly tacked on months after the picture completed principal photography at the behest of the studio chiefs. The movie has many lovely moments and just as many dead spots, but those moments are worth spending the 104 minutes. At one point, Turner says she's going to Liverpool to discover the Beatles, then she gives Cage a song for him to sing that turns out to be "She Loves You." Due to one fairly explicit scene and some rough language, kids should be teenagers before being allowed to see the film.

p, Paul R. Gurian; d, Francis Coppola; w, Jerry Leichtling, Arlene Sarner; ph, Jordan Cronenweth (DeLuxe Color); m, John Barry; ed, Barry Malkin; prod d, Dean Tavoularis; art d, Alex Tavoularis; set d, Marvin March; cos, Theadora Van Runkle.

Fantasy/Comedy   (PR:C MPAA:PG-13)

PEKIN CENTRAL†   (1986, Fr.) 95m Forum/Melody Movies Prod. c (Trans: Peking Central)

Yves Renier (Yves), Christine Citti (Valerie), Marco Bisson (Bruno), Sophie Deschamps, Beatrice Lord, Jacques Pibarot, Francoise Taguet, Hubert Watrinet, Pascale Bailly, Alain Tasma, Cai Xinming, Camille de Casabianca.

Armed with a fake script, director de Casabianca managed to obtain a filming permit from the Chinese government. Then she took a small cast and crew with her to make this romantic comedy-drama, the first film ever shot by a Westerner in Communist China. The story deals with a woman (Citti) who follows her journalist boy friend to China, but their relationship crumbles in the exotic setting, and she drifts into an affair with a photographer. He, too, is not interested in a serious relationship, and she eventually returns to Paris sadder and wiser. Director de Casabianca is the daughter of editor Denise de Casabianca and director Alain Cavalier, with whom she scripted the latter's THERESE.

p, Bernard Verley; d&w, Camille de Casabianca; ph, Raymond Depardon; m, Michel Hardy, Camille de Casabianca; ed, Denise de Casabianca.

Drama/Comedy   (PR:C MPAA:NR)

PEKING OPERA BLUES†   (1986, Hong Kong) 98m Cinema City/Golden Princess c

Lin Ching Hsia, Sally Yeh, Cherie Chung, Mark Cheng.

Three of the most popular actresses in Hong Kong are gathered for this lightweight film, set at the turn of the century. Lin is featured as the daughter of a Chinese general who finds herself involved with a revolutionary movement that sends her on a mission to rob her father's safe. The other two stars have smaller parts, Chung in her patented dumb Dora bit and Yeh as the stage-struck daughter of an opera manager who is prevented from taking to the stage by the conventions of the time.

p&d, Claudie Chung; w, To Kwok Wai; ph, Poon Hung Seng; m, James Wong; ed, David Wu; art d, Vicent Wai, Ho Kim Sing, Leung Chi Hing; cos, Ng Po Ling.

Comedy   (PR:C MPAA:NR)

PEQUENA REVANCHA†   (1986, Venezuela) 95m Alfredo J. Anzola c (Trans: Little Revenge)

Eduardo Emiro Garcia, Elisa Escamez, Carlos Sanchez, Pedro Duran, Carmencita Padron, Yoleigret Falcon, Cecilia Todd.

In an unnamed Latin American country, the repressive government begins taking steps to eliminate the traces of opposition in the peasant population. But as they do so, they actually have the opposite effect, galvanizing the resistance and creating martyrs. The story is told through the eyes of one 12-year-old boy whose dog is run over by an army jeep. This begins his political awareness, a process continued when a playmate's father is arrested and soldiers come to the school asking the children to report everything their parents say or do.

p, Alfredo J. Anzola; d, Olegario Barrera; w, Olegario Barrera, Laura Antillano; ph, Alfredo J. Anzola, Carlos Bricano, Jorge Naranjo; ed, Olegario Barrera, Marisa Bafile.

Drama   (PR:C MPAA:NR)

PERDOA ME POR ME TRAIRES†   (1986, Braz.) (Trans: Forgive Me for Your Betrayal)

Vera Fischer, Nuno Leal Maia, Rubens Correa, Lidia Bronde, Henriette Morineau, Sadi Cabral, Zaira Zambelli.

d, Braz Chediak; w, Gilvan Pereira, Nelson Rodrigues Filho, Jofre Rodrigues, Braz Chediak (based on the story by Nelson Rodriguez Filho); ph, Helio Silva; m, Chico Buarque; ed, Rafael Valverde; art d, Joffre Rodriguez.

PERILS OF P.K., THE zero   (1986) 90m P.K./Joseph Green c

Naura Hayden, Kaye Ballard, Sheila MacRae, Heather MacRae, Larry Storch, Norma Storch, Dick Shawn, Sammy Davis, Jr., Altovise Davis, Louise Lasser, Prof. Irwin Corey, Virginia Graham, Jackie Mason, Joey Heatherton, Anne Meara, Al Nuti, Mike Murphy.

This isn't really so much a feature film as it is a home movie for Las Vegas denizens. Hayden plays a former film star who now makes a living by doffing her clothes at adult parties. She harbors a desire to return to the limelight, something she confides regularly to her psychiatrist, Shawn. Hayden attempts to get a top movie star to appear in a film with her, though she ends up in a mental are cameo appearances by such performers as Larry Storch, Sheila MacRae (who also coproduced), Professor Irwin Corey, and the inimitable Sammy Davis, Jr. The majority of the gags are so old even Pee-Wee Herman wouldn't touch 'em. What's more, none of the bits is even remotely funny. Hayden, best known for penning such self-help books as *Astro-Logical Love* and *How to Satisfy a Woman Every Time & Have Her Beg For More*, somehow conned a group of investors out of $1.5 million to produce this vanity project, then enlisted a corps of her show-biz pals as costars. Three words to aptly describe this film: avoid, avoid, avoid.

p, Sheila MacRae, Marge Cowan; d, Joseph Green; w, Naura Hayden; ph, Paul Glickman; ed, Naura Hayden; md, Dunn Pearson; m/l, Naura Hayden.

Comedy   (PR:O MPAA:NR)

PERROS DE LA NOCHE†   (1986, Arg.) 85m c (Trans: Dogs of the Night)

Emilio Bardi, Gabriela Flores, Hector Bidone, Gustavo Belatti, Enrique Alonso, Mario Alarcon, Neomi Morelli, Raquel Albeniz.

This realistic social-consciousness film details the plight of an impoverished brother and sister as they attempt to work their way out of the slums. The thickheaded brother, Bardi, turns to petty crimes, is caught, and put in jail. His sister, Flores, earns a little money working at menial jobs as she waits for Bardi to be released from jail. Upon his release, Bardi decides to promote his sister as a stripper, and they travel from seedy club to seedy club, making a few dollars and learning a lot about life. Flores hates what her brother has forced her to do, but continues until she is infatuated club owner puts a stop to the dancing/prostitution to claim the girl for himself.

p&d, Teo Kofman; w, Pedro Espinosa, Enrique Medina, Teo Kofman (based on the book by Enrique Medina); ph, Julio Lencina; m, Tarrago Ros, Leion Gieco; ed, Norbert Rapado; set d, Miguel Angel Lumaldo, Enrique Bordolini; cos, Angelica Fuentes.

Drama   (PR:O MPAA:NR)

PERVOLA: TRACKS IN THE SNOW†   (1986, Netherlands) 95m Cinephile/ Maya c

Gerard Thoolen (Simon van Oyen), Bram van der Vlugt (Hein van Oyen), Melle van Essen (Aapo), Jan Willem Hees (Van Oyen, Sr.), Thom Hoffman (Ron), Jaap Hoogstra (Olga), Brigitte Kaandorp (Truusje), Phons Leussink (Adelaar), Mircea Krishan (German), Adrian Brine (Englishman), Suzanne Colin (French Lady), Rolf Leenders (Bald Man), Gunvor Asen (Housekeeper), Anna van Beers (Maid), Ingvall Pryts (Coachman), Hennie Velthuis (Working Woman), Hans Holtkamp (Soldier).

This tale of fraternal tension is told in flashback. The father of the two brothers is a wealthy stockbroker who decides to retire and move to a village in the north, leaving his business to be split evenly between his sons, Thoolen and van der Vlugt. Van der Vlugt, however, cheats his brother, tells him he has been disinherited because of his homosexuality, and keeps all the money for himself. Years later on his deathbed, the father asks to see both his sons. Thoolen is eager for a reconciliation, but van der Vlugt is equally eager to keep him from finding out what he has done. They travel north but the old man dies in van der Vlugt's arms before Thoolen can get there. Their father's last request is to be buried in the town of Pervola, even farther north, but van der Vlugt is reluctant to carry out the arduous trip. Thoolen, however, orders a heavy sledge built and prepares to leave. Van der Vlugt is afraid that his brother might yet learn the truth, so he agrees to go along. Along the way they are harassed by wolves, blizzards, and a civil war fought between black-uniformed, shave-headed government troops and white-uniformed rebel guerilas on skis, but these are only minor distractions compared to the conflict building between the two men. Van der Vlugt lets his secret slip and Thoolen finds he has reserves of inner strength and character he didn't know he had. By the time they finish their journey, the two have virtually exchanged personalities. Shot in Roros, Norway under incredibly difficult conditions (electric cables would freeze and snap in the -40 degree cold), the film creates its own world, taking place in an imaginary country that is stocked with its own city names, its own language, and even its own matchbooks. Further, the time setting of the film is left ambivalent, though if pressed the director would say it's sometime in the 1920s. Opening in the Netherlands in 1985, the film played several major cities in the U.S. and Canada in 1986. (In Dutch; English subtitles).

p, Jan Musch, Orlow Seunke, Tijs Tinbergen; d, Orlow Seunke; w, Orlow Seunke, Dirk Ayelt Kooiman, Maarten Koopman, Gerard Thoolen; ph, Theo Bierkens; m, Maarten Koopman; ed, Orlow Seunke, Dorith Vinken; art d, Misjel Vermeiren; cos, Anna Verhoeven; makeup, Nancy Baudoux; spec eff, Petter Borgli.

Drama   (PR:C   MPAA:NR)

PESTI VE TME†   (1986, Czech.) 98m Barrandov c

Marek Vasut *(Vilda Jakub)*, Josef Nedorost *(Kurt Schaller)*, Josef Vinklar *(Krakowski)*, Eliska Balzerova *(Ema Gabrielova)*, Jaroslav Tomsa *(Coach)*, Robert Vrchota *(Restaurant Headwaiter)*, Jana Krausova *(Blanka)*, Pavel Novy *(Tommy)*, Ferdinand Kruta *(Dedek)*, Vladislav Kowalski *(Dr. Vicha)*, Josef Stefl *(Dr. Herman)*, Cestmir Randa *(Fiedler)*, Evelyna Steimarova *(Zrzka)*, Ladislav Lakomy.

d, Jaroslav Soukup; w, Jaroslav Vokral, Jaroslav Soukup, Drahoslav Makovicka; ph, Richard Valenta; m, Zdenek Bartak; ed, Jiri Brozek; art d, Jiri Matolin; cos, Jan Kropacek.

PIAOBO QIYU†   (1986, China) 96m China Film Corp./Shanghai Film
Studios c (Trans: Strange Encounters)

Wang Shihuai *(The Wanderer)*, Xue Shujie *(Wildcat)*, Li Wei *(Bandit Chief)*, Liu Xinyi *(Knight Errant)*, Lu Qing *(Ghost Brother)*, Wa Ling *(Wife)*, Yuo *(Despot)*.

A young student wanders the countryside and falls in with a band of robbers who fight against the local evil warlord. He falls in love with the brigand chief's daughter, but she has eyes only for a dashing Robin Hood type with a habit of showing up in the nick of time. Filmed in 1982, the film only made its way to the West in 1986, meeting with overwhelming indifference heightened by a sudden outpouring of vastly superior films from the Chinese mainland.

p, Zhang Ianmin; d, Yu Benzheng; w, Ai Wu (based on the book *Going To The South*); ph, Peng Enli; m, Yang Shaolin.

Drama   (PR:A   MPAA:NR)

PICARDIA MEXICANA NUMERO DOS†   (1986, Mex.) 95m Cima/
Peliculas Mexicanas c (Trans: Mexican Picaresque, Part II)

Vicente Fernandez *(Nicho)*, Marcela Delgado *(Rosita)*, Hector Suarez *(Macaco)*, Lalo *(Sireno)*, Pedro Weber *(Don Tilo Aguilar)*.

The sequel to a successful comedy (in turn based on a successful humor book) centers on three vegetable deliverymen and their romantic adventures.

d, Rafael Villasenor Kuri; d, Pedro Urdimulas (based on the book by Armando Jimenez); ph, Jose Luis Lemus; ed, Max Sanchez.

Comedy   (PR:C   MPAA:NR)

PIMEYS ODOTTA†   (1986, Finland) 78m Finnkino/Villealfa c (Trans:
Waiting for Darkness)

Pekka Valkeejarvi *(Mack)*, Riita Havukainen *(The Singer)*, Ritva Sorvali *(The Blonde Girl Friend)*, Arno Virtanen *(Police Lieutenant)*, Turo Pajala *(Mack's Friend)*.

Another *film noir* parody, this time from Finland (of all places). Valkeejarvi is a young man who is approached by a sleazy police lieutenant who wants him to follow his wife and prove that she is sleeping with another man. Soon Valkeejarvi finds himself sinking ever deeper into a morass of lies, false identities, and murder.

p&d, Pauli Pentti; w, Antti Lindquist, Pauli Pentti; ph, Heikki Katajisto (Kodakcolor); m, Rauol Bjorkenheim; ed, Anne Lakanen.

Crime/Comedy   (PR:C   MPAA:NR)

PING PONG†   (1986, Brit.) 103m Film Four International/Picture Palace
Film c

David Yip *(Mike Wong)*, Lucy Sheen *(Elaine Choy)*, Robert Lee *(Mr. Chen)*, Lam Fung *(Ah Ying)*

When a wealthy Chinese businessman dies in a phone booth in London, his lawyer (Sheen) sets about trying to fulfill the requirements of the old man's will, of which she is the executor. One demand is that his son (Yip), a thoroughly Anglicized restaurant owner who speaks no Chinese, change his cuisine to traditional Cantonese. An old friend is left a farm in the countryside with the stipulation that he visit it regularly, despite the fact that the man has never in his life stepped outside of London's Chinatown. Another requirement of the man's will is that at least one of his children accompany his body back to his native village in China for burial. Apparently inspired by the success of DIM SUM, this film fell short of the mark and proved a box office disappointment.

p, Malcolm Craddock, Michael Guest; d, Po-chih Leong; w, Jerry Liu; ph, Nick Knowland; m, Richard Harvey; ed, David Spiers; prod d, Colin Pigott.

Comedy/Drama   (PR:C   MPAA:NR)

PINK CHIQUITAS, THE†   (1986, Can.) 86m SC Entertainment/Shapiro
Entertainment c

Frank Stallone *(Tony Mareda, Jr./Tony Mareda, Sr.)*, Cris Pirrie *(Clip Bacardi)*, McKinlay Robinson *(Trudy)*, Elizabeth Edwards *(Mary Anne Kowalski)*, Claudia Udy *(Helen)*, Don Lake *(Barnie Drum)*, John Hemphill *(Ernie Bodine)*, Gerald Isaac *(Dwight Wright)*, Cindy Valentine *(Stella Dumbrowski)*, Diana Platts *(Anita)*, Robert Bredin *(Dennis McDougal)*, Sharon Dyer *(Grindle)*, Peter McBurnie *(Jesse Cornfield)*, T.J. Scott *(Dave)*, Kevin Frankoff *(Ken)*, Heather Smith *(Hitchhiker)*, Eartha Kitt *(Voice of Betty, the Meteor)*, Harold Bachan *(Doctor)*, Marlow Vella *(Tony Mareda, Jr. [Child])*, Bob Aaron *(Tourist Dad)*, Marcia Bennett *(Tourist Mom)*, Andrew Paul Bernard, Christopher Tugnett *(Kids)*, David Rigby, Danny Addario, Michael Gerace, Angelo Christou, Durango Coy, Shaun Taylor, Brock Jolliffe *(Hitmen)*, Linda Arbuckle *(Kaye)*, Jan Anderson *(Snack Bar Cashier)*, Alan Fox *(Cashier's Assistant)*, Anne Sketchley *(Madge)*, Michael O'Farrell *(Scoutmaster)*, Jason Shoot, Chris Shoot, Paul Hembruff *(Cubs)*, Jean Currie *(Female Citizen)*, Gloria Wrona, Valerie Miller *(Go Go Girls)*, Julian Grant *(TV Security Guard)*, Dorin Ferber *(Belly Dancer)*; The Pink Chiquitas: Michelle Baker *(Marcia Aguiar)*, Susan Booth *(Brigitte Biller)*, Astrid Brandt *(Ingrid Bower)*, Lisa Chiverton *(Carol Chin)*, Nancy Hammond *(Lolita David)*, Susan Haskell *(Topaz Hasfal)*, Tracy Hunt *(Lorrie Howe)*, Cynthia Kereluk *(Jennifer Kent)*, Sherry Lee *(Konnie Krome)*, Caroline Neilson *(Marcia Levine)*, Cynara Pitimac *(Renata Nobrega)*, Rosanna Torre *(Jane Sowerby)*, Ildiko Sinka *(Danita Tynes)*; Zombie Beach Party III: Mike Ferguson, Don Richardson, Elverez Ryan *(Zombies)*, Nick Campbell, Colin Gleason, Carrie Gleason-Kennedy, Karen Kennedy, Karen Mair, Mike Simone *(Zombie Victims)*, Sharolyn Sparrow *(Jungle Girl)*.

A pink meteorite with Eartha Kitt's voice and the ability to turn otherwise decent women into gun-toting, sex-starved bimbos falls on the tiny town of Beansville, and only Stallone (Frank, that is) and his weatherman sidekick can save the Earth from being taken over by these heavily armed amazons. That's actually the premise of this Canadian science-fiction spoof, laden with references to everything from THE GODFATHER to 1950s monster movies. Songs and musical numbers include: "Like a Legend in My Time," "I did the Wrong Thing to the Right Girl," "Nobody Told Me," "You and I," "Flame" (Frank Stallone, Tom Marolda, performed by Frank Stallone), "She's Hot" (Frank Stallone, Tom Marolda, performed by Frank Stallone, Eartha Kitt), "Pink Chiquita" (Frank Stallone, Tom Marolda, performed by Frank Stallone, Tom Marolda), "The Boy From Ipanema" (Antonio Carlos Jobim, performed by Eartha Kitt), "Uska Dara" (traditional, performed by Eartha Kitt), "Peter Gunn" (Henry Mancini, performed by The Art of Noise), "Give Me Everything You Got" (Paul J. Zaza, performed by Cindy Valentine).

p, Nicolas Stiliadis; d&w, Anthony Currie (based on a concept by Nick Rotundo, Anthony Currie); ph, Nicolas Stiliadis (Kodak Color); m, Paul J. Zaza; ed, Stephen F. Withrow; art d, Danny Addario; set d, Bora Bulajic; ch, Roland Kirouac; m/l, Frank Stallone, Tom Marolda, Antonio Carlos Jobim, Henry Mancini, Paul J. Zaza; makeup, Nicole Demers; stunts, T.J. Scott.

Science Fiction/Comedy   Cas.   (PR:C-O   MPAA:PG-13)

PINKY'S GANG   (SEE: BALLERUP BOULEVARD, 1986, Neth.)

PIRATES***   (1986, Fr./Tunisia) 124m Carthago –Accent–Cominco/Cannon
c

Walter Matthau *(Capt. Thomas Bartholomew Red)*, Cris Campion *(Frog)*, Damien Thomas *(Don Alfonso)*, Richard Pearson *(Padre)*, Charlotte Lewis *(Dolores)*, Olu Jacobs *(Boumako)*, David Kelly *(Surgeon)*, Roy Kinnear *(Dutch)*, Bill Fraser *(Governor)*, Jose Santamaria *(Master at Arms)*, Ferdy Mayne *(Capt. Linares)*, Anthony Peck, Anthony Dawson, Richard Dieux, Jacques Maury *(Spanish Officers)*, Robert Dorning *(Commander of Marines)*, Luc Jamati *(Pepito Gonzalez)*, Emilio Fernandez *(Angelito)*, Wladyslaw Komar *(Jesus)*, Georges Trillat *(Pockmarked Sailor)*, Georges Montillier *(Duenna)*, John Gill *(Carpenter)*, David Foxxe *(Cook)*, Brian Maxine *(Boatswain)*, Raouf Ben Amor *(Armoury Guard)*, Eugeniusz Priwieziencew *(Hunchback)*, Roger Ashton-Griffiths *(Moonhead)*, Ian Dury *(Meat Hook)*, Bill Stewart *(Ginge)*, Sydney Bromley *(Diddler)*, Cardew Robinson *(Lawyer)*, Daniel Emilfork *(Hendrik)*, Carole Fredericks *(Surprise)*, Allen Horst *(Fiddler)*, Denis Fontayne *(Sailor)*, Michael Elphick, Angelo Casadei *(Sentries)*, Antonio Spoletini *(Palace Guard)*, Bill Mac-

Care *(Jailer)*, Smilja Mihailovitch *(New Duenna)*, Bernard Musson *(Passenger)*, Josine Comelas *(Passenger's Wife)*.

In 1974, when almost no one in Hollywood was interested in *film noir*, Polanski released CHINATOWN, a picture which effectively twisted the genre. Twelve years later Polanski has done the same with the swashbuckler. This time, however, nobody has paid any attention. The picture opens with Matthau, a grungy, bearded, peg-legged pirate who is feared by all who live at sea, and Campion, a handsome blonde French sailor, sailing on a tiny raft through the vast blue ocean. Nearly driven mad by hunger and exposure, Matthau imagines Campion to be a pig and attempts to take a bite out of him. Before he can feast, however, a Spanish galleon—the Neptune—is sighted. With some effort, the pair climb aboard as a mutiny is being put down by Thomas and his evil Spaniard lieutenants. Matthau and Campion are tossed into the brig along with another prisoner, Jacobs, a cook who previously tried to poison the Spaniards. Jacobs whets Matthau's appetite for greed by informing him that in the very next room sits a priceless gold Aztec throne which is being transported by Thomas via the orders of aging governor Fraser. While Matthau is contemplating ways to steal the throne, Campion is thinking of Lewis, the governor's beautiful niece who is also on board. Later, in the messroom, Matthau attempts to start a mutiny by tossing a rat in the soup. Thomas, with his heavily armed aides standing beside him, easily puts down the revolt and sentences Matthau and Campion to be hanged. Before doing so, Thomas invites the pair to lunch and serves them their rat, forcing each to eat half. After each take a few bites, Lewis implores Thomas to send them away. While standing on deck awaiting their hanging, Matthau and Campion manage to break free and incite a mutiny. After a great deal of sword-play, the Spaniards are rounded up and imprisoned. Meanwhile, Campion personally takes Lewis into custody, thereby preventing her from being raped by any of a number of sex-starved shipmates. Having taken charge of the ship and waving the pirate flag, Matthau steers its course to a familiar island. Matthau underestimates the cunning of the Spaniards who retake their ship and sail away, leaving Matthau and many of the rebel sailors behind.

Determined to take the throne as his own, Matthau buys himself a ship and sets sail for Maracaibo where governor Fraser resides. Holding Lewis as a hostage, Matthau gains entrance into the governor's bedroom, where he forces him to sign an affidavit which releases the throne into the pirate's care. Matthau and Campion nearly get away with their scheme, but are again captured and thrown into prison. They are visited in prison by Lewis—who has come to love the honorable Campion—before she must set sail with Thomas and the throne. Led by Jacobs, a group of Matthau's followers break the pair out of prison during an explosive nighttime raid. Matthau takes another ship and sets off after Thomas. A chase begins at sea with Matthau weighing his ship down in order to appear as if his is too slow to catch up. After the weight is cut loose, Matthau's ship rapidly shortens the distance between his and Thomas' ships. By nightfall, he catches Thomas and all swords are drawn. A swashbuckling battle of mammoth proportions follows amidst flames, smoke, and musket shots. Matthau and Jacobs load the throne onto a lifeboat, while Campion battles Thomas in front of the fearful Lewis. Thomas manages to slip away into his own lifeboat with Lewis, leaving Campion behind shouting for him to return and "fight like a man." Campion and Lewis—who simply are not meant to be together—exchange longing looks across the water as the distance between them grows greater. The following morning Matthau and Campion are adrift in the ocean as they were at the film's start, though now Matthau is seated upon his golden throne.

Polanski's first film since 1980's TESS, PIRATES was conceived, from start to finish, as a big-budget epic in the spirit of the classic Errol Flynn swashbucklers. Unable to make a film without adding a personal touch, however, Polanski (with long-time screenwriting collaborator Brach) crafted a rather unorthodox pirate tale. The film's pirate hero is not the athletic, bare-chested Hollywood type, but a decrepit Matthau who is filthy, greedy, peg-legged, and has a cannibalistic streak—a portrait which is probably far more accurate with regard to actual pirates than was Hollywood's idea. The plot is a simple one, allowing Polanski great freedom to play with his characters and to give his audience rousing fight scenes. Although the film is a bit slow and talky in spots, it fills the long-ignored gap in Hollywood-style swashbuckling pictures since the 1940s and 1950s. Polanski paid special attention to his sets, hiring the brilliant Guffroy as his set designer and painstakingly building his $1,000,000 galleon, the Neptune, over an old barge. Unfortunately for Polanski, the moviegoing public has either forgotten those great old films that PIRATES spoofs or has never seen a swashbuckler in the first place (unless one is so desperate as to count the saccharine PIRATES OF PENZANCE and THE PIRATE MOVIE, or the dismal SWASHBUCKLER). As 1985 saw PALE RIDER, SILVERADO, RUSTLER'S RHAPSODY, and LUST IN THE DUST put a final nail in the coffin for the western genre, so too will the monumental failure of PIRATES keep filmmakers from investing in another swashbuckler. Costing over $30,000,000 (plus nearly $10,000,000 for advertising), the long-awaited film was the opening-night attraction at the Cannes Film Festival and was shown stateside in 1200 theaters in mid-July. Within weeks, however, PIRATES sank out of sight, a victim of almost unanimously negative reviews. PIRATES was announced as far back as 1976 by Polanski as a Jack Nicholson-Isabelle Adjani vehicle. After passing through the hands of nearly every major studio in Hollywood, the project was dropped by American backers when Polanski fled the U.S. due to his much-publicized statutory rape charge. Polanski finally got backing from the wealthy Ben Ammar and a distribution deal with the Dino De Laurentiis Group. One of the film's original backers, MGM/UA, sold back to Ammar its $10,000,000 investment when company stockholders complained of the studio's involvement with Polanski (legally a fugitive from justice)—stating that MGM/UA "shouldn't be involved with such an individual." Regardless of Polanski's personal life, PIRATES is a wonderfully entertaining epic which provides a dose of the action and laughs missing from most Hollywood films today. Photographed in a picturesque widescreen process, PI-

RATES, like the CinemaScope pictures of the 1940s and 1950s, loses much of its energy when reduced to the limitations of a video monitor.

p, Tarak Ben Ammar; d, Roman Polanski; w, Gerard Brach, Roman Polanski, John Brownjohn; ph, Witold Sobocinski (Panavision, Satpec, Eclaircolor); m, Philippe Sarde; ed, Herve de Luze, William Reynolds; art d, Pierre Guffroy; cos, Anthony Powell; ch, William Hobbs.

Adventure   Cas.   (PR:C   MPAA:PG-13)

PISINGANA†   (1986, Colombia) FOCINE

Julie Pedraza, Carlos Barbosa, Consuelo Luzardo.

d, Leopoldo Pinzon; w, German Pinzon; ph, Victor Jorge Ruiz.

PISMA MERTVOGO CHELOVEKA†   (1986, USSR) 86m Lenfilm/Sovexportfilm bw-c (Trans: Letters from a Dead Man)

Rolan Bykov *(The Professor)*, I. Ryklin, V. Michailov, A. Sabinin, V. Lobanov, N. Griakalova, V. Maiorova, V. Dvorzhecki, S. Smirnova, N. Alkanov.

Some time after the end of the world, a few survivors huddle in an underground bunker, passing time in futile work and Russian roulette. One of the survivors is Bykov, a Nobel Prize winner, who constantly writes letters in his head to a son who is most likely long dead. Bykov, too, is not long for this world, but before cancer can kill him he hides in a pile of corpses that are then tossed outside, into the bleak, blasted landscape. There he puts on his gas mask and finds the ruins of a Protestant church, where a minister cares for a number of mute children. The two adults decorate a Christmas tree and celebrate the holiday with the children before equipping them with gas masks and sending them out across a desert to an uncertain future. Shot before the reactor accident at Chernobyl, it was released in the Soviet Union after that accident and the publicity made for lines around the block in Moscow. The film also played successfully in a number of European festivals, winning the Grand Prix at Mannheim.

d, Konstantin Lopushanski; w, Konstantin Lopushanski, Vjacheslav Rybakov, Boris Strugacki; ph, Nikolai Prokopcev; m, Alexander Zhurbin; art d, Elena Amshinskaya, Viktor Ivanov.

Science Fiction   (PR:C   MPAA:NR)

PLACE AT THE COAST, THE†   (1986, Aus.) Daedalus Films c (AKA: THE BEE-EATER)

John Hargreaves, Heather Mitchell, Tushka Hose.

p, Hilary Furlong; d, George Ogilvie; ph, Jeff Darling.

PLACE OF WEEPING*   (1986, South Africa) 90m NW c

James Whyle *(Philip Seago)*, Gcina Mhlophe *(Gracie)*, Charles Comyn *(Tokkie Van Rensburg)*, Norman Coombes *(Father Eagen)*, Michelle Du Toit *(Maria Van Rensburg)*, Ramolao Makhene *(Themba)*, Patrick Shai *(Lucky)*, Siphiwe Khumalo *(Joseph)*, Kernels Coertzen *(Prosecutor Dick Van Heerden)*, Doreen Mazibuko *(Ana)*, Thoko Ntshinga *(Joseph's Widow)*, Jeremy Taylor *(Tokkie's Son Pieter)*, Nicole Jourdan *(Tokkie's Daughter Elize)*.

On a South African farm Khumalo, a poor black worker, asks his white employer (Comyn) if he can have an increase in weekly rations. Comyn, a brutal individual who hates the blacks, responds by destroying Khumalo's sack of flour and telling the man to leave. That evening Khumalo sneaks back to the farm to steal a chicken for his family. When Comyn hears a noise outside, he finds Khumalo and savagely beats him to death. The next morning, when the workers find the corpse, Comyn accuses them of killing one of their own. The laborers are too frightened to speak out but one woman, Mhlophe, refuses to bow under Comyn's power. She begins seeking out the truth, and confronts Comyn, who cuts all workers' rations in retaliation. Whyle, a liberal white reporter, comes to the small village, initially to report on the fighting among rebel factions in the nearby mountains. After meeting Mhlophe, he agrees to help her uncover Comyn's crime no matter what the consequences. Later Mhlophe is kidnapped by Shai, the leader of one of the rebel bands. He and his men bring Mhlophe to their hideout and there try to persuade her that only direct and violent action against Comyn will bring justice. Whyle, in the meantime, confronts a local prosecutor about Khumalo's murder. The prosecutor is a corrupt man, however, and has a close business and personal relationship with Comyn. As a result, Whyle is later forced from his car and sadistically pummeled by Comyn and a gang of thugs. He struggles back to the home of Coombes, a local priest who has befriended him, and Mhlophe goes into hiding. A few days go by and Comyn decides to drive his family into town. They are stopped en route by Shai and his men, and though Comyn makes a run for it, the rebels take aim and fire.

Mhlophe is this film's stoic center, a portrait of dignity in the face of violent retaliation that looms over her search for the truth. She brings a quiet but assured presence to the character that overcomes some of the other characters' weaknesses. Though Whyle gives good support, most of the other characters are stock portraits, particularly Comyn's relentlessly cruel farmer. Writer/director Roodt emphasizes the human factor within Mhlophe's harsh story without giving a preachy anti-apartheid message. Instead, he wisely lets the characters and their situation speak for themselves, allowing the inherent political message to surface only in the viewers mind. Shot in 16mm, then blown up to 35mm, Roodt makes an effective use of his camera and editing patterns. He portrays violent actions in a stylized manner, utilizing distorted camera angles, closeups, and rapid editing to heighten the emotional impact. Roodt also knows how to use a long take, achieving some interesting visuals with an helicopter-mounted camera that tracks Whyle's car as he drives into town. Roodt's style suits his material and will please an aesthetically minded audience. His techniques, however, are right out of the director's recent past. Roodt, only 24 years old when PLACE OF WEEPING was made, is a veteran of South Africa's lucrative exploitation film business. His best-known work previous to this was an action film called MR. T.N.T. Though American audiences may wonder how a film like PLACE OF WEEPING could have come out of South Africa, the truth of the matter is this is not an atypical work from that racially torn country. Black revenge films are popular attractions, and not censored in the least by the government. Most aren't as inherently political as PLACE OF WEEPING, which was clearly made with an international market in mind. The film's producer, Singh, is of Indian heritage and thus is officially considered "colored" under the apartheid laws, but this hasn't kept him from working in the South African film industry.

p, Anant Singh; d, Darrell Roodt; w, Darrell Roodt, Les Volpe; ph, Paul Witte; ed, David Heitner; art d, Dave Barkham.

Drama   Cas.   (PR:C-O MPAA:PG)

PLACIDO†   (1986, Cuba) 92m ICAIC c

Jorge Villalon, Mirta Ibarra, Rosita Fornes, Miguel Benavides, Ramoncito Veloz, Miguel Gutierrez, Orlando Casin.

In the 19th Century, a mulatto poet comes to see the inherent injustice of the slave system in Cuba and starts writing about it. The authorities are not happy with this criticism, so they arrest him on charges of fomenting a rebellion, then torture and finally execute him. Based on a historical incident.

d, Sergio Giral; w, Sergio Giral, Sergio Fulled; ph, Raul Ridriguez; m, Sergio Vittier; ed, Nelson Rodriguez.

Historical/Biography   (PR:C MPAA:NR)

PLASTIKKPOSEN†   (1986, Nor.) Norsk (Trans: The Magic Bag)

Jon Skolmen, Sverre Anker Ousdal.

p, Wenche Solum; d, Hans Otto Nicolayssen; w, Jon Skolmen, Kerry Crabbe; ph, Halvor Naess.

PLATOON**   (1986) 111m Hemdale/Orion c

Tom Berenger (Sgt. Barnes), Willem Dafoe (Sgt. Elias), Charlie Sheen (Chris), Forest Whitaker (Big Harold), Francesco Quinn (Rhah), John C. McGinley (Sgt. O'Neill), Richard Edson (Sal), Kevin Dillon (Bunny), Reggie Johnson (Junior), Keith David (King), Johnny Depp (Lerner), David Neidorf (Tex), Mark Moses (Lt. Wolfe), Chris Pedersen (Crawford), Corkey Ford (Manny), Corey Glover (Francis), Bob Orwig (Gardner), Tony Todd (Warren), Kevin Eshelman (Morehouse), James Terry McIlvain (Ace), J. Adam Glover (Sanderson), Ivan Kane (Tony), Paul Sanchez (Doc), Dale Dye (Capt. Harris), Peter Hicks (Parker), Basile Achara (Flash), Steve Barredo (Fu Sheng), Chris Castillejo (Rodriguez), Andrew B. Clark (Tubbs), Bernardo Manalili (Village Chief), Than Rogers (Village Chief's Wife), Li Thi Van (Village Chief's Daughter), Clarisa Ortacio (Old Woman), Romy Sevilla (One-Legged Man), Mathew Westfall (Terrified Soldier), Nick Nickelson, Warren McLean (Mechanized Soldiers), Li Mai Thao (Rape Victim), Ron Barracks (Medic), Oliver Stone (Officer in Bunker).

The darkness is shattered as the transport plane's hatch slowly opens to reveal the intense heat and choking orange dust of Vietnam, 1967. Sheen, an 18-year-old

college dropout, is among the new recruits who have just arrived "in country." Stacked near the plane are the bodies of soldiers making the return trip home in rubber bags. The haunted face of a seasoned veteran stares right through Sheen as he boards the bus that will take him to his unit. Sheen's platoon is a group divided against itself. On one side is sergeant Berenger, a horribly scarred veteran of several tours of duty who believes in total war—a morally corrupt, remorseless

killing machine. The men who follow him seek clear-cut solutions to the complicated realities they face. On the other side is veteran sergeant Dafoe. Equally skilled in the ways of death, Dafoe still retains some semblance of humanity and he attempts to impose a sense of compassion and responsibility on his men. Their differences apply during leisure time as well. Berenger's men escape via beer and bourbon, while Dafoe's men have discovered marijuana and other drugs. Sheen is drawn to both these charismatic soldiers—darkness and light—in what he calls the "battle for possession of my soul." The platoon is interracial, and while the men may be of different colors and ethnic backgrounds, they all share one common trait—they are from the most poor and uneducated families in the U.S. When David, a black soldier with only a few more weeks left on his tour, learns that college-boy Sheen volunteered for duty because he didn't think it was "fair" for the underprivileged to do all the fighting, he shakes his head in disbelief and says, "You gotta be rich in the first place to think like that." Although he freezes at the sight of the enemy, Sheen survives his first firefight—other new guys are not as lucky. The platoon's next mission takes them into a small village which is suspected of harboring Viet Cong. The platoon discovers a deserted enemy outpost with a network of tunnels underneath. Two men are killed by a booby-trap while Dafoe takes his .45 and a flashlight and crawls into the tunnel. After a brief skirmish with a fleeing Vietnamese soldier, Dafoe resurfaces and declares the tunnels deserted as well. As the men regroup they find that one of their comrades has disappeared. Berenger and his unit find the soldier tied to a tree with his throat cut. The booby-traps, and now this death, have sent shock waves through the platoon. Fear and anger seethe inside the men as they enter the Vietnamese village. Berenger's unit arrives first and the men begin enacting revenge by killing farm animals. Sheen discovers a few villagers hiding and he screams for them to come out. One of the villagers is a young retarded man with a strange smile on his face. Sheen's anger, outrage, and fear causes him to shoot at the retarded man's feet, making him "dance." Dillon, a frighteningly amoral teenager, delights at Sheen's actions and urges him on. Sheen regains his composure and breaks down sobbing. Dillon takes over and finishes the job by bashing in the retarded man's skull with the butt of his rifle—even "superlifer" McGinley is horrified by Dillon. Meanwhile, Berenger and other men discover a cache of enemy weapons and enough rice to feed a small army. Berenger interrogates the village elder and his wife, but the sergeant becomes frustrated by the language problem and becomes incensed at what he perceives as meaningless babbling coming from the woman. Without warning, Berenger executes the woman and then grabs her small daughter and holds a pistol to the child's head in an effort to force the elder to reveal where the VC have gone. Some of the men goad Berenger on, while most are sickened by his actions. Dafoe arrives and screams his outrage at the scene. He and Berenger engage in a vicious fistfight that the platoon has to break up. Berenger vows to kill Dafoe, while orders are received to torch the village. The men set fire to the huts, destroy the weapons, and blow up the rice supplies. Ironically, the men who have just annihilated the village assist the Vietnamese by carrying their belongings, helping those too sick to walk, and letting the children ride on their shoulders. Back at the base camp, their commanding officer, Dye (a retired Marine captain and Vietnam vet who served as technical advisor on the production) promises to get to the bottom of the incident.

On their next mission, Berenger hunts down Dafoe in the brush and shoots him. Sheen arrives on the scene shortly thereafter and only suspects the truth, but as the platoon is being airlifted out of the overrun landing zone, he spots a wounded Dafoe running from scores of enemy troops. Before a helicopter can be sent to rescue the sergeant, Dafoe is killed by the Viet Cong. Sheen is determined to get revenge on Berenger—his comrades agree that something should be done—but when Berenger confronts them, they all back down save Sheen. Sheen attacks the sergeant, but he is quickly beaten back. Berenger must be talked out of stabbing Sheen. On their next mission, the platoon is sent to dig in at an area where the VC are likely to attack. Unbeknownst to them they are being used to bait the enemy out into the open. Most of the men have a "bad feeling" about the operation, and their worst fears are confirmed when hundreds of VC attack in the middle of the night. The camp is overrun by the enemy and Dye is finally forced to call an air-strike in on his own men. Sheen, crazy with fear and badly wounded, encounters Berenger during the confused battle and the sergeant raises a shovel to kill him. At that moment the air-strike hits and the concussion turns everything black. In the morning there are craters filled with hundreds of dead bodies—most of the platoon is dead. Sheen is alive, as is Berenger. Berenger is badly wounded and he orders Sheen to find him a medic. Sheen raises his rifle

and points it at Berenger. "Do it," Berenger sneers, and Sheen pulls the trigger, killing the sergeant. Another platoon arrives on the scene to bulldoze the enemy corpses into mass graves and evacuate the American wounded. Sheen is among those wounded badly enough to leave and he is carried away by a helicopter.

PLATOON is a shattering experience. Writer-director Stone, a Vietnam veteran, used his first-hand knowledge to create what will surely be looked upon as the most realistic war film ever made. PLATOON's success lies in the mass of detail Stone brings to the screen. He bombards the senses with vivid sights and sounds that have the feel of actual experience. Stone captures the heat, the dampness, the bugs, the jungle rot, and most important, the confusion and fear experienced by the average soldier. The soldiers of PLATOON do perform heroic actions on occasion, but the heroism isn't motivated by love of country or belief in an ideal—it is motivated by pure terror, by desperation, by a desire to end the madness one way or another. Never before in a war film has stark terror among soldiers been such a tangible, motivating force. Stone does not blink when gazing at the horrors of war, but he does not linger either. The pivotal point in the film—the destruction of the Vietnamese village—is extremely difficult to watch because of the shocking truths to be found there. Stone shows us the series of events that lead up to the near-massacre, and because we watch the insanity and tension build up before our eyes, we come away with a better understanding of how "nice American boys" could have participated in such horror. There is nothing appealing in Stone's war, it doesn't have a "recruitment flavor." Most of the men are resigned to doing their time and trying to stay alive. Few know or care why they are there. The men brandish the word "politics" as if it explains everything. "It just politics, man," they are heard to say frequently, and it is obvious that the word is merely a catchphrase the soldiers picked up somewhere to use as a focus for their confusion and frustration. The performances Stone gets from his ensemble cast are uniformly excellent. Military advisor Dye subjected the actors to a 14-day boot camp in the Philippine jungles, forcing them live as if they were real soldiers fighting in Vietnam—no hotels, no limos, no catered dinners. Dafoe and Berenger, both cast against type here, received Best Supporting Actor nominations for their roles. Sheen is fine as Oliver Stone's alter-ego—the film's main character and narrator—but the real revelations are among some of the less prominent players. Dillon, younger brother of Matt, is absolutely chilling as the disaffected teenager who actually *likes* the horror and insanity of Vietnam. "You get to do what you want, nobody f_____ with you, and you only gotta worry about dyin'." David is also superb as the black soldier who befriends Sheen, and is lucky enough to receive orders allowing him to go home only hours before the apocalyptic final battle. Quinn (Anthony's son), Whitaker, McGinley, and Johnson turn in memorable performances as well. While PLATOON has no equal when it comes to capturing the reality of men in combat, it falters when Stone attempts to apply greater meaning to his vision. As he proved in his equally excellent SALVADOR, Stone is a master at building intense situations, but he is a less-than-subtle screenwriter. Although he claims to have known sergeants like Berenger and Dafoe while serving in Vietnam, the film's metaphysical battle between the forces of good (Dafoe) and evil (Berenger) is heavyhanded and clumsy, as is Sheen's totally unnecessary voice-over narration, presented in the form of letters to his grandmother. Stone dilutes the power of his own visuals by inserting the fairly vapid narration to drive his points home. The narration is at its most disastrous in the final scene where Sheen is being evacuated away from the last battle. Rather than letting Georges Delerue's music and Sheen's acting say it all—Stone inserts a well-intentioned, but maudlin passage: "Those of us who did make it have an obligation to build again, to teach others what we know and to try with what's left of our lives to find a goodness and a meaning to this life." Stone should have more confidence in his imagery, for it is much more powerful than mere words. He is a very visceral filmmaker who, if he wins the struggle to mature and refine his vision, may become a major artistic talent. Stone had written the script for PLATOON ten years before, and although many in Hollywood respected the work, none would produce it. Upon receiving financing for SALVADOR from Hemdale, a progressive British production company, Stone knew he had finally found financing for his Vietnam film. On an incredibly low budget of $6.5 million, Stone brought his cast and crew to the Philippines and shot PLATOON in a swift 54 days. To everyone's surprise, the film was a massive hit with the critics and the public, grossing over $127,551,000 (as of this writing) and winning Best Picture, Best Director, Best Editing, and Best Sound Academy Awards. The audience that Stone knew would be the most judgmental—Vietnam veterans—hailed the film as well. Although some complained that

the actions portrayed in the film were extreme and atypical, most found it incredibly realistic and, most of all, accurate. What makes PLATOON an important film is the starkly realistic portrayal of men at war. Those mindless minions who thrilled to the cartoonish exploits of RAMBO, MISSING IN ACTION, or TOP GUN should see PLATOON and be jolted back to the reality of the hardship, suffering, and death that is war. Simplistic military fantasies which boast warped (and often, Department of Defense approved) views of honor, heroism, and bloodshed, appear offensive and insidious when compared to the chaotic, terrifying, and tragic reality of PLATOON. Georges Delerue's haunting arrangement of Samuel Barber's "Adagio for Strings" is a striking contrapuntal force in the film, which has three songs of the times: "White Rabbit" (Grace Slick, performed by Jefferson Airplane), "Okie from Muskogee" (Merle Haggard, performed by Haggard), "Tracks of My Tears" (William Robinson, Marvin Tarplin, Warren Moon, performed by Smokey Robinson and The Miracles).

p, Arnold Kopelson; d&w, Oliver Stone; ph, Robert Richardson (CFI Color); m, Samuel Barber; ed, Claire Simpson; prod d, Bruno Rubeo; md, Georges Delerue; art d, Rodel Cruz, Doris Sherman Williams; spec eff, Yves De Bono; m/l, Grace Slick, Merle Haggard, William Robinson, Marvin Tarplin, Warren Moon; makeup, Gordon J. Smith; stunts, Gil Arceo.

War (PR:O MPAA:R)

PLAY DEAD† (1986) 86m United Construction/Troma c

Yvonne De Carlo *(Hester)*, Stephanie Dunnam *(Audrey)*, David Cullinane *(Jeff)*, Glenn Kezer *(Otis)*, Ron Jackson *(Richard)*, David Ellzey *(Stephen)*, Jo Livingston *(Pathologist)*, Carolyn Greenwood *(Monique)*, Jeff McVey *(Eric)*, Robert Hibbard *(Policeman)*, Desmond Dhooge *(Dog Trainer)*, John Carroll Perry *(Sam)*, Alex Bond Winslow *(Clarisse)*, Harry Gibbs *(Funeral Attendant)*, Greta *(The Dog)*.

Dog breeds come and go from fashion—Rin Tin Tin started the German Shepherd boom, and for a period in the 1920s the Chow Chow was so popular that the breed was threatened by the inbreeding of "puppy mills" whose only concern was to produce enough dogs to keep up with demand. Recently Shar Pei, homely, wrinkle-skinned dogs, have been the rage, commanding huge prices, but without doubt 1981 was the year of the Rottweiler (in movies at least). Sort of a Doberman with lots more bulk, the Rottweiler was featured in two movies that year, the misspelled ROTWEILER: DOGS OF HELL, a wretched 3-D horror film from the C.B. DeMille of North Carolina, Earl Owensby, and this Texas-made film, which languished in some film vault until Michael Herz and Lloyd Kaufman of Troma rescued it for direct release to video. The story has De Carlo, a wealthy woman, embittered by the fact that the only man she ever loved ditched her to marry her sister. Both of them are dead now, so the vengeful De Carlo has to content herself with killing their children. She gives her niece a Rottweiler, then casts spells to make it attack. The finale finds her on the receiving end of the dog's fangs. Mercifully, there do not appear to be any more Rottweiler films looming in the distance to further defame the breed. Troma had released a black comedy made by the same Texas team, ELLIE in 1984. The producer's strategy was the same in each case: sign an aging "name" actress and bathe her in blood. ELLIE starred Shelley Winters.

p, Francine C. Rudine; d, Peter Wittman; w, Lothrop W. Jordan; ph, Robert E. Bethard (TVC Color); m, Bob Farrar; ed, Eugenie Nicoloff; art d, Robert A. Burns; makeup, Susan Posnick; stunts, Randy "Fife"; dog trainer, James C. Catalano.

Horror **Cas.** (PR:O MPAA:R)

PLAYING AWAY† (1986, Brit.) 100m Insight/Film Four International c

Norman Beaton *(Willie-Boy)*, Robert Urquhart *(Godfrey)*, Helen Lindsay *(Marjorie)*, Nicholas Farrel *(Derek)*, Brian Bovell *(Stuart)*, Gary Beadle *(Errol)*.

This is a comedy with a point. A small English village hopes to top off its "Third World Week" festivities with a cricket match against a West Indian team from South London. The invitation is made and accepted, but both sides have second thoughts about the contest, mutually afflicted as they are by the sticky wicket of prejudice and ignorance. The action cuts back and forth between the two factions as they prepare for, and dread, the upcoming confrontation, which is as much a clash of cultures as a sporting event. In the end, though, the cricketers on both sides—and their supporters—knock narrow-mindedness for "six" (cricket's equivalent of a grand slam homer). PLAYING AWAY is one of a number of recent British films dealing with the cultural conflicts that have arisen in increasingly multi-racial Britain.

p, Vijay Amarnani; d, Horace Ove; w, Caryl Phillips; ph, Nic Knowland; m, Simon Webb; ed, Graham Whitlock; art d, Pip Gardner.

Comedy (PR:A-C MPAA:NR)

PLAYING BEATIE BOW† (1986, Aus.) 93m South Australia Film/CEL c

Imogen Annesley *(Abigail)*, Peter Phelps *(Judah/Robert)*, Mouche Phillips *(Beatie Bow)*, Nikki Coghill *(Dovey)*, Moya O'Sullivan *(Granny)*, Don Barker *(Samuel)*, Lyndel Rowe *(Kathy)*, Barbara Stephens *(Justine)*, Damian Janko *(Gibbie)*, Phoebe Salter *(Natalie)*, Su Cruickshank *(Madam)*, Henry Salter *(Swanton)*, Jo England *(Doll)*, Edward Caddick *(Legless)*, Edwin Hodgeman *(Sir)*.

It's BACK TO THE FUTURE down under, or rather back to the Australian past of 1873 as a 16-year-old girl (Annesley), unhappy with a number of typical adolescent problems, follows a strange-looking little girl and ends up in the grimy, industrial Sydney of the 19th Century. There she doesn't seem too unhappy, especially when she falls in love with Phelps, the older brother of the girl she followed, but after a number of adventures—including a run-in with white slavers—she manages to get back to her own time. A box office disappointment, the film is rumored to be the last production for the South Australia Film Corporation, once the standard bearer for Australian cinema.

p, Jock Blair; d, Donald Crombie; w, Peter Gawler (based on the novel by Ruth Park); ph, Geoffrey Simpson (Eastmancolor); m, Garry McDonald, Laurie Stone; ed, A.J. Prowse; prod d, George Liddle.

Drama/Comedy   (PR:A-C MPAA:NR)

PLAYING FOR KEEPS*½   (1986) 103m Miramax/UNIV c

Daniel Jordano *(Danny)*, Matthew Penn *(Spikes)*, Leon W. Grant *(Silk)*, Mary B. Ward *(Chloe)*, Marisa Tomei *(Tracy)*, Jimmy Baio *(Steinberg)*, Harold Gould *(Rockerfeller)*, Kim Hauser *(Marie)*, Robert Milli *(Cromwell)*, John Randolf Jones *(Sheriff Billy Sullivan)*, Bruce Kluger *(Gene Epstein)*, Anthony Marciona *(Ronnie Long)*, Glen Robert Robillard *(Joel)*, J.D. Rosenbaum *(Davey Beck)*, Frank Scasso *(Van Go Go)*, Lisa Schultz *(Jill)*, Doug Warhit *(Larry Diamond)*, Michael May, Charles Picerni, Jr., William Burton, Peter Antico, Brad Orrison *(Flyers)*, John Anzaloni *(Guitar Player, Silk's Band)*, Anthony Arcure *(Diner Customer)*, Kevin Hagan *(Chief Deputy)*, Harrison Balthaser, Joseph R. Burns, Charles Morelli *(Deputies)*, Jack Banning, Ronnie Baron, Robert Berger, Joel Blake, Frank Rollins Harrison, Steven Hurwitz, David Lile, Jerry McGee, Donald Sharton, Sel Vitella *(Executives)*, Raymond Barry *(Mr. Hatcher, Chloe's Father)*, John Bennes, Ruth Judd *(Employment Counselors)*, Hildy Brooks *(Danny's Mom)*, Bonnie Jean Brown, Gena D'Orazio, Madelaine Carol, Edna Chew, Liz McLellan, Lenore Pemberton *(Spikes' Fantasy Dancers)*, Anita Ehrler, Edie Fleming, Monique Mannen *(Silk's Fantasy Dancers)*, Teresa Burns, Peter Carew, Paul Finan, Jean Spillane, Susan Steed, Pat De Vita *(Phone Callers)*, Timothy Carhart *(Emmett)*, Sheila Coonan *(Edna)*, John Corcoran *(Sam, Luncheonette Owner)*, William Cosgriff, Willy Switkes *(Mint Buyers)*, Agnes Cummings *(Supermarket Checker)*, Frank Faldermeyer *(Kidnaped Priest)*, Clement Fowler *(Banker Williams)*, Martha Frei *(78 Pound Lady)*, Germaine Goodson, Carol Schuberg *(Background Singers, Silk's Band)*, Jery Hewitt *(Backhoe Driver)*, Hal Holden *(Irate Bank Customer)*, Philip Kraus *(Art Lewis)*, Jerry Leonti *(Principal Canelli)*, Bonnie Lewis *(Lady Who Finds Cheap Steaks)*, David Lipman *(Bank Buddy)*, Tom McDermott *(Paint Store Salesman)*, Court Miller *(Claiborne)*, Katherine Elizabeth Neuman *(Danny's First Girl Friend)*, William Newman *(Joshua)*, Joseph J. O'Brien *(Equipment Store Manager)*, Max Olivas *(Head Flyer)*, Albert Rutherford *(Supermarket Manager)*, Donna Moore *(Keyboard Player, Silk's Band)*, Jeff Pope *(Drummer, Silk's Band)*, William Soose *(Man With Dog)*, Larry Swansen *(Steinberg's Priest)*, Raymond Thorne *(Perkins)*, Vickie Weinstein *(Secretary)*, Kelly Wolf *(Valedictorian)*, Louise Woolf *(Luncheonette Waitress)*.

Three buddies just out of high school (Jordano, Penn, and Grant) don't know what to do with themselves until Jordano learns that his family has inherited a ramshackle hotel somewhere in the Catskills. With his two friends, he cooks up a scheme to open a rock 'n' roll hotel, complete with Mick Jagger Suite, as a resort

for teenagers. Of course, they find the building in worse shape than they imagined, and it takes a lot of work to get it in shape, most of it to the tune of various rock songs. Also complicating matters is the $8000 in back taxes owed on the building, which they raise by impersonating Boy Scouts and selling cookies. They are opposed by the locals—understandably disconcerted by this threatened invasion of headbangers—and by some slimy industrialists in cahoots with the slimy town-council president to turn the area in a dump for toxic waste. The boys are joined by local farm girl Ward and by Gould, a former Wall Street bigwig and ex-convict who now lives in the hotel. They work together, sometimes through elaborate schemes, to obtain the materials needed. They also uncover the chemical dumping scheme and use it to turn public sentiment their way. Everything ends happily as the hotel opens right on time.

It seems hard to believe that a film like this could attract any kind of audience. Too youth-oriented for adults and too insipid for youths (perhaps insipid youths are the target audience), the film barely saw a wide release before disappearing into that limbo where unsuccessful films wait for video release. Of the three leads (ethnically balanced with a white, a black, and a Latino), only Jordano occasionally comes across well. Gould, the one familiar face here, steals the picture as a

lovable confidence man. The hopeful producers, ready for a smash hit, went to the trouble of preparing a half-hour special featuring musical acts from the movie, along with music videos of songs from the soundtrack. The music is easily the best thing here, including: "Life to Life" (Pete Townshend, performed by Pete Townshend), "It's Not Over" (John Van Tongeren, Robbie Nevil, Phil Galdston, performed by Chris Thompson), "Distant Drums" (Peter Frampton, Jed Lieber, Steve Broughton Lunt, performed by Peter Frampton), "It's Gettin' Hot" (George Acogny, Daniel Bechet, Alan Brewer, performed by Eugene Wilde), "Best Kept Secret" (China Crisis, performed by China Crisis); "We Love You (Maximus)" (Orchestral Manoeuvers in the Dark, performed by Orchestral Manoeuvers in the Dark), "Think We're Gonna Make It" (Alan Brewer, Rick Wakeman, performed by Hinton Battle), "Don't Look Back (Hello, Goodbye)" (Phil Collins, performed by Phil Collins), "Celebrate" (Sendal, Nichol, McIntosh, performed by Loose Ends), "Here To Stay" (George Acogny, Daniel Bechet, Julian Littman, performed by Sister Sledge), "Say the Word" (Simon Le Bon, Nick Rhodes, performed by Arcadia), "Make a Wish" (Alan Brewer, performed by Joe Cruz), "Stand By Me" (Ben E. King, Jerry Lieber, Michael Stoller, performed by Julian Lennon), "Muscles" (Michael Jackson, performed by Diana Ross), "I'm So Excited" (Anita Pointer, June Pointer, Ruth Pointer, Trevor Lawrence, performed by The Pointer Sisters), "These Dreams of You" (Anna Pepper, performed by Anna Pepper), "Jumpin' Jack Flash" (Mick Jagger, Keith Richards).

p, Alan Brewer, Bob Weinstein, Harvey Weinstein; d, Bob Weinstein, Harvey Weinstein; w, Bob Weinstein, Harvey Weinstein, Jeremy Leven; ph, Eric Van Haren Noman (Panavision, Precision Color); m, George Acogny, Daniel Bechet; ed, Gary Karr, Sharyn Ross; prod d, Waldemar Kalinowski; md, Alan Brewer; art d, Steve Miller; set d, Florence Fellman; cos, Aude Bronson-Howard; ch, Lynnette Barkley, Ronn Forella, Alison Pearl; m/l, Pete Townshend, John Van Tongeren, Robbie Nevil, Phil Galdston, Peter Frampton, Jed Lieber, Steve Broughton Lunt, George Acogny, Daniel Bechet, Alan Brewer, China Crisis, Orchestral Maneuvers in the Dark, Rick Wakeman, Phil Collins, Sendall, Nichol, McIntosh, Daniel Bechet, Julian Littman, Simon Le Bon, Nick Rhodes, Ben E. King, Jerry Lieber, Michael Stoller, Michael Jackson, Anita Pointer, June Pointer, Ruth Pointer, Trevor Lawrence, Anna Pepper, Mick Jagger, Keith Richards; makeup, Jeanne Van Phue.

Comedy/Drama   (PR:C MPAA:PG-13)

POBRE MARIPOSA†   (1986, Arg.) 118m Instituto Nacional de Cinematografia c (Trans: Poor Butterfly)

Graciela Borges *(Clara)*, Lautaro Mirua *(Julio)*, Pepe Seriano *(Shloime)*, Victor Laplace *(Jose)*, Cipe Lincovsky *(Juana)*, Ana Maria Piccio *(Irma)*, Cacho Fontana *(Luis)*, Augusto Bonardo *(Armando)*, Bibi Andersson *(Gertrud)*, F. Fernan Gomes *(Pereyra)*, Duilie Marzio *(Bruno)*, China Zorrilla *(Tia Amelia)*.

In the period between the end of WW II and the rise to power of Juan Peron in October of 1945, a variety of factions fought for dominance on the Argentine political front. It is against this background the POBRE MARIPOSA is set, with Borges a radio personality who is forced to face her own roots when her Jewish father obtains a list of top Nazi war criminals who are now filtering into the country.

p, Ben Silberstein; d, Raul de la Torre; w, Aida Bortnik, Raul de la Torre; ph, Marcelo Camorine; ed, Carlos Macias; art d, Jorge Sarudiansky; cos, Tita Tamanes, Rosa Zamborain.

Drama   (PR:C-O MPAA:NR)

POLICE***   (1986, Fr.) 113m GAU-TF1/GAU c

Gerard Depardieu *(Mangin)*, Sophie Marceau *(Noria)*, Richard Anconina *(Lambert)*, Pascale Rocard *(Marie Vedret)*, Sandrine Bonnaire *(Lydie)*, Franck Karoui *(Rene)*, Jonathan Leina *(Simon Slimane)*, Meaachou Bentahar *(Claude)*.

A gritty, realistic expose of the volatile Parisian criminal underworld which stars French superstar Depardieu as a brawny, animalistic cop who crosses over to the other side of the law whenever a case calls for it. The film opens with a long, purposely tedious interrogation scene as Depardieu plays a game of cat-and-mouse with a nervous North African drug dealer. Filmed in a series of intercutting close-ups, the scene sets the style and pacing for the rest of the film—director Pialat's interest is not in plot devices or action, but in the emotional intensity of his characters. Depardieu follows his leads to drug dealer, Leina, a Tunisian who has come to Paris with his many brothers and his one—streetwise and sensual—teenage sister, Marceau. Depardieu apprehends both of them and throws them into jail. Indifferent to Marceau's unconscious sexuality, Depardieu interrogates her in a ruthless, vulgar, and plainly sadistic manner, treating her as if she is any other hardened criminal. She fights back, casually lying and telling him anything he wants to hear. A mob lawyer, Anconina—who socializes with Leina and his brothers, and is enamored of Marceau—arranges to release the imprisoned teen but not Leina. Marceau, who is anything but the senseless girl she is perceived to be, sets a deceitful plan in motion to steal a cache of drug money. One of her brothers is roughed up, as is Anconina, by people who think they have information. She, however, keeps her scheme to herself. Gradually, Depardieu is lured into Marceau's spell. He reveals himself to her, explaining that he has two children from a wife who not long ago died of cancer. Underneath his seemingly cold, masculine policeman persona, Depardieu is a lonely, sensitive man who finds himself falling in love with Marceau. They are passionately attracted to each other, spending all night together talking in his car, and later making love in the nearly empty police station. Because of love, Depardieu crosses the blurred line between cop and criminal and agrees to help Marceau out of her spot with the drug dealers. As much as he tries to separate his love for her from his life on the right side of the law, however, he cannot convince Marceau to spend her life loving a cop. They are not meant for each other and Marceau lets him know it—walking out on him after filling his head with a pack of lies.

If not wholly successful, POLICE displays a restrained style which is rare in filmmaking today. Director Pialat not only allows his *actors* the freedom of improvisation, but also allows their *characters* to exist freely. He passes no judgment on their frequent amorality—the cops and the criminals, the North Africans and the French, the lawyers and their clients, the whores and the lovers are all thrown into the same category of people trying to exist on the streets of Paris. Everyone has reasons and, whether morally right or wrong, they are *their* reasons. It is this that interests Pialat and not the explosiveness of the action or the twisting of the plot. Unfortunately, with this narrative freedom come frequent lapses in the film. Certain scenes drag, others never seem to come together in their improvisation. Pialat's photography is as free as his script, employing a great deal of handheld, *cinema verite*-style camera work which, because it is used in excess, quickly becomes unnerving. All the film's weaknesses, however, are pulled together by the actors. Depardieu is excellent, though his abrupt change from brute to sensitive lover is a conspicuous turn since we are given no clue to his real feelings in the film's beginning. Acting opposite Depardieu is the equally superb Marceau who proves her range by turning in a performance which is completely contrary to her role as the charming and innocent teenager in LA BOUM. Together these two provide the film with all the energy it needs, playing off each other with a sexual tension that is ready to destroy them both. One interesting side note to POLICE is a particulary touching scene in which Depardieu purchases a newspaper at a Champs-Elysees magazine stand. He notices a copy of *Passion* with a cover photo of the late filmmaker Francois Truffaut. There is a lengthy reverential pause as he looks at the cover. It is a heartfelt homage to the director who, in real life, was a great admirer of Pialat's films. Depardieu's reaction to the photo seems equally honest, as he was a friend of Truffaut and star of two of his films, THE WOMAN NEXT DOOR and THE LAST METRO. POLICE was released in 1985 in France (see the 1986 MPG Annual), but did not see a U.S. release until this year. (In French; English subtitles.)

p, Emmanuel Schlumberger; d, Maurice Pialat; w, Catherine Breillat, Sylvie Danton, Jacques Fieschi, Maurice Pialat (based on an original story by Catherine Breillat); ph, Luciano Tovoli (Eastmancolor); m, Henryk Mikolaj Gorecki; ed, Yann Dedet; art d, Constantin Mejinsky; cos, Malika Brahim; makeup, Thi Loan N'Guyen.

Crime   (PR:O MPAA:NR)

POLICE ACADEMY 3: BACK IN TRAINING*½   (1986) 82m WB c

Steve Guttenberg *(Sgt. Mahoney)*, Bubba Smith *(Sgt. Hightower)*, David Graf *(Sgt. Tackleberry)*, Michael Winslow *(Sgt. Jones)*, Marion Ramsey *(Sgt. Hooks)*, Leslie Easterbrook *(Lt. Callahan)*, Art Metrano *(Commandant Mauser)*, Tim Kazurinsky *(Cadet Sweetchick)*, Bobcat [Bob] Goldthwait *(Cadet Zed)*, George Gaynes *(Commandant Lassard)*, Shawn Weatherly *(Cadet Adams)*, Scott Thomson *(Sgt. Copeland)*, Bruce Mahler *(Sgt. Fackler)*, Lance Kinsey *(Lt. Proctor)*, Brian Tochi *(Cadet Nogata)*, Debralee Scott *(Cadet Fackler)*, Ed Nelson *(Gov. Neilson)*, Andrew Paris *(Cadet Kirkland)*, George R. Robertson *(Chief Hurst)*, Georgina Spelvin *(The Hooker)*, David Huband *(Chief Hodges)*, R. Christopher Thomas, David Elliott *(Cadets)*, Arthur Batanides *(Mr. Kirkland)*; The Evaluation Committee: Jack Greley *(Mr. Matthews)*, Rita Tuckett *(Mrs. Tyler)*, Chas Lawther *(Mr. Delanny)*, Lyn Jackson *(Mrs. Chick)*; Mary Ann Coles *(Mrs. Hurst)*, Sam Stone *(Cabbie)*, Grant Cowan *(Line-Up Room Victim)*, Bruce Pirie *(Line-Up Room Cop)*, Doug Lennox *(Axe Murderer)*, Teddy Abner *(Tommy)*, Marcia Watkins *(Sarah)*, Pam Hyatt *(Sarah's Mother)*, Fran Gebhard *(Woman at Cafe)*, Les Nirenberg *(Man with Cigar)*, Susan Denyck *(Basketball Player)*, Glo-

ria Summers *(Maid)*, Fred Livingstone *(Elderly Man)*, Gladys O'Conner *(Woman at Phone Booth)*, Elias Zarod *(Hotel Manager)*, Gary Flannagan *(Bartender)*, Pierre Berube *(Boy on Bicycle)*, Peter Colvey, Alex Pauljak *(Gang Members)*, Anton Tyukodi *(Purse Snatcher)*.

Sure, the humor is witless and the gags are often inane, but given the quality of its predecessors, POLICE ACADEMY 3: BACK IN TRAINING has the dubious honor of being the funniest of the series to date. We're not talking Marx Brothers

or Ernst Lubitsch kind of funny, but within the severe limitations of the surprisingly successful POLICE ACADEMY films, this third outing has more amusing moments than the first two.

The bare-bones plot finds governor Nelson cutting back on funding for police academies, meaning only one of the state's two such institutions will be allowed to remain open. An evaluation committee is set up and Gaynes, head of the Good Police Academy, appeals to graduates Guttenberg, Smith, Winslow, Graf, and Ramsey to help train new recruits. Meanwhile Metrano, head of the Bad Police Academy does what he can to sabotage his rival's chances. He gets new recruits Kazurinsky and Goldthwait (left over from POLICE ACADEMY 2), along with the other would-be cops, sent out on patrol long before they're ready to hit the streets. Naturally, this leads to assorted mayhem, and the veteran cops suspect something is amiss. In a few subplots, Japanese recruit Tochi falls madly in love with one of his instructors, while Winslow (The man with the magic mouth) gets to repeat his kung-fu movie lip-sync bit *twice* (a routine first introduced in POLICE ACADEMY 2). Eventually Metrano's evil intentions are found out, while one of his henchmen is double crossed by Spelvin, Guttenberg's pal from the first POLICE ACADEMY film (Spelvin is, of course, better known for her work in the porno film THE DEVIL IN MISS JONES). When Nelson is taken hostage at a chi-chi fund raiser, the boys and girls of the Good Police Academy come in to save the day, rescuing their beloved institution for 1987's edition POLICE ACADEMY 4: CITIZENS ON PATROL.

Guttenberg and his cohorts make little more than cameo appearances in what is really a bunch of gag sequences strung together and labeled "comedy film." By now the characters (such as they are) are more or less established as an ensemble, so there are a few laughs from the stronger, albeit moronic ones. Of course there are still a few breast jokes, and some homophobic humor, but the coarser buffoonery of the first two films has been toned down significantly. This is the first "PG" film in the series (following an "R" and a "PG-13" respectively), which undoubtedly accounts for the stronger emphasis on slapstick. After all, the humor is at an adolescent level, so there's no point in making a movie that its potential audience can't see. Oh, one might quibble about the various ineptitudes and stupidities of a POLICE ACADEMY film, but there's no denying the series' popularity. The third film brought the POLICE ACADEMY films' worldwide box-office total to the $380 million mark. You can argue quality, you can argue taste, but you can't argue the phenomenal success of these cheaply made joke-fests. This would be the last film for director Jerry Paris, who died shortly after POLICE ACADEMY 3's completion. Songs and musical numbers include: "Team Thing" (Tena Clark, Tony Warren), "Luv Got Me Dancen On My Kneez" (Andy Hernandez, performed by Kid Creole and the Cocanuts), "This is What Love is All About" (Tena Clark, Lorenzo Pryor), "Wounded in Love" (Lauren Wood, Rick Chudakoff, performed by Lauren Wood), "El Bimbo" (Claude Ganem, performed by Jean-Marc Dompierre and his Orchestra).

p, Paul Maslansky; d, Jerry Paris; w, Gene Quintano (based on characters created by Neal Israel, Pat Proft); ph, Robert Saad (Technicolor); m, Robert Folk; ed, Bud Molin; prod d, Trevor Williams; art d, Rhiley Fuller; set d, Sean Kirby; m/l, Tena Clark, Tony Warren, Andy Hernandez, Lorenzo Pryor, Lauren Wood, Rick Chudakoff, Claude Ganem; makeup, Ken Brooke.

Comedy   Cas.   (PR:C-O MPAA:PG)

POLTERGEIST II**½   (1986) 90m UA/MGM c

JoBeth Williams *(Diane Freeling)*, Craig T. Nelson *(Steve Freeling)*, Heather O'Rourke *(Carol Anne Freeling)*, Oliver Robins *(Robbie Freeling)*, Zelda Rubinstein *(Tangina Barrons)*, Will Sampson *(Taylor)*, Julian Beck *(Reverend Henry Kane)*, Geraldine Fitzgerald *(Gramma Jess)*, John P. Whitecloud *(Old Indian)*, Noble Craig *(Vomit Creature)*, Susan Peretz *(Daughter)*, Helen Boll *(Mother)*, Kelly Jean Peters *(Young Jess)*, Jaclyn Bernstein *(Young Diane)*, Robert Lesser, Jamie Abbott, Ann Louise Baradach, Syd Beard, David Beaman, Hayley Taylor-Block, Pamela Gordon, Chelsea Hertford, Whitby Hertford, Rocky Krakoff, Carrie Lorraine, Kathy Wagner *(Kane's People)*.

Although much improved thematically when compared with the first film (the childlike awe of the original has been replaced by a very adult fear of impotence), POLTERGEIST II is terribly disjointed and dramatically unfulfilling. The forces of evil which had demolished the Freeling house in the original film have followed the family in search of the blonde, blue-eyed little girl, O'Rourke. Nelson and his

family have fled to Grandma's (Fitzgerald) house in Arizona. Their insurance company will not cover the ghostly implosion of their house in California. In dire need of funds Nelson, who used to be a successful real-estate agent, has now become a door-to-door vacuum cleaner salesman. The humiliation has sapped the energy of this basically weak man and he allows his hair to grow long and his drinking problem to become worse. The children have adjusted well since their experience, although young Robins is forced to go to the mall and watch television at a department store because his parents are too frightened to allow another set in the house (little O'Rourke was sucked into another dimension by the last set they owned). Fitzgerald and O'Rourke share a very special bond, and the elderly woman whispers to her granddaughter that they are both gifted with special powers, explaining that they can "see things others cannot see." Soon afterwards, Fitzgerald dies peacefully in her sleep, but she does not depart this world without calling O'Rourke on her play phone to say goodbye and tell her not to worry. The family is then visited by a soft-spoken Indian, Sampson, who was seen during the credits inhaling smoky spirits during a tribal rite atop a desert butte. He explains that Rubinstein, the wise midget who had helped the family overcome the evil spirits in the first film, has sent him to protect them. Nelson wants no part of this as he herds his family out of grandma's house after being attacked by another poltergeist. Sampson tells them that they must stay and fight off the evil power attempting to destroy them. Having nowhere else to go, the family stays, and Sampson begins teaching Nelson how to fight back. One bright, sunny day, the family is visited by a deathly looking old man dressed in the black suit and hat of a preacher (played brilliantly by the late Julien Beck). Although it is still sunny, a rainstorm suddenly bursts forth upon the stranger's arrival. Beck has his sights set on little O'Rourke, and he uses his Southern charm to try and enter the house. Nelson steps inside and speaks to the creepy man with the skull-like face through the screen door. Not to be dissuaded, Beck begins to prey on Nelson's weaknesses and low self-esteem: "Who do your wife and children turn to with their problems?," he says, referring to Sampson. "You feel that you're not man enough to hold this family together." Just as the preacher begins to ensnare Nelson in his trap, O'Rourke calls to her father from inside the house. The voice of his loved one snaps Nelson back to reality and he commands Beck to

leave his house. Beck's face changes from one of benign concern to evil hatred as he screams through the screen door, "You are gonna die in there! All of you! You are gonna die!" Just as quickly, Beck recovers his Southern-gentleman manners and bids Nelson good day. As he walks off, softly singing a hymn, he suddenly vaporizes and the sun shower stops.

Soon after, Rubinstein arrives to inform the family that she has discovered that Beck was once a warped religious leader in the 1800s who had buried his followers alive on the very site on which the Freeling's house was later built. The spirits of his followers had become intrigued with the life they felt in little O'Rourke when she passed into their dimension, and they have followed her. Beck is out to bring the girl back in order to placate his rebellious flock. After a near-fatal

poltergeist attack which sees young Robins almost entombed by yards of wire spewing forth from his braces, Sampson tells the family that they must return to the site of their house in Cuesta Verde and confront their tormentor. Uneasy at the thought of returning to the place he fears most, Nelson begins drinking heavily again. After swallowing the worm which floats in the bottom of his bottle of tequila, Nelson becomes possessed by the evil spirit of Beck and tries to kill his own family. Despite the fact that he is strangling her, Williams tells her husband that she loves him and this breaks the spell. Nelson begins convulsing horribly and vomits forth a horrible monster that has been growing inside him. Williams and Nelson rescue their children from the monster and barely make it out of the house alive. They return to California. Aided by Rubinstein and Sampson, the family members climb into the pit that once was their home and enter a fire to journey to "the other side" where they will finally do battle with their evil poltergeist. Sampson warns the family to hold onto each other at all costs or one or more may slip away into eternity forever. While in the vaporous void, the family is attacked by a monstrous demon and O'Rourke is jerked away from their grasp. Through the fire in the pit Sampson thrusts his Indian lance, tempered with his spiritual fire, and Nelson grabs the weapon and hurls it at the demon, killing it. When the monster lets loose of the little girl, she suddenly shoots toward the horizon into a blinding light and vanishes. Sampson, staring into the fire, moans: "We've lost her . . . " But as the anguished family floats helplessly, out of the blinding light comes their daughter, guided back to her family by the spirit of her grandmother, Fitzgerald. Sampson reaches into the fire and pulls the family back from the nether world.

Although the film moves along at a rapid clip, it is poorly constructed and haphazardly executed. According to star Nelson, several additional scenes developing the relationship between him and his family, wound up on the cutting room floor, leaving the film to lurch from special-effects sequence to special-effects sequence with little character insight in between. The confrontation scene between Nelson and Beck—the founder of the avant-garde "Living Theater" of the 1950s—is the very core of the film, and is its one redeeming moment. Despite his very brief appearance (Beck died soon after filming), Beck's bone-chilling presence dominates this film. His scene with Nelson is a marvel of screen acting. Filmed almost entirely in close-up, Beck's cadaverous visage shifts from a creepy civility to malevolent evil and back again with disarming subtlety. It is a tribute to Beck's considerable talents that in his all too brief appearance he manages to create an embodiment of evil so terrifying as to burn his image into the viewer's brain long after the rest of the film is justifiably forgotten. If anyone has nightmares after viewing this film they will be of Beck's face and not of the overdone and poorly integrated special effects. Famous Swiss painter H.R. Giger, creator of the monster in ALIEN, designed the "Vomit Creature" (it's billed that way in the credits, honest) which is seen ever so briefly as it slithers across the floor. (In its mature metamorphosis, the Creature is played by Johnson, wearing a monster suit; the actor is a paraplegic, who lost both legs and one arm in the Vietnam War.) The climactic battle of good against evil that presumably both films have been leading up to is over in a matter of minutes and is wholly unspectacular. Sampson's constant urgings that the family that stays together slays (demons) together becomes annoyingly trite. Director Gibson and his cast do inject a healthy amount of humor into the proceedings, and that aspect of the film is refreshing, but be it last-minute editorial tinkering or a basic flaw in the screenplay, POLTERGEIST II seems confused and forced. A minor note of annoyance: the teenage daughter of the Freeling family, played by the late Dominique Dunne in the first film, is missing from the sequel and never even mentioned. Soon after the release of POLTERGEIST, Dunne was murdered, her ex-boy friend found guilty of the crime, served less than three years in prison and now works as a chef in a swanky Los Angeles restaurant. While it is commendable that the producers of the sequel didn't try to substitute another performer in the role, it is a grievous disservice to the memory of that fine young actress to totally ignore the fact that her character ever existed. Yet another sequel, POLTERGEIST III, is being filmed in Chicago, this time featuring only O'Rourke and Rubinstein from the original cast.

p&w, Mark Victor, Michael Grais; d, Brian Gibson; ph, Andrew Laszlo (Panavision, Metrocolor); m, Jerry Goldsmith; ed, Thom Noble; prod d, Ted Haworth; set d, Roy Barnes, Greg Papalia; spec eff, Richard Edlund.

Horror   **Cas.**   **(PR:O MPAA:PG-13)**

POMNALUI NUNSOGI†   (1987, N. Korea) 100m Korfilm c (Tran: Thaw)

Cho Ji Sun, An Su Bok, Kim Ryong Rin, Kum Jun Sik, So Gyong Sop.

Two Koreans living in Japan plan to marry, but the girl's rich parents call off the wedding when they find a more suitable spouse for their daughter than the poor lad she loves. A rare North Korean film that attacks the Japanese rather than the Americans.

d, Rim Chang Bom, Ko Hak Rim; w, Lin Chun Gu; ph, Kwak Chol Sam, Liu Hui Song.

Drama   **(PR:A MPAA:NR)**

POPULATION: ONE†   (1986) 70m American Scenes c

Tomata DuPlenty (Himself), Sheela Edwards (Sheela), Jane Gaskill, Gorilla Rose, Mike Doud, Beck Campbell, Tommy Gear, Susan Ensley.

After the Americans finally manage to blow up the world, DuPlenty sits in his underground shelter watching scenes of U.S. history on his TV screens and gradually going bonkers. A surreal, oddly constructed film that has virtually no chance of reaching more than a small audience.

p, Bianca Daalder; d&w, Renee Daalder; ph, Jurg Victor Walther; m, Daniel

Schwartz; ed, Woody Wilson, Renee Daalder, Carel Struycken, Bianca Daalder; art d & set d, Keith Barrett; animation, Dominic Orlando.

Science Fiction/Fantasy (PR:O MPAA:NR)

POR UN VESTIDO DE NOVIA† (1986, Mex.) 86m Potosi/Peliculas Mexicanas c (Trans: All Because of a Wedding Dress)

Pedro Infante, Jr. *(Reynaldo)*, Arturo Martinez, Jr. *(Lauro)*, Monica Prado *(Marsela)*, Victor Alcocer *(Don Rafael Garza)*, Socorro Bonilla *(Bertha)*, Ana Luisa Petuffo *(Mother)*, Rodolfo de Anda, Juan Gallardo, Humberto Elizondo, Bruno Rey, Paty Maldonado.

Infante and Martinez are former best friends who come to blows over a woman, Prado. She refuses to marry Martinez and chooses, instead, to wed Infante. In the midst of their efforts to win the girl is a story about a gang of murderers who wreak havoc on the community and must be stopped. The film's bang-'em-up climax connects these two stories in a church where the wedding between Infante and Prado is taking place.

d, Arturo Martinez; w, (based on an original story and song by Vicente Fernandez); ph, Augustin Lara; m, Luis Arcaraz.

Drama/Crime (PR:O MPAA:NR)

POSITIVE I.D.† (1986) 104m A.C. Anderson/Anderson Film c

Stephanie Rascoe *(Julie Kenner)*, John Davies *(Don Kenner)*, Steve Fromholz, Gail Cronauer.

An independent film from Fort Worth, Texas about a woman, Rascoe, who is unable to recover from a rape which took place one year earlier. She becomes withdrawn, easily frazzled, obsessed with washing herself, and unreceptive to her husband Davies' sexual desires. She then finds a reason to live—she learns that she can get a new identity for herself. She applies for a new birth certificate and takes up residence in a remote inner-city hotel where she can exist under her new name. She reveals none of this to her family, taking great effort to keep her false identity papers freezer-wrapped in the refrigerator. She becomes obsessed with the idea of tracking down her rapist and giving him the vengeance he deserves, in a climactic eruption of violence.

p,d&w, Andy Anderson; ph, Paul Barton; ed, Robert J. Castaldo, Andy Anderson.

Drama (PR:O MPAA:NR)

POTERYALSYA SLON† (1986, USSR) 74m Soviet Film-Central Studio for Popular Science/Goskino c (Trans: An Elephant Got Lost)

Sasha Komarov *(Yegorska)*, Maxim Sidorov, Slava Galiullin, Vera Panassenkova *(The Other Children)*, Raissa Ryassanova *(Yegorska's Mother)*.

A Soviet children's film which stars young Komarov as a lad living in Siberia who befriends an escaped circus elephant that is being hunted by poachers. The boy's mother, a game warden, allows him to keep the elephant at home, though none of Komarov's school-mates believe his story. The elephant is finally taken away where it belongs, making for a sad but positive parting scene.

d, Yevgeni Ostashenko; w, Arkadi Krassilschohikov, Yevgeni Ostashenko; ph, Pavel Filimonovi; m, Sandor Kallosh; set d, Alexander Petrov.

Children's (PR:AA MPAA:NR)

POTOMOK BELOGO BARSSA (SEE: DESCENT OF THE SNOW LEOPARD, THE, 1986, U.S.S.R.)

POUVOIR INTIME (SEE: INTIMATE POWER, 1986, Can.)

POWER*** (1986) 111m Lorimar-Polar/FOX c

Richard Gere *(Pete St. John)*, Julie Christie *(Ellen Freeman)*, Gene Hackman *(Wilfred Buckley)*, Kate Capshaw *(Sydney Bettterman)*, Denzel Washington *(Arnold Billings)*, E.G. Marshall *(Sen. Sam Hastings)*, Beatrice Straight *(Claire Hastings)*, Fritz Weaver *(Wallace Furman)*, Michael Learned *(Gov. Andrea Stannard)*, J.T. Walsh *(Jerome Cade)*, E. Katherine Kerr *(Irene Furman)*, Polly Rowles *(Lucille DeWitt)*, Matt Salinger *(Phillip Aarons)*, Tom Mardirosian *(Sheikh)*, Omar Torres *(Roberto Cepeda)*, Ricardo Gallarzo *(Interpreter)*, Jessica James *(Helen)*, Glenn Kezer *(Frank McKusker)*, Douglas Newell *(David Garber)*, Scott Harlan *(Ralph Andropwicz)*, Nick Flynn *(Wilson Jacobs)*, Ed Van Nuys *(Charles Whiting)*, Noel Harrison *(Leonard Thompson)*, Jackson Beck *(The Voice)*, Leila Danette *(Poor Woman)*, Kevin Hagen *(Cop)*, Timothy Jecko *(Business Executive)*, Margaret Barker *(Wealthy Matron)*, D.B. Sweeney *(College Student)*, Linda DeNiro *(Desk Clerk)*, Lynn Klugman *(Video Technician)*, John Robert Evans *(1st Senator)*, Elizabeth Kendrick *(Receptionist)*, Jim Hartz, Roger Grimsby, Margaret Hall, Brad Holbrook, Donna Hanover, Frank Casey, Kristi Witker *(Commentators)*, Marvin Scott *(Anchorman)*, Daryl Edwards *(Waiter)*, Martha Pinson *(Assistant)*, Jack Zahniser *(Pilot)*, Burke Pearson *(City Clerk)*, Janet Sarno *(Moderator)*, Robert Fieldsteel, Gregory Wagrowski*(Assistant Directors)*, Ron Stein *(Stunt Cameraman)*, Robert Kruger*(Barry)*.

The electoral process has always been a matter of selling a candidate to the public as though his/her style of leadership was a sort of "new and improved" brand. In past eras, campaigns were conceived and plotted in the legendary smoke-filled rooms, but with the vast array of technologies available today the marketing of political candidates has become a highly competitive, multi-million dollar industry. Sidney Lumet's POWER examines this often ruthless world through the eyes of Gere, a much sought-after campaign strategist with an admirable eighty per-

cent success rate. The film opens at a political rally in an unnamed Latin American country. A car bomb goes off, wounding one of the supporters, and Torres, the would-be leader, rushes to the victim's aid. Torres cradles the dying man's head in his lap, getting blood all over his shirt. All of this action is captured by a camera crew, while Gere stands to the side, excitedly shouting for more closeups. Torres and Gere are hustled into a waiting car and we learn that Gere is running this campaign. The footage will be terrific, Gere exclaims, and instructs Torres to wear the bloodied shirt during any public appearance.

That night Gere flies back to his New York office to begin pre-campaign work with his American clients. He also finds time for a quick dalliance with Capshaw, Gere's full-time assistant and part-time girl friend. Weaver, an ineffectual but wealthy businessman, wants to be governor of New Mexico but is a little put off

by Gere's methods. The two sit in a darkened television studio as Gere explains the realities of modern-day campaigning. "You are paying me to make you a new life," Gere informs Weaver, "and in order for me to do that I've got to be in charge of all the elements that go into it . . . that means framing the overall strategy as well as deciding all the specifics. The look of the campaign. The look of the billboards, bumper stickers, what colors they're going to be . . . " Weaver tries to bring up his policies for New Mexico, but these are quickly dismissed as irrelevant. "I'm sure they're great but they're not important," Gere explains. "My job is to get you in. Once you're there you do whatever your conscience tells you to do."

Now Gere begins a nationwide crisscross to juggle his candidates and their individual needs. Learned is the governor of Washington, who may have trouble getting reelected. Following her victory in the last election, Learned had left her husband and children for her campaign manager. Gere must now combat Learned's tainted reputation while working to create a new image. In Ohio, Gere is shocked to learn his old friend, Senator Hastings (Marshall) has decided against running for another term. A longstanding figure in Washington, Marshall cites failing health as an explanation, though Gere remains suspicious of this surprise announcement. Gere is soon contacted by Washington, a representative of businessman Walsh. Walsh wants Marshall's senate seat and knows Gere can put him there. After some reluctance, Gere agrees to accept the job, although he has some reservations about Washington's connections with foreign oil interests and Walsh's vehement opposition to one of Marshall's solar-energy bills. Racing back and forth among candidates, Gere finds himself occasionally running into Christie, his ex-wife, who works as a journalist. Gere also crosses paths with Hackman, his one-time mentor, whose troubles with alcohol ruined a fine career. After speaking on the phone with a client, Gere accidentally finds that his office has been bugged. He begins investigating this and other unusual incidents, while Christie—who is good friends with Marshall's wife, Straight—looks into the reasons behind the senator's retirement. Meanwhile Salinger, a college professor, decides to enter the Ohio race as an independent candidate. Hackman becomes his advisor, and promptly works on changing the young idealist's image.

Eventually Christie and Gere learn that Marshall has decided to retire because of an indiscretion by Straight. She had entered into a business deal with Washington, but when this soured the stage was set for scandal. Marshall—threatened with a connection to foreign interests—has knuckled under to blackmail by resigning from political life, and Walsh's chances seem assured. Gere quits Walsh's campaign, then confronts Salinger before an important debate. He tells the candidate his feelings on the business of elections and image making, a business which has made Gere a wealthy man. "Prove me wrong!" Gere implores Salinger. Salinger speaks his mind during the debate, and his common-sense ideas surprise many. On election night Gere and Christie sit up watching the returns. Learned regains her seat, but Weaver, despite Gere's valiant efforts, loses his election. Walsh loses his three-way race as well, but amazingly comes in last, with Salinger showing a strong finish in second place.

The diverse elements of the plot are fairly complicated, but Lumet is a strong director who knows how to effectively weave these components together. Lumet jumps back and forth between locales and characters with Gere as the all-important connecting factor. Gere, in one of his better performances, runs on controlled adrenaline, taking out his frustrations by pounding along on a portable drum pad as a cassette of Benny Goodman's "Sing, Sing, Sing" blasts through his Walkman. Showing a little grey hair at the temples, Gere exudes a combination of charm, wit, and sheer arrogance as he throws himself into a job he so passionately loves. Gere's turn of conscience, imploring Salinger to forgo glitter for honest politics, is the film's weakest point. It's an unbelievable character twist for a man who has made his fortune molding and marketing human life. Gere's best moments come during times of near crisis. When Weaver is thrown from a horse while filming an expensive commercial, Gere's mind quickly goes into motion. He freezes the image on the video monitor, thereby turning Weaver into a genuine Western bronco rider. Potential tragedy turns into a victorious moment thanks to the miracle of modern technology. In a sense, the expensive hardware that helps sell the candidates is just as important to POWER as Gere is. Lumet portrays the production of commercials, computers compiling information, electronic listening devices, and even Gere's private airplane as integral parts of the election. In a fitting epilog to the story, Lumet's camera explores the machines used to package and promote candidates while a rousing version of "The Stars and Stripes Forever" blares on the soundtrack. The theme of image versus reality is a disturbing one, and Lumet uses this coda to neatly summarize his point. The secondary roles are well cast, with Washington and Learned giving the most assured characterizations. Capshaw gets lost somewhere in the frenzy, though this is her best performance to date. The only real waste is Hackman. Like Capshaw's, his role is often enveloped by the film's pace, and his relationship with Gere is dealt with only in a peripheral manner. His story of failure would undoubtedly have given POWER a slightly more human touch, and it's a shame Hackman's talents are subordinated to other concerns.

p, Reene Schisgal, Mark Tarlov; d, Sidney Lumet; w, David Himmelstein; ph, Andrzej Bartkowiak (Panavision, Technicolor); m, Cy Coleman; ed, Andrew Mondshein; prod d, Peter Larkin; art d, William Barclay; set d, Thomas C. Tonery; cos, Anna Hill Johnstone; spec eff, Laurencio Cordero; makeup, Joe Cranzano.

| Drama | Cas. | (PR:O MPAA:R) |

PPONG (SEE: BBONG, 1986, Korea)

PPPERFORMER, THE† (1986, Neth.) 87m De Roje He-Added/Cannon c

Freek de Jonge, Rosita Tamara, Johnny Van Elk, Jan Raub, Jugo Van Den Berge, Jelle de Jonge.

Dutch stage comedian Freek de Jonge is the center of this film as a stuttering performer who, in a surrealistic manner, relates his life as a circus clown to his curious young son. Following a dreamlike line of logic, the film combines narrative, personal storytelling, and filmed excerpts of de Jonge's stage show. (In Dutch; English subtitles.)

p, Dirk Schreiner; d, Casper Verbrugge; w, Casper Verbrugge, Freek de Jonge (based on the play "De Bedevaart" by Freek de Jonge); ph, Jules V.D. Steenhoven; m, William Breuker, Hennie Vrienten; ed, Ot Louw; art d, Hella de Jonge.

| Comedy | (PR:A MPAA:NR) |

PRAY FOR DEATH½ (1986) 92m Transworld Entertainment–American Distribution Group c

Sho Kosugi (Akira Saito), James Booth (Limehouse), Donna Kei Benz (Aiko Saito), Michael Constantine (Mr. Newman), Norman Burton (Lt. Anderson), Kane Kosugi (Takeshi Saito), Shane Kosugi (Tomoya Saito), Matthew Faison (Sgt. Daley), Parley Baer (Sam Green), Robert Ito (Koga), Alan Amiel (Vinnie Seline), Woody Watson (Cohen), Charles Gruber (Sgt. Trumble), Nik Hagler (Pirelli), Chris Wycliff (Joe Benson), Jude Stephen (Dr. Smith), Rodney Rincon (Sanchez), Marlene Mankey (The Nurse), Yosh (Shoji).

In PRAY FOR DEATH, Ninja hero Kosugi wipes out an entire army of American gangsters with such grace and efficiency that it must make DEATH WISH star Charles Bronson drool with envy. After some impressive opening credits, the film begins with a standard Ninja fighting scene which, as it turns out, is actually a film that two young Japanese boys—Shane and Kane Kosugi—are watching on television. Their mother, the pretty Benz, calls them to dinner. Awed by the performance of their Ninja heroes, the boys ask their father, Kosugi, if Ninjas still exist, a question he evades. Later, he and his wife decide that they will move to America and open a fruit business. Before he leaves, however, Kosugi visits an ominous temple where he remembers his past as a Ninja warrior and his battle

with his brother, which ended fatally for the latter. Kosugi's adopted father tells him to forget his past guilt and presents him with a prized warrior's helmet. The family arrives in America and finds that the house/storefront they purchased from the friendly and aging Baer needs a great deal of repair work. Unbeknownst to Kosugi, part of the storefront is used by a local gang to fence stolen property. Later that evening, one member of the gang arrives to hide a priceless necklace, pocketing the jewelry instead. When his contact arrives the following day and finds that the necklace is not there, he accuses Baer of its theft and kills him. With the necklace still missing, gang boss Constantine orders his top assistant, Booth, to find it. Booth assumes that Kosugi has stolen it and, in retaliation, kidnaps one of his sons. Kosugi, who refrains from donning his Ninja gear, fights back as the battle rapidly escalates. Kosugi goes on the offensive and infiltrates Booth's waterfront hideout, promising that he will make the villain "pray for death" if he does not leave his family in peace. Booth, who is something of a lunatic and refuses to be intimidated, kills Kosugi's wife and tries to do the same to one of his sons. Driven by inner fury, Kosugi ignores police lieutenant Burton's warnings, and plans his vengeance. He psychologically and physically prepares himself to return to Ninja form. He pulls his Ninja garb from storage, sharpens his sword, and heads for Constantine's gang headquarters. Vaulting over security gates, flinging "death stars" into guards' faces, slicing and dicing his enemies with less mess than a Veg-O-Matic, and drop-kicking his way to the main offices, Kosugi kills everyone in sight—except Booth, who escapes in an old pickup truck. Kosugi follows in his little Honda Accord and the chase eventually leads to an abandoned warehouse where hundreds of mannequins are stored and, like their human counterparts, are sliced, kicked, and impaled with "death stars." The climactic battle pits the heavily armored Kosugi against the chainsaw-wielding Booth. The gruesome, though bloodless, finale has Booth "praying for death" before being halved by a large circular buzzsaw. Afterwards, Kosugi, who is dressed again in his conventional suit and tie, brings his children to their mother's gravesite, vowing to stay in America to keep her company.

Ninja films exist primarily for one reason—to thrill certain impressionable audiences who are awestruck by the physical feats performed by the Ninja warriors. In this respect, the Ninja film is perhaps the only genre to be uncorrupted by feeble Hollywood attempts to legitimize with commercialization and artistry. With the exception of Sam Peckinpah and his 1975 film THE KILLER ELITE, no major director has attempted a Ninja film, as they have westerns or horror films. Ninja films receive no critical attention, are rarely reviewed by the press, and usually play only in the seediest of theaters. This is mainly because the films project nothing but highly stylized and carefully choreographed fight scenes, which owe their debt to the kabuki theatricality of the Japanese stage. PRAY FOR DEATH, however, has a minimum of fighting, instead concentrating on creating real characters and a believable script. The performances are all surprisingly adept—considering that actors in action films of this sort are ordinarily wooden, at best—and the photography is impeccable. Equally surprising is the restraint with respect to showing gore, something from which director Hessler's horror films of the 1960s didn't shy away. PRAY FOR DEATH isn't merely a good Ninja film, it's a good film, period. The audience cannot help but genuinely sympathize with Kosugi and his family. The novelty of an American locale and American villains also helps. PRAY FOR DEATH is a perfect film for someone who has never seen a Ninja film and wants to quench a curiosity. It's intense in spots, mainly the finale, but it has a ritualistic beauty which makes it oddly fascinating. Includes the song "Back to the Shadows" (performed by Peggy Abernathy).

p, Don Van Atta; d, Gordon Hessler; w, James Booth; ph, Roy H. Wagner (Foto-Kem Color); m, Thomas Chase, Steve Rucker; ed, Bill Butler, Steve Butler; art d, Adrian Gorton; cos, Ed Fincher; spec eff, Wayne Beauchamp; ch, Sho Kasugi; makeup, Kevin Board.

| Martial Arts/Drama | Cas. | (PR:O MPAA:R) |

PRENSES† (1986, Turkey) Omur-Varlik (Trans: Princess)

Serpil Cakmakli, Tunc Okan, Mahmut Hekimoglu, Guzin Dogan.

d&w, Sinan Cetin; ph, Aytekin Cakmakci.

PRETTY IN PINK*** (1986) 96m PAR c

Molly Ringwald (Andie Walsh), Harry Dean Stanton (Jack Walsh), Jon Cryer (Phil "Duckie" Dale), Andrew McCarthy (Blane McDonough), Annie Potts (Iona), James Spader (Steff McKee), Jim Haynie (Donnelly), Alexa Kenin (Jena), Kate Vernon (Benny), Andrew "Dice" Clay (Bouncer), Emily Longstreth (Kate), Margaret Colin (English Teacher), Jamie Anders (Terrence), Gina Gershon (Girl Friend in Gym Class), Bader Howar (Sales Girl), Christian Jacobs (Boy in Record Store), Audre Johnson (Benny's Mom), Melanie Manos (Girl at Party), Maggie Roswell (Mrs. Dietz), Dweezil Zappa (Simon), Jimmer Podrasky, Tommy Blatnik, Timothy J., Terry Wilson (The Rave-Ups), Bruno, Jeffrey Hollie, Kevin Ricard, David Sutton, Kevin Williams, Rock Deadrick (Talk Back), Karen Laine (Girl at Prom), Kristy Swanson (Duckette), Kevin D. Lindsay (Kevin).

The best teenage film to come off the John Hughes assembly line since 1984's SIXTEEN CANDLES, PRETTY IN PINK was, not accidentally, directed by someone other than Hughes—first-timer Deutch, who has here made an impressive debut with the Hughes-penned script. Ringwald (who also starred in SIXTEEN CANDLES and THE BREAKFAST CLUB) is cast as a kid from the wrong side of the tracks. She's a self-confident high school senior who dresses in handmade clothes, works in a record store, and lives in a modest home with her unemployed father, Stanton. Her mother deserted the family years earlier, leaving Ringwald to handle most of the household duties while Stanton tries to overcome the depression of losing the wife he still loves. Times are tough for Ringwald in school. She and her less-fortunate friends are tormented by the

"richies"—the wealthy students who make up the majority of the student body. Although Ringwald is poor, she's not *that* poor. She drives around in a sporty, though dented, car and has an answering machine on her bedroom phone—conveniences usually not had by the financially downtrodden. Ringwald's worst fear—and a fear that hits most every high school student—is that she won't get invited to the senior prom. Her best friend, the outlandish and romantic Cryer, talks matter-of-factly with Stanton about marrying Ringwald, but he never thinks of taking her to the prom—a social event that most of the poor kids avoid. Surprisingly, to her, she is asked to go to prom by the charming McCarthy, a "richie" who's not as snobbish as the rest of his elitist friends. When Cryer learns that Ringwald is associating with McCarthy—who represents everything Cryer and Ringwald are against—he goes into a rage. Initially, Cryer hides his rejection with jokes. Upon hearing the name of his competition, he goes into hysterics: "His name is Blaine?! Blaine?! That's a major appliance. That's not a name!" His real feelings emerge, however, and he tells her, with all the conviction in the world, "I would have died for you." He completely breaks off his friendship with Ringwald.

In the meantime, McCarthy's best friend, Spader, is even less accepting. Spader, a disgustingly wealthy psychopath who is more suited to the company of

Leopold and Loeb than McCarthy, calls Ringwald a "mutant" and threatens to break off his friendship with McCarthy. Having fallen head-over-heels for McCarthy—who indeed proves not to be an insensitive snob—Ringwald prepares herself for the prom. Stanton buys her an inexpensive pink dress which she plans to remake into something more fashionable. She confides in a coworker, Potts, a 30ish leather-clad woman who sees in Ringwald the teenager she once was in the 1960s. Potts relives her own memories of her senior prom and gives Ringwald the dress that she wore. Ringwald then combines the two dresses to create her own unique fashion.

McCarthy is having second thoughts about endangering his friendship with Spader. He avoids contact with Ringwald, refusing to return her phone calls, and eventually backing out on their prom date. Rather than sit home alone on the big night, Ringwald dolls herself up in pink and goes by herself to the prom. Waiting out front for her is Cryer, who is equally fashion conscious. They go in together, walking arm-in-arm. McCarthy sees her, apologizes, and tells her that he loves

her before leaving the prom. Cryer, in an act of pure nobility, tells her to go after him. Ringwald runs outside and catches McCarthy in the parking lot, where they kiss in a final clinch.

Following the disastrous WEIRD SCIENCE, which Hughes wrote and directed, PRETTY IN PINK marks a return to the form he displayed with his first film, SIXTEEN CANDLES. As in all of his films, PRETTY IN PINK touches a chord with today's teens (as well as anyone who has been that age), but at the same time seems to pander somewhat to the audience's expectations. The film's success rides on Ringwald who, at 18 years, has become the paragon of the 1980's teenager. Instead of being a stereotypical chesty blonde who serves only to turn on gullible young virgins, Ringwald is cute, though not gorgeous, intelligent, insecure, and individualistic. In short, Ringwald has become the ideal modern teenager. Similar to Corey Haim's character in this year's LUCAS, Ringwald's characters are real people who reflect the ways, mannerisms, and speech of today's youth. Interestingly, however, the finest moments in PRETTY IN PINK come, not from the script (which is more problematic than praiseworthy), but from Deutch's careful direction. While the script contains trite and unbelievable dialog, the superbly convincing performances make up for these faults. Many of the film's most effective moments come simply from the expressions and quiet looks that the characters give each other. Though much of the credit for PRETTY IN PINK went to Hughes, it seems rightly to belong to Deutch, whose directorial debut was unfairly overlooked by critics. What makes this film so watchable is that there isn't a bad performance in sight. Ringwald is excellent, especially in her scenes with Stanton, who has proven that his great performance in PARIS, TEXAS was far from an accident. Cryer's energy is phenomenal, McCarthy is genuinely likable, and Spader is excellent as the thoroughly reprehensible rich kid. The biggest surprise comes from Potts, who manages to play her supporting character with such verve that she nearly steals every scene she's in. As Ringwald's confidante, she is first seen as a tough punk, then as a devotee of 1960s nostalgia—sporting a beehive hairdo—and then, finally, as a relatively normal woman donning mildly conservative attire. One of the biggest objections to the film is its ending (a problem which also hurt LUCAS). As originally filmed, Cryer and Ringwald end up together, just as one is led to believe they would through the entire film. It's only natural, since they have been friends forever and have both told each other how much they care for one another. After screening the film for a test audience, however, the filmmakers decided to give its teen audience what they wanted—Ringwald ending up with heartthrob McCarthy—even if it was contrary to the rest of the film. Like all Hughes' products, PRETTY IN PINK fills the soundtrack with a bevy of rock songs, including the title track "Pretty in Pink" (The Psychedelic Furs, performed by the Psychedelic Furs), which was remixed from the 1981 single. Other songs are, "If You Leave" (Orchestral Manoeuvers in the Dark), "Wouldn't It Be Good" (Nik Kershaw, performed by Danny Hutton Hitters), "What's it Gonna Be" (Maggie Lee, performed by Maggie Lee), "Love" (John Lennon, performed by Jon Cryer), "Round, Round" (Neville Keighly, performed by Belouis Some), "Pursuit" (Winston Sharples), "Rave-Up/Shut-Up" (Jimmer Podrasky, Doug Leonard, performed by The Rave-Ups), "Positively Lost Me" (Jimmer Podrasky, performed by The Rave-Ups), "Copacabana (At The Copa)" (Barry Manilow, B. Sussman, J. Feldman, performed by Barry Manilow), "Thieves Like Us" (New Order, Artur Baker, performed by New Order), "Elegia" (New Order, performed by New Order), "Shell Shock" (New Order, John Robie, performed by New Order), "Whisper/Touch" (Dean Chamberlain, performed by Code Blue), "Bring On the Dancing Horses" (Echo and the Bunnymen), "Do Wot You Do" (Michael Hutchence, Andrew Farris, performed by INXS), "Try a Little Tenderness" (Harry Woods, Jimmy Campbell, Reg Connelly, performed by Otis Redding), "Cherish" (Terry Kirkman, performed by The Association), "Please Please Please Let Me Get What I Want" (Morrissey, Johnny Marr, performed by The Smiths), "Rudy" (Bruno, performed by Talk Back), "Left of Center" (Suzanne Vega, Steve Addabbo, performed by Suzanne Vega), "Get to Know You" (Jesse Johnson). PRETTY IN PINK is dedicated, in part, to one of the film's young actresses, Alexa Kenin, who died in 1985. She had a major role in the 1982 Clint Eastwood film HONKYTONK MAN.

p, Lauren Shuler; d, Howard Deutch; w, John Hughes; ph, Tak Fujimoto (Technicolor); m, Michael Gore; ed, Richard Marks; prod d, John W. Corso; ch, Kenny Ortega; m/l, The Psychedelic Furs, Orchestral Manoevers in the Dark, Nik Kershaw, Maggie Lee, John Lennon, Neville Keighly, Winston Sharples, Jimmer Podrasky, Doug Leonard, Barry Manilow, B. Sussman, J. Feldman, New Order, Arthur Baker, John Robie, Dean Chamberlain, Echo and the Bunnymen, Michael Hutchence, Andrew Farris, Harry Woods, Jimmy Campbell, Reg Connelly, Terry Kirkman, Morrissey, Johnny Marr, Bruno, Suzanne Vega, Steve Addabbo, Jesse Johnson.

Drama   Cas.   **(PR:C MPAA:PG-13)**

PROKA†   (1986, Yugo.) 100m Kosovafilm/Jugoslavija c

Xhevat Qorra *(Proka)*, Ahdrijana Videnovic *(Girl Neighbor)*, Abdurrahan Shala *(Mayor)*, Faruk Negolli *(Stoka, Mayor's Aide)*, Dorota Kaminska *(Proka's Sister)*.

A Yugoslavian political tale of a village idiot, Qorra, who becomes the scapegoat for the entire village. Because he is such a hard worker many locals become jealous. The town's mayor also takes a dislike to him, ordering him imprisoned. Trouble escalates for Qorra as he is locked away in a monastery and tortured.

d, Isa Qosja; w, Eqrem Basha; ph, Arim Spashu; m, Krist Lekaj; ed, Agron Vula; cos, Violeta Xhaferi.

Drama   **(PR:NR MPAA:NR)**

PROMISES TO KEEP†   (1986, Aus.) Laughing Kookaburra

John Lone, Wendy Hughes.

p, Jane Scott; d, Phillip Noyce; w, Jan Sharp; ph, Peter James.

PRUNELLE BLUES†   (1986, Fr.) 82m Sara–Cinergie/UGC c

Michel Boujenah *(Freddy)*, Valerie Steffen *(Florence)*, Vincent Lindon *(Fernand)*, Karim Allaoui *(Albert)*, Michel Aumont *(Cade)*, Jean-Claude Bourbault, Genevieve Brunel, Robert Bahr, Gilette Barbier, Jean-Pierre Laurent, Alain Floret, Guy Guerri, Alain-Jacques Adiba, Christian Duval, Bruno Moynot.

Boujenah, the Cesar-winning actor of last year's French comedy THREE MEN AND A CRADLE, stars in this comic thriller as the manager of a sleazy porno movie theater. Surrounded by photographs of female flesh, he has his heart set on the one live girl in the theater—Steffan, a stripper who entertains the audience between shows. Boujenah inadvertently gets involved in underworld affairs, during which he is mistaken for the person who stole a gang's drug shipment. It is actually Steffan the gang is looking for, giving Boujenah ample opportunity to defend the girl he loves.

p, Alain Sarde; d&w, Jacques Otmezguine (based on his novel); ph, Yves Dahan (Eastmancolor); m, Hubert Rostaing, Yvan Julian; ed, Yves Deschamps; art d, Katia Vischkof.

Crime/Comedy   **(PR:O   MPAA:NR)**

PSYCHO III*   (1986) 93m UNIV c

Anthony Perkins *(Norman Bates)*, Diana Scarwid *(Maureen Coyle)*, Jeff Fahey *(Duane Duke)*, Roberta Maxwell *(Tracy Venable)*, Hugh Gillin *(Sheriff Hunt)*, Lee Garlington *(Myrna)*, Robert Alan Browne *(Statler)*, Gary Bayer *(Father Brian)*, Patience Cleveland *(Sister Margaret)*, Juliette Cummins *(Red)*, Steve Guevara *(Deputy Leo)*, Kay Heberle *(Ruthie)*, Donovan Scott *(Kyle)*, Karen Hensel *(Sister Catherine)*, Jack Murdock *(Lou)*, Katt Shea Ruben *(Patsy Boyle)*, Hugo L. Stanger *(Harvey Leach)*, Lisa Ives *(Belltower Nun)*, Angele Ritter *(Bartender)*, Diane Rodriguez *(Nun)*, Virginia Gregg *(Mother's Voice)*.

It's only natural that Anthony Perkins should make his directorial debut with a PSYCHO sequel, directing himself in the role for which he will forever be

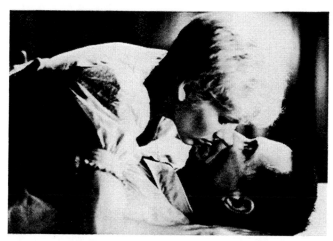

remembered. Understanding the Norman Bates character probably better than anyone (including Alfred Hitchcock and novelist Robert Bloch, as Perkins has lived in his shadow for 26 years), Perkins is here given his chance to interpret the story.

Beginning one month after the end of PSYCHO II, this film picks up with Mrs. Spool (played by Claudia Bryar in the 1983 film), Norman's "real" mother, still missing. As PSYCHO III opens, a blood-curdling scream is heard, exclaiming "There is no God." A pretty novice, Scarwid, is kneeling before an altar praying for a sign from above. Distressed, she climbs to the top of a bell tower (the same one used in Hitchcock's VERTIGO) and threatens to jump. When another nun intervenes, she is accidentally pushed to her death. Scarwid is told by a surviving nun that she will "burn in hell" for what she's done. Scarwid is then seen wandering through the desert dressed in street clothes. Along comes Fahey, a somewhat sleazy musician, who offers her a lift. A blinding rainstorm forces them to pull off the road, during which time Fahey tries to seduce Scarwid, unaware that she is a virginal nun. Fahey later stops at the Bates Motel, a rundown establishment which Perkins is trying to rejuvenate. He's bought a new ice machine and has booked four rooms for an upcoming high-school homecoming party. He hires Fahey to help run things. While at a local diner, Perkins is cornered by investigative reporter Maxwell, who is doing a story on the insanity plea. As Perkins nervously evades her questions, Scarwid enters. Wearing a short blonde haircut and carrying a suitcase engraved with the letters *M.C.*, Perkins is reminded of Marion Crane (played by Janet Leigh in the original). His shower victim from 26 years earlier. As he stares at Scarwid, he flashes back to the brutal shower scene. Scarwid then asks if there is anywhere nearby to spend the night. Naturally, she winds up in the infamous Cabin No. 1 at the Bates Motel. Her initial shock at finding Fahey as the manager is calmed when he proves much friendlier than the previous night. (He does, however, overcharge her for the room, pocketing the difference.) Perkins tries to keep himself under control,

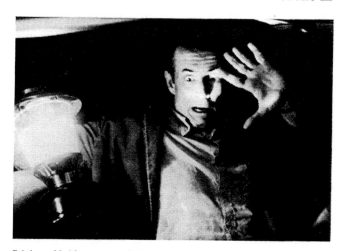

fighting with his memory of the murdered Marion Crane. He discusses the problem with "mother," who is still propped up at her bedroom window, and who wants very much to get rid of that "whore" Scarwid. Meanwhile, Scarwid is also being tormented by the thoughts of her own "mother"—the Virgin Mary—to whom she has devoted her life. Battling with his other self, Perkins peers through the hole in his office wall to watch Scarwid undress and head for the shower. He then grabs a knife and transforms into "mother." Slowly, "mother" enters the cabin where Scarwid sits in her steamy bathtub. "Mother," with knife in hand, rips back the shower curtain. But Scarwid lies nearly lifeless in a pool of red water, blood pumping from her slit wrists. "Mother" stands motionless as the dazed Scarwid looks up. Her point of view is distorted and foggy. She imagines the Virgin Mary standing above her, holding out a crucifix in her hand. Scarwid whispers, "Please forgive me."

Scarwid later awakens in a hospital where Perkins is introduced to her as the man who saved her life. When Scarwid apologizes for leaving the bathroom such a mess, Perkins replies with a grin, "I've seen it worse." Infatuated with Scarwid, Perkins invites her to stay at the motel to recuperate. While Perkins is engaged in another argument with "mother," Fahey is entertaining a blonde he picked up at

a bar. After an evening of sexual play (which is reminiscent of the Perkins-Kathleen Turner romance in CRIMES OF PASSION), the barely dressed girl makes a telephone call in the phone booth outside the motel. Before she can make her connection, she is butchered by "mother." In the morning, the phone booth is sparkling clean. Later that evening, Perkins and Scarwid are having dinner in a fancy restaurant, drinking, dancing, and sharing an occasional romantic glance. Afterwards, in cabin No. 1, Perkins and Scarwid awkwardly embrace and exchange a kiss, neither of them having had any sexual experience. Rather than make love, they just lay together on the bed. The same evening, during the raucous homecoming party, "mother" claims another victim—this time it's a young woman who is killed while sitting on the toilet (a modern counterpart to the shower scene, though far inferior). When the police arrive the following morning to look for the girl (who has been carefully stuffed into the ice machine, buried under thousands of cubes), they find nothing suspicious. Maxwell, who is also on the scene, isn't convinced and presses the issue. The sheriff, Gillin, nearly finds the body when he pops a couple of blood-stained ice cubes into his mouth, while Perkins nervously looks on. Scarwid then provides Perkins with an alibi, claiming that she was with him all night. Maxwell talks Scarwid into coming with her, leaving a heartbroken Perkins behind. He retreats to his house, only to find that the mummified corpse of his mother is missing. A note tells him that she is waiting in cabin No. 12. As Perkins steps inside the barely lit cabin, he finds her propped up in front of the television watching a "Woody Woodpecker" cartoon. A demented Fahey, with thoughts of blackmail on his mind, has kidnaped "mother." He is less than reverent, even kissing the rotting corpse's cheek, referring to her as "momma." Not to be manipulated, Perkins pounds Fahey senseless with a guitar.

While discussing her vocation with a priest, Scarwid decides that she is meant to stay with Perkins and returns to the motel. Perkins' battle with Fahey, however, is not finished. As he prepares to sink Fahey's car and body in the swamp, Fahey sits up in the back seat. Not quite dead, he wrestles Perkins until both of them are submerged in the murky water. Perkins manages to escape to his house as Scarwid arrives. At the top of the staircase (the same one where Martin Balsam met his end in the original), Scarwid reaches out her hands to Perkins, apologizing for leaving him. Forever haunted by his past, Perkins hears "mother" cry out. Frightened, he accidentally pushes Scarwid backwards. She tumbles down the stairs and impales herself on a statue of Cupid—her neck pierced by the lover's arrow. Driven by angry rage, Perkins yells at "mother's" corpse. Meanwhile, Maxwell is poking around downstairs. She finds a shrine of candles surrounding the dead body of Scarwid, who lies peacefully on the couch. She is then met by Perkins, dressed in "mother's" wig and dress, a demented grin stretching across his face. Perkins talks in "mother's" voice, asking why Maxwell cannot leave "my poor son alone." As Maxwell tries to get away from Perkins, she explains that Mrs. Spool was really his aunt. Spool was in love with her sister's husband (Perkins' father), killed Mr. and Mrs. Bates in a jealous rage, and then kidnaped little Norman. Finally realizing that "mother" is the one who has been responsible for all his problems and, worse yet, is the one who took Scarwid away from him, Perkins attacks "mother's" corpse. As he stabs her, sawdust pours out onto the floor. He completely butchers the body, beheading it as "mother's" wretched voice trails off. The police arrive and cart the leering Perkins away. Handcuffed and locked in the back seat of a patrol car, Perkins declares that he is finally free . . . from "mother." He still has something to remember her by, however—her stiffened arm, which he discreetly pulls from under his coat.

Richard Franklin's 1983 sequel to PSYCHO was commendable because it revered Hitchcock. A devoted follower of the "master of suspense," Franklin employed Hitchcock's techniques adroitly. He knew just when to pull the strings of suspense, tension, and fear. Perkins is also blessed with the same ability, knowing just how to manipulate his audience's fears. Where PSYCHO III differs from PSYCHO II, however, is in Perkins' wicked, malicious sense of humor. Hitchcock has long been known for his black humor (THE TROUBLE WITH HARRY, FAMILY PLOT), an element which is missing from most of today's homages/rip-offs. With Perkins behind the camera as well as in front, the element of the comic macabre is in high gear. The scene of the sheriff eating bloodstained ice cubes while he is questioning Perkins about the missing girl is one of pure black-comic genius, and one Hitchcock would surely have found wonderful. Later, as Perkins must remove the body from the machine, he is met with another grim but humorous moment. The corpse has frozen and rigor mortis has set in, leaving Perkins no choice but to snap its arm in order to remove it. Early in the film, Perkins is at his kitchen table stuffing a bird (this *is* his hobby, after all) while munching on his lunch at the same time. When Scarwid accepts a ride from Fahey, there is a plastic Jesus statue on the dashboard which gets knocked over inadvertently while Scarwid is being seduced. Later, when Fahey has kidnaped "mother," Perkins goes mad because "Woody Woodpecker's" incessantly staccato laugh is blaring forth from the television, a laugh that Perkins associates with "mother" laughing at him. Perkins has packed his film with references to the original—all done in a tongue-in-cheek manner. Perkins is having some fun with PSYCHO III.

In addition PSYCHO III has some exceptional stylistic moments which show a solid directorial command. Perkins is not just some actor who is given a chance to direct. He has a style and it is unfortunate that it has taken this long to put him behind the camera. Like Orson Welles and Clint Eastwood, Perkins knows his own persona. He knows how to photograph and light himself for the proper effect. In keeping with his comic tone, Perkins is constantly leering like a loon—something of a parody of the original character. But to counter this, Perkins gives Norman Bates a love interest. For the first time in his life, he has someone other than "mother." We even get to see Norman hold a woman close and kiss her. No one would have ever imagined in 1960 that Norman Bates would fall in love; stranger yet, that somebody would fall in love with *Norman*. PSYCHO III is not a Hitchcock imitation, homage, or rip-off; it merely uses his characterizations and colors them with Perkins' style and personality. What is so exciting about PSYCHO III is that Perkins is not afraid to take chances with his style or his material. Risking the wrath of religious groups, Perkins has made Scarwid a nun who has fallen from grace. She thinks her life has been saved by the Virgin Mary, but the credit is actually due to Norman—a schizophrenic murderer. To equate the infamous Norman Bates with the Virgin Mary took some guts on Perkins' part. Jean-Luc Godard caught much more flak with his HAIL, MARY (1985) for far less risque religious views.

Unfortunately, PSYCHO III does have its faults. There are two gory murder scenes which are better suited to third-rate slasher films than to a picture of this caliber. While both of the murders could have remained disturbing if done well (the phone booth killing had the victim stepping on broken pieces of glass, while the toilet killing had the potential for a taboo-breaking, modern equivalent of the shower scene), they relied instead on gratuitous gore and spurting blood. Reportedly, Perkins was pressured into including such shots by Universal studio heads who felt kids today expected such gore in the movies. Although both PSYCHO sequels were well done, this will, it's hoped, be the last of Norman Bates (at least for another 26 years, until he is as old as his mother). Perkins might even get the acclaim due him, should he tackle a different project. PSYCHO II did mediocre

business, and PSYCHO III did even worse. If Universal fears a fourth PSYCHO would be an even greater bust, then we can be assured of not seeing Norman for a while. Songs include "Catherine Mary" (Carter Burwell, Steve Bray, Stanton-Miranda, performed by Stanton-Miranda), "Dirty Street" (Burwell, Bray, performed by Bray, Stanton-Miranda), "Scream Of Love" (Burwell, Bray, David Sanborn).

p, Hilton A. Green; d, Anthony Perkins; w, Charles Edward Pogue (based on the characters created by Robert Bloch); ph, Bruce Surtees; m, Carter Burwell; ed, David Blewitt; prod d, Henry Bumstead; set d, Mickey S. Michaels; cos, Peter V. Saldutti, Marla Denise Schlom; spec eff, Karl G. Miller, Louis R. Cooper, Dan Lester, Syd Dutton, Bill Taylor; m/l, Carter Burwell, Steve Bray, Stanton-Miranda, David Sanborn; makeup, Mark Reedall, Michael Westmore; stunts, Bob Yerkes.

Horror/Comedy   **Cas.**   **(PR:O MPAA:R)**

PULSEBEAT*   (1986, Span.) 92m Calepas International c

Daniel Greene *(Roger)*, Lee Taylor Allan *(Annie)*, Bob Small *(Alvin)*, Alice Moore *(The Bat)*, Helga Line *(Marlene)*, Alex Intriago *(Adrian)*, Carole James *(Cyndi)*, Miguel De Grandy *(Vincent)*, Earleen Carey *(Leyna)*, Peter Lupus *(Greg Adonis)*.

Anything but invigorating, this partially dubbed snorer tells the story of two rival health clubs. The owner of the Rejuvenarium, Spanish actress Line, is playing rough with the owner of Roger's Gym, Greene, by luring away all of his top aerobics instructors. And boy does that make him mad! Then she plants a spy, Intriago, in his gym, which really gets Greene's dander up. Now if that's not enough to keep audiences glued to their seats, the slam-bang "Aerobithon" finale—groups of people performing competitive exercises—should do the trick. To top it all off, Line is really Greene's long-missing mother. And you thought PERFECT was a dog. The only thing of interest is the appearance of Peter Lupus as Greg Adonis. Lupus, you may remember, played strongman Willy Armitage in television's "Mission: Impossible" and appeared in the short-lived series "Police Squad!," a summer replacement series from the producers of AIRPLANE.

p, Jose Frade; d, Marice Tobias; w, Steven Siebert; ph, George Herrero; m, Walter Murphy; ed, Matt Cope; art d, Alfonso L. Barajas; cos, Frank Carretti; ch, Bill Williams.

Drama   **Cas.**   **(PR:O MPAA:NR)**

Q

QINGCHUN JI†

(1986, China) 95m China Film/Peking Youth Studio c
(Trans: Sacrifice of Youth)

Li Fengxu, Feng Yuanzheng, Song Tao, Guo Jianguo, Yu Da.

QINGCHUN JI is the second feature from Luanxin, a Chinese woman director. It is set during the chaos of the Cultural Revolution and tells the story of Fengxu, a 17-year-old girl who is deported from Peking for "re-education" in the country. She is placed on a farm run by an old man and his aged mother. There she must accustom herself to country ways. She finds that sexual attitudes of the farmers, especially the girls her age, are far more liberal than those in the city. Try as she may, Fengxu is never really accepted by the locals, who have built a cultural wall between themselves and Peking. She eventually leaves the country, but not without learning something about the community and about herself. QINGCHUN JI is one of a number of recent Chinese films that explore and criticize, not only the Cultural Revolution, but the treatment minorities have received in China.

d, Zhang Luanxin; w, Zhang Luanxin (based on the novel *You Yige Meilide Difang (There Was That Beautiful Place)* by Zhang Manling); ph, Mu Deyuan, Deng Wei; m, Liu Suola, Qu Xiasong; ed, Zhao Qihua; art d, Li Yongxin, Wang Yanjin.

Drama   **(PR:A-C MPAA:NR)**

QINGCHUN NUCHAO†

(1986, Hong Kong) Golden Harvest c (Trans: Grow Up in Anger)

Chen Yalun, Huang Yaohui.

d&w, Cai Jiguang

QUE ME MATEN DE UNA VEZ†

(1986, Mex.) 100m Peliculas Mexicanas/ Circo, Maroma y Teatro c (Trans: Let Them Kill Me Once And For All)

Jose Angel Espinosa [Ferrosquilla] *(Blind Matias)*, Sonia Linar *(Desiree)*, Humberto Cabanas *(Julio)*, Juan Antonio Llanes *(El Secretitos)*, Ruben Calderon *(Dr. Fausto)*, Luis Caso *(Alberto)*, Mar Castro *(Beatriz)*.

A collection of six allegories about vanity, all directed by Blancarte and connected by the film's guitar-playing storyteller, Espinosa. The more memorable episodes include a tale about a ghost who is fighting in the Mexican Revolution and a troubadour who has fallen hopelessly in love with his donkey.

p, Sonia Linar; d, Oscar Blancarte; w, Oscar Blancarte, Oscar Torrero; ph, Oscar Torrero Salcido; m, Joaquin Lopez Chapman; ed, Sigfrido Garcia Munoz, Sigfrido Garcia, Jr.

Drama   **(PR:NR MPAA:NR)**

QUEEN CITY ROCKERS†

(1986, New Zealand) 90m Challenge Film Corp. c

Matthew Hunter *(Ska)*, Mark Pilisi, Peter Bland, Kim Willoughby, Rebecca Saunders, Ricky Bribiesca, Pevise Viafale.

Rock 'n' roll and violence abound in this teenage drama about Hunter, a young street punk, who has become tired of his life on the edge. Within a couple of days, he falls in love with a rich society girl, sees his best friend murdered, and is nearly killed himself. When Hunter finds that his sister is working for a sleazy local mob boss, the enemy of the teenagers' gang, violence breaks out. Hunter and his friends launch an assault on the mobster's club. Later, at a rock concert sponsored by the mobster, an all-out war erupts as the entire young audience takes revenge on the mob boss. Hunter and his pals finally clear out for a better life, away from the decay and stench of the violence-stained neighborhood.

p, Larry Parr; d, Bruce Morrison; w, Bill Baer; ph, Kevin Hayard; m, Dave McArtney.

Action   **(PR:O MPAA:NR)**

QUI A TIRE SUR NOS HISTOIRES D'AMOUR?†

(1986, Can.) 91m J.A. La Maison Des Quatres–Telefilm Canada–Societe Generale du Cinema du Quebec/J.A. LaPointe c (Trans: A Question Of Loving)

Monique Mercure *(Madeline)*, Guylaine Normandine *(Renee)*, August Schellenberg *(Fabien)*, Claude Gauthier *(Michel)*.

After a middle-aged woman's daughter returns home from college for the summer, mother and daughter discover they have certain similarities, as well as a number of differences. In an effort to compete with her daughter, the mother engages in a variety of demanding activities, including the search for a satisfying lover.

d&w, Louise Carre; ph, Jean Charles Tremblay, Pierre Duceppe, Christiane Guernon, Michel Caron; m, Marc O'Farrell; ed, Louise Cote, Teresa De Luca; set d, Vianney Gauthier, Jean Kazemirchuk, Pierre Gauthier.

Drama   **(PR:NR MPAA:NR)**

QUI TROP EMBRASSE†

(1986, Fr.) 84m Les Films de l'Atalante c

Anne Wiazemsky, Tonie Marshall, Andrzej Seweryn, Michel Gautier.

Modern-day promiscuity is the subject of this low-budget feature starring Wiazemsky, who made a name for herself in Jean-Luc Godard's 1967 film WEEKEND. The film is set in Paris. It follows two men and two women as they jump from bed to bed, jealous of their mates' lovers but still taking on lovers of their own.

p, Gerard Vaugeois; d, Jacques Davila; w, Jacques Davila, Michel Gautier; ph, Jean-Marie Dreujou; m, Bruno Coulais; ed, Paul Vecchiali.

Drama   **(PR:O MPAA:NR)**

QUICKSILVER*

(1986) 101m IndieProd/COL c

Kevin Bacon *(Jack Casey)*, Jami Gertz, *(Terri)*, Paul Rodriguez *(Hector Rodriguez)*, Rudy Ramos *(Gypsy)*, Andrew Smith *(Gabe Kaplan)*, Gerald S. O'Laughlin *(Mr. Casey)*, Larry Fishburne *(Voodoo)*, Louis Anderson *(Tiny)*, Charles McCaughan *(Airborne)*, David Harris *(Apache)*, Whitney Kershaw *(Rand)*, Joshua Shelley *(Shorty)*, Georgann Johnson *(Mrs. Casey)*, Nelson Vails *(Messenger in Maroon Beret)*, Lou Dinos *(Cha Cha)*, Michael Kaye *(Dedicated)*, Joel Weiss *(Educated)*, Leila Kane *(Maria Rodriguez)*, Daniel Leegant *(Chip)*, John Walter Davis *(Ax)*, Gregory Wagrowski *(Rolf)*, Frank D'Annibale *(Grocery Store Owner)*, Jimmy Romano *(Spider)*, Patricia Allison *(Nurse)*, Abel Fernandez *(Guyamo)*, Patricia West-Del Ruth *(Secretary Ad Agency)*, Joe Leahy, Michael Fox *(Brokers at Lunch)*, Richard Warlock *(Cab Driver)*, Jacque Lynn Colton *(Waitress)*, Joseph Hieu, Michael Paul Chan *(Asian Gang Members)*, Joseph Peck *(Counterman)*, George Moffatt *(Bum)*, Robert Cotney *(Waiter)*, Valerie McIntosh, Shirley Walker *(Hookers)*, Launa Morosan *(Bar Flirt)*, Vanessa Newman *(Nector's Niece)*, Michael O'Rourke *(Public Trader)*, Irwin Schier *(Broker)*, Martin Aparijo, Woody Itson, Franz Krotochvil *(Bicycle Messengers)*, William J. Napoli, John E. Cappiello, Alan J. Sondag, Jim Henry, Reid Steiner *(Options Traders)*.

QUICKSILVER isn't a movie. It's actually a series of rock videos occasionally willing to tolerate a slight dalliance into story progression. The premise is wholly

fabricated, the style pure MTV, and the characters all pressed from Hollywood cliche cutters. Bacon, a successful stock trader with a bad mustache, manages in the course of a few hours to lose a fortune on the market. Having lost both his company's money, and his parents' savings, Bacon decides to shave the fuzz from his lip, drop out of Yuppiedom, and take up a working class trade. He gets a job working with the Quicksilver Messenger Service, a bicycle courier outfit that delivers messages, packages, and other items for businesses around the city. The location is never identified, though it looks like San Francisco. Apparently there's only one qualification to work for Quicksilver. You have to be a "type." Fishburne is the Angry Black Man, Rodriguez is the Wants-to-Make-Good-in-America Mexican, and Gertz is the Tough-But-Naive-Street-Hardened Girl With a Secret. Bacon fits well into their world as the Good-Guy-Who-Learns-About-Life-and-the-Nobility-of-the-Lower-Class. Of course, all is not sunshine and light for Ramos, a nefarious drug dealer, who occasionally uses Quicksilver messengers to run dope for him. Fishburne gets caught up in Ramos' dirty dealings and ends up getting killed. Hoping to see better things for himself, Rodriguez dreams of opening his own hot dog stand. With Bacon's help, he fills out a bank loan application, but Rodriguez is turned down after showing up to his interview wearing a powder blue tuxedo. Eventually, Bacon agrees to return to the stock exchange and invest Rodriguez' savings on the floor. While Bacon's trying to make his pal some cash, Rodriguez is at the hospital where his wife is having a baby. Meanwhile, Ramos is putting the pressure on Gertz, whom he's been using to run dope. She wants out, but Ramos won't release her. Bacon, returning from his not-too-surprising success on the trading floor, engages Ramos in a bicycle versus automobile chase. The plucky peddler manages to fool Ramos while driving through a multi-tiered structure, and the villain hurtles to his death when his car runs through a barricade. Bacon returns to the stock market with a New Understanding of Mankind, and treats Gertz (who now plans on becoming a paramedic) to a meal at Rodriguez's new hot dog stand.

There are a number of problems with QUICKSILVER, like the patronizing attitudes it holds towards its working class characters. Bacon is presented as a

good guy who just needs to get his head together following his terrific monetary loss. After he rubs elbows with Mexicans, blacks, and street kids, everything is hunky-dory. Bacon can reestablish himself in the Yuppie world, a better man for having "experienced" what life is like on the other side. This condescending viewpoint, colors the film's utterly routine point of view. It's another watered-down reworking of the ROCKY victory formula, with bicycles and the stock exchange replacing the boxing ring. Bacon is not much more than passable in a role that only requires him to look handsome and occasionally furrow his brow. That a stock trader could turn overnight into an expert cycler is taken for granted. In reality, Bacon spent *four months* training with Nelson Vails, a silver medalist in sprint cycling at the 1984 Olympics, who also served as the film's technical consultant. Most of the other actors merely go through the motions. Only Rodriguez gives his part any life, though it's a wasted effort on a stereotyped character. But then, QUICKSILVER isn't about human conflict, it's about making money. Producer Melnick had worked with Bacon on his previous film, FOOTLOOSE, a 1984 feature about a young man who brings rock 'n' roll to an uptight small town. The soundtrack sold an impressive 8 million albums, and undoubtedly Melnick thought he could do the same with QUICKSILVER. Donnelly, a first-time director working from his own screenplay, employs a number of rock video techniques within his film, including fast cutting, fancy camera angles, and carefully staged dance numbers. In the course of the film, we are treated to a gang of cyclers happily performing stunts while music blares on the soundtrack. We also get three finely cut chase sequences, and, in one of the film's silliest scenes, a pas de deux between dancer and bicycle. Bacon's girl friend Kershaw, who conveniently pops up whenever a little friction is needed, is a ballet dancer. While she practices to sensitive music, Bacon glides about their loft apartment on his bike, and picks Kershaw up on the handlebars. The two perform a variety of difficult moves, all of which are supposed to be totally spontaneous. Even before QUICKSILVER's theatrical release, the film spawned two rock videos ("Quicksilver Lightning" [Giorgio Moroder, Dean Pitchford, performed by Roger Daltry] and "One Sunny Day/Dueling Bikes from Quicksilver" [Ray Parker, Jr., performed by Ray Parker, Jr., Helen Terry]), which were telecast on MTV. In addition, Bacon served as an "MTV guest veejay" to promote the film. The commercial intent was blatant but the public wasn't buying. QUICKSILVER was a box-office washout, and the soundtrack album also did poorly. The film's other songs: "Love Song from QUICKSILVER (Through the Night)" (John Parr, Geoff Lyth, performed by John Parr, Marilyn Martin), "Shortcut to Somewhere" (Tony Banks, Fish, performed Tony Banks, Fish), "Nothing at All" (Peter Frampton, performed by Peter Frampton), "Casual Thing" (Allee Willis, Peter R. Melnick, Greg Mathieson, performed by Fiona), "The Motown Song" (Larry John McNally, performed by Larry John McNally), "Suite Streets from QUICKSILVER (Opening Title Sequence)" (Thomas Newman), "Reelin' and Rockin' " (Roy Milton, Dootsie Williams, performed by Roy Milton), "Mama (He Treats Your Daughter Mean)" (Johnny Wallace, Herbert J. Lance, Charles Singleton, performed by Ruth Brown).

p, Michael Rachmil, Daniel Melnick; d&w, Tom Donnelly; ph, Thomas Del Ruth (Metrocolor); m, Tony Banks; ed, Tom Rolf; prod d, Charles Rosen; md, Becky Mancuso; art d, James Shanahan; set d, Marvin March; cos, Betsy Cox; spec eff, Dennis Dion; ch, Grover Dale; m/l, Giorgio Moroder, Dean Pitchford, John Parr, Geoff Lyth, Bill Wolfer, Dean Pitchford, Tony Banks, Fish, Peter Frampton, Allee Willis, Peter R. Melnick, Greg Mathieson, Larry John McNally, Thomas Newman, Roy Milton, Dootsie Williams, Johnny Wallace, Herbert J. Lance, Charles Singleton; makeup, Christina Smith; stunts, Greg Walker.

Drama   Cas.   (PR:A-C MPAA:PG)

QUIET COOL**½   (1986) 80m Robert Shaye/New Line Cinema c

James Remar *(Joe Dillon)*, Adam Coleman Howard *(Joshua Greer)*, Daphne Ashbrook *(Katy Greer)*, Jared Martin *(Mike Prior)*, Nick Cassavetes *(Valence)*, Fran Ryan *(Ma)*.

In the lush forests of northern California, marijuana planters control an entire community through a combination of money and terror. Their fields are hidden under camouflage netting and protected by booby traps. As the film opens, a surveyor leads the corrupt sheriff Martin to the site of one patch, but when they get there they find Cassavetes and three other men waiting. The sheriff tells the hapless surveyor that no one likes a snitch, and the man is killed. The murder is

witnessed by Howard, the teenage son of a pair of former hippies who live in the woods. He runs back to tell his parents, but the killers are after him. They kill his mother and father, then toss Howard off a cliff. Back in town, Ashbrook, Howard's aunt, is worried over the disappearance of her brother and his wife and son, so she calls New York cop Remar, her former lover. He immediately flies out and starts investigating, ignoring Martin's warnings. During a foray into the hills, Remar narrowly escapes capture after becoming trapped in a razor blade-studded net, but he is saved by Howard. The boy survived being thrown off a cliff and is now engaged in a private battle against the growers. They team up and escape the bad guys through Remar's fancy motorcycle riding. Later, they go to the cabin where Howard had lived with his parents, where Ashbrook is waiting for them. Unfortunately, Cassavetes and his men are also waiting, and in the ensuing gunfight the house is set afire and Ashbrook killed. Remar and Howard escape into a cellar and sit out the fire, then prepare for battle. They infiltrate the growers' main camp. Remar places dynamite under the shack where Cassavetes plays cards with some of the other villains. At the same time, Howard runs a heavy rope through the bunkhouse where most of the men sleep and attaches one end to a thick log and the other to a jeep. The dynamite charge doesn't go off, so Remar tosses a stick in by hand, while Howard starts up the jeep and wipes out the bunkhouse. Then the two heroes kill everyone but Cassavetes, who manages to escape. Back in town, the two walk down the street like a pair of Wild West gunfighters until they face Cassavetes and Martin. A minute later both villains are dead, Martin from a bullet from Remar, and Cassavetes impaled on a grappling hook from Howard. Next Remar goes for a showdown with Ryan, the rumored chief of the whole operation, who has been passing herself off as the kindly Ma who runs the local diner and saloon. She gets the drop on Remar and is about to shoot him but Howard shoots her first.

Marijuana growers have actually taken over some remote parts of the U.S., an amazing and frightening situation, and it is surprising that no one had made a film about the topic before—the subject seems a natural for exploitation. Almost as surprising is that QUIET COOL is as good as it is. Remar, long known as one of the screen's best villains, makes the transition to hero with aplomb. He should be seeing more of these roles in the future. Howard is also mildly impressive in a role that easily could have become a ludicrous "jungle boy" type. Ashbrook has little to do but get killed. On the villainous side, Cassavetes stands out as a scary murderer (he shoves a lit joint into a lackey's ear for getting high on the job). He is one of a trio of color-coded killers, he with black hair, another with white hair, and a third with red hair. Well cut and superbly photographed, the film still did only mediocre business in a limited release, emerging on cassette just a few months after release.

p, Robert Shaye, Gerald T. Olson; d, Clay Borris; w, Clay Borris, Susan Vercellino; ph, Jacques Haitkin (DeLuxe Color); m, Jay Ferguson; ed, Bob Brady.

Action/Crime   Cas   (PR:O MPAA:R)

QUILOMBO***   (1986, Braz.) 114m CDK/New Yorker Films c

Antonio Pompeo *(Zumbi)*, Zeze Motta *(Dandara)*, Toni Tornado *(Ganga Zumba)*, Vera Fischer *(Ana de Ferro)*, Antonio Pitanga *(Acaiuba)*, Maurico do Valle *(Domingos Jorge Velho)*, Daniel Filho *(Carrilho)*, Joao Nogueira *(Rufino)*, Jorge Coutinho *(Sale)*, Grande Otelo *(Baba)*, Jofre Soares *(Caninde)*.

A spectacular, brilliantly colored historical epic that explores the beginnings of Quilombo de Palmares, the Brazilian slave nation in the mid-1600s. Director Diegues described the nation as "the first democratic society that we know of in the Western hemisphere." The picture begins as the slaves revolt and violently murder their Portuguese owners. Taking to the forests of northeastern Brazil, the slaves form a nation, free from the oppression of slave owners. They are soon joined by other oppressed peoples such as Jews and poor white farmers. A government is created and a leader elected—Ganga Zumba, played by Tornado. The Portuguese, however, retaliate and attempt to conquer the nation. Battles follow, and each time the well-equipped Portuguese are defeated by the Palmares' jungle traps and ambushes. While Tornado speaks of negotiations with the Portuguese, his godson Pompeo stirs up more radical emotions in the people, arguing that they must fight for their freedom. Eventually, the Portuguese defeat the rebels and many of the Palmares are returned to slavery. The film informs us, however, that factions of the Palmares took to the forests and continued to live for hundreds of years after their nation was destroyed.

Diegues previously scored on American art-house screens with BYE BYE BRA-ZIL and XICA. Here, he manages to mix historical recreation with the myth and folklore of the Palmares that has been handed down through the centuries. Exquisitely photographed and lavishly produced, QUILOMBO is a fine example of the newly revitalized Brazilian film industry—one that has produced, over the last few years, such films as DONA FLOR AND HER TWO HUSBANDS, PIXOTE, GABRIELA, and KISS OF THE SPIDER WOMAN. QUILOMBO was one of Brazil's most expensively budgeted films. Designer and costumer Ripper paid a great deal of attention to authentic sets, weapons, and clothing to give the period the proper atmosphere. The film has a great deal of action, culminating with some intense battle sequences, but it often falls flat and seems more concerned with recreating the period than in following through on its storyline. More than examining a historic period, QUILOMBO, like Diegues' other films, comments on the present state of Brazil as well as the nation's possible future. Released in Brazil in 1984, though it didn't come to the United States until this year. (In Portuguese; English subtitles.)

p, Augusto Arraes; d&w, Carlos Diegues; ph, Lauro Escorel Filho; ed, Mair Tavares; m/l, Gilberto Gil, Walid Salomao.

Historical   (PR:O MPAA:NR)

R

RAD* (1986) 91m Taliafilm II/Tri-Star c

Bill Allen *(Cru)*, Lori Laughlin *(Christian)*, Talia Shire *(Mrs. Jones)*, Ray Walston *(Burton Timmer)*, Alfie Wise *(Eliott Dole)*, Jack Weston *(Duke Best)*, Bart Conner *(Bart Taylor)*, Marta Kober *(Becky)*, Jamie Clarke *(Luke)*, Laura Jacoby *(Wesley Jones)*, H.B. Haggerty *(Sgt. Smith)*, Chad Hayes *(Rex Reynolds)*, Carey Hayes *(Rod Reynolds)*, Kellie McQuiggin *(Foxy)*, Beverly Hendry *(Tiger)*.

When Olympic gymnasts Kurt Thomas and Mitch Gaylord made their acting debuts, at least they had the good sense to choose projects that made efficient use

of their medal-winning athletic skills (GYMKATA and AMERICAN ANTHEM, respectively). However, their teammate Bart Conner apparently is not blessed with the same sort of smarts (or agent). In RAD he takes the nondescript role of a BMX bike champion (for the uninitiated, BMX bicycles are those small, rugged vehicles that 12-year-olds who hang out in front of the 7-11 always do tricks on). What's more, the former national hero assumes the role of movie bad guy! A small town, in an effort to gain publicity and raise money, decides to build a BMX racing course, dubbed "Hell Track." Allen is a local kid who loves BMX riding. Not realizing the officials behind the competition are more corrupt than the Nixon administration, Allen enters try-outs for the race convinced he has a chance to beat Connor, the factory sponsored champ. Allen's mother Shire doesn't like the idea, preferring her son prepare for his college entrance exams. Of course Allen does want to go to college, but as he confides to Laughlin, another factory-sponsored rider (and handy love interest), "those professionals are so *awesome*!" Shire learns that Allen has disobeyed her after seeing him on a television broadcast of the qualifying races. Although angry, Shire allows Allen to go on to the main competition after he makes a promise to eventually attend college. In the meantime, BMX big shot Weston tries everything he can to discourage Allen. The whole town rallies behind Allen, including giving him the financial sponsorship he needs to compete in the big race. When the big day arrives, Connor arranges for two teammates to help fix things in his favor but Allen's pluck and determination challenge Connor's unethical demeanor. The bike champ suddenly changes face, and offers a fair contest to the newcomer. Allen wins (surprised?), learning a few things about himself while picking up a measly $100,000. Connor has also been taught an important lesson, and in clear defiance of his bosses, joins up with Allen in the end.

Looking for an exciting film about a committed bicyclist? Then check out PEE-WEE'S BIG ADVENTURE. RAD (a term short for "radical," which is a new way of saying hunky-dory) is a boring, inconsequential bit of tripe that never drums up any of its promised excitement. The film really contains nothing more than a bunch of good looking bike stunts filled out by a few stock characters and plot developments used countless of times in other sports films. If the law of diminishing returns ever applied to a film director, then undoubtedly RAD's guiding force, Hal Needham, would be an unsurpassed applicant. The brains behind such schlock as THE VILLAIN, CANNONBALL RUN (both dismal installments), and STROKER ACE hits a new low with this barely released, filmed-in-Canada project. To his credit, RAD isn't nearly as obnoxious as Needham's previous work but it's still hard to get excited over a bunch of kids bouncing their bikes on one tire. The film was made through the auspices of Shire's own production company, proving she can find a job even when Sylvester Stallone isn't doing a ROCKY picture. The mixed cast of fresh-faced kids and seasoned veterans proceed through the banal events with some competence. Connor is absolutely terrible. His function is merely to lend some bankable name

value to the project. Someone else obviously is doing Connor's BMX riding. His acting is so bad its nearly entertaining. You can practically hear the gold medalist saying "what's my motivation, Mr. Needham?" The best thing about the film is the opening credits, created by John Schwartzman. Bikes and riders fly slow-motion through a brilliantly sunlit sky, seemingly in defiance of gravity. In its own way, this sequence holds an eerie resemblance to Leni Riefenstahl's documentary of the 1936 Berlin Olympics, OLYMPIA. If worse comes to worse, and you actually have to sit through RAD, try counting all the commercial endorsements. There are enough to keep any sharp-eyed viewer awake for the film's 91-minute running time. Songs include: "Break the Ice" (S. Shifrin, B. Marlette, performed by John Farnham), "Love Theme from RAD" (J. Di Pasquale, O. Brayfield, performed by John Farnham), "Thunder in Your Heart" (G. Sklerov, L. Macaluso, performed by John Farnham), "Baby Come Back" (Eddy Grant, performed by Jimmy Haddock), "Send Me an Angel" (D. Steery, R. Zatoski, performed by Real Life), "Riverside" (J. Kaney, S. Marshall, performed by the Beat Farmers), "Music You Can Dance To" (Ron Mael, Russell Mael, performed by Sparks), "Wind Me Up" (L. Chase, D. Currier, performed by 3 Speed), "Get Strange" (M. Kemmler, M. Loehr, performed by Hubert Kah), "Caught in the Crossfire" (John Brennan, Tom Griffith, performed by The Charm Kings).

p, Robert L. Levy, Sam Bernard; d, Hal Needham; w, Bernard, Geoffrey Edwards; ph, Richard Leiterman (Technicolor); m, James Di Pasquale; ed, Carl Kress; art d, Shirley Inget; set d, Cindy Gordon, Clay Weiler, Grant S. Goodman; cos, Jerry Allen; m/l, S. Shifrin, B. Marlette, J. DiPasquale, O. Brayfield, G. Sklerov, L. Macaluso, Eddy Grant, D. Steery, R. Zatoski, J. Kaney, S. Marshall, Ron Mael, Russell Mael, L. Chase, D. Currier, M. Kemmler, M. Loehr, John Brennan, Tom Griffith.

Sports/Action **Cas.** **(PR:A-C MPAA:PG)**

RADIOACTIVE DREAMS*½ (1986) 95m ITM/De Laurentiis Entertainment Group c

John Stockwell *(Phillip)*, Michael Dudikoff *(Marlowe)*, Lisa Blount *(Miles)*, George Kennedy *(Spade Chandler)*, Don Murray *(Dash Hammer)*, Michele Little *(Rusty Mars)*, Norbert Weisser *(Sternwood)*, Paul Keller Galan *(Chester)*, Demian Slade *(Harold)*, Chris Andew *(Brick Bardo)*, Hilary Shapiro *(Biker Leader)*, Glory Fiormonti *(2nd Biker)*, Sue Saad *(Punk District Singer)*, Kimberly McKillip *(Sadie, Hippie Chick)*, Mark Brown *(Greaser)*, Nathan Stein *(Corky the Surf Mutant)*, Chris Desjardins *(Punk Singer)*, Johnny B. Frank *(New Wave Singer)*, Madelynn Von Ritz *(Hippie Club Singer)*, Eve Muller *(Punk Henchwoman/Hippie Chick)*, Damon Webb *(Marlowe at Age 3)*, Garette Ratliff *(Phillip at Age 4)*, Joan Selesnow *(Mother)*, James Welch *(Father)*, Terry McGovern *(Micky)*, Reni Santoni *("Red" Hairstylist/Voice of Adult Harold)*, Archie Hahn *(Voice of Adult Chester)*.

A fitfully interesting post-nuclear comedy which tries to do too much and, therefore, accomplishes little. The year is 1996. Just before the world destroys itself in an all-out nuclear war, fathers Murray and Kennedy lock their young sons in a fallout shelter. After the initial destruction, the adults desert the boys, leaving them with a huge store of food, clothes from the 1940s, and a large supply of detective novels written by Dashiel Hammett and Raymond Chandler. By 2010, the boys, Stockwell and Dudikoff, have grown into young adults whose lingo, fashion sense, and worldview have been developed entirely from detective novels. Stockwell calls himself "Phillip," while Dudikoff calls himself "Marlowe." After years of living in the bomb shelter, the two finally find their way out. Dressed in their best 1940s suits and driving a vintage car, the boys set out for adventure, with Stockwell providing the standard *film noir* narration. Soon they pick up Blount, a tough blonde on the run named "Miles Archer." Dudikoff, the dumber member of the duo, immediately falls in love with Blount, but all she wants is her gun, and it's a .38 pistol. Blount succeeds in stealing the gun and deserting the boys, but doesn't realize that in doing so she's lost a pair of very important keys. The boys soon learn that the keys belong to the launch controls of the only remaining MX missile on Earth. The holder of the keys can rule the post-nuclear world.

From here the film becomes one long chase with every power-hungry fringe group vying for possession of the keys. Stockwell and Dudikoff find themselves fighting off groups of renegades from every popular American teen milieu of the 20th Century. The post-nuclear world is made up of red-haired bikers (whose affiliations are vague), 1950s greasers, 1960s "surf mutants" and homicidal hippies, two hilariously foul-mouthed little boys with greasy hair and John Travolta SATURDAY NIGHT FEVER suits known as the "Disco Mutants," and the obligatory punkers and New Wavers (representing the 1970s and 80s). The film builds to a huge, very confusingly choreographed showdown between the leaders of all the various groups in a abandoned warehouse. Thrown in for good measure are Stockwell's and Dudikoff's fathers, Murray and Kennedy (who have been posing as rifle-toting creatures with faces like lizards), and they, too, are after the keys. Eventually all the groups kill one another off, leaving Stockwell and Dudikoff to do a bizarre soft-shoe dance number at the close.

Filmed in 1984, but unreleased until De Laurentiis added it to its distribution schedule in 1986, RADIOACTIVE DREAMS is a sprawling comic-book style movie that really falls flat. While some scenes are memorable and directed with flair by Pyun, the film is haphazardly paced, sketchily developed, confusing, and looks too much like a hybrid of BLADE RUNNER and THE ROAD WARRIOR. The last half of the film is nothing more than a lengthy rock video set to a dozen lame tunes that grate on the nerves. The black humor is rarely biting, insightful, or in fact, remotely funny, and Pyun's running gag of naming nearly every character after a Hammett or Chandler character becomes pointless and annoying very quickly. Kennedy and Murray are mere walk-ons, Blount's talents are wasted, and Dudikoff, as the dunce, is almost insufferable. Only Stockwell comes across as somewhat likable, but the odds are stacked against him. Director Pyun, a Hawaiian filmmaker who studied under Japanese director Akira Kurosawa with Toshiro Mifune's sponsorship, apparently learned little from the master.

Songs include: "Nightmare" (Michael McCarty, Jill Jaxx, Judith Nee, performed by Jaxx), "Daddy's Gonna Boogie Tonight" (Pete Robinson, Cathy Wilmore, performed by Robinson), "Radioactive Dreams" (James Saad, Tony Riparetti, Steve Le Gassick, performed by Sue Saad), "She'll Burn You" (Gary Pickus), "All Talk" (performed by Lynn Carey), "Young Thing" (Robinson, Wilmore, performed by Cherri Delight), "Tickin' of the Clock" (performed by The Monte Carlos), "Psychedelic Man" (Steve Longo, Rose Wampier, performed by Shari Saba), "Eat You Alive" (Pam Reswick, Steve Wertel, performed by Lisa Lee), "Guilty Pleasures" (James Saad, Riparetti, performed by Sue Saad), "Turn Away" (James Saad, Riparetti, Le Gassick, performed by Mary Ellen Quinn), "She's a Fire" (James Saad, Riparetti, Le Gassick, performed by Sue Saad), "Zim Bim Zowie" (Pickus, Allan Roy Scott, performed by Darryl Phinessee).

p, Thomas Karnowski, Moctesuma Esparza; d&w, Albert Pyun; ph, Charles Minsky (Deluxe Color); m, Pete Robinson; ed, Dennis O'Connor; prod d, Chester Kaczenski; set d, Bob Ziembicki; cos, Christine Boyar; spec eff, R.J. Hohman; ch, Michelle Simmons; m/l, James Saad, Tony Riparetti, Steve Le Gassick, Sue Saad, Gary Pickus, Michael McCarty, Jill Jaxx, Judith Nee, Lynn Carey, The Monte Carlos; makeup, Greg Cannom, Ve Neill.

Science Fiction/Comedy   Cas.   **(PR:O MPAA:R)**

RAFAGA DE PLOMO†   (1986, Mex.) 87m Casablanca–Televicine–Videocine c (Trans: Burst of Lead)

Fernando Almada *(Fernando Trevino)*, Mario Almada *(Mateo Trevino)*, Jorge Reynosa *(Tony Snake)*, Javier Garcla *(Rene)*, Hilda Aguirre *(Diana)*, Marta Elena Cervantes *(Elsa)*, Eleazar Garcia, Jr., Carlos Cardan, Adelberto Arvizu, Ricardo Noriega, Gabriela de Leon, Jorge Guerra.

In conflict with the local sheriff Garcia over the affections of Garcia's wife and daughter, hero Almada (Mario, that is) finds himself framed and arrested for slaughtering all the people in a saloon. His brother Fernando helps him break out and the two arm themselves to get even with Garcia and his boss, local drug czar Reynosa, who lives in a house full of snakes.

p, Eduardo Galindo; d, Pedro Galindo, 3rd; w, Pedro Galindo, Carlos Valdemar; ph, Miguel Arana; m, Ricardo Carrion; ed, Carlos Savage.

Crime/Action   **(PR:C-O MPAA:NR)**

RAGE†   (1986, It./Span.) 91m Tiber International–Arco/Gel International c

Conrad Nichols *(Rage)*, Stelio Candelli, Werner Pochat, Taida Urruzola, Chris Huerta.

Another post-apocalyptic fantasy, this time with WW II vintage vehicles surviving instead of the usual souped-up 1960s models that frequent these films. A small group of survivors receive a radio signal from Alpha Base, the site of uranium reserves and much technical data. Nichols, along with a sidekick and a skimpily clad girl, set out to find Alpha Base after taking a map from a local bad guy cleverly named "Slash" because of the scar on his face. They have to avoid his minions until they find Alpha Base, where the only thing of use is a Bible they take home to rebuild civilization with. A sequel to RUSH, this film was shot in 1984 and actually got a theatrical release.

p, Paolo Ferrara; d, Anthony Richmond [Tonino Ricci]; w, Jaime Comas Gil, Eugenio Benito; ph, Gianni Bergamini (Luciano Vittori Color); m, Stelvio Cipriani; ed, Vincenzo Tomassi; set d, Javier Fernandez; stunts, Roland Zamperla.

Science Fiction   **(PR:O MPAA:NR)**

RAGING VENDETTA†   (1986, Phil.) Cinex Films–F. Puzon Film Enterprises c

Rudy Fernandez, Mario Montenegro, Charlie Davao, Dexter Doria, Laarni Enriquez.

A young man finds his mother having sex with a notorious local gangster, and in the ensuing struggle she dies. The young man refuses to tell his policeman father the truth, so he is locked up for the killing, but he escapes with the help of another gangster, who takes him to the island headquarters of the drug-running operation. There, after a bloody gun battle, the hero dies after learning that his real father was really the gangster all along.

d, Efren C. Pinon; w, Carlo J. Caparas; ph, Jun Rasca; m, Ernani Cuenco.

Action/Crime   **(PR:C-O MPAA:NR)**

RAI†   (1986, Alg.) 94m ENAPROC c

Abdelkader Tadjer *(Rachid)*, Salima *(Mother)*, Hamid Lourari *(Friend)*.

A minor Algerian criminal gets out of jail and is horrified to learn that his parents have gotten a divorce. His father sets him straight about his shrewish mother, explaining that she drove him to a life of crime, adding that she has loose morals and is sleeping with her boss. All this is too much for the young man, and he takes to drinking, but his friends help him get his life in order.

d&w, Said Ali Fettar; ph, Ali Yahyaoui; m, Farid Balkhirrat; ed, Rachid Ben Allal.

Drama   **(PR:C MPAA:NR)**

RAMS AND MAMMOTHS   (SEE: OVNI IN MAMUTI; 1986, Yugo.)

RAO SAHEB†   (1986, Ind.) 130m PBC c

Anupam Kher, Tanvi, Vijaya Mehta, Mangesh Kulharni, Chandrakant Gokhale, Nilu Phule, Tatoba Wellingkar, Vasant Ingale, Arvind Gadgil.

At the turn of the century, a wealthy Indian gentleman thoroughly anglicized, having been educated in Britain, tries to maintain his Western ideals despite their inappropriateness in the face of ancient tradition. He lives with his insane brother and a long-time widowed aunt (played by shaven-headed director Mehta, who also runs her own theater company), and later, with a young couple. He tries to push his European ideas of sexual equality on the two, succeeding only in building a sexual attraction between himself and the wife. When her husband dies, he tries to convince her to resist the strictures of widowhood that have confined Mehta for most of her life, and she expects him to propose to her. He doesn't, and she goes into lifelong mourning. Based on a classic Indian novel which was previously made into a play.

p, Vinay Welling; d, Vijaya Mehta; w, Vijaya Mehta, Aneel Chaudhari (based on a novel by Jaywant Dalvi); ph, Adeep Tandon; m, Bhaskar Chandavarkar; ed, Suresh Avdhoot; prod d, Shyam Bhutkar, Pramod Pawar; set d, Ravindra Sathe, Vijay Shinde.

Drama   **(PR:A MPAA:NR)**

RATBOY✱✱½   (1986) 104m Malpaso/WB c

Sondra Locke *(Nikki Morrison)*, Robert Townsend *(Manny)*, Christopher Hewett *(Acting Coach)*, Larry Hankin *(Jewell)*, Sydney Lassick *(Dial-A-Prayer)*, Gerrit Graham *(Billy Morrison)*, Louie Anderson *(Omer Morrison)*, S.L. Baird *(Ratboy)*, Billie Bird *(Psychic)*, John Witherspoon *(Heavy)*, Charles Bartlett, Lee de Broux, Jeffrey Josephson, Peter Looney *(Catullus Cops)*, Tiger Haynes *(Derelict Ralph)*, Gary Riley *(Bill)*, Gordon Anderson *(Ratboy's Voice)*, Nina Blackwood *(MTV Vee-Jay)*, Damita Jo Freeman *(Louise)*, Lisa Cloud *(Zu Zu)*, Courtney Gadny *(Kid in Car)*, Winifred Freedman *(Girl Friend)*, Lisa Figuerosa *(Trudy)*, Diane Delan *(Aurora)*, Brett Halsey *(Mr. Manes)*, Steve Bassett, Lloyd Nelson *(Reporters at Dump)*, Don Sparks *(Cameraman)*, Durk Pearson, Sandy Shaw *(Merv's Guests)*, Michael Canavan *(Production Assistant)*, Theresa DePaolo *(Theater Reporter)*, Virginia Peters *(Beggar Woman)*, Grant Loud *(Diver)*, Ed Williams *(Lake Reporter)*, Albert Michel, Jr. *(Gang Leader)*, M.C. Gainey *(Police Officer)*, Sam Ingraffia *(Studio Guard)*, Dahlia Pujol *(Singing Bag Lady)*, Clifford Shegog *(Heavy's Bodyguard)*, Casey Sander, Bob Yerkes, Mike Johnson *(Stagehands)*, Jon Lovitz, Bill Maher, George McGrath, Diz McNally, Wendi Morrison, Jonathan Schmock, Julie Silliman, James Vallely, Kathleen Wilhoite, Karen Witter, Don Woodard *(Party Guests)*.

Actress Sondra Locke's directorial debut is an odd little film, that—while suffering slightly from a dose of easy sentimentality—turns out to be a clever enough

fable on the plight of the exploited. Locke plays an ambitious Los Angeles window dresser who dreams of striking it rich some day. On an excursion to the local garbage dump in search of some unique items to spice up her new Daliesque window display, Locke happens upon two transients who have discovered a bizarre-looking boy who looks a lot like a rat (actually played by a 4-foot 8-inch woman, Baird, who, ironically, is a former "Mouseketeer" from the "Mickey Mouse Club"). The ratboy lives in the garbage dump and has set up living quarters hidden among the trash. The two bums hold the ratboy captive with plans to sell him to the highest bidder. Seizing the opportunity, Locke cons the men by telling them she's a journalist who can make their discovery famous. She whisks the ratboy away from the men and then, with the help of her dim-witted brothers (Graham and Anderson) and a clever street-hustler (Townsend), she launches into an exploitation campaign of her own. To get the ratboy to be a good sport and play along, Locke treats him with kindness and compassion— things he has never known. After winning the ratboy's confidence, Locke arranges for her find to take acting and elocution lessons (all he can do is squeak a few words), attend a Hollywood party, have a meeting with a big producer, get a spot on the "Merv Griffin Show," and talk with MTV "Vee-Jay" Nina Blackwood. Locke then holds a massive press conference at a swanky movie theater. At the press conference, ratboy becomes frightened by the spotlights (they remind him of the police helicopter searchlights he used to hide from) and he runs away.

With ratboy loose in the streets of L.A., half the hustlers in town and the police are out looking for him. Locke finally realizes what a selfish heel she's been to the trusting ratboy and she repents her exploitative ways at the fade.

Tired of being considered an extension of her "significant other" Clint Eastwood's movie machine, actress Locke searched for a project of her own. She had read Rob Thompson's script earlier while looking for a star vehicle, but rejected it because the character she would play was not challenging enough. The concept, however, stayed with her until she finally decided to direct and star in the film. Without using Eastwood, Locke convinced Warner Brothers executives to let her helm the project. Worried about directing and acting at the same time while having to develop a rapport with a crew of strangers, Locke turned to Eastwood's crack Malpaso production team—all of whom she had worked with in the past on various Eastwood projects. Her confidence in her crew (one of the finest in the business) allowed her to relax a bit and focus her concentration on her directing and acting. Although Eastwood was quite supportive, he rarely visited the set and left Locke to do things on her own. The resulting film is a notable enough debut (it took a certain amount of courage to select the offbeat topic), although it suffers from some haphazard scripting and surface treatment of the underlying implications of the material. Locke attempted to portray the dichotomy between her character's compassion for and exploitation of the ratboy, and she succeeds at times, but overall the film fails to dig deeply. The character of the ratboy is underdeveloped—perhaps it should have been allowed to speak more—and has little personality other than that of "victim." Graham and Anderson are quite funny as Locke's inept brothers, and Townsend nearly steals the movie as the streetwise hustler who babysits the ratboy and offers him advice like: " . . . get a nose job, get your hair fixed, get your teeth fixed, shave some of that hair off your hands, and be yourself." The ratboy design by Rick Baker (AMERICAN WEREWOLF IN LONDON) is quite good, although some critics felt that the ratboy resembled director Roman Polanski! Despite the fact that they gave Locke approval to make the film, Warner Brothers apparently didn't know what to do with it once it was finished and gave it a very scant release. Songs include: "Personality" (Lloyd Price, Howard Logan, performed by Price), "Hollywood Boulevard Street Rap" (Steve Dorff, Milton L. Brown, performed by The L.A. Dream Team), "Out of Control" (Steve Dorff, Steve Diamond, performed by The Waters), "Gotta Get Rich" (Steve Dorff, Steve Diamond, performed by Craig Morris), "Pretty Face" (Steve Dorff, John Bettis, Phil Brown, performed by Brown), "Looking For Trouble" (Sam Lorber, Dave Innis, performed by T.J. Seals), "I Get Mental" (Dennis Matkosky, Danny Sembello, David Batteau, performed by Lynn Davis), "Don't Follow Me" (Marc O'Connell, Shari Saba, performed by Saba), "In the Name of Love" (Steve Dorff, Phil Brown, performed by Brown), "Throw Down" (Dennis Matkosky, Richard Wolf, performed by Brenda Russell), "Tangled Up In You" (Steve Dorff, John Bettis, Phil Brown performed by Brown), "The Heart I Left Behind" (Steve Dorff, Milton L. Brown, performed by Craig Morris), "Night Games" (Don Stalker, Steve Berg, performed by Don Stalker and Berg), "Entrega" (Dahlia Pujol, performed by Pujol).

p, Fritz Manes; d, Sondra Locke; w, Rob Thompson; ph, Bruce Surtees (Panavision, Technicolor); m, Lennie Niehaus; ed, Joel Cox; prod d, Edward Carfagno; set d, Cloudia; spec eff, Wayne Edgar; makeup, Michael Hancock, Greg Nelson; stunts, Wayne Van Horn.

Drama (PR:C MPAA:PG-13)

RATTIS† (1986, Swed.) 82m Kanalfilm–Swedish Film Institute/Swedish Film Institute c (AKA:RATTY)

An animated feature about a poor, put-upon rat named Ratty who falls in love with a lovely she-rat named Rosetta. However, his parents and siblings do everything in their power to break up the lovers. Later the couple is accosted by a motorcycle gang and Rosetta goes off with them. On the waterfront, Ratty finds biker rodents attacking her, so he beats them up and he and Rosetta pledge their undying love for each other.

p, Lisbet Gabrielsson; d&w, Lennart Gustafsson; ph, Mikael Gerdin, Anders Holt; m, Markus Wikstrom, Bie Carlsson, Johan Stern, Stefan Axelsson, Ylva-Li Bjork, Urban Wrethagen; anim, Lennart Gustafsson, Jonas Adner, Ylva-Li Bjork.

Animation (PR:A MPAA:NR)

RAVEN† (1986, Swed.) 78m Svensk Filmindustri–Clas Lindberg Film–Movie Makers Sweden AB–Tonservice Lothner & Lothner c (Trans: The Fox)

Licka Sjoman (Monika), Goran Dyhrssen (Kaare), Willie Andreasson (Monica's Father), Allan Svensson (Police Sergeant), Gustav Kling (The Hunter).

A young man suspected of arson escapes the asylum where he has been sent, and his girl friend asks her policeman father for permission to try to bring him in herself. She goes to his parents' home in the forest and finds him there. Later, she learns that he has murdered both his mother and father.

p, Bert Sundberg, Lasse Lundberg; d&w, Clas Lindberg; ph, Ole Fredrik Haug, Bertil Rosengren (Eastmancolor); m, Bo Anders Persson; ed, Lasse Lundberg.

Drama (PR:O MPAA:NR)

RAW DEAL ** (1986) 97m International Film/DEG c

Arnold Schwarzenegger (Kaminski), Kathryn Harrold (Monique), Sam Wanamaker (Patrovita), Paul Shenar (Rocca), Robert Davi (Max), Ed Lauter (Baker), Darren McGavin (Shannon), Joe Regalbuto (Baxter), Mordecai Lawner

(Marcellino), Steven Hill (Lamanski), Blanche Baker (Amy Kaminski), Robey (Lamanski's Girl), Victor Argo (Dangerous Man), George Wilbur, Denver Mattson (Killers), John Malloy (Trager), Lorenzo Clemons (Sergeant), Dick Durock (Dingo), Frank Ferrara (Spike), Thomas Rosales (Jesus), Jack Hallett (Carson), Leon Rippy (Man in Tux), Jay Butler (Rice), Norman Maxwell (Fake State Trooper), Tony DiBenedetto (Rudy), Tom Hull (Metzger), Mary Canon (Saleswoman), Gary Houston, Gregory Noonan (Patrovita Thugs), Steve Holt (Blair), Cedric Guthrie (Agent with Shannon), Gary Olsen (Lamanski's Driver), Brooks Gardner (Elevator Operator), Pat Miller (Kinks Cashier), Jery Hewitt (Stickman), James Eric (Byron), Ralph Foody (Captain), Howard Elfman (Bomb Squad), John Hately (Trooper [Double]), Joel Kramer (Brenner [Double]), Jeff Ramsay, Bill McIntosh, Ted Grossman (Bodyguards), Kent Hays (Drunken Player), Greg Walker (Rudy [Double]), Cliff Happy (Tony's Bodyguard), Mike Adams (Patrovita's Bodyguard), Dean Smith (Patrovita's Double), Alex Ross (Station Wagon Driver), Socorro Santiago (Nurse at Center), Richard McGough (Baker's Partner), Sharon Rice (Jogger), R. Pickett Bugg (Lookout Gangster), John Clark (Newscaster), Scott Blount (Performer), Phil Adams, Chuck Hart, Larry Holt, Ken Sprunt (FBI Agents).

Arnold Schwarzenegger's summer action film probably contains the highest body count in any 1986 film, but unfortunately RAW DEAL doesn't measure up to the

strapping star's previous work. The story opens at a secluded cabin where the FBI is protecting a man scheduled to testify against crime boss Wanamaker. The powerful mobster brings in three of his top hitmen, who subsequently annihilate everyone inside the hideout. Among the dead is the son of FBI agent McGavin, who now wants revenge. To this end, McGavin looks up Schwarzenegger, a former FBI man himself, who had been forced into retirement because of his penchant for violence. Schwarzenegger—now working as a small-town sheriff and trapped in a loveless marriage to the alcoholic Baker—agrees to infiltrate Wanamaker's organization, following the promise of reinstatement as a federal agent as reward for his work. After faking his own death, Schwarzenegger adopts a phony guise and heads to Chicago. Once there, he does a number on one of Wanamaker's rivals, which makes a strong impression on the mobster. Wanamaker allows Schwarzenegger into his organization, although Davi, a mob underling, is suspicious of this new man. He sends Harrold after Schwarzenegger, instructing the beautiful woman to ply the truth out of Wanamaker's well-dressed new boy. Meanwhile Schwarzenegger helps recover a substantial amount of drugs and cash taken during a police raid. Wanamaker is further impressed by Schwarzenegger, who is now considered a full-fledged member of the elite circle. Davi discovers that Schwarzenegger has been using a bogus name, and through a crooked district attorney (Regalbuto), learns Schwarzenegger has been working with McGavin. Next Davi takes Schwarzenegger to a cemetery, explaining that they are about to knock off another victim. To his horror, Schwarzenegger sees that McGavin is the intended hit. Davi is able to get off a shot, hitting McGavin, but Schwarzenegger kills the mobster. McGavin, who is severely wounded, tells his friend the time has come to complete his mission. What follows is the film's big pay-off, as Schwarzenegger arms himself to the teeth, then turns Wanamaker's headquarters into kindling wood. Mafia goons drop like flies, Schwarzenegger avenges McGavin's son, then reunites with his friend for a happy freeze-frame ending.

What's lacking amidst the tough-guy posturings and flying bullets is Schwarzenegger's usual tongue-in-cheek humor. The plot is understandably short on subtleties, and a few well-placed laughs would have been a welcome relief from the violent proceedings. There is some unintentional comedy that comes with the huge gaps in plot logic. When Scharwzenegger sends one bad guy through the plate-glass window of an exclusive shop, customers outside the store walk by as though nothing unusual has just happened. Though big-city living does harden one's attitude, it seems unlikely that mall patrons would be blase about flying bodies and loaded guns. Irvin's direction is rudimentary for an action film and adds little excitement to the proceedings. There's not much suspense, with good guys and bad guys clearly drawn, and the final shootout is all too routine. Surprisingly, this was Irvin's followup to his much acclaimed 1985 drama TURTLE DIARY (when some people make a genre change, they go all the way!). Schwarzenegger is okay in his part, but he's done the same thing much better before. While women played a key part in his earlier films (Linda Hamilton in THE TERMINATOR and Rae Dawn Chong in COMMANDO), Harrold is a surprisingly bland love interest. Baker's role is almost negligible, an unappealing character who is quickly dropped from sight. But then again, characters aren't the attraction here; shootouts and car chases are. Considering Schwarzenegger's box-office clout among action fans, one would expect the former Mr. Universe to give them a little more fun than the elementary and ultimately boring ingredients that comprise RAW DEAL. Songs include: "One Way Rider" (Rodney Crowell, performed by Ricky Skaggs), "If Looks Could Kill" (Jack Conrad, Bob Garrett, performed by Pamala Stanley), "Immigrant in Love" (Vito DeStefano), "O Marie" (Traditional), "Trapped" (Colonel Abrams, Marston Freeman, performed by Colonel Abrams), "I've Seen That Face Before (Libertango)" (Astor Piazzolla, Natalie Delon, Dennis Wilkey, performed by Grace Jones), "Stand Alone" (Reed Neilsen, performed by Stone Fury).

p, Martha Schumacher; d, John Irvin; w, Gary M. DeVore, Norman Wexler (based on a story by Luciano Vincenzoni, Sergio Donati); ph, Alex Thomson (J-D-C Widescreen, Technicolor); m, Tom Bahler, Albhy Caluten, Chris Boardman, Jerry Hey, Randy Kerber, Steve Lukather, Joel Rosenbaum, Claude Gaudette; ed, Anne V. Coates; prod d, Giorgio Postiglione; art d, Maher Ahmad; set d, Hilton Rosemarin; cos, Clifford Capone; spec eff, Joe Lombardi; m/l, Rodney Crowell, Jack Conrad, Bob Garrett, Vito DeStefano, Colonel Abrams, Marston Freeman, Astor Piazzolla, Natalie Delon, Barry Renolds, Dennis Wilkey, Reed Nielsen; makeup, Barbara Page.

Crime/Action   **Cas.**   **(PR:O MPAA:R)**

RAW TUNES†   (1986) 72m Changing Horses c

Gary Levy *(Johnny Columbus)*, Dan Lewk *(Laird Bonnet)*, Malcolm Hurd, Steve Peterman, Mitchell Laurence, Jim Purcell.

Two Los Angeles graduate film students wrote, produced, directed, edited, and starred in this feature, shot for just $24,000. The film deals with a lousy rock 'n' roll band that collapses on the road. Although the movie actually was screened at a festival, release appears a very remote possibility.

p,d&w, Gary Levy, Dan Lewk; ph, Randy Sellars (Cine Craft Color); m, Dan Lewk, Julie Christensen, Gary Levy; ed, Gary Levy, Dan Lewk.

Comedy   **(PR:C-O MPAA:NR)**

REBEL LOVE*¹/₂   (1986) 80m Raven Cliff/Troma Team c

Jamie Rose *(Columbine Cromwell)*, Terence Knox *(Hightower/McHugh)*, Fran Ryan *(Granny Plug)*, Carl Spurlock *(Yankee Sergeant)*, Rick Waln *(Yankee Corporal)*, Larry Larson *(Aaron Cromwell)*, Charles Hill *(Rebel Captain)*, Harry Howell *(Gen. Clarence Mason)*, Thom Gossom, Jr. *(Pompeii, a Slave)*, Jimmy Rosser *(Unfriendly Farmer)*.

A well-intentioned but nonetheless amateurish romance set near the Indiana-Kentucky border during the Civil War. Knox is an actor who is hired to work as a spy for the Confederates. In the meantime, Rose, a war widow, spends her days listening to stories of past romances told by local merchant Ryan, an aging tramp who has been married nine times. The following morning Rose opens her front door to find Knox lying there unconscious, having been thrown from his horse

during the previous night's thunderstorm. She takes an interest in him, partly because she needs his love, and partly because she needs help around the farm. Eventually she falls in love with Knox, who is pretending to be an Irish stove salesman to cover his spy identity. Her idyllic life is shaken when some Union soldiers come looking for Knox. She hides him and gets rid of the soldiers, but in the process learns Knox's true identity. Angry that she had been lied to, she orders him to leave. Before he can go, the soldiers return unexpectedly and try to rape Rose. Knox comes to her aid, killing one of the men, as she kills the other. Knox tells her that he must leave, but promises that he'll return someday. Rose later learns from Ryan that Knox has been killed. Having rid herself of the memory of her dead husband, Rose decides to pack her things and leave the farmhouse behind, traveling into town with Ryan.

A low-budget feature filmed entirely in Alabama, REBEL LOVE is an attempt to re-create the passions of a Harlequin romance. There's no psychological depth here, but there is the sort of romantic tragedy which thrills fans of romance novels. Rather than allow Rose and Knox to come together in a Hollywood-style

final clinch, director Bagby has Knox die, leaving Rose with a few days' worth of highly romantic memories that she can treasure for the rest of her life. Although the film revolves around Rose and Knox, it is Ryan who provides the only interesting moments. At the film's end, Rose, who is searching for answers about romance, asks why Ryan speaks only of her first husband. Ryan explains that he was her first love and, although she was with him only a short while, it was he who made her respect herself and feel beautiful. Yes, it's trite, but Ryan manages to pull it off with a convincing performance. Ryan, a character actress who is best remembered as the mother of Jesse and Frank James in THE LONG RIDERS (she may, however, be best known to some as the mother of the giant Jack in the Hungry Jack biscuit TV commercials), is wonderful in a part which deserves to have an entire script written around it, rather than a mere ten minutes. Knox is barely convincing as a spy, much less as an actor working as a spy, and even less as an actor working as a spy but pretending to be an Irishman. Knox's dialog is bad enough without handicapping him with a fake brogue. Rose couldn't play the part with any less conviction if she tried. Although she does manage, for a few seconds, to resemble something along the lines of a mid-1800s frontierswoman, she generally fails to hide the fact that she is an actress from the 1980s. Beside making no apparent attempt to use the speech of the day, Rose strikes a pose which would have been better suited for her ill-fated 1986 television series "Lady Blue," in which she was cast as a hard-as-nails Chicago cop. Bagby, whose Raven Cliff Productions generated the project, must be commended for his desire to start off his film career (this is his first film) on a dramatic note. Rather than follow the example of most commercial independents Bagby claims that he "wanted to start off with something commercial, but we wanted it to stand apart from the crash/slash/burn items you see, to be different." There's no high art in REBEL LOVE, nor is there any real significance, but if it's a harmless, standard romance you want, then this is a perfect choice. Oddly, REBEL LOVE was released on videocassette this year, with a theatrical release set for 1987.

p, John Quenelle; d&w, Milton Bagby, Jr.; ph, Joseph A. Whigham (Panavision, TVC Color); m, Bobby Horton; ed, Mellena Bridges; prod d, Bill Teague; set d, Netta Bank; cos, Deborah Brunson; makeup, Marnie Ross Schlitt.

Historical/Romance   **Cas.**   **(PR:C-O MPAA:NR)**

RECRUITS zero   (1986) 82m Concorde

Steve Osmond *(Steve)*, Doug Annear *(Mike)*, Alan Deveau *(Howie)*, John Canada Terrell *(Winston)*, Lolita David *(Susan)*, Tracey Tanner *(Brazil)*, Annie McAuley *(Tanya)*, Tony Travis *(Stonewall)*, Mike McDonald *(Magruder)*, Colleen Karney *(Sgt. S)*, Jason Logan *(Mayor Bagley)*, Caroline Tweedle *(Mrs. Bagley)*, Mark Blutman *(Clint)*, John Mikl Thor *(Thunderhead)*, Tom Melissis, Frank Savage, Adrien Dorual, Terence Howson, Al Therrian, Bob Segarini, Bruce Bell, Kimberly McCoy, John Wing, Jr., Frank G. Thompson, David Sisak, Dianne Turgeon, Judi Embden, Lisa Shoesmith, Linda Nantel, Dave Strapko, Mike Strapko, Goran Kalezic, Mike Dolgy, Christian Liedtke, Charles Wiener, Norbert Kausen, Bo Staude, Sasha Mote Dolgy, Frank G. Thompson, Dominique St. Croix, Paul Webster, Karen Wood, Elizabeth Harden.

Okay, so POLICE ACADEMY made *mucho dinero* and spawned a successful string of films. Does that justify the all-too-many idiotic copycats of what was a moronic film to start with? RECRUITS follows its predecessor by openly stealing the plot and development with unashamed zeal. In a small town, a crooked police captain is determined to grab political control by publicly disgracing the mayor. First he hires a gang of oddballs and misfits to be the new police recruits. Next, a phony assassination is to be staged when the governor arrives for a personal appearance, thus showing the mayor's incompetence. However, the city's main police force succumbs to food poisoning at a beach party and is knocked out of service completely. Evil gangs run amok but the recruits band together to save the day. The mayor is restored to good grace, the new cops are heroes, and you return the tape to your local video store with a mixture of boredom and annoyance registered on your face.

Is anything original in this? That question is easily answered with a loud, resounding *No!* The jokes are based chiefly on women's breasts and men's groins, with plenty of the former on significant display. There's also a painfully bad parody of Clint Eastwood, and an acknowledged reference to Eddie Murphy's wonderful barroom takeover from 48 HOURS. To no one's surprise, this was produced by the same team that gave us the equally hapless LOOSE SCREWS in 1985. Their hallmark qualities of tasteless humor, inept production values, bad acting, and oodles of sub-sophomoric humor are firmly in place. They don't even bother to list who plays who in the title or closing credits, one sign of the film's low price. Without mincing words, this is just plain idiotic. Not only was there heavy emphasis on POLICE ACADEMY in the film's ad campaign ("You've failed POLICE ACADEMY, now graduate to RECRUITS!" among other slogans); RECRUITS was shot in the Toronto area, the same location site used by this film's role model. When you're going to rip someone off, you may as well do it right.

p, Maurice Smith; d, Rafal Zielinski; w, Charles Wiener, B.K. Roderick; ph, Peter Czerski; m, Steve Parsons; ed, Stephan Fanfara; art d, Craig Richards; set d, Nick White; cos, Eva Gord; makeup, Deni Delory.

Comedy   **Cas.**   **(PR:O MPAA:R)**

REDONDO†   (1986, Mex.) Cinematografica Redondo c (Trans: Round)

Alfredo Sevilla, Diana Bracho, Fernando Balzaretti, Angeles Gonzalez, Lei Quintana, Javier Garcia Galiano, Jaime Ramos, Emilio Garcia Riera, Brigida Alexander.

Complex account of an aspiring young writer who leaves his home and family to move to a strange city to write his novel—the story of an order of 17th Century

Mexican nuns. His own life, his fantasy life, the life of his characters, and the film made from the novel all intermingle. REDONDO, which spent two years in production, was the first presentation of young filmmaker Raul Busteros.

p,d&w, Raul Busteros (based on the novel by Paco Ignacio Taibo); ph, Mario Luna, Juan Carlos Martin; m, Carlos Lopez; ed, Fernando Pardo, Juan Manuel Vargas.

Drama   **(PR:C MPAA:NR)**

REFORM SCHOOL GIRLS*   (1986) 94m NW–Balcor c

Linda Carol *(Jenny)*, Wendy O. Williams *(Charlie)*, Pat Ast *(Edna)*, Sybil Danning *(Sutter)*, Charlotte McGinnis *(Dr. Norton)*, Sherri Stoner *(Lisa)*, Denise Gordy *(Claudie)*, Laurie Schwartz *(Nicky)*, Tiffany Helm *(Fish)*, Darcy DeMoss *(Knox)*.

Only rarely do self-conscious films striving for cult status succeed. ROCK AND ROLL HIGH SCHOOL and REPO MAN do because they contain enough unique energy, style, and humor to stand on their own as cult items, without ever

pandering to the purposely bad dialog, acting, and obnoxious situations most pre-fab cult films strive for. True cult films (of the "bad" variety—there are good ones as well) are those where the filmmaker sincerely has tried to make a "good" film, but the results have turned out to be hopelessly hokey and unintentionally funny. Cult audiences delight in giggling at the earnest-but-inept efforts of would-be cinematic geniuses. REFORM SCHOOL GIRLS is one of those self-consciously bad films that not only shoots for "cult" status, but also enters another dangerous cinematic ground: the genre parody. Sometimes the genre parody works, if a good genre is selected. Unfortunately, REFORM SCHOOL GIRLS focuses on a genre that is practically a self-parody by definition: the women-in-prison film (WOMEN IN CAGES, BIG DOLL HOUSE, CAGED HEAT).

Carol stars as a nice-but-wayward girl who is tossed into a nasty reform school after helping a boy friend rob a convenience store. She is shocked to find that her section is dominated by a mean-spirited lesbian inmate dressed in black leather underwear (Williams) who is allowed to run wild by the obese dorm matron, Ast.

Williams and her gang of female thugs are constantly at odds with the other girl gangs in the reform school. Carol tries not to get involved, but she can't help but defend another new inmate, Stoner, a weak and childlike teen who clutches a stuffed rabbit for comfort. Ast is so mean, however, that she snatches the stuffed animal away from Stoner and locks it in her desk. Later, when the desperate Stoner tries to steal the rabbit back, the sadistic Ast burns the stuffed toy before the horrified girl's eyes. If that isn't enough, Ast puts Stoner and Carol on hard labor in the sweltering farm fields. While Williams and her girls lie in the shade sipping iced tea, Stoner, Carol, and the others are refused food and water. Some of the nicer girls discover a kitten in the fields and smuggle it back to the dorm where they give it to Stoner for comfort. But Ast eventually finds the animal and crushes it under her shoe. Eventually, Stoner is driven to suicide by Ast's cruelty and Williams' sexual pestering. Fed up with the deadends she finds when trying to alert state officials to the horror, Carol starts an uprising against Ast and warden Danning (who dresses like a Gestapo officer, smokes a cigar, carries a shotgun, and reads from the Bible over the intercom) and change finally comes to the reform school.

Loaded with ridiculous scenes, silly dialog, and gratuitous violence and nudity (though not half as explicit as it could have been), REFORM SCHOOL GIRLS tries very hard to live up to the expectations of the genre, while poking fun at it at the same time. The only problem here is that little is funny. Ast gets some scenery-chewing mileage out of her sadistic matron character, but she is the only performer who is consistently amusing as she glowers into the camera and pounds her heavy way down the reform school corridors. Danning, a veteran of bad "B" productions, seems disinterested and could have phoned in her part—most of her scenes take place on a single set (her office). Carol and Stoner try hard to look earnest, while Williams, lead singer and driving force behind the obnoxious punk rock group "The Plasmatics," is much too old for the part (if it matters) and literally snarls her way through the film. Williams also contributes to the film's soundtrack, as do Girlschool, Girl's Night Out, and Etta James, who sings "So Young, So Bad, So What?" Writer-director DeSimone is a veteran of the women-in-prison genre, having helmed CONCRETE JUNGLE in 1982, and there is little difference between his approaches to the two films, except that here he has an already-exploitative situation stretched to the limit with actors that wink at the camera. Not for the easily offended.

p, Jack Cummins; d&w, Tom DeSimone; ph, Howard Wexler (Technicolor); m, Tedra Gabriel, Martin Schwartz; ed, Michael Spence; prod d, Becky Block; set d, Tom Talbert.

Prison/Comedy   **Cas.**   **(PR:O MPAA:R)**

REGALO DI NATALE†   (1986, It.) 100m Sacis–Due A Film–DMV/RAI-1 c
(Trans: Christmas Present)

Diego Abatantuono *(Franco)*, Gianni Cavina *(Ugo)*, Alessandro Haber *(Lele)*, Carlo Delle Piane *(Santia)*, George Eastman *(Stefano)*, Kristina Sevieri *(Martina)*.

Directed by one of Italy's most insightful social satirists, REGALO DI NATALE centers around five men involved in a Christmas Eve card game. Though initiated as a friendly gathering and reunion, each man harbors secret wishes of becoming the big winner, thus bettering his financial situation and future at the expense of the men he supposedly considers to be friends.

p, Antonio Avati; d, Pupi Avati; w, Pupi Avati; ph, Pasquale Rachini (Telecolor); m, Riz Ortolani; ed, Amedeo Salfa; art d, Giuseppe Pirrotta.

Drama   **(PR:C MPAA:NR)**

REI DO RIO†   (1986, Braz.) 90m Producoes Cinematograficas L.C. Barreto/
Embrafilme c (Trans: King of Rio)

Nuno Leal, Maia, Nelson Xavier, Milton Concalves, Amparo Grisales, Andrea Beltran, Marcia Barreto.

After winning the lottery, a man starts out to build a criminal empire, and 15 years later he is the top gangster in Brazil. Trouble comes when his daughter falls in love with the son of an old enemy, the man with whom he split the lottery prize.

d, Fabio Barreto; w, Jorge Duran, Jose Joffily, Fabio Barreto; ed, Raimundo Higino.

Comedy   **(PR:C-O MPAA:NR)**

REIS 222†   (1986, USSR) 120m Lenfilm c (Trans: Flight 222)

Larisa Polyakova *(Irina)*, Aleksandr Babanov *(Strelkov)*, Aleksander Kolesnikov *(Misha)*, Aleksandr Ivanov *(Zhigalin)*, Nikolai Alyoshin *(Kurzanov)*, Vilnis Paulovitch *(Bekkeris)*.

Defection, a subject previously avoided by Soviet filmmakers, is the focus of this film, perhaps a direct reaction to the 1985 U.S. release, WHITE NIGHTS. A Russian athlete in the U.S. defects, and Soviet officials order his wife to leave the country immediately before she can do the same. U.S. officials stop the plane from leaving and a war of words develops over the whole thing, with the other passengers on the plane rallying patriotically and the Americans looking to score a propaganda victory, exactly what the Russians are trying to avoid.

d&w, Sergei Mikaelyan; ph, Sergei Astakhov; m, Sergei Banevitch; art d, Elizaveta Urlina.

Drama   **(PR:A MPAA:NR)**

REPORTER X† (1986, Portugal) 100m c

Joaquim de Almeida, Paula Guedes, Fernando Heitor, Eunice Munoz, Susana Borges, Anamar, Mario Vieges, Jorge Silva, Filipe Ferrer.

Feature debut of young director Nascimento is a thriller that blurs the line between fiction and reality while paying tribute to the *noir* films of the 1940s. A journalist known only as Reporter X returns from London to cover the story of a headless corpse found on a lonely dock road in Lisbon. The head turns up in a hat box, but it is only a mask. Reporter X then finds himself involved with a mysterious Moroccan woman and her mother, who know the secret formula for a plague that can destroy life on Earth.

p&d, Jose Nascimento; w, Jose Nascimento, Manuel Joao Gomes, Edgar Pera; ph, Manuel Costa e Silva; m, Antonio Emiliano; ed, Ana Luisa Guimaraes, Jose Nascimento.

Drama/Thriller (PR:O MPAA:NR)

REQUIEM POR UN CAMPESINO ESPANOL† (1986, Span.) Nemo/Venus
c (Trans: Requiem for a Spanish Peasant)

Antonio Farrandis, Antonio Banderas, Fernando Fernan Gomez, Terele Pavez, Simon Andreu, Emilio Gutierrez Caba.

d, Francesc Betriu; w, Gustau Hernandez, Francesc Betriu, Raul Artigot (based on the novel by Ramon J. Sender); ph, Raul Artigot.

RETURN** (1986) 80m Silver c

Karlene Crockett *(Diana Stoving)*, John Walcutt *(Day Whittaker)*, Lisa Richards *(Ann Stoving)*, Frederic Forrest *(Brian Stoving)*, Anne Lloyd Francis *(Eileen Sedgely)*, Lenore Zann *(Susan)*, Thomas Rolapp *(Lucky)*, Harry Murphy *(MDC Officer)*, Lee Stetson *(Daniel Montross)*, Ariel Aberg-Riger *(Diana at Three)*.

A rather generic-looking film adaptation of the Donald Harington novel *Some Other Place. The Right Place* where supernatural phenomena are used to motivate a rather mundane murder mystery. The film begins in an Arkansas mountain range where we see a little girl playing near a waterfall. With the girl is her protector, a robust outdoorsman. The two are startled by the sound of someone crawling on the cliff overhead. The man goes for his rifle, but before he can arm himself, he is shot and killed by the unseen assassin. Years later, the little girl, now grown (Crockett) agrees to aid a young southern man, Walcutt, who has been possessed by the spirit of the man killed in the opening scene—Crockett's grandfather. Crockett was contacted by Francis, a leading professor in the areas of hypnosis, spirit-channeling, and age regression. Francis puts Walcutt under hypnosis and Crockett is shocked to see the shy southerner's voice and mannerisms suddenly transform into those of a robust old northerner. Crockett quizzes Walcutt with questions only her grandfather could answer and is amazed to find that his responses are correct. When Walcutt is brought out of hypnosis, both he and Crockett decide to investigate her grandfather's murder. After visiting Vermont where Crockett's grandfather was born, the two travel to the scene of the crime in Arkansas. Crockett and Walcutt fall in love along the way. Meanwhile, Crockett's mother, Richards, learns of her daughter's quest and enlists the aid of her husband, Forrest, to help her stop the investigation. Richards meets with professor Francis and confesses that her daughter is the product of an incestuous relationship between herself and her father (Crockett's dead grandfather). Richards and Forrest race to the Arkansas mountain range in time to witness Walcutt assume the identity of the dead man. Before the spirit can reveal the truth to Crockett, Forrest tries to shoot Walcutt/spirit, but misses. Crockett finally learns of her true parentage and that it was her mother, Richards, who had murdered her grandfather after he had kidnaped the child (Crockett) and fled into the mountains. Satisfied that the truth has been told, the spirit leaves Walcutt's body forever.
    Director Silver has made several fiction films for PBS, and while they may have been acclaimed as good adaptations of literary works, his visual style is strictly small-screen. RETURN plods along at a secure pace, highlights the picturesque scenery, and never takes any chances when it comes to visual composition, lighting, or editing. The performances are merely serviceable, with Forrest—a volatile actor who could have punched some life into the film—wasted in a cameo. Considering the topicality of spirit channeling, one would think that the exploitation value of the subject would have spurred director SIlver to liven up his film a bit. Instead, RETURN is simply a bland movie-of-the-week.

p, Andrew Silver, Yong-Hee Silver; d&w, Andrew Silver (based on the novel *Some Other Place. The Right Place* by Donald Harington); ph, Janos Zsombolyai; m, Ragnar Grippe, Michael Shrieve; ed, Gabrielle Gilbert.

Mystery (PR:O MPAA:R)

REVENGE zero (1986) 100m United Entertainment c

Patrick Wayne *(Michael Hogan)*, John Carradine *(Sen. Bradford)*, Bennie Lee McGowan *(Gracie Moore)*, Josef Hanet *(Dr. White)*, Stephanie Kropke *(Liz)*, Fred Graves *(Dean Bayley)*, Charles Ellis *(Ron)*, David Stice *(Deputy)*, John Bliss *(Psychiatrist)*, Andrea Adams *(Reporter)*.

Another straight-to-videocassette horror film, this one a shot-on-film sequel to the shot-on-video BLOOD CULT. The confused plot—which only serves as filler between the gore sequences—involves a cult which worships dogs, the "Cult of Caninus" no less. Predictably, the members of this doggy-cult are all upstanding citizens of a small community and their leader, Carradine, happens to be a senator. It seems the cult members want the land owned by a poor widow woman, McGowan, to perform one of their mumbo-jumbo sacred rites. The distraught McGowan is aided by stranger-in-town Wayne and together they try to fend off the crazed hound-enthusiasts.
    Simpleminded, mean-spirited, and downright laughable in spots, REVENGE is about as pathetic as it gets. Carradine, who should stop embarrassing himself and retire, is obviously reading his lines from cue-cards. Wayne, who turned in the best performance of his career in last year's campy western comedy RUSTLER'S RHAPSODY, is too dull an actor to inspire much faith. The violence is from the repulsive and gratuitous Herschel Gordon Lewis school of gore and the filmmakers even stoop so low as to intercut a shot of a woman having her leg amputated with a shot of her ignorant boy friend cutting up some sausage for breakfast. Detestable.

p, Linda Lewis; d&w, Christopher Lewis; ph, Steve McWilliams; m, Rod Slane; ed, James Lenertz; spec eff, DFX Studio; stunts, David Stice.

Horror Cas. (PR:O MPAA:NR)

REVENGE FOR JUSTICE† (1986, Phil.) 95m Saga Film International/Sittis
Film Exchange c

Rudy Fernandez *(Bobby)*, Donna Villa *(Malou)*, George Estregan *(Police Lieutenant)*, Yusuf Salim *(Police Sergeant)*, Ronnie Lazaro *(Sergeant's Younger Brother)*, Johnny Wilson *(Crime Syndicate Boss)*, Paquito Diaz, Max Alvarado, Rodolfo "Boy" Garcia, Dick Israel, Philip Gamboa, Dave Brodett.

Another Filipino blood-and-guts actioner starring Fernandez as a young gunsmith obsessed with dispensing personal justice in honor of his father, a cop who was killed by gangsters when Fernandez was just a child. On his off-hours Fernandez fashions a devastating weapon with the power of a bazooka which he uses in his vigilante stalkings. As is to be expected, Fernandez is hunted both by mobsters and law enforcement officers anxious to stop his wanton "justice." Finally the mob goes too far and kills his girl. This makes Fernandez mad enough to become a one-man army and attack their countryside fortress. English-dubbed from the original Tagalog.

p, Hadja Sitti Aiza Ummar; d, Manuel "Fyke" Cinco; w, Dave Brodett; ph, Edmund Cupcupin (Eastmancolor); m, Jimmy Fabregas; ed, Augusto Salvador.

Action/Crime (PR:O MPAA:NR)

REVENGE OF THE TEENAGE VIXENS FROM OUTER SPACE, THE*½
(1986) 84m Malamute c

Lisa Schwedop *(Carla)*, Howard Scott *(Paul Morelli)*, Amy Crumpacker *(Stephanie)*, Sterling Ramberg *(Danny)*, Julian Schembri *(Jack Morelli)*, Peter Guss *(John)*, Anne Lilly *(Mary Jo)*, Lisa McGregor, Kim Wickenburg, Susanne Dailey, Sarah Barnes *(The Vixens)*, Paul Fleming *(Danny's Father)*, Jerry Crisman *(The Governor)*, Katie Green *(Julie)*, Katie McGee *(Jane)*, Catherine Holmes *(Linda)*, Bob Yarnall *(Mike)*, Eric Kohl *(Steve)*, Charlie Benditt *(Pete)*, Kim Kramer *(Helen)*, Al Snipp *(The Scientist)*, Ellie Lichter *(Danny's Mother)*, Dean Silverstone *(Will Brady)*, Rollie Harbst *(Mr. Andrews)*, Cheryl Read *(Woman with Dog)*, Ken Levy *(Angry Brother)*, Ruth Silverstone *(Mrs. Brady)*, Sharon Harbst *(Mrs. Andrews)*, Pat Schroeppel *(Woman in Crowd)*, Mike Dornheim *(Man in Crowd)*, Bonnie McKnight *(Girl in Car)*, Steve Thompson *(Boy in Car)*, Diana Kinderis *(1st Dancer)*, Julie Dreher *(2nd Dancer)*, Stephen Swanson *(Baby Paul)*, Ruth Bond *(Secretary)*, Mike Hickman *(Todd)*, Evelyn Bishop *(Mia)*, Sarah Leach *(Girl)*, Cyndi Sprankle *(Yogurt Girl)*, Stephen Devito, Scott Dickson, Parto Karimi, Lara Pewsnar *(Frozen Teenagers)*, Ryan Johnson *(The Poor Sap)*, Todd Mansfield *(A Teenager)*, China *(Malamute)*.

A super-low-budget independent science fiction spoof shot around Seattle, THE REVENGE OF THE TEENAGE VIXENS FROM OUTER SPACE concerns a quartet of semi-voluptuous women who come down from their manless planet to check out the action on Earth after a teen magazine accidentally gets delivered there. They set about seducing all the boys in the local high school, making enemies of the Earth girls led by Crumpacker. Meanwhile, Schwedop and Scott, two school kids, are falling in love and noticing all the strange events going on around them. After being seduced by one of the vixens, Scott's biology-teacher father tells his son that the boy's mother is actually a space vixen who came to Earth 16 years before (after getting a hold of the censored bottom half of Elvis Presley's appearance on the "Ed Sullivan Show"). Crumpacker tries to organize the Earth girls to get rid of the vixens, but they all get turned into giant vegetables. The vixens go on a rampage, angered by the opposition and the sexual inexperience of the local boys, and soon they are turning whole towns into giant summer squashes and the like. Scott goes to the old school where the aliens are hiding out (marked by a big sign that says "Old School") and confronts his mother, Lilly, who has come back to chaperon the younger vixens. She rejects him and he leaves, but when bombers are coming to nuke the whole area, he goes back with Schwedop and her disc jockey friend to rescue his father, who wants to leave with Lilly. Those two fly away (and into the propeller of a plane), while the rest end up zapped to whatever distant planet the vixens call home.
    This could have easily been a very bad film, but the actors play it straight and it ends up a pleasant little spoof. The effects are delightfully cheesy as hapless teenagers are turned into giant carrots and pea pods and pickles—all with big round eyes. One angry father holds up the jar holding his pickle son and demands revenge, while another parent isn't so lucky as his tomato daughter was stepped on in the dark. Schwedop and Scott, while no great shakes as actors, are likable and believable teenagers, and, in fact, the whole film is commendable in that it is filled with genuine-looking teens. With no nudity, little foul language, and only silly violence, the film is also much more harmless than most of its type. Soundtrack includes "Sho'guns and Lovers," "Joe the Ripper" (Louis X. Erlanger), "Shot Down," "Lighthouse," "The Night Loves On," "Change Your Mind,"

(Lane James), and "Talk to Me," "Say What You Mean," "Sign of the Times," "Life of the Party," and "Thinking of You" (Gary Schmidt).

p, Michelle Lichter, Jeff Farrell; d, Jeff Farrell; w, Michelle Lichter, Jeff Farrell; ph, Jeff Farrell; ed, Michelle Lichter; m/l, Louis X. Erlanger, Lane James, Gary Schmidt; makeup, Michelle Lichter.

Science Fiction/Comedy   Cas.   (PR:C MPAA:NR)

REZHOU†   (1986, Chi.) 131m Shanghai/China c (Trans: Sunrise)

Fang Shu (*Lulu Chen*), Wang Shi-huai, Yan Xiang, Wang Futang, Wan Fuli.

A Hollywood-style melodrama based on a 1935 play by Cao Yu about a woman named Lulu (Fang) who turns her back on her husband, children, and traditional life style in order to take a job as a nightclub singer. She lives life to the fullest, has a number of lovers, and eventually commits suicide after finding no other way out of this life of sin. REZHOU won two Golden Rooster awards in its home country—Best Script and Best Supporting Actress (Wan Fuli).

d, Yu Benzheng; w, Cao Yu, Wan Fang (based on the play by Cao Yu); ph, Zhu Yongde (Scopecolor); m, Xu Jingxin.

Drama   (PR:NR MPAA:NR)

RHOSYN A RHITH   (SEE: COMING UP ROSES, 1986, Wales)

RIH ESSED   (SEE: MAN OF ASHES, 1986, Tunisia)

RIISUMINEN†   (1986, Fin.) 88m Jorn Donner c (Trans: The Undressing)

Eeva Eloranta, Erkki Saarela, Aarno Laitinen, Alpo Suhonen.

Based on a successful 1984 Finnish stage play, RIISUMINEN features Saarela as a respectable minister of the government who has softened his left-wing stance and begun to compromise his political principles. Preparing for a trip to Denmark he unexpectedly meets Eloranta, his former mistress. Despite the fact that he is now married and has much to lose politically if their tryst is revealed, he immediately takes Eloranta to an expensive hotel suite to resurrect the affair they had 10 years before. After sex, the two engage in an lengthy argument with Eloranta on the attack. She accuses him of becoming complacent and comfortable in his role as minister, having sold out his values for respectability. She also condemns him as a chauvinist and reveals—much to his surprise—that she has raised a daughter she had by him. Except for the opening scenes, the entire film is played out in the claustrophobic hotel suite with both Eloranta and Saarela totally naked through much of the film (as was the case in the stage production) which is not only realistic in terms of two lovers spending a carnal afternoon together, but symbolic of the emotions and ideas laid bare during the encounter. The film was both praised and condemned in Europe because of its sexual and political frankness.

p, Jorn Donner; d, Lauri Torhonen; w, Lauri Torhonen, Raija Oranen (based on the play by Raija Oranen); ph, Esa Vuorinen (Fujicolor); m, Hector; ed, Tuula Mehtonen.

Drama   (PR:O MPAA:NR)

RIVERBED, THE†   (1986, U.S./Neth.) 95m VPRO/Film International c

John Beuscher (*The Man*), Elaine Grove (*Mother*), Sharon Bellanoff-Smith (*Daughter*).

A low-budget feature that will probably never see a general release in the U.S. (although it has played festivals), THE RIVERBED tells, with next to no dialog, the story of a Depression-era drifter (Beuscher) who takes a job with Grove, a widow. Her daughter, Bellanoff-Smith, is mentally retarded and fantasizes endlessly about water in all its forms. Grove asks Beuscher to marry her daughter and take her away, and he agrees. The marriage is never consummated, though, and Beuscher simply cares for her the best he can. In the end he carries her—perhaps sleeping, perhaps dead already—into a pond and lets her sink. Born in St. Louis, director Reichman began shooting this film in 1983, but it was not until 1985 that Dutch TV gave her the money to complete the filming.

p,d,&w, Rachel Reichman; ph, Steven Giuliano; m, Josh Colow; ed, Rachel Reichman.

Drama   (PR:C MPAA:NR)

ROBINSONIADA ANU CHEMI INGLISELI PAPA†   (1986, USSR) 70m Georgia Film Studio c-bw (Trans: Robinsoniad; Or, My English Grandfather)

Janzi Lolaschwili (*Christopher Hughes*), Nineli Chankwetadse (*Anna*), Guram Pirchalawa (*Revolutionary*), Gudze Duzduli (*Landowner*).

Lolaschwili is a stubborn British telegraph operator stationed in Caucasian Georgia during the Bolshevik revolution who refuses to allow the military upheaval to interfere with his job. When his presence becomes a nuisance and he is forced to leave his post, Lolaschwili settles underneath a telegraph pole, claiming that ten feet surrounding each pole is British property. The story is told in flashback by the Englishman's grandson and his now-ancient lover of the era.

d, Nana Dschordschadse; w, Irakli Kwirikadze; ph, Lewan Paataschwili; m, Enri Lolaschwili; ed, Nana Dschordschadse; art d, Wachtang Kurna.

Comedy   (PR:C MPAA:NR)

ROCINANTE†   (1986, Brit.) 93m Cinema Action–Channel Four TV/Cinema Action c

John Hurt (*Bill*), Maureen Douglass (*Jess*), Ian Dury (*The Jester*), Jimmy Jewel (*The Projectionist*), Carol Gilles (*Molly*), David Travena (*Joe*), Tony Rohr (*Stan*), Nicky Bee (*Charlie*), Richard Worthy (*Estate Manager*), Jill Lamede (*Mrs. Matheson*), Adam Daye (*Charles Matheson*), Gillian Heasman (*Gillian*).

A picaresque tale that finds a modern-day Quixote (Hurt) wandering a Britain embroiled in the 1984 miners' strike. Hurt, a romantic idealist, "squats" in an aging movie house and delights in the images of the tranquil British countryside that unreel there. When the theater is to be demolished, Hurt takes to the road, hitching a ride with Douglass in a van that is outfitted with a computer and several curious maps. She is convinced that the National Coal Board's attempt to close down "uneconomic" pits is just the tip of an iceberg of government manipulation and secrecy made possible by computer technology. Because she is not just a theorist and is actively undertaking to disrupt this system, the police are after her. At a particularly anxious moment, she and Hurt are forced to part company. As Hurt continues his travels, he hooks up with Dury, a "jester" who introduces the reclusive dreamer to the downside of Not-So-Merry Old England.

It is not surprising that the National Union of Mineworkers strike of 1984-5 should loom so large in a film that concerns itself with modern British politics, nor is it surprising that such a film would be produced by Cinema Action, a company with a reputation for involvement in risky political documentaries. In 1984 a badly divided NUM (long the symbolic backbone of British trade unionism) attempted to fight the forced closures of many pits, but the strike that resulted was not supported by the entire membership of the union. Many local branches refused to go out, and in the north of England in particular, violence resulted from attempts to cross picket lines and confrontations between strikers and the police.

ROCINANTE, which takes its name from Don Quixote's horse, includes a couple of interesting casting choices: Douglass is a real-life miner's wife who stood on the picket lines, and Dury the rocker who looked for "reasons to be cheerful" with the Blockheads.

p, Gustav Lamche; d&w, Ann Guedes, Eduardo Guedes; ph, Thaddeus O'Sullivan (Eastmancolor); m, Jurgen Knieper; ed, Eduardo Guedes, Richard Taylor; art d, Caroline Amies; cos, Jo Thompson.

Drama   (PR:A-C MPAA:NR)

ROCKIN' ROAD TRIP**   (1986) 101m Triad Entertainment Group/Troma c

Garth McLean (*Martin Biggs*), Margaret Currie (*Nicole Miller*), Katherine Harrison (*Samantha Miller*), Steve Boles (*Wally Beckman*), Marty Tucker (*Lenny Drake*), Graham Smith (*Ivan the Angry Punk*), Leland Grantt (*Curtis Little*), Peter Bruno (*Boston Cabbie*), Alan Marx (*Roach*), Will Brown (*Gillis*), Rusty Owens (*Tucker Benson*), Denise Williams (*Terri*), Catherine Williams (*Claudia*), Sally Nussbaumer (*Mrs. Miller*), Jack Chatham (*Mr. Eugene Miller*), Bob Bloodworth (*Isaac M. Tunstall*), Duke Ernsberger (*Wayne*), Leon Rippy (*Earl Reese*), Mykle Mariette (*Leonard*), Simon Frederick (*North Carolina Cabbie*), Lars Lundgren (*Biker/Old Woman at Circus*), Cedric Guthrie (*Clubowner*), Pat Miller (*Jewel Thief*), Vivian Tedford (*Policewoman*), Boston Kunick (*Blind Man*), Mickey Henderson, Aaron Lewis, Chuck King (*Moving Men*), Guadalcanal Diary (*Band*), Albert Dulin (*Older Guy at Club*), Kim Saunders (*Waitress at Club*), Chester Corson (*Boston Cab Dispatcher*), Mark Ferri, Willie Stratford (*Van Guys*), Terry Loughlin (*Music Store Manager*), Michelle Brattain (*Music Store Clerk*), James Eric (*Bartender*), Mark Burton (*Kid in Bar/Unicyclist and Juggler*), Sadie Corson (*Old Woman at Elevator*), Rebecca Koon (*Doris the Waitress*), Kris McGary (*Girl in Parking Lot/Gospel Singer*), Kim DeCoste (*Girl in Parking Lot*), Fritz Goforth, Jeff Kluttz (*Guys in Pickup Truck*), Katy O'Toole (*Little Girl in Lobby*), Karen Bell-Holland (*Waitress in Diner*), Chuck Bibby (*Bus Driver*), Tim Bost (*Faith Healer*), Alpha Trivette (*Stage Manager*), Stewart Lippe (*Christian Juggler*), Mario Griego (*TV Director*), George Gray (*Tunstall's Partner*), Mike Clark (*1st Medic*), Cyndy Prevette (*TV Announcer*), Judy Ardis (*Lady in Cab*), Don Simandl (*Sign-Reading Pedestrian*), Billy Barber, Andy Leung, Mark Petro, Jason Metz (*Break Dancing Kids*), Tim Bost (*Older Salesman in Motel Bar*), Joe Alvarado, S.B. Bundy, Darrell Huffman, Dennis Richards (*Gun Club Members*), Cindy Roper (*Angry Girl at Airport*), Heidi Rinehardt (*Little Girl's Mommy*), Betty White (*Maid in Motel*), Dick Langdon (*Fainting Driver*), Ellis Boatman (*Pastor Bob*), Louise Barrett (*Woman with Bad Back*), Greg Plough, Mike Bigham (*TV Cameramen*), Howard Lineberger (*Clown*), Terry Kester (*Drunk at Circus*), Elizabeth Bundy (*Gypsy Fortune Teller*), Mike Nations (*Swami*), Elberta Coulter (*Old Woman's Friend*), Mark Rose, Mark Sams (*Medics*), Robert McMillin, Karen Detter (*Deputies*).

A mildly amusing low-budget effort about a kid from Boston, McLean, who falls in love with Harrison in a local bar. He's in for a bit of a surprise when he finds that Harrison is part of a package deal that includes a band called Cherry Suicide, fronted by her sister Currie. Hounded by a gang of inept jewel thieves, the band leaves town bound for Florida. Along the way they make a stop in North Carolina and take a gig playing at a religious carnival. It's all rather mindless, padded out with a collection of oddball characters including a blind philosopher, Boles, and a gun-toting punk rocker, Smith. The film is filled with music from a number of gutsy American rock bands, including critical favorites Guadalcanal Diary, Love Tractor, and Pylon. Songs include "Gilbert Takes the Wheel" (Murray Attaway, John Poe, Rhett Crowe, Jeff Walls, performed by Guadalcanal Diary), "Pillow Talk," "Watusi Rodeo," "Ghosts on the Road" (Attaway, Poe, Walls, performed by Guadalcanal Diary); "Greedy Dog," "Spin Your Partner," (Love Tractor, performed by Love Tractor); "Crazy," "M Train" (Pylon, performed by Pylon); "Wolves at Bay" (Marianna Pace, perfromed by Pace); "Red Dress" (Ellis, performed by The Heartfixers), "This Is

It!'' ''Slippin' Away,'' ''Summertime Blues'' (Keller-Simpson, performed by The Cheryl Wilson Band, as ''Cherry Suicide'').

p, William Olsen, Michael Rothschild; d, William Olsen; w, William Olsen, Nancy Sterling (based on a story by William Olsen); ph, Austin McKinney (TVC Color); m, Ricky Keller; ed, David H. Lloyd; prod d, James Eric; art d, Jerry Colbert; set d, Geoffrey Rayle, Leanne McIntyre; cos, Elizabeth Hale; spec eff, Mykle Mariette; ch, Allison Pearle; m/l, Murray Attaway, John Poe, Rhett Crowe, Jeff Walls, Love Tractor, Pylon, Marianna Pace; makeup, Elizabeth Hale; stunts, Lars Lundgren.

Comedy   **Cas.**   **(PR:C-O MPAA:PG-13)**

ROKUMEIKAN†   (1986, Jap.) Marugen/Toho (Trans: Rokumeikan, High Society of Meiji)

Bunta Sugawara, Ruriko Asaoka, Koji Ishizaka, Kiichi Nakai, Kyoko Kishida, Yasuko Sawaguchi.

d, Kon Ichikawa; w, Shin-ya Hidaka (based on the novel by Yukio Mishima); ph, Setsuo Kobayashi; art d, Shinobu Muraki.

ROLLER BLADE zero   (1986) 97m NW c

Suzanne Solari *(Sister Sharon Cross)*, Jeff Hutchinson *(Marshall Goodman)*, Shaun Michelle *(Hunter/Sister Fortune)*, Katina Garner *(Mother Speed)*, Sam Mann *(Waco)*, Robby Taylor *(The Deputy/Dr. Saticoy)*, Chris Douglas-Olen Ray *(Chris Goodman)*, Michelle Bauer, Barbara Peckinpaugh, Lisa Marie.

This unimaginative spin off the now-tired MAD MAX cliches takes place in post-nuclear Los Angeles, where Garner is the wheelchair-bound leader of some beautiful roller-skating women. The evil opposing leader, Taylor (you know he's bad just by his leather outfit), is trying to get hold of a magic crystal Garner owns. He sends his gorgeous assistant Michelle to work undercover in Garner's band, then pilfer the magic crystal when the time is right. Eventually Michelle discovers Taylor doesn't care who gets killed, just as long as he gets his hands on that crystal. Meanwhile, one of Garner's girls, Solari, catches onto Michelle's secret assignment. The two duke it out in a roller-skating fight for life, but while they're knocking heads, Taylor steals the crystal. Michelle gives up her life so Solari won't get killed by Taylor and is exonerated. Taylor tries to hightail it out of the scene via a rocket-powered skateboard, but Solari manages to catch up with him. Good naturally triumphs, but the troublesome crystal is destroyed along with Taylor.

When it's not just plain silly, ROLLER BLADE is an incompetently made bore. Gangs of skateboarding and roller-skating punks simply don't hold the same sort of threat motorcycle-bound nasties do, and the wretched performances here don't help matters much. The tired special effects and Jackson's woefully clunky direction further diminish what little impact there is to the story. In a dying gasp to throw some life into the film, Jackson gives us a preponderance of naked female flesh, some of which is provided by minor porno actresses who are obviously between jobs.

p&d, Donald G. Jackson; w, Donald G. Jackson, Randall Frakes (based on a story by Donald G. Jackson); ph, Donald G. Jackson; m, Robert Garrett; ed, Ron Amick; set d, Donald G. Jackson, Ron Amick; spec eff, Tony Tremblay, Ron Amick; stunts, Clifford Davidson.

Action/Science Fiction   **Cas.**   **(PR:O MPAA:NR)**

ROMANCE†   (1986, It.) 88m M.V.M./International Movie c

Walter Chiari *(Father)*, Luca Barbareschi *(Andrea)*, Julia Hiebaum Colombo *(Young Girl)*, Patrizia Fachini *(Andrea's Wife)*, Regina Nitsch *(German Tourist)*, Mario Buffa Moncalvo, Fernanda Alene, Giancarlo Garbelli, Lia Lenzini.

The second feature of director Mazzucco (SUMMERTIME [1985]) explores the relationship between a father and a son who haven't seen each other in years. Sensing that he's near death, Chiari sends for his son, Barbareschi, to visit him at the remote mountain retreat the family had used as a summer home. Plagued by a restless urge to find some truth in his life, Chiari had abandoned his family 20 years before and hadn't been heard from since. Barbareschi, now a successful Milanese career man who has rebelled against his father's walkout by creating a

perfect family life for himself, goes to Chiari out of curiosity. Over the next three days the two men get reacquainted and discover that they have little in common. Chiari considers his son's pursuits superficial, while Barbareschi sees Chiari's life as self-absorbed and morbid. During their discussions they begin to chip away at each others' fears and anxieties until they come to an understanding.

p, Paolo Pagnoni, Camilla Nesbitt; d, Massimo Mazzucco; w, Massimo Mazzucco, Lucia Zei; ph, Fabio Cianchetti (Luciano Vittori Color); m, Andrea Centazzo; ed, Rene Condoluci.

Drama   **(PR:O MPAA:NR)**

ROMANTICHNA-ISTORIJA†   (1986, Bulgaria) 98m Bulgariafilm c (Trans: Romantic Story)

Irene Krivoshieva *(Zhana)*, Ivan Ivanov *(Ivan Chunov ''Condor'')*, Vladimir Kolev *(Zhoro)*.

The romance of an unpleasant couple who imagine themselves to be like Romeo and Juliet is followed from the early 1970s right into the 1980s. Ivanov is an arrogant male chauvinist who expects his girl friend, Krivoshieva, to obey him at all times. He strings her along by constantly postponing any talk of marriage. Finally, years later, when he is ready to marry, she decides she wants more freedom in the relationship. Angered, he leaves only to return 10 years later having become involved in some shady dealings which have made him rich. This time she marries him, but their troubles are only beginning.

d, Miaden Nikolov; w, Aleksander Tomov (based on his short story ''Condor''); ph, Georgi Georgiov; m, Aleksander Burzitsov; ed, Catherine Stanley; art d, Vladimir Lokarski.

Romance   **(PR:C-O MPAA:NR)**

ROOM WITH A VIEW, A**   (1986, Brit.) 115m Cinecom c

Maggie Smith *(Charlotte Bartlett)*, Helena Bonham Carter *(Lucy Honeychurch)*, Denholm Elliott *(Mr. Emerson)*, Julian Sands *(George Emerson)*, Daniel Day Lewis *(Cecil Vyse)*, Simon Callow *(Rev. Beebe)*, Judi Dench *(Miss Lavish)*, Rosemary Leach *(Mrs. Honeychurch)*, Rupert Graves *(Freddy Honeychurch)*, Patrick Godfrey *(Mr. Eager)*, Fabia Drake *(Catherine Alan)*, Joan Henley *(Teresa Alan)*, Maria Britneva *(Mrs. Vyse)*, Amanda Walker *(The Cockney Signora)*, Peter Cellier *(Sir Harry Otway)*, Mia Fothergill *(Minnie Beebe)*, Patricia Lawrence *(Mrs. Butterworth)*, Mirio Guidelli *(Santa Croce Guide)*, Matyelock Gibbs, Kitty Aldridge *(The New Charlotte and Lucy)*, Freddy Korner *(Mr. Floyd)*, Elizabeth Marangoni *(Miss Pole)*, Lucca Rossi *(Phaeton)*, Isabella Celani *(Persephone)*, Luigi Di Fiori *(Murdered Youth)*.

Made for only $3 million, this Merchant-Ivory production was nominated for eight Oscars and won three. After years of producing beautiful, but often boring,

pictures, the team of James Ivory, Ismail Merchant, and Ruth Prawer Jhabvala finally tapped the commercial vein and they will probably never have to struggle for financing again. The three have been cited in the *Guinness Book Of Records* for having the longest writer-producer-director association in movie history, approaching a quarter of a century in 1986. California-born Ivory, India-born Merchant, and German-born Jhabvala would seem an unlikely trio to have brought forth HEAT AND DUST, THE EUROPEANS, THE BOSTONIANS, among other films. Gathering good notices and generally adequate box-office receipts, they continued to make movies that delighted themselves. Now, with A ROOM WITH A VIEW, they have delighted millions of others.

The droll comedy of manners and morals begins in 1907. The young women of Thorstein Veblen's ''leisure class'' are still struggling under the yoke of Victorian prudishness. The idea of an unattached woman traveling to Europe would be scandalous, so when Carter (in her second film after the mildly received LADY JANE) goes off to Italy, it's in the company of Smith, her maiden cousin and spinster chaperon. They arrive in Florence and take up residence at the Pensione Bertolini, a typical hostelry of the time catering to the British. This is sort of the mini-version of ''the Grand Tour'' that every young Englishwoman of stature took to expand her cultural parameters. At the hotel, they meet a potpourri of other guests. Elliott is a rough-hewn but charming businessman who came up the hard way and won't let anyone forget it. Still, he is a charming person and his

good, strong attitudes are seen in the personage of his young son, Sands, an executive with the British Rail System. Sands is a liberal man, given to somewhat eccentric thoughts (for the time) and living every moment of his life with elan and eclat. It's evident from the start that Sands finds Carter pleasing to gaze upon. At first, she responds with aloofness. Later, she escapes her cousin's watchful eye to visit the church of Santa Croce, where many of Italy's greatest artists are buried beneath the floor. On the Piazza Signorina, Carter witnesses a fight that ends in the stabbing murder of Di Fiori. She swoons and falls into the arms of the nearby Sands, who takes her back to the hotel.

There are others staying at the pensione. Drake and Henley are a pair of sisters who, at first, seem as tense as Smith but who do have a raffish sense of humor. Callow is a young reverend who is about to become vicar in the country church attended by Carter and Smith. Dench is a romance novelist who finds in Carter a wonderful virginal heroine for her next book. Callow likes the way Carter plays Beethoven, a composer that sweet young women of the day were supposed to forego. He says that "if she ever takes to living as she plays, it will be very exciting—both for us and for her." Carter and the others go off to a visit to Fiesole, the town high above Florence. Sands takes the opportunity to kiss Carter, which Smith witnesses. Smith puts her foot down and insists they leave for England at once.

Back in Surrey, where Carter lives with mother Leach and ne'er do-well brother Graves, their existence is pastoral and proper. Their manor house is surrounded by well-kept gardens, perfect fields, and all of the accoutrements of the good life. With the passion of Sands out of the way, Carter settles into her relationship with Lewis, a twit to whom she is engaged. Lewis is the epitome of the aesthete, a man who loves to spend his time reading books to women and doesn't seem to realize that there is more to a woman than a willing ear. It turns out that there is a vacant villa in the area and Carter suggests Drake and Henley as possible tenants. Graves has another idea. On a recent trip to London, he met a father and son who he thinks might make good neighbors, none other than Elliot and Sands, as eccentric a pair as Graves has ever encountered. He means it to be a good joke, but the two accept and move into the area. Sands and Graves become good friends and play many jolly games of tennis at the house. Carter tries to avoid paying attention to Sands, but there is no doubt her feelings are beginning to mount for the charming young man. Further, the more she sees of Lewis, the less she cares for him. One afternoon in the garden, Sands repeats his kiss with Carter, which is missed by the dozing Lewis sitting nearby. In a scene that has little to do with the picture but is, perhaps, it's best moment, Graves, Sands, and Callow decide to have a bit of a drench in the pond. They shed their clothing and have a riotous time wallowing nude in the water, a celebration of the shedding of inhibitions. Carter must now make a decision. Does she take the safe and sound and surely dull life with Lewis, or does she allow her feelings for Sands to emerge? She can't have it both ways, but she does break off her engagement with the foppish Lewis and plans to go to Greece with Drake and Henley. Smith and Elliot intervene and Carter and Sands are reunited. They marry and spend their blissful honeymoon in Florence, at the same pensione where they met. Naturally, the room they occupy is the one with a view.

E.M. Forster began writing this novel in 1901 and it was published in 1908, when he was 29. The filmmakers began work on the script in 1980, even though Ivory was tired of period pictures, having just directed HEAT AND DUST and THE BOSTONIANS. With such a low budget, the picture was scheduled to shoot in just nine weeks, but due to bad weather, it came in at ten. The acting is superb; from two-time Oscar winner Smith to the smallest role, there's not a false note. Hard to believe that this movie cost so little because the costumes and sets are dazzling. The one picture that fell below Merchant and Ivory's standards was THE WILD PARTY (not written by Jhabvala, based on a poem by Joseph Moncure March), which was their one contact with the "studio system" and was a great disappointment. Carter compensates for her lack of experience with her breathtaking beauty and innocence. She is the great granddaughter of former British Prime Minister Herbert Henry Asquith as well as the niece of director Anthony Asquith (PYGMALION, THE BROWNING VERSION, THE WINS-LOW BOY, THE IMPORTANCE OF BEING EARNEST, among many). Lewis, who will be remembered as the punk in MY BEAUTIFUL LAUNDRETTE, is astounding as the prig, and Elliot's work was good enough to merit an Oscar nomination as Best Supporting Actor. In addition to Elliot's nomination, the Motion Picture Academy nominated Smith for Best Actress, Ivory for Best Director, Pierce-Roberts for Best Cinematography, the film for Best Picture, and

presented Oscars to Jhabvala for Best Screenplay Based on Material from Another Medium, Quaranta, Ackland-Snow, Savegar, and Altramura for Best Art Direction—Set Direction, and Beavan and Bright for Best Costume Design. It took more than two decades for the team to gain such recognition. We can only hope it won't take that long next time out. The full frontal nudity is what gives this a "caution".

p, Ismail Merchant; d, James Ivory; w, Ruth Prawer Jhabvala (based on the novel by E.M. Forster); m, Richard Robbins; ed, Humphrey Dixon; prod d, Gianni Quaranta, Brian Ackland-Snow; cos, Jenny Beavan, John Bright; makeup, Christine Beveridge.

Comedy   Cas.   (PR:C   MPAA:PG-13)

ROSA LUXEMBURG†   (1986, Ger.) 122m Bioskop–Pro-ject–Regina Ziegler
–Baren–Westdeutscher Rundfunk c

Barbara Sukowa *(Rosa Luxemburg)*, Daniel Olbrychski *(Leo Jogiches)*, Otto Sander *(Karl Liebknecht)*, Adelheid Arndt *(Luise Kautsky)*, Jurgen Holtz *(Karl Kautsky)*, Doris Schade *(Clara Zetkin)*, Hannes Jaenicke *(Kostja Zetkin)*, Jan-Paul Biczycki *(August Bebel)*, Karin Baal *(Mathilde Jacob)*, Winfried Glatzeder *(Paul Levi)*, Regina Lemnitz *(Gertrud)*, Barbara Lass *(Rosa's Mother)*, Dagna Drozdek *(Rosa at Age 6)*.

Feminist filmmaker Margarethe von Trotta directed this biographical sketch of the early 20th Century revolutionist and spokesperson for the left-wing Spartacus League. The film opens with Sukowa, as Luxemburg, incarcerated in a Polish prison in 1905. Important events in her life are then detailed, showing her as a peaceful person who openly criticizes the Kaiser and his militaristic regime. These actions result in her repeated arrest. She is brutally murdered in 1919 while under arrest and being transported to prison, her body tossed into Berlin's Landwehrkanal. This film is a fictionalized account of Luxemburg's life derived from letters she had written. Originally, the late Rainer Werner Fassbinder had hoped to make a film about her, but he died at the outset of the project and von Trotta took over. ROSA LUXEMBURG won the German Film Prize for Best Film, while Sukowa received the Gold Film Band for her performance. She also shared the Best Actress Award at Cannes. (In German; English subtitles.)

p, Eberhard Junkersdorf, Martin Wiebel; d&w, Margarethe von Trotta; ph, Franz Rath; m, Nicolas Economou; ed, Dagmar Hirtz; set d, Bernd Lopel, Karel Vacek.

Biography/Drama   (PR:O   MPAA:NR)

ROSE†   (1986, Hong Kong) 99m Manshi Yonfan/Golden Harvest c

Chow Yan-fat, Maggie Cheung.

A melodramatic romance based on a love story popular among teenage girls in Hong Kong. Chow plays a dual role, as both the admired older brother of Cheung and as her lover and husband-to-be. Filmed in Paris. (In Cantonese; English subtitles.)

p&d, Manshi Yonfan (based on the novel by Yik Shue).

Romance   (PR:C   MPAA:NR)

ROUND MIDNIGHT***   (1986, Fr./U.S.) 133m PECF-Little Bear/WB. c

Dexter Gordon *(Dale Turner)*, Francois Cluzet *(Francis Borier)*, Gabrielle Haker *(Berangere)*, Sandra Reaves-Phillips *(Buttercup)*, Lonette McKee *(Darcey Leigh)*, Christine Pascal *(Sylvie)*, Herbie Hancock *(Eddie Wayne)*, Bobby Hutcherson *(Ace)*, Pierre Trabaud *(Francis's Father)*, Frederique Meininger *(Francis's Mother)*, Liliane Rovere *(Mme. Queen)*, Hart Leroy Bibbs *(Hershell)*, Ged Marlon *(Beau)*, Benoit Regent *(Psychiatrist)*, Victoria Gabrielle Platt *(Chan)*, Arthur French *(Booker)*, John Berry *(Ben)*, Martin Scorsese *(Goodley)*, Philippe Noiret *(Redon)*, Alain Sarde *(Terzian)*, Eddy Mitchell *(A Drunk)*; Blue Note: Billy Higgins *(Drums)*, Bobby Hutcherson *(Vibes)*, Eric Le`Lann *(Trumpet)*, John McLaughlin *(Guitar)*, Pierre Michelot *(Bass)*, Wayne Shorter *(Tenor Saxophone)*; Davout Studio: Ron Carter *(Bass)*, Billy Higgins *(Drums)*, Palle Mikkelborg *(Trumpet)*, Wayne Shorter *(Soprano Saxophone)*, Mads Vinding *(Bass)*; Lyon: Cheikh Fall *(Percussion)*, Michel Perez *(Guitar)*, Wayne Shorter *(Soprano Saxophone)*, Mads Vinding *(Bass)*, Tony Williams *(Drums)*, New York: Ron Carter *(Bass)*, Freddie Hubbard *(Trumpet)*, Cedar Walton *(Piano)*, Tony Williams *(Drums)*; Charles Belonzi, Marpessa Djian, Patrick Massieu, Jacques Poitrenaud, Jimmy Slyde, Pascale Vignal, Arnaud Chevrier, Guy Louret, Philippe Moreau, Luc Sarot, Pascal Tedes, Noel Simsolo.

It is meaningless to call ROUND MIDNIGHT the greatest jazz film ever made, simply because the competition is uniformly weak. ROUND MIDNIGHT's lasting value does not lie merely in its vivid portrayal of the bebop milieu, but in its delicate, subtle, and poignant examination of the turbulent forces within a man who is compelled to create his art—to give of himself—on a nightly basis despite the personal consequences. Dedicated to jazz greats Lester Young and Bud Powell, the film begins in 1959 as black bebop jazzman Dale Turner (Gordon), "the greatest tenor saxophone player in the world," decides to leave the "cold eyes" of New York City and move to Paris. Alcoholic, ill, and—it is hinted—a former heroin addict, Gordon is watched like a hawk by Reaves-Phillips, a stout, forceful woman who forbids him to drink, gets him to the gigs on time, and withholds his pay for fear he will spend it on drugs or liquor. Gordon plays nightly at the famous Blue Note jazz club in Paris to a packed house of adoring fans who appreciate and understand his bebop music. Many other black American expatriates play there as well, with Hutcherson desperately trying to assuage his homesickness by preparing elaborate southern-style meals in his dingy hotel room.

Gordon's fellow musicians are aware of his health problems and all take great pains to keep watch over him and prevent him from drinking (during one number Gordon slyly tries to swipe the glass of bourbon resting on the edge of Hancock's piano while the pianist performs his solo. Gently, Hancock slides the glass out of Gordon's reach while continuing to play one-handed).

On the street outside the Blue Note is a young Frenchman, Cluzet, crouched near the air vent in the driving rain listening to Gordon play. A commercial artist

with little money ("If I had any cash, I'd be inside!" he screams at a panhandler), Cluzet is a devoted fan of jazz in general and of Gordon in particular. Separated from his wife—who left him and their young daughter (Haker) for another man—Cluzet's obsession with Gordon's music is such that he leaves his child home alone at night to go to the Blue Note and listen to the music. One night after the show, Cluzet stands across the street from the club trying to work up enough nerve to speak to his idol. Gordon manages to slip past his keepers and saunters up to the young Frenchman and asks "Hey, man. Can you buy me a beer?" Cluzet immediately agrees and they adjourn to the local tavern. While Cluzet excitedly tells Gordon that "Your music has changed my life," all the musician can think about is getting another drink. Gordon repays the Frenchman by informing club owner Berry that Cluzet is a friend; this gets him into the Blue Note for free. Unfortunately, this new friendship does not curb Gordon's self-destructive instincts and he escapes several times to go on drinking binges (he usually snatches tips off the club tables since he has no money of his own). After one particularly nasty escapade, Cluzet finds Gordon in jail and bails him out. He takes the musician back to his hotel room and asks Hutcherson if anything had happened during his performance that would have set him off. Hutcherson's reply: "When you have to explore every night, even the most beautiful things you find can be the most painful." Sensing that Gordon will kill himself if given the chance, Cluzet decides to have the musician move in with him. Because his apartment is not big enough for three people, Cluzet asks his estranged wife, Pascal, to lend him the money for a bigger place. While it is obvious that there is still deep feeling between the two, Cluzet is unthinkingly cruel to Pascal and tells her that she never inspired him as much as Gordon's music. Despite the hurt, Pascal sends him the money. The change of abode, however, does little good at first. Gordon continues to sneak out and get drunk. Cluzet traces his friend to a hospital and eavesdrops on Gordon's conversation with a psychiatrist. Gordon tells the doctor that, although he sleeps, he never rests: "There's always the

dreams . . . about music . . . expanding the music. I'm tired of everything except the music." Gordon's self-destruction continues until one night Cluzet breaks down and cries over the drunken musician. The next morning Gordon awakens Cluzet with breakfast in bed. "Never. Never again, man. Don't cry for me." "What else can I do when you're killing yourself?" Cluzet responds. "I'll stop," Gordon promises. "You never stopped before," says Cluzet disgustedly. "I never promised anyone before."

In the weeks that follow, Gordon makes a supreme effort to behave. His health improves, his performances improve, and he begins composing and recording again. With his newfound trustworthiness, Gordon demands to be paid directly, and Berry and Reaves-Phillips reluctantly agree. Gordon cooks meals for Cluzet and Haker, and the three go on an outing to the beach. Gordon's new energy is tinged with self-doubt, however: "I keep wondering if I still have something to give." When Cluzet brings the musician along for a trip to his parents' house to celebrate Haker's birthday, Gordon becomes withdrawn and distant. Homesick and feeling dislocated, Gordon decides to return to New York. A wary Cluzet accompanies him to the U.S. and they are greeted by the owner of the Birdland jazz club, Scorsese (in an amazingly hyper performance—the man embodies New York City). The manic Scorsese takes them to a seedy, rundown hotel where many a jazz man has passed on and rattles off all the little details he has taken care of for Gordon: union dues, legal fees, fines, and tells him to get to the gig on time. During his opening night at Birdland, Gordon dedicates a new song to his young daughter, Platt, in honor of her birthday (he announces she's 15, but she's only 14). After the performance father and daughter share a meal, but the conversation is strained—Gordon doesn't really know his own child. Later at the hotel, Gordon confesses his neglect and implores Cluzet, "Don't let that happen to you and Berangere." Worried about a drug dealer that he spots lurking the halls of the hotel, Cluzet buys two tickets back to Paris and begs Gordon to go back with him. Gordon makes a vague agreement to meet Cluzet at the airport. As they walk along the East River Gordon muses, "You know, Lady Francis, there is not enough kindness in the world." Gordon never makes the flight, and Cluzet returns to Paris alone. Weeks later he receives a telegram from Scorsese that Gordon has died. While viewing some home movies of their happy times in Paris, Cluzet remembers something that Gordon once said: "I hope we'll all live long enough to see an avenue named after Charlie Parker . . . Lester Young park . . . Duke Ellington square . . . maybe, even, a street called Dale Turner."

The irony of ROUND MIDNIGHT is that it took a Frenchman to make the most accurate, understated, intelligent film yet about a distinctly American art form—jazz. Hollywood's efforts have been undistinguished at best (employing the jazz milieu merely as a backdrop for hackneyed melodramatics), and downright infuriating at worst, due to ignorance of the music and the virtual disregard of black musicians as the creators and driving force of jazz. Director Tavernier is a true jazz enthusiast and his passion for the music and its creators is evident in every frame of ROUND MIDNIGHT. Production designer Trauner (CHILDREN OF PARADISE) recreated Paris' famous Blue Note jazz club in perfect detail. Tavernier insisted on casting actual musicians as his actors and that the music be recorded live on the set with the cameras rolling—not post-dubbed. Using a two-camera setup and verbally instructing his camera operators where to move during the jazz performances, Tavernier captured in rich detail the complex relationships among musicians at work. How they watch each other intently to gauge in what direction the improvisations will flow, their musical searching, the expansion of the sound, and their exhilaration upon discovering new ground: these all occur before our eyes. The creative process has never before been captured with such spontaneity and skill in a narrative film. At other times Tavernier employs a more formal, studied visual style where his camera executes complicated moving shots that require meticulous planning and rehearsal. These shots serve as a cinematic counterpoint to the spontaneous musical improvisation occurring on stage; thus the viewer is treated to two very different virtuoso talents within the same shot. ROUND MIDNIGHT is filled with references to jazz greats, and the Dale Turner character is an amalgamation of many musicians, particularly Lester Young (who would address those he respected, male or female, as "Lady") and Bud Powell, with Dexter Gordon evoking much of his own experience. The plot of the film is based loosely on the last years of brilliant bebop pianist Powell's life. Suffering from mental illness (the man was practically catatonic and would go for days without speaking—he only came to life when sitting before a piano) and working in Paris, Powell was taken in and cared for by French jazz fan and critic Francis Paudras (who has a cameo in the film as a patron tape-recording one of Gordon's performances). Powell regained his faculties briefly and he eventually returned to New York, but the pressures proved too great and he died a few years later. Tavernier changed the pianist to a saxophone player and—with Paudras' help—screened films of surviving saxophone players from that era in a search for an artist who looked right for the role. Although the director considered casting Sonny Rollins, Rollins looked "the picture of health" and wouldn't be convincing as an ill musician plagued by personal demons. When Tavernier saw footage of Dexter Gordon, he knew he had his man. The towering (6-foot-5-inch") musician was a contemporary of Powell's; he had the right looks, the humor, and the movement that Tavernier was looking for. In addition, Gordon had a respected musical reputation and had lived in Europe for over 14 years. There was one slight problem however; Gordon had disappeared and Paudras didn't even know if the saxophonist was still alive. Word drifted through the jazz world and soon Gordon surfaced (he'd been living in Mexico and suffering from ill health). After talks with Tavernier, Gordon was convinced that the Frenchman sincerely wanted to "do it right" and Gordon signed on. The musician became obsessed with setting the record straight about what it means to be a jazz musician. He contributed much of the dialog and made suggestions for changes in the script. For example, Tavernier wanted to use a completely American band for Gordon's Blue Note performances. Gordon informed the director that such a thing was never done and that at least one member of the rhythm section should be French—so Tavernier brought in bass player Pierre Michelot (who had played with Bud Powell). Tavernier and Hancock (who not only acted, but composed the score—he won an Oscar) had also decided on a particularly complex arrangement for Gordon's opening-night performance. Gordon vetoed the idea and stated that such an arrangement would never be attempted on the first night with a strange band, so it was decided to use the simpler "As Time Goes By." While Gordon's technical advice greatly enhances the film, it is his superb performance (nominated for a Best Actor Oscar) as the tortured jazzman that lies at the heart of this film. His odd gait, sly wit, gentle mugging, and his thoughtful, slow delivery of his lines in a quiet, raspy voice virtually personifies the jazz music that is almost impossible to describe, but demands to be heard. Gordon felt that he was representing all the great artists who lived and died for their music and his devotion to their memory shines in his performance ("I have to carry with me the image of people like Charlie Parker and Lester Young, who never had the chance to express what I'm doing now," he is quoted as saying). Some have belittled his achievement by claiming that he was merely playing himself, but Tavernier has stated in interviews that there were several times when he had restrained Gordon from reacting as he normally would, instead behaving as the nearly defeated Dale Turner would (according to Tavernier, Gordon is an incredibly forceful and independent man who would not sit still for the kinds of controls that the characters in the film employ on "Dale Turner"). The role took much out of Gordon, and when the film was completed the musician asked Tavernier, "Lady Bertrand, how long do you think it's going to take me to get over this movie?" But ROUND MIDNIGHT contains much more than one superb performance. Young French actor Cluzet is excellent as well, and he too had trouble getting over the shooting of the movie. Tavernier reports that Cluzet so admired Gordon and was so absorbed by his character that he too began drinking heavily and fretting over the fate of his friend as if the real-life Gordon were about to die. Tavernier was finally forced to snap the actor back to reality by declaring that Gordon was a survivor: "Dexter in four years from now will be recording a new album, and *you* will be in the gutter." The relationship between these two very different men is exquisitely captured in all its joy, humor, and pain. Tavernier does not romanticize his main characters, for Cluzet is shown to be selfish and even cruel to those who love him (Haker and Pascal, although it is clear that Haker—a wonderful young actress—understands her father's obsessions and perhaps is more mature than he is), and, despite the brief respite, Gordon's demons finally destroy him. Relationships form the core of this film and Tavernier observes them with subtlety and elegance. The pace is unhurried and his camera lingers on the moment. Facial expressions and physical gestures are just as important as any words spoken or music played. Most important, Tavernier captures passion: passion for music, for art, for life itself. However, Tavernier is too perceptive to allow himself the illusion that this passion comes easily and without a price—there is no "ROCKY" ending here. The road to true creativity is paved with frustration, heartbreak, restlessness, self-doubt, and sacrifice. Be-bop, is an extremely demanding genre where the musician is compelled to stand before an audience and give them something that they've never heard before on a nightly basis. This urge, this necessity, that compels these musicians to give of their very souls—regardless of the recognition, fame, money, or personal consequence—is conveyed vividly by Tavernier with a beauty and grace that equals the music itself. Songs include "Round Midnight" (Thelonious Monk, Cootie Williams, Bernie Hanighen, performed by Bobby McFerrin), "As Time Goes By" (Herman Hupfeld), "Society Red" (Dexter Gordon), "Fairweather" (Kenny Dorham, performed by Chet Baker), "Now's the Time" (Charlie Parker), "Una Noche Con Francis" (Bud Powell), "Autumn in New York" (Vernon Duke), "Minuit Aux Champs Elysees" (Henri Renaud), "Body and Soul" (Edward Heyman, Robert Sour, Frank Eyton, Johnny Green), "I Cover the Waterfront" (Edward Heyman, Johnny Green, performed by Guy Marchand), "Watermelon Man" (Herbie Hancock), "The Peacocks" (Jimmy Rowles), "It's Only a Paper Moon" (Billy Rose, E.Y. Harburg, Harold Arlen), "Tivoli" (Dexter Gordon), "How Long Has This Been Going On?" (Ira Gershwin, George Gershwin, performed by Lonette McKee, also performed by Jimmy Gourley), "Put it Right Here" (Bessie Smith, performed by Sandra Reaves-Phillips), "Rhythm-A-Ning" (Thelonious Monk), "I Love Paris" (Cole Porter), "I Love a Party" (Herbie Hancock, Chan Parker), "What is This Thing Called Love?" (Cole Porter, performed by Bobby McFerrin), "Chan's Song (Never Said)" (Herbie Hancock, Stevie Wonder, performed by Bobby McFerrin).

p, Irwin Winkler; d, Bertrand Tavernier; w, Bertrand Tavernier, David Rayfiel (based on incidents in the lives of Francis Paudras, Bu Powell); ph, Bruno de Keyzer (Panavision, Eastmancolor); m, Herbie Hancock; ed, Armand Psenny; prod d, Alexandre Trauner; art d, Pierre Duquesne; set d, Philippe Turlure; cos, Jacqueline Moreau; m/l, Thelonious Monk, Cootie Williams, Bernie Hanighen, Herman Hupfeld, Dexter Gordon, Kenny Dorham, Charlie Parker, Bud Powell, Vernon Duke, Henri Renaud, Edward Heyman, Robert Sour, Frank Eyton, Johnny Green, Herbie Hancock, Jimmy Rowles, Billy Rose, E.Y. Harburg, Harold Arlen, Ira Gershwin, George Gershwin, Bessie Smith, Cole Porter, Chan Parker, Stevie Wonder; makeup, Paul Lemarinel.

Drama   **Cas. (PR:C MPAA:R)**

ROYAL WARRIORS†   (1986, Hong Kong) 93m D&B Films c

Michelle Kheng, Michael Wong.

Another big-budget police actioner from Hong Kong which sees Royal Hong Kong police force swing into action against the sleazy denizens of the underworld. Actress Kheng was a former Miss Malaysia.

p, John Sham; d&w, Chung Chi Man; ph, Chung Chi Man.

Crime   **(PR:C-O MPAA:NR)**

RUE DU DEPART†   (1986, Fr.) 95m Films Plain Chant-Films Ariane-Soprofilms-TF 1 Films/AAA c (Trans: Street of Departures)

Ann-Gisel Glass *(Clara Lombart)*, Christine Boisson *(Mimi)*, Francois Cluzet *(Paul Triana)*, Roger Coggio *(Cedonazzi)*, Jean-Pierre Sentier *(Boris)*, Gerard Depardieu *(Dr. Lombart)*, Hugues Quester, Jean-Pierre Bacri, Maurice Barrier, Gerard Darmon, Henri Deus, Daniel Laloux, Jean-Claude Lecas, Roger Mirmont, Chantal Neuwirth, Bruno Pradal, Marie-Helene Rudel.

With an original screenplay seemingly inspired by recent French film adaptations of David Goodis novels (Jean-Jacques Beineix's THE MOON IN THE GUTTER), RUE DU DEPART is set in the seamy milieu of the docks of Le Havre. Glass (DETECTIVE) stars as the young daughter of a bourgeois doctor, Depardieu, who decides to flee her stifling home and hide out among the denizens of the Parisian underworld. She meets Boisson, a streetwalker trying to break free from her sadistic pimp, Sentier. The pimp takes a liking to Glass, however, and menacingly tries to add the girl to his stable of streetwalkers. Glass also befriends Cluzet (ROUND MIDNIGHT), an escaped convict bent on revenge for the death of his father, after which he plans to sail away never to be seen again. Cluzet is wounded during his successful vendetta, and Glass turns to her father for medical help. Depardieu complies and Cluzet repays him by saving Glass from Sentier. In retaliation, Sentier kills Boisson. In the end, Glass joins Cluzet on his romantic journey to parts unknown.

p, Philippe Diaz; d, Tony Gatlif; w, Tony Gatlif, Marie-Helene Rudel; ph, Bernard Zitzermann (Eastmancolor); m, Charles Benarroch; ed, Claudine Bouche; art d, Denis Champenois; cos, Rose-Marie Nelka; m/l, Sapho; makeup, Maite Alonso.

Drama   **(PR:O MPAA:NR)**

RUNNING OUT OF LUCK zero   (1986) 80m Nitrate/CBS Records Group c

Mick Jagger *(Himself)*, Jerry Hall *(Herself)*, Rae Dawn Chong *(Slave Girl)*, Dennis Hopper *(Video Director)*, Angelo Di Biase *(Angelo)*, Raul Gazzola *(Spiderman)*, Andre Gasparelli, Vanessa, Luanu *(Transvestites)*, Tonico Pereira *(Truck Driver)*, Marcia De Souza *(Mick's Dancing Partner)*, Ritchie *(Himself)*, Angela Castro *(Blonde-Wig Whore)*, Tony Tornado, Jorge Coutinho, Geraldo Rosa *(Bunkhouse Card Players)*, Zeni Pereira *(Matriarch)*, Sandro Solviatt, Telma Reston *(Odd Couple)*, Marcelo Madureira *(The Boy)*, Waldir Onofre *(The Guard)*, Paulao, Marcos Comka, Rui Pollanah, Jose Dumont *(Prison Card Players)*, Paulo Henrique Souto *(Transvestite in Prison)*, Ita Morena *(Guitar Player)*, Rosana Campos *(Casino Girl)*, John Proctor *(Casino Manager)*, Laura Procter *(Varig Sales Girl)*, Tarita, Vicky Schneider, Carmita, Luma *(Girls on Yacht)*, Mis Viana *(Doorman)*, Norma Benguell, Carlos Krueber, Paulo Cesar Pereio, Grande Otelo, James Villiers, Nicholas Ball, Johnny Shannon, Jim Broadbent.

For the last 10 years or so rock personality Mick Jagger, the lead singer of the now-defunct Rolling Stones, has been running out of talent and it's never been more obvious than in this straight-to-video release. Apparently running out of ways to occupy his time, Jagger decided to act in and serve as executive producer on a feature film/rock video with songs from his latest album, "She's the Boss." Besides putting his own mug on screen, Jagger cast his girl friend (Texan model Hall), QUEST FOR FIRE star Chong, and the inimitable Hopper. The film's plot is as follows, if you can believe it. Jagger and Hall are in Rio de Janeiro to film a rock video called "Running Out of Luck" (ooh, dig the reflexivity) directed by Hopper. An angry Hall storms back to New York City and Jagger, fed up with Hopper's megalomania, bolts off the set with three heavily made-up extras. Well, poor Jagger soon discovers that they are transvestites who want to kill him (don't ask why, just accept it). They beat him senseless, stuff him into the back of a meat truck, and then put another body into a car which they push into the bay. The truck drives off and Jagger is deposited many miles away on a banana plantation as a sex slave. In the meantime, the sunken car has been found and the entire world assumes that Jagger is dead. Hall runs off with a stuffy senator, sending Jagger into a state of depression for a couple of seconds.

It is on the plantation that Jagger meets slave girl Chong, falls in love with her, and decides that he must escape (even though he seems right at home as a sex slave). Penniless and without any identification, Jagger must find a way to get back to Rio. Not to fret, Chong is full of luck. She finds a coin in a pay telephone, puts it in a slot machine, and hits the jackpot. With handfuls of slot machine slugs, the pair makes it to a Rio casino where Jagger wins more money. He's caught cheating, however, and thrown into prison. Chong helps him escape by putting poison on her breast, and thereby killing an anxious prison guard who kisses her there. Rather than go back to Los Angeles and deal with the problems of fame, Jagger wholes up in a remote hotel and practices new songs with a new band.

RUNNING OUT OF LUCK is an attempt by Jagger to make more than your typical rock video. Instead of filming a half-dozen different three-minute films, why not shoot an entire feature of music clips, strung together by one big narrative string? Well, the answer is simple—he doesn't know how. In the hope of alleviating this problem, he hired rock video ace Temple, a young British director who burst onto the scene in 1980 with the effective Sex Pistol's film THE GREAT ROCK 'N' ROLL SWINDLE. 1986 saw the release of Temple's excellent epic musical ABSOLUTE BEGINNERS, which shows more talent in any one scene than can be found in all of RUNNING OUT OF LUCK. In fact, Temple shows more talent in 1986's Janet Jackson video "When I Think Of You" (which draws heavily on the opening scene of ABSOLUTE BEGINNERS) than in all of RUNNING OUT OF LUCK. There is one, and only one, fun scene in this film. Jagger, with no money or ID, tries to persuade two elderly store owners to let him use their telephone. He tries to prove that he is "Mick Jagger, a famous rock star." He digs through a bin of used records and, after coming across countless Julio Iglesias records and one album by rival rock group The Who, he finds an

old Rolling Stones album. He puts it on the turntable and lip-synchs to "Jumpin'
Jack Flash" and "Brown Sugar"—two Rolling Stones songs known by almost
everyone in the world, except for this old couple. Other than this scene the film is
worthless. Don't waste precious time watching it—life is too short. In fact, don't
even waste time looking at the videocassette box on the rental store shelf.

Jagger, in his first film since 1970's X-rated PERFORMANCE (he started
filming FITZCARRALDO in 1980 with Werner Herzog before being replaced by
Klaus Kinski), cannot seem to get out from under his mammoth ego. Hall is a
throwaway who gets about five minutes of screen time. Chong bares her breasts
every now and again. Hopper, who has found time to appear in a number of
major releases this year (from BLUE VELVET to TEXAS CHAINSAW MAS-
SACRE II), unfortunately also found time to do this film. He tries, but simply
cannot overcome the inane "crazed director" dialog that he is forced to spout.
RUNNING OUT OF LUCK was scheduled for release in 1985 in conjunction
with Jagger's album "She's the Boss." When the album died quickly, the movie
disappeared for a while and has now finally emerged on video. Reportedly, it was
as a straight-to-video release, although it did get a one-night premiere showing in
some theaters. Songs include: "Running Out of Luck," "½ a Loaf," "Turn the
Girl Loose," "Hard Woman," "Secrets," "Just Another Night" (Mick Jagger,
performed by Jagger), "Lonely at the Top" (Jagger, Keith Richards, performed
by Jagger), "Jumpin' Jack Flash," "Brown Sugar" (Jagger, Richards, performed by The Rolling Stones), "Lucky in Love," "She's the Boss" (Jagger,
Carlos Alomar, performed by Jagger).

d, Julien Temple; w, Julien Temple, Mick Jagger; ph, Oliver Stapleton; m, Luis
Jardim; ed, Richard Bedford; prod d, Marcos Flaksman; cos, Tina Bossidy;
makeup, Angelo Di Biase, Carlos Prieto; ch, Jose Possi.

Drama   Cas.   (PR:O MPAA:NR)

RUNNING SCARED**½   (1986) 107m UA/MGM c

Gregory Hines (Ray Hughes), Billy Crystal (Danny Costanzo), Steven Bauer
(Frank), Darlanne Fluegel (Anna Costanzo), Joe Pantoliano (Snake), Dan
Hedaya (Capt. Logan), Jonathan Gries (Tony), Tracy Reed (Maryann), Jimmy
Smits (Julio Gonzales), John DiSanti (Vinnie), Larry Hankin (Ace).

A rather mundane cop film which is given a big boost by the comedic pairing of
Gregory Hines and Billy Crystal. The two play veteran Chicago cops who have
grown tired of chasing bad guys. The partners are frustrated because months of

detective work are frequently wasted by judges who let criminals off with light
sentences, and are disappointed with an indifferent public which couldn't care
less about their efforts to keep the streets safe. After being forced to take a
Florida vacation by their commander, Hines and Crystal begin to enjoy fun in the
sun and talk seriously of retiring. As luck would have it, Crystal inherits $40,000
from his aunt's estate. The partners decide to give their notice, retire to the
Sunshine State, and buy the beachside bar they saw for sale. With only 30 days
left to go before retirement, Hines and Crystal become obsessed with destroying
infamous drug dealer Smits' crime empire. Smits doesn't roll over and play dead,
however; he fights back hard. The crime-fighting duo think they've finally got
Smits cornered at O'Hare airport, but the criminal gives them the slip, leading to
a bizarre car chase down Chicago's "El" tracks (not on trains, in cars). Smits
retaliates by kidnaping Crystal's ex-wife, Fluegel, holding her hostage in Chicago's new glass behemoth, the Helmut Jahn-designed State of Illinois Building.
Hines and Crystal come to the rescue and a violent shootout erupts in the
cavernous rotunda. In the end, the baddies are defeated, with Hines and Crystal
changing their minds and deciding to stay cops after all.

Admittedly the plot isn't much, and the action scenes border on the ludicrous,
but the easy rapport between Hines and Crystal is worth the price of admission.
Wisecracking their way through tough situations and bickering like an old married couple, Hines and Crystal succeed in creating a new buddy team that ranks
with the likes of Robert Redford and Paul Newman. Much of their dialog was
improvised, with Hines—until now considered primarily a dancer—quite able to
keep up comedically with veteran stand-up comedian Crystal. Why Hollywood
has consistently pigeonholed the multi-talented Hines in hoofer roles is a mystery,
for he made an impressive film debut as a wisecracking coroner in WOLFEN
(1981). Although many in the press have claimed otherwise, RUNNING
SCARED is not the film debut of Billy Crystal, for he starred in the best-

forgotten Joan Rivers-directed fiasco RABBIT TEST (as the world's first pregnant man) in 1978. Crystal is wonderful in this film, and despite his small stature,
is quite convincing as a tough Chicago cop (he and Hines lifted weights to beef
up). The chemistry between the two actors keeps the rather predictable plot from
becoming stale, for the audience is never sure how the two will react in any typical
situation (instead of yelling "Freeze!" when bursting into a room, Crystal calmly
asks, "Did we come at a bad time?"). The film is theirs and theirs alone. Director
Hyams, a former Chicagoan, could have used a bit more restraint on the action
scenes—the "El" chase is pretty ridiculous and the editing is poor (endless teeth-
jarring shots from inside the cars as they rumble down the tracks)—and the few
scenes without Hines and Crystal on screen together are terribly dull. Hyams
must have been a bit disappointed with the rather mild winter Chicago had when
the crew was in town filming, because he had his crew spray every inch of every
shot with a fake snow which looks more like fire-extinguisher foam than an act of
nature. The effect is downright silly, especially when actors slog through it and
puffy mounds of the stuff stick to the tops of their shoes (it looks the worst
during the State of Illinois scene). Hyams' Chicago roots are evident, however,
for he selected several good locations that haven't been seen on the screen before.
RUNNING SCARED was a hit at the box office ($16.4 million in rentals) and it
is likely we'll see more of the Hines-Crystal team, for they spoke of their desire to
do another film together before they had even finished the first one.

p, David Foster, Lawrence Turman; d, Peter Hyams; w, Gary DeVore, Jimmy
Huston (based on a story by Gary DeVore); ph, Peter Hyams (Panavision,
Metrocolor); m, Rod Temperton; ed, James Mitchell; prod d, Albert Brenner; set
d, George P. Gaines; stunts, Carey Loftin, Bill Couch, Sr.

Crime/Action   Cas.   (PR:C-O MPAA:R)

RUTHLESS PEOPLE***½   (1986) 93m BV-Touchstone-Silver Screens
                                               Partners II/Touchstone c

Danny DeVito (Sam Stone), Bette Midler (Barbara Stone), Judge Reinhold (Ken
Kessler), Helen Slater (Sandy Kessler), Anita Morris (Carol), Bill Pullman (Earl),
William G. Schilling (Police Commissioner), Art Evans (Lt. Bender), Clarence
Felder (Lt. Walters), J.E. Freeman (Bedroom Killer).

Just when you thought that the ZAZ Brothers (AIRPLANE!'s Zucker,
Abrahams and Zucker) might have lost their touch, with TOP SECRET, here
they come with RUTHLESS PEOPLE, a wacky, tasteless, hilarious re-working
of O'Henry's classic short story "The Ransom of Red Chief." O. Henry was

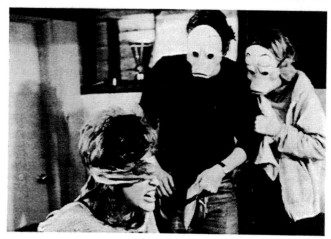

responsible for the plots of many pictures, credited and otherwise. He is not
credited in this film and first-time screenwriter Launer says he didn't consciously
take the idea from the famed short story. Instead, he drew his inspiration from
the Patty Hearst kidnaping by the Symbionese Liberation Army in 1974. Nevertheless, it does bear more than a slight resemblance to O. Henry's story about two

drifters who kidnap a young boy in the old West. After the boy proves to be a terror, the drifters have to pay the boy's father to take him off their hands.

This movie begins as millionaire garment manufacturer DeVito is having dinner with Morris, his sultry mistress, at a swank southern California restaurant. He is planning to murder Midler, his overweight and shrewish wife, and is unaware that the sexy Morris is cheating on him with her hunky, clunky beau, Pullman, a man who is functioning about three bricks shy of a load. DeVito abhors Midler, who is doing a role similar to the one she scored with in DOWN AND OUT IN BEVERLY HILLS, even with the same first name. He longs for the day when she dies and he can take up permanently with Morris. DeVito

becomes hyper about the murder-to-be and leaves before they finish eating. He intends to use chloroform to knock Midler out, then toss her off a precipice.

Before DeVito can kill Midler, she is kidnaped by a sweet young couple, Reinhold and Slater, who are seeking revenge against DeVito. Slater had come up with an idea for a skirt made of Spandex. She told it to DeVito, who used the idea to make a fortune, without paying her one cent in royalties. The couple, who live in a typical suburban residence, reckon that it cost them about half a million dollars, which is exactly what they ask in ransom. When they phone DeVito for the money, they also say that Midler will be tortured and killed if he breathes one word of the kidnaping to the police or the press. Watching DeVito's face as he receives these instructions from the "desperate" kidnapers is worth the price of admission because his relieved expression shows that all of his troubles are now apparently over. Naturally, DeVito's next call is to the police and to every single press source he can reach.

Meanwhile, Midler is making it very tough on Reinhold and Slater. She is one of those Bel Airheads who might say, if you blew in her ear, "thanks for the refill." She is held in the basement of their house and becomes increasingly appalled when her husband won't pay the ransom. The price keeps going down, winding up at a pittance of the original, and she comments, near the end, "Do I understand this correctly? I've been marked down? I've been kidnaped by K-Mart." DeVito is happy as can be, never realizing that Morris and Pullman fully intended to blackmail him. When the cops question DeVito, he plays the distraught spouse perfectly, down to tears, although he admits later that Midler was not the most wonderful wife when he says "Gandhi would have strangled her." Midler continues making life terrible for the confused Reinhold and Slater. Since she has nothing better to do, Midler uses her incarceration in the basement to watch every television exercise show, and as a result she begins slimming down rapidly. As she loses weight, her attitude sweetens, and she and Slater are no longer antagonistic. When Slater shows Midler her designs for clothing, Midler is impressed by the young woman's talent. Then she learns the real reason why she was kidnaped and she throws her lot in with her abductors.

The plot now adds more twists. DeVito is accused of having murdered Midler and he must buy her back to prove she's alive. The trio of Midler, Reinhold, and Slater come up with a devious ploy. They insist that DeVito pay them all the money he has under his own name. Then Reinhold flees with the cops chasing him. Meanwhile, there's a serial killer on the loose in Los Angeles, played by Freeman. When Reinhold stages his own murder, Midler identifies the body of one of Freeman's victims as her kidnaper. Midler, Reinhold, and Slater wind up with the money and DeVito winds up without Morris. Greed is the key here. All of the people are, indeed, ruthless, including the police chief, Schilling, who is involved in yet another subplot.

Madonna had been the first choice for the Midler role but the story called for the couple to have been married 15 years, which would have made Madonna pre-pubescent when she wed . . . a true stretch of the imagination. Midler got the job after the filmmakers saw her on *The Tonight Show* in a garish dress singing a special-material tune about obesity. The art direction is excellent and the DeVito/Midler home is a tribute to bad taste. In the beginning, Midler appears to be a female impersonator. Then, as she slims down and her raucous voice (which is entirely too loud for indoor use) calms, she actually become attractive, after a fashion. Every actor in the movie seems to have a comic moment, because the laughs are piled on top of each other. Call it rude, crude and lewd, but you also have to call it very funny.

p, Michael Peyser; d, Jim Abrahams, David Zucker, Jerry Zucker; w, Dale Launer; ph, Jan DeBont (DeLuxe Color); m, Michel Colombier; ed, Arthur

Schmidt; art d, Donald Woodruff; set d, William Teegarden; cos, Rosanna Norton; anim, Sally Cruikshank.

Comedy   (PR:C-O MPAA:R)

RYDER, P.I. zero   (1986) 92m Long Island Entertainment Group/YGB–Reel Movies c

Dave Hawthorne *(Sky Ryder)*, Bob Nelson *(Eppie)*, Frances Raines *(Valerie)*, John Mulrooney *(Gang Leader)*, Bob Woods *(Prof. Throckmorton)*, Howard Stern *(Ben Wah)*, Kim Lurie *(Maria)*, Chuck Rader *(Detective Hoolihan)*.

Shot on an obviously low budget, this lame detective spoof features Hawthorne as an overweight investigator who teams up with the nerdish Nelson. Completely incompetent, the two manage to get involved in some heavy dealings in spite of their own idiocies. After rescuing Raines from some swarthy bikers (who later prove to be government drug agents), the boys investigate a trail that leads to Latin American dope dealers. These diabolical types are after some land Raines owns down there, and Hawthorne does what he can to help the lady out. Romance blooms between detective and client and the case is solved without much trouble.

RYDER, P.I. suffers from a terminal case of the ludicrous. The assumption here seems to be that if an idea is dumb, then it's also funny. The film lurches from one unfunny episode to another, tossing in bad movie-star impersonations and television parodies in an effort to stir things up. Hawthorne is tolerable but not particularly funny, while Nelson is merely annoying. Playing a news broadcaster is popular New York disc jockey Howard Stern in a thankfully brief cameo appearance. This was originally shot on videotape, then transferred to film before its release. The picture quality suffers from the process, another inept factor in a mindless, forgettable feature.

p, Karl Hosch; d, Karl Hosch, Chuck Walker; w, Karl Hosch, Chuck Walker, Dave Hawthorne, Bob Nelson (based on a story by Karl Hosch, Chuck Walker); ph, Phil Arfman; m, Kevin Kelly; ed, Keith Brooke; art d, Kenneth Hosch.

Comedy/Crime   (PR:C-O MPAA:PG-13)

S

SACRIFICE, THE**** (1986, Fr./Swed.) 145m Swedish Film Institute-Argos-Film Four International-Josephson & Nykvist-Swedish Television-SVT 2-Sandrew Film & Teater-French Ministry of Culture/Orion Classics c (OFFRET-SACRIFICATIO)

Erland Josephson *(Alexander)*, Susan Fleetwood *(Adelaide)*, Valerie Mairesse *(Julia)*, Allan Edwall *(Otto)*, Gudrun Gisladottir *(Maria)*, Sven Wollter *(Victor)*, Filippa Franzen *(Marta)*, Tommy Kjellqvist *(Little Man)*.

The last film by one of Russia's greatest filmmakers, Andrei Tarkovsky, was also his first to receive any form of widespread recognition in the U.S. Like all of

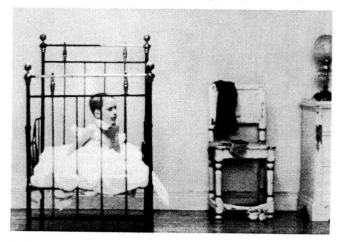

Tarkovsky's work, it tackles complex themes and concerns that the majority of directors (with the possible exceptions of Ingmar Bergman and Robert Bresson) would never approach. THE SACRIFICE is about a number of things, none of which are obvious, nor which remain wholly consistent from one viewer, or viewing, to the next. As such, it is a poetic vision filled with symbolism peculiar to Tarkovsky's imagination. It is also a visually stunning, hauntingly beautiful, brilliant piece of art.

THE SACRIFICE opens with Josephson and his 6-year-old son Kjellqvist busily planting a tree along the sandy, barren shore of the small island where Josephson and his family are vacationing. A respected drama critic and former actor, Josephson is celebrating his birthday with a gathering of close friends and immediate family. These include Josephson's English wife Fleetwood, his grown daughter Franzen, his best friend and doctor Wollter (who has been having an affair with Fleetwood), and the local mailman, Edwall, a quasi-mystic who claims his main preoccupation to be the collection of moments. During this party it is announced on the radio that WW III has begun; the complete destruction of Europe by nuclear arms is certain. Fleetwood becomes hysterical (she has already been upset by Wollter's recent plans to move to Australia), while the others contemplatively sip brandy as the shocking news takes effect. When he is away from the others, Josephson gets down on his hands and knees to ask forgiveness from his creator. He begs that the terrible events that are transpiring be undone; he promises to do anything—give up all his possessions, even part with his beloved "Little Man"—if only things are put back to normal. Later that evening Edwall visits Josephson with a solution to the tragedy at hand. It requires that Josephson sleep with one of his housekeepers, Gisladottir, a sexually innocent witch endowed with the mystical powers necessary to procure divine intervention. Sneaking away on Edwall's bicycle in the quiet of the night, Josephson rides to Gisladottir's hut. He asks to sleep with her, implying that he will kill himself if she does not comply. As they make love, they mystically levitate several feet into the air, slightly turning. The next morning everything appears to be back to normal. Fleetwood, Franzen, and Wollter are casually dining on the lawn when Josephson sneaks back. To meet his end of the bargain he made the previous evening, he sets the house and all his possessions on fire. His wife and friend think he has lost his sanity and call an ambulance to take him away. In a single shot lasting at least 10 minutes, Josephson frantically tries to elude the grasp of the ambulance attendants and his puzzled family. Only Gisladottir offers any sympathy to Josephson's predicament, but her attempts to reach him before the ambulance takes him away are futile. As the vehicle travels down the road, it passes Kjellqvist watering the tree planted the previous day as his father told him to do each day to make his gift to the earth a meaningful one. THE SACRIFICE ends at the point where it began; the camera rests on the symbolic tree with "Little Man" laying under it, a hopeful testament to future generations of mankind living in harmony with nature.

Tarkovsky died on December 29, 1986, less than a year after this movie was completed. While making THE SACRIFICE, the cancer that would eventually kill him was already far advanced. He knew that this would probably be his last film; as such it is the plea of a dying man for the rest of mankind to reconsider the damages done to our planet before it is too late. He seems to be saying that with all the astounding steps forward science is continually making, there is nothing to compensate man's spiritual essence, creating a gap between intellectual

consciousness and the environment that ultimately will be disastrous. In the film, after the roar of modern jets disrupts the serenity of the island, Josephson notes, "Each time another scientific breakthrough is made, it is immediately put to the use of evil." The simple planting and care of the small tree becomes a more beneficial gift to the planet and to future generations of mankind—represented by Kjellqvist—than the whole of science can ever offer. In Josephson's mind, scientific development is only paving the way for nuclear disaster. For this reason, it is never certain whether the nuclear disaster in THE SACRIFICE is actually occurring or is part of Josephson's nightmare while temporarily unconscious after Kjellqvist playfully knocks him down. Thus, his burning of the house becomes either a supreme sacrifice or the work of a crazy man. In either case, by the end of the film, Josephson is viewed as insane in the eyes of the rest of the world.

This was the second appearance for Josephson in a Tarkovsky film. In NOSTALGIA (1984), he played an eccentric man who publicly sets himself on fire. In that film, too, he was labeled as insane, while Tarkovsky viewed him as possessing mystical and spiritual insight. Josephson is perhaps best known for his appearances in several Ingmar Bergman films, notably HOUR OF THE WOLF (1968), SCENES FROM A MARRIAGE (1974), and AUTUMN SONATA (1978). Tarkovsky is also indebted to Ingmar Bergman for the use of the island of Faro—Bergman's home, where the Swede shot a number of films—and for the cinematography by longtime Bergman cohort Sven Nykvist. The formalistic camera work and theatricality common to Bergman films is present here as well, though Tarkovsky's cinematic vision is THE SACRIFICE'S strongest asset and artistic force. As in his earlier films, particularly THE MIRROR, Tarkovsky has combined several types of footage. Most notably, the stark black-and-white portraits of nuclear devastation enhance the already-compelling visuals. The masterful use of sound is also essential to the overall poetic impact; noises like the boom of jets abruptly disrupt the viewer, while the almost-continual eerie chanting heightens the sense of mystery and the occult. Tarkovsky's superb combination of the cinematic elements makes THE SACRIFICE a beautiful film to watch, even if one finds the abstract symbolism and thematic content unappealing. This film won four major awards at the Cannes Film Festival, namely the Special Jury Prize, Best Artistic Contribution to the Cinema for its cinematography, the Fipresci Prize, and the Ecumenical Award. It also won the Golden Sheaf at the Valladolid Festival. (In Swedish; English subtitles.)

p, Katinka Farago; d&w, Andrei Tarkovsky; ph, Sven Nykvist (Eastmancolor); m, Johann Sebastian Bach, Watazumido Shuoo; ed, Andrei Tarkovsky, Michal Leszczylowski; art d, Anna Asp; cos, Inger Pehrsson; spec eff, Svenska Stuntgruppen, Lars Hoglund, Lars Palmqvist, Richard Roberts, Johan Toren; makeup, Kjell Gustavsson, Florence Fouquier.

Drama (PR:C MPAA:PG)

SALOME zero (1986, Fr./It.) 97m Cannon Production-TF 1-Dedalus/ Cannon Group c

Tomas Milian *(Herod)*, Pamela Salem *(Herodias)*, Tim Woodward *(Nerva)*, Jo Champa *(Salome)*, Fabrizio Bentivoglio *(Yokanaan)*, Jean-Francois Stevenin *(Nerva's Aide)*, Fabio Carfora *(Narraboth)*, Richard Paul Majewski *(Nelim)*, Feodor Chaliapin *(Messenger)*, Paul Muller, *(Doctor)*, Lorenzo Piani *(Phillip)*, Fabiana Torrente *(Salome as a Child)*, Valerie Racz *(Princess)*, Alex Serra *(High Priest)*, Andrea Flamini *(Imperial Legionnaire)*, Nicola D'Erama *(First Guest)*, Jorge Krimer *(Second Guest)*, Paolo Paolini *(First Dignitary)*, Leslie Thomas *(Second Dignitary)*, Massimo Sarchielli *(First Assassin)*, Salem Mohamed Badr *(Second Assassin)*, Annie Edel *(The Mother Goddess)*, Sergio Doria *(Horseman)*, Ikky Maas, Cleo Sebastian, Michael Popper, Noel Wallace *(Dancers)*, David Cameron, Daniele Melani *(Gladiators)*.

The biblical story of King Herod and Salome is by no means new to the screen. Theda Bara took a shot at the legendary nymph back in the twenties, while Rita Hayworth, along with Charles Laughton as Herod, made the glossy Hollywood version in 1953. But never have the characters and supposed events been so confusing and crassly misrepresented as in this poor excuse to waste valuable celluloid. The credits state that the screenplay has been *freely* adapted from Oscar Wilde's play of the same name, apparently allowing for the prophet John the Baptist to become Yokanaan, the Emperor's soldier to don 20th Century Russian military coats and drive motorcycles, for Herod's male subjects to wear chastity belts, and for Salome to passionately lust after the prophet. Not that these inventions would be so bad, but when woven into the dull plot they become laughable attempts at creativity. As SALOME opens, Champa is brought back to Judea by the Emperor's representative Woodward. Milian, as Herod, who has become king by slaying Champa's father and taking Salem, Champa's mother, as a wife, now wants the young beauty as his bed partner. He offers her anything she could possibly desire if she will dance for him. Eventually Champa does perform the legendary "Dance of the Seven Veils" for the lustful Milian. Her only request is that the prophet Bentivoglio, kept chained in the dungeon, be slain. This is the one thing Milian doesn't want, but he does it anyway. Meanwhile, the Emperor's soldiers have infiltrated the palace, killing everyone in sight, including Milian and Salem. Woodward, who has fallen in love with Champa, has her killed, too, after noting her necrophilic passion for the dead Bentivoglio. Champa, a 19-year-old actress from Brooklyn, has the sensual profile to play a decent Salome, but her speech and movements quickly dispel any enchantment she may possess. Even the supposedly erotic "Dance of the Seven Veils" becomes just a tedious display of flesh, as do all the amateurishly choreographed dances. The set, the score, and some of the costume designs in SALOME have an enticing surreal quality; however, these do not a movie make—a nightmare, yes; a movie, no.

p, Henry Lange; d, Claude d'Anna; w, Claude d'Anna (based on the play by Oscar Wilde); ph, Pasqualino DeSantis (Panavision, Fotocinema Color); m,

Egisto Macchi; ed, Robert Perpignani; prod d, Giantito Burcheillaro; cos, Adriana Spadaro; ch, Christopher Bruce.

Religious/Drama   **Cas.**   **(PR:O MPAA:R)**

SALVADOR****   (1986, Brit.) 123m Hemdale c

James Woods *(Richard Boyle)*, James Belushi *(Dr. Rock)*, Michael Murphy *(Ambassador Thomas Kelly)*, John Savage *(John Cassady)*, Elpedia Carrillo *(Maria)*, Tony Plana *(Maj. Max)*, Colby Chester *(Jack Morgan)*, Cynthia Gibb *(Cathy Moore)*, Will MacMillian *(Col. Hyde)*, Valerie Wildman *(Pauline Axelrod)*, Jose Carlos Ruiz *(Archbishop Romero)*, Jorge Luke *(Col. Julio Figueroa)*, Juan Fernandez *(Army Lieutenant)*, Salvador Sanchez *(Human Rights Leader)*, Rosario Zuniga *(His Assistant)*, Martin Fuentes *(Maria's Brother)*, Gary Farr *(Australian Reporter)*, Gilles Milinaire *(French Reporter)*, Ramon Menendez *(Maj. Max's Assistant)*, John Doe *(Roberto, Restaurant Owner)*, Leticia Valenzuela *(Woman Rebel)*, Roberto Sosa, Jr. *(Rebel Youth)*, Daria Okugawa *(Dog Attendant)*, Sue Ann McKean *(Cop in San Francisco)*, Joshua Gallejos *(Immigration Officer on Bus)*, Maria Rubell *(Boyle's Baby)*, Tyrone Jones *(Landlord San Francisco)*, Sean Stone *(Boyle's Baby)*, Danna Hansen *(Sister Stan)*, Sigridur Gudmunds *(Sister Burkit)*, Erica Carlson *(Sister Wagner)*, Karla Glover *(Kelly Assistant)*, Jule Conn *(WAC at Party)*, Ma. Del Carmen Sanchez *(Maria's Grandmother)*, Arturo Bonilla *(Romero Assassin)*, "Chiquilin" Zepeda, Nicholas Jasso *(Death Squad)*, Jose Chavez Trowe *(Jail Guard)*, Hector Tellez *(Mayor at Nun's Burial)*, Jorge Reynoso *(Jefe at Customs Shed)*, Jorge Pol, Cesar Sobrevals, Bruno Rubeo, Bob Morones *(Customs Officers)*, Juliana Urquisa *(Wilma)*, Queta Carrasco *(Bruja)*, Ma. De Los Angeles Urquiza *(Mamma Moncha at Panama Club)*, Tomas Leal, Rene Perevra *(Rapists)*, Arturo Rodriguez Doring *(Young Student Killed)*, Yair De Rubin *(Maria's Son)*, Claudia Hernandez *(Maria's Daughter)*, Humberto Elizondo, Mario Arevalo *(Road Block Thugs)*, Gerardo Quiroz, Israel Leon *(Carlos' Friends)*, Mauricio Martinez *(Executed Lieutenant)*, Xochitl Del Rosario *(Messenger on Horse)*, Augustin Bernal *(Bodyguard to Maj. Max)*, John MacDevitt *(GI in Salvador)*, Bill Hoag *(2nd Immigration Officer)*, Waldeir DeSouza *(U.S. Customs Official)*, Angel Vargas *(Tic Tac Monster in Cafe)*, Miguel Ehrenberg *(Capt. Marti)*.

Who would have expected that two of the year's most powerful and profound films would have come from screenwriter Oliver Stone, whose previous work at the typewriter, SCARFACE and YEAR OF THE DRAGON among them, glori-

fied violence and demonstrated little in the way of humanity or compassion. Perhaps it was the directors of his screenplays who couldn't find the human niche in Stone's basically unappealing characters, for in SALVADOR Stone presents us with yet another unappealing protagonist ("I'm an assh_____!" he freely admits), but this time it works—mostly due to an incredible performance from James Woods. In addition to Stone finally coming into his own as a director and successfully having his character tread the fine line between antihero and repugnant weasel, the writer-director has made the first important film about the tragedy of El Salvador. Although there have been other major films recounting the situation in Latin America (MISSING in Chile, and UNDER FIRE in Nicaragua), none has conveyed the chaos, tension, and fear within the region as vividly as SALVADOR. Based on the experiences of real-life journalist Richard Boyle (who Stone says is much more "scummy" than the character Woods plays), SALVADOR begins in 1980 as the unemployed Woods awakens to find himself being evicted from his San Francisco apartment. Despite the fact that he is a veteran journalist who has covered the world's hot-spots over the last 20 years (Vietnam, Lebanon, Central America, "I was the last journalist out of Cambodia," he tells anyone who will listen), Woods cannot get work because of his repugnant personality. Drinking, drugs, and an inability to be polite have put Woods on the outs with just about everybody in the business. After finding that his Italian wife has taken their son and left him, Woods decides to head to El Salvador with his buddy, Belushi, an unemployed disk-jockey. Promising Belushi drink, drugs, and an endless supply of inexpensive virginal whores, Woods cons his friend into coming to a place where he can make some quick money covering the "little guerrilla war." Once they cross the border, however, things begin to get dangerous. They are waylaid at the border by government troops, and after witnessing the summary execution of a student who didn't have his papers, the hysterical Belushi becomes convinced that they will be killed. Luckily, Woods knows the colonel in charge and after a night of whoring with the soldiers,

Woods and Belushi are free to go. Woods resurrects his relationship with local girl Carrillo, while Belushi wanders the city in a drunken, drugged stupor. Looking for work, Woods hooks up with an old friend, photojournalist Savage, and together they go to the dump where the right-wing death squads take their victims. Hundreds of bodies rot in the hot sun and Woods is sickened by the sight. Later that day, Ronald Reagan is elected President of the United States. Right-wing Salvadorans such as Plana (playing a character based on Roberto D'Aubuisson), the leader of the death squads, perceive the election as a virtual endorsement of their activities and the slaughter of dissenters immediately increases and becomes even more blatant. The assassination of outspokenly liberal Catholic archbishop Romero (played by Ruiz) is quickly followed by the rape and murder of three American nuns and a Catholic layperson (Gibb). Woods, who knew and liked Gibb, is shaken by the killings. Realizing that there is little hope for the country ("Butchers on the Right, God knows what on the Left, and a gutless center," says U.S. ambassador Murphy), Woods decides to do what he can and get his girl friend Carrillo and her children to the U.S. Unfortunately, they have no papers, and Woods cannot convince any of the U.S. officials to give her any. After covering a battle between government troops and the rebels where Savage is killed (due to his obsession with getting the perfect shot—like Robert Capa), he finally decides to fake their papers and try to escape. Because of his blunt criticism of Plana, word has spread that Woods is not to leave the country alive. He is detained near the border by some of Plana's undercover guard and beaten senseless. Belushi places a frantic call to outgoing ambassador Murphy, who in turn contacts Salavadoran top brass and threatens them with annihilation if they do not let Woods go. Just as the death squad is about to kill Woods, word comes that he is to be spared. After sharing a meal and a few beers with his torturers (suddenly "foe" has become "friend"), the nervous Woods continues on his way. He and his "family" make it through customs and across the border, only to have immigration officers detain their bus and send Carrillo and her children back to El Salvador where they will face certain doom.

A scant plot synopsis cannot fully convey the vivid events which explode into every frame of SALVADOR. Not only does director Stone successfully convey the chaos and horror of life in El Salvador, he also shows us the rebirth of the conscience of a jaded, cynical, self-absorbed journalist whose problems pale in comparison to the atrocities being suffered by people for whom he genuinely cares. Woods is superb as the journalist who discovers his lost humanity amidst the horror and it is a tribute to his considerable skills as an actor that he is able to hold the viewer to his basically repugnant character throughout the film. The scene where he goes to confession for the first time in 30 years (as a gesture for Carrillo) and tries to barter with the priest by telling him it will be "a little tough" to change his sordid ways is a brilliant piece of acting that was almost entirely improvised. Woods also manages to make a few clumsily scripted and directed scenes involving lengthy speechmaking (much explanation of U.S. policy and the right-wing dictatorship in El Salvador presented in conversational dialog) quite palatable. While Woods' character is one of the most challenging and fascinating individuals to hit the screen in some time, it is Stone's vivid portrayal of El Salvador that gives the film its devastating tone. While the director's sympathies are decidedly anti-Reagan, he is fairly evenhanded and sees no easy military or political solution possible (during the battle between government troops and the rebels, Woods witnesses a rebel soldier summarily executing prisoners; "Is this your sense of justice? You'll become just like them!" he screams). The power of the film lies in its simple-but-detailed portrayal of the chaotic events of 1980-81. Stone successfully imparts the confusion, horror, senselessness, and despair felt in El Salvador, while jaded, blind Americans—government, military, and press—blithely ignore the realities. The film is vivid and full of small details as it relates the events of that period: the annihilation of a truly democratic party (anyone not right-wing is considered communist); the same American military and State Department officials who participated in the Vietnam and Cambodia debacles resurfacing in El Salvador; the genteel network press people who are too vapid (or afraid) to ask tough questions of Salvadoran leaders and American representatives; and those frustrated individuals, both government and press, both Salvadoran and American, who do care and try to help the people as best they can. Stone's camera is like a photojournalist, always on the move, running, swirling, probing, trying to "get close to the truth," as Savage says (but the truth does not sell in Hollywood; Stone had to obtain financing from Hemdale, the bold British production company). Here, and in PLATOON as well, Stone proves that he knows how to build and sustain a tense scene. In SALVADOR sudden, violent death lurks just outside every frame, threatening to burst in at any moment. From the time Woods and Belushi cross the border to the end, where the immigration officers expel Carrillo, the tension never stops (Costa-Gavras did much the same with the sound of gunfire cracking in the distance throughout MISSING). Some would say that Stone heaps too much on the viewer, that Woods sees too many of the shocking events in SALVADOR (the film does falter in a few minor areas—mainly due to some last-minute editing by Stone to bring the film closer to two hours from its original two-and-a-half-hours). Perhaps they do not realize how small El Salvador really is and how much killing took place on a daily basis during those years (50,000 murdered, 500,000 fled the country—a startling 15-20 percent of the population). "They kill people here!" blurts Belushi when he learns of their destination. Indeed they do. By the tens of thousands. Stone offers no solutions and does little preaching in SALVADOR. He simply shows the tragic reality that was 1980-81 in that country and leaves it to reverberate in our minds.

p, Gerald Green, Oliver Stone; d, Oliver Stone; w, Oliver Stone, Richard Boyle; ph, Robert Richardson; m, Georges Delerue; ed, Claire Simpson; prod d, Bruno Rubeo; art d, Melo Hinojosa; cos, Kathryn Greko Morrison; spec eff, Yves De Bono.

Drama Cas. **(PR:O MPAA:R)**

SAMUEL LOUNT† (1986, Can.) 95m Moonshine Prods c

R.H. Thomson (*Samuel Lount*), Linda Griffiths (*Elizabeth Lount*), Cedric Smith (*William Lyon Mackenzie*), Donald Davis (*Bishop Strachan*), David Fox (*David Wilson*), Andrew Gillies (*Sir Francis Bond Head*).

An ill-fated populist revolt in Canada in 1837 against restrictive land-ownership rules is the obscure subject of this low-budget historical epic. Agitated by journalist Smith, a large group of landless settlers begin marching on Toronto. Thomson, as the title personage, is a blacksmith and pacifist who reluctantly emerges as their leader and who is hanged for treason when the government crushes the uprising.

p, Elvira Lount; d, Laurence Keane; w, Phil Savath, Laurence Keane; ph, Marc Champion; m, Kitaro; ed, Richard Martin; art d, Kim Steer; cos, Olga Dimitrov.

Historical **(PR:A-C MPAA:NR)**

SAN ANTONITO† (1986, Colombia) 80m Focine c (Trans: Little Saint Anthony)

Carlos Jaramillo, Angela Calderon, Nubia Tapia, Margarita Maria Munoz, Ana Arango de Mejia.

A young man from a remote village is sent off to the city to study for the priesthood. He moves into a boarding house where the ladies who run it take him under their wings, buying his clothes and feeding him, while he leads their evening prayers. They are eventually disillusioned, however, when they learn that he is a profligate little crook.

d, Pepe Sanchez; w, Pepe Sanchez, Dunav Kuzmanich; ph, Carlos Sanchez; m, Juan Lanz; ed, Gabriel Gonzalez; cos, Susana Carrie, Rosario Lozano.

Drama **(PR:C MPAA:NR)**

SAN O RUZI† (1986) 96m Zagreb-Centar/Centar-Kinematografi Zagreb c (Trans: The Dream Of A Rose)

Rade Serbedzija, Fabijan Sovagovic, Iva Marjanovic, Ljubo Zecevic, Anja Sovagovic, Vlatko Dulic.

An innocent foundry worker is enmeshed in intrigue after finding, and keeping, a sackful of cash in the market square late one night. Near the money lay two dead men, indicating the recent occurrence of some horrible crime. Though the new-found money would relieve Serbedzija's impoverished condition, he keeps from spending any of it for fear of police and gangster retaliation.

d, Zoran Tadic; w, Pavao Pavlicic; ph, Goran Trbuljak; m, Alfi Kabiljo; ed, Vesna Kreber; art d, Ante Nola; cos, Lada Gamulin.

Crime/Drama **(PR:C MPAA:NR)**

SAPIRHURIN† (1986, USSR) 84m Georgia c (Trans: The Step)

Mirab Ninidze (*Alexei*), Ira Chichinadze (*Landlady*), Levan Abashidze (*Mito*), Nino Tarhanishvili (*Girl*).

Student Ninidze moves to the city hoping to find a job and to make something of his life. He takes a room in the boardinghouse of the eccentric Chichinadze, where he is never allowed a moment's peace or privacy. After failing to land a job, disappointed and exhausted from his encounters with neurotic people, Ninidze seeks refuge in the serenity and solitude of nature.

d, Alexander Rekhviascwili; w, Dato Chubiniswili, Alexander Rekhviascwili; ph, Archil Filipaswili; ed, Alexander Rekhviascwili.

Comedy **(PR:C MPAA:NR)**

SAPORE DEL GRANO† (1986, It.) 100m Antea-RAI-3 c (Trans: A Taste of Corn)

Lorenzo Lena (*Lorenzo*), Marco Mestriner (*Duilio*), Alba Mottura (*Cecilia*), Mattia Pinoli (*Grandpa*), Egidio Termine (*Bruno*), Marina Vlady (*Stepmother*), Paolo Garlato (*Father*), Elisabetta Barbini (*Grandma*), Elena Barbalich, Efisio Coletti, Maria Baldo, Michele Pastres.

A young school boy develops a homosexual attraction to his student teacher, Lena, who, away from the city on his first job, finds life in the small village rather lonely and boring. He welcomes the attention from the boy as a relief from his tedium, but when the boy's family notices his attraction to the teacher, the innocent friendship is stopped. Marina Vlady, the star of Jean-Luc Godard's TWO OR THREE THINGS I KNOW ABOUT HER, has a small role as the student's stepmother.

p, Chantal Bergamo, Enzo Porcelli; d&w, Gianni Da Campo; ph, Emilio Bestetti (Eastmancolor); m, Franco Piersanti; ed, Fernanda Indoni; art d, Stefano Nicolao.

Drama **(PR:O MPAA:NR)**

SARRAOUNIA† (1986, Burkina Faso) 130m Soleil O c

Lynn Watts, Jean Roger Milo, Jean-Pierre Sentier, Feodor Atkin, Jean-Pierre Casteldi.

A lavish African epic which details the rise of Sarraounia, a legendary tribal warrior-queen in the late 1800s. In a male-dominated society, she commands the respect of all the villagers because of her unmatched physical prowess and her powers of sorcery. The stability of her tribe is threatened, however, when two French army officers defy their Parisian commanders and launch an attack on her people. After the death of a number of her associates and the destruction of her fortress, Sarraounia manages to emerge victorious and provide her followers with the sort of folklore than would make her immortal. Filmed in the African country of Burkino Faso (formerly Upper Volta) by Hondo, a Mauritanian who worked as a filmmaker for a number of years in Paris (WEST INDIES, 1979).

p&d, Med Hondo; w, Med Hondo, Abdul War (based on a book by Abdoulaye Mamani); m, Pierre Akendengue.

Drama **(PR:O MPAA:NR)**

SAUVE-TOI, LOLA† (1986 Fr./Can.) 105m Onyx-Cinepix-Films A2-Telefilm Canada-CNC-Sofimage-Sofica Conseil-Gestimage/AAA Classic c (Trans: Run for Your Life, Lola)

Carole Laure (*Lola Friedlander*), Jeanne Moreau (*Marie-Aude*), Dominique Labourier (*Cathy*), Sami Frey (*Dr. Tobman*), Robert Charlebois (*Ferdinand*), Jacques Francois (*Charles*), Jean-Yves Gauthier (*Bertrand Benoit*), Guy Bedos (*Tsoukolvsky*), Isabelle Pasco (*Marielle*), Philippe Khorsand (*Maurice*).

A tragicomedy that is set in a cancer clinic run by Frey and visited by Laure, a young lawyer who must undergo extended treatment. While inside, Laure meets a number of interesting patients, including a diplomat's wife, Moreau, and the financially burdened Labourier, the latter of whom Laure soon takes as her friend.

d, Michel Drach; w, Jacques Kirsner (based on the novel by Ania Francos); ph, Robert Alazraki (Fujicolor); m, Lewis Furey; ed, Henri Lanoe; art d, Nicole Rachline; makeup, Daniele Vuarin, Arlette Pipart.

Comedy/Drama **(PR:O MPAA:NR)**

SAVING GRACE*** (1986) 112m EM/COL c

Tom Conti (*Pope Leo XIV*), Fernando Rey (*Cardinal Stefano Biondi*), Erland Josephson (*Monsignor Francesco Ghezzi*), Giancarlo Giannini (*Abalardi*), Donald Hewlett (*Monsignor Colin McGee*), Edward James Olmos (*Ciolino*), Patricia Mauceri (*Lucia*), Angelo Evans (*Giuliano*), Marta Zoffoli (*Isabella*), Guido Alberti (*Cardinal Augusto Morante*), Massimo Sarchielli (*Fortunato*), Massimo Serato (*Monsignor Betti*), Agnes Nobercourt (*Woman With Sick Boy*), Jorge Krimer (*Secretary, Sistine Chapel*), Robert Sommer (*Mr. Carver*), Tom Felleghy (*Ambassador*), Margherita Horowitz (*Nun Interpreter*), Domenico Modena (*Tonino*), Angelo Panarella (*Bastiano*), Julian Jenkyns (*Tourist Group Leader*), Peter Boom (*Tourist*), Carlo Monni (*Pizzeria Owner*), Claudio Masin (*Carabiniere at Montepetra*), Fernando Cartocci (*Truck Driver*), Eric Galati (*Radio Priest*), Tessa Passante (*Vatican Switchboard Operator*), Benito Pucciariello (*Montepetra Bartender*), Natale Nazzareno (*Rigio Guard*), Francesca Roberti, Mauro Sacripanti (*Reporters*), Paolo Merosi, Fabio Caretti (*Acolytes*), Judy Natalucci (*Mrs. Carver*), Ettore Martini (*Bishop*), Joe Chevalier (*Man Robbed in Rigio*), Italo Furlan, Phillip Dacchille, Don Sciarrino (*Monitor Room Guards*).

One year after his election to the papacy, Pope Leo XIV (Conti) fears that his title's trappings have led him away from the real troubles of the people. Conti's feeling of helplessness is further fueled when he meets Zoffoli, a young deaf girl who has hitchhiked to the Vatican, hoping Conti would provide her village with a priest. After discussing his troubles with Rey, a high-ranking cardinal, Conti dons everyday clothing and goes to work in the Vatican garden. When a speech he is to memorize accidentally blows out of his hands, Conti ventures outside the gates to fetch it. He ends up locked out and decides to use this serendipitous event to his advantage. After telephoning Rey to explain that he will be absent, Conti hitchhikes to Montepetra, Zoffoli's home village. Now wearing a beard, he is virtually unrecognized as the Catholic church's Most Holy Father and is able to move about freely. Zoffoli agrees to keep Conti's identity a secret, and the pontiff takes a room in the girl's home. Conti learns the poverty-ridden village is

ruled by Olmos, a repugnant hoodlum who has been faking typhus, thus putting the village under strict quarantine. Food packages are now shipped in, and Olmos is determined this is how things will always be. While visiting Montepetra's abandoned church, Conti is confronted by Evans, a young punk who works for Olmos. Though the boy puts on a good show, Conti sees through the sneer and takes a liking to him. In his travels around the village Conti encounters Giannini, a slightly drunken sheepherder. This nonbeliever instantly recognizes Conti for who he is, though Giannini remains mum about Conti's position.

Back at the Vatican, things are not going well for Rey or his colleagues Josephson and Hewlett. They have been accounting for Conti's absence by claiming illness, but this cover story is quickly wearing thin. Adding to their worries are the periodic phone calls from Conti, explaining that until his work is done he won't tell them where he is or when he'll be back. Conti learns that an aqueduct, destroyed by an earthquake, is deliberately kept in disrepair so Olmos can maintain the status quo. When Conti attempts to rebuild the structure, Olmos has it burned. Conti refuses to give up, though, and enlists the help of the town's women and children. Evans also lends a hand, telling Olmos he will no longer do the hoodlum's work. Giannini, it is learned, was once the village priest but left the cloth over a crisis of conscience. Conti's deeds are slowly restoring his faith, and work on the conduit continues. Evans is killed when Olmos dynamites the aqueduct, but the people remain undeterred. Conti has shown them what they are capable of and the structure is finished. The village is self-sufficient once more and Conti returns to the Vatican in time to deliver his Easter message.

This amiable story works well, thanks largely to the collective talents of its cast. Conti, while a bit young for the part, gives a personable edge to his character that is warm and appealing. His chemistry with Evans (the cocky young man from Robert Duvall's ANGELO MY LOVE), Giannini, and Mauceri (Zoffoli's mother) is particularly good. The sequence in which Maurceri, a former prostitute who does not know Conti's identity, expresses a sexual longing for her houseguest, is sensitively handled but without any false emotions. The international casting works nicely, with Rey and Josephson (an Ingmar Bergman regular) providing some nice moments with their brief roles. Young's direction is low key, emphasizing the story's humanist values rather than the religious aspects. By doing this, Young creates a story of more universal appeal, a small but well-told parable that is perfect for family viewing. (Considering he had both SAVING GRACE and EXTREMITIES on his 1986 filmography, Young certainly had one of the most varied years in his career.) This was shot on location in the small Italian village of Craco, where local residents pitched in as both on-camera extras and behind the scenes crew members. Interestingly, Young had dealt with the subject of faked typhus in Italy in a television documentary shot several years earlier in Palermo. Because the subject was so harsh, the work never was broadcast, but Young ended up incorporating many of that film's ideas and images into SAVING GRACE.

p, Herbert F. Solow; d, Robert M. Young; w, David S. Ward, Richard Kramer (based on the novel by Celia Gittelson); ph, Reynaldo Villalobos (Technovision, Technicolor); m, William Goldstein; ed, Michael Kelly, Peter Zinner; prod d, Giovanno Natalucci; set d, Joe Chevalier; cos, Vittoria Guaita; spec eff, Eros Bacciucchi, Adriano Pischiutta; makeup, Giancarlo Del Brocco.

Comedy/Drama   Cas.   (PR:A MPAA:PG)

SAY YES*   (1986) 90m Faunt Le Roy/Cinetel c

Lissa Layng (Annie), Art Hindle (Luke), Logan Ramsey (George), Jonathan Winters (W.D. Westmoreland), Maryedith Burrell (Gladys), Jensen Collier (Belinda), Jacque Lynn Colton (Message Taker), Devon Ericson (Cynthia), Art La Fleur (Ernest), Laurie Prange (First Bride), Anne Ramsey (Major), Paula Trueman (Lady On Bus), John Milford (Sailor).

A man having to find a wife in just 24 hours is a plot nearly as old as the movies, and SAY YES does little to breathe new life into the hoary old chestnut. Winters is an eccentric billionaire who decides he wants to make a change in his will. Rather than leave his fortune to his son Ramsey, Winters decides to give the bulk of the estate to his beloved grandson Hindle. Winters hopes Hindle will give up his playboy life style, as well as his concert pianist career. The only condition is that the inheritance is that Hindle must be married before his quickly approaching thirty-fifth birthday. Winters suddenly dies and Ramsey, who is confined to a

wheelchair, is naturally unhappy with the situation, particularly when it looks as if Hindle is actually going to make it down the aisle. An unexpected romance between Hindle's intended and the best man changes things drastically. Left standing at the altar with only half a day left to go, Hindle must quickly come up with a new bride. He puts in a call to Ericson, an old girl friend, but she has gotten married herself to spite Hindle. Realizing the vast wealth she can get her hands on, Ericson immediately sets out to kill her new husband. Hindle also telephones Collier, a vain film actress, who promises to fly around the world so that she can be the lucky consort. With his gloating father in hot pursuit, Hindle leaves the church and suddenly runs into Layng, a Midwestern girl who has just arrived in New York with a head full of dreams. Hindle is hopelessly smitten with Layng's charming smile, and though time is running out, the poor little rich boy suddenly realizes he's found his girl. Hindle beseeches Layng with a marriage proposal, which she turns down. He then follows her to the YWCA and eventually persuades Layng to visit his father's plush mansion. Ramsey, who finds his son's predicament to be highly amusing, offers Layng her own corporation in hopes of discouraging her further. But despite the unusual circumstances, the marriage will take place and Ramsey gallantly offers to arrange the ceremony. Following the hastily read vows, the three attend a post-wedding supper where Layng indulges in an excessive amount of champagne. That night, while watching Hindle perform in a concert, Layng becomes ill. She makes a quick trip to the ladies room, then has a chat with Ramsey outside in the foyer. Ramsey accidentally reveals that the priest who performed the wedding ceremony was defrocked, thus making the union technically invalid. Layng, undeterred by the loss of her dress in a struggle, manages to disrupt the concert and gets word to Hindle that they've been duped. She's then hauled off by the cops, but Hindle rushes to the police station to bail Layng out. Hindle manages to free Layng, but his own emotional state ends up getting him in the pokey. Collier suddenly arrives to marry Hindle, but the much beleaguered man will not change his mind. With only minutes to go until midnight, Layng finds a Salvation Army minister to perform the wedding ceremony. The clock strikes the crucial hour, but there is still a chance. Knowing that daylight saving time doesn't apply at sea, Hindle and Layng charter a leaky vessel and end up sinking. It appears they have married too late to get the dough, but the next morning the defrocked priest arrives, telling the couple he has been reinstated. Since this acquittal is retroactive, Hindle and Layng's union is legal and they are entitled to the inheritance.

There's nothing to SAY YES other than a tired sequence of unremarkable events. Winters' cameo stints, which show every indication of being improvised on the spot, are the only amusing moments, though his work is hardly belly-laugh material. Neither Hindle nor Layng shows an ability for light comedy and their romance has no spark. Like Yust's script and direction, they merely go through the motions in an apparent hope that something will click. In a real show of desperation for laughs, Yust resorts to that last comedic bastion: wholly gratuitous nudity. There's also a lot of trouble in clarifying the nature of major events, with Winters' death and the actual timing of Hindle's birthday being the biggest goofs. SAY YES feels like the sort of thing only a mother could love, and for good reason. The script was written specifically for Layng (her previous undistinguished work includes bits in WHOSE LIFE IS IT ANYWAY? and NIGHT OF THE COMET, as well as a never-released western) and her mother, Rosemary Le Roy Layng, became the film's coproducer. Though filmed in 1983, SAY YES remained in limbo for three years before its eventual release. The title song, "Say Yes" (David Jackson, Jill Gaynes, performed by Joe Pizzulo, Gloria Kaye), is the sole one.

p, Larry Yust, Rosemary Le Roy Layng; d&w, Larry Yust, Peter S. Ferrara; ph, Isidore Mankofsky (United Color); m, Steve Le Gassick, Tony Riparetti, James Saad, Ron Grant; ed, Margaret Morrison; set d, John Retsek; cos, Patti Callicott; m/l, David Jackson, Jill Gaynes; makeup, Patricia Messina, Helen Little, Byrd Holland.

Comedy   Cas.   (PR:O MPAA:PG-13)

SCALPS†   (1986, It.) Beatrice Film–Multivideo/Filmexport

Vassili Karis, Karen Wood, Beny Cardoso, Charlie Bravo.

A "spaghetti" western set in New Mexico circa 1875 which sees a wealthy rancher lust after the daughter of a local Indian chief. When the chief refuses to negotiate a deal with the rancher for his daughter, the angry rancher dispatches his gunslingers into the Indian village and they kidnap her. The squaw manages to escape, but she is badly wounded in the process. She stumbles upon the farm of a man whose wife and children were slaughtered by Indians and begs for help. Although bitter toward the Indian race, the farmer tends the squaw's wounds and then hides her from the rancher and his posse when they trail her to his door. The rancher suspects that the farmer is lying and he sets up camp near the farm. Knowing that they will return, the farmer decides to escape with the Indian woman. While on the run they meet an Indian warrior who had been betrothed to the squaw. She tells the warrior that she is in love with the white man, but the warrior refuses to concede. The warrior and the farmer fight a duel over the woman and the farmer wins. Shamed because the white man did not kill him, the warrior commits suicide. Soon afterwards, the rancher and his men catch up with the fugitive couple and capture them. Again the two escape, but this time they manage to defeat the rancher. The farmer and the Indian woman eventually return to the farm. The Indian woman places flowers on the graves of the farmer's family as a symbol of peace and understanding between the races.

d, Werner Knox; w, Bruno Mattei, Roberto Di Girolamo (based on a story by Italo Gasperini, Richard Harrison); ph, Julio Burgos, Luigi Ciccarese; m, Luigi Ceccarelli.

Western   (PR:O MPAA:NR)

SCENE OF THE CRIME*** (1986, Fr.) 90m T. Films–Films A2/Kino International c (LE LIEU DU CRIME)

Catherine Deneuve *(Lili)*, Danielle Darrieux *(Grandmother)*, Wadeck Stanczak *(Martin)*, Nicolas Giraudi *(Thomas)*, Victor Lanoux *(Maurice)*, Jean Bousquet *(Grandfather)*, Claire Nebout *(Alice)*, Jacques Nolot *(Father Sorbier)*, Jean-Claude Adelin, Christine Paolini, Philippe Landoulsi, Michel Grimaud.

In the French countryside we meet a criminal mind usually seen only in Claude Chabrol's provincial upper-class thrillers. Giraudi, a wiry 13-year-old, is picking flowers for his mother in a remote cemetery when he is accosted by Stanczak, a handsome but disheveled criminal. Stanczak threatens to kill the boy if he doesn't return before nightfall with some money. Stanczak surprisingly doesn't react in fear. He's a mischievous, rebellious, insolent youngster who cares only for Deneuve, his mother, and a divorcee who runs a lakeside nightclub and is greatly influenced by her mother, Darrieux. Giraudi manages to get some money from Bousquet, his half-deaf grandfather, who prefers retreating to his fishing boat rather than dealing with his family's problems. When Giraudi returns to Stanczak's hideout, he is greeted by a Stanczak's accomplice, who is convinced that the boy informed on them. When Giraudi is nearly strangled to death by the accomplice, Stanczak comes to the boy's defense and kills his partner. Giraudi is free to go home. Later that evening, Stanczak wanders into Deneuve's nightclub, where he eventually passes out in a drunken stupor. Deneuve, who is intrigued by the stranger, puts him up in a nearby hotel. When she returns the following morning, he has gone—picked up by a third accomplice, the frightening Nebout, a tough moll who had been a childhood friend to Stanczak and the dead man. In the meantime, Giraudi is being readied for his first communion. His entire family will attend the ceremony celebrated by his school. The family, including his hated bourgeois father, Lanoux, is temporarily united, although Giraudi refuses to behave like a nice boy. Only his mother understands him. Both of them are connected by a maternal, Oedipal bond (not unlike the mythical connection seen in Jean Cocteau's films) that underlies all of their actions. Deneuve later seeks out Stanczak, finds him and brings him back to her bedroom—bonded in love with the man who saved her boy's life. Realizing that she has not lived her life the way she wished, Deneuve plans to run away with Stanczak instead of turning him in to the police. Nebout, however, refuses to lose both of her men and hunts down Stanczak, shooting him at Deneuve's house before driving her sports car at full speed into a brick wall. The police arrest Deneuve as an accomplice. Having finally broken all ties with her family and her son, she is hauled off to prison. Giraudi, meanwhile, has come to accept his father, who now does all he can to make the boy happy.

The film was directed and written by three former critics for *Cahier du Cinema*, the intellectual film magazine that also employed Jean-Luc Godard, Francois Truffaut, and Claude Chabrol. SCENE OF THE CRIME attempts to do many, perhaps too many, things in its 90 minutes. Director Techine (who hit it big last year with RENDEZVOUS) manages to interweave his three main characters—Deneuve, Stanczak, and Giraudi—beautifully. Each are dependent on each other in different ways, living for one another and owing their very existence to one another. So much happens in the plot, however, that character nuances are lost in a rush to cram in more information. As a result, the film is a multilayered thriller with an uneasy sexual tension, though some of its many layers (the father's role, for example) are underdeveloped. Deneuve, whose excellence as an actress is superceded only by her beauty, is a marvel to watch as she casts aside (as best as nature will allow) her elegant looks to portray a plain, simple, provincial woman. Not since THE LAST METRO in 1980 has she had a role of such depth, erasing unpleasant memories of THE HUNGER and this year's LOVE SONGS. Darrieux, the *grande dame* of French cinema (having appeared in such great films as MAYERLING, THE EARRINGS OF MADAME DE . . . , LE PLAISIR, and THE YOUNG GIRLS OF ROCHEFORT in 1968 with Deneuve), is also excellent as the grandmother. The character has managed to keep a firm hold over her rebellious family, while defeating almost impossible odds to get them all to sit down together at the dinner table. Giraudi shows great promise, as does Stanczak (who starred in Techine's RENDEZVOUS). Both have the ability to capture an audience's eye. Also making a lasting impression in a small role is Nebout, whose intense, glassy-eyed gaze is haunting and unforgettable. (In French; English subtitles.)

p, Alain Terzian; d, Andre Techine; w, Andre Techine, Pascal Bonitzer, Olivier Assayas; ph, Pascal Marti (Eastmancolor); m, Philippe Sarde; ed, Martine Giordano; art d, Jean-Pierre Kohut-Svelko; makeup, Ronaldo Ribeiro de Abreu.

Thriller (PR:C-O MPAA:NR)

SCENY DZIECIECE Z ZYCIA PROWINCJI† (1986, Pol.) 153m Film Polski Zodiak Film Unit c (Trans: Childhood Scenes of Provincial Life)

Dariusz Siatkowski, Ewa Wisniewska, Beata Paluch, Henryk Bista, Eugenia Herman, Bronislaw Pawlik, Jerzy Trela, Jan Jankowski, Leon Niemczyk.

Former screenwriter and actor Zygaldo turned to directing with this study of class structures in modern-day Poland. The film focuses on a wealthy family and the young man who has moved into their household to tutor their attractive daughter. The movie had its premiere at the Gdansk Film Festival in 1986.

d, Tomasz Zygaldo; w, Andrzej Mencwel, Tomasz Zygaldo (based on a novel by Andrzej Mencwel); ph, Zdzislaw Kacmarek; m, Robert Schumann; set d, Roman Wolniec.

Drama (PR:O MPAA:NR)

SCHIAVE BIANCHE, VIOLENZA IN AMAZZONIA (SEE: WHITE SLAVE, 1986, It.)

SCHETIKA ME TON VASSILI† (1986, Gr.) 75m Stavros Tsiolis c (Trans: In Relation with Vassilis)

Tassos Denegris *(Professor)*, Constantinos Tzoumas, Katerina Tsioli, Loukia Pistola, Eva Vlahakou, Maria Argyraki, Costas Stavropoulos, Christos Vacaloupoulos, Christos Hatzakis.

Alienation in modern society is the focus of this film as university professor Denegris withdraws completely from contact with the outside world to protest against the futility of human communication.

p&d, Stavros Tsiolis; w, Stavros Tsiolis, Constantine Tzoumas, Christos Vacalopoulos; ph, Vassilis Kapsouros; ed, Costas Jordanides.

Drama (PR:C MPAA:NR)

SCHLEUSE 17† (1986, Ger.) 68m Munich Film Academy bw (Trans: Lock 17)

Roxane, John Cooper, George Lentz, Oliver Strietzel.

Following their successful million-dollar heist, three Americans are beset with troubles, beginning with the fatal wounding of one the gang. One thief stays to comfort his dying friend, while the other, only concerned with his own safety, departs for Paris. After the wounded thief dies, his friend meets and falls in love with a tour guide. He travels with her to Paris, where, after a violent encounter, he kills his former partner. He and the woman then try to flee from the police. This was the first feature for director Lentz, a recent graduate of the Munich Film Academy.

d&w, Sebastian Lentz; ph, Jo Heim; m, Paul Hornyak.

Crime/Thriller (PR:O MPAA:NR)

SCHMUTZ† (1986, Aust.) 100m Paulus Manker c

Fritz Schediwy *(Joseph Schmutz)*, Hans Michael Rehberg *(Chief Inspector)*, Siggi Schwientek *(Girl)*, Josefine Platt, Mareile Geisler, Axel Bohmert, Gunther Bothur, Constanzia Hochle, Hanno Poschl.

Schediwy is a security guard posted to guard an abandoned building, first with another man, then by himself. He slowly goes mad patrolling the empty edifice, killing intruders and a demolition worker before killing himself.

p,d&w, Paulus Manker; ph, Walter Kindler; m, Yollo; ed, Maria Homolkova; cos, Erika Navas.

Drama (PR:O MPAA:NR)

SCHOOL FOR VANDALS† (1986, Brit.) 80m Children's Film Unit–Film Four International c

Jennifer Barrand *(Sharon)*, Jeremy Coster *(Rupert)*, Samantha McMillan *(Tiger Lily)*, Nicholas Mott *(Bill)*, Deakin Glynn *(Deakin)*, Anne Dyson *(Miss Duff)*, Charles Kay *(Neil)*, Peter Bayliss *(Sir Oswald Kane)*.

In a small country town, a couple buys a school where they intend to send their children when the new educational year commences. Due to a lack of funding the doors of the school stand a good chance of never opening. In order to raise some much-needed cash, their two children and some of their friends resort to kidnaping Dyson, a kindly old lady who thoroughly enjoys being a hostage. This is the sixth production of England's Children's Film Unit, a production company devoted to teaching youngsters the art and craft of filmmaking. The majority of crew members are between ages 12 and 14, and the kids also had a hand in creating the screenplay.

p, Joanie Blaikie; d, Colin Finbow; w, Colin Finbow, children of the Children's Film Unit; ph, Titus Bicknell, Will Grove-White, Orlando Wells, Leigh Melrose (Kodak Color); m, David Hewson; ed, Colin Finbow; prod d, Griselda Wallace.

Children's (PR:AAA MPAA:NR)

SCHWARZ UND OHNE ZUCKER† (1986, Ger.) 94m Optische Werke-Lutz Konermann bw (Trans: Black and Without Sugar)

Edda Backman, Lutz Konermann, Kolbrun Halldorsdottir, Gudjon Petersen, Hanna Maria Kardottir, Throstur Gudjartson, Gudjon Ketilsson, Herbert Linkesch, Thorgeir Gunnarsson, Franca Mannetti, Niki Lauda, Ayrton Senna.

After leaving an Icelandic street theater group on tour in Europe, a woman performer begins hitchhiking and meets a man and begins a rather difficult relationship with him.

d&w, Lutz Konermann; ph, Tom Fahrmann; m, Adrian Vonwiller.

Romance/Comedy (PR:C MPAA:NR)

SCORPION† (1986) 98m Summons/Crown International c

Tonny Tulleners *(Steve Woods)*, Don Murray *(Gifford Leese)*, Robert Logan *(Gordon Thomas)*, Allen Williams *(Phil Keller)*, Kathryn Daley *(Jackie Wielmon)*, Ross Elliott *(Sam Douglas)*, John Anderson *(Neal G. Koch)*, Bart Braverman *(Mehdi)*, Thom McFadden *(Lt. Woodman)*, Billy Hayes *(Wolfgang Stoltz)*, Adam Pearson *(Jack Devlin)*, Ari Barak *(Hanis)*, Adam Ageli *(1st Faued)*, John La Zar *(2nd Faued)*, Pamela Bryant *(Flight Attendant)*, Lisa Pontrelli *(Leese's Secretary)*, Joseph Whipp *(Leese's Aide)*, Stephen Riead *(Young Steve)*, Thomas Riead *(Young Phil)*, Jack Lightsy *(1st Police Guard)*, Kelela Wright *(Police Guard's Wife)*, Douglas Joho *(Leese's Guard)*, Gloria Thomas *(Leese's Maid)*, Michael J. Epps *(2nd Police Guard)*, William Moy *(3rd Police Guard)*, William Griffith *(George Cauffman, District Attorney)*, Tom Cassell

(Deputy District Attorney), Douglas Happ (Cessna Pilot), Bill Sherwood (Agent in Cessna), Bob Golden (Helicopter Pilot), Leroy Tardy (DIA Agent), Bart McManus (Douglas' Aide), Jane Gierlich (Mrs. Douglas), Lawrence Cohen (Douglas' Driver), Wendy West (Mother in Park), Shawn Player (Harbor Patrol), Cam Colee (Young Flute Player); Washington Conference Room: Robert Colbert (Brig. Gen. James Hagen), Robert Darnell (Lt. Tom Miller), Allan Thomas (Col. John Forbes), Tom Bowen, Thomas L. Eden, George M. Mc-Combs, Robert Schulman, Joseph G. Stone (Political Officials); Los Angeles International Airport: Tony Martineau (Pilot), Tom Serrano, Duke Jubran, Anna Ortega (Terrorists), Raymond Patterson, Stephen Woods (Reporters), Joy Rinaldi (Passenger Leaving Plane), Byron Nelson (FBI Agent), Larry Genova, Heather Cameron, Tom Hess (Ticket Agents); Jeffrey Rizzo, Pedro Velis (Police Officers), Lisa Jensen, Kim Capone, Alex Potts, Anita Marie Potts (Waiting Relatives); Airport Conference Room: Anthony Vatsula (Austin), Jack Ettelson, Jim Gazely, Buz Levy, John Nugent, Rick Rounsavelle, Bernd Schulze, James Sheridan, Peter Yanovitch (Special Agents and Police); The Hospital: Marty Imsland (Dr. Grant), Herb Mitchell (Dr. Ghys), Patricia Murray (Head Nurse), William Utay (Pathologist), Vivian Patrick (Dr. Ghy's Secretary), Dimitra Mina (Nurse Receptionist), Ann Godron, Erika Hess, Elizabeth Nelson (Nurses), Colleen Nelson (Candy Striper), Harvey Whitaker (1st Policeman), Robert Hinshaw (2nd Policeman); The Ship: Erik White (Ship's Purser), Brad Wilson (Ship's Photographer), Steve Mattson (Waiter), Robert Storick (Busboy), Arielle Gorris, Rebecca Shinall (Girls in Stateroom); Spain: Richard Bravo (Tough Guy), Louis Alexander (Male Patron), J. Victor Lopez (Bartender), Sonia Vera (Female Patron); Jose Martin Munoz, Alumo Jimenez Martin (Men Outside Cantina), Luis Marugon (Man on Donkey), Felix Martin (Priest), Carmen More (Madrid Ticket Agent), Luisa Leschin, Kathleen Hernandez (Madrid Telephone Operators); Amsterdam: Clemens Meuleman (Pietor Geerlings); Hawaii: Wayne Ward (Hotel Manager), Taia Chard (Hotel Clerk), Peter Kamealoha Clark (Detective Kikoa), Vincent Kahaloa, Frederick A.C. Maikai, Jr. (Police Officers), Patrick Bishop (Cab Driver), Nabawa Abou-Seif (Victim); Restaurant: Alfredo Sedo (Alfredo), Dea McCallister (Morning Hostess), Marianne Fornstedt (Evening Hostess).

In the mid-1960s, Tonny Tulleners met Chuck Norris in a martial arts competition and beat him soundly, so two decades later we get to see him follow in Norris's footsteps in becoming a movie star. The plot has Tulleners as a Defense Intelligence Agency operative assigned to protect an Arab terrorist who is about to tell all he knows. Unfortunately, while Tulleners is out, the bad guys get to his charge and kill him, along with one of Tulleners' friends. Now armed with a strong revenge motive, Tulleners goes out to chase down the terrorists, disarm them, and then beat them up with his bare hands.

p,d&w, William Riead; ph, Bill Philbin; m, Sean Murray; ed, Gigi Coello; art d, Heather Cameron; spec eff, Wayne Beauchamp; makeup, Jan Thielbar; stunts, Dar Robinson.

Action **(PR:O MPAA:R)**

SCREAMPLAY*½ (1986) 85m Boston Movie/Troma c

Rufus Butler Seder (Edgar Allen), Eugene Seder (Al Weiner), Cheryl Hirshman (Harriet Weiner), James McCann (Sonny Weiner), Clif Sears (Bus Driver), Johanna Wagner (Coffee Shop Waitress), Lonny McDougall (Transvestite), George Kuchar (Martin), Basil J. Bova (Tony Cassano), George Cordeiro (Sgt. Joe Blatz), Ed Callahan (Kevin Kleindorf), M. Lynda Robinson (Nina Ray), Katy Bolger (Holly), Bob White (Lot), Jim Connor (Nicky Blair), Catherine Haag (Starlet), Mijo Johnson (Secretary), Bob Wilson (Irv Weiner), Theodore Braun, Flip Johnson (Policemen), H. Paul Smith (Sgt. Flaherty), Ellen Holbrook (Chemist), Linda Chisom, Alice Grossman, Rebecca Harclerode, Paul Hawkins, Dan Lavender, Karen McCann, Terri Nordone, Karl Erich Nussbaum (Bus Station Extras), Rob E. Murphy, Dennis M. Piana, Max Piana, Pip Shepley (Coffee Shop Extras), Carolyn Ayotte, Katherine Hogan, Armand Saiia (Hollywood Blvd. Extras), Deborah Bornstein, Patrick Conlan, Veronica Lewis, Justin Sean O'Connor, Steve Rasch, Carolyn Romberg (Reporters), Sam the Dog (Rocky).

An incredibly low-budget (under $25,000) film debut from writer-director-editor-matte painter-star Rufus Butler Seder. The picture manages to be fascinating despite its hopelessly cheap production (the entire movie was shot in a warehouse in Boston). Filmed in a very self-conscious 1940s B-movie style, SCREAMPLAY

features Seder as an aspiring young screenwriter who comes to Hollywood seeking fame and fortune. While in a coffee shop, he meets an agent who promises to add the youngster to his stable of talent if he can produce a good horror film script quickly. After being attacked in the men's room by a transvestite on roller skates, Seder is rescued by Kuchar, an avant-garde filmmaker, who happens to be the caretaker of the seedy Welcome Apartments. Needing a place to live and having little money, Seder accepts a job as the building's janitor in exchange for an apartment. As he goes about his duties, Seder meets some of the eccentric residents of the apartment building. Among them are Robinson, a former starlet who is starved for sex and giving acting lessons to hopeful actress Bolger; White, a drug-addled religious zealot who insists on expelling the demons inside Seder; and Callahan, another agent. Seder begins using the strange residents of the building in his writing and incorporates their characters into his horror screenplay. His script, for example, shows Robinson drowned in her bathtub and White burned alive in his apartment. One day, Seder discovers that his unfinished script has been stolen. Soon the murders described in the pages of his screenplay begin happening in real life. After a nasty confrontation with Kuchar, Seder is forced to vacate his apartment and move in with Bolger. Later, Kuchar shows up to collect more than the rent from the actress. In an effort to catch the killer, Seder finishes his script by creating a climax where he is murdered.

Even though Seder's character is named "Edgar Allen," apparently after Edgar Allen Poe, the feel of the film is closer to that of Edgar G. Ulmer, king of the Poverty Row Hollywood filmmakers. Like any creative filmmaker, Seder rises to the challenge of his low budget by employing such tried-and-true effects as rear-screen projection, forced perspective, and multiple exposures to create a unique and vivid cinematic universe. Seder's evocation of the seedy little dramas made by Ulmer and his colleagues is very intentional, as the casting of avant-garde filmmaker Kuchar suggests. Kuchar's films are outrageously sleazy parodies of the turgid melodramas of the 1940s and 50s. His casting in SCREAMPLAY as a particularly loathsome creep confirms the director's self-consciously campy intentions.

p, Dennis M. Piana; d, Rufus Butler Seder; w, Ed Greenberg, Rufus Butler Seder; ph, Dennis M. Piana; m, Basil Bova, George Cordeiro; ed, Rufus Butler Seder; art d, Cheryl Hirshman; set d, Roberta Murphy, Catherine Shaddix; cos, Catherine Shaddix; spec eff, Cheryl Hirshman, Catherine Shaddix; stunts, Theodore Braun.

Horror **(PR:O MPAA:NR)**

SCREAMTIME** (1986, Brit.) 89m Manson International/Rugged c

Framing Episode: Vincent Russo (Ed), Michael Gordon (Bill), Marie Scinto (Marie), Kevin Smith (Shop Owner); Killer Punch: Robin Bailey (Jack Grimshaw), Ann Lynn (Lena), Johnathon Morris (Damien), Dione Inman (Suzy), Boscoe Hogan (Doctor), John Styles (Punch Voice); Scream House: Ian Saynor (Tony), Yvonne Nicholson (Susan), Lally Bowers (Mrs. Kingsley), Veronica Doran (Miss Burns), Brenda Kempner (Woman); Garden of Blood: Dora Bryan (Emma), Jean Anderson (Mildred), David Van Day (Gavin), Matthew Peters (Tim), Phillip Bloomfield (Colin), Gary Linley (Frank), Kim Thompson (Lady Anne).

Premiering in 1983, regionally released in 1985, then revised and released on videocassette in 1986. The heyday of the horror anthology—mostly a British phenomenon dating back to DEAD OF NIGHT (1945)—was around 1970, with films such as TALES FROM THE CRYPT, ASYLUM, and THE HOUSE THAT DRIPPED BLOOD offering three to five little shockers framed by one connecting story. Here the tradition is revived for an inferior effort, opening with two lowlifes (Vincent Russo, Michael Gordon) stealing three videocassettes from a Times Square shop, the three being "Killer Punch," "Scream House," and "Garden of Blood." They take a subway to Brooklyn and go to the apartment of a girl (Scinto) to watch their new tapes. The first story concerns a Punch and Judy puppeteer (Bailey) whose wife and stepson are constantly badgering him to abandon his financially unrewarding career and move to Canada with them, a step they are going to take regardless. Things finally reach a head when the stepson (Morris) burns down Bailey's portable stage. Later, while sitting on the beach, Morris is attacked by an unseen assailant and beaten to death with a stick. Bailey's wife, not knowing what has happened to her son, threatens to leave him if he doesn't burn his puppets. That night she too is beaten to death. Bailey calls a doctor and tries to warn him about Mr. Punch, whom he thinks has killed her, and soon the doctor is similarly killed. Next morning Morris' girl friend comes by the house looking for him and is attacked by Bailey, the Punch doll on his hand clutching a heavy stick. He chases her to a dump, and finally dies when he falls into the crushing jaws of a garbage truck.

The first episode over, Russo takes out the tape and says, "Dey're British movies, I can tell by da way dey talk." The second tape is inserted, and it is the story of a young couple (Saynor and Nicholson) who move into a big house. Almost immediately Nicholson begins having strange hallucinations: a boy riding his bike on the lawn, bloody bodies throughout the house, and a man running through the halls with a knife. A seance turns up nothing, and one day she sees the murders in their entirety, a lunatic slasher killing everyone in the house. It proves too much and her mind snaps. In the last scene, the house has been sold to a family and Saynor has come for something left behind. He sees all the signs his wife had seen (though he doesn't realize what they are) and when he gets back into his car, his throat is cut from ear to ear by an escaped lunatic who then proceeds to enter the house.

The tapes are changed and the last episode comes up, in which a young man (Van Day), eager to make some extra money, takes a job as gardener and handyman for two old spinsters (Bryan and Anderson) in an old house. They tell him about the legends associated with the house, and about the fairies who live in the garden. He is more interested, however, in the chest from which he sees them take his pay. He returns in the middle of the night with two friends to rob the place, but strange things happen. One friend is attacked by a garden gnome come to life; another is pulled underground by the ghosts of the men buried there, victims of the fairies and a 16th-Century femme fatale. She appears before Van Day and kisses him before he is pinned to the wall by flying knives and killed. The segment ends with Bryan and Anderson showing a new prospective gardener about the place.

Not a shock or scare to be found anywhere, but the film does manage to generate some suspense in parts. The third episode is the best, building to an unfortunately flat conclusion. The first segment works only thanks to the acting skill of Bailey, and the second doesn't work at all. The most interesting thing about the film is the framing episode, which includes some nudity. This seems to have been added just for video release to punch things up a little.

p&d, Al Beresford; w, Michael Armstrong; ph, Don Lord, Alan Pudney, Mike Spera (Rank Color); m, KPM; art d, Adrian Atkinson, Martin Atkinson, Brian Savegar; cos, Ruth Collier, Imogen Magnus; spec eff, Nick Maley.

Horror   Cas.   (PR:O MPAA:R)

SCREEN TEST zero   (1986) 83m CineTel c

Michael Allan Bloom *(Terry)*, Robert Bundy *(Clayton)*, Paul Leuken *(Dan)*, David Simpatico *(Stevie)*, Cynthia Kahn *(Cindi)*, Mari Laskarin *(Theresa)*, Katharine Sullivan *(Sally-Ann)*, William Dick *(Dr. De Sade)*, Monique Gabrielle *(Roxanne)*, Vito D'Ambrosio *(Guido)*, David Katz *(The Boss)*, Cindy Froberg *(Gemini)*, Floyd May *(Floyd)*, Karen Vaccaro *(Nancy)*, John Cazzaza, Felipe Bermudez, Shawn Hisp *(Men in John)*, Caroline Cygan *(Woman Being Interviewed)*, Mark Bedard *(Reporter)*, Eddie Ross *(Bouncer)*, Michelle Bauer *(Dancer/Ninja Girl)*, Theresa Wolfe *(Sorority Girl)*, Richard Fulman *(Cobra Gang Leader)*, Vincent Shavers, Mitchell Moore, Burdett Tatum *(Cobra Gang Members)*, Jo Ann Auster, Lisa Smith Taylor *(Soap Stars)*, James C. Moore, Chris Field *(Amphibioids)*, Mike Dempsey, Dominic Streddo *(Porn Critics)*, Patricia Campbell, Johanna Kenney, Julie Polich *(Brownies)*, Michael Sheppard *(Man in Prepuce Men's Room)*, Sheila Goodbody *(Spinster at Auditions)*, Michelle Madda *(Punk Girl at Auditions)*, Jack Conway *(Bar MC)*, Dean Rosner *(Master Surgeon)*, Karen Wheeler *(Surgical Nurse)*, John Marshall Jones *(Italian Henchman)*, Flo Spink *(Boss' Mother)*, Michael Cariosia *(Boss' Bodyguard)*, Michelle Schlifke, Dana Lee Noth *(Little Girls)*, Adam Schlifke *(Little Boy)*, Lucien Madda *(Priest)*, Rita Fanelli *(Italian Woman at Wedding)*, Deborah Blaisdel *(Dancer)*, Lisa Hunter *(Anchor Woman)*.

Once again teenagers run wild across the land of sexual fantasy in this cheerfully tasteless low-budget comedy. Bloom, Bundy, Leuken, and Simpatico are four pals who simply can't connect with women. One day they come up with the ultimate solution. By holding auditions, then pretending to shoot a pornographic

video, the four are convinced they will meet some fabulous females. After going through preliminary motions, the gang hires the best-looking girls and begins its phony production. For some reason, the guys can afford lights, a camera, and studio space, but they simply don't have the funds for a tape to record their epic. So much for logic. Problems arise when it turns out their star, Laskarin, is actually daughter of mobster Katz. Katz's goon D'Ambrosio is sent after the boys, but when he is outwitted, Katz takes matters into his own hands. He arrives at the makeshift studio, then demands the tape be turned over as soon as it is returned from the lab. The cover is blown off the scam and now the boys must come up with something fast. Fortunately, everyone is sympathetic to their cause and their stars agree to help shoot a real video. Also joining the endeavor is Dick, a kinky doctor who had turned up at the auditions. Though his hopes of being a porno star had been rebuffed, Dick has persuaded some other medicos to invest in this fledgling production. Once real shooting is completed, the final product accidentally gets a television broadcast, which Katz views. Things don't appear to look good for Our Heroes, but it turns out Katz loves the movie and wants to promote their budding careers as filmmakers.

Bad? You bet. Shot in 1983 (under the working title COME AGAIN), the film certainly has a poor attitude towards women, and there's a tinge of racist humor within its catalog of bad jokes. SCREEN TEST is not without its moments, though. The acting is acceptable, considering some of the embarrassment the cast has to go through (Dick spends most of the film in a revealing leather outfit, complete with chains and a hood) and the photography is competent. Granted, this is largely witless, but it's hard not to crack a smile during "Sneak Preverts," a parody of Roger Ebert and Gene Siskel discussing pornographic sex toys. The songs, written and performed by two obscure bands from the Chicago area (where the film was shot on location), include: "Come Around," "Keep You Satisfied" (Don Harrow, performed by Walking London), "Summer Daze," "Got to Be Mine" (Harrow, Rich Parenti, performed by Walking London), "Jumpstart" (Parenti, Brett Brdas, Mike Scukanec, Sal Salamone, performed by The Quimbees), "Waking with You" (Michael Block, performed by The Quimbees).

p, Sam Auster, Laura Auster; d, Sam Auster; w, Sam Auster, Laura Auster; ph, Jeff Jur; ed, Carol Eastman; art d, Laura Auster; m/l, Don Harrow, Rich Parenti, Brett Brdas, Mike Scukanec, Sal Salamone, Michael Block; makeup, Jamie Sue Weiss.

Comedy   Cas.   (PR:O MPAA:R)

SCUOLA DI LADRI†   (1986, It.) 84m C.G. Silver–Maura International/
                                C.D.I.–Filmexport Group c (Trans: School for Thieves)

Paolo Villaggio, Lino Banfi, Massimo Boldi *(The Three Nephews)*, Enrico Maria Salerno *(Uncle)*, Barbara Scarpa, Antonio Barros, Corrado Monteforte, Claudio Boldi.

Three overweight middle-aged losers are summoned by their rich uncle, a successful con man and thief. He offers to train the trio in the ways of crime, but after they pull off a successful heist, the old man takes all the money and retires to a tropical island. He leaves behind a message which advises his nephews to never trust anyone.

p, Mario Cecchi Gori, Vittorio Cecchi Gori; d, Neri Parenti; w, Franco Castellano, Pipolo [Giuseppe Moccia] (based on a story by Parenti, Castellano, Pipolo); ph, Alessandro D'Eva; m, Bruno Zambrini; ed, Sergio Montanari; art d, Mario Ambrosino.

Comedy   (PR:A-C MPAA:NR)

SE SUFRE PERO SE GOZA†   (1986, Mex.) 87m Producciones Films
                         Seneca/Peliculas Mexicanas c (Trans: It Hurts But It Feels Good)

Rafael Inclan *(Perioache Echevarria)*, Evita Munoz *(Rene)*, Guillermo Rivas *(Matuta)*, Carmelita Gonzalez *(Dona Luz)*, Manuel Ibanez *(Don Juliano)*, Rosella *(Rosita)*.

Low-grade Mexican sex comedy about two characters (Inclan and Rivas) who go after the big bucks (or pesos) by managing women wrestlers who have to take off their bikini tops when they lose.

p&d, Julio Ruiz Llaneza; w, Rene Cardona, Sr., Fernando Oses; ph, Ruben Mendoza; ed, Raul Dominguez.

Comedy   (PR:O MPAA:NR)

SEA SERPENT, THE zero   (1986, Span.) 92m Calepas International c

Timothy Bottoms *(Capt. Pedro Barrios)*, Taryn Power *(Margaret Roberts)*, Jared Martin *(Lenares)*, Ray Milland *(Prof. Timothy Wallace)*, Gerard Tichy, Carole James, Jack Taylor, Leon Klimovsky, Paul Benson.

Filmed in Spain and Portugal in 1984, THE SEA SERPENT never made it to the big screen in the U.S. and instead went straight to videocassette in 1986. Boasting an incredibly silly monster that looks like a hand puppet, the film opens as a U.S. jet fighter in trouble is forced to dump an atomic bomb into the ocean. The explosion awakens the aforementioned sea serpent which has been snoozing on the bottom of the sea. The next day Spanish fishermen are dismayed to find thousands of dead fish floating in the area (oh yeah, nobody noticed the atomic explosion) and some folks suspect radiation. The owner of one of the fishing boats instructs his captain to go get checked for radiation poisoning, and to replace him, the owner assigns Bottoms, a controversial captain whose last boat was sunk due to his drunkenness. One crew member, Martin, is particularly unhappy about the arrangement because his brother was killed on the last boat that Bottoms captained. That night, during Bottoms' watch, the sea serpent (accompanied by a virtual note-for-note rip-off of John Williams' JAWS score) rams the boat, putting several holes in the hull. Of course only Bottoms saw the monster, of course nobody believes him, and of course they think he was drunk. The boat sinks, one lifeboat load of crew members is eaten by the sea monster (for close-ups of the monster gobbling victims, a large cheap-looking head and neck of the monster is substituted for the hand-puppet—this so the actors can climb into the mouth and push themselves down its throat—very similar to the rug-monster in THE CREEPING TERROR), and Bottoms is soon facing a tribunal. In an unintentionally hilarious courtroom scene (every time one lawyer asks a question the other lawyer yells "Objection!" and the judge patiently explains his ruling), the prosecution persuades the tribunal that Bottoms was drunk—his claims of seeing a sea serpent don't help much—and his captain's license is revoked. Meanwhile, in Lisbon, a rich American socialite, Power, witnesses her brother-in-law friend being consumed by the sea serpent during a walk on the beach. Authorities think Power is crazy so they put her in the mental ward of a hospital. Bottoms reads the account in the newspaper and hurries to Lisbon. He convinces Power that he too has seen the monster and together they try to prove its existence. Attempting to add some validity to their claims, the couple contact an eccentric American paleontologist, Milland, and persuade him to help them. Meanwhile, the sea serpent attacks a lighthouse and snakes its way up the tower. Constricting like a python, the sea serpent destroys the lighthouse, killing the watchman. Milland examines all the sightings and recent unusual sea occurrences and discovers a definite pattern to the monster's movements. The paleontologist predicts where the monster will show up next and the tiny troupe goes to the spot. Joined by former enemy Martin—who has finally seen the sea serpent himself—the monster-hunters arrive in time to witness the critter attack a train passing across a bridge. An oil car falls off the bridge into the water and ignites, scalding the monster. The burning serpent heads off for Africa and a possible sequel while the vindicated Bottoms and Power start a romance.

Some films are so silly they look as if they were made for children; this film looks as if it was made *by* children. From the laughable monster to the extraordinarily poor dubbing, THE SEA SERPENT is a total disaster. The film takes forever to get moving, with endless scenes of pointless discussion to pad out the appearances of the monster. This is one of those films where a scene ends with a character leaving a room (usually opening and closing a door), then walking to a car, driving, parking, walking from a parking lot into a building, then walking down a hall, opening a door, and finally reaching the person they are to converse with in the next scene. The dialog is ridiculously banal and all the characters seem to be suffering from acute stupidity. Which brings us to one reason films like this exist, the special effects. As stated above, the sea serpent looks like a refugee from Mr. Rogers' "Magic Kingdom," but the miniature work is worse. While the lighthouse is passable and the train trestle is fairly convincing, the train that runs across it is so obviously a toy (with little wisps of white smoke puffing out the smokestack) that the rest of the fragile illusion is shattered. Sadly, this travesty goes down as the last film appearance of veteran actor Ray Milland.

p, Jose Frade; d, Gregory Greens; w, Gordon A. Osburn; ph, Raul Cutler (Photofilm Madrid color); m, Robin Davis; ed, Anthony Red; art d, Joseph Galic.

Horror   Cas.   (PR:A   MPAA:NR)

SECANGKIR KOPI PAHIT†   (1986, Indonesia) 99m Sanggar–Inter Studio c
(Trans: Bitter Coffee)

Alex Komang *(Oleh Togar)*, Rina Hassim *(Lola)*, Sylvia Widiantono, Ray Sahetapy.

Komang leaves his village for life in the big city of Jakarta, finding a job as a reporter. He botches a sensitive story; then his father dies, prompting him to return to his home.

p, Bambang Widitomo, Nyoohansiang; d&w, Teguh Karya; ph, Tantra Suryadi; m, Eros Djarot; ed, Ed Kamarullah; art d, Benny Benhardi.

Drama   (PR:C   MPAA:NR)

SECOND VICTORY, THE†   (1986, Brit.) 112m Melaleuka/J&M c

Anthony Andrews *(Maj. Hanlon)*, Max von Sydow *(Dr. Huber)*, Helmut Griem *(Karl Fischer)*, Mario Adorf *(Dr. Sepp Kunzli)*, Birgit Doll *(Anna Kunzli)*, Wolfgang Reichmann *(Max Holzinger)*, Renee Soutendijk *(Traudi Holzinger)*, Immy Schell *(Liesl Holzinger)*, Gunther Maria Halmer *(Rudy Winkler)*, Wolfgang Preiss *(Father Albertus)*, Jaques Breuer *(Johann Wikivill)*.

In the aftermath of WW II, British troops under Andrews' command occupy a remote village in the Austrian Alps. A shell-shocked Austrian veteran of the Eastern Front mistakes a British sergeant for a Russian and shoots him dead, but Andrews receives no cooperation from local police chief Griem as he pursues the killer, because the veteran is policeman's nephew. Another plot centers on lawyer Adorf, whose sympathies did not lay with the Nazis, but who was not above legally finagling the property of Jews shipped off to death camps. His niece, Doll, is having an affair with Andrews, but when her uncle commits suicide when his crimes are exposed, she holds the British officer responsible. Director Thomas is best known for producing and directing a score and a half of the CARRY ON films.

p&d, Gerald Thomas; w, Morris West; ph, Alan Hume (Rank Color); m, Stanley Myers.

Drama   (PR:C   MPAA:NR)

SECVENTE†   (1986, Rom.) 98m Romaniafilm c (Trans: Sequences)

Geo Barton, Ion Vilcu, Emilia Dobrin-Besoiu, Mircea Diaconu, Dragos Pislaru, Alexandru Tatos, Florin Mihailescu.

A film crew divides its time between making state-sponsored films about glorious socialism and their own more interesting project, encountering myriad difficulties. The climax of the film comes when two elderly men hired as extras in a cafe scene are seated across from each other. Slowly, one comes to realize the other is the man who tortured him in a Nazi concentration camp.

d&w, Alexandru Tatos; ph, Florin Mihailescu; ed, Iulia Vincenz; art d, Nicolae Schiopu, Andrei Both; cos, Svetlana Mihailescu, Andreea Haznas.

Drama   (PR:C   MPAA:NR)

SEMBRA MORTO . . . MA E SOLO SVENUTO†   (1986, It.) 91m Tecno
Image c (Trans: He Looks Dead . . . But He Just Fainted)

Sergio Castellitto *(Romano Duranti)*, Marina Confalone *(Marina Duranti)*, Mario Prosperi *(Alfio)*, Marco Giardina *(Commissioner)*, Susanne Rust *(Jasmine)*, Claudio Spadaro *(Police Agent)*, Anita Zagaria.

Strange, bittersweet story concerns a brother and sister (Castellito and Confalone) on the far side of thirty who live together in the family apartment. Castellito makes ends meet by dognaping and Confalone by taking in typing, but their orderly existence is upset by the arrival of Prosperi as their new neighbor. He seduces Confalone then hides a kilo of cocaine in her refrigerator. This leads to much confusion and chasing about when the refrigerator is replaced and Castellito finds the cocaine. The finale finds Castellito as the top dog race bookie, but still dabbling in ransoming off pedigreed animals. When his sister shows up pregnant and has to be rushed to the hospital, he is forced to miss a ransom meeting. As a result, he is murdered.

p, Alessandro Verdecchi; d, Felice Farina; w, Gianni di Gregorio, Sergio Castellitto, Felice Farina (based on a story by Castellitto); ph, Renato Tafuri (Luciano Vittori Color, Eastmancolor); m, Lamberto Macchi; ed, Roberto Schiavone; art d, Valentino Salvati.

Comedy/Drama   (PR:C-O   MPAA:NR)

SEN TURKULERINI SOYLE†   (1986, Turkey) Uzman c (Trans: Sing Your
Songs)

Kadir Inanir, Sibel Turnagoll, Serif Goen, Tunca Yonder.

d, Serif Goren; w, Tirgay Aksoy; ph, Aytekin Cakmakci.

SENSI†   (1986, It.) 101m Dania–Filmes International–Globe–National
Cinematografica/D.M.V. c (Trans: Evil Senses)

Gabriele Lavia *(Manuel)*, Monica Guerritore *(Vittoria)*, Mimsy Farmer *(Micol)*, Lewis Eduard Ciannelli, Dario Mazzoli, Gioia Maria Scola, Jean Mass.

Lavia is a professional killer who is sought after by bad-news heavies who believe he is in possession of a list they think should be theirs. They track him from London to Rome, where he takes up residency in ex-girl friend Farmer's brothel. He begins a relationship with Guerritore, a rich, bored housewife who is a prostitute in the best BELLE DE JOUR tradition. She is also actually working for the people who want Lavia dead, but that's okay, he knew it all along.

p, Pietro Innocenzi; d, Gabriele Lavia; w, Gabriele Lavia, Dardano Sacchetti, Vincenzo Manino, Gianfranco Clerici (based on a story by Gabriele Lavia); ph, Mario Vulpiani (Luciano Vittori Color); m, Fabio Frizzi; ed, Daniele Alabiso; art d, Giovanni Agostinucci.

Drama   (PR:O   MPAA:NR)

SENZA SCRUPOLI†   (1986, It.) Grandangolo Coop/FOX c (Trans: Without
Scruples)

Sandra Wey, Marzio Honorato, Antonio Marsina, Cinzia De Ponti, Sandra Canale, Vincenzo Cavaliere, Giuseppe Mendolicchio.

A woman is raped and finds no one the least bit sympathetic. She comes to believe the only person who understands her is the rapist, so she decides to track him down and kill him, but not before having sex with him again. Yet another of the endless stream of so-called "erotic dramas" that now seem to dominate Italian cinema.

d, Tonino Valerii; w, Riccardo Ghione, Tonino Valerii (based on a story by Mino Roli); ph, Giulio Albonico (Telecolor); m, James Senese, Joe Amoroso; ed, Antonio Siciliano.

Drama   (PR:O   MPAA:NR)

SEPARATE VACATIONS*½   (1986, Can.) 82m RSL–Playboy/RSL c

David Naughton *(Richard Moore)*, Jennifer Dale *(Sarah Moore)*, Mark Keyloun *(Jeff Ferguson)*, Laurie Holden *(Karen)*, Blanca Guerra *(Alicia)*, Suzie Almgren *(Helen Gilbert)*, Lally Cadeau *(Shelley)*, Jackie Mahon *(Annie Moore)*, Lee-Max Walton *(Donald Moore)*, Jay Woodcroft *(Bobby Moore)*, Tony Rosato *(Harry Blender)*, Colleen Embree *(Robyn)*, Sherry Miller *(Sandy)*, Laura Henry *(Nancy)*, Carolyn Dunn, Rebecca Jones, Bonnie Kristian Squire *(Girls at Pool)*, Harvey Atkin *(Henry Gilbert)*, Jose Escandon *(Roberto)*, Miguel Angel Fuentes *(Tiny)*, Jaime Segal *(Singer in Disco)*, Robbi Baker *(Hostess at Lodge)*, Paco Mauri *(Rent-a-Car Man)*, Nancy Cser *(Stewardess)*, Jorge Victoria *(Immigration Officer)*, Jessica Booker *(Grandmother)*, Fred Rahn *(Grandfather)*.

Naughton and Dale are a long-married couple with three kids who find the stress of it all getting to them. Naughton is continually attracted to other women—who all appear willing—and when the opportunity to travel to Mexico on business presents itself (he's an architect designing a library that looks like a Mayan pyramid), he doesn't hesitate to cancel out on a family ski trip. Dale, of course, takes this decision as a personal rejection, so she goes off on her trip with the kids and the babysitter with a chip on her shoulder. After an unsuccessful attempt at sex with a fellow passenger in the airplane restroom, Naughton abandons any plans of looking at ruins in the jungle and heads for Puerta Vallarta to pick up some women. Of course, now that he feels he can have an affair with impunity, no one is interested. He suffers a series of humiliating rejections, not to mention a narrow escape from an angry pimp, and another encounter with the woman from the plane, who wants her insurance-salesman lover to join them in bed. Meanwhile, Dale has attracted a young ski instructor (Keyloun) who reminds her of Naughton, but she continually resists his advances. Naughton comes back from Mexico and learns from the babysitter (whom Keyloun has earlier rejected) where his wife is. He drives there and acts like an idiot, punching out Keyloun and trying to drag off Dale. She tells him she doesn't love him anymore and that he should find a lawyer, but both later have second thoughts and reconcile. Discussing it later, Naughton comes to the conclusion that the problem with their marriage is their kids, so they decide to take an apartment to which they can escape (dumping the kids at grandma's) and to return the romance to their marriage.

An annoying, unfunny comedy with very little going for it. Naughton is too unsympathetic to be the center of the film and Dale can't act well enough to do it herself. The script has the subtlety of dirty story told by a junior-high-schooler, and the plot is thoroughly familiar, reworking THE SEVEN YEAR ITCH, among others. Perhaps the funniest moment in the film comes when Naughton and a Mexican woman watch from his hotel balcony as the sun rises over the ocean. Unfortunately, Puerta Vallarta is on the western coast of Mexico. Songs include: "On the Brink" (Tony Macaulay, performed by Sandy MacLelland) and "Take It Like a Man" (Mel Ayres, performed by Jaime Segal).

p, Robert Lantos, Stephen J. Roth; d, Michael Anderson; w, Robert Kaufman; ph, Francois Protat; ed, Ron Wisman; prod d, Csaba Kertesz; set d, Murray Sumner; cos, Laurie Drew; m/l, Mel Ayres, Tony Macaulay; makeup, Marie Angele Brietner-Protat.

Comedy   **Cas.**   **(PR:O   MPAA:R)**

SEPARATI IN CASA†   (1986, It.) 100m Eidoscope/COL c (Trans: Separated at Home)

Riccardo Pazzaglia (Husband), Simona Marchini (Carolina), Massimiliano Pazzaglia (Luciano), Marina Confalone, Lucio Allocca (Lawyers), Elisabeth Gutierrez, Riccardo Perrotti, Natalia Bizzi, Serena Bennato, Maria Carolina Alba, Maria Rosaria Forte, Luigi Uzzo, Gino Ciotola, Sergio Simonelli, Domitilla Cavazza, Ughetta Lanari, Giovanni Moxedano, Aldo De Martino.

A married couple with a teenage son finally decides to separate. Since neither can afford new living accommodations, they work out a complicated arrangement to share the house. Eventually the son manages to persuade his parents that they still love each other and everything resolves happily.

p, Mario Orfini, Emilio Bolles; d&w, Riccardo Pazzaglia; ph, Nino Celeste (Telecolor); m, Riccardo Pazzaglia; ed, Anna Napoli; art d, Giovanni Agostinucci.

Comedy   **(PR:C   MPAA:NR)**

SERE CUALQUIER COSA PERO TE QUIERO**   (1986, Arg.) Instituto Nacional de Cinematografia Argentina c (Trans: I May Be Anything, But I Love You)

Luis Brandoni, Nene Malbran, Dora Baret, Micaela Brandoni, Carlos Moreno, Marcelo Alexandre, Alberto Busaid, Mabel Manzotti.

Baret is a lonely spinster who lives in a big, antique-filled house she inherited when her father died. She calls a plumber, Brandoni, to repair a toilet, but he soon makes a shambles of her whole house. She resists his crude overtures for a while, then slowly succumbs to his slightly idiotic charm and his good-natured bragging. To prove to her that he isn't a total loser, he enters the big bicycle race and she supports him through his training, buying a bicycle for him and allowing him to work out in her home. One of his seedier friends offers to arrange for him to win the race by sleeping with the wife of the judge. Brandoni can't go through with it, but Baret comes home to find this other woman anyway and immediately puts the picture together and tosses him out. Brandoni enters the race and loses badly, but as he crawls across the finish line, Baret is there to forgive him at the happy ending.

Not one of the better films to come out of Argentina since the recent wave of liberalization, this comedy does have a certain amount of charm. Brandoni manages to be sympathetic even when he is at his worst, and the loneliness of Baret, the factor that makes the unlikely romance possible, is well conveyed in her performance.

d, Carlos Galettini; w, Irene Ickowicz, Sergio De Cecco, Carlos Galettini; ph, Juan Carlos Lenardi; m, Jose Luis Castineira de Dios; set d, Guillermo de la Torre.

Comedy   **(PR:C-O   MPAA:NR)**

SES†   (1986, Turkey) Seref c (Trans: The Voice)

Tariik Akan, Nur Suter, Kamuran Usluser, Guler Okten.

d, Zeki Okten; w, Fehmi Yasar; ph, Orham Oguz.

SETTE CHILI IN SETTE GIORNI†   (1986, It.) 112m C.G. Silver/COL c (Trans: Seven Kilos in Seven Days)

Carlo Verdone (Alfio Tamburini), Renato Pozzetto (Silvano Barocchi), Tiziana Pini (Snob), Silvia Annichiarico.

Two failed medical school graduates return from an Eastern bloc country with a concoction that promises to take off seven kilos of fat in as many days. They connive to open a fat farm and attract a varied clientele, including an American rock star and a boxer. The formula turns out to add weight, and the two seem doomed to failure. The singer, however, says the treatment improved her voice, saving the young entrepreneurs.

p, Mario Cecchi Gori, Vittorio Cecchi Gori; d, Luca Verdone; w, Leonardo Benvenuti, Piero De Bernardi (based on a story by Luca Verdone, Carlo Verdone, Leonardo Benvenuti, Piero De Bernardi); ph, Danilo Desideri (Technicolor); m, Pino Donaggio; ed, Antonio Siciliano.

Comedy   **(PR:C   MPAA:NR)**

SEVEN MINUTES IN HEAVEN**½   (1986) 90m Zoetrope-FR/WB c

Jennifer Connelly (Natalie Becker), Byron Thames (Jeff Moran), Maddie Corman (Polly Franklin), Alan Boyce (Casey), Michael Zaslow (Bob Becker, Natalie's Father), Polly Draper (Aileen Jones, Jeff's Mother), Marshall Bell (Gerry Jones, Jeff's Stepfather), Billy Wirth (Zoo Knudsen), Terry Kinney (Zoo's Teammate), Spalding Gray (Dr. Rodney), Michael Higgins (Sen. Peterson), Denny Dillon (Aunt Gail), Lauren Holly (Lisa), Paul Martell (Tim Williams), Margo Skinner (Lenore Franklin, Polly's Mother), Matthew Lewis (Stew Franklin, Polly's Father), Brian Freilino (Natalie's Teacher), Patricia O'Connell (Lingerie Saleslady), Don Koll (Vice-President), Vivien Straus (Pet Store Saleslady), Vincent Capolupo (Polly's Admirer), James Bigwood (Journalist), Ed O'Ross (Mall Security), Van Brooks (Stadium Cop), Antony Bishop (Pet Store Man), Tim Waldrip (Richie Franklin, Polly's Brother), Eddie Cipot (Zoo's Teammate), Erna Rossman (Zoo's Fan), Jane Bernstein (Teacher).

An endearing and tender view of teenagers and their first steps into sexual relationships. The film takes place in a modest, traditional town and revolves

around three close friends. Connelly is a beautiful and intelligent aspiring politician whose chief concerns involve action in government, not in her bedroom. Her best friend, Corman, is obsessed with sex and desperately wants to unravel the mysteries of it for herself. A friend to both of them is Thames, a bratty but likable kid who is seen not as a boy, but as a friend—a role which frustrates him. After an argument at home, Thames turns to Connelly and asks to stay at her house. Connelly, whose father is away on business and whose mother is dead, reluctantly gives in to Thames, responding to his presence in a sisterly fashion. In the meantime, Connelly has been asked on a date by Boyce, a handsome, interesting womanizer. Corman is heartbroken, having hoped that she would be asked out by him. While Connelly and Boyce exchange some harmless kisses, Corman and Thames eagerly and curiously watch porno videotapes. Connelly refuses to give in to Boyce's pressure to bed, but rather than get angry Boyce is understanding. Assuming that Connelly has lost her virginity to Boyce, Corman becomes jealous and angry. Corman sees Connelly as having it all—brains, beauty, a promising future, and now a boy friend. Connelly is chosen as a "Future Leader" and is invited to Washington as part of a group meeting at the White House, where she meets a friendly and informative young Presidential aide. While Connelly is in Washington, Corman has taken off for New York City in the hope of seeing a baseball star with whom she's infatuated. Having met him quite by chance and spending an afternoon "making out" in the back seat of his car, Corman has become obsessed with thoughts of losing her virginity to him. Corman goes to Shea Stadium to watch him play, makes a fool out of herself by waving a red negligee in front of him, and is escorted out by security guards. A likable photographer, Kinney, rescues her from the guards by pretending to be a friend of hers. He brings her back to his Manhattan loft, feeds her, and lets her stay the night. Not surprisingly, she now wants to get under the covers with him. He's the voice of reason, however, and explains that she should save herself for someone special. Connelly and Corman, both returning from their trips, run into each other at the airport and quickly forget all about their argument. They return to their pleasant little town where all their problems are eventually resolved. Connelly, who has decided that she wants to be president, breaks up with Boyce when she learns that he has another girl, Thames reconciles with his parents, and Corman decides that she likes Thames as both a boy and a friend.

There's little in SEVEN MINUTES IN HEAVEN that hasn't been seen before, and though that may take away from the film's originality, it surely doesn't diminish its charm. Produced by Roos, a Francis Coppola associate and one-time legendary casting director, and directed by first-timer Feferman, the film captures those awkward days of growing up when one begins to confront sexual curiosity. Previous to these characters' encounters, they were never faced with life decisions based on sexual or romantic feelings. For the first (and surely not last) time in her life, Connelly must decide between sex and her career goals. Corman, for all her big talk, is faced with many of the same inhibitions as Connelly. The characters are placed in awkward situations which succeed because they are played by two exceptional actresses. Connelly, who has been seen before in ONCE UPON A TIME IN AMERICA, is one of the most gorgeous and talented young actresses working today. Corman, a New York stage actress, perfectly typifies the high school girl with all her insecurities, curiosity, energy, and adorable teenage looks. The real surprise in the film is Kinney, a Chicago stage actor, whose performance as the insightful photographer gives the film a needed base of good sense and reality. Putting Corman's feelings into perspective, Kinney treats her like a kid sister rather than taking advantage of her vulnerabilities and eagerness. Kinney shines when he is put on the spot by Corman, who asks him what it feels like to have an orgasm during intercourse. Instead of giving a smart-aleck answer, he supplies an eloquent, philosophical one. Appearing in only one scene, Kinney takes command of the entire film. It is his speech and his performance that comment on the scenes that came before and mold the scenes that come after. Although the talk in SEVEN MINUTES IN HEAVEN is frank, it is never degrading or exploitative. Rather, it has a harmless innocence to it. Although the entire film revolves around sexual awakening, there is no nudity, no demeaning photography, and not the slightest hint of any ill intentions. Songs include: "Dear You" (Robert Kraft, performed by Josie Aiello), "Ready or Not" (Robert Kraft, Franne Golde, performed by Josie Aiello), "Inner Logic" (Robert Kraft, Franne Golde, Bette Midler, performed by Josie Aiello), "Little Boy Sweet" (Franne Golde, Peter Ivers, performed by Josie Aiello).

p, Fred Roos; d, Linda Feferman; w, Jane Bernstein, Linda Feferman; ph, Steven Fierberg (Technicolor); m, Robert Kraft; ed, Marc Laub; prod d, Vaughan Edwards; art d, Thomas A. Walsh; set d, Debra Schutt; cos, Dianne Finn-Chapman; m/l, Robert Kraft, Franne Golde, Bette Midler, Peter Ivers; makeup, Hollywood DiRusso; stunts, E. Mourino.

Comedy/Drama **Cas.** **(PR:C MPAA:PG-13)**

SEX APPEAL** (1986) 84m Vestron/Platinum c

Louie Bonanno *(Tony Cannelloni)*, Tally Brittany *(Corrine)*, Marcia Karr *(Christina Cannelloni)*, Jerome Brenner *(Joseph Cannelloni)*, Marie Sawyer *(Louise Cannelloni)*, Philip Campanaro *(Ralph)*, Jeff Eagle *(Donald Cromronic)*, Gloria Leonard, Molly Morgan [Merle Michaels], Veronica Hart, Candida Royalle, Taija Rae, Stasia Micula [Samantha Fox], Kim Kafkaloff [Sheri St. Claire], Jill Kumer, Norris O'Neil, Stephen Raymond, Edwina Thorne, Cindy Joy, Terry Powers, Ron Chalon, Robin Leonard, Janice Doskey, Johnny Nineteen, Larry Catanzano, Anne Tylar, Suzanne Vale.

A hardcore pornographic feature from 1980, FASCINATION, is remade here as an R-rated sex comedy with a raft of porno stars and starlets getting to keep their clothes on for once (more or less). Bonanno is a hapless Jewish boy from New Jersey who buys a book on sex appeal to perk up his lonely life. His first step is to move out of his parents' house and into a Manhattan apartment. His superintendent and next door neighbor, Eagle, also happens to be a writer desperate to sell something. Bonanno turns his apartment into a seduction den complete with Japanese erotic prints and African fertility statues, then sets about finding a woman to seduce. His first attempt is with a woman from work, and she seems willing enough, but her husband crashes through the door and makes love to his wife on Bonanno's bed, with the lad watching helplessly. Other attempts end in similar disaster; one non-stop talker has to be folded up with the Murphy bed when his mother shows up unexpectedly; another squeals so loudly at the slightest touch that she is impossible to make love to. All the while Eagle has been listening through the wall and turning Bonanno's misadventures into a series of magazine articles about the "New Jersey Casanova" which have become wildly successful. At the same time, Bonanno's father and sister decide to use the apartment for their own respective trysts. Of course, it all falls apart when everyone shows up at the same time, and Eagle reveals that Bonanno is the New Jersey Casanova. Rejected by everyone, he finally wins the girl of his dreams, model Brittany from down the hall.

Basically a bedroom farce, there's nothing especially bad about this film: technical credits are acceptable to good, the script is so standard it's foolproof, and the performances adequate. It never takes off, though, and never delivers the big laughs. A few of the supporting roles are well done, especially Morgan (who performs her X-rated exploits under the name Merle Michaels), who shows a surprising comic talent as the non-stop talker. The original hardcore feature, FASCINATION, was produced and written by Chuck Vincent and directed by Larry Revene. Here Vincent takes over the directing chores while Revene takes over the camera. Hart and Morgan both appeared in FASCINATION, and excerpts from the film can be glimpsed briefly on Bonanno's home video system.

p&d, Chuck Vincent; w, Chuck Vincent, Craig Horrall (based on the film FASCINATION written by Vincent, Jimmy James); ph, Larry Revene; m, Ian Shaw, Kai Joffee; ed, Marc Ubell [Chuck Vincent]; cos, Robert Pusilo Studio.

Comedy **Cas.** **(PR:O MPAA:R)**

SEX O'CLOCK NEWS, THE zero (1986) 80m Chase-Prism c

Doug Ballard *(Bill McFarland)*, Lydia Mahan *(Maggie Neil)*, Wayne Knight *(Bill Wright)*, Kate Weiman *(Wanda Barrett)*, Rob Bartlett *(Marty Cohen)*, Philip McKinley *(Stormy Knight)*, Joy Bond *(Shelley Coates)*, Bruce Brown *((Game Show Host)*, Judith Drake *(Mary Ferrdip)*, Jerry Winsett *(Harve Gibbons)*, Don Pardo *(Announcer)*, Hetty Galen *(Rose Bancry)*, Robert Trebor *(Mr. Rajah)*, Anthony Picciano *(Barney Ferrdip)*, Karin Brown, Megan Mitchell *(Daughters)*, Teri Gair *(Hostess)*, Sherwyn Cloth *(TV Producer)*, Leigh Burgess *(Blonde)*, Shanton Granger *(Policeman)*, Captain Sticky *(Superman)*, Robert Sapoff *(Doctor)*, Harry Spillman *(Spokesman)*, Earl Hammond, Sandy Marshall, Joan Shepard, Peter Newland, Gary Alexander, Shelley Carroll, Jim Hunter, Mike Paskil *(Announcers)*.

No sense in mincing words about this, THE SEX O'CLOCK NEWS is just plain bad. The film is a parody of an evening newscast, complete with a few jabs at local events, national stories, and even the "Entertainment Tonight" style of journalism. There's also some commercial spoofs and previews of upcoming programs on the television station "KSEX" tossed in for good measure. With call letters like that, along with the film's sledgehammer subtle title, it's not too hard to figure out what the comic emphasis is here. Bared breasts, flatulence, and kinky encounters figure heavily in the punchlines as the skits parade across the screen. The bits include an Indian kids' show host ("Mr. Rajah's Neighborhood") who goes to Plato's Retreat; a flamboyantly gay weatherman; and a game show where a family plays for a chance to send their father to the electric chair. Captain Sticky, a favorite of the old NBC show "Real People," also makes an appearance as a retired Superman. Singer Bo Diddley also pops up as does famed announcer Don Pardo, who provides a narration for THE SEX O'CLOCK NEWS' opening, a coming attraction teaser for a movie titled THE GYNECOLOGIST FROM HELL. This actually could be pretty amusing in a tasteless sort of way, but what follows is merely a tired display of wretched excess. The unattractive and unfunny cast merely go through the motions, Vanderbes' direction is third rate, and the production qualities are strictly bottom of the barrel. THE GROOVE TUBE ranks as a masterpiece in comparison. Songs include: "Check Out the Sex O'Clock News" (Leigh Crizoe, Sherwyn Cloth, performed by R.J. Funk and Jam Trak), "Steppin' Out" (Andy Shernoff, performed by The Dictations), "Do Your Thing" (Bo Diddley, performed by Bo Diddley).

p&d, Romano Vanderbes; w, Sherry Cloth, Paul Laikin, Cary Bayer, Victor Zimet, Romano Vanderbes; ph, Oliver Wood, Robert Megginson; ed, Victor Zimet; m/l, Leigh Crizoe, Sherwyn Cloth, Andy Shernoff, Bo Diddley; makeup, Suzen Poshek.

Comedy **Cas.** **(PR:O MPAA:R)**

SEY SARSILIYOR† (1986, Turkey) Odak c (Trans: Saripinar 1914)

Sener Sen, Levent Yilmaz, Erol Durak, Orhan Cgman.

d, Atif Yilmaz; w, Baris Pirhasan (based on a novel by Resat Nuri Guntekin); ph, Orhan Oguz.

SHADOW OF VICTORY*** (1986, Neth.) 112m Matthijs van Heyningen-Sigma Filmproduction II (IN DE SCHADUW VAN DE OVERWINNING)

Jeroen Krabbe *(Peter van Dijk)*, Edwin de Vries *(Blumberg)*, Linda van Dyck, Marieke van der Pol, Rijk de Gooyer, Ton Lutz.

This fictionalized account of actual WW II events set in Amsterdam is an enlightening and engaging exploration of the Nazi invasion of the Netherlands. De Vries and Krabbe are two men with vastly different methods of dealing with the German occupation of their country. The former is a highly educated Jew with a nonviolent bent that borders on collaboration. His goal is to secure the safe passage of Jews out of the country, an activity that requires him to work closely with Nazi officials. Ultimately de Vries fails, and resigns himself to a menial job for the Nazis. Krabbe, on the other hand, is a leader in the Dutch resistance. He is a man of action, who bombs buildings and murders Nazis while keeping a wife and two mistresses. Krabbe's death mirrors the way he lived, fought, and loved. After being captured by a Nazi official, Krabbe ignites a bomb that blows both him and the German to bits. Both de Vries and Krabbe are based on actual WW II figures; de Vries on the peaceful theologian Friedrich Weinreb, and Krabbe on the resistance hero Gerrit van der Veen. While van der Veen was posthumously recognized as a hero, Weinreb served a term in jail for participating in what was wrongfully considered Nazi collaboration. His memoirs served as the basis for SHADOW OF VICTORY. (In Dutch; English subtitles.)

d, Ate de Jong; w, Ate de Jong, Edwin de Vries; ph, Eddy van der Enden; m, Hennie Vrienten; ed, Ton Ruys; art d, Ben van Os, Jan Roelfs.

War/Drama **(PR:O MPAA:NR)**

SHADOW PLAY* (1986) 98m Millenium/NW c

Dee Wallace Stone *(Morgan Hanna)*, Cloris Leachman *(Millie Crown)*, Ron Kuhlman *(John Crown)*, Barry Laws *(Jeremy Crown)*, Al Strobel *(Byron)*, Delia Slavi *(Bette)*, Susan Dixon *(Zelda)*, Al Strobel *(Byron Byron)*, Glen Baggerly *(Archie)*, Juleen Murray *(Sarah)*, Michele Mariana *(Lois)*, Bob Griggs *(Conroy)*, Marjorie Card Hughes *(Sophie)*, Richard Wilshire *(Dr. Feldman)*, George Stokes *(Marty)*, Mya Chamberlin *(Girl in Lighthouse)*, Steven Rock-Savage *(Tony)*.

This uninvolving story of the supernatural follows Stone, a struggling writer, who must come to terms with a devastating moment from her past. Seven years previously, her lover (Laws) fell to his death from a lighthouse. Now Stone is returning to the site of that freak accident, hoping she will be able to finish a play she is writing. Leachman, her dead lover's mother, welcomes Stone into her home and then some creepy things start happening. Stone begins seeing Laws every time

she looks around, and the accident keeps replaying in her dreams. She continues with her play—which is an exploration of her feelings towards this incident—by rehearsing it as a work-in-progress with some local actors. This monotonous plot line repeats itself over and over, with an occasional break in the pattern provided by Strobel, a one-armed tarot-card reader. Eventually it's learned that Laws' brother Kuhlman, who secretly loved Stone, was responsible for Laws' plunge and has kept his secret all these years. Finally knowing the truth, Stone can return to New York with play in hand.

Watching SHADOW PLAY is an exercise in steadfast patience. One keeps waiting for something interesting to happen, but the payoff doesn't come until the not-so-surprising climax. In the meantime, we are subject to Stone's sad-eyed looks and occasional screaming, Leachman's awful histrionics, and Shadburne's painfully slow direction. Shadburne may have been trying for mood effects by keeping this at a sluggish pace, but all she achieves is tedium. There's no buildup of suspense, just an occasional glimmer of some unearthly vision. The juxtaposition of Stone's play (a pretentious experimental work that consists of bad rhyming and hokey imagery) with her psychological state never gels. SHADOW PLAY was shot on location on a island off the coast of Washington State and marked Shadburne's feature debut. Working as a coproducer was Shadburne's husband, Will Vinton, who is well known for his own work in the art of Claymation filmmaking. Includes the song "Beautiful Music Tonight" (Jon Newton, performed by Taber Shadburne).

p, Dan Biggs, Susan Shadburne, Will Vinton; d&w, Susan Shadburne; ph, Ron Orieux; m, Jon Newton; ed, Konji Yamamoto; art d, Steve Karatzas; spec eff, Will Vinton Productions, Bruce McKean; m/l, Jon Newton; makeup, Elisabeth Scott.

Mystery   Cas.   (PR:O   MPAA:R)

SHADOWS RUN BLACK zero   (1986) 89m Mesa/Troma c

William J. Kulzer *(Rydell King)*, Elizabeth Trosper *(Judy Cole)*, Shea Porter *(Morgan Cole)*, George J. Engelson *(Priest)*, Dianne Hinkler *(Helen Cole)*, Julius Metoyer *(Billy)*, Terry Congie *(Lee Faulkner)*, Kevin Costner *(Jimmy Scott)*, Lee Bishop *(Police Officer)*, Jacqueline Rochelle Brodley *(Girl in Forest)*, Carl Nubile *(Boy in Forest)*, Nealie Gerard *(Prostitute)*, Gerard Thomas *(Janitor)*, Brianne Siddall *(Girl at Police Counter)*, Richard Escobedo *(Arresting Officer)*, Marc Christopher *(Detective at Station)*, Olwen Armstrong *(Lady Attorney)*, Hank Robinson *(Capt. Dorsey)*, James M. Cooper *(Policeman at Counter)*, John "Magic" Wright *(Magician)*, Paul Wright *(Bass Player)*, Rhonda Selesnow *(Girl Stabbed in Chest)*, Joe Marmo *(Coroner)*, William Solony *(Weightlifter)*, Kim Patterson *(Franklin)*, David Gaines *(Man Watching Television)*, Ann Hull *(Girl Killed in Kitchen)*, Joseph Long *(Detective at Interrogation)*, Vince McKay *(Sgt. Bishop)*, Wendy Tolkin *(Georgie)*, Barbara Peckinpaugh *(Sandy)*, Eric Robert Louzil *(Baby in Crib)*, Tim Mallacy *(Biker in Jail)*, Rick Searles *(Photographer at Pool)*, Sanford Barr, Ron Halpern *(Ambulance Attendants)*, Martha Garcia *(Witness in Hallway)*, Herbie Katz *(Press Photographer)*, Keith Doyle *(News Cameraman)*, Mary Beth McKenzie *(Newscaster)*, Dennis Vanetta *(Newscaster on Television)*, Jonathan Pleuka *(Policeman in Hallway)*.

Filmed in 1981 and never released theatrically (although both CineWorld and Troma announced release at different times), SHADOWS RUN BLACK wound up going straight to videocassette in 1986. Notable only because a young Kevin Costner (SILVERADO) appears briefly in an unbilled performance, this incredibly cheap-looking film is one step above a porno movie because of its shocking amount of full frontal nudity. Although it pretends to be a police thriller about a serial killer, SHADOWS RUN BLACK is nothing more than an excuse to parade several well-endowed young women naked before the camera while they wait to be murdered in a variety of bloody ways. When the filmmakers don't even bother giving the victims a name and bill the actresses as "Girl Stabbed in Chest" and "Girl Killed in Kitchen," you can expect a totally gratuitous flesh-and-blood-fest. The plot, such as it is, sees a young woman, Trosper, stand by helplessly as all her girl friends are being murdered. The case is being investigated by over-emphatic cop Kulzer, and he zeros in on Costner as his chief suspect. Costner is

innocent, of course, because it is Kulzer himself (surprise, surprise) who is killing the girls. The crazed Kulzer thinks the "loose" girls have corrupted his recently kidnapped daughter and for some reason he has identified Trosper with his missing daughter and feels as if he must save her (go figure).

Not only is the film repugnant in its exploitation of women, but it is hopelessly inept in nearly every other department. The photography is muddy, the lighting appears to be from one harshly bright source (probably a "sun-gun"), the acting is atrocious, and the pacing is torturously slow. Incredibly, Costner's talents do bubble to the surface and he manages to create the only believable character in the film. One can only assume that Costner is not billed in the credits because he doesn't want his filmography sullied by such trash.

p, Eric Louzil; d, Howard Heard; w, Craig Kusaba, Duke Howard (based on a story by Craig Kusaba); ph, John Sprung (United Color); ed, Raul Davalos, Davide Ganzino; stunts, William J. Kulzer.

Crime/Thriller   Cas.   (PR:O   MPAA:NR)

SHANGHAI SURPRISE   (1986, Brit.) 96m Handmade–Vista/MGM c

Sean Penn *(Glendon Wasey)*, Madonna *(Gloria Tatlock)*, Paul Freeman *(Walter Faraday/Father Burns)*, Richard Griffiths *(Willie Tuttle)*, Philip Sayer *(Justin Kronk)*, Clyde Kusatsu *(Joe Go)*, Kay Tong Lim *(Mei Gan)*, Sonserai Lee *(China Doll)*, Victor Wong *(Ho Chong)*, Prof. Toru Tanaka *(Yamagani San)*, Michael Aldridge *(Mr. Burns)*, Sarah Lam *(China Doll's Maid)*, George She *(Wu Ch'en She)*, Won Gam Bor *(Rickshaw King)*, To Chee Kan *(China Doll's Boatman)*, David Li *(Doorman at Zig-Zag Club)*, Keith Bonnard *(Maitre'D at Zig-Zag Club)*, Claire Lutter, Pamela Yang, *(Prostitutes)*, Michael Chow, Samuel Tsao *(Street Barkers)*, Philip Tan *(Ship's Officer)*, George Harrison *(Nightclub Singer)*.

SHANGHAI SURPRISE, like this year's superior Roman Polanski film PIRATES, has been victimized by a rash of fashionable criticism based more on hyped publicity and controversial personalities than on the film itself. PIRATES was mercilessly lambasted by critics who felt that Polanski (a fugitive from U.S. justice) deserved to be raked over the coals. SHANGHAI SURPRISE has also been attacked by critics who may have been determined to knock Hollywood bad boy Penn (he has a penchant for punching reporters) and his phenomenally popular rock-singer wife Madonna off of their media-constructed pedestals. After Penn and Madonna's headline-making wedding, they announced that they would be appearing together in a movie. The movie press apparently decided it was time to shake up their idyllic existence. In other words, SHANGHAI SURPRISE was doomed before it even opened. While no masterpiece, SHANGHAI SURPRISE is a tolerable period adventure film which, had it been released in the late 1930s, would have been relegated to the bottom half of a double bill.

The film opens in 1937, the year of the Japanese occupation of China, as drug kingpin Freeman is trying to escape with a shipment of opium, which becomes known as "Faraday's Flowers." Kay Tong Lim, a Chinese army officer, demands that the "flowers" be turned over to him. While searching Freeman's possessions, Kay Tong Lim falls victim to a booby trap called a "Shanghai Surprise" that blows his hands off. Freeman is chased into the bay by army guards and shot. One year later, the story picks up as Madonna, an innocent missionary, convinces Penn, a sleazy American who has bought a shipment of glow-in-the-dark nudie neckties, to help her find the missing opium. Madonna and the missionary head want to send the opium to injured Chinese soldiers who are in need of a painkiller since their morphine supply has been depleted. Penn, who is penniless and stranded, agrees to help, in exchange for a ticket back to Los Angeles. Penn, who speaks fluent Chinese, and Madonna make a number of contacts, including Griffiths, a Sydney Greenstreet-type reporter who was with Freeman the night he was shot; Sayer, a snoopy, nervous gentleman who always has a little too much information; Wong, a deal-making insurance salesman who forces his clients to buy useless policies (like Penn who has his ankles insured) in exchange for information; and Kusatsu, a powerful underworld businessman who loves baseball and implores Penn to help him improve his pitching.

Penn's life is endangered a few times, especially by Kay Tong Lim, who interrogates him with torture. Later, Penn meets with Griffiths and Sayer, who show him a photo of Kay Tong Lim and a newspaper clip which reads, "Is this the man who looted the royal tombs?" Penn meets with Lee, a beautiful princess who calls herself China Doll and knows the whereabouts of the tomb's "flowers." Kay Tong Lim has already tried, unsuccessfully, to get the "flowers" from Lee, whom he also tortured in the process. After spending the night in Lee's bed, Penn returns to a jealous Madonna, who removes her virginal missionary attire and crawls into bed with him. Penn then tells Madonna that the "flowers" that Kay Tong Lim are after are jewels, not opium. Madonna meets with Lee to ask for the jewels, which she then plans to use to buy the needed opium. When Lee asks why the mission doesn't buy guns instead, Madonna replies with all seriousness, "Guns cause pain, opium cures pain." She is given the jewels, but later, during a confrontation with Kay Tong Lim, the jewels are stolen. Madonna and Penn manage to get away after Kay Tong Lim again falls prey to a "Shanghai Surprise," which this time blows off his artificial hands. Madonna and Penn return to the mission with the jewels, only to have them stolen away by Father Burns, the head missionary, who is actually Freeman in disguise. He flees to a Los Angeles-bound ship, but is followed by Madonna and Penn. It is then revealed that Lee has tricked Freeman and that the jewels are only painted baubles. Rather than allow Madonna to leave his life, Penn, at the last minute, gets off the departing ship and has his crates of glow-in-the-dark ties unloaded. As the ship, with Freeman aboard, sails out of port, Penn discovers that his crates are filled with the opium "flower" that existed after all.

A no-expenses-spared production from Britain's Handmade Films, SHANG-HAI SURPRISE performed abominably at the box-office. According to MGM's marketing head, Greg Morrison, the studio "had done a lot of research on the movie and a lot of research in advertising and we found that there simply was no substantial interest in the film.'' Rather than open the film in New York and Los Angeles—two expensive markets that have the ability to ruin a film—SHANG-HAI SURPRISE was opened in the Midwest, Northeast, and Canada. Before long, the film had bombed out of the theaters and was destined for a life on the video store shelves. Penn was critically attacked for not pulling off his supposed attempt at Clark Gable, and Madonna was laughed at for playing a missionary after building her career on sexuality. The film was further panned for being predictable and unrealistic. The Penn-Madonna empire had successfully been toppled by the very people—the critics—who created it in the first place. This would have been justified if SHANGHAI SURPRISE was indeed the dog the critics all said it was. In the 1930s, Hollywood's ''dream factories'' cranked out endless films of this sort—''star vehicles'' that would give the audience a chance to see their favorites on screen. At that time, it didn't really matter what the stars did, just as long as they were on screen. SHANGHAI SURPRISE, however, makes the fatal mistake of assuming (like PIRATES did) that today's more sophisticated audiences want a return of classical Hollywood-style movie making. Many viewers won't even watch a great Hollywood film like IT'S A WONDER-FUL LIFE unless it's in color, much less a second-rate Hollywood film—which is all SHANGHAI SURPRISE is. It has all the markings of being another entry in the CHARLIE CHAN series.

Penn and Madonna both do a fine job with their roles, the supporting roles are excellent, the direction is passable, the camera work and art direction are accomplished, and the script mindless and predictable. There's nothing to create outrage, and there's nothing to stimulate excitement, which is probably why there was no ''substantial interest'' in SHANGHAI SURPRISE. Since Madonna has such a strong following among young girls, parents would be well-advised to think twice before subjecting impressionable preteens to some of this film's tough language (which is no racier than Madonna's songs) and talk of torture. Songs include ''Shanghai Surprise'' (George Harrison, performed by Harrison, Vicki Brown), ''Breath Away from Heaven'' ''Someplace Else'' (Harrison, performed by Harrison), ''Hottest Gong in Town'' (Harrison, performed by The Zig Zaggers), ''Zig-Zag'' (Harrison, Jeff Lynne, performed by The Gaslight Orchestra).

p, John Kohn; d, Jim Goddard; w, John Kohn, Robert Bentley (based on the novel *Faraday's Flowers* by Tony Kenrick); ph, Ernest Vincze (Technicolor); m, George Harrison, Michael Kamen; ed, Ralph Sheldon; prod d, Peter Mullins; art d, David Minty, John Siddall; set d, Jack Stephens; cos, Judy Moorcroft; spec eff, David Watkins, Dave Beavis; m/l, George Harrison, Jeff Lynne; makeup, Christine Beveridge, Graham Freeborn.

Adventure   Cas.   (PR:C   MPAA:PG-13)

SHE'S GOTTA HAVE IT***   (1986) 84m Spike Lee Joint–Forty Acres and a Mule Filmworks/Island bw-c

Tracy Camila Johns *(Nola Darling)*, Tommy Redmond Hicks *(Jamie Overstreet)*, John Canada Terrell *(Greer Childs)*, Spike Lee *(Mars Blackmon)*, Raye Dowell *(Opal Gilstrap)*, Joie Lee *(Clorinda Bradford)*, Epatha Merkinson *(Dr. Jamison)*, Bill Lee *(Sonny Darling)*, Cheryl Burr *(Ava)*, Aaron Dugger *(Noble)*, Stephanie Covington *(Keva)*, Renata Cobbs *(Shawn)*, Cheryl Singleton *(Toby)*, Monty Ross, Lewis Jordan, Erik Dellums, Reggie Hudlin, Eric Payne, Marcus Turner, Gerard Brown, Ernest Dickerson, Eric Wilkins, Fab Five Freddy Braithwaite, Scott Sillers, Geoffrey Garfield *("Dogs")*, Kathy Banks *(Receptionist)*, Steve Nicks *(Soundman)*, Pamm Jackson *(Female Walk-On)*.

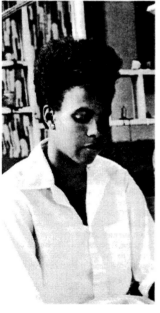

The mid-1980s have been very good to the Hollywood alternative of independent filmmakers, especially Spike Lee, a 29-year-old black New York University graduate, who has won deserved international acclaim for his first feature film. Like fellow NYU graduate Jim Jarmusch (STRANGER THAN PARADISE and DOWN BY LAW), Lee has found commercial and critical success with a small

black-and-white film that combines some very personal ideas with innovative filmmaking techniques.

SHE'S GOTTA HAVE IT is a sex comedy that stars Johns as a young, black Brooklyn woman whose bed is a shrine visited with great frequency by three very different boy friends. She can't, however, pick the one she likes the best. First there is Hicks, a sensitive, well-mannered sort who smothers Johns with an overly possessive attitude and talks of marriage. Then there's Terrell, a self-absorbed fashion model who brags that he is a ''sculptor'' and that Johns was ''but a mere lump of clay'' before meeting him. The most likeable character is the third beau, Lee, as Mars Blackmon, a bike-riding unemployed street punk who has an arrow carved into his hair, wears an 18-karat gold nameplate around his neck, prides himself on his $50 Air Jordan high-top gym shoes, and always manages to make Johns laugh. Also playing a part in Johns' life is Dowell, a lesbian friend determined to get the uninterested Johns into bed. Each man is extremely jealous of Johns' other bedmates—a rivalry that comes to a head during a Thanksgiving dinner at Johns' apartment, attended by all three boy friends. They each vie for Johns' affections by praising her cooking and verbally assaulting one another. Lee, who has previously described Terrell as having a ''16-piece Chicken McNugget head,'' humorously abuses him even more by calling him a ''pseudo-Negro'' and a ''Celtics fan,'' the latter insult referring to the Boston basketball team that boasts perhaps the best player in the game—the white Larry Bird—who gets a humorous roast from Lee. Terrell and Hicks, in return, don't have many nice things to say about each other or about Lee. Disgusted with their bickering, Johns threatens to throw them all out. By the end of the evening, however, it is Hicks who stays with her.

Unable to cope with her promiscuity, Hicks takes another lover, and finally turns his back completely on Johns. Realizing that he is the one she wants, Johns breaks up with Terrell, who is less than gracious, and Lee, who begs ''please baby, please baby, please baby, baby, baby, please'' in his rapid-fire delivery to get her to reconsider. She decides to become temporarily celibate and then tells Hicks that she loves him, in the hope that they will soon get back together. At the film's end, Johns explains (after a passage of some time) to the audience why her romance with Hicks failed: ''He wanted a wife—that mythic old-fashioned girl next door, but it's more than that. It's about control—my body, my mind. Who's gonna own it—them or me? I am not a one-man woman.'' She then turns away and curls back up in her bed.

Combining humor, drama, and documentary techniques, Lee has created an energetic film that takes an unflinching look at modern sexuality—specifically black sexuality. ''I decided,'' Lee says, ''it would be a good idea to do a film about a young black woman who's really leading her life like a man, in control, with three men dangling at her fingertips.'' While brutally honest in some parts, the attack on certain types of black men and the pick-up lines they use are filmed in a particularly humorous fashion. A montage sequence of ''dogs,'' Lee's name for these men, has one man looking directly into the camera saying ''You so fine baby, I drink a tub of your bath water.'' Another, dignified, dog brags, ''I got my BA from Morehouse, my MBA from Harvard, I own a new BMW 318I. I make 53 'thou' a year, after taxes . . . and I want you to want me.'' The film is filled with scenes of the main characters speaking to the camera, commenting on the story and their rival characters—bringing to the film a sense of authenticity it might not otherwise have. Because of the use of documentary techniques, the audience more readily accepts the fictional material. Lee's most commendable act as director is to avoid passing moral judgment on Johns' character. She admits that she is not ''a one-man woman'' and because of her honesty, she appears as an admirable heroine instead of a nymphomaniac.

Budgeted at a slim $175,000, SHE'S GOTTA HAVE IT was filmed in just 12 days using Super 16mm film (instead of the more popular regular 16mm), which makes a better blow-up to 35mm, the professional film distribution gauge. Although the film's small budget and tight schedule is apparent on the screen (some sloppy editing, lighting, and sound, and an occasional flat acting performance), SHE'S GOTTA HAVE IT still bursts forth with energy and a love of filmmaking. Lee, as both a director and actor, has more fun in this movie than is usually seen in a Hollywood film and used the budgetary restrictions to his advantage in the form of necessary invention. Rather than playing only the art-house market that the film seemed originally aimed at, SHE'S GOTTA HAVE IT played across the country. It not only attracted art crowds, but also average moviegoers who paid more attention to the humor than the low-budget look of the film. It grossed over $5 million at the box office, and also hit it big at the video stores. An international success, as well, SHE'S GOTTA HAVE IT played the Cannes Film Festival, earning Lee the Best New Director award. The film's title, for fans of trivia, is derived from the 1956 Frank Tashlin film, THE GIRL CAN'T HELP IT.

p, Shelton J. Lee; d&w, Spike Lee; ph, Ernest Dickerson; m, Bill Lee; ed, Spike Lee; prod d, Wynn Thomas; m, Bill Lee; art d, Ron Paley; set d, Clarence Jones; cos, John Michael Reefer.

Comedy/Drama   **Cas.**   **(PR:O MPAA:R)**

SHIN YOROKOBIMO KANASHIMIMO IKUTOSHITSUKI†   (1986, Jap.)
129m Shochiku-Tokyo Broadcasting System-Hakuhodo/Shochiku c (Trans: Big Joys, Small Sorrows)

Go Kato *(Yoshiaki)*, Reiko Ohara *(Asako)*, Hayao Okamoto *(Eisuke)*, Kuni Konishi *(Kenso)*, Hitoshi Ueki *(Kunio)*, Misako Konno *(Yukiko)*, Kiichi Nakai *(Daimon)*, Ken Tanaka *(Nagao)*, Yoko Shinoyama *(Masako)*.

A sentimental sequel to one of Japan's premier post-WW II directors' 1957 film about a family of lighthouse keepers who are continually uprooted from one oceanic outpost to be stationed at another, their long bouts of lonely light tending interrupted by joyous visits with old friends who are in the same profession. Each time the family moves—in a transit that circumnavigates virtually the entire Japanese coastline—its members receive a ceremonious visit from the patriarch of the clan, the father (Ueki) of the lighthouse keeper (Kato). The changing social ambience of Imperial Japan is observed in the interruptions of the lengthy light-tending vigils as the militarists become ascendant, but the story concentrates largely on the pleasures and travails—which result mostly from the forces of nature—experienced by the family.

p, Nobuyoshi Ohtani, Soya Hikida, Kazuo Watanabe, Masatake Wakita; d&w, Keisuke Kinoshita; ph, Kozo Okazaki (Vistavision); m, Chuji Kinoshita; ed, Yoshi Sugihara.

Drama/Comedy   **(PR:A MPAA:NR)**

SHOKUTAKU NO NAI IE†   (1986, Jap.) Marugen-Shochiku Fuji c (Trans: The Empty Table)

Tatsuya Nakadai, Mayuini Ogawa, Kiichi Nakai, Kie Nakai, Takayuki Takemoto, Azusa Maya.

d, Masaki Kobayshi; w, (based on the novel by Fumiko Enji); ph, Kuzo Okazaki; m, Toru Takemitsu.

SHOOT FOR THE SUN**   (1986, Brit.) 81m BBC c

Jimmy Nail *(Geordie)*, Brian Cox *(Duffy)*, Sara Clee *(Sadie)*, Billy McColl, Bill Simpson.

On bleak Edinburgh back streets that Arthur Frommer would never dream of wandering, first-time Scottish director Knox delves into the demimonde of heroin trafficking. Nail is the supplier for sleazy dealers who meet him in bathrooms or lurk in dark doorways. Cox, his partner, steps forward when muscle needs to be applied, though the menacing Nail is plenty capable of doing his own enforcing. When Nail discovers that dealer/addict McColl has been holding out on him, he uses an axe to break into his apartment and sets him straight. After a drinking session, Cox and Nail end up in a stupor by a tree rope-swing on the edge of a graveyard. While Nail swings and Cox reclines, they talk. Cox is anxious to leave dealing behind and return to "honest plunder," but Nail reminds him that robbery landed them in prison. When Cox says that their dealing could result in the same fate, Nail retorts that he hasn't heard Cox complaining about the new carpet he and his wife are planning to buy with his earnings.

McColl goes to work with new diligence, wanting to prove himself capable of peddling the larger amounts of heroin Nail has given him. His wife even leaves their daughter with her mother so she can help with the big push. McColl sells enough to make his payment to Nail and decides to keep more of the next batch for himself by cutting it with baby powder. Meanwhile, Cox and Nail prepare to meet with their London supplier, who has ventured north to make the delivery in the back of a laundromat. Outside in a car, two men look on, telling jokes and passing the time like a couple of post-FRENCH CONNECTION cops on a stakeout. However, when they rip off the London supplier on his southbound train, it becomes clear that they aren't cops at all. In fact, they are gangsters trying to move in on Nail's territory. Later, Cox runs into a 12-year-old to whom McColl has been selling. It is the last straw for Cox, who drunkenly confronts his partner in the hallway outside the apartment Nail shares with his mother. Nail hunts down McColl and his wife and finds them strung out in a shelter in a park. He shoves McColl around and takes everything he is holding, but before he leaves he gives McColl a small quantity of heroin, which his wife uses to shoot up. Nail, however, has cut the stuff with bleaching powder and McColl's wife dies.

While shopping for carpeting with his wife, Cox is approached by the gangsters, who make him the proverbial offer that can't be refused. Later, Nail's mother sits at the window of their apartment watching and worrying, knowing that, despite her son's assurances, he can be up to no good. She waves good-bye to him, and he does the same without even turning around as he walks below. Confronted by the gangsters, he is told that his time is up. It seems that Cox won't be leaving the business after all, but Nail will.

Director Knox gives a documentary-like feel to his film and the performances are convincing, particularly those of Cox and Nail. Yet the characters lack the complexity necessary to demonstrate why they've become involved in this sordid way of life. Why do the dealers deal? Certainly the limited expectations and prospects experienced by many in the United Kingdom can be offered as an

explanation, but it shouldn't be up to the viewer to supply the characters' motivations. In one scene an angry Nail exits from a posh restaurant after dealing with a condescending waiter and wrestles with a fake palm tree, nearly climbing it before smashing it to plastic bits. But if this is meant to offer the restrictions of class as the root of Nail's predicament, the idea isn't developed any further. SHOOT FOR THE SUN also offers little insight into the plight of the addict. Even a film like Jerry Schatzberg's PANIC IN NEEDLE PARK gives more of a sense of the obsessiveness of heroin addiction. Here love is *shown* to be unable to compete with addiction and Knox even attempts to manipulate the audience to *feel* that this is so, but his heavy-handed efforts lack substance.

Despite its grim subject matter there are a number of funny moments in the film, many of them provided by the gangsters, though thick Scottish accents make it difficult to understand them and much of the film's dialog. Originally shot in 16mm.

p, Andree Molyneaux; d, Ian Knox; w, Peter McDougall; ph, Remi Adefarasin; m, Michael Kamen, Ray Cooper; ed, Robin Sales; prod d, Stuart Walker; cos, Rita Reekie.

Crime/Drama   **(PR:C-O MPAA:NR)**

SHORT CHANGED†   (1986, Aus.) 104m Magpie/Greater Union c

Wanjun Carpenter *(Tommy at Age 2)*, Susan Leith *(Alison)*, David Kennedy *(Stuart)*, Steve Dodd *(Old Drunk)*, Athol Compton *(Bruiser)*, Mac Silva *(First Friend)*, Sylvia Scott *(Nan)*, Timothy Hornibrook *(Preacher)*, Ronald Merritt *(Uncle)*, Ken Radley *(Sergeant—Land Rights March)*, Jim Holt *(Serizio)*, Donnie Pryor *(Policeman—City Lockup)*, Jamie Agius *(Tommy)*, Ray Meagher *(Marshall)*, Adam Scougall *(Peter)*, David Slingsby *(Christian Brother)*, Max Worrall *(Sgt. Bill)*, Mark Little *(Curly)*, Robert Merritt, Jr. *(Light One)*, Michael Thompson *(Dark One)*, Dora Batt *(Neighbor)*, Shane Tickner *(Young Boy)*, Amanda Nikkenin *(Young Girl)*, Rhys McConnochie *(School Principal)*, Donnis Bartley *(Crying Woman)*, Len Brown *(Landlord)*, Alan McQueen *(Cummings)*, Nicholas Papademetriou *(Nick)*, Ron Haddrick *(Garrick)*, "Lucky" Wikramanayake *(Gopowalla)*, Denis MacKay *(Edwards)*, Daphne Grey *(Judge)*, Lindel Rowe *(Counsellor)*, Jenny Vuletic *(Real Estate Assistant)*, Louise Christie *(Mother at Zoo)*, James Robertson *(Brian)*, Heilan Robertson *(Shirley)*, Ross Bombaci *(Italian Proprietor)*, Ollie Hall *(Officer Collins)*, Michael Gow *(Sinclair)*.

Kennedy plays an aborigine married to a white woman, Leith, the daughter of a powerful businessman. After Kennedy's father dies in prison, and the pressures

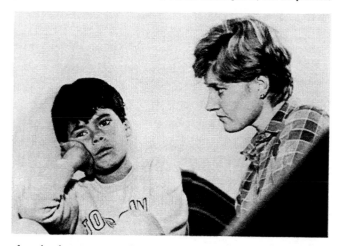

of marriage become too great, he returns to the bush and the pastoral existence to which he is more accustomed. Seven years later he returns to the city hoping to be reunited with his son, an assimilated ten-year-old unaware that his father is an aborigine. An arduous legal battle ensues between Kennedy and Leith over the father's legal right to see the boy. This was the first singly helmed feature for director Ogilvie, an established theater director and codirector with George Miller of MAD MAX: BEYOND THE THUNDERDOME. Screenwriter Merritt is one of a handful of successful aborigine writers.

p, Ross Matthews; d, George Ogilvie; w, Robert J. Merritt (based on a screenplay by Ken Quinnell, Robert J. Merritt); ph, Peter Levy (Eastmancolor); m, Chris Neal; ed, Richard Francis-Bruce; prod d, Kristian Fredrikson; set d, Alethea Deane; makeup, Liz Fardon.

Drama   **(PR:C MPAA:NR)**

SHORT CIRCUIT*½   (1986) 99m Tri-Star c

Ally Sheedy *(Stephanie Speck)*, Steve Guttenberg *(Newton Crosby)*, Fisher Stevens *(Ben Jabituya)*, Austin Pendleton *(Howard Marner)*, G.W. Bailey *(Skroeder)*, Brian McNamara *(Frank)*, Tim Blaney *(Voice of No. 5)*, Marvin McIntyre *(Duke)*, John Garber *(Otis)*, Penny Stanton *(Mrs. Cepeda)*, Vernon Weddle *(Gen. Washburne)*, Barbara Tarbuck *(Sen. Mills)*, Tom Lawrence *(Mr. Marner's Aide)*, Fred Slyter *(Norman)*, Billy Ray Sharkey *(Zack)*, Robert Krantz, Jan Speck *(Reporters)*, Marguerite Heppy *(Barmaid)*, Howard Krik *(Farmer)*, Marjorie Card Hughes *(Farmer's Wife)*, Herb Smith *(Gate Guard)*, Jack Thompson, William Striglos, Mary Reckley, Lisa Mclean, Eleanor C. Heutschy *(Party Guests)*.

E.T. goes mechanical is essentially what this inane comedy from director John Badham is all about. Guttenberg, stretching his comic range not far beyond a POLICE ACADEMY film, stars as a robotics technician for a government con-

tractor. At a special outdoor demonstration, the company's most sophisticated robots, which are capable of doing anything from mixing a drink to destroying a tank, are put on display for army officials. An approaching thunderstorm ends the day's activities, but as it turns out, things are just beginning. Before the five robots can be put away, one is struck by lightning. This bolt of electrical power brings the robot to life, and the creature goes off to discover the surrounding world. When it's learned the robot, known simply as "Number 5," is missing, an all-out search begins. Bailey, Guttenberg's boss, would prefer to destroy Number 5 rather than let the robot run loose. Along with his assistant Stevens, an Indian scientist who mangles the English language with incredible word configurations, Guttenberg begins his own hunt for the missing contraption. In the meantime, Number 5 has managed to sneak aboard a snack truck owned by Sheedy, a nature lover with a flighty personality. She lives in a house filled to the rafters with small animals and major appliances, not too shabby considering her source of income. When Sheedy discovers Number 5 on the premises, she is convinced he's a space alien and sets out to teach him all about Earth (its assumed by all that Number 5 is a boy because he's equipped with a masculine voice). Number 5 zips through every book in the house, watches countless hours of television, and rapidly becomes a dynamic expert in American pop culture. Government baddies close in, Sheedy and Guttenberg meet, and Number 5 manages to elude his would-be captors time and again. Eventually, we are treated to the big showdown, and it appears the military bad guys have succeeded in blowing the lovable robot to smithereens. But that wouldn't make for much of a happy ending, so as Guttenberg and Sheedy go riding off into the sunset, they are overjoyed to discover that Number 5 has cleverly outfoxed the government goonies and is still in one adorable piece.

Like the computer hardware of Guttenberg's workplace, SHORT CIRCUIT is a carefully programmed film designed to evoke certain responses. The plot line is as simple as they come: girl meets robot, girl loses robot, girl gets robot and boy friend is a class project. Of course the standard slapstick sequences of Number 5 making a disaster of Sheedy's home are included, along with some expected chase sequences and shoot-outs with the cartoonish bad guys. There's even a subplot involving Sheedy's jealous ex-boy friend, whom Number 5 chivalrously fends off. In addition to these components (which really are nothing more than rehashed moments from old Disney comedies), SHORT CIRCUIT also pays heed to the consumer-oriented Yuppie audience. Because Number 5 receives much of his information from television, we handily are subjected to a barrage of commercial endorsements. The majority of these are for well-known products from major companies, though that should come as no surprise. Care for John Wayne or the Three Stooges? Well, Number 5 does, and consequently moviegoers are treated to the robot's oh-so-cute impersonations of these popular film stars from the past (that an electronic intelligence turns into a Three Stooges fan doesn't say much for state-of-the-art computer technology). When Number 5 switches around a radio dial while searching for some music to listen to, he skips the classical and jazz stations, going straight for the hard-driving rock 'n' roll. It may not be as aesthetically pleasing, but who ever heard of an orchestral video? Badham's direction is as mechanical as his star. Setups are obvious, telegraphing exactly what will happen within any given sequence long before it ends. Anyone who thinks Number 5 really gets blown away before the so-called surprise conclusion could conceivably be considered brain dead. One scene has Sheedy and Number 5 do a few dance steps while watching a videotape of Badham's 1977 film SATURDAY NIGHT FEVER. Though undoubtedly an in-joke for the director and his friends, the clips are a pointed reminder that once upon a time Badham knew how to make an intelligent film with flesh-and-blood characters. The performances here, as Dorothy Parker once said, run an emotional gamut from A to B. Sheedy spends most of her time looking earnest and annoyingly insisting over and over: "Number 5 is alive!" Guttenberg smiles, looks charming, drives around a lot in a van, and occasionally pleads with the solid-faced military bad guys. Only Stevens shows any real life, though at times the laughs generated by his Indian character are tinged by xenophobic arrogance. Originally his role as sidekick was to be played straight. This was changed when Badham thought it might be funnier to make Stevens one of those foreign geniuses who are whizzes

at technology but have only a rudimentary understanding of the English language. The human actors are secondary, for the real star of the show is Number 5. Developed by Syd Mead (who also worked on such futuristic films as TRON, BLADE RUNNER, and ALIENS), Number 5 is equipped with camera eyes and flash-shield eyebrows that do a fairly effective job of emoting. He's really pretty charming, considering that Number 5 is a machine, though his unusual antics aren't enough to carry a feature-length motion picture. (Badham and his robot-design team went to Japan to investigate robotics.) SHORT CIRCUIT is really nothing more than a single joke stretched out over 99 minutes, and probably would have worked better as a one-hour television adventure. The film likely will best be appreciated by children, though some wholly unnecessary gags based on Number 5's use of four-letter words might make some parents wary. Songs include: "Who's Johnny (SHORT CIRCUIT Theme)" (Peter Wolf, Inia Wolf, performed by El DeBarge), "Come and Follow Me (No. 5's Theme from SHORT CIRCUIT)" (David Shire, Will Jennings, Max Carl, performed by Max Carl, Marcy Levy).

p, David Foster, Lawrence Turman; d, John Badham; w, S.S. Wilson, Brent Maddock; ph, Nick McLean (Panavision, Metrocolor); m, David Shire; ed, Frank Morriss; art d, Dianne Wager; set d, Garrett Lewis; spec eff, Syd Mead, Eric Allard; m/l, Peter Wolf, Inia Wolf, David Shire, Will Jennings, Max Carl.

Comedy   Cas.   (PR:A-C MPAA:PG)

SHTAY ETZBA'OT M'TZIDON†   (1986, Israel) 91m Israeli Defense Forces Film Unit/Marathon c (Trans: Ricochets)

Ronnie Pinkovitz *(Gadi)*, Shaul Mizrahi *(Tuvia)*, Alon Aboutboul *(Georgie)*, Ossie Hillel *(Mickey)*.

A young lieutenant in the Israeli army, Pinkovitz, goes directly from officer's training school to occupied Lebanon to replace a battle-scarred officer who was killed during the incursion. The self-assured novice soon discovers that war truly is hell, that it brings no resolution to political conflicts save death and destruction. Like many another, the picture details the lives—and deaths—of members of a small military unit functioning as a cog in a large, and largely unseen, war-making juggernaut. The soldiers under Pinkovitz's command have varied reactions to the conflict. One of them, a Druse, has divided loyalties, as his people are on both sides of the border. Another has an unexpressed attraction to a pretty Lebanese girl. And another tries to make friends with a young Lebanese boy. Through it all, the dulling drill and routine of military life are pervasive. Like rain—which falleth alike on the just and on the unjust—warfare and occupation injure everyone. A striking anti-war document originally made, strangely, as a training film for Israeli troops and filmed in Lebanon during the time of the actual occupation. The picture was later distributed theatrically in Israel. The title song, penned by Benny Nagari and Eli Madorski, was performed by Boaz Ofri. Filmed in 16mm.

p, Eli Dori; d, Eli Cohen; w, Eli Cohen, Tzvika Kertzner, Baruch Nevo; ph, Yehiel Ne'eman (Eastmancolor); m, Benny Nagari; ed, Avigdor Weill; m/l, Benny Nagari, Eli Madorski.

War   (PR:C MPAA:NR)

SHTO U SENIKI BYLO   (SEE: CHTO U SENJKI BYLO, 1986, USSR)

SHUKUJI†   (1986, Jap.) Shochiku c (Trans: Congratulatory Speech)

Ichiro Zaitsu, Michiko Hayashi, Ryoichi Yamaguchi, Yuki Kudo, Taketoshi Naito, Takehiko Maeda, Yuko Kazu.

d, Tomio Kuriyama; w, Masakuhi Takahashi; ph, Hirosuke Yasuda; m, Shigemori Shigeta.

SID AND NANCY**   (1986, Brit.) 111m Zenith-Initial/Goldwyn c

Gary Oldman *(Sid Vicious)*, Chloe Webb *(Nancy Spungen)*, Drew Schofield *(Johnny Rotten)*, David Hayman *(Malcolm McLaren)*, Debby Bishop *(Phoebe)*, Tony London *(Steve)*, Perry Benson *(Paul)*, Ann Lambton *(Linda)*, Kathy Burke *(Brenda)*, Mark Monero *(Clive)*, Michele Winstanley *(Olive)*, Graham Fletcher Cook *(Wally)*, Jude Alderson *(Ma Vicious)*, Sara Sugarman *(Abby)*, Stuart Fox *(Rock Head)*, Peter McCarthy *(Hugh Kares)*, Tenpole Tudor *(Receptionist)*, Pete Lee Wilson *(Duke Bowman)*, Courtney Love *(Gretchen)*, Jeanny McCarthy *(Trell)*, John Snyder *(Vito)*, Ron Moseley, Jr. *(Wax Max)*, Fox Harris *(Old Stain)*, Xander Berkeley *(Bowery Snax)*, Biff Yeager *(Detective)*, Sandy Baron *(Hotelier)*, Milton Selzer *(Granpa Spungen)*, Gloria Leroy *(Granma Spungen)*, Sy Richardson *(Caseworker)*.

The sad, sordid, pathetic lives of Sex Pistols bassist Sid Vicious and his groupie American girl friend Nancy Spungen would normally be considered dubious material for a movie romance, but director Alex Cox (REPO MAN) and cowriter Abbe Wool have done just that. Boasting superb performances from Oldman as Sid and Webb as Nancy, the film begins in 1978 as police arrive at New York's Chelsea Hotel to find the body of Webb in the bathroom and Oldman staring like a zombie and holding a knife (filmed in the actual room at the Chelsea where the death occurred). He is dragged through a media circus to a police station for questioning. Flashback to 1977 when the couple first meet at the home of Lambton, a friend of Oldman and Johnny Rotten's (Schofield) who works as a dominatrix. Webb is a loud, whining, American rock 'n' roll groupie with a heroin habit who has wound up in London at the height of the punk-rock movement. She is impressed when she learns that Lambton's guests are from the infamous Sex Pistols (although she thinks Oldman is Schofield and vice versa) and she goes to see them play that night. Later, she tries to sleep with Schofield, but he declares sex "boring" and leaves her to Oldman. Oldman echoes Schofield's assertion, calling sex "boring, hippie s_____," but then allows her to

stay. A few days later Oldman spots Webb in a pub and follows her when she runs out yelling and crying. She tells Oldman that another rocker had taken her money but never delivered the heroin promised. She scrapes her knuckles on a brick wall in anger and frustration. He grabs her hand and looks at the bloody knuckles. "That looks like it hurts," he tells her sympathetically. She angrily pulls her hand away. He looks at her and calmly states, "So does this," and brutally slams his head into the brick wall. Incredibly, Webb seems to understand and appreciate the gesture (one critic likened this to a prehistoric mating ritual). Oldman gives Webb money to buy heroin for both of them. Although she is a full-blown junkie, Oldman has never done hard drugs before. Soon both are high and making love.

At daybreak, Webb prepares to leave (as most rock stars would have preferred), but Oldman wants her to stay. In a matter of weeks Oldman and Webb are a steady item, much to the dismay of the other band members who dislike the obnoxious, junkie American and the effect she has had on Oldman. When The Sex Pistols' manager, Malcolm McLaren (Hayman) decides to launch a tour of America, Webb is not allowed to come along. The American tour is an unmitigated disaster (they are booked in redneck clubs in Texas; Oldman accidentally walks through a plate-glass door and is hospitalized) and the band breaks up, with Schofield returning to England and Oldman going to New York (he overdoses on booze and pills on the plane and must be taken off on a stretcher). Webb returns to New York to live with Oldman at the Chelsea Hotel and become his manager. She divides her time between scoring gigs for Oldman, and scoring heroin for both of them. Their heroin addiction worsens and Oldman's limited musical talent becomes more and more apparent as he stands on stage holding the lyrics to songs in front of him as he attempts to sing. They make a brief attempt to kick their addiction by taking trips to a methadone clinic, but Oldman shoots up again when Webb is away. Eventually what was left of Oldman's career dries up and he and Webb spend all their time shooting up and staring at television. In her drugged stupor, Webb becomes obsessed that they both die in a "blaze of glory" and talks incessantly of death. When Oldman passes out with a lighted cigarette in his hand and starts a huge fire in their room, Webb just sits and stares as the flames grow. Neither makes a move to escape death, and they are rescued by the fire department and moved to another room. Days pass without either realizing it and they bicker constantly until one evening Webb becomes violent and insists that they go out in a "blaze of glory." She stumbles around the room breaking things and screaming. Oldman is so fed up he grabs a pocketknife and sarcastically asks her, "Is this what you want?" Webb stumbles toward him and is stabbed in the stomach—although Oldman doesn't seem to realize it. Too stoned to feel the pain and too pathetic to care, Webb crawls into bed next to Oldman. Later in the night, the bedclothes covered with her blood, she stirs from her stupor and staggers to the bathroom where she dies on the floor (she was 20 years old). Early in the morning their pusher shows up, sees Webb's body, and leaves. The police arrive soon after to see a stunned Oldman sitting on the bed with the knife in his hand. The zombie-like Oldman goes through painful withdrawal in his holding cell and he is eventually released on bail (paid by McLaren). Oldman wanders through a garbage heap to a lonely pizza joint. After eating, he encounters some black children with a boom-box, dancing. They encourage him to join them and he dances with them until a yellow cab pulls up. Oldman looks in the cab and sees Webb, as radiant as she has ever looked. Oldman gets in the cab and it pulls off into the mist (Sid Vicious died four months later, at the age of 21, of a heroin overdose—following a suicide attempt—before his case came to trial).

SID AND NANCY does not seek to be a history of The Sex Pistols, or of the punk-rock movement. It does not canonize Sid Vicious and Nancy Spungen, nor does it glamorize their horrible self-destruction. Director Cox simply looks at them as sad, pathetic human beings and finds some value in their relationship. The original title of the film was "Love Kills" and it is that notion that Cox explores here (the title was changed by the studio for commercial reasons). Cox

highlights the irony that Sid, whom the punk movement canonized as its martyr, its icon, had a deeply conventional streak—a need to love and be loved—which moved him to maintain a romantic relationship with Nancy until he died. This despite the fact that he was at the forefront of the nihilistic, anarchic punk movement which had nothing but disdain and contempt for any notion of love or dependence. Frequently in the film, Cox shows Sid and Nancy ignoring (or rebelling against) the punk code. In one scene they kiss passionately in front of a mirror where the words "No Feelings" are scrawled in lipstick. They are separate from the chaos around them as the London police descend on a boatload of punkers at the docks, and they seem to float through the violence unnoticed and untouched. Cox also shows the couple in some bitingly funny domestic situations with Sid the dutiful husband doing dishes, vacuuming his mother's apartment floor, and cleaning up after the spoiled Jewish-American-Princess Nancy. While they may have rejected the letter of the punk movement in favor of each other, it was their love that proved destructive. Cox understands the brutal give-and-take—the mental and emotional games—that take place in an intense love relationship. He also understands that Sid and Nancy's idealistic visions of themselves—their status as "stars"—served to erode their spirit. No one in the film understands this better than McLaren (played in a superbly creepy manner by Hayman, an eerie look-alike), who has turned Sid into a role model. In a scene where he vetoes the band's decision to fire Sid in favor of a bass player who can actually play (Sid was a notoriously bad musician), Hayman points out Sid's importance to the band, "Sidney is more than a mere bass player . . . he's a fabulous disaster. He's a symbol . . . a metaphor . . . he embodies the dementia of a nihilistic generation. He's a star!"

Often Cox shows us Sid and Nancy's romantic view of themselves. In one sequence they kiss passionately in an alley as garbage rains down on them in slow motion (a punk version of a Hollywood love scene). In another sequence, which is quite funny, Sid happens upon a group of street urchins roughing up another child for money. Sid tells them to stop and they ask who the hell is he to be telling them what to do? "I'm Sid Vicious," he states. Cox then employs a cartoon-like fast-motion technique as the terrified children scamper off as Sid would like to imagine they would (he spends much of the film staring at cartoons, playing with toys, etc.). But cold, hard reality comes crashing down on all these romantic reveries, as in a painfully realistic scene where Sid meets Nancy's family. The scene speaks volumes as the conflicting urges for acceptance and rebellion clash inside the punks while their darkly romantic appeal can be seen through the eyes of Nancy's younger siblings. The confusion and pain felt by Nancy's parents and grandparents as they gently kick the couple out (they cut the weekend visit short by lying about having to suddenly go out of town) is heart-wrenching. Cox skillfully combines the comedy inherent in the situation with the mournful sadness of the elders and creates a vivid and poignant scene. Although Cox often displays a quirky black humor, the horror of drug addiction is always at the forefront and never glamorized or made light of. Cox avoided any detailed portrayal of the ritualistic preparation of the drugs and instead concentrated on the miserable, destructive illness that follows. SID AND NANCY is terribly realistic and very hard to watch at times as the couple sink further and further into the abyss, hoping for death. Cox makes no excuses and does not moralize or judge. He never softens Sid and Nancy's basically revolting image and behavior (she a screeching, self-absorbed harpy, he an dim-witted, inarticulate, virtually talentless, emaciated mess), but presents them as they were and finds hope in the fact that they could share a love—even if it was self-destructive—for it made them human.

Enough can't be said about the performances of Oldman and Webb. Both stage actors (he from Britain, she from the U.S.), Oldman—who lost 30 pounds to approximate Sid's emaciated state—and Webb researched their roles thoroughly by watching what little film footage there was of Sid and Nancy and talking with people who knew them. Webb met Nancy's younger sister and found new insight into her family life and personality, while Oldman met with Sid's mother, Anne Beverley, who presented the actor with Sid's chain necklace and studded-leather bracelet, which he wore throughout the movie. Both actors talked with heroin addicts and wanted to give an accurate portrayal of the ravages heroin has on the mind, spirit, and body. Oldman and Webb are so successful in their roles that they become Sid and Nancy and never does the viewer feel that they are acting (reportedly Oldman had trouble shaking himself out of the mindset once the film was completed). The songs in the film were all sung by the actors—there was no attempt to lip-synch to the original recordings—and the music was played by original Sex Pistols bass player Glen Matlock (who, ironically, Sid Vicious had replaced), the man who wrote the Sex Pistols classics "God Save the Queen," "Anarchy in the U.K.," and "Pretty Vacant." SID AND NANCY will certainly be tough going for any viewer unfamiliar with the punk movement and unprepared for the revolting amount of cynicism, ignorance, anger, and self-abuse that went hand-in-hand with it, but the film's value lies in its honest, unflinching gaze at a social phenomenon that most adults still do not fathom. Those who are presupposed to moral outrage and hasty judgment shouldn't even bother seeing the film, for its outrageous surface will merely confirm what they already think, and that is a pity, for those are the people who would benefit most from the grueling experience of SID AND NANCY.

p, Eric Fellner; d, Alex Cox; w, Alex Cox, Abbe Wool; ph, Roger Deakins; m, Pray for Rain, The Pogues, Joe Strummer; ed, David Martin; prod d, Andrew McAlpine; art d, J. Ray Fox, Lynda Burbank, cos, Cathy Cook, Theda De Ramus; m/l, Glen Matlock, Joe Strummer, Shane McGowan, Dan Wul; makeup, Peter Frampton.

Drama/Biography   Cas.   (PR:O MPAA:R)

SIESTA VETA†   (1986, Czech.) 93m Slovak-Bratislava-Koliba c (Trans: The Sixth Sentence)

Erika Ozsda (Bozena Slancikova-Timrava), Elo Romancik (Slancik), Brigita

Bobulova *(Slancikova)*, Tatiana Radeva *(Irena)*, Matus Olha *(Bohus)*, Miroslav Hesek *(Palo Racko)*, Stefan Kozka *(Ludovit)*, Ivan Romancik *(Cierny)*, Zuzana Vackova *(Olga)*, Eva Pavlikova *(Betka Mrzacka)*, Peter Bzduch *(Misko Kramarik)*, Jirina Jiraskova *(Ema)*.

The filmed biography of a famed Slovak writer, whose larger-than-life story is epitomized by the title (she herself stated that any life can be summed up in five sentences). As the author, Ozada's tale is recounted, appropriately, in six episodes. The daughter of a poor clergyman, the perceptive Ozada is bemused by her liberal maiden aunt Radeva's efforts to aid the downtrodden peasants by passing out books to the largely illiterate locals. Ozada is a radical by nature, an observer and supporter of the peasantry, who accompanies her aunt on these paradoxical literary forays with endearing indulgence, recording the people in her mind's eye. Later, when her first book is published, her characters prove to be so recognizable that the author is threatened with bodily harm. Her faith in and love for the peasantry prevail even through a traumatic experience in which, following a wild rustic wedding party, the incognito writer is raped. Ozada ages gracefully through the episodes, retaining a strong sense of irony mixed with compassion for the victims of poverty and oppression in this turn-of-the-century period piece.

d, Stefan Uher; w, Zuzana Tatarova, Hana Cielova, Stefan Uher (based on a story by Zuzana Tatarova, Hana Cielova); ph, Stanislav Szomolanyi; m, Svetozar Stur; ed, Maximilian Remen; art d, Roman Rjachovsky; cos, Milan Corba, Irena Tonkovicova; makeup, Jozef Skopek.

Biography   **(PR:O MPAA:NR)**

SIKAT SAFAR†   (1986, Egypt) 114m Abdel Malik El Khamisi c (Trans: The Travel Path)

Nour El Sherif *(Zarlu)*, Noura *(Noemi)*, Abdel Salam Mohamed *(Old Man)*, Hasam Mustapha, Aida Abdelaziz.

Obsessed with elevating their financial status, the inhabitants of a contemporary Egyptian village greet the return of a prodigal, El Sherif, whose garish suit and trappings proclaim his new-found wealth after a stint of employment abroad. Laden with Western appliances—every nicety from television sets to toasters—he is hailed as a hero by the town's indigent inhabitants (whose country is plagued by inflation and unemployment) and is gulled into joining a local business venture. He and his partner are both greatly taken with local beauty Noura, but rather than pursue his romantic attachment, he follows the bad advice of local sycophants and marries his business partner's daughter. Eventually, El Sherif does get together with the girl he truly loves, but it costs him all his possessions. He finds himself faced with the same situation that caused him to leave home in the first place: poverty. He leaves the girl he loves to repeat the cycle, journeying abroad for a job. The light side of a vexing social problem is pleasantly presented in this ironic comedy, El Deek's second feature film.

p, Abdel Malik El Khamisi; d&w, Bashir El Deek; ph, Tarak El Telmisani; ed, Adel Mounir; art d, Rogdi Hamed.

Comedy   **(PR:A MPAA:NR)**

SILENT LOVE†   (1986, Hong Kong) 98m D&B c

Season Ma *(Ah Yeung)*, Lau Ching Wan.

Young Ma is the mute—but not hearing-impaired—leader of a group of deaf-mute young houseboat-dwellers moored in the shadow of the Royal Hong Kong Yacht Club. She and her gang make a living by picking pockets. She meets a surly, disaffected youth just released from a long prison sentence, and a friendship blossoms. The prospect of romance is dampened when war erupts among competing gangs. Ma signs and mimes the popular song "Needing You Every Moment" by composer Lam. (In Cantonese; English subtitles.)

p, Dickson Poon; d, David Chiang; m, Lam.

Drama   **(PR:A MPAA:NR)**

SILK*   (1986, Phil.) 83m Premiere International/Concorde c

Cec Verrell *(Jenny "Silk" Sleighton)*, Bill McLaughlin *(Tom Stevens)*, Joe Mari Avellana *("Yashi" Kobayashi)*, Frederick Bailey *(Brown)*, Nick Nicholson *(Tyler)*, David Light *(Carnahan)*, Rex Cutter *(Walker)*, Ronnie Patterson *(Vernon)*, Peter Shilton *(Austin)*, Henry Strzalkowski *(Stromberg)*, Leo Martinez *(Yamamoto Tanaka)*, Joonie Gamboa *(Chen)*, Vicky Suba *(Lily)*, Zenaida Amador *(Mrs. Tokuda)*, Vic Diaz *(Tokuda)*, Berto Spoor *(Musgrave)*, Majid Jadali *(Knox)*, Sam Lombardo *(Hospital Attendant)*, Bill Kipp, Steve Rogers, Warren McLean, Jack Starr, Willy Williams, Bill Baldridge *(Officers)*, Don Gordon *(Haskell)*, Joe Zucchero *(Travis)*, Bobby Greenwood *(Prosecutor)*, Junix Inocian *(Polo Makena)*, Dick Reyes *(Security Chief)*, Mike Monty *(Frampton)*, Jerry Bailey *(Sgt. Keno)*, Mark Cohen *(Reporter)*, Richard Harlow *(Judge)*, Steve Cook *(Jazz)*, James Crumrine *(Douglas)*, Chantal Manz *(Wendy)*, Roger Noble *(Murchison)*, Ramon D'Salva *(Governor)*, Zenon Gil *(Councilman)*, Randy Hrobar *(Reilly)*, Paul Holmes *(P.R. Man)*, Tony Williams *(Roswell)*.

Move over McGarrett and Magnum; the toughest cop in Hawaii is now Silk Sleighton (Verrell). Her investigation of a heroin-smuggling ring leads her past the drug traffickers and into a more insidious racket, one in which people who die outside hospitals have their identities bought from their relatives so that Asian gangsters can enter the U.S. Along the way Verrell also learns that her policeman boy friend, McLaughlin, has hired a pair of dope-addicted psychotics he served with in the Army to kill criminals who walk out of court on technicalities. These two killers are also hired by Shilton, head of the identity-selling ring, after Verrell dispatches his regular hitmen. When the police get too close to cracking the ring, the criminals decide to murder their latest ID recipient to cover their tracks. The

cops already have the man under surveillance, and they close in on the killers. Things go sour and Verrell ends up being taken hostage. Shilton demands safe passage to the airport and out of the country, but the police surround the place, and in a bloody shoot-out, almost everyone but Verrell dies.

More like a TV cop show than a shot-in-the-Philippines exploitation title, SILK has little going for it. The plot is unfathomable, the acting lousy, and the action dull. On the other hand, Verrell is an interesting heroine and it is unusual to find a woman the center of an action film like this. If only there were some worthwhile action in which she could participate. Shot in 1985 and unreleased theatrically in the U.S.

p&d, Cirio H. Santiago; w, Frederick Bailey (based on a story by Cirio H. Santiago, Frederick Bailey and a character created by Claudine St. James); ph, Ricardo Remias; m, Willie Cruz; ed, Pacifico Sanchez, Jr.; prod d, Joe Mari Avellana; makeup, Teresa Mercader, Norma Remias.

Crime/Action   **Cas.**   **(PR:O MPAA:R)**

SINCERELY CHARLOTTE***   (1986, Fr.) 92m Les Films de la Tour-FR3/New Line c (SIGNE CHARLOTTE)

Isabelle Huppert *(Charlotte)*, Niels Arestrup *(Mathieu)*, Christine Pascal *(Christine)*, Nicolas Wostrikoff *(Freddy)*, Jean-Michel Ribes *(Roger)*, Philippe Delevingne *(Mathieu's Friend)*, Laurence Mercier *(Christine's Mother)*, Frederic Bourboulon *(Workman)*, Berangere Gros *(Marie-Cecile)*, Chantal Bronner *(Marie)*, Justine Heynemann *(Emilie)*, Baptiste Heynemann *(Vincent)*, Michel Fortin *(Inspector)*, Tina Lara *(Nurse)*, Luc Beraud *(Doctor)*, Josiane Comellas *(Jacquelina)*, Eduardo Manet *(Emilio)*, Ronald Chammah *(Nando)*, Caroline Faro *(Irene the Baby Sitter)*, Claude Menard *(Girl on Train)*, Laurence Masliah *(American Woman)*, Francois Borysse *(Man in Restaurant)*, Herman Braun *(Charlotte's Husband)*, Francoise Berleand, Henri Lassa, Alex Nemo, Adolphe Viezzi, Tina Sportolaro.

In her first film as director, Caroline Huppert, the older sister of actress Isabelle, has fashioned an entertaining tale of romantic temptation and crumbled memo-

ries. Huppert stars as a *femme fatale* club singer with punkish blonde hair, brightened with a streak of red. Angered that her boy friend has not shown up to hear her sing, she goes to his apartment and finds him dead. Confused, she turns to Arestup, a former lover with whom she had lived for six years, but has not seen in four. Arestup is now happily engaged to Pascal, a pretty-but-safe schoolteacher and mother. Upon seeing Huppert, Arestup rediscovers emotions that he had long forgotten. He wrestles with his desire for her and his devotion to his fiancee. He agrees to let Huppert spend the night in a guest house which he uses as a music studio. Huppert fails to mention that her boy friend is dead, only that she cannot return to him. Rather than explain Huppert's presence to Pascal—and assuming that she will soon be leaving—Arestup keeps her presence a secret. She stays longer than planned, however, and eventually Pascal finds out. By then Huppert has left and Arestup thinks that he has heard the last of her. He then learns that her lover has been murdered. Huppert phones from a small town outside of Paris and asks Arestup to send some money, swearing that she did not kill her lover. Arestup tells his fiancee that he is going to help Huppert, promising to return in just a few days. The situation becomes complicated and Arestup finds himself falling in love with Huppert all over again. After they steal some money and a car, Huppert and Arestup are nearly killed in an automobile accident. They escape from the hospital, leaving their money and papers behind, and hide out temporarily in a small town. Unbeknownst to Arestup, Huppert calls Pascal and asks her to wire more money. Out of concern for her fiance, she agrees. Pascal arrives in town and gives Huppert the money, declining an opportunity to see Arestup. When asked why she agreed to help, Pascal answers "Mathieu (Arestup) protects you . . . and I protect him. That's all." Pascal also gives her the keys to her parents' country cottage. Arestup and Huppert hide out there and,

after a night of lovemaking, plan to cross the border into Spain. Determined to keep Arestup, Pascal arrives at the cottage with her son. Arestup, however, has made up his mind—he's leaving with Huppert, even though she has admitted that she did kill her lover. Realizing that she cannot split this family apart, Huppert quietly sneaks away and hitches a ride to Spain. Arestup chases after her, his heart broken by her for the second time. The film's coda leaps forward two years and shows Arestup dropping his wife Pascal and their *two* children off at the train station for a vacation. After seeing them off, he spots Huppert on another train, happily married to a debonair gentlemen.

Played by a lesser actress than Huppert, SINCERELY CHARLOTTE (which was filmed in 1984, but released in 1986) could have been a disaster. It teeters on the edge of being an intriguing look at a confused man and being a ridiculous sexual romp. Fortunately, the Huppert sisters both have enough talent to make the situation not only believable, but thoroughly enjoyable. Director Huppert, who is debuting as film director but has a decade of experience in theater and television, injects just enough quirkiness and humor into her direction to pull the film along. Actress Huppert turns in what initially appears to be a simple performance, but is extremely complex in its range. Huppert, one of the best actresses working today, manages to make a deceitful, unloving, destructive, lawbreaking murderess into the type of woman every man would want as a lover. Although she is dangerous, she is full of life, energy, unpredictability, and sensuality. It comes as no surprise that Arestup is magnetically attracted to Huppert's lethal personality. Playing a character who walks such a fine line is difficult, but Huppert succeeds quite well. Arestup is also excellent, making the audience sympathize with him even though he has ditched his fiancee and her child. Although many films show man's attraction to the femme fatale, they never seem to capture the emotion of a man after he has fallen prey to one. This film, however, has done so in the scene in which Arestup realizes that Huppert has left him. It is a scene which lasts for barely a minute, but it is one of rare brilliance. In addition to Huppert's acting, the audience is also treated to an upbeat love song called "Souvenirs Chiffonnes" (Philippe Sarde, Caroline Huppert) which she sings over the film's opening credits. (In French; English subtitles.)

p, Adolphe Viezzi, Jean Ardy; d, Caroline Huppert; w, Caroline Huppert, Luc Beraud, Joelle Goron; ph, Bruno de Keyzer; m, Philippe Sarde; ed, Anne Boissel, Jacqueline Thiedot; prod d, Patrice Mercier; cos, Corinne Jorry; makeup, Paul Le Marinel; m/l, Philippe Sarde, Caroline Huppert.

Drama/Comedy   Cas.   **(PR:C-O MPAA:NR)**

SININEN IMETTAJA†   (1986,Fin.) 95m Gironfilmi Oy-Lulea–Finnish Film Foundation/Finnkino bw-c (Trans: The Blue Wet-Nurse)

Niilo Hyttinen *(Joel Strom)*, Aino-Maija Tikkanen *(Kerttu)*, Kaija Kiiski *(The Muse)*, Aino Lahdenpera *(Strom's Mother)*, Jaako Raulamo, Esko Hukkanen.

The Lapland tundra is home to deaf-mute artist Hyttinen, who pursues his muse in the face of adversity—primarily the need to sustain life through the necessities of food, shelter, clothing, and other such distractions from his art. Real-life artist Hyttinen's own works are shown in occasional color sequences. The wet-nurse of the title is nature itself, the artist's inspiration.

d, Markku Lehmuskallio; w, Markku Lehmuskallio, Helmi Paula Pulkkinen, Niilo Hyttinen; ph, Pekka Martevo; m, Pekka Jalkanen; ed, Juhu Gartz; prod d, Seija Kiiski.

Drama   **(PR:A MPAA:NR)**

SIZZLE BEACH, U.S.A. zero   (1986) 93m Troma c

Terry Congie *(Janice)*, Leslie Brander *(Sheryl)*, Roselyn Royce *(Dit)*, Kevin Costner.

It never fails. When a once-unknown actor attains some prominence, a previously unreleasable feature suddenly takes on a whole new value. Such is the case with SIZZLE BEACH, U.S.A., a silly beach picture which emphasizes female nudity, bad fashions from the 1970s, and an early appearance by a young actor named Kevin Costner (TESTAMENT, SILVERADO, THE UNTOUCHABLES [1987]).

Shot sometime in the late 1970s, the mindless story features Congie, Brander, and

Royce as three girls who want to make it big in Los Angeles. One is determined to be an actress, one wants to be an aerobics instructor, and the third wants to be a singer. In order to pursue these chosen fields, the three take to hanging out with whomever can help them. These liaisons lead to various stages of nudity, pitifully few laughs, and a brief appearance by Costner as a horse trainer. Eventually the girls end up living in a house on the title beach with Royce's cousin in a none-too-thrilling climax to a dramatically unchallenging feature.

Inept from the opening titles to the closing credits, SIZZLE BEACH, U.S.A. has just about everything you'd expect. The acting, including Costner's, isn't much, the plot is worthless, and nudity is the real star attraction. The clothing, the language, and a prominent picture of President Jimmy Carter date the picture, which would have spent eternity collecting dust on the shelf had it not been for the sudden rise of bit-player Costner. Leave it to the folks at Troma pictures, ever vigilant in ways of turning an exploitative buck, to grab onto a salable star's early entry, thus resurrecting the picture from total obscurity.

p, Eric Louzil; d, Richard Brander; w, Craig Kusaba; ph, John Sprang; m, The Beach Towels, Rick Dunham, Melodye Condos; ed, Howard Heard; m/l, The Beach Towels, Rick Dunham, Melodye Condos.

Comedy   **(PR:O MPAA:R)**

SKUPA MOYA, SKUPI MOY†   (1986, Bulgaria) 107m Bulgarafilm "Boyana" Studio c (Trans: My Darling, My Darling)

Marianna Dimitrova *(Anna)*, Plamen Sirakov *(Ivan)*, Ivan Donev *(Glado)*, Raya Buchvarova *(Raya)*, Andrei Todorov *(Andro)*, Anton Radichev *(Mitko)*, Stoyan Stoev *(Grigor)*, Anna Cuncheva *(Minka)*, Bozhidar Iskrenov *(Bozho)*, Katya Todorova *(Neighbor)*, Blagovest Argirov *(Blago)*, Svetoslav Argirov *(Svet)*, Penka Armanakova *(Pepa)*.

Reserved, gorgeous rustic Dimitrova, with her carefree husband Sirakov and their children, moves to Sofia. Unable to get an apartment in the crowded city, they find temporary shelter at the villa managed by an acquaintance. Sirakov gets a day job at a factory, while Dimitrova takes on a night-shift task in a textile mill, an arrangement that allows them to divide the care of their children. The inevitable occurs when a coworker of Dimitrova falls hard for her and pursues her, arousing the suspicions of her ordinarily good-natured spouse. To compound the problem, their friend is about to evict them from the villa. When they learn of the death of Dimitrova's mother, the family journeys again to the country for the funeral. Arriving anew in Sofia following the tragedy, they are now old hands, aware of the pitfalls they are likely to encounter.

d, Eduard Zahariev; w, Eduard Zahariev, Plamen Maslarov (based on motifs in the novel *The Saintly Anna* by Alexander Tomov); ph, Stefan Trifonov; m, Mitko Schtorev; ed, Magda Krusteva; set d, Georgi Gutsev.

Drama   **(PR:C MPAA:NR)**

SKY BANDITS   (1986, Brit.) 93m London Front/Galaxy International c

Scott McGinnis *(Barney)*, Jeff Osterhage *(Luke)*, Ronald Lacey *(Fritz)*, Miles Anderson *(Bannock)*, Valerie Steffen *(Yvette)*, Ingrid Held *(Mitsou)*, Keith Buckley *(Comdr. von Schlussel)*, Terrence Harvey *(Col. Canning)*, Ten Maynard *(Big Jake)*.

The story of two not-very-successful bank robbers in the waning days of the Old West (Osterhage and McGinnis). When the law finally catches up with them they have to choose between prison and the Army, so before you can say "The War To End All Wars," they are in the trenches in France. They manage to join a British fighter squadron commanded by Anderson whose sole objective is to down a massive, fantastic German dirigible that regularly wreaks havoc over the Allied lines. The fliers always bear the brunt of their actions, and every landing is a crash, though the planes are constantly put together in ever more outlandish fashion by resident aeronautical genius Lacey, a Britisher who has had his head shaken in so many crash landings that he now speaks with a German accent. Naturally Osterhage and McGinnis pick up flying in no time, and before long they have managed to move their girl friends into their tent with them. Of course, the two heroes eventually become the only ones who can stop the zeppelin's predations, so they try their old bank-robbing technique and drop dynamite on the monster airship. It blows up in a big way, and next thing we know the pair is back in the West, blowing up banks like before.

The leads are wooden and the script inane (with brief exceptions), but the flying scenes are hilarious, with the most unlikely looking bags of canvas, string, and cannibalized parts lumbering down the runway. The real star, though, is the gargantuan dirigible. A fantastic creation complete with a balcony from which the commander shouts curses, the airship is so tall the top disappears in the clouds when it is tied to the ground. Unfortunately, impressive hardware can't carry a story by itself. Predictably, the film disappeared after a very short theatrical run.

p, Richard Herland; d, Zoran Perisic; w, Thom Keyes; ph, David Watkin (Rank Color); m, Alfie Kabiljo; ed, Peter Tanner; prod d, Tony Woollard; art d, Charles Bishop; set d, Hugh Scaife; cos, Betsy Hermann; spec eff, Ian Wingrove; stunts, Marc Boyle.

Adventure/War   **(PR:A-C MPAA:PG13)**

SKY PIRATES†   (1986, Aus.) 95m Roadshow c

John Hargreaves *(Harris)*, Meredith Phillips *(Melanie Mitchell)*, Max Phipps *(Savage)*, Bill Hunter *(O'Reilly)*, Simon Chilvers *(Rev. Mitchell)*, Alex Scott *(Gen. Hackett)*, David Parker *(Hayes)*, Adrian Wright *(Valentine)*, Peter Cummins *(Col. Brien)*, Tommy Dysart *(Barman)*, Wayne Cull *(Logan)*, Alex Menglett *(Sullivan)*, Nigel Bradshaw *(Spencer)*.

An Australian attempt to produce a RAIDERS OF THE LOST ARK-style action-adventure, this film was long delayed in post-production before being released to overwhelming indifference down under. Hargreaves is the hero, a tough pilot flying his C-47 across the Pacific with a cargo of VIPs and a mysterious artifact from Easter Island with amazing powers. The artifact begins to exert its influence during the flight and zaps the whole plane into a weird time warp, where rusting ships litter the horizon. Hargreaves manages to get the plane back to its own time, fight off the villains, return the magical artifact (possibly left by outer-space visitors), and get the girl, all in just over an hour and a half.

p, John Lamond, Michael Hirsh; d, Colin Eggleston; w, John Lamond; ph, Garry Wapshott (Panavision); m, Brian May; ed, John Lamond, Michael Hirsh; prod d, Kristian Fredrickson; spec eff, Dennis Nicholson; stunts, Max Aspin.

Action/Adventure   **(PR:C MPAA:NR)**

SLADKE STAROSTI†   (1986, Czech.) Koliba c (Trans: Sweet Worries)

Emil Horvath, Jr., Antonin Duchoslav, Irena Kacirkova, Andrej Hryc.

d, Juraj Herz; w, Juraj Herz, Jozef Pasteka; ph, Dodo Simoncic.

SLEEPWALK†   (1986, U.S./Ger.) 75m Driver-Ottoskop c

Suzanne Fletcher *(Nicole)*, Ann Magnuson *(Isabelle)*, Dexter Lee *(Jimmy)*, Steven Chen *(Dr. Gou)*, Tony Todd *(Barrington)*, Richard Boes *(The Thief)*, Ako *(Ecco Ecco)*, Harvey Perr *(Matt)*, Jim Stark *(Detective)*, Roberta Wright *(Renee)*, Simon Daillie *(Cross Me Kid)*.

An atmospheric thriller directed by Driver, the producer of fellow New Yorker Jim Jarmusch's STRANGER THAN PARADISE. Fletcher stars as a bilingual computer operator who relieves her daily routine by translating an ancient Chinese manuscript into English. The manuscript was stolen and, as she soon finds out, cursed. A Japanese girl who steals the manuscript's first page is found dead. Fletcher's friend loses all her hair after coming in contact with the book, and worst of all for Fletcher, her son is kidnaped. An American independent film (Driver's second after YOU ARE NOT I) with West German financial backing, SLEEPWALK found an audience in Europe quicker than in the States, and Driver released the picture overseas before showing it in New York.

p&d, Sara Driver; w, Sara Driver, Lorenzo Mans; ph, Franz Prinzi, Jim Jarmusch; m, Phil Kline; ed, Li Shin Yu; art d, Robert Cooney, Andrea Degette.

Mystery   **(PR:NR MPAA:NR)**

SLOANE zero   (1986) 95m Venture International c

Robert Resnik *(Philip Sloane)*, Debra Blee *(Cynthia Thursby)*, Raul Aragon *(Pete Saimi)*, Victor Ordonez *(Sal)*, Carissa Carlos *(Naili Saimi)*, Jonee Gamboa *(Chan Se)*, Ann Milhench *(Janice Thursby)*, Charles Black *(Arthur Margolis)*, George Mahlberg *(Richard Thursby)*.

After some Filipino thugs hired by crime kingpin Gamboa kill Milhench's husband (Mahlberg) and take her off to the Philippines, the poor girl's father is faced with only one course of action. He calls in Resnik, an impossibly handsome ex-cop (and Milhench's former beau), to rescue the girl. Once in Manila, Resnik hooks up with Mahlberg's tough-as-nails sister Blee and his buddy Aragon and the search begins. Several car chases, explosions, double crosses, and shoot outs later, Aragon is dead, Blee is understandably aggravated with Resnik, and Milhench is safe. Resnik has the last word, as he pilots a chopper to do in the evil Gamboa.

    SLOANE tries so hard to be the ultimate action flick, it ends up resembling Woody Allen's spy spoof, WHAT'S UP, TIGER LILY? Much like that comedy's hero—Phil Moscowitz—Resnik is "a lovable rogue," while Gamboa's unintentionally funny delivery often resembles Allen's nefarious miscreant Shepherd Wong. The situation is simple and dealt with in a wholly ludicrous manner. Just try and keep a straight face when hordes of pygmy cannibals descend from the cave where Milhench is being held. Resnik is annoying in the lead, looking far too young for his character, considering all the exciting experiences he's supposed to have had. The technical end matches the artistic qualities, complete with poor vocal dubbings and badly lit, often out-of-focus photography.

p, Daniel Rosenthal, David Feder; d, Daniel Rosenthal, Richard Belding; w, Aubrey K. Rattan; ph, John Hart (Metrocolor); m, Phil Marshall; ed, 3-D Editorial, Andrew Horvitch; prod d, Robert Lee.

Action   **Cas.**   **(PR:O MPAA:NR)**

SMART ALEC†   (1986) 87m American Twist-Boulevard c

Ben Blass *(Alec Carroll)*, Natasha Kautsky *(Julie)*, Zsa Zsa Gabor *(Herself)*, Orson Bean *(Arthur Fitzgerald)*, Antony Alda *(Rodney)*, Kerry Remsen *(Samantha Gibbs)*, Lucinda Crosby *(Carla Rochester)*, David Hedison *(Frank Wheeler)*, Bill Henderson *(Bert)*.

Supporting himself as a film production assistant by day, Blass is an aspiring director who desperately wants to raise money to produce a film of his own script. He goes to a variety of investors, before ending up with Bean, an older man who is attracted to Blass. Bean agrees to fund the project provided a part can be written for his favorite actress, Zsa Zsa Gabor. Blass, in the meantime, is having other difficulties as he vainly attempts to get screen star Kautsky to appear in his opus. Gabor eventually lets Blass know of Bean's ulterior motives, and the would-be filmmaker is able to extract himself from a potentially unpleasant situation.

p&d, Jim Wilson; w, Rob Sullivan, Jim Wilson; ph, John Huneck; m, Stephen

Hunter, Jan King, Morgan Cavett, Bruce Langhorne; ed, James Addison, Brian Lee Ross; art d, Nancy Arnold; cos, Sunny Chayes.

Comedy   **(PR:O MPAA:NR)**

SMICH SE LEPI NA PATY†   (1986, Czech.) 94m Barrandov c (Trans: Laughter Sticks to Your Heels)

Vlastimil Brodsky *(Joska Platejz)*, Petr Cepek *(Fanda)*, Josef Kemr *(Kroupa)*, Miroslav Vladyka *(Jarda)*, Ladislav Krivacek *(Mirek)*, Pavel Novy *(Lada)*, Jirina Bohdalova *(Helena)*, Karel Hermanek *(Brousek)*, Vilma Cibulkova *(Brouskova)*, Ema Cerna *(Postmistress)*, Klara Jernekova *(Hejna)*, Josef Novotny, Sr. *(1st Novotny)*, Josef Novotny, Jr. *(2nd Novotny)*, Richard Novotny *(3rd Novotny)*, Jaroslava Ticha *(Kroupova)*, Sarka Cetlova *(Hanicka)*, Jan Hartl *(Jenda)*, Jitka Asterova *(Dana)*.

d, Hynek Bocan; w, Pavel Fiala, Hynek Bocan (based on a story by Pavel Fiala); ph, Ivan Spaleta; m, Petr Skoumal; ed, Dalibor Lipsky; art d, Zbynek Hloch; cos, Jarmila Konecna; makeup, Frantisek Pilny.

SMILE OF THE LAMB, THE***   (1986, Israel) 93m Dotan-Aroch c (HIUCH HA'GDI)

Tuncel Kurtiz *(Hilmi)*, Rami Danon *(Laniado)*, Makhram Khouri *(Katzman)*, Dan Muggia *(Sheffer)*, Iris Hoffman *(Shosh)*.

This interesting study of Jewish-Palestinian relations from the Israeli cinema opens as Houri, a military governor in charge of a West Bank village, decides to take decisive action against some local terrorists. He puts the rotting corpse of a dead donkey in the middle of the hot town square, hoping the stink will drive out hidden PLO members. Danon, a sympathetic Israeli doctor, takes the side of the Palestinians and deliberately disobeys Houri's orders by having the carcass removed. Kurtiz, a peculiar Arab hermit who lives in a cave outside the village, becomes friendly with Danon and the two build a close relationship. Danon is entertained by Kurtiz' stories but this friendship ultimately comes to a tragic end. When Kurtiz' adopted son, a member of the PLO, is killed the eccentric character takes Danon as a willing hostage. The captive will be freed, Kurtiz insists, only when the Israelis pull out of the West Bank.

    Director Dotan deals with several of Israel's most critical issues in a wise, humanistic manner which avoids any hard-line political statement. The unusual camaraderie which builds between Danon and Kurtiz supersedes any differences brought on by their respective backgrounds, quietly suggesting that Israel's problems are not as unsolvable as some might insist. Another of the film's strong points are the marvelous stories Kurtiz spins. Part truth and part fable, these tales are deftly handled under Dotan's direction. Elements of fantasy are incorporated into the narrative with a lyrical grace that greatly adds to the warmth generated by Kurtiz' narration. Kurtiz, a Turkish actor, gives an endearing performance in his offbeat role. He brings much heart to the curious recluse, and develops a natural chemistry with Danon in their scenes together. SMILE OF THE LAMB received the award as Best Picture in Israel's equivalent of the Academy Awards, while Kurtiz won an acting prize at the world-renowned Berlin Film Festival.

p, Jonathan Aroch; d, Shimon Dotan; w, Shimon Dotan, Shimon Riklin, Anath Levi-Bar (based on a novel by David Grossman); ph, Danny Schneuer; m, Ilan Virtzberg; ed, Netaya Anbar; set d, Charles Leon; cos, Rona Doron.

Drama   **(PR:O MPAA:NR)**

SMRT KRASNYCH SRNCU†   (1986, Czech.) 94m Barrandov c (Trans: The Death of Beautiful Deer)

Karel Hermanek *(Daddy Leo Popper)*, Marta Vancurova *(Mommy Herma Popperova)*, Marcel Valter *(Prdelka)*, Jiri Strach *(Jirka)*, Jan Jirasek *(Hugo)*, Rudolf Hrusinsky, *(Karel Prosek)*, Jiri Krampol *(Jenda Hejtmanek)*, Ladislav Potmesil *(Director Koralek)*, Dana Vlkova *(Irma Koralkova)*, Ladislav Trojan *(1st Inspector)*, Jan Preucil *(2nd Inspector)*, Lubor Tokos *(Nejezchleba the Foreman)*, Jana Synkova *(Gutova the Secretary)*.

d&w, Karel Kachyna (based on the book by Ota Pavbl); ph, Vladimir Smutny; m, Lubos Fiser; ed, Jiri Brozek; art d, Karel Lier; cos, Irena Greiflova; makeup, Frantisek Cizek.

SNO-LINE*   (1986) 89m Vandom c

Vince Edwards *(Steve King)*, Paul Smith *(Duval)*, June Wilkinson *(Audrey)*, Phil Foster *(Ralph Salerno)*, Louis Guss *(Gus)*, Carey Clark *(Michael)*, Charity Ann Zachary *(Tina)*, Gary Lee Love *(Eddie)*, Edward Talbot Matthews III *(Frankie)*, Billy J. Holman *(Bedford)*, Scott Strozer, Maggie Egan, Dominic Barto, Roy Morgan, Kelly Nichols, Gary Angelle, Michele Ewing, Fredrika Duke, Cassandra Edwards, Kay Elrod.

Filmed in Texas in 1984 and given only limited release in Beaumont and Corpus Christi (where the film was shot) in 1985, SNO-LINE wound up going to videocassette for general release. Basically a routine gangster film with an overabundance of subplots, the film stars Edwards as a ruthless mafioso about to make a big cocaine deal with the hulking Smith (who turned in a memorable performance as the vicious Turkish prison guard in MIDNIGHT EXPRESS), who sends his female agent, Wilkinson, to infiltrate Edwards' organization. Unfortunately, Edwards has stiff competition from a redneck gangster, Holman, whose headquarters are located in the midst of a swamp and guarded by an small army of greasy-looking good ol' boys. To spoil the cocaine deal, Holman has the 300-pound Smith kidnaped and holds him hostage. Meanwhile, Edwards (who has struck up a relationship with the wily Wilkinson) encounters other problems. His crime organization, which includes a casino and a diary business which works as a front for his drug dealing (his milkmen deliver drugs as well), is under seige from a group of four unknown terrorists who are waylaying his milkmen and robbing them of the proceeds. As it turns out, the young Turks all work at Edwards' country club and have learned the ins and outs of his crime organization by eavesdropping. The golf-pro gang members decide to end their crime days by robbing Edwards' lucrative casino.

While Edwards is tied up trying to rescue Smith from Holman, the golf pros rob his casino and make off with a few million (including the cash that was to pay for the cocaine). Edwards' thugs uncover the culprits when one of the dumber members of the gang, Matthews, displays his new wealth by giving away large amounts of cocaine to women he meets in a bar (Edwards' goons catch him in bed with Edwards' wife—but that's another subplot). Matthews is the weakest link in the gang and he soon spills his guts about the identity of the other members. Soon two more members of the country-club gang are murdered, leaving only the sincere Clark and his vapid girl friend Zachary alive. They decide to scram out of the country with the money, but Clark is forced to throw the briefcase full of loot at Edwards' enforcers in order to make good their escape. After a tedious car chase the young couple manage to hop a speedboat out of town. Edwards gets his money back and finally makes the deal with Smith. When Smith opens the briefcase, however, he finds only a thin layer of bills resting atop pages from the phone book. Guns are flashed and Edwards is shot in the back by Wilkinson. The film then returns to Clark and Zachary stranded in their speedboat (it ran out of gas). Clark reveals that he had stashed most of the money in her duffel bag and the happy couple are rescued by Smith (who is cruising in his yacht), who does not know who they are but hopes they know how to play chess—his favorite pastime.

This would have been strictly summer drive-in fare if the film had ever gotten wider release, and taken as such, SNO-LINE is at least tolerable. The action scenes are passable and the huge Smith manages to bring some entertainment value to the film as he gleefully takes on half-a-dozen armed men by himself. Most of the performers, however, are barely competent, with veterans like Edwards and Wilkinson scarcely able to elicit any discernible personality in their roles. Only character actor Guss evokes some much-needed humor as Edwards' loyal right-hand man who has a penchant for white golf caps, loud Hawaiian shirts, and Bermuda shorts. The makers of SNO-LINE know little about constructing or pacing a successful action film. Hilliard's script is so complicated and there are so many characters and subplots that little screen time is available to fully develop any one character or situation. Director O'Neons' insistence on cross-cutting among several different subplots totally diffuses any dramatic tension and only serves to bore and confuse the viewer. One gets the impression that O'Neons and Hilliard were attempting "epic" status by intermingling so many different story lines, but all they succeeded in doing was diluting their already weak ideas.

p, Robert Burge; d, Douglas F. O'Neons; w, Robert Hilliard; ph, Gary Thieltges (United Color); m, Richard Bellis; ed, Beth Conwell; prod d, Chuck Stewart.

Crime   **Cas.**   **(PR:O MPAA:R)**

SOBREDOSIS†   (1986, Arg.) c (Trans: Overdose)

Federico Luppi, Dora Baret, Gabriel Lenn.

Family conflicts arise when some parents discover their offspring are involved with drugs.

d, Fernando Ayala.

Drama   **(PR:O MPAA:NR)**

SOLARBABIES zero   (1986) 94m Brooksfilms–MGM-UA Entertainment Co.
                                                                              c

Richard Jordan (Grock), Jami Gertz (Terra), Jason Patric (Jason), Lukas Haas (Daniel), James Le Gros (Metron), Claude Brooks (Rabbit), Peter DeLuise (Tug), Peter Kowanko (Gavial), Adrian Pasdar (Darstar), Sarah Douglas (Shandray), Charles Durning (The Warden).

SOLARBABIES is a cookbook film of unlikely ingredients, incorporating parts of the MAD MAX trilogy, with sections of E.T., ROLLERBALL, DUNE, and a smattering of biker films as well. The story opens in that handy catch-all time period "the future" where the world has been transformed into a vast desert, thanks to the nefarious doings of an organization known as "The Protectorate." Orphaned children and teenagers now live in special camps, where they are being reeducated to accept the Protectorate's policies. Their only outlet is a hockey-like game played on rollerskates. The Solarbabies, comprising teenagers Gertz, Brooks, Le Gros, Patric, Pasdar, and youngster Haas (the boy from 1985's WITNESS) is one of the teams in this futuristic sporting event. Haas is contacted by Bodhi, a sort of magic glowing bowling ball, which wants to help the plucky band save the world. Bodhi (which is the word for a personal illumination Buddhists believe results from an eight-part road to salvation) tells the kids to skate their little hearts out of prison and through the desert in order to restore the earth to its former state of moist grandeur. Since it's only natural for futuristic teens to listen to mysterious shining spheres, the Solarbabies head out for the unknown. Jordan, a standard nasty sneering cop, heads out after the Solarbabies and provides the expected difficulties the kids have to face. Bodhi doesn't get off with a picnic either, as the magic overgrown lightbulb must do battle with a Protectorate robot. Ultimately though, the global tap gets turned back on and Our Heroes live you know how ever after.

Produced through the auspices of Mel Brooks' appropriately titled company Brooksfilms, and filmed on location in Spain, SOLARBABIES initially had been scheduled for a summer release. Realizing what a dog they had on their hands, MGM/UA held back, then dumped it out in the rush of big-budget Christmas movies. The film was swallowed in the rush, then forgotten, and for good reason:

it stinks. The acting is lame and the rehashed script is just too silly to be taken seriously. Director Johnson showed some flair for comedy in the 1983 remake of TO BE OR NOT TO BE, but he sure doesn't have a handle on science fiction, as SOLARBABIES so painfully proves. The film drags on and on until its obvious and none-too-thrilling conclusion. A film to punish the kids with if their behavior grows intolerable.

p, Irene Walzer, Jack Frost Sanders; d, Alan Johnson; w, Walon Green, Douglas Anthony Metrov; ph, Peter MacDonald (Metrocolor); m, Maurice Jarre; ed, Conrad Buff; prod d, Anthony Pratt; art d, Don Dossett; set d, Graham Sumner; cos, Bob Ringwood; spec eff, Richard Edlund; m/l, Smokey Robinson.

Science Fiction   **Cas.**   **(PR:A-C MPAA:PG-13)**

SOLDIER'S REVENGE*½   (1986) 88m Continental c

John Savage (Frank Morgan), Maria Socas (Baetriz), Edgardo Moreira (Ricardo), Frank Cane (Gomez), Paul Lambert (Gen. Burns), Sebastian Larrie (Tiny), George Wellurtz (Sheriff), Jack Arndt (Realtor), Albert Uris (Carlos), Brian McKlunn (Uncle Benjamin), Fiona Keyne (Amy), Daniel Warr (Pilot), George Kenny (Priest), Edward Jordan (Bearded Rebel), George Candi (Villa Guard), Elizabeth Palmer (Ticket Office Woman), James Murry (Cooley), Hellen Gavin (Tiny's Girl Friend), George Simpson, Michael Casanova (Policemen at Airport), Deborah Chin (Vietnamese Girl), Joseph M. Ibanez (Border Officer), Albert May (Bartender), Cona McDonald (Waitress), Dale Howser, Dan Bogart, Steven Cook, David Walsh, Peter Porteous, George Murdoch, Wayne Montanio, Robert Brenner, Ray Shaffer, John Findlater (Bar Thugs), Daniel Leibiker, Nestor Rosen, Cletus Rogers, John Erquiaga, Annelaine Briden, Deborah Cody (Bar People).

Savage is a Vietnam veteran who turned against the war after he was shot down and saw the carnage wreaked by bombs dropped from his plane. He told a magazine about the unsavory secret operations in which he participated and has been branded a traitor by many in his hometown in Texas. After the death of his mother, he returns home to clear up her affairs and sell the farm, but the locals continually harass him, even though he is simply trying to mind his own business. Meanwhile, a plane full of weapons for a Central American revolution has put down at the local airstrip for repairs and the pilot quits. Socas is accompanying the load because her father has been kidnaped by the revolutionaries and they have demanded the arms as ransom. Socas tries to interest Savage in flying the cargo for her, but he is unmoved. However, after busting up a bar where he has been attacked by a dozen creeps, Savage is pursued to the airport. There he and Socas create a diversion and escape in the airplane. Not long after they get into the air, Savage tells Socas that he loves her. Because they don't have enough fuel to make it all the way, they radio to the revolutionaries and ask them to help secure an airfield in a neighboring country so they can refuel. At first all comes off without a hitch, but an army patrol arrives and the plane is wrecked. Quickly the crates are loaded onto a truck and driven across the border, wiping out tanks, helicopters, and scores of soldiers along the way. Once inside the revolution-torn country, however, Savage and Socas are locked up and it is discovered that her father was killed trying to get away. Savage easily escapes and then frees Socas. With chief revolutionary Moreira—who also loves Socas—in pursuit, Savage, Socas, and her uncle and niece head for the waterfront, where the uncle has a boat. The uncle is killed, and while Socas and the little girl head for the boat, Savage stands face to face with Moreira and persuades him not to shoot him. Both men put down their weapons and Savage heads out to sea with Socas.

In a year that gave us the most intelligent look at the conflicts in Central America yet—SALVADOR—SOLDIER'S REVENGE is a idiotic fantasy for pacifists who still like to see trucks blown up. Savage wanders through the film offering a next-to-pointless narration and racing down overwhelming odds every few minutes. No mention is made of the politics involved in revolution, instead we get Savage whining about how no one can win a war. Shot in the U.S. and Argentina in 1984, the film appears on videocassette without ever gracing a theater screen.

p, J.C. Crespo; d, David Worth; w, Lee Stull, David Worth (based on a story by Eduard Sarlui); ph, Leonard Solis, Stephen Sealy; m, Don Great, Gary Rist; ed,

Raja Gosnell; prod d, George March; art d, Robert Summer; set d, Alan Bald, Charles Stone, Ed Berry; cos, Gloria von Hartenstein; makeup, Olga Brown.

War/Drama   Cas.   (PR:C   MPAA:NR)

SOMETHING WILD*½   (1986) 113m Religioso Primitiva/Orion c

Jeff Daniels *(Charles Driggs)*, Melanie Griffith *(Audrey Hankel)*, Ray Liotta *(Ray Sinclair)*, Margaret Colin *(Irene)*, Tracey Walter *(The Country Squire)*, Dana Preu *("Peaches")*, Jack Gilpin *(Larry Dillman)*, Su Tissue *(Peggy Dillman)*, Kristin Olsen *(Tracy)*, John Sayles *(Motorcycle Cop)*, John Waters *(Used Car Guy)*, Charles Napier *(Irate Chef)*, The Feelies *(The Willies)*, Kenneth Utt *("Dad")*, Adelle Lutz *("Rose")*, George Schwartz *(Counter Man)*, Leib Lensky *(Frenchy)*, Maggie T. *(Country Squire Bulldog)*, Patricia Falkenhain *(Charlie's Secretary)*, Sandy McLeod *(Graves' Secretary)*, Robert Ridgely *(Richard Graves)*, Buzz Kilman *(TV Newscaster)*, Jim Roche *(Motel Philosopher)*, The Texas Kid *(Hitchhiking Cowboy)*, Byron D. Hutcherson, Eleana Hutcherson *(Hitchhiking Kids)*, Thomas Cavano *(Guitar Player)*, Dorothy Demme, Emma Bryne *(Junk Store Gals)*, Max the Dog *(Himself)*, Mary Ardella Drew *(Donna Penski)*, Joseph Lee Davis *(James Williams)*, Edward Saxon *(Kevin Stroup)*, James Hurd, Joanna Kitchen-Hurd *(Stylish Reunion Couple)*, Gary Goetzman *(Guido Paonessa)*, Chloe Amateau *(Chloe)*, Dung Chau *(Robbery Victim)*, The Crew *(Gas Station Rappers)*, Steve Scales *("Nelson")*, John Montgomery *(Harmonica Slim)*, Heather Shaw *(Choir Girl)*, Vic Blair *(Cowboy Maitre D')*, D. Stanton Miranda *("Darlene")*, Ding-A-Ling *(Motorcycle Dog)*, Johnny Marrs *(Motorcycle Driver)*, George Henry Wyche, Jr., Marilee K. Smith, Jeffery R. Rioux, Jeff Herig *(Police Officers)*, Gil Lazier *(Homicide Detective)*, Anna Levine *(The Girl in 3F)*, "Sister Carol" East *("Dottie")*.

After the disappointment of SWING SHIFT and a detour to direct the rock concert film STOP MAKING SENSE, Jonathan Demme (MELVIN AND HOWARD) has returned to the highways and byways of America with a vengeance.

One bright Friday afternoon in lower Manhattan, Daniels, a successful young tax consultant, skips out of the tiny diner where he ate lunch without paying the check. Before he is 10 steps away from the eatery he is stopped by Griffith, a strange vision decked out in pseudo-African jewelry, goofy plastic sunglasses, and a black Louise Brooks wig (she calls herself "Lulu" after Brooks' character in PANDORA'S BOX). Griffith saw Daniels walk out on the check and tells him so. He nervously feigns ignorance and offers to rectify his mistake. A sly smile spreads across Griffith's face and she accuses him of being a "closet rebel." Before Daniels is fully cognizant of what is happening to him, he finds himself in Griffith's bizarre convertible (decorated with all manner of voodoo items), being driven to New Jersey. Griffith produces a bottle of bourbon and takes several long pulls while zooming down the road. Daniels is on the verge of hysteria—protesting that he has an important meeting scheduled for that afternoon—before

he finally decides to relax and play along. Griffith stops at a motel and demands money from Daniels for a room. Daniels stammers that the only cash he has is what he was going to deposit in his family's Christmas Club account. Griffith snatches the money and in a flash Daniels finds himself handcuffed to the bed with a phone held to his ear as he lies to his boss regarding his whereabouts. An

afternoon of carnality behind him, Daniels phones his wife and tells her that he'll be away on business.

Most of his inhibitions gone, Daniels decides to spend the weekend with this crazy, sexy woman. They cruise into Pennsylvania singing, drinking, and picking up hitchhikers. Griffith stops at a vintage clothing shop (run jointly by director Demme's mother and the mother of Talking Heads guru David Byrne) and buys Daniels a funky new wardrobe (Hawaiian shirt, shiny suit). Suddenly Daniels finds himself calling Griffith by her real name, Audrey, and standing on the doorstep of her mother's house, being introduced as her husband ("See Mama? Just the kind of man you said I should marry."). Wanting to appear a good sport in Griffith's eyes, Daniels plays along as Griffith invents their successful life together for the benefit of her mother (played superbly by Preu). Preu, however, is no dummy and she realizes that Griffith has invented the whole thing just to please her. While doing the dinner dishes with Daniels, she reveals that she knows the truth and quietly tells him, "You look out for that girl." When Griffith enters the kitchen, Daniels is stunned to see her with short blonde hair and a lovely summer dress—the picture of reserved suburbia.

Once again, before he has a chance to grasp what is happening, Daniels finds himself at Griffith's 10-year high school reunion, being introduced as her husband. Just as he begins to relax and get silly, Daniels sees, much to his horror, Gilpin, an ambitious toady who works for his company. As Daniels stutters out an excuse of why he's here with a strange woman, Griffith interrupts and introduces herself as his mistress. Instead of being shocked, Gilpin gives Daniels a respectful "You-sly-old-dog" look. Having survived that crisis, it is now Griffith's turn to bump into the last person on Earth she wants to see—her estranged husband, Liotta. Dressed in jeans, cowboy boots, and a black T-shirt, Liotta tells Griffith that he just got out of prison (armed robbery). While Griffith tries desperately to get away from him, Liotta uses his oily charm to ingratiate himself with Daniels and they wind up cruising around town in Liotta's car (accompanied by Liotta's date, Colin). After ditching Colin, Liotta tricks Daniels into participating in holding up a convenience store. Liotta cracks the clerk in the face with his gun and then gives Daniels a few hits in the face for good measure. He then takes Griffith and Daniels as his captives and drives them to a motel where he interrogates them. Daniels is finally forced to admit to Griffith that he is divorced and his kids live with their mother; he was just using his fictitious family as an out to get away from her if he had to. Because Daniels is an accomplice in the robbery, Liotta knows he won't talk and lets him go. Rather than return home in total defeat and humiliation, Daniels decides to follow Liotta and rescue Griffith. Eventually, Daniels corners Liotta and Griffith in a crowded restaurant where a group of police officers is sitting in a nearby booth. Daniels forces Liotta to hand over his car keys and wallet and he leaves the eatery with a shocked Griffith. After some bickering, Daniels and Griffith return to New York. The enraged Liotta finally manages to leave the restaurant without causing a fuss and he immediately steals a car and heads after them. He breaks into Griffith's lower Manhattan apartment and finds nothing, but remembering where Daniels said he lived, Liotta finds the address and heads to the suburbs. Meanwhile, Griffith and Daniels arrive at Daniels' house. Griffith is shocked to find that it is virtually empty—no sign of Daniels' marriage remains—only bags and cups from fast-food restaurants dot the floor. While Griffith takes a nap in the bedroom, Daniels drifts off in the den. He awakens to a tremendous crash when Liotta throws a lawn chair through the sliding glass door. After a violent struggle, Liotta handcuffs Daniels to the pipes under the bathroom sink. Bruised and battered, Daniels summons up enough strength to pull apart the pipes and free himself. He attacks Liotta, but again winds up on the floor, this time with the intruder's switchblade. When Daniels rises, knife in hand, Liotta runs right into the blade. Shock and confusion register on Liotta's face as the blade sinks into his stomach. "Damn . . . Charlie," Liotta says to Daniels as if their little game has just gone a bit too far. The police and ambulances arrive and cart off Liotta's dead body. Daniels has a broken arm and the police take Griffith away for questioning. Griffith disappears from Daniels' life.

Back in his normal world, Daniels decides to leave the firm despite the fact that he has just been promoted to vice-president. He eats lunch at the same diner where he first met Griffith and for old times' sake, he skips out on the check. Once again, 10 steps from the door, he is caught, this time by the waitress, East, who stops him to collect the bill. As Daniels feigns ignorance and pays his bill, he sees a beautiful blonde woman in a lovely dress and a big white hat. To his surprise the woman is Griffith. She smiles at him and leads him to her new car. This time she lets him drive.

Director Jonathan Demme is one of the few American filmmakers of his generation who does not spend his career trying to recapture his childhood in the manner of George Lucas, Steven Spielberg, or Joe Dante. These directors make films inspired by other films or television shows that they enjoyed while growing up. It seems as if they have spent their entire lives *watching* without ever *seeing*. Demme is different. Since his early films, he has demonstrated a superior eye for the American landscape and its people. With a keen wit and an optimistic compassion for the strength and resilience of Americans, Demme has created several vivid characters that have the ring of truth about them. But Demme's America is not a blindly hopeful one. He also recognizes the darkness behind the smiles, the hopelessness behind the bright slogans, the failure that comes with success, the claustrophobia within the vast landscape. Demme grapples with the problems, desires, and needs of his generation as adults.

With a script from first-time screenwriter Frye and superior performances from his principal cast, Demme has created a vivid, unique film in SOMETHING WILD that defies easy categorization. Smart and successful in the business world, Daniels has failed as a husband and father. He carries the guilt of those who grew up defiant and rebellious toward the establishment in the 1960s and early 1970s, who have since sold their idealism down the river for a high-paying job in the mainstream—a yuppie. Daniels plays games with his conscience by telling himself that he's " . . . a rebel. I just channeled my rebellion into the mainstream," and doing daring things like skipping out on a $4 lunch check. Only when he meets Griffith does he realize that his life has become a lonely trap of his own design (he can't even admit to himself that he has failed in his most important personal relationships). Griffith, however, lives in a trap of her own. Younger than Daniels, she is a woman who has been searching for something her entire life but is unsure of what she is looking for. During this phase of her life, she has embraced African culture (at one point we see her reading a biography of Winnie Mandella) and surrounds herself with African music, jewelry, and art. This obsession is just one more fad in a parade of fads she has embraced in an effort to be forever "hip" and avoid the appearance of being a respectable adult. Never does she demonstrate any understanding or appreciation of the African experience—it's just fashion. Because Daniels has always avoided passing fads in favor of tradition, he is fascinated by Griffith, and she with him. These wounded people form a bond. Although they use each other for selfish means (he to forget his family's collapse, she to prove that she's made something of her life to her mother and high school class), they eventually come to love and respect each other because together they form an emotionally complete person. Enter Liotta, the dark intangible that hovers outside of happiness. Although chillingly amoral and explosively violent, Liotta is not portrayed as a monster. Liotta is one of those loners who never fit in and has accepted his fate by becoming the most notorious member of his community. Griffith's rebellious nature must have been drawn to the darkly charming and dangerous aspects of Liotta's character and she latched onto him for as long as it amused her. He, however, is hurt by her rejection and cannot stand to see her in the company of a straight-arrow like Daniels. At first, however, Daniels is enthralled with Liotta and feels privileged to be in his company. Liotta is the kind of guy Daniels must have feared but admired in high school. Liotta understands this and plays on Daniels' urge for acceptance. It is at this point that the film turns from quirky comedy to deadly serious. These three people are all searching for the same thing—happiness. Daniels and Griffith see it in each other and Liotta sees it in them. Because he knows he can never share in that happiness, Liotta wants to destroy it. In the end, when the smoke clears, Daniels and Griffith meet each other half way. He does not wish to return to his staid existence; she seems to bury "Lulu" in favor of a more conventional persona. Where they go from here is an unanswerable question, but at least they are both willing to take a chance on one another.

In SOMETHING WILD Demme keeps the narrative twisting and turning so that the viewer can never predict what will happen next. He draws us in with humor and then grabs us by the throat, bringing us face-to-face with the failures of the American dream. The American cinema hasn't seen characters this well drawn and complex in quite some time. No one is purely good or purely evil. They are emotional human beings trying to make some sense out of their existence. Demme's eye and ear for detail are sharp as ever and he turns SOMETHING WILD into one of the those rare films that seems alive. Minor characters, bits, extras, and locations all vibrate with authenticity—each person and place has a story to tell. Demme's America is not just a fantasy land created by Hollywood; it is an actual place where emotions, ambitions, and dreams are played out among the motels, restaurants, and houses that dot the landscape.

Songs include: "Loco De Amor" (David Byrne, F.A.S., performed by Byrne and Celia Cruz), "Si Por Mi Llueve" (Cheo Feliciano, performed by Feliciano), "Wozani Mahipi" (N.S. Bopare, E. Piliso, performed by The Mahotella Queens), "Feel It" (Manley Buchanan, Herbie Miller, performed by Big Youth), "With You or Without You" (Steve Jones, performed by Jones), "Highlife" (Sonny Okossun, performed by Okossun), "Ooh! Aah!" (Ashley Cooper, Sidonia Thorpe, Harold Baile, Richard Walters, Alvin Campbell, Louis Marriot, Franklyn Campbell, performed by The Fabulous Five), "Nice Up Dancee" (L. Palmer, L. McQueen, J. White, performed by Natural Beauty), "Medicine Show" (M. Jones, D. Letts, performed by Big Audio Dynamite), "Wild Thing" (Chip Taylor, performed by The Troggs), "Nobody Move Nobody Get Hurt" (Yellowman, performed by Yellowman), "Yahooo Eeeee!" (Wazmo Nariz, performed by Nariz), "Minuet in G Major" (Johann Sebastian Bach, performed by Dana Preu), "Temptation" (New Order, performed by New Order), "Ever Fallen in Love" (Pete Shelley, performed by Fine Young Cannibals), "You Can Turn a Light On" (Lisa Chadwick, performed by Chadwick, D.C. Stringer), "I'm a Believer" (Neil Diamond, performed by The Feelies), "Before the Next Teardrop Falls" (N. Peters, Vivian Keith, performed by The Feelies, lead vocal by Gary Goetzman), "Crazy Rhythm," "Loveless Love" (Glen Mercer, Bill Million, performed by The Feelies), "Fame" (Carlos Alomar, David Bowie, John Lennon, performed by The Feelies), "Not My Slave" (Danny Elfman, performed by Oingo Boingo), "More Fun in the New World" (John X. Doe, Exene Cervenka, peformed by X), "Spring Rain" (Robert Forester, Grant McLennan, performed by The Go-Betweens), "The Candle Goes Away" (Bill Garvey, performed by Q. Lazarus), "The Future's So Bright I Gotta Wear Shades" (Pat McDonald, performed by Timbuk 3), "Total Control" (Martha Davis, Jeff Jourad, performed by The Motels), "Let the Big Dog Eat" (Bill Wharton, performed by Wharton), "Riding in a UFO" (David Bean, performed by The Judy's), "One More Cup of Coffee" (F. Ennui, Thomas Corey, performed by Electric Sheep), "Man with a Gun" (Jerry Harrison, performed by Harrison), "Co-Il" (Sam Dotson, Ronald Harris, Ricky Harris, Jerry Johnson, performed by The Crew), "Slipping (Into Something)" (Glen Mercer, Bill Million, performed by The Feelies), "Testimonial" (Tina Baker, Mitch Kaplan, performed by Baker), "Secrets" (Stanton-Miranda, performed by Stanton-Miranda, Stephen Vitello), "I Really Love You" (Robert Dockett, Joan York, performed by Jiggs & Co.), "Time Talks" (Scott Rogness, performed by Rogness), "One Day at a Time" (Marijohn Wilkin, Kris Kristofferson, performed by The Community Holiness Church Choir), "Black Sheep of the Family," "Long Legged Woman" (Danny Darst, performed by Darst), "Someone Like You" (John X. Doe, Exene Cervenka, performed by The Knitters), "Zero, Zero Seven Charlie" (James Brown, Ali Campbell, Robin Campbell, Earl Falconer, Norman Hassan, Brian Travers, Michael Virtue, Terence Wilson, performed by UB40), "My Watercolors" (Chuck Napier, performed by Napier), "Pili-Pili" (Jasper Van't Hof, performed by Van't Hof), "Cherokee Chief" (Jerry Harrison, performed by Harrison), "Ethnicolor" (Jean-Michel Jarre, performed by Jarre), "You Don't Have to Cry" (Arthur Baker, Little Steven, performed by Jimmy Cliff), "Wild Thing" (Chip Taylor, performed by Sister Carol), "R.U.O.K.?" ("Rev." Jim Roche).

p, Jonathan Demme, Kenneth Utt; d, Jonathan Demme; w, E. Max Frye; ph, Tak Fujimoto (Du Art color, Deluxe); m, John Cale, Laurie Anderson; ed, Craig McKay; prod d, Norma Moriceau; art d, Steve Lineweaver; set d, Billy Reynolds; m/l, David Byrne, F.A.S., Cheo Feliciano, N.S. Bopare, E. Piliso, Manley Buchanan, Herbie Miller, Steve Jones, Sonny Okossun, Ashley Cooper, Sidonia Thorpe, Harold Baile, Richard Walters, Alvin Campbell, Louis Marriot, Franklyn Campbell, L. Palmer, L. McQueen, J. White, M. Jones, D. Letts, Chip Taylor, Yellowman, Wazmo Nariz, Johann Sebastian Bach, New Order, Pete Shelley, Lisa Chadwick, Neil Diamond, N. Peters, Vivian Keith, Glen Mercer, Bill Million, Carlos Alomar, David Bowie, John Lennon, Danny Elfman, John X. Doe, Exene Cervenka, Robert Forester, Grant McLennan, Bill Garvey, Pat McDonald, Martha Davis, Jeff Jourad, Bill Wharton, David Bean, F. Ennui, Thomas Corey, Jerry Harrison, Sam Dotson, Ronald Harris, Ricky Harris, Jerry Johnson, Tina Baker, Mitch Kaplan, Robert Dockett, Joan York, Scott Rogness, Marijohn Wilkin, Kris Kristofferson, Danny Darst, James Brown, Ali Campbell, Robin Campbell, Earl Falconer, Norman Hassan, Brian Travers, Michael Virtue, Terence Wilson, Chuck Napier, Jasper Van't Hof, Jean-Michel Jarre, Arthur Baker, Little Steven, "Rev." Jim Roch; makeup, Richard Dean; stunts, John Robotham.

Drama/Comedy **(PR:O MPAA:R)**

SONHO SEM FIM† (1986, Braz.) 112m Cinefilmes/Embrafilme c (Trans: Endless Dream)

Carlos Alberto Riccelli, Debora Bloch, Fernanda Torres, Marieta Severo, Imara Reis, Emmanoel Cavalcanti.

Based on the life of one of Brazil's pioneering filmmakers, Eduardo Abelim, SONHO SEM FIM is an interesting look at the problems of creating a film industry in a country already preened on glossy Hollywood productions. Set in the early 20th Century, Riccelli, as Abelim, is shown first as a cab driver and then a stunt car driver before attempting a career acting in movies. This initial effort is disastrous, prompting Riccelli to head back home. Bu' a wealthy woman, with whom he has an affair aboard a boat, lends him the needed money to make his own productions. With a handful of friends as cast and crew he makes a couple of films which are criticized by Brazilian audiences for being amateurish. But Riccelli refuses to stop; at the film's end the political revolution in his country allows him the chance to continue making documentaries. This was the first directorial effort for the cinematographer of the International hit BYE-BYE BRASIL (1980).

p, Luciola Villela; d, Lauro Escorel Filho; w, Walter Lima, Jr., Nelson Nadotti, Escorel Filho; ph, Jose Tadeu Ribeiro; m, Antonio Adolfo; ed, Gilberto Santeiro; prod d, Adrian Cooper; cos, Rita Murtinho.

Biography **(PR:C MPAA:NR)**

SOREKARA† (1986, Jap.) 130m Toei bw (Trans: And Then)

Yusaku Matsuda *(Daisuke)*, Miwako Fujitani *(Michiyo)*, Kaoru Kobayashi *(Hiraoka)*, Chishu Ryu *(Father)*, Mitsuko Kusabue *(Sister-in-Law)*, Katsuo Nakamura *(Brother)*.

Set in 1909, the film follows Matsuda as the second son of a wealthy Japanese family who refuses to bow to tradition and find a respectable job and start a family. Passionate about literature, theater, and opera, Matsuda pursues his interests, much to the annoyance of his family. His life changes, however, when

Kobayashi—an old college friend—and his wife Fujitani return home from To-kyo. Kobayashi explains to Matsuda that he'd lost his banking job because he failed to spot the shady bookkeeping of a subordinate. Although unemployed himself, Kobayashi is shocked by Matsuda's lack of discipline and his frivolous attitude. What Kobayashi does not realize is that Matsuda has just added a new passion to his life, Kobayashi's wife, Fujitani. Matsuda and Fujitani were lovers in their college days, and now the bored housewife looks for a rekindling of the romance. Matsuda's struggle to decide whether to fulfill his desire and scandalize his friend and family, or to deny his own happiness, makes up the crux of the film.

p, Mitsuru Kurosawa, Sadatoshi Fujimine; d, Yoshimitsu Morita; w, Tomomi Tsutsui (based on the novel by Soseki Natsume); ph, Yonezo Maeda, Kazuo Yabe; m, Shigaru Umnhoyoshi; ed, Akira Suzuki; art d, Isutomu Imamura; cos, Michiko Kitamura.

Drama   **(PR:C MPAA:NR)**

SORORITY HOUSE MASSACRE zero   (1986) 74m Concorde c

Angela O'Neill (*Beth*), Wendy Martel (*Linda*), Pamela Ross (*Sara*), Nicole Rio (*Tracy*), John C. Russell (*Bobby*), Marcus Vaughter (*Andy*), Vincent Bilancio (*John*), Joe Nassi (*Craig*), Mary Anne (*Mrs. Lawrence*), Gillian Frank (*Dr. Lindsey*), Joseph Mansier (*Technician*), Axel Roberts (*Larry*), Fitzhough Houston (*Detective Gilbert*), Marsha Carter (*Nurse*), Maureen Hawkes (*Professor*), Alan Engster (*Night Orderly*), Phyllis Frank (*Teacher*), Thomas R. Mustin (*Steve*), Susan Bollman (*Cindy*), Ray Spinka (*Shop Owner*), Hammer (*Gas Station Woman*), Todd Darling (*U-Hauler*), Jon Hofferman (*U-Helper*), Patrick Fahey, Bob Moore (*Policemen*), Hillary Hollingsworth (*Laura*), Aimee Brooks (*Cathy*), Kara Joy (*Janet*), Ivory Berry (*Susan*), Shirley Aldridge (*Mother*), Scott Martin (*Father*).

Since just about every holiday around has been used up by slasher films, SORORITY HOUSE MASSACRE forgoes a festive theme in its title. That doesn't stop writer-director Frank from conjuring up images of HALLOWEEN (the John Carpenter film, not October 31), blatantly ripping off that film's plot, characters and camera style with unashamed abandon. The skimpy story line follows O'Neill, a girl in her late teens, who goes off to visit some friends living in a college sorority house. The girl is disturbed by dreams of a mad killer who slaughters a family, then tries to attack a little girl. Meanwhile, over at a nearby insane asylum, trouble is brewing. Russell, one of the longtime residents, is also being plagued with bad dreams. After some scientific mumbo jumbo (it's hard to pad these things out to 74 minutes, isn't it?) Russell manages to escape and starts heading you-know-where. Back at the sorority house, it's learned this abode was the scene of a horrible mass murder years before. Seems a crazed young man murdered his entire family, though a little girl managed to escape and it doesn't take much thought to calculate what this all means. Before long Russell is knocking off sorority sisters and their boy friends left and right. O'Neill, who has finally caught up to what the audience figured out a long time ago, manages to evade the knife-wielding lug time and again. Just like HALLOWEEN's psycho-slasher, Russell seemingly can't be killed, though a well-placed knife to his throat courtesy of O'Neill finally does the trick.

If Frank had tried something that was even borderline original, this might be tolerable. Instead she simply goes through the motions, generating nothing more than a bad Xerox copy of Carpenter's far superior work. There's no suspense, no excitement, just a lot of bloody knives to break up the tedium.

p, Ron Diamond; d&w, Carol Frank; ph, Marc Reshovsky; m, Michael Wetherwax; ed, Jeff Wishengra; art d, Susan Emshwiller; set d, Gene Serdena; makeup, Dennis Curcio.

Horror   **Cas.**   **(PR:O MPAA:R)**

SOUL MAN½   (1986) 101m NW–Balcor/NW c

C. Thomas Howell (*Mark Watson*), Arye Gross (*Gordon Bloomfeld*), Rae Dawn Chong (*Sarah Walker*), James Earl Jones (*Prof. Banks*), Melora Hardin (*Whitney Dunbar*), Leslie Nielsen (*Mr. Dunbar*), James B. Sikking (*Bill Watson*), Max Wright (*Dr. Aronson*), Jeff Altman (*Ray McGrady*), Jonathan [Fudge] Leonard (*George Walker*).

This sometimes amiable comedy is the funny version of BLACK LIKE ME, the true-life book and film about John Howard Griffin, a man who dyed his skin dark so he could learn what it was like to feel and be treated like a black man. Howell and best pal Gross are UCLA seniors who have been accepted to law school at prestigious Harvard. Howell is from an upper-middle-class family and when Sikking, his father, talks the education situation over with his analyst, Wright (a neurotic every bit as wacky as the psychiatrist in THE MEN'S CLUB), they decide it would be better for Sikking's son if the boy had to put himself through Harvard. Howell is desperate to raise the $54,000 needed to finance his education, but can't find any way to obtain the money. Then he hears that a scholarship is available to a needy black student in the Los Angeles area and that it has gone unclaimed. (This plot twist caused a great deal of annoyance in the black community where people felt it suggested that there were no qualified blacks in L.A.) Howell takes some experimental suntan pills and succeeds in darkening his skin enough to be accepted into Harvard on that scholarship, thus beating out Chong, a truly qualified black woman who is also at Harvard while she raises her son alone. Once in school, he persuades everyone that he is black (despite what must be the worst curly wig ever created, plus the fact that he makes no attempt at changing his white speech pattern, and mannerisms). It's never explained why the school didn't bother to verify his records, which would have blown the whistle on the scheme right away. Howell runs into prejudice as two students are always tossing off ''black'' jokes, a running gag that tires very

quickly. Howell meets Chong and falls hard for her. At the same time, nympho-maniac Hardin (who is as WASPish as Diane Keaton in ANNIE HALL) falls for him and thinks that he will be a marvelous lover because he's black and has ''suffered through 400 years of oppression.'' At a funny dinner table sequence where Howell meets Hardin's family, she says that she is more than passingly interested in black men, and ''I happen to *love* civil rights.'' Howell feels awful when he realizes that he took the scholarship away from the deserving Chong, who must now struggle to keep her grades up while working to pay for her schooling as well as to support her son. In the end, Howell is unmasked. His parents find out what he's doing and Chong learns he isn't really black. Howell apologizes to his John Houseman-like law professor Jones (who is as stentorian as he can be, almost mimicking himself). Jones says the school won't press any charges and Howell promises to donate money to a black law-student's fund. There are some good moments, as when Howell betrays his white inability for athletics when they want him to play basketball. Gross steals the picture. He has the best lines and makes the most of them, especially in a scene before a student tribunal where he defends Howell. Ronald Reagan, Jr., the ballet dancer-turned-TV commentator does a small bit in the film as a white-bread athlete, thus insuring that the first family would see the movie and give it ''thumbs up.'' Many other people also saw this movie, and it scored at the box office, then in video release. It was marginally better than WATERMELON MAN (which had a reverse story of a white bigot waking up black one day), but it might have been terrific if the makers hadn't opted for some cliched characters and the easy way out of the racial problems. The picture was denounced by the Black American Law Students Association at UCLA and rankled the L.A. Chapter of the NAACP, among others. But they may have overreacted because it never does worse than mildly poke fun.

p, Steve Tisch; d, Steve Miner; w, Carol Black; ph, Jeffrey Jur; m, Tom Scott; ed, David Finfer; prod d, Gregg Fonseca.

Comedy   **Cas.**   **(PR:C MPAA:PG-13)**

SPACECAMP   (1986) 107m ABC/FOX c

Kate Capshaw (*Andie*), Lea Thompson (*Kathryn*), Kelly Preston (*Tish*), Larry B. Scott (*Rudy*), Leaf Phoenix (*Max*), Tate Donovan (*Kevin*), Tom Skerritt (*Zach*), Barry Primus (*Brennan*), Terry O'Quinn (*Launch Director*), Mitchell Anderson (*Banning*), T. Scott Coffey (*Gardener*), Daryl Roach (*NASA No. 1*), Peter Scranton (*NASA No. 2*), Rocky Krakoff (*Boy on Rooftop*), Hollye Rebecca Suggs (*Young Andie*), Terry White (*NASA No. 3*), Susan Becton (*Senior Counselor*), D. Ben Casey (*Rudy's Father*), Kathy Hanson (*Girl*), Ron Harris (*Tom the Technician*), Scott Holcomb (*Hideo Takamini*), Kevin Gage (*Counselor No. 2*), Saundra McGuire (*Rudy's Mother*), Bill Phillips (*Kathryn's Father*), Jon Steigman (*Bully in Dorm*), Adrian Wells (*Rudy's Brother*); Frank Welker (*Voice*).

SPACECAMP, an adventure story of a teacher and her teenaged students who get launched into space, had a double stigma which hung ominously over its summer release. The first was the January 28 explosion of the space shuttle Challenger, in which the entire crew, including Christa McAuliffe, a civilian teacher, were tragically killed. The national mourning following the tragedy was deeply felt by many, and an escapist fantasy about an accidental shuttle launch couldn't have hit the theaters at a worse time. SPACECAMP's second significant problem was more elementary: it's not a very good movie. Plagued by cliched characters, ridiculous situations, and a bombastic John Williams score, SPACE-CAMP failed to attract an audience and quickly disappeared from theaters before its eventual reemergence on videocassette. SpaceCamp is a real-life independently run organization where young people learn the fundamentals of operating outer-space hardware. Though not affiliated directly with NASA, the two organizations work together and astronauts regularly take part in the teaching programs (interestingly, camp enrollment increased significantly following the Challenger explosion).

In this fictionalized version, Skerritt is a former space jockey who now runs the institution. His wife Capshaw, while waiting for her turn to ride the shuttle, is set to teach a new group of campers, an assignment she accepts with some reluctance. Capshaw has good reason to feel this way, for her assigned throng is nothing more than a composite group of teenage movie ''types.'' Thompson is the determined girl who wants to be an astronaut; Preston is a bejeweled blonde whose airhead demeanor belies her intelligence; Scott is a would-be scientist, but

more importantly serves as the group's token minority; Donovan is the bored pretty boy, more interested in Thompson than anything else; and Phoenix is the obnoxious runt who spouts STAR WARS' jargon like a running faucet. Phoenix also befriends a hopelessly cute robot (what kid-science fiction adventure is

complete without one of those?) which ultimately results in a good deal of trouble. After going through a series of drills, Capshaw and her kids are selected to sit aboard an actual space shuttle while its rockets are being tested. The robot (appropriately named "Jinx") decides to fulfill Phoenix's dreams of flying in space by tapping into NASA computers and arranging for the shuttle to launch. Jinx's tinkerings go exactly as planned, sending Capshaw and company into space. Considering the psychological ramifications involved, the group handles the accidental launching quite well. Because their radio is only equipped for short-range communication, the hardy bunch must figure out on their own how to return to Earth. Realizing they don't have much air left, Capshaw and kids head off to a yet-unfinished space station to pick up some additional oxygen. Capshaw dons a space suit and jet pack, then zips out after the spare air. When she proves to be a bit too large to reach the oxygen tanks, Phoenix is pressed into service. He's fitted into a space suit, then encouraged with a healthy dose of Luke Skywalkerisms as he makes his way to Capshaw. When Phoenix goes flying out of control, Capshaw rescues him and brings the plucky lad back to the shuttle. Of course he repays this favor when Capshaw has an accident with an oxygen tank and is knocked unconscious. With their fearless leader now out of the picture, it's up to the kids to bring home the bird. They naturally have to face a few imbroglios before landing, but the kids take on these hurdles without much trouble. Their landing is letter-perfect, proving once more there's nothing like American teenage know-how or contrived Hollywood screenplays to beat back a crisis.

If NASA's official policies are even closely approximated by SPACECAMP, then it's no wonder Cape Canaveral has had such a myriad of problems with their equipment in the wake of the Challenger tragedy. The film presents an amazingly high number of stupidities which we are asked to accept as NASA's standard operating procedure. Jinx, the mischievous R2D2 clone, is allowed free run within high security areas, yet no one thinks twice about the potential damage this talking hardware might cause. Furthermore, would NASA authorities really allow a group of green kids in a rocket while its engines are firing? These are two of the film's most contrived elements, yet the story would be nowhere without them. It doesn't get any better once the kids are in space. There's hardly a moment of panic as the group proves time and again that apparently it's easier to fly a space shuttle than to take a drivers' ed course. Most important, everyone Learns Something About Him or Herself, which was SpaceCamp's ultimate goal to start with. It's hardly a new theme, and all the stock shuttle footage or good looking special effects proffered can't disguise SPACECAMP's tired treatment of the well-worn ideas. Winer, making his directorial debut, injects a good deal of implied excitement within his scenes by having the kids encourage each other, but he can't escape one undeniable fact: realistic space travel is pretty dull. This was

accurately captured in Stanley Kubrick's 2001: A SPACE ODYSSEY and Philip Kaufman's THE RIGHT STUFF, but Winer directs like he's in the middle of a George Lucas extravaganza. Of course John Williams' music, as subtle as the composer's STAR WARS score, adds to that feeling (which undoubtedly was the intent). But this isn't STAR WARS, it's not even FLASH GORDON. SPACE-CAMP is just a conglomeration of overworked notions, coupled with a wholly unmemorable ensemble.

Marketing SPACECAMP proved to be a dicey task. Just how do you sell a film about a shuttle accident when the real-life events are still fresh in everyone's minds? SPACECAMP completed production in November of 1985, but the Challenger explosion two months later put the film's release on hold. A number of release dates were tossed around, including Christmas of 1986 and summer of 1987. Ultimately SPACECAMP hit theaters in June of 1986. There was also talk about dedicating SPACECAMP to the late Challenger crew, but Leonard Goldberg, the film's executive producer, vehemently turned down this suggestion. "I felt terrible about Challenger and the crew," he said, "but this is not a film about them. I felt it could easily be interpreted as exploitative, and I didn't want any part of it." A fine stance, to be certain, but the film's advertising campaign wasn't exactly above reproach. SPACECAMP's television commercials prominently featured a scene in which one young actor screams "we're going to explode!" moments before the gang is launched into space. The exploitative connection was blatantly obvious and these poorly conceived commercials were quickly withdrawn.

p, Patrick Bailey, Walter Coblenz; d, Harry Winer; w, W. W. Wicket, Casey T. Mitchell (based on a story by Patrick Bailey and Larry B. Williams); ph, William Fraker (Panavision, MGM color); m, John Williams; ed, John W. Wheeler, Timothy Board; prod d, Richard MacDonald; art d, Richard J. Lawrence, Leon Harris; set d, Richard C. Goddard; cos, Patricia Norris; spec eff, Chuck Gaspar; makeup, Zoltan, Katalin Elek.

Drama   **Cas.**   **(PR:A MPAA:PG)**

SPERIAMO CHE SIA FEMMINA   (SEE: LET'S HOPE IT'S A GIRL, 1986, It.)

SPIKER*   (1986) 104m Seymour Borde c

Patrick Houser, Kristi Ferrell, Jo McDonnel, Natasha Shneider, Stephan Burns, Christopher Allport, Michael Parks, Ken Michelman, Eric Matthew, Philip Mogul, Jan Ivan Dorin, Tim R. Ryan, Mark Hesse, Sandy-Alexander Champion, Doug Beal.

NORTH DALLAS FORTY looked at the tainted world of professional football; then came THE NATURAL with its story of a baseball player who struggles against corruption and his own inner demons to emerge victorious. Now comes SPIKER, which takes an unflinching look at the world of men's volleyball, and it's a hard-fought battle for any viewer to stay awake for the duration. Parks is the tough-as-nails coach who molds a group of green kids into a lean, mean Olympic volleyball playin' machine. Along the way come a few personal crises amidst the teammates, and some matches against foreign opponents, but to no real surprise SPIKER never amounts to anything substantial. Unlike other sports films, there's no climactic Big Game, just a lot of repetition as potential team members come and go. Cast includes members of the U.S. National Volleyball Team.

p&d, Roger Tilton; w, Marlene Matthews (based on a story by Roger Tilton, Marlene Matthews); ph, Robert A. Sherry; m, Jeff Barry; ed, Richard S. Brummer.

Sports   **(PR:C-O MPAA:R)**

SPIRITS OF THE AIR†   (1986, Aus.) Meaningful Eye Contact c

Michael Lake, Melissa Davis.

A religious fanatic and her disabled brother live in a small, run-down house in the desert.

p, Andrew McPhail; d, Alexander Proyas; w, Alexander Proyas, Peter Smalley; ph, David Knus.

Comedy   **(PR:NR MPAA:NR)**

SPOSERO SIMON LE BON†   (1986, It.) Numero Uno c (Trans: I'll Marry Simon Le Bon)

Barbara Blanc, Federica Izzo, Francesca Florio, Luca Lionello, Gianmarco Tognazzi, Saverio Tani, Anita Bartolucci, Gabriele Tozzi, Ezio Marano, Isabella Guidotti

The adolescent adventures of three Italian high school girls, two of whom worship Simon Le Bon, lead singer for the rock group Duran Duran. Eventually they settle down to start their adult lives, though one girl persists in calling her fiance "Simon."

d, Carlo Cotti; w, Cesare Frugoni, Francesco Massaro, Dino Tedesco, Lello Gurrado (based on a book by Clizia Gurrado); ph, Beppe Maccari (Telecolor); m, The Group's Power; ed, Raimondo Crociani.

Comedy   **(PR:C MPAA:NR)**

SPRING SYMPHONY½   (1986, W.Ger./E.Ger.) 103m Allianz-Peter Schamoni-ZDF-DEFA/Greentree c (FRUHLINGSSINFONIE)

Nastassja Kinski *(Clara Wieck)*, Herbert Gronemeyer *(Robert Schumann)*, Rolf Hoppe *(Friedrich Wieck)*, Anja-Christine Preussler *(Clara as a Child)*, Edda

Seippel *(Schumann's Mother)*, Andre Heller *(Felix Mendelssohn)*, Gidon Kremer *(Nicolo Paganini)* Bernhard Wicki *(Baron von Fricken)*, Sonja Tuchmann *(Baroness von Fricken)*, Margit Geissler *(Christerl)*, Uwe Muller *(Becker)*, Gunter Kraa *(Karl Banck)*, Inge Marschall *(Clemenza Wieck)*, Helmut Oskamp *(Alwien Wieck)*, Wolfgang Greese *(Presiding Judge)*, Gesa Thoma *(Nanni)*, Kitty Mattern *(Princess Starnitz)*, Walter Schuster *(Professor Fischhof)*, Peter Schamoni *(Publisher Hartel)*, H.G. Rohrig *(Music Director Dorn)*, Friedrich W. Bauschulte *(Fraternity Brother)*, Gert Holtenau *(Attorney)*, Marie Colbin *(Parisian Lady)*, Hanna Freitag, Ursula Gerstel *(Chamber Maids)*, Jochen Bott, H.H. Hochmann *(Innkeepers)*, Sylvio Michael Heufelder *(Von der Luhe)*, Hans-Eberhard Gabel *(Fencing Master)*.

This is a film with a fatally reverent tone about the love affair between famed composer Robert Schumann and Clara Wieck, one of the most highly-praised pianists of her day and later Schumann's wife and a major interpreter of his

compositions. The picture is set in Germany during the early 1800's. It begins with the teenage virtuoso Schumann, played with calculated intensity by Gronemeyer, being taken under the wing of piano instructor Hoppe. Besides training Gronemeyer, Hoppe also sets rigorous exercises and practice schedules for his prepubescent daughter Clara, played by the pretty young Preussler. Having determined that his daughter will someday be the greatest of pianists, Hoppe is neurotically possessive of her. He rarely lets her alone, pays no attention to teaching her any worldly knowledge, sleeps in the same bed with her, and even bathes her. Having little contact with others, Preussler comes to idolize Gronemeyer. As Clara (now played by Kinski) grows into a young woman of 16, Gronemeyer is attracted, to her. Most of her time is spent traveling with her father to recitals throughout Europe. She earns the praise of everyone from Goethe to Mendelssohn to Paganini to Chopin. Meanwhile, Gronemeyer, who has partially crippled his hands due to overly strenuous rehearsals, spends his days composing brilliant works that conservative music critics fail to appreciate. As Kinski gains more and more attention as a virtuoso, she regularly includes Gronemeyer's compositions in her repertoire, incurring the wrath of her father who is becoming intensely jealous of Gronemeyer's presence. Gronemeyer declares his love for Kinski by writing the "Spring Symphony" (Symphony No.1 in B flat, Op. 38) for her. Kinski and Gronemeyer finally decide to wed, but Hoppe refuses to give his permission. The case is taken to court where Hoppe questions Schumann's sanity, making accusations that mental health problems run in his family. Character witnesses support Schumann, however, and the judge rules for the marriage. The film ends with their wedding, though a cryptic narration track continues over a few photographs of the real Schumann and Wieck. We are told that Wieck gave birth to eight children, that Schumann died at age 46 in a mental asylum (justifying Hoppe's accusations), and that Wieck outlived her husband by 40 years. The narrator fails to mention that Wieck also went on to be the greatest interpreter of Johannes Brahms' works, as well as his companion until her death. While the romance between Schumann and Wieck is especially interesting and intense, Schamoni's direction is less-than-inspired. While this sort of reverence may please most classical music devotees who will hunt this film out, it does not make a very interesting picture. One never gets from the film the creative sparks and flashes of genius that must have existed in the characters' lives. As a result, SPRING SYMPHONY is as staid and conventional as the music of the day that Schumann and his progressive contemporaries were fighting. Kinski, as exotic and radiant as always, brings a touch of authenticity to her character—in some scenes appearing as innocent and victimized as she did in TESS (1980), while at other times (usually when behind the piano) appearing as possessed as her father Klaus Kinski in FITZCARRALDO (1982). One of the chief problems with SPRING SYMPHONY is the scale and complexity of its subject. Schamoni is telling the story of not just one musical genius, but of two—a task which overwhelms the script and direction, touching on both of the characters' lives but never getting inside either of them. Unfortunately, because of time restrictions, Schamoni can only include so much, though watching the film one feels that he's included nothing, at least nothing that provides any insight. For example, the real conflict that surrounded Wieck—that of being a woman in the male-oriented music world—never really surfaces in the film. Her struggle is best understood in an excerpt from her diary, dated 1839: "I once thought that I possessed creative talent, but I have given up on this idea; a woman must not desire to compose—not one has been able to do it, and why should I expect to? It would be arro-

gance, although, indeed, my father led me into it in earlier days.'' Music includes portions of the music of Robert Schumann and Niccolo Paganini, interpreted by a number of accomplished performers—Babette Hierholzer, Dietrich Fischer-Dieskau, Wilhelm Kempf, Gidon Kremer, Ivo Pogorelich, Manfred Rosenberg, the Berliner Hymnentafel, the Staatskapelle Dresden, Wolfgang Sawallisch. Released in Berlin in 1983 and London in 1984, though it did not achieve a wide release in the US until 1986. Dubbed into English.

d&w, Peter Schamoni; ph, Gerard Vandenberg (Fujicolor); m, Robert Schumann; ed, Elfie Tillack; art d, Alfred Hirschmeier; set d, Alfred Hirschmeier; cos, Christiane Dorst, Elisabeth Schewe; makeup, Viktor Leitenbauer, Henriette Schorgmeyer.

Musical Biography   Cas.   **(PR:A-C MPAA:PG-13)**

SPRINGEN†   (1986, Bel.) 96m Visie c (Trans: Jumping)

Mark Verstaete *(Pieter Paul)*, Herbert Flack *(Axel)*, Ingrid de Vos, Maja van den Broccke, Emy Starr.

At a rest home for wealthy and eccentric senior citizens, patients are given the unique opportunity to live out fantasies or events from their pasts. One individual wins a court case he actually lost years before, another enjoys a safari hunt, a third has a triumphant moment on stage, and one person even witnesses global nuclear destruction. (In Flemish.)

p, Roland Verhavert; d, Jean-Pierre de Decker; w, Jean-Pierre de Decker, Stijn Coninx, Fernand Auwera (based on a novel by Fernand Auwera); ph, Michel van Laer; m, Dirk Brosse; ed, Ludo Troch.

Comedy   **(PR:O MPAA:NR)**

SQUADRA SELVAGGIA†   (1986, It.) Euramerica International/Gel International c (Trans: Wild Team)

Antonio Sabato, Ivan Rassimov, Werner Pochath, Julia Fursich, Sal Borgese, Gabriella Giogelli, Gustavo Adolfo Matos, Franco Fantasia, Diego Verdegiglio, Geoffrey Copleston, Andrea Aureli, Duccio Dugoni, Dante Fioretti, Giovanni Gargano, Alex Serra, Ghezzi Pier Luigi.

A crack team of mercenaries is hired to rescue the hostage son of a Latin American leftist leader. The boy is held by the government of the leader's country. They succeed in their mission, but the leftist leader is killed, and the mercenaries take the son out of the country to be a new symbol of freedom for the people. Not shown in the U.S., but certain to turn up in video stores before long.

d, Umberto Lenzi; w, Roberto Leoni; ph, Giancarlo Ferrando; m, Sergio Cipriani; ed, Daniele Alabisio.

Action/Adventure   **(PR:O MPAA:NR)**

SRECNA NOVA '49†   (1986, Yugo.) 130m Vardar–Union–Makedonija-Gradski Kina c (Trans: Happy New Year '49)

Svetozar Cvetkovic *(Dragoslav)*, Meto Jovanovski *(Kosta)*, Vladica Milosavljevic *(Girl)*, Kusko Kostovski *(Inspector)*, Aco Djorcev, Petar Arsovski, Goce Todorovski, Milica Stojanova, Mite Grozdanov, Ivan Bekjarev.

This impressive second feature film from accomplished documentary filmmaker Stole Popov was a multiple winner at the Pula Festival of Yugoslav films, where it collected honors for Best Picture, Screenplay, Music, and Makeup, and shared the award for Best Supporting Player. Set shortly after WW II, SRECNA NOVA '49 contrasts the lives of two brothers with vastly different perspectives toward life. Cvetkovic is a political idealist, who serves a short jail term after being wrongly accused of spying for the Russians. His brother, Jovanovski, is a survivalist and entrepreneur engaged in the black market. This supports the self-fulfilling life style that his family abhors, and for which they disown him. The film concludes with Cvetkovic committing suicide when he discovers his brother and his girl friend Milosavljevic, involved in an affair.

d, Stole Popov; w, Gordan Mihic; ph, Miso Samoilovski; m, Ljupco Konstantinov; ed, Laki Cemcev; art d, Nikola Lazarevski; cos, Jasminka Jesic.

Drama   **(PR:O MPAA:NR)**

STAMMHEIM****   (1986, Ger.) 107m Bioskop-Thalia Theater–Weltvertrieb im Filmverlag der Autoren c

Ulrich Pleitgen *(Presiding Judge)*, Ulrich Tukur *(Andreas Baader)*, Therese Affolter *(Ulrike Meinhof)*, Sabine Wagner *(Gudrun Ensslin)*, Hans Kremer *(Jan-Carl Raspe)*, Peter Danzelsen, Hans Christian Rudolph, Holger Mahlich, Marina Wandruszka *(Defense Attorneys)*, Horst Mendroch, Gunther Flesch *(States Attorneys)*, Fred Hospowsky *(New Presiding Judge)*, Fred Maertens, Matthias Bramberger, *(Public Defenders)*, Hans Michael Rehberg *(Federal Attorney)*, Dominique Horwitz, Gunther Heising, Rainer Philippi, Angela Buddecke, Circe, Michael Schonborn, Eric Schildkraut, Klaus Schreiber, Silvia Fenz, Lothar Rehfeldt *(Witnesses)*, Alexander Duda *(Reporter)*.

The controversial winner of the 1986 Berlin Film Festival's Golden Bear Award, STAMMHEIM is based on the much-publicized Baader-Meinhof terrorist trials that shook the very foundation of Germany from 1975-77. Based on the trial transcripts, the film takes place almost entirely in the Stammheim Prison in Stuttgart, West Germany, as the five defendants—Andreas Baader, Ulrike Meinhof, Gudrun Ensslin, Jan-Carl Raspe, and Holger Meins—are brought before the judge and accused of the murder of four U.S. servicemen in a terrorist bombing attack. After a hunger strike at the trial's start, Meins dies. The next to die is Meinhof, an apparent suicide. As the trial stretches on Baader, Ensslin, and Raspe continuously disrupt the proceedings with accusations that they are being purposely undernourished and spied upon. The trial proceeds at the most tense of levels—Baader and his defending lawyers refusing to abide by the rules of German law, while the prosecution struggles to retain a sense of order. Many months into the trial, the presiding judge is removed, defense attorneys and prosecutors come and go, witnesses appear to tell their stories, and Baader, Ensslin, and Raspe waver in their nearly unfaltering resistance. On April 7, 1977, the chief prosecutor is murdered. On April 28, 1977, the three terrorists are sentenced to life imprisonment. Before long, Baader, Raspe, and Ensslin are found dead in their prison cells—suicides according to the German government, murder victims according to left-wing supporters.

Although STAMMHEIM is set almost entirely in a courtroom and based on court transcripts, it is as far from what one might expect. Rather than having the order and rigidity of a trial, the film explodes with the dynamics of the verbal battle between the defendants and the prosecutors. More than just a courtroom drama, STAMMHEIM is an examination of human nature and what happens to people when they refuse to buckle to the pressure of their oppressors. Whether or not the Baader-Meinhof group was guilty is not important to the film. What is important is to watch the accused fight against a political and judicial system that they believe is wrong. Not surprisingly, this film split as many opinions as the trial itself did. At a press screening at the Zoo Palast Theater in Berlin, a squad of riot police was brought into the lobby because of fears that demonstrators would incite a riot. When the film was awarded the Golden Bear, festival judge Gina Lollobrigida, who was outspoken in her dislike for the film, refused to acknowledge it during the awards ceremony. STAMMHEIM was produced without any subsidies from German television, which is usually very liberal with its financial support. Much of the funding came from the Thalia Theater ensemble, which put the film together as a labor of love—providing the money, the actors, and shooting on an extremely low-budget in a Hamburg warehouse. Also released this year was THE JOURNEY (DIE REISE), a Swiss-German coproduction based on a book by Berward Vesper, the husband of Gudrun Ensslin. (In German; English subtitles.)

p, Eberhard Junkersdorf, Jurgen Flimm; d, Reinhard Hauff; w, Stefan Aust; ph, Frank Bruhne, Gunter Wulff; m, Marcel Wengler; ed, Heidi Handorf; set d, Dieter Flimm.

Docu-drama (PR:C MPAA:NR)

STAND BY ME*½ (1986) 87m COL c

Wil Wheaton (*Gordie Lachance*), River Phoenix (*Chris Chambers*), Corey Feldman (*Teddy Duchamp*), Jerry O'Connell (*Vern Tessio*), Richard Dreyfuss (*The Writer*), Kiefer Sutherland (*Ace Merrill*), Casey Siemaszko (*Billy Tessio*), Gary Riley (*Charlie Hogan*), Bradley Gregg (*Eyeball Chambers*), Jason Oliver (*Vince Desjardins*), Marshall Bell (*Mr. Lachance*), Frances Lee McCain (*Mrs. Lachance*), Bruce Kirby (*Mr. Quidacioluo*), William Bronder (*Milo Pressman*), Scott Beach (*Mayor Grundy*), John Cusack (*Denny Lachance*), Madeleine Swift (*Waitress*), Popeye (*Chopper*), Geanette Bobst (*Mayor's Wife*), Art Burke (*Principal Wiggins*), Matt Williams (*Bob Cormier*), Andy Lindberg (*Lardass Hogan*), Dick Durock (*Bill Travis*), O.B. Babbs, Charlie Owens (*Lardass Hecklers*), Kenneth Hodges, John Hodges (*Donnelley Twins*), Susan Thorpe (*Fat Lady*), Korey Scott Pollard (*Moke*), Rick Elliott (*Jack Mudgett*), Kent Lutrell (*Ray Brower*), Chance Quinn (*Gordon's Son*), Jason Naylor (*His Friend*).

From the moment we hear the Ben E. King-Mike Stoller-Jerry Lieber hit "Stand By Me," we think we are in for a bath of nostalgia, but we are wrong. This film is a lot more than that. It's a little bit of *Huck Finn*, some of *Penrod and Sam*, a taste of "Leave it to Beaver," with a dash of *The Hardy Boys*. The year is 1959. It's summer and four best friends are spending their time hanging around their tree house, smoking, cursing, and making comments about Annette Funicello's burgeoning bust on "The Mickey Mouse Club." These 12-year-olds mince no words (which gives this movie an R rating, although the swearing is true to life) and there are a few moments when they sound far wiser than their age.

The picture is framed by the reminiscences of Dreyfuss, a writer, the grown-up version of Wheaton. When he hears about a friend's death, he recalls that summer when the boys were all so close. We then plunge into flashback with Dreyfuss narrating. The boys sit in their tree house in Castle Rock, Oregon (population about 1300), talk about life and love, smoke cigarettes, and, in

general, do what boys do. Wheaton is a smart lad. His father, Bell, hates the fact that he pals with the others, calling them "a thief and two feebs"—Wheaton is playing penny-ante poker with Phoenix, a somewhat older, take-charge kind of kid, and Feldman, an erratic boy whose father is in a mental hospital. Feldman adores his dad, nevertheless, and believes the man was a hero at the D-Day landing in WW II. The fourth member of the quartet is pudgy O'Connell, the type of rotund boy who is always forgetting the secret password that allows him entry into the tree house. O'Connell arrives with the news that he knows where there is a dead body. Several days before, a boy disappeared while gathering blueberries in the forest. O'Connell knows where the body is because he heard Siemaszko, his older brother, discussing it with a pal. The body is next to some railroad tracks in the forest. The boy must have been hit by a train as he walked along the tracks. A group of older boys, part of a tough knife-carrying gang, don't want to report the body because they found it while they were out for a spin in a stolen car and if they were questioned, they'd have to tell about the car. The younger boys, knowing the older boys will stay away, think it might be neat if they found the body. They could all be famous, maybe even be mentioned on the radio. They plan to make the 20-mile hike into the forest and reap the rewards. But they first have to lie to their parents about where they will be for the two days they'll be away.

Wheaton is currently disturbed because his older brother, Cusack (seen briefly in flashback) died accidentally a short time before. His father, who adored Cusack, has no hopes for Wheaton, a literary dreamer with none of the athletic ability of his football-playing older brother. The other three boys love to hear Wheaton tell stories and there is a diversionary fantasy scene in which he relates the tale of a grossly obese boy everyone ridiculed. The boy enters a pie-eating contest and deliberately begins throwing up, thus sending everyone at the contest retching. It's a funny and tasteless segment that the very kids who aren't allowed to see this movie because of the R rating would love. Phoenix, who is somewhat more mature than the others, is the closest to being a leader because he has natural smarts, though he doesn't do that well in school. He's the product of a drunken father and has an older brother who has been in trouble with the law, so in the minds of the townsfolk he will walk down the same path. Feldman wears glasses and his twisted ear is a result of having been abused by his psychotic father. Feldman likes living on the edge and does anything he can to show how macho he is. O'Connell (in a wonderful feature debut after years of doing commercials and modeling) is on the nose as the cliched "fat kid" afraid of just about everything.

The boys go off on their search for the body, stopping along the way to talk, getting caught on a long railroad trestle as a train rushes toward them, singing songs, and being rowdy. When they get to the body, they are met there by the older boys, led by mean Sutherland (son of Donald and star of BAY BOY) and it looks as though the older kids will wipe the floor with the younger boys, who want to reveal the location of the body to the public. Before that can happen, one of the young boys produces a gun and the older boys have to back off in the face of superior firepower. The picture ends as the boys make their way back to town and part, planning to meet the following day. Dreyfuss is seen at his word processor polishing off the final words of his story before going out to play with his kids. The words he writes are "I never had any friends later on like the ones I had when I was 12. Jesus, does anyone?"

Based on the short story "The Body," which appeared in Stephen King's collection "Different Seasons," the movie represented a reunion for director Reiner and Dreyfuss. Both were instrumental in starting an improvisational troupe in Los Angeles when they were barely out of high school. The excellent adaptation was written by the same two men who did the unheralded STARMAN. The picture was shot in Oregon and on Mount Shasta in California for about $8 million, making it a small film by the current Hollywood standard. STAND BY ME utilized many songs to help evoke the era. They include: "Rockin' Robin" (Jimmie Thomas, performed by Bobby Day) "Lollipop" (Bev-

erly Ross, Julius Dixon, performed by The Chordettes), "Book of Love" (War-
ren Davis, George Malone, Charles Patrick, performed by The Monotones),
"Mr. Lee" (Laura Webb, Jannie Pought, Emma Ruth Pought, Helen Gathers,
Heather Dixon, performed by The Bobbettes), "Sorry (I Ran All the Way
Home)" (H. Giosasi, A. Zwirn), "Have Gun Will Travel" (B. Herrmann),
"Whispering Bells" (Fred Lowry, C.E. Quick, performed by The Del Vikings),
"Let the Good Times Roll" (Leonard Lee, performed by Shirley and Lee),
"Great Balls of Fire" (Otis Blackwell, Jack Hammer, performed by Jerry Lee
Lewis), "Get A Job" (The Silhouettes, performed by The Silhouettes), "Every-
day" (N. Petty, C. Hardin, performed by Buddy Holly), "Come Go with Me"
(C.E. Quick, performed by The Del Vikings), "Come Softly to Me" (Gretchen
Christopher, Gary Troxel, Barbara Ellis, performed by The Fleetwoods), "Hush-
A-Bye" (Doc Pomus, Mort Shuman, performed by The Mystics) "Yakety Yak"
(Jerry Lieber, Mike Stoller, performed by The Coasters). STAND BY ME is a
lovely movie that should have been rated PG or PG-13 so the kids it was about
could have seen it.

p, Andrew Scheinman, Bruce A. Evans, Raynold Gideon; d, Rob Reiner; w,
Raynold Gideon, Bruce A. Evans (based on the novella *The Body* by Stephen
King); ph, Thomas Del Ruth (Panavision, Technicolor); m, Jack Nitzsche; ed,
Robert Leighton; md, Celest Ray; prod d, Dennis Washington; set d, Richard
MacKenzie; cos, Sue Moore; spec eff, Richard L. Thompson, Henry Millar;
makeup, Monty Westmore; stunts, Rick Barker.

Comedy   **Cas.**   **(PR:C   MPAA:R)**

STAR CRYSTAL*½   (1986) 92m Star Crystal-Eric Woster/New World c

C. Jutson Campbell, Faye Bolt, John Smith, Taylor Kingsley, Marcia Linn, Eric
Moseng, Lance Bruckner, Thomas William, Don Kingsley, Robert Allen, Emily
Longstreth, Lisa Goulian, Charles Linza, Frank Alexander.

A "routine" expedition to Mars picks up a strange rock that breaks open back at
the ship, sprouting a slimy creature that soon grows big enough to turn off
everybody's air supply one night. Some time later the derelict ship is recovered
and brought to a space station. A crew of two men and three women is aboard
the infested shuttlecraft when a defective generator in the space station goes
haywire, about to explode. The shuttle crew blast off and get away before the
station blows up, then settle in for a long, 18-month voyage back to Earth. Soon
the creature becomes active again and within minutes kills two of the women and
one of the men, leaving behind shriveled (but not very real looking) corpses and
lots of slime. The survivors huddle in the control room and watch tapes of the
wiped-out expedition to study their adversary. They learn that it uses a crystal as
a combination power source and computer, and they soon realize that it can also
access their own computer. The creature is using the computer to research the
New Testament, so when the film's hero goes after it for a showdown, the
creature uses telekinetic powers to pin him to the wall. He also uses it on the
surviving female crew member when she sneaks up behind him with a knife. The
creature later begins to speak, telling them his name is Gar, and everyone becomes friends. Since Gar needs the spaceship to get back home (even though he'd
been buried in the Martian soil for 300,000 years), he'll just drop them off at a
supply depot to catch another shuttle heading towards Earth. The other shuttle
never shows, though (maybe it was destroyed in a meteor storm earlier), and soon
they realize that the spaceship is their only means of survival. Gar tells them he
will stay behind and attempt to use the crystal to convert the supply depot ship to
get him home, but he doesn't seem optimistic. He waves a sad goodbye as the
ship departs.

STAR CRYSTAL is mostly a rip-off of ALIEN, with some overtones from
E.T. tossed in. The film does benefit from good special effects, but the story is
badly constructed—killing off two complete sets of characters before finally
settling on the shuttle refugees, then killing off the better part of them in a few
moments, leaving us with two people whose lips never seem to match the words
they're speaking. Presumably the two leads are played by Campbell and Bolt, but
the film's credits never identify any characters. Though hardly innovative, at least
the film is innocuous.

p, Eric Woster; d&w, Lance Lindsay (based on a story by Eric Woster, Lance
Lindsay); ph, Robert Carameco; m, Doug Katsaros; ed, Eric Woster; prod d,
Steve Sardanis; set d, Jay Burkhart; cos, Mary Ann Bozer; spec eff, Lewis
Abernathy, Chuck Comisky, Ken Diaz, Eric Woster; makeup, Lou Lazzara,
Blake Shephard, Kathy Tessalone.

Science Fiction   **Cas.**   **(PR:O   MPAA:R)**

STAR TREK IV: THE VOYAGE HOME**   (1986) 119m Paramount
                                                            Pictures c

William Shatner *(Capt. James T. Kirk)*, Leonard Nimoy *(Mr. Spock)*, DeForest
Kelley *(Dr. Leonard "Bones" McCoy)*, James Doohan *(Chief Engineer Mont-
gomery "Scotty" Scott)*, George Takei *(Sulu)*, Walter Koenig *(Chekov)*, Nichelle
Nichols *(Commander Uhura)*, Majel Barrett *(Dr. Christine Chapel)*, Jane Wyatt
(Amanda, Spock's Mother), Catherine Hicks *(Dr. Gillian Taylor)*, Mark Lenard
(Sarek), Robin Curtis *(Lt. Saavik)*, Robert Ellenstein *(Fed. Council President)*,
John Schuck *(Klingon Ambassador)*, Brock Peters *(Cartwright)*, Scott DeVenney
(Bob Briggs), Madge Sinclair *(Capt. of the U.S.S. Saratoga)*, Jane Wiedlin
(Trillya).

The fourth STAR TREK is, so far, the best and surely the funniest. The films
have taken in almost a half-billion dollars and show no signs of flagging, if the
quality of this picture is any indication. Of all the STAR TREK movie plots, this
is the silliest. But it is also the most satisfying because we are allowed to laugh,
not in ridicule, but along with the characters who have spanned more than two
decades in America's memory. The film is a triumph of manufacture over design,

because any synopsis could make the plot seem inane. STAR TREK IV is more of
a Save the Whales movie than a science-fiction fantasy. The last time we saw the
crew of the *Enterprise*, Spock had been resurrected, but his fabulous mind had
been wiped clean of memory. The *Enterprise* had been destroyed, and the crew
was alive but downtrodden.

As the story begins, the crew is coming home aboard a Klingon ship to face a
variety of charges. They have been accused by Schuck, the representative of the
Klingons, of destroying property, mutiny, and other assorted crimes. Schuck

wants them extradited to Klingon for having killed a character in STAR TREK II.
At the same time, there is an eerie sound coming from space. It's emanating from
a probe that is now in the Earth's area and is creating terrible weather problems.
The crew figures the sound is a duplication of the cry of the humpbacked whale.
But what does it mean? They realize the huge space probe is looking for a whale
to chat with and if the probe doesn't find one, it will destroy Earth and then
move on. By this time, centuries of hunters have murdered all the whales. To save
the world of the 23rd Century the crew must get back to the 20th Century, find a
couple of the sweet-voiced whales, and transport them to the future. (Actually,
the space-probe is little more than a plot device, because at the film's conclusion
the probe disappears just as mysteriously as it arrived.)

The crew arrives in San Francisco, 1986, and conceals the spaceship under a
cloak of invisibility in a local park. By this time, Nimoy is beginning to get his
memory back. He and Shatner go off to find the needed whales. At the same
time, the others try to locate a source of nuclear power so they can whip their
spaceship around the sun with the necessary speed to warp them back to the 23rd
Century. Nobody notices that Shatner is dressed in a space uniform and that
Nimoy is in a long gown. (The film was shot with hidden cameras in San
Francisco, and that city is so used to strange people in weird outfits that the cast
hardly merited a second glance from the local residents.) The crew are assigned
various tasks. One group will hunt for whales. Another will seek gear for their
ship, which was damaged in the boomerang trip around the sun that whisked
them to the 20th Century. Koenig and Takei learn that there are "nuclear wes-
sels" (as Koenig pronounces them) in the harbor, a likely source of enough
plutonium for their power. Naturally, the two are considered spies, and they are
chased by naval security men. Koenig is injured and taken to a hospital under
heavy guard. Kelley, the ship's doctor, sneaks into the area to save his pal's life as
he mumbles about the rudimentary medical techniques the 1986 doctors are
using. Doohan, the ship's Scotsman, is out searching for material with which to
build a whale tank. The rest of the crew members are making what repairs they
can.

Nimoy and Shatner go to the local aquarium where they have learned that a
pair of whales, George and Gracie, reside. The whales are lovingly tended by the
attractive Hicks. She is doing everything she can to keep the whales in captivity,
but the powers in charge feel that they can no longer afford to feed these
magnificent creatures, which are thus about to be released into the open sea.

Hicks fears for their lives because the whales are not accustomed to the ocean and, no doubt, will be hunted by either the Russians or Japanese. As Shatner and Hicks get to know each other, a mild romance begins to form (the romance will probably be continued in the next STAR TREK movie, to be directed by Shatner, as part of his deal with the studio). Against Hicks' wishes, the whales are released and the space people have to go after them. They manage to beam the creatures into the massive space ship just seconds before Soviet harpoons would have killed them. Then it's off for the bumpy voyage around the sun again and back to the 23rd Century. The space probe hears the song of the whales, is satisfied that Earth retains some semblance of civilization, and goes off without destroying the planet. At the conclusion, Shatner and the others do have to face a tribunal, but they are cleared of all charges save Shatner's insubordination. For that, the admiral is demoted to captain—a rank he happily accepts, because he and his crew can now take possession of a new starship, also named *Enterprise*. They gleefully exit together, looking forward to more adventures where no man has ever gone before.

Shatner and Nimoy demonstrate comedic byplay that goes past Hope and Crosby and sometimes into Cheech and Chong. Good verbal jokes emerge from the multi-authored screenplay, but audiences will be aided by prior knowledge of the characters, such as the fact that Spock cannot tell a lie and that Kelley is a grump. However, even if you have never seen a STAR TREK film or TV episode, you should still enjoy the film. Less hardware and more humanity contribute greatly to the overall effect. Nimoy had a doubly difficult job because he needed a two-hour makeup session daily in addition to his chores as director. There are a few technical glitches, but there is no faulting his handling of the actors, practically all of whom have spent at least a third of their careers playing these characters. They've gained some weight, and age is creeping up on them, but the film makes no attempt to keep the actors in a never-never land of perpetual youth. In 1967, actress Jane Wyatt appeared in a segment as Nimoy's human mother. She reprises that role here, much to the delight of the dedicated fans.

The movie cost about $24 million and made a profit in record time as it cleaned up at the box office. The anachronistic jokes are the ones that get the big laughs, just as they did in PEGGY SUE GOT MARRIED and BACK TO THE FUTURE. It's always easy to poke fun using hindsight. The making of the movie was not without some controversy. Majel Barrett, wife of creator Roddenberry, had done a number of scenes as the medical director for the star fleet, but they were mostly cut for the release print, which caused her to complain at a Trekkie convention in the Midwest. There are a few character holes in the picture as well, such as what happened to Vulcan Curtis? She was left behind when the crew went on the voyage home, and no explanation was given as to her fate. David Grober and his Motion Picture Maribe company arranged the scene where Nimoy jumps into the aquarium tank to talk to George and Gracie and find out how they feel about things. Those were not real whales, by the way, but then again, JAWS didn't use a real shark. Oscar-nominated for screenplay, musical score, sound effects, and cinematography, but the picture failed to win in any category.

p, Harve Bennett; d, Leonard Nimoy; w, Harve Bennett, Steve Meerson, Peter Krikes, Nicholas Meyer (based on a story by Leonard Nimoy and Harve Bennett and the TV series created by Gene Roddenberry); ph, Don Peterman (Panavision, Techniclor); m, Leonard Rosenman; ed, Peter E. Berger; prod d, Jack T. Collis; art d, Joe Aubel, Pete Smith; set d, Dan Gluck, James Bayliss, Richard Berger; cos, Robert Fletcher; spec eff, Michael Lanteri.

Fantasy/Science Fiction **(PR:A-C MPAA:PG)**

STEWARDESS SCHOOL zero (1986) 84m Summa Entertainment Group/COL c

Brett Cullen *(Philo Henderson)*, Mary Cadorette *(Kelly Johnson)*, Donald Most *(George Bunkle)*, Sandahl Bergman *(Wanda Polanski)*, Wendie Jo Sperber *(Jolean Winters)*, Judy Landers *(Sugar Dubois)*, Dennis Burkley *("Snake" Pellino)*, Julia Montgomery *(Pimmie Polk)*, Corinne Bohrer *(Cindy Adams)*, Rob Paulsen *(Larry Falkwell)*, William Bogert *(Roger Weidermeyer)*, Sherman Hemsley *(Mr. Buttersworth)*, Vicki Frederick *(Miss Grummet)*, Alan Rosenberg *(Mad Bomber)*, Rod McCary *(Capt. Biff)*, Vito Scotti *(Carl Stromboli)*, Yuliis Ruval *(Beautiful Blonde)*, Earl Boen *(Mr. Adams)*, Toni Sawyer *(Mrs. Adams)*, Joe Dorsey *(Captain)*, Casey Sander *(Dudley)*, John Allen *(Bubba Brock)*, Brooke Bundy *(Mrs. Polk)*, Gloria LeRoy *(Grandma Polk)*, Leslie Huntly *(Allison)*, Pilar Del Rey *(Sarah Stromboli)*, Mark Neely *(FAA Inspector)*, Barbara Whinnery *(Gushy Woman)*, Paul Eiding *(Cab Driver)*, Ruth Manning *(Nurse)*, Paul Barselou *(Dr. Mackie)*, Richard Lineback *(Sgt. Striker)*, Ron Ross *(Stanley Peterson)*, Lenore Woodward *(Poodle Lady)*, Anita Dangler *(Dowager)*, Timothy Hoskins *(Boy)*, Bert Hinchman *("Hip" Man)*, Rowena Balos *("Hip" Woman)*, John O'Leary *(Older Man)*, Paddi Edwards *(Older Woman)*, Larry Grennan *(Kent)*, Felix Nelson *(Judge)*, William O'Connell, Richard Erdman *(Attorneys)*, Tom Ashworth *(Bailiff)*, Justin Lord *(Co-Pilot)*, William Erwin *(Orchestra Conductor)*, Conrad Dunn *(Referee)*, Billy Varga *(Flight Manager)*, Joan Lemmo *(Butch)*, Robert Towers *(Cuddles)*, Dian Gallup, Denise Gallup *(Twins)*, Fran Ryan *(Fainting Lady)*, Marie Denn *(Lady in Elevator)*, Theodore Wilson *(Probation Officer)*, Kathleen O'Haco *(Masked Marvel)*, Linda Lutz *(Laughing Woman)*, Andrew J. Kuehn *(Man at Elevator)*, Carole Kean, Lela Rochon, Lenora Logan *(School Instructors)*, Hartley Silver *(Man in Plane)*, Phyllis Cowan *(Girl at Party)*, Suzanne Dunn, Priscilla Linn *(Stewardesses)*, Paul Bradley *(Butler)*, Cathleen MacIntosh *(Woman in Plane)*, Viola Kates Stimpson *(Blind Lady)*, David Sterago *(Navigator)*, Alexandra Rodzianko *(Student)*.

First POLICE ACADEMY ripped off the success of AIRPLANE! by placing a group of zany misfits within the confines of its title institution. The surprising success of that lowbrow cop comedy inspired several look-alike projects, including STEWARDESS SCHOOL, which technically brings the rip-off cycle full circle. STEWARDESS SCHOOL takes a look at some would-be airline attendants who get involved in sky-high hijinx. It's strictly by the-book material, complete with the now-familiar characters and standard formula, told in an unimaginative and thankfully short manner. Cullen is a student at pilots' school who gets thrown out thanks to the antics of his party-animal pal Most. Because Cullen is nearly blind without his glasses, Most suggests they skip flying planes and instead become professional flight attendants. In addition to seeing the world's great cities, Most is convinced that this is the best way to meet good-looking women. They enroll in stewardess school, along with several other equally dubious students. Bergman is a lady wrestler looking for a man; Landers is a prostitute trying to reform; Cadorette is a hapless klutz and Cullen's love interest; and Bohrer is a rich punker sent to school by her parents, who hope she will forget her biker boy friend. Also in this circle of misfits are Sperber, an overweight girl trying to lose some excess pounds; and Polk, a saccharine blonde whose mother and grandmother were both stewardesses. The school is run by a no-nonsense trainer who is determined to break this group, a role that's adequately filled by Frederick. After a variety of exploits and antics (if you stayed awake for POLICE ACADEMY you can fill in this part of the synopsis yourself) the students manage to pass the course. Bogert, the school's director, swings a deal to assign this group to Stromboli Airlines, a low-budget air carrier run by Scotti. For their maiden voyage, the group must deal with a group of blind passengers (Sherman Hemsley of the television sitcoms "The Jeffersons" and "Amen" is the most prominent in this band), a psychotic bomber, a drugged passenger, an unknown FAA inspector, as well as Frederick, who is making an on-board judgment of the flight attendants' capabilities. Enter the crises (pilots rendered unconscious, coupled with a bomb blowing a hole in the plane's fuselage) and everyone bands together to save the day. The gang is exonerated of any wrongdoing at a subsequent trial, becoming a group of heroes everyone loves.

So what? STEWARDESS SCHOOL runs down the plot trail like a checklist, making sure each expected scene is in its proper slot while we witness characters go through the required interactions. The usual breast jokes, homophobic jokes, flatulence gags, and cheesecake sexual humor with a new addition to the stew, zany blind people. It's never funny, merely sophomoric and dull. Unlike his costars Henry Winkler and Ron Howard from the popular sitcom "Happy Days," Most shows no talent beyond his time as a TV stooge. The only significant change he has made is changing his billing from "Donny" to the more mature sounding (if not acting) "Donald." The other cast members run through their anticipated motions without much trouble, cheerfully fulfilling their forgettable jobs. Hemsley is appropriately obnoxious, though the jabs taken at blind people are tasteless. Fans of Sam Peckinpah's THE WILD BUNCH will recognize producer Phil Feldman as the man who butchered that classic western on its initial release. Songs include: "Stew School" (Robert Folk, Ken Blancato, performed by Keith Landry), "Sea Cruise" (Huey Smith, performed by Frankie Ford), "Girl on Fire" (Mark Gibbons, Jerry Winn, performed by Magnum), and the finale from Pyotr Ilich Tchaikovsky's "1812 Overture" as performed by the American Chamber Symphony.

p, Phil Feldman; d&w, Ken Blancato; ph, Fred J. Koenekamp (Panavision, DeLuxe color); m, Robert Folk; ed, Lou Lombardo, Kenneth C. Paonessa; prod d, Daniel A. Lomino; set d, Sue Lomino; cos, Wayne Finkleman; spec eff, John Stirber; m/l, Robert Folk, Ken Blancato, Huey Smith, Mark Gibbons, Jerry Winn; makeup, Christina Smith, Bari Dreiband-Burman; stunts, Bill Couch, Jimmy Lynn Davis.

Comedy **Cas.** **(PR:O MPAA:R)**

STILL POINT, THE† (1986, Aus.) 82m Colosimo Film Prod. c

Nadine Garner *(Sarah)*, Lyn Semmler *(Barbara)*, Robin Cuming *(Grandfather)*, Alex Menglet *(Paul)*, Steve Bastoni *(David)*, Kirsty Grant *(Simone)*.

A number of 1986 films dealt with the deaf, most notably CHILDREN OF A LESSER GOD which featured Marlee Matlin's Oscar-winning performance. In this Australian offering, Garner is a deaf 14-year-old girl whose normal pubescent rebellion is intensified by her handicap and her parents' divorce.

p, Rosa Colosimo; d, Barbara Boyd-Anderson; w, Rosa Colosimo, Barbara Boyd-Anderson; ph, Kevin Anderson (Cinevex Color); m, Pierre Pierre; ed, Zbigniew Friederich; art d, Paddy Reardon.

Drama **(PR:C MPAA:NR)**

STONE BOY† (1986, Phil.) Cinex-D'Wonder/F. Puzon Film Enterprises c

Nino Muhlach, Jimi Melendrez, Isabel Rivas, Cecille Castillo.

A cartoon-like fantasy featuring Rocco the Wonder Boy, born of a mortal mother and the god she enchanted. The boy possesses extraordinary strength, which he uses to protect innocent villagers from the devious plotting of a mad scientist bent on creating a super race. The experiments go awry and transform the townspeople into vampire bats. Rocco saves the day, fighting off the deadly representatives of evil, and earning the chance to meet his father.

d, J. Erastheo Navoa; w, Joeben Miraflor; ph, Hermo Santos; m, Ernani Cuenco.

Fantasy/Adventure **(PR:A MPAA:NR)**

STOOGEMANIA* (1986) 83m Thomas Coleman-Michael Rosenblatt/Atlantic c-bw

Josh Mostel *(Howard F. Howard)*, Melanie Chartoff *(Beverly)*, Mark Holton *(Son of Curly)*, Sid Caesar *(Dr. Fixyer Minder)*, Josh Miller *(Young Howard)*, Thom Sharp *(Bob Smoynck)*, Nancy Lenehan *(Connie Smoynck)*, Jeremy Workman *(Smoynck Son)*, Patrick DeSantis *(Moe Jr.)*, Armin Shimerman *(Larry II)*, Paul "Mousie" Garner *(Arcade Owner)*, Victoria Jackson *(Nurse Grabatit)*,

Tony Goodstone *(Mr. Crull)*, Ron House *(Stooge Hills Director)*, Alan Shearman *(Justice of the Peace)*, Harvey Vernon *(Beverly's Dad)*, Gracia Lee *(Beverly's Mom)*, Bill Kirchenbauer *(Gower)*, James Avery *(Gulch)*, Annie Gagen *(Prostitstooge)*, Richard Brestoff *(Indian Doctor)*, Bridget Holloman *(Sexy Nurse)*, Daneen Maniscalco *(Frantic Nurse)*, Terrie M. Robinson *(Dancing Nurse)*, Christoper Metas *(Intern)*, Carmelo Maniscalco *(Orderly)*, Leslie Wilshire *(Bridesmaid)*, Tom Tangen, Neil Jano, Irving Wasserman, Grace Townsend, Jim Geoghan, Mark Major *(Stoogemaniacs)*, Leigh French, Danny Mora, Tracy Newman, Philip Proctor, Wendy Cutler *(Television Voices)*, Wendell Craig *(Announcer)*, The Three Stooges: Moe Howard, Larry Fine, Curly Howard, Shemp Howard.

Consider the Three Stooges. These rough-house comedians (Moe Howard, Larry Fine, and alternately Curly Howard, Shemp Howard, Joe Besser, and Curly-Joe De Rita) made close to 200 shorts between 1934 and 1958, as well as appearing in a few feature films and later inspiring a television cartoon series. They were popular enough to remain steadily employed during their heyday, but the team's 1980s cult following is nothing short of phenomenal. Reruns of their old shorts remain a staple for many television stations, while such Stooge memorabilia as books, videotapes, and even Moe Howard's canceled checks, have earned a respectable dollar for marketeers. It was inevitable that some filmmaker would try to cash in on the insatiable fans of the Stooges, and that's exactly what STOOGEMANIA attempts to do. Mostel (son of the late Zero Mostel) is a self-admitted Stooge freak, who is obsessed with the antics of Moe, Larry, and Curly/Shemp. He sees the Stooges everywhere he goes, a handy excuse to work in numerous clips from Stooges shorts. This obsession gets Mostel fired from his job, and in trouble with the parents of his fiancee, Chartoff. In hopes of breaking his Stooge obsession, Mostel goes to Caesar, a doctor specializing in such cases. Caesar (doing a variation on one of his old "Show of Shows" characters) gives Mostel a heavy dose of sedatives, which knocks Mostel out when he meets Chartoff and her parents (Vernon and Lee) for lunch. Vernon dismisses Mostel as "too silly," but Chartoff decides to elope with her beloved. They go to a justice of the peace, but the wedding degenerates into slapstick mayhem as Mostel goes through another Stooge hallucination. Eventually Mostel ends up on "Stooge Row," a ghetto inhabited largely by die-hard Stooge freaks (inexplicably, there's also a Harpo Marx impersonator hanging around, pure sacrilege to any Marx Brothers fan). The inhabitants dress like Stooges, reenact Stooge routines, and sink deeper into Stooge oblivion. Mostel seems to have hit rock bottom when suddenly a van comes to pick up the Stooge Row denizens. The hapless comedy fanatics are taken to "Stooge Hills," a sort of Betty Ford Center for diehard Stoogemaniacs. There residents learn hammers are not for hitting people in the head, nutcrackers are not to be used on someone's nose, and there is a strict policy of no "nyucking." When graduation ceremonies are held for the reformed Stoogeaholics, all appears well until a Three Stooges short is shown on the video monitor. Rather than prove everyone cured, the film triggers a mass relapse and the place is reduced to a pie-throwing frenzy. Mostel is back to his old habits but Chartoff doesn't care. She and her beloved are finally married in a wedding attended by all the Stoogemaniacs.

Criticizing STOOGEMANIA for its low-brow humor would be, to say the least, a foolish notion. This is the very element that made the team so popular, and while certainly not for every taste, it's what Stooge fans crave. (The film is completely accurate in portraying men as the majority of Stooge fans. It's a well-known fact that males, rather than females, prefer the Three Stooges, thus giving further support to Ashley Montagu's theories on the natural superiority of women.) The Stooge Row and Stooge Hills sequences actually have some clever moments, though the concept probably would have worked better as a 10-minute "Saturday Night Live" sketch. Moronic humor aside, STOOGEMANIA is technically a piece of trash. There are numerous attempts to match STOOGEMANIA's set design with Three Stooges' shorts, then use the old footage to further this film's plot. The matching looks like a bad cut and paste job and, if anything, only goes to show the original Stooge material wasn't all that much to start with. There's also some poorly done colorization of the old films that appears sporadically throughout STOOGEMANIA. The switch from black-and-white Stooges to colorized Stooges doesn't make a whole lot of sense, but then again neither does the film.

These quibbles shouldn't matter to STOOGEMANIA's potential audience, however. After all, they're the ones who made this film possible. The songs, all written by Hummie Mann and Gary Tigerman, include: "Stoogemaniac" (performed by Britt Bacon), "Play the Piano" (performed by Jimmie Woods), "School's Out" (performed by Debbie James), "Stooge Row" (performed by Gary Tigerman). STOOGEMANIA saw a few screenings in 1985, before going on to a more general release in 1986 via the miracle of videocassettes.

p, Chuck Workman, James Ruxin; d, Chuck Workman; w, Jim Geoghan, Chuck Workman; ph, Christopher Tufty (United Color), m, Hummie Mann, Gary Tigerman; ed, Ruxin; art d, Charles D. Tomlinson; set d, Tom Talbert; cos, Joseph Porro, Leslie Wilshire; spec eff, John Keim, Escott O. Norton; m/l, Hummie Mann, Gary Tigerman; makeup, John Maldonado.

Comedy   Cas.   (PR:A   MPAA:PG)

STORIA D'AMORE†   (1987, It.) 109m Pont Royal Film TV/Instituto Luce/Italnoleggio Cinematografico/RAI-3 c (Trans: A Story of Love)

Valeria Golino *(Bruna)*, Bals Roca-Rey *(Sergio)*, Livio Panieri *(Mario)*, Luigi Diberti *(Father)*, Gabriella Giorgelli *(Sergio's Mother)*, Teresa Ricci *(Amalia)*, Franca Scognetti *(Soror Assunta)*, Pierpaolo Benigni *(Giovanni)*, Massimiliano Martoriat *(Marco)*.

Golino plays an 18-year-old girl who has worked cleaning offices since she was 13 years old, a job that requires waking up at 3 o'clock every morning and an extraordinary amount of time riding the bus. Because of these early hours she

makes the acquaintance of Roca-Rey, who soon becomes her live-in lover, only to be replaced when Golino falls in love with the younger Panieri. Because Golino remains fond of Roca-Rey, she moves out of her parents' home so she can set up house with both her male friends in a vacant building. STORIA D'AMORE marks the return to feature film production after an 11-year absence for one-time promising director Francesco Maselli. The film won the Special Grand Jury Award at the Venice International Film Festival, where Golino was honored with the Silver Lion for Best Actress.

p, Carlo Tuzii; d&w, Francesco Maselli; ph, Maurizio Dell'Orco (Luciano Vittori color); m, Giovanna Salviucci Marini; ed, Carla Simoncelli; art d, Marco Dentici; cos, Lina Nerli Taviani.

Drama   (PR:O   MPAA:NR)

STREETS OF GOLD***½   (1986) 95m Roundhouse FOX c

Klaus Maria Brandauer *(Alek Neuman)*, Adrian Pasdar *(Timmy Boyle)*. Wesley Snipes *(Roland Jenkins)*, Angela Molina *(Elena Gitman)*, Elya Baskin *(Klebanov)*, Rainbow Harvest *(Brenda)*, Adam Nathan *(Grisha)*, John Mahoney *(Linehan)*, Jaroslav Stremien *(Malinovsky)*, Dan O'Shea *(Vinnie)*, Mike Beach *(Sonny)*, John McCurry *(Bobby Rainey)*, Jimmy Nickerson *(Suvorov)*, Jeff Ward *(Preston)*, Pete Antico *(Balsamo)*, Dan Nutu *(Semyon)*, Liya Glaz *(Polina)*, Elizbieta Czyzewska *(Mrs. Peshkov)*, Yacov Levitan *(Mr. Peshkov)*, Alexander Yampolsky *(Dimitri)*, David S. Chandler *(Intern)*, Rene Rivera *(Attendant)*, Frances Foster *(Nurse)*, The Hallelujah Orchestra: Lillian Covner, Henry Covner, Shalom Kovnator, Boris Monastrisky, Nathan Isaacson *(Russian Band)*, Bill Cobbs, Gregory Holtz, Sr. *(Dishwashers at Klebenov's)*, Grafton Trew *(Cook at Klebenov's)*, Ramon Rodriguez *(Cook's Helper)*, Paul Davidovsky *(Russian Friend)*, Paul Herman *(Patron at Gennaro's)*, Frank Patton *(Policeman at Tenement)*, John Garcia, Hechter Ubarry, Thomas Mendola *(Neighbors at Tenement)*, Jud Henry Baker, Luther Rucker *(Bouncers at Bootleg Arena)*, Eddie Mustafa Muhammad *(Timmy's Opponent at Trials)*, Kevin Mahon *(Roland's Opponent at Trials)*, Vern De Paul *(Referee at Trials)*, Jack Wilkes *(Policeman at Elena Attack)*, James Babchak *(Medic at Elena Attack)*, Al Bernstein *(ESPN Commentator)*, Gene LeBell *(Referee at Arena)*, Marty Denkin *(Ring Announcer)*, Mike Radner *(Ring Doctor)*.

Sylvester Stallone's 1976 hit ROCKY spawned numerous imitations that quickly became a tired mini-genre of their own. STREETS OF GOLD starts off as a refreshing change from that well-worn formula, but quickly dispenses with originailty in favor of those all-too-familiar cliches. Brandauer is a Soviet Jewish defector living in Brighton Beach. In Russia, Brandauer had been a champion

boxer, but was never allowed to compete in Olympic matches because of Soviet anti-semitism. Now he lives in a boarding house in "Little Odessa" (an area of Brooklyn populated by Russian Jews), works as a dishwasher, and drowns his sorrows in alcohol. One night he attends an illegal boxing match and is surprised by the talents of Snipes, a young black fighter. After the bout, Brandauer deliberately picks a fight with Snipes, then dodges every punch thrown his way. Snipes is unimpressed, but the next day Pasdar, an Irish kid who witnessed the incident, approaches Brandauer. He too is a fighter and, awed by what he has seen, asks the older man to be his coach. Brandauer agrees and puts Pasdar through a rigorous training schedule. Snipes, on learning what Brandauer is capable of, seeks the Russian's help as well, setting off some jealous feelings in Pasdar. Eventually the two come to an understanding, while Brandauer takes a renewed interest in life.

When the Soviet boxing team is scheduled to arrive in town for some exhibition matches, Brandauer arranges for his boys to take part in the bouts. This is not just a chance for Pasdar and Snipes to go against some talented opponents, but it is also a chance for Brandauer to gain some satisfaction from his Soviet coach. A few nights before the fight Snipes is cut during a street fracas and must drop out of the competition. Pasdar, representing both his coach and his friend, goes against a tough Russian fighter and takes a brutal beating. With the encouragement of Brandauer and Snipes, as well as his own determination to succeed, Pasdar makes a stunning comeback in the final round. He beats his Soviet counterpart and stands triumphantly in the ring as Snipes and Brandauer join him.

Brandauer gives a well-rounded portrait of a man on the skids, showing a bitter

edge that is not without sympathy. In the wrong hands, this character could easily have turned into a boring stereotype, but Brandauer is an intelligent and talented individual who avoids the obvious. He was first offered the role in 1982 after his success with MEPHISTO, though he ultimately had to wait four years for STREETS OF GOLD to begin production. Pasdar and Snipes are interesting complements to Brandauer's leadership, and give a lot of heart to their physically exhausting roles. Both Pasdar and Snipes went into rigorous training for their boxing sequences, and their fighting looks like the real thing. Concentrating on the three men, STREETS OF GOLD grows into a mildly absorbing character study and, had the film continued in that direction, it could have been an offbeat sleeper. Instead, the carefully built relationships degenerate into just another ROCKY variation as the climactic fight approaches. The tensions between Pasdar and Snipes are dropped, Brandauer's Soviet coach becomes a handy villain, and what was meant to be an amateur bout turns into a glorious metaphor. Everything falls into place, right down to that old standby, the freeze frame finale.

It's a shame first-time director Roth didn't stick with his own material; the first two-thirds of his film show good promise. Roth accurately captures the flavor of "Little Odessa" and seems genuinely concerned about the bonds between his three protagonists. One underdeveloped relationship involves Molina, Brandauer's Russian landlady. Though she clearly cares about the man, Roth disappointingly leaves their romance unexplored (Molina is probably best remembered for her role in Luis Bunuel's THAT OBSCURE OBJECT OF DESIRE). A touch of jingoism also rears its head toward the closing moments, while the racial conflicts between Pasdar and Snipes are quietly glossed over. By avoiding the complicated issues and going for rudimentary plot elements, Roth ultimately unravels what could have been an entertaining and memorable feature debut. Roth formerly worked as an independent producer, with such varied films as TUNNELVISION, AMERICATHON, THE STONE BOY, BACHELOR PARTY, and OFF BEAT on his resume. The original script, based on a story treatment by Dezso Magyar (a coproducer on STREETS OF GOLD), was penned by Heywood Gould, and was subsequently rewritten by Richard Price. Price's script was next put in the hands of Tom Cole, who turned out the final draft, though all three men received writing credit for their work.

p, Joe Roth, Harry Ufland; d, Joe Roth; w, Heywood Gould, Richard Price, Tom Cole (based on a story by Dezso Magyar); ph, Arthur Albert (Panavision, Deluxe Color); m, Jack Nitzche; ed, Richard Chew; prod d, Marcos Flaksman; art d, Bill Pollock; set d, Victor Kempster; cos, Jeffrey Kurland; ch, Jimmy Nickerson; makeup, Katie Bihr; tech adv, Emile Griffith.

Drama/Sports   Cas.   (PR:C MPAA:R)

STRIPPER*½   (1986) 90m FOX c

Janette Boyd *(Herself)*, Sara Costa *(Herself)*, Kimberly Holcomb *(Danyel,* Loree Menton *(Mouse)*, Lisa Suarez *(Gio)*, Ellen Claire McSweeney *(Shakti Om)*, Jamal Rofeh *(Club Owner)*.

A phony documentary of dubious intentions, STRIPPER gives its audience all the titillation of a cheap strip show without making any attempt to explore the characters it films. It pretends to show a random sampling of strippers (all of whom are strippers in real life, one of the few authentic aspects of the film), but there is clearly a director's hand behind the camera, pulling all the strings. Scenes are re-created for the camera and, most objectionable of all, so is the entire climactic Las Vegas strip contest. Although some scenes offer insight into the world of stripping, one can hardly trust anything that anyone says. How can the audience be expected to believe the strippers when we've already been duped about the authenticity of the entire project? Directed by the man who produced the fine documentary PUMPING IRON (which gave the film world its first glimpse of Arnold Schwarzenegger), Jerome Gary should take another look at that film—a real documentary—and stop passing off his exploitation as legitimate.

p, Jerome Gary, Geoff Bartz, Melvyn J. Estrin; d, Jerome Gary; ph, Ed Lachman; m, Buffy Sainte-Marie, Jack Nitzsche; ed, Geoff Bartz, Bob Eisenhardt, Lawrence Silk.

Docu-drama   Cas.   (PR:O MPAA:R)

SUIVEZ MON REGARD†   (1986, Fr.) 80m Protecrea/UGC c (Trans: Follow My Gaze)

Pierre Arditi, Feodor Atkine, Stephane Audran Jean-Pierre Bacri, Christian Barbier, Macha Beranger, Richard Berry, Jean-Pierre Bisson, Jean-Claude Brialy, Patrick Bruel, Jean Carmet, Claude Chabrol, Farid Chopel, Charlelie Couture, Darry Cowl, Gerard Darmon, Michel Duchaussoy, Roger Dumas, Andrea Ferreol, Michel Galabru, Veronique Genest, Hippolyte Girardot, Julie Jezequel, Riton Liebman, Vincent Lindon, Leo Malet, Macha Meril, Roger Mirmont, Tom Novembre, Dominique Pinon, Annette Poivre, Robin Renucci, Mort Shuman, Beth Todd, Patrice Valota, Jacques Weber, Zabou, Jean Curtelin, Joel Santoni, Brigitte Lahaie, Caroline Lang, Charly Chemouni, Jezabel Capri.

A collection of short comedy skits starring many of France's most popular actors and directors, this is the first film directed by Curtelin, who wrote the script for 1985's L'ADDITION. Besides Curtelin, the players include director Claude Chabrol; his wife, Stephan Audran; Brialy; Darmon and Pinon (the murderous duo from 1981's DIVA); and Lang, one of the stars of Robert Bresson's 1984 masterpiece L'ARGENT.

p, Dagmar Meyniel; d&w, Jean Curtelin; ph, Michel Cenet; m, Tom Novembre, Charlelie Couture; ed, Martine Barraque.

Comedy   (PR:NR MPAA:NR)

SUMMER*½   (1986, Fr.) 98m Films du Losange/Orion Classics c (LE RAYON VERT; GB: THE GREEN RAY)

Marie Riviere *(Delphine)*, Lisa Heredia *(Manuella)*, Beatrice Romand *(Beatrice)*, Rosette *(Francoise)*, Eric Hamm, *(Edouard)*, Vincent Gauthier *(Jacques)*, Carita *(Lena)*, Joel Comarlot *(Joel)*, Amira Chemakhi, Sylvia Richez, Basile Gervaise, Virginie Gervaise, Rene Hernandez, Dominique Riviere, Claude Jullien, Alaric Jullien, Laetitia Riviere, Isabelle Riviere, Marcello Pezzutto, Irene Skobline, Gerard Quere, Brigitte Poulain, Gerard Leleu, Liliane Leleu, Vanessa Leleu, Huger Foote, Maria Couto-Palos, Isa Bonnet, Yves Doyhamboure, Dr. Friedrich Gunther Christlein, Paulette Christlein, Marc Vivas.

SUMMER is the fifth in Rohmer's series of "Comedies and Proverbs" which began in 1981 with THE AVIATOR'S WIFE, both films starring the lovely Riviere. Having grown into her early twenties, Riviere has been made a lead actress for Rohmer, who likes to use the same "family" of actors in each of his films. It's August in Paris—the time when Parisians go on holiday and leave their city to the throngs of tourists. Riviere, however, can't find anywhere to go. She has been squeezed out of a planned trip to Greece when her girl friend decides to go with her new boy friend. Depressed, lonely, and loveless, Riviere is determined to take her vacation before the start of her fall semester at college. Her friend Rosette invites her to Cherbourg with her family, but she feels like an outsider and returns to Paris. Embarrassed at being in Paris during the tourist season, she looks for another way out. She tries a former lover's mountain resort, but that is no good either. She then accepts a friend's invitation to stay in her vacated Biarritz apartment. It is here, on the beach, that Riviere meets Carita, a voluptuous blonde girl from Sweden. Carita makes every effort to pull Riviere from her sad mood. Riviere and Carita, however, are complete opposites. Where Carita wants to roam the beach, topless and in search of any handsome man, Riviere wears a one-piece swimsuit and has no intention of picking up a one-night stand. Riviere wants romantic love or nothing at all. Later, in a train station, Riviere meets Gauthier, a dark-haired handsome man, to whom she becomes attracted. They stay together in the coastal town of Saint Jean-de-Luz. While strolling along one afternoon, Riviere overhears a conversation about Jules Verne's novel *Le Rayon Vert* (the film's French title) and how that title relates to a meteorological phenomenon (known in the U.S. as "a flash of green") which occurs when the sun sets on the horizon line. At the very moment the sun passes out of sight, a burst of green light bends across the horizon. According to Verne's legend, whoever witnesses this occurrence gains the power of supreme insight into his own emotions, as well as the emotions of the people who are with him. Riviere and Gauthier sit down along the seashore and watch anxiously as the sun goes down. As Riviere sees the "green ray" she gasps in astonishment and her hand innocently covers her mouth—her search for a truly passionate love has ended, at least for that summer.

Rohmer, since his rise to prominence in the late 1950's as a director in the critic-based French New Wave, has consistently delivered small but wonderful episodes of romantic Parisian love which cost very little to produce and always find an enthusiastic following. Although he has been often criticized for being "talky" and "tedious," these charges reveal more about the reviewer's dramatic expectations and intellectual limitations than they do about Rohmer. Rather than filming events or spectacles, Rohmer films people—usually lovelorn Parisians on a stubborn quest. In one of Rohmer's best-known films, 1971's CLAIRE'S KNEE, the male protagonist is literally driven by his romanticized desire to touch the knee of a pretty young woman named Claire. In 1982's LE BEAU MARIAGE, a young student (Romand, who appears in both SUMMER and CLAIRE'S KNEE, as well) decides she wants to be married, picks out a suitable "husband," and then becomes a victim of her own determination. In SUMMER, Riviere is equally determined—determined not to be stuck in Paris, determined to take her vacation, and determined to find a lover who will bring her happiness, even if her determination makes her unhappy. Discussing the director's intentions, Riviere explains, "He had seen some women alone on the beach on holiday and he noticed sometimes that women were looking for men in newspaper advertisements. He wanted to explore this loneliness of young women who are not ugly, who have nothing wrong with them, but who are still alone." Filming with his typically small crew and shooting on 16mm film (a process less expensive and more intimate than the standard 35mm), Rohmer continues to make extremely low-budget films that perform exceedingly well on the art-house circuit. Paying less attention to the technical polish evident in his previous film, FULL MOON IN PARIS, and relying more on improvisational acting, Rohmer has, in SUMMER, made one of his most refreshing and natural films to date. The film was awarded the Golden Lion at the Venice Film Festival, although the French Cesars mysteriously overlooked it in all categories. (In French; English subtitles.)

p, Margaret Menegoz; d&w, Eric Rohmer; ph, Sophie Maintigneux; m, Jean-Louis Valero; ed, Maria-Luisa Garcia.

Drama   **(PR:O MPAA:R)**

SUMMER AT GRANDPA'S, A†   (1986, Taiwan) 102m Marble Road c
                                      (TUNG-TUNG-TE-CHIA-CH'I)

Koo Chuen *(Grandpa)*, Mei Fong *(Grandma)*, Wang Chi-kwang *(Tung-Tung)*, Shu Cheng-lee *(Ting-Ting)*, Lin Hsiao-ling *(Pi-yun)*.

A 12-year-old boy and his little sister are packed off to the country to stay with their grandparents when their mother grows ill. They adapt to the country life, watching turtles, swimming in the waterhole, and looking for a lost cow. Successful on the international festival circuit, the film had only a brief run in Taiwan. (In Hokkien, Taiwanese, and Mandarin; English subtitles.)

p, Chang Hwa-kun; d, Hou Hsiao-hsien; w, Chu Tien-wen; ph, Chen Kwen-hou; m, Edward Yang; ed, Liao Ching-song.

Comedy   **(PR:A MPAA:NR)**

SUMMER NIGHT WITH GREEK PROFILE, ALMOND EYES AND SCENT OF BASIL†   (1986, It.) 95m A.M.A.–Leone
                                      Films–Medusa–Reteitalia/Medusa c

Mariangela Melato *(The Signora)*, Michele Placido *(Giuseppe Catania)*, Roberto Herlitzka *(Salvatore Cantalamessa)*, Massimo Wertmuller *(His Assistant)*.

Another political allegory from Wertmuller features Melato (recapitulating much the same role she had in SWEPT AWAY) as a wealthy industrialist fed up with the numerous kidnappings of her kind. She decides to turn the tables by applying the same tactics on Sicilian bandit leader Placido. Her strategy is temporarily successful; the bandits pay the $100,000.00 ransom, but pull one last trick by hijacking Melato's car, which also contains the money. Themes on the relationship between sex and power, common to most Wertmuller films, are dealt with here when Melato becomes the bedmate of a blindfolded Placido. (In Italian; English subtitles.)

p, Gianni Minervini; d&w, Lina Wertmuller; ph, Camillo Bazzoni (Cinecitta Color); m, Lello Greco, Lina Wertmuller; ed, Luigi Zitta; art d, Enrico Job; cos, Valentino.

Comedy/Crime   **(PR:O MPAA:NR)**

SUN ON A HAZY DAY, THE†   (1986, Syria) 90m National Film
                                      Organization c

Rafik El Soubeil *(Old Man)*, Jihad Sahd *(Adil)*, Mouna Wasef *(Prostitute)*, Jada El Charnaa *(Nour)*.

Sahd plays a wealthy adolescent whose affinity for the life of the lower classes eventually leads him to denounce his background. The youth falls in love with prostitute Wasef while learning the "knife dance" from elderly Sobeil. Sahd's father resents the influence Soubeil has upon his son and vents his rage against the old man. Set during Syria's colonial period in the 1930s, THE SUN ON A HAZY DAY is an allegory of that country's stirring desire for independence.

d, Mohamed Chahin; w, Mohamed Chahin, Mohamed Mouri Farouge (based on the novel by Hana Mina); ph, George Houry; m, Soulhi el Wadi; ed, Haithan Kouatili.

Drama   **(PR:O MPAA:NR)**

SUNSET STRIP zero   (1985) 82m Westwind c

Tom Eplin *(Mark Jefferson)*, Cheri Cameron Newell *(Carol Wyatt)*, John Mayall *(Roger Lucas)*, John Smith *(Jake)*, Danny Williams *(John Moran)*, George Derby *(Nick)*, Al Hansen *(Lt. Dole)*, Miles Clayton *(Martin)*, Rita Rogers *(Mrs. Peters)*, Vincent Dark *(Vinnie)*, Jack Fisher *(Lt. Donnegan)*, Lew Hopson *(Cappy)*, Dawn Deegan *(Turquoise)*, Dutch Van Dalsem *(Bud)*, James Wing Woo *(Charlie Wu)*, Dustin Nguyen *(Chinese Youth)*, Danny Wong *(Chinese Man)*, Anne Marie Bledsoe *(Judy)*, Richard Coca *(Jimmy)*, Rene Elizondro *(Rana)*, Mae Asada *(Oriental Woman)*, Shelly Hubbard *(Dancer)*, Liza Cochrell *(Stripper)*, Jeff Jourard *(Band Member)*, David Earle *(Blond Youth)*, Michael Montes *(Street Tough)*.

Technical ineptitude abounds in this bottom-of-the-barrel crime drama about a hotshot photographer, Eplin, who gets mixed up in an underworld of prostitution and gunrunning. The sleazy, neon-lit night life of Hollywood's Sunset Strip—with its prostitutes, sex clubs, and two-bit criminals—serves as the backdrop as club owner Mayall fights to keep the mob from closing his doors for good. Eplin offers to help Mayall by photographing an illegal payoff. Mayall is murdered, and the mob leader thinks that Eplin has some incriminating information. The police think Eplin is guilty of Mayall's murder. With the help of Eplin's former girl friend, Newell, the photographer tries to find out who's really responsible. Eventually the path leads to mob boss Williams, who is trying to use the club as a front to ship arms to South America. A corrupt police detective is involved in the plan. By the finale, the bad guys are dead, and the heroic Eplin and his friends are just fine.

Unconvincing, unrealistic, mindless, pedestrian, and unintentionally funny are just a few of the ways to describe SUNSET STRIP. There isn't the least bit of credibility in the characters; the story is ridiculously far-fetched; the chase scenes

are pathetic; and the special effects are even worse. It's difficult to imagine a film in which all the facets of production are worthless; it's even more difficult to know where to begin criticizing such a film; but it's most difficult to watch it for 82 minutes. If director Webb and his editor understood the concept of "sound synchronization" and the use of a "presence track," then SUNSET STRIP would have been a bit more tolerable. For their benefit, synchronous sound is when the actors move their lips and sound comes out in correspondence with their lip movements. Also for their benefit, a presence track is a constant atmospheric background soundtrack which runs throughout a scene in order to prevent sound drop-out. Other terms that the filmmakers would benefit from understanding are: match cut, continuity, and special effects. Eplin and Newell do what they can with their roles, which isn't much as they've been written so poorly. Williams and his criminal goons are laughable—again, because of the writing more than the acting. Only Mayall, the legendary British blues musician who started the careers of many rock-'n'-roll greats, comes through the film unscathed. He's the only convincing character in the entire picture, thereby making everyone else seem even more one-dimensional. Unfortunately, for the sake of the picture, Mayall's character gets killed within the first 10 minutes. Like a previous effort by the producers, the strung-together CALIFORNIA GIRLS (1984), this picture sat on the shelf for years, never finding a sucker to pick it up for theatrical release. It finally appeared in video stores. Songs include "Sunset Strip" (Elliott Solomon, Rick Thibodeau, Dave Flynn, Ron Cobner, performed by The Edge), "Do What You Can to Survive," "Savin' My Love" (Thibodeau, Solomon, Flynn, performed by The Edge), "Killers" (David Storrs, performed by Storrs, Ice-T), "Party Rock" (Storrs, performed by Storrs), "World Cruise" (Nicki Jones, performed by The Flames), "Somebody Loves You" (Jones, Jeff Jourard, performed by The Flames), "Final Notice" (Jones, Jeff Jourard, performed by The Flames), "Here Comes The Night" (Bobby Bennett, performed by Bennett), "Slave Trader" (Bob Blanajaar, Rob Simpson).

p, William Webb, Monica Webb; d, William Webb; w, William Webb, Brad Munson; ph, Eric Anderson; m, David Storrs, Elliott Solomon, Rick Thibodeau, Robbie Barton, Ron Codner, Mike Egizi; ed, David Schwartz; art d, Riley Morgan; set d, Don Fernandez; m/l, David Storrs, Elliott Solomon, Rick Thibodeau, Robbie Barton, Nicki Jones, Jeff Jourard, Bobby Bennett, Bob Blanajaar, Rob Simpson.

Crime   **Cas.**   **(PR:O MPAA:NR)**

SUNUS PALAIDUNAS†   (1986, USSR) 80m Lietuvos c (Trans: The
                                      Prodigal Son)

Markunas Rimas *(Vilius)*, Petras Vazdiks *(Petras)*, Brone Braskyte *(Liuda)*.

When Rimas, a Lithuanian stone carver, hurts himself in an accident, he goes to live with his older brother Vazdiks. Once Rimas settles in, he finds his values challenged by the well-off Vazdiks. Unlike the always-dreaming artistic sibling, Vazdiks has a good job and material possessions, coupled with a wife, two children, and a mistress.

d&w, Marijonas Giedrys; ph, Jonas Tomasevicius; m, Jusras Sirvimoskas; art d, Algimantas Sirigzda.

Drama   **(PR:C MPAA:NR)**

SUPER CITIZEN†   (1986, Taiwan) 97m Cinema City c

Lin Chih Chyi *(Li Shicheong)*, Chen Bor Jeng *(Rolly)*, Wang Yeu, Su Ming Ming, Lin Shou Ling.

Idealistic young Lin Chih Chyi leaves the security of his country home for the seedier sections of Taipei in search of his sister. He doesn't find her, but his nightly sojourns in the city's hot spots give him an education on the realities of Taipei.

p, Karl Maka, Dean Shek, Raymond Wong, Wang Ying Hsiang; d, Wan Jen; w, Wan Jen, Liao Cheng Song; ph, Lin Horng Jong; m, Li Show Chaun; ed, Liao Cheng Song; art d, Tsai Jen Bin.

Drama   **(PR:O MPAA:NR)**

SUURI ILLUSIONI†   (1986, Fin.) 92m Elokuvatuottajat Oy-Finnish Film
                                      Institute/Finnkino c (Trans: The Grand Illusion)

Pekka Valkeejarvi *(Hart)*, Stina Ekblad *(Caritas)*, Markku Toikka *(Hellas)*, Rea Mauranen *(Madama Spindel)*.

In the 1920s, Helsinki divinity student Valkeejarvi forsakes his studies for the decadence of cabaret life. He becomes involved with the beautiful Ekblad and poet Toikka, creating a threesome obsessed with drinking, sex, and the need for self-enlightenment.

p, Claes Olsson, Matti Penttila; d, Tuija-Maija Niskanen; w, Anja Kauranen (based on the novel by Mika Waltari); ph, Kari Sohlberg (Eastmancolor); m, Kaija Saariaho; ed, Irma Salmela; prod d, Erkki Saarainen; cos, Sari Salmela.

Drama   **(PR:O MPAA:NR)**

SUSMAN†   (1986, India) Association of Cooperation and Apex Societies of
                                      Handloom c (Trans: The Essence)

Neena Gupta, Om Puri, Shabana Azmi, Kulbusham Kharbanda, Pallavi Joshi, Ravi Jhankal.

This Indian feature, from one of that country's leading directors, chronicles life amidst a family of tie-and-dye weavers. Told in an anecdotal manner, the story revolves around one weaver who has others working under him, while his uncle in turn provides work for him. When the man's wife secretly takes some silk to make their daughter's wedding sari, it causes trouble for the uncle from an important designer. The weaver refuses to take any more work from his uncle, but the wife—who does not let pride stand in her way—takes jobs her husband will not. In the meantime, the daughter grows frustrated by the emptiness she finds in her marriage. Though her husband uses modern technology in his business, their village is still a poor one. The daughter returns to her hometown, only to find worker riots causing untold violence. (In Hindi.)

d, Shyam Benegal; ph, Ashok Mehta; m, Vanraj Bhatia.

Drama (PR:O MPAA:NR)

SVESAS KAISLIBAS† (1986, USSR) 93m Riga c (Trans: Other People's Passions)

Zane Ianchevska (*Marite*), Alguirdas Paulavitchus (*Antanas*), Via Artmane (*Anna*), Vizme Ozolinia (*Ausma*), Leonid Obolensky (*Old Man*).

Shortly after the Soviet government comes into power in Russia, 17-year-old Ianchevska, a poor peasant girl, is sent by her family to work on a Latvian farm. She is appalled by what she finds there and the story is told through her eyes. Paulavitchus is an ambitious farmhand who virtually runs the place, since the head of the house is woefully senile. Paulavitchus is having an affair with Artmane, the farmer's much younger wife, and at the same time wants to marry her daughter Ozolinia. When he discovers Ozolinia is pregnant he dreams of taking over the farm, but his hopes are dashed when she has an abortion.

d&w, Ianas Streitch; ph, Hari Kukels; m, Uldis Stabulnieks; ed, Ianas Streitch; art d, Gunars Balodis.

Drama (PR:O MPAA:NR)

SWEET LIBERTY**½ (1986) 107m UNIV c

Alan Alda (*Michael Burgess*), Michael Caine (*Elliott James*), Bob Hoskins (*Stanley Gould*), Michelle Pfeiffer (*Faith Healy*), Lise Hilboldt (*Gretchen Carlsen*), Lillian Gish (*Cecelia Burgess*), Saul Rubinek (*Bo Hodges*), Lois Chiles (*Leslie*), Linda Thorson (*Grace*), Diane Agostini (*Nurse*), Anthony Alda (*Film Crew Member*), Alvin Alexis (*Male Student*), Christopher Bregman (*Running Boy*), Leo Burmeister (*Hank*), Cynthia Burr (*Asst. Camera*), Timothy Carhart (*Eagleton*), Bryan Clark (*Gov. Swayze*), Bonnie Deroski (*Female Student*), Frank Ferrara (*Lopert*), Michael Flanagan (*Frank Stirling*), Dann Florek (*Jesse*), David Gideon (*Camera Operator*), Katherine Gowan (*TV Interviewer*), Terry Hinz, Kevin McClarnon (*FX Men*), John Leonidas, William Parry (*Teamsters*), Christopher Loomis (*Cinematographer*), John C. McGinley (*Floyd*), Polly Rowles (*Mrs. Delvechio*), Fred Sanders (*Soundman*), Robert Schenkkan (*Pilot*), Larry Shue (*Edson*), Steven Stahl (*Hotel Clerk*), Lynne Thigpen (*Claire*), Richard Whiting (*Johnny Delvechio*), Robert Zarem (*Publicist*).

Movies about the making of movies are a tricky proposition. When they succeed, as in DAY FOR NIGHT, they are a revelation. When they almost succeed, as in

this, they can be a disappointment. Alda, who wrote and directed the picture, plays a somewhat stuffy professor at a small North Carolina college. He is divorced, and having a relationship with fellow teacher Hilboldt, but he is loath to make a serious commitment. Alda's eccentric mother, Gish, lives in the area and thrives on the memory of a long-ago boy friend whom she blames for everything that's happened to her. A movie company has purchased Alda's Revolutionary War novel and descends on the small town to shoot it. The film company is led by director Rubinek, a send-up character resembling any of the *au courant* young filmmakers. Rubinek has his cast, crew, and screenwriter with him, and Alda is shocked to learn that great liberties have been taken with his historically accurate script. Rubinek says that in order to make a commercially successful film in this day and age, one must follow three rules . . . Defy Authority, Destroy Property, and Take People's Clothes Off! Alda meets screenwriter Hoskins (in a superb portrayal based loosely on screenwriter Don Segall, a pal of Alda's who actually read for the part of himself and lost it to Hoskins. Segall worked with Alda on TV's "Four Seasons" series and taped a few of his conversations so Hoskins could listen to the way he spoke and catch the nuances.) Alda helps Hoskins with the script rewrite in an attempt to bring it closer to the novel. Alda also meets Pfeiffer and falls madly in love

with her. They first encounter each other when she is in costume and has totally assumed the character of the woman in the book, going so far as to speak in 18th-Century dialog. Later, when he visits her room and finds her in jeans, smoking a cigarette and berating her agent on the phone in four-letter words, he remarks that she is two people. She smiles and says "If all I could be was two people, I'd be out of business." Caine plays the male lead, a British rake who loves stealing the hearts of American women. He is an actor from the old school, doing his own stunts and living on the edge. Caine drives too fast, drinks too much, and takes a fancy to Chiles, wife of the college president. He goes so far as to steal a helicopter and take her for a spin around the area.

As the first day for shooting approaches, Alda tries to exert some influence. He hangs around, complains, and gets into the director's hair. Too many subplots muddle what could have been a delicious parody of moviemaking. Hilboldt has a brief affair with Caine until the actor's wife shows up, ending Caine's fling. There's a nice scene where the principals go on a roller-coaster ride and then get drunk and waltz down the main street late at night uttering some vague philosophical truths that sound better when one has had a few too many. In the end, Alda gets even with the film company by doing the three things Rubinek said had to be in a film. The actors playing the Revolutionaries take their clothes off during the expensive battle scene, Alda blows up some property, and authority is surely defied.

There are a few moments that ring false to anyone who knows movies. For example, the actors are all amateurs and the chances of them being used in scenes with TNT are slim, especially after the John Landis TWILIGHT ZONE disaster that took the lives of Vic Morrow and two Asian children. Since the studio is attempting to make a teenage sex farce out of Alda's novel, why would they then hire a man as long in the tooth as Caine? Hilboldt is given very little to do, her part being the least defined. Pfeiffer is excellent in the best-defined role as the star who takes a lover on almost every film.

The picture was shot on Long Island at Sag Harbor, which was an actual watering spot for armies in the Revolutionary War. The village of Southhampton was also used and a part of the local hospital was converted to represent the fencing studio for Alda and Hilboldt. Gish, who was in her late 80s when she made the picture, was appearing in her 105th film in a career that spanned more than 7 decades. The shame of the movie is that it could have been terrific, but Alda wore too many hats, and there was nobody to tell him what went wrong. He claims that it took him 2½ years to get this movie made. Perhaps he should have taken 3½. The sexual scenes are mild and subtle, just like Alda's acting.

p, Martin Bregman; d&w, Alan Alda; ph, Frank Tidy (Panavision); m, Bruce Broughton; ed, Michael Economou; prod d, Ben Edwards; art d, Christopher Nowak; set d, John Alan Hicks; cos, Jane Greenwood; m/l, Howie Rice, Allan Rich; makeup, Irving Buchman, Fern Buchner; stunts, Victor Paul.

Comedy (PR:A-C MPAA:PG)

T

TABARANAKATHE†   (1986, India) National Film Development c (Trans: The Story of Tabarana)

Ramomoorthy, Savitramma, C.R. Sinha Vishwanath Rao.

An office clerk for the city government has difficulties in trying to obtain his long-overdue pension. When he takes another job working in a coffee factory, his financial burdens are still not relieved.

p,d&w, Girish Kasaravalli; ph, Madhu Ambat.

Drama   **(PR:C-O MPAA:NR)**

TAGEDIEBE†   (1986, Ger.) 100m Renz–Marcel Gisler Filmprouduktion bw (Trans: Hanging Out)

Dina Leipzig *(Lola)*, Rudolf Nadler *(Max)*, Lutz Deisinger *(Laurids)*, Matthieu Hornung *(Matthieu)*, Marcel Gisler *(Karl)*.

Marcel Gisler's film debut is a slight and plotless study of three young, directionless people who share a Berlin apartment. Leipzig has recently left her small family, Nadler is a self-proclaimed "artist," and Deisinger is a flautist. Each of the threesome deliberately attempts to avoid involved relationships and any form of commitment. Even the flat the three share is only a temporary arrangement. (In German; English subtitles.)

d&w, Marcel Gisler; ph, Rudiger Weiss; m, Marcel Gisler, ed, Catherine Steghens.

Drama   **(PR:O MPAA:NR)**

TAHOUNET AL SAYED FABRE†   (1986, Algeria) 124m ENAPROC c (Trans: Mr. Fabre's Mill)

Jacques Dufilho *(Fabre)*, Ezzat El Allaili *(Ali)*, Sid-Ahmed Agouni *(Captain)*, Abdelmoneim Madbouli *(Party Man)*.

This film centers on events in a poor Algerian village as its inhabitants prepare for a visit from that country's president. Representatives of the federal government insist a giant wall be built to hide the overcrowded slums from the president. But the good-hearted city council members beg that the money be used to build new houses, a stance for which they are promptly sent to prison. TAHOUNET AL SAYED FABRE won the Silver Tanit at the Carthage Film Festival.

d, Ahmed Rachedi; w, Ahmed Rachedi, Commandant Azzeddine, Boukalfa Hamza; ph, Rachid Merabtine; m, Noutil Fadel; ed, Rachid Mazouza.

Drama   **(PR:C MPAA:NR)**

TAI-PAN*   (1986) 127m DEG c

Bryan Brown *(Dirk Struan/"Tai-Pan")*, Joan Chen *(May-May)*, John Stanton *(Brock)*, Tim Guinee *(Culum)*, Bill Leadbitter *(Gorth)*, Russell Wong *(Gordon)*, Katy Behean *(Mary)*, Kyra Sedgwick *(Tess)*, Janine Turner *(Shevaun)*, Norman Rodway, *(Quance)*, John Bennett *(Orlov)*, Derrick Branche *(Vargas)*, Chang Cheng *(Jin Qua)*, Patrick Ryecart *(Capt. Glessing)*, Nicholas Gecks *(Horatio)*, Carol Gillies *(Mrs. Brock)*, Michael C. Gwynne *(Cooper)*, Bert Remsen *(Tillman)*, Barbara Keogh *(Mrs. Quance)*, Lisa Lu *(Ah Gip)*, Rosemary Dunham *(Mrs. Fotheringill)*, Robert Easton *(Zergeyev)*, Zhang Jie *(Lin)*, Rob Spendlove *(Nagrek)*, Chen Shu *(Chen Sheng)*, Kwang Pan *(Kwang Kuo)*, Chan Lub Bun *(Elderly Chinese Woman)*, Chan Koon Tai *(Wung)*, Richard Foo *(Lin Din)*, Siu Kam *(Executioner)*, Job Stewart *(Dr. Gonzales)*, Jovita Adrineda *(Servant Girl)*, Patty Toy *(Poxed Whore)*, Joycelyne Lew *(Beaten Whore)*, Denise Kellogg *(Nude Model)*, Charles Woods, Pat Gorman, Bob Appleby, Ian Sheridan, Mac Wheater *(British Merchants)*, Leslie Peterkin *(Piper)*, Vic Armstrong, *(Drunken Sailor)*, Dickey Beer, Billy Horrigan, Bronco McLoughlin *(Brock's Crew)*.

With the rise of television miniseries, epic filmmaking seems to have switched from three-hour big-screen productions to ten-hour extravaganzas designed specifically for the video tube. In a sense, this is a better way to unfold a story, as the additional length allows for proper coverage of multiple characters over several years. Granted, most miniseries are barely worth their usually overblown treatment, but in theory the marriage of epic and television is a good one. This story of Hong Kong's development as a trading port is simply too complex for a film that runs just over two hours. With its myriad players, numerous subplots, and broad time span, TAI-PAN quickly degenerates into a confusing, often ludicrous drama.

Brown plays Dirk Struan, a robust Scotsman who runs a trading fleet along Chinese ports. Dubbed "Tai-Pan" by all who know him, Brown is forced to leave when the local officials are fed up with his use of opium as a tool for bribes. Brown heads off to a rocky island called Hong Kong, where he intends to build his own port. Meanwhile, and there's a lot of that going on here), his Chinese mistress Chen is in lots of trouble with her people for sleeping with a white man. Brown's son Guinee suddenly arrives from Scotland, announcing that the rest of the family have all dropped dead from plague. Brown is also having some troubles with Stanton, a cruel rival whose brutish son Leadbitter has a penchant for beating prostitutes. Adding to these interfamily squabbles is Sedgwick, Stanton's daughter, who falls in love with Guinee. Then there's Behean, a minister's daughter who sleeps with elderly Chinese men for fun and profit. And what

about Turner, the American Southern belle whose primary function is to wear low-cut gowns and make Chen jealous? Rodway is an expatriate British artist who now stays in a brothel, wears a cute beard, and does nude studies of the whores with whom he lives. Somewhere in between these subplots, Stanton tries unsuccessfully to drive Brown out of business, Chen has a miscarriage, and Hong Kong turns from a rocky shore to a thriving city in a matter of seconds. There's also a costume ball, some jealousy and sleeping around, and a few fisticuffs. Finally Brown and Stanton duke it out in the middle of a hurricane. A lot of the major characters get killed, Guinee takes his father's position as Tai-Pan, and 150 years later Hong Kong has lots of glass and steel buildings. The end. Really.

Go on, just try to keep track of all the plot lines. TAI-PAN's slam-bang pacing is impossible to follow, so if you insist on seeing the film, have fun with the dialog. Chen's mispronunciations and misuse of the English language rival the permutations created by Leo Gorcey in his Bowery Boys comedies. Occidentals don't fare any better. Their lines are full of flowery words that push through the outside of the stupidity envelope. On finding Behean in a tryst with her Chinese lover, the astonished Brown exclaims: "This is not the Mary Sinclair I know!" For his part, Brown plays the material with the utmost seriousness, plowing valiantly through the plot twists while rarely changing his facial expression. Chen is beautiful and often removes her top, but that's about it. She's not much of an actress, though this native-born Chinese won her country's equivalent of an Oscar for her work in the film LITTLE FLOWER. Stanton and Leadbitter are appropriately brutish, though their performances aren't what you'd call subtle. But then, there's no room for that foolish notion in TAI-PAN: everything is Big. More than 3000 costumes are used by the huge cast of extras, the set design is authentic, and when a head gets chopped off you don't miss a lick. But Duke's direction, for all the film's bluster, is surprisingly bland. He knows how to photograph goodlooking sets and can stage an effective fight scene, but there's not much passion in these events. TAI-PAN simply runs pell-mell through the complications, and though it's only two hours and seven minutes long, it feels like sitting through a ten-hour miniseries in one stretch. This was the first American production to be filmed in China, made with the cooperation of government authorities. Despite this unique feature, there's nothing in TAI-PAN's look that distinguishes China from any other area. Believe it or not, according to publicity material, the production actually engaged a Chinese astrologer to pick the best day to begin shooting. In addition to choosing this all-important day, the sage advisor exclaimed: " . . . money will come in abundance and safety will be guaranteed." Perhaps the wizened old man looked at the wrong stars that day, for TAI-PAN proved to be a financial disaster. Shot on a $25 million budget, the American box-office receipts garnered a scant return.

p, Raffaella De Laurentiis; d, Daryl Duke; w, John Briley, Stanley Mann (based on the novel by James Clavell); ph, Jack Cardiff (J-D-C Widescreen, Technicolor); m, Maurice Jarre; ed, Antony Gibbs; md, Maurice Jarre; prod d, Tony

Masters; art d, Benjamin Fernandez, Pierluigi Basile; set d, Giorgio Desideri; cos, John Bloomfield, Edward Percival; spec eff, Kit West; makeup, Giannetto De Rossi; stunts, Vic Armstrong.

Historical/Drama   **Cas.**   **(PR:O MPAA:R)**

TAKE IT EASY†   (1986, Den.) 103m Crone-Danish Film Institute/
                                            Metronome c

Nikolaj Egelund *(Herbert)*, Martin Elley *(Allan)*, Maurice Weddington *(U.S. Army Captain)*, Eddie Skoller *(Leo Mathisen)*, Mek Pek Falk *(Erik Parker)*, Kasper Winding *(Erik "Spjat" Kragh)*, Jesper Thilo *(Henry Hagemann)*, Gert Rostock *(Carlo Jensen)*, Helle Hertz *(Herbert's Mother)*, Tommy Kentner *(Victor)*, Nadia Klovedal Reich *(Anita)*, Jeanne Boel *(Blonde)*, Louise Frevert *(Bitten)*, Masja Dessau *(Miss Andersson)*, Stig Hoffmeyer *(Greengrocer)*, Ole Ernst *(Vedel)*.

In the immediate aftermath of WW II in Denmark, a group of youths become peripherally involved in the black market. Their goal is to get close to their hero, boogie-woogie piano player Skoller, who performs in a dive frequented by U.S. and British soldiers. Director Hom based the film closely on his own experiences as a devotee of Danish jazz pianist Leo Mathisen, whose records still sell big in Copenhagen.

p, Nina Crone; d&w, Jesper Hom; ph, Peter Klitgaard (Agfacolor); m, Leo Mathisen; ed, Anders Refn; prod d, Soren Krag Sorensen; md, Kenny Drew, Kasper Winding; cos, Evelyn Olsson.

Drama/Comedy   **(PR:O MPAA:NR)**

TAMPOPO*½   (1986, Jap.) 114m Itami c (Trans: Dandelion)

Ken Watanabe, Tsutomu Yamazaki, Nobuko Miyamoto, Koji Yakusho, Rikiya Yasuoka, Kinzo Sakura, Shuji Otaki.

A hilarious comedy from Japan that concerns itself exclusively with food. The film begins in a movie theater where we (the viewing audience) sit looking at the audience in the film. In walks a suave-looking yakuza (gangster) dressed in white accompanied by his girl friend and an entourage of goons. The gangster and his girl sit in the front row, while the henchman set up a table and fill it with delectable food-stuffs. As the gangster munches on a morsel, he suddenly notices us (the viewing audience) watching him. He leans forward (into the camera) and asks "What are you eating?" The gangster then tells us of his hatred of talking and noise in movie theaters—especially people who crinkle wrappers and eat too loudly. Of course, a man sitting behind him is eating too noisily, and the gangster angrily threatens to kill the confused man if he continues. The gangster then sits down to enjoy the show, urging us to do the same. After this prologue, TAMPOPO proper begins. The film is basically a string of comic vignettes concerning food and its consumption. The story centers on a heroic truck driver and his sidekick as they teach a young widow named Tampopo how to improve her noodle shop business. The trucker is drawn to this hapless woman who can barely keep her business afloat. He takes pity on her young son who gets regularly beaten-up everyday after school. The truck driver quickly wins the widow's confidence and then assembles a group of men expert in everything from soup stock to redecoration to help her become the best noodle-seller in town (shades of THE SEVEN SAMURAI here). But TAMPOPO is the kind of film that drifts away from its main characters to follow the lives of some interesting people who happen to wander by in the background. One hilarious vignette shows an elderly noodle master teaching his eager young charge the zen way to eat noodles. Another portrays a junior executive besting his stodgy peers by being able to read French in a fancy restaurant. He knowledgeably orders fine cuisine after all his superiors have ordered exactly what the boss had ignorantly selected. A third take deals with a crazed old woman who gets her kicks by squeezing food in the supermarket. In addition, the gangster from the opening scene uses food in a variety of imaginative ways during a love-making session with his girl.
    TAMPOPO is a wonderfully funny and creative film that provides a cornucopia of comical characters in absurd situations. These loony elements combine to offer some perceptive observations about humans and their joy, fear, and passion for food. This is the second feature from director Itami. He had previously taken on Japanese burial rites in his first film, THE FUNERAL (1984). TAMPOPO satirizes filmmaking with references to THE SEVEN SAMURAI, American westerns, Steven Spielberg, and Japanese yakuza films, while owing a heavy debt to Luis Bunuel's films for its basic structure. In his first two films, Itami has moved to the forefront of irreverent young directors who have put a comedic spotlight on Japanese institutions. His work follows in the tradition of satirizing the family in Sogo Ishii's THE CRAZY FAMILY and the news media in Yojiro Takita's COMIC MAGAZINE. All these filmmakers have discovered some very funny and disturbing truths about Japanese life.

p, Yasushi Tamaoki, Seigo Hosogoe; d&w, Juzo Itami; ph, Masaki Tamura; m, Kunihiko Murai; ed, Akira Suzuki; art d, Takeo Kimura.

Comedy   **(PR:C-O MPAA:NR)**

TAROT†   (1986, Ger.) 115m Moana-Anthea/AAA Classic c

Vera Tschechowa *(Charlotte)*, Hanns Zischler *(Edouard)*, Rudiger Vogler *(Otto)*, Katharina Bohm *(Ottilie)*, William Berger *(Mittler)*, Kerstin Eiblmaier, Martin Kern, Peter Moland, George Tabori.

Having its basis in the Goethe's provocative novel *Die Wahlverwandtschaten*, TAROT is an emotionless exercise in intellectual discourse. A film director, his actress fiancee, their writer friend, and a student with musical aspirations gather at the forest home of the director, where they pose existential questions regarding personal desires, the individual's relation to society, and the immortality of the

human soul. Zischler, a prominent German film critic, and Vogler previously appeared together in Wim Wenders' 1976 film KINGS OF THE ROAD. Fittingly introduced into this film is a clip from Eric Rohmer's FULL MOON IN PARIS (1984). (In German; English subtitles.)

p, Hans Brockman; d, Rudolph Thome; w, Hans Zihlmann (based on the novel *Die Wahlverwandtschaten* by Johann Wolfgang von Goethe); ph, Martin Schafer; m, Christoph Oliver; ed, Dorte Volz; art d, Anamarie Michnevich; cos, Gioia Raspe.

Drama   **(PR:A MPAA:NR)**

TAXI BOY†   (1986, Fr.) 93m President-UGC-TF1-Marie
                                        Coline-Cinedeal-Conil/UGC c

Claude Brasseur *(Petrus)*, Richard Berry *(Manuel)*, Charlotte Valandrey *(Corrine)*, Evelyne Didi *(Marthe)*, Isaach de Bankole *(Toure)*, Alex Descas *(Pascal)*, Marie-Christine Darah *(Martine)*, Raymond Jourdan *(Miguel)*, Alain Floret *(Henri)*.

A debut feature from screenwriter Paige which stars Berry as a Parisian taxi driver and taxi dancer who has high hopes of opening a tango school. Also dreaming of a way out of his unwanted life style is Brasseur, a gambler who is being hounded by some card players he cheated. Rounding out the leading players is Valandrey (who, in 1985, made a spectacular debut in RED KISS), the teenage daughter of Brasseur who returns to her father after a long absence. The film's technical advisor is Luc Besson, the director of the Cesar-winning 1985 film SUBWAY.

p, Alain Depardieu; d&w, Alain Paige; ph, Renato Berta (Panavision, Fujicolor); m, Charlelie Couture; ed, Sophie Schmitt; art d, Jean-Pierre Kohut-Svelko; tech adv, Luc Besson.

Drama   **(PR:NR MPAA:NR)**

TE AMO†   (1986, Arg.) c (Trans: I Love You)

Ulises Dumont, Betiana Blum, Pepe Soriano.

A young girl goes through the usual teenage troubles.

d, Eduardo Calcagno.

Drama   **(PR:NR MPAA:NR)**

TELEPHONE CALLS, THE†   (1986, Iran) Center for the Propagation of
                                                    Islamic Thoughts and Arts c

Mohammad Kassebi, Reza Cheraghi.

d, Mohammad-Reza Honarmand; w, Mohsen Makhmalbaf; ph, Homayun Paivar; m, Ali Gholamali; ed, Manoochehr Oliai.

TENEMENT†   (1986) 91m Laurel/Shapiro Entertainment c (AKA: GAME
                                        OF SURVIVAL)

Joe Linn *(Sam Washington)*, Paul Caldron *(Hector)*, Corrine Chateau *(Carol)*, Mina Bern Bonas *(Ruth)*.

Roberta Findlay has long been active in exploitation filmmaking, producing, along with her husband Michael (later decapitated in a bizarre helicopter accident atop the Pan Am Building in New York), one of the most successful frauds in the history of cinema, SNUFF, a film alleged to have a real murder recorded as its finale. It was obviously a fake job, but that didn't stop it from garnering incredible publicity and making a sizeable profit. After years of obscurity, toiling in the pornographic ghetto, Findlay is back with this violent film about a vicious gang that besieges an apartment building to gain revenge against the residents who earlier called the police on them.

p, Walter E. Sear; d, Roberta Findlay; w, Joel Bender, Rick Marx; ph, Roberta Findlay; m, Walter E. Sear, William Fischer; ed, Walter E. Sear.

Crime/Action   **(PR:O MPAA:NR)**

TENUE DE SOIREE   (SEE: MENAGE, 1986, Fr.)

TEO EL PELIRROJO†   (1986, Span.) 94m Penya Amaya c (Trans: Teo the
                                                    Redhead)

Alvaro de Luna *(Teo)*, Juan Diego Botto *(Santiago)*, Maria Luisa San Jose *(Viviana)*, Ovidi Montllor *(Luis)*, Luis Escobar *(Grandfather)*, Concha Leza *(Aunt Maria)*, Sarai Hermosa *(Valeriana)*, Daniel Barros *(Matias)*.

A young boy (Botto) inherits his grandfather's farm when the old man dies, and he gradually comes to idolize the massive foreman (de Luna), who has a way with animals and finds little Botto when he gets lost in the hills. Things turn tragic when de Luna is put in jail for drunkenness and turns vengeful upon his release, killing those responsible.

p, Pedro Roman; d&w, Paco Lucio; ph, Federico Ribes (Eastmancolor); m, Jan Garbarek, Rosita Perrer; ed, Luis Manuel del Valle; prod d, Luis Valles.

Drama   **(PR:C MPAA:NR)**

TERROR Y ENCAJES NEGROS†   (1986, Mex.) 90m Conacite II c (Trans:
                                                            Terror and Black Lace)

Gonzalo Vega, Maribel Guardia, Jaime Moreno, Olivia Collins, Claudia Guzman, Martha Ortiz, Roberto Cobo.

Written and directed by Luis Bunuel's former scriptwriting partner Alcoriza

(LOS OLVIDADOS, THE EXTERMINATING ANGEL), TERROR Y EN-CAJES NEGROS is a claustrophobic horror film set in an apartment building. A seemingly meek resident who plays clarinet with the local chamber ensemble is in reality a hair fetishist who keeps his collection of female locks hidden away in a closet. Meanwhile, in the penthouse apartment lives a jealous man and his wife. This man is so worried that his beautiful bride will be unfaithful that he practically keeps her a prisoner in the apartment. Of course, the frustrated woman eventually sneaks out for a liaison with another man, but when she returns home she stumbles upon the musician trying to dispose of the body of a new victim. The crazed fetishist then goes after the woman, chasing her throughout the apartment building, in an effort to silence her.

d&w, Luis Alcoriza; ph, Xavier Cruz; m, Pedro Placencia; ed, Federico Landero.

Horror/Thriller (PR:O MPAA:NR)

TERRORVISION**½ (1986) 82m Altar/Empire c

Diane Franklin *(Suzy Putterman)*, Gerrit Graham *(Stanley Putterman)*, Mary Woronov *(Raquel Putterman)*, Chad Allen *(Sherman Putterman)*, Jonathan Gries *(O.D.)*, Jennifer Richards *(Medusa)*, Alejandro Rey *(Spiro)*, Bert Remsen *(Grampa)*, Randi Brooks *(Cherry)*, Ian Patrick Williams *(Nulty)*, Sonny Carl Davis *(Norton)*, William Paulson *(Pluthar)*, John Leamer *(Chauffeur)*.

Horror and science-fiction parodies tread on unfirm ground because most of the films they attempt to poke fun at are already jokes themselves, so what audiences continue to be presented with is lame slapstick with their favorite monsters, from

ABBOTT AND COSTELLO MEET FRANKENSTEIN to TRANSYLVANIA 6-5000. Occasionally one manages to be a qualified success, like DARK STAR, YOUNG FRANKENSTEIN, or DEATH RACE 2000, usually by having a greater respect for its subject or by going after some larger target than others of its ilk. Somewhere between these lies TERRORVISION, surely as dumb a monster movie as has come down the pike recently, but it takes potshots at so many easy targets it can't help but hit a few.

The all-American nuclear family endangered here is made up father Graham, mother Woronov, Cyndi Lauper-look-alike daughter Franklin, and son Allen. Also living in the house is Grampa (Remsen) who has his own bunker, espouses lizard tails as a self-regenerating food source for survival, and has Allen as a devoted and well-trained disciple. The perfect consumers, the family buys a Do-It-Yourself 100 satellite dish, but it attracts a strange signal. It seems that on a distant planet, affectionate monsters known as "hungrybeasts" are kept as pets, but sometimes they mutate into voracious, omnivorous threats to all life on the planet. When this happens, the creatures are turned into pure energy and zapped off to the farthest corner of the galaxy. Unfortunately, a freak alignment of planets deflects the signal to Earth (cue for a special-effects shot of a bolt of energy bouncing among a quartet of planets like a cosmic pinball). Now the signal has been caught by the Puttermans dish and it waits inside the TV.

That night the family breaks up to go their separate ways, Franklin on a date with heavy-metal freak Gries, and Graham and Woronov to meet the couple they contacted through classified ads for swingers. Remsen and Allen are left at home to watch horror movies hosted by Medusa (Richards), a provocative, big-breasted woman with a snake wig (clearly modeled on syndicated TV horror hostess Elvira [Cassandra Peterson]). At one point the station starts to go and is replaced by the staring eye of the hungrybeast, and for a moment they think it is another monster movie. They manage to get the set back to Medusa, and both fall asleep on the sofa. The monster comes out of the TV and comes face-to-face with Remsen and Allen. They scream and it scares the monster back into the TV. The two decide that the vision must have been a burglar in a mask, so they go to the bunker and arm themselves to the teeth with M-16s, submachine guns, and grenades. Patrolling the house, they find a satellite dish repairman in the back yard, and after deciding he's no threat, they go back into the house. The monster promptly pops out of the repairman's monitor and devours him, then zaps back into the house to make short work of Remsen.

Allen locks himself in the bunker until his parents return, their swinging partners Rey and Brooks in tow. Allen tries to convince them of the monster's existence, but they don't believe him, locking him in the bunker with the monster, which can grow the heads of people it has eaten to reassure future prey. It isn't long before the monster has killed all four swingers. Allen manages to blast his

way out of the bunker just as sister Franklin and date Gries return. Allen tells them of the monster, but they too don't believe him, especially when they go upstairs and find all four swingers in bed together, telling them they're fine. Gries turns on the TV to a program they keep picking up, which turns out to be Pluthar from the planet Pluton warning them about the hungrybeast and telling them that the only way to save Earth is to destroy all TV sets for the next 200 years. People think that Pluthar's plea is only another movie. The creature appears again and is about to eat Gries when the heavy-metal freak's studded wristband triggers a fond memory of its life as a pet. Before long the three survivors have taught the thing to talk and eat frozen pizzas and watch TV himself (its favorite movie is EARTH VS. THE FLYING SAUCERS). They decide to make a million dollars off the monster, so they call Richards at the TV studio and tell her there's a party in order to lure her over to have a look. Pluthar appears again, warning about the monster, and this sets the creature off again. Gries is the first to go, then the policeman who comes to arrest Allen for making prank phone calls about the monster. Suddenly Pluthar arrives and explains about the hungrybeast. When Allen and Franklin ask about their parents, he is dismayed to learn that it has eaten humans, fearing he'll lose his job over it. The two Earth kids are about to lead the alien to the monster when Richards arrives. She assumes that the alien in a spacesuit with a ray gun must be abducting the kids, so she sneaks up behind him and bops him in the head. His helmet cracks and he yells about losing pressure before his head explodes all over the inside of his helmet. The monster attacks and finishes them all off, the world apparently doomed.

While hardly a cinematic triumph, TERRORVISION does have a lot of good laughs and one of the funniest monsters in memory. The creation took up to a dozen people to operate. The creator, Empire's resident monster maker John Buechler, went to a great deal of trouble to make a creature that could be both cute and dangerous, and he succeeded admirably. Indeed, the monster gives a rather good performance as it insatiably gobbles up everyone in sight. Just as good is Woronov, who has been the best thing in many a bad movie, here doing another variation of the character she played in the hilarious EATING RAOUL. Graham is appropriately sleazy, and Rey has a terrific scene in which he asks Woronov if her husband "is a manly man," then goes on to explain that because he is Greek, he likes boys. It is hard to be upset when these people go into the monster's maw. The failings of the film are its attempt to go after too many targets without the script to carry the effort, and a relentlessly cartoonish style that starts to get tiresome. Filmed in Empire's Italian studios, the film did respectable business during a brief theatrical run before going to its real home, video.

p, Albert Band; d&w, Ted Nicolaou; ph, Romano Albani (Technicolor Roma Color); m, Richard Band; ed, Tom Meshelski; prod d&art d, Giovanni Natalucci; cos, Kathie Clark; spec eff, John Buechler and Mechanical and Makeup Imageries; m/l, The Fibonaccis.

Science Fiction/Comedy Cas. (PR:O MPAA:R)

TERRY ON THE FENCE† (1986, Brit.) 70m Eyeline–Children's Film and Television Foundation/RANK c

Jack McNicholl *(Terry)*, Neville Watson *(Les)*, Tracey Ann-Morris *(Tracey)*, Jeff Ward *(Mick)*, Matthew Barker *(Denis)*, Brian Coyle *(Plastic-Head)*, Susan Jameson *(Mum)*, Martin Fisk *(Dad)*, Margery Mason *(Gran)*.

Mixed-up runaway McNicholl becomes temporarily involved with a tough teen-age gang and its lawless activities before repenting. The emotional changes McNicholl experiences are juxtaposed with those of gangleader Watson, whose crass, hate-filled attitude softens during the course of the film.

p, Frank Godwin, Harold Orton; d&w, Frank Godwin (based on the novel by Bernard Ashley); ph, Ronald Maasz; m, Harry Robinson; ed, Gordon Grimward; prod d, Maurice Fowler; stunts, Alan Stuart.

Children's/Drama (PR:A MPAA:NR)

TEXAS CHAINSAW MASSACRE PART 2, THE zero (1986) 95m Cannon c

Dennis Hopper *(Lt. "Lefty" Enright)*, Caroline Williams *(Vanita "Stretch" Brock)*, Bill Johnson *(Leatherface)*, Jim Siedow *(Drayton Sawyer the Cook)*, Bill Moseley *(Chop-Top)*, Lou Perry *(L.G. McPeters)*, Barry Kinyon *(Mercedes Driver)*, Chris Douridas *(Gunner)*, Kinky Friedman *(Sports Anchor)*, Joe Bob Briggs [John Bloom] *(Gonzo Moviegoer)*, Ken Evert *(Grandpa)*, Tobe Hooper.

1986 was a banner year for director Tobe Hooper—not only did he totally botch an expensive remake of William Cameron Menzies' 1953 science fiction cult-classic INVADERS FROM MARS, but he went on to prove that he couldn't even make a sequel to *his own* 1974 cult-classic THE TEXAS CHAINSAW MASSA-CRE. Hooper's original film has an undeserved reputation as a mindlessly bloody gorefest where chain saws are wielded, madly dismembering cast members. Nothing could be further from the truth. Back in 1974, Hooper understood the power of *implied* violence. He staged the lead-up to the violence so effectively that he did not need nauseating closeups of gore, he let the audience *imagine* it. Apparently Hooper has forgotten everything he ever knew about horror, for this sequel is one long, disgustingly graphic bloodbath with no redeeming value whatever. The problems begin with the script, by the respected L.M. Kit Carson (PARIS, TEXAS), which wasn't finished by the time shooting started. Carson demonstrated that he understood little of what made the first film such a successfully frightening examination of the horror of the American family. Instead, he opted for a bloody "satire" where yuppies would be the fodder for gratuitous special makeup effects (sounds like a "laff riot," right?).

The film opens as a pair of yuppies (actually they're not even yuppies, they're college preppies) zoom through Texas in their new Mercedes Benz, guzzling beer

and shooting road signs while chatting on their car phone to a local female disk jockey, Williams. Suddenly the Mercedes is confronted by a pickup truck which contains three members of the "Sawyer family." As Williams listens in horror on the phone, "Leatherface" (Johnson) makes quick work of the two boys with his

whirring chainsaw. The murders come to the attention of ex-Texas Ranger Hopper (in an awful performance), a man obsessed with the chainsaw killings of the previous film, in which two of the victims were his nephew (a cripple who was murdered by a chainsaw) and his niece (who survived, but is now insane). Hopper contacts the disk jockey and uses her as bait to bring the insane family out of hiding. The family has undergone a few changes since 1974. Dad (played by original cast member Siedow) has started a mobile barbecue business and sells his very special cuts of meat (mostly human) to hungry football fans and state fair devotees. Having abandoned the house from the first film, the family now lives in a maze of tunnels underneath a closed amusement park. Leatherface and Grandpa are still around, so too, after a fashion, is Leatherface's brother, the hitchhiker from the first film. Although he was run over and killed in 1974, his corpse was salvaged, preserved, and turned into a life-sized muppet that is carried around like a rag doll by the third brother, Moseley. Moseley was serving in Vietnam when the events of the first film took place, but he returned with a metal plate in his head and proved to be just as crazy as the rest of the family.

The family members finally take the bait; they destroy the radio station and kidnap Williams. Hopper, who is insane himself, gives chase and traces them to the abandoned amusement park. Arming himself with his own chainsaws—for which he has designed a pair of six-shooter-type holsters—Hopper spends much of the rest of the film wandering around the tunnels screaming for vengeance. Meanwhile, Leatherface has fallen in love with Williams (he demonstrates this in a particularly nauseating manner which is better left undescribed in these pages) and is a bit agitated when the rest of the family subjects her to the exact, excruciatingly long, help-grandpa-hit-her-in-the-head-with-a-hammer dinner table scene from the first film. After what seems like an eternity, Hopper finally stumbles upon the family's living quarters and has a chainsaw duel to the death with Leatherface. Williams escapes and makes it to the surface with Moseley in hot pursuit. The distraught woman manages to seize a chainsaw and dispatch the last member of the family before going insane herself and waving the chainsaw in the air a la Leatherface at the conclusion of the first film.

It is hard to believe that this film was made by the same man who directed the

original. This fiasco was slapped together in a hurry to complete the trio of Hooper films for which Cannon had contracted. Because the first two were big-budget flops (the insufferable LIFEFORCE and the insipid INVADERS FROM MARS), Cannon wasn't real keen on the idea of dropping another bundle on Hooper, so they gave him a small $2.5 million budget (it's all relative; compared to the first film, which was made for $160,000, it's a fortune; compared to what he spent on his two previous films, $25 million and $12 million respectively, it's a paltry sum) and told him that the film had to be in 1800 theaters on August 22— Cannon had presold the booking and Hooper had eight weeks to shoot (Cannon upscaled the investment to a reported $6 million during production). From the concept to the casting, CHAINSAW II was an ill-conceived mess. Although every one of the original cast members was willing to participate in the sequel, all were snubbed except Siedow. Because the profit sharing of the first film was awash in controversy and the original cast members never saw any of the nearly $75 million that the film has grossed over the last 12 years, they took care to demand a bit more than scale for the sequel. This seemed to annoy both Hooper and Cannon, and negotiations with the original cast ceased. Perhaps the most significant addition to the sequel was the participation of gore-effects master Tom Savini. Savini does some terrifically nauseating work here, but it simply doesn't belong. In his haste, Hooper took the easy path and went for out-and-out gore rather than making a carefully constructed horror film that would claw at the mind instead of the gut. The film quickly fell behind schedule and over budget. Reportedly Hooper used three separate camera crews shooting simultaneously, with the cast members and Savini not having a clue as to what was expected of them, because screenwriter Carson was in his hotel room hacking out the script on a day-by-day basis. The film feels as if Hooper himself has nothing but contempt for the original movie and has gone out of his way to tear it down. And therein may lie the clue to this disaster. The 1974 film was Hooper's first feature, and to this date, the best thing he has ever done. He may have gotten himself hooked up with darlings of mainstream genre work like Stephen King (SALEM'S LOT) and Steven Spielberg (POLTERGEIST) in the hope that he would be universally hailed a "master of horror," but to most of the world he's still the guy who directed the infamous THE TEXAS CHAINSAW MASSACRE. Perhaps in his bid for respectability, Hooper began to resent his association with TEXAS CHAINSAW, and decided to bury it forever by finally living up to his undeserved reputation as a gore-freak and rub the mainstream's nose in this bloody, sadistic, disgusting, totally mindless film that would offend everyone, including the fans of the original. Unfortunately, in doing so he may have destroyed his own career, for who in Hollywood would have confidence in a director, with a string of expensive flops behind him, who cannot even handle a sequel to the film on which he made his reputation?

p, Menahem Golan, Yoram Globus; d, Tobe Hooper; w, L.M. Kit Carson; ph, Richard Kooris (TVC Color); m, Tobe Hooper, Jerry Lambert; ed, Alain Jakubowicz; prod d, Cary White; art d, Daniel Miller; set d, Pat Welsome; cos, Carin Hooper; spec eff, Tom Savini.

Horror   Cas.   (PR:O MPAA:NR)

TEYZEM†   (1986, Turkey) Burc c (Trans: My Aunt)

Mujde Ar, Yasar Alptekin, Nevin Aypar, Necati Bilgic.

d, Halit Refig; w, Umit Unal; ph, Ertunc Senkay.

THANATOS†   (1986, Mex.) 92m Gecisa International/Peliculas Mexicanas c

Nuria Bages (Alejandra), Ricardo Sanchez de la Barquera (Viches), Gabriela Araujo (Norma), Alejandro Rabago (Captain).

After losing his job, a television personality makes a deal with the devil in this Mexican variation on the Faust legend.

p, Maria Luisa Medina Pulido, Cristian Gonzalez, Pia Ana Corti; d, Cristian Gonzalez; w, Cristian Gonzalez, Juan Carlos Martin; ph, J. C. Martin; m, Edgar Sosa Corona; ed, Sigfrido Garcia Munoz.

Horror   (PR:O MPAA:NR)

THAT'S LIFE**½   (1986) 102m Paradise Cove-Ubilam/COL c

Jack Lemmon (Harvey Fairchild), Julie Andrews (Gillian Fairchild), Sally Kellerman (Holly Parrish), Robert Loggia (Father Baragone), Jennifer Edwards (Megan Fairchild Bartlet), Rob Knepper (Steve Larwin), Matt Lattanzi (Larry Bartlet), Chris Lemmon (Josh Fairchild), Cynthia Sikes (Janice Kern), Dana Sparks (Fanny Ward), Emma Walton (Kate Fairchild), Felicia Farr (Mme. Carrie), Theodore Wilson (Corey), Nicky Blair (Andre), Jordan Christopher (Dr. Keith Romanis), Biff Elliot (Belmont), Hal Riddle (Phil Carlson), Harold Harris (Harold), Sherry P. Sievert (Receptionist), Joe Lopes (Band Leader), James Umphlett, Frann Bradford (Party Guests), Jess G. Henecke (Jesse Grant), Lisa Kingston (Lisa), Ken Gehrig (Injured Man in E.R.), Donna McMullen (Woman in E.R.), Scott L. McKenna (Anesthesiologist), Dr. Charles Schneider (Dr. Gerald Spelner), Cora Bryant, Robin Foster (Histotechnologists), Eddie Vail (Surfer), Deborah Figuly (Surfer Girl), Ernie Anderson (T.V. Announcer), Harry Birrell (Radio Announcer), Chutney Walton (Chutney), Honey Edwards (Honey).

Those advanced birthdays with zeros at the end of them can be traumatic. In 10, Blake Edwards examined the problem with Dudley Moore. In S.O.B., he satirized the Hollywood establishment and how it feels to be over the hill. Here, he eschews the show-business scene and uses Lemmon in a different way. Woody Allen dealt with mortality in HANNAH AND HER SISTERS by considering a religious conversion when he thought he was dying. Lemmon does something similar with lesser comedic results. He's a successful and famous architect living

in a fabulous Malibu home with his long-time wife, Andrews, a beloved singer. The picture begins as Andrews has just had a node removed from her throat and Christopher, her doctor, doesn't know whether a biopsy will prove it to be cancerous. Since the action in the film takes place over a weekend, the movie keeps cutting back to the lab technician who is working on the tissue sample (this situation of waiting for word of a biopsy was handled brilliantly by author Phillip Wylie in *Opus 21*). Andrews will not tell Lemmon about the test. He is experiencing a crisis of his own, since this weekend marks his 60th birthday.

Lemmon is the extension of Felix Ungar in THE ODD COUPLE. He is a hypochondriac, very self-involved, and can't see that he should be happy with his

lot. Although he talks offhandedly about his sagging features and all his little ailments, it's not hard to see that he is teetering on the edge of a breakdown. The family is preparing for his birthday party and the kids arrive. Jennifer Edwards is the very pregnant daughter who used to be a ballerina and now feels fat and ugly and wishes her husband, Lattanzi, would pay more attention to her. Walton is a saxophonist studying at Julliard in New York City. Walton's boy friend, Knepper, has not been heard from and she fears he has run off with some else. Chris Lemmon is a star of a TV program resembling the Miami Vice-type TV shows. He arrives with knockout starlet Sparks on his arm. Jack Lemmon is becoming unsure of his sexual prowess and feels certain that he doesn't have it anymore when he visits the site of a half-built mansion he's designed for comely client Sikes. She wants to pay him a little bonus on his fee by offering herself. He tries but fails, thus convincing himself that he has had it sexually. He talks to his doctor and is told that he should seek professional therapy. Lemmon then tries a local priest and, through the opening in the confessional, he and Loggia the priest, realize that they were once college buddies. Loggia, in a terrific cameo, also suggests that Lemmon seek a therapist. Desperate to find the answer to the meaning of his life, he consults a local fortune teller, goes to bed with her, and receives a bit more than he bargained for, crab lice. The role is played by Farr, Lemmon's real-life wife. So we watch two parallel stories, waiting for the results of Andrews' biopsy and Lemmon's handling of his 60th birthday.

The party is held in a tent on the mansion property and Lemmon is starting to get a grip on himself as he sees his adoring wife and children and friends surrounding him. He realizes that life isn't so bad after all, despite his having the feeling that he's failed somewhere because he didn't become this era's Frank Lloyd Wright. Andrews has been told not to sing for a while, but the guests ask her to do a song in Lemmon's honor, and she steps up in front of the band just as doctor Christopher walks in and gives her an "okay" sign. She realizes that she is going to live, she steps off the podium, breaks down, and the picture ends with everyone happy and content.

The movie was made with Edwards' own money, about $1.8 million worth, at their own home, and was definitely a family affair. Edwards' daughter, Jennifer, plays the pregnant daughter, and for a good reason. When the girl married against her father's wishes many years before, he was conspicuously absent

during her pregnancy. He felt that he'd like a second chance, so he cast her in the role. Walton is Andrews' daughter by first husband Tony Walton, an award-winning designer, and Chris Lemmon is Jack Lemmon's son. This nepotism did not harm the movie in any way because all three children are good performers in their own right. Seen briefly in the picture is noted restaurateur Nicky Blair, who owns 1986's hottest Southern California dining spot. Edwards asked Blair if he thought he could handle the role of an Italian bachelor who is a fun-loving and successful restaurant owner. Blair, who is both of those things, stepped in and did a good job. Rounding out the cast is Kellerman, as a local real estate shark and pal of Andrews', who keeps trying to put the house on the market.

The script, such as it was, was only 13 pages in length. It was cowritten with Edwards' analyst, Wexler, after Edwards discovered he was suffering from a disease known as Epstein-Barr Syndrome, which is debilitating and makes patients think they are dying. The dialog was generally improvised and it's quality depended entirely on the actors. Andrews must be a heckuva woman because she is portrayed as something akin to Joan of Arc and seems too good to be true. This was Edwards' 31st directorial assignment, his 18th as a producer, and the 36th film in which he contributed to the script. Lots of good satire, but one wishes a script had been written, and that some better editing had been done. Music included "Life In a Looking Glass" (Henry Mancini, Leslie Bricusse, performed by Tony Bennett), "Having a Party" (Sam Cooke, performed by Sam Cooke), "Rock Camping" (performed by Ernie West), "Justice" (Jocko Marcellino, Bruce MacPherson, performed by the Magistrates). Why they didn't use "That's Life" is not known.

p, Tony Adams; d, Blake Edwards; w, Milton Wexler, Blake Edwards; ph, Anthony Richmond (Panavision, DeLuxe Color); m, Henry Mancini; ed, Lee Rhoads; set d, Tony Marando; cos, Tracy Tynan; m/l, Henry Mancini, Leslie Bricusse, Sam Cooke, Jocko Marcellino, Bruce MacPherson; makeup, Deborah Figuly.

Comedy (PR:C MPAA:PG-13)

THERESE**** (1986, Fr.) 90m AFC/Films A2–Circle c

Catherine Mouchet *(Therese Martin)*, Aurore Prieto *(Celine)*, Sylvie Habault *(Pauline)*, Ghislaine Mona *(Marie)*, Helene Alexandridis *(Lucie)*, Clemence Massart *(Prioress)*, Nathalie Bernart *(Aimee)*, Beatrice DeVigan *(The Singer)*, Noele Chantre *(The Old Woman)*, Anna Bernelat *(The Cripple)*, Sylvaine Massart *(The Nurse)*, M.C. Brown-Sarda *(The Gatekeeper)*, M. L. Eberschweiler *(The Painter)*, Josette Lefevre, Gilberte Laurain *(The Nuns)*, Jean Pelegri *(Father)*, Michel Rivelin *(Pranzini)*, Quentin *(Child in the Chorus)*, Pierre Baillot *(The Priest)*, Jean Pieuchot *(The Bishop)*, Georges Aranyossy *(The Cardinal)*, Armand Meppiel *(The Pope)*, Lucien Folet *(Old Man with Flowers)*, Pierre Maintigneux *(Convent Doctor)*, Guy Faucon *(Aimee's Fiance)*, Joel Le Francois *(The Young Doctor)*, Veronique Muller, Jacqueline Bouvyer *(Novices)*, Jacqueline Lagrain *(Violinist)*, Simone Dubocq *(Embroideress)*, Evy Carcassonne *(Picture Framer)*, Renee Cretien *(Les Petales)*.

In 1897, a young French girl named Therese Martin died of tuberculosis in a Carmelite convent in Liseux. Twenty-eight years later, she was canonized and has since become known as "the Little Flower of Jesus." Her diaries, written while in the convent, have been translated into numerous languages and have served as the basis for this film, directed by Cavalier and written by his daughter de Casabianca. THERESE stars Mouchet as the third of four sisters to enter Liseux. A novice, Mouchet faces the cold, hard life of the convent with great spiritual devotion, suffering in silent physical deterioration. At age 15, determined to become a nun, she makes a personal appeal to the Pope, who grants her wish. Believing, as all Carmelite nuns do, that she is the bride of Jesus Christ, Mouchet devotes her life to His name. Rather than viewing her "marriage" with Jesus in strictly spiritual terms, Mouchet, in a schoolgirl manner, sees Him as more of a boy friend with whom she is infatuated. Her physical condition weakens, confining her to bed under the care of her fellow nuns and novices—all of whom have come to deeply love the simple girl. After terrible spells of coughing, she dies of tuberculosis.

Out of respect for this young saint whose simple and pure devotion led to her canonization, director Cavalier and screenwriter de Casabianca have fashioned a beautiful and sensitive film. Constructed in a series of tableaux, THERESE is a sparse film. There is very little music (only snatches of Offenbach and Faure), a limited use of dialog, and, most strikingly, a set constructed in a minimal style that recalls the films of Robert Bresson. Rather than lose his fragile Therese character to the clutter of an intricate and elaborate convent set, Cavalier places her against the plain grey backdrop of the sound stage. Scenes played in Mouchet's bedroom show only her bed in a pool of light. Her room is not separated from the others by a wall, but merely by the dark of an unlit patch of the sound stage. Cavalier has stated, "I wished to get away from the mass of images and sounds with which I am bombarded every day. I took real pleasure in trying to enhance the features of a face or make the most hidden movements of a body perceptible." As skilled as the direction or script may be, THERESE depends almost wholly on Mouchet. It is the face of Therese Martin on which the film rests. In order for the film to succeed Cavalier had to find the perfect actress for the role. Fortunately, he found her in Mouchet, whose simple, pure face is to THERESE what Maria Falconetti was to Carl Dreyer's PASSION OF JOAN OF ARC in 1928. Mouchet, like Falconetti, is able to radiate that same quality that one associates with sainthood. THERESE is not merely a film about spirituality, it *is* spiritual. In a question-and-answer session after its Chicago Film Festival showing (attended by Cavalier and the 27-year-old Mouchet), a Carmelite priest in the audience thanked Mouchet for her performance. Having devoted his life to the study of Therese Martin—reading her diaries, reading about her life, and praying to her—he told Mouchet that it was not until seeing this film that he fully understood what the saint was about. While putting Therese's devotion on the screen, Mouchet still comes across as a normal young woman. She is not all reverence and seriousness, preferring instead to giggle with her friends. Cavalier's convent, while harsh and cold, is not without the happiness and warmth that the nuns exchange in their lives together. One specific nun, a feeble elderly creature whom Mouchet is assigned to care for, ignores the strict rules and keeps a picture of her long-dead husband—a secret which Mouchet has no intention of revealing. When the same nun asks Mouchet for a kiss, the young girl reverently obliges. The nun, however, wants "a real kiss, the kind that warms you up." These nuns and this convent are in direct opposition to the severe portrait painted in 1965 by Jacques Rivette is his film THE NUN (LA RELIGIEUSE), a film that was temporarily banned in France because of its unflattering look inside the convent. (Coincidentally, THE NUN was edited by Denise de Casabianca, the wife of Cavalier.) Cavalier hadn't made a film since 1980's UN ETRANGE VOYAGE and, as a result, has been practically forgotten. He had planned to film a biography of Therese Martin in 1972 with Isabelle Adjani (then a barely-known actress). It was not until he saw Mouchet at Paris' Conservatoire, performing a scene from Georges Bernanos' *Death of Mouchette*, which Bresson filmed as MOUCHETTE, that he again began to think of the film—although he did not cast Mouchet. After searching for two years to find a suitable lead actress, Cavalier went back to Mouchet and offered her the part. As scriptwriter, he employed his 28-year-old daughter, herself a filmmaker (this year's PEKIN CENTRAL) and actress (UN ETRANGE VOYAGE and Sam Fuller's French film THIEVES AFFAIR). Conceived as a small film for a limited audience, THERESE surprised even Cavalier when it won the prestigious Jury Prize at the Cannes Film Festival. The Cesar Awards also showered the film with honors, naming it as Best Picture, Cavalier as Best Director, Mouchet as Best Young Female Hopeful, Cavalier and de Casabianca for Best Script, and Isabelle Dedieu for Best Editing. The film also received nominations for photography (an excellent job by the brilliant Rousselot who is best known for his camerawork on DIVA), sound, and costumes. (In French; English subtitles.)

p, Maurice Bernart; d, Alain Cavalier; w, Cavalier, Camille De Casabianca; ph, Philippe Rousselot (Eclair Color); ed, Isabelle Dedieu; art d, Bernard Evein; cos, Yvette Bonnay.

Biography   **(PR:C MPAA:NR)**

'38†   (1986, Aus./Ger.) 103m Satel–Almaro c

Tobias Engel *(Martin Hoffman)*, Sunnyi Melles *(Carola Hell)*, Heinz Trixner *(Toni Drechsler)*, Lotte Ledl *(Mother)*, Ingrid Burkhard *(Frau Schostal)*, Josef Frolich *(Kemetter)*, David Camerum *(Col. Jovanic)*, Romuald Pekny *(Sovary)*, Maria Singer *(Frau Pekarek)*, Miguel Hertz-Hestranek *(Ferry)*, Michael Kehlmann *(Hebenstein)*, Walter Starz *(Stolnau)*, Ulf Dieter Kusdas *(Andi)*.

An Oscar nominee for Best Foreign Film, '38 is an Austrian-German coproduction that is set in Austria in 1938 in the days before the German *Anschluss*. As Austria's government was being crippled by the Nazi's, the Austrian stage was also undergoing change as its Jewish actors lived in fear of their oppressors. Engel is an Austrian Jew and a journalist in Vienna whose life changes when he falls in love with a beautiful young actress, Melles. Nothing, however, can prevent the rise of the Nazi government in Austria. Similar in some ways to the winner of the 1982 Oscar for Best Foreign Film, MEPHISTO, which explored the Hungarian stage and the rise of Nazism, '38 is also an interesting companion to WELCOME IN VIENNA, a 1986 Austrian film which examines that country in the days just after the Nazi defeat. (In German; English subtitles.)

p, Otto-Boris Dworak, Jan Syrovy; d&w, Wolfgang Gluck (based on the novel *What Else Vienna Was* by Friedrich Torberg); ph, Gerard Vandenberg; m, Bert Grund; ed, Heidi Handorf; art d, Herwig Libowwitzky.

Drama/War   **(PR:O MPAA:NR)**

37:2 LE MATIN   (SEE: BETTY BLUE, 1986, Fr.)

THOMAS EN SENIOR OP HET SPOOR VAN BRUTE BEREND†   (1986, Neth.) 108m Castor c (Trans: Thomas and Senior on the Trail of Brutal Bernard)

Bart Steenbeek *(Thomas)*, Lex Goudsmit *(Senior)*, Henk van Ulsen *(Professor)*, Jerome Reehuis *(Advertising Man)*.

The friendship between an old man and a boy is threatened by the boy's new friends at school, but an adventure involving a treasure map brings them together. Made at the same time as a TV series with the same characters.

d, Karst van der Meulen; ph, Fred Tammes; m, Tonny Eyk; ed, Karst van der Meulen; art d, Harry Ammerlaan.

Children's   **(PR:AA MPAA:NR)**

THRASHIN'*½   (1986) 92m Fries Entertainment c

Josh Brolin *(Corey Webster)*, Robert Rusler *(Tommy Hook)*, Pamela Gidley *(Chrissy)*, Brooke McCarter, Jr. *(Tyler)*, Josh Richman *(Radley)*, Brett Marx *(Bozo)*, David Wagner *(Little Stevie)*, Chuck McCann *(Sam Flood)*, Tony Alva *(T.A.)*, Mark Munski *(Monk)*, Sherilyn Fenn *(Velvet)*, Zachary *(Skate Club Announcer)*, Rocky Giordani *(Skate Club Bouncer)*, Steve Whittaker *(Bus Driver)*, Per Welinder *(Per, Venice Freestyler)*, Mondo Beck, Christian Hosoi, Jesse Martinex, Masao Miyashior, Steve Olson, Johnny Ray, Eddie Reategui, Steve Steadham *(Daggers)*, Ruben Blue *(Dagger Photographer)*, Steve Caballero, Tony Hawk, Christian Hosoi, Lester Kasai, Allen Losi, Tony Magnussem, Mike McGill, Billy Ruff, Kevin Staab *(Pool Skaters)*, Jaks Team, Madrid Team *(Downhill Skaters)*, Beau Brown, Natas Kaupas, Dennis Martinez *(Utility Ramp*

Locals), Matt Bernard, Eric Dressen, Peter Ducammun, Gator Rogowski, Kipp Woods *(Utility Daggers)*, Kelly Doyle, Pleasant Gehman *(Daggerettes)*.

In 1961, WEST SIDE STORY told of gang rivalry between "The Jets" and "The Sharks," and what happened when one gang leader's sister fell in love with the opposing gang leader. Well, THRASHIN' is just that . . . on skateboards. The gangs this time are "The Ramp Locals," some kids from the affluent Valley headed by clean-cut Brolin (son of James), and "The Daggers," a gang of hardcore punk rockers in leather led by Rusler. Rusler's kid sister, the pretty blonde Gidley, is visiting from Indiana and ends up falling for Brolin. Naturally, Rusler doesn't want kid sister anywhere near someone from the Valley. Deciding to fight for the right to Gidley, Brolin and Rusler engage in a violent battle they call "jousting." By the time the police arrive, Brolin's arm is broken. Also busted is his chance to win the "L.A. Massacre," a dangerous 20-mile downhill race through a mountain road in which skateboarders can reach speeds of 60 mph. The winner of the Massacre gets a corporate sponsorship. After a big fight between Brolin and Gidley, the latter decides to pack her things and return to her Hoosier hometown. Brolin, however, is determined to race, and does so with a cast on his forearm. Gidley reconsiders, comes back to L.A., and arrives at the finish line in time to see Brolin win. The happy couple joyfully reunite, while Rusler gives a nod of approval and congratulates the winner.

While not very original or even very skillful, THRASHIN' (a skateboarding term for aggressive, gutsy skating) isn't nearly as bad as it sounds. In fact, the term "totally awesome" may be used by some L.A. youngsters to describe it. The film takes a look—albeit a surface look—at a strange subculture which began in Los Angeles and has since spread through the entire country: groups of youths, many of them hardcore punk rockers, who identify themselves as skateboarders, much like previous generations had bikers and surfers. Unfortunately, it doesn't get any deeper than that. Director Winters (who had a fairly large role as an actor in WEST SIDE STORY, playing A-Rab) has managed to pull together a number of elements in a reasonably adroit manner. All the actors are accomplished, especially Gidley in her first role. A model and winner of an Australian beauty pageant which named her the Most Beautiful Woman in the World (a rather grand assumption), Gidley is not only beautiful (in an ordinary "hometown girl" sense), but quite an accomplished actress, combining a virginal quality with a hardened, tomboy edge. There's also a fine supporting cast that includes Richman and Marx as fellow "Ramp Locals." Complementing the acting is some phenomenal camera work, much of it shot from a camera attached to the front of a skateboard. While the actors perform their gymnastics in a cement "pool," on a ramp, or racing down Hollywood Boulevard's sidewalks (at speeds up to 40 mph), the camera zooms along with them. THRASHIN' is a great film for people who love skateboarding and is far better than 1978's dismal SKATEBOARD. Although the romance and subculture portions of the film are well done, they aren't nearly enough to support the film alone, making this one a poor bet for those uninterested in the sport. Surprisingly, for a film which, initially, seems exploitative (the ad reads "Skate or Die") there is no nudity (in fact, the love scene between Brolin and Gidley is quite tender), very little foul language, and no graphic violence. Special mention must be given to the numerous skateboard performers and doubles (the actors did some, though not all, of their routines) who add so much to the film's action sequences. Songs include "Thrashin' " (Larry Lee, Alan Sacks, Jodi Sacks-Micheli, performed by Meat Loaf), "That's Good" (Gerald Casale, Alan Mothersbaugh, Mark Mothersbaugh, performed by Devo), "Tequila" (Chuck Rio), "Arrow Through My Heart" (Mike Piccirillo, Garry Geotzman, performed by Jimmy Demers), "Dancin' in Jamaica" (Mike Piccirillo, Garry Geotzman, performed by The Tribe), "Want You" (Vicki Peterson, performed by The Bangles), "Black Eyed Blonde" (Anthony Kiedis, Michael Balzary, Cliff Martinez, performed by The Red Hot Chili Peppers), "Don't Think Twice" (Britta Phillips, Ned Liebman, Derek Meade, performed by France Joli), "Touch the Sky" (Bernie Shannahan, performed by White Sister), "Playground" (Dennis Greaves, Michael Lister, performed by The Truth), "Hey" (Lee Ving, performed by Fear), "Maniac" (Rosie Flores, performed by The Screaming Sirens), "Let the Love Begin" (Gloria Sklerov, Lenny Macaluso, performed by Jimmy Demers, Carol Sue Hill), "Wild in the Streets" (Garland Jeffreys, performed by The Circle Jerks), "Burnin' (for You)" (T. Quinn, L. Hester, performed by Rebel Faction), "Staring Down the Demons"

(Don Kirkpatrick, Randy Sharp, performed by Animotion), "Couldn't Care More" (David Steele, Roland Gift, performed by The Fine Young Cannibals).

p, Alan Sacks; d, David Winters; w, Alan Sacks, Paul Brown; ph, Chuck Colwell; m, Barry Goldberg; ed, Lorenzo DeStefano, Nicholas Smith; prod d, Katheryn Hardwick; set d, Beau Peterson; cos, Bernadette O'Brien; spec eff, John C. Hartigan, Frank Munos; m/l, Larry Lee, Alan Sacks, Jodi Sacks-Micheli, Gerald Casale, Alan Mothersbaugh, Mark Mothersbaugh, Chuck Rio, Mike Piccirillo, Garry Geotzman, Vicki Peterson, Anthony Kiedis, Michael Balzary, Cliff Martinez, Britta Phillips, Ned Liebman, Derek Meade, Bernie Shannahan, Dennis Greaves, Michael Lister, Lee Ving, Rosie Flores, Gloria Sklerov, Lenny Macaluso, Garland Jeffrys, T. Quinn, L. Hester, Don Kirkpatrick, Randy Sharp, David Steele, Roland Gift; makeup, Yvonne DePatis; stunts, Tony Epper, Ronnie Ross.

Sports/Romance   Cas.   **(PR:A-C MPAA:PG-13)**

THREE AMIGOS*   (1986) 103m Orion c

Chevy Chase *(Dusty Bottoms)*, Steve Martin *(Lucky Day)*, Martin Short *(Ned Nederlander)*, Patrice Martinez *(Carmen)*, Philip Gordon *(Rodrigo)*, Michael Wren *(Cowboy)*, Fred Asparagus *(Bartender)*, Gene Hartline, William Kaplan *(Silent Movie Bandidos)*, Sophia Lamour *(Silent Movie Senorita)*, Santos Morales *(Telegrapher)*, Joe Mantegna *(Harry Flugleman)*, Jon Lovitz *(Morty)*, Philip E. Hartmann *(Sam)*, Tino Insana *(Studio Guard)*, Craig Berenson *(Telegram Delivery Boy)*, Kai Wulff *(German)*, Josh Gallegos *(Bar Patron)*, Norbert Weisser *(German's Friend)*, Brian Thompson *(German's Other Friend)*, Hector Elias *(Pedro)*, Hector Morales *(Carlos)*, Abel Franco *(Papa Sanchez)*, Betty Carvalho *(Mama Sanchez)*, Benita *(Rosita)* Dyana Ortelli *(Juanita)*, Humberto Ortiz *(Pablo)*, Jorge Cervera, Candy Castillo, Jeff O'Haco *(Bandidos)*, Alfonso Arau *(El Guapo)*, Loyda Ramos *(Conchita)*, Tony Plana *(Jefe)*, Carl LaFong *(Tortoise)*, Randy Newman *(Singing Bush)*, Rebecca Underwood *(Hot Senorita)*.

Once again operating under his "Bigger is Better" style of comedy direction, John Landis presents yet another multi-million dollar extravaganza which fea-

tures some overpaid "Saturday Night Live" veterans, excessively broad slapstick, and, of course, plenty of explosions. Chase, Martin, and Short are "The Three Amigos," a trio of washed-up Western movie heroes during the silent era. When the Amigos demand to be paid in cash rather than in perequisites, cigar-chomping studio head Mantegna responds by giving Chase, Martin, and Short their walking papers. Meanwhile, down Mexico way, trouble is brewing in the village of Santa Poco. Arau, a notorious bandido undergoing a midlife crisis, has worked out his own problems by terrorizing the place, and the petrified townsfolk have nowhere to turn. When Martinez, a pretty villager, watches a Three Amigos film, she decides these celluloid cowboys are the only ones who can help. She sends a telegram to Hollywood, offering 100,000 pesos to Chase, Martin, and Short if they will help put an end to Arau's reign. Since The Three Amigos always turn down rewards in their movies, Martinez is convinced she won't have to put up the proffered money. But back in Hollywood, the three out-of-work amigos are in desperate need of cash. When the telegraph reader misinterprets Martinez' plea for help as a personal-appearance request, Chase, Martin, and Short are convinced their money woes have ended. They steal their gaudy costumes, which have been repossessed by the studio, and travel south with heady dreams of a much-needed career boost. Once in Santa Poco, they entertain villagers with showbiz antics (Short, playing a former child star, tells a group of uninterested youngsters how he was once praised by none other than Dorothy Gish), then confront Arau and his gang. Though convinced the bandido and his men are part of a publicity show, the Amigos receive a rude awakening after discovering the bullets whizzing past their heads are the real thing. When Arau nabs Martinez, Chase, Martin, and Short at last have a chance to perform some real-life heroics. They ride pell-mell through the desert, then sneak into Arau's headquarters. Following some predictably zany danger, the Amigos rescue Martinez courtesy of a none-too-safe biplane (supplied by rabid German Amigo fan Wulff), then successfully rouse the villagers to retaliate against Arau's nefarious ways.

Chase, Martin, and Short attempt to yuk it up here like a trio of latter-day Ritz Brothers (whose ARGENTINE NIGHTS [1940] may have inspired the scripters). Prodded by Landis' slam-bang direction, the effect isn't so much a comedy as it is an exercise in excess. The Three Amigos are singing cowboys during the silent

era, bedecked in spangly outfits that would cause even Cisco Kid to sneer. We're supposed to laugh because these are big comedy stars in funny suits who get into dangerous, slapstick-filled intrigues. Somewhere in the planning stage one all-important factor was left out: humor. The concept is a funny one, yet no one seems to have the faintest idea of what to do with it. Some potentially good bits, such as a singing bush and a musical number crooned around a deliberately phony set (complete with animals joining in harmony) are dragged out well beyond their capacity to entertain. Martin cowrote the script along with songwriter Randy Newman ("Short People") and ex-"Saturday Night Live" producer Lorne Michaels, so they must shoulder much of the blame. Landis, a hit-and-mostly-miss comedy director known for resorting to broad slapstick chases, four-letter-word punch lines, and—when all else fails—plenty of explosions, indulges in these favored elements like a pig wallowing in mud on a hot day. Between his direction and the initially lame screenplay, THE THREE AMIGOS never really stands a chance. The lead performances don't help much either. Martin resorts to his standard snide mugging, while Chase looks surprisingly bored. Only Short, here making his first major film appearance, is tolerable. He comes off as a likable young man, and clearly deserves more substantial material than this (his previous work included a wonderful stint on SCTV, appearing in one of the lesser casts of "Saturday Night Live," and a small role in the forgettable 1979 feature LOST AND FOUND). Another of the film's many problems is the stereotyped portrayal of Mexican peasants. Other than Martinez, the Mexicans are seen as an uneducated group, who rarely bathe and speak with exaggerated accents. This is played for laughs and comes off as what it is, a crass attempt at xenophobic humor. The film's original title was to have been THE THREE CABALLEROS in honor of the famed Disney cartoon/live action feature of 1944. When Disney Studios demanded $177,000 for rights to their title, this idea was dropped and the new name was selected.

p, Lorne Michaels, George Folsey, Jr.; d, John Landis; w, Steve Martin, Lorne Michaels, Randy Newman; ph, Ronald W. Browne (Technicolor); m, Elmer Bernstein; ed, Malcolm Campbell; prod d, Richard Sawyer; set d, Mark Faybus, Stan Tropp; cos, Deborah Nadoolman; spec eff, Roy Arbogast; ch, Shirley Kirkes; m/l, Randy Newman; makeup, Frank Griffin, Mark Reedall, Leonard Engelman, Ric Sagliani; stunts, Jerry Gatlin.

Comedy   Cas.   **(PR:C MPAA:PG)**

3:15, THE MOMENT OF TRUTH**   (1986) 85m Romax-Jones Kenner-Brody/Dakota Entertainment c (AKA: 3:15)

Adam Baldwin *(Jeff Hannah)*, Deborah Foreman *(Sherry Havilland)*, Rene Auberjonois *(Principal Horner)*, Ed Lauter *(Moran)*, Scott McGinnis *(Chris)*, Danny De La Paz *(Cinco)*, John Scott Clough *(Jim)*, Mario Van Peebles *(Whisperer)*, Jesse Aragon *(Smiley)*, Wendy Barry *(Lora)*, Bradford Bancroft *(Whitey)*, Joseph Brutsman *(Norman)*, Wayne Crawford *(Draper)*, Lori Eastside *(Patch)*, Jeb Ellis-Brown *(Ponch)*, Panchito Gomez *(Chooch)*, Nancy Locke Hauser *(Mrs. Havilland)*, Wings Hauser *(Mr. Havilland)*, John Achorn *(Teacher in Hallway)*, Lisa Adams *(Woman at Club)*, Mary Betten *(Mrs. Barts)*, Kendall Carly Browne *(French Teacher)*, Jodi Buss *(Student with Rumor)*, Dean Devlin *(Gum Chewer)*, John Doe *(Drunk at Club)*, Candy Galvane *(Messenger)*, David Harper *(Payoff Guy)*, Van Quattro *(Plainclothes Cop)*, Ivan E. Roth *(Freak)*, Christina Beck, Erin Linn Berlin, Bobby Brat, Gina Gershon *(Cobrettes)*, Derek Baker, Rusty Cundieff, Robert Dash, David Dunson, Kevin Simon, Ronnie Smith, Barry Wilson *(M-16s)*, Donald Hahn, Tony Lee, Master Ho Sik Pak, Phil Villanuevo, Michael Yamasaki, Calvin Yeshida, Paul Yi, David Yu *(Tams)*, Carol Ginsburg, Norine Ginsburg, Elizabeth Harmon, Fred Leyro, Mark Slama, Greta Young *(Students in Courtyard)*.

Filmed in 1984, but released two years later, 3:15, THE MOMENT OF TRUTH is an uneven film that plays like a cross between THE WARRIORS and HIGH NOON. Baldwin is a member of the Cobras, a tough street gang run by De La Paz. Tired of the gang life, Baldwin quits and within a year has settled down to a fairly normal high school existence. He has a loyal girl friend (Foreman) and appears to have forgotten his former days. De La Paz now controls the school (which seems evenly divided between eccentrically garbed gang members and wholesome creamcheese students). Auberjonois, the whiny principal, is determined to put an end to De La Paz's domination. He brings in Lauter, a local police man, and arranges for a surprise bust during school hours. De La Paz and his boys are arrested, but during all the confusion a rumor circulates that Baldwin is a police informant. From his jail cell De La Paz marks the former gang member as a dead man, while Baldwin's friends rally around him. Foreman, disgusted by these events, tries to break from Baldwin but she is beaten by a jealous group of female gang members. Baldwin rescues Foreman, who still winds up in the hospital. Baldwin sees some graffiti telling him when he is to meet De La Paz. The time for this showdown is, of course, 3:15 on a day when school only meets for morning classes. Just like Gary Cooper, Baldwin finds his friends deserting him like rats from a sinking ship, forcing him to go solo against De La Paz and company. Meanwhile Foreman slips out of the hospital, hoping she can help Baldwin. In the school's empty locker room Baldwin fights off the gang, but is finally overwhelmed and prepares for a beating. Suddenly Brutsman, a nerdy student who has admired Baldwin all along, bursts in with a baseball bat in hand. Brutsman is shot, but Baldwin escapes. Eventually he and De La Paz must go it alone. Foreman materializes just in time to lend a hand, and Baldwin emerges victorious. The police arrive, Brutsman is rushed to the hospital, and Baldwin is allowed to deck the namby-pamby principal who allowed the drug situation to get so out of hand.

Director Gross had previously written Walter Hill's 1982 film 48 HOURS, and probably should have studied a few of his mentor's earlier works. 3:15 would have benefited from a more consistent sense of visual style, like Hill maintained in such films as THE LONG RIDERS, SOUTHERN COMFORT, and his own gang film THE WARRIORS. Gross' ending, as the camera weaves through the labyrinth of gym lockers and school hallways, is suspenseful but events leading up to this climactic confrontation lack any real magnetism. Baldwin, though a bit too old for his part, is strong in the lead and De La Paz is appropriately psychotic as the villain. Foreman's character seems as unfocused as the actress' career (she's done everything from the critically acclaimed VALLEY GIRL to the trashy MY CHAUFFEUR), while Auberjonois is decidedly annoying. Its hard just to figure out what kind of school is portrayed here. On one hand, its bathrooms and outside walls are covered by gang graffiti and seems to attract a variety of hoodlums, most of whom are dark-skinned. On the other hand, the institution also boasts of clean hallways, an expensive looking language lab, and a neatly dressed, largely white student body. Gross seems to have combined elements of both worlds, grafting the punky, knife toting crowd of exploitation fare onto the mythical Shermer High from a John Hughes film. Songs include: "Out of Control" (Bob Cordi, Joe Esposito, performed by Cordi, Esposito), "Touchy Situation" (Larry Lee, Robert Ferraro, performed by Robert Ferraro), "Lined Up" (David Allen, Barry Andrews, Carl Marsh, performed by Shreikback), "The Right Time," "No Hesitation" (Chris Farren, performed by Farren), "Oh Lucille" (Larry Lee, Robert Ferraro, performed by Robert Ferraro), "Baby Your World Is Crashing Down" (Barry Goldberg, Jack Sherman, performed by Ruth Daniels), "Mystery" (Larry Lee, Mitchell Froom, Robert Ferraro, performed by Frankie Swan), "Human Race" (Jack Sherman, Barry Goldberg, performed by Jack Sherman, Ruth Daniels), "Something's Gotta Change" (Dubois Daniels, performed by Ruth Daniels).

p, Dennis Brody, Robert Kenner; d, Larry Gross; w, Sam Bernard, Michael Jacobs; ph, Misha Suslov (CFI Color); m, Gary Chang; ed, Steven Kemper; prod d, Paul Ahrens; set d, Anne Huntley; cos, Nina Padovano; m/l, Bob Cordi, Joe Esposito, Larry Lee, Robert Ferraro, David Allen, Barry Andrews, Carl Marsh, Chris Farren, Barry Goldberg, Jack Sherman, Mitchell Froom, Dubois Daniels; stunts, Dan Bradley.

Action/Drama **Cas.** **(PR:O MPAA:R)**

THRONE OF FIRE, THE† (1986, It.) 89m Visione Cinematografica-Cannon Group c

Sabrina Siani *(Princess Valkari)*, Peter McCoy [Pietro Torrisi] *(Siegfried)*, Harrison Muller *(Morak)*, Benny Carduso, Peter Caine, Dan Collins, Stefano Abbati.

Another Italian sword and sorcery epic that makes it to video without ever gracing an American screen. Muller is the son the devil's messenger, and potential evil overlord of the world. Before he can claim the title, though, he has to marry princess Siani and take the throne during an eclipse. Fortunately for the world, the forces of good have a muscleman champion in the person of McCoy, who can even turn invisible. Guess who wins.

p, Ettore Spagnuolo; d, Franco Prosperi; w, Nino Marino (based on a story by Nino Marino, Giuseppe Buricchi); ph, Guglielmo Mancori (Telecolor); m, Carlo Rustichelli; ed, Alessandro Lucidi; art d, Franco Cuppini; cos, Silvio Laurenzi; spec eff, Paolo Ricci.

Fantasy/Adventure **Cas.** **(PR:O MPAA:NR)**

THUNDER RUN* (1986) 91m Lynn-Davis-Panache/Cannon c

Forrest Tucker *(Charlie Morrison)*, John Ireland *(George Adams)*, John Sheperd *(Chris)*, Jill Whitlow *(Kim)*, Wally Ward *(Paul)*, Cheryl M. Lynn *(Jilly)*, Marilyn O'Connor *(Maggie Morrison)*, Graham Ludlow *(Mike)*, Alan Rachins *(Carlos)*, Tom Dugan *(Wolf)*.

The late Forrest Tucker stars in this obvious rip-off of the MAD MAX films. We find Tucker, a veteran truck driver who is now retired, in the middle of the desert trying to make something of a unproductive cobalt mine. He is aided by his loving grandson, Sheperd, and the latter's obnoxious teenage friends who try to con some sucker into purchasing the worthless property. Enter Ireland, an old buddy of Tucker who served with him in the Korean War. Ireland offers the vulnerable old trucker $250,000 to transport some plutonium across Nevada and Arizona to a high-security installation. Tucker takes the job, but little does he know that some incredibly well-armed terrorists are out to steal the radioactive cargo. From here on the film collapses into a less-than-thrilling ROAD WARRIOR chase through the desert with Tucker and Sheperd trying to fend off the terrorists, who just happen to have an unlimited supply of heat-seeking missiles. At one point, Sheperd jettisons the trailer of the semi-truck into the pursuing terrorists—appearing to give the baddies what they want—only to reveal that the plutonium somehow was transferred to the safety of the cab. Eventually Tucker and his grandson defeat the terrorists and crash the gate at their destination.

Slow, stupid, and ridiculous, THUNDER RUN deserved the fate it got at the box office. Dumped on the market with nary a whimper by Cannon, the film died a quick death and appeared on video shortly thereafter. Almost half the film is devoted to the insufferable antics of Sheperd and his teenage friends as they goof around at the cobalt mine. The rest of the movie is the uninspired and frequently ridiculous chase scene that is more aggravating by virtue of its ineptitude than thrilling. Shot in 1985, this was the last feature film appearance by Forrest Tucker, who died of cancer in 1986 a few weeks after collapsing during the unveiling ceremony of his star in the Hollywood Walk of Fame.

p, Carol Lynn, Lawrence Applebaum; d, Gary Hudson; w, Charles Davis, Carol Heyer (based on a story by Carol Lynn, Clifford Wenger, Sr.); ph, Harvey Genkins (DeLuxe color); m, Matthew McCauley, Jay Levy; ed, Burton Lee Harry; art d, Carol Heyer; spec eff, Clifford Wenger, Sr.; stunts, Rod Amateau.

Action **Cas.** **(PR:C MPAA:PG-13)**

THUNDER WARRIOR** (1986, It.) 84m European International/Trans World Entertainment c (AKA: THUNDER)

Bo Svenson *(Sheriff Bill Cook)*, Mark Gregory *(Thunder)*, Raymund Harmstorf *(Barry)*, Valeria Ross *(Sheila)*, Antonio Sabato *(Thomas)*, Giovanni Vettorazzo, Paolo Malco, Richard Harley, Slim Smith.

Shot in Arizona's Monument Valley and the Grand Canyon circa 1983, this Italian action epic was never released theatrically in the U.S., but turned up as a videocassette release in 1986. Gregory (1990: THE BRONX WARRIORS) stars as a Navajo Indian who returns to his ancestral home to discover that his tribal burial ground is being violated by construction workers building an observatory. Outraged that the treaty his grandfather had signed with the white man over 100 years before has been broken, Gregory tries to stop the construction by himself and ends up in a brawl with one of the workers, Sabato. Gregory takes his case to the local sheriff, Svenson, but his pleas are ignored. Adopting a different tactic, Gregory stages a sit-in at the local bank which is financing the construction. The bankers are neither enlightened nor amused by Gregory's protest, and the young Navajo is not only ejected from the bank, but from the county as well. Gregory is beaten up by the still-angry Sabato and his construction worker buddies. When Gregory dares to protest, deputy sheriff Harmstorf gives him another beating for good measure. Having been beaten and humiliated by most of the state of Arizona, Gregory finally snaps and decides to wage a one-man war against his enemies. His hit-and-run tactics spur several different posse groups and local law enforcement agents to try to track him down, but the Navajo proves too clever for them and soon he becomes something of a legend with the townsfolk. All this adds up to a sequel, THUNDER WARRIOR II, available in 1987 at a video store near you.

Not as bad as it could be, THUNDER WARRIOR has the benefit of John Ford's favorite location—the beautiful Monument Valley and the surrounding area. The muscle-bound Gregory does a competent job as the exasperated Navajo who finally decides to force the white man to honor his grandfather's treaty, and Svenson lends his usual dependable support. Director De Angelis (who in the inexplicable tradition of the Italian cinema goes under the name "Larry Ludman" for U.S. release) handles the action scenes with some flair, although someone should notify him that extended use of slow motion is by now only favored by the likes of Brian De Palma.

p, Fabrizio De Angelis; d, Larry Ludman [Fabrizio De Angelis]; w, David Parker, Jr., Larry Ludman [Fabrizio De Angelis] (based on a story by David Parker, Jr.); ph, Sergio Salvati (Telecolor); m, Francesco De Masi; ed, Eugenio Alabiso; art d&cos, Massimo Lentini; spec eff, Giovanni Corridori; stunts, Alan Petit.

Action **Cas.** **(PR:O MPAA:R)**

TIEMPO DE SILENCIO† (1986, Span.) 95m Lolafilms-Morgana c (Trans: Time of Silence)

Imanol Arias *(Pedro)*, Victoria Abril *(Dorita)*, Charo Lopez *(Charo/Mother)*, Francisco Rabal *(Muecas)*, Juan Echanove *(Matias)*, Francisco Algora, Joaquin Hinojosa, Diana Penalver, Enriqueta Claver.

TIEMPO DE SILENCIO is adapted from the popular novel by Luis Martin Santos about life under the fascism of Franco. Arias plays a young doctor researching cancer while spending his nights flirting with Abril and gallivanting with Madrid's elite. Possessed by the idealistic desire to perform good deeds, Arias' convictions are finally tested when a poor, young girl dies during an abortion. He is blamed for the death by the girl's boy friend even though he did not perform the operation, but was only trying to save her. The title refers to the overall political climate in Spain during the late 1940s, when it was better to remain quiet than voice any opinions.

d, Vicente Aranda; w, Vicente Aranda, Antonio Rabinat (based on the novel by Luis Martin Santos); ph, Juan Amoros (Eastmancolor); ed, Teresa Font; set d, Josep Rosell; cos, Gumersindo Andres.

Drama **(PR:C MPAA:NR)**

TIMING†   (1986, Can.) 75m Weinthal–Pan Can c

Eric Weinthal, Heather-Lynn Meacock

Debut feature from Weinthal, who also stars in this story of two young drama students who have a short-lived love affair.

p,d,w&ed, Eric Weinthal.

Drama   (PR:NR MPAA:NR)

TIME TO LIVE AND A TIME TO DIE, A†   (1986, Taiwan) 145m Central
Motion Picture-Yi Fu Films c (TONG NIEN WANG SHI)

T'ien Feng, Nei Fang, T'ang Ju-yun, Hsiao Ai, Yu An-shun, Wu Su-ying, Ch'en Shu-fang *(Adults)*, Chang Ning, Luo Tse-chung, Luo Ch'eng-ye, Chiang Chia-pao, Luo Hsun-lin, Liu Kuo-pin *(Children)*, Yen Sheng-huai, Chou Tung-hung, Chen Han-wen, Hu Hsiang-ping, Lin Chung-wen, Kao Chung-li, Tao Te-chen, Chen-Chin-chen, Chiang-Chiapao.

Drawing on his youth in Taiwan, director Hou Hsiao-hsien has come up with a warm and fond remembrance of his adolescent years from 1958 to 1966. As time passes, so do the young boy's loved ones. First his father succumbs to tuberculosis and is found dead at the kitchen table. The boy's mother is the next to go, losing a battle with cancer. The last family member to die is the grandmother, a sweet but senile woman who has a habit of wandering far from home and getting lost. Hou Hsiao-hsien photographs his film in long takes with his camera placed at an unobtrusive distance, giving the film a calm, subtle, matter-of-fact tone which has won praise from critics all over the world. A TIME TO LIVE AND A TIME TO DIE (the original title translates as "Memories of Childhood") is the third part of an unofficial trilogy which was begun in 1983 with THE BOYS FROM FENGKUEI and then followed in 1984 with A SUMMER AT GRANDPA'S. (In Mandarin; English subtitles.)

p, Lin Tong-fei; d, Hou Hsiao-hsien [Hou Xiaoxian]; w, Chou Tien-wen, Hou Hsiao-hsien; ph, Li Ping-pin; m, Wu Ch'u-ch'u; ed, Wang Ch'i-yang; prod d, Lin Chung-wen; cos, Chou Ching-wen.

Drama   (PR:C MPAA:NR)

TINGBUDAODE SHUOHUA   (SEE: SILENT LOVE, 1986, Hong Kong)

TITAN SERAMBUT DIBELAH TUJUH†   (1986, Indonesian) 99m Bustal
Nawawi-Kofina/Prasidi Teta c (Trans: The Narrow Bridge)

Dewi Irawan *(Ibrahim)*, Rachmat Hidaya *(Pak Sulaiam)*, Soekarno M. Noor *(Pak Harun)*, Soultan Saladin *(Arsad)*, Darussalam *(The Traveler)*, Menzano *(Syamsu)*, Sum Hutabarat *(Syamsu's Wife)*, Youtine Raisi *(Suleha, Harun's Wife)*, Firman D.A. *(Ukan, Harun's Friend)*, Marlia Hardi *(Maimunah)*.

In a remote village, a young schoolteacher who tries to promote more modern ways, finds himself accused of attempted rape by the wife of the local chieftain. At the same time, an innocent girl is charged with immoral conduct after she fends off an amorous attack by the local mosque-keeper. Everyone is properly shamed by their behavior when a wandering Moslem preacher comes through and shows them the errors of their ways.

d, Chaerul Uman; w, Asrul Sani, Chaerul Uman (based on a film by Asrul Sani); ph, M. Soleh Ruslani; m, Franki Raen; ed, Cassim Abas; set d, Rajul Kahfi.

Drama   (PR:C MPAA:NR)

TO DENDRO POU PLIGONAME†   (1986, Gr.) 76m Demos Avdeliodis c
(Trans: The Tree We Were Hurting)

Yannis Avdeliodis, Nicos Mioteris, Marina Delivoria, Takis Agoris, Demos Avdeliodis.

Two boys vacationing on the island of Chios in 1960 have a number of minor adventures and destroy a gum tree.

p,d&w, Demos Avdeliodis; ph, Philippos Koutsaftis; m, Demetris Papademetriou; ed, Costas Foundas; cos, Maria Avdeliodis.

Drama   (PR:A MPAA:NR)

TO SLEEP SO AS TO DREAM†   (1986, Jap.) 81m Shibata Organization bw
(YUME MIRUYONI NEMURITAI)

Moe Kamura *(Bellflower)*, Shiro Sano *(Uotsuka)*, Koji Otake *(Kobayashi)*, Akira Oizumi, Morio Agata, Kazunari Ozawa *(The Three Magicians)*, Fujiko Fukamizu *(Madame Cherry-Blossom)*, Yoshio Yoshida *(Matsunosuke, the Director)*, Shunsui Matsuda *(Akagaki, the Benshi)*, Tsuneo Nakamoto, Tatsuo Nakamoto *(The White Masks)*, Kyoko Kusajima *(Old Lady of the Comb Shop)*.

The feature film debut (16mm b&w) of 29-year-old director Kaizo Hayashi is a homage to the films of Japan's silent era. The film opens in the 1950s as an elderly former movie actress, Fujiko Fukamizu (in reality a leading lady of the 1930s), screens the final chapter of an old silent samurai serial called "The Eternal Mystery." Unfortunately, the final reel is missing and the frustrated actress hires two bumbling detectives, Sano and Otake, to find the beautiful young actress who starred in the serial. As the detectives dig deeper and deeper into the mystery they soon become embroiled in a film within a film (the "reel" intermingled with the "real") until it is eventually revealed that the young actress in the serial is none other than Fukamizu herself. TO SLEEP SO AS TO DREAM contains no spoken dialog and the conversations are translated silent movie style—via title cards. Several stars from Japan's cinematic past, especially actors who worked with director Kenji Mizoguchi, have small roles. The film was shown at the Cannes and New York Film Festivals. (In Japanese; English subtitles.)

p, Kaizo Hayashi, Takashige Ichise; d&w, Kaizo Hayashi; ph, Yuichi Nagata; m, Hidehiko Urayama, Yoko Kumagai, Moe Kamura, Morio Agata; ed, Yuichi Nagata, Kaizo Hayashi.

Drama   (PR:A MPAA:NR)

TOBY MCTEAGUE**   (1986, Can.) 95m Filmline International–Spectrafilm
c

Winston Rekert *(Tom McTeague)*, Yannick Bisson *(Toby McTeague)*, Timothy Webber *(Edison Crowe)*, Stephanie Morgenstern *(Sara)*, Andrew Bednarski *(Sam McTeague)*, Liliane Clune *(Jenny Lessard)*, George Clutesi *(Chief George Wild Dog)*, Evan Adams *(Jacob)*, Hamish McEwan *(Mike Lynn)*, Anthony Levinson *(Peter)*, Mark Kulik *(Ben)*, Joanne Vanicola *(Girl Punker)*, Tom Rack *(Faulkner)*, Dick McGrath *(Games Announcer No.l)*, Doug Price *(Games Announcer, No.2)*, Ian Findlay *(TV Reporter)*.

This film plays like one of those after-school specials, where unhappy adolescents manage to triumph in some area while simultaneously inspiring adults to straighten up their act for the good of all concerned. Bisson is the troubled

teenager in question, living with his father (Rekert) and little brother (Bednarski) in a small town in the far north of Canada. Rekert makes his living raising sled dogs, and his teams are the best in the province. Unfortunately, the economy of the town has been declining, and the bank is threatening to come in and take the dogs. To add to Rekert's problems, Bisson is at an age where he is beginning to rebel against his father, but he is too immature to really succeed in most of his fights. A new teacher arrives in town (with her own computer) and soon awes the students with her knowledge, in addition to catching Rekert's eye. Things get so tense at home for Bisson that he takes off into the hills, and there meets an old Indian chief Clutesi, his father's mentor, and the wise old man teaches him the ways of nature, especially of dogs. Bisson returns home, and his father finally allows him to race his top team in the provincial championship race. They

desperately need to win the race for the $6000 prize money to save the kennel. Needless to say, Bisson wins it after Clutesi turns up out of nowhere and gives him a wonder dog that leads the team to victory.

While films like this are fine for showing depressed teenagers that there is some hope for them, it is unlikely to attract anyone except parents who pick it off the video shelves over their kid's objections. Bisson is reasonably effective in his role, but no one else really seems to be involved in the story, especially Rekert, around whom the story could center more interestingly (father, failing in business, now challenged by son in one area he does best). On the other hand, the photography of the bleak northern landscape is beautiful and the dogs are a lot of fun, though these things aren't enough to interest anyone above the "age of acne."

p, Nicolas Clermont; d, Jean-Claude Lord; w, Jeff Maguire, Djordje Milicevic, Jamie Brown (based on a story by Jeff Maguire, Djordje Milicevic); ph, Rene Verzier; m, Claude Demers; ed, Yves Langlois; prod d, Jocelyn Joly; cos, Michele Hamel; spec eff, Bill Orr; stunts, Jerome Tiberghien.

Drama   Cas.   (PR:A MPAA:PG)

TOKIMEDI NI SHISU†   (1986, Jap.) 105m Nikkatsu (Trans: Deaths in Tokimeki) c

Kenji Sawada *(Kudo, the Man)*, Kanako Higuchi *(Kozue)*, Naoki Sugiura *(Okura)*.

Sawada stars as a professional assassin sequestered in a lonely Japanese country house with a concubine and a guard appointed by the assassin's mysterious employers. Everyday the assassin performs his ritualistic routine of exercising, driving, eating, and drinking in preparation for the day that his employers will need him again. Finally, Sawada is sent to assassinate a Japanese religious leader. When the day of the murder comes, Sawada's plan goes awry and he kills himself in shame and frustration. The film ends with the implication that Sawada's employers hoped for just such an outcome. Directed by the promising young newcomer Yoshimitsu Morita (best known in the West for THE FAMILY GAME, 1984).

p, Hiroshi Okada, Shogo Hosokoshi, Shin Omori; d&w, Yoshimitsu Morita (based on a novel by Kenji Maruyama); ph, Yonezo Maeda; m, Osamu Shiomura; prod d, Katsumi Nakazawa.

Crime/Drama   (PR:O MPAA:NR)

TOMB, THE†   (1986) 84m Trans World Entertainment c

Cameron Mitchell *(Prof. Howard Phillips)*, John Carradine *(Mr. Androheb)*, Sybil Danning *(Jade)*, Susan Stokey *(Helen)*, Richard Alan Hench *(David Manners)*, Michelle Bauer *(Nefratis)*, David Pearson *(John Banning)*, George Hoth *(Dr. Stewart)*, Stu Weltman, Frank McDonald, Victor Von Wright, Jack Frankel, Peter Conway, Brad Arrington, Emanuel Shipow, Craig Hamann, Kitten Natividad, Dawn Wildsmith.

Archaeologists do their usual bit here by defiling an ancient Egyptian tomb, then dying horribly as the princess who rests within sprouts fangs and goes after them and certain artifacts that will maintain her life. A number of inside jokes and some above-average special effects garnered fair notices for this picture, which was planned for theatrical release until the company holding the rights went out of business and the film emerged on video.

p, Fred Olen Ray, Ronnie Hadar; d, Fred Olen Ray; w, Kenneth J. Hall, T.L. Lankford; ph, Paul Elliott; m, Drew Neumann; ed, Miriam L. Preissel; art d, Maxine Shepard; cos, Elizabeth A. Reid; spec eff, Bret Mixon; makeup, Makeup and Effects Lab; stunts, John Stewart.

Horror   Cas.   (PR:O MPAA:NR)

TOMMASO BLU†   (1986, It./Ger.) 90m Florian Furtwangler Filmproductions c

Alessandro Haber, Antonella Porfido, Marina Eugeni.

An immensely disturbing film starring Haber as a factory worker disillusioned with his years of forced mechanical labor. Seeing that he, along with his family and his entire world, have become as structured as the machine he operates, he desperately attempts an escape from his predicament to regain the youth and vitality that have deserted him. Instead, his unfulfilling association with a younger crowd leaves him even more isolated. Haber received a City of Taormina Prize for his performance as the man facing a midlife crisis.

d, Florian Furtwangler; w, Tommaso Di Ciaula, Peter Kammerer, Florian Furtwangler (based on the novel *Tuta Blue* by Di Ciaula); ph, James Jacobs; m, Peer Raben.

Drama   (PR:O MPAA:NR)

TONG NIEN WANG SHI   (SEE: A TIME TO LIVE AND A TIME TO DIE, 1986, Taiwan)

TONGS—A CHINATOWN STORY†   (1986, Hong Kong) 98m Pan Pacific-D&B Films c

Simon Yam, Larry Tan, Anthony Gioia, Christopher O'Connor, Ouitan Han, Daisey Yong.

Two brothers escape Mainland China and reach New York, where they become involved in rival gangs. One brother eventually comes to the attention of the Tong, the oriental crime syndicate. Shot on location in New York. Exists in both an English-language and subtitled version. (In Cantonese; English subtitles.)

d, Philip Chan; w, Peter C. M. Chan, Neil P. Mainiello, Felipe Luciano.

Crime   (PR:O MPAA:NR)

TOP GUN**   (1986) 110m Paramount Pictures c

Tom Cruise *(Lt. Pete Mitchell)*, Anthony Edwards *(Lt. Nick Bradshaw)*, Kelly McGillis *(Charlotte Blackwood)*, Tom Skerritt *(Cmdr. Mike Metcalf)*, Val Kilmer *(Tom Kasanzky)*, Michael Ironsides *(Dick Wetherly)*, Rick Rossovich *(Ron Kerner)*, Barry Tubb *(Henry Ruth)*, Whip Hubley *(Rick Neven)*, Clarence Gilyard,

Jr. *(Evan Gough)*, Tim Robbins *(Sam Wills)*, John Stockwell *(Cougar)*, James Tolkan *(Stinger)*, Meg Ryan *(Carole)*.

The most successful movie of 1986. This paean to hotshot Navy fighter pilots and high technology attracted mass audiences despite the oldest plot in airplane films and characters so vapid they vanish from the mind as soon as the house lights

come up. Cruise is a fighter pilot aboard an aircraft carrier in the Indian Ocean. While playing a game of "tag" in the air with some enemy pilots (unnamed, but they fly MIGs and have big red stars in the middle of their oxygen masks), Cruise manages to maneuver his plane so that it is upside down only feet above the enemy. When the other pilot looks up, Cruise gives him the finger while his weapons man (Edwards) snaps a picture. The enemy pilot is so disconcerted by this unorthodox flying that he breaks off the game and hightails it back to his base. Back on the carrier, the incident makes Cruise an instant celebrity. Since the previous top pilot of his group has lost his nerve, "the edge," Cruise is tagged to return to California for advanced fighter training at Miramar Naval Air Station, near San Diego. Here he will train with the best pilots from other squadrons, flying against instructors and firing electronic missiles tracked by computer. The best student from each class wins the prized "Top Gun" award, and the privilege to remain at Miramar as an instructor. Cruise sizes up his competition and determines that his chief rival is Kilmer. In simulated combat, Cruise shoots down an instructor but gets in trouble because he flew beneath the 10,000 foot altitude floor on the exercise. Cruise also comes in for much criticism for his individualistic flying style, for which he earned the nick name "Maverick." Still, he manages to keep neck-and-neck with Kilmer on the overall score. Meanwhile, Cruise has initiated an affair with McGillis, a civilian consultant and expert on the physics of high speed airplane performance. He is attracted to her because of her looks, but she is interested in him because of his encounter over the Indian Ocean, in which he became the first aviator to see the latest enemy plane up close. Back in the air, Cruise cuts too close to another plane and has his engines fail in the backwash. In a flat spin, he and Edwards eject, but only Cruise survives. Badly shaken by his friend's death, Cruise loses the edge and falls out of contention for the Top Gun award, which goes to Kilmer. Meanwhile, McGillis leaves him without a word and moves to Washington. Back on his carrier in the Indian Ocean, this time with Kilmer a squadron mate, an international incident is in the offing. A crippled U.S. ship is threatened by enemy planes, so the F-14s scramble to protect the craft. Real shooting starts, and the Americans take some casualties

until Cruise finally manages to pull himself together and blow the bad guys out of the sky. A hero again, Cruise is offered a teaching job at Miramar, which he accepts and where McGillis is waiting for him.

The story is a familiar one and has been done in many variations in films like WINGS OF THE NAVY (1939). What TOP GUN contributes to the genre is a greater-than-ever emphasis on hardware and an almost homoerotic attraction for male bodies, preferably sweaty. Cruise is the only character whose motivations or background are explained, and that is an unsatisfactory tale about how his aviator father disappeared over Vietnam 20 years before. Fortunately for Cruise, Skerritt, the top instructor at Miramar, flew with his father and fills Cruise in on his dad's fate. The romance with McGillis is unconvincing, and their poorly defined respective ages make their relationship seem to veer from mother-son to rutting teenagers to tender adults. But in the final analysis, everything that happens on the ground is extraneous to the real heart of the film, the flying sequences. Much praised, the flying footage seamlessly intercuts live action shots of planes with special effects models. But for all the skill of their execution, the flying scenes are often confusing, rarely giving any idea of where planes are in relation to each other. Jets streak by and pilots spin their heads around yelling "Where'd he go? Where'd he go?" until the beepers aboard their planes go off telling them they've been shot down. The producers went to the Navy with the project and received complete cooperation, provided certain changes were made (including one that places the final battle over international waters rather than land). The Navy made five different types of planes available, in addition to a variety of other services ranging from technical advisors to air-sea rescue operations. However, taxpayers didn't bankroll the film. The filmmakers received a bill for $1.1 million from the Navy. The armed forces are not always so cooperative with filmmakers. The Air Force refused to help with IRON EAGLE, and the Army turned down PLATOON and HEARTBREAK RIDGE. In HEART-BREAK RIDGE, director Clint Eastwood simply changed the story to concern the more cooperative Marines. The Navy was handsomely rewarded for its trouble as it watched enlistments soar when the film became a hit. Some theater owners actually asked the Navy to put recruiters in their lobbies to catch young men coming out with the sound of jets still ringing in their ears. The Dutch Air Force, among others, reported much the same phenomenon when the film played there. One of the slickest films ever made, TOP GUN is a facile movie in which Americans get to kill Russians with impunity, proving their inherent superiority, plus they get the girl.

p, Don Simpson, Jerry Bruckheimer; d, Tony Scott; w, Jim Cash, Jack Epps, Jr.; ph, Jeffrey Kimball (Metrocolor); m, Harold Faltermeyer; ed, Billy Weber, Chris Lebenzon; prod d, John F. DeCuir, Jr.; set d, Robert B. Benton; spec eff, Gary Gutierrez.

Drama/War   Cas.   (PR:A-C MPAA:PG)

TOP OF THE WHALE†   (1986, Fr.) 90m bw-c

Willeke Van Ammelrooy (Eve), Jean Badin (Luis), Fernando Bordeu (Narcisso), Herbert Curiel (Adam), Amber De Grauw (Eden).

Another eclectic slice of life from Ruiz, the Chilean exile living in France, whose films are predictable only in the sense that one always knows that he will see something wholly unpredictable on the screen. Structured (if such a thing can be said of a Ruiz film) similarly to Ruiz's SANS IN MIROIR (also released this year), TOP OF THE WHALE has its characters wandering around on a surreal Latin American estate reacting to and interacting with a series of strange occurrences. Van Ammelrooy is an indecisive woman who cannot make up her mind whether she loves an anthropologist who is able to decipher the language of an nearly extinct Indian tribe, or a millionaire who refuses to furnish his magnificent estate. Ruiz photographed the film in color, sepiatone, and black-and-white, while his characters speak in five different languages. TOP OF THE WHALE received a short, uneventful New York release in 1986. (In Danish, English, Spanish, French, and German; English subtitles.)

p, Monica Tegelaar, Kees Kasander; d&w, Raul Ruiz; ph, Henri Alekan, Theo Bierkens; m, Jorge Arriagada; ed, Valeria Sarmiento.

Fantasy   (PR:NR MPAA:NR)

TORMENT*   (1986) 85m NW c

Taylor Gilbert (Jennifer), William Witt (Father), Eve Brenner (Mrs. Courtland), Warren Lincoln (Michael), Najean Cherry (Helen), Stan Weston (Bogartis), Doug Leach (Officer Tilman).

A slasher movie with a trace of intelligence may be the kindest way to consider this low-budget would-be psychological thriller. A killer, Witt, is loose in San Francisco, murdering young women, and Lincoln is the detective assigned to bring him in. Lincoln is engaged to Gilbert, who is being stalked by the killer. The detective takes Gilbert out to meet his mother, Brenner, and the two do not hit it off. Lincoln leaves the two together in his mother's big dark house and returns to his investigation. That night Witt breaks into the house and stands over Gilbert's bed. Brenner spots him as he is leaving and calls the police, but they find nothing and assume she imagined the episode, something she has been known to do. Early the next morning the maid arrives and Witt carves her up with a kitchen knife, then hides himself and the body. Gilbert leaves for a while and Witt shows up again, threatening to shoot Brenner. The older woman stabs him in the hand and hides in the den, and when Gilbert returns she thinks Brenner has lost her mind. The doorbell rings and Brenner screams that it's the killer, and when Gilbert opens the door, it is, but Gilbert puts her arms around him and calls him daddy. Yes, that's right, Witt is Gilbert's father. Brenner tries to convince Gilbert that her father is a murderer, but she refuses to believe it until Witt tells her himself, asking for her help in killing Lincoln to get him off his back. Gilbert tries to call Lincoln for help, and when Witt realizes his own daughter has betrayed him, he is determined to kill both women. They fight him off with guns and spears and arrows, but he keeps coming back for more, and Gilbert is unable to kill her own father. Brenner calls the sheriff, and when he arrives Witt cleaves him in two with an axe. Finally, with an almost superhuman effort, the two women succeed in killing Witt, just as Lincoln and the rest of the cops arrive.

Shot in San Francisco on a tiny budget, the film has a few good moments, but the plot becomes so convoluted and the point of view changes so often that the whole thing becomes a mess, though because of some good production values, a good-looking mess.

p,d&w, Samson Aslanian, John Hopkins; ph, Stephen Carpenter (Monaco Labs Color); m, Christopher Young; ed, John Penney, Earl Ghaffari, Bret Shelton; art d, Chris Hopkins.

Thriller   Cas.   (PR:O MPAA:R)

TORPIDONOSTCI†   (1986, USSR) 92m Lenfilm c (Trans: Torpedo Bombers)

Rodion Nakhapietov, Alexei Zharkov.

Soviet bravery during the Nazi invasion has long been a staple of Soviet cinema, and this is yet another example. The men of a torpedo plane squadron enact their own personal dramas, then fly off to bravely die fighting for Mother Russia. Interestingly, many of the minor roles in this film were filled by actors from MOI DRUG IVAN LAPSHIN who had been brought in from remote republics for that film, then found themselves in Leningrad unable to get work.

d, Simon Aronovitch; m, Svetlana Karmelita (based on a novel by Yuri Gherman); ph, Vladimir Ilyin; art d, Isa Kaplan.

War   (PR:A MPAA:NR)

TOUCH AND GO*   (1986) 101m Tri-Star c

Michael Keaton (Bobby Barbato), Maria Conchita Alonso (Denise DeLeon), Ajay Naidu (Louis DeLeon), Maria Tucci (Dee Dee), Max Wright (Lester), Lara Jill Miller (Courtney), D.V. de Vincentis (Lupo), Michael Zelniker (McDonald), Jere Burns (Levesolie), Dens Duffy (Lynch), Steve Pint (Green), Lara Jill Miller (Courtney), Clair Dolan, Carri Lyn Levinson, Charlotte Ross (Courtney's Girl Friends), Jean Bates (Lady at Mortuary), Lynda Weismeir, Cynthia Cypert (Girls in Bar), Earl Boby (Writer), Ed Meekat (Diner Waiter), Nick De Mauro (Maintenance Man), Ron Stokes (Sportscaster), Richard McNally, Mark Jacobs, Ford Lee (Reporters), Ron Presson (Bus Driver), Drake Collier (Doorman), Alex Ross (Variety Store Owner), Jean Lafette, Bill Morrison, Ron Pace, Kristin Collins York (Bar Patrons), Wayne McGinnis, Joseph Mazowics, Tim O'Donnell (Officials), Jack White, Dan Miller, Michael F. Kelley, Mark Nahan, Steve Grannelli, Louis Nicolan, Scott Berg, Jon Scott Rafeld, Kevin Boke, Eric Repas, Luc Boleau, J. Paul Timmons, Vincent Carter, Victor Venasky, Bob Clasby, Mike Wehrmann, Claude Cohen, Robert Udell, Craig Danger, Adam Peck, John Blom (The Chicago Eagles), Eric Troy Adams, Blair Hughes, Robert Bayer, Tim Jarin, Steve Cameron, Stephen Kelly, Allan Clelano, Michael Koble, Dan Coblifin, Mike McGee, Craig Cullen, Edward Mertz, Robert Destocki, Douglas Newsham, Dennis Gilbert, Rod Frith, Jay Green, Steve Zawslak, Ian Hendry (The Opposing Teams).

Though not entirely successful, TOUCH AND GO is a sweet little comedy that works thanks to the strong performances of its three leads, and a conscious effort to avoid standard plot twists. Keaton is a star hockey player living in Chicago, where he is the toast of the town. Fans cheer his name and women practically throw themselves in Keaton's path. One night, as Keaton walks to his car after a game, he's accosted by four muggers. Keaton manages to fight them off, then grabs 11-year-old Naidu, the gang's youngest member. The cocky lad manages to talk Keaton out of going to the police, instead persuading the athlete to take him home. Once there, Keaton gives Naidu his telephone number, instructing the boy to pass the number on to his absent mother. Naidu tells Keaton there's nothing to eat in the house, and against his better judgment, Keaton takes the boy out for a bite. Finally, they return to Naidu's apartment where they find Alonso, the boy's worried mother. She thanks Keaton, though she has no idea her son's benefactor is a Chicago celebrity. Keaton returns to his car and finds the windshield has been smashed. As he drives away, de Vincentis, the teenaged gang leader, howls maniacally from a nearby rooftop. After de Vincentis breaks into his apartment, Alonso decides the time has come to leave this neighborhood. Despite her son's protests, she ships Naidu off to the suburbs to stay with Alonso's cousins Tucci and Wright. Next, in an effort to apologize for the whole incident, she meets Keaton at the stadium. Alonso insists on treating Keaton to an expensive dinner.

Keaton acquiesces to this spirited woman's request, and the two cap their date by making love in Keaton's high-rise apartment. Keaton is not used to waking up with his bed partners. He tries to evade Alonso the next morning but she surprises him by making breakfast. Hoping to avoid any emotional commitment, Keaton awkwardly explains himself and the terribly insulted Alonso leaves. Meanwhile, Naidu is unhappy with his situation. He takes a train back to Chicago and gets back in touch with Keaton. Keaton drives Naidu and his mother back to the suburbs, where Tucci and Wright are holding a birthday party for their daughter Miller. Everyone recognizes Keaton, who becomes a reluctant guest at the affair. Naidu sneaks some champagne, which makes him sick, and he throws up on an expensive couch. Wright is furious, and Keaton, who has taken a strong dislike to the man, offers to pay for the damage. He drives Naidu and Alonso back to Chicago, then makes sure they get back to their apartment safely. As he says goodnight, both Keaton and Alonso feel somewhat uncomfortable as they avoid a strong urge to kiss. Later, Naidu sneaks aboard the team bus when Keaton's club heads north for a game in Minnesota. Keaton allows Naidu to stay in his hotel room, but makes arrangements for him to fly home following the game. That night de Vincentis breaks into Alonso's apartment and beats her up. Tucci calls Keaton, who meets her with Naidu at the airport the next day. Naidu angrily lashes out at his older friend when Keaton says he has to go to Los Angeles for a game. Realizing he does care for Alonso, Keaton abandons his team and returns to Chicago. At the hospital, Tucci tells him that Naidu has gone out to get revenge. Keaton catches up with the boy and together they track down de Vincentis. Using the fighting skills he has perfected in the hockey arena, Keaton subdues de Vincentis just before the police arrive. Knowing his glory days won't last forever, Keaton helps set up Alonso in a business partnership as the two finally allow their deeper feelings to surface.

Keaton, Alonso, and Naidu take an undeniably slight story and make it something warm and thoughtful with their fine performances. Holding back on his usual wisecracking, Keaton effectively stretches his range to create a more rounded character than previous roles allowed. Certainly he's funny, but Keaton also shows depth by portraying the athlete as a confused man who wants something more in life, even if he's not sure what that might be. Although Alonso is obviously typecast as the unwed Hispanic mother, she brings a wonderful effervescent quality to the part. This is an emotional woman who often lets her feelings rush ahead of logic, yet she maintains a strong and assured sense of dignity. In one of the film's funniest moments, Alonso follows Keaton into a men's bathroom, unaware of where she is as she breathlessly tries to apologize and invite Keaton to dinner. Alonso's energy, coupled with Keaton's ill-at-ease feelings over the situation, make this unlikely and offbeat sequence a real charmer. Keaton's relationship with Naidu is another of TOUCH AND GO's strong points. Naidu isn't just some child actor essaying the mannerisms of a street kid. He comes off very naturally, an arrogant and brash youngster with a sweet touch of naivete. Naidu and Keaton have a wonderful rapport within their love-hate relationship, an unaffected chemistry that feels warm and honest. However, the film does have its weak points. Alonso's relationship with Tucci and Wright is never firmly established, and these incidental characters are mostly a story intrusion. By the film's logic, Keaton must play for the only hockey team that has an inordinate number of home games and plays only when it's convenient for the star to show up. Fortunately, these false moments are overshadowed by the relationships among the three leads, and some interesting story turns. Mandel's direction gives the film a light touch, letting relationships develop with a sparing use of long takes. Allowing the Keaton-Alonso romance to develop on a tentative level works well, making their final kiss a wonderful payoff. There is much animosity between the two, though this is an obvious facade disguising deeper feelings. Some critics were disturbed by the violent confrontation of de Vincentis and Alonso but the scene takes a chance by jarring audience expectations. Though certainly disturbing, Alonso's assault is never exploited. Surprisingly, though the film was shot in 1984, Universal Pictures was convinced the film would never sell. The final print was completed in 1985, but TOUCH AND GO sat on the shelf for another year before Tri-Star picked it up for release (Mandel managed to complete shooting F/X in the interim). It quickly came and left theaters at the end of the summer, an undeserved fate for such an enjoyable feature. Undoubtedly TOUCH AND GO will see more audiences through its videocassette release. Songs here include: "Tangent Tears" (performed by Mr. Mister), "Signals" (Greg Phillinganes, Richard Page, John Lang, Nathan East, performed by Greg Phillinganes), "Playing with Fire" (Jackie Jackson, Pamela Phillips Oland, Jack Wargo, performed by Greg Phillinganes). Despite the often frank dialogue (the reason behind the film's "R" rating) TOUCH AND GO is acceptable viewing for older children.

p, Stephen Friedman; d, Robert Mandel; w, Alan Ormsby, Bob Sand, Harry Colomby; ph, Richard H. Kline (AstroLabs, Movielab); m, Sylvester Levay; ed, Walt Mulconery; prod d, Charles Rosen; set d, James Payne, Jean Akan; cos, Bernie Pollack; m/l, Greg Phillinganes, Richard Page, John Lang, Nathan East, Jackie Jackson, Pamela Phillips Oland, Jack Wargo; makeup, Robert Mills; stunts, Bill Couch; hockey advisor, Jack White; hockey coordinator, Michael F. Kelly.

Comedy/Romance   Cas.   (PR:C-O MPAA:R)

TOUGH GUYS**   (1986, US) 102m Silver Screen Partners II-Bryna Prods./
                                                                Touchstone-BV c

Burt Lancaster *(Harry Doyle)*, Kirk Douglas *(Archie Long)*, Charles Durning *(Deke Yablonski)*, Alexis Smith *(Belle)*, Dana Carvey *(Richie Evans)*, Darlanne Fluegel *(Skye Foster)*, Eli Wallach *(Leon B. Little)*, Monty Ash *(Vince)*, Billy Barty *(Philly)*, Simmy Bow *(Schultz)*, Darlene Conley *(Gladys Ripps)*, Nathan Davis *(Jimmy Ellis)*, Matthew Faison *(Man in Gay Bar)*, Corkey Ford *(Gang Leader)*, Rick Garcia *(Federale Captain)*, Graham Jarvis *(Richie's Boss)*, Doyle L. McCormack *(Train Engineer)*, Bob Maxwell *(Syms)*, Steven Memel *(Derek)*,

Jeanne Mori *(Female Officer)*, Scott Nemes *(Yogurt Boy)*, Ernie Sabella *(Hotel Clerk)*, Darryl Shelly *(Gang Member No. 2)*, Hillary Shepard *(Sandy)*, Jake Steinfeld *(Howard)*, Charles Sweigart *(Jarvis)*, Eleanor Zee *(Restaurant Hostess)*, Ron Ryan *(Prison Guard)*, Ruth De Sosa *(Teller No. 1)*, John Mariano *(Teller No. 2)*, Larry Mintz *(Bank Robber No. 1)*, Dick Hancock *(Bank Robber No. 2)*, John Demy *(Policeman in Park)*, Grant Aleksander *(Bartender at Mickey's)*, Kenny Ransom *(Gang Member No. 3)*, Joe Seely *(Gang Member No. 4)*, Michael F. Kelly *(Ambulance Attendant No. 1)*, Jeffrey Lynn Johnson *(Ambulance Attendant No. 2)*, Hugo Stanger *(Old Man)*, Jimmy Lennon *(Himself)*, Philip Culotta *(Slam Dancer)*, Donald Thompson *(Boy Scout)*, Lisa Pescia *(Customer No. 1)*, Jeff Levine *(Customer No. 2)*, Seth Kaufman *(Customer No. 3)*, Michele Marsh *(Newscaster)*, Todd Hollowell *(Himself)*, Steven Greenstein *(Bartender at Virgina's Bar)*, Thomas F. Maguire *(Armored Car Guard)*, Ellen Albertini Dow *(Old Lady)*, Scanlon Gail *(Sym's Assistant)*, James Clark *(Brakeman)*, Skip Stellrecht *(Reporter No. 1)*, David Michael O'Neil *(Reporter No. 2)*, James Deeth *(Helicopter Pilot)*, Denver Matteson *(Border Patrol Captain)*, Flea, Anthony Kiedis, Cliff Martinez, Hillel Slovak *(Red Hot Chili Peppers)*.

Teaming Kirk Douglas and Burt Lancaster for their sixth film together (following I WALK ALONE, 1948; GUN FIGHT AT THE OK CORRAL, 1957; THE DEVIL'S DISCIPLE, 1959; THE LIST OF ADRIAN MESSENGER, 1963; and SEVEN DAYS IN MAY, 1964) must have seemed like a good idea to the folks at

Disney Studio's Touchstone division. After all, the actors were good friends in real life. They had recently worked together on stage in 1982's "The Boys of Autumn," in which Douglas and Lancaster played aging versions of Huck Finn and Tom Sawyer, and both stole the show with their appearance at the 1985 Oscar ceremonies. How could anything they performed together go wrong? Yet their appealing chemistry is not enough to redeem TOUGH GUYS, a contrived and shallow comedy that doesn't do justice to the talent of either star. Douglas and Lancaster play a pair of old-time criminals, jailed for 30 years after committing the last train robbery in the US. Once paroled, the two are surprised at the prison gates by Wallach, a mysterious and near-sighted gunman who unsuccessfully tries to blow their heads off. The pair manage to escape, then go meet Carvey, their parole officer. The youthful criminologist admits he idolizes the pair (framed newspaper headlines of their famous train robbery hang in his office), and explains the terms of their parole. Lancaster, the older of the two, must go to a nursing home while Douglas is offered a chance at menial employment. Neither will be allowed to contact the other for three years, a jarring fact that doesn't sit well with either man. Lancaster feels humiliated by this treatment, but fortunately runs into Smith, an old flame who also lives in the nursing home. Douglas gets picked up by a healthy young aerobics instructor (Fluegel), who introduces him to the Los Angeles nightclub scene and engages the older man in all-night sex marathons. However Douglas, realizing his age and modern times just aren't mixing, leaves Fluegel and rapidly goes through a series of low-paying jobs. Eventually, he and Lancaster hook up once more while Durning, the lawman who arrested them three decades before, follows the pair around town. He is convinced that Douglas and Lancaster will return to a life of crime, a hunch that inevitably comes true. Douglas and Lancaster go to Davis, a former colleague, and try to rustle up some of their old gang. This proves to be fruitless, so the duo decide to pull a heist of their own. Lancaster feigns a heart attack, which attracts the attention of an armored car security guard. Once the guard is in a vulnerable position, Douglas and Lancaster pull out their guns and make off with the goods. Unfortunately, the vehicle has no substantial loot, but at least the caper puts them back in the holdup business. Despite the warnings of Carvey, Douglas and Lancaster decide to go after some real action. They plan to hijack the *Gold Coast Flyer*, the very train they tried to rob 30 years before, which is about to make a much publicized final run. After taking over the train, the pair is surprised once again by Wallach. The gunman explains he had been assigned to kill Douglas and Lancaster many years ago, and now he intends to fulfill his long overdue commitment. Instead, they persuade Wallach to become a partner in the hijacking. Meanwhile outside the locomotive Durning beseeches his long-time adversaries to give up. Carvey, who sneaks aboard the train, lends his hand to Douglas and Lancaster and the chase is on. En route, the criminals talk Carvey out of joining up in a life of crime, though the pair have every intention of pulling off their heist. Durning is convinced he will again capture the two, because the railroad tracks come to an end a few hundred feet from the Califor-

nia/Mexico border. Undeterred, Douglas and Lancaster drive the locomotive off its tracks, through the border gates, and straight into the Mexican desert. During watches helplessly while Douglas and Lancaster exit from the train, exuberant at what they have just pulled off. A Mexican patrol arrives to investigate but Douglas and Lancaster show the band they still have plenty of spunk left and kick the head man in the groin.

TOUGH GUYS tries to be a crime comedy while making an important statement about the dignity of senior citizens. It's not an unlikely mixture (the wonderful 1979 film GOING IN STYLE dealt with this same theme) but the script by Orr and Cruickshank only deals with issues on a surface level. Douglas' and Lancaster's confrontations with old and new are dealt with in broad strokes, simplifying problems that demand a more considered treatment. The film also suffers from rudimentary plot developments that congeal almost as soon as the hardened criminals become free men. While cashing their parole checks, Douglas and Lancaster foil a bank holdup. No one seems to notice when the two pocket the robbers' pistols and the episode is never referred to again. It's an implausible occurrence that typifies many of the script's troubles. In another scene Douglas enjoys a drink at one of his old hangouts, which is now a gay bar. He is stupefied when a man asks him to dance, and Lancaster has to rescue his old pal. These men have been locked up in an all-male prison for 30 years, yet are hopelessly naive about homosexuality. This unlikely gag plays exactly for what it is, a pitiful attempt at cheap humor. Kanew, who previously directed 1984's REVENGE OF THE NERDS (as well as Douglas' 1982 film EDDIE MACON'S RUN), shows little sense for comic setups in his direction. Put Douglas behind a yogurt stand, toss in a bratty child to give the man a hard time, and you know the little whelp will be wearing his food by the end of the sequence. Fluegel's seduction of Douglas is equally predictable. One closeup of her face gazing at the virile older man is all it takes to get the all-too obvious point across. But the blame can't be laid entirely on Orr, Cruickshank or Kanew. Surely Douglas and Lancaster must have read the script before beginning the project. No one forced them to go through some of their more embarrassing scenes, such as Douglas' brief foray into modern fashion. Lancaster's scenes with Smith do have some touching moments, but he did the same thing a lot better in ATLANTIC CITY (1981). The veteran actors make a good screen team, but this film isn't the right vehicle for their respective talents. Interestingly enough, Orr and Cruickshank wrote their script after seeing Douglas and Lancaster on the 1985 Oscar show. The writers had one previous collaboration, a forgettable 1985 exploitation feature called BREAKING ALL THE RULES. They still decided to draft a screenplay specifically for Douglas and Lancaster, despite the overwhelming probability their script wouldn't sell. It's a well known fact in Hollywood that unknown screenwriters shouldn't write on spec with major stars in mind. But amazingly, Orr and Cruickshank beat the odds. Producer Joe Wizan got their work to Douglas and Lancaster, who agreed to do the film if the characters would be rewritten to suit their personalities. Wallach's character was originally to have been played by Adolph Caesar, who succumbed to a heart attack only one day into production. At age 69 and 72, Douglas and Lancaster exhibited remarkably hardy constitutions in their often physically demanding roles. Both performed the majority of their own stunts in the climactic chase, including running around on top of the moving train. *The Gold Coast Flier*, moved at a speed between 15 and 20 miles per hour. The Flier, provided by an Oregon train museum, was outfitted with protective straps along the side in case either man fell. Douglas told one interviewer of the experience: "It was a lot of fun. I've always done most of my own stunts and I think Burt has always done most of his . . . People are so hip these days, they know when you're using doubles; they sense it when it's the stunt man hiding his face . . . I would have been cheating the people if I hadn't been up there myself." Songs include: "Bill Bailey Won't You Please Come Home" (Hughie Cannon), "Because of You" (Arthur Hammerstein, Dudley Wilkinson), "Don't Get Around Much Anymore" (Bob Russell, Duke Ellington, performed by Bing Crosby), "Set It Straight" (The Red Hot Chili Peppers, performed by The Red Hot Chili Peppers), "Nasty" (James Harris III, Terry Lewis, Janet Jackson, performed by Janet Jackson), "Androgynous" (Hillary Shepard, Louise Goffin, Dennis Herring, performed by The American Girls), "So Hip it Hurts" (Martin Frye, Mark White, performed by ABC), "Tuff Enuff" (Kim Wilson, performed by The Fabulous Thunderbirds), "Rags to Riches" (Richard Adler, Jerry Ross, performed by Michael Stanton), "Work That Body" (Diana Ross, Paul Jabara, Raymond Chew, performed by Phyllis St. James), "String of

Pearls" (Jerry Grey), "Moonlight Serenade" (Mitchell Parish, Glenn Miller), "Let's Have Some Fun" (Jesse Johnson, performed by Jesse Johnson).

p, Joe Wizan; d, Jeff Kanew; w, James Orr, Jim Cruickshank; ph, King Baggot (Panavision, DeLuxe Color); m, James Newton Howard; ed, Kaja Fehr; prod d, Todd Hallowell; set d, Jeff Haley; cos, Erica Phillips; spec eff, Chuck Gaspar, Joe D. Day, Stan Parks; makeup, Robert J. Schiffer; stunts, Conrad E. Palmisano.

Comedy/Crime Cas. (PR:C MPAA:PG)

TRACKS IN THE SNOW (SEE: PERVOLA—TRACKS IN THE SNOW, 1986, Neth.)

TRAMP AT THE DOOR† (1986, Can.) 80m CanWest-Burbank-Telefilm Canada/Simcom International c

Ed McNamara *(Gustave)*, August Schellenberg *(Albert)*, Monique Mercure *(Madeleine)*, Joanna Schellenberg *(Gabrielle)*, Eric Peterson *(Lemieux)*, Jean Louis Hebert *(Hebert)*.

Low-budget drama, told from a child's point of view, about a ragged stranger who shows up at a remote Manitoba farm in 1934. He claims to be a distant relative and proceeds to fulfill all manner of psychological needs for each family member.

p, Stan Thomas, Don Brinton; d&w, Allan Kroeker (based on a story by Gabrielle Roy); ph, Ron Orieux; m, Randolph Peters; ed, Lara Mazur; art d, Bonnie von Helmolt.

Drama (PR:A-C MPAA:NR)

TRANSFORMERS: THE MOVIE, THE* (1986) 86m Sunbow-Marvel/DEG c

Voices: Orson Welles *(Planet Unicron)*, Robert Stack *(Ultra Magnus)*, Leonard Nimoy *(Galvatron)*, Eric Idle *(Wreck Gar)*, Judd Nelson *(Hot Rod/Rodimus Prime)*, Lionel Stander *(Kup)*, John Moschitta *(Blurr)*, Norm Alden *(Kranix)*, Jack Angel *(Astrotrain)*, Michael Bell *(Prowl/Scrapper/Swoop/Junkion)*, Gregg Berger *(Grimlock)*, Susan Blu *(Arcee)*, Arthur Burghardt *(Devastator)*, Corey Burton *(Spike/Brawn/Shockwave)*, Roger C. Carmel *(Cyclonus/Quintesson Leader)*, Rege Cordic *(Quintesson Judge)*, Peter Cullen *(Prime/Ironhide)*, Scatman Crothers *(Jazz)*, Bud Davis *(Dirge)*, Walker Edmiston *(Inferno)*, Paul Eiding *(Perceptor)*, Ed Gilbert *(Blitzwing)*, Dan Gilvezan *(Bumblebee)*, Buster Jones *(Blaster)*, Stan Jones *(Scourge)*, Casey Kasem *(Cliffjumper)*, Chris Latta *(Starscream)*, David Mendenhall *(Daniel)*, Don Messick *(Gears)*, Hal Rayle *(Shrapnel)*, Clive Revill *(Kickback)*, Neil Ross *(Bonecrusher/Hook/Springer/Slag)*, Frank Welker *(Soundwave/Megatron/Rumble/Frenzy/Wheelie/Junkion)*.

Unlike other toy-inspired children's animations, such as THE CARE BEARS or MY LITTLE PONY, THE TRANSFORMERS: THE MOVIE doesn't try to appeal to just one market. Rather, this film attempts to have something for everyone, from tots to teens, and the result is a boring mess. Transformers are a popular series of robot toys (and comic books, and video tapes, and lunchboxes, and pillowcases, and so on into marketing infinity) boasting the not-so-unique ability to change size, shape, and function to whatever form best suits the mo-

ment. If you think this sounds vaguely familiar, you're not wrong: the Transformers share this same dexterous ability with their chief competitors, the Gobots. This latter group of toys was also featured in a 1986 motion picture, released a few months before THE TRANSFORMERS. Perhaps not so coincidentally, the two films share more than just metamorphosing machines as stars. Like GOBOTS: BATTLE OF THE ROCKLORDS, THE TRANSFORMERS: THE MOVIE also features rancid animation techniques, a story that will bore anyone over age ten, and a few overpaid celebrities essaying the lead voices. Unlike other toy-inspired animations, however, this film was rated PG rather than the expected G. This is due to the surprising amount of violence within the story which might upset younger children. There's also a gratuitous use of four-letter words, which the kids will enjoy, but which might cause their parents to blush.

The story takes place in the year 2005. As in the videotapes and television cartoon series, the heroic Transformers are locked into yet another life-or-death battle with their archenemies, the Decepticons. These evil creatures are fought off by some Earthly creatures known as Autobots, sending the severely demoralized Decepticons off into outer space. Now enters Unicron, a powerful force about the size of a planet, which is capable of destroying anything it wants to (Unicron is voiced by Orson Welles, but out of respect to the director of CITIZEN KANE and TOUCH OF EVIL the obvious girth jokes will be avoided). Unicron helps to rejuvenate the Decepticon leader, giving him a new body and a new moniker (Galvatron), as well as outfitting him with the voice of Leonard Nimoy. It's all-out war between the new, improved Decepticons and the Autobots, but enter a young Transformer named Hot Rod (guess what he can change into?), voiced by Judd Nelson. Several plot twists later, the film turns into a battle between Charles Foster Kane, Mr. Spock, and a Brat Packer. Guess who wins? A final word on this entirely forgettable feature. Though heavily advertised as the final screen work for the legendary Orson Welles, several posthumous works of his still awaited release in 1987.

p, Joe Bacal, Tom Griffin; d, Nelson Shin, Kozo Morishita; w, Ron Friedman, Flint Dille (based on the Hasbro toy The Transformers); m, Vince DiCola; ed, David Hankins; spec eff, Masayuki Kawachi, Shoji Sato; anim, Toei Animation Co.

Animated/Science Fiction   Cas.   (PR:A-C   MPAA:PG)

TRANSITTRAUME†   (1986, Ger.) 95m Pentafilm–Second German Television c (Trans: Transit Dreams)

Marita Marschall, Pascal Lavy, Gerald Uhlig, Edith Neitzel, Kurt Raab, Peter Heusch.

Two girls who resemble each other closely, one from East Berlin and the other from West Berlin, trade identities to see how the other side lives. Their stories are intercut with old newsreel footage that documents the way the two Germanys have drifted away from each other over the last 40 years. One of the codirectors, Wensierski, himself defected from the East not long before making this film.

p, Hartmut Jahn; d&w, Hartmut Jahn, Peter Wensierski; ph, Carlos Bustamente; m, Bernhard Voss.

Comedy   (PR:NR   MPAA:NR)

TRAS EL CRISTAL   (SEE: CAGED GLASS, 1986)

TRAVELLING NORTH†   (1986, Aus.) 96m View/CEL c

Leo McKern (Frank), Julia Blake (Frances), Graham Kennedy (Freddy), Henri Szeps (Saul), Michele Fawdon, Diane Craig, Andrea Moor, Drew Forsythe, John Gregg.

Although an Australian by birth, Leo McKern had never made a film in that country before this well-received effort based on a successful play. He plays a 70-year-old widower who retires and persuades a lady friend (Blake) to move with him to a clifftop home on the tropical northern shore of Australia. For a time they are happy, but soon McKern's health starts to deteriorate and he grows irritable. Tensions mount and threaten to divide them, but in the end they reconcile, marry, and enjoy a brief period of happiness before he dies.

p, Ben Gannon; d, Carl Schultz; w, David Williamson (based on his play); ph, Julian Penny (Eastmancolor); ed, Henry Dangar; prod d, Owen Paterson; md, Alan John.

Drama   (PR:C-O   MPAA:NR)

TRE SUPERMEN A SANTO DOMINGO†   (1986, It.) 71m Barbatoja/Uniexport c (Trans: Three Supermen in Santo Domingo)

Daniel Stephen, Sal Borgese, Steve Martin, Gena Gas.

A bunch of Soviet-backed hoods operating out of the title island are in possession of perfect printing plates and currency paper. Their plan is to subvert the entire world's monetary system, creating havoc for capitalists everywhere. An FBI agent-cum-superman and two other highly mercenary superguys make their way to Santo Domingo, where they capture a gorgeous girl-gangster and force her to assist them in battling both reds and mobsters. They succeed in expropriating the spurious currency and its means of manufacture and speed away from the island in a yacht. Followed by both American and Russian submarines, they luck out when each undersea craft interferes with the other's pursuit, leaving the trio free to frolic with the counterfeit bills and the lightly clad beauties who are eager to assist in their divestiture.

d, Italo Martinenghi; w, Italo Martinenghi, Adalberto Albertini, Antonio C. Corti (based on a story by Italo Martinenghi); ph, Pier Giorgio Albertini (Fotocinema Color); m, Paolo Colombo.

Comedy/Adventure   (PR:C   MPAA:NR)

TRICK OR TREAT**   (1986) 97m De Laurentiis Entertainment Group c

Marc Price (Eddie Weinbauer), Tony Fields (Sammi Curr), Lisa Orgolini (Leslie Graham), Doug Savant (Tim Hainey), Elaine Joyce (Angie Weinbauer), Glen

Morgan (Roger Mockus), Gene Simmons (Nuke), Ozzy Osbourne (Rev. Aaron Gilstrom), Elise Richards (Genie Wooster), Richard Pachorek (Ron Avery), Clare Nono (Maggie Wong-Hernandez), Alice Nunn (Mrs. Cavell), Larry Sprinkle (Marv McCain), Charles Martin Smith (Mr. Wimbley), Claudia Templeton (Hysterical Survivor), Denny Pierce, Ray Shaffer, Brad Thomas (Goons), Terry Loughlin (Senator), Graham Smith (Stan), Kevin Yahger (Lead Guitarist), Amy Bertolette (Fairy), Leroy Sweet, Barry Bell, Steve Boles (Cops), James D. Nelson (Dave the Partier), Richard Doyle (Voice).

A fairly clever send-up of both heavy-metal rock music and the paranoid parental-action groups that want it banned. The first directorial effort by actor Charles Martin Smith (AMERICAN GRAFFITI, NEVER CRY WOLF, STARMAN) stars Price, best known as "Skippy" on the hit television series "Family Ties," as

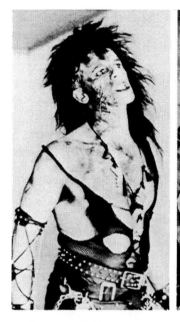

an alienated, nerdy high-schooler whose only refuge is heavy-metal music. His room is wallpapered with pictures and posters of his favorite heavy-metal rock stars, mainly Sammi Curr (Fields) who just happens to have graduated from the very high school Price attends. When Fields' offer to play a concert at his alma mater is denied by school officials, Price is crushed. Things get worse, however, when, to Price's horror, Fields is killed in a hotel fire. Despondent, Price visits his friend Simmons, a local heavy-metal DJ. In an effort to cheer Price up, Simmons gives Price the last, unreleased recording by Fields, which the disc jockey plans to debut at midnight on Halloween. Being an educated heavy-metal devotee, Price takes the record home and plays it backwards to find those evil satanic messages that most television evangelists claim warp young peoples' minds. Sure enough, Price unleashes the fire-scarred spirit of Fields. At first Fields is the dream weapon of every picked-on high-schooler in existence as he helps Price get revenge on the preppie jock-types who torment him. But Fields doesn't stop there, and he begins terrorizing Price's friends. Eventually Price becomes disillusioned with his idol and decides to rid the neighborhood of the heavy-metal menace.

While not exactly frightening, TRICK OR TREAT is a well-meaning, humorous look at the kind of rock music that isn't worth the attention paid to it by lonely teens, worried parents, and the exploitative media. Smith (who appears on screen in a cameo as a schoolteacher) pokes fun at all groups equally, including the television evangelists, by casting heavy-metal head-banger supremo Ozzy Osbourne as the TV preacher leading the witch-hunt (Fields reaches into the television set and throttles the guy). Smith seems to find the music relatively harmless until, that is, people begin to take it way too seriously.

The entire project evolved because of a call to producers Soisson and Murphey (NIGHTMARE ON ELM STREET PART II) from movie mogul Dino De Laurentiis. De Laurentiis had liked their work and wanted a film called "Trick or Treat" in theaters by Halloween. With nothing more than that to go on, Soisson and Murphey found young screenwriter Topham and bought his heavy-metal-inspired horror tale. Hearing that actor Smith was interested in directing, the producers hired him and the picture was set to roll. Shot in seven weeks on the DEG lot in South Carolina, TRICK OR TREAT boasts little in the way of special effects other than an incredibly detailed gargoyle puppet built by Kevin Yahger (seen on screen for a matter of seconds), the aforementioned hand-reaching-into-the-television scene, and some assorted lightning-like opticals. Smith's direction borrows heavily from other horror films, mainly HALLOWEEN and CARRIE, but he does show a sensitivity toward humanity sorely lacking in most modern horror films. Young actor Price is quite good as the alienated teen (one can't help but think director Smith gave him some tips from his own portrayal as the ultimate nerd, Toad, in AMERICAN GRAFFITI), and Fields is excellent as the crazed rocker brought back to life. Simmons and Osbourne are mere cameos (and the latter—although the character is funny—is miscast).

TRICK OR TREAT is bound to disappoint both hardcore heavy-metal and horror fans, but its quirky humor and compassionate sensibility are much more refreshing than your average mean-spirited slasher film. The music, mostly pro-

vided by heavy-metal band Fastway, is pretty awful and used sparingly. Songs include: "Stand Up," "Tear It Down," "Don't Stop the Fight," "Get Tough," "Hold on to the Night," "Trick or Treat," "After Midnight" (Fastway, performed by Fastway), "Scream Until You Like It" (Paul Sabu, Charles Esposito, Neil Citron, performed by Only Child), "Grey, Grey, Grey" (Mick Muhlfriedel, Marina Del Rey, performed by See Jane Run), "Tot" (Paul Sabu, performed by Only Child), "The Haunted House of Rock" (Jalil Hutchins, Pete Harris, Nigel Green, performed by Whodini), "It's Up to You Now" (Diana Blair, performed by Diana Blair), "Heartbreakin' Lie" (Diana Blair, Pat Anthony, performed by Diana Blair).

p, Michael S. Murphey, Joel Soisson; d, Charles Martin Smith; w, Michael S. Murphey, Joel Soisson, Rhet Topham (based on a story by Rhet Topham); ph, Robert Elswit (Technicolor); m, Christopher Young; ed, Jane Schwartz Jaffe; prod d, Curt Schnell; art d, Colin D. Irwin; set d, Doug Mowat; spec eff (makeup), Kevin Yahger; m/l, Fastway, Paul Sabu, Charles Esposito, Neil Citron, Mick Muhlfriedel, Marina Del Rey, Jalil Hutchins, Pete Harris, Nigel Green, Diana Blair, Pat Anthony; stunts, Dan Bradley.

Horror (PR:O MPAA:R)

TRIKAL† (1986, India) 139m Blaze c (Trans: Past, Present, Future)

Leela Naidu *(Dona Maria Souza-Soares)*, Sushma Prakash *(Ana)*, Neena Gupta *(Milagrenia)*, Dalip Tahil *(Leon)*, Naseeruddin Shah *(Ruiz Pereira in 1985)*, Nikhil Bhagat *(Ruiz Pereira in 1961)*, Makqsoom Alie *(Erasmo)*, Anita Kanwar *(Ana's Mother Sylvia)*, K.K. Raina *(Ana's Father Lucio)*, Soni Razdan *(Aurora)*, Keith Stevenson *(Dr. Pereira)*, Ila Arun *(Cook)*, Kulbhushan Kharbanda *(Vijay Singh Rane/Kushtora Ran)*, Remo Fernandes, Alisha Chinai *(Offscreen Singers)*.

Shah returns to his run-down (but once opulent) home of many memories on the Portuguese-controlled island of Goa where he spent his youth during the period when the island's long time occupiers were preparing to depart. Amidst the turmoil of the turnover of Goa to Indian rule 24 years previously, a youthful Shah (played in flashback by Bhagat) had seduced and abandoned pretty servant girl Gupta; now he seeks atonement. The seduction occurred in the setting of a prospective wedding as Prakash, granddaughter of rich old Naidu, became betrothed to silly young Alie, although her heart belonged to another. Continuing in flashback, we discover that Prakash's lover is concealed in the basement of the house, where the freedom fighter has fled to avoid Portuguese reprisals. During the engagement celebration, Prakash's ancient grandfather expires, which so upsets his wife, Naidu, that the ceremony is cancelled while the widow tries in vain to summon up the spirit of her spouse. Spirits do indeed arrive, but not the wanted one; instead, the shades of long-dead victims of the autocratic family appear. When the engagement party finally does resume, it is interrupted again when Prakash passes out—a condition resulting from her pregnancy—to the discomfiture of her hapless intended, Alie (who knows he is not the responsible party). A rare comedy (albeit in a setting of social unrest) from one of India's best-known directors, with a fine cast. (In Hindi.)

p, Freni M. Variava, Lalit M. Bljlani; d&w, Shyam Benegal; ph, Ashok Mehta; m, Vanraj Bhatia; ed, Bhanudas Divkar.

Comedy (PR:C MPAA:NR)

TRO HAB OG KARLIGHED (SEE: TWIST AND SHOUT, 1986, Swed.)

TROLL*½ (1986) 86m Empire c

Noah Hathaway *(Harry Potter, Jr.)*, Michael Moriarty *(Harry Potter, Sr.)*, Shelley Hack *(Anne Potter)*, Jenny Beck *(Wendy Potter)*, Sonny Bono *(Peter Dickinson)*, Phil Fondacaro *(Malcolm Malory/Torok the Troll)*, Brad Hall *(William Daniels)*, Anne Lockhart *(Young Eunice St. Clair)*, Julia Louis-Dreyfus *(Jeannette Cooper)*, Gary Sandy *(Barry Tabor)*, June Lockhart *(Eunice St. Clair)*, Robert Hathaway, James Beck *(Policemen)*, Dale Wyatt *(Dickinson's Girl Friend)*, Barbara Sciorilli, Viviana Giusti, Jessie Carfora *(Fairies)*, Debra Dion, Charles Band *(Young Couple on TV)*, Jacquelyn Band, Albert Band *(Older Couple on TV)*.

Those folks at Empire Pictures don't waste anything. They've taken the title "ghoulies" from 1985's horror epic and made them trolls and goblins in 1986. This fairly lame entry sees two of the more inept cinematic parents ever to hit the screen, Moriarty and Hack, move their family to a new apartment in San Francisco. Their kids, older boy Hathaway and his cute little sister Beck, play while mom and dad move dad's massive record collection. Beck wanders down into the laundry room and encounters an ugly troll. The troll wears a ring with a green stone and he uses the magical jewel to take the little girl's identity. That night Beck behaves strangely by gobbling her food and basically acting like a wild animal. Moriarty and Hack attribute their daughter's bizarre behavior to the "big move" and decide not to worry. Hathaway, however, does become concerned when his little sister throws him across the room.

While her parents go about their business, Beck wanders the apartment building transforming other residents into goblins and their apartments into fairy kingdoms overrun with foliage. Eventually the distraught Hathaway turns to June Lockhart, the strange old lady who lives upstairs. Guess what? Lockhart's really a witch and she's been doing battle with this troll for centuries. She informs Hathaway that his family moved into the building on Walpurgis night—when the witches' when all manner of strange things can happen. Lockhart and Hathaway team up to rescue his sister (who is being held captive in the fourth dimension, or some such nonsense) and defeat the troll. For some reason Lockhart transforms herself into a much younger incarnation (played by the actress' daughter Anne), but it doesn't do much good because the troll turns her into an ugly tree stump. This leaves Hathaway to complete the mission on his own, which he does.

Incredibly dull, with a cast made up mostly of actors from "Love Boat" limbo, TROLL is bit easier to take than an Amtrak ride through Oklahoma, but not by much. Except for another quirky performance from Moriarty—whose solo dance number to Blue Cheer's heavy metal rendition of Eddie Cochran's classic "Summertime Blues" (Cochran, Jerry Capehart) is almost worth the price of admission—and two likable performances from the children, the acting in TROLL borders on the pathetic. Boasting two of the most annoying members of one of the "Saturday Night Live" troupes (the ever-smug Hall and the cutesy-poo Louis-Dreyfus), "WKRP In Cinncinati" station manager Sandy, ex-"Charlie's Angel" Hack, "Lost in Space" mom Lockhart *and* her daughter Anne, and worst, of all, Sonny Bono, TROLLS would be insufferable if most of them weren't killed off in short order. The special effects, supervised by director Buechler, who was the effects man on GHOULIES, are pretty poor, with the same slimy glop he used on 1985's creatures smeared all over these as well. Once again the rubber creatures are simply constructed with a limited amount of movement—they look like stiff hand puppets—and the seams from their molds are clearly visible on some models. The script by film-book author Naha *(The Science Fictionary,* and *Horrors—From Scream to Screen)* is pretty simpleminded and there isn't a frightening moment in the entire film. Empire Pictures guru Albert Band (which is a pseudonym for Alfredo Antonini) and other members of his family can be spotted in a bad science fiction-film parody that Hathaway watches on television.

p, Albert Band; d, John Buechler; w, Ed Naha; ph, Romano Albani (Technicolor); m, Richard Band; ed, Lee Percy; set d, Gayle Simon; cos, Jill Ohanneson; spec eff, Buechler, Mechanical & Makeup Imageries.

Horror Cas. (PR:C MPAA:PG-13)

TROPPO FORTE† (1986, It.) 101m Scena/Titanus c (Trans: Too Strong)

Carlo Verdone *(Oscar)*, Stella Hall *(Nancy)*, Alberto Sordi *(Lawyer)*, John Steiner, Mario Brega, Sal Da Vinci.

Verdone is a biker and failed tough-guy who is rejected when he auditions for a bit in an American feature shooting in Rome. He decides to stage an accident by crashing into the producer's car in order to get insurance money. When he carries his plan out, the driver of the car turns out to be the leading actress. Her face is cut up by flying glass and she loses her job. Verdone, feeling guilty, takes her into his apartment while he prepares his suit against the producer. His lawyer, Sordi, dies before the case comes to court, and Verdone loses. The actress returns home to Texas with her turkey farmer husband, leaving Verdone to continue fantasizing about getting into the movies.

p, Augusto Caminito; d, Carlo Verdone; w, Carlo Verdone, Rodolfo Sonego, Alberto Sordi; ph, Danilo Desideri (Eastmancolor); m, Antonello Venditti; ed, Nino Baragli; ed, Nino Baragli; art d, Franco Velchi.

Comedy (PR:NR MPAA:NR)

TRUE STORIES**½ (1986) 89m True Stories Ventures/WB c

David Byrne *(Narrator)*, John Goodman *(Louis Fyne)*, Swoosie Kurtz *(Miss Rollings, the Laziest Woman in the World)*, Spalding Gray *(Earl Culver)*, Alix Elias *(The Cute Woman)*, Annie McEnroe *(Kay Culver)*, Roebuck "Pops" Staples *(Mr. Tucker)*, Umberto "Tito" Larriva *(Ramon)*, John Ingle *(The Preacher)*, Jo Harvey Allen *(The Lying Woman)*, Matthew Posey *(The Computer Guy)*, Amy Buffington *(Linda Culver)*, Richard Downlearn *(Larry Culver)*, Capucine DeWulf *(The Little Girl on the Road)*.

David Byrne, "Rock's Renaissance Man" (so sayeth a *Time* magazine cover story), makes his feature film directorial debut with a fitfully successful look at America. The film is marred by a lack of focus and an overkill of rock videos. Byrne himself plays the narrator, a friendly outsider dressed in a polyester urban cowboy suit and a ridiculously huge Stetson hat ("They sell a lot of these around here, but I never see anybody else wearing them"). He talks to the camera as he drives along in a big red convertible pointing out the sights of Virgil, Texas, a new town of 40,000 about to stage its "Celebration of Specialness" as part of the state's sesquicentennial. Virtually plotless, the film follows Byrne as he takes us on a tour of Virgil and its inhabitants. We meet Kurtz, the "Laziest Woman in the World," who never gets out of bed and is fed by a machine which spoons

food into her mouth; Allen, the "Lying Woman," who spices up her mundane work day with dozens of incredible stories such as "I had an affair with the 'real' Rambo," or "I wrote 'Billie Jean' and half of Elvis' songs"; civic leader Gray and his wife McEnroe who haven't spoken directly to each other in 15 years ("Linda, will you ask your mother to pass the mustard?" Gray asks his daughter); Elias, the "Cute Woman," whose house is an amazing array of little-girlish frill; Ingle, a paranoid preacher who sees conspiracy around every corner ("Have you ever noticed that toilet paper and Kleenex run out at the same time?"); and the man who comes closest to being the film's main character, Goodman, a large, lovable, panda-bear of a man who is looking for "Matrimony with a capital 'M.' " We follow Byrne to the Virgil shopping mall where a strange fashion show is being held, featuring clothing with brick-wall patterns and suits and dresses made of astroturf (this scene seems to go on forever). There is the dinner at civic leader Gray's house where the host launches into an impassioned dissertation on American capitalism using vegetables as props— one of the film's highlights. The film climaxes with the highlight of Virgil's "Celebration of Specialness," a talent show where Goodman lives out his fantasy and becomes a country-and-western singer crooning "People Like Us" to a live and television audience. Lazy-woman Kurtz hears his soulful singing and falls in love. The film ends with Goodman and Kurtz married and Byrne leaving Virgil in his big red convertible. Before zooming out of sight he turns to the camera and informs us that "This car isn't leased. It's privately owned."

Supposedly culled from bizarre clippings found in newspapers like "The Weekly World News" and other favorite grocery check-out line periodicals, TRUE STORIES tries to provide a fond, kindly glimpse of the heartland of America, but winds up suffering from its own self-conscious hipness. Byrne barely avoids a New Yorker's condescending attitude toward these "simple folk," attempting to show us that they aren't so weird after all. Unfortunately, when half the characters are named "The Cute Woman," "The Lying Woman," "The Computer Guy," and "The Laziest Woman in the World," you can expect fairly one-dimensional character portrayals. Byrne allows only enough screen time to expand his character. Otherwise, most of the citizens of Virgil exist in quirky little bits between the plethora of musical interludes that repeatedly grind the film to a halt. The actors all do amazingly well with the little they are given to work with, but it's hard to be more than a stereotype in less than 10 minutes of screen time. While Byrne does seem to have a fond curiosity for the people he finds in Virgil, he gently attacks their "shopping mall mentality" with his flat monotone voice and his insistence on highlighting the banal. "The radio reception is great here!" he remarks as he cruises through the desert. Unfortunately, Byrne's criticism of American consumerism is hard to swallow when the film stops again and again for a dozen poorly integrated rock videos designed to sell high-priced soundtrack albums and an expensive movie tie-in book. Do Byrne, Beth Henley, and Stephen Tobolowsky really merit an oversized paperback book of their screenplay illustrated with lots of glossy photos of Ed Lachman's superior cinematography before the film was even released? Is there much difference between a Virgilite who buys a suit made of astroturf and an oh-so-hip yuppie who listens to the TRUE STORIES soundtrack album on compact disk while reading the published screenplay? In TRUE STORIES music is a liberating force that frees people to relax and express themselves, but don't most of us have to pay to hear it? At what point does Byrne find American capitalism distasteful? TRUE STORIES raises many such questions but doesn't really explore any of them. The film is much like the very things Byrne seems to disdain. It's amusing, disposable fluff to be enjoyed while it lasts and then immediately forgotten. Byrne has imbued his film with the pretense that it is something more than a slick comedy with music, but he never gets beneath the surface of his concept. Songs include: "Road Song" (Meredith Monk, performed by Capucine DeWulf), "Cocktail Desperado" (David Byrne, Terry Allen, performed by Allen and The Panhandle Mystery Band), "Mail Melodies" (Carl Finch, performed by Finch), "Soy De Tejas" (Steve Jordan, performed by Jordan, Rio Jordan), "Ze Pereira" (Jeffrey Barnes, performed by Banda Eclipse), "Buster's Theme" (Carl Finch, performed by Finch), "Esta Para Um Rei Negro" (Zuzuca, performed by Jeffery Barnes, Banda Eclipse), "Wild Wild Life," "Love For Sale," "City of Dreams" (performed by The Talking Heads).

p, Gary Kurfirst; d, David Byrne; w, David Byrne, Beth Henley, Stephen Tobolowsky; ph, Ed Lachman (Technicolor); m, David Byrne, The Talking Heads; ed, Caroline Biggerstaff; prod d, Barbara Ling; cos, Elizabeth McBride;

ch, Meredith Monk, Dee McCandless, Gene Menger; m/l, David Byrne, Terry Allen, Meredith Monk, Steve Jordan, Carl Finch, Jeffrey Barnes, Zuzuca.

Comedy   Cas.   **(PR:A MPAA:PG)**

TUNG-NIEN WANG-SHIH   (SEE: A TIME TO LIVE AND A TIME TO DIE, 1986, Taiwan)

TUNG-TUNG-TE-CHIA-CH'I   (SEE: SUMMER AT GRANDPA'S, 1986, Taiwan)

TUNTEMATON SOTILAS†   (1986, Fin.) 193m Arctic–Kinosto–Finnish Film Foundation/Carlton-Raoul Katz c (Trans: The Unknown Soldier)

Mika Makela *(Rahikainen)*, Pertti Koivula *(Lahtinen)*, Pirkka-Pekka Petelius *(Heitanen)*, Tero Niva *(Vanhala)*, Pauli Poranen *(Lehto)*, Hannu Kiviola *(Riitaoja)*, Pekka Ketonen *(Lt. Kariluoto)*, Paavo Liiski *(Rokka)*, Risto Tuorila *(Koskela)*.

A single machine-gun platoon is followed through Finland's so-called "Continuation War" with the USSR over the contested province of Karelia, a war that made Finland an ally of Nazi Germany during WW II. The picture tracks the soldiers through their induction, their training, and their bloody missions as they doggedly attempt to obey orders to repeat the success of the Finns who had earlier repulsed attacks by ill-equipped Soviet forces. Brought in at a big-budget (for Finland) cost of $3 million, the picture is a remake of a briefer film made in 1956. This version, which was coscripted by the author of the best-selling novel, follows the book more closely than its predecessor.

p&d, Rauni Mollberg; w, Rauni Mollberg, Vaino Linna, Veikko Aaltonen (based on the novel by Vaino Linna); ph, Esa Vuorinen (Eastmancolor); ed, Olli Soinio; prod d, Ensio Suominen.

War/Drama   **(PR:C MPAA:NR)**

TWELFTH NIGHT†   (1986, Aus.) 120m Twelfth Night c

Gillian Jones *(Viola/Sebastian)*, Ivar Kants *(Orsino)*, Jacqy Phillips *(Olivia)*, Peter Cummins *(Malvolio)*, Kerry Walker *(The Fool)*, John Wood *(Sir Toby Belch)*, Geoffrey Rush *(Sir Andrew Aguecheek)*, Tracy Harvey *(Sarah)*, Stuart McCreery *(Antonio)*, Odile Le Clezio *(Olivia's Maid)*, Igor Sas, Russel Kiefel.

An Australian-accented, modern-dress movie made from a stage production of Shakespeare's famed comedy of romantic intrigue. The transvested heroine is nearly topped by another cross-dresser in the person of player Walker in the male role of The Fool. Director-scripter Armfield alters the bard substantially to suit the circumstances as Malvolio's (Cummins') cross-gaiters become yellow shorts and socks, a color abhorrent to the heroine (Phillips) he unsuccessfully pursues. Made on a shoestring budget, but pleasantly played.

p, Don Catchlove; d&w, Neil Armfield (based on the play by William Shakespeare); ph, Louis Irving (Agfacolor); m, Allen John; ed, Nicholas Beauman; prod d, Stephen Curtis; m/l, Allen John, William Shakespeare.

Comedy   **(PR:A MPAA:NR)**

27 HORAS†   (1986, Span.) 77m Elias Querejeta c (Trans: 27 Hours)

Martxelo Rubio *(Jon)*, Maribel Verdu *(Maite)*, Jon San Sebastian *(Patxi)*, Antonio Banderas, Michel Duperrer, Andre Falcon, Josu Balbuena, Silvia Arrese-Igor.

Dispossessed youth in the Basque region of Spain, where both unemployment and separatist feelings run high, but where young people have begun to drop out and turn on. To support his hard-drug habit—and that of his girl friend—one youth subsists on petty thefts, occasional labor, and money he begs from his parents. His best friend implores him to give up dope, but the high-school dropout persists. When the girl overdoses and dies, the young addict goes on a 27-hour drug toot and—despite his friend's attempts to dissuade him—follows her to the mortuary slab.

p, Elias Querejeta; d, Montxo Armendariz; w, Montxo Armendariz, Elias Querejeta; ph, Javier Aguirresarobe; m, Angel Illarramedi, Imanol Larzabal, Carol Jimenez, Luis Mendo; ed, Juan I. San Mateo; set d, Inigo Altolaguirre.

Drama   **(PR:C MPAA:NR)**

TWIST AGAIN A MOSCOU†   (1986, Fr.) 103m Gaumont International-Renn-Films A2-Camera One/AMLF c (Trans: Twist Again in Moscow)

Philippe Noiret *(Igor Tatiatev)*, Christian Clavier *(Youri)*, Marina Vlady *(Natasha Tatiatev)*, Martin Lamotte *(Pikov)*, Agnes Soral *(Tatiana)*, Bernard Blier *(Minister)*.

A luxurious—by local standards—hotel in Moscow, which houses foreign business travelers and tourists, is administered by the swindler Noiret. Black market deals and handouts for special services have enabled the duplicitous hotel director to live a lavish life style, albeit at the expense of being forced by his cohorts to assist in the illicit transport of Jewish dissidents to the West. Noiret's brother Clavier, an admirer of Western ways, is promoting a rock 'n'roll show, which brings the posh establishment to the attention of the authorities. Party inspector Lamotte arrives—along with some KGB agents—searching for irregularities, and what follows is a farcical cover-up of myriad misdeeds. A high-budget picture lensed largely on location in Yugoslavia. (In French.)

p, Alain Poure; d, Jean-Marie Poure; w, Jean-Marie Poure, Martin Lamotte, Christian Clavier; ph, Pascal Lebegue (Panavision, Eastmancolor); m, Michel

Goglat; ed, Catherine Kelber; art d, Pierre Guffroy; cos, Catherine Leterrier; stunts, Remy Julienne.

Comedy   **(PR:C MPAA:NR)**

TWIST & SHOUT**½   (1986, Den.) 99m Per Holst-Palle Fogtdal-Danish
    Film Institute-Children's Film Council-Danmarks Radio/Miramax c (TRO,
    HAB OG KARLIGHED; Trans: Faith, Hope And Charity)

Adam Tonsberg *(Bjorn)*, Lars Simonsen *(Erik)*, Camilla Soeberg *(Anna)*, Ulrikke Juul Bondo *(Kirsten)*, Thomas Nielsen *(Henning)*, Lone Lindorff *(Bjorn's Mother)*, Arne Hansen *(Bjorn's Father)*, Aase Hansen *(Erik's Mother)*, Bent Mejding *(Erik's Father)*, Malene Schwarz, Kurt Ravn, Grethe Mogensen, Troels Munk, Elga Olga, Helle Spaangard, Finn Gimlinge, Bent Brian, Rudolf Brink, Ingelise Ullner, Jytte Strandberg, Nina Christoffersen, Thyge Andersen, Poul Lunvad, Ole Borg, Rubber Band, Per Morgensen.

Reportedly the highest grossing film in Denmark's history, TWIST AND SHOUT is set in 1963 during a time when the music of The Beatles filled the streets, and teenagers found themselves growing up a bit too fast. Tonsberg and Simonsen are the closest of friends, standing by each other through good times

and bad. Of the two Simonsen is the worse off—his mother is mentally ill and confined to her bedroom, his father is perversely repressive, and, as a result, Simonsen has been browbeaten into a pathetic excuse for a young man. The one girl he has an eye for, a prissy rich girl played by Bondo, is dead set on getting Tonsberg to marry her. Tonsberg, however, is infatuated with Soeberg, a vision of beauty, maturity and intelligence. In the hopes of hitching Tonsberg, Bondo throws a ritzy party for all of her friends, but kicks Tonsberg out when he arrives with Soeberg on his arm. Tonsberg and Soeberg fall deeply in love, promising never to leave each other. In the meantime, Simonsen is discovering what his mother is really like. He finds that she is not as crazy as his father has led him to believe. He secretly reads library books to her, though his father strictly forbade this. When his father uncovers the hidden books, he explains that mother wanted to be a poet but went mad in the process. His reason for keeping her confined to the house is, supposedly, to keep her from getting any sicker. Tonsberg, however, learns the real reason upon spotting Simonsen's father visiting a local prostitute. Just when everything is looking great for Tonsberg and Soeberg, they learn that life isn't as happy and carefree as it is in a Beatles song. Soeberg is pregnant and "Love Me Do" has, for the previously innocent lovers, developed a darker meaning. Soeberg decides on an abortion and Tonsberg borrows the necessary money from Bondo, who makes him agree to vacation with her in exchange. After undergoing a painful and primitive illegal abortion, Soeberg cannot bear to see Tonsberg again. He leaves with Bondo and her family on vacation and the pair plan to marry, although it is clear that he still has Soeberg in his heart. Later, during an engagement ceremony, Tonsberg calls the wedding off and helps Simonsen in his escalating battle with his father. Tonsberg leads the way to the prostitute's house and Simonsen, who has found an inner strength that helps him and his mother survive, confronts his now-degraded father. After these tests of adolescence, all that remains is the friendship that Tonsberg and Simonsen will always share.

TWIST AND SHOUT is one of those films which is so well-intentioned and honest that it seems cynical to find fault in it. The film opens in a Danish fantasy world in which nothing matters but getting a Beatles haircut, dancing to their songs, and forming a Beatles cover band. Life is easy and love is truly romantic. In the first half of his film, director August has painted a charming but honest landscape of content, problem-free teenagers. His message is then shouted loud and clear as he warns that all is not a Beatles song and that everything has its dark side. The quiet, candlelight romance has produced a baby and, as a result, everything that is good crumbles. Unfortunately, August drives the point home far too often. (The epitome of this is the excruciatingly long abortion scene in which August shows us that abortion is—gasp!—traumatic and painful.) Everything that happens in the latter half of TWIST AND SHOUT is pure convention and easily predictable by everyone except the characters in the film. Tonsberg and Soeberg end their romance after the abortion, but there is no real reason to believe these two supposedly inseparable lovers would not continue to fight to be together. They profess that they believe in an undying love and then give up in midstream. Tonsberg then runs off to Bondo to carry on in a relationship that even Bondo knows will not last and which, not surprisingly, doesn't. The result is

a film which promises so much honesty and then deteriorates into predictable melodrama. The performances are excellent, however, and save the film when the script turns into a trite rant on how these kids have been robbed of their childhood. Tonsberg, Soeberg, Bondo and Aase Hansen as Simonsen's mother are all superb, but it is Simonsen who shines. His character, the best written of them all, walks a thin line in life—both family and social, and manages to do so with a gift of acting grace. One cannot help but feel for him when he chooses to be humiliated by his friends rather than not have any friends at all. The relationship he shares with his mother is also wonderful, as he thoughtfully spends time helping her recover in secret from his father's sadistic demands. In the end, TWIST AND SHOUT is not a bad film, just a disappointing one. Songs include: "Twist and Shout" (Bert Russell, Phil Medley,), "Love Me Do," "Please, Please Me," "Thank You Girl" (John Lennon, Paul McCartney), "The Banana Boat Song" (Erik Darling, Bob Carey, Alan Arkin), "Be My Baby" (Jeff Barry, Ellie Greenwich, Phil Spector, performed by The Ronettes) Released theatrically in Danish, with English subtitles, although the videotape release has been excellently dubbed into English.

p, Ib Tardini; d, Bille August; w, Bille August, Bjarne Rather (based on Rather's novels); ph, Jan Weincke (Eastmancolor); m, Bo Holten; ed, Janus Billeskov Jansen; prod d, Soren Kragh Sorensen; cos, Francoise Nicolet, Manon Rasmussen; m/l, John Lennon, Paul McCartney, Bert Russell, Phil Medley, Erik Darling, Bob Carey, Alan Arkin, Jeff Barry, Ellie Greenwich, Phil Spector.

Drama   **Cas.**   **(PR:O MPAA:R)**

TWO FRIENDS   (1986, Aus.) 76m ABC c

Emma Coles *(Louise)*, Kris Bidenko *(Kelly)*, Kris McQuade *(Louise's Mother Janet)*, Debra May *(Kelly's Mother Chris)*, Peter Hehir *(Kelly's Stepfather Malcolm)*, Tony Barry *(Kelly's Father Charlie)*, Steve Bisley *(Kevin)*, Sean Travers *(Matthew)*, Kerry Dwyer *(Alison)*, Giovanni Marangoni *(Renato)*, Stephen Leeder *(Jim)*, Paul Mason *(Father at Funeral)*, Martin Armiger *(Philip)*, Lisa Rogers *(Little Helen)*, Amanda Frederickson *(Kate)*, Rory Delaney *(Wally)*, Emily Stocker *(Soula)*.

The disparate life styles of two girls, Coles and Bidenko, are made evident at the outset. Both products of affluent—though broken—homes, Coles' character is refined and relatively well adapted to society, whereas Bidenko lives in a beachhouse commune and leads the life of a punk-rocker clone, complete with dyed mohawk hairstyle. The film opens in winter with Coles and her mother McQuade attending the funeral of a girl—a former friend—who overdosed on drugs, and segues in flashback to a happier time in the previous spring. Coles and Bidenko are seen to be inseparable high-schoolers, virtual duplicates of one another. With the best of intentions, Bidenko's stepfather decides that the private school Coles plans to attend is too elitist for his stepdaughter, who will, he attests, be better served by broader social contacts. The girls thus blossom in different directions, and a reasonable inference is that Bidenko's character may quickly be coffin-bound as well. There are no villains in this touching tale, only well-meaning people—both adults and youngsters—whose decisions do not always work out for the best. Made for Australian television, this is a first feature film for director Campion, a recent graduate from the Australian Film and Television School, and was well received at the Cannes Film Festival (where three of her short films had also been screened).

p, Jan Chapman; d, Jane Campion; w, Helen Garner; ph, Julian Penney (Eastmancolor); ed, Bill Russo; prod d, Janet Patterson.

Drama   **(PR:C MPAA:NR)**

TYPHOON CLUB†   (1986, Jap.) 115m Kuzui c

Yuichi Mikami *(Kyoichi)*, Shigeru Kurebayashi *(Ken)*, Toshiyuki Matsunaga *(Akira)*, Yuki Kudoh *(Rie)*, Yuka Ohnishi *(Michiko)*, Akiko Aizawa *(Yasuko)*, Ryuko Tendoh *(Yumi)*, Yuriko Fuchizaki *(Midori)*, Tomokazu Miura *(Umemiya)*.

The big winner at the 1985 Tokyo Film Festival's "Young Cinema" competition (there was a three-way split of the $1.5 million in prize money awarded to help finance the winner's next project—TYPHOON CLUB received the lion's share: $750,000), TYPHOON CLUB is a Japanese version of John Hughes' THE BREAKFAST CLUB. Set in a junior high school near Tokyo which has been besieged by a typhoon, the film explores the thoughts and emotions of a group of confused teens trapped inside for four days. The jumble of feelings thrashing around in the repressed teens surfaces during their isolation and they feel free to act on their impulses (political, social, moral, sexual), far away from the disapproving stare of strict Japanese society. Director Shinji Somai has made four films since 1980, and shot TYPHOON CLUB in 1984. The film lay on the shelf until the 1985 Tokyo Film Festival where the attention it garnered finally spurred distributor interest.

p, Tutomu Yamamoto; d, Shinji Somai; w, Yuji Katch; ph, Akihiro Itoh; ed, Isao Tomita.

Drama   **(PR:C-O MPAA:NR)**

U

UC HALKA YIRMIBES†   (1986, Turkey) Hakan (Trans: Three Rings Twenty-Five)

Hulya Avsar, Hakan Balamir, Huseyin Peyda, Guin Oziek.

d&w, Bilge Olgac (based on a novel by Muzaffer Izgu); ph, Vecihi Ener.

UEMURA NAOMI MONOGATARI†   (1986, Jap.) 140m Dentsu–Mainichi Hoso/Toho c

Toshiyuki Nishida *(Naomi Uemura)*, Chieko Baisho *(His Wife)*, Masato Furuoya, Go Wakabayashi, Muga Takewaki, Ryo Ikebe.

The filmed biography of famed Japanese explorer Naomi Uemura, a loner whose fragile ego compelled him to theretofore unimaginable feats of physical derring-do, including the first solo trip to the North Pole (overland by dogsled) and the first solo traverse of the Greenland icecap (by the same means). A formidable climber, Uemura scaled many of the world's major mountains as well, including Everest and Aconcagua, before losing his life on a solitary ascent of Alaska's Mount McKinley in the winter of 1984. A hastily assembled search party of internationally famed climbers—also attempting a winter ascent of the dangerous peak—discovered Uemura's last bivouac site (the lone climber had jettisoned his tent to save weight) near the mountain's forbidding "Windy Corner," where he had cached some frozen meat for his planned safe descent. Uemura's body was never found, and the search party concluded that the unbelayed climber had simply been blown off the mountain.

The episodic picture interrupts scenes of climbing and snow-traversing with sequences depicting the explorer (played by Nishida) at home in Japan with his uninterestingly submissive wife Baisho. Nishida plays the heroic loner as a hyper-active, somewhat simple fellow in the Douglas Fairbanks mold. Actress Baisho is best known for her continuing role in the TORA-SAN comedy series.

p, Juichi Tanaka, Haruyuki Takahashi, Hiroshi Takayama; d, Junya Sato; w, Yoshiki Iwama, Junya Sato (based on books by Naomi Uemura); ph, Hiroyuki Namiki, Etsuo Akutsu; m, William Ackerman.

Adventure/Biography   (PR:A MPAA:NR)

UMA RAPARIGA NO VERAO   (1986, Port.) 90m Tropico Filmes, Soc. de Producao c

Diogo Doria, Isabel Galhardo, Joaquim Leitao, Jose Manuel Mendes, Joao Perry, Virgilio Castelo, Madalena Pinto Leite, Alexandra Guimaraes.

A coming-of-age film featuring a girl in late adolescence eagerly awaiting her escape from the constraints of family life. Romanticizing the world of working self-dependence, she deplores her family's continuing treatment of her as a little girl. Shot in 16mm; a first feature from writer-director Goncalves, a sometime cinema-school instructor.

p, Jose Bogalheiro e Zita; d&w, Vitor Goncalves; ph, Daniel DelNegro, Mario de Carvalho; ed, Ana Luisa Guimaraes.

Drama   (PR:A MPAA:NR)

UMBRELLA WOMAN, THE   (SEE: GOOD WIFE, THE, 1986, Aus.)

UMUT SOKAGI†   (1986, Turkey) Umut (Trans: The Street of Hope)

Kadir Inanir, Sehnaz Dilan, Kazim Kartal, Bulent Bilgic.

d, Serif Goren; w, Ilhan Engin; ph, Aytekin Cakmackci.

UMUTLU SAFAKLLAR†   (1986, Turkey) Murat (Trans: The Dawn of Hope)

Hulya Avsar, Autac Arman, Ihsan Yuce.

d, Sureyya Duru; w, Vedat Turkali; ph, Ali Ugur.

UN COMPLICATO INTRIGO DI DONNE, VICOLI E DELITTI   (SEE: CAMORRA, 1986, It.)

UN HOMBRE DE EXITO†   (1986, Cuba) 110m Instituto Cubano del Artes e Industria Cinematografico c (Trans: A Successful Man)

Cesar Evora *(Javier)*, Raquel Revuelta *(Raquel)*, Daisy Granados *(Rita)*, Jorge Trinchot *(Dario)*, Mabel Roche *(Leana)*, Carlos Cruz *(Puig)*, Rubens de Falco, Miguel Navarro, Angel Espasande, Omar Valdes, Jorge Ali.

An epic film recounting details of a 30-year period in pre- and post-revolution Cuba, the story (which borrows its theme from Robert Louis Stevenson's novel *The Master of Ballantrae*) tells of two brothers, one of them (Trinchot) taking the high road to revolution, the other (Evora) opting for the low path to personal wealth. The picture focuses on the latter brother, who, from his student days, strives for success, even as his sibling, Trinchot, develops an awareness of the problems plaguing the mass of his fellow Cubans. Evora revels in the pleasures of pre-Castro Cuba—an island where sybaritic delights abounded for the wealthy, with more nightclubs per square mile than any other—while his idealistic brother distributes revolutionary leaflets and blows up dictator Batista's minions with homemade bombs.

The full resources of the nationalized Cuban cinema industry were put behind writer-director Solas, whose interest in architecture is obvious (in an interview by Marta Alvear [Tete Vasconcelos], Solas announced his intention of renewing his revolution-interrupted architecture studies, even if it meant going to night school for 10 years). Prominently featured is actress Revuelta, a stage impresario and talented player who also appeared in Solas' LUCIA, a three-part picture released in Cuba in 1968.

p, Humberto Hernandez; d&w, Humberto Solas; ph, Livio Delgado; m, Luigi Nono; ed, Nelson Rodriguez.

Historical Drama   (PR:C MPAA:NR)

UN HOMBRE VIOLENTE**   (1986, Mex.) 91m Cinematografica Sol/ Peliculas Mexicanas c (Trans: A Violent Man)

Valentin Trujillo *(Julian Carrera)*, Mario Almada *(Don Emilio)*, Rafael Inclan *(Charly)*, Maribel Guardia *(Lucia Castillano)*, Gilberto Trujillo *(Carlos)*, Victoria Ruffo *(Susana)*, Chelo, Gilberto de Anda, Victor Alcocer, Humberto Elizondo, Juan Gallardo, Los Cadetes de Linar, Los Humildes.

The body count runs high in this gory story of strike and counterstrike set in contemporary Mexico. *Machismo* mandates that automobile repairman V. Trujillo (who also helmed the picture) must avenge the violent death of his father at the hands of a robber. So begins a family feud worthy of the Hatfields and McCoys as the initial killer's kin exact reciprocal revenge. The picture recounts V. Trujillo's metamorphosis from a peaceful partner in a family business to an accomplished killer in a style reminiscent of BONNIE AND CLYDE (1967) with its car chases and, even, with bluegrass music (harmonica and guitar) to accompany the excitement. Some well-known Mexican players make cameo appearances, and two musical groups are featured. Inclan does well in a comic-relief sidekick role in a generally well-made action film. Nepotism worthy of Hollywood's heyday: the director-star's brother is a featured player, and writer-producer de Anda's family was everywhere on the sets and locations.

p, Gilberto de Anda; d, Valentin Trujillo; w, Gilberto de Anda; ph, Antonio de Anda; m, Ernesto Cortazar; ed, Sergio Soto.

Action   (PR:O MPAA:NR)

UN OASPETE LA CINA†   (1986, Rum.) 93m c "Bucharest" Studios

Gyorgy Csapo, Ruxandra Bucescu, Constantin Codrescu, Adela Marculescu, Paul Lavric, Geo Costiniu.

Problems with class in a nominally classless society as the daughter of a respected professor marries a young worker. The disapprobation of her parents persists even after the wedding, causing the young couple many problems. Their love for each other, coupled with the youth's talent—he's an inventor—manages to overcome all obstacles.

d, Mihai Constantinescu; w, Ion Bucheru; ph, Petre Petrescu; m, Temistocle Popa; art d, Dodu Balasoiu; cos, Svetlana Mihailescu.

Comedy/Drama   (PR:A-C MPAA:NR)

UN RAGAZZO COME TANTI†   (1986, It.) TV Cine 2000/Film Compass c (Trans: A Boy Like the Others)

Stefano Mioni *(Pino)*, Stefania Lupi, Antonio Graziano, Valter Toschi, Annamaria Porta, Edy Biagetti, Giorgio Mascia, Massimo Popolizio, Rita Pensa, Federico di Nepi.

Hoping to find a better life, young Mioni travels from a poverty-ridden southern province of Italy to Rome, where he is soon disheartened by harsh reality. Alone and friendless, the rural youth learns the lessons necessary for survival. He becomes embroiled in black-market activities, then in prostitution and petty theft, and finally in narcotics deals. His descent ends when he accidentally meets someone whose friendship blossoms into a genuine relationship. The two principals reinforce one another's inner resources, paving the way for renewed hope.

d&w, Gianni Minello; ph, Silvio Fraschetti (Luciano Vittori Color); m, Enrico Pieranunzi; ed, Emanuele Foglietti.

Drama   (PR:O MPAA:NR)

UNA CASA IN BILICO†   (1986, It.) 83m Angio/AIRONE c (Trans: A Tottering House)

Marina Vlady *(Maria)*, Riccardo Cucciolla *(Teo)*, Luigi Pistilli *(Giovanni)*, Armando Bandini, Stefania Graziosi, Daniela Igliozzi.

An aging household is formed when a former lover wills the womanizing Pistilli her apartment and the old raconteur quickly invites his introverted friend Cucciolla and displaced Russian Vlady to share the bounty. Despite their disparate personalities and many clashes, the three form a close bond—a virtual family relationship—that opens the world to them. The compassionate Vlady pursues the quest of helping a young Russian girl rejoin her parents in the U.S. To this end, she persuades reluctant clock-collector Cucciolla to wed the girl, giving her the Italian citizenship that will be a first step toward her reunion. An automobile accident reduces the threesome to two, but the survivors carry on in this warm, well-acted geriatric drama. A charming low-budget effort, well-photographed in 16mm and blown up for theatrical release. Exhibited at the Locarno Film Festival.

p, Roberta Fainello; d, Antonietta De Lillo, Giorgio Magliulo; w, Giuditta Rinaldi, Antonietta De Lillo, Giorgio Magliulo; ph, Giorgio Magliulo; m, Franco Piersanti; ed, Mirko Garrone; art d, Paola Bizzarri; cos, Sandra Montagna.

Drama/Comedy   (PR:C MPAA:NR)

UNA DOMENICA SI†   (1986, It.) Duea/Medusa–D.M.V. c (Trans: A Good Sunday)

Nik Novecento, Dario Parisini, Davide Celli, Elena Sofia Ricci, Fiorenza Tessari, Mario Mazzarotto, Marcello Cesena, Ferdinando Orlandi, Caterina Raganelli, Simply Red.

Three young men—recent military conscripts—are granted leave from their barren barracks existence on a sunny Sunday. One of the three friends, Davide, has been invited to spend the day at the resplendent home of wealthy Alfonso, a co-conscript; the other two go to a railroad station to welcome Elena, Dario's fiancee, who is accompanied by Nik's blind date, Giovanna. The latter disdains her intended date and joins some other friends rather than making the group a foursome. Viewing himself as the odd man out, Nik deserts his remaining friends, followed by the sympathetic Dario, who leaves the disgruntled Elena in order to remonstrate with his barracks-mate. The two decide to join their friend Davide, and Nik becomes much taken with a young woman whom he invites to a concert that evening, discovering to his delight that she is willing to spend the entire night with him. Meanwhile, the distraught Dario has been searching desperately for his beloved Elena. When the latter has second thoughts and seeks and finds Dario, Nik becomes aware that he must sacrifice his own night of bliss by returning to the barracks to answer roll call for his absent friend.

d, Cesare Bastelli; w, Cesare Bornazzini, Roberto Gandus, Giancarlo Scarchilli; ph, Pasquale Rachini (Telecolor); m, Riz Ortolani; ed, Amedeo Salfa.

Drama   **(PR:C MPAA:NR)**

UNA DONNA SENZA NOME†   (1986, It.) Produzione Cinematografica Televisiva c (Trans: A Woman Without Name)

Lisbeth Hummel *(Bella Pouldsatter)*, Gigi Reder, Pierangelo Pozzato, Georgia Forese.

Joining the domestic staff of a wealthy horse-breeder after having spent the first 28 years of her life in the protective cloisters of a convent, the beautiful, intelligent Hummel becomes the object of her much older master's desire. During the excitement attending their nuptial banquet, the old man dies, leaving her a wealthy widow. The former foundling returns to the convent of her childhood to seek the advice of its sagacious prioress on how to handle her new-found wealth. Hummel adopts a child, on whom she dotes, and marries for a second time. Her churlish new husband proves to be a mistake, and she quickly and cleverly finds a way to become a widow again. Succumbing to the compulsion to have a real family—something she has never experienced—she weds yet again, this time choosing a domineering brute, who quickly and conveniently dies. Hummel's several sallies into mayhem have been witnessed by her farm bailiff, who unsuccessfully attempts to extort a sexual liaison in return for his silence. While attending a horserace, the wealthy widow meets her fourth husband. Their idyllic life is punctuated by her pregnancy and the birth of her natural child. Believing herself finally to have found fulfillment, Hummel is shocked by the accidental discovery that her "perfect" spouse is in league with the bailiff, and the two plan to kill her for her money.

d&w, Luigi Russo; ph, John Wilder (Telecolor); m, Antonio Vivaldi, Wolfgang Amadeus Mozart.

Murder/Mystery   **(PR:O MPAA:NR)**

UNA NOTTE DI PIOGGIA†   (1986, It.) Cooperativa Coala Spettacoli/Pereio-Falcao (Trans: One Rainy Night)

Paolo Cesare Pereio *(Giorgio Ferrari)*, Adriana Falcao.

Nuclear physicist Pereio—whose laboratory was destroyed just as he was achieving a breakthrough in his quest for an antidote to radiation poisoning—finds employment with the multinational conglomerate Western Company. He learns of a secret experiment to test his antidote on some unknowing humans who have formed an independent community—one with its own laws and its own religion—in the isolated mountains of the Abruzzi region of Italy. Pereio is torn by the knowledge that the experiment may result in the death of everyone in the unique community.

d&w, Romeo Costantini; ph, Alessandro Carlotto, Gaetano Valle; m, Gianfranco Plenizio; ed, Enzo Meniconi.

Drama   **(PR:C MPAA:NR)**

UNA SPINA NEL CUORE†   (1986, It.) Faso–Producteurs Associes/Titanus (Trans: A Thorn in the Heart)

Anthony Delon, Sophie Duez, Antonella Lualdi, Gastone Moschin, Angelo Infanti, Carola Stagnaro, Leonardo Treviglio.

Teased beyond endurance by a lovely young woman who refuses to establish a relationship with him, a young man undertakes an investigation of her past dalliances. Among her many lovers is a devilish doctor who has erroneously diagnosed her as having a fatal ailment, a revelation that has shaped her flighty character. The truth comes out, but too late, as her capriciousness is now too deeply ingrained for her to change.

d, Alberto Lattuada; w, Alberto Lattuada, Franco Ferrini, Enrico Oldoini (based on the novel by Piero Chiara); ph, Luigi Kuveiller; m, Armando Trovaioli; ed, Ruggero Mastroianni.

Drama   **(PR:O MPAA:NR)**

UNA STORIA AMBIGUA†   (1986, It.) Cineglobo/Cineglobo-Uniexport c (Trans: An Ambiguous Story)

Minnie Minoprio, Gabriele Gori, Beba Balteano, Piero Gerlini, Manola D'Amato, Marco Manni, Paolo Merosi, Serena Bisio.

In a suburb of Rome during the 1930s, the young nephew of a Fascist official visits the latter's villa and finds himself enmeshed in a web of decadence. The self-important official's neglected wife, a countess, plays erotic games with the youth, but intends to discard him following the first signs of boredom. Her daughter—the young man's cousin—who at first treated him coldly, finally throws herself at him, confessing her love for him. Overwhelmed by it all, the panicky youth flees the villa, and its inhabitants revert to their former state of dissatisfaction.

d, Mario Bianchi; w, Pietro Regnoli, Andrew Bianco (based on a story by Pietro Regnoli); ph, Pasquale Fanetti (Luciano Vittori Color); m, Carlo Mezzano; ed, Cesare Bianchini.

Drama   **(PR:O MPAA:NR)**

UNA TENERA FOLLIA†   (1986, It.) Anthony Film International c (Trans: A Tender Folly)

Saverio Vallone, Sonia Viviani, Alex Damiani, Margie Newton, Yari Porzio, Laura Papi, Milvia Coloma, Mimmo Postiglione, Pippo Barone.

Engaged to a doting, possessive heiress, a young architecture student begins an innocent but ego-bolstering flirtation with another girl. His duplicity comes to light at the same time that his building-contractor father faces financial ruin. His fiancee shames the youth at a party and the other girl unceremoniously rejects him, leaving him alone and facing the prospect of poverty. The heiress still adores him, though; to prove it, she tears up his father's credit notes (she was the major creditor) and the two go on to romance and riches.

d&w, Nini Grassia; ph, Luigi Ciccarese (Luciano Vittori Color); m, Enzo Malepasso; ed, Vanio Amici.

Comedy/Romance   **(PR:O MPAA:NR)**

UNCONSCIOUS   (SEE: FEAR, 1986)

UNDER THE CHERRY MOON zero   (1986) 98m WB bw

Prince *(Christopher Tracy)*, Jerome Benton *(Tricky)*, Kristin Scott-Thomas *(Mary Sharon)*, Steven Berkoff *(Mr. Sharon)*, Francesca Annis *(Mrs. Wellington)*, Emmanuelle Sallet *(Katy)*, Alexandra Stewart *(Mrs. Sharon)*, Pamela Ludwig, Barbara Stall, Karen Geerlings *(The Girl Friends)*, Victor Spinetti, Myriam Tadesse, Moune De Vivier *(The Jaded Three)*, Amoury DesJardins *(Young Boy at Party)*, Garance Tosello *(Young Girl at Party)*, Sylvain Levignac *(Eddy)*, Guy Cuevas *(Lou)*, Patrice Malenec *(Larry Minders)*, Azouz Saieb *(Mary's Minder)*, Jean Allaz *(Sharon Butler)*, Rosette Taubert *(Sharon Maid)*, John Rico *(Mary's Chauffeur)*, Veronique DeNoyel, Lydie Diakhate, Patricia Poulain, Catherine Allard, Nicky South, Christine Christen-Giguet, Beatrice Berthet *(Party People)*, Maurice Lenorman *(Maitre D')*, Sam Karmann *(Police Inspector)*, John Cooper *(Mrs. Wellington's Butler)*, Jobby Valente *(Champagne Lady)*, Alexa Fioroni *(The Dancer)*, Lionel Turchi, Roger Capello, Scott Allen, Juan Villalobos, Patrick Carocci, Richard Gow, Daniel Bensadoun *(Musicians)*, Maurice Simon *(Pianist)*, Jean Marie Julien *(Violinist)*, Nicolas Monard *(Photographer)*, Michael Kotzritzki *(Doorman)*, Claude Copola *(Uniformed Policeman)*, Monica Quigley *(Bombshell Blonde)*, Giselle Finazzo *(Voluptuous Brunette)*.

In 1984, rock music sensation Prince surprised nearly everyone in the movie business with the overwhelming success of his debut film PURPLE RAIN. The semi-autobiographical tale, shot on a tiny budget, took in an astonishing $50

million at the box office, and spawned a best-selling soundtrack album that was awarded an Oscar for best score. Prince was described in artistic terms generally reserved for multi-talented geniuses. Although PURPLE RAIN received a mixed critical reaction, his future in motion pictures seemed assured. With UNDER THE CHERRY MOON Prince managed to obliterate his former accolades. This followup feature takes all the narcissistic and misogynistic ideas of PURPLE

RAIN, and whips them into an empty-headed froth. The result is foolish nonsense that serves as Prince's homage to himself. The story takes place along the coast of southern France. "Once upon a time," we are told, "there lived a bad boy named Christopher Tracy. Only one thing mattered to Christopher: money. The women he knew came in all sizes, shapes and colors and they were all very rich. . . . Somewhere along the way, he learned the true meaning of love." Prince plays Christopher Tracy, dressing like a cross between Valentino and Little Richard, a pianist in an expensive restaurant, but his real occupation is hustling wealthy women who are seemingly helpless whenever he flashes a seductive smile. His sidekick Benton (who had a similar position for Morris Day in PURPLE RAIN) helps Prince out in these conquests, consistently encouraging the mascara-adorned lothario towards his various conquests. Through a newspaper article, the two learn of a wealthy young heiress (Thomas) who is about to inherit $50 million in honor of her twenty-first birthday. They crash her coming out party, where Prince catches Thomas' attention. Both he and Benton try to woo the comely lass by publicly humiliating her, and amazingly she falls for this ploy. Berkoff, her father (looking just as nasty as he did in RAMBO and BEVERLY HILLS COP), is not particularly thrilled that his daughter is dating someone prettier than herself, so he sends his goons out to stop the romance. After some sneaking around and a candlelit tryst in a cave, Prince comes to realize he actually loves Thomas, though his sudden turnabout seems no different than his previous

attitude towards Thomas. As Thomas is about to leave the country on her father's private plane, Prince drives past barricades and carries off his girl. He hides her, but Berkoff and company catch up with them. As Prince flees the thugs, running towards Thomas' waiting arms, he is shot and killed. In the film's epilog Benton, having been set up with a Miami apartment complex by Thomas, reads a letter from the poor little rich girl who is managing to cope despite the tragic events.

UNDER THE CHERRY MOON amounts to a lot of preening, strutting, doe-eyed glances and other pseudo-erotic moves by its star/director. Mary Lambert, the film's original director and a veteran of rock videos, had been scheduled to make this film her feature debut. But Prince had her fired and took over the chore himself (Lambert did receive the title of "creative consultant"). One might expect someone in the rock world would pick up a few tricks watching music videos, but Prince doesn't show even a rudimentary sense of visual style. His sequences are lifeless, consisting largely of master shots stitched together, with an occasional lap dissolve or fadeout to break up the monotony. One scene, in which Prince and Benton break up a genteel restaurant crowd with some funky music, is filled with moments that could build into something exciting. Instead, Prince merely uses a longshot of cavorting bodies as he sings atop a piano. The scene's lack of imagination seems to sum up his sense of camera placement. Prince does know how to shoot his own face, which is seen time and again in loving closeup. With his Maybelline eyes, slicked back hair, and pouty lips, along with a wardrobe that looks like something from a Liberace lawn sale, Prince has pretenses of being an erotic god with a magical power women cannot withstand. One look and they are putty in his hands. Even the license plate on his car reads "LOVE." Prince obviously considers his constant preening and emphasis on material goods seductive. The whole film plays exactly for what it is, one long essay in ego massaging. His acting skills equal what his direction calls for, while Thomas (in a bland and unpromising screen debut) serves as little more than a prop. Prince and Benton have a minor running war over who "loves" Thomas more, but these two are clearly confusing love with lust. Women are treated as something to seek out and conquer, with their value clearly depending on how beautiful, rich, and sexually willing they are. While women aren't thrown in trash bins like they were in PURPLE RAIN, in Prince's world women are still simple objects of entertainment and easily disposable. His alluring glances never differ from one woman to the next. They are obviously well perfected moves. In the final sequence Benton verbally abuses his French girl friend who then chases him while Prince lets the

camera give us an ample look beneath her skirt. This final moment is typical of the film's degrading and archaic attitudes. One can't help but feel when Prince is shot in the end he's finally getting what he deserves. Ballhaus' photography of the art deco sets is the film's only redeeming value, though his talent is clearly wasted. Warner Brothers had this shot in color, but they acquiesced to Prince's request that the film be printed in black and white. Just where this whole mess takes place is really hard to establish. Although shot in France, hardly anyone speaks the native language. The rich folks all speak with crisp upper crust British accents, while Prince and Benton use a variation of black American dialect. French people speak in subtitles, and no one seems to notice these incredible differences. But logic isn't the primary intent of UNDER THE CHERRY MOON. The picture is all Prince with his fancy clothes, hedonistic glances, and plenty of his music on the soundtrack. With his self-centered attitude and greasy hair, Prince isn't a magnetic sexual idol. He's rock 'n' roll's answer to Jerry Lewis. The songs, which were released on the album "Parade" rather than a standard movie soundtrack, include: "An Honest Man," "Do U Lie," "Mia Boca," "New Position," "I Wonder U," "Alexa De Paris," "Girls & Boys," "Love or Money," "Love Can Be So Nice," "Venus De Milo," "Old Friends for Sale," "Anotherloverholeinyohead," "Kiss," "Sometimes it Snows in April," "Mountains" (Prince, performed by Prince and The Revolution), "Christopher Tracy's Parade," "Under the Cherry Moon" (John L. Nelson, Prince, performed by Prince and The Revolution).

p, Bob Cavallo, Joe Ruffalo, Steve Fargnoli; d, Prince; w, Becky Johnston; ph, Michael Ballhaus (Technicolor, b&w); m, Prince & The Revolution; ed, Eva Gardos; prod d, Richard Sylbert; art d, Damien Lafranchi; set d, Ian Whittaker; cos, Marie France; spec eff, Maurice Zisswiller; m/l, Prince and The Revolution, John L. Nelson; makeup, Robyn Lynch.

Romance   Cas.   (PR:O   MPAA:PG-13)

UNTERMEHMEN GEIGENKASTEN†   (1986, Ger.) 85m
Johannisthal-DEFA c (Trans: Operation Violin Case)

Alexander Heidenreich *(Ole)*, Dirk Bartsch *(Andreas)*, Peggy Steiner *(Marie)*, Matthias Krohse *(Jens)*, Swetlana Schonfeld *(Ole's Mother)*, Gerd Grasse *(Ole's Father)*, Peter Bause *(Lt. Vogel)*, Fred Delmare *(Grandpa Tonnchen)*, Andreas Schumann *(Herr Neumann)*, Gerd Hartmut Schreier *(Herr Franke)*.

Heidenreich, an adventurous youngster, test-pilots a fantastic flying machine of his own design, launching it from a steep hill. The experiment puts him in a hospital bed, where the bored boy has nothing to do but watch television. Becoming obsessively interested in a Sherlock Holmes film, Heidenreich eschews inventions and resolves to become a detective. His school chums poke fun at the beleaguered boy's ambition, except for Bartsch, who decides to play Watson to Heidenreich's Holmes. Since a violin case played a critical role in the film the bedridden boy admired, the two lads beg their parents to let them take fiddle lessons so that they can lay their hands on the appropriate prop. Suitably accoutered, the sleuths venture forth, seeking a mystery to solve. They happen upon a real burglary-in-progress. Do they solve the case? Elementary, my dear Bartsch. Screened at the Berlin Film Fest.

p, Siegfried Kabitzke; d, Gunter Friedrich; w, Anne Gossens; ph, Gunter Heimann; m, Bernd Menzel; ed, Vera Nowark; set d, Marlene Willmann.

Children's/Adventure   (PR:AA   MPAA:NR)

UPHILL ALL THE WAY*   (1986) 86m Melroy-Guardian/NW c

Roy Clark *(Ben Hooker)*, Mel Tillis *(Booger Skaggs)*, Glen Campbell *(Capt. Hazleton)*, Trish Van Devere *(Widow Quinn)*, Richard Paul *(Dillman)*, Burt Reynolds *(Poker Player)*, Elaine Joyce *(Miss Jesse)*, Jacque Lynn Colton *(Lucinda)*, Burl Ives *(Sheriff John Catledge)* Frank Gorshin *(Pike)*, Sheb Wooley *(Anson Sudro)*, Burton Gilliam *(Corporal)*, Gailard Sartain *(Private)*, Rockne Tarkington *(Leon)*, Christopher Weeks *(Sam Osmond)*, Pedro Gonzalez-Gonzalez *(Chicken Carlos)*, Danny Kwan, Jim Lau *(Chinese Washers)*, Jo Perkins *(Mrs. Sudro)*, David Logan Rankin *(Tom Sudro)*, Noah Davison *(Charlie Sudro)*, Vanessa Blanchard *(Velma)*, Blue Deckery *(Cowboy Gambler)*, Paul Meszel *(Merchant Gambler)*, Chet Warner *(Tap Dancer)*, Tommy Collins *(Newspaper Vendor)*, Ed Geldary *(Conductor)*.

Imagine a sketch from the television show "Hee-Haw" expanded to an hour and a half and you'll have UPHILL ALL THE WAY, a painfully unfunny cornball-comedy chase featuring country stars Roy Clark and Mel Tillis. They play a pair of bungling con men, roving through the Texas countryside in the early 1900s. After losing their money in a card game (where Burt Reynolds makes a brief cameo appearance as a hotshot gambler), Clark and Tillis enjoy the company of some ladies-for-hire. Unable to pay for services rendered, Clark and Tillis are quickly booted from the establishment. Hoping to get some money, they go to a local bank to apply for a loan. Because they are carrying a shotgun, Clark and Tillis are mistaken for bank robbers. This mistaken identity gag builds as the two con men steal a car from a traveling salesman, then heist the uniforms and horses from two unwitting soldiers. In the meantime, Sheriff Ives and Clark's and Tillis' increasingly large group of unintended victims pile into a car and begin pursuit. Clark and Tillis are stopped by Campbell, another Army officer, but they manage to outwit him and end up in a small store run by Wooley. The store is under siege by a seemingly endless stream of Mexican bandidos, so Clark and Willis pick up guns and join the battle. Ives and his eclectic posse arrive to finish off the outlaws, while Clark and Willis escape down the river. The two are declared heroes but decide to remain anonymous, continuing their winsome way down the road.

Laurel and Hardy these guys ain't. UPHILL ALL THE WAY is wholly predictable, unfolding in a connect-the-dots manner that can be deciphered long

before events come to an end. Clark and Tillis are amiable, as is the majority of the cast, but their meager acting abilities don't stretch through a feature-length film. Essentially, this is a one-joke comedy with the same gag repeated over and over and over. Though competently handled in the technical department, the film is a crashing bore. "Hee-Haw" fans might be interested but anyone else will undoubtedly want to avoid this minor nonsense. Songs include: "Uphill All the Way" (Mel Tillis, performed by Tillis, Roy Clark, Glen Campbell), "Is We Goin' Somewheres" (Sam Weedman, performed by Clark, Tillis), "The Unlikely Posse" (Carl Jackson, performed by Campbell, Jackson), "Never Thought I'd Be an Outlaw" (Zack Van Arsdale, performed by Waylon Jennings), "Wild Winds" (Dave Hanner, performed by Campbell), "Stonin' Around" (Tillis, performed by Clark, Tillis).

p, Burr Smidt, David L. Ford; d&w, Frank Q. Dobbs; ph, Roland [Ozzie] Smith (DeLuxe Color); m, Dennis M. Pratt; ed, Chuck Weiss; prod d, Hal Metheny; set d, Pat O'Neal; cos, Ruby K. Manis; spec eff, Joe Quinlivan; m/l, Mel Tillis, Sam Weedman, Carl Jackson, Zack Van Arsdale, Dave Hanner; makeup, Bob Clark; stunts, Dave Cass.

Comedy   **Cas.**   **(PR:C   MPAA:PG)**

USUGESHO†   (1986, Jap.) Gosha–Shochiku (Trans: Face Powder)

Ken Ogata, Katsuyo Asari, Mariko Fuji, Takuzo Kawatani, Kon Omura, Haruko Asano.

d, Hideo Gosha; w, Motomu Furuta (based on a novel by Nozomu Nishimura; ph, Fujio Morita.

UTEKAJME, UZ IDE!†   (1986, Czech.) 92m Bratislava c

Marian Zednikovic *(Sysel)*, Milan Lasica *(Dr. Mahm)*, Zuzana Bydzovska *(Syslova)*, Andrej Hryc *(Rawwal)*, Slava Sabova *(Andrejka)*, Milan Kis *(Jarko)*, Ladislav Gerendas *(Sano)*, Julius Satinsky *(Detective)*, Jiri Menzel *(Zverolekar)*, Miroslav Noga *(Apprentice)*, Tomas Zednikovic *(Dodo)*.

d, Dusan Rapos; w, Jozef Slovak, Jozef Heriban; ph, Vladimir Jesina; m, Dusan Rapos, Jozef Slovak; ed, Maximilian Remen; art d, Roman Rjachovsky; cos, Tatiana Balkovicova; makeup, Juraj Steiner.

V

VA BANQUE†　　　　　　　　　　(1986, Ger.) 105m Fuzzi-Roxy c

Grazyna Dylong *(Helen)*, Winfried Glatzeder *(Stefan)*, Achim Reichel *(Paul)*, Claus-Dieter Reents *(Alfred S.)*, Joschka Fischer *(Puhdy)*, Mink DeVille, Joy Rider, Rolf Zacher, Maximilian Ruethlein, Aurelio Malfa, Vera Muller, Helmut Stauss, Dorothea Moritz, Rio Reiser, Kevin Coyne.

A trio of normally law-abiding citizens, Glatzeder, Dylong, and Reichel, are forced into a complex robbery in the hopes of alleviating their personal financial woes. Glatzeder, a taxi-driving lawyer, masterminds the successful heist of an armored car by using information gathered through his friendship with one of the drivers.

p, Manuela Stehr; d&w, Diethard Kuster; ph, Wolfgang Pilgrim; m, Achim Reichel, Toni Nissl; ed, Karl Brandenburg; set d, Albrecht Konrad.

Drama　　　　　　　　　　　　　　　**(PR:C MPAA:NR)**

VAKVILAGBAN†　　　(1986, Hung.) 87m Hungarian Television–Mafilm-Dialog Studio/Hungarofilm c (Trans: Blind Endeavor)

Andor Lukats *(Sandor)*, Gyorgy Dorner *(Karoly)*, Kati Sir *(Eva)*, Hedy Temessy *(Karoly's Mother)*, Judit Meszlery *(Sandor's Wife)*, Cecilia Esztergalyos *(Secretary)*, Lajos Szabo, Janos Degi, Gyorgy Kolgyessi *(Brigade Members)*.

The seemingly unrelated, tragic stories of two desperate men are interwoven to create an impression of the general inner turmoil resulting from Hungary's massive number of social ailments. The elder of the two, Lukats, spends an evening celebrating with his fellow factory workers. As he becomes increasingly drunker, he boisterously relates his problems with an unhappy family life and an unfulfilling job. His continued drinking only enlightens Lukats to a starker revelation of his predicament. The other story centers around Dorner's efforts to break from the tyrannical hold of his mother to marry the woman he loves. After spending a frustrating weekend in the mountains, with his lover, Donner finally realizes the necessity of standing up to his mother. Winner of a Special Jury Prize at the Karlovy Vary Film Festival, VAKVILAGBAN was originally produced for television. This was the seventh feature film for its female director, Livia Gyarmathy.

d, Livia Gyarmathy; w, Gyula Marosi, Ildiko Korody, Pal Belohorszky; ph, Ferenc Pap (Fujicolor); m, Ferenc Balazs; ed, Eva Karmento, Eva Palotai; set d, Gabor Ballo; cos, Erzsebet Mialkovszky.

Drama　　　　　　　　　　　　　　　**(PR:C MPAA:NR)**

VALHALLA†　　　(1986, Den.) 88m Swan–Interpresse Metronome–Palle Fogtdal–Danish Film Institute/J&M c

Voices: Stephen Thorne *(Thor)*, Allan Corduner *(Loke)*, Suzanne Jones *(Roskva)*, Alexander Jones *(Chalfe)*, Michael Elphick *(Udgaardsloki)*, John Hollis *(Hymer)*, Mark Jones *(Odin)*, Thomas Eje *(Quark)*, Benny Hansen, Jesper Klein, Claus Ryskjar, Geoffrey Matthews, Percy Edwards.

This fantasy is an animated reworking of well-known Norse myths and legends. Two Viking youngsters are taken by Thor, God of Thunder and his assistant Loki to work as servants amidst the ruling deities. There the children meet Quark, a giant, who helps relieve them from living under Thor's harsh conditions. When the hammer-wielding Norseman discovers their hideaway, he takes the trio to a land where giants dwell. Quark instigates a battle between giants and gods and the children ultimately lend a hand in rescuing Thor. Among the animators on this project is Borge Ring, who won an Oscar in 1986 for his winsome cartoon short ANNA AND BELLA.

d, Peter Madsen; w, Peter Madsen, Henning Kure (based on Nordic myths and design and characters from the "Valhalla" comic strip by Peter Madsen, Kure, Hans Rancke-Madsen, Per Vadmand, Soren Hakonsson); m, Ron Goodwin; ed, Lidia Sablone; art d, Peter Madsen; anim, Borge Ring.

Animation/Fantasy　　　　　　　　　　**(PR:A MPAA:NR)**

VALKOINEN KAAPIO†　　(1986, Fin.) 104m Panfilm Humaloja & Innanen/ Finnish Film Foundation (Trans: The White Dwarf) c

Kari Heiskanen, Lilga Kovanko, Jaana Raski, Jaakko Pakkasvirta, Esko Salminen, Riitta Selin, Kimm Gunnel.

A mining engineer survives a nuclear blast in the tundra of Lapland by taking refuge in a mine shaft. He later finds he is dying of leukemia as a result of radiation contamination.

p, Heikki Innanen; d&w, Timo Humaloja (based on a story by Bo Carpelan); ph, Pertti Mutanen (Eastmancolor); m, Johnny Lee Michaels; ed, Tapio Suominen; art d, Mattheus Marttila.

Drama　　　　　　　　　　　　　　　**(PR:C MPAA:NR)**

VAMP**　　　　　　　　　　　　　　(1986) 93m NW c

Chris Makepeace *(Keith)*, Sandy Baron *(Vic)*, Robert Rusler *(A.J.)*, Dedee Pfeiffer *(Amaretto)*, Gedde Watanabe *(Duncan)*, Grace Jones *(Katrina)*, Billy Drago *(Snow)*, Brad Logan *(Vlad)*, Lisa Lyon *(Cimmaron)*, Jim Boyle *(Fraternity Leader)*, Larry Spinak, Eric Welch, Stuart Rogers *(Students)*, Gary Swailes *(Sock Salesman)*, Ray Ballard *(Coffee Shop Proprietor)*, Paunita Nichols *(Maven)*,

Trudel Williams *(Dragon Girl)*, Marlon McGann *(Hard Hat)*, Thomas Bellin *(Shorty)*, Bryan McGuire *(Pool Player)*, Leila Hee Olsen *(Seko)*, Hilary Carlip *(Jett)*, Francine Swift *(Dominique)*, Tricia Brown *(Candi)*, Naomi Shohan, Janeen Davis *(Bartendresses)*, Ytossie Patterson, Tanya Papanicolas *(Waitresses)*, Robin Kaufman *(Little Girl)*, Hy Pike *(Desk Clerk)*, Pops *(Dead Man in Car)*, Bob Schott *(Gang Leader)*, Adam Barth, Bill Morphew *(Dragons)*, Simmy Bow *(Bum)*, Roger Hampton, Andy Rivas *(Police)*, Julius Leflore *(Garbage Truck Driver)*, Greg Lewis *(Bus Driver)*, Dar Robinson *(Security Guard)*, Mitch Carter, Cathy Cavadini, Deborah Fallender, Greg Finley, David McCharen, Jan Rabson, Marilyn Schreffler, Dennis Tufano *(Voices)*.

Combining out-and-out horror with comedy is always a risky proposition. In most cases the horror becomes so gruesome that the film is no longer funny, or the humor is so moronic that it diffuses the horror. VAMP suffers somewhat from the above symptoms, but the film's basic problem is its sluggishness. The movie begins at the University of Southern California. Best buddies Makepeace

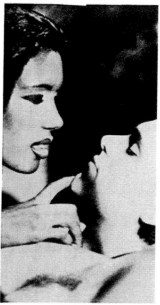

and Rusler decide to pledge a fraternity, but being no-nonsense guys, they grow impatient with their frat brothers' archaic and silly mumbo-jumbo initiation rites (they really couldn't care less about the frat, they want to sleep in the nice rooms, eat decent meals, and watch cable television). Stopping in the middle of their ridiculous ceremony, Rusler and Makepeace make the dim-witted frat brothers an offer—they will do anything to make the frat's upcoming party the hit of the campus. Although Rusler and Makepeace are thinking of booze and munchies, the frat brothers declare that they want a stripper. The friends accept the challenge and immediately run into a problem—they don't have a car. Desperate for wheels, they agree to befriend nerdy rich kid Watanabe (for one week only) if he lets them borrow one of his cars (a red Cadillac with a license plate that says "One of Nine"). Watanabe agrees, but demands that he be allowed to come along for the ride. The boys drive to downtown Los Angeles, where they almost get into an accident at an intersection. Rusler, who's driving, makes an evasive move and the car does a doughnut in the intersection. Oddly, the car keeps spinning until suddenly it is dusk and the car is parked in a seedy neighborhood. After a run-in with a gang of albino men whose girl friends are black, the boys enter the "After Dark Club." While Makepeace sits in embarrassed silence next to the dorky Watanabe, who hoots and slobbers over the strippers, Rusler pretends he doesn't know them and sits at the bar. After an incredibly erotic dance number by Jones, the star attraction, Rusler decides she is the stripper they will hire for the frat party. A waitress takes him backstage to meet Jones. Meanwhile, Makepeace sits trying to figure out why a cute young waitress, Pfeiffer (sister of Michelle), acts as if she knows him. Backstage, Rusler waits in Jones' exotic dressing room, which is adorned with pictures of herself. Jones appears, and without a word (and nary a thing on) she seduces the young man. Unfortunately, Jones happens to be a 2000-year-old Egyptian vampire and she bites Rusler on the neck (very graphically) and feasts on his blood. Soon Makepeace discovers that all the employees of the club are vampires as well, save Pfeiffer (she's new), and he tries to escape with the girl and the drunken Watanabe in tow. Makepeace encounters his buddy, Rusler, now among the undead, but still retaining his ironic sense of humor. Rusler begs Makepeace to kill him and tells him how ("They gave me a list . . . I've got it here somewhere"). Rusler hands his friend a jagged piece of wood, but Makepeace can't do it. Rusler grows impatient and does it himself. After another run-in with the albino gang, Makepeace, Pfeiffer, and Watanabe zoom off in their car, only to discover that Watanabe has become a vampire as well. After dispatching Watanabe (the car is set ablaze and explodes), Makepeace and Pfeiffer hide in the sewer system (during which she reveals that they knew each other in the fifth grade). There they discover the resting place of the vampires, which they set ablaze. Just as they are about to make good their escape, Jones appears and holds Pfeiffer hostage. Makepeace, who had acquired a bow and arrow from a pawnshop during the ordeal, manages to shoot an arrow into Jones' mouth, pinning her to the wall. As luck would have it, dawn breaks and Makepeace makes sure that sunlight destroys Jones. Makepeace and Pfeiffer are about to leave when they are confronted by a final vampire, the club's huge bouncer. Suddenly, from behind, the vampire is killed. When the body falls it reveals Rusler. He holds up the supposedly wooden stake with which he had killed himself and shrugs: "Formica." Rusler walks his friends to the nearest manhole and jokes that maybe spending his nights as a vampire won't be so bad after all. He says goodbye as Makepeace and Pfeiffer surface in the bright sunlight.

With the exception of its clever premise (vampires working in a nightclub where their victims come to them) and Jones' magnetic presence, VAMP has little fresh to offer. The humor is mostly of the sophomoric teen sex comedy variety, although veteran comedian Baron does add some class to the proceedings as the club owner and emcee. The violence, handled fairly well by special makeup artist Greg Cannom, is graphic and gruesome, and there is a fair amount of stripper bump-and-grind. Jones' erotic dance sequence is the showstopper. Wearing only a body painting by New York graffiti artist Keith Haring (and three strategically placed wire coils) and using a Haring-designed male-torso chair as a prop, Jones slinks about the stage to one of her own songs. Actually, Jones has surprisingly little to do in the film—she never speaks a word—and only appears in a half dozen scenes. First-time director Wenk tries to strike a balance between laughs and chills, but the film has an empty, almost listless quality as if the inspiration ran out shortly after Jones was revealed to be a vampire. Once the cleverness runs out, we are left to watch a rather mundane modern vampire film where the visual design elements have been fussed over more than the script (most of the film seems lit with trendy green and magenta neon). Reportedly, the shooting of the film was incredibly disorganized, with effects-artist Cannom having to rethink his designs on short notice after being informed that some of his key scenes would be shot in one day. To add to the tension, the L.A. neighborhood selected for the exterior scenes was particularly nasty and some crew members were afraid to go to work. It really wasn't worth it; VAMP bombed at the box office ($2.2 million in rentals) and hit the video stores very quickly. Songs include: "Bad Case of Lovin' You" (Moon Martin), "Volare" (Domenico Modugno, Mitchell Parish, performed by Bobby Rydell), "I'm in the Mood For Love" (Jimmy McHugh, Dorothy Fields), "Jealous Heart" (Andrew Kastner, Mark Campbell, Howard Benson, performed by Jack Mack & The Heart Attack), "Vamp" (Jonathan Elias, Grace Jones, performed by Jones), "Excite Me" (Larry Klug, performed by Fantasy Workshop), "Meaning of Love" (Devon James, performed by Devon LaCrosse), "Domestic #1 & #2-The Donna Reed Show Theme" (William Loose, John Seely), "A Song For Kim" (Johnette Napolitano, Jim Mankey, performed by Dream 6), "Now I Ride Alone" (Steve Wynn, performed by The Dream Syndicate), "One Thing on My Mind" (Ziggy Evans), "That Old Black Magic" (Harold Arlen, Johnny Mercer, performed by Louis Prima).

p, Donald P. Borchers; d&w, Richard Wenk (based on a story by Donald P. Borchers, Richard Wenk); ph, Elliot Davis (Metrocolor); m, Jonathan Elias; ed, Marc Grossman; prod d, Alan Roderick-Jones; art d, Carol Clements, Philip Aja; set d, Katherine J. Carmichael; cos, Betty Pecha Madden; spec eff, Greg Cannom, Image Engineering, Inc., Peter Chesney, Jarn Heil, Tom Chesney, Chris Chesney, Joseph Viskocil, Apogee, Inc.; ch, Russell Clark; stunts, Dar Robinson; makeup, Pamela S. Westmore, Robin Beauchesne, Teresa Austin, Joann Gair; anim, Clint Colver.

Horror/Comedy **Cas.** **(PR:O MPAA:R)**

VASECTOMY: A DELICATE MATTER zero (1986) 90m Vandom International/Seymour Borde & Associates c

Paul Sorvino *(Gino)*, Abe Vigoda *(Detective Edwards)*, Cassandra Edwards *(Anna)*, Lorne Greene *(Theo Marshall)*, Gary Raff *(George)*, Ina Balin *(Regine)*, Frank Aletter *(Mr. Cromwell)*, Catherine Battistone *(Mrs. Ellison)*, Suzanne Charney *(Mildred)*, John Moskoff *(Francis)*, Janet Wood *(Marie)*.

Where do people get ideas like this, and just how do they get them turned into motion pictures? Sorvino plays a banker summoned to the deathbed of his boss Greene. Greene doesn't want the institution to fall into the hands of some covetous relations, and makes Sorvino a lucrative offer. Sorvino will inherit $500,000 if he can help Greene's son Raff renounce his philandering life style and keep the bank profitable. In the meantime Sorvino's wife Edwards, the mother of eight children, informs her spouse there will not be a ninth member to their brood. Furthermore, unless Sorvino agrees to undergo a vasectomy, there will be a vast difference in the couple's sex life. Of course, Sorvino isn't too keen on the idea, but the thought of spending the rest of his married life sleeping on the couch isn't all that appealing either.

The comedy arises from Sorvino's reactions between these two conflicts, but the material is insufferable. There's no wit to this at all, merely a string of tasteless jokes revolving around the implications of a vasectomy. Burge, who produced, directed, and cowrote this trash, shows no sense for comedy in the least. Sorvino has never been more dismal, and the supporting cast simply flounders along behind him. VASECTOMY: A DELICATE MATTER died the miserable box office death it so richly deserved, opening and closing with little notice by anyone.

p, Robert Burge, Lou Wills; d, Robert Burge; w, Robert Burge, Robert Hilliard; ph, Gary Thieltges (United Color Labs); m, Fred Karlin; ed, Beth Conwell.

Comedy **(PR:O MPAA:R)**

VECERNJA ZVONA† (1986, Yugo.) 127m Jadran-Jugoart-Montenegroexport c (Trans: Evening Bells)

Rade Serbedzija *(Tomislav)*, Petar Bozovic, Neda Arneric, Tatjana Blagojevic, Miodrag Krivokapic, Mustafa Nadarevic.

Yugoslavian historical odyssey, based on an award-winning novel by screenwriter Kovac, which covers 22 years in the life of political leader Serbedzija. Beginning when he is just a boy, the film follows Serbedzija through WW II, during which he is rescued from a concentration camp by his wife, who becomes the mistress of a fascist officer in order to get him out. Serbedzija, however, sees her as a collaborator and eventually drives her to suicide. After the war Serbedzija is caught in the chaos of the Stalin era and is imprisoned. In prison Serbedzija is killed under mysterious circumstances. Director Zafranovic was named best director and Serbedzija best actor at the Pula Film Festival.

p, Sulejman Kapic; d, Lordan Zafranovic; w, Mirko Kovac (based on his novel *Entrance to the Womb*); ph, Andrija Pivcevic (Agfa Gevaert Color); m, Vladimir Kraus-Rajteric; ed, Andrija Zafranovic; art d, Ivica Sporcic; cos, Ruta Knezevic.

Drama **(PR:O MPAA:NR)**

VELKA FILMOVA LOUPEZ† (1986, Czech.) 82m Barrandov c (Trans: The Great Movie Robbery)

Oldrich Kaiser *(Kaiser/Kral)*, Jiri Labus *(Labus/Lambas)*, Jaroslav Moucka *(Sef)*, Jiri Nemecek *(Septal)*, Karel Hermanek *(Hezoun)*, Ladislav Gerendas *(Doctor)*, Zdenek Srstka *(Vocko)*, Dagmar Veskrnova *(Assistant Director)*, Vladimir Hrabanek *(Lojza)*, Lubomir Lipsky *(Janitor)*, Jiri Kodet *(Director)*.

d, Oldrich Lipsky, Zdenek Podskolsky; w, Matin Bezouska, Dusan Kukal, Oldrich Lipsky, Oldrich Kaiser, Jiri Labus (based on a story by Oldrich Lipsky); ph, Emil Sirotek; m, Vitezslav Hadl, Zdenek Borovec; ed, Dalibor Lipsky; art d, Jindrich Goetz; cos, Jan Kropacek; makeup, Stanislav Petrek.

VENDETTA** (1986) 88m Concorde c

Karen Chase *(Laurie Collins)*, Lisa Clarson *(Bobo)*, Lisa Hullana *(China)*, Linda Lightfoot *(Wanda)*, Sandy Martin *(Kay Butler)*, Michelle Newkirk *(Bonnie Cusak)*, Marianne Taylor *(Star)*, Marshall Teague *(Paul Donahue)*, Kin Shriner *(Steve Nelson)*, Roberta Collins *(Miss Dice)*, Greg Bradford *(Joe-Bob)*, Mark von Zech *(Randy)*, Pleasant Gehman, Rose Flores, Kerry O'Brian, Marsky Reins, Boom Boom Dixon *(Screaming Sirens)*, Holly Butler *(The Movie Star)*, Bruce Logan *(Director)*, Hoke Howell *(Deputy Curly)*, Will Hare *(Judge Waters)*, Mark Rosenblatt *(Bailiff)*, Charles Joseph Martin *(Willie)*, Marta Kober *(Sylvia)*, Renee Jacque Kino *(Amy)*, Cynthia Harrison *(Debra)*, Kelita Kelly *(Sandy)*, Reggie Bennett *(Conchita)*, Kim Collins *(Betty)*, Ginger Johnston *(Dakota)*, Jack Kosslyn *(Warden Haines)*, Ken Solomon *(Coroner)*, Dave Nicholson *(District Attorney)*, Eugene Robert Glazer *(David Greene)*, Joshua Brooks, J.W. Fails *(Parking Attendants)*, Gamy L. Taylor *(Judge)*, Adzine Melliti *(Gino)*, Joanelle Nadine Romero *(Elena)*, Dixie Lee *(Rosie)*, Durga McBroom *(Widow)*, Topaz *(Disc Jockey)*, Tracette St. Julian *(Celebrity Take-Off)*, Carol Porter, Kathleen Stevens, Lynell Carter, Patti Burdo, Patrice Davis, Shawni Davis *(Girls in Shower)*.

Fighting off a rape attempt, young Newkirk kills her assailant and ends up in jail for two years on a manslaughter charge. She quickly runs afoul of butch lesbian drug-dealer Martin and her gang when she rejects Martin's pass; that night she is attacked, pumped full of heroin, and tossed off a railing to her death. Her sister, Chase, a professional movie stuntwoman, tries to have the authorities look into the case, but they simply write it off as suicide. Chase steals a judge's car and leads police on a merry chase before they capture her, and she is sent to the same prison. There she soon learns who was responsible for the death of her sister, and she goes about killing them one by one after vicious fights in which her stunt training gives her an edge. As Martin sees her closest associates dying off, she grows frightened, and when she learns that Chase was Newkirk's sister, she tries to have Chase killed. Chase survives a couple of attempts before a fight gets her thrown into solitary and gets Martin's privileges as trusty revoked. While a corrupt guard goes to Chase's cell and tries to rape her, Martin and her remaining followers start a massive fight in the mess hall during a talent show. Chase manages to beat up the guard and escape, killing another of Martin's girls by kicking her down a flight of stairs. Back at the riot, chief of security Collins orders a tranquilizer gas released, and soon almost all the bad girls are fast asleep. Martin manages to slip out, though, and runs into Chase. They fight savagely until Martin is knocked out and Collins shows up with a shotgun. Martin gets up and is about to club Chase with a wrench when Collins blows her away. Collins, who has figured out Chase's mission of vengeance, tells her that she will have the rest of her life to think about what she's done, and it looks for a second that she will have to do serious time for the murders she's committed, but no, in the very next scene she's released from prison and picked up by her boy friend.

The ending betrays what until then had been one of the more intelligent women-in-prison films (as such things go). Chase seriously sets about avenging her sister at the beginning, but the first killing is almost accidental. By the third killing, she is having second thoughts about it all, and actually lets go of a girl she has by the throat. Unfortunately for the girl, once released, she attacks Chase, who kicks her into the shower where she cracks her head open on the tile. After that, it is only when attacked that she fights back, though her encounters usually end with the other person dead. The performances are way above average for this kind of thing, with Martin stealing every scene she's in, not to mention getting all the best lines. Collins has a smallish part as the head of prison security, but her appearance here is more in the way of an homage to all the other women-in-prison movies in which she has appeared, including THE BIG DOLL HOUSE, WOMEN IN CAGES, and the genre's best, RENEGADE GIRLS. As is usual for these films, any similarity between this prison and the real thing is strictly coincidental; the women here can wear just about any outlandish costume they can devise, and they have almost free run of the place. Of course, all the obligatory scenes are there: long showers, rapist guards, brutal beatings, and more showers; plus, this prison allows conjugal visits, so we can have more sex scenes. Let's face it, these films are as seedy as they come, but for fans of exploitation, the ultimate extension of what they want. For a film to deliver all of it, and toss in a not-too-heavy message as well, is more than many more presumptuous films have achieved. Songs include "The Wait" (Tracette St. Julian, Miriam Cutler, Elliot Wolff, performed by Duke Mooseekian), "Love Slave" (Rosie Flores, Pleasant Gehman, performed by Screaming Sirens), "Head for the Hills" (Gehman, performed by Screaming Sirens), "Friend" (Joanelle Nadine Romero, Jesse Galesi, performed by Romero).

p, Jeff Begun, Ken Solomon, Ken Dalton; d, Bruce Logan; w, Emil Farkas, Simon Maskell, Laura Cavestani, John Adams; ph, Robert New (Filmhouse Color); m, David Newman; ed, Glenn Morgan; art d, Chris Clarens; set d, Timothy Ford; cos, Meg Mayer; m/l, Tracette St. Julian, Miriam Cutler, Elliot Wolff, Rosie Flores, Pleasant Gehman, Joanelle Nadine Romero, Jesse Galesi; makeup, Michael Spatola.

Prison/Action	Cas.	(PR:O MPAA:R)

VENENO PARA LAS HADAS†   (1986, Mex.) 90m Instituto Mexicano de Cinematografia-Sindicato de Trabajadores de la Produccion Cinematografica/Peliculas Mexicanas c (Trans: Poison for Fairies)

Ana Patricia Rojo *(Veronica)*, Elsa Maria *(Flavia)*.

Set in an expensive private school, VENENO PARA LAS HADAS examines the potential for tragedy when childhood fantasies are taken too far. Rojo stars as the new girl in school who becomes absorbed in the occult and considers herself a witch. Her best friend Maria participates in witchcraft, mainly to please Rojo. The girls become obsessed with wiping out "fairies," the traditional enemy of witches. Each girl creates her own brand of special poison with which to kill the fairies. The film is shot entirely from a child's viewpoint, and adults, when they are shown, are seen only in part (arms, legs, hands) or from the back.

d&w, Carlos Enrique Toboada; ph, Guadalupe Garcia; m, Carlos Jimenez Mabarak; ed, Carlos Savage.

Drama		(PR:O MPAA:NR)

VERY CLOSE QUARTERS*   (1986) 101m Cable Star Ltd. c

Shelley Winters *(Galina)*, Paul Sorvino *(Kiril)*, Theodore Bikel *(Victor)*, Farley Granger *(Pavel)*, Lee Taylor Allen *(Vera)*, Ellen Barber *(Luda)*, Frederick Allen *(Vadik)*, Dennis Boutsikaris *(Alex)*, Kathleen Doyle *(Irena)*.

This dreadful attempt at comedy was filmed in 1983 and never saw the light of day until Vestron Video dusted it off and released it on videocassette. As is the case with most straight-to-video releases, it should have stayed perched high on a studio shelf awaiting a tragic warehouse fire. Virtually plotless, VERY CLOSE QUARTERS makes a laughable attempt at depicting living conditions in modern-day Moscow where 31 people share a cramped communal flat (sounds hilarious, eh?). As the mass of Soviet citizens elbow each other for breathing room, a story of sorts emerges. Winters—an unwed mother who doesn't want her pretty young daughter, Lee Taylor Allen, to suffer the same fate—tries to play matchmaker for her child. The target of Winters' obsession is Allen's wealthy-but-alcoholic boss, Sorvino. Allen, however, has her own ideas, and—being an irreverent young Soviet—she enjoys pretending that she's having a lesbian affair with Barber, a local artist, just to annoy the neighbors. Also threatening to destroy Winters' matchmaking is handsome young comrade Frederick Allen, who is in love with her daughter.
    Boring, obnoxious, and bereft of any comic value, VERY CLOSE QUARTERS is maddeningly inept. The filmmakers make no attempt to capture the look or flavor of life in the Soviet Union and the actors all speak in their normal American voices—this film could be set in Brooklyn. Most of the jokes play on the fact that 31 people are sharing the same bathroom, and this gets quite tiresome. While most of the cast members can attribute their bland performances to inexperience, there is no excuse for the blatant overacting of veterans Winters, Sorvino, Bikel, and Granger. The stifling, claustrophobic (the entire film takes place on one set—save for the last shot) feel of this film, combined with the total lack of entertainment value, will have viewers ready to leap out the nearest window to escape.

p, Harold Sobel, Jack Bean; d, Vladimir Rif; w, Vladimir Rif, Dennis Pearlstein; ph, Mikhail Suslov (Guffanti Color); m, Jay Chattaway; ed, Lorenzo Marinelli, Rudolph Marinelli; prod d, Mikhail Fishgoit; art d, Hilda Stark.

Comedy	Cas.	(PR:O MPAA:R)

VESELE VANOCE PREJI CHOBOTNICE†   (1986, Czech.) 100m Barrandov c (The Octopuses Wish You a Merry Christmas)

Dagmar Veskrnova *(Holan's Mom)*, Pavel Zednicek *(Holan's Father)*, Zaneta Fuchsova *(Eva)*, Milan Simacek *(Her Brother Honzik)*, Miroslav Machacek *(Research)*, Boris Rosner *(Andreadis)*, Vladimir Kratina *(Sculptor Mertlik)*, Jaroslav Moucka *(Old Man Nekvasil)*, Jiri Kodet *(Rudla Fara)*, Jirina Bohdalova (Voice of the Green Octopus), Frantisek Filipovsky (Voice of the Blue Octopus).

d, Jindrich Polak; w, Ota Hofman, Jindrich Polak; ph, Emil Sirotek; m, Angelo Michajlov; ed, Dalibor Lipsky; art d, Jindirch Goetz; cos, Sarka Hejnova; makeup, Jiri Budin.

VIAJE A NINGUNA PARTE†   (1986, Span.) 135m Ganesh Cinematograficas c (Trans: Voyage to Nowhere)

Jose Sacristan *(Carlos Galvan)*, Laura del Sol *(Juanita Plaza)*, Juan Diego *(Sergio Maldonado)*, Maria Luisa Ponte *(Julia Iniesta)*, Fernando Fernan Gomez *(Gal-*

van's *Father)*, Gabino Diego, Nuria Gallardo, Queta Claver, Agustin Gonzalez, Miguel Rellan, Emma Cohen, Carlos Lemos, Simon Andreu.

Sacristan stars as an elderly actor living in a nursing home who tells his psychiatrist of past glories when he was a member of a traveling actors troupe in the 1950s. Many members of his family were part of the troupe as well, including Sacristan's father, Gomez, and his 17-year-old illegitimate son, who, although homely and untalented, was allowed to come along. In flashback it is revealed that even though Sacristan has taken a lover from among the troupe—the beautiful Del Sol (THE HIT)—he still becomes involved in some complicated relationships with various local women as the troupe moves from town to town. After years of starving, the troupe breaks up and the members go their separate ways. Some travel to Madrid in search of movie stardom. While most wind up working as extras, Sacristan becomes a star. After seven years on top, his fame fades and he winds up in the old folks home. Sacristan's psychiatrist notes that the movie-star portion of the actor's tale is merely part of the delusions that the old man has surrounded himself with in his waning years.

p, Maribel Martin, Julian Mateos; d&w, Fernando Fernan Gomez; ph, Jose Luis Alcaine; m, Pedro Iturralde; ed, Pablo G. del Amo; set d&cos, Julio Esteban.

Drama		(PR:C-O MPAA:NR)

VIOLATED*   (1986) 88m Cinematronics c

J.C. Quinn *(Kevin McBane)*, April Daisy White *(Lisa Robb)*, John Heard *(Skipper)*, D. Balin *(Jack Diamond)*, Kaye Dowd *(Shirley Robb)*, Lisanne Falk *(Judy Engels)*, Elizabeth Kaitan *(Liz Grant)*, Carol Francis *(Katy Carson)*, Samantha Fox *(Joan)*, Jonathan Ward *(Danny Robb)*, Carl Gordon *(District Attorney)*, Alec Massey *(Frank Lyon)*, Charles Gilbert *(Zimmerman)*, Claude Vincent *(Manley)*, Richard Cannistraro *(Derrick Solo)*, Bill Galarno *(Dave)*, Randy Jurgensen *(Police Sergeant)*, Shifra Meyrow, Jill McWhirten, Cathy Perry, Nancy Cozzini, Peter Mele, Gunther Stern, John Hermann, Ed Malloy, Jake Packard, Sharon Cane, Mari Thronsen, Pam Anderson, Laura Bennett, Candy Middleton, Whitney Badin, Lynn Kelly, Cindy Shapiro, Hannah Price *(Party Guests)*.

Looking suspiciously like a film that was never finished, VIOLATED went straight to video after two years without a theatrical release. White is a young actress who is invited to a party at minor gangster Balin's house. There she is raped by senior gangster Massey, along with Balin and Balin's lesbian wife. At home she tries to hide her bruises, but her nosy aunt calls first the police, then the New York Post, which splashes the story across the front page. Subpoenaed to testify before a grand jury, she is thoroughly discredited by false testimony. Meanwhile, White begins an affair with Quinn, a policeman who is full of good advice. Later, after Balin cheats Massey in a marijuana smuggling scheme, the mob hires a hitman to kill him. Heard is the contact man, and who should the professional killer be but Quinn, apparently moonlighting. He kills Balin just as White is about to do the same, while Heard murders Massey and Balin's widow.
    After moving so ponderously and introducing so many extraneous characters, the way this movie wraps itself up in about ten minutes is confusing, but a relief. A few likable performances, particularly those of Quinn and White, are about all this movie has going for it. Stealing his scenes, though, is Heard—a talented actor who apparently will take any job offered him—as a twitchy low-level thug who contacts Quinn, then asks him how to get into this line of work, fantasizing about killing women who deserve it and bragging about a woman he once killed. Great dollops of nudity of the most gratuitous kind; the peak is reached when White has a long conversation in her bedroom with her little brother while topless. Hardly art, but mostly harmless.

p&d, Richard Cannistraro; w, Richard Cannistraro, Bennet Sims (based on a story by Cannistraro); ph, Skip Roessel (TVC Color); m, Lee Shapiro; ed, Michael R. Miller; prod d, Karen Morse; art d, Howard Kling; cos, Kathleen McCoy.

Crime/Drama	Cas.	(PR:O MPAA:NR)

VIOLENT BREED, THE*   (1986, It.) 91m Visione Cinematografica-Cannon/MGM-UA Home Video c

Henry Silva *(Kirk Cooper)*, Harrison Muller *(Mike Martin)*, Woody Strode *(Paolo)*, Carole Andre, Debora Keith, Danika.

Shot in 1983 and picked up for distribution in the U.S. by Cannon Films, who later changed their minds and released it straight to video in 1986, THE VIOLENT BREED is yet another of those anonymous jungle action pictures from Italy which invariably feature aging black actor Woody Strode. Strode, Silva, and Muller are three commandos who launch a secret mission into Southeast Asia to rescue a group of refugee children. At a crucial moment in the operation, Strode betrays his comrades without explanation. Years later, Silva, now in the CIA, orders Muller to return to Southeast Asia in search of Strode. It is learned that Strode is now running drugs and arms for the KGB *and* the Mafia. With the help of a young prostitute, Muller finds Strode's secret camp. Face to face with Strode, Muller, representing the United States government, offers him a better price for the drugs than he's getting from the Soviets or the Mafia. This causes confusing battle scenes among the U.S., Mafia, and Soviets, and the movie ends with Strode, Silva, and Muller as buddies again.
    A totally ludicrous amalgamation of Vietnam war films, political conspiracy thrillers, and gangster movies, THE VIOLENT BREED makes little sense among the poorly staged shootouts. It lurches from scene to scene with no sense of order or cohesion. Silva is barely in the film, Muller isn't worth watching, and for some reason Strode's voice is dubbed. Even the most undiscriminating action freaks will be bored by this one.

p, Ettore Spagnuolo; d, Fernando DiLeo; w, Fernando DiLeo, Nino Marino; ph,

Roberto Gerardi (Technicolor); m, Paolo Rustichelli; ed, Arnold Jury; spec eff, Paolo Ricci; stunts, Gil Galimberti.

Action   Cas.   (PR:O MPAA:NR)

VIOLETS ARE BLUE**   (1986) 88m Rastar/COL c

Sissy Spacek (*Gussie Sawyer*), Kevin Kline (*Henry Squires*), Bonnie Bedelia (*Ruth Squires*), John Kellogg (*Ralph Sawyer*), Jim Standiford (*Addy Squires*), Augusta Dabney (*Ethel Sawyer*), Kate McGregor-Stewart (*Sara Mae*), Adrian Sparks (*George*), Annalee Jefferies (*Sally*), Mike Starr (*Tony*), Brian Sargis (*Squid*), Keith Sargis (*Bryant*), Michael Mack (*Ben*), Erin Malooly (*Erin*), Megan Malooly (*Kathleen*), Kathleen Fannon (*Girl's Mother*), Doug Roberts (*Lloyd Lynch*).

Opening with a prologue set in 1969, VIOLETS ARE BLUE features Kline and Spacek as two lovers who pledge eternal devotion despite their separation when Kline goes off to college. Spacek ends up leaving their small, oceanside Maryland town as well, and becomes an airline stewardess. Through a picture montage we learn Spacek graduates from passing dinner trays on airplanes to international

acclaim as a photojournalist. Now, some 15 years later, she returns for a much needed vacation to the home of Kellogg and Dabney, her parents. Kline, who inherited the local newspaper after his father passed away, is married to Bedelia and father of Standiford, an adolescent son. After seeing Spacek at a boat race, Kline meets his former love at the newspaper office and invites her to dinner. Bedelia is none-too-pleased with the developing situation and is further intimidated after Spacek arrives. Kline walks Spacek home and before long the two rekindle their long dormant romance. Kline and Spacek begin spending more time together and accidentally uncover the makings of a local scandal. Following a lovemaking session on a small island, Kline and Spacek witness a group of businessmen poisoning some wild ponies. If the herd dies, these men will be allowed to build a condominium on the island, a project Kline has been vehemently opposing. Spacek takes some pictures of this illegal activity, which Kline prints on his paper's front page. Convinced they work well together, Spacek pulls a few strings and gets Kline a juicy writing assignment for a national magazine. She will photograph the children of Lebanon, and Kline will write the accompanying story. Bedelia is furious with her husband, but Kline refuses to answer her charges of infidelity. However, torn between what his life could have been and what reality has dealt him, Kline ultimately decides not to accompany Spacek to Beirut. He returns to Bedelia, while Spacek, through the view of her airplane window, watches the wild ponies run free.

How's that for a meaningful and symbolic ending? It's typical of the film's glossy style, projecting importance when there's really no depth beneath the surface. Issues are raised, then ignored when their usefulness in the plot ceases. The importance of memory, familial relationships, and the disappointment of unfulfilled dreams all make cameo appearances but under Fisk's bland direction no one idea ever takes hold. Kline and Spacek lack the chemistry to make their romance believable, never generating any real passion during the course of their affair. Kline walks around mope-eyed, carrying the burden of his past aspirations and current problems with the real estate developers as though bearing a deep, personal cross. Kline gives a one-note performance, a real surprise considering the ardor he brought to his romantic lead in SOPHIE'S CHOICE. Spacek, on the other hand, is too lighthearted to be taken seriously as an international photojournalist and other woman. The character has no bite, and there are moments when Spacek seems entirely oblivious to what's going on. Bedelia and Kellogg fare better, bringing some depth to their largely wasted performances. Fisk, Spacek's real-life off-screen spouse, gives his star plenty of flattering soft focus closeups, and treats her character's often inconsiderate behavior with kid gloves. It is Bedelia, rather than Spacek, who comes off looking like an unprincipled woman when she dares to question Kline's relationship with his old flame. With the exception of the two name stars, there's nothing about VIOLETS ARE BLUE that separates it from any number of prosaic made-for-television romances.

p, Marykay Powell; d, Jack Fisk; w, Naomi Foner; ph, Ralf Bode (DeLuxe Color); m, Patrick Williams; ed, Edward Warschilka; prod d, Peter Jamison; art d, Bo Welch; set d, Jane Bogart; cos, Joe I. Tompkins; spec eff, Ken Speed; makeup, Brenda Todd, Mickey Scott.

Romance   Cas.   (PR:C-O MPAA:PG-13)

VIRUS HAS NO MORALS, A***   (1986, Ger.) 82m Rosa von Praunheim c (EIN VIRUS KENNT KEINE MORAL)

Rosa von Praunheim (*Rudiger, Club Owner*), Dieter Dicken (*Christian*), Maria Hasenaecker (*Dr. Blut*), Christian Kesten (*Student*), Eva Kurz (*Carola*), Regina Rudnick (*Therapist*), Thilo von Trotha (*Mother*).

It would be hard to imagine anyone making a comedy about a deadly serious subject like AIDS, but that is exactly what camp filmmaker and gay spokesman Rosa von Praunheim has successfully accomplished in A VIRUS HAS NO MORALS. Not only is this an extremely funny movie, it also presents a provocative perusal of AIDS-related topics such as treatment, prevention, government policies, media misrepresentation, research, and life styles of AIDS victims. Using nonprofessional actors, von Praunheim presents cartoon caricatures in fantastic sketches. The director himself has a role as the owner of a gay sauna concerned only with the effects the AIDS epidemic will have on his business. He contracts the disease and finds the repercussions on his hedonistic existence an impossible irritation. His live-in lover, a singer in a church choir, also becomes infected. An AIDS researcher referred to as Dr. Blut travels to Africa to discover the disease's source. She becomes infected after a gorilla rapes her. An opportunistic journalist, whose son has AIDS, busily creates erroneous rumors just for the sake of scandal. A nurse at the treatment center sleeps with bisexual men hoping to catch the disease so she can spread it throughout the entire population. There is also a gay terrorist group continously popping into the film. Their approach is a combative, aggressive one, demanding that AIDS victims and the gay population fight both the disease and the popularized mythology surrounding it. The government's solution to the epidemic is to put all AIDS victims into camps much like leper colonies; and this is where we see all the characters at the film's close.

A VIRUS HAS NO MORALS was shot with a gritty garishness, abstract camera angles, and is sloppily edited. This is just von Praunheim's camp style, which surrealistically heightens the humor of situations. The use of nonprofessionals allows the actors to obsessively indulge in their caricatured roles in a way image-conscious professionals could not. Though von Praunheim does not present any solutions, he does show that the AIDS epidemic is not hopeless. His criticism of present approaches, specifically an inattentive and uncaring government, is thought-provoking, but, if nothing else, A VIRUS HAS NO MORALS may prove that laughter is the best medicine. (In German; English subtitles.)

p,d&w, Rosa von Praunheim; ph, Elfi Mikesch; m, Maran Gosov, The Bermudas; ed, Michael Schaeffer, Rosa von Praunheim.

Comedy   (PR:O MPAA:NR)

VISA U.S.A.†   (1986, Colombia/Cuba) 90m Focine–ICAIC c

Armando Gutierrez (*Adolfo*), Marcela Agudelo (*Patricia*), Raul Eguron Cuesta (*Papa Adolfo*), Lucy Martinez Tello (*Mama Adolfo*), Elios Fernandez (*Papa Patricia*), Vicky Hernandez (*Mama Patricia*), Diego Alvarez (*Pedro Guillermo*), Maria Lucia Castrillion (*Adriana*), Gellver de Currea Lugo (*Moncho*), Gerardo Calero (*Felmo*).

Feeling trapped and restless on his father's failing chicken farm, 20-year-old Gutierrez dreams of escaping Colombia and going to the U.S. to become a radio and television announcer. To save money for his trip, Gutierrez works in a local record store and gives English lessons to high school students. He falls in love with one of his students, Agudelo, a senior and the daughter of an upper-middle class family. Of course her parents do not approve of the son of a lowly chicken farmer and they discourage the relationship. When Gutierrez requests a tourist visa for the U.S., he is denied it because his older brother went there on such a visa, found a good job, and never returned. Desperate, Gutierrez spends his savings on a counterfeit passport and visa. Upon learning that the boy's visa request was denied, Agudelo's father seizes the opportunity and sends his daughter on a trip to New York in the hope that she will forget Gutierrez. Using his phony documents, however, Gutierrez attempts to travel with his love. Unfortunately, his false papers are detected and Gutierrez barely escapes arrest. Rather than go on to the U.S. alone, Agudelo decides to stay in Colombia and help Gutierrez realize his dream in their own country.

p, Guillermo Calle Delgado; d&w, Lisandro Duque; ph, Raul Perez Ureta; m, Leo Brouwer; ed, Nelson Rodriguez.

Drama   (PR:C MPAA:NR)

VISAGE PALE†   (1986, Can.) 103m Yuri Yoshmura–Gagnon c (Trans: Pale Face)

Luc Matte, Denis Lacroix, Allison Odjig.

A retired Canadian hockey player goes north and becomes friendly with an Indian man who is killed when he defends the white from some local thugs. The Indian's sister then becomes involved with the outlander, though their disparate political views make for a trying relationship.

d, Claude Gagnon.

Drama   (PR:O MPAA:NR)

VLCI BOUDA†   (1986, Czech.) 92m Barrandov c (Trans: Wolf Chalet)

Miroslav Machacek (*Daddy*), Stepankova Cervenkova (*Babeta*), Tomas Platy (*Dingo*), Rita Dudusova (*Gitka*), Hana Mrozkovy (*Lenka*), Ivana Mrozkovy (*Linda*), Radka Slavikova (*Emilka*), Jitka Zelenkova (*Brona*), Simona Rackova (*Gaba*), Frantisek Stanek (*Petr*), Jan Bidlas (*Jan*), Petr Horacek (*Alan*), Norbert Pycha (*Marcipan*), Roman Fiser (*Jozka*), Jan Kacer (*Jan's Father*), Nina Diviskova *(Jan's Mother)*, Jiri Krampol *(Alan's Father)*, Antonin Vrablik *(Lumberjack)*.

d, Vera Chytilova; w, Daniela Fischerova, Vera Chytilova; ph, Jaromir Sofr; m, Michael Kocab; ed, Jiri Brozek; art d, Ludvik Siroky; cos, Sarka Hejnova; makeup, Jana Dolejsi.

VOGLIA DI GUARDARE† (1986, It.) Filmirage/Vip International c (Trans: The Desire to Watch)

Jenny Tamburi, Marino Mase, Sebastiano Somma, Laura Gemser, Aldina Martano, Lilli Carati.

A bored housewife has an affair with a mysterious playboy. Her lover insists their trysts be held at an artist's studio, which is in fact a brothel owned by the playboy's other mistress. When the playboy begins to fall in love with the housewife, the jilted lover reveals to her rival that the whole affair has been engineered by her husband, who has watched everything through a secret mirror in the studio.

d, Joe D'Amato; w, Donatella Donnati (based on a story by Aristide Massaccesi); ph, Aristide Massaccesi (Telecolor); m, Guido Anelli, Stefano Mainetti.

Drama   **(PR:O MPAA:NR)**

VYHRAVAT POTICHU† (1986, Czech.) Barrandov c (Trans: Winning Discreetly)

Filip Blazek, Roman Bednar, Filip Zelezny, Pavel Novy, Lenka Tedrmerova.

d, Drahuse Kralova; w, Jan Kruta, Drahuse Kralova; ph, Vladimir Smutny.

VYITI ZAMUZH ZA KAPITANA† (1986, USSR) 88m Lenfilm c (Trans: To Marry the Captain)

Viktor Proskourine *(Capt. Blinov)*, Vera Glagoleva *(Elena Juravilova)*, Nikolai Rybnikov *(Liadov)*, Vera Vassilieva *(Woman Friend)*.

A Soviet romantic comedy starring Proskourine as a prudish KGB agent in charge of a frontier post who falls in love with a beautiful divorcee, Glagoleva, while on leave to visit his mother in the country. The somewhat conniving young divorcee begs the KGB officer to assist her in her battle against an annoying neighbor with whom she shares a bathroom. She has him pose as her lover, but soon she finds that he has really fallen in love with her. He follows her to work and becomes jealous of another man in her life. Discouraged, Proskourine returns to the frontier, but Glagoleva finally decides to marry him.

d, Vitaly Melnikov; w, Valentin Tchernykh; ph, Boris Liznev (Sovcolor); m, Isaak Schwarz; art d, Bedla Manevitch.

Romance/Comedy   **(PR:C MPAA:NR)**

W

WAEBULLEO† (1986, S. Korea)

I Heui-song, Na Jong-mi.

d, Jang Yeong-il; w, Yun Sam-yuk.

WALKMAN BLUES† (1986, Ger./Brit.) 91m Basis-Film Verleigh-Second German Television-Channel Four Television c

Heikko Deutschmann, Jennifer Capraru, Madeleine Daevers, Jorg Doring, Sema Engin, Werner Koller.

In wintry contemporary Berlin, Walkman-wearing Deutschmann travels to and from his nighttime job in a slaughterhouse, saying nothing, knowing no one. We observe his tours of the city, his domicile in a shabby loft (where he writes to his girl friend in a distant area), and his limited social life, which centers around popular music, but we learn little of the headphoned hero. Instead, we gain a sense of the city of Berlin in this visually oriented experimental picture by documentarist Behrens, whose S-BAHN PICTURES (1982) was highly regarded, winning a German Film Prize. Filmed in 16mm, WALKMAN BLUES won the Saarbrucken Film Fest Max Ophuls Prize.

d&w, Alfred Behrens; ph, Claus Deubel, Martin-Theo Krieger; m, Peter Radszuhn, Marius des Mestre, Heikoo Deutschmann; ed, Gabriele Herms, Heidi Heisuck; set d, Klaus-Jurgen Pfeiffer, Irene Kraft.

Drama (PR:A MPAA:NR)

WAY IT IS, THE† (1986) 80m Spring bw

Kai Eric (*Orpheus*), Boris Major (*Eurydice*), Vincent Gallo (*Vic*), Jessica Stutchbury (*Vera*), Mark Boone, Jr. (*Hank*), Steve Buscemi (*Willy*), Rockets Redglare (*Frank*), Daniel Rosen (*Dave*), Edwige Belmore (*Rebecca*), Brett Bartlett (*Ann*).

A modern version of the myth of Orpheus and Eurydice which takes place in New York City's East Village among characters named Hank, Willy, and Vic. Apparently a send-up of European art films, THE WAY IT IS makes use of a variety of film techniques and revels in its improvisation. The filmmakers themselves describe this as "an offbeat, tongue-in-cheek comedy."

p, Daniel Sales, Eric Mitchell; d&w, Eric Mitchell; ph, Bobby Bukowski; m, Vincent Gallo; ed, Bob Gould, Sue Graef.

Comedy (PR:NR MPAA:NR)

WEEKEND WARRIORS zero (1986) 85m Movie Store c

Chris Lemmon (*Vince Tucker*), Vic Tayback (*Sgt. Burge*), Lloyd Bridges (*Col. Archer*), Graham Jarvis (*Congressman Balljoy*), Daniel Greene (*Phil McCracken*), Marty Cohen (*Decola*), Brian Bradley (*Cory Seacomb*), Matt McCoy (*Ames*), Alan Campbell (*Duckworth*), Tom Villard (*Mort Seblinsky*), Jeff Meyer (*Tom Dawson*), Mark Taylor (*Capt. Cabot*), Gail Barle (*Nurse Nancy*), Camille Saviola (*Betty Beep*), Jeff Calhoun (*Choreographer*), Brenda Strong (*Danielle*), Bruce Belland (*Svenson*), Thomas J. Astor, Rick Hickman (*Airmen*), Dalton Cathey, Joe Hart (*Cops*), Jeff Allin (*Cop in Chase*), Monique Gabrielle (*Showgirl in Plane*), Gretchen Gray (*Balljoy's Girl Friend*), Bob Libman (*Aircraft Commander*), Randal Patrick (*Kramer*), Stephen F. Schmidt (*Anderson*), Lou Tiano (*Pledge's Pilot*), Wanda H. Tilson (*Mrs. Burdge*), Kelly Reed (*A.P.*), Gene Wood (*L.A.F.F. Speaker*), Greg Aikens (*Smythe*), Stephen M. Bottroff (*Romanian Ambassador*), Clay Wright (*Aircraft Consultant*).

About ten minutes into WEEKEND WARRIORS your mind will start to go numb. This is a warning sign not to proceed any further or you will risk permanent brain damage. In fact, just reading this synopsis may cause dizziness, nausea, or, if you're lucky, memory loss. The problem with the film begins with the fact that it was directed by television game show host and "Love Boat" refugee Bert Convy. If that isn't enough to scare you off, the turning point in the film involves a bet as to whether or not baked-bean-induced flatulence is ignitable. Okay, if you're determined to stick this out, then here's the story. Set in 1961, the film follows the "zany" antics of a bunch of movie-biz employees who have joined the National Guard to avoid the draft. For one weekend a month these "wackos" assemble at a nearby Hollywood base camp where they are subjected to the fire-breathing rages of sergeant Tayback and the eccentricities of their commanding officer, Bridges, who was a star of "B" westerns and frequently slips into dialog from his glory days on the silver screen. The narrator of the story is struggling screenwriter Lemmon (real-life son of actor Jack) and he introduces us to his buddies: a bisexual gossip columnist; the members of a doo-wop singing group; a makeup man who does mortuary work on the side; a huge bodybuilder type who talks like Elmer Fudd; and others too insipid to mention. The aforementioned flatulence scene occurs just as an uptight congressman, Jarvis, passes through the mess hall for an inspection. Justifiably outraged, Jarvis threatens to put the post on active duty if they do not shape up in time for an upcoming visit by the Romanian ambassador. Lemmon and his pals decide to stage a real Hollywood-style extravaganza that will dazzle both the congressman and the Soviet-bloc ambassador. The gang borrows several truckloads of props from a nearby film studio with which to spruce up the base; they hire a marching band, a baton twirler, and UCLA's ROTC unit to march in their place; and then they stage the dramatic "rescue" of a midget dressed like a baby. Of course everyone

is suitably impressed and our heroes are allowed to remain merely "weekend" warriors.

What the above synopsis omitted was the plethora of totally tasteless (and unfunny) jokes which mainly concentrate on every possible aspect of sex, flatulence (yes, there's more than just that one instance), and verbal vulgarity (the amount of gratuitous swearing is astounding—one gets the impression that director Convy and his cast from television's vast wasteland wanted to be "naughty" and use words that they always wanted to say on TV but couldn't). Honestly, there isn't one moment in this alleged comedy which anyone over the age of seven would find even remotely funny. Director Convy and writers Belland and Rogosin rip off everything from young Lemmon's father's military comedy OPERATION MAD BALL to ANIMAL HOUSE and STRIPES. Convy is a wretched director who can't even compose a simple shot, pace a sequence, or control an out-of-sync performance—this film would look bad on TV! No attempt is made to capture the look or feel of California in 1961 (everyone's hair is too long for starters) and there seems to be no reason to set the film in 1961, other than to inundate the soundtrack with a dozen popular songs from that era. The performers are mostly bland and annoying, with the exceptions of Lemmon (who looks trapped) and Bridges (who tries hard). Offensive, boring, and incredibly stupid, WEEKEND WARRIORS is simply insufferable. Songs include "Pretty Little Angel Eyes" (Tommy Boyce, Curtis Lee, performed by Curtis Lee), "Tossin' and Turnin' " (Malou Rene, Ritchie Adams, performed by Bobby Lewis), "Let's Twist Again" (Karl Mann, Dave Appell), "Louie, Louie" (Richard Berry), "The U.S. Air Force" (Robert Crawford), "Summertime Blues" (Eddie Cockran, Jerry Capehart), "Let the Good Times Roll" (Leonard Lee), "Wipe Out" (The Surfaris).

p, Hannah Hempstead; d, Bert Convy; w, Bruce Belland, Roy M. Rogosin; ph, Charles Minsky; m, Perry Botkin; ed, Raja Gosnell; prod d, Chester Kaczenski; cos, Susie Desanto; m/l, Tommy Boyce, Curtis Lee, Malou Rene, Ritchie Adams, Karl Mann, Dave Appell, Richard Berry, Robert Crawford, Eddie Cockran, Jerry Capehart, Leonard Lee, The Surfaris; stunts, Wally Crowder.

Comedy Cas. (PR:O MPAA:R)

WELCOME IN VIENNA**** (1986, Aust.) 126m Thalia-ORF-ZDF-SSR-Austrian Federal Ministry of Education, Arts and Sports bw

Gabriel Barylli (*Freddy Wolff*), Nicolas Brieger (*Sgt. Adler*), Claudia Messner (*Claudia Schutte*), Hubert Mann (*Capt. Karpeles*), Karlheinz Hackl (*Treschensky*), Liliana Nelska (*Russian Woman*), Kurt Sowinetz (*Stodola*), Joachim Kemmer (*Lt. Binder*), Heinz Trixner (*Oberst Schutte*).

WELCOME IN VIENNA is the first and only film made on the subject of Austrian and German emigres to the U.S. who joined the U.S. Army and then returned to their homeland in 1944 with the American liberating forces. Beauti-

fully photographed in a grainy black-and-white (which gives a documentary visual quality), the film opens on Christmas Eve, 1944, as the American forces are holed up in a barn in the middle of a snowy field. The two main characters are Barylli, an Austrian Jew who has longed for this return home, and Brieger, a German intellectual who fled to the States in fear of the Nazis and has now become sympathetic to the Communists. Heading their command is a tough-talking, hard-drinking German-American, Kemmer, who has a firm belief in Teutonic anti-Semitism. In the battle that follows, a German deserter, Hackl, is captured—a man who, as it turns out, is an opportunistic Viennese and Nazi former friend of Barylli's. Time jumps ahead to May 1945 in Salzburg on the final day of the war as the liberating forces descend on the city. The first girl that Barylli lays eyes on is Messner, a pretty, bicycle-riding Austrian girl whose father is a colonel in the "Abwehr"—the Nazi counter-intelligence. She informs U.S. authorities that her father is willing to surrender his information, but only if the U.S. receives him with full honors. Barylli has returned to Austria—his home—though he soon finds that things have changed. Thousands of Jews have disappeared, and as many buildings have been reduced to rubble. When he tries to locate his family's apartment, he finds it almost completely destroyed and learns that his family's possessions had been sold on the street. The "home" that he hoped to find no longer exists. He works his way up in the ranks of the new government, taking a cultural job because of his smattering knowledge of theater and literature. He falls in love with Messner, who is yet another representation of that Austria "home" that he cannot recapture. Although she loves him dearly she uses him as a means to further her career on the stage. Brieger, in the meantime, has become disillusioned in his admiration of Stalin's Communist rule, while Hackl, still the opportunist, has moved into a position of power in the black

market. As the film ends, Barylli has lost Messner to the stage and must now decide whether or not to return to America.

Funded by Austrian dollars, directed by Austrian Corti, and written by an Austrian expatriate living in Paris, Troller, WELCOME IN VIENNA is the first film, according to its filmmakers, that has accurately dealt with Austria's unflattering role during World War II. Labelled as the first innocent victim of Nazi aggression, Austria buckled under to Nazi forces with barely a struggle. From 1938 through the war years, there was no noticeable Resistance movement in Austria and anti-Semitism ran high, as it did in Germany. With a reported ten percent of its adult population members of the Nazi party, there existed little opposition to Hitler's aggression against the Jews. Rather than use these facts to condemn the population, Corti and Troller simply bring to light very real situations of the day. Accused of "behaving like a nest-fouler," Corti retaliates, "I feel that he who never looks down at what is underneath befouls his own nest." Describing his intentions further, Corti was quoted in an interview with film historian Francis Courtade as saying, "We did not want to make a movie about Good and Bad but intended to highlight facts and situations of a historic period of time and to display how everybody responds or, maybe, must respond to them, in his or her very special way." Echoing Jean Renoir's line of dialog that "Everybody has their reasons" from RULES OF THE GAME, Corti has presented an exceptional look at the human condition. Every element of the film rings of a desire to tell the truth—from the newsreel quality of the film stock to the locations to the unfaltering performances. Unfortunately, because of the political subject matter of the film and the general audience's distinct ignorance of world history, WELCOME IN VIENNA will probably never receive an American release. The film is also saddled with an inherent difficulty in distinguishing the Austrians from the Germans, because of most audiences' unfamiliarity with the difference in dialects. To most American ears, they all sound German, adding some initial confusion, especially in the early battle sequences as German and Austrian soldiers in the American Army are fighting German troops. WELCOME IN VIENNA was shown on the festival circuit where it earned a Best Director award at the San Sebastian film festival and the top honor of the Golden Hugo at the Chicago International Film Festival. (In German; English subtitles.)

d, Axel Corti; w, Axel Corti, Georg Stefan Troller; ph, Gernot Roll; m, Hans Georg Koch, Franz Schubert; ed, Ulrike Pahl, Claudia Rieneck; prod d, Matija Barl; set d, Fritz Hollergschwandtner; cos, Uli Fessler; makeup, Ellen Just, Adolf Uhrmacher.

War Drama (PR:O MPAA:NR)

WELCOME TO 18* (1986) 89m Summer Release/American Distribution Group c

Courtney Thorne-Smith (Lindsey), Mariska Hargitay (Joey), Jo Ann Willette (Robin), Cristen Kauffman (Talia), E. Erich Anderson (Roscoe), John Putch (Corey), Jeff MacGregor, Brian Bradley, Michael MacRae, Eli Cummins, Graham Ludlow, Micole Mercurio, Brandis Kemp, Cletus Young, Clay Stone, Michael Greene, Max Trumpower, Mickey Jones, Deanna Booher, Bob Gould.

If MODERN GIRLS wasn't bad enough, 1986 gave us yet another teenage sex comedy that substitutes a group of inane girls for the usual bunch of vapid guys. Thorne-Smith, Willette, and Hargitay (a blonde, a redhead, and a brunette respectively) all hop in a convertible and head off to work at a Nevada dude ranch immediately after graduation from high school. Unfortunately, the girls are forbidden to consort with the muscle-beach males who work there. During their first week of work the girls meet Kauffman, a rich Lake Tahoe gal. When our heroines are shortchanged on their first paycheck, they quit and go off to Kauffman's mansion. There they meet Kauffman's seedy mobster boy friend Anderson, and he agrees to get the girls phony I.D.'s so that they can work in the casinos. The girls end up staying in a lonely mountaintop motel and are inadvertently embroiled in a wild party attended by drug peddlers and the girls are mistaken for prostitutes. The cops break the party up and Thorne-Smith,

Hargitay, and Willette are hauled off to jail with the rest. The slimy Anderson bails the girls out, but then steals their car and holds it as collateral. Realizing that they must get their new friend Kauffman away from Anderson, the girls hatch a plan to get in on a local high-roller poker game so that they can win enough money to get their car back. Thorne-Smith winds up winning $35,000 in the game and the girls manage to snatch both their car and Kauffman away from Anderson's evil clutches and zoom off to San Francisco in time to register for fall classes at college.

Once again the teen exploitation genre seems to be turning toward a trend where girls prove to be as gross, stupid, and uncontrollably lustful as boys. Save for the likable young actresses in the cast (Hargitay is the daughter of Jayne Mansfield and Mickey Hargitay), there is not an inkling of intelligence in WELCOME TO 18 (the title presumably refers to the loss of virginity and/or innocence about the big, bad world out there). Using the time-honored exploitation device of seeming to preach against such abuses as teen sex, drug use, and gambling—while exploiting the hell out of such vices for the titillation of the audience—WELCOME TO 18 pretends to be a socially redeeming teen comedy. Not surprisingly, it is just as bad as the myriad trash that came before it, although a certain amount of restraint was required to land a PG-13 rating.

p, David C. Thomas; d, Terry Carr; w, Terry Carr, Judith Sherman Wolin; ph, Stephen L. Posey (Metrocolor); m, Tony Berg; ed, Lois Freeman-Fox; prod d, Steven Legler; set d, Don Ferguson.

Comedy/Drama Cas. (PR:O MPAA:PG-13)

WELCOME TO THE PARADE† (1986, Can.) 82m Northern Outlaw c

Paul James

James is a poor little rich boy, bored silly with his empty life. He gives nothing but grief to his family, and finally moves out of his parents' home after an argument over drugs. From there James heads to a rundown hotel, whose clientele consists mainly of dope dealers and prostitutes. Next he attempts to rob a coke dealer, a mistake for which James nearly pays with his life.

p, Peter Gentile; d&w, Stuart Clarfield; ph, Jon Joffin; m, Robb Wright, Mark Lalama, Paul James; ed, Stuart Clarfield; art d, Frank Gentile.

Drama (PR:O MPAA:NR)

WERTHER† (1986, Span.) 110m Pilar Miro P.C. c

Eusebio Poncela (Werther), Mercedes Sampietro (Carlota), Feodor Atkine (Alberto), Vicky Pena (Beatriz), Emilio Gutierrez Caba (Federico), Luis Hostalot (Jerusalen).

An adaptation of Goethe's 18th Century novel, updated to a modern Spanish setting. Poncela stars as the title character, a southerner who moves north to take a job teaching Greek. He falls in love with a student's mother—a female surgeon who has left her husband. The romance comes to a tragic end, however, when Poncela commits suicide believing his lover has gone back to her husband. This is the first film in four years for Miro, who temporarily headed the government's cinema unit before resigning over a conflict related to a controversial subsidy policy. WERTHER was cowritten by Mario Camus whose 1984 film THE HOLY INNOCENTS won international acclaim.

p&d, Pilar Miro; w, Pilar Miro, Mario Camus (based on the novel The Sorrows of Young Werther by Johann Wolfgang Goethe); ph, Hans Burmann; m, Jules Massenet; ed, Jose Luis Matesanz; art d, Gil Parrondo, Fernando Saez.

Drama (PR:NR MPAA:NR)

WESTLER (SEE: EAST OF THE WALL, 1986, Ger.)

WHAT COMES AROUND zero (1986) 86m Jerry Reed/A.W.O. Associates c

Jerry Reed (Joe Hawkins), Barry Corbin (Leon), Bo Hopkins (Tom Hawkins), Arte Johnson (Malone), Nancy (Esther Houston), Ernest Dixon (Big Jay), Hugh Jarrett (Ralph), Buck Ford (Chester).

This isn't so much a film as it is a vanity project for its executive producer/director/star, country singer Jerry Reed. He plays—surprise, surprise—a country singer who's been in the business for a quarter of a century. His years on the road have taken a toll, for Reed is a burnt-out, pill-popping booze hound. Reed's personal manager has used the star's addled state to his advantage, cheating Reed out of $8 million and putting the funds into a secret Swiss bank account. Reed's brother Hopkins catches onto the scam after snatching the singer off a tour. Reed regains his senses, and—with his brother—has revenge by destroying a shopping mall owned by his crooked manager.

To be kind, Reed is a talented singer who is at his best when he sticks to vinyl. Though passable as an actor, he shows no competence behind the camera. The already cliched story is so lamely told that it's hard to care about any of Reed's trials and tribulations.

p, Ted Evanson; d, Jerry Reed; w, Peter Herrecks (based on a story by Gary Smith, Dave Franklin); ph, James Pergola; m, Al Delory; ed, William Carruth; prod d, Don K. Ivey.

Drama Cas. (PR:C MPAA:NR)

WHAT HAPPENED NEXT YEAR† (1986, Syria) 140m National Film Organization c

Najah Safkouni (Mounir), Naila El Atrache (Lamia), Hala Al Faucal (Haifa).

Safkouni is a young orchestra conductor who returns to his native Syria after studying abroad. His attempts at creating a national symphony orchestra are constantly frustrated by a cultural ministry which has little interest in supporting such ideas. Safkouni's personal life is turbulent as well. He tries to maintain a relationship with divorcee Al Faucal, but her failed marriage drove her to a suicide attempt and she is afraid to commit herself again. Also on hand is Safkouni's young maid, El Atrache, who is oversexed and obsessed with her handsome boss. Eventually, Safkouni satisfies his professional frustrations by forming his own small ensemble which plays both classical and modern music.

d&w, Samir Zikra; ph, Hanna Warde; m, Ziad Rahbani; ed, Zouheir Daye; art d, L. Arslan, R. Hoshos.

Drama   (PR:O MPAA:NR)

WHAT WAITS BELOW*   (1986) 88m Adams Apple/Blossom c

Robert Powell *(Wolfson),* Timothy Bottoms *(Maj. Stevens),* Lisa Blount *(Leslie Peterson),* Richard Johnson *(Ben Gannon),* Anne Heywood *(Frida Shelley),* A.C. Weary *(Lt. George Barwell),* Liam Sullivan *(Lemurian Elder),* Jackson Bostwick *(Hunter),* Richard Beauchamp *(Santos Arias).*

After fleeing enemy soldiers in Nicaragua, mercenary Powell hooks up with American army officer Bottoms for a new assignment. Powell is soon working with Bottoms on a radio device contacting submarines but new troubles quickly develop. When anthropologists located near the army base open up some previously sealed caves, they inadvertently expose a hidden culture of underground dwellers who have been undisturbed for hundreds of years (these folks are played by albinos). The submarine radio transmitter is hard on this race's highly sensitive ears and violence quickly erupts. Powell ultimately reseals the caves, thus protecting the culture from the modern man's intrusion.

This tale of spelunking intrigues is about as exciting as watching the formation of stalagmites. The dangers are largely implied, with only remotely electrifying sequences popping up now and again. Powell and Bottoms are passable but not much more in their undemanding roles. Shot on location in the caves of Alabama and Tennessee in 1983, the film saw a few test screenings in 1984, then received a general release on videocassette some two years later.

p, Sandy Howard, Robert D. Bailey; d, Don Sharp; w, Christy Marx, Robert Vincent O'Neil (based on a story by Ken Barnett); ph, Virgil Harper (Bellevue Pathe Quebec Color); m, Michel Rubini, Denny Jaeger; ed, John R. Bowey; art d, Stephen Marsh; spec eff, Robert D. Bailey; makeup, William Munns.

Action/Adventure   **Cas.**   (PR:C MPAA:PG)

WHATEVER IT TAKES**   (1986) 93m Aquarius c

Tom Mason *(Jeff Perchick),* Martin Balsam *(Hap Perchicksky),* Chris Weatherhead *(Lee Bickford),* James Rebhorn *(Michael Manion),* Maura Shea *(Eren Haberfield),* Bill Bogert *(Timmy Shaughnessy),* Rosetta Lenoire *(Millie),* Joey Ginza *(Curley),* Fred Morsell *(Mr. Bunyon),* Edward Binns *(Mr. Kingsley),* Thomas Barbour *(Hilbourne).*

Mason, a Vietnam veteran, works as a cabdriver to support both himself and the small restaurant run by his father, Balsam. His real ambition is to become a syndicated cartoonist, a dream which seems doomed by the hard blows reality hands Mason. Balsam is about to lose his diner because of bad business and a rent increase. Another problem in the young man's life is his former girl friend Weatherhead, who is now involved with a once-idealistic lawyer. Mason's latest romance is with his on-again, off-again sweetheart Shea.

Told in anecdotal style, WHATEVER IT TAKES is too rambling. The performances often make up for the plot inconsistencies, but don't redeem this minor independent film. Producer/director/editor/cowriter Demchuk is himself a cartoonist and the film is a semi-autobiographical work.

p, Bob Demchuk, Walter J. Scherr; d, Bob Demchuk; w, Chris Weatherhead, Bob Demchuk; ph, John Drake; m, Garry Sherman; ed, Bob Demchuk; prod d, Maher Ahmad.

Drama   (PR:O MPAA:NR)

WHEN THE WIND BLOWS†   (1986, Brit.) Meltdown-British Screen-Film
                    Four International-TVC London-Penguin Books/KRG c

Voices: Peggy Ashcroft *(Hilda),* John Mills *(Jim).*

Adapted from a popular comic book and BBC radio play, this British animated feature tells the story of an old married couple in the days following nuclear holocaust. The film's title song was performed by David Bowie.

p, John Coates; d, Jimmy T. Murakami; w, Raymond Briggs; m, Roger Waters.

Animated   (PR:C MPAA:NR)

WHERE ARE THE CHILDREN? zero   (1986) 92m COL c

Jill Clayburgh *(Nancy Eldridge),* Max Gail *(Clay Eldridge),* Harley Cross *(Michael Eldridge),* Elisabeth Harnois *(Missy Eldridge),* Elizabeth Wilson *(Dorothy Prentiss),* Barnard Hughes *(Jonathan Knowles),* Frederic Forrest *(Courtney Parrish),* James Purcell *(Robin Legler),* Clifton James *(Chief Coffin),* Eriq La Salle *(Deputy Bernie Miles),* Joseph Hindy *(Detective Morello),* Devin Ratray *(Neil Kenney),* Zev Braun *(J.D. Quill),* Christopher Murney *(Lenny Barron),* Ted O'Brien *(Newscaster),* Dan Lounsbery *(Mailman Jenks),* Evan Malmuth *(Gas Station Attendant),* Bruce Malmuth *(Restaurant Owner),* Ruth Edinberg *(Ellen Kenney),* Louis Zorich *(Kragopoulos),* Axel Van Dereck *(Richard Kenney),* Peter Kovner *(Policeman),* D. Neal Brown *(Desk Sergeant),* Mike Stines *(1st TV Reporter),* Lori Michaels *(2nd TV Reporter),* Carol Higgins Clark *(3rd TV Reporter),* Doug Riley *(Policeman),* Dan Malmuth *(Motel Manager),* Paul O'Brien

(Officer Campbell), Robert Pena *(Day Sergeant),* Coleen Cavanaugh *(Woman in Crowd).*

You know a movie's in deep trouble when it resorts to child molestation to raise a few scares. WHERE ARE THE CHILDREN? isn't just a bad suspense drama; it's an appalling exercise in depravity. Clayburgh is the oh-so-happy mother of two kids (Cross and Harnois) who lives in sheer bliss with her husband Gail. Any intelligent moviegoer knows that someone this chipper is ripe for tragedy, which arrives on schedule when Cross and Harnois are kidnaped by Forrest, a psychopath who's been watching Clayburgh's nuclear family through a telescope. Forrest locks the kiddies up in his house, then delights in torturing the tots with drugs and sex-abuse. While Clayburgh turns frantic, Forrest takes a further twisted step by calling a local radio station with some goods on the lady's past: Clayburgh had been married once before, but was imprisoned for killing the two children of that marriage. She had been released on a technicality, but with this old skeleton out

of the closet, Clayburgh is now the chief suspect in the new disappearance. Only Hughes, a psychiatrist, believes Clayburgh is innocent. After he examines the poor woman, we are treated to some further lurid details of Clayburgh's past: Her first husband had a penchant for kinky activities; he forced Clayburgh to dress up as a little girl before giving her a good spanking. Once the kids arrived, they became the object of his demented desires. Clayburgh attempted to take the children away from this sicko, but he responded by murdering the kids, then apparently killing himself. Numbed by these horrifying events, Clayburgh simply accepted the blame for the murders, though she was totally innocent. Once this secret is out in the open, it's only a matter of time before Clayburgh figures out what the audience already knows: Forrest is that former spouse. One quick dash to the kidnaper's house later, Clayburgh saves the kids and does in Forrest once and for all.

WHERE ARE THE CHILDREN? went unreleased for quite some time after its completion, and for good reason. As a suspense film, the construction is ridiculously simplistic, but the added element of child molestation makes this often unwatchable. Hiding beneath a beard and bad fake paunch, Forrest gives a frighteningly psychotic performance. His scenes with the children have a perverse element which will nauseate anyone except actual child molesters; critics complained these moments work as an instructional film in sexual abuse. Clayburgh does nothing to further her career with her one-note hysterical performance, while the supporting players slog through as best they can. Gail is acceptable and Hughes is good, as always, though one wishes these players had been given something with a little substance rather than this mess. With his direction in the 1981 action film NIGHTHAWKS, Malmuth showed a good understanding of suspense, but none of that talent is evident here. Instead, he switches back and forth between exposition and Forrest's psycho-babble in a rudimentary hack fashion. Nothing builds, except revulsion in audience members willing to stick it out through this loathsome effort.

p, Zev Braun; d, Bruce Malmuth; w, Jack Sholder (based on the novel by Mary Higgins Clark); ph, Larry Pizer (Panavision, Metrocolor); m, Sylvester Levay; ed, Roy Watts; prod d, Robb Wilson King; set d, Jane Cavedon; cos, Mary Ellen Winston; spec eff, Image Engineering, Inc.; makeup, Kathy Shorkey-Doak.

Drama   (PR:O MPAA:R)

WHERE THE RIVER RUNS BLACK½**   (1986) 100m Ufland-Roth/MGM
                                                        UA c

Charles Durning *(Father O'Reilly),* Alessandro Rabelo *(Lazaro),* Ajay Naidu *(Segundo),* Peter Horton *(Father Mahoney),* Conchata Ferell *(Mother Marta),* Dana Delany *(Sister Ana),* Chico Diaz *(Raimundo),* Divana Brandao *(Eagle Woman),* Castulo Guerra *(Orlando Santos),* Marcelo Rabelo *(Lazaro—4 Years Old),* Ariel Coelho *(Francisco),* Paulo Sergio Oliveira *(Jose),* Mario Borges *(Brother Carlos),* Francois Thijm *(Luis),* Geraldo Salles *(Priest in Confessional),* Sandro Soviatt *(Calmanero),* Raimundo Carvalho *(Waika Man),* Jose Richardo Matos *(Ice Cream Vendor),* David C. Russel *(Floyd Jenkins),* Telmo Maia *(Miner in Truck),* Paulo Quindere *(Man Getting Shoeshine).*

Another addition to the rash of "noble savage" films that have hit movie screens in the last few years (THE EMERALD FOREST, THE MISSION), WHERE THE RIVER RUNS BLACK is a well-intentioned but hopelessly cliched, pretentious, and slow-moving drama set in the jungles of Brazil. Durning, a priest from

the city, paddles up the Rio Negro deep into the jungle to visit his spiritual protege, Horton, an idealistic young priest who wants to build a hospital among the natives at his jungle outpost. Durning admires Horton's ambition, but he informs the disappointed priest that the church's money would be better spent in the city. After Durning returns to civilization, Horton paddles up stream to "where the water turns black." He is amazed to see fresh-water dolphins frolicking in the dark water, but he is even more amazed by the beautiful young native woman, Brandao, swimming along side the creatures. Without a word the native woman seduces the vulnerable priest. On his way back to his mission, Horton is killed by a huge anaconda (God really enforces those celibacy vows). Of course, their brief tryst produces a baby and Brandao raises the child with the friendly dolphins acting as protectors. Ten years later, gold is found in the area and with it come the exploiters of the land. A canoe-load of city dwellers happens upon Brandao's hut and their leader, Guerra, tries to rape the native woman. She resists and is shot. The boy, Rabelo, is tossed to the crocodiles but is saved by his dolphin buddies. Soon after, Durning visits the mission only to find that Horton has died (you'd think Durning would get out of the rectory a bit more often). The natives tell of the tryst between the priest and the mystical dolphin woman and the spiritual child they produced. Durning goes to where the river runs black and finds only the remains of the murdered woman (the boy hides in the brush). Later, some poachers capture one of the dolphins and kidnap Rabelo and bring them to civilization. Durning hears of this, rescues the boy and forces the poachers to return the dolphin to the river. Durning names the boy Lazaro (because he is Horton risen from the dead) and takes him to the local orphanage run by strict Mother Superior Ferrell (who acts as if she is in a Dickens novel). Rabelo is considered a problem child and he is paired with another problem child, Naidu, an older Brazilian street kid who is made responsible for the jungle boy. The boys become fast friends. Rabelo learns quickly and soon he is reading from the Bible and playing soccer. One day the orphanage is visited by a local politician running for governor. As it turns out the man is none other than Guerra—

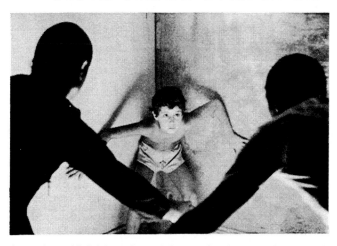

the murderer of Rabelo's mother. Rabelo recognizes the man and vows to kill him. That night Rabelo escapes the orphanage (with Naidu tagging along) and traces Guerra to a rally the next day. Rabelo tries to spear Guerra with a sharp wooden pole, but he misses. Naidu is captured by Guerra's people and sent off to be a slave in his gold mine. Rabelo rescues his friend and then returns to his jungle home. Meanwhile, Durning has deduced that the boy has returned to the jungle and goes off to find him. As Durning's canoe approaches, Guerra pops out of nowhere and grabs Rabelo. The struggle winds up in the water where Rabelo's dolphin friends cause severe intestinal damage on the villainous Guerra. The evil politician begs for help, but Durning lets the man drown. The priest decides to let the boy stay where he belongs—in the jungle among the dolphins.

Basically a children's film, WHERE THE RIVER RUNS BLACK suffers from television "After-School-Special" plotting where reason, reality and detail are dismissed in favor of simplicity. Director Cain's build-up is so slow (lingering on

the beautiful jungle atmosphere) that it gives the audience too much time to ponder over the sizable plot holes (why does Durning wait 10 years to return to the mission?). Cinematographer Ruiz-Anchia does a superior job capturing the mood and feel of the Amazonian jungle, but director Cain insists on highlighting lots of mystical native mumbo jumbo which is supposed to explain the unexplainable. The acting is uniformly mediocre with Durning spending the whole film looking compassionate, young Rabelo batting his big brown eyes at everyone he meets, and Guerra behaving almost cartoon-like as the glowering villain. With the exception of the dolphins, the special effects work by Donald Pennington is pretty poor with both the anaconda and the crocodile looking laughably synthetic. There is really nothing very bad or inept in WHERE THE RIVER RUNS BLACK, but there simply isn't anything fresh or particularly interesting either. A sad note: Co-writer Jimenez, who wrote the script for the chilling American teenager film RIVER'S EDGE (shown at film festivals in 1986 and given a general release in 1987), fell off a cliff while hiking during the writing of WHERE THE RIVER RUNS BLACK and lost the use of his legs.

p, Joe Roth, Harry Ufland; d, Christopher Cain; w, Peter Silverman, Neal Jimenez (based on the novel *Lazaro* by David Kendall); ph, Juan Ruiz-Anchia (Metrocolor); m, James Horner; ed, Richard Chew; prod d, Marcos Flaksman; art d, Paulo Flaksman; spec eff, Donald Pennington.

Adventure/Drama   Cas.   (PR:A MPAA:PG)

WHITE SLAVE*½   (1986, It.) 89m Cinevega c (AKA: AMAZONIA—THE CATHERINE MILES STORY)

Elvire Audray *(Cathy Miles)*, Will [Alvaro] Gonzales *(Umu Kai)*, Dick Marshall, Andrew Louis Coppola, Dick Campbell, Alma Vernon, Grace Williams.

Another Italian exploitation product that comes to American shores without a theatrical release. Allegedly based on a true story, the plot has Audray as the 18-year-old daughter of the owners of a giant rubber plantation along the Amazon. She returns home from school in England and joins her parents and her aunt and uncle for a picnic up the river. Suddenly both parents fall down dead from blowgun darts, and a smaller dose of dart poison paralyzes Audray. Guarnira Indians appear and revive her, then after cutting off the heads of her parents, lead her back to their camp. She is bought by one Indian, but when he finds she is a virgin, he treats her like a child (in this culture, females are ceremonially deflowered at age four). She tries to escape and he beats her, causing Gonzales, the Indian who led the party that found her, to challenge him to a duel. Gonzales kills him and wins Audray, but he is gentle with her, seeming to genuinely love her. Still, Audray forces herself to hate him because she thinks he killed her parents, whose heads hang among the tribe's trophies. One day she steals the heads and buries them, a crime among the tribe, though Gonzales looks the other way. He learns English and tells Audray that he did not kill her parents, that it was her aunt and uncle who hired some other Indians to do it, then killed them, all while Gonzales and his party watched. Suddenly a helicopter swoops down on the village and opens fire with a machine gun. The men in the chopper talk about the bounty the company is going to pay them for wiping out this group as they methodically cut off hands for the count. Gonzales and Audray are the only survivors, and the two of them board a canoe and head down the river. At her parent's former home, she climbs onto the dock and silently creeps through the house until she reaches the room where her aunt and uncle sleep. They awaken to find this half-naked, half-savage girl at the foot of their bed, and she sticks them both with paralyzing curare before lopping off their heads with a hatchet. She returns to Gonzales, who has been waiting in the canoe, but when he sees the blood on her hands, he knows they can never be together, for it is a taboo in his tribe for a woman to kill. She returns to shore while he goes to the middle of the river and sinks his canoe, committing suicide over his lost love. Audray turns herself in to the police and at a trial she is remanded to an insane asylum for eight years, after which she returns to England, marries and has children.

Certainly a cut above most of the Italian jungle epics that fill video store shelves, this film is not overly patronizing, nor does it substitute non-stop violence for plot, though the whole middle of the film does tend to drag as Audray's life among the savages is detailed. Her performance is surprisingly good, considering she has to play her part topless for most of the film. The direction is nothing special, a lot of stock footage nature shots don't match the look of the rest of the film and detract further, but the inherent fascination of the old-fashioned carried-off-by-savages tale is still present and should guarantee an audience for this mildly interesting effort.

d, Roy Garrett [Mario Gariazzo]; w, Franco Prosperi; ph, Silvano Ippoliti (Staco color); m, Franco Campanino; ed, Gianfranco Amicucci; spec eff, Aldo Gasparri.

Adventure/Drama   Cas.   (PR:O MPAA:NR)

WHOOPEE BOYS, THE*   (1986) 88m Adam Fields–David Obst/Paramount c

Michael O'Keefe *(Jake Bateman)*, Paul Rodriguez *(Barney)*, Denholm Elliott *(Col. Hugh Phelps)*, Carole Shelley *(Henrietta Phelps)*, Andy Bumatai *(Roy Raja)*, Eddie Deezen *(Eddie Lipshitz)*, Marsha Warfield *(Officer White)*, Elizabeth Arlen *(Shelley)*, Karen A. Smythe *(Clorinda Antonucci)*, Joe Spinell *(Guido Antonucci)*, Robert Gwaltney *(Humping the Butler)*, Lucinda Jenney *(Olivia Farragut)*, Dan O'Herlihy *(Judge Sternhill)*, Stephen Davies *(Strobe Fennebrest)*, Taylor Negron *(Whitey)*, Greg Germann *(Tipper)*.

If you can imagine a comedy starring your totally obnoxious 10-year-old cousin and his equally insufferable best friend, then you've got a good idea of the level of humor in THE WHOOPIE BOYS. O'Keefe and Rodriguez star as two New York City hustlers who get fed up with freezing New York winters and decide to head for Palm Beach, Florida, for a change of scenery. The foul-mouthed Rodriguez and his pal crash a swanky society party and meet Jenney, a beautiful heiress who runs a "School for the Exceptionally Poor and Talented" that is in deep financial trouble. O'Keefe is quite taken with the girl. When he learns that she can only collect her inheritance if she marries a perfect gentleman approved by O'Herlihy, her uncle, he decides to become a gentleman. Vying for Jenney's hand in marriage is wealthy snob Davies. He is also a successful condominium developer and wants to turn Jenney's school property into time-share condos. O'Keefe and Rodriguez enroll in the Phelps Institute of Etiquette, located in the midst of a swamp and run by Elliott and Shelley, a couple who have been booted out of high society. In addition to our uncouth duo, several other slobs are enrolled. Among them are Warfield, a black woman police officer prone to bursts of physical violence; Bumatai, a rich Indian who wants to assimilate in America; Arlen, a female psycho who admires Lizzie Borden; Deezen, a stereotypical nerd character; and Smythe, a pregnant Mafia princess. Elliott takes a liking to our main boors and teaches them all the secrets of being truly great gentlemen, including fencing, skeet shooting, and how to eat at swanky restaurants for free. Eventually the vulgar friends graduate and O'Keefe returns to Palm Beach to claim Jenney's hand. They infiltrate the stuffy O'Herlihy's weekend garden party with Rodriguez posing as a butler. O'Keefe does battle with his rival Davies in a stupid and predictable climax.

THE WHOOPIE BOYS redefines the phrase "toilet humor". There is not one moment of wit that anyone over the age of 11 would find remotely funny. Most of the truly tasteless humor comes from L.A. stand-up comic Rodriguez as he spouts intolerable racial slurs, revolting sexual innuendo, and plays obnoxious practical jokes. Director Byrum apparently was so enthralled with the comedic talents of his stars—many of them stand-up comics—that he allowed them to improvise at will. Who knows if the script by REVENGE OF THE NERDS writers Zacharias and Buhai ever had anything resembling wit? This may explain the sloppy visuals and wretched editing of this ugly film as the crew scrambled desperately to cover the action without interrupting the flow of comedic inspiration. Unfortunately, there is more true comedic inspiration during recess at a grade-school playground. The level of humor in THE WHOOPIE BOYS is so aggravating that it makes films like PORKY'S and POLICE ACADEMY look like masterpieces of cinematic wit. Paramount knew it had a stinker on its hands and the film got a very limited release in Los Angeles and some southern states before fading into well-deserved obscurity.

p, Adam Fields, Peter Macgregor-Scott; d, John Byrum; w, Steve Zacharias, Jeff Buhai, David Obst; ph, Ralf Bode (Technicolor); m, Jack Nitzsche; ed, Eric Jenkins; prod d, Charles Rosen; set d, Don Ivey; cos, Patricia Norris.

Comedy   **(PR:O   MPAA:R)**

WILD BEASTS†   (1986, It.) 92m Shumba/Euramco c (AKA: SAVAGE
                                                              BEASTS)

Lorraine de Selle *(Laura Schwarz)*, John Aldrich *(Dr. Rupert Berner)*, Ugo Bologna *(Nat)*, Louisa Lloyd *(Suzy)*.

Further proof (as if any is needed) that PCP (angel dust) is bad for you is on display in this Italian nature-on-the-rampage movie. A large quantity of the drug makes its way into the sewers and ground-water supply of a German city, where it turns all the zoo animals into man-eating killers. Hordes of sewer rats are also affected and they go on a tear as well. The high points include an attack on a ballet class by a polar bear. In the end it is up to biologist Aldrich, cop Bologna, and obligatory beautiful-lady-journalist de Selle to save humanity by turning flamethrowers on the rampant critters. Shot in 1982, the film predictably debuts here on videocassette.

p, Federico Prosperi; d&w, Franco E. Prosperi, Lewis E. Ciannelli; ph, Guglielmo Mancori (Luciano Vittori Color); m, Daniele Patucchi; ed, Mario Morra; spec eff, Cataldo Galiano, Alvaro Passeri; makeup, Maurizio Trani.

Action/Horror   **Cas.**   **(PR:O   MPAA:NR)**

WILD WIND, THE†   (1986, Yugo./USSR/U.S.) 100m Film Danas/Moldava
                                              Film/Croatia Film/Noble c

Svetozar Cvetkovic *(Svetozar)*, George Montgomery *(Maj. Mestrovic)*, Victor Proskurin *(Soviet Officer)*, Jay North, Dale Cummings, Albert Paulsen, Greg Finley, Michael Christian, Svetlana Toma, Milan Puzic, Drag Felba, Walter Kray, Ljuba Poliscuk, Dusan Janicijevic.

Escaped Russian POWs and American OSS agents team up with Communist Yugoslav guerrillas to blow up a strategic bridge and capture the armored train that has been terrorizing the area.

p, Ika Panajotovic; d, Alex Petko [Aleksandar Petkovic]; w, Zivojin Pavlovic (based on his novel *The Wild Wind*); ph, Vadim Jakovljev (Eastmancolor); m, Evgenij Doga; art d, Nemanja Petrovic; cos, Emilija Kovacevic.

War   **(PR:A-C   MPAA:NR)**

WILDCATS*   (1986) 107m Hawn-Sylbert/WB c

Goldie Hawn *(Molly McGrath)*, Swoosie Kurtz *(Verna)*, Robyn Lively *(Alice McGrath)*, Brandy Gold *(Marian McGrath)*, James Keach *(Frank McGrath)*, Jan Hooks *(Stephanie)*, Bruce McGill *(Dan Darwell)*, Nipsey Russell *(Ben Edwards)*, Mykel T. Williamson *(Levander "Bird" Williams)*, Tab Thacker *(Finch)*, Wesley Snipes *(Trumaine)*, Nick Corri *(Cerulo)*, Woody Harrelson *(Krushinski)*, Willie J. Walton *(Marvel)*, Rodney Hill *(Peanut)*, Lindsey Orr *(Central Player)*, Albert Michel *(Alonzo)*, Eddie Frescas *(Translator)*, M. Emmet Walsh *(Coes)*, Ellia English *(Marva)*, Jenny Havens *(Jeannie)*, Tony Salome *(Mr. Remo)*, George Wyner *(Principal Walker)*, Noel De Souza *(Doctor)*, Ann Doran *(Mrs. Chat-*

ham), Gloria Stuart *(Mrs. Connoly)*, Pilar Delano *(Angelique)*, Bruce French *(Mayhew)*, Royce Wallace *(Judge)*, Hakeem *(Boy)*, Lee Weaver *(Maurice)*, L.L. Cool J. *(Rapper)*, Vincent Isaac *(Companion No.1)*, Stan Foster *(Companion No.2)*, Dap "Sugar" Willie *(Poolhall Man No.1)*, Chino "Fats" Williams *(Poolhall Man No.2)*, John Vargas *(Poolhall Man No.3)*, David Kanakes *(Goon No.1)*, David Nieker *(Goon No.2)*, Tom E. Willman *(Prescott Assistant Coach)*, Gwen McGee *(Bird's Girl)*, Tan'ya Harris *(Central Cheerleader)*, Deborah Webber, Gary Austin *(Spectators)*, Richard B. Brown, Sylvester Blaylock *(Referees)*, Steven L. Carlson *(Prescott Quarterback)*.

With its painfully forced premise and utterly routine execution, WILDCATS quickly degenerates into a witless star vehicle that challenges THE BEST OF TIMES as 1986's worst football comedy. Hawn, a divorced mother of two, is the girl's track coach at Prescott High School, an institution located in one of Chicago's better neighborhoods. Hoping to follow in her father's footsteps, Hawn asks to become head football coach when the position suddenly becomes available. Her request is laughed off and instead, through the dealings of colleague McGill, Hawn is made football coach of the inner-city Central High. Hawn accepts the job with the expected amount of grit, and enters the formidable ghetto school where she is greeted by principal Russell. When Hawn confronts her new team, she is greeted with nothing but disdain. Eventually she earns their respect and Hawn sets out to build a first-class team. In doing so, she neglects her homelife and her ex-husband Keach threatens to take custody of Lively and Gold, their children. Forced to choose between children or coaching, Hawn agrees to give up football when the season ends. Her team, which has snapped into shape under Hawn's guiding hand, is disappointed by her decision and lets the coach know it. Hawn sees the light, tells off Keach and begins preparations for the inevitable Big Game against Prescott High. To no one's surprise, Hawn's team is victorious, proving to McGill that women are just as capable as men at coaching a football team.

WILDCATS seems to operate under the assumption that audiences will accept the film's improbabilities simply because this is a Goldie Hawn comedy. Thus, to fill out the wafer thin premise, we are presented with a street hustler turned quarterback, a William "Refrigerator" Perry look-a-like, Lively's foray into punk haircuts, a few flashes of nudity, and that handy save-all device: four-letter word punchlines. These are just a few of WILDCATS' simplistic devices. Central High School is one of those mythical Hollywood inner-city institutions where racial tensions are virtually nonexistent. Age requirements are also pretty liberal, because not one of the Wildcats appears remotely close to adolescence. Ritchie's comedy direction is perfunctory setup and delivery, a hack job any reasonably talented television director could easily match. With this and THE GOLDEN CHILD as his 1986 offerings, Ritchie seems dead set on further destroying the reputation he earned with such wonderful satires as THE CANDIDATE, SMILE and THE BAD NEWS BEARS. Hawn, whose production company was responsible for developing WILDCATS, gives a by-the-numbers performance. When it's time to show grit and determination, Hawn buckles down. If there's a problem with her children, Hawn develops worried mom distress lines along her forehead. Keach and Kurtz, as Hawn's sister and encouraging friend, do what they can, though both are capable of much better than what the script here offers them. There's no challenge to WILDCATS, only a few stock situations, characters, and plot developments reworked into a mindless and wholly unmemorable bit of fluff. Although the story takes place during the fall football season, the film was shot on location in Chicago in the midst of a torrid summer heat wave. For the climactic game between Central and Prescott, the cast was required to wear winter clothing despite the overwhelming temperatures. Consequently, everyone from Hawn to the trombone player of the high school marching band sweated uncomfortably for the shooting's duration. Songs on the soundtrack include: "Good Hands" (Hawk Wolinski, James Newton Howard, performed by The Isley Brothers), "Show Me How It Works" (Hawk Wolinski, James Newton

Howard, David Pack, performed by Mavis Staples), "Razzle Dazzle" (Hawk Wolinski, James Newton Howard, performed by Michael Jeffries), "Penetration" (Hawk Wolinski, James Newton Howard, performed by Brenda Russell), "Love Lives Alone" (Hawk Wolinski, James Newton Howard, David Pack, performed by Tata Vega), "Football Rap" (James Todd Smith, performed by L.L. Cool J), "Rock It" (Hawk Wolinski, James Newton Howard, performed by Sidney Justin), "We Stand Alone" (Hawk Wolinski, James Newton Howard, Joe Cocker, performed by Joe Cocker), "Hard to Say" (Hawk Wolinski, James Newton Howard, David Pack, performed by James Ingram), "Stormy Monday" (Aaron T. Walker, performed by T-Bone Walker), "She Blinded Me With Science" (Thomas Dolby, Joe Kerr).

p, Anthea Sylbert; d, Michael Ritchie; w, Ezra Sacks; ph, Donald E. Thorin (Technicolor); m, Hawk Wolinski, James Newton Howard; ed, Richard A. Harris; prod d, Boris Leven; art d, Steve Berger; set d, Phil Abramson; cos, Wayne A. Finkelman, Nick Scarano, Jennifer Parsons; spec eff, Cliff Wenger; ch, Joel Hall, Paula Tracy Smuin; m/l, Hawk Wolinsky, James Newton Howard, David Pack, James Todd Smith, Aaron T. Walker, Thomas Dolby, Joe Kerr; makeup, Cheri Minns; stunts, Donna Garrett, Kay H.Whipple.

Comedy/Sports   **Cas.**   **(PR:C-O   MPAA:R)**

WINDRIDER†   (1986, Aus.) 92m Barron Films/Hoyts c

Tom Burlinson (P.C. Simpson), Nicole Kidman (Jade), Charles Tingwell (Simpson, Sr.), Jill Perryman (Miss Dodge), Simon Chilvers, Kim Bullad, Matt Parkinson, Penny Brown.

This teenage romance from down under features Burlinson as the windsurfing crazed son of rich guy Tingwell. The old man outwardly disapproves of Burlinson's all-consuming passion for the sport, though Tingwell actually harbors hidden pride in his son's achievements. Burlinson gets involved with Kidman, a beautiful rock 'n' roll singer. The affair sees some rocky moments when Burlinson narrowly escapes a shark attack, and his personality turns a bit caustic. When the day arrives for a big surfing contest, Burlinson is fooled by a challenger and ends up going to the wrong starting location. Eventually he makes it to the right place and the story comes to a happy resolution for everyone. This is the first directorial effort for Vincent Monton, who previously worked as one of Australia's top cinematographers (NEWSFRONT, ROAD GAMES, and HEATWAVE, among others).

p, Paul Barron; d, Vincent Monton; w, Everett de Roche, Bonnie Harris; ph, Joe Pickering (Eastmancolor); m, Kevin Peak; ed, John Scott; art d, Phil Monaghan.

Romance   **(PR:C   MPAA:NR)**

WINDSCHADUW†   (1986, Neth.) 71m Frans van de Staak/Film International c (WINDSHADE)

Gerrart Klieverik (Man), Isabelle Guillaume (Woman).

An abstract piece of filmmaking which juxtaposes images of two people trapped in a circular search for elusive contentment against peaceful pastoral images. The soundtrack consists of two poems from one of The Netherlands' foremost poets, Gerrit Kouwenaar, read by the poet himself.

p&d, Frans van de Staak; w, Frans van de Staak, Gerrit Kouwenaar; ph, Mat van Hensbergen; m, Bernard Hunnekink; ed, Frans van de Staak, Jan Dop.

Drama   **(PR:C   MPAA:NR)**

WIRED TO KILL*   (1986) 96m Franky Schaeffer/American Distribution Group c

Emily Longstreth (Rebecca), Devin Hoelscher (Steve), Merritt Butrick (Reegus), Frank Collison (Sly), Garth Gardner (Loady), Tom Lister, Jr. (Sleet), Kim Milford (Rooster), Michael Wollet (Zero), Kristina David (Mother), Don Blakely (Sergeant), Dorothy Patterson (Grandmother), J.P. Bumstead.

Back to the depopulated future again, this time an epidemic causing the collapse of civilization (as we know it). Parts of the city are quarantine zones, and they have been taken over by gangs who prey on the hapless families in the area. One such family is that of Hoelscher, who all become the victims of Butrick and his gang. After they rob the place and break his legs, he calls the cops, so they kill grandma and badly injure mom. Now Hoelscher is confined to a wheelchair and mad, so, with girl friend Longstreth, he goes about thinning the gang's numbers. A booby-trapped motorcycle, a walkman that can fry brains, and battery acid sold as crack eliminate some bad guys, but when Butrick kidnaps Longstreth and forces her to perform "Romeo and Juliet" with him, Hoelscher sets loose his personal robot, Winston. The finale finds the remaining bad guys aboard their garbage truck (everyone drives garbage trucks in this particular future) blowing up in a big ball of flame.

Perhaps not as offensive as some films in the science fiction-vengeance vein, this may be the dullest yet. The simple fact that our hero, Hoelscher, is stuck in a wheelchair for most of the film rather restricts his opportunities for heroism. The performances are wooden, but the cinematography is superb, creating a shadowy, threatening city. Too bad it's wasted in this mindless vengeance actioner.

p, Jim Buchfuehrer; d&w, Franky Schaeffer; ph, Tom Fraser (Foto-Kem color); m, Russell Ferrante; ed, Daniel Agulian, Franky Schaeffer; art d, Diana Williams, Gay Redinger; set d, Ainslee Colt DeWolf; cos, Dorothy Bulac; spec eff, Bruce Hayes.

Science Fiction   **(PR:O   MPAA:R)**

WISDOM**   (1986) 108m Gladden Entertainment/FOX c

Demi Moore (Karen Simmons), Emilio Estevez (John Wisdom), Tom Skerritt (Lloyd Wisdom), Veronica Cartwright (Samantha Wisdom), William Allen Young (John Williamson, F.B.I. Agent), Richard Minchenberg (Cooper, F.B.I. Agent), Ernie Brown (Motel Manager), Bill Henderson (Theo), Gene Ross (Sheriff), Liam Sullivan (Jake Perry), Charlie Sheen (City Burger Manager), Hal Fishman (Network Anchorman), Chuck Henry (Local Anchorman), Nick Shields (Gun Salesman), Barbara Stamm (Loan Officer at Bank No.1), Santos Morales (Al Gomez), Gus Corrado (Yuppie Employer), Golden Henning (Katie), Rene Sprattling (Carol), Kate McKinnon (Nancy), Tim Sapunor (Matt), Charlie Holliday (Bob), Ron Presson (Guard at Bank No.1), Estee Chandler (Female Teller), Jeff Boudov (Minnesota Bank Teller), Thomas Will-Ellis, David DeFrancesca (Albuquerque Officers), Leon Corcos (Leon), Janet Rotblatt (Elderly Lady on Street), Erika Lincoln (Woman on Street), Sid Conrad (Farmer), Henry Proach (Old Man on Street), Matt Robinson (Young Man), Bob Devon Jones (Teacher), Jimmy Walker Lane (Night Manager at Mini-Mart), Walter Edward Smith, John Deaderick (Bank Customers), Beau Dare (FBI Agent), Gil Parra (Swat Team Leader), Jamie Namson (Helicopter Pilot).

Writing, directing, and starring in WISDOM, the 23-year-old Estevez may have proven his ambitiousness but he has not yet proven his talent. Having already seen one of his scripts produced—THAT WAS THEN . . . THIS IS NOW (1985), which he also starred in—Estevez decided to wear three hats for this film. It's a well-intentioned project that shows a certain promise and visual eye, but fails to really come together as anything more than an expensive film-school

thesis project. Estevez stars as John Wisdom, a 23-year-old street kid who is having trouble finding his niche in society because of a police record. As a teenager, he got drunk with some friends, stole a car, and was placed on probation for four years. He's a clean-cut kid and is trying desperately to find a job. In addition to being honest, he's also a little stupid, writing on his job applications that he has been convicted of a crime. Discouraged, he finally lies on a job form and is hired at a fast-food stand. Estevez's terrible past catches up with him, however, and when the truth leaks out, he is fired. Having no future as a burger-flipper, he looks to the crime world for other options. After seeing a television report on bank loan foreclosures, Estevez becomes inspired. With his girl friend Moore (Estevez's then real-life fiancee), Estevez begins a crime spree which entails robbing banks, not for their money, but in order to destroy their loan records. Sporting an Uzi submachine gun and a U.S. flag on the back of his jacket, this squeaky-clean defender of justice travels across the heartland, becoming a modern-day folk hero for millions of financially downtrodden Americans. This game soon turns tragic when Moore accidentally kills a police officer. State police and the FBI are on their trail, which stretches across five states. Although Estevez and Moore have become national heroes, this is not what they want—they have convictions and are fighting for a cause. They don't want to become media darlings, but they have to take the bad with the good. In the end, the law prevails and these good kids are killed by those nasty police. But wait, it was only a dream—with Estevez sitting in his bathtub pondering his future.

WISDOM is not a very good film, but unlike most Hollywood films today, it shows some promise. Somewhere underneath the clumsiness and inexperience lies a talented filmmaker that is trying to get out. Estevez has been criticized for being too young to direct a film (these nay-sayers have apparently forgotten that Orson Welles was only 25 when he did CITIZEN KANE), which seems rather senseless since people twice his age are consistently making films that are twice as bad. Having emerged as the brightest talent from the much-overrated "Brat Pack," Estevez proves that he isn't going to sit back and rest on his pretty face and rave reviews. Rather, Estevez is willing to take some risks. WISDOM has plot problems a mile long, merely passable performances, and some downright silly dialog. Underneath its "Robin Hood" theme is a rather typical 1980s mentality mixed with a dash of 1960s radicalism. When it's not being BONNIE AND CLYDE or BADLANDS (which starred Estevez's father, Martin Sheen), WISDOM smacks of the 1980s fascination with social causes. It's the decent, hard-working folks being victimized by the heartless government. It's the ultimate 1980s boxing match with Bruce Springsteen in one corner and Ronald Reagan in the other. And, of course, it's Estevez and Moore—the outlaw lovers—who see all of this clearly and work to rectify the entire system. But Estevez's criminal stance as John Wisdom feels fabricated and calculated. There is

in a lobster tank. Then he comes up with the ultimate idea. He assigns each of them to kill the other. The two leave town right away in search of some senior member of the mob who can get them off the hook. They arrive in Atlantic City and check into a hotel, using a credit card belonging to Albano, the hulking ex-wrestler. The hotel casino is managed by Keitel, doing a very fine impression of Robert De Niro. The movie then goes into a stall mode and mucks about until DeVito incredibly finds a mattress stuffed with money and their lives are saved.

no real criminal menace, as there was with Sheen's character in BADLANDS. Estevez is just a good kid trying to do right. Unfortunately for Estevez the director this duality doesn't work—you can't be a great guy and a wanted criminal at the same time. Estevez the writer just can't commit himself to the character. Rather than paint him as an antihero, he makes him a victim of circumstance. Yes, he stole a car, but he was drunk when he did it. Yes, he breaks into banks, but it's in the name of the people. Yes, Moore killed a cop, but it was an accident. And yes, they die in the end, but it was only a dream. In WISDOM, the characters really want to be criminals, but they just don't seem to want to commit any crimes. Like John Wisdom, Estevez the filmmaker has the image down pat, but the talent is lagging behind. Robert Wise, credited as the film's executive producer, is reputed to have been engaged to keep his experienced eye on WISDOM. Songs include: "Home Again" (performed by Oingo Boingo), "Whiskey in My Beer" (Gary Austin, performed by Austin), "Moonbright Misty Night" (Ron Gertz, performed by Scott Wojahn), "Tears Run Down," "Rock Me Baby" (Danny Elfman, performed by Elfman).

p, Bernard Williams; d&w, Emilio Estevez; ph, Adam Greenberg (DeLuxe Color); m, Danny Elfman; ed, Michael Kahn; prod d, Dennis Gassner; art d, Dins Danielsen; set d, Richard Hoover; cos, Jonathan Kinsey; spec eff, Richard Helmer; m/l, Gary Austin, Ron Gertz, Danny Elfman; makeup, Kyle Tucy; stunts, Bud Davis.

Crime   (PR:O MPAA:R)

WISE GUYS**   (1986) 91m MGM/UA c

Danny DeVito *(Harry Valentini)*, Joe Piscopo *(Moe Dickstein)*, Harvey Keitel *(Bobby Dilea)*, Ray Sharkey *(Marco)*, Dan Hedaya *(Anthony Castelo)*, Captain Lou Albano *(Frank The Fixer)*, Julie Bovasso *(Lil Dickstein)*, Patti LuPone *(Wanda Valentini)*, Antonia Rey *(Aunt Sadie)*, Mimi Cecchini *(Grandma Valentini)*.

Piscopo must have seen too many Jerry Lewis movies, because his gnawing on the scenery is surpassed only by Albano's. DeVito does a fairly good job holding himself in check. During one scene, the two men are in the hotel penthouse and DeVito is having his back rubbed by a blonde while Piscopo's in the Jacuzzi with another attractive woman. When a knock came at the door, DeVito thought it was a waiter with caviar and champagne as scripted, but when the actor opened the door, he handed a note to DeVito that read "Rhea's in labor." Rhea is Rhea ("Cheers") Perlman and she was expecting the couple's second child. DeVito rushed to the hospital and got there before his wife did. Lots and lots of foul language. It was 13 years since DePalma made his last comedy. Perhaps, if he can curb his customary excesses, he should do more. TV viewers will recall that DeVito's character on TV's "Taxi" was named De Palma. In a small role as DeVito's loving wife, note Patti LuPone, who was so spectacular on Broadway in "Evita".

p, Aaron Russo; d, Brian DePalma; w, George Gallo; ph, Fred Schuler (Technicolor); m, Ira Newborn; ed, Jerry Greenberg; prod d, Edward Pisoni; art d, Paul Bryan Eads; set d, Leslie Bloom.

Comedy   Cas.   (PR:C-O MPAA:R)

WITCHFIRE*   (1986) 100m Panda/Shapiro c

Shelley Winters *(Lydia)*, Gary Swanson *(The Hunter)*, Francesca De Sapio *(Hattie)*, Corinne Neuchateau *(Julietta)*, Al Shannon *(Harold)*, James Mendenhall *(Jarnigan)*, David Mendenhall *(Hunter's Son)*, Paula Shaw *(Nurse Hemmings)*.

An often funny, though just as often tasteless, comedy comes from an unlikely source, Brian DePalma. DeVito and Piscopo play best pals who live next door to each other in a seedy New Jersey row of tract houses. They both work in the lowest echelon of the Mafia (though Piscopo is supposed to be Jewish.) Their jobs include taking care of the laundry for local godfather Hedaya. Another of their tasks is going to the track to bet on horses for their boss. Why they are errand boys isn't explained though, as the mob runs bookmaking establishments that could handle the bets. At the track, if the horse wins there must be a report to the IRS. Since Hedaya's bets have been losers lately, DeVito puts the money on a different horse, one he is positive will win Of course, it doesn't, and the godfather is enraged because he is out about a quarter of a million on the $10 thousand he was wagering. Hedaya wants to kill them right away, and he has a bit of fun by suspending Piscopo over a pit of snapping dogs and dunking DeVito

When a psychiatrist dies in a car wreck, three of his female patients—Winters, De Sapio, and Neuchateau, all completely bonkers—refuse to believe that he is dead. They are taken to the funeral for verification, and they promptly escape, led by Winters. She fancies herself a witch and conducts seances to contact their deceased doctor at an abandoned mansion in the woods. Meanwhile, Swanson and his son, David Mendenhall, are hunting in the woods. Swanson wanders in on the women, who promptly club him on the head and tie him up. He escapes however, and hides his son—who is unconscious after falling into a ditch—under some brush. He is recaptured by the women, who now have his shotgun. Young Mendenhall regains consciousness and leads police to the house, now in flames with Neuchateau and De Sapio standing outside. Swanson tries to rescue Winters but fails, and the building collapses with her still inside. After everyone goes home (or back to the asylum, as the case may be), a cellar door in the smoking ruins opens up, and Winters is still alive.

Mercifully, despite the open-ended conclusion, no sequel appears in the offing. Actress Winters also acted as associate producer on this film, and picked much of the cast herself from the ranks of the Actor's Studio in New York, where she once trained. Her performance is the centerpiece of the film, the only thing of interest, and the thing that dooms it. Her best line comes when she tells Swanson, "I may be insane, but I'm not stupid." Perhaps not, but people who rent this tape (it went straight to video without a theatrical release) can't say the same.

p, James R. Orr; d, Vincent J. Privitera; w, Vincent J. Privitera, James R. Orr; m, Dave Puchan; ed, Gregg McGee.

Thriller   **Cas.**   **(PR:O MPAA:NR)**

WO CHE-YANG KUO-LE YI-SHENG   (SEE: KUEI-MEI, 1986, Taiwan)

WO ERH HAN-SHENG†   (1986, Taiwan) 96m Central c (Trans: Hang-Sheng, My Son)

Chiang Hsia, Tuan Chung-yi, Li Hsing-wen.

The second film by Chang Yi this year (KUEI-MEI, A WOMAN is the other), both based on short stories by his wife Hsiao Sa. In this one a loving mother strives to maintain her relationship with her son as he rejects everything he believes she stands for.

d, Chang Yi; w, Hsiao Sa, Chang Yi (based on a story by Hsiao Sa); ph, Yang Wei-han; m, Chang Hung-yi; ed, Wang Chin-ch'en.

Drama   **(PR:NR MPAA:NR)**

WOHIN MIT WILLFRIED?†   (1986, Ger.) 81m Dieter Koster–Sender Freies c (Trans: What to Do with Willfried?)

Geseke Piper (Valerie), Gisela Probst (Susanne), Dagmar Biener (Doris), Rainer Hunold (Paul), Dorothea Moritz (Frau Frisch), Christoph M. Ohrt (Walker), Beate Tober (Rose), Alexander Hauft (Freddy), Dorothee Kremps-Ehrlich (Gundula), Peter Schlesinger (Stallkeeper), Horst Pinnow (Cowboy).

A mail carrier and his family get a winning raffle ticket and journey to the office of the ticket-sponsor's advertising agency where they find, to their surprise, that they have won a white stallion named Willfried. Young Piper's best friend has just discovered boys, and has deserted her for one of them. Piper is thus pleased with the attention she gains through her new prize, which is the subject of much publicity. The one problem is that their urban tenement building is an inappropriate environment for a horse. Quartered in the courtyard, the steed gets wet when a rainstorm strikes, so the compassionate child leads the animal indoors, where it promptly defecates on a stairway. The advertising agency refuses to redeem the stallion, which has served its publicity purposes, and the rental cost of a stable stall would be prohibitive. The family members decide to use the deserted summer house of a family friend as a shelter for the beast, and to that effect they sneak Willfried onto a suburb-bound train. Their white-elephant white horse is not easily concealed, and only many adventures later do they hit upon a solution to their equine difficulties: the parents join the Berlin Wild West Club (a real organization) where the steed is welcome and horsefeed comes from the coffers of the club. (In German.)

p, Frauke Klinkers, Pierre Le Page; d, Dieter Koster; w, Hannelore Conradsen, Dieter Koster; ph, Wolfhard Osswold; ed, Dagmar Bleasing; set d, Mandus Kohler.

Children's/Comedy   **(PR:AA MPAA:NR)**

WOLF AT THE DOOR, THE†   (1986, Fr./Den.) 102m Dagmar–Henning Dam Kargaard–Cameras Continentales–Famous French Films–TF-1–Danish Film Institute–Danish Radio and Television– French Ministry of Cultural Affairs/Manson c (OVIRI)

Donald Sutherland (Paul Gauguin), Valerie Merea (Annah-la-Javanaise), Max von Sydow (August Strindberg), Sofie Grabol (Judith Molard), Merete Voldstedlund (Mette Gauguin), Jorgen Reenberg (Edward Brandes), Yves Barsack (Edgar Degas), Thomas Antoni (Jourdan), Fanny Bastien (Juliette Huet), Jean Yanne (William Molard), Ghita Norby (Ida Molard), Kristina Dubin (Aline Gauguin), Henrik Larsen (Julien Leclercq), Bill Dunn, Morten Grunwald, Hans Henrik Lehrfeldt, Jean-Claude Flamant, Solbjorg Hojfeldt, Jesper Bruun Rasmussen, Anthony Michael, Chili Turell.

The late-19th-Century painter, Paul Gauguin, is brought to life in this biography which concentrates on an 18-month period in the artist's life, beginning with his return to Paris from Tahiti and ending with his trip back to the tropics. Finding no critical success in Paris, and dejected by a series of failed love relationships, Gauguin decides to return to the island—not alone, but with an entourage of fellow artists and writers. The title refers to fellow painter Edgar Degas' description of Gauguin as a wolf, which—he explains in reference to Gauguin's wild nature—"would rather starve than wear a collar like his domesticated and well-fed counterpart, the dog." WOLF AT THE DOOR was released in 1986 in Copenhagen and was entered in the Venice Film Festival, and was picked up for a U.S. release in 1987.

p&d, Henning Carlsen; w, Christopher Hampton (based on a story by Henning Carlsen, Jean-Claude Carriere); ph, Mikael Salomon (Eastmancolor); m, Ole Schmidt; ed, Janus Billeskov Jansen; art d, Andre Guerin, Karl-Otto Hedal; cos,

Charlotte Clason, Ole Glaesner, Annelise Hauberg; makeup, Birte Christensen, Birthe Lyngsoe.

Biography   **(PR:O MPAA:NR)**

WOMEN'S PRISON MASSACRE zero   (1986, It./Fr.) 89m Beatrice–Les Films de Chauvin/Flor c

Laura Gemser (Emanuelle), Gabriele Tinti (Crazy Boy Henderson), Lorraine de Selle (Warden), Ursula Flores, Maria Romano, Antonella Giacomini, Raul Cabrera, Roberto Mura, Michael Laurant, Francoise Perrot, Franca Stoppi, Flo Astaire, Pierangelo Pozzato, Jacques Stany, Carlo De Mejo.

While investigating a drug-smuggling ring, Gemser gets too close to the crooked district attorney who has her framed for pushing and locked up. Prison life is a series of degradations, like having to stick her face in the sink as long as she can, and fending off repeated attempts on her life by the prison's toughest inmate. Meanwhile, the police have captured four killers, led by Tinti (Gemser's real-life husband), and hold them at the women's prison (which actually resembles a crumbling old chateau more than a correctional facility) pending their execution. The four manage to get hold of some hostages and demand $5 million in ransom. While the corrupt district attorney tries to stage a raid that fails miserably, the criminals force Gemser and another prisoner to play Russian Roulette. In the meantime, rape and murders abound before Tinti finally makes his move. He is wounded while trying to escape and beaten by the lawman he had wounded earlier and held hostage. The last scene has Gemser going back to jail.

In a year which saw an extraordinary number of women-in-prison films, this one must be at the very bottom of a very deep barrel. It is a sequel to 1984's CAGED WOMEN, making the total number of sequels in the Italian-French "Emanuelle" series (not to be confused with the exclusively French "Emmanuelle" series spelled with two m's somewhere in the teens). Shot on what looks like a minuscule budget (actually at the same time as CAGED WOMEN), the film has only a dozen or so prisoners and about four guards. There is some attempt to give the film style, with occasionally interesting lighting or camera moves, but mostly there are the usual elements of the genre—rape, murder, and naked girls taking showers. Some amusement can be derived from the bad dubbing, which has tough gals snarling lines like "Take my advice and go die" in one of those generic European accents, and a credit sequence that includes things like stockings by Arditi and upholstery by Bruno Schiami (though no upholstery is noticeable in this prison). Mostly, however, this film is simply an ordeal to sit through. Surprisingly, and unlike many of the women-in-prison films released this year, WOMEN'S PRISON MASSACRE actually saw a theatrical release before going to home video.

p, Jean Lefait; d, Gilbert Roussel; w, Claudio Fragasso, Olivier Lefait; ph, Henry Froger (Telecolor); m, Luigi Ceccarelli; ed, Gilbert Kikoine.

Prison   **Cas.**   **(PR:O MPAA:R)**

WORKING GIRLS*   (1986) 90m Lizzie Borden–Alternate Current/ Miramax Films c

Louise Smith (Molly), Ellen McElduff (Lucy), Amanda Goodwin (Dawn), Marusia Zach (Gina), Janne Peters (April), Helen Nicholas (Mary).

Although prostitution in the movies has had a long and varied history, never has any film dealt directly with the woman behind the illusion of the prostitute. The usual story shows the working girl as either a toughened streetwalker who takes to prostitution out of desperation, or the girl with a heart of gold who has learned to survive by making men feel comfortable. Seldom do these portraits ever amount to anything beyond a caricature or stereotype. The screen prostitute exists to reinforce the viewers' ingrained image of the fallen woman. The fact that a real person exists behind this professional mask is unimportant. WORKING GIRLS concentrates on the daily routine of a modern-day Manhattan prostitute in a detached, clinical manner. The film thus breaks away from old myths to create an insightful and, in many ways, disturbing interpretation of what has been called the "world's oldest profession."

Smith plays a Yale graduate, nearing 30, who temporarily works in a Manhattan brothel to help make ends meet. Her day begins a few minutes before eight o'clock. The alarm goes off, though Smith has already awakened in dreadful anticipation of her day's work. She tenderly wakens her lesbian lover and her lover's daughter. The three have a light breakfast while attending to their normal rituals in preparation for the day. This scene creates the mood of the routine that permeates the entire film, making Smith's job as a prostitute seem like any other job. The Manhattan brothel she works in appears as a normal office. The girls dress like secretaries, and harmlessly chat about their personal lives, the job, and their general disdain for their boss, as they patiently wait for the day to end so they can go home. On this particular day Smith works with Goodwin and Zach, the latter a sweet Latino girl who is saving her money so she can start her own business. Goodwin is a crass student with far fetched ideas of someday becoming a lawyer. McElduff, the boss, or their "pimp" as the girls call her, comes in late. Her delayed arrival allows the girls to lie about the actual amount of money they take in and thus keep more for themselves. When she does finally arrive, she behaves like a typical boss, complaining about the order of the "office" and the girls' disrespect for her rigid rules. The shift for these three girls ends but because McElduff only has two girls coming in for the night shift, one a newcomer, she begs Smith to stay a little longer. However, no one relieves Smith, so she is forced to remain the entire shift, a particularly busy one. Frustrated, overworked, and at the point of tears, Smith quits her job as she prepares to leave for the night. Presumably, she will take up the offer of an elderly customer willing to pay her well if she services only him. Her line of work would not change, but the amount of time, labor, and overall hassle would be reduced. The film ends as it began with the alarm ringing a little before eight and Smith in bed with her arm around her lover.

WORKING GIRLS is director Borden's second feature. Her first, BORN IN FLAMES (1983), had an extreme feminist perspective that met with varied responses. However, critics generally agreed that the director possessed a unusually sharp eye for detail. This same quality pervades WORKING GIRLS, and in the absence of any distinguishing plot, is the main force in maintaining interest. The camera studiously follows Smith and the other girls as they attend to their labors, giving significance to otherwise small and unimportant events. In this sense, the film is very much an anthropological study, concentrating upon everyday rituals that are, in fact, the distinguishing features of a culture. By focusing on these small details, Borden succeeds in stripping away the myths relating to prostitution, showing it to be just another way to make a living.

Borden spent six months of research preparing for WORKING GIRLS, interviewing and studying middle-class prostitutes much like the ones in the film. Surprisingly, she discovered that highly educated girls, like Smith in the film, often resort to such work to help support themselves. None of the actresses in WORKING GIRLS had any previous film appearances. Their acting experience was limited to small theater productions in New York. Borden had each of the girls apply for a job at a brothel before filming. This helped create the realistic, down-to-earth quality of their characters. These portrayals possess none of the stereotypes popular in media representations of prostitutes, and, as a result, are frighteningly realistic. Borden managed to finance the film on a tiny budget, though this is not evident in the final product. Instead of renting or building a set, she remodeled her own apartment in the image of the Manhattan brothels she had visited. It has the appearance of any homogenized office, where the slightest bit of disarray or uncleanliness disrupts the sterile order.

Perhaps the most unusual quality of WORKING GIRLS is its matter-of-fact attitude toward sex. There are a large number of sex scenes in the movie, none of which is the slightest bit erotic or romantic. Instead, the sex scenes are coldly clinical. The clients are viewed as paying customers, nothing more. They are treated by the girls in the manner that will secure the most profit, as long as the girls are not forced to do anything they don't want to do. Although a large number of men do appear in the film, and are endowed with original personality traits, none of them possess much real attractiveness. They are completely dependent upon the women, who knowingly manipulate them without bruising their egos. Such treatment offers the rather hopeless supposition that it is impossible for men and women to relate on a healthy or very personal level. Borden places the blame, at least in this film, on men, who are too wrapped up in themselves and their own sexual insecurities. WORKING GIRLS does not have an MPAA rating, but because of its subject matter theater owners restricted attendance to those over the age of 18.

p, Lizzie Borden, Andi Gladstone; d, Lizzie Borden; w, Lizzie Borden, Sandra Kay; ph, Judy Irola (Eastmancolor); m, David van Tieghem; ed, Lizzie Borden; prod d, Kurt Ossenfort.

Drama (PR:O MPAA:NR)

WRAITH, THE* (1986) Alliance-John Kemeny/New Century-Vista c

Charlie Sheen *(The Wraith/Jake Kesey)*, Nick Cassavetes *(Packard Walsh)*, Sherilyn Fenn *(Keri Johnson)*, Randy Quaid *(Sheriff Loomis)*, Matthew Barry *(Billy Hankins)*, David Sherrill *(Skank)*, Jamie Bozian *(Gutterboy)*, Clint Howard *(Rughead)*, Griffin O'Neal *(Oggie Fisher)*, Chris Nash *(Minty)*, Vickie Benson *(Waitress)*, Jeffrey Sudzin *(Redd)*, Peder Melhuse *(Murphy)*, Michael Hungerford *(Stokes)*, Steven Eckholdt *(Boy in Daytona)*, Elizabeth Cox *(Girl in Daytona)*, Dick Alexander *(Sandeval)*, Christopher Bradley *(Jamie)*, Joan H. Reynolds *(Policewoman)*.

A ridiculous mishmash of drag racing, ghosts, and science fiction, THE WRAITH swiftly disappeared, sparing Charlie Sheen a lot of embarrassment. Off in the Arizona desert, a gang of tough kids led by Cassavetes race against all comers, betting the cars on the outcome. Sheen shows up in town on a motor scooter one day and immediately falls in love with Fenn, Cassavetes' girl friend. Everyone seems to recall Sheen's face, but no one can quite place it. At about the same time, a mysterious and very fast black car starts turning up on the highways outside of town. The gang goes up against it in a race, but their designated driver, O'Neal, crashes in flames. When they reach his body, it is totally intact. Eventually it is revealed that Sheen is the reincarnation of a boy killed by the gang sometime before the action of the film, and now he has been returned to life by some aliens and sent back with a fast car to get revenge. Of course, the final duel is between him and Cassavetes, and guess who loses, leaving Sheen to drive off with Fenn, who is apparently from outer space herself.

If that synopsis confused you, you know exactly how audiences felt. The performances range from poor to lousy (although to be fair, Sheen isn't *too* bad), mostly the fault of an incomprehensible script that instead of working anything out, simply throws in another bone to keep the audience's collective mind away from the stupidity of the story. The director is obviously working outside his milieu, which consists of ski films and features with titles of things you eat or drink, SIX PACK (writer), HOT DOG—THE MOVIE (writer and second unit director), and HAMBURGER (director). The best thing here are the cars, because they don't have to say anything, just stand around looking fast. Sheen's car is played by a specially built Dodge pace car that cost over $1.5 million. Because the car was so valuable, seven models, including two built on dune buggy frames for stunt work, had to be built so the main car would remain intact. What the film does have going for it is some excellent cinematography by the television commercial-trained Reed Smoot, but that isn't enough to save this idiotic movie. Songs include "Where's the Fire?" (Tim Feehan, performed by Feehan), "Secret Loser" (Ozzy Osbourne, Jake E. Lee, Bob Daisley, performed by Osbourne), "Hearts vs. Heads" (Stan Bush, Andy DiTaranto, performed by Bush), "Wake

Up Call" (Arthur Baker, Tina B., Tommy Mandel, performed by Ian Hunter), "Smokin' in the Boys Room" (Cub Koda, Michael Lutz, performed by Motley Crue), "Addicted to Love" (Robert Palmer, performed by Palmer), "Scream of Angels" (Nick Gilder, Eric Nelson, performed by Gilder), "Power Love" (Norman Swan, performed by Lion), "Those Were the Days" (Ray Coburn, performed by Honeymoon Suite), "Never Surrender" (Swan, Douglas Aldrich, performed by Lion), "Matter of the Heart" (Adam Mitchell, Philip Allen Brown, performed by Bonnie Tyler), "Hold On Blue Eyes" (Haden Gregg, Mark Tiemens, John David Souther, performed by LaMarca), "Rebel Yell" (Billy Idol, Steve Stevens, performed by Idol), "Young Love, Hot Love" (Randall Nicklaus, performed by Jill Michaels), "Bad Mistake" (Jeffrey Wilson, Steve Woodard, performed by James House).

p, John Kemeny; d&w, Mike Marvin; ph, Reed Smoot (Metrocolor); m, Michael Hoenig, J. Peter Robinson; ed, Scott Conrad, Gary Rocklin; art d, Dean Tschetter; set d, Michele Starbuck; cos, Elinor Bardach, Glenn Ralston; spec eff, Phil Cory; m/l, Tim Feehan, Ozzy Osbourne, Jake E. Lee, Bob Daisley, Stan Bush, Andy DiTaranto, Arthur Baker, Tina B., Tommy Mandel, Cub Koda, Michael Lutz, Robert Palmer, Nick Gilder, Eric Nelson, Norman Swan, Ray Coburn, Douglas Aldrich, Adam Mitchell, Philip Allen Brown, Haden Gregg, Mark Tiemens, John David Souther, Billy Idol, Steve Stevens, Randall Nicklaus, Jeffrey Wilson, Steve Woodard; makeup, Kathryn Miles Logan; stunts, Buddy Joe Hooker.

Horror/Drama (PR:C MPAA:PG-13)

WRONG WORLD† (1986, Aus.) 95m Seon Film Enterprises c

Richard Moir *(David Trueman)*, Jo Kennedy *(Mary)*, Nicolas Lathouris *(Rangott)*, Robbie McGregor *(Robert)*, Esben Storm *(Laurence)*, Tim Robinson *(Psychiatrist)*, Cliff Ellen *(Old Man)*.

Moir is a doctor whose initial desire to become "the Albert Schweitzer of Bolivia" has given way to disillusionment, drifting, and morphine addiction. He finally returns home to Australia where a friend commits him to a clinic. There he meets Kennedy, a fellow addict, and the two escape and hit the road. A relationship slowly develops between the two, but it's doomed to fail. Kennedy won the Best Actress prize at the Berlin Film Festival for this film, which had a hard time finding a general release in its own country and didn't receive a single nomination in the Australian Film Awards.

p, Bryce Menzies; d, Ian Pringle; w, Doug Ling, Ian Pringle; ph, Ray Argall (Fujicolor); m, Eric Gradman; ed, Ray Argall; prod d, Christine Johnson.

Drama (PR:O MPAA:NR)

WYROK SMIERCI (SEE: DEATH SENTENCE, 1986, Pol.)

X

X† (1986, Norway) 93m Elinor–Filmgruppe 84–Christiania/Norsk Film–Frieda Ohrvik c

Jorn Christiansen *(Jon)*, Flora *(Bettina Banoun)*, Atle Mostad, Sigrid Huun, Sven Henriksen, Hege Schoyen, Are Storstein, Caspar Evensen, Trond Lybekk, Ola Solum, Holy Toy, Garden of Delight, Backstreet Girls.

A look at the on-again, off-again relationship between a 19-year-old photographer (Christiansen) and a 14-year-old runaway (Banoun).

p, Laila Mikkelsen, Ola Solum, Odvar Einarson; d&w, Odvar Einarson; ph, Svein Krovel (Eastmancolor); m, Andrej Nebb, Holy Toy; ed, Inger-Lise Langfeldt; prod d, Torun Muller.

Drama   **(PR:O MPAA:NR)**

XIANGNU XIAOXIAO† (1986, China) Peking Youth c (Trans: Hunan Girl Xiaoxiao)

Na Renhua, Deng Xiaoguang, Ni Meiling, Liu Qing.

d, Xie Fei, Niao Lan; w, Zhang Xian.

YAKO—CAZADOR DE MALDITOS† (1986, Mex.) 101m
Galubi-Torrente-Dynamic/Peliculas Mexicanas c (Trans: Yako—Hunter of the
Damned) c

Eduardo Yanez *(Jose Luis/Yako)*, Diane Ferretti *(Diana)*, Gregorio Casals
(Texas), Pedro Weber *(Chatanooga)*, Roberto Montiel, Gabriela Goldshmied,
Humberto Elzondo, Bob Nelson.

A honeymoon camping trip turns sour for Yanez and Ferretti when they are
attacked by a gang. Yanez is tied to a tree and Ferretti is raped and murdered.
Yanez survives and goes after the villains, killing them all with his bare hands or
with primitive weapons he fashions himself.

p, Raul Galindo; d, Ruben Galindo; w, Ruben Galindo, Carlos Valdemar; ph,
Victor Manuel Herrera; m, Pedro Galarra; ed, Enrique Murillo.

Action/Crime **(PR:O MPAA:NR)**

YAMASHITA SHONEN MONOGATARI† (1986, Japan) Kinema
Tokyo-The World-Toho c

Kenichi Migita, Atsushi Watanabe, Kaori Shima, Tamao Nakamura, Tomisaburo Wakayama.

d, Shukei Matsubayashi; ph, Yudai Kato.

YARI NO GONZA† (1986, Jap.) 121m Shochiko Hyogensha c (Trans:
Gonza The Spearman)

Hiromi Goh *(Gonza Sasano)*, Shima Iwashita *(Osai)*, Shohej Hino *(Bannojo
Kawazura)*, Misako Tanaka *(Oyuki)*, Haruko Kalo *(Oyaki's Governess)*, Takashi
Tsumura *(Ichinoshin Asaka)*, Kaori Mizushima *(Okiku)*.

A Japanese *jidai-geki* (period) film set during the Edo period. Goh stars as the
most handsome and trusted samurai of Tsumura, a shogun. While Tsumura is
away on a visit to the capital city, his wife, Iwashita, arranges for Goh to marry
her daughter, Mizushima, who loves him. Goh, however, is already betrothed to
the sister of a fellow samurai, but his ambition moves him to break off the
engagement. Goh looks forward to becoming a member of the shogun's family,
and he is desperate to learn the secrets of the special tea ceremony in which only
the truly privileged can participate. Worried that Goh will marry the other girl
instead, Iwashita impulsively agrees to show the samurai the tea ceremony before
the wedding in the hope that this will influence him to marry her daughter.
Iwashita is caught revealing the secrets (which is illegal) and soon rumors abound
that she and Goh have committed adultery. The couple are forced to flee the
castle, pursued by the shogun's samurai. Although the rumors are untrue, several
days on the run draw the man and woman to each other and they do make love.
Shortly thereafter, the couple is cornered by the samurai on a crowded bridge and
killed.

p, Kiyoshi Iwashita, Tomiyuki Motomochi, Masatake Wakita; d, Masahiro Shinoda; w, Taeko Tomioka (based on a play by Monzaemon Chikamatsu); ph,
Kazuo Miyagawa (Eastmancolor); m, Toru Takemitsu; ed, Sachiko Yamachi; set
d, Kiyoshi Awazu.

Drama **(PR:C-O MPAA:NR)**

YE SHAN (SEE: IN THE WILD MOUNTAINS, 1986, China)

YELLOW EARTH*** (1986, China) 89m World Entertainment Release c

Xue Bai *(Ciu Qiao)*, Wang Xueqi *(Gu Qing)*, Tan Tuo *(The Father)*, Liu Qiang
(Hanhan).

One of a handful of Chinese films made by a group of young directors labeled
"the fifth generation" to filter onto western screens. Originally made in 1984,
YELLOW EARTH first received recognition at the 1985 Hawaii Film Festival,
where it took prizes for Best Film and Best Cinematography. But Communist
Party officials decided it adversely portrayed China and refused to allow its entry
in any major festival. The film is set during the skirmishes between China and
Japan prior to WW II. Xueqi plays a communist soldier studying the local folk
songs in the Shaanxi province. He wanders into one village during the wedding
celebration of a 13-year-old girl to a much older man. The area is so impoverished that the people cannot afford to serve fish, the traditional wedding food.
Although they lack material wealth and are close to starvation because their land
is exhausted from centuries of planting, the people are rich in traditional folk
songs. Xueqi settles in the house of Tuo, a farmer who continues to plough his
barren land in the hope that this will reward him with a good crop. Along with
Tuo are his 10-year-old son, and 14-year-old daughter, Bai, rumored to have the
most beautiful voice in the province. The taciturn family slowly begins to open up
to Xueqi as he helps them with their chores, ploughing the land and helping Bai
carry buckets of water the mile and a half from the river. Xueqi explains to them
that it is the way of the Communist Party to work together, that the traditional
division of labor between men and women has become obsolete. He teaches
young Qiang the Communist Party song, and is even allowed to hear the father
bellow a sorrowful dirge when he sells his daughter. As Bai is of marriage age, her
father has searched for a worthy mate, one who will bring him a large dowry to
relieve his debt. Bai fearfully awaits the day when she will be forced to marry a
man she does not know, much less love. As Xueqi explains the equality to be

found as a member of the Communist Party, she begs him to take her away so
she can escape her unhappy fate. Xueqi refuses her request and leaves to rejoin
his troop. The two children desperately attempt to accompany him. He persuades
them to return home with promises of a quick return to take them away. But
before he can carry out his promise, Bai takes her ceremonial wedding vows.
With the ideals of a better life inside her head, she soon flees her husband to join
the army, only to drown in the rugged river she carelessly attempts to navigate.
Because the Chinese film industry has remained virtually unknown to western
audiences, films like YELLOW EARTH enter our theaters like a breath of fresh
air, offering revelations of a unique land and culture. Along with these fresh
insights comes an approach to the film medium that is a departure from the
western norm. In one sense, YELLOW EARTH has all the attributes of an old-
fashioned Hollywood drama, wallowing in sentimentality. Xeuqi is the perfect
rendering of the traditional hero, and the characters continuously burst into song
to explain story elements the plot fails to clarify. But a departure from this
format comes when Xueqi is unable to completely fulfill his role as the hero,
making YELLOW EARTH a sharp and subtle social satire with the early Communist Party as its victim. Xueqi has the chance to apply his abundance of
optimistic rhetoric to actually create change. But he backs down, like the political
party that promises to feed its starving people, but only provides ideals and not
food. The pacing is not above criticism as shots of the landscape, though immensely beautiful, are juxtaposed against one another without a sense of rhythm,
though this can be easily overlooked considering the many other fine attributes of
this film. The songs are all pleasing melodies never intruding into the plot, while
the colorful and exotic rituals are fascinating to western eyes.

d, Chen Kaige, w, Zhang Ziliang (based on a short essay "Sanwen" by Ke Lan);
ph, Zhang Yimou.

Drama **(PR:A MPAA:NR)**

YEOJAEUI BANRAN† (1986, S. Korea) c (Trans: Female Rebellion)

Jo Yon-Weon, Han Jin-Heui.

d, Kim Hyeong-myeong; w, Kang Jeong-su.

YES, DET ER FAR!† (1986, Den.) 81m Nordisk-Regnar Grasten-Per Holst
Filmproduktion-Danish Film Institute/Regnar Grasten c (Trans: Yes, It's Your
Dad)

Jarl Friis-Mikkelsen *(Carlo)*, Ole Stephensen *(Walter)*, Kirsten Rolffes *(Viola van
Heimweh)*, Ewa Carlsson *(Charlotta)*, Linda Lauersen *(Barbara)*, Flemming
[Bamse] Jorgensen *(Ewald)*, Erik Paaske, Jess Ingerslev *(Crooks)*, Claus Nissen
(The Bodyguard), Kirsten Lehfeldt, Preben Kristensen, Thomas Eje, Erik
Stephensen, Olaf Nielsen, Gerda Gilbo, Jorn Hjorting.

The sequel to the wildly successful (in Denmark, at least), if critically savaged,
WALTER & CARLO: OP PA FARS HAT, this film returns television stars Friis-
Mikkelsen and Stephenson in their neo-Lewis & Martin roles, this time getting
involved in smuggling coffee from Sweden.

p, Bo Christensen; d, John Hilbard; w, Jarl Friis-Mikkelsen, Ole Stephensen,
John Hilbard; ph, Claus Loof (Eastmancolor); m, Jan Glasel; ed, Edda Urup;
prod d, Henning Bahs; cos, Pia Myhrdal; spec eff, Henning Bahs.

Comedy **(PR:A MPAA:NR)**

YIDDISH CONNECTION† (1986, Fr.) 84m AFC-FR 3 Films-UGC-TOP
1-Cinergie/UGC c

Charlie Aznavour *(Aaron Rapoport)*, Ugo Tognazzi *(Moshe di Cremona)*, Andre
Dussollier *(The Seminarian)*, Vincent Lindon *(Zvi)*, Charlie Chemouny *(Samy)*,
Genevieve Minch, Roland Blanche, Jean-Claude Dauphin, Bill Dunn, Caroline
Chaniolleau, Alain Sarde, Jean-Francois Perrier, Alicia Alonso, Anne Berger.

In this comedy caper, based on a screen story by French singer-actor Charles
Aznavour, four Jewish men and a Catholic priest concoct an elaborate scheme to
heist the contents of a safe. Tognazzi (best known to American audiences for the
LA CAGE AUX FOLLES films) runs a delicatessen and wants some cash for his
family; Linden hopes to raise the money to pay for his girl friend's new nose; and
Chemouny is a would-be recording star. Aznavour is a junkman who becomes
involved with these characters. They hook up with Dussollier, a former safecracker who is now a man of the cloth. Together the group plans to break into a
safe stuffed with American bucks, hoping this will bring an end to their respective
money woes.

p, Maurice Bernart; d, Paul Boujenah; w, Didier Kaminka (based on a story by
Charles Aznavour); ph, Yves Dahan (Eastmancolor); m, George Garvarentz; ed,
Eva Zora; art d, Michele Abbe-Vannier.

Comedy/Crime **(PR:C-O MPAA:NR)**

YILANLARIN OCU† (1986, Turkey) Emek c (Trans: Revenge of the
Serpents)

Kadir Inanir, Serpil Cakmakli, Nur Surer, Fatma Girik.

d, Serif Goren; w, Yavuzer Gfetinkaya (based on a novel by Fakir Baykurt); ph,
Aytekin Cakmakci.

YOUNG COMPOSER'S ODYSSEY, A** (1986, USSR) 105m Gruzia c
(ACHALGAZRDA KOMPOZITORIS MOGZAUROBA)

Giya Peradze *(Leko Tatasheli)*, Levan Abashidze *(Nikusha Chachanidze)*, Zubar
Kipishidze *(Elisbar Chetereli)*, Rusudan Kvilvidze *(Thekla Chetereli)*, Ruslan
Mikaberidze *(Shalva Chetereli)*, Lili Yoseliani *(Elfimiya Chetereli)*, Teimuraz

Dshaparidze *(Georgi Ozcheli)*, Ketevan Orachelashvili *(Guranducht)*, Zinaida Kverenchchiladze *(Gulkan)*, Chabua Amiredshibi *(David Itrieli)*, Teimuraz Bichinashvili *(Rostom)*.

In 1907 pre-revolutionary Russia, a young musician sets out to document the folk songs of his country. During this journey he comes across many different people, both amusing and frightening. His tour is constantly overshadowed by the threat of Czarist troops roaming the countryside, looking for anyone who might pose a threat to the already precarious monarchy. In a horrifying mistake, the map of the student's journey is confused with a list of potential radicals. The people he has visited are put under arrest and killed, and the film ends with a mass seizure instigated by the Czar's men during a community religious celebration.

Though a potentially interesting idea, A YOUNG COMPOSER'S ODYSSEY suffers from a plodding development and several tiresome characters. The on-site locations are effectively used, however, accurately portraying the beauty of the Soviet countryside. (Film festival screening.)

d, Georgi Shengelaya; w, Erlom Achwlediani, Georgi Shengelaya (based on the novel *The Nameless Wind* by Otar Chcheidze); ph, Levan Paatashvili; m, Gustav Mahler; ed, S. Machaidze; set d, Boris Chakaya, Nikolai Shengelaya.

Drama (PR:O MPAA:NR)

YOUNG EINSTEIN†
(1986, Aus.) Einstein Entertainment c

Yahoo Serious, Odile Le Clezio, John Howard.

Serious (hardly his real name) wrote, directed, and stars in this comedy. He plays a young genius from Tasmania in the early 20th Century who comes up with the theory of relativity before Einstein and rock 'n' roll before Elvis.

p, Yahoo Serious, David Roach; d, Yahoo Serious; w, David Roach, Yahoo Serious; ph, Jeff Darling.

Comedy (PR:NR MPAA:NR)

YOUNGBLOOD**
(1986) 109m Guber-Peters/MGM-UA c

Rob Lowe *(Dean Youngblood)*, Cynthia Gibb *(Jessie Chadwick)*, Patrick Swayze *(Derek Sutton)*, Ed Lauter *(Coach Murray Chadwick)*, Jim Youngs *(Kelly Youngblood)*, Eric Nesterenko *(Blane Youngblood)*, George Finn *(Racki)*, Fionnula Flanagan *(Miss McGill)*, Ken James *(Frazier)*, Peter Faussett *(Huey)*, Walker Boone *(Assistant Coach)*, Keanu Reeves *(Hoover)*, Martin Donlevy *(Referee Hannah)*, Harry Spiegel *(Thunder Bay Coach)*, Rod Sapiensze *(Thunder Bay Assistant Coach)*, Bruce Edwards *(Thunder Bay Trainer)*, Lorraine Foreman *(Teacher)*, Catherine Bray, Jain Dickson *(Bar Girls)*, Barry Swatik *(Starting Guard)*, Michael Legros, Murray Evans *(Linesmen)*, Jason Warren, Warren Dukes, Sid Lynas *(Fans)*, Jamie McAllister, Jay Hanks. Frank Cini, Greg Salter, Howie McCarrol, Jr. *(Young Fans)*, Charlie Wasley *(Young Dean)*, Ricky Davis *(Young Kelly)*, Joe Bowen *(Radio Announcer)*, Peter Zezel, Kevin Hunter, Neil Trineer, Steve Thomas, Jules Jardine, Dave Sharp, Jeff Palmateer, Tim Salmon, Brian Meharry, Mark Laniel, Nick Calabrese, John Coranci, Claudic Russo, Bruno Pullara, Kevin Robinson, Rob Watson, Dave Mezzaros, Davin Kimber *(Hamilton Mustangs)*, James Richmond, Gerry Iuliano, Steve Torkos, Vito Cramarosa, Sebastiani Bianchi, Paul Cavalini, Andy Gribble, Johnny Braybrook, Don Campbell, Rick Dibiase, Steve Trearty, Fred Fioruni, Michael Winger *(Thunder Bay Bombers)*.

Though titled YOUNGBLOOD, the real name of this film is "More of the Same Old Thing." That all-too-familiar pattern of redemption through athletics as seen in such fare as the ROCKY films, THE KARATE KID, and AMERICAN FLYERS is reworked for brat packer Rob Lowe, who takes the part of an ice hockey

player. After being given the opportunity to try out for a semi-professional team, Lowe packs his things and leaves his father Nesterenko and brother Youngs. Once he hits the ice Lowe quickly makes an enemy of Finn, an overgrown, swarthy competitor with a penchant for severe body checking. Because Lowe is the faster of the two, he makes the team, while Finn is cut from the squad. Swayze, another team member, leads his fellow players in hazing Lowe, then proceeds to get the rookie plastered at a local bar. Romantic interest for the newcomer first arrives in the form of Flanagan, Lowe's sexually aggressive landlady. Next Lowe meets Gibb, the daughter of his coach Lauter. The two young

people hit it off, though Gibb is a bit hesitant about dating one of her father's players. This reluctance is soon shaken, and before long the kids are making love in Lowe's bedroom. In the meantime, Finn has been picked up by another team and now wants a little revenge. His underhanded tactics lead to an on-ice confrontation which results in a fractured skull for Swayze. Lowe decides to quit rather than fight, and returns to Nesterenko's farm. Youngs, a failed hockey player himself, is furious with Lowe for having given up such an opportunity. Faster than you can say "rock video montage," Youngs puts Lowe back in training and the newly determined lad returns to his old team just in time for The Big Game. Lowe takes revenge on Finn for the steel plate put in Swayze's head as result of Finn's actions, then scores the last-second game-winning goal, before finally skating a permanent way into Gibb's heart.

Lowe, whose good looks and unscarred face aren't exactly what you'd expect of a hockey player, is acceptable in the unchallenging lead role. YOUNGBLOOD is nothing more than a star vehicle for the young actor, and he does the job with

the proper amount of emotional angst and sultry good looks. Some of the supporting players, particularly Swayze and Youngs, give performances that are better than what the cliched material requires, though this doesn't give the story much of a lift. Nesterenko, the former Chicago Black Hawks star who makes an unremarkable acting debut in YOUNGBLOOD, also served as the film's hockey consultant. Markle's direction gives Lowe plenty of close-ups that look like a layout from the teenybopper magazine *Tiger Beat*. That's not too surprising considering that young adolescent females comprise the majority of Lowe's fans, yet the startlingly graphic sex scenes make YOUNGBLOOD questionable entertainment for its target audience. The encounter between Lowe and Gibb is simply gratuitous, an unneeded element that needlessly intrudes into the story. Like so many youth-oriented films, there's plenty of fancy backlighting, quickly cut montages, and a hard-pounding rock score. These techniques may be boring on the big screen, but cut down to MTV size, they well serve their purpose as promotional rock videos. Songs here include: "Ain't Gonna Walk the Line" (Tena Clark, performed by Kit Brooks), "I'm a Real Man" (John Hiatt, performed by Hiatt), "Soldier of Fortune" (Marc Jordan, John Capik, performed by Jordan), "Footsteps" (Nick Gilder, Jeff Silverman, performed by Gilder), "Something Real" (Richard Page, John Lang, Steve George, performed by Mr. Mister), "Don't Look Now" (William Orbit, Laurie Mayer, performed by Torch Song), "Winning Is Everything" (Steve Plunkett, Steve Lynch, Steven Isham, Keith Richards, Randy Rand, performed by Autograph), "On San Francisco Bay" (Max Hoffman), "Get Ready" (William [Smokey] Robinson, performed by Diana Ross and the Supremes), "Talk Me Into It" (Diane Warren, performed by Gloria Jones), "Cut You Down to Size" (Craig Chiquico, Mickey Thomas, performed by Starship), "Stand in the Fire" (Warren, performed by Thomas).

p, Peter Bart, Patrick Wells; d, Peter Markle; w, Markle (based on a story by Peter Markle, John Whitmore); ph, Mark Irwin (Metrocolor); m, William Orbit, Torchsong; ed, Stephen E. Rivkin, Jack Hofstra; art d, Alicia Keywan; set d, Angelo Stea; cos, Eileen Kennedy; m/l, Tena Clark, John Hiatt, Marc Jordan, John Capik, Nick Gilder, Jeff Silverman, Richard Page, John Lang, Steve George, William Orbit, Laurie Mayer, Steve Plunkett, Steve Lynch, Steven Isham, Keith Richards, Randy Rand, Max Hoffman, William [Smokey] Robinson, Dianne Warren, Craig Chiquico, Mickey Thomas; makeup, Kathleen Graham; stunts, Bobby Hannah; tech adv, Eric Nesterenko.

Sports/Drama Cas. (PR:O MPAA:R)

YU QING SAO†
(1986, Taiwan) 104m Cosmos c (Trans: Jade Love)

Yang Hulshan *(Yu Ch'ing)*, Ruan Shengtian *(Ch'ing-sheng)*, Ling Dingfeng *(Li Jung-jung)*, Fu Juan *(Chin Yen-fei)*.

A young boy (Ling) discovers that his new nanny (Yang) has a secret lover who is afflicted with ill health. Ling becomes a friend to the lover (Ruan) and introduces him to an actress acquaintance. Without trying, Ling has brought into Ruan's life the woman who will replace Yang. The distraught Yang kills Ruan then and herself.

p, Li Xing; d, Zhang Yi; w, (based on a short story by Bai Xianyong); ph, Lin Zirong; m, Zhang Hongyi; ed, Lin Shanliang; prod d, Zou Zhiliang; cos, Song Shu Lanying.

Drama (PR:O MPAA:NR)

YUME MIRUYONI NEMURITAI (SEE: TO SLEEP SO AS TO DREAM, 1986, Jap.)

YUPPIES, I GIOVANI DI SUCCESSO† (1986, It.) 96m Filmauro c (Yuppies, Youngsters Who Succeed)

Jerry Cala *(Gianluca)*, Christian De Sica *(Sandro)*, Massimo Boldi *(Lorenzo)*, Ezio Greggio *(Car Salesman)*, Corinne Clery *(Francoise)*, Federica Moro *(Magazine Editor)*, Sharon Gusberti *(Amanda)*, Valeria d'Obici *(Virginia)*, Guido Nicheli, Ugo Bologna, Cinzia de Ponti, Jinny Steffan, Manuela Romano, Renzo Marignano, Sergio Vastano, Hester Rode, Isaac George, Francesca Colombo.

Another in the long list of Italian sex comedies, this film focuses on the romantic escapades of four friends. De Sica and Boldi, married men with children, get the chance for some innocent skirt chasing when their families leave for a week's vacation. At the same time, Cala and Greggio are having their problems with members of the opposite sex. Several performers in this comedy hail from Italian television.

p, Luigi de Laurentiis, Aurelio de Laurentiis; d, Carlo Vanzina; w, Enrico Vanzina, Carlo Vanzina; ph, Luigi Kuveiller (Technicolor); m, Detto Mariano; ed, Raimondo Crociani.

Comedy (PR:O MPAA:NR)

Z

ZA KUDE PUTOVATE† (1986, Bulgaria) 90m Bulgariafilm c (Trans: Where Are You Going?)

Stoyan Alexiev, Georgi Kaloyanchev, Katerina Evro, Yossif Surchadijev.

A young scientist becomes disillusioned with his work, so he disappears under a table during a staff meeting, locks his wife out of their home, and throws out his telephone before leaving for the countryside. There he finds a remote village where he lives with a goatherd and lets his fancy run free, as he has done throughout the picture; this was all a withdrawal daydream fostered by the boring meeting.

d, Rangel Vulchanov; w, Georgi Danailov, Rangel Vulchanov; ph, Radoslav Spassov; m, Kiril Donchev; art d, Georgi Todorov.

Comedy (PR:C MPAA:NR)

ZA SRECU JE POTREBNO TROJE† (1986, Yugo.) 102m Jadran–Centar c (Trans: Three's Happiness)

Miki Manojlovic (*Drago*), Mira Furlan (*Zdenka*), Dubravka Ostojic (*Nina*), Bogdan Diklic (*Jozo*), Vanja Drach (*Ivan*), Ksenija Pajic (*Joagoda*).

After his release from prison, a man takes up residence with a female factory worker while he tries to regain his former love, now the mistress of a rich man.

p, Milan Samec; d, Rajko Grlic; w, Rajko Grlic, Dubravka Ugresic; ph, Zivko Zalar (Eastmancolor); m, Vlatko Stefanovski, Bogdan Arsovski; art d, Dinka Jericevic.

Drama/Comedy (PR:C MPAA:NR)

ZABRAVOTE TOZI SLOCHAI† (1986, Bulgaria) 100m Bojana Studio/ Bulgariafilm c (Trans: Forget That Case)

Filip Trifonov (*Magistrate Andreev*), Boris Loukanov (*Petrov*), Lyubomir Kabakchiev (*Sarafov*), Tsvetana Maneva (*Maria*), Ruth Spassova (*Petrov's Wife*), Tanya Shahova (*Elena*).

A young magistrate in a provincial town finds nothing but discouragement and stonewalling as he tries to discover why his predecessor has been imprisoned. Even the jailed man seems unwilling to assist the investigation.

d, Krassimir Spassov; w, Krassimir Spassov, Georgi Danailov (based on the stage play "The Autumn of an Investigating Magistrate" by Georgi Danailov); ph, Radoslav Spassov; m, Kiril Donchev; prod d, Georgi Todorov.

Drama (PR:C MPAA:NR)

ZABY A INE RYBY† (1986, Czech.) 71m Slovenska Filmova Tvorba Bratislava c

Branislav Kralik (*Martin Kovac*), Gabriela Skrabakova (*Lyda*), Martin Susina ("*Chrust*"), Peter Hain (*Jakub*), Igor Klacansky (*Karol*), Jindrich Khain (*Benko*), Imre Fazekas (*Hanus*), Peter Paulinyi (*Bozko*), Daniela Bambasova (*Letkova*), Peter Pilz (*Igor*), Rudolf Mancik (*Milan*), Ladislav Gegyi (*Dodo Janos*), Ladislav Pecho (*Juro Bilka*), Zuzana Husarova (*Kveta*), Jana Grmanova (*Zuzana*).

d, Julius Jarabek; w, Karol Hlavka, Jan Navratil; ph, Viktor Svoboda; m, Jan Lehotsky; ed, Roman Varga; art d, Jan Svoboda; cos, Tatiana Kovacevicova.

ZAKAZANE UVOLNENIE† (1986, Czech.) 79m Slovenska Filmova Tvorba Bratislava c

Ivan Romancik (*Karol Puffler*), Olga Solarova (*Eva Pufflerova*), Jan Kroner (*Igor Krska*), Karol Spisak (*Matasovsky*), Jan Gresso (*Trebaticky*), Martin Sulik (*Frco*), Ivona Krajcovicova (*Ivona*), Gabo Zelenay (*Coach Lisanik*), Ivan Matulik (*Valuch*), Pavol Mikulik (*Dr. Takac*), Milos Pietor (*Frank*).

d, Juraj Libosit; w, Dagmar Ditrichova, Peter Malec; ph, Vincent Rosinec; m, Pavel Danek, Gabor Presser; ed, Roman Varga; art d, Roman Rjachovsky; cos, Milos Pietor.

ZAKONNY BRAK† (1986, USSR) 93m Mosfilm c (Trans: Marriage of Convenience)

Natalia Belokhvostikova (*Olga*), Igor Kostolevsky (*Igor*).

Sent from Moscow to a remote town with his theater troupe, an actor falls in love with a nurse during the opening days of WW II, and since both want to return to Moscow—access to which is restricted to married couples—he proposes a marriage of convenience. Of course, true love blossoms just as the boy is sent off to the war.

d, Albert Mkrtchyan; w, Afanasy Belov; ph, Mikhail Koroptsov; m, Isaak Schwarz; prod d, Valentin Poliakov.

Romance/Drama (PR:C MPAA:NR)

ZANGIR† (1986, Pakistan) c (Trans: The Chain)

A young man takes on the corrupt establishment, killing all the people who wronged him. This is one of the few Pakistani films to be successful in its own country this year.

d, Pervaiz Malik.

Action/Drama (PR:C MPAA:NR)

ZAZZENNYJ FONAR† (1986, USSR) 87m Armenfilm c (Trans: The Lit Lantern)

Vladimir Kocarjan (*Vano*), Violeta Gevorkjan (*Vera*), Abesalom Loria (*Mkrtum*), Leonid Sarkisov (*Gasparelli*), Genrich Alaverdjan (*Bankutuzjan*), Karpos Martirosjan (*Pakule*).

Kocarjan is an impoverished pot-and-pan salesman whose passion for drawing loses him his job. Rather than tell his wife, he wanders the countryside with other salesmen, and eventually finds that his true calling is that of an artist. Based on the life of turn-of-the-century folk artist Vano Khodzhabekov.

d&w, Agasi Ajvazjan; ph, Levon Atojano; m, Tigran Mansurjan; art d, Grigor Torosjan.

Biography (PR:A MPAA:NR)

ZELENA LETA† (1986, Czech.) Barrandov c (Trans: Green Years)

Miroslav Noga, Lucie Noskova, Karel Chromik, Jiri Sedlacek.

d, Milan Muchna; w, Vladimir Tichy, Josef Silhavy, Milan Muchna; ph, Mahulena Bocanova.

ZIMNI VECHER V GAGRAKH† (1986, USSR) Mosfilm c (Trans: A Winter Night in Gagra)

Evgeny Evstigneev, Aleksandr Pankratov-Chyorny, Natalya Gundareva, Sergei Nikonenko, Pyotr Scherbakov.

A once-popular tap dancer is now relegated to teaching dance, but when television shows one of his old films, he is suddenly the object of widespread public acclaim.

d, Karen Shaknazarov; w, Aleksandr Borodyansky, Vladimir Shevtzik; m, Anatoly Kroll; art d, Valery Filipov.

Musical Comedy (PR:A MPAA:NR)

ZKROCENI ZLEHO MUZE† (1986, Czech.) 106m Barrandov c

Magda Vasaryova (*Tereza Burianova*), Karol Strasburger (*Tommi Donberg*), Nelly Gaierova (*Aunt Nelly*), Blanka Waleska (*Aunt Blanka*), Stella Zazvorkova (*Aunt Andulka*), Milos Kopecky (*Bayer*), Dagmar Veskrnova (*Krausova*), Jan Preucil (*Nadvornik*), Radoslav Brzobohaty (*Hradecky*), Julius Satinsky (*Viktor*), Vaclav Postranecky (*Mikes*), Sepp Laine (*Linkola*), Alp Suhonen (*Parkkinen*), Adriana Briedzinska (*Laura*).

d, Marie Polednakova; w, Krel Cop, Marie Polednakova; ph, Peter Polak; m, Michael Kocab; ed, Miroslav Hajek; art d, Jiri Matolin; cos, Libuse Prazakova.

ZONE ROUGE† (1986, Fr.) 114m Revcom-TF 1–AAA-Revcom c (Trans: Red Zone)

Sabine Azema (*Claire Rousset*), Richard Anconina (*Jeff Montellier*), Helene Surgere (*Claire's Mother*), Jacques Nolot (*Pierre Rousset*), Dominique Reymond (*Cheylard*), Pierre Frejek, Thierry Rode, Jean Reno, Bernard Freyd, Jean-Pierre Bagot, Philippe Vacher, Christin Pereira, Jean-Pierre Bisson, Henri Villon, Daniel Langlet, Jean Bouise.

Azema is a schoolteacher who pays a visit to her sickly ex-husband in a small village just outside Lyons. As with a number of other townsfolk, her ex-husband seems to have taken ill after drinking some tainted water. When much of the village is destroyed by fire and no proper explanation given, Azema grows suspicious. Together with insurance investigator Anconina, Azema learns that the water supply has been polluted with chemicals. Bit by bit, they uncover a wide-ranging scale of corruption that implicates many of the local authorities and endangers their own lives. The first film produced by Revcom Films, a newly-formed division of Editions Mondiales, a media and publishing enterprise in France.

p, Jean Bolvary; d, Robert Enrico; w, Robert Enrico, Alain Scoff (based on the novel *Brulez-les Tous* by G.J. Arnaud); ph, Didier Tarot (Fujicolor); m, Gabriel Yared; ed, Patricia Neny; art d, Jean-Claude Gallouin; spec eff, Georges Demetrau.

Thriller (PR:NR MPAA:NR)

ZONE TROOPERS† (1986) 88m Empire Pictures c

Tim Thomerson (*Sgt. Patrick "Sarge" Stone*), Timothy Van Patten (*Joey Verona*), Art La Fleur (*Cpl. George "Mittens" Mittinsky*), Biff Manard (*Dolan*), William Paulson (*The Alien*).

Imagine if you will an episode of the TV series "Combat" scrambled together with an episode of "The Outer Limits" and you'll have a good grip on this odd little low-budget item. The film takes place in 1944, somewhere on the Italian front. Thomerson is leading a platoon that's cut off behind the German lines, when they notice their radio and compasses going crazy. Later, a German ambush wipes out most of the men, leaving only Thomerson, Van Patten, La Fleur, and correspondent Manard. La Fleur and Manard are captured by the SS and taken to a small camp where they see a strange creature in a cage, an alien visitor. Meanwhile, Thomerson and Van Patten have discovered an enormous alien spacecraft half-buried in the ground. They sneak aboard and check it out and find a dead alien strapped in the pilot's seat, and the copilot's seat empty. Van Patten reads pulp science fiction magazines, so he immediately realizes what the ship is, but Thomerson thinks it's some new German secret weapon and, indeed, the Germans show up in force to investigate. Thomerson and Van Patten manage to blow up the ship and escape. Back at the SS camp, Hitler shows up to see for himself and La Fleur actually decks him before Thomerson and Van Patten turn up and free them, along with the alien creature. Later, with the Germans closing in on the fugitives and about to wipe them out, a huge ship lands and takes the alien aboard. The Americans plead for help against the superior German force, but the aliens refuse to get involved. Just when things look their blackest, though, the ship returns and zaps the Nazis with their ray gun. Van Patten is killed in the fighting, but the rest survive, agreeing that they can never tell this story.

The film gleefully joins two sets of cliches from two genres together. As a result, the science fiction elements suffer, and the aliens seem almost incidental to the war story. Thomerson does a good crusty sergeant and Van Patten is appealing as the bright-eyed kid who believes in such things. Production values are not so high and the film is barely convincing as a period piece, but the crashed spaceship is an impressive sight. The film's main problems are the lack of a strong central character and bad pacing, which makes for a rather dull movie.

p, Paul De Meo; d, Danny Bilson; w, Danny Bilson, Paul De Meo; ph, Mac Ahlberg (Technicolor); m, Richard Band; ed, Ted Nicolaou; spec eff, John Buechler.

Science Fiction/War   Cas.   (PR:A MPAA:PG)

ZONING*   (1986, Ger.) 89m Scala Z/Cine International c

Norbert Lamla, Hubertus Gertzen, Vernika Wolff, Rainer Frieb, Dieter Meier, Eleonore Weisgerber.

This film has pretensions of being a thrilling crime drama, but it is almost completely unwatchable because of ridiculous conception, a trite screenplay, lifeless acting, and inefficient technical attributes. Lamla and Gertzen are a pair of vengeance minded thieves who hide inside a large office building (the State of Illinois Building in Chicago), robbing people in elevators, washrooms, and hallways. The thieves had worked on the construction of the building so they know all the structure's intricacies. They were fired and have decided to seek revenge. The two spend four days inside the building without ever leaving. They use a room in the basement, which the building authorities know nothing about, as a hiding place. Never changing clothes and generally looking conspicuous, the pair somehow manage to escape detection by a complex security system. Wolff, one of the cleaning girls, uncovers their hiding place, but instead of reporting them she agrees to assist the thieves in return for part of their take. Dissatisfied with the bundle stolen from the building's inhabitants, Gertzen wants to tap into the computer system. To accomplish this, they must get some specific information from an office. While obtaining this information, they are spotted by a window washer. Lamla chases the worker and is wounded in a fight. By this time, leaving the building becomes more of a problem than anticipated and with Wolff's help one of them makes it out, hiding in a laundry delivery truck.

The makers of this movie obviously had very little knowledge of, or didn't care about, the art of making movies. The plot unfolds ludicrously, forcing situations just to make the movie last longer. In addition, all the signs are in English (the movie does take place in Chicago), while the characters only speak German. All in all, it's hard to watch this movie with a straight face, though it's supposed to be serious. Even the score by the usually quite good Tangerine Dream manages to be irritating. (In German; English subtitles.)

d, Ulrich Krenkler; w, Ulrich Krenkler, Angelika Hacker; ph, Nikolaus Starkmeth; m, Tangerine Dream; ed, Ute Albrecht-Lovell; art d, Thomas V. Klier, P. Ranody.

Crime   (PR:C MPAA:NR)

ZUODIAN YUANYANG   (SEE: CUODIAN YUANYANG, 1986, Hong Kong)

ZUGURT AGA†   (1986, Turkey) Mine c

Sen, Erdal Ozyagcilar, Nilgun Nazli, Can Kilukisa.

d, Nesli Colgecen; w, Yavuz Turgul; ph, Selcuk Taylaner.

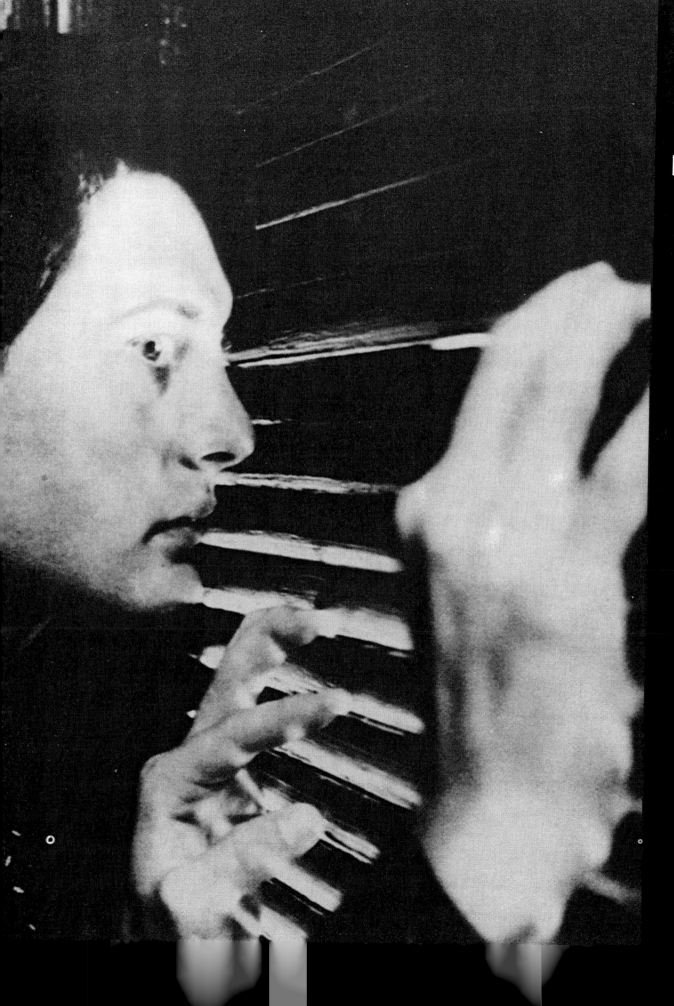

Allen

Benigni

Bonham Carter

JOAN ALLEN

As a veteran of Chicago's acclaimed Steppenwolf Theatre, JOAN ALLEN established herself as an actress of considerable depth and skill. After a small role in COMPROMISING POSITIONS (1985), Allen made her mark in movies this year with two very different performances. As the blind girl Reba in MANHUNTER, Allen brought new dimensions to the portrayal of the sightless. Aggressive, confident, and sexy, this blind woman is in control of her life and makes her own choices; her affliction is merely an inconvenience. The psychotic killer in MANHUNTER, Tom Noonan, is in awe of Allen, and it is she who seduces him. Although in the end she is victimized by Noonan, Allen's character is not made a victim because of her blindness. In a movie filled with fine acting, Allen's vivid performance nearly steals MANHUNTER. A few months later, Allen appeared again as one of Kathleen Turner's best friends in PEGGY SUE GOT MARRIED. Shown as a modest, proper, mature, and brainy high-schooler, Allen's character grows up to be the ideal housewife. She marries her high-school sweetheart, produces the proper number of children, and maintains a perfect household. Although her peers are getting divorced, finding careers, and leading more "exciting" life styles, Allen is perfectly content and happy in her chosen role as wife and mother. In a time when such characters are looked upon as victims or merely unenlightened, Allen plays the part with an appealing elegance, confidence, and compassion. Her sublime performance makes the other women in the film appear mystified by life's choices, while she knew exactly what she wanted all along. As an actress, Allen is able to convey the essence of her characters and turn them into completely captivating human beings.

ROBERTO BENIGNI

A household name in Italy, this 34-year-old native of Tuscany was a complete unknown in America until this year. Benigni played his first role at age 16 when he walked on stage during a political rally and pretended to be a candidate, getting the attention of a number of television cameras. As a result, Benigni was asked to join an experimental theater troupe in Rome. A film career eventually followed when he took a role in a film by Bernardo Bertolucci's brother Giuseppe (BERLINGUER, TI VOGLIO BENE). He has appeared in six other Italian films, including LA LUNA by Bernardo Bertolucci and a documentary about himself entitled TUTTOBENIGNI. He has also directed two films, TU MI TURBI in 1981 and NON CE RESTA CHE PIANGERE in 1984. Starring as, appropriately enough, an Italian immigrant in Jim Jarmusch's DOWN BY LAW, Benigni has taken American film audiences by storm. His hilarious performance is the highlight of the film and depends on a brilliant sense of comic timing, a wonderfully expressive face, and a humorous massacre of the English language. Arriving in New Orleans for his first day of shooting, Benigni reportedly knew only one word of English, a handicap for some but for him an advantage. In the film, his character carries a pocket-sized spiral notebook in which he scribbles down a variety of English phrases such as "Buzz off" and "I am a good egg." In real life, this notebook was an actual source for Benigni, containing many phrases Jarmusch taught him. The initial meeting between Jarmusch and Benigni took place at a film festival in Salsomaggiore where Jarmusch was showing his previous picture, STRANGER THAN PARADISE. Able to communicate only in broken French, the two hit it off and agreed to work together. The result was superb, and will, it's hoped, set the stage for American audiences to see more of Benigni.

LEOS CARAX [Alex Dupont]

The most interesting new director to come out of France since Jean-Jacques Beineix (DIVA, and this year's BETTY BLUE), the 26-year-old Carax first received international attention in 1985 with his stark black-and-white romantic tale BOY MEETS GIRL. Employing many of the stylistic techniques introduced by the French New Wave directors—Jean-Luc Godard, Francois Truffaut, and others—and with much the same energy, Carax has made it clear that he is a directorial force to be noticed, one willing to take cinematic chances. His new film, MAUVAIS SANG ("Bad Blood"), is a pulp-novelish, mythical tale of an unnamed fatal disease which is contracted by "making love to those you don't love." The thinly veiled disease is AIDS, but Carax's interests are more romantic than social. Like those directors who have influenced him, Carax is a romantic whose films revolve around lovers. Rather than tell a simple love story by traditional means, however, Carax invents as he goes along. In the same way that lovers disregard the world around them, so does Carax disregard filmmaking rules. Godard, apparently recognizing Carax's talents, has cast him as an actor in his upcoming adaptation of Shakespeare's "King Lear."

HELENA BONHAM CARTER

Another overnight success story, the 20-year-old Bonham Carter is a superb actress who has arrived on the international scene this year without any previous film credits to her name (as Marlee Matlin, Beatrice Dalle, Cathy Tyson, and Catherine Mouchet have done). A Londoner, Bonham Carter is the great-grand-daughter of former British Prime Minister Henry Asquith and the great-niece of film director Anthony Asquith. Studying at Westminster, Bonham Carter had little intention of pursuing an acting career until one of her teachers talked her into it. She appeared only in school productions until being cast in a television play entitled "A Pattern of Roses." When Trevor Nunn saw her he tried to cast her in the lead role in LADY JANE. At first, she held firm to her plans to attend a university, but eventually Nunn persuaded her to play the role of England's legendary Lady Jane Grey, who ruled her country for nine days before being executed. Although she was exceptional—combining a childlike innocence with an air of royalty—the film couldn't find an audience. On the last day of shooting, however, director James Ivory spotted Bonham Carter and cast her as the lead in his upcoming film A ROOM WITH A VIEW. Although she was excellent in both roles, and although A ROOM WITH A VIEW earned eight Oscar nominations, Bonham Carter came away without even a nomination. There can be little doubt, however, that she'll soon get all the attention that she deserves.

BEATRICE DALLE

Playing the title character in the latest Jean-Jacques Beineix film, BETTY BLUE, Dalle has entered the international film scene with the same eye-popping intensity as Brigitte Bardot in . . . AND GOD CREATED WOMAN in 1956. A French sex-kitten of mythical proportions, the 21-year-old Dalle had no previous film experience. Born in Brest and raised in Le Mans, she moved to Paris, lived the bohemian life of a young punk in and around the Les Halles area, and married at age 18. While crossing the Place de la Republique, Dalle was spotted by a photographer who took a series of shots of her. Later, while casting BETTY BLUE, Dominique Besnehard saw Dalle's face on a magazine cover. Beineix was won over by her wide eyes and exotic mouth. "She has this gift," Beineix has said, "this blessing of being able to appear and exist in front of the camera without doing or saying anything, simply being herself." People seem to agree with Beineix's description: BETTY BLUE was France's eighth most successful film at the box office in 1986 and earned Dalle a Best Actress nomination at the

French Cesars. She has since appeared in a French crime picture (appropriately cast as a famed French actress) entitled ON A VOLE CHARLIE SPENCER!

DANIEL DAY LEWIS

The grandson of one-time Ealing Studio head Sir Michael Balcon, and the son of Poet Laureate C. Day Lewis and actress Jill Balcon, Daniel Day Lewis crossed the Atlantic on film with a rather loud stateside bang this year. Both films he appeared in found wide, though varied, audiences. A ROOM WITH A VIEW reached a large commercial audience, earning eight Oscar nominations, while MY BEAUTIFUL LAUNDRETTE found its niche in lengthy art house runs. Playing a homosexual young tough with bleached hair in LAUNDRETTE, Day Lewis struck a very different pose in ROOM as a rich, repressed dilettante. Day Lewis didn't originally plan to enter acting. After running away from school at age 13, he followed his sister's lead and went to school at Beadales. Following the advice of his grandfather, who encouraged his acting career, he joined the Bristol Old Vic. He has since appeared in a number of British stage plays, including "A Midsummer Night's Dream" (in the West End), "Look Back In Anger" and "Dracula" (with the Little Theater Company), "Another Country" (at the Queen's Theater), and "Romeo and Juliet" (with the Royal Shakespeare Company). His film career dates to 1982 with a small role in GANDHI and another in 1984's THE BOUNTY, as well as a BBC television film entitled, A FROST IN MAY. Day Lewis is one of a number of young British actors who, with the recent rejuvenation of British cinema, are rising to the top, including Tim Roth, Tracy Ullman, Helena Bonham-Carter, Gary Oldman, and Cathy Tyson.

LUCY DEAKINS

In THE BOY WHO COULD FLY, Lucy Deakins gave a

multifaceted performance as a young girl faced with complex, and often overwhelming, emotions. In a single role, Deakins had to deal with an autistic neighbor, a father's suicide, responsibilities in caring for her younger brother, her newly discovered sexuality, and the realities of being a lonely kid in a strange environment. Such an intricate part would be demanding for any actress, but Deakins was faced with a further challenge, as the success of the film's unique story depended largely on her ability to carry the majority of scenes. This difficult task was accomplished with beautiful sensitivity by Deakins, who showed an incredible emotional range within her performance. Born on December 18, 1970, Deakins took up acting at age 11. Her teacher was highly impressed with Deakins' natural abilities, and though the girl was only in the class for a day, she was sent to audition for the prestigious New York Circle Repertory Theatre. Deakins was cast in the play "So What Are We Going to Do Now?," a part of the Circle Repertory's Young Playwright's Festival, then won a small part on the daytime television soap opera "As the World Turns." Despite this hectic life, Deakins kept up her high-school studies full time and maintained an A average. The daughter of a New York University Shakespeare teacher and a Columbia University sociolinguistics professor, Deakins followed THE BOY WHO COULD FLY with a part in "The Hands of Its Enemy," a new play by CHILDREN OF A LESSER GOD's author Mark Medoff.

KEVIN DILLON

The younger brother of actor Matt Dillon, 20-year-old KEVIN DILLON originally wanted to study art, but when an agent spotted him at a premiere of Matt's film TEX, Kevin's acting career began. Prominently featured as the school bully in last year's Catholic school comedy HEAVEN HELP US, Dillon went on to appear in Oliver Stone's Vietnam film PLA-

Dalle

Day Lewis

Deakins

Dillon

Friels

Gibb

TOON. Although it is difficult to single out one performance from a superb ensemble supporting cast, Dillon is unforgettable as the teenage soldier "Bunny," a dim-witted, totally amoral creature who sees the war as a place to have a good, uninhibited time. His matter-of-fact attitude toward death and his wanton murder of a retarded Vietnamese civilian is hideous, pathetic, and terribly sad. Dillon proves himself a skillful actor here, for he manages to convey the lamentable ignorance of his character without ever becoming condescending or judgmental. As horrible as he may be, Bunny is always shown to be a human being, and never a stereotypical monster. Bunny is a tragic character because he has become so warped and aberrant while still in his teens. Although the war has become his playground, Bunny was spawned in the United States and he is America's nightmare. With both HEAVEN HELP US and PLATOON, Dillon has shown that he can take basically unsympathetic parts and inject a sense of understanding and vulnerability (usually masked by bravado) into the characters, making them much more vivid than if they had been played in a more conventional manner. His insightful and intelligent approach to his performances indicates that Dillon is capable of playing much more than a swaggering young brute, and this young actor should be given a chance to expand his repertoire.

JACK EPPS, JR. and JIM CASH

TOP GUN was the most successful movie of 1986, catapulting the team of Jack Epps, Jr. and Jim Cash to the first ranks of screenwriters despite a cliche-ridden script and shallow characters. A couple of months after that film's Spring release, LEGAL EAGLES hit the theaters with Robert Redford, Daryl Hannah, Debra Winger, and another Cash-Epps screenplay, and the two were firmly entrenched, wildly successful (those two films earned the pair in the neighborhood of $2 million), and had another script in production (THE SECRET OF MY SUCCESS). All this, and the two have seen each other only twice in the last ten years. They met in 1971 when Epps joined a Michigan State University screenwriting class taught by Cash. The teacher was impressed by Epps' talent, and within a couple of years Epps was writing for television in Hollywood. In 1976 he was on a motorcycle trip across the country and he stopped in East Lansing to talk to his old teacher. Over a bowl of chili in the student cafeteria they worked out ten script ideas, then returned to their respective homes most of a continent away from each other to work on them. Using computer modems to zap each day's work to the other, and racking up $1000 phone bills, they had soon written and sold five scripts, none of them produced (including the increasingly remote-looking DICK TRACY for Warren Beatty). Now successful, they show little inclination to change their working methods. Cash still teaches at Michigan State and concentrates on the dialog (a skill he learned by listening to audio tapes of classic films), while Epps stays in Los Angeles participating in meetings and working out structure. When the two met face-to-face some time ago for the first time in years, Cash brought along a pair of telephones so the two could talk to each other in the way they always have.

COLIN FRIELS

An extremely versatile actor, Friels appeared in two films this year, in roles which are polar opposites. In MALCOLM (the better of the two), Friels plays a reckless, lovable, mischievous social misfit who understands everything about technology and very little about people. In KANGAROO, a bearded Friels plays the fictionalized persona of British author D.H. Lawrence during his short stay in Australia in 1922. While his role in KANGAROO is miscast and strangely under-written, Friels does the best he can with it. It is in MALCOLM that Friels shines. Finishing his studies at Australia's National Institute of Dramatic Art in 1976, Friels appeared in theater, television, and film, being widely sought after in all three mediums. His theatrical work includes "Hamlet," "Macbeth," and "The Man From Muckinupin" (for the Sydney Theater Company), and "King Lear" and "Zastrozzi" (for the Nimrod Theater Company). He appeared in five Australian films before 1986, including BUDDIES and MONKEY GRIP (both 1983). It is for his work in MALCOLM that Friels received his most attention, including a Best Actor award from the Australian Film Institute. Upon the completion of his two pictures this year, Friels returned to the stage to star opposite Lauren Bacall in the Tennessee Williams play "Sweet Bird Of Youth."

CYNTHIA GIBB

Although she struggled mightily to inject some flair into two of the year's more dismal efforts, YOUNGBLOOD and MODERN GIRLS, she was unable to overcome their insipid concepts. In SALVADOR, however, she emerged as a completely different actress. Her startling maturity and confidence as the likable Catholic layperson drew viewers to her like a magnet, and the fact that she was one of the few wholly sympathetic characters in the film added greatly to her appeal. Gibb plays the ill-fated character (she is later raped and murdered by a Salvadoran death squad) as a dedicated, compassionate, and very earnest young woman, yet she is charmed by James Woods' sleazy journalist and seems to be genuinely fond of him. Her optimistic view of Woods as a redeemable soul helps the audience warm up to his dislikable character. If Gibb can find some good in him, perhaps he isn't so bad after all. Gibb transforms what could have been a mundane role—that of innocent victim—into that of a complex, vivid individual whom viewers really care about. It would have been easy to play the part as a devoted saint who thinks of nothing other than her mission to help the poor and oppressed, but Gibb injects a subtle sensuality into the character, thus making her more human. It is a performance that promises good things to come. The daughter of a ballet instructor (her mother), Gibb studied dance and voice and worked as a model while still in her teens. Woody Allen spotted her picture in a fashion magazine and cast her in a small role in STARDUST MEMORIES. From there Gibb appeared for two years as "Suzi Wyatt Carter" on the daytime soap opera "Search For Tomorrow" before joining the cast of the syndicated television program "Fame" and from there finding her way back into feature films via YOUNGBLOOD.

KERRI GREEN

Appearing last year in supporting roles in both THE GOONIES and SUMMER RENTAL (as John Candy's daughter), Green, a 19-year-old redhead hailing from Woodcliffe Lake, New Jersey has finally received a chance to prove her talents in a worthwhile film. As the best friend of young Corey Haim in this year's LUCAS, Green played a teenager trapped between her friendship with Haim and her blossoming romance with Charlie Sheen. Looking like a real teenager (rather than one of the pre-packaged cutouts that appear in so many Hollywood productions), Green is wholly convincing in her role. With only a minimum of acting experience, Green is able to draw on her real life as a teenager. Her first step towards acting was in a junior high school version of "You're a Good Man, Charlie Brown," in which she was cast as . . . Woodstock!—a far cry from the charming teenager in LUCAS. A high school gymnast, Green pursued a modeling career in New York, receiving some bit parts on daytime TV soaps before landing her role in THE GOONIES.

Rather than running off to Hollywood, Green has chosen to juggle her film career with her Ivy League studies, a decision that will undoubtedly help her bring even more realism to her future roles.

HEMDALE

While it is unusual to single out an entire production company for an accolade, Hemdale, an independent British company, has taken some unusual chances recently and produced some of the best films of the year. With producer John Daly at the helm— with assistance from Gerald Green, Derek Gibson, and American Arnold Kopelson— Hemdale has produced a string of impressive films notable for their serious, important, and challenging subject matter. Early in 1986, both Oliver Stone's powerful drama about turmoil in Central America, SALVADOR, and James Foley's disturbing crime film, AT CLOSE RANGE, were released. Although both films met with mixed reviews and poor box office, they were among the most unique and affecting films of the year and neither would have been produced by a Hollywood studio (the screenplay for AT CLOSE RANGE bounced around for years without a taker). Then came PLATOON, Oliver Stone's intensely personal look at the Vietnam war from a "grunt's-eye-view." Again, Stone's screenplay passed through the Hollywood halls for nearly *a decade*, before the writer-director presented it to Hemdale after they had produced his film SALVADOR. Hemdale went to bat for Stone once again and this time it paid off both artistically and financially. PLATOON was hailed as the best film of the year, won four Oscars—including Best Picture, and became one of the top box office draws of the year. Also appearing late in 1986 from Hemdale was HOOSIERS, the sensitive look at small town basketball starring Gene Hackman, Barbara Hershey, and Dennis Hopper, who won an Oscar nomination for his performance (AT CLOSE

RANGE, PLATOON, and HOOSIERS were released in the U.S. by Orion). Begun in 1967 by Daly in partnership with actor David Hemmings (who dropped out in 1976, leaving Daly as sole proprietor), Hemdale currently has more than $100 million invested in productions. It appears that Hemdale is continuing a string of challenging, controversial films, for in 1987 RIVER'S EDGE, a disturbing look at modern American teenagers, is to be released by Island Pictures, another brave distributor working independent of Hollywood.

Green

PAUL HOGAN

One man is singlehandedly responsible for raising Australian tourism 40 percent ("I'll slip another shrimp on the barbie"), creating the most successful television show in Australian history ("The Paul Hogan Show," syndicated in 24 countries), and creating the most successful foreign film ever released in the U.S., the most successful film in Australian history, the most successful fall release ever, and the second most successful film of 1986 (after TOP GUN), CROCODILE DUNDEE. Of course, we're talking Paul Hogan (or "Hoges" to his Australian fans). Hogan spent years drifting through a series of blue-collar jobs, ending with working as a rigger on a bridge over Sydney harbor. On a dare from coworkers, he went on the TV show "New Faces," a vicious version of "The Gong Show." Billing himself as a tap-dancing, blindfolded knife thrower, Hogan walked out on stage, dropped his knives to the floor, and began lambasting the judges. He was an overnight smash, and was soon doing a regular spot on a news show in which he would attack anything that came into his head. People driving over the still-under-construction bridge would stop to look for Hogan, still working the rigging. Eventually he took on his own show, then tackled a series of specials before doing DUNDEE with much of the same crew with which he has always

Hogan

Kensit

worked. In that film he plays an Outback guide and adventurer (and part-time poacher) who is brought to New York by a journalist, and once there proves to be a good man in any world. While hardly a sophisticated comedy, CROCODILE DUNDEE hit a chord with audiences around the world and became a phenomenon. A national institution in Australia, Hogan is certainly the Australian best-known to the rest of the world, and the inevitable-looking CROCODILE DUNDEE II (for which Hogan admits to working on a script, but to which he still will not commit) will probably cement that reputation.

PATSY KENSIT

The 17-year-old star of ABSOLUTE BEGINNERS, this energetic and alluring blonde-haired beauty is no stranger to films. In 1974 when she was just a tot, she played Pamela Buchannan in THE GREAT GATSBY. In 1976, she played opposite Elizabeth Taylor, Jane Fonda, and Ava Gardner in George Cukor's film, THE BLUE BIRD. After her 1979 role in the Harrison Ford picture, HANOVER STREET, Kensit spent her time in television. Concentrating on a musical career in a band called Eighth Wonder (which she formed with her brother), Kensit is gaining some attention in England, and a song she penned and sings, "Having It All," is featured in ABSOLUTE BEGINNERS. Kensit simply burns up the screen with her presence in the film, completely capturing the elusive, wild, headstrong character of "Crepe Suzette" as Colin MacInnes (the author of the original 1959 novel) wrote it. When she needs to play sultry, she does just that. When the role calls for cute, tough, or romantic, she seems to perform effortlessly. It's not as if Kensit is playing Suzette, but as if MacInnes wrote Suzette as Kensit. Her most spectacular scene has her working behind the scenes of a ritzy fashion show until she gets her chance to show off her new, improvised-on-the-spot fashions, dancing across the stage with unharnessable energy. If Kensit doesn't continue in films, it will only be because her success as a singer will get in the way.

HANIF KUREISHI

Born in 1956, Kureishi is a rising British playwright born of a Pakistani father and an English mother. When he was 18, his first play was performed at the Royal Court Theatre (to earn a living, he spent his free time writing pornography under a pseudonym). He continues to work in the theater, having written "The Mother Country" (for the Riverside Theatre), "Outskirts" (for the Royal Shakespeare Company), "Borderline" (for the Royal Court), and adapted Bertolt Brecht's "Mother Courage" (for both Radio Three and the Royal Shakespeare Company). In 1985, he was approached by Channel Four TV to contribute a script to their heralded "Films on Four" series. After visiting Pakistan, Kureishi returned with the script that would eventually be made by Stephen Frears as MY BEAUTIFUL LAUNDRETTE. Released theatrically (rather than solely on TV), the film deals with a subject close to Kureishi —the identity crisis of being half Pakistani and half English. As racial tensions and class inequities between the two have been explosive, the conflict of dual loyalties is central to his work. The combination of Kureishi's brave, honest script and Frears' gutsy, electric direction has resulted in one of the better British films of late. With the published screenplay of MY BEAUTIFUL LAUNDRETTE, and an autobiographical essay entitled *The Rainbow Sign*, Kureishi has found acclaim in the U.S. He received an Oscar nomination for his script. His next project is another collaboration with Frears, again dealing with the Pakistani-England conflict, entitled SAMMY AND ROSIE GET LAID.

ED LACHMAN

A 38-year-old native of New Jersey, Lachman has been involved in film all his life (his father owned a movie theater), but has only recently begun to make a name for himself. Although he has photographed films for two New Yorkers recently—David Byrne's TRUE STORIES this year and Susan Seidelman's DESPERATELY SEEKING SUSAN in 1985—Lachman's previous involvement in film was with European directors. After spending a year at Harvard, Lachman studied French at the University of Tours before finally earning a Bachelor of Fine Arts degree in painting at Ohio University. It was German director Werner Herzog who gave him his first film break, employing him as cameraman on his documentaries HOW MUCH WOOD WOULD A WOODCHUCK CHUCK? (1975-6) and LA SOUFRIERE (in which Lachman photographed from the mouth of a live volcano) and on the feature film STROSZEK (with Lachman doing the American photography). Lachman's list of film credits (as assistant or second-unit camera) reads as a veritable who's-who of great directors—Wim Wenders' LIGHTNING OVER WATER (a documentary, of sorts, on director Nicholas Ray), TOKYO-GA (a documentary on Yasujiro Ozu) and THE AMERICAN FRIEND; Jean-Luc Godard's PASSION; Bernardo Bertolucci's LA LUNA, and Nicholas Roeg's INSIGNIFICANCE. With TRUE STORIES, Lachman's talent is clearly in the forefront. A mediocre film, TRUE STORIES received much of its praise because of its "look"—a high-gloss Polaroid snapshot view of America. Using bright primary colors, and a primitive rear screen projection technique, Lachman gave the film much of its style. The rock-video portions of the film came easily to Lachman, as he had already worked in that genre for The Rolling Stones, Tina Turner, and Elvis Costello. One of the most technically and compositionally inventive cinematographers at work today, Lachman surely will continue to impress.

DALE LAUNER

With RUTHLESS PEOPLE, his first produced screenplay, Dale Launer showed a real gift for comedy construction as he skillfully wove together a variety of characters and subplots, while incorporating seemingly throwaway details into the film's intricate plot. His combination of a millionaire lout, his boorish wife, two down-and-outers, a serial killer, blackmail, kidnaping, and cheap clown masks (among other surprises) wasted nothing, creating a wild farce that took twist after unexpected twist. Launer's background is somewhat eclectic; he studied a variety of subjects at California State University during the 1970s before winding up in the school's film program. The original story for RUTHLESS PEOPLE was penned in 1980, while Launer supported himself through a variety of odd jobs including automobile restoration and stereo sales (the latter occupation was held by Judge Reinhold's character in the film). A later draft was read by executive producers Richard Wagner and Joanna Lancaster, who fell in love with the project. They approached the directing team of Jim Abrahams, David Zucker, and Jerry Zucker (AIRPLANE!, TOP SECRET), with whom Wagner had previously worked, and the three were equally enthused with Launer's work. Although RUTHLESS PEOPLE's classic narrative structure was far removed from their well-known scattershot joke style, Abrahams and the Zuckers felt this would be an excellent change of pace for them, and agreed for the first time to do someone else's script. Unlike their other films, in RUTHLESS PEOPLE there was little improvisation on set, a direct result of Launer's elaborate plot development.

SPIKE LEE
[Shelton Jackson Lee]

Making his independent film SHE'S GOTTA HAVE IT on a microscopic budget, 29-year-old Spike Lee has made a thundering entrance into the Hollywood perspective. A graduate of New York University, Lee first gained attention with his award-winning student film JOE'S BED STUY BARBERSHOP: WE CUT HEADS. When no offers from Hollywood followed, Lee decided to direct, write, and star in his own independent feature. He prepared "Messenger" for production, a story of a black Brooklyn family whose main character was a bicycle messenger. With $18,000 from the New York State Council for the Arts, and $20,000 from the American Film Institute, Lee was ready. Last minute changes resulted in Lee's decision to film SHE'S GOTTA HAVE IT instead. When the AFI withdrew its grant, Lee was forced to scrounge money wherever he could find it. With a shooting schedule of only 12 days, Lee completed the project. The result is one of the year's freshest, most ebullient films, both technically innovative and brutally funny. Not only has Lee found critical and popular acclaim, thereby assuring himself further attention, but he has also made strong headways as a black filmmaker. Countering the cockeyed look at black culture that Steven Spielberg foisted upon the public in THE COLOR PURPLE, Lee brings his culture to the screen in an honest manner. His next film, a musical at an all-black college in Atlanta, has a considerably larger budget, $3,000,000, and the backing of a major distributor in Island Pictures. There is no doubt that Lee will be a driving force in American filmmaking; the only question is whether he will continue to spend as much time in front of the camera as he does behind it.

RAY LIOTTA

The most startling big-screen debut of the year belongs to Ray Liotta, the actor who played Melanie Griffith's estranged ex-con husband Ray Sinclair in Jonathan Demme's quirky SOMETHING WILD. It is Liotta's creepy charm and volatile demeanor that suddenly twists Demme's screwball comedy into a des-

Lee

Liotta

perate life-or-death struggle. Liotta's powerful performance commands the last half of the film, but he does not play the character as a monster. Rather, Liotta infuses his dangerous ex-con with an intelligence, a sense of humor, and a subtle sadness not found in most villainous portrayals. Liotta's Ray is an outsider who returns from prison to find his wife with another man and who tries to get her back the only way he knows how—by force. Liotta plays Ray as a human being—albeit a dangerous one—and to some extent we have all known someone like him. A native of New Jersey, Liotta studied acting at the University of Miami where he played a variety of roles including Stanley in "A Streetcar Named Desire," and George in "Of Mice and Men." After graduating, Liotta made the rounds in New York and wound up serving drinks during intermission for the Shubert organization. Eventually, Liotta landed a regular role as "Joey Perrini" in the television soap-opera "Another World"—a part he played for three years. Movie roles proved elusive, however. At college, Liotta met and became close friends with another young actor, Steven Bauer (who would later go on to star opposite Al Pacino in SCARFACE). Bauer later married actress Melanie Griffith (daughter of Tippi Hedren), and when director Demme cast Griffith, Liotta saw his chance for a movie role and read for the role of Ray. Demme called the actor on Superbowl Sunday to tell him he got the part. Liotta garnered raves for his performance in SOMETHING WILD (even from those who didn't care for the film), which would seem to ensure that this exciting young actor will be around for quite some time.

MARY ELIZABETH MASTRANTONIO

A veteran stage actress who had appeared in a number of musicals, including "Amadeus," Mary Elizabeth Mastrantonio was no novice when she played the part of Al

Mastrantonio

Matlin

Oldman

Pacino's sister in Brian De Palma's bloody SCARFACE (1983). Unfortunately, her solid performance was practically buried beneath a hail of cocaine and gunfire in that bloated gangster epic. Mastrantonio's next major appearance was on the small screen as Fascist dictator Benito Mussolini's daughter Edda in the ABC mini-series "Mussolini" starring George C. Scott. Again, Mastrantonio's talents were hidden by tedious excess. Finally, the actress was given a role that would display her considerable skills, that of Carmen, Tom Cruise's manipulative girl friend, in Martin Scorsese's THE COLOR OF MONEY. On screen with Paul Newman through the majority of the film, Mastrantonio more than holds her own. Tough, clever, and very sexy, Carmen is a survivor who uses her confident facade to cover her inexperience and vulnerability. She shamelessly manipulates the dim-witted Cruise character to her advantage and even tries to hustle the hustler himself, Newman. She and Newman share a passion for money that transcends mere emotion and they work together in an attempt to control their meal-ticket, Cruise. Mastrantonio brings great insight, style, and sensitivity to a role that could easily have become boorish and unsympathetic. A native of Oak Park, Illinois (a Chicago suburb), Mastrantonio was quite at home in THE COLOR OF MONEY, for it was shot in and around the Windy City. Mastrantonio's adept performance earned her an Oscar nomination for Best Supporting Actress.

MARLEE MATLIN

Despite a lack of professional experience or years of training, Marlee Matlin brought depth and raw honesty to her Oscar-winning role in CHILDREN OF A LESSER GOD. Barely out of her teens when shooting began, this deaf actress gave a fiery performance which belied her youth. Matlin—who was born and raised in the north suburbs of Chicago—was struck by roseola (also known as "baby measles") when she was just eighteen months old. The illness left her with only twenty percent hearing in her left ear, and total deafness in her right. As a child, Matlin attended schools for the hearing-impaired, and also became involved with the Children's Theater of the Deaf. Her acting talents blossomed and she was awarded lead roles in such productions as "The Wizard of Oz," "Peter Pan," and "Mary Poppins." Matlin then attended John Hersey High School in Arlington Heights, Illinois, where she participated in the institution's program for the hearing-impaired. Matlin's interest in theater never waned, and though she attended college under a criminal law program, Matlin eventually auditioned for a production of "Children of a Lesser God," staged by Chicago's much-praised Immediate Theater Company. Matlin received a secondary role, and a videotape of this professional debut eventually led to her being cast in the film's lead opposite William Hurt. In addition to her versatility with sign language, Matlin is able to speak, and is an accomplished lip reader. Her natural gift for acting overcomes her physical disabilities, and Matlin's sensual looks are well-graced by the movie camera. Although CHILDREN OF A LESSER GOD gave Matlin a true-to-life role, her performance could signal a breakthrough for handicapped actors. Given someone of Matlin's talents, roles usually assigned to able-bodied players could conceivably be rewritten to accommodate a disabled performer, as was the case with arthritis-crippled Lionel Barrymore years before.

CATHERINE MOUCHET

Cast as one of the most beloved saints in religious history, the 27-year-old Mouchet —in her film debut—gave such a remarkable interpretation of the role that she helped carry the film (THERESE) to international success. A stage actress at the Conservatoire National d'Art Dramatique in Paris, Mouchet caught director Alain Cavalier's attention while doing a reading from Georges Bernanos' "Death of Mouchette." During the performance, Mouchet held a water balloon between her legs which she perforated. As she delivered her lines, the water slowly trickled to the end of the stage. This image so struck Cavalier that he chose Mouchet for the lead. What she brings to her role is a convincing and spiritually moving sense of conviction. She doesn't merely imitate the mannerisms of a saint, she appears to become saintly. Throughout the film, one feels as if one is watching a divinely blessed young girl. Her pure, radiant, peaceful face is captivating. A consummate actress, Mouchet's off-screen personality is far more self-assured and knowledgeable than her simple Therese, which makes one believe she can overcome any the typecasting that this role could bring.

GARY OLDMAN

Britain's most promising young actor, Gary Oldman, made his starring film debut playing the infamous Sid Vicious in Alex Cox's uncompromising SID AND NANCY. The son of a housewife and a welder, Oldman found escape from his mundane South London roots through movies. Inspired by Malcolm McDowell's performance in IF . . ., Oldman decided to become an actor. Oldman graduated from the Rose Bruford College of Speech and Drama and entered the legitimate theater where he was awarded Drama Magazine's Best Actor Award in 1985 for his performance in "The Pope's Wedding" by Edward Bond (Oldman shared the award with Anthony Hopkins). For SID AND NANCY, director Cox auditioned many Sid Vicious look-alikes, but wisely opted to go for acting talent instead. Oldman, who admits to not having paid much attention to the punk movement during his adolescence, lost 30 pounds from his already thin frame in order to approximate the emaciated body of the Sex Pistols' bassist. Although Oldman's physical resemblance to Sid Vicious was marginal, the actor turned in a *tour de force* performance and managed to *become* Vicious (as did Chloe Webb become Nancy Spungen). It is a tribute to Oldman's acting skills that he managed to wring some sympathy and understanding out of his wholly pathetic character without resorting to melodramatics. Oldman pulled no punches and played the notorious heroin-addicted punker as a near-catatonic zombie—a walking testament to the ravages of drug addiction. Oldman's sensitive and honest portrayal of Sid Vicious—a character who could easily have become a cartoon—is nothing less than brilliant. In his next film, Oldman played yet another famous Britisher, homosexual playwright Joe Orton, a man who was brutally murdered at the height of his popularity by his long-time lover Kenneth Halliwell in director Stephen Frears' PRICK UP YOUR EARS.

RIVER PHOENIX

Rob Reiner's STAND BY ME was the sleeper hit of the summer of 1986, and a great deal of its strength came from the performance of River Phoenix as the doomed Chris Chambers, a sensitive kid whose ambitions are being killed by a no-good family and a corrupt society, but who is the natural leader of a quartet of friends who go to find a dead body. In Peter Weir's MOSQUITO COAST, Phoenix played the son of a lunatic inventor who takes his family to Central America to bring ice and civilization to the natives in a botched adaptation of Paul Theroux's novel. Moving his character down the Oedipal path from blind adoration of his father through a slow realization of his madness, and finally to rejection, Phoenix's Charlie Fox was the heart of the novel, but is a mere sidelight in Weir's film, and Phoenix was denied the acclaim he deserved. The son of 1960s-style society dropouts, Phoenix was himself taken to Latin America as a small child, and

spent some years living in a small Venezualan village working alongside his missionary parents. When he was seven they returned to the U.S. and settled in Los Angeles, where he began appearing in commercials three years later. Soon he was doing feature roles in miniseries ("Celebrity" and "Robert Kennedy and His Times"), had a regular role in a series ("Seven Brides for Seven Brothers"), and made his feature debut at fourteen in EXPLORERS (1985) (a brother and sister, Leaf and Summer, respectively, have also made feature appearances). Amazingly level-headed by all accounts, Phoenix is still leaving his future open and may drop out of acting to pursue other interests —like rock'n'roll. If that happens, it will be Hollywood's loss.

CHARLIE SHEEN

Son of actor Martin Sheen and younger brother of actor-writer-director Emilio Estevez, Charlie Sheen faced stiff competition from his own family when it came to recognition in Hollywood. Although he has been acting since the age of nine (he made his debut in his father's television film THE EXECUTION OF PRIVATE SLOVIK), it was not until this year that young Sheen made his mark as the central character in Oliver Stone's PLATOON. His portrayal of the naive young soldier who dropped out of college to volunteer for duty in Vietnam won him raves from both director Stone and critics alike (Stone immediately cast him in his next film, this time as a young Wall Street inside trader in the tentatively titled WALL STREET). The actor convincingly conveys the emotional range from inexperienced innocent to hardened veteran. His resemblance to his father —both in appearance and in voice—brought back memories of his father's stunning performance in Francis Coppola's Vietnam epic APOCALYPSE NOW. Young Sheen has a relaxed, natural screen presence that is quite appealing; he exudes confidence as

an actor, yet never falls into cockiness or bravado that his brother Estevez sometimes demonstrates. Because of all the publicity surrounding PLATOON, many forgot that Sheen appeared in three other films in 1986: LUCAS, FERRIS BUELLER'S DAY OFF, and THE WRAITH. While THE WRAITH is instantly forgettable, Sheen's performances in LUCAS and FERRIS BUELLER'S DAY OFF are truly noteworthy. As a popular high-school football star who befriends the title character in LUCAS, Sheen is perfectly cast. His scene in the laundry room with Kerri Green is captivating as he gently tries to strike up a romance with the shy girl. In FERRIS BUELLER'S DAY OFF, Sheen has a memorable cameo as a burned-out greaser type who charms Ferris' up-tight sister near the police station near the end of the film. His successful seduction of the stuck-up girl is one last guffaw in a frequently funny movie, and Sheen practically steals the film in his one brief sequence. With his talent and with directors like Oliver Stone behind him, Charlie Sheen will prove to be a star of the future.

BILL SHERWOOD

With his quirky independent feature PARTING GLANCES, Bill Sherwood received some well-deserved kudos from both critics and filmgoers. His spirited look at part of New York City's gay community was an art-house hit, showing once again what a talented writer/director can do despite the limitations of a small budget. Sherwood was a music student at Juilliard, but grew frustrated with the restrictions of the music world. He entered Hunter College as an English major, but eventually switched to the film school, where he met several people who would later crew on PARTING GLANCES. After graduate work at the University of Southern California, Sherwood returned to New York and was hired by Italtoons, where he worked procuring foreign rights for American television programs. Gradu-

Phoenix

Sheen

Stone

Sutherland

ally Sherwood received editing jobs cutting trailers, and then directed an award-winning short film, VARIATIONS ON A SENTENCE BY PROUST. This was followed by a job with CBS News, where Sherwood used his office space to work on screenplays, hoping to eventually produce his own feature film. His office mate was Kathy Kinney, whom Sherwood later cast in one of PARTING GLANCES' major roles. Sherwood left this job to direct some rock videos, and when a production deal on one of his scripts fell through, Sherwood decided to develop a screenplay on his own. He wrote PARTING GLANCES keeping in mind that the budget would have to be kept at a minimum, then enlisted the help of numerous friends to work on the project. The result was a film that belied its meager beginnings. Sherwood's storytelling abilities—coupled with an often kinetic camera style and an intelligent use of background music—showed a real understanding of the medium's various elements, resulting in one of the year's more engaging directorial debuts.

OLIVER STONE

Perhaps the biggest surprise of the year was the emergence of screenwriter Oliver Stone as a major director, with both SALVADOR and PLATOON. After the series of revoltingly mindless right-wing xenophobic fantasies featuring the likes of Sylvester Stallone and Chuck Norris, Stone's thoughtful and realistic examination of complicated world issues is most welcome. Although he is sometimes a clumsy writer with problems in the subtlety department, Stone's films have undeniable power, and he knows how to sustain an intense situation. Scenes in both SALVADOR and PLATOON are excruciatingly nerve-wracking and Stone skillfully conveys the palpable tension that leads to quick, violent death in the world's hottest spots. Stone can direct actors, as well, getting superb performances from James Woods in SAL-

VADOR, and from Tom Berenger, Willem Dafoe, and the entire ensemble cast of PLATOON. A Vietnam veteran, Stone is politically liberal (although some left-wing academic film critics have branded PLATOON as the ultimate Reagan-era pro-war film!) and has his eye on how America affects the rest of the world. As a scriptwriter (MIDNIGHT EXPRESS, SCARFACE, YEAR OF THE DRAGON among others), Stone's work has concentrated on the violent aspects of the human character. Other directors seem to have buried Stone's character studies underneath a hail of bullets. With Stone directing his own material, he has embraced causes rather than developing a weapons fetish, and although the films are still violent, the violence is not gratuitous, and he never loses sight of his characters in favor of flashy action. After several years of movies reflecting unthinking patriotism and blind conservatism, Stone's brave cinematic foray into controversial American policy issues is most refreshing—despite his flaws. Stone's next film, tentatively titled WALL STREET, takes on the insider-trading scandals.

ELISEO SUBIELA

With the fall of its military government in 1983, Argentina was swept by political reforms which were inevitably reflected in that country's cinema. Directors suddenly had untold creative freedom and their films, including Luis Puenzo's Oscar-winning THE OFFICIAL STORY, became subject to international attention. Eliseo Subiela's is a strong voice in this new wave of Argentine filmmaking, but unlike his colleagues, he avoided an overtly political message with his highly acclaimed MAN FACING SOUTHEAST. Subiela's interest in film began as a child, and by age seventeen he had directed his first film, a documentary about Hospital Nacional Borda. He returned to that insane asylum some twenty-four years later to shoot MAN FACING

SOUTHEAST, and incorporated many of the hospital's patients into his cast. Subiela's surreal imagery has earned him comparisons to Luis Bunuel, among others, but the director has acknowledged other influences in his work, citing the importance of authors Gabriel Garcia Marquez and Jorge Luis Borges, and the mystical tradition in Argentine art. In his second feature film, Subiela combined these elements within the structural tradition of Hollywood psychological dramas, a move he deliberately made so the film would be accessible to a wider audience. "People give me two hours of their life. I don't have the right to bore them," Subiela told one interviewer. The director toured worldwide with MAN FACING SOUTHEAST on the festival circuit in 1986, and was awarded the International Critics Prize at the Toronto Film Festival for this thoughtful, caring work.

KIEFER SUTHERLAND

Terrifying as the "two-bit dime store hoodlum" Ace Merrill in Rob Reiner's STAND BY ME—with a pack of cigarettes rolled up in his T-shirt sleeve, homemade tattoos, and a way of bullying even his own gang into doing what he wants them to do—Sutherland became the quintessential "big kid," the sort feared by every 12-year-old. The role could have been played by many actors, but Sutherland brought it a venomous verisimilitude that still revealed the fear within every bully. The son (and look-alike) of Donald Sutherland, Kiefer made his feature debut in 1983's MAX DUGAN RETURNS, then a year later won the lead in BAY BOY, playing a young man in a Canadian coastal village who struggles with the onset of adulthood and the expectations of parents who want him to go into the priesthood. This year he could be seen in a small part as one of the ring of teenage thieves in AT CLOSE RANGE and the lead in the Canadian CRAZY MOON as a young man more in synch with the 1930s than the 1980s and in love with a deaf girl. Sutherland will swing even more into the public eye, and he is shows signs of being as good an actor as his father.

JULIEN TEMPLE

Born in 1953 in London, Temple came onto the scene during England's punk-rock heyday directing the infamous bad boys, The Sex Pistols, in the 1980 near-documentary THE GREAT ROCK 'N' ROLL SWINDLE. Rather than concentrating on documentaries or features, Temple built a reputation as one of music's top rock-video directors. His Rolling Stones video for the song "Undercover" attempted to combine a short narrative with the music. Videos for Culture Club ("Do You Really Want to Hurt Me") and David Bowie ("Jazzin' for Blue Jean") continued his success. He also codirected a feature length concert film, THE SECRET POLICEMAN'S OTHER BALL, which was little more than a transposition from stage to screen. A BBC television film, IT'S ALL TRUE, followed in 1983. Another union with The Rolling Stones' Mick Jagger resulted in the disastrous RUNNING OUT OF LUCK, a feeble attempt at combining rock video with a feature-length narrative. Temple apparently learned something from the RUNNING OUT OF LUCK fiasco, because his next film, this year's ABSOLUTE BEGINNERS, is an astounding addition to the genre of musicals. Adapting the cultish 1959 youth novel by British author Colin MacInnes, and employing the musical talents of some of today's greatest performers, Temple has fashioned a picture unique to this generation. Understanding the techniques of Vincente Minnelli, and Stanley Donen, and influenced by MGM—the former masters of the musical—Temple has updated and modernized many of those long-forgotten ideas. He has helped rejuvenate a genre by combining the innovative and energetic techniques of rock-video with a narrative feature-length structure (some-

thing David Byrne was unable to do in TRUE STORIES). Although ABSOLUTE BEGINNERS was a financial disaster, Temple seems to have enough creativity to bounce back.

CATHY TYSON

A 21-year-old Liverpudlian (though born in Kingston-on-Thames, Surrey), Tyson found fame after being cast opposite Bob Hoskins in MONA LISA, as the title character, of sorts. The daughter of a black barrister from Trinidad and a white English social worker (and the niece of actress Cicely Tyson), Tyson dropped out of school at age 17. Without formal training, she stepped onto the stage of Liverpool's Everyman's Theatre performing in "The Blitz Show" and "The Tempest." She then landed a place in The Royal Shakespeare Company. Far from an instant success, she worked her way through the ranks, appearing in "Golden Girls," "Hamlet," and "Love's Labour's Lost," before winning her part in MONA LISA. It was when "Golden Girls" was brought to London's Barbican Theatre, that MONA LISA director Neil Jordan spotted Tyson. In MONA LISA she turns in a remarkable performance as the independent, enigmatic, high-class prostitute with whom Hoskins falls in love. In addition to holding her own against the powerfully charismatic Hoskins, she creates a character who has a mysterious power over the people around her. Extremely photogenic, Tyson completely fulfills the expectations of a modern-day Mona Lisa, giving us a glimpse of the person behind the famous painted smile and embodying the romantic lyrics of the Nat "King" Cole song.

CHLOE WEBB

Like her costar Gary Oldman, actress Chloe Webb actually *becomes* Nancy Spungen in SID AND NANCY. This American stage actress' portrayal of the whining, obnoxious, demanding, heroin-addicted rock groupie is so vivid that viewers can hardly imagine Webb playing anyone else, but that grossly underrates this

actress' talents. Devoted to acting since she was accepted into the Boston Conservatory of Music and Drama at the age of 16, Webb has appeared in major stage productions from coast to coast. She cowrote and appeared in "Forbidden Broadway," which had successful runs in both New York and Los Angeles. For her film debut in SID AND NANCY, Webb spent months researching rock groupies, heroin addiction, and Nancy Spungen. She met real groupies and absorbed their life style and characteristics. Webb contacted a man who had written a book about heroin addiction and she accompanied him on visits to real-life junkies. Webb also felt the need to contact a member of the Spungen family to get a firsthand account of Nancy's early years (in addition to reading Nancy's mother's book *And I Don't Want to Live This Life*), and she contacted Nancy's sister, Susan. Susan Spungen gave the actress pictures taken of Nancy through the years and told her of Nancy's inner strengths and of her all-consuming desire to be loved. The research paid off, for Webb adeptly balances Nancy's repulsive behavior with a little girl's yearning for attention and approval. Both Webb and Oldman managed to capture the contradictions of these pitiful and outrageous people, and to convey the humanity buried beneath the punk facade. SID AND NANCY contained two of the most difficult acting jobs of the year and both performers succeeded brilliantly. Hopefully film producers will soon give Webb a role completely removed from Nancy Spungen.

FOREST WHITAKER

People may think it nearly impossible for a young supporting player to steal a scene from the likes of Paul Newman, but that is just what young black actor Forest Whitaker did in Martin Scorsese's THE COLOR OF MONEY. Whitaker appeared in the pivotal scene of the film where Newman, having decided to pick up the cue again after 25 years,

Temple

Tyson

Webb

Whitaker

Wiest

gets cleverly hustled by the apparently dim-witted Whitaker. As Newman loses game after game to the large black youth, he thinks he's got the kid suckered, but as it turns out it is Newman who's being suckered. Whitaker takes him down and never once steps out of his dull, friendly, street-kid character, which both infuriates and humiliates Newman. The hulking Whitaker has great screen presence and exudes quiet confidence—he commands the frame. Some have hailed him as a natural, but Whitaker seems much too intelligent an actor to go on mere instinct, and his educational background proves it. Having gotten to college on a football scholarship, Whitaker then transferred to USC where he was awarded two more scholarships: one for the conservatory music program to study classical music and opera, and another for the conservatory theatrical program. Whitaker also landed the Sir John Gielgud scholarship for the Drama School London at Berkeley. He had small movie roles in FAST TIMES AT RIDGEMONT HIGH and VISION QUEST in addition to several television appearances before landing memorable supporting roles in two of the most popular movies of 1986, THE COLOR OF MONEY and PLATOON. With any luck, Whitaker will soon be cast in larger roles and have a chance to really expand his talents.

DIANNE WIEST

Although Dianne Wiest has had secondary roles in such films as IT'S MY TURN, I'M DANCING AS FAST AS I CAN, INDEPENDENCE DAY, FALLING IN LOVE, and FOOTLOOSE, it was her Oscar-winning role in Woody Allen's HANNAH AND HER SISTERS which brought her the attention she deserved. As Mia Farrow's airheaded younger sister Holly, Wiest effectively stole scene after scene with an engaging performance. She injected both comedy and a tinge of sadness into her character, making this frustrated personality one with whom audiences could easily sympathize. Wiest, who also had a small role in Allen's 1985 film THE PURPLE ROSE OF CAIRO, studied theater at the University of Maryland before joining the American Shakespeare Company. After touring with that group, Wiest moved to New York to further her career, and eventually joined the Washington D.C. Arena Stage Theatre. In her four years with this ensemble Wiest amassed an impressive list of roles, including parts in the plays "Heartbreak House," "Our Town," "Inherit the Wind," and "The Dybbuk." Wiest toured the Soviet Union with the company, then worked with other theater groups in a variety of classical and modern works including "Hedda Gabler," "A Doll's House," "Agamemnon," and "Leave It To Beaver is Dead." Wiest also appeared as Desdemona opposite James Earl Jones in a Broadway production of "Othello" and won several important awards for her performance in the New York Shakespeare Festival's "The Art of Dining." In addition to her gift for acting, Wiest has proven herself to be a talented director with her 1985 staging of the play "Not About Heroes," which featured Ed Herrmann in the lead. Originally produced in association with the Williamstown, Massachusetts theater festival, the show received much acclaim and eventually opened off-Broadway.

Ackerman, Mildred

Died 10 Jan. 1986, Cambridge, Mass., age 65.

Filmmaker-Dancer. After training with the Martha Graham Dance School and appearing in "Naughty Naught" (off-Broadway) during the late 1940s as a dancer, took up filmmaking (studied at Massachusetts Institute of Technology) and made the film TEA PARTY; edited three films, LOOKING FOR RENAISSANCE ROME, PALLADIO THE ARCHITECT, FRANK STELLA AT THE FOGG.

Ackles, Kenneth V.

(Kenneth Vincent Ackles)

Died 5 Nov. 1986, Pasadena, Tex., age 70.

Stage/Film/TV Actor-Wrestler. Born in New York, studied acting under Lee Strasberg and Sanford Meisner; wrestled in U.S. (gaining a championship) and Europe; appeared on the New York stage in "Li'l Abner," "The Lower Depths," "Scarecrow," and "Lulu: Free Spirit"; film credits include BODYHOLD, RACHEL, RACHEL, DEATH WISH, NIGHT OF THE JUGGLER; TV appearances included "Your Show of Shows," the soap operas "Guiding Light" and "Edge of Night," and the TV movie "Izzy and Moe."

Acremant, Germaine

Died 24 Aug. 1986, Neuilly, France, age 97.

Novelist-Playwright. Wrote 1921 best-selling novel *Ces Dames Aux Chapeaux Verts [The Ladies in the Green Hats]*, a tale of provincial life and manners, later adapted by her into a play which became the basis for three French films; her novel *La Sarrazine* was filmed in 1927 by Julien Duvivier with the title LE TOURBILLON DE PARIS.

Aherne, Brian

(Brian de Lacy Aherne)

Born 2 May 1902, King's Norton, England; died 10 Feb. 1986, Venice, Fla.

Film/Stage Actor. Started acting on amateur basis at age 3; studied at Italia Conti School, made stage debut at age 8; toured in England and Australia and made his U.S. stage debut in 1931 in "The Barretts of Wimpole Street"; U.S. film debut was in SONG OF SONGS in 1933, followed by THE CONSTANT NYMPH, SYLVIA SCARLETT, BELOVED ENEMY, MERRILY WE LIVE, JUAREZ (Oscar nominated), MY SON, MY SON, THE LADY IN QUESTION, FOREVER AND A DAY, TITANIC (1953); toured during 1957-1958 season in "My Fair Lady"; later became licensed pilot; first of his two wives was Joan Fontaine.

Albertine, Charles

Died 18 May 1986, Los Angeles, Calif., age 57.

Composer/Arranger. Originally from Passaic, N.J., played clarinet at New York City's Radio City Music Hall before becoming a composer and arranger for big bands such as Harry James, Sammy Kaye, Percy Faith, Les and Larry Elgart; composed the theme for TV's "American Band-

stand"; did title song for THE LONG SHIPS (1964).

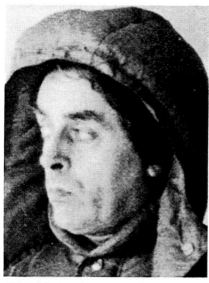

Alcott, John

Died 28 July 1986, Cannes, France, age 55.

Cinematographer. A native of London, started out as a focus puller before doing partial cinematography on 2001: A SPACE ODYSSEY (1968); advanced to full cinematographer status on A CLOCKWORK ORANGE (1971); won an Oscar in 1975 for BARRY LYNDON; other films include MARCH OR DIE, WHO IS KILLING THE GREAT CHEFS OF EUROPE?, FORT APACHE, THE BRONX, UNDER FIRE, GREYSTOKE: THE LEGEND OF TARZAN, LORD OF THE APES, RITES OF SUMMER, DECEIT; responsible for technical development of Super Techniscope (relabeled System 35).

Alda, Robert

(Alphonso Giuseppe Giovanni Roberto D'Abruzzo)

Born 26 Feb. 1914, New York City, N.Y.; died 3 May 1986, Los Angeles, Calif.

Stage/Film/TV Actor. Studied architecture and had minor position as draftsman in architectural firm before switching to show business, debuting in vaudeville in 1933, radio in 1934, TV in 1937; first and biggest film role was RHAPSODY IN BLUE (1945), which led to a contract with Warner Brothers and appearances in such films as CLOAK AND DAGGER, THE BEAST WITH FIVE FINGERS, NORA PRENTISS, APRIL SHOWERS; made his Broadway debut in "Guys and Dolls" in 1950, winning a Tony award; other films include IMITATION OF LIFE (1959), THE GIRL WHO KNEW TOO MUCH, I WILL, I WILL . . . FOR NOW;

TV efforts include "The Gentleman from Seventh Avenue" (1958) and "Supertrain" (1979); father of actor Alan Alda, star of TV's "M*A*S*H".

Aldrich, Richard

(Richard Stoddard Aldrich)

Born 17 Aug. 1902, Boston, Mass.; died 31 March 1986, Williamsburg, Va.

Broadway Producer. Produced over 30 plays on the Broadway stage including "The Moon is Blue" (filmed in 1953); married stage star Gertrude Lawrence; wrote a biography about his wife after her death from cancer in 1952; was an adviser on the musical film based on her life, STAR (1968).

Allan, Lewis

(Abel Meeropol)

Died 30 Oct. 1986, Longmeadow, Mass., age 83.

Songwriter. A New York native, composed Billie Holiday classic "Strange Fruit," as well as songs for stage, film, TV, radio; composed title song for Oscar-winning short THE HOUSE I LIVE IN, sung by Frank Sinatra; adopted sons of Julius and Ethel Rosenberg after their execution for passing atomic secrets to the Russians.

Allen, Hilda

Died 3 Mar. 1986, Regina, Canada, age 79.

Stage/Film Actress-Stage Director. Greatly influenced development of theater in Saskatchewan; actress and stage director in the Regina area, principally concerned with annual presentation of "The Trial of Louis Riel," a summer tourist attraction; appeared for the first time on film in 1984 in PORTRAITS OF CANADA, a Walt Disney production.

Alston, George D.

Died 14 Aug. 1986, San Gabriel, Calif., age 67.

Scenic Artist. Worked from 1945 through 1960 as head scenic artist at the Monogram Pictures ranch location; brother of producer Howard P. Alston.

Alvarez, Luis

Died 2 May 1986.

Film Actor. Appeared in MANHUNT IN THE JUNGLE (1958) and THE REDEEMER (1965).

Ameripoor, Alex

(Eskandar Ameripoor)

Died 6 June 1986, Culver City, Calif., age 49.

Cinematographer-Film Editor. Born in Iran, also known as Gaston Palau, Alex Ameri, Ali Ameri, Peter Guilfhoyle; worked in various capacities (second unit cameraman, camera operator, assistant, occasional actor) before becoming a cinematographer and editor for exploitation filmmaker Herschell Gordon Lewis, working on such films as ALLEY TRAMP, BLAST-OFF GIRLS, SHE-DEVILS ON WHEELS, and THE GORE-GORE GIRLS; made several TV and documentary films in Iran.

Amy, George J.

Born Oct. 1903, Brooklyn, N.Y.; died 18 Dec. 1986, Los Angeles, Calif.

Film Editor. Entered the motion picture business in New York in 1918, starting out as script clerk and assistant editor at Famous Players Lasky before reaching professional editor status in 1921; worked mainly for Warner Bros. on such films as BURN 'EM UP BARNES, THE BROWN DERBY, THE GORILLA, CABIN IN THE COTTON, DOCTOR X, FOOTLIGHT PARADE, GOLD DIGGERS OF 1933, THE MYSTERY OF THE WAX MUSEUM, CAPTAIN BLOOD, THE CHARGE OF THE LIGHT BRIGADE, THE GREEN PASTURES, DODGE CITY, THE OLD MAID, THE LETTER, SANTA FE TRAIL, THE SEA HAWK, VIRGINIA CITY, DIVE BOMBER, his Oscar-nominated YANKEE DOODLE DANDY, ACTION IN THE NORTH ATLANTIC, AIR FORCE (received an Oscar), UNCERTAIN GLORY, OBJECTIVE BURMA (Oscar nominated), LIFE WITH FATHER, THE BLUE VEIL; directed films such as KID NIGHTINGALE, GAMBLING ON THE HIGH SEAS, GRANNY GET YOUR GUN; went to CBS-TV in 1956 as coordinator in film-editing department, securing

Emmy nomination for work on "Schlitz Playhouse" anthology series.

Anderson, Bo

(Burt Anderson)

Died 29 March 1986, Hollywood, Calif., age 63.

Stand-in-Stunt Man-Film Actor. Was a stand-in for Broderick Crawford and Sean McClory, as well as a stunt man.

Andrews, Ann

Born 13 Oct. 1895, Los Angeles, Calif.; died 23 Jan. 1986, New York City, N.Y.

Stage/Film Actress. Made stage debut in Los Angeles in 1916 and Broadway debut the following year; theater endeavors include "Blind Youth," "The Hottentot," "Her Temporary Husband," "The Captive," "The Royal Family," "Dinner at Eight," "Dark Victory," "Our Betters," "Serena Blandish," and "Blithe Spirit"; essayed films just once in 1931's THE CHEAT.

Andrews, V.C.

(Virginia Cleo Andrews)

Died 19 Dec. 1986, Virginia Beach, Va.

Novelist. Confined to a wheelchair; wrote seven novels, including *Petals on the Wind, Seeds of Yesterday, My Sweet Audrina, Heaven, Dark Angel*; at her death, *Flowers in the Attic*, her first novel, was being made into a film.

Angel, Heather

(Heather Grace Angel)

Born 9 Feb. 1909, Oxford, England; died 13 Dec. 1986, Santa Barbara, Calif.

Film/Stage Actress. Came from scholarly family (father was chemistry professor at Oxford), attended London Polytechnic of Dramatic Arts for theatrical training and made stage debut in 1926, appearing in "A Midsummer Night's Dream," and "A Christmas Eve"; toured England, India, Egypt, and the Orient with repertory company of the Old Vic from 1926 through 1930; made British film debut in CITY OF SONG (U.S. title: FAREWELL TO LOVE) in 1931; other films include THE HOUND OF THE BASKERVILLES, PILGRIMAGE, CHARLIE CHAN'S GREATEST CASE, BERKELEY SQUARE, SPRINGTIME FOR HENRY, THE INFORMER, THE MYSTERY OF EDWIN DROOD, LAST OF THE MOHICANS, DANIEL BOONE, five Bulldog Drummond second features, PRIDE AND PREJUDICE, THAT HAMILTON WOMAN, SUSPICION, LIFEBOAT, PREMATURE BURIAL; did voices for two Disney films, ALICE IN WONDERLAND, PETER PAN; TV credits include "Perry Mason," "Mr. Novak," "Family Affair," and miniseries "Backstairs at the White House"; had three husbands, Ralph Forbes, Henry Wilcoxon, and stage director Robert B. Sinclair.

Anthony, Bob

Died 19 Nov. 1986, Leonia, N.J., age 71.

Singer. Sang with many big bands such as Tommy Dorsey (replaced Frank Sinatra), Harry James, Eddy Duchin; appeared on Broadway musical stage in "Pal Joey"; made one film, JOHNNY CONCHO; later did some TV talk shows and then became a columnist for *The Sporting News*.

Anthony, David

(William Dale Smith)

Died 31 March 1986, Los Angeles, Calif., 56.

Novelist. Born in Weirton, W. Va., served in the Army during the Korean War, then went to Antioch College and into newspaper work; under the name David Anthony wrote the novel that was the source for the 1974 film THE MIDNIGHT MAN; also wrote *The Organization, Blood on the Harvest Moon, Stud Game, Naked in December*; helped develop the films THIEF and EYE OF THE NEEDLE as a story analyst for United Artists; had recently finished another novel, *War Games*.

Arlen, Harold

(Hyman Arluck)

Born 15 Feb. 1905, Buffalo, N.Y.; died 23 Apr. 1986, New York City, N.Y.

Songwriter. Came from a religious family (father was a cantor); by the age of seven sang in the synagogue; took piano lessons in the classical vein with some instruction from mother; quit high school to start a three-man band, performing triple duty as singer, arranger, and pianist; worked as a rehearsal pianist then began composing for such Broadway shows as "9:15 Revue," "Earl Carroll's Vanities," "You Said It"; composed songs for performers at Harlem's Cotton Club such as Ethel Waters, Aida Ward, Lena Horne; many of his melodies were written with lyricist collaborators such as Ted Koehler, E.Y. Harburg, Ira Gershwin, Johnny Mercer; went to Hollywood during the Depression, writing such standards as "Get Happy," "Between the Devil and the Deep Blue Sea," "I Love a Parade," "It's Only a Paper Moon," "Stormy Weather," "I've Got the World on a String," "Let's Fall in Love," "In the Shade of the Old Apple Tree," "Over the Rainbow" (earned an Oscar), "Blues in the Night," "That Old Black Magic," "My Shining Hour," "Ac-cent-tchu-ate the Positive," "The Man That Got Away"; composed for many films, including THE WIZARD OF OZ, LOVE AFFAIR, ANDY HARDY MEETS DEBUTANTE, BLUES IN THE NIGHT, STAR SPANGLED RHYTHM, CABIN IN THE SKY, HERE COME THE WAVES, KISMET, CASBAH, MR. IMPERIUM, THE FARMER TAKES A WIFE, and 1954 version of A STAR IS BORN.

Arnaz, Desi

(Desiderio Alberto Arnaz y de Acha III)

Born 2 March 1917, Santiago, Cuba; died 2 Dec. 1986, Del Mar, Calif.

Bandleader-Film/TV Actor-TV Producer/Executive. Came from wealthy Cuban family (father was a member of Cuban senate and one-time mayor of Santiago); fled to U.S. in 1933 during revolution; while attending a Miami Beach high school joined a rhumba band and was noticed by Xavier Cugat who gave him a chance with his orchestra; toured with Cugat for six months, then returned to Miami Beach to form his own band and introduced the popular dance "Conga" to the U.S.; appeared on Broadway in 1939 in "Too Many Girls" and won a chance at Hollywood in the 1940 film version whose cast included RKO contract player Lucille Ball, whom he married four months later; signed a two-year contract with RKO and bought a five-acre California ranch and named it Desilu (the first appearance of the name that would become famous in his later TV years); made four films under the RKO banner—FOUR JACKS AND A JILL, FATHER TAKES A WIFE, and THE NAVY COMES THROUGH—before jumping to MGM to do BATAAN; in 1945, after a two-year stretch in the Army, organized a new band and introduced his trademark song "Babalu"; another film, CUBAN PETE, followed, as well as more records and a job with Bob Hope's radio show; in 1948, Lucille Ball was offered the chance to put her radio show "My Favorite Husband" on TV after her second successful year, and insisted that Arnaz be signed on to play her husband; the show, which became "I Love Lucy," was a fantastic success; changed the show in 1957 to once-a-month viewing spot called "The Lucille Ball-Desi Arnaz Show" to devote more time to heading Desilu Productions; bought his old studio (RKO) to create an entertainment empire containing 35 sound stages and a 40-acre backlot, producing such series as "Our Miss Brooks," "Make Room for Daddy," "The Line-up," "December Bride," "Those Whiting Girls," and "The Untouchables"; made two features with Lucille Ball, THE LONG, LONG TRAILER and FOREVER DARLING, before divorcing her in 1960; sold his part of the Desilu empire to Lucille Ball and retired except for producing TV's "The Mothers-In-Law" in 1967 and a few TV appearances; last film appearance in 1982's THE ESCAPE ARTIST, directed by Francis Ford Coppola.

Arthur, Robert

(Robert Arthur Feder)

Born 1 Nov. 1909, New York City, N.Y.; died 28 Oct. 1986, Beverly Hills, Calif.

Film Producer. After attending University of Southern California, worked in the oil industry, then joined MGM as a screenwriter in 1937; in 1947 switched to Universal as line producer on comedy films featuring Abbott and Costello and Francis the talking mule, which were among Universal's biggest moneymakers and launched his career; other films produced: THE BIG HEAT, THE LONG GRAY LINE, MAN OF A THOUSAND FACES, OPERATION PETTICOAT, COME SEPTEMBER, LOVER COME BACK, THAT TOUCH OF MINK, FATHER GOOSE, SHENANDOAH, HELLFIGHTERS, SWEET CHARITY, and his final film, ONE MORE TRAIN TO ROB, in 1971.

Atwater, Edith

Born 22 Apr. 1911, Chicago, Ill.; died 14 March 1986, Los Angeles, Calif.

Stage/Film Actress. Came from wealthy family and attended two theatrical schools before doing regional theater in New Jersey, New York, and Chicago; debuted on Broadway in 1931 in "Springtime for Henry"; her first film was WE WENT TO COLLEGE (1936), followed by THE GORGEOUS HUSSY, THE BODY SNATCHER, C-MAN, TERESA, SWEET SMELL OF SUCCESS, SWEET BIRD OF YOUTH, STRANGE BEDFELLOWS, TRUE GRIT, NORWOOD, STAND UP AND BE COUNTED, OUR TIME, FAMILY PLOT; appeared on TV in "Dr. Kildare," "Peyton Place," "The Rockford Files," "Family Ties"; had three husbands, all actors (Hugh Marlowe, Joseph Allen, Jr., and Kent Smith).

Austin, Bud

(Harold "Bud" Augenblick)

Born 31 Dec. 1924; died 31 May 1986, Los Angeles, Calif., age 66.

TV Executive/Producer-Film Producer. Served as a lieutenant in the U.S. Army during WW II and became a film syndicator upon his release; main thrust of his career was in TV, involved with such organizations as Goodson-Todman (who specialized in quiz shows), Filmways ("The Beverly Hillbillies," "Green Acres"); was coproducer on two films, MIKEY AND NICKY and JOHNNY DANGEROUSLY.

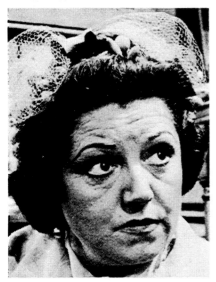

Baddeley, Hermione

(Hermione Clinton-Baddeley)

Born 13 Nov. 1906, Brosely, England; died 19 Aug. 1986, Los Angeles, Calif.

Stage/TV/Film Actress. Descendant of Sir Henry Clinton (British commander-in-chief in who captured New York from George Washington during the Revolutionary War); debuted on the London stage in 1918; her first appearance on the British screen was in 1926 (A DAUGHTER IN REVOLT); other film credits include CASTE, LOVE, LIFE AND LAUGHTER, KIPPS, BRIGHTON ROCK (also did the stage version), QUARTET, PASSPORT TO PIMLICO, SCROOGE (U.S.: A CHRISTMAS CAROL), TOM BROWN'S SCHOOL DAYS, THE PICKWICK PAPERS, ROOM AT THE TOP (Oscar nominated), MARY POPPINS, HARLOW, THE BLACK WINDMILL, and C.H.O.M.P.S in 1979; first appeared on the New York stage in 1960; selected by Tennessee Williams for his play "The Milk Train Doesn't Stop Here Anymore" in 1962; persuaded by Norman Lear to join the cast of TV's "Maude" as Bea Arthur's housekeeper.

Baehr, Nicholas E.

Died 31 May 1986, Burbank, Calif., age 61.

TV/Film Writer-Playwright. Main thrust of his career was in television, starting out in the New York area writing for such programs as "U.S. Steel Hour," "Kraft Theater," "Omnibus," "Philco Goodyear Playhouse," as well as Jackie Gleason's "The Honeymooners"; plays include "The Great Excitement," "The Palmer Way"; did one film THE INCIDENT (based on his TV script) in 1967.

Baker, Hylda

Died 3 May 1986, Lancashire, England, age 78.

Stage/Film/TV/Variety Actress-Comedienne. Began appearing in stage productions at age 10, later developing touring shows which she produced and directed; films include SATURDAY NIGHT AND SUNDAY MORNING, UP THE JUNCTION, OLIVER.

Baker-Bergen, Stuart

(Stuart Bergen, Jr.)

Died 9 May 1986, New Orleans, La., age 40.

Stage/Film Actor-Playwright-Composer. Started performing at age five, playing piano, guitar, and ukulele before going to New York to work with various theatrical groups over a 10-year period; toured Europe and the Middle East, then returned to New Orleans and appeared in a few films shot on location there such as TIGHTROPE and THE TOY; also wrote plays, including one based on the life of Louis Armstrong.

Ballard, Jack

Died 27 Jun. 1986, Beverly Hills, Calif., age 71.

Production Manager-Studio Executive. Former Vice President in Charge of Production Management for Paramount Pictures. Films supervised include: THE ODD COUPLE, ROSEMARY'S BABY, PLAZA SUITE, LOVE STORY, CATCH-22, THE GODFATHER, SAVE THE TIGER; left Paramount in 1972 to deal in the area of acquisition and development of film projects.

Barrett, William E.

(William Edmund Barrett)

Born 16 Nov. 1900, New York City, N.Y.; died 14 Sept. 1986, Denver, Colo.

Author. Attended Manhattan College and entered the business world as an advertising manager for Westinghouse Co.; became a licensed pilot and wrote several books on the subject; first novel published in 1938 (*Woman on Horseback*); best known for the *Left Hand of God* (went through 10 translations and 50,000 copies by 1963; filmed in 1955) and the novella *Lilies of the Field* (filmed in 1963) among the 18 novels and approximately 200 short stories he wrote.

Baseleon, Michael

Died 9 Oct. 1986, Lenox, Mass., age 61.

Stage/TV/Film Actor. Korean War veteran, mainly appeared on TV; films include MAN ON A STRING, PASSOVER PLOT, UPTIGHT, A MAN CALLED HORSE; was appearing on-stage in "Antony and Cleopatra" when he died.

Baskerville, David

Died 27 Dec. 1986, Denver, Colo., age 69.

Conductor-Composer-Author-Educator. Began his career with a dance band while studying at the University of Washington and went on to conduct for NBC, Paramount, 20th Century Fox, and the Nelson Riddle organization; appeared with the Los Angeles Philharmonic as a trombonist; specialized in consulting for the film industry (Walt Disney Productions was one of his clients); for Radio City Music Hall's 50th anniversary in 1982, appeared as guest conductor; was honored by ASCAP for his book *Music Business Handbook and Career Guide* as well as establishing the music department at the University of Colorado.

Bassett, John F.

(John Frederick Bassett)

Died 14 May 1986, Toronto, Canada, age 47.

Sports Executive-Athlete-Film Producer. A native of Toronto who brought the Ottawa Nationals (a hockey team) to Toronto; produced such Canadian-originated films as FLICK, FRANKENSTEIN ON CAMPUS, ROWDY MAN, PAPERBACK HERO and coproduced SPRING FEVER.

Bauer, Alfred

Died 19 Oct. 1986, Berlin, West Germany, age 75.

Film Historian-Founding Director of Berlin International Film Festival. A Bavarian native, studied law and art history at the University of Wurzburg, graduating with a doctorate degree in film law; started with UFA film company before joining the German army during WW II; after the war, worked for the British as a consultant on film and compiled information on all sound films made in Germany between the years of 1929 and 1950; in 1951, was selected by the Allies to put together a film festival aimed at reviving the industry, creating jobs, and attracting capital and producers; it gained worldwide importance and stirred interest in postwar film movements; retired in 1976 and was honored by many countries for his efforts.

Bay, Howard

Born 3 May 1912, Centralia, Wash.; died 21 Nov. 1986, New York City, N.Y.

Stage/Film Designer. Attended five schools, including Carnegie Institute of Technology, for his art training; primarily a stage designer, he worked on approximately 170 productions, including "There's a Moon Tonight," "The Little Foxes," "The Corn Is Green," "The Moon Is Down," "Ten Little Indians," "Catherine Was Great," "Show Boat," "Come Back, Little Sheba" "Toys in the Attic" (1960, won a Tony), "Man of La Mancha"; film credits include THE EXILE, UP IN CENTRAL PARK, GO, MAN, GO, A MIDSUMMER NIGHT'S DREAM; served as president of United Scenic Artists (the union of costume, scenic and lighting designers) for many years.

Beard, Cecil A.

Died 28 Dec. 1986, Silver City, New Mexico, age 79.

Film Cartoonist. Hailing from Texas, worked for Walt Disney Productions on such films as SNOW WHITE AND THE SEVEN DWARFS and BAMBI before working on such comic books as *Dennis the Menace, Bugs Bunny, Roadrunner* and *Fox and Crow*.

Beauvais, Peter

Died 16 Dec. 1986, age 70.

German TV Director-Actor. In 1973 directed the German TV film "In the Reservation"; during the 1950s appeared in the films MAN ON A TIGHTROPE and NIGHT PEOPLE.

Becher, John C.

(John Conrad Becher)

Born 13 Jan. 1915, Milwaukee, Wisc.; died 20 Sept. 1986, Hollywood, Calif.

Stage/TV/Film Actor. Studied at both Milwaukee State Teachers College and the Goodman Theatre in Chicago before being drafted into the army during WW II, assigned to the special services school in Lexington, Virginia, where he trained actors (such as Red Skelton and Melvyn Douglas) on how to handle the conditions they would face when entertaining troops in combat zones; though he had done some regional theater, he did not act on the New York stage until 1946; appeared in "Brigadoon" and "Picnic" and toured in "The Solid Gold Cadillac"; started in TV during its early days doing top-rated shows such as "Philco Television Playhouse," "Goodyear Theatre," and "U.S. Steel Hour"; film credits include THE WRONG MAN, THE ODD COUPLE, UP THE SANDBOX, HONKY TONK FREEWAY, GREMLINS, MURPHY'S ROMANCE.

Beery, Rita Gilman

(Rita Beery)

Died 14 Nov. 1986, age 88.

Film Actress. Appeared in the 1944 film DARK WATERS.

Behrens, Frank

Died 15 Dec. 1986, age 67

Film/TV/Radio Actor. Appeared in the film WAKE ME WHEN IT'S OVER (1960).

Benda, Helen

Died 24 Dec. 1986, age 83

Film Actress. Made the film HEAVENLY DAYS in 1944.

Benedict, Max P.

Died 20 April 1986, London, England, age 65.

Film Editor. Left his native Vienna during WW II to work for the British government, then became a script researcher for filmmakers Roy and John Boulting; editing credits include SEVEN DAYS TO NOON, TOWN ON TRIAL, LUCKY JIM, TROUBLE IN THE SKY, WHISTLE DOWN THE WIND, GUNS AT BATASI, RAPTURE, THE BLUE MAX, FATHOM, THE MAGUS, THE OBLONG BOX, SHAFT IN AFRICA, FIREPOWER; also translated plays, reviewed films, and lectured on his discipline at the National Film School.

Bergner, Elisabeth

(Elisabeth Ettel)

Born 22 Aug. 1897, Drohobycz, Poland (now U.S.S.R); died 12 May 1986, London, England.

Stage/Film Actress. Started her theatrical career in Zurich, Switzerland (1919), after training in Vienna, Austria; at first acted mainly in Shakespeare plays; played Rosalind in "As You Like It" in 1920 (a role she would play opposite Laurence Olivier in the 1936 British film version); other efforts included "Hannele," "A Doll's House," "Saint Joan," "The Circle of Chalk," and "The Constant Nymph"; following the Nazi rise to power in Germany, she moved to Paris in 1933 and then to London; debuted in London in "Escape Me Never" and brought it to New York in 1935, filming it the same year; other efforts included "The Boy David," (written specifically for her by James M. Barrie) "The Two Mrs. Carrolls," "The Duchess of Malfi," "A Long Day's Journey Into Night," and "The Madwoman of Chaillot"; first appeared on screen in Germany in 1923 in DER EVANGELIMANN, then appeared in NJU, DER GEIGER VON FLORENZ, LIEBE, DONA JUANA, QUEEN LOUISE, ARIANE, DER TRAUMENDE MUND; started a series of films in English with perhaps one of her best known performances in CATHERINE THE GREAT; also made DREAMING LIPS and a STOLEN LIFE in 1939, then came to the U.S. for PARIS CALLING; with the exception of CRY OF THE BANSHEE (1970, British), her other films were foreign.

Bernardi, Herschel

Born 30 Oct. 1923, New York City, N.Y.; died 9 May 1986, Los Angeles, Calif.

Stage/TV/Film Actor. Started his career on the Yiddish stage and made two Yiddish films he did in the late 1930s, GREEN FIELDS, YANKEL THE BLACKSMITH; his Hollywood career started in 1945 with MISS SUSIE SLAGLE'S (billed as Harold Bernardi), and included STAKEOUT ON DOPE STREET, IRMA LA DOUCE, A COLD WIND IN AUGUST, THE GEORGE RAFT STORY, LOVE WITH THE PROPER STRANGER, THE HONEY POT; supplied voices in two animated films, 1001 ARABIAN NIGHTS, THE MAN FROM BUTTON WILLOW; earned an Emmy in 1959 for his role as Lt. Jacoby in "Peter

Gunn"; perhaps best known for his starring roles in "Fiddler on the Roof" (more than 700 performances) and "Zorba"; appeared in many TV productions and had his own series, "Arnie" (1970-71); supplied voices for Charlie the Tuna and the Jolly Green Giant; brother Jack is also an actor.

Bernhard, Gosta

Died 4 Jan. 1986, Stockholm, Sweden, age 75.

Stage/Film Actor-Director-Writer-Manager. Started a slapstick-type comedy theater that led to many 1950s comedy films based on a country-rustic type army draftee; did a more serious film, POKER (1951), which starred noted Swedish actor, Stig Jarrel; delved into many areas of show business and wrote a book about his life.

Bird, Dick

Died 28 Sept. 1986, Regina, Saskatchewan, Canada, age 94.

Cinematographer. Moved from his native England to Vermont where, in 1910, as a teenager, started using a motion camera with a hand-crank, shooting footage of Barney Oldfield's record-setting race at Daytona Beach and selling the footage to a newsreel company; worked for local and Hollywood film companies, then began making regional documentaries for the Saskatchewan provincial government, and did nature features in the 1940s through the 1960s.

Bjornstrand, Gunnar

Born 13 Nov. 1909, Stockholm, Sweden; died 24 May 1986, Stockholm, Sweden.

Film/Stage Actor. A giant of the Swedish cinema, best known for his work in Ingmar Bergman films; had an actor father; after his debut film in 1931 in THE FALSE MILLIONAIRE, decided to join Stockholm's Royal Dramatic Theater School where Ingmar Bergman was his classmate; made at least 24 films (out of approximately 160) before he started working with Ingmar Bergman (in 1946), giving him worldwide recognition in such films as NIGHT IS MY FUTURE, SAWDUST AND TINSEL, DREAMS, SMILES OF A SUMMER NIGHT,

THE SEVENTH SEAL, WILD STRAWBERRIES, THE MAGICIAN, THROUGH A GLASS DARKLY, WINTER LIGHT, PERSONA, AUTUMN SONATA, FANNY AND ALEXANDER; he also worked for directors Olof and Gustaf Mo-

lander, Arne Mattson, Hasse Ekman (son of Gosta Ekman and father of Gosta Ekman, Jr., both prominent Swedish actors), Lars-Erik Kjellgren, Mai Zetterling.

Block, Irving A.

Died 3 May 1986, Los Angeles, Calif., age 73.

Documentary Producer. Art professor at California State University (Northridge), for 17 years produced documentaries on famous artists including REMBRANDT: POET OF LIGHT, GOYA, WORLD OF RUBENS; did model work and painting for science-fiction and horror films; stepped into TV for work on "Ripley's Believe It or Not."

Blumenthal, Herman Allen

Died 30 March 1986, Los Angeles, Calif., age 69.

Art Director-Production Designer. After entry into the film business in 1934, worked on such films as THE THREE FACES OF EVE, JOURNEY TO THE CENTER OF THE EARTH (Oscar nominated), THE RIGHT APPROACH, VOYAGE TO THE BOTTOM OF THE SEA, CLEOPATRA (won Oscar in 1963), KISSES FOR MY PRESIDENT, MORITURI, THE SATAN BUG, STAGECOACH, THE ONE AND ONLY, GENUINE, ORIGINAL FAMILY BAND, HELLO DOLLY! (won him his second Oscar in 1968), THE ONLY GAME IN TOWN, PIECES OF DREAMS, THE LOLLY MADONNA WAR, WHAT'S UP, DOC?, THE BETSY, ZORRO, THE GAY BLADE.

Blunk, John

Died 31 Jan. 1986, Woodland Hills, Calif., age 78.

Film Editor. Had an 18-year career at Primrose, 20th Century Fox, MGM, Revue; edited WOLF LARSEN in 1958.

Bolton, Joe

(Joseph Reeves Bolton, Jr.)

Born 8 Sept. 1910, Flushing, N.Y.; died 13 Aug. 1986, Santa Monica, Calif.

Children's Show Host/Announcer-Film Actor. Started out as a weatherman/announcer at WPIX New York (1948); mainly worked as a host of a children's show presenting "Three Stooges" shorts in his character of Officer Joe Bolton; later played the same role in two "Three Stooges" features, STOP! LOOK! AND LAUGH! and "THE THREE STOOGES MEET THE GUNSLINGER.

Bomba, Raymond V.

Died 24 June 1986, Encino, Calif., age 79.

Film Sound Editor. Hailing from Beeville, Texas, started working in 1942 at Columbia Pictures; founded a trade association in 1953, garnering awards from the association for his work on THE ENEMY BELOW, VON RYAN'S EXPRESS, PATTON, THE FRENCH CONNECTION.

Bonnell, Lee

Died 12 May 1986, Santa Monica, Calif., age 67.

Insurance Executive-Film Actor. Grew up in Royal Center, Ind., where he entered a national radio talent contest, winning the male part opposite Josephine Cottle (later renamed Gale Storm), leading to a contract at RKO and a chance to marry Storm; his films include STRANGER ON THE THIRD FLOOR, MEN AGAINST THE SKY, LADY SCARFACE, THE SAINT IN PALM SPRINGS, LOOK WHO'S LAUGHING, THE NAVY COMES THROUGH, ARMY SURGEON; served in the U.S. Coast Guard during WW II, resuming his career with CRIMINAL COURT, SAN QUENTIN, THE CHECKERED COAT, SMART WOMAN, JIGGS & MAGGIE IN SOCIETY; left films to go into the life insurance business.

Boren, Lamar

Died 15 Jan. 1986, La Jolla, Calif., age 68.

Underwater Cinematographer. Veteran of 40 years in the film industry; worked on TV in Lloyd Bridges' "Sea Hunt" and the TV and film versions of "Flipper"; in film, worked on THUNDERBALL, YOU ONLY LIVE TWICE, LADY IN CEMENT, BREWSTER MC CLOUD, DAY OF THE DOLPHIN.

Boretz, Allen

Born 31 Aug. 1900, New York, N.Y.; died 21 May 1986, Branford, Conn.

Screenwriter-Playwright-Composer. After attending college in New York, became a songwriter, getting some of his lyrics into the 1930 version of "Garrick Gaieties"; cowrote "The School Teacher" with character actor Ned Glass; did the 1937 Broadway 500-performance smash "Room Service," which was filmed with the Marx Brothers in 1938 and as a musical called STEP LIVELY in 1944; other films included IT AIN'T HAY, UP IN ARMS, BATHING BEAUTY, COPACABANA, IT HAD TO BE YOU, MY GIRL TISA, THE GIRL FROM JONES BEACH; continued his writing despite being blacklisted during the 1950s.

Bose, Nitin

Died 13 Apr. 1986, Calcutta, India, age 89.

Film Director. Started as a cameraman in 1925, photographed DENA PAONA; went on to direct over 50 Indian and Bengali motion pictures, including CHANDIDAS, KASHINATH, BHAGYA CHAKRA (pioneered "playback" system in India for this film), DIDI (all of 1930s vintage).

Boustedt, Christer

Died 10 Sept. 1986, Gavle, Sweden, age 47.

Jazz Saxophone Player-Film Actor. Dixieland/jazz saxophonist, appeared in a 1976 road film, SVEN KLANG'S QUINTET, which inspired Bertrand Tavernier to do 'ROUND MIDNIGHT in 1986.

Boyt, John Thomas

Born 19 Apr. 1921, Newark, N.J.; died 5 Nov. 1986, New York City, New York.

Costume/Set Designer-TV Script Writer-Art Director. Started his career on the N.Y. stage in 1946, doing costume design for "A Flag is Born"; other stage efforts included "Playboy of the Western World" (sets and costumes), "Years Ago" (costumes), Antony and Cleopatra" (men's costumes), and "Western Symphony" (set design for ballet); film work included the design on: SPLENDOR IN THE GRASS, THE TAKING OF PELHAM ONE TWO THREE, DOG DAY AFTERNOON; on TV, worked as an art director before writing teleplays in 1949; headed the costume department at NBC during 1952; taught at the State University of New York.

Bradshaw, Jon

Died 25 Nov. 1986, Los Angeles, Calif., age 48.

Screenwriter-Author-Magazine Contributing Editor. Hailed from New York City but moved to London before returning to Los Angeles in 1977; contributed nonfiction articles to many publications in the U.S. and Europe; had three scripts in development

("Dreams That Money Can Buy," a biography of blues singer Libby Holman; "The Moderns," cowritten with Alan Rudolph to be directed by Rudolph in 1987; "Rafferty"); books included *Fast Company* and *The Cruelest Game.*

Braine, John

(John Gerard Braine)

Died 28 Oct. 1986, London, England, age 64.

Author-Playwright. Born in Bradford, England, where he was a provincial librarian while writing his most famous book *Room at the Top* (published 1957, filmed 1959) which put him at the center of a new group of novelists, "The Angry Young Men"; wrote a sequel, *Life at the Top* (filmed 1965); also wrote a play and TV series, "Man at the Top," which later became a film.

Bremen, Lennie

(Leonard Bremen)

Died 21 March 1986, Hollywood, Calif., age 71.

Film Character Actor. Acted on the stage in Works Progress Administration theater groups and on Broadway before going to Los Angeles in 1942 to work at Warner Bros.; first film was PRIDE OF THE MARINES; others included BUCK PRIVATES COME HOME, LINDA BE GOOD, HENRY THE RAINMAKER, THE INSPECTOR GENERAL, M, TROPICAL HEAT WAVE, NEW YORK CONFIDENTIAL, THE MAN WITH THE GOLDEN ARM, DOUBLE TROUBLE, SWINGIN' ALONG, LOVE WITH THE PROPER STRANGER, WHO'S MINDING THE MINT, P.J., THE FRONT PAGE, LITTLE MISS MARKER, . . . ALL THE MARBLES.

Briggs, Donald P.

Born 28 Jan. 1911, Chicago, Ill.; died 3 Feb. 1986, Woodland Hills, Calif.

Film/Stage/Radio Actor. Started his career in Chicago radio, moving to California to do the heroic radio character "Frank Merriwell" on national hookup; went into films in the mid-1930s for such efforts as LOVE BEFORE BREAKFAST, CAPTAINS COURAGEOUS, MAN OF THE PEOPLE, THE FIRST HUNDRED YEARS, THEY WON'T FORGET, ALL-AMERICAN SWEETHEART, FIT FOR A KING, CRIME SCHOOL, MEN ARE SUCH FOOLS, COWBOY FROM BROOKLYN, WINGS OF THE NAVY, THE HARDYS RIDE HIGH, WHISPERING ENEMIES, PANAMA LADY, EX-CHAMP, FORGOTTEN WOMAN, UNEXPECTED FATHER, HOT STEEL.

Britton, Aileen

Died 19 Apr. 1986, Sydney, Australia, age unknown.

Film/Stage/TV Actress. Had her start in films in 1937 in TALL TIMBERS, an Australian film directed by that country's pioneer filmmaker, Ken G. Hall; because Australia's film industry was quiescent until the mid-1970s, she worked on stage, later returning to movies and appearing in BORN TO RUN,

MY BRILLIANT CAREER, NOW AND FOREVER, THE BEE EATER (a 1986 release); also handled some TV chores such as "Seven Little Australians," "The Sullivans," and "Cyclone Tracey," a miniseries that had not yet been presented.

Brodus, Tex

(Richard Brodus)

Died 9 May 1986, Woodland Hills, Calif., age 81.

Film/Stage Actor-Dancer. Made appearances in 42ND STREET, FOOTLIGHT PARADE, and other musicals.

Brooke, Walter

Died 20 Aug. 1986, Los Angeles, Calif., age 71.

Stage/Film/TV/Radio Actor. Born in New York, appeared in such plays as "Romeo and Juliet," "The Eagle With Two Heads," "The Second Man," "Hide and Seek," and "Twilight Walk"; started in films during the 1940s; credits include BULLET SCARS, C MAN, CONQUEST IN SPACE, EXECUTIVE SUITE, THE PARTY CRASHERS, BLOODLUST, THE WONDERFUL WORLD OF THE BROTHERS GRIMM, THE GRADUATE, SERGEANT RYKER, MAROONED, TORA!

TORA! TORA!, LAWMAN, FUN WITH DICK AND JANE, NORTH DALLAS FORTY, OMEN II, STIR CRAZY, JAGGED EDGE; his appearances on TV approach the 500-role category in such shows as "Paper Chase," "Cagney and Lacey," "Simon and Simon" plus a host of TV-movies; was extremely active in film industry unions.

Brown, Harry

(Harry Peter McNab Brown, Jr.)

Born 30 Apr. 1917, Portland, Me.; died 2 Nov. 1986, Los Angeles, Calif.

Screenwriter. After attending Harvard, worked at *Time* and *The New Yorker* and wrote two volumes of poetry; went into the army during WW II, and his war experiences compelled him to write the novel *Walk in the Sun,* which was filmed in 1946; other film efforts include THE OTHER LOVE, ARCH OF TRIUMPH, WAKE OF THE RED WITCH, SANDS OF IWO JIMA, KISS TOMORROW GOODBYE, ONLY THE VALIANT, A PLACE IN THE SUN (garnered a cowriting Oscar), BUGLES IN THE AFTERNOON, THE SNIPER, EIGHT IRON MEN, ALL THE BROTHERS WERE VALIANT, MANY RIVERS TO CROSS, THE VIRGIN QUEEN, D-DAY, THE SIXTH OF JUNE, OCEANS 11; his novel *The Stars in Their Courses* was the basis for EL DORADO.

Bruhn, Erik

Died 1 Apr. 1986, Toronto, Canada, age 57.

Ballet Dancer-Film Dancer-Actor. Born in Copenhagen, started ballet training at age nine and joined the Royal Ballet in his late teens; specialized in parts for the great classical ballets and danced with some of the greatest female dancers of the period; in 1949-

1950, was a guest artist with the American Ballet Theater and later had a role in HANS CHRISTIAN ANDERSEN; became a permanent part of the American Ballet Theater in 1951.

Bubbles, John W.

(John William Sublett)

Born 19 Feb. 1902, Louisville, Ky.; died 18 May 1986, Los Angeles, Calif.

Stage/Film Tap Dancer/Actor. Originated the art of rhythm tap dancing and brought it to the heights of popularity on both stage and screen; started out singing at the age of seven and formed a partnership dancing with Ford Lee Washington (later renamed "Buck"), resulting in the act "Buck and Bubbles" that lasted for 40 years; went into "Porgy and Bess" as Sportin' Life; other stage credits included "Frolics of 1922," "Ziegfeld Follies of 1931," "Virginia," "Carmen Jones"; the two did such films as VARSITY SHOW OF 1937, CABIN IN THE SKY, ATLANTIC CITY and A SONG IS BORN; offered tap instruction to such stars as Fred Astaire and Eleanor Powell; with the death of Buck death in 1955, Bubbles didn't work in show business for 10 years, but he bounced back with USO shows starring Bob Hope, a stint with Anna Maria Alberghetti, and as the opening act for Judy Garland's "Judy at the Palace"; did TV bits with Johnny Carson, Perry Como and Lucille Ball; retired in 1967 after a stroke left him partially paralyzed.

Buckley, Hal

Died 17 March 1986, Los Angeles, Calif., age 49.

Stage/Film/TV Performer. Started out in such off-Broadway productions as "Greenwich Village U.S.A.," "The Cradle Will Rock," "Ernest in Love,"; after a 1966 move to Los Angeles, worked in such films as SURFARI (narration only), KELLY'S HEROES, SHAMPOO; worked on TV in "O.K. Crackerby" and the "Marco Polo" miniseries; had recently completed a novel entitled *Beyond the Misty Space*.

Busch, Bob

Died 29 Sept. 1986, Santa Monica, Calif., age 69.

Film Dialog/Casting Director-Stage Actor. After graduating from Harvard and the drama school at Yale, went on stage in "Romeo and Juliet"; did the stage managing chores for the same play in 1948; assisted Max Liebman and Imogene Coca on TV's "Your Show of Shows" before going to Los Angeles to work with Sanford Meisner's drama group and a four-year stint (starting in 1958) at 20th Century Fox as a screen test director; did dialog directing on KITTEN WITH A WHIP, THE GREATEST STORY EVER TOLD, HOW TO SAVE A MARRIAGE—AND RUIN YOUR LIFE, GOOD NEIGHBOR SAM; went to Hawaii to work on the TV series "Hawaii Five-O" as a location casting director; while there he started up a cheesecake company which he later moved to Los Angeles.

Bustos Venegas, Jorge

Died in early 1986 at Cuernavaca, Mexico, age unknown.

Film Editor/Actor. Went into the Mexican film industry at the urging of his father, a film distributor, in the 1929 film PAYASADAS DE LA VIDA; received Mexico's equivalent of the Oscar for three films, TRES RASTROS DE MUJER, LA BESTIA MAGNIFICA, LA ESCONDIDA; switched to film editing (had two brothers in the same discipline) for a total career lasting approximately 50 years.

Cabot, Susan

(Harriet Shapiro)

Born 9 July 1927, Boston, Mass.; died 10 Dec. 1986, Encino, Calif.

Film Actress. Appeared in films during a 10-year period starting in 1950 with ON THE ISLE OF SAMOA; other films included TOMAHAWK, THE ENFORCER, FLAME OF ARABY, SON OF ALI BABA, BATTLE AT APACHE PASS, DUEL AT SILVER CREEK, THE SAGA OF THE VIKING WOMEN AND THEIR VOYAGE TO THE WATERS OF THE GREAT SERPENT, ONE AND ONLY, SORORITY GIRL, WAR OF THE SATELLITES, MACHINE GUN KELLY, WASP WOMAN; had a highly publicized romance with

Jordan's King Hussein in the late 1950s; was found beaten to death in her home and her son was arrested for the crime.

Caesar, Adolph

Died 6 March 1986, Los Angeles, Calif., age 52.

Black Stage/Film Actor. Born in the Harlem section of New York City, joined the Navy, then studied drama at New York University; was an announcer for years, then joined the Negro Ensemble Co. in 1970 for such productions as "The River Niger," "Square Root of the Soul," and "The Brownsville Raid"; worked with repertory groups such as the Minnesota Theater Co., Inner-City Repertory Co. (Los Angeles), Lincoln Center Repertory Co., and the American Shakespeare Co.; first appeared on the screen in CHE (1969), then returned to the stage until the late 1970s when he

did low-budget films (THE HITTER, FIST OF FEAR, TOUCH OF DEATH) before achieving his greatest success in A SOLDIER'S STORY (from the stage play for which he collected two awards), which earned him an Oscar nomination; appeared in THE COLOR PURPLE and was working on TOUGH GUYS with Burt Lancaster and Kirk Douglas when he collapsed on the set of a heart attack and died a short time later.

Cagney, James

(James Francis Cagney, Jr.)

Born 17 July 1899, New York City, N.Y.; died 30 Mar. 1986, Stanfordville, N.Y.

Film/Stage Actor-Dancer. One of the true greats of the silver screen, a dynamic personality with an

electric presence (once said he played his roles on his toes to project an energetic image); his father was a saloon owner who gambled away the family money while his mother (though in ill-health) held the family together; often held down several jobs at once to help support the family; his father died during the Spanish influenza epidemic of 1918; grew up in a tough, ethnically mixed (Jewish, Hungarian, Irish, Italian, German) neighborhood; the four Cagney brothers took a public speaking class at a settlement house and when one of the brothers was unable to appear in a play, Jimmy reluctantly took the part (baseball and boxing were his passions); the satisfaction received from his first outing sparked a lifetime interest in acting; while working in a department store, heard from a fellow employee that a revue needed a replacement; he wasn't enthusiastic about the part (which called for him to impersonate a female), but since the pay was more than double his clerk salary, he opted for the opportunity; during auditions, got a part in "Pitter Patter," a Broadway musical, by watching and then imitating the other hopefuls; his stipend was increased but he had to do valet services for the star and sometimes baggage handling for the whole company while understudying the lead; in the company at that time were two people who would be associated with him for many years, Allen Jenkins (appeared in many of his films as comic relief) and Frances Willard "Billie" Vernon (who later became his wife and appeared with him in a vaudeville act called "Vernon and Nye"); he toured in vaudeville, appeared in an act authored by Hugh Herbert and temporarily replaced a man named Archie Leach (later renamed Cary Grant in Hollywood) in a trio act; Cagney and his wife toured together in "Lew Fields' Ritz Girls of 1922" and then went to Los Angeles for their first try at films, which did not work out; appeared in a variety of stage productions and started a tap dancing school in New Jersey, giving him the chance to choreograph a satirical revue ("The Grand Street Follies of 1928") as well as dance and act in it; appeared in "Maggie the Magnificent" (1929) which teamed him for the first—but not the last—time with Joan Blondell; through the good offices of Al Jolson, was offered, along with Blondell, a part in the film version of "Penny Arcade," renamed SINNER'S HOLIDAY, followed by roles in DOORWAY TO HELL and OTHER MEN'S WOMEN (at the time, Warner Brothers worked their people on a six-day week schedule with no breaks between pictures); almost got the lead part in THE FRONT PAGE, but producer Howard Hughes thought he was too short; career took an upturn with a bit part in THE MILLIONAIRE, in which Cagney's two minutes on screen were so impressive they won him his first leading role in Warner Brothers' PUBLIC ENEMY, which featured the famous grapefruit scene with Mae Clarke; shortly thereafter he staged the first of his many walkouts in a tug of war with Warners over low pay; upon his return, he starred in SMART MONEY, BLONDE CRAZY, TAXI, THE CROWD ROARS, WINNER TAKE ALL; was assigned to do BLESSED EVENT, but walked out again, forcing Warners to replace him with Lee Tracy; Cagney threatened to give up his film career and become a doctor and the studio finally gave in to his salary demands; he returned to star in HARD TO HANDLE, PICTURE SNATCHER, THE MAYOR OF HELL, FOOTLIGHT PARADE, LADY KILLER, JIMMY THE GENT, HE WAS HER MAN, HERE COMES THE NAVY, THE ST. LOUIS KID, DEVIL DOGS OF THE AIR, G-MEN, THE IRISH IN US, A MIDSUMMER NIGHT'S DREAM, FRISCO KID, CEILING ZERO, GREAT GUY, SOMETHING TO SING ABOUT, the last two films done for Grand National during one of his revolts against Jack Warner; on coming back to Warners, received a new contract with some unique "perks" including the privilege of ending the studio relationship if working conditions were not to his liking; made BOY MEETS GIRL, ANGELS WITH DIRTY FACES, THE OKLAHOMA KID, EACH DAWN I DIE, THE ROARING TWENTIES (a semi-documentary about prohibition which marked the end of Warners run of gangster films), THE FIGHT-ING 69TH, TORRID ZONE, CITY FOR CON-QUEST, THE STRAWBERRY BLONDE, THE BRIDE CAME C.O.D., CAPTAINS OF THE CLOUDS (his first color film), and his Oscar-winning portrayal of George M. Cohan in YANKEE DOODLE DANDY (Cohan had personally selected Cagney for the role), showing Cagney at the top of his talent in both acting and dancing; he then made JOHNNY COME LATELY, THE TIME OF YOUR LIFE (both produced by his brother William), BLOOD ON THE SUN, 13 RUE MADE-LEINE, WHITE HEAT, THE WEST POINT STORY, KISS TOMORROW GOODBYE, COME FILL THE CUP, WHAT PRICE GLORY, A LION IS IN THE STREETS, RUN FOR COVER, LOVE ME OR LEAVE ME, MISTER ROBERTS, THE SEVEN LITTLE FOYS (a cameo role as George M. Cohan), TRIBUTE TO A BAD MAN, THESE WILDER YEARS, MAN OF A THOU-SAND FACES (bringing the life of Lon Chaney, Sr. to the screen); he directed but did not act in SHORT CUT TO HELL, then made NEVER STEAL ANYTHING SMALL, SHAKE HANDS WITH THE DEVIL, THE GALLANT HOURS (in which his adopted son, James Cagney, Jr., who died in 1984, had a small part), ONE, TWO, THREE; at this point, he decided to abandon his film career; though he supplied the narration on an anti-Communist documentary and the 1968 film ARIZONA BUSHWHACKERS, both for his old friend A.C. Lyles, he stuck to his guns in retirement, though he was offered numerous film roles; he spent his time at his four residences which included a house on Martha's Vineyard and a farm in Millbrook, N.Y., where he still exercised to keep in shape, raised horses, collected carriages, played classical guitar, continued his interest in painting; he was honored by the American Film Institute with a Life Achievement Award in 1974 and gave a memorable speech, sprinkled with humor and thoughts about the nature of art; became afflicted with diabetes and other ailments during his later years so that doctors recommended a return to acting; in 1981 he made RAGTIME (at first it was to be a small part but it was enlarged to fit his still potent charisma) and in 1984 he appeared a TV film, "Terrible Joe Moran"; he was a gentle man, unlike his film image, who seldom smoked or drank, had the same wife for 64 years, and brought great pleasure to quite a few generations.

Caldwell, Don

Died 16 Aug. 1986, Sherman Oaks, Calif., age 51.

Film/TV Extra-Actor. Made over 400 appearances as an extra, but did have a speaking role in LOOKIN' TO GET OUT and in the TV productions "Moviola: The Scarlett O'Hara War," "The Day the Bubble Burst," "The Thorn Birds."

Callahan, Mushy

(Vincent Morris Scheer)

Born 4 Nov. 1904, New York City, N.Y.; died 14 June 1986, Los Angeles, Calif.

Film Actor-Stand-In-Fight Choreographer-Former Junior Welterweight Boxing Champion-Boxing Referee. Held the junior welterweight boxing title in the late 1920s before going to Warner Bros. in 1934, first as a prop man and grip, then as a boxing instructor to studio stars; helped stage fights for films such as KID GALAHAD, THEY MADE ME A CRIMINAL, CITY FOR CONQUEST, GEN-TLEMAN JIM, JIM THORPE—ALL AMERI-CAN, THE WINNING TEAM; also worked on REBEL WITHOUT A CAUSE and was helping to train James Dean for SOMEBODY UP THERE LIKES ME until Dean's death when he was re-placed by Paul Newman; other films included CHAMPION, FROM HERE TO ETERNITY, THE SAND PEBBLES, and the ballet movements in the musical OKLAHOMA; his final effort before retirement was assisting James Earl Jones on THE GREAT WHITE HOPE; had small parts in films such as MADISON SQUARE GARDEN, THE PERSONALITY KID, THE IRISH IN US, HOUSE OF STRANGERS, THE IRON MAN, STOP, YOU'RE KILLING ME, SOME LIKE IT HOT, ELMER GANTRY, JUDGMENT AT NUREMBURG, HELLO DOLLY!; served as stand-in for Karl Malden (GYPSY), Stanley Hollo-way (MY FAIR LADY), and Jason Robards, Jr. (ANY WEDNESDAY).

Campbell, Muriel

(Muriel Campbell Douglas)

Died 1 July 1986, Warren, Ct., age 75.

Stage/Film Actress. Appeared mostly in summer stock and Broadway theater, although she did ap-pear in two films, the Marx Brothers' ANIMAL CRACKERS and SHE MARRIED A COP; stage efforts included a number of short-run plays along with one very successful run in "Having Wonderful Time" in 1937.

Canning, Victor

Born 16 June 1911, Plymouth, Devonshire, Eng-land; died 21 Feb. 1986, Cirencester, England.

Novelist. Adventure novels were his forte, but also wrote several comedic and historical novels; started in 1934 with *Mr. Finchley Discovers England* (inau-gurating a series based on that character); after a six-year hitch in the Royal Artillery during WW II he continued writing, producing several novels which were turned into films: *Panther's Moon* (filmed in 1950 as SPY HUNT), THE GOLDEN SALAMANDER (filmed in 1950), *Bird of Prey* (1953 as ASSASSIN), *The House of the Seven Flies* (1959 as THE HOUSE OF THE SEVEN HAWKS), *A Handful of Silver* (1965 as MASQUERADE), *Twist of the Knife* (1970 as SHARK), *The Limbo Line* (1969), *The Scorpio Letters* (1967 as a TV film) and *The Rainbird Pattern* (1976 as Alfred Hitchcock's last film, FAMILY PLOT).

Canty, Marietta

Died 9 July 1986, Hartford, Ct., age 80.

Film/Stage/Radio Actress. Appeared in several productions on Broadway in the 1930s such as "Run, Little Chillun!," "Co-Respondent Un-known," "No Time For Comedy,"; some of her films (usually as a maid or cook) include THE LADY IS WILLING, THE MAGNIFICENT DOPE, SILVER QUEEN, THE SPOILERS, IRISH EYES ARE SMILING, LADY IN THE DARK, SUNDAY DINNER FOR A SOLDIER, HOME SWEET HOMICIDE, THE SEARCHING WIND, DEAR RUTH, THE SEA OF GRASS, DEAR WIFE, MOTHER IS A FRESHMAN, MY FOOLISH HEART, A STREET NAMED DE-SIRE, THE BAD AND THE BEAUTIFUL, A MAN CALLED PETER and her final film, RE-BEL WITHOUT A CAUSE, in 1955; left the screen to take care of her father and participate in civic activities.

Canutt, Yakima

(Enos Edward Canutt)

Born 28 Nov. 1895, Colfax, Wash.; died 24 May 1986, North Hollywood, Calif.

Film Stuntman-Actor-Stunt Choreographer-Film Di-rector-Second Unit Director-Screenwriter. Started out at age 17 in Wild West shows; received the name of Yakima from a newspaper reporter who con-nected him with the valley in the state of Washing-ton; earned five world cowboy championships; after serving in the Navy during WW I, began working as an extra and stuntman in silent pictures; a produc-tion supervisor at Universal liked his athletic ability and put him in a string of westerns, sometimes in starring roles, while he continued to do stunt work on the side and staged an exciting horse fight that was reused in various westerns up to the late 1930s; his voice had been weakened by the influenza epi-demic in the late 1910s so he was not suited to play the hero in sound pictures; he continued to work occasionally as a supporting player, but concentrated on stunt work; taught John Wayne and Gene Autry

riding and stunt abilities; worked out the details on many stunts that would become standard in action vehicles; silent film work included THE FORBID-DEN RANGE, THE CACTUS CURE, THE HUMAN TORNADO, WHITE THUNDER, DE-SERT GREED, THE THREE OUTCASTS; sound credits include BAR L RANCH, CANYON HAWKS, THE CHEYENNE KID, THE MAN FROM UTAH, RANDY RIDES ALONE, THE STAR PACKER, WINDS OF THE WASTELAND, RIDERS OF THE WHISTLING SKULL, ROARIN' LEAD, OVERLAND STAGE RAID-ERS, COWBOYS FROM TEXAS, GONE WITH THE WIND, STAGECOACH, THE GREAT TRAIN ROBBERY (1941), FOR WHOM THE BELL TOLLS; films directed include SHERIFF OF CIMARRON, CARSON CITY RAIDERS, LAW-LESS RIDER; RIDERS OF THE GOLDEN GULCH (also story writer and actor); his stunt ex-pertise was used on RIDERS OF DESTINY, THE LIGHT THAT FAILED, ONE MILLION, B.C. (1940), EL CID, WHERE EAGLES DARE, as well as numerous other films; he handled the second unit direction of the climactic chariot race in the 1959 version of BEN HUR; was honored by the Motion Picture Academy in 1966 for his innovations in the stunt field, especially in the area of safety, and for raising the profession to a "fine science."

Capell, Peter

Died 3 March 1986, Munich, West Germany, age 73.

Stage/Film Actor-Radio Actor-Producer. A native of Berlin, came to the U.S. in 1933 for radio and theatrical work; from 1941 through 1947 was exec-utive producer of "The Voice of America"; ap-peared on stage in "Lamp at Midnight," "Blood Wedding," "The Sun And I," "Sands of the Negev," and "Hedda Gabler"; started his film ca-reer in 1952 with WALK EAST ON BEACON, and went on to appear in PATHS OF GLORY, I AIM AT THE STARS, ARMORED COMMAND, ONE, TWO, THREE, THE COUNTERFEIT TRAITOR, WILLY WONKA AND THE CHOC-OLATE FACTORY and in 1984, THE LITTLE DRUMMER GIRL; after 1955, most of his film work was done in Europe where he had returned;

his fluency in German and English enabled him to do quite a bit of dubbing.

Carey, Denis

Born 3 Aug. 1909, London, England; died 28 Sept. 1986, London, England.

Stage Actor/Director/Producer-Film/TV Actor. Started as a clerk in an income tax office before switching to the stage in 1921; appeared at the Gate and Abbey theaters in Dublin in such productions as "Deirdre, Is Life Worth Living," "The Resurrection," and "Murder in the Cathedral," repeating the latter role for his New York debut in 1938; toured theaters in Great Britain from 1940 through 1946; started to do some direction in 1947; appeared in the films CHILDREN OF CHANCE (1949) and THE DAY OF THE JACKAL (1973); when the American Shakespeare Theater was started, he was its first artistic director in 1955.

Carlile, Robert

Died 4 May 1986, Dublin, Ireland, age 40.

Stage/Film/TV Actor. Born in Cork, did local theatricals before stage work with the Edwards-MacLiammoir Dublin Gate Theater Co. and Gemini Productions; joined the Abbey Theater sometime in the 1960s for a run of approximately 100 roles, interspersed with TV and film appearances.

Carmel, Roger C.

Found dead 11 Nov. 1986, Hollywood, Calif., age 54.

Stage/Film/TV Actor. Started his stage work in the mid-1950s in such efforts as "The Plough and the Stars," "The Picture of Dorian Gray," "Hamlet," and "Purlie Victorious"; film appearances included THE GREATEST SHOW ON EARTH, STAGE STRUCK, NORTH BY NORTHWEST, A HOUSE IS NOT A HOME, GOODBYE CHARLIE, THE ART OF LOVE, ALVAREZ KELLY, GAMBIT, THE VENETIAN AFFAIR, SKULL-DUGGERY, BREEZY, THUNDER AND LIGHT-FOOT, HARDLY WORKING; had numerous TV roles on such shows as "Naked City," "Alfred

Hitchcock Presents," "Route 66," "I Spy," "Batman," "The Defenders," and "Star Trek"; supplied the voice for "Smokey the Bear" in TV commercials.

Carr, Frankie

(Frank Carozza)

Died 20 March 1986, Las Vegas, Nev., age 61.

Nightclub/TV Performer-Film Actor. Formed a musical comedy group during the 1950s called the Novelties; toured hotels and nightclubs; performed on TV for Ed Sullivan, Arthur Godfrey and other variety shows; appeared in several Jerry Lewis films; opened a Las Vegas night club which burned down in 1985.

Celi, Adolfo

Born 27 July 1922, Messina, Italy; died 19 Feb. 1986, Siena, Italy.

Film Actor/Director/Writer-Stage Actor/Director. Educated in Rome, made his film debut in 1946 with UN AMERICANO IN VACANZA, followed by NATALE AL CAMPO, PROIBITO RUBARE, EMIGRANTES; went to South America for a 15-year stretch as a stage actor/director in both Argentina and Brazil; his appearance in THAT MAN FROM RIO in 1963 revived his film career and upon returning to Europe he worked in more than 80 films, including THUNDERBALL, VON RYAN'S EXPRESS, THE AGONY AND THE ECSTASY, SLALOM, EL GRECO, GRAND PRIX, OPERATION KID BROTHER, THE HONEY POT, THE BOBO, MIDAS RUN, L'ALIBI (both cowrote and codirected), L'EMANUELLE, IN SEARCH OF GREGORY, MURDERS IN THE RUE MORGUE (1971), FRAGMENT OF FEAR, HITLER: THE LAST TEN DAYS, THE DEVIL IS A WOMAN, MON-SIGNOR; directed CIACARA, ALIBA, TICO TICO NO FUBA.

Chapman, Ted

Died 19 Aug. 1986, Studio City, Calif., age 63.

Stage/Film/TV Actor. Appeared in a revival of "The Rope Dancers" in 1959, followed by "What A Killing," "Red Roses For Me," "Gogo Loves You"; also appeared in films (BANANAS and DON'T ANSWER THE PHONE) and did extensive work in TV commercials.

Childress, Alvin

Died 19 Apr. 1986, Inglewood, Calif., age 78.

TV/Stage/Film Actor. Raised in Mississippi, attended Rust College, then went to New York for his stage debut in "Savage Rhythm" (late 1931); worked with the Federal Theater project and did some theatrical instructing at the American Negro Theater; other stage efforts included "Brown Sugar," "Haiti," "Natural Man," "Anna Lucasta" (appeared in the film version 14 years later), "Rain"; some of his films included KEEP PUNCHING (1939), THE MAN IN THE NET, THUNDERBOLT AND LIGHTFOOT, DARK-TOWN STRUTTERS (1975), THE DAY OF THE LOCUST, THE BINGO LONG TRAVELING ALL STARS AND MOTOR KINGS; best known for his portrayal of "Amos" in the popular but controversial TV series "Amos 'n' Andy," a part he took after helping with the original casting of

the show; did a stint as a Los Angeles County social worker after the cancellation of the series but went back into show business for the later films; later TV efforts included appearances on "Sanford and Son" and "The Jeffersons."

Christopher, David

Died 20 June 1986, age unknown.

Film Actor. Appeared in the 1984 film, HOT MOVES.

Clark, Mamo

Died 18 Dec. 1986, Panorama City, Calif., age 72.

Film Actress-Author. Born on the island of Maui, studied at the University of Southern California, making her screen debut opposite Clark Gable in MUTINY ON THE BOUNTY (1935), billed simply as Mamo; went on to appear in THE HURRI-CANE, WALLABY JIM OF THE ISLANDS, AIR DEVILS, BOOLOO, HAWAII CALLS, MUTINY ON THE BLACKHAWK, GIRL FROM GOD'S COUNTRY, ONE MILLION B.C., SEVEN SIN-NERS; in recent years, had received a degree in cinematography from The University of California at Los Angeles, and worked on a book about the Hawaiian Islands called *Except Their Sun*.

Coffin, Winnie

Died 18 Dec. 1986, Birmingham, Mich., age 75.

TV/Film Actress. After beginning her career at age 50, appeared on TV in such shows as "Bonanza," "Perry Mason," "Gunsmoke," "The Tonight Show," "The Red Skelton Show" and in several Walt Disney films.

Colonna, Jerry

(Gerald Luigi Colonna)

Born 17 Sept. 1904, Boston, Mass.; died 21 Nov. 1986, Woodland Hills, Calif.

Radio/TV/Film Comedian-Actor-Musician. After high school, had a job as a longshoreman while studying trombone and drums at night and organizing his own jazz band; played with some of the big bands of the time such as Ozzie Nelson, Benny Goodman, Artie Shaw; played in the CBS radio staff orchestra; went to Hollywood in 1937 for his screen debut in 52ND STREET; in 1938, signed a contract with Bob Hope (after earlier appearances with Fred Allen, Walter O'Keefe, Bing Crosby, Red Skelton) and stayed with him for 25 years; other films include ROSALIE, COLLEGE SWING, LITTLE MISS BROADWAY, GARDEN OF THE MOON, VALLEY OF THE GIANTS, NAUGHTY BUT NICE, ROAD TO SINGAPORE, MELODY AND MOONLIGHT, SIS HOPKINS, ICE CAPADES, STAR-SPANGLED RHYTHM, IT'S IN THE BAG!, ATLANTIC CITY (1944), MAKE MINE MUSIC, ROAD TO RIO, ANDY HARDY COMES HOME, ROAD TO HONG KONG; started accompanying Bob Hope on his U.S.O. tours in 1941; had three recordings that sold well, "Sweet Adeline," "Down by the Old Mill Stream," and "Ebb Tide"; wrote the novel *The Loves of Tullio* in 1970.

Colt, Samuel

(Samuel Barrymore Colt)

Died 1 Aug. 1986, Beverly Hills, Calif., age 76.

Actor-Film/Stage Producer. Grandson of the founder of the U.S. Rubber Co., great nephew to the inventor of the Colt revolver, and son of the stage and film star, Ethel Barrymore; appeared in A STAR IS BORN, THE MATING SEASON, THREE BRAVE MEN and his mother's final film, JOHNNY TROUBLE.

Coluche

(Michel Colucci)

Born 28 Oct. 1944, Paris, France; died 19 June 1986, Grasse, France.

Standup Comedian-Film Actor. One of France's top comedians; appeared in nightclubs and made 15 films, including BANZAI, TCHAO PANTIN (for which he won France's best actor award in 1984), and MY BEST FRIEND'S GIRL; announced plans to run for President in 1981 and when polls showed he could win 15 percent of the vote, French politicians became highly critical of him and he withdrew; in 1985 he started a free meals program for France's poor; a motorcycle enthusiast (he set a world speed record in 1985), his death was the result of a cycling accident.

Como, Rossella

Died 20 Dec. 1986, Rome, Italy, age 47.

Film/Stage/TV Actress. Born in an artistic neighborhood in Rome, began a TV career in 1956, later taking a small part in POVERI MA BELLI; other films include NONNA SABELLA, LAZZARELLA, SEVEN HILLS OF ROME, 8-1/2, THE TALL WOMEN, WE MARRIED TO HAVE FUN; appeared on stage in "Six Characters in Search of an Author" by Luigi Pirandello; originated and starred in a variety show which toured through South America.

Connell, Polly

(Polly Mallitz Connell)

Died 14 Jan. 1986, Burbank, Calif., age 73.

Literary Agent-Story Analyst-Film/Stage/Radio Actress. Hailing from New Orleans, came to California to get theatrical training from Max Reinhardt and secured a bit part in SPRING PARADE (1940); went on the stage and then became California's first female disc jockey; went to work for Walt Disney studios as a story analyst (sparked the production of "OLD YELLER" and "MARY POPPINS") and voice-over specialist (did the Dale voice for "Chip and Dale" cartoons, as well as the voice of Bambi's mother); left to start up a literary section in a talent agency and helped develop the talent of writers such as Stephen J. Cannell, creator of the TV series "The A-Team" and "Hardcastle and McCormick."

Cook, Dick

Died 3 Feb. 1986, Honolulu, Hawaii, age 58.

Radio Announcer/Personality-Film Actor. A native of Boston, appeared on the CBS "Let's Pretend" radio show at the age of nine; did radio work in Ohio and then became the announcer for George Gobel's TV show; made appearances in several films and worked as a disk jockey in both Los Angeles and Honolulu.

Cooper, Lady Diana

(Diana Olivia Winifred Maud Manners)

Born 29 Aug. 1892; died 16 June 1986, London, England.

Film Actress-Socialite. Beautiful but eccentric socialite who appeared in one silent film, THE MIRACLE, 1912, then did a 12-year promotional world tour for it; made one other film, GLORIOUS ADVENTURE in 1921; was married to the distinguished British diplomat, Alfred Duff Cooper.

Cooper, Edna Mae

Died 27 June 1986, Woodland Hills, Calif., age 85.

Film Actress-Pilot. Started her career in the late 1910s in such silent films (many for Cecil B. DeMille) as THE WHISPERING CHORUS, OLD WIVES FOR NEW, MALE AND FEMALE, PUTTING IT OVER, WHY CHANGE YOUR WIFE?, BEAUTY AND THE BAD MAN, GROUNDS FOR DIVORCE, SALLY, IRENE AND MARY, THE KING OF KINGS, CODE OF THE AIR, GEORGE WASHINGTON COHEN, SAY IT WITH SABLES; became a pilot who set a world refueling record for women; made her final film in 1956, which was also DeMille's last, THE TEN COMMANDMENTS.

Coppola, Gian Carlo

Died 26 May 1986, Annapolis, Maryland, age 23.

Film Second Unit Director. Worked in various capacities on the films of his father, Francis Coppola; was associate producer on RUMBLE FISH and THE OUTSIDERS; killed in a boating accident.

Cotner, Carl

Died 14 Nov. 1986, Buena Park, Calif., age 70.

Music Director-Film Stand-In. Started a 50-year career in association with Gene Autry as both musical arranger and occasional stand-in; appeared in the film MELODY RANCH.

Courtot, Marguerite

Born 1897, Summit, N.J.; died 28 May 1986, Long Beach, Calif.

Silent Film Actress. Born in Summit, N.J., made her on-screen debut in THE WAR CORRESPONDENT (1913), followed by THE OCTOROON, A CELEBRATED CASE, THE BAREFOOT BOY, VENTURES OF MARGUERITE, THE PRETENDERS, THE SECRET ROOM, THE VANDERHOFF AFFAIR, THE KISS, THE DEAD ALIVE, FEATHERTOP, ROLLING STONES, THE NATURAL LAW, CRIME AND PUNISHMENT, THE UNBELIEVER, ROARING OAKS, THE PERFECT LOVER, THE TEETH OF THE TIGER, THE UNBELIEVER, BOUND AND GAGGED, PIRATE GOLD, VELVET FINGERS, ROGUES AND ROMANCE, SILAS MARNER, RAINBOW, THE CRADLE BUSTER, DOWN

TO THE SEA IN SHIPS (1923), JAQUELINE, OR BLAZING BARRIERS, OUTLAWS OF THE SEA, THE STEADFAST HEART, MEN, WOMEN AND MONEY.

Cowling, Bruce

Died 22 Aug. 1986, age unknown.

Film Actor. Entered films in the mid-1940s in such efforts as TILL THE CLOUDS ROLL BY, HIGH BARBAREE, IT HAPPENED IN BROOKLYN, SONG OF THE THIN MAN, BATTLEGROUND, THE STRATTON STORY, AMBUSH, DEVIL'S DOORWAY, A LADY WITHOUT PASSPORT, CAUSE FOR ALARM, THE PAINTED HILLS, THE BATTLE AT APACHE PASS, GUN BELT, CANNIBAL ATTACK, MASTERSON OF KANSAS, TO HELL AND BACK.

Craig, Helen

Born 13 May 1912, San Antonio, Texas; died 20 July 1986, New York City, N.Y.

Stage/Film/TV/Radio Actress. Started with small roles in local repertory theater in San Antonio, and after training with four teachers, including Dame May Whitty and Josephine Dillon (at the time the wife of Clark Gable), went on to work in theatrical companies throughout the nation; made her New York debut in 1936 in "Russet Mantle" and met her future husband, John Beal, to whom she was married for more than 50 years; other theatrical efforts included "New Faces of 1936," "American Primitive," and "Julius Caesar"; originated the title role in "Johnny Belinda" (1940); films include THE KEYS OF THE KINGDOM, THE SNAKE PIT, THEY LIVE BY NIGHT, THE SPORTING CLUB, RANCHO DELUXE, HEROES; made numerous appearances on TV, beginning in 1938 ("The Donovan Affair") and 1939 ("The Dangerous Corner") both of which were done "live" before the kinescope or videotape eras.

Crawford, Broderick

(William Broderick Crawford)

Born 9 Dec. 1911, Philadelphia, Penn.; died 26 Apr. 1986, Rancho Mirage, Calif.

Film/Stage/TV Actor. Came from an acting background (grandparents were opera singers, father was a vaudeville performer and mother was a film comedienne); after appearing in his parents' vaudeville act, became a stevedore then a seaman before getting work on radio; his theatrical debut came in London where Noel Coward saw him, liked his stage presence and recommended him to Alfred Lunt and Lynn Fontanne who put him into their production of "Point Valaine"; made his film debut in 1937 in WOMAN CHASES MAN, then made SUBMARINE D-1, and THE WOMAN'S TOUCH; had his big theatrical success in "Of Mice and Men" which had a run of over 300 performances; returned to Hollywood for such films as BEAU GESTE, THE REAL GLORY, ETERNALLY YOURS, SLIGHTLY HONORABLE,

WHEN THE DALTONS RODE, SEVEN SIN-NERS, THE BLACK CAT (1941), TIGHT SHOES, BUTCH MINDS THE BABY, LAR-CENY, INC.; spent WW II in the air force, then returned in 1946 for a few films (THE BLACK ANGEL, SLAVE GIRL, SEALED VERDICT, BAD MEN OF TOMBSTONE, ANNA LU-CASTA) before getting the Oscar-winning role as Willie Stark in ALL THE KING'S MEN; subsequent films were BORN YESTERDAY and THE SWINDLE, before he moved on to TV and starred in "Highway Patrol" for four years; later films included LONE STAR, NIGHT PEOPLE, DOWN THREE DARK STREETS, THE FASTEST GUN ALIVE, BETWEEN HEAVEN AND HELL, UP FROM THE BEACH, RED TOMAHAWK, TER-ROR IN THE WAX MUSEUM, THE PRIVATE FILES OF J. EDGAR HOOVER, A LITTLE RO-MANCE and several films made in Spain or Italy; also did a few TV films ("The Challenge," "The Phantom of Hollywood," "Mayday at 40,000 Feet," "Supertrain") and appeared as a guest host on "Saturday Night Live."

Crothers, Scatman

(Benjamin Sherman Crothers)

Born 23 May 1910, Terre Haute, Ind.; died 26 Nov. 1986, Van Nuys, Calif.

Entertainer/Actor. Began his career in high school playing the drums and guitar while singing in local speakeasies; formed a band and toured around the Midwest eventually gravitating to Los Angeles where he became the first black to appear on a Los Angeles TV series ("Dixie Showboat"); began his film career in 1951 with YES SIR, MR. BONES; other film efforts include MEET ME AT THE

FAIR, RETURN OF GILBERT AND SULLI-VAN, EAST OF SUMATRA, WALKING MY BABY BACK HOME, BETWEEN HEAVEN AND HELL, TARZAN AND THE TRAPPERS, THE SINS OF RACHEL CADE, THE GREAT WHITE HOPE, LADY SINGS THE BLUES, THE FORTUNE, THE KING OF MARVIN GAR-DENS, ONE FLEW OVER THE CUCKOO'S NEST, THE SHOOTIST, SIL-VER STREAK, THE SHINING, BRONCO BILLY, TWO OF A KIND; probably best known for his role as Louie the garbageman on TV's "Chico and the Man."

Cunningham, Sarah

Died 24 March 1986, Los Angeles, Calif., age 67.

Stage/Film/TV Actress. Came from South Carolina and moved to New York for work on the stage in "The Visit," "Mme. Columbe," "Toys in the Attic," "Fair Game," "My Sweet Charlie"; commuted between Broadway and Hollywood for such films as NAKED CITY, THE COWBOYS, I NEVER PROMISED YOU A ROSE GARDEN, FUN WITH DICK AND JANE, FRANCES, JAG-GED EDGE; appeared in numerous TV shows and TV films, including "The Family Kovack," "F. Scott Fitzgerald in Hollywood," and "Belle Starr"; married for more than 40 years to actor John Randolph.

Curran, Paul

Died 1 Dec. 1986, London, England, age 73.

Stage/Film Actor. Originally from Scotland, the main thrust of his career was in stage work, particularly with the National Theater of Britain in such efforts as "The Front Page," "School for Scandal"; his few films include JOHN PAUL JONES, THE WILD AFFAIR, DECLINE AND FALL . . . OF A BIRD WATCHER, JABBERWOCKY, THE HUMAN FACTOR.

Da Silva, Howard

(Harold Silverblatt)

Born 4 May 1909, Cleveland, Oh.; died 16 Feb. 1986, Ossining, N.Y.

Film/Stage Actor-Stage Producer-Writer-Director. Worked in steel mills to pay for his education at the Carnegie Institute of Technology before going to New York to study with Eva Le Galliene's repertory company; appeared in regional theaters and did some teaching and directing; appeared in a one-performance production of "Ten Million Ghosts," a fiasco that proved valuable because it introduced him to Orson Welles, who cast him in "The Cradle Will Rock"; other stage work included "Casey Jones," "Abe Lincoln in Illinois," "Two on an Island," and the original production of "Oklahoma"; his first film was ONCE IN A BLUE MOON, but his film career did not really get going until he made ABE LINCOLN IN ILLINOIS, which was followed by such efforts as THE SEA WOLF, NAVY BLUES, SERGEANT YORK, KEEPER OF THE FLAME, TONIGHT WE

RAID CALAIS, THE LOST WEEKEND, THE BLUE DAHLIA, TWO WEEKS BEFORE THE MAST, BLAZE OF NOON, UNCONQUERED, THE GREAT GATSBY (both the 1949 version with Alan Ladd and the 1974 remake with Robert Redford), THEY LIVE BY NIGHT, TRIPOLI, FOURTEEN HOURS; was blacklisted during the 1950s and unable to work in films for nine years, filling in with stage work, both acting and directing; resumed his film career in 1962 with DAVID AND LISA, then appeared in IT'S A MAD, MAD, MAD, MAD WORLD, NEVADA SMITH, 1776, and his final film, GARBO TALKS in 1974; did several TV productions, including "Missiles of October," "Smile, Jenny, You're Dead," and "Power," and "Verna: U.S.O. Girl," which won him an Emmy for best supporting actor in 1978.

Damiani, Leo

Born 29 July 1912, St. Paul, Minn.; died 4 Nov. 1986, Burbank, Calif.

Orchestra Conductor/Organizer-Film Technical Adviser. After Juilliard School training, a move to California, and WW II army service, founded a symphony in Burbank where he conducted for 15 years; did a nine-year stint as resident conductor of the Las Vegas Symphony; was guest conductor for symphonies in the U.S. and all over the world; conducted for the Walt Disney Studios and trained Charlton Heston for his part as a conductor in COUNTERPOINT.

Davies, Janet

Died 22 Sept., 1986; age unknown.

British TV/Film/Stage Actress. Appeared in the films INTERLUDE (1968) and WHAT'S NEXT (1979).

Dassault, Marcel

Died 18 Apr. 1986, Neuilly, France, age 94.

Airplane Designer/Manufacturer-Motion Picture Financier/Producer. French billionaire known mainly for designing the Mirage jet fighter planes; also was involved in newspaper publishing, politics (was a senior deputy in the National Assembly), broadcasting; financed or produced such films as LA GIFLE, LA BOUM, LE TEMPS DES VA-CANCES, JAMAIS AVANT LE MARIAGE, L'ETE DE NOS 15 ANOS, BORSALINO, THE LAST METRO, THE RETURN OF MARTIN GUERRE, L'AMOUR EN DOUCE.

De Beauvoir, Simone

(Simone Lucie Ernestine Marie Bertrand de Beauvoir)

Born 9 Jan. 1908, Paris, France; died 14 Apr. 1986, Paris, France.

Author-Philosopher-Social Activist. Was a teacher of philosophy at various colleges and universities before taking up writing in 1943, producing such novels as *All Men Are Mortal* and *The Blood of Others* (filmed in 1984 by Claude Chabrol); best known for her feminist book, *The Second Sex* and the autobiographical *Memoirs of a Dutiful Daughter*); had a 50-year relationship with existentialist philosopher Jean-Paul Sartre; was the subject of a 1979 documentary.

De Bretagne, Joseph

Died 4 Dec. 1986, Cagnes-sur-Mer, France, age 86.

Film Sound Engineer. A pioneer in sound engineering in France, worked with many leading directors on such films as ROMAN HOLIDAY, BITTER VICTORY, THE VIKINGS, PARIS BLUES.

Debney, Louis

Died 8 Apr. 1986, Glendale, Calif., age 70.

Film Production Executive. As a teenager in 1934 started in the cutting department at Walt Disney Studios, working on SNOW WHITE AND THE SEVEN DWARFS; was assistant director on many films, including PETER PAN and PERRI; as an associate TV producer, helped in the production of "The Mickey Mouse Club" (100 episodes) and "Zorro" (80 episodes); after other chores on both TV and films, coordinated "The Wonderful World of Disney."

Deering, Olive

Died 22 March 1986, New York, N.Y., age 67.

Stage/Film Actress. Began her career with a bit part in "Girls in Uniform" (1933), then appeared in such plays as "Searching for the Sun," "Daughters of Atreus," "The Eternal Road," "Richard II," and "The Devil's Advocate"; film credits include GENTLEMAN'S AGREEMENT, AIR HOSTESS, SAMSON AND DELILAH, CAGED, THE TEN COMMANDMENTS (1956), SHOCK TREATMENT, HOWZER; worked on numerous radio and TV shows; a brother, Alfred Ryder, was also actor.

Denton, Jack

Died 18 Nov. 1986, Sun Valley, Calif., age 61.

Radio/TV Personality-Disk Jockey-Film Actor-Columnist-Musician-Comedy Writer. After high school worked as a drummer, became a comedian and at age 22 began writing for Milton Berle; worked in Milwaukee as a disk jockey, talk show host, columnist for the *Milwaukee Sentinel*, and held announcing jobs around the country; played Franklin Delano Roosevelt on both stage and TV; appeared in the films THE HELLCATS, SPLASH.

DeRue, Carmen

(Carmen Faye DeRue)

Died 28 Sept. 1986, North Hollywood, Calif., age 78.

Silent Screen Child Star. Billed as Baby DeRue, she first played the part of an Indian boy in Cecil B. DeMille's THE SQUAW MAN (1913); her father Eugene DeRue was given a part as an extra in the film and went on to become a director who originated the art of dubbing (he died in 1985 at age 100); other films, in which she often played boys, include BREWSTER'S MILLIONS (1916), ACQUITTED, GRETCHEN, THE GREENHORN, THE LITTLE SCHOOL MA'AM, FAN FAN, MASTERMINDS, FLIRT, CARMEN'S WILD RIDE, RURAL LOVE AFFAIR, BROKEN DOLL, CARMEN'S WASH DAY, THE GIRL WITH THE CHAMPAGNE EYES, BABES IN THE WOODS.

Diaz Gimeno, Rosita

Died summer, 1986, New York, N.Y., age 75.

Film Actress. Started her career In Madrid before the Spanish Civil War in such films as SUSANA TIENE UN SECRETO, EL BANDIDO DE RONDA, ANGELINA O EL HONOR DE UN BRIGADIER (filmed in Hollywood in 1935); after the war lived in exile in the U.S.; did films in Mexico such as EL ULTIMO AMOR DE GOYA, ME ENAMORE DE UNA SIRENA.

Dobie, Laurence

Died 20 Feb. 1986, London, England, age 58.

Playwright-Screenwriter. Wrote the play "The Tinker" (filmed as YOUNG AND WILLING) while working as a London newspaper copy editor; other plays were "Golden River," "Penny Whistle."

Dollar, William

Died 28 Feb. 1986, Flourtown, Pa., age 78.

Ballet Dancer/Choreographer/Teacher. Born in East St. Louis, Ill., studied under prominent dance teachers Michel Fokine and George Balanchine; worked for various ballet companies before joining Balanchine's American Ballet Theater; appeared in THE GOLDWYN FOLLIES (1938) as Vera Zorina's ballet partner; went to Monte Carlo as ballet master and did choreography in Brazil and Japan; started a ballet company in Iran in the 1950s.

Dornacker, Jane

Died 22 Oct. 1986, New York City, N.Y., age 40.

Helicopter Traffic Reporter-Film Actress. Moved from Albuquerque (her birthplace) to San Francisco working as a comedienne, songwriter, actress, then forming an all-female rock band, Leila and the Snakes; appeared in THE RIGHT STUFF; died when the helicopter she was reporting from crashed into the Hudson River.

Drivas, Robert

Died 29 June 1986, New York City, N.Y., age 50.

Stage Actor/Director-Film/TV Actor. Studied theater in Chicago and Miami, doing Miami stage work (Tennessee Williams had him play the lead in "Sweet Bird of Youth" for the Miami debut) before debuting in New York in 1958 in "The Firstborn"; other stage appearances included "The Wall," "Lorenzo," "Irregular Verb to Love"; plays directed included "The Ritz," "Legend"; debuted on screen in COOL HAND LUKE, then made THE ILLUSTRATED MAN, WHERE IT'S AT, ROAD MOVIE, GOD TOLD ME TO; worked in the Yale University repertory company in the 1970s; TV appearances included "Armstrong Circle Theater," "U.S. Steel Hour," "The Defenders," "East Side/West Side," "Naked City."

Duncan, Vivian

Died 19 Sept. 1986, Los Angeles, Calif., age 84.

Stage Performer-Film Actress. With her younger sister Rosetta, performed as the Duncan Sisters in Los Angeles clubs before they debuted on Coney Island in 1917; went to San Francisco where they were spotted by Florenz Ziegfeld who put them in some of his shows; their act, "Topsy and Eva," was popular throughout the country and was filmed in IT'S A GREAT LIFE (1930); was married to film actor Nils Asther.

Dupe, Gilbert

Died 24 July 1986, Cannes, France, age 86.

Novelist-Film Screenwriter/Producer. Wrote numerous novels, several of which were turned into films, including LA FERME DU PENDU, LE BATEAU A SOUPE, TEMPETE SUR LES MAUVENTS (also served as director); operated a legitimate theater in Paris.

Dwyer, Leslie

Born 1906; died 29 Dec. 1986, London, England.

Film/Stage/TV Actor. As a teenager, appeared in the silent film THE FIFTH FORM AT ST. DOMINIC'S, then had a role in THE FLAG LIEUTENANT (1932) before starting the main thrust of his career in 1942 with THE GOOSE STEPS OUT and IN WHICH WE SERVE; she then appeared in WINGS AND THE WOMAN, THE YOUNG MR. PITT, THE LAMP STILL BURNS, THE WAY AHEAD, VACATION FROM MARRIAGE, NIGHT BOAT TO DUBLIN, THIS MAN IS MINE, WHEN THE BOUGH BREAKS, THE BAD LORD BYRON, NOW BARABBAS WAS A ROBBER, LILLI MARLENE, JUDGMENT DEFERRED, HOLIDAY WEEK, MY WIFE'S LODGER, THE GOOD DIE YOUNG, ROOM IN THE HOUSE, NOT SO DUSTY, THIRTY NINE STEPS (the 1960 version), and SOPHIE'S PLACE; appeared in a two-year run of Terence Rattigan's play "Flare Path" during WW II.

Eaton, Marjorie

Died 25 Apr. 1986, age 86.

Film Character Actress. Appeared in ANNA AND THE KING OF SIAM, THE TIME OF THEIR LIVES, WITNESS FOR THE PROSECUTION, THE ATOMIC BRAIN, MARY POPPINS, THE TROUBLE WITH ANGELS, HAIL HERO, HAMMERSMITH IS OUT, THE ATTIC, STREET MUSIC, and CRACKERS in 1984 to round out an approximately 40-picture career.

Eccles, Donald

Died early 1986, Sussex, England, age 77.

British Stage/Film/TV Actor. Made his stage debut in New York in 1930 in "The Last Enemy"; worked with Malvern Festival and Royal Shakespeare Company; more recent efforts include "Hadrian the Seventh," "A Family and a Fortune," and Tennessee Williams' "Night of the Iguana"; film appearances began in 1960 with TASTE OF MONEY and included A MIDSUMMER NIGHT'S DREAM, THE WICKER MAN, THE DRESSER; TV films included "Coming Out of the Ice," "The Master of Ballantrae."

Edwards, Guy

Died 2 May 1986, Los Angeles, Calif., age 51.

Stage/Film/TV Actor. Appeared in a tour of "Boys in the Band" and WEEKEND WITH THE BABYSITTER, as well as other film and TV productions.

Elledge, Charles

(Charles Cowles Elledge)

Died 30 Aug. 1986, Charlotte, N.C., age 78.

Stage/Film Actor. An itinerant teller of stories about mountain people in the Carolinas, performed for over 30 years in "Horn in the West," an outdoor drama put on during the summer season; appeared in films such as SOMEBODY MOVED MY MOUNTAIN, HOT SUMMER IN BAREFOOT COUNTY, THE GARDENER'S SON, VISIONS OF SUGAR PLUMS, as well as one Hollywood film in 1958, THUNDER ROAD.

Ellin, Stanley

(Stanley Bernard Ellin)

Born 6 Oct. 1916, New York City, N.Y.; died 31 July 1986, Brooklyn, N.Y.

Novelist-Screenwriter. Graduated from a Brooklyn school of higher learning; had various jobs before doing a one-year stretch in the Army during WW II; several of his novels were adapted into films such as *Dreadful Summit* (THE BIG NIGHT), *The Key to Nicholas Street* (WEB OF PASSION), *House of Cards* (filmed under that title), *The Bind* (SUNBURN), as was a short story, "The Best of Everything" (NOTHING BUT THE BEST); *The Eighth Circle* earned the Edgar Award from the Mystery Writers of America; his last novel, *Very Old Money,* was published in 1985.

Engle, Morris

Died 22 Jan. 1986, Washington, D.C., age 84.

Businessman-Stage/Film Actor. Ran a grocery store and was a beer truck driver before becoming a restaurateur in Washington, D.C.; did local stage work and appeared in ALL THE PRESIDENT'S MEN and SCORPIO.

Englund, Bryan

Died 25 Feb. 1986, New York City, N.Y., age 30.

Film/TV Actor. Came from a show business family (father: producer George Englund; mother: actress Cloris Leachman; grandmother: actress Mabel Albertson; great-uncle: actor Jack Albertson); appeared in CRAZY MAMA, THE PROWLER and TV-films such as "Someone I Touched," "A Christmas to Remember," "Dixie: Changing Habits," "Ernie Kovacs: Between the Laughter."

Erickson, Leif

(William Wycliffe Anderson)

Born 27 Oct. 1911, Alameda, Calif.; died 29 Jan. 1986, Pensacola, Fla.

Film/TV Actor. While still in grammar school, decided to become a singer after attending an opera performance; quit high school to join a repertory company then toured before becoming a vocalist and trombonist with Ted Fio Rito's band, appearing with the ensemble in 1933's SWEETHEART OF SIGMA CHI; appeared on stage in "A Midsummer Night's Dream," followed by an 8-month vaudeville stint with Olsen and Johnson before beginning his actual film career in WANDERER OF THE WASTELAND (billed as Glenn Erickson) and continuing with NEVADA, DESERT GOLD, COLLEGE HOLIDAY, CONQUEST, WAIKIKI WEDDING, THE THRILL OF A LIFETIME, H.M. PULHAM, ESQ., NIGHT MONSTER; debuted on Broadway in "Golden Boy," then had roles in "Margin for Error," "Retreat to Pleasure," "The Cream in the Well;" was a photographer for the Navy during WW II; after the war, returned to the stage and had his biggest success with "Tea and Sympathy" (would repeat his role in the 1956 film); other film credits include SORRY WRONG NUMBER, JOAN OF ARC, THE SNAKE PIT, THE LADY GAMBLES, JOHNNY STOOL PIGEON, STELLA, DALLAS, WITH A SONG IN MY HEART, CARBINE WILLIAMS, TROUBLE ALONG THE WAY, ON THE WATERFRONT, THE YOUNG LIONS, THE CARPETBAGGERS, TWILIGHT'S LAST

GLEAMING, HUNTER'S MOON; in his later years, moved on to TV, starring for four years in "High Chaparral" and appearing in TV films "Terror in the Sky," "The Deadly Dream," "The Family Rico," "The Daughters of Joshua Cabe," "Wild Times."

Erskine, Chester

Born 29 Nov. 1905, Hudson, N.Y.; died 7 Apr. 1986, Beverly Hills, Calif.

Stage Actor-Stage/Film Producer-Director-Writer. After theatrical training at American Academy of Dramatic Arts in New York City, played numerous minor roles, toured in Shakespeare productions, then sold new material to vaudeville acts before directing "Harlem," "Subway Express," and his big success, "The Last Mile"; throughout his career billed as "Chester Erskin" without the last "e"; other early stage credits include THE "Stepdaughters of War," "De Luxe," "Siege,"; went to Hollywood in 1931 to work with director Lewis Milestone on two films, RAIN (as assistant director) and HALLELUJAH, I'M A BUM; supplied the story for MASTER OF MEN, then produced, wrote and directed MIDNIGHT and directed FRANKIE AND JOHNNIE; other credits (as writer, producer, or director) include THE SAILOR TAKES A WIFE, THE EGG AND I, ALL MY SONS, TAKE ONE FALSE STEP, ANDROCLES AND THE LION, THE BELLE OF NEW YORK, A GIRL IN EVERY PORT, ANGEL FACE, SPLIT SECOND, WITNESS TO MURDER, THE WONDERFUL COUNTRY, THE INVINCIBLE SIX; as creative consultant, helped Katharine Hepburn put together the PBS documentary "The Spencer Tracy Legacy: A Tribute by Katharine Hepburn."

Escalada, Tito

(Roberto "Tito" Escalada)

Born 4 July 1916, Buenos Aires, Argentina; died 5 Dec. 1986, Buenos Aires, Argentina.

Film/Stage/TV Actor. Started out as a house painter before working on Argentine radio in soap operas; debuted on screen in DOCE MUJERES (1939), starting a 50-film career which peaked with SAFO, HISTORIA DE UNA PASION in 1943; other credits include EL CRIMEN DE ORIBE, 24 HORAS EN LA VIDA DE UNA MUJER, MADAME BOVARY (1947), AYER FUE PRIMAVERA; received Argentina's Oscar equivalent in 1955.

Essex, Jon

Died 21 July 1986, Detroit, Mich., age 62.

Theater Press Agent-Film/TV Actor. Served as assistant manager for a Cleveland theater and then as a press agent for Detroit's Fisher and the Schubert theaters; occasionally worked in both films and TV.

Estrada Aguirre, Jose

Died 23 Aug. 1986, Mexico City, Mexico, age 48.

Film/Stage Director. Began his theatrical career staging the first presentation of Samuel Beckett's play in Mexico, inaugurating a 30-play directorial stint; among the 70 films he directed are: CAYO DE LA GLORIA EL DIABLO and LA PACHANGA which received Mexico's version of the Oscar in 1981.

Falkenberg, Paul

Died 13 Jan. 1986, New York City, N.Y., age 80.

Film Editor-Associate Producer-Documentary Director-Writer. Started his career as a film editor for prominent German directors from the 1920s through the 1930s (editor on THE TRUNKS OF MR. O.F., sound editor on Fritz Lang's 1933 classic M); came to the U.S. in 1938 to work for various companies (McGraw Hill, United Jewish Appeal, United Nations, ABC-TV); established his own organization, producing art documentaries for 35 years; became a professor of film at C.W. Post College, New York University, Columbia University and wrote articles for scholarly cinema publications.

Farr, Derek

Born 7 Feb. 1912, Chiswick, England; died 22 March 1986, London, England.

Film/Stage/TV Actor. Had a career as a schoolmaster before going into show business, making his stage debut in 1937 and film debut in 1939 with CLOUDS OVER EUROPE; received star billing in his third film, QUIET WEDDING, then did VOICE IN THE NIGHT before going into the British armed forces for three years during WW II; came back to films and made THE SPELL OF AMY NUGENT, WANTED FOR MURDER, BOND STREET, CODE OF SCOTLAND YARD, CONSPIRACY IN TEHERAN, QUIET WEEKEND, THE STORY OF SHIRLEY YORKE, MAN ON THE RUN, SILENT DUST, THE SILK NOOSE, MURDER WITHOUT CRIME, RELUCTANT HEROES, LITTLE BIG SHOT, DOUBLE CONFESSION, BANG! YOU'RE DEAD, EIGHT O'CLOCK WALK, FRONT PAGE STORY, YOUNG WIVE'S TALE, THE DAM BUSTERS, DOCTOR AT LARGE, THE MAN IN THE ROAD, TOWN ON TRIAL, THE CIRCLE, ATTEMPT TO KILL, THE PROJECTED MAN, POPE JOAN.

Fernandez, Emilio

Born 26 March 1904, El Seco, Mexico; died 6 Aug. 1986, Mexico City, Mexico.

Film Director/Actor/Writer. Known as "El Indio" because of his Indian mother, took part in the Mexican Revolution of the 1920s, achieving the rank of lieutenant colonel; upon being sentenced to 20 years imprisonment in 1923, escaped to the U.S. and went to Washington, D.C., then to Hollywood, where he worked as a busboy and landed small film roles; in 1933, amnesty was declared and he returned to Mexico, gaining recognition as an actor in such films as LA BUENAVENTURA, CRUZ DIABLO, ADIOS, NICANOR, AMOR CON AMOR SE PAGA, JANITZIO, ALLA EN EL RANCHO GRANDE, EL FANFARRON; he began directing in 1941 and helmed such productions as PASSION ISLAND, PORTRAIT OF MARIA (earned the top prize at the Cannes Film Festival in 1943), FLOR SILVESTRE (earning a prize at the Locarno Festival), THE PEARL (honored at San Sebastian), LAS ABANDONADAS, PEPITA JIMENEZ, ENAMORADA, RIO ESCONDIDO, PUEBLERINA, LA MALQUERIDA, DUELO EN LAS MONTANAS, UN DIA DE VIDA, VICTIMAS DEL PECADO, LA BIENAMADA, ACAPULCO, TU Y EL MAR, LA RED, LA REBELION DE LOS COLGADOS; his films, which primarily explored the world of the Indian peasant, gradually decreased in popularity during the late 1950s, which led him to age assistant director jobs (he worked for John Huston on THE NIGHT OF THE IGUANA, THE UNFORGIVEN) and to return to acting, appearing in THE REWARD, THE APPALOOSA, A COVENANT WITH DEATH, RETURN OF THE SEVEN, THE WAR WAGON, THE WILD BUNCH, PAT GAR-

RETT AND BILLY THE KID, BRING ME THE HEAD OF ALFREDO GARCIA, BREAKOUT, LUCKY LADY, POLITICAL ASYLUM and his final film in 1984, UNDER THE VOLCANO.

Festa Campanile, Pasquale

Born 28 July 1927, Melfi, Italy; died 24 Feb. 1986, Rome, Italy.

Film Director/Screenwriter-Novelist. Took legal training before entering the newspaper field and then writing short stories, plays and novels; first screenplay, FADDIJA, was written in 1950, and followed by WILD LOVE, POOR BUT BEAUTIFUL, YOUNG HUSBANDS, ROCCO AND HIS BROTHERS, THE LOVE MAKERS, THE ASSASSIN, THE CONJUGAL BED, THE FOUR DAYS OF NAPLES, THE LEOPARD (honored at Cannes in 1963); in 1962, collaborated on a musical comedy which was filmed in 1973 as RUGANTINO; directed and wrote the scripts for WHITE VOICES (codirected), ADULTERY ITALIAN STYLE, THE GIRL AND THE GENERAL, A MAIDEN FOR A PRINCE, WHEN WOMEN HAD TAILS; pictures which he directed only include LA COSTANZA DELLA REGIONE, THE CHASTITY BELT, DROP DEAD MY LOVE, CHECK TO THE QUEEN, THE MALE BLACKBIRD, SOLDIER OF FORTUNE, THE RETURN OF CASANOVA, HOW TO LOSE A WIFE AND FIND A LOVER, THE GIGOLO FROM NAPLES, THE GOOD THIEF, THE BIG VAGABOND, HAND IN GLOVE, THE RICH AND THE POOR, SCANDAL OF AN UNKNOWN MAN; recently he made two of his novels into films, THE THIEF and THE GIRL FROM TRIESTE.

Fisher, Al

(Al Fichera)

Died 16 July 1986, Fort Lauderdale, Fla., age 69.

Comedian-Dancer-Singer-Film Actor. A 1948 chance encounter with comic Lou Marks led to the formation of the comedy act, "Fisher and Marks"; they toured clubs dates in the U.S. and Europe, and appeared in the films MISTER ROCK AND ROLL and COUNTRY MUSIC HOLIDAY.

Flanagan, Neil

Died 4 June 1986, North Hollywood, Calif., age 52.

Stage/TV/Film Actor. Mainly known for performing in the off-Broadway theater; helped to start up the Circle Repertory and appeared in their productions of "Exiles," "Hot l Baltimore"; appeared on Broadway in "Sheep on the Runway," "The Secret Affairs of Mildred Wild," "Beethoven's Tenth"; won Obie awards for "The Madness of Lady Bright" and his contribution to the off-Broadway theater scene; film appearances included TORTURE DUNGEON, GURU, THE MAD MONK, MOMENT BY MOMENT, S.O.B. and a TV movie, "Casino."

Fotopoulos, Mimis

Died 29 Oct. 1986, Athens, Greece, age 73.

Film/Stage Actor/Comedian. Started his 55-year career in 1931 on the stage in rural theaters which led to work with leading Greek theatrical troupes; started up his own acting company in 1952; debuted on screen in 1948 with ANTHROPI, ANTHROPI, followed by GIRL OF THE MOUNTAINS, THE FORTUNE TELLER, THE GROUCH among his more than 100 films; wrote four collections of poetry and a popular opera.

Francis, Ivor

Died 22 Oct. 1986, Sherman Oaks, Calif., age 68

Stage/Film/TV/Radio Character Actor-Drama Coach. Originally from Toronto, Canada, where he did broadcasting as a teenager; after WW II Royal Air Force service, moved to New York and had a regular role on the soap opera "Ma Perkins"; appeared on Broadway in "The Will and the Way," "J.B.," "The Fun Couple," "A Rainy Day in Newark," "Lorenzo," "The Investigation"; films include A TIGER WALKS, I LOVE MY WIFE, PIECES OF DREAMS, HONKY, THE LATE LIZ, THE STEAGLE, THE WORLD'S GREATEST ATHLETE, SUPERDAD, BUSTING, THE PRISONER OF SECOND AVENUE, THE WACKIEST WAGON TRAIN IN THE WEST, THE NORTH AVENUE IRREGULARS; extensive TV credits include "Mary Hartman, Mary Hartman," "Kojak," "The Waltons," "The Odd Couple," and telefilms such as "In Name Only," "Hunters Are For Killing," "Outrage," "Mc-Naughton's Daughter," "Spider-Man," "Will There Really Be A Morning"; best known for his role as Prof. Dragan on "Room 222"; taught the art of stagecraft in New York and Los Angeles; was the father of TV soap opera star Genie Francis.

Francois, Camille

Died 10 March 1986, Paris, France, age 84.

Lyricist-Poet-Film Company Administrator-Writer-Actor. Primarily a writer of operettas and poetry, his one foray into films was as the administrator for the film company that produced RULES OF THE GAME, a project in which he also acted and worked on the script.

Frank, Anne Ray

Died 1 Apr. 1986, Los Angeles, Calif., age unknown.

Dancer-Film/Radio Writer. Billed as Anne Ray, danced in early 1930s Hollywood musicals, most notably as one of the group that danced on airplane wings in FLYING DOWN TO RIO; wrote for the screen and for such radio shows as "Corliss Archer" and "The Dinah Shore Show"; formerly married to Melvin Frank, film director/writer.

Franklin, Hugh

Died 26 Sept. 1986, Torrington, Conn., age 70.

Stage/Film/TV Actor. Primarily a stage actor with appearances in "Harriet," "One-Man Show," "Medea," "I Know My Love,"; retired for 10 years to run a food store; returned to do "The Best Man," "A Shot in the Dark," "Arturo Ui," "The Devils," "The Joyous Season," "Alice in Wonderland," "The Play's The Thing"; his films include THE CURSE OF THE LIVING CORPSE, WHAT'S SO BAD ABOUT FEELING GOOD? and a TV movie, "The Borgia Stick."

Franklin, Mark

Died 9 Oct. 1986, age 39.

Composer-Musician-Film Actor. Appeared in the film SEMI-TOUGH.

Frees, Paul

Born 22 June 1920, Chicago, Ill.; died 1 Nov. 1986, Tiboron, Calif.

Voice-Over Specialist-Film Actor/Narrator. Won a radio impersonation contest and, billed as "Buddy Green," worked in vaudeville and then returned to radio, working on such shows as "Suspense" and "Escape"; went into films in the late 1940s, starting out in bit parts in FORCE OF EVIL, RED LIGHT, HUNT THE MAN DOWN, HIS KIND OF WOMAN, A PLACE IN THE SUN, THE THING, THE BIG SKY, THE LAS VEGAS STORY, MILLION DOLLAR MERMAID, THE STAR, RIOT IN CELL BLOCK 11, SUDDENLY, PRINCE OF PLAYERS, THE HARDER THEY FALL, JET PILOT, SPACE MASTER X-7; decided to use his vocal talents in many areas of show business, becoming practically a one-man industry, eventually earning over $1 million a year; narrated or provided voice-overs for THE TOAST OF NEW ORLEANS, WHEN WORLDS COLLIDE, WAR OF THE WORLDS, THE TIME MACHINE, UTOPIA, THE MONOLITH MONSTERS, A PUBLIC AFFAIR, THE ST. VALENTINE'S DAY MASSACRE, WILD IN THE STREETS, THE SHAGGY DOG (also appeared as a psychiatrist); directed and wrote an exploitation film called THE BEATNIKS; supplied voices for animated films such as THE SNOW QUEEN, GAY PURR-EE, THE INCREDIBLE MR. LIMPET, THE MAN CALLED FLINTSTONE, CRICKET ON THE HEARTH, MR. MAGOO'S HOLIDAY FESTIVAL, THE LAST UNICORN, TWICE UPON A TIME; some of his prodigious TV output (aside from voice-overs for commercial characters such as the Pillsbury "Doughboy," "Mr. Goodwrench" for General Motors, "Toucan Sam" for Kellogg's cereals) includes "The Hobbit," "Frosty the Snowman," "Rudolph the Red-Nosed Reindeer," the voice of the character of John Beresford Tipton on "The Millionaire," "The Beatles," "Jackson Five," "The Osmonds," as well as narrating "Shogun," the miniseries.

Gabel, Martin

Born 19 June 1912, Philadelphia, Pa.; died 22 May 1986, New York City, N.Y.

Stage/Film Actor/Director-Stage Producer. Studied English at Lehigh University, attended New York's American Academy of Dramatic Arts and made his stage debut in Chicago in "Three Men on a Horse"; his Broadway debut was in "Man Bites Dog" (1933), followed by "The Sky's the Limit," then a starring role in "Dead End"; became associated with Orson Welles' Mercury Players in such productions as "Ten Million Ghosts," "Julius Caesar," "Danton's Death" (where he met his future wife Arlene Francis); helped raise $100,000 to put on a play that would roll on for 3,224 performances, the classic "Life With Father"; also appeared in "Medicine Show" (with a cast that included Alfred Ryder and Olive Deering, his real-life brother and sister); "King Lear," "The Little Blue Light," "Reclining Figure," "Will Success Spoil Rock Hunter," "Big Fish, Little Fish" (earned him a Tony); plays coproduced include: "Cafe Crown," "The Assassin," "The Survivors," "Twentieth Century," "Tiger at the Gates"; stepped into films in a directorial capacity on THE LOST MOMENT in 1947, then acted in FOURTEEN HOURS, M (1951), DEADLINE—U.S.A., THE THIEF, TIP ON A DEAD JOCKEY, GOODBYE CHARLIE, MARNIE, LORD LOVE A DUCK, DIVORCE AMERICAN STYLE, LADY IN CEMENT, THERE WAS A CROOKED MAN, THE FRONT PAGE (1974), THE FIRST DEADLY SIN; on TV was a regular panelist with his wife on "What's My Line?" and appeared in "Tiger at the Gates," "Smile, Jenny, You're Dead" and "Contract on Cherry Street," and narrated "Vincent Van Gogh, A Self Portrait," and "The Making of the President."

Gallardo, Adrian

Died 27 July 1986, San Diego, Calif., age 60.

Composer-Singer-Film Actor. Started out in Mexican films and came to California to play minor parts in American films; as a singer with a mariachi band, toured the U.S. and Europe and made several records.

Gautier, Jean-Jacques

Died 20 April 1986, Paris, France, age 77.

Drama Critic-Novelist. After studying journalism, worked at two papers *Echo de Paris* and *Le Figaro* (when the latter paper moved to Lyons during WW II, he wired his theater stories from Paris); his books *History of a Crime* and *The Well of Three Truths* were turned into films.

Genet, Jean

Born 19 Dec. 1910, Paris, France; died 14 April 1986, Paris, France.

Poet-Novelist-Playwright. Mother deserted him at birth and he was raised by peasants; spent four years in reform school as a youngster and became an itinerant wanderer between WW I and WW II before beginning a literary career during which he would produce a number of highly controversial books, including *Our Lady of the Flowers*, *Miracle of the Rose*, *Pompes Funebres*, *Querelle*, characterized by a lyrical style and eroticism, describing the world of homosexuals, thieves, prostitutes and corruption; much of his work was banned in many areas because of its pornographic and controversial nature; other works include *A Thief's Journal* and the plays, "Deathwatch," "The Maids," "The Blacks," "The Balcony," "The Screens"; films based on his works include THE BALCONY, DEATHWATCH, MADEMOISELLE, THE MAIDS, QUERELLE; he personally wrote and directed UN CHANT D'AMOUR, a short film that was banned.

Geniat, Gilberte

Died 28 June 1986, Paris, France, age 70.

Stage/Film Actress. Mainly a stage actress who appeared in many Jean Anouilh plays; film credits include LA BELLE AMERICAINE, DIARY OF A CHAMBERMAID, LA PRISONNIERE, THE LADY IN THE CAR WITH GLASSES AND A GUN, A VERY CURIOUS GIRL, SUCH A GORGEOUS KID LIKE ME and a small part in 1984's AMERICAN DREAMER.

Genna, Irene

Died 6 Feb. 1986, Rome, Italy, age 55.

Film Actress. Appeared in many films starting in 1948, including GIUSEPPE VERDI, LA SCHIAVA DEL PECCATO, VERGINITA; married Italian matinee idol Amedeo Nazzari in 1956 and left the screen five years later.

Gershenson, Stephen N.

Died 23 July 1986, Houston, Tex., age 38.

Screenwriter. Wrote screenplays for films such as GOING FOR BROKE, THE MONEY HONEY, MAGIC'S IN THE MUSIC.

Gheraldi, Cesarina

Died 21 Jan. 1986, Rome, Italy, age 70.

Stage/Film/Radio/TV Actress. First went on the stage in 1929 and appeared in the first Italian production of Bertolt Brecht's "Mother Courage"; later specialized in the plays of Luigi Pirandello; appeared in a few films such as PERSIANE CHIUSE and ENGAGEMENT ITALIANO.

Gibney, Louise

(Lillian Harrington)

Died 22 Sept. 1986, Santa Maria, Calif., age 90.

Silent Film/Stage Actress. Debuted in the "Ziegfeld Follies" in Boston before entering films in such efforts as THE BEAUTIFUL CHEAT, MOTHER,

MY OLD DUTCH and one sound epic, Cecil B. DeMille's SIGN OF THE CROSS; after being forced to leave the screen because of her high-pitched voice, appeared in local theater under the name of Lillian Chesterton.

Gil, Rafael

Born 22 May 1913, Spain; died 10 Sept. 1986, Madrid, Spain.

Film Director. Entered films in 1935 as a codirector with Gonzalo Memedez Pidal on three films, LA SEMENA SANTA DE MURCIA, SEMANA SANTA EN CARTAGENA, CINCO MINUTOS DE ESPANOLADA; started his solo directorial career in 1941 with EL HOMBRE QUE SE QUISO MATAR, followed by VIAJE SIN DESTINO, HUELLA DE LUZ, ELCISA ESTA DEBAJO DE UN ALMENDRO, LECCIONES DE BUEN AMOR, EL CLAVO, LA PRODIGA, MARE NOSTRUM (1948), LA CALLE SIN SOL, LA SENORA DE FATIMA, DE MADRID AL CIELO, CINCUENTA ANOS DEL REAL MADRID, LA GUERRA DE DIOS (won the Venice Film Festival Silver Lion), EL BESO DE JUDAS, MURIO HACE QUINCE ANOS, EL CANTO DEL GALLO, VIVA LO IMPOSIBLE!, ROGELIA, SAMBA, ES MI HOMBRE, CAMINO DEL ROCIO, VERDE DONCELLA, SANGRE EN EL RUEDO, EL RELICARIO, EL SOBRE VERDE, LA GUERILLA, Y AL TERCER ANO RESUSCITO.

Gillmore, Margalo

Born 31 May 1897, London, England; died 30 June 1986, New York City, New York.

Stage/Film Actress. Born to theatrical parents (her father Frank Gilmore founded Actors Equity), debuted on the stage in 1917 in "The Scrap of Paper,"; went on to appear in numerous stage productions, including "The Habitual Husband," "Ned McCobb's Daughter," "Marco's Millions," "Berkeley Square," "The Barretts of Wimpole Street," "The Women," "Life with Father," "Outrageous Fortune" and "Sail Away," her final theatrical effort; she made her first film appearance in WAYWARD in 1932 then returned to the stage until the 1950s when she went back to Hollywood and made THE HAPPY YEARS, PERFECT STRANGERS, CAUSE FOR ALARM, ELOPEMENT, THE LAW AND THE LADY, SKIRTS AHOY, SCANDAL AT SCOUR, WOMAN'S WORLD, GABY, HIGH SOCIETY, UPSTAIRS AND DOWNSTAIRS, THE TROUBLE WITH ANGELS; published her autobiography *Four Flights Up* in 1964.

Gilmore, Virginia

(Sherman Virginia Poole)

Born 26 July 1919, El Monte, Calif.; died 28 March 1986, Santa Barbara, Calif.

Stage/Film Actress. After involvement in local theater as a teenager, attended universities in California and Vienna; debuted on Broadway in "Those Endearing Young Charms" in 1943, then appeared in "The World's Full of Girls," "Dear Ruth," "Truckline Cafe," "The Grey-Eyed People," "Critic's Choice"; debuted on screen in WINTER CARNIVAL in 1939 and appeared in LADDIE, MANHATTAN HEARTBEAT, JENNIE, SWAMP WATER, WESTERN UNION, BERLIN CORRESPONDENT, THE LOVES OF EDGAR ALLAN POE, ORCHESTRA WIVES, THE PRIDE OF THE YANKEES, SON OF FURY, SUNDOWN JIM, THAT OTHER WOMAN, CHETNIKS, WONDER MAN, THE CARTER CASE, CLOSE-UP, WALK EAST ON BEACON (1952); TV appearances included "Philco Television Playhouse," "Kraft Television Theater," "Studio One" and a series, "We're On," with Yul Brynner who was, at the time, her husband; taught drama at Yale and was a leading figure in Alcoholics Anonymous.

Gipe, George

Died 6 Sept. 1986, Glendale, Calif., age 53.

Screenwriter. Hailing from Baltimore, worked in various capacities in TV, then wrote for newspapers and magazines; wrote the screenplays for two Steve Martin comedies, DEAD MEN DON'T WEAR PLAID, THE MAN WITH TWO BRAINS; wrote movie-adaptation books such as "Gremlins," "Melvin and Howard," "Back to the Future."

Gobert, Boy

(Boy Christian Klee Gobert)

Born 5 June 1925, Hamburg, Germany; died 30 May 1986, Vienna, Austria.

Stage Actor/Director-Film Actor. Came from an aristocratic, political family and appeared on stages throughout Germany in Shakespearean plays and other dramas; his more than 50 film appearances include DIE WILDEN 50ER, THE REST IS SILENCE, DIE FLEDERMAUS, LADY HAMILTON, KAMIKAZE '89; was the director of a theater in Hamburg starting in 1969.

Gonzalez, Arturo

Died 3 Sept. 1986, Madrid, Spain, age 84.

Producer/Distributor. Produced such films as AMOR A LA ESPANOLA, LAS QUE TIENEN QUE SERVIR, EL HALCON Y LA PRESA; coproduced THE GOOD, THE BAD, AND THE UGLY, LA MUERTE TENIA UN PRECIO.

Goodman, Benny

(Benjamin David Goodman)

Born 30 May 1909, Chicago, Il.; died 13 June 1986, New York City, N.Y.

Bandleader-Clarinetist-Composer-Film Actor. Born on the west side of Chicago (the eighth of 12 children from poor immigrant parents), received his first clarinet on loan from a synagogue; played in neighborhood and local bands and after one year of high school joined Ben Pollack's band in California; later left to do work on radio and to make records on a freelance basis while supplying the music for "Free for All" in 1931; formed his own band, worked for Billy Rose, and served as replacement for Guy Lombardo at the Roosevelt Grill then went to Hollywood to appear at the Palomar Ballroom where his "swing" style achieved widespread popularity; had a hand in song writing or adaptation on such musical pieces as "Stomping at the Savoy," "Don't Be That Way," "Lullaby in Rhythm," "Flying Home," "Soft Winds" and others; broke the race barrier by adding black musicians to his band, including Teddy Wilson and Lionel Hampton; made his first film appearance in THE BIG BROADCAST OF 1937 and went on to appear with his band in HOLLYWOOD HOTEL, THE POWERS GIRL, SYNCOPATION, THE GANG'S ALL HERE, STAGE DOOR CANTEEN, SWEET AND LOWDOWN, A SONG IS BORN; supplied the clarinet music for Walt Disney's MAKE MINE MUSIC; a film based on his life, THE BENNY GOODMAN STORY, was made in 1956 with Steve Allen in the title role.

Gordon, George

Died 24 May 1986, Apple Valley, Calif., age 79.

Animation Writer/Director. Started out in 1930 with the Paul Terry Studio in New Rochelle, N.Y., helping produce more than 50 of the "Terrytoon" cartoons; switched to MGM in 1937 and worked on "Barney the Bear" and "Tom and Jerry" among others; during WW II made armed services training films; afterwards, did commercials ("Chiquita Banana"), industrial, and documentary films.

Grant, Cary

(Alexander Archibald "Archie" Leach)

Born 18 Jan. 1904, Bristol, England; died 29 Nov. 1986, Davenport, Iowa.

Film/Stage Actor. Master of the light touch, was born to wife of a pants presser and ran away from home at age 13 to join an acrobatic act; was brought back before he had a chance to perform, but rejoined the troupe a year-and-a-half later as an apprentice; toured Europe and the U.S. where the act appeared in a musical called "Good Times" in 1920; when the group returned to Europe, he stayed in the U.S., taking odd jobs and appearing on Broadway in productions such as "Better Times," "Golden Dawn," "Polly," "Boom-Boom," "The Street Singer," "A Wonderful Night," "Nikki"; went to Hollywood where he was rechristened Cary Grant and made his first film, THIS IS THE NIGHT, followed by SINNERS IN THE SUN, MERRILY WE GO TO HELL, DEVIL AND THE DEEP, BLONDE VENUS, HOT SATURDAY, MADAME BUTTERFLY, SHE DONE HIM WRONG (with Mae West, the first film in which he received some notice in the romantic department), WOMAN ACCUSED, THE EAGLE AND THE HAWK, GAMBLING SHIP, I'M NO ANGEL, ALICE IN WONDERLAND (1933); in 1934, married his first wife, actress Virginia Cherrill, divorcing her a year later; his film career was going strong with pictures like THIRTY DAY PRINCESS, BORN TO BE BAD, KISS AND MAKE UP, LADIES SHOULD LISTEN, ENTER MADAME, WINGS IN THE DARK, THE LAST OUTPOST, SYLVIA SCARLETT, BIG BROWN EYES, SUZY, WEDDING PRESENT, WHEN YOU'RE IN LOVE, ROMANCE AND RICHES, AMAZING QUEST OF ERNEST BLISS, TOPPER, TOAST OF NEW YORK, THE AWFUL TRUTH, BRINGING UP BABY, HOLIDAY, GUNGA DIN, ONLY ANGELS HAVE WINGS, IN NAME ONLY, HIS GIRL FRIDAY, MY FAVORITE WIFE, THE HOWARDS OF VIRGINIA, THE PHILADELPHIA STORY, PENNY SERENADE (received an Oscar nomination for best actor), SUSPICION (1941, his first of many films with Alfred Hitchcock); in 1942 he became an American citizen and made Cary Grant his legal name; went on to make THE TALK OF THE TOWN, ONCE UPON A HONEYMOON, DESTINATION TOKYO, ONCE UPON A TIME, NONE BUT THE LONELY HEART (1944, received an Oscar nomination for what is generally considered his finest dramatic role), ARSENIC AND OLD LACE, NIGHT AND DAY, NOTORIOUS, THE BACHELOR AND THE BOBBY SOXER, THE BISHOP'S WIFE, MR. BLANDINGS BUILDS

HIS DREAM HOUSE, EVERY GIRL SHOULD BE MARRIED (with Betsy Drake, whom he married a year later and divorced in 1960), I WAS A MALE WAR BRIDE, CRISIS, PEOPLE WILL TALK, ROOM FOR ONE MORE, MONKEY BUSINESS, DREAM WIFE, TO CATCH A THIEF, THE PRIDE AND THE PASSION, AN AFFAIR TO REMEMBER, KISS THEM FOR ME, INDISCREET (picked by Grant as his best film), HOUSEBOAT, NORTH BY NORTHWEST, OPERATION PETTICOAT, THE GRASS IS GREENER, THAT TOUCH OF MINK, CHARADE, FATHER GOOSE, and his final film WALK, DON'T RUN; divorced his fourth wife, Dyan Cannon, in 1968 after three years of marriage, then engaged in a losing battle to gain custody of his only child, Jennifer; was honored in 1970 by the Academy of Motion Picture Arts & Sciences with a special award for his lifetime work; married his close companion for several years, Englishwoman Barbara Harris, in 1981; served on the boards of Faberge, Hollywood Park, Western Airlines, MGM/UA and MGM Grand Hotels; would occasionally do personal appearances, talking about his films and showing film clips.

Greene, Joe

Died 16 June 1986, Pasadena, Calif., age 71.

Songwriter-Novelist-Film Score Composer. Associated for many years with Hoagy Carmichael and Stan Kenton; wrote or helped write "And Her Tears Flowed Like Wine," "Across the Alley from the Alamo," "Don't Let the Sun Catch You Cryin' "; wrote musical scores for A PUBLIC AFFAIR, ON HER BED OF ROSES, A BOY . . . A GIRL, CHILDISH THINGS, TIGER BY THE TAIL, THE NARROW CHUTE; his novels include *The Golden Platter* and *House of Pleasure*.

Greenfield, Howard

Died 4 March 1986, Los Angeles, Calif., age late 40s.

Songwriter. Composed more than 450 songs, including "Breaking in a Brand New Broken Heart," "Breaking Up Is Hard to Do," "Calendar Girl," "Everybody's Somebody's Fool," "Little Devil," "Frankie," "Where the Boys Are" (cowritten with Neil Sedaka and popularized by Connie Francis and the basis for the 1960 film), "Love Will Keep Us Together" (awarded a 1975 Grammy), "My Heart Has a Mind of Its Own," "You Never Done It Like That," "Two Less Lonely People in the World," "The Hungry Years," "Happy Birthday, Sweet Sixteen"; wrote theme songs for films such as THE NIGHT OF THE GENERALS, THE VICTORS, MURDERER'S ROW, KISS THE GIRLS AND MAKE THEM DIE, and TV shows such as "Gidget," "Bewitched," "Hazel," "The Flying Nun."

Gregg, Virginia

Died 15 Sept. 1986, Encino, Calif., age 69.

Radio/Film/TV Actress. Originally from Harrisburg, Illinois, moved to Pasadena, California, as a youngster; studied music at college and played with the Pasadena Symphony before going into radio for hundreds of shows such as a "One Man's Family," "The Jack Benny Show," "Lux Radio Theater," "Lum 'N Abner," "Sam Spade," "Dragnet" (beginning a long association with actor-producer Jack Webb through both film and TV versions of the top-rated police show as well as some of his other projects); began appearing in films in mid 1940s, including NOTORIOUS, BODY AND SOUL, GENTLEMAN'S AGREEMENT, CASBAH, I'LL CRY TOMORROW, LOVE IS A MANY-SPLENDORED THING, THE D.I., THE HANGING TREE, OPERATION PETTICOAT, SPENCER'S MOUNTAIN, JOY IN THE MORNING, A BIG HAND FOR THE LITTLE LADY, MADIGAN, HEAVEN WITH A GUN, S.O.B., HEIDI'S SONG; was the voice of Norman Bates' mother in PSYCHO and the two sequels; appeared in TV shows such as "The Waltons," "Baretta," "Cannon," "Ironside," "The Streets of San Francisco," "Happy Days"; TV movie credits include "Prescription: Murder," "Along Came a Spider," "Quarantined," "The Other Man," "Crowhaven Farm," "The D.A.: Conspiracy to Kill," "Emergency" "Chase," "You Lie So Deep, My Love," "Man From Atlantis," "Little Women" "Forbidden Love."

Grosz, Paul

Died 11 July 1986, Crystal Lake, N.Y., age 75.

Film Art Director. Worked in art direction for Universal, 20th Century Fox, Paramount, United Artists and other organizations.

Guardia, Bob

(Albert H. Guardia)

Died 15 Nov. 1986, Elko, Nevada, age 65

Film Actor-Police Officer. Was in on the start of the "Our Gang" shorts comedy series as a member of the cast; left show business to become a member of the Reno Police Department and more recently had a position with Elko County Sheriff's Department as a court bailiff.

Haacke, Kathe

Died 5 May 1986, age unknown.

Stage/Film Actress. Appeared in the silent German film ALGOL in 1920, as well as the sound films THE DAY AFTER THE DIVORCE and INDECENT (both German productions), and the French/German coproduction DANIELLA BY NIGHT (1962).

Hagstrom, Lasse

Died 14 March 1986, age 49.

Film Editor. After working on the films of Kjell Grede, went on to edit films of other Swedish directors, then broadened his scope by working for

the Norwegian directors Anja Breien and Lasse Glomm; suggested using the music of Mozart in Bo Widerberg's 1967 lyrical film ELVIRA MADIGAN.

Halop, Florence

Born 23 Jan. 1923, Queens, N.Y.; died 15 July 1986, Los Angeles, Calif.

Radio/TV/Film Actress. Entered show business at age four when brother Billy Halop (one of the "Dead End Kids") suggested her for a radio role which led to frequent appearances on such shows as "Bobby Benson and the H-Bar-O Ranch," "Miss Duffy," "The Jimmy Durante Show"; made one film, NANCY DREW-REPORTER, in 1939; TV work included "Meet Millie," "All in the Family," "Barney Miller," "Alice," "St. Elsewhere," "Night Court" (in which she was most recently appearing as the bailiff) and TV movies "But I Don't Want to Get Married" and "Queen of the Stardust Ballroom."

Hamilton, Murray

Died 1 Sept. 1986, Washington, N.C., age 63.

Film/Stage/TV Actor. Originally from Washington, N.C., went to New York in 1945 to appear on stage in "Strange Fruit," "Mister Roberts," "The Chase," "Stockade," "Critic's Choice," "Forty Carats"; first appeared on the screen in BRIGHT VICTORY, then made TOWARD THE UNKNOWN, JEANNE EAGELS, THE SPIRIT OF ST. LOUIS, DARBY'S RANGERS, HOUSEBOAT, NO TIME FOR SERGEANTS, ANATOMY OF A MURDER, THE FBI STORY, THE HUSTLER, THE CARDINAL, PAPA'S DELICATE CONDITION, SECONDS, THE GRADUATE, NO WAY TO TREAT A LADY, THE

BOSTON STRANGLER, SERGEANT RYKER, IF IT'S TUESDAY, THIS MUST BE BELGIUM, THE WAY WE WERE, THE DROWNING POOL, JAWS, CASEY'S SHADOW, THE AMITYVILLE HORROR, 1941, BRUBAKER, HYSTERICAL, and his final film, released in 1985 (though filmed in 1982), TOO SCARED TO SCREAM; his TV exposure was considerable in such shows as "Mission: Impossible," "McCloud," "Cannon," "Streets of San Francisco," "Police Story," "Barnaby Jones," "Murder She Wrote," and the telefilms "Vanished," "A Tattered Web," "The Harness," "The Failing of Raymond," "Deadly Harvest," "Incident on a Dark Street," "Murdock's Gang," "Rich Man, Poor Man," "Swan Song," "Summer Girl".

Hamlin, George

Died 5 July 1986, Bronx, N.Y., age 65.
Stage/Film Actor-Stage Producer/Director. A Chicago native, attended Principia College in Elsah, Illinois; directed and acted in regional theater and assisted in Broadway productions; 1961 through 1980 was the producer-director at the drama center of Harvard College; appeared in Woody Allen's ZELIG and the TV movie "Bill".

Hand, David

Died 11 Oct. 1986, San Luis Obispo, Calif., age 86.
Animation Director. Studied at the Chicago Academy of Fine Arts, then moved West to work for Max Fleischer and Eastman Kodak before joining Walt Disney Studios in 1931, working on about 60 short cartoons (including the Oscar winner of 1932, FLOWERS AND TREES), before being assigned the job of supervising director on Disney's first feature-length cartoon, SNOW WHITE AND THE SEVEN DWARFS; performed the same function on BAMBI and the wartime patriotic piece, VICTORY THROUGH AIR POWER; after the war, went to England to organize an animation department for J. Arthur Rank and produced some cartoons and shorts before his return to the U.S. in 1951; with his wife, cowrote a book, *Living Dolls*, in 1983.

Harris, Dermot

Died 12 Nov. 1986, Chicago, Ill., age 47.
Record/Film Producer. Native of Limerick, Ireland, and brother of actor Richard Harris; produced records (including Neil Diamond's "Jonathan Livingston Seagull"), and served as associate producer on his brother's films MAN IN THE WILDERNESS and ECHOES OF A SUMMER.

Harris, Howard

Died 22 March 1986, Santa Monica, Calif., age 74.
Film/TV Comedy Writer. Worked out comedy material for many personalities such as Phil Baker, Joe Penner, and W.C. Fields; was staff writer for TV shows such as "The Tonight Show," "The Jimmy Durante Show," "The Phil Silvers Show," "Gilligan's Island," "Petticoat Junction," "Here's Lucy"; wrote for Jackie Gleason on "The Honeymooners" and Groucho Marx on "You Bet Your Life"; wrote the script for Marx's COPACABANA and did some work on the Marx Brothers' A NIGHT IN CASABLANCA; was writer or co-writer on the following films: HIGHER AND HIGHER, LINDA BE GOOD, THE NOOSE HANGS HIGH.

Hatley, T. Marvin

(Thomas Marvin Hatley)
Died 26 Aug. 1986, California, age 81.
Film Actor-Music Director. Acted and wrote scores for shorts and features at Hal Roach Studios; was involved in the scoring and/or musical direction of several Laurel and Hardy films including WAY OUT WEST, BLOCKHEADS (both Oscar-nominated for his music), PACK UP YOUR TROUBLES (also acted in it), CHUMP AT OXFORD, SAPS AT SEA, ZENOBIA, GENERAL SPANKY, PICK A STAR, TOPPER, MERRILY WE LIVE, THERE GOES MY HEART, BROADWAY LIMITED; appeared in OUR RELATIONS.

Hayden, Sterling

(Sterling Relyea Walter)

Born 26 March 1916, Montclair, N.J.; died 23 May 1986, Sausalito, Calif.

Film Actor-Author. Took the last name of Hayden from his stepfather; left high school before graduation to work on a schooner and stayed at sea until financial difficulties forced him to take a job as a model, which led to a movie contract in 1941 and his first two films, VIRGINIA and BAHAMA PASSAGE (billed in each as "Stirling" Hayden), both starring Madeline Carroll whom he married the same year; during WW II, was in the Marine Corps and the Office of Strategic Services (during which time he legally had his name changed to John Hamilton), operating in Greece and Yugoslavia, running guns to partisans while also briefly becoming a member of the Communist Party (an action which resulted in his testifying against his compatriots in the House Unamerican Activities Committee hearings in the 1950s); divorced Carroll and resumed his film career in 1947 with BLAZE OF NOON, followed by VARI-

ETY GIRL, EL PASO, MANHANDLED, THE ASPHALT JUNGLE, JOURNEY INTO LIGHT, FLAMING FEATHER, DENVER AND RIO GRANDE, THE GOLDEN HAWK, HELLGATE, FLAT TOP, THE STAR, KANSAS PACIFIC, TAKE ME TO TOWN, FIGHTER ATTACK, CRIME WAVE, JOHNNY GUITAR, PRINCE VALIANT, ARROW IN THE DUST, NAKED ALIBI, SUDDENLY, SO BIG, TIMBERJACK, BATTLE TAXI, THE ETERNAL SEA, SHOTGUN, THE LAST COMMAND, TOP GUN (1955), THE COME-ON, THE KILLING, CRIME OF PASSION, FIVE STEPS TO DANGER, THE IRON SHERIFF, VALERIE, GUN BATTLE AT MONTEREY, ZERO HOUR!, TERROR IN A TEXAS TOWN, TEN DAYS TO TULARA, DR. STRANGELOVE: OR HOW I LEARNED TO STOP WORRYING AND LOVE THE BOMB, SWEET HUNTERS, HARD CONTRACT, LOVING, LE SAUT DE L'ANGE, LE GRAND DEPART, THE GODFATHER, THE LONG GOODBYE, THE LAST DAYS OF MAN ON EARTH, DEADLY STRANGERS, CRY ONION, 1900, KING OF THE GYPSIES, WINTER KILLS, THE OUTSIDER, NINE TO FIVE, VENOM, GAS; was the subject of a 1983 documentary, PHAROS OF CHAOS, filmed on the barge he owned in Paris; appeared on TV in "The Blue and the Gray," "A Sound of Different Drummers," "The Last Man," "Old Man," "Carol of Another Christmas"; wrote an autobiography, *Wanderer*, in 1963 based on the 1959 voyage he took to Tahiti with his children, breaking a court order after winning custody of them from second wife Betty Ann DeNoon; wrote the novel, *Voyage*, in 1976; appeared on the stage only once, in the 1973 production "Are You Now or Have You Ever Been"; was married to Catherine McConnell (since 1960) at the time of his death.

Haynes, Hilda

Died 4 March 1986, New York City, N.Y., age 72.
Stage/Film/TV Actress. Was part of the American Negro Theater which presented such productions as "Three's a Family" and "On Strivers' Row" in the 1940s; joined the cast of "A Streetcar Named Desire" during its original run, then worked in "King of Hearts," "The Wisteria Trees," "Trouble in Mind," "Take a Giant Step," "The Irregular Verb to Love," "Golden Boy," "Purlie Victorious" (also appeared in the film version in 1963, retitled GONE ARE THE DAYS), "The Great White Hope"; other film credits include TAXI (1953), STAGE STRUCK, HOME FROM THE HILL, DIARY OF A MAD HOUSEWIFE, THE RIVER NIGER, TIME AFTER TIME; TV-film credits include "Sarah T.—Portrait of a Teenage Alcoholic," "F. Scott Fitzgerald in Hollywood," "The Boy in the Plastic Bubble," "Panic in Echo Park," "The Greatest Thing That Almost Happened," "The Miracle Worker"; was active in theatrical union and organization activities.

Haynes, Lloyd

Died 31 Dec. 1986, Coronado, Calif., age 52.
TV/Film Actor. Studied acting in Los Angeles and worked as a TV crewman before landing his role as the star of the TV series "Room 222"; appeared in the TV films "Assault on the Wayne," "Look What's Happened to Rosemary's Baby," "Harold Robbins' '79 Park Avenue," "Born to be Sold"; latest effort had been playing the mayor on the soap opera "General Hospital"; movie work consisted of ICE STATION ZEBRA, THE MAD ROOM, TARZAN'S JUNGLE REBELLION, THE GREATEST, GOOD GUYS WEAR BLACK.

Heathcote, Thomas

Died 5 Jan. 1986, London, England, age 68.
Stage/TV/Film Actor. Worked mainly with the "Old Vic" theater company in England; film appearances include DANCE HALL, CLOUDBURST, THE SWORD AND THE ROSE, THE LARGE ROPE, MALTA STORY, PARATROOPER, LAND OF FURY, DOCTOR AT SEA, ABOVE US THE WAVES, BATTLE HELL, EYEWITNESS (1956), THE LAST MAN TO HANG, TIGER IN THE SMOKE, A NIGHT TO REMEMBER, TREAD SOFTLY STRANGER, VILLAGE OF THE DAMNED, OPERATION SNAFU, A MAN FOR ALL SEASONS, FIVE MILLION YEARS TO EARTH, THE FIXER, JULIUS CAESAR (1970), ISLAND OF THE BURNING DAMNED, LUTHER, DIRTY KNIGHT'S WORK and 1984's SWORD OF THE VALIANT; his TV work consisted of "The Onedin Line" (a British miniseries) and "Softly Softly."

Heidt, Horace

Born 21 May 1901, Alameda, Calif.; died 1 Dec. 1986, Los Angeles, Calif.
Band Leader-Composer-Film Actor. Attended Culver Military Academy and University of California at

Berkeley, where a back injury thwarted a budding football career; hearing Guy Lombardo on the radio inspired him to start his own band, working in San Francisco then moving on to New York, touring Europe, and spending several years at the Drake Hotel in Chicago inaugurating the radio program "Answers by the Dancers"; was involved with several other radio efforts before achieving his greatest success with "Pot O' Gold," one of the first shows to give money away; the show served as the inspiration for the 1941 film POT O' GOLD, which starred Paulette Goddard and Fred MacMurray and featured Heidt and his band; continued in radio work until the late 1950s when he retired and served briefly as the mayor of Van Nuys, California.

Helpmann, Robert

(Robert Murray Helpman)

Born 9 Apr. 1909, Mount Gambier, South Australia; died 28 Sept. 1986, Sydney, Australia.

Ballet Dancer-Choreographer-Author-Actor-Director-Producer. Started his theatrical career as an actor/dancer (after studying with visiting Anna Pavlova) in his native Australia, went to London and after a few acting jobs joined Sadler's Wells Ballet School (now the Royal Ballet) in 1933; became their principal dancer and stayed with them until 1950 (often dancing with Margot Fonteyn), alternating dancing with acting on either stage (which occasionally included directing/acting chores) or films; some of his acting efforts on the British stage included "Precipice," "Caesar and Cleopatra," "The Millionairess," "Nekrassov," plus a generous portion of Shakespearean plays; repeated many of his plays in New York; first appeared on the screen in ONE OF OUR AIRCRAFT IS MISSING (1942), then made HENRY V, CARAVAN, THE RED SHOES (which he also choreographed), THE TALES OF HOFFMANN, THE IRON PETTICOAT, THE BIG MONEY, 55 DAYS AT PEKING, THE SOLDIER'S TALE, THE QUILLER MEMORANDUM, CHITTY CHITTY BANG BANG, ALICE'S ADVENTURES IN WONDERLAND, DON QUIXOTE (also co-directed it with Rudolph Nureyev), PATRICK, THE MANGO TREE, and 1984's SECOND TIME LUCKY (the last four all being made in Australia).

Henley, David

Died 30 July 1986, London, England, age 93.

Talent Agent-Acting Teacher-Trade Union Executive-Film Producer. Started out as an actor, then became general secretary of the British actors' union; worked for the Myron Selznick talent agency, later setting up an acting school for J. Arthur Rank; produced a few films in the 1950s through 1960s such as THE DEVIL'S PASS, MAKE MINE A DOUBLE, STRANGLEHOLD, BLAZE OF GLORY, THE CROOKED ROAD (1965), THE YELLOW HAT.

Herbert, Frank

(Frank Patrick Herbert)

Born 8 Oct. 1920, Tacoma, Wash.; died 11 Feb. 1986, Madison, Wis.

Novelist-Journalist. Studied psychology in college, worked as a reporter, writer, editor in newspapers and magazines before publishing his first novel, *Dragon in the Sea*, in 1955; published *Dune* in 1965, an immensely popular novel which was the first of a six-book series and was the basis for the film of the same name in 1984.

Herbert, Tim

Died 20 June 1986, Los Angeles, Calif., age 71.

Stage/Film/TV Actor-Comedian. Coming from vaudevillian parents, also went in the business, appearing in numerous stage productions; film credits include DON'T WORRY, WE'LL THINK OF A TITLE, A GUIDE FOR THE MARRIED MAN, THEY SHOOT HORSES, DON'T THEY?, SOYLENT GREEN, EARTHQUAKE; TV efforts include work on such shows as "Bonanza," "Chico and the Man," "Bracken's World," "The Lucy Show," plus the TV films "But I Don't Want to Get Married," "Duel," "Ellery Queen: Don't Look Behind You," "Goodnight My Love," "Terror on the 40th Floor."

Hewitt, Alan

(Alan Everett Hewitt)

Born 21 Jan. 1915, New York City, N.Y.; died 7 Nov. 1986, New York City, N.Y.

Stage/Film/Radio/TV Actor-Union Official. After graduation from Dartmouth College, did regional and summer theater before his Broadway debut in 1935 with Alfred Lunt and Lynn Fontanne in "The Taming of the Shrew;" also appeared in "Amphitryon 38," "The Sea Gull," "Love for Love," "The Golden Journey," "The Masque of Kings," "The Virginian," "The American Way," "Death of a Salesman," "Ondine"; appeared on the screen in A PRIVATE'S AFFAIR, THE ABSENT-MINDED PROFESSOR, BACHELOR IN PARADISE, DAYS OF WINE AND ROSES, FOLLOW THAT DREAM, THAT TOUCH OF MINK, SON OF FLUBBER, THE MISADVENTURES OF MERLIN JONES, HOW TO MURDER YOUR WIFE, THE MONKEY'S UNCLE, THE BROTHERHOOD, THE HORSE IN THE GRAY FLANNEL SUIT, SWEET CHARITY, THE COMPUTER WORE TENNIS SHOES, R.P.M., THE BAREFOOT EXECUTIVE, NOW YOU SEE HIM, NOW YOU DON'T, THE SENIORS; TV credits include a

recurring role in "My Favorite Martian," as well as the TV films "Wake Me When the War is Over," "The D.A.: Murder One," "The Legend of Lizzie Borden," "Captains and the Kings" (a miniseries), "Tail Gunner Joe"; was a member of the actors' union council; recorded over 220 books for the blind.

Hewitt, Virginia

(Virginia Hewitt Meer)

Died 21 July 1986, Los Angeles, Calif., age 58.

TV/Stage/Film Actress. Mainly known for her role in the early TV series "Space Patrol" (1950 to 1956); started out as a model and regional theater actress before appearing in MY DEAR SECRETARY, followed by THE FLYING SAUCER, BOWERY BATTALION, THE PEOPLE AGAINST O'HARA; after retirement, ran a chandelier shop with her husband who designed many pieces for prominent personalities.

Hickman, Bill

Died 24 Feb. 1986, Indio, Calif., age 65.

Film Stuntman-Actor. After a start as a child actor in the "Our Gang" comedy series, became a stuntman and sometime director, though he continued acting in such films as TO PLEASE A LADY, FIXED BAYONETS, THE JOKER IS WILD, HOUSEBOAT, POINT BLANK, BULLITT, THE LOVE BUG, PATTON, THE FRENCH CONNECTION (also directed the second unit on the latter two), HICKEY AND BOGGS, WHAT'S UP, DOC?, THE SEVEN UPS.

Higby, Mary Jane

Died 1 Feb. 1986, New York City, N.Y., age 70.

Radio/Film Actress-Author. Primarily known as a prolific radio actress, who was a part of radio shows like "Shell Chateau" (dubbed singer Nadine Conner's speaking voice), "Joe Palooka," "John's Other Wife," "Linda's Other Love," "Listening Post," "Parties at Pickfair," "Perry Mason," "The Romance of Helen Trent," "Stella Dallas," "The Story of Mary Marlin," "This Is Nora Drake," "Rosemary," and starred in "Thanks For Tomorrow," and "When a Girl Marries"; also wrote short stories and appeared in the 1969 film THE HONEYMOON KILLERS.

Hill, Roland E.

Born 5 Feb. 1895, East Liverpool, Ohio; died 10 Nov. 1986, Woodland Hills, Calif.

Architect-Aircraft Designer-Film Art/Set Director. After college years at Exeter and Princeton and a stint with the Army Air Service during WW I, studied architecture in U.S. and France; designed the airship *Shenandoah* and went to Los Angeles where he designed numerous mansions; worked for First National Studios, which later became part of Warner Bros., on early films like QUEEN KELLY and THE JAZZ SINGER; specializing in ship architecture, he assisted on or directed the model work for CAPTAIN BLOOD, ACTION IN THE NORTH ATLANTIC, CAPTAIN HORATIO HORNBLOWER; was art director on three Oscar-winning Warner Bros. shorts; during the 1950s, designed submarine interiors for the *Nautilus* in 20,000 LEAGUES UNDER THE SEA; devoted his later years to Disneyland projects, especially the overall design of the Sleeping Beauty Castle.

Hippe, Laura

Died 21 Oct. 1986, age unknown.

Film Actress. Appeared in the films LOGAN'S RUN, THE SWINGING BARMAIDS (both 1976), and MAUSOLEUM (1983).

Hirschler, Kurt

Died May 1986, Los Angeles, Calif., age 54.

Film/TV Editor. Started out as an assistant on SPLENDOR IN THE GRASS, then edited such films as ENTER THE DRAGON, RUNNING, WHISPER MY NAME; edited TV movies "Fast Friends," "Young Love, First Love," "Forbidden Love," "Still the Beaver," "Getting Physical"; directed "Come Walk the World," a religious series.

Hobson, Laura Z.

(Laura Kean Zametkin)

Died 28 Feb. 1986, New York City, New York, age 85.

Author. After attending Cornell University, married publishing executive Francis Thayer Hobson; started out writing advertising copy for the *New York Evening Post*, then went to *Time* Magazine, rising to copy chief; cowrote western novels with husband and then after a 1935 divorce, published her first short story; her second novel *Gentleman's Agreement* was made into an Academy Award-winning film in 1947; other novels include *The Other Father, The Celebrity, First Papers, The Tenth Month* (made into a TV-movie), *Consenting Adult, Over and Above, Untold Millions*; was involved in the screenplay for HER TWELVE MEN in 1954; published the first volume of her autobiography, *Laura Z*, and was working on the second at the time of her death.

Hoeree, Arthur

Died June 1986, Paris, France, age 88.

Composer-Musicologist. A multi-talented person in such disciplines as film criticism, film editing, screenwriting, composing; wrote music for stage, radio, and (usually in collaboration with Arthur Honegger) films, including RAPT, L'OR DANS LA MONTAGNE, LES BATISSEURS, LES DEMONS DE L'AUBE.

Hoffenberg, Mason

Died 1 June 1986, New York City, N.Y., age 64.

Author. Was coauthor (with Terry Southern) of *Candy*, made into a 1968 film: hailing from New York City, also wrote other books (usually under a pseudonym).

Hoffman, Beth Webb

Died 25 July 1986, Studio City, Calif., age 89.

Silent Film Actress. Was a bathing beauty for Mack Sennett and appeared in D.W. Griffith's classic INTOLERANCE.

Holmes, Leroy

(Alvin Holms)

Born 22 Sept. 1913, Pittsburgh, Pa.; died 27 July 1986, Los Angeles, Calif.

Composer-Arranger-Conductor. After studying at Northwestern School of Music and the Juilliard School, started his own band in 1934, then became an arranger for Vincent Lopez and Harry James; after WW II military service and a short return stint with James, went to Hollywood to score films and radio shows, mainly working for MGM Records (with other work for United Artists and radio); compositions include "The New Dixieland Parade," "Sahara," "Pennsylvania Turnpike," "One Stop Boogie"; arranged and worked on recordings with such pop artists as Art Lund, Helen Forrest, Shirley Bassey, Nelson Eddy; wrote the musical score for various films including SMILE in 1975.

Howell, Teddy

(Edward Howell)

Died 20 Aug. 1986, Sydney, Australia, age 84.

Stage/Radio/TV/Film Actor. Started his over 70-year show business career at the age of eight in an act with his father and brother; was most noted for a 31-year stint with a radio serial called "Fred and Maggie Everybody," which he wrote, produced and acted in with his wife; appeared on Australian TV in "A Country Practice" and in the film CAREFUL, HE MIGHT HEAR YOU.

Huie, William Bradford

Born 13 Nov. 1910, Hartselle, Ala.; died 22 Nov. 1986, Guntersville, Ala.

Author. After attending the University of Alabama, became a reporter (in Birmingham) and a magazine editor for *American Mercury*; his first novel, *Mud on the Stars*, was published in 1942; films made from his novels include THE REVOLT OF MAMIE STOVER, WILD RIVER, THE OUTSIDER, THE AMERICANIZATION OF EMILY, THE KLANSMAN, and the TV movie "The Execution of Private Slovik."

Hurst, Brian Desmond

Born 12 Feb. 1900, Castle Reagh, Ireland; died 26 Sept. 1986, London, England.

Film Director-Screenwriter. After a Paris education, went to Hollywood in 1925 where he picked up the directing essentials from John Ford; returned to England in 1934 and did directing or writing (or both) on such films as BUCKET OF BLOOD, NORAH O'NEALE, SENSATION, GLAMOROUS NIGHT, THE TENTH MAN,

PRISON WITHOUT BARS, THE FUGITIVE, THE LION HAS WINGS, SUICIDE SQUADRON, THE ALIBI, THE HUNDRED POUND WINDOW, HUNGRY HILL, THE MARK OF CAIN, THE GAY LADY, A CHRISTMAS CAROL (1951), TOM BROWN'S SCHOOLDAYS, MALTA STORY, SIMBA, THE BLACK TENT, BEHIND THE MASK, DANGEROUS EXILE, HIS AND HERS, THE PLAYBOY OF THE WESTERN WORLD.

Isherwood, Christopher

Born 26 Aug. 1904, Bisley, Cheshire, England; died 4 Jan. 1986, Los Angeles, Calif.

Novelist-Film/Stage Writer. After attending Cambridge University, where he wrote the novels *All the Conspirators* and *The Memorial*, went to Germany in 1929 where exposure to the growing Nazi movement provided the inspiration for the stories that would be the basis of the 1952 play "I Am a Camera" (from which came the 1955 British film version and then the musical "Cabaret" which was filmed in 1972; came to America in 1939 (with W.H. Auden, with whom he had collaborated on such plays as "Dog Beneath the Skin," "The Ascent of F6," "On the Frontier") to do screenplays for films such as RAGE IN HEAVEN, FOREVER AND A DAY, ADVENTURE IN BALTIMORE, THE GREAT SINNER, DIANE, THE LOVED ONE, THE SAILOR FROM GIBRALTAR; he cowrote the TV movie FRANKENSTEIN: THE TRUE STORY; other books include *The Last of Mr. Norris, Journey to a War* (with W. H. Auden), *Prater Violet, Down There on a Visit, A Meeting by the River, Christopher and His Kind, Kathleen and Frank: The Autobiography of a Family*; in his later years he was often a guest lecturer at colleges. He made a screen appearance in a bit part in the 1981 film RICH AND FAMOUS.

James, Claire

Died 18 Jan. 1986, Woodland Hills, Calif., age 65.

Film Actress. A Minneapolis native and the first runner-up in the 1938 Miss America beauty pageant, she appeared in the following films: FORTY LITTLE MOTHERS, BLONDIE ON A BUDGET, ROAD TO SINGAPORE, THEY DRIVE BY NIGHT, NAVY BLUES, ZIEGFELD GIRL, I WAKE UP SCREAMING, CONEY ISLAND, VOODOO MAN, ROAD TO UTOPIA, SADDLE SERENADE, FREDDIE STEPS OUT, VACATION DAYS, ONE TOO MANY, ONLY THE VALIANT, THE REVOLT OF MAMIE STOVER, CAPRICE; using the name of Carol Stevens, made SABOTEUR, GOOD SAM, MAIDSTONE.

Jensen, Soren

Died 21 March 1986, Sonora, Calif., age unknown.

Film Stunt Pilot. Worked on such films as APOCALYPSE NOW, BLUE THUNDER, RED DAWN, INDIANA JONES AND THE TEMPLE OF DOOM, RUNAWAY TRAIN (nominated for 2 stunt awards), INVASION U.S.A.

Jerome, Suzanne

(Susan Willis)

Died 4 Dec. 1986, Cornwall, England, age 26.

Stage/TV/Film Actress. Appeared in films (OCTOPUSSY), stage ("Oh, Calcutta"), TV ("Benny Hill Show").

Johnson, Carlton

Died 22 Dec. 1986, Los Angeles, Calif., age 52.

Dancer-Choreographer. Danced on TV on such shows as "The Carol Burnett Show," "The Danny Kaye Show," "The Sammy Davis, Jr. Show," and in films such as SWEET CHARITY and THE WIZ; danced in and choreographed DOCTOR DETROIT and choreographed IT'S A MAD, MAD, MAD, MAD WORLD and THE BLUES BROTHERS; taught dance and did choreography for many show-business acts.

Jones, Darby

Died 30 Nov. 1986, Los Angeles, Calif., age 76.

Film Actor. A Los Angeles native, started at the age of nine in bit parts leading to roles in TARZAN THE FEARLESS, TARZAN AND HIS MATE, THE VIRGINIA JUDGE, TARZAN ESCAPES,

SWING HIGH, SWING LOW, A DAY AT THE RACES, GONE WITH THE WIND, STANLEY AND LIVINGSTONE, MARYLAND, CONGO MAISIE, SAFARI, SUNDOWN, VIRGINIA, WHITE CARGO, I WALKED WITH A ZOMBIE, PASSPORT TO SUEZ, ZOMBIES ON BROADWAY, THE MACOMBER AFFAIR, ROPE OF SAND, ZAMBA, WHITE GODDESS, SOMETHING OF VALUE, PORGY AND BESS.

Jones, Peaches

Died 10 July 1986, Pasadena, Calif., age early 30s.

Stuntwoman-Actress. Was one of the first black stuntwomen, entering the business in the mid-1960s; worked as a stuntwoman on various features such as BUCK AND THE PREACHER; had minor roles in the 1972 films THE LIMIT and MELINDA; on TV, was the double for Teresa Graves in the series, "Get Christie Love"; quit the business in the mid-1970s.

Joyce, Anna

Died 23 Nov. 1986, Hialeah, Fla., age 74.

Silent Film Child Actress. Born in Mamaroneck, N.Y., the oldest of 11 children; appeared in THE GHOST IN THE GARRET.

Kark, Raymond

Died 28 June 1986, age unknown.

Film Actor. Appeared in COLD TURKEY, YOUR THREE MINUTES ARE UP, RUBY, SKATEBOARD.

Kass, Ronald S.

Died 17 Oct. 1986, Los Angeles, Calif., age 51.

Record Company Executive-Film Producer. Born in Philadelphia, he spent his formative years in Chicago and Los Angeles. After starting out in a European branch of a record company, he worked as an executive for Apple Records, MGM Records, Warner Bros. Records (the last-mentioned in the British Isles), coproduced or produced MELODY, THE OPTIMIST, NAKED YOGA; for TV, JANE EYRE; for his wife of the time, Joan Collins, produced or coproduced for films (THE STUD, THE BITCH) and for TV (FALLEN ANGELS).

Kay, Beatrice

(Hannah Beatrice Kuper)

Born 21 Apr. 1907, New York City, N.Y.; died 8 Nov. 1986, North Hollywood, Calif.

Stage/Radio/Film/TV Actress-Singer. The great-grandniece of Samuel Gompers, the union pioneer of the late 1800s through the early 1900s, moved to Louisville before the age of 6 at which time she entered show business as a professional (she had done amateur performing before), assuming the role of "Little Lord Fauntleroy" in a local stock company; in early roles, used the names "Honey Kuper" and "Honey Day"; at the Fort Lee, N.J. film studios where silent pictures were produced, she doubled for Madge Evans; she appeared on Broadway in "What's in a Name" (which starred James J. Corbett, the former boxing champion), "Secrets," "Jarnegan," (1928, with Richard Bennett, his daughter Joan in her stage debut, Wynne Gibson, Henry O'Neill), "Provincetown Follies" (at this time, she was advised to rest her voice, but didn't, and as a result developed the raspy voice that added a certain something to her presentation), "Behind the Red Lights" (with Hardie Albright and Edward Andrews), "Tell Me, Pretty Maiden" (a failure of a play with Doris Nolan); her radio show had a four-year run in the early 1940s; she headlined in nightclubs (toured the world, appearing at Paris' Moulin Rouge, Ciro's in Los Angeles, The Fairmont Hotel in San Francisco); her records sold in the millions, featuring her singing in a belt-'em-out "Gay 90s" style, particularly her rendition of "Mention My Name in Sheboygan," which sold 12,000,000 copies: other hits were such ditties as "The Strawberry Blonde," "Only a Bird in a Gilded Cage," "My Mother Was a Lady"; she appeared on screen in DIAMOND HORSESHOE (she had made her mark at the original nightclub in 1939; run by Billy Rose, the club was where she made her mark singing "Ta Ra Ra Boom De Ay" over 1,100 times), UNDERWORLD, U.S.A., A TIME FOR DYING; she ran a guest ranch for awhile, semiretired to Hollywood, then reentered the business after a disastrous home fire; TV appearances included "Bonanza," "Hawaiian Eye," and the Milton Berle and Rosemary Clooney shows, as well as various other commitments.

Kean, Betty

(Betty Wynn Kean)

Born 15 Dec. 1920, Hartford, Ct.; died 29 Sept. 1986, Hollywood, Calif.

Stage/Film/Nightclub/TV Actress-Performer. Worked both singly and with her sister Jane (born 1928), especially on the nightclub circuit; appeared on Broadway in "Music Hall Varieties," "Crazy with the Heat," "The Sun Field," "Ziegfeld Follies of 1943," "Call Me Mister," "Along Fifth Avenue," "Ankles Aweigh," and touring with "No, No, Nanette," "Irene," "Bye Bye Birdie," "High Spirits," "Call Me Mister"; on screen in MOONLIGHT MASQUERADE, GALS,INCORPORATED, SING A JINGLE, HI,GOOD-LOOKIN', MURDER IN THE BLUE ROOM, MY GAL LOVES MUSIC, SLIGHTLY TERRIFIC, THE SEDUCTION, DREAMSCAPE; TV efforts include such shows as "The Ed Sullivan Show," "The Jackie Gleason Show," "Naked City," "The Jack Paar Show," "The Johnny Carson Show," "The Cavalcade of Stars," "That Girl" (with her husband, Lew Parker), "Happy Days," "Police Woman," "The Love Boat," "The Facts of Life."

Keenan, Paul

Died 11 Dec. 1986, Boston, Mass., age 30.

TV/Film Actor. Primarily known for his recurring roles in TV's "Days of Our Lives" and "Dynasty," also appeared in the telefilms SECRETS OF A MOTHER AND DAUGHTER and SUMMER FANTASY; appeared in at least one theatrically released film, HONKY TONK FREEWAY.

King, Dennis, Jr.

Died 24 Aug. 1986, Las Vegas, Nev., age unknown.

Stage/TV/Film Actor. From a show business background (his father had an over-50-year career on the stage and appeared on the screen in THE VAGABOND KING, PARAMOUNT ON PARADE, FRA DIAVOLO, and BETWEEN TWO WORLDS), he too went on the stage in more than 20 shows, including "The Trojan Horse," "Kiss Them For Me," "The Playboy of the Western World," "Parlor Story," "The Cradle Will Rock"; on screen in THE SCARLET COAT, THE RESTLESS BREED, LET'S MAKE LOVE; TV saw him in "Playhouse 90," "Lux Video Theater," "Hallmark Hall of Fame," and "Perry Mason"; after a hip injury he turned to radio in a management capacity in several cities.

King, Diana

Died 31 July 1986, age unknown.

Film/Stage/TV Actress. Appeared on screen in ONCE A CROOK, THE MAN IN GREY, THE SPELL OF AMY NUGENT, A FAREWELL TO ARMS (1957), THE MAN WHO WOULDN'T TALK, TEENAGE BAD GIRL, OFFBEAT, DIE, DIE,MY DARLING, THEY CAME FROM BEYOND SPACE, SCHIZO, BLACK CARRION.

Klein, Irving

Died 27 Oct. 1986, Sherman Oaks, Calif., age 97.

Stage Singer-Dancer-Film Stuntman. Former vaudevillian (with "The Four Aces" singing/dancing act from 1903 through 1944), appeared on screen as either a western stuntman or as a double for Adolphe Menjou.

Klingman, Lawrence L.

Died 20 Oct. 1986, Carlsbad, Calif., age 68.

Reporter-Author-Public Relations/Dance Organization Executive. Hailing from Chicago, wrote copy for the U.S. Army in WW I, worked for the *Philadelphia Inquirer* and helped edit news for International News Service; in partnership with Gerald Green wrote the novel *His Majesty O'Keefe*, which was filmed in 1953 with Burt Lancaster; served as executive of dance companies.

Knight, Ted

(Tadeus Wladyslaw Konopka)

Born 7 Dec. 1923, Terryville, Ct.; died 26 Aug. 1986, Pacific Palisades, Calif.

TV/Radio/Film/Stage Actor. Dropped out of high school for WW II service; studied acting in Hartford and did local theater work; had various jobs (disk jockey, announcer, puppeteer/ventriloquist, singer, pantomimist) before going to New York for both radio and TV appearances in "Big Town," "Suspense," "Lux Video Theater"; appeared on screen in more than 300 roles including those in CAGE OF EVIL, PSYCHO, THIRTEEN FIGHTING MEN, TWELVE HOURS TO KILL, CRY FOR HAPPY, TWO RODE TOGETHER, HITLER, SWINGIN' ALONG, THIRTEEN WEST STREET, THE CANDIDATE, YOUNG DILLINGER, COUNTDOWN, M, CADDY SHACK; also appeared in Los Angeles local theaters and many TV performances before hitting it big as the pompous, know-it-all Ted Baxter newscaster character on "The Mary Tyler Moore Show" (which garnered him two Emmys); also appeared on a short-lived "Ted Knight Show" and the more

successful "Too Close for Comfort" which was revived in syndication (a new season was being planned with the renamed show which had been taped to run through April of 1987); debuted on Broadway in 1977 in "Some of My Best Friends"; used his vocal ability in both commercials and cartoon voice-overs.

Kohner, Frederick

Died 6 July 1986, Brentwood, Calif., age 81.

Film/Stage Writer-Novelist. Born in Teplitz-Schoenau, Czechoslovakia, he studied at both Paris' Sorbonne and the University of Vienna, writing a doctoral dissertation that later became a book, *Film is Art*; became a reporter in Hollywood, (1920s), then covered filmmaking for two European newspapers until the rise of Nazism caused him to settle permanently in California; wrote screenplays for SINS OF MAN, MAD ABOUT MUSIC (Oscar-nominated for the cowritten original story), IT'S A DATE, THE MEN IN HER LIFE, JOHNNY DOUGHBOY, TAHITI HONEY, THE LADY AND THE MONSTER, LAKE PLACID SERENADE, PAN-AMERICANA, THREE DARING DAUGHTERS, NANCY GOES TO RIO, HOLLYWOOD STORY, NEVER WAVE AT A WAC, TOY TIGER, and three "Gidget" films (GIDGET, GIDGET GOES HAWAIIAN, GIDGET GOES TO ROME) derived from his original novel based on his daughter's growing up years which spawned five more books plus a TV series and telefilms; wrote other books including *Seven Rooms in Hollywood, Cher Papa, The Continental Kick, The Gremmie, Kiki of Montparnasse, The Magician of Sunset Boulevard* (a biography of his brother, Paul, a talent agent whose daughter, Su-

san, had a brief acting career in the mid-1950s to early 1960s).

Kosloff, Maurice

Died 22 Jan. 1986, Hollywood, Calif., age 81.

Dance Director-Film Producer. Ran a dance studio that catered to such stars as Fredric March, Betty Grable, Mickey Rooney, June Haver, Jackie Coogan; produced two films, THE HOODLUM, MOVIE STUNTMEN.

Lambert, Douglas

Died 17 Dec. 1986, London, England, age 50.

Stage/TV/Film Actor. Born in New York, he debuted on Broadway in "The Dark at the Top of the Stairs," appeared in "A Mighty Man is He," plus a London production of "The Boys in the Band"; TV credits include "Bonanza," "Wagon Train," "Rawhide," "Dr. Kildare," "The Oppenheimer Affair," "The Rothko Conspiracy," "Strange Medicine," five years on "General Hospital," and "Inside Story," a British miniseries; appeared on the big screen in SUNDAY BLOODY SUNDAY, GOT IT MADE, MOONRAKER, SATURN 3, RAGTIME, THE HUNGER.

Lanchester, Elsa

(Elizabeth Sullivan)

Born 28 Oct. 1902, London, England; died 26 Dec. 1986, Woodland Hills, Calif.

Film/Stage/TV Actress. Was educated privately and had dance training with Isadora Duncan and Margaret Morris; organized a children's dancing class that became the Children's Theatre; made her London debut in 1922 in "Thirty Minutes in a Street" then appeared in "The Insect Play," "The Way of the World," "The Duenna," "The Pool," "Mr. Prohack," "Outskirts," "Little Lord Fauntleroy," "Payment Deferred" (1931); appeared briefly on the New York stage before returning to London for repertory appearances with the Old Vic/Sadler's Wells; her film debut was in the British silent ONE OF THE BEST in 1927, followed by THE CONSTANT NYMPH, THE LOVE HABIT,

THE STRONGER SEX, POTIPHAR'S WIFE, THE OFFICER'S MESS, THE PRIVATE LIFE OF HENRY VIII, THE PRIVATE LIFE OF DON JUAN, DAVID COPPERFIELD, NAUGHTY MARIETTA, THE BRIDE OF FRANKENSTEIN, THE GHOST GOES WEST, REMBRANDT, THE BEACHCOMBER, LADIES IN RETIREMENT, SON OF FURY, TALES OF MANHATTAN, FOREVER AND A DAY, PASSPORT TO DESTINY, THE SPIRAL STAIRCASE, THE RAZOR'S EDGE, NORTHWEST OUTPOST, THE BISHOP'S WIFE, THE BIG CLOCK, THE SECRET GARDEN, COME TO THE STABLE (Oscar-nominated), THE INSPECTOR GENERAL, BUCCANEER'S GIRL, MYSTERY STREET, THE PETTY GIRL, FRENCHIE, DREAMBOAT, LES MISERABLES (1952), ANDROCLES AND

THE LION, GIRLS OF PLEASURE ISLAND, HELL'S HALF ACRE, THREE RING CIRCUS, THE GLASS SLIPPER, WITNESS FOR THE PROSECUTION (Oscar-nominated), BELL, BOOK AND CANDLE, HONEYMOON HOTEL, MARY POPPINS, PAJAMA PARTY, THAT DARN CAT, EASY COME, EASY GO, BLACKBEARD'S GHOST, RASCAL, ME NATALIE, WILLARD, TERROR IN THE WAX MUSEUM, ARNOLD, MURDER BY DEATH, DIE LAUGHING; married to actor Charles Laughton; TV appearances include "The John Forsythe Show," "Nanny and the Professor," "The Bill Cosby Show" and the TV movie IN NAME ONLY; did revue sketches, toured nightclubs, had a one-woman show, and also made records; wrote two books, *Charles Laughton and I* and *Elsa Lanchester Herself* in which she discussed her husband's homosexuality.

Lane, Lauri Lupino

Died 4 June 1986, London, England, age 64.

Stage/Vaudeville/Film/TV Actor. A member of a distinguished theatrical family (father: actor Lupino Lane; cousin: actor/director Ida Lupino) played on stage in England and the continent; film credits include A KING IN NEW YORK, CARRY ON LOVING, THE GREAT WALTZ (1972).

Lane, Rusty

Died 10 Oct. 1986, age unknown

Film Character Actor. Appeared in such films as THE HOUSE ON 92ND STREET, BEYOND A REASONABLE DOUBT (1956), BIGGER THAN LIFE, THE HARDER THEY FALL, FURY AT SHOWDOWN, JOHNNY TREMAIN, PORTLAND EXPOSE, THE SHADOW ON THE WINDOW, DAMN CITIZEN, I WANT TO LIVE!, THE RAWHIDE TRAIL, FATE IS THE HUNTER, THE NEW INTERNS, YOUNGBLOOD HAWKE.

Lang, Andre

Died 4 Oct. 1986, Paris, France, age 94.

Critic-Author-Film/Stage Writer. Began writing film criticism in the early 1920s and wrote more than 30 plays; screenwriting credits include TARAKANOWA, THE END OF THE WORLD, LES MISERABLES (1936), ANNE-MARIE, LE SEPTIEME CIEL, VOLPONE.

Lang, Philip J.

(Philip Joseph Lang)

Born 17 Apr. 1911, Bronx, N.Y.; died 22 Feb. 1986, Bradford, Ct.

Orchestrator-Composer-Author-Film Music Director. After studying music, joined the Merchant Marine during WW II; upon returning, orchestrated "Billion Dollar Baby," "Annie Get Your Gun," "High Button Shoes," "Make a Wish," "Two on the Aisle," Can-Can," "Fanny," "My Fair Lady," "Li'l Abner," "Goldilocks," "Camelot," "Carnival," "Subways Are For Sleeping," "Mr. President," "Hello, Dolly!" "Mame," "I Do! I Do!" "George M!" "Annie"; also worked in films (music director on THE NIGHT THEY RAIDED MINSKY'S and orchestrations on HELLO DOLLY!) and TV ("Omnibus," "Hallmark Hall of Fame," "David Susskind Show"); wrote a book about his discipline and taught at the college level.

Lavery, Emmet

(Emmet Godfrey Lavery)

Born 8 Nov. 1902, Poughkeepsie, N.Y.; died 1 Jan. 1986, Tarzana, Calif.

Stage/Film Writer. Earned a law degree, but began writing plays in the 1930s, producing such efforts as "The First Legion," "Monsignor's Hour," "The Gentleman From Athens," "Brother Petroc's Return"; film credits include: HITLER'S CHILDREN, ARMY SURGEON, BEHIND THE RISING SUN, FOREVER AND A DAY (as one of several screenwriters), NIGHT IN PARADISE, GUILTY OF TREASON, THE COURT-MARTIAL OF BILLY MITCHELL; wrote screen versions of his plays "The Magnificent Yankee" and "The First Legion"; cowrote an opera, "Tarquin"; ran unsuccessfully for Congress in 1946.

Lawrence, Jody

Died 10 July 1986, age 55.

Film Actress. Appeared in films from 1951 through 1962 such as THE SON OF DR. JEKYLL, THE BRIGAND, CAPTAIN JOHN SMITH AND POCAHONTAS, THE LEATHER SAINT, THE SCARLET HOUR, STAGECOACH TO DANCER'S ROCK.

Lee, Carl

Died 17 Apr. 1986, New York City, N.Y., age 52.

Stage/Film/TV Actor-Stage Director. Son of stage/film actor Canada Lee, he studied acting in New York (which included sessions with Stella Adler) and appeared in the Obie-winning "The Connection," as well as the 1962 film version of the play; other theatrical efforts include "Shakespeare in Harlem," "The Marrying Maiden," "Ceremonies in Dark Old Men"; film credits include HUMAN DESIRE, THE COOL WORLD (also coscripted), THE LANDLORD, POUND, WEREWOLVES ON WHEELS, SUPERFLY, GORDON'S WAR, EXPOSED.

Lerner, Alan Jay

Born 31 Aug. 1918, New York City, N.Y.; died 14 June 1986, New York City, N.Y.

Lyricist-Playwright. Born to a prominent retailing family (the Lerner Shops), studied music at Juilliard before going to Choate and Harvard; wrote radio scripts; in 1942, met Frederick Loewe and they decided to collaborate; their first effort was a Detroit presentation of "Life of the Party," followed by "What's Up," "The Day Before Spring," "Brigadoon" (filmed in 1954), "Paint Your Wagon" (filmed in 1969), "My Fair Lady" (filmed in 1964), "Camelot" (filmed in 1967), "On a Clear Day You Can See Forever" (filmed in 1970), "Coco," after juggling "Gigi" for the theater, Loewe retired to France; other motion picture credits include AN AMERICAN IN PARIS (which gained him an Oscar), ROYAL WEDDING, GIGI (a complete musical for the screen which won nine Oscars), THE LITTLE PRINCE; married eight times.

Leven, Boris

Born 13 Aug. 1908, Moscow, Russia; died 11 Oct. 1986, Los Angeles, Calif.

Film Production Designer-Art Director. Studied architecture in New York and Southern California after emigrating from Russia in 1927; worked for Paramount, Major Pictures, 20th Century-Fox, Universal; credits include: ALEXANDER'S RAGTIME BAND (Oscar nominated), DOWN ON THE FARM, ROAD DEMON, THE FLYING DEUCES, THE SHANGHAI GESTURE (Oscar nominated); GIRL TROUBLE, LIFE BEGINS AT 8:30; TALES OF MANHATTAN, HELLO, FRISCO, HELLO, DOLL FACE, HOME SWEET HOMICIDE, SHOCK, I WONDER WHO'S KISSING HER NOW, THE SHOCKING MISS PILGRIM, MR. PEABODY AND THE MERMAID, CRISS CROSS, THE LOVABLE CHEAT, SEARCH FOR DANGER, DESTINATION MURDER, EXPERIMENT ALCATRAZ, A MILLIONAIRE FOR CHRISTY, THE PROWLER, THE SECOND WOMAN, TWO DOLLAR BETTOR, SUDDEN FEAR, DONOVAN'S BRAIN, FORT ALGIERS, INVADERS FROM MARS, THE LONG WAIT, THE SILVER CHALICE, GIANT (Oscar nominated), THUNDER IN THE SUN, SEPTEMBER STORM, WEST SIDE STORY, THE SOUND OF MUSIC, THE SAND PEBBLES, STAR!, THE ANDROMEDA STRAIN, TWO FOR THE SEESAW, STRAIT-JACKET, A DREAM OF KINGS, HAPPY BIRTHDAY, WANDA JUNE, THE NEW CENTURIONS, JONATHAN LIVINGSTON SEAGULL, SHANKS, MANDINGO, NEW YORK, NEW YORK, THE LAST WALTZ, THE KING OF COMEDY, FLETCH, THE COLOR OF MONEY.

Lewis, Buddy

Died 22 Nov. 1986, Los Angeles, Calif., age 69.

Stage/Nightclub/Film Character Actor-Comedian. Played secondary roles in CHICAGO CONFIDENTIAL, TARAWA BEACHHEAD, ROUST-

ABOUT, HARLOW (as Al Jolson), SWEET CHARITY, 2000 YEARS LATER, WOMEN AND BLOODY TERROR, LAST OF THE RED HOT LOVERS.

Lifar, Serge

Died 15 Dec. 1986, Lausanne, Switzerland, age 81.

Dancer-Choreographer. A native of Kiev, Russia, he studied at the school run by Vaslav Nijinsky's sister, then went to Paris in 1923 to join Serge Diaghilev's ballet troupe; choreographed his first ballet in 1929, then became ballet master of the Paris Opera, performing and creating new ballets; did choreography for the films BALLERINA, THE LIVING CORPSE; made appearances in CRIME DOES NOT PAY and THE TESTAMENT OF ORPHEUS; wrote books on dance and founded two schools of ballet.

Linares, Marcelo Lopez

Died 10 Jan. 1986, Mexico City, Mexico, age 64.

Film/Stage/TV Actor. Screen credits include EL PADRECIT, FUEGO NEGRO; appeared on stage in "A Flea in Her Ear" and "Mi Mujer Muerde la Rosca".

Lipsky, Oldrich

Died 20 Oct. 1986, age 62.

Film Director-Actor-Producer-Writer. Active in Czechoslovakian films since the early 1950s; best known for his western spoof LEMONADE JOE; others include THE MAN FROM THE FIRST CENTURY, HAPPY END, I KILLED EINSTEIN, GENTLEMEN, ADELE HASN'T HAD HER SUPPER YET.

Livingston, Charles D.

Died 28 July 1986, Sarasota, Fla., age 83.

Radio Producer-Director-Actor. After acting on stage and radio, became a producer/director for WXYZ, Detroit, Michigan for the radio serials "The Lone Ranger," "The Green Hornet," "Sergeant Preston of the Yukon" (all three being the source material for both movie and TV efforts); went to Hollywood in 1954 to act as a consultant on the TV series based on "The Lone Ranger" character.

Long, Edmund

Died 24 July 1986, Toronto, Canada, age 52.

TV/Film Cinematographer. Primarily involved with projects for the Canadian Broadcasting Corporation, but did handle the cinematography for the big screen on WHERE DID ALL THE FLOWERS GO? (a documentary) and THE ROWDYMAN.

Long, Ronald

Died 23 Oct. 1986, Burbank, Calif., age 75.

Stage/Film Actor. Born in London, England (where he acted with the Old Vic), he came to New York to appear in such stage efforts as "A Pin to See the Peep Show," "Nature's Way," and "The Cherry Orchard"; was seen on the big screen in TWO LOVES, THE NOTORIOUS LANDLADY, THE MAN FROM THE DINER'S CLUB and ASSAULT ON A QUEEN; appeared on TV in "I Dream of Jeannie" and a telefilm, WONDER WOMAN.

Loos, Anne

Died 3 May 1986, Los Angeles, Calif., age 70.

Film/Stage Actress. After preliminary stock work in Carmel, Calif., entered the film business in 1942 to debut in HITLER'S CHILDREN, followed by TWO SENORITAS FROM CHICAGO, EVER SINCE VENUS, JAM SESSION, MR. WINKLE GOES TO WAR, ONCE UPON A TIME, ONE MYSTERIOUS NIGHT, TOGETHER AGAIN, LEAVE IT TO BLONDIE, OVER 21, PILLOW TO POST, THE WOMAN IN THE WINDOW, TOMORROW IS FOREVER, HANNAH LEE, PUSHOVER, NEVER SAY GOODBYE, THE SOLID GOLD CADILLAC, THE MUSIC MAN; had a recurring part on TV in "Meet Mr. McNulty" with Ray Milland, and appeared in the TV movie "All My Darling Daughters" and its sequel, "My Darling Daughters' Anniversary".

Lopez, J. Victor

Died 28 March 1986, Los Angeles, Calif., age 39.

Stage/Film/TV Actor. Appeared on stage in "Equus," "The Gingerbread Lady," "The Time of the Cuckoo"; movie credits include 10, MEGAFORCE, DEADLY FORCE; was frequently on TV in such shows as "Falcon Crest" (a recurring role), "Man from Atlantis," "Dynasty," "Matt Houston," "Crazy Like a Fox," and the TV movies A SMALL KILLING, FANTASIES, TOMORROW'S CHILD.

Lormer, Jon

Died 19 March 1986, Burbank, Calif., age 80.

Stage/Film/TV Actor. Was a director/teacher at New York's American Theater Wing as well as an actor in "American Holiday," "Murder in the Cathedral," "Class of '29," "The Sun and I"; early TV appearances include "Playhouse 90," "Ellery Queen," "Studio One," "Ford Theater," "Matinee Theater" and the soap opera "Search for Tomorrow"; went to Hollywood in 1958 for appearances in such films as I WANT TO LIVE, GIRLS ON THE LOOSE, THE MATCHMAKER, RALLY 'ROUND THE FLAG, BOYS, THE COMANCHEROS, DEAD RINGER, ONE MAN'S WAY, YOUNGBLOOD HAWKE, ZEBRA IN THE KITCHEN, DIMENSION 5, THE SINGING NUN, THE SAND PEBBLES, A FINE MADNESS, IF HE HOLLERS, LET HIM GO, THE LEARNING TREE, GETTING STRAIGHT, DOCTORS' WIVES, THE MAN, ROOSTER COGBURN, THE BOOGENS, CREEPSHOW; appeared regularly on "Perry Mason," "Lassie," "The Real McCoys," "Peyton Place," "The Lawman," "Star Trek," "Highway to Heaven" and appeared in the TV movies FRANKENSTEIN, THE GUN AND THE PULPIT, THE LEGEND OF LIZZIE BORDEN, CONSPIRACY OF TERROR, ARTHUR HAILEY'S THE MONEYCHANGERS, LOOSE CHANGE, THE GOLDEN GATE MURDERS, BEGGARMAN, THIEF.

Love, Bessie

(Juanita Horton)

Born 10 Sep. 1898 (some sources say 1891), Midland, Texas; died 26 Apr. 1986, London, England.

Film/Stage/TV Actress. One of the busiest actresses of the silent screen, she started work as a teenager for D. W. Griffith's company as a Piedmont girl in BIRTH OF A NATION, INTOLERANCE, REGGIE MIXES IN, SISTER OF SIX, STRANDED, THE ARYAN, WEE LADY BETTY, POLLY ANN, THE DAWN OF UNDERSTANDING, THE GREAT ADVENTURE, CUPID FORECLOSES, THE MIDLANDERS, PEGEEN, THE SEA LION, PURPLE DAWN, THE VILLAGE BLACKSMITH, THE GHOST PATROL, HUMAN WRECKAGE, ST. ELMO, THE KING ON MAIN STREET, THE LOST WORLD, RUBBER TIRES, A HARP IN HOCK, ANYBODY HERE SEEN KELLY?, THE MATI-

NEE IDOL, SALLY OF THE SCANDALS; sound film credits include THE BROADWAY MELODY, THE GIRL IN THE SHOW, THE IDLE RICH, CHASING RAINBOWS, CONSPIRACY, GOOD NEWS, SEE AMERICA THIRST, MORALS FOR WOMEN, LIVE AGAIN, ATLANTIC FERRY, JOURNEY TOGETHER, THE MAGIC BOX, THE BAREFOOT CONTESSA, THE LIGHT TOUCH, THE STORY OF ESTHER COSTELLO, LOSS OF INNOCENCE, THE ROMAN SPRING OF MRS. STONE, PROMISE HER ANYTHING, ISADORA (1968), ON HER MAJESTY'S SECRET SERVICE, CATLOW, SUNDAY BLOODY SUNDAY, THE RITZ, RAGTIME, REDS, THE HUNGER; wrote the play "The Homecoming" in 1958.

Lyons, Collette

(Collette Lyons Hearst)

Died 5 Oct. 1986, age 78.

Stage/Film Actress-Comedienne. Appeared on stage in the 1939 version of "George White's Scandals," "Hold On To Your Hats" (with Al Jolson), "Vickie," "Artists and Models" (1943), a 1946 revival of "Show Boat" as well as productions of "New Moon" and "The Desert Song"; films are DANCE, CHARLIE, DANCE, HOTEL HAYWIRE, 52ND STREET, WOMAN AGAINST THE WORLD, THREE TEXAS STEERS, BLONDE RANSOM, THE DOLLY SISTERS, FRISCO SAL, BLONDIE'S BIG DEAL, THE LONE WOLF AND HIS LADY, WHEN YOU'RE SMILING, WABASH AVENUE, THE REBEL SET, RETURN TO PEYTON PLACE; formerly married to George Hearst of the great newspaper family.

Lys, Lya

(Natalia Lyecht)

Died 2 June 1986, Newport Beach, Calif., age 78.

Film Actress. A native of France, appeared in the avant-garde films UN CHIEN ANDALOU and L'AGE D'OR before traveling to the U.S. and appearing in such films as CLEAR ALL WIRES, JIMMY AND SALLY, LIVES OF A BENGAL LANCER, THE GREAT GAMBINI, MY DEAR MISS ALDRICH, THE YOUNG IN HEART, CONFESSIONS OF A NAZI SPY, THE RETURN OF DR. X., MURDER IN THE AIR; retired from show business in the early 1940s.

Maas, Ernest

Died 21 July 1986, Los Angeles, Calif., age 94.

Documentary Filmmaker-Screenwriter. Mainly known for documentaries such as UNCLE SAM OF FREEDOM RIDGE (1920); wrote the screenplay for THE SHOCKING MISS PILGRIM; headed Paramount Studio's New York branch (both newsreel and short subject departments).

MacDonald, John D.

(John Dann MacDonald)

Born 24 July 1916, Sharon, Pa.; died 28 Dec. 1986, Milwaukee, Wis.

Novelist. Earned a master's degree from Harvard before going into the Army during WW II where he began writing short stories (some of which were published upon his release in 1945); his first novel, *The Brass Cupcake*, was published in 1950, and he wrote a total of 77 novels, including 21 featuring the Travis McGee character; films based on his novels were MAN-TRAP, CAPE FEAR, KONA COAST, DARKER THAN AMBER, and in 1984 A FLASH OF GREEN.

MacEwen, Walter

Died 15 Apr. 1986, Woodland Hills, Calif.

Film Producer. A native of Scotland, worked for British-International and Gainsborough Pictures until 1930 when he came to the U.S. to serve as a reader at Warner Bros., eventually becoming head of the story department; went to Paramount and later to Jesse L. Lasky Productions; during the 1940s produced ALWAYS IN MY HEART, THE BIG SHOT, HENRY ALDRICH GETS GLAMOUR, NIGHT PLANE FROM CHUNGKING, THE GOOD FELLOWS, HENRY ALDRICH SWINGS IT, SALUTE FOR THREE, HENRY

ALDRICH'S LITTLE SECRET, NATIONAL BARN DANCE, THE MAN IN HALF-MOON STREET, THE MIRACLE OF THE BELLS; in the late 1940s, returned to Warner Bros. and rose to vice president of production before the 1969 takeover by Kinney Services.

Mack, Helen

(Helen McDougal)

Died 13 Aug. 1986, Beverly Hills, Calif., age 72.

Film Actress-Radio Director/Producer. A Rock Island, Illinois native, went to a theatrical children's school in New York before taking child's parts on Broadway ("The Dybbuk") and in silent films made on the East Coast (UNDER THE RED ROBE, GRIT, ZAZA, THE LITTLE RED SCHOOL HOUSE, PIED PIPER MALONE); her Hollywood career started in 1931 with THE STRUGGLE, and continued with THE SILENT WITNESS, WHILE PARIS SLEEPS, BLIND ADVENTURE, THE CALIFORNIA TRAIL, CHRISTOPHER BEAN, FARGO EXPRESS, MELODY CRUISE, SON OF KONG, SWEEPINGS, ALL OF ME, COLLEGE RHYTHM, KISS AND MAKE UP, THE LEMON DROP KID (1934), YOU BELONG TO ME, CAPTAIN HURRICANE, FOUR HOURS TO KILL, THE RETURN OF PETER GRIMM, THE MILKY WAY, FIT FOR A KING, I PROMISE TO PAY, THE LAST TRAIN FROM MADRID, THE WRONG ROAD, YOU CAN'T BUY LUCK, I STAND ACCUSED, KING OF THE NEWSBOYS, SECRETS OF A NURSE, CALLING ALL MARINES, GAMBLING SHIP, MYSTERY OF THE WHITE ROOM, GIRLS OF THE ROAD, HIS GIRL FRIDAY, POWER DIVE, AND NOW TOMORROW, STRANGE HOLIDAY, DIVORCE; went into radio in 1940s as director/producer on "A Date With Judy" and "Meet Corliss Archer"; wrote one play, "The Matinee Dance."

MacRae, Gordon

Born 12 March 1921, East Orange, N.J.; died 24 Jan. 1986, Lincoln, Neb.

Film/TV/Radio/Stage Actor-Singer. Acted on the radio as a child and then worked in a revue headed by Ray Bolger; first appeared on the stage in "Junior Miss" and was encouraged by NBC bandleader Horace Heidt, who helped him begin a successful recording career; worked on radio in "The Railroad Hour" then on Broadway in "Three to Make Ready"; went into films in such efforts as THE BIG PUNCH, LOOK FOR THE SILVER LINING, BACKFIRE, THE DAUGHTER OF ROSIE O'GRADY, RETURN OF THE FRONTIERSMAN, TEA FOR TWO, THE WEST POINT STORY, ON MOONLIGHT BAY, STARLIFT, ABOUT FACE, BY THE LIGHT OF THE SILVERY MOON, THE DESERT SONG, THREE SAILORS AND A GIRL, OKLAHOMA, THE BEST THINGS IN LIFE ARE FREE, CAROUSEL, THE PILOT; appeared on TV in "The Colgate Comedy Hour" and "The Gordon MacRae

Show''; often teamed with former wife, Sheila MacRae, in summer stock and nightclub appearances.

Magidson, Herb

Born 7 Jan. 1906, Braddock, Pa.; died 2 Jan. 1986, Beverly Hills, Calif.

Lyricist. Began writing songs for stage presentations, including "Earl Carroll's Vanities of 1928," "The Songwriter," "The Vanderbilt Revue," "George White's Music Hall Varieties"; films which used his lyrics included THE GAY DIVORCEE, GIFT OF GAB, GEORGE WHITE'S 1935 SCANDALS, HERE'S TO ROMANCE, HATS OFF, LIFE OF THE PARTY, RADIO CITY REVELS, SLEEPY TIME GAL, HERS TO HOLD, SING YOUR WAY HOME, DO YOU LOVE ME?, SONG OF THE THIN MAN; most well-known songs include "The Continental" (Oscar winner from THE GAY DIVORCEE), "Roses in December," "Say a Prayer for the Boys Over There" (from HERS TO HOLD, Oscar nominated), "I'll Buy That Dream," "You're Not So Easy to Forget," "I'll Dance at Your Wedding," "Enjoy Yourself (It's Later Than You Think)," "Conchita Lopez."

Malamud, Bernard

Born 26 Apr. 1914, Brooklyn, N.Y.; died 18 March 1986, New York City, N.Y.

Author. Inspired to become a writer by his father's stories of life in czarist Russia, he attended college in New York, then taught high school English before becoming an instructor at Oregon State University, and more recently a professor of literature at Bennington College in Vermont; published *The Natural* in 1952 (filmed 1984), *The Fixer* in 1966 (received the Pulitzer Prize and the National Book Award; filmed 1968); other fiction pieces include *The Assistant*, *The Magic Barrel* (a collection of stories for which he received the National Book Award for fiction), *A New Life*, *Idiots First* (stories), *Pictures of Fidelman: An Exhibition*, *The Tenants*, *Rembrandt's Hat* (another story collection), *Dubin's Lives*.

Malkames, Don

Died 24 Nov. 1986, Yonkers, N.Y., age 82.

Cinematographer-Inventor-Film Historian. Worked for small studios and on independent productions, photographing VICTIMS OF PERSECUTION, CRY MURDER, BEWARE, HI-DE-HO, CITIZEN SAINT, MIRACLE IN HARLEM, JIGSAW (1949), PROJECT X (1949), SARUMBA, SO YOUNG, SO BAD, ST. BENNY THE DIP, THAT MAN FROM TANGIER, THE BURGLAR, PIE IN THE SKY; invented a film process and a newsreel camera.

Maltagliati, Evi

Died 27 April 1986, Rome, Italy, age 77.

Stage/Film/TV Actress. A native of Florence, went into the theater in 1923 and appeared in "A Mid-

summer Night's Dream" and "Tombola"; her few film appearances include THE BETROTHED, BURIED ALIVE, WOMEN ALONE, ULYSSES, SULEIMAN THE CONQUEROR, THE HEAD OF THE FAMILY, ROMA BENE.

Maron, Alfred

Died 28 Sept. 1986, age 74.

Stage/Film Actor. An Englishman, he appeared in THE HARASSED HERO, THE MAN IN THE ROAD, HELL, HEAVEN OR HOBOKEN, CLUE OF THE TWISTED CANDLE, and FIDDLER ON THE ROOF.

Marshall, Ray

Died 20 Sept. 1986, Sydney, Australia, age 66.

Film/TV Actor. Appeared in the following Australian films: CADDIE, MONEY MOVERS, STIR, NEWSFRONT, and in 1986, CACTUS; seen on TV in "A Country Practice" and "Sons and Daughters" among many efforts.

Martell, Jack

Died 29 March 1986, Los Angeles, Calif., age 67.

Film Costumer. A New York City native, came West in the 1920s and entered the film business in the 1940s, working mainly for MGM on such films as BEN HUR, THE GALLANT HOURS, THE GREATEST STORY EVER TOLD, THE PROFESSIONALS, IN COLD BLOOD, A MAN CALLED HORSE, THE BAD NEWS BEARS IN BREAKING TRAINING, MATILDA; his TV credits include work on "Roots," for which he received an Emmy nomination.

Mason, Hal

Died 10 Oct. 1986, Los Angeles, Calif., age 69.

Animator-Writer-Producer-Director. Worked with Walter Lantz on his cartoon characters Oswald Rabbit, Andy Panda, and Woody Woodpecker; for TV commercials created the Hamm's Beer bear, the Pillsbury Dough Boy, Mr. Clean, the Frito Bandito; wrote the 1982 TV special entitled "Chipmunks Christmas."

Maston, Jerry

Died 24 July 1986, Los Angeles, Calif., age 46.

Film Set Decorator-Floral Arranger-Stage Actor. Appeared in dramas and musicals in the New York area; went West in 1970 to work as a set decorator on such films as MAME, FUNNY LADY, WHAT'S UP DOC?, THE POSEIDON ADVENTURE, A WEDDING, SWING SHIFT, ROCKY III, BEVERLY HILLS COP; TV credits include "Love Boat," "The Incredible Hulk," and "Little House on the Prairie."

Maurer, Norman

Died 23 Nov. 1986, Los Angeles, Calif., age 60.

Film Producer-Cartoon Consultant-Writer-Comic Book Illustrator. Started in the comic book business while still a teenager, illustrating such comics as "Daredevil Comics," "Boy Comics," "The Little Wiseguys," "Dennis the Menace" (as a ghostwriter for Hank Ketcham), and a series of "Three Stooges" comic books; in 1956, went into the film industry as a producer; worked on several "Three Stooges" features and THE ANGRY RED PLANET, WHO'S MINDING THE MINT?, THE MAD ROOM; further involvement with the "Three Stooges" included managing the trio for 15 years and writing, producing, and directing several pilot films; in 1975, joined Hanna-Barbera as a writer-story editor; went to CBS as a cartoon consultant.

McCabe, Leo

Died 23 Feb. 1986, Dublin, Ireland, age 71.

Stage/Film Actor. A native of Dublin, formed his own theater group, appearing in "Edward My Son" and "Of Mice and Men"; was on the big screen in THE HOUSE OF ROTHSCHILD, THE INFORMER, BELOVED ENEMY, POLO JOE, LITTLE MISS MOLLY, THE QUARE FELLOW, OF HUMAN BONDAGE (1964), BLUES FOR LOVERS.

McCall, Mary C., Jr.

Died 3 Apr. 1986, Woodland Hills, Calif., age 81.

Screenwriter. A native New Yorker, graduated from Vassar then studied at Trinity College in Dublin, Ireland; had various writing jobs before her novel *Revolt* was sold to Warner Bros. (filmed as SCARLET DAWN), initiating a 25-year screenwriting career, working on such films as MORGAN'S MARAUDERS, IT'S TOUGH TO BE FAMOUS, STREET OF WOMEN, BABBITT, A MIDSUMMER'S NIGHT'S DREAM, THE WOMAN IN RED (1935), DR. SOCRATES, CRAIG'S WIFE, MAISIE, CONGO MAISIE, KATHLEEN, DU BARRY WAS A LADY, THE SULLIVANS, KEEP YOUR POWDER DRY, MR. BELVEDERE GOES TO COLLEGE, DANCING IN THE DARK, SLIM CARTER, JUKE BOX RHYTHM; also wrote for such TV shows as "The Millionaire," "Ford Theater," "Dr. Hudson's Secret Journal," "Sea Hunt," "Third Man," "I Dream of Jeannie"; was a member of the Writer's Guild of America and served three terms as its president.

McCarthy, Frank

Born 8 June 1912, Richmond, Va.; died 1 Dec. 1986, Woodland Hills, Calif.

Film Producer-Press Agent-Government/Army Official. Worked as a reporter and press agent before earning a master's degree from Virginia Military Institute and going to work for the war department; worked up through the ranks to become an aide to Chief of Staff Gen. George C. Marshall in 1941, and reached the rank of brigadier general; retired from the service and became an executive producer for 20th Century-Fox (1949-1962; 1965-1972) and Universal (1963-1965; 1972-1977); during these periods, was responsible for such films as DECISION BEFORE DAWN (1951, nominated for an Academy Award), SAILOR OF THE KING, A GUIDE FOR THE MARRIED MAN, PATTON (which won 7 Academy Awards, including Best Picture), MAC ARTHUR, CUTTER AND BONE, PENNIES FROM HEAVEN, ZOOT SUIT, DEAD MEN DON'T WEAR PLAID, THE MAN WITH TWO BRAINS, REACHING OUT, THE STING II; also produced the telefilm, "Fireball Forward"; was heavily involved in academic, military, charitable institutions.

McCarthy, Winnie

Died 20 Apr. 1986, age unknown.

Film Actress. Appeared in the film TO BE OR NOT TO BE (1983).

McKenna, Siobhan

(Siobhan Giollamhuire Nic Cionnaith McKenna)

Born 24 May 1922, Belfast, Northern Ireland, died 16 Nov. 1986, Dublin, Ireland.

Stage/Film Actress. Came from educated parents in a household where only Gaelic was spoken; after attending convent schools and university, appeared at a Gaelic theater in Galway (1940-42) and then the

Abbey Theater in Dublin (1943-46); debuted in London in 1947 in "The White Steed," then appeared in "Berkeley Square," "Fading Mansion," "Ghosts," "Heloise," "Saint Joan"; made her American debut in 1955 in New York in "The Chalk Garden," then appeared in "The Rope Dancers," and played the lead in "Hamlet" (1959); film appearances include HUNGRY HILL, DAUGHTER OF DARKNESS, THE LOST PEOPLE, THE ADVENTURERS, KING OF KINGS, THE PLAYBOY OF THE WESTERN WORLD, OF HUMAN BONDAGE (1964), DOCTOR ZHIVAGO, and MEMED MY HAWK in 1984; appeared on TV "Hallmark Hall of Fame" productions "The Letter," "What Every Woman Knows," "Cradle Song"; was married to Hollywood actor Denis O'Dea who died in 1978.

McIntire, Tim

Died 15 Apr. 1986, Los Angeles, Calif., age 42.

Film/TV Actor. From show business parents (actor John McIntire, actress Jeanette Nolan), appeared in the following films: SHENANDOAH, FOLLOW ME BOYS, THE STERILE CUCKOO, THE 1,000 PLANE RAID, KID BLUE, ALOHA, BOBBY AND ROSE, A BOY AND HIS DOG, WIN, PLACE OR STEAL, THE GUMBALL RALLY, THE KILLER INSIDE ME, THE CHOIRBOYS, AMERICAN HOT WAX (contains his most-noted part as disk jockey Alan Freed),

BRUBAKER, FAST-WALKING, SACRED GROUND; also wrote and performed the music for JEREMIAH JOHNSON and provided the voice of the dog and the music for A BOY AND HIS DOG; was prolific in the area of voice-overs for TV commercials.

McLendon, Gordon

Died 14 Sept. 1986, Lake Dallas, Tex., age 65.

Radio Broadcaster-Film Producer/Actor. Famed for creating colorful baseball game descriptions from Western Union wire reports, built a 458-station radio network from one station in Dallas; produced one film, ESCAPE TO VICTORY in 1981, and appeared in another, THE KILLER SHREWS in 1959.

McNamara, Ed

Died 11 Oct. 1986, Toronto, Canada, age 65.

Film/TV/Stage/Radio Actor. Worked in local theater and radio in the Toronto area and on Canadian network TV before appearing in films such as SILVER STREAK, THE HOUSE BY THE LAKE, THE BLACK STALLION, and 1985's STITCHES.

Meadows, Robert

Died 17 May 1986, New York City, N.Y., age 29.

Stage/Film/TV Actor-Dancer. Appeared mainly on stage in such efforts as a revival of "On Your

Toes," was in the touring production of "Chicago" and "Oklahoma," and with American Ballet Theater II, Boston Ballet, and Diamond Dance Co.; appeared on screen in WUNDERKIND, TOOTSIE; one of his TV outings was "Alice in Wonderland," which appeared on PBS.

Mendez, Francisco

Died 7 July 1986, New York City, N.Y., age 35.

Stage/Film Actor. Hailing from Puerto Rico, acted in approximately 15 Spanish plays; actively represented the Hispanic community; appeared in such Spanish language films as LOS HIJOS DEL VICIO, LA MASACRE DE PONCE, EL SALTO, TECATO ASI ME LLAMAN.

Merkel, Una

Born 10 Dec. 1903, Covington, Ky.; died 2 Jan. 1986, Los Angeles, Calif.

Film/Stage Actress. A spirited performer, she went to school in Philadelphia and New York City, took dance lessons, and studied acting under Tyrone Power's mother; had a few small parts in silent films (including serving as a stand-in for Lillian

Gish in D.W. Griffith's WAY DOWN EAST); debuted on the New York stage in 1925 in "Two By Two" followed by "Pigs," "Two Girls Wanted," "The Gossipy Sex," "Coquette"; director Griffith remembered her from the bits she did in his silents and had her play Ann Rutledge in ABRAHAM LINCOLN in 1930; this was followed by THE BAT WHISPERS, EYES OF THE WORLD, SIX CYLINDER LOVE, THE MALTESE FALCON (1931), COMMAND PERFORMANCE, WICKED, THE SECRET WITNESS, DON'T BET ON WOMEN, DADDY LONG LEGS, THE BARGAIN, PRIVATE LIVES, REDHEADED WOMAN, SHE WANTED A MILLIONAIRE, MAN WANTED, THEY CALL IT SIN, HUDDLE, IMPATIENT MAIDEN, MEN ARE SUCH FOOLS, REUNION IN VIENNA, WHISTLING IN THE DARK (1933), BEAUTY FOR SALE, BOMBSHELL, HER FIRST MATE, THE WOMEN IN HIS LIFE, 42ND STREET, MIDNIGHT MARY, BROADWAY TO HOLLYWOOD, DAY OF RECKONING, CLEAR ALL WIRES, THE SECRET OF MADAME BLANCHE, THE WOMEN IN HIS LIFE, PARIS INTERLUDE, THIS SIDE OF HEAVEN, MURDER IN THE PRIVATE CAR, THE CAT'S PAW, THE MERRY WIDOW, BULLDOG DRUMMOND STRIKES BACK, HAVE A HEART, EVELYN PRENTICE, BIOGRAPHY OF A BACHELOR GIRL, ONE NEW YORK NIGHT, MURDER IN THE FLEET, BABY FACE HARRINGTON, IT'S IN THE AIR, RIFFRAFF, THE NIGHT IS YOUNG, BROADWAY MELODY OF 1936, SPEED, WE WENT TO COLLEGE, BORN TO DANCE, DON'T TELL THE WIFE, THE GOOD OLD SOAK, SARATOGA, TRUE CONFESSION, CHECKERS, FOUR GIRLS IN WHITE, ON BOR-

ROWED TIME, DESTRY RIDES AGAIN, SOME LIKE IT HOT (1939), COMIN' ROUND THE MOUNTAIN, THE BANK DICK, SANDY GETS HER MAN, CRACKED NUTS, DOUBLE DATE, ROAD TO ZANZIBAR, TWIN BEDS, THE MAD DOCTOR OF MARKET STREET, THIS IS THE ARMY, SWEETHEARTS OF THE U.S.A., IT'S A JOKE, SON!, THE BRIDE GOES WILD, THE MAN FROM TEXAS, KILL THE UMPIRE, MY BLUE HEAVEN, EMERGENCY WEDDING, RICH, YOUNG AND PRETTY, A MILLIONAIRE FOR CHRISTY, GOLDEN GIRL, WITH A SONG IN MY HEART, THE MERRY WIDOW, I LOVE MELVIN, THE KENTUCKIAN, BUNDLE OF JOY, THE KETTLES IN THE OZARKS, THE FUZZY PINK NIGHTGOWN, THE GIRL MOST LIKELY, THE MATING GAME, THE PARENT TRAP, SUMMER AND SMOKE (1961, won an Academy Award nomination), SUMMER MAGIC, A TIGER WALKS, SPINOUT; returned to the theater in 1944 in "Three's A Family" then didn't work for nine years until taking a part in "The Remarkable Mr. Pennypacker"; further efforts included "The Ponder Heart" (awarded a Tony), "Take Me Along," "Listen to the Mockingbird"; appeared on some of the early TV drama shows such as "Studio One," "Kraft Theater," "Playhouse 90," "Climax".

Michtom, Rose

Died 1 Apr. 1986, Los Angeles, Calif., age 89.

TV/Film Actress. A performer who entered show business at age 65, working mainly on TV shows such as "Get Smart," "McMillan and Wife," "Rhoda," "Too Close for Comfort," and "Laverne and Shirley"; appeared in the films THE STING, CHINATOWN, SHAMPOO, THE FORTUNE, IN GOD WE TRUST, YOUNG DOCTORS IN LOVE.

Miles, Sally

Died 2 Dec. 1986, London, England, age 53.

Stage/Film Actress-Director-Manager. The daughter of Sir Bernard Miles and Josephine Wilson, both prominent members of the British theatrical community; founded and managed a playhouse and did a number of one-woman shows (for which she wrote or adapted material); started a rural repertory company and a London theater club; appeared in PRIVATE'S PROGRESS (1956).

Milland, Ray

(Reginald Alfred John Truscott-Jones)

Born 3 Jan. 1907, Neath, Wales; died 10 March 1986, Torrance, Calif.

Film/Stage/TV Actor-Film Director. Born in Wales and took the last name of his stepfather, Mullane, when his parents divorced (was known as Jack Mullane in the early part of his film career); briefly studied architecture, then left school for London to attend the Household Cavalry for three years, during which time he became an excellent horseman and marksman and served as a guard to the Royal Family; after leaving the service, a chance visit to a film studio led to the offer of a film part, although the picture was scrapped due to bad weather on location; was then offered the chance to be a sharpshooter on THE INFORMER (1929), which led to a role in THE FLYING SCOTSMAN, billing himself as Raymond Milland; after one more British film (THE LADY FROM THE SEA) he went to Hollywood where he had two unbilled parts in WAY FOR A SAILOR and PASSION FLOWER; shortened his first name to Ray for THE BACHELOR FATHER, followed by JUST A GIGOLO, AMBASSADOR BILL, BOUGHT, BLONDE CRAZY, THE MAN WHO PLAYED GOD, POLLY OF THE CIRCUS, PAYMENT DEFERRED; returned to England to make ORDERS IS ORDERS and THIS IS THE LIFE, and turned to professional bridge playing and steeplechase riding for extra income; in 1932, married showgirl Muriel Weber, who would be his wife for the next 53 years; returned to Hollywood in 1934 and began filming again with MANY HAPPY RETURNS, then BOLERO, CHARLIE CHAN IN LONDON, WE'RE NOT DRESSING, MENACE, FOUR HOURS TO KILL, THE GILDED LILY, ALIAS MARY DOW, ONE HOUR LATE, THE

GLASS KEY (1935), THE RETURN OF SOPHIE LANG, THE JUNGLE PRINCESS, NEXT TIME WE LOVE, THE BIG BROADCAST OF 1937, EASY LIVING, THREE SMART GIRLS, WISE GIRL, EBB TIDE, WINGS OVER HONOLULU, BULLDOG DRUMMOND ESCAPES, HER JUNGLE LOVE, SAY IT IN FRENCH, MEN WITH WINGS, HOTEL IMPERIAL, EVERYTHING HAPPENS AT NIGHT, BEAU GESTE, FRENCH WITHOUT TEARS, UNTAMED, DOCTOR TAKES A WIFE, IRENE, SKYLARK, I WANTED WINGS, ARISE, MY LOVE, THE MAJOR AND THE MINOR, THE LADY HAS PLANS, STAR SPANGLED RHYTHM, THE CRYSTAL BALL, FOREVER AND A DAY, 'TILL WE MEET AGAIN, THE UNINVITED, LADY IN THE DARK, MINISTRY OF FEAR, THE LOST WEEKEND (1945, which earned him a Best Actor Oscar), KITTY, THE TROUBLE WITH WOMEN, THE WELL-GROOMED BRIDE, CALIFORNIA, THE IMPERFECT LADY, VARIETY GIRL, GOLDEN EARRINGS, SO EVIL MY LOVE, SEALED VERDICT, THE BIG CLOCK, MISS TATLOCK'S MILLIONS, ALIAS NICK BEAL, IT HAPPENS EVERY SPRING, A WOMAN OF DISTINCTION, COPPER CANYON, A LIFE OF HER OWN, CIRCLE OF DANGER (also produced), NIGHT INTO MORNING, CLOSE TO MY HEART, RHUBARB, SOMETHING TO LIVE FOR, THE THIEF, BUGLES IN THE AFTERNOON, JAMAICA RUN, LET'S DO IT AGAIN, DIAL M FOR MURDER, A MAN ALONE (also directed), THE GIRL IN THE RED VELVET SWING, THE RIVER'S EDGE, THREE BRAVE MEN, HIGH FLIGHT, THE SAFECRACKER (also directed), THE PREMATURE BURIAL, PANIC IN YEAR ZERO (also directed), "X"—THE MAN WITH THE X-RAY EYES, THE CONFESSION, ROSE ROSSE PER IL FUHRER, HOSTILE WITNESS (also directed), LOVE STORY, COMPANY OF KILLERS, THE THING WITH TWO HEADS, EMBASSY, FROGS, THE BIG GAME, THE HOUSE IN NIGHTMARE PARK, TERROR IN THE WAX MUSEUM, THE STUDENT CONNECTION, GOLD, ESCAPE TO WITCH MOUNTAIN, OIL, THE SWISS CONSPIRACY, THE LAST TYCOON, ACES HIGH, SLAVERS, THE UNCANNY, I GABIANI VOLANO BASSI, SPREE, OLIVER'S STORY, BATTLESTAR GALACTICA, BLACKOUT, THE CONCORDE AFFAIR, A GAME FOR VULTURES, LA RAGAZZA IN PIGIAMA GALLO, THE ATTIC, SURVIVAL RUN, COCAINE, THE SEA SERPENT. In 1966, made his debut on Broadway at the age of 60 in "Hostile Witness" (starred in the film the following year); had two TV series, "Meet Mr. McNulty" and "Markham," as well as several TV films including "River of Gold," "Black Noon," "The Dead Don't Die," "Ellery Queen," "Rich Man, Poor Man," "Look What's Happened to Rosemary's Baby," "Mayday at 40,000 Feet,"

"Seventh Avenue," "Testimony of Two Men," "The Dream Merchants," "Our Family Business," "The Royal Romance of Charles and Diana," "Starflight: The Plane That Couldn't Land," "Cave-In."

Miller, Court

(J. Courtlandt Miller)

Died 7 March 1986, Portland, Maine, age 34.

Stage/TV/Film Actor. Studied acting under Uta Hagen before appearing in "Torch Song Trilogy," "The First," "Spookhouse"; was seen on TV in "Rage of Angels" (a miniseries), as well as many commercials; film credits include GARBO TALKS, CAT'S EYE, and THE NEW KIDS.

Miller, Merle

Born 17 May 1919, Montour, Iowa; died 10 June 1986, Danbury, Conn.

Author-Screenwriter. After attending universities in Iowa and London, worked as a reporter for the *Philadelphia Record*; during WW II, worked for *Yank* magazine as an editor; worked for *Time* and *Harper's Monthly* and published his first book, *Island 49*, in 1945, followed by *We Dropped the A-Bomb, That Winter, The Sure Thing, The Judges and the Judged, Reunion, A Gay and Melancholy Sound, A Day in Late September, Only You, Dick Daring, On Being Different, What Happened, Plain Speaking: An Oral Biography of Harry S. Truman, Lyndon: An Oral Biography of Lyndon Baines Johnson,*; wrote the screenplays for THE RAINS OF RANCHIPUR, KINGS GO FORTH, TANK FORCE, CAREER BED.

Minnelli, Vincente

Born 28 Feb. 1903, Chicago, Ill.; died 25 July 1986, Beverly Hills, Calif.

Stage Art Director-Costume/Scenic Designer-Film Director. Coming from an itinerant show business family (father and uncle ran a summer tent show in which his mother starred), appeared on the stage at the age of three; went to Chicago as a teenager to work for Marshall Field & Co. as a window dresser, then left to become a photographer's assistant; took a job with Balaban & Katz theaters designing costumes for stage shows, which led to his being sent to New York to work as a set and costume designer for the Paramount-Publix chain; moved on to Radio City Music Hall as art director for the stage shows; first gained notoriety with the Broadway musical "At Home Abroad," which he co-directed; went on to do "Ziegfeld Follies of 1936," "The Show Is On," "Hooray for What" and "Very Warm for May"; went to Hollywood in 1940, working for MGM as a director of musical numbers in such films as STRIKE UP THE BAND, BABES ON BROADWAY, PANAMA HATTIE; first directorial chore was on CABIN IN THE SKY (with an all-black cast); then made a non-musical, I DOOD IT; when Arthur Freed and Roger Edens formed a unit within MGM to produce musicals, Minnelli was hired to direct MEET ME IN ST. LOUIS, starring Judy Garland, whom he married a year later in 1945, and the following year the couple's daughter Liza was born; went on to make THE CLOCK, YOLANDA AND THE THIEF, ZIEGFELD FOLLIES (codirected with five other uncredited directors), UNDERCURRENT, TILL THE CLOUDS ROLL BY (directed Judy Garland's sequence only), THE PIRATE, MADAME BOVARY, FATHER OF THE BRIDE, AN AMERICAN IN PARIS (1951, won an Oscar for best picture), FATHER'S LITTLE DIVIDEND, LOVELY TO LOOK AT, THE STORY OF THREE LOVES (directing one sequence on each of the latter two), THE BAD AND THE BEAUTIFUL, THE BAND WAGON, THE LONG, LONG TRAILER, BRIGADOON, THE COBWEB, KISMET, LUST FOR LIFE, TEA AND SYMPATHY, DESIGNING WOMAN, THE SEVENTH SIN (uncredited), GIGI (earning a Best Director Oscar); THE RELUCTANT DEBUTANTE, SOME CAME RUNNING, HOME FROM THE HILL, BELLS ARE RINGING, THE FOUR HORSEMEN OF THE APOCALYPSE, TWO WEEKS IN ANOTHER TOWN, THE COURTSHIP OF EDDY'S FATHER, GOODBYE CHARLIE, THE

SANDPIPER, ON A CLEAR DAY YOU CAN SEE FOREVER, A MATTER OF TIME.

Ministeri, George

(George Mirisola Ministeri)

Died 29 Jan. 1986, South Boston, Mass., age 72.

Film Actor-Comic-Acrobat. Appeared on screen in THE WIZARD OF OZ (as a Munchkin), THE TERROR OF TINY TOWN, TARZAN FINDS A SON; appeared as a comic with a trio and in his own act, both as comic and acrobat.

Mirkin, Abraham

Died 28 July 1986, Philadelphia, Pa., age 68.

Film Actor-Model-Nightclub Owner. As a teenager was offered the chance to appear as a "Little Johnny" for Philip Morris cigarette promotions; held the job from 1935-40, gaining exposure which led to appearances in OIL FOR THE LAMPS OF CHINA, THE WIZARD OF OZ (as the Munchkin mayor), GHOST CATCHER, DRAGONSEED; later ran a nightclub, a bar, and an ice cream parlor.

Mollison, Clifford

Died 5 June 1986, Cyprus, age 89.

Stage/Film Actor-Stage Producer-Singer-Dramatist. Started his stage career in 1913, inaugurating a 60-year run in such efforts as "A Safety Match," "Loyalties," "R.U.R." "Lilies of the Field," "The Forest," "A Midsummer Night's Dream," "The River," "The Show," "Love's a Terrible Thing," "The Blue Mazurka," "The Girl Friend," "Bees and Honey"; seen on the screen in the British films ALMOST A HONEYMOON, THE LUCKY NUMBER, MEET MY SISTER, A SOUTHERN MAID, FREEDOM OF THE SEAS, THE LUCK OF A SAILOR, MISTER CINDERS, RADIO FOLLIES, REGAL CAVALCADE, GIVE HER A RING, BLIND FOLLY, A CHRISTMAS CAROL (1951), THE BABY AND THE BATTLESHIP, MARY HAD A LITTLE, THE V.I.P.s, OH! WHAT A LOVELY WAR.

Morris, Rolland

(Rolland "Rusty" Morris)

Died 14 May 1986, Los Angeles, Calif., age 63.

Stage/Radio/TV/Film Actor. Hailing from Colorado, first appeared on the stage in San Francisco, then worked in radio before serving in the Navy during WW II; returned to radio and had roles in many top shows such as "Mayor of the Town," "Halls of Ivy," "This is Your FBI," "Lux Radio Theater," "Doctor Christian," and "The Railroad Hour"; screen credits include THE ACCUSED, PAID IN FULL, AS YOU WERE, I WANT YOU, ON MOONLIGHT BAY, STRANGERS ON A TRAIN, SHE'S WORKING HER WAY THROUGH COLLEGE, FLAT TOP, FIGHTER ATTACK, FRANCIS GOES TO WEST POINT; appeared on TV in "Death Valley Days," "The Ray Bolger Show," "The Ann Sothern Show,"

"Omnibus," "Ruggles," and had a continuing part as Hugh Devon on the NBC soap opera, "From These Roots"; served as confidential secretary to playwright Jerome Lawrence.

Morton, Gregory

Died 28 Jan. 1986, Los Angeles, Calif., age 74.

Stage/Film Actor-Musician-Author. Accomplished violinist and stage actor, appeared on Broadway in "The Eternal Road," "King Lear," "Nathan the Wise," "War President," "Mayor of Zalamea," "A Flag Is Born," "Romeo and Juliet," "Sherlock Holmes," "Sands of the Negev"; his screen appearances include THE VAGABOND KING, THE FIEND WHO WALKED THE WEST, THE FLIGHT THAT DISAPPEARED, THE INTERNS, BYE BYE BIRDIE, JOHNNY COOL, THE NEW INTERNS, SYNANON, COUNTERPOINT, THE DESTRUCTORS, PANIC IN THE CITY, THE MEPHISTO WALTZ, THE ADULTERESS; had a role in the TV film "Brave New World."

Moyer, Ray

Died 6 Feb. 1986, Woodland Hills, Calif., age 87.

Film Set Decorator. A native of Santa Barbara, California, spent a year in the Army during WW I before being hired in 1919 as a prop man at MGM; later worked for Rex Ingram's studio, First National, Warner Bros., and RKO before settling in at Paramount in 1933; film credits include LET'S FACE IT, HERE COME THE WAVES, STANDING ROOM ONLY, 'TILL WE MEET AGAIN, LOVE LETTERS, BRING ON THE GIRLS, CALIFORNIA, NIGHT HAS A THOUSAND EYES, SEALED VERDICT, THE GREAT GATSBY (1949), UNION STATION, THE BIG CARNIVAL, THE GREATEST SHOW ON EARTH, JUST FOR YOU, HOUDINI, THE SAVAGE, LOVE IN A GOLDFISH BOWL, POCKETFUL OF MIRACLES, THE DISORDERLY ORDERLY, GOOD NEIGHBOR SAM, THE PATSY, THE GLORY GUYS, THE SONS OF KATIE ELDER, PARADISE, HAWAIIAN STYLE, PICTURE MOMMY DEAD, RED TOMAHAWK, THE WAR WAGON, THE GREEN BERETS, THE ODD COUPLE, UPTIGHT, WILL PENNY, TRUE GRIT, CATCH-22, BIG JAKE, LAWMAN, DEADLY TRACKERS, PAT GARRETT AND BILLY THE KID; won Oscars for SAMSON AND DELILAH, SUNSET BOULEVARD, CLEOPATRA (1963), and earned nominations for LADY IN THE DARK, LOVE LETTERS, KITTY, SABRINA, RED GARTERS, THE TEN COMMANDMENTS, FUNNY FACE, BREAKFAST AT TIFFANY'S, THE GREATEST STORY EVER TOLD.

Mulot, Claude

Died 13 Oct. 1986, Saint-Tropez, France, age 44.

Film Director. After assisting the noted French directors Christian-Jacque and Claude Chabrol, directed comedies, action-oriented films and exploitation type pictures (sometimes using the name of Frederic Lansac); his credits include THE BLOOD ROSE (also cowrote), THE BLOOD LETTING, BLACK VENUS.

Mustapha, Niazi

Died late 1986, Cairo, Egypt, age 78.

Film Director. His latest effort, EL KORADATI, brought to an end a career consisting of approximately 150 films, mainly dealing in the area of suspense; before starting his prolific output, had studied film in Germany during the 1920s.

Nathan, Adele

(Adele Gutman Nathan)

Died 24 Jul. 1986, New York, N.Y., age 86.

Children's Author-Pageant Organizer-Theater Producer/Manager- Film Actress. Wrote 14 children's books, mainly dealing with history; organized a Baltimore theater group; appeared in Warren Beatty's REDS (1981).

Nazarro, Ray

(Raymond Nazarro)

Born 25 Sept. 1902, Boston, Mass.; died 8 Sept. 1986, Los Angeles, Calif.

Film Director-Author. Started his career in films as a stand-in for Mary Pickford; co-wrote the story for JIMMY THE GENT; became a director in 1945 with OUTLAWS OF THE ROCKIES followed by many others (at least six each year), including SONG OF THE PRAIRIE, TEXAS PANHANDLE COWBOY BLUES, THE DESERT HORSEMAN, GALLOPING THUNDER, THROW A SADDLE ON A STAR, OVER THE SANTA FE TRAIL, LAST DAYS OF BOOT HILL, SIX-GUN LAW, WEST OF SONORA, BLAZING TRAIL, EL DORADO PASS, HOEDOWN, SMOKY MOUNTAIN MELODY, FLAME OF STAMBOUL, WAR CRY, CRIPPLE CREEK, GUN BELT, LONE GUN, TOP GUN, THE PHANTOM STAGECOACH, THE HIRED GUN, APACHE TERRITORY, EINER FRISST DEN ANDERN (DOG EAT DOG, codirected with Albert Zugsmith), ARRIVEDERCI COWBOY (his final picture in 1967); also directed TV shows such as "Fury," "The Durango Kid," "Buffalo Bill, Jr.".

Neagle, Anna

(Florence Marjorie Robertson)

Born 20 Oct. 1904, Forest Gate, England; died 3 June 1986, Surrey, England.

Film/Stage Actress-Film Producer. One of the leading lights of the British stage and screen, she wanted to go on stage from childhood, but her parents were against it and she became a dance teacher; her parents relented and she took chorus work in "Charlot's Revue," then appeared in "Rose Marie," "The Desert Song," "One Damn Thing After Another" "This Year of Grace," and "Wake Up and Dream," a role she repeated in 1929 in her New York City debut; entered films in 1930 with SHOULD A DOCTOR TELL?, which led to changing her name from Marjorie Robertson to Anna Neagle; she then appeared in THE CHINESE BUNGALOW; she returned to the stage for "Stand Up and Sing" in which she was spotted by Herbert Wilcox, who put her in GOODNIGHT VIENNA, the film that began a long professional and personal relationship (the two married in 1943); her other films are THE FLAG LIEUTENANT, THE LITTLE DAMOZEL, BITTER SWEET, THE RUNAWAY QUEEN, NELL GWYN, PEG OF OLD DRURY, BACKSTAGE, THE SHOW GOES ON, GIRLS IN THE STREET, VICTORIA THE GREAT, SIXTY GLORIOUS YEARS, NURSE EDITH CAVELL, IRENE, NO, NO, NANETTE, SUNNY, WINGS AND THE WOMAN, FOREVER AND A DAY, THE YELLOW CANARY, A YANK IN LONDON, PICCADILLY INCIDENT, THE COURTNEY AFFAIR, SPRING IN PARK LANE, ELIZABETH OF LADYMEAD, MAYTIME IN MAYFAIR, ODETTE, THE LADY WITH A LAMP, FOUR AGAINST FATE, LET'S MAKE UP, KING'S RHAPSODY, TEENAGE BAD GIRL, NO TIME FOR TEARS, THE MAN WHO WOULDN'T TALK, THE LADY IS A SQUARE; produced the films DANGEROUS YOUTH, WONDERFUL THINGS, THE HEART OF A MAN; on stage, appeared in "Peter Pan," "Emma," "The Glorious Days," "The More the Merrier," "Person Unknown,"; in order to help her husband, who went bankrupt in 1964, she sold some jewelry and real estate and returned to the stage in "Charlie Girl" (a musical that racked up over 2,050 performances as well as a subsequent Australian tour); was awarded the Order of the British Empire in 1969; lately, had been in a production of "Cinderella".

Nichols, Dandy

(Daisy Waters)

Died 6 Feb. 1986, London, England, age 78

Film/TV Actress. Best known for her role in Britain's long-running TV comedy "Till Death Us Do Part," appeared on the London stage in "Plunder," "Ten Times Table," and in New York, "Home"; her film efforts include HUE AND CRY, NICHOLAS NICKLEBY, THE FALLEN IDOL, THE WINSLOW BOY, HERE COME THE HUGGETTS, THE HISTORY OF MR. POLLY, THE GIRL IN THE PAINTING, SCOTT OF THE ANTARCTIC, DON'T EVER LEAVE ME, NOW BARABBAS WAS A ROBBER, TONY DRAWS A HORSE, DANCE HALL, THE CLOUDED YELLOW, WHITE CORRIDORS, THE HOLLY AND THE IVY, MR. LORD SAYS NO, MY SON, THE VAMPIRE, HUNDRED HOUR HUNT, THE PICKWICK PAPERS, TWILIGHT WOMEN, BOTH SIDES OF THE LAW, THE WEDDING OF LILLI MARLENE, MEET MR. LUCIFER, THE INTRUDER, TIME IS MY ENEMY, THE CROWDED SKY, MAD ABOUT MEN, WHERE THERE'S A WILL, THE DEEP BLUE SEA, A TIME TO KILL, TEARS FOR SIMON, NOT SO DUSTY, THE GENTLE TOUCH, BLONDE SINNER, TOWN ON TRIAL, THE VIKINGS, COSMIC MONSTERS, CARRY ON SERGEANT, A CRY FROM THE STREETS, DON'T TALK TO STRANGE MEN, CROOKS ANONYMOUS, LADIES WHO DO, THE LEATHER BOYS, ACT OF MURDER, HELP!, THE AMOROUS ADVENTURES OF MOLL FLANDERS, THE KNACK . . . AND HOW TO GET IT, THE EARLY BIRD, CARNABY, M.D., GEORGY GIRL, HOW I WON THE WAR, THE BIRTHDAY PARTY, CARRY ON DOCTOR, ALF 'N' FAMILY, THE BED SITTING ROOM, FIRST LOVE, THE ALF GARNETT SAGA, O LUCKY MAN!, CONFESSIONS OF A WINDOW CLEANER, THREE FOR ALL, THE PLAGUE DOGS (voice only), BRITANNIA HOSPITAL.

Nofal, Emil

Died 18 July 1986, Johannesburg, South Africa, age 60.

Film Producer-Director-Writer. Was one of the best-known South African director/writers, with such credits as KIMBERLY JIM, WILD SEASON, MY WAY, THE SUPER-JOCKS, DIE KANDIDAAT, KATRINA.

Nye, Ben, Sr.

Died 9 Feb. 1986, Santa Monica, Calif., age 79.

Film Makeup Artist. From Broken Bow, Nebraska, he started out as a commercial artist, took a position as a reproducer of sheet music for the music department at 20th Century-Fox, then entered the studio's makeup apprenticeship program; did the makeup for such films as JESSE JAMES, IN OLD CHICAGO, SUEZ, GONE WITH THE WIND, REBECCA, INTERMEZZO, FOR WHOM THE BELL TOLLS, FALLEN ANGEL, LEAVE HER TO HEAVEN, SENTIMENTAL JOURNEY, THE BRASHER DOUBLOON, CALL NORTHSIDE 777, FOREVER AMBER, THE GHOST AND MRS. MUIR, A LETTER TO THREE WIVES, THE SNAKE PIT, MOTHER IS A FRESHMAN, YOU'RE MY EVERYTHING, THE MUDLARK, ALL ABOUT EVE, DAVID AND BATHSHEBA, I'D CLIMB THE HIGHEST MOUNTAIN, WITH A SONG IN MY HEART, GENTLEMEN PREFER BLONDES, NIAGARA, THE PRESIDENT'S LADY, THE EGYPTIAN, OKLAHOMA, GOOD MORNING, MISS DOVE, THE MAN IN THE GREY FLANNEL SUIT, THE KING AND I, PEYTON PLACE, THE LONG HOT SUMMER, THE FLY, NORTH TO ALASKA, SEVEN THIEVES, WILD RIVER, VOYAGE TO THE BOTTOM OF THE SEA, STATE FAIR, CLEOPATRA (1963), THE SOUND OF MUSIC, THE FLIGHT OF THE PHOENIX, VON RYAN'S EXPRESS, OUR MAN FLINT, THE SAND PEBBLES, THE FLIM-FLAM MAN, HOMBRE, DOCTOR DOLITTLE, PLANET OF THE APES and others; worked on the TV series "Lost in Space," "Time Tunnel," "Voyage to the Bottom of the Sea".

Owens, Harry

Died 12 Dec. 1986, Eugene, Ore., age 84

Music Composer/Conductor-Film Actor. Mainly known for composing the Oscar-winning song "Sweet Leilani," immortalized by Bing Crosby in the film WAIKIKI WEDDING, 1937; appeared with his orchestra in the film COCOANUT GROVE and supplied songs for the film as well; other films include IT'S A DATE, SONG OF THE ISLANDS, LAKE PLACID SERENADE.

Page, Bradley

Died early 1986, age in the 80s.

Film Actor. With his small mustache and smooth, polished looks, generally played shifty crooks or mob bosses in films of the 1930s and 1940s such as ATTORNEY FOR THE DEFENSE, FINAL EDITION, LOVE AFFAIR, NIGHT AFTER NIGHT, THE CHIEF, FROM HELL TO HEAVEN, GOLDIE GETS ALONG, HOLD THE PRESS, LOVE IS LIKE THAT, THE SUNDOWN RIDER, THIS DAY AND AGE, AGAINST THE LAW, CRIME OF HELEN STANLEY, THE FIGHTING RANGER, GENTLEMEN ARE BORN, GOOD DAME, HE WAS HER MAN, I HATE WOMEN, HELL BENT FOR LOVE, MILLION DOLLAR RANSOM, NAME THE WOMAN, ONCE TO EVERY BACHELOR, SEARCH FOR BEAUTY, SHADOWS OF SING SING, SIX OF A KIND, TAKE THE STAND, CAPPY RICKS RETURNS, CHAMPAGNE FOR BREAKFAST, CHINATOWN SQUAD, FORCED LANDING, KING SOLOMON OF BROADWAY, MR. DYNAMITE, THE NUT FARM, ONE HOUR LATE, PUBLIC MENACE, RED HOT TIRES, SHADOW OF A DOUBT, UNWELCOME STRANGER, CHEERS OF THE CROWD, THE PRINCESS COMES ACROSS, THREE OF A KIND, TWO IN A CROWD, WEDDING PRESENT, WOMAN TRAP, CRASHING HOLLYWOOD, DON'T TELL THE WIFE, FIFTY ROADS TO TOWN, HER HUSBAND LIES, HIDEAWAY, MUSIC FOR MADAME, THE OUTCASTS OF POKER FLAT, SUPER SLEUTH, THERE GOES MY GIRL, THE TOAST OF NEW YORK, TROUBLE IN MOROCCO, YOU CAN'T BEAT LOVE, AFFAIRS OF ANNABEL, ANNABEL TAKES A TOUR, CRIME RING, FUGITIVES FOR A NIGHT, GO CHASE YOURSELF, THE LAW WEST OF TOMBSTONE, NIGHT SPOT, FIXER DUGAN, TWELVE CROWDED HOURS, CAFE HOSTESS, ENEMY AGENT, GIRL FROM HAVANA, BADLANDS OF DAKOTA, ROARING FRONTIERS, BEYOND THE SACRAMENTO, FOOTLIGHT FEVER, SCATTERGOOD BAINES, SCATTERGOOD MEETS BROADWAY, THE BIG STORE, FRECKLES COMES HOME, ISLE OF MISSING MEN, PRIDE OF THE ARMY, SONS OF THE PIONEERS, TOP SERGEANT, THE TRAITOR WITHIN, FIND THE BLACKMAILER, SHERLOCK HOLMES IN WASHINGTON, WHAT'S BUZZIN COUSIN?, THE CARTER CASE.

Painchaud, Brian

(Brian Roger Painchaud)

Film Actor. At the age of 10, headed the cast of the Canadian film, WHO HAS SEEN THE WIND (1980).

Palmer, Lilli

(Lillie Marie Peiser)

Born 24 May 1914, Posen, Germany (now Poland); died 27 Jan. 1986, Los Angeles, Calif.

Stage/Film Actress-Novelist-Painter. A multi-talented person who at age 10 was doing amateur acting in Berlin; while in high school took acting lessons from Ilka Gruning, who was later to be a character actress in Hollywood; in 1932 began working in stage productions, then went to Paris, where she worked at the Moulin Rouge; traveled to England and appeared in such films as CRIME UNLIMITED, FIRST OFFENCE, WOLF'S CLOTHING, THE SECRET AGENT, WHERE THERE'S A WILL (1937), SILENT BARRIERS, COMMAND PERFORMANCE, THE MAN WITH A HUNDRED FACES (1938); debuted on the British stage in "Road to Gandahar" then appeared in "The Tree of Eden," "Little Ladyship," "You, of All People," "Ladies in Action," "No Time for Comedy" (playing with Rex Harrison, whom she would marry in 1943); concurrent with her plays, continued in films with BLIND FOLLY, SUICIDE LEGION, CHAMBER OF HORRORS, A GIRL MUST LIVE, THE GENTLE SEX, THUNDER ROCK, NOTORIOUS, BEWARE OF PITY, CLOAK AND DAGGER, BODY AND SOUL, MY GIRL TISA, NO MINOR VICES, HER MAN GILBEY, THE WICKED CITY; made her New York stage debut in 1949 in "My Name is Aquilon," then appeared in "Caesar and Cleopatra," "Bell, Book and Candle,"; returned to films for THE LONG DARK HALL, PICTURA, ADVENTURES IN ART (as narrator), THE FOUR POSTER (1952), MAIN STREET TO BROADWAY, OH!, MY PAPA, THE DEVIL IN SILK, IS ANNA ANDERSON ANASTASIA?, BETWEEN TIME AND ETERNITY, THE NIGHT OF THE STORM, THE GLASS TOWER, MODIGLIANI OF MONTPARNASSE; at this point, having divorced Rex Harrison, married Carlos Thompson, then made EINE FRAU DIE WEISS, WAS SIE WILL, MAEDCHEN IN UNIFORM, MRS. WARREN'S PROFESSION, LEVIATHAN, LIFE TOGETHER, BUT NOT FOR ME, CONSPIRACY OF HEARTS, THE PLEASURE OF HIS COMPANY, THE COUNTERFEIT TRAITOR, MIDNIGHT MEETING, END OF MRS. CHENEY, MIRACLE OF THE WHITE STALLIONS, EIN FRAUENARZT KLAGT AN, DIE LETZEN ZWEI VON RIO BRAVO, TORPEDO BAY, DARK JOURNEY, ADORABLE JULIA, SEX CAN BE DIFFICULT, FINDEN SIE, DASS CONSTANZE SICH RICHTIG VERHALT?, OF WAYWARD LOVE, AND SO TO BED, MONSIEUR, LE TONNERRE DE DIEU, THE AMOROUS ADVENTURES OF MOLL FLANDERS, OPERATION CROSSBOW, DER KONGRESS AMUSIERT SICH, LE VOYAGE DU PERE, AN AFFAIR OF STATE, ZWEI GIRLS VOM ROTEN STERN, PAARUNGEN, OEDIPUS THE KING, JACK OF DIAMONDS, THE HIGH COMMISSIONER, THE DANCE OF DEATH, SEBASTIAN, ONLY THE COOL, DE SADE, HARD CONTRACT, THE HOUSE THAT SCREAMED, NIGHT HAIR CHILD, MURDERS IN THE RUE MORGUE, LOTTE IN WEIMAR, THE BOYS FROM BRAZIL, SOCIETY LIMITED, THE HOLCROFT COVENANT; she appeared in the TV film, "Hauser's Memory"; first writing attempt was her autobiography, *Change Lobsters and Dance*, followed by some well-received novels, *Red Raven* (semi-autobiographical), *A Time to Embrace*, and *Night Music*.

Palmer, Norman

Born 1921, Plymouth, England; died 25 Nov. 1986, Duarte, Calif.

Film/TV Actor. Served in the Royal Navy during the WW II years and ran a dental technician's laboratory (worked in local theater while doing so), then began acting ins such films as ST. IVES, NEW YORK, NEW YORK, THE BETSY, MOMMIE DEAREST; TV appearances include parts in "Hart to Hart," "The Love Boat," "Lou Grant," "Hotel," "Remington Steele."

Paris, Jerry

Born 25 July 1925, San Francisco, Calif.; died 31 Mar. 1986, Los Angeles, Calif.

Film/Stage/TV Actor-Director-Writer-Producer. Educated at New York University and UCLA before service in the Navy; upon discharge, studied at Hollywood's Actors Lab and New York's Actors

Studio then appeared in such films as MY FOOLISH HEART, SWORD IN THE DESERT, CYRANO DE BERGERAC, FLYING MISSILE, OUTRAGE, BRIGHT VICTORY, CALL ME MISTER, SUBMARINE COMMAND, BONZO GOES TO COLLEGE, MONKEY BUSINESS, FLIGHT TO TANGIER, THE GLASS WALL, SABRE JET, THE WILD ONE, THE CAINE MUTINY, DRIVE A CROOKED ROAD, PRISONER OF WAR, GOOD MORNING, MISS DOVE, MARTY, THE NAKED STREET, UNCHAINED, THE VIEW FROM POMPEY'S HEAD, D-DAY, THE SIXTH OF JUNE, I'VE

LIVED BEFORE, NEVER SAY GOODBYE, MAN ON THE PROWL, ZERO HOUR, THE FEMALE ANIMAL, THE LADY TAKES A FLYER, THE NAKED AND THE DEAD, SING, BOY, SING, CAREER, NO NAME ON THE BULLET, THE GREAT IMPOSTOR; TV credits included "The Whiting Girls," "Michael Shayne," "Steve Canyon," and "The Untouchables" before he took his best-known part as the neighbor-dentist on "The Dick Van Dyke Show"; he began directing on that show and went on to be the only director on "Happy Days"; other TV directing assignments included "The Odd Couple," "That Girl," "The Partridge Family," "Love, American Style" and the TV films "But I Don't Want to Get Married" (also acted), "The Feminist and the Fuzz," "Two On a Bench," "What's A Nice Girl Like You . . . ?," "Call Her Mom," "Evil Roy Slade" (also acted), "The Couple Takes a Wife," "Every Man Needs One" (also acted), "Only With Married Men," "How to Break Up a Happy Divorce," "Make Me an Offer"; co-wrote the screen story on THE CARETAKERS; acted in and directed DON'T RAISE THE BRIDGE, LOWER THE RIVER, NEVER A DULL MOMENT, LEO AND LOREE; directed HOW SWEET IT IS, VIVA MAX, THE GRASSHOPPER, STAR SPANGLED GIRL, POLICE ACADEMY 2: THEIR FIRST ASSIGNMENT, POLICE ACADEMY 3: BACK IN TRAINING.

Patil, Smita

Died 13 Dec. 1986, Bombay, India, age 32.

Film Actress. Had a job as a TV newsreader before beginning a film career that included appearances in JAIT RE JAIT, NISHANT, MANTHAN, BHUMIKA, CHAKRA, UMBARTHA, SADGATI, AKALER SANDHANEY, CHIDAMBARAM and many others; four more awaited release at her death.

Paynter, Corona

Died 29 July 1986, Los Angeles, Calif., age 88.

Stage/Film Actress-Performer. A personal discovery of Florenz Ziegfeld, appeared in a couple of his "Follies", did a London revue, then came back to appear in "The Greenwich Village Follies" and

"Tantrum" (1924); worked in the silent film EVERY MOTHER'S SON.

Phoenix, Pat

Died 17 Sept. 1986, Manchester, England, age 62.

TV/Film Actress. Mainly known for her role on British TV's "Coronation Street," appeared in the film THE L-SHAPED ROOM.

Polacco, Cesare

Died 2 Mar. 1986, Rome, Italy, age 85.

Stage/TV/Film Actor. Appeared in many stage plays and TV movies ("Anna Karenina," "The Betrothed") as well as commercials, appeared in the film THE WANDERING JEW (1948).

Poole, Roy

Died 1 July 1986, Mount Kisco, N.Y., age 62.

Stage/Film/TV Actor. Born in San Bernardino, Calif., attended Stanford University, and served in the Army during WW II, appeared in numerous stage productions, including "Under Milk Wood," "The Cretan Woman," "The Clandestine Marriage," "The Firstborn," "Macbeth," "I Knock at the Door," "The Quare Fellow," "Flowering Cherry," "The Balcony," "St. Joan," "Quartermaine's Terms" (won the off-Broadway Obie award); films include EXPERIMENT IN TERROR, UP THE DOWN STAIRCASE, GAILY, GAILY, 1776, SOMETIMES A GREAT NOTION, MANDINGO, NETWORK, THE BETSY, BRUBAKER, THE END OF AUGUST, A STRANGER IS WATCHING; was featured in the following TV films: "The Whole World is Watching," "The Face of Fear," "The Autobiography of Miss Jane Pittman," "A Cry in the Wilderness," "The Ordeal of Patty Hearst," "Act of Violence," "Ohms," "Hellinger's Law," "The Winds of War."

Preminger, Otto

(Otto Ludwig Preminger)

Born 5 Dec. 1905 (some sources say 1906), Vienna, Austria; died 23 April, 1986, New York, N.Y.

Film/Stage Actor-Director-Producer. Born to a prominent family (his father was a successful lawyer who was once the equivalent of the attorney-general of the Hapsburg empire), he ignored his father's wish that he become a lawyer and opted for the stage, first as an actor, then as a director/manager when still only 19; after directing the film DIE GROSSE LIEBE (1931) he was invited to the U.S. by Joseph M. Schenck to direct in Hollywood; while in transit, was asked by Gilbert Miller to stop in New York to direct "Libel" (a piece that he had already done six months before in Austria); also gave Miller help in his direction of "Victoria Regina" and spent much time attending movie theaters in an effort to improve his English; when he reached Hollywood, had a learning period before directing two minor films, UNDER YOUR SPELL and DANGER—LOVE AT WORK; as he could not get along with Darryl F. Zanuck, Fox studio head, he went back to Broadway to work on such

plays as "Outward Bound," "Margin for Error" (also acted, a double chore that he would repeat in the 1943 film version), "My Dear Children" "Beverly Hills," "Cue for Passion," "The More the Merrier"; returned to the west coast in 1942 to act in two films (THE PIED PIPER and THEY GOT ME COVERED) before resuming film director status on such films as MARGIN FOR ERROR, IN THE MEANTIME, DARLING, LAURA, WHERE DO WE GO FROM HERE? (acted only), ROYAL SCANDAL, FALLEN ANGEL, CENTENNIAL SUMMER, FOREVER AMBER, DAISY KENYON, THE LADY IN ERMINE, THE FAN, WHIRLPOOL, WHERE THE SIDEWALK ENDS, THE THIRTEENTH LETTER; took time out for more Broadway work on "Four Twelves are 48" and "The Moon is Blue" (would film this in 1953); then back to filming on ANGEL FACE, STALAG 17 (acted only), THE MOON IS BLUE, RIVER OF NO RETURN, CARMEN JONES, THE MAN WITH THE GOLDEN ARM, THE COURT MARTIAL OF BILLY MITCHELL, SAINT JOAN, BONJOUR TRISTESSE, PORGY AND BESS, ANATOMY OF A MURDER, EXODUS, ADVISE AND CONSENT, THE CARDINAL, IN HARM'S WAY, BUNNY LAKE IS MISSING, HURRY SUNDOWN, SKIDOO, TELL ME THAT YOU LOVE ME, JUNIE MOON, SUCH GOOD FRIENDS, ROSEBUD, THE HUMAN FACTOR.

Presnell, Robert, Jr.

Died 14 June 1986, Sherman Oaks, Calif., age 71.

Radio/TV/Film Writer-Radio Director. A native of Illinois and the son of producer/screenwriter Robert Presnell, Sr., after attending college in the U.S. and Europe, worked as a reporter in Milwaukee before going to New York and serving as producer, writer, and director on radio shows while also writing short stories for magazines; moved to Hollywood in the mid-1940s, continuing with radio work for Orson Welles and "I Love a Mystery" before writing screenplays for such films as MAN IN THE ATTIC, A LIFE IN THE BALANCE, THE RAWHIDE YEARS, SCREAMING EAGLES, LEGEND OF THE LOST, CONSPIRACY OF HEARTS, LET NO MAN WRITE MY EPITAPH, 13 WEST ST, THE THIRD DAY; wrote TV episodes for "The Twilight Zone," "Dr. Kildare," "High Chaparral," "Wild Wild West," "McCloud," "Banacek" as well as TV movies like "Smash-Up on Interstate 5," "All My Darling Daughters" (cowriter of original story only), "Ritual of Evil," "The Secret Night Caller," "Damien: The Leper Priest"; published a novel, Edgell's Island and belonged to the Writers Guild of America/West, serving on the board of directors and the arbitration board.

Priestley, Robert

Died 27 Nov. 1986, San Diego, Calif., age 86.

Film Set Designer. Worked for most of the major studios on such films as ONCE UPON A TIME, SECRET COMMAND, COUNTER-ATTACK, THE FIGHTING GUARDSMAN, SERGEANT MIKE, GILDA, MYSTERIOUS INTRUDER, THE THRILL OF BRAZIL, THE WALLS CAME TUMBLING DOWN, INTRIGUE, THE TENDER YEARS, THE FABULOUS DORSEYS, ON OUR MERRY WAY, LULU BELLE, MAN-EATER FROM KUMAON, PITFALL, THE GIRL FROM MANHATTAN, UNKNOWN ISLAND, OUTPOST IN MOROCCO, MRS. MIKE, WITHOUT HONOR, COVER-UP, APACHE CHIEF, CRAZY OVER HORSES, SIROCCO, AFRICAN TREASURE, NO HOLDS BARRED, JALOPY, MAN IN THE DARK, PARIS PLAYBOYS, THE EDDY DUCHIN STORY, PICNIC (earned an Oscar), SAYONARA (earned an Oscar), CAT ON A HOT TIN ROOF, THE HIGH COST OF LOVING, SOME CAME RUNNING, THE COMANCHEROS, ADVENTURES OF A YOUNG MAN, WALK, DON'T RUN, IN THE HEAT OF THE NIGHT.

Proach, Henry

Died 22 June 1986, Los Angeles, Calif., age 66.

Stage/Film/TV Actor. Was one of the mainstays of the Living Theater headed by Julian Beck and

Judith Malina and appeared in many of their productions; some of his theater efforts include "Many Loves," "The Cave at Machpeleh," "The Connection," "The Marrying Maiden," "In the Jungle of Cities," "The Apple," "Man Is Man," "The Brig," "The Wicked Cooks," "The Cuban Thing," "Sheep on the Runway"; some of his films include THE INCIDENT, DIRTY LITTLE BILLY, and WISDOM (a film that had not been released at his death); was on TV in "Pretty Boy Floyd," "The Fourth Wise Man," "The Bet," the TV movie "Gideon's Trumpet."

Quinn, Frank P.

Died 23 May 1986, Miami, Florida, age 73.

Newspaper Reporter-Public Relations Executive-Film Actor. From Bayonne, N.J., he started at the New York Daily Mirror, serving as amusement editor and then theater and film critic until the paper closed in 1963; while functioning as a reporter, appeared in the film TEACHER'S PET; later handled public relations for various organizations.

Ramirez, Carlos

(Carlos Julio Ramirez)

Died 11 Dec. 1986, Miami, Fla., age 73.

Film/Stage Singer-Actor. Generally known for his specialty numbers in musicals of the 1940s and 1950s; born in Tocaim, Colombia, and started singing at age 8 on passenger trains, later appearing in opera at New York's Carnegie Hall and in Buenos Aires; debuted on Broadway in 1941 in the revue "Crazy with the Heat"; film credits include BATHING BEAUTY, TWO GIRLS AND A SAILOR, ANCHORS AWEIGH, WHERE DO WE GO FROM HERE?, EASY TO WED, LATIN LOVERS (dubbed Ricardo Montalban's singing voice), and NIGHT AND DAY.

Reddick, Cecil

Died 10 Dec. 1986, Los Angeles, Calif., age 56.

Stage/Film/TV Actor. Hailing from New York, moved to Los Angeles in 1966 to become the producer-director of the Evergreen Stage Company; appeared in the films UNHOLY ROLLERS and VAN NUYS BLVD.

Reed, Dean

Died 17 June 1986, East Germany, age 47.

Peace Activist-Singer-Actor. Born in Denver, became a recording artist before going to South America, then Europe, where he appeared in approximately 18 films, including THE BOUNTY HUNTERS, ADIOS SABATA, EL CANTOR (also directed this East German effort), and SING, MEIN COWBOY, SING (also wrote and directed); was the subject of a 1985 documentary AMERICAN REBEL; very popular in the Soviet Union.

Reed, Donna

(Donna Belle Mullenger)

Born 27 Jan. 1921, Denison, Iowa; died 14 Jan. 1986, Beverly Hills, Calif.

Film/TV Actress. After winning a beauty contest in Iowa, went to Los Angeles to study at City College where she was named a campus queen, gaining the notice of film talent scouts; signed with MGM and, billed as Donna Adams, made two films, BABES ON BROADWAY and THE GET-AWAY; taking the name Reed, she appeared in THE BUGLE SOUNDS, SHADOW OF THE THIN MAN, MOKEY, CALLING DR. GILLESPIE, APACHE TRAIL, THE COURTSHIP OF ANDY HARDY, EYES IN THE NIGHT, THOUSANDS CHEER, THE HUMAN COMEDY, DR. GILLESPIE'S CRIMINAL CASE, THE MAN FROM DOWN UNDER, GENTLE ANNIE, SEE HERE, PRIVATE HARGROVE, MRS. PARKINGTON, THE PICTURE OF DORIAN GRAY, THEY WERE EXPENDABLE, FAITHFUL IN MY FASHION, IT'S A WONDERFUL LIFE, GREEN DOLPHIN STREET, BEYOND GLORY, CHICAGO DEADLINE, SCANDAL SHEET, SATURDAY'S HERO, HANGMAN'S KNOT, RAIDERS OF THE SEVEN SEAS, TROUBLE ALONG THE WAY, THE CADDY, FROM HERE TO ETERNITY (awarded Best Supporting Actress Oscar), GUN FURY, THREE HOURS TO KILL, THE LAST TIME I SAW PARIS, THEY RODE WEST, THE FAR HORIZONS, RANSOM!, THE BENNY GOODMAN STORY, BACKLASH, BEYOND MOMBASA, THE WHOLE TRUTH, PEPE; appeared on TV in "The Donna Reed Show" (coproduced with her second husband, Tony Owen) and the TV movies "The Best Place to Be," "Deadly Lessons"; temporarily replaced Barbara Bel Geddes on "Dallas," then filed suit against the show's producers when she was released upon the return of Bel Geddes.

Rhodes, Leah

Died 17 Oct. 1986, Burbank, Calif., age 84.

Film Costume Designer. A native of Port Arthur, Tex., went west to work under Orry-Kelly at Warner Bros.; headed the costume department when Orry-Kelly went into the Army during WW II; worked from the 1940s through the 1960s on such films as MURDER ON THE WATERFRONT, OLD ACQUAINTANCE, NORTHERN PURSUIT, MISSION TO MOSCOW, THE CONSPIRATORS, THE DESERT SONG, EXPERIMENT PERILOUS, PASSAGE TO MARSEILLES, GOD IS MY CO-PILOT, HOTEL BERLIN, CONFIDENTIAL AGENT, SARATOGA TRUNK, THE BIG SLEEP, CLOAK AND DAGGER, MY REPUTATION, THE VOICE OF THE TURTLE, KEY LARGO, MY GIRL TISA, ONE SUNDAY AFTERNOON, JUNE BRIDE, ADVENTURES OF DON JUAN (shared an Oscar with fellow designers Travilla and Marjorie Best), NIGHT UNTO NIGHT, WHITE HEAT, TASK FORCE, CHAIN LIGHTNING, TEA FOR TWO, I'LL SEE YOU IN MY DREAMS, STRANGERS ON A TRAIN, ROOM FOR ONE MORE, THE WINNING TEAM, KINGS GO FORTH, THE FOX, FIVE CARD STUD.

Ritz, Harry

(Herschel Joachim)

Born 22 May 1906, Newark, N.J.; died 29 Mar. 1986, San Diego, Calif.

Stage/Film Comedian-Actor. The last of the madcap Ritz Brothers to die (Al in 1965, Jimmy in 1985), entered vaudeville out of high school; teamed with his brothers in 1925 in the musical "Florida Girl" and worked in various versions of "Earl Carroll's Vanities," as well as "Continental Varieties"; the brothers entered films in 1934 with a short, "Hotel Anchovy"; in 1936 and 1937 performed in their first features, SING, BABY, SING, ONE IN A MILLION, ON THE AVENUE, YOU CAN'T HAVE EVERYTHING, and LIFE BEGINS IN COLLEGE, which were followed by THE GOLDWYN FOLLIES, KENTUCKY MOONLIGHT, STRAIGHT, PLACE AND SHOW, PACK UP YOUR TROUBLES, THE GORILLA, THE THREE MUSKETEERS, ARGENTINE NIGHTS, BEHIND THE EIGHT BALL, HI'YA, CHUM, NEVER A DULL MOMENT; in their later years, they worked primarily in clubs and on TV, though Harry and Jimmy had minor roles in BLAZING STEWARDESSES, WON TON TON,

THE DOG WHO SAVED HOLLYWOOD; Harry alone appeared in SILENT MOVIE.

Roberts, Morgan

Died 17 June 1986, age unknown.

Film Actor. Appeared in SOMETHING OF VALUE, LET'S DO IT AGAIN, WHICH WAY IS UP?, THE HUNTER, BUSTIN' LOOSE.

Robins, Barry

Died 1 April 1986, Los Angeles, Calif., age 41.

Stage/TV/Film Actor. Hailing from Brooklyn, studied acting and singing before landing the part of the crown prince in a touring production of "The King and I" in 1964; also toured in "Annie Get Your Gun," "Fanny," "Camelot," "South Pacific," "The Boys from Syracuse," "Milk and Honey," "Li'l Abner"; appeared in the film BLESS THE BEASTS AND CHILDREN; TV appearances included "Twelve O'Clock High," "Rat Patrol," "Columbo."

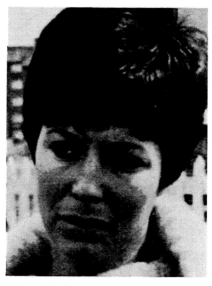

Robins, Toby

Died 21 Mar. 1986, London, England, age 55.

Stage/Film Actress. A Toronto, Canada native, worked in Canadian, American, and British theater in such productions as "Measure for Measure," "The Taming of the Shrew," "Cyrano de Bergerac," "Before You Go," "The Aspern Papers"; film appearances included GAME FOR THREE LOSERS, THE NAKED RUNNER, FRIENDS, PAUL AND MICHELLE, FOR YOUR EYES ONLY, SCANDALOUS.

Robinson, Bartlett

(Bart Robinson)

Died 26 Mar. 1986, Fallbrook, Calif., age 73.

Stage/Radio/Film/TV Actor. Born in New York City, went to Los Angeles for radio work, then alternated radio, stage, and film work; stage efforts consisted of "Sweet River," "Naughty-Naught 'OO," "The Merchant of Yonkers" and "Hello Dolly," "Point of No Return," "The Prescott Proposals"; radio credits include "Backstage Wife," "Ellen Randolph," "Perry Mason," "Portia Faces Life," "Pretty Kitty Kelly," "The Romance of Helen Trent"; the big screen used his talents in TOWARD THE UNKNOWN, BATTLE HYMN, THE SPIRIT OF ST. LOUIS, GIRL IN THE WOODS, I WANT TO LIVE, NO TIME FOR SERGEANTS, STRANGER IN MY ARMS, WARLOCK, ALL HANDS ON DECK, A DISTANT TRUMPET, READY FOR THE PEOPLE, WHERE LOVE HAS GONE, THE BIRDS AND THE BEES, JOY IN THE MORNING, THE FORTUNE COOKIE, THE BAMBOO SAUCER, LIVE A LITTLE, LOVE A LITTLE, SLEEPER; TV appearances included "Mona McCluskey," "Wendy and Me," and the TV movies "Trial Run" and "The New Adventures of Heidi".

Robinson, Dar

(Dar Allen Robinson)

Died 21 Nov. 1986, Page, Ariz., age 39.

Film Stuntman. A man whose ability made him one of the industry's highest paid stuntmen, he worked on such films as PAPILLON, DOC SAVAGE, THE MAN OF BRONZE, ROLLERBALL, ST. IVES, STUNTS, NIGHTHAWKS, SHARKY'S MACHINE, STICK, TURK 182!, LETHAL WEAPON, CYCLONE, HIGH POINT; died while performing a stunt for MILLION DOLLAR INDUSTRY; held numerous world records for stunts; known for working out his stunts beforehand with mathematical calculations and careful thought.

Roddy, James D.

Died 25 Aug. 1986, Los Angeles, Calif., age 38.

Stage/Film Dancer-Choreographer. Originally from Omaha, Neb., studied at the Juilliard School in New York City before his stage stints in "See-Saw," "Liza at the Winter Garden," and touring in "A Chorus Line"; did some stage directing and choreography in southern California; appeared in HISTORY OF THE WORLD, PART I, PENNIES FROM HEAVEN, THE TOY, THE BEST LITTLE WHOREHOUSE IN TEXAS.

Roediger, Rolf

Died 24 Dec. 1986, Los Angeles, Calif., age 57.

TV/Film Puppeteer. After a career as a ballet dancer in Germany, came to Los Angeles to work for a puppet manufacturer, developing puppets for world's fairs and amusement parks; designed the puppets for the "H.R. Pufnstuf" TV show that led to the PUFNSTUF film.

Romm, Harry A.

Born 1896, Philadelphia, Pa.; died 27 Aug. 1986, Port Washington, N.Y.

Stage/Vaudeville Performer-Talent Agent-Radio/Film Producer. Started in vaudeville and then became a talent agent, discovering or developing performers such as Ted Healy, Frank Sinatra, Dean Martin, Jerry Lewis, Dinah Shore, the Boswell Sisters, Glenn Miller, Benny Goodman, Artie Shaw, Woody Herman, Harry James, as well as sports personalities such as Babe Ruth, Lou Gehrig, Lefty Gomez; brought together "The Three Stooges" and managed them for over 20 years (including the producing chore on their 1959 feature, HAVE ROCKET, WILL TRAVEL); also produced SWING PARADE OF 1946, LADIES OF THE CHORUS, SENIOR PROM, HEY BOY! HEY GIRL!, HEY, LET'S TWIST, TWO TICKETS TO PARIS.

Rose, Sherman A.

Died 22 Sept. 1986, Los Angeles, Calif., age 71.

Film Editor-Director. A Massachusetts native, came to Los Angeles in 1935, getting work as an editor on the William Boyd "Hopalong Cassidy" series (produced by his uncle, Harry Sherman); also edited THE MYSTERIOUS RIDER, HERITAGE OF THE DESERT, CHEROKEE STRIP, THE LIGHT OF WESTERN STARS, THE LLANO KID, PARSON OF PANAMINT, SILVER QUEEN, LOST CANYON, RAMROD, THE SENATOR WAS INDISCREET, TWO DOLLAR BETTOR, FOR MEN ONLY, THE RETURN OF DRACULA, SON OF A GUNFIGHTER; handled both the directorial and editing chores on three 1950s films, TARGET EARTH, MAGNIFICENT ROUGHNECKS, TANK BATTALION; worked briefly in TV before retiring to start a black-and-white still photography studio.

Rubin, Benny

Born 1899, Boston, Mass.; died 15 July 1986, Los Angeles, Calif.

Stage/Film/TV Actor-Comedian-Screenwriter. Began tap dancing as a youngster and by age 14 was working in local revues and vaudeville; specialized in ethnic comedy and made his film debut in 1929 with NAUGHTY BABY, then went on to make MARIANNE, IT'S A GREAT LIFE, HOT CURVES, CHILDREN OF PLEASURE, LEATHERNECKING, LORD BYRON OF BROADWAY, LOVE IN THE ROUGH, MONTANA MOON, SUNNY SKIES, THEY LEARNED ABOUT WOMEN, GEORGE WHITE'S 1935 SCANDALS, GO INTO YOUR DANCE, ADVENTURES OF JANE ARDEN, FIGHTING MAD, THE HEADLEYS AT HOME, THE FIGHTING 69TH, LET'S MAKE MUSIC, LUCKY PARTNERS, NO NO NANETTE, DOUBLE TROUBLE, HERE COMES MR. JORDAN, OBLIGING YOUNG LADY, SUNNY, ZIS BOOM BAH, THE BASHFUL BACHELOR, BROADWAY, COLLEGE SWEETHEARTS, MR. WISE GUY, HOLLOW TRIUMPH, THE NOOSE HANGS HIGH, THE SELLOUT, JUST THIS ONCE, EASY TO LOVE, THE GLASS WEB, TANGIER INCIDENT, TORCH SONG, ABOUT MRS. LESLIE, EL ALAMEIN, THE LAW VS. BILLY THE KID, MASTERSON OF KANSAS, SUSAN SLEPT HERE, YANKEE PASHA, THE TENDER TRAP, MEET ME IN LAS VEGAS, EIGHTEEN AND ANXIOUS, UP IN SMOKE, WILL SUCCESS SPOIL ROCK HUNTER?, IN THE MONEY, PARTY GIRL, A

HOLE IN THE HEAD, PLEASE DON'T EAT THE DAISIES, THE ERRAND BOY, POCKETFUL OF MIRACLES, THE DISORDERLY ORDERLY, A HOUSE IS NOT A HOME, THAT FUNNY FEELING, GHOST IN THE INVISIBLE BIKINI, THOROUGHLY MODERN MILLIE, THE SHAKIEST GUN IN THE WEST, ANGEL IN MY POCKET, WHICH WAY TO THE FRONT?, HOW TO FRAME A FIGG, THE SHAGGY D.A., WON TON TON, THE DOG WHO SAVED HOLLYWOOD; also helped write the scripts for BRIGHT LIGHTS, THE GIRL

FRIEND, THE TRAVELING SALESLADY, HIGH FLIERS, ON AGAIN-OFF AGAIN; was a regular guest on both Jack Benny's radio and TV shows and appeared in "I Dream of Jeanie," "Gunsmoke," "What's Happening?," and a TV film, "The Return of the World's Great Detective"; his last appearance was in "Glitter," a TV mini-series.

Rubinoff, David

Born 13 Sept. 1896, Grodno, Russia; died 6 Oct. 1986, Columbus, Ohio.

Concert Violinist-Film Actor. Was playing both the balalaika and the violin at the age of 5 and graduated from Warsaw's Royal Conservatory of Music at the age of 14; Victor Herbert took an interest in him and brought him to the U.S. where he attended school; played the violin on the Eddie Cantor Chase and Sanborn radio show; appeared in the films THANKS A MILLION and YOU CAN'T HAVE EVERYTHING.

Ryan, Thomas C.

Died 25 Nov. 1986, New York, N.Y., age 54.

Screenwriter-Producer. Started out as an assistant to Otto Preminger on such films as SAINT JOAN, EXODUS, and ANATOMY OF A MURDER and cowrote the script for Preminger's HURRY SUNDOWN; wrote the screenplay for THE PAD AND HOW TO USE IT and wrote and coproduced THE HEART IS A LONELY HUNTER.

Sanchez, Marcelino

Born 5 Dec. 1957, Cayey, Puerto Rico; died 21 Nov. 1986, Los Angeles, Calif.

Stage/TV/Film Actor. Acted in both New York and Los Angeles, as well as a production of "Hair" that toured in Spain; appeared in the films THE WARRIORS and 48 HOURS (with a name change to James Marcelino); TV appearances include "Hill Street Blues," "CHIPS," "The Color Game," as well as a TV film, "Death Penalty."

Scheffer, Dick

Died 24 Nov. 1986, Amsterdam, Netherlands, age 57.

Film/TV/Stage/Radio Actor. Some of the Dutch actor's films include THE LIFT and FLODDER, in a career that started in 1950.

Schock, Rudolf

Born 4 Sept. 1915; died 14 Nov. 1986, Duren, West Germany.

Opera Singer-Film Actor. Used his opera singing talent in various media such as film (HOUSE OF THE THREE GIRLS, YOU ARE THE WORLD FOR ME, THE HAPPY WANDERER, THE WORLD IS BEAUTIFUL), opera (appeared at Salzburg, Bayreuth, London's Covent Garden, and Vienna in productions of "Ariadne," "The Magic Flute," "Madame Butterfly," and had a successful tour of Australia), operetta, radio, and television; his films and recordings were very popular in Germany and Austria.

Schuster, Harold

Born 1 Aug. 1902, Cherokee, Iowa; died 19 July 1986, Westlake Village, Calif.

Film Editor-Film/TV Director. Held various jobs in the film industry while attending the University of Southern California; appeared as an extra in silent feature films and shorts, became a second cameraman and then an editor, working on such films as FOUR DEVILS, FROZEN JUSTICE, RENEGADES, SUCH MEN ARE DANGEROUS, WOMEN ARE EVERYWHERE, AMBASSADOR BILL, DON'T BET ON WOMEN, THE MAN WHO CAME BACK, CHANDU THE MAGICIAN, DEVIL'S LOTTERY, PASSPORT TO HELL, BERKELEY SQUARE, ZOO IN BUDAPEST, ALL MEN ARE ENEMIES, HELLDORADO; began directing in 1937 with WINGS OF THE MORNING (the first color film made in England), then helmed such films as DINNER AT THE RITZ, EXPOSED, SWING THAT CHEER, DIAMOND FRONTIER, ONE HOUR TO LIVE, FRAMED, MA, HE'S MAKING EYES AT ME, SOUTH TO KARANGA, ZANZIBAR, PIRATES OF THE SEVEN SEAS, SMALL TOWN DEB, A

VERY YOUNG LADY, GIRL TROUBLE, ON THE SUNNY SIDE, THE POSTMAN DIDN'T RING, BOMBER'S MOON (co-directed with Edward Ludwig, using the name of Charles Fuhr), MY FRIEND FLICKA (his best known film), MARINE RAIDERS, BREAKFAST IN HOLLYWOOD, THE TENDER YEARS, SO DEAR TO MY HEART, KID MONK BARONI, JACK SLADE, LOOPHOLE, SECURITY RISK, FINGER MAN, PORT OF HELL, THE RETURN OF JACK SLADE, TARZAN'S HIDDEN JUNGLE, DRAGON WELLS MASSACRE, PORTLAND EXPOSE; entered TV during the 1950s and worked on such shows as "Playhouse of Stars," "Ellery Queen," "The Line-Up," "Wire Service," "The Gray Ghost," "Wichita Town," "Man with a Camera," "The Californians," "The Outlaws," "U.S. Marshal," "Border Patrol," "Death Valley Days," "Twilight Zone," "Tombstone Territory," "Zane Grey Theater," "21 Beacon St.," "Laramie," "Surfside Six," "Lassie."

Scott, Ken

Died 2 Dec. 1986, Los Angeles, Calif., age 58.

Film Actor. Film credits include A GUY NAMED JOE, SEE HERE, PRIVATE HARGROVE, STOPOVER TOKYO, THE THREE FACES OF EVE, THE WAY TO THE GOLD, THE BRAVADOS, THE FIEND WHO WALKED THE WEST, FROM HELL TO TEXAS, BELOVED INFIDEL, FIVE GATES TO HELL, THIS EARTH IS MINE, WOMAN OBSESSED, DESIRE IN THE DUST (1960), THE FIERCEST HEART, PIRATES OF TORTUGA, THE SECOND TIME AROUND, POLICE NURSE, RAIDERS FROM BENEATH THE SEA, THE NAKED BRIGADE, FANTASTIC VOYAGE, THE MURDER GAME, THE ST. VALENTINE'S DAY MASSACRE, PSYCH-OUT, THE ROOMMATES; appeared in the TV movie "The Amazing Howard Hughes."

Seiter, Robert

Died 12 Jan. 1986, St. Petersburg, Fla., age 76.

TV/Film Editor-Film Actor. Hailing from New York City, came to California in the latter part of the 1920s, acting in such silent films as OUT ALL NIGHT (1927), CHICAGO AFTER MIDNIGHT, RED LIPS (1928); also served as cameraman on some films and edited ONLY THE VALIANT (1951) and A PUBLIC AFFAIR (1962); moved into TV, editing shows such as "Leave It To Beaver," "Medic," and "Green Acres."

Seymour, John D.

(John Russell Davenport Seymour)

Born 24 Oct. 1897, Boston, Mass.; died 10 July 1986, New York City, New York.

Stage/Film/TV/Radio Actor. Came from an acting family (uncle was actor Harry Davenport; niece was actress Anne Seymour), entered show business in touring companies before making his Broadway debut in 1919 in "A Young Man's Fancy," then went on to appear in "One Night in Rome," "Richard III," "She Stoops to Conquer," "Mr. Moneypenny," "Sweet Adeline," "Cyrano de Bergerac," "Solitaire," "The Moon is Down," "Light Up the Sky," "The Sacred Flame," "Pal Joey," "The King and I," and a revival of "Life with Father," leading up to his final outing in 1975, "We Interrupt This Program"; was seen in PATTERNS (had also appeared in the TV version) and THE SPORTING CLUB.

Shaw, Glen Byam

(Glencairn Alexander Byam Shaw)

Born 13 Dec. 1904, London, England; died 29 April 1986, London, England.

Stage/Film Actor-Stage/Opera Director. Came from an artistic family (both parents were painters) and married actress Angela Baddeley; made his acting debut in the London theater in "At Mrs. Beams," followed by "The Cherry Orchard," "Down Hill," and "The Spook Sonata"; made his New York debut in "And So to Bed," then appeared in "The Lady From the Sea," "The Hell Within," "Queen of Scots," "Ghosts," and "Parnell" before becoming a director of both plays and operas; films appeared in include THE VAGA-

BOND QUEEN (1931, Brit.) and LOOK BACK IN ANGER.

Shull, Charles E.

Died 24 March 1986, Simi, Calif., age 56.

TV/Film/Stage Actor. Worked in TV as a Richmond, Virginia news director until 1960 then entered the acting field and appeared in the films FOXES, THE ESCAPE ARTIST, FRANCES, REAL GENIUS and in TV's "Hart to Hart," "Baretta," "The Fall Guy," "Little House on the Prairie," and TV films "Thursday's Game," "Target Risk," "The Ordeal of Patty Hearst," "Scruples," "Prime Suspect," "Portrait of a Showgirl."

Smith, Justin

Died 27 Feb. 1986, Santa Monica, Calif., age 66.

Film/TV Actor-Drama Teacher. A Syracuse, New York native, went into show business as a dancer after college and U.S. Navy service; appeared on TV in "The Kate Smith Show," "Pulitzer Playhouse"; film credits include THE JAZZ SINGER (1953), POLICE NURSE, THE YOUNG SWINGERS, WHAT A WAY TO GO, WILD ON THE BEACH, HOW TO SUCCEED IN BUSINESS WITHOUT REALLY TRYING; in 1967, opened an acting studio and coached Hollywood talents such as Raquel Welch, David and Keith Carradine, Sharon Tate, Penny Marshall; became a gay rights activist in the 1970s.

Smith, Kate

(Kathryn Elizabeth Smith)

Born 1 May 1907, Greenville, Va.; died 17 June 1986, Raleigh, N.C.

Singer-Film Actress. Started performing at the age of five (she had refused to speak until she was four) in a Washington, D.C. church choir; at the age of 10 her entertaining of WW I soldiers earned her a commendation from Gen. John J. Pershing; in her midteens, Eddie Dowling, a stage actor-director, put her into "Honeymoon Lane," a musical that lasted for 353 performances; record representative Ted Collins noticed her in a performance of "Flying High," and decided to promote her, starting a professional relationship which would last until his death in 1964; Collins got Smith her first radio show (where she picked up her theme song "When the Moon Comes Over the Mountain" and her opening and closing trademarks, "Hello Everybody" and "Thanks for Listenin'"); in 1938, she began an hour-long daytime show and was soon radio's highest paid female performer; after extensively revising the tune (it had been in the musical "Yip Yip Yaphank," 1918), Irving Berlin gave her exclusive rights to sing the song that would become so identified with her, "God Bless America"; ap-

peared in the films HELLO EVERYBODY and THIS IS THE ARMY; in the 1950s, had a television show, "The Kate Smith Hour"; in her later

years concentrated primarily on concerts; in 1982, President Ronald Reagan awarded her the Medal of Freedom (he had appeared with her in THIS IS THE ARMY).

Smith, William Craig

Died 22 Aug. 1986, Burbank, Calif., age 67.

TV/Film Art Director. Hailing from Philadelphia, started at a local experimental TV station before WW II army service; returned to Philadelphia, continuing there until 1949, when he went to New York to join NBC and worked as art director on "Armstrong Circle Theater," "Requiem for a Heavyweight," "Gilligan's Island," "The Twilight Zone," "The Wild Wild West," "Hawaii Five-O," "Gunsmoke"; also worked on such feature films as THE LAST TYCOON, EXORCIST II: THE HERETIC, THE ONE AND ONLY, THE PROPHECY, RAISE THE TITANIC, S.O.B., VICTOR/VICTORIA (shared an Oscar with Rodger Maus and Tim Hutchinson).

Smrz, Brett

Died 21 Sept. 1986, Los Angeles, Calif., age 26.

Film/TV Stuntman. Did stuntwork in Los Angeles and New York for the last ten years; worked in TV's "V" and the films TURK 182, ROCKY III, TAPS, THEY ALL LAUGHED and BEAT STREET; was killed doing a stunt which required a seven-floor leap when he bounced off the edge of a protective airbag and hit the ground.

Stark, Col. Richard S.

(Richard Salisbury Stark)

Died 12 Dec. 1986, Sotogrande, Spain, age 75.

Radio/TV Announcer-Film Actor. A native of Grand Rapids, Michigan, in the period from 1916 through 1921, acted in silent films such as THE WEDDING MARCH, HEARTS OF HUMANITY and OUT OF THE WRECK; attended Cornell University and after graduation, went into radio for a 31-year run to 1949 working primarily as an announcer; appeared on stage in "A Midsummer Night's Dream; served in both WW II and in Viet Nam as an officer in the Marine Corps Reserve; after 1949, went into TV as announcer on such shows as "Perry Como Show," "Fireside Theatre," "What's My Line," "Masquerade," "Down You Go"; studied architecture and received a degree from the Pratt Institute in 1957.

Starrett, Charles

Born 28 March 1903, Athol, Mass.; died 22 March 1986, Borrego Springs, Calif.

Film Actor. While playing for the Dartmouth College football team, was used as an extra in the 1926 silent THE QUARTERBACK; after initial work in both vaudeville and local theaters, went to Hollywood and appeared as first or second romantic lead in such films as THE ROYAL FAMILY OF BROADWAY, FAST AND LOOSE, TOUCHDOWN, THE VIKING (1931), SILENCE, THE

AGE FOR LOVE, SKY BRIDE, THE MASK OF FU MANCHU, SWEETHEART OF SIGMA CHI (1933), RETURN OF CASEY JONES, MURDER ON THE CAMPUS, GENTLEMEN ARE BORN, THE SILVER STREAK (1935), THREE ON A HONEYMOON, SONS OF STEEL, SO RED THE ROSE; switched to westerns in the mid 1930s, appearing in such films as CODE OF THE RANGE, WESTBOUND MAIL, THE MAN FROM SUNDOWN; in 1940 became famous playing The Durango Kid, appearing in 66 films as such, including THE DURANGO KID, RETURN OF THE DURANGO KID, GALLOPING THUNDER, THE FIGHTING FRONTIERSMAN, THE LONE HAND TEXAN, BUCKAROO FROM POWDER RIVER, EL DORADO PASS, QUICK ON THE TRIGGER, LARAMIE, THE BLAZING TRAIL, TEXAS DYNAMO, STREETS OF GHOST TOWN, BONANZA TOWN, PECOS RIVER and the last of the series THE KID FROM BROKEN GUN; helped to found the Screen Actors Guild.

Stephens, Harvey

Died 22 Dec. 1986, Laguna Hills, Calif., age 85.

Film/Stage Actor. Worked in Walter Hampden's repertory company and toured before hitting Broadway in "Other Men's Wives," "Dishonored Lady," "Conquest," "The Party's Over," "Wife Insurance," "Over Twenty-One," "South Pacific"; had a prolific film career, appearing in such films as THE CHEAT, JIMMY AND SALLY, PADDY, THE NEXT BEST THING, WORST WOMAN IN PARIS, EVELYN PRENTICE, AFTER OFFICE HOURS, BABY FACE HARRINGTON, MURDER MAN, ORCHIDS TO YOU, ROBIN HOOD OF EL DORADO, TOUGH GUY (1936), KING OF GAMBLERS, MAID OF SALEM, THE TEXANS, BEAU GESTE (1939), THE HOUSE OF FEAR (1939), THE OKLAHOMA KID, ABE LINCOLN IN ILLINOIS, THE FIGHTING 69TH, WHEN THE DALTONS RODE, SERGEANT YORK, THE LADY IS WILLING, THE STORY OF DR. WASSELL, THE GIRL IN THE RED VELVET SWING, THE YOUNG LIONS, THE BAT, NORTH BY NORTHWEST, and his last effort, JOY IN THE MORNING (1965).

Stevens, Paul

(Paul Steven Gattoni)

Born 17 June 1924, Los Angeles, Calif.; died 4 June 1986, New York City, New York. Stage/TV/Film Actor.

Attended both the University of Southern California and the Pasadena Playhouse; made his debut on Broadway in "The Merchant of Venice" (1953), followed by "Oliver Twist," "As You Like It," "Romeo and Juliet," "Ivanov"; film credits include EXODUS, THE MASK, ADVISE AND CONSENT, MARLOWE, PATTON, CORKY, MELINDA, RAGE, BATTLE FOR THE PLANET OF THE APES; appeared on TV in "Playhouse 90," "Bonanza," "Mission: Impossible," "The Rockford Files," a recurring part in the soaper, "Another World" (1977-1985), as well as three TV movies, "Get Christie Love!" "Law of the Land," "In the Glitter Palace."

Stevenson, Robert

Born 31 March 1905, Buxton, England; died 30 Apr. 1986, Santa Barbara, Calif.

Film Director-Writer. A man who had a three-stage directorial career, working in British films, American films, and mainly on Walt Disney family pictures; graduated from Cambridge; began as a writer on such films as LATIN LOVE (1930), LOVE ON WHEELS, MICHAEL AND MARY, THE OFFICE GIRL, THE RINGER, EARLY TO BED, FAITHFUL HEART, F.P. 1, HEART SONG, THE BATTLE, THE GAIETY GIRLS; early directorial attempts were HAPPY EVER AFTER (1932), FALLING FOR YOU (also wrote), LITTLE FRIEND (produced only), LADY JANE GREY (1936, also wrote), THE MAN WHO LIVED AGAIN, KING SOLOMON'S MINES (1937), NON-STOP NEW YORK, TO THE VICTOR, THE TWO OF US, THE WARE CASE, RETURN TO YESTERDAY (also wrote), then proceeded to Hollywood to both direct and write his first American film TOM BROWN'S SCHOOL DAYS (1940), followed by BACK STREET, JOAN OF PARIS, FOREVER AND A DAY (coproduced and directed), YOUNG MAN'S FANCY, JANE EYRE (cowrote); during WW II, did filming for Frank Capra's military unit; returned to direct DISHONORED LADY, TO THE ENDS OF THE EARTH, WALK SOFTLY STRANGER, THE WOMAN ON PIER 13, MY FORBIDDEN PAST, THE LAS VEGAS STORY; worked in TV on such shows as "Gunsmoke," "General Electric Theater," "Ford Theater," "Cavalcade of America" and "Alfred Hitchcock Presents"; in 1956, signed with Walt Disney Studios, working exclusively for that company until his retirement in the late 1970s; his Disney fare started with JOHNNY TREMAIN and continued with OLD YELLER, DARBY O'GILL AND THE LITTLE PEOPLE, KIDNAPPED (also wrote), THE ABSENT-MINDED PROFESSOR, IN SEARCH OF THE CASTAWAYS, SON OF FLUBBER, MARY POPPINS (received an Oscar nomination), THE MISADVENTURES OF MERLIN JONES, THE MONKEY'S UNCLE, THAT DARN CAT, THE GNOME-MOBILE, BLACKBEARD'S GHOST, THE LOVE BUG, BEDKNOBS AND BROOMSTICKS, HERBIE RIDES AGAIN, THE ISLAND AT THE TOP OF THE WORLD, ONE OF OUR DINOSAURS IS MISSING, THE SHAGGY D.A.

Stewart, Paul

(Paul Sternberg)

Born 13 March 1908, New York City, N.Y.; died 17 Feb. 1986, Los Angeles, Calif.

Radio/Stage/Film Actor-Stage Director. After studying law, opted for an acting career; started on the stage in his early teens in such plays as "Two Seconds," "East of Broadway," "Bulls, Bears and Asses," "Wine of Choice," "Native Son," "Mister Roberts"; directed stage productions "Alternate Current," "Twilight Walk," "Sing Me No Lullaby"; performed prodigiously on radio (close to 5,000 performances) during the period from 1934-1944, and also directed some daytime serials; his radio credits include "Buck Rogers in the 25th Century," "Cavalcade of America," "David Harum," "Easy Aces," "Life Can Be Beautiful," "Mr. District Attorney," and Orson Welles' "Mercury Theater," which initiated a long-lived professional association and led to his screen debut in CITIZEN KANE; other films include JOHNNY EAGER,

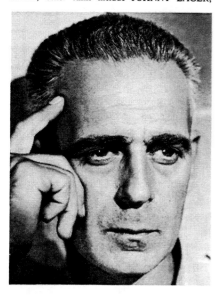

GOVERNMENT GIRL, MR. LUCKY, CHAMPION, EASY LIVING, ILLEGAL ENTRY, TWELVE O'CLOCK HIGH, THE WINDOW, EDGE OF DOOM, WALK SOFTLY, STRANGER, APPOINTMENT WITH DANGER, THE BAD AND THE BEAUTIFUL, CARBINE WILLIAMS, DEADLINE-U.S.A., LOAN SHARK, WE'RE NOT MARRIED, THE JOE LOUIS STORY, THE JUGGLER, DEEP IN MY HEART, PRISONER OF WAR, CHICAGO SYNDICATE, THE COB-

WEB, KISS ME DEADLY, HELL ON FRISCO BAY, THE WILD PARTY, TOP SECRET AFFAIR, KING CREOLE, A CHILD IS WAITING, THE GREATEST STORY EVER TOLD, IN COLD BLOOD, JIGSAW (1968), HOW TO COMMIT MARRIAGE, MURPH THE SURF, BITE THE BULLET, THE DAY OF THE LOCUST, W.C. FIELDS AND ME (as Florenz Ziegfeld), OPENING NIGHT, REVENGE OF THE PINK PANTHER, NOBODY'S PERFEKT, S.O.B., TEMPEST; appeared in the TV films "Carter's Army," "City Beneath the Sea," "The Dain Curse," "The Nativity," "Power," "Emergency Room," and directed episodes for such TV series as "The Defenders," "Twilight Zone," "Peter Gunn," "Checkmate," "M-Squad," "Hawaiian Eye."

Stock, Nigel

Born 21 Sept. 1919, Malta; died 23 June 1986, London, England.

Film/Stage Actor. Originally from Malta, started on the London stage in 1931 (at the age of 12) in small parts before landing a major role in 1937 in "Tobacco Road"; served in the army during WW II, then returned to the stage in "The Caine Mutiny Court Martial," "Uncle Vanya," "The Browning Version"; in the U.S. appeared in "You Never Can Tell," "Mixed Doubles"; started his film career in 1937 with LANCASHIRE LUCK, BREAK THE NEWS!, NORTH SEA PATROL, GOODBYE MR. CHIPS!, SONS OF THE SEAS, IT ALWAYS RAINS ON SUNDAY, BRIGHTON ROCK, THE LADY WITH A LAMP, FOUR AGAINST FATE, MALTA STORY, AUNT CLARA, THE DAM BUSTERS, THE NIGHT MY NUMBER CAME UP, EYEWITNESS, PURSUIT OF THE GRAF SPEE, THE SILENT ENEMY, NEVER LET GO, VICTIM, DAMN THE DEFIANT!, THE PASSWORD IS COURAGE, THE GREAT ESCAPE, TO HAVE AND TO HOLD, NOTHING BUT THE BEST, WEEKEND AT DUNKIRK, MCGUIRE GO HOME, THE NIGHT OF THE GENERALS, THE LOST CONTINENT, THE LION IN WINTER, CROMWELL, THE NELSON AFFAIR, RUSSIAN ROULETTE, OPERATION DAYBREAK, THE MIRROR CRACK'D, RED MONARCH, YELLOWBEARD, YOUNG SHERLOCK HOLMES; played Winston Churchill in the 6-hour TV miniseries "A Man Called Intrepid"; in 1983, he toured in a one-man show called "221-B"; also played Dr. Watson in a British TV series based on the Sherlock Holmes stories.

Strauch, Joseph, Jr.

Died 31 May 1986, Age 56

Film Actor. As a youngster, doubled for Spanky McFarland in the popular series, "The Little Rascals" and can be seen as Smiley Burnette's nephew in the Gene Autry oaters UNDER FIESTA STARS, BELLS OF CAPISTRANO, CALL OF THE CANYON, HEART OF THE RIO GRANDE, HOME IN WYOMIN'; appeared in

such other films as THIS TIME FOR KEEPS, BENEATH WESTERN SKIES and IF WINTER COMES.

Streatfield, Noel

Died 11 Sept. 1986, London, England, age 90.

Author. She was the writer of the original story on which WELCOME, MR. WASHINGTON was based, as well as the novel which was the basis for AUNT CLARA.

Stucker, Stephen

Died 13 Apr. 1986, Hollywood, Calif., age 36.

Film Actor. Appeared in CARNAL MADNESS, CRACKING UP, AIRPLANE, AIRPLANE II: THE SEQUEL, TRADING PLACES, BAD MANNERS.

Sultan, Arne

Died 17 March 1986, Studio City, Calif., age 60.

TV Producer/Writer-Screenwriter-Comedian. A Brooklyn native, started in show business as a stand-up comedian in the resorts in New York's Catskill Mountains; went into television as a writer for Martha Raye, Steve Allen, "The Chevy Show," and "The Judy Garland Show"; did double duty as executive producer and writer on "Get Smart" (for which he received an Emmy); produced "He and She," "The Sandy Duncan Show," "Barney Miller," "The Governor and J.J. (cocreator and producer), "The Partners" (cocreator and executive producer); cowrote with Marvin Worth the stories for the films BOYS' NIGHT OUT, PROMISE HER ANYTHING, THREE ON A COUCH; collaborated with two others on the script for THE NUDE BOMB; with Earl Barret, reworked British TV series for their American variants "Too Close for Comfort" (later "The Ted Knight Show") and "Check It Out"; coauthored with Barret the play "Wife Begins at 40"; also did double duty on a couple of telefilms, "Poor Devil" (executive producer and cowriter) and "It Couldn't Happen to a Nicer Guy" (producer and cowriter).

Sutherland, Esther

Died 31 Dec. 1986, Los Angeles, Calif., age 54.

Stage/Film/TV Actress-Musician/Singer. Appeared on stage (toured in "Under Papa's Picture" as well as "Get on Board," "Lenny," and "Funny You Should Ask") and in films (RIVERRUN, BLACK BELT JONES, TRUCK TURNER, THE COMMITMENT, THE GOODBYE GIRL, NINE TO FIVE, STIR CRAZY, YOUNG DOCTORS IN LOVE) as well as on TV ("The Jeffersons," "Lou Grant," "Hill Street Blues," "Archie Bunker's Place," "Kojak").

Sweet, Blanche

(Sarah Blanche Sweet)

Born 18 June 1896, Chicago, Ill.; died 6 Sept. 1986, New York N.Y.

Film/Stage Actress. One of the last remaining greats from the silent era, she started out on the stage at a very young age and made her first film in 1909 (A MAN WITH THREE WIVES); later that year worked with D.W. Griffith (the man who put her name in the cinema history books) on A CORNER IN WHEAT; that was followed by appearances in many one- and two-reelers, including ALL ON ACCOUNT OF THE MILK, THE DAY AFTER, CHOOSING A HUSBAND, A ROMANCE OF THE WESTERN HILLS, THE ROCKY ROAD, THE LONEDALE OPERATOR, THE WHITE ROSE OF THE WILDS, THE PRIMAL CALL, THE BLIND PRINCESS AND THE POET, A WOMAN SCORNED, THE ETERNAL MOTHER, MAN'S LUST FOR GOLD, THE PAINTED LADY, OIL AND WATER, THE HERO OF LITTLE ITALY, THE COMING OF ANGELO, TWO MEN ON THE DESERT, THE MASSACRE and Griffith's first feature picture JUDITH OF BETHULIA, the film that made her a star; she then appeared in STRONGHEART, THE PAINTED LADY, HOME SWEET HOME, THE WARRENS OF VIRGINIA, THE SECRET ORCHARD, THE CASE OF BECKY, THE SECRET SIN, THE DUPE, PUBLIC OPINION, THE STORM, THE RAGAMUFFIN, THOSE WITHOUT SIN, SILENT PARTNER, THE HUSHED HOUR, HELP WANTED-MALE, ANNA CHRISTIE, IN THE PALACE OF THE KING, TESS OF THE D'URBERVILLES, THE NEW COMMANDMENT, BLUEBEARD'S SEVEN WIVES, THE LADY FROM HELL, THE WOMAN IN WHITE, and the talkies THE WOMAN RACKET, SHOW GIRL IN HOLLYWOOD, THE SILVER HORDE; as her film career waned, she went into vaudeville, later being coached by her second husband, Raymond Hackett, also a former film star; did a few plays, including the original production of "The Petrified Forest," followed by "There's Always a Breeze," "Aries is Rising," "Those Endearing Young Charms"; played a bit part in THE FIVE PENNIES (1959).

Talbot, Brud

(Joseph Talbot)

Died 20 Nov. 1986, Boston, Mass., age 46.

Film Actor-Producer-Director. Started out as a producer on an award-winning featurette called THE BOY WHO OWNED A MELEPHANT before switching to acting in FORCE OF IMPULSE, WITHOUT EACH OTHER, FINGER ON THE TRIGGER; later returned to producing for TV ("Around the World of Mike Todd"); produced "Soundblast 66," a concert extravaganza; acted as administrator for Dana Films and Cinemation Industries; coproduced THE BLACK PEARL.

Taranto, Nino

Died 23 Feb. 1986, Naples, Italy, age 79.

Film/Stage/Vaudeville/TV Actor-Comedian. Started his career in vaudeville, appeared in numerous stage productions, then entered the film industry, appearing in such movies as DOVE STA ZAZA?, LA CINTURA DI CASTITA, ANNI FACILI, THE TWO COLONELS, among others.

Tarkovsky, Andrei

Born 1932, Moscow, USSR; died 29 Dec. 1986, Paris, France.

Film Director. Though he had a limited output, he was highly regarded by both critics and his fellow directors; before entering the film business studied music and Arabic and worked as a geological prospector; made two short films, THERE WILL BE NO LEAVE TONIGHT (1959) and VIOLIN AND ROLLER (1961) while at the Soviet State Film School where he had studied under prominent filmmaker Mikhail Romm; his first feature film, MY NAME IS IVAN, won a Golden Lion at the Venice Film Festival; his film ANDREI RUBLEV (shot in 1966) won the International Critics Prize at the Cannes Film Festival; he then directed SOLARIS, THE MIRROR, and STALKER (his last film made in the USSR); his final two films, NOSTALGHIA (1984) and SACRIFICE (1986, made when he already knew he was dying of cancer) were done in exile (technically he did not defect until after making NOSTALGHIA, which was shot primarily in

Italy); the downbeat nature of his films made them unpopular with the Soviet bureaucracy.

Taylor, Dwight

Born 1 Jan. 1902, New York, N.Y.; died Dec. 31, 1986, Woodland Hills, Calif.

Playwright-Screenwriter-Author. Born into a show business family (his father, Charles A. Taylor, a playwright; his mother, Laurette Taylor, an actress), he grew up in an atmosphere surrounded by the literary and media lights of the time; after turning down a reporter's job, went to work for *The New Yorker* magazine; wrote the plays "Don't Tell George," "Lipstick," and "The Gay Divorce" (which used the music of Cole Porter and was the genesis for the film THE GAY DIVORCEE); went to Hollywood as a screenwriter on such productions as NUMBERED MEN, SECRETS OF A SECRETARY, ARE YOU LISTENING?, IF I WERE FREE, TODAY WE LIVE, LADY BY CHOICE, LONG LOST FATHER, PARIS IN SPRING, TOP HAT, FOLLOW THE FLEET, GANGWAY, HEAD OVER HEELS IN LOVE, AMAZING MR. WILLIAMS, WHEN TOMORROW COMES, RHYTHM ON THE RIVER, KISS THE BOYS GOODBYE, I WAKE UP SCREAMING, NIGHTMARE (1942), THE THIN MAN GOES HOME, CONFLICT, SOMETHING TO LIVE FOR, WE'RE NOT MARRIED, PICKUP ON SOUTH STREET, SPECIAL DELIVERY (1955), BOY ON A DOLPHIN, INTERLUDE (1957); in 1950, again in association with Cole Porter, was the cowriter of the stage musical "Out of This World"; scripted such TV shows as "Climax," "77 Sunset Strip," "Playhouse of Stars," "The Thin Man," "Batman"; books authored include *Joy Ride*, *What Sank the Dreamboat*, *Blood and Thunder*.

Teitel, Carol

(Carolyn Sally Kahn)

Born 1 Aug. 1929, Brooklyn, N.Y.; died 27 July 1986, Camden, N.J.

Stage/Film Actress. Studied acting with Leo Bulgakov, William Hansen, Lee Strasberg; made her stage debut in 1942 at Master Institute, then appeared in "Billy the Kid," "Pullman Car Hiawatha," "Galileo," "Marat/Sade," "The Keymaker" (a play written by her husband, Norman), "A Flea in Her Ear," among many others; had a minor part in an Electronovision filming of Richard Burton's HAMLET; appeared on TV in "The Catholic Hour" and "The Eternal Light" as well as a TV film, "My Old Man"; nominated for an Emmy for her work in "Woman of Valor."

Tenoudji, Edmond

Died 28 Apr. 1986, Paris, France, age 83.

Film Executive/Producer. Hailing from Algeria, after WW II, produced, coproduced, or distributed approximately 250 films, including his first production effort, Orson Welles' OTHELLO; produced the work of many major directors, including Henri-Georges Clouzot, Roger Vadim, Luis Bunuel.

Termini, Charles

Died 30 Sept. 1986, Burbank, Calif., age 77.

Film Camera Assistant. Originally from Sicily, Italy, started in the business in 1926 as a film stripper before going to Hollywood in 1939; served as a camera assistant on KISMET, THE YEARLING, NATIONAL VELVET, AROUND THE WORLD IN 80 DAYS, SAYONARA, MUTINY ON THE BOUNTY (1962), THE GREATEST STORY EVER TOLD, DOCTORS' WIVES; worked closely with James Wong Howe on THE MOLLY MCGUIRES, FUNNY LADY, and other projects.

Terry, Sonny

(Saunders Terrill)

Died 11 March 1986, Mineola, N.Y., age 74.

Blues Singer-Harmonica Player-Film Actor. Overcame an accident in his youth that blinded him, becoming a brilliant harmonica player, touring with medicine shows by the age of 19; through the Depression, worked with guitarists Gary Davis and Blind Boy Fuller (both of whom were also blind); then began a near-50-year professional relationship with vocalist-guitarist Brownie McGhee recording

and performing (worked mainly in the "Piedmont Blues" format); appeared in "Cat on a Hot Tin Roof" on Broadway, THE JERK (a Steve Martin film comedy) and Steven Spielberg's THE COLOR PURPLE.

Thomson, Beatrix

Died early 1986, England, age 85.

Stage/Film Actress-Playwright. Formerly married to Claude Rains, mainly worked in British theater although she was seen in the U.S. in "The Constant Nymph," "Out of the Sea" (in which she appeared with her husband), "Unknown Warrior," "The Subway," "The Artist and the Shadow," "Monsieur Brotonneau," "The Princess in the Cage," "Wisdom Teeth," "Duet by Accident" (also wrote); appeared on the screen in THE DREYFUS CASE (1931), CROWN VS STEVENS, THE STORY OF SHIRLEY YORKE; her other plays include "Wooden Shoes," "Love for Sale," "Son of Adam," "Woman Alive," "Special Delivery."

Torres, Dr. Donald R.

Died 22 March 1986, Los Angeles, Calif., age 49.

Film Dancer/Actor-Spiritual Adviser. Appeared in several films including A STAR IS BORN (1954); became a spiritual adviser to various entertainers such as Peggy Lee after founding the Triune Science of Being.

Tracy, Steve

Died 27 Nov. 1986, Tampa, Fla., age 34.

TV/Stage/Film Actor. Mainly seen on TV in "Little House on the Prairie" (had recurring role as Percival Dalton), "James at 15," "Quincy"; film credits include NATIONAL LAMPOON'S CLASS REUNION, SAVE THE LAST DANCE FOR ME, FOREVER YOUNG.

Tubens, Joe

Died 25 Apr. 1986, New York City, New York, age unknown.

Stage/Film/TV Hair Designer. Worked on 27 Broadway shows including "Promises, Promises," "Butterflies are Free," "Applause," "Sugar," "Coco" as well as for such films as STAR, LAST EMBRACE, FUNNY GIRL, THE BOSTON STRANGLER, THE EXORCIST, LUNA, SATURDAY NIGHT FEVER, HAIR, THE KING OF COMEDY; was hair designer for 11 Tony Award broadcasts, as well as for the Johnny Carson, Mike Douglas and Dick Cavett shows; did hair styling for ballet companies and private clients such as Myrna Loy, Gloria Swanson, Katharine Hepburn.

Tucker, Forrest

(Forrest Meredith Tucker)

Born 12 Feb. 1919, Plainfield, Ind.; died 25 Oct. 1986, Woodland Hills, Calif.

Film/Stage Actor. Appeared in burlesque before serving in the Army for two years; visiting Hollywood, got a part in THE WESTERNER; then appeared in THE HOWARDS OF VIRGINIA, EMERGENCY LANDING, NEW WINE, HONOLULU LU, CANAL ZONE, CAMP NUTS, TRAMP, TRAMP, TRAMP, SHUT MY BIG MOUTH, PARACHUTE NURSE, THE SPIRIT OF STANFORD, KEEPER OF THE FLAME, BOSTON BLACKIE GOES HOLLYWOOD, MY SISTER EILEEN, SUBMARINE RAIDER, COUNTER ESPIONAGE; after a second hitch in the Army during WW II, appeared in THE MAN WHO DARED, TALK ABOUT A LADY, RENEGADES, DANGEROUS BUSINESS, NEVER SAY GOODBYE (1946), THE YEARLING, GUNFIGHTERS, ADVENTURES IN SILVERADO, THE PLUNDERERS, MONTANA BELLE, CORONER CREEK, TWO GUYS FROM TEXAS, THE BIG CAT, BRIMSTONE, THE LAST BANDIT, SANDS OF IWO JIMA, HELLFIRE, THE NEVADAN, ROCK ISLAND TRAIL, CALIFORNIA PASSAGE, FIGHTING COAST GUARD, OH, SUSANNA, CROSSWINDS, HOODLUM EMPIRE, THE WILD BLUE YONDER, FLAMING FEATHER, WARPATH, BUGLES IN THE AFTERNOON, HURRICANE SMITH, RIDE THE MAN DOWN, PONY EXPRESS, SAN ANTONE, FLIGHT NURSE, JUBILEE TRAIL, LAUGHING ANNE, TROUBLE IN THE GLEN,

RAGE AT DAWN, FINGER MAN, THE VANISHING AMERICAN (1955), NIGHT FREIGHT, THE BREAK IN THE CIRCLE, STAGECOACH TO FURY, THREE VIOLENT PEOPLE, THE QUIET GUN, THE DEERSLAYER, THE ABOMINABLE SNOWMAN, GIRL IN THE WOODS, COSMIC MONSTERS, THE CRAWLING EYE, AUNTIE MAME (1958), GUNSMOKE IN TUCSON, FORT MASSACRE, COUNTERPLOT, DON'T WORRY, WE'LL THINK OF A TITLE, THE SILENT TREATMENT, THE NIGHT THEY RAIDED MINSKY'S, BARQUERO, CHISUM, THE WILD McCULLOCHS, THE WACKIEST WAGON TRAIN IN THE WEST, FINAL CHAPTER-WALKING TALL, CARNAUBA, RARE BREED, THUNDER RUN, OUTTAKES (1985); appeared on the stage in a touring production of "The Music Man," then appeared on Broadway in "Fair Game for Lovers"; mainly known for his role on the TV series "F Troop"; also did the TV series "Dusty's Trail" and the TV films, "Alias Smith and Jones," "Welcome Home, Johnny Bristol," "Footsteps," "Jarrett," "Once an Eagle," "The Incredible Rocky Mountain Race," "Black Beauty," "A Real American Hero," "The Rebels," "The Adventures of Huckleberry Finn," "Blood Feud"; married three times.

Tucker, Lorenzo

Born 27 June, 1907, Philadelphia, Pa.; died 19 Aug. 1986, Hollywood, Calif.

Stage/Film Actor. Known as "The Black Valentino" when he appeared in Oscar Micheaux all-black films between 1928 and 1934; went to Temple University and photographic trade schools; made appearances with Bessie Smith on countrywide tours; was seen on Broadway in "Make Me Know It" (1929), "The Constant Sinner," "Ol' Man Satan," "Hummin' Sam," as well as tours of "Harvey," "Bell, Book and Candle," "Born Yesterday," "Springtime for Henry," "Porgy and Bess," and a two-year stint in a London production of "Anna Lucasta" in 1952; his films are WAGES OF SIN, FOOL'S ERRAND, BEWITCHING EYES, EASY STREET, WHEN MEN BETRAY, DAUGHTER OF THE CONGO, THE BLACK KING, VEILED ARISTOCRATS, HARLEM AFTER MIDNIGHT, TEMPTATION, THE UNDERWORLD, MIRACLE IN HARLEM, STRAIGHT TO HEAVEN, BOY, WHAT A GIRL!, ONE ROUND JONES, SEPIA CINDERELLA, REAT, PETITE AND GONE.

Tuttle, Lurene

Died 28 May 1986, Encino, Calif., age 79.

Radio/TV/Film Actress. Did stock theater on the West Coast before breaking into radio in 1934 to appear with Dick Powell on "Hollywood Hotel" starting a prolonged career on the airwaves (averaging 15 appearances per week) in such shows as "The Adventures of Ozzie and Harriet," "Dr. Christian," "Suspense," "Duffy's Tavern," "The Saint," "The

Great Gildersleeve," "Maisie," "The Red Skelton Show," "Sam Spade," "Strange Wills," "Those We Love"; appeared in the films STAND UP AND CHEER, TOM, DICK AND HARRY, HEAVEN ONLY KNOWS, HOMECOMING (1948), MACBETH (1948), MR. BLANDINGS BUILDS HIS DREAM HOUSE, GOODBYE MY FANCY, TOMORROW IS ANOTHER DAY, THE WHIP HAND, DON'T BOTHER TO KNOCK, NEVER WAVE AT A WAC, ROOM FOR ONE MORE, THE AFFAIRS OF DOBIE GILLIS, NIAGARA, THE GLASS SLIPPER, SINCERELY YOURS, SLANDER, SWEET SMELL OF SUCCESS, UNTAMED YOUTH, MA BARKER'S KILLER BROOD, PSYCHO, NIGHTMARE IN THE SUN, THE RESTLESS ONES, THE FORTUNE COOKIE, THE GHOST AND MR. CHICKEN, THE HORSE IN THE GRAY FLANNEL SUIT, THE MANITOU, THE CLONUS HORROR, NUTCRACKER FANTASY, TESTAMENT (1983); for a two-year period (1953 to 1955), she appeared opposite Leon Ames in TV's "Life with Father," as well as other TV shows such as "Father of the Bride," "Gunsmoke," "Perry Mason," "Bonanza," "The Beverly Hillbillies," "Trapper John, M.D." "The Love Boat," "Dynasty," "Julia," and the TV films, "Mrs. Sundance," "Live Again, Die Again," "Law and Order," "Crash," "White Mama," "For the Love of It," "The Adventures of Huckleberry Finn" (1981), "Return of the Beverly Hillbillies," "Shooting Stars".

Vallee, Rudy

(Hubert Pryor Vallee)

Born 28 July 1901, Island Point, Vt.; died 3 July 1986, North Hollywood, Calif.

Singer-Actor-Songwriter. Became interested in music at a young age, learning to play drums, piano, clarinet, saxophone; attended the University of Maine and Yale, and upon graduating formed his own band, The Connecticut Yankees; had his own radio show in 1929 on which he and his band performed "My Time Is Your Time," which later became his theme song; was the first singer to be dubbed a crooner; appeared on stage in both the 1931 and 1935 versions of "George White's Scandals," as well as "The Man in Possession"; made his debut on screen in 1929 in THE VAGABOND LOVER, fol-

lowed by GLORIFYING THE AMERICAN GIRL, INTERNATIONAL HOUSE, GEORGE WHITE'S SCANDALS, SWEET MUSIC, GOLD DIGGERS IN PARIS, SECOND FIDDLE, TIME OUT FOR RHYTHM, TOO MANY BLONDES, THE PALM BEACH STORY, HAPPY GO LUCKY, IT'S IN THE BAG, MAN ALIVE, PEOPLE ARE FUNNY, THE FABULOUS SUZANNE, THE BACHELOR AND THE BOBBY-SOXER, I REMEMBER MAMA, SO THIS IS NEW YORK, MY DEAR SECRETARY, UNFAITHFULLY YOURS, MOTHER IS A FRESHMAN, THE BEAUTIFUL BLONDE FROM BASHFUL BEND, FATHER

WAS A FULLBACK, MAD WEDNESDAY, THE ADMIRAL WAS A LADY, RICOCHET ROMANCE, GENTLEMEN MARRY BRUNETTES, THE HELEN MORGAN STORY, LIVE A LITTLE, LOVE A LITTLE, SUNBURST, THE NIGHT THEY RAIDED MINSKY'S (narration only), THE PHYNX, HOW TO SUCCEED IN BUSINESS WITHOUT REALLY TRYING (1976, repeating his 1961 Broadway success), WON TON TON: THE DOG WHO SAVED HOLLYWOOD; had his own TV show and was seen in "Jenny Kissed Me" on "Matinee Theater" in 1956; wrote two books about his life, *Vagabond Dreams Come True* (1929) and *My Time Is Your Time* (1962); was married four times—third wife was actress Jane Greer.

Van Dyke, Willard

(Willard Ames Van Dyke)

Born 5 Dec. 1906, Denver, Colo.; died 23 Jan. 1986, Jackson, Tenn.

Film Documentary Maker-Still Photographer. A still photographer who made documentaries on social issues such as migrant workers, was an apprentice to photographer Edward Weston, and founded an organization of prominent still photographers; worked for Pare Lorentz on the 1938 documentary THE RIVER later directing THE CHILDREN MUST LEARN, VALLEYTOWN, THE BRIDGE, SAN FRANCISCO, THE PHOTOGRAPHER, SKYSCRAPER, RICE; became head of the film library at the Museum of Modern Art in New York City and was also artist in residence at Harvard; more recently had presented one-man shows of his still photography.

Vigran, Herbert

Died 28 Nov. 1986, Los Angeles, Calif., age 76.

Film/Stage/Radio/TV Character Actor. After graduation from law school, decided to take up acting; appeared on the Broadway stage in the 1930s in such presentations as "Achilles Had a Heel," "Cyrano de Bergerac," "Happy Valley, Limited," "Having Wonderful Time"; debut film was VAGABOND LADY (1935), followed by DEATH FROM A DISTANCE, IT ALL CAME TRUE, STRANGER ON THE THIRD FLOOR, MILLION DOLLAR BABY, MURDER BY INVITATION, REG'LAR FELLERS, SECRETS OF A CO-ED, THE GHOST SHIP, IT AIN'T HAY, SWEET ROSIE O'GRADY, HER ADVENTUROUS NIGHT, ALL MY SONS, FIGHTING MAD, THE NOOSE HANGS HIGH, TEXAS, BROOKLYN AND HEAVEN, HOUSE OF STRANGERS, THE JUDGE, TELL IT TO THE JUDGE, LET'S DANCE, MRS. O'MALLEY AND MR. MALONE, SIDE STREET, NIGHT INTO MORNING, APPOINTMENT WITH DANGER, ABBOTT AND COSTELLO MEET THE INVISIBLE MAN, BEDTIME FOR BONZO, HALF ANGEL, THE IRON MAN, JUST FOR YOU, SOMEBODY LOVES ME, THE ROSE BOWL STORY, THE BAND WAGON, LET'S DO IT AGAIN, THE GIRL NEXT DOOR, DRAGNET, THE LONG, LONG TRAILER, LUCKY ME, SUSAN SLEPT HERE, WHITE CHRISTMAS, 20,000 LEAGUES UNDER THE SEA, I DIED A THOUSAND TIMES, ILLEGAL, THAT CERTAIN FEELING, CALLING HOMICIDE, A CRY IN THE NIGHT, OUR MISS BROOKS, THESE WILDER YEARS, THREE FOR JAMIE DAWN, GUNSIGHT RIDGE, PUBLIC PIGEON NO. 1, THE MIDNIGHT STORY, THE VAMPIRE, THE CASE AGAINST BROOKLYN, GO, JOHNNY, GO, PLUNDERERS OF PAINTED FLATS, THE ERRAND BOY, THE BRASS BOTTLE, THE CANDIDATE, SEND ME NO FLOWERS, THE UNSINKABLE MOLLY BROWN, THAT FUNNY FEELING, DID YOU HEAR THE ONE ABOUT THE TRAVELING SALESLADY?, SUPPORT YOUR LOCAL GUNFIGHTER, CANCEL MY RESERVATION, CHARLOTTE'S WEB, BENJI, HOW TO SEDUCE A WOMAN, MURPH THE SURF, HAWMPS, THE SHAGGY D.A., FIRST MONDAY IN OCTOBER; his radio stints included "California Caravan," "The Damon Runyon Theatre," "Family Skeleton," "Father Knows Best," had the title character role in "The Sad Sack"; TV featured him in "Superman," "I Love Lucy,"

"Gunsmoke," plus the TV movies "Vanished," "Emergency," "Chase," "Babe," "The Loneliest Runner," "Testimony of Two Men," "Kill Me If You Can," "I Was a Mail Order Bride".

Vohrer, Alfred

Born 1918, Stuttgart, Germany; died Feb. 1986.

Film Director. Was a director of German westerns from the late 1950s through the 1970s, sometimes using the characters from the books of German author Karl May; films include SCHMUTZIGER ENGEL, MEIN BRAUTE, VERBRECHEN NACH SCHULSCHLUSS, WINNETOU UND SEIN FREUND OLD FIREHAND, THE YOUNG GO WILD, THE DEAD EYES OF LONDON, THE DOOR WITH SEVEN LOCKS, THE INN ON THE RIVER, THE SQUEAKER, FRONTIER HELLCAT, FLAMING FRONTIER.

von Radvanyi, Geza

Born 26 Sept. 1907, Kaschau, Hungary; died 27 Nov. 1986, Budapest, Hungary.

Film Director-Screenwriter. Inspired by French director Julien Duvivier, entered the directing field in the early 1940s working on such films as INFERNO GIALLO, IT HAPPENED IN EUROPE (1947, the only film of his that received worldwide recognition), WOMEN WITHOUT NAMES, L'ETRANGE DESIR DE MONSIEUR BARD, SPECIAL DELIVERY (writer only), DER ARZT VON STALINGRAD, THE HOUSE IN THE TIROL, ANGEL ON EARTH, DAS RIESENRAD, MAEDCHEN IN UNIFORM (1965), IT DOESN'T ALWAYS HAVE TO BE CAVIAR, UNCLE TOM'S CABIN (1969, wrote and directed).

Wallis, Hal B.

(Harold Brent Wallis)

Born 14 Sept. 1898, Chicago, Ill.; died 5 Oct. 1986, Rancho Mirage, Calif.

Film Producer. Family finances forced him to leave school at age 14, taking various jobs, finally landing one as a theater manager, which led to a position in the Warner Bros. publicity department where he rose to department head in three months; in 1928, became production head at First National (after Warners took over), giving him a chance to put out such films as THE DAWN PATROL, LITTLE CAESAR, FIVE STAR FINAL, SALLY (an early Technicolor film); Darryl F. Zanuck joined the studio in 1933 and was given the job of production head, with Wallis being demoted to producer status, during which time he made ONE WAY PASSAGE, I AM A FUGITIVE FROM A CHAIN GANG, MYSTERY OF THE WAX MUSEUM, GOLD DIGGERS OF 1933; when Zanuck left to start 20th Century Pictures a year later, Wallis regained the production head's status, handling such pictures as DANGEROUS (Bette Davis won her first Academy Award for her role in this), CAPTAIN BLOOD, A MIDSUMMER NIGHT'S DREAM (winner of two Oscars), KID GALAHAD, THE LIFE OF EMILE ZOLA, THE PRINCE AND THE PAUPER (1937), THE ADVENTURES OF ROBIN HOOD, THE DAWN PATROL (1938), JEZEBEL, THE SISTERS, DARK VICTORY, JUAREZ, THE OLD MAID, THE PRIVATE LIVES OF ELIZABETH AND ESSEX, THE ROARING TWENTIES, ALL THIS AND HEAVEN TOO, A DISPATCH FROM REUTERS, DR. EHRLICH'S MAGIC BULLET, KNUTE ROCKNE—ALL AMERICAN, SANTA FE TRAIL, THE SEA HAWK, THE BRIDE CAME C.O.D., THE MALTESE FALCON, DIVE BOMBER, THE GREAT LIE, ONE FOOT IN HEAVEN, SERGEANT YORK (coproduced with Jesse L. Lasky), THE SEA WOLF, THE STRAWBERRY BLONDE, CAPTAINS OF THE CLOUDS, CASABLANCA (winner of three Oscars), DESPERATE JOURNEY, KING'S ROW, THE MALE ANIMAL, THE MAN WHO CAME TO DINNER, NOW, VOYAGER, THEY DIED WITH THEIR BOOTS ON, YANKEE DOODLE

DANDY, AIR FORCE, PRINCESS O'ROURKE, THIS IS THE ARMY, WATCH ON THE RHINE, PASSAGE TO MARSEILLE, SARATOGA TRUNK; in 1944 formed his own production company which released through Paramount, making

LOVE LETTERS, YOU CAME ALONG, THE SEARCHING WIND, THE STRANGE LOVE OF MARTHA IVERS, DESERT FURY, SO EVIL MY LOVE, SORRY, WRONG NUMBER, DARK CITY, THE FILE ON THELMA JORDAN, THE FURIES, SEPTEMBER AFFAIR, SAILOR BEWARE, THAT'S MY BOY, JUMPING JACKS, THE STOOGE, THREE RING CIRCUS, ARTISTS AND MODELS, COME BACK LITTLE SHEBA, ABOUT MRS. LESLIE, THE ROSE TATTOO, THE RAINMAKER, GUNFIGHT AT THE O.K. CORRAL, THE SAD SACK, WILD IS THE WIND, HOT SPELL, KING CREOLE, LAST TRAIN FROM GUN HILL, ALL IN A NIGHT'S WORK, BLUE HAWAII, SUMMER AND SMOKE, WIVES AND LOVERS, FUN IN ACAPULCO, BECKET (1964, Brit.), ROUSTABOUT, BOEING BOEING, THE SONS OF KATIE ELDER, BAREFOOT IN THE PARK, FIVE CARD STUD, TRUE GRIT, NORWOOD, ANNE OF THE THOUSAND DAYS, MARY, QUEEN OF SCOTS, RED SKY AT MORNING, THE NELSON AFFAIR, ROOSTER COGBURN; married twice to actresses Louise Fazenda and Martha Hyer; 121 Oscar nominations and 32 Oscars were garnered by the films with which he was associated.

Ward, Charles

Died 11 July 1986, Glendale, Calif., age 33.

Ballet Dancer-Film Actor. Worked as a dancer with the American Ballet Theater, on Broadway in "Dancin'," and appeared in the films THE TURNING POINT and STAYING ALIVE.

Warners, Robert

Died 17 April 1986, New York City, N. Y., age 29.

Stage/Film/TV Singer-Dancer. Made his stage debut in "Dancin'," and appeared in "One More Song/One More Dance," "Woman of the Year," and a national tour of "Chorus Line"; film credits include CAN'T STOP THE MUSIC, THE BEST LITTLE WHOREHOUSE IN TEXAS; appeared on TV in "Night of 100 Stars," "Face of the '80s," and a Miss America pageant.

Watkins, Toney Davis

Died 28 June 1986, Philadelphia, Pa., age 39.

Singer-Film Actor. Started singing at age 16 with Duke Ellington, working as a featured performer

from 1965 to 1974; also worked with Louis Bellson, Lena Horne, and Mercer Ellington; appeared on the Broadway stage in "The Wiz" and on film in HAIR.

Watson, Waldon O.

Died 15 Aug. 1986, Fullerton, Calif., age 79.

Film Sound Director. Worked at Universal Studios from 1959 through 1972 (after entering the industry in 1934 with Republic); earned Oscars for his work on FLOWER DRUM SONG, THAT TOUCH OF MINK, CAPTAIN NEWMAN, M.D., FATHER GOOSE, SHENANDOAH, GAMBIT, THOROUGHLY MODERN MILLIE; also won Oscars for helping develop Sensurround and the acoustical design of a scoring stage at Universal.

Webster, Hugh

Died 31 May 1986, Owen Sound, Ontario, Canada, age 58.

Film/Radio/TV Actor. A native of Scotland, came to Canada in 1948 and worked at odd jobs before entering show business, working in radio, TV, and films; film credits include KING OF THE GRIZZLIES, FORTUNE AND MEN'S EYES, THE REINCARNATE, RIP-OFF, GET BACK, MR. PATMAN, NOTHING PERSONAL, AGENCY, IF YOU COULD SEE WHAT I HEAR, NEVER CRY WOLF.

Welles, Paola Mori

(Countess di Girafalco)

Died 12 Aug. 1986, Las Vegas, Nev., age 57.

Film Actress. The Italian-born widow of Orson Welles; appeared in films such as CROSSED SWORDS and MR. ARKADIN; died of injuries suffered in a car crash.

White, Theodore H.

(Theodore Harold White)

Born 6 May 1915, Boston, Mass.; died 15 May 1986, New York City, N.Y.

Journalist-Author. Graduated from Harvard and went to China on a fellowship, submitting articles to newspapers before accepting a post as the head of the China bureau for *Time* magazine in 1939; continued in that post until the end of WW II, then wrote for many publications, including *The New Republic*, *The Reporter*, *Collier's* and *Harpers*; published his first book in 1946, then wrote the novels *The Mountain Road* (filmed in 1960) and *The View from the 40th Floor*, which gave him financial security for the remainder of his life; followed the John F. Kennedy/Richard M. Nixon election campaign and wrote *Making of the President* in 1960, which won him a pulitzer Prize (and credit for first coining the term "Camelot" to refer to that era; also wrote *Caesar at the Rubicon*, *Breach of Faith: The Fall of Richard Nixon*, and an autobiography, *In Search of History*.

Wieck, Dorothea

Born 3 Jan. 1905, Davos, Switzerland; died 23 Feb. 1986, Berlin, West Germany.

Stage/Film Actress. Started training as an actress in her mid-teens and debuted on the German screen in 1926 in HEIMLICHE SUNDER, followed by such films as KLETTERMAXE, STURMFLUT, VALENCIA, MAEDCHEN IN UNIFORM, ANNA UND ELISABETH; in 1933, came to the U.S. and appeared in CRADLE SONG, MISS FANE'S BABY IS STOLEN; returned to Germany for DER STUDENT VON PRAG, PRIVATE LIFE OF LOUIS XIV, DIE GELBE FLAGGE, ANDREAS SCHLUTER, PANIK, DER GRUNE SALON, HERZ DER WELT, DAS FRAULEIN VON SCUDERI, DAS FORSTHAUS IM TIROL, SCHACHNOVELLE; made two other U.S. films, MAN ON A TIGHTROPE and A TIME TO LOVE AND A TIME TO DIE.

Wilson, Margery

Died 21 Jan. 1986, Alhambra, Calif., age 89.

Silent Film Actress-Director. Debuted as Brown Eyes in INTOLERANCE (1916), followed by THE HONORABLE ALGY, THE PRIMAL LURE, THE SIN YE DO, THE RETURN OF "DRAW" EGAN, THE GUNFIGHTER, WOLF LOWRY, WILD SUMAC, THE BRIDE OF HATE, THE HARD ROCK BREED, THE LAW OF THE GREAT NORTHWEST, MARKED CARDS, OLD LOVES FOR NEW, WITHOUT HONOR, DESERT GOLD, THE BLOOMING ANGEL, THE HOUSE OF WHISPERS; directed, as well as appeared in THAT SOMETHING (1921) and INSINUATION (1922); retired to write self-improvement books; had an autobiography published in the 1950s.

Wilson, Teddy

Born 24 Nov. 1912, Austin, Tex; died 31 July 1986, New Britain, Conn.

Jazz Pianist-Film Actor. Played with Louis Armstrong and Benny Goodman; appeared in

HOLLYWOOD HOTEL and THE BENNY GOODMAN STORY.

Wottitz, Walter

Died 1 Nov. 1986, Brysur-Marne, France, age 75.

Cinematographer. Active in the French film industry since the early 1930s; received an Oscar in tandem with Jean Bourgoin for the second-unit cinematography on THE LONGEST DAY (1962); some of his other films include THE VIKINGS, THE TRAIN, UP FROM THE BEACH, THE UP-

PER HAND, 24 HOURS IN A WOMAN'S LIFE, LEATHER AND NYLON, THOSE DARING YOUNG MEN IN THEIR JAUNTY JALOPIES, A COP, THE CAT, LA CAGE, DIRTY MONEY.

Wright, Tony

Born 1925; died spring, 1986, London, England.

Film Actor. Appeared in French and English films such as BAD BLONDE, followed by THE AMAZING MR. CALLAHAN, JACQUELINE, JUMPING FOR JOY, TIGER IN THE SMOKE, THE SPANIARD'S CURSE, THE BEASTS OF MARSEILLES, BROTH OF A BOY, AND THE SAME TO YOU, FACES IN THE DARK, THE HOUSE IN MARSH ROAD, IN THE WAKE OF A STRANGER, ATTEMPT TO KILL, PORTRAIT OF A SINNER, JOURNEY INTO NOWHERE, THE LIQUIDATOR, THE MAN WHO HAUNTED HIMSELF, KIDNAPPED, THE CREEPING FLESH, HOSTAGES, CAN I COME TOO?.

Wynn, Keenan

(Francis Xavier Aloysius James Jeremiah Keenan Wynn)

Born 27 July 1916, New York, N.Y.; died 14 Oct. 1986, Brentwood, Calif.

Film/Stage/TV/Radio Actor. From a show business family (father was legendary comedian-actor Ed Wynn, mother was actress Hilda Keenan); started as a prop boy in Maine, appeared in stock productions, then went on to Broadway in "Ten Minute Alibi," "Remember the Day," "The Stag at Bay," "The Little Inn," "Feather in the Breeze," "Hitch Your Wagon!," "Two for the Show," "The More the Merrier," "Johnny on the Spot," "Strip for Action" (1942); that same year, signed with MGM (where both father and grandfather [Shakespearean actor Frank Keenan] had preceded him), appearing in NORTHWEST RANGERS (1934), FOR ME AND MY GAL, SOMEWHERE I'LL FIND YOU, LOST ANGEL, MARRIAGE IS A PRIVATE AFFAIR, SEE HERE, PRIVATE HARGROVE, SINCE YOU WENT AWAY, ZIEGFELD FOLLIES, BETWEEN TWO WOMEN, WITHOUT LOVE, WEEKEND AT THE WALDORF, THE CLOCK, THE THRILL OF BRAZIL, THE COCKEYED MIRACLE, EASY TO WED, NO LEAVE, NO LOVE, SONG OF THE THIN MAN, THE HUCKSTERS, MY DEAR SECRETARY, B.F'S DAUGHTER, THE THREE MUSKETEERS, NEPTUNE'S DAUGHTER, THAT MIDNIGHT KISS, LOVE THAT BRUTE, ANNIE GET YOUR GUN, ROYAL WEDDING, THREE LITTLE WORDS, TEXAS CARNIVAL, KIND LADY, MR. IMPERIUM, IT'S A BIG COUNTRY, ANGELS IN THE OUTFIELD, THE BELLE OF NEW YORK, PHONE CALL FROM A STRANGER, FEARLESS FAGAN, SKY FULL OF MOON, DESPERATE SEARCH, HOLIDAY

FOR SINNERS, ALL THE BROTHERS WERE VALIANT, BATTLE CIRCUS, CODE TWO, KISS ME KATE, MEN OF THE FIGHTING LADY, TENNESSEE CHAMP, THE LONG, LONG TRAILER, THE GLASS SLIPPER, THE MARAUDERS, RUNNING WILD, SHACK OUT ON 101, THE NAKED HILLS, THE MAN IN THE GREY FLANNEL SUIT, JOHNNY CONCHO, JOE BUTTERFLY, THE GREAT MAN, THE FUZZY PINK NIGHTGOWN, TOUCH OF EVIL, A TIME TO LOVE AND A TIME TO DIE, THE DEEP SIX, THE PERFECT FURLOUGH, A HOLE IN THE HEAD, THAT KIND OF WOMAN, THE ABSENT-MINDED PROFESSOR (the first of several Disney efforts in which he was invariably a comic villain), KING OF THE ROARING TWENTIES, THE SCARFACE MOB, THE BAY OF SAINT MICHEL, SON OF FLUBBER, DR. STRANGELOVE: OR HOW I LEARNED TO STOP WORRYING AND LOVE THE BOMB, MAN IN THE MIDDLE, NIGHTMARE IN THE SUN, STAGE TO THUNDER ROCK, HONEYMOON HOTEL, THE AMERICANIZATION OF EMILY, THE PATSY, BIKINI BEACH, THE GREAT RACE, PROMISE HER ANYTHING, AROUND THE WORLD UNDER THE SEA, THE NIGHT OF THE GRIZZLY, STAGECOACH (1966), WELCOME TO HARD TIMES, RUN LIKE A THIEF, WARNING SHOT, POINT BLANK, THE WAR WAGON, FINIAN'S RAINBOW, ONCE UPON A TIME IN THE WEST, SMITH, MC KENNA'S GOLD, THE MONITORS, 80 STEPS TO JONAH, VIVA MAX!, LOVING, THE ANIMALS, B.J. LANG PRESENTS, PRETTY MAIDS ALL IN A ROW, JAMAICAN GOLD, BLACK JACK, THE MAN WITH THE ICY EYES, CANCEL MY RESERVATION, THE MECHANIC, SNOWBALL EXPRESS, HOLLYWOOD KNIGHT, NIGHT TRAIN TO TERROR, HERBIE RIDES AGAIN, THE INTERNECINE PROJECT, THE DEVIL'S RAIN, THE LEGEND OF EARL DURAND, THE MAN WHO WOULD NOT DIE, NASHVILLE, A WOMAN FOR ALL MEN, HE IS MY BROTHER, THE KILLER INSIDE ME, THE SHAGGY D.A., HIGH VELOCITY, ORCA, LASERBLAST, THE LUCIFER COMPLEX, COACH, THE DARK, PIRANHA, THE BUSHIDO BLADE, MONSTER, THE CLONUS HORROR, JUST TELL ME WHAT YOU WANT, THE GLOVE, SUNBURN, THE LAST UNICORN (voice only), WAVELENGTH, BEST FRIENDS, HYSTERICAL, BOOMERANG, PRIME RISK, BLACK MOON RISING, TALES FROM THE DARKSIDE, HYPER SAPIEN (his most recent film, unreleased at the time of his death); radio credits include "The Amazing Mr. Smith," "The Goldbergs," "The Undecided Molecule," "The Shadow"; TV credits include "Playhouse 90," "Omnibus," "Requiem for a Heavyweight" (with his father), "The Last Tycoon," "The Troublemakers," "No Time at All," "The Power and the Glory," and the TV movies "The Young Lawyers," "The House on Greenapple Road," "Assault on the Wayne," "Cannon," "Terror in the Sky," "Assignment: Munich," "Hijack," "Hit Lady," "Sex and the Married Woman," "The Bastard," "The Billion Dollar Threat," "Mom, The Wolfman and Me," "The Monkey Mission," "Call to Glory"; enjoyed racing airplanes, autos, and motorcycles, the noise of which caused the actor to go deaf in both ears; two sons are currently in the film industry—Tracy Keenan Wynn is a writer and director, and Edmund Keenan Wynn is an actor and writer.

Yergin, Irving

Died 24 Aug. 1986, Los Angeles, Calif., age 79.

Publicist-Editor-Novelist. Began as a police reporter with the *Chicago Tribune* and the *Chicago Times*, then became a publicist for Warner Bros. in the 1930s; served as editor of *The Hollywood Reporter* for one year, then concentrated on writing stories and screenplays and doing freelance publicity work; wrote the novel that became the film THE MURDER GAME.

AWARDS INDEX

This section covers the major film industry awards given in 1986. Represented here are 24 film festivals from 17 countries and 17 awards listings for industry organizations and professional associations from 7 countries. Whenever possible, we have included nominees as well as winners, and in the case of festivals, we have often listed all competing films. Some festivals are noncompetitive, and in these instances, we have provided as extensive a list of the films presented as possible. We have also noted honorary awards as well as competitive ones, scientific and technical awards as well as artistic ones. Included are the honors awarded by the following festivals: the Asia-Pacific Film Festival, the Berlin International Film Festival, the Cannes Film Festival, the Carthage Film Festival, the Chicago International Film Festival, Dutch Film Days, the Gijon Film Festival for Young People, the Havana International Festival of New Latin American Cinema, Hungaro Film Week, the Karlovy Vary Film Festival, the Leipzig International Documentary and Short Film Festival, the Locarno International Film Festival, the Montreal World Film Festival, the New York Film Festival, the Pula Festival of Yugoslav Feature Films, the Rio De Janeiro International Film Festival, the San Sebastian Film Festival, the Sitges Film Festival, the Taormina Film Festival, the Thessaloniki Greek Film Festival, the Toronto Festival of Festivals, the Valladolid Film Festival, the Venice International Film Festival, and the Women's International Film Festival in Creteil.

In addition to the festivals, the index includes the following: Academy of Motion Picture Arts and Sciences Awards, the American Cinematographers Award, the Australian Film Institute Awards, the Cesar Awards of the French film industry, the David Di Donatello Awards, the Directors Guild of America Awards, the French Film Critics Awards, the Italian Film Journalists Awards, the Genie Awards of the Academy of Canadian Cinema and Television, the German Film Prizes, the Golden Globe Awards, the London Film Critics Awards, the Los Angeles Film Critics Association Awards, the National Board of Review D.W. Griffith Awards, the National Society of Film Critics Awards, the New York Film Critics Awards, and the Writers Guild of America Awards.

59TH AWARDS OF THE ACADEMY OF MOTION PICTURE ARTS AND SCIENCES

Best Picture
CHILDREN OF A LESSER GOD, PAR. Produced by Burt Sugarman and Patrick Palmer.
HANNAH AND HER SISTERS, Orion. Produced by Robert Greenhut.
THE MISSION, WB. Produced by Fernando Ghia and David Puttnam.
PLATOON, Orion. Produced by Arnold Kopelson.
A ROOM WITH A VIEW (Brit.), Cinecom. Produced by Ismail Merchant.

Best Actor
Dexter Gordon for 'ROUND MIDNIGHT (U.S./Fr.).
Bob Hoskins for MONA LISA (Brit.).
William Hurt for CHILDREN OF A LESSER GOD.
Paul Newman for THE COLOR OF MONEY.
James Woods for SALVADOR.

Best Actress
Jane Fonda for THE MORNING AFTER.
Marlee Matlin for CHILDREN OF A LESSER GOD.
Sissy Spacek for CRIMES OF THE HEART.
Kathleen Turner for PEGGY SUE GOT MARRIED.
Sigourney Weaver for ALIENS.

Best Supporting Actor
Tom Berenger for PLATOON.
Michael Caine for HANNAH AND HER SISTERS.
Willem Dafoe for PLATOON.
Denholm Elliott for A ROOM WITH A VIEW.
Dennis Hopper for HOOSIERS.

Best Supporting Actress
Tess Harper for CRIMES OF THE HEART.
Piper Laurie for CHILDREN OF A LESSER GOD.
Mary Elizabeth Mastrantonio for THE COLOR OF MONEY.
Maggie Smith for A ROOM WITH A VIEW.
Dianne Wiest for HANNAH AND HER SISTERS.

Best Direction
Woody Allen for HANNAH AND HER SISTERS.
David Lynch for BLUE VELVET.
Roland Joffe for THE MISSION.
James Ivory for A ROOM WITH A VIEW.
Oliver Stone for PLATOON.

Best Screenplay Based on Material from Another Medium
CHILDREN OF A LESSER GOD by Hesper Anderson and Mark Medoff.
THE COLOR OF MONEY by Richard Price.
CRIMES OF THE HEART by Beth Henley.
A ROOM WITH A VIEW by Ruth Prawer Jhabvala.
STAND BY ME by Raynold Gideon and Bruce A. Evans.

Best Screenplay Written Directly for the Screen
CROCODILE DUNDEE by Paul Hogan, Ken Shadie, and John Cornell, from the story by Paul Hogan.
HANNAH AND HER SISTERS by Woody Allen.
MY BEAUTIFUL LAUNDRETTE (Brit.) by Hanif Kureishi.

PLATOON by Oliver Stone.
SALVADOR by Oliver Stone and Richard Boyle.

Best Cinematography
THE MISSION, Chris Menges.
PEGGY SUE GOT MARRIED, Jordan Cronenweth.
PLATOON, Robert Richardson.
A ROOM WITH A VIEW, Tony Pierce-Roberts.
STAR TREK IV: THE VOYAGE HOME, Don Peterman.

Best Song
"Glory of Love" from THE KARATE KID PART II. Music by Peter Cetera and David Foster; lyrics by Cetera and Diane Nini.
"Life in a Looking Glass" from THAT'S LIFE! Music by Henry Mancini; lyrics by Leslie Bricusse.
"Mean Green Mother From Outer Space" from THE LITTLE SHOP OF HORRORS. Music by Alan Menken; lyrics by Howard Ashman.
"Somewhere Out There" from AN AMERICAN TAIL. Music by James Horner and Barry Mann; lyrics by Cynthia Weil.
"Take My Breath Away" from TOP GUN. Music by Giorgio Moroder; lyrics by Tom Whitlock.

Best Original Score
Jerry Goldsmith for HOOSIERS.
Herbie Hancock for 'ROUND MIDNIGHT (U.S./Fr.).
James Horner for ALIENS.
Ennio Morricone for THE MISSION.
Leonard Rosenman for STAR TREK IV: THE VOYAGE HOME.

Best Film Editing
ALIENS, Ray Lovejoy.
HANNAH AND HER SISTERS, Susan E. Morse.
THE MISSION, Jim Clark.
PLATOON, Claire Simpson.
TOP GUN, Billy Weber and Chris Lebenzon.

Best Art Direction—Set Decoration
ALIENS, Peter Lamont; Crispan Sallis.
THE COLOR OF MONEY, Boris Leven; Karen A. O'Hara.
HANNAH AND HER SISTERS, Stuart Wurtzel; Carol Joffe.
THE MISSION, Stuart Craig; Jack Stephens.
A ROOM WITH A VIEW, Gianni Quaranta and Brian Ackland-Snow; Brian Savegar and Elio Altramura.

Best Costume Design
THE MISSION, Enrico Sabbatini.
OTELLO (Ital.), Anna Anni.
PEGGY SUE GOT MARRIED, Theadora Van Runkle.
PIRATES, Anthony Powell.
A ROOM WITH A VIEW, Jenny Beavan and John Bright.

Best Makeup
THE CLAN OF THE CAVE BEAR, Michael G. Westmore and Michele Burke.
THE FLY, Chris Walas and Stephan Dupuis.
LEGEND, Rob Bottin and Peter Robb-King.

Best Sound
ALIENS, Graham V. Harttone, Nicolas Le Messurier, Michael A. Carter, and Roy Charman.
HEARTBREAK RIDGE, Les Fresholtz, Dick Alexander, Vern Pooer, and William Nelson.
PLATOON, John (Doc) Wilkinson, Richard Rogers, Charles (Bud) Grenzbach, and Simon Kaye.
STAR TREK IV: THE VOYAGE HOME, Terry Porter, Dave Hudson, Mel Metcalfe, and Gene S. Cantamessa.
TOP GUN, Donald O. Mithcell, Kevin O'Connell, Rick Kline, and William B. Kaplan.

Best Sound Effects Editing
ALIENS, Don Sharpe.
STAR TREK IV: THE VOYAGE HOME, Mark Mangini.
TOP GUN, Cecelia Hall and George Watters II.

Best Visual Effects
ALIENS, Robert Skotak, Stan Winston, John Richardson, and Suzanne Benson.
LITTLE SHOP OF HORRORS, Lyle Conway, Bran Ferren, and Martin Gutteridge.
POLTERGEIST II: THE OTHER SIDE, Richard Edlund, John Bruno, Garry Waller, and William Neil.

Best Foreign-Language Film
THE ASSAULT (Neth.), Fons Rademakers.
BETTY BLUE (Fr.), Jean-Jacques Beineix.
THE DECLINE OF THE AMERICAN EMPIRE (Can.), Denys Arcand.
MY SWEET LITTLE VILLAGE (Czech.), Jiri Menzel.
38 (Aust.), Wolfgang Gluck.

Short Subjects
Best Animated Film
THE FROG, THE DOG AND THE DEVIL (New Zealand), New Zealand National Film Unit. Produced by Hugh MacDonald and Martin Townsend.
A GREEK TRAGEDY, CineTe pvba. Produced by Linda Van Tulden and Willem Thijssen.
LUXO JR., Pixar. Produced by John Lasseter and William Reeves.

Best Live-Action Film

EXIT (Ital.), RAI-UNO. Produced by Stefano Reali and Pino Quartullo.
LOVE STRUCK, Rainy Day. Produced by Fredda Weiss.
PRECIOUS IMAGES, Calliope. Produced by Chuck Workman.

Documentaries

Best Short Documentary
DEBONAIR DANCERS. Produced by Alison Nigh-Strelich.
THE MASTERS OF DISASTER, Indiana University Audio Visual Center.
Produced by Sonya Friedman.
RED GROOMS: SUNFLOWER IN A HOTHOUSE, Polaris Entertainment.
Produced by Thomas L. Neff and Madeline Bell.
SAM. Produced by Aaron D. Weisblatt.
"WOMEN—FOR AMERICA, FOR THE WORLD," *Educational Film and Video Project. Produced by Vivienne Verdon-Roe.*

Best Feature Documentary
ARTIE SHAW: TIME IS ALL YOU'VE GOT, Bridge. Produced by Brigitte Berman.
CHILE: HASTA CUANDO? Produced by David Bradbury.
DOWN AND OUT IN AMERICA. Produced by Joseph Feury and Milton Justice.
ISSAC IN AMERICA: A JOURNEY WITH ISSAC BASHEVIS SINGER, Amram Nowak Associates. Produced by Kirk Simon.
WITNESS TO APARTHEID, Developin News. Produced by Sharon I. Sopher.

Honorary Award

Ralph Bellamy, for his unique artistry and his distinguished service to the profession of acting.

Irving G. Thalberg Memorial Award

Steven Spielberg.

Scientific and Technical Awards

Scientific and Engineering Award
Bran Ferren, Charles Harrison, and Kenneth Wisner of Associates & Ferren, for the concept and design of an advanced optical printer.
Richard Benjamin Grant and Ron Grant of Auricle Control Systems, for their invention of the Film Composer's Time Processor.
MGM Laboratories and Technical Film Systems, for the design and engineering of a continuous Feed Printer.
Robert Greenberg, Joel Hynek, and Eugene Mamut, of R/Greenberg Associates, and Dr. Alfred Thumin, Elan Lipschitz, and Darryl A. Armour of the Oxberry Division of Richmark Camera Service, for the design and development of the RGA/Oxberry Compu-Quad Special Effects Optical Printer.
Dr. Fritz Sennheiser of Sennheiser Electronic, for the invention of an interference tube directional microphone.
Boss Film, for the design and development of a zoom aerial (ZAP) 65m optical printer.
William L. Frederick and Hal Needham, for the design and development of the Shotmaker Elite camera car and crane.
Technical Achievement Award
Lee Electric (Lighting) Ltd., for the design and development of an electronic, flicker-free, discharge lamp control system.
Peter D. Parks of Oxford Scientific Films' Image Quest Division, for the development of a live aerocompositor for special effects photography.
Matt Sweeney and Lucinda Strub, for the development of an automatic capsule gun for motion picture special effects.
Carl E. Holmes of Carl E. Holmes Co. and Alexander Bryce of the Burbank Studios, for the development of a mobile D.C. power supply unit for motion picture production photography.
Bran Ferren of Associates & Ferren, for the invention of a laser synchro-cue system for applications in the motion picture industry.
John L. Baptista of MGM Laboratories, for the development and installation of a computerized silver recovery operation.
David W. Samuelson, for the development of programs incorporated into a portable computer for motion picture cinematographers based on new algorithms developed with W.B. Pollar.
Hal Landaker and Alan Landaker of the Burbank Studios, for the development of the Beat System low-frequency cue track for motion picture production sound recording.
Medal of Commendation
E.M. (Al) Lewis in appreciation for outstanding service and dedication in upholding the standards of the Academy of Motion Picture Arts and Sciences.

1ST AMERICAN SOCIETY OF CINEMATOGRAPHERS' AWARD

Nominees

James Crabe for THE KARATE KID PART II.
Jordan Cronenweth for PEGGY SUE GOT MARRIED.
Christopher Menges for THE MISSION.
Tony Pierce-Roberts for A ROOM WITH A VIEW.
Don Peterman for STAR TREK IV: THE VOYAGE HOME.

31ST ASIA-PACIFIC FILM FESTIVAL

Best Film

MEMENTOS (Indonesia.), Teguh Karya.

Best Direction

Chang Yi for KUEI MEI, A WOMAN (Taipei).

Best Actress

Lee Mi-suk for PPONG (S.K.).

Best Actor

Minoru Chiaki for GREY SUNSET (Jap.).

Best Supporting Actress

Betty King for MY NAME AIN'T SUZIE (Hong Kong).

Best Supporting Actor

Krailas Kriankrai for KHAMSINGH—THE FIGHTER (Thai.).

Best Cinematography

George Kamarullah for MEMENTOS (Indo.).

Best Screenplay

Ikuo Sekimoto and Kaoru Kaisuragi for FOUR SISTERS (Jap.).

Best Music

Choi Chang-kwon for PPONG (S.K.).

Best Editing

Jphari Ibrahim for JASMIN 2 (Malaysia).

Best Sound Effects

Ng Kwokwah for DREAM LOVERS (Hong Kong).

Best Art Direction

MAYURI (India).

Best Short Film

TAMAN NEGARA (Malaysia), produced by Filem Negara.

Special Journalist's Award

Hwu In-tzyy for REUNION (Taipei).

Special Award of Jury

THE TIME TO LIVE AND THE TIME TO DIE (Taiwan), Hou Hsiao Hsien.

Special Acting Awards

Kim God-gi for GOD-GI (S.K.).
Wong Yue Man for GOODBYE MOTHER (Hong Kong).
Season Ma for SILENT LOVE (Hong Kong).

AUSTRALIAN FILM INSTITUTE AWARDS

Best Film

THE FRINGE DWELLERS, produced by Sue Milliken.
MALCOLM, produced by Nadia Tass and David Parker.
THE MORE THINGS CHANGE, produced by Jim Robb.
SHORT CHANGED, produced by Ross Matthews.

Best Direction

Bruce Beresford for THE FRINGE DWELLERS.
Paul Cox for CACTUS.
George Ogilvie for SHORT CHANGED.
Nadia Tass for MALCOLM.

Best Actor

Colin Friels for MALCOLM.
Robert Menzies for CACTUS.
Barry Otto for THE MORE THINGS CHANGE.
Reb Brown for DEATH OF A SOLDIER.

Best Actress

Helen Buday for FOR LOVE ALONE.
Judy Davis for KANGAROO.
Judy Morris for THE MORE THINGS CHANGE.
Justine Saunders for THE FRINGE DWELLERS.

Best Supporting Actor

Maurie Fields for DEATH OF A SOLDIER.
John Hargreaves for MALCOLM.
Mark Little for SHORT CHANGED.
John Walton for KANGAROO.

Best Supporting Actress

Kylie Belling for THE FRINGE DWELLERS.
Lindy Davies for MALCOLM.
Victoria Longley for THE MORE THINGS CHANGE.
Kerry Walker for TWELFTH NIGHT.

Best Original Screenplay

Robert Merritt for SHORT CHANGED.
David Parker for MALCOLM.
Yahoo Serious and David Roach for YOUNG EINSTEIN.
Moya Wood for THE MORE THINGS CHANGE.

Best Adapted Screenplay

Bruce Beresford and Rhoisin Beresford for THE FRINGE DWELLERS.
Peter Gawler for PLAYING BEATIE BOW.
Evans Jones for KANGAROO.
Stephen Wallace for FOR LOVE ALONE.

Best Cinematography

Russell Boyd for BURKE AND WILLS.
Jeff Darling for YOUNG EINSTEIN.
Peter James for THE RIGHT HAND MAN.
Don McAlpine for THE FRINGE DWELLERS.

Best Original Music

Peter Best for THE MORE THINGS CHANGE.
William Motzing and Martin Armiger for YOUNG EINSTEIN.
Nathan Waks for FOR LOVE ALONE.

Best Costume Design
George Liddle for BURKE AND WILLS and PLAYING BEATIE BOW.
Terry Ryan for KANGAROO.
Jeannie Tate for FOR LOVE ALONE.

Best Editing
Richard Francis-Bruce for SHORT CHANGED.
Andrew Prowse for PLAYING BEATIE BOW.
Ken Sallows for MALCOLM.
Tim Wellburn for THE FRINGE DWELLERS.

Best Production Design
Neil Angwin for THE RIGHT-HAND MAN.
Larry Eastwood for DEAD-END DRIVE-IN.
George Liddle for PLAYING BEATIE BOW.
John Stoddart for FOR LOVE ALONE.

Best Sound
BURKE AND WILLS, Syd Butterworth, Phil Haywood, Ron Purvis, and Lee Smith.
MALCOLM, Roger Savage, Craig Carter, Dean Gawen, and Paul Clark.
PLAYING BEATIE BOW, Rob Cutcher, Frank Lipson, Glen Newman, James Currie, Peter Smith, and David Harrison.
YOUNG EINSTEIN, Roger Savage, Bruce Lamshed, Steve Burgess, Geoff Grist, Annie Breskin, and Peter Fenton.

Best Documentary
CHILE: HASTA CUANDO?, David Bradbury.

Short Film Awards
Best Fiction Film
THE MOONCALF, Ian Rochford.
Best Experimental Film
MY LIFE WITHOUT STEVE, Gillian Leahy.
Best Animated Film
THE HUGE ADVENTURES OF TREVOR, A CAT, John Taylor.

Raymond Longford Award for longtime contribution to the Australian Film Industry:
Barry Jones.

Special Achievement Award
CROCODILE DUNDEE, for its international contribution to the Australian Film Industry.

36TH BERLIN INTERNATIONAL FILM FESTIVAL

Prizes of the International Jury
Golden Bear
STAMMHEIM (Ger.), Reinhard Hauff.
Silver Bears
Special Jury Prize
THE MASS IS OVER (It.), Nanni Moretti.
Best Direction
Georgi Shengelaya for A YOUNG COMPOSER'S ODYSSEY (USSR).
Best Actress
Marcelia Cartaxo for HOUR OF THE STAR (Braz.).
Charlotte Valandrey for RED KISS (Fr.).
Best Actor
Tuncel Kurtiz for THE SMILE OF THE LAMB (Israel).
Special Prize for Outstanding Style
YARI NO GONZA (Jap.), Masahiro Shinoda.
Outstanding Single Achievement
Gabriel Beristain for the photography of CARAVAGGIO (Brit.).
Special Mention
PASO DOBLE (Rum.), Dan Pita.
Golden Bear for Short Film
TOM GOES TO THE BAR (U.S.), Dean Parisot.
Silver Bear for Short Film
AUGUSTA FEEDS (Hung.), Csaba Varga.

FIPRESCI Prizes
Best in Competition
STAMMHEIM (Ger.), Reinhard Hauff.
Best in Forum
SHOAH (Fr.), Claude Lanzmann.
Special Mentions
A TIME TO LIVE AND A TIME TO DIE (Taiwan), Hou Hsiao-Hsien.
THE WOMAN FROM THE PROVINCES (Pol.), Andrezej Baranski.
Competing Films
ANNE TRISTER (Can.), Lea Pool.
AT CLOSE RANGE (U.S.), James Foley.
AUSTRALIAN DREAM (Aus.), Jacki McKimmie.
BERLIN AFFAIR (It./Ger.), Liliana Cavani.
CAMORRA (It.), Lina Wertmuller.
CARAVAGGIO (Brit.), Derek Jarman.
ELSO KETSZAZ EVEM (Hung.), Gyula Maar.
FLIGHT NORTH (Ger./Fin.), Ingemo Engstrom.
GILSODOM (North Korea), Im Kwon-Taak.
HEIDENLOCHER (Aust./Ger.), Wolfram Paulus.
HOUR OF THE STAR (Braz.), Suzana Amaral.
HOUSE BY THE RIVER (E. Ger.), Roland Graf.
L'AUBE (Fr.), Miklos Jancso.
LOVE ME! (Swed.), Kay Pollack.

MANIA (Gr.), George Panoussopoulos.
THE MASS IS OVER (It.), Nanni Moretti.
MON BEAU-FRERE A TUE SOEUR (Fr.), Jacques Rouffio.
PASO DOBLE (Rum.), Dan Pita.
RED KISSES (Fr./Ger.), Vera Belmont.
SKUPA MOYA, SKUPI MOY (Bulgaria), Eduard Zahariev.
THE SMILE OF THE LAMB (Israel), Shimon Dotan.
STAMMHEIM (Ger.), Reinhard Hauff.
TEO EL PELIRROJO (Span.), Paco Lucio.
YARI NO GONZA (Jap.), Masahiro Shinoda
A YOUNG COMPOSER'S ODYSSEY (USSR), Georgi Shengelaya.

BRITISH ACADEMY OF FILM AND TELEVISION AWARDS

Best Picture
HANNAH AND HER SISTERS (U.S.), Woody Allen.
MISSION, Roland Joffe.
MONA LISA, Neil Jordan.
A ROOM WITH A VIEW, James Ivory.

Best Actor
Woody Allen for HANNAH AND HER SISTERS (U.S.).
Michael Caine for HANNAH AND HER SISTERS (U.S.).
Paul Hogan for CROCODILE DUNDEE (Aus.).
Bob Hoskins for MONA LISA.

Best Actress
Mia Farrow for HANNAH AND HER SISTERS (U.S.).
Meryl Streep for OUT OF AFRICA (U.S.).
Maggie Smith for A ROOM WITH A VIEW.
Cathy Tyson for MONA LISA.

Best Direction
Woody Allen for HANNAH AND HER SISTERS (U.S.).
Roland Joffe for THE MISSION.
Neil Jordan for MONA LISA.
James Ivory for A ROOM WITH A VIEW.

Best Original Screenplay
CROCODILE DUNDEE (Aus.) by Paul Hogan, Ken Shadie, and John Cornell.
HANNAH AND HER SISTERS (U.S.) by Woody Allen.
THE MISSION by Robert Bolt.
MONA LISA by Neil Jordan and David Leland.

Best Adapted Screenplay
CHILDREN OF A LESSER GOD (U.S.) by Hesper Anderson and Mark Medoff.
THE COLOR PURPLE (U.S.) by Menno Meyjes.
OUT OF AFRICA (U.S.) by Kurt Luedtke.
RAN (Jap./Fr.) by Akira Kurosawa, Hideo Oguni, and Masato Ide.
A ROOM WITH A VIEW by Ruth Prawer Jhabvala.

Best Supporting Actor
Ray McAnally for THE MISSION.
Klaus Maria Brandauer for OUT OF AFRICA (U.S.).
Simon Callow for A ROOM WITH A VIEW.
Denholm Elliott for A ROOM WITH A VIEW.

Best Supporting Actress
Rosanna Arquette for AFTER HOURS (U.S.).
Judi Dench for A ROOM WITH A VIEW.
Barbara Hershey for HANNAH AND HER SISTERS (U.S.).
Rosemary Leach for A ROOM WITH A VIEW.

Best Musical Score
THE MISSION, Ennio Morricone.
OUT OF AFRICA (U.S.), John Barry.
A ROOM WITH A VIEW, Richard Robbins.
'ROUND MIDNIGHT (U.S./Fr.), Herbie Hancock.

Best Cinematography
THE MISSION, Chris Menges.
OUT OF AFRICA (U.S.), David Watkins.
RAN (Jap./Fr.), Takao Saito and Masaharu Ueda.
A ROOM WITH A VIEW, Tony Pierce-Roberts.

Best Production Design
ALIENS (U.S.), Peter Lamont.
THE MISSION, Stuart Craig.
RAN (Jap./Fr.), Yoshiro Muraki and Shinobu Muraki.
A ROOM WITH A VIEW, Gianni Quaranta and Brian Ackland-Snow.

Best Costume Design
THE MISSION, Enrico Sabbatini.
OUT OF AFRICA (U.S.), Milena Canonero.
RAN (Jap./Fr.), Emi Wada.
A ROOM WITH A VIEW, Jenny Bevan and John Bright.

Best Editing
HANNAH AND HER SISTERS, Susan E. Morse.
THE MISSION, Jim Clark.
MONA LISA, Lesley Walker.
A ROOM WITH A VIEW, Humphrey Dixon.

Best Sound
ALIENS (U.S.).

DREAMCHILD.
LABYRINTH (U.S.).
THE MISSION.

Best Makeup
ALIENS (U.S.), Peter Robb-King.
DREAMCHILD, Jenny Shircore.
RAN (Jap./Fr.), Shohichiro Meda, Tameyuki Aimi, Chihako Naito, and Noriko Takemizawa.

Best Foreign Language Film
BETTY BLUE (Fr.), Jean-Jacques Beneix.
GINGER AND FRED (It.), Federico Fellini.
OTELLO (It.), Franco Zefferelli.
RAN (Jap.), Akira Kurosawa.

British Film Institute Fellowship Award
Federico Fellini.

39TH CANNES INTERNATIONAL FILM FESTIVAL

Prizes of the International Jury
Golden Palm
THE MISSION (Brit.), Roland Joffe.
Special Jury Prize
THE SACRIFICE (Swed.), Andrei Tarkovsky.
Jury Prize
THERESE (Fr.), Alain Cavalier.
Best Director
Martin Scorsese for AFTER HOURS (U.S.).
Best Actor
Bob Hoskins for MONA LISA (Brit.).
Michel Blanc for TENUE DE SOIREE (Fr.).
Best Actress
Barbara Sukowa for ROSA LUXEMBURG (Ger.).
Fernanda Torres for EU SEI QUE VOU TE AMAR (Braz.).
Best Artistic Contribution
Sven Nykvist for the cinematography of THE SACRIFICE (Swed.).
Camera D'Or for Best First Feature
Claire Devers for BLACK AND WHITE (Fr.).
Short Films
Golden Palm
PEEL (Aus.), Jane Campion.
Jury Prize
GAIDOUK (USSR), Y. Katsap and L. Gorokhov.
THE LITTLE MAGICIANS (Switz.), Vincent Mercier and Yves Robert.

FIPRESCI Prizes
Best Competing Film
THE SACRIFICE (Swed.), Andrei Tarkovsky.
Best Non-competing Film
THE DECLINE OF THE AMERICAN EMPIRE (Can.), Denys Arcand.

Ecumenical Prize
THE SACRIFICE (Swed.), Andrei Tarkovsky.
Ecumenical Special Mention
THERESE (Fr.), Alain Cavalier.

Competing Films
AFTER HOURS (U.S.), Martin Scorsese.
BORIS GODOUNOV (USSR), Sergei Bondarchuk.
DOWN BY LAW (U.S.), Jim Jarmusch.
EU SEI QUE VOU TE AMAR (Braz.), Arnaldo Jabor.
FOOL FOR LOVE (U.S.), Robert Altman.
THE FRINGE DWELLERS (Aus.), Bruce Beresford.
GENESIS (India/Fr./Switz.), Mrinal Sen.
I LOVE YOU (It.), Marco Ferreri.
THE LAST IMAGE (Fr./Tunisia), Mohammed Lakhdar-Hamina.
MAX MON AMOUR (Fr.), Nagisa Oshima.
MENAGE (Fr.), Bertrand Blier.
THE MISSION (Brit.), Roland Joffe.
MONA LISA (Brit.), Neil Jordan.
OTELLO (It.), Franco Zeffirelli.
POBRE MARIPOSA (Arg.), Raul de la Torre.
ROSA LUXEMBURG (Ger.), Margarethe von Trotta.
RUNAWAY TRAIN (U.S.), Andrei Konchalovsky.
THE SACRIFICE (Swed.), Andrei Tarkovsky.
SCENE OF THE CRIME (Fr.), Andre Techine.
THERESE (Fr.), Alain Cavalier.

11TH CARTHAGE FILM FESTIVAL

Feature Films
Gold Tanit
MAN OF ASHES (Tunisia), Nouri Bouzid.
Silver Tanit
TAHO UNET AL SAYED FABRE (Algeria), Ahmed Rachedi.
Bronze Tanit
NYAMANTON (Mali), Cheik Omar Sissoko.
Best Actor
Khald Ksouri for MAN OF ASHES (Tunisia).
Best Actress
Naila El Atrache for WHAT HAPPENED NEXT YEAR (Syria).

Short Films
Gold Tanit
RAPHIA (Gabon), Paul Mouketa.
Silver Tanit
HAMMAM DHAHAB (Tunisia), Moncef Dhouib.
Bronze Tanit
DAY BY DAY (Syria), Oussama Mohamed.
Opera Prima
LE SINGE FOU (Gabon), Henry Josef Koumba.

12TH CESAR AWARDS OF THE FRENCH FILM INDUSTRY

Best Film/Best Director
BETTY BLUE, Jean-Jacques Beineix. Produced by Claudie Ossard.
JEAN DE FLORETTE, Claude Berri. Produced by Berri.
MELO, Alain Resnais. Produced by Marin Karmitz.
MENAGE, Bertrand Blier. Produced by Rene Cleitman.
THERESE, Alain Cavalier. Produced by Maurice Bernart.

Best First Feature
BLACK AND WHITE, Claire Dever.
BLACK MIC-MAC, Thomas Guilou.
I HATE ACTORS, Gerard Krawczyk.
LA FEMME DE MA VIE, Regis Wargnier.

Best Foreign Film
AFTER HOURS (U.S.), Martin Scorsese.
HANNAH AND HER SISTERS (U.S.), Woody Allen.
THE MISSION (Brit.), Roland Joffe.
THE NAME OF THE ROSE (U.S.), Jean-Jacques Annaud.
OUT OF AFRICA (U.S.), Sydney Pollack.

Best Actor
Jean-Hugues Anglade for BETTY BLUE.
Daniel Auteuil for JEAN DE FLORETTE.
Michel Blanc for MENAGE.
Andre Dussollier for MELO.
Christophe Malavoy for LA FEMME DE MA VIE.

Best Actress
Sabine Azema for MELO.
Juiliette Binoche for MAUVAIS SANG.
Jane Birkin for LA FEMME DE MA VIE.
Beatrice Dalle for BETTY BLUE.
Miou-Miou for MENAGE.

Best Supporting Actor
Pierre Arditi for MELO.
Jean Carmet for THE FUGITIVES.
Gerard Darmon for BETTY BLUE.
Claude Pieplu for LE PALTOQUET.
Jean-Louis Trintignant for LA FEMME DE MA VIE.

Best Supporting Actress
*Emmanuelle Beart for JEAN DE FLORETTE.**
Clementine Celarie for BETTY BLUE.
Danielle Darrieux for SCENE OF THE CRIME.
Marie Dubois for DESCENTE AUX ENFERS.
Jeanne Moreau for LE PALTOQUET.

Best Young Male Hopeful
Isaach de Bankole for BLACK MIC-MAC.
Cris Campion for PIRATES.
Jean-Philippe Ecoffey for GARDIEN DE LA NUIT.
Remi Martin for FAMILY COUNCIL.

Best Young Female Hopeful
Marianne Basler for ROSA LA ROSE, FILLE PUBLIQUE.
Dominique Blanc for LA FEMME DE MA VIE.
Julie Delpy for MAUVAIS SANG.
Catherine Mouchet for THERESE.

Best Screenplay
THE FUGITIVES by Francis Veber.
JEAN DE FLORETTE by Claude Berri and Gerard Brach.
MENAGE by Bertr and Blier.
THERESE by Alain Cavalier and Camille de Casabianca.

Best Score
Serge Gainsbourg for MENAGE.
Herbie Hancock for 'ROUND MIDNIGHT.
Jean-Claude Petit for JEAN DE FLORETTE.
Gabriel Yared for BETTY BLUE.

Best Cinematography
Jean-Yves Escoffer for MAUVAIS SANG.
Bruno Nuytten for JEAN DE FLORETTE.
Philippe Rousselot for THERESE.
Charlie Van Damme for MELO.

Best Production Design
Bernard Evein for THERESE.
Pierre Guffroy for PIRATES.
Jacques Saulnier for MELO.
Alexandre Trauner for 'ROUND MIDNIGHT.

Best Sound
Bernard Bats and Dominique Hennequin for MENAGE.
Michel Desrois and William Flageollet for 'ROUND MIDNIGHT.
Pierre Gamet and Dominique Hennequin for JEAN DE FLORETTE.
Alain Lachassagne and Dominique Dalmasso for THERESE.

Best Editing
Isabelle Dedieu for THERESE.
Claudine Merlin for MENAGE.
Monique Prim for BETTY BLUE.
Armand Psenny for 'ROUND MIDNIGHT.

Best Costumes
Yvette Bonnay for THERESE.
Catherine Leterrier for MELO.
Anthony Powell for PIRATES.

Best Short Film
LA COULA, Roger Guillot.

Best Poster
BETTY BLUE, designed by Christian Blondel.

Special Career Cesar
Jean-Luc Godard.

*Beart actually appears in MANON DES SOURCES, the sequel to JEAN DE FLORETTE, though both films were released as one in France under the latter title.

22ND CHICAGO INTERNATIONAL FILM FESTIVAL

Prizes of the International Jury
Gold Hugo
WELCOME IN VIENNA (Aust.), Axel Corti.
Silver Hugo
DECLINE OF THE AMERICAN EMPIRE (Can.), Denys Arcand.
THERESE (Fr.), Alain Cavalier.
Gold Plaques
Special Jury Prize
COMING UP ROSES (Wales), Stephen Bayly.
Best Performance
Anna Linden for LOVE ME!
Best Script
Geza Beremenya and Ferenc Andras for THE GREAT GENERATION (Hung.).
Silver Plaque
Best First Feature
BAD COMPANY (Arg.), Jose Santiso.

Oscar Getz World Peace Medal
GILSODOM (S. K.), Im Kwon-Taek.

Most Popular Film
ANOTHER LOVE STORY (Arg.), Americo Ortiz de Zarate.

Competing Films
ABEL (Neth.), Alex van Warmerdam.
BACKLASH (Aus.), Bill Bennett.
BAR 51 (Israel), Amos Guttman.
CHIDAMBARAM (India), G. Aravindan.
COMING UP ROSES (Wales), Stephen Bayly.
THE DECLINE OF THE AMERICAN EMPIRE (Can.), Denys Arcand.
DREAM OF NORTHERN LIGHTS (Norway), Lasse Glomm.
FLIGHT NORTH (Fin./Ger.), Ingemo Engstrom.
GILSODOM (S.K.), Im Kwon-Taek.
THE GREAT GENERATION (Hung.), Ferenc Andras.
THE JOURNEY (Ger.), Markus Imhoof.
LITTLE FLAMES (It.), Peter Del Monte.
LOVE ME! (Swed.), Kay Pollak.
MAN LOOKING SOUTHEAST (Arg.), Eliseo Subiela.
THE MASS IS OVER (It.), Nanni Moretti.
MISS MARY (Arg.), Maria Luisa Bemberg.
RAMS AND MAMMOTHS (Yugo.), Filip Robar-Dorin.
SHOOT FOR THE SUN (Scotland), Ian Knox.
THERESE (Fr.), Alain Cavalier.
WELCOME IN VIENNA (Aust.), Axel Corti.
A YOUNG COMPOSER'S ODYSSEY (USSR), Georgi Shengelaya.

31ST DAVID DI DONATELLO AWARDS

Awards for Italian Films
Best Picture
GINGER AND FRED, Federico Fellini.
LET'S HOPE IT'S A GIRL, Mario Monicelli.
THE MASS IS OVER, Nanni Moretti.
Best Direction
Federico Fellini for GINGER AND FRED.
Mario Monicelli for LET'S HOPE IT'S A GIRL.
Nanni Moretti for THE MASS IS OVER.
Best Actor
Nanni Moretti for THE MASS IS OVER.
Marcello Mastroianni for GINGER AND FRED.
Francesco Nuti for BLAME IT ON PARADISE.
Best Actress
Giulietta Masina for GINGER AND FRED.

Angela Molina for CAMORRA.
Liv Ullmann for LET'S HOPE IT'S A GIRL.
Best Supporting Actor
Bernard Blier for LET'S HOPE IT'S A GIRL.
Ferruccio De Ceresa for THE MASS IS OVER.
Franco Fabrizi for GINGER AND FRED.
Philippe Noiret for LET'S HOPE IT'S A GIRL.
Best Supporting Actress
Athina Cenci for LET'S HOPE IT'S A GIRL.
Isa Danieli for CAMORRA.
Stefania Sandrelli for LET'S HOPE IT'S A GIRL.
Best Producer
Giovanni Di Clemente for LET'S HOPE IT'S A GIRL.
Best Cinematography
Giuseppe Lanci for CAMORRA.
Best Screenplay
LET'S HOPE IT'S A GIRL by Mario Monicelli, Tullio Pinelli, Suso Cecchi d'Amici, Leonardo Benvenuti, and Piero De Bernardi.
Best Costume
Danilo Donati for GINGER AND FRED.
Best Set Design
Enrico Job for CAMORRA.
Best Score
Nicola Piovani for GINGER AND FRED.
Riz Ortolani for GRADUATION PARTY.
Best Editing
Ruggero Mastroianni for LET'S HOPE IT'S A GIRL.
Best First Film
Enrico Montesano for I LIKE MYSELF.

Foreign Film Awards
Best Picture
OUT OF AFRICA (U.S.), Sydney Pollack.
RAN (Jap./Fr.), Akira Kurosawa.
ANOTHER TIME, ANOTHER PLACE (Brit.), Michael Radford.
Best Direction
John Huston for PRIZZI'S HONOR.
Akira Kurosawa for RAN (Jap./Fr.).
Emir Kusturica for WHEN FATHER WAS AWAY ON BUSINESS (Yugo.).
Sydney Pollack for OUT OF AFRICA (U.S.).
Best Actor
William Hurt for KISS OF THE SPIDER WOMAN (U.S./Braz.).
Jack Nicholson for PRIZZI'S HONOR (U.S.).
Robert Redford for OUT OF AFRICA (U.S.).
Best Actress
Phyllis Logan for ANOTHER TIME, ANOTHER PLACE (Brit.).
Miranda Richardson for DANCE WITH A STRANGER (Brit.).
Meryl Streep for OUT OF AFRICA (U.S.).
Best Producer
Steven Spielberg, Frank Marshall, and Kathleen Kennedy for THE FUTURE (U.S.).
Best Screenplay
BACK TO THE FUTURE (U.S.) by Robert Zemeckis and Bob Gale.

Rene Clair Award
Federico Fellini.

Luchino Visconti Memorial Lifetime Achievement Award
Ingmar Bergman.

38TH DIRECTORS GUILD OF AMERICA AWARDS

Outstanding Feature Film Achievement
Woody Allen for HANNAH AND HER SISTERS.
Randa Haines for CHILDREN OF A LESSER GOD.
James Ivory for A ROOM WITH A VIEW (Brit.).
Rob Reiner for STAND BY ME.
Oliver Stone for PLATOON.

D.W. Griffith Award for outstanding achievement and contribution to film
Elia Kazan.

Frank Capra Award in recognition of outstanding service to the industry by an assistant director or unit production manager
Henry E. "Bud" Brill.

6TH DUTCH FILM DAYS AWARDS

Best Film
ABEL, Alex van Warmerdam.

Best Direction
Alex van Warmerdam for ABEL.

Best Actor
John Kraykamp for THE ASSAULT and THE POINTSMAN.

Best Actress
Geert de Jong for MAMA IS MAD.

Best Score
Vincent van Warmerdam for ABEL.

Best Short
REQUIEM, Fjef Lagro.

Best Documentary
PASSIONS, produced by Olivier Koning.

Export Prize
Orlow Seunke for TASTE OF WATER and PERVOLA.

City of Utrecht Prize
Jos Stelling.

Dutch Film Critics Prize
ABEL, Alex van Warmerdam.

Special Jury Prize
Jos Stelling, producer of THE POINTSMAN.

Production Prize
Jos van der Linden for THE ASSAULT.

FRENCH FILM CRITICS UNION AWARDS

Melies Prize for Best Domestic Film
THERESE, Alain Cavalier.

Moussinac Prize for Best Foreign Film
HANNAH AND HER SISTERS (U.S.), Woody Allen.

Literary Prize
Henri Langlois: 300 Ans de Cinema.

13TH GENIE AWARDS OF THE ACADEMY OF CANADIAN CINEMA AND TELEVISION

Best Picture
DANCING IN THE DARK, produced by Anthony Kramreither.
THE DECLINE OF THE AMERICAN EMPIRE, produced by Rene Malo and Roger Frappier.
JOHN AND THE MISSUS, produced by Peter O'Brian and John Hunter.
LOYALTIES, produced by Ronald Lillie and William Johnston.
POUVOIR INTIME, produced by Claude Bonin.

Best Actor
Pierre Curzi for THE DECLINE OF THE AMERICAN EMPIRE.
Remy Girard for THE DECLINE OF THE AMERICAN EMPIRE.
Gordon Pinsent for JOHN AND THE MISSUS.
Winston Rekert for THE BLUE MAN.
Kenneth Welsh for LOYALTIES.

Best Actress
Dorothee Berryman for THE DECLINE OF THE AMERICAN EMPIRE.
Jackie Burroughs for JOHN AND THE MISSUS.
Tantoo Cardinal for LOYALTIES.
Martha Henry for DANCING IN THE DARK.
Helen Shaver for LOST!
Marie Tifo for POUVOIR INTIME.

Best Supporting Actor
Gabriel Arcand for THE DECLINE OF THE AMERICAN EMPIRE.
Robert Gravel for POUVOIR INTIME.
Roland Hewgill for JOHN AND THE MISSUS.
Tom Jackson for LOYALTIES.
Yves Jacques for THE DECLINE OF THE AMERICAN EMPIRE.

Best Supporting Actress
Lucie Laurier for ANNE TRISTER.
Andree Pelletier for BACH ET BOTTINE.
Louise Portal for THE DECLINE OF THE AMERICAN EMPIRE.
Genevieve Rioux for THE DECLINE OF THE AMERICAN EMPIRE.
Marie Tifo for LES FOUS DE BASSAN.

Best Art Direction/Production Design
Michel Proulx for LES FOUS DE BASSAN.
Michel Proulx for POUVOIR INTIME.
Lillian Sarafinchan for DANCING IN THE DARK.
Francois Seguin for EXIT.

Best Cinematography
Alain Dostie for LES FOUS DE BASSAN.
Guy Dufaux for EQUINOXE.
Pierre Mignot for ANNE TRISTER.
Pierre Mignot for EXIT.
Rene Verzier for MORNING MAN.
Rene Verzier for TOBY MCTEAGUE.

Best Direction
Denys Arcand for THE DECLINE OF THE AMERICAN EMPIRE.
Leon Marr for DANCING IN THE DARK.
Yves Simoneau for POUVOIR INTIME.
John N. Smith for SITTING IN LIMBO.
Anne Wheeler for LOYALTIES.

Best Film Editing
Andre Corriveau for POUVOIR INTIME.
Monique Fortier for THE DECLINE OF THE AMERICAN EMPIRE.
Michael Jones for THE ADVENTURE OF FAUSTUS BIDGOOD.

Best Costume Design
Michele Hamel for EXIT.
Louise Jobin for POUVOIR INTIME.
Wendy Partridge for LOYALTIES.

Nicole Pelletier for LES FOUS DE BASSAN.

Best Score
Marie Bernard and Richard Gregoire for EXIT.
Michael Conway Baker for JOHN AND THE MISSUS.
Marvin Dolgay for THE BLUE MAN.

Best Original Song
Robert Joy and Andy Jones for "Show Goin' On," from THE ADVENTURE OF FAUSTUS BIDGOOD.
Danielle Messia for "De La Main Gauche," from ANNE TRISTER.
Peter Pringle and Kevin Hunter for "Cold as Ice," from TOBY MCTEAGUE.
Gilles Vigneault for "Les Iles de L'Enfance," from EQUINOXE.
Paul Zaza and Peter Simpson for "Out of the Fire," from BULLIES.

Best Sound
Richard Besse, Jean-Pierre Joutel, and Adrian Croll for THE DECLINE OF THE AMERICAN EMPIRE.
Peter Clements, David Appleby, and Don White for ABDUCTED.
Richard Nichol, Hans Domes, Jean-Pierre Joutel, and Shelley Craig for SITTING IN LIMBO.
Gordon Thompson, Michael O'Farrell, David Appleby, and Don White for THE PINK CHIQUITAS.

Best Sound Editing
Paul Dion, Diane Boucher, and Andy Malcolm for THE DECLINE OF THE AMERICAN EMPIRE.
Paul Dion, Jules Le Noir, and Andy Malcolm for POUVOIR INTIME.
Michael O'Farrell, Alison Clark, Sharon Lackie, Alison Grace, and Peter McBurnie for THE PINK CHIQUITAS.
Peter Thillaye, Sharon Lackie, and Peter McBurnie for LOYALTIES.

Best Original Screenplay
Denys Arcand for THE DECLINE OF THE AMERICAN EMPIRE.
Andy Jones and Michael Jones for THE ADVENTURE OF FAUSTUS BIDGOOD.
Sharon Riis for LOYALTIES.
Yves Simoneau and Pierre Curzi for POUVOIR INTIME.

Best Adapted Screenplay
Leon Marr for DANCING IN THE DARK.
Gordon Pinsent for JOHN AND THE MISSUS.
Peter Rowe for LOST!

Shorts and Documentaries

Best Documentary
?O, ZOO!, produced by Philip Hoffman.
DADS & KIDS, produced by Christian Bruyere.
RANCH; THE ALAN WOOD RANCH PROJECT, produced by Steven Denure and Chris Lowry.
RETURN TO DEPARTURE: THE BIOGRAPHY OF A PAINTING OR WATCHING PIGMENT DRY AND OTHER REALISMS, produced by Kirk Tougas.
LES TRACES DU REVE, produced by Jacques Vallee.

Best Live-Action Short Drama
I NEED A MAN LIKE YOU TO MAKE MY DREAMS COME TRUE, produced by Daria Stermac and Kalli Paakspuu.
IT'S A PARTY!, produced by Peg Campbell and Peggy Thompson.
NION IN THE KABARET DE LA VITA, produced by Jeremy Podeswa.
TRANSIT, produced by Jean-Roch Marcotte.
WHERE'S PETE?, produced by Michael Scott.

Best Animated Short
EVERY DOG'S GUIDE TO COMPLETE HOME SAFETY, produced by Les Drew.
GET A JOB, produced by Derek Mazur, Michael Scott, and Brad Caslor.
TABLES OF CONTENT, produced by Wendy Tilby.

The Air Canada Award for outstanding contribution to the business of filmmaking in Canada
Garth H. Drabinsky.

The Outstanding Canadian Film Achievement of Expo '86
TAMING OF THE DEMONS, produced by Paul Krivicky.

GERMAN FILM AWARDS

German Film Prize
ROSA LUXEMBURG, Margarethe von Trotta.

Gold Film Band
Barbara Sukowa for her performance in ROSA LUXEMBURG.

Silver Film Band
THE BLIND DIRECTOR, Alexander Kluge.
MEN, Doris Dorrie.

Other Winners
Ilse Kubaschewski, Lonny van Laak, Winnie Markus, Peter Pasetti, Ernst Schroder, Herbert Weissbach, Hilde Weissner, and Ilse Werner.

German Cross of Merit for longstanding service to film and television
Manfred Durniok.

Nominated Films
THE BLIND DIRECTOR, Alexander Kluge.
GOETHE IN D, Manfred Vosz.
HIDEOUTS, Wolfram Paulus.

FORBIDDEN, Anthony Page.
MEN, Doris Dorrie.
PEOPLE DIE AT HOME, Klaus Gietinger and Leo Hiemer.
ROSA LUX EMBURG, Margarethe von Trotta.
SUGARBABY, Percy Adlon.

24TH GIJON FILM FESTIVAL FOR YOUNG PEOPLE

Prizes of the International Jury
Best Feature
MY LIFE AS A DOG (Swed.), Lasse Hallstrom.
Best Short Film
POLIBKY PANA PIPA (Czech.).
Best Director
Lasse Hallstrom for MY LIFE AS A DOG (Swed.).
Best Actress
Tania Lattarjet for TROP TARD BALTHAZAR (Fr.).
Best Actor
Alvaro de Lunda for TEO EL PELIRROJO (Span.).
Best Screenplay
Reidar Jonsson for MY LIFE AS A DOG (Swed.).
Best Special Effects
PERINBABA (Span.).
Special Mention
HOW YOUNG WE WERE (USSR).

Prizes of the Juvenile Jury
Best Feature
JOEY'S SECRET (Ger.), Roland Emmerich.
Best Short Film
REKSIO I SROKA (Pol.), Romulad Klys.
Best Rendering of a Young Character
Joshua Morrell for JOEY'S SECRET (Ger.).

Prizes of the Film Critics Jury
Best Feature
MY LIFE AS A DOG (Swed.), Lasse Hallstrom.
Best Short Film
KRESADLO (Czech.).

Prizes of the Publicists Jury
Best of the Festival
MY LIFE AS A DOG (Swed.), Lasse Hallstrom.
Special Mention
TROP TARD BALTHAZAR (Fr.).

Prizes of the International Organization of Catholic Critics Jury
First Prize
HOLDING ONTO AIR (Yugo.).
Special Mention
TEO EL PELIRRO JO (Span.).
TROP TARD BALTHAZAR (Fr.).

44TH GOLDEN GLOBE AWARDS

Best Motion Picture—Drama
CHILDREN OF A LESSER GOD, PAR.
THE MISSION, WB.
MONA LISA (Brit.), Island.
PLATOON, Orion.
A ROOM WITH A VIEW, Cinecom.
STAND BY ME, COL.

Best Actress—Drama
Julie Andrews for DUET FOR ONE.
Anne Bancroft for 'NIGHT, MOTHER.
Farrah Fawcett for EXTREMITIES.
Marlee Matlin for CHILDREN OF A LESSER GOD.
Sigourney Weaver for ALIENS.

Best Actor—Drama
Harrison Ford for THE MOSQUITO COAST.
Dexter Gordon for 'ROUND MIDNIGHT (U.S./Fr.).
Bob Hoskins for MONA LISA (Brit.).
William Hurt for CHILDREN OF A LESSER GOD.
Jeremy Irons for THE MISSION.
Paul Newman for THE COLOR OF MONEY.

Best Motion Picture—Musical or Comedy
CRIMES OF THE HEART, DEG.
CROCODILE DUNDEE (Aus.), FOX/PAR.
DOWN AND OUT IN BEVERLY HILLS, BV.
HANNAH AND HER SISTERS, Orion.
LITTLE SHOP OF HORRORS, WB.
PEGGY SUE GOT MARRIED, Tri-Star.

Best Actress—Musical or Comedy
Julie Andrews for THAT'S LIFE!
Melanie Griffith for SOMETHING WILD.
Bette Midler for DOWN AND OUT IN BEVERLY HILLS.
Sissy Spacek for CRIMES OF THE HEART.
Kathleen Turner for PEGGY SUE GOT MARRIED.

Best Actor—Musical or Comedy
Matthew Broderick for FERRIS BUELLER'S DAY OFF.

Jeff Daniels for SOMETHING WILD.
Danny DeVito for RUTHLESS PEOPLE.
Paul Hogan for CROCODILE DUNDEE.
Jack Lemmon for THAT'S LIFE!

Best Foreign-Language Film
THE ASSAULT (Neth.), Fons Rademaker.
BETTY BLUE (Fr.), Jean-Jacques Beineix.
GINGER AND FRED (It.), Federico Fellini.
OTELLO (It.), Franco Zeffirelli.
THREE MEN AND A CRADLE (Fr.), Coline Serreau.

Best Supporting Actress
Linda Kozowlski for CROCODILE DUNDEE.
Mary Elizabeth Mastrantonio for THE COLOR OF MONEY.
Maggie Smith for A ROOM WITH A VIEW.
Cathy Tyson for MONA LISA.
Dianne Wiest for HANNAH AND HER SISTERS.

Best Supporting Actor
Tom Berenger for PLATOON.
Michael Caine for HANNAH AND HER SISTERS.
Dennis Hopper for BLUE VELVET.
Dennis Hopper for HOOSIERS.
Ray Liotta for SOMETHING WILD.

Best Director
Woody Allen for HANNAH AND HER SISTERS.
James Ivory for A ROOM WITH A VIEW.
Roland Joffe for THE MISSION.
Rob Reiner for STAND BY ME.
Oliver Stone for PLATOON.

Best Screenplay
Woody Allen for HANNAH AND HER SISTERS.
Robert Bolt for THE MISSION.
David Lynch for BLUE VELVET.
Neil Jordan and David Leland for MONA LISA.
Oliver Stone for PLATOON.

Best Original Score
LITTLE SHOP OF HORRORS, Miles Goodman.
THE MISSION, Ennio Morricone.
THE MOSQUITO COAST, Maurice Jarre.
'ROUND MIDNIGHT, Herbie Hancock.
TOP GUN, Harold Faltermeyer.

Best Original Song
"Glory of Love" from THE KARATE KID, PART II.
"Life Through a Looking Glass" from THAT'S LIFE.
"Somewhere Out There" from AN AMERICAN TAIL.
"Sweet Freedom" from RUNNING SCARED.
"Take My Breath Away" from TOP GUN.
"They Don't Make Them Like They Used To" from TOUGH GUYS.

Cecil B. DeMille Award for Outstanding Contribution to the Entertainment Industry
Anthony Quinn.

8TH HAVANA INTERNATIONAL FESTIVAL OF NEW LATIN AMERICAN CINEMA

First Prize
HOUR OF THE STAR (Braz.), Suzana Amaral.
UN HOMBRE DE EXITO (Cuba), Humberto Solas.

Second Prize
MISS MARY (Arg.), Maria Luisa Bemb erg.

Third Prize
EL IMPERIO DE LA FORTUNA (Mex.), Arturo Ripstein.

Special Jury Prize
MALANDRO (Braz.), Ruy Guerra.

Opera Prima for First Work
LA BODA DEL ACORDEONISTA (Colombia), Luis F. Bollia.
GERONIMA (Arg.), Raul Tosso.

Honorable Mention
LA GRAN FIESTA (Puerto Rico), Roberto Gandara and Marcos Zurinaga.

Best Actress
Fernanda Torres for EU SEI QUE VOI TE AMAR (Braz.).
Julie Christie for MISS MARY (Arg.).

Best Actor
Ernesto Gomez Cruz for EL IMPERIO DE LA FORTUNA (Mex.).

Best Art Direction
Cesar Argudillo for MISS MARY (Arg.).
Derubin Jacome for UN HOMBRE DE EXITO (Cuba).

Best Editor
Mals Tabares for MALANDRO (Braz.).

Best Cinematography
Angel Goded for EL IMPERIO DE LA FORTUNA (Mex.).
Livio Delgado for UN HOMBRE DE EXITO (Cuba).

Best Music
Chico Buarque for MALANDRO (Braz.).

18TH HUNGARO (HUNGARIAN) FILM WEEK AWARDS

Prizes of the Main Jury
  Grand Prix
    HABOLINA, Sandor Sara.
  Special Jury Prize
    THE WALL DRILLER, Gyorgy Szomjas.
  Best Director
    Peter Gothar for TIME.
    Geza Beremenyl for THE DISCIPLES.
  Best Documentary
    COWBOYS, Pal Schiffer.
  Best Actor
    Peter Andorai for THE WALL DRILLER.

Prizes of the Professional Jury
  Best Director
    Peter Gothar for TIME.
    Peter Timar for SOUND EROTICISM.
  Best Actor
    Janos Ban for THE WALL DRILLER.
    Frigyes Hollosy for THE PICTURE HUNTERS and THE DISCIPLES.
  Best Actress
    Eva Ruttkai for TIME.
  Best Screenplay
    Peter Esterhazy for TIME.
  Best Photography
    Sandor Kardos for THE DISCIPLES and SOUND EROTICISM.
  Best Documentary
    COWBOYS, Pal Schiffer.

Lifetime Achievement Awards
    Geza Radvanyi.
    Peter Bacso.
    Miklos Jancso.

ITALIAN FILM JOURNALISTS AWARDS

Best Film
    LET'S HOPE IT'S A GIRL, Mario Monicelli.

Best Actor
    Marcello Mastroianni for GINGER AND FRED.

Best Actress
    Giulietta Masina for GINGER AND FRED.

Best Foreign Film
    OUT OF AFRICA (U.S.), Sidney Pollack

Best Foreign Actor
    Phillipe Noiret for LET'S HOPE IT'S A GIRL.

Best Foreign Actress
    Angela Molina for CAMORRA.

Best Supporting Actress
    Isa Danieli for CAMORRA.

Best Debuting Actor
    Elvio Porta for CAMORRA.

Best Screenplay
    LET'S HOPE IT'S A GIRL by Mario Monicelli, Tullio Pinelli, Suso Cecchi d'Amici, Leonardo Benvenuti, and Piero De Bernardi.

Best Cinematography
    Marcello Gatti for INGANNI.

Best Editing
    Ruggero Mastroianni for LET'S HOPE IT'S A GIRL.

Best Score
    Toney Esposito for CAMORRA.

Best Art Direction
    Dante Ferretti for GINGER AND FRED.

Best Costume Design
    Danilo Donati for GINGER AND FRED.

Best Producer
    Fulvio Lucisano.

Special Ribbon for Poetic Subject Matter
    INGANNI, Luigi Faccini.

25TH KARLOVY VARY (CZECHOSLOVAKIA) FILM FESTIVAL AWARDS

Crystal Globe
    A STREET TO DIE (Aus.), Bill Bennett.

Special Jury Prize
    BLACK TANNER (Switz.), Xavier Koller.

Jury Prizes
    LIANJIA FUNU (Chi.), Huang Jianzhung.
    TE AMO (Arg.), Eduardo Calcagno.
    POMNALUI NUNSOGI (North Korea), Rim Chang Bom and Ko-Hak Rim.

Special Jury Awards
    DA OBICHACH NA INAT (Bulgaria), Nikolai Volev.

VAKVILAGBAN (Hung.), Livia Gyarmathy.

Best Actor
    Leonid Filatov for CHICHERIN (USSR).

Best Actress
    Jane Fonda, Meg Tilly, and Anne Bancroft for AGNES OF GOD (U.S.).

Rose of Lidice Prize
    ZASTIHLA ME NOC (Czech.), Juraj Herz.

A.M. Brousil Prize for Best First Film.
    NEW DELHI TIMES (India), Ramesh Sharma.

LOS ANGELES FILM CRITICS ASSOCIATION AWARDS
(Includes winners and runner-ups only)

Best Picture
    HANNAH AND HER SISTERS, Woody Allen.
    BLUE VELVET, David Lynch.

Best Director
    David Lynch for BLUE VELVET.
    Woody Allen for HANNAH AND HER SISTERS.

Best Actor
    Bob Hoskins for MONA LISA.
    Dexter Gordon for 'ROUND MIDNIGHT (U.S./Fr.).

Best Actress
    Sandrine Bonnaire for VAGABOND (Fr.).
    Marlee Matlin for CHILDREN OF A LESSER GOD.

Best Foreign Film
    VAGABOND (Fr.), Agnes Varda.
    MY BEAUTIFUL LAUNDRETTE (Brit.), Stephen Frears.

Best Supporting Actor
    Dennis Hopper for BLUE VELVET and HOOSIERS.
    Michael Caine for HANNAH AND HER SISTERS and MONA LISA.

Best Supporting Actress (Tie)
    Cathy Tyson for MONA LISA (Brit.).
    Dianne Wiest for HANNAH AND HER SISTERS.

Best Cinematography
    Chris Menges for THE MISSION (Brit.).
    Bruno De Keyzer for 'ROUND MIDNIGHT (U.S./Fr.).

Best Music
    Herbie Hancock, Dexter Gordon, and the ensemble for 'ROUND MID-NIGHT (U.S./Fr.).
    Ennio Morricone for THE MISSION (Brit.).

Career Achievement Award
    John Cassavetes.

New Generation Award
    Spike Lee.

Special Awards
    Fox International Theater for consistently venturesome film programming.
    Chuck Workman and the Directors Guild of America for the short subject PRECIOUS IMAGES.

Group Statement: *"The Los Angeles Film Critics Association strongly opposes the alteration of films by editing, computer color and other means that subvert the look, the content and the original intent of the filmmakers. Because so many people first see films on television or home-video, and not on a theater screen, it is also particularly damaging when movies photographed in a wide-screen format are adapted for television by panning and scanning, eliminating almost one-third of the original image."*

29TH LEIPZIG INTERNATIONAL DOCUMENTARY AND SHORT FILM FESTIVAL

Prizes of the International Jury
  Feature Length
    Golden Dove
      JOE POLOWSKY—AN AMERICAN DREAMER (Ger.), Wolfgang Pfeiffer.
    Silver Dove
      ACTA GENERAL DE CHILE (Span.), Miguel Littin.
      HALF LIFE (Aus.), Dennis O'Rourke.
  Short Films
    Golden Dove
      CHILDREN OF FUSTAT (Fin.), Heiki Partanen.
    Silver Dove
      MARISKA'S BAND (Yugo.), Peter Krelja.
      HIPPOCRATES' NEW OATH (East Germany), Gisela Schulz and Walter Heinz.
  Animated Films
    Golden Dove
      BREAK! (USSR), G. Bardin.
    Honorary Golden Dove
      THE GENERALS (Brit./Neth./Gr./Ger.), Heynowski, Scheumann, Kade, and Hellmich.
    Support Prize
      CHURCH OF LIBERATION (Braz.), Silvio De-Rin.

Special Jury Prize
GANZ UNTEN (Ger.), Jorg Gfrorer.

FIPRESCI Prize
JOE POLOWSKY—AN AMERICAN DREAMER (Ger.), Wolfgang Pfeiffer.

FICC Film Clubs Prize
JOE POLOWSKY—AN AMERICAN DREAMER (Ger.), Pfeiffer.

39TH LOCARNO INTERNATIONAL FILM FESTIVAL

Prizes of the International Jury
Golden Leopard
JEZIORO BODENSKIE (Pol.), Janusz Zaorski.
Silver Leopard
40 SQUARE METERS OF GERMANY (Ger.), Tevfik Baser.
Bronze Leopard
MOJ DRUG IVAN LAPCHIN (USSR), Alexei Guerman.
LAMB (Brit.), Colin Gregg.
Special Mentions
KALI PATRITHA SYNTROPHE (Gr.), Lefteris Xanthopoulos.
DIAPASON (Arg.), Jorge Polaco.
Fernanda Torres for her performance in COM LICENCA, EU VOU A LUTA (Braz.).

FIPRESCI Prize
MOJ DRUG IVAN LAPCHIN (USSR), Guerman.
Special Mentions
KAYAKO NO TAMENI (Jap.), Kohei Oguri.
40 SQUARE METERS OF GERMANY (Ger.), Baser.

International Federation of Art Cinemas Prize
DIE FALSCHE (Ger.), Werner Masten.

Youth Prizes
First Prize
LAMB (Brit.), Gregg.
Second Prize
JEZIORO BODENSKIE (Pol.), Zaorski.
Third Prize
DEBSHISHU (India), Uptalendu Chakraborty.

Ecumenical Prize
LAMB (Brit.), Gregg.
Special Mention
40 SQUARE METERS OF GERMANY (Ger.), Baser.
DEBSHISHU (India), Chakraborty.

LONDON FILM CRITICS AWARDS

Best Picture
AFTER HOURS (U.S.), Martin Scorsese.
HANNAH AND HER SISTERS (U.S.), Woody Allen.
KISS OF THE SPIDER WOMAN (U.S./Braz.), Hector Babenco.
MY BEAUTIFUL LAUNDRETTE, Stephen Frears.
PRIZZI'S HONOR (U.S.), John Huston.
A ROOM WITH A VIEW, James Ivory.

Best Actor
Klaus Maria Brandauer for OUT OF AFRICA (U.S.).
Denholm Elliott for A ROOM WITH A VIEW.
Bob Hoskins for MONA LISA and SWEET LIBERTY.
William Hurt for KISS OF THE SPIDER WOMAN (U.S./Braz.).
Jack Nicholson for PRIZZI'S HONOR (U.S.).
Cathy Tyson for MONA LISA.
Jon Voight for RUNAWAY TRAIN.

Best Director
Woody Allen for HANNAH AND HER SISTERS (U.S.).
John Boorman for THE EMERALD FOREST (U.S.).
John Huston for PRIZZI'S HONOR (U.S.).
James Ivory for A ROOM WITH A VIEW.
Akira Kurosawa for RAN (Jap./Fr.).
Martin Scorsese for AFTER HOURS (U.S.).

Best Screenplay
HANNAH AND HER SISTERS (U.S.) by Woody Allen.
A ROOM WITH A VIEW by Ruth Prawer Jhabvala.
MONA LISA by Neil Jordan and David Leland.
MY BEAUTIFUL LAUNDRETTE by Hanif Kureishi.
AFTER HOURS (U.S.) by Joseph Minion.
DREAMCHILD by Dennis Porter.

Best Foreign-Language Film
RAN (Jap./Fr.), Akira Kurosawa.

Special Awards for Outstanding Contribution to the Cinema
Lillian Gish.
Chris Menges.
Alexandre Trauner.

Music Award
John Barry for the score of OUT OF AFRICA (U.S.).

10TH MONTREAL WORLD FILM FESTIVAL AWARDS

Prizes of the International Jury
Grand Prix of the Americas
BETTY BLUE (Fr.), Jean-Jacques Beineix.
Special Jury Award
MY SWEET LITTLE VILLAGE (Czech.), Jiri Menzel.
Jury Award
LAPUTA (Ger.), Helma Sanders-Brahms.
Best Actress
Krystyna Janda for LAPUTA (Ger.).
Best Actor
Dennis Hopper for BLUE VELVET (U.S).
Best Short
TABLES OF CONTENT (Can.), Wendy Tilby.
Special Award
Carlos Saura for his dance film trilogy, which includes BLOOD WEDDING, CARMEN, and EL AMOR BRUJO.

FIPRESCI Prize
BLACK TANNER (Switz.), Xavier Koller.
Special Mention
LAPUTA (Ger.), Sanders-Brahms.

Ecumenical Awards
Best Film
MY SWEET LITTLE VILLAGE (Czech.), Menzel.
Special Mention
SOREKARA (Jap.), Yoshimitsu Morita.

Competing Films
AGHAAT (India), Govind Nihalani.
THE AMERICAN WAY (Brit.), Maurice Phillips.
BETTY BLUE (Fr.), Jean-Jacques Beineix.
BLUE VELVET (U.S.), David Lynch.
CACTUS (Aus.), Paul Cox.
DEMONS (Swed.), Carsten Brandt.
DER WILDE CLOWN (Ger.), Josef Rodl.
DREAM OF NORTHERN LIGHTS (Norway), Lasse Glomm.
EL AMOR BRUJO (Span.), Carlos Saura.
EQUINOXE (Can.), Arthur Lamothe.
THE WALL DRILLER (Hung.), Gyorgy Szomjas.
IN THE WILD MOUNTAINS (Chi.), Yan Xueshu.
LAPUTA (Ger.), Helma Sanders-Brahms.
LET'S HOPE IT'S A GIRL (It./Fr.), Mario Monicelli.
LOYALTIES (Can.), Anne Wheeler.
MY SWEET LITTLE VILLAGE (Czech.), Jiri Menzel.
SARRAOUNIA (Burkina Faso), Med Hondo.
SOREKARA (Jap.), Yoshimitsu Morita.
TIEMPO DE SILENCIO (Span.), Vicente Aranda.
TUTTA COLPA DEL PARADISO (It.), Francesco Nuti.
ZAKONNY BRAK (USSR), Albert Mkrtchan.

NATIONAL BOARD OF REVIEW D.W. GRIFFITH AWARDS

Best Picture
A ROOM WITH A VIEW (Brit.), James Ivory.
Remainder of Top 10 Films (in order of preference)
HANNAH AND HER SISTERS, Woody Allen.
MY BEAUTIFUL LAUNDRETTE (Brit.), Stephen Frears.
THE FLY, David Cronenberg.
STAND BY ME, Rob Reiner.
THE COLOR OF MONEY, Martin Scorsese.
CHILDREN OF A LESSER GOD, Randa Haines.
'ROUND MIDNIGHT (U.S./Fr.), Bertrand Tavernier.
PEGGY SUE GOT MARRIED, Francis Coppola.
THE MISSION (Brit.), Roland Joffe.

Best Foreign-Language Film
OTELLO (It.), Franco Zeffirelli.
Best Foreign-Language Film Runner-Ups (in order of preference)
MISS MARY (Arg.), Maria Luisa Bemberg.
GINGER AND FRED (It.), Federico Fellini.
MENAGE (Fr.), Bertrand Blier.
MEN (Ger.), Doris Dorrie.

Best Actor
Paul Newman for THE COLOR OF MONEY.

Best Actress
Kathleen Turner for PEGGY SUE GOT MARRIED.

Best Director
Woody Allen for HANNAH AND HER SISTERS.

Best Supporting Actor
Daniel Day Lewis for MY BEAUTIFUL LAUNDRETTE (Brit.) and A ROOM WITH A VIEW (Brit.).

Best Supporting Actress
Dianne Wiest for HANNAH AND HER SISTERS.

NATIONAL SOCIETY OF FILM CRITICS AWARDS

Best Picture
BLUE VELVET, David Lynch.

Best Director
David Lynch for BLUE VELVET.

Best Actor
Bob Hoskins for MONA LISA.

Best Actress
Chloe Webb for SID AND NANCY (Brit.).

Best Supporting Actor
Dennis Hopper for BLUE VELVET.

Best Supporting Actress
Dianne Wiest for HANNAH AND HER SISTERS.

Best Screenplay
MY BEAUTIFUL LAUNDRETTE (Brit.) by Hanif Kureishi.

Best Cinematography
Frederick Elmes for BLUE VELVET.

Best Documentary
MARLENE (Ger.), Maximilian Schell.

52ND NEW YORK FILM CRITICS CIRCLE AWARDS

(listed in order of votes received)

Best Picture
HANNAH AND HER SISTERS, Woody Allen, on fifth ballot.
PLATOON, Oliver Stone.
BLUE VELVET, David Lynch.
A ROOM WITH A VIEW (Brit.), James Ivory.

Best Director
Woody Allen for HANNAH AND HER SISTERS.
Oliver Stone for PLATOON and SALVADOR.
David Lynch for BLUE VELVET.

Best Actress
Sissy Spacek for CRIMES OF THE HEART.
Kathleen Turner for PEGGY SUE GOT MARRIED.
Chloe Webb for SID AND NANCY.

Best Actor
Bob Hoskins for MONA LISA.
Paul Newman for THE COLOR OF MONEY.
Jeff Goldblum for THE FLY.
Dexter Gordon for 'ROUND MIDNIGHT.

Best Screenplay
MY BEAUTIFUL LAUNDRETTE by Hanif Kureishi.
HANNAH AND HER SISTERS by Woody Allen.
A ROOM WITH A VIEW by Ruth Prawer Jhabvala, based on the novel by E.M. Forster.

Best Supporting Actress
Dianne Wiest for HANNAH AND HER SISTERS.

Best Supporting Actor
Daniel Day Lewis for A ROOM WITH A VIEW.

Best Cinematography
Tony Pierce-Roberts for A ROOM WITH A VIEW.

Best Foreign-Language Film
THE DECLINE OF THE AMERICAN EMPIRE (Can.), Denys Arcand.

Best Documentary
MARLENE, Maximilian Schell.

24TH NEW YORK FILM FESTIVAL

The New York Film Festival is noncompetitive, so there are no official entries. The following is a list of the films presented:
THE BLIND DIRECTOR (Ger.), Alexander Kluge.
CACTUS (Aus.), Paul Cox.
CHARLOTTE AND LULU (Fr.), Claude Miller.
DANCING IN THE DARK (Can.), Leon Marr.
THE DECLINE OF THE AMERICAN EMPIRE (Can.), Denys Arcand.
DIRECTED BY WILLIAM WYLER (U.S.), Aviva Slesin.
DOWN BY LAW (U.S.), Jim Jarmusch.
INTERNATIONAL SWEETHEARTS OF RHYTHM (U.S.) Greta Schiller, Andrea Weiss
ISAAC IN AMERICA (U.S.), Amram Nowack.
MALANDRO (Braz.), Ruy Guerra.
MARLENE (Ger.), Maximilian Schell.
MENAGE (Fr.), Bertrand Blier.
NO END (Pol.), Krzysztof Kieslowski.
PEGGY SUE GOT MARRIED (U.S.), Francis Coppola.
POLICE (Fr.), Maurice Pialat.
'ROUND MIDNIGHT (U.S./Fr.), Bertrand Tavernier.
THE SACRIFICE (Swed.), Andrei Tarkovsky.

SCENE OF THE CRIME (Fr.), Andre Techine.
SID AND NANCY (Brit.), Alex Cox.
THERESE (Fr.), Alain Cavalier.
A TIME TO LIVE AND A TIME TO DIE (Taiwan), Hou Hsiao-Hsien.
TO SLEEP SO AS TO DREAM (Jap.), Kaizo Hayashi.
TRUE STORIES (U.S.), David Byrne.
A ZED AND TWO NOUGHTS (Brit.), Peter Greenaway.

33RD PULA FESTIVAL OF YUGOSLAV FEATURE FILMS

Jury Prizes
Large Golden Arena
HAPPY NEW YEAR—1949, Stole Popov.
Best Director
Lordan Zafranovic for EVENING BELLS.
Best Screenplay
HAPPY NEW YEAR—1949 by Gordan Mihic.
Best Actress
Mira Furlan for THE BEAUTY OF VICE.
Best Actor
Rade Serbedzija for EVENING BELLS.
Best Supporting Players
Nada Djuevski for THE GOLDEN APPLE.
Dusan Kostovski for HAPPY NEW YEAR—1949.
Best Cinematography
Goran Trbuljak for THE DREAM OF A ROSE.
Best Music
Ljupoe Konstantinov for HAPPY NEW YEAR—1949.
Best Art Direction
Dinka Jericevic for THREE'S HAPPINESS.
Best Editing
Andrija Zafranovic for EVENING BELLS.
Best Sound
Matjaz Janezic for CORMORANT.
Best Makeup
Radmila Ivatovic for HAPPY NEW YEAR—1949.

3RD RIO DE JANEIRO INTERNATIONAL FILM FESTIVAL

Prizes of the International Jury
Golden Tucan for Best Film
MY BEAUTIFUL LAUNDRETTE (Brit.), Stephen Frears.
Best Director
Ruy Guerra for MALANDRO (Braz./Fr.).
Best Actor
Peter Thiel for MANDEN I MANEN (Den.).
Best Actress
Sabine Azema for MELO (Fr.).
First Jury Prize
LA MANSION DE ARAUCAIME (Colombia), Carlos Mayol.
Second Jury Prize
BAIXO GAVEA (Braz.), Haroldo Marinho Barbosa.
LA FEMME DE MA VIE (Fr.), Regis Wargnier.

FIPRESCI Prize
GERONIMA (Arg.), Raul Tosso.

OCIC Catholic Prize
GERONIMA (Arg.), Tosso.

SAN SEBASTIAN FILM FESTIVAL

Prizes of the International Jury
Gold Shell for Best Film
LA MITAD DEL CIELO (Span.), Manuel Gutierrez.
Special Jury Prize
THE GREAT GENERATION (Hung.), Ferenc Andras.
Best Direction
Axel Corti for WELCOME IN VIENNA (Aust.).
Best Actor
Ernesto Gomez Cruz for EL IMPERIO DE LA FORTUNA (Mex.).
Best Actress
Angela Molina for LA MITAD DEL CIELO (Span.)
Silver Shell
27 HORAS (Span.), Montxo Armendariz.
NINGUEN NO YAKUSOKU (Jap.), Yoshishige Yoshida.
Best Short Film
A ESPERA (Braz.), Mauricio Farias and Luis Fernando Carvalho.

FIPRESCI Prize
NINGUEN NO YAKUSOKU (Jap.), Yoshishige Yoshida.

OCIC Catholic Prize
MAN LOOKING SOUTHEAST (Arg.), Eliseo Subiela.

Ciga Hotel Prize
MAN LOOKING SOUTHEAST (Arg.), Eliseo Subiela.
ENAS ISICHOS THANATOS (Gr.), Frieda Liappa.

Guipuzcoa Cultural Prize
NINGUEN NO YAKUSOKU (Jap.), Yoshishige Yoshida.

SITGES (SPAIN) FANTASY FILM FESTIVAL

Jury Prizes
Best Film
BLUE VELVET (U.S.), David Lynch.
Best Director
Sergei Paradjanov and Dodo Abashidze for THE LEGEND OF SURAM FORTRESS (USSR).
Best Actor
Juanjo Poigcorbe for MES ENLLA DE LA PASION (Span.).
Best Actress
Caroline Williams for THE TEXAS CHAINSAW MASSACRE, PART II (U.S.).
Best Cinematography
Frederick Elmes for BLUE VELVET (U.S.).
Best Soundtrack
Richard Band for FROM BEYOND (U.S.).
Best Special Effects
John Naulin and Anthony Doublin for FROM BEYOND (U.S.).
Best Short
STREET OF CROCODILES (Brit.), the Quay brothers.
Non-Official Critics Jury Award
FROM BEYOND (U.S.), Stuart Gordon.

22ND TAORMINA (SICILY) FILM FESTIVAL

Prizes of the International Jury
Gold Charybdis
MAN OF ASHES (Tunisia), Nouri Bouzid.
Silver Charybdis
MALA YUNTA (Arg.), Jose Santiso.
Bronze Charybdis
EAT THE PEACH (Brit.), Peter Ormrod.
Gold Polyhymina Mask for Best Performance
Tom Conti for HEAVENLY PURSUITS (Brit.).
Silver Polyhymina Mask
Micheline Presle for BEAU TEMPS MAIS ORAGEUX EN FIN DE JOURNEE (Fr.).
Bronze Polyhymina
Marian Rolle for ALMACITA DI DESOLATA (Dutch Antilles).

Italian Film Critics Association Award
DESERT BLOOM (U.S.), Eugene Corr.
THE DECLINE OF THE AMERICAN EMPIRE (Can.), Denys Arcand.

Italian Film Journalists Association Award
BEAU TEMPS MAIS ORAGEUX EN FIN DE JOURNEE (Fr.), Gerard Frot-Coutaz.
F/X (U.S.), Robert Mandel.

City of Taormina Awards
Franco Bruno for the direction of BLACK TUNNEL (Ital.).
Gianni Garko for his performance in BLACK TUNNEL (Ital.).
Alessandro Haber for his performance in TOMASSO BLU (Ger.).

Filmcritica Magazine Award
BEAU TEMPS MAIS ORAGEUX EN FIN DE JOURNEE (Fr.), Frot-Coutaz.

27TH THESSALONIKI GREEK FILM FESTIVAL

Best Picture
CARAVAN SARAI, Tassos Psarras.
KNOCK OUT, Pavlos Tassios.

Best Director
Pavlos Tassios for KNOCK OUT.

Best New Director
Lefteris Xanthopoulos for HAPPY HOMECOMING COMRADE.

Best Photography
Nikos Smaragdis for A QUIET DEATH.

Best Actress
Eleonora Stathopoulou for A QUIET DEATH.

Best Actor
George Kimoulis for KNOCK OUT.

Best Supporting Actress
Mirca Kalatzopoulou for CARAVAN SARAI.

Best Supporting Actor
Fanis Hinas for KNOCK OUT.

Best Screenplay
THE PHOTOGRAPH by Nikos Papatakis.

Best Music
Eleni Karaindrou for HAPPY HOMECOMING COMRADE.

Best Sets
Antonis Halkias for CARAVAN SARAI.

Best Costumes
Anastasia Arseni for CARAVAN SARAI.

Best Editor
Takis Yannopoulos for A QUIET DEATH.

Best Soundtrack
A QUIET DEATH.

Best Special Effects
Yannis Samiotis for A QUIET DEATH.

Best Shorts
ADAM, Jordan Ananiadis.
A PERFECT TIME, Evris Papanikolas.
A SUNDAY, Anna Grigoriou.

Special Citation
Tassos Pallatsidis for CARAVAN SARAI.

11TH TORONTO FESTIVAL OF FESTIVALS

John Labatt Classic Prize for Most Popular Film (Audience Poll)
THE DECLINE OF THE AMERICAN EMPIRE (Can.), Denys Arcand.

Four Seasons International Critics Award
MAN FACING SOUTHEAST (Arg.), Eliseo Subiela.

Best Canadian Film
THE DECLINE OF THE AMERICAN EMPIRE (Can.), Arcand.

The Toronto Festival of Festivals is noncompetitive, so there are no official entries. However, films presented in major categories included:

Gala Features
CHILDREN OF A LESSER GOD (U.S.), Randa Haines.
THE DECLINE OF THE AMERICAN EMPIRE (Can.), Denys Arcand.
DOWN BY LAW (U.S.), Jim Jarmusch.
MALANDRO (Braz./Fr.), Ruy Guerra.
'NIGHT, MOTHER (U.S.), Tom Moore.
RICOCHETS (Israel), Eli Cohen.
'ROUND MIDNIGHT (U.S./Fr.), Bertrand Tavernier.
THAT'S LIFE (U.S.), Blake Edwards.
WHERE THE RIVER RUNS BLACK (U.S.), Chris Cain.

Canadian Features
THE ADVENTURE OF FAUSTUS BIDGOOD, Michael Jones and Andy Jones.
ANNE TRISTER, Lea Pool.
CLOSE TO HOME, Rick Beairsto.
CONFIDENTIAL, Bruce Pittman.
DANCING IN THE DARK, Leon Marr.
EVIXION, Bachar Chbib.
HENRI, Francois Labonte.
LOYALTIES, Anne Wheeler.
OVERNIGHT, Jack Darcus.
POUVOIR INTIME, Yves Simoneau.
SITTING IN LIMBO, John N. Smith.
WELCOME TO THE PARADE, Stuart Clarfield.

Canadian Documentaries
THE FINAL BATTLE, Donald Brittain.
PASSIFLORA, Fernand Belanger and Dagmar Gueissaz Teufal.
RICHARD CARDINAL: CRY FROM THE DIARY OF A METIS CHILD, Alanis Obomsawin.

31ST VALLADOLID (SPAIN) FILM FESTIVAL

Prizes of the International Jury
Golden Sheaf for Best Picture
MONA LISA (Brit.), Neil Jordan.
THE SACRIFICE (Swed.), Andrei Tarkovsky.
Silver Sheaf
EL DISPUTADO VOTO DEL SENOR CAYO (Span.), Antonio Gimenez-Rico.
Francois Truffaut Prize for Best First Film
A KING AND HIS MOVIE (Arg.), Carlos Sorin.
Best Photography
Sven Nykvist for THE SACRIFICE (Swed.).
Best Actress
Meryl Streep for HEARTBURN (U.S.).
Best Actor
Bob Hoskins for MONA LISA (Brit.).
Short Film Awards
Golden Sheaf
A GREEK TRAGEDY (Bel.), Nicole Van Goethem.
Silver Sheaf
FENYEK VIRRADAT ELLOTT (Hung.), Sandor Kekesi.

43RD VENICE INTERNATIONAL FILM FESTIVAL

Prizes of the International Jury
Golden Lion
SUMMER (Fr.), Eric Rohmer.
Special Grand Jury Award
STORIA D'AMORE (It.), Francesco Maselli.
CUZAJA, BELAJA I RJABOJ (USSR), Sergei Soloviev.
Silver Lion for Best First Film
A KING AND HIS MOVIE (Arg.), Carlos Sorin.
Best Actor
Carlo Delle Piane for REGALO DI NATALE (It.).

Best Actress
Valeria Golino for STORIA D'AMORE (It.).
Special Award
X (Norway), Oddvar Einarson.

FIPRESCI Prize
Best Film
SUMMER (Fr.), Eric Rohmer.
Special Mention
ACTA GENERAL DE CHILE (Span.), Miguel Littin.

OCIC Catholic Award
Best Film
SUMMER (Fr.), Eric Rohmer.
Special Mention
DAS SCHWEIGEN DES DICHTERS (Ger.), Peter Lilienthal.

Competing Films
AMOROSA (Swed.), Mai Zetterling.
CUZAJA, BELAJA I RJABOJ (USSR), Sergei Soloviev.
DAS SCHWEIGEN DES DICHTERS (Ger.), Peter Lilienthal.
EL HERMANO BASTARDO DE DIOS (Span.), Benito Rabal.
FATHERLAND (Brit.), Ken Loach.
IDO VAN (Hung.), Peter Gothar.
THE JOURNEY (Switz.), Markus Imhoof.
KINEMA NO TENCHI (Jap.), Yamada Yoji.
A KING AND HIS MOVIE (Arg.) Carlos Sorin.
KRANI MENJA, MOJ TALISMAN (USSR), Roman Balajan.
LA PURITAINE (Fr.), Jacques Doillon.
LINNA (Fin.), Jaakko Pakkasvirta.
O MELISSOKOMOS (Gr.), Theo Angelopoulos.
ON VALENTINE'S DAY (U.S.), Ken Harrison.
OVIRI—THE WOLF AT THE DOOR (Den.), Henning Carlsen.
REGALO DI NATALE (It.), Pupi Avati.
ROMANCE (It.), Massimo Mazzucco.
A ROOM WITH A VIEW (Brit.), James Ivory.
'ROUND MIDNIGHT (U.S./Fr.), Bertrand Tavernier.
STORIA D'AMORE (It.), Francesco Maselli.
SUMMER (Fr.), Eric Rohmer.
WERTHER (Span.), Pilar Miro.
X (Norway), Oddvar Einarson.

8TH WOMEN'S INTERNATIONAL FILM FESTIVAL IN CRETEIL

Jury Prizes
Grand Prize
PUZEZ DOTEK (Pol.), Magdalena Lazrakiewicz.
Directing Prize
Suzana Amaral for HOUR OF THE STAR (Braz.).
Acting Prizes
Louise Marleau for ANNE TRISTER (Can.).
Jukka-Pekka Palo for FLIGHT NORTH (Ger./Fin.).
Public Prizes
Best Fiction Film
ANNE TRISTER (Can.), Lea Pool.
Best Documentary
LAS MADRES—THE MOTHERS OF PLAZA DE MAYO (U.S.), Susana Munoz and Lourdes Portillo.

39TH WRITERS GUILD OF AMERICA AWARDS

Best Screenplay Written Directly for the Screen
Woody Allen for HANNAH AND HER SISTERS.
Neil Jordan and David Leland for MONA LISA.
David Lynch for BLUE VELVET.
Oliver Stone for PLATOON.
Oliver Stone and Richard Boyle for SALVADOR.

Best Screenplay Adapted from Another Medium
Hesper Anderson and Mark Medoff for CHILDREN OF A LESSER GOD.
Howard Ashman for LITTLE SHOP OF HORRORS.
Raynold Gideon and Bruce A. Evans for STAND BY ME.
Ruth Prawer Jhabvala for A ROOM WITH A VIEW.
Paul Mazursky and Leon Capetanos for DOWN AND OUT IN BEVERLY HILLS.

Laurel Award for lifetime contribution to the cinema
Woody Allen.

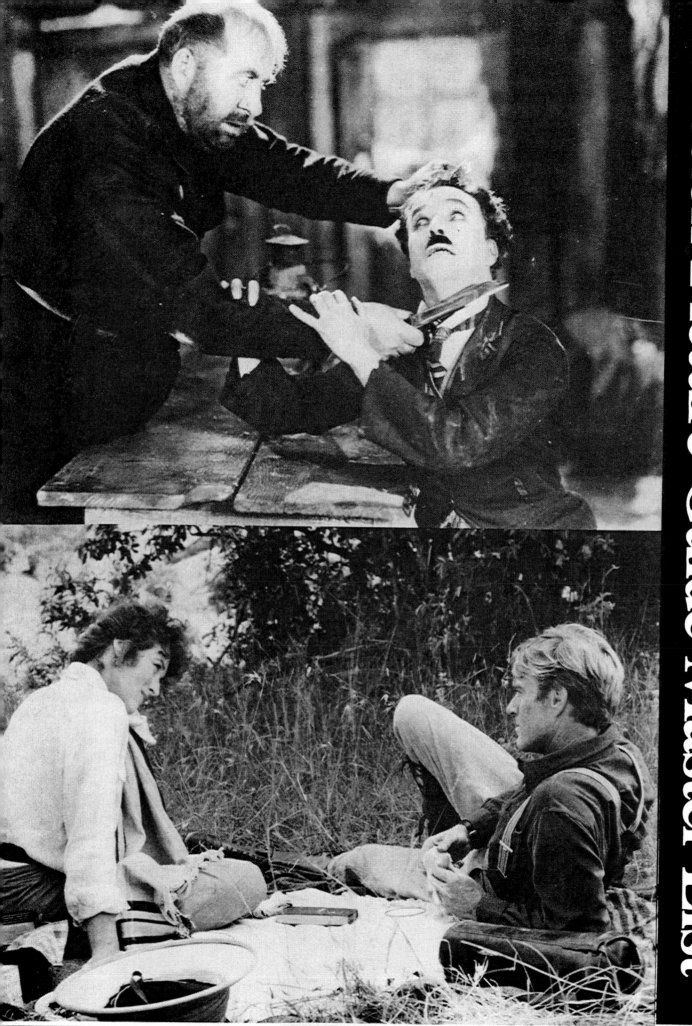

MOTION PICTURE GUIDE MASTER LIST

The following is an alphabetical listing of the titles of all the films in the ten movie entry volumes of the Motion Picture Guide (MPG) (1910–1984). Immediately following this list is a listing of all the films which appear in the MPG 1986 Annual (the films of 1985).

The list includes the year of release of the film and the parental recommendation (AAA: must for children; AA: good for children; A: acceptable for children; C: cautionary; O: objectionable) for the film. Italics denote that the film is available on cassette.

Those films which do not include a year of release are cross references for films which appear in the volumes under another title. A "SEE:" notation appears with those titles in the MPG volumes to indicate the title under which the film has been reviewed. Those titles which have no PR rating are from the MPG miscellaneous lists. Miscellaneous talkies (1930–1984) are listed in Volume IX. Miscellaneous silents (1910–1929) are listed in Volume X.

-A-

A, 1976
A L'HORIZON DU SUD, 1924
A L'OMBRE DE VATICAN, 1922
A L'OMBRE DES TOMBEAUX, 1927
A LA GARE, 1925
A NOS AMOURS, 1984, O
A NOUS LA LIBERTE, 1931, A
A-HAUNTING WE WILL GO, 1942, AA
AARON LOVES ANGELA, 1975, O
AARON SLICK FROM PUNKIN CRICK, 1952, AA
ABABIAN KNIGHT, AN, 1920, A
ABANDON SHIP, 1957, C-O
ABANDONED, 1953, A
ABANDONMENT, THE, 1916
ABAR—THE FIRST BLACK SUPERMAN, 1977
ABBOTT AND COSTELLO IN HOLLYWOOD, 1945, AAA
ABBOTT AND COSTELLO IN THE FOREIGN LEGION, 1950, A
ABBOTT AND COSTELLO IN THE NAVY
ABBOTT AND COSTELLO LOST IN ALASKA
ABBOTT AND COSTELLO MEET CAPTAIN KIDD, 1952, A
ABBOTT AND COSTELLO MEET DR. JEKYLL AND MR. HYDE, 1954, A
ABBOTT AND COSTELLO MEET FRANKENSTEIN, 1948, A
ABBOTT AND COSTELLO MEET THE INVISIBLE MAN, 1955, A
ABBOTT AND COSTELLO MEET THE KILLER, BORIS KARLOFF, 1949, A
ABBOTT AND COSTELLO MEET THE MUMMY, 1955, A
ABBY, 1974, O
ABC OF LOVE, THE, 1919
ABDICATION, THE, 1974, C-O
ABDUCTION, 1975, O
ABDUCTORS, THE, 1957, A
ABDUCTORS, THE, 1972
ABDUL THE DAMNED, 1935, C
ABDULLAH'S HAREM, 1956, O
ABE LINCOLN IN ILLINOIS, 1940, AA
ABIE'S IMPORTED BRIDE, 1925, A
ABIE'S IRISH ROSE, 1928, A
ABIE'S IRISH ROSE, 1946, C
ABILENE TOWN, 1946, A
ABILENE TRAIL, 1951, A
ABLEMINDED LADY, THE, 1922, A
ABOMINABLE DR. PHIBES, THE, 1971, O
ABOMINABLE SNOWMAN OF THE HIMALAYAS, THE, 1957, A
ABORTION, 1924
ABOUT FACE, 1942, A
ABOUT FACE, 1952, A
ABOUT MRS. LESLIE, 1954, A
ABOUT TRIAL MARRIAGE
ABOVE ALL LAW
ABOVE AND BEYOND, 1953, A
ABOVE SUSPICION, 1943, A
ABOVE THE CLOUDS, 1934, A
ABOVE US THE WAVES, 1956, A
ABRAHAM LINCOLN, 1924, A
ABRAHAM LINCOLN, 1930, AAA
ABRAHAM OUR PATRIARCH, 1933
ABROAD WITH TWO YANKS, 1944, A
ABSENCE OF MALICE, 1981, O
ABSENT, 1928, A
ABSENT-MINDED PROFESSOR, THE, 1961, AAA
ABSENTEE-NRA, THE, 1915, A
ABSINTHE, 1914
ABSOLUTE QUIET, 1936, C
ABSOLUTION, 1981, O
ABSURD—ANTROPOPHAGOUS 2, 1982
ABUSED CONFIDENCE, 1938, C-O
ABYSMAL BRUTE, THE, 1923, A
ACAPULCO GOLD, 1978, O

ACCATTONE!, 1961, O
ACCENT ON LOVE, 1941, A
ACCENT ON YOUTH, 1935, A
ACCEPTABLE LEVELS, 1983, C
ACCESS CODE, 1984
ACCESSION TO THE THRONE, 1913
ACCIDENT, 1967, O
ACCIDENT, 1983
ACCIDENTAL DEATH, 1963, C
ACCIDENTAL HONEYMOON, THE, 1918
ACCIDENTS WILL HAPPEN, 1938, A
ACCOMPLICE, 1946, A
ACCOMPLICE, THE, 1917
ACCORDING TO HOYLE, 1922, A
ACCORDING TO LAW, 1916, A
ACCORDING TO MRS. HOYLE, 1951, A
ACCORDING TO THE CODE, 1916, A
ACCOUNT RENDERED, 1957, A
ACCURSED, THE, 1958, A
ACCUSED
ACCUSED, 1925
ACCUSED, 1936, A
ACCUSED OF MURDER, 1956, A
ACCUSED, THE, 1949, C
ACCUSED, THE, 1953
ACCUSED—STAND UP, 1930, A
ACCUSING FINGER, THE, 1936, A
ACE ELI AND RODGER OF THE SKIES, 1973, A
ACE HIGH, 1918
ACE HIGH, 1969, O
ACE IN THE HOLE
ACE OF ACES, 1933, C
ACE OF ACES, 1982, O
ACE OF ACTION, 1926, A
ACE OF CACTUS RANGE, 1924
ACE OF CADS, THE, 1926, A
ACE OF CLUBS, THE, 1926
ACE OF HEARTS, THE, 1916, C
ACE OF HEARTS, THE, A
ACE OF SPADES, THE, 1935, A
ACE OF THE LAW, A
ACE OF THE SADDLE, 1919
ACE, THE
ACES AND EIGHTS, 1936, A
ACES HIGH, 1977, C
ACES WILD, 1937, A
ACID EATERS, THE, 1968
ACQUITTAL, THE, 1923, A
ACQUITTED, 1929, C
ACQUITTED, A
ACROSS 110TH STREET, 1972, O
ACROSS THE ATLANTIC, 1928
ACROSS THE BADLANDS, 1950, A
ACROSS THE BORDER, 1922
ACROSS THE BRIDGE, 1957, C
ACROSS THE CONTINENT, 1913
ACROSS THE CONTINENT, 1922, A
ACROSS THE DEAD-LINE, 1922, A
ACROSS THE DEADLINE, 1925, AA
ACROSS THE DEADLINE, 1976, AAA
ACROSS THE DIVIDE, 1921
ACROSS THE GREAT DIVIDE, 1921
ACROSS THE GREAT DIVIDE, 1976, AAA
ACROSS THE PACIFIC, 1914
ACROSS THE PACIFIC, 1926, A
ACROSS THE PACIFIC, 1942, A
ACROSS THE PLAINS, 1928
ACROSS THE PLAINS, 1939, A
ACROSS THE RIO GRANDE, 1949, A
ACROSS THE RIVER, 1965, C
ACROSS THE SIERRAS, 1941, A
ACROSS THE SINGAPORE, 1928
ACROSS THE WIDE MISSOURI, 1951, A
ACT OF LOVE, 1953, C
ACT OF MURDER, 1965, C
ACT OF MURDER, AN, 1948, C
ACT OF REPRISAL, 1965

ACT OF THE HEART, 1970, O
ACT OF VENGEANCE, 1974, O
ACT OF VIOLENCE, 1949, C
ACT ONE, 1964, A
ACT, THE, 1984, O
ACTION, 1921
ACTION CRAVER, THE, 1927, A
ACTION FOR SLANDER, 1937, A
ACTION GALORE, 1925, A
ACTION IN ARABIA, 1944, A
ACTION IN THE NORTH ATLANTIC, 1943, A
ACTION OF THE TIGER, 1957, A
ACTION STATIONS, 1959, A-C
ACTOR'S REVENGE, AN, 1963, O
ACTORS AND SIN, 1952, C
ACTRESS, THE, 1928, A
ACTRESS, THE, 1953, A
ADA, 1961, C
ADALEN 31, 1969, C
ADAM AND EVA, 1923, A
ADAM AND EVE, 1958, O
ADAM AND EVELYNE, 1950, A
ADAM AND EVIL, 1927, A
ADAM AT 6 A.M., 1970, O
ADAM BEDE
ADAM HAD FOUR SONS, 1941, A
ADAM'S RIB, 1923, A
ADAM'S RIB, 1949, A
ADAM'S WOMAN, 1972, C
ADDING MACHINE, THE, 1969, C
ADDRESS UNKNOWN, 1944, A
ADELE, 1919, A
ADELE HASN'T HAD HER SUPPER YET, 1978, C
ADERYN PAPUR, 1984, A-C
ADIEU PHILLIPINE, 1962, C
ADIOS AMIGO, 1975, C
ADIOS GRINGO, 1967, A
ADIOS SABATA, 1971, A
ADMIRABLE CRICHTON, THE, 1918, A
ADMIRABLE CRICHTON, THE, 1957, A
ADMIRAL NAKHIMOV, 1948, C
ADMIRAL WAS A LADY, THE, 1950, A
ADMIRAL'S SECRET, THE, 1934, A
ADMIRALS ALL, 1935, A
ADOLESCENT, THE, 1978, C
ADOLESCENTS, THE, 1967, C
ADOLF HITLER—MY PART IN HIS DOWNFALL, 1973, A
ADOPTED SON, THE, 1917, A
ADOPTION, THE, 1978, O
ADORABLE, 1933, A
ADORABLE CHEAT, THE, 1928, A
ADORABLE CREATURES, 1956, O
ADORABLE DECEIVER, THE, 1926, A
ADORABLE JULIA, 1964, C
ADORABLE LIAR, 1962, C
ADORABLE SAVAGE, THE, 1920
ADORATION, 1928, A
ADRIFT, 1971, O
ADULTERESS, THE, 1959, O
ADULTERESS, THE, 1976
ADULTEROUS AFFAIR, 1966, A
ADVANCE TO THE REAR, 1964, A
ADVENTURE, 1925, A
ADVENTURE, 1945, A
ADVENTURE FOR TWO, 1945, A
ADVENTURE GIRL, 1934
ADVENTURE IN BALTIMORE, 1949, AAA
ADVENTURE IN BLACKMAIL, 1943, A
ADVENTURE IN DIAMONDS, 1940, A
ADVENTURE IN HEARTS, AN, 1919, A
ADVENTURE IN MANHATTAN, 1936, A
ADVENTURE IN MUSIC, 1944
ADVENTURE IN ODESSA, 1954, C
ADVENTURE IN SAHARA, 1938, A
ADVENTURE IN THE HOPFIELDS, 1954, AA
ADVENTURE IN WASHINGTON, 1941, C

ADVENTURE ISLAND, 1947, A
ADVENTURE LIMITED, 1934, A
ADVENTURE MAD, 1928
ADVENTURE OF SALVATOR ROSA, AN, 1940, A
ADVENTURE OF SHERLOCK HOLMES' SMARTER BROTHER, THE, 1975, AA
ADVENTURE SHOP, THE, 1918, A
ADVENTURE'S END, 1937, A
ADVENTURER, THE
ADVENTURER, THE, 1917
ADVENTURER, THE, 1920
ADVENTURER, THE, 1928, A
ADVENTURERS, THE, 1951, C
ADVENTURERS, THE, 1970, O
ADVENTURES AT RUGBY
ADVENTURES IN IRAQ, 1943, A
ADVENTURES IN SILVERADO, 1948, A
ADVENTURES OF A BOY SCOUT, THE, 1915
ADVENTURES OF A MADCAP, 1915
ADVENTURES OF A ROOKIE, 1943, A
ADVENTURES OF A YOUNG MAN, 1962, A
ADVENTURES OF AN OCTOBERITE, THE, 1924
ADVENTURES OF ARSENE LUPIN, 1956, A
ADVENTURES OF BARRY McKENZIE, 1972, C-O
ADVENTURES OF BUCKAROO BANZAI: ACROSS THE 8TH DIMENSION, THE, 1984, C-O
ADVENTURES OF BUFFALO BILL, 1917
ADVENTURES OF BULLWHIP GRIFFIN, THE, 1967, AAA
ADVENTURES OF CAPTAIN FABIAN, 1951, A
ADVENTURES OF CAPTAIN KETTLE, THE, 1922, A
ADVENTURES OF CAROL, THE, 1917, AA
ADVENTURES OF CASANOVA, 1948, A
ADVENTURES OF CHICO, THE, 1938
ADVENTURES OF DON COYOTE, 1947, A
ADVENTURES OF DON JUAN, 1949, A
ADVENTURES OF FRONTIER FREMONT, THE, 1976, AAA
ADVENTURES OF GALLANT BESS, 1948, AAA
ADVENTURES OF GERARD, THE, 1970, A
ADVENTURES OF HAJJI BABA, 1954, C
ADVENTURES OF HAL 5, THE, 1958, A
ADVENTURES OF HUCKLEBERRY FINN
ADVENTURES OF HUCKLEBERRY FINN, THE, 1960, AAA
ADVENTURES OF ICHABOD AND MR. TOAD, 1949, AAA
ADVENTURES OF JACK LONDON
ADVENTURES OF JANE ARDEN, 1939, A
ADVENTURES OF JANE, THE, 1949, A
ADVENTURES OF KITTY COBB, THE, 1914, A
ADVENTURES OF KITTY O'DAY, 1944, A
ADVENTURES OF LUCKY PIERRE, THE, 1961
ADVENTURES OF MARCO POLO, THE, 1938, A
ADVENTURES OF MARK TWAIN, THE, 1944, AAA
ADVENTURES OF MARTIN EDEN, THE, 1942, A
ADVENTURES OF MICHAEL STROGOFF
ADVENTURES OF MR. PICKWICK, THE, 1921, A
ADVENTURES OF PC 49, THE, 1949, A
ADVENTURES OF PICASSO, THE, 1980, O
ADVENTURES OF PINOCCHIO. THE, 1978
ADVENTURES OF PRINCE ACHMED, THE, 1926
ADVENTURES OF QUENTIN DURWARD, THE
ADVENTURES OF ROBIN HOOD, THE, 1938, AAA
ADVENTURES OF ROBINSON CRUSOE, THE, 1954, AA
ADVENTURES OF RUSTY, 1945, A
ADVENTURES OF SADIE, THE, 1955, A
ADVENTURES OF SCARAMOUCHE, THE, 1964, C
ADVENTURES OF SHERLOCK HOLMES, THE, 1939, A
ADVENTURES OF STAR BIRD, 1978
ADVENTURES OF TARTU, 1943, A
ADVENTURES OF THE MASKED PHANTOM, THE, 1939
ADVENTURES OF THE WILDERNESS FAMILY, THE, 1975, AAA
ADVENTURES OF TOM SAWYER, THE, 1938, AAA
ADVENTURES OF YOUNG ROBIN HOOD, 1983
ADVENTURESS, THE, 1946, A
ADVENTUROUS BLONDE, 1937, A
ADVENTUROUS KNIGHTS, 1935
ADVENTUROUS SEX, THE, 1925, A
ADVENTUROUS SOUL, THE, 1927, A
ADVENTUROUS YOUTH, 1928, A
ADVERSARY, THE, 1970
ADVERSARY, THE, 1973, A
ADVICE TO THE LOVELORN, 1933, A
ADVISE AND CONSENT, 1962, C
AELITA, 1929
AERIAL GUNNER, 1943, A
AERODROME, THE, 1983
AFFAIR AT AKITSU, 1980, O
AFFAIR BLUM, THE, 1949, C
AFFAIR IN HAVANA, 1957, O
AFFAIR IN MONTE CARLO, 1953, A
AFFAIR IN RENO, 1957, A
AFFAIR IN TRINIDAD, 1952, C
AFFAIR LAFONT, THE, 1939, O
AFFAIR OF SUSAN, 1935, A
AFFAIR OF THE FOLLIES, AN, 1927, A
AFFAIR OF THE SKIN, AN, 1964, O
AFFAIR OF THREE NATIONS, AN, 1915
AFFAIR TO REMEMBER, AN, 1957, A

AFFAIR WITH A STRANGER, 1953, A
AFFAIRS IN VERSAILLES
AFFAIRS OF A GENTLEMAN, 1934, A
AFFAIRS OF A MODEL, 1952, O
AFFAIRS OF A ROGUE, THE, 1949, A
AFFAIRS OF ADELAIDE, 1949, C
AFFAIRS OF ANATOL, THE, 1921, C
AFFAIRS OF ANNABEL, 1938, A
AFFAIRS OF CAPPY RICKS, 1937, A
AFFAIRS OF CELLINI, THE, 1934, C
AFFAIRS OF DOBIE GILLIS, THE, 1953, A
AFFAIRS OF DR. HOLL, 1954, A
AFFAIRS OF GERALDINE, 1946, A
AFFAIRS OF JIMMY VALENTINE
AFFAIRS OF JULIE, THE, 1958, C
AFFAIRS OF MARTHA, THE, 1942, A
AFFAIRS OF MAUPASSANT, 1938, A
AFFAIRS OF MESSALINA, THE, 1954, O
AFFAIRS OF ROBIN HOOD, THE, 1981
AFFAIRS OF SUSAN, 1945, A
AFFECTIONATELY YOURS, 1941, A
AFFINITIES, 1922
AFGANISTAN, 1929
AFLAME IN THE SKY, 1927, A
AFRAID OF LOVE, 1925, C
AFRAID TO FIGHT, 1922, A
AFRAID TO LOVE, 1927, A
AFRAID TO TALK, 1932, C
AFRICA SCREAMS, 1949, AA
AFRICA—TEXAS STYLE!, 1967, AA
AFRICAN FURY
AFRICAN INCIDENT, 1934
AFRICAN MANHUNT, 1955, A
AFRICAN QUEEN, THE, 1951, AA
AFRICAN TREASURE, 1952, A
AFRICAN, THE, 1983, C
AFTER A MILLION, 1924, A
AFTER BUSINESS HOURS, 1925, A
AFTER DARK, 1915
AFTER DARK, 1915
AFTER DARK, 1923
AFTER DARK, 1924, AA
AFTER FIVE, 1915, A
AFTER HIS OWN HEART, 1919
AFTER MANY DAYS, 1919, C
AFTER MANY YEARS, 1930, A
AFTER MARRIAGE, 1925, A
AFTER MIDNIGHT, 1921, A
AFTER MIDNIGHT, 1927, A
AFTER MIDNIGHT WITH BOSTON BLACKIE, 1943, A
AFTER OFFICE HOURS, 1932, A
AFTER OFFICE HOURS, 1935, A
AFTER SIX DAYS, 1922
AFTER THE BALL, 1914
AFTER THE BALL, 1924, A
AFTER THE BALL, 1932, C
AFTER THE BALL, 1957, A
AFTER THE DANCE, 1935, A
AFTER THE FALL OF NEW YORK, 1984, O
AFTER THE FOG, 1929, C
AFTER THE FOX, 1966, A
AFTER THE REHEARSAL, 1984, C-O
AFTER THE SHOW, 1921, A
AFTER THE STORM, 1928, A
AFTER THE THIN MAN, 1936, A
AFTER THE VERDICT, 1929, A
AFTER THE WAR, 1918
AFTER TOMORROW, 1932, A
AFTER TONIGHT, 1933, A
AFTER YOU, COMRADE, 1967, A
AFTER YOUR OWN HEART, 1921
AFTERGLOW, 1923
AFTERMATH, 1914
AFTERMATH, THE, 1980
AFTERWARDS, 1928, A
AGAINST A CROOKED SKY, 1975, C
AGAINST ALL FLAGS, 1952, A
AGAINST ALL ODDS, 1924, A
AGAINST ALL ODDS, 1984, C-O
AGAINST THE LAW, 1934, C
AGAINST THE TIDE, 1937, A
AGAINST THE WIND, 1948, A
AGATHA, 1979, C
AGATHA CHRISTIE'S ENDLESS NIGHT
AGE FOR LOVE, THE, 1931, A
AGE OF CONSENT, 1932, C
AGE OF CONSENT, 1969, O
AGE OF DESIRE, THE, 1923
AGE OF ILLUSIONS, 1967, O
AGE OF INDISCRETION, 1935, C
AGE OF INFIDELITY, 1958, O
AGE OF INNOCENCE, 1934, C
AGE OF INNOCENCE, 1977, O
AGE OF INNOCENCE, THE, 1924
AGE OF PISCES, 1972
AGE OF THE MEDICI, THE, 1979, C
AGENCY, 1981, O
AGENT 8 3/4, 1963, C
AGENT FOR H.A.R.M., 1966, C
AGGIE APPLEBY, MAKER OF MEN, 1933, A
AGITATOR, THE, 1949, A
AGONY AND THE ECSTASY, THE, 1965, A

AGOSTINO, 1962, C
AGUIRRE, THE WRATH OF GOD, 1977, O
AH YING, 1984, A
AH, WILDERNESS!, 1935, AAA
AHEAD OF THE LAW, 1926, A
AIDA, 1954, A
AIMEZ-VOUS BRAHMS
AIN EL GHEZAL
AIN'T LOVE FUNNY?, 1927, A
AIN'T MISBEHAVIN', 1955, A
AIR CADET, 1951, A
AIR CIRCUS, THE, 1928, A
AIR DEVILS, 1938, A
AIR EAGLES, 1932, C
AIR FORCE, 1943, A
AIR HAWK, THE, 1924, A
AIR HAWKS, 1935, A
AIR HOSTESS, 1933, A
AIR HOSTESS, 1949, A
AIR LEGION, THE, 1929, A
AIR MAIL, 1932, A
AIR MAIL PILOT, THE, 1928, A
AIR MAIL, THE, 1925, A
AIR PATROL, 1962, C
AIR PATROL, THE, 1928, A
AIR POLICE, 1931, A
AIR RAID WARDENS, 1943, AAA
AIR STRIKE, 1955, A
AIRBORNE, 1962, A
AIRPLANE II: THE SEQUEL, 1982, C
AIRPLANE!, 1980, C
AIRPORT, 1970, C
AIRPORT '77, 1977, C
AIRPORT '79
AIRPORT 1975, 1974, C
AL CAPONE, 1959, C-O
AL CHRISTIE'S "MADAME BEHAVE"
AL JENNINGS OF OKLAHOMA, 1951, A
ALABAMA'S GHOST, 1972
ALABASTER BOX, AN, 1917
ALADDIN AND HIS LAMP, 1952, AA
ALADDIN AND THE WONDERFUL LAMP, 1917
ALADDIN FROM BROADWAY, 1917, A
ALADDIN'S OTHER LAMP, 1917, AA
ALAKAZAM THE GREAT!, 1961, AAA
ALAMBRISTA!, 1977, C
ALAMO, THE, 1960, AA
ALARM CLOCK ANDY, 1920, A
ALARM ON 83RD STREET, 1965
ALARM, THE, 1917
ALASKA, 1944, A
ALASKA HIGHWAY, 1943, A
ALASKA PASSAGE, 1959, A
ALASKA PATROL, 1949, A
ALASKA SEAS, 1954, A
ALASKAN, THE, A
ALBANY NIGHT BOAT, THE, 1928, A
ALBERT, R.N., 1953, A
ALBINO, 1980
ALBUQUERQUE, 1948, A
ALCATRAZ ISLAND, 1937, A
ALCHEMIST, THE, 1981
ALERT IN THE SOUTH, 1954, A
ALEX AND THE GYPSY, 1976, C
ALEX IN WONDERLAND, 1970, C
ALEX JOSEPH & HIS WIVES, 1978
ALEX THE GREAT, 1928, A
ALEXANDER GRAHAM BELL
ALEXANDER HAMILTON, 1931, A
ALEXANDER NEVSKY, 1939, C
ALEXANDER THE GREAT, 1956, A
ALEXANDER'S RAGTIME BAND, 1938, AAA
ALF GARNETT SAGA, THE, 1972
ALF 'N' FAMILY, 1968, C
ALF'S BABY, 1953, A
ALF'S BUTTON, 1920, A
ALF'S BUTTON, 1930, AA
ALF'S BUTTON AFLOAT, 1938, A
ALF'S CARPET, 1929, A
ALFIE, 1966, O
ALFIE DARLING, 1975, O
ALFRED THE GREAT, 1969, C
ALFREDO, ALFREDO, 1973, O
ALGIERS, 1938, C
ALGOL, 1920
ALI BABA, 1954, A
ALI BABA AND THE FORTY THIEVES, 1918, A
ALI BABA AND THE FORTY THIEVES, 1944, AAA
ALI BABA GOES TO TOWN, 1937, AAA
ALI BABA NIGHTS, 1953
ALIAS A GENTLEMAN, 1948, A
ALIAS BIG SHOT, 1962, C
ALIAS BILLY THE KID, 1946, AA
ALIAS BOSTON BLACKIE, 1942, A
ALIAS BULLDOG DRUMMOND, 1935, A
ALIAS FRENCH GERTIE, 1930, A
ALIAS JESSE JAMES, 1959, A
ALIAS JIMMY VALENTINE, 1915
ALIAS JIMMY VALENTINE, 1920, A
ALIAS JIMMY VALENTINE, 1928, A
ALIAS JOHN LAW, 1935, A
ALIAS JOHN PRESTON, 1956, A

ALIAS JULIUS CAESAR, 1922, A
ALIAS LADYFINGERS
ALIAS MARY BROWN, 1918, A
ALIAS MARY DOW, 1935, A
ALIAS MARY FLYNN, 1925
ALIAS MARY SMITH, 1932, A
ALIAS MIKE MORAN, 1919, A
ALIAS MISS DODD, 1920
ALIAS MR. TWILIGHT, 1946
ALIAS MRS. JESSOP, 1917, A
ALIAS NICK BEAL, 1949, A
ALIAS PHIL KENNEDY, 1922
ALIAS THE BAD MAN, 1931, A
ALIAS THE CHAMP, 1949, A
ALIAS THE DEACON, 1928, A
ALIAS THE DEACON, 1940, A
ALIAS THE DOCTOR, 1932, A
ALIAS THE LONE WOLF, 1927, A
ALIAS THE NIGHT WIND, 1923, A
ALIBI, 1929, C
ALIBI, 1931, A
ALIBI FOR MURDER, 1936, A
ALIBI IKE, 1935, AA
ALIBI INN, 1935, A
ALIBI, THE, 1916
ALIBI, THE, 1939, C
ALIBI, THE, 1943, C
ALICE ADAMS, 1923, A
ALICE ADAMS, 1935, A
ALICE DOESN'T LIVE HERE ANYMORE, 1975, O
ALICE GOODBODY, 1974
ALICE IN THE CITIES, 1974, A
ALICE IN WONDERLAND, 1916
ALICE IN WONDERLAND, 1931
ALICE IN WONDERLAND, 1933, AAA
ALICE IN WONDERLAND, 1951, AAA
ALICE IN WONDERLAND, 1951, A
ALICE OF WONDERLAND IN PARIS, 1966
ALICE THROUGH A LOOKING GLASS, 1928
ALICE'S ADVENTURES IN WONDERLAND, 1972, A
ALICE'S RESTAURANT, 1969, O
ALICE, OR THE LAST ESCAPADE, 1977, C
ALICE, SWEET ALICE, 1978, O
ALICIA OF THE ORPHANS
ALIEN, 1979, O
ALIEN BLOOD, 1917
ALIEN CONTAMINATION, 1981
ALIEN ENCOUNTER, 1979
ALIEN ENEMY, AN, 1918, C
ALIEN FACTOR, THE, 1978
ALIEN FACTOR, THE, 1984, C
ALIEN SOULS, 1916, A
ALIEN THUNDER, 1975, C
ALIEN ZONE, 1978
ALIEN'S RETURN, THE, 1980
ALIEN, THE, 1915, A
ALIENS
ALIENS FROM ANOTHER PLANET, 1967
ALIENS FROM SPACESHIP EARTH, 1977
ALIKI—MY LOVE, 1963
ALIMONY, 1924, A
ALIMONY, 1949, C
ALIMONY MADNESS, 1933, C
ALISON'S BIRTHDAY, 1979
ALIVE AND KICKING, 1962, AA
ALIVE ON SATURDAY, 1957, A
ALL ABOARD, 1927, A
ALL ABOUT EVE, 1950, A
ALL AMERICAN, THE
ALL AROUND FRYING PAN, 1925
ALL ASHORE, 1953, AA
ALL AT SEA, 1929
ALL AT SEA, 1935, A
ALL AT SEA, 1939, A
ALL AT SEA, 1958, A
ALL AT SEA, 1970, A
ALL BY MYSELF, 1943, A
ALL COPPERS ARE..., 1972
ALL CREATURES GREAT AND SMALL, 1975, AAA
ALL DOLLED UP, 1921, A
ALL FALL DOWN, 1962
ALL FOR A GIRL, 1915, A
ALL FOR A HUSBAND, 1917
ALL FOR A WOMAN, 1921
ALL FOR MARY, 1956, A
ALL HALLOWE'EN, 1952
ALL HANDS ON DECK, 1961, A
ALL I DESIRE, 1953, A
ALL IN, 1936, A
ALL IN A NIGHT'S WORK, 1961, C
ALL MAN, 1916, A
ALL MAN, 1918, A
ALL MEN ARE APES, 1965
ALL MEN ARE ENEMIES, 1934, A
ALL MEN ARE LIARS, 1919, A
ALL MINE TO GIVE, 1957, AA
ALL MY SONS, 1948, C
ALL NEAT IN BLACK STOCKINGS, 1969, C
ALL NIGHT, 1918, A
ALL NIGHT LONG, 1961, C
ALL NIGHT LONG, 1981, C
ALL NUDITY SHALL BE PUNISHED, 1974, O

ALL OF A SUDDEN NORMA, 1919, A
ALL OF A SUDDEN PEGGY, 1920
ALL OF ME, 1934, C
ALL OF ME, 1984, A-C
ALL OVER THE TOWN, 1949, AA
ALL OVER TOWN, 1937, A
ALL QUIET ON THE WESTERN FRONT, 1930, C
ALL RIGHT, MY FRIEND, 1983, A
ALL ROADS LEAD TO CALVARY, 1921, C
ALL SCREWED UP, 1976, O
ALL SORTS AND CONDITIONS OF MEN, 1921, A
ALL SOULS EVE, 1921, A
ALL THAT GLITTERS, 1936, A
ALL THAT HEAVEN ALLOWS, 1955, A
ALL THAT I HAVE, 1951
ALL THAT JAZZ, 1979, O
ALL THAT MONEY CAN BUY
ALL THE BROTHERS WERE VALIANT, 1923, A
ALL THE BROTHERS WERE VALIANT, 1953, A
ALL THE FINE YOUNG CANNIBALS, 1960, C
ALL THE KING'S HORSES, 1935, A
ALL THE KING'S MEN, 1949, C
...ALL THE MARBLES, 1981, C
ALL THE OTHER GIRLS DO!, 1967, C
ALL THE PRESIDENT'S MEN, 1976, C
ALL THE RIGHT MOVES, 1983, C
ALL THE RIGHT NOISES, 1973, O
ALL THE SAD WORLD NEEDS, 1918, A
ALL THE WAY HOME, 1963, A
ALL THE WAY UP, 1970, A
ALL THE WAY, BOYS, 1973, C
ALL THE WINNERS, 1920, A
ALL THE WORLD TO NOTHING, 1919, A
ALL THE WORLD'S A STAGE, 1917, C
ALL THE YOUNG MEN, 1960, A
ALL THE YOUNG WIVES, 1975
ALL THESE WOMEN, 1964, O
ALL THINGS BRIGHT AND BEAUTIFUL, 1979, AAA
ALL THIS AND HEAVEN TOO, 1940, A
ALL THROUGH THE NIGHT, 1942, A
ALL WOMAN, 1918, A
ALL WOMAN, 1967, O
ALL WOMEN HAVE SECRETS, 1939, A
ALL WRONG, 1919, A
ALL'S FAIR IN LOVE, 1921, A
ALL-AMERICAN BOY, THE, 1973, 0
ALL-AMERICAN CHUMP, 1936, A
ALL-AMERICAN CO-ED, 1941, A
ALL-AMERICAN SWEETHEART, 1937, A
ALL-AMERICAN, THE, 1932, A
ALL-AMERICAN, THE, 1953, A
ALL-AROUND REDUCED
    PERSONALITY—OUTTAKES, THE, 1978, A
ALLEGHENY UPRISING, 1939, A
ALLEGRO NON TROPPO, 1977, A
ALLERGIC TO LOVE, 1943, A
ALLEY CAT, 1984, O
ALLEY CAT, THE, 1929, A
ALLEY OF GOLDEN HEARTS, THE, 1924, A
ALLIES
ALLIGATOR, 1980, O
ALLIGATOR NAMED DAISY, AN, 1957, A
ALLIGATOR PEOPLE, THE, 1959, C
ALLOTMENT WIVES, INC., 1945, A
ALLURING GOAL, THE, 1930, A
ALMA, WHERE DO YOU LIVE?, 1917
ALMIGHTY DOLLAR, THE, 1916
ALMOST A BRIDE
ALMOST A DIVORCE, 1931, A
ALMOST A GENTLEMAN, 1938
ALMOST A GENTLEMAN, 1939, A
ALMOST A HONEYMOON, 1930, A
ALMOST A HONEYMOON, 1938, A
ALMOST A HUSBAND, 1919, A
ALMOST A LADY, 1926, A
ALMOST ANGELS, 1962, AAA
ALMOST HUMAN, 1927
ALMOST HUMAN, 1974, O
ALMOST MARRIED, 1919, A
ALMOST MARRIED, 1932, C
ALMOST MARRIED, 1942, A
ALMOST PERFECT AFFAIR, AN, 1979, C
ALMOST SUMMER, 1978, A
ALMOST TRANSPARENT BLUE, 1980, O
ALMOST YOU, 1984, C
ALOHA, 1931, A
ALOHA OE, 1915
ALOHA, BOBBY AND ROSE, 1975, C
ALOMA OF THE SOUTH SEAS, 1926, A
ALOMA OF THE SOUTH SEAS, 1941, A
ALONE AGAINST ROME, 1963, C
ALONE IN LONDON, 1915, A
ALONE IN NEW YORK, 1914
ALONE IN THE DARK, 1982, O
ALONE IN THE STREETS, 1956, C
ALONE ON THE PACIFIC, 1964, AAA
ALONG CAME JONES, 1945, A
ALONG CAME LOVE, 1937, A
ALONG CAME RUTH, 1924, A
ALONG CAME SALLY, 1933
ALONG CAME SALLY, 1934, A
ALONG CAME YOUTH, 1931, A

ALONG THE GREAT DIVIDE, 1951, C
ALONG THE NAVAJO TRAIL, 1945, A
ALONG THE OREGON TRAIL, 1947, A
ALONG THE RIO GRANDE, 1941, A
ALONG THE SUNDOWN TRAIL, 1942
ALPHA BETA, 1973, C
ALPHA INCIDENT, THE, 1976
ALPHABET CITY, 1984, O
ALPHABET MURDERS, THE, 1966, A
*ALPHAVILLE, A STRANGE CASE OF LEMMY
    CAUTION*, 1965, A
ALRAUNE, 1952, O
ALSACE, 1916
ALSINO AND THE CONDOR, 1983, C
ALSTER CASE, THE, 1915, A
ALTAR CHAINS, 1916, C
ALTAR STAIRS, THE, 1922, A
ALTARS OF DESIRE, 1927, A
ALTEMER LE CYNIQUE, 1924
ALTERED STATES, 1980, O
ALTERNATIVE, 1976
ALTERNATIVE MISS WORLD, THE, 1980
ALVAREZ KELLY, 1966, A
ALVIN PURPLE, 1974, C
ALVIN RIDES AGAIN, 1974, O
ALWAYS A BRIDE, 1940, A
ALWAYS A BRIDE, 1954, A
ALWAYS A BRIDESMAID, 1943, A
ALWAYS ANOTHER DAWN, 1948, A
ALWAYS AUDACIOUS, 1920, A
ALWAYS GOODBYE, 193A
ALWAYS GOODBYE, 193A
ALWAYS IN MY HEART, 194A, A
ALWAYS IN THE WAY, 1915
ALWAYS IN TROUBLE, 1938, AA
ALWAYS LEAVE THEM LAUGHING, 1949, A
ALWAYS RIDIN' TO WIN, 1925
ALWAYS THE WOMAN, 1922, A
ALWAYS TOGETHER, 1947, A
ALWAYS VICTORIOUS, 1960, A
AM I GUILTY?, A
AMADEUS, 1984, C
AMANITA PESTILENS, 1963
AMANTI
AMARCORD, 1974, O
AMARILLY OF CLOTHESLINE ALLEY, 1918, A
AMATEUR ADVENTURESS, THE, 1919, A
AMATEUR CROOK, 1937, A
AMATEUR DADDY, 193A
AMATEUR DEVIL, AN, 1921, A
AMATEUR GENTLEMAN, 1936, A
AMATEUR GENTLEMAN, THE, 1920, A
AMATEUR GENTLEMAN, THE, 1926, A
AMATEUR ORPHAN, AN, 1917
AMATEUR WIDOW, AN, 1919, A
AMATEUR WIFE, THE, 1920, A
AMATEUR, THE, 1982, C
AMAZING ADVENTURE, THE
AMAZING COLOSSAL MAN, THE, 195A
AMAZING DOBERMANS, THE, 1976, AAA
AMAZING DR. CLITTERHOUSE, THE, 1938, C
AMAZING GRACE, 1974, A
AMAZING IMPOSTER, THE, 1919, A
AMAZING LOVE SECRET, 1975
AMAZING LOVERS, 1921, A
AMAZING MONSIEUR FABRE, THE, 1952, A
AMAZING MR. BEECHAM, THE, 1949, A
AMAZING MR. BLUNDEN, THE, 197C
AMAZING MR. FORREST, THE, 194A
AMAZING MR. WILLIAMS, 1939, A
AMAZING MR. X, THE
AMAZING MRS. HOLLIDAY, 1943, AAA
AMAZING PARTNERSHIP, THE, 1921, A
AMAZING QUEST OF ERNEST BLISS, THE
AMAZING TRANSPARENT MAN, THE, 1960, C
AMAZING TRANSPLANT, THE, 1970
AMAZING VAGABOND, 1929, A
AMAZON QUEST, 1949, A
AMAZONS, THE, 1917, A
AMBASSADOR BILL, 1933, A
AMBASSADOR'S DAUGHTER, THE, 1956, A
AMBASSADOR, THE, 1984
AMBITION, 1916, A
AMBUSH, 1939, A
AMBUSH, 1950, A
AMBUSH AT CIMARRON PASS, 1958, A
AMBUSH AT TOMAHAWK GAP, 1953, C
AMBUSH BAY, 1966, C
AMBUSH IN LEOPARD STREET, 196C
AMBUSH TRAIL, 1946, A
AMBUSH VALLEY, 1936, A
AMBUSHED, 1926
AMBUSHERS, THE, 1967, A
AME D'ARTISTE, 1925
AMELIE OR THE TIME TO LOVE, 1961, A
AMERICA, 1924, A
AMERICA—THAT'S ALL, 1917
AMERICA, AMERICA, 1963, A
AMERICAN ARISTOCRACY, 1916, A
AMERICAN BEAUTY, 1927, A
AMERICAN BEAUTY, THE, 1916

AMERICAN BUDS, 1918, AA
AMERICAN CITIZEN, AN, 1914
AMERICAN CONSUL, THE, 1917, A
AMERICAN DREAM, AN, 1966, O
AMERICAN DREAMER, 1984, A-C
AMERICAN EMPIRE, 1942, A
AMERICAN FRIEND, THE, 1977
AMERICAN GAME, THE, 1979
AMERICAN GENTLEMAN, AN, 1915
AMERICAN GIGOLO, 1980, O
AMERICAN GRAFFITI, 1973, C
AMERICAN GUERRILLA IN THE PHILIPPINES, AN, 1950, A
AMERICAN HOT WAX, 1978, A
AMERICAN IN PARIS, AN, 1951, AAA
AMERICAN LIVE WIRE, AN, 1918, A
AMERICAN LOVE, 1932, A
AMERICAN MADNESS, 1932, A
AMERICAN MAID, 1917, A
AMERICAN MANNERS, 1924, A
AMERICAN MATCHMAKER, 1940
AMERICAN METHODS, 1917, A
AMERICAN NIGHTMARE, 1984, O
AMERICAN NIGHTMARE, 1981
AMERICAN PLUCK, 1925
AMERICAN POP, 1981, O
AMERICAN PRISONER, THE, 1929, A
AMERICAN RASPBERRY, 1980
AMERICAN ROMANCE, AN, 1944, A
AMERICAN SOLDIER, THE, 1970, C
AMERICAN SUCCESS COMPANY, THE, 1980, C
AMERICAN TABOO, 1984, O
AMERICAN TRAGEDY, AN, 1931, C
AMERICAN VENUS, THE, 1926, A
AMERICAN WAY, THE, 1919, A
AMERICAN WEREWOLF IN LONDON, AN, 1981, O
AMERICAN WIDOW, AN, 1917, A
AMERICAN WIFE, AN, 1965, O
AMERICANA, 1981, C
AMERICANIZATION OF EMILY, THE, 1964, C
AMERICANO, THE, 1917, A
AMERICANO, THE, 1955, A
AMERICATHON, 1979, C
AMES D'ENFANTS, 1929
AMES D'ORIENT, 1919
AMIN—THE RISE AND FALL, 1982, O
AMITYVILLE 3-D, 1983, O
AMITYVILLE HORROR, THE, 1979, O
AMITYVILLE II: THE POSSESSION, 1982, O
AMONG HUMAN WOLVES, 1940, A
AMONG THE LIVING, 1941, C
AMONG THE MISSING, 1934, A
AMONG THE RUINS, 1923
AMONG VULTURES, 1964, A
AMOROUS ADVENTURES OF DON QUIXOTE AND SANCHO PANZA, THE, 1976
AMOROUS ADVENTURES OF MOLL FLANDERS, THE, 1965, C
AMOROUS MR. PRAWN, THE, 1965, A
AMOS 'N' ANDY, 1930, A
AMOUR, AMOUR, 1937, A
AMOURS, DELICES ET ORGUES, 1925
AMPHIBIOUS MAN, THE, 1961, AA
AMPHYTRYON, 1937, A
AMSTERDAM AFFAIR, THE, 1968, C
AMSTERDAM KILL, THE, 1978, O
AMY, 1981, AAA
ANASTASIA, 1956, A
ANATAHAN, 1953, A
ANATOMIST, THE, 1961, C
ANATOMY OF A MARRIAGE (MY DAYS WITH JEAN-MARC AND MY NIGHTS WITH FRANCOISE), 1964, O
ANATOMY OF A MURDER, 1959, C
ANATOMY OF A PSYCHO, 1961, C
ANATOMY OF A SYNDICATE
ANATOMY OF LOVE, 1959, C
ANCE A LA CARTE, 1938, A
ANCE IS SACRED
ANCHORS AWEIGH, 1945, AAA
ANCIENT HIGHWAY, THE, 1925, A
ANCIENT MARINER, THE, 1925, A
AND A STILL, SMALL VOICE, 1918, A
AND BABY MAKES THREE, 1949, A
AND GOD CREATED WOMAN, 1957, O
AND HOPE TO DIE, 1972, C
...AND JUSTICE FOR ALL, 1979, O
AND MILLIONS WILL DIE, 1973, C
AND NOW FOR SOMETHING COMPLETELY DIFFERENT, 1972, PG
AND NOW MIGUEL, 1966, AA
AND NOW MY LOVE, 1975, C
AND NOW THE SCREAMING STARTS, 1973, O
AND NOW TOMORROW, 1944, A
AND NOW TOMORROW, 1952
AND ONE WAS BEAUTIFUL, 1940, A
...AND PIGS MIGHT FLY
AND QUIET FLOWS THE DON, 1960, A
AND SO THEY WERE MARRIED
AND SO THEY WERE MARRIED, 1936, AA
AND SO TO BED, 1965, O
AND SOON THE DARKNESS, 1970, O

AND SUDDEN DEATH, 1936, A
AND SUDDENLY IT'S MURDER!, 1964, C
AND THE ANGELS SING, 1944, A
AND THE LAW SAYS, 1916
AND THE SAME TO YOU, 1960, A
AND THE SHIP SAILS ON, 1983, A
AND THE WALL CAME TUMBLING DOWN, 1984
AND THE WILD, WILD WOMEN, 1961, C-O
AND THEN THERE WERE NONE
AND THEN THERE WERE NONE, 1945, A
AND THERE CAME A MAN, 1968, AAA
AND WOMEN SHALL WEEP, 1960, C
ANDERSON TAPES, THE, 1971, C-O
ANDRE CORNELIS, 1918
ANDRE CORNELIS, 1927
ANDREA, 1979
ANDREI KOZHUKHOV, 1917
ANDREI ROUBLOV, 1973, A
ANDREW'S RAIDERS
ANDROCLES AND THE LION, 1952, A
ANDROID, 1982, O
ANDROMEDA STRAIN, THE, 1971, A
ANDY, 1965, A
ANDY HARDY COMES HOME, 1958, AAA
ANDY HARDY GETS SPRING FEVER, 1939, AAA
ANDY HARDY MEETS DEBUTANTE, 1940, AAA
ANDY HARDY'S BLONDE TROUBLE, 1944, AAA
ANDY HARDY'S DOUBLE LIFE, 1942, AAA
ANDY HARDY'S PRIVATE SECRETARY, 1941, AAA
ANDY WARHOL'S DRACULA, 1974
ANDY WARHOL'S FRANKENSTEIN, 1974
ANGEL, 1937, C
ANGEL, 1982, C
ANGEL, 1984, O
ANGEL AND SINNER, 1947, C
ANGEL AND THE BADMAN, 1947, A
ANGEL BABY, 1961, C
ANGEL CHILD, 1918, A
ANGEL CITIZENS, 1922
ANGEL COMES TO BROOKLYN, AN, 1945, AA
ANGEL ESQUIRE, 1919, A
ANGEL FACE, 1953, C
ANGEL FACTORY, THE, 1917
ANGEL FOR SATAN, AN, 1966
ANGEL FROM TEXAS, AN, 1940, A
ANGEL IN EXILE, 1948, A
ANGEL IN MY POCKET, 1969, AA
ANGEL LEVINE, THE, 1970, A
ANGEL OF BROADWAY, THE, 1927, A
ANGEL OF CROOKED STREET, THE, 1922, A
ANGEL OF H.E.A.T., 1982
ANGEL OF THE WARD, THE, 1915
ANGEL OF VIOLENCE
ANGEL ON MY SHOULDER, 1946, A
ANGEL ON THE AMAZON, 1948, A
ANGEL PASSED OVER BROOKLYN, AN
ANGEL STREET
ANGEL UNCHAINED, 1970, C
ANGEL WHO PAWNED HER HARP, THE, 1956, A
ANGEL WITH THE TRUMPET, THE, 1950, C
ANGEL WORE RED, THE, 1960, A
ANGEL'S HOLIDAY, 1937, A
ANGEL, ANGEL, DOWN WE GO, 1969, O
ANGELA, 1955, A
ANGELA, 1977, O
ANGELE, 1934, C
ANGELIKA
ANGELINA, 1948, C
ANGELO, 1951, C
ANGELO IN THE CROWD, 1952, A
ANGELO MY LOVE, 1983, O
ANGELS, 1976
ANGELS ALLEY, 1948, A
ANGELS BRIGADE, 1980, O
ANGELS DIE HARD, 1970, O
ANGELS FROM HELL, 1968, O
ANGELS HARD AS THEY COME, 1971, O
ANGELS IN DISGUISE, 1949, A
ANGELS IN THE OUTFIELD, 1951, AAA
ANGELS OF DARKNESS, 1956, O
ANGELS OF THE STREETS, 1950, C
ANGELS ONE FIVE, 1954, A
ANGELS OVER BROADWAY, 1940, A
ANGELS WASH THEIR FACES, 1939, A
ANGELS WITH BROKEN WINGS, 1941, A
ANGELS WITH DIRTY FACES, 1938, C
ANGELS' WILD WOMEN, 1972
ANGI VERA, 1980, C
ANGOISSE, 1917
ANGRY BREED, THE, 1969, O
ANGRY GOD, THE, 1948
ANGRY HILLS, THE, 1959, A
ANGRY ISLAND, 1960, A
ANGRY MAN, THE, 1979, C
ANGRY RED PLANET, THE, 1959, A
ANGRY SILENCE, THE, 1960, C
ANIMAL CRACKERS, 1930, AAA
ANIMAL FARM, 1955, A
ANIMAL HOUSE
ANIMAL KINGDOM, THE, 1932, A
ANIMALS, THE, 1971, O
ANITA GARIBALDI, 1954, C

ANKLES PREFERRED, 1927, A
ANN CARVER'S PROFESSION, 1933, A
ANN VICKERS, 1933, A
ANN'S FINISH, 1918, A
ANNA, 1951, C-O
ANNA, 1981, A
ANNA AND THE KING OF SIAM, 1946, A
ANNA ASCENDS, 1922, A
ANNA CHRISTIE, 1923, C
ANNA CHRISTIE, 1930, C
ANNA CROSS, THE, 1954, A
ANNA KARENINA, 1914
ANNA KARENINA, 1935, A
ANNA KARENINA, 1948, A
ANNA LUCASTA, 1949, C
ANNA LUCASTA, 1958, C
ANNA OF BROOKLYN, 1958, C
ANNA OF RHODES, 1950, A
ANNA THE ADVENTURESS, 1920, A
ANNABEL LEE, 1921, A
ANNABEL TAKES A TOUR, 1938, A
ANNABELLE LEE, 1972
ANNABELLE'S AFFAIRS, 1931, A
ANNAPOLIS, 1928, A
ANNAPOLIS FAREWELL, 1935, A
ANNAPOLIS SALUTE, 1937, A
ANNAPOLIS STORY, AN, 1955, A
ANNE AGAINST THE WORLD, 1929, A
ANNE DEVLIN, 1984, C
ANNE OF GREEN GABLES, 1919, A
ANNE OF GREEN GABLES, 1934, A
ANNE OF LITTLE SMOKY, 1921, A
ANNE OF THE INDIES, 1951, A
ANNE OF THE THOUSAND DAYS, 1969, C-O
ANNE OF WINDY POPLARS, 1940, A
ANNE ONE HUNDRED, 1933, A
ANNE-MARIE, 1936, A
ANNEXING BILL, 1918, A
ANNIE, 1982, AAA
ANNIE GET YOUR GUN, 1950, AAA
ANNIE HALL, 1977, C-O
ANNIE LAURIE, 1916
ANNIE LAURIE, 1927, A
ANNIE LAURIE, 1936, A
ANNIE OAKLEY, 1935, AAA
ANNIE, LEAVE THE ROOM, 1935, A
ANNIE-FOR-SPITE, 1917
ANNIVERSARY, THE, 1968, O
ANONYMOUS AVENGER, THE, 1976
ANONYMOUS VENETIAN, THE, 1971, C
ANOTHER CHANCE
ANOTHER COUNTRY, 1984, C
ANOTHER DAWN, 1937, A
ANOTHER FACE, 1935, A
ANOTHER LANGUAGE, 1933, A
ANOTHER MAN'S BOOTS, 1922, A
ANOTHER MAN'S POISON, 1952, C
ANOTHER MAN'S SHOES, 1922
ANOTHER MAN'S WIFE, 1924, A
ANOTHER MAN, ANOTHER CHANCE, 1977, C-O
ANOTHER PART OF THE FOREST, 1948, C
ANOTHER SCANDAL, 1924, A
ANOTHER SHORE, 1948, A
ANOTHER SKY, 1960, A
ANOTHER THIN MAN, 1939, A
ANOTHER TIME, ANOTHER PLACE, 1958, A
ANOTHER TIME, ANOTHER PLACE, 1983, C
ANOTHER TIME, ANOTHER PLACE, 1984, O
ANSWER THE CALL, 1915
ANSWER, THE, 1916, A
ANSWER, THE, 1918, A
ANTARCTICA, 1984, A
ANTHING ONCE, 1917, A
ANTHONY ADVERSE, 1936, A
ANTHONY OF PADUA, 1952, O
ANTI-CLOCK, 1980, C-O
ANTICS OF ANN, THE, 1917, A
ANTIGONE, 1962, A
ANTIQUE DEALER, THE, 1915
ANTOINE ET ANTOINETTE, 1947, A
ANTOINETTE SABRIER, 1927
ANTON THE TERRIBLE, 1916, A
ANTONIO DAS MORTES, 1970, C-O
ANTONY AND CLEOPATRA, 1973, A
ANTS IN HIS PANTS, 1940, AA
ANY BODY...ANY WAY, 1968
ANY GUN CAN PLAY, 1968, C
ANY MAN'S WIFE, 1936, A
ANY NIGHT, 1922
ANY NUMBER CAN PLAY, 1949, A
ANY NUMBER CAN WIN, 1963, A
ANY WEDNESDAY, 1966, C-O
ANY WHICH WAY YOU CAN, 1980, C
ANY WIFE, 1922, C
ANY WOMAN, 1925, A
ANY WOMAN'S MAN
ANYBODY HERE SEEN KELLY?, 1928
ANYBODY'S BLONDE, 1931, A
ANYBODY'S WAR, 1930, A
ANYBODY'S WOMAN, 1930, A
ANYONE CAN PLAY, 1968, O
ANYONE FOR VENICE?

ASSIGNED TO DANGER, 1948, A
ASSIGNMENT ABROAD, 1955
ASSIGNMENT IN BRITTANY, 1943, A
ASSIGNMENT K, 1968, A
ASSIGNMENT OUTER SPACE, 1960, C
ASSIGNMENT REDHEAD
ASSIGNMENT TERROR, 1970, C-O
ASSIGNMENT TO KILL, 1968, C
ASSIGNMENT, THE, 1978
ASSIGNMENT—PARIS, 1952, A
ASSIGNMENT: KILL CASTRO
ASSISTANT, THE, 1982, C
ASSOCIATE, THE, 1982, A
ASTERO, 1960, A
ASTHORE, 1917, A
ASTONISHED HEART, THE, 1950, C
ASTOUNDING SHE-MONSTER, THE, 1958, C
ASTRO-ZOMBIES, THE, 1969, C
ASTROLOGER, THE, 1975
ASTROLOGER, THE, 1979
ASYLUM, 1972, O
ASYLUM FOR A SPY, 1967
ASYLUM OF SATAN, 1972
AT
AT 3:25
AT BAY, 1915
AT DAWN WE DIE, 1943, A
AT DEVIL'S GORGE, 1923, A
AT FIRST SIGHT, 1917
AT GUNPOINT, 1955, A
AT LONG LAST LOVE, 1975, A
AT PINEY RIDGE, 1916
AT SWORD'S POINT, 1951, A
AT THE CIRCUS, 1939, AAA
AT THE CROSSROADS, 1922
AT THE EARTH'S CORE, 1976, C
AT THE EDGE OF THE WORLD, 1929
AT THE END OF THE WORLD, 1921
AT THE GREY HOUSE
AT THE MERCY OF MEN, 1918
AT THE MERCY OF TIBERIUS
AT THE OLD CROSSED ROADS, 1914
AT THE RIDGE, 1931, A
AT THE SIGN OF THE JACK O'LANTERN, 1922
AT THE STAGE DOOR, 1921, A
AT THE STROKE OF NINE, 1957, A
AT THE TORRENT'S MERCY, 1915
AT THE VILLA ROSE, 1920, A
AT WAR WITH THE ARMY, 1950, A
AT YALE
ATCH ME A SPY, 1971, A-C
ATHENA, 1954, A
ATLANTIC, 1929, A
ATLANTIC ADVENTURE, 1935, A
ATLANTIC CITY, 1944, A
ATLANTIC CITY, 1981, C-O
ATLANTIC CONVOY, 1942, A
ATLANTIC FERRY, 1941, A
ATLANTIC FLIGHT, 1937, A
ATLANTIS, 1913
ATLANTIS, THE LOST CONTINENT, 1961, A
ATLAS, 1960, C-O
ATLAS AGAINST THE CYCLOPS, 1963, A
ATLAS AGAINST THE CZAR, 1964, A
ATOLL K
ATOM AGE VAMPIRE, 1961, C
ATOM, THE, 1918, A
ATOMIC AGENT, 1959
ATOMIC BRAIN, THE, 1964, O
ATOMIC CITY, THE, 1952, A
ATOMIC KID, THE, 1954, A
ATOMIC MAN, THE, 1955, A
ATOMIC SUBMARINE, THE, 1960, A
ATOMIC WAR BRIDE, 1966
ATONEMENT, 1920
ATONEMENT OF GOSTA BERLING, THE
ATOR, THE INVINCIBLE, 1984
ATOR: THE FIGHTING EAGLE, 1983
ATRAGON, 1965, A
ATTA BOY, 1926, A
ATTA BOY'S LAST RACE, 1916, A
ATTACK AND RETREAT
ATTACK AT NOON SUNDAY, 1971
ATTACK OF THE 50 FOOT WOMAN, 1958, A
ATTACK OF THE CRAB MONSTERS, 1957, A
ATTACK OF THE GIANT LEECHES, 1959, C-O
ATTACK OF THE KILLER TOMATOES, 1978, C
ATTACK OF THE MAYAN MUMMY, 1963, C
ATTACK OF THE MUSHROOM PEOPLE, 1964, A
ATTACK OF THE PUPPET PEOPLE, 1958, A
ATTACK OF THE ROBOTS, 1967, C
ATTACK ON THE IRON COAST, 1968, A
ATTACK!, 1956, O
ATTEMPT TO KILL, 1961, A
ATTENTION, THE KIDS ARE WATCHING, 1978, C
ATTIC, THE, 1979, C-O
ATTILA, 1958, C
ATTORNEY FOR THE DEFENSE, 1932, A
AU BONHEUR DES DAMES, 1929
AU DELA DES LOIS HUMAINES, 1920
AU HASARD, BALTHAZAR, 1970, C-O
AU PAIR GIRLS, 1973

AU PARADIS DES ENFANTS, 1918
AU SEUIL DU HAREM, 1922
AUCTION BLOCK, THE, 1917, C
AUCTION BLOCK, THE, 1926, A
AUCTION MART, THE, 1920, A
AUCTION OF SOULS, 1922
AUCTION OF VIRTUE, THE, 1917
AUCTIONEER, THE, 1927, A
AUDACIOUS MR. SQUIRE, THE, 1923, A
AUDREY, 1916, A
AUDREY ROSE, 1977, C
AUGUST WEEK-END, 1936, A
AUGUSTINE OF HIPPO, 1973, A
AULD LANG SYNE, 1917, A
AULD LANG SYNE, 1929, A
AULD LANG SYNE, 1937, A
AULD ROBIN GRAY, 1917, A
AULD ROBIN GRAY, 1917
AUNT CLARA, 1954, A
AUNT FROM CHICAGO, 1960, C
AUNT RACHEL, 1920, A
AUNTIE MAME, 1958, A
AUNTIE'S ANTICS, 1929
AURORA LEIGH, 1915
AUSTERLITZ, 1960, A
AUTHOR! AUTHOR!, 1982, A
AUTOCRAT, THE, 1919, A
AUTOPSY, 1980
AUTOUR D'UN BERCEAU, 1925
AUTOUR DU MYSTERE, 1920
AUTUMN, 1916
AUTUMN CROCUS, 1934, A
AUTUMN LEAVES, 1956, C
AUTUMN MARATHON, 1982, A
AUTUMN OF PRIDE, THE, 1921, A
AUTUMN SONATA, 1978, O
AUX JARDINS DE MURCIE, 1923
AVALANCHE, 1928, A
AVALANCHE, 1946, A
AVALANCHE, 1975
AVALANCHE, 1978, O
AVALANCHE EXPRESS, 1979, C
AVALANCHE, THE, 1915
AVALANCHE, THE, 1919, C
AVANTI!, 1972, C
AVE MARIA, 1918, A
AVE MARIA, 1984, O
AVENGER OF THE SEVEN SEAS, 1960
AVENGER OF VENICE, 1965
AVENGER, THE, 1924, A
AVENGER, THE, 1931, A
AVENGER, THE, 1933, A
AVENGER, THE, 1962, C
AVENGER, THE, 1966, C
AVENGERS, THE, 1942, A
AVENGERS, THE, 1950, A
AVENGING CONSCIENCE, THE, 1914, C
AVENGING FANGS, 1927, A
AVENGING HAND, THE, 1915
AVENGING HAND, THE, 1936, A
AVENGING RIDER, THE, 1928, A
AVENGING RIDER, THE, 1943, A
AVENGING SHADOW, THE, 1928, A
AVENGING TRAIL, THE, 1918, A
AVENGING WATERS, 1936, A
AVERAGE WOMAN, THE, 1924, A
AVIATOR SPY, THE, 1914
AVIATOR'S WIFE, THE, 1981, O
AVIATOR, THE, 1929, A
AWAKENING OF BESS MORTON, THE, 1916
AWAKENING OF HELENA RICHIE, THE, 1916
AWAKENING OF JIM BURKE, 1935, A
AWAKENING OF RUTH, THE, 1917
AWAKENING, THE, 1917, C
AWAKENING, THE, 1928, A
AWAKENING, THE, 1938, A
AWAKENING, THE, 1958, AA
AWAKENING, THE, 1980, O
AWAY ALL BOATS, 1956, A
AWAY GOES PRUDENCE, 1920, A
AWAY IN THE LEAD, 1925
AWFUL DR. ORLOFF, THE, 1964, O
AWFUL TRUTH, THE, 1925, A
AWFUL TRUTH, THE, 1929, A
AWFUL TRUTH, THE, 1937, A
AWOL, 1973
AXE, 1977
AYLWIN, 1920, A
AZAIS, 1931, A
AZTEC MUMMY, THE, 1957, O
AZURE EXPRESS, 1938, A

–B–
"B"...MUST DIE, 1973
B. F.'S DAUGHTER, 1948, A
B.J. LANG PRESENTS, 1971
B.S. I LOVE YOU, 1971, O
BAB THE FIXER, 1917
BAB'S BURGLAR, 1917, A
BAB'S CANDIDATE, 1920, A
BAB'S DIARY, 1917, A

BAB'S MATINEE IDOL, 1917
BABBITT, 1924, A
BABBITT, 1934, A
BABBLING TONGUES, 1917, A
BABE COMES HOME, 1927, A
BABE RUTH STORY, THE, 1948, AAA
BABES IN ARMS, 1939, AAA
BABES IN BAGDAD, 1952, A
BABES IN THE WOODS, 1917
BABES IN TOYLAND, 1934, AAA
BABES IN TOYLAND, 1961, AAA
BABES ON BROADWAY, 1941, AAA
BABES ON SWING STREET, 1944, A
BABETTE, 1917
BABETTE GOES TO WAR, 1960, C
BABETTE OF THE BALLY HOO, 1916
BABIES FOR SALE, 1940, A
BABO 73, 1964
BABY AND THE BATTLESHIP, THE, 1957, A
BABY BLUE MARINE, 1976, C
BABY CYCLONE, THE, 1928
BABY DOLL, 1956, O
BABY DOLLS, 1982
BABY FACE, 1933, O
BABY FACE HARRINGTON, 1935, A
BABY FACE MORGAN, 1942, A
BABY FACE NELSON, 1957, O
BABY LOVE, 1969, O
BABY MAKER, THE, 1970, O
BABY MINE, 1917, A
BABY MINE, 1928, A
BABY MOTHER, THE
BABY NEEDS A NEW PAIR OF SHOES, 1974
BABY, IT'S YOU, 1983, C-O
BABY, TAKE A BOW, 1934, AA
BABY, THE, 1973, C-O
BABY, THE RAIN MUST FALL, 1965, C
BABYLON, 1980, O
BABYSITTER, THE, 1969
BACCHANALE, 1970
BACCHANTES, THE, 1963, A
BACHELOR AND THE BOBBY-SOXER, THE, 1947, AAA
BACHELOR APARTMENT, 1931, C
BACHELOR APARTMENTS, 1920
BACHELOR BAIT, 1934, A
BACHELOR BRIDES, 1926
BACHELOR DADDY, 1941, A
BACHELOR DADDY, THE, 1922
BACHELOR FATHER, 1931, A
BACHELOR FLAT, 1962, A
BACHELOR GIRL, THE, 1929, A
BACHELOR HUSBAND, THE, 1920
BACHELOR IN PARADISE, 1961, A
BACHELOR IN PARIS, 1953, A
BACHELOR MOTHER, 1933, C
BACHELOR MOTHER, 1939, A
BACHELOR OF ARTS, 1935, A
BACHELOR OF HEARTS, 1958, A
BACHELOR PARTY, 1984, O
BACHELOR PARTY, THE, 1957, C
BACHELOR'S AFFAIRS, 1932, A
BACHELOR'S BABY, 1932, C
BACHELOR'S BABY, A, 1922
BACHELOR'S BABY, THE, 1927, A
BACHELOR'S CHILDREN, A, 1918
BACHELOR'S CLUB, THE, 1929
BACHELOR'S DAUGHTERS, THE, 1946, A
BACHELOR'S FOLLY
BACHELOR'S PARADISE, 1928, A
BACHELOR'S ROMANCE, THE, 1915
BACHELOR'S WIFE, A, 1919
BACHELORS' CLUB, THE, 1921, A
BACK AT THE FRONT, 1952, A
BACK DOOR TO HEAVEN, 1939, A
BACK DOOR TO HELL, 1964, A
BACK FIRE, 1922, A
BACK FROM ETERNITY, 1956, C
BACK FROM SHANGHAI, 1929
BACK FROM THE DEAD, 1957, C-O
BACK HOME AND BROKE, 1922, A
BACK IN CIRCULATION, 1937, A
BACK IN THE SADDLE, 1941, A
BACK OF THE MAN, 1917
BACK PAGE, 1934
BACK PAY, 1922
BACK PAY, 1930, A
BACK ROADS, 1981, O
BACK ROOM BOY, 1942, A
BACK STREET, 1932, A
BACK STREET, 1941, A
BACK STREET, 1961, A
BACK STREETS OF PARIS, 1962, C-O
BACK TO BATAAN, 1945, A
BACK TO GOD'S COUNTRY, 1919
BACK TO GOD'S COUNTRY, 1927
BACK TO GOD'S COUNTRY, 1953, A
BACK TO LIBERTY, 1927
BACK TO LIFE, 1925
BACK TO NATURE, 1936, A
BACK TO OLD VIRGINIA, 1923
BACK TO THE WALL, 1959, O

BACK TO YELLOW JACKET, 1922
BACK TRAIL, 1948, A
BACK TRAIL, THE, 1924, A
BACKBONE, 1923
BACKFIRE, 1950, A
BACKFIRE, 1965, C
BACKFIRE!, 1961, A
BACKGROUND, 1953, C
BACKGROUND TO DANGER, 1943, A
BACKLASH, 1947, A
BACKLASH, 1956, A
BACKSTAGE, 1927, A
BACKSTAGE, 1937, A
BACKSTAIRS, 1921
BACKTRACK, 1969, A
BAD AND THE BEAUTIFUL, THE, 1952, C
BAD BASCOMB, 1946, AA
BAD BLONDE, 1953, C
BAD BOY, 1935, A
BAD BOY, 1938, A
BAD BOY, 1939, A
BAD BOY, 1949, A
BAD BOYS, 1917
BAD BOYS, 1983, O
BAD BUNCH, THE, 1976
BAD CHARLESTON CHARLIE, 1973, A
BAD COMPANY, 1925
BAD COMPANY, 1931, A
BAD COMPANY, 1972, A
BAD DAY AT BLACK ROCK, 1955, A
BAD FOR EACH OTHER, 1954, A
BAD GEORGIA ROAD, 1977
BAD GIRL, 1931, C
BAD GIRL, 1959
BAD GUY, 1937, A
BAD LANDS, 1939, A
BAD LANDS, THE, 1925
BAD LITTLE ANGEL, 1939, AA
BAD LORD BYRON, THE, 1949, A
BAD MAN FROM BODIE, 1925
BAD MAN FROM RED BUTTE, 1940, A
BAD MAN OF BRIMSTONE, 1938, A
BAD MAN OF DEADWOOD, 1941, A
BAD MAN'S BLUFF, 1926
BAD MAN'S MONEY
BAD MAN'S RIVER, 1972, A
BAD MAN, THE, 1923
BAD MAN, THE, 1930, A
BAD MAN, THE, 1941, A
BAD MANNERS, 1984, C
BAD MEN OF MISSOURI, 1941, A
BAD MEN OF THE BORDER, 1945, A
BAD MEN OF THE HILLS, 1942, A
BAD MEN OF THUNDER GAP, 1943, A
BAD MEN OF TOMBSTONE, 1949, C
BAD MEN'S MONEY, 1929
BAD NEWS BEARS GO TO JAPAN, THE, 1978, C
BAD NEWS BEARS IN BREAKING TRAINING, THE,
    1977, C
BAD NEWS BEARS, THE, 1976, C
BAD ONE, THE, 1930, C
BAD SEED, THE, 1956, C
BAD SISTER, 1931, A
BAD SISTER, 1947, A
BADGE 373, 1973, O
BADGE OF HONOR, 1934, A
BADGE OF MARSHAL BRENNAN, THE, 1957, A
BADGER'S GREEN, 1934, A
BADGER'S GREEN, 1949, A
BADLANDERS, THE, 1958, A
BADLANDS, 1974, O
BADLANDS OF DAKOTA, 1941, A
BADLANDS OF MONTANA, 1957, A
BADMAN'S COUNTRY, 1958, A
BADMAN'S GOLD, 1951, A
BADMAN'S TERRITORY, 1946, A
BAFFLED, 1924, A
BAG AND BAGGAGE, 1923
BAGDAD, 1949, A
BAHAMA PASSAGE, 1941, A
BAILOUT AT 43,000, 1957, A
BAIT, 1950, A
BAIT, 1954, C
BAIT, THE, 1916
BAIT, THE, 1921, A
BAITED TRAP, 1926
BAKER'S HAWK, 1976, A
BAKER'S WIFE, THE, 1940, C
BAL TABARIN, 1952, A
BALACLAVA
BALACLAVA
BALALAIKA, 1939, A
BALCONY, THE, 1963, O
BALKAN EXPRESS, 1983
BALL AT SAVOY, 1936, A
BALL AT THE CASTLE, 1939, A
BALL OF FIRE, 1941, A
BALL OF FORTUNE, THE, 1926
BALLAD IN BLUE
BALLAD OF A GUNFIGHTER, 1964, A
BALLAD OF A HUSSAR, 1963, A
BALLAD OF A SOLDIER, 1960, A

BALLAD OF BILLIE BLUE, 1972
BALLAD OF CABLE HOGUE, THE, 1970, C
BALLAD OF COSSACK GLOOTA, 1938, A
BALLAD OF GREGORIO CORTEZ, THE, 1983, C-O
BALLAD OF JOSIE, 1968, A
BALLAD OF NARAYAMA, 1961, C
BALLAD OF NARAYAMA, THE, 1984, C
BALLERINA, 1950, A
BALLET GIRL, THE, 1916, A
BALLOON GOES UP, THE, 1942, A
BALLYHOO BUSTER, THE, 1928
BALTHAZAR
BALTIC DEPUTY, 1937, A
BALTIMORE BULLET, THE, 1980, C
BAMBI, 1942, AAA
BAMBOLE!, 1965, C
BAMBOO BLONDE, THE, 1946, A
BAMBOO GODS AND IRON MEN, 1974
BAMBOO PRISON, THE, 1955, A
BAMBOO SAUCER, THE, 1968, A
BANANA MONSTER, THE
BANANA PEEL, 1965, C
BANANA RIDGE, 1941, A
BANANAS, 1971, C
BAND OF ANGELS, 1957, A
BAND OF ASSASSINS, 1971
BAND OF OUTSIDERS, 1966, C-O
BAND OF THIEVES, 1962, A
BAND PLAYS ON, THE, 1934, A
BAND WAGGON, 1940, A
BAND WAGON, THE, 1953, A
BANDBOX, THE, 1919
BANDE A PART
BANDIDO, 1956, A
BANDIDOS, 1967, A
BANDIT BUSTER, THE, 1926
BANDIT KING OF TEXAS, 1949, A
BANDIT OF SHERWOOD FOREST, THE, 1946, AA
BANDIT OF ZHOBE, THE, 1959, A
BANDIT QUEEN, 1950, A
BANDIT RANGER, 1942, A
BANDIT TAMER, THE, 1925
BANDIT TRAIL, THE, 1941, A
BANDIT'S BABY, THE, 1925
BANDIT'S DOUBLE, THE, 1917
BANDIT'S SON, THE, 1927, A
BANDIT, THE, 1949, A
BANDITS IN ROME, 1967
BANDITS OF CORSICA, THE, 1953, A
BANDITS OF DARK CANYON, 1947, A
BANDITS OF EL DORADO, 1951, A
BANDITS OF ORGOSOLO, 1964, A
BANDITS OF THE AIR, 1925
BANDITS OF THE BADLANDS, 1945, A
BANDITS OF THE WEST, 1953, A
BANDITS ON THE WIND, 1964, A
BANDOLERO!, 1968, A
BANDOLERO, THE, 1924
BANG BANG KID, THE, 1968, A
BANG THE DRUM SLOWLY, 1973, A
BANG! YOU'RE DEAD, 1954, C
BANG, BANG, YOU'RE DEAD, 1966, A
BANISHED, 1978, C
BANJO, 1947, AA
BANJO ON MY KNEE, 1936, A
BANK ALARM, 1937, A
BANK DICK, THE, 1940, A
BANK HOLIDAY, 1938, C
BANK MESSENGER MYSTERY, THE, 1936, A
BANK RAIDERS, THE, 1958, A
BANK SHOT, 1974, A
BANKER'S DAUGHTER, THE, 1914
BANNERLINE, 1951, A
BANNING, 1967, C
BANTAM COWBOY, THE, 1928, A
BANZAI, 1983, C-O
BAR 20, 1943, A
BAR 20 JUSTICE, 1938, A
BAR 20 RIDES AGAIN, 1936, A
BAR L RANCH, 1930, A
BAR MITSVE, 1935
BAR NOTHIN', 1921, A
BAR SINISTER, THE, 1917, A
BAR SINISTER, THE, 1955, A
BAR Z BAD MEN, 1937, A
BAR-C MYSTERY, THE, 1926
BARABBAS, 1962, C
BARB WIRE, 1922
BARBADOS QUEST
BARBARA, 1970
BARBARA FRIETCHIE, 1915
BARBARA FRIETCHIE, 1924
BARBARELLA, 1968, O
BARBARIAN AND THE GEISHA, THE, 1958, A
BARBARIAN, THE, 1921
BARBARIAN, THE, 1933, C
BARBAROSA, 1982, C
BARBARY COAST, 1935, A
BARBARY COAST GENT, 1944, A
BARBARY PIRATE, 1949, A
BARBARY SHEEP, 1917
BARBED WIRE

BARBED WIRE, 1927, A
BARBED WIRE, 1952, A
BARBER OF SEVILLE, 1949, A
BARBER OF SEVILLE, THE, 1947, A
BARBER OF SEVILLE, THE, 1973, A
BARBER OF STAMFORD HILL, THE, 1963, A
BARBERINA, 1932, A
BARCAROLE, 1935, A
BARDELYS THE MAGNIFICENT, 1926
BARE FISTS, 1919
BARE KNEES, 1928
BARE KNUCKLES, 1921
BARE KNUCKLES, 1977
BARE KNUCKLES, 1978, O
BARE-FISTED GALLAGHER, 1919
BAREE, SON OF KAZAN, 1918
BAREE, SON OF KAZAN, 1925
BAREFOOT BATTALION, THE, 1954, A
BAREFOOT BOY, 1938, A
BAREFOOT BOY, THE, 1923
BAREFOOT CONTESSA, THE, 1954, A
BAREFOOT EXECUTIVE, THE, 1971, AAA
BAREFOOT IN THE PARK, 1967, A
BAREFOOT MAILMAN, THE, 1951, A
BAREFOOT SAVAGE
BARGAIN WITH BULLETS, 1937
BARGAIN, THE, 1914
BARGAIN, THE, 1921
BARGAIN, THE, 1931, A
BARGAINS, 1923
BARGEE, THE, 1964, C
BARKER, THE, 1917
BARKER, THE, 1928
BARKER, THE, 1928, A
BARKLEYS OF BROADWAY, THE, 1949, A
BARN OF THE NAKED DEAD Zero, 1976, O
BARNABY, 1919
BARNABY RUDGE, 1915
BARNACLE BILL, 1935, A
BARNACLE BILL, 1941, A
BARNACLE BILL, 1958
BARNES MURDER CASE, THE, 1930, A
BARNSTORMER, THE, 1922
BARNSTORMERS, THE, 1915
BARNUM WAS RIGHT, 1929, A
BARNYARD FOLLIES, 1940, A
BAROCCO, 1925
BAROCCO, 1976, O
BARON BLOOD, 1972, C
BARON MUNCHAUSEN, 1962, A
BARON OF ARIZONA, THE, 1950, A
BARONESS AND THE BUTLER, THE, 1938, A
BARQUERO, 1970, O
BARRACUDA, 1978, C
BARRANCO, 1932, A
BARRETTS OF WIMPOLE STREET, THE, 1934, A
BARRETTS OF WIMPOLE STREET, THE, 1957, A
BARRICADE, 1939, A
BARRICADE, 1950, A
BARRICADE, THE, 1917
BARRICADE, THE, 1921
BARRIER, 1966, A
BARRIER, THE, 1926, A
BARRIER, THE, 1937, A
BARRIERS BURNED AWAY, 1925
BARRIERS OF FOLLY, 1922
BARRIERS OF SOCIETY, 1916
BARRIERS OF THE LAW, 1925, A
BARRY LYNDON, 1975, C-O
BARRY MC KENZIE HOLDS HIS OWN, 1975
BARS OF HATE, 1936, A
BARS OF IRON, 1920
BARTLEBY, 1970, A
BARTON MYSTERY, THE, 1920
BARTON MYSTERY, THE, 1932, A
BASHFUL BACHELOR, THE, 1942, A
BASHFUL BUCCANEER, 1925, A
BASHFUL ELEPHANT, THE, 1962, A
BASILEUS QUARTET, 1984, O
BASKET CASE, 1982, O
BASKETBALL FIX, THE, 1951, A
BAT PEOPLE, THE, 1974, C
BAT WHISPERS, THE, 1930, A
BAT, THE, 1926, A
BAT, THE, 1959, C
BATAAN, 1943, C
BATHING BEAUTY, 1944, A
BATMAN, 1966, AA
BATTLE AT APACHE PASS, THE, 1952, A
BATTLE AT BLOODY BEACH, 1961, A
BATTLE BENEATH THE EARTH, 1968, A
BATTLE BEYOND THE STARS, 1980, C
BATTLE BEYOND THE SUN, 1963, O
BATTLE CIRCUS, 1953, A
BATTLE CRY, 1955, A
BATTLE CRY, 1959, A
BATTLE CRY OF PEACE, THE, 1915, A
BATTLE CRY, THE
BATTLE FOR MUSIC, 1943
BATTLE FOR THE PLANET OF THE APES, 1973, A
BATTLE HELL, 1956, A
BATTLE HYMN, 1957, A

BATTLE IN OUTER SPACE, 1960, A
BATTLE OF ALGIERS, THE, 1967, C
BATTLE OF AUSTERLITZ
BATTLE OF BALLOTS, THE, 1915
BATTLE OF BILLY'S POND, 1976
BATTLE OF BLOOD ISLAND, 1960, A
BATTLE OF BRITAIN, THE, 1969
BATTLE OF BROADWAY, 1938, A
BATTLE OF EL ALAMEIN, 1971
BATTLE OF GALLIPOLI, 1931, A
BATTLE OF GETTYSBURG, 1914, A
BATTLE OF GREED, 1934, A
BATTLE OF HEARTS, 1916
BATTLE OF LIFE, THE, 1916, A
BATTLE OF LOVE'S RETURN, THE, 1971, A
BATTLE OF MONS, 1929
BATTLE OF PARIS, THE, 1929, A
BATTLE OF ROGUE RIVER, 1954, A
BATTLE OF SHILOH, THE, 1914
BATTLE OF THE AMAZONS, 1973, A
BATTLE OF THE BULGE, 1965, A
BATTLE OF THE CORAL SEA, 1959, A
BATTLE OF THE EAGLES, 1981
BATTLE OF THE NERETVA, 1971, A
BATTLE OF THE RAILS, 1949, A
BATTLE OF THE RIVER PLATE, THE
BATTLE OF THE SEXES, THE, 1914, A
BATTLE OF THE SEXES, THE, 1928, A
BATTLE OF THE SEXES, THE, 1960, A
BATTLE OF THE VI
BATTLE OF THE VILLA FIORITA, THE, 1965, A
BATTLE OF THE WORLDS, 1961, A
BATTLE OF WATERLOO, THE, 1913
BATTLE STATIONS, 1956, A
BATTLE STRIPE
BATTLE TAXI, 1955, A
BATTLE ZONE, 1952, A
BATTLE, THE, 1934, A
BATTLEAXE, THE, 1962, A
BATTLEGROUND, 1949, A
BATTLER, THE, 1919
BATTLER, THE, 1925
BATTLES OF CHIEF PONTIAC, 1952, A
BATTLES OF THE CORONEL AND FALKLAND
  ISLANDS, THE, 1928, A
BATTLESHIP POTEMKIN, THE, 1925, C
BATTLESTAR GALACTICA, 1979, A
BATTLETRUCK, 1982, C
BATTLIN' BILL, 1927
BATTLIN' BUCKAROO, 1924
BATTLING BATES, 1923
BATTLING BELLHOP, THE
BATTLING BOOKWORM, 1928
BATTLING BUCKAROO, 1932, A
BATTLING BUDDY, 1924
BATTLING BUNYON, 1925
BATTLING BURKE, 1928
BATTLING BUTLER, 1926, A
BATTLING FOOL, THE, 1924
BATTLING JANE, 1918
BATTLING KID, 1926
BATTLING KING, 1922
BATTLING MARSHAL, 1950, A
BATTLING MASON, 1924
BATTLING ORIOLES, THE, 1924
BAVU, 1923
BAWBS O' BLUE RIDGE, 1916
BAWDY ADVENTURES OF TOM JONES, THE, 1976, O
BAXTER, 1973, C
BAY BOY, 1984, C
BAY OF ANGELS, 1964, C
BAY OF SAINT MICHEL, THE, 1963, A
BAYOU, 1957, A
BE A LITTLE SPORT, 1919
BE CAREFUL, MR. SMITH, 1935
BE MINE TONIGHT, 1933, A
BE MY GUEST, 1965, A
BE MY VALENTINE, OR ELSE...
BE MY WIFE, 1921
BE YOURSELF, 1930, A
BEACH BALL, 1965, A
BEACH BLANKET BINGO, 1965, A
BEACH BUNNIES, 1977
BEACH COMBER, THE
BEACH GIRLS, 1982, C-O
BEACH GIRLS AND THE MONSTER, THE, 1965, C
BEACH HOUSE, 1982
BEACH HOUSE PARTY
BEACH OF DREAMS, 1921
BEACH PARTY, 1963, A
BEACH PARTY, ITALIAN STYLE
BEACH RED, 1967, A
BEACHCOMBER, THE, 1938, A
BEACHCOMBER, THE, 1955, A
BEACHHEAD, 1954, A
BEADS OF ONE ROSARY, THE, 1982, A
BEALE STREET MAMA, 1946
BEANS, 1918
BEAR ISLAND, 1980, C
BEAR'S WEDDING, THE, 1926
BEAR, THE, 1963, AA
BEAR, THE, 1984, C

BEARCAT, THE, 1922
BEARS AND I, THE, 1974, C
BEARTOOTH, 1978
BEAST FROM 20,000 FATHOMS, THE, 1953, C
BEAST FROM THE HAUNTED CAVE, 1960, C
BEAST IN THE CELLAR, THE, 1971, C
BEAST MUST DIE, THE, 1974, A
BEAST OF BABYLON AGAINST THE SON OF
  HERCULES
BEAST OF BLOOD, 1970, C-O
BEAST OF BORNEO, 1935
BEAST OF BUDAPEST, THE, 1958, C
BEAST OF HOLLOW MOUNTAIN, THE, 1956, A
BEAST OF MOROCCO
BEAST OF THE CITY, THE, 1932, C-O
BEAST OF THE DEAD
BEAST OF THE YELLOW NIGHT, 1971
BEAST OF YUCCA FLATS, THE, 1961, C
BEAST THAT KILLED WOMEN, 1965
BEAST WITH A MILLION EYES, THE, 1956, A
BEAST WITH FIVE FINGERS, THE, 1946, C
BEAST WITHIN, THE, 1982, O
BEAST, THE, 1916
BEAST, THE, 1975, O
BEASTMASTER, THE, 1982, C
BEASTS, 1983
BEASTS OF BERLIN, 1939, C
BEASTS OF MARSEILLES, THE, 1959, C
BEAT GENERATION, THE, 1959, C
"BEAT" GIRL
BEAT STREET, 1984, A-C
BEAT THE BAND, 1947, A
BEAT THE DEVIL, 1953, A
BEATEN, 1924
BEATING THE GAME, 1921, A
BEATING THE ODDS, 1919
BEATNIKS, THE, 1960, O
BEAU BANDIT, 1930, A
BEAU BROADWAY, 1928
BEAU BROCADE, 1916
BEAU BRUMMEL, 1924, A
BEAU BRUMMELL, 1954, A
BEAU GESTE, 1926, A
BEAU GESTE, 1939, A
BEAU GESTE, 1966, A
BEAU IDEAL, 1931, A
BEAU JAMES, 1957, A
BEAU PERE, 1981, O
BEAU REVEL, 1921, C
BEAU SABREUR, 1928, A
BEAUTE FATALE, 1923
BEAUTE QUI MEURT, 1917
BEAUTIFUL ADVENTURE, 1932, A
BEAUTIFUL ADVENTURE, THE, 1917
BEAUTIFUL AND DAMNED, THE, 1922, A
BEAUTIFUL BLONDE FROM BASHFUL BEND, THE,
  1949, A
BEAUTIFUL BUT BROKE, 1944, A
BEAUTIFUL BUT DEADLY
BEAUTIFUL BUT DUMB, 1928, A
BEAUTIFUL CHEAT, THE, 1926, A
BEAUTIFUL CHEAT, THE, 1946, A
BEAUTIFUL CITY, THE, 1925
BEAUTIFUL GAMBLER, THE, 1921, A
BEAUTIFUL JIM
BEAUTIFUL KITTY, 1923, A
BEAUTIFUL LIAR, THE, 1921, A
BEAUTIFUL LIE, THE, 1917
BEAUTIFUL MRS. REYNOLDS, THE, 1918
BEAUTIFUL PRISONER, THE, 1983, C
BEAUTIFUL SINNER, THE, 1924
BEAUTIFUL STRANGER, 1954, C
BEAUTIFUL SWINDLERS, THE, 1967, O
BEAUTIFULLY TRIMMED, 1920
BEAUTY AND BULLETS, 1928, A
BEAUTY AND THE BAD MAN, 1925
BEAUTY AND THE BANDIT, 1946, A
BEAUTY AND THE BARGE, 1937, A
BEAUTY AND THE BEAST, 1947, A
BEAUTY AND THE BEAST, 1963, C
BEAUTY AND THE BODY, 1963
BEAUTY AND THE BOLSHEVIK, 1923
BEAUTY AND THE BOSS, 1932, A
BEAUTY AND THE DEVIL, 1952, A
BEAUTY AND THE ROGUE, 1918
BEAUTY FOR SALE, 1933, A
BEAUTY FOR THE ASKING, 1939, A
BEAUTY FROM NIVERNAISE, THE
BEAUTY IN CHAINS, 1918
BEAUTY JUNGLE, THE, 1966, C
BEAUTY MARKET, THE, 1920
BEAUTY ON PARADE, 1950, A
BEAUTY PARLOR, 1932, A
BEAUTY PRIZE, THE, 1924
BEAUTY PROOF, 1919
BEAUTY SHOP, THE, 1922
BEAUTY SHOPPERS, 1927
BEAUTY'S DAUGHTER, 1935
BEAUTY'S SORROWS, 1931
BEAUTY'S WORTH, 1922
BEBO'S GIRL, 1964, A
BECAUSE, 1918

BECAUSE, 1921
BECAUSE I LOVED YOU, 1930, C
BECAUSE OF EVE, 1948, C-O
BECAUSE OF HIM, 1946, A
BECAUSE OF THE CATS, 1974
BECAUSE OF THE WOMAN, 1917
BECAUSE OF YOU, 1952, A
BECAUSE THEY'RE YOUNG, 1960, C
BECAUSE YOU'RE MINE, 1952, AA
BECKET, 1923
BECKET, 1964, C
BECKONING FLAME, THE, 1916
BECKONING ROADS, 1920
BECKONING TRAIL, THE, 1916
BECKY, 1927
BECKY SHARP, 1935, C
BED AND BOARD, 1971, C
BED AND BREAKFAST, 1930, A
BED AND BREAKFAST, 1936, A
BED AND SOFA, 1926
BED OF ROSES, 1933, A
BED OF VIOLENCE, 1967
BED SITTING ROOM, THE, 1969, C
BEDAZZLED, 1967, C
BEDELIA, 1946, A
BEDEVILLED, 1955, C
BEDFORD INCIDENT, THE, 1965, C
BEDKNOBS AND BROOMSTICKS, 1971, AAA
BEDLAM, 1946, C
BEDROOM EYES, 1984, O
BEDROOM WINDOW, THE, 1924, A
BEDSIDE, 1934, A
BEDSIDE MANNER, 1945, A
BEDTIME FOR BONZO, 1951, AA
BEDTIME STORY, 1938, A
BEDTIME STORY, 1942, A
BEDTIME STORY, 1964, C
BEDTIME STORY, A, 1933, AA
BEEN DOWN SO LONG IT LOOKS LIKE UP TO ME,
  1977, A
BEES IN PARADISE, 1944, A
BEES, THE, 1978, C
BEETLE, THE, 1919
BEFORE DAWN, 1933, A
BEFORE HIM ALL ROME TREMBLED, 1947, A
BEFORE I HANG, 1940, A
BEFORE I WAKE
BEFORE MIDNIGHT, 1925
BEFORE MIDNIGHT, 1934, A
BEFORE MORNING, 1933, A
BEFORE THE REVOLUTION, 1964, C
BEFORE THE WHITE MAN CAME, 1920
BEFORE WINTER COMES, 1969, C
BEG, BORROW OR STEAL, 1937, A
BEGGAR GIRL'S WEDDING, THE, 1915
BEGGAR IN PURPLE, A, 1920
BEGGAR OF CAWNPORE, THE, 1916
BEGGAR ON HORSEBACK, 1925, A
BEGGAR PRINCE, THE, 1920
BEGGAR STUDENT, THE, 1931, A
BEGGAR STUDENT, THE, 1958, A
BEGGAR'S HOLIDAY, 1934
BEGGAR'S OPERA, THE, 1953, C
BEGGARS IN ERMINE, 1934, A
BEGGARS OF LIFE, 1928, A-C
BEGGING THE RING, 1979
BEGINNING OF THE END, 1957, C
BEGINNING OR THE END, THE, 1947, A
BEGUILED, THE, 1971, A-O
BEHAVE YOURSELF, 1951, C
BEHEMOTH, THE SEA MONSTER, 1959, A
BEHIND CITY LIGHTS, 1945, A
BEHIND CLOSED DOORS, 1929
BEHIND CLOSED SHUTTERS, 1952, O
BEHIND GREEN LIGHTS, 1935, A
BEHIND GREEN LIGHTS, 1946, A
BEHIND JURY DOORS, 1933, A
BEHIND LOCKED DOORS, 1948, A
BEHIND LOCKED DOORS, 1976, O
BEHIND MASKS, 1921
BEHIND OFFICE DOORS, 1931, A
BEHIND PRISON BARS, 1937
BEHIND PRISON GATES, 1939, A
BEHIND PRISON WALLS, 1943, A
BEHIND SOUTHERN LINES, 1952
BEHIND STONE WALLS, 1932, A
BEHIND THAT CURTAIN, 1929, C
BEHIND THE ALTAR, 1929
BEHIND THE CURTAIN, 1924
BEHIND THE DOOR
BEHIND THE DOOR, 1920
BEHIND THE EIGHT BALL, 1942, A
BEHIND THE EVIDENCE, 1935, A
BEHIND THE FRONT, 1926, A
BEHIND THE HEADLINES, 1937, A
BEHIND THE HEADLINES, 1953
BEHIND THE HEADLINES, 1956, A
BEHIND THE HIGH WALL, 1956, C
BEHIND THE IRON CURTAIN
BEHIND THE IRON MASK, 1977, C
BEHIND THE LINES, 1916
BEHIND THE MAKEUP, 1930, C

BEHIND THE MASK, 1917
BEHIND THE MASK, 1932, C
BEHIND THE MASK, 1946, A
BEHIND THE MASK, 1958, C
BEHIND THE MIKE, 1937, A
BEHIND THE NEWS, 1941, A
BEHIND THE RISING SUN, 1943, C
BEHIND THE SCENES, 1914
BEHIND THE SHUTTERS, 1976
BEHIND TWO GUNS, 1924
BEHIND YOUR BACK, 1937, A
BEHOLD A PALE HORSE, 1964, C
BEHOLD MY WIFE, 1920
BEHOLD MY WIFE, 1935, C
BEHOLD THE MAN, 1921
BEHOLD THIS WOMAN, 1924
BEILIS CASE, THE, 1917
BEING RESPECTABLE, 1924
BEING THERE, 1979, C
BEING, THE, 1983, C
BELA LUGOSI MEETS A BROOKLYN GORILLA, 1952, A
BELGIAN, THE, 1917
BELIEVE IN ME, 1971, O
BELIEVE ME, XANTIPPE, 1918
BELL BOY 13, 1923
BELL JAR, THE, 1979, O
BELL OF HELL, THE, 1973
BELL' ANTONIO, 1962, C-O
BELL, BOOK AND CANDLE, 1958, A
BELL-BOTTOM GEORGE, 1943, A
BELLA DONNA, 1915
BELLA DONNA, 1923
BELLA DONNA, 1934, A
BELLA DONNA, 1983, C
BELLAMY TRIAL, THE, 1929, C
BELLAMY: MESSAGE GIRL MURDERS, 1980
BELLBOY, THE, 1960, AA
BELLE DE JOUR, 1968, O
BELLE LE GRAND, 1951, A
BELLE OF ALASKA, 1922
BELLE OF BROADWAY, THE, 1926
BELLE OF NEW YORK, THE, 1919
BELLE OF NEW YORK, THE, 1952, A
BELLE OF OLD MEXICO, 1950, A
BELLE OF THE NINETIES, 1934, C
BELLE OF THE SEASON, THE, 1919
BELLE OF THE YUKON, 1944, A
BELLE SOMMERS, 1962
BELLE STARR, 1941, A
BELLE STARR'S DAUGHTER, 1947, A
BELLES OF ST. CLEMENTS, THE, 1936, A
BELLES OF ST. TRINIAN'S, THE, 1954, AA
BELLES ON THEIR TOES, 1952, AAA
BELLISSIMA, 1952, C
BELLMAN, THE, 1947, C
BELLS, 1981, O
BELLS ARE RINGING, 1960, AA
BELLS GO DOWN, THE, 1943, A
BELLS OF CAPISTRANO, 1942, A
BELLS OF CORONADO, 1950, AA
BELLS OF ROSARITA, 1945, AAA
BELLS OF SAN ANGELO, 1947, A
BELLS OF SAN FERNANDO, 1947, A
BELLS OF SAN JUAN, 1922
BELLS OF ST. MARY'S, THE, 1928
BELLS OF ST. MARY'S, THE, 1945, AAA
BELLS, THE, 1914
BELLS, THE, 1918
BELLS, THE, 1926
BELLS, THE, 1931, C
BELONGING, 1922
BELOVED, 1934, A
BELOVED ADVENTURESS, THE, 1917
BELOVED BACHELOR, THE, 1931, A
BELOVED BLACKMAILER, THE, 1918
BELOVED BRAT, 1938, A
BELOVED BRUTE, THE, 1924
BELOVED CHEATER, THE, 1920
BELOVED ENEMY, 1936, C
BELOVED IMPOSTER, 1936, A
BELOVED IMPOSTER, THE, 1918
BELOVED INFIDEL, 1959, A
BELOVED JIM, 1917
BELOVED ROGUE, THE, 1927, A
BELOVED ROGUES, 1917
BELOVED TRAITOR, THE, 1918
BELOVED VAGABOND, THE, 1912
BELOVED VAGABOND, THE, 1923
BELOVED VAGABOND, THE, 1936, A
BELOVED, THE, 1972
BELOW THE BELT, 1980, C
BELOW THE BORDER, 1942, A
BELOW THE DEAD LINE, 1921
BELOW THE DEADLINE, 1929
BELOW THE DEADLINE, 1936, A
BELOW THE DEADLINE, 1946, A
BELOW THE HILL, 1974
BELOW THE LINE, 1925, A
BELOW THE RIO GRANDE, 1923
BELOW THE SEA, 1933, A

BELOW THE SURFACE, 1920
BELPHEGOR THE MOUNTEBANK, 1921
BELT AND SUSPENDERS MAN, THE, 1970
BELSTONE FOX, THE, 1976, AAA
BEN, 1972, A
BEN BLAIR, 1916
BEN HUR, 1959, A
BEN-HUR, 1925, A
BEND OF THE RIVER, 1952, C
BENEATH THE 12-MILE REEF, 1953, A
BENEATH THE CZAR, 1914
BENEATH THE PLANET OF THE APES, 1970, AA
BENEATH WESTERN SKIES, 1944, A
BENGAL BRIGADE, 1954, A
BENGAL TIGER, 1936, A
BENGAZI, 1955, A-C
BENJAMIN, 1968, O
BENJAMIN, 1973, AA
BENJI, 1974, AAA
BENNIE THE HOWL, 1927
BENNY GOODMAN STORY, THE, 1956, AA
BENSON MURDER CASE, THE, 1930, A
BENTLEY'S CONSCIENCE, 1922
BENVENUTA, 1983, C
BEQUEST TO THE NATION
BERKELEY SQUARE, 1933, A
BERLIN AFTER DARK, 1929
BERLIN ALEXANDERPLATZ, 1933, A
BERLIN CORRESPONDENT, 1942, A
BERLIN EXPRESS, 1948, C
BERLIN VIA AMERICA, 1918
BERMONDSEY KID, THE, 1933, A
BERMUDA AFFAIR, 1956, A
BERMUDA MYSTERY, 1944, A
BERNADETTE OF LOURDES, 1962, A
BERNARDINE, 1957, AA
BERSERK, 1967, O
BERTHA, THE SEWING MACHINE GIRL, 1927, A
BESIDE THE BONNIE BRIER BUSH
BEST BAD MAN, THE, 1925
BEST DEFENSE, 1984, O
BEST FOOT FORWARD, 1943, A
BEST FRIENDS, 1975, O
BEST FRIENDS, 1975
BEST FRIENDS, 1982, A
BEST HOUSE IN LONDON, THE, 1969, O
BEST LITTLE WHOREHOUSE IN TEXAS, THE, 1982, O
BEST MAN WINS, 1948, AA
BEST MAN WINS, THE, 1935, A
BEST MAN, THE, 1917
BEST MAN, THE, 1919
BEST MAN, THE, 1964, C
BEST OF ENEMIES, 1933, A
BEST OF ENEMIES, THE, 1962, A
BEST OF EVERYTHING, THE, 1959, C-O
BEST OF LUCK, THE, 1920
BEST OF THE BADMEN, 1951, A
BEST PEOPLE, THE, 1925
BEST THINGS IN LIFE ARE FREE, THE, 1956, AA
BEST WAY, THE, 1978, C
BEST YEARS OF OUR LIVES, THE, 1946, A
BEST, THE, 1979
BETES...COMES LES HOMMES, 1923
BETHUNE, 1977
BETRAYAL, 1929
BETRAYAL, 1932, A
BETRAYAL, 1939, A
BETRAYAL, 1983, O
BETRAYAL FROM THE EAST, 1945, AA
BETRAYAL, THE
BETRAYAL, THE, 1929
BETRAYAL, THE, 1948, A
BETRAYAL, THE, 1958, A
BETRAYAL: THE STORY OF KAMILLA
BETRAYED, 1916
BETRAYED, 1917
BETRAYED, 1954, C
BETRAYED WOMEN, 1955, C
BETSY ROSS, 1917
BETSY'S BURGLAR, 1917
BETSY, THE, 1978, C
BETTA THE GYPSY, 1918
BETTER 'OLE, THE, 1926, A
BETTER A WIDOW, 1969, O
BETTER DAYS, 1927
BETTER HALF, THE, 1918
BETTER LATE THAN NEVER, 1983, C
BETTER MAN WINS, THE, 1922
BETTER MAN, THE, 1914
BETTER MAN, THE, 1915
BETTER MAN, THE, 1921
BETTER MAN, THE, 1926
BETTER TIMES, 1919
BETTER WAY, THE, 1926
BETTER WIFE, THE, 1919
BETTER WOMAN, THE, 1915
BETTINA LOVED A SOLDIER, 1916
BETTY AND THE BUCCANEERS, 1917
BETTY BE GOOD, 1917
BETTY CO-ED, 1946, A
BETTY OF GRAYSTONE, 1916
BETTY TAKES A HAND, 1918

BETTY TO THE RESCUE, 1917
BETWEEN DANGERS, 1927
BETWEEN FIGHTING MEN, 1932, A
BETWEEN FRIENDS, 1924
BETWEEN HEAVEN AND HELL, 1956, A
BETWEEN MEN, 1916
BETWEEN MEN, 1935, A
BETWEEN MIDNIGHT AND DAWN, 1950, C
BETWEEN THE LINES, 1977, C
BETWEEN TIME AND ETERNITY, 1960, A
BETWEEN TWO HUSBANDS, 1922
BETWEEN TWO WOMEN, 1937, C
BETWEEN TWO WOMEN, 1944, A
BETWEEN TWO WORLDS
BETWEEN TWO WORLDS, 1944, A
BETWEEN US GIRLS, 1942, C
BEULAH, 1915
BEVERLY HILLS COP, 1984, O
BEVERLY OF GRAUSTARK, 1926, A
BEWARE, 1919
BEWARE, 1946, A
BEWARE MY BRETHREN, 1972
BEWARE OF BACHELORS, 1928
BEWARE OF BLONDES, 1928
BEWARE OF BLONDIE, 1950, AA
BEWARE OF CHILDREN, 1961, A
BEWARE OF LADIES, 1937, A
BEWARE OF MARRIED MEN, 1928
BEWARE OF PITY, 1946, A
BEWARE OF STRANGERS, 1918
BEWARE OF THE BRIDE, 1920
BEWARE OF THE LAW, 1922
BEWARE OF WINDOWS, 1927
BEWARE SPOOKS, 1939, A
BEWARE THE BLACK WIDOW, 1968
BEWARE! THE BLOB, 1972, A
BEWARE, MY LOVELY, 1952, C
BEWITCHED, 1945, C
BEYOND, 1921, A
BEYOND A REASONABLE DOUBT, 1956, C
BEYOND ALL ODDS, 1926
BEYOND AND BACK, 1978, A
BEYOND ATLANTIS, 1973, O
BEYOND CONTROL, 1971
BEYOND EVIL, 1980, A
BEYOND FEAR, 1977, C
BEYOND GLORY, 1948, A
BEYOND GOOD AND EVIL, 1984, O
BEYOND LONDON LIGHTS, 1928
BEYOND MOMBASA, 1957, A-C
BEYOND PRICE, 1921, A
BEYOND REASONABLE DOUBT, 1980, C
BEYOND REASON, 1977
BEYOND THE BLUE HORIZON, 1942, A
BEYOND THE BORDER, 1925
BEYOND THE CITIES, 1930, A
BEYOND THE CROSSROADS, 1922
BEYOND THE CURTAIN, 1960, A
BEYOND THE DOOR, 1975, O
BEYOND THE DOOR II, 1979, O
BEYOND THE DREAMS OF AVARICE, 1920
BEYOND THE FOG, 1981, O
BEYOND THE FOREST, 1949, C
BEYOND THE LAST FRONTIER, 1943, A
BEYOND THE LAW, 1918
BEYOND THE LAW, 1930
BEYOND THE LAW, 1934, A
BEYOND THE LAW, 1967
BEYOND THE LAW, 1968, C
BEYOND THE LIMIT, 1983, C
BEYOND THE LIVING
BEYOND THE MOON, 1964
BEYOND THE PECOS, 1945, A
BEYOND THE POSEIDON ADVENTURE, 1979, A-C
BEYOND THE PURPLE HILLS, 1950, A
BEYOND THE RAINBOW, 1922
BEYOND THE REEF, 1981, O
BEYOND THE RIO GRANDE, 1930, A
BEYOND THE RIVER, 1922
BEYOND THE ROCKIES, 1926
BEYOND THE ROCKIES, 1932, A
BEYOND THE ROCKS, 1922, A
BEYOND THE SACRAMENTO, 1941, A
BEYOND THE SHADOWS, 1918
BEYOND THE SIERRAS, 1928
BEYOND THE TIME BARRIER, 1960, C
BEYOND THE TRAIL, 1926
BEYOND THE UNIVERSE, 1981
BEYOND THE VEIL, 1925
BEYOND THE WALL
BEYOND THIS PLACE, 1959, C
BEYOND TOMORROW, 1940, A
BEYOND VICTORY, 1931, C
BHOWANI JUNCTION, 1956, C
BIBI, 1977
BIBLE...IN THE BEGINNING, THE, 1966, AA
BICYCLE THIEF, THE, 1949, A-C
BID FOR FORTUNE, A, 1917, A
BIDDY, 1983, A
BIFF BANG BUDDY, 1924
BIG ADVENTURE, THE, 1921
BIG AND THE BAD, THE, 1971, C

BIG BAD MAMA, 1974, O
BIG BAD WOLF, THE, 1968
BIG BIRD CAGE, THE, 1972, O
BIG BLOCKADE, THE, 1942, A
BIG BLUFF, THE, 1933, C
BIG BLUFF, THE, 1955, C
BIG BONANZA, THE, 1944, C
BIG BOODLE, THE, 1957, C
BIG BOSS, THE, 1941, A
BIG BOUNCE, THE, 1969, O
BIG BOY, 1930, A
BIG BOY RIDES AGAIN, 1935
BIG BRAIN, THE, 1933, A
BIG BRAWL, THE, 1980, C
BIG BROADCAST OF 1936, THE, 1935, AA
BIG BROADCAST OF 1937, THE, 1936, AA
BIG BROADCAST OF 1938, THE, 1937, AA
BIG BROADCAST, THE, 1932, AA
BIG BROTHER, 1923
BIG BROWN EYES, 1936, A
BIG BUS, THE, 1976, A
BIG BUSINESS, 1930, A
BIG BUSINESS, 1934, A
BIG BUSINESS, 1937, A
BIG BUSINESS GIRL, 1931, A
BIG BUST-OUT, THE, 1973
BIG CAGE, THE, 1933, A
BIG CALIBRE, 1935
BIG CAPER, THE, 1957, C
BIG CARNIVAL, THE, 1951, O
BIG CAT, THE, 1949, C
BIG CATCH, THE, 1968, A
BIG CHANCE, THE, 1933, A
BIG CHANCE, THE, 1957, A
BIG CHASE, THE, 1954, A
BIG CHIEF, THE, 1960, AA
BIG CHILL, THE, 1983, C
BIG CIRCUS, THE, 1959, A
BIG CITY, 1937, A
BIG CITY, 1948, AA
BIG CITY BLUES, C
BIG CITY, THE, 1928, A
BIG CITY, THE, 1963, A
BIG CLOCK, THE, 1948, C
BIG COMBO, THE, 1955, O
BIG COUNTRY, THE, 1958
BIG CUBE, THE, 1969, O
BIG DADDY, 1969, O
BIG DAN, 1923
BIG DAY, THE, 1960, A
BIG DEAL ON MADONNA STREET, THE, 1960, A
BIG DIAMOND ROBBERY, THE, 1929
BIG DOLL HOUSE, THE, 1971, O
BIG DOLL HOUSE, THE, 1971
BIG DRIVE, THE, 1928
BIG EXECUTIVE, 1933, A
BIG FELLA, 1937, A
BIG FIGHT, THE, 1930
BIG FISHERMAN, THE, 1959, A-C
BIG FIX, THE, 1947, A
BIG FIX, THE, 1978, C
BIG FOOT, 1973, O
BIG FRAME, THE, 1953, A
BIG FUN CARNIVAL, THE, 1957
BIG GAMBLE, THE, 1931, A
BIG GAMBLE, THE, 1961, A
BIG GAME, 1921, C
BIG GAME, THE
BIG GAME, THE, 1936, A
BIG GAME, THE, 1972, C
BIG GUNDOWN, THE, 1968, A
BIG GUNS
BIG GUSHER, THE, 1951, A
BIG GUY, THE, 1939, A
BIG HAND FOR THE LITTLE LADY, A, 1966, A
BIG HANGOVER,THE, 1950, A-C
BIG HAPPINESS, 1920
BIG HEART, THE
BIG HEARTED HERBERT, 1934, A
BIG HEAT, THE, 1953, C
BIG HOP, THE, 1928
BIG HOUSE, THE, 1930, C
BIG HOUSE, U.S.A., 1955, O
BIG JACK, 1949, C
BIG JAKE, 1971, O
BIG JIM GARRITY, 1916
BIG JIM McLAIN, 1952, C
BIG JOB, THE, 1965, A
BIG KILLING, THE, 1928
BIG KNIFE, THE, 1955, O
BIG LAND, THE, 1957, A
BIG LEAGUER, 1953, A
BIG LIFT, THE, 1950, A-C
BIG LITTLE PERSON, THE, 1919
BIG MEAT EATER, 1984, O
BIG MONEY, 1918
BIG MONEY, 1930, A
BIG MONEY, THE, 1962, A
BIG MOUTH, THE, 1967, AA
BIG NEWS, 1929, A
BIG NIGHT, THE, 1951, C

BIG NIGHT, THE, 1960, C
BIG NOISE, THE, 1928
BIG NOISE, THE, 1936, A
BIG NOISE, THE, 1944, AA
BIG OPERATOR, THE, 1959, O
BIG PAL, 1925, A
BIG PARADE, THE, 1925, A
BIG PARTY, THE, 1930, A
BIG PAYOFF, THE, 1933, A
BIG POND, THE, 1930, A
BIG PUNCH, THE, 1921, A
BIG PUNCH, THE, 1948, A
BIG RACE, THE, 1934, AA
BIG RED, 1962, AA
BIG RED ONE, THE, 1980, C
BIG SCORE, THE, 1983, C
BIG SEARCH, THE
BIG SHAKEDOWN, THE, 1934, A
BIG SHOT, THE, 1931, A
BIG SHOT, THE, 1937, A
BIG SHOT, THE, 1942, A
BIG SHOW, THE, 1926
BIG SHOW, THE, 1937, A
BIG SHOW, THE, 1961, A
BIG SHOW-OFF, THE, 1945, C
BIG SISTER, THE, 1916
BIG SKY, THE, 1952, A
BIG SLEEP, THE, 1946, C
BIG SLEEP, THE, 1978, C
BIG SOMBRERO, THE, 1949, A
BIG SPLASH, THE, 1935, A
BIG STAKES, 1922
BIG STAMPEDE, THE, 1932, A
BIG STEAL, THE, 1949, C
BIG STORE, THE, 1941, AA
BIG STREET, THE, 1942, A
BIG STUNT, 1925
BIG SWITCH, THE, 1970, O
BIG TIMBER, 1917
BIG TIMBER, 1924
BIG TIMBER, 1950, A-C
BIG TIME, 1929, A
BIG TIME, 1977
BIG TIME OR BUST, 1934, A
BIG TIMER, 1932
BIG TIMERS, 1947
BIG TIP OFF, THE, 1955, C
BIG TOWN, 1932, C
BIG TOWN, 1947, AA
BIG TOWN AFTER DARK, 1947, AA
BIG TOWN CZAR, 1939, C
BIG TOWN GIRL, 1937, A
BIG TOWN IDEAS, 1921, A
BIG TOWN ROUND-UP, 1921
BIG TOWN SCANDAL, 1948, AA
BIG TRAIL, THE, 1930, A
BIG TREES, THE, 1952, A-C
BIG TREMAINE, 1916, A
BIG WEDNESDAY, 1978, A-C
BIG WHEEL, THE, 1949, A-C
BIG ZAPPER, 1974
BIGAMIST, THE, 1916
BIGAMIST, THE, 1921, A
BIGAMIST, THE, 1953, C
BIGGER MAN, THE
BIGGER SPLASH,A, 1984, O
BIGGER THAN BARNUM'S, 1926
BIGGER THAN LIFE, 1956, C
BIGGEST BUNDLE OF THEM ALL, THE, 1968, A
BIGGEST SHOW ON EARTH, THE, 1918
BIJOU, 1972
BIKINI BEACH, 1964, A
BIKINI PARADISE, 1967
BILL AND COO, 1947, AAA
BILL APPERSON'S BOY, 1919
BILL CRACKS DOWN, 1937, A
BILL FOR DIVORCEMENT, A, 1922
BILL HENRY, 1919
BILL OF DIVORCEMENT, 1940, C
BILL OF DIVORCEMENT, A, 1932, A-C
BILL'S LEGACY, 1931, A
BILLIE, 1965, A
BILLION DOLLAR BRAIN, 1967, C
BILLION DOLLAR HOBO, THE, 1977, A
BILLION DOLLAR SCANDAL, 1932, A
BILLION DOLLAR THREAT, THE, 1979
BILLIONS, 1920
BILLY AND THE BIG STICK, 1917
BILLY BUDD, 1962, C
BILLY IN THE LOWLANDS, 1979, A-C
BILLY JACK, 1971, O
BILLY JACK GOES TO WASHINGTON, 1977, C
BILLY JIM, 1922, A
BILLY LIAR, 1963, A-C
BILLY ROSE'S DIAMOND HORSESHOE
BILLY ROSE'S JUMBO
BILLY THE KID, 1930, A
BILLY THE KID, 1941, A
BILLY THE KID IN TEXAS, 1940, A
BILLY THE KID OUTLAWED, 1940
BILLY THE KID RETURNS, 1938, A
BILLY THE KID TRAPPED, 1942, A

BILLY THE KID VS. DRACULA, 1966, A
BILLY THE KID WANTED, 194A
BILLY THE KID'S FIGHTING PALS, 1941, A
BILLY THE KID'S GUN JUSTICE, 1940
BILLY THE KID'S RANGE WAR, 1941, A
BILLY THE KID'S ROUNDUP, 1941, A
BILLY THE KID'S SMOKING GUNS, 1942
BILLY TWO HATS, 1973, C
BILLY'S SPANISH LOVE SPASM, 1915
BIM, 1976
BIMBO THE GREAT, 1961
BING BANG BOOM, 1922
BINGO BONGO, 198A, AA
*BINGO LONG TRAVELING ALL-STARS AND MOTOR
   KINGS, THE*, A-C
BIO-HAZARD, 1984
BIOGRAPHY OF A BACHELOR GIRL, 1935, A
BIONIC BOY, THE, 1977, R
BIQUEFARRE, 1983, A
BIRCH INTERVAL, 1976, A
BIRD OF PARADISE, 1932
BIRD OF PARADISE, 1951, C
BIRD OF PREY, A, 1916
BIRD OF PREY, THE, 1918
BIRD WATCH, THE, 1983
BIRD WITH THE CRYSTAL PLUMAGE, THE, 1970, C
BIRDMAN OF ALCATRAZ, 1962, C
BIRDS AND THE BEES, THE, 1965, A
BIRDS COME TO DIE IN PERU, 1968, C
BIRDS DO IT, 1966, A
BIRDS OF A FEATHER, 1931, AA
BIRDS OF A FEATHER, 1935, A
BIRDS OF PREY
BIRDS OF PREY, 1927
BIRDS' CHRISTMAS CAROL, THE, 1917
BIRDS, THE, 1963, C
BIRDS, THE BEES AND THE ITALIANS, THE, 1967, O
BIRDY, 1984, O
BIRTH CONTROL, 1917
BIRTH OF A BABY, 1938, C
BIRTH OF A MAN, THE, 1916
BIRTH OF A NATION, THE, 1915, C
BIRTH OF A RACE, 1919
BIRTH OF A SOUL, THE, 1920
BIRTH OF CHARACTER, THE, 1916
BIRTH OF PATRIOTISM, THE, 1917
BIRTH OF THE BLUES, 1941, A
BIRTHDAY PARTY, THE, 1968, C
BIRTHDAY PRESENT, THE, 1957, C
BIRTHRIGHT, 1924
BIRTHRIGHT, 1939
BISCUIT EATER, THE, 1940, AA
BISCUIT EATER, THE, 1972, AAA
BISHOP MISBEHAVES, THE, 1933, AA
BISHOP MURDER CASE, THE, 1930, A
BISHOP OF THE OZARKS, THE, 1923
BISHOP'S EMERALDS, THE, 1919
BISHOP'S SECRET, THE, 1916
BISHOP'S WIFE, THE, 1947, A
BIT O'HEAVEN, A
BIT OF HEAVEN, A, 1928
BIT OF JADE, A, 1918
BIT OF KINDLING, A, 1917
BITCH, THE, 1979
BITE THE BULLET, 1975, C
BITER BIT, THE, 1937, A
BITS OF LIFE, 1921
BITTER APPLES, 1927
BITTER CREEK, 1954, A
BITTER HARVEST, 1963, C
BITTER RICE, 1950, O
BITTER SPRINGS, 1950, A
BITTER SWEET, 1933, A
BITTER SWEET, 1940, A
BITTER SWEETS, 1928
BITTER TEA OF GENERAL YEN, THE, 1933, C
BITTER TEARS OF PETRA VON KANT, THE, 1970
BITTER TRUTH, 1917
BITTER VICTORY, 1958, C
BITTERSWEET LOVE, 1976, C
BIZARRE, 1969
BIZARRE BIZARRE, 1939, A
BIZET'S CARMEN, 1984, A-C
BLACK 13, 1954, A
BLACK ABBOT, THE, 1934, A
BLACK ACE, THE, 1928
BLACK ACES, 1937, A
BLACK AND WHITE IN COLOR, 1976, C
BLACK ANGEL, 1946, A
BLACK ANGELS, THE, 1970, O
BLACK ARROW, 1948, A
BLACK BAG, THE, 1922
BLACK BANDIT, 1938
BLACK BART, 1948, C
BLACK BEAUTY, 1921, AAA
BLACK BEAUTY, 1933, AAA
BLACK BEAUTY, 1946, AA
BLACK BEAUTY, 1971, AA
BLACK BELLY OF THE TARANTULA, THE, 1972, O
BLACK BELT JONES, 1974, O
BLACK BELT JONES, 1974

BLACK BIRD DESCENDING: TENSE ALIGNMENT, 1977
BLACK BIRD, THE, 1926, A
BLACK BIRD, THE, 1975, A-C
BLACK BOOK, THE, 1949, A
BLACK BOOMERANG, THE, 1925
BLACK BUTTERFLIES, 1928
BLACK BUTTERFLY, THE, 1916
BLACK CAESAR, 1973, O
BLACK CAMEL, THE, 1931, A
BLACK CARGOES OF THE SOUTH SEAS, 1929
BLACK CARRION, 1984
BLACK CASTLE, THE, 1952, C
BLACK CAT, THE, 1934, C
BLACK CAT, THE, 1941, A
BLACK CAT, THE, 1966, O
BLACK CAT, THE, 1984, O
BLACK CHARIOT, 1971
BLACK CHRISTMAS, 1974, O
BLACK CIRCLE, THE, 1919
BLACK COFFEE, 1931, A
BLACK CONNECTION, THE, 1974
BLACK CROOK, THE, 1916
BLACK CYCLONE, 1925, AAA
BLACK DAKOTAS, THE, 1954, A-C
BLACK DEVILS OF KALI, THE
BLACK DIAMOND, THE, 1927
BLACK DIAMONDS, 1932, A
BLACK DIAMONDS, 1940, A
BLACK DOLL, THE, 1938, A
BLACK DRAGONS, 1942, A
BLACK EAGLE, 1948, A
BLACK EYE, 1974, O
BLACK EYES, 1939, A
BLACK FANTASY, 1974
BLACK FEAR, 1915
BLACK FEATHER, 1928
BLACK FIST, 1977
BLACK FOREST, THE, 1954
BLACK FRIDAY, 1916
BLACK FRIDAY, 1940, A
BLACK FURY, 1935, C
BLACK GATE, THE, 1919
BLACK GESTAPO, THE, 1975, O
BLACK GIRL, 1972, A
BLACK GLOVE, 1954, A
BLACK GODFATHER, THE, 1974
BLACK GOLD, 1924
BLACK GOLD, 1928
BLACK GOLD, 1947, A
BLACK GOLD, 1963, A-C
BLACK GUNN, 1972, O
BLACK HAND, THE, 1950, C
BLACK HAND GANG, THE, 1930, A
BLACK HEART, THE, 1915
BLACK HEAT, 1976
BLACK HILLS, 1929
BLACK HILLS, 1948, A
BLACK HILLS AMBUSH, 1952, A-C
BLACK HILLS EXPRESS, 1943, A
BLACK HOLE, THE, 1979, A-C
BLACK HOOKER, 1974
BLACK HORSE CANYON, 1954, A
BLACK ICE, THE, 1957, A
BLACK IS WHITE, 1920
BLACK ISLAND, 1979
BLACK JACK
BLACK JACK, 1927
BLACK JACK, 1973, C
BLACK JACK, 1979, AA
BLACK JESUS, 1971
BLACK JOY, 1977, A-C
BLACK KING, 1932, A
BLACK KLANSMAN, THE, 1966, O
BLACK LASH, THE, 1952, A
BLACK LEGION, THE, 1937, C
BLACK LIGHTING, 1924
BLACK LIKE ME, 1964, C
BLACK LIMELIGHT, 1938, A
BLACK LOLITA, 1975
BLACK MAGIC, 1929
BLACK MAGIC, 1949, C
BLACK MAMA, WHITE MAMA, 1973, O
BLACK MARBLE, THE, 1980, C-O
BLACK MARKET BABIES, 1946, A
BLACK MARKET RUSTLERS, 1943, A
BLACK MASK, 1935, A
BLACK MEMORY, 1947, A
BLACK MIDNIGHT, 1949, AA
BLACK MOON, 1934, C
BLACK MOON, 1975, C
BLACK NARCISSUS, 1947, A-C
BLACK NIGHT, THE, 1916
BLACK OAK CONSPIRACY, 1977, C
BLACK ORCHID, 1952
BLACK ORCHID, 1959, C
BLACK ORCHIDS, 1917
BLACK ORPHEUS, 1959, C
BLACK OXEN, 1924
BLACK PANTHER'S CUB, THE, 1921
BLACK PANTHER, THE, 1977, O

BLACK PARACHUTE, THE, 1944, A
BLACK PARADISE, 1926
BLACK PATCH, 1957, C
BLACK PEARL, THE, 1928
BLACK PEARL, THE, 1977
BLACK PIRATE, THE, 1926, A
BLACK PIRATES, THE, 1954, C
BLACK PIT OF DOCTOR M, 1958, O
BLACK PLANET, THE, 1982
BLACK RAINBOW, 1966
BLACK RAVEN, THE, 1943, A
BLACK RIDER, THE, 1954, A
BLACK RODEO, 1972, C
BLACK ROOM, THE, 1935, C
BLACK ROOM, THE, 1983
BLACK ROOM, THE, 1984, O
BLACK ROSE, THE, 1950, A
BLACK ROSES, 1921
BLACK ROSES, 1936, A
BLACK SABBATH, 1963, O
BLACK SAIL, THE, 1929
BLACK SAMSON, 1974, O
BLACK SAMURAI, 1977
BLACK SCORPION, THE, 1957, C
BLACK SHADOWS, 1920
BLACK SHAMPOO, 1976, O
BLACK SHEEP, 1921
BLACK SHEEP, 1935, A
BLACK SHEEP OF THE FAMILY, THE, 1916
BLACK SHEEP OF WHITEHALL, THE, 1941, A
BLACK SHEEP, A, 1915
BLACK SHEEP, THE, 1920
BLACK SHIELD OF FALWORTH, THE, 1954, A-C
BLACK SIX, THE, 1974, Adven
BLACK SLEEP, THE, 1956, C
BLACK SPIDER, THE, 1920
BLACK SPIDER, THE, 1983, O
BLACK SPURS, 1965, A
BLACK STALLION RETURNS, THE, 1983, A-C
BLACK STALLION, THE, 1979, AAA
BLACK STARLET, 1974
BLACK STORK, THE, 1917
BLACK STREETFIGHTER, 1976
BLACK SUN, THE, 1979, A
BLACK SUNDAY, 1961, O
BLACK SUNDAY, 1977, C
BLACK SWAN, THE, 1942, A
BLACK TEARS, 1927
BLACK TENT, THE, 1956, A
BLACK THUNDERBOLT, THE, 1922
BLACK TIDE, 1958
BLACK TIGHTS, 1962, A
BLACK TORMENT, 1984
BLACK TORMENT, THE, 1965, A
BLACK TRASH, 1978
BLACK TUESDAY, 1955, C
BLACK TULIP, THE, 1921
BLACK TULIP, THE, 1937, A
BLACK VEIL FOR LISA, A, 1969, C
BLACK WATCH, THE, 1929, C
BLACK WATERS, 1929, A
BLACK WHIP, THE, 195A
BLACK WIDOW, 1951, A
BLACK WIDOW, 1954, C
BLACK WINDMILL, THE, 1974, C
BLACK WOLF, THE, 1917
BLACK ZOO, 1963, C
BLACKBEARD THE PIRATE, 1952, A-C
BLACKBEARD'S GHOST, 1968, AA
BLACKBIRDS, 1920
BLACKBOARD JUNGLE, THE, 1955, C
BLACKENSTEIN, 1973, O
BLACKIE'S REDEMPTION, 1919
BLACKJACK, 1978
BLACKJACK KETCHUM, DESPERADO, 1956, A
BLACKLIST, 1916
BLACKMAIL, 1920
BLACKMAIL, 1929, A
BLACKMAIL, 1939, A
BLACKMAIL, 1947, A
BLACKMAILED, 1951, A
BLACKMAILER, 1936, A
BLACKMAILERS, THE, 1915
BLACKOUT, 1940, A
BLACKOUT, 1950, A
BLACKOUT, 1954, A-C
BLACKOUT, 1978, A-C
BLACKSNAKE, 1973
BLACKWELL'S ISLAND, 1939, A
BLACULA, 1972, O
BLADE, 1973, O
BLADE O' GRASS, 1915
BLADE RUNNER, 1982, O
BLADES OF THE MUSKETEERS, 1953, A
BLADYS OF THE STEWPONY, 1919
BLAME IT ON RIO, 1984, O
BLAME IT ON THE NIGHT, 1984, C
BLAME THE WOMAN, 1932, A
BLANCHE, 1971, PC
BLANCHE FURY, 1948, A-C
BLANCHETTE, 1921
BLANCHEVILLE MONSTER, 1963

BLARNEY, 1926
BLARNEY KISS, 1933, A
BLASPHEMER, THE, 1921
BLAST OF SILENCE, 1961, C
BLAST-OFF
BLAST-OFF GIRLS, 1967
BLASTED HOPES, 1924
BLAZE AWAY, 1922
BLAZE O' GLORY, 1930, A
BLAZE OF GLORY, 1963, A
BLAZE OF NOON, 1947, A-C
BLAZING ACROSS THE PECOS, 1948
BLAZING ARROWS, 1922
BLAZING BARRIERS
BLAZING BARRIERS, 1937, A
BLAZING BULLETS, 1951
BLAZING DAYS, 1927, A
BLAZING FOREST, THE, 1952, A-C
BLAZING FRONTIER, 1944, A
BLAZING GUNS, 1935
BLAZING GUNS, 1943, A
BLAZING JUSTICE, 1936
BLAZING LOVE, 1916
BLAZING MAGNUM, 1976
BLAZING SADDLES, 1974, C-O
BLAZING SIX SHOOTERS, 1940, A
BLAZING SIXES, 1937, A
BLAZING STEWARDESSES, 1975
BLAZING SUN, THE, 1950, A
BLAZING THE WESTERN TRAIL, 1945
BLAZING TRAIL, THE, 1921, A
BLAZING TRAIL, THE, 1949, A
BLEAK HOUSE, 1920
BLEAK HOUSE, 1922
BLEAK MOMENTS, 1972, C
BLESS 'EM ALL
BLESS 'EM ALL, 1949, A
BLESS THE BEASTS AND CHILDREN, 1971, A-C
BLESS THEIR LITTLE HEARTS, 1984, O
BLESS THIS HOUSE, 1972
BLESSED EVENT, 1932, A-C
BLESSURE D'AMOUR, 1916
BLIGHTY, 1927
BLIND ADVENTURE, 1933, A
BLIND ADVENTURE, THE, 1918
BLIND ALIBI, 1938, A
BLIND ALLEY
BLIND ALLEY, 1939, C
BLIND ALLEYS, 1927, A
BLIND BARGAIN, A, 1922, C
BLIND BOY, THE, 1917, A
BLIND CIRCUMSTANCES, 1922
BLIND CORNER
BLIND DATE, 1934, A
BLIND DATE, 1984, O
BLIND DATE, 1959
BLIND DEAD, THE, 1972, O
BLIND DESIRE, 1948, A
BLIND FOLLY, 1939, C
BLIND FOOLS, 1940
BLIND GODDESS, THE, 1926, A
BLIND GODDESS, THE, 1948, A
BLIND HEARTS, 1921, A
BLIND HUSBANDS, 1919, A
BLIND JUSTICE, 1917
BLIND JUSTICE, 1934, A
BLIND LOVE, THE, 1920
BLIND MAN'S BLUFF, 1936, AA
BLIND MAN'S BLUFF, 1952, A
BLIND MAN'S BLUFF, 1967
BLIND MAN'S EYES, 1919
BLIND MAN'S HOLIDAY, 1917
BLIND MAN'S LUCK, 1917
BLIND RAGE, 1978
BLIND SPOT, 1932, A
BLIND SPOT, 1947
BLIND SPOT, 1958, A
BLIND TERROR
BLIND TRAIL, 1926
BLIND WIVES, 1920
BLIND YOUTH, 1920
BLINDFOLD, 1928
BLINDFOLD, 1966, A
BLINDFOLDED, 1918
BLINDING TRAIL, THE, 1919
BLINDMAN, 1972, O
BLINDNESS OF DEVOTION, 1915
BLINDNESS OF DIVORCE, THE, 1918
BLINDNESS OF LOVE, THE, 1916
BLINDNESS OF VIRTUE, THE, 1915
BLINKER'S SPY-SPOTTER, 1971
BLINKEYES, 1922
BLINKY, 1923
BLISS OF MRS. BLOSSOM, THE, 1968, C
BLITHE SPIRIT, 1945, A
BLIZZARD, THE, 1924
BLOB, THE, 1958, A-C
BLOCK BUSTERS, 1944, A
BLOCK SIGNAL, THE, 1926
BLOCKADE, 1928, A
BLOCKADE, 1929, A
BLOCKADE, 1938, A

BLOCKED TRAIL, THE, 1943
BLOCKHEADS, 1938, AAA
BLOCKHOUSE, THE, 1974, A
BLOND CHEAT, 1938, A
BLONDE ALIBI, 1946, A
BLONDE BAIT, 1956, A
BLONDE BANDIT, THE, 1950, A-C
BLONDE BLACKMAILER, 1955, A
BLONDE BOMBSHELL
BLONDE COMET, 1941, A
BLONDE CONNECTION, THE, 1975
BLONDE CRAZY, 1931, A
BLONDE DYNAMITE, 1950, A
BLONDE FEVER, 1944, A
BLONDE FOR A DAY, 1946, A
BLONDE FOR A NIGHT, A, 1928
BLONDE FROM BROOKLYN, 1945, A
BLONDE FROM PEKING, THE, 1968, A
BLONDE FROM SINGAPORE, THE, 1941, A
BLONDE GODDESS, 1982
BLONDE ICE, 1949, C
BLONDE IN A WHITE CAR
BLONDE INSPIRATION, 1941, A
BLONDE NIGHTINGALE, 1931, A
BLONDE OR BRUNETTE, 1927
BLONDE PICKUP, 1955, A
BLONDE RANSOM, 1945, A
BLONDE SAINT, THE, 1926
BLONDE SAVAGE, 1947, A
BLONDE SINNER, 1956, C
BLONDE TROUBLE, 1937, A
BLONDE VAMPIRE, THE, 1922
BLONDE VENUS, 1932, C-O
BLONDES AT WORK, 1938, A
BLONDES BY CHOICE, 1927
BLONDES FOR DANGER, 1938, A
BLONDIE, 1938, AA
BLONDIE BRINGS UP BABY, 1939, AA
BLONDIE FOR VICTORY, 1942, A
BLONDIE GOES LATIN, 1941, AA
BLONDIE GOES TO COLLEGE, 1942, AA
BLONDIE HAS SERVANT TROUBLE, 1940, AA
BLONDIE HITS THE JACKPOT, 1949, AA
BLONDIE IN SOCIETY, 1941, AA
BLONDIE IN THE DOUGH, 1947, AA
BLONDIE JOHNSON, 1933, A
BLONDIE KNOWS BEST, 1946, AA
BLONDIE MEETS THE BOSS, 1939, AA
BLONDIE OF THE FOLLIES, 1932, A-C
BLONDIE ON A BUDGET, 1940, AA
BLONDIE PLAYS CUPID, 1940, AA
BLONDIE TAKES A VACATION, 1939, AA
BLONDIE'S ANNIVERSARY, 1947, AA
BLONDIE'S BIG DEAL, 1949, AA
BLONDIE'S BIG MOMENT, 1947, AA
BLONDIE'S BLESSED EVENT, 1942, AA
BLONDIE'S HERO, 1950, AA
BLONDIE'S HOLIDAY, 1947, AA
BLONDIE'S LUCKY DAY, 1946, AA
BLONDIE'S REWARD, 1948, AA
BLONDIE'S SECRET, 1948, AA
BLOOD, 1974, C
BLOOD AND BLACK LACE, 1965, O
BLOOD AND GUNS, 1979
BLOOD AND GUTS, 1978, O
BLOOD AND LACE, 1971, O
BLOOD AND ROSES, 1961, C-O
BLOOD AND SAND, 1922, C
BLOOD AND SAND, 1941, C
BLOOD AND SOUL, 1923
BLOOD AND STEEL, 1925
BLOOD AND STEEL, 1959, A
BLOOD ARROW, 1958, A-C
BLOOD BARRIER, THE, 1920
BLOOD BATH, 1966, C
BLOOD BATH, 1976, O
BLOOD BEACH, 1981, C
BLOOD BEAST FROM OUTER SPACE, 1965, C
BLOOD BEAST TERROR, THE, 1967, C
BLOOD BOND, THE, 1925
BLOOD COUPLE, 1974
BLOOD CREATURE
BLOOD DEBTS, 1983
BLOOD DEMON, 1967, O
BLOOD DRINKERS, THE, 1966, P
BLOOD FEAST, 1963, O
BLOOD FEAST, 1976, O
BLOOD FEUD, 1979, O
BLOOD FROM THE MUMMY'S TOMB, 1972, O
BLOOD IN THE STREETS, 1975, C
BLOOD LEGACY
BLOOD MANIA, 1971, O
BLOOD MONEY, 1921
BLOOD MONEY, 1933, C
BLOOD MONEY, 1974, O
BLOOD MONSTER, 1972
BLOOD NEED NOT BE SPILLED, 1917
BLOOD OF A POET, THE, 1930, C
BLOOD OF DRACULA, 1957, O
BLOOD OF DRACULA'S CASTLE, 1967, O
BLOOD OF FRANKENSTEIN, 1970, O

BLOOD OF FU MANCHU, THE, 1968, O
BLOOD OF GHASTLY HORROR
BLOOD OF HIS FATHERS, 1917
BLOOD OF JESUS, 1941
BLOOD OF THE IRON MAIDEN, 1969
BLOOD OF THE TREVORS
BLOOD OF THE VAMPIRE, 1958, O
BLOOD ON MY HANDS
BLOOD ON SATAN'S CLAW, THE, 1970, O
BLOOD ON THE ARROW, 1964, C
BLOOD ON THE MOON, 1948, A
BLOOD ON THE SUN, 1945, C
BLOOD ORANGE, 1953, A
BLOOD ORGY OF THE SHE-DEVILS, 1973, O
BLOOD RELATIVES, 1978, O
BLOOD ROSE, THE, 1970, O
BLOOD SEEKERS, THE, 1971
BLOOD SHIP, THE, 1927
BLOOD SIMPLE, 1984, O
BLOOD SONG, 1982
BLOOD SPATTERED BRIDE, THE, 1974, O
BLOOD SUCKERS
BLOOD TEST, 1923
BLOOD THIRST, 1965
BLOOD TIDE, 1982, O
BLOOD WATERS OF DOCTOR Z, 1982, O
BLOOD WEDDING, 1981, A
BLOOD WILL TELL, 1917
BLOOD WILL TELL, 1927
BLOOD, SWEAT AND FEAR, 1975, C-O
BLOODBATH AT THE HOUSE OF DEATH, 1984, C-O
BLOODBROTHERS, 1978, O
BLOODEATERS, 1980, C
BLOODHOUND, THE, 1925
BLOODHOUNDS OF BROADWAY, 1952, A
BLOODLESS VAMPIRE, THE, 1965
BLOODLINE, 1979, O
BLOODLUST, 1959, O
BLOODRAGE, 1979
BLOODSTALKERS, 1976
BLOODSUCKERS
BLOODSUCKING FREAKS, 1982, O
BLOODTHIRSTY BUTCHERS, 1970, O
BLOODY BIRTHDAY, 1980
BLOODY BROOD, THE, 1959, O
BLOODY EAST, THE, 1915
BLOODY KIDS, 1983, O
BLOODY MAMA, 1970, O
BLOODY PIT OF HORROR, THE, 1965, O
BLOOMFIELD, 1971, C
BLOOMING ANGEL, THE, 1920
BLOSSOM TIME
BLOSSOMS IN THE DUST, 1941, A
BLOSSOMS ON BROADWAY, 1937, A
BLOT, THE, 1921, A
BLOW BUGLES BLOW, 1936
BLOW OUT, 1981, O
BLOW TO THE HEART, 1983, O
BLOW YOUR OWN HORN, 1923
BLOW YOUR OWN TRUMPET, 1958, A
BLOW-UP, 1966, O
BLOWING WILD, 1953, C
BLOWN SKY HIGH, 1984
BLUE, 1968, C
BLUE ANGEL, THE, 1930, O
BLUE ANGEL, THE, 1959, O
BLUE BANDANNA, THE, 1919
BLUE BIRD, THE, 1940, AA
BLUE BIRD, THE, 1976, AA
BLUE BLAZES, 1922
BLUE BLAZES, 1926
BLUE BLAZES RAWDEN, 1918
BLUE BLOOD, 1922
BLUE BLOOD, 1925, A
BLUE BLOOD, 1951, AA
BLUE BLOOD, 1973, O
BLUE BLOOD AND RED, 1916
BLUE BONNET, THE, 1920
BLUE CANADIAN ROCKIES, 1952, A
BLUE COLLAR, 1978, O
BLUE COUNTRY, THE, 1977, C-O
BLUE DAHLIA, THE, 1946, C
BLUE DANUBE, 1932, A
BLUE DANUBE, THE, 1928
BLUE DEMON VERSUS THE INFERNAL BRAINS, 1967, O
BLUE DENIM, 1959, C-O
BLUE EAGLE, THE, 1926
BLUE ENVELOPE MYSTERY, THE, 1916
BLUE EXPRESS, 1929
BLUE FIN, 1978, A
BLUE GARDENIA, THE, 1953, C
BLUE GRASS OF KENTUCKY, 1950, AA
BLUE HAWAII, 1961, A
BLUE IDOL, THE, 1931, A
BLUE JEANS, 1917
BLUE LAGOON, THE, 1949, A-C
BLUE LAGOON, THE, 1980, O
BLUE LAMP, THE, 1950, C
BLUE LIGHT, THE, 1932, A
BLUE MAX, THE, 1966, C
BLUE MONEY, 1975

BLUE MONTANA SKIES, 1939, AA
BLUE MOON, THE, 1920
BLUE MOUNTAIN MYSTERY, THE, 1922
BLUE MURDER AT ST. TRINIAN'S, 1958, AA
BLUE PARROT, THE, 1953, A
BLUE PEARL, THE, 1920
BLUE PETER, THE
BLUE PETER, THE, 1928
BLUE SCAR, 1949, A
BLUE SEXTET, 1972
BLUE SIERRA, 1946, AA
BLUE SKIES, 1929
BLUE SKIES, 1946, AA
BLUE SKIES AGAIN, 1983, A
BLUE SMOKE, 1935, A
BLUE SQUADRON, THE, 1934, A
BLUE STEEL, 1934, A
BLUE STREAK MCCOY, 1920
BLUE STREAK O'NEIL, 1926
BLUE STREAK, THE, 1917
BLUE STREAK, THE, 1926, A
BLUE SUMMER, 1973
BLUE SUNSHINE, 1978, A
BLUE THUNDER, 1983, C
BLUE VEIL, THE, 1947, A
BLUE VEIL, THE, 1951, A
BLUE, WHITE, AND PERFECT, 1941, A
BLUE-EYED MARY, 1918
BLUEBEARD, 1944, A
BLUEBEARD, 1972, O
BLUEBEARD'S 8TH WIFE, 1923
BLUEBEARD'S CASTLE, 1969
BLUEBEARD'S EIGHTH WIFE, 1938, A-C
BLUEBEARD'S SEVEN WIVES, A
BLUEBEARD'S TEN HONEYMOONS, 1960, A-C
BLUEBEARD, 1963
BLUEBEARD, JR.
BLUEBIRD, THE, 1918
BLUEPRINT FOR MURDER, A, 1953, CA
BLUEPRINT FOR ROBBERY, 1961, A
BLUES BROTHERS, THE, 1980, C-O
BLUES BUSTERS, 1950, AA
BLUES FOR LOVERS, 1966, A
BLUES IN THE NIGHT, 1941, A
BLUFF, 1916
BLUFF, 1921
BLUFF, 1924, A
BLUFFER, THE, 1919
BLUME IN LOVE, 1973, O
BLUSHING BRIDE, THE, 1921, A
BLUSHING BRIDES, 1930, A
BMX BANDITS, 1983, AA
BOADICEA, 1926
BOARDING HOUSE, 1984
BOARDING HOUSE BLUES, 1948
BOARDWALK, 1979, C-O
BOASTER, THE, 1926
BOAT FROM SHANGHAI, 1931, A
BOAT, THE
BOATNIKS, THE, 1970, AAA
BOB AND CAROL AND TED AND ALICE, 1969, O
BOB HAMPTON OF PLACER, 1921, A
BOB MATHIAS STORY, THE, 1954, AA
BOB'S YOUR UNCLE, 1941, A
BOB, SON OF BATTLE
BOBBED HAIR, 1922
BOBBED HAIR, 1925
BOBBIE JO AND THE OUTLAW, 1976, C-O
BOBBIE OF THE BALLET, 1916
BOBBIKINS, 1959, A
BOBBY DEERFIELD, 1977, C
BOBBY WARE IS MISSING, 1955, A
BOBO, THE, 1967, A-C
BOCCACCIO, 1936, A
BOCCACCIO '70, 1962, O
BOD SQUAD, THE, 1976
BODEN'S BOY, 1923
BODY AND SOUL, 1920
BODY AND SOUL, 1925
BODY AND SOUL, 1927
BODY AND SOUL, 1931, A
BODY AND SOUL, 1947, C
BODY AND SOUL, 1981, C
BODY BEAUTIFUL, 1928
BODY BENEATH, THE, 1970
BODY DISAPPEARS, THE, 1941, A
BODY DOUBLE, 1984, O
BODY FEVER, 1981
BODY HEAT, 1981, C
BODY IS A SHELL, THE, 1957
BODY PUNCH, THE, 1929
BODY ROCK, 1984, C
BODY SAID NO!, THE, 1950, AA
BODY SNATCHER, THE, 1945, A
BODY STEALERS, THE, 1969, A
BODYGUARD, 1948, A
BODYGUARD, THE, 1976
BODYHOLD, 1950, A
BOEFJE, 1939, AA
BOEING BOEING, 1965, C
BOER WAR, THE, 1914
BOESMAN AND LENA, 1976

BOY WHO CAUGHT A CROOK, 1961, AA
BOY WHO CRIED WEREWOLF, THE, 1973, A-C
BOY WHO STOLE A MILLION, THE, 1960, AA
BOY WHO TURNED YELLOW, THE, 1972, AA
BOY WITH THE GREEN HAIR, THE, 1949, AA
BOY WITH TWO HEADS, THE, 1974
BOY WOODBURN, 1922
BOY! WHAT A GIRL, 1947, A
BOY'S REFORMATORY, 1939, A
BOY, A GIRL AND A BIKE, A, 1949, A
BOY, A GIRL, AND A DOG, A, 1946, A
BOY, DID I GET A WRONG NUMBER!, 1966, AA
BOY...A GIRL, A, 1969, O
BOYD'S SHOP, 1960, A
BOYS FROM BRAZIL, THE, 1978, C-O
BOYS FROM BROOKLYN, THE
BOYS FROM SYRACUSE, 1940, A
BOYS IN BROWN, 1949, AA
BOYS IN COMPANY C, THE, 1978, O
BOYS IN THE BAND, THE, 1970, O
BOYS OF PAUL STREET, THE, 1969, A
BOYS OF THE CITY, 1940, A
BOYS OF THE OLD BRIGADE, THE, 1916
BOYS OF THE OTTER PATROL, 1918
BOYS TOWN, 1938, AAA
BOYS WILL BE BOYS, 1921
BOYS WILL BE BOYS, 1936, A
BOYS WILL BE GIRLS, 1937, AA
BOYS' NIGHT OUT, 1962, C
BOYS' RANCH, 1946, A
BOYS, THE, 1962, C
BRACE UP, 1918
BRACELETS, 1931, A
BRADY'S ESCAPE, 1984, C
BRAIN EATERS, THE, 1958, C
BRAIN FROM THE PLANET AROUS, THE, 1958, C
BRAIN MACHINE, THE, 1955, A
BRAIN MACHINE, THE, 1972
BRAIN OF BLOOD, 1971, C
BRAIN THAT WOULDN'T DIE, THE, 1959, O
BRAIN, THE, 1965, A
BRAIN, THE, 1969, A
BRAINSTORM, 1965, C
BRAINSTORM, 1983, C-O
BRAINWASH, 1982
BRAINWASHED, 1961, A-C
BRAINWAVES, 1983, O
BRAMBLE BUSH, THE, 1919
BRAMBLE BUSH, THE, 1960, O
BRANCHES, 1971
BRAND, 1915
BRAND OF CAIN, THE, 1935
BRAND OF COWARDICE, 1925
BRAND OF COWARDICE, THE, 1916, A
BRAND OF FEAR, 1949, A
BRAND OF HATE, 1934
BRAND OF LOPEZ, THE, 1920
BRAND OF SATAN, THE, 1917
BRAND OF THE DEVIL, 1944, A
BRAND OF THE OUTLAWS, 1936
BRAND X, 1970
BRAND'S DAUGHTER, 1917
BRAND, THE, 1919
BRANDED, 1920
BRANDED, 1931, A
BRANDED, 1951, A
BRANDED A BANDIT, 1924, A
BRANDED A COWARD, 1935, A
BRANDED A THIEF, 1924
BRANDED MAN, 1922
BRANDED MAN, 1928
BRANDED MEN, 1931, A
BRANDED SOMBRERO, THE, 1928
BRANDED SOUL, A, 1917
BRANDED SOUL, THE, 1920
BRANDED WOMAN, THE, 1920, A
BRANDING BROADWAY, 1918, A
BRANDING FIRE, 1930
BRANDING IRON, THE, 1920, A
BRANDY FOR THE PARSON, 1952, A
BRANDY IN THE WILDERNESS, 1969
BRANNIGAN, 1975, A-C
BRASA DORMIDA, 1928
BRASHER DOUBLOON, THE, 1947, A
BRASIL ANNO 2,000, 1968, A
BRASS, 1923
BRASS BOTTLE, THE, 1914
BRASS BOTTLE, THE, 1923
BRASS BOTTLE, THE, 1964, A
BRASS BOWL, THE, 1924
BRASS BUTTONS, 1919
BRASS CHECK, THE, 1918
BRASS COMMANDMENTS, 1923
BRASS KNUCKLES, 1927
BRASS LEGEND, THE, 1956, A
BRASS MONKEY
BRASS RING, THE, 1975
BRASS TARGET, 1978, A-C
BRAT, THE, 1919, A
BRAT, THE, 1930, A
BRAT, THE, 1931, A
BRAVADOS, THE, 1958, C

BRAVE AND BOLD, 1918, A
BRAVE BULLS, THE, 1951, A
BRAVE DON'T CRY, THE, 1952, A
BRAVE ONE, THE, 1956, AAA
BRAVE WARRIOR, 1952, A
BRAVEST WAY, THE, 1918, A
BRAVEHEART, 1925
BRAWN OF THE NORTH, 1922
BRAZEN BEAUTY, 1918, A
BRAZIL, 1944, A
BREAD, 1918, A
BREAD, 1924
BREAD AND CHOCOLATE, 1978, A
BREAD OF LOVE, THE, 1954, A
BREAD, LOVE AND DREAMS, 1953, O
BREAK IN THE CIRCLE, THE, 1957, A
BREAK OF DAY, 1977, A
BREAK OF HEARTS, 1935, A
BREAK THE NEWS, 1938, A
BREAK THE NEWS TO MOTHER, 1919
BREAK TO FREEDOM
BREAK, THE, 1962, A
BREAK-UP, THE, 1930
BREAKAWAY, 1956, A
BREAKDOWN, 1953, A
BREAKER MORANT, 1980, A-C
BREAKER! BREAKER!, 1977, C
BREAKER, THE, 1916, A
BREAKERS AHEAD, 1918
BREAKERS AHEAD, 1935, A
BREAKERS AHEAD, 1938, A
BREAKFAST AT SUNRISE, 1927
BREAKFAST AT TIFFANY'S, 1961, A
BREAKFAST FOR TWO, 1937, A
BREAKFAST IN BED, 1978, C
BREAKFAST IN HOLLYWOOD, 1946, A
BREAKFAST IN PARIS, 1981
BREAKHEART PASS, 1976, C
BREAKIN', 1984, A-C
BREAKIN' 2: ELECTRIC BOOGALOO, 1984, A-C
BREAKING AWAY, 1979, C-O
BREAKING GLASS, 1980, C-O
BREAKING HOME TIES, 1922
BREAKING INTO SOCIETY, 1923
BREAKING OF BUMBO, 1972
BREAKING POINT, 1976, C
BREAKING POINT, THE, 1921, C
BREAKING POINT, THE, 1924, A
BREAKING POINT, THE, 1950, A
BREAKING POINT, THE, 1961, A
BREAKING THE ICE, 1938, A
BREAKING THE SOUND BARRIER, 1952, A
BREAKOUT, 1959
BREAKOUT, 1960, A
BREAKOUT, 1975, C
BREAKOUT, 1984, AA
BREAKTHROUGH, 1950, A
BREAKTHROUGH, 1978, C
BREATH OF A SCANDAL, THE, 1924
BREATH OF LIFE, 1962, A
BREATH OF SCANDAL, A, 1960, A
BREATH OF THE GODS, THE, 1920
BREATHLESS, 1959, O
BREATHLESS, 1983, O
BREATHLESS MOMENT, THE, 1924
BRED IN OLD KENTUCKY, 1926
BRED IN THE BONE, 1915
BREED APART, A, 1984, A-C
BREED OF COURAGE, 1927
BREED OF MEN, 1919, A
BREED OF THE BORDER, 1933, A
BREED OF THE BORDER, THE, 1924
BREED OF THE SEA, 1926
BREED OF THE SUNSETS, 1928, A
BREED OF THE TRESHAMS, THE, 1920
BREED OF THE WEST, 1930
BREEZING HOME, 1937, A
BREEZY, 1973, O
BREEZY BILL, 1930
BREEZY JIM, 1919
BRENDA OF THE BARGE, 1920, A
BREWSTER McCLOUD, 1970, C
BREWSTER'S MILLIONS, 1914, A
BREWSTER'S MILLIONS, 1921, A
BREWSTER'S MILLIONS, 1935, A
BREWSTER'S MILLIONS, 1945, A
BRIBE, THE, 1949, C
BRIDAL CHAIR, THE, 1919, A
BRIDAL PATH, THE, 1959, A
BRIDAL SUITE, 1939, A
BRIDE AND THE BEAST, THE, 1958, C
BRIDE BY MISTAKE, 1944, A
BRIDE CAME C.O.D., THE, 1941, A
BRIDE COMES HOME, 1936, A
BRIDE COMES TO YELLOW SKY, THE
BRIDE FOR A NIGHT, A, 1923, A
BRIDE FOR HENRY, A, 1937, A
BRIDE FOR SALE, 1949, A
BRIDE GOES WILD, THE, 1948, A
BRIDE IS MUCH TOO BEAUTIFUL, THE, 1958, O
BRIDE OF FEAR, THE, 1918, A
BRIDE OF FRANKENSTEIN, THE, 1935, C

BRIDE OF GLOMDAL, THE, 1925
BRIDE OF HATE, THE, 1917, A
BRIDE OF THE DESERT, 1929, A
BRIDE OF THE GORILLA, 1951, A
BRIDE OF THE LAKE, 1934, A
BRIDE OF THE MONSTER, 1955, A
BRIDE OF THE REGIMENT, 1930, A
BRIDE OF THE STORM, 1926, A
BRIDE OF VENGEANCE, 1923
BRIDE OF VENGEANCE, 1949, A
BRIDE WALKS OUT, THE, 1936, A
BRIDE WITH A DOWRY, 1954, A
BRIDE WORE BLACK, THE, 1968, C
BRIDE WORE BOOTS, THE, 1946, A
BRIDE WORE CRUTCHES, THE, 1940, A
BRIDE WORE RED, THE, 1937, A
BRIDE'S AWAKENING, THE, 1918, A
BRIDE'S CONFESSION, THE, 1921
BRIDE'S PLAY, THE, 1922
BRIDE'S SILENCE, THE, 1917, A
BRIDE, THE, 1973, C-O
BRIDEGROOM FOR TWO, 1932, A
BRIDES ARE LIKE THAT, 1936, A
BRIDES OF BLOOD, 1968, O
BRIDES OF DRACULA, THE, 1960, O
BRIDES OF FU MANCHU, THE, 1966, A
BRIDES TO BE, 1934, A
BRIDGE AT REMAGEN, THE, 1969, C
BRIDGE IN THE JUNGLE, THE, 1971
BRIDGE OF SAN LUIS REY, THE, 1929, A
BRIDGE OF SAN LUIS REY, THE, 1944, A
BRIDGE OF SIGHS, 1936, A
BRIDGE OF SIGHS, THE, 1915
BRIDGE OF SIGHS, THE, 1922
BRIDGE OF SIGHS, THE, 1925
BRIDGE ON THE RIVER KWAI, THE, 1957, C
BRIDGE TO THE SUN, 1961, A
BRIDGE TOO FAR, A, 1977, C
BRIDGE, THE, 1961, A
BRIDGES AT TOKO-RI, THE, 1954, A
BRIDGES BURNED, 1917
BRIDGES TO HEAVEN, 1975
BRIEF ECSTASY, 1937, A
BRIEF ENCOUNTER, 1945, A
BRIEF MOMENT, 1933, A
BRIEF RAPTURE, 1952, C
BRIEF VACATION, A, 1975, C
BRIG, THE, 1965
BRIGADIER GERARD, 1915
BRIGADOON, 1954, A
BRIGAND OF KANDAHAR, THE, 1965, A
BRIGAND, THE, 1952, A
BRIGGS FAMILY, THE, 1940, A
BRIGHAM YOUNG—FRONTIERSMAN, 1940, A
BRIGHT COLLEGE YEARS, 1971
BRIGHT EYES, 1934, AAA
BRIGHT LEAF, 1950, A
BRIGHT LIGHTS, 1925, A
BRIGHT LIGHTS, 1931, A
BRIGHT LIGHTS, 1935, A
BRIGHT LIGHTS OF BROADWAY, 1923
BRIGHT ROAD, 1953, A
BRIGHT SHAWL, THE, 1923
BRIGHT SKIES, 1920
BRIGHT VICTORY, 1951, A
BRIGHTHAVEN EXPRESS, 1950
BRIGHTON ROCK, 1947, C
BRIGHTON STRANGLER, THE, 1945, AA
BRIGHTY OF THE GRAND CANYON, 1967, A
BRILLIANT MARRIAGE, 1936, A
BRIMSTONE, 1949, A
BRIMSTONE AND TREACLE, 1982, C
BRING HIM IN, 1921, A
BRING ME THE HEAD OF ALFREDO GARCIA, 1974, O
BRING ON THE GIRLS, 1945, A
BRING YOUR SMILE ALONG, 1955, A
BRINGIN' HOME THE BACON, 1924
BRINGING HOME FATHER, 1917
BRINGING UP BABY, 1938, A
BRINGING UP BETTY, 1919
BRINGING UP FATHER, 1928
BRINGING UP FATHER, 1946, A
BRINK OF LIFE, 1960, C-O
BRINK'S JOB, THE, 1978, A-C
BRINK, THE, 1915
BRITANNIA MEWS
BRITANNIA OF BILLINGSGATE, 1933, A
BRITISH AGENT, 1934, A
BRITISH INTELLIGENCE, 1940, A
BRITTANIA HOSPITAL, 1982, C
BRITTON OF THE SEVENTH, 1916
BROAD COALITION, THE, 1972
BROAD DAYLIGHT, 1922
BROAD ROAD, THE, 1923
BROADMINDED, 1931, A
BROADWAY, 1929, A
BROADWAY, 1942, A
BROADWAY AFTER DARK, 1924, A
BROADWAY AFTER MIDNIGHT, 1927
BROADWAY AND HOME, 1920
BROADWAY ARIZONA, 1917
BROADWAY BABIES, 1929, A

BROADWAY BAD, 1933, A
BROADWAY BIG SHOT, 1942, A
BROADWAY BILL, 1918
BROADWAY BILL, 1934, A
BROADWAY BILLY, 1926, A
BROADWAY BOOB, THE, 1926
BROADWAY BROKE, 1923
BROADWAY BUBBLE, THE, 1920
BROADWAY BUCKAROO, 1921
BROADWAY BUTTERFLY, A, 1925
BROADWAY COWBOY, THE, 1920
BROADWAY DADDIES, 1928
BROADWAY DANNY ROSE, 1984, A-C
BROADWAY DRIFTER, THE, 1927
BROADWAY FEVER, 1929
BROADWAY GALLANT, THE, 1926
BROADWAY GOLD, 1923
BROADWAY GONDOLIER, 1935, A
BROADWAY HOOFER, THE, 1929, A
BROADWAY HOSTESS, 1935, A
BROADWAY JONES, 1917
BROADWAY LADY, 1925
BROADWAY LIMITED, 1941, A
BROADWAY LOVE, 1918
BROADWAY MADNESS, 1927
BROADWAY MADONNA, THE, 1922
BROADWAY MELODY OF '38, 1937, A
BROADWAY MELODY OF 1936, 1935, A
BROADWAY MELODY OF 1940, 1940, A
BROADWAY MELODY, THE, 1929, A
BROADWAY MUSKETEERS, 1938, A
BROADWAY NIGHTS, 1927
BROADWAY OR BUST, 1924
BROADWAY PEACOCK, THE, 1922
BROADWAY RHYTHM, 1944, A
BROADWAY ROSE, 1922, A
BROADWAY SAINT, A, 1919
BROADWAY SCANDAL, 1918, A
BROADWAY SCANDALS, 1929, A
BROADWAY SERENADE, 1939, A
BROADWAY SPORT, THE, 1917
BROADWAY THROUGH A KEYHOLE, 1933, A
BROADWAY TO CHEYENNE, 1932, A
BROADWAY TO HOLLYWOOD, 1933, A
BROKEN ARROW, 1950, A
BROKEN BARRIER
BROKEN BARRIERS, 1919
BROKEN BARRIERS, 1924
BROKEN BARRIERS, 1928
BROKEN BLOSSOMS, 1919, A
BROKEN BLOSSOMS, 1936, A
BROKEN BUTTERFLY, THE, 1919
BROKEN CHAINS, 1916, C
BROKEN CHAINS, 1922
BROKEN CHAINS, 1925
BROKEN COMMANDMENTS, 1919
BROKEN DISHES, 1930
BROKEN DOLL, A, 1921, A
BROKEN DREAMS, 1933, A
BROKEN ENGLISH, 1981, O
BROKEN FETTERS, 1916
BROKEN GATE, THE, 1920
BROKEN GATE, THE, 1927
BROKEN HEARTED, 1929
BROKEN HEARTS, 1926, A
BROKEN HEARTS, 1933
BROKEN HEARTS OF BROADWAY, THE, 1923
BROKEN HEARTS OF HOLLYWOOD, 1926, A
BROKEN HOMES, 1926
BROKEN HORSESHOE, THE, 1953, A
BROKEN JOURNEY, 1948, A
BROKEN LANCE, 1954, A
BROKEN LAND, THE, 1962, A
BROKEN LAW, THE, 1915
BROKEN LAW, THE, 1924
BROKEN LAW, THE, 1926
BROKEN LAWS, 1924
BROKEN LOVE, 1946, A
BROKEN LULLABY, 1932, A
BROKEN MASK, THE, 1928
BROKEN MELODY, 1938, A
BROKEN MELODY, THE, 1916
BROKEN MELODY, THE, 1920
BROKEN MELODY, THE, 1929, A
BROKEN MELODY, THE, 1934, A
BROKEN ROAD, THE, 1921
BROKEN ROMANCE, A, 1929, A
BROKEN ROSARY, THE, 1934, A
BROKEN SHADOWS, 1922
BROKEN SILENCE, THE, 1922
BROKEN SPUR, THE, 1921
BROKEN STAR, THE, 1956, A
BROKEN STRINGS, 1940
BROKEN THREADS, 1917
BROKEN THREADS, 1919
BROKEN TIES, 1918
BROKEN VIOLIN, THE, 1923
BROKEN VIOLIN, THE, 1927
BROKEN WING, THE, 1923
BROKEN WING, THE, 1932, A
BROMLEY CASE, THE, 1920
BRONC BUSTER, THE

BRONC STOMPER, THE, 1928
BRONCHO BUSTER, THE, 1927
BRONCHO TWISTER, 1927, A
BRONCO BILLY, 1980, C
BRONCO BULLFROG, 1972, A
BRONCO BUSTER, 1952, A
BRONENOSETS POTEMKIN
BRONX WARRIORS
BRONTE SISTERS, THE, 1979, A
BRONZE BELL, THE, 1921, A
BRONZE BRIDE, THE, 1917
BRONZE BUCKAROO, THE, 1939, A
BROOD, THE, 1979, C
BROODING EYES, 1926
BROOKLYN ORCHID, 1942, A
BROTH FOR SUPPER, 1919
BROTH OF A BOY, 1959, A
BROTHER ALFRED, 1932, A
BROTHER CARL, 1972
BROTHER FROM ANOTHER PLANET, THE, 1984, O
BROTHER JOHN, 1971, A
BROTHER OF THE WIND, 1972
BROTHER ON THE RUN, 1973
BROTHER ORCHID, 1940, A
BROTHER RAT, 1938, A
BROTHER RAT AND A BABY, 1940, A
BROTHER SUN, SISTER MOON, 1973, A
BROTHER, CRY FOR ME, 1970
BROTHERHOOD OF DEATH, 1976
BROTHERHOOD OF SATAN, THE, 1971, C-O
BROTHERHOOD OF THE YAKUZA
BROTHERHOOD, THE, 1968, C-O
BROTHERLY LOVE, 1928
BROTHERLY LOVE, 1970, O
BROTHERS, 1929
BROTHERS, 1930, A
BROTHERS, 1977, C
BROTHERS, 1984, O
BROTHERS AND SISTERS, 1980, A
BROTHERS DIVIDED, 1919
BROTHERS IN LAW, 1957, A
BROTHERS IN THE SADDLE, 1949, A
BROTHERS KARAMAZOV, THE, 1958, C-O
BROTHERS O'TOOLE, THE, 1973, A
BROTHERS OF THE WEST, 1938, A
BROTHERS RICO, THE, 1957, C
BROTHERS UNDER THE SKIN, 1922
BROTHERS, THE, 1948, A
BROWN DERBY, THE, 1926
BROWN IN HARVARD, 1917
BROWN OF HARVARD, 1926, A
BROWN ON RESOLUTION
BROWN SUGAR, 1922
BROWN SUGAR, 1931, A
BROWN WALLET, THE, 1936, A
BROWNING VERSION, THE, 1951, A
BRUBAKER, 1980, C-O
BRUCE LEE AND I, 1976, C-O
BRUCE LEE—TRUE STORY, 1976, C-O
BRUISED BY THE STORMS OF LIFE, 1918
BRUISER, THE, 1916
BRUSHFIRE, 1962, A
BRUTAL JUSTICE, 1978
BRUTE AND THE BEAST, THE, 1968, C
BRUTE BREAKER, THE, 1919
BRUTE CORPS, 1972
BRUTE FORCE, 1947, C
BRUTE MAN, THE, 1946, A
BRUTE MASTER, THE, 1920
BRUTE, THE, 1925
BRUTE, THE, 1927, A
BRUTE, THE, 1952, C
BUBBLE, THE, 1967, A
BUBBLES, 1920
BUCCANEER'S GIRL, 1950, A
BUCCANEER, THE, 1938, A
BUCCANEER, THE, 1958, A
BUCHANAN RIDES ALONE, 1958, A
BUCHANAN'S WIFE, 1918
BUCK AND THE PREACHER, 1972
BUCK BENNY RIDES AGAIN, 1940, A
BUCK PRIVATES, 1928
BUCK PRIVATES, 1941, AAA
BUCK PRIVATES COME HOME, 1947, AAA
BUCK ROGERS
BUCK ROGERS IN THE 25TH CENTURY, 1979, A-C
BUCKAROO BANZAI
BUCKAROO FROM POWDER RIVER, 1948, A
BUCKAROO KID, THE, 1926
BUCKAROO SHERIFF OF TEXAS, 1951, A
BUCKET OF BLOOD, 1934, O
BUCKET OF BLOOD, A, 1959, A
BUCKIN' THE WEST, 1924
BUCKING BROADWAY, 1918
BUCKING THE BARRIER, 1923
BUCKING THE LINE, 1921
BUCKING THE TIGER, 1921
BUCKING THE TRUTH, 1926, A
BUCKSHOT JOHN, 1915
BUCKSKIN, 1968, A
BUCKSKIN FRONTIER, 1943, A
BUCKSKIN LADY, THE, 1957, A

BUCKTOWN, 1975, C
BUDDHA, 1965, C
BUDDIES, 1983, A
BUDDY BUDDY, 1981, C
BUDDY HOLLY STORY, THE, 1978, A-C
BUDDY SYSTEM, THE, 1984, A-C
BUECHSE DER PANDORA
BUFFALO BILL, 1944, AAA
BUFFALO BILL AND THE INDIANS, OR SITTING BULL'S HISTORY LESSON, 1976, C
BUFFALO BILL IN TOMAHAWK TERRITORY, 1952, A
BUFFALO BILL ON THE U.P. TRAIL, 1926
BUFFALO BILL RIDES AGAIN, 1947, A
BUFFALO BILL, HERO OF THE FAR WEST, 1962, A
BUFFALO GUN, 1961, A
BUFFALO RIDER, 1978
BUG, 1975, A-C
BUGLE CALL, THE, 1916
BUGLE CALL, THE, 1927
BUGLE SOUNDS, THE, 1941, A
BUGLER OF ALGIERS, THE, 1916
BUGLES IN THE AFTERNOON, 1952, A
BUGS BUNNY'S THIRD MOVIE—1001 RABBIT TALES, 1982, AAA
BUGS BUNNY, SUPERSTAR, 1975, AAA
BUGS BUNNY/ROAD-RUNNER MOVIE, THE
BUGSY MALONE, 1976, AAA
BUILD MY GALLOWS HIGH
BUILD THY HOUSE, 1920
BUILDERS OF CASTLES, 1917
BUILT FOR RUNNING, 1924
BULL BUSTER, THE, 1975
BULL DODGER, THE, 1922
BULLDOG BREED, THE, 1960, A
BULLDOG COURAGE, 1922, A
BULLDOG COURAGE, 1935
BULLDOG DRUMMOND, 1923, A
BULLDOG DRUMMOND, 1929, A
BULLDOG DRUMMOND AT BAY, 1937, A
BULLDOG DRUMMOND AT BAY, 1947
BULLDOG DRUMMOND COMES BACK, 1937, A
BULLDOG DRUMMOND ESCAPES, 1937, A
BULLDOG DRUMMOND IN AFRICA, 1938, A
BULLDOG DRUMMOND STRIKES BACK, 1934, A
BULLDOG DRUMMOND STRIKES BACK, 1947
BULLDOG DRUMMOND'S BRIDE, 1939, A
BULLDOG DRUMMOND'S PERIL, 1938, A
BULLDOG DRUMMOND'S REVENGE, 1937, A
BULLDOG DRUMMOND'S SECRET POLICE, 1939, A
BULLDOG EDITION, 1936, A
BULLDOG JACK
BULLDOG PLUCK, 1927, A
BULLDOG SEES IT THROUGH, 1940, A
BULLDOGS OF THE TRAIL, THE, 1915
BULLET CODE, 1940, A
BULLET FOR A BADMAN, 1964, A
BULLET FOR BILLY THE KID, 1963
BULLET FOR JOEY, A, 1955, A
BULLET FOR PRETTY BOY, A, 1970, C
BULLET FOR SANDOVAL, A, 1970, C
BULLET FOR STEFANO, 1950, A
BULLET FOR THE GENERAL, A, 1967, C
BULLET IS WAITING, A, 1954, A
BULLET MARK, THE, 1928, A
BULLET SCARS, 1942, A
BULLET-PROOF, 1920
BULLETS AND BROWN EYES, 1916
BULLETS AND JUSTICE, 1929
BULLETS AND SADDLES, 1943
BULLETS FOR BANDITS, 1942
BULLETS FOR O'HARA, 1941, A
BULLETS FOR RUSTLERS, 1940, A
BULLETS OR BALLOTS, 1936, A
BULLFIGHTER AND THE LADY, 1951, A
BULLFIGHTERS, THE, 1945, A
BULLIN' THE BULLSHEVIKI, 1919, A
BULLITT, 1968, C
BULLSHOT, 1983, A-C
BULLWHIP, 1958, A
BULLY, 1978
BUMMER, 1973
BUNCH OF KEYS, A, 1915
BUNCH OF VIOLETS, A, 1916
BUNCO SQUAD, 1950, A
BUNDLE OF JOY, 1956, A
BUNGALOW 13, 1948, A
BUNKER BEAN, 1936, A
BUNNY LAKE IS MISSING, 1965, C
BUNNY O'HARE, 1971, C
BUNTY PULLS THE STRINGS, 1921, A
BUONA SERA, MRS. CAMPBELL, 1968, C
BURDEN OF PROOF, THE, 1918
BURDEN OF RACE, THE, 1921
BUREAU OF MISSING PERSONS, 1933, A
BURG THEATRE, 1936, A
BURGLAR AND THE LADY, THE, 1914
BURGLAR BY PROXY, 1919
BURGLAR, THE, 1917
BURGLAR, THE, 1956, A
BURGLAR-PROOF, 1920
BURGLARS, THE, 1972, C
BURGOMASTER OF STILEMONDE, THE, 1928

BURIDAN, LE HEROS DE LA TOUR DE NESLE, 1924
BURIED ALIVE, 1939, A
BURIED ALIVE, 1951, C
BURIED ALIVE, 1984, O
BURIED GOLD, 1926
BURIED TREASURE, 1921, A
BURKE AND HARE, 1972, O
BURMA CONVOY, 1941, A
BURN, 1970, O
BURN 'EM UP BARNES, 1921, A
BURN 'EM UP O'CONNER, 1939, A
BURN WITCH BURN, 1962, O
BURNING AN ILLUSION, 1982, C
BURNING BRIDGES, 1928
BURNING CROSS, THE, 1947, C
BURNING DAYLIGHT, 1914
BURNING DAYLIGHT, 1920
BURNING DAYLIGHT, 1928
BURNING GOLD, 1927
BURNING GOLD, 1936, A
BURNING HILLS, THE, 1956, A
BURNING QUESTION, THE
BURNING QUESTION, THE, 1919
BURNING SANDS, 1922, A
BURNING THE CANDLE, 1917
BURNING THE WIND, 1929
BURNING TRAIL, THE, 1925
BURNING UP, 1930, A
BURNING UP BROADWAY, 1928
BURNING WORDS, 1923
BURNING YEARS, THE, 1979, O
BURNING, THE, 1981, O
BURNOUT, 1979
BURNT EVIDENCE, 1954, O
BURNT FINGERS, 1927
BURNT IN, 1920
BURNT OFFERINGS, 1976, C-O
BURNT WINGS, 1916
BURNT WINGS, 1920
BURY ME AN ANGEL, 1972, O
BURY ME DEAD, 1947, C
BURY ME NOT ON THE LONE PRAIRIE, 1941, A
BUS IS COMING, THE, 1971, C-O
BUS RILEY'S BACK IN TOWN, 1965, A
BUS STOP, 1956, A
BUSH CHRISTMAS, 1947, AA
BUSH CHRISTMAS, 1983, AA
BUSH LEAGUER, THE, 1927
BUSH PILOT, 1947
BUSHBABY, THE, 1970, AA
BUSHER, THE, 1919
BUSHIDO BLADE, THE, 1982, O
BUSHRANGER, THE, 1928
BUSHWHACKERS, THE, 1952, A
BUSINESS AND PLEASURE, 1932, A
BUSINESS IS BUSINESS, 1915
BUSINESS OF LIFE, THE, 1918
BUSINESS OF LOVE, THE, 1925
BUSMAN'S HOLIDAY, 1936, A
BUSMAN'S HONEYMOON, 1940, A
BUSSES ROAR, 1942, A
BUSTER AND BILLIE, 1974
BUSTER KEATON STORY, THE, 1957, A
BUSTER, THE, 1923
BUSTIN' LOOSE, 1981, O
BUSTIN' THRU, 1925
BUSTING, 1974, C
BUSYBODY, THE, 1967, A
BUT NOT FOR ME, 1959, A
BUT NOT IN VAIN, 1948, A
BUT THE FLESH IS WEAK, 1932, A
BUT WE'RE AFRAID TO ASK, 1972, O
BUT YOUR TEETH ARE IN MY NECK, THE, 1967, C
BUTCH AND SUNDANCE: THE EARLY DAYS, 1979, C
BUTCH CASSIDY AND THE SUNDANCE KID, 1969, A
BUTCH MINDS THE BABY, 1942, A
BUTCHER BAKER (NIGHTMARE MAKER), 1982, O
BUTCHER, THE
BUTLER'S DILEMMA, THE, 1943, A
BUTLEY, 1974, O
BUTTER AND EGG MAN, THE, 1928
BUTTERCUP CHAIN, THE, 1971, O
BUTTERFIELD 8, 1960, O
BUTTERFLIES ARE FREE, 1972, A
BUTTERFLIES IN THE RAIN, 1926
BUTTERFLY, 1924
BUTTERFLY, 1982, O
BUTTERFLY AFFAIR, THE, 1934
BUTTERFLY GIRL, THE, 1917
BUTTERFLY GIRL, THE, 1921
BUTTERFLY ON THE SHOULDER, A, 1978, C-O
BUTTERFLY RANCH
BUTTERFLY RANGE, 1922
BUTTERFLY, THE, 1915
BUTTONS, 1927
BUY ME THAT TOWN, 1941, A
BUZZARD'S SHADOW, THE, 1915
BUZZY AND THE PHANTOM PINTO, 1941
BUZZY RIDES THE RANGE, 1940
BWANA DEVIL, 1953, A
BY APPOINTMENT ONLY, 1933, A
BY BERWIN BANKS, 1920

BY CANDLELIGHT, 1934, A
BY DESIGN, 1982, O
BY DIVINE RIGHT, 1924
BY HOOK OR BY CROOK
BY HOOK OR CROOK, 1918
BY LOVE POSSESSED, 1961, O
BY PROXY, 1918, A
BY RIGHT OF BIRTH, 1921
BY RIGHT OF POSSESSION, 1917, A
BY RIGHT OF PURCHASE, 1918
BY THE LAW, 1926
BY THE LIGHT OF THE SILVERY MOON, 1953, A
BY THE SHORTEST OF HEADS, 1915
BY THE WORLD FORGOT, 1918, A
BY WHOSE HAND?, 1916, A
BY WHOSE HAND?, 1927, A
BY WHOSE HAND?, 1932, A
BY YOUR LEAVE, 1935, A
BYE BYE BARBARA, 1969, A
BYE BYE BIRDIE, 1963
BYE-BYE BRAVERMAN, 1968, A
BYE-BYE BRASIL, 1980, C-O
BYE-BYE BUDDY, 1929
BYPASS TO HAPPINESS, 1934, A

–C–

C'MON, LET'S LIVE A LITTLE, 1967
C-MAN, 1949, A
C. C. AND COMPANY, 1971, O
C.B. HUSTLERS, 1978
C.H.O.M.P.S., 1979, AAA
C.H.U.D., 1984, O
C.O.D., 1915
C.O.D., 1932, A
C.O.D., 1983
CAARAVAN TRAIL, THE, 1946
CABARET, 1927
CABARET, 1972, CMPAA
CABARET GIRL, THE, 1919, A
CABIN IN THE SKY, 1943, A
CABIN IN THE COTTON, 1932, A-C
CABARET, THE, 1918, A
CABINET OF CALIGARI, THE, 1962, A
CABINET OF DR. CALIGARI, THE, 1921, A
CABIRIA
CABIRIA, 1914, G
CABOBLANCO, 1981
CACCIA TRAGICA
CACTUS CRANDALL, 1918
CACTUS CURE, THE, 1925
CACTUS FLOWER, 1969, C
CACTUS IN THE SNOW, 1972, A
CACTUS KID, THE, 1934
CACTUS TRAILS, 1925
CACTUS TRAILS, 1927
CADDIE, 1976, C
CADDY SHACK, 1980, C-O
CADDY, THE, 1953, A
CADET GIRL, 1941, A
CADET-ROUSSELLE, 1954, A
CADETS ON PARADE, 1942
CAESAR AND CLEOPATRA, 1946, A
CAESAR THE CONQUEROR, 1963, C
CAFE COLETTE, 1937, A
CAFE DE PARIS, 1938
CAFE ELECTRIC, 1927
CAFE EXPRESS, 1980, C
CAFE FLESH, 1982
CAFE HOSTESS, 1940, A
CAFE IN CAIRO, A, 1924
CAFE MASCOT, 1936, A
CAFE METROPOLE, 1937, A-C
CAFE SOCIETY, 1939, A
CAGE OF EVIL, 1960, A-C
CAGE OF GOLD, 1950, A
CAGE OF NIGHTINGALES, A, 1947, A
CAGED, 1950, O
CAGED FURY, 1948, A
CAGED FURY, 1984, O
CAGED HEAT
CAGED VIRGINS, 1972
CAGED WOMEN, 1984, O
CAGLIOSTRO, 1920
CAGLIOSTRO, 1928
CAGLIOSTRO, 1975, C
CAHILL, UNITED STATES MARSHAL, 1973, C
CAILLAUX CASE, THE, 1918
CAIN AND MABEL, 1936, A
CAIN'S WAY, 1969, O
CAINE MUTINY, THE, 1954, A
CAIO, 1967
CAIRO, 1942, A
CAIRO, 1963, A
CAIRO ROAD, 1950, A
CAL, 1984, O
CALABUCH, 1956, A
CALAMITY JANE, 1953
CALAMITY JANE AND SAM BASS, 1949
CALAMITY THE COW, 1967, AA
CALCULATED RISK, 1963, A
CALCUTTA, 1947, A
CALEB PIPER'S GIRL, 1919

CALENDAR GIRL, 1947, A
CALENDAR, THE, 1931, A
CALENDAR, THE, 1948, A
CALENDER GIRL, THE, 1917
CALGARY STAMPEDE, THE, 1925
CALIBRE 38, 1919
CALIBRE 45, 1924
CALIFORNIA, 1927, A
CALIFORNIA, 1946, A
CALIFORNIA, 1963, A
CALIFORNIA CONQUEST, 1952, A
CALIFORNIA DOLLS
CALIFORNIA DREAMING, 1979, C
CALIFORNIA FIREBRAND, 1948, A
CALIFORNIA FRONTIER, 1938, A
CALIFORNIA GIRLS, 1984, O
CALIFORNIA GOLD RUSH, 1946
CALIFORNIA IN '49, 1924
CALIFORNIA JOE, 1944, A
CALIFORNIA MAIL, THE, 1929
CALIFORNIA MAIL, THE, 1937, A
CALIFORNIA OR BUST, 1927, A
CALIFORNIA PASSAGE, 1950, A
CALIFORNIA ROMANCE, A, 1922, A
CALIFORNIA SPLIT, 1974, C
CALIFORNIA STRAIGHT AHEAD, 1925
CALIFORNIA STRAIGHT AHEAD, 1937
CALIFORNIA SUITE, 1978, A-C
CALIFORNIA TRAIL, THE, 1933, A
CALIFORNIAN, THE, 1937, A
CALIGARI'S CURE, 1983
CALL A MESSENGER, 1939, A
CALL FROM THE WILD, THE, 1921, A
CALL HER SAVAGE, 1932, A
CALL HIM MR. SHATTER, 1976, O
CALL IT A DAY, 1937
CALL IT LUCK, 1934, A
CALL ME BWANA, 1963, A
CALL ME BY MY RIGHTFUL NAME, 1973
CALL ME GENIUS, 1961, A
CALL ME MADAM, 1953, A
CALL ME MAME, 1933
CALL ME MISTER, 1951, A
CALL NORTHSIDE 777, 1948
CALL OF COURAGE, THE, 1925
CALL OF HER PEOPLE, THE, 1917
CALL OF HIS PEOPLE, THE, 1922
CALL OF HOME, THE, 1922
CALL OF THE BLOOD, 1948, A
CALL OF THE CANYON, 1942, A
CALL OF THE CANYON, 1923
CALL OF THE CIRCUS, 1930, A
CALL OF THE CUMBERLANDS, THE, 1915
CALL OF THE DANCE, THE, 1915
CALL OF THE DESERT, 1930
CALL OF THE EAST, THE, 1917
CALL OF THE EAST, THE, 1922, C
CALL OF THE FLESH, 1930, A
CALL OF THE FOREST, 1949
CALL OF THE HEART, 1928
CALL OF THE HILLS, THE, 1923
CALL OF THE JUNGLE, 1944, A
CALL OF THE KLONDIKE, 1950, A
CALL OF THE KLONDIKE, THE, 1926
CALL OF THE MATE, 1924
CALL OF THE NIGHT, 1926
CALL OF THE NORTH, THE, 1914, A
CALL OF THE NORTH, THE, 1921
CALL OF THE PIPES, THE, 1917
CALL OF THE PRAIRIE, 1936, A
CALL OF THE ROAD, THE, 1920
CALL OF THE ROCKIES, 1931
CALL OF THE ROCKIES, 1938, A
CALL OF THE ROCKIES, 1944
CALL OF THE SEA, THE, 1915
CALL OF THE SEA, THE, 1919
CALL OF THE SEA, THE, 1930
CALL OF THE SOUL, THE, 1919
CALL OF THE SOUTH SEAS, 1944, A
CALL OF THE WEST, 1930
CALL OF THE WILD, 1935, AA
CALL OF THE WILD, 1972, A
CALL OF THE WILD, THE, 1914
CALL OF THE WILD, THE, 1923, A
CALL OF THE WILDERNESS, THE, 1926
CALL OF THE YUKON, 1938, A
CALL OF YOUTH, THE, 1920, A
CALL OF YOUTH, THE, 1921
CALL OUT THE MARINES, 1942, A
CALL THE MESQUITEERS, 1938
CALL, THE, 1938, A
CALLAHANS AND THE MURPHYS, THE, 1927, A
CALLAN, 1975
CALLAWAY WENT THATAWAY, 1951
CALLBOX MYSTERY, THE, 1932, A
CALLED BACK, 1914
CALLED BACK, 1933
CALLING ALL CARS, 1935
CALLING ALL CROOKS, 1938, A
CALLING ALL HUSBANDS, 1940, A
CALLING ALL MA'S
CALLING ALL MARINES, 1939, A

CALLING BULLDOG DRUMMOND, 1951, A-C
CALLING DR. DEATH, 1943, A
CALLING DR. GILLESPIE, 1942, A
CALLING DR. KILDARE, 1939, A
CALLING HOMICIDE, 1956
CALLING OF DAN MATTHEWS, THE, 1936
CALLING PAUL TEMPLE, 1948, A
CALLING PHILO VANCE, 1940, A
CALLING THE TUNE, 1936
CALLING WILD BILL ELLIOTT, 1943, A
CALLING, THE
CALLIOPE, 1971
CALM YOURSELF, 1935, A
CALTIKI, THE IMMORTAL MONSTER, 1959, C
CALVAIRE D'AMOUR, 1923
CALVARY, 1920
CALVERT'S VALLEY, 1922
CALYPSO, 1959, A-C
CALYPSO HEAT WAVE, 1957, A
CALYPSO JOE, 1957, A
CAMBRIC MASK, THE, 1919
CAMEL BOY, THE, 1984, AAA
CAMELOT, 1967, A-C
CAMELS ARE COMING, THE, 1934, A
CAMEO KIRBY, 1923
CAMEO KIRBY, 1930
CAMERA BUFF, 1983, A
CAMERAMAN, THE, 1928, A
CAMERONS, THE, 1974
CAMILLE, 1916
CAMILLE, 1917
CAMILLE, 1921
CAMILLE, 1927, A
CAMILLE, 1937, A-C
CAMILLE 2000, 1969, O
CAMILLE OF THE BARBARY COAST, 1925
CAMMINA CAMMINA, 1983, AA
CAMOUFLAGE KISS, A, 1918
CAMP ON BLOOD ISLAND, THE, 1958
CAMPBELL'S KINGDOM, 1957, A
CAMPBELLS ARE COMING, THE, 1915, A
CAMPER JOHN, 1973
CAMPSITE MASSACRE, 1981
CAMPUS CONFESSIONS, 1938, A
CAMPUS FLIRT, THE, 1926, A
CAMPUS HONEYMOON, 1948
CAMPUS KNIGHTS, 1929, A
CAMPUS RYTHM, 1943, A
CAMPUS SLEUTH, 1948, A
CAMPY KIDS FROM BOOT CAMP, 1942
CAN A WOMAN LOVE TWICE?, 1923
CAN HIERONYMUS MERKIN EVER FORGET MERCY
   HUMPPE AND FIND TRUE HAPPINESS?, 1969
CAN I DO IT 'TIL I NEED GLASSES?, 1977
CAN SHE BAKE A CHERRY PIE?, 1983, C
CAN THIS BE DIXIE?, 1936, A
CAN YOU HEAR ME MOTHER?, 1935, A
CAN'T HELP SINGING, 1944, A
CAN'T STOP THE MUSIC, 1980, C
CAN-CAN, 1960, A-C
CANADIAN MOUNTIES VS. ATOMIC INVADERS
CANADIAN PACIFIC, 1949, A
CANADIAN, THE, 1926
CANADIANS, THE, 1961, A
CANAL ZONE, 1942, A
CANARIES SOMETIMES SING, 1930, A
CANARIS, 1955, C
CANARY MURDER CASE, THE, 1929, A
CANCEL MY RESERVATION, 1972, A
CANCELLED DEBT, THE, 1927
CANDIDATE FOR MURDER, 1966, A
CANDIDATE, THE, 1964, C
CANDIDATE, THE, 1972, A-C
CANDIDE, 1962, A
CANDLELIGHT IN ALGERIA, 1944, A
CANDLES AT NINE, 1944
CANDLESHOE, 1978, AAA
CANDY, 1968, O
CANDY GIRL, THE, 1917
CANDY KID, THE, 1928
CANDY MAN, THE, 1969
CANDY SNATCHERS, THE, 1974
CANDY STRIPE NURSES, 1974
CANDY TANGERINE MAN, THE, 1975
CANDYTUFT, I MEAN VERONICA, 1921
CANICULE
CANNABIS, 1970, O
CANNERY ROW, 1982, C-O
CANNIBAL ATTACK, 1954, A
CANNIBAL GIRLS, 1973, C
CANNIBALISTIC HUMANOID UNDERGROUND
   DWELLING
CANNIBALS IN THE STREETS, 1982, O
CANNIBALS, THE, 1970, O
CANNON AND THE NIGHTINGALE, THE, 1969
CANNON FOR CORDOBA, 1970, C-O
CANNONBALL, 1976, C
CANNONBALL EXPRESS, 1932
CANNONBALL RUN II, 1984, O
CANNONBALL RUN, THE, 1981, A
CANON CITY, 1948, A
CANTERBURY TALE, A, 1944, A

CANTERVILLE GHOST, THE, 1944, AAA
CANTOR'S DAUGHTER, THE, 1913
CANTOR'S SON, THE, 1937, A
CANVAS KISSER, THE, 1925
CANYON AMBUSH, 1952, A
CANYON CITY, 1943, A
CANYON CROSSROADS, 1955, A
CANYON HAWKS, 1930, A
CANYON OF ADVENTURE, THE, 1928
CANYON OF LIGHT, THE, 1926
CANYON OF MISSING MEN, THE, 1930, A
CANYON OF THE FOOLS, 1923
CANYON PASSAGE, 1946, A
CANYON RAIDERS, 1951, A
CANYON RIVER, 1956, A
CANYON RUSTLERS, 1925
CAP'N ABE'S NIECE, 1919
CAPE CANAVERAL MONSTERS, 1960, A
CAPE FEAR, 1962, O
CAPE FORLORN
CAPER OF THE GOLDEN BULLS, THE, 1967, A
CAPETOWN AFFAIR, 1967, C
CAPITAL PUNISHMENT, 1925
CAPITOL, THE, 1920
CAPONE, 1975, O
CAPPY RICKS, 1921, A
CAPPY RICKS RETURNS, 1935, A
CAPRICE, 1913
CAPRICE, 1967, A
CAPRICE OF THE MOUNTAINS, 1916, A
CAPRICES OF KITTY, THE, 1915, A
CAPRICIOUS SUMMER, 1968, C
CAPRICORN ONE, 1978, C
CAPTAIN ALVAREZ, 1914
CAPTAIN APACHE, 1971, C
CAPTAIN APPLEJACK, 1931, A
CAPTAIN BILL, 1935, A
CAPTAIN BLACK JACK, 1952, A
CAPTAIN BLOOD, 1924
CAPTAIN BLOOD, 1935, A
CAPTAIN BOYCOTT, 1947
CAPTAIN CALAMITY, 1936, A
CAPTAIN CARELESS, 1928, A
CAPTAIN CAREY, U.S.A, 1950, A
CAPTAIN CAUTION, 1940, A
CAPTAIN CELLULOID VS THE FILM PIRATES, 1974
CAPTAIN CHINA, 1949, A
CAPTAIN CLEGG, 1962
CAPTAIN COURTESY, 1915, A
CAPTAIN COWBOY, 1929
CAPTAIN DIEPPE
CAPTAIN EDDIE, 1945, AA
CAPTAIN FLY-BY-NIGHT, 1922
CAPTAIN FROM CASTILE, 1947
CAPTAIN FROM KOEPENICK, 1933, A
CAPTAIN FROM KOEPENICK, THE, 1956, A
CAPTAIN FURY, 1939, A
CAPTAIN GRANT'S CHILDREN, 1939, AA
CAPTAIN HORATIO HORNBLOWER, 1951, A
CAPTAIN HURRICANE, 1935, A
CAPTAIN IS A LADY, THE, 1940, A
CAPTAIN JANUARY, 1924, A
CAPTAIN JANUARY, 1935, AAA
CAPTAIN JINKS OF THE HORSE MARINES, 1916
CAPTAIN JOHN SMITH AND POCAHONTAS, 1953
CAPTAIN KIDD, 1945, A
CAPTAIN KIDD AND THE SLAVE GIRL, 1954, A
CAPTAIN KIDD, JR., 1919
CAPTAIN KIDDO, 1917
CAPTAIN KRONOS: VAMPIRE HUNTER, 1974, O
CAPTAIN LASH, 1929, A
CAPTAIN LIGHTFOOT, 1955, A
CAPTAIN MACKLIN, 1915
CAPTAIN MIDNIGHT
CAPTAIN MILKSHAKE, 1970, O
CAPTAIN MOONLIGHT, 1940, A
CAPTAIN NEMO AND THE UNDERWATER CITY,
   1969, A
CAPTAIN NEWMAN, M.D., 1963, C
CAPTAIN OF HIS SOUL, 1918
CAPTAIN OF THE GRAY HORSE TROOP, THE,
   1917, A
CAPTAIN OF THE GUARD, 1930, A
CAPTAIN PIRATE, 1952, A
CAPTAIN SALVATION, 1927, A
CAPTAIN SCARLET VS. THE MYSTERIONS, 1982
CAPTAIN SCARLETT, 1953, A
CAPTAIN SINDBAD, 1963, A
CAPTAIN SIROCCO
CAPTAIN SWAGGER, 1928
CAPTAIN SWIFT, 1914, A
CAPTAIN SWIFT, 1920
CAPTAIN THUNDER, 1931
CAPTAIN TUGBOAT ANNIE, 1945
CAPTAIN'S CAPTAIN, THE, 1919, A
CAPTAIN'S COURAGE, A, 1926, A
CAPTAIN'S KID, THE, 1937, A
CAPTAIN'S ORDERS, 1937
CAPTAIN'S PARADISE, THE, 1953
CAPTAIN'S TABLE, THE, 1936, A
CAPTAIN'S TABLE, THE, 1960, A
CAPTAINS COURAGEOUS, 1937, AAA

CAPTAINS OF THE CLOUDS, 1942, A-C
CAPTIVATION, 1931, A
CAPTIVE, 1980
CAPTIVE CITY, 1952, A
CAPTIVE CITY, THE, 1963, C
CAPTIVE GIRL, 1950, A
CAPTIVE GOD, THE, 1916, A
CAPTIVE HEART, THE, 1948, C
CAPTIVE OF BILLY THE KID, 1952, A
CAPTIVE WILD WOMAN, 1943, A
CAPTIVE WOMEN, 1952, A
CAPTIVE, THE, 1915, A
CAPTURE OF BIGFOOT, THE, 1979
CAPTURE THAT CAPSULE, 1961
CAPTURE, THE, 1950
CAPTURED, 1933, A
CAPTURED IN CHINATOWN, 1935
CAR 99, 1935, A
CAR OF CHANCE, THE, 1917
CAR OF DREAMS, 1935, A
CAR, THE, 1977, C
CARAVAN, 1934, A
CARAVAN, 1946, A
CARAVAN TO VACCARES, 1974, C
CARAVANS, 1978, C
CARBINE WILLIAMS, 1952, A
CARBON COPY, 1981, C
CARD, THE
CARD, THE, 1922
CARDBOARD CAVALIER, THE, 1949, A
CARDBOARD LOVER, THE, 1928
CARDIAC ARREST, 1980, O
CARDIGAN, 1922, A
CARDINAL RICHELIEU, 1935, A
CARDINAL RICHELIEU'S WARD, 1914
CARDINAL, THE, 1936, A
CARDINAL, THE, 1963, C
CAREER, 1939, A
CAREER, 1959, C
CAREER BED, 1972
CAREER GIRL, 1944, A
CAREER GIRL, 1960
CAREER OF KATHERINE BUSH, THE, 1919
CAREER WOMAN, 1936, A
CAREERS, 1929, A
CAREFREE, 1938, A
CAREFUL, HE MIGHT HEAR YOU, 1984, A-C
CAREFUL, SOFT SHOULDERS, 1942, A
CARELESS AGE, 1929, A
CARELESS LADY, 1932, A
CARELESS WOMAN, THE, 1922
CARELESS YEARS, THE, 1957
CARESSED, 1965
CARETAKER, THE
CARETAKERS DAUGHTER, THE, 1952, A
CARETAKERS, THE, 1963, C
CAREY TREATMENT, THE, 1972, C
CARGO TO CAPETOWN, 1950
CARHOPS, 1980
CARIB GOLD, 1955
CARIBBEAN, 1952, A
CARIBBEAN MYSTERY, THE, 1945, A
CARIBOO TRAIL, THE, 1950, A
CARLTON-BROWNE OF THE F.O.
CARMELA, 1949, A
CARMEN
CARMEN, 1915, A
CARMEN, 1916
CARMEN, 1917
CARMEN, 1928
CARMEN, 1931
CARMEN, 1946, A
CARMEN, 1949
CARMEN, 1983, C
CARMEN JONES, 1954, C
CARMEN OF THE KLONDIKE, 1918, A
CARMEN OF THE NORTH, 1920
CARMEN, BABY, 1967, O
CARNABY, M.D., 1967, C
CARNAL KNOWLEDGE, 1971, O
CARNAL MADNESS, 1975
CARNATION KID, 1929
CARNEGIE HALL, 1947, A
CARNIVAL, 1921
CARNIVAL, 1931, A
CARNIVAL, 1935, A
CARNIVAL, 1946, A
CARNIVAL, 1953, A
CARNIVAL BOAT, 1932, A
CARNIVAL GIRL, THE, 1926, A
CARNIVAL IN COSTA RICA, 1947, A
CARNIVAL IN FLANDERS, 1936, A
CARNIVAL LADY, 1933, A
CARNIVAL OF BLOOD, 1976, C
CARNIVAL OF CRIME, 1929
CARNIVAL OF SINNERS, 1947, A
CARNIVAL OF SOULS, 1962, C
CARNIVAL QUEEN, 1937, A
CARNIVAL ROCK, 1957, A
CARNIVAL STORY, 1954, A
CARNY, 1980, O
CAROLINA, 1934, A

CAROLINA BLUES, 1944
CAROLINA CANNONBALL, 1955, A
CAROLINA MOON, 1940, A
CAROLINE CHERIE, 1968, C
CAROLLIE CHERIE, 1951, A
CAROLYN OF THE CORNERS, 1919, A
CAROUSEL, 1956
CARPET FROM BAGDAD, THE, 1915, A
CARPETBAGGERS, THE, 1964, C
CARRIE, 1952, C
CARRIE, 1976, O
CARRINGTON SCHOOL MYSTERY, THE, 1958
CARRINGTON V.C.
CARROTS, 1917
CARRY ON, 1927
CARRY ON 'ROUND THE BEND, 1972
CARRY ON ABROAD, 1974
CARRY ON ADMIRAL, 1957
CARRY ON AGAIN, DOCTOR, 1969, C
CARRY ON BEHIND, 1975
CARRY ON CABBIE, 1963, C
CARRY ON CAMPING, 1969, C
CARRY ON CLEO, 1964, C
CARRY ON CONSTABLE, 1960, C
CARRY ON COWBOY, 1966, A
CARRY ON CRUISING, 1962
CARRY ON DICK, 1975
CARRY ON DOCTOR, 1968, C
CARRY ON EMANUELLE, 1978, O
CARRY ON ENGLAND, 1976, A
CARRY ON GIRLS, 1974
CARRY ON HENRY VIII, 1970, O
CARRY ON JACK, 1963, A
CARRY ON LOVING, 1970, C-O
CARRY ON MATRON, 1973
CARRY ON NURSE, 1959, A
CARRY ON REGARDLESS, 1961, C
CARRY ON SCREAMING, 1966, A
CARRY ON SERGEANT, 1959, A
CARRY ON SPYING, 1964, A
CARRY ON TEACHER, 1962, A
CARRY ON TV
CARRY ON UP THE JUNGLE, 1970, A
CARRY ON VENUS
CARRY ON, UP THE KHYBER, 1968, A
CARS THAT ATE PARIS, THE, 1974, O
CARSON CITY, 1952, A
CARSON CITY CYCLONE, 1943, A
CARSON CITY KID, 1940, AA
CARSON CITY RAIDERS, 1948, A
CARTER CASE, THE, 1947, A
CARTHAGE IN FLAMES, 1961, C-O
CARTOUCHE, 1957, A
CARTOUCHE, 1962, A
CARVE HER NAME WITH PRIDE, 1958, A
CARWASH, 1976, C
CARYL OF THE MOUNTAINS, 1936, AA
CASA MANANA, 1951, A
CASA RICORDI
CASABLANCA, 1942, A
CASANOVA, 1927
CASANOVA, 1976, O
CASANOVA '70, 1965
CASANOVA AND COMPANY
CASANOVA BROWN, 1944, A
CASANOVA IN BURLESQUE, 1944, A
CASANOVA'S BIG NIGHT, 1954, A
CASBAH, 1948, C
CASE AGAINST BROOKLYN, THE, 1958, A
CASE AGAINST FERRO, THE, 1980, C
CASE AGAINST MRS. AMES, THE, 1936, A
CASE AT LAW, A, 1917
CASE FOR PC 49, A, 1951, A
CASE FOR THE CROWN, THE, 1934, A
CASE OF BECKY, THE, 1921
CASE OF CHARLES PEACE, THE, 1949
CASE OF CLARA DEANE, THE, 1932, A
CASE OF DR. LAURENT, 1958
CASE OF GABRIEL PERRY, THE, 1935, A
CASE OF JONATHAN DREW, THE
CASE OF LADY CAMBER, THE, 1920
CASE OF LENA SMITH, THE, 1929
CASE OF MRS. LORING
CASE OF PATTY SMITH, THE, 1962, C-O
CASE OF SERGEANT GRISCHA, THE, 1930
CASE OF THE 44'S, THE, 1964, C
CASE OF THE BLACK CAT, THE, 1936
CASE OF THE BLACK PARROT, THE, 1941, A
CASE OF THE CURIOUS BRIDE, THE, 1935, A
CASE OF THE FRIGHTENED LADY, THE, 1940
CASE OF THE HOWLING DOG, THE, 1934, A
CASE OF THE LUCKY LEGS, THE, 1935, A
CASE OF THE MISSING MAN, THE, 1935, A
CASE OF THE RED MONKEY, 1955, A
CASE OF THE STUTTERING BISHOP, THE, 1937, A
CASE OF THE VELVET CLAWS, THE, 1936, A
CASE VAN GELDERN, 1932, C
CASEY AT THE BAT, 1916
CASEY AT THE BAT, 1927, A
CASEY JONES, 1927
CASEY'S MILLIONS, 1922
CASEY'S SHADOW, 1978, A

CASH McCALL, 1960, C
CASH ON DELIVERY, 1956, A
CASH ON DEMAND, 1962, C
CASINO DE PARIS, 1957, C
CASINO MURDER CASE, THE, 1935, A
CASINO ROYALE, 1967, A
CASQUE D'OR, 1956, C
CASS, 1977
CASS TIMBERLANE, 1947, C
CASSANDRA CROSSING, THE, 1977, C
CASSIDY, 1917, A
CASSIDY OF BAR 20, 1938, A
CAST A DARK SHADOW, 1958, A
CAST A GIANT SHADOW, 1966, A-C
CAST A LONG SHADOW, 1959, C
CASTAWAY COWBOY, THE, 1974, AAA
CASTE, 1930, A
CASTILIAN, THE, 1963, C
CASTLE, 1917
CASTLE IN THE AIR, 1952, A
CASTLE IN THE DESERT, 1942, A
CASTLE KEEP, 1969, C
CASTLE OF BLOOD, 1964, O
CASTLE OF CRIMES, 1940, A
CASTLE OF DREAMS, 1919
CASTLE OF EVIL, 1967, C
CASTLE OF FU MANCHU, THE, 1968, C
CASTLE OF PURITY, 1974, C-O
CASTLE OF TERROR
CASTLE OF THE LIVING DEAD, 1964, C
CASTLE OF THE MONSTERS, 1958, C
CASTLE ON THE HUDSON, 1940, C
CASTLE SINISTER, 1932, C
CASTLE, THE, 1969, C
CASTLES FOR TWO, 1917
CASTLES IN SPAIN, 1920
CASTLES IN THE AIR, 1919
CASTLES IN THE AIR, 1923
CAT AND MOUSE
CAT AND MOUSE, 1958
CAT AND MOUSE, 1978
CAT AND THE CANARY, THE, 1927, A
CAT AND THE CANARY, THE, 1939
CAT AND THE CANARY, THE, 1979, C
CAT AND THE FIDDLE, 1934, A
CAT ATE THE PARAKEET, THE, 1972, A
CAT BALLOU, 1965, A-C
CAT BURGLAR, THE, 1961, C
CAT CREEPS, THE, 1930
CAT CREEPS, THE, 1946, AA
CAT FROM OUTER SPACE, THE, 1978, AAA
CAT GANG, THE, 1959
CAT GIRL, 1957, C
CAT IN THE SACK, THE, 1967, C
CAT MURKIL AND THE SILKS, 1976
CAT O'NINE TAILS, 1971, O
CAT ON A HOT TIN ROOF, 1958, C
CAT PEOPLE, 1942, C
CAT PEOPLE, 1982, O
CAT WOMEN OF THE MOON, 1953, A
CAT'S PAJAMAS, THE, 1926, A
CAT'S PAW, THE, 1934, C
CAT, THE, 1959, C
CAT, THE, 1966
CAT, THE, 1975, C
CATACLYSM, 1980
CATACOMBS
CATALINA CAPER, THE, 1967, A
CATAMOUNT KILLING, THE, 1975, C
CATCH AS CATCH CAN, 1927, A
CATCH AS CATCH CAN, 1937, A
CATCH AS CATCH CAN, 1968, C
CATCH ME IF YOU CAN, 1959
CATCH ME A SPY, 1971, A-C
CATCH MY SMOKE, 1922
CATCH MY SOUL, 1974, C
CATCH US IF YOU CAN
CATCH-22, 1970, O
CATERED AFFAIR, THE, 1956, A
CATHERINE, 1924
CATHERINE & CO., 1976, O
CATHERINE THE GREAT, 1934, C
CATHY'S CHILD, 1979, C
CATHY'S CURSE, 1977, O
CATLOW, 1971
CATMAN OF PARIS, THE, 1946, A
CATSKILL HONEYMOON, 1950
CATSPAW, THE, 1916
CATTLE ANNIE AND LITTLE BRITCHES, 1981, C
CATTLE DRIVE, 1951, AA
CATTLE EMPIRE, 1958
CATTLE KING, 1963, A
CATTLE QUEEN, 1951, A
CATTLE QUEEN OF MONTANA, 1954, A
CATTLE RAIDERS, 1938
CATTLE STAMPEDE, 1943, A
CATTLE THIEF, THE, 1936, A
CATTLE TOWN, 1952, A
CAUGHT, 1931, A
CAUGHT, 1949, C
CAUGHT BLUFFING, 1922
CAUGHT CHEATING, 1931

CAUGHT IN THE ACT, 1918
CAUGHT IN THE ACT, 1941, A
CAUGHT IN THE DRAFT, 1941, AA
CAUGHT IN THE FOG, 1928, A
CAUGHT IN THE NET, 1960, AA
CAUGHT PLASTERED, 1931, A
CAUGHT SHORT, 1930, A
CAULDRON OF BLOOD, 1971, C
CAULDRON OF DEATH, THE, 1979, O
CAUSE FOR ALARM, 1951, C
CAUSE FOR DIVORCE, 1923
CAVALCADE, 1933, A
CAVALCADE OF THE WEST, 1936, A
CAVALIER OF THE STREETS, THE, 1937
CAVALIER OF THE WEST, 1931, A
CAVALIER, THE, 1928, A
CAVALIER, THE, 1928
CAVALLERIA RUSTICANA
CAVALRY, 1936, A
CAVALRY COMMAND, 1963, A
CAVALRY SCOUT, 1951, A
CAVANAUGH OF THE FOREST RANGERS, 1918
CAVE GIRL, THE, 1921
CAVE OF OUTLAWS, 1951, A
CAVE OF THE LIVING DEAD, 1966, A
CAVELL CASE, THE
CAVEMAN, 1981, C
CAVEMAN, THE, 1915
CAVEMAN, THE, 1926, A
CAVERN, THE, 1965, A
CAXAMBU, 1968
CAYMAN TRIANGLE, THE, 1977, C-O
CE COCHON DE MORIN, 1924
CE PAUVRE CHERI, 1923
CECILIA OF THE PINK ROSES, 1918
CECROPIA MOTH, THE, 1916
CEDDO, 1978, C
CEILNG ZERO, 1935
CELEBRATED CASE, A, 1914, A
CELEBRATED SCANDAL, A, 1915
CELEBRITY, 1928
CELESTE, 1982, A
CELESTE OF THE AMBULANCE CORPS, 1916
CELESTIAL CITY, THE, 1929
CELIA, 1949, A
CELINE AND JULIE GO BOATING, 1974, C
CELL 2455, DEATH ROW, 1955, C
CELLAR OF DEATH, THE, 1914
CENSUS TAKER, THE, 1984, O
CENTENNIAL SUMMER, 1946, AA
CENTERFOLD GIRLS, THE, 1974
CENTO ANNI D'AMORE, 1954, C
CENTRAL AIRPORT, 1933, A
CENTRAL PARK, 1932, A
CENTURION, THE, 1962, A
CEREBROS DIABOLICOS, 1966, A
CEREBROS INFERNAL
CEREMONY, THE, 1963, C
CERTAIN RICH MAN, A, 1921
CERTAIN SMILE, A, 1958, C-O
CERTAIN YOUNG MAN, A, 1928
CERTAIN, VERY CERTAIN, AS A MATTER OF FACT... PROBABLE, 1970, O
CERVANTES
CESAR, 1936, A
CESAR AND ROSALIE, 1972, C
CH OF BLUE, A, 1965, C
CHA-CHA-CHA BOOM, 1956
CHACALS, 1918
CHAD HANNA, 1940, A-C
CHAFED ELBOWS, 1967
CHAIN GANG, 1950, C
CHAIN GANG WOMEN, 1972
CHAIN INVISIBLE, THE, 1916
CHAIN LIGHTING, 1927
CHAIN LIGHTNING, 1922, A
CHAIN LIGHTNING, 1950, A
CHAIN OF CIRCUMSTANCE, 1951
CHAIN OF EVENTS, 1958, A-C
CHAIN OF EVIDENCE, 1957, A
CHAIN REACTION, 1980, C
CHAINED, 1927
CHAINED, 1934, C
CHAINED FOR LIFE, 1950, C
CHAINED HEAT, 1983, O
CHAINS OF BONDAGE, 1916
CHAINS OF EVIDENCE, 1920
CHAIRMAN, THE, 1969
CHALICE OF COURAGE, THE, 1915
CHALICE OF SORROW, 1916
CHALK GARDEN, THE, 1964, A
CHALK MARKS, 1924
CHALLENGE, 1974
CHALLENGE ACCEPTED, THE, 1918, A
CHALLENGE FOR ROBIN HOOD, A, 1968, A
CHALLENGE OF CHANCE, THE, 1919, A
CHALLENGE OF MC KENNA, THE, 1983
CHALLENGE OF THE LAW, THE, 1920
CHALLENGE OF THE RANGE, 1949, A
CHALLENGE THE WILD, 1954
CHALLENGE TO BE FREE, 1976, A
CHALLENGE TO LASSIE, 1949, AAA

CHALLENGE TO LIVE, 1964, O
CHALLENGE, THE
CHALLENGE, THE, 1916
CHALLENGE, THE, 1922
CHALLENGE, THE, 1939, A
CHALLENGE, THE, 1948, A
CHALLENGE, THE, 1982, C
CHALLENGERS, THE, 1968
CHAMBER OF HORRORS, 1929
CHAMBER OF HORRORS, 1941, A
CHAMBER OF HORRORS, 1966, O
CHAMBER OF MYSTERY, THE, 1920
CHAMELEON, 1978, C
CHAMP FOR A DAY, 1953, A
CHAMP, THE, 1931, AA
CHAMP, THE, 1979, AA
CHAMPAGNE, 1928, A
CHAMPAGNE CHARLIE, 1936, A
CHAMPAGNE CHARLIE, 1944, A
CHAMPAGNE FOR BREAKFAST, 1935, A
CHAMPAGNE FOR CAESAR, 1950, AAA
CHAMPAGNE MURDERS, THE, 1968, C
CHAMPAGNE WALTZ, 1937, A
CHAMPION, 1949, C
CHAMPION OF LOST CAUSES, 1925, A
CHAMPIONS, 1984, C
CHAN IS MISSING, 1982, C
CHANCE AT HEAVEN, 1933, A
CHANCE MEETING, 1954, A
CHANCE MEETING, 1960, C
CHANCE OF A LIFETIME, 1950, A
CHANCE OF A LIFETIME, THE, 1916
CHANCE OF A LIFETIME, THE, 1943, A
CHANCE OF A NIGHT-TIME, THE, 1931, A
CHANCES, 1931, A
CHANDLER, 1971
CHANDU ON THE MAGIC ISLAND, 1934
CHANDU THE MAGICIAN, 1932, A
CHANEL SOLITAIRE, 1981, C
CHANG, 1927, C
CHANGE FOR A SOVEREIGN, 1937, A
CHANGE OF HABIT, 1969, C-O
CHANGE OF HEART, 1934, A
CHANGE OF HEART, 1938
CHANGE OF HEART, 1943
CHANGE OF HEART, 1962, A
CHANGE OF MIND, 1969, C
CHANGE OF SEASONS, A, 1980, C-O
CHANGE PARTNERS, 1965
CHANGELING, THE, 1980, O
CHANGES, 1969, O
CHANGING HUSBANDS, 1924
CHANGING WOMAN, THE, 1918
CHANNEL CROSSING, 1934, A
CHANNING OF THE NORTHWEST, 1922
CHANNINGS, THE, 1920
CHANSON FILMEES, 1918
CHANT OF JIMMIE BLACKSMITH, THE, 1980, O
CHANTE-LOUVE, 1921
CHAPERON, THE, 1916
CHAPMAN REPORT, THE, 1962, O
CHAPPAQUA, 1967, O
CHAPPY—THAT'S ALL, 1924
CHAPTER IN HER LIFE, A, 1923
CHAPTER TWO, 1979, C
CHARADE, 1953, A
CHARADE, 1963, A-C
CHARGE AT FEATHER RIVER, THE, 1953, C
CHARGE IT, 1921, A
CHARGE IT TO ME, 1919
CHARGE OF THE GAUCHOS, THE, 1928
CHARGE OF THE LANCERS, 1953, A
CHARGE OF THE LIGHT BRIGADE, THE, 1936, A
CHARGE OF THE LIGHT BRIGADE, THE, 1968
CHARGE OF THE MODEL-T'S, 1979, AA
CHARING CROSS ROAD, 1935, A
CHARITY
CHARITY ANN, 1915
CHARITY CASTLE, 1917
CHARITY?, 1916, A
CHARLATAN, THE, 1916
CHARLATAN, THE, 1929, A
CHARLES AND LUCIE, 1982, A
CHARLES XII, PARTS 1 & 2, 1927
CHARLES, DEAD OR ALIVE, 1972
CHARLESTON, 1978, A
CHARLEY AND THE ANGEL, 1973
CHARLEY MOON, 1956, A
CHARLEY VARRICK, 1973, C
CHARLEY', BIG-
CHARLEY'S AUNT, 1925
CHARLEY'S AUNT, 1930
CHARLEY'S AUNT, 1941, AA
CHARLEY-ONE-EYE, 1973, C
CHARLIE BUBBLES, 1968, C
*CHARLIE CHAN AND THE CURSE OF THE DRAGON
    QUEEN*, 1981, A
CHARLIE CHAN AT MONTE CARLO, 1937, A
CHARLIE CHAN AT THE CIRCUS, 1936, A
CHARLIE CHAN AT THE OLYMPICS, 1937, A
CHARLIE CHAN AT THE OPERA, 1936, A

CHARLIE CHAN AT THE RACE TRACK, 1936, A
CHARLIE CHAN AT THE WAX MUSEUM, 1940
CHARLIE CHAN AT TREASURE ISLAND, 1939, A
CHARLIE CHAN CARRIES ON, 1931, A
CHARLIE CHAN IN BLACK MAGIC, 1944, A
CHARLIE CHAN IN EGYPT, 1935, A
CHARLIE CHAN IN HONOLULU, 1938, A
CHARLIE CHAN IN LONDON, 1934, A
CHARLIE CHAN IN PANAMA, 1940, A
CHARLIE CHAN IN PARIS, 1935
CHARLIE CHAN IN RENO, 1939, A
CHARLIE CHAN IN RIO, 1941, A
CHARLIE CHAN IN SHANGHAI, 1935, A
CHARLIE CHAN IN THE CITY OF DARKNESS, 1939, A
CHARLIE CHAN IN THE SECRET SERVICE, 1944, A
CHARLIE CHAN ON BROADWAY, 1937, A
CHARLIE CHAN'S CHANCE, 1932, A
CHARLIE CHAN'S COURAGE, 1934, A
CHARLIE CHAN'S GREATEST CASE, 1933, A
CHARLIE CHAN'S MURDER CRUISE, 1940, A
CHARLIE CHAN'S SECRET, 1936, A
CHARLIE CHAN: HAPPINESS IS A WARM CLUE, 1971
CHARLIE MC CARTHY, DETECTIVE, 1939, A
CHARLIE, THE LONESOME COUGAR, 1967, AAA
CHARLOTTE, 1917
CHARLOTTE'S WEB, 1973, AAA
CHARLTON-BROWN OF THE F.O.
CHARLY, 1968, A-C
CHARM SCHOOL, THE, 1921, A
CHARMER, THE, 1917
CHARMER, THE, 1925, A
CHARMING DECEIVER, THE, 1921
CHARMING DECEIVER, THE, 1933, A
CHARMING SINNERS, 1929, A
CHARRIOTS OF FIRE, 1981, AAA
CHARRO, 1969, A
CHARTER PILOT, 1940, A
CHARTROOSE CABOOSE, 1960
CHASE A CROOKED SHADOW, 1958, A
CHASE FOR THE GOLDEN NEEDLES
CHASE ME CHARLIE, 1918
CHASE, THE, 1946, A
CHASE, THE, 1966, O
CHASER, THE, 1928, A
CHASER, THE, 1938
CHASERS, THE
CHASING DANGER, 1939, A
CHASING RAINBOWS, 1919
CHASING RAINBOWS, 1930, A
CHASING THE MOON, 1922, A
CHASING THROUGH EUROPE, 1929
CHASING TROUBLE, 1926
CHASING TROUBLE, 1940, A
CHASING YESTERDAY, 1935, A
CHASTITY, 1923
CHASTITY, 1969, C
CHASTITY BELT, THE, 1968, C
CHATEAU HISTORIQUE, 1923
CHATO'S LAND, 1972, O
CHATTANOOGA CHOO CHOO, 1984, A-C
CHATTEL, THE, 1916
CHATTERBOX, 1936, A
CHATTERBOX, 1943, A
CHATTERBOX, 1977
CHE!, 1969, C
CHE?, 1973, O
CHEAP DETECTIVE, THE, 1978, C
CHEAP KISSES, 1924
CHEAPER BY THE DOZEN, 1950, AAA
CHEAPER TO KEEP HER, 1980, O
CHEAPER TO MARRY, 1925
CHEAT, THE, 1915
CHEAT, THE, 1923
CHEAT, THE, 1931, C-O
CHEAT, THE, 1950
CHEATED HEARTS, 1921, A
CHEATED LOVE, 1921
CHEATER REFORMED, THE, 1921, A
CHEATER, THE, 1920
CHEATERS, 1927, A
CHEATERS, 1934, A
CHEATERS AT PLAY, 1932, A
CHEATERS, THE, 1945, A
CHEATERS, THE, 1961, O
CHEATING BLONDES, 1933, A
CHEATING CHEATERS, 1919
CHEATING CHEATERS, 1927, A
CHEATING CHEATERS, 1934
CHEATING HERSELF, 1919
CHEATING THE PUBLIC, 1918
CHECHAHCOS, THE, 1924
CHECK AND DOUBLE CHECK
CHECK YOUR GUNS, 1948, A
CHECKERBOARD, 1969, O
CHECKERED COAT, THE, 1948, A
CHECKERED FLAG OR CRASH, 1978, C
CHECKERED FLAG, THE, 1963, C
CHECKERS, 1913, A
CHECKERS, 1919
CHECKERS, 1937, A
CHECKMATE, 1935, A

CHECKMATE, 1973, O
CHECKMATE, THE, 1917
CHECKPOINT, 1957, A
CHEECH AND CHONG'S NEXT MOVIE, 1980, O
CHEECH AND CHONG'S NICE DREAMS, 1981, O
CHEECH AND CHONG'S THE CORSICAN BROTHERS,
    1984, O
CHEER BOYS CHEER, 1939, A
CHEER LEADER, THE, 1928
CHEER THE BRAVE, 1951
CHEER UP AND SMILE, 1930, A
CHEER UP!, 1936, A
CHEERFUL FRAUD, THE, 1927
CHEERFUL GIVERS, 1917
CHEERING SECTION, 1977
CHEERLEADERS BEACH PARTY, 1978
CHEERLEADERS, THE, 1973
CHEERS FOR MISS BISHOP, 1941, A
CHEERS OF THE CROWD, 1936, A
CHELSEA GIRLS, THE, 1967, O
CHELSEA LIFE, 1933, A
CHELSEA STORY, 1951, A
CHEREZ TERNII K SVEZDAM, 1981, A
CHEROKEE FLASH, THE, 1945, A
CHEROKEE KID, THE, 1927
CHEROKEE STRIP, 1937, A
CHEROKEE STRIP, 1940, A
CHEROKEE STRIP, THE, 1925
CHEROKEE UPRISING, 1950, A
CHERRY HILL HIGH, 1977
CHERRY RIPE, 1921
CHESS PLAYER, THE, 1930
CHESS PLAYERS, THE, 1978, C
CHESTY ANDERSON, U.S. NAVY, 1976, O
CHETNIKS, 1943, A
CHEYENNE, 1929
CHEYENNE, 1947, A
CHEYENNE AUTUMN, 1964, A
CHEYENNE CYCLONE, THE, 1932, A
CHEYENNE KID, THE, 1930, A
CHEYENNE KID, THE, 1933, A
CHEYENNE KID, THE, 1940, A
CHEYENNE RIDES AGAIN, 1937, A
CHEYENNE ROUNDUP, 1943, A
CHEYENNE SOCIAL CLUB, THE, 1970, C
CHEYENNE TAKES OVER, 1947, A
CHEYENNE TORNADO, 1935, A
CHEYENNE TRAILS, 1928
CHEYENNE WILDCAT, 1944, A
CHICAGO, 1928, A
CHICAGO 70, 1970, C
CHICAGO AFTER MIDNIGHT, 1928, A
CHICAGO CALLING, 1951, A
CHICAGO CONFIDENTIAL, 1957
CHICAGO DEADLINE, 1949, A
CHICAGO KID, THE, 1945, A
CHICAGO KID, THE, 1969
CHICAGO SYNDICATE, 1955, A
CHICHINETTE ET CIE, 1921
CHICK, 1928
CHICK, 1936, A
CHICKEN A LA KING, 1928
CHICKEN CASEY, 1917, A
CHICKEN CHRONICLES, THE, 1977, C
CHICKEN EVERY SUNDAY, 1948, A
CHICKEN IN THE CASE, THE, 1921
CHICKEN WAGON FAMILY, 1939, A
CHICKENS, 1921, A
CHICKIE, 1925
CHIEF CRAZY HORSE, 1955, A
CHIEF, THE, 1933, A
CHIFFY KIDS GANG, THE, 1983
CHIGNON D'OR, 1916
CHILD AND THE KILLER, THE, 1959, C
CHILD BRIDE, 1937
CHILD FOR SALE, A, 1920, A
CHILD IN JUDGEMENT, A, 1915
CHILD IN PAWN, A, 1921
CHILD IN THE HOUSE, 1956, A
CHILD IS A WILD THING, A, 1976, O
CHILD IS BORN, A, 1940, A
CHILD IS WAITING, A, 1963, A
CHILD OF DESTINY, THE, 1916
CHILD OF DIVORCE, 1946, A
CHILD OF GOD, A, 1915
CHILD OF M'SIEU, 1919, A
CHILD OF MANHATTAN, 1933, C
CHILD OF MYSTERY, A, 1916
CHILD OF THE BIG CITY, 1914
CHILD OF THE PARIS STREETS, A, 1916
CHILD OF THE PRAIRIE, A, 1925
CHILD OF THE WILD, A, 1917
CHILD THOU GAVEST ME, THE, 1921
CHILD UNDER A LEAF, 1975, O
CHILD'S PLAY, 1954, A
CHILD'S PLAY, 1972
CHILD'S PLAY, 1984
CHILD, THE, 1977, O
CHILDHOOD OF MAXIM GORKY, 1938
CHILDISH THINGS, 1969, O
CHILDREN—FLOWERS OF LIFE, 1919
CHILDREN GALORE, 1954, A

CHILDREN IN THE HOUSE, THE, 1916
CHILDREN NOT WANTED, 1920
CHILDREN OF BABYLON, 1980, O
CHILDREN OF BANISHMENT, 1919
CHILDREN OF CHANCE, 1930, A
CHILDREN OF CHANCE, 1949, A
CHILDREN OF CHANCE, 1950, A
CHILDREN OF CHAOS, 1950, C
CHILDREN OF COURAGE, 1921
CHILDREN OF DESTINY, 1920
CHILDREN OF DIVORCE, 1927
CHILDREN OF DREAMS, 1931, A
CHILDREN OF DUST, 1923
CHILDREN OF EVE, THE, 1915
CHILDREN OF FATE, 1926
CHILDREN OF FATE, 1928
CHILDREN OF GIBEON, THE, 1920
CHILDREN OF GOD'S EARTH, 1983, C
CHILDREN OF HIROSHIMA, 1952, C-O
CHILDREN OF JAZZ, 1923
CHILDREN OF PARADISE, 1945, C
CHILDREN OF PLEASURE, 1930, A
CHILDREN OF RAGE, 1975, O
CHILDREN OF SANCHEZ, THE, 1978, O
CHILDREN OF STORM, 1926
CHILDREN OF THE CORN, 1984, C-O
CHILDREN OF THE DAMNED, 1963, O
CHILDREN OF THE FEUD, 1916
CHILDREN OF THE FOG, 1935
CHILDREN OF THE GHETTO, THE, 1915
CHILDREN OF THE NEW DAY, 1930
CHILDREN OF THE NIGHT, 1921, A
CHILDREN OF THE RITZ, 1929
CHILDREN OF THE SEA, 1926
CHILDREN OF THE WHIRLWIND, 1925
CHILDREN PAY, THE, 1916
CHILDREN SHOULDN'T PLAY WITH DEAD THINGS,
    1972, O
CHILDREN'S HOUR, THE, 1961, C
CHILDREN, THE, 1949, AAA
CHILDREN, THE, 1980, O
CHILDRENS GAMES, 1969
CHILL, THE, 1981
CHILLY SCENES OF WINTER, 1982, C
CHILTERN HUNDREDS, THE
CHIMES AT MIDNIGHT, 1967, C
CHIMES, THE, 1914
CHIMMIE FADDEN, 1915, A
CHIMMIE FADDEN OUT WEST, 1915, A
CHINA, 1943, C
CHINA 9, LIBERTY 37, 1978, O
CHINA BOUND, 1929
CHINA CLIPPER, 1936, A
CHINA CORSAIR, 1951, C
CHINA DOLL, 1958, C
CHINA GATE, 1957, C
CHINA GIRL, 1942, A
CHINA IS NEAR, 1968, C-O
CHINA PASSAGE, 1937, A
CHINA SEAS, 1935, A
CHINA SKY, 1945
CHINA SLAVER, 1929
CHINA SYNDROME, THE, 1979, A
CHINA VENTURE, 1953, C
CHINA'S LITTLE DEVILS, 1945, C
CHINATOWN, 1974, O
CHINATOWN AFTER DARK, 1931, A
CHINATOWN AT MIDNIGHT, 1949, C
CHINATOWN CHARLIE, 1928
CHINATOWN NIGHTS, 1929, A
CHINATOWN NIGHTS, 1938, A
CHINATOWN SQUAD, 1935
CHINCERO
CHINESE BOXES, 1984, O
CHINESE BUNGALOW, THE, 1926, A
CHINESE BUNGALOW, THE, 1930, A
CHINESE CAT, THE, 1944, A
CHINESE DEN, THE, 1940, A
CHINESE PARROT, THE, 1927
CHINESE PUZZLE, THE, 1919
CHINESE PUZZLE, THE, 1932, A
CHINESE RING, THE, 1947, A
CHINESE ROULETTE, 1977, O
CHINO, 1976, A-C
CHIP OF THE FLYING U, 1914
CHIP OF THE FLYING U, 1926
CHIP OF THE FLYING U, 1940, A
CHIP OFF THE OLD BLOCK, 1944, A
CHIPS, 1938
CHIQUTTO PERO PICOSO, 1967, A
CHISUM, 1970, A
CHITTY CHITTY BANG BANG, 1968, AAA
CHIVALROUS CHARLEY, 1921
CHIVATO, 1961, A-C
CHLOE IN THE AFTERNOON, 1972, O
CHOCOLATE SOLDIER, THE, 1915
CHOCOLATE SOLDIER, THE, 1941, A
CHOICE OF ARMS, 1983, C
CHOICES, 1981
CHOIRBOYS, THE, 1977, O
CHOOSE ME, 1984, O
CHOPPER SQUAD, 1971

CHOPPERS, THE, 1961, C-O
CHORUS CALL, 1979
CHORUS GIRL'S ROMANCE, A, 1920, A
CHORUS KID, THE, 1928
CHORUS LADY, THE, 1924
CHORUS OF TOKYO, 1931
CHOSEN SURVIVORS, 1974
CHOSEN, THE, 1978, O
CHOSEN, THE, 1982, A
CHOUCHOU POIDS PLUME, 1925
CHOUQUETTE ET SON AS, 1920
CHRIS AND THE WONDERFUL LAMP, 1917, A
CHRISMAS THAT ALMOST WASN'T, THE, 1966, A
CHRIST STOPPED AT EBOLI
CHRISTIAN LICORICE STORE, THE, 1971
CHRISTIAN THE LION, 1976, AAA
CHRISTIAN, THE, 1914, A
CHRISTIAN, THE, 1915
CHRISTIAN, THE, 1923
CHRISTIE JOHNSTONE, 1921
CHRISTINA, 1929
CHRISTINA, 1974, C
CHRISTINE, 1959, C
CHRISTINE, 1983
CHRISTINE JORGENSEN STORY, THE, 1970, O
CHRISTINE KEELER AFFAIR, THE, 1964, O
CHRISTINE OF THE BIG TOPS, 1926
CHRISTINE OF THE HUNGRY HEART, 1924
CHRISTMAS CAROL, A, 1938, AAA
CHRISTMAS CAROL, A, 1951, AAA
CHRISTMAS EVE, 1913
CHRISTMAS EVE, 1947, A
CHRISTMAS HOLIDAY, 1944, A
CHRISTMAS IN CONNECTICUT, 1945, AAA
CHRISTMAS IN JULY, 1940, A
CHRISTMAS KID, THE, 1968, C
CHRISTMAS STORY, A, 1983, A
CHRISTMAS TREE, THE, 1966, AA
CHRISTMAS TREE, THE, 1969, A
CHRISTOPHE COLOMB, 1919
CHRISTOPHER BEAN, 1933, A
CHRISTOPHER COLUMBUS, 1949, A
CHRISTOPHER STRONG, 1933, C
CHRISTUS, 1917
CHROME AND HOT LEATHER, 1971, O
CHRONICLE OF ANNA MAGDALENA BACH,
    1968, A-C
CHRONICLE OF THE MAY RAIN, 1924
CHRONICLES OF THE GRAY HOUSE, THE, 1923
CHRONOPOLIS, 1982
CHRYSANTHEMUMS, 1914
CHU CHIN CHOW, 1923
CHU CHIN CHOW, 1934, A
CHU CHU AND THE PHILLY FLASH, 1981, A
CHUBASCO, 1968, A
CHUKA, 1967, C
CHUMP AT OXFORD, A, 1940, A
CHURCH MOUSE, THE, 1934, A
CHUSHINGURA, 1963, C
CIAO MANHATTAN, 1973
CIGARETTE GIRL, 1947, A
CIGARETTE GIRL FROM MOSSELPROM, 1924
CIGARETTE GIRL, THE, 1917
CIGARETTE MAKER'S ROMANCE, A, 1920
CIMARRON, 1931
CIMARRON, 1960, O
CIMARRON KID, THE, 1951, A
CINCINNATI KID, THE, 1965
CINDERELLA, 1915, A
CINDERELLA, 1926
CINDERELLA, 1937, A
CINDERELLA, 1950, AAA
CINDERELLA AND THE MAGIC SLIPPER, 1917
CINDERELLA JONES, 1946
CINDERELLA LIBERTY, 1973, C-O
CINDERELLA MAN, THE, 1918
CINDERELLA OF THE HILLS, 1921
CINDERELLA SWINGS IT, 1942, A
CINDERELLA'S TWIN, 1920
CINDERFELLA, 1960, A
CINDERS, 1926
CINDY AND DONNA, 1971
CINEMA GIRL'S ROMANCE, A, 1915
CINEMA MURDER, THE, 1920
CIPHER BUREAU, 1938, A
CIPHER KEY, THE, 1915
CIRCE THE ENCHANTRESS, 1924
CIRCLE CANYON, 1934, A
CIRCLE OF DEATH, 1935
CIRCLE OF DANGER, 1951, C
CIRCLE OF DECEIT, 1982, O
CIRCLE OF DECEPTON, 1961, C
CIRCLE OF IRON, 1979
CIRCLE OF LOVE, 1965, C-O
CIRCLE OF POWER
CIRCLE OF POWER, 1984
CIRCLE OF TWO, 1980, O
CIRCLE, THE, 1925
CIRCLE, THE, 1959, C
CIRCULAR STAIRCASE, THE, 1915
CIRCUMSTANIAL EVIDENCE, 1954, C
CIRCUMSTANTIAL EVIDENCE, 1920

CIRCUMSTANTIAL EVIDENCE, 1929
CIRCUMSTANTIAL EVIDENCE, 1935
CIRCUMSTANTIAL EVIDENCE, 1945, C
CIRCUS
CIRCUS, 1919
CIRCUS ACE, THE, 1927, A
CIRCUS BOY, 1947
CIRCUS CLOWN, 1934, A
CIRCUS COWBOY, THE, 1924
CIRCUS CYCLONE, THE, 1925
CIRCUS DAYS, 1923, A
CIRCUS FRIENDS, 1962, AA
CIRCUS GIRL, 1937, A
CIRCUS JIM, 1921
CIRCUS JOYS, 1923
CIRCUS KID, THE, 1928, A
CIRCUS LURE, 1924
CIRCUS MAN, THE, 1914, A
CIRCUS OF FEAR
CIRCUS OF HORRORS, 1960
CIRCUS OF LIFE, THE, 1917
CIRCUS OF LOVE, 1958, C
CIRCUS QUEEN MURDER, THE, 1933, C
CIRCUS ROMANCE, A, 1916
CIRCUS ROOKIES, 1928
CIRCUS SHADOWS, 1935
CIRCUS WORLD, 1964, A
CIRCUS, THE, 1928, A
CISCO KID, 1931, AA
CISCO KID AND THE LADY, THE, 1939, A
CISCO KID RETURNS, THE, 1945, A
CISCO PIKE, 1971, O
CITADEL OF CRIME, 1941, C
CITADEL, THE, 1938, A
CITIES AND YEARS, 1931
CITIZEN KANE, 1941, A
CITIZEN SAINT, 1947, AA
CITIZEN SOLDIER, 1984
CITIZENS BAND, 1977
CITY ACROSS THE RIVER, 1949, C
CITY AFTER MIDNIGHT, 1957, C
CITY BENEATH THE SEA, 1953, C
CITY DESTROYED, A, 1922
CITY GIRL, 1930
CITY GIRL, 1938, C
CITY GIRL, THE, 1984, O
CITY GONE WILD, THE, 1927, A
CITY HEAT, 1984, O
CITY IN DARKNESS
CITY LIGHTS, 1931, A
CITY LIMITS, 1934, A
CITY LIMITS, 1941
CITY LOVERS, 1982, C
CITY NEWS, 1983, C
CITY OF BAD MEN, 1953, A
CITY OF BEAUTIFUL NONSENSE, THE, 1919
CITY OF BEAUTIFUL NONSENSE, THE, 1935, A
CITY OF CHANCE, 1940, C
CITY OF COMRADES, THE, 1919
CITY OF DIM FACE, THE, 1918
CITY OF FAILING LIGHT, THE, 1916
CITY OF FEAR, 1959, C
CITY OF FEAR, 1965, C
CITY OF ILLUSION, THE, 1916
CITY OF MASKS, THE, 1920
CITY OF MISSING GIRLS, 1941
CITY OF PAIN, 1951, C
CITY OF PLAY, 1929, C
CITY OF PURPLE DREAMS, 1928
CITY OF PURPLE DREAMS, THE, 1918, A
CITY OF SECRETS, 1963, O
CITY OF SHADOWS, 1929
CITY OF SHADOWS, 1955, A
CITY OF SILENT MEN, 1921, A
CITY OF SILENT MEN, 1942
CITY OF SONG
CITY OF SONGS
CITY OF TEARS, THE, 1918
CITY OF TEMPTATION, 1929
CITY OF THE DEAD
CITY OF THE DEAD
CITY OF THE WALKING DEAD, 1983, O
CITY OF TORMENT, 1950, C
CITY OF WOMEN, 1980, O
CITY OF YOUTH, 1938, C
CITY OF YOUTH, THE, 1928
CITY ON A HUNT
CITY ON FIRE, 1979, O
CITY PARK, 1934, A
CITY SENTINEL
CITY SPARROW, THE, 1920
CITY STORY, 1954, C
CITY STREETS, 1931, A
CITY STREETS, 1938, A
CITY THAT NEVER SLEEPS, 1953, A
CITY THAT NEVER SLEEPS, THE, 1924
CITY UNDER THE SEA, 1965, A
CITY WITHOUT MEN, 1943, A
CITY, FOR CONQUEST, 1941, A
CITY, THE, 1916
CITY, THE, 1926
CIVILIAN CLOTHES, 1920
CIVILIZATION, 1916, A

COLT .45, 1950, A
COLT COMRADES, 1943, A
COLUMBUS, 1923
COLUMN SOUTH, 1953, A
COMA, 1978, A
COMANCHE, 1956, A
COMANCHE STATION, 1960, A
COMBAT, 1927
COMBAT SQUAD, 1953, A
COMBAT, THE, 1916
COMBAT, THE, 1926
COME 'N' GET IT
COME ACROSS, 1929
COME AGAIN SMITH, 1919
COME AND GET IT, 1929
COME AND GET IT, 1936, A
COME BACK BABY, 1968, O
COME BACK CIHARLESTON BLUE, 1972, O
COME BACK LITTLE SHEBA, 1952, A-C
COME BACK PETER, 1952, A
COME BACK PETER, 1971
*COME BACK TO THE 5 & DIME, JIMMY DEAN,
    JIMMY DEAN*, 1982, O
COME BLOW YOUR HORN, 1963, A-C
COME CLOSER, FOLKS, 1936
COME DANCE WITH ME, 1950
COME DANCE WITH ME, 1960, C-O
COME FILL THE CUP, 1951, C
COME FLY WITH ME, 1963, A
COME LIVE WITH ME, 1941, A
COME NEXT SPRING, 1956, AA
COME ON COWBOYS, 1924
COME ON DANGER, 1942, A
COME ON DANGER!, 1932, A
COME ON GEORGE, 1939, A
COME ON IN, 1918
COME ON OVER, 1922, AA
COME ON RANGERS, 1939, A
COME ON TARZAN, 1933, A
COME ON, COWBOY!, 1948
COME ON, COWBOYS, 1937, A
COME ON, LEATHERNECKS, 1938
COME ON, MARINES, 1934, A
COME ON, THE, 1956, A
COME ONE, COME ALL, 1970
COME OUT FIGHTING, 1945, A
COME OUT OF KITCHEN, 1919
COME OUT OF THE PANTRY, 1935, AA
COME SEPTEMBER, 1961, A
COME SPY WITH ME, 1967, A
COME THROUGH, 1917
COME TO MY HOUSE, 1927
COME TO THE STABLE, 1949, AA
COME-BACK, THE, 1916
COMEBACK TRAIL, THE, 1982, O
COMEBACK, THE, 1982, C
COMEDIANS, THE, 1977, C
COMEDY MAN, THE, 1964, A
COMEDY OF HORRORS, THE, 1964, A
COMES A HORSEMAN, 1978, A-C
COMES MIDNIGHT, 1940
COMET OVER BROADWAY, 1938
COME TOGETHER, 1971
COMFORT AND JOY, 1984, A-C
COMIC, THE, 1969, A
COMIG OUT PARTY, 1934, A
COMIN' AT YA!, 1981, O
COMIN' ROUND THE MOUNTAIN, 1936
COMIN' ROUND THE MOUNTAIN, 1940, AA
COMIN' ROUND THE MOUNTAIN, 1951, AAA
COMIN' THRO' THE RYE, 1916
COMIN' THRO' THE RYE, 1923
COMIN' THRU' THE RYE, 1947, A
COMING AN' GOING, 1926, A
COMING APART, 1969
COMING ATTRACTIONS
COMING HOME, 1978, C-O
COMING OF AGE, 1938, A
COMING OF AMOS, THE, 1925, A
COMING OF THE LAW, THE, 1919
COMING POWER, THE, 1914
COMING THROUGH, 1925
COMING, THE, 1983
COMING-OUT PARTY, A-C
COMMANCHE TERRITORY, 1950, A
COMMANCHEROS, THE, 1961, A
COMMAND DECISION, 1948, A
COMMAND PERFORMANCE, 1931, A
COMMAND PERFORMANCE, 1937, A
COMMAND, THE, 1954, A
COMMANDING OFFICER, THE, 1915, A
COMMANDMENTS, THE, 1956, AA
COMMANDO, 1962, C
COMMANDO CODY, 1953
COMMANDOS STRIKE AT DAWN, THE, 1942
COMMISSIONAIRE, 1933, A
COMMITMENT, THE, 1976, C
COMMITTEE, THE, 1968, C
COMMON CAUSE, THE, 1918
COMMON CLAY, 1919
COMMON CLAY, 1930, A
COMMON GROUND, 1916

COMMON LAW WIFE, 1963, O
COMMON LAW, THE, 1916, A
COMMON LAW, THE, 1923, A
COMMON LAW, THE, 1931
COMMON LEVEL, A, 1920
COMMON PROPERTY, 1919
COMMON SENSE, 1920
COMMON SENSE BRACKETT, 1916
COMMON SIN, THE, 1920
COMMON TOUCH, THE, 1941, A
COMMUNION
COMMUTER HUSBANDS, 1974
COMMUTORS, THE, 1915
COMPANEROS, 1970, C
COMPANION, THE, 1976
COMPANIONATE MARRIAGE, THE, 1928
COMPANIONS IN CRIME, 1954
COMPANY OF KILLERS, 1970, A
COMPANY SHE KEEPS, THE, 1950, C
COMPANYY OF COWARDS
COMPASSION, 1927
COMPELLED, 1960
COMPETITION, THE, 1980, C
COMPLIMENTS OF MR. FLOW, 1941, A
COMPROMISE, 1925, A
COMPROMISED, 1931, A
COMPROMISED DAPHINE
COMPROMISED!, 1931, A
COMPULSION, 1959, C-O
COMPULSORY HUSBAND, THE, 1930, A
COMPULSORY WIFE, THE, 1937, A
COMPUTER FREE-FOR-ALL, 1969, C
COMPUTER WORE TENNIS SHOES, THE, 1970, AAA
COMRADE JOHN, 1915
COMRADE X, 1940, A
COMRADES, 1928
COMRADESHIP, 1919
CON ARTISTS, THE, 1981, O
CON MEN, THE, 1973, A
CONAN THE BARBARIAN, 1982, C-O
CONAN THE DESTROYER, 1984, C
CONCEALED TRUTH, THE, 1915
CONCEIT, 1921
CONCENTRATIN' KID, THE, 1930, A
CONCENTRATION CAMP, 1939, A
CONCERNING MR. MARTIN, 1937, A
CONCERT, THE, 1921
CONCORDE, THE—AIRPORT '79, A-C
CONCRETE JUNGLE, THE, 1962, C
CONCRETE JUNGLE, THE, 1982, O
CONDEMNED, 1923
CONDEMNED, 1929, C
CONDEMNED MEN, 1940
CONDEMNED OF ALTONA, THE, 1963
CONDEMNED TO DEATH, 1932, A
CONDEMNED TO LIFE
CONDEMNED TO LIVE, 1935, A
CONDEMNED WOMEN, 1938, A
CONDOR, 1984
CONDORMAN, 1981, AAA
CONDUCT UNBECOMING, 1975, A-C
CONDUCTOR 1492, 1924
CONDUCTOR, THE, 1981, A-C
CONE OF SILENCE
CONEY ISLAND, 1928
CONEY ISLAND, 1943, A
CONEY ISLAND PRINCESS, A, 1916
CONFESS DR. CORDA, 1960, C
CONFESSION, 1918
CONFESSION, 1937, A
CONFESSION, 1955
CONFESSION, THE, 1920
CONFESSION, THE, 1964
CONFESSION, THE, 1970, C
CONFESSIONAL, THE, 1977, O
CONFESSIONS, 1925
CONFESSIONS FROM A HOLIDAY CAMP, 1977, A
CONFESSIONS OF A CO-ED, 1931, A
CONFESSIONS OF A NAZI SPY, 1939, C
CONFESSIONS OF A NEWLYWED, 1941, A
CONFESSIONS OF A POLICE CAPTAIN, 1971, A
CONFESSIONS OF A POP PERFORMER, 1975, O
CONFESSIONS OF A QUEEN, 1925
CONFESSIONS OF A ROGUE, 1948
CONFESSIONS OF A WIFE, 1928
CONFESSIONS OF A WINDOW CLEANER, 1974, O
CONFESSIONS OF AMANS, THE, 1977, C-O
CONFESSIONS OF AN OPIUM EATER, 1962, C
CONFESSIONS OF BOSTON BLACKIE, 1941, A
CONFESSIONS OF FELIX KRULL, THE, 1957, C-O
CONFESSIONS OF TOM HARRIS, 1972
CONFESSOR, 1973, A
CONFETTI, 1927
CONFIDENCE, 1922
CONFIDENCE, 1980, C-O
CONFIDENCE GIRL, 1952, A
CONFIDENCE MAN, THE, 1924
CONFIDENTIAL, 1935, A
CONFIDENTIAL AGENT, 1945, C
CONFIDENTIAL CONNIE, 1953, A
CONFIDENTIAL LADY, 1939
CONFIDENTIAL REPORT

CONFIDENTIALLY YOURS, 1983, A-C
CONFIRM OR DENY, 1941, A
CONFLAGRATION
CONFLICT, 1937, A
CONFLICT, 1939, O
CONFLICT, 1945, A
CONFLICT OVER WINGS
CONFLICT, THE, 1916
CONFLICT, THE, 1921, A
CONFORMIST, THE, 1971, C
CONGESTION, 1918
CONGO CROSSING, 1956, A
CONGO MAISIE, 1940, A
CONGO SWING
CONGRESS DANCES, 1932
CONGRESS DANCES, 1957
CONJUGAL BED, THE, 1963, O
CONJURE WOMAN, THE, 1926
CONNECTICUT YANKEE AT KING ARTHUR'S
    COURT, A, 1921, A
*CONNECTICUT YANKEE IN KING ARTHUR'S COURT,
    A*, 1949, A
CONNECTICUT YANKEE, A, 1931, AAA
CONNECTING ROOMS, 1971, A
CONNECTION, THE, 1962, O
CONQUERED CITY, 1966, C
CONQUERED HEARTS, A
CONQUERING HORDE, THE, 1931, A
CONQUERING POWER, THE, 1921, A
CONQUERING THE WOMAN, 1922
CONQUEROR OF CORINTH
CONQUEROR WORM, THE, 1968, O
CONQUEROR, THE, 1916
CONQUEROR, THE, 1917
CONQUEROR, THE, 1956, A-C
CONQUERORS, THE, 1932, A
CONQUEST, 1929, A
CONQUEST, 1937, C
CONQUEST, 1984, O
CONQUEST OF CANAAN, THE, 1921
CONQUEST OF CHEYENNE, 1946, A
CONQUEST OF COCHISE, 1953, A
CONQUEST OF MYCENE, 1965, A-C
CONQUEST OF SPACE, 1955, A
CONQUEST OF THE AIR, 1940, A
CONQUEST OF THE CAUCASUS, 1913
CONQUEST OF THE EARTH, 1980, A
CONQUEST OF THE PLANET OF THE APES, 1972, A
CONRACK, 1974, A
CONRAD IN QUEST OF HIS YOUTH, 1920
CONSCIENCE, 1915
CONSCIENCE, 1917
CONSCIENCE BAY, 1960, C
CONSCIENCE OF JOHN DAVID, THE, 1916
CONSOLATION MARRIAGE, 1931, A
CONSPIRACY, 1939, A
CONSPIRACY IN TEHERAN, 1948, A
CONSPIRACY OF HEARTS, 1960, AAA
CONSPIRACY Zero, 1930, A
CONSPIRACY, THE, 1914, A
CONSPIRATOR, 1949, A-C
CONSPIRATORS, THE
CONSPIRATORS, THE, 1944, A
CONSTANCE, 1984, O
CONSTANT FACTOR, THE, 1980, C-O
CONSTANT NYMPH, THE, 1928
CONSTANT WOMAN, THE, 1933
CONSTANTINE AND THE CROSS, 1962, C-O
CONTACT MAN, THE
CONTEMPT, 1963, C-O
CONTENDER, THE, 1944, A
CONTEST GIRL
CONTINENTAL DIVIDE, 1981, A-C
CONTINENTAL EXPRESS, 1939, A
CONTINENTAL GIRL, A, 1915
CONTINENTAL TWIST
CONTRABAND
CONTRABAND, 1925
CONTRABAND LOVE, 1931, A
CONTRABAND SPAIN, 1955, A
CONTRACT, THE, 1982
CONVENTION CITY, 1933
CONVENTION GIRL, 1935, A
CONVENTION GIRLS, 1978
CONVERSATION PIECE, 1976, C
CONVERSATION, THE, 1974, A-C
CONVICT 99, 1919
CONVICT 99, 1938, A
CONVICT 993, 1918
CONVICT KING, THE, 1915
CONVICT STAGE, 1965, A
CONVICT'S CODE, 1930, A
CONVICT'S CODE, 1939, A
CONVICTED, 1931, A
CONVICTED, 1938, A
CONVICTED, 1950, A
CONVICTED WOMAN, 1940, A
CONVICTS AT LARGE, 1938, A
CONVICTS FOUR, 1962, A
CONVOY, 1927, A
CONVOY, 1940, A
CONVOY, 1978, C

CONVOY BUDDIES, 1977
COOGAN'S BLUFF, 1968, C-O
COOK OF CANYON CAMP, THE, 1917
COOL AND THE CRAZY, THE, 1958, C-O
COOL BREEZE, 1972, C
COOL HAND LUKE, 1967, C
COOL IT, CAROL!, 1970, O
COOL MIKADO, THE, 1963, A
COOL ONES THE, 1967, A
COOL SOUND FROM HELL, A, 1959
COOL WORLD, THE, 1963, C-O
COOLEY HIGH, 1975
COONSKIN, 1975, C
COP HATER, 1958, C
COP KILLERS, 1984
COP, A, 1973, O
COP, THE, 1928
COP-OUT, 1967, C-O
COPACABANA, 1947, A
COPPER CANYON, 1950, A
COPPER SKY, 1957, A
COPPER, THE, 1930, A
COPPERHEAD, THE, 1920
COPS AND ROBBERS, 1973, A
COPTER KIDS, THE, 1976
COQUETTE, 1929, C
COQUETTE, THE, 1915
CORA, 1915
CORAL, 1915
CORDELIA, 1980, C-O
CORDELIA THE MAGNIFICENT, 1923
CORINTHIAN JACK, 1921
CORKY, 1972
CORKY OF GASOLINE ALLEY, 1951, AA
CORN IS GREEN, THE, 1945, A
CORNBREAD, EARL AND ME, 1975, C
CORNER GROCER, THE, 1917
CORNER IN COLLEENS, A, 1916, A
CORNER IN COTTON, A, 1916
CORNER MAN, THE, 1921
CORNER, THE, 1916
CORNERED, 1924
CORNERED, 1932, A
CORNERED, 1945, C
CORONADO, 1935
CORONER CREEK, 1948
CORPORAL KATE, 1926, A
CORPSE CAME C.O.D., THE, 1947, A
CORPSE GRINDERS, THE, 1972, O
CORPSE OF BEVERLY HILLS, THE, 1965, O
CORPSE VANISHES, THE, 1942, C
CORPUS CHRISTI BANDITS, 1945, A
CORREGIDOR, 1943, C
CORRIDOR OF MIRRORS, 1948, A
CORRIDORS OF BLOOD, 1962, C-O
CORRUPT, 1984, O
CORRUPT ONES, THE, 1967, C
CORRUPTION, 1917
CORRUPTION, 1933, A
CORRUPTION, 1968, O
CORRUPTION OF CHRIS MILLER, THE, 1979, O
CORRUPTION OF THE DAMNED, 1965
CORSAIR, 1931, C
CORSAIR, THE, 1914
CORSICAN BROTHERS, THE, 1920
CORSICAN BROTHERS, THE, 1941, A
CORVETTE K-225, 1943
CORVETTE SUMMER, 1978, C-O
CORVINI INHERITANCE, 1984
COSH BOY
COSMIC MAN, THE, 1959, A
COSMIC MONSTERS, 1958, A
COSMO JONES, CRIME SMASHER, 1943
COSSACK WHIP, THE, 1916
COSSACKS IN EXILE, 1939, A
COSSACKS OF THE DON, 1932, A
COSSACKS, THE, 1928
COSSACKS, THE, 1960
COST OF BEAUTY, THE, 1924
COST OF HATRED, THE, 1917
COST, THE, 1920, A
COSTELLO CASE, THE, 1930, A
COTTAGE ON DARTMOOR
COTTAGE TO LET
COTTER, 1972
COTTON AND CATTLE, 1921
COTTON CLUB, THE, 1984, O
COTTON COMES TO HARLEM, 1970, O
COTTON KING, THE, 1915, A
COTTON QUEEN, 1937, A
COTTONPICKIN' CHICKENPICKERS, 1967, C
COUCH, THE, 1962, C-O
COUNSEL FOR CRIME, 1937
COUNSEL FOR ROMANCE, 1938
COUNSEL FOR THE DEFENSE, 1925
COUNSEL'S OPINION, 1933, A
COUNSELLOR-AT-LAW, 1933, A
COUNT DRACULA, 1971, C-O
COUNT DRACULA AND HIS VAMPIRE BRIDE,
   1978, C-O
COUNT FIVE AND DIE, 1958, A
COUNT OF BRAGELONNE, THE

COUNT OF LUXEMBOURG, THE, 1926
COUNT OF MONTE CRISTO, 1976, A
COUNT OF MONTE CRISTO, THE, 1913
COUNT OF MONTE CRISTO, THE, 1934, AAA
COUNT OF MONTE-CRISTO, 1955, A
COUNT OF TEN, THE, 1928
COUNT OF THE MONK'S BRIDGE, THE, 1934
COUNT OF TWELVE, 1955
COUNT THE HOURS, 1953
COUNT THREE AND PRAY, 1955, A
COUNT YORGA, VAMPIRE, 1970, O
COUNT YOUR BLESSINGS, 1959, A-C
COUNT YOUR BULLETS, 1972, O
COUNTDOWN, 1968, A
COUNTDOWN AT KUSINI, 1976, C
COUNTDOWN TO DANGER, 1967, AA
COUNTER BLAST, 1948
COUNTER TENORS, THE
COUNTER-ATTACK, 1945, A
COUNTER-ESPIONAGE, 1942, A
COUNTERFEIT, 1919, A
COUNTERFEIT, 1936, A
COUNTERFEIT COMMANDOS, 1981, O
COUNTERFEIT CONSTBLE, THE, 1966, A-C
COUNTERFEIT KILLER, THE, 1968, A
COUNTERFEIT LADY, 1937, A
COUNTERFEIT LOVE, 1923
COUNTERFEIT PLAN, THE, 1957, A
COUNTERFEIT TRAITOR, THE, 1962, A-C
COUNTERFEITERS OF PARIS, THE, 1962, C
COUNTERFEITERS, THE, 1948, A
COUNTERFEITERS, THE, 1953, A
COUNTERPLOT, 1959, A
COUNTERPOINT, 1967, A-C
COUNTERSPY MEETS SCOTLAND YARD, 1950, A
COUNTESS CHARMING, THE, 1917
COUNTESS DRACULA, 1972, O
COUNTESS FROM HONG KONG, A, 1967, C
COUNTESS OF MONTE CRISTO, THE, 1934, A
COUNTESS OF MONTE CRISTO, THE, 1948, A
COUNTRY, 1984, C
COUNTRY BEYOND, THE, 1926
COUNTRY BEYOND, THE, 1936, A
COUNTRY BLUE, 1975
COUNTRY BOY, 1966, A
COUNTRY BOY, THE, 1915
COUNTRY BRIDE, 1938, A
COUNTRY COUSIN, THE, 1919
COUNTRY CUZZINS, 1972
COUNTRY DANCE
COUNTRY DOCTOR, THE, 1927
COUNTRY DOCTOR, THE, 1936, A
COUNTRY DOCTOR, THE, 1963, A
COUNTRY FAIR, 1941, A
COUNTRY FLAPPER, THE, 1922
COUNTRY GENTLEMEN, 1937, A
COUNTRY GIRL, THE, 1954, A-C
COUNTRY KID, THE, 1923, AA
COUNTRY MAN, 1982, C
COUNTRY MOUSE, THE, 1914, A
COUNTRY MUSIC, 1972
COUNTRY MUSIC HOLIDAY, 1958, A
COUNTRY THAT GOD FORGOT, THE, 1916
COUNTRY TOWN, 1971
COUNTY CHAIRMAN, THE, 1914, A
COUNTY CHAIRMAN, THE, 1935, A
COUNTY FAIR, 1933, A
COUNTY FAIR, 1937
COUNTY FAIR, 1950
COUNTY FAIR, THE, 1920
COUNTY FAIR, THE, 1932, A
COUP DE FOUDRE
COUP DE GRACE, 1978, C
COUP DE TETE
COUP DE TORCHON, 1981, O
COUPLE OF DOWN AND OUTS, A, 1923
COUPLE ON THE MOVE, A, 1928
COURAGE
COURAGE, 1921, A
COURAGE, 1924
COURAGE, 1930, A
COURAGE AND THE MAN, 1915
COURAGE FOR TWO, 1919
COURAGE OF BLACK BEAUTY, 1957, AA
COURAGE OF LASSIE, 1946, AAA
COURAGE OF MARGE O'DOONE, THE, 1920
COURAGE OF SILENCE, THE, 1917
COURAGE OF THE COMMONPLACE, 1917
COURAGE OF THE NORTH, 1935
COURAGE OF THE WEST, 1937, A
COURAGE OF WOLFHEART, 1925
COURAGEOUS AVENGER, THE, 1935, A
COURAGEOUS COWARD, THE, 1919
COURAGEOUS COWARD, THE, 1924
COURAGEOUS DR. CHRISTIAN, THE, 1940, A
COURAGEOUS FOOL, 1925
COURAGEOUS MR. PENN, THE, 1941, A
COURIER OF LYONS, 1938, A
COURRIER SUD, 1937, A
COURT CONCERT, THE, 1936
COURT JESTER, THE, 1956, AAA
COURT MARTIAL, 1954, A

COURT MARTIAL, 1962, A-C
COURT MARTIAL OF MAJOR KELLER, THE,
   1961, A-C
COURT-MARTIAL, 1928
COURT-MARTIAL OF BILLY MITCHELL, THE,
   1955, A
COURT-MARTIALED, 1915
COURTESAN, THE, 1916
COURTIN' TROUBLE, 1948, A
COURTIN' WILDCATS, 1929, A
COURTNEY AFFAIR, THE, 1947, A
COURTSHIP OF ANDY HARDY, THE, 1942, A
COURTSHIP OF EDDY'S FATHER, THE, 1963, AA
COURTSHIP OF MILES STANDISH, THE, 1923, A
COUSIN KATE, 1921
COUSIN PONS, 1924
COUSIN, COUSINE, 1976
COUSINE DE FRANCE, 1927
COUSINS IN LOVE, 1982, O
COUSINS, THE, 1959, C-O
COVE OF MISSING MEN, 1918
COVENANT WITH DEATH, A, 1966
COVER GIRL, 1944, AA
COVER GIRL KILLER, 1960, C-O
COVER GIRL MODELS, 1975
COVER ME BABE, 1970, O
COVER-UP, 1949, A
COVERED TRAIL, THE, 1924, A
COVERED TRAILER, THE, 1939, AA
COVERED WAGON DAYS, 1940, A
COVERED WAGON RAID, 1950, A
COVERED WAGON TRAILS, 1930, A
COVERED WAGON TRAILS, 1930
COVERED WAGON TRAILS, 1940, A
COVERED WAGON, THE, 1923, A
COVERGIRL, 1984, O
COVERT ACTION, 1980, O
COW AND I, THE, 1961, A
COW COUNTRY, 1953, A
COW TOWN, 1950, A
COWARD, THE, 1914
COWARD, THE, 1915
COWARD, THE, 1927, A
COWARDICE COURT, 1919
COWARDS, 1970, C-O
COWBOY, 1958, A
COWBOY ACE, A, 1921
COWBOY AND THE BANDIT, THE, 1935, A
COWBOY AND THE BLONDE, THE, 1941, A
COWBOY AND THE COUNTESS, THE, 1926
COWBOY AND THE FLAPPER, THE, 1924
COWBOY AND THE INDIANS, THE, 1949
COWBOY AND THE KID, THE, 1936, A
COWBOY AND THE LADY, THE, 1915
COWBOY AND THE LADY, THE, 1922
COWBOY AND THE LADY, THE, 1938, A
COWBOY AND THE OUTLAW, THE, 1929
COWBOY AND THE PRIZEFIGHTER, 1950, A
COWBOY AND THE SENORITA, 1944, A
COWBOY BLUES, 1946, A
COWBOY CANTEEN, 1944, A
COWBOY CAVALIER, 1929
COWBOY CAVALIER, 1948, A
COWBOY CAVALIER, THE, 1928
COWBOY COMMANDOS, 1943, A
COWBOY COP, THE, 1926
COWBOY COUNSELOR, 1933
COWBOY COURAGE, 1925
COWBOY FROM BROOKLYN, 1938, A
COWBOY FROM LONESOME RIVER, 1944, A
COWBOY FROM SUNDOWN, 1940
COWBOY GRIT, 1925
COWBOY HOLIDAY, 1934, A
COWBOY IN AFRICA
COWBOY IN MANHATTTAN, 1943, A
COWBOY IN THE CLOUDS, 1943, A
COWBOY KID, THE, 1928
COWBOY KING, THE, 1922
COWBOY MILLIONAIRE, 1935, A
COWBOY MUSKETEER, THE, 1925
COWBOY PRINCE, THE, 1924
COWBOY PRINCE, THE, 1930
COWBOY QUARTERBACK, 1939, A
COWBOY SERENADE, 1942, A
COWBOY STAR, THE, 1936, A
COWBOYS FROM TEXAS, 1939, A
COWBOYS, THE, 1972, A-C
COYOTE FANGS, 1924
COYOTE TRAILS, 1935, A
CPTAINN HATES THE SEA, THE, 1934, A
CRAB, THE, 1917, A
CRACK IN THE MIRROR, 1960
CRACK IN THE WORLD, 1965
CRACK O'DAWN, 1925
CRACK-UP, 1946, A
CRACK-UP, THE, 1937, A
CRACKED NUTS, 1931, AA
CRACKED NUTS, 1941, A
CRACKERJACK
CRACKERJACK, THE, 1925
CRACKERS, 1984, A-C
CRACKING UP

CRACKING UP, 1977, O
CRACKLE OF DEATH, 1974
CRACKSMAN, THE, 1963, A
CRADLE BUSTER, THE, 1922, A
CRADLE OF COURAGE, THE, 1920
CRADLE OF THE WASHINGTONS, THE, 1922
CRADLE SNATCHERS, THE, 1927
CRADLE SONG, 1933, A
CRADLE, THE, 1922, A
CRAIG'S WIFE, 1928, A
CRAIG'S WIFE, 1936, A-C
CRAINQUEBILLE, 1922
CRANES ARE FLYING, THE, 1960, A
CRASH, 1977, C-O
CRASH, THE, 1932, A
CRASH DIVE, 1943
CRASH DONOVAN, 1936, A
CRASH DRIVE, 1959, A-C
CRASH LANDING, 1958, A
CRASH OF SILENCE, 1952, A
CRASH, THE, 1928
CRASHIN' THROUGH, 1924
CRASHIN' THRU, 1923, A
CRASHIN' THRU DANGER, 1938, A
CRASHING BROADWAY, 1933, A
CRASHING COURAGE, 1923
CRASHING HOLLYWOOD, 1937, A
CRASHING LAS VEGAS, 1956, A
CRASHING THROUGH, 1928
CRASHING THRU, 1939, A
CRASHING THRU, 1949, A
CRASHOUT, 1955, C
CRATER LAKE MONSTER, THE, 1977, A
CRAVING, THE, 1916
CRAVING, THE, 1918, A
CRAWLING ARM, THE, 1973
CRAWLING EYE, THE, 1958, C
CRAWLING HAND, THE, 1963, A
CRAWLING MONSTER, THE
CRAWLING TERROR, THE, 1958
CRAZE, 1974, C
CRAZIES, THE, 1973, O
CRAZY DESIRE, 1964, C
CRAZY FOR LOVE, 1960, C-O
CRAZY HOUSE, 1943
CRAZY HOUSE, 1975
CRAZY JACK AND THE BOY
CRAZY JOE, 1974, O
CRAZY KNIGHTS, 1944, A
CRAZY MAMA, 1975
CRAZY OVER HORSES, 1951, A
CRAZY PAGE, A, 1926
CRAZY PARADISE, 1965, O
CRAZY PEOPLE, 1934, A
CRAZY QUILT, THE, 1966, A
CRAZY RAY, THE
CRAZY THAT WAY, 1930, A
CRAZY TO MARRY, 1921, A
CRAZY WORLD OF JULIUS VROODER, THE,
  1974, C-O
CRAZYLEGS, ALL AMERICAN, 1953
CREAKING STAIRS, 1919
CREAM OF THE EARTH
CREAM OF THE EARTH
CREATION, 1922, A
CREATION OF THE HUMANOIDS, 1962, C
CREATURE CALLED MAN, THE, 1970, C
CREATURE FROM BLACK LAKE, THE, 1976, C
CREATURE FROM THE BLACK LAGOON, 1954, A
CREATURE FROM THE HAUNTED SEA, 1961, C
CREATURE OF DESTRUCTION, 1967
CREATURE OF THE WALKING DEAD, 1960, C
CREATURE WALKS AMONG US, THE, 1956, A
CREATURE WASN'T NICE, THE, 1981, A
CREATURE WITH THE ATOM BRAIN, 1955, O
CREATURE WITH THE BLUE HAND, 1971, O
CREATURE'S REVENGE, THE
CREATURES
CREATURES OF DARKNESS, 1969
CREATURES OF THE TORIC PLANET
CREATURES THE WORLD FORGOT, 1971, O
CREEPER, THE, 1948, O
CREEPER, THE, 1980, O
CREEPING FLESH, 1973, O
CREEPING TERROR, THE, 1964, C
CREEPS
CREEPSHOW, 1982, O
CREMATOR, THE, 1973, O
CREMATORS, THE, 1972, C
CREPUSCULE D'EPOUVANTE, 1921
CRESCENDO, 1972, C
CREST OF THE WAVE, 1954, A
CRICKET OF THE HEARTH, THE, 1968
CRICKET ON THE HEARTH, THE, 1923
CRICKET, THE, 1917
CRIES AND WHISPERS, 1972, C
CRIES IN THE NIGHT, 1964
CRIES IN THE NIGHT, 1982
CRIME AFLOAT, 1937, A
CRIME AGAINST JOE, 1956
CRIME AND PASSION, 1976, C-O
CRIME AND PUNISHMENT, 1913

CRIME AND PUNISHMENT, 1917, A
CRIME AND PUNISHMENT, 1929
CRIME AND PUNISHMENT, 1935, A
CRIME AND PUNISHMENT, 1935, C
CRIME AND PUNISHMENT, 1948, A
CRIME AND PUNISHMENT, 1975, A
CRIME AND PUNISHMENT, U.S.A., 1959, A
CRIME AND THE PENALTY, 1916
CRIME AT BLOSSOMS, THE, 1933, A
CRIME AT PORTA ROMANA, 1980, O
CRIME AT THE DARK HOUSE, 1940, A-C
CRIME BOSS, 1976, C
CRIME BY NIGHT, 1944, A
CRIME DOCTOR, 1943, A
CRIME DOCTOR'S COURAGE, THE, 1945, A
CRIME DOCTOR'S DIARY, THE, 1949, A
CRIME DOCTOR'S GAMBLE, 1947, A
CRIME DOCTOR'S MAN HUNT, 1946, A
CRIME DOCTOR'S STRANGEST CASE, 1943, A
CRIME DOCTOR'S WARNING, 1945
CRIME DOCTOR, THE, 1934, A
CRIME DOES NOT PAY, 1962, C-O
CRIME IN THE STREETS, 1956, C-O
CRIME NOBOBY SAW, THE, 1937, A
CRIME OF DR. CRESPI, THE, 1936, C
CRIME OF DR. FORBES, 1936, A
CRIME OF DR. HALLET, 1938, A
CRIME OF HELEN STANLEY, 1934
CRIME OF MONSIEUR LANGE, THE, 1936, C-O
CRIME OF PASSION, 1957
CRIME OF PETER FRAME, THE, 1938, A
CRIME OF STEPHEN HAWKE, THE, 1936, A-C
CRIME OF THE CENTURY, 1946
CRIME OF THE CENTURY, THE, 1933, A
CRIME OF THE FUTURE, 1969, O
CRIME OF THE HOUR, 1918
CRIME ON THE HILL, 1933, A
CRIME OVER LONDON, 1936, A
CRIME PATROL, THE, 1936, A
CRIME RING, 1938, A
CRIME SCHOOL, 1938, AA
CRIME TAKES A HOLIDAY, 1938, A
CRIME UNLIMITED, 1935, A
CRIME WAVE, 1954
CRIME WITHOUT PASSION, 1934, A
CRIME, INC., 1945, A
CRIMES OF PASSION, 1984, O
CRIMINAL AT LARGE, 1932, A
CRIMINAL CODE, 1931, A
CRIMINAL CONVERSATION, 1980, C
CRIMINAL COURT, 1946, A
CRIMINAL INVESTIGATOR, 1942
CRIMINAL LAWYER, 1937
CRIMINAL LAWYER, 1951, A
CRIMINAL LIFE OF ARCHIBALDO DE LA CRUZ,
  THE, 1962, O
CRIMINAL, THE
CRIMINAL, THE, 1916
CRIMINALS OF THE AIR, 1937, A
CRIMINALS WITHIN, 1941, A
CRIMSON ALTAR, THE
CRIMSON BLADE, THE, 1964, A
CRIMSON CANARY, 1945, A
CRIMSON CANDLE, THE, 1934, A-C
CRIMSON CANYON, THE, 1928
CRIMSON CHALLENGE, THE, 1922, A
CRIMSON CIRCLE, THE, 1922, A
CRIMSON CIRCLE, THE, 1930, A
CRIMSON CIRCLE, THE, 1936, A
CRIMSON CITY, THE, 1928, A
CRIMSON CLUE, 1922
CRIMSON CROSS, THE, 1921
CRIMSON CULT, THE, 1970, O
CRIMSON DOVE, THE, 1917, A
CRIMSON EXECUTIONER, THE
CRIMSON GARDENIA, THE, 1919
CRIMSON GHOST, THE
CRIMSON GOLD, 1923
CRIMSON KEY, THE, 1947, A
CRIMSON KIMONO, THE, 1959
CRIMSON PIRATE, THE, 1952
CRIMSON ROMANCE, 1934, C
CRIMSON RUNNER, THE, 1925, A
CRIMSON SHOALS, 1919
CRIMSON SKULL, THE, 1921
CRIMSON TRAIL, THE, 1935
CRIMSON WING, THE, 1915
CRINOLINE AND ROMANCE, 1923, A
CRIPPLE CREEK, 1952, A
CRIPPLED HAND, THE, 1916
CRISIS, 1950, A
CRISIS, THE, 1915
CRISS CROSS, 1949, C
CRITIC'S CHOICE, 1963, A
CRITICAL AGE, THE, 1923, A
CROCODILE, 1979, O
CROISIERES SIDERALES, 1941, A
CROMWELL, 1970, A
CROOK OF DREAMS, 1919
CROOK'S ROMANCE, A, 1921
CROOK, THE, 1971, A
CROOKED ALLEY, 1923

CROOKED ALLEY, 1923, A
CROOKED BILLET, THE, 1930, A
CROOKED CIRCLE, 1932, A
CROOKED CIRCLE, THE, 1958, A-C
CROOKED LADY, THE, 1932, A
CROOKED RIVER, 1950, A
CROOKED ROAD, 1932
CROOKED ROAD, THE, 1940, A
CROOKED ROAD, THE, 5,BC
CROOKED ROMANCE, A, 1917
CROOKED SKY, THE, 1957, A
CROOKED STRAIGHT, 1919
CROOKED STREETS, 1920, A
CROOKED TRAIL, THE, 1936, A
CROOKED WAY, THE, 1949, A-C
CROOKED WEB, THE, 1955, A
CROOKS AND CORONETS
CROOKS ANONYMOUS, 1963, A-C
CROOKS CAN'T WIN, 1928
CROOKS IN CLOISTERS, 1964
CROOKS TOUR, 1940, A
CROOKY, 1915
CROONER, 1932
CROQUETTE, 1927
CROSBY CASE, THE, 1934, A
CROSS AND THE SWITCHBLADE, THE, 1970, A
CROSS BEARER, THE, 1918
CROSS BREED, 1927, A
CROSS CHANNEL, 1955, A-C
CROSS COUNTRY, 1983, O
CROSS COUNTRY CRUISE, 1934, A-C
CROSS COUNTRY ROMANCE, 1940, A
CROSS CREEK, 1983, C
CROSS CURRENTS, 1916
CROSS CURRENTS, 1935, A
CROSS MY HEART, 1937, A
CROSS MY HEART, 1946, A
CROSS OF IRON, 1977, O
CROSS OF LORRAINE, THE, 1943, C-O
CROSS OF THE LIVING, 1963, C-O
CROSS, 1922
CROSS ROADS, 1930
CROSS STREETS, 1934, A
CROSS-EXAMINATION, 1932, A
CROSS-UP, 1958, A
CROSSED SIGNALS, 1926
CROSSED SWORDS, 1954, A
CROSSED SWORDS, 1978, A
CROSSED TRAILS, 1924
CROSSED TRAILS, 1948, A
CROSSED WIRES, 1923
CROSSFIRE, 1933, A
CROSSFIRE, 1947, C
CROSSING TRAILS, 1921, A
CROSSPLOT, 1969, C
CROSSROADS
CROSSROADS, 1938, A
CROSSROADS, 1942, A
CROSSROADS OF NEW YORK, THE, 1922
CROSSROADS OF PASSION, 1951, A
CROSSROADS TO CRIME, 1960, C
CROSSTALK, 1982, O
CROSSTRAP, 1962, C
CROSSWAYS, 1928
CROSSWINDS, 1951, A
CROUCHING BEAST, THE, 1936, A
CROW HOLLOW, 1952, A-C
CROW'S NEST, THE, 1922
CROWD INSIDE, THE, 1971, C
CROWD ROARS, THE, 1932, A-C
CROWD ROARS, THE, 1938, A
CROWD, THE, 1928, A
CROWDED DAY, THE, 1954, A
CROWDED PARADISE, 1956, C
CROWDED SKY, THE, 1960, A
CROWED HOUHE, 1925
CROWN JEWELS, 1918
CROWN OF LIES, THE, 1926
CROWN OF THORNS, 1934
CROWN PRINCE'S DOUBLE, THE, 1916
CROWN VS STEVENS, 1936, A
CROWNING EXPERIENCE, THE, 1960, A
CROWNING GIFT, THE, 1967, A
CROWNING TOUCH, THE, 1959, A
CROXLEY MASTER, THE, 1921
CRUCIAL TEST, THE, 1916
CRUCIBLE OF HORROR, 1971, C
CRUCIBLE OF LIFE, THE, 1918
CRUCIBLE OF TERROR, 1971, O
CRUCIBLE, THE, 1914
CRUCIFIX OF DESTINY, THE, 1920
CRUCIFIX, THE, 1934, A
CRUEL SEA, THE, 1953, A
CRUEL SWAMP
CRUEL TOWER, THE, 1956, A
CRUEL TRUTH, THE, 1927
CRUISE MISSILE, 1978
CRUISE OF THE HELLION, THE, 1927
CRUISE OF THE JASPER B, 1926
CRUISE OF THE MAKE-BELIEVES, THE, 1918
CRUISER EMDEN, 1932, A
CRUISIN' 57, 1975

CRUISIN' DOWN THE RIVER, 1953, A
CRUISING, 1980, O
CRUISKEEN LAWN, 1922
CRUNCH, 1975
CRUSADE AGAINST RACKETS, 1937, A
CRUSADE OF THE INNOCENT, 1922
CRUSADER, THE, 1922
CRUSADER, THE, 1932, A
CRUSADERS OF THE WEST, 1930
CRUSADES, THE, 1935, A
CRUZ BROTHERS AND MISS MALLOY, THE, 1979
CRY BABY KILLER, THE, 1958, C
CRY BLOOD, APACHE, 1970, O
CRY DANGER, 1951, A
CRY DOUBLE CROSS
CRY DR. CHICAGO, 1971, O
CRY FOR HAPPY, 1961, C
CRY FOR JUSTICE, THE, 1919
CRY FOR ME, BILLY
CRY FREEDOM, 1961, A
CRY FROM THE STREET, A, 1959, AAA
CRY HAVOC, 1943, A
CRY IN THE NIGHT, A, 1956, C
CRY MURDER, 1936, A
CRY OF BATTLE, 1963, A
CRY OF THE BANSHEE, 1970, O
CRY OF THE BEWITCHED
CRY OF THE CITY, 1948, C
CRY OF THE HUNTED, 1953, A
CRY OF THE PENGUINS, 1972, A
CRY OF THE WEAK, THE, 1919
CRY OF THE WEREWOLF, 1944, C-O
CRY TERROR, 1958, A-C
CRY TO THE WIND, 1979
CRY TOUGH, 1959, A
CRY UNCLE, 1973
CRY VENGEANCE, 1954, A
CRY WOLF, 1947, A
CRY WOLF, 1968, AA
CRY, THE BELOVED COUNTRY, 1952, A
CRYPT OF DARK SECRETS, 1976
CRYPT OF THE LIVING DEAD, 1973, C
CRYSTAL BALL, THE, 1943
CRYSTAL CUP, THE, 1927, A
CRYSTAL GAZER, THE, 1917
CUB REPORTER, THE, A
CUB, THE, 1915, A
CUBA, 1979, C
CUBA CROSSING, 1980, O
CUBAN FIREBALL, 1951, A
CUBAN LOVE SONG,THE, 1931, A
CUBAN PETE, 1946, A
CUBAN REBEL GIRLS, 1960
CUCKOO CLOCK, THE, 1938, A
CUCKOO IN THE NEST, THE, 1933
CUCKOO PATROL, 1965
CUCKOOS, THE, 1930, AA
CUJO, 1983
CUL-DE-SAC, 1966, C-O
CULPEPPER CATTLE COMPANY, THE, 1972, C
CULT OF THE COBRA, 1955, A-C
CULT OF THE DAMNED
CUMBERLAND ROMANCE, A, 1920, A
CUP FEVER, 1965, AA
CUP OF FURY, THE, 1920
CUP OF KINDNESS, A, 1934, A
CUP OF LIFE, THE, 1915
CUP OF LIFE, THE, 1921
CUP-TIE HONEYMOON, 1948, A
CUPID BY PROXY, 1918, A
CUPID FORECLOSES, 1919
CUPID IN CLOVER, 1929
CUPID'S BRAND, 1921
CUPID'S FIREMAN, 1923
CUPID'S KNOCKOUT, 1926
CUPID'S ROUND-UP, 1918
CUPID'S RUSTLER, 1924
CUPID, THE COWPUNCHER, 1920
CUPS OF SAN SEBASTIAN, THE
CURE FOR LOVE, THE, 1950, A
CURFEW BREAKERS, 1957, C
CURIOUS CONDUCT OF JUDGE LEGARDE, THE, 1915
CURIOUS DR. HUMPP, 1967, O
CURIOUS FEMALE, THE, 1969, O
CURLY TOP, 1935, AAA
CURLYTOP, 1924
CURSE OF BIGFOOT, THE, 1972, C
CURSE OF DRACULA, THE
CURSE OF DRINK, THE, 1922, A
CURSE OF EVE, THE, 1917
CURSE OF FRANKENSTEIN, THE, 1957, O
CURSE OF GREED, THE, 1914
CURSE OF IKU, THE, 1918
CURSE OF KILIMANJARO, 1978
CURSE OF THE AZTEC MUMMY, THE, 1965, A-C
CURSE OF THE BLOOD GHOULS, 1969, O
CURSE OF THE CAT PEOPLE, THE, 1944, C-O
CURSE OF THE CRIMSON ALTAR
CURSE OF THE CRYING WOMAN, THE, 1969, C
CURSE OF THE DEMON, 1958, O
CURSE OF THE DEVIL, 1973, O
CURSE OF THE DOLL PEOPLE, THE, 1968, C-o

CURSE OF THE FACELESS MAN, 1958, C
CURSE OF THE FLY, 1965, C
CURSE OF THE GHOULS
CURSE OF THE GOLEM
CURSE OF THE HEADLESS HORSEMAN, 1972
CURSE OF THE LIVING CORPSE, THE, 1964 KID, THE, 1951, AAA
CURSE OF THE MAYAN TEMPLE, 1977
CURSE OF THE MOON CHILD, 1972
CURSE OF THE MUMMY'S TOMB, THE, 1965, C
CURSE OF THE MUSHROOM PEOPLE
CURSE OF THE PINK PANTHER, 1983, A
CURSE OF THE STONE HAND, 1965, C
CURSE OF THE SWAMP CREATURE, 1966, C
CURSE OF THE UNDEAD, 1959, C
CURSE OF THE VAMPIRE
CURSE OF THE VAMPIRES, 1970, O
CURSE OF THE VOODOO, 1965, O
CURSE OF THE WEREWOLF, THE, 1961, O
CURSE OF THE WRAYDONS, THE, 1946, A-C
CURSED MILLIONS, 1917
CURTAIN, 1920
CURTAIN AT EIGHT, 1934, A
CURTAIN CALL, 1940, A
CURTAIN CALL AT CACTUS CREEK, 1950, AA
CURTAIN FALLS, THE
CURTAIN RISES, THE, 1939, A
CURTAIN UP, 1952, A
CURTAINS, 1983, O
CURUCU, BEAST OF THE AMAZON, 1956, C
CUSTARD CUP, THE, 1923
CUSTER MASSACRE, THE
CUSTER OF THE WEST, 1968, C
CUSTER'S LAST FIGHT, 1925
CUSTOMARY TWO WEEKS, THE, 1917
CUSTOMS AGENT, 1950, A
CUTTER AND BONE, 1981, O
CUTTING LOOSE, 1980
CY WHITTAKER'S WARD, 1917
CYBORG 2087, 1966, A
CYCLE OF FATE, THE, 1916
CYCLE SAVAGES, 1969, O
CYCLE, THE, 1979, A-C
CYCLES SOUTH, 1971
CYCLONE BLISS, 1921
CYCLONE BOB, 1926
CYCLONE BUDDY, 1924
CYCLONE CAVALIER, 1925
CYCLONE COWBOY, THE, 1927
CYCLONE FURY, 1951
CYCLONE HIGGINS, D.D., 1918
CYCLONE JONES, 1923
CYCLONE KID, 1931, A
CYCLONE KID, THE, 1942, A
CYCLONE OF THE RANGE, 1927, A
CYCLONE OF THE SADDLE, 1935
CYCLONE ON HORSEBACK, 1941, A
CYCLONE PRAIRIE RANGERS, 1944
CYCLONE RANGER, 1935, A
CYCLONE RIDER, THE, 1924
CYCLONE, THE, 1920, A
CYCLOPS, 1957
CYCLOTRODE X, 1946, A
CYNARA, 1932, A-C
CYNTHIA, 1947, AA
CYNTHIA IN THE WILDERNESS, 1916
CYNTHIA'S SISTER, 1975
CYNTHIA-OF-THE-MINUTE, 1920
CYRANO DE BERGERAC, 1950, AA
CYTHEREA, 1924
CYTHEREA, 1924, A
CZAR OF BRODWAY, THE, 1930, A
CZAR WANTS TO SLEEP, 1934, A
CZECH MATE, 1984

-D-

D'ARTAGNAN, 1916
D-DAY, THE SIXTH OF JUNE, 1956, A
D.C. CAB, 1983, C
D.I., THE, 1957, A
D.O.A., 1950, A
D.W. GRIFFITH'S "THAT ROYLE GIRL"
DAD AND DAVE COME TO TOWN, 1938, A
DAD'S ARMY, 1971, A
DAD'S GIRL, 1919
DADDIES, 1924
DADDY, 1917
DADDY, 1923, A
DADDY LONG LEGS, 1919, A
DADDY LONG LEGS, 1931, AAA
DADDY LONG LEGS, 1955, AAA
DADDY'S DEADLY DARLING, 1984, O
DADDY'S GIRL
DADDY'S GIRL, 1918
DADDY'S GONE A-HUNTING, 1925
DADDY'S GONE A-HUNTING, 1969, C
DADDY'S LOVE, 1922
DADDY-O, 1959, C
DAFFODIL KILLER
DAFFY
DAFFY DUCK'S MOVIE: FANTASTIC ISLAND, 1983
DAGGERS OF BLOOD
DAGORA THE SPACE MONSTER, 1964, A

DAISIES, 1967, C-O
DAISY KENYON, 1947, A-C
DAISY MILLER, 1974, C-O
DAKOTA, 1945, A
DAKOTA INCIDENT, 1956, A
DAKOTA LIL, 1950, A
DALEKS—INVASION EARTH 2155 A.D., 1966, A
DALLAS, 1950, A
DALTON GANG, THE, 1949, A
DALTON GIRLS, THE, 1957, A
DALTON THAT GOT AWAY, 1960, A
DALTON'S WOMEN, THE, 1950, A
DALTONS RIDE AGAIN, THE, 1945, A
DAM BUSTERS, THE, 1955, A
DAMAGED GOODS, 1915, A
DAMAGED GOODS, 1917
DAMAGED GOODS, 1919
DAMAGED GOODS, 1937, C
DAMAGED HEARTS, 1924
DAMAGED LIVES, 1937, C
DAMAGED LOVE, 1931, C
DAME CHANCE, 1926, A
DAMES, 1934, A
DAMES AHOY, 1930, AAA
DAMIEN'S ISLAND, 1976
DAMIEN—OMEN II, 1978, O
DAMN CITIZEN, 1958, A
DAMN THE DEFIANT!, 1962, A
DAMN YANKEES, 1958, A
DAMNATION ALLEY, 1977, C
DAMNED DON'T CRY, THE, 1950, A-C
DAMNED, THE
DAMNED, THE, 1948, C
DAMON AND PYTHIAS, 1914, A
DAMON AND PYTHIAS, 1962, A
DAMSEL IN DISTRESS, A, 1919, A
DAMSEL IN DISTRESS, A, 1937, A
DAN, 1914, A
DAN CANDY'S LAW
DAN MATTHEWS, 1936, A
DAN'S MOTEL, 1982, O
DANCE BAND, 1935, A
DANCE HALL, 1929, A
DANCE HALL, 1941, AA
DANCE HALL, 1950, A
DANCE HALL RACKET, 1956
DANCE LITTLE LADY, 1954, A
DANCE MADNESS, 1926
DANCE MAGIC, 1927
DANCE MALL HOSTESS, 1933, A
DANCE OF DEATH, THE, 1938, A
DANCE OF DEATH, THE, 1971, C
DANCE OF LIFE, THE, 1929, A
DANCE OF THE DWARFS, 1983, C
DANCE OF THE VAMPIRES
DANCE PRETTY LADY, 1932, A
DANCE TEAM, 1932, AA
DANCE WITH ME, HENRY, 1956, A
DANCE, CHARLIE, DANCE, 1937, A
DANCE, FOOLS, DANCE, 1931, A-C
DANCE, GIRL, DANCE, 1933, A
DANCE, GIRL, DANCE, 1940, A
DANCER AND THE KING, THE, 1914
DANCER OF BARCELONA, 1929
DANCER OF PARIS, THE, 1926
DANCER OF THE NILE, THE, 1923
DANCER'S PERIL, THE, 1917, A
DANCERS IN THE DARK, 1932, A
DANCERS, THE, 1925
DANCERS, THE, 1930, A
DANCIN' FOOL, THE, 1920
DANCING CHEAT, THE, 1924
DANCING CO-ED, 1939
DANCING DAYS, 1926
DANCING DYNAMITE, 1931, A
DANCING FEET, 1936, A
DANCING GIRL, THE, 1915
DANCING HEART, THE, 1959, A
DANCING IN MANHATTAN, 1945, A
DANCING IN THE DARK, 1949, A
DANCING LADY, 1933, A
DANCING MAN, 1934, A
DANCING MASTERS, THE, 1943, A
DANCING MOTHERS, 1926, A
DANCING ON A DIME, 1940, A
DANCING PIRATE, 1936, A
DANCING SWEETIES, 1930, A
DANCING WITH CRIME, 1947, A
DANCING YEARS, THE, 1950, AA
DANDY, 1973
DANDY DICK, 1935, A
DANDY IN ASPIC, A, 1968, A
DANDY, THE ALL AMERICAN GIRL, 1976, A
DANGER, 1923
DANGER AHEAD, 1921
DANGER AHEAD, 1923
DANGER AHEAD, 1935, A
DANGER AHEAD, 1940, A
DANGER BY MY SIDE, 1962, A-C
DANGER FLIGHT, 1939, AAA
DANGER GAME, THE, 1918

DANGER GIRL, THE, 1926
DANGER IN THE PACIFIC, 1942, A
DANGER IS A WOMAN, 1952, C-O
DANGER ISLAND
DANGER LIGHTS, 1930, AA
DANGER LINE, THE, 1924
DANGER MAN, THE, 1930
DANGER MARK, THE, 1918, A
DANGER ON THE AIR, 1938, A
DANGER ON WHEELS, 1940, A
DANGER PATH, THE
DANGER PATROL, 1928
DANGER PATROL, 1937, A
DANGER POINT, THE, 1922, A
DANGER QUEST, 1926
DANGER RIDER, 1925
DANGER RIDER, 1925
DANGER RIDER, THE, 1928
DANGER ROUTE, 1968, A
DANGER SIGNAL, 1945, A
DANGER SIGNAL, THE, 1915, A
DANGER SIGNAL, THE, 1925
DANGER SIGNALS, 1917
DANGER STREET, 1928
DANGER STREET, 1947, A
DANGER TOMORROW, 1960, A-C
DANGER TRAIL, 1928
DANGER TRAIL, THE, 1917
DANGER TRAILS, 1935, A
DANGER VALLEY, 1921, A
DANGER VALLEY, 1938
DANGER WITHIN
DANGER WITHIN, 1918
DANGER WOMAN, 1946, A
DANGER ZONE, 1951, C
DANGER ZONE, THE, 1918
DANGER ZONE, THE, 1925
DANGER! WOMEN AT WORK, 1943, A
DANGER, GO SLOW, 1918
DANGER—LOVE AT WORK, 1937, A
DANGER: DIABOLIK, 1968, A
DANGEROUS, 1936, A-C
DANGEROUS ADVENTURE, A, 1922
DANGEROUS ADVENTURE, A, 1937, A
DANGEROUS AFFAIR, A, 1919
DANGEROUS AFFAIR, A, 1931, A
DANGEROUS AFTERNOON, 1961, A-C
DANGEROUS AGE, A, 1960, A
DANGEROUS AGE, THE, 1922, A
DANGEROUS APPOINTMENT, 1934
DANGEROUS ASSIGNMENT, 1950
DANGEROUS BLONDE, THE, 1924
DANGEROUS BLONDES, 1943, A
DANGEROUS BUSINESS, 1920
DANGEROUS BUSINESS, 1946, A
DANGEROUS CARGO, 1939, A
DANGEROUS CARGO, 1954, C
DANGEROUS CHARTER, 1962, A
DANGEROUS CORNER, 1935, A
DANGEROUS COWARD, THE, 1924
DANGEROUS CROSSING, 1953, A
DANGEROUS CURVE AHEAD, 1921
DANGEROUS CURVES, 1929, AA
DANGEROUS DAVIES—THE LAST DETECTIVE,
  1981, A
DANGEROUS DAYS, 1920
DANGEROUS DUB, THE, 1926
DANGEROUS DUDE, THE, 1926
DANGEROUS EXILE, 1958, A
DANGEROUS FEMALE
DANGEROUS FINGERS
DANGEROUS FISTS, 1925
DANGEROUS FLIRT, THE, 1924
DANGEROUS FRIEND
DANGEROUS FRIENDS, 1926
DANGEROUS GAME, A, 1922
DANGEROUS GAME, A, 1941, A
DANGEROUS GROUND, 1934, A
DANGEROUS HOLIDAY, 1937, AA
DANGEROUS HOUR, 1923, A
DANGEROUS HOURS, 1920
DANGEROUS INNOCENCE, 1925
DANGEROUS INTRIGUE, 1936, A
DANGEROUS INTRUDER, 1945, A
DANGEROUS KISS, THE, 1961, A
DANGEROUS LADY, 1941, A
DANGEROUS LIES, 1921
DANGEROUS LITTLE DEMON, THE, 1922
DANGEROUS LOVE AFFAIR
DANGEROUS MAID, THE, 1923
DANGEROUS MEDICINE, 1938, A
DANGEROUS MILLIONS, 1946, A
DANGEROUS MISSION, 1954, A-C
DANGEROUS MOMENT, THE, 1921
DANGEROUS MONEY, 1924
DANGEROUS MONEY, 1946, A
DANGEROUS MOONLIGHT
DANGEROUS NAN McGREW, 1930, A
DANGEROUS NUMBER, 1937, A
DANGEROUS ODDS, 1925
DANGEROUS PARADISE, 1930, A
DANGEROUS PARADISE, THE, 1920

DANGEROUS PARTNERS, 1945, A
DANGEROUS PASSAGE, 1944, A
DANGEROUS PASTIME, 1922
DANGEROUS PATHS, 1921
DANGEROUS PLEASURE, 1925
DANGEROUS PROFESSION, A, 1949, A
DANGEROUS RELATIONS, 1973
DANGEROUS SEAS, 1931, A
DANGEROUS SECRETS, 1938, A
DANGEROUS TALENT, THE, 1920
DANGEROUS TO KNOW, 1938, A
DANGEROUS TO MEN, 1920, A
DANGEROUS TOYS, 1921
DANGEROUS TRAFFIC, 1926
DANGEROUS TRAILS, 1923
DANGEROUS VENTURE, 1947, A
DANGEROUS VOYAGE
DANGEROUS WATERS, 1919
DANGEROUS WATERS, 1936, A
DANGEROUS WHEN WET, 1953, A
DANGEROUS WOMAN, 1929, A
DANGEROUS YEARS, 1947, A
DANGEROUS YOUTH, 1958, A
DANGEROUSLY THEY LIVE, 1942, A
DANGEROUSLY YOURS, 1933, A
DANGEROUSLY YOURS, 1937, A
DANGERS OF THE ENGAGEMENT PERIOD, 1929
DANIEL, 1983, C
DANIEL BOONE, 1936, AAA
DANIEL BOONE THRU THE WILDERNESS, 1926
DANIEL BOONE, TRAIL BLAZER, 1957, AA
DANIEL DERONDA, 1921
DANIELLA BY NIGHT, 1962, C
DANNY, 1979
DANNY BOY, 1934, A
DANNY BOY, 1941, A
DANNY BOY, 1946, AAA
DANS LA RAFALE, 1916
DANS LES GRIFFES DU MANIAQUE
DANSE MACABRE
DANTE'S INFERNO, 1924, A
DANTE'S INFERNO, 1935
DANTON
DANTON, 1931, A
DANTON, 1983, O
DAPHNE AND THE PIRATE, 1916, A
DAPHNE, THE, 1967, A-C
DARBY AND JOAN, 1919
DARBY AND JOAN, 1937, A
DARBY O'GILL AND THE LITTLE PEOPLE,
  1959, AAA
DARBY'S RANGERS, 1958
DAREDEVIL, 1919
DAREDEVIL DRIVERS, 1938, A
DAREDEVIL IN THE CASTLE, 1969, A
DAREDEVIL KATE, 1916
DAREDEVIL'S REWARD, 1928, A
DAREDEVIL, THE, 1918
DAREDEVIL, THE, 1920
DAREDEVIL, THE, 1971
DAREDEVILS OF EARTH, 1936, A
DAREDEVILS OF THE CLOUDS, 1948, A
DARING CABALLERO, THE, 1949, A
DARING CHANCES, 1924, A
DARING DANGER, 1922
DARING DANGER, 1932, A
DARING DAUGHTERS, 1933
DARING DAYS, 1925
DARING DEEDS, 1927
DARING DOBERMANS, THE, 1973, AA
DARING GAME, 1968, A
DARING HEARTS, 1919
DARING LOVE, 1924
DARING OF DIANA, THE, 1916
DARING YEARS, THE, 1923
DARING YOUNG MAN, THE, 1935
DARING YOUNG MAN, THE, 1942, A
DARING YOUTH, 1924, A
DARK ALIBI, 1946, A
DARK ANGEL, THE, 1925, A
DARK ANGEL, THE, 1935, A
DARK ANGEL, THE, 1935, A
DARK AT THE TOP OF THE STAIRS, THE, 1960, C
DARK AUGUST, 1975
DARK AVENGER, THE
DARK CASTLE, THE, 1915
DARK CITY, 1950, A
DARK COMMAND, THE, 1940, A
DARK CORNER, THE, 1946, C
DARK CRYSTAL, THE, 1982, A
DARK DELUSION, 1947, A
DARK DREAMS, 1971
DARK END OF THE STREET, THE, 1981, O
DARK ENDEAVOUR, 1933
DARK ENEMY, 1984, A
DARK EYES, 1938, O
DARK EYES, 1980
DARK EYES OF LONDON
DARK EYES OF LONDON, 1961, A
DARK HAZARD, 1934, A
DARK HORSE, THE, 1932, A
DARK HORSE, THE, 1946, A

DARK HOUR, THE, 1936, A
DARK INTERVAL, 1950, C
DARK INTRUDER, 1965, C
DARK IS THE NIGHT, 1946, C-O
DARK JOURNEY, 1937, A
DARK LANTERN, A, 1920
DARK LIGHT, THE, 1951, C
DARK MAN, THE, 1951, A
DARK MANHATTAN, 1937, C
DARK MIRROR, THE, 1946, C
DARK MIRROR, THE, A
DARK MOUNTAIN, 1944, A
DARK ODYSSEY, 1961, C
DARK OF THE SUN, 1968, A
DARK PASSAGE, 1947, A
DARK PAST, THE, 1948, A
DARK PLACES, 1974, A
DARK PURPOSE, 1964
DARK RED ROSES, 1930, A
DARK RIVER, 1956, O
DARK ROAD, THE, 1917, A
DARK ROAD, THE, 1948
DARK SANDS, 1938, AA
DARK SECRET, 1949, A
DARK SECRETS, 1923
DARK SHADOWS
DARK SIDE OF TOMORROW, THE, 1970, O
DARK SILENCE, THE, 1916
DARK SKIES
DARK STAIRWAY, THE, 1938, A
DARK STAIRWAYS, 1924, A
DARK STAR, 1975, C
DARK STAR, THE, 1919
DARK STREETS, 1929, A
DARK STREETS OF CAIRO, 1940, A
DARK SUNDAY, 1978
DARK SWAN, THE, 1924
DARK TOWER, THE, 1943
DARK VENTURE, 1956, A
DARK VICTORY, 1939, A
DARK WATERS, 1944, A
DARK WORLD, 1935, A
DARK, THE, 1979, O
DARK, THE
DARKENED ROOMS, 1929
DARKENED SKIES, 1930, A
DARKENING TRAIL, THE, 1915
DARKER THAN AMBER, 1970, O
DARKEST AFRICA, 1936, A
DARKEST HOUR, THE, 1920
DARKEST LONDON, 1915, A
DARKEST RUSSIA, 1917
DARKNESS AND DAYLIGHT, 1923
DARKNESS BEFORE DAWN, THE, 1915
DARKTOWN STRUTTERS, 1975, C
DARLING, 1965, O
DARLING LILI, 1970, C
DARLING MINE, 1920, A
DARLING OF NEW YORK, THE, 1923
DARLING OF PARIS, THE, 1917, A
DARLING OF THE RICH, THE, 1923, A
DARLING, HOW COULD YOU!, 1951, A
DARTS ARE TRUMPS, 1938, A
DARWIN ADVENTURE, THE, 1972, A
DARWIN WAS RIGHT, 1924
DAS BOOT, 1982, C-O
DAS CABINETT DES CALIGARI
DAS LETZTE GEHEIMNIS, 1959, C
DASHING THRU, 1925
DATE AT MIDNIGHT, 1960
DATE BAIT, 1960, O
DATE WITH A DREAM, A, 1948, A
DATE WITH DEATH, A, 1959, A
DATE WITH DISASTER, 1957, C
DATE WITH JUDY, A, 1948, AA
DATE WITH THE FALCON, A, 1941, A
DATELINE DIAMONDS, 1966, A
DAUGHTER ANGELE, 1918
DAUGHTER IN REVOLT, A, 1927, A
DAUGHTER OF CLEOPATRA
DAUGHTER OF DARKNESS, 1948, O
DAUGHTER OF DAWN, THE, 1920
DAUGHTER OF DAWN, THE, 1924
DAUGHTER OF DECEIT, 1977, A-C
DAUGHTER OF DESTINY, 1917
DAUGHTER OF DEVIL DAN, 1921
DAUGHTER OF DR. JEKYLL, 1957, A
DAUGHTER OF ENGLAND, A, 1915
DAUGHTER OF EVE, A, 1919
DAUGHTER OF EVIL, 1930, O
DAUGHTER OF FRANCE, A, 1918
DAUGHTER OF LOVE, A, 1925, A
DAUGHTER OF LUXURY, A, 1922
DAUGHTER OF MACGREGOR, A, 1916
DAUGHTER OF MARYLAND, A, 1917
DAUGHTER OF MATA HARI
DAUGHTER OF MINE, 1919, A
DAUGHTER OF ROSIE O'GRADY, THE, 1950, AA
DAUGHTER OF SHANGHAI, 1937, A
DAUGHTER OF THE CITY, A, 1915
DAUGHTER OF THE CONGO, A, 1930
DAUGHTER OF THE DON, THE, 1917

DAUGHTER OF THE DON, THE, 1918
DAUGHTER OF THE DRAGON, 1931, A
DAUGHTER OF THE GODS, A, 1916
DAUGHTER OF THE JUNGLE, 1949, A
DAUGHTER OF THE LAW, A, 1921
DAUGHTER OF THE OLD SOUTH, A, 1918
DAUGHTER OF THE PEOPLE, A, 1915
DAUGHTER OF THE POOR, A, 1917
DAUGHTER OF THE SANDS, 1952, C-O
DAUGHTER OF THE SEA, A, 1915, A
DAUGHTER OF THE SIOUX, A, 1925
DAUGHTER OF THE SUN GOD, 1962
DAUGHTER OF THE TONG, 1939, A
DAUGHTER OF THE WEST, 1949, A
DAUGHTER OF THE WILDS, 1917
DAUGHTER OF THE WOLF, A, 1919
DAUGHTER OF TWO WORLDS, A, 1920
DAUGHTER PAYS, THE, 1920, A
DAUGHTERS COURAGEOUS, 1939, A
DAUGHTERS OF DARKNESS, 1971, O
DAUGHTERS OF DESIRE, 1929
DAUGHTERS OF DESTINY, 1954, C
DAUGHTERS OF MEN, A
DAUGHTERS OF PLEASURE, 1924
DAUGHTERS OF SATAN, 1972
DAUGHTERS OF THE NIGHT, 1924
DAUGHTERS OF THE RICH, 1923
DAUGHTERS OF TODAY, 1924, A
DAUGHTERS OF TODAY, 1933, A
DAUGHTERS WHO PAY, 1925, A
DAVID, 1979, C
DAVID AND BATHSHEBA, 1951, C
DAVID AND GOLIATH, 1961
DAVID AND JONATHAN, 1920, A
DAVID AND LISA, 1962, A-C
DAVID COPPERFIELD, 1913
DAVID COPPERFIELD, 1935, A
DAVID COPPERFIELD, 1970, A
DAVID GARRICK, 1913
DAVID GARRICK, 1916
DAVID GOLDER, 1932, A
DAVID HARDING, COUNTERSPY, 1950, A
DAVID HARUM, 1915, A
DAVID HARUM, 1934, A
DAVID HOLZMAN'S DIARY, 1968, C-O
DAVID LIVINGSTONE, 1936, A
DAVY, 1958, A
DAVY CROCKETT, 1916
DAVY CROCKETT AND THE RIVER PIRATES,
   1956, AAA
DAVY CROCKETT AT THE FALL OF THE ALAMO,
   1926
DAVY CROCKETT, INDIAN SCOUT, 1950, AAA
DAVY CROCKETT, KING OF THE WILD FRONTIER,
   1955, AAA
DAWN, 1917, A
DAWN, 1919
DAWN, 1928, C
DAWN, 1979, C
DAWN AT SOCORRO, 1954, A
DAWN EXPRESS, THE, 1942, A
DAWN MAKER, THE, 1916
DAWN OF A TOMORROW, THE, 1915, A
DAWN OF A TOMORROW, THE, 1924
DAWN OF FREEDOM, THE, 1916
DAWN OF LOVE, THE, 1916
DAWN OF REVENGE, 1922
DAWN OF THE DEAD, 1979, O
DAWN OF THE EAST, 1921, A
DAWN OF THE MUMMY, 1981
DAWN OF THE TRUTH, THE, 1920
DAWN OF UNDERSTANDING, THE, 1918
DAWN ON THE GREAT DIVIDE, 1942, A
DAWN OVER IRELAND, 1938, A
DAWN PATROL, THE, 1930, A
DAWN PATROL, THE, 1938, C
DAWN RIDER, 1935, A
DAWN TRAIL, THE, 1931, A
DAWN, THE
DAY AFTER HALLOWEEN, THE, 1981, O
DAY AFTER THE DIVORCE, THE, 1940
DAY AFTER, THE
DAY AND THE HOUR, THE, 1963, A
DAY AT THE BEACH, A, 1970, O
DAY AT THE RACES, A, 1937, AA
DAY DREAMS, 1919
DAY FOR NIGHT, 1973, A-C
DAY IN COURT, A, 1965, O
DAY IN THE DEATH OF JOE EGG, A, 1972, O
DAY IT CAME TO EARTH, THE, 1979
DAY MARS INVADED EARTH, THE, 1963, C
DAY OF ANGER, 1970, O
DAY OF DAYS, THE, 1914, A
DAY OF FAITH, THE, 1923
DAY OF FURY, A, 1956, A
DAY OF RECKONING, 1933, O
DAY OF THE ANIMALS, 1977, C
DAY OF THE BAD MAN, 1958, A
DAY OF THE DOLPHIN, THE, 1973, A
DAY OF THE EVIL GUN, 1968, A

DAY OF THE HANGING, THE
DAY OF THE JACKAL, THE, 1973, C
DAY OF THE LANDGRABBERS
DAY OF THE LOCUST, THE, 1975, C-O
DAY OF THE NIGHTMARE, 1965, C
DAY OF THE OUTLAW, 1959, A
DAY OF THE OWL, THE, 1968, C
DAY OF THE TRIFFIDS, THE, 1963, C
DAY OF THE WOLVES, 1973, A-C
DAY OF TRIUMPH, 1954, A
DAY OF WRATH, 1948, C
DAY SANTA CLAUS CRIED, THE, 1980
DAY SHE PAID, THE, 1919
DAY THAT SHOOK THE WORLD, THE, 1977, A-C
DAY THE BOOKIES WEPT, THE, 1939, A
DAY THE EARTH CAUGHT FIRE, THE, 1961, A
DAY THE EARTH FROZE, THE, 1959, AA
DAY THE EARTH GOT STONED, THE, 1978
DAY THE EARTH STOOD STILL, THE, 1951, A
DAY THE FISH CAME OUT, THE, 1967, C
DAY THE HOTLINE GOT HOT, THE, 1968, A
DAY THE LORD GOT BUSTED, THE, 1976
DAY THE SCREAMING STOPPED, THE
DAY THE SKY EXPLODED, THE, 1958, A
DAY THE SUN ROSE, THE, 1969, A
DAY THE WAR ENDED, THE, 1961, A-C
DAY THE WORLD CHANGED HANDS, THE
DAY THE WORLD ENDED, THE, 1956
DAY THEY ROBBED THE BANK OF ENGLAND, THE,
   1960, A
DAY TIME ENDED, THE, 1980, A
DAY TO REMEMBER, A, 1953, A
DAY WILL COME, A, 1960
DAY WILL DAWN, THE
DAY-TIME WIFE, 1939, A-C
DAYBREAK, 1918
DAYBREAK, 1931, A
DAYBREAK, 1940, A
DAYDREAK, 1948, C-O
DAYDREAMER, THE, 1966, AAA
DAYDREAMER, THE, 1975, A
DAYLIGHT ROBBERY, 1964, AA
DAYS AND NIGHTS, 1946, C
DAYS OF 36, 1972, C
DAYS OF BUFFALO BILL, 1946
DAYS OF GLORY, 1944, A
DAYS OF HEAVEN, 1978
DAYS OF JESSE JAMES, 1939, A
DAYS OF OLD CHEYENNE, 1943, A
DAYS OF OUR LIFE, 1914
DAYS OF WINE AND ROSES, 1962, C
DAYTIME WIVES, 1923
DAYTON'S DEVILS, 1968, A
DAYTONA BEACH WEEKEND Zero, 1965
DAZZLING MISS DAVISON, THE, 1917
DE L'AMOUR, 1968, C
DE SADE, 1969, O
DE STILTE ROND CHRISTINE M...
DEAD ALIVE, THE, 1916
DEAD AND BURIED, 1981, O
DEAD ARE ALIVE, THE, 1972, O
DEAD CERT, 1974
DEAD CERTAINTY, A, 1920, A
DEAD DON'T DREAM, THE, 1948, A
DEAD END, 1937, C
DEAD END KIDS ON DRESS PARADE, 1939, A
DEAD EYES OF LONDON
DEAD GAME, 1923
DEAD HEART, THE, 1914
DEAD HEAT ON A MERRY-GO-ROUND, 1966, A
DEAD KIDS, 1981, O
DEAD LINE, THE, 1920
DEAD LINE, THE, 1926
DEAD LUCKY, 1960, C
DEAD MAN'S CHEST, 1965, A-C
DEAD MAN'S CURVE, 1928, A
DEAD MAN'S EVIDENCE, 1962
DEAD MAN'S EYES, 1944, A
DEAD MAN'S FLOAT, 1980
DEAD MAN'S GOLD, 1948, A
DEAD MAN'S GULCH, 1943, A
DEAD MAN'S SHOES, 1939, A
DEAD MAN'S TRAIL, 1952, A
DEAD MAN, THE, 1914
DEAD MARCH, THE, 1937, C
DEAD MELODY, 1938, C
DEAD MEN ARE DANGEROUS, 1939, A
DEAD MEN DON'T MAKE SHADOWS, 1970
DEAD MEN DON'T WEAR PLAID, 1982, C
DEAD MEN TELL, 1941, A
DEAD MEN TELL NO TALES, 1920
DEAD MEN TELL NO TALES, 1939
DEAD MEN WALK, 1943, A
DEAD MOUNTAINEER HOTEL, THE, 1979, C
DEAD OF NIGHT, 1946, O
DEAD OF NIGHT, 1972
DEAD OF SUMMER, 1970, C-O
DEAD ON COURSE, 1952, A-C
DEAD ONE, THE, 1961, O
DEAD OR ALIVE, 1921
DEAD OR ALIVE, 1944, A
DEAD OR ALIVE, 1968

DEAD PEOPLE, 1974, O
DEAD PIGEON ON BEETHOVEN STREET, 1972, C
DEAD RECKONING, 1947, C
DEAD RINGER, 1964, A-C
DEAD RUN, 1961, C
DEAD SOUL, THE, 1915
DEAD TO THE WORLD, 1961, A
DEAD WOMAN'S KISS, A, 1951, A
DEAD ZONE, THE, 1983, O
DEAD-SHOT BAKER, 1917
DEADFALL, 1968, C
DEADHEAD MILES, 1982, A-C
DEADLIER SEX, THE, 1920
DEADLIER THAN THE MALE, 1957, C
DEADLIER THAN THE MALE, 1967, C
DEADLIEST SIN, THE, 1956
DEADLINE, 1948, A
DEADLINE, 1984
DEADLINE AT DAWN, 1946, A
DEADLINE AT ELEVEN, 1920
DEADLINE FOR MURDER, 1946, A
DEADLINE, THE, 1932, A
DEADLINE—U.S.A., 1952, C
DEADLOCK, 1931, A
DEADLOCK, 1943, A
DEADLOCK, 1961
DEADLY AFFAIR, THE, 1967, A-C
DEADLY AND THE BEAUTIFUL, 1974
DEADLY AS THE FEMALE
DEADLY AUGUST, 1966
DEADLY BEES, THE, 1967, C
DEADLY BLESSING, 1981, O
DEADLY CHINA DOLL, 1973, O
DEADLY CIRCLE, THE
DEADLY COMPANIONS, THE, 1961, C
DEADLY DECISION
DEADLY DECOYS, THE, 1962, A-C
DEADLY DUO, 1962, A
DEADLY ENCOUNTER, 1979
DEADLY EYES, 1982, O
DEADLY FEMALES, THE, 1976, O
DEADLY FORCE, 1983, O
DEADLY GAME, THE, 1941
DEADLY GAME, THE, 1955, A
DEADLY GAME, THE, 1974
DEADLY GAMES, 1982
DEADLY GAMES, 1980
DEADLY HARVEST, 1972
DEADLY HERO, 1976, O
DEADLY HONEYMOON, 1974
DEADLY IS THE FEMALE
DEADLY MANTIS, THE, 1957, A
DEADLY NIGHTSHADE, 1953, A
DEADLY RECORD, 1959, A
DEADLY SILENCE
DEADLY SPAWN, THE, 1983, O
DEADLY STRANGERS, 1974, C
DEADLY TRACKERS, 1973, O
DEADLY TRAP, THE, 1972
DEADLY WEAPONS, 1974
DEADSHOT CASEY, 1928
DEADWOOD COACH, THE, 1924
DEADWOOD PASS, 1933, A
DEADWOOD '76, 1965, C
DEAF SMITH AND JOHNNY EARS, 1973, C
DEAFULA, 1975
DEAL OF THE CENTURY, 1983, C
DEALING: OR THE BERKELEY-TO-BOSTON
   FORTY-BRICK
DEAR BRAT, 1951, A
DEAR BRIGETTE, 1965, A
DEAR DETECTIVE, 1978, C
DEAR FOOL, A, 1921
DEAR HEART, 1964, A
DEAR INSPECTOR
DEAR JOHN, 1966
DEAR MARTHA
DEAR MR. PROHACK, 1949, A
DEAR MR. WONDERFUL, 1983, C
DEAR MURDERER, 1947, C
DEAR OCTOPUS
DEAR RUTH, 1947, A
DEAR WIFE, 1949, AA
DEAR, DEAD DELILAH, 1972, O
DEARIE, 1927
DEATH AT A BROADCAST, 1934, A
DEATH AT DAWN, 1924
DEATH BAY, 1926
DEATH BITE
DEATH BLOW
DEATH BY INVITATION, 1971
DEATH COLLECTOR, 1976, O
DEATH CORDS
DEATH CROONS THE BLUES, 1937, A
DEATH CURSE OF TARTU, 1967, C-O
DEATH DANCE, THE, 1918
DEATH DRIVER, 1977
DEATH DRIVES THROUGH, 1935, A
DEATH DRUMS ALONG THE RIVER
DEATH FLIES EAST, 1935, A
DEATH FORCE, 1978
DEATH FROM A DISTANCE, 1936, A

DEATH FROM OUTER SPACE
DEATH GAME, 1977, O
DEATH GOES NORTH, 1939, A
DEATH HUNT, 1981, C
DEATH IN SMALL DOSES, 1957, C
DEATH IN THE AIR, 1937
DEATH IN THE GARDEN, 1977, O
DEATH IN THE SKY, 1937, C
DEATH IN VENICE, 1971, C
DEATH IS A NUMBER, 1951, A-C
DEATH IS A WOMAN
DEATH IS CALLED ENGELCHEN, 1963, C
DEATH JOURNEY, 1976
DEATH KISS, THE, 1933, A
DEATH MACHINES, 1976, O
DEATH MAY BE YOUR SANTA CLAUS, 1969
DEATH OF A BUREAUCRAT, 1979, A-C
DEATH OF A CHAMPION, 1939, A
DEATH OF A CYCLIST
DEATH OF A GUNFIGHTER, 1969, C
DEATH OF A JEW
DEATH OF A SALESMAN, 1952, O
DEATH OF A SCOUNDREL, 1956, C
DEATH OF A STRANGER, 1976
DEATH OF AN ANGEL, 1952, A
DEATH OF HER INNOCENCE
DEATH OF MARIO RICCI, THE, 1983, C
DEATH OF MICHAEL TURBIN, THE, 1954, A
DEATH OF TARZAN, THE, 1968, C
DEATH OF THE APEMAN
DEATH OF THE DIAMOND, 1934, A
DEATH OF THE GODS, 1917
DEATH ON CREDIT, 1976
DEATH ON THE MOUNTAIN, 1961, O
DEATH ON THE NILE, 1978, C
DEATH ON THE SET
DEATH OVER MY SHOULDER, 1958, A-C
DEATH PLAY, 1976, C
DEATH RACE, 1978, C-O
DEATH RACE 2000, 1975, O
DEATH RAY, THE, 1925
DEATH RIDERS, 1976
DEATH RIDES A HORSE, 1969
DEATH RIDES THE PLAINS, 1944, A
DEATH RIDES THE RANGE, 1940, A
DEATH SCREAMS, 1982
DEATH SENTENCE, 1967, O
DEATH SHIP, 1980, O
DEATH SMILES ON A MURDER, 1974
DEATH TAKES A HOLIDAY, 1934, C
DEATH TOOK PLACE LAST NIGHT, 1970, O
DEATH TRAP, 1962, C
DEATH TRAP, 1967
DEATH TRAP, 1976
DEATH TRAP, 1982
DEATH VALLEY, 1927
DEATH VALLEY, 1946, A
DEATH VALLEY, 1982, O
DEATH VALLEY GUNFIGHTER, 1949, A
DEATH VALLEY MANHUNT, 1943, A
DEATH VALLEY OUTLAWS, 1941, A
DEATH VALLEY RANGERS, 1944, A
DEATH VENGEANCE, 1982, O
DEATH WEEKEND
DEATH WISH, 1974
DEATH WISH II, 1982, O
DEATHCHEATERS, 1976, C
DEATHDREAM, 1972, O
DEATHGAMES, 1981
DEATHHEAD VIRGIN, THE, 1974
DEATHLINE, 1973, O
DEATHLOCK, THE, 1915
DEATHMASTER, THE, 1972, O
DEATHSHEAD VAMPIRE
DEATHSPORT, 1978, O
DEATHSTALKER, 1983
DEATHSTALKER, THE, 1984, O
DEATHTRAP, 1982
DEATHWATCH, 1966, O
DEATHWATCH, 1980, O
DEATM GOES TO SCHOOL, 1953, A
DEBT OF HONOR, 1922, A
DEBT OF HONOR, 1936, A
DEBT OF HONOR, A, 1916
DEBT OF HONOR, THE, 1918
DEBT, THE
DEBT, THE, 1917
DEBTOR TO THE LAW, A, 1924
DECAMERON NIGHTS, 1924, A
DECAMERON NIGHTS, 1953, A
DECEIT, 1923
DECEIVER, THE, 1920
DECEIVER, THE, 1931, A
DECEIVERS, THE
DECEMBRISTS, 1927
DECEPTION, 1918
DECEPTION, 1921
DECEPTION, 1933, A
DECEPTION, 1946, A-C
DECIDING KISS, THE, 1918
DECISION AGAINST TIME, 1957
DECISION AT SUNDOWN, 1957, C

DECISION BEFORE DAWN, 1951, A
DECISION OF CHRISTOPHER BLAKE, THE, 1948, A
DECKS RAN RED, THE, 1958, A-C
DECLASSE, 1925
DECLINE AND FALL... OF A BIRD WATCHER,
   1969, C
DECOY, 1946, C-O
DECOY FOR TERROR, 1970, O
DECOY, 1963
DECOY, THE, 1916
DEDEE, 1949, C
DEEDS MEN DO, THE
DEEDS OF DARING, 1924
DEEMSTER, THE, 1917
DEEP BLUE SEA, THE, 1955, C
DEEP DESIRE OF GODS
DEEP END, 1970, O
DEEP IN MY HEART, 1954, AA
DEEP IN THE HEART, 1983, O
DEEP IN THE HEART OF TEXAS, 1942, A
DEEP PURPLE, THE, 1915
DEEP PURPLE, THE, 1920
DEEP RED, 1976, O
DEEP SIX, THE, 1958, A
DEEP THRUST—THE HAND OF DEATH, 1973, O
DEEP VALLEY, 1947, C
DEEP WATERS, 1920
DEEP WATERS, 1948, A
DEEP, THE, 1977, O
DEER HUNTER, THE, 1978, O
DEERSLAYER, 1943, O
DEERSLAYER, THE, 1923
DEERSLAYER, THE, 1957, A
DEFEAT OF HANNIBAL, THE, 1937, C
DEFEAT OF THE CITY, THE, 1917
DEFECTOR, THE, 1966, C
DEFENCE OF SEVASTOPOL, 1911
DEFEND MY LOVE, 1956, A-C
DEFEND YOURSELF, 1925
DEFENDERS OF THE LAW, 1931, A
DEFENSE HESTS, THE, 1934, A
DEFENSE OF VOLOTCHAYEVSK, THE, 1938, A
DEFIANCE, 1980, C
DEFIANT DAUGHTERS
DEFIANT ONES, THE, 1958, C
DEFINITE OBJECT, THE, 1920
DEFYING DESTINY, 1923
DEFYING THE LAW, 1922
DEFYING THE LAW, 1924
DEFYING THE LAW, 1935
DEGREE OF MURDER, A, 1969, O
DELAVINE AFFAIR, THE, 1954, A
DELAY IN MARIENBORN
DELAYED ACTION, 1954, A
DELICATE BALANCE, A, 1973, C
DELICATE DELINQUENT, THE, 1957, A
DELICIOUS, 1931, A
DELICIOUS LITTLE DEVIL, THE, 1919
DELIGHTFUL HOGUE, 1929, A
DELIGHTFULLY DANGEROUS, 1945
DELINQUENT DAUGHTERS, 1944, C
DELINQUENT PARENTS, 1938, A
DELINQUENTS, THE, 1957, C
DELIRIUM
DELIRIUM, 1979, O
DELIVER US FROM EVIL, 1975
DELIVERANCE, 1928
DELIVERANCE, 1972, O
DELIVERY BOYS, 1984, O
DELTA FACTOR, THE, 1970, C
DELTA FOX, 1979
DELUGE, 1933, A
DELUGE, THE, 1925
DELUSION
DELUSIONS OF GRANDEUR, 1971, C
DELUXE ANNIE, 1918
DEMENTED, 1980, O
DEMENTIA, 1955, O
DEMENTIA 13, 1963, C
DEMETRIUS AND THE GLADIATORS, 1954, C
DEMI-BRIDE, THE, 1927
DEMI-PARADISE, THE
DEMOBBED, 1944, A
DEMOCRACY, 1918
DEMOCRACY, 1920
DEMOLITION, 1977
DEMON BARBER OF FLEET STREET, THE, 1939
DEMON FOR TROUBLE, A, 1934, A
DEMON FROM DEVIL'S LAKE, THE, 1964, A
DEMON LOVER, THE, 1977, O
DEMON PLANET, THE
DEMON POND, 1980, C
DEMON RIDER, THE, 1925
DEMON SEED, 1977, O
DEMON WITCH CHILD, 1974
DEMON, THE, 1918
DEMON, THE, 1926
DEMON, THE, 1981, O
DEMON, THE, 1965
DEMONIAQUE, 1958, C-O
DEMONIOS EN EL JARDIN
DEMONOID

DEMONS IN THE GARDEN, 1984, O
DEMONS OF LUDLOW, THE, 1983, O
DEMONS OF THE DEAD, 1976
DEMONS OF THE MIND, 1972, O
DEMONSTRATOR, 1971, O
DEMOS
DEN OF DOOM
DENIAL, THE, 1925
DENNY FROM IRELAND, 1918
DENTIST IN THE CHAIR, 1960, A
DENTIST ON THE JOB
DENVER AND RIO GRANDE, 1952, A
DENVER DUDE, THE, 1927
DENVER KID, THE, 1948
DEPARTMENT STORE, 1935, A
DEPORTED, 1950, A
DEPRAVED, THE, 1957, A-C
DEPTH CHARGE, 1960, A-C
DEPUTY DRUMMER, THE, 1935, A
DEPUTY MARSHAL, 1949, A
DER FREISCHUTZ, 1970, A
DER GOLEM
DER LETZTE MANN
DER MUDE TOD
DER VERLORENE SCHATTEN
DERANGED, 1974, O
DERBY DAY
DERBY WINNER, THE, 1915
DERELICT, 1930, A
DERELICT, THE, 1917
DERELICT, THE, 1937, A
DERELICTS, 1917
DERSU UZALA, 1976, A
DES VOLKES HELDENGANG
DESERT ATTACK, 1958, A
DESERT BANDIT, 1941, A
DESERT BLOSSOMS, 1921, A
DESERT BRIDE, THE, 1928
DESERT BRIDEGROOM, A, 1922
DESERT DEMON, THE, 1925
DESERT DESPERADOES
DESERT DRIVEN, 1923
DESERT DUST, 1917
DESERT DUST, 1927
DESERT FLOWER, THE, 1925, A
DESERT FOX, THE, 1951, A
DESERT FURY, 1947, C
DESERT GOLD, 1919
DESERT GOLD, 1926
DESERT GOLD, 1936, A
DESERT GREED, 1926
DESERT GUNS, 1936, A
DESERT HAWK, THE, 1924
DESERT HAWK, THE, 1950, A
DESERT HELL, 1958, A
DESERT HONEYMOON, A, 1915
DESERT HORSEMAN, THE, 1946, A
DESERT JUSTICE, 1936, A
DESERT LAW, 1918
DESERT LEGION, 1953, A
DESERT LOVE, 1920
DESERT MADNESS, 1925
DESERT MAN, THE, 1917
DESERT MESA, 1935, A
DESERT MICE, 1960, A
DESERT NIGHTS, 1929
DESERT OF LOST MEN, 1951, A
DESERT OF THE LOST, THE, 1927
DESERT OF THE TARTARS, THE, 1976, C
DESERT OUTLAW, THE, 1924
DESERT PASSAGE, 1952, A
DESERT PATROL, 1938, A
DESERT PATROL, 1962, C
DESERT PHANTOM, 1937, A
DESERT PIRATE, THE, 1928, A
DESERT PURSUIT, 1952, A
DESERT RATS, THE, 1953, A
DESERT RAVEN, 1965, A
DESERT RIDER, 1923
DESERT RIDER, THE, 1929, A
DESERT SANDS, 1955, A
DESERT SCORPION, THE, 1920
DESERT SECRET, THE, 1924
DESERT SHEIK, THE, 1924
DESERT SONG, THE, 1929, A
DESERT SONG, THE, 1943, A
DESERT SONG, THE, 1953, A
DESERT TRAIL, 1935, A
DESERT VALLEY, 1926
DESERT VENGEANCE, 1931
DESERT VIGILANTE, 1949, A
DESERT VULTURES, 1930
DESERT WARRIOR, 1961, A
DESERT WOOING, A, 1918
DESERT'S CRUCIBLE, THE, 1922
DESERT'S PRICE, THE, 1926, A
DESERT'S TOLL, THE, 1926, A
DESERTED AT THE ALTAR, 1922, A
DESERTER, 1934, A
DESERTER AND THE NOMADS, THE, 1969, O
DESERTER, THE, 1916
DESERTER, THE, 1971

DIALOGUE, 1967, A
DIAMANT NOIR, 1922
DIAMOND BANDIT, THE, 1924
DIAMOND CARLISLE, 1922
DIAMOND CITY, 1949, A
DIAMOND COUNTRY
DIAMOND CUT DIAMOND
DIAMOND EARRINGS
DIAMOND FRONTIER, 1940
DIAMOND HANDCUFFS, 1928
DIAMOND HEAD, 1962, C
DIAMOND HORSESHOE, 1945, A
DIAMOND HUNTERS
DIAMOND JIM, 1935, A
DIAMOND MAN, THE, 1924
DIAMOND NECKLACE, THE, 1921, A
DIAMOND QUEEN, THE, 1953, A
DIAMOND RUNNERS, THE, 1916
DIAMOND SAFARI, 1958, A
DIAMOND STUD, 1970, C
DIAMOND STUD, 1970
DIAMOND TRAIL, 1933, A
DIAMOND WIZARD, THE, 1954
DIAMONDS, 1975, C
DIAMONDS ADRIFT, 1921, A
DIAMONDS AND CRIME
DIAMONDS AND PEARLS, 1918
DIAMONDS ARE FOREVER, 1971, C
DIAMONDS FOR BREAKFAST, 1968, C
DIAMONDS OF THE NIGHT, 1968, C
DIANA AND DESTINY, 1916
DIANA OF DOBSON'S, 1917
DIANA OF THE CROSSWAYS, 1922
DIANA OF THE FOLLIES, 1916
DIANE, 1955, A-C
DIANE OF STAR HOLLOW, 1921, A
DIANE OF THE GREEN VAN, 1919
DIANE'S BODY, 1969
DIARY FOR MY CHILDREN, 1984, O
DIARY OF A BACHELOR, 1964, O
DIARY OF A BAD GIRL, 1958, C
DIARY OF A CHAMBERMAID, 1946, A
DIARY OF A CHAMBERMAID, 1964, O
DIARY OF A CLOISTERED NUN, 1973, O
DIARY OF A COUNTRY PRIEST, 1954, A
DIARY OF A HIGH SCHOOL BRIDE, 1959, C-O
DIARY OF A LOST GIRL, 1929
DIARY OF A MAD HOUSEWIFE, 1970, C-O
DIARY OF A MADMAN, 1963, C-O
DIARY OF A NAZI, 1943, C
DIARY OF A REVOLUTIONIST, 1932, A
DIARY OF A SCHIZOPHRENIC GIRL, 1970, A
DIARY OF A SHINJUKU BURGLAR, 1969, O
DIARY OF AN ITALIAN, 1972, C
DIARY OF ANNE FRANK, THE, 1959, A
DIARY OF FORBIDDEN DREAMS
DIARY OF MAJOR THOMPSON, THE
DIARY OF OHARU
DICE OF DESTINY, 1920
DICE WOMAN, THE, 1927
DICK BARTON AT BAY, 1950, A
DICK BARTON STRIKES BACK, 1949, A
DICK BARTON—SPECIAL AGENT, 1948, A
DICK CARSON WINS THROUGH, 1917
DICK DEADEYE, 1977
DICK TRACY, 1945, A-C
DICK TRACY MEETS GRUESOME, 1947, A-C
DICK TRACY VS. CUEBALL, 1946, C
DICK TRACY'S DILEMMA, 1947, C
DICK TURPIN, 1925, A
DICK TURPIN, 1933
DICK TURPIN'S RIDE TO YORK, 1922
DICK'S FAIRY, 1921
DICKY MONTEITH, 1922
DICTATOR, THE, 1922, A
DICTATOR, THE, 1935, A
DID I BETRAY?
DID YOU HEAR THE ONE ABOUT THE TRAVELING
DIDN'T YOU HEAR, 1983
DIE FASTNACHTSBEICHTE, 1962, A
DIE FLAMBIERTE FRAU
DIE FLEDERMAUS, 1964, A
DIE GANS VON SEDAN, 1962, A
DIE GEHEIMNISSE EINER SEELE
DIE HAMBURGER KRANKHEIT, 1979, C
DIE LAUGHING, 1980, O
DIE MANNER UM LUCIE, 1931, A
DIE NIBELUNGEN
DIE NIBELUNGEN
DIE SCREAMING, MARIANNE, 1970, O
DIE SISTER, DIE, 1978
DIE UNENDLICHE GESCHICHTE
DIE, BEAUTIFUL MARYANNE, 1969
DIE, DIE, MY DARLING, 1965, O
DIE, MONSTER, DIE, 1965, C
DIFFERENT SONS, 1962, O
DIFFERENT STORY, A, 1978, O
DIFFICULT LOVE, A
DIFFICULT YEARS, 1950, C
DIG THAT JULIET
DIG THAT URANIUM, 1956, A

DIGBY, THE BIGGEST DOG IN THE WORLD, 1974, AAA
DILLINGER, 1945, C-O
DILLINGER, 1973, O
DILLINGER IS DEAD, 1969, O
DIMBOOLA, 1979, O
DIME WITH A HALO, 1963, A
DIMENSION 5, 1966, A
DIMKA, 1964, AA
DIMPLES, 1916, A
DIMPLES, 1936, AAA
DINER, 1982, C-O
DING DONG WILLIAMS, 1946, A
DINGAKA, 1965, A
DINKY, 1935, A
DINNER AT EIGHT, 1933, C
DINNER AT THE RITZ, 1937, A
DINNER FOR ADELE
DINO, 1957, A
DINOSAURUS, 1960, AA
DINTY, 1920, A
DION BROTHERS, THE
DIPLOMACY, 1916
DIPLOMACY, 1926
DIPLOMANIACS, 1933, A
DIPLOMAT'S MANSION, THE, 1961, C
DIPLOMATIC CORPSE, THE, 1958, A
DIPLOMATIC COURIER, 1952, A
DIPLOMATIC LOVER, THE, 1934, A
DIPLOMATIC MISSION, A, 1918
DIPLOMATIC PASSPORT, 1954, A
DIRIGIBLE, 1931, A
DIRT GANG, THE, 1972, O
DIRTIEST GIRL I EVER MET, THE, 1973
DIRTY DINGUS MAGEE, 1970, C
DIRTY DOZEN, THE, 1967, C-O
DIRTY GAME, THE, 1966, C
DIRTY GERTY FROM HARLEM, USA, 1946
DIRTY HANDS, 1976, O
DIRTY HARRY, 1971, O
DIRTY HEROES, 1971, A
DIRTY KNIGHT'S WORK, 1976, C
DIRTY LITTLE BILLY, 1972, O
DIRTY MARY, CRAZY LARRY, 1974, O
DIRTY MONEY, 1977, C
DIRTY O'NEIL, 1974, O
DIRTY OUTLAWS, THE, 1971, O
DIRTY TRICKS, 1981, C
DIRTY WORK, 1934, A
DIRTYMOUTH, 1970, O
DISAPPEARANCE OF THE JUDGE, THE, 1919
DISAPPEARANCE, THE, 1981, C
DISASTER, 1948, A
DISBARRED, 1939
DISC JOCKEY, 1951, A
DISC JOCKEY JAMBOREE
DISCARD, THE, 1916
DISCARDED LOVERS, 1932, A
DISCARDED WOMAN, THE, 1920
DISCIPLE OF DEATH, 1972, O
DISCIPLE, THE, 1915
DISCIPLES OF DEATH, 1975
DISCO 9000, 1977
DISCO FEVER, 1978
DISCO GODFATHER, 1979
DISCONTENTED HUSBANDS, 1924
DISCONTENTED WIVES, 1921
DISCORD, 1933, A
DISCOVERIES, 1939, A
DISCREET CHARM OF THE BOURGEOISIE, THE, 1972, C
DISEMBODIED, THE, 1957, C
DISGRACED, 1933, A
DISHONOR BRIGHT, 1936, A
DISHONORED, 1931, C
DISHONORED, 1950, A
DISHONORED LADY, 1947, C
DISHONORED MEDAL, THE, 1914, A
DISILLUSION, 1949, A
DISOBEDIENT, 1953, O
DISORDER, 1964
DISORDER AND EARLY TORMENT, 1977, A
DISORDERLY CONDUCT, 1932, A
DISORDERLY ORDERLY, THE, 1964, A
DISPATCH FROM REUTERS, A, 1940, A
DISPUTED PASSAGE, 1939, A
DISRAELI, 1916
DISRAELI, 1921
DISRAELI, 1929, A
DISTANCE, 1975, O
DISTANT DRUMS, 1951, A
DISTANT JOURNEY, 1950, C
DISTANT TRUMPET, 1952, A
DISTANT TRUMPET, A, 1964, A
DISTRICT ATTORNEY, THE, 1915
DITES 33
DIVA, 1982, C
DIVE BOMBER, 1941, A-C
DIVIDED HEART, THE, 1955, A
DIVIDEND, THE, 1916, A
DIVINE EMMA, THE, 1983, A
DIVINE GIFT, THE, 1918

DIVINE LADY, THE, 1929
DIVINE MR. J., THE, 1974, O
DIVINE NYMPH, THE, 1979
DIVINE SACRIFICE, THE, 1918
DIVINE SINNER, 1928
DIVINE SPARK, THE, 1935, A
DIVINE WOMAN, THE, 1928, A
DIVING GIRLS OF JAPAN
DIVING GIRLS' ISLAND, THE
DIVORCE, 1923, A
DIVORCE, 1945, A
DIVORCE AMERICAN STYLE, 1967, C
DIVORCE AMONG FRIENDS, 1931, C
DIVORCE AND THE DAUGHTER, 1916
DIVORCE COUPONS, 1922
DIVORCE GAME, THE, 1917, A
DIVORCE IN THE FAMILY, 1932, A
DIVORCE MADE EASY, 1929
DIVORCE OF CONVENIENCE, A, 1921
DIVORCE OF LADY X, THE, 1938, A
DIVORCE TRAP, THE, 1919, A
DIVORCE, ITALIAN STYLE, 1962, A
DIVORCED, 1915
DIVORCEE, THE, 1917
DIVORCEE, THE, 1919
DIVORCEE, THE, 1930, C
DIVORCONS, 1915
DIXIANA, 1930, A
DIXIE, 1943, A
DIXIE DUGAN, 1943, A
DIXIE DYNAMITE, 1976, C
DIXIE FLYER, THE, 1926, A
DIXIE HANDICAP, THE, 1925
DIXIE JAMBOREE, 1945, A
DIXIE MERCHANT, THE, 1926
DIZZY DAMES, 1936, A
DIZZY LIMIT, THE, 1930
DJANGO, 1966, O
DJANGO KILL, 1967, O
DK. JEKYLL AND THE WOLFMAN, 1971
DO AND DARE, 1922, O
DO IT NOW, 1924
DO NOT DISTURB, 1965, A
DO NOT THROW CUSHIONS INTO THE RING, 1970, O
DO THE DEAD TALK?, 1920
DO UNTO OTHERS, 1915
DO YOU KEEP A LION AT HOME?, 1966, AA
DO YOU KNOW THIS VOICE?, 1964
DO YOU LIKE WOMEN?
DO YOU LOVE ME?, 1946, A
DO YOUR DUTY, 1928, A
DOBBIN, THE, 1939
DOBERMAN GANG, THE, 1972, C
DOC, 1914
DOC, 1971, O
DOC HOOKER'S BUNCH, 1978
DOC SAVAGE... THE MAN OF BRONZE, 1975, A
DOCK BRIEF, THE
DOCKS OF NEW ORLEANS, 1948, A
DOCKS OF NEW YORK, 1945, A
DOCKS OF NEW YORK, THE, 1928
DOCKS OF SAN FRANCISCO, 1932, A
DOCTEUR LAENNEC, 1949, A
DOCTEUR POPAUL, 1972, O
DOCTOR AND THE BRICKLAYER, THE, 1918
DOCTOR AND THE GIRL, THE, 1949, C
DOCTOR AND THE WOMAN, THE, 1918
DOCTOR AT LARGE, 1957, A
DOCTOR AT SEA, 1955, A
DOCTOR BEWARE, 1951, C
DOCTOR CRIMEN, 1953, C
DOCTOR DEATH: SEEKER OF SOULS, 1973, O
DOCTOR DETROIT, 1983, O
DOCTOR DOLITTLE, 1967
DOCTOR FAUSTUS, 1967, C
DOCTOR FROM SEVEN DIALS, THE
DOCTOR IN CLOVER
DOCTOR IN DISTRESS, 1963, A
DOCTOR IN LOVE, 1960, A
DOCTOR IN THE HOUSE, 1954, A
DOCTOR IN TROUBLE, 1970, A
DOCTOR JACK, 1922, C
DOCTOR MONICA, 1934, A
DOCTOR OF DOOM, 1962, O
DOCTOR OF ST. PAUL, THE, 1969, C
DOCTOR PHIBES RISES AGAIN, 1972, C-O
DOCTOR SYN, 1937, A
DOCTOR TAKES A WIFE, 1940, AA
DOCTOR X, 1932, A
DOCTOR ZHIVAGO, 1965, A-C
DOCTOR'S DIARY, A, 1937, A
DOCTOR'S DILEMMA, THE, 1958, A
DOCTOR'S ORDERS, 1934, C
DOCTOR'S SECRET, 1929, A
DOCTOR'S WOMEN, THE, 1929
DOCTOR, YOU'VE GOT TO BE KIDDING, 1967
DOCTORS AND NURSES, 1983
DOCTORS DON'T TELL, 1941, A
DOCTORS WEAR SCARLET
DOCTORS' WIVES, 1931, C
DOCTORS' WIVES, 1971, O
DOCTORS, THE, 1956, A

DOCUMENT SECRET, 1916
DODESKA-DEN, 1970, C
DODGE CITY, 1939, A
DODGE CITY TRAIL, 1937, A
DODGING A MILLION, 1918
DODGING THE DOLE, 1936, A
DODSWORTH, 1936, A
DOES IT PAY?, 1923
DOG AND THE DIAMONDS, THE, 1962, AA
DOG DAY, 1984, O
DOG DAY AFTERNOON, 1975, O
DOG EAT DOG, 1963
DOG JUSTICE, 1928
DOG LAW, 1928, A
DOG OF FLANDERS, A, 1935, AAA
DOG OF FLANDERS, A, 1959, A
DOG OF THE REGIMENT, 1927, A
DOG'S BEST FRIEND, A, 1960, AAA
DOG, A MOUSE AND A SPUTNIK, A
DOGPOUND SHUFFLE, 1975, A
DOGS, 1976, O
DOGS OF HELL
DOGS OF WAR, THE, 1980, O
DOING THEIR BIT, 1918, A
DOING TIME, 1979, A
DOLEMITE, 1975, O
DOLL FACE, 1945, A
DOLL SQUAD, THE, 1973
DOLL THAT TOOK THE TOWN, THE, 1965
DOLL'S EYE, 1982
DOLL'S HOUSE, A, 1917
DOLL'S HOUSE, A, 1918, A
DOLL'S HOUSE, A, 1922
DOLL'S HOUSE, A, 1973
DOLL'S HOUSE, A, 1973, A
DOLL, THE, 1962, A
DOLL, THE, 1964, C
DOLLAR, 1938, A
$ (DOLLARS), 1971, O
DOLLAR AND THE LAW, THE, 1916
DOLLAR DEVILS, 1923, A
DOLLAR DOWN, 1925
DOLLAR FOR DOLLAR, 1920
DOLLAR MARK, THE, 1914, A
DOLLAR-A-YEAR MAN, THE, 1921
DOLLARS AND SENSE, 1920, A
DOLLARS AND THE WOMAN, 1916
DOLLARS AND THE WOMAN, 1920
DOLLARS FOR A FAST GUN, 1969, A
DOLLARS IN SURREY, 1921
DOLLS, THE
DOLLY, 1929
DOLLY DOES HER BIT, 1918
DOLLY GETS AHEAD, 1931, A
DOLLY SISTERS, THE, 1945, AA
DOLLY'S VACATION, 1918, A
DOLORES, 1928
DOLORES, 1949, A
DOLWYN
DOMANI A TROPPO TARDI
DOMBEY AND SON, 1917
DOMENICA D'AGOSTO
DOMESTIC MEDDLERS, 1928
DOMESTIC RELATIONS, 1922
DOMESTIC TROUBLES, 1928
DOMESTIC-AGITATOR, 1920
DOMINANT SEX, THE, 1937, A
DOMINIQUE, 1978
DOMINO KID, 1957, A
DOMINO PRINCIPLE, THE, 1977, O
DON CAESAR DE BAZAN, 1915
DON CHICAGO, 1945, A
DON DARE DEVIL, 1925
DON DESPERADO, 1927
DON GIOVANNI, 1955, A
DON GIOVANNI, 1979, A
DON IS DEAD, THE, 1973, O
DON JUAN, 1926, A
DON JUAN, 1956, A
DON JUAN ET FAUST, 1923
DON JUAN OF THE WEST, 1928
DON JUAN QUILLIGAN, 1945, A
DON JUAN'S THREE NIGHTS, 1926
DON JUAN, 1934
DON MIKE, 1927, A
DON Q, SON OF ZORRO, 1925, A
DON QUICKSHOT OF THE RIO GRANDE, 1923
DON QUIXOTE, 1916
DON QUIXOTE, 1923, A
DON QUIXOTE, 1935, A
DON QUIXOTE, 1961, A
DON QUIXOTE, 1973, A
DON RICARDO RETURNS, 1946, A
DON X, 1925, A
DON'S PARTY, 1976, C-O
DON'T, 1925
DON'T ANSWER THE PHONE, 1980, O
DON'T BE A DUMMY, 1932, A
DON'T BET ON BLONDES, 1935, A
DON'T BET ON LOVE, 1933, A
DON'T BET ON WOMEN, 1931, A
DON'T BLAME THE STORK, 1954, A

DON'T BLAME YOUR CHILDREN, 1922
DON'T BOTHER TO KNOCK, 1952, O
DON'T BOTHER TO KNOCK, 1964
DON'T BUILD YOUR HAPPINESS ON YOUR WIFE
    AND CHILD (1917, USSR)
DON'T CALL IT LOVE, 1924
DON'T CALL ME A CON MAN, 1966
DON'T CALL ME LITTLE GIRL, 1921, A
DON'T CHANGE YOUR HUSBAND, 1919
DON'T CRY WITH YOUR MOUTH FULL, 1974, A
DON'T CRY, IT'S ONLY THUNDER, 1982, O
DON'T DOUBT YOUR HUSBAND, 1924
DON'T DOUBT YOUR WIFE, 1922
DON'T DRINK THE WATER, 1969, A
DON'T EVER LEAVE ME, 1949, A
DON'T EVER MARRY, 1920
DON'T FENCE ME IN, 1945, A
DON'T GAMBLE WITH LOVE, 1936, A
DON'T GAMBLE WITH STRANGERS, 1946, A
DON'T GET ME WRONG, 1937, A
DON'T GET PERSONAL, 1922, A
DON'T GET PERSONAL, 1936, A
DON'T GET PERSONAL, 1941, A
DON'T GIVE UP THE SHIP, 1959, A
DON'T GO IN THE HOUSE, 1980, O
DON'T GO INTO THE WOODS, 1980
DON'T GO NEAR THE PARK, 1981
DON'T GO NEAR THE WATER, 1975
DON'T JUST LIE THERE, SAY SOMETHING!, 1973
DON'T JUST STAND THERE, 1968, A
DON'T KNOCK THE ROCK, 1956, A
DON'T KNOCK THE TWIST, 1962, A
DON'T LEAVE YOUR HUSBAND
DON'T LET THE ANGELS FALL, 1969, A
DON'T LOOK IN THE BASEMENT, 1973, O
DON'T LOOK NOW, 1969, A
DON'T LOOK NOW, 1973, O
DON'T LOSE YOUR HEAD, 1967, C
DON'T MAKE WAVES, 1967, A
DON'T MARRY, 1928, A
DON'T MARRY FOR MONEY, 1923, A
DON'T NEGLECT YOUR WIFE, 1921
DON'T OPEN THE DOOR, 1974
DON'T OPEN THE WINDOW, 1974, O
DON'T OPEN TILL CHRISTMAS, 1984, O
DON'T PANIC CHAPS!, 1959, A
DON'T PLAY US CHEAP, 1973
DON'T PLAY WITH MARTIANS, 1967, A
DON'T RAISE THE BRIDGE, LOWER THE RIVER,
    1968, A
DON'T RUSH ME, 1936, A
DON'T SAY DIE, 1950, A
DON'T SCREAM, DORIS DAYS!
DON'T SHOOT, 1922
DON'T TAKE IT TO HEART, 1944, A
DON'T TALK TO STRANGE MEN, 1962, C
DON'T TELL EVERYTHING, 1921, A
DON'T TELL THE WIFE, 1927
DON'T TELL THE WIFE, 1937, A
DON'T TEMPT THE DEVIL, 1964, A
DON'T TOUCH MY SISTER
DON'T TOUCH THE LOOT
DON'T TOUCH WHITE WOMEN!, 1974, C
DON'T TRUST YOUR HUSBAND, 1948, C
DON'T TURN THE OTHER CHEEK, 1974, C
DON'T TURN'EM LOOSE, 1936, A
DON'T WORRY, WE'LL THINK OF A TITLE, 1966, A
DON'T WRITE LETTERS, 1922
DON'T YOU CRY
DONA FLOR AND HER TWO HUSBANDS, 1977, O
DONATELLA, 1956, A
DONDI, 1961, AAA
DONKEY SKIN, 1975, C-O
DONOVAN AFFAIR, THE, 1929, A
DONOVAN'S BRAIN, 1953, C
DONOVAN'S REEF, 1963, A
DONZOKO
DOOLINS OF OKLAHOMA, THE, 1949, A
DOOMED AT SUNDOWN, 1937, AA
DOOMED BATTALION, THE, 1932, A
DOOMED CARAVAN, 1941
DOOMED CARGO, 1936, A
DOOMED TO DIE, 1940, A
DOOMSDAY, 1928
DOOMSDAY AT ELEVEN, 1963, A-C
DOOMSDAY MACHINE, 1967, A
DOOMSDAY VOYAGE, 1972, O
DOOMWATCH, 1972, C
DOOR BETWEEN, THE, 1917
DOOR THAT HAS NO KEY, THE, 1921
DOOR TO DOOR, 1984, C
DOOR WITH SEVEN LOCKS, THE
DOOR-TO-DOOR MANIAC
DOORSTEPS, 1916, A
DOORWAY TO HELL, 1930, O
DOP DOCTOR, THE
DORA THORNE, 1915
DORIAN GRAY, 1970, O
DORIAN'S DIVORCE, 1916
DORM THAT DRIPPED BLOOD, THE, 1983, O
DORMANT POWER, THE, 1917
DOROTHY VERNON OF HADDON HALL, 1924

DOS COSMONAUTAS A LA FUERZA, 1967, A
DOSS HOUSE, 1933, A-C
DOT AND THE BUNNY, 1983, AA
DOTTED LINE, THE
DOUBLE ACTION DANIELS, 1925
DOUBLE AFFAIR, THE
DOUBLE AGENT 73, 1974
DOUBLE AGENTS, THE
DOUBLE ALIBI, 1940, A
DOUBLE BED, THE, 1965, C
DOUBLE BUNK, 1961, A
DOUBLE CON, THE
DOUBLE CONFESSION, 1953, C
DOUBLE CRIME IN THE MAGINOT LINE, 1939, A
DOUBLE CROSS, 1941, A
DOUBLE CROSS, 1956, A-C
DOUBLE CROSS ROADS, 1930, A
DOUBLE CROSSBONES, 1950, AA
DOUBLE CROSSED, 1917
DOUBLE DANGER, 1938, AA
DOUBLE DARING, 1926
DOUBLE DATE, 1941, AA
DOUBLE DEAL, 1939
DOUBLE DEAL, 1950
DOUBLE DEALING, 1923
DOUBLE DECEPTION, 1963, A-C
DOUBLE DOOR, 1934, C-O
DOUBLE DYNAMITE, 1951, A
DOUBLE EVENT, THE, 1921
DOUBLE EVENT, THE, 1934, A
DOUBLE EXPOSURE, 1944, A
DOUBLE EXPOSURE, 1954, A-C
DOUBLE EXPOSURE, 1982, O
DOUBLE EXPOSURES, 1937, A
DOUBLE FISTED, 1925
DOUBLE HARNESS, 1933, A-C
DOUBLE INDEMNITY, 1944, C
DOUBLE INITIATION, 1970
DOUBLE JEOPARDY, 1955, A
DOUBLE LIFE OF MR. ALFRED BURTON, THE,
    1919, A
DOUBLE LIFE, A, 1947, C-O
DOUBLE MAN, THE, 1967, C
DOUBLE MCGUFFIN, THE, 1979, A
DOUBLE NEGATIVE, 1980, O
DOUBLE NICKELS, 1977, C
DOUBLE O, THE, 1921
DOUBLE OR NOTHING, 1937, A
DOUBLE OR QUITS, 1938, A
DOUBLE SPEED, 1920
DOUBLE STANDARD, THE, 1917
DOUBLE STOP, 1968
DOUBLE SUICIDE, 1970, O
DOUBLE TAKE, 1972
DOUBLE TROUBLE, 1915
DOUBLE TROUBLE, 1941, A
DOUBLE TROUBLE, 1967, A
DOUBLE TROUBLE, 1962
DOUBLE WEDDING, 1937, A
DOUBLE, THE, 1916
DOUBLE, THE, 1963, A
DOUBLE-BARRELED JUSTICE, 1925
DOUBLE-BARRELLED DETECTIVE STORY, THE,
    1965, A
DOUBLE-DYED DECIEVER, A, 1920
DOUBLE-ROOM MYSTERY, THE, 1917
DOUBLES, 1978, C
DOUBLING FOR ROMEO, 1921, A
DOUBLING WITH DANGER, 1926, A
DOUBTING THOMAS, 1935, A
DOUCE
DOUGH BOYS, 1930, AAA
DOUGHBOYS IN IRELAND, 1943, A
DOUGHGIRLS, THE, 1944, A
DOUGHNUTS AND SOCIETY, 1936, A
DOUGLAS FAIRBANKS IN ROBIN HOOD
DOULOS—THE FINGER MAN, 1964, C
DOVE, THE, 1927
DOVE, THE, 1974, AA
DOWN AMONG THE SHELTERING PALMS, 1953, A
DOWN AMONG THE Z MEN, 1952, A
DOWN ARGENTINE WAY, 1940
DOWN BY THE RIO GRANDE, 1924, A
DOWN CHANNEL, 1929
DOWN DAKOTA WAY, 1949
DOWN GRADE, THE, 1927, A
DOWN HOME, 1920
DOWN IN ARKANSAW, 1938, A
DOWN IN SAN DIEGO, 1941, A
DOWN LAREDO WAY, 1953, A
DOWN MEMORY LANE, 1949, A
DOWN MEXICO WAY, 1941, A
DOWN MISSOURI WAY, 1946, A
DOWN ON THE FARM, 1920
DOWN ON THE FARM, 1938, A
DOWN OUR ALLEY, 1939, A
DOWN OUR STREET, 1932, A
DOWN RIO GRANDE WAY, 1942
DOWN RIVER, 1931, A
DOWN TEXAS WAY, 1942, A
DOWN THE ANCIENT STAIRCASE, 1975, O
DOWN THE STRETCH, 1927, A

DOWN THE STRETCH, 1936, A
DOWN THE WYOMING TRAIL, 1939, A
DOWN THREE DARK STREETS, 1954, C
DOWN TO EARTH, 1917, A
DOWN TO EARTH, 1932, A
DOWN TO EARTH, 1947, A
DOWN TO THE SEA, 1936, A
DOWN TO THE SEA, 1975
DOWN TO THE SEA IN SHIPS, 1923, A
DOWN TO THE SEA IN SHIPS, 1949, AAA
DOWN TO THE SEA IN SHIPS, 1937
DOWN TO THEIR LAST YACHT, 1934, A
DOWN UNDER DONOVAN, 1922
DOWN UNDER THE SEA
DOWN UPON THE SUWANNEE RIVER, 1925, A
DOWNFALL, 1964, C
DOWNHILL
DOWNHILL
DOWNHILL RACER, 1969, C
DOWNSTAIRS, 1932, A
DOWNSTREAM, 1929
DOZENS, THE, 1981, C
DR. BLACK AND MR. HYDE, 1976, O
DR. BLOOD'S COFFIN, 1961, O
DR. BROADWAY, 1942, C
DR. BULL, 1933, A
DR. BUTCHER, M.D., 1982, O
DR. CHRISTIAN MEETS THE WOMEN, 1940
DR. COPPELIUS, 1968, AA
DR. CRIPPEN, 1963, C
DR. CYCLOPS, 1940, A
DR. EHRLICH'S MAGIC BULLET, 1940, A
DR. FRANKENSTEIN ON CAMPUS, 1970
DR. GILLESPIE'S CRIMINAL CASE, 1943, A
DR. GILLESPIE'S NEW ASSISTANT, 1942, A
DR. GOLDFOOT AND THE BIKINI MACHINE, 1965, C
DR. GOLDFOOT AND THE GIRL BOMBS, 1966
DR. HECKYL AND MR. HYPE, 1980, O
DR. JEKYLL AND MR. HYDE, 1920, A
DR. JEKYLL AND MR. HYDE, 1932, O
DR. JEKYLL AND MR. HYDE, 1941
DR. JEKYLL AND SISTER HYDE, 1971, A
DR. JEKYLL'S DUNGEON OF DEATH, 1982, O
DR. JIM, 1921, A
DR. JOSSER KC, 1931, A
DR. KILDARE GOES HOME, 1940, A
DR. KILDARE'S CRISIS, 1940, A
DR. KILDARE'S STRANGE CASE, 1940, A
DR. KILDARE'S VICTORY, 1941, A
DR. KILDARE'S WEDDING DAY, 1941, A
DR. KNOCK, 1936, A
DR. MABUSE'S RAYS OF DEATH, 1964, A
DR. MABUSE, DER SPIELER
DR. MABUSE, THE GAMBLER, 1922
DR. MACDONALD'S SANATORIUM, 1920
DR. MINX, 1975, O
DR. MORELLE—THE CASE OF THE MISSING
  HEIRESS, 1949, A
DR. NEIGHBOR, 1916
DR. NO, 1962, C
DR. O'DOWD, 1940, A
DR. POPAUL
DR. RAMEAU, 1915
DR. RENAULT'S SECRET, 1942, C
DR. RHYTHM, 1938, AA
DR. SIN FANG, 1937, A
DR. SOCRATES, 1935, A-C
DR. STRANGELOVE: OR HOW I LEARNED TO STOP
DR. SYN, ALIAS THE SCARECROW, 1975, AA
DR. TARR'S TORTURE DUNGEON, 1972, O
DR. TERROR'S GALLERY OF HORRORS, 1967
DR. TERROR'S HOUSE OF HORRORS, 1965, O
DR. WAKE'S PATIENT, 1916
DR. WHO AND THE DALEKS, 1965, A
DRACULA, 1931, C-O
DRACULA, 1969, O
DRACULA, 1979, C
DRACULA A.D. 1972, 1972, O
DRACULA AND SON, 1976, C
DRACULA AND THE SEVEN GOLDEN VAMPIRES,
  1978, O
DRACULA HAS RISEN FROM HIS GRAVE, 1968, O
DRACULA SUCKS, 1979
DRACULA TODAY
DRACULA VERSUS FRANKENSTEIN, 1972, O
DRACULA'S DAUGHTER, 1936, O
DRACULA'S DOG, 1978, O
DRACULA'S GREAT LOVE, 1972, O
DRACULA, 1958
DRACULA—PRINCE OF DARKNESS, 1966, O
DRAEGERMAN COURAGE, 1937, A
DRAFT 258, 1917
DRAG, 1929, A
DRAG HARLAN, 1920
DRAGNET, 1954, A
DRAGNET, 1974, A
DRAGNET NIGHT, 1931, A
DRAGNET PATROL, 1932, A
DRAGNET, THE, 1928, A
DRAGNET, THE, 1936
DRAGON DIES HARD, THE, 1974
DRAGON FLIES, THE

DRAGON HORSE, THE
DRAGON INN, 1968, C
DRAGON MASTER
DRAGON MURDER CASE, THE, 1934, A
DRAGON OF PENDRAGON CASTLE, THE, 1950
DRAGON PAINTER, THE, 1919
DRAGON SEED, 1944, A
DRAGON SKY, 1964, A
DRAGON WELLS MASSACRE, 1957, A
DRAGON'S GOLD, 1954
DRAGON, THE, 1916
DRAGONFLY SQUADRON, 1953, A
DRAGONFLY, 1976
DRAGONFLY, THE, 1955, A
DRAGONSLAYER, 1981, C-O
DRAGONWYCH, 1946
DRAGSTRIP GIRL, 1957, A
DRAGSTRIP RIOT, 1958, C
DRAKE CASE, THE, 1929, A
DRAKE THE PIRATE, 1935, A
DRAMA OF JEALOUSY
DRAMA OF THE RICH, 1975, A-C
DRAMATIC LIFE OF ABRAHAM LINCOLN, THE
DRAMATIC SCHOOL, 1938, A-C
DRANGO, 1957, A
DRAUGHTSMAN'S CONTRACT, THE, 1983, O
DREADING LIPS, 1958, C
DREAM CHEATER, THE, 1920
DREAM COME TRUE, A, 1963, A
DREAM DOLL, THE, 1917
DREAM GIRL, 1947, A
DREAM GIRL, THE, 1916
DREAM LADY, THE, 1918
DREAM MAKER, THE, 1963, A
DREAM MELODY, THE, 1929, A
DREAM NO EVIL, 1984
DREAM NO MORE, 1950, A
DREAM OF A COSSACK, 1982, A
DREAM OF BUTTERFLY, THE, 1941
DREAM OF KINGS, A, 1969, C
DREAM OF LOVE, 1928
DREAM OF PASSION, A, 1978, C
DREAM OF SCHONBRUNN, 1933, A
DREAM OF THE RED CHAMBER, THE, 1966, A
DREAM ON, 1981, O
DREAM ONE, 1984, O
DREAM OR TWO AGO, A, 1916
DREAM STREET, 1921, A
DREAM TOWN, 1973, C
DREAM WIFE, 1953, A
DREAM WOMAN, THE, 1914
DREAMBOAT, 1952, AA
DREAMER, 1979, A
DREAMER, THE, 1936, A
DREAMER, THE, 1947
DREAMER, THE, 1970, O
DREAMING, 1944, A
DREAMING LIPS, 1937, C
DREAMING OUT LOUD, 1940, A
DREAMS, 1960, C
DREAMS COME TRUE, 1936, A
DREAMS IN A DRAWER, 1957, A
DREAMS OF GLASS, 1969, C
DREAMS OF YOUTH, 1923
DREAMS OF YOUTH, 1928
DREAMS THAT MONEY CAN BUY, 1948, C
DREAMSCAPE, 1984, C-O
DREAMWORLD
DREARY HOUSE, 1928
DREI VON DER TANKSTELLE
DRESS PARADE, 1927, A
DRESSED TO KILL, 1941, A
DRESSED TO KILL, 1946, A
DRESSED TO KILL, 1928
DRESSED TO KILL, 1980, O
DRESSED TO THRILL, 1935, A
DRESSER, THE, 1983, C
DRESSMAKER FROM PARIS, THE, 1925
DREYFUS CASE, THE, 1931, A
DREYFUS CASE, THE, 1940, A
DRIFT FENCE, 1936
DRIFTER, 1975
DRIFTER, THE, 1916, A
DRIFTER, THE, 1929
DRIFTER, THE, 1932
DRIFTER, THE, 1944, A
DRIFTER, THE, 1966, C
DRIFTERS, THE
DRIFTERS, THE, 1919
DRIFTIN' KID, THE, 1941, A
DRIFTIN' RIVER, 1946, A
DRIFTIN' SANDS, 1928, A
DRIFTIN' THRU, 1926
DRIFTING, 1923
DRIFTING, 1932, A
DRIFTING, 1984, O
DRIFTING ALONG, 1946, A
DRIFTING KID, THE, 1928
DRIFTING ON, 1927
DRIFTING SOULS, 1932
DRIFTING WEEDS
DRIFTING WESTWARD, 1939

DRIFTWOOD, 1916
DRIFTWOOD, 1924
DRIFTWOOD, 1928
DRIFTWOOD, 1947, A
DRILLER KILLER, 1979, O
DRINK, 1917
DRIVE A CROOKED ROAD, 1954, C
DRIVE, HE SAID, 1971, O
DRIVE-IN, 1976, O
DRIVE-IN MASSACRE, 1976, O
DRIVEN
DRIVEN, 1923
DRIVEN FROM HOME, 1927, A
DRIVER'S SEAT, THE, 1975, O
DRIVER, THE, 1978, O
DRIVERS TO HELL
DRIVIN' FOOL, THE, 1923
DROLE DE DRADE
DROP DEAD, DARLING
DROP DEAD, MY LOVE, 1968, C
DROP THEM OR I'LL SHOOT, 1969, O
DROPKICK, THE, 1927, A
DROWNING POOL, THE, 1975, C
DRUG MONSTER, THE, 1923
DRUG STORE COWBOY, 1925
DRUG TRAFFIC, THE, 1923, A
DRUGGED WATERS, 1916
DRUM, 1976, O
DRUM BEAT, 1954, A
DRUM TAPS, 1933, A
DRUMMER OF VENGEANCE, 1974, O
DRUMS, 1938, A
DRUMS ACROSS THE RIVER, 1954, A
DRUMS ALONG THE MOHAWK, 1939, AAA
DRUMS IN THE DEEP SOUTH, 1951, A
DRUMS O' VOODOO, 1934
DRUMS OF AFRICA, 1963, A
DRUMS OF DESTINY, 1937, A
DRUMS OF FATE, 1923
DRUMS OF FU MANCHU, 1943, A
DRUMS OF JEOPARDY, 1931, A
DRUMS OF JEOPARDY, THE, 1923
DRUMS OF LOVE, 1928
DRUMS OF TABU, THE, 1967, A
DRUMS OF TAHITI, 1954, A
DRUMS OF THE CONGO, 1942, A
DRUMS OF THE DESERT, 1927
DRUMS OF THE DESERT, 1940, A
DRUNKEN ANGEL, 1948, C
DRUNKENNESS AND ITS CONSEQUENCES, 1913
DRUSILLA WITH A MILLION, 1925
DRY BIKINI, THE
DRY MARTINI, 1928
DRY ROT, 1956
DRY SUMMER, 1967, A
DRY VALLEY JOHNSON, 1917
DRYLANDERS, 1963, A
DU BARRY WAS A LADY, 1943, A
DU BARRY, WOMAN OF PASSION, 1930, A-C
DU RIRE AUX LARMES, 1917
DU SOLLIST NICHT EHEBRECHEN
DUAL ALIBI, 1947
DUB, THE, 1919
DUBARRY, 1915
DUBEAT-E-O, 1984, O
DUBLIN NIGHTMARE, 1958, A-C
DUCH IN ORANGE SAUCE, 1976, C
DUCHESS AND THE DIRTWATER FOX, THE, 1976, C
DUCHESS OF BUFFALO, THE, 1926
DUCHESS OF DOUBT, THE, 1917
DUCHESS OF IDAHO, THE, 1950
DUCHESS OF SEVEN DIALS, THE, 1920
DUCK RINGS AT HALF PAST SEVEN, THE, 1969, O
DUCK SOUP, 1933, AA
DUCK, YOU SUCKER!, 1972, C
DUCKS AND DRAKES, 1921, A
DUDE BANDIT, THE, 1933, A
DUDE COWBOY, 1941, A
DUDE COWBOY, THE, 1926, A
DUDE GOES WEST, THE, 1948, A
DUDE RANCH, 1931, A
DUDE RANGER, THE, 1934, A
DUDE WRANGLER, THE, 1930
DUDES ARE PRETTY PEOPLE, 1942, A
DUDS, 1920
DUE SOLDI DI SPERANZA
DUEL, 1928
DUEL AT APACHE WELLS, 1957, A
DUEL AT DIABLO, 1966, A
DUEL AT EZO, 1970, C
DUEL AT SILVER CREEK, THE, 1952, A
DUEL IN DURANGO
DUEL IN THE JUNGLE, 1954, A
DUEL IN THE SUN, 1946, C-O
DUEL OF CHAMPIONS, 1964, A
DUEL OF THE TITANS, 1963, A
DUEL ON THE MISSISSIPPI, 1955, A
DUEL WITHOUT HONOR, 1953, A
DUEL, THE, 1964, A
DUELLISTS, THE, 1977, O
DUET FOR CANNIBALS, 1969, O
DUET FOR FOUR, 1982, C

DUFFY, 1968, C
DUFFY OF SAN QUENTIN, 1954, A
DUFFY'S TAVERN, 1945, A
DUGAN OF THE BAD LANDS, 1931, A
DUGAN OF THE DUGOUTS, 1928
DUGI BRODOVI
DUKE COMES BACK, THE, 1937, A
DUKE IS THE TOPS, THE, 1938, A
DUKE OF CHICAGO, 1949, A
DUKE OF CHIMNEY BUTTE, THE, 1921
DUKE OF THE NAVY, 1942, A
DUKE OF WEST POINT, THE, 1938, A
DUKE STEPS OUT, THE, 1929, A
DUKE WORE JEANS, THE, 1958, A
DUKE'S SON
DULCIE'S ADVENTURE, 1916
DULCIMA, 1971, A
DULCIMER STREET, 1948, A
DULCINEA, 1962, C
DULCY, 1923, A
DULCY, 1940, A
DUMB GIRL OF PORTICI, 1916, A
DUMBBELLS IN ERMINE, 1930, A
DUMBO, 1941, AAA
DUMMY TALKS, THE, 1943, A
DUMMY, THE, 1917
DUMMY, THE, 1929, A-C
DUNCAN'S WORLD, 1977
DUNE, 1984, C-O
DUNGEON OF DEATH, THE, 1915
DUNGEON, THE, 1922
DUNGEONS OF HARROW, 1964, O
DUNKIRK, 1958, A
DUNWICH HORROR, THE, 1970, C
DUPE, THE, 1916, A
DUPED, 1925
DUPLICITY OF HARGRAVES, THE, 1917
DURAND OF THE BAD LANDS, 1917
DURAND OF THE BAD LANDS, 1925
DURANGO KID, THE, 1940, A
DURANGO VALLEY RAIDERS, 1938, A
DURANT AFFAIR, THE, 1962
DURING ONE NIGHT, 1962, C
DUSK TO DAWN, 1922
DUST, 1916
DUST BE MY DESTINY, 1939, A
DUST FLOWER, THE, 1922, A
DUST OF DESIRE, 1919, A
DUST OF EGYPT, THE, 1915
DUSTY AND SWEETS McGEE, 1971, O
DUSTY ERMINE
DUTCHMAN, 1966, C
DUTY FIRST, 1922
DUTY'S REWARD, 1927
DWELLING PLACE OF LIGHT, THE, 1920
DYBBUK THE, 1938
DYNAMITE, 1930, A
DYNAMITE, 1948, A
DYNAMITE, 1972
DYNAMITE ALLEN, 1921
DYNAMITE BROTHERS, THE, 1974
DYNAMITE CANYON, 1941, A
DYNAMITE DAN, 1924, A
DYNAMITE DELANEY, 1938
DYNAMITE DENNY, 1932, A
DYNAMITE JACK, 1961, A
DYNAMITE JOHNSON, 1978, A
DYNAMITE PASS, 1950, A
DYNAMITE RANCH, 1932
DYNAMITE SMITH, 1924
DYNAMITERS, THE, 1956, A

-E-

E.T. THE EXTRA-TERRESTRIAL, 1982, AAA
EACH DAWN I DIE, 1939, A
EACH MAN FOR HIMSELF
EACH PEARL A TEAR, 1916, A
EACH TO HIS KIND, 1917, A
EADIE WAS A LADY, 1945, A
EAGER BEAVERS
EAGER LIPS, 1927, A
EAGLE AND THE HAWK, THE, 1933, C
EAGLE AND THE HAWK, THE, 1950, A
EAGLE HAS LANDED, THE, 1976
EAGLE IN A CAGE, 1971, A
EAGLE OF THE SEA, THE, 1926
EAGLE OVER LONDON, 1973, C
EAGLE ROCK, 1964, A
EAGLE SQUADRON, 1942, A
EAGLE WITH TWO HEADS, 1948, A
EAGLE'S BROOD, THE, 1936, A
EAGLE'S CLAW, THE, 1924, A
EAGLE'S FEATHER, THE, 1923, A
EAGLE'S MATE, THE, 1914, A
EAGLE'S NEST, 1915
EAGLE'S WING, 1979, A
EAGLE'S WINGS, THE, 1916
EAGLE, THE, 1918, A
EAGLE, THE, 1925, A
EARL CARROLL SKETCHBOOK, 1946, A
EARL CARROLL'S VANITIES, 1945, A
EARL OF CHICAGO, THE, 1940, A

EARL OF PAWTUCKET, THE, 1915, A
EARL OF PUDDLESTONE, 1940, A
EARLY AUTUMN, 1962, C
EARLY BIRD, THE, 1925, A
EARLY BIRD, THE, 1936, A
EARLY BIRD, THE, 1965, A
EARLY BIRDS, 1923
EARLY TO BED, 1933, A
EARLY TO BED, 1936, A
EARLY TO WED, 1926, A
EARLY WORKS, 1970, O
EARRINGS OF MADAME DE..., THE, 1954, C-O
EARTH, 1930, A
EARTH CRIES OUT, THE, 1949, A
EARTH DIES SCREAMING, THE, 1964, A
EARTH ENTRANCED, 1970, C
EARTH VS. THE FLYING SAUCERS, 1956
EARTH VS. THE SPIDER, 1958, A
EARTH WOMAN, THE, 1926
EARTHBOUND, 1920
EARTHBOUND, 1940, A
EARTHBOUND, 1981, C
EARTHLING, THE, 1980, C
EARTHQUAKE, 1974, A
EARTHQUAKE MOTOR, THE, 1917
EARTHWORM TRACTORS, 1936
EASIEST WAY, THE, 1917
EASIEST WAY, THE, 1931, C
EAST CHINA SEA, 1969, C
EAST END CHANT
EAST IS EAST, 1916, A
EAST IS WEST, 1922, A
EAST IS WEST, 1930, C
EAST LYNNE, 1913, A
EAST LYNNE, 1916, A
EAST LYNNE, 1921
EAST LYNNE, 1925
EAST LYNNE, 1931, A
EAST LYNNE ON THE WESTERN FRONT, 1931, A
EAST MEETS WEST, 1936, A
EAST OF BORNEO, 1931, A
EAST OF BROADWAY, 1924, A
EAST OF EDEN, 1955, C-O
EAST OF ELEPHANT ROCK, 1976, O
EAST OF FIFTH AVE., 1933, C
EAST OF JAVA, 1935, A
EAST OF KILIMANJARO, 1962
EAST OF PICADILLY
EAST OF SHANGHAI
EAST OF SUDAN, 1964, A
EAST OF SUEZ, 1925, C
EAST OF SUMATRA, 1953, A
EAST OF THE RIVER, 1940, A
EAST SIDE KIDS, 1940, A
EAST SIDE KIDS MEET BELA LUGOSI, THE
EAST SIDE OF HEAVEN, 1939, A
EAST SIDE SADIE, 1929, A
EAST SIDE, WEST SIDE, 1927
EAST SIDE, WEST SIDE, 1949, A-C
EAST SIDE—WEST SIDE, 1923, C
EASTER SUNDAY
EASTER PARADE, 1948, AAA
EASTWARD HO, 1919
EASY COME, EASY GO, 1928, A
EASY COME, EASY GO, 1947, A
EASY COME, EASY GO, 1967, A
EASY GO
EASY GOING, 1926
EASY GOING GORDON, 1925, A
EASY LIFE, THE, 1963, C
EASY LIFE, THE, 1971, C
EASY LIVING, 1937, A
EASY LIVING, 1949, A
EASY MILLIONS, 1933, A
EASY MONEY, 1917
EASY MONEY, 1922
EASY MONEY, 1925, A
EASY MONEY, 1934
EASY MONEY, 1936, A
EASY MONEY, 1948, A
EASY MONEY, 1983, C-O
EASY PICKINGS, 1927, A
EASY RICHES, 1938, A
EASY RIDER, 1969, O
EASY ROAD, THE, 1921, A
EASY STREET, 1930
EASY TO GET, 1920, A
EASY TO LOOK AT, 1945, A
EASY TO LOVE, 1934, A
EASY TO LOVE, 1953, A
EASY TO MAKE MONEY, 1919, A
EASY TO TAKE, 1936, A
EASY TO WED, 1946, A
EASY VIRTUE, 1927, A
EASY WAY
EAT MY DUST!, 1976, A
EATEN ALIVE, 1976, O
EATING RAOUL, 1982, O
EAVESDROPPER, THE, 1966, C
EBB TIDE, 1922, A
EBB TIDE, 1932, A
EBB TIDE, 1937, A

EBIRAH, HORROR OF THE DEEP
EBOLI, 1980, A
EBONY, IVORY AND JADE, 1977
ECHO MURDERS, THE, 1945, A
ECHO OF A DREAM, 1930, A-C
ECHO OF BARBARA, 1961, C
ECHO OF DIANA, 1963, A-C
ECHO OF YOUTH, THE, 1919
ECHO, THE, 1964, C
ECHOES, 1983, O
ECHOES OF A SUMMER, 1976, A
ECHOES OF SILENCE, 1966, C
ECLIPSE, 1962, C
ECSTACY OF YOUNG LOVE, 1936
ECSTASY, 1940, O
ED HILLS, THE, 1956, A
EDDIE AND THE CRUISERS, 1983, C
EDDIE CANTOR STORY, THE, 1953, AA
EDDIE MACON'S RUN, 1983, A-C
EDDY DUCHIN STORY, THE, 1956, A
EDEN AND RETURN, 1921
EDEN CRIED, 1967, A
EDGAR ALLAN POE'S CASTLE OF BLOOD
EDGAR ALLAN POE'S CONQUEROR WORM
EDGAR ALLAN POE'S "THE OBLONG BOX"
EDGE O'BEYOND, 1919, A
EDGE OF DARKNESS, 1943, A
EDGE OF DIVORCE
EDGE OF DOOM, 1950, C
EDGE OF ETERNITY, 1959, A
EDGE OF FURY, 1958, O
EDGE OF HELL, 1956, A
EDGE OF THE ABYSS, THE, 1915, A
EDGE OF THE CITY, 1957, A
EDGE OF THE LAW, 1917
EDGE OF THE WORLD, THE, 1937, A
EDGE OF YOUTH, THE, 1920
EDGE, THE, 1968, C
EDISON, THE MAN, 1940, AAA
EDITH AND MARCEL, 1984, A
EDMUND KEAN—PRINCE AMONG LOVERS
EDUCATED EVANS, 1936, A
EDUCATING FATHER, 1936, A
EDUCATING RITA, 1983, A
EDUCATION DE PRINCE, 1927
EDUCATION OF ELIZABETH, THE, 1921, A
EDUCATION OF NICKY, THE, 1921, A
EDUCATION OF SONNY CARSON, THE, 1974
EDVARD MUNCH, 1976, C
EDWARD AND CAROLINE, 1952
EDWARD, MY SON, 1949, C
EEGAH!, 1962, C
EERIE WORLD OF DR. JORDAN. THE
EFFECT OF GAMMA RAYS ON MAN-IN-THE-
EFFECTS, 1980, O
EFFI BRIEST, 1974, O
EFFICIENCY EDGAR'S COURTSHIP, 1917, A
EGG AND I, THE, 1947, AAA
EGG CRATE WALLOP, THE, 1919
EGGHEAD'S ROBOT, 1970, A
EGLANTINE, 1972, A
EGON SCHIELE—EXCESS AND PUNISHMENT,
  1981, O
EGYPT BY THREE, 1953
EGYPTIAN. THE, 1954, A-C
EIGER SANCTION, THE, 1975, C
EIGHT ARMS TO HOLD YOU
EIGHT BELLS, 1916
EIGHT BELLS, 1935, A
EIGHT GIRLS IN A BOAT, 1932, A
EIGHT GIRLS IN A BOAT, 1934, C
EIGHT IRON MEN, 1952
EIGHT O'CLOCK WALK, 1954, A
EIGHT ON THE LAM, 1967, A
18 MINUTES, 1935
1812, 1912
1812, 1944, A
EIGHTEEN AND ANXIOUS, 1957, C
EIGHTEEN IN THE SUN, 1964, C
80 STEPS TO JONAH, 1969, A
80,000 SUSPECTS, 1963, C
EIGHTH DAY OF THE WEEK, THE, 1959, C-O
EILEEN OF THE TREES
EINE DU BARRY VON HEUTE
EINE LIEBE IN DEUTSCHLAND
EL, 1955, C-O
EL ALAMEIN, 1954, A-C
EL BRUTO
EL CID, 1961
EL CONDOR, 1970, O
EL DIABLO RIDES, 1939, A
EL DORADO, 1967, A-C
EL DORADO PASS, 1949, A
EL GRECO, 1966, A
EL NORTE, 1984, O
EL PASO, 1949, A
EL PASO KID, THE, 1946, A
EL PASO STAMPEDE, 1953, A
EL RELICARIO, 1926
EL SUPER, 1979
EL TOPO, 1971, O
ELDER BROTHER, THE, 1937, A

ELDER MISS BLOSSOM, THE
ELDER VASILI GRYAZNOV, 1924
ELDORADO, 1921
ELECTRA, 1962, A
ELECTRA GLIDE IN BLUE, 1973, C
ELECTRIC BOOGALOO: BREAKIN' 2
ELECTRIC CHAIR, THE, 1977
ELECTRIC DREAMS, 1984, A-C
ELECTRIC HORSEMAN, THE, 1979, A-C
ELECTRONIC MONSTER. THE, 1960, C
ELEMENT OF CRIME, THE, 1984, O
ELEPHANT BOY, 1937, AA
ELEPHANT CALLED SLOWLY, AN, 1970, A
ELEPHANT GUN, 1959, A
ELEPHANT MAN, THE, 1980, A-C
ELEPHANT STAMPEDE, 1951, A
ELEPHANT WALK, 1954, A
ELEVENTH COMMANDMENT, 1933, A
ELEVENTH COMMANDMENT, THE, 1924, A
ELEVENTH HOUR, THE, 1922, A
ELEVENTH HOUR, THE, 1923, A
ELEVENTH bEARb THE, 1928
ELI ELI, 1940, A
ELIANE, 1919
ELIMINATOR, THE
ELIMINATOR, THE, 1982
ELINOR NORTON, 1935, A
ELISABETH OF AUSTRIA, 1931, A
ELISABETH REIGNE D'ANGLETERRE
ELISO, 1928
ELIZA COMES TO STAY, 1936, A
ELIZA FRASER, 1976, C
ELIZA'S HOROSCOPE, 1975, O
ELIZABETH OF ENGLAND
ELIZABETH OF LADYMEAD, 1949, A
ELIZABETH THE QUEEN
ELLA CINDERS, 1926, A
ELLERY QUEEN AND THE MURDER RING, 1941, A
ELLERY QUEEN AND THE PERFECT CRIME, 1941, A
ELLERY QUEEN'S PENTHOUSE MYSTERY, 1941, A
ELLERY QUEEN. MASTER DETECTIVE, 1940, A
ELLIE, 1984, O
ELLIS ISLAND, 1936
ELMER, 1977
ELMER AND ELSIE, 1934, A
ELMER GANTRY, 1960, C
ELMER THE GREAT, 1933
ELOPE IF YOU MUST, 1922, A
ELOPEMENT, 1951, A
ELUSIVE CORPORAL, THE, 1963, A
ELUSIVE ISABEL, 1916, A
ELUSIVE PIMPERNEL, THE
ELUSIVE PIMPERNEL, THE, 1919, A
ELVIRA MADIGAN, 1967, O
ELVIS! ELVIS!, 1977, A
ELYSIA, 1933
EMBALMER, THE, 1966, C
EMBARRASSING MOMENTS, 1930, A
EMBARRASSING MOMENTS, 1934, A
EMBARRASSMENT OF RICHES, THE, 1918, A
EMBASSY, 1972, C
EMBERS, 1916
EMBEZZLED HEAVEN, 1959, A
EMBEZZLER, THE, 1954, A
EMBLEMS OF LOVE, 1924
EMBODIED THOUGHT, THE, 1916
EMBRACEABLE YOU, 1948, A
EMBRACERS, THE, 1966, C
EMBRYO, 1976, C
EMERALD OF THE EAST, 1928, A
EMERGENCY, 1962, A
EMERGENCY CALL, 1933, A
EMERGENCY CALL, 1953
EMERGENCY HOSPITAL, 1956, A
EMERGENCY LANDING, 1941, A
EMERGENCY SQUAD, 1940, A
EMERGENCY WARD
EMERGENCY WEDDING, 1950
EMERGENCY! 1953
EMIGRANTS, THE, 1972, A
EMIL, 1938, AA
EMIL AND THE DETECTIVE, 1931, AA
EMIL AND THE DETECTIVES, 1964, AA
EMILY
EMILY, 1976, O
EMMA, 1932, A
EMMA MAE, 1976, O
EMPEROR AND A GENERAL, THE, 1968, O
EMPEROR AND THE GOLEM, THE, 1955, A
EMPEROR AND THE NIGHTINGALE, THE, 1949
EMPEROR JONES, THE, 1933, C
EMPEROR OF PERU
EMPEROR OF THE NORTH POLE, 1973, C
EMPEROR WALTZ, THE, 1948, AA
EMPEROR'S CANDLESTICKS, THE, 1937, A
EMPIRE BUILDERS, 1924
EMPIRE OF DIAMONDS, THE, 1920
EMPIRE OF NIGHT, THE, 1963, C
EMPIRE OF THE ANTS, 1977, C
EMPIRE STRIKES BACK, THE, 1980, A
EMPLOYEE'S ENTRANCE, 1933, A
EMPRESS AND I, THE, 1933, A

EMPRESS WU, 1965, A
EMPRESS, THE, 1917
EMPTY ARMS, 1920
EMPTY CAB, THE, 1918
EMPTY CANVAS, THE, 1964, O
EMPTY CRADLE, THE, 1923
EMPTY HANDS, 1924, A
EMPTY HEARTS, 1924
EMPTY HOLSTERS, 1937
EMPTY POCKETS, 1918
EMPTY SADDLE, THE, 1925
EMPTY SADDLES, 1937, A
EMPTY STAR, THE, 1962, A
EN PLONGEE, 1927
EN RADE, 1927
EN RAEDSOM NAT, 1914
ENCHANTED APRIL, 1935, A
ENCHANTED BARN, THE, 1919
ENCHANTED COTTAGE, THE, 1924, A
ENCHANTED COTTAGE, THE, 1945, A
ENCHANTED FOREST, THE, 1945, AAA
ENCHANTED HILL, THE, 1926, A
ENCHANTED ISLAND, 1958, A
ENCHANTED ISLAND, THE, 1927, A
ENCHANTED VALLEY, THE, 1948, A
ENCHANTING SHADOW, THE, 1965, A
ENCHANTMENT, 1917
ENCHANTMENT, 1921, A
ENCHANTMENT, 1948, A
ENCORE, 1951, A
ENCOUNTER WITH THE UNKNOWN, 1973, C
ENCOUNTERS IN SALZBURG, 1964, C
ENCOUNTERS OF THE DEEP, 1984
END OF A DAY, THE, 1939, A
END OF A PRIEST, 1970, C
END OF AUGUST, 1974
END OF AUGUST AT THE HOTEL OZONE, THE, 1967, C
END OF AUGUST, THE, 1982, C-O
END OF BELLE, THE
END OF DESIRE, 1962, A
END OF INNOCENCE, 1960, O
END OF MRS. CHENEY, 1963, A
END OF ST. PETERSBURG, THE, 1927
END OF SUMMER, THE
END OF THE AFFAIR, THE, 1955, A
END OF THE GAME, 1976, C-O
END OF THE GAME, THE, 1919, A
END OF THE LINE, THE, 1959, A-C
END OF THE RAINBOW, THE, 1916
END OF THE RIVER, THE, 1947, A
END OF THE ROAD, 1944, A
END OF THE ROAD, THE, 1915
END OF THE ROAD, THE, 1923
END OF THE ROAD, THE, 1936, A
END OF THE ROAD, THE, 1954, A
END OF THE ROPE, 1923
END OF THE TOUR, THE, 1917
END OF THE TRAIL, 1932, A
END OF THE TRAIL, 1936, A
END OF THE TRAIL, THE, 1916, A
END OF THE WORLD, 1977, C
END OF THE WORLD, 1978, C
END OF THE WORLD, THE, 1930, A
END OF THE WORLD, THE, 1962
END PLAY, 1975, C
END, THE, 1978, O
ENDANGERED SPECIES, 1982, O
ENDGAME, 1984
ENDLESS LOVE, 1981, O
ENDLESS NIGHT, 1971, C
ENDLESS NIGHT, THE, 1963, C
ENDSTATION 13 SAHARA
ENEMIES OF CHILDREN, 1923, A
ENEMIES OF PROGRESS, 1934, A
ENEMIES OF THE LAW, 1931, A
ENEMIES OF WOMEN, THE, 1923, A
ENEMIES OF YOUTH, 1925, A
ENEMY AGENT, 1940
ENEMY AGENTS MEET ELLERY QUEEN, 1942, A
ENEMY BELOW, THE, 1957, A
ENEMY FROM SPACE, 1957, A
ENEMY GENERAL, THE, 1960, A
ENEMY OF MEN, AN, 1925, A
ENEMY OF THE LAW, 1945, A
ENEMY OF THE PEOPLE, AN, 1978, A
ENEMY OF THE POLICE, 1933, A
ENEMY OF WOMEN, 1944, C
ENEMY SEX, THE, 1924, A
ENEMY TO SOCIETY, AN, 1915
ENEMY TO THE KING, AN, 1916
ENEMY, THE
ENEMY, THE, 1916
ENEMY, THE, 1927, C
ENEMY, THE SEA, THE
ENERGETIC EVA, 1916
ENFORCER FROM DEATH ROW, THE, 1978
ENFORCER, THE, 1951, C
ENFORCER, THE, 1976, O
ENGAGEMENT ITALIANO, 1966
ENGINEER PRITE'S PROJECT, 1918
ENGLANO MADE ME, 1973, C

ENGLISH WITHOUT TEARS
ENGLISHMAN'S HOME, AN
ENGLISHMAN'S HONOUR, AN, 1915
ENIGMA, 1983, C
ENJO, 1959, O
ENLIGHTEN THY DAUGHTER, 1917
ENLIGHTEN THY DAUGHTER, 1934, A
ENOCH ARDEN, 1914
ENOCH ARDEN, 1915
ENOUGH ROPE, 1966
ENSIGN PULVER, 1964, A
ENTENTE CORDIALE, 1939, A
ENTER ARSENE LUPIN, 1944, A
ENTER INSPECTOR DUVAL, 1961
ENTER LAUGHING, 1967, A
ENTER MADAME, 1922, A
ENTER MADAME, 1935, A
ENTER THE DEVIL, 1975
ENTER THE DRAGON, 1973, O
ENTER THE NINJA, 1982, O
ENTERTAINER, THE, 1960, A
ENTERTAINER, THE, 1975, A-C
ENTERTAINING MR. SLOANE, 1970, O
ENTICEMENT, 1925
ENTITY, THE, 1982, O
ENTRE NOUS, 1983, C
ENVIRONMENT, 1917
ENVIRONMENT, 1922, A
ENVOY EXTRAORDINARY, THE, 1914
ENVY, 1917, A
EPILOGUE, 1967, A
EPISODE, 1937, A
EQUINOX, 1970, C-O
"E QUUS", 1977, O
ER LOVE A STRANGER, 1958, A
ER WAVE AT A WAC, 1952, A
ERASERHEAD, 1978, O
ERASMUS WITH FRECKLES
ERENDIRA, 1984, O
ERIC SOYA'S "17", 1967, O
ERIK THE CONQUEROR, 1963, C
ERMINE AND RHINESTONES, 1925
ERNEST HEMINGWAY'S ADVENTURES OF A YOUNG MAN
ERNEST HEMINGWAY'S THE KILLERS, 1964
ERNEST MALTRAVERS, 1920
ERNEST MALTRAVERS, 1920, A
ERNESTO, 1979, O
EROICA, 1966, C
EROTIKON, 1920
EROTIKON, 1929
EROTIQUE, 1969, C
ERRAND BOY, THE, 1961, A
ERSTWHILE SUSAN, 1919, A
ESCAPADE, 1932, A
ESCAPADE, 1935, A
ESCAPADE, 1955, A
ESCAPADE IN JAPAN, 1957, A
ESCAPE, 1930, A
ESCAPE, 1940, A
ESCAPE, 1948, A
ESCAPE 2000, 1983, 0
ESCAPE ARTIST, THE, 1982, C
ESCAPE BY NIGHT, 1937, A
ESCAPE BY NIGHT, 1954, A-C
ESCAPE BY NIGHT, 1965, C
ESCAPE DANGEROUS, 1947, A
ESCAPE FROM ALCATRAZ, 1979, C
ESCAPE FROM ANGOLA, 1976
ESCAPE FROM CRIME, 1942, A
ESCAPE FROM DEVIL'S ISLAND, 1935, A
ESCAPE FROM EAST BERLIN, 1962, A
ESCAPE FROM EL DIABLO, 1983
ESCAPE FROM FORT BRAVO, 1953, A
ESCAPE FROM HELL ISLAND
ESCAPE FROM HONG KONG, 1942, A
ESCAPE FROM NEW YORK, 1981, O
ESCAPE FROM RED ROCK, 1958, A
ESCAPE FROM SAN QUENTIN, 1957, A
ESCAPE FROM SEGOVIA, 1984, C
ESCAPE FROM TERROR, 1960, A
ESCAPE FROM THE DARK
ESCAPE FROM THE PLANET OF THE APES, 1971, C
ESCAPE FROM THE SEA, 1968, AA
ESCAPE FROM YESTERDAY, 1939, A
ESCAPE FROM ZAHRAIN, 1962, A
ESCAPE IN THE DESERT, 1945, A
ESCAPE IN THE FOG, 1945, A
ESCAPE IN THE SUN, 1956, A
ESCAPE LIBRE
ESCAPE ME NEVER, 1935, A
ESCAPE ME NEVER, 1947, A
ESCAPE ROUTE
ESCAPE TO ATHENA, 1979, C
ESCAPE TO BERLIN, 1962, A
ESCAPE TO BURMA, 1955, A
ESCAPE TO DANGER, 1943, A
ESCAPE TO GLORY, 1940, A
ESCAPE TO PARADISE, 1939, A
ESCAPE TO THE SUN, 1972, C
ESCAPE TO WITCH MOUNTAIN, 1975, AA
ESCAPE 2000, 1983, O

ESCAPE, THE, 1914, C
ESCAPE, THE, 1926
ESCAPE, THE, 1928, A
ESCAPE, THE, 1939, A
ESCAPED CONVICT, THE, 1927
ESCAPED FROM DARTMOOR, 1930, C
ESCORT FOR HIRE, 1960, A-C
ESCORT WEST, 1959, A
ESMERALDA, 1915, A
ESPIONAGE, 1937, A
ESPIONAGE AGENT, 1939, A
ESSANAY-CHAPLIN REVUE OF 1916, THE, 1916
ESSENTIAL SPARK OF JEWISHNESS, THE, 1912
ESTHER AND THE KING, 1960, A
ESTHER REDEEMED, 1915
ESTHER WATERS, 1948, C
ETERNAL CITY, THE, 1915, A
ETERNAL CITY, THE, 1923
ETERNAL FEMININE, THE, 1931
ETERNAL FLAME, THE, 1922
ETERNAL GRIND, THE, 1916, A
ETERNAL HUSBAND, THE, 1946, C
ETERNAL LIGHT, THE, 1919
ETERNAL LOVE, 1917, A
ETERNAL LOVE, 1929, A
ETERNAL LOVE, 1960, A
ETERNAL MAGDALENE, THE, 1919, A
ETERNAL MASK, THE, 1937, A-C
ETERNAL MELODIES, 1948, A
ETERNAL MOTHER, THE, 1917
ETERNAL MOTHER, THE, 1921
ETERNAL PEACE, 1922
ETERNAL QUESTION, THE, 1916
ETERNAL RETURN, THE, 1943, A
ETERNAL SAPHO, THE, 1916, A
ETERNAL SEA, THE, 1955, A
ETERNAL SIN, THE, 1917, C
ETERNAL STRUGGLE, THE, 1923, A
ETERNAL SUMMER, 1961, A
ETERNAL TEMPTRESS, THE, 1917, A
ETERNAL THREE, THE, 1923, A
ETERNAL TRIANGLE, THE, 1917
ETERNAL WALTZ, THE, 1959, A
ETERNAL WOMAN, THE, 1929, A
ETERNALLY YOURS, 1939, A
ETERNITY OF LOVE, 1961, C
ETHAN, 1971
ETRE AIME POUR SOI-MEME, 1920
ETRE OU NE PAS ETRE, 1922
EUGENE ARAM, 1914, A
EUGENE ARAM, 1915, A
EUGENE ARAM, 1924
EUNION, 1936, A
EUREKA, 1983, O
EUREKA STOCKADE
EUROPE 51
EUROPEANS, THE, 1979, A
EVA, 1918
EVA, 1962, O
EVANGELINE, 1914
EVANGELINE, 1919
EVANGELINE, 1929, A
EVANGELINE, 1929, A
EVANGELIST, THE, 1915
EVE, 1968, A
EVE IN EXILE, 1919
EVE KNEW HER APPLES, 1945, A
EVE OF ST. MARK, THE, 1944, A-C
EVE WANTS TO SLEEP, 1961, A
EVE'S DAUGHTER, 1918, A
EVE'S DAUGHTER, 1916, Brit.
EVE'S LEAVES, 1926
EVE'S LOVER, 1925, A
EVE'S SECRET, 1925, A
EVEL KNIEVEL, 1971
EVELYN PRENTICE, 1934, C
EVEN AS EVE, 1920
EVEN AS YOU AND I, 1917, A
EVEN BREAK, AN, 1917
EVENING CLOTHES, 1927, A
EVENINGS FOR SALE, 1932, A
EVENSONG, 1934, A
EVENT, AN, 1970, C
EVENTS, 1970, O
EVER IN MY HEART, 1933, C
EVER SINCE EVE, 1921
EVER SINCE EVE, 1934, A
EVER SINCE EVE, 1937, A
EVER SINCE VENUS, 1944, A
EVERGREEN, 1934, A
EVERLASTING WHISPER, THE, 1925
EVERY BASTARD A KING, 1968, C
EVERY DAY IS A HOLIDAY, 1966, A
EVERY DAY'S A HOLIDAY, 1938, A
EVERY DAY'S A HOLIDAY, 1965
EVERY DAY'S A HOLIDAY, 1954
EVERY GIRL SHOULD BE MARRIED, 1948, A
EVERY GIRL'S DREAM, 1917
EVERY HOME SHOULD HAVE ONE
EVERY LITTLE CROOK AND NANNY, 1972, C
EVERY MAN A KING
EVERY MAN FOR HIMSELF, 1980, O

EVERY MAN FOR HIMSELF AND GOD AGAINST
  ALL, 1975, A
EVERY MAN'S WIFE, 1925, A
EVERY MOTHER'S SON, 1919
EVERY MOTHER'S SON, 1926, C
EVERY NIGHT AT EIGHT, 1935, A
EVERY PICTURE TELLS A STORY, 1984, C
EVERY SATURDAY NIGHT, 1936, A
EVERY SPARROW MUST FALL, 1964, C
EVERY WHICH WAY BUT LOOSE, 1978
EVERY WOMAN'S PROBLEM, 1921, A
EVERYBODY DANCE, 1936, A
EVERYBODY DOES IT, 1949, A
EVERYBODY GO HOME!, 1962
EVERYBODY SING, 1938, A
EVERYBODY'S ACTING, 1926
EVERYBODY'S BABY, 1939, A
EVERYBODY'S DANCIN', 1950, A
EVERYBODY'S DOING IT, 1938, A
EVERYBODY'S GIRL, 1918, A
EVERYBODY'S HOBBY, 1939
EVERYBODY'S OLD MAN, 1936, A
EVERYBODY'S SWEETHEART, 1920, A
EVERYDAY, 1976
EVERYMAN'S LAW, 1936, A
EVERYMAN'S PRICE, 1921, A
EVERYTHING BUT THE TRUTH, 1920
EVERYTHING BUT THE TRUTH, 1956, AA
EVERYTHING FOR SALE, 1921
EVERYTHING HAPPENS AT NIGHT, 1939, A
EVERYTHING HAPPENS TO ME, 1938, A
EVERYTHING I HAVE IS YOURS, 1952, A
EVERYTHING IN LIFE, 1936, A
EVERYTHING IS RHYTHM, 1940, A
EVERYTHING IS THUNDER, 1936, A
EVERYTHING OKAY, 1936
EVERYTHING YOU ALWAYS WANTED TO KNOW
  ABOUT SEX, BUT WERE AFRAID TO ASK
EVERYTHING'S DUCKY, 1961, A
EVERYTHING'S ON ICE, 1939, A
EVERYTHING'S ROSIE, 1931, A
EVERYWOMAN, 1919
EVERYWOMAN'S HUSBAND, 1918
EVICTORS, THE, 1979, O
EVIDENCE, 1915, A
EVIDENCE, 1918, A
EVIDENCE, 1922
EVIDENCE, 1929, A
EVIDENCE OF POWER, 1979
EVIL COME, EVIL GO
EVIL DEAD, THE, 1983, O
EVIL EYE, 1964
EVIL EYE OF KALINOR, THE, 1934
EVIL EYE, THE, 1917
EVIL FINGERS, 1975
EVIL GUN
EVIL IN THE DEEP
EVIL MIND
EVIL OF FRANKENSTEIN, THE, 1964, A
EVIL THAT MEN DO, THE
EVIL THAT MEN DO, THE, 1984, O
EVIL THEREOF, THE, 1916
EVIL UNDER THE SUN, 1982, A
EVIL WOMEN DO, THE, 1916
EVIL, THE, 1978, O
EVILS OF THE NIGHT, 1983
EVILSPEAK, 1982, O
EX-BAD BOY, 1931, A
EX-CHAMP, 1939, A
EX-FLAME, 1931, A
EX-LADY, 1933, A
EX-MRS. BRADFORD, THE, 1936
EXALTED FLAPPER, THE, 1929, A
EXCALIBUR, 1981, C-O
EXCESS BAGGAGE, 1928, A
EXCESS BAGGAGE, 1933, A
EXCHANGE OF WIVES, 1925
EXCITEMENT, 1924, A
EXCITERS, THE, 1923, A
EXCLUSIVE, 1937, A
EXCLUSIVE RIGHTS, 1926
EXCLUSIVE STORY, 1936, A
EXCUSE ME, 1916
EXCUSE ME, 1925
EXCUSE MY DUST, 1920, A
EXCUSE MY DUST, 1951, AAA
EXCUSE MY GLOVE, 1936, A
EXECUTIONER PART II, THE, 1984, O
EXECUTIONER, THE, 1970, C
EXECUTIVE ACTION, 1973, C
EXECUTIVE SUITE, 1954, A
EXILE, 1917
EXILE EXPRESS, 1939, A
EXILE, THE, 1931, C-O
EXILE, THE, 1947
EXILED TO SHANGHAI, 1937, A
EXILES, THE, 1923, A
EXILES, THE, 1966
EXIT SMILING, 1926, A
EXIT THE DRAGON, ENTER THE TIGER, 1977, O
EXIT THE VAMP, 1921, A
EXODUS, 1960, C

EXORCISM AT MIDNIGHT, 1966, C-O
EXORCISM'S DAUGHTER, 1974, O
EXORCIST II: THE HERETIC, 1977, O
EXORCIST, THE, 1973, O
EXOTIC ONES, THE, 1968, O
EXPENSIVE HUSBANDS, 1937, A
EXPENSIVE WOMEN, 1931, C
EXPERIENCE, 1921
EXPERIENCE PREFERRED... BUT NOT ESSENTIAL,
  1983, C
EXPERIMENT ALCATRAZ, 1950, A
EXPERIMENT IN TERROR, 1962, C
EXPERIMENT PERILOUS, 1944
EXPERIMENT, THE, 1922, A
EXPERIMENTAL MARRIAGE, 1919
EXPERT'S OPINION, 1935, A
EXPERT, THE, 1932, A
EXPIATION, 1918
EXPIATION, 1922
EXPLOSION, 1969, O
EXPLOSIVE GENERATION, THE, 1961, C
EXPOSED, 1932, A
EXPOSED, 1938, A
EXPOSED, 1947, A
EXPOSED, 1983, O
EXPOSURE, 1932
EXPRESSO BONGO, 1959, C
EXQUISIT THIEF, THE, 1919
EXQUISITE SINNER, THE, 1926, A
EXTERMINATING ANGEL, THE, 1967, O
EXTERMINATOR 2, 1984, O
EXTERMINATOR, THE, 1980, O
EXTERMINATORS, THE, 1965, A-C
EXTORTION, 1938, A
EXTRA DAY, THE, 1956, A
EXTRA EXTRA, 1922
EXTRA GIRL, THE, 1923, A
EXTRAORDINARY ADVENTURES OF MR. WEST IN
  THE LAND OF THE BOLSHEVIKS (1924, USSR)
EXTRAORDINARY SEAMAN, THE, 1969, A
EXTRAVAGANCE, 1916
EXTRAVAGANCE, 1919, A
EXTRAVAGANCE, 1921
EXTRAVAGANCE, 1930, A
EXTREME CLOSE-UP, 1973
EYE CREATURES, THE, 1965, A-C
EYE FOR AN EYE, AN, 1915
EYE FOR AN EYE, AN, 1966
EYE FOR AN EYE, AN, 1975
EYE FOR AN EYE, AN, 1981, O
EYE FOR EYE, 1918, A
EYE OF ENVY, THE, 1917
EYE OF GOD, THE, 1916
EYE OF THE CAT, 1969, C
EYE OF THE DEVIL, 1967, C
EYE OF THE NEEDLE, 1981, C-O
EYE OF THE NEEDLE, THE, 1965, C
EYE OF THE NIGHT, THE, 1916, A
EYE WITNESS, 1950, A-C
EYEBALL, 1978, O
EYES BEHIND THE STARS, 1972
EYES IN THE NIGHT, 1942, A
EYES OF A STRANGER, 1980, O
EYES OF ANNIE JONES, THE, 1963, A
EYES OF FATE, 1933, A
EYES OF FIRE, 1984, O
EYES OF HELL
EYES OF HOLLYWOOD, 1925
EYES OF JULIA DEEP, THE, 1918, A
EYES OF LAURA MARS, 1978, 0
EYES OF MYSTERY, THE, 1918
EYES OF TEXAS, 1948, A
EYES OF THE AMARYLLIS, THE, 1982, A-C
EYES OF THE DESERT, 1926
EYES OF THE FOREST, 1923
EYES OF THE HEART, 1920, A
EYES OF THE JUNGLE, 1953
EYES OF THE SOUL, 1919
EYES OF THE TOTEM, 1927
EYES OF THE UNDERWORLD, 1929, A
EYES OF THE UNDERWORLD, 1943, A
EYES OF THE WORLD, THE, 1917
EYES OF THE WORLD, THE, 1930, C
EYES OF YOUTH, 1919
EYES RIGHT, 1926, A
EYES THAT KILL, 1947, A
EYES WITHOUT A FACE
EYES, THE MOUTH, THE, 1982
EYES, THE SEA AND A BALL, 1968, A
EYEWITNESS, 1956, A
EYEWITNESS, 1981, O
EYEWITNESS, 1970

-F-

F MAN, 1936, A
F.I.S.T., 1978, A-C
F.J. HOLDEN, THE, 1977, O
F.P. 1, 1933
F.P. 1 DOESN'T ANSWER, 1933, A
FABIAN OF THE YARD, 1954, A
FABIENNE, 1920
FABIOLA, 1923

FABIOLA, 1951, A-C
FABLE, A, 1971, O
FABULOUS ADVENTURES OF MARCO POLO, THE
FABULOUS BARON MUNCHAUSEN, THE
FABULOUS DORSEYS, THE, 1947, A
FABULOUS JOE, THE, 1946
FABULOUS SENORITA, THE, 1952, A
FABULOUS SUZANNE, THE, 1946, A
FABULOUS TEXAN, THE, 1947, A
FABULOUS WORLD OF JULES VERNE, THE, 1961, AA
FACE A L'OCEAN, 1920
FACE AT THE WINDOW, THE, 1920, A
FACE AT THE WINDOW, THE, 1932, C
FACE AT THE WINDOW, THE, 1939, C
FACE AT YOUR WINDOW, 1920
FACE BEHIND THE MASK, THE, 1941, C
FACE BEHIND THE SCAR, 1940, A
FACE BETWEEN, THE, 1922
FACE IN THE CROWD, A, 1957, C
FACE IN THE DARK, 1918
FACE IN THE FOG, 1922
FACE IN THE FOG, A, 1936, A
FACE IN THE NIGHT
FACE IN THE RAIN, A, 1963, A
FACE IN THE SKY, 1933, A
FACE OF A FUGITIVE, 1959, A
FACE OF A STRANGER, 1964, A-C
FACE OF ANOTHER, THE, 1967, O
FACE OF EVE, THE
FACE OF EVIL
FACE OF FEAR
FACE OF FEAR, 1964
FACE OF FIRE, 1959, C
FACE OF FU MANCHU, THE, 1965, O
FACE OF MARBLE, THE, 1946, A
FACE OF TERROR, 1964, C
FACE OF THE SCREAMING WEREWOLF, 1959, A
FACE OF THE WORLD, 1921
FACE ON THE BARROOM FLOOR, THE, 1923
FACE ON THE BARROOM FLOOR, THE, 1932, A
FACE TO FACE, 1920
FACE TO FACE, 1952, A
FACE TO FACE, 1967, O
FACE TO FACE, 1976, O
FACE TO THE WIND
FACE VALUE, 1918
FACE VALUE, 1927
FACE, THE
FACELESS MAN, THE
FACELESS MEN, THE
FACELESS MONSTERS
FACES, 1934, A
FACES, 1968, O
FACES IN THE DARK, 1960, A
FACES IN THE FOG, 1944, A
FACES OF CHILDREN
FACING THE MUSIC, 1933
FACING THE MUSIC, 1941, A
FACTORY MAGDALEN, A, 1914, A
FACTS OF LIFE, THE
FACTS OF LIFE, THE, 1960, A
FACTS OF LOVE, 1949, A
FACTS OF MURDER, THE, 1965, O
FADE TO BLACK, 1980
FADE-IN, 1968
FADED FLOWER, THE, 1916
FAGASA, 1928
FAHRENHEIT 451, 1966, C
FAIL SAFE, 1964, C
FAILURE, THE
FAILURE, THE, 1915
FAINT PERFUME, 1925
FAIR AND WARMER, 1919
FAIR BARBARIAN, THE, 1917
FAIR CHEAT, THE, 1923
FAIR CO-ED, THE, 1927, A
FAIR ENOUGH, 1918, A
FAIR EXCHANGE, 1936, A
FAIR IMPOSTER, A, 1916
FAIR LADY, 1922
FAIR MAID OF PERTH, THE, 1923
FAIR PLAY, 1925, A
FAIR PRETENDER, THE, 1918, A
FAIR WARNING, 1931, A
FAIR WARNING, 1937, A
FAIR WEEK, 1924
FAIR WIND TO JAVA, 1953, A
FAIRY AND THE WAIF, THE, 1915
FAIRY TALES, 1979
FAITH
FAITH, 1916
FAITH, 1919
FAITH, 1920, A
FAITH AND ENDURIN', 1918
FAITH AND FORTUNE, 1915
FAITH FOR GOLD, 1930
FAITH HEALER, THE, 1921, A
FAITH OF A CHILD, THE, 1915
FAITH OF THE STRONG, 1919
FAITHFUL, 1936, A
FAITHFUL CITY, 1952, A
FAITHFUL HEART, 1933, A

FAITHFUL HEART, THE
FAITHFUL HEART, THE, 1922
FAITHFUL HEARTS
FAITHFUL IN MY FASHION, 1946, A
FAITHFUL WIVES, 1926
FAITHLESS, 1932
FAITHLESS LOVER, 1928
FAITHLESS SEX, THE, 1922
FAKE'S PROGRESS, 1950, A
FAKE, THE, 1927, C
FAKE, THE, 1953, A
FAKE-OUT, 1982
FAKER, THE, 1929
FAKERS, THE
FAKING OF THE PRESIDENT, THE, 1976
FALCON AND THE CO-EDS, THE, 1943, A
FALCON FIGHTERS, THE, 1970, C
FALCON IN DANGER, THE, 1943, A
FALCON IN HOLLYWOOD, THE, 1944, A
FALCON IN MEXICO, THE, 1944, A
FALCON IN SAN FRANCISCO, THE, 1945, A
FALCON OUT WEST, THE, 1944
FALCON STRIKES BACK, THE, 1943, A
FALCON TAKES OVER, THE, 1942, A
FALCON'S ADVENTURE, THE, 1946, A
FALCON'S ALIBI, THE, 1946, A
FALCON'S BROTHER, THE, 1942, A
FALCON'S GOLD, 1982
FALL GIRL, THE
FALL GUY, 1947, C
FALL GUY, THE
FALL GUY, THE, 1930, A
FALL OF A NATION, THE, 1916
FALL OF A SAINT, THE, 1920
FALL OF EVE, THE, 1929, A
FALL OF ROME, THE, 1963, C
FALL OF THE HOUSE OF USHER, THE
FALL OF THE HOUSE OF USHER, THE, 1928
FALL OF THE HOUSE OF USHER, THE, 1952, C
FALL OF THE HOUSE OF USHER, THE, 1980, O
FALL OF THE ROMAN EMPIRE, THE, 1964, O
FALL OF THE ROMANOFFS, THE, 1917
FALLEN ANGEL, 1945, A
FALLEN ANGEL, THE, 1918
FALLEN ANGELS
FALLEN IDOL, A, 1919
FALLEN IDOL, THE, 1949, A
FALLEN SPARROW, THE, 1943, C
FALLEN STAR, A, 1916
FALLGUY, 1962
FALLING FOR YOU, 1933
FALLING IN LOVE
FALLING IN LOVE, 1984, C
FALLING IN LOVE AGAIN, 1980, C
FALLS, THE, 1980
FALSE ALARM, THE, 1926
FALSE AMBITION, 1918
FALSE BRANDS, 1922, A
FALSE CODE, THE, 1919
FALSE COLORS, 1914, A
FALSE COLORS, 1943, A
FALSE EVIDENCE, 1919, A
FALSE EVIDENCE, 1922, A
FALSE EVIDENCE, 1937, A-C
FALSE FACE
FALSE FACES, 1919, A
FALSE FACES, 1932, A
FALSE FACES, 1943, A
FALSE FATHERS, 1929, A
FALSE FRIEND, THE, 1917, A
FALSE FRIENDS, 1926
FALSE FRONTS, 1922
FALSE GODS, 1919
FALSE KISSES, 1921
FALSE MADONNA, 1932, A
FALSE MAGISTRATE, THE, 1914
FALSE MORALS, 1927
FALSE PARADISE, 1948, A
FALSE PLAY
FALSE PRETENSES, 1935, A
FALSE PRIDE, 1926
FALSE RAPTURE, 1941, A
FALSE ROAD, THE, 1920
FALSE SHAME
FALSE TRAILS, 1924
FALSE WIRELESS, THE, 1914
FALSE WITNESS
FALSE WOMEN, 1921
FALSTAFF
FAME, 1936, A
FAME, 1980, C
FAME AND FORTUNE, 1918, A
FAME IS THE SPUR, 1947, A
FAME STREET, 1932, A
FAMILY AFFAIR, 1954
FAMILY AFFAIR, A, 1937, AAA
FAMILY CLOSET, THE, 1921
FAMILY CUPBOARD, THE, 1915, A
FAMILY DIARY, 1963, A
FAMILY DOCTOR
FAMILY ENFORCER, 1978
FAMILY GAME, THE, 1984, C

FAMILY HONEYMOON, 1948, A
FAMILY HONOR, 1973, O
FAMILY HONOR, THE, 1917
FAMILY HONOR, THE, 1920
FAMILY JEWELS, THE, 1965, A
FAMILY KILLER, 1975
FAMILY LIFE, 1971, O
FAMILY NEXT DOOR, THE, 1939, A
FAMILY PLOT, 1976, C
FAMILY SECRET, THE, 1924, A
FAMILY SECRET, THE, 1951, A
FAMILY SKELETON, THE, 1918, A
FAMILY STAIN, THE, 1915
FAMILY UPSTAIRS, THE, 1926
FAMILY WAY, THE, 1966, O
FAMILY, THE, 1974, O
FAMILY—PART TWO, 1978, AAA
FAMOUS FERGUSON CASE, THE, 1932, A
FAMOUS MRS. FAIR, THE, 1923
FAN FAN, 1918
FAN'S NOTES, A, 1972, C
FAN, THE, 1949, A
FAN, THE, 1981, C-O
FANATIC
FANATIC, THE
FANATICS, 1917
FANCHON THE CRICKET, 1915, A
FANCY BAGGAGE, 1929, A
FANCY DRESS, 1919, A
FANCY PANTS, 1950, A
FANDANGO, 1970, O
FANFAN THE TULIP, 1952, A
FANGELSE
FANGS, 1974
FANGS OF DESTINY, 1927
FANGS OF FATE, 1925
FANGS OF FATE, 1928
FANGS OF JUSTICE, 1926, A
FANGS OF THE ARCTIC, 1953, A
FANGS OF THE WILD, 1928, A
FANGS OF THE WILD, 1954, A
FANGS OF THE WOLF, 1924
FANGS OF WOLFHEART, 1925
FANNY, 1948, A-C
FANNY, 1961, A-C
FANNY AND ALEXANDER, 1983, C-O
FANNY BY GASLIGHT
FANNY FOLEY HERSELF, 1931, A
FANNY HAWTHORNE, 1927
*FANNY HILL: MEMOIRS OF A WOMAN OF
  PLEASURE*, 1965, O
FANTAISIE DE MILLARDAIRE, 1919
FANTASIES, 1981, O
FANTASM, 1976, O
FANTASMA, 1914
FANTASTIC COMEDY, A, 1975, C
FANTASTIC INVASION OF THE PLANET EARTH,
  THE
FANTASTIC INVENTION, THE
FANTASTIC PLANET, 1973, O
FANTASTIC THREE, THE, 1967, A
FANTASTIC VOYAGE, 1966, A
FANTASTICA, 1980, C-O
FANTASY MAN, 1984, C
FANTOMAS, 1966
FANTOMAS STRIKES BACK, 1965, A
FANTOMAS, THE CROOK DETECTIVE, 1914
FANTOMAS, THE FALSE MAGISTRATE
FAR CALL, THE, 1929, A
FAR COUNTRY, THE, 1955, A
FAR CRY, THE, 1926, A
FAR FROM DALLAS, 1972, C
FAR FROM POLAND, 1984, C
FAR FROM THE MADDING CROWD, 1915, A
FAR FROM THE MADDING CROWD, 1967
FAR FRONTIER, THE, 1949, A
FAR HORIZONS, THE, 1955, A
FAR SHORE, THE, 1976, O
FAR WESTERN TRAILS, 1929
FARARUV KONEC
FAREWELL AGAIN
FAREWELL PERFORMANCE, 1963, A-C
FAREWELL TO ARMS, A, 1932, A
FAREWELL TO ARMS, A, 1957, C
FAREWELL TO CINDERELLA, 1937, A
FAREWELL TO LOVE, 1931, A
FAREWELL, DOVES, 1962
FAREWELL, FRIEND, 1968, O
FAREWELL, MY BELOVED, 1969, O
FAREWELL, MY LOVELY, 1975, C-O
FAREWELL, MY LOVELY, 1944
FARGO, 1952, A
FARGO EXPRESS, 1933, A
FARGO KID, THE, 1941, A
FARGO, 1964
FARM GIRL
FARMER IN THE DELL, THE, 1936
FARMER TAKES A WIFE, THE, 1935, A
FARMER TAKES A WIFE, THE, 1953, A
FARMER'S DAUGHTER, THE, 1928
FARMER'S DAUGHTER, THE, 1940, A

FARMER'S DAUGHTER, THE, 1947, AA
FARMER'S OTHER DAUGHTER, THE, 1965, A
FARMER'S WIFE, THE, 1928, A
FARMER'S WIFE, THE, 1941, A
FARMER, THE, 1977, O
FASCINATING YOUTH, 1926
FASCINATION, 1922
FASCINATION, 1931
FASCIST, THE, 1965, A
FASHION HOUSE OF DEATH
FASHION MADNESS, 1928
FASHION MODEL, 1945, A
FASHION ROW, 1923
FASHIONABLE FAKERS, 1923
FASHIONS FOR WOMEN, 1927
FASHIONS IN LOVE, 1929, A-C
FASHIONS OF 1934, 1934, A
FAST AND FEARLESS, 1924
FAST AND FURIOUS, 1927
FAST AND FURIOUS, 1939
FAST AND LOOSE, 1930, A
FAST AND LOOSE, 1939, A
FAST AND LOOSE, 1954, A
FAST AND SEXY, 1960, A
FAST AND THE FURIOUS, THE, 1954, A
FAST BREAK, 1979, A
FAST BULLETS, 1936
FAST CHARLIE... THE MOONBEAM RIDER, 1979, C
FAST COMPANIONS, 1932, A
FAST COMPANY, 1918
FAST COMPANY, 1929, A
FAST COMPANY, 1938
FAST COMPANY, 1953, A
FAST COMPANY, 1979
FAST FIGHTIN', 1925
FAST KILL, 1973
FAST LADY, THE, 1963, A
FAST LIFE, 1929, A
FAST LIFE, 1932
FAST MAIL, THE, 1922
FAST ON THE DRAW, 1950, A
FAST SET, THE, 1924
FAST TIMES AT RIDGEMONT HIGH, 1982, O
FAST WORKER, THE, 1924
FAST WORKERS, 1933, A
FAST-WALKING, 1982, O
FASTEST GUITAR ALIVE, THE, 1967, A
FASTEST GUN ALIVE, 1956, A
FASTEST GUN, THE
FAT ANGELS, 1980, C
FAT CHANCE, 1982
FAT CITY, 1972, C
FAT MAN, THE, 1951
FAT SPY, 1966, A
FATAL 30, THE, 1921
FATAL DESIRE, 1953, C
FATAL FINGERS, 1916, A
FATAL GAMES, 1983
FATAL HOUR, THE, 1920
FATAL HOUR, THE, 1937, A
FATAL HOUR, THE, 1940, A
FATAL LADY, 1936
FATAL MARRIAGE, THE
FATAL MISTAKE, THE, 1924
FATAL NIGHT, THE, 1915
FATAL NIGHT, THE, 1948
FATAL PLUNGE, THE, 1924
FATAL WITNESS, THE, 1945
FATALNA KLATWA, 1913
FATE, 1921
FATE AND THE CHILD, 1917
FATE IS THE HUNTER, 1964, A
FATE OF A FLIRT, THE, 1925
FATE TAKES A HAND, 1962, A
FATE'S BOOMERANG, 1916
FATE'S PLAYTHING, 1920, A
FATHER, 1967, A
FATHER AND SON, 1916
FATHER AND SON, 1929, A
FATHER AND SON, 1934, A
FATHER AND THE BOYS, 1915
FATHER BROWN
FATHER BROWN, DETECTIVE, 1935, A
FATHER CAME TOO, 1964
FATHER DEAR FATHER, 1973
FATHER FROST, 1924
FATHER GOOSE, 1964, AAA
FATHER IS A BACHELOR, 1950, A
FATHER IS A PRINCE, 1940, A
FATHER MAKES GOOD, 1950, A
FATHER O'FLYNN, 1919, A
FATHER O'FLYNN, 1938, A
FATHER OF A SOLDIER, 1966, C
FATHER OF THE BRIDE, 1950, AA
FATHER SERGIUS, 1918
FATHER STEPS OUT, 1937, A
FATHER STEPS OUT, 1941
FATHER TAKES A WIFE, 1941, A
FATHER TAKES THE AIR, 1951, A
FATHER TOM, 1921
FATHER WAS A FULLBACK, 1949, A
FATHER'S DILEMMA, 1952, A

FATHER'S DOING FINE, 1952, A
FATHER'S LITTLE DIVIDEND, 1951
FATHER'S SON, 1931, A
FATHER'S SON, 1941, A
FATHER'S WILD GAME, 1950, A
FATHERHOOD, 1915
FATHERS AND SONS, 1960, A
FATHERS OF MEN, 1916
FATHOM, 1967, A
FATSO, 1980, A
FATTY FINN, 1980, A-C
FAUBOURG MONTMARTE, 1924
FAUSSES INGENUES
FAUST, 1922
FAUST, 1926, C
FAUST, 1963, A
FAUST, 1964, A
FAVOR TO A FRIEND, A, 1919
FAZIL, 1928
FBI CODE 98, 1964, A
FBI CONTRO DR. MABUSE
FBI GIRL, 1951
FBI STORY, THE, 1959, C
FEAR, 1946, C
FEAR, 1956, O
FEAR AND DESIRE, 1953, C
FEAR CHAMBER, THE, 1968, C
FEAR CITY, 1984, O
FEAR EATS THE SOUL, 1974, O
FEAR FIGHTER, THE, 1925
FEAR IN THE NIGHT, 1947, C-O
FEAR IN THE NIGHT, 1972, C
FEAR IS THE KEY, 1973, C
FEAR MARKET, THE, 1920
FEAR NO EVIL, 1981, O
FEAR NO MORE, 1961, C
FEAR NOT, 1917
FEAR O' GOD, 1926, A
FEAR O'GOD, 1926
FEAR SHIP, THE, 1933, A
FEAR STRIKES OUT, 1957, C
FEAR WOMAN, THE, 1919
FEAR, THE, 1967, O
FEAR-BOUND, 1925
FEARLESS DICK, 1922
FEARLESS FAGAN, 1952, AA
FEARLESS FRANK, 1967
FEARLESS LOVER, THE, 1925, A
FEARLESS RIDER, THE, 1928
FEARLESS VAMPIRE KILLERS, OR PARDON ME
FEARMAKERS, THE, 1958, A
FEAST OF FLESH
FEAST OF LIFE, THE, 1916
FEATHER IN HER HAT, A, 1935, A
FEATHER YOUR NEST, 1937, A
FEATHER, THE, 1929, A
FEATHERED SERPENT, THE, 1934, A
FEATHERED SERPENT, THE, 1948, A
FEATHERTOP, 1916
FECONDITE, 1929
FEDERAL AGENT, 1936, A
FEDERAL AGENT AT LARGE, 1950, A
FEDERAL BULLETS, 1937, A
FEDERAL FUGITIVES, 1941, A
FEDERAL MAN, 1950, A
FEDERAL MAN-HUNT, 1939, A
FEDERICO FELLINI'S 8 1/2
FEDORA, 1918
FEDORA, 1946, A
FEDORA, 1978, C
FEEDBACK, 1979, C
FEEL MY PULSE, 1928
FEELIN' GOOD, 1966, A
FEELIN' UP, 1983
FEET FIRST, 1930, A
FEET OF CLAY, 1917
FEET OF CLAY, 1924
FEET OF CLAY, 1960, A
FELIANA L'ESPIONNE, 1924
FELIX O'DAY, 1920
FELLER NEEDS A FRIEND, 1932, A
FELLINI SATYRICON, 1969, C-O
FELLINI'S CASANOVA
FELLINI'S ROMA
FEMALE, 1933, A
FEMALE ANIMAL, THE, 1958
FEMALE BUNCH, THE, 1969, O
FEMALE BUTCHER, THE, 1972, O
FEMALE FIENDS, 1958, A
FEMALE FUGITIVE, 1938, A
FEMALE JUNGLE, THE, 1955, C
FEMALE OF THE SPECIES, 1917, A
FEMALE ON THE BEACH, 1955, A-C
FEMALE PRINCE, THE, 1966, C
FEMALE PRISONER, THE
FEMALE RESPONSE, THE, 1972, O
FEMALE SWINDLER, THE, 1916
FEMALE TRAP, THE
FEMALE TROUBLE, 1975, O
FEMALE, THE, 1924
FEMALE, THE, 1960, C
FEMININE TOUCH, THE

FEMININE TOUCH, THE, 1941, A
FEMMES D'UN ETE
FEMMINA, 1968, C
FEMMINE DI LUSSO
FENCE RIDERS, 1950, A
FERN, THE RED DEER, 1977
FERNANDEL THE DRESSMAKER, 1957, A
FEROCIOUS PAL, 1934, AAA
FERRAGUS, 1923
FERRY ACROSS THE MERSEY, 1964, A
FERRY TO HONG KONG, 1959, A
FETTERED, 1919
FETTERED WOMAN, THE, 1917
FEU, 1927
FEU MATHIAS PASCAL
FEUD GIRL, THE, 1916
FEUD MAKER, 1938, A
FEUD OF THE RANGE, 1939, A
FEUD OF THE TRAIL, 1938
FEUD OF THE WEST, 1936, A
FEUD WOMAN, THE, 1926
FEUD, THE, 1919
FEUDIN' FOOLS, 1952, A
FEUDIN' RHYTHM, 1949
FEUDIN', FUSSIN' AND A-FIGHTIN', 1948, A
FEVER HEAT, 1968, A
FEVER IN THE BLOOD, A, 1961, A
FEW BULLETS MORE, A, 1968, A
FFOLKES, 1980, C
FIANCAILLES, 1926
FIANCES, THE, 1964, A
FIASCO IN MILAN, 1963, A
FIBBERS, THE, 1917
FICKLE FINGER OF FATE, THE, 1967, A
FICKLE WOMAN
FICKLE WOMEN, 1920, A
FIDDLER ON THE ROOF, 1971, AAA
FIDDLERS THREE, 1944, A
FIDDLIN' BUCKAROO, THE, 1934, A
FIDELIO, 1961, A
FIDELIO, 1970, A
FIDELITE, 1924
FIELD OF HONOR, THE, 1917
FIELD OF HONOR, THE, 1922, A
FIELDS OF HONOR
FIELDS OF HONOR, 1918
FIEND, 1980, O
FIEND OF DOPE ISLAND, 1961, C
FIEND WHO WALKED THE WEST, THE, 1958, O
FIEND WITH THE SYNTHETIC BRAIN
FIEND WITHOUT A FACE, 1958, C-O
FIEND, THE, 1971
FIENDISH GHOULS, THE
FIENDISH PLOT OF DR. FU MANCHU, THE, 1980, C
FIENDS OF HELL, 1914
FIENDS, THE
FIERCEST HEART, THE, 1961, A
FIERY SPUR
FIESTA, 1947, A
FIEVRE, 1921
15 FROM ROM
50,000 B.C. (BEFORE CLOTHING), 1963, O
52 MILES TO MIDNIGHT
52 MILES TO TERROR
52ND STREET, 1937, A
55 DAYS AT PEKING, 1963
FIFTEEN MAIDEN LANE, 1936, A
FIFTEEN WIVES, 1934, A
FIFTH AVENUE, 1926
FIFTH AVENUE GIRL, 1939, A
FIFTH AVENUE MODELS, 1925
FIFTH COMMANDMENT, THE, 1915
FIFTH COMMANDMENT, THE, 1927
FIFTH FLOOR, THE, 1980, O
FIFTH FORM AT ST. DOMINIC'S, THE, 1921
FIFTH HORSEMAN IS FEAR, THE, 1968, C
FIFTH HORSEMAN, THE, 1924
FIFTH MAN, THE, 1914
FIFTH MUSKETEER, THE
FIFTY CANDLES, 1921, A
FIFTY FATHOMS DEEP, 1931, A
FIFTY MILLION FRENCHMEN, 1931, AA
FIFTY ROADS TO TOWN, 1937, A
FIFTY-FIFTY, 1916
FIFTY-FIFTY, 1925
FIFTY-FIFTY GIRL, THE, 1928, A
FIFTY-SHILLING BOXER, 1937, A
FIG LEAVES, 1926
FIGARO, 1929
FIGHT FOR FREEDOM, A OR EXILED TO SIBERIA, 1914
FIGHT FOR HONOR, A, 1924
FIGHT FOR LIFE, THE, 1940
FIGHT FOR LOVE, A, 1919
FIGHT FOR MILLIONS, THE, 1913
FIGHT FOR ROME, 1969, A
FIGHT FOR THE 'ULTIMATUM' FACTORY, 1923
FIGHT FOR THE GLORY, 1970, C
FIGHT FOR YOUR LADY, 1937, A
FIGHT FOR YOUR LIFE Zero, 1977, O
FIGHT NEVER ENDS, THE, 1947
FIGHT TO THE FINISH, A, 1925

FIGHT TO THE FINISH, A, 1937, A
FIGHT TO THE LAST, 1938, C
FIGHT, THE, 1915
FIGHTER ATTACK, 1953, A
FIGHTER PILOTS, 1977
FIGHTER SQUADRON, 1948, A
FIGHTER'S PARADISE, 1924, A
FIGHTER, THE, 1921, A
FIGHTER, THE, 1952, A
FIGHTERS IN THE SADDLE
FIGHTERS OF THE SADDLE, 1929
FIGHTIN' COMEBACK, THE, 1927
FIGHTIN' DEVIL, 1922
FIGHTIN' MAD, 1921
FIGHTIN' ODDS, 1925
FIGHTIN' REDHEAD, THE, 1928
FIGHTIN' THRU, 1924
FIGHTING 69TH, THE, 1940, A
FIGHTING ACE, THE
FIGHTING AMERICAN, THE, 1924, A
FIGHTING BACK
FIGHTING BACK, 1917
FIGHTING BACK, 1948, A
FIGHTING BACK, 1983, C
FIGHTING BILL CARSON, 1945, A
FIGHTING BILL FARGO, 1942, A
FIGHTING BLACK KINGS, 1977
FIGHTING BLADE, THE, 1923
FIGHTING BOB, 1915, A
FIGHTING BOOB, THE, 1926, A
FIGHTING BREED, THE, 1921, A
FIGHTING BUCKAROO, THE, 1926
FIGHTING BUCKAROO, THE, 1943, A
FIGHTING CABALLERO, 1935, A
FIGHTING CARAVANS, 1931, A
FIGHTING CHAMP, 1933, A
FIGHTING CHANCE, THE, 1920
FIGHTING CHANCE, THE, 1955
FIGHTING CHEAT, THE, 1926, A
FIGHTING COAST GUARD, 1951, A
FIGHTING COBBLER, THE, 1915
FIGHTING CODE, THE, 1934, A
FIGHTING COLLEEN, A, 1919
FIGHTING COURAGE, 1925
FIGHTING COWARD, THE, 1924, A
FIGHTING COWBOY, 1930
FIGHTING COWBOY, 1933, A
FIGHTING CRESSY, 1919
FIGHTING CUB, THE, 1925, A
FIGHTING DEATH, 1914
FIGHTING DEMON, THE, 1925
FIGHTING DEPUTY, THE, 1937, A
FIGHTING DESTINY, 1919
FIGHTING DEVIL DOGS, 1938
FIGHTING DOCTOR, THE, 1926
FIGHTING EAGLE, THE, 1927
FIGHTING EDGE, 1926, A
FIGHTING EDGE, THE, 1926
FIGHTING FAILURE, THE, 1926
FIGHTING FATE, 1925
FIGHTING FATHER DUNNE, 1948, A
FIGHTING FOOL, THE, 1932, A
FIGHTING FOOLS, 1949, A
FIGHTING FOR GOLD, 1919
FIGHTING FOR JUSTICE, 1924
FIGHTING FOR JUSTICE, 1932
FIGHTING FOR LOVE, 1917, A
FIGHTING FRONTIER, 1943, AA
FIGHTING FRONTIERSMAN, THE, 1946
FIGHTING FURY
FIGHTING FURY, 1924
FIGHTING GENTLEMAN, THE, 1932, A
FIGHTING GOB, THE, 1926
FIGHTING GRIN, THE, 1918
FIGHTING GRINGO, THE, 1917
FIGHTING GRINGO, THE, 1939, A
FIGHTING GUARDSMAN, THE, 1945, A
FIGHTING GUIDE, THE, 1922
FIGHTING HEART, A, 1924
FIGHTING HEART, THE, 1925
FIGHTING HEARTS, 1922
FIGHTING HERO, 1934, A
FIGHTING HOMBRE, THE, 1927
FIGHTING HOPE, THE, 1915
FIGHTING JACK, 1926
FIGHTING JIM GRANT, 1923
FIGHTING KENTUCKIAN, THE, 1949, A
FIGHTING KENTUCKIANS, THE, 1920
FIGHTING KID, THE, 1922
FIGHTING LADY, 1935
FIGHTING LAWMAN, THE, 1953, A
FIGHTING LEGION, THE, 1930, A
FIGHTING LOVE, 1927
FIGHTING LOVER, THE, 1921
FIGHTING LUCK, 1926
FIGHTING MAD, 1917
FIGHTING MAD, 1939, A
FIGHTING MAD, 1948, A
FIGHTING MAD, 1957, A-C
FIGHTING MAD, 1976, C
FIGHTING MAN OF THE PLAINS, 1949, A
FIGHTING MARINE, THE, 1926

FIGHTING MARSHAL, THE, 1932, AA
FIGHTING MUSTANG, 1948
FIGHTING O'FLYNN, THE, 1949, A
FIGHTING ODDS, 1917, A
FIGHTING PARSON, THE, 1933, A
FIGHTING PEACEMAKER, THE, 1926
FIGHTING PILOT, THE, 1935
FIGHTING PIMPERNEL, THE, 1950, A
FIGHTING PIONEERS, 1935, A
FIGHTING PLAYBOY, 1937, A
FIGHTING PRINCE OF DONEGAL, THE, 1966, AAA
FIGHTING RANGER, 1926
FIGHTING RANGER, THE, 1922
FIGHTING RANGER, THE, 1934, A
FIGHTING RANGER, THE, 1948, A
FIGHTING REDHEAD, THE, 1950, A
FIGHTING RENEGADE, 1939, AA
FIGHTING ROMEO, THE, 1925
FIGHTING ROOKIE, THE, 1934, A
FIGHTING SAP, THE, 1924
FIGHTING SEABEES, THE, 1944, C
FIGHTING SHADOWS, 1935, A
FIGHTING SHEPHERDESS, THE, 1920
FIGHTING SHERIFF, THE, 1925
FIGHTING SHERIFF, THE, 1931, A
FIGHTING SMILE, THE, 1925, A
FIGHTING STALLION, THE, 1926
FIGHTING STALLION, THE, 1950, A
FIGHTING STOCK, 1935, A
FIGHTING STRAIN, THE, 1923
FIGHTING STRANGER, THE, 1921
FIGHTING STREAK, THE, 1922
FIGHTING SULLIVANS, THE
FIGHTING TERROR, THE, 1929, A
FIGHTING TEXAN, 1937, A
FIGHTING TEXANS, 1933, A
FIGHTING THE FLAMES, 1925
FIGHTING THOROBREDS, 1926
FIGHTING THOROUGHBREDS, 1939, A
FIGHTING THREE, THE, 1927
FIGHTING THROUGH, 1934
FIGHTING THRU, 1931, A
FIGHTING TO LIVE, 1934
FIGHTING TROOPER, THE, 1935, A
FIGHTING TROUBLE, 1956, A
FIGHTING VALLEY, 1943, A
FIGHTING VIGILANTES, THE, 1947, A
FIGHTING WILDCATS, THE, 1957, A-C
FIGHTING YOUTH, 1925
FIGHTING YOUTH, 1935, A
FIGUREHEAD, THE, 1920
FIGURES DON'T LIE, 1927
FIGURES IN A LANDSCAPE, 1970, C
FILE 113, 1932, A
FILE OF THE GOLDEN GOOSE, THE, 1969, C
FILE ON THELMA JORDAN, THE, 1950, A-C
FILES FROM SCOTLAND YARD, 1951, A
FILLE D'ARTISTE, 1916
FILLE DE RIEN, 1921
FILLING HIS OWN SHOES, 1917
FILM WITHOUT A NAME, 1950, A
FINAL APPOINTMENT, 1954, A
FINAL ASSIGNMENT, 1980, C
FINAL CHAPTER—WALKING TALL, 1977, O
FINAL CHORD, THE, 1936, C
FINAL CLOSEUP, THE, 1919
FINAL COLUMN, THE, 1955, A
FINAL COMEDOWN, THE, 1972, O
FINAL CONFLICT, THE, 1981, O
FINAL COUNTDOWN, THE, 1980, C
FINAL CURTAIN, THE, 1916, A
FINAL CUT, THE, 1980, O
FINAL EDITION, 1932, A
FINAL EXAM, 1981, O
FINAL EXTRA, THE, 1927
FINAL HOUR, THE, 1936, A
FINAL JUDGEMENT, THE, 1915
FINAL OPTION, THE, 1983, O
FINAL PAYMENT, THE, 1917
FINAL PROGRAMME, THE
FINAL RECKONING, THE, 1932, A
FINAL TERROR, THE, 1983, O
FINAL TEST, THE, 1953, A
FINAL WAR, THE, 1960, C
FINALLY SUNDAY
FINCHE DURA LA TEMPESTA
FIND THE BLACKMAILER, 1943, A
FIND THE LADY, 1936, A
FIND THE LADY, 1956, C
FIND THE WITNESS, 1937, A
FIND THE WOMAN, 1918
FIND THE WOMAN, 1922
FIND YOUR MAN, 1924
FINDERS KEEPERS, 1921
FINDERS KEEPERS, 1928
FINDERS KEEPERS, 1951, AA
FINDERS KEEPERS, 1966, A
FINDERS KEEPERS, 1984, C-O
FINDERS KEEPERS, LOVERS WEEPERS, 1968, O
FINE CLOTHES, 1925
FINE FEATHERS, 1915, A
FINE FEATHERS, 1915

FINE FEATHERS, 1921, A
FINE FEATHERS, 1937
FINE MADNESS, A, 1966, C
FINE MANNERS, 1926, A
FINE PAIR, A, 1969, C
FINGER MAN, 1955, A
FINGER OF GUILT, 1956, A
FINGER ON THE TRIGGER, 1965, A
FINGER POINTS, THE, 1931, C
FINGER PRINTS, 1923, A
FINGER PRINTS, 1927
FINGERMAN, THE, 1963, C
FINGERPRINTS DON'T LIE, 1951, A
FINGERS, 1940, A
FINGERS, 1978, O
FINGERS AT THE WINDOW, 1942, C
FINIAN'S RAINBOW, 1968
FINISHING SCHOOL, 1934, A
FINN AND HATTIE, 1931, A
FINNEGAN'S BALL, 1927, A
FINNEGANS WAKE, 1965, A
FINNEY, 1969, A
FINNIS TERRAE, 1929
FINO A FARTI MALE, 1969, O
FIRE AND ICE, 1983, C
FIRE AND STEEL, 1927
FIRE AND SWORD, 1914, A
FIRE AND SWORD, 1982
FIRE BRIDE, THE, 1922
FIRE BRIGADE, THE, 1926
FIRE CAT, THE, 1921
FIRE DOWN BELOW, 1957, C
FIRE EATER, THE, 1921
FIRE FLINGERS, THE, 1919
FIRE HAS BEEN ARRANGED, A, 1935, A
FIRE IN THE FLESH, 1964, A
FIRE IN THE STONE, THE, 1983, AA
FIRE IN THE STRAW, 1943, A
FIRE MAIDENS FROM OUTER SPACE, 1956, A
FIRE OVER AFRICA, 1954, A
FIRE OVER ENGLAND, 1937
FIRE PATROL, THE, 1924
FIRE RAISERS, THE, 1933
FIRE SALE, 1977, A-C
FIRE WITHIN, THE, 1964, O
FIREBALL 590, 1966, A
FIREBALL JUNGLE, 1968, C
FIREBALL, THE, 1950, A
FIREBIRD 2015 AD, 1981, O
FIREBIRD, THE, 1934, A
FIREBRAND JORDAN, 1930, A
FIREBRAND TREVISON, 1920
FIREBRAND, THE, 1918
FIREBRAND, THE, 1922
FIREBRAND, THE, 1962, C
FIREBRANDS OF ARIZONA, 1944, A
FIRECHASERS, THE, 1970, C
FIRECRACKER, 1981, 0
FIRECREEK, 1968, C
FIRED WIFE, 1943
FIREFLY OF FRANCE, THE, 1918
FIREFLY OF TOUGH LUCK, THE, 1917
FIREFLY, THE, 1937, A
FIREFOX, 1982, C
FIREMAN SAVE MY CHILD, 1954, A
FIREMAN'S BALL, THE, 1968, C
FIREMAN, SAVE MY CHILD, 1927, A
FIREMAN, SAVE MY CHILD, 1932, A
FIREPOWER, 1979, O
FIRES OF CONSCIENCE, 1916, A
FIRES OF FATE, 1923, A
FIRES OF FATE, 1932, A
FIRES OF INNOCENCE, 1922, A
FIRES OF REBELLION, 1917
FIRES OF YOUTH, 1917
FIRES OF YOUTH, 1918
FIRES OF YOUTH, 1924
FIRES ON THE PLAIN, 1962, O
FIRESTARTER, 1984, O
FIRETRAP, THE, 1935
FIRING LINE, THE, 1919
FIRM MAN, THE, 1975, C
FIRM OF GIRDLESTONE, THE, 1915, A
1ST NOTCH, THE, 1977
FIRST 100 YEARS, THE, 1938, A
FIRST A GIRL, 1935, A
FIRST AID, 1931, A
FIRST AND THE LAST, THE
FIRST AUTO, THE, 1927
FIRST BABY, 1936, A
FIRST BLOOD, 1982, O
FIRST BORN, THE, 1921
FIRST BORN, THE, 1928
FIRST COMES COURAGE, 1943, A
FIRST DEADLY SIN, THE, 1980, O
FIRST DEGREE, THE, 1923
FIRST FAMILY, 1980, O
FIRST GENTLEMAN, THE
FIRST GREAT TRAIN ROBBERY, THE
FIRST HUNDRED YEARS
FIRST KISS, THE, 1928
FIRST LADY, 1937, A

FIRST LAW, THE, 1918
FIRST LEGION, THE, 1951, A
FIRST LOVE, 1921
FIRST LOVE, 1939, A
FIRST LOVE, 1970, C-O
FIRST LOVE, 1977, O
FIRST MAN INTO SPACE, 1959, A
FIRST MARINES
FIRST MEN IN THE MOON, 1964, A
FIRST MEN IN THE MOON, THE, 1919
FIRST MONDAY IN OCTOBER, 1981
FIRST MRS. FRASER, THE, 1932, A
FIRST NAME: CARMEN, 1984, O
FIRST NIGHT, 1937, A
FIRST NIGHT, THE, 1927
FIRST NUDIE MUSICAL, THE, 1976, O
FIRST OF THE FEW, THE
FIRST OFFENCE, 1936, A
FIRST OFFENDERS, 1939
FIRST REBEL, THE
FIRST SPACESHIP ON VENUS, 1960, A
FIRST START, 1953, A
FIRST TASTE OF LOVE, 1962, C
FIRST TEXAN, THE, 1956
FIRST TIME ROUND, 1972
FIRST TIME, THE, 1952, A
FIRST TIME, THE, 1969, C
FIRST TIME, THE, 1978, O
FIRST TIME, THE, 1983, O
FIRST TO FIGHT, 1967, C
FIRST TRAVELING SALESLADY, THE, 1956, A
FIRST TURN-ON?, THE, 1984, O
FIRST WIFE
FIRST WOMAN, THE, 1922
FIRST YANK INTO TOKYO, 1945, C
FIRST YEAR, THE, 1926, A
FIRST YEAR, THE, 1932
FIRSTBORN, 1984, C
FISH HAWK, 1981, AA
FISH THAT SAVED PITTSBURGH, THE, 1979
FISHERMAN'S WHARF, 1939, AA
FIST IN HIS POCKET, 1968, O
FIST OF FEAR, TOUCH OF DEATH, 1980, O
FIST OF FURY
FISTFUL OF CHOPSTICKS, A
FISTFUL OF DOLLARS, A, 1964, C
FISTFUL OF DYNAMITE, A
FISTS OF FURY, 1973
FIT FOR A KING, 1937, A
FITZCARRALDO, 1982, C
FITZWILLY, 1967
$5,000 REWARD
$5,000 REWARD, 1918
$5,000,000 COUNTERFEITING PLOT, THE, 1914, A
$50,000 Reward, 1924
5 MINUTES TO LOVE
5 SINNERS, 1961, C-O
5,000 FINGERS OF DR. T. THE, 1953, AAA
FIVE, 1951, C
FIVE AGAINST THE HOUSE, 1955, C
FIVE AND TEN, 1931, A
FIVE AND TEN CENT ANNIE, 1928
FIVE ANGLES ON MURDER, 1950, A
FIVE ANGRY WOMEN, 1975
FIVE ASHORE IN SINGAPORE
FIVE BAD MEN, 1935
FIVE BLOODY GRAVES
FIVE BOLD WOMEN, 1960, A
FIVE BRANDED WOMEN, 1960, C
FIVE CAME BACK, 1939, A
FIVE CARD STUD, 1968, C
FIVE DAYS
FIVE DAYS FROM HOME, 1978, C
FIVE DAYS ONE SUMMER, 1982, A
FIVE DAYS TO LIVE, 1922
FIVE DOLLAR BABY, THE, 1922
FIVE EASY PIECES, 1970, C-O
FIVE FAULTS OF FLO, THE, 1916
FIVE FINGER EXERCISE, 1962, A
FIVE FINGERS, 1952, A
FIVE FINGERS OF DEATH, 1973, O
FIVE GATES TO HELL, 1959, O
FIVE GIANTS FROM TEXAS, 1966, C
FIVE GOLDEN DRAGONS, 1967, O
FIVE GOLDEN HOURS, 1961, A
FIVE GRAVES TO CAIRO, 1943, A
FIVE GUNS TO TOMBSTONE, 1961, A
FIVE GUNS WEST, 1955, A
FIVE LITTLE PEPPERS AND HOW THEY GREW,
   1939, AA
FIVE LITTLE PEPPERS AT HOME, 1940, AA
FIVE LITTLE PEPPERS IN TROUBLE, 1940, A
FIVE MAN ARMY, THE, 1970, C
FIVE MILES TO MIDNIGHT, 1963, O
FIVE MILLION YEARS TO EARTH, 1968, A
FIVE MINUTES TO LIVE, 1961, C
FIVE NIGHTS, 1915
FIVE OF A KIND, 1938, AA
FIVE OF THE JAZZBAND
FIVE ON THE BLACK HAND SIDE, 1973, A
FIVE PENNIES, THE, 1959, A
FIVE POUND MAN, THE, 1937, C

FIVE SINISTER STORIES, 1919
FIVE STAR FINAL, 1931, C
FIVE STEPS TO DANGER, 1957, A
FIVE THE HARD WAY, 1969, O
FIVE THOUSAND AN HOUR, 1918
FIVE TO ONE, 1963, C
FIVE WEEKS IN A BALLOON, 1962, A
FIVE WILD GIRLS, 1966, O
FIXATION
FIXED BAYONETS, 1951, A
FIXED BY GEORGE, 1920
FIXER DUGAN, 1939, A
FIXER, THE
FIXER, THE, 1968, O
FLAG LIEUTENANT, THE, 1919
FLAG LIEUTENANT, THE, 1926
FLAG LIEUTENANT, THE, 1932
FLAME, 1975
FLAME AND THE ARROW, THE, 1950, A
FLAME AND THE FLESH, 1954, C
FLAME BARRIER, THE, 1958, C
FLAME IN THE HEATHER, 1935, A
FLAME IN THE STREETS, 1961, A
FLAME OF ARABY, 1951
FLAME OF CALCUTTA, 1953, A
FLAME OF HELLGATE, THE, 1920
FLAME OF LIFE, THE, 1923
FLAME OF LOVE, THE, 1930, A
FLAME OF NEW ORLEANS, THE, 1941, A-C
FLAME OF PASSION, THE, 1915
FLAME OF SACRAMENTO
FLAME OF STAMBOUL, 1957, A
FLAME OF THE ARGENTINE, 1926
FLAME OF THE BARBARY COAST, 1945, A
FLAME OF THE DESERT, 1919
FLAME OF THE ISLANDS, 1955, A
FLAME OF THE WEST, 1945, A
FLAME OF THE YUKON, THE, 1917
FLAME OF THE YUKON, THE, 1926
FLAME OF TORMENT
FLAME OF YOUTH, 1920
FLAME OF YOUTH, 1949, A
FLAME OF YOUTH, THE, 1917
FLAME OVER INDIA, 1960, A
FLAME OVER VIETNAM, 1967, A
FLAME WITHIN, THE, 1935, C
FLAME, THE, 1920
FLAME, THE, 1948, A
FLAMENCA LA GITANE, 1928
FLAMES, 1917, A
FLAMES, 1926
FLAMES, 1932, A
FLAMES OF CHANCE, THE, 1918, A
FLAMES OF DESIRE, 1924
FLAMES OF FEAR, 1930, A
FLAMES OF JOHANNIS, THE, 1916
FLAMES OF PASSION, 1922, A
FLAMES OF PASSION, 1923
FLAMES OF THE FLESH, 1920, A
FLAMES OF WRATH, 1923
FLAMING BARRIERS, 1924, A
FLAMING BULLETS, 1945, A
FLAMING CLUE, THE, 1920
FLAMING CRISIS, THE, 1924
FLAMING DESIRE
FLAMING FEATHER, 1951, A
FLAMING FOREST, THE, 1926
FLAMING FORTIES, THE, 1924
FLAMING FRONTIER, 1958
FLAMING FRONTIER, 1968, A
FLAMING FRONTIER, THE, 1926
FLAMING FURY, 1926
FLAMING FURY, 1949, A
FLAMING GOLD, 1934, A
FLAMING GUNS, 1933, A
FLAMING HEARTS, 1922
FLAMING HOUR, THE, 1922
FLAMING LEAD, 1939, A
FLAMING OMEN, THE, 1917
FLAMING PASSION
FLAMING SIGNAL, 1933, A
FLAMING STAR, 1960, C-O
FLAMING SWORD, 1915
FLAMING TEEN-AGE, THE, 1956, A
FLAMING URGE, THE, 1953
FLAMING WATERS, 1925, A
FLAMING YOUTH, 1923
FLAMINGO, 1947
FLAMINGO AFFAIR, THE, 1948, A
FLAMINGO KID, THE, 1984, C
FLAMINGO ROAD, 1949, C
FLANAGAN BOY, THE
FLANNELFOOT, 1953, A
FLAP, 1970, A
FLAPPER WIVES, 1924
FLAPPER, THE, 1920, A
FLARE-UP SAL, 1918
FLAREUP, 1969, O
FLASH AND THE FIRECAT, 1976
FLASH GORDON, 1936, AAA
FLASH GORDON, 1980, AA
FLASH O'LIGHTING, 1925

FLASH OF FATE, THE, 1918
FLASH OF GREEN, A, 1984, A-C
FLASH OF THE FOREST, 1928
FLASH THE SHEEPDOG, 1967, AA
FLASH, THE, 1923
FLASHDANCE, 1983
FLASHING FANGS, 1926
FLASHING GUNS, 1947, A
FLASHING HOOFS, 1928
FLASHING SPURS, 1924
FLASHING STEEDS, 1925
FLASHLIGHT, THE, 1917, A
FLASHPOINT, 1984, C
FLAT TOP, 1952, A
FLAT TWO, 1962, A-C
FLATTERY, 1925
FLATTERY, 1925, A
FLAVOR OF GREEN TEA OVER RICE, THE
FLAW, THE, 1933, A
FLAW, THE, 1955, A
FLAXY MARTIN, 1949, A
FLEA IN HER EAR, A, 1968, C
FLEDGLINGS, 1965, O
FLEET'S IN, THE, 1928
FLEET'S IN, THE, 1942, AA
FLEETWING, 1928
FLEMISH FARM, THE, 1943, A
FLESH, 1932, C
FLESH AND BLOOD, 1922
FLESH AND BLOOD, 1951, C
FLESH AND BLOOD SHOW, THE, 1974, O
FLESH AND FANTASY, 1943, A-C
FLESH AND FLAME
FLESH AND FURY, 1952, A
FLESH AND SPIRIT, 1922
FLESH AND THE DEVIL, 1926, A
FLESH AND THE FIENDS, THE
FLESH AND THE SPUR, 1957, C
FLESH AND THE WOMAN, 1954, O
FLESH EATERS, THE, 1964, O
FLESH FEAST, 1970, O
FLESH GORDON, 1974
FLESH IS WEAK, THE, 1957, O
FLESH MERCHANT, THE, 1956, O
FLESHBURN, 1984, O
FLETCH, 1984, C
FLEUR D'AMOUR, 1927
FLEUR DE PARIS, 1916
FLICK
FLICKER UP, 1946
FLIGHT, 1929, A
FLIGHT, 1960
FLIGHT ANGELS, 1940, A
FLIGHT AT MIDNIGHT, 1939, A
FLIGHT COMMAND, 1940, A
FLIGHT COMMANDER, THE, 1927
FLIGHT FOR FREEDOM, 1943, A
FLIGHT FROM ASHIYA, 1964, A
FLIGHT FROM DESTINY, 1941
FLIGHT FROM FOLLY, 1945, A
FLIGHT FROM GLORY, 1937, A
FLIGHT FROM SINGAPORE, 1962, A
FLIGHT FROM TERROR
FLIGHT FROM TREASON, 1960
FLIGHT FROM VIENNA, 1956, A
FLIGHT INTO NOWHERE, 1938
FLIGHT LIEUTENANT, 1942, A
FLIGHT NURSE, 1953, A
FLIGHT OF THE DOVES, 1971, AA
FLIGHT OF THE DUCHESS, THE, 1916
FLIGHT OF THE EAGLE, 1983, A-C
FLIGHT OF THE LOST BALLOON, 1961, C
FLIGHT OF THE PHOENIX, THE, 1965, C
FLIGHT OF THE SANDPIPER, THE
FLIGHT THAT DISAPPEARED, THE, 1961, A
FLIGHT TO BERLIN, 1984, O
FLIGHT TO FAME, 1938, A
FLIGHT TO FURY, 1966, C
FLIGHT TO HONG KONG, 1956, C
FLIGHT TO MARS, 1951, A
FLIGHT TO NOWHERE, 1946, C
FLIGHT TO TANGIER, 1953, A
FLIM-FLAM MAN, THE, 1967, A
FLIPOTTE, 1920
FLIPPER, 1963, AAA
FLIPPER'S NEW ADVENTURE, 1964, AAA
FLIRT, THE, 1916
FLIRT, THE, 1922, A
FLIRTATION WALK, 1934, AA
FLIRTING WIDOW, THE, 1930, A
FLIRTING WITH DANGER, 1935, A
FLIRTING WITH DEATH, 1917
FLIRTING WITH FATE, 1916, A
FLIRTING WITH FATE, 1938, A
FLIRTING WITH LOVE, 1924
FLITTERWOCHEN IN DER HOLLE
FLOATING COLLEGE, THE, 1928, A
FLOATING DUTCHMAN, THE, 1953, A
FLOATING WEEDS, 1970, A
FLOOD, 1915
FLOOD TIDE, 1935, A
FLOOD TIDE, 1958, C

FOXHOLE IN CAIRO, 1960, A
FOXTROT, 1977, C-O
FOXY DROWN, 1974, O
FOXY LADY, 1971, A
FQIEDA, 1947, A
FRA DIAVOLO
FRAGE 7
FRAGMENT OF AN EMPIRE, 1930
FRAGMENT OF FEAR, 1971, C-O
FRAGRANCE OF WILD FLOWERS, THE, 1979, C
FRAIL WOMEN, 1932, C
FRAILTY, 1921, C
FRAME UP, THE, 1917, A
FRAME UP, THE, 1923
FRAME-UP THE, 1937, A
FRAME-UP, THE
FRAME-UP, THE, 1915
FRAMED, 1927
FRAMED, 1930, A
FRAMED, 1940
FRAMED, 1947, C
FRAMED, 1975
FRAMEUP, THE, 1916
FRAMING FRAMERS, 1918
FRANCES, 1982
FRANCHETTE; LES INTRIGUES, 1969, O
FRANCHISE AFFAIR, THE, 1952, A
FRANCIS, 1949
FRANCIS COVERS THE BIG TOWN, 1953, AA
FRANCIS GOES TO THE RACES, 1951, A
FRANCIS GOES TO WEST POINT, 1952, AA
FRANCIS IN THE HAUNTED HOUSE, 1956
FRANCIS IN THE NAVY, 1955, A
FRANCIS JOINS THE WACS, 1954, AA
FRANCIS OF ASSISI, 1961, A
FRANCOISE
FRANK'S GREATEST ADVENTURE
FRANKENSTEIN, 1931, C-O
FRANKENSTEIN 1970, 1958, C
FRANKENSTEIN AND THE MONSTER FROM HELL, 1974, O
FRANKENSTEIN CONQUERS THE WORLD, 1964, C
FRANKENSTEIN CREATED WOMAN, 1965, O
FRANKENSTEIN MEETS THE SPACE MONSTER, 1965, C
FRANKENSTEIN MEETS THE WOLF MAN, 1943, C
FRANKENSTEIN MUST BE DESTROYED!, 1969, C-O
FRANKENSTEIN VS. THE GIANT DEVILFISH
FRANKENSTEIN'S BLOODY TERROR, 1968, C
FRANKENSTEIN'S DAUGHTER, 1958, C-O
FRANKENSTEIN'S ISLAND, 1982
FRANKENSTEIN, THE VAMPIRE AND CO., 1961, C
FRANKENSTEIN-ITALIAN STYLE, 1977, O
FRANKIE AND JOHNNY, 1936, A-C
FRANKIE AND JOHNNY, 1966, A
FRANKWEILER, 1973, AA
FRANTIC, 1961, C
FRASIER, THE SENSUOUS LION, 1973, AA
FRATERNITY ROW, 1977, O
FRAU IM MOND
FRAULEIN, 1958, C
FRAULEIN DOKTOR, 1969, C-O
FREAKS, 1932, O
FREAKS!, 1966
FREAKY FRIDAY, 1976, AA
FRECKLED RASCAL, THE, 1929, A
FRECKLES, 1917
FRECKLES, 1928
FRECKLES, 1935, A
FRECKLES, 1960, A
FRECKLES COMES HOME, 1942, A
FREDDIE STEPS OUT, 1946, A
FREDDY UNTER FREMDEN STERNEN, 1962, A
FREE AIR, 1922
FREE AND EASY, 1930, A
FREE AND EASY, 1941, A
FREE AND EQUAL, 1924
FREE FOR ALL, 1949, A
FREE GRASS, 1969, O
FREE KISSES, 1926
FREE LIPS, 1928, A
FREE LOVE, 1930
FREE SOUL, A, 1931, C
FREE SPIRIT
FREE TO LOVE, 1925
FREE, BLONDE AND 21, 1940, A
FREE, WHITE AND 21, 1963, C
FREEBIE AND THE BEAN, 1974, O
FREEDOM FOR US
FREEDOM OF THE PRESS, 1928, A
FREEDOM OF THE SEAS, 1934, A
FREEDOM RADIO
FREEDOM TO DIE, 1962, A
FREEWHEELIN', 1976, A
FREEZE BOMB, 1980
FREEZE OUT, THE, 1921
FREIBURG PASSION PLAY, 1924
FREIGHTERS OF DESTINY, 1932, A
FRENCH CANCAN, 1956, A
FRENCH CONNECTION II, 1975, O
FRENCH CONNECTION, THE, 1971, O
FRENCH CONSPIRACY, THE, 1973, A

FRENCH DOLL, THE, 1923, A
FRENCH DRESSING, 1927, C
FRENCH DRESSING, 1964, A
FRENCH GAME, THE, 1963, C
FRENCH HEELS, 1922
FRENCH KEY, THE, 1946, A
FRENCH LEAVE, 1937, A
FRENCH LEAVE, 1948, A
FRENCH LIEUTENANT'S WOMAN, THE, 1981, O
FRENCH LINE, THE, 1954
FRENCH MISTRESS, 1960, A
FRENCH POSTCARDS, 1979
FRENCH QUARTER, 1978, O
FRENCH TOUCH, THE, 1954, A
FRENCH WAY, THE, 1952, A
FRENCH WAY, THE, 1975, O
FRENCH WITHOUT TEARS, 1939, A
FRENCH, THEY ARE A FUNNY RACE, THE, 1956, A
FRENCHIE, 1950, A
FRENCHMAN'S CREEK, 1944, A
FRENZIED FLAMES, 1926
FRENZY, 1946
FRENZY, 1972, C-O
FRESH EVERY HOUR
FRESH FROM PARIS, 1955, A
FRESHIE, THE, 1922, A
FRESHMAN LOVE, 1936, A
FRESHMAN YEAR, 1938, A
FRESHMAN, THE
FRESHMAN, THE, 1925, A
FREUD, 1962, A-C
FRIC FRAC, 1939, A
FRIDAY FOSTER, 1975, O
FRIDAY ON MY MIND, 1970
FRIDAY THE 13TH, 1916, A
FRIDAY THE 13TH, 1934, A
FRIDAY THE 13TH, 1980, O
FRIDAY THE 13TH PART II, 1981, O
FRIDAY THE 13TH PART III, 1982, O
FRIDAY THE 13TH—THE FINAL CHAPTER, 1984, O
FRIDAY THE 13TH... THE ORPHAN, 1979, O
FRIEND HUSBAND, 1918
FRIEND OF THE FAMILY, 1965, A
FRIEND OR FOE, 1982
FRIEND WILL COME TONIGHT, A, 1948, A
FRIEND WILSON'S DAUGHTER, 1915
FRIENDLIEST GIRLS IN THE WORLD, THE
FRIENDLY ENEMIES, 1925
FRIENDLY ENEMIES, 1942, A
FRIENDLY HUSBAND, A, 1923, A
FRIENDLY KILLER, THE, 1970, C-O
FRIENDLY NEIGHBORS, 1940, A
FRIENDLY PERSUASION, 1956, A
FRIENDS, 1971, O
FRIENDS AND HUSBANDS, 1983, C
FRIENDS AND LOVERS
FRIENDS AND LOVERS, 1931, A
FRIENDS AND NEIGHBORS, 1963, A
FRIENDS FOR LIFE, 1964, A
FRIENDS OF EDDIE COYLE, THE, 1973, O
FRIENDS OF MR. SWEENEY, 1934
FRIGHT
FRIGHT, 1971, O
FRIGHTENED BRIDE, THE, 1952, A
FRIGHTENED CITY, THE, 1961, A
FRIGHTENED LADY
FRIGHTENED LADY, THE
FRIGHTENED MAN, THE, 1952, A
FRIGHTMARE, 1974, O
FRIGHTMARE, 1983, O
FRIGID WIFE
FRINGE OF SOCIETY, THE, 1918
FRISCO JENNY, 1933, A
FRISCO KID, 1935, A
FRISCO KID, THE, 1979, C
FRISCO LILL, 1942, A
FRISCO SAL, 1945, A
FRISCO SALLY LEVY, 1927
FRISCO TORNADO, 1950, A
FRISCO WATERFRONT, 1935, A
FRISKY, 1955, A
FRISKY MRS. JOHNSON, THE, 1920
FRIVOLOUS SAL, 1925
FRIVOLOUS WIVES, 1920
FROG, THE, 1937, A
FROGGY'S LITTLE BROTHER
FROGMEN, THE, 1951
FROGS, 1972, C
FROM A BROADWAY TO A THRONE, 1916
FROM A ROMAN BALCONY, 1961, C
FROM BEYOND THE GRAVE, 1974, C
FROM BROADWAY TO CHEYENNE, 1932
FROM HEADQUARTERS, 1919
FROM HEADQUARTERS, 1929
FROM HEADQUARTERS, 1933, A
FROM HELL IT CAME, 1957, C
FROM HELL TO HEAVEN, 1933, C
FROM HELL TO TEXAS, 1958, C
FROM HELL TO VICTORY, 1979, C
FROM HERE TO ETERNITY, 1953, C-O
FROM NASHVILLE WITH MUSIC, 1969
FROM NOON TO THREE, 1976, C

FROM NOW ON, 1920
FROM RAGS TO RICHES
FROM RUSSIA WITH LOVE, 1963, A
FROM SHOPGIRL TO DUCHESS, 1915
FROM SPARKS—FLAMES, 1924
FROM THE DESK OF MARGARET TYDING, 1958
FROM THE EARTH TO THE MOON, 1958
FROM THE GROUND UP, 1921, A
FROM THE LIFE OF THE MARIONETTES, 1980, O
FROM THE MANGER TO THE CROSS, 1913, A
FROM THE MIXED-UP FILES OF MRS. BASIL E.
FROM THE TERRACE, 1960, C
FROM THE VALLEY OF THE MISSING, 1915
FROM THE WEST, 1920
FROM THIS DAY FORWARD, 1946, A
FROM TOP TO BOTTOM, 1933, A
FROM TWO TO SIX, 1918
FROMONT JEUNNE ET RISLER AINE, 1921
FRONT LINE KIDS, 1942, AA
FRONT PAGE STORY, 1954, A
FRONT PAGE STORY, A, 1922, A
FRONT PAGE WOMAN, 1935, A
FRONT PAGE, THE, 1931
FRONT PAGE, THE, 1974, C-O
FRONT, THE, 1976, C
FRONTIER AGENT, 1948, A
FRONTIER BADMEN, 1943, A
FRONTIER CRUSADER, 1940
FRONTIER DAYS, 1934, A
FRONTIER FEUD, 1945
FRONTIER FIGHTERS, 1947
FRONTIER FUGITIVES, 1945
FRONTIER FURY, 1943, A
FRONTIER GAL, 1945, A
FRONTIER GAMBLER, 1956
FRONTIER GUN, 1958, A
FRONTIER GUNLAW, 1946
FRONTIER HELLCAT, 1966, A
FRONTIER INVESTIGATOR, 1949, A
FRONTIER JUSTICE, 1936, A
FRONTIER LAW, 1943, A
FRONTIER MARSHAL, 1934, A
FRONTIER MARSHAL, 1939, A
FRONTIER MARSHAL IN PRAIRIE PALS
FRONTIER OF THE STARS, THE, 1921
FRONTIER OUTLAWS, 1944, A
FRONTIER OUTPOST, 1950, A
FRONTIER PHANTOM, THE, 1952, A
FRONTIER PONY EXPRESS, 1939
FRONTIER REVENGE, 1948, A
FRONTIER SCOUT, 1939, A
FRONTIER TOWN, 1938, A
FRONTIER TRAIL, THE, 1926
FRONTIER UPRISING, 1961, A
FRONTIER VENGEANCE, 1939, A
FRONTIER WOMAN, 1956
FRONTIERS OF '49, 1939, A
FRONTIERSMAN, THE, 1927
FRONTIERSMAN, THE, 1938, A
FRONTIERSMAN, THE, 1968
FROU FROU, 1914
FROU-FROU, 1955, A
FROZEN ALIVE, 1966, A
FROZEN DEAD, THE, 1967, C
FROZEN FATE, 1929
FROZEN GHOST, THE, 1945
FROZEN JUSTICE, 1929, A
FROZEN LIMITS, THE, 1939, A
FROZEN RIVER, 1929, A
FROZEN SCREAM, 1980
FROZEN WARNING, THE, 1918
FRUIT IS RIPE, THE, 1961, C
FRUIT OF DIVORCE, THE
FRUITFUL VINE, THE, 1921
FRUITS OF DESIRE, THE, 1916, A
FRUITS OF PASSION, 1919
FRUSTRATIONS, 1967, O
FU MANCHU AND THE KISS OF DEATH
FUEGO
FUEL OF LIFE, 1917
FUGITIVE AT LARGE, 1939, A
FUGITIVE FROM A PRISON CAMP, 1940, A
FUGITIVE FROM JUSTICE, A, 1940, A
FUGITIVE FROM MATRIMONY, 1919
FUGITIVE FROM SONORA, 1943, A
FUGITIVE GIRLS, 1975
FUGITIVE IN THE SKY, 1937
FUGITIVE KILLER, 1975
FUGITIVE KIND, THE, 1960, C
FUGITIVE LADY, 1934, C
FUGITIVE LADY, 1951, O
FUGITIVE LOVERS, 1934
FUGITIVE OF THE PLAINS, 1943
FUGITIVE ROAD, 1934, A
FUGITIVE SHERIFF, THE, 1936
FUGITIVE VALLEY, 1941, A
FUGITIVE, THE, 1916
FUGITIVE, THE, 1925
FUGITIVE, THE, 1933, A
FUGITIVE, THE, 1940, A
FUGITIVE, THE, 1947, C
FUGITIVES, 1929, A

FUGITIVES FOR A NIGHT, 1938, C
FULL CIRCLE, 1935, A
FULL CIRCLE, 1977, O
FULL CONFESSION, 1939, C
FULL HOUSE, A, 1920
FULL MOON HIGH, 1982, A-C
FULL MOON IN PARIS, 1984, O
FULL OF LIFE, 1956, A
FULL OF PEP, 1919
FULL SPEED, 1925
FULL SPEED AHEAD, 1936, A
FULL SPEED AHEAD, 1939, A
FULL TREATMENT, THE
FULLER BRUSH GIRL, THE, 1950, AAA
FULLER BRUSH MAN, 1948, AAA
FULLER REPORT, THE, 1966
FUN AND FANCY FREE, 1947, AAA
FUN AND GAMES, 1973
FUN AT ST. FANNY'S, 1956, AA
FUN HOUSE, THE, 1977
FUN IN ACAPULCO, 1963, A
FUN LOVING
FUN ON A WEEKEND, 1979, AA
FUN ON THE FARM, 1926
FUN WITH DICK AND JANE, 1977, C-O
FUNDOSHI ISHA
FUNERAL FOR AN ASSASSIN, 1977
FUNERAL HOME, 1982, O
FUNERAL IN BERLIN, 1966, C
FUNHOUSE, THE, 1981, O
FUNNY FACE, 1957, AA
FUNNY FARM, THE, 1982, C
FUNNY GIRL, 1968
FUNNY LADY, 1975, A
FUNNY MONEY, 1983, O
FUNNY PARISHIONER, THE
FUNNY THING HAPPENED ON THE WAY TO THE
   FORUM,
*FUNNY THING HAPPENED ON THE WAY TO THE
   FORUM, A*, 1966, C
FUNNYMAN, 1967, C
FUOCO FATUO
FUR COLLAR, THE, 1962
FURESSHUMAN WAKADISHO
FURIA, 1947, O
FURIES, THE, 1930, A
FURIES, THE, 1950, C
FURIN KAZAN
FURNANCE, THE, 1920
FURTHER ADVENTURES OF THE FLAG
   LIEUTENANT, 1927, A
FURTHER ADVENTURES OF THE WILDERNESS
FURTHER EXPLOITS OF SEXTON BLAKE, THE
   -MYSTERY OF THE S.S. OLYMPIC, THE (1919, Brit.)
FURTHER UP THE CREEK!, 1958
FURY, 1922
FURY, 1936, C
FURY AND THE WOMAN, 1937, A
FURY AT FURNACE CREEK, 1948, A
FURY AT GUNSIGHT PASS, 1956, O
FURY AT SHOWDOWN, 1957, O
FURY AT SMUGGLERS BAY, 1963, A
FURY BELOW, 1938, A
FURY IN PARADISE, 1955, A
FURY OF HERCULES, THE, 1961, A
FURY OF THE CONGO, 1951, AA
FURY OF THE JUNGLE, 1934, O
FURY OF THE PAGANS, 1963, C
FURY OF THE VIKINGS
FURY OF THE WILD, 1929
FURY ON THE BOSPHOROUS, 1965
FURY, THE, 1978, O
FUSS AND FEATHERS, 1918
FUSS OVER FEATHERS, 1954, AAA
FUTARI NO MUSUCKO
FUTUREWORLD, 1976, C
FUZZ, 1972, O
FUZZY PINK NIGHTGOWN, THE, 1957, A
FUZZY SETTLES DOWN, 1944, A
FYRE, 1979

-G-

G-MAN'S WIFE
G-MEN, 1935, A
G.I. BLUES, 1960, A
G.I. EXECUTIONER, THE, 1971
G.I. HONEYMOON, 1945
G.I. JANE, 1951, A
G.I. WAR BRIDES, 1946, A
GABLE AND LOMBARD, 1976, O
GABLES MYSTERY, THE, 1931, A
GABLES MYSTERY, THE, 1938, A
GABRIEL OVER THE WHITE HOUSE, 1933, C
GABRIELA, 1984, O
GABY, 1956, A
GAIETY GEORGE
GAIETY GIRL, THE, 1924
GAIETY GIRLS, THE, 1938, A
GAILY, GAILY, 1969, C-O
GAL WHO TOOK THE WEST, THE, 1949, A
GAL YOUNG UN, 1979
GALAXINA, 1980

GALAXY EXPRESS, 1982, A
GALAXY OF TERROR, 1981, O
GALIA, 1966, C
GALILEO, 1968, A
GALILEO, 1975
GALLANT BESS, 1946
GALLANT BLADE, THE, 1948, A
GALLANT DEFENDER, 1935, A
GALLANT FOOL, THE, 1926, A
GALLANT FOOL, THE, 1933, A
GALLANT HOURS, THE, 1960, A
GALLANT JOURNEY, 1946, A
GALLANT LADY, 1934, A
GALLANT LADY, 1942, A
GALLANT LEGION, THE, 1948, A
GALLANT ONE, THE, 1964, A
GALLANT SONS, 1940, A
GALLERY OF HORRORS
GALLEY SLAVE, THE, 1915
GALLIPOLI, 1981, A-C
GALLOPER, THE, 1915
GALLOPIN' THROUGH
GALLOPING ACE, THE, 1924, A
GALLOPING COWBOY, THE, 1926
GALLOPING DEVIL, THE
GALLOPING DEVILS, 1920
GALLOPING DUDE
GALLOPING DYNAMITE, 1937, A
GALLOPING FISH, 1924
GALLOPING FURY, 1927
GALLOPING GALLAGHER, 1924, A
GALLOPING GOBS, THE, 1927, A
GALLOPING JINX, 1925
GALLOPING KID, THE, 1922, A
GALLOPING KID, THE, 1932
GALLOPING LOVER, THE, 1929
GALLOPING MAJOR, THE, 1951
GALLOPING ON, 1925
GALLOPING ROMEO, 1933, A
GALLOPING THRU, 1923, A
GALLOPING THRU, 1932, A
GALLOPING THUNDER, 1927
GALLOPING THUNDER, 1946
GALLOPING VENGENCE, 1925
GALS, INCORPORATED, 1943, A
GAMBIT, 1966
GAMBLE FOR LOVE, A, 1917
GAMBLE IN LIVES, A, 1920
GAMBLE IN SOULS, A, 1916
GAMBLE WITH HEARTS, A, 1923, A
GAMBLER AND THE LADY, THE, 1952, A
GAMBLER FROM NATCHEZ, THE, 1954
GAMBLER OF THE WEST, THE, 1915
GAMBLER WORE A GUN, THE, 1961, A
GAMBLER'S ADVOCATE, 1915
GAMBLER'S CHOICE, 1944, A
GAMBLER, THE, 1958, C
GAMBLER, THE, 1974, O
GAMBLERS ALL, 1919
GAMBLERS, THE, 1914
GAMBLERS, THE, 1919
GAMBLERS, THE, 1929, A
GAMBLERS, THE, 1969, A
GAMBLERS, THE 1948
GAMBLIN' MAN
GAMBLING, 1934, A
GAMBLING DAUGHTERS, 1941, A
GAMBLING FOOL, THE, 1925
GAMBLING HOUSE, 1950, A
GAMBLING IN SOULS, 1919, A
GAMBLING LADY, 1934, A
GAMBLING ON THE HIGH SEAS, 1940, A
GAMBLING SAMURAI, THE, 1966, C
GAMBLING SEX, 1932, A
GAMBLING SHIP, 1933, A
GAMBLING SHIP, 1939, A
GAMBLING TERROR, THE, 1937, A
GAMBLING WITH SOULS, 1936
GAMBLING WIVES, 1924, A
GAME CHICKEN, THE, 1922
GAME FIGHTER, A, 1924
GAME FOR SIX LOVERS, A, 1962, A
GAME FOR THREE LOSERS, 1965, A
GAME FOR VULTURES, A, 1980, O
GAME IS OVER, THE, 1967, O
GAME OF CHANCE, A, 1932, A
GAME OF DANGER
GAME OF DEATH, A, 1945, A
GAME OF DEATH, THE, 1979, O
GAME OF LIBERTY, THE
GAME OF LIFE, THE, 1922, A
GAME OF LOVE, THE, 1954, C
GAME OF TRUTH, THE, 1961, C
GAME OF WITS, A, 1917
GAME SHOW MODELS, 1977
GAME THAT KILLS, THE, 1937, A
GAME WITH FATE, A, 1918
GAME'S UP, THE, 1919
GAMEKEEPER, THE, 1980, A
GAMERA THE INVINCIBLE, 1966, A
GAMERA VERSUS BARUGON, 1966, A
GAMERA VERSUS GAOS, 1967, A

GAMERA VERSUS GUIRON, 1969, A
GAMERA VERSUS MONSTER K, 1970, A
GAMERA VERSUS VIRAS, 1968
GAMERA VERSUS ZIGRA, 1971, A
GAMES, 1967, O
GAMES FOR SIX LOVERS
GAMES MEN PLAY, THE, 1968, O
GAMES THAT LOVERS PLAY, 1971, O
GAMES, THE, 1970
GAMESTERS, THE, 1920
GAMLET
GAMMA PEOPLE, THE, 1956, A
GAMMERA THE INVINCIBLE
GANDHI, 1982, A
GANG BULLETS, 1938, A
GANG BUSTER, THE, 1931, A
GANG BUSTERS, 1955, A
GANG SHOW, THE
GANG THAT COULDN'T SHOOT STRAIGHT, THE,
   1971
GANG WAR, 1928
GANG WAR, 1940, C
GANG WAR, 1958, C-O
GANG WAR, 1962, A
GANG'S ALL HERE, 1941, A
GANG'S ALL HERE, THE
GANG'S ALL HERE, THE, 1943, A
GANG, THE, 1938, A
GANGA
GANGS INCORPORATED
GANGS OF CHICAGO, 1940, A
GANGS OF NEW YORK, 1938, A
GANGS OF SONORA, 1941, A
GANGS OF THE WATERFRONT, 1945, A
GANGSTER STORY, 1959, A
GANGSTER VIP, THE, 1968, C
GANGSTER'S BOY, 1938, A
GANGSTER'S BRIDE, THE
GANGSTER'S DEN, 1945
GANGSTER'S ENEMY NO. 1
GANGSTER'S REVENGE
GANGSTER, THE, 1947, C
GANGSTERS OF NEW YORK, THE, 1914, O
GANGSTERS OF THE FRONTIER, 1944, A
GANGSTERS, THE, 1914
GANGWAY, 1937, A
GANGWAY FOR TOMORROW, 1943, A
GANJA AND HESS, 1973, O
GAOL BREAK, 1936, A
GAOLBREAK, 1962, A
GAP, THE
GAPPA THE TRIFIBIAN MONSTER, 1967
GARAKUTA
GARBAGE MAN, THE, 1963, C
GARBO TALKS, 1984, C
GARDEN MURDER CASE, THE, 1936
GARDEN OF ALLAH, THE, 1916
GARDEN OF ALLAH, THE, 1927
GARDEN OF ALLAH, THE, 1936, C
GARDEN OF EDEN, 1954, O
GARDEN OF EDEN, THE, 1928
GARDEN OF EVIL, 1954, C
GARDEN OF KNOWLEDGE, THE, 1917, O
GARDEN OF LIES, THE, 1915
GARDEN OF RESURRECTION, THE, 1919, A
GARDEN OF THE DEAD, 1972, O
GARDEN OF THE FINZI-CONTINIS, THE, 1976, C
GARDEN OF THE MOON, 1938, A
GARDEN OF WEEDS, THE, 1924
GARDENER, THE
GARDIENS DE PHARE, 1929
GARMENT JUNGLE, THE, 1957, A
GARMENTS OF YOUTH, 1921
GARNET BRACELET, THE, 1966, A
GARRISON FOLLIES, 1940, A
GARRISON'S FINISH, 1923, A
GARRYOWEN, 1920
GARTER GIRL, THE, 1920
GARU, THE MAD MONK
GAS, 1981, O
GAS HOUSE KIDS, 1946, A
GAS HOUSE KIDS GO WEST, 1947, A
GAS HOUSE KIDS IN HOLLYWOOD, 1947, A
GAS PUMP GIRLS, 1979
GAS, OIL AND WATER, 1922
GAS-S-S-S!, 1970, O
GASBAGS, 1940
GASLIGHT, 1940, C
GASLIGHT, 1944, C
GASOLINE ALLEY, 1951, AA
GASOLINE COWBOY, 1926
GASOLINE GUS, 1921, A
GASU NINGEN DAIICHIGO
GATE CRASHER, THE, 1928, A
GATE OF FLESH, 1964, O
GATE OF HELL, 1954, C-O
GATES OF BRASS, 1919
GATES OF DOOM, THE, 1917
GATES OF DUTY, 1919
GATES OF EDEN, THE, 1916
GATES OF GLADNESS, 1918
GATES OF HELL, THE, 1983, O

GIANT CLAW, THE, 1957, A
GIANT FROM THE UNKNOWN, 1958, C
GIANT GILA MONSTER, THE, 1959, A
GIANT LEECHES, THE
GIANT OF HIS RACE, A, 1921
GIANT OF MARATHON, THE, 1960, O
GIANT OF METROPOLIS, THE, 1963, A
GIANT SPIDER INVASION, THE, 1975, A
GIANTS A' FIRE
GIBRALTAR
GIBRALTAR ADVENTURE
GIDEON OF SCOTLAND YARD, 1959, A
GIDEON'S DAY
GIDGET, 1959
GIDGET GOES HAWAIIAN, 1961, A
GIDGET GOES TO ROME, 1963, A
GIFT
GIFT FOR HEIDI, A, 1958
GIFT GIRL, THE, 1917
GIFT HORSE, THE
GIFT O' GAB, 1917
GIFT OF GAB, 1934
GIFT OF LOVE, THE, 1958, A
GIFT SUPREME, THE, 1920
GIFT, THE
GIFT, THE, 1983, O
GIGANTES PLANETARIOS, 1965
GIGANTIS, 1959, A
GIGI, 1958, A
GIGOLETTE, 1920
GIGOLETTE, 1935, A-C
GIGOLETTES OF PARIS, 1933, A
GIGOLO, 1926
GIGOT, 1962, A
GILBERT AND SULLIVAN
GILDA, 1946, C
GILDED BUTTERFLY, THE, 1926, A
GILDED CAGE, THE, 1916, A
GILDED CAGE, THE, 1954, A
GILDED DREAM, THE, 1920, A
GILDED FOOL, THE, 1915
GILDED HIGHWAY, THE, 1926, A
GILDED LIES, 1921
GILDED LILY, THE, 1921, A
GILDED LILY, THE, 1935, AA
GILDED SPIDER, THE, 1916, A
GILDED YOUTH, A, 1917
GILDERSLEEVE ON BROADWAY, 1943, A
GILDERSLEEVE'S BAD DAY, 1943, A
GILDERSLEEVE'S GHOST, 1944, A
GIMME AN 'F', 1984, O
GIMMIE, 1923, A
GINA, 1961, C
GINGER, 1919
GINGER, 1935, A
GINGER, 1947, A
GINGER, 1972
GINGER IN THE MORNING, 1973, A
GINGHAM GIRL, THE, 1927
GINSBERG THE GREAT, 1927, A
GION MATSURI
GIORDANO BRUNO, 1973, O
GIORNI DI FUOCO
GIPSY BLOOD
GIPSY CAVALIER, A, 1922
GIRARA, 1967, G
GIRDLE OF GOLD, 1952, A
GIRL AGAINST NAPOLEON, A
GIRL ALASKA, THE, 1919
GIRL AND THE CRISIS, THE, 1917
GIRL AND THE GAMBLER, THE, 1939, A
GIRL AND THE GENERAL, THE, 1967, C
GIRL AND THE HUGLER, THE, 1967, AA
GIRL AND THE JUDGE, THE, 1918
GIRL AND THE LEGEND, THE, 1966, A
GIRL AND THE PALIO, THE
GIRL ANGLE, THE, 1917
GIRL AT BAY, A, 1919
GIRL AT HOME, THE, 1917
GIRL BY THE ROADSIDE, THE, 1918
GIRL CAN'T HELP IT, THE, 1956, C
GIRL CAN'T STOP, THE, 1966, C
GIRL CRAZY, 1932, A
GIRL CRAZY, 1943, AAA
GIRL CRAZY, 1965
GIRL DODGER, THE, 1919
GIRL DOWNSTAIRS, THE, 1938, A
GIRL FEVER, 1961, A
GIRL FOR JOE, A
GIRL FRIEND, THE, 1935, A
GIRL FRIENDS, THE
GIRL FROM ALASKA, 1942
GIRL FROM AVENUE A, 1940, A
GIRL FROM BEYOND, THE, 1918
GIRL FROM BOHEMIA, THE, 1918
GIRL FROM CALGARY, 1932, A
GIRL FROM CARTHAGE, THE, 1924
GIRL FROM CHICAGO, THE, 1927, A
GIRL FROM CHINA, THE
GIRL FROM CONEY ISLAND, THE
GIRL FROM DOWNING STREET, THE, 1918, A
GIRL FROM GAY PAREE, THE, 1927

GIRL FROM GOD'S COUNTRY, 1940, A
GIRL FROM GOD'S COUNTRY, THE, 1921
GIRL FROM HAVANA, 1940, A
GIRL FROM HAVANA, THE, 1929, A
GIRL FROM HIS TOWN, THE, 1915, A
GIRL FROM HONG KONG, 1966, A
GIRL FROM IRELAND
GIRL FROM JONES BEACH, THE, 1949, AA
GIRL FROM LORRAINE, A, 1982, O
GIRL FROM MANDALAY, 1936, A
GIRL FROM MANHATTAN, 1948, A
GIRL FROM MAXIM'S. THE, 1936, A
GIRL FROM MEXICO, 1930
GIRL FROM MEXICO, THE, 1939, A
GIRL FROM MISSOURI, THE, 1934
GIRL FROM MONTEREY, THE, 1943, A
GIRL FROM MONTMARTRE, THE, 1926
GIRL FROM NOWHERE, THE, 1919
GIRL FROM NOWHERE, THE, 1921
GIRL FROM PARIS, THE
GIRL FROM PETROVKA, THE, 1974, A
GIRL FROM POLTAVA, 1937, A
GIRL FROM PORCUPINE, THE, 1921
GIRL FROM RECTOR'S, THE, 1917
GIRL FROM RIO, THE, 1927, A
GIRL FROM RIO, THE, 1939, A
GIRL FROM ROCKY POINT, THE, 1922
GIRL FROM SAN LORENZO, THE, 1950, A
GIRL FROM SCOTLAND YARD, THE, 1937, A
GIRL FROM STARSHIP VENUS, THE, 1975, O
GIRL FROM TENTH AVENUE, THE, 1935, A
GIRL FROM THE MARSH CROFT, THE, 1935, A
GIRL FROM THE OUTSIDE, THE, 1919
GIRL FROM THE WEST, 1923, A
GIRL FROM TOBACCO ROW, THE, 1966
GIRL FROM TRIESTE, THE, 1983, C
GIRL FROM VALLADOLIO, 1958, A
GIRL FROM WOOLWORTH'S, THE, 1929, A
GIRL GAME, 1968, C
GIRL GETTERS, THE, 1966, C
GIRL GLORY, THE, 1917
GIRL GRABBERS, THE, 1968, O
GIRL HABIT, 1931, A
GIRL HAPPY, 1965, A
GIRL HE DIDN'T BUY, THE, 1928
GIRL HE LEFT BEHIND, THE, 1956, A
GIRL HUNTERS, THE, 1963, C-O
GIRL I ABANDONED, THE, 1970, C-O
GIRL I LEFT BEHIND ME, THE, 1915
GIRL I LOVED, THE, 1923
GIRL I MADE, THE
GIRL IN 313, 1940, A
GIRL IN 419, 1933
GIRL IN A MILLION, A, 1946, A
GIRL IN BLACK STOCKINGS, 1957
GIRL IN BLUE, THE, 1974
GIRL IN BOHEMIA, A, 1919
GIRL IN DANGER, 1934, A
GIRL IN DISTRESS, 1941, A
GIRL IN EVERY PORT, A, 1928, A
GIRL IN EVERY PORT, A, 1952, A
GIRL IN GOLD BOOTS, 1968, O
GIRL IN HIS HOUSE, THE, 1918
GIRL IN HIS POCKET
GIRL IN HIS ROOM, THE, 1922
GIRL IN LOVER'S LANE, THE, 1960
GIRL IN NUMBER 29, THE, 1920
GIRL IN OVERALLS, THE
GIRL IN PAWN
GIRL IN POSSESSION, 1934, A
GIRL IN ROOM 13, 1961, A
GIRL IN ROOM 17, THE
GIRL IN THE BIKINI, THE, 1958
GIRL IN THE CASE, 1944, A
GIRL IN THE CHECKERED COAT, THE, 1917
GIRL IN THE CROWD, THE, 1934, A
GIRL IN THE DARK, THE, 1918, A
GIRL IN THE FLAT, THE, 1934, A
GIRL IN THE GLASS CAGE, THE, 1929, A
GIRL IN THE HEADLINES, THE
GIRL IN THE INVISIBLE BIKINI, THE
GIRL IN THE KREMLIN, THE, 1957, A
GIRL IN THE LEATHER SUIT
GIRL IN THE LIMOUSINE, THE, 1924
GIRL IN THE NEWS, THE, 1941, A
GIRL IN THE NIGHT, THE, 1931, A
GIRL IN THE PAINTING, THE, 1948, A
GIRL IN THE PICTURE, THE, 1956, A
GIRL IN THE PULLMAN, THE, 1927
GIRL IN THE RAIN, 1927
GIRL IN THE RAIN, THE, 1920
GIRL IN THE RED VELVET SWING, THE, 1955, C
GIRL IN THE SHOW, THE, 1929, A
GIRL IN THE STREET, 1938, A
GIRL IN THE TAXI, 1937, A
GIRL IN THE TAXI, THE, 1921
GIRL IN THE WEB, THE, 1920
GIRL IN THE WOODS, 1958
GIRL IN TROUBLE, 1963, C
GIRL IN WHITE, THE, 1952, A
GIRL IS MINE, THE, 1950, A
GIRL LIKE THAT, A, 1917

GIRL LOVES BOY, 1937
GIRL MADNESS
GIRL MERCHANTS
GIRL MISSING, 1933, A
GIRL MOST LIKELY, THE, 1957, AA
GIRL MUST LIVE, A, 1941, A
GIRL NAMED MARY, A, 1920
GIRL NAMED TAMIRO, A, 1962, A
GIRL NEXT DOOR, THE, 1953, A
GIRL O' MY DREAMS, 1935, A
GIRL O'DREAMS, THE, 1918
GIRL OF GOLD, THE, 1925
GIRL OF LONDON, A, 1925, A
GIRL OF LOST LAKE, THE, 1916
GIRL OF MY DREAMS
GIRL OF MY DREAMS, THE, 1918
GIRL OF MY HEART, 1920, A
GIRL OF THE GOLDEN WEST, 1930, A
GIRL OF THE GOLDEN WEST, THE, 1915, A
GIRL OF THE GOLDEN WEST, THE, 1923, A
GIRL OF THE GOLDEN WEST, THE, 1938, AA
GIRL OF THE GYPSY CAMP, THE, 1925
GIRL OF THE LIMBERLOST, 1934, A
GIRL OF THE LIMBERLOST, A, 1924
GIRL OF THE LIMBERLOST, THE, 1945, A
GIRL OF THE MOORS, THE, 1961, C-O
GIRL OF THE MOUNTAINS, 1958, C-O
GIRL OF THE NIGHT, 1960, C-O
GIRL OF THE NILE, THE, 1967
GIRL OF THE OZARKS, 1936, A
GIRL OF THE PORT, 1930, A
GIRL OF THE RIO, 1932, A
GIRL OF THE SEA, 1920
GIRL OF THE SUNNY SOUTH, THE, 1913
GIRL OF THE TIMBER CLAIMS, THE, 1917
GIRL OF THE WEST, 1925
GIRL OF THE YEAR
GIRL OF TODAY, THE, 1918
GIRL ON A CHAIN GANG, 1966, O
GIRL ON A MOTORCYCLE, THE, 1968, O
GIRL ON APPROVAL, 1962, A
GIRL ON THE BARGE, THE, 1929, A
GIRL ON THE BOAT, THE, 1962, A
GIRL ON THE BRIDGE, THE, 1951, A
GIRL ON THE CANAL, THE, 1947, A
GIRL ON THE FRONT PAGE, THE, 1936, A
GIRL ON THE MOON, THE
GIRL ON THE PIER, THE, 1953, A
GIRL ON THE RUN, 1961, A
GIRL ON THE SPOT, 1946, A
GIRL ON THE STAIRS, THE, 1924, A
GIRL OVERBOARD, 1929, A
GIRL OVERBOARD, 1937, A
GIRL PHILIPPA, THE, 1917
GIRL PROBLEM, THE, 1919
GIRL RUSH, 1944, A
GIRL RUSH, THE, 1955, A
GIRL SAID NO, THE, 1930
GIRL SAID NO, THE, 1937, A
GIRL SHY, 1924, A
GIRL SMUGGLERS, 1967, O
GIRL STROKE BOY, 1971, C
GIRL SWAPPERS, THE
GIRL THIEF, THE, 1938, AA
GIRL TROUBLE, 1933
GIRL TROUBLE, 1942, A
GIRL WAS YOUNG, THE
GIRL WHO CAME BACK, THE, 1918
GIRL WHO CAME BACK, THE, 1923
GIRL WHO CAME BACK, THE, 1935, A
GIRL WHO COULDN'T GROW UP, THE, 1917
GIRL WHO COULDN'T QUITE, THE, 1949, A
GIRL WHO COULDN'T SAY NO, THE, 1969, A
GIRL WHO DARED, THE
GIRL WHO DARED, THE, 1920, A
GIRL WHO DARED, THE, 1944, A
GIRL WHO DID NOT CARE, THE
GIRL WHO DIDN'T THINK, THE, 1917
GIRL WHO DOESN'T KNOW, THE, 1917
GIRL WHO FORGOT, THE, 1939, A
GIRL WHO HAD EVERYTHING, THE, 1953, A
GIRL WHO KNEW TOO MUCH, THE, 1969, O
GIRL WHO LOVES A SOLDIER, THE, 1916, A
GIRL WHO RAN WILD, THE, 1922
GIRL WHO STAYED AT HOME, THE, 1919, A
GIRL WHO TOOK THE WRONG TURNING, THE,
  1915, A
GIRL WHO WON OUT, THE, 1917
GIRL WHO WOULDN'T QUIT, THE, 1918, A
GIRL WHO WOULDN'T WORK, THE, 1925, A
GIRL WHO WRECKED HIS HOME, THE, 1916
GIRL WITH A JAZZ HEART, THE, 1920
GIRL WITH A PISTOL, THE, 1968, A
GIRL WITH A SUITCASE, 1961, A
GIRL WITH GREEN EYES, 1964, A-C
GIRL WITH IDEAS, A, 1937
GIRL WITH NO REGRETS, THE, 1919
GIRL WITH THE CHAMPAGNE EYES, THE, 1918
GIRL WITH THE FABULOUS BOX, THE, 1969
GIRL WITH THE GOLDEN EYES, THE, 1962, C
GIRL WITH THE GREEN EYES, THE, 1916
GIRL WITH THE HAT-BOX, 1927

GIRL WITH THE JAZZ HEART, THE, 1920
GIRL WITH THE RED HAIR, THE, 1983, A
GIRL WITH THREE CAMELS, THE, 1968, A
GIRL WITHOUT A ROOM, 1933, A
GIRL WITHOUT A SOUL, THE, 1917, A
GIRL WOMAN, THE, 1919
GIRL'S DESIRE, A, 1922
GIRL'S FOLLY, A, 1917, A
GIRL, A GUY AND A GOB, A, 1941, A
GIRL, THE BODY, AND THE PILL, THE, 1967, O
GIRL-SHY COWBOY, THE, 1928
GIRLFRIENDS, 1978, A-C
GIRLS, 1919
GIRLS ABOUT TOWN, 1931
GIRLS ARE FOR LOVING, 1973
GIRLS AT SEA, 1958, A
GIRLS CAN PLAY, 1937, A
GIRLS DEMAND EXCITEMENT, 1931, A
GIRLS DISAPPEAR
GIRLS DON'T GAMBLE, 1921, A
GIRLS FOR RENT, 1974
GIRLS FROM THUNDER STRIP, THE, 1966, O
GIRLS GONE WILD, 1929, A
GIRLS HE LEFT BEHIND, THE
GIRLS IN ACTION
GIRLS IN ARMS
GIRLS IN CHAINS, 1943, A
GIRLS IN PRISON, 1956, C
GIRLS IN THE NIGHT, 1953, C
GIRLS IN THE STREET, 1937, A
GIRLS IN UNIFORM,, 1932
GIRLS IN UNIFORM, 1965
GIRLS MEN FORGET, 1924
GIRLS NEVER TELL
GIRLS NEXT DOOR, THE, 1979
GIRLS NIGHT OUT, 1984, O
GIRLS OF 42ND STREET, 1974
GIRLS OF LATIN QUARTER, 1960, A
GIRLS OF PLEASURE ISLAND, THE, 1953, A
GIRLS OF SPIDER ISLAND
GIRLS OF THE BIG HOUSE, 1945, A
GIRLS OF THE ROAD, 1940, C
GIRLS ON PROBATION, 1938, A
GIRLS ON THE BEACH, 1965, A
GIRLS ON THE LOOSE, 1958
GIRLS PLEASE!, 1934, A
GIRLS UNDER TWENTY-ONE, 1940, A
GIRLS WHO DARE, 1929, A
GIRLS WILLS BE BOYS, 1934, A
GIRLS! GIRLS! GIRLS!, 1962, A
GIRLS' DORMITORY, 1936, A
GIRLS' SCHOOL, 1938, A
GIRLS' SCHOOL, 1950, A
GIRLS' TOWN, 1942, A
GIRLS' TOWN, 1959, C
GIRLS, THE, 1972, O
GIRLY
GIRO CITY, 1982, C
GIT ALONG, LITTLE DOGIES, 1937, A
GIT!, 1965
GITANELLA, 1924
GIU LA TESTA
GIULIETTA DEGLI SPIRITI
GIULIO CEASRE IL CONQUISTATORE DELLE
  GALLIE
GIULLI, 1927
GIUSEPPE VENDUTO DAI FRATELLI
GIVE A DOG A HONE, 1967, A
GIVE A GIRL A BREAK, 1953, A
GIVE AND TAKE
GIVE AND TARE, 1929, A
GIVE HER A RING, 1936, A
GIVE HER THE MOON, 1970, A
GIVE ME A SAILOR, 1938, A
GIVE ME MY CHANCE, 1958, C
GIVE ME THE STARS, 1944, A
GIVE ME YOUR HEART, 1936, A
GIVE MY REGARDS TO BROAD STREET, 1984, A-C
GIVE MY REGARDS TO BROADWAY, 1948, A
GIVE OUT, SISTERS, 1942, A
GIVE US THE MOON, 1944, A
GIVE US THIS DAY
GIVE US THIS DAY, 1913
GIVE US THIS NIGHT, 1936, A
GIVE US WINGS, 1940, A
GIVE'EM HELL, HARRY!, 1975, A
GIVEN WORD, THE, 1964, A
GIVING BECKY A CHANCE, 1917
GLAD EYE, THE, 1920
GLAD EYE, THE, 1927
GLAD RAG DOLL, THE, 1929, O
GLAD TIDINGS, 1953, A
GLADIATOR OF ROME, 1963, C
GLADIATOR, THE, 1938, AAA
GLADIATORERNA
GLADIATORS 7, 1964, O
GLADIATORS, THE, 1970, C-O
GLADIOLA, 1915, A
GLAMOROUS NIGHT, 1937, C
GLAMOUR, 1931, A
GLAMOUR, 1934, C
GLAMOUR BOY, 1941, AA

GLAMOUR BOY, 1940
GLAMOUR FOR SALE, 1940, A
GLAMOUR GIRL, 1938, A
GLAMOUR GIRL, 1947, A
GLASS ALIBI, THE, 1946, A
GLASS BOTTOM BOAT, THE, 1966, A
GLASS CAGE, THE
GLASS CAGE, THE, 1964, O
GLASS HOUSES, 1922
GLASS HOUSES, 1972, O
GLASS KEY, THE, 1935, C
GLASS KEY, THE, 1942, O
GLASS MENAGERIE, THE, 1950, A
GLASS MOUNTAIN, THE, 1950, A
GLASS OF WATER, A, 1962, A
GLASS SLIPPER, THE, 1955, A
GLASS SPHINX, THE, 1968, A
GLASS TOMB, THE, 1955, A
GLASS TOWER, THE, 1959, A
GLASS WALL, THE, 1953, A
GLASS WEB, THE, 1953, A
GLEAM O'DAWN, 1922, A
GLEN AND RANDA, 1971
GLEN OR GLENDA, 1953, O
GLENISTER OF THE MOUNTED, 1926
GLENN MILLER STORY, THE, 1953, AAA
GLENROWAN AFFAIR, THE, 1951, C
GLIMPSE OF PARADISE, A, 1934, A
GLIMPSES OF THE MOON, THE, 1923
GLITTERBALL, THE, 1977
GLOBAL AFFAIR, A, 1964, A
GLOIRE ROUGE, 1923
GLORIA, 1980, O
GLORIANA, 1916
GLORIFYING THE AMERICAN GIRL, 1930
GLORIOUS ADVENTURE, THE, 1918
GLORIOUS ADVENTURE, THE, 1922, A
GLORIOUS FOOL, THE, 1922
GLORIOUS LADY, THE, 1919
GLORIOUS SACRIFICE
GLORIOUS TRAIL, THE, 1928
GLORIOUS YOUTH, 1928
GLORY, 1917
GLORY, 1955, AAA
GLORY ALLEY, 1952, C
GLORY AT SEA, 1952, A
GLORY BOY, 1971, O
GLORY BRIGADE, THE, 1953, C
GLORY GUYS, THE, 1965, C
GLORY OF CLEMENTINA, THE, 1922
GLORY OF FAITH, THE, 1938, A
GLORY OF LOVE, THE
GLORY OF YOLANDA, THE, 1917
GLORY STOMPERS, THE, 1967, O
GLORY TRAIL, THE, 1937, A
GLOVE, THE, 1979
GLOVE, THE, 1980, O
GLOW OF LIFE, THE, 1918
GLOWING AUTUMN, 1981, A-C
GNOME-MOBILE, THE, 1967, AAA
GO AND GET IT, 1920
GO CHASE YOURSELF, 1938, A
GO DOWN DEATH, 1944
GO FOR A TAKE, 1972
GO FOR BROKE, 1951, A
GO GET 'EM GARRINGER, 1919
GO GET HIM, 1921
GO INTO YOUR DANCE, 1935, A
GO KART GO, 1964, AAA
GO NAKED IN THE WORLD, 1961, O
GO STRAIGHT, 1921
GO STRAIGHT, 1925
GO TELL IT ON THE MOUNTAIN, 1984, A
GO TELL THE SPARTANS, 1978, O
GO TO BLAZES, 1962, A
GO WEST, 1925, A
GO WEST, 1940, A
GO WEST, YOUNG LADY, 1941, A
GO WEST, YOUNG MAN, 1919, A
GO WEST, YOUNG MAN, 1936, C
GO, JOHNNY, GO!, 1959, A
GO, MAN, GO!, 1954, A
GO-BETWEEN, THE, 1971, A-C
GO-GET-'EM HAINES, 1936
GO-GETTER, THE, 1923
GO-GETTER, THE, 1937, A
GO-GO SET
GOAT GETTER, 1925, A
GOAT, THE, 1918
GOBEN NO TSUBAKI
GOBS AND GALS, 1952, A
GOD AND THE MAN, 1918, A
GOD BLESS DR. SHAGETZ, 1977
GOD BLESS OUT RED, WHITE AND BLUE, 1918
GOD FORGIVES—I DON'T!, 1969, O
GOD GAME, THE
GOD GAVE HIM A DOG
GOD GAVE ME TWENTY CENTS, 1926
GOD IN THE GARDEN, THE, 1921, A
GOD IS MY CO-PILOT, 1945, A
GOD IS MY PARTNER, 1957, A
GOD IS MY WITNESS, 1931, A

GOD OF LITTLE CHILDREN, 1917
GOD OF MANKIND, 1928
GOD OF VENGEANCE, THE, 1914
GOD TOLD ME TO, 1976, O
GOD'S BLOODY ACRE, 1975
GOD'S CLAY, 1919
GOD'S CLAY, 1928
GOD'S COUNTRY, 1946, A
GOD'S COUNTRY AND THE LAW, 1921
GOD'S COUNTRY AND THE MAN, 1931, A
GOD'S COUNTRY AND THE MAN, 1937, A
GOD'S COUNTRY AND THE WOMAN, 1916
GOD'S COUNTRY AND THE WOMAN, 1937
GOD'S CRUCIBLE, 1917
GOD'S CRUCIBLE, 1921
GOD'S GIFT TO WOMEN, 1931, A
GOD'S GOLD, 1921
GOD'S GOOD MAN, 1921
GOD'S GREAT WILDERNESS, 1927
GOD'S GUN, 1977, O
GOD'S HALF ACRE, 1916, A
GOD'S LAW AND MAN'S, 1917
GOD'S LITTLE ACRE, 1958, O
GOD'S MAN, 1917
GOD'S OUTLAW, 1919, A
GOD'S PRODIGAL, 1923
GOD'S STEPCHILDREN, 1937
GOD'S WITNESS, 1915
GOD, MAN AND DEVIL, 1949
GODDESS OF LOST LAKE, THE, 1918
GODDESS OF LOVE, THE, 1960, O
GODDESS, THE, 1958, C-O
GODDESS, THE, 1962
GODFATHER, THE, 1972, O
GODFATHER, THE, PART II, 1974, O
GODLESS GIRL, THE, 1929, C
GODLESS MEN, 1921
GODS MUST BE CRAZY, THE, 1984, C
GODS OF FATE, 1916
GODSEND, THE, 1980, O
GODSON, THE, 1972, C-O
GODSPELL, 1973, C
GODY MOLODYYE
GODZILLA
GODZILLA TAI MOTHRA
GODZILLA VERSUS THE COSMIC MONSTER, 1974, C
GODZILLA VERSUS THE SEA MONSTER, 1966, C
GODZILLA VERSUS THE SMOG MONSTER, 1972
GODZILLA VS. MEGALON, 1976, C
GODZILLA VS. THE THING, 1964, C
GODZILLA'S REVENGE, 1969
GODZILLA, RING OF THE MONSTERS, 1956, C
GOFORTH
GOG, 1954, A
GOHA, 1958, O
GOIN' ALL THE WAY, 1982
GOIN' COCONUTS, 1978, A
GOIN' DOWN THE ROAD, 1970, O
GOIN' HOME, 1976, AAA
GOIN' SOUTH, 1978, O
GOIN' TO TOWN, 1935, C
GOIN' TO TOWN, 1944, A
GOING APE!, 1981, A
GOING BERSERK, 1983, O
GOING CROOKED, 1926
GOING GAY
GOING HIGHBROW, 1935, A
GOING HOLLYWOOD, 1933, A
GOING HOME, 1971, O
GOING IN STYLE, 1979, C
GOING MY WAY, 1944, AAA
GOING PLACES, 1939, A
GOING PLACES, 1974, O
GOING SOME, 1920
GOING STEADY, 1958, A
GOING STRAIGHT, 1916
GOING STRAIGHT, 1933, A
GOING THE LIMIT, 1925, A
GOING THE LIMIT, 1926
GOING TO TOWN
GOING UP, 1923
GOING WILD, 1931, A
GOJIRA TAI MOSUHA
GOJUMAN-NIN NO ISAN
GOKE, BODYSNATCHER FROM HELL, 1968, O
GOLD, 1932, A
GOLD, 1934, C
GOLD, 1974, O
GOLD AND GRIT, 1925
GOLD AND THE GIRL, 1925, A
GOLD AND THE WOMAN, 1916
GOLD CURE, THE, 1919
GOLD CURE, THE, 1925
GOLD DIGGERS IN PARIS, 1938, A
GOLD DIGGERS OF 1933, 1933, A
GOLD DIGGERS OF 1935, 1935, A
GOLD DIGGERS OF 1937, 1936, A
GOLD DIGGERS OF BROADWAY, 1929, A
GOLD DIGGERS, THE, 1923, A
GOLD DIGGERS, THE, 1984
GOLD DUST GERTIE, 1931
GOLD EXPRESS, THE, 1955, A

GOLD FEVER, 1952, A
GOLD FOR THE CAESARS, 1964, C
GOLD FROM WEEPAH, 1927
GOLD GRABBERS, 1922
GOLD GUITAR, THE, 1966, A
GOLD HEELS, 1924
GOLD HUNTERS, THE, 1925
GOLD IS WHERE YOU FIND IT, 1938
GOLD MADNESS, 1923, A
GOLD MINE IN THE SKY, 1938, A
GOLD OF NAPLES, 1957, C-O
GOLD OF THE SEVEN SAINTS, 1961, A
GOLD RACKET, THE, 1937, A
GOLD RAIDERS, THE, 1952
GOLD RUSH, THE, 1925, A
GOLD WEST, THE, 1932
GOLDEN ARROW, THE, 1936, A
GOLDEN ARROW, THE, 1964, A
GOLDEN ARROW, THE, 1949
GOLDEN BED, THE, 1925
GOLDEN BEETLE, THE, 1914
GOLDEN BIRD, THE
GOLDEN BLADE, THE, 1953, A
GOLDEN BOX, THE, 1970
GOLDEN BOY, 1939, A
GOLDEN BULLET
GOLDEN CAGE, THE, 1933, A
GOLDEN CALF, THE, 1930, AA
GOLDEN CHANCE, THE, 1915, A
GOLDEN CLAW, THE, 1915
GOLDEN CLOWN, THE, 1927
GOLDEN COACH, THE, 1953, A-C
GOLDEN COCOON, THE, 1926
GOLDEN DAWN, 1930, A
GOLDEN DAWN, THE, 1921
GOLDEN DEMON, 1956, C-O
GOLDEN DISK
GOLDEN DREAMS, 1922
GOLDEN EARRINGS, 1947, C
GOLDEN EYE, THE
GOLDEN FETTER, THE, 1917
GOLDEN FLAME, THE, 1923
GOLDEN FLEECE, THE, 1918
GOLDEN FLEECING, THE, 1940, A
GOLDEN GALLOWS, THE, 1922
GOLDEN GATE GIRL, 1941, C
GOLDEN GIFT, THE, 1922, A
GOLDEN GIRL, 1951, AA
GOLDEN GLOVES, 1940, A
GOLDEN GLOVES STORY, THE, 1950, A
GOLDEN GLOVES, 1939
GOLDEN GOAL, THE, 1918
GOLDEN GOD, THE, 1917
GOLDEN GODDESS, THE, 1916
GOLDEN GOOSE, THE, 1966
GOLDEN HANDS OF KURIGAL, THE, 1949
GOLDEN HARVEST, 1933, A
GOLDEN HAWK, THE, 1952, A
GOLDEN HEAD, THE, 1965, A
GOLDEN HEIST, THE
GOLDEN HELMET
GOLDEN HOOFS, 1941, AAA
GOLDEN HORDE, THE, 1951, A
GOLDEN IDIOT, THE, 1917
GOLDEN IDOL, THE, 1954, AA
GOLDEN IVORY
GOLDEN LADY, THE, 1979, O
GOLDEN LINK, THE, 1954, A
GOLDEN MADONNA, THE, 1949, A
GOLDEN MARIE
GOLDEN MASK, THE, 1954, A
GOLDEN MISTRESS, THE, 1954, A
GOLDEN MOUNTAINS, 1958, A
GOLDEN NEEDLES, 1974, O
GOLDEN NYMPHS, THE
GOLDEN PLAGUE, THE, 1963, A
GOLDEN PRINCESS, THE, 1925
GOLDEN RABBIT, THE, 1962, A
GOLDEN RENDEZVOUS, 1977, O
GOLDEN ROSARY, THE, 1917
GOLDEN RULE KATE, 1917
GOLDEN SALAMANDER, 1950, A
GOLDEN SEA, THE, 1919
GOLDEN SEAL, THE, 1983, AAA
GOLDEN SHACKLES, 1928
GOLDEN SHOWER, THE, 1919
GOLDEN SILENCE, 1923
GOLDEN SNARE, THE, 1921
GOLDEN STALLION, THE, 1949, A
GOLDEN STRAIN, THE, 1925
GOLDEN THOUGHT, A, 1924
GOLDEN TRAIL, THE, 1920
GOLDEN TRAIL, THE, 1927
GOLDEN TRAIL, THE, 1940, A
GOLDEN TRAIL, THE 1937
GOLDEN VOYAGE OF SINBAD, THE, 1974, AAA
GOLDEN WEB, THE, 1920
GOLDEN WEB, THE, 1926
GOLDEN WEST, THE, 1932, A
GOLDEN YUKON, THE, 1927
GOLDENGIRL, 1979, O
GOLDFINGER, 1964, C-O

GOLDFISH, THE, 1924, A
GOLDIE, 1931
GOLDIE GETS ALONG, 1933, A
GOLDSTEIN, 1964, O
GOLDTOWN GHOST RIDERS, 1953, A
GOLDWYN FOLLIES, THE, 1938, A
GOLEM, 1980, C
GOLEM, THE, 1914
GOLEM, THE, 1937, C
GOLEM: HOW HE CAME INTO THE WORLD, THE, 1920, C
GOLF WIDOWS, 1928
GOLFO
GOLGOTHA, 1937
GOLIATH AGAINST THE GIANTS, 1963, A
GOLIATH AND THE BARBARIANS, 1960, A
GOLIATH AND THE DRAGON, 1961, A
GOLIATH AND THE SINS OF BABYLON, 1964, A
GOLIATH AND THE VAMPIRES, 1964, C
GOLIATHON, 1979, C
GONE ARE THE DAYS, 1963, A
GONE IN 60 SECONDS, 1974, C
GONE TO EARTH
GONE TO GROUND, 1976
GONE TO THE DOGS, 1939, A
GONE WITH THE WEST, 1976
GONE WITH THE WIND, 1939, A
GONG SHOW MOVIE, THE, 1980, C
GONKS GO BEAT, 1965
GONZAQUE, 1923
GOOD AND EVIL, 1921
GOOD AND NAUGHTY, 1926, A
GOOD AS GOLD, 1927
GOOD BAD BOY, 1924
GOOD BAD GIRL, THE, 1931, C
GOOD BAD MAN, THE, 1916, A
GOOD BEGINNING, THE, 1953, A
GOOD COMPANIONS, 1933, A
GOOD COMPANIONS, THE, 1957, A
GOOD DAME, 1934, A
GOOD DAY FOR A HANGING, 1958, A
GOOD DAY FOR FIGHTING
GOOD DIE YOUNG, THE, 1954, C
GOOD DISSONANCE LIKE A MAN, A, 1977, C
GOOD EARTH, THE, 1937, A
GOOD FAIRY, THE, 1935, A
GOOD FELLOWS, THE, 1943, A
GOOD FOR NOTHING, THE, 1917
GOOD GIRLS GO TO PARIS, 1939, A
GOOD GRACIOUS ANNABELLE, 1919
GOOD GUYS AND THE BAD GUYS, THE, 1969, A-C
GOOD GUYS WEAR BLACK, 1978, O
GOOD HUMOR MAN, THE, 1950, A
GOOD INTENTIONS, 1930, A
GOOD LITTLE DEVIL, A, 1914, A
GOOD LOSER, THE, 1918
GOOD LUCK, MISS WYCKOFF, 1979, O
GOOD LUCK, MR. YATES, 1943, A
GOOD MEN AND BAD, 1923
GOOD MEN AND TRUE, 1922
GOOD MORNING JUDGE, 1928
GOOD MORNING, BOYS
GOOD MORNING, DOCTOR
GOOD MORNING, JUDGE, 1943, A
GOOD MORNING, MISS DOVE, 1955, A
GOOD MORNING... AND GOODBYE, 1967, O
GOOD NEIGHBOR SAM, 1964
GOOD NEWS, 1930, A
GOOD NEWS, 1947, AA
GOOD NIGHT, PAUL, 1918, A
GOOD OLD DAYS, THE, 1939, A
GOOD OLD SOAK, THE, 1937, A
GOOD PROVIDER, THE, 1922
GOOD REFERENCES, 1920
GOOD SAM, 1948, A
GOOD SOLDIER SCHWEIK, THE, 1963
GOOD SPORT, 1931, A
GOOD TIME CHARLEY, 1927
GOOD TIME GIRL, 1950, O
GOOD TIMES, 1967, A
GOOD WOMEN, 1921
GOOD, THE BAD, AND THE BEAUTIFUL, THE, 1975
GOOD, THE BAD, AND THE UGLY, THE, 1967, O
GOOD-BAD WIFE, THE, 1921
GOOD-BY GIRLS, 1923
GOOD-BYE KISS, THE, 1928, A
GOOD-BYE, BILL, 1919, A
GOOD-FOR-NOTHING, THE, 1914, A
GOODBYE, 1918
GOODBYE AGAIN, 1933, A
GOODBYE AGAIN, 1961, C
GOODBYE BROADWAY, 1938, A
GOODBYE BRUCE LEE: HIS LAST GAME OF DEATH
GOODBYE CHARLIE, 1964, C
GOODBYE COLUMBUS, 1969, O
GOODBYE CRUEL WORLD, 1983
GOODBYE EMMANUELLE, 1980, O
GOODBYE FRANKLIN HIGH, 1978, A
GOODBYE GEMINI, 1970, O
GOODBYE GIRL, THE, 1977, C
GOODBYE LOVE, 1934, A
GOODBYE MR. CHIPS, 1939, AAA

GOODBYE MR. CHIPS, 1969, A
GOODBYE PEOPLE, THE, 1984, A-C
GOODBYE PORK PIE, 1981, C
GOODBYE TO THE HILL
GOODBYE, MOSCOW, 1968, O
GOODBYE, MY FANCY, 1951, A
GOODBYE, MY LADY, 1956, AA
GOODBYE, NORMA JEAN, 1976, O
GOODNIGHT SWEETHEART, 1944, A
GOODNIGHT VIENNA
GOODNIGHT, LADIES AND GENTLEMEN, 1977, C-O
GOONA-GOONA, 1932
GOOSE AND THE GANDER, THE, 1935, A
GOOSE GIRL, THE, 1915, A
GOOSE GIRL, THE, 1967, C-O
GOOSE HANGS HIGH, THE, 1925
GOOSE STEP
GOOSE STEPS OUT, THE, 1942, A
GOOSE WOMAN, THE, 1925, C
GORATH, 1964, C
GORBALS STORY, THE, 1950, C
GORDEYEV FAMILY, THE, 1961, O
GORDON IL PIHATA NERO
GORDON'S WAR, 1973, O
GORGEOUS HUSSY, THE, 1936, AA
GORGO, 1961, A
GORGON, THE, 1964
GORILLA, 1964, C
GORILLA AT LARGE, 1954, C
GORILLA GREETS YOU, THE, 1958, C
GORILLA MAN, 1942, A
GORILLA SHIP, THE, 1932, A
GORILLA, 1944
GORILLA, THE, 1927
GORILLA, THE, 1931, A
GORILLA, THE, 1939, A
GORKY PARK, 1983, O
GORP, 1980, O
GOSH, 1974
GOSPEL ACCORDING TO ST. MATTHEW, THE, 1966, A
GOSPEL ROAD, THE, 1973, A
GOSSIP, 1923
GOT IT MADE, 1974
GOT WHAT SHE WANTED, 1930, A
GOUPI MAINS ROUGES
GOVERNMENT GIRL, 1943, A
GOVERNOR'S BOSS, THE, 1915, A
GOVERNOR'S LADY, THE, 1923
GOWN OF DESTINY, THE, 1918
GOYOKIN, 1969, O
GRACE QUIGLEY
GRACIE ALLEN MURDER CASE, 1939, A
GRAD NIGHT, 1980
GRADUATE, THE, 1967, A
GRADUATION DAY, 1981
GRAFT, 1931, C
GRAFTERS, 1917
GRAIL, THE, 1923
GRAIN OF DUST, THE, 1928, A
GRAN VARIETA, 1955, A
GRANATOVYY BRASLET, 1966
GRAND BABYLON HOTEL, THE, 1916
GRAND CANARY, 1934, A
GRAND CANYON, 1949, A
GRAND CANYON TRAIL, 1948, A
GRAND CENTRAL MURDER, 1942, A
GRAND DUCHESS AND THE WAITER, THE, 1926, A
GRAND DUKE AND MR. PIMM
GRAND ESCAPADE, THE, 1946, A
GRAND EXIT, 1935, A
GRAND FINALE, 1936, A
GRAND HOTEL, 1932, A
GRAND ILLUSION, 1938, A
GRAND JURY, 1936, A
GRAND JURY, 1977
GRAND JURY SECRETS, 1939, A
GRAND LARCENY, 1922
GRAND MANEUVER, THE, 1956, C
GRAND NATIONAL NIGHT
GRAND OLD GIRL, 1935, A
GRAND OLE OPRY, 1940, A
GRAND PARADE, THE, 1930, A
GRAND PASSION, THE, 1918
GRAND PRIX, 1934, A
GRAND PRIX, 1966, O
GRAND SLAM, 1933, A
GRAND SLAM, 1968, A-C
GRAND SUBSTITUTION, THE, 1965, C
GRAND THEFT AUTO, 1977
GRANDAD RUDD, 1935, A
GRANDEE'S RING, THE, 1915
GRANDEUR ET DECADENCE, 1923
GRANDMA'S BOY, 1922, A
GRANDPA GOES TO TOWN, 1940, A
GRANDVIEW, U.S.A., 1984, O
GRANNY GET YOUR GUN, 1940, A
GRAPES OF WRATH, 1940, A
GRASP OF GREED, THE, 1916
GRASS EATER, THE, 1961, C
GRASS IS GREENER, THE, 1960, A
GRASS IS SINGING, THE

GRASS IS SINGING, THE, 1982, A
GRASS ORPHAN, THE, 1922
GRASSHOPPER, THE, 1970, O
GRAUSTARK, 1915
GRAUSTARK, 1925
GRAVE OF THE VAMPIRE, 1972, O
GRAVE ROBBERS FROM OUTER SPACE
GRAVESIDE STORY, THE
GRAVEYARD OF HORROR, 1971, O
GRAVY TRAIN, THE, 1974, O
GRAY DAWN, THE, 1922
GRAY HORIZON, THE, 1919
GRAY HORROR, THE, 1915
GRAY LADY DOWN, 1978, C
GRAY TOWERS MYSTERY, THE, 1919
GRAY WOLF'S GHOST, THE, 1919
GRAYEAGLE, 1977, C
GRAZIE ZIA
GRAZIELLA, 1926
GREASE, 1978, A
GREASE 2, 1982, C-O
GREASED LIGHTING, 1919
GREASED LIGHTING, 1928
GREASED LIGHTNING, 1977, C
GREASER'S PALACE, 1972, C
GREAT ACCIDENT, THE, 1920
GREAT ADVENTURE, THE, 1915, A
GREAT ADVENTURE, THE, 1918, A
GREAT ADVENTURE, THE, 1921
GREAT ADVENTURE, THE, 1955, AAA
GREAT ADVENTURE, THE, 1976
GREAT AIR ROBBERY, THE, 1920
GREAT ALLIGATOR, 1980, O
GREAT ALONE, THE, 1922
GREAT AMERICAN BROADCAST, THE, 1941, A
GREAT AMERICAN BUGS BUNNY-ROAD RUNNER
   CHASE, 1979, AAA
GREAT AMERICAN PASTIME, THE, 1956, A
GREAT ARMORED CAR SWINDLE, THE, 1964
GREAT AWAKENING, THE
GREAT BALLOON ADVENTURE, THE
GREAT BANK HOAX, THE, 1977, C
GREAT BANK ROBBERY, THE, 1969, A
GREAT BARRIER, THE
GREAT BIG THING, A, 1968, C
GREAT BIG WORLD AND LITTLE CHILDREN, THE,
   1962, A
GREAT BRADLEY MYSTERY, THE, 1917
GREAT BRAIN MACHINE, THE
GREAT BRAIN, THE, 1978, AA
GREAT BRITISH TRAIN ROBBERY, THE, 1967, A
GREAT CALL OF THE WILD, THE, 1976
GREAT CARUSO, THE, 1951, A
GREAT CATHERINE, 1968, AA
GREAT CHICAGO CONSPIRACY CIRCUS, THE
GREAT CITIZEN, THE, 1939
GREAT COMMANDMENT, THE, 1941, A
GREAT COUP, A, 1919
GREAT DAN PATCH, THE, 1949, AA
GREAT DAWN, THE, 1947, A
GREAT DAY, 1945, A
GREAT DAY IN THE MORNING, 1956, A
GREAT DAY, THE, 1921
GREAT DAY, THE, 1977
GREAT DECEPTION, THE, 1926
GREAT DEFENDER, THE, 1934, A
GREAT DIAMOND MYSTERY, THE, 1924
GREAT DIAMOND ROBBERY, 1953, A
GREAT DIAMOND ROBBERY, THE, 1914
GREAT DICTATOR, THE, 1940, AAA
GREAT DIVIDE, THE, 1916
GREAT DIVIDE, THE, 1925
GREAT DIVIDE, THE, 1930, A
GREAT DREAM, THE
GREAT ESCAPE, THE, 1963, A
GREAT EXPECTATIONS, 1917, A
GREAT EXPECTATIONS, 1934, AA
GREAT EXPECTATIONS, 1946, AAA
GREAT EXPECTATIONS, 1975, AAA
GREAT FEED, THE
GREAT FLAMARION, THE, 1945, A-C
GREAT FLIRTATION, THE, 1934, A
GREAT GABBO, THE, 1929, C
GREAT GAMBINI, THE, 1937, A
GREAT GAME, THE, 1918, A
GREAT GAME, THE, 1930, A
GREAT GAME, THE, 1953, A
GREAT GARRICK, THE, 1937, A
GREAT GATSBY, THE, 1926, A
GREAT GATSBY, THE, 1949, A
GREAT GATSBY, THE, 1974
GREAT GAY ROAD, THE, 1931, A
GREAT GEORGIA BANK HOAX
GREAT GILBERT AND SULLIVAN, THE, 1953, AAA
GREAT GILDERSLEEVE, THE, 1942, A
GREAT GOD GOLD, 1935, A
GREAT GUNDOWN, THE, 1977, O
GREAT GUNFIGHTER, THE
GREAT GUNS, 1941, AAA
GREAT GUY, 1936, A
GREAT GUY ROAD, THE, 1920
GREAT HADIO MYSTERY, THE

GREAT HOPE, THE, 1954, C
GREAT HOSPITAL MYSTERY, THE, 1937, A
GREAT HOTEL MURDER, 1935, A
GREAT IMPERSONATION, THE, 1921
GREAT IMPERSONATION, THE, 1935, A
GREAT IMPERSONATION, THE, 1942, A
GREAT IMPOSTER, THE, 1918
GREAT IMPOSTOR, THE, 1960, A
GREAT JASPER, THE, 1933
GREAT JESSE JAMES RAID, THE, 1953, A
GREAT JEWEL ROBBER, THE, 1950, A
GREAT JEWEL ROBBERY, THE, 1925
GREAT JOHN L. THE, 1945, A
GREAT K & A TRAIN ROBBERY, THE, 1926, A
GREAT LEAP, THE, 1914, A
GREAT LESTER BOGGS, THE, 1975
GREAT LIE, THE, 1941, A
GREAT LOCOMOTIVE CHASE, THE, 1956, AA
GREAT LOVE, THE, 1918, A
GREAT LOVE, THE, 1925, A
GREAT LOVER, THE, 1920
GREAT LOVER, THE, 1931, A
GREAT LOVER, THE, 1949, A
GREAT MACARTHY, THE, 1975, C-O
GREAT MAGARAZ, THE, 1915
GREAT MAIL ROBBERY, THE, 1927, A
GREAT MAN VOTES, THE, 1939, A
GREAT MAN'S LADY, THE, 1942, A
GREAT MAN, THE, 1957, A
GREAT MANHUNT, THE, 1951, A
GREAT MANHUNT, THE, 1949
GREAT MCGONAGALL, THE, 1975, O
GREAT MEN AMONG US, 1915
GREAT MIKE, THE, 1944, A
GREAT MISSOURI RAID, THE, 1950, A
GREAT MOMENT, THE, 1921
GREAT MOMENT, THE, 1944, A
GREAT MONKEY RIP-OFF, THE, 1979
GREAT MORGAN, THE, 1946
GREAT MR. HANDEL, THE, 1942, A
GREAT MR. NOBODY, THE, 1941, A
GREAT MUPPET CAPER, THE, 1981
GREAT McGINTY, THE, 1940, A
GREAT NIGHT, THE, 1922, A
GREAT NORTHFIELD, MINNESOTA RAID, THE,
   1972, O
GREAT O'MALLEY, THE, 1937, A
GREAT PHYSCIAN, THE, 1913
GREAT PLANE ROBBERY, 1950, A
GREAT PLANE ROBBERY, THE, 1940, A
GREAT POISON MYSTERY, THE, 1914
GREAT PONY RAID, THE, 1968, AA
GREAT POWER, THE, 1929, A
GREAT PRINCE SHAN, THE, 1924
GREAT PROBLEM, THE, 1916
GREAT PROFILE, THE, 1940, A
GREAT RACE, THE, 1965, A-C
GREAT REDEEMER, THE, 1920
GREAT RIDE, THE, 1978
GREAT RIVIERA BANK ROBBERY, THE, 1979
GREAT ROAD, THE, 1927
GREAT ROMANCE, THE, 1919
GREAT RUBY, THE, 1915
GREAT RUPERT, THE, 1950
GREAT SANTINI, THE, 1979
GREAT SCHNOZZLE, THE
GREAT SCOUT AND CATHOUSE THURSDAY, THE,
   1976, O
GREAT SENSATION, THE, 1925
GREAT SHADOW, THE, 1920, A
GREAT SINNER, THE, 1949, A
GREAT SIOUX MASSACRE, THE, 1965, A
GREAT SIOUX UPRISING, THE, 1953, A
GREAT SKYCOPTER RESCUE, THE, 1982
GREAT SMOKEY ROADBLOCK, THE, 1978, C
GREAT SPY CHASE, THE, 1966
GREAT SPY MISSION, THE
GREAT ST. LOUIS BANK ROBBERY, THE, 1959, C-O
GREAT ST. TRINIAN'S TRAIN ROBBERY, THE,
   1966, AA
GREAT STAGECOACH ROBBERY, 1945, A
GREAT STUFF, 1933, A
GREAT SWINDLE, THE, 1941, A
GREAT TEXAS DYNAMITE CHASE, THE, 1976, O
GREAT THAIN ROBBERY, THE, 1941, A
GREAT TRAIN ROBBERY, THE, 1979, A
GREAT TURF MYSTERY, THE, 1924
GREAT VAN ROBBERY, THE, 1963, O
GREAT VICTOR HERBERT, THE, 1939, AAA
GREAT VICTORY, WILSON OR THE KAISER?, THE,
   1918
GREAT WALDO PEPPER, THE, 1975, C
GREAT WALL OF CHINA, THE, 1970
GREAT WALL, THE, 1965, O
GREAT WALTZ, THE, 1938, AA
GREAT WALTZ, THE, 1972, AA
GREAT WAR, THE, 1927
GREAT WAR, THE, 1961, O
GREAT WELL, THE
GREAT WHITE HOPE, THE, 1970, C-O
GREAT WHITE TRAIL, THE, 1917
GREAT WHITE WAY, THE, 1924

GREAT WHITE, THE, 1982, O
GREAT YEARNING, THE, 1930, A
GREAT ZIEGFELD, THE, 1936, AAA
GREAT, MEADOW, THE, 1931
GREATER ADVISOR, THE, 1940
GREATER CLAIM, THE, 1921
GREATER GLORY, THE, 1926
GREATER LAW, THE, 1917, A
GREATER LOVE HATH NO MAN, 1915
GREATER LOVE, THE, 1919
GREATER NEED, THE, 1916, A
GREATER PROFIT, THE, 1921
GREATER SINNER, THE, 1919
GREATER THAN A CROWN, 1925
GREATER THAN ART, 1915
GREATER THAN FAME, 1920, A
GREATER THAN LOVE, 1920
GREATER THAN MARRIAGE, 1924
GREATER WILL, THE, 1915
GREATER WOMAN, THE, 1917
GREATEST BATTLE ON EARTH, THE
GREATEST BATTLE ON EARTH, THE
GREATEST LOVE OF ALL, THE, 1925
GREATEST LOVE, THE, 1920
GREATEST LOVE, THE, 1954, C
GREATEST MENACE, THE, 1923
GREATEST POWER, THE, 1917
GREATEST QUESTION, THE, 1920, A
GREATEST SHOW ON EARTH, THE, 1952
GREATEST SIN, THE, 1922
GREATEST STORY EVER TOLD, THE, 1965
GREATEST THING IN LIFE, THE, 1918, AAA
GREATEST TRUTH, THE, 1922
GREATEST WISH IN THE WORLD, THE, 1918, A
GREATEST, THE, 1977, C-O
GREATHEART, 1921
GREED, 1917
GREED, 1925, C
GREED IN THE SUN, 1965, O
GREED OF WILLIAM HART, THE, 1948, C-O
GREEK STREET
GREEK TYCOON, THE, 1978, C
GREEKS HAD A WORD FOR THEM, 1932, A
GREEN 1CE, 1981
GREEN BERETS, THE, 1968, C
GREEN BUDDHA, THE, 1954, C
GREEN CARAVAN, THE, 1922, A
GREEN CARNATION
GREEN CLOAK, THE, 1915
GREEN COCKATOO, THE, 1947, A
GREEN DOLPHIN STREET, 1947, A-C
GREEN EYE OF THE YELLOW GOD, THE, 1913
GREEN EYES, 1918
GREEN EYES, 1934, A
GREEN FIELDS, 1937, A
GREEN FINGERS, 1947, A
GREEN FIRE, 1955, C
GREEN FLAME, THE, 1920, A
GREEN FOR DANGER, 1946, A
GREEN GLOVE, THE, 1952, A
GREEN GOD, THE, 1918
GREEN GODDESS, THE, 1923
GREEN GODDESS, THE, 1930, A
GREEN GRASS OF WYOMING, 1948, AA
GREEN GRASS WIDOWS, 1928
GREEN GROW THE RUSHES, 1951, A
GREEN HELL, 1940, A
GREEN HELMET, THE, 1961, A
GREEN ICE, 1981, C
GREEN LIGHT, 1937, A
GREEN MAN, THE, 1957, A
GREEN MANSIONS, 1959, A
GREEN MARE, THE, 1961, O
GREEN ORCHARD, THE, 1916
GREEN PACK, THE, 1934, C
GREEN PASTURES, 1936, AA
GREEN PROMISE, THE, 1949, A
GREEN ROOM, THE, 1979, C-O
GREEN SCARF, THE, 1954, A
GREEN SLIME, THE, 1969, C
GREEN SPIDER, THE, 1916
GREEN STOCKINGS, 1916
GREEN SWAMP, THE, 1916
GREEN TEMPTATION, THE, 1922
GREEN TERROR, THE, 1919
GREEN TREE, THE, 1965, A
GREEN YEARS, THE, 1946, A
GREEN-EYED BLONDE, THE, 1957, C
GREEN-EYED MONSTER, THE, 1916
GREEN-EYED MONSTER, THE, 1921
GREENE MURDER CASE, THE, 1929, A
GREENGAGE SUMMER, THE
GREENWICH VILLAGE, 1944, A
GREENWICH VILLAGE STORY, 1963, C
GREENWOOD TREE, THE, 1930, A
GREGORIO, 1968
GREGORY'S GIRL, 1982
GREH, 1962, O
GRELL MYSTERY, THE, 1917
GREMLINS, 1984, O
GRENDEL GRENDEL GRENDEL, 1981, AAA
GRETCHEN, THE GREENHORN, 1916, A

GRETNA GREEN, 1915
GREY DAWN, THE
GREY DEVIL, THE, 1926, A
GREY FOX, THE, 1983, C
GREY PARASOL, THE, 1918
GREY STREAK, THE, 1927
GREY VULTURE, THE, 1926
GREYFRIARS BOBBY, 1961, AAA
GREYHOUND LIMITED, THE, 1929, A
GREYHOUND, THE, 1914, A
GREYSTOKE: THE LEGEND OF TARZAN
GREYSTOKE: THE LEGEND OF TARZAN, LORD OF THE APES, 1984, C
GRIBICHE, 1926
GRIDIRON FLASH, 1935, A
GRIEF STREET, 1931, A
GRIFFON OF AN OLD WARRIOR, 1916
GRIGSBY
GRIM COMEDIAN, THE, 1921
GRIM GAME, THE, 1919, A
GRIM JUSTICE, 1916
GRIM REAPER, THE, 1981, O
GRINGO, 1963
GRINNING GUNS, 1927
GRIP, 1915
GRIP OF IRON, THE, 1913
GRIP OF IRON, THE, 1920
GRIP OF JEALOUSY, THE, 1916
GRIP OF THE STRANGLER
GRIP OF THE YUKON, THE, 1928
GRISSLY'S MILLIONS, 1945, A
GRISSOM GANG, THE, 1971, C-O
GRIT, 1924, A
GRIT OF A JEW, THE, 1917, A
GRIT WINS, 1929, A
GRITOS EN LA NOCHE
GRIZZLY, 1976, C
GROOM WORE SPURS, THE, 1951, A
GROOVE ROOM, THE, 1974
GROOVE TUBE, THE, 1974, O
GROUCH, THE, 1961, A
GROUND ZERO, 1973, O
GROUNDS FOR DIVORCE, 1925
GROUNDS FOR MARRIAGE, 1950, A
GROUNDSTAR CONSPIRACY, THE, 1972, C
GROUP MARRIAGE, 1972
GROUP, THE, 1966, O
GROUPIE GIRL
GROVE, THE
GROWING BETTER, 1923
GROWING PAINS
GROWN-UP CHILDREN, 1963, A
GRUB STAKE, THE, 1923
GRUESOME TWOSOME, 1968, O
GRUMPY, 1923
GRUMPY, 1930, A
GUADALAJARA, 1943, A
GUADALCANAL DIARY, 1943, C
GUARD THAT GIRL, 1935, A
GUARDIAN OF THE WILDERNESS, 1977, AAA
GUARDIAN, THE, 1917
GUARDIANS OF THE WILD, 1928
GUARDING BRITAIN'S SECRETS
GUARDSMAN, THE, 1927
GUARDSMAN, THE, 1931, A
GUDRUN
GUERILLAS IN PINK LACE, 1964
GUERRE SECRET
GUERRILLA GIRL, 1953, C
GUESS WHAT HAPPENED TO COUNT DRACULA, 1970, O
GUESS WHAT WE LEARNED IN SCHOOL TODAY?, 1970, O
GUESS WHAT!?!
GUESS WHO'S COMING TO DINNER, 1967, C
GUEST AT STEENKAMPSKRAAL, THE, 1977, O
GUEST HOUSE, THE
GUEST IN THE HOUSE, 1944, A
GUEST OF HONOR, 1934, A
GUEST WIFE, 1945, A
GUEST, THE, 1963, C
GUEST, THE, 1984, A
GUESTS ARE COMING, 1965, A
GUEULE D'ANGE
GUIDE FOR THE MARRIED MAN, A, 1967, C
GUIDE, THE, 1965, A
GUILE OF WOMEN, 1921, A
GUILT, 1930, A
GUILT, 1967, O
GUILT IS MY SHADOW, 1950, O
GUILT IS NOT MINE, 1968, A
GUILT OF JANET AMES, THE, 1947, A
GUILT OF SILENCE, THE, 1918
GUILTY, 1922
GUILTY AS CHARGED
GUILTY AS HELL, 1932, A
GUILTY BYSTANDER, 1950, C
GUILTY CONSCIENCE, A, 1921
GUILTY GENERATION, THE, 1931
GUILTY HANDS, 1931, C
GUILTY MAN, THE, 1918
GUILTY MELODY, 1936, A

GUILTY OF LOVE, 1920, C
GUILTY OF TREASON, 1950, C
GUILTY ONE, THE, 1924
GUILTY OR NOT GUILTY, 1932
GUILTY PARENTS, 1934, C
GUILTY TRAILS, 1938, A
GUILTY, THE, 1947, C
GUILTY?, 1930, A
GUILTY?, 1956, A
GUINEA PIG, THE
GUINGUETTE, 1959, C
GULF BETWEEN, THE, 1918
GULLIVER IN LILLIPUT, 1923
GULLIVER'S TRAVELS, 1939, AAA
GULLIVER'S TRAVELS, 1977
GULLIVER'S TRAVELS BEYOND THE MOON, 1966, AAA
GUMBALL RALLY, THE, 1976, A
GUMBO YA-YA
GUMS, 1976
GUMSHOE, 1972, C
GUN BATTLE AT MONTEREY, 1957, C
GUN BELT, 1953, A
GUN BROTHERS, 1956, A
GUN CODE, 1940, A
GUN CRAZY, 1949, O
GUN DUEL IN DURANGO, 1957, A
GUN FEVER, 1958
GUN FIGHT, 1961, C
GUN FOR A COWARD, 1957, O
GUN FURY, 1953, A
GUN GLORY, 1957, A
GUN GOSPEL, 1927
GUN GRIT, 1936
GUN HAND, THE
GUN HAWK, THE, 1963, C
GUN JUSTICE, 1934, A
GUN LAW, 1929, A
GUN LAW, 1933, A
GUN LAW, 1938, A
GUN LAW JUSTICE, 1949, A
GUN LORDS OF STIRRUP BASIN, 1937, A
GUN MAN FROM BODIE, THE, 1941, A
GUN MOLL
GUN MOLL, 1938
GUN PACKER, 1938, A
GUN PLAY, 1936, A
GUN RANGER, THE, 1937, A
GUN RIDERS, THE, 1969, O
GUN RUNNER, 1949, A
GUN RUNNER, 1969, O
GUN RUNNER, THE
GUN RUNNER, THE, 1928, A
GUN RUNNERS, THE, 1958, A
GUN SHY, 1922
GUN SMOKE, 1931, A
GUN SMOKE, 1936, A
GUN SMOKE, 1945
GUN SMUGGLERS, 1948, A
GUN STREET, 1962
GUN TALK, 1948, A
GUN THAT WON THE WEST, THE, 1955, C
GUN THE MAN DOWN, 1957, C
GUN TOWN, 1946, A
GUN WOMAN, THE, 1918
GUN, THE, 1978, O
GUN-FIGHTIN' GENTLEMAN, A, 1919
GUN-HAND GARRISON, 1927
GUNFIGHT AT ABILENE
GUNFIGHT AT COMANCHE CREEK, 1964, A
GUNFIGHT AT DODGE CITY, THE, 1959
GUNFIGHT AT RED SANDS
GUNFIGHT AT THE O.K. CORRAL, 1957, C
GUNFIGHT IN ABILENE, 1967, C
GUNFIGHT, A, 1971, O
GUNFIGHTER, THE, 1917
GUNFIGHTER, THE, 1923
GUNFIGHTER, THE, 1950
GUNFIGHTERS OF ABILENE, 1960, A
GUNFIGHTERS OF CASA GRANDE, 1965, C
GUNFIGHTERS, THE, 1947, A
GUNFIRE, 1935
GUNFIRE, 1950, A
GUNFIRE AT INDIAN GAP, 1957, A
GUNG HO!, 1943, C
GUNGA DIN, 1939, C
GUNMAN FROM BODIE
GUNMAN HAS ESCAPED, A, 1948
GUNMAN'S CODE, 1946, A
GUNMAN'S WALK, 1958, C
GUNMAN, THE, 1952
GUNMEN FROM LAREDO, 1959, O
GUNMEN OF ABILENE, 1950, A
GUNMEN OF THE RIO GRANDE, 1965, C
GUNN, 1967, C
GUNNAR HEDE'S SAGA, 1922
GUNNERS AND GUNS, 1935
GUNNING FOR JUSTICE, 1948, A
GUNNING FOR VENGEANCE, 1946
GUNPLAY, 1951, A
GUNPOINT, 1966, A
GUNPOINT!

GUNRUNNERS, THE
GUNS, 1980, O
GUNS A'BLAZING
GUNS ALONG THE BORDER, 1952
GUNS AND GUITARS, 1936, A
GUNS AND THE FURY, THE, 1983, O
GUNS AT BATASI, 1964, C
GUNS FOR HIRE, 1932
GUNS FOR SAN SEBASTIAN, 1968, O
GUNS IN THE AFTERNOON
GUNS IN THE DARK, 1937, A
GUNS IN THE HEATHER, 1968, AA
GUNS OF A STRANGER, 1973, A
GUNS OF DARKNESS, 1962, C
GUNS OF DIABLO, 1964, C
GUNS OF FORT PETTICOAT, THE, 1957, A
GUNS OF HATE, 1948, A
GUNS OF LOOS, THE, 1928
GUNS OF NAVARONE, THE, 1961
GUNS OF THE BLACK WITCH, 1961, C
GUNS OF THE LAW, 1944, A
GUNS OF THE MAGNIFICENT SEVEN, 1969, C
GUNS OF THE PECOS, 1937, A
GUNS OF THE TIMBERLAND, 1960, A
GUNS OF THE TREES, 1964, O
GUNS OF WYOMING
GUNS, GIRLS AND GANGSTERS, 1958, C
GUNS, SIN AND BATHTUB GIN
GUNSAULUS MYSTERY, THE, 1921
GUNSIGHT RIDGE, 1957, A
GUNSLINGER, 1956, C
GUNSLINGERS, 1950, A
GUNSMOKE, 1947
GUNSMOKE, 1953, A
GUNSMOKE IN TUCSON, 1958, A
GUNSMOKE MESA, 1944, A
GUNSMOKE ON THE GUADALUPE, 1935
GUNSMOKE RANCH, 1937, A
GUNSMOKE TRAIL, 1938, A
GURU, THE, 1969
GURU, THE MAD MONK, 1971
GUS, 1976, AAA
GUSARSKAYA BALLADA
GUTS IN THE SUN, 1959, O
GUTTER GIRLS, 1964, O
GUTTER MAGDALENE, THE, 1916
GUTTERSNIPE, THE, 1922
GUV'NOR, THE
GUY CALLED CAESAR, A, 1962, A
GUY COULD CHANGE, A, 1946, A
GUY FAWKES, 1923
GUY FROM HARLEM, THE, 1977
GUY NAMED JOE, A, 1943, A
GUY WHO CAME BACK, THE, 1951, A
GUY, A GAL AND A PAL, A, 1945, A
GUYANA, CULT OF THE DAMNED, 1980, O
GUYS AND DOLLS, 1955, A
GWENDOLINE
GWYNETH OF THE WELSH HILLS, 1921
GYPSY, 1937, A
GYPSY, 1962, C
GYPSY AND THE GENTLEMAN, THE, 1958, O
GYPSY BLOOD, 1921
GYPSY COLT, 1954
GYPSY FURY, 1950, C
GYPSY GIRL, 1966
GYPSY MELODY, 1936, A
GYPSY MOTHS, THE, 1969, O
GYPSY OF THE NORTH, 1928, A
GYPSY PASSION, 1922
GYPSY ROMANCE, THE, 1926
GYPSY TRAIL, THE, 1918
GYPSY WILDCAT, 1944, A
GYPSY'S TRUST, THE, 1917

–H–

H-MAN, THE, 1959, O
H.A.R.M. MACHINE, THE
H.E.A.L.T.H.
H.M. PULHAM, ESQ., 1941, A
H.M.S. DEFIANT
H.M.S. PINAFORE, 1951
H.O.T.S., 1979, O
HA' PENNY BREEZE, 1950, A
HABIT, 1921
HABIT OF HAPPINESS, THE, 1916, A
HACELDAMA, 1919
HADAKA NO SHIMA
HADAKA NO TAISHO
HADLEY'S REBELLION, 1984, C
HAGBARD AND SIGNE, 1968, C-O
HAHAKIRI, 1963, O
HAIL, 1973, O
HAIL AND FAREWELL, 1936, A
HAIL MAFIA, 1965, O
HAIL THE CONQUERING HERO, 1944, A
HAIL THE HERO, 1924
HAIL THE WOMAN, 1921
HAIL TO THE CHIEF
HAIL TO THE RANGERS, 1943, A
HAIL, HERO!, 1969, C
HAINE, 1918

HAIR, 1979, C-O
HAIR OF THE DOG, 1962, A
HAIR TRIGGER BAXTER, 1926, A
HAIR TRIGGER CASEY, 1922
HAIR-TRIGGER CASEY, 1936
HAIRPINS, 1920, A
HAIRY APE, THE, 1944, A
HAKUCHI
HAKUJA DEN
HALCON Y LA PRESA, EL
HALDANE OF THE SECRET SERVICE, 1923, A
HALF A BRIDE, 1928, A
HALF A CHANCE, 1920
HALF A HERO, 1953, AA
HALF A HOUSE, 1979
HALF A ROGUE, 1916
HALF A SINNER, 1934, A
HALF A SINNER, 1940, A
HALF A SIXPENCE, 1967, A
HALF A TRUTH, 1922, A
HALF AN HOUR, 1920
HALF ANGEL, 1936, C
HALF ANGEL, 1951, A
HALF BREED, THE, 1916
HALF BREED, THE, 1922
HALF HUMAN, 1955, C-O
HALF MILLION BRIBE, THE, 1916
HALF PAST MIDNIGHT, 1948, A
HALF PINT, THE, 1960, AAA
HALF SHOT AT SUNRISE, 1930, A
HALF WAY TO HEAVEN, 1929, A
HALF WAY TO SHANGHAI, 1942, C
HALF-A-DOLLAR BILL, 1924
HALF-BREED, THE, 1952, A
HALF-MARRIAGE, 1929
HALF-NAKED TRUTH, THE, 1932, A
HALF-WAY GIRL, THE, 1925
HALF-WAY HOUSE, THE, 1945, C
HALFBREED, 1919
HALFWAY TO HELL, 1957
HALLELUJAH, 1929, A
HALLELUJAH AND SARTANA, SON OF...GOD, 1972
HALLELUJAH THE HILLS, 1963, C
HALLELUJAH TRAIL, THE, 1965, A
HALLELUJAH, I'M A BUM, 1933, A
HALLIDAY BRAND, THE, 1957, C
HALLOWEEN, 1978, O
HALLOWEEN II, 1981, O
HALLOWEEN III: SEASON OF THE WITCH, 1982, O
HALLS OF ANGER, 1970, O
HALLS OF MONTEZUMA, 1951, C
HALLUCINATION GENERATION, 1966, C
HALLUCINATORS, THE
HAM AND EGGS
HAM AND EGGS AT THE FRONT, 1927, A
HAMBONE AND HILLIE, 1984, A
HAMILE, 1965, C
HAMLET, 1913, A
HAMLET, 1921
HAMLET, 1948, A
HAMLET, 1962, A
HAMLET, 1964, A
HAMLET, 1966, C
HAMLET, 1969, A
HAMLET, 1976
HAMMER, 1972, O
HAMMER THE TOFF, 1952, A
HAMMERHEAD, 1968, C
HAMMERSMITH IS OUT, 1972, C
HAMMETT, 1982, C
HAMNSTED
HAMP
HAMPSTER OF HAPPINESS
HANA TO NAMIDA TO HONOO
HAND AT THE WINDOW, THE, 1918
HAND IN HAND, 1960
HAND IN THE TRAP, THE, 1963, C
HAND INVISIBLE, THE, 1919
HAND OF DEATH, 1962
HAND OF DESTINY, THE, 1914
HAND OF JUSTICE, THE, 1915
HAND OF NIGHT, THE, 1968, C
HAND OF PERIL, THE, 1916
HAND OF THE HUN, THE, 1917
HAND OF THE LAW, THE, 1915
HAND THAT ROCKS THE CRADLE, THE, 1917
HAND, THE, 1960, C
HAND, THE, 1981, O
HANDCUFFED, 1929, A
HANDCUFFS OR KISSES, 1921
HANDCUFFS, LONDON, 1955
HANDGUN
HANDICAP, THE, 1925
HANDLE WITH CARE
HANDLE WITH CARE, 1922, A
HANDLE WITH CARE, 1932, A
HANDLE WITH CARE, 1935, A
HANDLE WITH CARE, 1958, A
HANDLE WITH CARE, 1964
HANDS ACROSS THE BORDER, 1926, A
HANDS ACROSS THE BORDER, 1943, A
HANDS ACROSS THE ROCKIES, 1941

HANDS ACROSS THE TABLE, 1935, A
HANDS DOWN, 1918
HANDS OF A STRANGER, 1962, C
HANDS OF DESTINY, 1954, A
HANDS OF NARA, THE, 1922
HANDS OF ORLAC, THE, 1925
HANDS OF ORLAC, THE, 1964, A
HANDS OF THE RIPPER, 1971, O
HANDS OF THE STRANGLER
HANDS OFF, 1921
HANDS OFF, 1927
HANDS UP, 1917
HANDS UP, 1926, A
HANDSOME BRUTE, THE, 1925, A
HANDSOME SERGE
HANDY ANDY, 1921, A
HANDY ANDY, 1934, A
HANG YOUR HAT ON THE WIND, 1969, AA
HANG'EM HIGH, 1968, C
HANG-UP, THE, 1969
HANGAR 18, 1980, A
HANGING JUDGE, THE, 1918, A
HANGING TREE, THE, 1959, C
HANGING WOMAN, THE, 1976
HANGMAN WAITS, THE, 1947, C
HANGMAN'S HOUSE, 1928
HANGMAN'S KNOT, 1952, C
HANGMAN'S WHARF, 1950, A
HANGMAN, THE, 1959
HANGMEN ALSO DIE, 1943
HANGOVER
HANGOVER SQUARE, 1945, C
HANGUP, 1974
HANK WILLIAMS STORY, THE
HANK WILLIAMS: THE SHOW HE NEVER GAVE,
   1982, C
HANKY-PANKY, 1982, A-C
HANNAH K., 1983, C
HANNAH LEE, 1953, A
HANNAH—QUEEN OF THE VAMPIRES, 1972
HANNIBAL, 1960, A
HANNIBAL BROOKS, 1969, C
HANNIE CALDER, 1971, 0
HANOI HANNA—QUEEN OF CHINA
HANOVER STREET, 1979, C
HANS BRINKER AND THE SILVER SKATES, 1969
HANS CHRISTIAN ANDERSEN, 1952
HANSEL AND GRETEL, 1954, AA
HANSEL AND GRETEL, 1965, AA
HANTISE, 1922
HAPPENING, THE, 1967, C
HAPPIDROME, 1943
HAPPIEST DAYS OF YOUR LIFE, 1950, A
HAPPIEST MILLIONAIRE, THE, 1967, AA
HAPPILY EVER AFTER
HAPPINESS
HAPPINESS, 1917
HAPPINESS, 1924
HAPPINESS A LA MODE, 1919
HAPPINESS AHEAD, 1928
HAPPINESS AHEAD, 1934, A
HAPPINESS C.O.D., 1935, A
HAPPINESS CAGE, THE, 1972, C
HAPPINESS OF THREE WOMEN, THE, 1917
HAPPINESS OF THREE WOMEN, THE, 1954, A
HAPPINESS OF US ALONE, 1962, A
HAPPY, 1934, A
HAPPY ALEXANDER
HAPPY ANNIVERSARY, 1959, C
HAPPY AS THE GRASS WAS GREEN, 1973, A
HAPPY BIRTHDAY TO ME, 1981, O
HAPPY BIRTHDAY, DAVY, 1970, O
HAPPY BIRTHDAY, GEMINI, 1980
HAPPY BIRTHDAY, WANDA JUNE, 1971
HAPPY DAYS, 1930, A
HAPPY DAYS ARE HERE AGAIN, 1936, A
HAPPY DEATHDAY, 1969, C
HAPPY END, 1968, C-O
HAPPY ENDING, THE, 1925
HAPPY ENDING, THE, 1931, A
HAPPY ENDING, THE, 1969, C
HAPPY EVER AFTER
HAPPY EVER AFTER, 1932, A
HAPPY FAMILY, THE
HAPPY FAMILY, THE, 1936, A
HAPPY GO LOVELY, 1951, A
HAPPY GO LUCKY, 1943, AA
HAPPY GYPSIES
HAPPY HOOKER GOES TO HOLLYWOOD, THE,
   1980, O
HAPPY HOOKER GOES TO WASHINGTON, THE,
   1977, O
HAPPY HOOKER, THE, 1975, O
HAPPY IS THE BRIDE, 1958, A
HAPPY LAND, 1943, A
HAPPY LANDING, 1934, A
HAPPY LANDING, 1938, A
HAPPY MOTHER'S DAY... LOVE, GEORGE, 1973, C
HAPPY ROAD, THE, 1957
HAPPY THIEVES, THE, 1962, C
HAPPY THOUGH MARRIED, 1919
HAPPY TIME, THE, 1952, AAA

HAPPY WARRIOR, THE, 1917
HAPPY WARRIOR, THE, 1925
HAPPY YEARS, THE, 1950
HAPPY-GO-LUCKY, 1937, A
HAR HAR DU DITT LIV
HARAKIRI, 1919
HARASSED HERO, THE, 1954, A
HARBOR LIGHT YOKOHAMA, 1970, C-O
HARBOR LIGHTS, 1963
HARBOR OF MISSING MEN, 1950
HARBOR PATROL, 1924
HARBOUR LIGHTS, THE, 1914
HARBOUR LIGHTS, THE, 1923
HARD BOILED, 1919
HARD BOILED, 1926
HARD BOILED HAGGERTY, 1927
HARD BOILED MAHONEY, 1947, A
HARD BUNCH, THE
HARD CASH, 1921
HARD CHOICES, 1984, O
HARD CONTRACT, 1969
HARD COUNTRY, 1981, O
HARD DAY'S NIGHT, A, 1964, A
HARD DRIVER
HARD FEELINGS, 1981
HARD FISTS, 1927
HARD GUY, 1941, A
HARD HITTIN' HAMILTON, 1924
HARD HOMBRE, 1931, A
HARD KNOCKS, 1980, O
HARD MAN, THE, 1957
HARD ON THE TRAIL
HARD PART BEGINS, THE, 1973, C
HARD RIDE, THE, 1971, C
HARD ROAD, THE, 1970, O
HARD ROCK BREED, THE, 1918
HARD ROCK HARRIGAN, 1935, A
HARD STEEL, 1941
HARD TIMES, 1915, A
HARD TIMES, 1975, A-C
HARD TO GET, 1929, A
HARD TO GET, 1938, A
HARD TO HANDLE, 1933, A
HARD TO HOLD, 1984, A-C
HARD TRAIL, 1969
HARD WAY TO DIE, A, 1980
HARD WAY, THE, 1916, A
HARD WAY, THE, 1942, A-C
HARD WAY, THE, 1980
HARD, FAST, AND BEAUTIFUL, 1951, A
HARD-BOILED CANARY
HARDBODIES, 1984, O
HARDBOILED, 1929, A
HARDBOILED ROSE, 1929, A
HARDCORE, 1979, O
HARDER THEY COME, THE, 1973, C
HARDER THEY FALL, THE, 1956, O
HARDLY WORKING, 1981
HARDYS RIDE HIGH, THE, 1939, AAA
HAREM BUNCH; OR WAR AND PIECE, THE,
   1969, C-O
HAREM GIRL, 1952, A
HAREM HOLIDAY
HARISCHANDRA, 1913
HARLEM AFTER MIDNIGHT, 1934
HARLEM GLOBETROTTERS, THE, 1951, A
HARLEM IS HEAVEN, 1932, A
HARLEM ON THE PRAIRIE, 1938, A
HARLEM RIDES THE RANGE, 1939, A
HARLEQUIN, 1980, C-O
HARLOW, 1965, C
HARMON OF MICHIGAN, 1941, A
HARMONY AT HOME, 1930, A
HARMONY HEAVEN, 1930, A
HARMONY LANE, 1935, A
HARMONY ROW, 1933, A
HARMONY TRAIL
HAROLD AND MAUDE, 1971, A-C
HAROLD ROBBINS' THE BETSY
HAROLD TEEN, 1928, A
HAROLD TEEN, 1934, A
HARP IN HOCK, A, 1927
HARP KING, THE, 1920
HARP OF BURMA, 1967
HARPER, 1966, C
HARPER MYSTERY, THE, 1913
HARPER VALLEY, P.T.A., 1978, C
HARPOON, 1948, A
HARRAD EXPERIMENT, THE, 1973, O
HARRAD SUMMER, THE, 1974, O
HARRIET AND THE PIPER, 1920
HARRIET CRAIG, 1950, A-C
HARRIGAN'S KID, 1943, A
HARRY AND SON, 1984, C
HARRY AND TONTO, 1974, C
HARRY AND WALTER GO TO NEW YORK, 1976, C
HARRY BLACK AND THE TIGER, 1958, C
HARRY FRIGG
HARRY IN YOUR POCKET, 1973, C
HARRY TRACY—DESPERADO, 1982, C
HARRY'S WAR, 1981, C
HARSH FATHER, THE, 1911

HARUM SCARUM, 1965, A
HARVARD, HERE I COME, 1942, A
HARVEST, 1939, O
HARVEST MELODY, 1943, A
HARVEST MOON, THE, 1920
HARVEST OF HATE, THE, 1929, A
HARVESTER, THE, 1927
HARVESTER, THE, 1936, A
HARVEY, 1950, A
HARVEY GIRLS, THE, 1946, AAA
HARVEY MIDDLEMAN, FIREMAN, 1965, C
HAS ANYBODY SEEN MY GAL?, 1952, A
HAS MAN THE RIGHT TO KILL?, 1919
HAS THE WORLD GONE MAD, 1923, A
HASHIMURA TOGO, 1917
HASSAN, TERRORIST, 1968, O
HASTY HEART, THE, 1949, A
HAT CHECK GIRL, 1932
HAT CHECK HONEY, 1944, A
HAT, COAT AND GLOVE, 1934, A
HATARI!, 1962, A
HATCHET FOR A HONEYMOON, 1969, O
HATCHET MAN, THE, 1932, C-O
HATE, 1917
HATE, 1922
HATE FOR HATE, 1967, C
HATE IN PARADISE, 1938
HATE SHIP, THE, 1930, A
HATE TRAIL, THE, 1922
HATE WITHIN
HATER OF MEN, 1917, A
HATFUL OF RAIN, A, 1957, C
HATRED, 1941, A
HATS OFF, 1937, A
HATS OFF TO RHYTHM
HATTER'S CASTLE, 1948, C
HATTER'S GHOST, THE, 1982
HAUNTED, 1976, O
HAUNTED AND THE HUNTED
HAUNTED BEDROOM, THE, 1919
HAUNTED CASTLE, THE, 1921
HAUNTED GOLD, 1932, A
HAUNTED HONEYMOON
HAUNTED HOUSE OF HORROR
HAUNTED HOUSE, THE, 1917
HAUNTED HOUSE, THE, 1928, A
HAUNTED HOUSE, THE, 1940, A
HAUNTED MANOR, THE, 1916
HAUNTED MINE, THE, 1946
HAUNTED PAJAMAS, 1917, A
HAUNTED PALACE, THE, 1963
HAUNTED RANCH, THE
HAUNTED RANCH, THE, 1943, A
HAUNTED RANGE, THE, 1926, A
HAUNTED SHIP, THE, 1927
HAUNTED STRANGLER, THE, 1958, O
HAUNTED TRAILS, 1949
HAUNTING OF CASTLE MONTEGO
HAUNTING OF JULIA, THE, 1981, O
HAUNTING OF M, THE, 1979, C
HAUNTING OF ROSALIND, THE, 1973
HAUNTING SHADOWS, 1920
HAUNTING, THE, 1963, C-O
HAUNTS, 1977, O
HAVANA ROSE, 1951, A
HAVANA WIDOWS, 1933, A
HAVE A HEART, 1934
HAVE A NICE WEEKEND, 1975, O
HAVE ROCKET, WILL TRAVEL, 1959, A
HAVING A WILD WEEKEND, 1965
HAVING WONDERFUL CRIME, 1945, A
HAVING WONDERFUL TIME, 1938, A
HAVOC, 1925
HAVOC, THE, 1916
HAWAII, 1966, C
HAWAII BEACH BOY
HAWAII CALLS, 1938, A
HAWAIIAN BUCKAROO, 1938, A
HAWAIIAN NIGHTS, 1939, A
HAWAIIAN NIGHTS, 1934
HAWAIIANS, THE, 1970, C
HAWK OF POWDER RIVER, THE, 1948, A
HAWK OF THE HILLS, 1929
HAWK OF WILD RIVER, THE, 1952, A
HAWK THE SLAYER, 1980, A
HAWK'S NEST, THE, 1928
HAWK, THE, 1917
HAWK, THE, 1935
HAWKS AND THE SPARROWS, THE, 1967, C
HAWLEY'S OF HIGH STREET, 1933, A
HAWMPS!, 1976
HAWTHORNE OF THE U.S.A., 1919, A
HAXAN
HAY FOOT, 1942, A
HAY FOOT, STRAW FOOT, 1919
HAY, HAY, HAY, 1983
HAZARD, 1948, A
HAZARDOUS VALLEY, 1927, A
HAZEL KIRKE, 1916
HAZEL'S PEOPLE, 1978, C
HAZING, THE, 1978, C
HE COMES UP SMILING, 1918

HE COULDN'T SAY NO, 1938, A
HE COULDN'T TAKE IT, 1934
HE FELL IN LOVE WITH HIS WIFE, 1916
HE FOUND A STAR, 1941, A
HE HIRED THE BOSS, 1943, A
HE IS MY BROTHER, 1976
HE KNEW WOMEN, 1930, A
HE KNOWS YOU'RE ALONE, 1980, O
HE LAUGHED LAST, 1956, A
HE LEARNED ABOUT WOMEN, 1933
HE LOVED AN ACTRESS, 1938, A
HE MARRIED HIS WIFE, 1940, A
HE RAN ALL THE WAY, 1951
HE RIDES TALL, 1964, A
HE SNOOPS TO CONQUER, 1944, A
HE STAYED FOR BREAKFAST, 1940, A
HE WALKED BY NIGHT, 1948
HE WAS HER MAN, 1934, A-C
HE WHO GETS SLAPPED, 1916
HE WHO GETS SLAPPED, 1924, A
HE WHO LAUGHS LAST, 1925
HE WHO RIDES A TIGER, 1966, A
HE WHO SHOOTS FIRST, 1966, C
HE'S A COCKEYED WONDER, 1950, A
HE'S A PRINCE
HE'S MY GUY, 1943, A
HE, SHE OR IT!
HE-MAN'S COUNTRY, A, 1926, A
HEAD, 1968, A
HEAD FOR THE DEVIL
HEAD FOR THE HILLS
HEAD MAN, THE, 1928, A
HEAD OF A TYRANT, 1960
HEAD OF JANUS, THE, 1920
HEAD OF THE FAMILY, 1933, A
HEAD OF THE FAMILY, 1967
HEAD OF THE FAMILY, THE, 1922, A
HEAD OF THE FAMILY, THE, 1928, A
HEAD OFFICE, 1936, A
HEAD ON, 1971, O
HEAD ON, 1981
HEAD OVER HEELS
HEAD OVER HEELS, 1922
HEAD OVER HEELS IN LOVE, 1937
HEAD THAT WOULDN'T DIE
HEAD WINDS, 1925
HEAD, THE, 1961, O
HEADIN' EAST, 1937, A
HEADIN' FOR BROADWAY, 1980, C
HEADIN' FOR DANGER, 1928
HEADIN' FOR GOD'S COUNTRY, 1943, A
HEADIN' FOR THE RIO GRANDE, 1937, A
HEADIN' FOR TROUBLE, 1931, A
HEADIN' HOME, 1920
HEADIN' NORTH, 1921
HEADIN' NORTH, 1930, A
HEADIN' SOUTH, 1918, A
HEADIN' THROUGH, 1924
HEADIN' WEST, 1922
HEADIN' WESTWARD, 1929, A
HEADING FOR HEAVEN, 1947, A
HEADING WEST, 1946
HEADLESS EYES, THE, 1983
HEADLESS GHOST, THE, 1959, A
HEADLESS HORSEMAN, THE, 1922
HEADLEYS AT HOME, THE, 1939, A
HEADLINE, 1943, A
HEADLINE CRASHER, 1937, A
HEADLINE HUNTERS, 1955, A
HEADLINE HUNTERS, 1968, AAA
HEADLINE SHOOTER, 1933, A
HEADLINE WOMAN, THE, 1935, A
HEADLINES, 1925
HEADMASTER, THE, 1921
HEADS UP, 1925, A
HEADS UP, 1930, A
HEADS UP, CHARLIE, 1926
HEADS WE GO
HEADS WIN, 1919
HEALER, THE, 1935, A
HEALTH, 1980, C-O
HEAR ME GOOD, 1957, A
HEAR THE PIPERS CALLING, 1918
HEARSE, THE, 1980, A
HEART AND SOUL, 1917
HEART AND SOUL, 1950, A
HEART BANDIT, THE, 1924
HEART BEAT, 1979, O
HEART BUSTER, THE, 1924
HEART IN PAWN, A, 1919
HEART IS A LONELY HUNTER, THE, 1968, O
HEART LIKE A WHEEL, 1983, C
HEART LINE, THE, 1921
HEART O' THE HILLS, 1919
HEART O' THE WEST
HEART OF A CHILD, 1958
HEART OF A CHILD, THE, 1915
HEART OF A CHILD, THE, 1920
HEART OF A CLOWN
HEART OF A COWARD, THE, 1926, A
HEART OF A FOLLIES GIRL, THE, 1928, A
HEART OF A FOOL

HEART OF A GIRL, 1918
HEART OF A GYPSY, THE, 1919
HEART OF A HERO, THE, 1916
HEART OF A LION, THE, 1917
HEART OF A MAN, THE, 1959, A
HEART OF A NATION, THE, 1943, A
HEART OF A PAINTED WOMAN, THE, 1915
HEART OF A ROSE, THE, 1919
HEART OF A SIREN, 1925
HEART OF A TEMPTRESS
HEART OF A TEXAN, THE, 1922
HEART OF A WOMAN, THE, 1920
HEART OF ALASKA, 1924
HEART OF ARIZONA, 1938, A
HEART OF BROADWAY, THE, 1928
HEART OF EZRA GREER, THE, 1917
HEART OF GOLD, 1919
HEART OF HUMANITY, THE, 1919
HEART OF JENNIFER, THE, 1915
HEART OF JUANITA, 1919
HEART OF LINCOLN, THE, 1922
HEART OF MARYLAND, THE, 1915
HEART OF MARYLAND, THE, 1921, A
HEART OF MARYLAND, THE, 1927
HEART OF MIDLOTHIAN, THE, 1914
HEART OF NEW YORK, 1932, A
HEART OF NEW YORK, 1916
HEART OF NORA FLYNN, THE, 1916
HEART OF PARIS, 1939, A
HEART OF PAULA, THE, 1916
HEART OF RACHAEL, THE, 1918
HEART OF ROMANCE, THE, 1918
HEART OF SALOME, THE, 1927
HEART OF SISTER ANN, THE, 1915
HEART OF TARA, THE, 1916
HEART OF TEXAS RYAN, THE, 1917
HEART OF THE BLUE RIDGE, THE, 1915, A
HEART OF THE GOLDEN WEST, 1942, A
HEART OF THE HILLS, THE, 1916
HEART OF THE MATTER, THE, 1954, A-C
HEART OF THE NORTH, 1938, A
HEART OF THE NORTH, THE, 1921
HEART OF THE RIO GRANDE, 1942, A
HEART OF THE ROCKIES, 1937, A
HEART OF THE ROCKIES, 1951, A
HEART OF THE STAG, 1984, A
HEART OF THE SUNSET, 1918
HEART OF THE WEST
HEART OF THE WEST, 1937, A
HEART OF THE WILDS, 1918
HEART OF THE YUKON, THE, 1927
HEART OF TWENTY, THE, 1920
HEART OF VIRGINIA, 1948, A
HEART OF WETONA, THE, 1919
HEART OF YOUTH, THE, 1920
HEART PUNCH, 1932, A
HEART RAIDER, THE, 1923, A
HEART SONG, 1933, A
HEART SPECIALIST, THE, 1922
HEART STRINGS, 1917
HEART STRINGS, 1920
HEART THIEF, THE, 1927
HEART TO HEART, 1928
HEART TO LET, A, 1921
HEART TROUBLE, 1928, A
HEART WITHIN, THE, 1957, A
HEART'S CRUCIBLE, A, 1916
HEART'S DESIRE, 1917
HEART'S DESIRE, 1937, A
HEART'S HAVEN, 1922
HEART'S REVENGE, A, 1918
HEARTACHES, 1915
HEARTACHES, 1947, A
HEARTACHES, 1981, O
HEARTBEAT, 1946, A
HEARTBEEPS, 1981
HEARTBOUND, 1925
HEARTBREAK, 1931, A
HEARTBREAK KID, THE, 1972, C-O
HEARTBREAK MOTEL, 1978
HEARTBREAKER, 1983, C
HEARTBREAKERS, 1984, C-O
HEARTLAND, 1980, A
HEARTLESS HUSBANDS, 1925
HEARTS ADRIFT, 1914, A
HEARTS AFLAME, 1923
HEARTS AND FISTS, 1926, A
HEARTS AND FLOWERS, 1914
HEARTS AND MASKS, 1921
HEARTS AND SADDLES, 1919
HEARTS AND SPANGLES, 1926
HEARTS AND SPURS, 1925
HEARTS AND THE HIGHWAY, 1915
HEARTS ARE TRUMPS, 1920
HEARTS ASLEEP, 1919
HEARTS DIVIDED, 1936, A
HEARTS IN BONDAGE, 1936, A
HEARTS IN DIXIE, 1929, A
HEARTS IN EXILE, 1929, A
HEARTS O' THE RANGE, 1921
HEARTS OF HUMANITY, 1932, A
HEARTS OF HUMANITY, 1936, A

HEARTS OF LOVE, 1918
HEARTS OF MEN, 1915
HEARTS OF MEN, 1919, A
HEARTS OF MEN, 1928
HEARTS OF MEN, THE
HEARTS OF OAK, 1924, A
HEARTS OF THE WEST, 1925
HEARTS OF THE WEST, 1975, A
HEARTS OF THE WOODS, 1921
HEARTS OF THE WORLD, 1918, A
HEARTS OF YOUTH, 1921
HEARTS OR DIAMONDS?, 1918
HEARTS THAT ARE HUMAN, 1915
HEARTS UNITED, 1914
HEARTS UP, 1920
HEARTSEASE, 1919
HEARTSTRINGS, 1917
HEARTSTRINGS, 1923, A
HEAT, 1970, O
HEAT, 1972
HEAT AND DUST, 1983, C
HEAT LIGHTNING, 1934, A
HEAT OF DESIRE, 1984, O
HEAT OF MIDNIGHT, 1966, O
HEAT OF THE SUMMER, 1961, A
HEAT WAVE, 1935, A
HEAT'S ON, THE, 1943, A-C
HEATWAVE, 1954, A
HEATWAVE, 1983, O
HEAVEN CAN WAIT, 1943, A
HEAVEN CAN WAIT, 1978, C
HEAVEN IS ROUND THE CORNER, 1944, A
HEAVEN KNOWS, MR. ALLISON, 1957, A
HEAVEN ON EARTH, 1927
HEAVEN ON EARTH, 1931, A
HEAVEN ON EARTH, 1960, A
HEAVEN ONLY KNOWS, 1947, A
HEAVEN SENT
HEAVEN WITH A BARBED WIRE FENCE, 1939, A
HEAVEN WITH A GUN, 1969, C
HEAVEN'S GATE, 1980, O
HEAVENLY BODY, THE, 1943, A
HEAVENLY DAYS, 1944, A
HEAVENS ABOVE!, 1963, AA
HEAVY METAL, 1981, O
HEAVY TRAFFIC, 1974
HEDDA, 1975, A-C
HEDDA GABLER, 1917
HEEDLESS MOTHS, 1921
HEIDI, 1937, AAA
HEIDI, 1954, AAA
HEIDI, 1968, AAA
HEIDI AND PETER, 1955, AAA
HEIDI'S SONG, 1982, AA
HEIGHTS OF DANGER, 1962, A
HEIGHTS OF HAZARDS, THE, 1915
HEINZELMANNCHEN
HEIR OF THE AGES, THE, 1917
HEIR TO JENGHIS-KHAN, THE, 1928
HEIR TO JENGHIZ KHAN, THE
HEIR TO THE HOORAH, THE, 1916
HEIR TO TROUBLE, 1936, A
HEIR-LOONS, 1925
HEIRESS AT "COFFEE DAN'S", THE, 1917
HEIRESS FOR A DAY, 1918
HEIRESS, THE, 1949, A
HEIRLOOM MYSTERY, THE, 1936, A
HEIST, THE, 1979, A
HELD BY THE ENEMY, 1920
HELD BY THE LAW, 1927, A
HELD FOR RANSOM, 1914
HELD FOR RANSOM, 1938, A
HELD IN TRUST, 1920
HELD IN TRUST, 1949, A
HELD TO ANSWER, 1923, A
HELDEN
HELDEN—HIMMEL UND HOLLE
HELDINNEN, 1962, A
HELDORADO
HELEN MORGAN STORY, THE, 1959, A
HELEN OF FOUR GATES, 1920
HELEN OF TROY
HELEN OF TROY, 1956, A
HELEN'S BABIES, 1924, A
HELENE OF THE NORTH, 1915
HELICOPTER SPIES, THE, 1968, A
HELIOTROPE, 1920
HELL AND HIGH WATER, 1933, A
HELL AND HIGH WATER, 1954, A
HELL BELOW, 1933, A
HELL BELOW ZERO, 1954, A
HELL BENT, 1918
HELL BENT FOR 'FRISCO, 1931, A
HELL BENT FOR GLORY
HELL BENT FOR LEATHER, 1960, A
HELL BENT FOR LOVE, 1934, A
HELL BOATS, 1970, A
HELL BOUND, 1931, A
HELL BOUND, 1957, A
HELL CANYON OUTLAWS, 1957, A
HELL CAT, THE, 1918
HELL CAT, THE, 1934, A

HELL DIGGERS, THE, 1921
HELL DIVERS, 1932
HELL DRIVERS, 1958, A
HELL FIRE AUSTIN, 1932, A
HELL HARBOR, 1930
HELL HATH NO FURY, 1917
HELL HOUSE GIRLS, 1975
HELL IN KOREA, 1956, C
HELL IN NORMANDY, 1968
HELL IN THE CITY
HELL IN THE HEAVENS, 1934, A
HELL IN THE PACIFIC, 1968, O
HELL IS A CITY, 1960, A
HELL IS EMPTY, 1967, C
HELL IS FOR HEROES, 1962, C
HELL IS SOLD OUT, 1951, A
HELL MORGAN'S GIRL, 1917
HELL NIGHT, 1981, O
HELL ON DEVIL'S ISLAND, 1957, A
HELL ON EARTH, 1934, A
HELL ON FRISCO BAY, 1956, C
HELL ON WHEELS, 1967, A
HELL RAIDERS, 1968, A-C
HELL RAIDERS OF THE DEEP, 1954, A
HELL RIVER, 1977
HELL ROARIN' REFORM, 1919
HELL SHIP MUTINY, 1957, A
HELL SHIP, THE, 1920
HELL SHIP, THE, 1923
HELL SQUAD, 1958, A
HELL TO ETERNITY, 1960, A
HELL TO MACAO
HELL UP IN HARLEM, 1973, O
HELL WITH HEROES, THE, 1968, C
HELL'S 400, 1926
HELL'S ANGELS, 1930, C
HELL'S ANGELS ON WHEELS, 1967, O
HELL'S ANGELS '69, 1969, O
HELL'S BELLES, 1969, O
HELL'S BLOODY DEVILS, 1970, O
HELL'S BOARDER
HELL'S BORDER, 1922
HELL'S CARGO, 1935, A
HELL'S CARGO, 1939
HELL'S CHOSEN FEW, 1968, O
HELL'S CRATER, 1918
HELL'S CROSSROADS, 1957, A
HELL'S END, 1918
HELL'S FIVE HOURS, 1958, A
HELL'S HALF ACRE, 1954, A
HELL'S HEADQUARTERS, 1932
HELL'S HEROES, 1930, A
HELL'S HIGHROAD, 1925
HELL'S HIGHWAY, 1932, A
HELL'S HINGES, 1916, A
HELL'S HOLE, 1923
HELL'S HORIZON, 1955, A
HELL'S HOUSE, 1932, A
HELL'S ISLAND, 1930, A
HELL'S ISLAND, 1955
HELL'S KITCHEN, 1939, A
HELL'S OASIS, 1920
HELL'S OUTPOST, 1955, A
HELL'S PLAYGROUND, 1967, A
HELL'S RIVER
HELL'S VALLEY, 1931
HELL, HEAVEN OR HOBOKEN, 1958, A
HELL-BENT FOR HEAVEN, 1926
HELL-SHIP MORGAN, 1936
HELL-TO-PAY AUSTIN, 1916, A
HELLBENDERS, THE, 1967, A
HELLCAT, THE, 1928
HELLCATS OF THE NAVY, 1957, A
HELLCATS, THE, 1968, O
HELLDORADO, 1935, A
HELLDORADO, 1946, A
HELLER IN PINK TIGHTS, 1960, C
HELLFIGHTERS, 1968, A
HELLFIRE, 1949, A
HELLFIRE CLUB, THE, 1963, C
HELLGATE, 1952, A
HELLHOUNDS OF THE WEST, 1922
HELLION, THE, 1919
HELLION, THE, 1924
HELLIONS, THE, 1962, O
HELLO ANNAPOLIS, 1942, A
HELLO BEAUTIFUL
HELLO BILL, 1915
HELLO CHEYENE, 1928
HELLO DOWN THERE, 1969
HELLO GOD, 1951, A
HELLO LONDON, 1958
HELLO SISTER, 1930, A
HELLO SISTER!, 1933, C-O
HELLO SUCKER, 1941, A
HELLO SWEETHEART, 1935, A
HELLO TROUBLE, 1932, A
HELLO, DOLLY!, 1969, AAA
HELLO, ELEPHANT, 1954
HELLO, EVERYBODY, 1933, A
HELLO, FRISCO, HELLO, 1943, A
HELLO—GOODBYE, 1970, O

HELLSHIP BRONSON, 1928
HELLZAPOPPIN', 1941, A
HELP HELP POLICE, 1919
HELP I'M INVISIBLE, 1952, A
HELP ME...I'M POSSESSED, 1976
HELP WANTED, 1915
HELP WANTED—MALE, 1920, A
HELP YOURSELF, 1920
HELP YOURSELF, 1932, A
HELP!, 1965, A
HELTER SKELTER, 1949, A
HEMINGWAY'S ADVENTURES OF A YOUNG MAN
HENNESSY, 1975, C
HENRIETTE'S HOLIDAY, 1953, C
HENRY ALDRICH FOR PRESIDENT, 1941, A
HENRY ALDRICH GETS GLAMOUR, 1942, A
HENRY ALDRICH HAUNTS A HOUSE, 1943, A
HENRY ALDRICH PLAYS CUPID, 1944, A
HENRY ALDRICH SWINGS IT, 1943, A
HENRY ALDRICH'S LITTLE SECRET, 1944, A
HENRY ALDRICH, BOY SCOUT, 1944, A
HENRY ALDRICH, EDITOR, 1942, A
HENRY AND DIZZY, 1942, A
HENRY GOES ARIZONA, 1939, A
HENRY LIMPET
HENRY STEPS OUT, 1940, A
HENRY V, 1946, A
HENRY VIII
HENRY VIII AND HIS SIX WIVES, 1972, A
HENRY'S NIGHT IN, 1969
HENRY, KING OF NAVARRE, 1924
HENRY, THE RAINMAKER, 1949, A
HENTAI, 1966, O
HER ACCIDENTAL HUSBAND, 1923
HER ADVENTUROUS NIGHT, 1946, A
HER AMERICAN HUSBAND, 1918
HER AMERICAN PRINCE, 1916
HER ATONEMENT, 1915
HER BELOVED ENEMY, 1917
HER BELOVED VILLIAN, 1920
HER BENNY, 1920
HER BETTER SELF, 1917
HER BIG ADVENTURE, 1926
HER BIG NIGHT, 1926
HER BITTER CUP, 1916
HER BLEEDING HEART, 1916
HER BODY IN BOND, 1918
HER BODYGUARD, 1933, A
HER BOY, 1915, A
HER BOY, 1918
HER CARDBOARD LOVER, 1942, A
HER CODE OF HONOR, 1919
HER CONDONED SIN
HER COUNTRY FIRST, 1918
HER COUNTRY'S CALL, 1917
HER CROSS, 1919
HER DEBT OF HONOR, 1916
HER DECISION, 1918
HER DOUBLE CROSS, 1917
HER DOUBLE LIFE, 1916
HER ELEPHANT MAN, 1920, A
HER ENLISTED MAN
HER EXCELLENCY, THE GOVERNOR, 1917
HER FACE VALUE, 1921
HER FATAL MILLIONS, 1923, A
HER FATHER SAID NO, 1927
HER FATHER'S GOLD, 1916
HER FATHER'S KEEPER, 1917
HER FATHER'S SON, 1916
HER FAVORITE HUSBAND
HER FIGHTING CHANCE, 1917, A
HER FINAL RECKONING, 1918
HER FIRST AFFAIR, 1947, A
HER FIRST AFFAIRE, 1932, A
HER FIRST BEAU, 1941, A
HER FIRST ELOPEMENT, 1920
HER FIRST MATE, 1933, A
HER FIRST ROMANCE, 1940
HER FIRST ROMANCE, 1951
HER FIVE-FOOT HIGHNESS, 1920, A
HER FORGOTTEN PAST, 1933, A
HER GAME, 1919
HER GILDED CAGE, 1922, A
HER GOOD NAME, 1917
HER GREAT CHANCE, 1918, A
HER GREAT HOUR, 1916
HER GREAT MATCH, 1915
HER GREAT PRICE, 1916
HER GREATEST BLUFF, 1927
HER GREATEST LOVE, 1917
HER GREATEST PERFORMANCE, 1916
HER HALF BROTHER
HER HAPPINESS, 1915
HER HERITAGE, 1919, A
HER HIGHNESS AND THE BELLBOY, 1945, A
HER HONOR THE GOVERNOR, 1926
HER HONOR THE MAYOR, 1920
HER HOUR, 1917
HER HUSBAND LIES, 1937, A
HER HUSBAND'S AFFAIRS, 1947, A
HER HUSBAND'S FRIEND, 1920
HER HUSBAND'S HONOR, 1918

HER HUSBAND'S SECRET, 1925
HER HUSBAND'S SECRETARY, 1937, A
HER HUSBAND'S TRADEMARK, 1922
HER IMAGINARY LOVER, 1933, A
HER INDISCRETIONS, 1927
HER INSPIRATION, 1918
HER JUNGLE LOVE, 1938, A
HER KIND OF MAN, 1946, A
HER KINGDOM OF DREAMS, 1919
HER LAST AFFAIRE, 1935, A
HER LIFE AND HIS, 1917
HER LONELY SOLDIER, 1919, A
HER LORD AND MASTER, 1921
HER LOVE STORY, 1924
HER LUCKY NIGHT, 1945, A
HER MAD BARGAIN, 1921, A
HER MAD NIGHT, 1932, A
HER MAJESTY, 1922
HER MAJESTY LOVE, 1931, A
HER MAN, 1918
HER MAN, 1924, A
HER MAN, 1930, C
HER MAN GILBEY, 1949, A
HER MAN O'WAR, 1926
HER MARKET VALUE, 1925
HER MARRIAGE LINES, 1917
HER MARRIAGE VOW, 1924
HER MARTYRDOM, 1915
HER MASTER'S VOICE, 1936, A
HER MATERNAL RIGHT, 1916
HER MISTAKE, 1918
HER MOMENT, 1918
HER MOTHER'S SECRET, 1915
HER NAMLESS CHILD, 1915
HER NEW YORK, 1917
HER NIGHT OF NIGHTS, 1922
HER NIGHT OF ROMANCE, 1924
HER NIGHT OUT, 1932, A
HER OFFICAL FATHERS, 1917
HER ONE MISTAKE, 1918
HER ONLY WAY, 1918
HER OWN FREE WILL, 1924, A
HER OWN MONEY, 1922
HER OWN PEOPLE, 1917
HER OWN STORY, 1922
HER OWN STORY, 1926
HER OWN WAY, 1915
HER PANELLED DOOR, 1951, A
HER PENALTY, 1921
HER PRICE, 1918
HER PRIMITIVE MAN, 1944, A
HER PRIVATE AFFAIR, 1930, A
HER PRIVATE LIFE, 1929, A
HER PROPER PLACE, 1915
HER PURCHASE PRICE, 1919
HER RECKONING, 1915
HER REDEMPTION
HER REPUTATION, 1923
HER REPUTATION, 1931, A
HER RESALE VALUE, 1933, A
HER RIGHT TO LIVE, 1917
HER SACRIFICE, 1917
HER SACRIFICE, 1926
HER SECOND CHANCE, 1926
HER SECOND HUSBAND, 1918
HER SECOND MOTHER, 1940
HER SECRET, 1917
HER SECRET, 1919, A
HER SECRET, 1933
HER SHATTERED IDOL, 1915
HER SILENT SACRIFICE, 1917
HER SISTER, 1917
HER SISTER FROM PARIS, 1925
HER SISTER'S GUILT, 1916
HER SISTER'S SECRET, 1946, A
HER SOCIAL VALUE, 1921
HER SON, 1920
HER SOUL'S INSPIRATION, 1917
HER SPLENDID FOLLY, 1933, A
HER STORY, 1920, A
HER STORY, 1922
HER STRANGE DESIRE, 1931, A
HER STRANGE WEDDING, 1917
HER STURDY OAK, 1921
HER SUMMER HERO, 1928
HER TEMPORARY HUSBAND, 1923
HER TEMPTATION, 1917
HER TWELVE MEN, 1954, A
HER UNBORN CHILD, 1933
HER UNWILLING HUSBAND, 1920
HER VOCATION, 1915
HER WAYWARD SISTER, 1916
HER WEDDING NIGHT, 1930, A
HER WILD OAT, 1927
HER WINNING WAY, 1921, A
HERBIE GOES BANANAS, 1980, AAA
HERBIE GOES TO MONTE CARLO, 1977, AAA
HERBIE RIDES AGAIN, 1974, AAA
HERCULE CONTRE MOLOCH
HERCULES, 1959, C-O
HERCULES, 1983, A
HERCULES AGAINST THE MOON MEN, 1965, A

HERCULES AGAINST THE SONS OF THE SUN, 1964, A
HERCULES AND THE CAPTIVE WOMEN, 1963
HERCULES AND THE PRINCESS OF TROY, 1966
HERCULES AND THE TYRANTS OF BABYLON, 1964
HERCULES IN NEW YORK, 1970, A
HERCULES IN THE HAUNTED WORLD, 1964, C
HERCULES IN VALE OF WOE, 1962
HERCULES THE INVINCIBLE, 1963
HERCULES UNCHAINED, 1960, A
HERCULES VS-THE GIANT WARRIORS, 1965, A
HERCULES' PILLS, 1960, C
HERCULES, PRISONER OF EVIL, 1967
HERCULES, SAMSON & ULYSSES, 1964, A
HERE COME THE CO-EDS, 1945, AAA
HERE COME THE GIRLS, 1953, A
HERE COME THE HUGGETTS, 1948, A
HERE COME THE JETS, 1959
HERE COME THE MARINES, 1952
HERE COME THE NELSONS, 1952, A
HERE COME THE TIGERS, 1978, C
HERE COME THE WAVES, 1944, A
HERE COMES CARTER, 1936, A
HERE COMES COOKIE, 1935, A
HERE COMES ELMER, 1943, A
HERE COMES HAPPINESS, 1941, A
HERE COMES KELLY, 1943, A
HERE COMES MR. JORDAN, 1941, A
HERE COMES SANTA CLAUS, 1984, AAA
HERE COMES THAT NASHVILLE SOUND
HERE COMES THE BAND, 1935, A
HERE COMES THE BRIDE, 1919
HERE COMES THE GROOM, 1934, A
HERE COMES THE GROOM, 1951, A
HERE COMES THE NAVY, 1934, A
HERE COMES THE SUN, 1945, A
HERE COMES TROUBLE, 1936, A
HERE COMES TROUBLE, 1948, A
HERE HE COMES, 1926
HERE I AM A STRANGER, 1939, A
HERE IS A MAN
HERE IS MY HEART, 1934, A
HERE SURRENDER, 1916
HERE WE GO AGAIN, 1942, AA
HERE WE GO ROUND THE MULBERRY BUSH, 1968, C
HERE'S FLASH CASEY, 1937, A
HERE'S GEORGE, 1932, A
HERE'S THE KNIFE, DEAR: NOW USE IT
HERE'S TO ROMANCE, 1935, A
HERE'S YOUR LIFE, 1968, C-O
HEREDITY, 1918
HERETIC
HERITAGE, 1915
HERITAGE, 1920
HERITAGE, 1935, A
HERITAGE OF HATE, THE, 1916
HERITAGE OF THE DESERT, 1933, A
HERITAGE OF THE DESERT, 1939, A
HERITAGE OF THE DESERT, THE, 1924
HERKER VON LONDON, DER
HERO, 1982, C
HERO AIN'T NOTHIN' BUT A SANDWICH, A, 1977
HERO AT LARGE, 1980, A
HERO FOR A DAY, 1939, A
HERO FOR A NIGHT, A, 1927
HERO OF BABYLON, 1963, A
HERO OF OUR TIME, A, 1969
HERO OF SUBMARINE D-2, THE, 1916
HERO OF THE BIG SNOWS, A, 1926
HERO OF THE CIRCUS, THE, 1928
HERO OF THE HOUR, THE, 1917
HERO ON HORSEBACK, A, 1927
HERO'S ISLAND, 1962, A
HERO, THE
HERO, THE, 1923, A
HEROD THE GREAT, 1960, C
HEROES, 1977, A
HEROES AND HUSBANDS, 1922
HEROES ARE MADE, 1944, C-O
HEROES DIE YOUNG, 1960, C
HEROES FOR SALE, 1933, A
HEROES IN BLUE, 1927
HEROES IN BLUE, 1939, A
HEROES IN THE NIGHT, 1927
HEROES OF TELEMARK, THE, 1965, C
HEROES OF THE ALAMO, 1938, A
HEROES OF THE HILLS, 1938, A
HEROES OF THE RANGE, 1936, A
HEROES OF THE SADDLE, 1940, A
HEROES OF THE SEA, 1941
HEROES OF THE STREET, 1922
HEROES THREE, 1984
HEROES, THE
HEROES, THE, 1975
HEROIC LOVER, THE, 1929, A
HEROINA, 1965, C
HEROS SANS RETOUR
HEROSTRATUS, 1968, C
HEROWORK, 1977
HERR ARNES PENGAR
HERR DOKTOR, 1917

HERRSCHER OHNE KRONE
HERS TO HOLD, 1943, A
HESPER OF THE MOUNTAINS, 1916
HESTER STREET, 1975, C
HEX, 1973, O
HEY BABE?, 1984, A
HEY BOY! HEY GIRL!, 1959, A
HEY HEY COWBOY, 1927, A
HEY RUBE, 1928, A
HEY THERE, IT'S YOGI BEAR, 1964, AAA
HEY! HEY! U.S.A., 1938, A
HEY, GOOD LOOKIN', 1982, O
HEY, LET'S TWIST!, 1961, A
HEY, ROOKIE, 1944
HI DIDDLE DIDDLE, 1943, A
HI GAUCHO!, 1936, A
HI IN THE CELLAR
HI' YA, SAILOR, 1943, A
HI'YA, CHUM, 1943, A
HI, BUDDY, 1943, A
HI, GANG!, 1941, A
HI, GOOD-LOOKIN', 1944, A
HI, MOM!, 1970, O
HI, NEIGHBOR, 1942, A
HI, NELLIE!, 1934, A
HI-DE-HO, 1947, A
HI-JACKED, 1950, A
HI-JACKERS, THE, 1963, A
HI-JACKING RUSTLERS, 1926
HI-RIDERS, 1978, O
HI-YO SILVER, 1940, AA
HIAWATHA, 1913
HIAWATHA, 1952, AAA
HICKEY AND BOGGS, 1972, C
HICKVILLE TO BROADWAY, 1921
HIDDEN ACES, 1927
HIDDEN CHILDREN, THE, 1917
HIDDEN CODE, THE, 1920
HIDDEN DANGER, 1949, A
HIDDEN ENEMY, 1940, A
HIDDEN EYE, THE, 1945, A
HIDDEN FEAR, 1957, C
HIDDEN FIRES, 1918
HIDDEN FORTRESS, THE, 1959, C
HIDDEN GOLD, 1933, A
HIDDEN GOLD, 1940, A
HIDDEN GUNS, 1956, C
HIDDEN HAND, THE, 1916
HIDDEN HAND, THE, 1942, C
HIDDEN HOMICIDE, 1959, C
HIDDEN LAW, THE, 1916
HIDDEN LIGHT, 1920
HIDDEN LOOT, 1925
HIDDEN MENACE, THE, 1925
HIDDEN MENACE, THE, 1940, A
HIDDEN PEARLS, 1918
HIDDEN POWER, 1939, A
HIDDEN ROOM OF 1,000 HORRORS
HIDDEN ROOM, THE, 1949, A
HIDDEN SCAR, THE, 1916, A
HIDDEN SPRING, THE, 1917
HIDDEN TRUTH, THE, 1919
HIDDEN VALLEY, 1932, A
HIDDEN VALLEY OUTLAWS, 1944, A
HIDDEN VALLEY, THE, 1916
HIDDEN WAY, THE, 1926
HIDDEN WOMAN, THE, 1922
HIDE AND SEEK, 1964, A
HIDE IN PLAIN SIGHT, 1980, C
HIDE-OUT, 1934, A
HIDE-OUT, THE, 1930, A
HIDEAWAY, 1937, A
HIDEAWAY GIRL, 1937, A
HIDEAWAYS, THE
HIDEOUS SUN DEMON, THE, 1959, C
HIDEOUT, 1948, C
HIDEOUT, 1949, A
HIDEOUT IN THE ALPS, 1938, A
HIDEOUT IN THE SUN, 1960
HIDEOUT, THE, 1956, C
HIDING PLACE, THE, 1975, C-O
HIER ET AUJOURD'HUI, 1918
HIGGINS FAMILY, THE, 1938, A
HIGH, 1968, O
HIGH AND DRY, 1954, A
HIGH AND HANDSOME, 1925, A
HIGH AND LOW, 1963, C-O
HIGH AND THE MIGHTY, THE, 1954, A
HIGH ANXIETY, 1977, C
HIGH BARBAREE, 1947, A
HIGH BRIGHT SUN, THE
HIGH COMMAND, 1938, A
HIGH COMMISSIONER, THE, 1968, C-O
HIGH CONQUEST, 1947, A
HIGH COST OF LOVING, THE, 1958, A
HIGH COUNTRY CALLING, 1975
HIGH COUNTRY ROMANCE, 1915
HIGH COUNTRY, THE, 1981, A
HIGH EXPLOSIVE, 1943, A
HIGH FINANCE, 1917
HIGH FINANCE, 1933, A
HIGH FLIGHT, 1957, A

HIGH FLYER, THE, 1926
HIGH FLYERS, 1937, A
HIGH FURY, 1947, A
HIGH GEAR, 1933, A
HIGH GEAR JEFFREY, 1921
HIGH HAND, THE, 1915
HIGH HAND, THE, 1926
HIGH HAT, 1927
HIGH HAT, 1937, A
HIGH HEELS, 1921, A
HIGH HELL, 1958, C
HIGH INFIDELITY, 1965, O
HIGH JINKS IN SOCIETY, 1949, A
HIGH JUMP, 1959, A
HIGH LONESOME, 1950, A
HIGH NOON, 1952, C
HIGH PLAINS DRIFTER, 1973, O
HIGH PLAY, 1917
HIGH POCKETS, 1919
HIGH POWERED, 1945, A
HIGH PRESSURE, 1932, A
HIGH RISK, 1981, O
HIGH ROAD TO CHINA, 1983, C
HIGH ROAD, THE, 1915
HIGH ROLLING, 1977, O
HIGH SCHOOL, 1940, A
HIGH SCHOOL BIG SHOT, 1959, C
HIGH SCHOOL CAESAR, 1960, C
HIGH SCHOOL CONFIDENTIAL, 1958, O
HIGH SCHOOL GIRL, 1935, A
HIGH SCHOOL HELLCATS, 1958, O
HIGH SCHOOL HERO, 1927
HIGH SCHOOL HERO, 1946, A
HIGH SCHOOL HONEYMOON
HIGH SEAS, 1929, A
HIGH SIERRA, 1941, C
HIGH SIGN, THE, 1917
HIGH SOCIETY, 1932
HIGH SOCIETY, 1955, AA
HIGH SOCIETY, 1956, A
HIGH SOCIETY BLUES, 1930, A
HIGH SPEED, 1917, A
HIGH SPEED, 1920
HIGH SPEED, 1924
HIGH SPEED, 1932, A
HIGH SPEED LEE, 1923
HIGH STAKES, 1918
HIGH STAKES, 1931, A
HIGH STEPPERS, 1926
HIGH TENSION, 1936, A
HIGH TERRACE, 1957, A
HIGH TIDE, 1918
HIGH TIDE, 1947, A
HIGH TIDE AT NOON, 1957, A
HIGH TIME, 1960, A
HIGH TREASON, 1929, A
HIGH TREASON, 1937, A
HIGH TREASON, 1951, A
HIGH VELOCITY, 1977, C
HIGH VOLTAGE, 1929, A
HIGH WALL, THE, 1947, C
HIGH WIND IN JAMAICA, A, 1965, A
HIGH YELLOW, 1965, C-O
HIGH, WIDE AND HANDSOME, 1937, A
HIGH-BALLIN', 1978, C
HIGH-POWERED RIFLE, THE, 1960, A
HIGHBINDERS, THE, 1926
HIGHER AND HIGHER, 1943, A
HIGHEST BID, THE, 1916
HIGHEST BIDDER, THE, 1921
HIGHEST LAW, THE, 1921
HIGHEST TRUMP, THE, 1919
HIGHLAND FLING, 1936, A
HIGHLY DANGEROUS, 1950, A
HIGHPOINT, 1984, C
HIGHWAY 13, 1948, A
HIGHWAY 301, 1950, C
HIGHWAY DRAGNET, 1954, A
HIGHWAY OF HOPE, THE, 1917
HIGHWAY PATROL, 1938, A
HIGHWAY PICKUP, 1965, C
HIGHWAY TO BATTLE, 1961, A
HIGHWAY TO HELL, 1984, O
HIGHWAY WEST, 1941, A
HIGHWAYMAN RIDES, THE
HIGHWAYMAN, THE, 1951, C
HIGHWAYS BY NIGHT, 1942, A
HIJACK, 1975
HIKEN
HIKEN YABURI, 1969, C
HILARY'S BLUES, 1983
HILDA CRANE, 1956, A
HILDE WARREN AND DEATH, 1916
HILDUR AND THE MAGICIAN, 1969, AAA
HILL 24 DOESN'T ANSWER, 1955, A
HILL BILLY, THE, 1924
HILL IN KOREA, A
HILL, THE, 1965, O
HILLBILLY BLITZKRIEG, 1942, A
HILLBILLYS IN A HAUNTED HOUSE, 1967, A
HILLCREST MYSTERY, THE, 1918
HILLS HAVE EYES, THE, 1978, O

HILLS OF DONEGAL, THE, 1947, A
HILLS OF HATE, 1921
HILLS OF HOME, 1948, AAA
HILLS OF KENTUCKY, 1927, A
HILLS OF MISSING MEN, 1922, A
HILLS OF OKLAHOMA, 1950, A
HILLS OF OLD WYOMING, 1937, A
HILLS OF PERIL, 1927
HILLS OF UTAH, 1951, A
HILLS RUN RED, THE, 1967, C
HIM
HINDENBURG, THE, 1975, C
HINDERED, 1974
HINDLE WAKES
HINDLE WAKES, 1918
HINDLE WAKES, 1931, A
HINDLE WAKES, 1952
HINDU TOMB, THE
HINDU, THE, 1953, AA
HINOTORI, 1980, O
HINTON'S DOUBLE, 1917
HIPPODROME, 1961, C-O
HIPPOLYT, THE LACKEY, 1932, A
HIPS, HIPS, HOORAY, 1934, A
HIRED GUN
HIRED GUN, 1952
HIRED GUN, THE, 1957, A
HIRED HAND, THE, 1971, A
HIRED KILLER, THE, 1967, C
HIRED MAN, THE, 1918
HIRED WIFE, 1934, A
HIRED WIFE, 1940, A
HIRELING, THE, 1973, C
HIROSHIMA, MON AMOUR, 1959, C-O
HIS AND HERS, 1961, A
HIS AND HIS
HIS BACK AGAINST THE WALL, 1922
HIS BIRTHRIGHT, 1918
HIS BONDED WIFE, 1918
HIS BRIDAL NIGHT, 1919
HIS BROTHER'S GHOST, 1945, A
HIS BROTHER'S KEEPER, 1921
HIS BROTHER'S KEEPER, 1939, A-C
HIS BROTHER'S WIFE, 1916
HIS BROTHER'S WIFE, 1936, A-C
HIS BUDDY'S WIFE, 1925
HIS BUTLER'S SISTER, 1943, A
HIS CALL
HIS CAPTIVE WOMAN, 1929, A
HIS CHILDREN'S CHILDREN, 1923
HIS COUNTRY'S HONOUR
HIS DARKER SELF, 1924, A
HIS DAUGHTER'S DILEMMA, 1916
HIS DAUGHTER'S SECOND HUSBAND, 1916
HIS DEAREST POSSESSION, 1919
HIS DEBT, 1919
HIS DIVORCED WIFE, 1919
HIS DOG, 1927
HIS DOUBLE LIFE, 1933, A
HIS ENEMY THE LAW, 1918
HIS ENEMY'S DAUGHTER
HIS ENEMY'S DAUGHTER
HIS EXCELLENCY, 1952, A
HIS EXCITING NIGHT, 1938, A
HIS EYES, 1916
HIS FAMILY TREE, 1936, A
HIS FATHER'S SON, 1917, A
HIS FATHER'S WIFE, 1919
HIS FIGHTING BLOOD, 1935, A
HIS FIRST COMMAND, 1929, A
HIS FIRST FLAME, 1927
HIS FOREIGN WIFE, 1927
HIS FORGOTTEN WIFE, 1924
HIS GIRL FRIDAY, 1940, C
HIS GLORIOUS NIGHT, 1929
HIS GRACE GIVES NOTICE, 1924
HIS GRACE GIVES NOTICE, 1933, A
HIS GREAT CHANCE, 1923
HIS GREAT TRIUMPH, 1916
HIS GREATEST BATTLE, 1925
HIS GREATEST GAMBLE, 1934, A
HIS GREATEST SACRIFICE, 1921
HIS HOUR, 1924, A
HIS HOUSE IN ORDER, 1920
HIS HOUSE IN ORDER, 1928, A
HIS JAZZ BRIDE, 1926, A
HIS KIND OF WOMAN, 1951, C-O
HIS LAST BULLET, 1928
HIS LAST DEFENCE, 1919
HIS LAST DOLLAR, 1914, A
HIS LAST HAUL, 1928
HIS LAST RACE, 1923
HIS LAST TWELVE HOURS, 1953, A
HIS LORDSHIP, 1932, A
HIS LORDSHIP GOES TO PRESS, 1939, A
HIS LORDSHIP REGRETS, 1938, A
HIS LORDSHIP, 1936
HIS LUCKY DAY, 1929, A
HIS MAJESTY AND CO, 1935, A
HIS MAJESTY BUNKER BEAN
HIS MAJESTY BUNKER BEAN, 1918
HIS MAJESTY BUNKER BEAN, 1925

HIS MAJESTY O'KEEFE, 1953, A
HIS MAJESTY THE AMERICAN, 1919, A
HIS MAJESTY THE OUTLAW, 1924
HIS MAJESTY, KING BALLYHOO, 1931, A
HIS MAJESTY, THE SCARECROW OF OZ, 1914
HIS MASTER'S VOICE, 1925, A
HIS MOTHER'S BOY, 1917
HIS MYSTERY'S GIRL, 1923
HIS NEW YORK WIFE, 1926
HIS NIBS, 1921
HIS NIGHT OUT, 1935, A
HIS OFFICIAL FIANCEE, 1919
HIS OLD-FASHIONED DAD, 1917
HIS OTHER WIFE, 1921
HIS OTHER WOMAN
HIS OWN HOME TOWN, 1918
HIS OWN LAW, 1920
HIS OWN LAW, 1924
HIS OWN PEOPLE, 1918
HIS PAJAMA GIRL, 1921
HIS PARISIAN WIFE, 1919
HIS PEOPLE, 1925
HIS PICTURE IN THE PAPERS, 1916
HIS PRIVATE LIFE, 1928
HIS PRIVATE SECRETARY, 1933, A
HIS RISE TO FAME, 1927
HIS ROBE OF HONOR, 1918, A
HIS ROYAL HIGHNESS, 1918
HIS ROYAL HIGHNESS, 1932, A
HIS SECRETARY, 1925, A
HIS SISTER'S CHAMPION, 1916
HIS SUPREME MOMENT, 1925
HIS SUPREME SACRIFICE, 1922
HIS SWEETHEART, 1917
HIS TEMPORARY WIFE, 1920
HIS TIGER LADY, 1928
HIS TURNING POINT, 1915
HIS VINDICATION, 1915
HIS WIFE, 1915
HIS WIFE'S FRIEND, 1920
HIS WIFE'S GOOD NAME, 1916
HIS WIFE'S HUSBAND, 1913
HIS WIFE'S HUSBAND, 1922
HIS WIFE'S HUSBAND, 1922
HIS WIFE'S MONEY, 1920
HIS WIFE'S MOTHER, 1932, A
HIS WIFE'S LOVER, 1931
HIS WOMAN, 1931, A
HIS, HERS AND THEIRS
HISTOIRE D'ADELE H
HISTOIRE D'AIMER
HISTORY IS MADE AT NIGHT, 1937, C
HISTORY OF MR. POLLY, THE, 1949, A
HISTORY OF THE WORLD, PART 1, 1981, C-O
HIT, 1973, O
HIT AND RUN, 1924
HIT AND RUN, 1957, C
HIT AND RUN, 1982
HIT MAN, 1972, O
HIT OF THE SNOW, 1928
HIT OF THE SNOW, 1928
HIT OR MISS, 1919
HIT PARADE OF 1941, 1940, A
HIT PARADE OF 1943, 1943, A
HIT PARADE OF 1947, 1947, A
HIT PARADE OF 1951, 1950, A
HIT PARADE, THE, 1937, A
HIT THE DECK, 1930, A
HIT THE DECK, 1955, AA
HIT THE HAY, 1945, A
HIT THE ICE, 1943, A
HIT THE ROAD, 1941
HIT THE SADDLE, 1937, A
HIT-THE-TRAIL HOLLIDAY, 1918
HITCH HIKE LADY, 1936, A
HITCH HIKE TO HEAVEN, 1936, A
HITCH IN TIME, A, 1978, AA
HITCH-HIKER, THE, 1953, C-O
HITCHHIKE TO HAPPINESS, 1945, A
HITCHHIKE TO HELL, 1978
HITCHHIKERS, THE, 1972, O
HITCHIN' POSTS, 1920
HITLER, 1962, C
HITLER GANG, THE, 1944, A
HITLER'S CHILDREN, 1942, C
HITLER'S GOLD
HITLER'S MADMAN, 1943, A
HITLER, A FILM FROM GERMANY
HITLER—DEAD OR ALIVE, 1942, A
HITLER: THE LAST TEN DAYS, 1973, C
HITOKIRI
HITTER, THE, 1979
HITTIN' THE TRAIL, 1937, A
HITTING A NEW HIGH, 1937, A
HITTING THE HIGH SPOTS, 1918
HITTING THE TRAIL, 1918
HIYA, CHUM
HO, 1968, O
HOA-BINH, 1971, C-O
HOARDED ASSETS, 1918
HOAX, THE, 1972, C
HOBBS IN A HURRY, 1918

HOBSON'S CHOICE, 1920
HOBSON'S CHOICE, 1931, A
HOBSON'S CHOICE, 1954, A
HOEDOWN, 1950, A
HOFFMAN, 1970, A
HOG WILD, 1980, O
HOGAN'S ALLEY, 1925
HOLD 'EM YALE, 1928, A
HOLD BACK THE DAWN, 1941, A
HOLD BACK THE NIGHT, 1956, A
HOLD BACK TOMORROW, 1955, O
HOLD EVERYTHING, 1930, AA
HOLD ME TIGHT, 1933, A
HOLD MY HAND, 1938, A
HOLD ON, 1966, A
HOLD THAT BABY!, 1949, A
HOLD THAT BLONDE, 1945, A
HOLD THAT CO-ED, 1938, A
HOLD THAT GHOST, 1941, AAA
HOLD THAT GIRL, 1934, A
HOLD THAT HYPNOTIST, 1957, A
HOLD THAT KISS, 1938, A
HOLD THAT LINE, 1952, A
HOLD THAT LION, 1926
HOLD THAT RIVER, 1936
HOLD THAT WOMAN, 1940, A
HOLD THE PRESS, 1933, C
HOLD YOUR BREATH, 1924
HOLD YOUR HORSES, 1921
HOLD YOUR MAN, 1929, C
HOLD YOUR MAN, 1933, C
HOLD'EM JAIL, 1932, A
HOLD'EM NAVY!, 1937, A
HOLD'EM YALE, 1935
HOLD-UP A LA MILANAISE
HOLE IN THE HEAD, A, 1959
HOLE IN THE WALL, 1929, A-C
HOLE IN THE WALL, THE, 1921
HOLIDAY, 1930, A
HOLIDAY, 1938, A
HOLIDAY AFFAIR, 1949, A
HOLIDAY CAMP, 1947, C
HOLIDAY FOR HENRIETTA, 1955, A
HOLIDAY FOR LOVERS, 1959, A
HOLIDAY FOR SINNERS, 1952, C
HOLIDAY IN HAVANA, 1949, A
HOLIDAY IN MEXICO, 1946, A
HOLIDAY IN SPAIN
HOLIDAY INN, 1942, A
HOLIDAY ON THE BUSES, 1974
HOLIDAY RHYTHM, 1950, A
HOLIDAY WEEK, 1952, A
HOLIDAY'S END, 1937, A
HOLIDAYS WITH PAY, 1948, A
HOLLOW OF HER HAND, THE
HOLLOW TRIUMPH, 1948, A
HOLLY AND THE IVY, THE, 1954, A
HOLLYWOOD, 1923
HOLLYWOOD 90028, 1973
HOLLYWOOD AND VINE, 1945, AA
HOLLYWOOD BARN DANCE, 1947, A
HOLLYWOOD BOULEVARD, 1936, A
HOLLYWOOD BOULEVARD, 1976, O
HOLLYWOOD CANTEEN, 1944, A
HOLLYWOOD CAVALCADE, 1939, A
HOLLYWOOD COWBOY, 1937, A
HOLLYWOOD COWBOY, 1975
HOLLYWOOD HIGH, 1976
HOLLYWOOD HIGH, 1977, O
HOLLYWOOD HIGH PART II, 1984, O
HOLLYWOOD HOODLUM
HOLLYWOOD HOT TUBS, 1984, O
HOLLYWOOD HOTEL, 1937, AA
HOLLYWOOD KNIGHT, 1979
HOLLYWOOD KNIGHTS, THE, 1980, O
HOLLYWOOD MAN, THE, 1976
HOLLYWOOD MYSTERY, 1934, C
HOLLYWOOD OR BUST, 1956, A
HOLLYWOOD PARTY, 1934, AAA
HOLLYWOOD REPORTER, THE, 1926
HOLLYWOOD ROUNDUP, 1938, A
HOLLYWOOD SPEAKS, 1932, C-O
HOLLYWOOD STADIUM MYSTERY, 1938, A
HOLLYWOOD STORY, 1951, A
HOLLYWOOD STRANGLER MEETS THE SKIDROW
   SLASHER, THE, 1979
HOLLYWOOD STRANGLER, THE
HOLLYWOOD THRILL-MAKERS, 1954
HOLLYWOOD THRILLMAKERS
HOLOCAUST 2000
HOLY INNOCENTS, THE, 1984, O
HOLY MATRIMONY, 1943, A
HOLY MOUNTAIN, THE, 1973, O
HOLY ORDERS, 1917, A
HOLY SINNER, THE, 1929
HOLY TERROR
HOLY TERROR, A, 1931, A
HOLY TERROR, THE, 1937, A
HOMBRE, 1967, C
HOMBRE Y EL MONSTRUO, EL
HOME, 1915
HOME, 1916, A

HOME, 1919
HOME AND AWAY, 1956, A
HOME AND THE WORLD, THE, 1984, C
HOME AT SEVEN
HOME BEFORE DARK, 1958, C
HOME FOR TANYA, A, 1961, A
HOME FREE ALL, 1983, A
HOME FREE ALL, 1984, O
HOME FROM HOME, 1939
HOME FROM THE HILL, 1960, O
HOME IN INDIANA, 1944
HOME IN OKLAHOMA, 1946, A
HOME IN SAN ANTONE, 1949
HOME IN WYOMIN', 1942, A
HOME IS THE HERO, 1959, C
HOME JAMES, 1928
HOME MADE, 1927
HOME MAKER, THE, 1925
HOME MOVIES, 1979
HOME OF THE BRAVE, 1949, C
HOME ON THE HANGE, 1946, A
HOME ON THE PRAIRIE, 1939, A
HOME ON THE RANGE, 1935, A
HOME STRETCH, THE, 1921
HOME STRUCK, 1927, A
HOME STUFF, 1921, A
HOME SWEET HOME, 1914, A
HOME SWEET HOME, 1945, A
HOME SWEET HOME, 1981, O
HOME SWEET HOMICIDE, 1946, AAA
HOME TALENT, 1921
HOME TO DANGER, 1951, A
HOME TOWN GIRL, THE, 1919
HOME TOWN STORY, 1951, C
HOME TOWNERS, THE, 1928, A
HOME TRAIL, THE, 1918
HOME WANTED, 1919
HOME, SWEET HOME, 1933, A
HOME-KEEPING HEARTS, 1921
HOMEBODIES, 1974, O
HOMEBREAKER, THE, 1919
HOMECOMING, 1929
HOMECOMING, 1948, A
HOMECOMING, THE, 1973, C
HOMEMAKER, THE, 1919
HOMER, 1970, C
HOMER COMES HOME, 1920
HOMESICK, 1928, A
HOMESPUN FOLKS, 1920
HOMESPUN VAMP, A, 1922, A
HOMESTEADER, THE, 1922
HOMESTEADERS OF PARADISE VALLEY, 1947, A
HOMESTEADERS, THE, 1953, A
HOMESTRETCH, THE, 1947, A
HOMETOWN U.S.A., 1979, C
HOMEWARD BORNE, 1957
HOMEWARD BOUND, 1923
HOMEWORK, 1982, O
HOMICIDAL, 1961, O
HOMICIDE, 1949, C
HOMICIDE BUREAU, 1939, O
HOMICIDE FOR THREE, 1948, C
HOMICIDE SQUAD, 1931, A
HONDO, 1953, C
HONEST HUTCH, 1920
HONEST MAN, AN, 1918
HONESTY-THE BEST POLICY, 1926
HONEY, 1930, A
HONEY BEE, THE, 1920
HONEY POT, THE, 1967, A
HONEYBABY, HONEYBABY, 1974, C
HONEYCHILE, 1951, A
HONEYMOON, 1929, A
HONEYMOON, 1947, A
HONEYMOON ABROAD, 1929
HONEYMOON ADVENTURE, A
HONEYMOON AHEAD, 1927, A
HONEYMOON AHEAD, 1945, A
HONEYMOON DEFERRED, 1940, A
HONEYMOON DEFERRED, 1951, A
HONEYMOON EXPRESS, THE, 1926
HONEYMOON FLATS, 1928, A
HONEYMOON FOR THREE, 1935, A
HONEYMOON FOR THREE, 1941, A
HONEYMOON HATE, 1927
HONEYMOON HOTEL, 1946, A
HONEYMOON HOTEL, 1964, C
HONEYMOON IN BALI, 1939, A
HONEYMOON KILLERS, THE, 1969, O
HONEYMOON LANE, 1931, A
HONEYMOON LIMITED, 1936, A
HONEYMOON LODGE, 1943, A
HONEYMOON MACHINE, THE, 1961, A
HONEYMOON MERRY-GO-ROUND, 1939, AA
HONEYMOON OF HORROR, 1964, O
HONEYMOON OF TERROR, 1961, O
HONEYMOON RANCH, 1920
HONEYMOON'S OVER, THE, 1939, C
HONEYMOON, THE, 1917
HONEYMOONS WILL KILL YOU, 1966
HONEYPOT, THE, 1920
HONEYSUCKLE ROSE, 1980, C

HONG KONG, 1951, A
HONG KONG AFFAIR, 1958, A
HONG KONG CONFIDENTIAL, 1958, A
HONG KONG NIGHTS, 1935, A
HONKERS, THE, 1972, C
HONKY, 1971, O
HONKY TONK, 1929, A
HONKY TONK, 1941, C
HONKY TONK FREEWAY, 1981, C
HONKYTONK MAN, 1982, A-C
HONNEUR D'ARTISTE, 1917
HONOLULU, 1939, A
HONOLULU LU, 1941, A
HONOLULU-TOKYO-HONG KONG, 1963, A
HONOR AMONG LOVERS, 1931, A
HONOR AMONG MEN, 1924
HONOR BOUND, 1920
HONOR BOUND, 1928
HONOR FIRST, 1922
HONOR OF HIS HOUSE, THE, 1918
HONOR OF MARY BLAKE, THE, 1916
HONOR OF THE FAMILY, 1931, A
HONOR OF THE MOUNTED, 1932, A
HONOR OF THE PRESS, 1932, A
HONOR OF THE RANGE, 1934, A
HONOR OF THE WEST, 1939, A
HONOR SYSTEM, THE, 1917, A
HONOR THY NAME, 1916
HONOR'S ALTAR, 1916
HONOR'S CROSS, 1918
HONORABLE ALGY, THE, 1916
HONORABLE FRIEND, THE, 1916
HONOUR IN PAWN, 1916
HONOURABLE MURDER, AN, 1959, C
HONOURS EASY, 1935, A
HOOCH, 1977
HOODLUM EMPIRE, 1952, A
HOODLUM PRIEST, THE, 1961, C
HOODLUM SAINT, THE, 1946, A
HOODLUM THE, 1919, A
HOODLUM, THE, 1951, C
HOODMAN BLIND
HOODMAN BLIND, 1913
HOODMAN BLIND, 1923
HOODOO ANN, 1916
HOODOO RANCH, 1926
HOODWINK, 1981, C
HOOF MARKS, 1927
HOOFBEATS OF VENGEANCE, 1929, A
HOOK AND HAND, 1914
HOOK AND LADDER, 1924, A
HOOK AND LADDER NO. 9, 1927, A
HOOK, LINE AND SINKER, 1930, A
HOOK, LINE AND SINKER, 1969, A
HOOK, THE, 1962, C
HOOKED GENERATION, THE, 1969, O
HOOP-LA, 1919
HOOPER, 1978, A
HOOPLA, 1933, C
HOORAY FOR LOVE, 1935, A
HOOSIER HOLIDAY, 1943, A
HOOSIER ROMANCE, A, 1918
HOOSIER SCHOOLBOY, 1937, A
HOOSIER SCHOOLMASTER, 1914, A
HOOSIER SCHOOLMASTER, 1935, A
HOOSIER SCHOOLMASTER, THE, 1924
HOOTENANNY HOOT, 1963, A
HOOTS MON!, 1939, A
HOP, THE DEVIL'S BREW, 1916, A
HOPALONG CASSIDY, 1935, A
HOPALONG CASSIDY RETURNS, 1936
HOPALONG RIDES AGAIN, 1937, A
HOPE
HOPE CHEST, THE, 1918
HOPE OF HIS SIDE, 1935, A
HOPE, THE, 1920
HOPELESS ONES, THE
HOPPER, THE, 1918
HOPPITY GOES TO TOWN
HOPPY SERVES A WRIT, 1943, A
HOPPY'S HOLIDAY, 1947, A
HOPSCOTCH, 1980, C
HORIZONS WEST, 1952, A
HORIZONTAL LIEUTENANT, THE, 1962, A
HORLA, THE
HORN BLOWS AT MIDNIGHT, THE, 1945, AAA
HORNET'S NEST, 1923
HORNET'S NEST, 1970, O
HORNET'S NEST, THE, 1919
HORNET'S NEST, THE, 1955, A
HOROSCOPE, 1950, O
HORRIBLE DR. HICHCOCK, THE, 1964
HORRIBLE HOUSE ON THE HILL, THE
HORRIBLE MILL WOMEN, THE
HORROR CASTLE, 1965, O
HORROR CHAMBER OF DR. FAUSTUS, THE, 1962, O
HORROR CREATURES OF THE PREHISTORIC
   PLANET
HORROR EXPRESS, 1972, C
HORROR HIGH, 1974, O
HORROR HOSPITAL, 1973
HORROR HOTEL, 1960, C

HORROR HOTEL, 1976
HORROR HOUSE, 1970, O
HORROR ISLAND, 1941, A
HORROR MANIACS
HORROR OF DRACULA, THE, 1958, O
HORROR OF FRANKENSTEIN, THE, 1970
HORROR OF IT ALL, THE, 1964, A
HORROR OF PARTY BEACH, THE, 1964, C
HORROR OF THE BLOOD MONSTERS, 1970, O
HORROR OF THE STONE WOMEN
HORROR OF THE ZOMBIES, 1974, C
HORROR ON SNAPE ISLAND
HORROR PLANET, 1982, O
HORRORS OF SPIDER ISLAND
HORRORS OF THE BLACK MUSEUM, 1959, O
HORRORS OF THE BLACK ZOO
HORSE, 1965
HORSE FEATHERS, 1932, A
HORSE IN THE GRAY FLANNEL SUIT, THE,
     1968, AAA
HORSE NAMED COMANCHE, A
HORSE OF PRIDE, 1980, A
HORSE ON BROADWAY, A, 1926
HORSE SENSE, 1924
HORSE SHOES, 1927
HORSE SOLDIERS, THE, 1959, C
HORSE'S MOUTH, THE, 1953, A
HORSE'S MOUTH, THE, 1958, A
HORSE, MY HORSE
HORSE, THE, 1984, O
HORSEMAN OF THE PLAINS, A, 1928
HORSEMEN OF THE SIERRAS, 1950, A
HORSEMEN, THE, 1971, C
HORSEPLAY, 1933, A
HORSESHOE LUCK, 1924
HOSPITAL MASSACRE, 1982, O
HOSPITAL MASSACRE, 1984, O
HOSPITAL, THE, 1971, C
HOSTAGE, THE, 1917
HOSTAGE, THE, 1956, A
HOSTAGE, THE, 1966, A
HOSTAGES, 1943, A
HOSTILE COUNTRY, 1950, A
HOSTILE GUNS, 1967, A
HOSTILE WITNESS, 1968, A
HOT AND DEADLY, 1984, O
HOT ANGEL, THE, 1958, C
HOT BLOOD, 1956, A
HOT BOX, THE, 1972, O
HOT CAR GIRL, 1958, O
HOT CARGO, 1946, A
HOT CARS, 1956, A
HOT CHILD, 1974
HOT CURVES, 1930, A
HOT DOG...THE MOVIE, 1984, O
HOT ENOUGH FOR JUNE
HOT FOR PARIS, 1930, A
HOT FRUSTRATIONS
HOT HEELS, 1928
HOT HEIRESS, 1931, A
HOT HORSE
HOT HOURS, 1963, O
HOT ICE, 1952
HOT IN PARADISE
HOT LEAD, 1951, A
HOT LEAD AND COLD FEET, 1978, AA
HOT MILLIONS, 1968, C
HOT MONEY, 1936, A
HOT MONEY GIRL, 1962, C
HOT MONTH OF AUGUST, THE, 1969
HOT MOVES, 1984, O
HOT NEWS, 1928, A
HOT NEWS, 1936, A
HOT NEWS, 1953, A
HOT OFF THE PRESS, 1935
HOT PEPPER, 1933, A
HOT POTATO, 1976, O
HOT PURSUIT, 1981
HOT RHYTHM, 1944, A
HOT ROCK, THE, 1972, A-C
HOT ROD, 1950, A
HOT ROD GANG, 1958, A
HOT ROD GIRL, 1956, A
HOT ROD HULLABALOO, 1966, C
HOT ROD RUMBLE, 1957, C
HOT RODS TO HELL, 1967, C-O
HOT SATURDAY, 1932, A
HOT SHOTS, 1956, A
HOT SPELL, 1958, C-O
HOT SPOT
HOT SPUR, 1968, O
HOT STUFF, 1929, A
HOT STUFF, 1979, C
HOT SUMMER IN BAREFOOT COUNTY, 1974
HOT SUMMER NIGHT, 1957, A
HOT SUMMER WEEK, 1973, O
HOT T-SHIRTS, 1980
HOT TIMES, 1974, O
HOT TIP, 1935, A
HOT TOMORROWS, 1978, C
HOT WATER, 1924, A

HOT WATER, 1937, A
HOTEL, 1967, A
HOTEL BERLIN, 1945, A
HOTEL CONTINENTAL, 1932, A
HOTEL FOR WOMEN, 1939, A
HOTEL HAYWIRE, 1937, A
HOTEL IMPERIAL, 1927
HOTEL IMPERIAL, 1939, A
HOTEL MOUSE, THE, 1923, A
HOTEL NEW HAMPSHIRE, THE, 1984, C-O
HOTEL PARADISO, 1966
HOTEL RESERVE, 1946, A
HOTEL SAHARA, 1951, A
HOTEL SPLENDIDE, 1932, A
HOTEL VARIETY, 1933, A
HOTHEAD, 1963, C
HOTSPRINGS HOLIDAY, 1970, A
HOTTENTOT, THE, 1922
HOTTENTOT, THE, 1929, A
HOTWIRE, 1980
HOUDINI, 1953, A
HOUND OF THE BASKERVILLES, 1932, A
HOUND OF THE BASKERVILLES, THE, 1914
HOUND OF THE BASKERVILLES, THE, 1917
HOUND OF THE BASKERVILLES, THE, 1921
HOUND OF THE BASKERVILLES, THE, 1929
HOUND OF THE BASKERVILLES, THE, 1939, A
HOUND OF THE BASKERVILLES, THE, 1959, C
HOUND OF THE BASKERVILLES, THE, 1980, C
HOUND OF THE BASKERVILLES, THE, 1983, C
HOUND OF THE SILVER CREEK, THE, 1928
HOUND-DOG MAN, 1959, A
HOUNDS... OF NOTRE DAME, THE, 1980
HOUR BEFORE THE DAWN, THE, 1944, A
HOUR OF DECISION, 1957, A
HOUR OF GLORY, 1949
HOUR OF RECKONING, THE, 1927
HOUR OF THE GUN, 1967, C
HOUR OF THE TRIAL, THE, 1920
HOUR OF THE WOLF, THE, 1968, O
HOUR OF THIRTEEN, THE, 1952, A
HOURS OF LONELINESS, 1930, C
HOURS OF LOVE, THE, 1965, A
HOUSE ACROSS THE BAY, THE, 1940, A
HOUSE ACROSS THE LAKE, THE
HOUSE ACROSS THE STREET, THE, 1949, A
HOUSE AND THE BRAIN, THE, 1973
HOUSE AT THE END OF THE WORLD
HOUSE AT THE END OF THE WORLD
HOUSE BEHIND THE CEDARS, THE, 1927
HOUSE BROKEN, 1936
HOUSE BUILT UPON SAND, THE, 1917
HOUSE BY THE CEMETERY, THE, 1984, O
HOUSE BY THE LAKE, THE, 1977, O
HOUSE BY THE RIVER, 1950, C
HOUSE CALLS, 1978, C
HOUSE DIVIDED, A, 1919
HOUSE DIVIDED, A, 1932, C
HOUSE IN MARSH ROAD, THE, 1960
HOUSE IN NIGHTMARE PARK, THE
HOUSE IN THE SNOW-DRIFTS, THE, 1928
HOUSE IN THE SQUARE, THE
HOUSE IN THE WOODS, THE, 1957, C
HOUSE IS NOT A HOME, A, 1964, O
HOUSE NEXT DOOR, THE, 1914, A
HOUSE OF 1,000 DOLLS, 1967, O
HOUSE OF A THOUSAND CANDLES, THE, 1915
HOUSE OF A THOUSAND CANDLES, THE, 1936, A
HOUSE OF BAMBOO, 1955, C
HOUSE OF BLACKMAIL, 1953, C
HOUSE OF CARDS, 1969, C
HOUSE OF CARDS, 1934
HOUSE OF CONNELLY
HOUSE OF CRAZIES
HOUSE OF DANGER, 1934, A
HOUSE OF DARK SHADOWS, 1970, C-O
HOUSE OF DARKENED WINDOWS, THE, 1925
HOUSE OF DARKNESS, 1948, O
HOUSE OF DEATH, 1932, C
HOUSE OF DRACULA, 1945, A
HOUSE OF DREAMS, 1933
HOUSE OF DREAMS, 1963
HOUSE OF ERRORS, 1942, A
HOUSE OF EVIL, 1968, O
HOUSE OF EXORCISM, THE, 1976, O
HOUSE OF FEAR, 1929
HOUSE OF FEAR, THE, 1915
HOUSE OF FEAR, THE, 1939, A
HOUSE OF FEAR, THE, 1945, A
HOUSE OF FRANKENSTEIN, 1944, A
HOUSE OF FREAKS, 1973, O
HOUSE OF FRIGHT, 1961
HOUSE OF GLASS, THE, 1918
HOUSE OF GOD, THE, 1979
HOUSE OF GOD, THE, 1984, O
HOUSE OF GOLD, THE, 1918
HOUSE OF GREED, 1934, A
HOUSE OF HORROR, 1929
HOUSE OF HORRORS, 1946, C
HOUSE OF INTRIGUE, THE, 1959, A
HOUSE OF LIES, THE, 1916
HOUSE OF LIFE, 1953

HOUSE OF LONG SHADOWS, THE, 1983, O
HOUSE OF MARNEY, 1926
HOUSE OF MIRRORS, THE, 1916
HOUSE OF MIRTH, THE, 1918
HOUSE OF MORTAL SIN, THE
HOUSE OF MYSTERY, 1934, A
HOUSE OF MYSTERY, 1941, A
HOUSE OF MYSTERY, 1961, C
HOUSE OF MYSTERY, THE, 1938
HOUSE OF NUMBERS, 1957, A
HOUSE OF PERIL, THE, 1922
HOUSE OF PLEASURE
HOUSE OF PSYCHOTIC WOMEN, THE, 1973, O
HOUSE OF ROTHSCHILD, THE, 1934, A
HOUSE OF SCANDAL, THE, 1928
HOUSE OF SECRETS, 1929, O
HOUSE OF SECRETS, 1956
HOUSE OF SECRETS, THE, 1937, A
HOUSE OF SEVEN CORPSES, THE, 1974, C-O
HOUSE OF SEVEN GABLES
HOUSE OF SEVEN JOYS
HOUSE OF SHADOWS, 1977
HOUSE OF SHAME, THE, 1928
HOUSE OF SILENCE, THE, 1918
HOUSE OF STRANGE LOVES, THE, 1969, C
HOUSE OF STRANGERS, 1949, C
HOUSE OF TEARS, THE, 1915
HOUSE OF TEMPERLEY, THE, 1913, A
HOUSE OF THE ARROW, THE, 1930, A
HOUSE OF THE ARROW, THE, 1953, A
HOUSE OF THE ARROW, THE, 1940
HOUSE OF THE BLACK DEATH, 1965, O
HOUSE OF THE DAMNED, 1963, C
HOUSE OF THE DEAD, 1980
HOUSE OF THE GOLDEN WINDOWS, THE, 1916
HOUSE OF THE LIVING DEAD, 1973, C
HOUSE OF THE LOST CORD, THE, 1915, A
HOUSE OF THE MISSING GIRLS, 1974
HOUSE OF THE SEVEN GABLES, THE, 1940, A
HOUSE OF THE SEVEN HAWKS, THE, 1959, A
HOUSE OF THE SPANIARD, THE, 1936, A
HOUSE OF THE THREE GIRLS, THE, 1961, A
HOUSE OF THE TOLLING BELLS, THE, 1920
HOUSE OF TOYS, THE, 1920
HOUSE OF TRENT, THE, 1933, A
HOUSE OF UNREST, THE, 1931, A
HOUSE OF USHER, 1960, O
HOUSE OF WAX, 1953, C
HOUSE OF WHIPCORD, 1974, O
HOUSE OF WHISPERS, THE, 1920
HOUSE OF WOMEN, 1962, O
HOUSE OF YOUTH, THE, 1924, A
HOUSE ON 56TH STREET, THE, 1933, C
HOUSE ON 92ND STREET, THE, 1945, A
HOUSE ON CEDAR HILL, THE, 1926
HOUSE ON HAUNTED HILL, 1958, C
HOUSE ON SKULL MOUNTAIN, THE, 1974, C
HOUSE ON SORORITY ROW, THE, 1983, O
HOUSE ON STRAW HILL, THE, 1976
HOUSE ON TELEGRAPH HILL, 1951, C
HOUSE ON THE FRONT LINE, THE, 1963, A
HOUSE ON THE MARSH, THE, 1920, A
HOUSE ON THE SAND, 1967, C
HOUSE ON THE SQUARE, THE
HOUSE ON TRUBNAYA SQUARE, 1928
HOUSE OPPOSITE, THE, 1917
HOUSE OPPOSITE, THE, 1931, A
HOUSE RENT PARTY, 1946
HOUSE THAT CRIED MURDER, THE
HOUSE THAT DRIPPED BLOOD, THE, 1971, O
HOUSE THAT JAZZ BUILT, THE, 1921
HOUSE THAT SCREAMED, THE, 1970, O
HOUSE THAT VANISHED, THE, 1974, O
HOUSE WHERE DEATH LIVES, THE, 1982
HOUSE WHERE DEATH LIVES, THE, 1984, O
HOUSE WHERE EVIL DWELLS, THE, 1982, O
HOUSE WITH AN ATTIC, THE, 1964, A
HOUSE WITH THE GOLDEN WINDOWS, THE, 1916
HOUSE WITHOUT CHILDREN, THE, 1919
HOUSEBOAT, 1958, A
HOUSEHOLDER, THE, 1963, A
HOUSEKEEPER'S DAUGHTER, 1939, A
HOUSEMASTER, 1938, A
HOUSEWIFE, 1934, A
HOUSTON STORY, THE, 1956, A
HOVERBUG, 1970, AA
HOW ABOUT US?
HOW BAXTER BUTTED IN, 1925
HOW COME NOBODY'S ON OUR SIDE?, 1975, A
HOW COULD YOU UNCLE?, 1918
HOW COULD YOU, CAROLINE?, 1918
HOW COULD YOU, JEAN?, 1918
HOW DO I LOVE THEE?, 1970, C
HOW DO YOU DO?, 1946, A
HOW GREEN WAS MY VALLEY, 1941, A
HOW I WON THE WAR, 1967, C
HOW KITCHENER WAS BETRAYED, 1921
HOW LOW CAN YOU FALL?
HOW MANY ROADS
HOW MEN LOVE WOMEN, 1915
HOW MOLLY MADE GOOD, 1915, A
HOW MOLLY MALONE MADE GOOD

HOW NOT TO ROB A DEPARTMENT STORE, 1965, A
HOW SWEET IT IS, 1968, C-O
HOW THE WEST WAS WON, 1962, AAA
HOW TO BEAT THE HIGH COST OF LIVING, 1980, A
HOW TO COMMIT MARRIAGE, 1969, A
HOW TO EDUCATE A WIFE, 1924
HOW TO FRAME A FIGG, 1971, AA
HOW TO HANDLE WOMEN, 1928
HOW TO MAKE A DOLL, 1967
HOW TO MAKE A MONSTER, 1958, C
HOW TO MAKE IT
HOW TO MARRY A MILLIONAIRE, 1953, A
HOW TO MURDER A RICH UNCLE, 1957, A
HOW TO MURDER YOUR WIFE, 1965, A
HOW TO SAVE A MARRIAGE—AND RUIN YOUR
    LIFE, 1968, A
HOW TO SCORE WITH GIRLS, 1980
HOW TO SEDUCE A PLAYBOY, 1968, C
HOW TO SEDUCE A WOMAN, 1974, O
HOW TO STEAL A MILLION, 1966, A
HOW TO STUFF A WILD BIKINI, 1965, A
HOW TO SUCCEED IN BUSINESS WITHOUT REALLY
HOW TO UNDRESS IN FRONT OF YOUR HUSBAND,
    1937
HOW WILLINGLY YOU SING, 1975, A-C
HOW WOMEN LOVE, 1922
HOW'S ABOUT IT?, 1943, A
HOW'S CHANCES
HOWARD CASE, THE, 1936, A
HOWARDS OF VIRGINIA, THE, 1940, A
HOWDY BROADWAY, 1929
HOWLING, THE, 1981, O
HOWZER, 1973, A
HT CARGO, 1936, A
HU-MAN, 1975, C
HUCK AND TOM, 1918, A
HUCKLEBERRY FINN, 1920, A
HUCKLEBERRY FINN, 1931, AAA
HUCKLEBERRY FINN, 1939, AAA
HUCKLEBERRY FINN, 1960
HUCKLEBERRY FINN, 1974, AAA
HUCKSTERS, THE, 1947, A
HUD, 1963, O
HUDDLE, 1932, A
HUDSON'S BAY, 1940, A
HUE AND CRY, 1950, A
HUGGETTS ABROAD, THE, 1949, A
HUGHES AND HARLOW: ANGELS IN HELL, 1978
HUGO THE HIPPO, 1976
HUGON THE MIGHTY, 1918
HUGS AND KISSES, 1968, O
HUK, 1956, O
HULA, 1927
HULDA FROM HOLLAND, 1916
HULLABALOO, 1940, A
HULLABALOO OVER GEORGIE AND BONNIE'S
    PICTURES, 1979
HUMAN BEAST, THE
HUMAN CARGO, 1929
HUMAN CARGO, 1936, A
HUMAN COLLATERAL, 1920
HUMAN COMEDY, THE, 1943, A
HUMAN CONDITION, THE, 1959
HUMAN DESIRE, 1954, C
HUMAN DESIRE, THE, 1919
HUMAN DESIRES, 1924, A
HUMAN DRIFTWOOD, 1916
HUMAN DUPLICATORS, THE, 1965, A
HUMAN EXPERIMENTS, 1980, O
HUMAN FACTOR, THE, 1975, O
HUMAN FACTOR, THE, 1979, C
HUMAN GORILLA, 1948
HUMAN HEARTS, 1922
HUMAN HIGHWAY, 1982, O
HUMAN JUNGLE, THE, 1954, A
HUMAN LAW, 1926
HUMAN MONSTER, THE, 1940, O
HUMAN ORCHID, THE, 1916
HUMAN PASSIONS, 1919
HUMAN SIDE, THE, 1934, A
HUMAN STUFF, 1920, A
HUMAN SUFFERING, 1923
HUMAN TARGETS, 1932
HUMAN TERROR, THE, 1924
HUMAN TORNADO, THE, 1925
HUMAN TORNADO, THE, 1976, O
HUMAN VAPOR, THE, 1964, A
HUMAN WRECKAGE, 1923
HUMANITY, 1917
HUMANITY, 1933, A
HUMANIZING MR. WINSBY, 1916
HUMANOID, THE, 1979, C
HUMANOIDS FROM THE DEEP, 1980, O
HUMDRUM BROWN, 1918
HUMMING BIRD, THE, 1924
HUMONGOUS, 1982, O
HUMORESQUE, 1920
HUMORESQUE, 1946, A-C
HUMPHREY TAKES A CHANCE, 1950, A
HUN WITHIN, THE, 1918, A
HUNCH, THE, 1921, A

HUNCH, THE, 1967, AA
HUNCHBACK AND THE DANCER, THE, 1920
HUNCHBACK OF NOTRE DAME, THE, 1923, A
HUNCHBACK OF NOTRE DAME, THE, 1939, A-C
HUNCHBACK OF NOTRE DAME, THE, 1957, A-C
HUNCHBACK OF ROME, THE, 1963, C
HUNCHBACK OF THE MORGUE, THE, 1972, O
HUNDRA, 1984, C
HUNDRED HOUR HUNT, 1953, A
HUNDRED POUND WINDOW, THE, 1943, A
HUNDRETH CHANCE, THE, 1920
HUNGARIAN NABOB, THE, 1915
HUNGER, 1968, O
HUNGER OF THE BLOOD, THE, 1921
HUNGER, THE, 1983, O
HUNGRY EYES, 1918
HUNGRY HEART, A, 1917
HUNGRY HEART, THE, 1917
HUNGRY HEARTS, 1922, A
HUNGRY HILL, 1947, C
HUNGRY WIVES, 1973, O
HUNS WIHIN OUR GATES, 1918
HUNS, THE, 1962
HUNT THE MAN DOWN, 1950, A
HUNT TO KILL
HUNT, THE, 1967, O
HUNTED
HUNTED IN HOLLAND, 1961, AA
HUNTED MEN, 1930, A
HUNTED MEN, 1938, A
HUNTED WOMAN, THE, 1916
HUNTED WOMAN, THE, 1925
HUNTED, THE
HUNTED, THE, 1948, A
HUNTER OF THE APOCALYPSE
HUNTER, THE, 1980, C
HUNTERS OF THE GOLDEN COBRA, THE, 1984, A
HUNTERS, THE, 1958, A-C
HUNTIN' TROUBLE, 1924
HUNTING IN SIBERIA, 1962, A
HUNTING OF THE HAWK, THE, 1917
HUNTING PARTY, THE, 1977, O
HUNTINGTOWER, 1927, A
HUNTRESS OF MEN, THE, 1916
HUNTRESS, THE, 1923, A
HURRAY FOR BETTY BOOP, 1980
HURRICANE, 1929, A
HURRICANE, 1979
HURRICANE HAL, 1925
HURRICANE HORSEMAN, 1925
HURRICANE HORSEMAN, 1931, A
HURRICANE HUTCH IN MANY ADVENTURES, 1924
HURRICANE ISLAND, 1951
HURRICANE KID, THE, 1925, A
HURRICANE SMITH, 1942, A
HURRICANE SMITH, 1952, A
HURRICANE'S GAL, 1922
HURRICANE, THE, 1926, A
HURRICANE, THE, 1937, A
HURRICANE, THE 1964
HURRY SUNDOWN, 1967, O
HURRY UP OR I'LL BE 30, 1973, C
HURRY, CHARLIE, HURRY, 1941, A
HUSBAND AND WIFE, 1916
HUSBAND HUNTER, THE, 1920
HUSBAND HUNTER, THE, 1920
HUSBAND HUNTERS, 1927, A
HUSBAND'S HOLIDAY, 1931, A
HUSBANDS, 1970, C
HUSBANDS AND LOVERS, 1924, A
HUSBANDS AND WIVES, 1924
HUSBANDS FOR RENT, 1927, A
HUSH, 1921
HUSH MONEY, 1921, A
HUSH MONEY, 1931, A
HUSH-A-BYE MURDER
HUSH... HUSH, SWEET CHARLOTTE, 1964, O
HUSHED HOUR, THE, 1920
HUSSY, 1979
HUSTLE, 1975, O
HUSTLER SQUAD, 1976
HUSTLER SQUAD, THE
HUSTLER, THE, 1961, C
HUTCH OF THE U.S.A., 1924
HUTCH STIRS 'EM UP, 1923, A
HUTCH—U.S.A.
HVEM ER HUN?, 1914
HYDE PARK CORNER, 1935, A
HYPERBOLOID OF ENGINEER GARIN, THE, 1965, A
HYPNOTIC EYE, THE, 1960, O
HYPNOSIS, 1966, C-O
HYPNOTIST, THE
HYPNOTIZED, 1933, A
HYPOCRISY, 1916
HYPOCRITE, THE, 1921
HYPOCRITES, 1914, A
HYPOCRITES, THE
HYPOCRITES, THE, 1923
HYSTERIA, 1965, O
HYSTERICAL, 1983, O

-I-

I ACCUSE
I ACCUSE
I ACCUSE, 1916
I ACCUSE, 1958, A
I ACCUSE MY PARENTS, 1945, A
I ADORE YOU, 1933, A
I AIM AT THE STARS, 1960, A
I AM A CAMERA, 1955, A
I AM A CRIMINAL, 1939, A
I AM A FUGITIVE FROM A CHAIN GANG, 1932, 0
I AM A GROUPIE, 1970, O
I AM A THIEF, 1935, A
I AM CURIOUS GAY
I AM FRIGID...WHY?, 1973
I AM GUILTY, 1921
I AM NOT AFRAID, 1939, A
I AM SUZANNE, 1934, A
I AM THE CHEESE, 1983, A
I AM THE LAW, 1922
I AM THE LAW, 1938, A
I AM THE MAN, 1924
I AM THE WOMAN, 1921
I BECAME A CRIMINAL, 1947, A
I BELIEVE, 1916
I BELIEVE, 1918
I BELIEVE IN YOU, 1953, A
I BELIEVED IN YOU, 1934, A
I BOMBED PEARL HARBOR, 1961, A
I BURY THE LIVING, 1958, A
I CALL FIRST
I CAN EXPLAIN, 1922
I CAN GET IT FOR YOU WHOLESALE, 1951, A
I CAN'T ... I CAN'T
I CAN'T ESCAPE, 1934, A
I CAN'T GIVE YOU ANYTHING BUT LOVE, BABY,
    1940, A
I CHANGED MY SEX
I CHEATED THE LAW, 1949, A
I COLTELLI DEL VENDICATORE
I COMPAGNI
I CONFESS, 1953, A
I CONQUER THE SEA, 1936, A
I COULD GO ON SINGING, 1963, A
I COULD NEVER HAVE SEX WITH ANY MAN WHO
    HAS SO LITTLE REGARD FOR MY HUSBAND,
    1973, O
I COVER BIG TOWN, 1947, A
I COVER CHINATOWN, 1938, A
I COVER THE UNDERWORLD, 1955, A
I COVER THE UNDERWORLD
I COVER THE WAR, 1937, A
I COVER THE WATERFRONT, 1933, A
I CROSSED THE COLOR LINE
I DEAL IN DANGER, 1966, A
I DEMAND PAYMENT, 1938, A
I DIDN'T DO IT, 1945, A
I DIED A THOUSAND TIMES, 1955, A-C
I DISMEMBER MAMA, 1974, O
I DON'T CARE GIRL, THE, 1952, A
I DON'T WANT TO BE BORN
I DOOD IT, 1943, A
I DREAM OF JEANIE, 1952, A
I DREAM TOO MUCH, 1935, A
I DRINK YOUR BLOOD, 1971, O
I EAT YOUR SKIN, 1971, O
I ESCAPED FROM DEVIL'S ISLAND, 1973, O
I ESCAPED FROM THE GESTAPO, 1943, A
I EVEN MET HAPPY GYPSIES, 1968, A
I FLUNKED, BUT..., 1930
I FOUND STELLA PARISH, 1935, A
I GIORNI DELL'IRA
I GIVE MY HEART
I GIVE MY LOVE, 1934, A
I HAD SEVEN DAUGHTERS
I HATE BLONDES, 1981, A
I HATE MY BODY, 1975, A
I HATE WOMEN, 1934
I HATE YOUR GUTS
I HAVE LIVED, 1933, A
I HAVE SEVEN DAUGHTERS
I HEAR YOU CALLING ME, 1919
I KILLED EINSTEIN, GENTLEMEN, 1970, A
I KILLED GERONIMO, 1950, A
I KILLED THAT MAN, 1942, A
I KILLED THE COUNT
I KILLED WILD BILL HICKOK, 1956, A
I KNOW WHERE I'M GOING, 1947, A
I LED TWO LIVES
I LIKE IT THAT WAY, 1934, A
I LIKE MONEY, 1962, A
I LIKE YOUR NERVE, 1931, A
I LIVE FOR LOVE, 1935, A
I LIVE FOR YOU
I LIVE IN FEAR, 1967, A
I LIVE IN GROSVENOR SQUARE
I LIVE MY LIFE, 1935, A
I LIVE ON DANGER, 1942, A
I LIVED WITH YOU, 1933, A
I LOVE A BANDLEADER, 1945, A
I LOVE A MYSTERY, 1945, A
I LOVE A SOLDIER, 1944, A

I LOVE IN JERUSALEM
I LOVE MELVIN, 1953, A
I LOVE MY WIFE, 1970, O
I LOVE THAT MAN, 1933, A
I LOVE TROUBLE, 1947, A
I LOVE YOU, 1918, A
I LOVE YOU
I LOVE YOU AGAIN, 1940, A
I LOVE YOU, ALICE B. TOKLAS, 1968, O
I LOVE YOU, I KILL YOU, 1972, O
I LOVE YOU, I LOVE YOU NOT
I LOVED A WOMAN, 1933, A
I LOVED YOU WEDNESDAY, 1933, A
I MARRIED A COMMUNIST
I MARRIED A DOCTOR, 1936, A
I MARRIED A MONSTER FROM OUTER SPACE, 1958, O
I MARRIED A NAZI
I MARRIED A SPY, 1938, A
I MARRIED A WITCH, 1942, A
I MARRIED A WOMAN, 1958, A
I MARRIED AN ANGEL, A
I MARRIED TOO YOUNG
I MET A MURDERER, 1939, C-O
I MET HIM IN PARIS, 1937, A
I MET MY LOVE AGAIN, 1938, A
I MISS YOU, HUGS AND KISSES, 1978, C-O
I MISTERI DELLA GIUNGLA NERA
I NEVER PROMISED YOU A ROSE GARDEN, 1977, O
I NEVER SANG FOR MY FATHER, 1970, A-C
I NUOVI BARBARI
I NUOVI MOSTRI
I ONLY ASKED, 1958, A
I OUGHT TO BE IN PICTURES, 1982, C
I PASSED FOR WHITE, 1960, A
I PROMISE TO PAY, 1937, A
I PROMISE TO PAY, 1962
I REMEMBER LOVE, 1981
I REMEMBER MAMA, 1948, AAA
I RING DOORBELLS, 1946, A
I SAILED TO TAHITI WITH AN ALL GIRL CREW, 1969, A
I SAW WHAT YOU DID, 1965, C-O
I SEE A DARK STRANGER
I SEE ICE, 1938, A
I SELL ANYTHING, 1934, A
I SENT A LETTER TO MY LOVE, 1981, A
I SHALL RETURN
I SHOT BILLY THE KID, 1950, A
I SHOT JESSE JAMES, 1949, A
I SPIT ON YOUR GRAVE, 1962, O
I SPIT ON YOUR GRAVE, 1983, O
I SPY, 1933, A
I SPY, YOU SPY
I STAND ACCUSED, 1938, A
I STAND CONDEMNED, 1936, A
I START COUNTING, 1970, O
I STOLE A MILLION, 1939, A
I SURRENDER DEAR, 1948, A
I TAKE THIS OATH, 1940, A
I TAKE THIS WOMAN, 1931, A
I TAKE THIS WOMAN, 1940, A
I THANK A FOOL, 1962, A-C
I THANK YOU, 1941, A
I TITANI
I TRE VOLTI
I TRE VOLTI DELLA PAURA
I VAMPIRI
I VITELLONI
I WAKE UP SCREAMING, 1942, A
I WALK ALONE, 1948, C
I WALK THE LINE, 1970, A
I WALKED WITH A ZOMBIE, 1943, C-O
I WANNA HOLD YOUR HAND, 1978, A
I WANT A DIVORCE, 1940, A
I WANT HER DEAD
I WANT MY MAN, 1925
I WANT TO BE A MOTHER, 1937
I WANT TO FORGET, 1918, A
I WANT TO LIVE, O
I WANT WHAT I WANT, 1972, O
I WANT YOU, 1951, A
I WANTED WINGS, A
I WAS A CAPTIVE IN NAZI GERMANY, 1936, A
I WAS A COMMUNIST FOR THE F.B.I., C
I WAS A CONVICT, 1939, A
I WAS A MALE WAR BRIDE, A
I WAS A PRISONER ON DEVIL'S ISLAND, 1941, A
I WAS A SHOPLIFTER, 1950, A
I WAS A SPY, 1934, A
I WAS A TEENAGE ALIEN, 1980
I WAS A TEENAGE FRANKENSTEIN, 1958, C-O
I WAS A TEENAGE WEREWOLF, 1957, C-O
I WAS A ZOMBIE FOR THE F.B.I., 1982
I WAS AN ADVENTURESS, 1940, A
I WAS AN AMERICAN SPY, 1951, A
I WAS BORN, BUT..., 1932
I WAS FAITHLESS
I WAS FRAMED, 1942, A
I WAS HAPPY HERE
I WAS MONTY'S DOUBLE
I WILL, 1919

I WILL ...I WILL ...FOR NOW, 1976, C
I WILL REPAY
I WILL REPAY, 1917
I WONDER WHO'S KILLING HER NOW, 1975
I WONDER WHO'S KISSING HER NOW, 1947, A
I WOULDN'T BE IN YOUR SHOES, 1948, A
I'D CLIMB THE HIGHEST MOUNTAIN, 1951, A
I'D GIVE MY LIFE, 1936, A
I'D RATHER BE RICH, 1964, A
I'LL BE SEEING YOU, 1944, A
I'LL BE THERE, 1927
I'LL BE YOUR SWEETHEART, 1945, A
I'LL BE YOURS, 1947, A
I'LL CRY TOMORROW, 1955, A-C
I'LL FIX IT, 1934, A
I'LL GET BY, 1950, A
I'LL GET HIM YET, 1919, A
I'LL GET HIM YET, 1919
I'LL GET YOU, 1953, A
I'LL GET YOU FOR THIS
I'LL GIVE A MILLION, 1938, A
I'LL GIVE MY LIFE, 1959, A
I'LL LOVE YOU ALWAYS, 1935, A
I'LL NAME THE MURDERER, 1936
I'LL NEVER FORGET WHAT'S 'IS NAME, 1967, A-C
I'LL NEVER FORGET YOU, 1951, A
I'LL REMEMBER APRIL, 1945, A
I'LL SAVE MY LOVE
I'LL SAY SO, 1918
I'LL SEE YOU IN MY DREAMS, 1951, A
I'LL SELL MY LIFE, 1941, A
I'LL SHOW YOU THE TOWN, 1925
I'LL STICK TO YOU, 1933, A
I'LL TAKE ROMANCE, 1937, A
I'LL TAKE SWEDEN, 1965, A
I'LL TELL THE WORLD, 1934, A
I'LL TELL THE WORLD, 1945, AA
I'LL TURN TO YOU, 1946, A
I'LL WAIT FOR YOU, 1941, A
I'LL WALK BESIDE YOU, 1943, A
I'M A STRANGER, 1952, A
I'M ALL RIGHT, JACK, 1959, A
I'M AN EXPLOSIVE, 1933, A
I'M CRAZY ABOUT YOU
I'M DANCING AS FAST AS I CAN, 1982, C-O
I'M FROM ARKANSAS, 1944, A
I'M FROM MISSOURI, 1939, A
I'M FROM THE CITY, 1938, A
I'M GLAD MY BOY GREW TO BE A SOLDIER, 1915
I'M GOING TO BE FAMOUS, 1981
I'M GOING TO GET YOU ... ELLIOT BOY, 1971, O
I'M NO ANGEL, 1933, C
I'M NOBODY'S SWEETHEART NOW, 1940, A
I'M STILL ALIVE, 1940, A
I'PAGLIACCI, 1923
I'VE ALWAYS LOVED YOU, 1946, A
I'VE BEEN AROUND, 1935, A
I'VE GOT A HORSE, 1938, A
I'VE GOT YOUR NUMBER, 1934, A
I'VE GOTTA HORSE, 1965, A
I'VE LIVED BEFORE, 1956, A
I, JANE DOE, 1948, A
I, MAUREEN, 1978, A
I, MOBSTER, 1959, C-O
I, MONSTER, 1971, C
I, THE JURY, 1953, C-O
I, THE JURY, 1982, O
I, TOO, AM ONLY A WOMAN, 1963, C
I.N.R.I
IBANEZ' TORRENT
ICARUS XB-1
ICE, 1970, O
ICE CASTLES, 1978, A
ICE COLD IN ALEX
ICE FLOOD, THE, 1926, A
ICE FOLLIES OF 1939, 1939, A
ICE HOUSE, THE, 1969, O
ICE PALACE, 1960, A-C
ICE PIRATES, THE, 1984, A-C
ICE STATION ZEBRA, 1968, A
ICE-CAPADES, 1941, A
ICE-CAPADES REVUE, 1942, A
ICEBOUND, 1924, A
ICED BULLET, THE, 1917, A
ICELAND, 1942, A
ICEMAN, 1984, A-C
ICEMAN COMETH, THE, C
ICEMAN OF THE 16TH PRECINCT, THE, 1963, A
ICHABOD AND MR. TOAD
ICHIJOJI NO KETTO
IDAGINE SU UN CITTADINO AL DI DOPRA DI OGNI SOSPETTO
IDAHO, 1943, A
IDAHO KID, THE, 1937, A
IDAHO RED, 1929, A
IDAHO TRANSFER, 1975, C
IDEA GIRL, 1946, A
IDEAL HUSBAND, AN, 1948, A
IDEAL LODGER, THE, 1957, O
IDEAL LOVE, THE, 1921
IDEAL MARRIAGE, THE, 1970
IDENTIFICATION MARKS: NONE, 1969, A

IDENTIFICATION OF A WOMAN, 1983, C-O
IDENTIKIT
IDENTITY PARADE
IDENTITY UNKNOWN, 1945, A
IDENTITY UNKNOWN, 1960, A
IDIOT'S DELIGHT, 1939, A
IDIOT, THE, 1948, A
IDIOT, THE, 1960, O
IDIOT, THE, 1963, C-O
IDLE HANDS, 1920
IDLE HANDS, 1921, A
IDLE ON PARADE
IDLE RICH, THE, 1921, A
IDLE RICH, THE, 1929, A
IDLE TONGUES, 1924
IDLE WIVES, 1916
IDLER, THE, 1914
IDO ZERO DAISAKUSEN
IDOL DANCER, THE, 1920, A
IDOL OF PARIS, 1948, A
IDOL OF PARIS, THE, 1914
IDOL OF THE CROWDS, 1937, A
IDOL OF THE NORTH, THE, 1921, A
IDOL OF THE STAGE, THE, 1916, A
IDOL ON PARADE, 1959, A
IDOL, THE, 1966, O
IDOLMAKER, THE, 1980, A-C
IDOLS IN THE DUST
IDOLS OF CLAY, 1920
IERI, OGGI E DOMANI
IF, 1916, A
IF ..., 1968, O
IF A MAN ANSWERS, 1962, A
IF EVER I SEE YOU AGAIN, 1978, C
IF FOUR WALLS TOLD, 1922, A
IF HE HOLLERS, LET HIM GO, 1968, O
IF I HAD A MILLION, 1932, A
IF I HAD MY WAY, 1940, A
IF I MARRY AGAIN, 1925, A
IF I WERE BOSS, 1938, A
IF I WERE FREE, 1933, A
IF I WERE KING, 1920
IF I WERE KING, 1938, A
IF I WERE KING, 1930
IF I WERE QUEEN, 1922, A
IF I WERE RICH, 1936, A
IF I WERE SINGLE, 1927, A
IF I'M LUCKY, 1946, A
IF IT'S TUESDAY, THIS MUST BE BELGIUM, 1969, A
IF MARRIAGE FAILS, 1925
IF MY COUNTRY SHOULD CALL, 1916
IF ONLY JIM, 1921, A
IF PARIS WERE TOLD TO US, 1956, A
IF THIS BE SIN, 1950, A
IF THOU WERT BLIND, 1917, A
IF WINTER COMES, 1923
IF WINTER COMES, 1947, A
IF WOMEN ONLY KNEW, 1921, A
IF YOU BELIEVE IT, IT'S SO, 1922, A
IF YOU COULD ONLY COOK, 1936, A
IF YOU COULD SEE WHAT I HEAR, 1982, A
IF YOU DON'T STOP IT, YOU'LL GO BLIND, 1977
IF YOU FEEL LIKE SINGING
IF YOU KNEW SUSIE, 1948, A
IF YOUTH BUT KNEW, 1926, A
IGNORANCE, 1916
IGNORANCE, 1922
IGOROTA, THE LEGEND OF THE TREE OF LIFE, 1970, O
IKARIE XB 1
IKIMONO NO KIROUKU
IKIRU, 1960, A
IL BIDONE
IL BODONE
IL BUONO, IL BRUTTO, IL CATTIVO
IL COBRA
IL CONFORMIST
IL CONTE DI MONTECRISTO
IL DESERTO ROSSO
IL DESTINO
IL DIABOLICO DR. MABUSE
IL DISPREZZO
IL GATTOPARDO
IL GENERALE DELA-ROVERE
IL GIORNO DELLA CIVETTA
IL GIORNO E L'ORA
IL GRIDO, 1962, C
IL MAESTRO
IL MAESTRO DI DON GIOVANNI
IL MAGNIFICO CORNUTO
IL MITO
IL NEMICO DI MIA MOGLIE
IL POZZO DELLE TRE VERITA
IL RE DEI FAISARI
IL SEGNO DI VENERA
IL SEME DELL'UOMO
IL SEPOLCRO DEI RE
IL SOGNO DI BUTTERFLY
IL SUFFIT D'AIMER
IL TESORO DI ROMMEL
IL TROVATORE, 1914

IL VANGELO SECONDE MATTEO
ILL MET BY MOONLIGHT
ILL-STARRED BABBLE, 1915
ILLEGAL, 1932, A
ILLEGAL, 1955, C
ILLEGAL DIVORCE, THE
ILLEGAL ENTRY, 1949, A
ILLEGAL RIGHTS
ILLEGAL TRAFFIC, 1938, A
ILLIAC PASSION, THE, 1968, O
ILLICIT, 1931, C
ILLICIT INTERLUDE, 1954, O
ILLUMINATIONS, 1976, O
ILLUSION, 1929, A
ILLUSION OF BLOOD, 1966, O
ILLUSION OF LOVE, 1929
ILLUSION TRAVELS BY STREETCAR, THE, 1977, C
ILLUSTRATED MAN, THE, 1969, O
ILLUSTRIOUS PRINCE, THE, 1919
ILSA, HAREM KEEPER OF THE OIL SHEIKS, 1976
ILSA, SHE WOLF OF THE SS, 1975
IM LAUF DER ZEIT
IM STAHLNETZ DES DR. MABUSE
IMAGE MAKER, THE, 1917
IMAGE OF DEATH, 1977
IMAGES, 1972, C-O
IMAGINARY BARON, THE, 1927
IMAGINARY SWEETHEART
IMAGO, 1970
IMAR THE SERVITOR, 1914
IMERES TOU 36
IMITATION GENERAL, 1958, A
IMITATION OF LIFE, 1934, A
IMITATION OF LIFE, 1959, A
IMMEDIATE DISASTER
IMMEDIATE LEE, 1916, A
IMMIGRANT, THE, 1915, A
IMMORAL CHARGE, 1962, A
IMMORAL MOMENT, THE, 1967, C
IMMORTAL BACHELOR, THE, 1980, O
IMMORTAL BATTALION, THE
IMMORTAL FLAME, THE, 1916
IMMORTAL GARRISON, THE, 1957, A
IMMORTAL GENTLEMAN, 1935, A
IMMORTAL MONSTER
IMMORTAL SERGEANT, THE, 1943, A
IMMORTAL STORY, THE, 1969, C
IMMORTAL VAGABOND, 1931, A
IMMORTALS OF BONNIE SCOTLAND
IMP, THE, 1920
IMPACT, 1949, A
IMPACT, 1963, C
IMPASSE, 1969, O
IMPASSE DES VERTUS
IMPASSIVE FOOTMAN, THE
IMPATIENT MAIDEN, 1932, C
IMPATIENT YEARS, THE, 1944, A
IMPERFECT LADY, THE, 1947, A
IMPERFECT LADY, THE, 1935
IMPERFECT LOVER, THE, 1921
IMPERIAL VENUS, 1963, A
IMPERSONATION, THE, 1916
IMPERSONATOR, THE, 1962, C
IMPORTANCE OF BEING EARNEST, THE, 1952, A
IMPORTANT MAN, THE, 1961, O
IMPORTANT WITNESS, THE, 1933, A
IMPOSSIBLE CATHERINE, 1919, A
IMPOSSIBLE LOVER
IMPOSSIBLE MRS. BELLEW, THE, 1922, A
IMPOSSIBLE OBJECT, 1973, C-O
IMPOSSIBLE ON SATURDAY, 1966, A
IMPOSSIBLE SUSAN, 1918
IMPOSSIBLE WOMAN, THE, 1919, A
IMPOSSIBLE YEARS, THE, 1968, A
IMPOSTER, THE, 1918, A
IMPOSTER, THE, 1926
IMPOSTER, THE, 1944, A
IMPOSTORS, 1979, O
IMPRESSIVE FOOTMAN, THE
IMPROPER CHANNELS, 1981, C
IMPROPER DUCHESS, THE, 1936, A
IMPULSE, 1922, A
IMPULSE, 1955, C
IMPULSE, 1975, O
IMPULSE, 1984, O
IN
IN A LONELY PLACE, 1950, C
IN A MOMENT OF TEMPTATION, 1927
IN A MONASTERY GARDEN, 1935, A
IN A SECRET GARDEN
IN A YEAR OF THIRTEEN MOONS, 1980, O
IN AGAIN-OUT AGAIN, 1917, A
IN ANOTHER GIRL'S SHOES, 1917
IN BAD, 1918, A
IN BONDAGE, 1919
IN BORROWED PLUMES, 1926, A
IN BRONCHO LAND, 1926
IN CALIENTE, 1935, A
IN CASE OF ADVERSITY
IN CELEBRATION, 1975, O
IN COLD BLOOD, 1967, O
IN DARKNESS WAITING

IN DER HOLLE IST NOCH PLATZ
IN EARLY ARIZONA, 1938, A
IN ENEMY COUNTRY, 1968, A-C
IN EVERY WOMAN'S LIFE, 1924, A
IN FAST COMPANY, 1924, A
IN FAST COMPANY, 1946, A
IN FOLLY'S TRAIL, 1920, A
IN FOR THIRTY DAYS, 1919, A
IN FULL CRY, 1921
IN GAY MADRID, 1930, A
IN GOD WE TRUST, 1980, C-O
IN HARM'S WAY, 1965, A
IN HIGH GEAR, 1924, A
IN HIS BROTHER'S PLACE, 1919
IN HIS GRIP, 1921, A
IN HIS STEPS, 1936, A
IN HOLLAND, 1929
IN HOLLYWOOD WITH POTASH AND PERLMUTTER, 1924, A
IN HONOR'S WEB, 1919
IN JUDGEMENT OF, 1918
IN LIKE FLINT, 1967, A
IN LOVE, 1983
IN LOVE AND WAR, 1958, A
IN LOVE WITH LIFE, 1934, A
IN LOVE WITH LOVE, 1924
IN MACARTHUR PARK, 1977, C-O
IN MIZZOURA, 1914
IN MIZZOURA, 1919
IN MUSIC LAND, 1928
IN NAME ONLY, 1939, A
IN OLD AMARILLO, 1951, A
IN OLD ARIZONA, 1929, A
IN OLD CALIENTE, 1939, A
IN OLD CALIFORNIA, 1929, A
IN OLD CALIFORNIA, 1942, A
IN OLD CHEYENNE, 1931, A
IN OLD CHEYENNE, 1941, A
IN OLD CHICAGO, 1938, A
IN OLD COLORADO, 1941, A
IN OLD KENTUCKY, 1920, A
IN OLD KENTUCKY, 1927, A
IN OLD KENTUCKY, 1935, A
IN OLD LOS ANGELES, 1948
IN OLD MEXICO, 1938, A
IN OLD MISSOURI, 1940, A
IN OLD MONTANA, 1939, A
IN OLD MONTANA, 1939
IN OLD MONTEREY, 1939, A
IN OLD NEW MEXICO, 1945, AA
IN OLD OKLAHOMA, 1943, A
IN OLD SACRAMENTO, 1946, C
IN OLD SANTA FE, 1935, A
IN OUR TIME, 1944, C
IN PARIS, A.W.O.L., 1936
IN PERSON, 1935, A
IN PIENO SOLE
IN PRAISE OF OLDER WOMEN, 1978, O
IN PURSUIT OF POLLY, 1918
IN ROSIE'S ROOM
IN SEARCH OF A HERO, 1926
IN SEARCH OF A HUSBAND, 1915
IN SEARCH OF A SINNER, 1920, A
IN SEARCH OF A THRILL, 1923, A
IN SEARCH OF ANNA, 1978, O
IN SEARCH OF ARCADY, 1919
IN SEARCH OF GOLDEN SKY, 1984
IN SEARCH OF GREGORY, 1970, O
IN SEARCH OF HISTORIC JESUS, 1980, AA
IN SEARCH OF THE CASTAWAYS, 1962, AAA
IN SELF DEFENSE, 1947
IN SLUMBERLAND, 1917
IN SOCIETY, 1921
IN SOCIETY, 1944, AAA
IN SPITE OF DANGER, 1935, A
IN STRANGE COMPANY
IN THE BALANCE, 1917, A
IN THE BISHOP'S CARRIAGE, 1913
IN THE BLOOD, 1923, A
IN THE COOL OF THE DAY, 1963, C
IN THE COUNTRY, 1967, A
IN THE DARK, 1915
IN THE DAYS OF SAINT PATRICK, 1920, A
IN THE DAYS OF THE COVERED WAGON, 1924
IN THE DAYS OF THE MISSIONS
IN THE DAYS OF THE THUNDERING HERD, 1914
IN THE DAYS OF THE THUNDERING HERD
IN THE DEVIL'S BOWL
IN THE DEVIL'S GARDEN
IN THE DIPLOMATIC SERVICE, 1916
IN THE DOGHOUSE, 1964, A
IN THE FALL OF '55 EDEN CRIED
IN THE FIRST DEGREE, 1927
IN THE FRENCH STYLE, 1963, O
IN THE GLOAMING, 1919
IN THE GOOD OLD SUMMERTIME, 1949, AA
IN THE GRIP OF SPIES, 1914
IN THE GRIP OF THE SULTAN, 1915
IN THE HANDS OF THE LAW, 1917
IN THE HANDS OF THE LONDON CROOKS, 1913, A
IN THE HEADLINES, 1929, A
IN THE HEART OF A FOOL, 1920

IN THE HEAT OF THE NIGHT, 1967, C
IN THE HOLLOW OF HER HAND, 1918
IN THE HOUR OF HIS NEED, 1925
IN THE KINGDOM OF OIL AND MILLIONS, 1916
IN THE LINE OF DUTY, 1931, A
IN THE MEANTIME, DARLING, 1944, A
IN THE MONEY, 1934, A
IN THE MONEY, 1958, AA
IN THE NAME OF LIFE, 1947, O
IN THE NAME OF LOVE, 1925, A
IN THE NAME OF THE LAW, 1922
IN THE NAME OF THE PRINCE OF PEACE, 1914
IN THE NAVY, 1941, AAA
IN THE NEXT ROOM, 1930, A
IN THE NICK, 1960, A
IN THE NIGHT
IN THE NIGHT, 1920
IN THE PALACE OF THE KING, 1915
IN THE PALACE OF THE KING, 1923
IN THE PILLORY, 1924
IN THE RAPTURE, 1976
IN THE SHADOW, 1915
IN THE SHADOW OF BIG BEN, 1914
IN THE SOUP, 1936, A
IN THE SPIDER'S WEB, 1924
IN THE STRETCH, 1914, A
IN THE WAKE OF A STRANGER, 1960, C
IN THE WAKE OF THE BOUNTY, 1933, A
IN THE WATER, 1923
IN THE WEB OF THE GRAFTERS, 1916
IN THE WEST, 1923
IN THE WHIRLWIND OF REVOLUTION, 1922
IN THE WHITE CITY, 1983, C-O
IN THE WOODS
IN THE YEAR 2889, 1966, C
IN THIS CORNER, 1948, A
IN THIS OUR LIFE, 1942, C-O
IN TREASON'S GRASP, 1917
IN TROUBLE WITH EVE, 1964, A
IN WALKED EVE
IN WALKED MARY, 1920, A
IN WHICH WE SERVE, 1942, A
IN WRONG, 1919
IN-LAWS, THE, 1979, A
INADMISSIBLE EVIDENCE, 1968, C
INBETWEEN AGE, THE, 1958, A
INBREAKER, THE, 1974, O
INCENDIARY BLONDE, 1945, A
INCENSE FOR THE DAMNED, 1970, O
INCH'ALLAH, 1922
INCHON, 1981, O
INCIDENT, 1948, C
INCIDENT AT MIDNIGHT, 1966, A
INCIDENT AT PHANTOM HILL, 1966
INCIDENT IN AN ALLEY, 1962, A
INCIDENT IN SHANGHAI, 1937, A
INCIDENT, THE, 1967, O
INCOMING FRESHMEN, 1979
INCOMPARABLE BELLAIRS, THE
INCOMPARABLE MISTRESS BELLAIRS, THE, 1914
INCORRIGIBLE, 1980, C
INCORRIGIBLE DUKANE, THE, 1915, A
INCREDIBLE INVASION, THE, 1971, C-O
INCREDIBLE JOURNEY, THE, 1963, AAA
INCREDIBLE MELTING MAN, THE, 1978, O
INCREDIBLE MR. LIMPET, THE, 1964, AAA
INCREDIBLE PETRIFIED WORLD, THE, 1959, A
INCREDIBLE PRAYING MANTIS, THE
INCREDIBLE SARAH, THE, 1976, C
INCREDIBLE SHRINKING MAN, THE, 1957, A
INCREDIBLE SHRINKING WOMAN, THE, 1981, C
INCREDIBLE TWO-HEADED TRANSPLANT, THE, 1971, O
INCREDIBLY STRANGE CREATURES WHO STOPPED LIVING AND BECAME CRAZY MIXED-UP ZOMBIES, THE, 1965, O
INCREDIBLY STRANGE CREATURES, THE
INCUBUS, 1966, O
INCUBUS, THE, 1982, O
INDECENT, 1962, O
INDEPENDENCE DAY, 1976, C-O
INDEPENDENCE DAY, 1983, O
INDESTRUCTIBLE MAN, THE, 1956, A
INDESTRUCTIBLE WIFE, THE, 1919
INDIAN AGENT, 1948, A
INDIAN FIGHTER, THE, 1955, C
INDIAN LOVE CALL
INDIAN LOVE LYRICS, THE, 1923, A
INDIAN PAINT, 1965, AA
INDIAN SCOUT
INDIAN SUMMER
INDIAN SUMMER OF DRY VALLEY JOHNSON, THE, 1917
INDIAN TERRITORY, 1950, A
INDIAN TOMB, THE
INDIAN UPRISING, 1951, A
INDIANA JONES AND THE TEMPLE OF DOOM, 1984, C-O
INDIANAPOLIS SPEEDWAY, 1939, A
INDISCREET, 1931, C
INDISCREET, 1958, A-C
INDISCREET CORINNE, 1917

INDISCRETION, 1917
INDISCRETION, 1921
INDISCRETION OF AN AMERICAN WIFE, 1954, A-C
INDISCRETIONS OF EVE, 1932, A
INEVITABLE, THE, 1917
INEZ FROM HOLLYWOOD, 1924, A
INFAMOUS
INFAMOUS LADY, THE, 1928
INFAMOUS MISS REVELL, THE, 1921, A
INFATUATION, 1915, A
INFATUATION, 1925
INFELICE, 1915
INFERIOR SEX, THE, 1920, A
INFERNAL IDOL
INFERNAL MACHINE, 1933, A
INFERNO, 1953, O
INFERNO, 1980, O
INFERNO DEI MORTI-VIVENTI
INFIDEL, THE, 1922
INFIDELITY, 1917, A
INFINITE SORROW, 1922
INFORMATION KID
INFORMATION RECEIVED, 1962, C
INFORMER, THE, 1929, A
INFORMER, THE, 1935, C
INFORMERS, THE
INFRA SUPERMAN, THE
INFRA-MAN, 1975, C
INGAGI, 1931, C
INGEBORG HOLM, 1913
INGLORIOUS BASTARDS
INHERIT THE WIND, 1960, A
INHERITANCE, 1920
INHERITANCE IN PRETORIA, 1936, C
INHERITANCE, THE, 1951, A
INHERITANCE, THE, 1964, C
INHERITANCE, THE, 1978, O
INHERITED PASSIONS, 1916
INITIATION, THE, 1984, O
INJUN FENDER, 1973, O
INJUSTICE
INN FOR TROUBLE, 1960, A
INN IN TOKYO, AN, 1935
INN OF THE DAMNED, 1974, O
INN OF THE FRIGHTENED PEOPLE
INN OF THE SIXTH HAPPINESS, THE, 1958, AA
INNER CHAMBER, THE, 1915
INNER CHAMBER, THE, 1921, A
INNER CIRCLE, THE, 1946, A
INNER MAN, THE, 1922, A
INNER SANCTUM, 1948, A
INNER SHRINE, THE, 1917
INNER STRUGGLE, THE, 1916
INNER VOICE, THE, 1920
INNERVIEW, THE, 1974, O
INNOCENCE, 1923, A
INNOCENCE IS BLISS
INNOCENCE OF LIZETTE, THE, 1917
INNOCENCE OF RUTH, THE, 1916, A
INNOCENCE UNPROTECTED, 1971, C
INNOCENT, 1918, A
INNOCENT, 1921, A
INNOCENT ADVENTURESS, AN, 1919
INNOCENT AFFAIR, AN
INNOCENT AND THE DAMNED
INNOCENT BYSTANDERS, 1973, O
INNOCENT CHEAT, THE, 1921
INNOCENT LIE, THE, 1916, A
INNOCENT LOVE, 1928
INNOCENT MAGDALENE, AN, 1916, A
INNOCENT MAID, AN, 1934
INNOCENT MEETING, 1959, C
INNOCENT SINNER, THE, 1917, A
INNOCENT SINNERS, 1958, AAA
INNOCENT'S PROGRESS, 1918
INNOCENT, THE, 1979, O
INNOCENTS IN PARIS, 1955, A
INNOCENTS OF CHICAGO, THE
INNOCENTS OF PARIS, 1929, A
INNOCENTS WITH DIRTY HANDS
INNOCENTS, THE, 1961, C-O
INQUEST, 1931, C
INQUEST, 1939, C
INQUISITOR, THE, 1982, C-O
INSECT WOMAN, THE, 1964, C
INSECT, THE
INSEL DER AMAZONEN
INSEMINOID
INSEMINOID, 1980
INSEPARABLES, THE, 1929, A
INSIDE AMY, 1975, O
INSIDE DAISY CLOVER, 1965, O
INSIDE DETROIT, 1955, O
INSIDE INFORMATION
INSIDE INFORMATION, 1934, A
INSIDE INFORMATION, 1939, A
INSIDE JOB, 1946, A
INSIDE LOOKING OUT, 1977, C
INSIDE MOVES, 1980, C
INSIDE OF THE CUP, THE, 1921
INSIDE OUT
INSIDE OUT, 1975, C

INSIDE STORY, 1939, A
INSIDE STORY, THE, 1948, A
INSIDE STRAIGHT, 1951, O
INSIDE THE LAW, 1942, O
INSIDE THE LINES, 1918, A
INSIDE THE LINES, 1930, A
INSIDE THE MAFIA, 1959, O
INSIDE THE ROOM, 1935, C
INSIDE THE WALLS OF FOLSOM PRISON, 1951, C
INSIDIOUS DR. FU MANCHU, THE
INSINUATION, 1922
INSPECTOR CALLS, AN, 1954, O
INSPECTOR CLOUSEAU, 1968, A
INSPECTOR GENERAL, THE, 1937, A
INSPECTOR GENERAL, THE, 1949, AAA
INSPECTOR HORNLEIGH, 1939, A
INSPECTOR HORNLEIGH GOES TO IT
INSPECTOR HORNLEIGH ON HOLIDAY, 1939, A
INSPECTOR MAIGRET
INSPECTOR, THE
INSPIRATION, 1928
INSPIRATION, 1931, C
INSPIRATIONS OF HARRY LARRABEE, 1917
INSTANT COFFEE, 1974
INSTRUCTOR, THE, 1983
INSULT, 1932, C
INSURANCE INVESTIGATOR, 1951, C
INSURRECTION, THE, 1915
INTELLIGENCE MEN, THE
INTENT TO KILL, 1958, A
INTERFERENCE, 1928, A
INTERFERIN' GENT, THE, 1927
INTERIORS, 1978, C-O
INTERLOPER, THE, 1918
INTERLUDE
INTERLUDE, 1957, A
INTERLUDE, 1968, C
INTERMEZZO, 1937, A
INTERMEZZO: A LOVE STORY, 1939, A
INTERNATIONAL CRIME, 1938, A
INTERNATIONAL HOUSE, 1933, A
INTERNATIONAL LADY, 1941, A
INTERNATIONAL MARRIAGE, AN, 1916
INTERNATIONAL POLICE
INTERNATIONAL SETTLEMENT, 1938, A
INTERNATIONAL SQUADRON, 1941, A
INTERNATIONAL VELVET, 1978, AAA
INTERNECINE PROJECT, THE, 1974, O
INTERNES CAN'T TAKE MONEY, 1937, A
INTERNS, THE, 1962, O
INTERPLAY, 1970
INTERPOL
INTERRUPTED HONEYMOON, AN, 1948
INTERRUPTED HONEYMOON, THE, 1936, A
INTERRUPTED JOURNEY, THE, 1949, A-C
INTERRUPTED MELODY, 1955, A
INTERVAL, 1973, C
INTIMACY, 1966, O
INTIMATE LIGHTING, 1969, A
INTIMATE PLAYMATES, THE, 1976
INTIMATE RELATIONS, 1937, A
INTIMATE RELATIONS, 1948
INTIMATE RELATIONS, 1953
INTIMATE STRANGER, THE
INTIMNI OSVETLENI
INTO HER KINGDOM, 1926
INTO NO MAN'S LAND, 1928
INTO THE BLUE
INTO THE NIGHT, 1928, A
INTO THE PRIMITIVE, 1916
INTO THE STRAIGHT, 1950, C
INTOLERANCE, 1916, C
INTRAMUROS
INTRIGUE, 1916
INTRIGUE, 1917
INTRIGUE, 1921
INTRIGUE, 1947, A
INTRIGUE IN PARIS
INTRODUCE ME, 1925, A
INTRODUCTION TO MARRIAGE, 1930
INTRUDER IN THE DUST, 1949, C-O
INTRUDER, THE, 1932, A
INTRUDER, THE, 1955, C
INTRUDER, THE, 1962, C
INTRUSION OF ISABEL, THE, 1919
INVADER, THE
INVADERS FROM MARS, 1953, A
INVADERS, THE, 1929, A
INVADERS, THE, 1941, A
INVASION, 1965, A
INVASION 1700, 1965, C
INVASION EARTH 2150 A.D.
INVASION FORCE
INVASION FROM INNER EARTH, 1977
INVASION FROM THE MOON
INVASION OF ASTRO-MONSTERS
INVASION OF THE ANIMAL PEOPLE, 1962, A
INVASION OF THE ASTROS
INVASION OF THE BEE GIRLS, 1973, O
INVASION OF THE BLOOD FARMERS, 1972, O
INVASION OF THE BODY SNATCHERS, 1956, A
INVASION OF THE BODY SNATCHERS, 1978, C-O

INVASION OF THE BODY STEALERS
INVASION OF THE FLESH HUNTERS, 1981
INVASION OF THE FLYING SAUCERS
INVASION OF THE HELL CREATURES
INVASION OF THE SAUCER MEN, 1957, C
INVASION OF THE STAR CREATURES, 1962, A
INVASION OF THE VAMPIRES, THE, 1961, O
INVASION OF THE ZOMBIES
INVASION QUARTET, 1961, A
INVASION U.S.A., 1952, A
INVESTIGATION OF A CITIZEN ABOVE SUSPICION, 1970, O
INVESTIGATION OF MURDER, AN
INVINCIBLE GLADIATOR, THE, 1963, C
INVINCIBLE SIX, THE, 1970, A
INVISIBLE AGENT, 1942, A
INVISIBLE AVENGER, THE, 1958, A
INVISIBLE BOND, THE, 1920
INVISIBLE BOY, THE, 1957, AA
INVISIBLE CREATURE, THE
INVISIBLE DIVORCE, THE, 1920
INVISIBLE DR. MABUSE, THE, 1965, C
INVISIBLE ENEMY, 1938, A
INVISIBLE ENEMY, THE, 1916
INVISIBLE FEAR, THE, 1921, A
INVISIBLE GHOST, THE, 1941, C
INVISIBLE HORROR, THE
INVISIBLE INFORMER, 1946, A
INVISIBLE INVADERS, 1959, C
INVISIBLE KILLER, THE, 1940, A
INVISIBLE MAN RETURNS, THE, 1940, A
INVISIBLE MAN'S REVENGE, 1944, A
INVISIBLE MAN, THE, 1933, C
INVISIBLE MAN, THE, 1958, A
INVISIBLE MAN, THE, 1963, A
INVISIBLE MENACE, THE, 1938, A
INVISIBLE MESSAGE, THE
INVISIBLE OPPONENT, 1933, A
INVISIBLE POWER
INVISIBLE POWER, THE, 1914
INVISIBLE POWER, THE, 1921, A
INVISIBLE RAY, THE, 1936, C
INVISIBLE STRANGLER, 1984, C-O
INVISIBLE STRIPES, 1940, A
INVISIBLE WALL, THE, 1947, A
INVISIBLE WEB, THE, 1921
INVISIBLE WOMAN, THE, 1941, A
INVITATION, 1952, A
INVITATION TO A GUNFIGHTER, 1964, C
INVITATION TO A HANGING
INVITATION TO HAPPINESS, 1939, A
INVITATION TO MURDER, 1962, C
INVITATION TO THE DANCE, 1956, A
INVITATION TO THE WALTZ, 1935, A
INVITATION, THE, 1975, C-O
IO ... TU ... Y ... ELLA, 1933, A
IOLANTA
IPCRESS FILE, THE, 1965, A-C
IPHIGENIA, 1977, A
IPNOSI
IRELAND'S BORDER LINE, 1939, A
IRENE, 1926, A
IRENE, 1940, A
IRIS, 1915, A
IRISH AND PROUD OF IT, 1938, A
IRISH DESTINY, 1925, A
IRISH EYES, 1918
IRISH EYES ARE SMILING, 1944, A
IRISH FOR LUCK, 1936, A
IRISH GRINGO, THE, 1935
IRISH HEARTS
IRISH HEARTS, 1927, A
IRISH IN US, THE, 1935, A
IRISH LUCK, 1925
IRISH LUCK, 1939, A
IRISH MOTHER, AN
IRISH WHISKEY REBELLION, 1973, C
IRISHMAN, THE, 1978, A MP
IRMA LA DOUCE, 1963, C-O
IRO
IRON ANGEL, 1964, A
IRON COLLAR, THE
IRON CURTAIN, THE, 1948, A
IRON DUKE, THE, 1935, A
IRON FIST
IRON FIST, 1926
IRON GLOVE, THE, 1954, A
IRON HAND, THE, 1916
IRON HEART, THE, 1917
IRON HEART, THE, 1920
IRON HORSE, THE, 1924, A
IRON JUSTICE, 1915, C
IRON KISS, THE
IRON MAIDEN, THE
IRON MAJOR, THE, 1943, A
IRON MAN, THE, 1925, A
IRON MAN, THE, 1931, A
IRON MAN, THE, 1951, C
IRON MASK, THE, 1929, A
IRON MASTER, THE, 1933, A
IRON MISTRESS, THE, 1952, C
IRON MOUNTAIN TRAIL, 1953, A

IRON PETTICOAT, THE, 1956, A
IRON RIDER, THE, 1920
IRON RING, THE, 1917, A
IRON ROAD, THE
IRON SHERIFF, THE, 1957, A
IRON STAIR, THE
IRON STAIR, THE, 1933, A
IRON STRAIN, THE, 1915
IRON TO GOLD, 1922
IRON TRAIL, THE, 1921
IRON WOMAN, THE, 1916
IROQUOIS TRAIL, THE, 1950, A
IRRECONCILABLE DIFFERENCES, 1984, A-C
IRRESISTIBLE FLAPPER, THE, 1919
IRRESISTIBLE LOVER, THE, 1927, A
IS A MOTHER TO BLAME?, 1922
IS DIVORCE A FAILURE?, 1923, A
IS EVERYBODY HAPPY?, 1929, A
IS EVERYBODY HAPPY?, 1943, A
IS LIFE WORTH LIVING?, 1921
IS LOVE EVERYTHING?, 1924, A
IS MATRIMONY A FAILURE?, 1922
IS MONEY EVERYTHING?, 1923, A
IS MY FACE RED?, 1932, A
IS PARIS BURNING?, 1966, A
IS THAT NICE?, 1926, A
IS THERE JUSTICE?, 1931, A
IS THERE SEX AFTER DEATH, 1971
IS THIS TRIP REALLY NECESSARY?, 1970, O
IS WHEN IT SIZZLES, 1964, A
IS YOUR DAUGHTER SAFE?, 1927, C
IS YOUR HONEYMOON REALLY NECESSARY?,
   1953, A
IS ZAT SO?, 1927, A
ISAAC LITTLEFEATHERS, 1984, C
ISABEL, 1968, O
ISADORA, 1968, O
ISLAND AT THE TOP OF THE WORLD, THE,
   1974, AAA
ISLAND CAPTIVES, 1937, A
ISLAND CLAWS, 1981, O
ISLAND IN THE SKY, 1938, A
ISLAND IN THE SKY, 1953, A
ISLAND IN THE SUN, 1957, C
ISLAND MAN
ISLAND OF ALLAH, 1956, A
ISLAND OF DESIRE, 1952, C
ISLAND OF DESIRE, 1930
ISLAND OF DESIRE, THE, 1917
ISLAND OF DESPAIR, THE, 1926
ISLAND OF DOOM, 1933, A
ISLAND OF DOOMED MEN, 1940, C
ISLAND OF DR. MOREAU, THE, 1977, C
ISLAND OF INTRIGUE, THE, 1919, A
ISLAND OF LOST GIRLS, 1975
ISLAND OF LOST MEN, 1939, A
ISLAND OF LOST SOULS, 1933, C
ISLAND OF LOST WOMEN, 1959, A
ISLAND OF LOVE, 1963, A
ISLAND OF MONTE CRISTO
ISLAND OF PROCIDA, THE, 1952, C
ISLAND OF REGENERATION, THE, 1915, A
ISLAND OF ROMANCE, THE, 1922
ISLAND OF SURPRISE, THE, 1916
ISLAND OF TERROR, 1967, C
ISLAND OF THE BLUE DOLPHINS, 1964, AAA
ISLAND OF THE BURNING DAMNED, 1971, C
ISLAND OF THE BURNING DOOMED
ISLAND OF THE DAMNED, 1976, O
ISLAND OF THE DOOMED, 1968, C
ISLAND OF THE FISHMEN, THE
ISLAND OF WISDOM, THE, 1920
ISLAND RESCUE, 1952, A
ISLAND TRADER, 1982
ISLAND WIVES, 1922
ISLAND WOMAN
ISLAND WOMEN, 1958, A
ISLAND, THE, 1962, C
ISLAND, THE, 1980, O
ISLANDS IN THE STREAM, 1977, C
ISLE OF CONQUEST, 1919, A
ISLE OF DESTINY, 1940, A
ISLE OF DOUBT, 1922
ISLE OF ESCAPE, 1930, C
ISLE OF FORGOTTEN SINS, 1943, A
ISLE OF FORGOTTEN WOMEN, 1927, A
ISLE OF FURY, 1936, A
ISLE OF HOPE, THE, 1925, A
ISLE OF INTRIGUE, THE, 1918
ISLE OF LIFE, THE, 1916
ISLE OF LOST MEN, 1928, A
ISLE OF LOST SHIPS, 1929, A
ISLE OF LOST SHIPS, THE, 1923, A
ISLE OF LOST WRANGLERS
ISLE OF LOVE, THE, 1916
ISLE OF LOVE, THE, 1922
ISLE OF MISSING MEN, 1942, A
ISLE OF OBLIVION, 1917
ISLE OF RETRIBUTION, THE, 1926, A
ISLE OF SIN, 1963, C-O
ISLE OF THE DEAD, 1945, C
ISLE OF THE SNAKE PEOPLE

ISN'T IT ROMANTIC?, 1948, A
ISN'T LIFE A BITCH?
ISN'T LIFE WONDERFUL, 1924, A
ISN'T LIFE WONDERFUL, 1953, A
ISOBEL, 1920, A
ISTANBUL, 1957, A
IT, 1927, A
IT, 1967, O
IT AIN'T EASY, 1972, C-O
IT AIN'T HAY, 1943, AAA
IT ALL CAME TRUE, 1940, A-C
IT ALWAYS RAINS ON SUNDAY, 1949, C
IT CAME FROM BENEATH THE SEA, 1955, A
IT CAME FROM OUTER SPACE, 1953, A
IT CAME WITHOUT WARNING
IT CAN BE DONE, 1921, A
IT CAN BE DONE, 1929, A
IT CAN'T LAST FOREVER, 1937, A
IT COMES UP LOVE, 1943, A
IT COMES UP MURDER
IT CONQUERED THE WORLD, 1956, A
IT COULD HAPPEN TO YOU, 1937, A
IT COULD HAPPEN TO YOU, 1939, A
IT COULDN'T HAVE HAPPENED
IT COULDN'T HAVE HAPPENED—BUT IT DID,
   1936, A
IT FELL FROM THE SKY, 1980, C
IT GROWS ON TREES, 1952, A
IT HAD TO BE YOU, 1947, A
IT HAD TO HAPPEN, 1936, A
IT HAPPENED AT THE INN, 1945, A
IT HAPPENED AT THE WORLD'S FAIR, 1963, A
IT HAPPENED HERE, 1966, C
IT HAPPENED IN ATHENS, 1962, A
IT HAPPENED IN BROAD DAYLIGHT, 1960, A
IT HAPPENED IN BROOKLYN, 1947, A
IT HAPPENED IN CANADA, 1962, A
IT HAPPENED IN FLATBUSH, 1942, A
IT HAPPENED IN GIBRALTAR, 1943, A
IT HAPPENED IN HARLEM, 1945
IT HAPPENED IN HOLLYWOOD
IT HAPPENED IN HOLLYWOOD, 1937, A
IT HAPPENED IN HONOLULU, 1916
IT HAPPENED IN NEW YORK, 1935, A
IT HAPPENED IN PARIS, 1919
IT HAPPENED IN PARIS, 1935, A
IT HAPPENED IN PARIS, 1953, A
IT HAPPENED IN PARIS, 1938
IT HAPPENED IN PARIS, 1940
IT HAPPENED IN ROME, 1959, A
IT HAPPENED IN SOHO, 1948, C
IT HAPPENED ON 5TH AVENUE, 1947, A
IT HAPPENED ONE NIGHT, 1934, A
IT HAPPENED ONE SUMMER
IT HAPPENED ONE SUNDAY, 1944, A
IT HAPPENED OUT WEST, 1923
IT HAPPENED OUT WEST, 1937, A
IT HAPPENED TO ADELE, 1917
IT HAPPENED TO JANE, 1959, A
IT HAPPENED TO ONE MAN, 1941, A
IT HAPPENED TOMORROW, 1944, A
IT HAPPENS EVERY SPRING, 1949, AAA
IT HAPPENS EVERY THURSDAY, 1953, A
IT HAPPENS IN ROME
IT HURTS ONLY WHEN I LAUGH
IT IS FOR ENGLAND
IT IS THE LAW, 1924, A
IT ISN'T BEING DONE THIS SEASON, 1921
IT ISN'T DONE, 1937, A
IT LIVES AGAIN, 1978, O
IT LIVES BY NIGHT
IT MIGHT HAPPEN TO YOU, 1920
IT MUST BE LOVE, 1926, A
IT ONLY HAPPENS TO OTHERS, 1971, C
IT ONLY TAKES 5 MINUTES
IT PAYS TO ADVERTISE, 1919
IT PAYS TO ADVERTISE, 1931, A
IT RAINED ALL NIGHT THE DAY I LEFT, 1978
IT SEEMED LIKE A GOOD IDEA AT THE TIME,
   1975, O
IT SHOULD HAPPEN TO YOU, 1954, A
IT SHOULDN'T HAPPEN TO A DOG, 1946, A
IT SHOULDN'T HAPPEN TO A VET
IT STALKED THE OCEAN FLOOR
IT STARTED AT MIDNIGHT
IT STARTED IN NAPLES, 1960, C
IT STARTED IN PARADISE, 1952, A
IT STARTED IN THE ALPS, 1966, A
IT STARTED WITH A KISS, 1959, C
IT STARTED WITH EVE, 1941, A
IT TAKES A THIEF, 1960, C
IT TAKES ALL KINDS, 1969, C
IT THE TERROR FROM BEYOND SPACE, 1958, C
IT THE VAMPIRE FROM BEYOND SPACE
IT WON'T RUB OFF, BABY
IT'S A 2'6'' ABOVE THE GROUND WORLD, 1972, O
IT'S A BEAR, 1919, A
IT'S A BET, 1935, A
IT'S A BIG COUNTRY, 1951, AA
IT'S A BIKINI WORLD, 1967, A
IT'S A BOY, 1934, A
IT'S A COP, 1934, A

IT'S A DATE, 1940, A
IT'S A DEAL, 1930, A-C
IT'S A DOG'S LIFE
IT'S A GIFT, 1934, AAA
IT'S A GRAND LIFE, 1953, A
IT'S A GRAND OLD WORLD, 1937, A
IT'S A GREAT DAY, 1956, A
IT'S A GREAT FEELING, 1949, A
IT'S A GREAT LIFE, 1920
IT'S A GREAT LIFE, 1930, A
IT'S A GREAT LIFE, 1936, A
IT'S A GREAT LIFE, 1943, AA
IT'S A JOKE, SON, 1947, A
IT'S A KING, 1933, A
IT'S A MAD, MAD, MAD, MAD WORLD, 1963, AAA
IT'S A PLEASURE, 1945, A
IT'S A SMALL WORLD, 1935, A
IT'S A SMALL WORLD, 1950, A
IT'S A WISE CHILD, 1931, A
IT'S A WONDERFUL DAY, 1949, A
IT'S A WONDERFUL LIFE, 1946, AAA
IT'S A WONDERFUL WORLD, 1939, A
IT'S A WONDERFUL WORLD, 1956, A
IT'S ALIVE, 1968, C
IT'S ALIVE, 1974, O
IT'S ALIVE II
IT'S ALL HAPPENING
IT'S ALL IN YOUR MIND, 1938
IT'S ALL OVER TOWN, 1963, A
IT'S ALL YOURS, 1937, A
IT'S ALWAYS FAIR WEATHER, 1955, A
IT'S EASY TO MAKE MONEY, 1919
IT'S GREAT TO BE ALIVE, 1933, A
IT'S GREAT TO BE YOUNG, 1946, A
IT'S GREAT TO BE YOUNG, 1956, A
IT'S HAPPINESS THAT COUNTS, 1918, A
IT'S HARD TO BE GOOD, 1950, A
IT'S HOT IN HELL
IT'S HOT IN PARADISE, 1962, C
IT'S IN THE AIR, 1935, A
IT'S IN THE AIR, 1940, A
IT'S IN THE BAG, 1936, A
IT'S IN THE BAG, 1943, A
IT'S IN THE BAG, 1945, A
IT'S IN THE BLOOD, 1938, A
IT'S LOVE AGAIN, 1936, A
IT'S LOVE I'M AFTER, 1937, A
IT'S MAGIC
IT'S MY LIFE
IT'S MY TURN, 1980, C
IT'S NEVER TOO LATE, 1958, A
IT'S NEVER TOO LATE, 1984, O
IT'S NEVER TOO LATE TO MEND, 1917
IT'S NEVER TOO LATE TO MEND, 1937, A
IT'S NO LAUGHING MATTER, 1915, A
IT'S NOT CRICKET, 1937, A
IT'S NOT CRICKET, 1949, A
IT'S NOT THE SIZE THAT COUNTS, 1979, O
IT'S ONLY MONEY, 1962, A
IT'S ONLY MONEY, 1951
IT'S SAM SMALL AGAIN
IT'S THAT MAN AGAIN, 1943, A
IT'S THE OLD ARMY GAME, 1926, A
IT'S TOUGH TO BE FAMOUS, 1932, A
IT'S TRAD, DAD
IT'S TURNED OUT NICE AGAIN
IT'S WHAT'S HAPPENING
IT'S YOU I WANT, 1936, A
ITALIAN CONNECTION, THE, 1973, O
ITALIAN JOB, THE, 1969, A
ITALIAN MOUSE, THE
ITALIAN SECRET SERVICE, 1968, C
ITALIAN STRAW HAT, AN, 1927, A
ITALIAN, THE, 1915, A
ITALIANI BRAVA GENTE
ITALIANO BRAVA GENTE, 1965, A
ITCHING PALMS, 1923
IVAN GROZNYI
IVAN THE TERRIBLE, PART 1, 1947, A
IVAN'S CHILDHOOD
IVAN'S CHILDHOOD
IVANHOE, 1913, A
IVANHOE, 1952, A
IVANHOE
IVANOVO DETSTVO
IVORY HUNTER, 1952, A
IVORY HUNTERS, THE
IVORY SNUFF BOX, THE, 1915, A
IVORY-HANDLED GUN, 1935, A
IVY, 1947, A
IVY LEAGUE KILLERS, 1962

—J—

J'ACCUSE, 1919
J'ACCUSE, 1939, C-O
J'AI TUE, 1924
J'AVAIS SEPT FILLES
J'IRAI CRACHER SUR VOS TOMBES
J-MEN FOREVER, 1980, C
J.C., 1972
J.D.'S REVENGE, 1976, O
J.R.

J.W. COOP, 1971, A
JABBERWOCKY, 1977, O
JACK, 1925
JACK AHOY, 1935, A
JACK AND JILL, 1917, A
JACK AND THE BEANSTALK, 1917, A
JACK AND THE BEANSTALK, 1952, AAA
JACK AND THE BEANSTALK, 1970, AA
JACK CHANTY, 1915
JACK FROST, 1966, AAA
JACK KNIFE MAN, THE, 1920, A
JACK LONDON, 1943, A
JACK LONDON'S KLONDIKE FEVER
JACK MCCALL, DESPERADO, 1953, A
JACK O' CLUBS, 1924, A
JACK O'HEARTS, 1926, A
JACK OF ALL TRADES
JACK OF DIAMONDS, 1967, A
JACK OF DIAMONDS, THE, 1949, A
JACK OF HEARTS
JACK RIDER, THE, 1921, A
JACK SLADE, 1953, C
JACK SPURLOCK, PRODIGAL, 1918, A
JACK STRAW, 1920, A
JACK TAR, 1915, A
JACK THE GIANT KILLER, 1962, AA
JACK THE RIPPER, 1959, O
JACK'S WIFE
JACK, SAM AND PETE, 1919, A
JACKALS, THE, 1967, A
JACKASS MAIL, 1942, A
JACKIE, 1921
JACKIE ROBINSON STORY, THE, 1950, AA
JACKPOT, 1960, A
JACKPOT, 1982
JACKPOT, THE, 1950, A
JACKSON COUNTY JAIL, 1976, O
JACKTOWN, 1962, A
JACOB TWO-TWO MEETS THE HOODED FANG,
   1979, AAA
JACQUELINE, 1956, A
JACQUELINE SUSANN'S ONCE IS NOT ENOUGH
JACQUELINE, OR BLAZING BARRIERS, 1923, A
JACQUES BREL IS ALIVE AND WELL AND LIVING
   IN PARIS, 1975, A
JACQUES LANDAUZE, 1919
JACQUES OF THE SILVER NORTH, 1919
JADA, GOSCIE, JADA
JADE CASKET, THE, 1929
JADE CUP, THE, 1926
JADE HEART, THE, 1915
JADE MASK, THE, 1945, A
JAFFERY, 1915
JAGA WA HASHITTA
JAGUAR, 1956, A
JAGUAR, 1980, C
JAGUAR LIVES, 1979, C
JAGUAR'S CLAWS, 1917
JAIL BAIT, 1954, C
JAIL BAIT, 1977, O
JAIL BUSTERS, 1955, AA
JAIL HOUSE BLUES, 1942, A
JAILBIRD, THE, 1920, A
JAILBIRDS, 1939, A
JAILBIRDS, 1931
JAILBREAK, 1936, A
JAILBREAKERS, THE, 1960, A
JAILHOUSE ROCK, 1957, A
JAK BYC KOCHANA
JAKE THE PLUMBER, 1927, A
JALNA, 1935, A
JALOPY, 1953, AA
JALSAGHAR
JAM SESSION, 1944, A
JAMAICA INN, 1939, C
JAMAICA RUN, 1953, A
JAMAICAN GOLD, 1971
JAMBOREE
JAMBOREE, 1944, A
JAMBOREE, 1957, A
JAMES BROTHERS, THE
JAMESTOWN, 1923, A
JAN OF THE BIG SNOWS, 1922
JANE, 1915
JANE AUSTEN IN MANHATTAN, 1980, A
JANE EYRE, 1914
JANE EYRE, 1921, A
JANE EYRE, 1935, A
JANE EYRE, 1944, A
JANE EYRE, 1971, A
JANE GOES A' WOOING, 1919, A
JANE SHORE
JANE STEPS OUT, 1938, A
JANICE MEREDITH, 1924, A
JANIE, 1944, AA
JANIE GETS MARRIED, 1946, A
JANITOR, THE
JAPANESE NIGHTINGALE, A, 1918
JAPANESE WAR BRIDE, 1952, A
JASON AND THE ARGONAUTS, 1963, AA
JASPER LANDRY'S WILL
JASSY, 1948, A

JAVA HEAD, 1923, A
JAVA HEAD, 1935, C
JAVA SEAS
JAWS, 1975, C-O
JAWS 3-D, 1983, C-O
JAWS II, 1978, A-C
JAWS OF DEATH, THE
JAWS OF HELL, 1928
JAWS OF JUSTICE, 1933, A
JAWS OF SATAN, 1980, O
JAWS OF STEEL, 1927, A
JAWS OF THE JUNGLE, 1936, C
JAYHAWKERS, THE, 1959, A
JAZZ AGE, THE, 1929
JAZZ BABIES, 1932, A
JAZZ BOAT, 1960, A
JAZZ CINDERELLA, 1930, A
JAZZ GIRL, THE, 1926, A
JAZZ HEAVEN, 1929, A
JAZZ HOUNDS, THE, 1922
JAZZ MAD, 1928
JAZZ SINGER, THE, 1927, A
JAZZ SINGER, THE, 1953, A
JAZZ SINGER, THE, 1980, C
JAZZBAND FIVE, THE, 1932, A
JAZZBOAT
JAZZLAND, 1928, A
JAZZMAN, 1984, C
JAZZMANIA, 1923, A
JE T'AIME, 1974, C
JE T'AIME, JE T'AIME, 1972, C
JE VOUS SALUE, MAFIA
JEALOUS HUSBANDS, 1923, A
JEALOUSY
JEALOUSY, 1916
JEALOUSY, 1929, C
JEALOUSY, 1931, A
JEALOUSY, 1934, C
JEALOUSY, 1945, A
JEAN D'AGREVE, 1922
JEAN MARC OR CONJUGAL LIFE
JEAN O' THE HEATHER, 1916
JEANNE DORE, 1916
JEANNE EAGELS, 1957, C
JEANNE OF THE GUTTER, 1919
JEANNIE
JEDDA, THE UNCIVILIZED, 1956, A
JEDER FUR SICH UND GOTT GEGEN ALLE
JEEPERS CREEPERS, 1939, A
JEKYLL AND HYDE, 1982, O
JEKYLL AND HYDE PORTFOLIO, THE
JEKYLL AND HYDE TOGETHER AGAIN, 1972
JEKYLL'S INFERNO
JELF'S
JENIFER HALE, 1937, A
JENNIE
JENNIE, 1941, A
JENNIE GERHARDT, 1933, A
JENNIE LESS HA UNA NUOVA PISTOLA
JENNIE, WIFE/CHILD, 1968
JENNIFER, 1953, A
JENNIFER, 1978, C-O
JENNIFER (THE SNAKE GODDESS)
JENNIFER ON MY MIND, 1971, O
JENNY, 1969, A
JENNY BE GOOD, 1920, A
JENNY LAMOUR, 1948, A
JENNY LIND
JENSEITS DES RHIENS
JEOPARDY, 1953, A
JEREMIAH JOHNSON, 1972, C-O
JEREMY, 1973, A
JERICHO
JERK, THE, 1979, O
JERRICO, THE WONDER CLOWN
JERUSALEM DELIVERED, 1918
JERUSALEM FILE, THE, 1972, C
JES' CALL ME JIM, 1920
JESS, 1914
JESS OF MOUNTAIN COUNTRY, 1914
JESSE AND LESTER, TWO BROTHERS IN A PLACE
   CALLED TRINITY, 1972, A
JESSE JAMES, 1927, A
JESSE JAMES, 1939, A
JESSE JAMES AS THE OUTLAW, 1921, A
JESSE JAMES AT BAY, 1941, A
JESSE JAMES MEETS FRANKENSTEIN'S DAUGHTER,
   1966, A
JESSE JAMES UNDER THE BLACK FLAG, 1921, A
JESSE JAMES VERSUS THE DALTONS, 1954, A
JESSE JAMES' WOMEN, 1954, A
JESSE JAMES, JR., 1942, A
JESSE'S GIRLS, 1975
JESSICA, 1962, C
JESSICA, 1970
JESSIE'S GIRLS, 1976, O
JEST OF GOD, A
JESUS, 1979, A
JESUS CHRIST, SUPERSTAR, 1973, A
JESUS OF NAZARETH, 1928
JESUS TRIP, THE, 1971, C
JET ATTACK, 1958, A

JET JOB, 1952, A
JET MEN OF THE AIR
JET OVER THE ATLANTIC, 1960, A
JET PILOT, 1957, C
JET SQUAD
JET STORM, 1961, A
JETLAG, 1981, C
JETSTREAM
JEU DE MASSACRE
JEUNE FILLE, UN SEUL AMOUR, UNE
JEUNES FILLES EN UNIFORME
JEUX D'ADULTES
JEUX PRECOCES
JEW AT WAR, A, 1931
JEW SUSS
JEWEL, 1915
JEWEL IN PAWN, A, 1917
JEWEL ROBBERY, 1932, A
JEWEL, THE, 1933, A
JEWELS OF BRANDENBURG, 1947, A
JEWELS OF DESIRE, 1927, A
JEWISH DAUGHTER, 1933
JEWISH FATHER, 1934
JEWISH KING LEAR, 1935
JEWISH LUCK, 1925
JEWISH MELODY, THE, 1940
JEZEBEL, 1938, A
JEZEBELS, THE
JIG SAW, 1965, A
JIG SAW, 1979
JIGGS AND MAGGIE IN COURT, 1948
JIGGS AND MAGGIE IN JACKPOT JITTERS, 1949
JIGGS AND MAGGIE IN SOCIETY, 1948, AA
JIGGS AND MAGGIE OUT WEST, 1950, AA
JIGOKUHEN
JIGOKUMEN
JIGSAW, 1949, A
JIGSAW, 1968, O
JIGSAW MAN, THE, 1984, C
JIGSAW, 1965
JILT, THE, 1922, A
JILTED JANET, 1918
JIM BLUDSO, 1917
JIM GRIMSBY'S BOY, 1916, A
JIM HANVEY, DETECTIVE, 1937, A
JIM LA HOULETTE, ROI DES VOLEURS, 1926
JIM THE CONQUEROR, 1927, A
JIM THE MAN, 1967
JIM THE PENMAN, 1921, A
JIM THORPE—ALL AMERICAN, 1951, A
JIM, THE PENMAN, 1915
JIM, THE WORLD'S GREATEST, 1976, A
JIMMIE'S MILLIONS, 1925, A
JIMMY, 1916, A
JIMMY AND SALLY, 1933, A
JIMMY BOY, 1935, A
JIMMY ORPHEUS, 1966, C
JIMMY THE GENT, 1934, A
JIMMY THE KID, 1982, A
JIMMY VALENTINE
JIMMY'S MILLIONS
JIMMY, THE BOY WONDER, 1966
JINCHOGE
JINX, 1919
JINX JUMPER, THE, 1917
JINX MONEY, 1948, A
JINXED, 1982, O
JITTERBUGS, 1943, AAA
JIVARO, 1954, A
JIVE JUNCTION, 1944, A
JIVE TURKEY, 1976
JO THE CROSSING SWEEPER, 1918, C
JOAN AT THE STAKE, 1954, A
JOAN BEDFORD IS MISSING
JOAN OF ARC, 1948, A
JOAN OF FLANDERS
JOAN OF OZARK, 1942, A
JOAN OF PARIS, 1942, A
JOAN OF PLATTSBURG, 1918, A
JOAN OF THE ANGELS, 1962, O
JOAN OF THE WOODS, 1918, O
JOAN THE WOMAN, 1916, C
JOANNA, 1925, A
JOANNA, 1968, O
JOAQUIN MARRIETA
JOB LAZADASA
JOCASTE, 1927
JOCELYN, 1922
JOCK PETERSEN
JOCKEY OF DEATH, THE, 1916
JOE, 1970, O
JOE AND ETHEL TURP CALL ON THE PRESIDENT,
   1939, A
JOE AND MAXI, 1980
JOE BUTTERFLY, 1957, A
JOE DAKOTA, 1957, C
JOE HILL, 1971, C
JOE KIDD, 1972, C
JOE LOUIS STORY, THE, 1953, A
JOE MACBETH, 1955, C
JOE NAVIDAD
JOE PALOOKA

JOE PALOOKA IN FIGHTING MAD
JOE PALOOKA IN HUMPHREY TAKES A CHANCE
JOE PALOOKA IN THE BIG FIGHT, 1949, AA
JOE PALOOKA IN THE COUNTERPUNCH, 1949, AAA
JOE PALOOKA IN THE KNOCKOUT, 1947
JOE PALOOKA IN THE SQUARED CIRCLE, 1950, A
JOE PALOOKA IN TRIPLE CROSS, 1951, AA
JOE PALOOKA IN WINNER TAKE ALL, 1948, AA
JOE PALOOKA MEETS HUMPHREY, 1950, AA
JOE PALOOKA, CHAMP, 1946, AA
JOE PANTHER, 1976, AAA
JOE SMITH, AMERICAN, 1942, A
JOE'S BED-STUY BARBERSHOP: WE CUT HEADS, 1983
JOE, EL IMPLACABLE
JOEY, 1977
JOEY BOY, 1965, O
JOHANNA ENLISTS, 1918
JOHANNES, FILS DE JOHANNES, 1918
JOHANSSON GETS SCOLDED, 1945, A
JOHN AND JULIE, 1957, AAA
JOHN AND MARY, 1969, O
JOHN BARLEYCORN, 1914, A
JOHN ERMINE OF THE YELLOWSTONE, 1917
JOHN FORREST FINDS HIMSELF, 1920
JOHN GLAYDE'S HONOR, 1915, A
JOHN GOLDFARB, PLEASE COME HOME, 1964, A-C
JOHN HALIFAX, GENTLEMAN, 1915, A
JOHN HALIFAX—GENTLEMAN, 1938, A
JOHN HERIOT'S WIFE, 1920, A
JOHN LOVES MARY, 1949, A
JOHN MEADE'S WOMAN, 1937, C
JOHN NEEDHAM'S DOUBLE, 1916, A
JOHN OF THE FAIR, 1962, AAA
JOHN PAUL JONES, 1959, A
JOHN PETTICOATS, 1919
JOHN SMITH, 1922, A
JOHN WESLEY, 1954, AAA
JOHNNY ALLEGRO, 1949, A-C
JOHNNY ANGEL, 1945, A
JOHNNY APOLLO, 1940, A
JOHNNY BANCO, 1969, O
JOHNNY BELINDA, 1948, C-O
JOHNNY COME LATELY, 1943, A
JOHNNY COMES FLYING HOME, 1946, A
JOHNNY CONCHO, 1956, A
JOHNNY COOL, 1963, O
JOHNNY DANGEROUSLY, 1984, C
JOHNNY DARK, 1954, A
JOHNNY DOESN'T LIVE HERE ANY MORE, 1944, A
JOHNNY DOUGHBOY, 1943, AA
JOHNNY EAGER, 1942, C
JOHNNY FIRECLOUD, 1975
JOHNNY FRENCHMAN, 1946, A
JOHNNY GET YOUR GUN, 1919, A
JOHNNY GET YOUR HAIR CUT, 1927, A
JOHNNY GOT HIS GUN, 1971, O
JOHNNY GUITAR, 1954, C
JOHNNY HAMLET, 1972, O
JOHNNY HOLIDAY, 1949, A
JOHNNY IN THE CLOUDS, 1945, A
JOHNNY NOBODY, 1965, O
JOHNNY NORTH
JOHNNY O'CLOCK, 1947, A
JOHNNY ON THE RUN, 1953, AAA
JOHNNY ON THE SPOT, 1954, A
JOHNNY ONE-EYE, 1950, A
JOHNNY ORO
JOHNNY RENO, 1966, O
JOHNNY RING AND THE CAPTAIN'S SWORD, 1921, A
JOHNNY ROCCO, 1958, A
JOHNNY STEALS EUROPE, 1932, A
JOHNNY STOOL PIGEON, 1949, C
JOHNNY THE GIANT KILLER, 1953, AA
JOHNNY TIGER, 1966, A
JOHNNY TREMAIN, 1957, AAA
JOHNNY TROUBLE, 1957, A
JOHNNY VAGABOND
JOHNNY VIK, 1973, C
JOHNNY YUMA, 1967, O
JOHNNY, YOU'RE WANTED, 1956, A
JOHNNY-ON-THE-SPOT, 1919, A
JOHNSTOWN FLOOD, THE, 1926, A
JOHNSTOWN MONSTER, THE, 1971
JOI-UCHI
JOIN THE MARINES, 1937, A
JOKE OF DESTINY LYING IN WAIT AROUND THE
   CORNER LIKE A STREET BANDIT, A, 1984, C
JOKE OF DESTINY, A
JOKER IS WILD, THE, 1957, C
JOKER, THE, 1961, O
JOKERS, THE, 1967, A-C
JOKES MY FOLKS NEVER TOLD ME, 1979
JOLLY BAD FELLOW, A, 1964, C
JOLLY GENIE, THE, 1964
JOLLY OLD HIGGINS
JOLSON SINGS AGAIN, 1949, A
JOLSON STORY, THE, 1946, A
JOLT, THE, 1921, A
JONAH—WHO WILL BE 25 IN THE YEAR 2000,
   1976, C
JONAS: QUI AURA 25 ANS EN L'AN 2000

JONATHAN, 1973, O
JONATHAN LIVINGSTON SEAGULL, 1973, A
JONES FAMILY IN HOLLYWOOD, THE, 1939, A
JONI, 1980, A
JONIKO
JONIKO AND THE KUSH TA KA, 1969, AAA
JORDAN IS A HARD ROAD, 1915, A
JORY, 1972, A
JOSEPH AND HIS BRETHREN
JOSEPH AND HIS BRETHREN, 1915
JOSEPH ANDREWS, 1977, O
JOSEPH IN THE LAND OF EGYPT, 1914
JOSEPH IN THE LAND OF EGYPT, 1932
JOSEPH SOLD BY HIS BROTHERS
JOSEPHINE AND MEN, 1955, A
JOSETTE, 1938, A
JOSHUA, 1976, O
JOSSELYN'S WIFE, 1919
JOSSELYN'S WIFE, 1926, A
JOSSER IN THE ARMY, 1932, A
JOSSER JOINS THE NAVY, 1932, A
JOSSER ON THE FARM, 1934, A
JOSSER ON THE RIVER, 1932, A
JOTAI
JOUR DE FETE, 1952, A
JOURNAL OF A CRIME, 1934, C
JOURNEY, 1977, O
JOURNEY AHEAD, 1947, A
JOURNEY BACK TO OZ, 1974, AAA
JOURNEY AMONG WOMEN, 1977, O
JOURNEY BENEATH THE DESERT, 1967, A
JOURNEY FOR MARGARET, 1942, AA
JOURNEY INTO DARKNESS, 1968, A
JOURNEY INTO FEAR, 1942, A
JOURNEY INTO FEAR, 1976, O
JOURNEY INTO LIGHT, 1951, C
JOURNEY INTO MIDNIGHT, 1968, A
JOURNEY INTO NOWHERE, 1963, O
JOURNEY THROUGH ROSEBUD, 1972, O
JOURNEY TO FREEDOM, 1957, A
JOURNEY TO ITALY
JOURNEY TO LOVE, 1953, A
JOURNEY TO SHILOH, 1968, C
JOURNEY TO THE BEGINNING OF TIME, 1966, AAA
JOURNEY TO THE CENTER OF THE EARTH,
   1959, AAA
JOURNEY TO THE CENTER OF TIME, 1967, A
JOURNEY TO THE FAR SIDE OF THE SUN, 1969, A
JOURNEY TO THE LOST CITY, 1960, A
JOURNEY TO THE SEVENTH PLANET, 1962, C
JOURNEY TOGETHER, 1946, A
JOURNEY'S END, 1918, A
JOURNEY'S END, 1930, C
JOURNEY'S END, THE, 1921, A
JOURNEY, THE, 1959, A-C
JOURNEYS FROM BERLIN—1971, 1980, O
JOVITA, 1970, A
JOY, 1983, O
JOY AND THE DRAGON, 1916, A
JOY GIRL, THE, 1927, A
JOY HOUSE, 1964, O
JOY IN THE MORNING, 1965, O
JOY OF LEARNING, THE
JOY OF LIVING, 1938, A
JOY OF SEX, 1984, O
JOY PARADE, THE
JOY RIDE, 1935, A
JOY RIDE, 1958, C
JOY RIDE TO NOWHERE, 1978
JOY STREET, 1929, A
JOYOUS ADVENTURES OF ARISTIDE PUJOL, THE,
   1920, A
JOYOUS LIAR, THE, 1919, A
JOYOUS TROUBLEMAKERS, THE, 1920, A
JOYRIDE, 1977, O
JOYSTICKS, 1983, O
JUAREZ, 1939, A
JUAREZ AND MAXIMILLIAN
JUBAL, 1956, C
JUBILEE, 1978, O
JUBILEE TRAIL, 1954, A
JUBILEE WINDOW, 1935, A
JUBILO, 1919, A
JUCKLINS, THE, 1920
JUD, 1971, O
JUDAS CITY
JUDAS WAS A WOMAN
JUDEX, 1966, C
JUDGE AND THE ASSASSIN, THE, 1979, C
JUDGE AND THE SINNER, THE, 1964, C
JUDGE HARDY AND SON, 1939, AAA
JUDGE HARDY'S CHILDREN, 1938, AAA
JUDGE HER NOT, 1921, A
JUDGE NOT, 1920, A
JUDGE NOT OR THE WOMAN OF MONA DIGGINGS,
   1915, A
JUDGE PRIEST, 1934, AAA
JUDGE STEPS OUT, THE, 1949, A
JUDGE, THE, 1949, O
JUDGED BY APPEARANCES, 1916
JUDGEMENT, 1922
JUDGEMENT HOUSE, THE, 1917

JUDGEMENT, THE
JUDGMENT AT NUREMBERG, 1961, C
JUDGMENT BOOK, THE, 1935
JUDGMENT DEFERRED, 1952, A
JUDGMENT IN THE SUN
JUDGMENT OF THE HILLS, 1927, A
JUDGMENT OF THE STORM, 1924, A
JUDITH, 1965, C-O
JUDITH OF BETHULIA, 1914, C
JUDITH OF THE CUMBERLANDS, 1916, A
JUDO SAGA, 1965, C
JUDO SHOWDOWN, 1966, C
JUDY FORGOT, 1915, A
JUDY GOES TO TOWN
JUDY OF ROGUES' HARBOUR, 1920, A
JUDY'S LITTLE NO-NO, 1969, O
JUGGERNAUT, 1937, O
JUGGERNAUT, 1974, A-C
JUGGERNAUT, THE, 1915, A
JUGGLER, THE, 1953, C-O
JUKE BOX JENNY, 1942, AA
JUKE BOX RACKET, 1960, A
JUKE BOX RHYTHM, 1959, A
JUKE GIRL, 1942, A
JUKE JOINT, 1947
JULES AND JIM, 1962, C-O
JULES OF THE STRONG HEART, 1918, A
JULES VERNE'S ROCKET TO THE MOON
JULIA, 1977, A-C
JULIA MISBEHAVES, 1948, A
JULIA, DU BIST ZAUBER-HAFT
JULIE, 1956, A
JULIE DARLING, 1982, O
JULIE THE REDHEAD, 1963, A
JULIET OF THE SPIRITS, 1965, A-C
JULIETTA, 1957, A
JULIUS CAESAR, 1914
JULIUS CAESAR, 1952, A
JULIUS CAESAR, 1953, C
JULIUS CAESAR, 1970, A
JULY PORK BELLIES
JUMBO, 1962, AA
JUMP, 1971, A
JUMP FOR GLORY
JUMP INTO HELL, 1955, A
JUMPING FOR JOY, 1956, A
JUMPING JACKS, 1952, A
JUNCTION 88, 1940
JUNCTION CITY, 1952, A
JUNE BRIDE, 1948, A
JUNE FRIDAY, 1915, A
JUNE MADNESS, 1922, A
JUNE MOON, 1931, A
JUNGE LORD, DER
JUNGE SCHRIE MORD, EIN
JUNGE TORLESS, DER
JUNGLE ATTACK
JUNGLE BOOK, 1942, AAA
JUNGLE BOOK, THE, 1967, AAA
JUNGLE BRIDE, 1933, A
JUNGLE CAPTIVE, 1945, A
JUNGLE CHILD, THE, 1916, A
JUNGLE FIGHTERS
JUNGLE FLIGHT, 1947, A
JUNGLE GENTS, 1954, AA
JUNGLE GODDESS, 1948, A
JUNGLE GODS, 1927
JUNGLE HEAT, 1957, A
JUNGLE HELL, 1956
JUNGLE ISLAND
JUNGLE JIM, 1948, AAA
JUNGLE JIM IN THE FORBIDDEN LAND, 1952, AAA
JUNGLE LOVERS, THE, 1915
JUNGLE MAN, 1941, A
JUNGLE MAN-EATERS, 1954, AAA
JUNGLE MANHUNT, 1951, AAA
JUNGLE MOON MEN, 1955, AAA
JUNGLE OF CHANG, 1951, C
JUNGLE PATROL, 1948, A
JUNGLE PRINCESS, THE, 1923
JUNGLE PRINCESS, THE, 1936, A
JUNGLE QUEEN, 1946
JUNGLE RAMPAGE
JUNGLE SIREN, 1942, A
JUNGLE STREET
JUNGLE STREET GIRLS, 1963, A
JUNGLE TERROR
JUNGLE TRAIL OF THE SON OF TARZAN, 1923
JUNGLE TRAIL, THE, 1919, A
JUNGLE VIRGIN
JUNGLE WARRIORS, 1984, O
JUNGLE WOMAN
JUNGLE WOMAN, 1944, A
JUNGLE WOMAN, THE, 1926, A
JUNGLE, THE, 1914, A
JUNGLE, THE, 1952, AA
JUNIOR ARMY, 1943, AA
JUNIOR BONNER, 1972, A-C
JUNIOR MISS, 1945, AAA
JUNIOR PROM, 1946, AA
JUNKET 89, 1970, AAA
JUNKMAN, THE, 1982, C-O

JUNO AND THE PAYCOCK, 1930, A
JUPITER, 1952, A
JUPITER MENACE, THE, 1982
JUPITER'S DARLING, 1955, A
JURY OF FATE, THE, 1917
JURY OF ONE
JURY OF THE JUNGLE
JURY'S EVIDENCE, 1936, A
JURY'S SECRET, THE, 1938, A
JUST A BIG, SIMPLE GIRL, 1949, A
JUST A GIGOLO, 1931, A
JUST A GIGOLO, 1979, O
JUST A GIRL, 1916, A
JUST A MOTHER, 1923
JUST A SONG AT TWILIGHT, 1922, A
JUST A WIFE, 1920
JUST A WOMAN, 1925, A
JUST ACROSS THE STREET, 1952, A
JUST AROUND THE CORNER, 1921, A
JUST AROUND THE CORNER, 1938, AAA
JUST BE THERE, 1977
JUST BEFORE DAWN, 1946, A
JUST BEFORE DAWN, 1980, O
JUST BEFORE NIGHTFALL, 1975, A-C
JUST DECEPTION, A, 1917, C
JUST FOR A SONG, 1930, A
JUST FOR FUN, 1963, AA
JUST FOR THE HELL OF IT, 1968, O
JUST FOR THE HELL OF IT, 1968
JUST FOR TONIGHT, 1918, A
JUST FOR YOU, 1952, A
JUST GREAT
JUST IMAGINE, 1930, A
JUST JIM, 1915, A
JUST JOE, 1960, A
JUST LIKE A WOMAN, 1923, A
JUST LIKE A WOMAN, 1939, A
JUST LIKE A WOMAN, 1967, C
JUST LIKE HEAVEN, 1930, A
JUST MARRIED, 1928, A
JUST ME, 1950, A
JUST MY LUCK, 1933, A
JUST MY LUCK, 1936
JUST MY LUCK, 1957, A
JUST OFF BROADWAY, 1924, A
JUST OFF BROADWAY, 1929, A
JUST OFF BROADWAY, 1942, A
JUST ONCE MORE, 1963, O
JUST ONE MORE
JUST OUT OF COLLEGE, 1921, A
JUST OUT OF REACH, 1979, C
JUST OUTSIDE THE DOOR, 1921
JUST PALS, 1920
JUST PLAIN FOLKS, 1925
JUST SMITH
JUST SQAW, 1919
JUST SUPPOSE, 1926, A
JUST SYLVIA, 1918, A
JUST TELL ME WHAT YOU WANT, 1980, C
JUST TELL ME YOU LOVE ME, 1979
JUST THE TWO OF US, 1975
JUST THE WAY YOU ARE, 1984, C
JUST THIS ONCE, 1952, A
JUST TO BE LOVED
JUST TONY, 1922, A
JUST TRAVELIN', 1927
JUST WILLIAM, 1939, AA
JUST WILLIAM'S LUCK, 1948, A
JUST YOU AND ME, KID, 1979, C
JUSTE AVANT LA NUIT
JUSTICE, 1914
JUSTICE, 1914, A
JUSTICE, 1917
JUSTICE CAIN
JUSTICE D'ABORD, 1921
JUSTICE FOR SALE
JUSTICE OF THE FAR NORTH, 1925, A
JUSTICE OF THE RANGE, 1935, A
JUSTICE TAKES A HOLIDAY, 1933, A
JUSTINE, 1969, C
JUSTINE, 1969, O
JUVENILE COURT, 1938, A
JUVENILE JUNGLE, 1958, A
JUVENTUD A LA IMTEMPERIE

-K-

K—THE UNKNOWN, 1924, A
KADOYNG, 1974, AAA
KAGEMUSHA, 1980, C
KAGI
KAHUNA!, 1981
KAIDAN
KAIJU DAISENSO
KAIJU SOSHINGEKI
KAISER'S FINISH, THE, 1918, A
KAISER'S SHADOW, THE, 1918, A
KAISER, BEAST OF BERLIN, THE, 1918, A
KAITEI GUNKA
KAJA, UBIT CU TE
KAJIKKO
KALEIDOSCOPE, 1966, A-C
KALIA MARDAN, 1919

KAMIGAMI NO FUKAKI YOKUBO
KAMIKAZE '89, 1983, O
KAMILLA, 1984, A-C
KAMOURASKA, 1973, O
KANAL, 1961, C
KANCHENJUNGHA, 1966, A
KANGAROO, 1952, A
KANGAROO KID, THE, 1950, A
KANGAROO, THE, 1914
KANOJO
KANSAN, THE, 1943, A
KANSAS CITY BOMBER, 1972, O
KANSAS CITY CONFIDENTIAL, 1952, C-O
KANSAS CITY KITTY, 1944, A
KANSAS CITY PRINCESS, 1934, A
KANSAS CYCLONE, 1941, A
KANSAS PACIFIC, 1953, A
KANSAS RAIDERS, 1950, A
KANSAS TERRITORY, 1952, A
KANSAS TERRORS, THE, 1939, A
KAPHETZOU
KAPITANLEUTENANT PRIEN—DER STIER VON
   SCAPA FLOW
KAPO, 1964, O
KARAMAZOV, 1931, C
KARAMI-AI
KARATE KID, THE, 1984, A-C
KARATE KILLERS, THE, 1967
KARATE, THE HAND OF DEATH, 1961, C
KARE JOHN
KAREN, THE LOVEMAKER, 1970, O
KARIN, INGMAR'S DAUGHTER, 1920
KARL XII
KARMA, 1933, A
KATE PLUS TEN, 1938, A
KATERINA IZMAILOVA, 1969, A
KATHLEEN, 1938, A
KATHLEEN, 1941, AAA
KATHLEEN MAVOUREEN, 1938
KATHLEEN MAVOURNEEN, 1919, A
KATHLEEN MAVOURNEEN, 1930, A
KATHY O', 1958, A
KATHY'S LOVE AFFAIR
KATIA
KATIE DID IT, 1951, A
KATINA
KATKA'S REINETTE APPLES, 1926
KATOK I SKRIPKA
KATORGA, 1928
KAWAITA MIZUUMI
KAYA, I'LL KILL YOU, 1969, A
KAZABLAN, 1974, A
KAZAN, 1921
KAZAN, 1949, AA
KEAN, 1924
KEAN—THE MADNESS OF GENIUS
KEELER AFFAIR, THE
KEEP 'EM FLYING, 1941, AAA
KEEP 'EM ROLLING, 1934, A
KEEP 'EM SLUGGING, 1943, AA
KEEP FIT, 1937, A
KEEP GOING, 1926
KEEP HIM ALIVE
KEEP IT CLEAN, 1956, A
KEEP IT COOL
KEEP IT QUIET, 1934, A
KEEP IT UP, JACK!, 1975
KEEP MOVING, 1915, A
KEEP MY GRAVE OPEN, 1980, O
KEEP OFF! KEEP OFF!, 1975
KEEP PUNCHING, 1939
KEEP SMILING, 1925, A
KEEP SMILING, 1938, A
KEEP SMILING, 1938
KEEP TO THE RIGHT, 1920
KEEP YOUR POWDER DRY, 1945, A
KEEP YOUR SEATS PLEASE, 1936, A
KEEP, THE, 1983, O
KEEPER OF THE BEES, 1935, A
KEEPER OF THE BEES, 1947, A
KEEPER OF THE BEES, THE, 1925
KEEPER OF THE DOOR, 1919, A
KEEPER OF THE FLAME, 1942, A
KEEPER, THE, 1976, A
KEEPERS OF YOUTH, 1931, A
KEEPING COMPANY, 1941, A
KEEPING ON, 1981
KEEPING UP WITH LIZZIE, 1921, A
KEITH OF THE BORDER, 1918
KEK BALVANY
KELLY, 1981
KELLY AND ME, 1957, AA
KELLY OF THE SECRET SERVICE, 1936, A
KELLY OF THE U.S.A.
KELLY THE SECOND, 1936, A
KELLY'S HEROES, 1970, C-O
KEMPO SAMURAI
KENNEDY SQUARE, 1916, A
KENNEL MURDER CASE, THE, 1933, A
KENNER, 1969, C
KENNY AND CO., 1976, C
KENT THE FIGHTING MAN, 1916

KENT, THE FIGHTING MAN, 1916, A
KENTUCKIAN, THE, 1955, A
KENTUCKIANS, THE, 1921, A
KENTUCKY, 1938, AA
KENTUCKY BLUE STREAK, 1935, A
KENTUCKY CINDERELLA, A, 1917, A
KENTUCKY COLONEL, THE, 1920
KENTUCKY COURAGE
KENTUCKY DAYS, 1923, A
KENTUCKY DERBY, THE, 1922, A
KENTUCKY FRIED MOVIE, THE, 1977, O
KENTUCKY HANDICAP, 1926, A
KENTUCKY JUBILEE, 1951, A
KENTUCKY KERNELS, 1935, A
KENTUCKY MINSTRELS, 1934, A
KENTUCKY MOONSHINE, 1938, AAA
KENTUCKY PRIDE, 1925
KENTUCKY RIFLE, 1956, A
KENYA—COUNTRY OF TREASURE, 1964
KEPT HUSBANDS, 1931, C
KES, 1970, C
KETTLE CREEK
KETTLES IN THE OZARKS, THE, 1956, AAA
KETTLES ON OLD MACDONALD'S FARM, THE,
   1957, AAA
KETTO GENRYU JIMA
KEY LARGO, 1948, C
KEY MAN, THE, 1957, A
KEY OF THE WORLD, THE, 1918
KEY TO HARMONY, 1935, A
KEY TO POWER, THE, 1918
KEY TO THE CITY, 1950, A
KEY TO YESTERDAY, THE, 1914
KEY WITNESS, 1947, C
KEY WITNESS, 1960, O
KEY, THE, 1934, A
KEY, THE, 1958, O
KEYHOLE, THE, 1933, A
KEYS OF THE KINGDOM, THE, 1944, A
KEYS OF THE RIGHTEOUS, THE, 1918
KEYS, THE, 1917
KHARTOUM, 1966, C
KHYBER PATROL, 1954, A
KIBITZER, THE, 1929, A
KICK BACK, THE, 1922, A
KICK IN, 1917, A
KICK IN, 1922, A
KICK IN, 1931, C
KICK-OFF, THE, 1926, A
KICKING THE MOON AROUND
KID BLUE, 1973, C
KID BOOTS, 1926, A
KID BROTHER, THE, 1927, A
KID CANFIELD THE REFORM GAMBLER, 1922, A
KID COLOSSUS, THE
KID COMES BACK, THE, 1937, A
KID COURAGEOUS, 1935, A
KID DYNAMITE, 1943, AA
KID FOR TWO FARTHINGS, A, 1956, A
KID FROM AMARILLO, THE, 1951, A
KID FROM ARIZONA, THE, 1931, A
KID FROM BOOKLYN, THE, 1946, AA
KID FROM BROKEN GUN, THE, 1952, A
KID FROM CANADA, THE, 1957, AA
KID FROM CLEVELAND, THE, 1949, A
KID FROM GOWER GULCH, THE, 1949, A
KID FROM KANSAS, THE, 1941, C
KID FROM KOKOMO, THE, 1939, A
KID FROM LEFT FIELD, THE, 1953, AAA
KID FROM NOT SO BIG, THE, 1978
KID FROM SANTA FE, THE, 1940, AA
KID FROM SPAIN, THE, 1932, AA
KID FROM TEXAS, THE, 1939, AAA
KID FROM TEXAS, THE, 1950, C
KID GALAHAD, 1937, A-C
KID GALAHAD, 1962, A
KID GLOVE KILLER, 1942, C
KID GLOVES, 1929, C
KID IS CLEVER, THE, 1918
KID MILLIONS, 1934, AAA
KID MONK BARONI, 1952, C
KID NIGHTINGALE, 1939, A
KID RANGER, THE, 1936, A
KID RIDES AGAIN, THE, 1943, A
KID RODELO, 1966, C
KID SISTER, THE, 1927, A
KID SISTER, THE, 1945, A
KID VENGEANCE, 1977, C
KID'S CLEVER, THE, 1929, A
KID'S LAST FIGHT, THE
KID'S LAST RIDE, THE, 1941, A
KID, THE, 1916, A
KID, THE, 1921, AA
KIDCO, 1984, C
KIDDER & KO., 1918
KIDNAP OF MARY LOU, THE
KIDNAPPED, 1917, A
KIDNAPPED, 1938, AAA
KIDNAPPED, 1948, AAA
KIDNAPPED, 1960, AAA
KIDNAPPED, 1971, AA
KIDNAPPED, 1934

KIDNAPPERS, THE, 1964, A
KIDNAPPERS, THE, 1953
KIDNAPPING OF THE PRESIDENT, THE, 1980, O
KIEV COMEDY, A, 1963, C
KIGEKI DAI SHOGEKI
KIKI, 1926, A
KIKI, 1931, A
KIL 1
KILDARE OF STORM, 1918, A
KILL
KILL, 1968, C
KILL A DRAGON, 1967, O
KILL AND GO HIDE
KILL AND KILL AGAIN, 1981, O
KILL BABY KILL, 1966, O
KILL CASTRO
KILL HER GENTLY, 1958, O
KILL KILL KILL, 1972, O
KILL ME TOMORROW, 1958, C
KILL OR BE KILLED, 1950, C
KILL OR BE KILLED, 1967, C
KILL OR BE KILLED, 1980, C
KILL OR CURE, 1962, C
KILL SQUAD, 1982, O
KILL THE GOLDEN GOOSE, 1979
KILL THE UMPIRE, 1950, AA
KILL THEM ALL AND COME BACK ALONE, 1970, O
KILL, THE, 1968, O
KILL, THE, 1973
KILL-JOY, THE, 1917
KILLER APE, 1953, AA
KILLER AT LARGE, 1936, O
KILLER AT LARGE, 1947, O
KILLER BATS
KILLER BEHIND THE MASK, THE
KILLER DILL, 1947, C
KILLER DILLER, 1948
KILLER DINO
KILLER ELITE, THE, 1975, O
KILLER FISH, 1979, O
KILLER FORCE, 1975, O
KILLER GRIZZLY
KILLER INSIDE ME, THE, 1976, O
KILLER IS LOOSE, THE, 1956, O
KILLER LEOPARD, 1954, A
KILLER McCOY, 1947, A
KILLER ON A HORSE
KILLER SHARK, 1950, A
KILLER SHREWS, THE, 1959, C
KILLER THAT STALKED NEW YORK, THE, 1950, O
KILLER WALKS, A, 1952, A
KILLER WITH A LABEL
KILLER'S CAGE
KILLER'S CARNIVAL, 1965
KILLER'S DELIGHT, 1978
KILLER'S KISS, 1955, C
KILLER'S MOON, 1978
KILLER, THE
KILLER, THE
KILLER, THE, 1921, C
KILLERS ARE CHALLENGED
KILLERS FROM KILIMANJARO
KILLERS FROM SPACE, 1954, A
KILLERS OF KILIMANJARO, 1960, A
KILLERS OF THE PRAIRIE
KILLERS OF THE WILD, 1940, AAA
KILLERS THREE, 1968, O
KILLERS, THE, 1946, C
KILLERS, THE, 1964, C-O
KILLERS, THE, 1984, O
KILLING AT OUTPOST ZETA, THE, 1980
KILLING FIELDS, THE, 1984, O
KILLING GAME, THE, 1968, C
KILLING GROUND, THE, 1972
KILLING HEAT, 1984, O
KILLING HOUR, THE, 1982, O
KILLING KIND, THE, 1973, O
KILLING OF A CHINESE BOOKIE, THE, 1976, C
KILLING OF ANGEL STREET, THE, 1983, A
KILLING TOUCH, THE, 1983
KILLING URGE
KILLING, THE, 1956, C
KILLPOINT, 1984, O
KILMENY, 1915, A
KILROY ON DECK
KILROY WAS HERE, 1947, AA
KILTIES THREE, 1918, A
KIM, 1950, AA
KIMBERLEY JIM, 1965, A
KIN FOLK
KIND HEARTS AND CORONETS, 1949, A-C
KIND LADY, 1935, A
KIND LADY, 1951, O
KIND OF LOVING, A, 1962, A-C
KIND STEPMOTHER, 1936, AAA
KINDLED COURAGE, 1923, A
KINDLING, 1915, A
KINDRED OF THE DUST, 1922, A
KINFOLK, 1970, O
KING AND COUNTRY, 1964, C
KING AND FOUR QUEENS, THE, 1956, A
KING AND I, THE, 1956, AAA

KING AND THE CHORUS GIRL, THE, 1937, AA
KING ARTHUR WAS A GENTLEMAN, 1942, A
KING BLANK, 1983, O
KING CHARLES, 1913, A
KING COBRA
KING COWBOY, 1928
KING CREOLE, 1958, A
KING DINOSAUR, 1955, AA
KING FOR A NIGHT, 1933, C
KING FRAT, 1979
KING IN NEW YORK, A, 1957, A
KING IN SHADOW, 1961, A
KING KELLY OF THE U.S.A, 1934, A
KING KONG, 1933, A-C
KING KONG, 1976, C-O
KING KONG ESCAPES, 1968, C
KING KONG VERSUS GODZILLA, 1963, C
KING KONG'S COUNTERATTACK
KING LEAR, 1916, A
KING LEAR, 1971, C
KING MONSTER, 1977
KING MURDER, THE, 1932, 0
KING OEDIPUS
KING OF AFRICA
KING OF ALCATRAZ, 1938, C
KING OF BURLESQUE, 1936, A
KING OF CHINATOWN, 1939, O
KING OF COMEDY, THE, 1983, C
KING OF CRIME, THE, 1914
KING OF DIAMONDS, THE, 1918, A
KING OF DODGE CITY, 1941, A
KING OF GAMBLERS, 1937, A
KING OF HEARTS, 1936, AA
KING OF HEARTS, 1967, C
KING OF HOCKEY, 1936, AA
KING OF KINGS, 1961, AA
KING OF KINGS, THE, 1927, AA
KING OF MARVIN GARDENS, THE, 1972, C-O
KING OF PARIS, THE, 1934, A
KING OF THE ALCATRAZ
KING OF THE ARENA, 1933, A
KING OF THE BANDITS, 1948, A
KING OF THE BULLWHIP, 1950, C
KING OF THE CASTLE, 1925, A
KING OF THE CASTLE, 1936, A
KING OF THE CORAL SEA, 1956, C
KING OF THE COWBOYS, 1943, AAA
KING OF THE DAMNED, 1936, C
KING OF THE GAMBLERS, 1948, A
KING OF THE GRIZZLIES, 1970, AAA
KING OF THE GYPSIES, 1978, O
KING OF THE HERD, 1927, A
KING OF THE ICE RINK
KING OF THE JUNGLE, 1933, A
KING OF THE JUNGLELAND
KING OF THE KHYBER RIFLES, 1953, A
KING OF THE KHYBER RIFLES, 1929
KING OF THE LUMBERJACKS, 1940, A
KING OF THE MOUNTAIN, 1981, O
KING OF THE MOUNTAIN, 1964
KING OF THE NEWSBOYS, 1938, A
KING OF THE PACK, 1926
KING OF THE PECOS, 1936, A
KING OF THE PEOPLE, A, 1917
KING OF THE RITZ, 1933, A
KING OF THE ROARING TWENTIES—THE STORY OF
   ARNOLD ROTHSTEIN, 1961, C
KING OF THE RODEO, 1929, A
KING OF THE ROYAL MOUNTED, 1936, A
KING OF THE SADDLE, 1926, A
KING OF THE SIERRAS, 1938, A
KING OF THE STALLIONS, 1942, A
KING OF THE TURF, 1939, A
KING OF THE TURF, THE, 1926, A
KING OF THE UNDERWORLD, 1939, A-C
KING OF THE UNDERWORLD, 1952, A
KING OF THE WILD
KING OF THE WILD HORSES, 1947, A
KING OF THE WILD HORSES, THE, 1924, A
KING OF THE WILD HORSES, THE, 1934, A
KING OF THE WILD STALLIONS, 1959, AAA
KING OF THE ZOMBIES, 1941, C
KING ON MAIN STREET, THE, 1925
KING RAT, 1965, O
KING RICHARD AND THE CRUSADERS, 1954, A
KING SOLOMON OF BROADWAY, 1935, A
KING SOLOMON'S MINES, 1937, A
KING SOLOMON'S MINES, 1950, A
KING SOLOMON'S TREASURE, 1978, A
KING SPRUCE, 1920, A
KING STEPS OUT, THE, 1936, A
KING TUT-ANKH-AMEN'S EIGHTH WIFE, 1923, A
KING'S CREEK LAW, 1923, A
KING'S CUP, THE, 1933, A
KING'S DAUGHTER, THE, 1916, A
KING'S GAME, THE, 1916, A
KING'S HIGHWAY, THE, 1927
KING'S JESTER, THE, 1947, O
KING'S OUTCAST, THE
KING'S PIRATE, 1967, A
KING'S RHAPSODY, 1955, A
KING'S ROMANCE, THE

KING'S ROW, 1942, C-O
KING'S THIEF, THE, 1955, A
KING'S VACATION, THE, 1933, A
KING, MURRAY, 1969, O
KING, QUEEN, JOKER, 1921, A
KING, QUEEN, KNAVE, 1972, O
KING, THE
KINGDOM OF HUMAN HEARTS, THE, 1921
KINGDOM OF LOVE, THE, 1918, A
KINGDOM OF THE SPIDERS, 1977, C
KINGDOM OF TWILIGHT, THE, 1929
KINGDOM OF YOUTH, THE, 1918
KINGDOM WITHIN, THE, 1922, A
KINGFISH CAPER, THE, 1976, A
KINGFISHER CAPER, THE
KINGFISHER'S ROOST, THE, 1922, A
KINGFISHER, THE, 1982
KINGS AND DESPERATE MEN, 1984, C
KINGS GO FORTH, 1958, A
KINGS OF THE HILL, 1976
KINGS OF THE ROAD, 1976, C
KINGS OF THE SUN, 1963, O
KINKAID, GAMBLER, 1916, A
KINKY COACHES & THE POM POM PUSSYCATS,
   THE, 1981
KINO, THE PADRE ON HORSEBACK, 1977
KINSMAN, THE, 1919
KIPPERBANG, 1984, A-C
KIPPS
KIPPS, 1921, A
KIRA KIRALINA, 1927
KIRI NI MUSEBU YORU
KIRLIAN WITNESS, THE, 1978, O
KIRU
KISENGA, MAN OF AFRICA, 1952, C
KISMET, 1916
KISMET, 1920, A
KISMET, 1930, A
KISMET, 1944, A
KISMET, 1955, A
KISS AND KILL
KISS AND MAKE UP, 1934, A
KISS AND TELL, 1945, A
KISS BARRIER, THE, 1925, A
KISS BEFORE DYING, A, 1956, A
KISS BEFORE THE MIRROR, THE, 1933, A
KISS DADDY GOODBYE, 1981
KISS FOR CINDERELLA, A, 1926, A
KISS FOR CORLISS, A, 1949, A
KISS FOR SUSIE, A, 1917, A
KISS FROM EDDIE, A
KISS HER GOODBYE, 1959
KISS IN A TAXI, A, 1927
KISS IN THE DARK, A, 1925, A
KISS IN THE DARK, A, 1949, A
KISS IN TIME, A, 1921, A
KISS ME
KISS ME AGAIN, 1925, A
KISS ME AGAIN, 1931, A
KISS ME DEADLY, 1955, O
KISS ME GOODBYE, 1935, A
KISS ME GOODBYE, 1982, C
KISS ME KATE, 1953, AA
KISS ME, SERGEANT, 1930, A
KISS ME, STUPID, 1964, C
KISS MY BUTTERFLY
KISS MY GRITS, 1982
KISS OF DEATH, 1916
KISS OF DEATH, 1947, C-O
KISS OF EVIL, 1963, C
KISS OF FIRE, 1955, A
KISS OF FIRE, THE, 1940, A
KISS OF HATE, THE, 1916
KISS OF THE TARANTULA, 1975, O
KISS OF THE VAMPIRE, THE
KISS OR KILL, 1918
KISS THE BLOOD OFF MY HANDS, 1948, C-O
KISS THE BOYS GOODBYE, 1941, A
KISS THE BRIDE GOODBYE, 1944, A
KISS THE GIRLS AND MAKE THEM DIE, 1967, O
KISS THE GIRLS AND SEE THEM DIE, 1968
KISS THE OTHER SHEIK, 1968, C
KISS THEM FOR ME, 1957, A
KISS TOMORROW GOODBYE, 1950, C-O
KISS, THE, 1916, A
KISS, THE, 1921
KISS, THE, 1929, A
KISSED, 1922, A
KISSES, 1922, A
KISSES FOR BREAKFAST, 1941, A
KISSES FOR MY PRESIDENT, 1964, A
KISSES FOR THE PRESIDENT
KISSIN' COUSINS, 1964, A
KISSING BANDIT, THE, 1948, A
KISSING CUP, 1913
KISSING CUP'S RACE, 1920
KISSING CUP'S RACE, 1920, A
KISSING CUP'S RACE, 1930, A
KIT CARSON, 1928, A
KIT CARSON, 1940, A
KIT CARSON OVER THE GREAT DIVIDE, 1925
KITCHEN, THE, 1961, A

LA CHIENNE, 1975, C-O
LA CHINOISE, 1967, C-O
LA CHUTE DE LA MAISON USHER
LA CIBLE, 1925
LA CIGARETTE, 1919
LA CINEMA AU SERVICE DE L'HISTOIRE, 1927
LA CINTURA DI CASTITA
LA CIQUILLE ET LE CLERGYMAN, 1928
LA CITE FOUDROYEE, 1924
LA CITTA PRIGIONIERA
LA CITTA SI DIFENDE
LA CLE DE VOUTE, 1925
LA COLLECTIONNEUSE, 1971, C-O
LA CONGA NIGHTS, 1940, A
LA CONGIUNTURA
LA CORDE AU COU, 1926
LA COURSE AU FLAMBEAU, 1925
LA CROISADE, 1920
LA CROIX DES VIVANTS
LA CUCARACHA, 1961, A
LA DAME MASQUEE, 1924
LA DANSEUSE ORCHIDEE, 1928
LA DANSEUSE VOILEE, 1917
LA DECADE PRODIGIEUSE
LA DENTELLIERE
LA DETTE, 1920
LA DETTE DE SANG, 1923
LA DISTANCE, 1918
LA DIVINE CROISIERE, 1928
LA DIXIEME SYMPHONIE, 1918
LA DOLCE VITA, 1961, C
LA DOUBLE EXISTENCE DE LORD SAMSEY, 1924
LA DOULEUR, 1925
LA DUBARRY, 1914
LA FABULEUSE AVENTURE DE MARCO POLO
LA FAUTE D'ODETTE MARECHAL, 1920
LA FAUTE DE MONIQUE, 1928
LA FAUTEUIL 47, 1926
LA FEE DES NEIGES, 1920
LA FEMME AUX BOTTES ROUGES
LA FEMME AUX DEUX VISAGES, 1920
LA FEMME D'A COTE
LA FEMME DE MON POTE
LA FEMME DE NULLE PART, 1922
LA FEMME DU BOULANGERS
LA FEMME ET LE PANTIN, 1929
LA FEMME INCONNUE, 1923
LA FEMME INFIDELE, 1969, C
LA FEMME NUE
LA FEMME REVEE, 1929
LA FEMME SU VOISIN, 1929
LA FERME DU PENDU, 1946, C
LA FETE A HENRIETTE
LA FETE ESPAGNOLE, 1919
LA FEU FOLLET
LA FIANCEE DU DISPARU, 1921
LA FILLE BIEN GARDEE, 1924
LA FILLE DE L'EAU, 1924
LA FILLE DE MATA HARI, n(SE
LA FILLE DE PUISATIER
LA FILLE DES CHIFFONNIERS, 1922
LA FILLE DU DIABLE
LA FILLE DU PEUPLE, 1920
LA FILLE SANS VOILE
LA FIN DE MONTE, 1927
LA FIN DU MONDE
LA FLAMBEE DE REVES, 1924
LA FLAMME, 1925
LA FLAMME CACHE, 1918
LA FLUTE A SIX SCHTROUMPFS
LA FOLIE DES VAILLANTS, 1925
LA FOLIE DU DOUTE, 1923
LA FOLLE DES GRANDEURS
LA FONTAINE DES AMOURS, 1924
LA FORET QUI TUE, 1924
LA FORTUNA DI ESSERE DONNA
LA FUGA, 1966, O
LA FUGITIVE, 1918
LA FUGUE DE LILY, 1917
LA GALERIE DES MONSTRES, 1924
LA GLU, 1927
LA GOSSELINE, 1923
LA GOUTTE DE SANG, 1924
LA GRANDE BOUFFE, 1973, C-O
LA GRANDE BOURGEOISE, 1977, C
LA GRANDE ILLUSION
LA GRANDE PASSION, 1928
LA GUERRE EST FINIE, 1967, C-O
LA GUITARE ET LA JAZZ BAND, 1922
LA HABANERA, 1937, A
LA HIJA DEL ENGANO
LA HURLE, 1921
LA JALOUSIE DU BARBOUILLE, 1929
LA JOVEN
LA JUSTICIERE, 1925
LA KERMESSE HEROIQUE
LA LA LUCILLE, 1920
LA LAMA NEL CORPO
LA LEGENDE DE SOEUR BEATRIX, 1923
LA LINEA DEL CIELO
LA LUNE DANS LE CANIVEAU
LA LUTTE POUR LA VIE, 1920

LA MADONE DES SLEEPINGS, 1928
LA MAIN QUI A TUE, 1924
LA MAISON D'ARGILE, 1918
LA MAISON DU MALTAIS, 1927
LA MAISON DU SOLEIL, 1929
LA MAISON VIDE, 1921
LA MALDICION DE LA MOMIA AZTECA
LA MAMAM ET LA PUTAIN
LA MANDARINE
LA MANDRAGOLA
LA MARCA DEL MUERTO
LA MARCHAND DE PLAISIR, 1923
LA MARCHE DU DESTIN, 1924
LA MARCHE NUPTIALE, 1929
LA MARCHE TRIOMPHALE, 1916
LA MARIE DU PORT, 1951, C
LA MARIEE ETAIT EN NOIR
LA MARSEILLAISE, 1920
LA MARSEILLAISE, 1938, A
LA MARTYRE DE STE. MAXENCE, 1927
LA MASCOTTE DES POILUS, 1918
LA MATERNELLE, 1925
LA MATERNELLE, 1933, A
LA MEILLEURE MAITRESSE, 1929
LA MERVELILLEUSE VIE DE JEANNE D'ARC, 1929
LA MONTEE VERS L'ACROPOLE, 1920
LA MORT DU SOLEIL, 1922
LA MORT EN CE JARDIN
LA MORTADELLA
LA MORTE EN DIRECT
LA MORTE RISALE A IERI SERA
LA MORTE VIENE DALLA SPAZIO
LA MUERTA EN EST JARDIN
LA NAVE DE LOS MONSTRUOS, 1959, C-O
LA NEUVAINE DE COLETTE, 1925
LA NIEGE SUR LE PAS, 1924
LA NOTTE, 1961, C-O
LA NOTTE BRAVA, 1962, O
LA NOUVELLE ANTIGONE, 1916
LA NUIT AMERICAINE
LA NUIT DE LA REVANCHE, 1924
LA NUIT DE SAINT JEAN, 1922
LA NUIT DE VARENNES, 1983, O
LA NUIT DES GENERAUX
LA NUIT DU 11 SEPTEMBRE, 1922
LA NUIT DU 13, 1921
LA NUIT EST A NOUS, 1927
LA NUIT ROUGE, 1924
LA P'TITE DU SIXIEME, 1917
LA PAIX CHEZ SOI, 1921
LA PARISIENNE, 1958, C-O
LA PART DE L'OMBRE
LA PASSANTE, 1983, C
LA PEAU DOUCE
LA PENTE, 1928
LA PERE GORIOT, 1921
LA PERMISSION
LA PETIT SIRENE, 1984, C
LA PETITE CAFE
LA PETITE CHOCOLATIERE, 1927
LA PLANETE SAUVAGE
LA PORTEUSE DE PAIN, 1923
LA POSSESSION, 1929
LA POUPEE
LA POUPEE, 1920
LA POUPEE, 1920, A
LA PREUVE, 1921
LA PRINCESSE AUX CLOWNS, 1925
LA PRINCESSE MANDANE, 1928
LA PRISE DE POUVOIR PAR LOUIS XIV
LA PRISONNIERE, 1969, O
LA PROIE, 1917
LA PROIE DU VENT, 1927
LA PROMISE DE L'AUBE
LA PROVINCIALE
LA QUESTION
LA RAFALE, 1920
LA RESIDENCIA
LA RESURRECTION DU BOUIF, 1922
LA REVANCHE DU MAUDIT, 1929
LA RIPOSTE, 1922
LA RONDE, 1954, O
LA RONDE INFERNALE, 1927
LA ROSE ESCORCHEE
LA ROUE, 1923
LA ROUTE DE DEVOIR, 1918
LA ROUTE EST BELLE
LA RUE DES AMOURS FACILES
LA RUE DU PAVE D'AMOUR, 1923
LA RUSE, 1922
LA SIGNORA SENZA CAMELIE
LA SIN-VENTURA, 1922
LA SIRENE DE PIERRE, 1922
LA SIRENE DES TROPIQUES, 1928
LA SIRENE DU MISSISSIPPI
LA STRADA, 1956, A-C
LA STRADA PER FORT ALAMO
LA SULTANE DE L'AMOUR, 1919
LA SUPREME EPOEE, 1919
LA SYMPHONIE PASTORALE
LA SYMPHONIE PATHETIQUE, 1929
LA TENDA ROSSA

LA TENTATION, 1929
LA TERRA TREMA, 1947, A
LA TERRAZA
LA TERRE, 1921
LA TERRE DU DIABLE, 1921
LA TERRE PROMISE, 1925
LA TOSCA, 1918
LA TRAVIATA, 1968, A
LA TRAVIATA, 1982, A
LA TRUITE
LA VACCA E IL PRIGIONIERO
LA VACHE ET LE PRISONNIER
LA VALLEE DES PHARAOHS
LA VENGANZA DEL SEXO
LA VENGEANCE DE MALLET, 1920
LA VERITE, 1922
LA VESTALE DU GANGE, 1927
LA VIA LATTEA
LA VIACCIA, 1962, C-O
LA VICTOIRE EN CHANTANT
LA VIE CONTINUE, 1982, A
VIE D'UNE REINE, 1917
LA VIE DE BOHEME, 1916
LA VIE DE CHATEAU, 1967, A
LA VIE DEVANT SOI
LA VIE EST UN ROMAN
LA VIE MIRACULEIUSE DE THERESE MARTIN, 1929
LA VIERGE FOLLE, 1929
LA VIOLENZA E L'MORE
LA VIRGEN DE LA CARIDAD, 1930
LA VISITA, 1966, O
LA VIVANTE EPINGLE, 1921
LA VOGLIA MATTA
LA VOIE LACTEE
LA VOIX DE LA MER, 1921
LA VOYANTE, 1923
LA ZOME DE LA MORT, 1917
LABBRA ROSSE
LABORATORY, 1980
LABOUR LEADER, THE, 1917, A
LABURNUM GROVE, 1936, A
LABYRINTH
LABYRINTH, THE, 1915
LACE, 1928
LACEMAKER, THE, 1977, O
LACKEY AND THE LADY, THE, 1919
LACOMBE, LUCIEN, 1974, O
LAD AND THE LION, THE, 1917
LAD FROM OUR TOWN, 1941, A
LAD, THE, 1935, A
LAD: A DOG, 1962, AAA
LADDER JINX, THE, 1922
LADDER OF LIES, THE, 1920
LADDIE, 1920
LADDIE, 1926
LADDIE, 1935, AAA
LADDIE, 1940, AAA
LADDIE BE GOOD, 1928, A
LADIES AND GENTLEMEN, THE FABULOUS STAINS,
 1982, O
LADIES AT EASE, 1927, A
LADIES AT PLAY, 1926, A
LADIES BEWARE, 1927
LADIES COURAGEOUS, 1944, A
LADIES CRAVE EXCITEMENT, 1935, A
LADIES IN DISTRESS, 1938, A
LADIES IN LOVE, 1930, A
LADIES IN LOVE, 1936, A
LADIES IN RETIREMENT, 1941, C
LADIES IN WASHINGTON
LADIES LOVE BRUTES, 1930, A
LADIES LOVE DANGER, 1935, A
LADIES MAN, THE, 1961, A
LADIES MUST DRESS, 1927, A
LADIES MUST LIVE, 1921
LADIES MUST LIVE, 1940, A
LADIES MUST LOVE, 1933, A
LADIES MUST PLAY, 1930, A
LADIES OF LEISURE, 1926
LADIES OF LEISURE, 1930, A-C
LADIES OF THE BIG HOUSE, 1932, A
LADIES OF THE CHORUS, 1948, A
LADIES OF THE JURY, 1932, A
LADIES OF THE MOB
LADIES OF THE MOB, 1928, A
LADIES OF THE NIGHT CLUB, 1928
LADIES OF THE PARK, 1964, C
LADIES OF WASHINGTON, 1944, A
LADIES SHOULD LISTEN, 1934, A
LADIES THEY TALK ABOUT, 1933, A
LADIES TO BOARD, 1924, A
LADIES WHO DO, 1964, A
LADIES' DAY, 1943, A
LADIES' MAN, 1931, C
LADIES' MAN, 1947, A
LADIES' NIGHT IN A TURKISH BATH, 1928
LADS OF THE VILLAGE, THE, 1919
LADY AND GENT, 1932, A
LADY AND THE BANDIT, THE, 1951, A
LADY AND THE BEARD, THE, 1931
LADY AND THE BURGLAR, THE, 1915
LADY AND THE DOCTOR, THE

LADY AND THE MOB, THE, 1939, A
LADY AND THE MONSTER, THE, 1944, C
LADY AND THE OUTLAW, THE
LADY AND THE TRAMP, 1955, AAA
LADY AT MIDNIGHT, 1948, A
LADY AUDLEY'S SECRET, 1920
LADY BARNACLE, 1917
LADY BE CAREFUL, 1936, A
LADY BE GAY
LADY BE GOOD, 1928, A
LADY BE GOOD, 1941, A
LADY BEHAVE, 1937, A
LADY BEWARE
LADY BODYGUARD, 1942, A
LADY BY CHOICE, 1934, A
LADY CAROLINE LAMB, 1972, A
LADY CHASER, 1946, A
LADY CHATTERLEY'S LOVER, 1959, A
LADY CHATTERLEY'S LOVER, 1981, A
LADY CHATTERLY VS. FANNY HILL, 1980
LADY CLARE, THE, 1919
LADY COCOA, 1975
LADY CONFESSES, THE, 1945, A
LADY CONSENTS, THE, 1936, A
LADY CRAVED EXCITEMENT, THE, 1950, A
LADY DANCES, THE
LADY DOCTOR, THE, 1963, C
LADY DRACULA, THE, 1974, O
LADY ESCAPES, THE, 1937, A
LADY EVE, THE, 1941, A
LADY FIGHTS BACK, 1937, A
LADY FOR A DAY, 1933, A
LADY FOR A NIGHT, 1941, A
LADY FRANKENSTEIN, 1971, O
LADY FREDERICK
LADY FROM BOSTON, THE
LADY FROM CHEYENNE, 1941, A
LADY FROM CHUNGKING, 1943, A
LADY FROM HELL, THE, 1926, A
LADY FROM LISBON, 1942, A
LADY FROM LONGACRE, THE, 1921
LADY FROM LOUISIANA, 1941, A
LADY FROM NOWHERE, 1931, A
LADY FROM NOWHERE, 1936, A
LADY FROM SHANGHAI, THE, 1948, C
LADY FROM TEXAS, THE, 1951, A
LADY FROM THE SEA, THE, 1929, A
LADY GAMBLES, THE, 1949, A
LADY GANGSTER, 1942, A
LADY GENERAL, THE, 1965, A
LADY GODIVA, 1955, A
LADY GODIVA RIDES AGAIN, 1955, A
LADY GREY, 1980, O
LADY HAMILTON
LADY HAMILTON, 1969, O
LADY HAS PLANS, THE, 1942, A
LADY ICE, 1973, CA
LADY IN A CAGE, 1964, O
LADY IN A JAM, 1942, A
LADY IN CEMENT, 1968, O
LADY IN DANGER, 1934, A
LADY IN DISTRESS, 1942, A
LADY IN ERMINE, THE, 1927
LADY IN LOVE, A, 1920, A
LADY IN QUESTION, THE, 1940, A
LADY IN RED, THE, 1979, O
LADY IN SCARLET, THE, 1935, A
LADY IN THE CAR WITH GLASSES AND A GUN,
   THE, 1970, O
LADY IN THE DARK, 1944, A
LADY IN THE DEATH HOUSE, 1944, A
LADY IN THE FOG
LADY IN THE IRON MASK, 1952, A
LADY IN THE LAKE, 1947, A
LADY IN THE LIBRARY, THE, 1917
LADY IN THE MORGUE, 1938, A
LADY IS A SQUARE, THE, 1959, A
LADY IS FICKLE, THE, 1948, A
LADY IS WILLING, THE, 1934, A
LADY IS WILLING, THE, 1942, A
LADY JANE GREY, 1936, A
LADY JENNIFER, 1915
LADY KILLER, 1933, A
LADY KILLERS, THE
LADY L, 1965, C
LADY LIBERTY, 1972, C
LADY LIES, THE, 1929, A
LADY LUCK, 1936, A
LADY LUCK, 1946, A
LADY MISLAID, A, 1958, A
LADY NOGGS-PEERESS, 1929, A
LADY OBJECTS, THE, 1938, A
LADY OF BURLESQUE, 1943, C
LADY OF CHANCE, A, 1928, A
LADY OF DECEIT
LADY OF MONZA, THE, 1970, O
LADY OF MYSTERY
LADY OF QUALITY, A, 1913
LADY OF QUALITY, A, 1924
LADY OF RED BUTTE, THE, 1919
LADY OF SCANDAL, THE, 1930, A
LADY OF SECRETS, 1936, A

LADY OF THE BOULEVARDS
LADY OF THE DUGOUT, 1918
LADY OF THE HAREM, THE, 1926
LADY OF THE LAKE, THE, 1928, A
LADY OF THE NIGHT, 1925, A
LADY OF THE PAVEMENTS, 1929, A
LADY OF THE PHOTOGRAPH, THE, 1917
LADY OF THE ROSE
LADY OF THE SHADOWS
LADY OF THE TROPICS, 1939, C
LADY OF VENGEANCE, 1957, A
LADY ON A TRAIN, 1945, A
LADY ON THE TRACKS, THE, 1968, A
LADY OSCAR, 1979, C
LADY OWNER, THE, 1923
LADY PAYS OFF, THE, 1951, A
LADY POSSESSED, 1952, A
LADY RAFFLES, 1928
LADY REFUSES, THE, 1931, A
LADY REPORTER
LADY ROBINHOOD, 1925, A
LADY ROSE'S DAUGHTER, 1920
LADY SAYS NO, THE, 1951, A
LADY SCARFACE, 1941, A
LADY SINGS THE BLUES, 1972, O
LADY SURRENDERS, A, 1930, A
LADY SURRENDERS, A, 1947, A
LADY TAKES A CHANCE, A, 1943, A
LADY TAKES A FLYER, THE, 1958, A
LADY TAKES A SAILOR, THE, 1949, A
LADY TETLEY'S DEGREE, 1920
LADY TO LOVE, A, 1930, A
LADY TUBBS, 1935, A
LADY VANISHES, THE, 1938, A
LADY VANISHES, THE, 1980, C
LADY WANTS MINK, THE, 1953, A
LADY WHO DARED, THE, 1931, A
LADY WHO LIED, THE, 1925
LADY WINDERMERE'S FAN, 1916
LADY WINDERMERE'S FAN, 1925, A
LADY WINDERMERE'S FAN
LADY WITH A LAMP, THE, 1951, A
LADY WITH A PAST, 1932, A
LADY WITH RED HAIR, 1940, A
LADY WITH THE DOG, THE, 1962, A
LADY WITH THE LAMP, THE
LADY WITHOUT CAMELLIAS, THE, 1981, C-O
LADY WITHOUT PASSPORT, A, 1950, A
LADY'S FROM KENTUCKY, THE, 1939, A
LADY'S MORALS, A, 1930, A
LADY'S NAME, A, 1918
LADY'S PROFESSION, A, 1933, A
LADY, LET'S DANCE, 1944, A
LADY, STAY DEAD, 1982, O
LADY, THE, 1925
LADYBIRD, THE, 1927, A
LADYBUG, LADYBUG, 1963, C
LADYFINGERS, 1921
LADYKILLERS, THE, 1956, A-C
LAFAYETTE, 1963, AA
LAFAYETTE ESCADRILLE, 1958, A
LAFAYETTE, WE COME, 1918
LAFFIN' FOOL, THE, 1927, A
LAHOMA, 1920
LAILA
LAIR OF THE WOLF, THE, 1917
LAKE OF DRACULA, 1973, O
LAKE PLACID SERENADE, 1944, A
LAKE, THE, 1970, O
LAMA NEL CORPO, LA
LAMB AND THE LION, THE, 1919
LAMB, THE, 1915, A
LAMBETH WALK, THE, 1940, A
LAMENT OF THE PATH, THE
LAMP IN ASSASSIN MEWS, THE, 1962, A
LAMP IN THE DESERT, 1922
LAMP OF DESTINY, 1919
LAMP STILL BURNS, THE, 1943, A
LAMPLIGHTER, THE, 1921, A
LANCASHIRE LASS, A, 1915
LANCASHIRE LUCK, 1937, A
LANCELOT AND GUINEVERE
LANCELOT DU LAC
LANCELOT OF THE LAKE, 1975, C
LANCER SPY, 1937, A
LAND AND THE LAW
LAND BEYOND THE LAW, 1937, A
LAND BEYOND THE LAW, THE, 1927
LAND JUST OVER YONDER, THE, 1916
LAND O' LIZARDS, 1916
LAND OF FIGHTING MEN, 1938, A
LAND OF FURY, 1955, A
LAND OF HOPE AND GLORY, 1927, A
LAND OF HOPE, THE, 1921
LAND OF HUNTED MEN, 1943, A
LAND OF JAZZ, THE, 1920
LAND OF LONG SHADOWS, 1917
LAND OF MISSING MEN, THE, 1930, A
LAND OF MY FATHERS, 1921
LAND OF MYSTERY, THE, 1920
LAND OF NO RETURN, THE, 1981, A
LAND OF OZ

LAND OF PROMISE, THE, 1917
LAND OF SIX GUNS, 1940
LAND OF THE LAWLESS, 1927
LAND OF THE LAWLESS, 1947, A
LAND OF THE MINOTAUR, 1976, O
LAND OF THE MISSING MEN
LAND OF THE OPEN RANGE, 1941, A
LAND OF THE OUTLAWS, 1944, A
LAND OF THE PHARAOHS, 1955, A-C
LAND OF THE SILVER FOX, 1928, AA
LAND OF THE SIX GUNS, 1940, A
LAND OF WANTED MEN, 1932, A
LAND RAIDERS, 1969, C
LAND THAT TIME FORGOT, THE, 1975, A
LAND UNKNOWN, THE, 1957, A
LAND WE LOVE, THE
LAND WITHOUT MUSIC
LANDFALL, 1953, A
LANDLOPER, THE, 1918
LANDLORD, THE, 1970, C
LANDON'S LEGACY, 1916
LANDRU, 1963, O
LANDRUSH, 1946, A
LANDSLIDE, 1937, A
LANE THAT HAD NO TURNING, THE, 1922
LANGTAN
LARAMIE, 1949, A
LARAMIE KID, THE, 1935
LARAMIE MOUNTAINS, 1952, A
LARAMIE TRAIL, THE, 1944, A
LARCENY, 1948, A-C
LARCENY IN HER HEART, 1946, A
LARCENY LANE
LARCENY ON THE AIR, 1937, A
LARCENY STREET, 1941, A
LARCENY WITH MUSIC, 1943, A
LARCENY, INC., 1942, A
LARGE ROPE, THE
LARGE ROPE, THE, 1953, A
LARIAT KID, THE, 1929, A
LARIATS AND SIXSHOOTERS, 1931
LARMES DE CROCODILE, 1916
LAS CUATRO VERDADES
LAS RATAS NO DUERMEN DE NOCHE, 1974, O
LAS VEGAS 500 MILLIONS
LAS VEGAS FREE-FOR-ALL, 1968, C
LAS VEGAS HILLBILLYS, 1966, A
LAS VEGAS LADY, 1976, A
LAS VEGAS NIGHTS, 1941, A
LAS VEGAS SHAKEDOWN, 1955, A
LAS VEGAS STORY, THE, 1952, A
LASCA, 1919
LASCA OF THE RIO GRANDE, 1931, A
LASCIVIOUSNESS OF THE VIPER, THE, 1920
LASERBLAST, 1978, C
LASH OF DESTINY, THE, 1916
LASH OF JEALOUSY, THE
LASH OF PINTO PETE, THE, 1924
LASH OF POWER, THE, 1917
LASH OF THE LAW, 1926
LASH OF THE PENITENTES
LASH OF THE WHIP, 1924, A
LASH, THE, 1916
LASH, THE, 1930, A
LASH, THE, 1934, C
LASKY JEDNE PLAVOLASKY
LASS O' THE LOOMS, A, 1919, A
LASSIE FROM LANCASHIRE, 1938, AA
LASSIE'S GREAT ADVENTURE, 1963, AAA
LASSIE, COME HOME, 1943, AAA
LASSIE, THE VOYAGER, 1966
LASSITER, 1984, O
LAST ACT OF MARTIN WESTON, THE, 1970, C
LAST ACT, THE, 1916
LAST ADVENTURE, THE, 1968, A
LAST ADVENTURERS, THE, 1937, A
LAST AFFAIR, THE, 1976, O
LAST ALARM, THE, 1926, A
LAST ALARM, THE, 1940
LAST AMERICAN HERO, THE, 1973, C
LAST AMERICAN VIRGIN, THE, 1982, O
LAST ANGRY MAN, THE, 1959, A
LAST ASSIGNMENT, THE, 1936
LAST BANDIT, THE, 1949, A
LAST BARRICADE, THE, 1938, C
LAST BATTLE, THE
LAST BLITZKRIEG, THE, 1958, A
LAST BRIDGE, THE, 1957, O
LAST CARD, THE, 1921
LAST CASTLE, THE
LAST CHALLENGE, THE, 1916
LAST CHALLENGE, THE, 1967, A
LAST CHANCE, THE, 1921, A
LAST CHANCE, THE, 1926, A
LAST CHANCE, THE, 1937, A
LAST CHANCE, THE, 1945, A
LAST CHAPTER, THE, 1915, A
LAST CHASE, THE, 1981, A
LAST COMMAND, THE, 1928, A
LAST COMMAND, THE, 1955, A
LAST COMMAND, THE, 1942
LAST CONCERT, THE, 1915

LAST COUPON, THE, 1932, A
LAST CROOKED MILE, THE, 1946, A
LAST CURTAIN, THE, 1937, A
LAST DANCE, THE, 1930, A
LAST DAY OF THE WAR, THE, 1969, A
LAST DAYS OF BOOT HILL, 1947, A
LAST DAYS OF DOLWYN, THE, 1949
LAST DAYS OF MAN ON EARTH, THE, 1975, O
LAST DAYS OF MUSSOLINI, 1974, A
LAST DAYS OF PLANET EARTH
LAST DAYS OF POMPEII, THE, 1935, A
LAST DAYS OF POMPEII, THE, 1960, A
LAST DAYS OF SODOM AND GOMORRAH, THE
LAST DETAIL, THE, 1973, O
LAST DOOR, THE, 1921
LAST EDITION, THE, 1925, A
LAST EGYPTIAN, THE, 1914, A
LAST EMBRACE, 1979, O
LAST ESCAPE, THE, 1970, A
LAST EXPRESS, THE, 1938, A
LAST FEELINGS, 1981
LAST FIGHT, THE, 1983
LAST FIGHT, THE, 1983, O
LAST FLIGHT OF NOAH'S ARK, THE, 1980, AA
LAST FLIGHT, THE, 1931, A
LAST FOUR DAYS, THE
LAST FRONTIER UPRISING, 1947, A
LAST FRONTIER, THE, 1926
LAST FRONTIER, THE, 1955, A
LAST GAME, THE, 1964, C
LAST GAME, THE, 1983
LAST GANGSTER, THE, 1937, A
LAST GANGSTER, THE, 1944
LAST GENERATION, THE, 1971
LAST GENTLEMAN, THE, 1934, A
LAST GLORY OF TROY
LAST GRAVE, THE
LAST GREAT TREASURE, THE
LAST GRENADE, THE, 1970, C
LAST GUNFIGHTER, THE
LAST GUNFIGHTER, THE, 1961, A
LAST HARD MEN, THE, 1976, O
LAST HERO
LAST HILL, THE, 1945, A
LAST HOLIDAY, 1950, A
LAST HORROR FILM, THE, 1984, O
LAST HORSEMAN, THE, 1944, A
LAST HOUR, THE, 1923
LAST HOUR, THE, 1930, A
LAST HOUSE ON DEAD END STREET, 1977, O
LAST HOUSE ON THE LEFT, 1972, O
LAST HOUSE ON THE LEFT, PART II
LAST HUNT, THE, 1956, C
LAST HUNTER, THE, 1984, O
LAST HURRAH, THE, 1958, A
LAST JOURNEY, THE, 1936, A
LAST KIDS ON EARTH, THE, 1983
LAST LAP, 1928
LAST LAUGH, THE, 1924, A
LAST LOAD, THE, 1948, AAA
LAST MAN, 1932, A
LAST MAN ON EARTH, THE, 1924
LAST MAN ON EARTH, THE, 1964, O
LAST MAN TO HANG, THE, 1956, C
LAST MAN, THE, 1916
LAST MAN, THE, 1924
LAST MAN, THE, 1968, C
LAST MARRIED COUPLE IN AMERICA, THE, 1980, O
LAST MERCENARY, THE, 1969, C
LAST METRO, THE, 1981, C-O
LAST MILE, THE, 1932, A
LAST MILE, THE, 1959, C
LAST MOMENT, THE, 1923
LAST MOMENT, THE, 1928
LAST MOMENT, THE, 1954, A
LAST MOMENT, THE, 1966
LAST MOMENT, THE, 1976
LAST MOVIE, THE, 1971, O
LAST MUSKETEER, THE, 1952, A
LAST MUSKETEER, THE, 1952
LAST NIGHT AT THE ALAMO, 1984, O
LAST OF HIS PEOPLE, THE, 1919
LAST OF MRS. CHEYNEY, THE, 1929, A
LAST OF MRS. CHEYNEY, THE, 1937, A
LAST OF SHEILA, THE, 1973, C
LAST OF SUMMER
LAST OF THE AMERICAN HOBOES, THE, 1974
LAST OF THE BADMEN, 1957, A
LAST OF THE BUCCANEERS, 1950, A
LAST OF THE CARNABYS, THE, 1917
LAST OF THE CAVALRY, THE
LAST OF THE CLINTONS, THE, 1935, A
LAST OF THE COMANCHES, 1952, A
LAST OF THE COWBOYS, THE
LAST OF THE DESPERADOES, 1956, A
LAST OF THE DUANES, 1930, A
LAST OF THE DUANES, 1941, A
LAST OF THE DUANES, THE, 1919
LAST OF THE DUANES, THE, 1924
LAST OF THE FAST GUNS, THE, 1958, A
LAST OF THE INGRAHAMS, THE, 1917, A
LAST OF THE KNUCKLEMEN, THE, 1981, A

LAST OF THE LONE WOLF, 1930, A
LAST OF THE MAFFIA, THE, 1915
LAST OF THE MOHICANS, THE, 1920, A
LAST OF THE MOHICANS, THE, 1936, A
LAST OF THE PAGANS, 1936, A
LAST OF THE PONY RIDERS, 1953, A
LAST OF THE RED HOT LOVERS, 1972, A
LAST OF THE REDMEN, 1947, AA
LAST OF THE REDSKINS
LAST OF THE RENEGADES, 1966, A
LAST OF THE SECRET AGENTS?, THE, 1966, A
LAST OF THE VIKINGS, THE, 1962, A
LAST OF THE WARRENS, THE, 1936, A
LAST OF THE WILD HORSES, 1948, A
LAST OUTLAW, THE, 1927
LAST OUTLAW, THE, 1936, A
LAST OUTPOST, THE, 1935, A
LAST OUTPOST, THE, 1951, A
LAST PAGE, THE
LAST PARADE, THE, 1931, A
LAST PAYMENT, 1921
LAST PERFORMANCE, THE, 1929, C
LAST PICTURE SHOW, THE, 1971, C-O
LAST PLANE OUT, 1983
LAST PORNO FLICK, THE, 1974, O
LAST POSSE, THE, 1953, A
LAST POST, THE, 1929, C
LAST REBEL, THE, 1918
LAST REBEL, THE, 1961, C
LAST REBEL, THE, 1971, C
LAST REMAKE OF BEAU GESTE, THE, 1977, C
LAST REUNION, 1978
LAST RHINO, THE, 1961, AAA
LAST RIDE, THE, 1932, A
LAST RIDE, THE, 1944, A
LAST RITES, 1980, O
LAST ROMAN, THE
LAST ROSE OF SUMMER, THE, 1920, A
LAST ROSE OF SUMMER, THE, 1937, A
LAST ROUND-UP, THE, 1934, A
LAST ROUND-UP, THE, 1947, AA
LAST ROUNDUP, THE, 1929, A
LAST RUN, THE, 1971, A
LAST SAFARI, THE, 1967, A
LAST SENTENCE, THE, 1917
LAST SHOT YOU HEAR, THE, 1969, C
LAST STAGE, THE
LAST STAGECOACH WEST, THE, 1957, A
LAST STAND, THE, 1938, A
LAST STARFIGHTER, THE, 1984, C
LAST STOP ON THE NIGHT TRAIN, 1976
LAST STOP, THE, 1949, O
LAST STRAW, THE, 1920, A
LAST SUMMER, 1969, O
LAST SUNSET, THE, 1961, C-O
LAST TANGO IN ACAPULCO, THE, 1975
LAST TEN DAYS, THE, 1956, A
LAST THREE, 1942
LAST TIDE, THE, 1931
LAST TIME I SAW ARCHIE, THE, 1961, A
LAST TIME I SAW PARIS, THE, 1954, A
LAST TOMAHAWK, THE, 1965, A
LAST TOMB OF LIGEIA
LAST TRAIL, 1921, A
LAST TRAIL, THE, 1927, A
LAST TRAIL, THE, 1934, A
LAST TRAIN FROM BOMBAY, 1952, A
LAST TRAIN FROM GUN HILL, 1959, C
LAST TRAIN FROM MADRID, THE, 1937, A
LAST TYCOON, THE, 1976, C
LAST UNICORN, THE, 1982, AAA
LAST VALLEY, THE, 1971, A
LAST VICTIM, THE
LAST VOLUNTEER, THE, 1914, A
LAST VOYAGE, THE, 1960, A
LAST WAGON, THE, 1956, C
LAST WALTZ, THE, 1927
LAST WALTZ, THE, 1936, A
LAST WAR, THE, 1962, C
LAST WARNING, THE, 1929, A
LAST WARNING, THE, 1938, A
LAST WARRIOR, THE
LAST WAVE, THE, 1978, A
LAST WHITE MAN, THE, 1924
LAST WILL OF DR. MABUSE, THE
LAST WINTER, THE, 1983
LAST WITNESS, THE, 1925, A
LAST WOMAN OF SHANG, THE, 1964, A
LAST WOMAN ON EARTH, THE, 1960, A
LAST WORD, THE, 1979, A
LAST YEAR AT MARIENBAD, 1962, C
LATE AT NIGHT, 1946, A
LATE AUTUMN, 1973, A
LATE EDWINA BLACK, THE
LATE EXTRA, 1935, A
LATE GEORGE APLEY, THE, 1947, A
LATE LIZ, THE, 1971, A
LATE MATTHEW PASCAL, THE, 1925
LATE SHOW, THE, 1977, A-C
LATEST FROM PARIS, THE, 1928, A
LATIN LOVE, 1930, A
LATIN LOVERS, 1953, A

LATIN QUARTER
LATITUDE ZERO, 1969, AAA
LAUGH AND GET RICH, 1931, A
LAUGH IT OFF, 1939, A
LAUGH IT OFF, 1940, A
LAUGH PAGLIACCI, 1948, A
LAUGH YOUR BLUES AWAY, 1943, A
LAUGH, CLOWN, LAUGH, 1928, A
LAUGHING ANNE, 1954, A
LAUGHING AT DANGER, 1924, A
LAUGHING AT DANGER, 1940, A
LAUGHING AT DEATH, 1929
LAUGHING AT LIFE, 1933, A
LAUGHING AT TROUBLE, 1937, A
LAUGHING BILL HYDE, 1918
LAUGHING BOY, 1934, A
LAUGHING CAVALIER, THE, 1917
LAUGHING IN THE SUNSHINE, 1953, A
LAUGHING IRISH EYES, 1936, A
LAUGHING LADY, THE, 1930, A
LAUGHING LADY, THE, 1950, A
LAUGHING POLICEMAN, THE, 1973, O
LAUGHING SINNERS, 1931, C
LAUGHTER, 1930, A-C
LAUGHTER AND TEARS, 1921, A
LAUGHTER HOUSE, 1984, C
LAUGHTER IN HELL, 1933, A
LAUGHTER IN PARADISE, 1951, AA
LAUGHTER IN THE AIR
LAUNDRY GIRL, THE
LAURA, 1944, A
LAUTLOSE WAFFEN
LAVENDER AND OLD LACE, 1921, A
LAVENDER BATH LADY, THE, 1922, A
LAVENDER HILL MOB, THE, 1951, A
LAVIRINT SMRTI
LAW AND DISORDER, 1940, A
LAW AND DISORDER, 1958, A
LAW AND DISORDER, 1974, O
LAW AND JAKE WADE, THE, 1958, A
LAW AND LAWLESS, 1932, A
LAW AND LEAD, 1937, A
LAW AND ORDER, 1932, A
LAW AND ORDER, 1940, A
LAW AND ORDER, 1942, A
LAW AND ORDER, 1953, A
LAW AND ORDER, 1936
LAW AND ORDER, 1936
LAW AND THE LADY, THE, 1924
LAW AND THE LADY, THE, 1951, A
LAW AND THE MAN, 1928
LAW AND THE OUTLAW, 1925
LAW AND THE WOMAN, THE, 1922
LAW AND TOMBSTONE, THE
LAW BEYOND THE RANGE, 1935, A
LAW COMES TO GUNSIGHT, THE, 1947
LAW COMES TO TEXAS, THE, 1939, A
LAW COMMANDS, THE, 1938, A
LAW DECIDES, THE, 1916
LAW DEMANDS, THE
LAW DEMANDS, THE, 1924
LAW DIVINE, THE, 1920
LAW FOR TOMBSTONE, 1937, A
LAW FORBIDS, THE, 1924, A
LAW HUSTLERS, THE
LAW IN HER HANDS, THE, 1936, A
LAW IS THE LAW, THE, 1959, A
LAW MEN, 1944, A
LAW OF COMPENSATION, 1927
LAW OF COMPENSATION, THE, 1917
LAW OF FEAR, 1928
LAW OF MEN, THE, 1919
LAW OF NATURE, THE, 1919
LAW OF THE 45'S, 1935
LAW OF THE BADLANDS, 1950, A
LAW OF THE BARBARY COAST, 1949, A
LAW OF THE CANYON, 1947
LAW OF THE GOLDEN WEST, 1949, A
LAW OF THE GREAT NORTHWEST, THE, 1918
LAW OF THE JUNGLE, 1942, A
LAW OF THE LAND, THE, 1917, A
LAW OF THE LASH, 1947, A
LAW OF THE LAWLESS, 1964, A
LAW OF THE LAWLESS, THE, 1923, A
LAW OF THE MOUNTED, 1928, A
LAW OF THE NORTH, 1932, AA
LAW OF THE NORTH, THE, 1917
LAW OF THE NORTH, THE, 1918
LAW OF THE NORTH, THE, 1918
LAW OF THE NORTHWEST, 1943, A
LAW OF THE PAMPAS, 1939, A
LAW OF THE PANHANDLE, 1950, A
LAW OF THE PLAINS, 1929
LAW OF THE PLAINS, 1929
LAW OF THE PLAINS, 1938, A
LAW OF THE RANGE, 1941, A
LAW OF THE RANGE, THE, 1928, A
LAW OF THE RANGER, 1937, A
LAW OF THE RIO
LAW OF THE RIO GRANDE, 1931, A
LAW OF THE SADDLE, 1944, A
LAW OF THE SEA, 1932, A

LAW OF THE SNOW COUNTRY, THE, 1926, A
LAW OF THE TEXAN, 1938, A
LAW OF THE TIMBER, 1941, A
LAW OF THE TONG, 1931, A
LAW OF THE TROPICS, 1941, A
LAW OF THE UNDERWORLD, 1938, A
LAW OF THE VALLEY, 1944, A
LAW OF THE WEST, 1932
LAW OF THE WEST, 1949, A
LAW OF THE WILD, 1941
LAW OF THE YUKON, THE, 1920
LAW OF THE YUKON, THE, 1920
LAW OR LOYALTY, 1926
LAW OR LOYALTY, 1926
LAW RIDES AGAIN, THE, 1943, A
LAW RIDES WEST, THE
LAW RIDES, THE, 1936, A
LAW RUSTLERS, THE, 1923
LAW RUSTLERS, THE, 1923
LAW THAT DIVIDES, THE, 1919
LAW THAT DIVIDES, THE, 1919
LAW THAT FAILED, THE, 1917
LAW THAT FAILED, THE, 1917
LAW UNTO HIMSELF, A, 1916
LAW UNTO HIMSELF, A, 1916
LAW VS. BILLY THE KID, THE, 1954, A
LAW WEST OF TOMBSTONE, THE, 1938, A
LAW'S LASH, THE, 1928
LAW'S OUTLAW, THE, 1918
LAW, THE, 1940
LAW, THE, 1958
LAWBREAKERS, THE, 1960
LAWFUL CHEATERS, 1925, A
LAWFUL LARCENY, 1923, A
LAWFUL LARCENY, 1930, A
LAWLESS BORDER, 1935, A
LAWLESS BREED, THE, 1946, AA
LAWLESS BREED, THE, 1952, A
LAWLESS CLAN
LAWLESS CODE, 1949, A
LAWLESS COWBOYS, 1952, A
LAWLESS EIGHTIES, THE, 1957, C
LAWLESS EMPIRE, 1946, A
LAWLESS FRONTIER, THE, 1935, A
LAWLESS LAND, 1937, A
LAWLESS LEGION, THE, 1929, A
LAWLESS LOVE, 1918
LAWLESS MEN, 1924
LAWLESS NINETIES, THE, 1936, A
LAWLESS PLAINSMEN, 1942, A
LAWLESS RANGE, 1935, A
LAWLESS RIDER, THE, 1954, A
LAWLESS RIDERS, 1936, A
LAWLESS STREET, A, 1955, A
LAWLESS TRAILS, 1926
LAWLESS VALLEY, 1932
LAWLESS VALLEY, 1938, A
LAWLESS WOMAN, THE, 1931, A
LAWLESS, THE, 1950, A-C
LAWMAN, 1971, C
LAWMAN IS BORN, A, 1937, A
LAWRENCE OF ARABIA, 1962, C
LAWTON STORY, THE, 1949, A
LAWYER MAN, 1933, A
LAWYER'S SECRET, THE, 1931, A
LAWYER, THE, 1969, O
LAXDALE HALL
LAY THAT RIFLE DOWN, 1955, A
LAZARILLO, 1963, A
LAZY BONES
LAZY LIGHTNING, 1926, A
LAZY RIVER, 1934, A
LAZYBONES, 1925, A
LAZYBONES, 1935, A
LE 15E PRELUDE DE CHOPIN, 1922
LE AMICHE, 1962, C
LE AVVENTURE E GLI AMORI DI MIGUEL
  CERVANTES
LE BAL, 1984, A
LE BANDEAU SUR LES YEUX, 1917
LE BEAU MARIAGE, 1982, C-O
LE BEAU SERGE, 1959, C-O
LE BLE EN HERBE
LE BLED, 1929
LE BON PLAISIR, 1984, A-C
LE BONHEUR, 1966, C
LE BONHEUR CONJUGAL, 1922
LE BONHEUR DES AUTRES, 1919
LE BONHEUR DU JOUR, 1927
LE BOUCHER, 1971, O
LE BRASIER ARDENT, 1923
LE CABINET DE L'HOMME NOIR, 1924
LE CALVAIRE D'UNE REINE, 1919
LE CAPITAINE FRACASSE, 1929
LE CAPORAL EPINGLE
LE CARILLON DE MINUIT, 1922
LE CARNIVAL DES VERITES, 1920
LE CAVE SE REBIFFE
LE CERVEAU
LE CHANSON DU FEU, 1917
LE CHANT DE L'AMOUR TRIOMPHANT, 1923
LE CHARME DISCRET DE LA BOURGEOISIE

LE CHAT
LE CHAT DANS LE SAC
LE CHAUFFEUR DE MADEMOISELLE, 1928
LE CHEMIN D'ERONA, 1921
LE CHEMINEAU, 1917
LE CHEMINEAU, 1926
LE CHEVAL D'ORGEUIL
LE CHEVALIER DE GABY, 1920
LE CHIFFONNIER DE PARIS, 1924
LE CIEL EST A VOUS, 1957, A
LE CLOCHARD
LE COFFRET DE JADE
LE COMTE DE MONTE CRISTO
LE COMTE KOSTIA, 1925
LE CORBEAU
LE CORNIAUD
LE COSTAUD DES EPINETTES, 1923
LE COUPABLE, 1917
LE COUR DES GUEUX, 1925
LE CRABE TAMBOUR, 1984, O
LE CREPUSCULE DE COEUR, 1916
LE CRIME DE LORD ARTHUR SAVILLE, 1922
LE CRIME DE MONSIEUR LANGE
LE CRIME DES HOMMES, 1923
LE CRIME DU BOUIF, 1921
LE DANGER VIENT DE L'ESCAPE
LE DEDALE, 1917
LE DEDALE, 1927
LE DELAI, 1918
LE DENIER MILLIARDAIRE, 1934, A
LE DERNIER COMBAT, 1984, O
LE DESERT DES TARTARES
LE DESERT ROUGE
LE DESTIN EST MAITRE, 1920
LE DIABLE AU COEUR, 1928
LE DIABLE AU CORPS
LE DIABLE DANS LA VILLE, 1925
LE DIABLE PAR LA QUEUE
LE DIABLE PROBABLEMENT
LE DIABOLIQUE DOCTEUR MABUSE
LE DIAMANT VERT, 1917
LE DIEU DU HASARD, 1919
LE DISTRAIT
LE DOUBLE AMOUR, 1925
LE DROIT A LA VIE, 1917
LE DROIT DE TUER, 1920
LE FANTOME DE LA LIBERTE
LE FANTOME DU MOULIN ROUGE, 1925
LE FARCEUR
LE FATE
LE FERME DU CHOQUART, 1922
LE GAI SAVOIR, 1968, A
LE GAMIN DE PARIS, 1923
LE GARDIN DU FEU, 1924
LE GENDARME ET LES EXTRATERRESTRES, 1978, C
LE GENTILHOMME COMMERCANT, 1918
LE GENTLEMAN DE COCODY
LE GEOLE, 1921
LE GORILLE A MORDU L'ARCHEVEQUE
LE GRAND CHEF
LE GRAND JEU
LE JARDIN SUR L'ORONTE, 1925
LE JEUNE FOLLE
LE JOUER D'ECHECS
LE JOUER D'ECHES
LE JOUEUR
LE JOUR ET L'HEURE
LE JOUR SE LEVE
LE JOURNAL D'UNE CURE DE CAMPAGNE
LE JUGE ET L'ASSASSIN
LE JUIF ERRANT, 1926
LE LAC D'ARGENT, 1922
LE LION DES MOGOLS, 1924
LE LONG DES TROITTORS
LE LOTUS D'OR, 1916
LE LYS ROUGE, 1920
LE MAGNIFIQUE
LE MALHEUR QUI PASSE, 1916
LE MANOIR DE LA PEUR, 1927
LE MANS, 1971, A
LE MARIAGE DE FIGARO
LE MARIAGE DE MADEMOISELLE BEULEMANS, 1927
LE MARIAGE DE ROSINE, 1925
LE MAUVAIS GARCON, 1923
LE MENEUR DE JOIES, 1929
LE MEPRIS
LE MERAVIGLIOSE AVVENTURE DI MARCO POLO
LE MERCENARIRE
LE MERCHANT HOMME, 1921
LE MEURTIER DE THEODORE, 1921
LE MILLION
LE MIRACLE DES LOUPS
LE MIROIR A DEUX FACES
LE MONDAT
LE MONDE TREMBLERA, 1939, A
LE MYSTERE DE LA TOUR EIFFEL, 1927
LE NEGRE BLANC, 1925
LE NOCTURNE, 1917
LE NOCTURNE, 1919
LE NOEL D'UN VAGABOND, 1918
LE NOEL DU PERE LATHUILE, 1922
LE NOTTI BIANCHE

LE PASSAGER, 1928
LE PASSAGER DE LA PLUIE
LE PASSE DE MONIQUE, 1918
LE PASSE MURAILLE
LE PAYS BLEU
LE PENSEUR, 1920
LE PERE TRANQUEUIL
LE PETIT CAFE, 1919
LE PETIT CHOSE, 1923
LE PETIT MOINEAU DE PARIS, 1923
LE PETIT SOLDAT, 1965, C
LE PETIT THEATRE DE JEAN RENOIR, 1974, C
LE PLAISIR, 1954, C-O
LE PORION, 1921
LE PREMIERE IDYLLE DE BOUCOT, 1920
LE PRINCE CHARMANT, 1925
LE PRINCE JEAN, 1928
LE PUITS AUX TROIS VERITES
LE QUATTRO VERITA
LE RAVIN SANS FOND, 1917
LE RAYON INVISIBLE
LE REFLET DE CLAUDE MERCOEUR, 1923
LE REMOUS, 1920
LE RETOUR AUX CHAMPS, 1918
LE REVE, 1921
LE REVEIL, 1925
LE REVEIL DE MADDALONE, 1924
LE ROI DE CAMARGUE, 1921
LE ROI DE CIRQUE, 1925
LE ROI DE COEUR
LE ROI DE LA MER, 1917
LE ROI DE LA VITESSE, 1923
LE ROMAN D'UN JEUNE HOMME PAUVRE, 1927
LE ROMAN D'UN SPAHI, 1917
LE ROMAN D'UN TRICHEUR
LE ROUBLE A DEUX FACES
LE ROUGE AUX LEVRES
LE ROUGE ET LA NOIR
LE ROUTE DE CORINTH
LE SANG D'ALLAH, 1922
LE SANG D'UN POETE
LE SANG DES FINOEL, 1922
LE SCANDALE, 1918
LE SECRET DE CARGO, 1929
LE SECRET DE POLICHINELLE, 1923
LE SECRET DE ROSETTE LAMBERT, 1920
LE SECRET DU 'LONE STAR', 1920
LE SENS DE LA MORT, 1921
LE SERPENT
LE SIEGE DES TROIS, 1918
LE SILENCE EST D'OR
LE SOUFFLE AU COEUR
LE SOUS MARIN DE CRISTAL, 1928
LE TABLIER BLANC, 1917
LE TALISON, 1921
LE TAXI 313 x 7, 1922
LE TEMPS DES ASSASSINS
LE TESTAMENT DU DR. MABUSE
LE TOCSIN, 1920
LE TONNERRE, 1921
LE TORNOI, 1928
LE TORRENT, 1918
LE TOURBILLON DE PARIS, 1928
LE TRAIN SANS YEUX, 1928
LE TRAITEMENT DU HOQUET, 1918
LE VALSE DE L'ADIEU, 1928
LE VENENOSA, 1928
LE VENT D'EST
LE VERTIGE, 1917
LE VERTIGE, 1926
LE VICOMTE REGLE SES COMPTES
LE VIOL, 1968, O
LE VOILE BLEU
LE VOLEUR
LE VOYAGE EN AMERIQUE
LE VOYAGE IMAGINAIRE, 1926
LE VOYOU
LEAD KINDLY LIGHT
LEAD LAW
LEAD, KINDLY LIGHT, 1918, A
LEADBELLY, 1976, C-O
LEADVILLE GUNSLINGER, 1952, A
LEAGUE OF FRIGHTENED MEN, 1937, A
LEAGUE OF GENTLEMEN, THE, 1961, A-C
LEAH KLESCHNA, 1913
LEAH'S SUFFERING, 1917
LEAP INTO LIFE, 1924
LEAP INTO THE VOID, 1982, O
LEAP OF FAITH, 1931, A
LEAP TO FAME, 1918, A
LEAP YEAR, 1921
LEAP YEAR, 1932, A
LEARN, BABY, LEARN
LEARNIN' OF JIM BENTON, THE, 1917
LEARNING TO LOVE, 1925, A
LEARNING TREE, THE, 1969, O
LEASE OF LIFE, 1954, A
LEATHER AND NYLON, 1969, A-C
LEATHER BOYS, THE, 1965, O
LEATHER BURNERS, THE, 1943, A
LEATHER GLOVES, 1948, A
LEATHER SAINT, THE, 1956, A

LEATHER-PUSHERS, THE, 1940, A
LEATHERNECK, THE, 1929, A
LEATHERNECKING, 1930, A
LEATHERNECKS HAVE LANDED, THE, 1936, A
LEAVE HER TO HEAVEN, 1946, O
LEAVE IT TO BLANCHE, 1934, A
LEAVE IT TO BLONDIE, 1945, A
LEAVE IT TO GERRY, 1924
LEAVE IT TO HENRY, 1949, A
LEAVE IT TO ME, 1920
LEAVE IT TO ME, 1933, A
LEAVE IT TO ME, 1937, A
LEAVE IT TO SMITH, 1934, A
LEAVE IT TO SUSAN, 1919
LEAVE IT TO THE IRISH, 1944, A
LEAVE IT TO THE MARINES, 1951, A
LEAVENWORTH CASE, THE, 1923
LEAVENWORTH CASE, THE, 1936, A
LEAVES FROM SATAN'S BOOK, 1921
LEAVES OF MEMORY, 1914
LEBENSBORN
LEBENSZEICHEN
LEDA
LEECH WOMAN, THE, 1960, C
LEECH, THE, 1921, A
LEFT HAND BRAND, THE, 1924
LEFT HAND OF GEMINI, THE, 1972
LEFT HAND OF GOD, THE, 1955, A
LEFT, RIGHT AND CENTRE, 1959, A
LEFT-HANDED, 1972
LEFT-HANDED GUN, THE, 1958, C
LEFT-HANDED LAW, 1937, A
LEFT-HANDED WOMAN, THE, 1980, C-O
LEFTOVER LADIES, 1931, A
LEGACY, 1963
LEGACY, 1976, O
LEGACY OF A SPY
LEGACY OF BLOOD, 1973, O
LEGACY OF BLOOD, 1978, O
LEGACY OF HORROR, 1978
LEGACY OF MAGGIE WALSH
LEGACY OF SATAN, 1973
LEGACY OF THE 500,000, THE, 1964, A
LEGACY, THE, 1979, O
LEGAL LARCENY
LEGALLY DEAD, 1923, A
LEGEND IN LEOTARDS
LEGEND OF A BANDIT, THE, 1945, A
LEGEND OF ALFRED PACKER, THE, 1979
LEGEND OF BLOOD MOUNTAIN, THE, 1965
LEGEND OF BLOOD MOUNTAIN, THE, 1965, O
LEGEND OF BOGGY CREEK, THE, 1973, A-C
LEGEND OF CHAMPIONS, 1983
LEGEND OF COUGAR CANYON, 1974, A
LEGEND OF EARL DURAND, THE, 1974
LEGEND OF FRANK WOODS, THE, 1977
LEGEND OF FRENCHIE KING, THE, 1971, C
LEGEND OF GOSTA BERLING, 1928
LEGEND OF HELL HOUSE, THE, 1973, C
LEGEND OF HILLBILLY JOHN, THE
LEGEND OF HOLLYWOOD, THE, 1924, A
LEGEND OF HORROR, 1972
LEGEND OF LOBO, THE, 1962, AA
LEGEND OF LYLAH CLARE, THE, 1968, A-C
LEGEND OF NIGGER CHARLEY, THE, 1972, C
LEGEND OF ROBIN HOOD, THE
LEGEND OF SPIDER FOREST, THE, 1976, C
LEGEND OF THE BAYOU
LEGEND OF THE JUGGLER, 1978
LEGEND OF THE LONE RANGER, THE, 1981, C
LEGEND OF THE LOST, 1957, C
LEGEND OF THE SEA WOLF
LEGEND OF THE SEVEN GOLDEN VAMPIRES, THE
LEGEND OF THE TREE OF LIFE
LEGEND OF THE WEREWOLF, 1974
LEGEND OF THE WILD, 1981
LEGEND OF THE WOLF WOMAN, THE, 1977, O
LEGEND OF TOM DOOLEY, THE, 1959, A
LEGEND OF WITCH HOLLOW
LEGENDARY CURSE OF LEMORA
LEGION OF DEATH, THE, 1918
LEGION OF LOST FLYERS, 1939, A
LEGION OF MISSING MEN, 1937, A
LEGION OF TERROR, 1936, A
LEGION OF THE CONDEMNED, 1928
LEGION OF THE DOOMED, 1958, A
LEGION OF THE LAWLESS, 1940, A
LEGIONNAIRES IN PARIS, 1927
LEGIONS OF THE NILE, 1960, A
LEMON DROP KID, THE, 1934, A
LEMON DROP KID, THE, 1951, A
LEMON GROVE KIDS MEET THE MONSTERS, THE, 1966, C
LEMONADE JOE, 1966, A
LEMORA THE LADY DRACULA
LENA RIVERS, 1914
LENA RIVERS, 1925
LENA RIVERS, 1932, A
LEND ME YOUR EAR
LEND ME YOUR HUSBAND, 1924, A
LEND ME YOUR HUSBAND, 1935, A
LEND ME YOUR NAME, 1918

LEND ME YOUR WIFE, 1935, A
LENNY, 1974, C-O
LEO AND LOREE, 1980, A
LEO CHRONICLES, THE, 1972
LEO THE LAST, 1970, O
LEONOR, 1977, O
LEOPARD IN THE SNOW, 1979, A
LEOPARD LADY, THE, 1928, A
LEOPARD MAN, THE, 1943, O
LEOPARD WOMAN, THE, 1920
LEOPARD'S BRIDE, THE, 1916
LEOPARD, THE, 1963, A-C
LEOPARDESS, THE, 1923
LEPKE, 1975, O
LES ABYSSES, 1964, O
LES AMANTS
LES AMANTS DE VERONE
LES AMOURS DE ROCAMBOLE, 1924
LES ANGES DU PECHE
LES AVENTURES EXTRAORDINAIRES DE CERVANTES
LES BAS FONDS
LES BELLES-DE-NUIT, 1952, C
LES BICHES, 1968, O
LES BLEUS DE L'AMOUR, 1918
LES CAMARADES
LES CAPRICES DE MARIE
LES CARABINIERS, 1968, O
LES CHASSEUR DE CHEZ MAXIM'S, 1927
LES CHERES IMAGES, 1920
LES CHOSES DE LA VIE
LES CINQ GENTLEMEN MAUDITS, 1919
LES CLANDESTINS
LES CLOCHES DE CORNEVILLE, 1917
LES COMPERES, 1984, A
LES CONTES LES MILLES ET UNE NUITS, 1922
LES COUSINS
LES CREATURES, 1969, A
LES DAMES DE BOIS DE BOULOGNE
LES DAMES DE CROIX-MORT, 1917
LES DEMOISELLES DE ROCHEFORT
LES DEMONS DE MINUIT
LES DERNIERES VACANCES, 1947, A-C
LES DEUX AMOURS, 1917
LES DEUX BAISERS, 1920
LES DEUX GOSSES, 1924
LES DEUX MARQUISES, 1916
LES DEUX TIMIDES, 1929
LES DIABOLIQUES
LES DIEUX ONT SOIF, 1926
LES DOIGTS CROISES
LES ECRITS RESTENT, 1917
LES ELUS DE LA MER, 1925
LES ENFANTS DU PARADIS
LES ENFANTS TERRIBLES, 1952, A-C
LES ESPIONS
LES FELINS
LES FEMMES COLLANTES, 1920
LES FEMMES DES AUTRES, 1920
LES FOURCHAMBAULT, 1929
LES FRERES CORSES, 1917
LES GARCONS
LES GAULOISES BLEUES, 1969, A
LES GIRLS, 1957, A
LES GRANDES MANOEUVRES
LES GRANDS, 1924
LES HERITIERS DE L'ONCLE JAMES, 1924
LES HOMMES EN BLANC
LES INNOCENTS AUX MAINS SALES
LES JEUX INTERDIT
LES JEUX SONT FAITS, 1947, A-C
LES LACHES VIVENT D'ESPOIR
LES LARMES DU PARDON, 1919
LES LETTRES DE MON MOULIN
LES LIAISONS DANGEREUSES, 1961, O
LES LIENS DE SANG
LES LOUVES
LES LOUVES, 1925
LES MAINS FLETRIES, 1920
LES MAINS SALES, 1954, A-C
LES MAITRES DU TEMPS, 1982, A
LES MAUDITS
LES MISERABLES, 1918, A
LES MISERABLES, 1927
LES MISERABLES, 1935, A
LES MISERABLES, 1936, A
LES MISERABLES, 1952, A
LES MISERABLES, 1982, A
LES MORTS QUI PARLENT, 1920
LES MOUTTES, 1919
LES MYSTERES SU CIEL, 1920
LES NOCES DU SABLE
LES NOUVEAUX MESSIEURS, 1929
LES NUITS DE CARNAVAL, 1922
LES NUITS DE L'EVPOUVANTE
LES NUITS DE LA PLEINE LUNE
LES OGRESSES
LES OMBRES QUI PASSANT, 1924
LES OPPRIMES, 1923
LES PARENTS TERRIBLES, 1950, A
LES PEMPS DES AMANTS
LES PERLES DES COURONNE

LES PETITES MARIONETTES, 1918
LES PETITS, 1925
LES PETROLEUSES
LES PORTES DE LA NUIT
LES PREMIERES ARMES DE ROCAMBOLE, 1924
LES QUATRES CENTS COUPS
LES QUATRES VERITES
LES RANTZAU, 1924
LES RIPOUX
LES ROQUEVILLARD, 1922
LES SOEURS ENNEMIES, 1917
LES SOMNAMBULES
LES TERRES D'OR, 1925
LES TITANS
LES TRANSATLANTIQUES, 1928
LES TRAVAILLEURS DE LA MER, 1918
LES TRICHEURS
LES TRIPES AU SOLEIL
LES TROIS COURONNES DU MATELOT
LES TROIS GANTS DE LA DAMES EN NOIR, 1920
LES TROIS MASQUES, 1921
LES VACANCES DE MONSIEUR HULOT
LES VALSEUSES
LES VISITEURS DU SOIR
LES VOLEURS DE GLOIRE, 1926
LES YEUX D L'AIME, 1922
LES YEUX SANS VISAGE
LESBIAN TWINS
LESNAYA PESNYA
LESS THAN KIN, 1918
LESS THAN THE DUST, 1916
LESSON IN LOVE, A, 1960, C
LESSON, THE, 1917
LESSONS IN LOVE, 1921, A
LEST WE FORGET, 1918
LEST WE FORGET, 1934, C
LET 'EM HAVE IT, 1935, A
LET 'ER BUCK, 1925, A
LET 'ER GO GALLEGHER, 1928, A
LET FREEDOM RING, 1939, A
LET GEORGE DO IT, 1938
LET GEORGE DO IT, 1940, A
LET HIM BUCK, 1924
LET IT RAIN, 1927, A
LET JOY REIGN SUPREME, 1977, C
LET KATHY DO IT, 1916
LET ME EXPLAIN, DEAR, 1932, A
LET NO MAN PUT ASUNDER, 1924
LET NO MAN WRITE MY EPITAPH, 1960, A
LET THE BALLOON GO, 1977, A
LET THE PEOPLE LAUGH
LET THE PEOPLE SING, 1942, A
LET THEM LIVE, 1937, A
LET US BE GAY, 1930, A
LET US LIVE, 1939, A
LET WOMEN ALONE, 1925
LET'S BE FAMOUS, 1939, A
LET'S BE FASHIONABLE, 1920
LET'S BE HAPPY, 1957, A
LET'S BE RITZY, 1934, A
LET'S DANCE, 1950, A
LET'S DO IT
LET'S DO IT AGAIN, 1953, A
LET'S DO IT AGAIN, 1975, A
LET'S ELOPE, 1919
LET'S FACE IT, 1943, A
LET'S FALL IN LOVE, 1934, A
LET'S FINISH THE JOB, 1928
LET'S GET A DIVORCE, 1918
LET'S GET MARRIED, 1926, A
LET'S GET MARRIED, 1937, A
LET'S GET MARRIED, 1960, A
LET'S GET TOUGH, 1942, A
LET'S GO, 1923
LET'S GO COLLEGIATE, 1941, A
LET'S GO GALLAGHER, 1925
LET'S GO NATIVE, 1930, A
LET'S GO NAVY, 1951, A
LET'S GO PLACES, 1930, A
LET'S GO STEADY, 1945, A
LET'S GO, YOUNG GUY, 1967, A
LET'S HAVE A MURDER
LET'S HAVE FUN
LET'S HAVE FUN, 1943
LET'S KILL UNCLE, 1966, C
LET'S LIVE A LITTLE, A
LET'S LIVE AGAIN, 1948, A
LET'S LIVE TONIGHT, 1935, A
LET'S LOVE AND LAUGH
LET'S MAKE A MILLION, 1937, A
LET'S MAKE A NIGHT OF IT, 1937, A
LET'S MAKE IT LEGAL, 1951, A
LET'S MAKE LOVE, 1960, AA
LET'S MAKE MUSIC, 1940, A
LET'S MAKE UP, 1955, A
LET'S MAKE WHOOPEE
LET'S PRETEND
LET'S ROCK, 1958, A
LET'S SCARE JESSICA TO DEATH, 1971, C
LET'S SING AGAIN, 1936, A
LET'S TALK ABOUT WOMEN, 1964, C
LET'S TALK IT OVER, 1934, A

LET'S TRY AGAIN, 1934, A
LETTER FOR EVIE, A, 1945, A
LETTER FROM A NOVICE
LETTER FROM AN UNKNOWN WOMAN, 1948, A
LETTER FROM KOREA
LETTER OF INTRODUCTION, 1938, A
LETTER THAT WAS NEVER SENT, THE, 1962, A
LETTER TO THREE WIVES, A, 1948, A
LETTER, THE, 1929, A
LETTER, THE, 1940, A
LETTERS FROM MY WINDMILL, 1955, A
LETTING IN THE SUNSHINE, 1933, A
LETTY LYNTON, 1932, A-C
LETYAT ZHURAVIT
LEVIATHAN, 1961, O
LEW TYLER'S WIVES, 1926
LI'L ABNER, 1940, AAA
LI'L ABNER, 1959, AA
LI-HANG LE CRUEL, 1920
LIANG SHAN-PO YU CHU YING-TAI
LIANNA, 1983, O
LIAR'S DICE, 1980, O
LIAR'S MOON, 1982, O
LIAR, THE, 1918
LIARS, THE, 1964, A
LIBEL, 1959, A
LIBELED LADY, 1936, A
LIBERATION OF L.B. JONES, THE, 1970, O
LIBERTINE, THE, 1916
LIBERTY HALL, 1914
LIBIDO, 1973, O
LICENSED TO KILL
LICENSED TO LOVE AND KILL, 1979
LIDO MYSTERY, THE
LIE DETECTOR, THE
LIE, THE, 1918
LIEBESSPIELE
LIES, 1983
LIES, 1984, C
LIES MY FATHER TOLD ME, 1960, A
LIES MY FATHER TOLD ME, 1975, A
LIEUT. DANNY, U.S.A., 1916, A
LIEUTENANT DARING RN AND THE WATER RATS, 1924, A
LIEUTENANT DARING, RN, 1935, A
LIEUTENANT WORE SKIRTS, THE, 1956, A
LIFE, 1920
LIFE, 1928, A
LIFE AFTER DARK
LIFE AND DEATH OF COLONEL BLIMP, THE
LIFE AND DEATH OF LIEUTENANT SCHMIDT, 1917
LIFE AND LEGEND OF BUFFALO JONES, THE, 1976
LIFE AND LOVES OF BEETHOVEN, THE, 1937, A
LIFE AND LOVES OF MOZART, THE, 1959, C
LIFE AND PASSION OF CHRIST, 1921
LIFE AND TIMES OF CHESTER-ANGUS RAMSGOOD, THE, 1971, C
LIFE AND TIMES OF GRIZZLY ADAMS, THE, 1974, AAA
LIFE AND TIMES OF JUDGE ROY BEAN, THE, 1972, C
LIFE AT STAKE, A
LIFE AT THE TOP, 1965, C
LIFE BEGINS, 1932, C
LIFE BEGINS ANEW, 1938, A
LIFE BEGINS AT 17, 1958, C
LIFE BEGINS AT 40, 1935, AAA
LIFE BEGINS AT 8:30, 1942, A
LIFE BEGINS AT COLLEGE
LIFE BEGINS FOR ANDY HARDY, 1941, A
LIFE BEGINS IN COLLEGE, 1937, AA
LIFE BEGINS TOMORROW, 1952, C
LIFE BEGINS WITH LOVE, 1937, A
LIFE DANCES ON, CHRISTINE
LIFE FOR A LIFE, A, 1916
LIFE FOR RUTH
LIFE GOES ON, 1932, A-C
LIFE GOES ON, 1938
LIFE IN DANGER, 1964, A
LIFE IN DEATH, 1914
LIFE IN EMERGENCY WARD 10, 1959, C
LIFE IN HER HANDS, 1951, C
LIFE IN THE BALANCE, A, 1955, O
LIFE IN THE ORANGE GROVES, 1920
LIFE IN THE RAW, 1933, A
LIFE IS A BED OF ROSES, 1984, C
LIFE IS A CIRCUS, 1962, A
LIFE LINE, THE, 1919
LIFE LOVE DEATH, 1969, O
LIFE MASK, THE, 1918
LIFE OF A COUNTRY DOCTOR, 1961, A
LIFE OF A LONDON ACTRESS, THE, 1919
LIFE OF AN ACTRESS, 1927
LIFE OF AN ACTRESS, THE, 1915
LIFE OF BRIAN
LIFE OF EMILE ZOLA, THE, 1937, AA
LIFE OF GENERAL VILLA, THE, 1914
LIFE OF GENEVIEVE, THE, 1922
LIFE OF HER OWN, A, 1950, A-C
LIFE OF JIMMY DOLAN, THE, 1933, A
LIFE OF JOHN BUNYAN-PILGRIM'S PROGRESS, 1912
LIFE OF LORD KITCHENER, THE, 1917
LIFE OF MOSES, 1909

LIFE OF OHARU, 1964, C
LIFE OF RILEY, THE, 1927
LIFE OF RILEY, THE, 1949, A
LIFE OF ROBERT BURNS, THE, 1926, A
LIFE OF SHAKESPEARE, THE
LIFE OF THE COUNTRY DOCTOR
LIFE OF THE PARTY, 1934, A
LIFE OF THE PARTY, THE, 1920
LIFE OF THE PARTY, THE, 1930, A
LIFE OF THE PARTY, THE, 1937, A
LIFE OF VERGIE WINTERS, THE, 1934, C
LIFE OF "BIG TIM" SULLIVAN, THE, 1914
LIFE OR HONOR?, 1918
LIFE POD, 1980
LIFE RETURNS, 1939, C
LIFE STORY OF DAVID LLOYD GEORGE, THE, 1918
LIFE STUDY, 1973, O
LIFE UPSIDE DOWN, 1965, C
LIFE WITH BLONDIE, 1946, AAA
LIFE WITH FATHER, 1947, AAA
LIFE WITH HENRY, 1941, AAA
LIFE WITH THE LYONS
LIFE WITHOUT SOUL, 1916, A
LIFE'S A FUNNY PROPOSITION, 1919
LIFE'S A STAGE, 1929
LIFE'S BLIND ALLEY, 1916
LIFE'S CROSSROADS, 1928
LIFE'S DARN FUNNY, 1921, A
LIFE'S GREATEST GAME, 1924
LIFE'S GREATEST PROBLEM, 1919
LIFE'S GREATEST QUESTION, 1921
LIFE'S MOCKERY, 1928
LIFE'S SHADOWS, 1916
LIFE'S SHOP WINDOW, 1914
LIFE'S TEMPTATIONS, 1914
LIFE'S TWIST, 1920
LIFE'S WHIRLPOOL, 1916, A
LIFE'S WHIRLPOOL, 1917, A
LIFEBOAT, 1944, A
LIFEGUARD, 1976, C
LIFEGUARDSMAN, THE, 1916
LIFESPAN, 1975, C
LIFT, THE, 1965, O
LIFT, THE, 1983, C
LIFTED VEIL, THE, 1917
LIFTING SHADOWS, 1920, A
LIGEA
LIGHT
LIGHT, 1915
LIGHT ACROSSS THE STREET, THE, 1957, O
LIGHT AT DUSK, THE, 1916, A
LIGHT AT THE EDGE OF THE WORLD, THE, 1971, O
LIGHT BLUE
LIGHT FANTASTIC, 1964, A
LIGHT FANTASTIC, THE
LIGHT FINGERS, 1929, A
LIGHT FINGERS, 1957, A
LIGHT IN DARKNESS, 1917
LIGHT IN THE CLEARING, THE, 1921
LIGHT IN THE DARK, THE, 1922, A
LIGHT IN THE FOREST, THE, 1958, AAA
LIGHT IN THE PIAZZA, 1962, A
LIGHT IN THE WINDOW, THE, 1927, A
LIGHT OF HAPPINESS, THE, 1916
LIGHT OF HEART, THE
LIGHT OF THE WESTERN STARS, THE, 1925
LIGHT OF VICTORY, 1919, A
LIGHT OF WESTERN STARS, THE, 1918
LIGHT OF WESTERN STARS, THE, 1930, A
LIGHT OF WESTERN STARS, THE, 1940, A
LIGHT THAT FAILED, THE, 1916
LIGHT THAT FAILED, THE, 1923
LIGHT THAT FAILED, THE, 1939, A
LIGHT TOUCH, THE, 1951, C
LIGHT TOUCH, THE, 1955, A
LIGHT UP THE SKY, 1960, A
LIGHT WITHIN, THE
LIGHT WITHIN, THE, 1918
LIGHT WOMAN, A
LIGHT WOMAN, A, 1920
LIGHT YEARS AWAY, 1982, C
LIGHT, THE, 1916
LIGHT, 1919
LIGHTHOUSE, 1947, A
LIGHTHOUSE BY THE SEA, THE, 1924, A
LIGHTHOUSE KEEPER'S DAUGHTER, THE
LIGHTING, 1927
LIGHTING BILL, 1926
LIGHTNING BOLT, 1967, A
LIGHTING RIDER, THE, 1924
LIGHTING SPEED, 1928
LIGHTNIN', 1925
LIGHTNIN', 1930, A
LIGHTNIN' CRANDALL, 1937, A
LIGHTNIN' IN THE FOREST, 1948, C
LIGHTNIN' JACK, 1924
LIGHTNIN' SHOT, 1928
LIGHTNIN' SMITH RETURNS, 1931
LIGHTNING BILL CARSON, 1936, A
LIGHTNING BOLT, 1967, A
LIGHTNING CARSON RIDES AGAIN, 1938
LIGHTNING CONDUCTOR, 1938, A

LIGHTNING CONDUCTOR, THE, 1914, A
LIGHTNING FLYER, 1931, A
LIGHTNING GUNS, 1950, A
LIGHTNING LARIATS, 1927, A
LIGHTNING RAIDERS, 1945, A
LIGHTNING RANGE, 1934, A
LIGHTNING REPORTER, 1926, A
LIGHTNING ROMANCE, 1924, A
LIGHTNING STRIKES TWICE, 1935, A
LIGHTNING STRIKES TWICE, 1951, C
LIGHTNING STRIKES WEST, 1940, A
LIGHTNING SWORDS OF DEATH
LIGHTNING TRIGGERS, 1935
LIGHTS AND SHADOWS
LIGHTS O' LONDON, THE, 1914
LIGHTS OF HOME, THE, 1920
LIGHTS OF NEW YORK, 1928, A
LIGHTS OF NEW YORK, THE, 1916, A
LIGHTS OF NEW YORK, THE, 1922
LIGHTS OF OLD BROADWAY, 1925
LIGHTS OF OLD SANTA FE, 1944, A
LIGHTS OF THE DESERT, 1922, A
LIGHTS OF VARIETY
LIGHTS OUT
LIGHTS OUT, 1923
LIKE A CROW ON A JUNE BUG, 1972, C
LIKE A TURTLE ON ITS BACK, 1981, O
LIKE FATHER LIKE SON, 1961, C
LIKE FATHER, LIKE SON, 1965
LIKE WILDFIRE, 1917
LIKELY LADS, THE, 1976, A
LIKELY STORY, A, 1947, A
LIKENESS OF THE NIGHT, THE, 1921, A
LILA, 1962
LILA, 1968
LILA—LOVE UNDER THE MIDNIGHT SUN
LILAC DOMINO, THE, 1940, A
LILAC SUNBONNET, THE, 1922
LILAC TIME, 1928, A
LILACS IN THE SPRING
LILI, 1953, AA
LILI MARLEEN, 1981, O
LILI MARLENE
LILIES OF THE FIELD, 1930, O
LILIES OF THE FIELD, 1934, A
LILIES OF THE FIELD, 1963, A
LILIOM, 1930, C
LILIOM, 1935, A
LILITH, 1964, C
LILLI MARLENE, 1951, C
LILLIAN RUSSELL, 1940, A
LILLIES OF THE FIELD, 1924
LILLIES OF THE STREETS, 1925
LILLY TURNER, 1933, C
LILY AND THE ROSE, THE, 1915, A
LILY CHRISTINE, 1932, C
LILY OF KILARNEY
LILY OF KILLARNEY, 1929
LILY OF LAGUNA, 1938, C
LILY OF POVERTY FLAT, THE, 1915
LILY OF THE ALLEY, 1923, A
LILY OF THE DUST, 1924
LILY, THE, 1926
LIMBO
LIMBO, 1972, O
LIMBO LINE, THE, 1969, O
LIMEHOUSE BLUES, 1934, A-C
LIMELIGHT, 1952, A
LIMELIGHT, 1937
LIMIT, THE, 1972, C
LIMITE, 1930
LIMITED MAIL, THE, 1925
LIMONADOVY JOE
LIMOUSINE LIFE, 1918
LIMPING MAN, THE, 1931, A
LIMPING MAN, THE, 1936, A
LIMPING MAN, THE, 1953, A
LINCOLN CONSPIRACY, THE, 1977, A
LINCOLN HIGHWAYMAN, THE, 1920
LINDA, 1929, A
LINDA, 1960, A
LINDA BE GOOD, 1947, A
LINDA LOVELACE FOR PRESIDENT, 1975
LINE
LINE ENGAGED, 1935, A
LINE OF DUTY
LINE, THE, 1982, C
LINEUP, THE, 1934, A
LINEUP, THE, 1958, O
LINGERIE, 1928, A
LINKED BY FATE, 1919
LINKS OF JUSTICE, 1958, A
LIOLA
LION AND THE HORSE, THE, 1952, A
LION AND THE LAMB, 1931, A
LION AND THE MOUSE, THE, 1914
LION AND THE MOUSE, THE, 1919
LION AND THE MOUSE, THE, 1928, A
LION HAS WINGS, THE, 1940, A
LION HUNTERS, THE, 1951, AA
LION IN THE STREETS, A
LION IN WINTER, THE, 1968, A

LOS OLVIDADOS, 1950, O
LOS PLATILLOS VOLADORES, 1955, A
LOS SANTOS INOCENTES
LOSER TAKE ALL
LOSER TAKES ALL, 1956, A
LOSER'S END, 1934
LOSER'S END, THE, 1924, A
LOSERS, THE, 1968, O
LOSERS, THE, 1970, O
LOSIN' IT, 1983, O
LOSING GAME, THE
LOSING GROUND, 1982
LOSS OF FEELING, 1935, A
LOSS OF INNOCENCE, 1961, C
LOSS OF THE BIRKENHEAD, THE, 1914
LOST
LOST, 1983
LOST—A WIFE, 1925
LOST AND FOUND
LOST AND FOUND, 1979, A-C
LOST AND FOUND ON A SOUTH SEA ISLAND, 1923
LOST AND WON, 1915
LOST AND WON, 1917
LOST ANGEL, 1944, A
LOST AT SEA, 1926
LOST AT THE FRONT, 1927
LOST ATLANTIS
LOST BATALLION, THE, 1919
LOST BATTALION, 1961, A
LOST BATTALION, THE, 1921
LOST BOUNDARIES, 1949, A
LOST BRIDEGROOM, THE, 1916, A
LOST CANYON, 1943, A
LOST CHORD, THE, 1917, A
LOST CHORD, THE, 1925
LOST CHORD, THE, 1937, A
LOST CITY, THE, 1982
LOST COMMAND, THE, 1966, A-C
LOST CONTINENT, 1951, A
LOST CONTINENT, THE, 1968, A
LOST EXPRESS, THE, 1926
LOST FACE, THE, 1965, C
LOST HAPPINESS, 1948, A
LOST HONEYMOON, 1947, A
LOST HONOR OF KATHARINA BLUM, THE, 1975, C
LOST HORIZON, 1937, A
LOST HORIZON, 1973, A
LOST HOUSE, THE, 1915
LOST ILLUSION, THE
LOST IN A BIG CITY, 1923
LOST IN A HAREM, 1944, A
LOST IN ALASKA, 1952, AAA
LOST IN THE DARK, 1914
LOST IN THE LEGION, 1934, A
LOST IN THE STARS, 1974, A
LOST IN THE STRATOSPHERE, 1935, A
LOST IN TRANSIT, 1917
LOST JUNGLE, THE, 1934, A
LOST LADY, A, 1924, A
LOST LADY, A, 1934, A
LOST LADY, THE
LOST LAGOON, 1958, A
LOST LEADER, A, 1922
LOST LIMITED, THE, 1927, A
LOST MAN, THE, 1969, C
LOST MEN
LOST MISSILE, THE, 1958, A
LOST MOMENT, THE, 1947, A
LOST MONEY, 1919
LOST ON THE WESTERN FRONT, 1940, A
LOST ONE, THE, 1951, C
LOST PARADISE, THE, 1914
LOST PATROL, THE, 1929, A
LOST PATROL, THE, 1934, C
LOST PEOPLE, THE, 1950, A
LOST PRINCESS, THE, 1919
LOST RANCH, 1937, A
LOST RIVER
LOST ROMANCE, THE, 1921
LOST SEX, 1968, O
LOST SHADOW, THE, 1921
LOST SOULS, 1961, O
LOST SQUADRON, THE, 1932, C
LOST STAGE VALLEY
LOST TRAIL, THE, 1926
LOST TRAIL, THE, 1945, A
LOST TREASURE OF THE AMAZON
LOST TRIBE, THE, 1924
LOST TRIBE, THE, 1949, A
LOST VOLCANO, THE, 1950, AA
LOST WEEKEND, THE, 1945, C-O
LOST WOMEN
LOST WORLD OF LIBRA, THE, 1968
LOST WORLD OF SINBAD, THE, 1965, A
LOST WORLD, THE, 1925, A
LOST WORLD, THE, 1960, A
LOST ZEPPELIN, 1930, A
LOST ZEPPELIN, THE, 1929
LOST, LONELY AND VICIOUS, 1958, A
LOST-BAG BLUES, 1971
LOTNA, 1966, C
LOTTERY BRIDE, THE, 1930, A

LOTTERY LOVER, 1935, A
LOTTERY MAN, THE, 1916
LOTTERY MAN, THE, 1919
LOTUS BLOSSOM, 1921
LOTUS BLOSSOM, 1921
LOTUS EATER, THE, 1921
LOTUS LADY, 1930, A
LOTUS WOMAN, THE, 1916
LOUDEST WHISPER, THE
LOUDSPEAKER, THE, 1934, A
LOUDWATER MYSTERY, THE, 1921
LOUIE, THERE'S A CROWD DOWNSTAIRS
LOUISA, 1950, A
LOUISE, 1940, A
LOUISIANA, 1919, A
LOUISIANA, 1947, A
LOUISIANA GAL
LOUISIANA HAYRIDE, 1944, A
LOUISIANA HUSSY, 1960, C
LOUISIANA PURCHASE, 1941, A
LOUISIANA STORY, 1948, AAA
LOUISIANA TERRITORY, 1953, A
LOUISIANE, 1984, A-C
LOULOU, 1980, O
LOVABLE AND SWEET
LOVABLE CHEAT, THE, 1949, A
LOVE, 1916, A
LOVE, 1920
LOVE, 1927, C
LOVE, 1972, C
LOVE, 1982, C
LOVE 'EM AND LEAVE 'EM, 1926
LOVE -HATE -DEATH, 1918
LOVE -A LA CARTE, 1965, O
LOVE AFFAIR, 1932, A
LOVE AFFAIR, 1939, A
LOVE AFFAIR OF THE DICTATOR, THE
LOVE AFFAIR; OR THE CASE OF THE MISSING
   SWITCHBOARD OPERATOR, 1968, O
LOVE AFLAME, 1917, A
LOVE AFTER DEATH, 1968
LOVE AMONG THE MILLIONAIRES, 1930, A
LOVE AND AMBITION, 1917
LOVE AND ANARCHY, 1974, O
LOVE AND BULLETS, 1979, C
LOVE AND DEATH, 1975, A-C
LOVE AND GLORY, 1924
LOVE AND HATE, 1916
LOVE AND HISSES, 1937, A
LOVE AND JOURNALISM, 1916
LOVE AND KISSES, 1965, A
LOVE AND KISSES
LOVE AND LARCENY, 1963, A
LOVE AND LARCENY, 1983
LOVE AND LEARN, 1928, A
LOVE AND LEARN, 1947, A
LOVE AND MARRIAGE, 1966, C
LOVE AND MONEY, 1982, O
LOVE AND PAIN AND THE WHOLE DAMN THING,
   1973, C
LOVE AND SACRIFICE
LOVE AND SACRIFICE, 1936
LOVE AND THE DEVIL, 1929
LOVE AND THE FRENCHWOMAN, 1961, C-O
LOVE AND THE LAW, 1919
LOVE AND THE MIDNIGHT AUTO SUPPLY, 1978, C-O
LOVE AND THE WOMAN, 1919
LOVE AT FIRST BITE, 1979, C
LOVE AT FIRST SIGHT, 1930, A
LOVE AT FIRST SIGHT, 1977, A
LOVE AT NIGHT, 1961, C-O
LOVE AT SEA, 1936, A
LOVE AT SECOND SIGHT
LOVE AT THE WHEEL, 1921, A
LOVE AT TWENTY, 1963, C
LOVE AUCTION, THE, 1919, A
LOVE BAN, THE
LOVE BANDIT, THE, 1924
LOVE BEFORE BREAKFAST, 1936, A
LOVE BEGINS AT TWENTY, 1936, A
LOVE BIRDS, 1934, A
LOVE BOUND, 1932, A
LOVE BRAND, THE, 1923
LOVE BUG, THE, 1968, AAA
LOVE BURGLAR, THE, 1919
LOVE BUTCHER, THE, 1982, O
LOVE CAGE, THE
LOVE CALL, THE, 1919
LOVE CAPTIVE, THE, 1934, A
LOVE CHARM, THE, 1921, A
LOVE CHEAT, THE, 1919
LOVE CHILD, 1982, O
LOVE CHILDREN
LOVE COMES ALONG, 1930, A
LOVE COMES QUIETLY, 1974
LOVE CONTRACT, THE, 1932, A
LOVE CRAZY, 1941, A
LOVE CYCLES, 1969, C
LOVE DARES ALL
LOVE DEFENDER, THE, 1919
LOVE DOCTOR, THE, 1917
LOVE DOCTOR, THE, 1929, A

LOVE ETERNAL
LOVE ETERNE, THE, 1964, A
LOVE EXPERT, THE, 1920
LOVE FACTORY, 1969, C-O
LOVE FEAST, THE, 1966, O
LOVE FINDS A WAY
LOVE FINDS ANDY HARDY, 1938, AA
LOVE FLOWER, THE, 1920, A
LOVE FROM A STRANGER, 1937, C
LOVE FROM A STRANGER, 1947, A
LOVE GAMBLE, THE, 1925
LOVE GAMBLER, THE, 1922, A
LOVE GIRL, THE, 1916, A
LOVE GOD?, THE, 1969, A
LOVE HABIT, THE, 1931, A
LOVE HAPPY, 1949, A
LOVE HAS MANY FACES, 1965, C
LOVE HERMIT, THE, 1916
LOVE HOUR, THE, 1925
LOVE HUNGER, 1965, O
LOVE HUNGER, THE, 1919
LOVE HUNGRY, 1928
LOVE IN 4 DIMENSIONS, 1965, C
LOVE IN A BUNGALOW, 1937, A
LOVE IN A FOUR LETTER WORLD, 1970, O
LOVE IN A GOLDFISH BOWL, 1961, A
LOVE IN A HOT CLIMATE, 1958, A
LOVE IN A HURRY, 1919, A
LOVE IN A TAXI, 1980, A
LOVE IN A WOOD, 1915, A
LOVE IN BLOOM, 1935, A
LOVE IN COLD BLOOD
LOVE IN EXILE, 1936, A
LOVE IN GERMANY, A, 1984, O
LOVE IN HIGH GEAR, 1932
LOVE IN LAS VEGAS
LOVE IN MOROCCO, 1933, A
LOVE IN PAWN, 1953, A
LOVE IN THE AFTERNOON, 1957, A
LOVE IN THE DARK, 1922
LOVE IN THE DESERT, 1929, A
LOVE IN THE ROUGH, 1930, A
LOVE IN THE WELSH HILLS, 1921
LOVE IN THE WILDERNESS, 1920
LOVE IN WAITING, 1948, A
LOVE INSURANCE, 1920
LOVE IS A BALL, 1963, A
LOVE IS A CAROUSEL, 1970, O
LOVE IS A DAY'S WORK
LOVE IS A FUNNY THING, 1970, C
LOVE IS A HEADACHE, 1938, A
LOVE IS A MANY-SPLENDORED THING, 1955, A
LOVE IS A RACKET, 1932, A
LOVE IS A SPLENDID ILLUSION, 1970, O
LOVE IS A WEAPON
LOVE IS A WOMAN, 1967, C
LOVE IS AN AWFUL THING, 1922, A
LOVE IS BETTER THAN EVER, 1952, A
LOVE IS LIKE THAT, 1933, A
LOVE IS LIKE THAT, 1930
LOVE IS LOVE, 1919
LOVE IS MY PROFESSION, 1959, O
LOVE IS NEWS, 1937, A
LOVE IS ON THE AIR, 1937, A
LOVE ISLAND, 1952, A
LOVE ITALIAN STYLE
LOVE KISS, THE, 1930, A
LOVE LAUGHS AT ANDY HARDY, 1946, A
LOVE LETTER, THE, 1923, A
LOVE LETTERS, 1917
LOVE LETTERS, 1924
LOVE LETTERS, 1945, A
LOVE LETTERS, 1983, C
LOVE LETTERS OF A STAR, 1936, A
LOVE LIAR, THE, 1916, A
LOVE LIES, 1931, A
LOVE LIGHT, THE, 1921, A
LOVE LOTTERY, THE, 1954, A
LOVE MACHINE, THE, 1971, O
LOVE MADNESS
LOVE MADNESS, 1920
LOVE MAGGY, 1921
LOVE MAKERS, THE
LOVE MAKES 'EM WILD, 1927, A
LOVE MART, THE, 1927
LOVE MASK, THE, 1916
LOVE MASTER, THE, 1924
LOVE MATCH, THE, 1955, A
LOVE MATES, 1967, A
LOVE MATES, THE
LOVE ME, 1918
LOVE ME AND THE WORLD IS MINE, 1928, A
LOVE ME DEADLY, 1972, O
LOVE ME FOREVER, 1935, A
LOVE ME OR LEAVE ME, 1955, A
LOVE ME TENDER, 1956, A
LOVE ME TONIGHT, 1932, A
LOVE MERCHANT, THE, 1966, O
LOVE MERCHANTS
LOVE NEST, 1951, A
LOVE NEST, THE, 1922
LOVE NEST, THE, 1933, A

LOVE NET, THE, 1918
LOVE NEVER DIES, 1916
LOVE NEVER DIES, 1921
LOVE NOW . . . PAY LATER, 1966, C
LOVE NOW . . . PAY LATER, O
LOVE OF A STATE COUNCILLOR, 1915
LOVE OF AN ACTRESS, THE, 1914
LOVE OF JEANNE NEY, THE, 1927
LOVE OF PAQUITA, THE, 1927
LOVE OF SUNYA, THE, 1927
LOVE OF THREE QUEENS
LOVE OF WOMEN, 1924
LOVE OF WOMEN, THE, 1915
LOVE ON A BET, 1936, A
LOVE ON A BUDGET, 1938, A
LOVE ON A PILLOW, 1963, O
LOVE ON SKIS, 1933, A
LOVE ON THE DOLE, 1945, A
LOVE ON THE GROUND, 1984, C
LOVE ON THE RIO GRANDE, 1925
LOVE ON THE RIVIERA, 1964, C
LOVE ON THE RUN, 1936, A
LOVE ON THE RUN, 1980, A-C
LOVE ON THE SPOT, 1932, A
LOVE ON TOAST, 1937, A
LOVE ON WHEELS, 1932, A
LOVE ONE ANOTHER, 1922
LOVE OR FAME, 1919
LOVE OR JUSTICE, 1917
LOVE OR MONEY, 1920
LOVE OVER THE NIGHT, 1928
LOVE PARADE, THE, 1929, A-C
LOVE PAST THIRTY, 1934, A
LOVE PIKER, THE, 1923
LOVE PILL, THE, 1971
LOVE PIRATE, THE, 1923
LOVE PLAY
LOVE PROBLEMS, 1970, C
LOVE RACE
LOVE RACE, THE, 1931, A
LOVE RACKET, THE, 1929, A
LOVE REDEEMED
LOVE ROBOTS, THE, 1965, C
LOVE ROOT, THE
LOVE ROUTE, THE, 1915
LOVE SLAVES OF THE AMAZONS, 1957, A
LOVE SPECIAL, THE, 1921
LOVE SPECIALIST, THE, 1959, A
LOVE STARVED
LOVE STORM, THE, 1931, A
LOVE STORY
LOVE STORY, 1949, C
LOVE STORY, 1970, A-C
LOVE STORY OF ALIETTE BRUNTON, THE, 1924
LOVE STREAMS, 1984, C
LOVE SUBLIME, A, 1917
LOVE SWINDLE, 1918, A
LOVE TAKES FLIGHT, 1937, A
LOVE TEST, THE, 1935, A
LOVE THAT BRUTE, 1950, A
LOVE THAT DARES, THE, 1919
LOVE THAT LIVES, THE, 1917
LOVE THIEF, THE, 1916
LOVE THIEF, THE, 1926
LOVE THRILL, THE, 1927
LOVE THY NEIGHBOR, 1940, A
LOVE THY NEIGHBOUR, 1973
LOVE TIME, 1934, A
LOVE TOY, THE, 1926, A
LOVE TRADER, 1930, A
LOVE TRAIL, THE, 1916
LOVE TRAP, THE, 1923
LOVE TRAP, THE, 1929, A
LOVE UNDER FIRE, 1937, A
LOVE UNDER THE CRUCIFIX, 1965, A
LOVE UNDER THE ELMS, 1973
LOVE UP THE POLE, 1936, A
LOVE WAGER, THE, 1927
LOVE WAGER, THE, 1933, A
LOVE WALTZ, THE, 1930, A
LOVE WANGA, 1942
LOVE WATCHES, 1918
LOVE WITH THE PROPER STRANGER, 1963, C
LOVE WITHOUT QUESTION, 1920
LOVE'S A LUXURY
LOVE'S BATTLE, 1920
LOVE'S BLINDNESS, 1926, A
LOVE'S BOOMERANG, 1922
LOVE'S CONQUEST, 1918
LOVE'S CROSS ROADS, 1916
LOVE'S CRUCIBLE, 1916
LOVE'S CRUCIBLE, 1922
LOVE'S FLAME, 1920
LOVE'S GREATEST MISTAKE, 1927
LOVE'S HARVEST, 1920
LOVE'S INFLUENCE, 1922
LOVE'S LARIAT, 1916
LOVE'S LAW, 1917
LOVE'S LAW, 1918
LOVE'S MASQUERADE, 1922
LOVE'S OLD SWEET SONG, 1917, A
LOVE'S OLD SWEET SONG, 1923

LOVE'S OLD SWEET SONG, 1933, A
LOVE'S OPTION, 1928
LOVE'S PAY DAY, 1918
LOVE'S PENALTY, 1921, A
LOVE'S PILGRIMAGE TO AMERICA, 1916
LOVE'S PRISONER, 1919
LOVE'S PROTEGE, 1920
LOVE'S REDEMPTION, 1921, A
LOVE'S TOLL, 1916, A
LOVE'S WHIRLPOOL, 1924
LOVE'S WILDERNESS, 1924, A
LOVE, HATE AND A WOMAN, 1921
LOVE, HONOR AND ?, 1919
LOVE, HONOR AND BEHAVE, 1920
LOVE, HONOR AND BEHAVE, 1938, A
LOVE, HONOR AND GOODBYE, 1945, A
LOVE, HONOR AND OBEY, 1920, A
LOVE, HONOR AND OH, BABY, 1940, A
LOVE, HONOR, AND OH BABY, 1933, A
LOVE, LIFE AND LAUGHTER, 1934, A
LOVE, LIVE AND LAUGH, 1929, A
LOVE, SOLDIERS AND WOMEN
LOVE, THE ITALIAN WAY, 1964, C
LOVE, THE ONLY LAW
LOVE, VAMPIRE STYLE, 1971
LOVE—TAHITI STYLE
LOVE-INS, THE, 1967, C
LOVEBOUND, 1923
LOVED ONE, THE, 1965, C
LOVELESS, THE, 1982, O
LOVELETTERS FROM TERALBA ROAD, 1977
LOVELINES, 1984, O
LOVELORN, THE, 1927, A
LOVELY BUT DEADLY, 1983
LOVELY MARY, 1916
LOVELY TO LOOK AT
LOVELY TO LOOK AT, 1952, A
LOVELY WAY TO DIE, A, 1968, C
LOVELY WAY TO GO, A
LOVEMAKER, THE
LOVEMAKERS, THE
LOVER BOY
LOVER COME BACK, 1931, A
LOVER COME BACK, 1946, A
LOVER COME BACK, 1961, A
LOVER FOR THE SUMMER, A
LOVER OF CAMILLE, THE, 1924
LOVER'S ISLAND, 1925, A
LOVER'S LANE, 1924, A
LOVER'S NET, 1957, C
LOVER'S OATH, A, 1925, A
LOVER, WIFE
LOVERS AND LIARS, 1981, O
LOVERS AND LOLLIPOPS, 1956, A
LOVERS AND LUGGERS, 1938, A
LOVERS AND OTHER STRANGERS, 1970, C
LOVERS COURAGEOUS, 1932, A
LOVERS IN ARABY, 1924
LOVERS IN LIMBO
LOVERS IN QUARANTINE, 1925
LOVERS LIKE US
LOVERS MUST LEARN
LOVERS OF LISBON
LOVERS OF MONTPARNASSE, THE
LOVERS OF TERUEL, THE, 1962, A
LOVERS OF TOLEDO, THE, 1954, A
LOVERS OF VERONA, THE, 1951, A
LOVERS ON A TIGHTROPE, 1962, A
LOVERS' ROCK, 1966, A
LOVERS, HAPPY LOVERS, 1955, C
LOVERS, THE, 1959, O
LOVERS, THE, 1972, C
LOVERS?, 1927
LOVES AND ADVENTURES IN THE LIFE OF
    SHAKESPEARE (1914, Brit.)
LOVES AND TIMES OF SCARAMOUCHE, THE, 1976, C
LOVES OF A BLONDE, 1966, A
LOVES OF A DICTATOR
LOVES OF AN ACTRESS, 1928
LOVES OF ARIANE, THE
LOVES OF CARMEN, 1927
LOVES OF CARMEN, THE, 1948, C
LOVES OF COLLEEN BAWN, THE, 1924
LOVES OF EDGAR ALLAN POE, THE, 1942, A
LOVES OF HERCULES, THE, 1960, A
LOVES OF ISADORA, THE
LOVES OF JOANNA GODDEN, THE, 1947, A
LOVES OF LETTY, THE, 1920
LOVES OF MADAME DUBARRY, THE, 1938, A
LOVES OF MARY, QUEEN OF SCOTS, THE, 1923
LOVES OF RICARDO, THE, 1926, A
LOVES OF ROBERT BURNS, THE, 1930, A
LOVES OF SALAMMBO, THE, 1962, A
LOVES OF THREE QUEENS, THE, 1954, A
LOVESICK, 1983, C
LOVETIME, 1921
LOVEY MARY, 1926
LOVIN' FOOL, THE, 1926
LOVIN' MOLLY, 1974, O
LOVIN' THE LADIES, 1930, A
LOVING, 1970, C
LOVING COUPLES, 1966, O

LOVING COUPLES, 1980, O
LOVING FOOL, THE
LOVING LIES, 1924
LOVING MEMORY, 1970, O
LOVING YOU, 1957, A
LOW BLOW, THE, 1970
LOWER DEPTHS, THE, 1937, C
LOWER DEPTHS, THE, 1962, C
LOWLAND CINDERELLA, A, 1921
LOYAL HEART, 1946, AAA
LOYAL LIVES, 1923, A
LOYALTIES, 1934, A
LOYALTY, 1918
LOYALTY OF LOVE, 1937, A
LSD, I HATE YOU
LT. ROBIN CRUSOE, U.S.N., 1966, AAA
LUCETTE, 1924
LUCI DEL VARIETA
LUCIANO, 1963, C
LUCIFER COMPLEX, THE, 1978
LUCIFER PROJECT, THE
LUCIFER'S WOMEN, 1978
LUCK, 1923, A
LUCK AND PLUCK, 1919, A
LUCK AND SAND, 1925
LUCK IN PAWN, 1919
LUCK OF A SAILOR, THE, 1934, A
LUCK OF GERALDINE LAIRD, THE, 1920
LUCK OF GINGER COFFEY, THE, 1964, A-C
LUCK OF ROARING CAMP, THE, 1937, A
LUCK OF THE GAME
LUCK OF THE IRISH, 1948, A
LUCK OF THE IRISH, THE, 1920
LUCK OF THE IRISH, THE, 1937, A
LUCK OF THE NAVY
LUCK OF THE NAVY, THE, 1927
LUCK OF THE TURF, 1936, A
LUCK TOUCHED MY LEGS, 1930
LUCKIEST GIRL IN THE WORLD, THE, 1936, A
LUCKY
LUCKY 13
LUCKY BOOTS
LUCKY BOY, 1929, A
LUCKY BRIDE, THE, 1948, AA
LUCKY CARSON, 1921
LUCKY CISCO KID, 1940, A
LUCKY DAN, 1922
LUCKY DAYS, 1935, A
LUCKY DAYS, 1943
LUCKY DEVIL, 1925
LUCKY DEVILS, 1933, A
LUCKY DEVILS, 1941, C
LUCKY DOG, 1933, AAA
LUCKY FOOL, 1927
LUCKY GIRL, 1932, A
LUCKY HORSESHOE, THE, 1925, A
LUCKY IN LOVE, 1929, A
LUCKY JADE, 1937, A
LUCKY JIM, 1957, C
LUCKY JORDAN, 1942, A
LUCKY LADIES, 1932, A
LUCKY LADY, 1975, C-O
LUCKY LADY, THE, 1926
LUCKY LARKIN, 1930
LUCKY LARRIGAN, 1933, A
LUCKY LEGS, 1942, A
LUCKY LOSER, 1934, A
LUCKY LOSERS, 1950, C
LUCKY LUCIANO
LUCKY LUKE, 1971, A
LUCKY MASCOT, THE, 1951, A
LUCKY ME, 1954, A
LUCKY NICK CAIN, 1951, A
LUCKY NIGHT, 1939, A
LUCKY NUMBER, THE, 1933, A
LUCKY PARTNERS, 1940, A
LUCKY RALSTON
LUCKY SPURS, 1926
LUCKY STAR, 1929, A
LUCKY STAR, THE, 1980, A
LUCKY STIFF, THE, 1949, A
LUCKY SWEEP, A, 1932, A
LUCKY TERROR, 1936, A
LUCKY TEXAN, THE, 1934, A
LUCKY TO BE A WOMAN, 1955, C-O
LUCKY TO ME, 1939, AA
LUCRECE BORGIA, 1953, O
LUCRETIA BORGIA
LUCRETIA LOMBARD, 1923
LUCREZIA BORGIA, 1937, A
LUCY GALLANT, 1955, C
LUDWIG, 1973, O
LUGGAGE OF THE GODS, 1983, C
LULLABY, 1961, A
LULLABY OF BROADWAY, THE, 1951, A
LULLABY, THE
LULLABY, THE, 1924, A
LULU, 1962, O
LULU, 1978, O
LULU BELLE, 1948, A
LUM AND ABNER ABROAD, 1956, AA
LUMBERJACK, 1944, A

MAGIC CUP, THE, 1921
MAGIC EYE, THE, 1918
MAGIC FACE, THE, 1951, A
MAGIC FIRE, 1956, A
MAGIC FLAME, THE, 1927
MAGIC FOUNTAIN, THE, 1961, A
MAGIC GARDEN OF STANLEY SWEETHART, THE, 1970, O
MAGIC GARDEN, THE
MAGIC GARDEN, THE, 1927
MAGIC NIGHT, 1932, A
MAGIC OF LASSIE, THE, 1978, AA
MAGIC PONY, 1979
MAGIC SKIN, THE, 1915
MAGIC SPECTACLES, 1961, O
MAGIC SWORD, THE, 1962, A
MAGIC TOWN, 1947, AA
MAGIC VOYAGE OF SINBAD, THE, 1962, A
MAGIC WEAVER, THE, 1965, A
MAGIC WORLD OF TOPO GIGIO, THE, 1961, A
MAGICAL SPECTACLES
MAGICIAN OF LUBLIN, THE, 1979, C
MAGICIAN, THE, 1926
MAGICIAN, THE, 1959, C
MAGNET, THE, 1950, A
MAGNETIC MONSTER, THE, 1953, C
MAGNIFICENT ADVENTURE, THE, 1952
MAGNIFICENT AMBERSONS, THE, 1942, A
MAGNIFICENT BANDITS, THE, 1969, C
MAGNIFICENT BRUTE, THE, 1921
MAGNIFICENT BRUTE, THE, 1936, A
MAGNIFICENT CONCUBINE, THE, 1964, A
MAGNIFICENT CUCKOLD, THE, 1965, A
MAGNIFICENT DOLL, 1946, A
MAGNIFICENT DOPE, THE, 1942, A
MAGNIFICENT FLIRT, THE, 1928, A
MAGNIFICENT FRAUD, THE, 1939, A
MAGNIFICENT LIE, 1931, A
MAGNIFICENT MATADOR, THE, 1955, A
MAGNIFICENT MEDDLER, THE, 1917
MAGNIFICENT OBSESSION, 1935, A
MAGNIFICENT OBSESSION, 1954, A
MAGNIFICENT ONE, THE, 1974, A
MAGNIFICENT OUTCAST
MAGNIFICENT ROGUE, THE, 1946, A
MAGNIFICENT ROUGHNECKS, 1956, A
MAGNIFICENT SEVEN DEADLY SINS, THE, 1971, A-C
MAGNIFICENT SEVEN RIDE, THE, 1972, A
MAGNIFICENT SEVEN, THE, 1960, C
MAGNIFICENT SEVEN, THE, 1954
MAGNIFICENT SHOWMAN, THE
MAGNIFICENT SINNER, 1963, A
MAGNIFICENT TRAMP, THE, 1962, A
MAGNIFICENT TWO, THE, 1967, A
MAGNIFICENT YANKEE, THE, 1950, AA
MAGNUM FORCE, 1973, C-O
MAGOICHI SAGA, THE, 1970, C
MAGUS, THE, 1968, C
MAHANAGAR
MAHLER, 1974, A-C
MAHOGANY, 1975, C
MAID AND THE MARTIAN, THE
MAID FOR MURDER, 1963, A
MAID HAPPY, 1933, A
MAID OF BELGIUM, THE, 1917
MAID OF CEFN YDFA, THE, 1914
MAID OF SALEM, 1937, A
MAID OF THE MOUNTAINS, THE, 1932, A
MAID OF THE WEST, 1921, A
MAID TO ORDER, 1932, A
MAID'S NIGHT OUT, 1938, A
MAIDEN FOR A PRINCE, A, 1967, A
MAIDEN, THE, 1961, A
MAIDS, THE, 1975, C
MAIDSTONE, 1970, C
MAIGRET LAYS A TRAP, 1958, C
MAIL ORDER BRIDE, 1964, A
MAIL TRAIN, 1941, A
MAILBAG ROBBERY, 1957, A-C
MAILMAN, THE, 1923, A
MAIN ATTRACTION, THE, 1962, A
MAIN CHANCE, THE, 1966, A
MAIN EVENT, THE, 1927
MAIN EVENT, THE, 1938, A
MAIN EVENT, THE, 1979, A-C
MAIN STREET, 1923
MAIN STREET, 1956, A
MAIN STREET AFTER DARK, 1944, A
MAIN STREET GIRL
MAIN STREET KID, THE, 1947, A
MAIN STREET LAWYER, 1939, A
MAIN STREET TO BROADWAY, 1953, A
MAIN STREET, 1936
MAIN THING IS TO LOVE, THE, 1975, C
MAINSPRING, THE, 1916
MAINSPRING, THE, 1917
MAIS OU ET DONC ORNICAR, 1979, C
MAISIE, 1939, A
MAISIE GETS HER MAN, 1942, A
MAISIE GOES TO RENO, 1944, A
MAISIE WAS A LADY, 1941, A
MAISIE'S MARRIAGE, 1923

MAITRE EVORA, 1921
MAJDHAR, 1984, C
MAJESTY OF THE LAW, THE, 1915
MAJIN, 1968, A
MAJIN, THE HIDEOUS IDOL
MAJIN, THE MONSTER OF TERROR
MAJOR AND THE MINOR, THE, 1942, A
MAJOR BARBARA, 1941, A
MAJOR DUNDEE, 1965, C-O
MAJORITY OF ONE, A, 1961, A
MAKE A FACE, 1971, C
MAKE A MILLION, 1935, A
MAKE A WISH, 1937, A
MAKE AND BREAK
MAKE BELIEVE BALLROOM, 1949, A
MAKE HASTE TO LIVE, 1954, A
MAKE IT THREE, 1938, A
MAKE LIKE A THIEF, 1966, A
MAKE ME A STAR, 1932, A
MAKE ME AN OFFER, 1954, A
MAKE MINE A DOUBLE, 1962, A
MAKE MINE A MILLION, 1965, A
MAKE MINE MINK, 1960, A
MAKE MINE MUSIC, 1946, AA
MAKE WAY FOR A LADY, 1936, A
MAKE WAY FOR LILA, 1962, A
MAKE WAY FOR TOMORROW, 1937, A
MAKE YOUR OWN BED, 1944, A
MAKE-BELIEVE WIFE, THE, 1918
MAKE-UP, 1937, A
MAKER OF MEN, 1931, A
MAKERS OF MEN, 1925
MAKING A MAN, 1922, A
MAKING GOOD
MAKING GOOD
MAKING GOOD, 1923
MAKING IT, 1971, O
MAKING LOVE, 1982, O
MAKING OF A LADY, THE
MAKING OF BOBBY BURNIT, THE, 1914
MAKING OF MADDALENA, THE, 1916
MAKING OF O'MALLEY, THE, 1925
MAKING OVER OF GEOFFREY MANNING, THE, 1915
MAKING THE GRADE, 1921, A
MAKING THE GRADE, 1929, A
MAKING THE GRADE, 1984, O
MAKING THE HEADLINES, 1938, A
MAKING THE VARSITY, 1928, A
MAKO: THE JAWS OF DEATH, 1976, C
MAKUCHI
MALACHI'S COVE, 1973, AAA
MALAGA, 1962, A
MALAGA, 1954
MALATESTA'S CARNIVAL, 1973, O
MALAY NIGHTS, 1933, A
MALAYA, 1950, A
MALCOLM STRAUSS' SALOME
MALDONE, 1928
MALE AND FEMALE, 1919, A
MALE AND FEMALE
MALE AND FEMALE SINCE ADAM AND EVE, 1961, A
MALE ANIMAL, THE, 1942, A
MALE COMPANION, 1965, A
MALE HUNT, 1965, A
MALE SERVICE, 1966, O
MALE WANTED, 1923
MALEFICES
MALENCONTRE, 1920
MALENKA, THE VAMPIRE, 1972, O
MALEVIL, 1981, C
MALIBU
MALIBU BEACH, 1978, C
MALIBU HIGH, 1979, O
MALICE
MALICIOUS, 1974, O
MALIZIA
MALOU, 1983, C
MALPAS MYSTERY, THE, 1967, A
MALPERTIUS, 1972, C
MALTA STORY, 1954, A-C
MALTESE BIPPY, THE, 1969, A
MALTESE FALCON, THE, 1931, A
MALTESE FALCON, THE, 1941, A
MAMA LOVES PAPA, 1933, A
MAMA LOVES PAPA, 1945, A
MAMA RUNS WILD, 1938, A
MAMA STEPS OUT, 1937, A
MAMA'S AFFAIR, 1921
MAMA'S DIRTY GIRLS, 1974
MAMA'S GONE A-HUNTING, 1976
MAMAN COLIBRI, 1929
MAMBA, 1930, A
MAMBO, 1955, C
MAME, 1974, A
MAMI
MAMMA DRACULA, 1980, O
MAMMA ROMA, 1962, C
MAMMY, 1930, A
MAN ABOUT THE HOUSE, 1974
MAN ABOUT THE HOUSE, A, 1947, A
MAN ABOUT TOWN, 1932, A
MAN ABOUT TOWN, 1939, AA

MAN ABOUT TOWN, 1947, A
MAN ABOVE THE LAW, 1918, A
MAN ACCUSED, 1959, C
MAN AFRAID, 1957, A
MAN AGAINST MAN, 1961, C
MAN AGAINST WOMAN, 1932, A
MAN ALIVE, 1945, A
MAN ALONE, A, 1955, A
MAN ALONE, THE, 1923
MAN AND A WOMAN, A, 1966, A-C
MAN AND BEAST, 1917
MAN AND BOY, 1972, A
MAN AND HIS ANGEL, 1916
MAN AND HIS MATE
MAN AND HIS MATE, A, 1915, A
MAN AND HIS MONEY, A, 1919
MAN AND HIS SOUL, 1916
MAN AND HIS WOMAN, 1920, C
MAN AND MAID, 1925, A
MAN AND THE BEAST, THE, 1951, A
MAN AND THE MOMENT, THE, 1918, C
MAN AND THE MOMENT, THE, 1929, A
MAN AND THE MONSTER, THE, 1965, A
MAN AND THE WOMAN, A, 1917, A
MAN AND WIFE, 1923
MAN AND WOMAN, 1920
MAN AND WOMAN, 1921
MAN AT LARGE, 1941, A
MAN AT SIX
MAN AT THE CARLTON TOWER, 1961, C
MAN AT THE TOP, 1973, A
MAN BAIT, 1926, A
MAN BAIT, 1952, A
MAN BEAST, 1956, A
MAN BEHIND THE CURTAIN, THE, 1916
MAN BEHIND THE DOOR, THE, 1914, A
MAN BEHIND THE GUN, THE, 1952, A
MAN BEHIND THE MASK, THE, 1936, A
MAN BEHIND "THE TIMES", THE, 1917
MAN BENEATH, THE, 1919
MAN BETRAYED, A, 1937, A
MAN BETRAYED, A, 1941, A
MAN BETWEEN, THE, 1923
MAN BETWEEN, THE, 1953, A
MAN BY THE ROADSIDE, THE, 1923
MAN CALLED ADAM, A, 1966, C
MAN CALLED BACK, THE, 1932, C
MAN CALLED DAGGER, A, 1967, A
MAN CALLED FLINTSTONE, THE, 1966, AAA
MAN CALLED GANNON, A, 1969, A
MAN CALLED HORSE, A, 1970, O
MAN CALLED NOON, THE, 1973, C
MAN CALLED PETER, THE, 1955, AA
MAN CALLED SLEDGE, A, 1971, O
MAN CALLED SULLIVAN, A
MAN COULD GET KILLED, A, A
MAN CRAZY, 1927, A
MAN CRAZY, A
MAN DETAINED, C
MAN EATER, 1958
MAN EATER OF HYDRA
MAN ESCAPED, A, A
MAN FOLLOWING THE SUN
MAN FOR ALL SEASONS, A, A
MAN FOR HANGING, A, 1972
MAN FOUR-SQUARE, A, 1926, A
MAN FOUR-SQUARE, THE
MAN FRIDAY, A-C
MAN FROM ARIZONA, THE, 1932
MAN FROM BEYOND, THE, 1922, A
MAN FROM BITTER RIDGE, THE, 1955, A
MAN FROM BITTER ROOTS, THE, 1916
MAN FROM BLACK HILLS, THE, 1952, A
MAN FROM BLANKLEY'S, THE, 1930, A
MAN FROM BROADWAY, 1924
MAN FROM BRODNEY'S, THE, 1923
MAN FROM BUTTON WILLOW, THE, AA
MAN FROM C.O.T.T.O.N.
MAN FROM CAIRO, THE, 1953, A
MAN FROM CHEYENNE, A
MAN FROM CHICAGO, THE, A
MAN FROM COCODY, A
MAN FROM COLORADO, THE, 1948, A-C
MAN FROM DAKOTA, THE, 1940, A
MAN FROM DEATH VALLEY, THE, 1931, A
MAN FROM DEL RIO, 1956, A
MAN FROM DOWN UNDER, THE, 1943, A-C
MAN FROM DOWNING STREET, THE, 1922
MAN FROM FRISCO, 1944, A
MAN FROM FUNERAL RANGE, THE, 1918
MAN FROM GALVESTON, THE, 1964, A
MAN FROM GLENGARRY, THE, 1923
MAN FROM GOD'S COUNTRY, 1924
MAN FROM GOD'S COUNTRY, 1958, A
MAN FROM GUN TOWN, THE, 1936, A
MAN FROM HARDPAN, THE, 1927, A
MAN FROM HEADQUARTERS, 1928, A
MAN FROM HEADQUARTERS, 1942, A
MAN FROM HELL'S EDGES, 1932, A
MAN FROM HELL'S RIVER, 1922
MAN FROM HELL, THE, 1934, A
MAN FROM HOME, THE, 1914, A

MAN FROM HOME, THE, 1922
MAN FROM HONG KONG, 1975, O
MAN FROM LARAMIE, THE, 1955, C
MAN FROM LONE MOUNTAIN, THE, 1925
MAN FROM LOST RIVER, THE, 1921
MAN FROM MANHATTAN, THE, 1916
MAN FROM MARS, THE
MAN FROM MEDICINE HAT, THE
MAN FROM MEXICO, THE, 1914
MAN FROM MONTANA, 1941, A
MAN FROM MONTANA, THE, 1917, A
MAN FROM MONTEREY, THE, 1933, A
MAN FROM MONTREAL, THE, 1940, A
MAN FROM MOROCCO, THE, 1946, A
MAN FROM MUSIC MOUNTAIN, 1938, A
MAN FROM MUSIC MOUNTAIN, 1943, A
MAN FROM NEVADA, THE
MAN FROM NEVADA, THE, 1929
MAN FROM NEW MEXICO, THE, 1932, A
MAN FROM NEW YORK, THE, 1923
MAN FROM NOWHERE, A, 1920
MAN FROM NOWHERE, THE, 1916
MAN FROM NOWHERE, THE, 1930
MAN FROM NOWHERE, THE, 1976
MAN FROM NOWHERE, THE
MAN FROM O.R.G.Y., THE, 1970, O
MAN FROM OKLAHOMA, THE, 1926
MAN FROM OKLAHOMA, THE, 1945, AAA
MAN FROM OREGON, THE, 1915
MAN FROM PAINTED POST, THE, 1917, A
MAN FROM PLANET X, THE, 1951, A
MAN FROM RAINBOW VALLEY, THE, 1946, A
MAN FROM RED GULCH, THE, 1925
MAN FROM SNOWY RIVER, THE, 1983, C
MAN FROM SONORA, 1951
MAN FROM SUNDOWN, THE, 1939, A
MAN FROM TANGIER
MAN FROM TEXAS, THE, 1921
MAN FROM TEXAS, THE, 1939, A
MAN FROM TEXAS, THE, 1948, A
MAN FROM THE ALAMO, THE, 1953, A
MAN FROM THE BIG CITY, THE
MAN FROM THE BLACK HILLS, 1952
MAN FROM THE DINERS' CLUB, THE, 1963, A
MAN FROM THE EAST, A, 1974, C-O
MAN FROM THE EAST, THE, 1961, A
MAN FROM THE FIRST CENTURY, THE, 1961, A
MAN FROM THE FOLIES BERGERE, THE
MAN FROM THE PAST, THE
MAN FROM THE RIO GRANDE, THE, 1926
MAN FROM THE RIO GRANDE, THE, 1943, A
MAN FROM THE WEST, THE, 1926
MAN FROM THUNDER RIVER, THE, 1943, A
MAN FROM TORONTO, THE, 1933, A
MAN FROM TUMBLEWEEDS, THE, 1940, A
MAN FROM UTAH, THE, 1934, A
MAN FROM WYOMING, A, 1930, A
MAN FROM WYOMING, THE, 1924, A
MAN FROM YESTERDAY, THE, 1932, A
MAN FROM YESTERDAY, THE, 1949, O
MAN GETTER, THE
MAN GETTER, THE, 1923
MAN GOES THROUGH THE WALL, A
MAN HATER, THE, 1917, C
MAN HE FOUND, THE
MAN HUNT, 1933, A
MAN HUNT, 1936, A
MAN HUNT, 1941, A
MAN HUNT, THE, 1918, A
MAN HUNTER, THE, 1919
MAN HUNTER, THE, 1930, A
MAN HUNTERS, 1923
MAN HUNTERS OF THE CARIBBEAN, 1938, A
MAN I KILLED
MAN I LOVE, THE, 1929, A
MAN I LOVE, THE, 1946, A
MAN I MARRIED, THE, 1940, A
MAN I MARRY, THE, 1936, A
MAN I WANT, THE, 1934, A
MAN IN A COCKED HAT, 1960, A
MAN IN A LOOKING GLASS, A, 1965
MAN IN BLACK, THE, 1950, C-O
MAN IN BLUE, THE, 1925
MAN IN BLUE, THE, 1937, A
MAN IN GREY, THE, 1943, A-C
MAN IN HALF-MOON STREET, THE, 1944, A
MAN IN HIDING
MAN IN HOBBLES, THE, 1928, A
MAN IN MOTLEY, THE, 1916
MAN IN OUTER SPACE
MAN IN POSSESSION, THE
MAN IN POSSESSION, THE, 1915
MAN IN POSSESSION, THE, 1931, A-C
MAN IN THE ATTIC, 1953, C
MAN IN THE ATTIC, THE, 1915
MAN IN THE BACK SEAT, THE, 1961, A
MAN IN THE DARK, 1953, A
MAN IN THE DARK, 1963, A
MAN IN THE DINGHY, THE, 1951, A
MAN IN THE GLASS BOOTH, THE, 1975, A
MAN IN THE GREY FLANNEL SUIT, THE, 1956, A
MAN IN THE IRON MASK, THE, 1939, A

MAN IN THE MIDDLE, 1964, A-C
MAN IN THE MIRROR, THE, 1936, A
MAN IN THE MOON, 1961, A
MAN IN THE MOONLIGHT MASK, THE, 1958, A
MAN IN THE MOONLIGHT, THE, 1919
MAN IN THE NET, THE, 1959, A
MAN IN THE OPEN, A, 1919, A
MAN IN THE ROAD, THE, 1957, A
MAN IN THE ROUGH, 1928, A
MAN IN THE SADDLE, 1951, A
MAN IN THE SADDLE, THE
MAN IN THE SADDLE, THE, 1926
MAN IN THE SHADOW, 1957, A
MAN IN THE SHADOW, THE, 1926
MAN IN THE SHADOWS, THE, 1915
MAN IN THE SKY
MAN IN THE STORM, THE, 1969, A
MAN IN THE TRUNK, THE, 1942, A
MAN IN THE VAULT, 1956, A
MAN IN THE WATER, THE, 1963, A
MAN IN THE WHITE SUIT, THE, 1952, A
MAN IN THE WILDERNESS, 1971, O
MAN INSIDE, THE, 1916
MAN INSIDE, THE, 1958, C
MAN IS ARMED, THE, 1956, A
MAN IS TEN FEET TALL, A
MAN KILLER
MAN LIFE PASSED BY, THE, 1923
MAN MAD
MAN MADE MONSTER, 1941, A
MAN MISSING
MAN MUST LIVE, THE, 1925
MAN NEXT DOOR, THE, 1923
MAN NOBODY KNOWS, THE, 1925
MAN O' WARS MAN, THE, 1914
MAN OF A THOUSAND FACES, 1957, A
MAN OF ACTION, 1933
MAN OF ACTION, THE, 1923
MAN OF AFFAIRS, 1937, A
MAN OF AFRICA, 1956, A
MAN OF BRONZE
MAN OF BRONZE, THE, 1918
MAN OF CONFLICT, 1953, A
MAN OF CONQUEST, 1939, A
MAN OF COURAGE, 1922
MAN OF COURAGE, 1943, A
MAN OF EVIL, 1948, A
MAN OF FLOWERS, 1984, O
MAN OF HIS WORD, A, 1915
MAN OF HONOR, A, 1919
MAN OF IRON
MAN OF IRON, 1935, A
MAN OF IRON, 1981, C
MAN OF IRON, A
MAN OF LA MANCHA, 1972, C
MAN OF MARBLE, 1979, C-O
MAN OF MAYFAIR, 1931, A
MAN OF MUSIC, 1953, A
MAN OF MYSTERY, THE, 1917
MAN OF NERVE, A, 1925, A
MAN OF QUALITY, A, 1926
MAN OF SENTIMENT, A, 1933, A
MAN OF SHAME, THE, 1915
MAN OF SORROW, A, 1916
MAN OF STONE, THE, 1921
MAN OF THE FAMILY
MAN OF THE FOREST, 1926
MAN OF THE FOREST, 1933, A
MAN OF THE FOREST, THE, 1921
MAN OF THE HOUR
MAN OF THE HOUR, THE, 1940, A
MAN OF THE MOMENT, 1935, A
MAN OF THE MOMENT, 1955, A
MAN OF THE PEOPLE, 1937, A
MAN OF THE WEST, 1958, C-O
MAN OF THE WORLD, 1931, A
MAN OF TWO WORLDS, 1934, A
MAN OF VIOLENCE, 1970, O
MAN ON A MISSION, 1965
MAN ON A STRING, 1960, A
MAN ON A SWING, 1974, C
MAN ON A TIGHTROPE, 1953, A
MAN ON A TIGHTROPE, 1949
MAN ON AMERICA'S CONSCIENCE, THE
MAN ON FIRE, 1957, A
MAN ON THE BOX, THE, 1914
MAN ON THE BOX, THE, 1925, A
MAN ON THE EIFFEL TOWER, THE, 1949, A
MAN ON THE FLYING TRAPEZE, THE, 1935, A
MAN ON THE PROWL, 1957, A
MAN ON THE RUN, 1949, A
MAN ON THE RUN, 1964
MAN ON THE SPYING TRAPEZE, 1965
MAN OR GUN, 1958, A
MAN OUTSIDE, 1965
MAN OUTSIDE, THE, 1933, A
MAN OUTSIDE, THE, 1968, A
MAN POWER, 1927
MAN RUSTLIN', 1926
MAN SHE BROUGHT BACK, THE, 1922
MAN STOLEN, 1934, A
MAN TAMER, THE, 1921

MAN THE ARMY MADE, A, 1917, A
MAN THERE WAS, A, 1917
MAN THEY COULD NOT HANG, THE, 1939, C
MAN THEY COULDN'T ARREST, THE, 1933, A
MAN TO MAN, 1922, A
MAN TO MAN, 1931, A
MAN TO REMEMBER, A, 1938, A
MAN TRACKERS, THE, 1921
MAN TRAIL, THE, 1915
MAN TRAILER, THE, 1934, A
MAN TRAP, THE, 1917
MAN TROUBLE, 1930, A
MAN UNCONQUERABLE, THE, 1922
MAN UNDER COVER, THE, 1922
MAN UPSTAIRS, THE, 1926
MAN UPSTAIRS, THE, 1959, A
MAN WANTED, 1922
MAN WANTED, 1932, A
MAN WHO BEAT DAN DOLAN, THE, 1915
MAN WHO BOUGHT LONDON, THE, 1916
MAN WHO BROKE THE BANK AT MONTE CARLO,
    THE, 1935, A
MAN WHO CAME BACK, THE, 1924
MAN WHO CAME BACK, THE, 1931, C
MAN WHO CAME FOR COFFEE, THE, 1970, O
MAN WHO CAME TO DINNER, THE, 1942, A
MAN WHO CHANGED HIS MIND
MAN WHO CHANGED HIS NAME, THE, 1928, A
MAN WHO CHANGED HIS NAME, THE, 1934, A
MAN WHO CHANGED, THE
MAN WHO CHEATED HIMSELF, THE, 1951, A
MAN WHO COULD CHEAT DEATH, THE, 1959, C
MAN WHO COULD NOT LOSE, THE, 1914, A
MAN WHO COULD WORK MIRACLES, THE, 1937, A
MAN WHO COULD'T BEAT GOD, THE, 1915
MAN WHO COULDN'T WALK, THE, 1964, A
MAN WHO CRIED WOLF, THE, 1937, A
MAN WHO DARED, THE, 1920
MAN WHO DARED, THE, 1933, AA
MAN WHO DARED, THE, 1939, A
MAN WHO DARED, THE, 1946, A
MAN WHO DIED TWICE, THE, 1958, A
MAN WHO FELL TO EARTH, THE, 1976, C-O
MAN WHO FIGHTS ALONE, THE, 1924
MAN WHO FINALLY DIED, THE, 1967, A
MAN WHO FORGOT, THE, 1917, A
MAN WHO FORGOT, THE, 1919
MAN WHO FOUND HIMSELF, THE, 1915
MAN WHO FOUND HIMSELF, THE, 1925
MAN WHO FOUND HIMSELF, THE, 1937, A
MAN WHO HAD EVERYTHING, THE, 1920
MAN WHO HAD POWER OVER WOMEN, THE,
    1970, C
MAN WHO HAUNTED HIMSELF, THE, 1970, A
MAN WHO KILLED BILLY THE KID, THE, 1967, A
MAN WHO KNEW TOO MUCH, THE, 1935, C
MAN WHO KNEW TOO MUCH, THE, 1956, A
MAN WHO LAUGHS, THE, 1927, C
MAN WHO LAUGHS, THE, 1966, O
MAN WHO LIES, THE, 1970, C
MAN WHO LIKED FUNERALS, THE, 1959, A
MAN WHO LIVED AGAIN, THE, 1936, A
MAN WHO LIVED TWICE, 1936, A
MAN WHO LOST HIMSELF, THE, 1920
MAN WHO LOST HIMSELF, THE, 1941, A
MAN WHO LOST HIS WAY, THE
MAN WHO LOVED CAT DANCING, THE, 1973, C-O
MAN WHO LOVED REDHEADS, THE, 1955, A
MAN WHO LOVED WOMEN, THE, 1977, O
MAN WHO LOVED WOMEN, THE, 1983, O
MAN WHO MADE DIAMONDS, THE, 1937, A
MAN WHO MADE GOOD, THE, 1917, A
MAN WHO MADE GOOD, THE, 1917
MAN WHO MARRIED HIS OWN WIFE, THE, 1922
MAN WHO NEVER WAS, THE, 1956, A
MAN WHO PAID, THE, 1922
MAN WHO PAWNED HIS SOUL
MAN WHO PLAYED GOD, THE, 1922, A
MAN WHO PLAYED GOD, THE, 1932, A
MAN WHO PLAYED SQUARE, THE, 1924
MAN WHO RECLAIMED HIS HEAD, THE, 1935, A
MAN WHO RETURNED TO LIFE, THE, 1942, A
MAN WHO SAW TOMORROW, THE, 1922, A
MAN WHO SAW TOMORROW, THE, 1981
MAN WHO SHOT LIBERTY VALANCE, THE, 1962, A
MAN WHO STAYED AT HOME, THE, 1915
MAN WHO STAYED AT HOME, THE, 1919
MAN WHO STOLE THE SUN, THE, 1980, C
MAN WHO STOOD STILL, THE, 1916
MAN WHO TALKED TOO MUCH, THE, 1940, A
MAN WHO TALKS TO WHALES, THE, 1976
MAN WHO THOUGHT LIFE, THE, 1969, A
MAN WHO TOOK A CHANCE, THE, 1917
MAN WHO TURNED TO STONE, THE, 1957, C
MAN WHO TURNED WHITE, THE, 1919, A
MAN WHO UNDERSTOOD WOMEN, THE, 1959, A-C
MAN WHO VANISHED, THE, 1915
MAN WHO WAGGED HIS TAIL, THE, 1961, A
MAN WHO WAITED, THE, 1922
MAN WHO WALKED ALONE, THE, 1945, A
MAN WHO WALKED THROUGH THE WALL, THE,
    1964, A

MAN WHO WAS AFRAID, THE, 1917
MAN WHO WAS NOBODY, THE, 1960, C
MAN WHO WAS SHERLOCK HOLMES, THE, 1937, A
MAN WHO WASN'T THERE, THE, 1983, C
MAN WHO WATCHED TRAINS GO BY, THE
MAN WHO WOKE UP, THE, 1918
MAN WHO WON, THE, 1918
MAN WHO WON, THE, 1919
MAN WHO WON, THE, 1923
MAN WHO WON, THE, 1933, A
MAN WHO WOULD BE KING, THE, 1975, A-C
MAN WHO WOULD NOT DIE, THE, 1916
MAN WHO WOULD NOT DIE, THE, 1975, C
MAN WHO WOULDN'T DIE, THE, 1942, A
MAN WHO WOULDN'T TALK, THE, 1940, A
MAN WHO WOULDN'T TALK, THE, 1958, A
MAN WHO WOULDN'T TELL, THE, 1918
MAN WHO, THE, 1921, A
MAN WITH 100 FACES, THE, 1938, A
MAN WITH A CLOAK, THE, 1951, A
MAN WITH A GUN, 1958, C
MAN WITH A MILLION, 1954, A
MAN WITH BOGART'S FACE, THE, 1980, A-C
MAN WITH CONNECTIONS, THE, 1970, C
MAN WITH MY FACE, THE, 1951, A
MAN WITH NINE LIVES, THE, 1940, A
MAN WITH THE BALLOONS, THE, 1968, A
MAN WITH THE DEADLY LENS, THE
MAN WITH THE ELECTRIC VOICE, THE
MAN WITH THE GLASS EYE, THE, 1916
MAN WITH THE GOLDEN ARM, THE, 1955, O
MAN WITH THE GOLDEN GUN, THE, 1974, A
MAN WITH THE GREEN CARNATION, THE, 1960, A
MAN WITH THE GUN, 1955, C
MAN WITH THE ICY EYES, THE, 1971
MAN WITH THE MAGNETIC EYES, THE, 1945, C
MAN WITH THE SYNTHETIC BRAIN
MAN WITH THE TRANSPLANTED BRAIN, THE,
    1972, A
MAN WITH THE X-RAY EYES, THE
MAN WITH THE YELLOW EYES
MAN WITH THIRTY SONS, THE
MAN WITH TWO BRAINS, THE, 1983, O
MAN WITH TWO FACES, THE, 1934, A-C
MAN WITH TWO HEADS, THE, 1972, O
MAN WITH TWO LIVES, THE, 1942, A
MAN WITH TWO MOTHERS, THE, 1922
MAN WITH X-RAY EYES, THE
MAN WITHIN, THE, 1948
MAN WITHIN, THE, 1975
MAN WITHOUT A BODY, THE, 1957, A
MAN WITHOUT A CONSCIENCE, THE, 1925
MAN WITHOUT A COUNTRY, THE, 1917
MAN WITHOUT A COUNTRY, THE, 1925
MAN WITHOUT A FACE, 1964
MAN WITHOUT A FACE, THE, 1935, A
MAN WITHOUT A FACE, THE, 1975
MAN WITHOUT A GUN
MAN WITHOUT A HEART, THE, 1924
MAN WITHOUT A SOUL, THE
MAN WITHOUT A STAR, 1955, C
MAN WITHOUT DESIRE, THE, 1923, A
MAN WORTH WHILE, THE, 1921, A
MAN'S AFFAIR, A, 1949, A
MAN'S BEST FRIEND, 1935
MAN'S CASTLE, A, 1933, A
MAN'S COUNTRY, 1938, A
MAN'S COUNTRY, A, 1919
MAN'S DESIRE, 1919
MAN'S FATE, 1917
MAN'S FAVORITE SPORT (?), 1964, A
MAN'S FIGHT, A, 1927
MAN'S GAME, A, 1934, A
MAN'S HERITAGE
MAN'S HOME, A, 1921, A
MAN'S HOPE, 1947, A
MAN'S LAND, A, 1932, A
MAN'S LAW AND GOD'S, 1922, A
MAN'S LAW, A, 1917
MAN'S MAKING, THE, 1915
MAN'S MAN, A, 1917
MAN'S MAN, A, 1929, A
MAN'S MATE, A, 1924
MAN'S PAST, A, 1927
MAN'S PLAYTHING, 1920
MAN'S PREROGATIVE, A, 1915, A
MAN'S SHADOW, A, 1920, C
MAN'S SIZE, 1923
MAN'S WOMAN, 1917
MAN'S WORLD, A, 1918
MAN'S WORLD, A, 1942, A
MAN, A WOMAN AND A KILLER, A, 1975, O
MAN, A WOMAN, AND A BANK, A, 1979, C
MAN, THE, 1925
MAN, THE, 1972, A
MAN, WOMAN AND CHILD, 1983, A
MAN, WOMAN AND SIN, 1927
MAN, WOMAN AND WIFE, 1929
MAN, WOMAN, MARRIAGE
MAN—WOMAN—MARRIAGE, 1921
MAN-EATER
MAN-EATER OF HYDRA

MAN-EATER OF KUMAON, 1948, A
MAN-KILLER
MAN-MADE WOMEN, 1928, A
MAN-PROOF, 1938, A
MAN-TRAP, 1961, A
MANAGER OF THE B&A, THE, 1916
MANCHESTER MAN, THE, 1920, A
MANCHU EAGLE MURDER CAPER MYSTERY, THE,
    1975, A
MANCHURIAN CANDIDATE, THE, 1962, C-O
MANDABI, 1970, A
MANDALAY, 1934, A-C
MANDARIN MYSTERY, THE, 1937, A
MANDARIN'S GOLD, 1919
MANDINGO, 1975, O
MANDRAGOLA, 1966, A
MANDRAGOLA/THE LOVE ROOT
MANDY
MANFISH, 1956, A
MANGANINNIE, 1982, A
MANGO TREE, THE, 1981, O
MANHANDLED, 1924
MANHANDLED, 1949, A
MANHANDLERS, THE, 1975
MANHATTAN, 1924, A
MANHATTAN, 1979, C
MANHATTAN ANGEL, 1948, A
MANHATTAN BUTTERFLY, 1935
MANHATTAN COCKTAIL, 1928, A
MANHATTAN COCKTAIL, 1928
MANHATTAN COWBOY, 1928, A
MANHATTAN HEARTBEAT, 1940, A
MANHATTAN KNIGHT, A, 1920
MANHATTAN KNIGHTS, 1928, A
MANHATTAN LOVE SONG, 1934, A
MANHATTAN MADNESS, 1916, A
MANHATTAN MADNESS, 1925
MANHATTAN MADNESS, 1936
MANHATTAN MADNESS, 1943, Brit.
MANHATTAN MELODRAMA, 1934, A
MANHATTAN MERRY-GO-ROUND, 1937, A
MANHATTAN MOON, 1935, A
MANHATTAN MUSIC BOX
MANHATTAN PARADE, 1931, A
MANHATTAN SHAKEDOWN, 1939, A
MANHATTAN TOWER, 1932, A
MANHUNT
MANHUNT
MANHUNT IN SPACE, 1954
MANHUNT IN THE JUNGLE, 1958, A
MANHUNTER, 1983
MANIA, 1961, O
MANIAC, 1934, O
MANIAC, 1963, C
MANIAC, 1977, C
MANIAC, 1980, O
MANIAC MANSION, 1978, O
MANIAC, 1978, Ital.
MANIACS ARE LOOSE, THE
MANIACS ON WHEELS, 1951, A
MANICURE GIRL, THE, 1925
MANILA CALLING, 1942, A
MANINA
MANIPULATOR, THE, 1972
MANITOU, THE, 1978, C
MANJI
MANNEQUIN, 1926
MANNEQUIN, 1933, A
MANNEQUIN, 1937, A
MANNER MUSSEN SO SIEN
MANNISKOR MOTS OCH LJUV MUSIK UPPSTAR I
    HJARTAT
MANNY'S ORPHANS
MANOLETE, 1950, A
MANOLIS, 1962, A
MANON, 1950, A
MANON 70, 1968, O
MANON LESCAUT, 1914, A
MANON LESCAUT, 1926
MANOS, THE HANDS OF FATE, 1966, C
MANPOWER, 1941, A
MANSION OF ACHING HEARTS, THE, 1925
MANSION OF THE DOOMED, 1976, O
MANSLAUGHTER, 1922
MANSLAUGHTER, 1930, A
MANSON MASSACRE, THE, 1976
MANSTER, THE, 1962, A
MANSTER—HALF MAN, HALF MONSTER, THE
MANTIS IN LACE, 1968, O
MANTLE OF CHARITY, THE, 1918
MANTRAP, 1926
MANTRAP, 1953
MANTRAP, 1961
MANTRAP, THE, 1943, A
MANUELA
MANULESCU, 1933, A
MANUSCRIPT FOUND IN SARAGOSSA
MANXMAN, THE, 1916
MANXMAN, THE, 1929, A
MANY A SLIP, 1931, A
MANY HAPPY RETURNS, 1934, A
MANY RIVERS TO CROSS, 1955, A

MANY TANKS MR. ATKINS, 1938, A
MANY WATERS, 1931, A
MAOS SANGRENTAS
MARA MARU, 1952, A
MARA OF THE WILDERNESS, 1966, A
MARACAIBO, 1958, A
MARAT/SADE
MARATHON MAN, 1976, O
MARAUDERS, THE, 1947, A
MARAUDERS, THE, 1955, A
MARAUDERS, THE, 1962
MARBLE HEART, THE, 1915
MARBLE HEART, THE, 1916
MARCELLINI MILLIONS, THE, 1917
MARCH HARE, THE, 1919, A
MARCH HARE, THE, 1921
MARCH HARE, THE, 1956, A
MARCH OF THE SPRING HARE, 1969, O
MARCH OF THE WOODEN SOLDIERS, THE
MARCH ON PARIS 1914—OF GENERALOBERST
    ALEXANDER VON KLUCK—AND HIS MEMORY OF
    JESSIE HOLLADAY, 1977, C
MARCH OR DIE, 1977, C-O
MARCHA O MUERE
MARCHANDES D'ILLUSIONS
MARCHANDS DE FILLES
MARCIA O CREPA
MARCO, 1973, A
MARCO POLO, 1962, A
MARCO POLO JUNIOR, 1973, A
MARCO THE MAGNIFICENT, 1966, C
MARCUS GARLAND, 1925
MARDI GRAS, 1958, A
MARDI GRAS MASSACRE, 1978, O
MARE NOSTRUM, 1926, A
MARGARET DAY
MARGEM, A
MARGIE, 1940, A
MARGIE, 1946, AAA
MARGIN FOR ERROR, 1943, A
MARGIN, THE,, 1969, C
MARIA CANDELARIA
MARIA CHAPDELAINE
MARIA ELENA
MARIA MARTEN
MARIA MARTEN, 1928
MARIA ROSA, 1916
MARIA, THE WONDERFUL WEAVER
MARIAGE A L'ITALIENNE
MARIAGE D'AMOUR, 1917
MARIANNE
MARIANNE, 1929, A
MARIE ANTOINETTE, 1938, A
MARIE DES ILES
MARIE GALANTE, 1934, A
MARIE OF THE ISLES, 1960, A
MARIE WALEWSKA
MARIE, LTD., 1919
MARIE-ANN, 1978, A
MARIGOLD, 1938, A
MARIGOLD MAN, 1970, C
MARIGOLDS IN AUGUST, 1980, C
MARIGOLDS IN AUGUST, 1984, A
MARILYN, 1953, O
MARINE BATTLEGROUND, 1966, A
MARINE RAIDERS, 1944, A
MARINES ARE COMING, THE, 1935, A
MARINES ARE HERE, THE, 1938, A
MARINES COME THROUGH, THE, 1943, A
MARINES FLY HIGH, THE, 1940, A
MARINES, LET'S GO, 1961, A
MARION DE LORME, 1918
MARIONETTES, THE, 1918
MARIUS, 1933, C
MARIZINIA, 1962, A
MARIZINIA, THE WITCH BENEATH THE SEA
MARJORIE MORNINGSTAR, 1958, A-C
MARK IT PAID, 1933, A
MARK OF CAIN, THE, 1916
MARK OF CAIN, THE, 1917
MARK OF CAIN, THE, 1948, A
MARK OF THE APACHE
MARK OF THE AVENGER
MARK OF THE BEAST, 1923
MARK OF THE CLAW
MARK OF THE DEVIL, 1970, O
MARK OF THE DEVIL II, 1975, O
MARK OF THE GORILLA, 1950, A
MARK OF THE GUN, 1969
MARK OF THE HAWK, THE, 1958, A
MARK OF THE LASH, 1948, A
MARK OF THE PHOENIX, 1958, C
MARK OF THE RENEGADE, 1951, A
MARK OF THE SPUR, 1932
MARK OF THE VAMPIRE, 1935, C
MARK OF THE VAMPIRE, 1957
MARK OF THE WHISTLER, THE, 1944, A
MARK OF THE WITCH, 1970, C
MARK OF ZORRO, 1920, A
MARK OF ZORRO, THE, 1940, A
MARK TWAIN, AMERICAN, 1976
MARK, THE, 1961, A

MARKED BULLET, THE
MARKED CARDS, 1918
MARKED FOR MURDER, 1945, A
MARKED GIRLS, 1949, A
MARKED MAN, A, 1917
MARKED MAN, THE
MARKED MEN, 1920
MARKED MEN, 1940, A
MARKED MONEY, 1928, A
MARKED ONE, THE, 1963, A
MARKED TRAILS, 1944, A
MARKED WOMAN, 1937, C
MARKED WOMAN, THE, 1914
MARKET OF SOULS, THE, 1919
MARKET OF VAIN DESIRE, THE, 1916, A
MARKETA LAZAROVA, 1968, O
MARKO POLO
MARKOPOULOS PASSION, THE
MARKSMAN, THE, 1953, C
MARLIE THE KILLER, 1928
MARLOWE, 1969, A
MARNIE, 1964, C
MAROC 7, 1967, A
MAROONED, 1933, C
MAROONED, 1969, A
MAROONED HEARTS, 1920
MARQUIS DE SADE: JUSTINE
MARQUIS PREFERRED, 1929
MARQUITTA, 1927
MARRIAGE, 1927
MARRIAGE BARGAIN, THE, 1935
MARRIAGE BOND, THE, 1916
MARRIAGE BOND, THE, 1932, A
MARRIAGE BY CONRACT, 1928
MARRIAGE BY CONTRACT, 1928, A
MARRIAGE CAME TUMBLING DOWN, THE, 1968, A
MARRIAGE CHANCE, THE, 1922
MARRIAGE CHEAT, THE, 1924
MARRIAGE CIRCLE, THE, 1924, A
MARRIAGE CLAUSE, THE, 1926, A
MARRIAGE FOR CONVENIENCE, 1919
MARRIAGE FORBIDDEN
MARRIAGE IN THE SHADOWS, 1948, A
MARRIAGE IN TRANSIT, 1925
MARRIAGE IS A PRIVATE AFFAIR, 1944, A
MARRIAGE LIE, THE, 1918
MARRIAGE LINES, THE, 1921
MARRIAGE MAKER, THE, 1923
MARRIAGE MARKET, THE, 1917
MARRIAGE MARKET, THE, 1923
MARRIAGE MORALS, 1923
MARRIAGE OF A YOUNG STOCKBROKER, THE, 1971, A
MARRIAGE OF BALZAMINOV, THE, 1966, A
MARRIAGE OF CONVENIENCE, 1970, A
MARRIAGE OF CONVENIENCE, 1934
MARRIAGE OF CORBAL
MARRIAGE OF FIGARO, THE, 1963, A
MARRIAGE OF FIGARO, THE, 1970, A
MARRIAGE OF KITTY, THE, 1915, A
MARRIAGE OF MARIA BRAUN, THE, 1979, O
MARRIAGE OF MOLLY-O, THE, 1916
MARRIAGE OF THE BEAR, THE, 1928
MARRIAGE OF WILLIAM ASHE, THE, 1916
MARRIAGE OF WILLIAM ASHE, THE, 1921, A
MARRIAGE ON APPROVAL, 1934, A
MARRIAGE ON THE ROCKS, 1965, A-C
MARRIAGE PIT, THE, 1920
MARRIAGE PLAYGROUND, THE, 1929, A
MARRIAGE PRICE, 1919, A
MARRIAGE RING, THE, 1918
MARRIAGE SPECULATION, THE, 1917
MARRIAGE SYMPHONY
MARRIAGE WHIRL, THE, 1925
MARRIAGE, A, 1983, C
MARRIAGE—ITALIAN STYLE, 1964, O
MARRIAGE-GO-ROUND, THE, 1960, A
MARRIAGES ARE MADE, 1918
MARRIED ALIVE, 1927, A
MARRIED AND IN LOVE, 1940, A
MARRIED BACHELOR, 1941, A
MARRIED BEFORE BREAKFAST, 1937, A
MARRIED BUT SINGLE
MARRIED COUPLE, A, 1969, O
MARRIED FLAPPER, THE, 1922
MARRIED FLIRTS, 1924, A
MARRIED FOR MONEY, 1915
MARRIED IN HASTE, 1919
MARRIED IN HASTE, 1931
MARRIED IN HASTE, 1934
MARRIED IN HOLLYWOOD, 1929, A
MARRIED IN NAME ONLY, 1917
MARRIED LIFE, 1920
MARRIED LIFE, 1921
MARRIED LOVE
MARRIED PEOPLE, 1922
MARRIED TO A MORMAN, 1922, A
MARRIED TOO YOUNG, 1962, A
MARRIED VIRGIN, THE
MARRIED WOMAN, THE, 1965, C
MARRIED?, 1926
MARRY IN HASTE, 1924, A

MARRY ME, 1925
MARRY ME, 1932, A
MARRY ME, 1949, A
MARRY ME AGAIN, 1953, A
MARRY ME MARRY ME, 1969, A
MARRY THE BOSS' DAUGHTER, 1941, A
MARRY THE GIRL, 1928, A
MARRY THE GIRL, 1935, A
MARRY THE GIRL, 1937, A
MARRY THE POOR GIRL, 1921
MARRYING KIND, THE, 1952, A
MARRYING MONEY, 1915
MARRYING WIDOWS, 1934, C
MARS CALLING
MARS NEEDS WOMEN, 1966, A
MARSCHIER ODER KREIPER
MARSE COVINGTON, 1915
MARSEILLAISE
MARSEILLES CONTRACT, THE
MARSHAL OF AMARILLO, 1948, A
MARSHAL OF CEDAR ROCK, 1953, A
MARSHAL OF CRIPPLE CREEK, THE, 1947, A
MARSHAL OF GUNSMOKE, 1944, A
MARSHAL OF HELDORADO, 1950, A
MARSHAL OF LAREDO, 1945, A
MARSHAL OF MESA CITY, THE, 1939, A
MARSHAL OF MONEYMINT, THE, 1922, A
MARSHAL OF RENO, 1944, A
MARSHAL'S DAUGHTER, THE, 1953, A
MARSHALS IN DISGUISE, 1954
MARSHMALLOW MOON
MARTA OF THE LOWLANDS, 1914
MARTHA'S VINDICATION, 1916, A
MARTHE, 1919
MARTIAN IN PARIS, A, 1961, A
MARTIN, 1979, O
MARTIN LUTHER, 1953, AA
MARTIN LUTHER, HIS LIFE AND TIME, 1924
MARTIN ROUMAGNAC
MARTINACHE MARRIAGE, THE, 1917
MARTY, 1955, A
MARTYR SEX, THE, 1924
MARTYR, THE, 1976, C
MARTYRDOM OF PHILLIP STRONG, THE, 1916
MARTYRE, 1926
MARTYRS OF LOVE, 1968, A
MARTYRS OF THE ALAMO, THE, 1915, A
MARUJA
MARVELOUS MACISTE, THE, 1918
MARVIN AND TIGE, 1983, C
MARX BROTHERS AT THE CIRCUS
MARX BROTHERS GO WEST
MARY
MARY BURNS, FUGITIVE, 1935, A
MARY ELLEN COMES TO TOWN, 1920
MARY HAD A LITTLE, 1961, C
MARY JANE'S PA, 1917
MARY JANE'S PA, 1935, A
MARY LATIMER, NUN, 1920, A
MARY LAWSON'S SECRET, 1917
MARY LOU, 1948, A
MARY MORELAND, 1917
MARY NAMES THE DAY
MARY OF SCOTLAND, 1936, A
MARY OF THE MOVIES, 1923
MARY POPPINS, 1964, AAA
MARY REGAN, 1919
MARY RYAN, DETECTIVE, 1949, C
MARY STEVENS, M.D., 1933, A
MARY'S ANKLE, 1920
MARY'S LAMB, 1915
MARY, MARY, 1963, A-C
MARY, MARY, BLOODY MARY, 1975, O
MARY, QUEEN OF SCOTS, 1971, A-C
MARY-FIND-THE-GOLD, 1921
MARYA-ISKUSNITSA
MARYJANE, 1968, O
MARYLAND, 1940, A
MARYSE, 1917
MAS ALLA DE LAS MONTANAS
MASCULINE FEMININE, 1966, C-O
MASK OF DIIJON, THE, 1946, A-C
MASK OF DIMITRIOS, THE, 1944, A
MASK OF DUST
MASK OF FU MANCHU, THE, 1932, C
MASK OF FURY
MASK OF KOREA, 1950, A
MASK OF LOPEZ, THE, 1924
MASK OF RICHES
MASK OF THE AVENGER, 1951, A
MASK OF THE DRAGON, 1951, A
MASK OF THE HIMALAYAS
MASK OF THE KU KLUX KLAN, THE, 1923
MASK, THE, 1918
MASK, THE, 1921, A
MASK, THE, 1961, O
MASKED ANGEL, 1928, A
MASKED AVENGER, THE, 1922, A
MASKED BRIDE, THE, 1925
MASKED DANCER, THE, 1924
MASKED EMOTIONS, 1929, A
MASKED HEART, THE, 1917

MASKED LOVER, THE, 1928
MASKED PIRATE, THE
MASKED RAIDERS, 1949, A
MASKED RIDER, THE, 1916
MASKED RIDER, THE, 1941, A
MASKED STRANGER
MASKED WOMAN, THE, 1927
MASKS AND FACES, 1917
MASKS OF THE DEVIL, THE, 1928
MASOCH, 1980, O
MASON OF THE MOUNTED, 1932, A
MASQUE OF THE RED DEATH, THE, 1964, C
MASQUERADE, 1965, A
MASQUERADE BANDIT, THE, 1926
MASQUERADE IN MEXICO, 1945, C
MASQUERADE OF THIEVES, 1973
MASQUERADE, 1929, A
MASQUERADER, THE, 1922
MASQUERADER, THE, 1933, A
MASQUERADERS, THE, 1915, A
MASS APPEAL, 1984, C
MASSACRE, 1934, A
MASSACRE, 1956, A
MASSACRE AT CENTRAL HIGH, 1976, O
MASSACRE AT FORT HOLMAN
MASSACRE AT GRAND CANYON, 1965
MASSACRE AT THE ROSEBUD
MASSACRE CANYON, 1954, A
MASSACRE HILL, 1949, A
MASSACRE IN ROME, 1973, C
MASSACRE RIVER, 1949, A
MASSIVE RETALIATION, 1984, O
MASTER AND MAN, 1915
MASTER AND MAN, 1929
MASTER AND MAN, 1934, A
MASTER CRACKSMAN, THE, 1914, A
MASTER GUNFIGHTER, THE, 1975, C
MASTER MAN, THE, 1919
MASTER MIND, THE, 1914, A
MASTER MIND, THE, 1920, A
MASTER MINDS, 1949, A
MASTER OF BALLANTRAE, THE, 1953, A
MASTER OF BANKDAM, THE, 1947, C
MASTER OF BEASTS, THE, 1922
MASTER OF CRAFT, A, 1922, A
MASTER OF GRAY, THE, 1918
MASTER OF HIS HOME, 1917
MASTER OF HORROR, 1965, C-O
MASTER OF LASSIE
MASTER OF LOVE, THE, 1919
MASTER OF MEN, 1933, A
MASTER OF MEN, A, 1917
MASTER OF TERROR
MASTER OF THE HOUSE, 1925
MASTER OF THE HOUSE, THE, 1915
MASTER OF THE ISLANDS
MASTER OF THE RANGE, 1928
MASTER OF THE WORLD, 1935, A
MASTER OF THE WORLD, 1961, A
MASTER PASSION, THE, 1917
MASTER PLAN, THE, 1955, A
MASTER RACE, THE, 1944, C
MASTER SHAKESPEARE, STROLLING PLAYER, 1916
MASTER SPY, 1964, A
MASTER STROKE, A, 1920, A
MASTER TOUCH, THE, 1974, C
MASTERMIND, 1977, A
MASTERS OF MEN, 1923
MASTERSON OF KANSAS, 1954, A
MATA HARI, 1931, A
MATA HARI, 1965, C
MATA HARI'S DAUGHTER, 1954, A
MATALOS Y VUELVE
MATCH KING, THE, 1932, C
MATCH-BREAKER, THE, 1921
MATCH-MAKERS, THE, 1916
MATCHLESS, 1967, C
MATCHLESS, 1974, O
MATCHMAKER, THE, 1958, A
MATCHMAKING OF ANNA, THE, 1972, O
MATE DOMA IVA?
MATE OF THE SALLY ANN, THE, 1917
MATER DOLOROSA, 1917
MATERNAL SPARK, THE, 1917
MATERNITY, 1917
MATHIAS SANDORF, 1963, A
MATILDA, 1978, A
MATINEE IDOL, 1933, A
MATINEE IDOL, THE, 1928, A
MATINEE LADIES, 1927, A
MATING CALL, THE, 1928
MATING GAME, THE, 1959, A
MATING OF MARCELLA, THE, 1918
MATING OF MARCUS, THE, 1924, A
MATING OF MILLIE, THE, 1948, A
MATING OF THE SABINE WOMEN, THE
MATING SEASON, THE, 1951, A
MATING, THE, 1915
MATING, THE, 1918
MATKA JOANNA OD ANIOLOW
MATRIMANIAC, THE, 1916, A
MATRIMONIAL BED, THE, 1930, A

MATRIMONIAL MARTYR, A, 1916
MATRIMONIAL PROBLEM, A
MATRIMONIAL WEB, THE, 1921
MATRIMONIO ALL'ITALIANA
MATRIMONY, 1915
MATT, 1918
MATTER OF CHOICE, A, 1963, A
MATTER OF CONVICTION, A
MATTER OF DAYS, A, 1969, O
MATTER OF INNOCENCE, A, 1968, A
MATTER OF LIFE AND DEATH, A
MATTER OF LOVE, A, 1979
MATTER OF MORALS, A, 1961, O
MATTER OF MURDER, A, 1949, A
MATTER OF RESISTANCE, A
MATTER OF TIME, A, 1976, A-C
MATTER OF WHO, A, 1962, A
MAUPRAT, 1926
MAURIE, 1973, A
MAURIE, 1973
MAUSOLEUM, 1983, O
MAVERICK QUEEN, THE, 1956, A
MAVERICK, THE, 1952, A
MAX DUGAN RETURNS, 1983, A
MAXIME, 1962, O
MAXWELL ARCHER, DETECTIVE, 1942, C
MAY BLOSSOM, 1915, A
MAY MORNING, 1970
MAYA, 1966, A
MAYA, 1982, C
MAYBE IT'S LOVE, 1930, A
MAYBE IT'S LOVE, 1935, A
MAYBLOSSOM, 1917
MAYERLING, 1937, C-O
MAYERLING, 1968, C
MAYFAIR GIRL, 1933, A
MAYFAIR MELODY, 1937, A
MAYHEM
MAYOR OF 44TH STREET, THE, 1942, A
MAYOR OF CASTERBRIDGE, THE, 1921
MAYOR OF FILBERT, THE, 1919
MAYOR OF HELL, THE, 1933, C
MAYOR'S NEST, THE, 1932, A
MAYOR'S NEST, THE, 1941
MAYTIME, 1923
MAYTIME, 1937, A
MAYTIME IN MAYFAIR, 1952, A
MAZE, THE, 1953, C
MAZEL TOV, 1924
MAZEL TOV OU LE MARIAGE
MAZEL TOV, JEWS, 1941
MC CABE AND MRS. MILLER, 1971, O
MC CONNELL STORY, THE, 1955, A
MC CORD
MC CULLOCHS, THE
MC FADDEN'S FLATS, 1935, A
MC GLUSKY THE SEA ROVER
MC GUIRE, GO HOME, 1966, A
MC HALE'S NAVY, 1964, A
MC HALE'S NAVY JOINS THE AIR FORCE, 1965, A
MC KENNA OF THE MOUNTED, 1932, A
MC KENZIE BREAK, THE, 1970, C
MC LINTOCK, 1963, A
MC MASTERS, THE, 1970, O
MC Q, 1974, O
MC VICAR, 1982, C
MCFADDEN FLATS, 1927
MCGUIRE OF THE MOUNTED, 1923
ME, 1970, A
ME AND CAPTAIN KID, 1919
ME AND GOTT
ME AND M'PAL, 1916
ME AND MARLBOROUGH, 1935, A
ME AND ME MOKE
ME AND MY BROTHER, 1969, O
ME AND MY GAL, 1932, A
ME AND MY PAL, 1939, A
ME AND THE COLONEL, 1958, A
ME UND GOTT, 1918
ME, GANGSTER, 1928
ME, NATALIE, 1969, C
MEA CULPA, 1919
MEAL, THE, 1975, O
MEAN DOG BLUES, 1978, O
MEAN FRANK AND CRAZY TONY, 1976, O
MEAN JOHNNY BARROWS, 1976, O
MEAN MOTHER, 1974
MEAN STREETS, 1973, O
MEANEST GAL IN TOWN, THE, 1934, A
MEANEST MAN IN THE WORLD, THE, 1923
MEANEST MAN IN THE WORLD, THE, 1943, A
MEANWHILE BACK AT THE RANCH
MEANWHILE, FAR FROM THE FRONT
MEASURE OF A MAN, THE, 1916, A
MEASURE OF A MAN, THE, 1924, A
MEAT CLEAVER MASSACRE, 1977
MEATBALLS, 1979, C
MEATBALLS PART II, 1984, C
MEATEATER, 1979
MECHANIC, THE, 1972, O
MED MORD I BAGAGET
MEDAL FOR BENNY, A, 1945, A

MEDAL FOR THE GENERAL
MEDALS
MEDDLER, THE, 1925, A
MEDDLIN' STRANGER, THE, 1927
MEDDLING WOMEN, 1924
MEDEA, 1971, O
MEDIATOR, THE, 1916, A
MEDICINE BEND, 1916
MEDICINE MAN, THE, 1917
MEDICINE MAN, THE, 1930, A
MEDICINE MAN, THE, 1933, A
MEDICO OF PAINTED SPRINGS, THE, 1941, A
MEDIUM COOL, 1969, O
MEDIUM, THE, 1951, A
MEDJU JASTREBOVIMA
MEDUSA TOUCH, THE, 1978, C
MEET BOSTON BLACKIE, 1941, A
MEET DANNY WILSON, 1952, A
MEET DR. CHRISTIAN, 1939, A
MEET JOHN DOE, 1941, A
MEET MAXWELL ARCHER
MEET ME AFTER THE SHOW, 1951, A
MEET ME AT DAWN, 1947, A
MEET ME AT THE FAIR, 1952, A
MEET ME IN LAS VEGAS, 1956, A
MEET ME IN MOSCOW, 1966, A
MEET ME IN ST. LOUIS, 1944, AAA
MEET ME ON BROADWAY, 1946, A
MEET ME TONIGHT
MEET MISS BOBBY SOCKS, 1944, A
MEET MISS MARPLE
MEET MR. CALLAGHAN, 1954, A
MEET MR. LUCIFER, 1953, A
MEET MR. MALCOLM, 1954, A
MEET MR. PENNY, 1938, A
MEET MY SISTER, 1933, A
MEET NERO WOLFE, 1936, A
MEET SEXTON BLAKE, 1944, A
MEET SIMON CHERRY, 1949, A
MEET THE BARON, 1933, A
MEET THE BOY FRIEND, 1937, A
MEET THE CHUMP, 1941, A
MEET THE DUKE, 1949, A
MEET THE GIRLS, 1938, A
MEET THE MAYOR, 1938, A
MEET THE MISSUS, 1937, A
MEET THE MISSUS, 1940, A
MEET THE MOB, 1942, A
MEET THE NAVY, 1946, A
MEET THE NELSONS
MEET THE PEOPLE, 1944, A
MEET THE PRINCE, 1926
MEET THE PRINCE, 1926
MEET THE STEWARTS, 1942, A
MEET THE WIFE, 1931, A
MEET THE WILDCAT, 1940, A
MEET WHIPLASH WILLIE
MEETING AT MIDNIGHT
MEETINGS WITH REMARKABLE MEN, 1979, A
MEFIEZ-VOUS DE VOTRE BONNE, 1920
MEG, 1926, A
MEG O' THE WOODS, 1918
MEG OF THE SLUMS, 1916
MEGAFORCE, 1982, C
MEGLIO VEDOVA
MEIN KAMPF—MY CRIMES, 1940, C
MELANIE, 1982, C
MELBA, 1953, A
MELINDA, 1972, O
MELISSA OF THE HILLS, 1917
MELODIE EN SOUS-SOL
MELODIES, 1926
MELODY, 1971, AAA
MELODY AND MOONLIGHT, 1940, A
MELODY AND ROMANCE, 1937, A
MELODY CLUB, 1949, A
MELODY CRUISE, 1933, A
MELODY FOR THREE, 1941, A
MELODY FOR TWO, 1937, A
MELODY GIRL
MELODY IN SPRING, 1934, A
MELODY IN THE DARK, 1948, A
MELODY INN
MELODY LANE, 1929, A
MELODY LANE, 1941, A
MELODY LINGERS ON, THE, 1935, A
MELODY MAKER, 1946
MELODY MAKER, THE, 1933, A
MELODY MAN, 1930, A
MELODY OF LIFE
MELODY OF LOVE, 1954, A
MELODY OF LOVE, THE, 1928, A
MELODY OF MY HEART, 1936, A
MELODY OF THE PLAINS, 1937, A
MELODY OF YOUTH
MELODY PARADE, 1943, A
MELODY RANCH, 1940, A
MELODY TIME, 1948, AAA
MELODY TRAIL, 1935, AA
MELON AFFAIR, THE, 1979
MELTING MILLIONS, 1917
MELTING POT, THE

MELTING POT, THE, 1915
MELVIN AND HOWARD, 1980, C-O
MELVIN, SON OF ALVIN, 1984, O
MEMBER OF THE JURY, 1937, A
MEMBER OF THE TATTERSALL'S, A, 1919
MEMBER OF THE WEDDING, THE, 1952, A
MEMED MY HAWK, 1984, C
MEMENTO MEI, 1963, C
MEMOIRS, 1984, O
MEMOIRS OF A SURVIVOR, 1981, C
MEMOIRS OF PRISON, 1984, O
MEMORIAS DO CARCERE
MEMORY EXPERT, THE
MEMORY FOR TWO
MEMORY LANE, 1926, A
MEMORY OF LOVE, 1949
MEMORY OF US, 1974, A
MEN, 1924
MEN AGAINST THE SKY, 1940, A
MEN AGAINST THE SUN, 1953, A
MEN AND WOMEN, 1925
MEN ARE CHILDREN TWICE, 1953, A
MEN ARE LIKE THAT, 1930, A
MEN ARE LIKE THAT, 1931, A
MEN ARE NOT GODS, 1937, A-C
MEN ARE SUCH FOOLS, 1933, A
MEN ARE SUCH FOOLS, 1938, A
MEN BEHIND BARS
MEN CALL IT LOVE, 1931, C
MEN IN EXILE, 1937, A
MEN IN HER DIARY, 1945, A
MEN IN HER LIFE, 1931, A
MEN IN HER LIFE, THE, 1941, A
MEN IN THE RAW, 1923
MEN IN WAR, 1957, A-C
MEN IN WHITE, 1934, A
MEN LIKE THESE
MEN MUST FIGHT, 1933, A
MEN OF ACTION, 1935
MEN OF AMERICA, 1933, A
MEN OF BOYS TOWN, 1941, AA
MEN OF CHANCE, 1932, A
MEN OF DARING, 1927
MEN OF DESTINY
MEN OF IRELAND, 1938, A
MEN OF SAN QUENTIN, 1942, A
MEN OF SHERWOOD FOREST, 1957, A
MEN OF STEEL, 1926
MEN OF STEEL, 1932, A
MEN OF STEEL, 1937
MEN OF STEEL, 1980
MEN OF TEXAS, 1942, A
MEN OF THE DEEP
MEN OF THE DESERT, 1917
MEN OF THE FIGHTING LADY, 1954, A
MEN OF THE HOUR, 1935, A
MEN OF THE NIGHT, 1926
MEN OF THE NIGHT, 1934, A
MEN OF THE NORTH, 1930, A
MEN OF THE PLAINS, 1936, A
MEN OF THE SEA, 1938, A
MEN OF THE SEA, 1951, A
MEN OF THE SKY, 1931, A
MEN OF THE TENTH
MEN OF THE TIMBERLAND, 1941, A
MEN OF TOMORROW, 1935, A
MEN OF TWO WORLDS
MEN OF YESTERDAY, 1936, A
MEN OF ZANSIBAR, THE, 1922
MEN ON CALL, 1931, A
MEN ON HER MIND, 1944, A
MEN ON HER MIND, 1935
MEN PREFER FAT GIRLS, 1981, C
MEN SHE MARRIED, THE, 1916, A
MEN WHO FORGET, 1923
MEN WHO HAVE MADE LOVE TO ME, 1918
MEN WITH WINGS, 1938, A
MEN WITHOUT HONOUR, 1939, A
MEN WITHOUT LAW, 1930, A
MEN WITHOUT NAMES, 1935, A
MEN WITHOUT SOULS, 1940, A
MEN WITHOUT WOMEN, 1930, A
MEN WOMEN LOVE, 1926
MEN WOMEN LOVE
MEN, THE, 1950, C
MEN, WOMEN AND MONEY, 1919
MEN, WOMEN AND MONEY, 1924
MENACE, 1934, A
MENACE IN THE NIGHT, 1958, A
MENACE OF THE MUTE, THE, 1915
MENACE, 1934, Brit.
MENACE, THE, 1918
MENACE, THE, 1932, A-C
MENACING PAST, THE, 1922
MENILMONTANT, 1926
MENNESKER MODES OG SOD MUSIK OPSTAR I
    HJERTET
MENSCHEN AM SONNTAG
MENSCHEN IM NETZ
MENTIONED IN CONFIDENCE, 1917
MEPHISTO, 1981, O
MEPHISTO WALTZ, THE, 1971, C-O

MERCENARIES, THE
MERCENARY, THE, 1970, C
MERCHANT OF SLAVES, 1949, C
MERCHANT OF VENICE, THE, 1914
MERCHANT OF VENICE, THE, 1916, A
MERCY ISLAND, 1941, A
MERCY PLANE, 1940, A
MERELY MARY ANN, 1916
MERELY MARY ANN, 1920
MERELY MARY ANN, 1931, A
MERELY MR. HAWKINS, 1938, A
MERELY MRS. STUBBS, 1917
MERELY PLAYERS, 1918
MERES FRANCAISES, 1917
MERMAID, THE, 1966, A
MERMAIDS OF TIBURON, THE, 1962, A-C
MERRILL'S MARAUDERS, 1962, C-O
MERRILY WE GO TO HELL, 1932, A-C
MERRILY WE LIVE, 1938, A
MERRY ANDREW, 1958, AA
MERRY CAVALIER, THE, 1926
MERRY CHRISTMAS MR. LAWRENCE, 1983, O
MERRY COMES TO STAY, 1937, A
MERRY COMES TO TOWN
MERRY FRINKS, THE, 1934, A
MERRY MONAHANS, THE, 1944, A
MERRY WIDOW, THE, 1925, C
MERRY WIDOW, THE, 1934, A-C
MERRY WIDOW, THE, 1952, A
MERRY WIVES OF RENO, THE, 1934, A
MERRY WIVES OF TOBIAS ROUKE, THE, 1972, A
MERRY WIVES OF WINDSOR, THE, 1952, A
MERRY WIVES OF WINDSOR, THE, 1966, A
MERRY WIVES, THE, 1940, C
MERRY-G0-ROUND, 1948, A
MERRY-GO ROUND, THE, 1919
MERRY-GO-ROUND, 1923, A
MERRY-GO-ROUND OF 1938, 1937, A
MERTON OF THE MOVIES, 1924, A
MERTON OF THE MOVIES, 1947, A
MES FEMMES AMERICAINES
MESA OF LOST WOMEN, THE, 1956, A
MESDAMES ET MESSIEURS
MESQUITE BUCKAROO, 1939, A
MESSAGE FROM MARS, A, 1913, A
MESSAGE FROM MARS, A, 1921
MESSAGE FROM SPACE, 1978, A
MESSAGE OF HOPE, THE, 1923
MESSAGE OF THE MOUSE, THE, 1917
MESSAGE TO GARCIA, A, 1916
MESSAGE TO GARCIA, A, 1936, A
MESSAGE, THE
MESSALINA, 1924
MESSALINE, 1952, A
MESSENGER OF PEACE, 1950, A
MESSENGER OF THE BLESSED VIRGIN, 1930
MESSIAH OF EVIL
METAL MESSIAH, 1978
METALSTORM: THE DESTRUCTION OF JARED-SYN, 1983, C
METAMORPHOSES, 1978, A
METAMORPHOSIS, 1951
METEMPSYCO
METEOR, 1979, C
METEOR MONSTER
METROPOLIS, 1927, A
METROPOLITAN, 1935, A
METROPOLITAN SYMPHONY, 1929
MEURTRE EN 45 TOURS
MEXICALI KID, THE, 1938, A
MEXICALI ROSE, 1929, A
MEXICALI ROSE, 1939, A
MEXICAN HAYRIDE, 1948, A
MEXICAN MANHUNT, 1953, A
MEXICAN SPITFIRE, 1939, A
MEXICAN SPITFIRE AT SEA, 1942, A
MEXICAN SPITFIRE OUT WEST, 1940, A
MEXICAN SPITFIRE SEES A GHOST, 1942, A
MEXICAN SPITFIRE'S BABY, 1941, A
MEXICAN SPITFIRE'S BLESSED EVENT, 1943, A
MEXICAN SPITFIRE'S ELEPHANT, 1942, A
MEXICAN, THE
MEXICANA, 1945, A
MEXICO IN FLAMES, 1982, O
MI MUJER ES DOCTOR
MIAMI, 1924
MIAMI EXPOSE, 1956, A
MIAMI RENDEZVOUS
MIAMI STORY, THE, 1954, A
MIARKA, LA FILLE A L'OURSE
MIARKA, THE DAUGHTER OF THE BEAR
MICE AND MEN, 1916, A
MICHAEL, 1924
MICHAEL AND MARY, 1932, A
MICHAEL O'HALLORAN, 1923
MICHAEL O'HALLORAN, 1937, A
MICHAEL O'HALLORAN, 1948, A
MICHAEL SHAYNE, PRIVATE DETECTIVE, 1940, A
MICHAEL STROGOFF, 1960, A
MICHAEL STROGOFF, 1937
MICHEL STROGOFF, 1926
MICHELINE, 1920

MICHELLE, 1970, C
MICHIGAN KID, THE, 1928, A
MICHIGAN KID, THE, 1947, A
MICKEY, 1919, A
MICKEY, 1948, A
MICKEY ONE, 1965, C-O
MICKEY, THE KID, 1939, A
MICKI AND MAUDE, 1984, C
MICROBE, THE, 1919
MICROSCOPE MYSTERY, THE, 1916
MICROSCOPIA
MICROWAVE MASSACRE, 1983, O
MID-DAY MISTRESS, 1968, O
MIDAREGUMO
MIDARERU
MIDAS RUN, 1969, C
MIDAS TOUCH, THE, 1940, A
MIDCHANNEL, 1920
MIDDLE AGE CRAZY, 1980, O
MIDDLE AGE SPREAD, 1979, O
MIDDLE COURSE, THE, 1961, A
MIDDLE OF THE NIGHT, 1959, A-C
MIDDLE PASSAGE, 1978
MIDDLE WATCH, THE, 1930, A
MIDDLE WATCH, THE, 1939, A
MIDDLEMAN, THE, 1915
MIDDLETON FAMILY AT THE N.Y. WORLD'S FAIR, 1939, A
MIDINETTE, 1917
MIDLANDERS, THE, 1920
MIDNIGHT, 1922
MIDNIGHT, 1934, A
MIDNIGHT, 1939, A
MIDNIGHT, 1983, O
MIDNIGHT ACE, THE, 1928
MIDNIGHT ADVENTURE, THE, 1928
MIDNIGHT ALARM, THE, 1923
MIDNIGHT ALIBI, 1934, A
MIDNIGHT ANGEL, 1941, A
MIDNIGHT AT MADAME TUSSAUD'S
MIDNIGHT AT MAXIM'S, 1915
MIDNIGHT AT THE WAX MUSEUM, 1936, A
MIDNIGHT AUTO SUPPLY
MIDNIGHT BELL, A, 1921
MIDNIGHT BRIDE, THE, 1920
MIDNIGHT BURGLAR, THE, 1918
MIDNIGHT CLUB, 1933, A
MIDNIGHT COURT, 1937, A
MIDNIGHT COWBOY, 1969, O
MIDNIGHT DADDIES, 1929, A
MIDNIGHT EPISODE, 1951, A
MIDNIGHT EXPRESS, 1978, O
MIDNIGHT EXPRESS, THE, 1924, A
MIDNIGHT FACES, 1926
MIDNIGHT FIRES
MIDNIGHT FLOWER, THE, 1923
MIDNIGHT FLYER, THE, 1925
MIDNIGHT FOLLY, 1962, C
MIDNIGHT GAMBOLS, 1919
MIDNIGHT GIRL, THE, 1925
MIDNIGHT GUEST, THE, 1923
MIDNIGHT INTRUDER, 1938, A
MIDNIGHT KISS, THE, 1926
MIDNIGHT LACE, 1960, C
MIDNIGHT LADY, 1932, A
MIDNIGHT LIFE, 1928, A
MIDNIGHT LIMITED, 1926
MIDNIGHT LIMITED, 1940, A
MIDNIGHT LOVERS, 1926
MIDNIGHT MADNESS, 1918
MIDNIGHT MADNESS, 1928, A
MIDNIGHT MADNESS, 1980, C
MIDNIGHT MADONNA, 1937, A
MIDNIGHT MAN, 1917
MIDNIGHT MAN, THE, 1974, O
MIDNIGHT MANHUNT
MIDNIGHT MARY, 1933, A-C
MIDNIGHT MEETING, 1962, A
MIDNIGHT MELODY
MIDNIGHT MENACE
MIDNIGHT MESSAGE, THE, 1926, A
MIDNIGHT MOLLY, 1925
MIDNIGHT MORALS, 1932, A
MIDNIGHT MYSTERY, 1930, A
MIDNIGHT ON THE BARBARY COAST, 1929
MIDNIGHT PATROL, THE, 1918, A
MIDNIGHT PATROL, THE, 1932, A
MIDNIGHT PHANTOM, THE, 1935
MIDNIGHT PLEASURES, 1975, O
MIDNIGHT PLOWBOY, 1973
MIDNIGHT RAIDERS
MIDNIGHT ROMANCE, A, 1919, A
MIDNIGHT ROSE, 1928
MIDNIGHT SECRETS, 1924
MIDNIGHT SHADOW, 1939
MIDNIGHT SHADOWS, 1924
MIDNIGHT SPECIAL, 1931, A
MIDNIGHT STAGE, THE, 1919
MIDNIGHT STORY, THE, 1957, A
MIDNIGHT SUN, THE, 1926
MIDNIGHT TAXI, 1937, A
MIDNIGHT TAXI, THE, 1928, A

MIDNIGHT THIEVES, 1926
MIDNIGHT TRAIL, THE, 1918
MIDNIGHT WARNING, THE, 1932, A
MIDNIGHT WATCH, THE, 1927, A
MIDSHIPMAID GOB, 1932, A
MIDSHIPMAN EASY
MIDSHIPMAN JACK, 1933, A
MIDSHIPMAN, THE, 1925
MIDSHIPMAN, THE
MIDSTREAM, 1929, A
MIDSUMMER MADNESS, 1920, C
MIDSUMMER NIGHT'S DREAM, A, 1928
MIDSUMMER NIGHT'S DREAM, A, 1966, A
MIDSUMMER NIGHT'S DREAM, A, 1969, A
MIDSUMMER NIGHT'S DREAM, A, 1984, O
MIDSUMMER NIGHT'S SEX COMEDY, A, 1982, C-O
MIDSUMMER NIGHT'S DREAM, A, 1935, A
MIDSUMMERS NIGHT'S DREAM, A, 1961, AAA
MIDWAY, 1976, A
MIDWIFE, THE, 1961, A
MIGHT AND THE MAN, 1917
MIGHT MAKES RIGHT
MIGHTY BARNUM, THE, 1934, A
MIGHTY CRUSADERS, THE, 1961, A
MIGHTY DEBRAU, THE, 1923
MIGHTY GORGA, THE, 1969, A
MIGHTY JOE YOUNG, 1949, A
MIGHTY JUNGLE, THE, 1965, A
MIGHTY LAK' A ROSE, 1923
MIGHTY MCGURK, THE, 1946, A
MIGHTY MOUSE IN THE GREAT SPACE CHASE, 1983, AAA
MIGHTY TREVE, THE, 1937, AAA
MIGHTY TUNDRA, THE
MIGHTY URSUS, 1962, A
MIGHTY WARRIOR, THE
MIGHTY, THE, 1929, A
MIGNON, 1915
MIKADO, THE, 1939, A
MIKADO, THE, 1967, AAA
MIKE, 1926, A
MIKE'S MURDER, 1984, O
MIKEY AND NICKY, 1976, C-O
MILADY, 1923
MILADY O' THE BEAN STALK, 1918
MILCZACA GWIAZDA
MILDRED PIERCE, 1945, A
MILE A MINUTE
MILE A MINUTE LOVE, 1937, A
MILE A MINUTE MORGAN, 1924
MILE-A-MINUTE KENDALL, 1918
MILE-A-MINUTE MAN, THE, 1926
MILE-A-MINUTE ROMEO, 1923
MILESTONES, 1916
MILESTONES, 1920
MILESTONES, 1975, C
MILESTONES OF LIFE, 1915
MILITARY ACADEMY, 1940, A
MILITARY ACADEMY WITH THAT TENTH AVENUE GANG, 1950, A
MILITARY POLICEMAN
MILITARY SECRET, 1945, A
MILKMAN, THE, 1950, A
MILKY WAY, THE, 1922
MILKY WAY, THE, 1936, AA
MILKY WAY, THE, 1969, C
MILL OF THE STONE WOMEN, 1963, O
MILL ON THE FLOSS, 1939, A
MILL ON THE FLOSS, THE, 1915
MILL-OWNER'S DAUGHTER, THE, 1916
MILLER'S WIFE, THE, 1957, O
MILLERSON CASE, THE, 1947, A
MILLIE, 1931, A
MILLIE'S DAUGHTER, 1947, A
MILLION A MINUTE, A, 1916
MILLION BID, A, 1914
MILLION BID, A, 1927
MILLION DOLLAR BABY, 1935, A
MILLION DOLLAR BABY, 1941, A
MILLION DOLLAR COLLAR, THE, 1929, A
MILLION DOLLAR DOLLIES, THE, 1918
MILLION DOLLAR DUCK
MILLION DOLLAR HANDICAP, THE, 1925
MILLION DOLLAR HAUL, 1935
MILLION DOLLAR KID, 1944, A
MILLION DOLLAR LEGS, 1932, A
MILLION DOLLAR LEGS, 1939, A
MILLION DOLLAR MANHUNT, 1962, A
MILLION DOLLAR MERMAID, 1952, A
MILLION DOLLAR MYSTERY, 1927
MILLION DOLLAR PURSUIT, 1951, A
MILLION DOLLAR RACKET
MILLION DOLLAR RANSOM, 1934, A
MILLION DOLLAR ROBBERY, THE, 1914, A
MILLION DOLLAR WEEKEND, 1948, A
MILLION EYES OF SU-MURU, THE, 1967, A
MILLION FOR LOVE, A, 1928, A
MILLION FOR MARY, A, 1916
MILLION POUND NOTE
MILLION TO BURN, A, 1923
MILLION TO ONE, A, 1938, A
MILLION, THE, 1915

MILLION, THE, 1931, A
MILLIONAIRE BABY, THE, 1915
MILLIONAIRE COWBOY, THE, 1924
MILLIONAIRE FOR A DAY
MILLIONAIRE FOR A DAY, A, 1921
MILLIONAIRE FOR CHRISTY, A, 1951, A
MILLIONAIRE KID, 1936, A
MILLIONAIRE MERRY-GO-ROUND
MILLIONAIRE ORPHAN, THE, 1926
MILLIONAIRE PIRATE, THE, 1919
MILLIONAIRE PLAYBOY, 1940, A
MILLIONAIRE PLAYBOY, 1937
MILLIONAIRE POLICEMAN, THE, 1926
MILLIONAIRE VAGRANT, THE, 1917
MILLIONAIRE'S DOUBLE, THE, 1917
MILLIONAIRE, THE, 1921, A
MILLIONAIRE, THE, 1931, A
MILLIONAIRES, 1926
MILLIONAIRES IN PRISON, 1940, A
MILLIONAIRESS, THE, 1960, A
MILLIONARE, THE, 1927
MILLIONS, 1936, A
MILLIONS IN THE AIR, 1935, A
MILLIONS LIKE US, 1943, A
MILLS OF THE GODS, 1935, A
MILLSTONE, THE, 1917
MILOSC DWUDZIESTOLATKOW
MILPITAS MONSTER, THE, 1980
MIMI, 1935, A
MIMI TROTTIN, 1922
MIN AND BILL, 1930, A
MIN VAN BALTHAZAR
MINAMI NO SHIMA NI YUKI GA FURA
MIND BENDERS, THE, 1963, C-O
MIND OF MR. REEDER, THE
MIND OF MR. SOAMES, THE, 1970, A
MIND OVER MOTOR, 1923, A
MIND READER, THE, 1933, A
MIND SNATCHERS, THE
MIND THE PAINT GIRL, 1919
MIND YOUR OWN BUSINESS, 1937, A
MIND-THE-PAINT-GIRL, 1916
MINDWARP: AN INFINITY OF TERROR
MINE OF MISSING MEN, 1917
MINE OWN EXECUTIONER, 1948, C-O
MINE TO KEEP, 1923
MINE WITH THE IRON DOOR, THE, 1924
MINE WITH THE IRON DOOR, THE, 1936, A
MINESWEEPER, 1943, A
MINI WEEKEND
MINI-AFFAIR, THE, 1968, A
MINI-SKIRT MOB, THE, 1968, O
MINISTRY OF FEAR, 1945, C
MINIVER STORY, THE, 1950, A
MINNESOTA CLAY, 1966, C
MINNIE, 1922
MINNIE AND MOSKOWITZ, 1971, C
MINOTAUR, 1955
MINOTAUR, 1976
MINOTAUR, THE, 1961, A
MINOTAUR, WILD BEAST OF CRETE
MINSTREL BOY, THE, 1937, A
MINSTREL MAN, 1944, A
MINTS OF HELL, THE, 1919
MINUIT...PLACE PIGALLE, 1928
MINUTE TO PRAY, A SECOND TO DIE, A, 1968, C
MINX, THE, 1969, O
MIO FIGILIO NERONE
MIR VKHODYASHCHEMU
MIRACLE BABY, THE, 1923
MIRACLE CAN HAPPEN, A
MIRACLE IN HARLEM, 1948, A
MIRACLE IN MILAN, 1951, A
MIRACLE IN SOHO, 1957, A
MIRACLE IN THE RAIN, 1956, A
MIRACLE IN THE SAND
MIRACLE KID, 1942, A
MIRACLE MAKERS, THE, 1923, A
MIRACLE MAN, THE, 1919, A
MIRACLE MAN, THE, 1932, A
MIRACLE OF FATIMA
MIRACLE OF LIFE
MIRACLE OF LIFE, THE, 1915
MIRACLE OF LIFE, THE, 1926
MIRACLE OF LOVE, A, 1916
MIRACLE OF LOVE, THE, 1920
MIRACLE OF MANHATTAN, THE, 1921
MIRACLE OF MONEY, THE, 1920
MIRACLE OF MORGAN'S CREEK, THE, 1944, C
MIRACLE OF OUR LADY OF FATIMA, THE, 1952, A
MIRACLE OF SAN SEBASTIAN
MIRACLE OF SANTA'S WHITE REINDEER, THE,
    1963, A
MIRACLE OF THE BELLS, THE, 1948, A
MIRACLE OF THE HILLS, THE, 1959, A
MIRACLE OF THE WHITE REINDEER, THE
MIRACLE OF THE WHITE STALLIONS, 1963, AA
MIRACLE OF WOLVES, THE, 1925
MIRACLE ON 34TH STREET, THE, 1947, AAA
MIRACLE ON MAIN STREET, A, 1940, A
MIRACLE WOMAN, THE, 1931, A-C
MIRACLE WORKER, THE, 1962, A

MIRACLE, THE, 1912
MIRACLE, THE, 1959, A
MIRACLE, THE, 1948
MIRACLE-MAKER, 1922
MIRACLES DO HAPPEN, 1938, A
MIRACLES FOR SALE, 1939, A
MIRACOLO A MILANO
MIRACULOUS JOURNEY, 1948, A
MIRAGE, 1965, A-C
MIRAGE, 1972, C
MIRAGE, THE, 1920, A
MIRAGE, THE, 1924
MIRANDA, 1949, A
MIRANDY SMILES, 1918
MIRELE EFROS, 1912
MIRELE EFROS, 1939
MIRIAM
MIRIAM ROZELLA, 1924, C
MIRROR CRACK'D, THE, 1980, A-C
MIRROR HAS TWO FACES, THE, 1959, A
MIRROR OF LIFE, THE, 1916
MIRROR, THE, 1917
MIRRORS, 1978
MIRRORS, 1984, O
MIRTH AND MELODY
MISADVENTURES OF MERLIN JONES, THE,
    1964, AAA
MISBEHAVING HUSBANDS, 1941, A
MISBEHAVING LADIES, 1931, A
MISCHIEF, 1931, A
MISCHIEF, 1969, A
MISCHIEF MAKER, THE, 1916, A
MISERICORDE, 1917
MISFIT EARL, A, 1919
MISFIT WIFE, THE, 1920
MISFITS, THE, 1961, C
MISHPACHAT SIMCHON
MISLEADING LADY, THE, 1916
MISLEADING LADY, THE, 1920
MISLEADING LADY, THE, 1932, A
MISLEADING WIDOW, THE, 1919
MISMATES, 1926
MISS ADVENTURE, 1919
MISS AMBITION, 1918
MISS ANNIE ROONEY, 1942, A
MISS ARIZONA, 1919
MISS BLUEBEARD, 1925, A
MISS BREWSTER'S MILLIONS, 1926, A
MISS CHARITY, 1921
MISS CRUSOE, 1919, A
MISS DECEPTION, 1917
MISS DULCIE FROM DIXIE, 1919, A
MISS EDITH, DUCHESSE, 1928
MISS FANE'S BABY IS STOLEN, 1934, A
MISS FIX-IT
MISS GEORGE WASHINGTON, 1916
MISS GRANT TAKES RICHMOND, 1949, A
MISS HELYETT, 1927
MISS HOBBS, 1920, A
MISS INNOCENCE, 1918
MISS JACKIE OF THE ARMY, 1917
MISS JACKIE OF THE NAVY, 1916
MISS JESSICA IS PREGNANT, 1970, O
MISS JUDE
MISS LESLIE'S DOLLS, 1972
MISS LONDON LTD., 1943, A
MISS LULU BETT, 1921
MISS MELODY JONES, 1973
MISS MEND, 1926
MISS MINK OF 1949, 1949, A
MISS MISCHIEF MAKER, 1918
MISS MUERTE
MISS NOBODY, 1917
MISS NOBODY, 1920
MISS NOBODY, 1926, A
MISS PACIFIC FLEET, 1935, A
MISS PAUL REVERE, 1922
MISS PEASANT, 1916
MISS PETTICOATS, 1916
MISS PILGRIM'S PROGRESS, 1950, A
MISS PINKERTON, 1932, A
MISS PRESIDENT, 1935, A
MISS ROBIN CRUSOE, 1954, A
MISS ROBIN HOOD, 1952, A
MISS ROBINSON CRUSOE, 1917
MISS ROVEL, 1920
MISS SADIE THOMPSON, 1953, O
MISS SUSIE SLAGLE'S, 1945, A
MISS TATLOCK'S MILLIONS, 1948, A
MISS TULIP STAYS THE NIGHT, 1955, A
MISS U.S.A., 1917
MISS V FROM MOSCOW, 1942, A
MISSILE FROM HELL, 1960, A
MISSILE TO THE MOON, 1959, A
MISSING, 1918
MISSING, 1982, A-C
MISSING CORPSE, THE, 1945, A
MISSING DAUGHTERS, 1939, A
MISSING DAUGHTERS, 1939, A
MISSING EVIDENCE, 1939, A
MISSING GIRLS, 1936, A
MISSING GUEST, THE, 1938, A

MISSING HUSBANDS
MISSING IN ACTION, 1984, O
MISSING JUROR, THE, 1944, A
MISSING LADY, THE, 1946, A
MISSING LINK, THE, 1927
MISSING LINKS, THE, 1916
MISSING MILLION, THE, 1942, A
MISSING MILLIONS, 1922, A
MISSING NOTE, THE, 1961, AA
MISSING PEOPLE, THE, 1940, A
MISSING PERSONS
MISSING REMBRANDT, THE, 1932, A
MISSING TEN DAYS, 1941, A
MISSING THE TIDE, 1918, C
MISSING WITNESS
MISSING WITNESSES, 1937, A
MISSING WOMEN, 1951, A
MISSING, BELIEVED MARRIED, 1937, A
MISSION BATANGAS, 1968, A
MISSION BLOODY MARY, 1967, A
MISSION GALACTICA: THE CYLON ATTACK, 1979, A
MISSION HILL, 1982
MISSION IN MOROCCO, 1959
MISSION MARS, 1968, A
MISSION OF THE SEA HAWK, 1962
MISSION OVER KOREA, 1953, A
MISSION STARDUST, 1968, A
MISSION TO DEATH, 1966
MISSION TO HELL
MISSION TO HONG KONG
MISSION TO MOSCOW, 1943, A
MISSION, THE, 1984, O
MISSION: MONTE CARLO, 1981
MISSIONARY, THE, 1982, O
MISSISSIPPI, 1935, A
MISSISSIPPI GAMBLER, 1929, A
MISSISSIPPI GAMBLER, 1942, A
MISSISSIPPI GAMBLER, THE, 1953, C
MISSISSIPPI MERMAID, 1970, A
MISSISSIPPI RHYTHM, 1949, A
MISSISSIPPI SUMMER, 1971, C
MISSISSIPPI, 1931
MISSOURI BREAKS, THE, 1976, C-O
MISSOURI OUTLAW, A, 1942, A
MISSOURI TRAVELER, THE, 1958, A
MISSOURIANS, THE, 1950, A
MIST IN THE VALLEY, 1923
MISTAKEN ORDERS, 1926
MISTER 44, 1916
MISTER 880, 1950, AA
MISTER ANTONIO, 1929, A
MISTER BROWN, 1972, C
MISTER BUDDWING, 1966, C
MISTER CINDERELLA, 1936, A
MISTER CINDERS, 1934, A
MISTER CORY, 1957, A
MISTER FREEDOM, 1970, A
MISTER HOBO, 1936, A
MISTER MOSES, 1965, O
MISTER ROBERTS, 1955, A
MISTER ROCK AND ROLL, 1957, A
MISTER SCARFACE, 1977
MISTER TEN PERCENT, 1967, A
MISTER V
MISTER, YOU ARE A WIDOWER
MISTERIOUS DE ULTRATUMBA
MISTRESS FOR THE SUMMER, A, 1964, C
MISTRESS NELL, 1915, A
MISTRESS OF ATLANTIS, THE, 1932, A
MISTRESS OF SHENSTONE, THE, 1921, A
MISTRESS OF THE APES, 1981, O
MISTRESS OF THE WORLD, 1959, A
MISTRESS PAMELA, 1974
MISTY, 1961, AAA
MISUNDERSTOOD, 1984, C
MIT EVA DIE SUNDE AN
MITCHELL, 1975, O
MITYA, 1927
MIVTZA KAHIR
MIX ME A PERSON, 1962, C
MIXED BLOOD, 1916
MIXED BLOOD, 1984, O
MIXED COMPANY, 1974, C
MIXED DOUBLES, 1933, A
MIXED FACES, 1922, A
MLLE PAULETTE, 1918
MOANA, 1926
MOB TOWN, 1941, A
MOB, THE, 1951, C-O
MOBS INC, 1956, O
MOBY DICK, 1930
MOBY DICK, 1956, C
MOCCASINS, 1925
MOCKERY, 1927, C
MODEL AND THE MARRIAGE BROKER, THE, 1951, A
MODEL FOR MURDER, 1960, A
MODEL FROM MONTMARTE, THE, 1928
MODEL MURDER CASE, THE, 1964, A
MODEL SHOP, THE, 1969, C-O
MODEL WIFE, 1941, A
MODEL'S CONFESSION, THE, 1918
MODELS, INC., 1952, C

MODERATO CANTABILE, 1964, C
MODERN CAIN, A, 1925
MODERN CINDERELLA, A, 1917, A
MODERN DAUGHTERS, 1927
MODERN DAY HOUDINI, 1983
MODERN DU BARRY, A, 1928
MODERN ENOCH ARDEN, A, 1916
MODERN HERO, A, 1934, A
MODERN HERO, A 1941
MODERN HUSBANDS, 1919
MODERN JEAN VAL JEAN; OR A FRAME UP, A, 1930
MODERN LORELEI, A
MODERN LOVE, 1918
MODERN LOVE, 1929, A
MODERN MADNESS
MODERN MAGDALEN, A, 1915
MODERN MARRIAGE, 1923, A
MODERN MARRIAGE, A, 1962, O
MODERN MATRIMONY, 1923
MODERN MEPHISTO, A, 1914
MODERN MIRACLE, THE
MODERN MONTE CRISTO, A, 1917, A
MODERN MOTHER GOOSE, 1917
MODERN MOTHERS, 1928
MODERN MUSKETEER, A, 1917, A
MODERN OTHELLO, A, 1917
MODERN PROBLEMS, 1981, A-C
MODERN ROMANCE, 1981, C
MODERN SALOME, A, 1920, C
MODERN THELMA, A, 1916
MODERN TIMES, 1936, A
MODERN YOUTH, 1926
MODESTY BLAISE, 1966, A
MODIGLIANI OF MONTPARNASSE, 1961, A
MOGAMBO, 1953, A
MOGLIAMANTE
MOHAMMAD, MESSENGER OF GOD, 1976, C-O
MOHAN JOSHI HAAZIR HO, 1984, A
MOHAWK, 1956, A
MOHICAN'S DAUGHTER, THE, 1922
MOI AUSSI, J'ACCUSE, 1920
MOJAVE FIREBRAND, 1944, A
MOJAVE KID, THE, 1927
MOKEY, 1942, A
MOLE PEOPLE, THE, 1956, A
MOLE, THE
MOLESTER, THE
MOLLY
MOLLY AND I, 1920
MOLLY AND LAWLESS JOHN, 1972, A
MOLLY AND ME, 1929, A
MOLLY AND ME, 1945, A
MOLLY BAWN, 1916, A
MOLLY ENTANGLED, 1917, A
MOLLY LOUVAIN
MOLLY MAGUIRES, THE, 1970, C-O
MOLLY MAKE-BELIEVE, 1916
MOLLY O', 1921, A
MOLLY OF THE FOLLIES, 1919, A
MOLLY, GO GET 'EM, 1918
MOLLYCODDLE, THE, 1920, A
MOM AND DAD, 1948, O
MOMENT BEFORE, THE, 1916
MOMENT BY MOMENT, 1978, O
MOMENT OF DANGER
MOMENT OF INDISCRETION, 1958, A
MOMENT OF TERROR, 1969, C
MOMENT OF TRUTH
MOMENT OF TRUTH, THE, 1965, A
MOMENT TO MOMENT, 1966, A
MOMENTS, 1974, O
MOMMAN, LITTLE JUNGLE BOY
MOMMIE DEAREST, 1981, C-O
MON COEUR AU RALENTI, 1928
MON CURE CHEZ LES PAUVRES, 1925
MON CURE CHEZ LES RICHES, 1925
MON ONCLE
MON ONCLE, 1925
MON ONCLE ANTOINE
MON ONCLE BENJAMIN, 1923
MON ONCLE D'AMERIQUE, 1980, C
MON PREMIER AMOUR
MONA KENT
MONASTERY GARDEN
MONDAY'S CHILD, 1967, A-C
MONDO TRASHO, 1970, O
MONEY, 1915
MONEY, 1921
MONEY AND THE WOMAN, 1940, A
MONEY CHANGERS, THE, 1920
MONEY CORRAL, THE, 1919, A
MONEY FOR JAM
MONEY FOR NOTHING, 1932, A
MONEY FOR SPEED, 1933, A
MONEY FROM HOME, 1953, A
MONEY GOD, OR DO RICHES BRING HAPPINESS,
    THE, 1914
MONEY HABIT, THE, 1924, A
MONEY IN MY POCKET, 1962
MONEY ISN'T EVERYTHING
MONEY ISN'T EVERYTHING, 1918
MONEY ISN'T EVERYTHING, 1925, A

MONEY JUNGLE, THE, 1968, A
MONEY LENDER, THE, 1914
MONEY MAD, 1918
MONEY MAD, 1934, A
MONEY MADNESS, 1917
MONEY MADNESS, 1948, A
MONEY MAGIC, 1917, A
MONEY MANIAC, THE, 1921
MONEY MASTER, THE, 1915
MONEY MEANS NOTHING, 1932, A
MONEY MEANS NOTHING, 1934, A
MONEY MILL, THE, 1917
MONEY MONEY MONEY, 1923, A
MONEY MOVERS, 1978, O
MONEY ON THE STREET, 1930, A
MONEY ORDER, THE
MONEY TALKS, 1926
MONEY TALKS, 1933, A
MONEY TO BURN, 1922
MONEY TO BURN, 1926
MONEY TO BURN, 1940, A
MONEY TO BURN, 1981
MONEY TRAP, THE, 1966, C
MONEY, MONEY, MONEY
MONEY, THE, 1975, O
MONEY, WOMEN AND GUNS, 1958, A
MONGOLS, THE, 1966, A
MONGREL, 1982, O
MONITORS, THE, 1969, C
MONKEY BUSINESS, 1931, A
MONKEY BUSINESS, 1952, A
MONKEY GRIP, 1983, A
MONKEY HUSTLE, THE, 1976, C-O
MONKEY IN WINTER, A, 1962, A
MONKEY ON MY BACK, 1957, C
MONKEY TALKS, THE, 1927, A
MONKEY'S PAW, THE, 1923, A
MONKEY'S PAW, THE, 1933, C
MONKEY'S PAW, THE, 1948, A
MONKEY'S UNCLE, THE, 1965, AAA
MONKEYS, GO HOME, 1967, AAA
MONNA VANNA, 1923
MONOLITH MONSTERS, THE, 1957, A
MONOPOLIST, THE, 1915
MONSEIGNEUR, 1950, A
MONSIEUR, 1964, A
MONSIEUR BEAUCAIRE, 1924, A
MONSIEUR BEAUCAIRE, 1946, A
MONSIEUR COGNAC
MONSIEUR FABRE
MONSIEUR HULOT'S HOLIDAY
MONSIEUR LE DIRECTEUR, 1924
MONSIEUR LEBIDOIS PROPRIETAIRE, 1922
MONSIEUR LEBUREAU, 1920
MONSIEUR RIPOIS
MONSIEUR VERDOUX, 1947, O
MONSIEUR VINCENT, 1949, A
MONSIGNOR, 1982, O
MONSOON, 1953, C
MONSTER, O
MONSTER A GO-GO, 1965, C
MONSTER AND THE GIRL, THE, 1914
MONSTER AND THE GIRL, THE, 1941, C
MONSTER BARAN, THE
MONSTER CLUB, THE, 1981, C
MONSTER FROM THE GREEN HELL, 1958, A
MONSTER FROM THE OCEAN FLOOR, THE, 1954, A
MONSTER FROM THE SURF
MONSTER ISLAND, 1981, C
MONSTER MAKER, 1954
MONSTER MAKER, THE, 1944, C
MONSTER MEETS THE GORILLA
MONSTER OF HIGHGATE PONDS, THE, 1961, AAA
MONSTER OF LONDON CITY, THE, 1967, O
MONSTER OF PIEDRAS BLANCAS, THE, 1959, C
MONSTER OF TERROR
MONSTER OF THE ISLAND, 1953, A
MONSTER OF THE WAX MUSEUM
MONSTER ON THE CAMPUS, 1958, C
MONSTER THAT CHALLENGED THE WORLD, THE,
    1957, A
MONSTER WALKED, THE
MONSTER WALKS, THE, 1932, A
MONSTER WANGMAGWI, 1967, A
MONSTER YONGKARI
MONSTER ZERO, 1970, A
MONSTER, 1980
MONSTER, THE, 1925, A
MONSTERS ARE LOOSE
MONSTERS FROM THE MOON
MONSTERS FROM THE UNKNOWN PLANET, 1975, A
MONSTROID, 1980
MONSTROSITY
MONTANA, 1950, A
MONTANA BELLE, 1952, A
MONTANA BILL, 1921
MONTANA DESPERADO, 1951, A
MONTANA INCIDENT, 1952
MONTANA JUSTICE
MONTANA KID, THE, 1931, A
MONTANA MIKE
MONTANA MOON, 1930, A

MONTANA TERRITORY, 1952, A
MONTE CARLO, 1926
MONTE CARLO, 1930, AA
MONTE CARLO BABY, 1953, A
MONTE CARLO MADNESS
MONTE CARLO NIGHTS, 1934, A
MONTE CARLO OR BUST
MONTE CARLO STORY, THE, 1957, A
MONTE CASSINO, 1948, A
MONTE CRISTO, 1912
MONTE CRISTO, 1922
MONTE CRISTO'S REVENGE
MONTE WALSH, 1970, C
MONTE-CRISTO, 1929
MONTENEGRO, 1981, O
MONTENEGRO—OR PIGS AND PEARLS
MONTMARTE ROSE, 1929
MONTPARNASSE 19
MONTREAL MAIN, 1974, O
MONTY PYTHON AND THE HOLY GRAIL, 1975, O
MONTY PYTHON'S LIFE OF BRIAN, 1979, O
MONTY PYTHON'S THE MEANING OF LIFE, 1983, O
MONTY WORKS THE WIRES, 1921, O
MOON AND SIXPENCE, THE, 1942, A
MOON IN THE GUTTER, THE, 1983, O
MOON IS BLUE, THE, 1953, A-C
MOON IS DOWN, THE, 1943, C
MOON MADNESS, 1920, A
MOON MARIGOLDS, THE, 1972, C
MOON OF ISRAEL, 1927
MOON OVER BURMA, 1940, A
MOON OVER HARLEM, 1939
MOON OVER HER SHOULDER, 1941, A
MOON OVER LAS VEGAS, 1944, AA
MOON OVER MIAMI, 1941, A
MOON OVER MONTANA, 1946
MOON OVER THE ALLEY, 1980, O
MOON PILOT, 1962, AAA
MOON WALK
MOON ZERO TWO, 1970, A
MOON'S OUR HOME, THE, 1936, A
MOON-SPINNERS, THE, 1964, AAA
MOONBEAM MAN, THE
MOONCHILD, 1972, O
MOONFIRE, 1970, O
MOONFLEET, 1955, A
MOONLIGHT AND CACTUS, 1944, A
MOONLIGHT AND HONEYSUCKLE, 1921
MOONLIGHT AND MELODY
MOONLIGHT AND PRETZELS, 1933, A
MOONLIGHT FOLLIES, 1921
MOONLIGHT IN HAVANA, 1942, A
MOONLIGHT IN HAWAII, 1941, A
MOONLIGHT IN VERMONT, 1943, A
MOONLIGHT MASQUERADE, 1942, A
MOONLIGHT MURDER, 1936, A
MOONLIGHT ON THE PRAIRIE, 1936, A
MOONLIGHT ON THE RANGE, 1937, A
MOONLIGHT RAID
MOONLIGHT SONATA, 1938, A
MOONLIGHTER, THE, 1953, A
MOONLIGHTING, 1982, C
MOONLIGHTING WIVES, 1966, O
MOONRAKER, 1979, A
MOONRAKER, THE, 1958, A
MOONRISE, 1948, C
MOONRUNNERS, 1975, A
MOONSHINE COUNTY EXPRESS, 1977, C
MOONSHINE MENACE, THE, 1921
MOONSHINE MOUNTAIN, 1964, A
MOONSHINE TRAIL, THE, 1919
MOONSHINE VALLEY, 1922, A
MOONSHINE WAR, THE, 1970, C
MOONSHINER'S WOMAN, 1968, O
MOONSHOT
MOONSPINNERS, THE
MOONSTONE, THE, 1915
MOONSTONE, THE, 1934, A
MOONTIDE, 1942, A
MOONWOLF, 1966, A
MORAL CODE, THE, 1917
MORAL COURAGE, 1917
MORAL DEADLINE, THE, 1919
MORAL FABRIC, THE, 1916
MORAL FIBRE, 1921, A
MORAL LAW, THE, 1918
MORAL SINNER, THE, 1924
MORAL SUICIDE, 1918
MORALIST, THE, 1964, A
MORALS, 1921, A
MORALS FOR MEN, 1925
MORALS FOR WOMEN, 1931, A
MORALS OF HILDA, THE, 1916
MORALS OF MARCUS, THE, 1936, A
MORALS OF WEYBURY, THE, 1916
MORALS SQUAD, 1960
MORAN OF THE LADY LETTY, 1922, A
MORAN OF THE MARINES, 1928
MORAN OF THE MOUNTED, 1926
MORD UND TOTSCHLAG
MORDEI HA'OR
MORDER UNTER UNS

MORE, 1969, O
MORE AMERICAN GRAFFITI, 1979, C
MORE DEAD THAN ALIVE, 1968, C
MORE DEADLY THAN THE MALE, 1919
MORE DEADLY THAN THE MALE, 1961, C
MORE EXCELLENT WAY, THE, 1917
MORE PAY—LESS WORK, 1926
MORE THAN A MIRACLE, 1967, O
MORE THAN A SECRETARY, 1936, A
MORE THE MERRIER, THE, 1943, A
MORE TO BE PITIED THAN SCORNED, 1922
MORE TROUBLE, 1918, A
MORE TRUTH THAN POETRY, 1917
MORGAN, 1966, C
MORGAN LA SIRENE
MORGAN THE PIRATE, 1961, A
MORGAN'S LAST RAID, 1929, A
MORGAN'S MARAUDERS, 1929, A
MORGAN'S RAIDERS, 1918
MORGANE, THE ENCHANTRESS, 1929
MORGANSON'S FINISH, 1926
MORIARTY
MORITURI, 1965, C
MORMON MAID, A, 1917
MORMON PERIL, THE
MORNING CALL
MORNING DEPARTURE
MORNING GLORY, 1933, C
MORNING STAR, 1962, A
MORO WITCH DOCTOR, 1964, C
MOROCCO, 1930, C
MOROZKO
MORTADELLA
MORTAL SIN, THE, 1917
MORTAL STORM, THE, 1940, A
MORTE A VENEZIA
MORTGAGED WIFE, THE, 1918
MORTMAIN, 1915
MORTON OF THE MOUNTED
MORTUARY, 1983, O
MOSCOW, 1927
MOSCOW DISTRUSTS TEARS
MOSCOW DOES NOT BELIEVE IN TEARS, 1980, A
MOSCOW IN OCTOBER, 1927
MOSCOW NIGHTS
MOSCOW ON THE HUDSON, 1984, C-O
MOSCOW SHANGHAI, 1936, A
MOSCOW—CASSIOPEIA, 1974, A
MOSES, 1976, A
MOSES AND AARON, 1975, C
MOSQUITO SQUADRON, 1970, A
MOSS ROSE, 1947, A
MOST BEAUTIFUL AGE, THE, 1970, C
MOST DANGEROUS GAME, THE, 1932, C-O
MOST DANGEROUS MAN ALIVE, THE, 1961, A
MOST DANGEROUS MAN IN THE WORLD, THE
MOST IMMORAL LADY, A, 1929, A
MOST PRECIOUS THING IN LIFE, 1934, A
MOST WANTED MAN, THE, 1962, A
MOST WONDERFUL EVENING OF MY LIFE, THE,
  1972, A
MOSURA
MOTEL HELL, 1980, O
MOTEL, THE OPERATOR, 1940, C
MOTELE THE WEAVER
MOTH AND RUST, 1921
MOTH AND THE FLAME, THE, 1915, A
MOTH, THE, 1917
MOTH, THE, 1934, A
MOTHER, 1914, A
MOTHER, 1920
MOTHER, 1926
MOTHER, 1927
MOTHER AND DAUGHTER, 1965, A
MOTHER AND SON, 1931, C
MOTHER AND THE WHORE, THE, 1973, C
MOTHER CAREY'S CHICKENS, 1938, A
MOTHER DIDN'T TELL ME, 1950, A
MOTHER ETERNAL, 1921
MOTHER GOOSE A GO-GO, 1966, A
MOTHER HEART, THE, 1921
MOTHER INSTINCT, THE, 1917
MOTHER IS A FRESHMAN, 1949, A
MOTHER JOAN OF THE ANGELS?
MOTHER KNOWS BEST, 1928, A
MOTHER KNOWS BEST, 1949
MOTHER KUSTERS GOES TO HEAVEN, 1976, C-O
MOTHER LODE, 1982, C
MOTHER LOVE AND THE LAW, 1917
MOTHER MACHREE, 1922
MOTHER MACHREE, 1928
MOTHER O' MINE, 1921
MOTHER O'MINE, 1917
MOTHER OF DARTMOOR, THE, 1916
MOTHER OF HIS CHILDREN, THE, 1920
MOTHER OUGHT TO MARRY
MOTHER RILEY, 1952, A
MOTHER RILEY JOINS UP, 1939, A
MOTHER RILEY MEETS THE VAMPIRE
MOTHER RILEY'S JUNGLE TREASURE, 1951, A
MOTHER RILEY, HEADMISTRESS, 1950, A
MOTHER SHOULD BE LOVED, A, 1934

MOTHER SIR
MOTHER SUPERIOR
MOTHER WORE TIGHTS, 1947, A
MOTHER'S BOY, 1929, A
MOTHER'S DAY, 1980, O
MOTHER'S HEART, A, 1914
MOTHER'S MILLIONS
MOTHER'S ORDEAL, A, 1917
MOTHER'S SECRET, A, 1918
MOTHER'S SIN, A, 1918
MOTHER, I NEED YOU, 1918
MOTHER, JUGS & SPEED, 1976, O
MOTHERHOOD, 1915, C
MOTHERHOOD, 1917
MOTHERHOOD; LIFE'S GREATEST MIRACLE, 1928
MOTHERLOVE, 1916
MOTHERS CRY, 1930, A
MOTHERS OF MEN, 1917
MOTHERS OF MEN, 1920
MOTHERS OF TODAY, 1939, C
MOTHERS-IN-LAW, 1923, A
MOTHRA, 1962, A
MOTHS, 1913
MOTION TO ADJOURN, A, 1921
MOTIVE FOR REVENGE, 1935, A
MOTIVE WAS JEALOUSY, THE, 1970, C
MOTOR MADNESS, 1937, A
MOTOR PATROL, 1950, A
MOTOR PSYCHO, 1965, O
MOTORCYCLE GANG, 1957, C-O
MOTORING, 1927, A
MOTORING THRU SPAIN, 1929
MOTSART I SALVERI
MOUCHETTE, 1970, C
MOULDER OF MEN, 1927
MOULIN ROUGE, 1928, C
MOULIN ROUGE, 1934, A
MOULIN ROUGE, 1944, A
MOULIN ROUGE, 1952, A-C
MOUNTAIN CHARLIE, 1982
MOUNTAIN DESPERADOES
MOUNTAIN DEW, 1917
MOUNTAIN EAGLE, THE
MOUNTAIN EAGLE, THE
MOUNTAIN FAMILY ROBINSON, 1979, A
MOUNTAIN JUSTICE, 1930, A
MOUNTAIN JUSTICE, 1937, A
MOUNTAIN MADNESS, 1920
MOUNTAIN MAN
MOUNTAIN MEN, THE, 1980, O
MOUNTAIN MOONLIGHT, 1941, A
MOUNTAIN MUSIC, 1937, A
MOUNTAIN RAT, THE, 1914, A
MOUNTAIN RHYTHM, 1939, A
MOUNTAIN RHYTHM, 1942, AAA
MOUNTAIN ROAD, THE, 1960, A
MOUNTAIN WOMAN, THE, 1921
MOUNTAIN, THE, 1935, A
MOUNTAIN, THE, 1956, A
MOUNTAINS O'MOURNE, 1938, A
MOUNTAINS OF MANHATTAN, 1927
MOUNTED FURY, 1931, A
MOUNTED STRANGER, THE, 1930, A
MOURNING BECOMES ELECTRA, 1947, C
MOURNING SUIT, THE, 1975, C
MOUSE AND HIS CHILD, THE, 1977, A
MOUSE AND THE WOMAN, THE, 1981, O
MOUSE ON THE MOON, THE, 1963, AA
MOUSE THAT ROARED, THE, 1959, AAA
MOUTH TO MOUTH, 1978, C
MOUTHPIECE, THE, 1932, A
MOVE, 1970, C
MOVE OVER, DARLING, 1963, A
MOVIE CRAZY, 1932, A
MOVIE MOVIE, 1978, A-C
MOVIE STAR, AMERICAN STYLE, OR, LSD I HATE
  YOU, 1966, C
MOVIE STRUCK
MOVIE STUNTMEN, 1953, A
MOVIEMAKERS, 1970
MOVIETONE FOLLIES OF 1929
MOVIETONE FOLLIES OF 1930
MOVING FINGER, THE, 1963, C
MOVING GUEST, THE, 1927
MOVING IMAGE, THE, 1920
MOVING IN SOCIETY
MOVING TARGET, THE
MOVING VIOLATION, 1976, C
MOZAMBIQUE, 1966, A
MOZART
MOZART, 1940, A
MOZART STORY, THE, 1948, A
MR. ACE, 1946, A
MR. AND MRS. NORTH, 1941, A
MR. AND MRS. SMITH, 1941, A
MR. ARKADIN, 1962, C
MR. ASHTON WAS INDISCREET
MR. BARNES OF NEW YORK, 1914, A
MR. BARNES OF NEW YORK, 1922
MR. BELVEDERE GOES TO COLLEGE, 1949, A
MR. BELVEDERE RINGS THE BELL, 1951, A
MR. BIG, 1943, A

MR. BILL THE CONQUEROR
MR. BILLINGS SPENDS HIS DIME, 1923, A
MR. BILLION, 1977, A
MR. BINGLE, 1922
MR. BLANDINGS BUILDS HIS DREAM HOUSE,
  1948, A
MR. BOGGS STEPS OUT, 1938, A
MR. BROWN COMES DOWN THE HILL, 1966, A
MR. BUG GOES TO TOWN, 1941, AAA
MR. CELEBRITY, 1942, A
MR. CHEDWORTH STEPS OUT, 1939, A
MR. CHUMP, 1938, A
MR. COHEN TAKES A WALK, 1936, A
MR. DEEDS GOES TO TOWN, 1936, A
MR. DENNING DRIVES NORTH, 1953, A
MR. DISTRICT ATTORNEY, 1941, A
MR. DISTRICT ATTORNEY, 1946, A
MR. DISTRICT ATTORNEY IN THE CARTER CASE
MR. DODD TAKES THE AIR, 1937, A
MR. DOLAN OF NEW YORK, 1917
MR. DOODLE KICKS OFF, 1938, A
MR. DRAKE'S DUCK, 1951, A
MR. DREW
MR. DYNAMITE, 1935, A
MR. DYNAMITE, 1941, A
MR. EMMANUEL, 1945, A
MR. FAINTHEART
MR. FIX-IT, 1918, A
MR. FORBUSH AND THE PENGUINS
MR. FOX OF VENICE
MR. GILFIL'S LOVE STORY, 1920
MR. GOODE, THE SAMARITAN, 1916
MR. GREX OF MONTE CARLO, 1915
MR. GRIGGS RETURNS
MR. H. C. ANDERSEN, 1950, A
MR. HEX, 1946, A
MR. HOBBS TAKES A VACATION, 1962, AA
MR. HORATIO KNIBBLES, 1971
MR. HOT SHOT
MR. HULOT'S HOLIDAY, 1954, AAA
MR. IMPERIUM, 1951, A
MR. INNOCENT
MR. INVISIBLE
MR. JIM—AMERICAN, SOLDIER, AND GENTLEMAN
MR. JUSTICE RAFFLES, 1921, A
MR. KINGSTREET'S WAR, 1973
MR. KLEIN, 1976, C
MR. LEMON OF ORANGE, 1931, A
MR. LIMPET
MR. LOGAN, USA, 1918
MR. LORD SAYS NO, 1952, A
MR. LUCKY, 1943, A
MR. LYNDON AT LIBERTY, 1915
MR. MAGOO'S HOLIDAY FESTIVAL, 1970, AAA
MR. MAJESTYK, 1974, C
MR. MOM, 1983, A-C
MR. MOTO AND THE PERSIAN OIL CASE
MR. MOTO IN DANGER ISLAND, 1939, A
MR. MOTO ON DANGER ISLAND
MR. MOTO TAKES A CHANCE, 1938, A
MR. MOTO TAKES A VACATION, 1938, A
MR. MOTO'S GAMBLE, 1938, A
MR. MOTO'S LAST WARNING, 1939, A
MR. MUGGS RIDES AGAIN, 1945, A
MR. MUGGS STEPS OUT, 1943, A
MR. MUSIC, 1950, A
MR. NOBODY, 1927, A
MR. OPP, 1917
MR. ORCHID, 1948, A
MR. PATMAN, 1980, C
MR. PEABODY AND THE MERMAID, 1948, AA
MR. PEEK-A-BOO, 1951
MR. PERRIN AND MR. TRAILL, 1948, A
MR. PIM PASSES BY, 1921
MR. POTTER OF TEXAS, 1922
MR. POTTS GOES TO MOSCOW, 1953, A
MR. PULVER AND THE CAPTAIN
MR. QUILP, 1975, A
MR. QUINCEY OF MONTE CARLO, 1933, A
MR. RADISH AND MR. CARROT
MR. RECKLESS, 1948, A
MR. REEDER IN ROOM 13
MR. RICCO, 1975, C
MR. ROBINSON CRUSOE, 1932, A
MR. SARDONICUS, 1961, C
MR. SATAN, 1938, A
MR. SCOUTMASTER, 1953, A
MR. SEBASTIAN
MR. SKEFFINGTON, 1944, C
MR. SKITCH, 1933, A
MR. SMITH CARRIES ON, 1937, A
MR. SMITH GOES GHOST, 1940
MR. SMITH GOES TO WASHINGTON, 1939, AAA
MR. SOFT TOUCH, 1949, A
MR. STRINGFELLOW SAYS NO, 1937, A
MR. SUPERINVISIBLE, 1974, AAA
MR. SYCAMORE, 1975, A
MR. TOPAZE
MR. UNIVERSE, 1951, A
MR. WALKIE TALKIE, 1952, A
MR. WASHINGTON GOES TO TOWN, 1941, A
MR. WHAT'S-HIS-NAME, 1935, A

MR. WINKLE GOES TO WAR, 1944, A
MR. WISE GUY, 1942, A
MR. WONG AT HEADQUARTERS
MR. WONG IN CHINATOWN, 1939, A
MR. WONG, DETECTIVE, 1938, A
MR. WU, 1919, A
MR. WU, 1927, C
MRS. BALFANE, 1917
MRS. BLACK IS BACK, 1914, A
MRS. BROWN, YOU'VE GOT A LOVELY DAUGHTER, 1968, A
MRS. CASSELL'S PROFESSION, 1915
MRS. DANE'S CONFESSION, 1922
MRS. DANE'S DANGER, 1922
MRS. DANE'S DEFENCE, 1933, A
MRS. DANE'S DEFENSE, 1918
MRS. FITZHERBERT, 1950, A
MRS. GIBBONS' BOYS, 1962, A
MRS. LEFFINGWELL'S BOOTS, 1918
MRS. LORING'S SECRET
MRS. MIKE, 1949, A
MRS. MINIVER, 1942, A
MRS. O'MALLEY AND MR. MALONE, 1950, A
MRS. PARKINGTON, 1944, A
MRS. PLUM'S PUDDING, 1915
MRS. POLLIFAX-SPY, 1971, A
MRS. PYM OF SCOTLAND YARD, 1939, A
MRS. SLACKER, 1918, A
MRS. SOFFEL, 1984, C
MRS. TEMPLE'S TELEGRAM, 1920
MRS. THOMPSON, 1919, A
MRS. WARREN'S PROFESSION, A
MRS. WIGGS OF THE CABBAGE PATCH, 1914
MRS. WIGGS OF THE CABBAGE PATCH, 1919
MRS. WIGGS OF THE CABBAGE PATCH, 1934, A
MRS. WIGGS OF THE CABBAGE PATCH, 1942, AA
MS. 45, 1981, O
MUCEDNICI LASKY
MUCH TOO SHY, 1942, A
MUD
MUD HONEY
MUDDY RIVER, 1982, A
MUDHONEY
MUDLARK, THE, 1950, A
MUERTO 4-3-2-1-0
MUG TOWN, 1943, A
MUGGER, THE, 1958, A
MUHOMATSU NO ISSHO
MULE TRAIN, 1950, A
MULHALL'S GREAT CATCH, 1926
MUM'S THE WORD, 1918
MUMMY AND THE HUMMINGBIRD, THE, 1915
MUMMY'S BOYS, 1936, A
MUMMY'S CURSE, THE, 1944, A
MUMMY'S GHOST, THE, 1944, A
MUMMY'S HAND, THE, C
MUMMY'S SHROUD, THE, 1967, C
MUMMY'S TOMB, THE, 1942, C
MUMMY, THE, 1932, C-O
MUMMY, THE, 1959, C
MUMSIE, 1927, A
MUMSY, NANNY, SONNY, AND GIRLY, 1970, O
MUMU, 1961, A
MUNECOS INFERNALES
MUNITION GIRL'S ROMANCE, A, 1917, A
MUNKBROGREVEN
MUNSTER, GO HOME, 1966, A
MUPPET MOVIE, THE, 1979, AA
MUPPETS TAKE MANHATTAN, THE, 1984, AAA
MURDER, 1930, A
MURDER A LA MOD, 1968, C
MURDER AHOY, 1964, C
MURDER AMONG FRIENDS, 1941, A
MURDER AT 3 A.M., 1953, A
MURDER AT 45 R.P.M., 1965, C
MURDER AT COVENT GARDEN, 1932, A
MURDER AT DAWN, 1932, A
MURDER AT GLEN ATHOL, 1936, A
MURDER AT MIDNIGHT, 1931, A
MURDER AT MONTE CARLO, 1935, A
MURDER AT SCOTLAND YARD, 1952
MURDER AT SITE THREE, 1959, A
MURDER AT THE BASKERVILLES, 1941, A
MURDER AT THE BURLESQUE
MURDER AT THE CABARET, 1936, A
MURDER AT THE GALLOP, 1963, A
MURDER AT THE INN, 1934, A
MURDER AT THE VANITIES, 1934, A
MURDER AT THE WINDMILL
MURDER BY AGREEMENT
MURDER BY AN ARISTOCRAT, 1936, A
MURDER BY CONTRACT, 1958, C
MURDER BY DEATH, 1976, C
MURDER BY DECREE, 1979, C-O
MURDER BY INVITATION, 1941, A
MURDER BY MAIL
MURDER BY PHONE
MURDER BY PROXY
MURDER BY ROPE, 1936, A
MURDER BY TELEVISION, 1935, A
MURDER BY THE CLOCK, 1931, C
MURDER CAN BE DEADLY, 1963, A

MURDER CLINIC, THE, 1967, C
MURDER CZECH STYLE, 1968, A
MURDER FOR SALE
MURDER GAME, THE, 1966, A
MURDER GOES TO COLLEGE, 1937, A
MURDER IN EDEN, 1962, A
MURDER IN GREENWICH VILLAGE, 1937, A
MURDER IN MISSISSIPPI, 1965, C
MURDER IN MOROCCO
MURDER IN REVERSE, 1946, A
MURDER IN SOHO
MURDER IN THE AIR, 1940, A
MURDER IN THE BIG HOUSE
MURDER IN THE BIG HOUSE, 1942, A
MURDER IN THE BLUE ROOM, 1944, A
MURDER IN THE CATHEDRAL, 1952, A
MURDER IN THE CLOUDS, 1934, A
MURDER IN THE FAMILY, 1938, A
MURDER IN THE FLEET, 1935, A
MURDER IN THE FOOTLIGHTS
MURDER IN THE MUSEUM, 1934, C
MURDER IN THE MUSIC HALL, 1946, O
MURDER IN THE NIGHT, 1940, O
MURDER IN THE OLD RED BARN, 1936, O
MURDER IN THE PRIVATE CAR, 1934, A
MURDER IN THORTON SQUARE
MURDER IN TIMES SQUARE, 1943, O
MURDER IN TRINIDAD, 1934, O
MURDER IS MY BEAT, 1955, O
MURDER IS MY BUSINESS, 1946, O
MURDER IS NEWS, 1939, O
MURDER MAN, 1935, C
MURDER MISSISSIPPI
MURDER MOST FOUL, 1964, A
MURDER OF DR. HARRIGAN, THE, 1936, O
MURDER OF GENERAL GRYAZNOV, THE, 1921
MURDER ON A BRIDLE PATH, 1936, O
MURDER ON A HONEYMOON, 1935, A
MURDER ON APPROVAL, 1956, C
MURDER ON DIAMOND ROW, 1937, C
MURDER ON LENOX AVENUE, 1941
MURDER ON MONDAY, 1953, C
MURDER ON THE BLACKBOARD, 1934, A
MURDER ON THE BRIDGE
MURDER ON THE CAMPUS, 1934, A
MURDER ON THE CAMPUS, 1963, A
MURDER ON THE HIGH SEAS, 1938
MURDER ON THE ORIENT EXPRESS, 1974, C
MURDER ON THE ROOF, 1930, A
MURDER ON THE RUNAWAY TRAIN
MURDER ON THE SECOND FLOOR, 1932, A
MURDER ON THE SET, 1936, A
MURDER ON THE WATERFRONT, 1943, A
MURDER ON THE YUKON, 1940, A
MURDER OVER NEW YORK, 1940, A
MURDER REPORTED, 1958, O
MURDER RING, THE
MURDER SHE SAID, 1961, A
MURDER SOCIETY, THE
MURDER TOMORROW, 1938, A
MURDER WILL OUT, 1930, A
MURDER WILL OUT, 1939, A
MURDER WILL OUT, 1953, A
MURDER WITH MUSIC, 1941
MURDER WITH PICTURES, 1936, A
MURDER WITHOUT CRIME, 1951, A
MURDER WITHOUT TEARS, 1953, A
MURDER, HE SAYS, 1945, A
MURDER, INC.
MURDER, INC., 1960, O
MURDER, MY SWEET, 1945, C-O
MURDERER AMONG US
MURDERER DMITRI KARAMAZOV, THE
MURDERER LIVES AT NUMBER 21, THE, 1947, A
MURDERER, THE
MURDERERS AMONG US, 1948, O
MURDERERS ARE AMONGST US
MURDERERS' ROW, 1966, C
MURDERS IN THE RUE MORGUE, 1932, C
MURDERS IN THE RUE MORGUE, 1971, O
MURDERS IN THE ZOO, 1933, O
MURDOCK TRIAL, THE, 1914
MURIEL, 1963, A
MURIEL, OU LE TEMPS D'UN RETOUR
MURIETA, 1965, O
MURMUR OF THE HEART, 1971, O
MURPH THE SURF, 1974, C
MURPHY'S WAR, 1971, C-O
MURRI AFFAIR, THE
MUSCLE BEACH PARTY, 1964, AA
MUSEUM MYSTERY, 1937, A
MUSHROOM EATER, THE, 1976, O
MUSIC AND MILLIONS
MUSIC BOX KID, THE, 1960, C
MUSIC FOR MADAME, 1937, A
MUSIC FOR MILLIONS, 1944, AA
MUSIC GOES 'ROUND, THE, 1936, A
MUSIC HALL, 1934, A
MUSIC HALL PARADE, 1939, A
MUSIC HATH CHARMS, 1935, A
MUSIC IN MANHATTAN, 1944, A
MUSIC IN MY HEART, 1940, A

MUSIC IN THE AIR, 1934, A
MUSIC IS MAGIC, 1935, A
MUSIC LOVERS, THE, 1971, O
MUSIC MACHINE, THE, 1979, O
MUSIC MAKER, THE, 1936, A
MUSIC MAN, 1948, AA
MUSIC MAN, THE, 1962, AAA
MUSIC MASTER, THE, 1927
MUSIC ROOM, THE, 1963, A
MUSICAL MUTINY, 1970, A
MUSIK I MORKER
MUSS 'EM UP, 1936, A
MUST WE MARRY?, 1928
MUSTANG, 1959, A
MUSTANG COUNTRY, 1976, A
MUSUME TO WATASHI
MUTANT
MUTATIONS, THE, 1974, O
MUTE APPEAL, A, 1917
MUTHERS, THE, 1976
MUTINEERS, THE
MUTINEERS, THE, 1949, A
MUTINY, 1917
MUTINY, 1925, A
MUTINY, 1952, A
MUTINY AHEAD, 1935, A
MUTINY IN OUTER SPACE, 1965, A
MUTINY IN OUTER SPACE, 1958
MUTINY IN THE ARCTIC, 1941, A
MUTINY IN THE BIG HOUSE, 1939, A
MUTINY OF THE ELSINORE, THE, 1920
MUTINY OF THE ELSINORE, THE, 1939, A
MUTINY ON THE BLACKHAWK, 1939, A
MUTINY ON THE BOUNTY, 1935, A
MUTINY ON THE BOUNTY, 1962, C-O
MUTINY ON THE SEAS
MY AIN FOLK, 1944, A
MY AIN FOLK, 1974, A
MY AMERICAN UNCLE
MY AMERICAN WIFE, 1923, A
MY AMERICAN WIFE, 1936, A
MY APPLE
MY BABY IS BLACK, 1965, A
MY BEST FRIEND'S GIRL, 1984, O
MY BEST GAL, 1944, A
MY BEST GIRL, 1915
MY BEST GIRL, 1927, A
MY BILL, 1938, A
MY BLOOD RUNS COLD, 1965, O
MY BLOODY VALENTINE, 1981, O
MY BLUE HEAVEN, 1950, A
MY BODY HUNGERS, 1967, O
MY BODYGUARD, 1980, A
MY BOY, 1922, A
MY BOYS ARE GOOD BOYS, 1978, A
MY BREAKFAST WITH BLASSIE, 1983, O
MY BRILLIANT CAREER, 1980, O
MY BROTHER HAS BAD DREAMS, 1977, O
MY BROTHER JONATHAN, 1949, A
MY BROTHER TALKS TO HORSES, 1946, AAA
MY BROTHER'S KEEPER, 1949, A
MY BROTHER'S WEDDING, 1983, A
MY BROTHER, THE OUTLAW, 1951, A
MY BUDDY, 1944, A
MY CHILDHOOD, 1972, A
MY COUNTRY FIRST, 1916
MY COUSIN, 1918, A
MY COUSIN RACHEL, 1952, A
MY DAD, 1922, A
MY DARLING CLEMENTINE, 1946, A
MY DAUGHTER JOY
MY DAYS WITH JEAN MARC
MY DEAR MISS ALDRICH, 1937, A
MY DEAR SECRETARY, 1948, A-C
MY DEATH IS A MOCKERY, 1952, C-O
MY DINNER WITH ANDRE, 1981, A-C
MY DOG RUSTY, 1948, AAA
MY DOG SHEP, 1948
MY DOG, BUDDY, 1960, C
MY DREAM IS YOURS, 1949, A
MY ENEMY, THE SEA
MY FAIR LADY, 1964, AA
MY FATHER'S HOUSE, 1947, A
MY FATHER'S MISTRESS, 1970, C
MY FAVORITE BLONDE, 1942, A
MY FAVORITE BRUNETTE, 1947, A
MY FAVORITE SPY, 1942, A
MY FAVORITE SPY, 1951, A
MY FAVORITE WIFE, 1940, A
MY FAVORITE YEAR, 1982, C
MY FIGHTING GENTLEMAN, 1917
MY FIRST LOVE, 1978, O
MY FOOLISH HEART, 1949, A-C
MY FORBIDDEN PAST, 1951, C
MY FOUR YEARS IN GERMANY, 1918, A
MY FRIEND FLICKA, 1943, AAA
MY FRIEND FROM INDIA, 1927
MY FRIEND IRMA, 1949, A
MY FRIEND IRMA GOES WEST, 1950, A
MY FRIEND THE KING, 1931, A
MY FRIEND, THE DEVIL, 1922
MY FRIENDS NEED KILLING, 1984

MY GAL LOVES MUSIC, 1944, A
MY GAL SAL, 1942, A
MY GEISHA, 1962, A
MY GIRL TISA, 1948, A
MY GIRLFRIEND'S WEDDING, 1969
MY GUN IS QUICK, 1957, O
MY HANDS ARE CLAY, 1948, A
MY HEART BELONGS TO DADDY, 1942, A
MY HEART GOES CRAZY, 1953, A
MY HEART IS CALLING, 1935, A
MY HERO
MY HOBO, 1963, A
MY HOME TOWN, 1925
MY HOME TOWN, 1928, A
MY HUSBAND'S FRIEND, 1918
MY HUSBAND'S FRIEND, 1922
MY HUSBAND'S OTHER WIFE, 1919
MY HUSBAND'S WIVES, 1924, A
MY IRISH MOLLY
MY KIND OF TOWN, 1984, A
MY KINGDOM FOR A COOK, 1943, A
MY LADY FRIENDS, 1921
MY LADY INCOG, 1916, A
MY LADY OF WHIMS, 1925
MY LADY'S DRESS, 1917
MY LADY'S GARTER, 1920
MY LADY'S LATCHKEY, 1921
MY LADY'S LIPS, 1925
MY LADY'S SLIPPER, 1916
MY LAST DUCHESS
MY LEARNED FRIEND, 1943, A
MY LIFE IS YOURS
MY LIFE TO LIVE, 1963, A
MY LIFE WITH CAROLINE, 1941, A-C
MY LIPS BETRAY, 1933, A
MY LITTLE BOY, 1917
MY LITTLE CHICKADEE, 1940, A
MY LITTLE SISTER, 1919
MY LORD CONCEIT, 1921
MY LORD THE CHAUFFEUR, 1927, A
MY LOVE CAME BACK, 1940, A
MY LOVE FOR YOURS
MY LOVE LETTERS
MY LOVER, MY SON, 1970, O
MY LUCKY STAR, 1933, A
MY LUCKY STAR, 1938, A
MY MADONNA, 1915
MY MAIN MAN FROM STONY ISLAND
MY MAN, 1924
MY MAN, 1928, A
MY MAN GODFREY, 1936, A
MY MAN GODFREY, 1957, A
MY MARGO, 1969, C
MY MARRIAGE, 1936, A
MY MOTHER, 1933, A
MY NAME IS IVAN, 1963, O
MY NAME IS JULIA ROSS, 1945, A
MY NAME IS LEGEND, 1975
MY NAME IS NOBODY, 1974, O
MY NAME IS PECOS, 1966, C
MY NAME IS ROCCO PAPALEO
MY NEIGHBOR'S WIFE, 1925
MY NEW PARTNER, 1984, A
MY NIGHT AT MAUD'S, 1970, A
MY NIGHT WITH MAUD
MY NIGHTS WITH FRANCOISE
MY OFFICIAL WIFE, 1914
MY OFFICIAL WIFE, 1926
MY OLD DUCHESS, 1933, A
MY OLD DUTCH, 1915, A
MY OLD DUTCH, 1926
MY OLD DUTCH, 1934, A
MY OLD KENTUCKY HOME, 1922
MY OLD KENTUCKY HOME, 1938, A
MY OLD MAN'S PLACE
MY OUTLAW BROTHER
MY OWN PAL, 1926
MY OWN TRUE LOVE, 1948, A
MY OWN UNITED STATES, 1918
MY PAL, 1925
MY PAL GUS, 1952, A
MY PAL TRIGGER, 1946, AAA
MY PAL, THE KING, 1932, A
MY PAL, WOLF, 1944, A
MY PARTNER, 1916
MY PARTNER MR. DAVIS
MY PAST, 1931, A
MY PLEASURE IS MY BUSINESS, 1974
MY REPUTATION, 1946, A-C
MY SEVEN LITTLE SINS, 1956, A
MY SIDE OF THE MOUNTAIN, 1969, AAA
MY SIN, 1931, A-C
MY SISTER AND I, 1948, C
MY SISTER EILEEN, 1942, AA
MY SISTER EILEEN, 1955, AA
MY SISTER, MY LOVE
MY SIX CONVICTS, 1952, A-C
MY SIX LOVES, 1963, AA
MY SON, 1925, A
MY SON ALONE
MY SON IS A CRIMINAL, 1939, A

MY SON IS GUILTY, 1940, C
MY SON NERO
MY SON, JOHN, 1952, C
MY SON, MY SON, 1940, A
MY SON, THE HERO, 1943, A
MY SON, THE HERO, 1963, A
MY SON, THE VAMPIRE, 1963, A
MY SONG FOR YOU, 1935, A
MY SONG GOES ROUND THE WORLD, 1934, A
MY SOUL RUNS NAKED
MY SWEETHEART, 1918
MY TEENAGE DAUGHTER
MY THIRD WIFE BY GEORGE
MY THIRD WIFE GEORGE, 1968, A
MY TRUE STORY, 1951, A
MY TUTOR, 1983, O
MY TWO HUSBANDS
MY UNCLE, 1958, AAA
MY UNCLE ANTOINE, 1971, C
MY UNCLE FROM AMERICA
MY UNCLE, MR. HULOT
MY UNIVERSITY
MY UNMARRIED WIFE, 1918
MY WAY, 1974, A
MY WAY HOME, 1978, C
MY WEAKNESS, 1933, AAA
MY WIDOW AND I, 1950, C
MY WIFE, 1918
MY WIFE AND I, 1925
MY WIFE'S BEST FRIEND, 1952, A
MY WIFE'S ENEMY, 1967, A
MY WIFE'S FAMILY, 1932, A
MY WIFE'S FAMILY, 1941, A
MY WIFE'S FAMILY, 1962, A
MY WIFE'S HUSBAND, 1965, A
MY WIFE'S LODGER, 1952, A
MY WIFE'S RELATIVES, 1939, AAA
MY WILD IRISH ROSE, 1922
MY WILD IRISH ROSE, 1947, A
MY WOMAN, 1933, A
MY WORLD DIES SCREAMING, 1958, C
MYRT AND MARGE, 1934, A
MYRTE AND THE DEMONS, 1948
MYSTERE D'UNE VIE, 1917
MYSTERIANS, THE, 1959, A
MYSTERIES, 1979, C
MYSTERIES OF INDIA, 1922
MYSTERIES OF LONDON, THE, 1915
MYSTERIOUS AVENGER, THE, 1936, A
MYSTERIOUS CLIENT, THE, 1918
MYSTERIOUS CROSSING, 1937, A-C
MYSTERIOUS DESPERADO, THE, 1949, A
MYSTERIOUS DOCTOR, THE, 1943, C
MYSTERIOUS DR. FU MANCHU, THE, 1929, A
MYSTERIOUS GOODS, 1923
MYSTERIOUS HOUSE OF DR. C., THE, 1976, A
MYSTERIOUS INTRUDER, 1946, A
MYSTERIOUS INVADER, THE
MYSTERIOUS ISLAND, 1929, A
MYSTERIOUS ISLAND, 1941, A
MYSTERIOUS ISLAND, 1961, AA
MYSTERIOUS ISLAND OF CAPTAIN NEMO, THE,
  1973, AA
MYSTERIOUS ISLAND, THE 1973
MYSTERIOUS LADY, THE, 1928, A
MYSTERIOUS MISS TERRY, 1917
MYSTERIOUS MISS X, THE, 1939, A
MYSTERIOUS MR. DAVIS, THE, 1936, A
MYSTERIOUS MR. MOTO, 1938, A
MYSTERIOUS MR. MOTO OF DEVIL'S ISLAND
MYSTERIOUS MR. NICHOLSON, THE, 1947, A
MYSTERIOUS MR. REEDER, THE, 1940, A-C
MYSTERIOUS MR. TILLER, THE, 1917
MYSTERIOUS MR. VALENTINE, THE, 1946, A
MYSTERIOUS MR. WONG, 1935, C
MYSTERIOUS MRS. M, THE, 1917
MYSTERIOUS MRS. MUSSLEWHITE, THE
MYSTERIOUS RIDER, 1921
MYSTERIOUS RIDER, THE, 1927
MYSTERIOUS RIDER, THE, 1933, A
MYSTERIOUS RIDER, THE, 1938, A
MYSTERIOUS RIDER, THE, 1942, A
MYSTERIOUS SATELLITE, THE, 1956, A
MYSTERIOUS STRANGER, 1982
MYSTERIOUS STRANGER, THE, 1925
MYSTERIOUS STRANGER, THE 1937
MYSTERIOUS STRANGER, THE 1945
MYSTERIOUS WITNESS, THE, 1923, A
MYSTERY AT MONTE CARLO
MYSTERY AT THE BURLESQUE, 1950, A
MYSTERY AT THE VILLA ROSE, 1930, A
MYSTERY BRAND, THE, 1927
MYSTERY BROADCAST, 1943, A
MYSTERY CLUB, THE, 1926
MYSTERY HOUSE, 1938, A
MYSTERY IN MEXICO, 1948, A
MYSTERY IN SWING, 1940
MYSTERY JUNCTION, 1951, A
MYSTERY LAKE, 1953, A
MYSTERY LINER, 1934, A
MYSTERY MAN, 1944, A
MYSTERY MAN, THE, 1935, A

MYSTERY MANSION, 1984, C
MYSTERY OF A GIRL, THE, 1918
MYSTERY OF A HANSOM CAB, THE, 1915
MYSTERY OF A LONDON FLAT, THE
MYSTERY OF DIAMOND ISLAND, THE
MYSTERY OF EDWIN DROOD, THE, 1914
MYSTERY OF EDWIN DROOD, THE, 1935, C
MYSTERY OF KASPAR HAUSER, THE
MYSTERY OF MARIE ROGET, THE, 1942, A
MYSTERY OF MR. BERNARD BROWN, 1921, A
MYSTERY OF MR. WONG, THE, 1939, A
MYSTERY OF MR. X, THE, 1934, C
MYSTERY OF NO. 47, THE, 1917
MYSTERY OF RICHMOND CASTLE, THE, 1913
MYSTERY OF ROOM 13, 1941, A
MYSTERY OF ROOM 13, THE, 1915
MYSTERY OF SOULS, THE, 1911
MYSTERY OF THE 13TH GUEST, THE, 1943, A
MYSTERY OF THE BLACK JUNGLE, 1955, A
MYSTERY OF THE DIAMOND BELT, 1914
MYSTERY OF THE FATAL PEARL, THE, 1914
MYSTERY OF THE GLASS COFFIN, THE, 1912
MYSTERY OF THE GOLDEN EYE, THE, 1948, A
MYSTERY OF THE HOODED HORSEMEN, THE,
  1937, A
MYSTERY OF THE LOST RANCH, THE, 1925
MYSTERY OF THE MARIE CELESTE
MYSTERY OF THE OLD MILL, THE, 1914
MYSTERY OF THE PINK VILLA, THE, 1930, A
MYSTERY OF THE PINK VILLA, THE, 930, A
MYSTERY OF THE POISON POOL, THE, 1914, A
MYSTERY OF THE WAX MUSEUM, THE, 1933, C
MYSTERY OF THE WENTWORTH CASTLE, THE
MYSTERY OF THE WHITE ROOM, 1939, A
MYSTERY OF THE YELLOW ROOM, THE, 1919
MYSTERY OF THUG ISLAND, THE, 1966, A
MYSTERY OF TUT-ANK-AMEN'S EIGHTH WIFE, THE
MYSTERY ON BIRD ISLAND, 1954, C
MYSTERY ON MONSTER ISLAND
MYSTERY PLANE, 1939, A
MYSTERY RANCH, 1932, A
MYSTERY RANCH, 1934
MYSTERY RANGE, 1937, A
MYSTERY RIDER, 1928
MYSTERY ROAD, THE, 1921
MYSTERY SEA RAIDER, 1940, A
MYSTERY SHIP, 1941, A
MYSTERY STREET, 1950, C
MYSTERY SUBMARINE, 1950, A
MYSTERY SUBMARINE, 1963, A
MYSTERY TRAIN, 1931, A
MYSTERY VALLEY, 1928
MYSTERY WOMAN, 1935, A
MYSTIC CIRCLE MURDER, 1939, A
MYSTIC FACES, 1918
MYSTIC HOUR, THE, 1917
MYSTIC HOUR, THE, 1934, A
MYSTIC MIRROR, THE, 1928
MYSTIC, THE, 1925
MYSTIFIERS, THE
MYSTIQUE, 1981, O
MYTH, THE, 1965, O

-N-

N CITY, 1946, O
N. P., 1971, A
NA SEMI VETRAKH
NABONGA, 1944, A
NACHTS, WENN DER TEUFEL KAM
NACKT UNTER WOLFEN
NADA
NADA GANG, THE, 1974, A
NADA MAS QUE UNA MUJER, 1934, A
NADIA, 1984, C
NAGANA, 1933, A
NAGOOA
NAIDRA, THE DREAM WOMAN, 1914
NAKED ALIBI, 1954, A
NAKED AMONG THE WOLVES, 1967, C
NAKED AND THE DEAD, THE, 1958, O
NAKED ANGELS, 1969, O
NAKED APE, THE, 1973, C
NAKED AUTUMN, 1963, A
NAKED BRIGADE, THE, 1965, A
NAKED CHILDHOOD
NAKED CITY, THE, 1948, C
NAKED DAWN, THE, 1955, A
NAKED EARTH, THE, 1958, A
NAKED EDGE, THE, 1961, A-C
NAKED EVIL
NAKED FACE, THE, 1984, C
NAKED FLAME, THE, 1970, C
NAKED FURY, 1959, C
NAKED FURY, THE, 1964
NAKED GENERAL, THE, 1964, A
NAKED GODDESS, THE
NAKED GUN, THE, 1956
NAKED HEART, THE, 1955, A
NAKED HEARTS, 1916, A
NAKED HILLS, 1956
NAKED HOURS, THE, 1964, C
NAKED IN THE SUN, 1957, C

NEW LAND, THE, 1973, A
NEW LEAF, A, 1971, C-O
NEW LIFE STYLE, THE, 1970, O
NEW LIVES FOR OLD, 1925, A
NEW LOVE, 1968, O
NEW LOVE FOR OLD, 1918, A
NEW MEXICO, 1951, A
NEW MINISTER, 1922
NEW MONSTERS, THE
NEW MOON, 1930, A
NEW MOON, 1940, A
NEW MOON, THE, 1919, A
NEW MORALS FOR OLD, 1932, A
NEW MOVIETONE FOLLIES OF 1930, THE
NEW ONE-ARMED SWORDSMAN, THE
NEW ORLEANS, 1929, A
NEW ORLEANS, 1947, A
NEW ORLEANS AFTER DARK, 1958, C
NEW ORLEANS UNCENSORED, 1955, A
NEW SCHOOL TEACHER, THE, 1924
NEW TEACHER, THE, 1922, A
NEW TEACHER, THE, 1941
NEW TOYS, 1925
NEW WINE, 1941, A
NEW WIZARD OF OZ, THE
NEW YEAR'S EVE, 1923
NEW YEAR'S EVE, 1929, A
NEW YEAR'S EVIL, 1980, O
NEW YORK
NEW YORK, 1916, A
NEW YORK, 1927, A
NEW YORK APPELLE SUPER DRAGON
NEW YORK CONFIDENTIAL, 1955, C
NEW YORK IDEA, THE, 1920, A
NEW YORK LUCK, 1917
NEW YORK NIGHTS
NEW YORK NIGHTS, 1929, A
NEW YORK NIGHTS, 1984
NEW YORK PEACOCK, THE, 1917, A
NEW YORK TOWN, 1941, A
NEW YORK, NEW YORK, 1977, C
NEWLY RICH, 1931, AA
NEWMAN SHAME, THE, 1977
NEWMAN'S LAW, 1974, A
NEWS HOUNDS, 1947, A
NEWS IS MADE AT NIGHT, 1939, A
NEWS PARADE, THE, 1928, A
NEWSBOY'S HOME, 1939, A
NEWSFRONT, 1979, C
NEXT CORNER, THE, 1924
NEXT IN LINE
NEXT MAN, THE, 1976, O
NEXT OF KIN, 1942, A
NEXT OF KIN, 1983, O
NEXT ONE, THE, 1982, C
NEXT STOP, GREENWICH VILLAGE, 1976, C
NEXT TIME I MARRY, 1938, A
NEXT TIME WE LOVE, 1936, A
NEXT TO NO TIME, 1960, A
NEXT VICTIM, 1971
NEXT VOICE YOU HEAR, THE, 1950
NEXT!, 1971, O
NIAGARA, 1953, C
NICE GIRL LIKE ME, A, 1969, C
NICE GIRL?, 1941, A
NICE LITTLE BANK THAT SHOULD BE ROBBED, A,
    1958, A
NICE PEOPLE, 1922, A
NICE PLATE OF SPINACH, A
NICE WOMAN, 1932, A
NICHOLAS AND ALEXANDRA, 1971, C
NICHOLAS NICKLEBY, 1947, A
NICHT VERSOHNT ODER "ES HILFT NUR GEWALT,
    WO GEWALT HERRSCHT"
NICK CARTER IN PRAGUE
NICK CARTER, MASTER DETECTIVE, 1939, A
NICKEL QUEEN, THE, 1971, A
NICKEL RIDE, THE, 1974, C
NICKELODEON, 1976, C
NICOLE, 1972
NIGGER, THE, 1915
NIGHT, 1923
NIGHT AFFAIR, 1961, A
NIGHT AFTER NIGHT, 1932, C
NIGHT AFTER NIGHT AFTER NIGHT, 1970
NIGHT ALARM, 1935, A
NIGHT ALONE, 1938, A
NIGHT AMBUSH, 1958, A
NIGHT AND DAY, 1933, A
NIGHT AND DAY, 1946, A
NIGHT AND THE CITY, 1950, O
NIGHT ANGEL, THE, 1931, A
NIGHT AT THE OPERA, A, 1935, A
NIGHT AT THE RITZ, A, 1935, A
NIGHT BEAT, 1932, A
NIGHT BEAT, 1948, A
NIGHT BEFORE CHRISTMAS, A, 1963, A
NIGHT BEFORE THE DIVORCE, THE, 1942, A
NIGHT BIRD, THE, 1928
NIGHT BIRDS, 1931, A
NIGHT BOAT TO DUBLIN, 1946, A

NIGHT BRIDE, THE, 1927, A
NIGHT CALL NURSES, 1974, O
NIGHT CALLER FROM OUTER SPACE
NIGHT CALLER, THE
NIGHT CARGOES, 1963
NIGHT CHILD, 1975, O
NIGHT CLUB
NIGHT CLUB GIRL, 1944, A
NIGHT CLUB GIRL, 1947
NIGHT CLUB HOSTESS
NIGHT CLUB LADY, 1932, A
NIGHT CLUB MURDER
NIGHT CLUB QUEEN, 1934, A
NIGHT CLUB SCANDAL, 1937, A
NIGHT CLUB, THE, 1925, A
NIGHT COMERS, THE, 1971, C-O
NIGHT COMES TOO SOON, 1948, C
NIGHT COURT, 1932, A
NIGHT CRAWLERS, THE
NIGHT CREATURE, 1979, A
NIGHT CREATURES, 1962, A
NIGHT CROSSING, 1982, C
NIGHT CRY, THE, 1926, A
NIGHT DIGGER, THE, 1971, O
NIGHT EDITOR, 1946, A
NIGHT ENCOUNTER, 1963, A
NIGHT EVELYN CAME OUT OF THE GRAVE, THE,
    1973, O
NIGHT EXPRESS, THE
NIGHT FIGHTERS, THE, 1960, A
NIGHT FLIGHT, 1933, A
NIGHT FLIGHT FROM MOSCOW
NIGHT FLOWERS, 1979, O
NIGHT FLYER, THE, 1928, A
NIGHT FOR CRIME, A, 1942, A
NIGHT FREIGHT, 1955, A
NIGHT FULL OF RAIN, A
NIGHT GAMES, 1966, O
NIGHT GAMES, 1980, O
NIGHT GOD SCREAMED, THE, 1975
NIGHT HAIR CHILD, 1971, O
NIGHT HAS A THOUSAND EYES, 1948, C
NIGHT HAS EYES, THE
NIGHT HAWK, THE, 1921
NIGHT HAWK, THE, 1924
NIGHT HAWK, THE, 1938, A
NIGHT HEAVEN FELL, THE, 1958, O
NIGHT HOLDS TERROR, THE, 1955, C
NIGHT HORSEMAN, THE, 1921, A
NIGHT HUNT
NIGHT IN BANGKOK, 1966, A
NIGHT IN CAIRO, A
NIGHT IN CASABLANCA, A, 1946, A
NIGHT IN HAVANA
NIGHT IN HEAVEN, A, 1983, O
NIGHT IN HONG KONG, A, 1961, A
NIGHT IN JUNE, A, 1940, A
NIGHT IN MONTMARTE, A, 1931, A
NIGHT IN NEW ARABIA, A, 1917
NIGHT IN NEW ORLEANS, A, 1942, A
NIGHT IN PARADISE, A, 1946, A
NIGHT INTO MORNING, 1951, A
NIGHT INVADER, THE, 1943, C
NIGHT IS ENDING, THE
NIGHT IS MY FUTURE, 1962, A
NIGHT IS OURS, 1930, A
NIGHT IS THE PHANTOM
NIGHT IS YOUNG, THE, 1935, A
NIGHT JOURNEY, 1938, A
NIGHT KEY, 1937, A
NIGHT LIFE, 1927, A
NIGHT LIFE IN HOLLYWOOD, 1922, A
NIGHT LIFE IN RENO, 1931
NIGHT LIFE OF NEW YORK, 1925, A
NIGHT LIFE OF THE GODS, 1935, A
NIGHT LIKE THIS, A, 1932, A
NIGHT MAIL, 1935, C
NIGHT MAYOR, THE, 1932
NIGHT MESSAGE, THE, 1924
NIGHT MONSTER, 1942, A
NIGHT MOVES, 1975, C
NIGHT MUST FALL, 1937, O
NIGHT MUST FALL, 1964, O
NIGHT MY NUMBER CAME UP, THE, 1955, A-C
NIGHT NURSE, 1931, A-C
NIGHT NURSE, THE, 1977
NIGHT OF A THOUSAND CATS, 1974, O
NIGHT OF ADVENTURE, A, 1944, A
NIGHT OF ANUBIS
NIGHT OF BLOODY HORROR, 1969, O
NIGHT OF DARK SHADOWS, 1971, C
NIGHT OF EVIL, 1962, C
NIGHT OF JANUARY 16TH, 1941, A
NIGHT OF JUNE 13, 1932, A
NIGHT OF LOVE, THE, 1927, A
NIGHT OF LUST, 1965, C
NIGHT OF MAGIC, A, 1944, A
NIGHT OF MYSTERY, 1937, A
NIGHT OF MYSTERY, A, 1928, A
NIGHT OF NIGHTS, THE, 1939, A
NIGHT OF PASSION
NIGHT OF SAN LORENZO, THE

NIGHT OF TERROR, 1933, A
NIGHT OF TERRORS
NIGHT OF THE ASKARI, 1978, C
NIGHT OF THE ASSASSIN, THE, 1972
NIGHT OF THE BEAST
NIGHT OF THE BIG HEAT
NIGHT OF THE BLOOD BEAST, 1958, A
NIGHT OF THE BLOODY APES, 1968, O
NIGHT OF THE CLAW
NIGHT OF THE COBRA WOMAN, 1974, O
NIGHT OF THE COMET, 1984, C-O
NIGHT OF THE DARK FULL MOON
NIGHT OF THE DEMON
NIGHT OF THE DEMON
NIGHT OF THE DEMON, 1980
NIGHT OF THE EAGLE
NIGHT OF THE FLESH EATERS
NIGHT OF THE FOLLOWING DAY, THE, 1969, O
NIGHT OF THE FULL MOON, THE, 1954, C
NIGHT OF THE GARTER, 1933, A
NIGHT OF THE GENERALS, THE, 1967, O
NIGHT OF THE GHOULS, 1959
NIGHT OF THE GRIZZLY, THE, 1966, A
NIGHT OF THE HOWLING BEAST, 1977
NIGHT OF THE HUNTER, THE, 1955, O
NIGHT OF THE IGUANA, THE, 1964, O
NIGHT OF THE JUGGLER, 1980, O
NIGHT OF THE LAUGHING DEAD
NIGHT OF THE LEPUS, 1972, C
NIGHT OF THE LIVING DEAD, 1968, O
NIGHT OF THE PARTY, THE, 1934, A
NIGHT OF THE PROWLER, 1962
NIGHT OF THE PROWLER, THE, 1979, O
NIGHT OF THE QUARTER MOON, 1959, C
NIGHT OF THE SEAGULL, THE, 1970, C
NIGHT OF THE SHOOTING STARS, THE, 1982, O
NIGHT OF THE SILICATES
NIGHT OF THE SORCERORS, 1970
NIGHT OF THE STRANGLER, 1975
NIGHT OF THE TIGER, THE
NIGHT OF THE WITCHES, 1970, O
NIGHT OF THE ZOMBIES, 1981, O
NIGHT OF THE ZOMBIES, 1983, O
NIGHT OUT, A, 1916, A
NIGHT OWL, THE, 1926, A
NIGHT PARADE, 1929, A
NIGHT PASSAGE, 1957, A
NIGHT PATROL, 1984, O
NIGHT PATROL, THE
NIGHT PATROL, THE, 1926, A
NIGHT PEOPLE, 1954, A
NIGHT PLANE FROM CHUNGKING, 1942, A
NIGHT PORTER, THE, 1974, O
NIGHT RAIDERS, 1952, A
NIGHT RIDE, 1930, A
NIGHT RIDE, 1937, C
NIGHT RIDER, THE, 1932, A
NIGHT RIDERS OF MONTANA, 1951, A
NIGHT RIDERS, THE, 1920
NIGHT RIDERS, THE, 1939, A
NIGHT ROSE, THE, 1921
NIGHT RUNNER, THE, 1957, A
NIGHT SCHOOL, 1981, O
NIGHT SHADOWS, 1984, O
NIGHT SHIFT, 1982, C
NIGHT SHIP, THE, 1925, A
NIGHT SONG, 1947, A
NIGHT SPOT, 1938, A
NIGHT STAGE TO GALVESTON, 1952, A
NIGHT THE CREATURES CAME
NIGHT THE LIGHTS WENT OUT IN GEORGIA, THE,
    1981, C
NIGHT THE SILICATES CAME
NIGHT THE SUN CAME OUT, THE
NIGHT THE WORLD EXPLODED, THE, 1957, A
NIGHT THEY KILLED RASPUTIN, THE, 1962, C
NIGHT THEY RAIDED MINSKY'S, THE, 1968, C-O
NIGHT THEY ROBBED BIG BERTHA'S, THE, 1975, O
NIGHT TIDE, 1963, C
NIGHT TIME IN NEVADA, 1948, A
NIGHT TO DISMEMBER, A, 1983
NIGHT TO REMEMBER, A, 1942, A
NIGHT TO REMEMBER, A, 1958, A
NIGHT TRAIN, 1940, A
NIGHT TRAIN FOR INVERNESS, 1960, C
NIGHT TRAIN TO MEMPHIS, 1946, A
NIGHT TRAIN TO MUNDO FINE, 1966, A
NIGHT TRAIN TO MUNICH
NIGHT TRAIN TO PARIS, 1964, A
NIGHT UNTO NIGHT, 1949, A
NIGHT VISITOR, THE, 1970, C
NIGHT WAITRESS, 1936, A
NIGHT WALK
NIGHT WALKER, THE, 1964, C
NIGHT WAS OUR FRIEND, 1951, C-O
NIGHT WATCH, 1973, C
NIGHT WATCH, THE, 1926, A
NIGHT WATCH, THE, 1928, A
NIGHT WATCH, THE, 1964, A
NIGHT WE DROPPED A CLANGER, THE
NIGHT WE GOT THE BIRD, THE, 1961, C
NIGHT WIND, 1948, A

NIGHT WITHOUT PITY, 1962
NIGHT WITHOUT SLEEP, 1952, C
NIGHT WITHOUT STARS, 1953, A
NIGHT WON'T TALK, THE, 1952, C
NIGHT WORK, 1930, A
NIGHT WORK, 1939, A
NIGHT WORKERS, THE, 1917, A
NIGHT WORLD, 1932, A
NIGHT, THE
NIGHTBEAST, 1982, C-O
NIGHTBIRDS OF LONDON, THE, 1915
NIGHTFALL, 1956, A
NIGHTFLIGHT FROM MOSCOW
NIGHTHAWKS, 1978, O
NIGHTHAWKS, 1981
NIGHTINGALE SANG IN BERKELEY SQUARE, A, 1979
NIGHTINGALE, THE, 1914, A
NIGHTKILLERS, 1983
NIGHTMARE
NIGHTMARE, 1942, C
NIGHTMARE, 1956, C
NIGHTMARE, 1963, O
NIGHTMARE, 1981, O
NIGHTMARE ALLEY, 1947, C-O
NIGHTMARE BLOOD BATH, 1971
NIGHTMARE CASTLE, 1966, C
NIGHTMARE CITY
NIGHTMARE COUNTY, 1977
NIGHTMARE HONEYMOON, 1973, O
NIGHTMARE IN BLOOD, 1978, O
NIGHTMARE IN THE SUN, 1964, O
NIGHTMARE IN WAX, 1969, O
NIGHTMARE ON ELM STREET, A, 1984, O
NIGHTMARE WEEKEND
NIGHTMARES, 1983, O
NIGHTS IN A HAREM
NIGHTS OF CABIRIA, 1957, C
NIGHTS OF LUCRETIA BORGIA, THE, 1960, A
NIGHTS OF PRAGUE, THE, 1968, C
NIGHTS OF SHAME, 1961, O
NIGHTS WHEN THE DEVIL CAME
NIGHTSONGS, 1984, C
NIGHTWING, 1979, O
NIHON NO ICHIBAN NAGAI HI
NIJINSKY, 1980, C-O
NIKKI, WILD DOG OF THE NORTH, 1961, AAA
NIKOLAI STAVROGIN, 1915
NIKUTAI NO GAKKO
NINA, THE FLOWER GIRL, 1917, A
NINE, 1920
NINE AND THREE-FIFTHS SECONDS, 1925, A
NINE DAYS A QUEEN
NINE DAYS OF ONE YEAR, 1964, O
NINE FORTY-FIVE, 1934, A
NINE GIRLS, 1944, C
NINE HOURS TO RAMA, 1963, C
NINE LIVES ARE NOT ENOUGH, 1941, A
NINE LIVES OF FRITZ THE CAT, THE, 1974
NINE MEN, 1943, A
NINE MILES TO NOON, 1963, C
9/30/55, 1977, C
NINE O'CLOCK TOWN, A, 1918, A
NINE POINTS OF THE LAW, 1922
NINE TILL SIX, 1932, A
NINE TO FIVE, 1980, C-O
1984, 1956, A-C
1941, 1979, C-O
1900, 1976, C-O
1990: BRONX WARRIORS, 1983, C
90 DEGREES IN THE SHADE, 1966, O
99 AND 44/100% DEAD, 1974, C-O
99 RIVER STREET, 1953, C
99 WOUNDS, 1931, O
92 IN THE SHADE, 1975, C
NINE-TENTHS OF THE LAW, 1918
NINETEEN AND PHYLLIS, 1920, A
NINETY AND NINE, THE, 1916
NINETY AND NINE, THE, 1922, A
NINGEN NO JOKEN
NINGEN NO JOKEN II
NINGEN NO JOKEN III
NINJA III—THE DOMINATION, 1984, O
NINJA MISSION, 1984
NINJUTSU, SORYU HIKEN
NINOTCHKA, 1939
NINTH CIRCLE, THE, 1961, O
NINTH CONFIGURATION, THE, 1980, O
NINTH GUEST, THE, 1934, A
NINTH HEART, THE, 1980, A
NINTH OF JANUARY, 1925
NIOBE, 1915, A
NIPPER, THE
NIPPON KONCHUKI
NIPPON NO ICHIBAN NAGAI HI
NITCHEVO, 1926
NITWITS, THE, 1935, A
NIX ON DAMES, 1929, A
NO BABIES WANTED, 1928, A
NO BLADE OF GRASS, 1970, O
NO BRAKES
NO CHILDREN WANTED, 1918
NO CONTROL, 1927, A

NO DEADLY MACHINE
NO DEFENSE, 1921
NO DEFENSE, 1929, A
NO DEPOSIT, NO RETURN, 1976, AAA
NO DIAMONDS FOR URSULA, 1967
NO DOWN PAYMENT, 1957, C
NO DRUMS, NO BUGLES, 1971, A
NO ESCAPE, 1934, C
NO ESCAPE, 1936, C
NO ESCAPE, 1953, O
NO ESCAPE, 1943
NO EXIT, 1930
NO EXIT, 1962, O
NO FUNNY BUSINESS, 1934, A
NO GREATER GLORY, 1934, A
NO GREATER LOVE, 1915
NO GREATER LOVE, 1932, A
NO GREATER LOVE, 1944, O
NO GREATER LOVE THAN THIS, 1969, C
NO GREATER LOVE, 1931
NO GREATER LOVE, 1970
NO GREATER SIN
NO GREATER SIN, 1941, A
NO HANDS ON THE CLOCK, 1941, A
NO HAUNT FOR A GENTLEMAN, 1952, A
NO HIGHWAY
NO HIGHWAY IN THE SKY, 1951, A
NO HOLDS BARRED, 1952, A
NO KIDDING
NO KNIFE
NO LADY, 1931, A
NO LEAVE, NO LOVE, 1946, A
NO LIMIT, 1931, A
NO LIMIT, 1935, A
NO LIVING WITNESS, 1932, A
NO LONGER ALONE, 1978, C
NO LOVE FOR JOHNNIE, 1961, O
NO LOVE FOR JUDY, 1955
NO MAN IS AN ISLAND, 1962, C
NO MAN OF HER OWN, 1933, A
NO MAN OF HER OWN, 1950, A
NO MAN WALKS ALONE
NO MAN'S GOLD, 1926, A
NO MAN'S LAND
NO MAN'S LAND, 1918
NO MAN'S LAND, 1964, O
NO MAN'S LAW, 1925
NO MAN'S LAW, 1927, A
NO MAN'S RANGE, 1935, A
NO MAN'S WOMAN, 1921, A
NO MAN'S WOMAN, 1955, C
NO MARRIAGE TIES, 1933, A
NO MERCY MAN, THE, 1975, O
NO MINOR VICES, 1948, A
NO MONKEY BUSINESS, 1935, A
NO MORE EXCUSES, 1968
NO MORE LADIES, 1935, C
NO MORE ORCHIDS, 1933, A
NO MORE WOMEN, 1924, A
NO MORE WOMEN, 1934, A
NO MOTHER TO GUIDE HER, 1923, C
NO NAME ON THE BULLET, 1959, A
NO ONE MAN, 1932, A
NO ORCHIDS FOR MISS BLANDISH, 1948, O
NO OTHER WOMAN, 1928, A
NO OTHER WOMAN, 1933, A
NO PARKING, 1938, A
NO PLACE FOR A LADY, 1943, A
NO PLACE FOR JENNIFER, 1950, A
NO PLACE LIKE HOMICIDE
NO PLACE TO GO, 1927
NO PLACE TO GO, 1939, A
NO PLACE TO HIDE, 1956, A
NO PLACE TO HIDE, 1975, C-O
NO PLACE TO LAND, 1958, A-C
NO QUESTIONS ASKED, 1951, A
NO RANSOM, 1935, A
NO RESTING PLACE, 1952, A
NO RETURN ADDRESS, 1961, A
NO ROAD BACK, 1957, A
NO ROOM AT THE INN, 1950, A
NO ROOM FOR THE GROOM, 1952, A
NO ROOM TO DIE, 1969, O
NO ROSES FOR OSS 117, 1968, C
NO SAD SONGS FOR ME, 1950, A-C
NO SAFETY AHEAD, 1959, C
NO SEX PLEASE—WE'RE BRITISH, 1979, C
NO SLEEP TILL DAWN
NO SMALL AFFAIR, 1984, O
NO SMOKING, 1955, A
NO SURVIVORS, PLEASE, 1963, C
NO TIME FOR BREAKFAST, 1978, O
NO TIME FOR COMEDY, 1940, A
NO TIME FOR ECSTASY, 1963, O
NO TIME FOR FLOWERS, 1952, A
NO TIME FOR LOVE, 1943, A
NO TIME FOR SERGEANTS, 1958, A
NO TIME FOR TEARS, 1957, A
NO TIME FOR TEARS, 1951
NO TIME TO BE YOUNG, 1957, O
NO TIME TO DIE
NO TIME TO KILL, 1963, C

NO TIME TO MARRY, 1938, A
NO TOYS FOR CHRISTMAS
NO TRACE, 1950, A
NO TREE IN THE STREET, 1964, A
NO TRESPASSING, 1922, A
NO WAY BACK, 1949, C
NO WAY BACK, 1976, O
NO WAY OUT, 1950, A
NO WAY OUT, 1975, O
NO WAY TO TREAT A LADY, 1968, C-O
NO WOMAN KNOWS, 1921, A
NO, MY DARLING DAUGHTER, 1964, A
NO, NO NANETTE, 1930, A
NO, NO NANETTE, 1940, A
NO-GOOD GUY, THE, 1916
NO-GUN MAN, THE, 1924, A
NO. 13 DEMON STREET
NO. 5 JOHN STREET, 1921, A
NO. 96, 1974, C
NO. 99, 1920
NOAH'S ARK, 1928, A-C
NOBI
NOBODY, 1921, A
NOBODY HOME
NOBODY IN TOYLAND, 1958, A
NOBODY LIVES FOREVER, 1946, A
NOBODY LOVES A DRUNKEN INDIAN
NOBODY LOVES A FLAPPING EAGLE
NOBODY RUNS FOREVER
NOBODY WAVED GOODBYE, 1965, C
NOBODY'S BABY, 1937, A
NOBODY'S BRIDE, 1923, A
NOBODY'S CHILD, 1919, A
NOBODY'S CHILDREN, 1926
NOBODY'S CHILDREN, 1940, AAA
NOBODY'S DARLING, 1943, A
NOBODY'S FOOL, 1921, A
NOBODY'S FOOL, 1936, A
NOBODY'S GIRL, 1920
NOBODY'S KID, 1921, A
NOBODY'S MONEY, 1923, A
NOBODY'S PERFECT, 1968, A
NOBODY'S PERFEKT, 1981, C
NOBODY'S WIDOW, 1927, A
NOBODY'S WIFE, 1918, A
NOBORIRYU TEKKAHADA
NOCTURNA, 1979, O
NOCTURNE, 1946, C
NOISE IN NEWBORO, A, 1923, A
NOISY NEIGHBORS, 1929, A
NOMADIC LIVES, 1977
NOMADS OF THE NORTH, 1920, A
NOMANDIE, 1931
NON TIRATE IL DIAVOLO PER LA CODA
NON-CONFORMIST PARSON, A, 1919
NON-STOP FLIGHT, THE, 1926, A
NON-STOP NEW YORK, 1937, A
NONE BUT THE BRAVE, 1928, A
NONE BUT THE BRAVE, 1963, C
NONE BUT THE BRAVE, 1965, O
NONE BUT THE BRAVE, 1960
NONE BUT THE LONELY HEART, 1944, A
NONE SHALL ESCAPE, 1944, A
NONE SO BLIND, 1923
NONENTITY, THE, 1922, A
NOON SUNDAY, 1971
NOOSE
NOOSE FOR A GUNMAN, 1960, A
NOOSE FOR A LADY, 1953, A
NOOSE HANGS HIGH, THE, 1948, AAA
NOOSE, THE, 1928, C
NOR THE MOON BY NIGHT
NORA INU
NORA PRENTISS, 1947, A
NORAH O'NEALE, 1934, A
NORMA RAE, 1979, A-C
NORMAN CONQUEST, 1953, A
NORMAN LOVES ROSE, 1982, O
NORMAN...IS THAT YOU?, 1976, C
NORSEMAN, THE, 1978, C
NORTH AVENUE IRREGULARS, THE, 1979, A
NORTH BY NORTHWEST, 1959, A
NORTH DALLAS FORTY, 1979, C-O
NORTH FROM LONE STAR, 1941, A
NORTH OF 36, 1924, A
NORTH OF ALASKA, 1924
NORTH OF ARIZONA, 1935
NORTH OF FIFTY-THREE, 1917
NORTH OF HUDSON BAY, 1923, A
NORTH OF NEVADA, 1924, A
NORTH OF NOME, 1925
NORTH OF NOME, 1937, A
NORTH OF SHANGHAI, 1939, A
NORTH OF THE GREAT DIVIDE, 1950
NORTH OF THE RIO GRANDE, 1922, A
NORTH OF THE RIO GRANDE, 1937, A
NORTH OF THE ROCKIES, 1942
NORTH OF THE YUKON, 1939, A
NORTH SEA HIJACK
NORTH SEA PATROL, 1939, A
NORTH STAR, 1925

NORTH STAR, THE, 1943, A-C
NORTH STAR, THE, 1982
NORTH TO ALASKA, 1960, A
NORTH TO THE KLONDIKE, 1942, A
NORTH WEST FRONTIER
NORTH WIND'S MALICE, THE, 1920, A
NORTHEAST TO SEOUL, 1974
NORTHERN CODE, 1925, A
NORTHERN FRONTIER, 1935, A
NORTHERN LIGHTS, 1914
NORTHERN LIGHTS, 1978, A
NORTHERN PATROL, 1953, A
NORTHERN PURSUIT, 1943, A
NORTHFIELD CEMETERY MASSACRE, THE
NORTHVILLE CEMETERY MASSACRE, THE, 1976
NORTHWEST MOUNTED POLICE, 1940, A
NORTHWEST OUTPOST, 1947, A
NORTHWEST PASSAGE, 1940, A-C
NORTHWEST RANGERS, 1942, A
NORTHWEST STAMPEDE, 1948, A
NORTHWEST TERRITORY, 1952, A
NORTHWEST TRAIL, 1945, A
NORWOOD, 1970, A
NOSE ON MY FACE, THE
NOSFERATU, A SYMPHONY OF HORROR
NOSFERATU, A SYMPHONY OF TERROR
NOSFERATU, THE VAMPIRE, 1922, C
NOSFERATU, THE VAMPIRE, 1979, C-O
NOSFURATU, EINE SYMPHONIE DES GRAUENS
NOSTALGHIA, 1984, O
NOT A DRUM WAS HEARD, 1924
NOT A HOPE IN HELL, 1960
NOT A LADIES MAN, 1942
NOT AGAINST THE FLESH
NOT AS A STRANGER, 1955, A-C
NOT BUILT FOR RUNNIN', 1924
NOT DAMAGED, 1930, C
NOT EXACTLY GENTLEMEN
NOT FOR HONOR AND GLORY
NOT FOR PUBLICATION, 1927
NOT FOR PUBLICATION, 1984, C-O
NOT FOR SALE, 1924
NOT FOR SALE, 1924, A
NOT GUILTY, 1915
NOT GUILTY, 1919, A
NOT GUILTY, 1921, A
NOT MINE TO LOVE, 1969, A
NOT MY DAUGHTER, 1975
NOT MY SISTER, 1916, A
NOT NEGOTIABLE, 1918
NOT NOW DARLING, 1975, O
NOT OF THIS EARTH, 1957
NOT ON YOUR LIFE
NOT ON YOUR LIFE, 1965, C-O
NOT ONE TO SPARE
NOT QUITE A LADY, 1928, A
NOT QUITE DECENT, 1929, A
NOT RECONCILED, OR "ONLY VIOLENCE HELPS
    WHERE IT RULES", 1969, C
NOT SO DUMB, 1930, A
NOT SO DUSTY, 1936, A
NOT SO DUSTY, 1956, A
NOT SO LONG AGO, 1925, A
NOT SO QUIET ON THE WESTERN FRONT, 1930, A
NOT TONIGHT HENRY, 1961
NOT WANTED, 1949, A
NOT WANTED ON VOYAGE, 1957, A
NOT WANTED ON VOYAGE, 1938, Brit.
NOT WITH MY WIFE, YOU DON'T!, 1966, A
NOTCH NUMBER ONE, 1924
NOTEBOOKS OF MAJOR THOMPSON
NOTHING BARRED, 1961, A
NOTHING BUT A MAN, 1964, A
NOTHING BUT LIES, 1920
NOTHING BUT THE BEST, 1964, C
NOTHING BUT THE NIGHT, 1975, A
NOTHING BUT THE TRUTH, 1920, A
NOTHING BUT THE TRUTH, 1929, A
NOTHING BUT THE TRUTH, 1941, A
NOTHING BUT TROUBLE, 1944, AA
NOTHING ELSE MATTERS
NOTHING LASTS FOREVER, 1984, C
NOTHING LIKE PUBLICITY, 1936, A
NOTHING PERSONAL, 1980, A-C
NOTHING SACRED, 1937, A
NOTHING TO BE DONE, 1914
NOTHING TO LOSE
NOTHING TO WEAR, 1928, A
NOTHING VENTURE, 1948, AAA
NOTORIETY, 1922, A
NOTORIOUS, 1946, A
NOTORIOUS AFFAIR, 1930, A
NOTORIOUS BUT NICE, 1934, A
NOTORIOUS CLEOPATRA, THE, 1970, O
NOTORIOUS GALLAGHER
NOTORIOUS GENTLEMAN, 1945, C
NOTORIOUS GENTLEMAN, A, 1935, A
NOTORIOUS LADY, THE, 1927, A
NOTORIOUS LANDLADY, THE, 1962, A-C
NOTORIOUS LONE WOLF, THE, 1946, A
NOTORIOUS MISS LISLE, THE, 1920, A
NOTORIOUS MR. MONKS, THE, 1958, C

NOTORIOUS MRS. CARRICK, THE, 1924, A
NOTORIOUS MRS. SANDS, THE, 1920, A
NOTORIOUS SOPHIE LANG, THE, 1934, A
NOTRA PAUVRE COEUR, 1916
NOTRE DAME D'AMOUR, 1922
NOTRE DAME DE PARIS
NOTTI BIANCHE, LA
NOUS IRONS A PARIS, 1949, A
NOVEL AFFAIR, A, 1957, A
NOW ABOUT ALL THESE WOMEN
NOW AND FOREVER, 1934, A
NOW AND FOREVER, 1956, A
NOW AND FOREVER, 1983, O
NOW BARABBAS
NOW BARABBAS WAS A ROBBER, 1949, A
NOW I LAY ME DOWN
NOW I'LL TELL, 1934, A-C
NOW IT CAN BE TOLD
NOW OR NEVER, 1935
NOW THAT APRIL'S HERE, 1958, A
NOW WE'RE IN THE AIR, 1927, A
NOW YOU SEE HIM, NOW YOU DON'T, 1972, AAA
NOW, VOYAGER, 1942, A-C
NOWHERE TO GO, 1959, A
NOZ W WODZIE
NTH COMMANDMENT, THE, 1923, A
NTOM SUBMARINE, THE, 1941, A
NUDE BOMB, THE, 1980, A
NUDE HEAT WAVE
NUDE IN A WHITE CAR, 1960, C
NUDE IN HIS POCKET, 1962, A
NUDE ODYSSEY, 1962, A
NUDE...SI MUORE
NUDES ON CREDIT
NUGGET IN THE ROUGH, A, 1918
NUGGET NELL, 1919, A
NUISANCE, THE, 1933, A
NUIT DE VARENNES, LA
NUITS ROUGES
NUMBER 17, 1920, A
NUMBER ONE, 1969, C
NUMBER ONE, 1984, C
NUMBER SEVENTEEN, 1928, A
NUMBER SEVENTEEN, 1932, A
NUMBER SIX, 1962, A
NUMBER TWO, 1975
NUMBERED MEN, 1930, A
NUMBERED WOMAN, 1938
NUMERO DEUX
NUN AND THE SERGEANT, THE, 1962, A
NUN AT THE CROSSROADS, A, 1970, A
NUN OF MONZA, THE
NUN'S STORY, THE, 1959, A
NUN, THE, 1971, C
NUNZIO, 1978, O
NUR TOTE ZEUGEN SCHWEIGEN
NUREMBERG, 1961
NURSE AND MARTYR, 1915
NURSE EDITH CAVELL, 1939, A
NURSE FROM BROOKLYN, 1938, A
NURSE MARJORIE, 1920, A
NURSE ON WHEELS, 1964, O
NURSE SHERRI, 1978, O
NURSE'S SECRET, THE, 1941, A
NURSEMAID WHO DISAPPEARED, THE, 1939, A
NURSES FOR SALE, 1977
NUT FARM, THE, 1935, A
NUT, THE, 1921, A
NUT-CRACKER, THE, 1926, A
NUTCRACKER, 1982, O
NUTCRACKER, 1984
NUTCRACKER FANTASY, 1979, AAA
NUTTY PROFESSOR, THE, 1963, A
NUTTY, NAUGHTY CHATEAU, 1964, C
NVUIIRANDO NO WAKADAISHO
NYMPH, 1974
NYMPH OF THE FOOTHILLS, A, 1918
NYMPH OF THE WOODS, 1918
NYUJIRANDO NO WAKADAISHO

-O-

O LUCKY MAN!, 1973, O
O SLAVNOSTI A HOSTECH
O'FLYNN, THE
O'HARA'S WIFE, 1983, C
O'LEARY NIGHT
O'MALLEY OF THE MOUNTED, 1921, A
O'MALLEY OF THE MOUNTED, 1936, A
O'MALLEY RIDES ALONE, 1930
O'RILEY'S LUCK
O'ROURKE OF THE ROYAL MOUNTED
O'SHAUGHNESSY'S BOY, 1935, A
O, MY DARLING CLEMENTINE, 1943, A
O. HENRY'S FULL HOUSE, 1952, AAA
O.K. CONNERY
O.M.H.S.
O.S.S., 1946, C
O.U. WEST, 1925
OAD BACK,THE, 1937, A
OAKDALE AFFAIR, THE, 1919, A
OASIS OF FEAR, 1973
OASIS, THE, 1984, O

OATH OF THE BIBLE, THE
OATH OF VENGEANCE, 1944
OATH, THE, 1921
OATH-BOUND, 1922, A
OBEAH, 1935
OBEY THE LAW, 1926
OBEY THE LAW, 1933, A
OBEY YOUR HUSBAND, 1928, A
OBJECT—ALIMONY, 1929, A
OBJECTIVE 500 MILLION, 1966, C
OBJECTIVE, BURMA!, 1945, C
OBLIGIN' BUCKAROO, THE, 1927
OBLIGING YOUNG LADY, 1941, A
OBLONG BOX, THE, 1969, O
OBSESSED, 1951, C
OBSESSION
OBSESSION, 1954, C
OBSESSION, 1968, C
OBSESSION, 1976, C
OBVIOUS SITUATION, AN
OCCASIONALLY YOURS, 1920, A
OCCHI SENZA VOLTO
OCEAN BREAKERS, 1949, A
OCEAN WAIF, THE, 1916
OCEAN'S ELEVEN, 1960, A
OCHAZUKE NO AJI
OCTAGON, THE, 1980, O
OCTAMAN, 1971, O
OCTOBER
OCTOBER, 1928
OCTOBER MAN, THE, 1948, A
OCTOBER MOTH, 1960, O
OCTOMAN
OCTOPUSSY, 1983, C
ODD ANGRY SHOT, THE, 1979, C
ODD COUPLE, THE, 1968, A
ODD JOB, THE, 1978, O
ODD MAN OUT, 1947, C-O
ODD OBSESSION, 1961, O
ODDO, 1967
ODDS AGAINST
ODDS AGAINST HER, THE, 1919, A
ODDS AGAINST TOMORROW, 1959, C
ODE TO BILLY JOE, 1976, O
ODESSA FILE, THE, 1974, C
ODETTE, 1951, A-C
ODISSEA NUDA
ODONGO, 1956, A
ODYSSEY OF THE NORTH, AN, 1914, A
ODYSSEY OF THE PACIFIC, 1983, AA
OEDIPUS REX, 1957, A
OEDIPUS THE KING, 1968
OEVIL'S HAND, THE
OF BEDS AND BROADS
OF FLESH AND BLOOD, 1964, C
OF HUMAN BONDAGE, 1934, C-O
OF HUMAN BONDAGE, 1946, A
OF HUMAN BONDAGE, 1964, O
OF HUMAN HEARTS, 1938, A
OF LOVE AND DESIRE, 1963, O
OF MICE AND MEN, 1939, O
OF STARS AND MEN, 1961, AAA
OF UNKNOWN ORIGIN, 1983, O
OF WAYWARD LOVE, 1964, O
OFF LIMITS, 1953, A
OFF THE BEATEN TRACK
OFF THE DOLE, 1935, A
OFF THE HIGHWAY, 1925, A
OFF THE RECORD, 1939, A
OFF THE WALL, 1977, C
OFF THE WALL, 1983, O
OFF TO THE RACES, 1937, O
OFF YOUR ROCKER, 1980
OFF-SHORE PIRATE, THE, 1921, A
OFFBEAT, 1961, A
OFFENDERS, THE, 1924, A
OFFENDERS, THE, 1980, O
OFFENSE, THE, 1973, O
OFFERING, THE, 1966, C
OFFICE GIRL, THE, 1932, A
OFFICE GIRLS, 1974
OFFICE PICNIC, THE, 1974, C
OFFICE SCANDAL, THE, 1929, A
OFFICE WIFE, THE, 1930, A
OFFICER 13, 1933, A
OFFICER 444, 1926
OFFICER 666, 1914
OFFICER 666, 1920
OFFICER AND A GENTLEMAN, AN, 1982, O
OFFICER AND THE LADY, THE, 1941, A
OFFICER JIM, 1926, A
OFFICER O'BRIEN, 1930, A
OFFICER'S MESS, THE, 1931, A
OGGI, DOMANI E DOPODOMANI, 1968
OGNUNO PER SE
OGRE AND THE GIRL, THE, 1915
OGUE SONG, THE, 1930, A
OH BILLY BEHAVE, 1926
OH BOY!, 1938, A
OH BROTHERHOOD
OH CE BAISER, 1917

OH DAD, POOR DAD, MAMA'S HUNG YOU IN THE CLOSET AND I'M FEELIN' SO SAD, 1967, C
OH DADDY!, 1935, A
OH DOCTOR, 1937, A
OH GOD! BOOK II, 1980, A-C
OH GOD! YOU DEVIL, 1984, A-C
OH JOHNNY, HOW YOU CAN LOVE!, 1940, A
OH MARY BE CAREFUL, 1921
OH MY DARLING CLEMENTINE
OH NO DOCTOR!, 1934
OH ROSALINDA, 1956, A
OH WHAT A DUCHESS!
OH! CALCUTTA!, 1972, O
OH! FOR A MAN!, 1957
OH! SAILOR, BEHAVE!, 1930, AAA
OH! SUSANNA, 1951, A
OH! THOSE MOST SECRET AGENTS
OH! WHAT A LOVELY WAR, 1969, A-C
OH, ALFIE
OH, BABY, 1926
OH, BOY, 1919, A
OH, DOCTOR, 1924, A
OH, FOR A MAN!, 1930, A
OH, GOD!, 1977, A-C
OH, HEAVENLY DOG!, 1980, A
OH, JO, 1921
OH, JOHNNY, 1919, A
OH, KAY, 1928, A
OH, LADY, LADY, 1920, A
OH, MABEL BEHAVE, 1922
OH, MEN! OH, WOMEN!, 1957, A-C
OH, MR. PORTER!, 1937, A
OH, SUSANNA, 1937, A
OH, WHAT A NIGHT, 1926, A
OH, WHAT A NIGHT, 1935, A
OH, WHAT A NIGHT, 1944, A
OH, WHAT A NURSE, 1926, A
OH, YEAH!, 1929, A
OH, YOU BEAUTIFUL DOLL, 1949, A
OH, YOU TONY, A
OH, YOU WOMEN, 1919
OHAYO, 1962, A
OIL, 1977
OIL AND ROMANCE, 1925
OIL FOR THE LAMPS OF CHINA, 1935, A
OIL GIRLS, THE
OIL RAIDER, THE, 1934
OIL TOWN
OISEAUX DE PASSAGE, 1925
OKAY AMERICA, 1932, A
OKAY BILL, 1971, O
OKAY FOR SOUND, 1937, A
OKEFENOKEE, 1960
OKINAWA, 1952, A
OKLAHOMA, 1955, AAA
OKLAHOMA ANNIE, 1952, A
OKLAHOMA BADLANDS, 1948, A
OKLAHOMA BLUES, 1948, A
OKLAHOMA COWBOY, AN, 1929
OKLAHOMA CRUDE, 1973, O
OKLAHOMA CYCLONE, 1930, A
OKLAHOMA FRONTIER, 1939
OKLAHOMA JIM, 1931, A
OKLAHOMA JUSTICE, 1951, A
OKLAHOMA KID, THE, 1929, A
OKLAHOMA KID, THE, 1939, A
OKLAHOMA RAIDERS, 1944, A
OKLAHOMA RENEGADES, 1940, A
OKLAHOMA SHERIFF, THE, 1930, A
OKLAHOMA TERRITORY, 1960, A
OKLAHOMA TERROR, 1939, A
OKLAHOMA WOMAN, THE, 1956, C
OKLAHOMAN, THE, 1957, A
OLD ACQUAINTANCE, 1943, A-C
OLD AGE HANDICAP, 1928, A
OLD AND NEW, 1930
OLD ARM CHAIR, THE, 1920, A
OLD BARN DANCE, THE, 1938, A
OLD BILL AND SON, 1940, A
OLD BILL OF PARIS
OLD BILL THROUGH THE AGES, 1924, A
OLD BONES OF THE RIVER, 1938, A
OLD BOYFRIENDS, 1979, O
OLD CHISHOLM TRAIL, 1943, A
OLD CLOTHES, 1925, A
OLD CODE, THE, 1928, A
OLD CORRAL, THE, 1937, A
OLD CORRAL, THE, 1936
OLD COUNTRY, THE, 1921, A
OLD CURIOSITY SHOP, THE, 1913, A
OLD CURIOSITY SHOP, THE, 1921, A
OLD CURIOSITY SHOP, THE, 1935, A
OLD CURIOSITY SHOP, THE, 1975
OLD DAD, 1920
OLD DARK HOUSE, THE, 1932, A
OLD DARK HOUSE, THE, 1963, A
OLD DRACULA, 1975, C
OLD ENGLISH, 1930, A
OLD ENOUGH, 1984, C
OLD FAITHFUL, 1935, A
OLD FASHIONED BOY, AN, 1920, A
OLD FASHIONED YOUNG MAN, AN, 1917

OLD FOLKS AT HOME, THE, 1916, A
OLD FOOL, THE, 1923
OLD FRONTIER, THE, 1950, A
OLD GREATHEART
OLD GROUCHY
OLD HARTWELL'S CUB, 1918
OLD HEIDELBERG, 1915
OLD HOME WEEK, 1925, A
OLD HOMESTEAD, THE, 1916
OLD HOMESTEAD, THE, 1922
OLD HOMESTEAD, THE, 1935, A
OLD HOMESTEAD, THE, 1942, A
OLD HUTCH, 1936, A
OLD IRON, 1938, A
OLD IRONSIDES, 1926, A
OLD LADY 31, 1920
OLD LOS ANGELES, 1948, A
OLD LOUISIANA, 1938, A
OLD LOVES AND NEW, 1926, A
OLD LOVES FOR NEW, 1918
OLD MAC, 1961
OLD MAID'S BABY, THE, 1919, A
OLD MAID, THE, 1939, C
OLD MAN AND THE BOY, THE
OLD MAN AND THE SEA, THE, 1958, A
OLD MAN RHYTHM, 1935, A
OLD MAN, THE, 1932, A
OLD MOTHER RILEY, 1937, A
OLD MOTHER RILEY AT HOME, 1945, A
OLD MOTHER RILEY CATCHES A QUISLING
OLD MOTHER RILEY IN BUSINESS, 1940, A
OLD MOTHER RILEY IN PARIS, 1938
OLD MOTHER RILEY IN SOCIETY, 1940, A
OLD MOTHER RILEY MEETS THE VAMPIRE
OLD MOTHER RILEY MP, 1939, A
OLD MOTHER RILEY OVERSEAS, 1943, A
OLD MOTHER RILEY'S CIRCUS, 1941, A
OLD MOTHER RILEY'S GHOSTS, 1941, A
OLD MOTHER RILEY'S NEW VENTURE
OLD MOTHER RILEY, DETECTIVE, 1943, A
OLD NEST, THE, 1921
OLD OAKEN BUCKET, THE, 1921
OLD OKLAHOMA PLAINS, 1952, A
OLD OVERLAND TRAIL, 1953, A
OLD ROSES, 1935, A
OLD SAN FRANCISCO, 1927, A
OLD SCHOOL TIE, THE
OLD SHATTERHAND, 1968, A
OLD SHOES, 1927, A
OLD SOAK, THE, 1926, A
OLD SOLDIERS NEVER DIE, 1931, A
OLD SPANISH CUSTOM, AN, 1936, A
OLD SPANISH CUSTOMERS, 1932, A
OLD ST. PAUL'S
OLD SUREHAND, 1. TIEL
OLD SWEETHEART OF MINE, AN, 1923
OLD SWIMMIN' HOLE, THE, 1921, A
OLD SWIMMIN' HOLE, THE, 1941, A
OLD TESTAMENT, 1963
OLD TEXAS TRAIL, THE, 1944, A
OLD WEST, THE, 1952, A
OLD WIVES FOR NEW, 1918, C
OLD WIVES' TALE, THE, 1921, A
OLD WOOD CARVER, THE, 1913
OLD WYOMING TRAIL, THE, 1937, A
OLD YELLER, 1957, A
OLD-FASHIONED GIRL, AN, 1948, A
OLD-FASHIONED WAY, THE, 1934, A
OLDEST CONFESSION, THE
OLDEST LAW, THE, 1918, C
OLDEST PROFESSION, THE, 1968, O
OLE REX, 1961
OLGA'S GIRLS, 1964, O
OLIVE TREES OF JUSTICE, THE, 1967, A
OLIVER TWIST, 1912
OLIVER TWIST, 1916, A
OLIVER TWIST, 1922, A
OLIVER TWIST, 1933, A
OLIVER TWIST, 1951, AA
OLIVER TWIST, JR., 1921, A
OLIVER!, 1968, AAA
OLIVER'S STORY, 1978, C
OLLY, OLLY, OXEN FREE, 1978, A
OLSEN'S BIG MOMENT, 1934, A
OLSEN'S NIGHT OUT
OLTRAGGIO AL PUDORE
OLTRE IL BENE E IL MALE
OLYMPIC HERO, THE, 1928, A
OLYMPIC HONEYMOON
OMAHA TRAIL, THE, 1942, A
OMAR KHAYYAM, 1957, A
OMAR THE TENTMAKER, 1922
OMBRE BIANCHE
OMEGA MAN, THE, 1971, C
OMEGANS, THE, 1968
OMEN, THE, 1976, O
OMICRON, 1963, A
OMOO OMOO, THE SHARK GOD, 1949, A
ON A CLEAR DAY YOU CAN SEE FOREVER, 1970, AA
ON AGAIN—OFF AGAIN, 1937, A
ON AN ISLAND WITH YOU, 1948, A
ON ANY STREET

ON APPROVAL, 1930, A
ON APPROVAL, 1944, A
ON BITTER CREEK, 1915
ON BORROWED TIME, 1939, A
ON DANGEROUS GROUND, 1917
ON DANGEROUS GROUND, 1951, C
ON DANGEROUS PATHS, 1915
ON DRESS PARADE
ON FRIDAY AT ELEVEN
ON GOLDEN POND, 1981, A-C
ON GUARD
ON HER BED OF ROSES, 1966, C
ON HER HONOR, 1922
ON HER MAJESTY'S SECRET SERVICE, 1969, C
ON HER WEDDING NIGHT, 1915, A
ON HIS MAJESTY'S SECRET SERVICE
ON HIS OWN, 1939, A
ON LEAVE, 1918, A
ON MOONLIGHT BAY, 1951, AAA
ON MY WAY TO THE CRUSADES, I MET A GIRL WHO...
ON NE BADINE PAS AVEC L'AMOUR, 1924
ON OUR LITTLE PLACE
ON OUR MERRY WAY, 1948, A
ON OUR SELECTION, 1930, A
ON PROBATION
ON PROBATION, 1924, A
ON PROBATION, 1935, A
ON RECORD, 1917, A
ON SECRET SERVICE, 1933
ON SECRET SERVICE, 1936
ON SPECIAL DUTY
ON STAGE EVERYBODY, 1945, A
ON SUCH A NIGHT, 1937, A
ON THE AIR, 1934, A
ON THE AIR LIVE WITH CAPTAIN MIDNIGHT, 1979
ON THE AVENUE, 1937
ON THE BANKS OF ALLAN WATER, 1916, A
ON THE BANKS OF THE WABASH, 1923, A
ON THE BEACH, 1959, O
ON THE BEAT, 1962, A
ON THE BREAD LINE, 1915
ON THE BRINK
ON THE BUSES, 1972, C
ON THE CARPET
ON THE COMET, 1970, A
ON THE DIVIDE, 1928, A
ON THE DOTTED LINE
ON THE DOUBLE, 1961, A
ON THE FIDDLE
ON THE GO, 1925, A
ON THE GREAT WHITE TRAIL, 1938, A
ON THE HIGH CARD, 1921
ON THE HIGH SEAS, 1922, A
ON THE ISLE OF SAMOA, 1950, A
ON THE JUMP, 1918
ON THE LAM, 1972
ON THE LEVEL, 1917
ON THE LEVEL, 1930, A
ON THE LINE, 1984, O
ON THE LOOSE, 1951, A
ON THE MAKE
ON THE NICKEL, 1980, O
ON THE NIGHT OF THE FIRE
ON THE NIGHT STAGE, 1915
ON THE OLD SPANISH TRAIL, 1947, A
ON THE QUIET, 1918, A
ON THE RIGHT TRACK, 1981, C
ON THE RIVERA, 1951, A
ON THE ROAD AGAIN
ON THE RUN, 1958, A
ON THE RUN, 1967, A
ON THE RUN, 1969, A
ON THE RUN, 1983, C
ON THE SHELF
ON THE SPANISH MAIN, 1917
ON THE SPOT, 1940, A
ON THE STEPS OF THE ALTAR, 1916
ON THE STEPS OF THE THRONE, 1913
ON THE STROKE OF NINE
ON THE STROKE OF THREE, 1924, A
ON THE STROKE OF TWELVE, 1927
ON THE SUNNY SIDE, 1942, AA
ON THE SUNNYSIDE, 1936, A
ON THE THRESHOLD, 1925
ON THE THRESHOLD OF SPACE, 1956, A
ON THE TOWN, 1949, A
ON THE WARSAW HIGHROAD, 1916
ON THE WATERFRONT, 1954, O
ON THE YARD, 1978, O
ON THEIR OWN, 1940, A
ON THIN ICE, 1925, A
ON THIN ICE, 1933
ON TIME, 1924, A
ON TO RENO, 1928, A
ON TOP OF OLD SMOKY, 1953, A
ON TOP OF THE WORLD
ON TRIAL, 1917, A
ON TRIAL, 1928, A
ON TRIAL, 1939, A
ON VELVET, 1938
ON WINGS OF SONG

ON WITH THE DANCE, 1920, A
ON WITH THE SHOW, 1929, A
ON YOUR BACK, 1930, A
ON YOUR TOES, 1927
ON YOUR TOES, 1939, A
ON ZE BOULEVARD, 1927, A
ON-THE-SQUARE GIRL, THE, 1917
ONCE, 1974, C
ONCE A CROOK, 1941, A
ONCE A DOCTOR, 1937, A
ONCE A GENTLEMAN, 1930, A
ONCE A JOLLY SWAGMAN
ONCE A LADY, 1931, A
ONCE A PLUMBER, 1920, A
ONCE A RAINY DAY, 1968, A
ONCE A SINNER, 1931, A
ONCE A SINNER, 1952, A
ONCE A THIEF, 1935, A
ONCE A THIEF, 1950, A
ONCE A THIEF, 1965, C
ONCE A THIEF, 1961
ONCE ABOARD THE LUGGER, 1920, A
ONCE AND FOREVER, 1927
ONCE BEFORE I DIE, 1967, C
ONCE IN A BLUE MOON, 1936, A
ONCE IN A LIFETIME, 1925
ONCE IN A LIFETIME, 1932, A
ONCE IN A MILLION
ONCE IN A NEW MOON, 1935, A
ONCE IN PARIS, 1978, C
ONCE IS NOT ENOUGH, 1975, O
ONCE MORE, MY DARLING, 1949, A
ONCE MORE, WITH FEELING, 1960, A-C
ONCE THERE WAS A GIRL, 1945, C
ONCE TO EVERY BACHELOR, 1934, A
ONCE TO EVERY WOMAN, 1920
ONCE TO EVERY WOMAN, 1934, A
ONCE UPON A COFFEE HOUSE, 1965, A
ONCE UPON A DREAM, 1949, A
ONCE UPON A HONEYMOON, 1942, A
ONCE UPON A HORSE, 1958, A
ONCE UPON A SCOUNDREL, 1973, A
ONCE UPON A SUMMER
ONCE UPON A THURSDAY
ONCE UPON A TIME
ONCE UPON A TIME, 1918, A
ONCE UPON A TIME, 1922, A
ONCE UPON A TIME, 1922
ONCE UPON A TIME, 1944, A
ONCE UPON A TIME IN AMERICA, 1984, O
ONCE UPON A TIME IN THE WEST, 1969
ONCE YOU KISS A STRANGER, 1969, O
ONDATA DI CALORE
100 MEN AND A GIRL, 1937, AAA
100 RIFLES, 1969, O
1001 ARABIAN NIGHTS, 1959, AA
1 2 3 MONSTER EXPRESS, 1977, C
$100 A NIGHT, 1968, C
ONE A MINUTE, 1921, A
ONE AGAINST MANY, 1919
ONE AGAINST SEVEN
*ONE AND ONLY GENUINE ORIGINAL FAMILY
BAND, THE*, 1968, AA
ONE AND ONLY, THE, 1978, C
ONE APRIL 2000, 1952, A
ONE ARABIAN NIGHT, 1921, A
ONE ARABIAN NIGHT, 1923
ONE ARMED EXECUTIONER, 1980
ONE AWAY, 1980
ONE BIG AFFAIR, 1952, A
ONE BODY TOO MANY, 1944, A
ONE BORN EVERY MINUTE
ONE BRIEF SUMMER, 1971
ONE CHANCE IN A MILLION, 1927, A
ONE CHANCE TO WIN, 1976
ONE CLEAR CALL, 1922, A
ONE COLUMBO NIGHT, 1926, A
ONE CROWDED NIGHT, 1940, A
ONE DANGEROUS NIGHT, 1943, A
ONE DARK NIGHT, 1939, A
ONE DARK NIGHT, 1983, C
ONE DAY, 1916, A
ONE DAY IN THE LIFE OF IVAN DENISOVICH,
1971, A
ONE DEADLY SUMMER, 1984, O
ONE DESIRE, 1955, AA
ONE DOWN TWO TO GO, 1982, O
ONE EIGHTH APACHE, 1922
ONE EMBARRASSING NIGHT, 1930, A
ONE EXCITING ADVENTURE, 1935, A
ONE EXCITING NIGHT, 1922, A
ONE EXCITING NIGHT, 1945, A
ONE EXCITING NIGHT, 1946
ONE EXCITING WEEK, 1946, A
ONE FAMILY, 1930
ONE FATAL HOUR
ONE FLEW OVER THE CUCKOO'S NEST, 1975, O
ONE FOOT IN HEAVEN, 1941, AA
ONE FOOT IN HELL, 1960, A
ONE FOR ALL
ONE FOR THE BOOKS
ONE FRIGHTENED NIGHT, 1935, A

ONE FROM THE HEART, 1982, O
ONE GIRL'S CONFESSION, 1953, C
ONE GLORIOUS DAY, 1922
ONE GLORIOUS NIGHT, 1924
ONE GLORIOUS SCRAP, 1927, A
ONE GOOD TURN, 1936, A
ONE GOOD TURN, 1955, A
ONE HEAVENLY NIGHT, 1931, A
ONE HORSE TOWN
ONE HOUR, 1917
ONE HOUR BEFORE DAWN, 1920
ONE HOUR LATE, 1935, A
ONE HOUR OF LOVE, 1927, A
ONE HOUR PAST MIDNIGHT, 1924
ONE HOUR TO DOOM'S DAY
ONE HOUR TO LIVE, 1939
ONE HOUR WITH YOU, 1932, A-C
ONE HUNDRED AND ONE DALMATIANS, 1961, AAA
$100 A NIGHT, 1968, C
100 MEN AND A GIRL, 1937, AAA
ONE HUNDRED PERCENT PURE
100 RIFLES, 1969, O
125 ROOMS OF COMFORT, 1974, O
ONE HYSTERICAL NIGHT, 1930, A
ONE IN A MILLION, 1935, A
ONE IN A MILLION, 1936, AA
ONE INCREASING PURPOSE, 1927
ONE IS A LONELY NUMBER, 1972, C
ONE IS GUILTY, 1934
ONE JUMP AHEAD, 1955, A
ONE JUST MAN, 1955, A
ONE LAST FLING, 1949, A
ONE LAST RIDE, 1980
ONE LAW FOR BOTH, 1917, A
ONE LAW FOR THE WOMAN, 1924, A
ONE LIFE
ONE LITTLE INDIAN, 1973, AA
ONE MAD KISS, 1930, A
ONE MAN, 1979, C
ONE MAN AGAINST THE ORGANIZATION, 1977
ONE MAN DOG, THE, 1929, A
ONE MAN GAME, A, 1927
ONE MAN IN A MILLION, 1921
ONE MAN JURY, 1978, O
ONE MAN JUSTICE, 1937, A
ONE MAN TRAIL, 1926
ONE MAN'S JOURNEY, 1933, A
ONE MAN'S LAW, 1940, A
ONE MAN'S WAY, 1964, A
ONE MILE FROM HEAVEN, 1937, A
ONE MILLION B.C., 1940, A-C
ONE MILLION DOLLARS, 1915, A
ONE MILLION DOLLARS, 1965, A
$1,000,000 DUCK, 1971, AA
$1,000,000 RACKET, 1937, A
ONE MILLION IN JEWELS, 1923, A
ONE MILLION YEARS B.C., 1967, A
ONE MINUTE TO PLAY, 1926, A
ONE MINUTE TO ZERO, 1952, A
ONE MOMENT'S TEMPTATION, 1922
ONE MORE AMERICAN, 1918, A
ONE MORE RIVER, 1934, A
ONE MORE SPRING, 1935, A
ONE MORE TIME, 1970, A
ONE MORE TOMORROW, 1946, A
ONE MORE TRAIN TO ROB, 1971, A
ONE MYSTERIOUS NIGHT, 1944, A
ONE NEW YORK NIGHT, 1935, A
ONE NIGHT AT SUSIE'S, 1930, A
ONE NIGHT IN LISBON, 1941, A
ONE NIGHT IN PARIS, 1940, A
ONE NIGHT IN ROME, 1924
ONE NIGHT IN THE TROPICS, 1940, A
ONE NIGHT OF LOVE, 1934, A
ONE NIGHT STAND, 1976, O
ONE NIGHT WITH YOU, 1948, A
ONE NIGHT...A TRAIN, 1968, C
ONE OF MANY, 1917, A
ONE OF MILLIONS, 1914
ONE OF OUR AIRCRAFT IS MISSING, 1942, A
ONE OF OUR DINOSAURS IS MISSING, 1975, AA
ONE OF OUR GIRLS, 1914, A
ONE OF OUR SPIES IS MISSING, 1966, A
ONE OF THE BEST, 1927, A
ONE OF THE BRAVEST, 1925, A
ONE OF THE FINEST, 1919
ONE OF THE MANY
ONE OF THOSE THINGS, 1974
ONE ON ONE, 1977, A
ONE PAGE OF LOVE, 1979
ONE PLUS ONE, 1961, C-O
ONE PLUS ONE, 1969, O
ONE POTATO, TWO POTATO, 1964, C
ONE PRECIOUS YEAR, 1933, A
ONE PUNCH O'DAY, 1926, A
ONE RAINY AFTERNOON, 1936, A
ONE ROMANTIC NIGHT, 1930, A
ONE RUSSIAN SUMMER, 1973
ONE SHOT RANGER, 1925
ONE SHOT ROSS, 1917, A
ONE SINGS, THE OTHER DOESN'T, 1977, C-O
ONE SPLENDID HOUR, 1929, A

ONE SPY TOO MANY, 1966, A
ONE STEP TO HELL, 1969, C
ONE STOLEN NIGHT, 1923, A
ONE STOLEN NIGHT, 1929, A
ONE SUMMER LOVE, 1976, C
ONE SUMMER'S DAY, 1917, A
ONE SUNDAY AFTERNOON, 1933, A
ONE SUNDAY AFTERNOON, 1948, A
ONE THAT GOT AWAY, THE, 1958, A
ONE THIRD OF A NATION, 1939, A
1,000 CONVICTS AND A WOMAN, 1971, O
$1,000 A MINUTE, 1935, A
$1,000 A TOUCHDOWN, 1939, A
1,000 PLANE RAID, 1969, A
1,000 SHAPES OF A FEMALE, 1963, A
1001 ARABIAN NIGHTS, 1959, AA
ONE THOUSAND DOLLARS, 1918
ONE THRILLING NIGHT, 1942, A
ONE TOO MANY, 1950, A
ONE TOUCH OF NATURE, 1917
ONE TOUCH OF SIN, 1917
ONE TOUCH OF VENUS, 1948, A
ONE, TWO, THREE, 1961, A
123 MONSTER EXPRESS, 1977, C
ONE WAY OUT
ONE WAY OUT, 1955, A
ONE WAY PASSAGE, 1932, A
ONE WAY PENDULUM, 1965, A
ONE WAY STREET, 1925
ONE WAY STREET, 1950, A
ONE WAY TICKET TO HELL, 1955
ONE WAY TO LOVE, 1946, A
ONE WAY TRAIL, THE, 1931, A
ONE WAY WAHINI, 1965, C-O
ONE WEEK OF LIFE, 1919
ONE WEEK OF LOVE, 1922, A
ONE WILD NIGHT, 1938, A
ONE WILD OAT, 1951, A
ONE WILD WEEK, 1921, A
ONE WISH TOO MANY, 1956, A
ONE WITH THE FUZZ, THE
ONE WOMAN IDEA, THE, 1929
ONE WOMAN TO ANOTHER, 1927, A
ONE WOMAN'S STORY, 1949, A
ONE WOMAN, THE, 1918
ONE WONDERFUL NIGHT, 1914
ONE WONDERFUL NIGHT, 1922
ONE YEAR LATER, 1933, A
ONE YEAR TO LIVE, 1925, A
ONE-EYED JACKS, 1961, O
ONE-EYED SOLDIERS, 1967, C
ONE-MAN LAW, 1932
ONE-MAN MUTINY
ONE-MAN TRAIL, THE, 1921
ONE-PIECE BATHING SUIT, THE
ONE-ROUND HOGAN, 1927, A
ONE-THING-AT-A-TIME O'DAY, 1919
ONE-TRICK PONY, 1980, C
ONE-WAY TICKET, 1935, A
ONE-WAY TRAIL, THE, 1920
ONEICHAN MAKARI TORU
ONI NO SUMU YAKATA
ONI SHLI NA VOSTOK
ONIBABA, 1965, C
ONIMASA, 1983, O
ONION FIELD, THE, 1979, C-O
ONIONHEAD, 1958, A
ONKEL TOMS HUTTE
ONLY 38, 1923, A
ONLY A MILL GIRL, 1919, A
ONLY A SHOP GIRL, 1922, A
ONLY A WOMAN, 1966, A
ONLY ANGELS HAVE WINGS, 1939, A
ONLY EIGHT HOURS
ONLY GAME IN TOWN, THE, 1970, C
ONLY GIRL, THE
ONLY GOD KNOWS, 1974, A
ONLY MAN, THE, 1915
ONLY ONCE IN A LIFETIME, 1979, C
ONLY ONE NIGHT, 1942, C
ONLY ROAD, THE, 1918
ONLY SAPS WORK, 1930, A
ONLY SON, THE, 1914, A
ONLY THE BEST
ONLY THE BRAVE, 1930, A
ONLY THE FRENCH CAN
ONLY THE VALIANT, 1951, A
ONLY THING YOU KNOW, THE, 1971, C
ONLY THING, THE, 1925
ONLY TWO CAN PLAY, 1962, C
ONLY WAY HOME, THE, 1972, C
ONLY WAY OUT IS DEAD, THE, 1970
ONLY WAY OUT, THE, 1915
ONLY WAY, THE, 1926, A
ONLY WAY, THE, 1970, A
ONLY WHEN I LARF, 1968, A
ONLY WHEN I LAUGH, 1981, C
ONLY WOMAN, THE, 1924, A
ONLY YESTERDAY, 1933, C
ONNA GA KAIDAN O AGARUTOKI
ONNA GOROSHI ABURA JIGOKU
ONNA NO MIZUUMI

ONNA NO NAKANI IRU TANIN
ONNA NO REKISHI
ONNA NO UZU TO FUCHI TO NAGARE
ONNA NO ZA
ONNA UKIYOBURO
ONSEN GERIRA DAI SHOGEKI
ONWARD CHRISTIAN SOLDIERS, 1918, A
OOH, YOU ARE AWFUL
OPEN ALL NIGHT, 1924, A
OPEN ALL NIGHT, 1934, O
OPEN COUNTRY, 1922, C
OPEN DOOR, THE, 1919
OPEN PLACES, 1917
OPEN RANGE, 1927
OPEN ROAD, THE, 1940, A
OPEN SEASON, 1974, O
OPEN SECRET, 1948, A
OPEN SWITCH, THE, 1926
OPEN THE DOOR AND SEE ALL THE PEOPLE,
    1964, A
OPEN TRAIL, THE
OPEN YOUR EYES, 1919, C
OPENED BY MISTAKE, 1940, A
OPENED SHUTTERS, 1921
OPENED SHUTTERS, THE, 1914, A
OPENING NIGHT, 1977, C
OPENING NIGHT, THE, 1927
OPERACION GOLDMAN
OPERACION LOTO AZUL
OPERATION AMSTERDAM, 1960, A
OPERATION BIKINI, 1963, A
OPERATION BLUE BOOK
OPERATION BOTTLENECK, 1961, A
OPERATION BULLSHINE, 1963, A
OPERATION CAMEL, 1961, A
OPERATION CIA, 1965, A
OPERATION CONSPIRACY, 1957, A
OPERATION CROSS EAGLES, 1969, A
OPERATION CROSSBOW, 1965, A
OPERATION CUPID, 1960, A
OPERATION DAMES, 1959, C
OPERATION DAYBREAK, 1976, A
OPERATION DELILAH, 1966, A
OPERATION DIAMOND, 1948, A
OPERATION DIPLOMAT, 1953, A
OPERATION DISASTER, 1951, A
OPERATION EICHMANN, 1961, A
OPERATION ENEMY FORT, 1964
OPERATION GANYMED, 1977
OPERATION HAYLIFT, 1950, A
OPERATION KID BROTHER, 1967, A
OPERATION LOTUS BLEU
OPERATION LOVEBIRDS, 1968, A
OPERATION M
OPERATION MAD BALL, 1957, A
OPERATION MANHUNT, 1954, A
OPERATION MASQUERADE
OPERATION MERMAID
OPERATION MURDER, 1957, A
OPERATION PACIFIC, 1951, A
OPERATION PETTICOAT, 1959, A
OPERATION SAN GENNARO
OPERATION SECRET, 1952, A
OPERATION SNAFU, 1965, A
OPERATION SNAFU, 1970
OPERATION SNATCH, 1962, A
OPERATION ST. PETER'S, 1968, A
OPERATION STOGIE, 1960
OPERATION THIRD FORM, 1966, AA
OPERATION THUNDERBOLT, 1978, C
OPERATION UNDER COVER
OPERATION WAR HEAD
OPERATION X, 1951, A-C
OPERATION X, 1963, C
OPERATOR 13, 1934, A
OPERAZIA GOLDMAN
OPERAZIONE CROSSBOW
OPERAZIONE PARADISO
OPERAZIONE PAURA
OPERETTA, 1949, A
OPHELIA, 1964, C
OPIATE '67, 1967, C
OPPORTUNITY, 1918
OPPOSITE SEX, THE, 1956, A
OPTIMIST, THE
OPTIMISTIC TRAGEDY, THE, 1964, A
OPTIMISTS OF NINE ELMS, THE
OPTIMISTS, THE, 1973, A
OR POUR LES CESARS
ORA PRO NOBIS, 1917, A
ORACLE, THE
ORAZIO E COURIAZI
ORBITA MORTAL
ORCA, 1977, C
ORCHESTRA WIVES, 1942, A
ORCHIDS AND ERMINE, 1927
ORCHIDS TO YOU, 1935, A
ORDEAL BY INNOCENCE, 1984, C
ORDEAL OF ELIZABETH, THE, 1916
ORDEAL OF ROSETTA, THE, 1918
ORDEAL, THE, 1914, C
ORDEAL, THE, 1922, C

ORDER OF DEATH
ORDER TO KILL, 1974
ORDERED TO LOVE, 1963, O
ORDERS ARE ORDERS, 1959, A
ORDERS IS ORDERS, 1934, A
ORDERS TO KILL, 1958, A
ORDERS, THE, 1977, C-O
ORDET, 1957, A-C
ORDINARY PEOPLE, 1980, O
OREGON PASSAGE, 1958, A
OREGON TRAIL, 1945, A
OREGON TRAIL SCOUTS, 1947, A
OREGON TRAIL, THE, 1936, A
OREGON TRAIL, THE, 1959, A
ORFEU NEGRO
ORGANIZATION, THE, 1971, C
ORGANIZER, THE, 1964, A
ORGY OF BLOOD
ORGY OF THE DEAD, 1965, O
ORGY OF THE GOLDEN NUDES
ORIENT EXPRESS, 1934, A
ORIENT EXPRESS, 1952
ORIENTAL DREAM
ORIGINAL OLD MOTHER RILEY, THE
ORLAK, THE HELL OF FRANKENSTEIN, 1960, C-O
ORPHAN OF THE PECOS, 1938, A
ORPHAN OF THE RING
ORPHAN OF THE SAGE, 1928, A
ORPHAN OF THE WILDERNESS, 1937, A
ORPHAN SALLY, 1922
ORPHAN, THE, 1920
ORPHAN, THE, 1979
ORPHANS OF THE GHETTO, 1922
ORPHANS OF THE NORTH, 1940
ORPHANS OF THE STORM, 1922, A
ORPHANS OF THE STREET, 1939, AAA
ORPHEE
ORPHEUS, 1950, A
OSAKA MONOGATARI
OSCAR WILDE, 1960, C
OSCAR, THE, 1966, A
OSETROVNA
OSS 117—MISSION FOR A KILLER, 1966, C
OSSESSIONE, 1959, C
OSTATNI ETAP
OSTERMAN WEEKEND, THE, 1983, C-O
OSTRE SLEDOVANE VLAKY
OTCHI TCHORNIA
OTCHIY DOM
OTEL U POGIBSHCHEGO ALPINISTA
OTETS SOLDATA
OTHELLO, 1914
OTHELLO, 1922
OTHELLO, 1955, C
OTHELLO, 1960, A
OTHELLO, 1965, A
OTHER GIRL, THE, 1916
OTHER HALF, THE, 1919
OTHER KIND OF LOVE, THE, 1924, A
OTHER LOVE, THE, 1947, A
OTHER MAN'S WIFE, THE, 1919, A
OTHER MAN, THE, 1918, A
OTHER MEN'S DAUGHTERS, 1918, A
OTHER MEN'S DAUGHTERS, 1923
OTHER MEN'S SHOES, 1920
OTHER MEN'S WIVES, 1919
OTHER MEN'S WOMEN, 1931, A-C
OTHER ONE, THE, 1967, C
OTHER PEOPLE'S BUSINESS
OTHER PEOPLE'S MONEY, 1916
OTHER PEOPLE'S SINS, 1931, A
OTHER PERSON, THE, 1921, A
OTHER SELF, THE, 1918
OTHER SIDE OF BONNIE AND CLYDE, THE, 1968
OTHER SIDE OF MIDNIGHT, THE, 1977, O
OTHER SIDE OF PARADISE, THE
OTHER SIDE OF THE DOOR, THE, 1916
OTHER SIDE OF THE MOUNTAIN, THE, 1975
OTHER SIDE OF THE MOUNTAIN—PART 2, THE,
    1978, A
OTHER SIDE OF THE UNDERNEATH, THE, 1972, O
OTHER SIDE, THE, 1922
OTHER TOMORROW, THE, 1930, A
OTHER WOMAN'S STORY, THE, 1925
OTHER WOMAN, THE, 1918
OTHER WOMAN, THE, 1921
OTHER WOMAN, THE, 1931, A
OTHER WOMAN, THE, 1954, C-O
OTHER WOMEN'S CLOTHES, 1922
OTHER WOMEN'S HUSBANDS, 1926
OTHER, THE, 1912
OTHER, THE, 1972, O
OTKLONENIE
OTLEY, 1969, C
OTOKO TAI OTOKO
OTROKI VO VSELENNOI
OTTO E MEZZO
OUANGA, 1936, A
OUR BETTER SELVES, 1919
OUR BETTERS, 1933, C
OUR BLUSHING BRIDES, 1930, A
OUR DAILY BREAD, 1934, A

OUR DAILY BREAD, 1950, O
OUR DANCING DAUGHTERS, 1928, A
OUR FIGHTING NAVY
OUR GIRL FRIDAY
OUR HEARTS WERE GROWING UP, 1946, A
OUR HEARTS WERE YOUNG AND GAY, 1944, A
OUR HITLER, A FILM FROM GERMANY, 1980, O
OUR HOSPITALITY, 1923, A
OUR LADY OF FATIMA
OUR LEADING CITIZEN, 1922, A
OUR LEADING CITIZEN, 1939, A
OUR LITTLE GIRL, 1935, AAA
OUR LITTLE WIFE, 1918, A
OUR MAN IN HAVANA, 1960, A
OUR MAN IN JAMAICA, 1965
OUR MAN IN MARRAKESH, 1966
OUR MAN IN MARRAKESH, 1967
OUR MAN IN THE CARIBBEAN, 1962
OUR MEN IN BAGHDAD, 1967
OUR MISS BROOKS, 1956, AA
OUR MISS FRED, 1972, C
OUR MODERN MAIDENS, 1929, A
OUR MODERN MAIDENS, 1929, A
OUR MOTHER'S HOUSE, 1967, O
OUR MRS. McCHESNEY, 1918, A
OUR MUTUAL FRIEND, 1921
OUR NEIGHBORS—THE CARTERS, 1939, AAA
OUR RELATIONS, 1936, AA
OUR SILENT LOVE, 1969, A
OUR TIME, 1974, A
OUR TOWN, 1940, A
OUR VERY OWN, 1950, A
OUR VINES HAVE TENDER GRAPES, 1945, A
OUR WIFE, 1941, A
OUR WINNING SEASON, 1978, C
OURSELVES ALONE
OUT, 1982, C-O
OUT ALL NIGHT, 1927, A
OUT ALL NIGHT, 1933, A
OUT CALIFORNIA WAY, 1946, A
OUT OF A CLEAR SKY, 1918, A
OUT OF IT, 1969, A
OUT OF LUCK, 1919, A
OUT OF LUCK, 1923, A
OUT OF SEASON, 1975, C-O
OUT OF SIGHT, 1966, A
OUT OF SINGAPORE, 1932, C
OUT OF THE BLUE, 1931, A
OUT OF THE BLUE, 1947, A
OUT OF THE BLUE, 1982, O
OUT OF THE CHORUS, 1921
OUT OF THE CLOUDS, 1921
OUT OF THE CLOUDS, 1957, A
OUT OF THE DARKNESS, 1958
OUT OF THE DARKNESS, 1979
OUT OF THE DEPTHS, 1921
OUT OF THE DEPTHS, 1946, A
OUT OF THE DRIFTS, 1916, A
OUT OF THE DUST, 1920, C
OUT OF THE FOG, 1919
OUT OF THE FOG, 1941, C
OUT OF THE FOG, 1962
OUT OF THE FRYING PAN
OUT OF THE NIGHT
OUT OF THE NIGHT, 1918
OUT OF THE PAST, 1927, C
OUT OF THE PAST, 1933
OUT OF THE PAST, 1947, C
OUT OF THE RUINS, 1915
OUT OF THE RUINS, 1928
OUT OF THE SHADOW
OUT OF THE SHADOW, 1919, A
OUT OF THE SHADOWS, 1920
OUT OF THE SILENT NORTH, 1922, A
OUT OF THE STORM, 1920, A
OUT OF THE STORM, 1926
OUT OF THE STORM, 1948, A
OUT OF THE TIGER'S MOUTH, 1962, A
OUT OF THE WEST, 1926, A
OUT OF THE WRECK, 1917
OUT OF THIN AIR, 1969
OUT OF THIS WORLD, 1945, A
OUT OF TOWNERS, THE, 1970, A
OUT OF TOWNERS, THE, 1964
OUT TO WIN, 1923, A
OUT WEST WITH THE HARDYS, 1938, AAA
OUT WEST WITH THE PEPPERS, 1940, AAA
OUT WITH THE TIDE, 1928, A
OUT YONDER, 1920, A
OUTBACK, 1971, O
OUTBREAK OF HOSTILITIES, 1979
OUTCAST, 1917
OUTCAST, 1922
OUTCAST, 1928, C
OUTCAST, 1937, A
OUTCAST LADY, 1934, A
OUTCAST OF BLACK MESA, 1950, A
OUTCAST OF THE ISLANDS, 1952, A
OUTCAST SOULS, 1928
OUTCAST, THE, 1915
OUTCAST, THE, 1934, A
OUTCAST, THE, 1954, A

PANHANDLE, 1948, A
PANIC
PANIC, 1966, A
PANIC BUTTON, 1964, A
PANIC IN NEEDLE PARK, 1971, O
PANIC IN THE CITY, 1968, O
PANIC IN THE PARLOUR, 1957
PANIC IN THE STREETS, 1950, C
PANIC IN YEAR ZERO!, 1962, O
PANIC ON THE AIR
PANIC ON THE TRANS-SIBERIAN TRAIN
PANIQUE, 1947, C
PANTHEA, 1917
PANTHER ISLAND
PANTHER WOMAN, THE, 1919
PANTHER'S CLAW, THE, 1942, A
PANTHER'S MOON
PANTS, 1917
PAPA HULIN, 1916
PAPA SOLTERO, 1939
PAPA'S DELICATE CONDITION, 1963, A
PAPER BULLETS, 1941, A
PAPER CHASE, THE, 1973, A-C
PAPER DOLL'S WHISPER OF SPRING, A, 1926
PAPER GALLOWS, 1950, A
PAPER LION, 1968, A
PAPER MOON, 1973, A
PAPER ORCHID, 1949, C
PAPER PEOPLE, THE, 1969
PAPER TIGER, 1975, A-C
PAPERBACK HERO, 1973, O
PAPILLON, 1920
PAPILLON, 1973, O
PAR DESSUS LE MUR, 1923
PAR LE FER ET PAR LE FEU
PAR OU T'ES RENTRE? ON T'A PAS VUE SORTIR,
     1984, A
PARACHUTE BATTALION, 1941
PARACHUTE JUMPER, 1933, A
PARACHUTE NURSE, 1942, A
PARADE D'AMOUR
PARADE OF THE WEST, 1930, A
PARADES, 1972, O
PARADINE CASE, THE, 1947, A-C
PARADISE, 1926, A
PARADISE, 1928, A
PARADISE, 1982, O
PARADISE ALLEY, 1931, A
PARADISE ALLEY, 1962
PARADISE ALLEY, 1978, O
PARADISE AND PURGATORY, 1912
PARADISE CANYON, 1935, A
PARADISE EXPRESS, 1937, A
PARADISE FOR THREE, 1938, A
PARADISE FOR TWO
PARADISE FOR TWO, 1927
PARADISE GARDEN, 1917, C
PARADISE IN HARLEM, 1939
PARADISE ISLAND, 1930, A
PARADISE ISLE, 1937, A
PARADISE LAGOON
PARADISE POUR TOUS, 1982, C-O
PARADISE ROAD
PARADISE WITHOUT ADAM, 1918
PARADISE, HAWAIIAN STYLE, 1966, A
PARADISIO, 1962
PARADISO DELL'UOMO
PARALLAX VIEW, THE, 1974, O
PARALLELS, 1980, A-C
PARANOIA, 1968
PARANOIA, 1968
PARANOIAC, 1963, O
PARASITE, 1982, O
PARASITE MURDERS, THE
PARASITE, THE, 1925
PARATROOP COMMAND, 1959, A
PARATROOPER, 1954, A
PARBESZED
PARDNERS, 1917
PARDNERS, 1956, A
PARDON MY BRUSH, 1964
PARDON MY FRENCH, 1921
PARDON MY FRENCH, 1951, A
PARDON MY GUN, 1930, A
PARDON MY GUN, 1942, A
PARDON MY NERVE, 1922, A
PARDON MY PAST, 1945, A
PARDON MY RHYTHM, 1944, A
PARDON MY SARONG, 1942, AAA
PARDON MY STRIPES, 1942, A
PARDON MY TRUNK
PARDON OUR NERVE, 1939, A
PARDON US, 1931, AAA
PAREMA, CRERATURE FROM THE STARWORLD,
     1922
PARENT TRAP, THE, 1961, AA
PARENTAGE, 1918
PARENTS ON TRIAL, 1939, A
PARIS, 1924
PARIS, 1926
PARIS, 1929, A
PARIS AFTER DARK, 1923

PARIS AFTER DARK, 1943, A
PARIS ASLEEP
PARIS AT MIDNIGHT, 1926
PARIS AU MOIS D'AOUT
PARIS BELONGS TO US, 1962, A-C
PARIS BLUES, 1961, O
PARIS BOUND, 1929, A
PARIS BRULE-T-IL?
PARIS CALLING, 1941, A
PARIS DOES STRANGE THINGS, 1957, A
PARIS EN CINQ JOURS, 1926
PARIS EROTIKA
PARIS EXPRESS, THE, 1953, A
PARIS FOLLIES OF 1956, 1955, A
PARIS GIRLS, 1929
PARIS GREEN, 1920, A
PARIS HOLIDAY, 1958, A
PARIS HONEYMOON, 1939, A
PARIS IN SPRING, 1935, A
PARIS IN THE MONTH OF AUGUST, 1968, A
PARIS INTERLUDE, 1934, A
PARIS IS OURS
PARIS LOVE SONG
PARIS MODEL, 1953, A
PARIS NOUS APPARTIENT
PARIS OOH-LA-LA!, 1963, O
PARIS PICK-UP, 1963, C
PARIS PLANE, 1933, A
PARIS PLAYBOYS, 1954, A
PARIS QUI DORT, 1924
PARIS UNDERGROUND, 1945, A
PARIS VU PAR
PARIS WAS MADE FOR LOVERS
PARIS, TEXAS, 1984, C-O
PARISH PRIEST, THE, 1921
PARISIAN COBBLER, 1928
PARISIAN LOVE, 1925
PARISIAN NIGHTS, 1925
PARISIAN ROMANCE, A, 1916
PARISIAN ROMANCE, A, 1932, A
PARISIAN SCANDAL, A, 1921
PARISIAN TIGRESS, THE, 1919
PARISIAN, THE, 1931, A
PARISIENNE
PARK AVENUE LOGGER, 1937, A
PARK PLAZA 605
PARK ROW, 1952, A
PARLIAMO DI DONNE
PARLOR, BEDROOM AND BATH, 1920
PARLOR, BEDROOM AND BATH, 1931, A
PARMI LES VAUTOURS
PARNELL, 1937, A-C
PAROLE, 1936, A
PAROLE FIXER, 1940, A
PAROLE GIRL, 1933, A
PAROLE RACKET, 1937, A
PAROLE, INC., 1949, A
PAROLED FROM THE BIG HOUSE, 1938, A
PAROLED—TO DIE, 1938, A
PAROXISMUS
PARRISH, 1961, A
PARSIFAL, 1983, A
PARSON AND THE OUTLAW, THE, 1957, A
PARSON OF PANAMINT, THE, 1916, A
PARSON OF PANAMINT, THE, 1941, A
PARSON'S WIDOW, THE, 1920
PART 2, SOUNDER
PART 2, WALKING TALL
PART TIME WIFE, 1930, A
PART TIME WIFE, THE, 1925
PART-TIME WIFE, 1961
PARTED BY THE SWORD, 1915
PARTED CURTAINS, 1921
PARTING OF THE TRAILS, 1930
PARTINGS, 1962, A
PARTLY CONFIDENTIAL
PARTNER, THE, 1966, A
PARTNERS, 1932, A
PARTNERS, 1976, C
PARTNERS, 1982, O
PARTNERS AGAIN, 1926, A
PARTNERS AT LAST, 1916
PARTNERS IN CRIME, 1928, A
PARTNERS IN CRIME, 1937, A
PARTNERS IN CRIME, 1961
PARTNERS IN FORTUNE
PARTNERS IN TIME, 1946, A
PARTNERS OF FATE, 1921
PARTNERS OF THE NIGHT, 1920, A
PARTNERS OF THE PLAINS, 1938, A
PARTNERS OF THE SUNSET, 1922
PARTNERS OF THE SUNSET, 1948, A
PARTNERS OF THE TIDE, 1921, A
PARTNERS OF THE TRAIL, 1931, A
PARTNERS OF THE TRAIL, 1944, A
PARTNERS THREE, 1919
PARTS: THE CLONUS HORROR
PARTY CRASHERS, THE, 1958, A
PARTY GIRL, 1930, A
PARTY GIRL, 1958, C
PARTY GIRLS FOR THE CANDIDATE
PARTY HUSBAND, 1931, A

PARTY PARTY, 1983, C
PARTY WIRE, 1935, A
PARTY'S OVER, THE, 1966, O
PARTY, THE, 1968, A
PAS DE MENTALITE
PAS QUESTION LE SEMEDI
PASAZERKA
PASQUALE, 1916
PASQUALINO SETTEBELLEZZE
PASQUALINO: SEVEN BEAUTIES
PASS TO ROMANCE
PASSAGE FROM HONG KONG, 1941, A
PASSAGE HOME, 1955, A
PASSAGE OF LOVE
PASSAGE TO INDIA, A, 1984, C
PASSAGE TO MARSEILLE, 1944, A
PASSAGE WEST, 1951, A
PASSAGE, THE, 1979, O
PASSAGES FROM JAMES JOYCE'S FINNEGANS
     WAKE
PASSENGER TO LONDON, 1937, A
PASSENGER, THE, 1970, O
PASSENGER, THE, 1975, C
PASSERS-BY, 1916
PASSERS-BY, 1920
PASSIN' THROUGH
PASSING FANCY, 1933
PASSING OF MR. QUIN, THE, 1928, A
PASSING OF THE OKLAHOMA OUTLAWS, THE, 1915
PASSING OF THE THIRD FLOOR BACK, THE, 1918
PASSING OF THE THIRD FLOOR BACK, THE, 1936, A
PASSING OF WOLF MACLEAN, THE, 1924
PASSING SHADOWS, 1934, A
PASSING SHOW, THE
PASSING STRANGER, THE, 1954, A
PASSING THROUGH, 1977, O
PASSING THRU, 1921
PASSION, 1917
PASSION, 1920, A
PASSION, 1954, A
PASSION, 1968, O
PASSION, 1983, O
PASSION FLOWER, 1930, A
PASSION FLOWER, THE, 1921
PASSION FOR LIFE, 1951, A
PASSION FRUIT, 1921
PASSION HOLIDAY, 1963, C
PASSION IN THE SUN, 1964, O
PASSION ISLAND, 1927, A
PASSION ISLAND, 1943, A
PASSION OF A WOMAN TEACHER, THE, 1926
PASSION OF ANNA, THE, 1970, C
PASSION OF JOAN OF ARC, THE, 1928, A
PASSION OF LOVE, 1982, O
PASSION OF SLOW FIRE, THE, 1962, C
PASSION OF ST. FRANCIS, 1932
PASSION OF THE SUN
PASSION PIT, THE, 1965
PASSION PIT, THE, 1969
PASSION SONG, THE, 1928
PASSION STREET, U.S.A., 1964, C
PASSION'S PATHWAY, 1924
PASSION'S PLAYGROUND, 1920
PASSION, 1969
PASSIONATE ADVENTURE, THE, 1924, C
PASSIONATE DEMONS, THE, 1962, A
PASSIONATE FRIENDS, THE
PASSIONATE FRIENDS, THE, 1922, A
PASSIONATE PILGRIM, THE, 1921
PASSIONATE PLUMBER, 1932, A
PASSIONATE QUEST, THE, 1926
PASSIONATE SENTRY, THE, 1952, C
PASSIONATE STRANGER, THE
PASSIONATE STRANGERS, THE, 1968, C
PASSIONATE SUMMER, 1959, A
PASSIONATE SUNDAY
PASSIONATE THIEF, THE, 1963, A
PASSIONATE YOUTH, 1925, A
PASSIONE D'AMORE
PASSIONNEMENT, 1921
PASSKEY TO DANGER, 1946, A
PASSOVER PLOT, THE, 1976, C
PASSPORT HUSBAND, 1938, A
PASSPORT TO ADVENTURE
PASSPORT TO ALCATRAZ, 1940, A
PASSPORT TO CHINA, 1961, A
PASSPORT TO DESTINY, 1944, A
PASSPORT TO HEAVEN, 1943
PASSPORT TO HELL, 1932, A
PASSPORT TO HELL, 1940
PASSPORT TO OBLIVION
PASSPORT TO PARADISE, 1932
PASSPORT TO PIMLICO, 1949, A
PASSPORT TO SHAME
PASSPORT TO SUEZ, 1943, A
PASSPORT TO TREASON, 1956, A
PASSWORD IS COURAGE, THE, 1962, A
PAST OF MARY HOLMES, THE, 1933, A
PASTEBOARD CROWN, A, 1922
PASTEBOARD LOVER, THE
PASTEUR, 1922
PASTEUR, 1936, A

PERSONALITY, 1930, A
PERSONALITY KID, 1946, AA
PERSONALITY KID, THE, 1934, A
PERSONALS, THE, 1982, C
PERSONS IN HIDING,, 1939
PERSONS UNKNOWN
PERSUADER, THE, 1957, A
PERSUASIVE PEGGY, 1917, A
PERVYY DEN MIRA
PEST IN FLORENZ, 1919
PEST, THE, 1919, A
PETAL ON THE CURRENT, THE, 1919, C
PETE 'N' TILLIE, 1972, A-C
PETE KELLY'S BLUES, 1955, C
PETE'S DRAGON, 1977, AAA
PETER IBBETSON
PETER IBBETSON, 1935, A
PETER PAN, 1924, A
PETER PAN, 1953, AAA
PETER RABBIT AND TALES OF BEATRIX POTTER, 1971, AA
PETER THE CRAZY
PETER THE GREAT, 1923
PETERSEN, 1974, C
PETERVILLE DIAMOND, THE, 1942, A
PETEY WHEATSTRAW, 1978, O
PETIT ANGE, 1920
PETIT ANGE ET SON PANTIN, 1923
PETIT HOTEL A LOUER, 1923
PETITE FILLE, 1928
PETRIFIED FOREST, THE, 1936
PETS, 1974
PETTICOAT FEVER, 1936, A
PETTICOAT LARCENY, 1943, A
PETTICOAT LOOSE, 1922
PETTICOAT PILOT, A, 1918
PETTICOAT PIRATES, 1961, A
PETTICOAT POLITICS, 1941, A
PETTICOATS AND BLUEJEANS
PETTICOATS AND POLITICS, 1918
PETTIGREW'S GIRL, 1919
PETTY GIRL, THE, 1950, A
PETTY STORY, THE, 1974
PETULIA, 1968, C
PEYTON PLACE, 1957, C
PHAEDRA, 1962, C
PHANTASM, 1979, O
PHANTOM BROADCAST, THE, 1933, A
PHANTOM BUCCANEER, THE, 1916
PHANTOM BULLET, THE, 1926
PHANTOM BUSTER, THE, 1927
PHANTOM CARRIAGE, THE, 1921
PHANTOM CHARIOT, THE
PHANTOM CITY, THE, 1928
PHANTOM COWBOY, THE, 1935
PHANTOM COWBOY, THE, 1941, A
PHANTOM EXPRESS, THE, 1925
PHANTOM EXPRESS, THE, 1932, A
PHANTOM FIEND, 1966
PHANTOM FIEND, THE, 1935, A
PHANTOM FLYER, THE, 1928
PHANTOM FORTUNES, THE, 1916
PHANTOM FROM 10,000 LEAGUES, THE, 1956, A
PHANTOM FROM SPACE, 1953, A
PHANTOM GOLD, 1938, A
PHANTOM HONEYMOON, THE, 1919
PHANTOM HORSEMAN, THE
PHANTOM HORSEMAN, THE, 1924
PHANTOM HUSBAND, A, 1917
PHANTOM IN THE HOUSE, THE, 1929, A
PHANTOM JUSTICE, 1924
PHANTOM KID, THE, 1983
PHANTOM KILLER, 1942, A
PHANTOM LADY, 1944, C
PHANTOM LIGHT, THE, 1935, C
PHANTOM MELODY, THE, 1920
PHANTOM OF 42ND STREET, THE, 1945, A
PHANTOM OF CHINATOWN, 1940, A
PHANTOM OF CRESTWOOD, THE, 1932, A
PHANTOM OF LIBERTY, THE, 1974, O
PHANTOM OF PARIS, 1942
PHANTOM OF PARIS, THE, 1931, A
PHANTOM OF SANTA FE, 1937
PHANTOM OF SOHO, THE, 1967, C
PHANTOM OF TERROR, THE
PHANTOM OF THE AIS
PHANTOM OF THE DESERT, 1930, A
PHANTOM OF THE FOREST, THE, 1926
PHANTOM OF THE JUNGLE, 1955, A
PHANTOM OF THE MOULIN ROUGE, THE
PHANTOM OF THE NORTH, 1929, A
PHANTOM OF THE OPERA, 1943, A
PHANTOM OF THE OPERA, THE, 1925, A
PHANTOM OF THE OPERA, THE, 1929, A
PHANTOM OF THE OPERA, THE, 1962, C-O
PHANTOM OF THE PARADISE, 1974, A
PHANTOM OF THE PLAINS, 1945, A
PHANTOM OF THE RANGE, 1928, A
PHANTOM OF THE RANGE, THE, 1938, A
PHANTOM OF THE RUE MORGUE, 1954, C
PHANTOM OF THE TURF, 1928
PHANTOM PATROL, 1936, A

PHANTOM PICTURE, THE, 1916, A
PHANTOM PLAINSMEN, THE, 1942, A
PHANTOM PLANET, THE, 1961, A
PHANTOM PRESIDENT, THE, 1932, A
PHANTOM RAIDERS, 1940, A
PHANTOM RANCHER, 1940, A
PHANTOM RANGER, 1938, A
PHANTOM RANGER, THE
PHANTOM RIDER, THE, 1929, A
PHANTOM RIDERS, THE, 1918
PHANTOM SHADOWS, 1925
PHANTOM SHIP, 1937, A
PHANTOM SHOTGUN, THE, 1917
PHANTOM SPEAKS, THE, 1945, A
PHANTOM STAGE, THE, 1939, A
PHANTOM STAGECOACH, THE, 1957, A
PHANTOM STALLION, THE, 1954, A
PHANTOM STOCKMAN, THE, 1953
PHANTOM STRIKES, THE, 1939, A
PHANTOM THIEF, THE, 1946, A
PHANTOM THUNDERBOLT, THE, 1933, A
PHANTOM TOLLBOOTH, THE, 1970, AAA
PHANTOM VALLEY, 1948, A
PHANTOM'S SECRET, THE, 1917
PHANTOM, THE, 1916
PHANTOM, THE, 1922
PHAR LAP, 1984, C
PHARAOH'S CURSE, 1957, A
PHAROAH'S WOMAN, THE, 1961, A
PHASE IV, 1974, A
PHENIX CITY STORY, THE, 1955, C
PHFFFT!, 1954, A
PHIL-FOR-SHORT, 1919
PHILADELPHIA EXPERIMENT, THE, 1984, C
PHILADELPHIA HERE I COME, 1975
PHILADELPHIA STORY, THE, 1940
PHILIP
PHILIP HOLDEN -WASTER, 1916
PHILO VANCE RETURNS, 1947, A
PHILO VANCE'S GAMBLE, 1947, A
PHILO VANCE'S SECRET MISSION, 1947, A
PHOBIA, 1980, O
PHOBIA, 1981
PHOELIX, 1979
PHOENIX CITY STORY
PHONE CALL FROM A STRANGER, 1952, A-C
PHONY AMERICAN, THE, 1964, A
PHROSO, 1922
PHYLLIS OF THE FOLLIES, 1928, A
PHYNX, THE, 1970, C
PHYSICIAN, THE, 1928, C
PIAF—THE EARLY YEARS, 1982, A-C
PICCADILLY, 1932, A-C
PICCADILLY INCIDENT, 1948, A
PICCADILLY JIM, 1920
PICCADILLY JIM, 1936, A
PICCADILLY NIGHTS, 1930
PICCADILLY THIRD STOP, 1960, A
PICK A STAR, 1937, AAA
PICK-UP, 1933, A
PICK-UP, 1975
PICK-UP SUMMER, 1981, O
PICKPOCKET, 1963, A
PICKUP, 1951, A
PICKUP ALLEY, 1957, A
PICKUP IN ROME
PICKUP ON 101, 1972, C
PICKUP ON SOUTH STREET, 1953, C
PICKWICK PAPERS, THE, 1952, AA
PICNIC, 1955, A
PICNIC AT HANGING ROCK, 1975, C-O
PICNIC ON THE GRASS, 1960, C
PICTURE BRIDES, 1934, A
PICTURE MOMMY DEAD, 1966, O
PICTURE OF DORIAN GRAY, THE, 1915
PICTURE OF DORIAN GRAY, THE, 1916, C
PICTURE OF DORIAN GRAY, THE, 1917
PICTURE OF DORIAN GRAY, THE, 1945, C
PICTURE SHOW MAN, THE, 1980, C
PICTURE SNATCHER, 1933, A-C
PICTURES, 1982, A-C
PIDGIN ISLAND, 1916
PIE IN THE SKY, 1964, A
PIECE OF THE ACTION, A, 1977, C
PIECES, 1983, O
PIECES OF DREAMS, 1970, C
PIED PIPER MALONE, 1924
PIED PIPER OF HAMELIN, THE, 1917
PIED PIPER, THE, 1942, C
PIED PIPER, THE, 1972, C
PIED PIPER, THE, 1968
PIEGES
PIEL DE VERANO
PIER 13, 1940, A
PIER 13, 1932
PIER 23, 1951, A
PIER 5, HAVANA, 1959, A
PIERRE ET JEAN, 1924
PIERRE OF THE PLAINS, 1914, A
PIERRE OF THE PLAINS, 1942, A
PIERROT LE FOU, 1968, O
PIERROT PIERRETTE, 1924

PIGEON THAT TOOK ROME, THE, 1962; C
PIGEONS
PIGS, 1984, C
PIGS, THE
PIGSKIN PARADE, 1936, A
PIKOVAJA DAMA
PIKOVAYA DAMA
PILGRIM LADY, THE, 1947, A
PILGRIM, FAREWELL, 1980, C
PILGRIM, THE, 1923, A
PILGRIMAGE, 1933, A-C
PILGRIMAGE, 1972, C
PILGRIMS OF THE NIGHT, 1921
PILL, THE
PILLAR OF FIRE, THE, 1963, A
PILLARS OF SOCIETY, 1916
PILLARS OF SOCIETY, 1920
PILLARS OF SOCIETY, 1936, A
PILLARS OF THE SKY, 1956, A
PILLORY, THE, 1916
PILLOW OF DEATH, 1945, A
PILLOW TALK, 1959, A
PILLOW TO POST, 1945
PILOT NO. 5, 1943, A
PILOT, THE, 1979, C
PIMPERNEL SMITH, 1942, A
PIMPERNEL SVENSSON, 1953, A
PIMPLE'S THREE WEEKS, 1915
PIN UP GIRL, 1944, A
PINBALL PICK-UP
PINBALL SUMMER
PINCH HITTER, THE, 1917, A
PINCH HITTER, THE, 1925
PINK ANGELS, THE, 1971
PINK FLOYD—THE WALL, 1982, O
PINK GODS, 1922
PINK JUNGLE, THE, 1968, A
PINK MOTEL, 1983, O
PINK PANTHER STRIKES AGAIN, THE, 1976, A
PINK PANTHER, THE, 1964, A
PINK STRING AND SEALING WAX, 1950, A
PINK TIGHTS, 1920, A
PINKY, 1949, A
PINOCCHIO, 1940, AAA
PINOCCHIO, 1969, A
PINOCCHIO IN OUTER SPACE, 1965, AA
PINOCCHIO'S GREATEST ADVENTURE, 1974
PINOCCHIO'S STORYBOOK ADVENTURES, 1979
PINTO, 1920
PINTO BANDIT, THE, 1944, A
PINTO CANYON, 1940, AA
PINTO KID, THE, 1928
PINTO KID, THE, 1941, A
PINTO RUSTLERS, 1937, A
PIONEER BUILDERS
PIONEER DAYS, 1940, A
PIONEER JUSTICE, 1947, A
PIONEER MARSHAL, 1950, A
PIONEER SCOUT, THE, 1928, A
PIONEER TRAIL, 1938, A
PIONEER TRAILS, 1923
PIONEER'S GOLD, 1924
PIONEER, GO HOME
PIONEERS OF THE FRONTIER, 1940, A
PIONEERS OF THE WEST, 1927
PIONEERS OF THE WEST, 1929
PIONEERS OF THE WEST, 1940, A
PIONEERS, THE, 1941, A
PIPE DREAMS, 1976, C
PIPER'S PRICE, THE, 1917
PIPER'S TUNE, THE, 1962, AA
PIPER, THE
PIPES OF PAN, THE, 1923, C
PIPPI IN THE SOUTH SEAS, 1974, AAA
PIPPI ON THE RUN, 1977, AAA
PIRAHANA II: FLYING KILLERS
PIRANHA, 1978, O
PIRANHA II: THE SPAWNING, 1981, O
PIRANHA, PIRANHA, 1972
PIRATE AND THE SLAVE GIRL, THE, 1961, A
PIRATE HAUNTS, 1917
PIRATE MOVIE, THE, 1982, C
PIRATE OF THE BLACK HAWK, THE, 1961, A
PIRATE SHIP
PIRATE, THE, 1948, A
PIRATES OF BLOOD RIVER, THE, 1962, A
PIRATES OF CAPRI, THE, 1949, A
PIRATES OF MONTEREY, 1947, A
PIRATES OF PENZANCE, THE, 1983, A
PIRATES OF THE PRAIRIE, 1942, A
PIRATES OF THE SEVEN SEAS, 1941, A
PIRATES OF THE SKIES, 1939, A
PIRATES OF THE SKY, 1927, A
PIRATES OF TORTUGA, 1961, A
PIRATES OF TRIPOLI, 1955, A
PIRATES ON HORSEBACK, 1941, A
PISTOL FOR RINGO, A, 1966, C
PISTOL HARVEST, 1951, A
PISTOL PACKIN' MAMA, 1943, A
PISTOLERO
PIT AND THE PENDULUM, THE, 1961, C
PIT OF DARKNESS, 1961, A

PIT STOP, 1969, O
PIT, THE
PIT, THE, 1915
PIT, THE, 1984
PIT-BOY'S ROMANCE, A, 1917
PITFALL, 1948, C
PITFALL, THE, 1915
PITFALLS OF A BIG CITY, 1919
PITFALLS OF PASSION, 1927
PITTSBURGH, 1942, A
PITTSBURGH KID, THE, 1941, A
PITY ME NOT, 1960
PIXOTE, 1981, O
PIZZA TRIANGLE, THE, 1970, O
PLACE BEYOND THE WINDS, THE, 1916
PLACE CALLED GLORY, A, 1966
PLACE CALLED TRINITY, A, 1975
PLACE FOR LOVERS, A, 1969, C-O
PLACE IN THE SUN, A, 1916, C
PLACE IN THE SUN, A, 1951, C
PLACE OF HONOUR, THE, 1921, A
PLACE OF ONE'S OWN, A, 1945, A
PLACE OF THE HONEYMOONS, THE, 1920
PLACE TO GO, A, 1964, A
PLACE WITHOUT PARENTS, A, 1974
PLACES IN THE HEART, 1984, A-C
PLAGUE, 1978, C
PLAGUE DOGS, THE, 1982
PLAGUE DOGS, THE, 1984, C-O
PLAGUE OF THE ZOMBIES, THE, 1966, C
PLAGUE-M3: THE GEMINI STRAIN
PLAIN JANE, 1916
PLAINS OF HEAVEN, THE, 1982
PLAINSMAN AND THE LADY, 1946, A
PLAINSMAN, THE, 1937, C
PLAINSMAN, THE, 1966, A
PLAINSMAN, THE, 1964
PLAINSONG, 1982
PLAN 9 FROM OUTER SPACE, 1959, A
PLANET OF BLOOD, 1965
PLANET OF BLOOD, 1966
PLANET OF DINOSAURS, 1978, A
PLANET OF HORRORS
PLANET OF STORMS
PLANET OF THE APES, 1968, C
PLANET OF THE VAMPIRES, 1965, C
PLANET ON THE PROWL
PLANETS AGAINST US, THE, 1961, C
PLANK, THE, 1967, A
PLANTER'S WIFE, THE
PLANTER, THE, 1917
PLANTS ARE WATCHING US, THE
PLASTERED IN PARIS, 1928
PLASTIC AGE, THE, 1925, A
PLASTIC DOME OF NORMA JEAN, THE, 1966, C
PLATINUM BLONDE, 1931, A
PLATINUM HIGH SCHOOL, 1960, A
PLAY DEAD, 1981
PLAY DIRTY, 1969, C
PLAY GIRL, 1932, A
PLAY GIRL, 1940, A
PLAY GIRL, THE, 1928, A
PLAY IT AGAIN, SAM, 1972, C
PLAY IT AS IT LAYS, 1972, O
PLAY IT COOL, 1963, A
PLAY IT COOL, 1970, C
PLAY IT COOLER, 1961
PLAY MISTY FOR ME, 1971, O
PLAY SAFE, 1927, A
PLAY SQUARE, 1921
PLAY UP THE BAND, 1935
PLAYBACK, 1962, A
PLAYBOY OF PARIS, 1930, A
PLAYBOY OF THE WESTERN WORLD, THE, 1963, C
PLAYBOY, THE, 1942, AA
PLAYERS, 1979, A
PLAYERS, 1980
PLAYGIRL, 1954, A
PLAYGIRL AFTER DARK
PLAYGIRL AND THE WAR MINISTER, THE
PLAYGIRL KILLER
PLAYGIRL, 1968
PLAYGIRLS AND THE BELLBOY, THE, 1962, O
PLAYGIRLS AND THE VAMPIRE, 1964, O
PLAYGROUND, THE, 1965, O
PLAYING AROUND, 1930, A
PLAYING DEAD, 1915
PLAYING DOUBLE, 1923, A
PLAYING THE GAME
PLAYING THE GAME, 1918, A
PLAYING WITH FIRE, 1916
PLAYING WITH FIRE, 1921
PLAYING WITH SOULS, 1925
PLAYMATES, 1941, A
PLAYMATES, 1969, O
PLAYMATES, 1971
PLAYTHING OF BROADWAY, THE, 1921
PLAYTHING, THE, 1929, A
PLAYTHINGS, 1918
PLAYTHINGS OF DESIRE, 1924, A
PLAYTHINGS OF DESTINY, 1921, A
PLAYTHINGS OF HOLLYWOOD, 1931

PLAYTIME, 1963, C
PLAYTIME, 1973, AAA
PLAZA SUITE, 1971, A-C
PLEASANTVILLE, 1976, A
PLEASE BELIEVE ME, 1950, A
PLEASE DON'T EAT MY MOTHER, 1972
PLEASE DON'T EAT THE DAISIES, 1960, A
PLEASE GET MARRIED, 1919
PLEASE HELP EMILY, 1917
PLEASE MURDER ME, 1956, A
PLEASE SIR, 1971, A
PLEASE STAND BY, 1972, C
PLEASE TEACHER, 1937, A
PLEASE TURN OVER, 1960, C
PLEASE! MR. BALZAC, 1957, C
PLEASE, NOT NOW!, 1963, C
PLEASURE, 1933, A
PLEASURE BEFORE BUSINESS, 1927
PLEASURE BUYERS, THE, 1925
PLEASURE CRAZED, 1929, A
PLEASURE CRUISE, 1933, A
PLEASURE DOING BUSINESS, A, 1979
PLEASURE GARDEN, THE, 1925, A
PLEASURE GIRL
PLEASURE GIRLS, THE, 1966, C
PLEASURE LOVER
PLEASURE LOVERS, THE, 1964, C
PLEASURE MAD, 1923, C
PLEASURE OF HIS COMPANY, THE, 1961, A
PLEASURE PLANTATION, 1970, O
PLEASURE SEEKERS, 1920
PLEASURE SEEKERS, THE, 1964, A
PLEASURES AND VICES, 1962, C
PLEASURES OF THE FLESH, THE, 1965, C
PLEASURES OF THE RICH, 1926, A
PLEBIAN, 1915
PLEDGEMASTERS, THE, 1971, O
PLEIN SOLEIL
PLEIN SUD
PLEURE PAS LA BOUCHE PLEINE
PLEYDELL MYSTERY, THE, 1916, A
PLOT THICKENS, THE, 1936, A
PLOT THICKENS, THE, 1935
PLOT TO KILL ROOSEVELT, THE
PLOTTERS, THE, 1966
PLOUGH AND THE STARS, THE, 1936, A
PLOUGHMAN'S LUNCH, THE, 1984, O
PLOUGHSHARE, THE, 1915
PLOW GIRL, THE, 1916, A
PLOW WOMAN, THE, 1917
PLUCKED, 1969, C-O
PLUMBER, THE, 1980, C-O
PLUNDER, 1931, A
PLUNDER OF THE SUN, 1953, A
PLUNDER ROAD, 1957, A
PLUNDERER, THE, 1915, A
PLUNDERER, THE, 1924
PLUNDERERS OF PAINTED FLATS, 1959, A
PLUNDERERS, THE, 1948, A
PLUNDERERS, THE, 1960, A
PLUNGE INTO DARKNESS, 1977
PLUNGER, THE, 1920
PLUNGING HOOFS, 1929, A
PLYMOUTH ADVENTURE, 1952, AA
POACHER'S DAUGHTER, THE, 1960
POCATELLO KID, 1932, A
POCKET MONEY, 1972, A-C
POCKETFUL OF MIRACLES, 1961, AA
POCO—LITTLE DOG LOST, 1977
POCOMANIA, 1939, C
POE'S TALES OF HORROR
POET'S PUB, 1949, A
POI TI SPOSERO
POIL DE CAROTTE, 1926
POIL DE CAROTTE, 1932, A
POINT BLANK, 1967, O
POINT BLANK, 1962
POINT OF TERROR, 1971, O
POINT OF VIEW, THE, 1920
POINTED HEELS, 1930, A
POINTING FINGER, THE, 1919
POINTING FINGER, THE, 1922, A
POINTING FINGER, THE, 1934, A
POINTS WEST, 1929, A
POISON, 1924, A
POISON PEN, 1941, A
POISON PEN, THE, 1919
POISONED DIAMOND, THE, 1934
POISONED PARADISE: THE FORBIDDEN STORY OF
   MONTE CARLO, 1924
POITIN, 1979, A
POKER FACES, 1926
POLAR STAR, THE, 1919, A
POLICE ACADEMY, 1984, O
POLICE BULLETS, 1942, A
POLICE CALL, 1933, A
POLICE CAR 17, 1933
POLICE CONNECTION: DETECTIVE GERONIMO
POLICE COURT
POLICE DOG, 1955, A
POLICE DOG STORY, THE, 1961, A
POLICE NURSE, 1963

POLICE PATROL, THE, 1925, A
POLICE PYTHON 357, 1976, C
POLICEWOMAN, 1974
POLIKUSHKA, 1919
POLITIC FLAPPER, THE
POLITICAL ASYLUM, 1975, A
POLITICAL PARTY, A, 1933, A
POLITICIANS, THE, 1915
POLITICS, 1931, A
POLK COUNTY POT PLANE, 1977
POLLY ANN, 1917
POLLY FULTON
POLLY OF THE CIRCUS, 1917, A
POLLY OF THE CIRCUS, 1932, A
POLLY OF THE FOLLIES, 1922
POLLY OF THE MOVIES, 1927
POLLY OF THE STORM COUNTRY, 1920, A
POLLY PUT THE KETTLE ON, 1917
POLLY REDHEAD, 1917
POLLY WITH A PAST, 1920
POLLYANNA, 1920, A
POLLYANNA, 1960, AAA
POLO JOE, 1936, A
POLTERGEIST, 1982, C-O
POLYESTER, 1981, O
POM POM GIRLS, THE, 1976
POMOCNIK
PONCOMANIA
PONJOLA, 1923
PONTIUS PILATE, 1967, A
PONY EXPRESS, 1953, A
PONY EXPRESS RIDER, 1926, A
PONY EXPRESS RIDER, 1976, A
PONY EXPRESS, THE, 1925, A
PONY POST, 1940, A
PONY SOLDIER, 1952, A
POOKIE
POOL OF FLAME, THE, 1916
POOL OF LONDON, 1951, A
POOR ALBERT AND LITTLE ANNIE
POOR BOOB, 1919
POOR COW, 1968, C
POOR GIRL'S ROMANCE, A, 1926
POOR GIRLS, 1927
POOR LITTLE PEPPINA, 1916
POOR LITTLE RICH GIRL, 1936, A
POOR LITTLE RICH GIRL, 1965
POOR LITTLE RICH GIRL, A, 1917, A
POOR MEN'S WIVES, 1923, A
POOR MILLIONAIRE, THE, 1930
POOR NUT, THE, 1927
POOR OLD BILL, 1931, A
POOR OUTLAWS, THE
POOR PRETTY EDDIE, 1975
POOR RELATION, A, 1921
POOR RELATIONS, 1919, A
POOR RICH MAN, THE, 1918
POOR RICH, THE, 1934, A
POOR SCHMALTZ, 1915
POOR SIMP, THE, 1920
POOR WHITE TRASH
POOR WHITE TRASH II
POOR, DEAR MARGARET KIRBY, 1921
POP ALWAYS PAYS, 1940, A
POPDOWN, 1968
POPE JOAN, 1972, C
POPE OF GREENWICH VILLAGE, THE, 1984, O
POPE ONDINE STORY, THE
POPEYE, 1980, A
POPI, 1969, A
POPIOL Y DIAMENT
POPPIES OF FLANDERS, 1927, A
POPPY, 1917
POPPY, 1936, A
POPPY GIRL'S HUSBAND, THE, 1919, A
POPPY IS ALSO A FLOWER, THE, 1966, C
POPPY TRAIL, THE, 1920
POPSY POP, 1971, A
POPULAR SIN, THE, 1926
POR MIS PISTOLAS, 1969, A
POR UN PUNADO DE DOLARES
PORCELAIN LAMP, THE, 1921
PORGY AND BESS, 1959, A-C
PORI, 1930
PORK CHOP HILL, 1959, C
PORKY'S, 1982, O
PORKY'S II: THE NEXT DAY, 1983, O
PORRIDGE
PORT AFRIQUE, 1956, A
PORT DES LILAS
PORT O' DREAMS
PORT OF 40 THIEVES, THE, 1944, A
PORT OF CALL, 1963, C
PORT OF DESIRE, 1960, C
PORT OF DOOM, THE, 1913
PORT OF ESCAPE, 1955, A
PORT OF HATE, 1939, A
PORT OF HELL, 1955, A
PORT OF LOST DREAMS, 1935, A
PORT OF LOST SOULS, 1924
PORT OF MISSING GIRLS, 1938, A
PORT OF MISSING GIRLS, THE, 1928

PORT OF MISSING MEN, 1914, A
PORT OF MISSING WOMEN, THE, 1915
PORT OF NEW YORK, 1949, A
PORT OF SEVEN SEAS, 1938, A
PORT OF SHADOWS, 1938, A
PORT OF SHAME
PORT SAID, 1948, A
PORT SINISTER, 1953, A
PORTIA ON TRIAL, 1937, A
PORTLAND EXPOSE, 1957, A
PORTNOY'S COMPLAINT, 1972, O
PORTRAIT FROM LIFE
PORTRAIT IN BLACK, 1960, A-C
PORTRAIT IN SMOKE, 1957, O
PORTRAIT IN TERROR, 1965
PORTRAIT OF A HITMAN, 1984
PORTRAIT OF A MOBSTER, 1961, C
PORTRAIT OF A SINNER, 1961, C
PORTRAIT OF A WOMAN, 1946, A
PORTRAIT OF ALISON
PORTRAIT OF CHIEKO, 1968, A
PORTRAIT OF CLARE, 1951, A
PORTRAIT OF HELL, 1969, A
PORTRAIT OF INNOCENCE, 1948, A
PORTRAIT OF JASON, 1967
PORTRAIT OF JENNIE, 1949, A
PORTRAIT OF LENIN, 1967, A
PORTRAIT OF MARIA, 1946, C
PORTRAIT OF THE ARTIST AS A YOUNG MAN, A, 1979, A
PORTS OF CALL, 1925, A
POSEIDON ADVENTURE, THE, 1972, A
POSITIONS
POSITIONS OF LOVE
POSSE, 1975, C
POSSE FROM HEAVEN, 1975
POSSE FROM HELL, 1961, A
POSSESSED, 1931, A-C
POSSESSED, 1947, A-C
POSSESSION, 1919, A
POSSESSION, 1922
POSSESSION, 1981, O
POSSESSION OF JOEL DELANEY, THE, 1972, O
POST OFFICE INVESTIGATOR, 1949, A
POSTAL INSPECTOR, 1936, A
POSTMAN ALWAYS RINGS TWICE, THE, 1946, O
POSTMAN ALWAYS RINGS TWICE, THE, 1981, O
POSTMAN DIDN'T RING, THE, 1942, A
POSTMAN GOES TO WAR, THE, 1968, A
POSTMAN'S KNOCK, 1962, A
POSTMARK FOR DANGER, 1956, A
POSTORONNIM VKHOD VOSPRESHCHEN
POT CARRIERS, THE, 1962, A
POT LUCK, 1936, A
POT LUCK PARDS, 1924
POT O' GOLD, 1941, A
POT! PARENTS! POLICE!, 1975
POT-LUCK PARDS
POTASH AND PERLMUTTER, 1923
POTEMKIN
POTIPHAR'S WIFE
POTLUCK PARDS, 1934
POTS AND PANS PEGGIE, 1917
POTTER'S CLAY, 1922, A
POTTERS, THE, 1927, A
POTTERY GIRL'S ROMANCE, A, 1918
POUR EPOUSER GABY, 1917
POUR UNE NUIT, 1921
POURQUOI PAS!, 1979, C
POVERTY OF RICHES, THE, 1921, A
POWDER, 1916
POWDER MY BACK, 1928, A
POWDER RIVER, 1953, A
POWDER RIVER RUSTLERS, 1949, A
POWDER TOWN, 1942, A
POWDERSMOKE RANGE, 1935, A
POWER, 1928
POWER, 1934, A
POWER AND GLORY
POWER AND THE GLORY, THE, 1918
POWER AND THE GLORY, THE, 1933
POWER AND THE PRIZE, THE, 1956, A
POWER DIVE, 1941, A
POWER DIVINE, THE, 1923
POWER OF A LIE, THE, 1922
POWER OF DARKNESS, THE, 1918
POWER OF DECISION, THE, 1917, A
POWER OF EVIL, 1929
POWER OF EVIL, THE, 1916
POWER OF JUSTICE
POWER OF LIFE, THE, 1938
POWER OF LOVE, THE, 1922
POWER OF POSSESSION
POWER OF RIGHT, THE, 1919, A
POWER OF SILENCE, THE, 1928
POWER OF THE PRESS, THE, 1914
POWER OF THE PRESS, THE, 1928, A
POWER OF THE WEAK, THE, 1926, A
POWER OF THE WHISTLER, THE, 1945, A
POWER OVER MEN, 1929, A
POWER PLAY, 1978, C

POWER WITHIN, THE, 1921
POWER, THE, 1968, A
POWER, THE, 1984, O
POWERFORCE, 1983, O
POWERS GIRL, THE, 1942, A
POWERS THAT PREY, 1918
POZEGNANIA
PRACTICALLY YOURS, 1944, A
PRAIRIE BADMEN, 1946, A
PRAIRIE EXPRESS, 1957, A
PRAIRIE GUNSMOKE, 1942
PRAIRIE JUSTICE, 1938, A
PRAIRIE KING, THE, 1927
PRAIRIE LAW, 1940, A
PRAIRIE MOON, 1938
PRAIRIE MYSTERY, THE, 1922
PRAIRIE OUTLAWS, 1948
PRAIRIE PALS, 1942
PRAIRIE PIONEERS, 1941, A
PRAIRIE PIRATE, THE, 1925
PRAIRIE RAIDERS, 1947
PRAIRIE ROUNDUP, 1945, A
PRAIRIE RUSTLERS, 1945, A
PRAIRIE SCHOONERS, 1940, A
PRAIRIE STRANGER, 1941, A
PRAIRIE THUNDER, 1937, A
PRAIRIE TRAILS, 1920
PRAIRIE WIFE, THE, 1925, A
PRAIRIE, THE, 1948, A
PRAISE AGENT, THE, 1919, A
PRANKS, 1982
PRATLDWANDI
PRAYING MANTIS, 1982, C
PREACHERMAN, 1971, O
PREACHERMAN MEETS WIDDERWOMAN, 1973
PRECIOUS JEWELS, 1969
PRECIOUS PACKET, THE, 1916
PREHISTORIC MAN, THE, 1924, A
PREHISTORIC PLANET WOMEN
PREHISTORIC WOMEN, 1950, C
PREHISTORIC WOMEN, 1967, O
PREHISTORIC WORLD
PREJUDICE, 1922
PREJUDICE, 1949, A
PRELUDE TO ECSTASY, 1963, C
PRELUDE TO FAME, 1950, A
PRELUDE TO TAURUS, 1972
PREMATURE BURIAL, THE, 1962, C
PREMIERE
PREMONITION, 1972
PREMONITION, THE, 1976, C
PRENON: CARMEN
PREP AND PEP, 1928, A
PREPARED TO DIE, 1923, A
PREPPIES
PREPPIES, 1984, O
PRES DE CRIME, 1921
PRESCOTT KID, THE, 1936
PRESCRIPTION FOR ROMANCE, 1937, A
PRESENT ARMS
PRESENTING LILY MARS, 1943, A
PRESIDENT VANISHES, THE, 1934, A
PRESIDENT'S ANALYST, THE, 1967, O
PRESIDENT'S LADY, THE, 1953, A-C
PRESIDENT'S MYSTERY, THE, 1936, A
PRESIDENT, THE, 1918
PRESS FOR TIME, 1966, A
PRESSURE, 1976, C
PRESSURE OF GUILT, 1964, C
PRESSURE POINT, 1962, C
PRESTIGE, 1932, A
PRESUMPTION OF STANLEY HAY, MP, THE, 1925, A
PRETENDER, THE, 1918
PRETENDER, THE, 1947, A
PRETENDERS, THE, 1915
PRETENDERS, THE, 1916, A
PRETTY BABY, 1950, A
PRETTY BABY, 1978, O
PRETTY BOY FLOYD, 1960, C-O
PRETTY BUT WICKED, 1965, O
PRETTY CLOTHES, 1927, A
PRETTY LADIES, 1925, A
PRETTY MAIDS ALL IN A ROW, 1971, O
PRETTY MRS. SMITH, 1915, A
PRETTY POISON, 1968, C-O
PRETTY POLLY
PRETTY SISTER OF JOSE, 1915, A
PRETTY SMOOTH, 1919
PREVIEW MURDER MYSTERY, 1936, A
PREY OF THE DRAGON, THE, 1921
PREY, THE, 1920
PREY, THE, 1984, O
PRICE FOR FOLLY, A, 1915, A
PRICE MARK, THE, 1917, A
PRICE OF A GOOD TIME, THE, 1918
PRICE OF A PARTY, THE, 1924, A
PRICE OF A SONG, THE, 1935, A
PRICE OF APPLAUSE, THE, 1918
PRICE OF DIVORCE, THE, 1928
PRICE OF FAME, THE, 1916
PRICE OF FEAR, THE, 1928
PRICE OF FEAR, THE, 1956, A

PRICE OF FLESH, THE, 1962, O
PRICE OF FOLLY, THE, 1937, A
PRICE OF FREEDOM, THE
PRICE OF HAPPINESS, THE, 1916
PRICE OF HER HONOR, THE, 1927
PRICE OF HER SILENCE, THE, 1915
PRICE OF HER SOUL, THE, 1917
PRICE OF JUSTICE, THE, 1914
PRICE OF JUSTICE, THE, 1915
PRICE OF MALICE, THE, 1916
PRICE OF PLEASURE, THE, 1925
PRICE OF POSSESSION, THE, 1921
PRICE OF POWER, THE, 1916
PRICE OF POWER, THE, 1916
PRICE OF POWER, THE, 1969, C
PRICE OF PRIDE, THE, 1917
PRICE OF REDEMPTION, THE, 1920
PRICE OF SILENCE, THE, 1916
PRICE OF SILENCE, THE, 1917
PRICE OF SILENCE, THE, 1920, A
PRICE OF SILENCE, THE, 1960, A
PRICE OF SUCCESS, THE, 1925
PRICE OF THINGS, THE, 1930, A
PRICE OF WISDOM, THE, 1935, A
PRICE OF YOUTH, THE, 1922
PRICE SHE PAID, THE, 1917
PRICE SHE PAID, THE, 1924
PRICE WOMAN PAYS, THE, 1919
PRICE, THE, 1915
PRIDE, 1917
PRIDE AND PREJUDICE, 1940, A
PRIDE AND THE MAN, 1917
PRIDE AND THE PASSION, THE, 1957, C
PRIDE OF DONEGAL, THE, 1929, A
PRIDE OF JENNICO, THE, 1914, A
PRIDE OF KENTUCKY
PRIDE OF MARYLAND, 1951, A
PRIDE OF NEW YORK, THE, 1917
PRIDE OF PALOMAR, THE, 1922, A
PRIDE OF PAWNEE, THE, 1929
PRIDE OF ST. LOUIS, THE, 1952, AA
PRIDE OF SUNSHINE ALLEY, 1924, A
PRIDE OF THE ARMY, 1942, AA
PRIDE OF THE BLUE GRASS, 1954, A
PRIDE OF THE BLUEGRASS, 1939, AA
PRIDE OF THE BOWERY, 1941, A
PRIDE OF THE BOWERY, THE, 1946
PRIDE OF THE CLAN, THE, 1917, A
PRIDE OF THE FANCY, THE, 1920, A
PRIDE OF THE FORCE, THE, 1925, A
PRIDE OF THE FORCE, THE, 1933, A
PRIDE OF THE LEGION, THE, 1932, A
PRIDE OF THE MARINES, 1936, A
PRIDE OF THE MARINES, 1945, C
PRIDE OF THE NAVY, 1939, A
PRIDE OF THE NORTH, THE, 1920, A
PRIDE OF THE PLAINS, 1944, A
PRIDE OF THE WEST, 1938, A
PRIDE OF THE YANKEES, THE, 1942, AAA
PRIEST OF LOVE, 1981, O
PRIEST OF ST. PAULI, THE, 1970, C
PRIEST'S WIFE, THE, 1971, O
PRIMA DELLA REVOLUTIONA
PRIMA DONNA'S HUSBAND, THE, 1916
PRIMAL LAW, THE, 1921
PRIMAL LURE, THE, 1916, A
PRIME CUT, 1972, O
PRIME MINISTER, THE, 1941, A
PRIME OF MISS JEAN BRODIE, THE, 1969, C
PRIME TIME, THE, 1960, O
PRIMITIVE CALL, THE, 1917
PRIMITIVE LOVE, 1927
PRIMITIVE LOVE, 1966, O
PRIMITIVE LOVER, THE, 1922
PRIMITIVE WOMAN, THE, 1918
PRIMITIVES, THE, 1962, A
PRIMROSE PATH, 1940, C
PRIMROSE PATH, THE, 1915
PRIMROSE PATH, THE, 1925
PRIMROSE PATH, THE, 1934, A
PRIMROSE RING, THE, 1917
PRINCE AND BETTY, THE, 1919
PRINCE AND THE BEGGARMAID, THE, 1921, C
PRINCE AND THE DANCER, 1929
PRINCE AND THE PAUPER, THE, 1915, A
PRINCE AND THE PAUPER, THE, 1929
PRINCE AND THE PAUPER, THE, 1937, AAA
PRINCE AND THE PAUPER, THE, 1969, AA
PRINCE AND THE PAUPER, THE, 1978
PRINCE AND THE SHOWGIRL, THE, 1957, A
PRINCE CHAP, THE, 1916
PRINCE CHAP, THE, 1920
PRINCE EMBETE, 1920
PRINCE IN A PAWNSHOP, A, 1916, A
PRINCE OF A KING, A, 1923
PRINCE OF ARCADIA, 1933, AA
PRINCE OF AVENUE A., THE, 1920, A
PRINCE OF BROADWAY, THE, 1926
PRINCE OF DIAMONDS, 1930, A
PRINCE OF FOXES, 1949, C
PRINCE OF GRAUSTARK, THE, 1916
PRINCE OF HEADWAITERS, THE, 1927

PRINCE OF HEARTS, THE, 1929
PRINCE OF HIS RACE, THE, 1926
PRINCE OF INDIA, A, 1914, A
PRINCE OF LOVERS, A, 1922
PRINCE OF PEACE, THE, 1951, AAA
PRINCE OF PEANUTS
PRINCE OF PEP, THE, 1925
PRINCE OF PILSEN, THE, 1926, A
PRINCE OF PIRATES, 1953, A
PRINCE OF PLAYERS, 1955, C
PRINCE OF TEMPTERS, THE, 1926
PRINCE OF THE BLUE GRASS
PRINCE OF THE CITY, 1981, O
PRINCE OF THE PLAINS, 1927
PRINCE OF THE PLAINS, 1949, A
PRINCE OF THE SADDLE, 1926
PRINCE OF THIEVES, THE, 1948, A
PRINCE THERE WAS, A, 1921, A
PRINCE VALIANT, 1954, AA
PRINCE WHO WAS A THIEF, THE, 1951, A
PRINCE ZILAH, 1926
PRINCESS AND THE MAGIC FROG, THE, 1965, AAA
PRINCESS AND THE PIRATE, THE, 1944, A
PRINCESS AND THE PLUMBER, THE, 1930, A
PRINCESS CHARMING, 1935, A
PRINCESS COMES ACROSS, THE, 1936, A
PRINCESS FROM HOBOKEN, THE, 1927, A
PRINCESS JONES, 1921
PRINCESS O'HARA, 1935, A
PRINCESS O'ROURKE, 1943, A
PRINCESS OF BAGDAD, 1913
PRINCESS OF BROADWAY, THE, 1927
PRINCESS OF HAPPY CHANCE, THE, 1916, A
PRINCESS OF NEW YORK, THE, 1921
PRINCESS OF PARK ROW, THE, 1917
PRINCESS OF PATCHES, THE, 1917
PRINCESS OF THE DARK, 1928
PRINCESS OF THE DARK, A, 1917
PRINCESS OF THE NILE, 1954, AA
PRINCESS OLALA
PRINCESS ROMANOFF, 1915
PRINCESS VIRTUE, 1917
PRINCESS' NECKLACE, THE, 1917
PRINCESS, THE
PRINCESSE LULU, 1924
PRINCESSE MASHA, 1927
PRINSESSAN
PRINTEMPS D'AMOUR, 1927
PRINTER'S DEVIL, THE, 1923
PRIORITIES ON PARADE, 1942, A
PRISCA, 1921
PRISM, 1971, C
PRISM, 1971
PRISON BREAK, 1938, A
PRISON BREAKER, 1936, A
PRISON CAMP
PRISON FARM, 1938, A
PRISON GIRL, 1942, A
PRISON NURSE, 1938, A
PRISON SHADOWS, 1936, A
PRISON SHIP, 1945, C
PRISON TRAIN, 1938, A
PRISON WARDEN, 1949, A
PRISON WITHOUT BARS, 1939, A
PRISON WITHOUT WALLS, THE, 1917
PRISONER IN THE HAREM, THE, 1913
PRISONER OF CORBAL, 1939, C
PRISONER OF JAPAN, 1942, A
PRISONER OF SECOND AVENUE, THE, 1975, A-C
PRISONER OF SHARK ISLAND, THE, 1936, A
PRISONER OF THE CANNIBAL GOD, 1978
PRISONER OF THE IRON MASK, 1962, A
PRISONER OF THE PINES, 1918, A
PRISONER OF THE VOLGA, 1960, C
PRISONER OF WAR, 1954, C
PRISONER OF WAR, THE, 1918
PRISONER OF ZENDA, THE, 1915, A
PRISONER OF ZENDA, THE, 1922, A
PRISONER OF ZENDA, THE, 1937, A
PRISONER OF ZENDA, THE, 1952
PRISONER OF ZENDA, THE, 1979, A
PRISONER, THE, 1923, A
PRISONER, THE, 1955, C
PRISONERS, 1929, A
PRISONERS, 1975
PRISONERS IN PETTICOATS, 1950, A
PRISONERS OF LOVE, 1921, C
PRISONERS OF THE CASBAH, 1953, A
PRISONERS OF THE SEA, 1929
PRISONERS OF THE STORM, 1926
PRIVATE AFFAIRS, 1925
PRIVATE AFFAIRS, 1940, A
PRIVATE AFFAIRS OF BEL AMI, THE, 1947, A
PRIVATE AFFAIRS, 1935
PRIVATE ANGELO, 1949, A
PRIVATE BENJAMIN, 1980, O
PRIVATE BUCKAROO, 1942, A
PRIVATE COLLECTION, 1972, O
PRIVATE DETECTIVE, 1939, A
PRIVATE DETECTIVE 62, 1933, A
PRIVATE DUTY NURSES, 1972, O
PRIVATE ENTERPRISE, A, 1975, A

PRIVATE EYES, 1953, A
PRIVATE EYES, THE, 1980, A
PRIVATE FILES OF J. EDGAR HOOVER, THE, 1978, C
PRIVATE HELL 36, 1954, C
PRIVATE INFORMATION, 1952, A
PRIVATE IZZY MURPHY, 1926, A
PRIVATE JONES, 1933, A
PRIVATE LESSONS, 1981, O
PRIVATE LIFE
PRIVATE LIFE OF DON JUAN, THE, 1934, A
PRIVATE LIFE OF HELEN OF TROY, THE, 1927
PRIVATE LIFE OF HENRY VIII, THE, 1933, A-C
PRIVATE LIFE OF LOUIS XIV, 1936, A
PRIVATE LIFE OF SHERLOCK HOLMES, THE, 1970, C
PRIVATE LIVES, 1931, A
PRIVATE LIVES OF ADAM AND EVE, THE, 1961
PRIVATE LIVES OF ELIZABETH AND ESSEX, THE, 1939, A
PRIVATE NAVY OF SGT. O'FARRELL, THE, 1968, A
PRIVATE NUMBER, 1936, A
PRIVATE NURSE, 1941, A
PRIVATE PARTS, 1972, O
PRIVATE PEAT, 1918, A
PRIVATE POOLEY, 1962, C
PRIVATE POTTER, 1963, A-C
PRIVATE PROPERTY, 1960, O
PRIVATE RIGHT, THE, 1967
PRIVATE ROAD, 1971, O
PRIVATE SCANDAL, 1934, A
PRIVATE SCANDAL, A, 1921, A
PRIVATE SCANDAL, A, 1932, A
PRIVATE SCHOOL, 1983, O
PRIVATE SECRETARY, THE, 1935, A
PRIVATE SNUFFY SMITH
PRIVATE WAR OF MAJOR BENSON, THE, 1955, A
PRIVATE WORE SKIRTS, THE
PRIVATE WORLDS, 1935, A-C
PRIVATE'S AFFAIR, A, 1959, A
PRIVATE'S PROGRESS, 1956, A
PRIVATES ON PARADE, 1982, O
PRIVATES ON PARADE, 1984, O
PRIVATKLINIK PROF. LUND
PRIVILEGE, 1967, A
PRIVILEGED, 1982, C-O
PRIZE FIGHTER, THE, 1979, C
PRIZE OF ARMS, A, 1962, A
PRIZE OF GOLD, A, 1955, A
PRIZE, THE, 1952, A
PRIZE, THE, 1963, C
PRIZED AS A MATE!
PRIZEFIGHTER AND THE LADY, THE, 1933, A
PRO, THE
PROBATION, 1932, A
PROBATION WIFE, THE, 1919
PROBLEM GIRLS, 1953, A
PROCES DE JEANNE D'ARC
PRODIGAL DAUGHTER, THE, 1916
PRODIGAL DAUGHTERS, 1923
PRODIGAL GUN
PRODIGAL JUDGE, THE, 1922
PRODIGAL LIAR, THE, 1919
PRODIGAL SON, THE, 1923, A
PRODIGAL SON, THE, 1935
PRODIGAL SON, THE, 1964, C
PRODIGAL WIFE, THE, 1918, C
PRODIGAL, THE, 1931, A
PRODIGAL, THE, 1955, A-C
PRODIGAL, THE, 1984, A
PRODUCERS, THE, 1967, O
PROFESSIONAL BLONDE
PROFESSIONAL BRIDE
PROFESSIONAL GUN, A
PROFESSIONAL SOLDIER, 1936, A
PROFESSIONAL SWEETHEART, 1933, A
PROFESSIONALS, THE, 1960
PROFESSIONALS, THE, 1966, O
PROFESSOR BEWARE, 1938, A
PROFESSOR CREEPS, 1942
PROFESSOR TIM, 1957, A
PROFILE, 1954, A
PROFILE OF TERROR, THE
PROFIT AND THE LOSS, 1917, A
PROFITEER, THE, 1919
PROFITEERS, THE, 1919
PROFLIGATE, THE, 1917, C
PROHIBITION, 1915, A
PROJECT M7, 1953, A
PROJECT MOONBASE, 1953, A
PROJECT X, 1949, A
PROJECT X, 1968
PROJECT: KILL, 1976, O
PROJECTED MAN, THE, 1967, A
PROJECTIONIST, THE, 1970, A-C
PROLOGUE, 1970, C
PROM NIGHT, 1980, O
PROMISE AT DAWN, 1970, A
PROMISE HER ANYTHING, 1966, A
PROMISE HER ANYTHING, 1963
PROMISE OF A BED, A
PROMISE, THE, 1917
PROMISE, THE, 1969, A
PROMISE, THE, 1979, A-C

PROMISED LAND, THE, 1925
PROMISES IN THE DARK, 1979, C
PROMISES, PROMISES, 1963, O
PROMOTER, THE, 1952, A
PROPER TIME, THE, 1959
PROPERTY, 1979
PROPHECIES OF NOSTRADAMUS, 1974, C
PROPHECY, 1979, C-O
PROPHET'S PARADISE, THE, 1922
PROPHET, THE, 1976
PROSPERITY, 1932, A
PROSTITUTE, 1980, O
PROSTITUTION, 1965, C
PROTECT US, 1914
PROTECTION, 1929, A
PROTECTORS, BOOK 1, THE, 1981, O
PROTECTORS, THE
PROTOCOL, 1984, A-C
PROUD AND THE DAMNED, THE, 1972, C-O
PROUD AND THE PROFANE, THE, 1956, A-C
PROUD FLESH, 1925, A
PROUD HEART
PROUD ONES, THE, 1956, A
PROUD REBEL, THE, 1958, A
PROUD RIDER, THE, 1971, C
PROUD VALLEY, THE, 1941, A
PROUD, DAMNED AND DEAD
PROVIDENCE, 1977, O
PROWL GIRLS, 1968
PROWLER, THE, 1951, C-O
PROWLER, THE, 1981, O
PROWLERS OF THE NIGHT, 1926, A
PROWLERS OF THE SEA, 1928
PROXIES, 1921
PRUDENCE AND THE PILL, 1968, O
PRUDENCE ON BROADWAY, 1919
PRUDENCE THE PIRATE, 1916
PRUDES FALL, THE, 1924, A
PRUNELLA, 1918, A
PRUSSIAN CUR, THE, 1918
PSI FACTOR, 1980
PSYCH-OUT, 1968, O
PSYCHE 59, 1964, C
PSYCHIC KILLER, 1975, O
PSYCHIC LOVER, THE
PSYCHIC, THE, 1979, O
PSYCHO, 1960, O
PSYCHO A GO-GO!, 1965, O
PSYCHO FROM TEXAS, 1982, O
PSYCHO II, 1983, O
PSYCHO KILLERS
PSYCHO LOVER, 1969
PSYCHO SISTERS, 1972
PSYCHO-CIRCUS, 1967, O
PSYCHOMANIA, 1964, O
PSYCHOMANIA, 1974, O
PSYCHOPATH, THE, 1966, O
PSYCHOPATH, THE, 1973, O
PSYCHOTRONIC MAN, THE, 1980, O
PSYCHOUT FOR MURDER, 1971, O
PSYCOSISSIMO, 1962, O
PT 109, 1963, A
PT RAIDERS
PT RAIDERS
PUBERTY BLUES, 1983, O
PUBLIC AFFAIR, A, 1962, C
PUBLIC BE DAMNED, 1917
PUBLIC BE HANGED, THE
PUBLIC COWBOY NO. 1, 1937, A
PUBLIC DEB NO. 1, 1940, C
PUBLIC DEFENDER, 1917
PUBLIC DEFENDER, THE, 1931, A
PUBLIC ENEMIES, 1941, A
PUBLIC ENEMY'S WIFE, 1936, A
PUBLIC ENEMY, THE, 1931, O
PUBLIC EYE, THE, 1972, A
PUBLIC HERO No. 1, 1935, A
PUBLIC LIFE OF HENRY THE NINTH, THE, 1934
PUBLIC MENACE, 1935, C
PUBLIC NUISANCE NO. 1, 1936, A
PUBLIC OPINION, 1916
PUBLIC OPINION, 1935, A
PUBLIC PIGEON NO. 1, 1957, A
PUBLIC PROSECUTOR, 1917
PUBLIC STENOGRAPHER, 1935, C
PUBLIC WEDDING, 1937, A
PUBLICITY MADNESS, 1927
PUDD'NHEAD WILSON, 1916
PUDDIN' HEAD, 1941, AAA
PUEBLO TERROR, 1931
PUFNSTUF, 1970, AAA
PULCINELLA, 1925
PULGARCITO
PULP, 1972, C
PULSE OF LIFE, THE, 1917
PUMA MAN, THE, 1980
PUMPKIN, 1928
PUMPKIN EATER, THE, 1964
PUNCH AND JUDY MAN, THE, 1963, A
PUNISHMENT PARK, 1971, O
PUO UNA MORTA RIVIVERE PER AMORE?
PUPPET CROWN, THE, 1915, A

PUPPET MAN, THE, 1921, C
PUPPET ON A CHAIN, 1971, O
PUPPETS, 1926, A
PUPPETS OF FATE
PUPPETS OF FATE
PUPPETS OF FATE, 1921
PUPPY LOVE, 1919
PURCHASE PRICE, THE, 1932, O
PURE GRIT, 1923, A
PURE HELL OF ST. TRINIAN'S, THE, 1961, C
PURE S, 1976, O
PURITAN PASSIONS, 1923
PURITY, 1916
PURLIE VICTORIOUS
PURPLE CIPHER, THE, 1920, A
PURPLE DAWN, 1923
PURPLE GANG, THE, 1960, O
PURPLE HAZE, 1982, O
PURPLE HEART DIARY, 1951, A
PURPLE HEART, THE, 1944, C-O
PURPLE HEARTS, 1984, C-O
PURPLE HIGHWAY, THE, 1923
PURPLE HILLS, THE, 1961, O
PURPLE LADY, THE, 1916
PURPLE LILY, THE, 1918
PURPLE MASK, THE, 1955, A
PURPLE NOON, 1961, O
PURPLE PLAIN, THE, 1954, A-C
PURPLE RAIN, 1984, O
PURPLE RIDERS, THE
PURPLE TAXI, THE, 1977
PURPLE V, THE, 1943, O
PURPLE VIGILANTES, THE, 1938, A
PURSE STRINGS, 1933, A
PURSUED, 1925
PURSUED, 1934, A
PURSUED, 1947, C-O
PURSUERS, THE, 1961, A
PURSUING VENGEANCE, THE, 1916, A
PURSUIT, 1935, A
PURSUIT, 1975, O
PURSUIT OF D.B. COOPER, THE, 1981, C
PURSUIT OF HAPPINESS, THE, 1934, C
PURSUIT OF HAPPINESS, THE, 1971, O
PURSUIT OF PAMELA, THE, 1920, C
PURSUIT OF THE GRAF SPEE, 1957, A
PURSUIT OF THE PHANTOM, THE, 1914, A
PURSUIT TO ALGIERS, 1945, A
PUSHER, THE, 1960, O
PUSHERS, THE
PUSHING UP DAISIES, 1971
PUSHOVER, 1954, A
PUSHOVER, THE
PUSS AND KRAM
PUSS OCH KRAM
PUSS 'N' BOOTS, 1964, AAA
PUSS 'N' BOOTS, 1967, AAA
PUSSYCAT ALLEY, 1965, O
PUSSYCAT, PUSSYCAT, I LOVE YOU, 1970, O
PUSUIT OF POLLY
PUT 'EM UP, 1928
PUT ON THE SPOT, 1936, A
PUT UP OR SHUT UP, 1968, O
PUT UP YOUR HANDS, 1919
PUTNEY SWOPE, 1969, O
PUTTIN' ON THE RITZ, 1930, A
PUTTING IT OVER, 1919, A
PUTTING IT OVER, 1922, A
PUTTING ONE OVER, 1919
PUTTING THE BEE IN HERBERT, 1917
PUTYOVKA V ZHIZN
PUZZLE OF A DOWNFALL CHILD, 1970, O
PYGMALION, 1938, A
PYGMY ISLAND, 1950, A
PYRAMID, THE, 1976
PYRO, 1964, O
PYRO-THE THING WITHOUT A FACE
PYX, THE, 1973, O

-Q-

Q, 1982, O
Q PLANES
Q-SHIPS
*QUACKSER FORTUNE HAS A COUSIN IN THE
    BRONX*, 1970, A-C
QUADROON, 1972, O
QUADROPHENIA, 1979, O
QUAI DE GRENELLE
QUAI DES BRUMES
QUALIFIED ADVENTURER, THE, 1925, A
QUALITY OF FAITH, THE, 1916
QUALITY STREET, 1927, A
QUALITY STREET, 1937, A
QUAND NOUS ETIONS DEUX, 1929
QUANDO EL AMOR RIE, 1933
QUANTEZ, 1957, A
QUANTRILL'S RAIDERS, 1958, A
QUARANTINED RIVALS, 1927
QUARE FELLOW, THE, 1962, C-O
QUARTERBACK, THE, 1926, A
QUARTERBACK, THE, 1940, A
QUARTET, 1949, C

QUARTET, 1981, C
QUATERMASS AND THE PIT
QUATERMASS CONCLUSION, 1980, C
QUATERMASS EXPERIMENT, THE
QUATERMASS II
QUATRE-VINGT TREIZE, 1921
QUE LA BETE MEURE
QUE LA FETE COMMENCE
QUEBEC, 1951, A
QUEEN BEE
QUEEN BEE, 1955, C
QUEEN BOXER, THE, 1973
QUEEN CHRISTINA, 1933, A
QUEEN ELIZABETH, 1912, A
QUEEN FOR A DAY, 1951, A
QUEEN HIGH, 1930, A
QUEEN KELLY, 1929, A
QUEEN MOTHER, THE, 1916, A
QUEEN O' DIAMONDS, 1926, A
QUEEN O' TURF, 1922
QUEEN OF ATLANTIS
QUEEN OF BABYLON, THE, 1956, A
QUEEN OF BLOOD, 1966, O
QUEEN OF BROADWAY, 1942, A
QUEEN OF BROADWAY, 1943
QUEEN OF BURLESQUE, 1946, C
QUEEN OF CLUBS
QUEEN OF CRIME
QUEEN OF DESTINY
QUEEN OF HEARTS, 1936, A
QUEEN OF HEARTS, THE, 1918
QUEEN OF MY HEART, 1917, C
QUEEN OF OUTER SPACE, 1958, A
QUEEN OF SHEBA, 1953, C
QUEEN OF SHEBA MEETS THE ATOM MAN, THE,
    1963
QUEEN OF SHEBA, THE, 1921, A
QUEEN OF SIN AND THE SPECTACLE OF SODOM
    AND GOMORRAH, THE (1923, Aust.)
QUEEN OF SIN, THE
QUEEN OF SPADES, 1925
QUEEN OF SPADES, 1948, A-C
QUEEN OF SPADES, 1961, C
QUEEN OF SPADES, THE, 1916
QUEEN OF SPIES
QUEEN OF THE AMAZONS, 1947, A
QUEEN OF THE CANNIBALS
QUEEN OF THE CHORUS, 1928
QUEEN OF THE MOB, 1940, C
QUEEN OF THE MOULIN ROUGE, 1922
QUEEN OF THE NIGHTCLUBS, 1929, A-C
QUEEN OF THE NILE, 1964, C
QUEEN OF THE PIRATES, 1961, C
QUEEN OF THE SCREEN, 1916
QUEEN OF THE SEA, 1918
QUEEN OF THE SEAS, 1960
QUEEN OF THE SMUGGLERS, THE, 1914
QUEEN OF THE WEST
QUEEN OF THE WICKED, 1916, A
QUEEN OF THE YUKON, 1940, A
QUEEN WAS IN THE PARLOUR, THE
QUEEN X, 1917
QUEEN'S AFFAIR, THE
QUEEN'S EVIDENCE, 1919
QUEEN'S GUARDS, THE, 1963, C
QUEEN'S HUSBAND, THE
QUEEN'S SECRET, THE, 1919
QUEEN'S SWORDSMEN, THE, 1963, AAA
QUEENIE, 1921, A
QUEENS, THE, 1968, O
QUEER CARGO
QUEI DISPERATI CHE PUZZANO DI SUDORE E DI
    MORTE
QUEI TEMERARI SULLE LORO PAZZE, SCATENATE,
    SCALCINATE CARRIOLE
QUEIMADA
QUELLA VILLA ACCANTO AL CIMITERO
QUELLI CHE NON MUOIONO
QUELQU'UN DERRIERE LA PORTE
QUELQUES JOURS PRES
QUEMADA!
QUENTIN DURWARD, 1955, A
QUERELLE, 1983, O
QUERY, 1945, O
QUEST FOR FIRE, 1982, O
QUEST FOR LOVE, 1971, C
QUEST OF LIFE, THE, 1916, A
QUEST OF THE SACRED GEM, THE, 1914
QUEST, THE, 1915
QUESTI FANTASMI
QUESTION 7, 1961, C
QUESTION OF ADULTERY, A, 1959, C
QUESTION OF HONOR, A, 1922, A
QUESTION OF SILENCE, 1984, O
QUESTION OF SUSPENSE, A, 1961, C
QUESTION OF TRUST, A, 1920, A
QUESTION, THE, 1916, C
QUESTION, THE, 1917
QUESTION, THE, 1977, O
QUESTIONE DI PELLE
QUI A TUE, 1919
QUICK ACTION, 1921

QUICK AND THE DEAD, THE, 1963, O
QUICK CHANGE, 1925
QUICK GUN, THE, 1964, A
QUICK MILLIONS, 1931, C
QUICK MILLIONS, 1939, A
QUICK MONEY, 1938, A
QUICK ON THE TRIGGER, 1949, A
QUICK TRIGGER LEE, 1931
QUICK TRIGGERS, 1928
QUICK, BEFORE IT MELTS, 1964, A
QUICK, LET'S GET MARRIED, 1965, C
QUICKENING FLAME, THE, 1919
QUICKER'N LIGHTNIN', 1925, A
QUICKSAND, 1950, C
QUICKSANDS, 1917
QUICKSANDS, 1918, A
QUICKSANDS, 1923
QUICKSANDS OF LIFE, 1915
QUIEN SABE?
QUIET AMERICAN, THE, 1958, A
QUIET DAY IN BELFAST, A, 1974, C
QUIET GUN, THE, 1957, A
QUIET MAN, THE, 1952, A
QUIET PLACE IN THE COUNTRY, A, 1970, O
QUIET PLEASE, 1938, A
QUIET PLEASE, MURDER, 1942, A
QUIET WEDDING, 1941, A
QUIET WEEKEND, 1948, A
QUIET WOMAN, THE, 1951, A
QUILLER MEMORANDUM, THE, 1966, C
QUINCANNON, FRONTIER SCOUT, 1956, A
QUINCY ADAMS SAWYER, 1922
QUINCY ADAMS SAWYER AND MASON'S CORNER
    FOLKS (1912)
QUINTET, 1979, C-O
QUITTER, THE
QUITTER, THE, 1916
QUITTER, THE, 1929
QUITTERS, THE, 1934
QUO VADIS, 1951
QUO VADIS?, 1913, A
QUO VADIS?, 1925

-R-

R.P.M., 1970, C
R.S.V.P., 1921
R.S.V.P., 1984
RABBI AND THE SHIKSE, THE, 1976, A
RABBIT TEST, 1978, C-O
RABBIT TRAP, THE, 1959, A
RABBIT, RUN, 1970, O
RABBLE, THE, 1965, A
RABID, 1976, O
RACCONTI D'ESTATE
RACE FOR LIFE, A, 1928
RACE FOR LIFE, A, 1955, A
RACE FOR THE YANKEE ZEPHYR
RACE FOR YOUR LIFE, CHARLIE BROWN, 1977, AAA
RACE GANG
RACE STREET, 1948, C
RACE SUICIDE, 1916
RACE WILD, 1926
RACE WITH THE DEVIL, 1975, C
RACE, THE, 1916, A
RACERS, THE, 1955, A
RACHEL AND THE STRANGER, 1948, A
RACHEL CADE
RACHEL'S MAN, 1974
RACHEL, RACHEL, 1968, A-C
RACING BLOOD, 1926
RACING BLOOD, 1938, A
RACING BLOOD, 1954, A
RACING FEVER, 1964, C
RACING FOOL, THE, 1927
RACING FOR LIFE, 1924, A
RACING HEARTS, 1923, A
RACING LADY, 1937, A
RACING LUCK, 1924
RACING LUCK, 1935, A
RACING LUCK, 1948, A
RACING LUCK, 1935
RACING ROMANCE, 1926, A
RACING ROMANCE, 1927
RACING ROMANCE, 1937, A
RACING ROMEO, 1927, A
RACING STRAIN, 1919
RACING STRAIN, THE, 1933, A
RACING WITH THE MOON, 1984, C
RACING YOUTH, 1932
RACK, THE, 1956, A
RACKET MAN, THE, 1944, A
RACKET, THE, 1928, A
RACKET, THE, 1951, C
RACKETEER ROUND-UP, 1934
RACKETEER, THE, 1929, A
RACKETEERS IN EXILE, 1937, A
RACKETEERS OF THE RANGE, 1939, A
RACKETY RAX, 1932, A
RACQUET, 1979, O
RADAN
RADAR SECRET SERVICE, 1950, A

RADIO CAB MURDER, 1954, A
RADIO CITY REVELS, 1938, A
RADIO FLYER, THE, 1924
RADIO FOLLIES, 1935, A
RADIO LOVER, 1936, A
RADIO MURDER MYSTERY, THE
RADIO ON, 1980, C
RADIO PARADE OF 1935
RADIO PATROL, 1932, A
RADIO PIRATES, 1935, A
RADIO REVELS OF 1942
RADIO STAR, THE
RADIO STARS ON PARADE, 1945, A
RADIO-MANIA, 1923
RADIOGRAFIA D'UN COLPO D'ORO
RADISHES AND CARROTS
RADON
RADON THE FLYING MONSTER
RAFFERTY AND THE GOLD DUST TWINS, 1975, C-O
RAFFICA DI COLTELLI
RAFFLES, 1930, A
RAFFLES, 1939, A
RAFFLES, THE AMATEUR CRACKSMAN, 1917
RAFFLES, THE AMATEUR CRACKSMAN, 1925, A
RAFTER ROMANCE, 1934, A
RAG DOLL
RAG MAN, THE, 1925, A
RAGE, 1966, C
RAGE, 1972, C
RAGE, 1984
RAGE AT DAWN, 1955, A
RAGE IN HEAVEN, 1941, C
RAGE OF PARIS, THE, 1921, A
RAGE OF PARIS, THE, 1938, A
RAGE OF THE BUCCANEERS, 1963, A
RAGE TO LIVE, A, 1965, C
RAGE WITHIN, THE
RAGE, 1976
RAGE, THE, 1963
RAGGED ANGELS
RAGGED EARL, THE, 1914
RAGGED EDGE, THE, 1923, A
RAGGED HEIRESS, THE, 1922, A
RAGGED MESSENGER, THE, 1917, C
RAGGED PRINCESS, THE, 1916
RAGGED ROBIN, 1924
RAGGEDY ANN AND ANDY, 1977, AAA
RAGGEDY MAN, 1981, C
RAGGEDY QUEEN, THE, 1917
RAGING BULL, 1980, O
RAGING MOON, THE
RAGING TIDE, THE, 1951, A
RAGING WATERS
RAGMAN'S DAUGHTER, THE, 1974, C
RAGS, 1915, A
RAGS TO RICHES, 1922, A
RAGS TO RICHES, 1941, A
RAGTIME, 1927, A
RAGTIME, 1981, C
RAGTIME COWBOY JOE, 1940, A
RAID ON ROMMEL, 1971, C
RAID, THE, 1954, A-C
RAIDERS FROM BENEATH THE SEA, 1964, A
RAIDERS OF ATLANTIS, 1983
RAIDERS OF LEYTE GULF, 1963, A
RAIDERS OF OLD CALIFORNIA, 1957, A
RAIDERS OF RED GAP, 1944, A
RAIDERS OF SAN JOAQUIN, 1943, A
RAIDERS OF SUNSET PASS, 1943, A
RAIDERS OF THE BORDER, 1944, A
RAIDERS OF THE DESERT, 1941, A
RAIDERS OF THE LOST ARK, 1981, C-O
RAIDERS OF THE RANGE, 1942, A
RAIDERS OF THE SEVEN SEAS, 1953, A
RAIDERS OF THE SOUTH, 1947, A
RAIDERS OF THE WEST, 1942, A
RAIDERS OF TOMAHAWK CREEK, 1950, A
RAIDERS, THE, 1916
RAIDERS, THE, 1921, A
RAIDERS, THE, 1952, A
RAIDERS, THE, 1964, A
RAIL RIDER, THE, 1916
RAILROAD MAN, THE, 1965, A
RAILROAD WORKERS, 1948, A
RAILROADED, 1923, A
RAILROADED, 1947, C
RAILROADER, THE, 1919
RAILS INTO LARAMIE, 1954, A
RAILWAY CHILDREN, THE, 1971, A
RAIN, 1932, C-O
RAIN FOR A DUSTY SUMMER, 1971, C
RAIN OR SHINE, 1930, A
RAIN PEOPLE, THE, 1969, C-O
RAINBOW, 1921, A
RAINBOW 'ROUND MY SHOULDER, 1952, A
RAINBOW BOYS, THE, 1973, A
RAINBOW BRIDGE, 1972
RAINBOW GIRL, THE, 1917
RAINBOW ISLAND, 1944, A
RAINBOW JACKET, THE, 1954, A
RAINBOW MAN, 1929, A
RAINBOW ON THE RIVER, 1936, A

RAINBOW OVER BROADWAY, 1933, A
RAINBOW OVER TEXAS, 1946, A
RAINBOW OVER THE RANGE, 1940, A
RAINBOW OVER THE ROCKIES, 1947, A
RAINBOW PRINCESS, THE, 1916, A
RAINBOW RANCH, 1933, A
RAINBOW RANGE, 1929
RAINBOW RANGERS, 1924, A
RAINBOW RILEY, 1926
RAINBOW TRAIL, 1932, A
RAINBOW TRAIL, THE, 1918
RAINBOW TRAIL, THE, 1925, A
RAINBOW VALLEY, 1935, A
RAINBOW'S END, 1935, A
RAINBOW, THE, 1917
RAINBOW, THE, 1929
RAINBOW, THE, 1944, C
RAINMAKER, THE, 1926, A
RAINMAKER, THE, 1956, A
RAINMAKERS, THE, 1935, A
RAINS CAME, THE, 1939, A
RAINS OF RANCHIPUR, THE, 1955
RAINTREE COUNTY, 1957, C
RAISE MARX AND PASS THE AMMUNITION, 1970, A
RAISE THE ROOF, 1930
RAISE THE TITANIC, 1980, A-C
RAISIN IN THE SUN, A, 1961, A
RAISING A RIOT, 1957, A
RAISING THE ROOF, 1971
RAISING THE WIND, 1933
RAISING THE WIND, 1962
RAJAH'S AMULET, THE
RAKE'S PROGRESS, THE
RAKU FIRE, 5m
RALLY 'ROUND THE FLAG, BOYS!, 1958, C
RAMBLIN' GALOOT, THE, 1926
RAMBLIN' KID, THE, 1923
RAMBLING RANGER, THE, 1927
RAMON, 1972
RAMONA, 1916, A
RAMONA, 1928, A
RAMONA, 1936, A
RAMPAGE, 1963, A
RAMPAGE AT APACHE WELLS, 1966, A
RAMPANT AGE, THE, 1930, A
RAMPARTS WE WATCH, THE, 1940, A
RAMROD, 1947, A
RAMRODDER, THE, 1969, O
RAMSBOTTOM RIDES AGAIN, 1956, A
RAMSHACKLE HOUSE, 1924, A
RAMUNTCHO, 1919
RANCHERS AND RASCALS, 1925
RANCHERS, THE, 1923
RANCHO DELUXE, 1975
RANCHO GRANDE, 1938, A
RANCHO GRANDE, 1940, A
RANCHO NOTORIOUS, 1952, A
RANDOLPH FAMILY, THE, 1945, A
RANDOM HARVEST, 1942, A
RANDY RIDES ALONE, 1934, A
RANDY STRIKES OIL
RANGE BEYOND THE BLUE, 1947, A
RANGE BLOOD, 1924
RANGE BOSS, THE, 1917
RANGE BUSTERS, THE, 1940, A
RANGE BUZZARDS, 1925
RANGE COURAGE, 1927
RANGE DEFENDERS, 1937, A
RANGE FEUD, THE, 1931, A
RANGE JUSTICE, 1925
RANGE JUSTICE, 1949, A
RANGE LAND, 1949, A
RANGE LAW, 1931, A
RANGE LAW, 1944, A
RANGE PATROL, THE, 1923
RANGE PIRATE, THE, 1921
RANGE RAIDER, THE, 1927
RANGE RENEGADES, 1948, A
RANGE RIDERS
RANGE RIDERS, THE, 1927, A
RANGE TERROR, THE, 1925
RANGE VULTURES, 1925
RANGE WAR, 1939, A
RANGE WARFARE, 1935
RANGELAND, 1922
RANGER AND THE LADY, THE, 1940, A
RANGER AND THE LAW, THE, 1921
RANGER BILL, 1925
RANGER COURAGE, 1937, A
RANGER OF CHEROKEE STRIP, 1949, A
RANGER OF THE BIG PINES, 1925, A
RANGER OF THE NORTH, 1927, A
RANGER'S CODE, THE, 1933, A
RANGER'S OATH, 1928
RANGER'S ROUNDUP, THE, 1938, A
RANGER, THE, 1918
RANGERS OF CHEROKEE STRIP
RANGERS OF FORTUNE, 1940, AA
RANGERS RIDE, THE, 1948, A
RANGERS STEP IN, THE, 1937, A
RANGERS TAKE OVER, THE, 1942
RANGLE RIVER, 1939, A

RANGO, 1931, A
RANI RADOVI
RANK OUTSIDER, 1920, A
RANKS AND PEOPLE, 1929
RANSOM, 1928, A
RANSOM, 1956, A
RANSOM, 1975
RANSOM, 1977
RANSOM, THE, 1916, A
RANSON'S FOLLY, 1915, A
RANSON'S FOLLY, 1926, A
RAPE KILLER, THE, 1976
RAPE OF MALAYA
RAPE OF THE SABINES, THE
RAPE SQUAD
RAPE, THE, 1965, O
RAPE, THE, 1968
RAPID FIRE ROMANCE, 1926
RAPTURE, 1950, A
RAPTURE, 1965, C
RAQ LO B'SHABBAT
RARE BREED, 1984, A
RARE BREED, THE, 1966, A
RARIN' TO GO, 1924
RASCAL, 1969, AAA
RASCALS, 1938, AA
RASHOMON, 1951, A-C
RASPOUTINE, 1954, C
RASPUTIN
RASPUTIN, 1929
RASPUTIN, 1930
RASPUTIN, 1932, A
RASPUTIN, 1939, A
RASPUTIN AND THE EMPRESS, 1932, C
RASPUTIN THE MAD MONK, 1932
RASPUTIN, THE BLACK MONK, 1917
RASPUTIN, THE HOLY SINNER
RASPUTIN—THE MAD MONK, 1966, C
RAT, 1960, A
RAT FINK, 1965, C
RAT PFINK AND BOO BOO, 1966, A
RAT RACE, THE, 1960, A
RAT SAVIOUR, THE, 1977
RAT, THE, 1925, A
RAT, THE, 1938, A
RATATAPLAN, 1979, A
RATCATCHER, THE
RATED AT $10,000,000, 1915
RATIONING, 1944, A
RATON PASS, 1951, A
RATS, 1984
*RATS ARE COMING! THE WEREWOLVES ARE
   HERE!, THE*, 1972, O
RATS OF TOBRUK, 1951, A
RATS, THE, 1955, A
RATS, THE, 1982
RATTLE OF A SIMPLE MAN, 1964, C
RATTLER, THE, 1925
RATTLERS, 1976, C
RATTLERS, 1976
RAUTHA SKIKKJAN
RAVAGER, THE, 1970, O
RAVAGERS, THE, 1965, A
RAVAGERS, THE, 1979, A
RAVEN'S END, 1970, A
RAVEN, THE, 1915
RAVEN, THE, 1935, A
RAVEN, THE, 1948, A
RAVEN, THE, 1963, C
RAVISHING IDIOT, A, 1966, A
RAW COURAGE, 1984, O
RAW DEAL, 1948, A-C
RAW DEAL, 1977, A
RAW EDGE, 1956, A
RAW FORCE, 1982, O
RAW MEAT
RAW TIMBER, 1937, A
RAW WEEKEND, 1964, O
RAW WIND IN EDEN, 1958, A
RAWHIDE, 1926
RAWHIDE, 1938, A
RAWHIDE, 1951
RAWHIDE HALO, THE
RAWHIDE KID, THE, 1928, A
RAWHIDE MAIL, 1934
RAWHIDE RANGERS, 1941, A
RAWHIDE ROMANCE, 1934
RAWHIDE TERROR, THE, 1934
RAWHIDE TRAIL, THE, 1950
RAWHIDE TRAIL, THE, 1958, A
RAWHIDE YEARS, THE, 1956, A
RAYMIE, 1960, AAA
RAZOR'S EDGE, THE, 1946
RAZOR'S EDGE, THE, 1984, C-O
RAZORBACK, 1984, O
RE-CREATION OF BRIAN KENT, THE, 1925
RE-UNION
RE: LUCKY LUCIANO, 1974, O
REACH FOR GLORY, 1963, A
REACH FOR THE SKY, 1957, A
REACHING FOR THE MOON, 1917, A
REACHING FOR THE MOON, 1931, A

RENDEZVOUS 24, 1946, A
RENDEZVOUS AT MIDNIGHT, 1935, A
RENDEZVOUS WITH ANNIE, 1946, A
RENDEZVOUS, 1951
RENDEZVOUS, THE, 1923, A
RENEGADE GIRL, 1946, A
RENEGADE GIRLS, 1974, O
RENEGADE HOLMES, M.D., 1925
RENEGADE POSSE
RENEGADE RANGER, 1938, A
RENEGADE TRAIL, 1939, A
RENEGADE, THE, 1943
RENEGADES, 1930, A
RENEGADES, 1946, A
RENEGADES OF SONORA, 1948, A
RENEGADES OF THE RIO GRANDE, 1945, A
RENEGADES OF THE SAGE, 1949, A
RENEGADES OF THE WEST, 1932, A
RENFREW OF THE ROYAL MOUNTED, 1937, A
RENFREW OF THE ROYAL MOUNTED ON THE
   GREAT WHITE TRAIL
RENFREW ON THE GREAT WHITE TRAIL
RENO, 1923, A
RENO, 1930, A
RENO, 1939, A
RENO AND THE DOC, 1984, O
RENO DIVORCE, A, 1927
RENONCEMENT, 1917
RENT CONTROL, 1981, C
RENT FREE, 1922
RENTADICK, 1972, O
RENTED
REPEAT PERFORMANCE, 1947, A
REPENT AT LEISURE, 1941, A
REPENTANCE, 1922, A
REPLICA OF A CRIME
REPO MAN, 1984, O
REPORT ON TH EPARTY AND THE GUESTS, A,
   1968, A
REPORT TO THE COMMISSIONER, 1975, C
REPORTED MISSING, 1922, A
REPORTED MISSING, 1937, A
REPRIEVE
REPRIEVED
REPRISAL, 1956, A
REPTILE, THE, 1966, C
REPTILICUS, 1962, A
REPULSION, 1965, O
REPUTATION
REPUTATION, 1917
REPUTATION, 1921, A
REQUIEM FOR A GUNFIGHTER, 1965, A
REQUIEM FOR A HEAVYWEIGHT, 1962, C
REQUIEM FOR A SECRET AGENT, 1966, A
REQUINS, 1917
RESCUE SQUAD, 1935, A
RESCUE SQUAD, THE, 1963, A
RESCUE, THE, 1917, A
RESCUE, THE, 1929, A
RESCUERS, THE, 1977, AAA
RESCUING ANGEL, THE, 1919
RESERVED FOR LADIES, 1932, AA
RESPECTABLE BY PROXY, 1920
RESPONDENT, THE
REST CURE, THE, 1923, A
REST IS SILENCE, THE, 1960, C
RESTITUTION, 1918
RESTLESS
RESTLESS BREED, THE, 1957, A
RESTLESS NIGHT, THE, 1964, C
RESTLESS ONES, THE, 1965, A
RESTLESS SEX, THE, 1920
RESTLESS SOULS, 1919
RESTLESS SOULS, 1922
RESTLESS WIVES, 1924
RESTLESS YEARS, THE, 1958, A
RESTLESS YOUTH, 1928
RESURRECTION, 1912
RESURRECTION, 1918
RESURRECTION, 1927
RESURRECTION, 1931, A
RESURRECTION, 1963, A
RESURRECTION, 1980, C
RESURRECTION OF LOVE, 1922
RESURRECTION OF ZACHARY WHEELER, THE,
   1971, A
RESURRECTION SYNDICATE
RETALIATION, 1929
RETENEZ MOI...OU JE FAIS UN MALHEUR
RETRIEVERS, THE
RETURN FROM THE ASHES, 1965, A
RETURN FROM THE PAST
RETURN FROM THE SEA, 1954, A
RETURN FROM WITCH MOUNTAIN, 1978, AA
RETURN OF 18 BRONZEMEN, 1984
RETURN OF A MAN CALLED HORSE, THE, 1976, C
RETURN OF A STRANGER, 1962, C
RETURN OF A STRANGER, 1940
RETURN OF BOSTON BLACKIE, THE, 1927
RETURN OF BULLDOG DRUMMOND, THE, 1934, A
RETURN OF CAPTAIN INVINCIBLE, THE, 1983, C
RETURN OF CAROL DEANE, THE, 1938, A

RETURN OF CASEY JONES, 1933, A
RETURN OF COUNT YORGA, THE, 1971, C
RETURN OF DANIEL BOONE, THE, 1941, A
RETURN OF DR. FU MANCHU, THE, 1930, A
RETURN OF DR. MABUSE, THE, 1961, C
RETURN OF DR. X, THE, 1939, C
RETURN OF DRACULA, THE, 1958
RETURN OF EVE, THE, 1916
RETURN OF FRANK JAMES, THE, 1940, A
RETURN OF GILBERT AND SULLIVAN, 1952
RETURN OF JACK SLADE, THE, 1955, A
RETURN OF JESSE JAMES, THE, 1950, A
RETURN OF JIMMY VALENTINE, THE, 1936, A
RETURN OF MARTIN GUERRE, THE, 1983, C
RETURN OF MARY, THE, 1918
RETURN OF MAURICE DONNELLY, THE, 1915
RETURN OF MAXWELL SMART, THE
RETURN OF MONTE CRISTO, THE, 1946, A
RETURN OF MR. H, THE
RETURN OF MR. MOTO, THE, 1965, A
RETURN OF OCTOBER, THE, 1948, A
RETURN OF OLD MOTHER RILEY, THE
RETURN OF PETER GRIMM, THE, 1926, A
RETURN OF PETER GRIMM, THE, 1935, A
RETURN OF RAFFLES, THE, 1932, A
RETURN OF RIN TIN TIN, THE, 1947, AA
RETURN OF RINGO, THE, 1966, A
RETURN OF RUSTY, THE, 1946
RETURN OF SABATA, 1972, C
RETURN OF SOPHIE LANG, THE, 1936, A
RETURN OF TARZAN, THE, 1920
RETURN OF THE APE MAN, 1944, A
RETURN OF THE BADMEN, 1948, C
RETURN OF THE BLACK EAGLE, 1949, A
RETURN OF THE CISCO KID, 1939, A
RETURN OF THE CORSICAN BROTHERS
RETURN OF THE DRAGON, 1974, O
RETURN OF THE DURANGO KID, 1945
RETURN OF THE FLY, 1959, A
RETURN OF THE FROG, THE, 1938, A
RETURN OF THE FRONTIERSMAN, 1950, A
RETURN OF THE JEDI, 1983, A-C
RETURN OF THE LASH, 1947, A
RETURN OF THE LIVING DEAD
RETURN OF THE LONE WOLF
RETURN OF THE PINK PANTHER, THE, 1975, A-C
RETURN OF THE PRODIGAL, THE
RETURN OF THE RANGERS, THE, 1943, A
RETURN OF THE RAT, THE, 1929, A
RETURN OF THE SCARLET PIMPERNEL, 1938, A
RETURN OF THE SECAUCUS SEVEN, 1980, O
RETURN OF THE SEVEN, 1966, A
RETURN OF THE SOLDIER, THE, 1983, C
RETURN OF THE TERROR, 1934, C
RETURN OF THE TEXAN, 1952, A
RETURN OF THE TIGER, 1979
RETURN OF THE VAMPIRE, THE, 1944, A
RETURN OF THE VIGILANTES, THE
RETURN OF THE WHISTLER, THE, 1948, A
RETURN OF WILD BILL, THE, 1940, A
RETURN OF WILDFIRE, THE, 1948, A
RETURN OF "DRAW" EGAN, THE, 1916
RETURN TO BOGGY CREEK, 1977, AA
RETURN TO CAMPUS, 1975, C
RETURN TO MACON COUNTY, 1975, C-O
RETURN TO PARADISE, 1953, A
RETURN TO PEYTON PLACE, 1961, A
RETURN TO SENDER, 1963, A
RETURN TO THE HORRORS OF BLOOD ISLAND
RETURN TO THE LAND OF OZ, 1971
RETURN TO TREASURE ISLAND, 1954, A
RETURN TO WARBOW, 1958, A
RETURN TO YESTERDAY, 1940, A
RETURN, THE, 1980, C
RETURNING, THE, 1983, O
REUBEN, REUBEN, 1983, O
REUNION, 1932, A
REUNION IN FRANCE, 1942, A
REUNION IN RENO, 1951, A
REUNION IN VIENNA, 1933, A-C
REUNION, THE, 1977
REVEILLE, 1924
REVEILLE WITH BEVERLY, 1943, A
REVEILLE-TOI ET MEURS
REVELATION, 1918
REVELATION, 1924, A
REVELATIONS, 1916
REVENGE, 1918
REVENGE, 1928
REVENGE AT EL PASO, 1968, A
REVENGE AT MONTE CARLO, 1933, A
REVENGE IS MY DESTINY, 1971
REVENGE OF DRACULA
REVENGE OF FRANKENSTEIN, THE, 1958, C
REVENGE OF GENERAL LING
REVENGE OF KING KONG
REVENGE OF MILADY, THE
REVENGE OF THE BLOOD BEAST, THE
REVENGE OF THE CHEERLEADERS, 1976, O
REVENGE OF THE CREATURE, 1955, A
REVENGE OF THE DEAD
REVENGE OF THE DEAD, 1975

REVENGE OF THE GLADIATORS, 1962
REVENGE OF THE GLADIATORS, 1965, A
REVENGE OF THE LIVING DEAD
REVENGE OF THE NERDS, 1984, C-O
REVENGE OF THE NINJA, 1983, A-C
REVENGE OF THE PINK PANTHER, 1978, A-C
REVENGE OF THE SCREAMING DEAD
REVENGE OF THE SHOGUN WOMEN, 1982, O
REVENGE OF THE ZOMBIES, 1943, A
REVENGE OF UKENO-JO, THE
REVENGE RIDER, THE, 1935, A
REVENGE, 1936
REVENGE, 1971
REVENGE, 1979
REVENGEFUL SPIRIT OF EROS, THE, 1930
REVENGERS, THE, 1972, A-C
REVENUE AGENT, 1950, A
REVERSE BE MY LOT, THE, 1938, A
REVOLT, 1916
REVOLT AT FORT LARAMIE, 1957, A
REVOLT IN CANADA, 1964
REVOLT IN THE BIG HOUSE, 1958, A
REVOLT IN THE DESERT, 1932
REVOLT OF JOB, THE, 1984, O
REVOLT OF THE BOYARS, THE
REVOLT OF THE MERCENARIES, 1964, A
REVOLT OF THE ROBOTS
REVOLT OF THE SLAVES, THE, 1961, C
REVOLT OF THE ZOMBIES, 1936, C
REVOLUTION
REVOLUTIONARY, THE, 1970, A-C
REVOLUTIONIST, 1917
REVOLUTIONIST, THE, 1914
REVOLUTIONS PER MINUTE
REWARD OF FAITH, 1929
REWARD OF PATIENCE, THE, 1916
REWARD OF THE FAITHLESS, THE, 1917
REWARD, THE, 1915, A
REWARD, THE, 1965, A
REY DE AFRICA
RHAPSODIE IN BLEI
RHAPSODY, 1954, A
RHAPSODY IN BLUE, 1945, AA
RHINESTONE, 1984, C
RHINO, 1964, A
RHINOCEROS, 1974, A-C
RHODES, 1936, A
RHODES OF AFRICA
RHUBARB, 1951, A
RHYTHM HITS THE ICE
RHYTHM IN THE AIR, 1936, A
RHYTHM IN THE CLOUDS, 1937, A
RHYTHM INN, 1951, A
RHYTHM OF THE ISLANDS, 1943, A
RHYTHM OF THE RIO GRANDE, 1940, A
RHYTHM OF THE SADDLE, 1938, A
RHYTHM ON THE RANGE, 1936, A
RHYTHM ON THE RANGE, 1932
RHYTHM ON THE RIVER
RHYTHM ON THE RIVER, 1940, A
RHYTHM PARADE, 1943, A
RHYTHM RACKETEER, 1937, A
RHYTHM ROMANCE
RHYTHM ROUND-UP, 1945
RHYTHM SERENADE, 1943, A
RICE GIRL, 1963, C-O
RICH AND FAMOUS, 1981, O
RICH AND STRANGE, 1932, C
RICH ARE ALWAYS WITH US, THE, 1932, A
RICH BRIDE, THE
RICH BUT HONEST, 1927
RICH GIRL, POOR GIRL, 1921
RICH KIDS, 1979, C
RICH MAN'S DAUGHTER, A, 1918
RICH MAN'S FOLLY, 1931, A
RICH MAN'S PLAYTHING, A, 1917
RICH MAN, POOR GIRL, 1938, A
RICH MAN, POOR MAN, 1918
RICH MEN'S SONS, 1927
RICH MEN'S WIVES, 1922, A
RICH PEOPLE, 1929, A
RICH SLAVE, THE, 1921
RICH, FULL LIFE, THE
RICH, YOUNG AND DEADLY
RICH, YOUNG AND PRETTY, 1951, A-C
RICHARD, 1972, C
RICHARD III, 1913
RICHARD III, 1956, A-C
RICHARD TAUBER STORY, THE
RICHARD THE BRAZEN, 1917
RICHARD'S THINGS, 1981, O
RICHARD, THE LION-HEARTED, 1923
RICHELIEU
RICHELIEU, 1914
RICHES AND ROMANCE
RICHEST GIRL IN THE WORLD, THE, 1934, A
RICHEST GIRL, THE, 1918
RICHEST MAN IN THE WORLD, THE
RICHEST MAN IN TOWN, 1941, A
RICHTOFEN, 1932
RICKSHAW MAN, THE, 1960, C-O
RICOCHET, 1966, C

RICOCHET ROMANCE, 1954, AAA
RIDDLE GAWNE, 1918
RIDDLE OF THE SANDS, THE, 1984, C
RIDDLE RANCH, 1936
RIDDLE TRAIL, THE, 1928
RIDDLE: WOMAN, THE, 1920, A
RIDE 'EM COWBOY, 1936, A
RIDE 'EM COWBOY, 1942, AAA
RIDE 'EM COWGIRL, 1939, A
RIDE 'EM HIGH, 1927
RIDE A CROOKED MILE, 1938, C
RIDE A CROOKED TRAIL, 1958, A-C
RIDE A NORTHBOUND HORSE, 1969, AA
RIDE A VIOLENT MILE, 1957, C
RIDE A WILD PONY, 1976, AAA
RIDE BACK, THE, 1957, C
RIDE BEYOND VENGEANCE, 1966, O
RIDE CLEAR OF DIABLO, 1954, C
RIDE FOR YOUR LIFE, 1924, A
RIDE HIM, COWBOY, 1932, A
RIDE IN A PINK CAR, 1974
RIDE IN THE WHIRLWIND, 1966, C
RIDE LONESOME, 1959, C
RIDE ON VAQUERO, 1941, A
RIDE OUT FOR REVENGE, 1957, C
RIDE THE HIGH COUNTRY, 1962, C
RIDE THE HIGH IRON, 1956, A
RIDE THE HIGH WIND, 1967, A
RIDE THE MAN DOWN, 1952, C
RIDE THE PINK HORSE, 1947, C
RIDE THE TIGER, 1971
RIDE THE WILD SURF, 1964, A
RIDE TO HANGMAN'S TREE, THE, 1967, A
RIDE, KELLY, RIDE, 1941, A
RIDE, RANGER, RIDE, 1936, A
RIDE, RYDER, RIDE!, 1949, A
RIDE, TENDERFOOT, RIDE, 1940, A
RIDE, VAQUERO!, 1953, A
RIDER FROM NOWHERE
RIDER FROM TUCSON, 1950, A
RIDER IN THE NIGHT, THE, 1968, C
RIDER OF DEATH VALLEY, 1932, A
RIDER OF MYSTERY RANCH, 1924
RIDER OF THE KING LOG, THE, 1921
RIDER OF THE LAW, 1919
RIDER OF THE LAW, 1927
RIDER OF THE LAW, THE, 1935, A
RIDER OF THE PLAINS, 1931, A
RIDER ON A DEAD HORSE, 1962, C
RIDER ON THE RAIN, 1970, C
RIDERS AT NIGHT, 1923
RIDERS FROM NOWHERE, 1940, A
RIDERS FROM THE DUSK
RIDERS IN THE SKY, 1949, A
RIDERS OF BLACK HILLS
RIDERS OF BLACK MOUNTAIN, 1941, A
RIDERS OF BLACK RIVER, 1939, A
RIDERS OF BORDER BAY, 1925
RIDERS OF DESTINY, 1933, A
RIDERS OF MYSTERY, 1925, A
RIDERS OF PASCO BASIN, 1940, A
RIDERS OF RIO, 1931
RIDERS OF THE BADLANDS, 1941, A
RIDERS OF THE BLACK HILLS, 1938, A
RIDERS OF THE CACTUS, 1931, A
RIDERS OF THE DARK, 1928
RIDERS OF THE DAWN, 1920, A
RIDERS OF THE DAWN, 1937, A
RIDERS OF THE DAWN, 1945, A
RIDERS OF THE DEADLINE, 1943, A
RIDERS OF THE DESERT, 1932, A
RIDERS OF THE DUSK, 1949, A
RIDERS OF THE FRONTIER, 1939, A
RIDERS OF THE GOLDEN GULCH, 1932, A
RIDERS OF THE LAW, 1922
RIDERS OF THE LONE STAR, 1947
RIDERS OF THE NIGHT, 1918
RIDERS OF THE NORTH, 1931, A
RIDERS OF THE NORTHLAND, 1942, A
RIDERS OF THE NORTHWEST MOUNTED, 1943, A
RIDERS OF THE PONY EXPRESS, 1949
RIDERS OF THE PURPLE SAGE, 1918
RIDERS OF THE PURPLE SAGE, 1925, A
RIDERS OF THE PURPLE SAGE, 1931, A
RIDERS OF THE PURPLE SAGE, 1941, A
RIDERS OF THE RANGE, 1923
RIDERS OF THE RANGE, 1949, A
RIDERS OF THE RIO GRANDE, 1929, A
RIDERS OF THE RIO GRANDE, 1943, A
RIDERS OF THE ROCKIES, 1937, A
RIDERS OF THE SAGE, 1939
RIDERS OF THE SAND STORM, 1925
RIDERS OF THE SANTA FE, 1944, A
RIDERS OF THE STORM, 1929
RIDERS OF THE WEST, 1927
RIDERS OF THE WEST, 1942, A
RIDERS OF THE WHISTLING PINES, 1949, A
RIDERS OF THE WHISTLING SKULL, 1937, A-C
RIDERS OF VENGEANCE
RIDERS OF VENGEANCE, 1919, A
RIDERS OF VENGEANCE, 1928
RIDERS TO THE STARS, 1954, A

RIDERS UP, 1924
RIDGEWAY OF MONTANA, 1924, A
RIDIN' COMET, 1925
RIDIN' DEMON, THE, 1929
RIDIN' DOUBLE
RIDIN' DOWN THE CANYON, 1942, A
RIDIN' DOWN THE TRAIL, 1947, A
RIDIN' EASY, 1925
RIDIN' FOOL, 1924
RIDIN' FOOL, THE, 1931
RIDIN' FOR JUSTICE, 1932, A
RIDIN' GENT, A, 1926
RIDIN' KID, 1930
RIDIN' KID FROM POWDER RIVER, THE, 1924
RIDIN' LAW, 1930, A
RIDIN' LUCK, 1927
RIDIN' MAD, 1924, A
RIDIN' ON, 1936
RIDIN' ON A RAINBOW, 1941, A
RIDIN' PRETTY, 1925
RIDIN' RASCAL, THE, 1926
RIDIN' ROMEO, A, 1921
RIDIN' ROWDY, THE, 1927
RIDIN' STRAIGHT, 1926
RIDIN' STREAK, THE, 1925
RIDIN' THE LONE TRAIL, 1937, A
RIDIN' THE OUTLAW TRAIL, 1951, A
RIDIN' THE TRAIL, 1940
RIDIN' THE WIND, 1925, A
RIDIN' THROUGH
RIDIN' THRU, 1923
RIDIN' THRU, 1935
RIDIN' THUNDER, 1925
RIDIN' WEST, 1924
RIDIN' WILD, 1922, A
RIDIN' WILD, 1925
RIDING AVENGER, THE, 1936, A
RIDING DEMON
RIDING DOUBLE, 1924
RIDING FOOL, 1924
RIDING FOR FAME, 1928
RIDING FOR LIFE, 1926
RIDING HIGH, 1937, A
RIDING HIGH, 1943, A
RIDING HIGH, 1950, A
RIDING ON, 1937, A
RIDING ON AIR, 1937, AA
RIDING RENEGADE, THE, 1928
RIDING RIVALS, 1926
RIDING ROMANCE, 1926
RIDING SHOTGUN, 1954, A
RIDING SPEED, 1934, A
RIDING TALL
RIDING THE CALIFORNIA TRAIL, 1947
RIDING THE CHEROKEE TRAIL, 1941, A
RIDING THE SUNSET TRAIL, 1941, A
RIDING THE WIND, 1942, A
RIDING THROUGH NEVADA, 1942
RIDING THUNDER
RIDING TO FAME, 1927
RIDING TORNADO, THE, 1932, A
RIDING WEST, 1944, A
RIDING WILD, 1935
RIDING WITH DEATH, 1921, A
RIDING WITH DEATH, 1976
RIEL, 1979
RIFF RAFF GIRLS, 1962, O
RIFF-RAFF, 1936, A
RIFFRAFF, 1947, A
RIFIFFI A TOKYO
RIFIFI, 1956, A-C
RIFIFI FOR GIRLS
RIFIFI FRA LE DONNE
RIFIFI IN PARIS
RIFIFI IN TOKYO, 1963, A-C
RIFIFI INTERNAZIONALE
RIGHT AGE TO MARRY, THE, 1935, A
RIGHT APPROACH, THE, 1961, A
RIGHT CROSS, 1950, A-C
RIGHT DIRECTION, THE, 1916
RIGHT ELEMENT, THE, 1919
RIGHT HAND OF THE DEVIL, THE, 1963, C
RIGHT MAN, THE
RIGHT MAN, THE, 1925
RIGHT OF MARY BLAKE, THE, 1916
RIGHT OF THE STRONGEST, THE, 1924
RIGHT OF WAY, THE, 1915
RIGHT OF WAY, THE, 1920
RIGHT OF WAY, THE, 1931, A
RIGHT OFF THE BAT, 1915
RIGHT STUFF, THE, 1983, A-C
RIGHT THAT FAILED, THE, 1922, A
RIGHT TO BE HAPPY, THE, 1917
RIGHT TO HAPPINESS, THE, 1919
RIGHT TO LIE, THE, 1919, A
RIGHT TO LIVE, THE, 1921
RIGHT TO LIVE, THE, 1933, A
RIGHT TO LIVE, THE, 1935, A
RIGHT TO LIVE, THE, 1945
RIGHT TO LOVE, THE, 1920
RIGHT TO LOVE, THE, 1931, C
RIGHT TO ROMANCE, 1933, A-C

RIGHT TO STRIKE, THE, 1923
RIGHT TO THE HEART, 1942, A
RIGHT WAY, THE, 1921, A
RIGHTS OF MAN, THE, 1915
RIGOLETTO, 1949, A
RILEY OF THE RAINBOW DIVISION, 1928
RILEY THE COP, 1928, A
RILKA, 1918
RIM OF HELL, 1970
RIM OF THE CANYON, 1949, A
RIMFIRE, 1949, A
RIMROCK JONES, 1918
RING AND THE MAN, THE, 1914, A
RING AROUND THE CLOCK, 1953, A
RING AROUND THE MOON, 1936, A
RING OF BRIGHT WATER, 1969, A
RING OF FEAR, 1954, A
RING OF FIRE, 1961, A-C
RING OF SPIES
RING OF SPIES, 1964, A
RING OF TERROR, 1962, A
RING OF THE BORGIAS, THE, 1915
RING TWENTIES, THE, 1939, C
RING UP THE CURTAIN
RING, THE, 1927, A
RING, THE, 1952, A
RING-A-DING RHYTHM, 1962, A
RINGER, THE, 1928, A
RINGER, THE, 1932, A
RINGER, THE, 1953, A
RINGING THE CHANGES, 1929
RINGO AND HIS GOLDEN PISTOL, 1966, A
RINGS ON HER FINGERS, 1942, A
RINGSIDE, 1949, A
RINGSIDE MAISIE, 1941, A
RINGTAILED RHINOCEROS, THE, 1915
RINTY OF THE DESERT, 1928
RIO, 1939, A
RIO 70, 1970, C
RIO ABAJO
RIO BRAVO, 1959, A
RIO CONCHOS, 1964
RIO GRANDE, 1920
RIO GRANDE, 1939, A
RIO GRANDE, 1949
RIO GRANDE, 1950, A
RIO GRANDE PATROL, 1950, A
RIO GRANDE RAIDERS, 1946, A
RIO GRANDE RANGER, 1937, A
RIO GRANDE ROMANCE, 1936, A
RIO LOBO, 1970, A
RIO RATTLER, 1935
RIO RITA, 1929, A
RIO RITA, 1942, AAA
RIO VENGENCE
RIOT, 1969, O
RIOT AT LAUDERDALE
RIOT IN CELL BLOCK 11, 1954, C
RIOT IN JUVENILE PRISON, 1959, C
RIOT ON PIER 6
RIOT ON SUNSET STRIP, 1967, C
RIOT SQUAD, 1933
RIOT SQUAD, 1941, A
RIOTOUS BRUIN, THE
RIP OFF, 1977
RIP ROARIN' BUCKAROO, 1936
RIP ROARIN' ROBERTS, 1924
RIP ROARING LOGAN, 1928
RIP ROARING RILEY, 1935
RIP SNORTER, THE, 1925
RIP TIDE, 1934, A
RIP VAN WINKLE, 1914, A
RIP VAN WINKLE, 1921, A
RIP-OFF, 1971, O
RIP-TIDE, THE, 1923, A
RIPPED-OFF, 1971
RISATE DI GIOLA
RISE AGAINST THE SWORD, 1966, A
RISE AND FALL OF LEGS DIAMOND, THE, 1960, C
RISE AND RISE OF MICHAEL RIMMER, THE, 1970, C
RISE AND SHINE, 1941, A
RISE OF CATHERINE THE GREAT
RISE OF HELGA, THE
RISE OF JENNIE CUSHING, THE, 1917, C
RISE OF LOUIS XIV, THE, 1970, A
RISE OF SUSAN, THE, 1916
RISING DAMP, 1980, C
RISING GENERATION, THE, 1928
RISING OF THE MOON, THE, 1957, A
RISING TO FAME
RISK, THE, 1961, A
RISKY BUSINESS, 1920
RISKY BUSINESS, 1926
RISKY BUSINESS, 1939, A
RISKY BUSINESS, 1983, O
RISKY ROAD, THE, 1918, A
RITA, 1963, C
RITEN
RITUAL, THE, 1970, O
RITUALS
RITZ, THE, 1976, C-O
RITZY, 1927

RIVAL OF PERPETUA, THE, 1915
RIVALEN DER MANEGE
RIVALS, 1933
RIVALS, 1972, O
RIVALS, THE, 1963, A
RIVER BEAT, 1954, A
RIVER CHANGES, THE, 1956, A
RIVER GANG, 1945, A
RIVER HOUSE GHOST, THE, 1932, A
RIVER HOUSE MYSTERY, THE, 1935, A
RIVER LADY, 1948, A
RIVER NIGER, THE, 1976, O
RIVER OF EVIL, 1964
RIVER OF FOREVER, 1967, A-C
RIVER OF LIGHT, THE, 1921
RIVER OF MISSING MEN
RIVER OF NO RETURN, 1954, A
RIVER OF POISON
RIVER OF ROMANCE, 1929, A
RIVER OF ROMANCE, THE, 1916
RIVER OF STARS, THE, 1921
RIVER OF UNREST, 1937, A
RIVER RAT, THE, 1984, A
RIVER WOLVES, THE, 1934, A
RIVER WOMAN, 1929
RIVER WOMAN, THE, 1928, A
RIVER'S EDGE, THE, 1957
RIVER'S END, 1931, A
RIVER'S END, 1940, A
RIVER'S END, THE, 1920
RIVER, THE, 1928, A
RIVER, THE, 1951, A
RIVER, THE, 1961
RIVER, THE, 1984, A-C
RIVERBOAT RHYTHM, 1946, A
RIVERRUN, 1968, O
RIVERSIDE MURDER, THE, 1935, A
ROAD AGENT, 1926
ROAD AGENT, 1941, A
ROAD AGENT, 1952, A
ROAD BETWEEN, THE, 1917
ROAD CALLED STRAIGHT, THE, 1919
ROAD DEMON, 1938
ROAD DEMON, THE, 1921
ROAD GAMES, 1981, O
ROAD GANG, 1936
ROAD GANGS, ADVENTURES IN THE CREEP ZONE
ROAD HOME, THE, 1947, A
ROAD HOUSE, 1928, A
ROAD HOUSE, 1934
ROAD HOUSE, 1948, C
ROAD HUSTLERS, THE, 1968, C
ROAD IS FINE, THE, 1930, A
ROAD MOVIE, 1974, O
ROAD OF AMBITION, THE, 1920
ROAD OF DEATH, 1977
ROAD REBELS, 1963
ROAD SHOW, 1941, A
ROAD THROUGH THE DARK, THE, 1918
ROAD TO ALCATRAZ, 1945, A
ROAD TO ARCADY, THE, 1922
ROAD TO BALI, 1952
ROAD TO BROADWAY, THE, 1926
ROAD TO DENVER, THE, 1955, A
ROAD TO DIVORCE, THE, 1920
ROAD TO ETERNITY, 1962, O
ROAD TO FORT ALAMO, THE, 1966, C
ROAD TO FORTUNE, THE, 1930, A
ROAD TO FRANCE, THE, 1918
ROAD TO FRISCO
ROAD TO GLORY, THE, 1926
ROAD TO GLORY, THE, 1936, A-C
ROAD TO HAPPINESS, 1942, A
ROAD TO HONG KONG, THE, 1962, AA
ROAD TO LIFE, 1932, A
ROAD TO LONDON, THE, 1921, A
ROAD TO LOVE, THE, 1916
ROAD TO MANDALAY, THE, 1926, C
ROAD TO MOROCCO, 1942, AA
ROAD TO NASHVILLE, 1967
ROAD TO PARADISE, 1930, A
ROAD TO RENO, 1931, A
ROAD TO RENO, THE, 1938, A
ROAD TO RIO, 1947, AA
ROAD TO ROMANCE, THE, 1927
ROAD TO RUIN, 1934, O
ROAD TO RUIN, THE, 1913, A
ROAD TO RUIN, THE, 1928
ROAD TO SALINA, 1971, O
ROAD TO SHAME, THE, 1962, C-O
ROAD TO SINGAPORE, 1931, A
ROAD TO SINGAPORE, 1940, AA
ROAD TO THE BIG HOUSE, 1947, A
ROAD TO UTOPIA, 1945, AA
ROAD TO YESTERDAY, THE, 1925
ROAD TO ZANZIBAR, 1941, AA
ROAD WARRIOR, THE, 1982, O
ROAD, THE
ROADBLOCK, 1951, A
ROADHOUSE 66, 1984, C
ROADHOUSE GIRL
ROADHOUSE MURDER, THE, 1932, A

ROADHOUSE NIGHTS, 1930, A
ROADIE, 1980, A-C
ROADRACERS, THE, 1959, A
ROADS OF DESTINY, 1921
ROADSIDE IMPRESARIO, A, 1917
ROAMIN' WILD, 1936
ROAMING COWBOY, THE, 1937, A
ROAMING LADY, 1936, A
ROAR, 1981, A
ROAR OF THE CROWD, 1953, A
ROAR OF THE DRAGON, 1932, A
ROAR OF THE PRESS, 1941, A
ROARIN' BRONCS, 1927
ROARIN' GUNS, 1936, A
ROARIN' LEAD, 1937, A
ROARING ADVENTURE, A, 1925
ROARING BILL ATWOOD, 1926
ROARING CITY, 1951, A
ROARING FIRES, 1927
ROARING FORTIES, THE
ROARING FRONTIERS, 1941
ROARING GUNS, 1936
ROARING RAILS, 1924, A
ROARING RANCH, 1930, A
ROARING RANGERS, 1946
ROARING RIDER, 1926
ROARING ROAD, 1926
ROARING ROAD, THE, 1919, A
ROARING ROADS, 1935
ROARING SIX GUNS, 1937, A
ROARING TIMBER, 1937, A
ROARING TIMBERS
ROARING WESTWARD, 1949, A
ROB ROY
ROB ROY, 1922, A
ROB ROY, THE HIGHLAND ROGUE, 1954, A
ROBBER SYMPHONY, THE, 1937, A
ROBBERS OF THE RANGE, 1941
ROBBERS' ROOST, 1933, A
ROBBERY, 1967, A-C
ROBBERY UNDER ARMS, 1958, A
ROBBERY WITH VIOLENCE, 1958, A
ROBBO
ROBBY, 1968, AA
ROBE, THE, 1953, A
ROBERT'S ADVENTURE IN THE GREAT WAR, 1920
ROBERTA, 1935, A
ROBES OF SIN, 1924
ROBIN, 1979
ROBIN AND MARIAN, 1976, A-C
ROBIN AND THE SEVEN HOODS, 1964, A-C
ROBIN HOOD, 1913
ROBIN HOOD, 1922, A
ROBIN HOOD, 1973, AAA
ROBIN HOOD OF EL DORADO, 1936, C
ROBIN HOOD OF MONTEREY, 1947
ROBIN HOOD OF THE PECOS, 1941, A
ROBIN HOOD OF THE RANGE, 1943, A
ROBIN HOOD, 1938
ROBIN HOOD, 1952
ROBIN HOOD, JR., 1923
ROBIN OF TEXAS, 1947, A
ROBINSON CRUSOE
ROBINSON CRUSOE, 1916
ROBINSON CRUSOE, 1927, A
ROBINSON CRUSOE AND THE TIGER, 1972
ROBINSON CRUSOE ON MARS, 1964, A
ROBINSON CRUSOELAND
ROBINSON SOLL NICHT STERBEN
ROBO DE DIAMANTES
ROBO NO ISHI
ROBOT MONSTER, 1953, A
ROBOT VS. THE AZTEC MUMMY, THE, 1965, O
ROCAMBOLE, 1923
ROCCO AND HIS BROTHERS, 1961, C
ROCCO E I SUOI FRATELLI
ROCCO PAPALEO, 1974, O
ROCK 'N' ROLL HIGH SCHOOL, 1979, C
ROCK 'N' RULE, 1983
ROCK ALL NIGHT, 1957, A
ROCK AROUND THE CLOCK, 1956, A
ROCK AROUND THE WORLD, 1957, A
ROCK BABY, ROCK IT, 1957, A
ROCK ISLAND TRAIL, 1950, A
ROCK OF AGES, 1918
ROCK RIVER RENEGADES, 1942, A
ROCK YOU SINNERS, 1957, A
ROCK, PRETTY BABY, 1956, A
ROCK, ROCK, ROCK!, 1956, A
ROCK-A-BYE BABY, 1958, A
ROCKABILLY BABY, 1957, A
ROCKABYE, 1932, A
ROCKERS, 1980, O
ROCKET ATTACK, U.S.A., 1961
ROCKET FROM CALABUCH, THE
ROCKET MAN, THE, 1954, A
ROCKET TO NOWHERE, 1962, AAA
ROCKET TO THE MOON
ROCKETS GALORE
ROCKETS IN THE DUNES, 1960, AA
ROCKETSHIP X-M, 1950, A
ROCKIN' IN THE ROCKIES, 1945, A

ROCKING HORSE WINNER, THE, 1950, C-O
ROCKING MOON, 1926
ROCKS OF VALPRE, THE
ROCKS OF VALPRE, THE, 1919
ROCKY, 1948, A
ROCKY, 1976, A-C
ROCKY HORROR PICTURE SHOW, THE, 1975, O
ROCKY II, 1979, A-C
ROCKY III, 1982, A-C
ROCKY MOUNTAIN, 1950, A
ROCKY MOUNTAIN MYSTERY, 1935, A
ROCKY MOUNTAIN RANGERS, 1940, A
ROCKY RHODES, 1934, A
RODAN, 1958, A
RODEO, 1952, A
RODEO KING AND THE SENORITA, 1951, A
RODEO MIXUP, A, 1924
RODEO RHYTHM, 1941, AA
ROGER LA HONTE, 1922
ROGER TOUHY, GANGSTER!, 1944, A
ROGUE AND GRIZZLY, THE, 1982
ROGUE AND RICHES, 1920
ROGUE COP, 1954, C
ROGUE IN LOVE, A, 1916
ROGUE IN LOVE, A, 1922, A
ROGUE OF THE RANGE, 1937, A
ROGUE OF THE RIO GRANDE, 1930, A
ROGUE RIVER, 1951, A
ROGUE'S GALLERY, 1968
ROGUE'S GALLERY, 1942
ROGUE'S MARCH, 1952, A
ROGUE'S ROMANCE, A, 1919
ROGUE'S WIFE, A, 1915
ROGUE'S YARN, 1956, A
ROGUE, THE, 1976
ROGUES AND ROMANCE, 1920
ROGUES GALLERY, 1945, A
ROGUES OF LONDON, THE, 1915, A
ROGUES OF PARIS, 1913
ROGUES OF SHERWOOD FOREST, 1950, A
ROGUES OF THE TURF, 1923
ROGUES' REGIMENT, 1948, A
ROGUES' TAVERN, THE, 1936, A
ROLL ALONG, COWBOY, 1938, A
ROLL ON
ROLL ON TEXAS MOON, 1946, A
ROLL, THUNDER, ROLL, 1949, A
ROLL, WAGONS, ROLL, 1939, A
ROLLED STOCKINGS, 1927, A
ROLLER BOOGIE, 1979, C
ROLLERBALL, 1975, O
ROLLERCOASTER, 1977, C-O
ROLLIN' HOME TO TEXAS, 1941, A
ROLLIN' PLAINS, 1938, A
ROLLIN' WESTWARD, 1939, A
ROLLING CARAVANS, 1938, A
ROLLING DOWN THE GREAT DIVIDE, 1942, A
ROLLING HOME, 1926, A
ROLLING HOME, 1935, A
ROLLING HOME, 1948
ROLLING IN MONEY, 1934, A
ROLLING ROAD, THE, 1927
ROLLING STONES, 1916
ROLLING THUNDER, 1977, O
ROLLOVER, 1981, O
ROMA, 1972, O
ROMA CONTRO ROMA
ROMA RIVUOLE CESARE
ROMA, CITTA APERTA
ROMAINE KALBRIS, 1921
ROMAN HOLIDAY, 1953, A
ROMAN SCANDALS, 1933, A-C
ROMAN SPRING OF MRS. STONE, THE, 1961, C
ROMANCE, 1920
ROMANCE, 1930, A
ROMANCE AND ARABELLA, 1919, A
ROMANCE AND BRIGHT LIGHTS
ROMANCE AND RHYTHM
ROMANCE AND RICHES, 1937, A
ROMANCE AND RUSTLERS, 1925
ROMANCE FOR THREE
ROMANCE IN FLANDERS, A, 1937, Brit.
ROMANCE IN MANHATTAN, 1935, A
ROMANCE IN RHYTHM, 1934
ROMANCE IN THE DARK, 1938, A
ROMANCE IN THE RAIN, 1934, A
ROMANCE LAND, 1923, A
ROMANCE OF A HORSE THIEF, 1971, A
ROMANCE OF A MILLION DOLLARS, THE, 1926
ROMANCE OF A ROGUE, 1928
ROMANCE OF A RUSSIAN BALLERINA, 1913
ROMANCE OF ANNIE LAURIE, THE, 1920
ROMANCE OF BILLY GOAT HILL, A, 1916
ROMANCE OF HAPPY VALLEY, A, 1919, A
ROMANCE OF LADY HAMILTON, THE, 1919
ROMANCE OF OLD BAGDAD, A, 1922
ROMANCE OF RIO GRANDE
ROMANCE OF ROSY RIDGE, THE, 1947, A
ROMANCE OF SEVILLE, A, 1929, A
ROMANCE OF TARZAN, THE, 1918, A
ROMANCE OF THE AIR, A, 1919, A
ROMANCE OF THE LIMBERLOST, 1938, A

ROMANCE OF THE MAYFAIR, A, 1925
ROMANCE OF THE NAVY, A, 1915
ROMANCE OF THE NILE, 1924
ROMANCE OF THE REDWOODS, 1939, A
ROMANCE OF THE REDWOODS, A, 1917, A
ROMANCE OF THE RIO GRANDE, 1929, A
ROMANCE OF THE RIO GRANDE, 1941, A
ROMANCE OF THE ROCKIES, 1938, A
ROMANCE OF THE UNDERWORLD, 1928
ROMANCE OF THE UNDERWORLD, A, 1918
ROMANCE OF THE WASTELAND, 1924
ROMANCE OF THE WEST, 1946, A
ROMANCE OF WASTDALE, A, 1921
ROMANCE ON THE BEACH
ROMANCE ON THE HIGH SEAS, 1948, A
ROMANCE ON THE RANGE, 1942, A
ROMANCE ON THE RUN, 1938, A
ROMANCE PROMOTORS, THE, 1920
ROMANCE RANCH, 1924, A
ROMANCE RIDES THE RANGE, 1936, A
ROMANCE ROAD, 1925, A
ROMANCING THE STONE, 1984, C-O
ROMANOFF AND JULIET, 1961, A
ROMANTIC ADVENTURESS, A, 1920
ROMANTIC AGE, THE, 1927
ROMANTIC AGE, THE, 1934
ROMANTIC AGE, THE, 1949, Brit.
ROMANTIC COMEDY, 1983, A-C
ROMANTIC ENGLISHWOMAN, THE, 1975, O
ROMANTIC JOURNEY, THE, 1916
ROMANTIC ROGUE, 1927
ROMANY LASS, A
ROMANY LOVE, 1931
ROMANY RYE, THE, 1915
ROMANY, THE, 1923
ROME ADVENTURE, 1962, A
ROME EXPRESS, 1933, A
ROME WANTS ANOTHER CAESAR, 1974, A
ROME, OPEN CITY
ROMEO AND JULIET, 1916, A
ROMEO AND JULIET, 1916
ROMEO AND JULIET, 1936, C
ROMEO AND JULIET, 1954, A
ROMEO AND JULIET, 1955, A
ROMEO AND JULIET, 1966, A
ROMEO AND JULIET, 1968, A-C
ROMEO AND JULIET, 1968, C
ROMEO IN PYJAMAS
ROMEO, JULIET AND DARKNESS
ROMMEL'S TREASURE, 1962, A
ROMMEL-DESERT FOX
ROMOLA, 1925, A
ROMOLO E REMO
ROOF TREE, THE, 1921
ROOF, THE, 1933, A
ROOGIE'S BUMP, 1954, A
ROOK, THE
ROOKERY NOOK
ROOKIE COP, THE, 1939, A
ROOKIE FIREMAN, 1950, A
ROOKIE'S RETURN, THE, 1921, A
ROOKIE, THE, 1959, A
ROOKIES
ROOKIES, 1927
ROOKIES COME HOME
ROOKIES IN BURMA, 1943, A
ROOKIES ON PARADE, 1941, A
ROOM 43, 1959, A
ROOM AND BOARD, 1921
ROOM AT THE TOP, 1959, O
ROOM FOR ONE MORE, 1952, AA
ROOM FOR TWO, 1940, A
ROOM IN THE HOUSE, 1955, A
ROOM SERVICE, 1938, A
ROOM TO LET, 1949, A
ROOM UPSTAIRS, THE, 1948, C
ROOMATES, 1969
ROOMMATES, 1962, AA
ROOMMATES, 1971, O
ROOMMATES, THE, 1973, O
ROONEY, 1958, A
ROOSTER COGBURN, 1975, A
ROOT OF ALL EVIL, THE, 1947, A
ROOT OF EVIL, THE, 1919
ROOTIN' TOOTIN' RHYTHM, 1937, A
ROOTS OF HEAVEN, THE, 1958, C
ROPE, 1948, C-O
ROPE OF FLESH, 1965, O
ROPE OF SAND, 1949
ROPE, 1965
ROPED, 1919
ROPED BY RADIO, 1925
ROPIN' RIDIN' FOOL, A, 1925
ROSALEEN DHU, 1920
ROSALIE, 1937, A
ROSARY, THE, 1915
ROSARY, THE, 1922
ROSARY, THE, 1931
ROSE BOWL, 1936, A
ROSE BOWL STORY, THE, 1952, A
ROSE FOR EVERYONE, A, 1967, O
ROSE FRANCE, 1919

ROSE IN THE DUST, 1921
ROSE MARIE, 1936, AA
ROSE MARIE, 1954, AA
ROSE O' PARADISE, 1918
ROSE O' THE RIVER
ROSE O' THE SEA, 1922
ROSE OF BLOOD, THE, 1917
ROSE OF CIMARRON, 1952, A
ROSE OF GRENADE, 1916
ROSE OF KILDARE, THE, 1927
ROSE OF NOME, 1920
ROSE OF PARIS, THE, 1924, A
ROSE OF SANTA ROSA, 1947
ROSE OF THE ALLEY, 1916
ROSE OF THE BOWERY, 1927
ROSE OF THE DESERT, 1925
ROSE OF THE GOLDEN WEST, 1927
ROSE OF THE RANCHO, 1914, A
ROSE OF THE RANCHO, 1936, A
ROSE OF THE RIO GRANDE
ROSE OF THE RIO GRANDE, 1938, A
ROSE OF THE RIVER, 1919
ROSE OF THE SOUTH, 1916
ROSE OF THE TENEMENTS, 1926
ROSE OF THE WEST, 1919
ROSE OF THE WORLD, 1918, A
ROSE OF THE WORLD, 1925, A
ROSE OF THE YUKON, 1949, A
ROSE OF TRALEE, 1938, A
ROSE OF TRALEE, 1942, A
ROSE OF WASHINGTON SQUARE, 1939, A
ROSE TATTOO, THE, 1955, C-O
ROSE, THE, 1979, O
ROSE-MARIE, 1928
ROSEANNA McCOY, 1949, AA
ROSEBUD, 1975, C
ROSEBUD BEACH HOTEL, 1984, C-O
ROSELAND, 1977, C
ROSEMARY, 1915
ROSEMARY, 1960, C
ROSEMARY CLIMBS THE HEIGHTS, 1918
ROSEMARY'S BABY, 1968, O
ROSEMARY'S KILLER
ROSEN FUR DEN STAATSANWALT
ROSES ARE RED, 1947, A
ROSES BLOOM TWICE, 1977
ROSES FOR THE PROSECUTOR, 1961, A
ROSES OF PICARDY, 1918
ROSES OF PICARDY, 1927, A
ROSIE THE RIVETER, 1944, A
ROSIE!, 1967, A
ROSITA, 1923, A
ROSMUNDA E ALBOINO
ROSSINI, 1948, A
ROSSITER CASE, THE, 1950, A
ROTHSCHILD, 1938, A
ROTTEN APPLE, THE, 1963, O
ROTTEN TO THE CORE, 1956, C
ROTTERS, THE, 1921
ROTWEILER: DOGS OF HELL, 1984, O
ROUGE AND RICHES, 1920
ROUGED LIPS, 1923
ROUGH AND READY, 1918, A
ROUGH AND READY, 1927
ROUGH AND READY, 1930
ROUGH AND THE SMOOTH, THE
ROUGH COMPANY
ROUGH CUT, 1980, C
ROUGH DIAMOND, THE, 1921
ROUGH GOING, 1925
ROUGH HOUSE ROSIE, 1927, A
ROUGH LOVER, THE, 1918, A
ROUGH NIGHT IN JERICHO, 1967, O
ROUGH RIDERS OF CHEYENNE, 1945, A
ROUGH RIDERS OF DURANGO, 1951, A
ROUGH RIDERS' ROUNDUP, 1939, A
ROUGH RIDERS, THE, 1927, A
ROUGH RIDIN', 1924
ROUGH RIDIN' JUSTICE, 1945
ROUGH RIDIN' RED, 1928
ROUGH RIDIN' RHYTHM, 1937, A
ROUGH RIDING RANGER, 1935, A
ROUGH RIDING ROMANCE, 1919
ROUGH RIDING ROMEO
ROUGH ROMANCE, 1930, A
ROUGH SHOD, 1925, A
ROUGH SHOD FIGHTER, A, 1927
ROUGH SHOOT
ROUGH STUFF, 1925
ROUGH WATERS, 1930
ROUGH, TOUGH AND READY, 1945, A
ROUGH, TOUGH WEST, THE, 1952, A
ROUGHLY SPEAKING, 1945
ROUGHNECK, THE, 1919
ROUGHNECK, THE, 1924, A
ROUGHSHOD, 1949, A
ROULETTE, 1924, A
ROUND TRIP, 1967, C
ROUND UP, THE, 1920, A
ROUND UP, THE, 1969, O
ROUNDERS, THE, 1965, A-C
ROUNDING UP THE LAW, 1922

ROUNDTRIP
ROUNDUP TIME IN TEXAS, 1937
ROUNDUP, THE, 1941, A
ROUSTABOUT, 1964, A
ROVER, THE, 1967, C
ROVIN' TUMBLEWEEDS, 1939
ROVING ROGUE, A
ROWDY, THE, 1921, A
ROWDYMAN, THE, 1973, C
ROXIE HART, 1942, A
ROYAL AFFAIR, A, 1950, A
ROYAL AFFAIRS IN VERSAILLES, 1957, A
ROYAL AFRICAN RIFLES, THE, 1953, A
ROYAL AMERICAN, THE, 1927
ROYAL BED, THE, 1931, A
ROYAL BOX, THE, 1914
ROYAL BOX, THE, 1930, A
ROYAL CAVALCADE
ROYAL DEMAND, A, 1933, A
ROYAL DEMOCRAT, A, 1919
ROYAL DIVORCE, A, 1923
ROYAL DIVORCE, A, 1938, A
ROYAL EAGLE, 1936, A
ROYAL FAMILY OF BROADWAY, THE, 1930, A
ROYAL FAMILY, A, 1915, A
ROYAL FLASH, 1975, A-C
ROYAL FLUSH
ROYAL GAME, THE
ROYAL HUNT OF THE SUN, THE, 1969, A
ROYAL LOVE, 1915
ROYAL MOUNTED PATROL, THE, 1941
ROYAL OAK, THE, 1923, A
ROYAL PAUPER, THE, 1917
ROYAL RIDER, THE, 1929, A
ROYAL ROMANCE, 1917
ROYAL ROMANCE, A, 1930, A
ROYAL SCANDAL, 1929
ROYAL SCANDAL, A, 1945, C-O
ROYAL TRACK, THE
ROYAL WALTZ, THE, 1936, A
ROYAL WEDDING, 1951, A
ROZMARNE LETO
RUBA AL PROSSIMO TUO
RUBBER GUN, THE, 1977, C
RUBBER HEELS, 1927
RUBBER RACKETEERS, 1942, A
RUBBER TIRES, 1927, A
RUBE, THE, 1925
RUBY, 1971, C
RUBY, 1977, O
RUBY GENTRY, 1952, C-O
RUBY VIRGIN, THE
RUCKUS, 1981, C
RUDDIGORE, 1967
RUDE BOY, 1980, O
RUDYARD KIPLING'S JUNGLE BOOK
RUE CASES NEGRES
RUE DE LA PAIX, 1927
RUGGED O'RIORDANS, THE, 1949, A
RUGGED PATH, THE, 1918
RUGGED WATER, 1925, A
RUGGLES OF RED GAP, 1918
RUGGLES OF RED GAP, 1923, A
RUGGLES OF RED GAP, 1935, A
RULER OF THE ROAD, 1918
RULER OF THE WORLD
RULERS OF THE SEA, 1939, A
RULES OF THE GAME, THE, 1939, C
RULING CLASS, THE, 1972, O
RULING PASSION, THE, 1916
RULING PASSION, THE, 1922, A
RULING VOICE, THE, 1931, A
RUM RUNNERS, THE, 1923
RUMBA, 1935, A
RUMBLE FISH, 1983, O
RUMBLE ON THE DOCKS, 1956, A
RUMMY, THE, 1916
RUMPELSTILSKIN, 1915
RUMPELSTILTSKIN, 1965, A
RUMPELSTILZCHEN
RUN ACROSS THE RIVER, 1961, A
RUN FOR COVER, 1955, A-C
RUN FOR THE HILLS, 1953, A
RUN FOR THE ROSES, 1978, C
RUN FOR THE SUN, 1956, A
RUN FOR YOUR MONEY, A, 1950, A
RUN FOR YOUR WIFE, 1966, C
RUN HERO RUN
RUN HOME SLOW, 1965
RUN LIKE A THIEF
RUN LIKE A THIEF, 1968, C
RUN OF THE ARROW, 1957, C-O
RUN ON GOLD, A
RUN SHADOW RUN
RUN SILENT, RUN DEEP, 1958, A-C
RUN WILD, RUN FREE, 1969, A
RUN WITH THE DEVIL, 1963, A
RUN WITH THE WIND, 1966, O
RUN, ANGEL, RUN, 1969, O
RUN, RUN, JOE!, 1974
RUN, STRANGER, RUN
RUNAROUND, THE, 1931, A

RUNAROUND, THE, 1946, A
RUNAWAY, 1971
RUNAWAY, 1984, C-O
RUNAWAY BRIDE, 1930, A
RUNAWAY BUS, THE, 1954, A
RUNAWAY DAUGHTER
RUNAWAY DAUGHTERS, 1957, A
RUNAWAY DAUGHTERS, 1968
RUNAWAY EXPRESS, THE, 1926
RUNAWAY GIRL, 1966, C
RUNAWAY GIRLS, 1928, A
RUNAWAY LADIES, 1935, A
RUNAWAY PRINCESS, THE, 1929
RUNAWAY QUEEN, THE, 1935, A
RUNAWAY RAILWAY, 1965, AA
RUNAWAY ROMANY, 1917
RUNAWAY WIFE, THE, 1915
RUNAWAY, THE, 1917
RUNAWAY, THE, 1926, A
RUNAWAY, THE, 1964, A
RUNNER STUMBLES, THE, 1979, C
RUNNERS, 1983, A
RUNNING, 1979, C
RUNNING BRAVE, 1983, C
RUNNING FIGHT, THE, 1915, A
RUNNING HOT, 1984, O
RUNNING MAN, THE, 1963, A-C
RUNNING SCARED
RUNNING SCARED, 1972, C-O
RUNNING SCARED, 1980
RUNNING TARGET, 1956, A
RUNNING WATER, 1922, A
RUNNING WILD, 1927
RUNNING WILD, 1955, A
RUNNING WILD, 1973
RUNNING WITH THE DEVIL, 1973
RUPERT OF HENTZAU, 1915, A
RUPERT OF HENTZAU, 1923, A
RUSE OF THE RATTLER, THE, 1921
RUSH, 1984, C-O
RUSH HOUR, THE, 1927, A
RUSLAN I LUDMILA, 1915
RUSSIA, 1929
RUSSIA—LAND OF TOMORROW, 1919
RUSSIAN ROULETTE, 1975, C
RUSSIANS ARE COMING, THE RUSSIANS ARE
    COMING, THE, 1966, A
RUSTLE OF SILK, THE, 1923
RUSTLER'S END, THE, 1928
RUSTLER'S HIDEOUT, 1944, A
RUSTLER'S PARADISE, 1935, A
RUSTLER'S RANCH, 1926, A
RUSTLER'S ROUNDUP, 1946, A
RUSTLER'S VALLEY, 1937, A
RUSTLERS, 1949, A
RUSTLERS OF DEVIL'S CANYON, 1947, A
RUSTLERS OF THE BADLANDS, 1945
RUSTLERS OF THE NIGHT, 1921
RUSTLERS ON HORSEBACK, 1950, A
RUSTLERS' ROUNDUP, 1933, A
RUSTLING A BRIDE, 1919
RUSTLING FOR CUPID, 1926
RUSTY LEADS THE WAY, 1948, A
RUSTY RIDES ALONE, 1933, A
RUSTY SAVES A LIFE, 1949, A
RUSTY'S BIRTHDAY, 1949, A
RUTHLESS, 1948, A
RUTHLESS FOUR, THE, 1969, C
RUUSUJEN AIKA
RUY BLAS, 1948, A
RX MURDER, 1958, A
RYAN'S DAUGHTER, 1970, O
RYMDINVASION I LAPPLAND
RYSOPIS

-S-

S, 1974, C
S.O.B., 1981, O
S.O.S., 1928
S.O.S. COAST GUARD, 1937
S.O.S. ICEBERG, 1933, A
S.O.S. PACIFIC, 1960, A
S.O.S. PERILS OF THE SEA, 1925
S.O.S. TIDAL WAVE, 1939, A
S.T.A.B., 1976, O
S.W.A.L.K.
SA GOSSE, 1919
SA TETE, 1930
SAADIA, 1953, A
SABA, 1929
SABAKA
SABALEROS
SABATA, 1969, C
SABINA, THE, 1979, O
SABLE BLESSING, THE, 1916
SABLE LORCHA, THE, 1915, A
SABLES, 1928
SABOTAGE, 1937, O
SABOTAGE, 1939, A
SABOTAGE AT SEA, 1942, A
SABOTAGE SQUAD, 1942, A
SABOTAGE, 1932, Brit.

SABOTEUR, 1942, A
SABOTEUR, CODE NAME MORITURI
SABRA, 1970, C
SABRE AND THE ARROW, THE
SABRE JET, 1953, A
SABRINA, 1954, A
SABRINA FAIR
SABU AND THE MAGIC RING, 1957, A
SACCO AND VANZETTI, 1971, C
SACKCLOTH AND SCARLET, 1925
SACRED AND PROFANE LOVE, 1921
SACRED FLAME, THE, 1919
SACRED FLAME, THE, 1929, A
SACRED FLAME, THE, 1935, A
SACRED GROUND, 1984, C
SACRED HEARTS, 1984, A
SACRED KNIVES OF VENGEANCE, THE, 1974, O
SACRED RUBY, THE, 1920
SACRED SILENCE, 1919, A
SACRIFICE, 1917
SACRIFICE, 1929
SACRIFICE OF HONOR, 1938, A
SAD HORSE, THE, 1959, AA
SAD SACK, THE, 1957, A
SAD SACK, THE, 1963
SADDLE ACES, 1935
SADDLE BUSTER, THE, 1932, A
SADDLE CYCLONE, 1925
SADDLE HAWK, THE, 1925
SADDLE JUMPERS, 1927
SADDLE KING, THE, 1929
SADDLE LEATHER LAW, 1944
SADDLE LEGION, 1951, A
SADDLE MATES, 1928
SADDLE MOUNTAIN ROUNDUP, 1941, A
SADDLE PALS, 1947, A
SADDLE SERENADE, 1945
SADDLE THE WIND, 1958, A
SADDLE TRAMP, 1950, A
SADDLEMATES, 1941, A
SADDLES AND SAGEBRUSH, 1943
SADIE GOES TO HEAVEN, 1917
SADIE LOVE, 1920
SADIE MCKEE, 1934, A
SADIE THOMPSON, 1928, C
SADIE THOMPSON, 1928, C
SADIST THE, 1963, A
SADKO
SAFARI, 1940, A
SAFARI, 1956, A
SAFARI 3000, 1982, A-C
SAFARI DRUMS, 1953, A
SAFE AFFAIR, A, 1931, A
SAFE AT HOME, 1962, A
SAFE FOR DEMOCRACY
SAFE GUARDED, 1924
SAFE IN HELL, 1931, A
SAFE PLACE, A, 1971, A
SAFECRACKER, THE, 1958, A
SAFETY CURTAIN, THE, 1918
SAFETY FIRST, 1926, A
SAFETY IN NUMBERS, 1930, A
SAFETY IN NUMBERS, 1938, A
SAFETY LAST, 1923, A
SAFFO, VENERE DE LESBO
SAGA OF DEATH VALLEY, 1939, A
SAGA OF DRACULA, THE, 1975, O
SAGA OF GOSTA BERLING, THE, 1924
SAGA OF HEMP BROWN, THE, 1958, A
SAGA OF THE FLYING HOSTESS
SAGA OF THE ROAD, THE
SAGA OF THE VAGABONDS, 1964, A
SAGA OF THE VIKING WOMEN AND THEIR VOYAGE
    TO THE WATERS OF THE, 1957, A
SAGE BRUSH HAMLET, A, 1919
SAGE HEN, THE, 1921
SAGE-BRUSH LEAGUE, THE, 1919
SAGEBRUSH FAMILY TRAILS WEST, THE, 1940, A
SAGEBRUSH GOSPEL, 1924
SAGEBRUSH HEROES, 1945
SAGEBRUSH LADY, THE, 1925
SAGEBRUSH LAW, 1943, A
SAGEBRUSH POLITICS, 1930, A
SAGEBRUSH TRAIL, 1934, A
SAGEBRUSH TRAIL, THE, 1922
SAGEBRUSH TROUBADOR, 1935, A
SAGEBRUSHER, THE, 1920
SAGINAW TRAIL, 1953, A
SAGITTARIUS MINE, THE, 1972
SAHARA, 1919, C
SAHARA, 1943, C
SAHARA, 1984, C
SAHARA LOVE, 1926
SAID O'REILLY TO MACNAB
SAIGON, 1948, A
SAIKAKU ICHIDAI ONNA
SAIL A CROOKED SHIP, 1961, A
SAIL INTO DANGER, 1957, A
SAILING ALONG, 1938, A
SAILOR BE GOOD, 1933, A
SAILOR BEWARE, 1951, A
SAILOR BEWARE?

SAILOR FROM GIBRALTAR, THE, 1967, O
SAILOR IZZY MURPHY, 1927, A
SAILOR OF THE KING, 1953, A
SAILOR TAKES A WIFE, THE, 1946, A
SAILOR TRAMP, A, 1922
SAILOR WHO FELL FROM GRACE WITH THE SEA,
    THE, 1976, O
SAILOR'S DON'T CARE, 1940, A
SAILOR'S HOLIDAY, 1944, A
SAILOR'S LADY, 1940, A
SAILOR'S LUCK, 1933, A
SAILOR'S RETURN, THE, 1978, O
SAILOR'S SWEETHEART, A, 1927, A
SAILOR-MADE MAN, A, 1921, A
SAILORS DON'T CARE, 1928
SAILORS ON LEAVE, 1941, A
SAILORS THREE
SAILORS' HOLIDAY, 1929, A
SAILORS' WIVES, 1928
SAINT AND THE BRAVE GOOSE, THE, 1981
SAINT IN LONDON, THE, 1939, A
SAINT IN NEW YORK, THE, 1938, A
SAINT IN PALM SPRINGS, THE, 1941, A
SAINT JACK, 1979, O
SAINT JOAN, 1957, A-C
SAINT MEETS THE TIGER, THE, 1943, A
SAINT STRIKES BACK, THE, 1939, A
SAINT TAKES OVER, THE, 1940, A
SAINT'S ADVENTURE, THE, 1917
SAINT'S DOUBLE TROUBLE, THE, 1940, A
SAINT'S GIRL FRIDAY, THE, 1954, A
SAINT'S RETURN, THE
SAINT'S VACATION, THE, 1941, A
SAINT, DEVIL AND WOMAN, 1916
SAINTED DEVIL, A, 1924, A
SAINTED SISTERS, THE, 1948, A
SAINTLY SINNER, THE, 1917
SAINTLY SINNERS, 1962, A
SAINTS AND SINNERS, 1916
SAINTS AND SINNERS, 1949, A
SAJENKO THE SOVIET, 1929
SAL OF SINGAPORE, 1929, A
SALAMANDER, THE, 1915, A
SALAMANDER, THE, 1916
SALAMANDER, THE, 1983, O
SALAMMBO
SALAMMBO, 1925
SALARIO PARA MATAR
SALESLADY, 1938, A
SALESLADY, THE, 1916
SALESLADY?, 1968, A-C
SALLAH, 1965, C
SALLY, 1925, A
SALLY, 1929, A
SALLY AND SAINT ANNE, 1952, A
SALLY BISHOP, 1916
SALLY BISHOP, 1923
SALLY BISHOP, 1932, O
SALLY CASTLETON, SOUTHERNER, 1915
SALLY FIELDGOOD & CO., 1975, C-O
SALLY IN A HURRY, 1917
SALLY IN OUR ALLEY, 1916
SALLY IN OUR ALLEY, 1927, A
SALLY IN OUR ALLEY, 1931, A
SALLY OF THE SAWDUST, 1925, A
SALLY OF THE SCANDALS, A
SALLY OF THE SUBWAY, 1932, C
SALLY SHOWS THE WAY
SALLY'S HOUNDS, 1968, C
SALLY'S IRISH ROGUE
SALLY'S SHOULDERS, 1928
SALLY, IRENE AND MARY, 1925
SALLY, IRENE AND MARY, 1938, A
SALOME, 1919
SALOME, 1922, A
SALOME, 1923
SALOME, 1953, C
SALOME OF THE TENEMENTS, 1925
SALOME, WHERE SHE DANCED, 1945, C
SALOMY JANE, 1914, A
SALOMY JANE, 1923, A
SALOON BAR, 1940, C
SALT & PEPPER, 1968, C
SALT AND THE DEVIL
SALT IN THE WOUND, 1972
SALT LAKE RAIDERS, 1950, A
SALT LAKE TRAIL, 1926
SALT OF THE EARTH, 1917
SALT OF THE EARTH, 1954, C
SALT TO THE DEVIL, 1949, A
SALTO, 1966, O
SALTY, 1975, A
SALTY O'ROURKE, 1945, A-C
SALTY SAUNDERS, 1923
SALUTE, 1929, A
SALUTE FOR THREE, 1943, A
SALUTE JOHN CITIZEN, 1942, A
SALUTE THE TOFF, 1952, A
SALUTE TO A REBEL
SALUTE TO COURAGE
SALUTE TO ROMANCE
SALUTE TO THE MARINES, 1943, C

SALVAGE, 1921, A
SALVAGE GANG, THE, 1958, AA
SALVARE LA FACCIA
SALVATION HUNTERS, THE, 1925, A
SALVATION JANE, 1927, A
SALVATION JOAN, 1916
SALVATION NELL, 1921, A
SALVATION NELL, 1931, A
SALVATORE GIULIANO, 1966, O
SALZBURG CONNECTION, THE, 1972, C
SAM COOPER'S GOLD
SAM MARLOW, PRIVATE EYE
SAM SMALL LEAVES TOWN, 1937, A
SAM WHISKEY, 1969, C-O
SAM'S BOY, 1922
SAM'S SON, 1984, A-C
SAM'S SONG, 1971, O
SAMANTHA
SAMAR, 1962, C
SAMARITAN, THE
SAME TIME, NEXT YEAR, 1978, A-C
SAMMY GOING SOUTH
SAMMY SOMEBODY, 1976
SAMMY STOPS THE WORLD, 1978, C
SAMPO
SAMSON, 1914, A
SAMSON, 1915
SAMSON, 1961, A
SAMSON AND DELILAH, 1922
SAMSON AND DELILAH, 1949, C
SAMSON AND THE SEA BEAST, 1960
SAMSON AND THE SEVEN MIRACLES OF THE
    WORLD, 1963, A
SAMSON AND THE SLAVE QUEEN, 1963, A
SAMSON IN THE WAX MUSEUM
SAMSON VS. THE GIANT KING
SAMURAI
SAMURAI, 1945, A-C
SAMURAI, 1955, O
SAMURAI (PART II), 1967, C-O
SAMURAI (PART III), 1967, C-O
SAMURAI ASSASSIN, 1965, O
SAMURAI BANNERS
SAMURAI FROM NOWHERE, 1964, C
SAMURAI PIRATE
SAN ANTONE, 1953, C
SAN ANTONE AMBUSH, 1949, A
SAN ANTONIO, 1945, A-C
SAN ANTONIO KID, THE, 1944, A
SAN ANTONIO ROSE, 1941, A
SAN DEMETRIO, LONDON, 1947, C
SAN DIEGO, I LOVE YOU, 1944, A
SAN FERNANDO VALLEY, 1944, A
SAN FERRY ANN, 1965, A
SAN FRANCISCO, 1936, A
SAN FRANCISCO DOCKS, 1941, A
SAN FRANCISCO NIGHTS, 1928
SAN FRANCISCO STORY, THE, 1952, A
SAN QUENTIN, 1937, C
SAN QUENTIN, 1946, A
SANCTUARY, 1916, A
SANCTUARY, 1961, O
SAND, 1920, A
SAND, 1949, A
SAND BLIND, 1925
SAND CASTLE, THE, 1961, AAA
SAND PEBBLES, THE, 1966, C-O
SANDA TAI GAILAH
SANDAI KAIJU CHIKYU SAIDAI NO KESSEN
SANDERS, 1963, A
SANDERS OF THE RIVER, 1935, A-C
SANDFLOW, 1937, A
SANDOKAN THE GREAT, 1964, A
SANDPIPER, THE, 1965, C-O
SANDPIT GENERALS, THE
SANDRA, 1924
SANDRA, 1966, O
SANDS OF BEERSHEBA, 1966, O
SANDS OF FATE, 1914
SANDS OF IWO JIMA, 1949, C
SANDS OF SACRIFICE, 1917
SANDS OF THE DESERT, 1960, A
SANDS OF THE KALAHARI, 1965, O
SANDS OF TIME, THE, 1919
SANDU FOLLOWS THE SUN, 1965, AAA
SANDWICH MAN, THE, 1966, A
SANDY, 1918
SANDY, 1926, A
SANDY BURKE OF THE U-BAR-U, 1919
SANDY GETS HER MAN, 1940, AAA
SANDY IS A LADY, 1940, AAA
SANDY TAKES A BOW
SANDY THE SEAL, 1969, AAA
SANG D'UN POETE
SANG ET LUMIERES
SANGAREE, 1953, C
SANITORIUM
SANJURO, 1962, C
SANS FAMILLE, 1925
SANSHO THE BAILIFF, 1969, A
SANSONE
SANTA, 1932, O

SANTA AND THE THREE BEARS, 1970, AAA
SANTA CLAUS, 1960, AAA
SANTA CLAUS CONQUERS THE MARTIANS,
    1964, C-O
SANTA FE, 1951, A
SANTA FE BOUND, 1937, A
SANTA FE MARSHAL, 1940, A
SANTA FE PASSAGE, 1955, O
SANTA FE PETE, 1925
SANTA FE RIDES, 1937
SANTA FE SADDLEMATES, 1945, A
SANTA FE SATAN
SANTA FE SCOUTS, 1943, A
SANTA FE STAMPEDE, 1938, C
SANTA FE TRAIL, 1940, C
SANTA FE TRAIL, THE, 1930, A
SANTA FE UPRISING, 1946, A
SANTA'S CHRISTMAS CIRCUS, 1966, AAA
SANTEE, 1973, O
SANTIAGO, 1956, A
SANTO AND THE BLUE DEMON VS. THE MONSTERS
SANTO CONTRA BLUE DEMON EN LA ATLANTIDA,
    1968, O
SANTO CONTRA EL CEREBRO DIABOLICO, 1962, C
SANTO CONTRA EL DOCTOR MUERTE, 1974, O
SANTO CONTRA LA HIJA DE FRANKENSTEIN,
    1971, O
SANTO CONTRA LA INVASION DE LOS MARCIANOS,
    1966, O
SANTO EN EL MUSEO DE CERA, 1963, O
SANTO VERSUS THE MARTIAN INVASION
SANTO VS. FRANKENSTEIN'S DAUGHTER
SANTO Y BLUE DEMON CONTRA LOS MONSTRUOS
    ZERO, 1968, O
SAP FROM ABROAD, THE
SAP FROM SYRACUSE, THE, 1930, A
SAP, THE, 1926
SAP, THE, 1929, A
SAPHEAD, THE, 1921, A
SAPHO
SAPHO, 1917
SAPPHIRE, 1959, A
SAPPHO, 1913
SAPS AT SEA, 1940, A
SARABA MOSUKUWA GURENTAI
SARABAND, 1949, A
SARABAND FOR DEAD LOVERS
SARACEN BLADE, THE, 1954, A
SARAGOSSA MANUSCRIPT, THE, 1972, A
SARAH AND SON, 1930, A
SARAH AND THE SQUIRREL, 1983
SARATI-LE-TERRIBLE, 1923
SARATOGA, 1937, A
SARATOGA TRUNK, 1945, A-C
SARDINIA: RANSOM, 1968, C
SARDONICUS
SARGE GOES TO COLLEGE, 1947, A
SARONG GIRL, 1943, A
SARUMBA, 1950, A
SASAKI KOJIRO
SASAYASHI NO JOE
SASKATCHEWAN, 1954, A-C
SASOM I EN SPEGEL
SASQUATCH, 1978, A
SATAN AND THE WOMAN, 1928
SATAN BUG, THE, 1965, A
SATAN IN HIGH HEELS, 1962, O
SATAN IN SABLES, 1925
SATAN JUNIOR, 1919
SATAN MET A LADY, 1936, A
SATAN NEVER SLEEPS, 1962, C
SATAN SANDERSON, 1915
SATAN TOWN, 1926
SATAN TRIUMPHANT, 1917
SATAN'S BED, 1965, O
SATAN'S BLACK WEDDING, 1976
SATAN'S CHEERLEADERS, 1977, O
SATAN'S CHILDREN, 1975
SATAN'S CLAW
SATAN'S CRADLE, 1949, A
SATAN'S HARVEST, 1970
SATAN'S MISTRESS, 1982, O
SATAN'S PAWN
SATAN'S PRIVATE DOOR, 1917
SATAN'S SADIST, 1969, O
SATAN'S SATELLITES, 1958, AA
SATAN'S SISTER, 1925, A
SATAN'S SKIN
SATAN'S SLAVE, 1976, O
SATANAS, 1919
SATANIC RITES OF DRACULA, THE
SATANIST, THE, 1968
SATELLITE IN THE SKY, 1956, A
SATIN GIRL, THE, 1923
SATIN MUSHROOM, THE, 1969, C
SATIN WOMAN, THE, 1927
SATURDAY ISLAND
SATURDAY NIGHT, 1922, A
SATURDAY NIGHT AND SUNDAY MORNING, 1961, O
SATURDAY NIGHT AT THE BATHS, 1975, O
SATURDAY NIGHT BATH IN APPLE VALLEY
SATURDAY NIGHT FEVER, 1977, C-O

SATURDAY NIGHT IN APPLE VALLEY, 1965, C
SATURDAY NIGHT KID, THE, 1929, A
SATURDAY NIGHT OUT, 1964, A
SATURDAY NIGHT REVUE, 1937, A
SATURDAY THE 14TH, 1981, A
SATURDAY'S CHILDREN, 1929, A
SATURDAY'S CHILDREN, 1940, A
SATURDAY'S HERO, 1951, A
SATURDAY'S HEROES, 1937, A
SATURDAY'S MILLIONS, 1933, A
SATURN 3, 1980, C
SATYRICON
SAUCE FOR THE GOOSE, 1918
SAUL AND DAVID, 1968, A
SAUTERELLE
SAUVE QUI PEUT/LA VIE
SAVAGE ABDUCTION, 1975, O
SAVAGE AMERICAN, THE
SAVAGE BRIGADE, 1948, A
SAVAGE DAWN, 1984, O
SAVAGE DRUMS, 1951, A
SAVAGE EYE, THE, 1960, C-O
SAVAGE FRONTIER, 1953, A
SAVAGE GIRL, THE, 1932, A
SAVAGE GOLD, 1933, C
SAVAGE GUNS, THE, 1962, A
SAVAGE HARVEST, 1981, O
SAVAGE HORDE, THE, 1950, A
SAVAGE INNOCENTS, THE, 1960, A
SAVAGE IS LOOSE, THE, 1974, C
SAVAGE MESSIAH, 1972, O
SAVAGE MUTINY, 1953, A
SAVAGE OF THE SEA, 1925
SAVAGE PAMPAS, 1967, C
SAVAGE PASSIONS, 1927
SAVAGE SAM, 1963, A
SAVAGE SEASON, 1970
SAVAGE SEVEN, THE, 1968, O
SAVAGE SISTERS, 1974, O
SAVAGE STREETS, 1984, O
SAVAGE WEEKEND, 1983, O
SAVAGE WILD, THE, 1970, A
SAVAGE WILDERNESS
SAVAGE WOMAN, THE, 1918
SAVAGE!, 1973
SAVAGE, THE, 1917
SAVAGE, THE, 1926
SAVAGE, THE, 1953, A
SAVAGE, THE, 1975, C
SAVAGE?, 1962, A
SAVAGES, 1972, O
SAVAGES FROM HELL, 1968, O
SAVANNAH SMILES, 1983, AA
SAVE A LITTLE SUNSHINE, 1938, A
SAVE THE TIGER, 1973, C-O
SAVED BY RADIO, 1922
SAVED FROM THE HAREM, 1915
SAVED FROM THE SEA, 1920
SAVING THE FAMILY NAME, 1916, A
SAVVA, 1919
SAWDUST, 1923, A
SAWDUST AND TINSEL
SAWDUST DOLL, THE, 1919
SAWDUST PARADISE, THE, 1928
SAWDUST RING, THE, 1917
SAWDUST TRAIL, 1924, A
SAXON CHARM, THE, 1948, A
SAY HELLO TO YESTERDAY, 1971, C
SAY IT AGAIN, 1926
SAY IT IN FRENCH, 1938, A
SAY IT WITH DIAMONDS, 1927
SAY IT WITH DIAMONDS, 1935, A
SAY IT WITH FLOWERS, 1934, A
SAY IT WITH MUSIC, 1932, A
SAY IT WITH SABLES, 1928
SAY IT WITH SONGS, 1929, A
SAY ONE FOR ME, 1959, C
SAY YOUNG FELLOW, 1918, A
SAYONARA, 1957, C
SAYS O'REILLY TO MCNAB
SCALAWAG, 1973, A
SCALAWAG BUNCH, THE, 1976
SCALES OF JUSTICE, THE, 1914, A
SCALP MERCHANT, THE, 1977
SCALPEL, 1976, O
SCALPHUNTERS, THE, 1968, C-O
SCALPS, 1983, O
SCAMP, THE
SCANDAL, 1915, A
SCANDAL, 1917
SCANDAL, 1929, A
SCANDAL, 1964, A
SCANDAL '64
SCANDAL AT SCOURIE, 1953, A
SCANDAL FOR SALE, 1932, A
SCANDAL IN DENMARK, 1970, O
SCANDAL IN PARIS, 1929
SCANDAL IN PARIS, A, 1946, A
SCANDAL IN SORRENTO, 1957, O
SCANDAL INCORPORATED, 1956, A
SCANDAL MONGERS, 1918

SCANDAL PROOF, 1925
SCANDAL SHEET, 1931, A
SCANDAL SHEET, 1940, A
SCANDAL SHEET, 1952, C
SCANDAL STREET, 1925
SCANDAL STREET, 1938, A
SCANDAL, THE, 1923, A
SCANDAL?, 1929
SCANDALOUS, 1984, C
SCANDALOUS ADVENTURES OF BURAIKAN, THE,
  1970, C
SCANDALOUS JOHN, 1971, AA
SCANDALOUS TONGUES, 1922
SCANDALS
SCANDALS OF PARIS, 1935, A
SCANNERS, 1981, O
SCAPEGOAT, THE, 1959, A
SCAPPAMENTO APERTO
SCAR HANAN, 1925
SCAR OF SHAME, THE, 1927
SCAR, THE
SCAR, THE, 1919
SCARAB, 1982, O
SCARAB MURDER CASE, THE, 1936, A
SCARAB RING, THE, 1921, A
SCARAMOUCHE, 1923, A
SCARAMOUCHE, 1952, A
SCARAMOUCHE, 1964
SCARECROW, 1973, C-O
SCARECROW IN A GARDEN OF CUCUMBERS, 1972, C
SCARECROW, THE, 1982, C
SCARED STIFF, 1945, A
SCARED STIFF, 1953, A
SCARED TO DEATH, 1947, A
SCARED TO DEATH, 1981, O
SCAREHEADS, 1931, A
SCAREMAKER, THE
SCARF, THE, 1951, A
SCARFACE, 1932, O
SCARFACE, 1983, O
SCARFACE MOB, THE, 1962, A
SCARLET AND GOLD, 1925
SCARLET ANGEL, 1952, A
SCARLET BLADE, THE
SCARLET BRAND, 1932, A
SCARLET BUCCANEER, THE
SCARLET CAMELLIA, THE, 1965, C
SCARLET CAR, THE, 1918
SCARLET CAR, THE, 1923, A
SCARLET CLAW, THE, 1944, A
SCARLET CLUE, THE, 1945, A
SCARLET COAT, THE, 1955, A
SCARLET CRYSTAL, THE, 1917
SCARLET DAREDEVIL, THE, 1928
SCARLET DAWN, 1932, A
SCARLET DAYS, 1919, A
SCARLET DOVE, THE, 1928, A
SCARLET DROP, THE, 1918
SCARLET EMPRESS, THE, 1934, C
SCARLET HONEYMOON, THE, 1925
SCARLET HOUR, THE, 1956, A
SCARLET KISS, THE, 1920
SCARLET LADY, THE, 1922
SCARLET LADY, THE, 1928, A
SCARLET LETTER, THE, 1917
SCARLET LETTER, THE, 1926, A
SCARLET LETTER, THE, 1934, A
SCARLET LILY, THE, 1923, A
SCARLET OATH, THE, 1916
SCARLET PAGES, 1930, A
SCARLET PIMPERNEL, THE, 1917
SCARLET PIMPERNEL, THE, 1935, A
SCARLET RIVER, 1933, A
SCARLET ROAD, THE, 1916, A
SCARLET ROAD, THE, 1918
SCARLET SAINT, 1925
SCARLET SEAS, 1929, A
SCARLET SHADOW, THE, 1919
SCARLET SIN, THE, 1915, A
SCARLET SPEAR, THE, 1954, A
SCARLET STREET, 1945, C
SCARLET THREAD, 1951, A
SCARLET TRAIL, THE, 1919
SCARLET WEB, THE, 1954, A
SCARLET WEEKEND, A, 1932, A
SCARLET WEST, THE, 1925
SCARLET WOMAN, THE, 1916
SCARLET WOOING, THE, 1920
SCARLET YOUTH, 1928
SCARRED, 1984, O
SCARRED HANDS, 1923
SCARS OF DRACULA, THE, 1970, O
SCARS OF HATE, 1923
SCARS OF JEALOUSY, 1923, A
SCATTERBRAIN, 1940, A
SCATTERGOOD BAINES, 1941, A
SCATTERGOOD MEETS BROADWAY, 1941, A
SCATTERGOOD PULLS THE STRINGS, 1941, A
SCATTERGOOD RIDES HIGH, 1942, A
SCATTERGOOD SURVIVES A MURDER, 1942, A
SCAVENGER HUNT, 1979, C
SCAVENGERS, THE, 1959, A

SCAVENGERS, THE, 1969, O
SCENE OF THE CRIME, 1949, A
SCENES FROM A MARRIAGE, 1974, C-O
SCENIC ROUTE, THE, 1978, A
SCENT OF A WOMAN, 1976, O
SCENT OF MYSTERY, 1960, A
SCHATTEN UBER TIRAN-KOMMANDO SINAI
SCHEHERAZADE, 1965, A
SCHEMERS, THE, 1922
SCHIZO, 1977, O
SCHIZOID, 1980, O
SCHLAGER-PARADE, 1953, A
SCHLOCK, 1973, A
SCHNEEWEISSCHEN UND ROSENROT
SCHNEEWITTCHEN UND DIE SIEBEN ZWERGE
SCHNOOK, THE (SEE: SWINGIN' ALONG, 1962)
SCHOOL DAYS, 1921, A
SCHOOL FOR BRIDES, 1952, A
SCHOOL FOR DANGER, 1947, A
SCHOOL FOR GIRLS, 1935, A
SCHOOL FOR HUSBANDS, 1939, A
SCHOOL FOR HUSBANDS, A, 1917
SCHOOL FOR RANDLE, 1949, A
SCHOOL FOR SCANDAL, THE, 1914
SCHOOL FOR SCANDAL, THE, 1923
SCHOOL FOR SCANDAL, THE, 1930, A
SCHOOL FOR SCOUNDRELS, 1960, AA
SCHOOL FOR SECRETS, 1946, A
SCHOOL FOR SEX, 1966, O
SCHOOL FOR SEX, 1969, O
SCHOOL FOR STARS, 1935, A
SCHOOL FOR UNCLAIMED GIRLS, 1973, O
SCHOOL FOR VIOLENCE
SCHOOL FOR WIVES, 1925
SCHOOL OF LOVE
SCHOOLBOY PENITENTIARY
SCHOOLGIRL DIARY, 1947, A
SCHOOLMASTER, THE
SCHOONER GANG, THE, 1937, A
SCHWARZE NYLONS-HEISSE NACHTE
SCHWEIK'S NEW ADVENTURES, 1943, A
SCHWESTERN, ODER DIE BALANCE DES GLUECKS
SCIENTIFIC CARDPLAYER, THE, 1972, A
SCINTILLATING SIN
SCIPIO
SCOBIE MALONE, 1975, O
SCOFFER, THE, 1920
SCOOP, THE, 1934, A
SCOOP, THE,
SCORCHER, THE, 1927
SCORCHING FURY, 1952
SCORCHY, 1976, O
SCORE, THE
SCORING, 1980
SCORPIO, 1973, C
SCORPIO SCARAB, THE, 1972
SCORPION WITH TWO TAILS, 1982
SCORPION'S STING, THE, 1915
SCOTCH ON THE ROCKS, 1954, A
SCOTLAND YARD, 1930, A
SCOTLAND YARD, 1941, A
SCOTLAND YARD COMMANDS, 1937, A
SCOTLAND YARD DRAGNET, 1957, A
SCOTLAND YARD HUNTS DR. MABUSE, 1963, A
SCOTLAND YARD INSPECTOR, 1952, A
SCOTLAND YARD INVESTIGATOR, 1945, A
SCOTLAND YARD MYSTERY, THE
SCOTT JOPLIN, 1977, C
SCOTT OF THE ANTARCTIC, 1949, A
SCOUNDREL IN WHITE
SCOUNDREL, THE, 1935, C
SCOURGE, THE
SCOUTS OF THE AIR
SCRAGS, 1930
SCRAMBLE, 1970, AAA
SCRAMBLED WIVES, 1921
SCRAP IRON, 1921
SCRAP OF PAPER, THE, 1920
SCRAPPER, THE, 1917, A
SCRAPPIN' KID, THE, 1926
SCRATCH HARRY, 1969, O
SCRATCH MY BACK, 1920
SCREAM AND DIE
SCREAM AND SCREAM AGAIN, 1970, O
SCREAM BLACULA SCREAM, 1973, O
SCREAM BLOODY MURDER, 1972, O
SCREAM BLOODY MURDER, 1973
SCREAM FOR HELP, 1984, O
SCREAM FREE
SCREAM IN THE DARK, A, 1943, A
SCREAM IN THE NIGHT, 1943, A
SCREAM IN THE NIGHT, A, 1919
SCREAM IN THE STREETS, A, 1972
SCREAM OF FEAR, 1961, C
SCREAM OF THE BUTTERFLY, 1965, O
SCREAM, BABY, SCREAM, 1969, O
SCREAMERS, 1978, A
SCREAMING EAGLES, 1956, A
SCREAMING HEAD, THE
SCREAMING MIMI, 1958, A
SCREAMING SKULL, THE, 1958, A
SCREAMS OF A WINTER NIGHT, 1979, A

SCREAMTIME, 1983
SCREWBALLS, 1983, O
SCROOGE, 1935, AA
SCROOGE, 1970, AAA
SCROOGE, 1951, Brit.
SCRUBBERS, 1984, O
SCRUFFY, 1938, AA
SCUDDA-HOO? SCUDDA-HAY?, 1948, A
SCULPTOR'S DREAM, 1929
SCUM, 1979, O
SCUM OF THE EARTH, 1963, O
SCUM OF THE EARTH, 1976, O
SCUSI, FACCIAMO L'AMORE?
SCUTTLERS, THE, 1920
SE PERMETTETE, PARLIAMO DI DONNE
SE TUTTE LE DONNE DEL MONDO
SEA BAT, THE, 1930, A
SEA BEAST, THE, 1926, A
SEA CHASE, THE, 1955, A-C
SEA DEVILS, 1931, A
SEA DEVILS, 1937, A
SEA DEVILS, 1953, A
SEA FEVER
SEA FLOWER, THE, 1918
SEA FURY, 1929, A
SEA FURY, 1959, A
SEA GHOST, THE, 1931, A
SEA GOD, THE, 1930, A
SEA GULL, THE, 1968, A-C
SEA GYPSIES, THE, 1978, AAA
SEA HAWK, THE, 1924
SEA HAWK, THE, 1940, A
SEA HORNET, THE, 1951, A
SEA HORSES, 1926, A
SEA LEGS, 1930, A
SEA LION, THE, 1921, A
SEA MASTER, THE, 1917
SEA NYMPHS
SEA OF GRASS, THE, 1947, A-C
SEA OF LOST SHIPS, 1953, A
SEA OF SAND
SEA PANTHER, THE, 1918
SEA PIRATE, THE, 1967, A
SEA PROWLERS
SEA RACKETEERS, 1937, A
SEA RIDER, THE, 1920
SEA SHALL NOT HAVE THEM, THE, 1955, A-C
SEA SPOILERS, THE, 1936, A
SEA TIGER, 1952, A
SEA TIGER, THE, 1927, A
SEA URCHIN, THE, 1926
SEA WAIF, THE, 1918
SEA WALL, THE
SEA WIFE, 1957, A
SEA WOLF, THE, 1920
SEA WOLF, THE, 1926
SEA WOLF, THE, 1930, A
SEA WOLF, THE, 1941, C
SEA WOLVES, THE, 1981, A
SEA WOMEN, THE
SEA WYF AND BUSCUIT
SEA-WOLF, THE, 1913, A
SEABO, 1978, O
SEAFIGHTERS, THE
SEAGULLS OVER SORRENTO
SEAL OF SILENCE, THE, 1918
SEALED CARGO, 1951, A
SEALED ENVELOPE, THE, 1919
SEALED HEARTS, 1919
SEALED LIPS, 1915, A
SEALED LIPS, 1925
SEALED LIPS, 1941, A
SEALED LIPS, 1933
SEALED VALLEY, THE, 1915, A
SEALED VERDICT, 1948, A
SEANCE ON A WET AFTERNOON, 1964, C
SEARCH AND DESTROY, 1981, C
SEARCH FOR BEAUTY, 1934, A
SEARCH FOR BRIDEY MURPHY, THE, 1956, A
SEARCH FOR DANGER, 1949, A
SEARCH FOR THE EVIL ONE, 1967
SEARCH FOR THE MOTHER LODE
SEARCH OF THE CASTAWAYS
SEARCH, THE, 1948, A
SEARCHERS, THE, 1956, C
SEARCHING WIND, THE, 1946, A-C
SEAS BENEATH, THE, 1931, A
SEASIDE SWINGERS, 1965, AA
SEASON FOR LOVE, THE, 1963, A-C
SEASON OF PASSION, 1961, C
SEASON OF THE WITCH
SEATED AT HIS RIGHT, 1968, O
SEATS OF THE MIGHTY, THE, 1914, A
SEAWEED CHILDREN, THE
SEAWOLF, 1974
SEBASTIAN, 1968, A
SECLUDED ROADHOUSE, THE, 1926
SECOND BEST BED, 1937, A
SECOND BEST SECRET AGENT IN THE WHOLE
  WIDE WORLD, THE, 1965, A-C
SECOND BUREAU, 1936, A
SECOND BUREAU, 1937, A

SEPARATE WAYS, 1981, O
SEPARATION, 1968, A
SEPARATION, 1977
SEPIA CINDERELLA, 1947, A
SEPPUKU
SEPT FOIS FEMME
SEPT HOMMES EN OR
SEPTEMBER 30, 1955
SEPTEMBER AFFAIR, 1950, A
SEPTEMBER STORM, 1960, A
SEQUEL TO THE DIAMOND FROM THE SKY, 1916
SEQUOIA, 1934, A
SERAFINO, 1970, A
SERDTSE MATERI
SERENA, 1962, A-C
SERENADE, 1921
SERENADE, 1927
SERENADE, 1956, A
SERENADE FOR TWO SPIES, 1966, A
SERENADE OF THE WEST, 1937
SERENADE OF THE WEST, 1942
SERENITY, 1962, A
SERGE PANIN, 1922
SERGEANT BERRY, 1938, A
SERGEANT DEADHEAD, 1965, A
SERGEANT DEADHEAD THE ASTRONAUT
SERGEANT JIM, 1962, A
SERGEANT MADDEN, 1939, A
SERGEANT MIKE, 1945, A
SERGEANT MURPHY, 1938, A
SERGEANT RUTLEDGE, 1960, C
SERGEANT RYKER, 1968, A
SERGEANT STEINER
SERGEANT WAS A LADY, THE, 1961, A
SERGEANT YORK, 1941, A
SERGEANT, THE, 1968, O
SERGEANTS 3, 1962, A
SERIAL, 1980, O
SERIOUS CHARGE
SERPENT ISLAND, 1954, A
SERPENT OF THE NILE, 1953, A
SERPENT'S EGG, THE, 1977, O
SERPENT'S TOOTH, THE, 1917
SERPENT, THE, 1916, C
SERPENT, THE, 1973, A-C
SERPENTS OF THE PIRATE MOON, THE, 1973, O
SERPICO, 1973, C-O
SERVANT IN THE HOUSE, THE, 1920
SERVANT QUESTION, THE, 1920
SERVANT, THE, 1964, C
SERVANTS' ENTRANCE, 1934, A
SERVICE
SERVICE DE LUXE, 1938, A
SERVICE FOR LADIES
SERVICE FOR LADIES, 1927
SERVICE STAR, THE, 1918
SERVING TWO MASTERS, 1921
SERYOZHA
SESSION WITH THE COMMITTEE
SET FREE, 1918
SET FREE, 1927
SET, THE, 1970, O
SET-UP, THE, 1926
SET-UP, THE, 1949, C
SET-UP, THE, 1963, A
SETTE CONTRO LA MORTE
SETTE DONNE PER I MAC GREGOR
SETTE PISTOLE PER I MAC GREGOR
SETTE UOMINI D'ORO
SETTE VOLTE DONNA
SETTE WINCHESTER PER UN MASSACRO
SETTLED OUT OF COURT, 1925
SEVEN, 1979, O
SEVEN AGAINST THE SUN, 1968, A
SEVEN ALONE, 1975, AA
SEVEN ANGRY MEN, 1955, A
SEVEN BAD MEN
SEVEN BEAUTIES, 1976, O
SEVEN BRAVE MEN, 1936, A
SEVEN BRIDES FOR SEVEN BROTHERS, 1954, AA
SEVEN BROTHERS MEET DRACULA, THE
SEVEN CAPITAL SINS, 1962, O
SEVEN CHANCES, 1925, A
SEVEN CITIES OF GOLD, 1955, A-C
SEVEN CITIES TO ATLANTIS
SEVEN DARING GIRLS, 1962, A
SEVEN DAYS, 1925
SEVEN DAYS ASHORE, 1944, A
SEVEN DAYS IN MAY, 1964, C
SEVEN DAYS LEAVE, 1930, A
SEVEN DAYS LEAVE, 1942, A
SEVEN DAYS TO NOON, 1950, C
SEVEN DEADLY SINS, THE, 1953, A
SEVEN DIFFERENT WAYS
SEVEN DOORS OF DEATH, 1983
SEVEN DOORS TO DEATH, 1944, A
SEVEN DWARFS TO THE RESCUE, THE, 1965, A
SEVEN FACES, 1929, A
SEVEN FACES OF DR. LAO, 1964, A
SEVEN FOOTPRINTS TO SATAN, 1929, C
SEVEN GOLDEN MEN, 1969, A
SEVEN GRAVES FOR ROGAN

SEVEN GUNS FOR THE MACGREGORS, 1968, A
SEVEN GUNS TO MESA, 1958, A
SEVEN HILLS OF ROME, THE, 1958, A
SEVEN KEYS, 1962, A
SEVEN KEYS TO BALDPATE, 1917
SEVEN KEYS TO BALDPATE, 1925
SEVEN KEYS TO BALDPATE, 1930, A
SEVEN KEYS TO BALDPATE, 1935, A
SEVEN KEYS TO BALDPATE, 1947, A
SEVEN LITTLE FOYS, THE, 1955, AAA
SEVEN MEN FROM NOW, 1956, A
SEVEN MILES FROM ALCATRAZ, 1942, A
SEVEN MINUTES, THE, 1971, O
SEVEN NIGHTS IN JAPAN, 1976, C
SEVEN REVENGES, THE, 1967, C
SEVEN SAMURAI, THE, 1956, C
SEVEN SEAS TO CALAIS, 1963, A
SEVEN SECRETS OF SU-MARU, THE
SEVEN SINNERS, 1925
SEVEN SINNERS, 1940, A
SEVEN SINNERS, 1936
SEVEN SISTERS
SEVEN SISTERS, THE, 1915, A
SEVEN SLAVES AGAINST THE WORLD, 1965, A
SEVEN SWANS, THE, 1918
SEVEN SWEETHEARTS, 1942, A
SEVEN TASKS OF ALI BABA, THE, 1963, A
SEVEN THIEVES, 1960, A-C
SEVEN THUNDERS
SEVEN TIMES SEVEN, 1973
SEVEN UPS, THE, 1973, C
SEVEN WAVES AWAY
SEVEN WAYS FROM SUNDOWN, 1960, A
SEVEN WERE SAVED, 1947, A
SEVEN WOMEN, 1966, C
SEVEN WOMEN FROM HELL, 1961, A
SEVEN YEAR ITCH, THE, 1955, A-C
SEVEN YEARS BAD LUCK, 1921
SEVEN-PER-CENT SOLUTION, THE, 1977, C
SEVENTEEN, 1916
SEVENTEEN, 1940, A
SEVENTH BANDIT, THE, 1926
SEVENTH CAVALRY, 1956, A
SEVENTH CONTINENT, THE, 1968, A
SEVENTH CROSS, THE, 1944, C
SEVENTH DAWN, THE, 1964, A-C
SEVENTH DAY, THE, 1922, A
SEVENTH HEAVEN, 1927, A
SEVENTH HEAVEN, 1937, A-C
SEVENTH JUROR, THE, 1964, A
SEVENTH NOON, THE, 1915
SEVENTH SEAL, THE, 1958, C
SEVENTH SHERIFF, THE, 1923, A
SEVENTH SIN, THE, 1917
SEVENTH SIN, THE, 1957, A
SEVENTH SURVIVOR, THE, 1941, A
SEVENTH VEIL, THE, 1946, A-C
SEVENTH VICTIM, THE, 1943, A
SEVENTH VOYAGE OF SINBAD, THE, 1958, AA
SEVENTY DEADLY PILLS, 1964, AA
SEVERED ARM, 1973
SEVERED HEAD, A, 1971, O
SEX, 1920, A
SEX AGENT
SEX AND THE SINGLE GIRL, 1964, C
SEX AND THE TEENAGER
SEX AT NIGHT
SEX DU JOUR, 1976
SEX IS A WOMAN
SEX KITTENS GO TO COLLEGE, 1960, A
SEX LURE, THE, 1916
SEX MADNESS, 1929
SEX MADNESS, 1937
SEX RACKETEERS, THE
SEXORCISTS, THE
SEXTETTE, 1978, C
SEXTON BLAKE AND THE BEARDED DOCTOR,
   1935, A
SEXTON BLAKE AND THE HOODED TERROR,
   1938, A
SEXTON BLAKE AND THE MADEMOISELLE, 1935, A
SEXY GANG
SEZ O'REILLY TO MACNAB, 1938, A
SFIDA A RIO BRAVO
SGT. PEPPER'S LONELY HEARTS CLUB BAND,
   1978, A
SH? THE OCTOPUS, 1937, A
SHABBY TIGER, THE
SHACK OUT ON 101, 1955, A
SHACKLED, 1918
SHACKLED BY FILM, 1918
SHACKLED LIGHTING, 1925
SHACKLES OF FEAR, 1924
SHACKLES OF GOLD, 1922, A
SHACKLES OF TRUTH, 1917
SHADES OF SILK, 1979, O
SHADOW AND THE MISSING LADY, THE, MISS, A
SHADOW BETWEEN, THE, 1920
SHADOW BETWEEN, THE, 1932, A
SHADOW IN THE SKY, 1951, A
SHADOW LAUGHS, 1933
SHADOW MAN, 1953, A

SHADOW OF A DOUBT, 1935, A
SHADOW OF A DOUBT, 1943, C
SHADOW OF A MAN, 1955, A-C
SHADOW OF A WOMAN, 1946, A
SHADOW OF CHIKARA
SHADOW OF DOUBT, THE, 1916
SHADOW OF EGYPT, THE, 1924, A
SHADOW OF EVIL, 1921
SHADOW OF EVIL, 1967, A
SHADOW OF FEAR, 1956, A
SHADOW OF FEAR, 1963, A
SHADOW OF LIGHTING RIDGE, THE, 1921
SHADOW OF MIKE EMERALD, THE, 1935, A
SHADOW OF NIGHT, THE
SHADOW OF ROSALIE BYRNES, THE, 1920
SHADOW OF SUSPICION, 1944, A
SHADOW OF TERROR, 1945, A
SHADOW OF THE CAT, THE, 1961, A
SHADOW OF THE DESERT
SHADOW OF THE EAGLE, 1955, A
SHADOW OF THE EAST, THE, 1924
SHADOW OF THE HAWK, 1976, A
SHADOW OF THE LAW, 1930, A
SHADOW OF THE LAW, THE, 1926
SHADOW OF THE PAST, 1950, A
SHADOW OF THE THIN MAN, 1941, A
SHADOW ON THE WALL, 1950, A
SHADOW ON THE WALL, THE, 1925
SHADOW ON THE WINDOW, THE, 1957, A
SHADOW RANCH, 1930, A
SHADOW RANGER, 1926
SHADOW RETURNS, THE, 1946, A
SHADOW STRIKES, THE, 1937, A
SHADOW VALLEY, 1947, A
SHADOW VERSUS THE THOUSAND EYES OF DR.
   MABUSE, THE
SHADOW WARRIOR, THE
SHADOW, THE, 1916
SHADOW, THE, 1921
SHADOW, THE, 1936, A
SHADOW, THE, 1937, A
SHADOWED, 1946, A
SHADOWED EYES, 1939, A-C
SHADOWMAN, 1974, A
SHADOWS, 1915
SHADOWS, 1919
SHADOWS, 1922, A
SHADOWS, 1931, A-C
SHADOWS, 1960, O
SHADOWS AND SUNSHINE, 1916
SHADOWS FROM THE PAST, 1915
SHADOWS GROW LONGER, THE, 1962, A
SHADOWS IN AN EMPTY ROOM
SHADOWS IN THE NIGHT, 1944, A
SHADOWS OF CHINATOWN, 1926
SHADOWS OF CONSCIENCE, 1921, A
SHADOWS OF DEATH, 1945, A
SHADOWS OF FEAR
SHADOWS OF FORGOTTEN ANCESTORS, 1967, A
SHADOWS OF OUR FORGOTTEN ANCESTORS
SHADOWS OF PARIS, 1924
SHADOWS OF SING SING, 1934, A
SHADOWS OF SINGAPORE
SHADOWS OF SUSPICION, 1919
SHADOWS OF THE MOULIN ROUGE, THE, 1914
SHADOWS OF THE NIGHT, 1928, A
SHADOWS OF THE NORTH, 1923
SHADOWS OF THE ORIENT, 1937, A
SHADOWS OF THE PAST, 1919
SHADOWS OF THE SEA, 1922, A
SHADOWS OF THE WEST, 1921
SHADOWS OF THE WEST, 1949, A
SHADOWS OF TOMBSTONE, 1953, A
SHADOWS OF YOSHIWARA, THE
SHADOWS ON THE RANGE, 1946
SHADOWS ON THE SAGE, 1942, A
SHADOWS ON THE STAIRS, 1941, A
SHADOWS OVER CHINATOWN, 1946, A
SHADOWS OVER SHANGHAI, 1938, A
SHADY LADY, 1945, A
SHADY LADY, THE, 1929, A
SHAFT, 1971, O
SHAFT IN AFRICA, 1973, O
SHAFT'S BIG SCORE, 1972, O
SHAGGY, 1948, AA
SHAGGY D.A., THE, 1976, AAA
SHAGGY DOG, THE, 1959, AAA
SHAKE HANDS WITH MURDER, 1944, A
SHAKE HANDS WITH THE DEVIL, 1959, C
SHAKE, RATTLE, AND ROCK?, 1957, A
SHAKEDOWN, 1936, A
SHAKEDOWN, 1950, C
SHAKEDOWN, 1934
SHAKEDOWN, THE, 1929, A
SHAKEDOWN, THE, 1960, C
SHAKESPEARE WALLAH, 1966, A
SHAKIEST GUN IN THE WEST, THE, 1968, A
SHALAKO, 1968, O
SHALIMAR, 1978
SHALL THE CHILDREN PAY?
SHALL WE DANCE, 1937, A
SHALL WE FORGIVE HER?, 1917

SHAM, 1921, A
SHAME
SHAME, 1918
SHAME, 1921, A
SHAME, 1968, O
SHAME OF MARY BOYLE, THE
SHAME OF PATTY SMITH, THE
SHAME OF THE JUNGLE, 1980
SHAME OF THE SABINE WOMEN, THE, 1962, A
SHAME, SHAME, EVERYBODY KNOWS HER NAME,
  1969, O
SHAMEFUL BEHAVIOR?, 1926
SHAMELESS OLD LADY, THE, 1966, A
SHAMPOO, 1975, O
SHAMROCK AND THE ROSE, THE, 1927
SHAMROCK HANDICAP, THE, 1926
SHAMROCK HILL, 1949, AA
SHAMS OF SOCIETY, 1921, A
SHAMUS, 1959, AA
SHAMUS, 1973, C
SHAN-KO LIEN
SHANE, 1953, C
SHANGHAI, 1935, A
SHANGHAI BOUND, 1927
SHANGHAI CHEST, THE, 1948, A
SHANGHAI COBRA, THE, 1945, A
SHANGHAI DOCUMENT, A, 1929
SHANGHAI DRAMA, THE, 1945, A
SHANGHAI EXPRESS, 1932, O
SHANGHAI GESTURE, THE, 1941, C
SHANGHAI LADY, 1929, A
SHANGHAI MADNESS, 1933, A
SHANGHAI ROSE, 1929
SHANGHAI STORY, THE, 1954, A
SHANGHAIED, 1927
SHANGHAIED LOVE, 1931, A
SHANGRI-LA, 1961, O
SHANKS, 1974, A
SHANNON OF THE SIXTH, 1914
SHANNONS OF BROADWAY, THE, 1929, A
SHANTY TRAMP, 1967, O
SHANTYTOWN, 1943, A
SHANTYTOWN HONEYMOON, 1972
SHAPE OF THINGS TO COME, THE, 1979, A
SHARE AND SHARE ALIKE, 1925
SHARE OUT, THE, 1966, A
SHARK, 1970, C
SHARK GOD, THE
SHARK MASTER, THE, 1921, A
SHARK MONROE, 1918
SHARK REEF
SHARK RIVER, 1953, A
SHARK WOMAN, THE, 1941, A
SHARK'S TREASURE, 1975, A
SHARK, THE, 1920
SHARKFIGHTERS, THE, 1956, A
SHARKY'S MACHINE, 1928, O
SHARP SHOOTERS, 1928, A
SHARPSHOOTERS, 1938, A
SHATTER
SHATTERED DREAMS, 1922
SHATTERED FAITH, 1923
SHATTERED IDOLS, 1922, A
SHATTERED IDYLL, A, 1916
SHATTERED LIVES, 1925
SHATTERED REPUTATIONS, 1923, A
SHATTERHAND
SHE, 1916
SHE, 1917
SHE, 1925
SHE, 1935, A
SHE, 1965, A-C
SHE, 1983
SHE ALWAYS GETS THEIR MAN, 1962, A
SHE AND HE, 1967, A
SHE AND HE, 1969, O
SHE ASKED FOR IT, 1937, A
SHE BEAST, THE, 1966, C
SHE CAME TO THE VALLEY, 1979
SHE COULDN'T HELP IT, 1921
SHE COULDN'T SAY NO, 1930, A
SHE COULDN'T SAY NO, 1939, A
SHE COULDN'T SAY NO, 1941, A
SHE COULDN'T SAY NO, 1954, A
SHE COULDN'T TAKE IT, 1935, A
SHE DANCES ALONE, 1981, A
SHE DEMONS, 1958, A
SHE DEVIL, 1940
SHE DEVIL, 1957, A
SHE DEVIL, THE, 1918
SHE DIDN'T SAY NO?, 1962, A
SHE DONE HIM WRONG, 1933, C
SHE FREAK, 1967, O
SHE GETS HER MAN, 1935, A
SHE GETS HER MAN, 1945, A
SHE GOES TO WAR, 1929, A
SHE GOT HER MAN
SHE GOT WHAT SHE WANTED, 1930, A
SHE HAD TO CHOOSE, 1934, A
SHE HAD TO EAT, 1937, A
SHE HAD TO SAY YES, 1933, A
SHE HAD TO SAY YES, 1954

SHE HAS WHAT IT TAKES, 1943, A
SHE HIRED A HUSBAND, 1919
SHE KNEW ALL THE ANSWERS, 1941, A
SHE KNEW WHAT SHE WANTED, 1936, A
SHE KNOWS Y'KNOW, 1962, C
SHE LEARNED ABOUT SAILORS, 1934, A
SHE LEFT WITHOUT HER TRUNKS, 1916
SHE LET HIM CONTINUE
SHE LOVED A FIREMAN, 1937, A
SHE LOVES AND LIES, 1920, A
SHE LOVES ME NOT, 1934, A
SHE MADE HER BED, 1934, A
SHE MAN, THE, 1967, C
SHE MARRIED A COP, 1939, A
SHE MARRIED AN ARTIST, 1938, A
SHE MARRIED HER BOSS, 1935, A
SHE MONSTER OF THE NIGHT
SHE PLAYED WITH FIRE, 1957, C
SHE SHALL HAVE MURDER, 1950, A
SHE SHALL HAVE MUSIC, 1935, A
SHE SHOULD HAVE SAID NO, 1949
SHE SHOULDA SAID NO
SHE STEPS OUT
SHE STOOPS TO CONQUER, 1914
SHE WANTED A MILLIONAIRE, 1932, A
SHE WAS A HIPPY VAMPIRE
SHE WAS A LADY, 1934, A
SHE WAS ONLY A VILLAGE MAIDEN, 1933, A
SHE WENT TO THE RACES, 1945, A
SHE WHO DARES
SHE WOLVES, 1925
SHE WORE A YELLOW RIBBON, 1949, A
SHE WOULDN'T SAY YES, 1945, A
SHE WROTE THE BOOK, 1946, A
SHE'LL FOLLOW YOU ANYWHERE, 1971
SHE'LL HAVE TO GO
SHE'S A SHEIK, 1927, A
SHE'S A SOLDIER TOO, 1944, A
SHE'S A SWEETHEART, 1944, A
SHE'S BACK ON BROADWAY, 1953, A
SHE'S DANGEROUS, 1937, A
SHE'S FOR ME, 1943, A
SHE'S GOT EVERYTHING, 1938, A
SHE'S IN THE ARMY, 1942, A
SHE'S MY BABY, 1927
SHE'S MY LOVELY
SHE'S MY WEAKNESS, 1930, A
SHE'S NO LADY, 1937, A
SHE'S TOO MEAN TO ME, 1948
SHE'S WORKING HER WAY THROUGH COLLEGE,
  1952, A
SHE-CREATURE, THE, 1956, A
SHE-DEVIL ISLAND, 1936, A
SHE-DEVILS ON WHEELS, 1968, O
SHE-GODS OF SHARK REEF, 1958, A
SHE-WOLF OF LONDON, 1946, A
SHE-WOLF, THE, 1931, A
SHE-WOLF, THE, 1963, A
SHEBA, 1919
SHEBA BABY, 1975, C
SHED NO TEARS, 1948, A
SHEENA, 1984, C-O
SHEEP TRAIL, 1926
SHEEPDOG OF THE HILLS, 1941, A
SHEEPMAN, THE, 1958, A
SHEER BLUFF, 1921, A
SHEFFIELD BLADE, A, 1918, A
SHEHERAZADE
SHEIK OF ARABY, THE, 1922
SHEIK OF MOJAVE, THE, 1928
SHEIK STEPS OUT, THE, 1937, A
SHEIK'S WIFE, THE
SHEIK, THE, 1921, A
*SHEILA LEVINE IS DEAD AND LIVING IN NEW
  YORK*, 1975, A-C
SHELL FORTY-THREE, 1916
SHELL GAME, THE, 1918
SHELL SHOCK, 1964, C
SHELL SHOCKED SAMMY, 1923
SHELTERED DAUGHTERS, 1921
SHENANDOAH, 1965, C
SHENANIGANS
SHEP COMES HOME, 1949, AA
SHEPHERD GIRL, THE, 1965, A
SHEPHERD KING, THE, 1923
SHEPHERD LASSIE OF ARGYLE, THE, 1914
SHEPHERD OF THE HILL, THE, 1928
SHEPHERD OF THE HILLS, THE, 1920
SHEPHERD OF THE HILLS, THE, 1941, A
SHEPHERD OF THE HILLS, THE, 1964, A
SHEPHERD OF THE OZARKS, 1942, A
SHEPPER-NEWFOUNDER, THE
SHERIFF OF CIMARRON, 1945, A
SHERIFF OF FRACTURED JAW, THE, 1958, A
SHERIFF OF HOPE ETERNAL, THE, 1921
SHERIFF OF LAS VEGAS, 1944, A
SHERIFF OF MEDICINE BOW, THE, 1948
SHERIFF OF REDWOOD VALLEY, 1946, A
SHERIFF OF SAGE VALLEY, 1942, A
SHERIFF OF SUN-DOG, THE, 1922
SHERIFF OF SUNDOWN, 1944, A
SHERIFF OF TOMBSTONE, 1941, A

SHERIFF OF WICHITA, 1949, A
SHERIFF'S GIRL, 1926
SHERIFF'S LASH, THE, 1929
SHERIFF'S LONE HAND, THE
SHERIFF'S SECRET, THE, 1931
SHERIFF'S SON, THE, 1919
SHERLOCK BROWN, 1921, A
SHERLOCK HOLMES, 1916
SHERLOCK HOLMES, 1922, A
SHERLOCK HOLMES, 1932, A
SHERLOCK HOLMES AND THE DEADLY NECKLACE,
  1962, A
SHERLOCK HOLMES AND THE SECRET CODE
SHERLOCK HOLMES AND THE SECRET WEAPON,
  1942, A
SHERLOCK HOLMES AND THE SPIDER WOMAN,
  1944, A
SHERLOCK HOLMES AND THE VOICE OF TERROR,
  1942, A
SHERLOCK HOLMES FACES DEATH, 1943, O
SHERLOCK HOLMES GROSSTER FALL
SHERLOCK HOLMES IN WASHINGTON, 1943, A
SHERLOCK HOLMES' FATAL HOUR, 1931, A
SHERLOCK HOLMES, 1939
SHERLOCK, JR., 1924, A
SHERRY, 1920
SHICHININ NO SAMURAI
SHIELD FOR MURDER, 1954, A
SHIELD OF FAITH, THE, 1956, A
SHIELD OF HONOR, THE, 1927, A
SHIELD OF SILENCE, THE, 1925
SHIFTING SANDS, 1918
SHIFTING SANDS, 1922
SHILLINGBURY BLOWERS, THE, 1980, A
SHIN NO SHIKOTEI
SHINBONE ALLEY, 1971, A
SHINE GIRL, THE, 1916
SHINE ON, HARVEST MOON, 1938, A
SHINE ON, HARVEST MOON, 1944, A
SHINEL
SHINING ADVENTURE, THE, 1925
SHINING HOUR, THE, 1938, A-C
SHINING STAR
SHINING VICTORY, 1941, A
SHINING, THE, 1980, C-O
SHINJU TEN NO AMIJIMA
SHIP AHOY, 1942, A
SHIP CAFE, 1935, A
SHIP COMES IN, A, 1928
SHIP FROM SHANGHAI, THE, 1930, A
SHIP OF CONDEMNED WOMEN, THE, 1963, A
SHIP OF DOOM, THE, 1917
SHIP OF FOOLS, 1965, C
SHIP OF LOST MEN, THE, 1929
SHIP OF SOULS, 1925
SHIP OF WANTED MEN, 1933, A
SHIP THAT DIED OF SHAME, THE, 1956, A
SHIP WAS LOADED, THE
SHIPBUILDERS, THE, 1943, A
SHIPMATES, 1931, A
SHIPMATES FOREVER, 1935, A
SHIPMATES O' MINE, 1936, A
SHIPS OF HATE, 1931, A
SHIPS OF THE NIGHT, 1928
SHIPS THAT PASS IN THE NIGHT, 1921, A
SHIPS WITH WINGS, 1942, A
SHIPWRECK
SHIPWRECKED, 1926
SHIPYARD SALLY, 1940, A
SHIRALEE, THE, 1957, C
SHIRAZ, 1929
SHIRIKURAE MAGOICHI
SHIRLEY, 1922
SHIRLEY KAYE, 1917
SHIRLEY OF THE CIRCUS, 1922, A
SHIRLEY THOMPSON VERSUS THE ALIENS, 1968, O
SHIRO TO KURO
SHIVERS
SHIVERS, 1984, C
SHLOSHA YAMIN VE' YELED
SHNEI KUNI LEMEL
SHOCK, 1934, C
SHOCK, 1946, O
SHOCK CORRIDOR, 1963, O
SHOCK HILL, 1966
SHOCK PUNCH, THE, 1925
SHOCK TREATMENT, 1964, O
SHOCK TREATMENT, 1973, O
SHOCK TREATMENT, 1981, O
SHOCK TROOPS, 1968, O
SHOCK WAVES, 1977, O
SHOCK, 1979
SHOCK, THE, 1923, A
SHOCKER
SHOCKING MISS PILGRIM, THE, 1947, A
SHOCKING NIGHT, A, 1921, A
SHOCKPROOF, 1949, C
SHOD WITH FIRE, 1920
SHOE SHINE, 1947, C
SHOEBLACK OF PICCADILLY, THE, 1920, A
SHOEMAKER AND THE ELVES, THE, 1967, AAA
SHOES, 1916

SHOES OF THE FISHERMAN, THE, 1968, A
SHOES THAT DANCED, THE, 1918
SHOGUN ASSASSIN, 1980, O
SHOGUN ISLAND
SHONEN SSARUTOBI SASUKE
SHOOT, 1976, O
SHOOT FIRST, 1953, C-O
SHOOT FIRST, DIE LATER, 1973
SHOOT FIRST, LAUGH LAST, 1967, O
SHOOT IT: BLACK, SHOOT IT: BLUE, 1974, O
SHOOT LOUD, LOUDER... I DON'T UNDERSTAND,
  1966, O
SHOOT OUT, 1971, C
SHOOT OUT AT BIG SAG, 1962, C
SHOOT THE MOON, 1982, C-O
SHOOT THE PIANO PLAYER, 1962, C
SHOOT THE SUN DOWN, 1981
SHOOT THE WORKS, 1934, A
SHOOT TO KILL, 1947, C
SHOOT TO KILL, 1961, A
SHOOT-OUT AT MEDICINE BEND, 1957, A
SHOOTIN' FOR LOVE, 1923, A
SHOOTIN' IRONS
SHOOTIN' IRONS, 1927, A
SHOOTIN' SQUARE, 1924
SHOOTING HIGH, 1940, A
SHOOTING OF DAN MCGREW, THE, 1915, A
SHOOTING OF DAN MCGREW, THE, 1924
SHOOTING STARS, 1928
SHOOTING STRAIGHT, 1927
SHOOTING STRAIGHT, 1930, A
SHOOTING, THE, 1971, O
SHOOTIST, THE, 1976, O
SHOOTOUT
SHOOTOUT AT MEDICINE BEND
SHOP ANGEL, 1932, C
SHOP AROUND THE CORNER, THE, 1940, A
SHOP AT SLY CORNER, THE
SHOP GIRL, THE
SHOP ON HIGH STREET, THE
SHOP ON MAIN STREET, THE, 1966, C-O
SHOPGIRLS; OR, THE GREAT QUESTION, 1914
SHOPSOILED GIRL, THE, 1915, A
SHOPWORN, 1932, A
SHOPWORN ANGEL, 1938, A
SHOPWORN ANGEL, THE, 1928, A
SHORE ACRES, 1914
SHORE ACRES, 1920
SHORE LEAVE, 1925, A
SHORT CUT TO HELL, 1957, O
SHORT EYES, 1977, O
SHORT GRASS, 1950, C
SHORT IS THE SUMMER, 1968, O
SHORT SKIRTS, 1921
SHOT AT DAWN, A, 1934, C
SHOT GUN PASS
SHOT IN THE DARK, A, 1933, A
SHOT IN THE DARK, A, 1935, C
SHOT IN THE DARK, A, 1964, A-C
SHOT IN THE DARK, THE, 1941, C
SHOT IN THE NIGHT, A, 1923
SHOTGUN, 1955, O
SHOTGUN PASS, 1932, A
SHOTGUN WEDDING, THE, 1963, A-C
SHOULD A BABY DIE?, 1916
SHOULD A DOCTOR TELL?, 1923
SHOULD A DOCTOR TELL?, 1931, C
SHOULD A GIRL MARRY?, 1929, A
SHOULD A GIRL MARRY?, 1939, A
SHOULD A HUSBAND FORGIVE?, 1919
SHOULD A MOTHER TELL?, 1915
SHOULD A WIFE FORGIVE?, 1915, A
SHOULD A WIFE WORK?, 1922, A
SHOULD A WOMAN DIVORCE?, 1914, A
SHOULD A WOMAN TELL?, 1920, C
SHOULD HUSBANDS WORK?, 1939, AAA
SHOULD LADIES BEHAVE?, 1933, C-O
SHOULD SHE OBEY?, 1917
SHOULDER ARMS, 1917
SHOUT AT THE DEVIL, 1976, C
SHOUT, THE, 1978, O
SHOW BOAT, 1929, A
SHOW BOAT, 1936, A
SHOW BOAT, 1951, A
SHOW BUSINESS, 1944, AAA
SHOW FLAT, 1936, A
SHOW FOLKS, 1928, A
SHOW GIRL, 1928, A
SHOW GIRL IN HOLLYWOOD, 1930, A
SHOW GIRL, THE, 1927, A
SHOW GOES ON, THE, 1937, A
SHOW GOES ON, THE, 1938, C
SHOW OFF, THE, 1926
SHOW PEOPLE, 1928, A
SHOW THEM NO MERCY, 1935, C
SHOW, THE, 1927
SHOW-DOWN, THE, 1917
SHOW-OFF, THE, 1934, A
SHOW-OFF, THE, 1946, A
SHOWDOWN, 1963, A
SHOWDOWN, 1973, A
SHOWDOWN AT ABILENE, 1956, A

SHOWDOWN AT BOOT HILL, 1958, A
SHOWDOWN FOR ZATOICHI, 1968, C-O
SHOWDOWN, THE, 1928
SHOWDOWN, THE, 1940, A
SHOWDOWN, THE, 1950, A
SHOWDOWN, THE, 1940
SHOWGIRL IN HOLLYWOOD
SHOWOFF
SHOWTIME, 1948, A
SHRIEK IN THE NIGHT, A, 1933, A
SHRIEK OF ARABY, THE, 1923
SHRIEK OF THE MUTILATED, 1974, O
SHRIKE, THE, 1955, C
SHRINE OF HAPPINESS, THE, 1916
SHUBIN
SHULAMIS, 1931
SHULMATE, THE, 1915
SHUT MY BIG MOUTH, 1942, AAA
SHUT MY BIG MOUTH, 1946
SHUTTERED ROOM, THE, 1968, C-O
SHUTTLE OF LIFE, THE, 1920
SHUTTLE, THE, 1918
SI JAMAIS JE TE PINCE, 1920
SI PARIS NOUS ETAIT CONTE
SI VERSAILLES M'ETAIT CONTE
SIAVASH IN PERSEPOLIS, 1966, C
SIBERIA, 1926, A
SICILIAN CLAN, THE, 1970, O
SICILIAN CONNECTION, THE, 1977, O
SICILIANS, THE, 1964, A
SICK ABED, 1920
SICKLE AND HAMMER, 1921
SICKLE OR THE CROSS, THE, 1951
SIDDHARTHA, 1972, C
SIDE SHOW, 1931, A
SIDE STREET, 1929, A
SIDE STREET, 1950, C
SIDE STREET ANGEL, 1937, A
SIDE STREETS, 1934, A
SIDECAR RACERS, 1975, A
SIDEHACKERS, THE
SIDELONG GLANCES OF A PIGEON KICKER, THE,
  1970, O
SIDESHOW, 1950, C
SIDESHOW OF LIFE, THE, 1924, A
SIDESHOW, THE, 1928
SIDEWALKS OF LONDON, 1940, AA
SIDEWALKS OF NEW YORK, 1923
SIDEWALKS OF NEW YORK, 1931, AAA
SIDEWINDER ONE, 1977, C
SIDNEY SHELDON'S BLOODLINE
SIEGE, 1925
SIEGE, 1983, O
SIEGE AT RED RIVER, THE, 1954, C
SIEGE OF FORT BISMARK, 1968, C-O
SIEGE OF HELL STREET, THE
SIEGE OF PINCHGUT
SIEGE OF RED RIVER, THE
SIEGE OF SIDNEY STREET, THE, 1960, O
SIEGE OF SYRACUSE, 1962, C
SIEGE OF THE SAXONS, 1963, A
SIEGFRIED, 1924, C
SIEGFRIED'S DEATH
SIEGFRIEDS TOD
SIERRA, 1950, A
SIERRA BARON, 1958, A
SIERRA DE TERUEL
SIERRA PASSAGE, 1951, A
SIERRA STRANGER, 1957, C
SIERRA SUE, 1941, A
SIETE HOMBRES DE ORO
SIGHT UNSEEN, A, 1914
SIGMA III, 1966
SIGN, 1932, C-O
SIGN INVISIBLE, THE, 1918
SIGN OF AQUARIUS, 1970, O
SIGN OF FOUR, THE, 1932, C
SIGN OF FOUR, THE, 1983, C
SIGN OF THE CACTUS, THE, 1925
SIGN OF THE CLAW, THE, 1926
SIGN OF THE FOUR, THE, 1923
SIGN OF THE GLADIATOR, 1959, C
SIGN OF THE PAGAN, 1954, C
SIGN OF THE POPPY, THE, 1916
SIGN OF THE RAM, THE, 1948, A
SIGN OF THE ROSE, THE, 1922, A
SIGN OF THE SPADE, THE, 1916
SIGN OF THE VIRGIN, 1969, O
SIGN OF THE WOLF, 1941, AAA
SIGN OF VENUS, THE, 1955, C
SIGN OF ZORRO, THE, 1960, AAA
SIGN ON THE DOOR, THE, 1921
SIGNAL 7, 1984, O
SIGNAL FIRES, 1926
SIGNAL TOWER, THE, 1924, A
SIGNALS-AN ADVENTURE IN SPACE, 1970, A
SIGNED JUDGEMENT
SIGNORA SENZA CAMELIE
SIGNORE E SIGNORI
SIGNPOST TO MURDER, 1964, O
SIGNS OF LIFE, 1981, O
SILAS MARNER, 1916

SILAS MARNER, 1922
SILENCE, 1926
SILENCE, 1931, O
SILENCE, 1974, AAA
SILENCE HAS NO WINGS, 1971, A
SILENCE OF DEAN MAITLAND, THE, 1934, C-O
SILENCE OF DR. EVANS, THE, 1973, C
SILENCE OF MARTHA, THE
SILENCE OF THE DEAD, THE, 1913
SILENCE OF THE NORTH, 1981, C
SILENCE SELLERS, THE, 1917
SILENCE, THE, 1964, O
SILENCERS, THE, 1966, 0
SILENT ACCUSER, THE
SILENT ACCUSER, THE, 1914
SILENT ACCUSER, THE, 1924
SILENT AVENGER, THE, 1927
SILENT BARRIER, THE, 1920
SILENT BARRIERS, 1937, A
SILENT BATTLE, THE
SILENT BATTLE, THE, 1916
SILENT CALL, THE, 1921, A
SILENT CALL, THE, 1961, A
SILENT CODE, THE, 1935
SILENT COMMAND, THE, 1915
SILENT COMMAND, THE, 1923, A
SILENT CONFLICT, 1948, A
SILENT DEATH
SILENT DUST, 1949, A
SILENT ENEMY, THE, 1930, C
SILENT ENEMY, THE, 1959, C
SILENT EVIDENCE, 1922, A
SILENT FLUTE, THE
SILENT GUARDIAN, THE, 1926
SILENT HERO, THE, 1927
SILENT HOUSE, THE, 1929
SILENT INVASION, THE, 1962, A
SILENT LADY, THE, 1917
SILENT LIE, THE, 1917
SILENT LOVER, THE, 1926, A
SILENT MADNESS, 1984, O
SILENT MAN, THE, 1917
SILENT MASTER, THE, 1917
SILENT MEN, 1933
SILENT MOVIE, 1976, A-C
SILENT NIGHT, BLOODY NIGHT, 1974, O
SILENT NIGHT, DEADLY NIGHT, 1984, O
SILENT NIGHT, EVIL NIGHT
SILENT ONE, THE, 1984, O
SILENT PAL, 1925
SILENT PARTNER, 1944, C
SILENT PARTNER, THE, 1917
SILENT PARTNER, THE, 1923, A
SILENT PARTNER, THE, 1979, C-O
SILENT PASSENGER, THE, 1935, A
SILENT PLAYGROUND, THE, 1964, C-O
SILENT POWER, THE, 1926, A
SILENT RAGE, 1982, O
SILENT RAIDERS, 1954, C
SILENT RIDER, THE, 1918
SILENT RIDER, THE, 1927
SILENT RUNNING, 1972, C
SILENT SANDERSON, 1925
SILENT SCREAM, 1980, O
SILENT SENTINEL, 1929
SILENT SHELBY
SILENT SHELDON, 1925
SILENT STAR
SILENT STRANGER, THE, 1924
SILENT STRANGER, THE, 1975
SILENT STRENGTH, 1919
SILENT TRAIL, 1928
SILENT VOICE, THE
SILENT VOICE, THE, 1915, A
SILENT VOW, THE, 1922, A
SILENT WATCHER, THE, 1924
SILENT WIRES, 1924
SILENT WITNESS, 1942
SILENT WITNESS, THE, 1917
SILENT WITNESS, THE, 1932, C
SILENT WITNESS, THE, 1962, O
SILENT WOMAN, THE, 1918
SILENT YEARS, 1921
SILHOUETTES, 1982, C
SILICATES
SILK BOUQUET, THE, 1926
SILK EXPRESS, THE, 1933, A
SILK HAT KID, 1935, A
SILK HOSIERY, 1920
SILK HUSBANDS AND CALICO WIVES, 1920
SILK LEGS, 1927, A
SILK NOOSE, THE, 1950, A
SILK STOCKING SAL, 1924
SILK STOCKINGS, 1927
SILK STOCKINGS, 1957, A
SILK-LINED BURGLAR, THE, 1919
SILKEN AFFAIR, THE, 1957, A
SILKEN SHACKLES, 1926
SILKEN SKIN
SILKEN TRAP, THE
SILKS AND SADDLES, 1929, A
SILKS AND SADDLES, 1938

SIX HOURS TO LIVE, 1932, C
SIX IN PARIS, 1968, C-O
SIX INCHES TALL
SIX LESSONS FROM MADAME LA ZONGA, 1941, A
SIX MEN, THE, 1951, A
SIX OF A KIND, 1934, A
SIX P.M., 1946, A
SIX PACK, 1982, C
SIX PACK ANNIE, 1975, O
SIX SHOOTIN' ROMANCE, A, 1926
SIX SHOOTIN' SHERIFF, 1938, A
SIX WEEKS, 1982, C
SIX-DAY BIKE RIDER, 1934, A
SIX-FIFTY, THE, 1923
SIX-GUN DECISION, 1953
SIX-GUN LAW, 1948, AA
SIX-GUN RHYTHM, 1939, A
SIX-GUN TRAIL, 1938
SIX-SHOOTER ANDY, 1918
SIXTEEN
SIXTEEN CANDLES, 1984, A-C
SIXTEEN FATHOMS DEEP, 1934, A
SIXTEEN FATHOMS DEEP, 1948, A
SIXTEENTH WIFE, THE, 1917
SIXTH AND MAIN, 1977, C
SIXTH COMMANDMENT, THE, 1924
SIXTH MAN, THE
SIXTH OF JUNE, THE
SIXTH OF THE WORLD, A, 1926
SIXTY CENTS AN HOUR, 1923, A
SIXTY GLORIOUS YEARS, 1938, A
SKAMMEN
SKATEBOARD, 1978, C
SKATEBOARD MADNESS, 1980
SKATETOWN, U.S.A., 1979, A
SKATING-RINK AND THE VIOLIN, THE
SKAZA O KONKE-GORBUNKE
SKEDADDLE GOLD, 1927
SKELETON ON HORSEBACK, 1940, C
SKETCHES OF A STRANGLER
SKEZAG, 1971
SKI BATTALION, 1938, C
SKI BUM, THE, 1971, O
SKI FEVER, 1969, C
SKI PARTY, 1965, A
SKI PATROL, 1940, A
SKI RAIDERS, THE
SKI TROOP ATTACK, 1960, C
SKID KIDS, 1953, AAA
SKID PROOF, 1923, A
SKIDOO, 1968, C
SKIES ABOVE
SKIMPY IN THE NAVY, 1949, A
SKIN DEEP, 1922
SKIN DEEP, 1929, C
SKIN DEEP, 1978, O
SKIN GAME, 1971, C
SKIN GAME, THE, 1920
SKIN GAME, THE, 1931, C
SKIN GAME, THE, 1965, C
SKINNER STEPS OUT, 1929, A
SKINNER'S BABY, 1917
SKINNER'S BIG IDEA, 1928, A
SKINNER'S BUBBLE, 1917
SKINNER'S DRESS SUIT, 1917, A
SKINNER'S DRESS SUIT, 1926, A
SKINNING SKINNERS, 1921
SKIP TRACER, THE, 1979, C
SKIPALONG ROSENBLOOM, 1951, A
SKIPPER SURPRISED HIS WIFE, THE, 1950, A
SKIPPER'S WOOING, THE, 1922, A
SKIPPY, 1931, AAA
SKIRTS, 1921
SKIRTS, 1928
SKIRTS AHOY?, 1952, A
SKULL, THE, 1965, O
SKULL AND CROWN, 1938, AAA
SKULLDUGGERY, 1970, C
SKUPLIJACI PERJA
SKY ABOVE HEAVEN, 1964, C
SKY BANDITS, THE, 1940, A
SKY BEYOND HEAVEN
SKY BIKE, THE, 1967, AAA
SKY BRIDE, 1932, A
SKY CALLS, THE, 1959, A
SKY COMMANDO, 1953, A
SKY DEVILS, 1932, A
SKY DRAGON, 1949, A
SKY FULL OF MOON, 1952, A
SKY GIANT, 1938, A
SKY HAWK, 1929, A
SKY HIGH, 1922, A
SKY HIGH, 1952, A
SKY HIGH CORRAL, 1926
SKY IS RED, THE, 1952, O
SKY IS YOURS, THE
SKY LINER, 1949, A
SKY MONSTER, THE, 1914
SKY MURDER, 1940, A
SKY PARADE, 1936, A
SKY PATROL, 1939, A
SKY PILOT, THE, 1921, A

SKY PIRATE, THE, 1926
SKY PIRATE, THE, 1970, C
SKY PIRATES, 1977
SKY RAIDER, THE, 1925
SKY RAIDERS, 1931, A
SKY RAIDERS, THE, 1938, A
SKY RIDER, THE, 1928, A
SKY RIDERS, 1976, C
SKY SKIDDER, THE, 1929, A
SKY SPIDER, THE, 1931, A
SKY TERROR
SKY WEST AND CROOKED
SKY'S THE LIMIT, 1925
SKY'S THE LIMIT, THE, 1937, A
SKY'S THE LIMIT, THE, 1943, A
SKY-EYE, 1920
SKY-HIGH SAUNDERS, 1927, A
SKYBOUND, 1935
SKYDIVERS, THE, 1963, C
SKYJACKED, 1972, A
SKYLARK, 1941, A
SKYLARKS, 1936, A
SKYLIGHT ROOM, THE, 1917
SKYLINE, 1931, A
SKYLINE, 1984, C
SKYROCKET, THE, 1926, A
SKYSCRAPER, 1928
SKYSCRAPER SOULS, 1932, A
SKYSCRAPER WILDERNESS
SKYWATCH
SKYWAY, 1933, A
SKYWAYMAN, THE, 1920
SLA FORST, FREDE?
SLACKER, THE, 1917
SLADE
SLAM BANG JIM
SLAMMER
SLAMS, THE, 1973, O
SLANDER, 1916
SLANDER, 1956, A
SLANDER HOUSE, 1938, A
SLANDER THE WOMAN, 1923, A
SLANDER THE WOMAN, 1923, A
SLANDERERS, THE, 1924
SLAP IN THE FACE, 1974
SLAP SHOT, 1977, A
SLAPSTICK OF ANOTHER KIND, 1984, A-C
SLASHER, THE, 1953, O
SLASHER, THE, 1975, O
SLATTERY'S HURRICANE, 1949, C
SLAUGHTER, 1972, O
SLAUGHTER, THE, 1913
SLAUGHTER HOTEL, 1971, O
SLAUGHTER IN SAN FRANCISCO, 1981, O
SLAUGHTER OF THE VAMPIRES, THE
SLAUGHTER ON TENTH AVENUE, 1957, A-C
SLAUGHTER TRAIL, 1951, A
SLAUGHTER'S BIG RIP-OFF, 1973, O
SLAUGHTERDAY, 1981
SLAUGHTERHOUSE-FIVE, 1972, O
SLAVE, THE, 1917
SLAVE, THE, 1918
SLAVE, THE, 1963, A
SLAVE GIRL, 1947, A
SLAVE GIRL OF BABYLON, 1962
SLAVE GIRLS
SLAVE GIRLS OF SHEBA, 1960
SLAVE MARKET, THE, 1917
SLAVE OF DESIRE, 1923, A
SLAVE OF FASHION, A, 1925
SLAVE OF PASSION, SLAVE OF VICE, 1914
SLAVE OF THE CANNIBAL GOD, 1979, O
SLAVE OF VANITY, A, 1920
SLAVE SHIP, 1937, A
SLAVER, THE, 1927
SLAVERS, 1977, O
SLAVES, 1969, O
SLAVES OF BABYLON, 1953, A
SLAVES OF BEAUTY, 1927, A
SLAVES OF DESTINY, 1924, A
SLAVES OF PRIDE, 1920
SLAVES OF SCANDAL, 1924
SLAVEY STUDENT, THE, 1915
SLAYER, THE, 1982, O
SLAYGROUND, 1984, O
SLEEP, MY LOVE, 1948, A
SLEEPAWAY CAMP, 1983, O
SLEEPER, 1973, A-C
SLEEPERS EAST, 1934, A
SLEEPERS WEST, 1941, A
SLEEPING BEAUTY, 1959, AAA
SLEEPING BEAUTY, 1965, AAA
SLEEPING BEAUTY, THE, 1966, AAA
SLEEPING CAR, 1933, A
SLEEPING CAR MURDER THE, 1966, C-O
SLEEPING CAR TO TRIESTE, 1949, A
SLEEPING CARDINAL, THE
SLEEPING CITY, THE, 1950, C
SLEEPING DOGS, 1977, C
SLEEPING FIRES, 1917
SLEEPING LION, THE, 1919
SLEEPING MEMORY, A, 1917

SLEEPING PARTNER, 1961
SLEEPING PARTNERS, 1930, A
SLEEPING PARTNERS, 1964
SLEEPING TIGER, THE, 1954, C
SLEEPLESS NIGHTS, 1933, A
SLEEPWALKER, THE, 1922, A
SLEEPY LAGOON, 1943, A
SLEEPYTIME GAL, 1942, A
SLENDER THREAD, THE, 1965, C
SLEPOY MUZYKANT
SLEUTH, 1972, C-O
SLIDE, KELLY, SLIDE, 1927, A
SLIGHT CASE OF LARCENY, A, 1953, A
SLIGHT CASE OF MURDER, A, 1938, A
SLIGHTLY DANGEROUS, 1943, A
SLIGHTLY FRENCH, 1949, A
SLIGHTLY HONORABLE, 1940, A
SLIGHTLY MARRIED, 1933, A
SLIGHTLY SCANDALOUS, 1946, A
SLIGHTLY SCARLET, 1930, A
SLIGHTLY SCARLET, 1956, C
SLIGHTLY TEMPTED, 1940, A
SLIGHTLY TERRIFIC, 1944, A
SLIGHTLY USED, 1927, A
SLIM, 1937, C
SLIM CARTER, 1957, A
SLIM FINGERS, 1929, A
SLIM PRINCESS, THE, 1915, A
SLIM PRINCESS, THE, 1920
SLIM SHOULDERS, 1922, A
SLIME PEOPLE, THE, 1963, A
SLINGSHOT, 1971
SLINGSHOT KID, THE, 1927
SLIPPER AND THE ROSE, THE, 1976, AAA
SLIPPER EPISODE, THE, 1938, A
SLIPPY MCGEE, 1923, A
SLIPPY MCGEE, 1948, A
SLIPSTREAM, 1974, O
SLITHER, 1973, C
SLITHIS, 1978, C
SLOGAN, 1970, C
SLOTH, 1917
SLOW AS LIGHTING, 1923
SLOW DANCING IN THE BIG CITY, 1978, C
SLOW DYNAMITE, 1925
SLOW MOTION
SLOW MOVES, 1984, O
SLOW RUN, 1968, O
SLUMBER PARTY '57, 1977, O
SLUMBER PARTY IN A HAUNTED HOUSE
SLUMBER PARTY IN HORROR HOUSE
SLUMBER PARTY MASSACRE, THE, 1982, O
SLUMS OF TOKYO, 1930
SMALL BACHELOR, THE, 1927
SMALL BACK ROOM, THE
SMALL CHANGE, 1976, C
SMALL CIRCLE OF FRIENDS, A, 1980, O
SMALL HOTEL, 1957, A
SMALL HOURS, THE, 1962, O
SMALL MAN, THE, 1935, A
SMALL MIRACLE, THE
SMALL TOWN BOY, 1937, A
SMALL TOWN DEB, 1941, A
SMALL TOWN GIRL, 1936, A
SMALL TOWN GIRL, 1953, A
SMALL TOWN GIRL, A, 1917
SMALL TOWN GUY, THE, 1917
SMALL TOWN IDOL, A, 1921, A
SMALL TOWN IN TEXAS, A, 1976, C
SMALL TOWN LAWYER
SMALL TOWN STORY, 1953, A
SMALL VOICE, THE
SMALL WORLD OF SAMMY LEE, THE, 1963, C
SMALLEST SHOW ON EARTH, THE, 1957, A
SMART ALEC, 1951, A
SMART ALECKS, 1942, A
SMART BLONDE, 1937, A
SMART GIRL, 1935, A
SMART GIRLS DON'T TALK, 1948, A
SMART GUY, 1943, A
SMART MONEY, 1931, A
SMART POLITICS, 1948, A
SMART SET, A, 1919
SMART SET, THE, 1928, A
SMART SEX, THE, 1921
SMART WOMAN, 1931, A
SMART WOMAN, 1948, A
SMARTEST GIRL IN TOWN, 1936, A
SMARTY, 1934, A
SMASH AND GRAB
SMASH PALACE, 1982, O
SMASH-UP, THE STORY OF A WOMAN, 1947, C
SMASHED BACK, 1927
SMASHING BARRIERS, 1923
SMASHING BIRD I USED TO KNOW, THE
SMASHING THE CRIME SYNDICATE
SMASHING THE MONEY RING, 1939, A
SMASHING THE RACKETS, 1938, A
SMASHING THE SPY RING, 1939, A
SMASHING THROUGH
SMASHING THROUGH, 1918
SMASHING THROUGH, 1928, A

SOULS ON THE ROAD, 1921
SOULS TRIUMPHANT, 1915
SOUND AND THE FURY, THE, 1959, C-O
SOUND BARRIER, THE
SOUND OF FURY, THE, 1950, C
SOUND OF HORROR, 1966, C
SOUND OF LIFE, THE, 1962, A
SOUND OF MUSIC, THE, 1965, AAA
SOUND OF TRUMPETS, THE, 1963, A
SOUND OFF, 1952, A
SOUNDER, 1972, AAA
SOUNDER, PART 2, 1976, AA
SOUNDS OF HORROR, 1968
SOUP FOR ONE, 1982, O
SOUP TO NUTS, 1930, A
SOUP TO NUTS, 1982
SOURCE, THE, 1918
SOURDOUGH, 1977, AA
SOUS LA MENACE, 1916
SOUS LES TOITS DE PARIS
SOUTH AMERICAN GEORGE, 1941, A
SOUTH OF ALGIERS
SOUTH OF ARIZONA, 1938, A
SOUTH OF CALIENTE, 1951, A
SOUTH OF DEATH VALLEY, 1949, A
SOUTH OF DIXIE, 1944, A
SOUTH OF HELL MOUNTAIN, 1971
SOUTH OF MONTEREY, 1946
SOUTH OF NORTHERN LIGHTS, 1922, A
SOUTH OF PAGO PAGO, 1940, A
SOUTH OF PANAMA, 1928
SOUTH OF PANAMA, 1941, A
SOUTH OF RIO, 1949, A
SOUTH OF SANTA FE, 1924
SOUTH OF SANTA FE, 1932, A
SOUTH OF SANTA FE, 1942, A
SOUTH OF SONORA, 1930, A
SOUTH OF ST. LOUIS, 1949, A
SOUTH OF SUEZ, 1940, A
SOUTH OF SUVA, 1922, A
SOUTH OF TAHITI, 1941, A
SOUTH OF THE BORDER, 1939, A
SOUTH OF THE CHISHOLM TRAIL, 1947
SOUTH OF THE EQUATOR, 1924
SOUTH OF THE RIO GRANDE, 1932, A
SOUTH OF THE RIO GRANDE, 1945, A
SOUTH PACIFIC, 1958, A
SOUTH PACIFIC TRAIL, 1952, A
SOUTH RIDING, 1938, A
SOUTH SEA BUBBLE, A, 1928
SOUTH SEA LOVE, 1923, A
SOUTH SEA LOVE, 1927
SOUTH SEA ROSE, 1929, A
SOUTH SEA SINNER, 1950, A
SOUTH SEA WOMAN, 1953, A
SOUTH SEAS FURY
SOUTH TO KARANGA, 1940, A
SOUTHERN COMFORT, 1981, O
SOUTHERN DOUBLE CROSS, 1973
SOUTHERN JUSTICE, 1917
SOUTHERN LOVE
SOUTHERN MAID, A, 1933, A
SOUTHERN PRIDE, 1917
SOUTHERN ROSES, 1936, A
SOUTHERN STAR, THE, 1969, C
SOUTHERN YANKEE, A, 1948, AAA
SOUTHERNER, THE, 1945, A
SOUTHERNER, THE, 1931
SOUTHSIDE 1-1000, 1950, A
SOUTHWARD HO?, 1939, A
SOUTHWEST PASSAGE, 1954, A
SOUTHWEST TO SONORA
SOWERS AND REAPERS, 1917
SOWERS, THE, 1916
SOWING THE WIND, 1916
SOWING THE WIND, 1921
SOYLENT GREEN, 1973, C
SPACE AMOEBA, THE, 1970, A
SPACE CHILDREN, THE, 1958, A
SPACE CRUISER, 1977, A
SPACE DEVILS
SPACE FIREBIRD 2772, 1979, A
SPACE HUNTER: ADVENTURES IN THE FORBIDDEN
   ZONE
SPACE INVASION FROM LAPLAND
SPACE MASTER X-7, 1958, A
SPACE MEN
SPACE MEN APPEAR IN TOKYO
SPACE MISSION OF THE LOST PLANET
SPACE MONSTER, 1965, A
SPACE RAIDERS, 1983, C
SPACE RIDERS, 1984
SPACE SHIP, THE, 1935, A
SPACE STATION X
SPACE STATION X-14
SPACED OUT, 1981, O
SPACEFLIGHT IC-1, 1965, A
*SPACEHUNTER: ADVENTURES IN THE FORBIDDEN
   ZONE*, 1983, C
SPACEMAN AND KING ARTHUR, THE
SPACEMEN SATURDAY NIGHT
SPACESHIP

SPACESHIP TO VENUS
SPACEWAYS, 1953, A
SPAN OF LIFE, THE, 1914
SPANGLES, 1926
SPANGLES, 1928
SPANIARD'S CURSE, THE, 1958, A
SPANIARD, THE, 1925
SPANISH AFFAIR, 1958, A
SPANISH CAPE MYSTERY, 1935, A
SPANISH DANCER, THE, 1923
SPANISH EYES, 1930, A
SPANISH FLY, 1975, O
SPANISH GARDENER, THE, 1957, A
SPANISH JADE, 1922
SPANISH JADE, THE, 1915
SPANISH MAIN, THE, 1945, A
SPANISH SWORD, THE, 1962, A
SPARA FORTE, PIU FORTE...NON CAPISCO
SPARE A COPPER, 1940, A
SPARE THE ROD, 1961, A
SPARK DIVINE, THE, 1919
SPARKLE, 1976, C-O
SPARKS OF FLINT, 1921
SPARROWS, 1926, C
SPARROWS, 1926, C
SPARROWS CAN'T SING, 1963, A
SPARTACUS, 1960, C
SPARTAKIADA, 1929
SPASMO, 1976
SPASMS, 1983, O
SPATS TO SPURS
SPAWN OF THE DESERT, 1923, A
SPAWN OF THE NORTH, 1938, A
SPEAK EASILY, 1932, A
SPEAKEASY, 1929, A
SPECIAL AGENT, 1935, A-C
SPECIAL AGENT, 1949, A
SPECIAL AGENT K-7, 1937, A
SPECIAL DAY, A, 1977, C
SPECIAL DELIVERY, 1927, A
SPECIAL DELIVERY, 1955, A
SPECIAL DELIVERY, 1976, C
SPECIAL EDITION, 1938, A
SPECIAL EFFECTS, 1984, O
SPECIAL INSPECTOR, 1939, A
SPECIAL INVESTIGATOR, 1936, A
SPECIALIST, THE, 1975, O
SPECKLED BAND, THE, 1931, A
SPECTER OF FREEDOM, THE
SPECTER OF THE ROSE, 1946, C
SPECTOR OF FREEDOM
SPECTRE HAUNTS EUROPE, A, 1923
SPECTRE OF EDGAR ALLAN POE, 1973
SPECTRE OF EDGAR ALLAN POE, THE, 1974, O
SPEED, 1925
SPEED, 1936, A
SPEED BRENT WINS
SPEED CLASSIC, THE, 1928
SPEED COP, 1926, A
SPEED CRAZED, 1926, A
SPEED CRAZY, 1959, C
SPEED DEMON, 1933
SPEED DEMON, THE, 1925
SPEED DEVILS, 1935, A
SPEED GIRL, THE, 1921, A
SPEED KING, 1923, A
SPEED LIMIT 65
SPEED LIMIT, THE, 1926
SPEED LIMITED, 1940, A
SPEED LOVERS, 1968, A
SPEED MAD, 1925, A
SPEED MADNESS, 1925
SPEED MADNESS, 1932, A
SPEED MANIAC, THE, 1919
SPEED REPORTER, 1936, A
SPEED REPORTER, THE 1931
SPEED SPOOK, THE, 1924
SPEED TO BURN, 1938, A
SPEED TO SPARE, 1937, A
SPEED TO SPARE, 1948, A
SPEED WILD, 1925
SPEED WINGS, 1934, A
SPEEDING HOOFS, 1927
SPEEDING THROUGH, 1926
SPEEDING VENUS, THE, 1926
SPEEDTRAP, 1978, A
SPEEDWAY, 1929
SPEEDWAY, 1968, A
SPEEDY, 1928, A
SPEEDY MEADE, 1919
SPEEDY SMITH, 1927
SPEEDY SPURS, 1926
SPELL OF AMY NUGENT, THE, 1945, A
SPELL OF THE HYPNOTIST, 1956, A
SPELL OF THE YUKON, THE, 1916
SPELLBINDER, THE, 1939, A
SPELLBOUND
SPELLBOUND, 1916
SPELLBOUND, 1945, A-C
SPENCER'S MOUNTAIN, 1963, C
SPENDER OR THE FORTUNES OF PETER, THE, 1915
SPENDER, THE, 1919

SPENDERS, THE, 1921
SPENDTHRIFT, 1936, A
SPENDTHRIFT, THE, 1915, A
SPERMULA, 1976, O
SPESSART INN, THE, 1961, A
SPETTERS, 1983, O
SPHINX, 1981, C
SPHINX, THE, 1916
SPHINX, THE, 1933, A
SPICE OF LIFE, 1954, A
SPIDER, THE, 1916, C
SPIDER, THE, 1931, A
SPIDER, THE, 1940, A
SPIDER, THE, 1945, A
SPIDER, THE, 1958, A
SPIDER AND THE FLY, THE, 1916
SPIDER AND THE FLY, THE, 1952, A
SPIDER AND THE ROSE, THE, 1923, A
*SPIDER BABY, OR THE MADDEST STORY EVER
   TOLD*
SPIDER BABYZERO, 1968, O
SPIDER WEBS, 1927, A
SPIDER WOMAN
SPIDER WOMAN STRIKES BACK, THE, 1946, A
SPIDER'S WEB, THE, 1927
SPIDER'S WEB, THE, 1960, A
SPIDER'S WEB, THE, 1962
SPIDERS, THE, 1919
SPIELER, THE, 1929, A
SPIES, 1929, A
SPIES A GO-GO
SPIES AT WORK
SPIES OF THE AIR, 1940, A
SPIKES GANG, THE, 1974, C
SPIN A DARK WEB, 1956, A
SPIN OF A COIN
SPINAL TAP
SPINDLE OF LIFE, THE, 1917, A
SPINNER O' DREAMS, 1918
SPINOUT, 1966, A
SPIONE UNTER SICHE
SPIRAL BUREAU, THE, 1974
SPIRAL ROAD, THE, 1962, A
SPIRAL STAIRCASE, THE, 1946, C
SPIRAL STAIRCASE, THE, 1975, C-O
SPIRIT AND THE FLESH, THE, 1948, A
SPIRIT IS WILLING, THE, 1967, C
SPIRIT OF '17, THE, 1918
SPIRIT OF '76, THE, 1917
SPIRIT OF CULVER, THE, 1939, A
SPIRIT OF GOOD, THE, 1920
SPIRIT OF NOTRE DAME, THE, 1931, A
SPIRIT OF ROMANCE, THE, 1917
SPIRIT OF ST. LOUIS, THE, 1957, AAA
SPIRIT OF STANFORD, THE, 1942, A
SPIRIT OF THE BEEHIVE, THE, 1976, C
SPIRIT OF THE CONQUEROR, OR THE NAPOLEON
   OF LABOR, THE (1915)
SPIRIT OF THE DEAD
SPIRIT OF THE PEOPLE
SPIRIT OF THE U.S.A., THE, 1924
SPIRIT OF THE WEST, 1932, A
SPIRIT OF THE WIND, 1979, C
SPIRIT OF WEST POINT, THE, 1947, A
SPIRIT OF YOUTH, 1937, A
SPIRIT OF YOUTH, THE, 1929
SPIRITISM, 1965, C
SPIRITS OF THE DEAD, 1969, O
SPIRITUALIST, THE, 1948, A
SPITE BRIDE, THE, 1919
SPITE MARRIAGE, 1929, A
SPITFIRE, 1922
SPITFIRE, 1934, A
SPITFIRE, 1943, A
SPITFIRE, THE, 1914
SPITFIRE, THE, 1924, A
SPITFIRE OF SEVILLE, THE, A
SPITTIN' IMAGE, 1983
SPLASH, 1984, A-C
SPLATTER UNIVERSITY, 1984, O
SPLENDID COWARD, THE, 1918
SPLENDID CRIME, THE, 1926
SPLENDID FELLOWS, 1934, A
SPLENDID FOLLY, 1919
SPLENDID HAZARD, A, 1920
SPLENDID LIE, THE, 1922, A
SPLENDID ROAD, THE, 1925, A
SPLENDID ROMANCE, THE, 1918
SPLENDID SIN, THE, 1919, C
SPLENDID SINNER, THE, 1918
SPLENDOR, 1935, A
SPLENDOR IN THE GRASS, 1961, C
SPLINTERS, 1929, A
SPLINTERS IN THE AIR, 1937, A
SPLINTERS IN THE NAVY, 1931, A
SPLIT IMAGE, 1982, O
SPLIT SECOND, 1953, A
SPLIT, THE, 1968, O
SPLIT, THE, 1962
SPLITFACE
SPLITTING THE BREEZE, 1927, A
SPLITTING UP, 1981, C

SPLITZ, 1984, O
SPOILED ROTTEN, 1968, C-O
SPOILERS OF THE FOREST, 1957, A
SPOILERS OF THE NORTH, 1947, A
SPOILERS OF THE PLAINS, 1951, A
SPOILERS OF THE RANGE, 1939, A
SPOILERS OF THE WEST, 1927
SPOILERS, THE, 1914, A
SPOILERS, THE, 1923
SPOILERS, THE, 1930, A
SPOILERS, THE, 1942, A
SPOILERS, THE, 1955, C
SPOILS OF THE NIGHT, 1969, C-O
SPOOK BUSTERS, 1946, A
SPOOK CHASERS, 1957, A
SPOOK RANCH, 1925, A
SPOOK TOWN, 1944, A
SPOOK WHO SAT BY THE DOOR, THE, 1973, O
SPOOKS RUN WILD, 1941, A
SPORT OF A NATION
SPORT OF KINGS, 1947, A
SPORT OF KINGS, THE, 1921, A
SPORT OF KINGS, THE, 1931, A
SPORT OF THE GODS, THE, 1921
SPORT PARADE, THE, 1932, A
SPORTING AGE, THE, 1928
SPORTING BLOOD, 1916
SPORTING BLOOD, 1931, A
SPORTING BLOOD, 1940, A
SPORTING CHANCE, 1931, A
SPORTING CHANCE, A, 1919
SPORTING CHANCE, A, 1945, A
SPORTING CHANCE, THE, 1925
SPORTING CLUB, THE, 1971, O
SPORTING DOUBLE, A, 1922
SPORTING DUCHESS, THE, 1915
SPORTING DUCHESS, THE, 1920
SPORTING GOODS, 1928, A
SPORTING INSTINCT, THE, 1922
SPORTING LIFE
SPORTING LIFE, 1918
SPORTING LIFE, 1925
SPORTING LOVE, 1936, A
SPORTING LOVER, THE, 1926
SPORTING VENUS, THE, 1925
SPORTING WEST, 1925
SPORTING WIDOW, THE
SPORTING YOUTH, 1924
SPORTS KILLER, THE, 1976
SPORTSMAN'S WIFE, A, 1921
SPOT
SPOT OF BOTHER, A, 1938, A
SPOTLIGHT SADIE, 1919
SPOTLIGHT SCANDALS, 1943, A
SPOTLIGHT, THE, 1927
SPOTS ON MY LEOPARD, THE, 1974, A
SPOTTED LILY, THE, 1917
SPREADING DAWN, THE, 1917, A
SPREADING EVIL, THE, 1919
SPRING, 1948, A
SPRING AFFAIR, 1960, A
SPRING AND PORT WINE, 1970, C-O
SPRING BREAK, 1983, O
SPRING COMES WITH THE LADIES, 1932
SPRING FEVER, 1927
SPRING FEVER, 1983, C
SPRING HANDICAP, 1937, A
SPRING IN PARK LANE, 1949, A
SPRING IN THE AIR, 1934, A
SPRING IS HERE, 1930, A
SPRING MADNESS, 1938, A
SPRING MEETING, 1941, A
SPRING NIGHT, SUMMER NIGHT
SPRING PARADE, 1940, A
SPRING REUNION, 1957, A
SPRING SHOWER, 1932, A
SPRING SONG
SPRING TONIC, 1935, A
SPRINGFIELD RIFLE, 1952, A
SPRINGTIME, 1915, A
SPRINGTIME, 1948, A
SPRINGTIME FOR HENRY, 1934, A
SPRINGTIME IN TEXAS, 1945
SPRINGTIME IN THE ROCKIES, 1937, A
SPRINGTIME IN THE ROCKIES, 1942, A
SPRINGTIME IN THE SIERRAS, 1947, A
SPRINGTIME ON THE VOLGA, 1961, A
SPUDS, 1927, A
SPURS, 1930, A
SPURS AND SADDLES, 1927
SPURS OF SYBIL, THE, 1918
SPUTNIK, 1960, A
SPY 13
SPY 77
SPY BUSTERS
SPY CHASERS, 1956, A
SPY FOR A DAY, 1939, A
SPY HUNT, 1950, A
SPY IN BLACK, THE
SPY IN THE GREEN HAT, THE, 1966, A
SPY IN THE PANTRY
SPY IN THE SKY, 1958, A

SPY IN WHITE, THE
SPY IN YOUR EYE, 1966, A
SPY OF MME. POMPADOUR, 1929
SPY OF NAPOLEON, 1939, A
SPY RING, THE, 1938, A
SPY SHIP, 1942, A
SPY SQUAD, 1962
SPY TODAY, DIE TOMORROW, 1967
SPY TRAIN, 1943, A
SPY WHO CAME IN FROM THE COLD, THE,
  1965, A-C
SPY WHO LOVED ME, THE, 1977, C
SPY WITH A COLD NOSE, THE, 1966, A
SPY WITH MY FACE, THE, 1966, A
SPY, THE, 1914
SPY, THE, 1917
SPY, THE, 1931
SPYASHCHAYA KRASAVITSA
SPYLARKS, 1965, A
SPYS
SQUAD CAR, 1961, A
SQUADRON 633, 1964, A-C
SQUADRON LEADER X, 1943, A
SQUADRON OF HONOR, 1938, A
SQUALL, THE, 1929, A
SQUANDERED LIVES, 1920
SQUARE CROOKS, 1928
SQUARE DANCE JUBILEE, 1949, A
SQUARE DANCE KATY, 1950, A
SQUARE DEAL MAN, THE, 1917
SQUARE DEAL SANDERSON, 1919
SQUARE DEAL, A, 1917
SQUARE DEAL, A, 1918
SQUARE DECEIVER, THE, 1917
SQUARE JOE, 1921
SQUARE JUNGLE, THE, 1955, A
SQUARE OF VIOLENCE, 1963, A
SQUARE PEG, THE, 1958, A
SQUARE RING, THE, 1955, A
SQUARE ROOT OF ZERO, THE, 1964, C
SQUARE SHOOTER, 1935
SQUARE SHOOTER, THE
SQUARE SHOOTER, THE, 1920
SQUARE SHOULDERS, 1929, A
SQUARED CIRCLE, THE
SQUARES, 1972, A
SQUATTER'S DAUGHTER, 1933, A
SQUAW MAN'S SON, THE, 1917
SQUAW MAN, THE, 1914, A
SQUAW MAN, THE, 1918
SQUAW MAN, THE, 1931, A
SQUEAKER, THE, 1930, A
SQUEAKER, THE, 1937
SQUEALER, THE, 1930, A
SQUEEZE A FLOWER, 1970, A
SQUEEZE PLAY, 1981, O
SQUEEZE, THE, 1977, O
SQUEEZE, THE, 1980, O
SQUIBS, 1921, A
SQUIBS, 1935, A
SQUIBS WINS THE CALCUTTA SWEEP, 1922, A
SQUIBS' HONEYMOON, 1926, A
SQUIBS, MP, 1923, A
SQUIRE OF LONG HADLEY, THE, 1925
SQUIRE PHIN, 1921
SQUIRM, 1976, C
SQUIZZY TAYLOR, 1984, O
SSSSNAKE
SSSSSSSS, 1973, C
ST. BENNY THE DIP, 1951, A
ST. ELMO, 1923, A
ST. GEORGE AND THE 7 CURSES
ST. HELENS, 1981, A
ST. IVES, 1976, O
ST. LOUIS BLUES, 1939, A
ST. LOUIS BLUES, 1958, A
ST. LOUIS KID, THE, 1934, A
ST. LOUIS WOMAN, 1935
ST. MARTIN'S LANE
ST. VALENTINE'S DAY MASSACRE, THE, 1967, O
STABLE COMPANIONS, 1922
STABLEMATES, 1938, A
STACEY AND HER GANGBUSTERS
STACEY?, 1973, O
STACKED CARDS, 1926
STACY'S KNIGHTS, 1983, C
STADIUM MURDERS, THE
STAGE COACH DRIVER, 1924
STAGE DOOR, 1937, A-C
STAGE DOOR CANTEEN, 1943, A
STAGE FRIGHT, 1950, A-C
STAGE FROM BLUE RIVER
STAGE KISSES, 1927, A
STAGE MADNESS, 1927, A
STAGE MOTHER, 1933, A
STAGE ROMANCE, A, 1922
STAGE STRUCK, 1917
STAGE STRUCK, 1925
STAGE STRUCK, 1936, A
STAGE STRUCK, 1948, C
STAGE STRUCK, 1958, A-C
STAGE TO BLUE RIVER, 1951, A

STAGE TO CHINO, 1940, A
STAGE TO MESA CITY, 1947, A
STAGE TO THUNDER ROCK, 1964, A
STAGE TO TUCSON, 1950, A
STAGE WHISPERS
STAGECOACH, 1939, C
STAGECOACH, 1966, A-C
STAGECOACH BUCKAROO, 1942, A
STAGECOACH DAYS, 1938, A
STAGECOACH DRIVER, 1951
STAGECOACH EXPRESS, 1942, A
STAGECOACH KID, 1949, A
STAGECOACH LINE
STAGECOACH OUTLAWS, 1945, A
STAGECOACH TO DANCER'S PARK, 1962, A
STAGECOACH TO DENVER, 1946, A
STAGECOACH TO FURY, 1956, A
STAGECOACH TO HELL
STAGECOACH TO MONTEREY, 1944, A
STAGECOACH WAR, 1940, A
STAGEFRIGHT, 1983
STAIN IN THE BLOOD, THE, 1916
STAIN, THE, 1914, A
STAINLESS BARRIER, THE, 1917
STAIRCASE, 1969, C-O
STAIRS OF SAND, 1929, A
STAIRWAY FOR A STAR, 1947
STAIRWAY TO HEAVEN, 1946, A
STAKEOUT ON DOPE STREET, 1958, C
STAKEOUT?, 1962, A
STAKING HIS LIFE, 1918
STALAG 17, 1953, C
STALKER, 1982, C
STALKING MOON, THE, 1969, A
STALLION CANYON, 1949, A
STALLION ROAD, 1947, A
STAMBOUL, 1931, A
STAMBOUL QUEST, 1934, A
STAMPEDE, 1930
STAMPEDE, 1936, A
STAMPEDE, 1949, A
STAMPEDE THUNDER, 1925
STAMPEDE, 1960
STAMPEDE, THE, 1921
STAMPEDED
STAMPEDIN' TROUBLE, 1925
STAND AND DELIVER
STAND AND DELIVER, 1928, A
STAND AT APACHE RIVER, THE, 1953, A
STAND BY ALL NETWORKS, 1942
STAND BY FOR ACTION, 1942, A
STAND EASY
STAND UP AND BE COUNTED, 1972, C
STAND UP AND CHEER, 1934, A
STAND UP AND FIGHT, 1939, A-C
STAND UP VIRGIN SOLDIERS, 1977, O
STAND-IN, 1937, A
STANDING ROOM ONLY, 1944, A
STANLEY
STANLEY, 1973, O
STANLEY AND LIVINGSTONE, 1939, AA
STAR 80, 1983, O
STAR CHAMBER, THE, 1983, C-O
STAR CHILD
STAR CRASH
STAR DUST
STAR DUST, 1940, A
STAR DUST TRAIL, THE, 1924
STAR FELL FROM HEAVEN, A, 1936, AAA
STAR FOR A NIGHT, 1936, A
STAR IN THE DUST, 1956, A
STAR IN THE WEST
STAR INSPECTOR, THE, 1980, A
STAR IS BORN, A, 1937, C
STAR IS BORN, A, 1954, A-C
STAR IS BORN, A, 1976, C-O
STAR MAIDENS, 1976
STAR MAKER, THE, 1939, AA
STAR ODYSSEY, 1978
STAR OF HONG KONG, 1962, A
STAR OF INDIA, 1956, A
STAR OF INDIA, THE, 1913
STAR OF MIDNIGHT, 1935, A
STAR OF MY NIGHT, 1954, C
STAR OF TEXAS, 1953, A
STAR OF THE CIRCUS
STAR PACKER, THE, 1934, A
STAR PILOT, 1977, A
STAR REPORTER, 1939, A
STAR REPORTER, THE, 1921
STAR ROVER, THE, 1920
STAR SAID NO, THE
STAR SPANGLED GIRL, 1971, A
STAR SPANGLED RHYTHM, 1942, A
STAR TREK II: THE WRATH OF KHAN, 1982, A
STAR TREK III: THE SEARCH FOR SPOCK, 1984, A-C
STAR TREK: THE MOTION PICTURE, 1979, A
STAR WARS, 1977, A-C
STAR WITNESS, 1931, A
STAR!, 1968, A-C
STAR, THE, 1953, A
STARBIRD AND SWEET WILLIAM, 1975

STARCRASH, 1979, C
STARDUST, 1921, A
STARDUST, 1974, O
STARDUST MEMORIES, 1980, C
STARDUST ON THE SAGE, 1942, A
STARDUST, 1938
STARFIGHTERS, THE, 1964, A
STARHOPS, 1978, O
STARK FEAR, 1963, C
STARK LOVE, 1927
STARK MAD, 1929, A
STARK RAVING MAD, 1983
STARLIFT, 1951, A
STARLIGHT OVER TEXAS, 1938, A
STARLIGHT SLAUGHTER
STARLIGHT'S REVENGE, 1926
STARLIGHT, THE UNTAMED, 1925
STARLIT GARDEN, THE, 1923
STARMAN, 1984, C
STARS AND STRIPES FOREVER, 1952, AAA
STARS ARE SINGING, THE, 1953, A
STARS IN MY CROWN, 1950, A
STARS IN YOUR BACKYARD
STARS IN YOUR EYES, 1956, A
STARS LOOK DOWN, THE, 1940, A-C
STARS ON PARADE, 1944, A
STARS OVER ARIZONA, 1937, A
STARS OVER BROADWAY, 1935, A
STARS OVER TEXAS, 1946, A
STARSHIP INVASIONS, 1978, AA
STARSTRUCK, 1982, C
START CHEERING, 1938, A
START THE REVOLUTION WITHOUT ME, 1970, C-O
STARTING OVER, 1979, C-O
STARTING POINT, THE, 1919, A
STASTNY KONEC
STATE DEPARTMENT—FILE 649, 1949, A
STATE FAIR, 1933, A
STATE FAIR, 1945, A
STATE FAIR, 1962, A
STATE OF SIEGE, 1973, C
STATE OF THE UNION, 1948, A
STATE OF THINGS, THE, 1983, A
STATE PENITENTIARY, 1950, A
STATE POLICE, 1938, A
STATE POLICE 1948
STATE SECRET
STATE STREET SADIE, 1928, C
STATE TROOPER, 1933, A
STATE'S ATTORNEY, 1932, A
STATELESS
STATELINE MOTEL, 1976, O
STATION CONTENT, 1918
STATION MASTER, THE, 1928
STATION SIX-SAHARA, 1964, C
STATION WEST, 1948, A
STATUE, THE, 1971, O
STAVISKY, 1974, C
STAY AWAY, JOE, 1968, A
STAY HOME
STAY HUNGRY, 1976, O
STAYING ALIVE, 1983, C
STEADFAST HEART, THE, 1923, A
STEADY COMPANY, 1932, A
STEAGLE, THE, 1971, O
STEALERS, THE, 1920
STEAMBOAT BILL, JR., 1928, A
STEAMBOAT ROUND THE BEND, 1935, A
STEEL, 1980, C
STEEL AGAINST THE SKY, 1941, A
STEEL ARENA, 1973, C
STEEL BAYONET, THE, 1958, A
STEEL CAGE, THE, 1954, A
STEEL CLAW, THE, 1961, A
STEEL FIST, THE, 1952, A
STEEL HELMET, THE, 1951, C
STEEL HIGHWAY, THE
STEEL JUNGLE, THE, 1956, A
STEEL KEY, THE, 1953, A
STEEL KING, THE, 1919
STEEL LADY, THE, 1953, A
STEEL PREFERRED, 1926
STEEL TOWN, 1952, A
STEEL TRAP, THE, 1952, A
STEELHEART, 1921, A
STEELYARD BLUES, 1973, C
STEFANIA, 1968, O
STEFANIE IN RIO, 1963
STELLA, 1921
STELLA, 1950, A
STELLA DALLAS, 1925, A
STELLA DALLAS, 1937, A
STELLA MARIS, 1918, A
STELLA MARIS, 1925, A
STELLA PARISH
STELLA STAR
STELLE OF THE ROYAL MOUNTED, 1925
STEP BY STEP, 1946, A
STEP DOWN TO TERROR, 1958, A
STEP LIVELY, 1944, A
STEP LIVELY, JEEVES, 1937, A
STEP ON IT, 1922, A

STEPAN KHALTURIN, 1925
STEPCHILD, 1947, A
STEPCHILDREN, 1962, A
STEPFORD WIVES, THE, 1975, A-C
STEPHANIA
STEPHEN STEPS OUT, 1923, A
STEPMOTHER, THE, 1914
STEPMOTHER, THE, 1973
STEPPE, THE, 1963, A
STEPPENWOLF, 1974, O
STEPPIN' IN SOCIETY, 1945, A
STEPPIN' OUT, 1925
STEPPING ALONG, 1926, A
STEPPING FAST, 1923, A
STEPPING INTO SOCIETY
STEPPING LIVELY, 1924
STEPPING OUT, 1919
STEPPING OUT, 1931
STEPPING SISTERS, 1932, A
STEPPING STONE, THE, 1916
STEPPING TOES, 1938, A
STEPS TO THE MOON, 1963, A
STEPTOE AND SON, 1972, A-C
STEREO, 1969, O
STERILE CUCKOO, THE, 1969, C
STEVIE, 1978, A
STEVIE, SAMSON AND DELILAH, 1975
STICK 'EM UP, 1950, A
STICK TO YOUR GUNS, 1941, A
STICK TO YOUR STORY, 1926
STICK UP, THE, 1978, A
STICKS
STIGMA, 1972, O
STIGMATIZED ONE, THE
STILETTO, 1969, O
STILL ALARM, THE, 1926
STILL OF THE NIGHT, 1982, O
STILL ROOM IN HELL
STILL SMOKIN', 1983, O
STILL WATERS, 1915, A
STILL WATERS RUN DEEP, 1916, A
STING II, THE, 1983, C
STING OF DEATH, 1966, C
STING OF THE LASH, 1921, A
STING OF THE SCORPION, THE, 1923, A
STING OF VICTORY, THE, 1916
STING, THE, 1973, C
STINGAREE, 1934, A
STINGRAY, 1978, C
STIR, 1980, O
STIR CRAZY, 1980, C-O
STIRRUP CUP SENSATION, THE, 1924
STITCH IN TIME, A, 1919
STITCH IN TIME, A, 1967, A
STOCK CAR, 1955, A
STOCKS AND BLONDES, 1928, A
STOKER, THE, 1932, A
STOKER, THE, 1935, A
STOLEN AIRLINER, THE, 1962, AA
STOLEN ASSIGNMENT, 1955, A
STOLEN BRIDE, THE, 1927, A
STOLEN CHILD, THE, 1923
STOLEN DIRIGIBLE, THE, 1966, AAA
STOLEN FACE, 1952, A
STOLEN GOODS, 1915
STOLEN HARMONY, 1935, A
STOLEN HEAVEN, 1931, A
STOLEN HEAVEN, 1938, A
STOLEN HEIRLOOMS, THE, 1915
STOLEN HOLIDAY, 1937, A
STOLEN HONOR, 1918
STOLEN HONOURS, 1914
STOLEN HOURS, 1918
STOLEN HOURS, 1963, A-C
STOLEN IDENTITY, 1953, A
STOLEN KISS, THE, 1920
STOLEN KISSES, 1929, A
STOLEN KISSES, 1969, O
STOLEN LIFE, 1939, A
STOLEN LIFE, A, 1946, A-C
STOLEN LOVE, 1928
STOLEN MASTERPIECE, THE, 1914
STOLEN MOMENTS, 1920
STOLEN ORDERS, 1918
STOLEN PARADISE, 1941
STOLEN PARADISE, THE, 1917
STOLEN PLANS, THE, 1962, AA
STOLEN PLAY, THE, 1917
STOLEN PLEASURES, 1927, A
STOLEN RANCH, THE, 1926
STOLEN SACRIFICE, THE, 1916
STOLEN SECRETS, 1924
STOLEN SWEETS, 1934, A
STOLEN TIME
STOLEN TREATY, THE, 1917
STOLEN TRIUMPH, THE, 1916
STOLEN VOICE, 1915, A
STOLEN WEALTH
STONE, 1974, O
STONE BOY, THE, 1984, C
STONE COLD DEAD, 1980, O
STONE KILLER, THE, 1973, O

STONE OF SILVER CREEK, 1935, A
STONE RIDER, THE, 1923
STONY ISLAND, 1978, C
STOOGE, THE, 1952, A
STOOGES GO WEST
STOOL PIGEON, 1928
STOOL PIGEON, THE
STOOLIE, THE, 1972, C
STOP AT NOTHING, 1924
STOP FLIRTING, 1925
STOP ME BEFORE I KILL?, 1961, C
STOP PRESS GIRL, 1949, A
STOP THAT CAB, 1951, A
STOP THAT MAN, 1928, A
STOP THE WORLD—I WANT TO GET OFF, 1966, A
STOP THIEF, 1915
STOP THIEF, 1920, A
STOP TRAIN 349, 1964, A
STOP, LOOK, AND LISTEN, 1926
STOP, LOOK, AND LOVE, 1939, A
STOP, YOU'RE KILLING ME, 1952, A
STOPOVER FOREVER, 1964, A
STOPOVER TOKYO, 1957, A
STORIA DI UNA DONNA
STORIES FROM A FLYING TRUNK, 1979, AA
STORK, 1971, O
STORK BITES MAN, 1947, A
STORK CLUB, THE, 1945, A
STORK PAYS OFF, THE, 1941, A
STORK TALK, 1964, O
STORK'S NEST, THE, 1915, A
STORM AT DAYBREAK, 1933, A
STORM BOY, 1976, AAA
STORM BREAKER, THE, 1925
STORM CENTER, 1956, A
STORM DAUGHTER, THE, 1924, A
STORM FEAR, 1956, A
STORM GIRL, 1922
STORM IN A TEACUP, 1937, A
STORM IN A WATER GLASS, 1931, A
STORM OVER AFRICA
STORM OVER ASIA, 1929, A
STORM OVER BENGAL, 1938, A
STORM OVER LISBON, 1944, A
STORM OVER THE ANDES, 1935, A
STORM OVER THE NILE, 1955, A
STORM OVER THE PACIFIC
STORM OVER TIBET, 1952, A
STORM OVER WYOMING, 1950, A
STORM PLANET, 1962, A
STORM RIDER, THE, 1957, A
STORM SIGNAL, 1966
STORM WARNING, 1950, C-O
STORM WITHIN, THE
STORM, THE, 1916
STORM, THE, 1922, A
STORM, THE, 1930, A
STORM, THE, 1938, A
STORMBOUND, 1951, A
STORMSWEPT, 1923, A
STORMY, 1935, A
STORMY CROSSING, 1958, A-C
STORMY KNIGHT, A, 1917
STORMY SEAS, 1923, A
STORMY TRAILS, 1936, A
STORMY WATERS, 1928, A
STORMY WATERS, 1946, A
STORMY WEATHER, 1935, A
STORMY WEATHER, 1943, A
STORY OF A CHEAT, THE, 1938, O
STORY OF A CITIZEN ABOVE ALL SUSPICION
STORY OF A DRAFT DODGER
STORY OF A LOVE STORY
STORY OF A TEENAGER
STORY OF A THREE DAY PASS, THE, 1968, O
STORY OF A WOMAN, 1970, O
STORY OF ADELE H., THE, 1975, C-O
STORY OF ALEXANDER GRAHAM BELL, THE, 1939, AA
STORY OF ARNOLD ROTHSTEIN
STORY OF CINDERELLA, THE
STORY OF DAVID, A, 1960, A
STORY OF DR. EHRLICH'S MAGIC BULLET, THE
STORY OF DR. WASSELL, THE, 1944, A-C
STORY OF ESTHER COSTELLO, THE, 1957, C
STORY OF FLOATING WEEDS, A, 1934
STORY OF G.I. JOE, THE, 1945, A-C
STORY OF GILBERT AND SULLIVAN, THE
STORY OF JOSEPH AND HIS BRETHREN THE, 1962, A
STORY OF LOUIS PASTEUR, THE, 1936, AA
STORY OF MANDY, THE
STORY OF MANKIND, THE, 1957, A
STORY OF MOLLY X, THE, 1949, A
STORY OF MONTE CRISTO, THE
STORY OF ROBIN HOOD AND HIS MERRIE MEN, THE
STORY OF ROBIN HOOD, THE, 1952, AAA
STORY OF RUTH, THE, 1960, A
STORY OF SEABISCUIT, THE, 1949, A
STORY OF SEVEN WHO WERE HANGED, 1920
STORY OF SHIRLEY YORKE, THE, 1948, A

STORY OF SUSAN, THE, 1916
STORY OF TEMPLE DRAKE, THE, 1933, O
STORY OF THE BLOOD RED ROSE, THE, 1914
STORY OF THE COUNT OF MONTE CRISTO, THE, 1962, A
STORY OF THE CRUELTIES OF YOUTH, A
STORY OF THE ROSARY, THE, 1920
STORY OF THREE LOVES, THE, 1953, A
STORY OF VERNON AND IRENE CASTLE, THE, 1939, A
STORY OF VICKIE, THE, 1958, A
STORY OF WILL ROGERS, THE, 1952, A
STORY ON PAGE ONE, THE, 1959, C
STORY WITHOUT A NAME
STORY WITHOUT A NAME, THE, 1924
STORY WITHOUT WORDS, 1981, A
STORYVILLE, 1974
STOWAWAY, 1932, A
STOWAWAY, 1936, AAA
STOWAWAY GIRL, 1957, A
STOWAWAY GIRL, THE, 1916
STOWAWAY IN THE SKY, 1962, AA
STRAIGHT FROM PARIS, 1921
STRAIGHT FROM THE HEART, 1935, A
STRAIGHT FROM THE SHOULDER, 1921
STRAIGHT FROM THE SHOULDER, 1936, A
STRAIGHT IS THE WAY, 1921, A
STRAIGHT IS THE WAY, 1934, A
STRAIGHT JACKET, 1980
STRAIGHT ON TILL MORNING, 1974, O
STRAIGHT ROAD, THE, 1914, A
STRAIGHT SHOOTER, 1940, A
STRAIGHT SHOOTIN', 1927
STRAIGHT SHOOTING, 1917
STRAIGHT THROUGH, 1925
STRAIGHT TIME, 1978, O
STRAIGHT TO HEAVEN, 1939, A
STRAIGHT WAY, THE, 1916
STRAIGHT, PLACE AND SHOW, 1938, A
STRAIGHTAWAY, 1934, A
STRAIGHTFORWARD BOY, A, 1929
STRAIT-JACKET, 1964, O
STRAITJACKET, 1963
STRANDED, 1916
STRANDED, 1927, A
STRANDED, 1935, A
STRANDED, 1965, O
STRANDED IN ARCADY, 1917
STRANDED IN PARIS
STRANDED IN PARIS, 1926
STRANDED, 1967
STRANGE ADVENTURE, 1932, A
STRANGE ADVENTURE, A, 1956, A
STRANGE ADVENTURES OF MR. SMITH, THE, 1937, A
STRANGE AFFAIR, 1944, A
STRANGE AFFAIR OF UNCLE HARRY, THE
STRANGE AFFAIR, THE, 1968, O
STRANGE AFFECTION, 1959, A
STRANGE ALIBI, 1941, A
STRANGE AWAKENING, THE
STRANGE BARGAIN, 1949, A
STRANGE BEDFELLOWS, 1965, A-C
STRANGE BEHAVIOR
STRANGE BOARDERS, 1938, A
STRANGE BORDER, THE, 1920
STRANGE BREW, 1983, O
STRANGE CARGO, 1929, A
STRANGE CARGO, 1936, A
STRANGE CARGO, 1940, C
STRANGE CASE OF CLARA DEANE, THE, 1932, A
STRANGE CASE OF DISTRICT ATTORNEY M., 1930
STRANGE CASE OF DR. MANNING, THE, 1958, A
STRANGE CASE OF DR. MEADE, 1939, A
STRANGE CASE OF DR. RX, THE, 1942, A
STRANGE CASE OF PHILIP KENT, THE, 1916
STRANGE CONFESSION
STRANGE CONFESSION, 1945, A
STRANGE CONQUEST, 1946, A
STRANGE CONSPIRACY, THE
STRANGE DEATH OF ADOLF HITLER, THE, 1943, A
STRANGE DECEPTION, 1953, O
STRANGE DOOR, THE, 1951, A
STRANGE EVIDENCE, 1933, A
STRANGE EXPERIMENT, 1937, A
STRANGE FACES, 1938, A
STRANGE FASCINATION, 1952, A
STRANGE FETISHES OF THE GO-GO GIRLS
STRANGE FETISHES, THE, 1967, O
STRANGE GAMBLE, 1948, A
STRANGE HOLIDAY, 1945, A
STRANGE HOLIDAY, 1969, A
STRANGE IDOLS, 1922
STRANGE ILLUSION, 1945, A
STRANGE IMPERSONATION, 1946, A
STRANGE INCIDENT
STRANGE INTERLUDE, 1932, C
STRANGE INTERVAL
STRANGE INTRUDER, 1956, A
STRANGE INVADERS, 1983, O
STRANGE JOURNEY, 1946, A
STRANGE JOURNEY, 1966

STRANGE JUSTICE, 1932, A
STRANGE LADY IN TOWN, 1955, A
STRANGE LAWS
STRANGE LOVE OF MARTHA IVERS, THE, 1946, C
STRANGE LOVE OF MOLLY LOUVAIN, THE, 1932, A
STRANGE LOVERS, 1963, O
STRANGE MR. GREGORY, THE, 1945, A
STRANGE MRS. CRANE, THE, 1948, A
STRANGE ONE, THE, 1957, O
STRANGE ONES, THE,
STRANGE PEOPLE, 1933, A
STRANGE RIDER, THE, 1925
STRANGE ROADS
STRANGE SHADOWS IN AN EMPTY ROOM, 1977, O
STRANGE THINGS HAPPEN AT NIGHT, 1979
STRANGE TRANSGRESSOR, A, 1917
STRANGE TRIANGLE, 1946, A
STRANGE VENEGEANCE OF ROSALIE, THE, 1972, C
STRANGE VOYAGE, 1945, A
STRANGE WIVES, 1935, A
STRANGE WOMAN, THE, 1918
STRANGE WOMAN, THE, 1946, C
STRANGE WORLD, 1952, A
STRANGE WORLD OF PLANET X, THE
STRANGER AT MY DOOR, 1950, A
STRANGER AT MY DOOR, 1956, A
STRANGER CAME HOME, THE
STRANGER FROM ARIZONA, THE, 1938, A
STRANGER FROM PECOS, THE, 1943, A
STRANGER FROM PONCA CITY, THE, 1947
STRANGER FROM SANTA FE, 1945
STRANGER FROM SOMEWHERE, A, 1916
STRANGER FROM TEXAS, THE, 1940, A
STRANGER FROM VENUS, THE, 1954, A
STRANGER IN BETWEEN, THE, 1952, A
STRANGER IN CANYON VALLEY, THE, 1921
STRANGER IN HOLLYWOOD, 1968, A-C
STRANGER IN MY ARMS, 1959, A
STRANGER IN THE HOUSE, 1967
STRANGER IN THE HOUSE, 1975
STRANGER IN TOWN, 1932, A
STRANGER IN TOWN, 1957, A
STRANGER IN TOWN, A, 1943, A
STRANGER IN TOWN, A, 1968, C
STRANGER IS WATCHING, A, 1982, O
STRANGER KNOCKS, A, 1963, C
STRANGER OF THE HILLS, THE, 1922
STRANGER ON HORSEBACK, 1955, A
STRANGER ON THE PROWL, 1953, A-C
STRANGER ON THE THIRD FLOOR, 1940, C
STRANGER RETURNS, THE, 1968, A
STRANGER THAN FICTION, 1921, A
STRANGER THAN LOVE
STRANGER THAN PARADISE, 1984, O
STRANGER WALKED IN, A
STRANGER WORE A GUN, THE, 1953, A
STRANGER'S BANQUET, 1922, A
STRANGER'S GUNDOWN, THE, 1974, C
STRANGER'S HAND, THE, 1955, A
STRANGER'S MEETING, 1957, A
STRANGER'S RETURN, 1933, A
STRANGER, THE, 1913
STRANGER, THE, 1924, A
STRANGER, THE, 1946, C
STRANGER, THE, 1967, C-O
STRANGER, THE, 1940
STRANGER, THE, 1962
STRANGERS ALL, 1935, A
STRANGERS AT SUNRISE, 1969
STRANGERS CAME, THE
STRANGERS HONEYMOON
STRANGERS IN LOVE, 1932, A
STRANGERS IN THE CITY, 1962, A
STRANGERS IN THE HOUSE, 1949, C
STRANGERS IN THE NIGHT, 1944, A-C
STRANGERS KISS, 1984, C
STRANGERS MAY KISS, 1931, A
STRANGERS OF THE EVENING, 1932, A
STRANGERS OF THE NIGHT, 1923, A
STRANGERS ON A HONEYMOON, 1937, A
STRANGERS ON A TRAIN, 1951, C-O
STRANGERS WHEN WE MEET, 1960, C
STRANGERS, 1970
STRANGERS, THE, 1955, A
STRANGEST CASE, THE
STRANGLEHOLD, 1931, A
STRANGLEHOLD, 1962, A
STRANGLER OF THE SWAMP, 1945, A
STRANGLER'S WEB, 1966, A-C
STRANGLER, THE, 1941, C
STRANGLER, THE, 1964, C
STRANGLERS OF BOMBAY, THE, 1960, C
STRANGLING THREADS, 1923
STRATEGIC AIR COMMAND, 1955, A
STRATEGY OF TERROR, 1969, A
STRATHMORE, 1915
STRATTON STORY, THE, 1949, AA
STRAUSS' GREAT WALTZ, 1934, A
STRAUSS' SALOME
STRAUSS, THE WALTZ KING, 1929
STRAW DOGS, 1971, O
STRAW MAN, THE, 1953, A

STRAWBERRY BLONDE, THE, 1941, A
STRAWBERRY ROAN, 1933, A
STRAWBERRY ROAN, 1945, A
STRAWBERRY ROAN, THE, 1948, A
STRAWBERRY STATEMENT, THE, 1970, C
STRAWS IN THE WIND, 1924
STRAY DOG, 1963, A-C
STREAK OF LUCK, A, 1925
STREAM OF LIFE, THE, 1919
STREAMERS, 1983, O
STREAMLINE EXPRESS, 1935, A
STREET ANGEL, 1928, A
STREET BANDITS, 1951, A
STREET CALLED STRAIGHT, THE, 1920
STREET CORNER
STREET CORNER, 1948, C
STREET FIGHTER, 1959, A
STREET GANG
STREET GIRL, 1929, A
STREET GIRLS, 1975
STREET IS MY BEAT, THE, 1966, C
STREET LAW, 1981
STREET MUSIC, 1982, A-C
STREET OF ADVENTURE, THE, 1921
STREET OF CHANCE, 1930, A
STREET OF CHANCE, 1942, A
STREET OF DARKNESS, 1958, A
STREET OF FORGOTTEN MEN, THE, 1925
STREET OF ILLUSION, THE, 1928
STREET OF MEMORIES, 1940, A
STREET OF MISSING MEN, 1939, A
STREET OF MISSING WOMEN
STREET OF SEVEN STARS, THE, 1918
STREET OF SHADOWS
STREET OF SIN, THE, 1928, A
STREET OF SINNERS, 1957, A
STREET OF TEARS, THE, 1924
STREET OF WOMEN, 1932, A
STREET PARTNER, THE
STREET PEOPLE, 1976, O
STREET SCENE, 1931, C
STREET SINGER, THE, 1937, A
STREET SONG, 1935, A
STREET WITH NO NAME, THE, 1948, C-O
STREET, THE, 1927
STREETCAR NAMED DESIRE, A, 1951, C-O
STREETFIGHTER, THE
STREETS OF FIRE, 1984, C
STREETS OF GHOST TOWN, 1950, A
STREETS OF HONG KONG, 1979
STREETS OF ILLUSION, THE, 1917
STREETS OF LAREDO, 1949, A-C
STREETS OF LONDON, THE, 1929
STREETS OF NEW YORK, 1939, A
STREETS OF NEW YORK, THE, 1922, A
STREETS OF SAN FRANCISCO, 1949, A
STREETS OF SHANGHAI, 1927
STREETS OF SIN
STREETS OF SINNERS
STRENGTH OF DONALD MCKENZIE, THE, 1916
STRENGTH OF THE PINES, 1922
STRENGTH OF THE WEAK, THE, 1916
STRICTLY CONFIDENTIAL
STRICTLY CONFIDENTIAL, 1919
STRICTLY CONFIDENTIAL, 1959, A
STRICTLY DISHONORABLE, 1931, A-C
STRICTLY DISHONORABLE, 1951, A
STRICTLY DYNAMITE, 1934, A
STRICTLY FOR PLEASURE
STRICTLY FOR THE BIRDS, 1963, C
STRICTLY ILLEGAL, 1935, A
STRICTLY IN THE GROOVE, 1942, A
STRICTLY MODERN, 1930, A
STRICTLY PERSONAL, 1933, A
STRICTLY UNCONVENTIONAL, 1930, A
STRIFE, 1919
STRIFE ETERNAL, THE, 1915
STRIKE, 1925
STRIKE IT RICH, 1933, A
STRIKE IT RICH, 1948, A
STRIKE ME DEADLY
STRIKE ME DEADLY, 1963
STRIKE ME PINK, 1936, A
STRIKE UP THE BAND, 1940, AAA
STRIKE?, 1934, A
STRIKEBOUND, 1984, C-O
STRIKERS, THE
STRIKERS, THE, 1915
STRIKING BACK, 1981
STRING BEANS, 1918
STRIP TEASE MURDER, 1961, C-O
STRIP, THE, 1951, C
STRIP-TEASE
STRIPED STOCKING GANG, THE
STRIPES, 1981, O
STRIPPED FOR A MILLION, 1919
STRIPPER, THE, 1963, O
STRIPTEASE LADY
STRIVING FOR FORTUNE, 1926, A
STROKE OF MIDNIGHT, THE
STROKER ACE, 1983, C
STROMBOLI, 1950, C-O

STRONG BOY, 1929, A
STRONG MAN'S WEAKNESS, A, 1917
STRONG MAN, THE, 1917
STRONG MAN, THE, 1926, A
STRONG MEDICINE, 1981
STRONG WAY, THE, 1918
STRONGER LOVE, THE, 1916
STRONGER SEX, THE, 1931, A
STRONGER THAN DEATH, 1920
STRONGER THAN DESIRE, 1939, A
STRONGER THAN FEAR
STRONGER THAN THE SUN, 1980, A
STRONGER VOW, THE, 1919
STRONGER WILL, THE, 1928
STRONGEST MAN IN THE WORLD, THE, 1975, A
STRONGEST, THE, 1920
STRONGHOLD, 1952, A
STRONGROOM, 1962, A
STRUGGLE EVERLASTING, THE, 1918
STRUGGLE, THE, 1916
STRUGGLE, THE, 1921, A
STRUGGLE, THE, 1931, A-C
STRYKER, 1983, O
STUBBORNESS OF GERALDINE, THE, 1915
STUCK ON YOU, 1983, O
STUCKEY'S LAST STAND, 1980, C
STUD, THE, 1979, O
STUDENT BODIES, 1981, O
STUDENT BODY, THE, 1976, O
STUDENT NURSES, THE, 1970, O
STUDENT OF PRAGUE, THE, 1913
STUDENT OF PRAGUE, THE, 1927, A
STUDENT PRINCE IN OLD HEIDELBERG, THE, 1927
STUDENT PRINCE, THE, 1954, A
STUDENT ROMANCE
STUDENT TEACHERS, THE, 1973, O
STUDENT TOUR, 1934, A
STUDENT'S ROMANCE, THE, 1936, A
STUDIO GIRL, THE, 1918
STUDIO MURDER MYSTERY, THE, 1929, A
STUDIO ROMANCE
STUDS LONIGAN, 1960, A
STUDY IN SCARLET, A, 1914
STUDY IN SCARLET, A, 1933, A
STUDY IN TERROR, A, 1966, A
STUETZEN DER GESELLSCHAFT
STUNT MAN, THE, 1980, O
STUNT PILOT, 1939, A
STUNTS, 1977, C-O
SUB-A-DUB-DUB
SUBJECT WAS ROSES, THE, 1968, C
SUBMARINE, 1928
SUBMARINE ALERT, 1943, A
SUBMARINE BASE, 1943, A
SUBMARINE COMMAND, 1951, A
SUBMARINE D-1, 1937, A
SUBMARINE EYE, THE, 1917
SUBMARINE PATROL, 1938, A
SUBMARINE PIRATE, A, 1915, A
SUBMARINE RAIDER, 1942, A
SUBMARINE SEAHAWK, 1959, A
SUBMARINE ZONE
SUBMERSION OF JAPAN, THE
SUBSTITUTE WIFE, THE, 1925
SUBSTITUTION, 1970, O
SUBTERFUGE, 1969, A
SUBTERRANEANS, THE, 1960, C
SUBURBAN WIVES, 1973, O
SUBURBAN, THE, 1915, A
SUBURBIA, 1984, O
SUBVERSIVES, THE, 1967, C
SUBWAY EXPRESS, 1931, A
SUBWAY IN THE SKY, 1959, C
SUBWAY RIDERS, 1981, O
SUBWAY SADIE, 1926
SUCCESS
SUCCESS, 1923, A
SUCCESS AT ANY PRICE, 1934, A
SUCCESS IS THE BEST REVENGE, 1984, O
SUCCESSFUL ADVENTURE, THE, 1918
SUCCESSFUL CALAMITY, A, 1932, A
SUCCESSFUL FAILURE, A, 1917
SUCCESSFUL FAILURE, A, 1934, A
SUCH A GORGEOUS KID LIKE ME, 1973, O
SUCH A LITTLE PIRATE, 1918
SUCH A LITTLE QUEEN, 1914, A
SUCH A LITTLE QUEEN, 1914, A
SUCH A LITTLE QUEEN, 1921, A
SUCH GOOD FRIENDS, 1971, O
SUCH IS LIFE, 1929
SUCH IS LIFE, 1936, A
SUCH IS THE LAW, 1930, A
SUCH MEN ARE DANGEROUS
SUCH MEN ARE DANGEROUS, 1930, A
SUCH THINGS HAPPEN
SUCH WOMEN ARE DANGEROUS, 1934, A
SUCKER ... OR HOW TO BE GLAD WHEN YOU'VE
   BEEN HAD, THE
SUCKER MONEY, 1933, A
SUCKER, THE, 1966, A
SUDAN, 1945, A-C
SUDDEN BILL DORN, 1938, A

SUDDEN DANGER, 1955, A
SUDDEN DEATH, 1977
SUDDEN FEAR, 1952, A-C
SUDDEN FURY, 1975, C
SUDDEN GENTLEMAN, THE, 1917
SUDDEN IMPACT, 1983, O
SUDDEN JIM, 1917
SUDDEN MONEY, 1939, A
SUDDEN RICHES, 1916
SUDDEN TERROR, 1970, A
SUDDENLY, 1954, C
SUDDENLY IT'S SPRING, 1947, A
SUDDENLY, A WOMAN, 1967, O
SUDDENLY, LAST SUMMER, 1959, O
SUDS, 1920, A
SUE OF THE SOUTH, 1919
SUED FOR LIBEL, 1940, A
SUENO DE NOCHE DE VERANO
SUEZ, 1938, A
SUGAR CANE ALLEY, 1984, C
SUGAR COOKIES, 1973
SUGAR HILL, 1974, C
SUGARFOOT, 1951, A
SUGARLAND EXPRESS, THE, 1974, C
SUGATA SANSHIRO
SUICIDE BATTALION, 1958, A
SUICIDE CLUB, THE
SUICIDE CLUB, THE, 1914
SUICIDE FLEET, 1931, A
SUICIDE LEGION, 1940, C
SUICIDE MISSION, 1956, C
SUICIDE RUN
SUICIDE SQUADRON, 1942, A
SUITABLE CASE FOR TREATMENT, A
SUITOR, THE, 1963, C
SULEIMAN THE CONQUEROR, 1963, A
SULLIVAN'S EMPIRE, 1967, A
SULLIVAN'S TRAVELS, 1941, C
SULLIVANS, THE, 1944, A
SULT
SULTAN'S DAUGHTER, THE, 1943, A
SULTANA, THE, 1916
SUMARINE X-1, 1969, A
SUMMER AND SMOKE, 1961, C-O
SUMMER BACHELORS, 1926, A
SUMMER CAMP, 1979, O
SUMMER FIRES
SUMMER FLIGHT
SUMMER GIRL, THE, 1916
SUMMER HOLIDAY, 1948, AA
SUMMER HOLIDAY, 1963, A
SUMMER INTERLUDE
SUMMER LIGHTNING, 1933, A
SUMMER LIGHTNING, 1948
SUMMER LOVE, 1958, A
SUMMER LOVERS, 1982, O
SUMMER MADNESS
SUMMER MAGIC, 1963, AAA
SUMMER OF '42, 1971, O
SUMMER OF '64
SUMMER OF SECRETS, 1976, O
SUMMER OF THE SEVENTEENTH DOLL
SUMMER PLACE, A, 1959, C
SUMMER RUN, 1974, A
SUMMER RUN, 1974
SUMMER SCHOOL TEACHERS, 1977, O
SUMMER SOLDIERS, 1972, C
SUMMER STOCK, 1950, A
SUMMER STORM, 1944, C
SUMMER TALES
SUMMER TO REMEMBER, A, 1961, A
SUMMER WISHES, WINTER DREAMS, 1973, A
SUMMER'S CHILDREN, 1979, O
SUMMERDOG, 1977, AAA
SUMMERFIELD, 1977, O
SUMMERPLAY
SUMMERSKIN, 1962, C
SUMMERSPELL, 1983, C
SUMMERTIME, 1955, A-C
SUMMERTIME KILLER, 1973, C
SUMMERTREE, 1971, A
SUMURU
SUMURUN
SUMURUN, 1910
SUMURUN, 1921
SUN ABOVE, DEATH BELOW, 1969, C
SUN ALSO RISES, THE, 1957, C
SUN ALWAYS RISES, THE
SUN COMES UP, THE, 1949, AAA
SUN DEMON, THE
SUN DOG TRAILS, 1923
SUN IS UP, THE
SUN NEVER SETS, THE, 1939, A
SUN RISES AGAIN, THE
SUN SETS AT DAWN, THE, 1950, A
SUN SHINES BRIGHT, THE, 1953, A
SUN SHINES FOR ALL, THE, 1961, A
SUN SHINES FOR EVERYBODY, THE
SUN SHINES, THE, 1939, A
SUN TAN RANCH, 1948
SUN VALLEY CYCLONE, 1946, A
SUN VALLEY SERENADE, 1941, AA

SUN-UP, 1925
SUNA NO KAORI
SUNA NO ONNA
SUNBEAM, THE, 1916
SUNBONNET SUE, 1945, A
SUNBURN, 1979, C
SUNBURST, 1975
SUNDANCE CASSIDY AND BUTCH THE KID, 1975
SUNDAY BLOODY SUNDAY, 1971, O
SUNDAY DINNER FOR A SOLDIER, 1944, A
SUNDAY IN NEW YORK, 1963, C
SUNDAY IN THE COUNTRY, 1975, O
SUNDAY IN THE COUNTRY, A, 1984, A
SUNDAY LOVERS, 1980, O
SUNDAY PUNCH, 1942, A
SUNDAY SINNERS, 1941
SUNDAY TOO FAR AWAY, 1975, C
SUNDAYS AND CYBELE, 1962, C
SUNDOWN, 1924
SUNDOWN, 1941, C
SUNDOWN IN SANTA FE, 1948, A
SUNDOWN JIM, 1942, A
SUNDOWN KID, THE, 1942, A
SUNDOWN ON THE PRAIRIE, 1939, A
SUNDOWN RIDER, THE, 1933, AA
SUNDOWN RIDERS, 1948, A
SUNDOWN SAUNDERS, 1937, A
SUNDOWN SLIM, 1920
SUNDOWN TRAIL, 1931, A
SUNDOWN TRAIL, THE, 1919
SUNDOWN TRAIL, THE, 1975
SUNDOWN VALLEY, 1944, A
SUNDOWNERS, THE, 1950, A
SUNDOWNERS, THE, 1960, A
SUNFLOWER, 1970, A
SUNKEN ROCKS, 1919
SUNLIGHT'S LAST RAID, 1917
SUNNY, 1930, A
SUNNY, 1941, A
SUNNY JANE, 1917
SUNNY SIDE OF THE STREET, 1951, A
SUNNY SIDE UP, 1929, A
SUNNY SKIES, 1930, A
SUNNYSIDE, 1979, O
SUNNYSIDE UP, 1926
SUNRISE AT CAMPOBELLO, 1960, A
SUNRISE TRAIL, 1931, A
SUNRISE—A SONG OF TWO HUMANS, 1927, A
SUNSCORCHED, 1966, O
SUNSET BOULEVARD, 1950, C-O
SUNSET CARSON RIDES AGAIN, 1948
SUNSET COVE, 1978, O
SUNSET DERBY, THE, 1927, A
SUNSET IN EL DORADO, 1945, A
SUNSET IN THE WEST, 1950, A
SUNSET IN VIENNA
SUNSET IN WYOMING, 1941, A
SUNSET JONES, 1921
SUNSET LEGION, THE, 1928, A
SUNSET MURDER CASE, 1941, C
SUNSET OF A CLOWN
SUNSET OF POWER, 1936, A
SUNSET ON THE DESERT, 1942, AA
SUNSET PASS, 1929, A
SUNSET PASS, 1933, A
SUNSET PASS, 1946, A
SUNSET RANGE, 1935, A
SUNSET SERENADE, 1942, A
SUNSET SPRAGUE, 1920
SUNSET TRAIL, 1917
SUNSET TRAIL, 1932, A
SUNSET TRAIL, 1938, A
SUNSET TRAIL, THE, 1924
SUNSHINE AHEAD, 1936, A
SUNSHINE ALLEY, 1917
SUNSHINE AND GOLD, 1917
SUNSHINE BOYS, THE, 1975, A-C
SUNSHINE DAD, 1916
SUNSHINE HARBOR, 1922
SUNSHINE NAN, 1918
SUNSHINE OF PARADISE ALLEY, 1926
SUNSHINE RUN, 1979
SUNSHINE SUSIE
SUNSHINE TRAIL, THE, 1923, A
SUNSTRUCK, 1973, A
SUPER BUG, 1975
SUPER COPS, THE, 1974, O
SUPER DRAGON
SUPER DUDE
SUPER FUZZ, 1981, C
SUPER INFRAMAN, THE
SUPER SEAL, 1976
SUPER SLEUTH, 1937, A
SUPER SPEED, 1925
SUPER SPOOK, 1975, O
SUPER VAN, 1977, C
SUPER WEAPON, THE, 1976
SUPER-JOCKS, THE, 1980
SUPER-SEX, THE, 1922, A
SUPERARGO, 1968, A
SUPERARGO VERSUS DIABOLICUS, 1966, A
SUPERBEAST, 1972, O

SUPERBUG, SUPER AGENT, 1976, AAA
SUPERBUG, THE WILD ONE, 1977
SUPERCHICK, 1973, O
SUPERCOCK, 1975
SUPERDAD, 1974, AAA
SUPERFLY, 1972, O
SUPERFLY T.N.T., 1973, O
SUPERGIRL, 1984, C
SUPERMAN, 1978, AAA
SUPERMAN AND THE MOLE MEN, 1951, A
SUPERMAN AND THE STRANGE PEOPLE
SUPERMAN II, 1980, A
SUPERMAN III, 1983, A
SUPERNATURAL, 1933, A-C
SUPERSNOOPER
SUPERSONIC MAN, 1979, A
SUPERSONIC SAUCER, 1956
SUPERSPEED, 1935, A
SUPERSTITION, 1922
SUPERZAN AND THE SPACE BOY, 1972, AAA
SUPPORT YOUR LOCAL GUNFIGHTER, 1971, A
SUPPORT YOUR LOCAL SHERIFF, 1969, A
*SUPPOSE THEY GAVE A WAR AND NOBODY
   CAME?*, 1970, A
SUPREME KID, THE, 1976, C
SUPREME PASSION, THE, 1921
SUPREME SACRIFICE, THE, 1916
SUPREME SECRET, THE, 1958, A
SUPREME TEMPTATION, THE, 1916
SUPREME TEST, THE, 1915
SUPREME TEST, THE, 1923, A
SUPRISES OF AN EMPTY HOTEL, THE, 1916
SUR LA COUR
SUR LA ROUTE DE SALINA
SURABAYA CONSPIRACY, 1975
SURCOUF, LE DERNIER CORSAIRE
SURE FIRE, 1921
SURE FIRE FLINT, 1922, A
SURF II, 1984, O
SURF PARTY, 1964, A
SURF TERROR
SURF, THE
SURFTIDE 77, 1962, O
SURFTIDE 777
SURGEON'S KNIFE, THE, 1957, C
SURGING SEAS, 1924, A
SURPRISE PACKAGE, 1960, C
SURRENDER, 1927
SURRENDER, 1931, A
SURRENDER, 1950, C
SURRENDER—HELL?, 1959, C
SURROGATE, THE, 1984, O
SURVIVAL, 1930
SURVIVAL, 1976, C
SURVIVAL RUN, 1980, O
SURVIVAL, 1962
SURVIVAL, 1965
SURVIVE!, 1977, O
SURVIVOR, 1980, C-O
SURVIVORS, THE, 1983, C-O
SUSAN AND GOD, 1940, A
SUSAN LENOX—HER FALL AND RISE, 1931, C
SUSAN ROCKS THE BOAT, 1916
SUSAN SLADE, 1961, C
SUSAN SLEPT HERE, 1954, C
SUSAN'S GENTLEMAN, 1917
SUSANNA
SUSANNA PASS, 1949, A
SUSANNAH OF THE MOUNTIES, 1939, AAA
SUSIE SNOWFLAKE, 1916
SUSIE STEPS OUT, 1946, A
SUSPECT, 1961
SUSPECT, THE, 1916
SUSPECT, THE, 1944, C
SUSPECTED
SUSPECTED ALIBI
SUSPECTED PERSON, 1943, A
SUSPENCE, 1919
SUSPENDED ALIBI, 1957, A
SUSPENSE, 1930, C
SUSPENSE, 1946, A-C
SUSPICION, 1918
SUSPICION, 1941, A-C
SUSPICIOUS WIFE, A, 1914
SUSPICIOUS WIVES, 1921
SUSPIRIA, 1977, O
SUSUZ YAZ
SUTTER'S GOLD, 1936, A
SUZANNA, 1922, A
SUZANNE, 1916
SUZANNE, 1980, C
SUZY, 1936, C
SVALT
SVEGLIATI E UCCIDI
SVENGALI, 1931, A-C
SVENGALI, 1955, C
SVIRACHUT
SWALLOWS AND AMAZONS, 1977, AAA
SWAMP COUNTRY, 1966, O
SWAMP DIAMONDS
SWAMP FIRE, 1946, A
SWAMP THING, 1982, C

SWAMP WATER, 1941, A
SWAMP WOMAN, 1941, A
SWAMP WOMEN, 1956, A
SWAMP, THE, 1921, A
SWAN LAKE, THE, 1967, AAA
SWAN, THE, 1925
SWAN, THE, 1956, A
SWANEE RIVER, 1931
SWANEE RIVER, 1939, A-C
SWANEE SHOWBOAT, 1939
SWANN IN LOVE, 1984, C-O
SWAP MEET, 1979, O
SWAPPERS, THE, 1970, O
SWARM, THE, 1978, C
SWASHBUCKLER, 1976, O
SWASTIKA SAVAGES
SWAT THE SPY, 1918
SWEATER GIRL, 1942, A
SWEATER GIRLS, 1978
SWEDENHIELMS, 1935, A
SWEDISH MISTRESS, THE, 1964, O
SWEDISH WEDDING NIGHT, 1965, C
SWEENEY, 1977, O
SWEENEY 2, 1978, O
SWEENEY TODD, 1928
SWEENEY TODD. THE DEMON BARBER OF FLEET
   STREET
SWEEPING AGAINST THE WINDS, 1930
SWEEPINGS, 1933, A
SWEEPSTAKE ANNIE, 1935, A
SWEEPSTAKE RACKETEERS
SWEEPSTAKES, 1931, A
SWEEPSTAKES WINNER, 1939, A
SWEET ADELINE, 1926, A
SWEET ADELINE, 1935, A
SWEET ALOES
SWEET ALYSSUM, 1915
SWEET AND LOWDOWN, 1944, A
SWEET AND SOUR, 1964, A
SWEET AND TWENTY, 1919
SWEET BEAT, 1962, A
SWEET BIRD OF YOUTH, 1962, O
SWEET BODY OF DEBORAH, THE, 1969, O
SWEET BODY, THE
SWEET CHARITY, 1969, A
SWEET COUNTRY ROAD, 1981
SWEET CREEK COUNTY WAR, THE, 1979, A
SWEET DADDIES, 1926
SWEET DEVIL, 1937, A
SWEET DIRTY TONY
SWEET DREAMERS, 1981
SWEET ECSTASY, 1962, C
SWEET GENEVIEVE, 1947
SWEET GEORGIA, 1972
SWEET GINGER BROWN
SWEET HUNTERS, 1969, C
SWEET INNISCARRA, 1934, A
SWEET JESUS, PREACHER MAN, 1973, O
SWEET KILL
SWEET KITTY BELLAIRS, 1916
SWEET KITTY BELLAIRS, 1930, A
SWEET LAVANDER, 1920
SWEET LAVENDER, 1915
SWEET LIGHT IN A DARK ROOM, 1966, A
SWEET LOVE, BITTER, 1967, C
SWEET MAMA, 1930, A
SWEET MUSIC, 1935, A
SWEET NOVEMBER, 1968, A
SWEET REVENGE
SWEET RIDE, THE, 1968, C
SWEET ROSIE O'GRADY, 1926
SWEET ROSIE O'GRADY, 1943, A
SWEET SAVIOR, 1971
SWEET SIXTEEN, 1928, A
SWEET SIXTEEN, 1983, O
SWEET SKIN, 1965, O
SWEET SMELL OF LOVE, 1966, A
SWEET SMELL OF SUCCESS, 1957, C-O
SWEET SOUND OF DEATH, 1965
SWEET STEPMOTHER
SWEET SUBSTITUTE, 1964, C
SWEET SUGAR, 1972, O
SWEET SURRENDER, 1935, A
SWEET SUZY, 1973, O
SWEET TRASH, 1970, O
SWEET VIOLENCE
SWEET WILLIAM, 1980, O
SWEETHEART OF SIGMA CHI, 1933, A
SWEETHEART OF SIGMA CHI, 1946, A
SWEETHEART OF THE CAMPUS, 1941, A
SWEETHEART OF THE DOOMED, 1917
SWEETHEART OF THE FLEET, 1942, A
SWEETHEART OF THE NAVY, 1937, A
SWEETHEARTS, 1919
SWEETHEARTS, 1938, A
SWEETHEARTS AND WIVES, 1930, A
SWEETHEARTS OF THE U.S.A., 1944, A
SWEETHEARTS ON PARADE, 1930, A
SWEETHEARTS ON PARADE, 1953, A
SWEETHEARTS ON PARADE, 1944
SWEETIE, 1929, A
SWELL GUY, 1946, A

SWELL-HEAD, 1935, A
SWELL-HEAD, THE, 1927, A
SWELLHEAD, THE, 1930, A
*SWEPT AWAY...BY AN UNUSUAL DESTINY IN THE
   BLUE SEA OF AUGUST*, 1975, O
SWIFT SHADOW, THE, 1927
SWIFT VENGEANCE
SWIFTY, 1936, A
SWIM TEAM, 1979
SWIM, GIRL, SWIM, 1927
SWIMMER, THE, 1968, C
SWINDLE, THE, 1962, A
SWINDLER, THE, 1919
SWING, 1938
SWING AND SWAY
SWING FEVER, 1943, A
SWING HIGH, 1930, A
SWING HIGH, 1944
SWING HIGH, SWING LOW, 1937, A-C
SWING HOSTESS, 1944, A
SWING IN THE SADDLE, 1944, A
SWING IT BUDDY
SWING IT SAILOR, 1937, A
SWING IT SOLDIER, 1941, A
SWING IT, PROFESSOR, 1937, A
SWING OUT THE BLUES, 1943, A
SWING OUT, SISTER, 1945, A
SWING PARADE OF 1946, 1946, A
SWING SHIFT, 1984, A-C
SWING SHIFT MAISIE, 1943, A
SWING THAT CHEER, 1938, A
SWING THE WESTERN WAY, 1947
SWING TIME, 1936, AA
SWING YOUR LADY, 1938, A
SWING YOUR PARTNER, 1943, A
SWING, COWBOY, SWING, 1944
SWING, SISTER, SWING, 1938, A
SWING, TEACHER, SWING
SWINGER'S PARADISE, 1965, A
SWINGER, THE, 1966, A
SWINGIN' AFFAIR, A, 1963, A
SWINGIN' ALONG, 1962, A
SWINGIN' IN THE GROOVE, 1960
SWINGIN' MAIDEN, THE, 1963, A
SWINGIN' ON A RAINBOW, 1945, A
SWINGIN' SUMMER, A, 1965, A
SWINGING BARMAIDS, THE, 1976, O
SWINGING CHEERLEADERS, THE, 1974
SWINGING COEDS, THE, 1976
SWINGING FINK
SWINGING PEARL MYSTERY, THE
SWINGING SET
SWINGING THE LEAD, 1934, A
SWINGTIME JOHNNY, 1944, A
SWIRL OF GLORY
SWISS CONSPIRACY, THE, 1976, C
SWISS FAMILY ROBINSON, 1934, AAA
SWISS FAMILY ROBINSON, 1960, AAA
SWISS HONEYMOON, 1947, A
SWISS MISS, 1938, AAA
SWISS TOUR
SWITCH, THE, 1963, C
SWITCHBLADE SISTERS, 1975, O
SWORD AND THE DRAGON, THE, 1960, A
SWORD AND THE ROSE, THE, 1953, A
SWORD AND THE SORCERER, THE, 1982, O
SWORD IN THE DESERT, 1949, C
SWORD IN THE STONE, THE, 1963, AAA
SWORD OF ALI BABA, THE, 1965, A
SWORD OF DAMOCLES, THE, 1920
SWORD OF DOOM, THE, 1967, C-O
SWORD OF EL CID, THE, 1965, A
SWORD OF FATE, THE, 1921
SWORD OF HONOUR, 1938, A
SWORD OF LANCELOT, 1963, A
SWORD OF MONTE CRISTO, THE, 1951, A
SWORD OF PENITENCE, 1927
SWORD OF SHERWOOD FOREST, 1961, A
SWORD OF THE AVENGER, 1948, A
SWORD OF THE CONQUEROR, 1962, C
SWORD OF THE VALIANT, 1984, C
SWORD OF VALOR, THE, 1924, A
SWORD OF VENUS, 1953, A
SWORDKILL, 1984, C
SWORDS AND THE WOMAN, 1923
SWORDSMAN OF SIENA, THE, 1962, A
SWORDSMAN, THE, 1947, A
SWORN ENEMY, 1936, A
SYBIL, 1921
SYLVIA, 1965, O
SYLVIA AND THE GHOST
SYLVIA AND THE PHANTOM, 1950, A
SYLVIA GRAY, 1914, A
SYLVIA OF THE SECRET SERVICE, 1917
SYLVIA ON A SPREE, 1918
SYLVIA SCARLETT, 1936, A-C
SYLVIE AND THE PHANTOM
SYMBOL OF THE UNCONQUERED, 1921
SYMPATHY FOR THE DEVIL
SYMPHONIE FANTASTIQUE, 1947, A
SYMPHONIE PASTORALE, 1948, C
SYMPHONY FOR A MASSACRE, 1965, A

TAXI FOR TOBRUK, 1965, A
TAXI FOR TWO, 1929, A
TAXI MYSTERY, THE, 1926, A
TAXI NACH TOBRUK
TAXI TAXI, 1927, A
TAXI TO HEAVEN, 1944, A
TAXI!, 1932, A
TAZA, SON OF COCHISE, 1954, A
TE QUIERO CON LOCURA, 1935, A
TEA AND RICE, 1964, A
TEA AND SYMPATHY, 1956, C-O
TEA FOR THREE, 1927, A
TEA FOR TWO, 1950, A
TEA LEAVES IN THE WIND
TEA—WITH A KICK, 1923
TEACHER AND THE MIRACLE, THE, 1961, A
TEACHER'S PET, 1958, A
TEACHER, THE, 1974, C
TEACHERS, 1984, C-O
TEAHOUSE OF THE AUGUST MOON, THE, 1956, AA
TEAM-MATES, 1978
TEAR GAS SQUAD, 1940, A
TEARIN' INTO TROUBLE, 1927
TEARIN' LOOSE, 1925
TEARING THROUGH, 1925
TEARS, 1914
TEARS AND SMILES, 1917
TEARS FOR SIMON, 1957, A
TEARS OF HAPPINESS, 1974, A
TEASER, THE, 1925
TEASERS, THE, 1977
TECHNIQUE D'UN MEUTRE
TECKMAN MYSTERY, THE, 1955, A
TECNICA DI UN OMICIDO
TEDDY BEAR, THE
TEEN AGE TRAMP
TEEN KANYA
TEEN-AGE CRIME WAVE, 1955, C
TEEN-AGE STRANGLER, 1967, O
TEENAGE BAD GIRL, 1959, O
TEENAGE CAVEMAN, 1958, A
TEENAGE DELINQUENTS
TEENAGE DOLL, 1957, O
TEENAGE FRANKENSTEIN
TEENAGE GANG DEBS, 1966, O
TEENAGE GRAFFITI, 1977
TEENAGE HITCHHIKERS, 1975
TEENAGE LOVERS
TEENAGE MILLIONAIRE, 1961, A
TEENAGE MONSTER, 1958, A
TEENAGE MOTHER, 1967, O
TEENAGE PSYCHO MEETS BLOODY MARY
TEENAGE REBEL, 1956, A
TEENAGE TEASE, 1983
TEENAGE TEASERS, 1982
TEENAGE THUNDER, 1957, A
TEENAGE ZOMBIES, 1960, C
TEENAGER, 1975
TEENAGERS FROM OUTER SPACE, 1959, A
TEENAGERS IN SPACE, 1975, AA
TEETH, 1924
TEETH OF THE TIGER, THE, 1919
TEHERAN
TEL AVIV TAXI, 1957, A
TELEFON, 1977, C-O
TELEGIAN, THE
TELEGRAPH TRAIL, THE, 1933, A
TELEPHONE BOOK, THE, 1971
TELEPHONE GIRL, THE, 1927, A
TELEPHONE OPERATOR, 1938, A
TELEVISION SPY, 1939, A
TELEVISION TALENT, 1937, A
TELI SIROKKO
TELL ENGLAND
TELL IT TO A STAR, 1945, A
TELL IT TO SWEENEY, 1927
TELL IT TO THE JUDGE, 1949, A
TELL IT TO THE MARINES
TELL IT TO THE MARINES, 1918
TELL IT TO THE MARINES, 1926, A
TELL ME A RIDDLE, 1980, C
TELL ME IN THE SUNLIGHT, 1967, C-O
TELL ME LIES, 1968, O
TELL ME THAT YOU LOVE ME, 1983
TELL ME THAT YOU LOVE ME, JUNIE MOON,
   1970, A-C
TELL NO TALES, 1939, A
TELL THEM WILLIE BOY IS HERE, 1969, C
TELL YOUR CHILDREN
TELL-TALE HEART, THE, 1962, O
TELL-TALE HEART, THE, 1934
TELLING THE WORLD, 1928, A
TELLTALE STEP, THE, 1917
TEMPERAMENTAL WIFE, A, 1919
TEMPERED STEEL, 1918
TEMPEST, 1928, A
TEMPEST, 1932, C
TEMPEST, 1958, C
TEMPEST, 1982, C-O
TEMPEST AND SUNSHINE, 1916
TEMPEST, THE, 1980
TEMPETES, 1922

TEMPLE DRAKE
TEMPLE OF DUSK, THE, 1918
TEMPLE OF VENUS, THE, 1923
TEMPLE TOWER, 1930, A
TEMPO DI MASSACRO
TEMPORAL POWER, 1916
TEMPORARY GENTLEMAN, A, 1920
TEMPORARY MARRIAGE, 1923, A
TEMPORARY SHERIFF, 1926
TEMPORARY VAGABOND, A, 1920, A
TEMPORARY WIDOW, THE, 1930, C
TEMPTATION, 1915, A
TEMPTATION, 1916
TEMPTATION, 1923, A
TEMPTATION, 1930
TEMPTATION, 1935, A
TEMPTATION, 1936, A
TEMPTATION, 1946, A
TEMPTATION, 1962, C
TEMPTATION AND THE MAN, 1916
TEMPTATION HARBOR, 1949, A
TEMPTATION OF CARLTON EARLYE, THE, 1923
TEMPTATION'S HOUR, 1916
TEMPTATIONS OF A SHOP GIRL, 1927
TEMPTATIONS OF SATAN, THE, 1914
TEMPTER, THE, 1974, A-C
TEMPTER, THE, 1978, O
TEMPTRESS AND THE MONK, THE, 1963, C
TEMPTRESS, THE, 1920
TEMPTRESS, THE, 1926, A
TEMPTRESS, THE, 1949, A
TEN CENTS A DANCE, 1931, A
TEN CENTS A DANCE, 1945, A
TEN COMMANDMENTS, THE, 1923, A
TEN COMMANDMENTS, THE, 1956, AA
TEN DAYS, 1925
TEN DAYS IN PARIS
TEN DAYS THAT SHOOK THE WORLD, 1927, A
TEN DAYS TO TULARA, 1958, A
TEN DAYS' WONDER, 1972, O
TEN DOLLAR RAISE, THE, 1921, A
$10 RAISE, 1935, A
TEN GENTLEMEN FROM WEST POINT, 1942, A
TEN GLADIATORS, THE, 1960
TEN LAPS TO GO, 1938, A
TEN LITTLE INDIANS, 1965, A
TEN LITTLE INDIANS, 1975, C
TEN LITTLE NIGGERS
TEN MILLION DOLLAR GRAB, 1966
TEN MINUTE ALIBI, 1935, A
TEN MINUTES TO KILL, 1933
TEN MINUTES TO LIVE, 1932
TEN MODERN COMMANDMENTS, 1927
TEN NIGHTS IN A BAR ROOM, 1921
TEN NIGHTS IN A BARROOM
TEN NIGHTS IN A BARROOM, 1926
TEN NIGHTS IN A BARROOM, 1931, A
10 WORTH FREDERICK, 1958, A-C
10 RILLINGTON PLACE, 1971, O
TEN OF DIAMONDS, 1917
TEN SECONDS TO HELL, 1959, A
TEN TALL MEN, 1951, AA
10:30 P.M. SUMMER, 1966, O
TEN THOUSAND BEDROOMS, 1957, A
10,000 DOLLARS BLOOD MONEY, 1966, O
10 TO MIDNIGHT, 1983, O
10 VIOLENT WOMEN, 1982, O
TEN WANTED MEN, 1955, A-C
TEN WHO DARED, 1960, A
TENANT, THE, 1976, O
TENCHU, 1970, O
TENDER COMRADE, 1943, A
TENDER DRACULA OR CONFESSIONS OF A BLOOD
   DRINKER, 1974
TENDER FLESH, 1976, O
TENDER HEARTS, 1955, A
TENDER HOUR, THE, 1927, A
TENDER IS THE NIGHT, 1961, C
TENDER LOVING CARE, 1974
TENDER MERCIES, 1982, A-C
TENDER SCOUNDREL, 1967, C
TENDER TRAP, THE, 1955, A
TENDER WARRIOR, THE, 1971, AAA
TENDER YEARS, THE, 1947, A-C
TENDERFEET, 1928
TENDERFOOT GOES WEST, A, 1937, A
TENDERFOOT, THE, 1917
TENDERFOOT, THE, 1932, A
TENDERLOIN, 1928, A
TENDERLY
TENDRE POULET
TENDRE VOYOU
TENNESSEE BEAT, THE
TENNESSEE CHAMP, 1954, A
TENNESSEE JOHNSON, 1942, A
TENNESSEE'S PARDNER, 1916, A
TENNESSEE'S PARTNER, 1955, C
TENSION, 1949, O
TENSION AT TABLE ROCK, 1956, A
TENTACLES, 1977, C
TENTACLES OF THE NORTH, 1926
TENTH AVENUE, 1928

TENTH AVENUE ANGEL, 1948, A
TENTH AVENUE KID, 1938, A
TENTH CASE, THE, 1917
TENTH MAN, THE, 1937, A
TENTH VICTIM, THE, 1965, O
TENTH WOMAN, THE, 1924
TENTING TONIGHT ON THE OLD CAMP GROUND,
   1943, A
TENTS OF ALLAH, THE, 1923
TEOREMA, 1969, O
TERCENTENARY OF THE ROMANOV DYNASTY'S
TERESA, 1951, A
TERESA RAQUIN, 1915
TERM OF TRIAL, 1962, C
TERMINAL ISLAND, 1973, O
TERMINAL MAN, THE, 1974, C
TERMINAL STATION
TERMINATOR, THE, 1984, O
TERMS OF ENDEARMENT, 1983, A-C
TERRA EM TRANSE
TERRACE, THE, 1964, O
TERREUR, 1924
TERRIBLE BEAUTY, A
TERRIBLE ONE, THE, 1915
TERRIBLE REVENGE, A, 1913
TERRIFIED, 1963, O
TERROR, 1928
TERROR, 1979, O
TERROR ABOARD, 1933, A
TERROR AFTER MIDNIGHT, 1965, C
TERROR AT BLACK FALLS, 1962, C
TERROR AT HALFDAY
TERROR AT MIDNIGHT, 1956, O
TERROR BENEATH THE SEA, 1966, C
TERROR BY NIGHT, 1946, A
TERROR BY NIGHT, 1931
TERROR CASTLE
TERROR CIRCUS
TERROR EN EL ESPACIO
TERROR EYES, 1981, O
TERROR FACTOR, THE
TERROR FROM THE SUN
TERROR FROM THE UNKNOWN, 1983
TERROR FROM THE YEAR 5,000, 1958, A
TERROR FROM UNDER THE HOUSE, 1971, C
TERROR HOUSE, 1942, C
TERROR HOUSE, 1972, O
TERROR IN A TEXAS TOWN, 1958, A
TERROR IN THE CITY
TERROR IN THE CRYPT, 1963
TERROR IN THE HAUNTED HOUSE
TERROR IN THE JUNGLE, 1968, A
TERROR IN THE MIDNIGHT SUN
TERROR IN THE SWAMP, 1984
TERROR IN THE WAX MUSEUM, 1973, C
TERROR IS A MAN, 1959, C
TERROR ISLAND, 1920
TERROR MOUNTAIN, 1928
TERROR OF BAR X, THE, 1927, A
TERROR OF DR. CHANEY, THE
TERROR OF DR. MABUSE, THE, 1965, C
TERROR OF FRANKENSTEIN
TERROR OF GODZILLA
TERROR OF PUEBLO, THE, 1924
TERROR OF SHEBA
TERROR OF THE BLACK MASK, 1967, A
TERROR OF THE BLOODHUNTERS, 1962, A
TERROR OF THE HATCHET MEN
TERROR OF THE MAD DOCTOR, THE
TERROR OF THE PLAINS, 1934
TERROR OF THE TONGS, THE, 1961, O
TERROR OF TINY TOWN, THE, 1938, A
TERROR ON A TRAIN, 1953, A
TERROR ON BLOOD ISLAND
TERROR ON TIPTOE, 1936, A
TERROR ON TOUR, 1980, O
TERROR SHIP, 1954, A
TERROR STREET, 1953, A
TERROR STRIKES, THE
TERROR TRAIL, 1933, A
TERROR TRAIL, 1946
TERROR TRAIN, 1980, O
TERROR, THE, 1917
TERROR, THE, 1920
TERROR, THE, 1926
TERROR, THE, 1928, A
TERROR, THE, 1941, A
TERROR, THE, 1963, C
TERROR-CREATURES FROM THE GRAVE, 1967, O
TERRORE NELLO SPAZIO
TERRORISTS, THE, 1975, C
TERRORNAUTS, THE, 1967, A
TERRORS ON HORSEBACK, 1946, A
TESEO CONTRO IL MINOTAURO
TESHA, 1929, A
TESS, 1980, A-C
TESS OF THE D'URBERVILLES, 1924, A
TESS OF THE STORM COUNTRY, 1914, A
TESS OF THE STORM COUNTRY, 1922, A
TESS OF THE STORM COUNTRY, 1932, A
TESS OF THE STORM COUNTRY, 1961, A
TESSIE, 1925

TEST OF DONALD NORTON, THE, 1926
TEST OF HONOR, THE, 1919
TEST OF LOYALTY, THE, 1918
TEST OF PILOT PIRX, THE, 1978, C
TEST OF WOMANHOOD, THE, 1917
TEST PILOT, 1938, A
TEST, THE, 1915
TEST, THE, 1916
TESTAMENT, 1983, A
TESTAMENT OF DR. MABUSE, THE, 1943, C
TESTAMENT OF DR. MABUSE, THE, 1965
TESTAMENT OF ORPHEUS, 1962, C
TESTIGO PARA UN CRIMEN
TESTIMONY, 1920
TESTING BLOCK, THE, 1920, A
TESTING OF MILDRED VANE, THE, 1918
TEUFEL IN SEIDE
TEVYA, 1939, A
TEX, 1926
TEX, 1982, A
TEX RIDES WITH THE BOY SCOUTS, 1937, A
TEX TAKES A HOLIDAY, 1932, A
TEXAN MEETS CALAMITY JANE, THE, 1950, A
TEXAN'S HONOR, A, 1929
TEXAN, THE, 1920
TEXAN, THE, 1930, A
TEXAN, THE, 1932
TEXANS NEVER CRY, 1951, A
TEXANS, THE, 1938, A
TEXAS, 1922
TEXAS, 1941, A
TEXAS ACROSS THE RIVER, 1966, A
TEXAS BAD MAN, 1932, A
TEXAS BAD MAN, 1953, A
TEXAS BEARCAT, THE, 1925
TEXAS BUDDIES, 1932, A
TEXAS CARNIVAL, 1951, A
TEXAS CHAIN SAW MASSACRE, THE, 1974, O
TEXAS CITY, 1952, A
TEXAS COWBOY, A, 1929
TEXAS CYCLONE, 1932, A
TEXAS DESPERADOS
TEXAS DETOUR, 1978
TEXAS DYNAMO, 1950, A
TEXAS FLASH, 1928
TEXAS GUN FIGHTER, 1932, A
TEXAS JACK, 1935
TEXAS JUSTICE, 1942
TEXAS KID
TEXAS KID, OUTLAW
TEXAS KID, THE, 1944, A
TEXAS LADY, 1955, A
TEXAS LAWMEN, 1951, A
TEXAS LIGHTNING, 1981, O
TEXAS MAN HUNT, 1942, A
TEXAS MARSHAL, THE, 1941, A
TEXAS MASQUERADE, 1944, A
TEXAS PANHANDLE, 1945
TEXAS PIONEERS, 1932, A
TEXAS RAMBLER, THE, 1935
TEXAS RANGER, THE, 1931, A
TEXAS RANGERS RIDE AGAIN, 1940, A
TEXAS RANGERS, THE, 1936, A
TEXAS RANGERS, THE, 1951, A
TEXAS RENEGADES, 1940
TEXAS ROAD AGENT
TEXAS ROSE
TEXAS SERENADE
TEXAS STAGECOACH, 1940, A
TEXAS STAMPEDE, 1939, A
TEXAS STEER, A, 1915
TEXAS STEER, A, 1915
TEXAS STEER, A, 1927, A
TEXAS STREAK, THE, 1926
TEXAS TERROR, 1935, A
TEXAS TERROR, THE, 1926
TEXAS TERRORS, 1940, A
TEXAS TO BATAAN, 1942, A
TEXAS TOMMY, 1928
TEXAS TORNADO, 1934, A
TEXAS TORNADO, THE, 1928
TEXAS TRAIL, 1937, A
TEXAS TRAIL, THE, 1925
TEXAS TROUBLE SHOOTERS, 1942
TEXAS WILDCATS, 1939, A
TEXAS, BROOKLYN AND HEAVEN, 1948, A
TEXICAN, THE, 1966, A
THAIS, 1914, C
THAIS, 1917
THANK EVANS, 1938, A
THANK GOD IT'S FRIDAY, 1978, C
THANK HEAVEN FOR SMALL FAVORS, 1965, A
THANK YOU, 1925
THANK YOU ALL VERY MUCH, 1969, C
THANK YOU, AUNT, 1969, O
THANK YOU, JEEVES, 1936, A
THANK YOU, MR. MOTO, 1937, A
THANK YOUR LUCKY STARS, 1943, A
THANK YOUR STARS
THANKS A MILLION, 1935, A
THANKS FOR EVERYTHING, 1938, A
THANKS FOR LISTENING, 1937, A

THANKS FOR THE BUGGY RIDE, 1928, A
THANKS FOR THE MEMORY, 1938, A
THANOS AND DESPINA, 1970, C
THARK, 1932, A
THAT BRENNAN GIRL, 1946, A
THAT CERTAIN AGE, 1938, A
THAT CERTAIN FEELING, 1956, A
THAT CERTAIN SOMETHING, 1941, A
THAT CERTAIN THING, 1928
THAT CERTAIN WOMAN, 1937, A-C
THAT CHAMPIONSHIP SEASON, 1982, O
THAT COLD DAY IN THE PARK, 1969, O
THAT CURSED WINTER'S DAY, DJANGO &
   SARTANA TO THE LAST SHOT, 1970
THAT DANGEROUS AGE
THAT DARN CAT, 1965, AAA
THAT DEVIL QUEMADO, 1925
THAT DEVIL, BATEESE, 1918
THAT FORSYTE WOMAN, 1949, A-C
THAT FRENCH LADY, 1924
THAT FUNNY FEELING, 1965, C
THAT GANG OF MINE, 1940, A
THAT GIRL FROM BEVERLY HILLS
THAT GIRL FROM COLLEGE
THAT GIRL FROM PARIS, 1937, A
THAT GIRL IS A TRAMP, 1974
THAT GIRL MONTANA, 1921
THAT GIRL OKLAHOMA, 1926
THAT HAGEN GIRL, 1947, A-C
THAT HAMILTON WOMAN, 1941, A
THAT HOUSE IN THE OUTSKIRTS, 1980, C-O
THAT I MAY LIVE, 1937, A
THAT I MAY SEE, 1953
THAT KIND OF GIRL
THAT KIND OF GIRL, 1963, O
THAT KIND OF WOMAN, 1959, C
THAT LADY, 1955, C
THAT LADY IN ERMINE, 1948, A
THAT LUCKY TOUCH, 1975, A-C
THAT MAD MR. JONES
THAT MAN BOLT, 1973, O
THAT MAN FLINTSTONE
THAT MAN FROM RIO, 1964, A
THAT MAN FROM TANGIER, 1953, A
THAT MAN GEORGE, 1967, A-C
THAT MAN IN ISTANBUL, 1966, A-C
THAT MAN JACK, 1925
THAT MAN MR. JONES
THAT MAN OF MINE, 1947
THAT MAN'S HERE AGAIN, 1937, A
THAT MIDNIGHT KISS, 1949, A
THAT MODEL FROM PARIS, 1926
THAT MURDER IN BERLIN, 1929
THAT NAVY SPIRIT
THAT NAZTY NUISANCE, 1943, A
THAT NIGHT, 1957, A
THAT NIGHT IN LONDON
THAT NIGHT IN RIO, 1941, A-C
THAT NIGHT WITH YOU, 1945, A
THAT NIGHT'S WIFE, 1930
THAT OBSCURE OBJECT OF DESIRE, 1977, O
THAT OLD GANG OF MINE, 1925
THAT OTHER WOMAN, 1942, A
THAT RIVIERA TOUCH, 1968, A
THAT SINKING FEELING, 1979, A
THAT SOMETHING, 1921
THAT SORT, 1916
THAT SPLENDID NOVEMBER, 1971, C-O
THAT SUMMER, 1979, A-C
THAT TENDER AGE
THAT TENDER TOUCH, 1969, O
THAT TENNESSEE BEAT, 1966, A
THAT TEXAS JAMBOREE, 1946
THAT THEY MAY LIVE
THAT TOUCH OF MINK, 1962
THAT TOUCH OF MINK, 1962, C
THAT UNCERTAIN FEELING, 1941, A
THAT WAY WITH WOMEN, 1947, A
THAT WILD WEST, 1924
THAT WOMAN, 1922
THAT WOMAN, 1968, C-O
THAT WOMAN OPPOSITE
THAT WONDERFUL URGE, 1948, A
THAT'LL BE THE DAY, 1974, C
THAT'S A GOOD GIRL, 1933, A
THAT'S GOOD, 1919
THAT'S GRATITUDE, 1934, A
THAT'S MY BABY, 1926, A
THAT'S MY BABY, 1944, A
THAT'S MY BOY, 1932, A
THAT'S MY BOY, 1951, A
THAT'S MY DADDY, 1928
THAT'S MY GAL, 1947, A
THAT'S MY MAN, 1947, A
THAT'S MY STORY, 1937, A
THAT'S MY UNCLE, 1935, A
THAT'S MY WIFE, 1933, A
THAT'S RIGHT—YOU'RE WRONG, 1939, A
THAT'S THE SPIRIT, 1945, A
THAT'S THE TICKET, 1940, A
THAT'S THE WAY OF THE WORLD, 1975, C
THAT'S YOUR FUNERAL, 1974

THEATRE OF BLOOD, 1973, O
THEATRE OF DEATH, 1967, C-O
THEATRE ROYAL, 1943, A
THEATRE ROYAL, 1930
THEIR BIG MOMENT, 1934, A
THEIR COMPACT, 1917
THEIR HOUR, 1928
THEIR MAD MOMENT, 1931
THEIR MUTUAL CHILD, 1920
THEIR NIGHT OUT, 1933, A
THEIR ONLY CHANCE, 1978
THEIR OWN DESIRE, 1929, A
THEIR SECRET AFFAIR
THELMA, 1918
THELMA, 1922, A
THELMA JORDAN
THEM NICE AMERICANS, 1958, A
THEM?, 1954, C
THEN CAME THE WOMAN, 1926
THEN I'LL COME BACK TO YOU, 1916
THEN THERE WERE THREE, 1961, A-C
THEN YOU'LL REMEMBER ME, 1918
THEODORA, 1921
THEODORA GOES WILD, 1936, A
THEOREM
THERE AIN'T NO JUSTICE, 1939, A
THERE ARE NO VILLAINS, 1921
THERE GOES KELLY, 1945, A
THERE GOES MY GIRL, 1937, A
THERE GOES MY HEART, 1938, A
THERE GOES SUSIE
THERE GOES THE BRIDE, 1933, A
THERE GOES THE BRIDE, 1980, C
THERE GOES THE GROOM, 1937, A
THERE IS ANOTHER SUN
THERE IS NO 13, 1977, O
THERE IS STILL ROOM IN HELL, 1963, C-O
THERE WAS A CROOKED MAN, 1962, A
THERE WAS A CROOKED MAN, 1970, C
THERE WAS A YOUNG LADY, 1953, A
THERE WAS A YOUNG MAN, 1937, A
THERE WAS AN OLD COUPLE, 1967, A
THERE YOU ARE, 1926
THERE'S A GIRL IN MY HEART, 1949, A
THERE'S A GIRL IN MY SOUP, 1970, C
THERE'S ALWAYS A THURSDAY, 1957, A
THERE'S ALWAYS A WOMAN, 1938, A
THERE'S ALWAYS TOMORROW
THERE'S ALWAYS TOMORROW, 1956, A
THERE'S ALWAYS VANILLA, 1972, C
THERE'S MAGIC IN MUSIC, 1941, A
THERE'S MILLIONS IN IT, 1924
THERE'S NO BUSINESS LIKE SHOW BUSINESS,
   1954, A
THERE'S NO PLACE BY SPACE
THERE'S ONE BORN EVERY MINUTE, 1942, A
THERE'S SOMETHING ABOUT A SOLDIER, 1943, A
THERE'S SOMETHING FUNNY GOING ON
THERE'S THAT WOMAN AGAIN, 1938, AA
THERESE, 1963, O
THERESE AND ISABELLE, 1968, O
THERESE DESQUEYROUX
THERESE RAQUIN, 1928
THERESE UND ISABELL
THESE ARE THE DAMNED, 1965, C
THESE CHARMING PEOPLE, 1931, A
THESE DANGEROUS YEARS
THESE GLAMOUR GIRLS, 1939, A
THESE THIRTY YEARS, 1934, A
THESE THOUSAND HILLS, 1959, A
THESE THREE, 1936, C
THESE WILDER YEARS, 1956, A
THESEUS AGAINST THE MINOTAUR
THEY ALL COME OUT, 1939, A
THEY ALL DIED LAUGHING
THEY ALL KISSED THE BRIDE, 1942, A-C
THEY ALL LAUGHED, 1981, A
THEY ARE GUILTY
THEY ARE NOT ANGELS, 1948, A
THEY ASKED FOR IT, 1939, A
THEY CALL HER ONE EYE, 1974, O
THEY CALL IT SIN, 1932, A
THEY CALL ME BRUCE, 1982, C
THEY CALL ME HALLELUJAH, 1973
THEY CALL ME MISTER TIBBS, 1970, C
THEY CALL ME ROBERT, 1967, A
THEY CALL ME TRINITY, 1971, A
THEY CALLED HIM AMEN, 1972
THEY CAME BY NIGHT, 1940, A
THEY CAME FROM BEYOND SPACE, 1967, A
THEY CAME FROM WITHIN, 1976, O
THEY CAME TO A CITY, 1944, A
THEY CAME TO BLOW UP AMERICA, 1943, A
THEY CAME TO CORDURA, 1959, C-O
THEY CAME TO ROB LAS VEGAS, 1969, O
THEY CAN'T HANG ME, 1955, A
THEY DARE NOT LOVE, 1941, A
THEY DIDN'T KNOW, 1936, A
THEY DIED WITH THEIR BOOTS ON, 1942, A
THEY DON'T WEAR PAJAMAS AT ROSIE'S
THEY DRIVE BY NIGHT, 1938, C
THEY DRIVE BY NIGHT, 1940, A-C

THEY FLEW ALONE
THEY GAVE HIM A GUN, 1937, A
THEY GOT ME COVERED, 1943, A
THEY HAD TO SEE PARIS, 1929, A
THEY JUST HAD TO GET MARRIED, 1933, A
THEY KNEW MR. KNIGHT, 1945, A
THEY KNEW WHAT THEY WANTED, 1940, C
THEY LEARNED ABOUT WOMEN, 1930, A
THEY LIKE 'EM ROUGH, 1922
THEY LIVE BY NIGHT, 1949, C
THEY LIVE IN FEAR, 1944, A
THEY LOVE AS THEY PLEASE
THEY LOVED LIFE
THEY MADE HER A SPY, 1939, A
THEY MADE ME A CRIMINAL
THEY MADE ME A CRIMINAL, 1939, A
THEY MADE ME A FUGITIVE
THEY MADE ME A KILLER, 1946, A
THEY MEET AGAIN, 1941, A
THEY MET AT MIDNIGHT
THEY MET IN A TAXI, 1936, A
THEY MET IN ARGENTINA, 1941, A
THEY MET IN BOMBAY, 1941, A
THEY MET IN THE DARK, 1945, A
THEY MET ON SKIS, 1940, A
THEY MIGHT BE GIANTS, 1971, A
THEY NEVER COME BACK, 1932, A
THEY ONLY KILL THEIR MASTERS, 1972, C
THEY PASS THIS WAY
THEY RAID BY NIGHT, 1942, A
THEY RAN FOR THEIR LIVES, 1968, A
THEY RODE WEST, 1954, A
THEY SAVED HITLER'S BRAIN, 1964, C
THEY SHALL HAVE MUSIC, 1939, A
THEY SHALL PAY, 1921
THEY SHOOT HORSES, DON'T THEY?, 1969, O
THEY WANTED PEACE, 1940, A
THEY WANTED TO MARRY, 1937, A
THEY WENT THAT-A-WAY AND THAT-A-WAY,
    1978, C
THEY WERE EXPENDABLE, 1945, A
THEY WERE FIVE, 1938, A
THEY WERE NOT DIVIDED, 1951, A
THEY WERE SISTERS, 1945, A
THEY WERE SO YOUNG, 1955, A
THEY WERE TEN, 1961, A
THEY WHO DARE, 1954, A
THEY WON'T BELIEVE ME, 1947, C
THEY WON'T FORGET, 1937, C
THEY'RE A WEIRD MOB, 1966, A
THEY'RE COMING TO GET YOU, 1976
THEY'RE OFF
THEY'RE OFF, 1917
THEY'RE OFF, 1922
THEY'RE PLAYING WITH FIRE, 1984, O
THIEF, 1916
THIEF, 1981, O
THIEF IN PARADISE, A, 1925
THIEF IN THE DARK, A, 1928
THIEF OF BAGDAD, THE, 1924, A
THIEF OF BAGHDAD, THE, 1940, AAA
THIEF OF BAGHDAD, THE, 1961, A
THIEF OF DAMASCUS, 1952, A
THIEF OF HEARTS, 1984, C-O
THIEF OF PARIS, THE, 1967, A
THIEF OF VENICE, THE, 1952, A
THIEF WHO CAME TO DINNER, THE, 1973, A
THIEF, THE, 1915, A
THIEF, THE, 1920
THIEF, THE, 1952, C
THIEVES, 1919
THIEVES, 1977, A
THIEVES FALL OUT, 1941, A
THIEVES LIKE US, 1974, C
THIEVES' GOLD, 1918
THIEVES' HIGHWAY, 1949, C
THIEVES' HOLIDAY
THIN AIR
THIN ICE, 1919
THIN ICE, 1937, A
THIN LINE, THE, 1967, C
THIN MAN GOES HOME, THE, 1944, A
THIN MAN, THE, 1934, A
THIN RED LINE, THE, 1964, O
THING THAT CAME FROM ANOTHER WORLD, THE
THING THAT COULDN'T DIE, THE, 1958, C
THING WITH TWO HEADS, THE, 1972, C
THING WITHOUT A FACE, A
THING, THE, 1951, C
THING, THE, 1982, O
THINGS ARE LOOKING UP, 1934, A
THINGS ARE TOUGH ALL OVER, 1982, O
THINGS HAPPEN AT NIGHT, 1948, A
THINGS MEN DO, 1921
THINGS OF LIFE, THE, 1970, C
THINGS TO COME, 1936
THINGS WE LOVE, THE, 1918
THINGS WIVES TELL, 1926
THINK DIRTY, 1970, O
THINK FAST, MR. MOTO, 1937, A
THINK IT OVER, 1917
THIRD ALARM, THE, 1922, A

THIRD ALARM, THE, 1930, A
THIRD ALIBI, THE, 1961, A
THIRD CLUE, THE, 1934, A
THIRD DAY, THE, 1965, A
THIRD DEGREE, THE, 1914
THIRD DEGREE, THE, 1919
THIRD DEGREE, THE, 1926, A
THIRD EYE, THE, 1929
THIRD FINGER, LEFT HAND, 1940, A
THIRD GENERATION, THE, 1915
THIRD GENERATION, THE, 1920
THIRD KEY, THE, 1957, A
THIRD KISS, THE, 1919
THIRD LOVER, THE, 1963, O
THIRD MAN ON THE MOUNTAIN, 1959, A
THIRD MAN, THE, 1950, AAA
THIRD OF A MAN, 1962, C
THIRD PARTY RISK
THIRD ROAD, THE
THIRD SECRET, THE, 1964, C
THIRD STRING, THE, 1932, A
THIRD TIME LUCKY, 1931, A
THIRD TIME LUCKY, 1950, A
THIRD VISITOR, THE, 1951, A
THIRD VOICE, THE, 1960, A
THIRD WALKER, THE, 1978, C
THIRD WOMAN, THE, 1920
THIRST
THIRST, 1979, O
THIRSTY DEAD, THE, 1975, O
13 EAST STREET, 1952, A
THIRTEEN FIGHTING MEN, 1960, C
THIRTEEN FRIGHTENED GIRLS, 1963, A
THIRTEEN GHOSTS, 1960, A
THIRTEEN HOURS BY AIR, 1936, A
THIRTEEN LEAD SOLDIERS, 1948, A
13 MEN AND A GUN, 1938, A
13 RUE MADELEINE, 1946, A-C
THIRTEEN WEST STREET, 1962, O
THIRTEEN WOMEN, 1932, C
THIRTEEN, THE, 1937, A
THIRTEENTH CANDLE, THE, 1933, A
THIRTEENTH CHAIR, THE, 1919
THIRTEENTH CHAIR, THE, 1930, A
THIRTEENTH CHAIR, THE, 1937, A
THIRTEENTH GREEN, 1954
THIRTEENTH GUEST, THE, 1932, A
THIRTEENTH HOUR, THE, 1927
13TH HOUR, THE, 1947, A
THIRTEENTH JUROR, THE, 1927
THIRTEENTH LETTER, THE, 1951, C
THIRTEENTH MAN, THE, 1937, A
THIRTIETH PIECE OF SILVER, THE, 1920
—30—, 1959, A-C
THIRTY A WEEK, 1918
THIRTY DAYS
THIRTY DAYS, 1922, A
THIRTY FOOT BRIDE OF CANDY ROCK, THE,
    1959, AAA
30 IS A DANGEROUS AGE, CYNTHIA, 1968, A-C
39 STEPS, THE, 1935, A
THIRTY NINE STEPS, THE, 1960, C
THIRTY NINE STEPS, THE, 1978, C
THIRTY SECONDS OVER TOKYO, 1944, A
THIRTY-SIX HOURS
36 HOURS, 1965, C
THIRTY SIX HOURS TO KILL, 1936
THIRTY SIX HOURS TO LIVE
THIRTY YEARS BETWEEN, 1921
THIRTY YEARS LATER, 1928
THIRTY YEARS LATER, 1938
THIRTY-DAY PRINCESS, 1934, A
THIS ABOVE ALL, 1942, A
THIS ACTING BUSINESS, 1933, A
THIS ANGRY AGE, 1958, C
THIS COULD BE THE NIGHT, 1957, AA
THIS DAY AND AGE, 1933, A
THIS EARTH IS MINE, 1959, O
THIS ENGLAND, 1941, A
THIS FREEDOM, 1923
THIS GREEN HELL, 1936, A
THIS GUN FOR HIRE, 1942, C-O
THIS HAPPY BREED, 1944, A
THIS HAPPY FEELING, 1958, A
THIS HERO STUFF, 1919, A
THIS IMMORAL AGE
THIS IS A HIJACK, 1973, C
THIS IS ELVIS, 1982, A
THIS IS HEAVEN, 1929, A
THIS IS MY AFFAIR, 1937, A
THIS IS MY LOVE, 1954, O
THIS IS MY STREET, 1964, O
THIS IS NOT A TEST, 1962, A
THIS IS SPINAL TAP, 1984, C-O
THIS IS THE ARMY, 1943, AA
THIS IS THE LIFE, 1917
THIS IS THE LIFE, 1933, A
THIS IS THE LIFE, 1935, A
THIS IS THE LIFE, 1944, A
THIS IS THE NIGHT, 1932, A
THIS ISLAND EARTH, 1955, A
THIS LAND IS MINE, 1943, A

THIS LOVE OF OURS, 1945, C
THIS MAD WORLD, 1930, C
THIS MADDING CROWD, 1964, C
THIS MAN CAN'T DIE, 1970, O
THIS MAN IN PARIS, 1939, A
THIS MAN IS DANGEROUS
THIS MAN IS MINE, 1934, A
THIS MAN IS MINE, 1946, A
THIS MAN IS NEWS, 1939, A
THIS MAN MUST DIE, 1970, O
THIS MAN REUTER
THIS MAN'S NAVY, 1945, AA
THIS MARRIAGE BUSINESS, 1927, A
THIS MARRIAGE BUSINESS, 1938, A
THIS MODERN AGE, 1931, A-C
THIS OTHER EDEN, 1959, A
THIS PROPERTY IS CONDEMNED, 1966, O
THIS REBEL AGE
THIS REBEL BREED, 1960, O
THIS RECKLESS AGE, 1932, A
THIS SAVAGE LAND, 1969, A
THIS SIDE OF HEAVEN, 1934, AA
THIS SIDE OF THE LAW, 1950, C
THIS SPECIAL FRIENDSHIP, 1967, O
THIS SPORTING AGE, 1932, A
THIS SPORTING LIFE, 1963, O
THIS STRANGE PASSION TORMENTS
THIS STUFF'LL KILL YA!, 1971, O
THIS THING CALLED LOVE, 1929, C
THIS THING CALLED LOVE, 1940, O
THIS TIME FOR KEEPS, 1942, A
THIS TIME FOR KEEPS, 1947, AAA
THIS TIME FOREVER, 1981
THIS WAS A WOMAN, 1949, O
THIS WAS PARIS, 1942, C
THIS WAY PLEASE, 1937, AA
THIS WEEK OF GRACE, 1933, A
THIS WINE OF LOVE, 1948, AA
THIS WOMAN, 1924
THIS WOMAN IS DANGEROUS, 1952, A-C
THIS WOMAN IS MINE
THIS WOMAN IS MINE, 1941, A
THIS'LL MAKE YOU WHISTLE, 1938, A
THIS, THAT AND THE OTHER, 1970, O
THISTLEDOWN, 1938, A
THOMAS CROWN AFFAIR, THE, 1968, C
THOMASINE AND BUSHROD, 1974, O
THOR AND THE AMAZON WOMEN, 1960
THORNS AND ORANGE BLOSSOMS, 1922, A
THOROBRED, 1922
THOROUGHBRED, 1932, A
THOROUGHBRED, 1936, C
THOROUGHBRED, THE, 1916
THOROUGHBRED, THE, 1916
THOROUGHBRED, THE, 1925
THOROUGHBRED, THE, 1928
THOROUGHBRED, THE, 1930, A
THOROUGHBREDS
THOROUGHBREDS, 1945, AA
THOROUGHBREDS DON'T CRY, 1937, AA
THOROUGHBREDS, THE, 1977
THOROUGHLY MODERN MILLIE, 1967, A
THOSE CALLOWAYS, 1964, AA
THOSE DARING YOUNG MEN IN THEIR JAUNTY
    JALOPIES, 1969, A
THOSE DIRTY DOGS, 1974, C
THOSE ENDEARING YOUNG CHARMS, 1945, A
THOSE FANTASTIC FLYING FOOLS, 1967, AAA
THOSE HIGH GREY WALLS, 1939, C
THOSE KIDS FROM TOWN, 1942, A
THOSE LIPS, THOSE EYES, 1980, O
*THOSE MAGNIFICENT MEN IN THEIR FLYING
    MACHINES*, ACHI, A
THOSE PEOPLE NEXT DOOR, 1952, A
THOSE REDHEADS FROM SEATTLE, 1953, AA
THOSE THREE FRENCH GIRLS, 1930, A
THOSE WE LOVE, 1932, C
THOSE WERE THE DAYS, 1934, A
THOSE WERE THE DAYS, 1940, A
THOSE WERE THE HAPPY TIMES
THOSE WHO DANCE, 1924
THOSE WHO DANCE, 1930, A
THOSE WHO DARE, 1924
THOSE WHO JUDGE, 1924
THOSE WHO LOVE, 1929, A
THOSE WHO PAY, 1918
THOSE WHO TOIL, 1916
THOSE WITHOUT SIN, 1917, A
THOU ART THE MAN, 1915
THOU ART THE MAN, 1916
THOU ART THE MAN, 1920, A
THOU FOOL, 1926, A
THOU SHALT HONOR THY WIFE
THOU SHALT NOT
THOU SHALT NOT, 1914, A
THOU SHALT NOT, 1919
THOU SHALT NOT COVET, 1916
THOU SHALT NOT KILL, 1915
THOU SHALT NOT KILL, 1939, A
THOU SHALT NOT KILL
THOU SHALT NOT LOVE, 1922
THOU SHALT NOT STEAL, 1917

THUNDER ON THE HILL, 1951, A
THUNDER ON THE TRAIL
THUNDER OVER ARIZONA, 1956, A
THUNDER OVER HAWAII
THUNDER OVER SANGOLAND, 1955, A
THUNDER OVER TANGIER, 1957, A
THUNDER OVER TEXAS, 1934, A
THUNDER OVER THE PLAINS, 1953, A
THUNDER OVER THE PRAIRIE, 1941, A
THUNDER PASS, 1954, A
THUNDER PASS,
THUNDER RIDERS, 1928
THUNDER RIVER FEUD, 1942, A
THUNDER ROAD, 1958, C
THUNDER ROCK, 1944, A
THUNDER TOWN, 1946, A
THUNDER TRAIL, 1937, A
THUNDERBALL, 1965, A-C
THUNDERBIRD 6, 1968, A
THUNDERBIRDS, 1952, A
THUNDERBIRDS 6, 1968
THUNDERBIRDS ARE GO, 1968, A
THUNDERBOLT, 1929, A
THUNDERBOLT, 1936, A-C
THUNDERBOLT AND LIGHTFOOT, 1974, O
THUNDERBOLT STRIKES, THE, 1926
THUNDERBOLT'S TRACKS, 1927
THUNDERBOLT, THE, 1919
THUNDERBOLTS OF FATE, 1919
THUNDERCLAP, 1921
THUNDERCLOUD
THUNDERCLOUD, THE, 1919
THUNDERGAP OUTLAWS, 1947
THUNDERGATE, 1923
THUNDERGOD, 1928
THUNDERHEAD-SON OF FLICKA, 1945, AAA
THUNDERHOOF, 1948, A
THUNDERING CARAVANS, 1952, A
THUNDERING DAWN, 1923
THUNDERING FRONTIER, 1940, A
THUNDERING GUN SLINGERS, 1944, A
THUNDERING HERD, 1925
THUNDERING HERD, THE, 1934, A
THUNDERING HOOFS, 1922
THUNDERING HOOFS, 1924
THUNDERING HOOFS, 1941, A
THUNDERING JETS, 1958, A
THUNDERING ROMANCE, 1924
THUNDERING SPEED, 1926
THUNDERING THOMPSON, 1929
THUNDERING THROUGH, 1925
THUNDERING TRAIL, THE, 1951, A
THUNDERING TRAILS, 1943, A
THUNDERING WEST, THE, 1939, A
THUNDERING WHEELS
THUNDERSTORM, 1934, A
THUNDERSTORM, 1956, A
THURSDAY MORNING MURDERS, THE, 1976
THURSDAY'S CHILD, 1943, A
THX 1138, 1971, C
THY NAME IS WOMAN, 1924
THY NEIGHBOR'S WIFE, 1953, C
THY SOUL SHALL BEAR WITNESS
TI-CUL TOUGAS, 1977, C
TIARA TAHITI, 1962, A
...TICK...TICK...TICK..., 1970, A
TICKET OF LEAVE, 1936, A
TICKET OF LEAVE MAN, THE, 1937, A
TICKET TO CRIME, 1934, A
TICKET TO HEAVEN, 1981, C
TICKET TO PARADISE, 1936, A
TICKET TO PARADISE, 1961, A
TICKET TO TOMAHAWK, 1950, A
TICKET-OF-LEAVE MAN, THE, 1918
TICKLE ME, 1965, A
TICKLED PINK
TICKLISH AFFAIR, A, 1963, A
TIDAL WAVE, 1975, A-C
TIDAL WAVE, 1939
TIDAL WAVE, THE, 1918
TIDAL WAVE, THE, 1920
TIDE OF EMPIRE, 1929
TIDES OF BARNEGAT, THE, 1917
TIDES OF FATE, 1917, A
TIDES OF PASSION, 1925
TIE THAT BINDS, THE, 1923, A
TIERRA BRUTAL
TIES OF BLOOD, 1921
TIFFANY JONES, 1976, O
TIFFANY MEMORANDUM, 1966
TIGER AMONG US, THE
TIGER AND THE FLAME, THE, 1955, A-C
TIGER AND THE PUSSYCAT, THE, 1967, A-C
TIGER BAY, 1933, A
TIGER BAY, 1959, A
TIGER BY THE TAIL, 1970, C
TIGER BY THE TAIL, 1958
TIGER FANGS, 1943, A
TIGER FLIGHT, 1965, A
TIGER GIRL, 1955, A
TIGER IN THE SKY
TIGER IN THE SMOKE, 1956, A

TIGER LILY, THE, 1919
TIGER LOVE, 1924
TIGER MAKES OUT, THE, 1967, A-C
TIGER MAN
TIGER MAN, THE, 1918
TIGER OF BENGAL
TIGER OF ESCHNAPUR, THE
TIGER OF THE SEA, THE, 1918
TIGER OF THE SEVEN SEAS, 1964, A
TIGER ROSE, 1923
TIGER ROSE, 1930, A
TIGER SHARK, 1932, A-C
TIGER THOMPSON, 1924
TIGER TRUE, 1921
TIGER WALKS, A, 1964, C
TIGER WOMAN, THE, 1917, A
TIGER WOMAN, THE, 1945, A
TIGER'S CLAW, THE, 1923, A
TIGER'S COAT, THE, 1920
TIGER'S CUB, 1920
TIGHT LITTLE ISLAND, 1949
TIGHT SHOES, 1941, A
TIGHT SKIRTS
TIGHT SKIRTS, LOOSE PLEASURES, 1966, O
TIGHT SPOT, 1955, O
TIGHTROPE, 1984, C-O
TIGHTROPE TO TERROR, 1977
TIGRESS, THE, 1914, A
TIGRESS, THE, 1927
TIGRIS, 1913
TIJUANA STORY, THE, 1957, A
TIKI TIKI, 1971, AAA
TIKO AND THE SHARK, 1966, A
TIKOYO AND HIS SHARK
'TIL WE MEET AGAIN, 1940, A
TILL DEATH, 1978, C-O
TILL DEATH DO US PART
'TILL I COME BACK TO YOU, 1918
TILL MARRIAGE DO US PART, 1979, O
TILL THE CLOUDS ROLL BY, 1946, AA
TILL THE END OF TIME, 1946, A-C
TILL TOMORROW COMES, 1962, C
TILL WE MEET AGAIN, 1922
TILL WE MEET AGAIN, 1936, A
TILL WE MEET AGAIN, 1944, A
TILLERS OF THE SOIL
TILLIE, 1922, A
TILLIE AND GUS, 1933, A
TILLIE THE TOILER, 1927, A
TILLIE THE TOILER, 1941, A
TILLIE WAKES UP, 1917, A
TILLIE'S PUNCTURED ROMANCE, 1914, A
TILLIE'S PUNCTURED ROMANCE, 1928, A
TILLIE'S TOMATO SURPRISE, 1915, A
TILLIE, A MENONITE MAID, 1922
TILLY OF BLOOMSBURY, 1921
TILLY OF BLOOMSBURY, 1931, A
TILLY OF BLOOMSBURY, 1940, A
TILT, 1979, C
TIM, 1981, C
TIM DRISCOLL'S DONKEY, 1955, AA
TIMBER, 1942, A
TIMBER FURY, 1950, A
TIMBER QUEEN, 1944, A
TIMBER STAMPEDE, 1939, A
TIMBER TERRORS, 1935, A
TIMBER TRAIL, THE, 1948, A
TIMBER TRAMPS, 1975
TIMBER WAR, 1936, A
TIMBER WOLF, 1925
TIMBERESQUE, 1937
TIMBERJACK, 1955, A
TIMBERLAND TERROR, 1940
TIMBUCTOO, 1933, A
TIMBUKTU, 1959, A
TIME AFTER TIME, 1979, O
TIME AND THE TOUCH, THE, 1962, C
TIME BANDITS, 1981, A-C
TIME BOMB, 1961, A
TIME BOMB, 1953
TIME FLIES, 1944, A
TIME FOR ACTION
TIME FOR DYING, A, 1971, C
TIME FOR GIVING, A
TIME FOR HEROS, A
TIME FOR KILLING, A, 1967, A
TIME FOR LOVE, A, 1974
TIME FOR LOVING, A, 1971, A-C
TIME GENTLEMEN PLEASE?, 1953, A
TIME IN THE SUN, A, 1970, O
TIME IS MY ENEMY, 1957, A
TIME LIMIT, 1957, C
TIME LOCK, 1959, A
TIME LOCK NO. 776, 1915
TIME LOCKS AND DIAMONDS, 1917
TIME LOST AND TIME REMEMBERED, 1966, A
TIME MACHINE, THE, 1960, A
TIME OF DESIRE, THE, 1957, O
TIME OF FURY, 1968
TIME OF HIS LIFE, THE, 1955, A
TIME OF INDIFFERENCE, 1965, A
TIME OF RETURN, THE

TIME OF ROSES, 1970, C
TIME OF THE HEATHEN, 1962, C
TIME OF THE WOLVES, 1970, O
TIME OF THEIR LIVES, THE, 1946, AAA
TIME OF YOUR LIFE, THE, 1948, A-C
TIME OUT FOR LOVE, 1963, A
TIME OUT FOR MURDER, 1938, A
TIME OUT FOR RHYTHM, 1941, A
TIME OUT FOR ROMANCE, 1937, A
TIME OUT OF MIND, 1947, A
TIME RUNNING OUT, 1950
TIME SLIP, 1981, C
TIME TO DIE, A, 1983, O
TIME TO KILL, 1942, A
TIME TO KILL, A, 1955, A
TIME TO LOVE, 1927, A
TIME TO LOVE AND A TIME TO DIE, A, 1958, A-C
TIME TO REMEMBER, 1962, A
TIME TO RUN, 1974
TIME TO SING, A, 1968, A
TIME TRAP
TIME TRAVELERS, THE, 1964, A
TIME WALKER, 1982, A
TIME WITHOUT PITY, 1957, C
TIME, THE COMEDIAN, 1925
TIME, THE PLACE AND THE GIRL, THE, 1929, A
TIME, THE PLACE AND THE GIRL, THE, 1946, A
TIMERIDER, 1983, C
TIMES GONE BY, 1953, C
TIMES HAVE CHANGED, 1923
TIMES SQUARE, 1929, A
TIMES SQUARE, 1980, O
TIMES SQUARE LADY, 1935, A
TIMES SQUARE PLAYBOY, 1936, A
TIMESLIP
TIMETABLE, 1956, A
TIMID TERROR, THE, 1926
TIMOTHY'S QUEST, 1922, A
TIMOTHY'S QUEST, 1936, A
TIN DRUM, THE, 1979, O
TIN GIRL, THE, 1970, A
TIN GODS, 1926, A
TIN GODS, 1932, A
TIN HATS, 1926
TIN MAN, 1983, A
TIN PAN ALLEY, 1920
TIN PAN ALLEY, 1940, A
TIN STAR, THE, 1957, A
TINDER BOX, THE, 1968, AA
TINGLER, THE, 1959, C
TINKER, 1949, AA
TINKER, 1950
TINKER, TAILOR, SOLDIER, SAILOR, 1918
TINSEL, 1918
TINTED VENUS, THE, 1921
TINTORERA...BLOODY WATERS, 1977, O
TIOGA KID, THE, 1948, A
TIP ON A DEAD JOCKEY, 1957, A-C
TIP-OFF GIRLS, 1938, A
TIP-OFF, THE, 1929
TIP-OFF, THE, 1931, A
TIPPED OFF, 1923, A
TIPTOES, 1927
TIRE AU FLANC
TIRE AU FLANC, 1929
TIRED BUSINESS MAN, THE, 1927
TIREZ SUR LE PIANISTE
'TIS A PITY SHE'S A WHORE, 1973, O
TISH, 1942, A
TIT FOR TAT, 1922
TITANIC, 1953, A-C
TITFIELD THUNDERBOLT, THE, 1953, A
TITLE SHOT, 1982, C
TNT JACKSON, 1975, O
TO A FINISH, 1921
TO ALL A GOODNIGHT, 1980, O
TO BE A CROOK, 1967, A
TO BE A LADY, 1934, A
TO BE A MAN
TO BE FREE, 1972, O
TO BE OR NOT TO BE, 1942, A
TO BE OR NOT TO BE, 1983, C
TO BEAT THE BAND, 1935, A
TO BED OR NOT TO BED
TO BEGIN AGAIN, 1982, C
TO CATCH A COP, 1984, A
TO CATCH A SPY
TO CATCH A THIEF, 1936, A
TO CATCH A THIEF, 1955, C
TO CHASE A MILLION, 1967
TO COMMIT A MURDER, 1970, C
TO DIE IN PARIS, 1968
TO DOROTHY, A SON
TO EACH HIS OWN, 1946, A-C
TO ELVIS WITH LOVE
TO FIND A MAN, 1972, A
TO HAVE AND HAVE NOT, 1944, A-C
TO HAVE AND TO HOLD, 1916
TO HAVE AND TO HOLD, 1922, A
TO HAVE AND TO HOLD, 1951, A
TO HAVE AND TO HOLD, 1963, A
TO HELL AND BACK, 1955, A-C

TO HELL WITH THE KAISER, 1918
TO HELL YOU PREACH, 1972
TO HIM THAT HATH, 1918
TO HONOR AND OBEY, 1917
TO KILL A CLOWN, 1972, C-O
TO KILL A MOCKINGBIRD, 1962, C
TO KILL OR TO DIE, 1973, C
TO LIVE
TO LIVE IN PEACE, 1947, A
TO LOVE, 1964, O
TO LOVE, PERHAPS TO DIE, 1975
TO MARY—WITH LOVE, 1936, A
TO OBLIGE A LADY, 1931, A
TO OUR LOVES
TO PARIS WITH LOVE, 1955, A
TO PLEASE A LADY, 1950, A
TO PLEASE ONE WOMAN, 1920
TO SIR, WITH LOVE, 1967, A
TO THE DEATH, 1917
TO THE DEVIL A DAUGHTER, 1976, O
TO THE ENDS OF THE EARTH, 1948, A-C
TO THE HIGHEST BIDDER, 1918
TO THE LADIES, 1923
TO THE LAST MAN, 1923, A
TO THE LAST MAN, 1933, A
TO THE SHORES OF HELL, 1966, A
TO THE SHORES OF TRIPOLI, 1942, A
TO THE VICTOR, 1938, A
TO THE VICTOR, 1948, A
TO TRAP A SPY, 1966, A
TO WHAT RED HELL, 1929, A
TOAST OF DEATH, THE, 1915
TOAST OF NEW ORLEANS, THE, 1950, A
TOAST OF NEW YORK, THE, 1937, A
TOAST OF THE LEGION
TOAST TO LOVE, 1951, A
TOBACCO ROAD, 1941, A
TOBO, THE HAPPY CLOWN, 1965
TOBOR THE GREAT, 1954, AA
TOBRUK, 1966, A
TOBY TYLER, 1960, AAA
TOBY'S BOW, 1919
TODAY, 1917, A
TODAY, 1930, A
TODAY I HANG, 1942, A
TODAY IT'S ME...TOMORROW YOU?, 1968, C
TODAY WE KILL...TOMORROW WE DIE, 1971
TODAY WE LIVE, 1933, C
TODAY WE LIVE, 1963
TODD KILLINGS, THE, 1971, O
TODD OF THE TIMES, 1919
TOGETHER, 1918
TOGETHER, 1956, A
TOGETHER AGAIN, 1944, A
TOGETHER BROTHERS, 1974, C
TOGETHER FOR DAYS, 1972, C
TOGETHER IN PARIS
TOGETHER WE LIVE, 1935, A
TOGETHERNESS, 1970
TOILER, THE, 1932
TOILERS OF THE SEA, 1923
TOILERS OF THE SEA, 1936, A
TOILERS, THE, 1919
TOILERS, THE, 1928, A
TOKIO SIREN, A, 1920
TOKOLOSHE, 1973
TOKYO AFTER DARK, 1959, A
TOKYO FILE 212, 1951, A
TOKYO JOE, 1949, A
TOKYO MARCH, 1929
TOKYO ROSE, 1945, A
TOKYO STORY, 1972, C
TOL'ABLE DAVID, 1921, A
TOL'ABLE DAVID, 1930, A
TOLD AT THE TWILIGHT, 1917
TOLD IN THE HILLS, 1919
TOLL GATE, THE, 1920
TOLL GATE, THE, 1920, A
TOLL OF LOVE, THE, 1914
TOLL OF MAMON, 1914, A
TOLL OF THE DESERT, 1936, A
TOLL OF THE SEA, THE, 1922
TOM, 1973, O
TOM AND HIS PALS, 1926, A
TOM BROWN OF CULVER, 1932, AA
TOM BROWN'S SCHOOL DAYS, 1940, AA
TOM BROWN'S SCHOOLDAYS, 1916
TOM BROWN'S SCHOOLDAYS, 1951, AA
TOM HORN, 1980, O
TOM JONES, 1917
TOM JONES, 1963, O
TOM SAWYER, 1917
TOM SAWYER, 1930, AAA
TOM SAWYER, 1973, AAA
TOM SAWYER, 1938
TOM SAWYER, DETECTIVE, 1939, A
TOM THUMB, 1958, AAA
TOM THUMB, 1967, A
TOM'S GANG, 1927
TOM, DICK AND HARRY, 1941, A
TOMAHAWK, 1951, A
TOMAHAWK AND THE CROSS, THE

TOMAHAWK TRAIL, 1957, A
TOMAHAWK TRAIL, THE, 1950
TOMB OF LIGEIA, THE, 1965, C
TOMB OF THE CAT
TOMB OF THE LIVING DEAD
TOMB OF THE UNDEAD, 1972, O
TOMB OF TORTURE, 1966, O
TOMBOY, 1940, A
TOMBOY AND THE CHAMP, 1961, A
TOMBOY, THE, 1921
TOMBOY, THE, 1924
TOMBS OF HORROR
TOMBS OF THE BLIND DEAD, 1974
TOMBSTONE CANYON, 1932, A
TOMBSTONE TERROR, 1935, A
TOMBSTONE, THE TOWN TOO TOUGH TO DIE,
   1942, A
TOMCAT, THE, 1968, O
TOMCATS, 1977
TOMMY, 1975, C
TOMMY ATKINS, 1928
TOMMY STEELE STORY, THE
TOMMY THE TOREADOR, 1960, A
TOMORROW, 1972, C
TOMORROW AND TOMORROW, 1932, A
TOMORROW AT MIDNIGHT
TOMORROW AT SEVEN, 1933, A
TOMORROW AT TEN, 1964, C
TOMORROW IS ANOTHER DAY, 1951, A
TOMORROW IS FOREVER, 1946, A
TOMORROW IS MY TURN, 1962, C
TOMORROW MAN, THE, 1979
TOMORROW NEVER COMES, 1978, O
TOMORROW THE WORLD, 1944, A
TOMORROW WE LIVE, 1936, C
TOMORROW WE LIVE, 1942, A
TOMORROW'S CHILDREN, 1934
TOMORROW'S LOVE, 1925
TOMORROW'S YOUTH, 1935, A
TONG MAN, THE, 1919
TONGUES OF FLAME, 1919
TONGUES OF FLAME, 1924
TONGUES OF MEN, THE, 1916, A
TONGUES OF SCANDAL, 1927
TONI, 1928
TONI, 1968, C
TONIGHT A TOWN DIES, 1961, C
TONIGHT AND EVERY NIGHT, 1945, A
TONIGHT AT 8:30, 1953, A
TONIGHT AT TWELVE, 1929, A
TONIGHT FOR SURE, 1962, O
TONIGHT IS OURS, 1933, A
TONIGHT OR NEVER, 1931, A-C
TONIGHT THE SKIRTS FLY, 1956, C
TONIGHT WE RAID CALAIS, 1943, A
TONIGHT WE SING, 1953, A
TONIGHT'S THE NIGHT, 1932, A
TONIGHT'S THE NIGHT, 1954, A
TONIO KROGER, 1968, C
TONIO, SON OF THE SIERRAS, 1925
TONKA, 1958, AAA
TONS OF MONEY, 1924
TONS OF MONEY, 1931, A
TONS OF TROUBLE, 1956, AA
TONTO BASIN OUTLAWS, 1941, A
TONTO KID, THE, 1935
TONY AMERICA, 1918
TONY DRAWS A HORSE, 1951, A-C
TONY ROME, 1967, C
TONY RUNS WILD, 1926, A
TOO BAD SHE'S BAD, 1954, C
TOO BUSY TO WORK, 1932, A
TOO BUSY TO WORK, 1939, A
TOO DANGEROUS TO LIVE, 1939, A
TOO DANGEROUS TO LOVE
TOO FAT TO FIGHT, 1918
TOO HOT TO HANDLE, 1938, A-C
TOO HOT TO HANDLE, 1961, C
TOO HOT TO HANDLE, 1976
TOO LATE BLUES, 1962, C
TOO LATE FOR TEARS, 1949, O
TOO LATE THE HERO, 1970, C
TOO MANY BLONDES, 1941, A
TOO MANY CHEFS
TOO MANY COOKS, 1931, A
TOO MANY CROOKS, 1919
TOO MANY CROOKS, 1927
TOO MANY CROOKS, 1959, A
TOO MANY GIRLS, 1940, A
TOO MANY HUSBANDS, 1938, AA
TOO MANY HUSBANDS, 1940, A
TOO MANY KISSES, 1925
TOO MANY MILLIONS, 1918
TOO MANY MILLIONS, 1934, A
TOO MANY PARENTS, 1936, A
TOO MANY THIEVES, 1968, A
TOO MANY WINNERS, 1947, A
TOO MANY WIVES, 1927
TOO MANY WIVES, 1933, A
TOO MANY WIVES, 1937, A
TOO MANY WOMEN, 1942, A
TOO MANY WOMEN, 1931

TOO MUCH BEEF, 1936, A
TOO MUCH BUSINESS, 1922, A
TOO MUCH FOR ONE MAN
TOO MUCH HARMONY, 1933, A
TOO MUCH JOHNSON, 1920
TOO MUCH MARRIED, 1921
TOO MUCH MONEY, 1926
TOO MUCH SPEED, 1921, A
TOO MUCH WIFE, 1922
TOO MUCH YOUTH, 1925
TOO MUCH, TOO SOON, 1958, C
TOO SOON TO LOVE, 1960, C
TOO TOUGH TO KILL, 1935, A
TOO WISE WIVES, 1921
TOO YOUNG TO KISS, 1951, A
TOO YOUNG TO KNOW, 1945, A
TOO YOUNG TO LOVE, 1960, C
TOO YOUNG TO MARRY, 1931, A
TOO YOUNG, TOO IMMORAL!, 1962, O
TOOLBOX MURDERS, THE, 1978, O
TOOMORROW, 1970, A
TOOTSIE, 1982, C
TOP BANANA, 1954, A
TOP DOG, THE, 1918
TOP FLOOR GIRL, 1959, A
TOP GUN, 1955, A-C
TOP HAND, 1925
TOP HAT, 1935, A
TOP JOB
TOP MAN, 1943, A
TOP O' THE MORNING, 1949, A
TOP O' THE MORNING, THE, 1922
TOP OF NEW YORK, THE, 1925, A
TOP OF THE BILL
TOP OF THE FORM, 1953, A
TOP OF THE HEAP, 1972, O
TOP OF THE TOWN, 1937, A
TOP OF THE WORLD, 1955, A
TOP OF THE WORLD, THE, 1925
TOP SECRET
TOP SECRET AFFAIR, 1957, A
TOP SECRET!, 1984
TOP SENSATION
TOP SERGEANT, 1942, A
TOP SERGEANT MULLIGAN, 1928
TOP SERGEANT MULLIGAN, 1941, A
TOP SPEED, 1930, A
TOPA TOPA, 1938
TOPAZ, 1969, C
TOPAZE, 1933, C
TOPAZE, 1935, A
TOPEKA, 1953, A
TOPEKA TERROR, THE, 1945, A
TOPKAPI, 1964, A-C
TOPPER, 1937, A
TOPPER RETURNS, 1941, A
TOPPER TAKES A TRIP, 1939, A
TOPS IS THE LIMIT
TOPSY AND EVA, 1927
TOPSY-TURVY JOURNEY, 1970, A
TORA! TORA! TORA!, 1970, C
TORA-SAN PART 2, 1970, C
TORA-SAN'S CHERISHED MOTHER
TORCH BEARER, THE, 1916
TORCH SINGER, 1933, A
TORCH SONG, 1953, A
TORCH SONG, 953
TORCH, THE, 1950, A
TORCHBEARER, THE
TORCHLIGHT, 1984, O
TORCHY BLANE IN CHINATOWN, 1938, A
TORCHY BLANE IN PANAMA, 1938, A
TORCHY BLANE RUNS FOR MAYOR
TORCHY BLANE, THE ADVENTUROUS BLONDE
TORCHY GETS HER MAN, 1938, A
TORCHY PLAYS WITH DYNAMITE, 1939, A
TORCHY RUNS FOR MAYOR, 1939, A
TORMENT, 1924, A
TORMENT, 1947, A
TORMENT, 1950, Brit.
TORMENTED, 1960, C
TORMENTED, THE, 1978, O
TORN CURTAIN, 1966, C
TORN SAILS, 1920
TORNADO, 1943, A
TORNADO IN THE SADDLE, A, 1942
TORNADO RANGE, 1948, A
TORNADO, THE, 1924
TORPEDO ALLEY, 1953, A
TORPEDO BAY, 1964, C
TORPEDO BOAT, 1942, A
TORPEDO RUN, 1958, A-C
TORPEDOED, 1939, C
TORRENT, THE, 1921, A
TORRENT, THE, 1924
TORRENT, THE, 1926, A
TORRID ZONE, 1940, A
TORSO, 1974, O
TORSO MURDER MYSTERY, THE, 1940, C
TORTILLA FLAT, 1942, A
TORTURE CHAMBER OF DR. SADISM, THE
TORTURE DUNGEON, 1970, O

TORTURE GARDEN, 1968, O
TORTURE ME KISS ME, 1970, O
TORTURE SHIP, 1939, A
TORTURED HEART, A, 1916
TOTO AND THE POACHERS, 1958, AA
TOTO IN THE MOON, 1957, A
TOTO, VITTORIO E LA DOTTORESSA
TOTON, 1919
TOUCH AND GO, 1955, C
TOUCH ME NOT, 1974, C
TOUCH OF A CHILD, THE, 1918
TOUCH OF CLASS, A, 1973, C
TOUCH OF DEATH, 1962, A
TOUCH OF EVIL, 1958, C
TOUCH OF FLESH, THE, 1960, C
TOUCH OF HELL, A
TOUCH OF HER FLESH, THE, 1967, O
TOUCH OF HER LIFE, THE
TOUCH OF LARCENY, A, 1960, A
TOUCH OF LOVE, A
TOUCH OF SATAN, THE, 1971, O
TOUCH OF SATAN, THE, 1974
TOUCH OF THE MOON, A, 1936, A
TOUCH OF THE OTHER, A, 1970, O
TOUCH OF THE SUN, A, 1956, A
TOUCH WHITE, TOUCH BLACK
TOUCH, THE, 1971, O
TOUCHABLES, THE, 1968
TOUCHDOWN, 1931, A
TOUCHDOWN, ARMY, 1938, A
TOUCHE PAS A LA FEMME BLANCHE
TOUCHED, 1983, C
TOUCHED BY LOVE, 1980, A
TOUGH, 1974
TOUGH AS THEY COME, 1942, A
TOUGH ASSIGNMENT, 1949, A
TOUGH ENOUGH, 1983, C
TOUGH GUY, 1936, A
TOUGH GUY, THE, 1926
TOUGH KID, 1939, A
TOUGH TO HANDLE, 1937, A
TOUGHER THEY COME, THE, 1950, A
TOUGHEST GUN IN TOMBSTONE, 1958, A
TOUGHEST MAN ALIVE, 1955, A
TOUGHEST MAN IN ARIZONA, 1952, A
TOURIST TRAP, THE, 1979, C
TOUT VA BIEN, 1973, C
TOVARICH, 1937, AA
TOWARD THE UNKNOWN, 1956, A
TOWARDS THE LIGHT, 1918
TOWER OF EVIL, 1972
TOWER OF EVIL, 1981
TOWER OF IVORY
TOWER OF JEWELS, THE, 1920
TOWER OF LIES, THE, 1925, C
TOWER OF LONDON, 1939, A
TOWER OF LONDON, 1962, C
TOWER OF STRENGTH
TOWER OF TERROR, 1971
TOWER OF TERROR, THE, 1942, A
TOWERING INFERNO, THE, 1974, C
TOWING, 1978, C
TOWN CALLED BASTARD, A
TOWN CALLED HELL, A, 1971, O
TOWN LIKE ALICE, A, 1958, A
TOWN OF CROOKED WAYS, THE, 1920
TOWN ON TRIAL, 1957, C
TOWN SCANDAL, THE, 1923, A
TOWN TAMER, 1965, A
TOWN THAT CRIED TERROR, THE
TOWN THAT DREADED SUNDOWN, THE, 1977, O
TOWN THAT FORGOT GOD, THE, 1922
TOWN WENT WILD, THE, 1945, A
TOWN WITHOUT PITY, 1961, C-O
TOXI, 1952, A
TOY BOX, THE, 1971
TOY SOLDIERS, 1983
TOY SOLDIERS, 1984, O
TOY TIGER, 1956, AA
TOY WIFE, THE, 1938, A-C
TOY, THE, 1982, C
TOYGRABBERS, THE
TOYS ARE NOT FOR CHILDREN, 1972, O
TOYS IN THE ATTIC, 1963, C
TOYS OF FATE, 1918
TRACK OF THE CAT, 1954, C
TRACK OF THE MOONBEAST, 1976, C-O
TRACK OF THE VAMPIRE,
TRACK OF THUNDER, 1967, A
TRACK THE MAN DOWN, 1956, A
TRACKDOWN, 1976, O
TRACKED, 1928
TRACKED BY THE POLICE, 1927
TRACKED IN THE SNOW COUNTRY, 1925
TRACKED TO EARTH, 1922, A
TRACKING THE ZEPPELIN RAIDERS, 1916
TRACKS, 1922
TRACKS, 1977, O
TRACY RIDES, 1935
TRACY THE OUTLAW, 1928
TRADE WINDS, 1938, A
TRADER HORN, 1931, C

TRADER HORN, 1973, A
TRADER HORNEE, 1970, O
TRADING PLACES, 1983, C-O
TRAFFIC, 1915
TRAFFIC, 1972, AAA
TRAFFIC COP, THE, 1916, A
TRAFFIC COP, THE, 1926
TRAFFIC IN CRIME, 1946, A
TRAFFIC IN HEARTS, 1924
TRAFFIC IN SOULS, 1913, A
TRAGEDIES OF THE CRYSTAL GLOBE, THE, 1915
TRAGEDY AT MIDNIGHT, A, 1942, A
TRAGEDY OF A RIDICULOUS MAN, THE, 1982, A
TRAGEDY OF BASIL GRIEVE, THE
TRAGEDY OF LOVE, 1923
TRAGEDY OF YOUTH, THE, 1928, A
TRAIL BEYOND, THE, 1934, A
TRAIL BLAZERS, 1953
TRAIL BLAZERS, THE, 1940, A
TRAIL DRIVE, THE, 1934, A
TRAIL DUST, 1924
TRAIL DUST, 1936, A
TRAIL GUIDE, 1952, A
TRAIL MARRIAGE, 1929
TRAIL OF COURAGE, THE, 1928
TRAIL OF HATE, 1922
TRAIL OF KIT CARSON, 1945, A
TRAIL OF ROBIN HOOD, 1950, A
TRAIL OF TERROR, 1935, AA
TRAIL OF TERROR, 1944, A
TRAIL OF THE ARROW, 1952
TRAIL OF THE AXE, THE, 1922, A
TRAIL OF THE CIGARETTE, THE, 1920
TRAIL OF THE HAWK, 1935
TRAIL OF THE HORSE THIEVES, THE, 1929
TRAIL OF THE LAW, 1924
TRAIL OF THE LONESOME PINE, THE, 1914
TRAIL OF THE LONESOME PINE, THE, 1916
TRAIL OF THE LONESOME PINE, THE, 1936, A-C
TRAIL OF THE LONESOME, THE, 1923
TRAIL OF THE PINK PANTHER, THE, 1982, C
TRAIL OF THE RUSTLERS, 1950
TRAIL OF THE SHADOW, THE, 1917, C
TRAIL OF THE SILVER SPURS, 1941, A
TRAIL OF THE VIGILANTES, 1940, A
TRAIL OF THE YUKON, 1949, A
TRAIL OF VENGEANCE, 1937, A
TRAIL OF VENGEANCE, THE, 1924
TRAIL OF '98, THE, 1929, A
TRAIL RIDER, THE, 1925
TRAIL RIDERS, 1928
TRAIL RIDERS, 1942, AA
TRAIL STREET, 1947, A
TRAIL TO GUNSIGHT, 1944, AA
TRAIL TO LAREDO, 1948
TRAIL TO MEXICO, 1946
TRAIL TO RED DOG, THE, 1921
TRAIL TO SAN ANTONE, 1947, A
TRAIL TO VENGEANCE, 1945, A
TRAIL TO YESTERDAY, THE, 1918
TRAIL'S END, 1922, A
TRAIL'S END, 1935
TRAIL'S END, 1949, A
TRAILIN', 1921
TRAILIN' BACK, 1928
TRAILIN' TROUBLE, 1930
TRAILIN' TROUBLE, 1937
TRAILIN' WEST, 1936, A
TRAILING DANGER, 1947
TRAILING DOUBLE TROUBLE, 1940, A
TRAILING NORTH, 1933
TRAILING THE KILLER, 1932, A
TRAILING TROUBLE, 1930, A
TRAILING TROUBLE, 1937, A
TRAILS OF ADVENTURE, 1935
TRAILS OF DANGER, 1930
TRAILS OF DESTINY, 1926
TRAILS OF PERIL
TRAILS OF THE GOLDEN WEST, 1931
TRAILS OF THE WILD, 1935, A
TRAILS OF TREACHERY, 1928
TRAIN 2419
TRAIN GOES EAST, THE, 1949, A
TRAIN GOES TO KIEV, THE, 1961, A
TRAIN OF EVENTS, 1952, A
TRAIN RIDE TO HOLLYWOOD, 1975, A
TRAIN ROBBERS, THE, 1973, A
TRAIN ROBBERY CONFIDENTIAL, 1965, A
TRAIN TO ALCATRAZ, 1948, A
TRAIN TO TOMBSTONE, 1950, A
TRAIN WRECKERS, THE, 1925
TRAIN, THE, 1965, C
TRAINED TO KILL
TRAINER AND THE TEMPTRESS, 1925
TRAITOR, 1926
TRAITOR SPY
TRAITOR WITHIN, THE, 1942, A
TRAITOR'S GATE, 1966, A
TRAITOR, THE, 1936, A
TRAITOR, THE, 1957
TRAITORS, 1957, A
TRAITORS, THE, 1963, A

TRAITORS, THE, 1958, Brit.
TRAMP, TRAMP, TRAMP, 1926, A
TRAMP, TRAMP, TRAMP, 1942, A
TRAMPLERS, THE, 1966, C
TRANS-EUROP-EXPRESS, 1968, O
TRANSATLANTIC, 1931, A
TRANSATLANTIC, 1961, A
TRANSATLANTIC MERRY-GO-ROUND, 1934, A
TRANSATLANTIC TROUBLE
TRANSATLANTIC TUNNEL, 1935, A
TRANSCONTINENT EXPRESS
TRANSCONTINENTAL LIMITED, 1926
TRANSGRESSION, 1917
TRANSGRESSION, 1931, A
TRANSGRESSOR, THE, 1918
TRANSIENT LADY, 1935, A
TRANSPORT FROM PARADISE, 1967, A
TRANSPORT OF FIRE, 1931
TRAP DOOR, THE, 1980, O
TRAP ON COUGAR MOUNTAIN, 1972
TRAP, THE, 1918
TRAP, THE, 1919
TRAP, THE, 1922, A
TRAP, THE, 1947, A
TRAP, THE, 1959, A
TRAP, THE, 1967, A
TRAPEZE, 1932, A
TRAPEZE, 1956, A-C
TRAPP FAMILY, THE, 1961, A
TRAPPED, 1925
TRAPPED, 1931, A
TRAPPED, 1937, A
TRAPPED, 1949, A
TRAPPED, 1982
TRAPPED BY BOSTON BLACKIE, 1948, A
TRAPPED BY G-MEN, 1937, A
TRAPPED BY TELEVISION, 1936, A
TRAPPED BY THE LONDON SHARKS, 1916, A
TRAPPED BY THE MORMONS, 1922, C
TRAPPED BY THE TERROR, 1949, AAA
TRAPPED BY WIRELESS
TRAPPED IN A SUBMARINE, 1931, A
TRAPPED IN TANGIERS, 1960, A
TRAPPED IN THE AIR, 1922
TRAPPED IN THE SKY, 1939, A
TRAQUENARDS
TRAUMA, 1962, C
TRAUMSTADT
TRAVAIL, 1920
TRAVELIN' FAST, 1924
TRAVELIN' ON, 1922, A
TRAVELING EXECUTIONER, THE, 1970, O
TRAVELING HUSBANDS, 1931, O
TRAVELING LADY
TRAVELING SALESLADY, THE, 1935, A
TRAVELING SALESMAN, THE, 1916
TRAVELING SALESMAN, THE, 1921
TRAVELING SALESWOMAN, 1950, A
TRAVELLER'S JOY, 1951, A
TRAVELS WITH ANITA
TRAVELS WITH MY AUNT, 1972, C
TRE NOTTI D'AMORE
TRE NOTTI VIOLENTE
TRE PASSI NEL DELIRIO
TREACHERY ON THE HIGH SEAS, 1939, A
TREACHERY RIDES THE RANGE, 1936, A
TREAD SOFTLY, 1952, A
TREAD SOFTLY STRANGER, 1959, A
TREASON, 1917
TREASON, 1918
TREASON, 1933
TREASON, 1937
TREASON, 1950
TREASURE, 1918
TREASURE AT THE MILL, 1957, AAA
TREASURE CANYON, 1924
TREASURE HUNT, 1952, A
TREASURE ISLAND, 1917
TREASURE ISLAND, 1920, A
TREASURE ISLAND, 1934, A
TREASURE ISLAND, 1950, A-C
TREASURE ISLAND, 1972, A
TREASURE OF ARNE, THE
TREASURE OF FEAR
TREASURE OF HEAVEN, THE, 1916
TREASURE OF JAMAICA REEF, THE, 1976, C
TREASURE OF KALIFA
TREASURE OF LOST CANYON, THE, 1952, A
TREASURE OF MAKUBA, THE, 1967, A
TREASURE OF MATECUMBE, 1976, AA
TREASURE OF MONTE CRISTO, 1949, A
TREASURE OF MONTE CRISTO, THE
TREASURE OF PANCHO VILLA, THE, 1955, A
TREASURE OF RUBY HILLS, 1955, A
TREASURE OF SAN GENNARO, 1968, A
TREASURE OF SAN TERESA, THE
TREASURE OF SILVER LAKE, 1965, A
TREASURE OF TAYOPA, 1974
TREASURE OF THE AMAZON, 1983
TREASURE OF THE FOUR CROWNS, 1983, A
TREASURE OF THE GOLDEN CONDOR, 1953, A
TREASURE OF THE PIRANHA

TREASURE OF THE SEA, 1918
TREASURE OF THE SIERRA MADRE, THE, 1948, C
TREASURE OF THE YANKEE ZEPHYR, 1984, A-C
TREAT 'EM ROUGH, 1919
TREAT EM' ROUGH, 1942, A
TREATMENT, THE
TREE GROWS IN BROOKLYN, A, 1945, C
TREE OF KNOWLEDGE, THE, 1920
TREE OF LIBERTY
TREE OF WOODEN CLOGS, THE, 1979, A-C
TREE, THE, 1969, O
TRELAWNEY OF THE WELLS, 1916
TREMBLING HOUR, THE, 1919
TREMENDOUSLY RICH MAN, A, 1932, A
TRENCHCOAT, 1983, A
TRENT'S LAST CASE, 1920
TRENT'S LAST CASE, 1929
TRENT'S LAST CASE, 1953, A
TRES NOCHES VIOLENTAS
TRESPASSER, THE, 1929, A
TRESPASSER, THE, 1947, A
TRESPASSER, THE, 1946
TRESPASSERS, THE, 1976, O
TRI
TRI SESTRY
TRIAL, 1955, A
TRIAL AND ERROR, 1962, A
TRIAL BY COMBAT
TRIAL MARRIAGE, 1928
TRIAL OF BILLY JACK, THE, 1974, C
TRIAL OF JOAN OF ARC, 1965, C
TRIAL OF LEE HARVEY OSWALD, THE, 1964, A
TRIAL OF MADAM X, THE, 1948, A
TRIAL OF MARY DUGAN, THE, 1929, C
TRIAL OF MARY DUGAN, THE, 1941, A
TRIAL OF PORTIA MERRIMAN, THE
TRIAL OF SERGEANT RUTLEDGE, THE
TRIAL OF THE CATONSVILLE NINE, THE, 1972, A
TRIAL OF VIVIENNE WARE, THE, 1932, A
TRIAL WITHOUT JURY, 1950, A
TRIAL, THE, 1948, A
TRIAL, THE, 1963, C
TRIALS OF OSCAR WILDE, THE
TRIANGLE, 1971
TRIBES, 1970, A
TRIBUTE, 1980, C
TRIBUTE TO A BADMAN, 1956, C
TRICET JEDNA VE STINU
TRICK BABY, 1973, O
TRICK FOR TRICK, 1933, A
TRICK OF FATE, A, 1919
TRICK OF HEARTS, A, 1928
TRICK OR TREATS, 1982, O
TRICK OR TREATS, 1983
TRICKED
TRICKS, 1925
TRIFLERS, THE, 1920
TRIFLERS, THE, 1924
TRIFLING WITH HONOR, 1923
TRIFLING WOMEN, 1922
TRIGGER FINGER, 1924
TRIGGER FINGERS, 1946
TRIGGER FINGERS, 1939, A
TRIGGER HAPPY
TRIGGER LAW, 1944
TRIGGER PALS, 1939, A
TRIGGER SMITH, 1939, A
TRIGGER TOM, 1935
TRIGGER TRAIL, 1944, A
TRIGGER TRICKS, 1930, A
TRIGGER TRIO, THE, 1937, A
TRIGGER, JR., 1950, A
TRIGGERMAN, 1948
TRILBY, 1914
TRILBY, 1915, A
TRILBY, 1923
TRILOGY
TRIMMED, 1922
TRIMMED IN SCARLET, 1923
TRINITY, 1975
TRINITY AND SARTANA, 1972
TRINITY IS STILL MY NAME, 1971, A
TRIO, 1950, A
TRIP TO AMERICA, A
TRIP TO CHINATOWN, A, 1926
TRIP TO ITALY, A
TRIP TO MARS, A, 1920
TRIP TO PARADISE, A, 1921
TRIP TO PARIS, A, 1938, A
TRIP TO TERROR
TRIP WITH ANITA, A
TRIP WITH THE TEACHER, 1975
TRIP, THE
TRIP, THE, 1967, O
TRIPLE ACTION, 1925
TRIPLE CROSS, 1967, C-O
TRIPLE CROSS, THE
TRIPLE DECEPTION, 1957, A
TRIPLE ECHO, THE, 1973, O
TRIPLE IRONS, 1973, O
TRIPLE JUSTICE, 1940, A
TRIPLE PASS, 1928

TRIPLE THREAT, 1948, A
TRIPLE TROUBLE
TRIPLE TROUBLE, 1950, A
TRIPLEPATTE, 1922
TRIPOLI, 1950, A
TRISTANA, 1970, C
TRITIY TAYM
TRIUMPH, 1917
TRIUMPH, 1924
TRIUMPH OF ROBIN HOOD, THE, 1960
TRIUMPH OF SHERLOCK HOLMES, THE, 1935, A
TRIUMPH OF THE RAT, THE, 1926
TRIUMPH OF THE SCARLET PIMPERNEL
TRIUMPH OF THE WEAK, THE, 1918
TRIUMPH OF VENUS, THE, 1918
TRIUMPHS OF A MAN CALLED HORSE, 1983, O
TRIXIE FROM BROADWAY, 1919
TROCADERO, 1944, A
TROG, 1970, A
TROIKA, 1969, O
TROIS HOMMES A ABATTRE
TROIS JEUNES FILLES, 1928
TROIS VERITES
TROJAN BROTHERS, THE, 1946, A
TROJAN HORSE, THE, 1962, AA
TROJAN WAR, THE
TROJAN WOMEN, THE, 1971, C
TROLLENBERG TERROR, THE
TROMBA, THE TIGER MAN, 1952, C
TRON, 1982, A
TROOP TRAIN, THE
TROOPER 44, 1917
TROOPER HOOK, 1957, C
TROOPER O'NEIL, 1922
TROOPER, THE
TROOPERS THREE, 1930, AA
TROOPSHIP, 1938, C
TROPIC FURY, 1939, A
TROPIC HOLIDAY, 1938, A
TROPIC MADNESS, 1928
TROPIC ZONE, 1953, A
TROPICAL HEAT WAVE, 1952, A
TROPICAL LOVE, 1921
TROPICAL NIGHTS, 1928
TROPICAL TROUBLE, 1936, A
TROPICANA
TROPICS, 1969, O
TROTTIE TRUE
TROUBLE, 1922, A
TROUBLE, 1933, A
TROUBLE AHEAD, 1936, A
TROUBLE ALONG THE WAY, 1953, O
TROUBLE AT 16
TROUBLE AT MELODY MESA, 1949
TROUBLE AT MIDNIGHT, 1937, A
TROUBLE BREWING, 1939, A
TROUBLE BUSTER, THE, 1917
TROUBLE BUSTER, THE, 1925
TROUBLE BUSTERS, 1933
TROUBLE CHASER
TROUBLE CHASER, 1926
TROUBLE CHASERS, 1945
TROUBLE FOR EDGAR, 1915
TROUBLE FOR TWO, 1936, A
TROUBLE IN MOROCCO, 1937, A
TROUBLE IN PANAMA
TROUBLE IN PARADISE, 1932, C
TROUBLE IN STORE, 1955, A
TROUBLE IN SUNDOWN, 1939, A
TROUBLE IN TEXAS, 1937, A
TROUBLE IN THE AIR, 1948, A
TROUBLE IN THE GLEN, 1954, A
TROUBLE IN THE SKY, 1961, C
TROUBLE MAKERS, 1948
TROUBLE MAN, 1972, O
TROUBLE ON THE TRAIL, 1954
TROUBLE PREFERRED, 1949, A
TROUBLE SHOOTER, THE, 1924
TROUBLE TRAIL, 1924
TROUBLE WITH ANGELS, THE, 1966, AA
TROUBLE WITH EVE
TROUBLE WITH GIRLS (AND HOW TO GET INTO IT), THE, 1969, A
TROUBLE WITH HARRY, THE, 1955, A-C
TROUBLE WITH WIVES, THE, 1925
TROUBLE WITH WOMEN, THE, 1947, A
TROUBLE-FETE, 1964, O
TROUBLED WATERS, 1936, A
TROUBLED WATERS, 1964
TROUBLEMAKER, THE, 1964, O
TROUBLEMAKERS, 1917
TROUBLES OF A BRIDE, 1924
TROUBLES THROUGH BILLETS
TROUBLESOME DOUBLE, THE, 1971, AA
TROUBLESOME WIVES, 1928
TROUPER, THE, 1922
TROUPING WITH ELLEN, 1924
TROUSERS, 1920
TROUT, THE, 1982, O
TRUANT HUSBAND, THE, 1921
TRUANT SOUL, THE, 1917
TRUANT, THE

TRUANTS, THE, 1922
TRUCK BUSTERS, 1943, A
TRUCK STOP WOMEN, 1974, O
TRUCK TURNER, 1974, O
TRUCKER'S TOP HAND, 1924
TRUCKIN', 1975
TRUCKIN' BUDDY McCOY, 1983
TRUCKIN' MAN, 1975
TRUE AND THE FALSE, THE, 1955, O
TRUE AS A TURTLE, 1957, A
TRUE AS STEEL, 1924
TRUE BLUE, 1918
TRUE CONFESSION, 1937, A
TRUE CONFESSIONS, 1981, O
TRUE DIARY OF A WAHINE
TRUE GRIT, 1969, A
TRUE HEART SUSIE, 1919, A
TRUE HEAVEN, 1929
TRUE NOBILITY, 1916
TRUE STORY OF A WAHINE
TRUE STORY OF ESKIMO NELL, THE, 1975, O
TRUE STORY OF JESSE JAMES, THE, 1957, A
TRUE STORY OF LYNN STUART, THE, 1958, A
TRUE TILDA, 1920, A
TRUE TO LIFE, 1943, A
TRUE TO THE ARMY, 1942, AAA
TRUE TO THE NAVY, 1930, A
TRUFFLERS, THE, 1917
TRUMAN CAPOTE'S TRILOGY, 1969, A
TRUMPET BLOWS, THE, 1934, A
TRUMPET CALL, THE, 1915
TRUMPET ISLAND, 1920
TRUMPIN' TROUBLE, 1926
TRUNK CRIME
TRUNK MYSTERY, THE
TRUNK MYSTERY, THE, 1927
TRUNK TO CAIRO, 1966, C
TRUNK, THE, 1961, C
TRUNKS OF MR. O.F., THE, 1932, A
TRUST THE NAVY, 1935, A
TRUST YOUR WIFE
TRUST YOUR WIFE, 1921
TRUST, THE
TRUSTED OUTLAW, THE, 1937, A
TRUTH ABOUT HELEN, THE, 1915
TRUTH ABOUT HUSBANDS, THE, 1920
TRUTH ABOUT MEN, 1926
TRUTH ABOUT MURDER, THE, 1946, A
TRUTH ABOUT SPRING, THE, 1965, AA
TRUTH ABOUT WIVES, THE, 1923
TRUTH ABOUT WOMEN, THE, 1924
TRUTH ABOUT WOMEN, THE, 1958, A
TRUTH ABOUT YOUTH, THE, 1930, A
TRUTH AND JUSTICE, 1916
TRUTH IS STRANGER
TRUTH WAGON, THE, 1914, A
TRUTH, THE, 1920, A
TRUTH, THE, 1961, O
TRUTHFUL LIAR, THE, 1922
TRUTHFUL SEX, THE, 1926
TRUTHFUL TULLIVER, 1917
TRUTHFUL TULLIVER, 1917, A
TRUXTON KING, 1923
TRY AND FIND IT
TRY AND GET IT, 1924
TRY AND GET ME
TRYGON FACTOR, THE, 1969, C
TRYING, 1967, A
TSAR IVAN VASILYEVICH GROZNY, 1915
TSAR NIKOLAI II, 1917
TSAR'S BRIDE, THE, 1966, C
TSARSKAYA NEVESTA
TSUBAKI SANJURO
TU M'APPARTIENS, 1929
TU PERDONAS..YO NO
TU SERAS TERRIBLEMENT GENTILLE
TUCK EVERLASTING, 1981
TUCSON, 1949, A
TUCSON RAIDERS, 1944, A
TUDOR ROSE
TUGBOAT ANNIE, 1933, A
TUGBOAT ANNIE SAILS AGAIN, 1940, AA
TUGBOAT PRINCESS, 1936
TULIPS, 1981, C
TULSA, 1949, A
TULSA KID, THE, 1940, A
TUMBLEDOWN RANCH IN ARIZONA, 1941, A
TUMBLEWEED, 1953, A
TUMBLEWEED TRAIL, 1942
TUMBLEWEED TRAIL, 1946, A
TUMBLEWEEDS, 1925, A
TUMBLING RIVER, 1927, A
TUMBLING TUMBLEWEEDS, 1935, AA
TUNA CLIPPER, 1949, A
TUNDRA, 1936, A
TUNES OF GLORY, 1960, C
TUNNEL 28
TUNNEL OF LOVE, THE, 1958, C
TUNNEL TO THE SUN, 1968, C
TUNNEL, THE
TUNNELVISION, 1976, O
TURF CONSPIRACY, A, 1918

TURKEY SHOOT
TURKEY TIME, 1933, A
TURKISH CUCUMBER, THE, 1963, C
TURKISH DELIGHT, 1927
TURKSIB, 1930
TURLIS ABENTEUER
TURMOIL, THE, 1916
TURMOIL, THE, 1924
TURN BACK THE CLOCK, 1933, A
TURN BACK THE HOURS, 1928
TURN IN THE ROAD, THE, 1919
TURN OF THE CARD, THE, 1918
TURN OF THE ROAD, THE, 1915
TURN OF THE TIDE, 1935, A
TURN OF THE WHEEL, THE, 1918
TURN OFF THE MOON, 1937, A
TURN ON TO LOVE, 1969, O
TURN THE KEY SOFTLY, 1954, C
TURN TO THE RIGHT, 1922
TURNABOUT, 1940, A
TURNED OUT NICE AGAIN, 1941, A
TURNED UP, 1924
TURNERS OF PROSPECT ROAD, THE, 1947, A
TURNING POINT, THE, 1920
TURNING POINT, THE, 1952, C-O
TURNING POINT, THE, 1977, C
TURNING THE TABLES, 1919
TUSK, 1980
TUTTE LE ALTRE RAGAZZE LO FANNO
TUTTI A CASA
TUTTI FRUTTI
TUTTI PAZZI MENO IO
TUTTLES OF TAHITI, 1942, A
TUXEDO JUNCTION, 1941, A
TUXEDO WARRIOR, 1982
TVA LEVANDE OCH EN DOD
TWAS EVER THUS, 1915
TWELFTH NIGHT, 1956, A
12 ANGRY MEN, 1957, A
TWELVE CHAIRS, THE, 1970, A-C
TWELVE CROWDED HOURS, 1939, A
TWELVE GOOD MEN, 1936, A
TWELVE HOURS TO KILL, 1960, A
TWELVE MILES OUT, 1927, A
TWELVE O'CLOCK HIGH, 1949, C
TWELVE PLUS ONE, 1970, A
TWELVE POUND LOOK, THE, 1920
TWELVE TO THE MOON, 1960, A
TWELVE-HANDED MEN OF MARS, THE, 1964, A
TWENTIETH CENTURY, 1934, A
20TH CENTURY OZ, 1934, A
25TH HOUR, THE, 1967, C
24 HOURS, 1931, A
24 HOURS IN A WOMAN'S LIFE, 1968, C
24 HOURS TO KILL, 1966, C
24-HOUR LOVER, 1970, O
20 MILLION MILES TO EARTH, 1957, A
TWENTY MILLION SWEETHEARTS, 1934, A
TWENTY MULE TEAM, 1940, A
TWENTY PLUS TWO, 1961, C-O
TWENTY QUESTIONS MURDER MYSTERY, THE,
   1950, A
27A, 1974, O
27TH DAY, THE, 1957, A-C
20,000 EYES, 1961, C
20,000 LEAGUES UNDER THE SEA, 1954, A
20,000 MEN A YEAR, 1939, A
20,000 POUNDS KISS, THE, 1964, C
20,000 YEARS IN SING-SING, 1933, A
23 1/2 HOURS LEAVE, 1937, A
23 PACES TO BAKER STREET, 1956, C
TWENTY-ONE, 1918
TWENTY-ONE, 1923
TWENTY-ONE DAYS
TWENTY-ONE DAYS TOGETHER, 1940, A
TWICE A MAN, 1964, O
TWICE AROUND THE DAFFODILS, 1962, A
TWICE BLESSED, 1945, A
TWICE BRANDED, 1936, A
TWICE TOLD TALES, 1963, C
TWICE UPON A TIME, 1953, A
TWICE UPON A TIME, 1983, A
TWILIGHT, 1919
TWILIGHT FOR THE GODS, 1958, A
TWILIGHT HOUR, 1944, A
TWILIGHT IN THE SIERRAS, 1950, A
TWILIGHT OF HONOR, 1963, C
TWILIGHT OF THE DEAD
TWILIGHT ON THE PRAIRIE, 1944, A
TWILIGHT ON THE RIO GRANDE, 1947, A
TWILIGHT ON THE TRAIL, 1941, A
TWILIGHT PATH, 1965, C
TWILIGHT PEOPLE, 1972, O
TWILIGHT STORY, THE, 1962, O
TWILIGHT TIME, 1983, A
TWILIGHT WOMEN, 1953, C
TWILIGHT ZONE—THE MOVIE, 1983, C-O
TWILIGHT'S LAST GLEAMING, 1977, O
TWIN BEDS, 1920, A
TWIN BEDS, 1929, A
TWIN BEDS, 1942, A
TWIN FACES, 1937, A

TWIN FLAPPERS, 1927
TWIN HUSBANDS, 1934, A
TWIN KIDDIES, 1917
TWIN PAWNS, THE, 1919
TWIN SISTERS OF KYOTO, 1964, C
TWIN SIX O'BRIEN, 1926
TWIN TRIANGLE, THE, 1916
TWIN TRIGGERS, 1926
TWINKLE AND SHINE
TWINKLE IN GOD'S EYE, THE, 1955, A
TWINKLE, TWINKLE, KILLER KANE
TWINKLER, THE, 1916
TWINKLETOES, 1926, A
TWINKY
TWINS OF EVIL, 1971, O
TWINS OF SUFFERING CREEK, 1920
TWIST ALL NIGHT, 1961, A
TWIST AROUND THE CLOCK, 1961, A
TWIST OF FATE
TWIST OF SAND, A, 1968, A
TWIST, THE, 1976, C-O
TWISTED BRAIN
TWISTED LIVES
TWISTED NERVE, 1969, O
TWISTED RAILS, 1935
TWISTED ROAD, THE
TWISTED TRIGGERS, 1926
TWITCH OF THE DEATH NERVE, 1973, O
TWO, 1975, O
TWO A PENNY, 1968, O
TWO AGAINST THE WORLD, 1932, A
TWO AGAINST THE WORLD, 1936, A
TWO ALONE, 1934, A
TWO AND ONE TWO, 1934, A
TWO AND TWO MAKE SIX, 1962, C
TWO ARABIAN KNIGHTS, 1927
TWO ARE GUILTY, 1964, C
TWO BLACK SHEEP
TWO BLONDES AND A REDHEAD, 1947, A
TWO BRIDES, THE, 1919
TWO BRIGHT BOYS, 1939, A
TWO CAN PLAY, 1926
TWO CATCH TWO, 1979
TWO COLONELS, THE, 1963, A
TWO DAUGHTERS, 1963, A
TWO DAYS, 1929
TWO DOLLAR BETTOR, 1951, A
TWO ENEMIES
TWO ENGLISH GIRLS, 1972, O
TWO EYES, TWELVE HANDS, 1958, C
TWO FACES OF DR. JEKYLL
TWO FACES OF EVIL, THE, 1981
TWO FISTED, 1935, A
TWO FISTED AGENT
TWO FISTED BUCKAROO, 1926
TWO FISTED JUSTICE, 1924
TWO FISTED JUSTICE, 1943, A
TWO FISTED TENDERFOOT, A, 1924
TWO FISTED THOMPSON, 1925
TWO FLAGS WEST, 1950, A
TWO FLAMING YOUTHS, 1927, A
TWO FOR DANGER, 1940, A
TWO FOR THE ROAD, 1967, C
TWO FOR THE SEESAW, 1962, C
TWO FOR TONIGHT, 1935, A
TWO GALS AND A GUY, 1951, A
TWO GENTLEMEN SHARING, 1969, O
TWO GIRLS AND A SAILOR, 1944, A
TWO GIRLS ON BROADWAY, 1940, A
TWO GROOMS FOR A BRIDE, 1957, A
TWO GUN CABALLERO, 1931
TWO GUN LAW, 1937, A
TWO GUN MAN, THE, 1931, A
TWO GUN MURPHY, 1928
TWO GUN O'BRIEN, 1928
TWO GUN SAP, 1925
TWO GUN SHERIFF, 1941, A
TWO GUNS AND A BADGE, 1954, A
TWO GUYS FROM TEXAS, 1948, A
TWO HEADS ON A PILLOW, 1934, A
TWO HEARTS IN HARMONY, 1935, A
TWO HEARTS IN WALTZ TIME, 1934, A
TWO HUNDRED MOTELS, 1971, O
TWO IN A CROWD, 1936, A
TWO IN A MILLION
TWO IN A SLEEPING BAG, 1964, C
TWO IN A TAXI, 1941, A
TWO IN REVOLT, 1936, AAA
TWO IN THE DARK, 1936, A
TWO IN THE SHADOW, 1968, C
TWO IS A HAPPY NUMBER
TWO KINDS OF LOVE, 1920
TWO KINDS OF WOMEN, 1922
TWO KINDS OF WOMEN, 1932, C
TWO KOUNEY LEMELS, 1966, A
TWO LANCASHIRE LASSES IN LONDON, 1916
TWO LATINS FROM MANHATTAN, 1941, A
TWO LEFT FEET, 1965, O
TWO LETTER ALIBI, 1962, A
TWO LITTLE BEARS, THE, 1961
TWO LITTLE DRUMMER BOYS, 1928
TWO LITTLE IMPS, 1917

TWO LITTLE WOODEN SHOES, 1920
TWO LIVING, ONE DEAD, 1964, C
TWO LOST WORLDS, 1950, A
TWO LOVERS, 1928, A
TWO LOVERS, 1961, C
TWO MEN AND A GIRL
TWO MEN AND A MAID, 1929, A
TWO MEN AND A WOMAN, 1917
TWO MEN IN TOWN, 1973, O
TWO MEN OF SANDY BAR, 1916
TWO MINUTES TO GO, 1921, A
TWO MINUTES TO PLAY, 1937, A
TWO MINUTES' SILENCE, 1934, A
TWO MOONS, 1920
TWO MRS. CARROLLS, THE, 1947, A-C
TWO MUGS FROM BROOKLYN
TWO MULES FOR SISTER SARA, 1970, C
TWO NIGHTS WITH CLEOPATRA, 1953, C
TWO O'CLOCK COURAGE, 1945, C
TWO OF A KIND, 1951, C
TWO OF A KIND, 1983, C
TWO OF US, THE, 1938, A
TWO OF US, THE, 1968, A
TWO ON A DOORSTEP, 1936, A
TWO ON A GUILLOTINE, 1965, C
TWO ON THE TILES
TWO OR THREE THINGS I KNOW ABOUT HER,
   1970, O
TWO ORPHANS, THE, 1915
TWO OUTLAWS, THE, 1928
TWO PEOPLE, 1973, O
TWO ROADS
TWO RODE TOGETHER, 1961, C
TWO SECONDS, 1932, C
TWO SENORITAS
TWO SENORITAS FROM CHICAGO, 1943, A
TWO SHALL BE BORN, 1924
TWO SINNERS, 1935, A
TWO SISTERS, 1929
TWO SISTERS, 1938, A
TWO SISTERS FROM BOSTON, 1946, A
TWO SMART MEN, 1940, A
TWO SMART PEOPLE, 1946, A
TWO SOLITUDES, 1978, A
TWO SOULED WOMAN, THE
TWO SUPER COPS, 1978, C
TWO TEXAS KNIGHTS
TWO THOROUGHBREDS, 1939, A
TWO THOUSAND MANIACS, 1964, O
2,000 WEEKS, 1970, C
2,000 WOMEN, 1944, A
2000 YEARS LATER, 1969, O
2001: A SPACE ODYSSEY, 1968, A
TWO THOUSAND YEARS LATER, 1969
TWO TICKETS TO BROADWAY, 1951, A
TWO TICKETS TO LONDON, 1943, A
TWO TICKETS TO PARIS, 1962, A
TWO TIMES TWO
TWO TONS OF TURQUOISE TO TAOS, 1967
TWO VIOLENT MEN, 1964
TWO VOICES, 1966, C
TWO WEEKS, 1920
TWO WEEKS IN ANOTHER TOWN, 1962, O
TWO WEEKS IN SEPTEMBER, 1967, O
TWO WEEKS OFF, 1929, A
TWO WEEKS TO LIVE, 1943, A
TWO WEEKS WITH LOVE, 1950, A
TWO WEEKS WITH PAY, 1921
TWO WHITE ARMS
TWO WHO DARED, 1937, A
TWO WISE MAIDS, 1937, A
TWO WIVES AT ONE WEDDING, 1961, A
TWO WOMEN, 1919
TWO WOMEN, 1940, A
TWO WOMEN, 1961, C-O
TWO WORLD, 1930, A
TWO WORLDS OF ANGELITA, THE, 1982
TWO WORLDS OF CHARLY GORDON, THE
TWO YANKS IN TRINIDAD, 1942, A
TWO YEARS BEFORE THE MAST, 1946, C
TWO YEARS HOLIDAY
TWO'S COMPANY, 1939, A
TWO-BITS SEATS, 1917
TWO-EDGED SWORD, THE, 1916, A
TWO-FACED WOMAN, 1941, A
TWO-FISTED GENTLEMAN, 1936, A
TWO-FISTED JEFFERSON, 1922
TWO-FISTED JONES, 1925
TWO-FISTED JUSTICE, 1931, A
TWO-FISTED LAW, 1932, A
TWO-FISTED RANGERS, 1940, A
TWO-FISTED SHERIFF, 1937, A
TWO-FISTED SHERIFF, A, 1925
TWO-FISTED STRANGER, 1946
TWO-GUN BETTY, 1918
TWO-GUN CUPID
TWO-GUN JUSTICE, 1938, A
TWO-GUN LADY, 1956, A
TWO-GUN MAN FROM HARLEM, 1938
TWO-GUN MAN, THE, 1926
TWO-GUN OF THE TUMBLEWEED, 1927
TWO-GUN TROUBADOR, 1939, A

TWO-HEADED SPY, THE, 1959, C
TWO-LANE BLACKTOP, 1971, O
TWO-MAN SUBMARINE, 1944, A
TWO-MINUTE WARNING, 1976, O
TWO-SOUL WOMAN, THE, 1918
TWO-WAY STRETCH, 1961, A-C
TWONKY, THE, 1953, A
TYCOON, 1947, A
TYPHOON, 1940, A
TYPHOON LOVE, 1926
TYPHOON TREASURE, 1939, A
TYPHOON, THE, 1914, A
TYRANT FEAR, 1918
TYRANT OF RED GULCH, 1928
TYRANT OF SYRACUSE, THE
TYRANT OF THE SEA, 1950, A
TYRANT, THE, 1972
TYSTNADEN

-U-

U KRUTOGO YARA
U-47 LT. COMMANDER PRIEN, 1967, A
U-BOAT 29, 1939, A
U-BOAT PRISONER, 1944, A
U-TURN, 1973, C
U.P. TRAIL, THE, 1920
U.S.S. TEAKETTLE
UCCELLACCI E UCCELLINI
UCCIDERO UN UOMO
UCHUJIN TOKYO NI ARAWARU
UFO
UFO: TARGET EARTH, 1974, A
UGETSU, 1954, A
UGLY AMERICAN, THE, 1963, A-C
UGLY DACHSHUND, THE, 1966, AAA
UGLY DUCKLING, THE, 1920
UGLY DUCKLING, THE, 1959, A
UGLY ONES, THE, 1968, O
UKIGUSA
ULTIMATE CHASE, THE
ULTIMATE SOLUTION OF GRACE QUIGLEY, THE,
  1984, C
ULTIMATE THRILL, THE, 1974, A-C
ULTIMATE WARRIOR, THE, 1975, O
ULTIMATUM, 1940, A
ULTUS, THE MAN FROM THE DEAD, 1916
ULYSSES, 1955, C
ULYSSES, 1967, C
ULZANA'S RAID, 1972, O
UMBERTO D, 1955, C
UMBRELLA, THE, 1933, A
UMBRELLAS OF CHERBOURG, THE, 1964, A-C
UN AMOUR DE POCHE, 1957
UN AMOUR DE SWANN
UN AMOUR EN ALLEMAGNE
UN AVENTURIER, 1921
UN BON PETIT DIABLE, 1923
UN CARNET DE BAL, 1938, A
UN CHATEAU DE LA MORT LENTE, 1925
UN CRIME A ETE COMMIS, 1919
UN DIMANCHE A LA CAMPAGNE
UN DRAME SOUS NAPOLEON, 1921
UN FIL A LA PATTE, 1924
UN FILE
UN FILS D'AMERIQUE, 1925
UN HOMME ET UNE FEMME
UN HOMME PASSA, 1917
UN MARIAGE DE RAISON, 1916
UN OURS, 1921
UN ROMAN D'AMOUR ET D'AVENTURES, 1918
UN SEUL AMOUR
UN SOIR, 1919
UN TAXI MAUVE
UN UOMO, UN CAVALLO, UNA PISTOLA
UN, DEUX, TROIS, QUATRE?
UNA MOGLIE AMERICANA
UNA SIGNORA DELL'OVEST, 1942, A
UNAFRAID, THE, 1915
UNAKRSNA VATRA
UNASHAMED, 1932, A
UNASHAMED, 1938, O
UNATTAINABLE, THE, 1916
UNBEATABLE GAME, THE, 1925
UNBELIEVER, THE, 1918
UNBLAZED TRAIL, 1923
UNBROKEN PROMISE, THE, 1919
UNBROKEN ROAD, THE, 1915
UNCANNY ROOM, THE, 1915
UNCANNY, THE, 1977, C
UNCENSORED, 1944, A
UNCERTAIN GLORY, 1944, A
UNCERTAIN LADY, 1934, A
UNCHAINED
UNCHAINED, 1955, A
UNCHARTED CHANNELS, 1920
UNCHARTED SEAS, 1921
UNCHASTENED WOMAN, 1925, A
UNCIVILISED, 1937, A
UNCLAIMED GOODS, 1918
UNCLE DICK'S DARLING, 1920
UNCLE HARRY, 1945, C
UNCLE JASPAR'S WILL, 1922

UNCLE JOE SHANNON, 1978, C
UNCLE MOSES, 1932
UNCLE NICK, 1938
UNCLE SAM AWAKE, 1916
UNCLE SCAM, 1981, O
UNCLE SILAS
UNCLE TOM'S CABIN, 1914, A
UNCLE TOM'S CABIN, 1918
UNCLE TOM'S CABIN, 1927
UNCLE TOM'S CABIN, 1969, C
UNCLE VANYA, 1958, A
UNCLE VANYA, 1972, A
UNCLE VANYA, 1977, A
UNCLE, THE, 1966, A
UNCOMMON THIEF, AN, 1967, A
UNCOMMON VALOR, 1983, O
UNCONQUERED, 1917
UNCONQUERED, 1947, A
UNCONQUERED BANDIT, 1935
UNCONQUERED WOMAN, 1922
UND IMMER RUFT DAS HERZ
...UND MORGEN FAHRT IHR ZUR HOLIE
UNDEAD, THE, 1957, A
UNDEFEATED, THE, 1951
UNDEFEATED, THE, 1969, A
UNDER A CLOUD, 1937, A
UNDER A TEXAS MOON, 1930, A
UNDER AGE, 1941, A-C
UNDER AGE, 1964, O
UNDER ARIZONA SKIES, 1946, A
UNDER CALIFORNIA SKIES
UNDER CALIFORNIA STARS, 1948, A
UNDER CAPRICORN, 1949, C
UNDER COLORADO SKIES, 1947, A
UNDER COVER, 1916
UNDER COVER OF NIGHT, 1937, A
UNDER COVER ROGUE
UNDER CRIMSON SKIES, 1920
UNDER EIGHTEEN, 1932, A
UNDER FALSE COLORS, 1917
UNDER FIESTA STARS, 1941, A
UNDER FIRE, 1926, A
UNDER FIRE, 1957, A
UNDER FIRE, 1983, O
UNDER HANDICAP, 1917
UNDER MEXICALI SKIES
UNDER MEXICALI STARS, 1950, A
UNDER MILK WOOD, 1973, C
UNDER MONTANA SKIES, 1930, A
UNDER MY SKIN, 1950, A
UNDER NEVADA SKIES, 1946, A
UNDER NEW MANAGEMENT
UNDER NORTHERN LIGHTS, 1920
UNDER OATH, 1922
UNDER PRESSURE, 1935, A
UNDER PROOF, 1936, A
UNDER SECRET ORDERS, 1933, A
UNDER SECRET ORDERS, 1943, A-C
UNDER SOUTHERN SKIES, 1915
UNDER STRANGE FLAGS, 1937, A
UNDER SUSPICION, 1916
UNDER SUSPICION, 1918
UNDER SUSPICION, 1919
UNDER SUSPICION, 1919, A
UNDER SUSPICION, 1931, A
UNDER SUSPICION, 1937, A
UNDER TEN FLAGS, 1960, C
UNDER TEXAS SKIES, 1931, A
UNDER TEXAS SKIES, 1940, A
UNDER THE BANNER OF SAMURAI, 1969, C
UNDER THE BIG TOP, 1938, A
UNDER THE BLACK EAGLE, 1928
UNDER THE CLOCK
UNDER THE DOCTOR, 1976
UNDER THE GASLIGHT, 1914
UNDER THE GREENWOOD TREE, 1918
UNDER THE GREENWOOD TREE, 1930, A
UNDER THE GUN, 1951, A
UNDER THE LASH, 1921
UNDER THE PAMPAS MOON, 1935, A
UNDER THE RAINBOW, 1981, C
UNDER THE RED ROBE, 1915
UNDER THE RED ROBE, 1923, A
UNDER THE RED ROBE, 1937, A
UNDER THE ROOFS OF PARIS, 1930, A
UNDER THE ROUGE, 1925
UNDER THE SIGN OF CAPRICORN, 1971
UNDER THE SOUTHERN CROSS
UNDER THE SUN OF ROME, 1949, A
UNDER THE TABLE YOU MUST GO, 1969
UNDER THE TONTO RIM, 1928
UNDER THE TONTO RIM, 1933, A
UNDER THE TONTO RIM, 1947, A
UNDER THE TOP, 1919
UNDER THE VOLCANO, 1984, O
UNDER THE WESTERN SKIES, 1921
UNDER THE YOKE, 1918
UNDER THE YUM-YUM TREE, 1963, C-O
UNDER TWO FLAGS, 1916
UNDER TWO FLAGS, 1922
UNDER TWO FLAGS, l936, A-C
UNDER WESTERN SKIES, 1926

UNDER WESTERN SKIES, 1945, A
UNDER WESTERN STARS, 1938, A
UNDER YOUR HAT, 1940, A
UNDER YOUR SPELL, 1936, A
UNDER-COVER MAN, 1932, A
UNDER-PUP, THE, 1939, A
UNDERCOVER
UNDERCOVER AGENT, 1935, A
UNDERCOVER AGENT, 1939, A
UNDERCOVER DOCTOR, 1939, A
UNDERCOVER GIRL
UNDERCOVER GIRL, 1950, A
UNDERCOVER GIRL, 1957, A
UNDERCOVER MAISIE, 1947, A
UNDERCOVER MAN, 1936, A
UNDERCOVER MAN, 1942, A
UNDERCOVER MAN, THE, 1949, C
UNDERCOVER MEN, 1935
UNDERCOVER WOMAN, THE, 1946, A
UNDERCOVERS HERO, 1975, O
UNDERCURRENT, 1946, A-C
UNDERCURRENT, THE, 1919
UNDERDOG, THE, 1943, A
UNDERGROUND, 1928
UNDERGROUND, 1941, A
UNDERGROUND, 1970, C
UNDERGROUND ACES, 1981
UNDERGROUND AGENT, 1942, A
UNDERGROUND GUERRILLAS, 1944, A
UNDERGROUND RUSTLERS, 1941, A
UNDERGROUND U.S.A., 1980, O
UNDERNEATH THE ARCHES, 1937, A
UNDERSEA GIRL, 1957, A
UNDERSEA ODYSSEY, AN
UNDERSTANDING HEART, THE, 1927
UNDERSTUDY, THE, 1917
UNDERSTUDY, THE, 1922
UNDERTAKER AND HIS PALS, THE, 1966, O
UNDERTOW, 1930, A
UNDERTOW, 1949, A
UNDERTOW, THE, 1916
UNDERWATER CITY, THE, 1962, A
UNDERWATER ODYSSEY, AN
UNDERWATER WARRIOR, 1958, A
UNDERWATER!, 1955, C-O
UNDERWORLD, 1927, A
UNDERWORLD, 1937, A-C
UNDERWORLD AFTER DARK
UNDERWORLD INFORMERS, 1965, A
UNDERWORLD OF LONDON, THE, 1915
UNDERWORLD STORY, THE
UNDERWORLD TERROR, 1936
UNDERWORLD U.S.A., 1961, C
UNDINE, 1916
UNDISPUTED EVIDENCE, 1922
UNDRESSED, 1928
UNDYING FLAME, THE, 1917
UNDYING MONSTER, THE, 1942, A
UNE AVENTURE, 1922
UNE ETRANGERE, 1924
UNE FEMME DEUCE
UNE FEMME EST UNE FEMME
UNE FEMME INCONNUE, 1918
UNE FLEUR DANS LES RONCES, 1921
UNE HISTOIRE DE BRIGANDS, 1920
UNE HISTOIRE IMMORTELLE
UNE JEUNE FILLE
UNE MERE, UNE FILLE
UNE NUIT AGITEE, 1920
UNE PARISIENNE
UNE VIE SANS JOIE
UNEARTHLY STRANGER, THE, 1964, A
UNEARTHLY, THE, 1957, C
UNEASY MONEY, 1918
UNEASY PAYMENTS, 1927
UNEASY TERMS, 1948
UNEASY VIRTUE, 1931, A
UNEXPECTED FATHER, 1932, A
UNEXPECTED FATHER, 1939, A
UNEXPECTED GUEST, 1946, A
UNEXPECTED PLACES, 1918
UNEXPECTED UNCLE, 1941, A
UNFAIR SEX, THE, 1926
UNFAITHFUL, 1931, A
UNFAITHFUL WIFE, THE
UNFAITHFUL WIFE, THE, 1915
UNFAITHFUL, THE, 1947, A
UNFAITHFULLY YOURS, 1948, A-C
UNFAITHFULLY YOURS, 1984, C
UNFAITHFULS, THE, 1960, A
UNFINISHED BUSINESS, 1941, A
UNFINISHED DANCE, THE, 1947, A
UNFINISHED SYMPHONY, THE, 1953, A
UNFOLDMENT, THE, 1922
UNFORGIVEN, THE, 1960, C
UNFORSEEN, THE, 1917
UNFORTUNATE SEX, THE, 1920
UNGUARDED GIRLS, 1929
UNGUARDED HOUR, THE, 1925, A
UNGUARDED HOUR, THE, 1936, A
UNGUARDED MOMENT, THE, 1956, A
UNGUARDED WOMEN, 1924

UNHINGED, 1982, O
UNHOLY DESIRE, 1964, O
UNHOLY FOUR, THE, 1954, A
UNHOLY FOUR, THE, 1969, C
UNHOLY GARDEN, THE, 1931, A
UNHOLY LOVE, 1932, A
UNHOLY NIGHT, THE, 1929, A
UNHOLY PARTNERS, 1941, A
UNHOLY QUEST, THE, 1934, A
UNHOLY ROLLERS, 1972, O
UNHOLY THREE, THE, 1925, A
UNHOLY THREE, THE, 1930, C
UNHOLY WIFE, THE, 1957, A
UNIDENTIFIED FLYING ODDBALL, THE, 1979, A
UNIFORM LOVERS
UNINHIBITED, THE, 1968, C
UNINVITED GUEST, THE, 1923, A
UNINVITED GUEST, THE, 1924
UNINVITED, THE, 1944, C
UNION CITY, 1980, A
UNION DEPOT, 1932, A
UNION PACIFIC, 1939, A
UNION STATION, 1950, C
UNITED STATES SMITH, 1928
UNIVERSAL SOLDIER, 1971, C
UNIVERSITY OF LIFE, 1941, C
UNJUSTLY ACCUSED, 1913
UNKILLABLES, THE
UNKISSED BRIDE, 1966
UNKISSED BRIDE, THE
UNKNOWN 274, 1917
UNKNOWN BATTLE, THE
UNKNOWN BLONDE, 1934, A
UNKNOWN CAVALIER, THE, 1926, A
UNKNOWN DANGERS, 1926
UNKNOWN GUEST, THE, 1943, A
UNKNOWN ISLAND, 1948, A
UNKNOWN LOVE, THE, 1919
UNKNOWN LOVER, THE, 1925
UNKNOWN MAN OF SHANDIGOR, THE, 1967, A
UNKNOWN MAN, THE, 1951, C
UNKNOWN POWERS, 1979
UNKNOWN PURPLE, THE, 1923
UNKNOWN QUANTITY, THE, 1919
UNKNOWN RANGER, THE, 1936, A
UNKNOWN RIDER, THE, 1929
UNKNOWN SATELLITE OVER TOKYO
UNKNOWN SOLDIER, THE, 1926
UNKNOWN TERROR, THE, 1957, A
UNKNOWN TREASURES, 1926
UNKNOWN VALLEY, 1933, A
UNKNOWN WIFE, THE, 1921
UNKNOWN WOMAN, 1935, A
UNKNOWN WORLD, 1951, A
UNKNOWN, THE, 1915
UNKNOWN, THE, 1921, A
UNKNOWN, THE, 1927, C
UNKNOWN, THE, 1946, A
UNMAN, WITTERING AND ZIGO, 1971, C
UNMARRIED, 1920
UNMARRIED, 1939, A
UNMARRIED WIVES, 1924
UNMARRIED WOMAN, AN, 1978, C-O
UNMASKED, 1929
UNMASKED, 1929, A
UNMASKED, 1950, A
UNNAMED WOMAN, THE, 1925
UNO DEI TRE
UNPAINTED WOMAN, THE, 1919
UNPARDONABLE SIN, THE, 1916
UNPARDONABLE SIN, THE, 1919
UNPROTECTED, 1916
UNPUBLISHED STORY, 1942, A
UNRECONCILED
UNREST, 1920, A
UNRESTRAINED YOUTH, 1925
UNRUHIGE NACHT
UNSATISFIED, THE, 1964, A
UNSEEING EYES, 1923
UNSEEN ENEMIES, 1926
UNSEEN ENEMY, 1942, A
UNSEEN FORCES, 1920
UNSEEN HANDS, 1924
UNSEEN HEROES
UNSEEN, THE, 1945, A
UNSEEN, THE, 1981, O
UNSENT LETTER, THE
UNSER BOSS IST EINE DAME
UNSINKABLE MOLLY BROWN, THE, 1964, A
UNSTOPPABLE MAN, THE, 1961, A
UNSTRAP ME, 1968, O
UNSUITABLE JOB FOR A WOMAN, AN, 1982, C-O
UNSUSPECTED, THE, 1947, A
UNTAMEABLE, THE, 1923
UNTAMED, 1918
UNTAMED, 1929, A-C
UNTAMED, 1940, A
UNTAMED, 1955, C-O
UNTAMED BREED, THE, 1948, A
UNTAMED FRONTIER, 1952, A
UNTAMED FURY, 1947, A
UNTAMED HEIRESS, 1954, A

UNTAMED JUSTICE, 1929
UNTAMED LADY, THE, 1926, A
UNTAMED MISTRESS, 1960, O
UNTAMED WEST, THE
UNTAMED WOMEN, 1952, A
UNTAMED YOUTH, 1924
UNTAMED YOUTH, 1957, A
UNTAMED, THE, 1920
UNTER GEIERN
UNTIL SEPTEMBER, 1984, O
UNTIL THE DAY WE MEET AGAIN, 1932
UNTIL THEY GET ME, 1918
UNTIL THEY SAIL, l957, C
UNTITLED
UNTO EACH OTHER, 1929
UNTO THOSE WHO SIN, 1916
UNTOUCHABLES, THE
UNTOUCHED, 1956, A
UNVANQUISHED, THE
UNVEILING HAND, THE, 1919
UNWANTED, THE, 1924, A
UNWED MOTHER, 1958, C-O
UNWELCOME MOTHER, THE, 1916
UNWELCOME MRS. HATCH, THE, 1914
UNWELCOME STRANGER, 1935, A
UNWELCOME VISITORS
UNWELCOME WIFE, THE, 1915
UNWILLING AGENT, 1968, A
UNWILLING HERO, AN, 1921
UNWRITTEN CODE, THE, 1919
UNWRITTEN CODE, THE, 1944, A
UNWRITTEN LAW, THE, 1916
UNWRITTEN LAW, THE, 1925
UNWRITTEN LAW, THE, 1932, A
UP AND AT 'EM, 1922
UP AND GOING, 1922
UP FOR MURDER, 1931, A
UP FOR THE CUP, 1931, A
UP FOR THE CUP, 1950, A
UP FOR THE DERBY, 1933, A
UP FROM THE BEACH, 1965, A
UP FROM THE DEPTHS, 1915
UP FROM THE DEPTHS, 1979, O
UP FRONT, 1951, A
UP GOES MAISIE, 1946, A
UP IN ARMS, 1944, AA
UP IN CENTRAL PARK, 1948, A
UP IN MABEL'S ROOM, 1926
UP IN MABEL'S ROOM, 1944, A
UP IN MARY'S ATTICK, 1920
UP IN SMOKE, 1957, A
UP IN SMOKE, l978, O
UP IN THE AIR, 1940, A
UP IN THE AIR, 1969, AA
UP IN THE AIR ABOUT MARY, 1922
UP IN THE CELLAR, 1970, C
UP IN THE WORLD, 1957, A
UP JUMPED A SWAGMAN, 1965, A
UP JUMPED THE DEVIL, 1941
UP OR DOWN, 1917
UP PERISCOPE, 1959, A
UP POMPEII, 1971, O
UP POPS THE DEVIL, 1931, A
UP RIVER, 1979
UP ROMANCE ROAD, 1918
UP SHE GOES
UP THE ACADEMY, 1980, O
UP THE CHASTITY BELT, 1971, O
UP THE CREEK, 1958, A
UP THE CREEK, 1984, O
UP THE DOWN STAIRCASE, 1967, A-C
UP THE FRONT, 1972, C
UP THE JUNCTION, 1968, O
UP THE LADDER, 1925
UP THE MACGREGORS, 1967, A
UP THE RIVER, 1930, A
UP THE RIVER, 1938, A
UP THE ROAD WITH SALLIE, 1918
UP THE SANDBOX, 1972, C-O
UP TIGHT
UP TO HIS EARS, 1966, C
UP TO HIS NECK, 1954, A
UP TO THE NECK, 1933, A
UP WITH THE LARK, 1943, A
UP YOUR ALLEY, 1975
UP YOUR TEDDY BEAR, 1970, O
UPHEAVAL, THE, 1916
UPLAND RIDER, THE, 1928
UPLIFTERS, THE, 1919
UPPER CRUST, THE, 1917
UPPER HAND, THE, 1967, C
UPPER UNDERWORLD
UPPER WORLD, 1934, A
UPPERCRUST, THE, 1982
UPRISING, 1918
UPS AND DOWNS, 1981
UPSIDE DOWN, 1919
UPSTAGE, 1926
UPSTAIRS, 1919
UPSTAIRS AND DOWN, 1919
UPSTAIRS AND DOWNSTAIRS, 1961, A
UPSTART, THE, 1916

UPSTATE MURDERS, THE
UPSTREAM, 1927
UPTIGHT, 1968, O
UPTOWN NEW YORK, 1932, A
UPTOWN SATURDAY NIGHT, 1974, C
UPTURNED GLASS, THE, 1947, A-C
URANIUM BOOM, 1956, A
URBAN COWBOY, 1980, C
URGE TO KILL, 1960, C
URGENT CALL
URSUS
URSUS, IL GLADIATORE RIBELLE
URUBU, 1948
USCHI DAI SENSO
USED CARS, 1980, O
USURPER, THE, 1919
UTAH, 1945, A
UTAH BLAINE, 1957, A
UTAH KID, THE, 1930, A
UTAH KID, THE, 1944
UTAH TRAIL, 1938, A
UTAH WAGON TRAIN, 1951, A
UTILITIES, 1983, C-O
UTOPIA, 1952, A
UTU, 1984, O

–V–

V.D., 1961, O
V.I.P.s, THE, 1963, A
V1
VACATION DAYS, 1947, A
VACATION FROM LOVE, 1938, A
VACATION FROM MARRIAGE, 1945, A
VACATION IN RENO, 1946, A
VACATION, THE, 1971, C
VADO...L'AMMAZZO E TORNO
VAGABOND CUB, THE, 1929
VAGABOND KING, THE, 1930, A
VAGABOND KING, THE, 1956, A
VAGABOND LADY, 1935, A
VAGABOND LOVER, 1929, A
VAGABOND LUCK, 1919
VAGABOND PRINCE, THE, 1916
VAGABOND QUEEN, THE, 1931, A
VAGABOND TRAIL, THE, 1924
VAGABOND VIOLINIST
VAGABOND'S REVENGE, A, 1915
VAGHE STELLE DELL'ORSA
VALACHI PAPERS, THE, 1972, O
VALDEZ IS COMING, 1971, O
VALENCIA, 1926
VALENTINE GIRL, THE, 1917
VALENTINO, 1951, C
VALENTINO, 1977, C-O
VALERIE, 1957, C
VALIANT HOMBRE THE, 1948, A
VALIANT IS THE WORD FOR CARRIE, 1936, A-C
VALIANT, THE, 1929, A-C
VALIANT, THE, 1962, A
VALIANTS OF VIRGINIA, THE, 1916
VALLEY GIRL, 1983, C
VALLEY OF BLOOD, 1973
VALLEY OF BRAVERY, THE, 1926, A
VALLEY OF DEATH, THE
VALLEY OF DECISION, THE, 1916
VALLEY OF DECISION, THE, 1945, A
VALLEY OF DOUBT, THE, 1920
VALLEY OF EAGLES, 1952, A
VALLEY OF FEAR
VALLEY OF FEAR, 1947
VALLEY OF FEAR, THE, 1916
VALLEY OF FEAR, THE, 1917
VALLEY OF FIRE, 1951, A
VALLEY OF FURY
VALLEY OF GWANGI, THE, 1969, A
VALLEY OF HATE, THE, 1924
VALLEY OF HELL, THE, 1927
VALLEY OF HUNTED MEN, 1942, A
VALLEY OF HUNTED MEN, THE, 1928
VALLEY OF LOST HOPE, THE, 1915
VALLEY OF LOST SOULS, THE, 1923
VALLEY OF MYSTERY, 1967, A
VALLEY OF SILENT MEN, THE, 1922, A
VALLEY OF SONG
VALLEY OF TERROR, 1937
VALLEY OF THE DOLLS, 1967, O
VALLEY OF THE DRAGONS, 1961, A
VALLEY OF THE GHOSTS, 1928
VALLEY OF THE GIANTS, 1938, A
VALLEY OF THE GIANTS, THE, 1919
VALLEY OF THE GIANTS, THE, 1927
VALLEY OF THE HEADHUNTERS, 1953, A
VALLEY OF THE KINGS, 1954, C
VALLEY OF THE LAWLESS, 1936, A
VALLEY OF THE MOON, THE, 1914
VALLEY OF THE REDWOODS, 1960, A
VALLEY OF THE SUN, 1942, A
VALLEY OF THE SWORDS
VALLEY OF THE WHITE WOLVES
VALLEY OF THE ZOMBIES, 1946, C
VALLEY OF TOMORROW, THE, 1920
VALLEY OF VANISHING MEN, THE, 1924

VIOLENT ONES, THE, 1967, C
VIOLENT PLAYGROUND, 1958, A
VIOLENT ROAD, 1958, A
VIOLENT SATURDAY, 1955, O
VIOLENT STRANGER, 1957, A
VIOLENT STREETS
VIOLENT SUMMER, 1961, C
VIOLENT WOMEN, 1960, O
VIOLENT YEARS, THE, 1956, C-O
VIOLENZA PER UNA MONACA
VIOLETTE, 1978, O
VIOLETTES IMPERIALES, 1924
VIOLIN AND ROLLER, 1962, A
VIPER, THE, 1938, A
VIRGIN AND THE GYPSY, THE, 1970, O
VIRGIN AQUA SEX, THE
VIRGIN COCOTTE, THE
VIRGIN FOR THE PRINCE, A
VIRGIN ISLAND, 1960, C
VIRGIN LIPS, 1928
VIRGIN OF NUREMBURG, THE
VIRGIN OF SEMINOLE, THE, 1923
VIRGIN OF STAMBOUL, THE, 1920
VIRGIN PARADISE, A, 1921
VIRGIN PRESIDENT, THE, 1968, A
VIRGIN QUEEN, THE, 1923
VIRGIN QUEEN, THE, 1955, A-C
VIRGIN SACRIFICE, 1959, C
VIRGIN SOLDIERS, THE, 1970, O
VIRGIN SPRING, THE, 1960, C
VIRGIN WIFE, THE, 1926
VIRGIN WITCH, THE, 1973, O
VIRGIN'S SACRIFICE, A, 1922
VIRGIN, THE, 1924
VIRGINIA, 1941, A
VIRGINIA CITY, 1940, A
VIRGINIA COURTSHIP, A, 1921
VIRGINIA JUDGE, THE, 1935, A
VIRGINIA'S HUSBAND, 1928, A
VIRGINIA'S HUSBAND, 1934, AAA
VIRGINIAN OUTCAST, 1924
VIRGINIAN, THE, 1914, A
VIRGINIAN, THE, 1923, A
VIRGINIAN, THE, 1929, A
VIRGINIAN, THE, 1946, A-C
VIRIDIANA, 1962, C-O
VIRTOUS SINNERS, 1919
VIRTUE, 1932, C
VIRTUE'S REVOLT, 1924
VIRTUOUS HUSBAND, 1931, A
VIRTUOUS LIARS, 1924
VIRTUOUS MEN, 1919
VIRTUOUS MODEL, THE, 1919
VIRTUOUS OUTCAST, THE
VIRTUOUS SIN, THE, 1930, A
VIRTUOUS THIEF, THE, 1919
VIRTUOUS TRAMPS, THE
VIRTUOUS VAMP, A, 1919
VIRTUOUS WIFE, THE
VIRTUOUS WIVES, 1919
VIRUS, 1980, C
VISA TO CANTON
VISAGE D'ENFANTS, 1926
VISAGES VIOLES...AMES CLOSES, 1921
VISCOUNT, THE, 1967, C
VISIT TO A CHIEF'S SON, 1974, AA
VISIT TO A SMALL PLANET, 1960, A
VISIT, THE, 1964, C
VISITING HOURS, 1982, O
VISITOR, THE, 1973, C-O
VISITOR, THE, 1980, O
VISITORS FROM THE GALAXY, 1981, AA
VISITORS, THE, 1972, O
VISKINGAR OCH ROP
VITA PRIVATA
VITAL QUESTION, THE, 1916
VITE PERDUTE
VITELLONI, 1956, C
VIVA CISCO KID, 1940, A
VIVA ITALIA, 1978, O
VIVA KNIEVEL?, 1977, A
VIVA LAS VEGAS
VIVA LAS VEGAS, 1964, A
VIVA MARIA, 1965, C
VIVA MAX?, 1969, A
VIVA VILLA!, 1934, A-C
VIVA ZAPATA!, 1952, C
VIVACIOUS LADY, 1938, A
VIVE LA FRANCE, 1918
VIVEMENT DIMANCHE?
VIVERE PER VIVERE
VIVIAMO OGGI
VIVIETTE, 1918
VIVIR DESVIVIENDOSE
VIVO PER LA TUA MORTE
VIVRE, 1928
VIVRE POUR VIVRE
VIVRE SA VIE
VIXEN, 1970, O
VIXEN, THE, 1916
VIXENS, THE, 1969, O
VOGUES

VOGUES OF 1938, 1937, A
VOICE FROM THE MINARET, THE, 1923
VOICE IN THE DARK, 1921, A
VOICE IN THE MIRROR, 1958, A
VOICE IN THE NIGHT
VOICE IN THE NIGHT, 1934, A
VOICE IN THE NIGHT, A, 1941, A
VOICE IN THE WIND, 1944, A
VOICE IN YOUR HEART, A, 1952, C
VOICE OF BUGLE ANN, 1936, A
VOICE OF CONSCIENCE, THE, 1917
VOICE OF DESTINY, THE, 1918
VOICE OF LOVE, THE, 1916
VOICE OF MERRILL, THE
VOICE OF TERROR
VOICE OF THE CITY, 1929, A
VOICE OF THE HURRICANE, 1964, A
VOICE OF THE STORM, THE, 1929
VOICE OF THE TURTLE, THE, 1947, A
VOICE OF THE WHISTLER, 1945, C
VOICE OVER, 1983
VOICE WITHIN, THE, 1929
VOICE WITHIN, THE, 1945, A
VOICES, 1920
VOICES, 1973, O
VOICES, 1979, C
VOICES FROM THE PAST, 1915
VOLCANO, 1926, A
VOLCANO, 1953, A
VOLCANO, 1969
VOLCANO, THE, 1919
VOLGA AND SIBERIA, 1914
VOLGA BOATMAN, THE, 1926, A
VOLONTE, 1917
VOLPONE, 1947, A
VOLTAIRE, 1933, A
VOLUNTEER ORGANIST, THE, 1914
VOLUNTEER, THE, 1918
VON RICHTHOFEN AND BROWN, 1970, C
VON RYAN'S EXPRESS, 1965
VOODOO BLOOD BATH
VOODOO GIRL
VOODOO HEARTBEAT, 1972, O
VOODOO ISLAND, 1957, A
VOODOO MAN, 1944, A
VOODOO TIGER, 1952, A
VOODOO WOMAN, 1957, A
VOR SONNENUNTERGANG, 1961, A
VORTEX
VORTEX, 1982, O
VORTEX OF FATE, THE, 1913
VORTEX, THE, 1918
VORTEX, THE, 1927, A
VOSKRESENIYE
VOTE FOR HUGGETT, 1948, A
VOULEZ-VOUS DANSER AVEC MOI
VOW OF VENGEANCE, THE, 1923
VOW, THE, 1915
VOW, THE, 1947, A
VOYAGE BEYOND THE SUN
VOYAGE IN A BALLOON
VOYAGE OF SILENCE, 1968, A
VOYAGE OF THE DAMNED, 1976, A-C
VOYAGE TO AMERICA, 1952, A
VOYAGE TO PREHISTORY
VOYAGE TO THE BOTTOM OF THE SEA, 1961, A
VOYAGE TO THE END OF THE UNIVERSE, 1963, A
VOYAGE TO THE PLANET OF PREHISTORIC
   WOMEN, 1966, A
VOYAGE TO THE PREHISTORIC PLANET, 1965, A
VOYAGE, THE, 1974, 0
VOYNA I MIR
VRAZDA PO CESKU
VRAZDA PO NASEM
VREDENS DAG
VROODER'S HOOCH
VU DU PONT
VULCAN AFFAIR, THE
VULCANO
VULGAR YACHTSMEN, THE, 1926
VULTURE OF GOLD, THE, 1914
VULTURE, THE, 1937, A
VULTURE, THE, 1967, C
VULTURES IN PARADISE, 1984
VULTURES OF SOCIETY, 1916
VULTURES OF THE LAW
VYNALEZ ZKAZY
VZROSLYYE DETI

-W-

W, 1974, C
W. W. AND THE DIXIE DANCEKINGS, 1975, A
W.C. FIELDS AND ME, 1976, C
W.I.A. (WOUNDED IN ACTION), 1966, A
"W" PLAN, THE, 1931, A
WABASH AVENUE, 1950, A
WAC FROM WALLA WALLA, THE, 1952, A
WACKIEST SHIP IN THE ARMY, THE, 1961, A
WACKIEST WAGON TRAIN IN THE WEST, THE,
   1976, A
WACKO, 1983, C
WACKY WORLD OF DR. MORGUS, THE, 1962, A

WACKY WORLD OF MOTHER GOOSE, THE,,
   1967, AAA
WACO, 1952, A
WACO, 1966, C
WAGA KOI WAGA UTA
WAGER, THE, 1916
WAGES FOR WIVES, 1925, A
WAGES OF CONSCIENCE, 1927
WAGES OF FEAR, 1977
WAGES OF FEAR, THE, 1955, O
WAGES OF SIN, THE, 1918
WAGES OF SIN, THE, 1922
WAGES OF SIN, THE, 1929
WAGES OF VIRTUE, 1924
WAGNER, 1983, C-O
WAGON MASTER, THE, 1929, A
WAGON SHOW, THE, 1928
WAGON TEAM, 1952, A
WAGON TRACKS, 1919
WAGON TRACKS WEST, 1943, A
WAGON TRAIL, 1935, A
WAGON TRAIN, 1940, A
WAGON TRAIN, 1952
WAGON WHEELS, 1934, A
WAGON WHEELS WESTWARD, 1956, AA
WAGONMASTER, 1950, A
WAGONS ROLL AT NIGHT, THE, 1941, A
WAGONS WEST, 1952, A
WAGONS WESTWARD, 1940, A
WAHINE
WAIF, THE, 1915
WAIFS, 1918
WAIFS, THE, 1916
WAIKIKI WEDDING, 1937, A
WAIT 'TIL THE SUN SHINES, NELLIE, 1952, A
WAIT AND SEE, 1928
WAIT UNTIL DARK, 1967, O
WAITING AT THE CHURCH
WAITING FOR CAROLINE, 1969, C
WAITING FOR THE BRIDE
WAITING SOUL, THE, 1917
WAITING WOMEN
WAITRESS, 1982, O
WAJAN, 1938, A
WAKAMBA?, 1955, AA
WAKAMONO TACHI
WAKARE
WAKARETE IKURU TOKI MO
WAKE ISLAND, 1942, A
WAKE ME WHEN IT'S OVER, 1960, A
WAKE OF THE RED WITCH, 1949, A-C
WAKE UP AND DIE, 1967, C
WAKE UP AND DREAM, 1934, A
WAKE UP AND DREAM, 1946, A
WAKE UP AND DREAM, 1942
WAKE UP AND LIVE, 1937, AA
WAKE UP FAMOUS, 1937, A
WAKEFIELD CASE, THE, 1921
WAKING UP THE TOWN, 1925
WALK A CROOKED MILE, 1948, A
WALK A CROOKED PATH, 1969, O
WALK A TIGHTROPE, 1964, A-C
WALK CHEERFULLY, 1930
WALK EAST ON BEACON, 1952, A
WALK IN THE SHADOW, 1966, A
WALK IN THE SPRING RAIN, A, 1970, C
WALK IN THE SUN, A, 1945, C
WALK INTO HELL, 1957, A
WALK LIKE A DRAGON, 1960, O
WALK ON THE WILD SIDE, 1962, O
WALK PROUD, 1979, C
WALK SOFTLY, STRANGER, 1950, A
WALK TALL, 1960, A
WALK THE ANGRY BEACH, 1961, C
WALK THE DARK STREET, 1956, C
WALK THE PROUD LAND, 1956, A
WALK THE WALK, 1970, O
WALK WITH LOVE AND DEATH, A, 1969, C
WALK, DON'T RUN, 1966, A
WALK-OFFS, THE, 1920
WALKABOUT, 1971, C
WALKING BACK, 1928, A
WALKING DEAD, THE, 1936, A
WALKING DOWN BROADWAY, 1938, A
WALKING DOWN BROADWAY, 1935
WALKING HILLS, THE, 1949, A
WALKING MY BABY BACK HOME, 1953, A
WALKING ON AIR, 1936, A
WALKING ON AIR, 1946, AAA
WALKING STICK, THE, 1970, C
WALKING TALL, 1973, O
WALKING TALL, PART II, 1975, O
WALKING TARGET, THE, 1960, C
WALKOVER, 1969, C
WALKOWER
WALL BETWEEN, THE, 1916
WALL FLOWER, THE, 1922, A
WALL FOR SAN SEBASTIAN
WALL OF NOISE, 1963, A
WALL STREET, 1929, A
WALL STREET COWBOY, 1939, A
WALL STREET MYSTERY, THE, 1920

WALL STREET TRAGEDY, A, 1916
WALL STREET WHIZ, THE, 1925
WALL, THE
WALL-EYED NIPPON, 1963, A
WALLABY JIM OF THE ISLANDS, 1937, A
WALLET, THE, 1952, A
WALLFLOWER, 1948, A
WALLFLOWER, THE
WALLFLOWERS, 1928
WALLOP, THE, 1921, A
WALLOPING KID, 1926
WALLOPING WALLACE, 1924, A
WALLS CAME TUMBLING DOWN, THE, 1946, A
WALLS OF GOLD, 1933, C
WALLS OF HELL, THE, 1964, A
WALLS OF JERICHO, 1948, C
WALLS OF JERICHO, THE, 1914
WALLS OF MALAPAGA, THE, 1950, A
WALLS OF PREJUDICE, 1920, A
WALPURGIS NIGHT, 1941, A-C
WALTZ ACROSS TEXAS, 1982, A-C
WALTZ DREAM, A, 1926
WALTZ OF THE TOREADORS, 1962, A-C
WALTZ TIME, 1933, A
WALTZ TIME, 1946, A
WALTZES FROM VIENNA
WANDA, 1971, C
WANDA NEVADA, 1979, A-C
WANDER LOVE STORY
WANDERER BEYOND THE GRAVE, 1915
WANDERER OF THE WASTELAND, 1924
WANDERER OF THE WASTELAND, 1935, A
WANDERER OF THE WASTELAND, 1945, A
WANDERER OF THE WEST, 1927
WANDERER, THE, 1926
WANDERER, THE, 1969, A
WANDERERS OF THE WEST, 1941, A
WANDERERS, THE, 1979, O
WANDERING DAUGHTERS, 1923
WANDERING FIRES, 1925
WANDERING FOOTSTEPS, 1925
WANDERING GIRLS, 1927, A
WANDERING HUSBANDS, 1924
WANDERING JEW, THE, 1913
WANDERING JEW, THE, 1923
WANDERING JEW, THE, 1933, A
WANDERING JEW, THE, 1935, A
WANDERING JEW, THE, 1948, O
WANDERING STARS, 1927
WANDERLOVE, 1970, O
WANDERLUST
WANING SEX, THE, 1926, A
WANT A RIDE LITTLE GIRL?
WANTED, 1937, A
WANTED—A BROTHER, 1918
WANTED—A HOME, 1916
WANTED—A HUSBAND, 1919
WANTED—A MOTHER, 1918
WANTED—A WIDOW, 1916
WANTED—A WIFE, 1918
WANTED AT HEADQUARTERS, 1920
WANTED BY SCOTLAND YARD, 1939, A
WANTED BY THE LAW, 1924
WANTED BY THE POLICE, 1938, A
WANTED DEAD OR ALIVE, 1951
WANTED FOR MURDER, 1919, A
WANTED FOR MURDER, 1946, C
WANTED FOR MURDER, OR BRIDE OF HATE
WANTED MEN, 1931
WANTED MEN, 1936
WANTED WOMEN
WANTED, 1929
WANTED, 1933
WANTED—A COWARD, 1927, A
WANTED: JANE TURNER, 1936, A
WANTERS, THE, 1923, A
WANTON CONTESSA, THE
WAR
WAR AGAINST MRS. HADLEY, THE, 1942, A
WAR AND PEACE, 1915
WAR AND PEACE, 1956, A-C
WAR AND PEACE, 1968, A-C
WAR AND PEACE, 1983, C
WAR AND PIECE
WAR AND THE WOMAN, 1917
WAR ARROW, 1953, A
WAR BETWEEN MEN AND WOMEN, THE, 1972, A-C
WAR BETWEEN THE PLANETS, 1971, A
WAR BRIDE'S SECRET, THE, 1916
WAR BRIDES, 1916
WAR CORRESPONDENT, 1932, A
WAR DOGS, 1942, A
WAR DRUMS, 1957, A
WAR EXTRA, THE, 1914
WAR GAMES, 1970
WAR GAMES, 1983
WAR GODS OF THE DEEP
WAR HEAD
WAR HERO, WAR MADNESS
WAR HORSE, THE, 1927, A
WAR HUNT, 1962, C
WAR IS A RACKET, 1934, A-C

WAR IS HELL, 1964, A-C
WAR IS OVER, THE
WAR ITALIAN STYLE, 1967, A
WAR LORD, THE, 1965, O
WAR LORD, THE, 1937
WAR LOVER, THE, 1962, C-O
WAR MADNESS
WAR NURSE, 1930, A
WAR OF THE ALIENS
WAR OF THE BUTTONS, 1963, A
WAR OF THE COLOSSAL BEAST, 1958, A
WAR OF THE GARGANTUAS, THE, 1970, A
WAR OF THE MONSTERS, 1972, A
WAR OF THE PLANETS, 1977, A
WAR OF THE RANGE, 1933, A
WAR OF THE SATELLITES, 1958, A
WAR OF THE TONGS, THE, 1917
WAR OF THE WILDCATS
WAR OF THE WIZARDS, 1983, C
WAR OF THE WORLDS, THE, 1953, C
WAR OF THE WORLDS—NEXT CENTURY, THE,
1981, C
WAR OF THE ZOMBIES, THE, 1965, C-O
WAR PAINT, 1926, A
WAR PAINT, 1953, A
WAR PARTY, 1965, A
WAR SHOCK
WAR WAGON, THE, 1967, A
WAR'S WOMEN, 1916
WAR'S WOMEN, 1923
WARD 13
WARE CASE, THE, 1917, A
WARE CASE, THE, 1928
WARE CASE, THE, 1939, A
WARFARE OF THE FLESH, THE, 1917
WARGAMES, 1983, A
WARHEAD, 1974
WARKILL, 1968, O
WARLOCK, 1959, C
WARLOCK MOON, 1973
WARLORD OF CRETE, THE
WARLORDS OF ATLANTIS, 1978, AA
WARLORDS OF THE 21ST CENTURY
WARLORDS OF THE DEEP
WARM BODY, THE
WARM CORNER, A, 1930, AA
WARM DECEMBER, A, 1973, C
WARM IN THE BUD, 1970, A
WARMING UP, 1928, A
WARN LONDON?, 1934, A
WARN THAT MAN, 1943, A
WARNED OFF, 1928
WARNING FORM SPACE
WARNING SHADOWS, 1924
WARNING SHOT, 1967, A-C
WARNING SIGNAL, THE, 1926
WARNING TO WANTONS, A, 1949, A
WARNING, THE, 1915
WARNING, THE, 1927, A
WARNING, THE, 1928
WARPATH, 1951, A
WARREN CASE, THE, 1934, A
WARRENS OF VIRGINIA, THE, 1915, A
WARRENS OF VIRGINIA, THE, 1924, A
WARRING CLANS, 1963, C
WARRING MILLIONS, THE, 1915
WARRIOR AND THE SLAVE GIRL, THE, 1959, A
WARRIOR AND THE SORCERESS, THE, 1984, O
WARRIOR EMPRESS, THE, 1961, O
WARRIOR GAP, 1925
WARRIOR STRAIN, THE, 1919
WARRIOR'S HUSBAND THE, 1933, C
WARRIORS FIVE, 1962, A
WARRIORS OF THE WASTELAND, 1984, O
WARRIORS OF THE WIND, 1984, C
WARRIORS, THE, 1955, A-C
WARRIORS, THE, 1979, O
WARRIORS, THE, 1970
WAS HE GUILTY?, 1927
WAS IT BIGAMY?, 1925, A
WAS SHE GUILTY?, 1922
WAS SHE JUSTIFIED?, 1922
WAS SHE TO BLAME?, 1915
WASHINGTON AFFAIR, THE, 1978
WASHINGTON AT VALLEY FORGE, 1914, A
WASHINGTON B.C.
WASHINGTON COWBOY
WASHINGTON MASQUERADE, 1932, A
WASHINGTON MELODRAMA, 1941, A
WASHINGTON MERRY-GO-ROUND, 1932, A
WASHINGTON STORY, 1952, A
WASP WOMAN, THE, 1959, A
WASP, THE, 1918
WASTED LIVES, 1923
WASTED LIVES, 1925, A
WASTED LOVE, 1930
WASTED YEARS, THE, 1916
WASTER, THE, 1926
WASTREL, THE, 1963, C
WASTRELS, THE
WATASHI GA SUTETA ONNA
WATCH BEVERLY, 1932, A

WATCH HIM STEP, 1922, A
WATCH IT, SAILOR?, 1961, A
WATCH ON THE RHINE, 1943, A
WATCH THE BIRDIE, 1950, A
WATCH YOUR STEP, 1922, A
WATCH YOUR STERN, 1961, A
WATCH YOUR WIFE, 1926, A
WATCHED, 1974, O
WATCHER IN THE WOODS, THE, 1980, C
WATCHING EYES, 1921, A
WATER BABIES, THE, 1979, AAA
WATER CYBORGS
WATER FOR CANITOGA, 1939, A
WATER GIPSIES, THE
WATER GYPSIES, THE, 1932, A
WATER HOLE, THE, 1928
WATER LILY, THE, 1919
WATER RUSTLERS, 1939, A
WATER, WATER, EVERYWHERE, 1920
WATERFRONT, 1928
WATERFRONT, 1939, A
WATERFRONT, 1944, A
WATERFRONT AT MIDNIGHT, 1948, A
WATERFRONT LADY, 1935, A
WATERFRONT WOLVES, 1924
WATERFRONT WOMEN, 1952, A
WATERFRONT, 1952
WATERHOLE NO. 3, 1967, C
WATERLOO, 1970, C
WATERLOO BRIDGE, 1940
WATERLOO BRIDGE, 1931, C
WATERLOO ROAD, 1949, A
WATERMELON MAN, 1970, C
WATERSHIP DOWN, 1978, C-O
WATTS MONSTER, THE
WATUSI, 1959, A
WATUSI A GO-GO
WAVE, A WAC AND A MARINE, A, 1944, A
WAVELENGTH, 1983, C
WAX MODEL, THE, 1917
WAXWORKS, 1924
WAY AHEAD, THE, 1945, A
WAY BACK HOME, 1932, A
WAY BACK, THE, 1915
WAY DOWN EAST, 1920, A
WAY DOWN EAST, 1935, A
WAY DOWN SOUTH, 1939, A
WAY FOR A SAILOR, 1930, A
WAY MEN LOVE, THE
WAY OF A GAUCHO, 1952, A
WAY OF A GIRL, THE, 1925
WAY OF A MAID, THE, 1921, A
WAY OF A MAN WITH A MAID, THE, 1918
WAY OF A MAN, THE, 1921
WAY OF A WOMAN, 1919, A
WAY OF A WOMAN, THE, 1925
WAY OF ALL FLESH, THE, 1927, A
WAY OF ALL FLESH, THE, 1940, A
WAY OF ALL MEN, THE, 1930, A
WAY OF AN EAGLE, THE, 1918, A
WAY OF LIFE, THE
WAY OF LOST SOULS, THE, 1929, C
WAY OF THE STRONG, THE, 1919
WAY OF THE STRONG, THE, 1928, A
WAY OF THE TRANSGRESSOR, THE, 1923
WAY OF THE WEST, THE, 1934, A
WAY OF THE WORLD, THE, 1916
WAY OF THE WORLD, THE, 1920
WAY OF YOUTH, THE, 1934, A
WAY OUT, 1966, O
WAY OUT LOVE
WAY OUT WEST, 1930, A
WAY OUT WEST, 1937, AAA
WAY OUT, THE, 1918
WAY OUT, THE, 1956, A
WAY OUT, WAY IN, 1970, O
WAY TO LOVE, THE, 1933, A
WAY TO THE GOLD, THE, 1957, A
WAY TO THE STARS, THE
WAY WE LIVE NOW, THE, 1970, O
WAY WE LIVE, THE, 1946, A
WAY WE WERE, THE, 1973, C
WAY WEST, THE, 1967, A
WAY WOMEN LOVE, THE, 1920
WAY...WAY OUT, 1966, C-O
WAYLAID WOMEN
WAYS OF LOVE, 1950, C-O
WAYS OF THE WORLD, THE, 1915
WAYSIDE PEBBLE, THE, 1962, A
WAYWARD, 1932, A
WAYWARD BUS, THE, 1957, C
WAYWARD GIRL, THE, 1957, A
WE ACCUSE
WE AMERICANS, 1928
WE ARE ALL MURDERERS, 1957, C
WE ARE ALL NAKED, 1970, O
WE ARE IN THE NAVY NOW
WE ARE NOT ALONE, 1939, A-C
WE CAN'T HAVE EVERYTHING, 1918
WE DIVE AT DAWN, 1943, A
WE GO FAST, 1941, A
WE HAVE ONLY ONE LIFE, 1963, A

WE HAVE OUR MOMENTS, 1937, A
WE HUMANS
WE JOINED THE NAVY, 1962, A
WE LIVE AGAIN, 1934, C
WE MODERNS, 1925
WE OF THE NEVER NEVER, 1983, C
WE SHALL RETURN, 1963, A
WE SHALL SEE, 1964, C
WE SHOULD WORRY, 1918
WE STILL KILL THE OLD WAY, 1967, C
WE THREE
WE WANT TO LIVE ALONE
WE WENT TO COLLEGE, 1936, A
WE WERE DANCING, 1942, A
WE WERE STRANGERS, 1949, C
WE WHO ARE ABOUT TO DIE, 1937, A
WE WHO ARE YOUNG, 1940, A-C
WE WILL REMEMBER, 1966, C-O
WE WOMEN, 1925
WE'LL GROW THIN TOGETHER, 1979, C
WE'LL MEET AGAIN, 1942
WE'LL SMILE AGAIN, 1942, A
WE'RE ALL GAMBLERS, 1927, A
WE'RE GOING TO BE RICH, 1938, A
WE'RE IN THE ARMY NOW
WE'RE IN THE LEGION NOW, 1937, A
WE'RE IN THE MONEY, 1935, A
WE'RE IN THE NAVY NOW, 1926
WE'RE NO ANGELS, 1955, A-C
WE'RE NOT DRESSING, 1934, A
WE'RE NOT MARRIED, 1952, A
WE'RE ON THE JURY, 1937, A
WE'RE ONLY HUMAN, 1936, A
WE'RE RICH AGAIN, 1934, A
WE'VE GOT THE DEVIL ON THE RUN, 1934
WE'VE NEVER BEEN LICKED, 1943, A
WEAK AND THE WICKED, THE, 1954, A
WEAKER SEX, THE, 1917
WEAKER SEX, THE, 1949, A
WEAKER VESSEL, THE, 1919
WEAKNESS OF MAN, THE, 1916
WEAKNESS OF STRENGTH, THE, 1916
WEALTH, 1921, A
WEAPON, THE, 1957, C
WEAPONS OF DEATH, 1982
WEARY DEATH, THE
WEARY RIVER, 1929, A
WEATHER IN THE STREETS, THE, 1983, C
WEAVER OF DREAMS, 1918
WEAVERS OF FORTUNE, 1922, A
WEAVERS OF LIFE, 1917
WEB OF CHANCE, THE, 1919
WEB OF DANGER, THE, 1947, A
WEB OF DECEIT, THE, 1920
WEB OF DESIRE, THE, 1917
WEB OF EVIDENCE
WEB OF FATE, 1927, A
WEB OF FEAR, 1966, C
WEB OF LIFE, THE, 1917
WEB OF PASSION, 1961, C
WEB OF SUSPICION, 1959, A
WEB OF THE LAW, THE, 1923, A
WEB OF THE SPIDER, 1972, O
WEB OF VIOLENCE, 1966, C
WEB, THE, 1947, A
WEBS OF STEEL, 1925
WEBSTER BOY, THE, 1962, A
WEDDING BELLS
WEDDING BELLS, 1921
WEDDING BILL, 1927, A
WEDDING BREAKFAST
WEDDING GROUP
WEDDING IN WHITE, 1972, O
WEDDING MARCH, THE, 1927, A
WEDDING NIGHT, 1970, O
WEDDING NIGHT, THE, 1935, A
WEDDING OF LILLI MARLENE, THE, 1953, A
WEDDING ON THE VOLGA, THE, 1929
WEDDING PARTY, THE, 1969, O
WEDDING PRESENT, 1936, A
WEDDING PRESENT, 1963
WEDDING REHEARSAL, 1932, A
WEDDING RINGS, 1930, A
WEDDING SONG, THE, 1925, A
WEDDING, A, 1978, C
WEDDINGS AND BABIES, 1960, A
WEDDINGS ARE WONDERFUL, 1938, A
WEDLOCK, 1918
WEDNESDAY CHILDREN, THE, 1973, C
WEDNESDAY'S CHILD
WEDNESDAY'S CHILD, 1934, A
WEDNESDAY'S LUCK, 1936, A
WEE GEORDIE, 1956, A
WEE LADY BETTY, 1917
WEE MACGREGOR'S SWEETHEART, THE, 1922
WEE WILLIE WINKIE, 1937, AA
WEEK END HUSBANDS, 1924
WEEK-END MADNESS
WEEK-END MARRIAGE, 1932, A
WEEK-END, THE, 1920
WEEK-ENDS ONLY, 1932, A
WEEKEND, 1964, C

WEEKEND, 1968, O
WEEKEND A ZUYDCOOTE
WEEKEND AT DUNKIRK, 1966, A
WEEKEND AT THE WALDORF, 1945, A
WEEKEND BABYSITTER
WEEKEND FOR THREE, 1941, A
WEEKEND IN HAVANA, 1941, A
WEEKEND LOVER, 1969
WEEKEND MILLIONAIRE, 1937, A
WEEKEND MURDERS, THE, 1972, O
WEEKEND OF FEAR, 1966, C
WEEKEND OF SHADOWS, 1978, C
WEEKEND PASS, 1944, A
WEEKEND PASS, 1984, A
WEEKEND WITH FATHER, 1951, A
WEEKEND WITH LULU, A, 1961, A
WEEKEND WITH THE BABYSITTER, 1970, O
WEEKEND WIVES
WEEKEND WIVES, 1928, A
WEEKEND, ITALIAN STYLE, 1967, A
WEIRD LOVE MAKERS, THE, 1963, O
WEIRD ONES, THE, 1962, C
WEIRD WOMAN, 1944, A
WELCOME CHILDREN, 1921, A
WELCOME DANGER, 1929, A
WELCOME HOME
WELCOME HOME, 1925
WELCOME HOME, 1935, A
WELCOME HOME, BROTHER CHARLES, 1975
WELCOME HOME, SOLDIER BOYS, 1972, O
WELCOME KOSTYA?, 1965, AA
WELCOME STRANGER, 1924, A
WELCOME STRANGER, 1947, A
WELCOME STRANGER, 1941
WELCOME TO ARROW BEACH
WELCOME TO BLOOD CITY, 1977, O
WELCOME TO HARD TIMES, 1967, O
WELCOME TO L.A., 1976, O
WELCOME TO OUR CITY, 1922
WELCOME TO THE CLUB, 1971, O
WELCOME, MR. BEDDOES
WELCOME, MR. WASHINGTON, 1944, A
WELL DONE, HENRY, 1936, A
WELL, THE, 1951, A
WELL-DIGGER'S DAUGHTER, THE, 1946, C
WELL-GROOMED BRIDE, THE, 1946, A
WELLS FARGO, 1937, A
WELLS FARGO GUNMASTER, 1951, A
WELSH SINGER, A, 1915, A
WENT THE DAY WELL?
WEREWOLF IN A GIRL'S DORMITORY, 1961, C-O
WEREWOLF OF LONDON, THE, 1935, C
WEREWOLF OF WASHINGTON, 1973, C
WEREWOLF VS. THE VAMPIRE WOMAN, THE, 1970, O
WEREWOLF, THE, 1956, C-O
WEREWOLVES ON WHEELS, 1971, O
WEST 11, 1963, C
WEST IS EAST
WEST IS STILL WILD, THE, 1977
WEST IS WEST, 1920
WEST OF ABILENE, 1940, A
WEST OF ARIZONA, 1925
WEST OF BROADWAY, 1926
WEST OF BROADWAY, 1931, A
WEST OF CARSON CITY, 1940, A
WEST OF CHEYENNE, 1931, A
WEST OF CHEYENNE, 1938, A
WEST OF CHICAGO, 1922, A
WEST OF CHICAGO, 1922, A
WEST OF CIMARRON, 1941, A
WEST OF DODGE CITY, 1947
WEST OF EL DORADO, 1949, A
WEST OF MONTANA
WEST OF NEVADA, 1936, A
WEST OF PARADISE, 1928
WEST OF PINTO BASIN, 1940, A
WEST OF RAINBOW'S END, 1938, A
WEST OF SANTA FE, 1928, A
WEST OF SANTA FE, 1938, A
WEST OF SHANGHAI, 1937, A
WEST OF SINGAPORE, 1933, A
WEST OF SONORA, 1948, A
WEST OF SUEZ
WEST OF TEXAS, 1943, A
WEST OF THE ALAMO, 1946, A
WEST OF THE BRAZOS, 1950, A
WEST OF THE DIVIDE, 1934, A
WEST OF THE GREAT DIVIDE
WEST OF THE LAW, 1926, A
WEST OF THE LAW, 1942, A
WEST OF THE MOJAVE, 1925
WEST OF THE PECOS, 1922
WEST OF THE PECOS, 1935, A-C
WEST OF THE PECOS, 1945, A
WEST OF THE RAINBOW'S END, 1926, A
WEST OF THE RIO GRANDE, 1921
WEST OF THE RIO GRANDE, 1944
WEST OF THE ROCKIES, 1929, A
WEST OF THE ROCKIES, 1931, A
WEST OF THE SACRED GEM, THE, 1914
WEST OF THE SUEZ

WEST OF THE WATER TOWER, 1924
WEST OF TOMBSTONE, 1942, A
WEST OF WYOMING, 1950, A
WEST OF ZANZIBAR, 1928, A
WEST OF ZANZIBAR, 1954, A
WEST ON PARADE, 1934
WEST POINT, 1928, A
WEST POINT OF THE AIR, 1935, A
WEST POINT STORY, THE, 1950, A
WEST POINT WIDOW, 1941, A
WEST SIDE KID, 1943, A
WEST SIDE STORY, 1961, A-C
WEST TO GLORY, 1947, A
WEST VS. EAST, 1922
WESTBOUND, 1924, A
WESTBOUND, 1959, A
WESTBOUND LIMITED, 1937, A
WESTBOUND LIMITED, THE, 1923
WESTBOUND MAIL, 1937, A
WESTBOUND STAGE, 1940, A
WESTERN ADVENTURER, A, 1921
WESTERN BLOOD, 1918
WESTERN BLOOD, 1923
WESTERN CARAVANS, 1939, A
WESTERN CODE, 1932
WESTERN COURAGE, 1927, A
WESTERN COURAGE, 1935, A
WESTERN CYCLONE, 1943, A
WESTERN DEMON, A, 1922, A
WESTERN ENGAGEMENT, A, 1925
WESTERN FATE, 1924, A
WESTERN FEUDS, 1924
WESTERN FIREBRANDS, 1921, A
WESTERN FRONTIER, 1935, A
WESTERN GOLD, 1937, A
WESTERN GOVERNOR'S HUMANITY, A, 1915
WESTERN GRIT, 1924
WESTERN HEARTS, 1921, A
WESTERN HERITAGE, 1948, A
WESTERN HONOR
WESTERN JAMBOREE, 1938, A
WESTERN JUSTICE, 1923
WESTERN JUSTICE, 1935, A
WESTERN LIMITED, 1932, A
WESTERN LUCK, 1924, A
WESTERN MAIL, 1942, A
WESTERN METHODS, 1929
WESTERN MUSKETEER, THE, 1922, A
WESTERN PACIFIC AGENT, 1950, A
WESTERN PLUCK, 1926
WESTERN PROMISE, 1925
WESTERN RACKETEERS, 1935
WESTERN RENEGADES, 1949, A
WESTERN ROVER, THE, 1927, A
WESTERN SPEED, 1922
WESTERN THOROUGHBRED, A, 1922
WESTERN TRAILS, 1926
WESTERN TRAILS, 1938, A
WESTERN UNION, 1941, A
WESTERN VENGEANCE, 1924, A
WESTERN WALLOP, THE, 1924
WESTERN WHIRLWIND, THE, 1927, A
WESTERN YESTERDAYS, 1924
WESTERNER, THE, 1936, A
WESTERNER, THE, 1940, A
WESTERNERS, THE, 1919
WESTLAND CASE, THE, 1937, A
WESTMINSTER PASSION PLAY—BEHOLD THE MAN, THE, 1951, A
WESTWARD BOUND, 1931, A
WESTWARD BOUND, 1944, A
WESTWARD DESPERADO, 1961, C
WESTWARD HO, 1919
WESTWARD HO, 1936, A
WESTWARD HO, 1942, A
WESTWARD HO THE WAGONS?, 1956, A
WESTWARD PASSAGE, 1932, A
WESTWARD THE WOMEN, 1951, A
WESTWARD TRAIL, THE, 1948, A
WESTWORLD, 1973, C
WET GOLD, 1921, A
WET PAINT, 1926, A
WET PARADE, THE, 1932, C
WETBACKS, 1956, A
WHALE OF A TALE, A, 1977, AAA
WHALERS, THE, 1942, A
WHARF ANGEL, 1934, A
WHARF RAT, THE, 1916
WHAT A BLONDE, 1945, A
WHAT A CARRY ON?, 1949, A
WHAT A CARVE UP?, 1962, A
WHAT A CHASSIS?
WHAT A CRAZY WORLD, 1963, A
WHAT A LIFE, 1939, A
WHAT A MAN, 1930, A
WHAT A MAN, 1941
WHAT A MAN?, 1937, A
WHAT A MAN?, 1944, A
WHAT A NIGHT, 1928, A
WHAT A NIGHT?, 1931, A
WHAT A WAY TO GO, 1964, A-C
WHAT A WHOPPER, 1961, A

WHERE THERE'S A WILL, 1937, A
WHERE THERE'S A WILL, 1955, A
WHERE THERE'S LIFE, 1947, A
WHERE TRAILS BEGIN, 1927
WHERE TRAILS DIVIDE, 1937, A
WHERE TRAILS END, 1942
WHERE WAS I?, 1925
WHERE WERE YOU WHEN THE LIGHTS WENT
   OUT?, 1968, A-C
WHERE'S CHARLEY?, 1952, AA
WHERE'S GEORGE?
WHERE'S JACK?, 1969, A
WHERE'S POPPA?, 1970, C-O
WHERE'S SALLY?, 1936, A
WHERE'S THAT FIRE?, 1939, A
WHERE'S WILLIE?, 1978
WHEREVER SHE GOES, 1953, A
WHICH SHALL IT BE?, 1924
WHICH WAY IS UP?, 1977, O
WHICH WAY TO THE FRONT?, 1970, A
WHICH WILL YOU HAVE?
WHICH WOMAN?, 1918
WHIFFS, 1975, A
WHILE FIRE RAGED, 1914
WHILE I LIVE, 1947, A
WHILE JUSTICE WAITS, 1922
WHILE LONDON SLEEPS
WHILE LONDON SLEEPS, 1922
WHILE LONDON SLEEPS, 1926
WHILE NEW YORK SLEEPS, 1920, A
WHILE NEW YORK SLEEPS, 1938, A
WHILE NEW YORK SLEEPS, 1934
WHILE PARENTS SLEEP, 1935, A
WHILE PARIS SLEEPS, 1923
WHILE PARIS SLEEPS, 1932, A
WHILE PLUCKING THE DAISIES
WHILE SATAN SLEEPS, 1922, A
WHILE THE ATTORNEY IS ASLEEP, 1945, A
WHILE THE CITY SLEEPS, 1928, A
WHILE THE CITY SLEEPS, 1956, C
WHILE THE DEVIL LAUGHS, 1921
WHILE THE PATIENT SLEPT, 1935, A
WHILE THE SUN SHINES, 1950, A
WHILE THOUSANDS CHEER, 1940
WHIMS OF SOCIETY, THE, 1918
WHIP HAND, THE, 1951, A
WHIP WOMAN, THE, 1928, A
WHIP'S WOMEN, 1968, O
WHIP, THE, 1917
WHIP, THE, 1928
WHIPLASH, 1948, A
WHIPPED, THE, 1950, A
WHIPPING BOSS, THE, 1924
WHIPSAW, 1936, A
WHIRL OF LIFE, THE, 1915
WHIRLPOOL, 1934, A
WHIRLPOOL, 1949, A
WHIRLPOOL, 1959, A
WHIRLPOOL OF DESTINY, THE, 1916
WHIRLPOOL OF FLESH
WHIRLPOOL OF WOMAN, 1966, O
WHIRLPOOL OF YOUTH, THE, 1927
WHIRLPOOL, THE, 1918
WHIRLWIND, 1951, A
WHIRLWIND, 1968, C
WHIRLWIND HORSEMAN, 1938, A
WHIRLWIND OF PARIS, 1946, A
WHIRLWIND RAIDERS, 1948, A
WHIRLWIND RANGER, THE, 1924
WHIRLWIND RIDER, THE, 1935
WHIRLWIND, THE, 1933
WHISKEY MOUNTAIN, 1977
WHISKY GALORE
WHISPER MARKET, THE, 1920
WHISPERED NAME, THE, 1924
WHISPERERS, THE, 1967, C
WHISPERING CANYON, 1926
WHISPERING CHORUS, THE, 1918
WHISPERING CITY, 1947, A
WHISPERING DEATH
WHISPERING DEVILS, 1920
WHISPERING ENEMIES, 1939, A
WHISPERING FOOTSTEPS, 1943, A
WHISPERING GHOSTS, 1942, A
WHISPERING JOE, 1969, O
WHISPERING PALMS, 1923
WHISPERING SAGE, 1927
WHISPERING SHADOWS, 1922
WHISPERING SKULL, THE, 1944, A
WHISPERING SMITH, 1916
WHISPERING SMITH, 1926, A
WHISPERING SMITH, 1948, A
WHISPERING SMITH HITS LONDON
WHISPERING SMITH SPEAKS, 1935, A
WHISPERING SMITH VERSUS SCOTLAND YARD,
   1952, A
WHISPERING TONGUES, 1934, A
WHISPERING WINDS, 1929, A
WHISPERING WIRES, 1926
WHISPERING WOMEN, 1921
WHISPERS, 1920, A
WHISPERS, 1920, A

WHISTLE AT EATON FALLS, 1951, A
WHISTLE DOWN THE WIND, 1961, A
WHISTLE STOP, 1946, A-C
WHISTLE, THE, 1921
WHISTLER, THE, 1944, A
WHISTLIN' DAN, 1932, A
WHISTLING BULLETS, 1937, A
WHISTLING HILLS, 1951, A
WHISTLING IN BROOKLYN, 1943, A
WHISTLING IN DIXIE, 1942, A
WHISTLING IN THE DARK, 1933, A
WHISTLING IN THE DARK, 1941, A
WHISTLING JIM, 1925
WHITE AND UNMARRIED, 1921, A
WHITE ANGEL, THE, 1936, A
WHITE BANNERS, 1938, A
WHITE BLACK SHEEP, THE, 1926, A
WHITE BONDAGE, 1937, A
WHITE BUFFALO, THE, 1977, C-O
WHITE CAPTIVE
WHITE CARGO, 1929
WHITE CARGO, 1930, C
WHITE CARGO, 1942, C
WHITE CAT, THE
WHITE CHRISTMAS, 1954, AA
WHITE CIRCLE, THE, 1920
WHITE CLIFFS OF DOVER, THE, 1944, A-C
WHITE COCKATOO, 1935, A
WHITE COMANCHE, 1967
WHITE CORRIDORS, 1952, A
WHITE CRADLE INN
WHITE DAWN, THE, 1974, O
WHITE DEATH, 1936, A
WHITE DEMON, THE, 1932, C
WHITE DESERT, THE, 1925
WHITE DEVIL, THE, 1948, C
WHITE DOG, 1982, O
WHITE DOVE, THE, 1920
WHITE EAGLE, 1932, A
WHITE EAGLE, THE, 1928
WHITE ELEPHANT, 1984, C
WHITE ENSIGN, 1934, A
WHITE FACE, 1933, A
WHITE FANG, 1925
WHITE FANG, 1936, A
WHITE FEATHER, 1955, A
WHITE FIRE, 1953, A
WHITE FLAME, 1928
WHITE FLANNELS, 1927, A
WHITE FLOWER, THE, 1923, A
WHITE GODDESS, 1953, A
WHITE GOLD, 1927, A
WHITE GORILLA, 1947, A
WHITE HANDS, 1922, A
WHITE HEAT, 1926
WHITE HEAT, 1934, O
WHITE HEAT, 1949, C
WHITE HEATHER, THE, 1919
WHITE HELL, 1922
WHITE HEN, THE, 1921
WHITE HOPE, THE, 1915
WHITE HOPE, THE, 1922
WHITE HORSE INN, THE, 1959, A
WHITE HUNTER, 1936, A
WHITE HUNTER, 1965, A
WHITE HUNTRESS, 1957, A
WHITE LEGION, THE, 1936, A
WHITE LIES, 1920
WHITE LIES, 1935, A
WHITE LIGHTING, 1953, A
WHITE LIGHTNIN' ROAD, 1967, A
WHITE LIGHTNING, 1973, C
WHITE LILAC, 1935, A
WHITE LINE FEVER, 1975, C
WHITE LINE, THE, 1952, C
WHITE LIONS, 1981
WHITE MAN, 1924
WHITE MAN'S LAW, THE, 1918
WHITE MAN, THE
WHITE MASKS, THE, 1921
WHITE MICE, 1926
WHITE MOLL, THE, 1920
WHITE MONKEY, THE, 1925
WHITE MOTH, THE, 1924
WHITE NIGHTS, 1961, O
WHITE OAK, 1921, A
WHITE ORCHID, THE, 1954, A
WHITE OUTLAW, THE, 1925, A
WHITE OUTLAW, THE, 1929
WHITE PANTHER, THE, 1924
WHITE PANTS WILLIE, 1927, A
WHITE PARADE, THE, 1934, A
WHITE PEBBLES, 1927
WHITE PONGO, 1945, AA
WHITE RAT, 1972, O
WHITE RAVEN, THE, 1917
WHITE RENEGADE, 1931
WHITE RIDER, THE, 1920
WHITE ROSE OF HONG KONG, 1965, O
WHITE ROSE, THE, 1923, A
WHITE ROSETTE, THE, 1916
WHITE SAVAGE, 1943, A

WHITE SAVAGE, 1941
WHITE SCAR, THE, 1915
WHITE SHADOW, THE
WHITE SHADOWS, 1924
WHITE SHADOWS IN THE SOUTH SEAS, 1928, A
WHITE SHEEP, THE, 1924
WHITE SHEIK, THE, 1928
WHITE SHEIK, THE, 1956, C
WHITE SHOULDERS, 1922
WHITE SHOULDERS, 1931, A
WHITE SIN, THE, 1924
WHITE SISTER, 1973, O
WHITE SISTER, THE, 1915
WHITE SISTER, THE, 1923, A
WHITE SISTER, THE, 1933, A
WHITE SLAVE SHIP, 1962, C
WHITE SLAVE, THE, 1929
WHITE SLIPPERS
WHITE SQUAW, THE, 1956, A
WHITE STALLION, 1947, A
WHITE STAR, THE, 1915
WHITE TERROR, THE, 1915
WHITE THUNDER, 1925
WHITE TIE AND TAILS, 1946, A
WHITE TIGER, 1923
WHITE TOWER, THE, 1950, A
WHITE TRAP, THE, 1959, C
WHITE TRASH ON MOONSHINE MOUNTAIN
WHITE UNICORN, THE
WHITE VOICES, 1965, O
WHITE WARRIOR, THE, 1961, C
WHITE WITCH DOCTOR, 1953, A
WHITE WOMAN, 1933, C
WHITE YOUTH, 1920, A
WHITE ZOMBIE, 1932, O
WHITE, RED, YELLOW, PINK, 1966, O
WHITEFACE
WHITHER THOU GOEST, 1917
WHO AM I?, 1921
WHO ARE MY PARENTS?, 1922
WHO CAN KILL A CHILD
WHO CARES, 1925
WHO CARES?, 1919
WHO DARES WIN
WHO DONE IT?, 1942, A
WHO DONE IT?, 1956, C
WHO FEARS THE DEVIL, 1972, A
WHO GOES NEXT?, 1938, C
WHO GOES THERE?
WHO GOES THERE?, 1917
WHO HAS SEEN THE WIND, 1980, A
WHO IS GUILTY?, 1940, A
WHO IS HARRY KELLERMAN AND WHY IS HE
   SAYING THOSE TERRIBLE THINGS ABOUT ME?,
   1971, C
WHO IS HOPE SCHUYLER?, 1942, A
WHO IS KILLING THE GREAT CHEFS OF EUROPE?,
   1978, C
WHO IS KILLING THE STUNTMEN?
WHO IS THE MAN?, 1924
WHO IS TO BLAME?, 1918
WHO KILLED "DOC" ROBBIN?, 1948, AAA
WHO KILLED AUNT MAGGIE?, 1940, A
WHO KILLED FEN MARKHAM?, 1937, A
WHO KILLED GAIL PRESTON?, 1938, A
WHO KILLED JESSIE?, 1965, C
WHO KILLED JOE MERRION?, 1915
WHO KILLED JOHN SAVAGE?, 1937, A
WHO KILLED MARY WHAT'SER NAME?, 1971, O
WHO KILLED TEDDY BEAR?, 1965, O
WHO KILLED THE CAT?, 1966, A-C
WHO KILLED VAN LOON?, 1984, A
WHO KILLED WALTON?, 1918
WHO KNOWS?, 1918
WHO LOVED HIM BEST?, 1918
WHO RIDES WITH KANE?
WHO SAYS I CAN'T RIDE A RAINBOW?, 1971, AAA
WHO SHALL TAKE MY LIFE?, 1918
WHO SLEW AUNTIE ROO?, 1971, O
WHO VIOLATES THE LAW, 1915
WHO WANTS TO KILL JESSIE?
WHO WAS MADDOX?, 1964, A
WHO WAS THAT LADY?, 1960, A
WHO WAS THE OTHER MAN?, 1917
WHO WILL MARRY ME?, 1919
WHO WOULD KILL A CHILD
WHO'LL STOP THE RAIN?, 1978, C
WHO'S AFRAID OF VIRGINIA WOOLF?, 1966, O
WHO'S BEEN SLEEPING IN MY BED?, 1963, C
WHO'S CHEATING?, 1924
WHO'S CRAZY, 1965
WHO'S GOT THE ACTION?, 1962, A
WHO'S GOT THE BLACK BOX?, 1970, O
WHO'S MIDING THE MINT?, 1967, A
WHO'S MINDING THE STORE?, 1963, A
WHO'S THAT KNOCKING AT MY DOOR?, 1968, O
WHO'S WHO IN SOCIETY, 1915
WHO'S YOUR BROTHER?, 1919
WHO'S YOUR FATHER?, 1935, A
WHO'S YOUR FRIEND, 1925
WHO'S YOUR LADY FRIEND?, 1937, A
WHO'S YOUR NEIGHBOR?, 1917

WHO'S YOUR SERVANT?, 1920
WHO?, 1975, C
WHOEVER SLEW AUNTIE ROO?
WHOLE DAMN WAR, THE
WHOLE DARN WAR, THE, 1928
WHOLE SHOOTIN' MATCH, THE, 1979, C
WHOLE TOWN'S TALKING, THE, 1926
WHOLE TOWN'S TALKING, THE, 1935, A
WHOLE TRUTH, THE, 1958, A
WHOLLY MOSES, 1980, C
WHOM GOD HATH JOINED, 1919
WHOM SHALL I MARRY, 1926
WHOM THE GODS DESTROY, 1916
WHOM THE GODS DESTROY, 1934, A
WHOM THE GODS LOVE
WHOM THE GODS WOULD DESTROY, 1915
WHOM THE GODS WOULD DESTROY, 1919
WHOOPEE, 1930, AA
WHOSE CHILD AM I?, 1976
WHOSE LIFE IS IT ANYWAY?, 1981, C-O
WHOSE WIFE?, 1917
WHOSO DIGGETH A PIT, 1915
WHOSO FINDETH A WIFE
WHOSO IS WITHOUT SIN, 1916
WHOSO TAKETH A WIFE, 1916
WHOSOEVER SHALL OFFEND, 1919
WHY AMERICA WILL WIN, 1918
WHY ANNA?
WHY ANNOUNCE YOUR MARRIAGE?, 1922
WHY BE GOOD?, 1929, A
WHY BLAME ME?
WHY BOTHER TO KNOCK, 1964
WHY BRING THAT UP?, 1929, A
WHY CHANGE YOUR HUSBAND?
WHY CHANGE YOUR WIFE?, 1920
WHY DOES HERR R. RUN AMOK?, 1977, O
WHY GERMANY MUST PAY, 1919
WHY GIRLS GO BACK HOME, 1926
WHY GIRLS LEAVE HOME, 1921
WHY GIRLS LEAVE HOME, 1945, C
WHY I WOULD NOT MARRY, 1918
WHY KILL AGAIN?, 1965
WHY LEAVE HOME?, 1929, A
WHY MEN FORGET, 1921
WHY MEN LEAVE HOME, 1924
WHY MUST I DIE?, 1960, C
WHY NOT MARRY?, 1922
WHY NOT?
WHY PICK ON ME?, 1937, A
WHY ROCK THE BOAT?, 1974, O
WHY RUSSIANS ARE REVOLTING, 1970, O
WHY SAILORS GO WRONG, 1928
WHY SAILORS LEAVE HOME, 1930, A
WHY SAPS LEAVE HOME, 1932, A
WHY SHOOT THE TEACHER, 1977, C
WHY SMITH LEFT HOME, 1919
WHY SPY
WHY TRUST YOUR HUSBAND?, 1921
WHY WOMEN LOVE, 1925
WHY WOMEN REMARRY, 1923
WHY WORRY, 1923, A
WHY WOULD ANYONE WANT TO KILL A NICE GIRL
   LIKE YOU?
WHY WOULD I LIE, 1980, C
WICHITA, 1955, A
WICKED, 1931, A
WICKED AS THEY COME
WICKED DARLING, THE, 1919
WICKED DIE SLOW, THE, 1968, O
WICKED DREAMS OF PAULA SCHULTZ, THE,
   1968, C
WICKED GO TO HELL, THE, 1961, O
WICKED LADY, THE, 1946, A
WICKED LADY, THE, 1983, O
WICKED WIFE, 1955, O
WICKED WOMAN, 1953, O
WICKED WOMAN, A, 1934, C
WICKED, WICKED, 1973, O
WICKEDNESS PREFERRED, 1928
WICKER MAN, THE, 1974, O
WICKHAM MYSTERY, THE, 1931, A
WIDE BOY, 1952, A
WIDE OPEN, 1927
WIDE OPEN, 1930, A
WIDE OPEN FACES, 1938, A
WIDE OPEN TOWN, 1941, A
WIDE-OPEN TOWN, A, 1922, A
WIDECOMBE FAIR, 1928
WIDOW AND THE GIGOLO, THE
WIDOW BY PROXY, 1919
WIDOW FROM CHICAGO, THE, 1930, A-C
WIDOW FROM MONTE CARLO, THE, 1936, A
WIDOW IN SCARLET, 1932, A
WIDOW IN SCARLET, 1932
WIDOW IS WILLING, THE
WIDOW TWAN-KEE
WIDOW'S MIGHT, 1934, A
WIDOW'S MIGHT, THE, 1918
WIDOWS' NEST, 1977, O
WIE ER IN DE WELT
WIE ER IN DE WELT
WIEN TANZT

WIEN, DU STADT DER LIEDER
WIFE AGAINST WIFE, 1921, A
WIFE BY PROXY, A, 1917
WIFE HE BOUGHT, THE, 1918
WIFE HUNTERS, THE, 1922
WIFE IN NAME ONLY, 1923
WIFE LOST, 1928
WIFE NUMBER TWO, 1917
WIFE OF GENERAL LING, THE, 1938, A
WIFE OF MONTE CRISTO, THE, 1946, A
WIFE OF THE CENTAUR, 1924
WIFE OF THE PHARAOH, THE, 1922
WIFE ON TRAIL, A, 1917
WIFE OR COUNTRY, 1919
WIFE OR TWO, A, 1935, A
WIFE SAVERS, 1928, A
WIFE SWAPPERS, THE
WIFE TAKES A FLYER, THE, 1942, A
WIFE TRAP, THE, 1922
WIFE VERSUS SECRETARY, 1936, A
WIFE WANTED, 1946, A
WIFE WHO WASN'T WANTED, THE, 1925
WIFE'S AWAKENING, A, 1921, A
WIFE'S FAMILY, THE
WIFE'S RELATIONS, THE, 1928
WIFE'S ROMANCE, A, 1923
WIFE'S SACRIFICE, A, 1916
WIFE, DOCTOR AND NURSE, 1937, A
WIFE, HUSBAND AND FRIEND, 1939, A
WIFEMISTRESS, 1979, O
WILBY CONSPIRACY, THE, 1975, C
WILD 90, 1968, O
WILD AFFAIR, THE, 1966, O
WILD AND THE INNOCENT, THE, 1959, C
WILD AND THE SWEET, THE
WILD AND THE WILLING, THE
WILD AND WILLING
WILD AND WONDERFUL, 1964, A
WILD AND WOOLLY, 1917, A
WILD AND WOOLLY, 1937
WILD ANGELS, THE, 1966
WILD ARCTIC
WILD BEAUTY, 1927
WILD BEAUTY, 1946, A
WILD BILL HICKOK, 1923
WILD BLOOD, 1929, A
WILD BLUE YONDER, THE, 1952, A
WILD BORN, 1927
WILD BOY, 1934, A
WILD BOYS OF THE ROAD, 1933, A-C
WILD BRIAN KENT, 1936, A
WILD BULL'S LAIR, THE, 1925
WILD BUNCH, THE, 1969, O
WILD CARGO
WILD CAT OF PARIS, THE, 1919
WILD CHILD, THE, 1970, C-O
WILD COMPANY, 1930, A
WILD COUNTRY, 1947, A
WILD COUNTRY, THE, 1971, AA
WILD DAKOTAS, THE, 1956, A
WILD DRIFTER
WILD DUCK, THE, 1977, A
WILD DUCK, THE, 1983, C
WILD EYE, THE, 1968, O
WILD FOR KICKS
WILD FRONTIER, THE, 1947, A
WILD GAME
WILD GEESE, 1927
WILD GEESE CALLING, 1941, A-C
WILD GEESE, THE, 1978, O
WILD GIRL, 1932, A
WILD GIRL OF THE SIERRAS, A, 1916
WILD GIRL, THE, 1917
WILD GIRL, THE, 1925, A
WILD GOLD, 1934, A
WILD GOOSE CHASE, 1919
WILD GOOSE CHASE, THE, 1915, A
WILD GOOSE, THE, 1921, A
WILD GUITAR, 1962, A
WILD GYPSIES, 1969, O
WILD HARVEST, 1947, A
WILD HARVEST, 1962, O
WILD HEART, THE, 1952, C
WILD HEATHER, 1921
WILD HERITAGE, 1958, A
WILD HONEY, 1919, A
WILD HONEY, 1922, A
WILD HORSE, 1931, A
WILD HORSE AMBUSH, 1952, A
WILD HORSE CANYON, 1939, A
WILD HORSE HANK, 1979, A
WILD HORSE MESA, 1925
WILD HORSE MESA, 1932, A
WILD HORSE MESA, 1947, A
WILD HORSE PHANTOM, 1944, A
WILD HORSE RANGE, 1940
WILD HORSE RODEO, 1938, A
WILD HORSE ROUND-UP, 1937, A
WILD HORSE RUSTLERS, 1943, A
WILD HORSE STAMPEDE, 1943, A
WILD HORSE STAMPEDE, THE, 1926
WILD HORSE VALLEY, 1940, A

WILD HORSES, 1984, C
WILD IN THE COUNTRY, 1961, A
WILD IN THE SKY
WILD IN THE STREETS, 1968, C
WILD INNOCENCE, 1937, A
WILD IS MY LOVE, 1963, O
WILD IS THE WIND, 1957, A
WILD JUNGLE CAPTIVE
WILD JUSTICE, 1925
WILD LIFE, 1918
WILD LIFE, THE, 1984, C-O
WILD LOVE-MAKERS
WILD MAN OF BORNEO, THE, 1941, A
WILD MONEY, 1937, A
WILD MUSTANG, 1935, A
WILD McCULLOCHS, THE, 1975, O
WILD NORTH, THE, 1952, A
WILD OATS, 1915
WILD OATS, 1916
WILD OATS, 1919
WILD OATS LANE, 1926, A
WILD ON THE BEACH, 1965, A
WILD ONE, THE, 1953, A
WILD ONES ON WHEELS, 1967, C-O
WILD ORANGES, 1924
WILD ORCHIDS, 1929, A
WILD PACK, THE, 1972, O
WILD PARTY, THE, 1923
WILD PARTY, THE, 1956, C-O
WILD PARTY, THE, 1975, O
WILD PARTY, THE, 1929, A
WILD PRIMROSE, 1918
WILD RACERS, THE, 1968, A-C
WILD REBELS, THE, 1967, O
WILD RIDE, THE, 1960, C
WILD RIDERS, 1971, O
WILD RIVER, 1960, A-C
WILD ROVERS, 1971, C-O
WILD SCENE, THE, 1970, O
WILD SEASON, 1968, A
WILD SEED, 1965, A
WILD SIDE, THE
WILD STALLION, 1952, A
WILD STRAIN, THE, 1918
WILD STRAWBERRIES, 1959, O
WILD SUMAC, 1917
WILD TO GO, 1926
WILD WEED, 1949, A-C
WILD WEST, 1946, A
WILD WEST ROMANCE, 1928
WILD WEST SHOW, THE, 1928
WILD WEST WHOOPEE, 1931, A
WILD WESTERNERS, THE, 1962, A
WILD WHEELS, 1969, O
WILD WINSHIP'S WIDOW, 1917
WILD WOMEN, 1918
WILD WOMEN OF WONGO, THE, 1959, C
WILD WORLD OF BATWOMAN, THE, 1966, C
WILD YOUTH, 1918
WILD YOUTH, 1961, C
WILD, FREE AND HUNGRY, 1970, C
WILD, WILD PLANET, THE, 1967, A-C
WILD, WILD SUSAN, 1925
WILD, WILD WINTER, 1966, A
WILD, WILD WOMEN, THE
WILDCAT
WILDCAT, 1942, A
WILDCAT BUS, 1940, A
WILDCAT JORDAN, 1922
WILDCAT OF TUCSON, 1941, A
WILDCAT SAUNDERS, 1936
WILDCAT TROOPER, 1936, A
WILDCAT, THE, 1917
WILDCAT, THE, 1924
WILDCAT, THE, 1926
WILDCATS OF ST. TRINIAN'S, THE, 1980, A
WILDCATTER, THE, 1937, A
WILDE SEISON
WILDERNESS FAMILY PART 2
WILDERNESS MAIL, 1935, A
WILDERNESS TRAIL, THE
WILDERNESS TRAIL, THE, 1919
WILDERNESS WOMAN, THE, 1926, A
WILDFIRE, 1915
WILDFIRE, 1925
WILDFIRE, 1945, A
WILDFIRE; THE STORY OF A HORSE
WILDFLOWER, 1914
WILDNESS OF YOUTH, 1922
WILDWECHSEL
WILFUL YOUTH, 1927
WILL AND A WAY, A, 1922
WILL ANY GENTLEMAN?, 1955, A
WILL BILL HICKOK RIDES, 1942, A
WILL JAMES' SAND
WILL O' THE WISP, THE, 1914
WILL OF HER OWN, A, 1915
WILL OF THE PEOPLE, THE
WILL PENNY, 1968, A-C
WILL SUCCESS SPOIL ROCK HUNTER?, 1957, A-C
WILL TOMORROW EVER COME
WILL YOU BE STAYING FOR SUPPER?, 1919

WILL, THE, 1921
WILLARD, 1971, O
WILLIAM COMES TO TOWN, 1948, A
WILLIAM FOX MOVIETONE FOLLIES OF 1929
WILLIAM TELL, 1925
WILLIE AND JOE BACK AT THE FRONT
WILLIE AND PHIL, 1980, O
WILLIE AND SCRATCH, 1975
WILLIE DYNAMITE, 1973, O
WILLIE MCBEAN AND HIS MAGIC MACHINE,
   1965, AAA
WILLOW TREE, THE, 1920
WILLY, 1963, A
WILLY DYNAMITE
WILLY REILLY AND HIS COLLEEN BAWN, 1918
WILLY WONKA AND THE CHOCOLATE FACTORY,
   1971, A
WILSON, 1944, A
WILSON OR THE KAISER?
WIN THAT GIRL, 1928
WIN(K)SOME WIDOW, THE, 1914
WIN, LOSE OR DRAW, 1925
WIN, PLACE AND SHOW
WIN, PLACE, OR STEAL, 1975, A
WINCHESTER WOMAN, THE, 1919
WINCHESTER '73, 1950, C
WIND ACROSS THE EVERGLADES, 1958, C
WIND AND THE LION, THE, 1975, C
WIND BLOWETH WHERE IT LISTETH, THE
WIND CANNOT READ, THE, 1958, A
WIND FROM THE EAST, 1970, C
WIND OF CHANGE, THE, 1961, A
WIND, THE, 1928, C
WINDBAG THE SAILOR, 1937, A
WINDFALL, 1935, A
WINDFALL, 1955, A
WINDFLOWERS, 1968, C
WINDING ROAD, THE, 1920
WINDING STAIR, THE, 1925, A
WINDING TRAIL, THE, 1918
WINDING TRAIL, THE, 1921
WINDJAMMER, 1937, A
WINDJAMMER, THE, 1926
WINDJAMMER, THE, 1931, A
WINDMILL, THE, 1937, A
WINDOM'S WAY, 1958, A-C
WINDOW IN LONDON, A
WINDOW IN PICCADILLY, A, 1928
WINDOW TO THE SKY, A
WINDOW, THE, 1949, C
WINDOWS, 1980, O
WINDOWS OF TIME, THE, 1969, A
WINDS OF AUTUMN, THE, 1976
WINDS OF CHANCE, 1925
WINDS OF THE PAMPAS, 1927
WINDS OF THE WASTELAND, 1936, A
WINDSPLITTER, THE, 1971, C
WINDWALKER, 1980, C
WINDY CITY, 1984, C
WINE, 1924
WINE AND THE MUSIC, THE
WINE GIRL, THE, 1918
WINE OF LIFE, THE, 1924
WINE OF YOUTH, 1924
WINE, WOMEN AND HORSES, 1937, A
WINE, WOMEN, AND SONG, 1934, A
WING AND A PRAYER, 1944, A
WING TOY, 1921, A
WINGED DEVILS
WINGED HORSEMAN, THE, 1929
WINGED IDOL, THE, 1915
WINGED MYSTERY, THE, 1917
WINGED SERPENT
WINGED SERPENT, THE
WINGED VICTORY, 1944, A
WINGS, 1927, A
WINGS AND THE WOMAN, 1942, A
WINGS FOR THE EAGLE, 1942, A
WINGS IN THE DARK, 1935, A
WINGS OF A SERF, 1926
WINGS OF ADVENTURE, 1930, A
WINGS OF CHANCE, 1961, A
WINGS OF DANGER
WINGS OF EAGLES, THE, 1957, A
WINGS OF MYSTERY, 1963, AAA
WINGS OF THE HAWK, 1953, A
WINGS OF THE MORNING, 1937, A
WINGS OF THE MORNING, THE, 1919
WINGS OF THE NAVY, 1939, A
WINGS OF THE STORM, 1926, A
WINGS OF VICTORY, 1941, A
WINGS OF YOUTH, 1925
WINGS OVER AFRICA, 1939, A
WINGS OVER HONOLULU, 1937, A
WINGS OVER THE PACIFIC, 1943, A
WINGS OVER WYOMING
WINIFRED THE SHOP GIRL, 1916
WINK OF AN EYE, 1958, A
WINNER TAKE ALL, 1924
WINNER TAKE ALL, 1932, A
WINNER TAKE ALL, 1939, A
WINNER TAKE ALL, 1948

WINNER TAKES ALL, 1918
WINNER'S CIRCLE, THE, 1948, A
WINNER, THE
WINNER, THE, 1926
WINNERS OF THE WILDERNESS, 1927
WINNERS, THE
WINNETOU, PART I
WINNETOU, PART II
WINNETOU, PART III
WINNING, 1969, A-C
WINNING A CONTINENT, 1924
WINNING A WOMAN, 1925
WINNING GIRL, THE, 1919
WINNING GOAL, THE, 1929, A
WINNING GRANDMA, 1918
WINNING HIS FIRST CASE, 1914
WINNING OAR, THE, 1927
WINNING OF BARBARA WORTH, THE, 1926, A
WINNING OF BEATRICE, THE, 1918
WINNING OF SALLY TEMPLE, THE, 1917
WINNING OF THE WEST, 1922
WINNING OF THE WEST, 1953, A
WINNING POSITION
WINNING STROKE, THE, 1919, A
WINNING TEAM, THE, 1952, A
WINNING THE FUTURITY, 1926
WINNING TICKET, THE, 1935, A
WINNING WALLOP, THE, 1926
WINNING WAY, THE
WINNING WITH WITS, 1922
WINSLOW BOY, THE, 1950, A
WINSTANLEY, 1979, C
WINSTON AFFAIR, THE
WINTER A GO-GO, 1965, A
WINTER CARNIVAL, 1939, A
WINTER COMES EARLY, 1972
WINTER FLIGHT, 1984, C
WINTER KEPT US WARM, 1968, C
WINTER KILLS, 1979, O
WINTER LIGHT, THE, 1963, C
WINTER MEETING, 1948, A
WINTER OF OUR DREAMS, 1982, O
WINTER RATES
WINTER WIND, 1970, C
WINTER WONDERLAND, 1947, A
WINTER'S TALE, THE, 1968, A
WINTERHAWK, 1976, C
WINTERSET, 1936, A-C
WINTERTIME, 1943, A
WIRE SERVICE, 1942, A
WIRELESS, 1915
WIRETAPPERS, 1956, A
WISE BLOOD, 1979, O
WISE FOOL, A, 1921, A
WISE GIRL, 1937, A
WISE GIRLS, 1930, A
WISE GUY, THE, 1926
WISE GUYS, 1937, A
WISE GUYS, 1969, A
WISE HUSBANDS, 1920, A
WISE KID, THE, 1922
WISE VIRGIN, THE, 1924
WISE WIFE, THE, 1927
WISER AGE, 1962, C
WISER SEX, THE, 1932, A
WISHBONE CUTTER, 1978, C
WISHBONE, THE, 1933, A
WISHING MACHINE, 1971, AAA
WISHING RING MAN, THE, 1919
WISHING RING, THE, 1914, A
WISP O' THE WOODS, 1919
WISTFUL WIDOW OF WAGON GAP, THE, 1947, A
WISTFUL WIDOW, THE
WIT WINS, 1920
WITCH BENEATH THE SEA, THE
WITCH DOCTOR
WITCH WHO CAME FROM THE SEA, THE, 1976
WITCH WITHOUT A BROOM, A, 1967, C
WITCH WOMAN, THE, 1918
WITCH'S CURSE, THE, 1963, A
WITCH'S LURE, THE, 1921
WITCH'S MIRROR, THE, 1960, C
WITCH, THE, 1916
WITCH, THE, 1969, C
WITCHCRAFT, 1916
WITCHCRAFT, 1964, A
WITCHCRAFT THROUGH THE AGES, 1921
WITCHES CURSE, THE
WITCHES' BREW, 1980
WITCHES, THE
WITCHES, THE, 1969, C
WITCHES—VIOLATED AND TORTURED TO DEATH
WITCHFINDER GENERAL
WITCHING EYES, THE, 1929
WITCHING HOUR, THE, 1916
WITCHING HOUR, THE, 1921, A
WITCHING HOUR, THE, 1934, A
WITCHING, THE
WITCHMAKER, THE, 1969, C
WITH A SMILE, 1939, A
WITH A SONG IN MY HEART, 1952, A
WITH ALL HER HEART, 1920

WITH BRIDGES BURNED, 1915
WITH DAVY CROCKETT AT THE FALL OF THE
   ALAMO
WITH FIRE AND SWORD
WITH GENERAL CUSTER AT LITTLE BIG HORN
WITH GUNILLA MONDAY EVENING AND TUESDAY
WITH HOOPS OF STEEL, 1918
WITH JOYOUS HEART
WITH KIT CARSON OVER THE GREAT DIVIDE
WITH LOVE AND KISSES, 1937, A
WITH LOVE AND TENDERNESS, 1978, A
WITH NAKED FISTS, 1923
WITH NEATNESS AND DISPATCH, 1918
WITH SITTING BULL AT THE SPIRIT LAKE
   MASSACRE
WITH SIX YOU GET EGGROLL, 1968, A
WITH THIS RING, 1925
WITH WINGS OUTSPREAD, 1922
WITHIN PRISON WALLS
WITHIN THE CUP, 1918
WITHIN THE LAW
WITHIN THE LAW, 1917
WITHIN THE LAW, 1923
WITHIN THE LAW, 1939, A
WITHIN THESE WALLS, 1945, A
WITHOUT A HOME, 1939, A
WITHOUT A SOUL
WITHOUT A SOUL, 1916
WITHOUT A TRACE, 1983, A
WITHOUT APPARENT MOTIVE, 1972, O
WITHOUT BENEFIT OF CLERGY, 1921
WITHOUT CHILDREN
WITHOUT COMPROMISE, 1922
WITHOUT EACH OTHER, 1962, A
WITHOUT FEAR, 1922, A
WITHOUT HONOR, 1918
WITHOUT HONOR, 1949, A
WITHOUT HONORS, 1932, A
WITHOUT HOPE, 1914, A
WITHOUT LIMIT, 1921, A
WITHOUT LOVE, 1945, A
WITHOUT MERCY, 1925
WITHOUT ORDERS, 1926
WITHOUT ORDERS, 1936, A
WITHOUT PITY, 1949, C
WITHOUT REGRET, 1935, A
WITHOUT RESERVATIONS, 1946, A
WITHOUT RISK
WITHOUT WARNING
WITHOUT WARNING, 1952, C
WITHOUT WARNING, 1980, O
WITHOUT YOU, 1934, A
WITNESS CHAIR, THE, 1936, A
WITNESS FOR THE DEFENSE, THE, 1919
WITNESS FOR THE PROSECUTION, 1957, A
WITNESS IN THE DARK, 1959, A
WITNESS OUT OF HELL, 1967
WITNESS TO MURDER, 1954, C
WITNESS VANISHES, THE, 1939, A
WITNESS, THE, 1959
WITNESS, THE, 1982, C
WITS VS. WITS, 1920
WIVES AND LOVERS, 1963, A
WIVES AND OTHER WIVES, 1919
WIVES AT AUCTION, 1926
WIVES BEWARE, 1933, A
WIVES NEVER KNOW, 1936, A
WIVES OF MEN, 1918
WIVES OF THE PROPHET, THE, 1926
WIVES UNDER SUSPICION, 1938, A
WIZ, THE, 1978, C
WIZARD OF BAGHDAD, THE, 1960, C
WIZARD OF GORE, THE, 1970, O
WIZARD OF MARS, 1964, C
WIZARD OF OZ, THE, 1925, A
WIZARD OF OZ, THE, 1939, AAA
WIZARD OF THE SADDLE, 1928
WIZARD, THE, 1927
WIZARDS, 1977, C
WOLF AND HIS MATE, THE, 1918
WOLF BLOOD, 1925
WOLF CALL, 1939, A
WOLF DOG, 1958, AA
WOLF FANGS, 1927
WOLF HUNTERS, THE, 1926
WOLF HUNTERS, THE, 1949, A
WOLF LAKE, 1979
WOLF LARSEN, 1958, A
WOLF LARSEN, 1978, A
WOLF LAW, 1922, A
WOLF LOWRY, 1917
WOLF MAN, 1924
WOLF MAN, THE, 1924
WOLF MAN, THE, 1941, C
WOLF OF DEBT, THE, 1915
WOLF OF NEW YORK, 1940, A
WOLF OF WALL STREET THE, 1929, C
WOLF PACK, 1922, A
WOLF RIDERS, 1935
WOLF SONG, 1929, A-C
WOLF WOMAN, THE, 1916
WOLF'S CLOTHING, 1927, A

WOLF'S CLOTHING, 1936, A
WOLF'S FANGS, THE, 1922
WOLF'S TRACKS, 1923
WOLF'S TRAIL, 1927
WOLF, THE, 1914
WOLF, THE, 1919
WOLF-MAN, THE, 1915
WOLFE OR THE CONQUEST OF QUEBEC, 1914
WOLFEN, 1981, O
WOLFHEART'S REVENGE, 1925
WOLFMAN, 1979, O
WOLFPACK
WOLFPEN PRINCIPLE, THE, 1974, AA
WOLVERINE, THE, 1921, A
WOLVES, 1930, A
WOLVES OF THE AIR, 1927
WOLVES OF THE BORDER, 1918
WOLVES OF THE BORDER, 1923
WOLVES OF THE CITY, 1929
WOLVES OF THE DESERT, 1926
WOLVES OF THE NIGHT, 1919
WOLVES OF THE NORTH, THE, 1921
WOLVES OF THE RAIL, 1918
WOLVES OF THE RANGE, 1921
WOLVES OF THE RANGE, 1943, A
WOLVES OF THE ROAD, 1925
WOLVES OF THE SEA, 1938, A
WOLVES OF THE STREET, 1920
WOLVES OF THE UNDERWORLD, 1935, A
WOMAN, 1919
WOMAN ABOVE REPROACH, THE, 1920
WOMAN ACCUSED, 1933, A-C
WOMAN AGAINST THE WORLD, 1938, A
WOMAN AGAINST THE WORLD, A, 1928
WOMAN AGAINST WOMAN, 1938, A
WOMAN ALONE, A
WOMAN ALONE, A, 1917
WOMAN ALONE, THE
WOMAN AND OFFICER 26, THE, 1920
WOMAN AND THE BEAST, THE, 1917
WOMAN AND THE HUNTER, THE, 1957, A
WOMAN AND THE LAW, 1918
WOMAN AND THE PUPPET, THE, 1920
WOMAN AND WIFE, 1918
WOMAN AND WINE, 1915, A
WOMAN AT HER WINDOW, A, 1978, O
WOMAN BENEATH, THE, 1917
WOMAN BETWEEN, 1931, C
WOMAN BETWEEN FRIENDS, THE, 1918
WOMAN BETWEEN, THE, 1931
WOMAN BETWEEN, THE, 1937
WOMAN BREED, THE, 1922
WOMAN CHASES MAN, 1937, A
WOMAN COMMANDS, A, 1932, A
WOMAN CONDEMNED, 1934
WOMAN CONQUERS, THE, 1922
WOMAN DECIDES, THE, 1932, A
WOMAN DESTROYED, A
WOMAN DISPUTED, THE, 1928
WOMAN DOCTOR, 1939, A
WOMAN EATER, THE, 1959, C
WOMAN ETERNAL, THE, 1918
WOMAN FLAMBEE, A
WOMAN FOR ALL MEN, A, 1975
WOMAN FOR CHARLEY, A
WOMAN FOR JOE, THE, 1955, A
WOMAN FROM CHINA, THE, 1930
WOMAN FROM HEADQUARTERS, 1950, A
WOMAN FROM HELL, THE, 1929
WOMAN FROM MONTE CARLO, THE, 1932, A
WOMAN FROM MOSCOW, THE, 1928
WOMAN FROM TANGIER, THE, 1948, A
WOMAN GAME, THE, 1920
WOMAN GIVES, THE, 1920
WOMAN GOD CHANGED, THE, 1921, A
WOMAN GOD FORGOT, THE, 1917
WOMAN GOD SENT, THE, 1920
WOMAN HATER, 1949, A
WOMAN HATER, THE, 1925
WOMAN HE LOVED, THE, 1922
WOMAN HE MARRIED, THE, 1922
WOMAN HE SCORNED, THE, 1930, A
WOMAN HUNGRY, 1931, C
WOMAN HUNT, 1962, C
WOMAN HUNT, THE, 1975, O
WOMAN I LOVE, THE, 1929
WOMAN I LOVE, THE, 1937, A
WOMAN I STOLE, THE, 1933, A
WOMAN IN 47, THE, 1916
WOMAN IN BLACK, THE, 1914
WOMAN IN BONDAGE, 1932
WOMAN IN BONDAGE, 1943
WOMAN IN BROWN
WOMAN IN CHAINS, 1932, A
WOMAN IN CHAINS, THE, 1923
WOMAN IN COMMAND, THE, 1934, A
WOMAN IN DISTRESS, 1937, A
WOMAN IN FLAMES, A, 1984, O
WOMAN IN GREEN, THE, 1945, A
WOMAN IN HER THIRTIES, A
WOMAN IN HIDING, 1949, A-C
WOMAN IN HIDING, 1953, A

WOMAN IN HIS HOUSE, THE
WOMAN IN HIS HOUSE, THE, 1920
WOMAN IN PAWN, A, 1927
WOMAN IN POLITICS, THE, 1916
WOMAN IN QUESTION, THE
WOMAN IN RED, THE, 1935, A
WOMAN IN RED, THE, 1984, C
WOMAN IN ROOM 13, THE, 1920
WOMAN IN ROOM 13, THE, 1932, A
WOMAN IN THE CASE, 1935
WOMAN IN THE CASE, A, 1916
WOMAN IN THE CASE, THE, 1945
WOMAN IN THE DARK, 1934, A
WOMAN IN THE DARK, 1952, A
WOMAN IN THE DUNES, 1964, O
WOMAN IN THE HALL, THE, 1949, A
WOMAN IN THE NIGHT, A, 1929
WOMAN IN THE RAIN, 1976
WOMAN IN THE SUITCASE, THE, 1920
WOMAN IN THE WINDOW, THE, 1945, C
WOMAN IN WHITE, THE, 1917
WOMAN IN WHITE, THE, 1929
WOMAN IN WHITE, THE, 1948, C
WOMAN INSIDE, THE, 1981, O
WOMAN IS A WOMAN, A, 1961, A
WOMAN IS THE JUDGE, A, 1939, A
WOMAN MICHAEL MARRIED, THE, 1919
WOMAN NEXT DOOR, THE
WOMAN NEXT DOOR, THE, 1915
WOMAN NEXT DOOR, THE, 1981, O
WOMAN OBSESSED, 1959, A-C
WOMAN OF AFFAIRS, A, 1928, A
WOMAN OF ANTWERP
WOMAN OF BRONZE, THE, 1923
WOMAN OF DARKNESS, 1968, O
WOMAN OF DISTINCTION, A, 1950, A
WOMAN OF DOLWYN
WOMAN OF EXPERIENCE, A, 1931, A
WOMAN OF FLESH, A, 1927
WOMAN OF HIS DREAM, THE, 1921
WOMAN OF IMPULSE, A, 1918
WOMAN OF LIES, 1919
WOMAN OF MYSTERY, A, 1957, A
WOMAN OF MYSTERY, THE, 1914, A
WOMAN OF NO IMPORTANCE, A, 1921
WOMAN OF PARIS, A, 1923, C
WOMAN OF PLEASURE, 1924
WOMAN OF PLEASURE, A, 1919
WOMAN OF REDEMPTION, A, 1918
WOMAN OF ROME, 1956, O
WOMAN OF SIN, 1961, A
WOMAN OF STRAW, 1964, C
WOMAN OF THE DUNES
WOMAN OF THE IRON BRACELETS, THE, 1920
WOMAN OF THE NORTH COUNTRY, 1952, A
WOMAN OF THE RIVER, 1954, O
WOMAN OF THE SEA, A, 1926
WOMAN OF THE TOWN, THE, 1943, A
WOMAN OF THE WORLD, A
WOMAN OF THE WORLD, A, 1925
WOMAN OF THE YEAR, 1942, AA
WOMAN OF TOKYO, 1933
WOMAN OF TOMORROW, 1914
WOMAN ON FIRE, A, 1970, O
WOMAN ON PIER 13, THE, 1950, A
WOMAN ON THE BEACH, THE, 1947, A
WOMAN ON THE INDEX, THE, 1919
WOMAN ON THE JURY, THE, 1924
WOMAN ON THE MOON, THE, 1929, A
WOMAN ON THE RUN, 1950, A
WOMAN ON TRIAL, THE, 1927, A
WOMAN PAYS, THE, 1915
WOMAN POSSESSED,A, 1958, A
WOMAN PURSUED, 1931
WOMAN RACKET, THE, 1930, A
WOMAN REBELS , A, 1936, A-C
WOMAN REDEEMED, A, 1927
WOMAN TAMER
WOMAN TEMPTED, THE, 1928, A
WOMAN THE GERMANS SHOT, 1918
WOMAN THERE WAS, A, 1919
WOMAN THEY ALMOST LYNCHED, THE, 1953, A
WOMAN THOU GAVEST ME, THE, 1919
WOMAN TIMES SEVEN, 1967, C-O
WOMAN TO WOMAN, 1923
WOMAN TO WOMAN, 1929, A
WOMAN TO WOMAN, 1946, A
WOMAN TRAP, 1929, A
WOMAN TRAP, 1936, A
WOMAN UNAFRAID, 1934, A
WOMAN UNDER COVER, THE, 1919
WOMAN UNDER OATH, THE, 1919
WOMAN UNDER THE INFLUENCE, A, 1974, C
WOMAN UNTAMED, THE, 1920
WOMAN WANTED, 1935, A
WOMAN WHO BELIEVED, THE, 1922
WOMAN WHO CAME BACK, 1945, A
WOMAN WHO DARED, 1949, A
WOMAN WHO DARED, A
WOMAN WHO DARED, THE, 1916
WOMAN WHO DID NOT CARE, THE, 1927, A
WOMAN WHO DID, A, 1914

WOMAN WHO DID, THE, 1915
WOMAN WHO FOOLED HERSELF, THE, 1922, A
WOMAN WHO GAVE, THE, 1918
WOMAN WHO INVENTED LOVE, THE, 1918
WOMAN WHO LIED, THE, 1915
WOMAN WHO OBEYED, THE, 1923
WOMAN WHO SINNED, A, 1925, A
WOMAN WHO TOUCHED THE LEGS, THE, 1926
WOMAN WHO UNDERSTOOD, A, 1920
WOMAN WHO WALKED ALONE, THE, 1922, A
WOMAN WHO WAS FORGOTTEN, THE, 1930
WOMAN WHO WAS NOTHING, THE, 1917
WOMAN WHO WOULDN'T DIE, THE, 1965, A
WOMAN WISE, 1928, A
WOMAN WITH A DAGGER, 1916
WOMAN WITH FOUR FACES, THE, 1923
WOMAN WITH NO NAME, THE
WOMAN WITH RED BOOTS, THE, 1977, O
WOMAN WITH THE FAN, THE, 1921
WOMAN WITHOUT A FACE
WOMAN WITHOUT CAMELLIAS, THE
WOMAN WOMAN, 1919
WOMAN'S ANGLE, THE, 1954, A
WOMAN'S AWAKENING, A, 1917
WOMAN'S BUSINESS, 1920, A
WOMAN'S DARING, A, 1916
WOMAN'S DEVOTION, A, 1956, A
WOMAN'S EXPERIENCE, A, 1918
WOMAN'S FACE, A, 1939, A
WOMAN'S FACE, A, 1941, A-C
WOMAN'S FAITH, A, 1925
WOMAN'S FIGHT, A, 1916
WOMAN'S FOOL, A, 1918
WOMAN'S HEART, A, 1926
WOMAN'S HONOR, A, 1916
WOMAN'S LAW, 1927
WOMAN'S LAW, THE, 1916
WOMAN'S LIFE, A, 1964, A
WOMAN'S MAN, 1920, A
WOMAN'S MAN, A, 1934
WOMAN'S PAST, A, 1915
WOMAN'S PLACE, 1921, A
WOMAN'S PLACE, A
WOMAN'S POWER, A, 1916
WOMAN'S RESURRECTION, A, 1915
WOMAN'S REVENGE, A
WOMAN'S SACRIFICE, A
WOMAN'S SECRET, A, 1924, A
WOMAN'S SECRET, A, 1949, A
WOMAN'S SIDE, THE, 1922
WOMAN'S TEMPTATION, A, 1959, A
WOMAN'S TRIUMPH, A, 1914
WOMAN'S URGE, A, 1966
WOMAN'S VENGEANCE, A, 1947, A
WOMAN'S VENGEANCE, A, 1939
WOMAN'S WAY, A, 1916
WOMAN'S WAY, A, 1928
WOMAN'S WEAPONS, 1918
WOMAN'S WOMAN, A, 1922
WOMAN'S WORLD, 1954, A-C
WOMAN, THE, 1915, A
WOMAN, WAKE UP, 1922
WOMAN-PROOF, 1923
WOMAN-WISE, 1937, A
WOMANEATER
WOMANHANDLED, 1925, A
WOMANHOOD, 1917
WOMANHOOD, 1934, A
WOMANLIGHT, 1979, C
WOMANPOWER, 1926, A
WOMBLING FREE, 1977, AAA
WOMEN AND BLOODY TERROR, 1970, O
WOMEN AND DIAMONDS, 1924
WOMEN AND GOLD, 1925
WOMEN AND WAR, 1965, C
WOMEN ARE LIKE THAT, 1938, A
WOMEN ARE STRONG, 1924
WOMEN ARE TROUBLE, 1936, A
WOMEN AREN'T ANGELS, 1942, A
WOMEN EVERYWHERE, 1930, A
WOMEN FIRST, 1924
WOMEN FOR SALE, 1975
WOMEN FROM HEADQUARTERS
WOMEN GO ON FOREVER, 1931, A
WOMEN IN A DRESSING GOWN, 1957, A
WOMEN IN BONDAGE, 1943, A
WOMEN IN CAGES, 1972
WOMEN IN CELL BLOCK 7, 1977, O
WOMEN IN CHAINS, THE
WOMEN IN HIS LIFE, THE, 1934, A
WOMEN IN LIMBO
WOMEN IN LOVE, 1969, O
WOMEN IN PRISON
WOMEN IN PRISON, 1938, A
WOMEN IN PRISON, 1957, O
WOMEN IN THE NIGHT, 1948, A
WOMEN IN THE WIND, 1939, A
WOMEN IN WAR, 1940, A
WOMEN IN WAR, 1965
WOMEN LOVE DIAMONDS, 1927
WOMEN LOVE ONCE, 1931, A
WOMEN MEN FORGET, 1920

WOMEN MEN LIKE, 1928
WOMEN MEN LOVE, 1921
WOMEN MEN MARRY, 1922
WOMEN MEN MARRY, 1931, A
WOMEN MEN MARRY, THE, 1937, A
WOMEN MUST DRESS, 1935, A
WOMEN OF ALL NATIONS, 1931, A-C
WOMEN OF DESIRE, 1968, O
WOMEN OF GLAMOUR, 1937, A
WOMEN OF NAZI GERMANY
WOMEN OF PITCAIRN ISLAND, THE, 1957, A
WOMEN OF RYAZAN, 1927
WOMEN OF THE NORTH COUNTRY
WOMEN OF THE PREHISTORIC PLANET, 1966, A
WOMEN OF TWILIGHT
WOMEN ON THE FIRING LINE, 1933
WOMEN THEY TALK ABOUT, 1928, A
WOMEN WHO DARE, 1928
WOMEN WHO GIVE, 1924
WOMEN WHO PLAY, 1932, A
WOMEN WHO WAIT
WOMEN WHO WIN, 1919
WOMEN WITHOUT MEN
WOMEN WITHOUT NAMES, 1940, A
WOMEN WON'T TELL, 1933, A
WOMEN'S PRISON, 1955, A-C
WOMEN'S WARES, 1927
WOMEN'S WEAPONS
WOMEN, THE, 1939, C
WOMEN, THE, 1969
WON BY A HEAD, 1920, A
WON IN THE CLOUDS, 1928
WON TON TON, THE DOG WHO SAVED
   HOLLYWOOD, 1976, A
WON'T WRITE HOME, MOM—I'M DEAD, 1975
WONDER BAR, 1934, A
WONDER BOY, 1951, A
WONDER CHILD
WONDER KID
WONDER MAN, 1945, AA
WONDER MAN, THE, 1920
WONDER OF WOMEN, 1929, A
WONDER PLANE
WONDER WOMEN, 1973, C
WONDERFUL ADVENTURE, THE, 1915
WONDERFUL CHANCE, THE, 1920
WONDERFUL COUNTRY, THE, 1959, A
WONDERFUL DAY
WONDERFUL LAND OF OZ, THE, 1969, AAA
WONDERFUL LIFE
WONDERFUL STORY, THE, 1932, A
WONDERFUL THING, THE, 1921
WONDERFUL THINGS?, 1958, A
WONDERFUL TO BE YOUNG?, 1962, A
WONDERFUL WIFE, A, 1922, A
WONDERFUL WOOING, THE
*WONDERFUL WORLD OF THE BROTHERS GRIMM,
   THE*, 1962, A-C
WONDERFUL YEAR, THE, 1921
WONDERFUL YEARS, THE
WONDERS OF ALADDIN, THE, 1961, AA
WONDERS OF THE SEA, 1922
WONDERWALL, 1969, O
WOOD NYMPH, THE, 1916
WOODEN HORSE, THE, 1951, A
WOODEN SHOES, 1917, A
WOODPIGEON PATROL, THE, 1930
WOOING OF PRINCESS PAT, THE, 1918
WOORUZHYON I OCHEN OPASEN
WORD, THE
WORDS AND MUSIC, 1929, A
WORDS AND MUSIC, 1948, A
WORDS AND MUSIC BY..., 1919
WORK IS A FOUR LETTER WORD, 1968, C
WORKING GIRLS, 1931, A
WORKING GIRLS, THE, 1973, O
WORKING MAN, THE, 1933, A
WORKING OF A MIRACLE, THE, 1915
WORKING WIVES
WORLD ACCORDING TO GARP, THE, 1982, C-O
WORLD ACCUSES, THE, 1935, A
WORLD AFLAME, THE, 1919
WORLD AGAINST HIM, THE, 1916
WORLD AND HIS WIFE, THE
WORLD AND HIS WIFE, THE, 1920
WORLD AND ITS WOMAN, THE, 1919
WORLD AND THE FLESH, THE, 1932, A
WORLD AND THE WOMAN, THE, 1916
WORLD APART, THE, 1917
WORLD AT HER FEET, THE, 1927
WORLD CHANGES, THE, 1933, A
WORLD FOR RANSOM, 1954, C-O
WORLD FOR SALE, THE, 1918
WORLD GONE MAD, THE, 1933, A
WORLD IN HIS ARMS, THE, 1952, A-C
WORLD IN MY CORNER, 1956, A
WORLD IN MY POCKET, THE, 1962, A
WORLD IS FULL OF MARRIED MEN, THE, 1980, O
WORLD IS JUST A 'B' MOVIE, THE, 1971, O
WORLD MOVES ON, THE, 1934, A
WORLD OF APU, THE, 1960, A
WORLD OF FOLLY, A, 1920

WORLD OF HANS CHRISTIAN ANDERSEN, THE,
   1971, AAA
WORLD OF HENRY ORIENT, THE, 1964, C
WORLD OF SPACE, THE
WORLD OF SUZIE WONG, THE, 1960, O
WORLD OF TODAY, THE, 1915
WORLD OWES ME A LIVING, THE, 1944, A
WORLD PREMIERE, 1941, A
WORLD TEN TIMES OVER, THE
WORLD TO LIVE IN, THE, 1919
WORLD WAR III BREAKS OUT
WORLD WAS HIS JURY, THE, 1958, A
WORLD WITHOUT A MASK, THE, 1934, A
WORLD WITHOUT END, 1956, A
WORLD'S A STAGE, THE, 1922
WORLD'S APPLAUSE, THE, 1923
WORLD'S CHAMPION, THE, 1922, A
WORLD'S DESIRE, THE, 1915
WORLD'S GREAT SNARE, THE, 1916
WORLD'S GREATEST ATHLETE, THE, 1973, AAA
WORLD'S GREATEST LOVER, THE, 1977, A-C
WORLD'S GREATEST SINNER, THE, 1962, O
WORLD'S GREATEST SWINDLES
WORLD, THE FLESH AND THE DEVIL, THE, 1914
WORLD, THE FLESH, AND THE DEVIL, THE, 1932, A
WORLD, THE FLESH, AND THE DEVIL, THE, 1959, A
WORLDLINGS, THE, 1920, A
WORLDLY GOODS, 1924
WORLDLY GOODS, 1930, A
WORLDLY MADONNA, THE, 1922
WORLDS APART, 1921
WORLDS APART, 1980, C
WORLDS OF GULLIVER, THE
WORM'S EYE VIEW, 1951, A
WORMWOOD, 1915
WORRYING AND LOVE THE BOMB, 1964, C
WORST SECRET AGENTS
WORST WOMAN IN PARIS, 1933, A
WORTHY DECEIVER
WOULD YOU BELIEVE IT, 1929
WOULD YOU BELIEVE IT?, 1930, AAA
WOULD YOU FORGIVE?, 1920
WOULD-BE GENTLEMAN, THE, 1960, A
WOZZECK, 1962, A
WRAITH OF THE TOMB, THE
WRANGLER'S ROOST, 1941, A
WRATH, 1917
WRATH OF GOD, THE, 1972, C-O
WRATH OF JEALOUSY, 1936, A
WRATH OF LOVE, 1917
WRATH OF THE GODS, THE or THE DESTRUCTION
   OF SAKURA JIMA, 1914, A
WRECK OF THE HESPERUS, 1948
WRECK OF THE HESPERUS, THE, 1927
WRECK OF THE MARY DEARE, THE, 1959, A
WRECK, THE, 1919
WRECK, THE, 1927
WRECKAGE, 1925
WRECKER OF LIVES, THE, 1914
WRECKER, THE, 1928
WRECKER, THE, 1933, A
WRECKERS, THE
WRECKING CREW, 1942, A
WRECKING CREW, THE, 1968, C
WRECKING YARD, THE
WRESTLER, THE, 1974, C
WRESTLING QUEEN, THE, 1975
WRIGHT IDEA, THE, 1928
WRITING ON THE WALL, THE, 1916
WRITTEN LAW, THE, 1931, A
WRITTEN ON THE SAND
WRITTEN ON THE WIND, 1956, C
WRONG ARM OF THE LAW, THE, 1963, A
WRONG BOX, THE, 1966, A
WRONG DAMN FILM, THE, 1975, C-O
WRONG DOERS, THE, 1925
WRONG DOOR, THE, 1916
WRONG IS RIGHT, 1982, O
WRONG KIND OF GIRL, THE
WRONG MAN, THE, 1956, A
WRONG MR. RIGHT, THE, 1939
WRONG MR. WRIGHT, THE, 1927
WRONG NUMBER, 1959, A
WRONG ROAD, THE, 1937, A
WRONG WOMAN, THE, 1915
WRONG WOMAN, THE, 1920
WRONGLY ACCUSED
WRONGS RIGHTED, 1924
WU-HOU
WUSA, 1970, C
WUTHERING HEIGHTS, 1920
WUTHERING HEIGHTS, 1939, C
WUTHERING HEIGHTS, 1970, A
WYLIE
WYOMING, 1928
WYOMING, 1940, A
WYOMING, 1947, A
WYOMING BANDIT, THE, 1949, A
WYOMING HURRICANE, 1944
WYOMING KID, THE
WYOMING MAIL, 1950, A
WYOMING OUTLAW, 1939, A

WYOMING RENEGADES, 1955, A
WYOMING ROUNDUP, 1952
WYOMING TORNADO, 1929
WYOMING WHIRLWIND, 1932
WYOMING WILDCAT, 1941, A
WYOMING WILDCAT, THE, 1925

-X-

X
X MARKS THE SPOT, 1931, A
X MARKS THE SPOT, 1942, A
"X"—THE MAN WITH THE X-RAY EYES, 1963, C
X THE UNKNOWN, 1957, A-C
X Y & ZEE, 1972, O
X-15, 1961, A
X-RAY
XANADU, 1980, C
XICA, 1982, O
XICA DA SILVA
XOCHIMILCO
XTRO, 1983, O

-Y-

...Y EL DEMONIO CREO A LOS HOMBRES
YA KUPIL PAPU
YA SHAGAYU PO MOSKVE
YABU NO NAKA NO KURONEKO
YABUNIRAMI NIPPON
YAGYU BUGEICHO
YAGYU SECRET SCROLLS
YAKUZA, THE, 1975, O
YAMANEKO SAKUSEN
YAMBAO
YANCO, 1964, A
YANG KWEI FEI
YANGTSE INCIDENT
YANK AT ETON, A, 1942, A
YANK AT OXFORD, A, 1938, A
YANK IN DUTCH, A
YANK IN ERMINE, A, 1955, A
YANK IN INDO-CHINA, A, 1952, A
YANK IN KOREA, A, 1951, A
YANK IN LIBYA, A, 1942, A
YANK IN LONDON, A, 1946, A
YANK IN THE R.A.F., A, 1941, A
YANK IN VIET-NAM, A, 1964, A
YANK ON THE BURMA ROAD, A, 1942, A
YANKEE AT KING ARTHUR'S COURT, THE
YANKEE BUCCANEER, 1952, A
YANKEE CLIPPER, THE, 1927, A
YANKEE CONSUL, THE, 1924
YANKEE DON, 1931, A
YANKEE DOODLE DANDY, 1942, AAA
YANKEE DOODLE, JR., 1922
YANKEE FAKIR, 1947, A
YANKEE FROM THE WEST, A, 1915
YANKEE GIRL, THE, 1915
YANKEE GO-GETTER, A, 1921
YANKEE IN KING ARTHUR'S COURT, A
YANKEE MADNESS, 1924
YANKEE PASHA, 1954, A
YANKEE PLUCK, 1917
YANKEE PRINCESS, A, 1919
YANKEE SENOR, THE, 1926, A
YANKEE SPEED, 1924
YANKEE WAY, THE, 1917
YANKS, 1979, C-O
YANKS AHOY, 1943, A
YANKS ARE COMING, THE, 1942, A
YAQUI DRUMS, 1956, AA
YAQUI, THE, 1916
YASMINA, 1926
YATO KAZE NO NAKA O HASHIRU
YAWARA SEMPU DOTO NO TAIKETSU
YE BANKS AND BRAES, 1919, A
YEAR 2889
YEAR OF LIVING DANGEROUSLY, THE, 1982, C
YEAR OF THE CRICKET
YEAR OF THE HORSE
YEAR OF THE HORSE, THE, 1966, AA
YEAR OF THE TIGER, THE
YEAR OF THE YAHOO, 1971, O
YEAR ONE, 1974, A
YEARLING, THE, 1946, AA
YEARNING, 1964, C
YEARS BETWEEN, THE, 1947, A
YEARS OF THE LOCUST, THE, 1916
YEARS WITHOUT DAYS
YEKATERINA IVANOVNA, 1915
YELLOW BACK, THE, 1926, A
YELLOW BALLOON, THE, 1953, A
YELLOW BULLET, THE, 1917
YELLOW CAB MAN, THE, 1950, A
YELLOW CANARY, THE, 1944, A
YELLOW CANARY, THE, 1963, A
YELLOW CARGO, 1936, A
YELLOW CLAW, THE, 1920
YELLOW CONTRABAND, 1928
YELLOW DOG, 1973, A-C
YELLOW DOG, THE, 1918
YELLOW DUST, 1936, A
YELLOW FIN, 1951, A

YELLOW FINGERS, 1926, A
YELLOW GOLLIWOG, THE
YELLOW HAIR AND THE FORTRESS OF GOLD, 1984, O
YELLOW HAIRED KID, THE, 1952
YELLOW HAT, THE, 1966, A
YELLOW JACK, 1938, A
YELLOW LILY, THE, 1928
YELLOW MASK, THE, 1930, A
YELLOW MEN AND GOLD, 1922
YELLOW MOUNTAIN, THE, 1954, A
YELLOW PASSPORT, THE
YELLOW PASSPORT, THE, 1916
YELLOW PAWN, THE, 1916
YELLOW ROBE, THE, 1954, A
YELLOW ROLLS-ROYCE, THE, 1965, C
YELLOW ROSE OF TEXAS, THE, 1944, A
YELLOW SANDS, 1938, A
YELLOW SKY, 1948, A
YELLOW SLIPPERS, THE, 1965, A
YELLOW STAIN, THE, 1922, A
YELLOW STOCKINGS, 1928
YELLOW STOCKINGS, 1930, AA
YELLOW STREAK, A, 1915
YELLOW STREAK, A, 1927
YELLOW SUBMARINE, 1958, A
YELLOW TAIFUN, THE, 1920
YELLOW TEDDYBEARS, THE
YELLOW TICKET, THE, 1918
YELLOW TICKET, THE, 1931, A
YELLOW TOMAHAWK, THE, 1954, A
YELLOW TRAFFIC, THE, 1914
YELLOW TYPHOON, THE, 1920
YELLOWBACK, THE, 1929
YELLOWBEARD, 1983, C-O
YELLOWNECK, 1955, A
YELLOWSTONE, 1936, A
YELLOWSTONE KELLY, 1959, A
YENTL, 1983, C
YES OR NO?, 1920
YES SIR, MR. BONES, 1951, A
YES SIR, THAT'S MY BABY, 1949, A
YES, GIORGIO, 1982, C
YES, MADAM?, 1938, A
YES, MR. BROWN, 1933, A
YES, MY DARLING DAUGHTER, 1939, A
YESTERDAY, 1980, C
YESTERDAY'S ENEMY, 1959, O
YESTERDAY'S HERO, 1979, C-O
YESTERDAY'S HERO, 1937
YESTERDAY'S HEROES, 1940, A
YESTERDAY'S WIFE, 1923, A
YESTERDAY, TODAY, AND TOMORROW, 1964, O
YETI, 1977, A
YIDDLE WITH HIS FIDDLE, 1937, A
YIELD TO THE NIGHT
YIN AND YANG OF DR. GO, THE, 1972
YNGSJOMORDET
YO YO, 1967, A
YODELIN' KID FROM PINE RIDGE, 1937, A
YOG-MONSTER FROM SPACE, 1970, A
YOICKS!, 1932, AA
YOJIMBO, 1961, O
YOKE OF GOLD, A, 1916
YOKEL BOY, 1942, A
YOL, 1982, O
YOLANDA, 1924
YOLANDA AND THE THIEF, 1945, A
YOLANTA, 1964, A
YONGKARI MONSTER FROM THE DEEP, 1967, A
YOR, THE HUNTER FROM THE FUTURE, 1983, A
YORK STATE FOLKS, 1915
YOSAKOI JOURNEY, 1970, C
YOSAKOI RYOKO
YOSEI GORASU
YOSEMITE TRAIL, THE, 1922
YOSIE GORATH
YOTSUYA KAIDAN
YOU AND I
YOU AND ME, 1938, A-C
YOU AND ME, 1975
YOU ARE GUILTY, 1923
YOU ARE IN DANGER
YOU ARE THE WORLD FOR ME, 1964, A
YOU BELONG TO ME, 1934, A
YOU BELONG TO ME, 1941, A
YOU BELONG TO MY HEART
YOU BETTER WATCH OUT, 1980, O
YOU CAME ALONG, 1945, A
YOU CAME TOO LATE, 1962, A
YOU CAN'T BEAT LOVE, 1937, A
YOU CAN'T BEAT THE IRISH, 1952, A
YOU CAN'T BEAT THE LAW
YOU CAN'T BEAT THE LAW, 1928
YOU CAN'T BELIEVE EVERYTHING, 1918
YOU CAN'T BUY EVERYTHING, 1934, A
YOU CAN'T BUY LUCK, 1937, A
YOU CAN'T CHEAT AN HONEST MAN, 1939, A
YOU CAN'T DO THAT TO ME
YOU CAN'T DO WITHOUT LOVE, 1946, A
YOU CAN'T ESCAPE, 1955, A
YOU CAN'T ESCAPE FOREVER, 1942, A

YOU CAN'T FOOL AN IRISHMAN, 1950, A
YOU CAN'T FOOL YOUR WIFE, 1923
YOU CAN'T FOOL YOUR WIFE, 1940, A
YOU CAN'T GET AWAY WITH IT, 1923
YOU CAN'T GET AWAY WITH MURDER, 1939, A-C
YOU CAN'T HAVE EVERYTHING, 1937, A
YOU CAN'T HAVE EVERYTHING, 1972
YOU CAN'T KEEP A GOOD MAN DOWN, 1922
YOU CAN'T RATION LOVE, 1944, A
YOU CAN'T RUN AWAY FROM IT, 1956, A
YOU CAN'T RUN FAR
YOU CAN'T SEE 'ROUND CORNERS, 1969, A
YOU CAN'T SLEEP HERE
YOU CAN'T STEAL LOVE
YOU CAN'T TAKE IT WITH YOU, 1938, A
YOU CAN'T TAKE MONEY
YOU CAN'T WIN 'EM ALL
YOU CAN'T WIN 'EM ALL, 1970, C
YOU DON'T NEED PAJAMAS AT ROSIE'S
YOU FIND IT EVERYWHERE, 1921
YOU FOR ME, 1952, A
YOU GOTTA STAY HAPPY, 1948, A
YOU HAVE TO RUN FAST, 1961, A
YOU JUST KILL ME
YOU KNOW WHAT SAILORS ARE, 1928
YOU KNOW WHAT SAILORS ARE, 1954, A
YOU LIGHT UP MY LIFE, 1977, C
YOU LIVE AND LEARN, 1937, A
YOU LUCKY PEOPLE, 1955, A
YOU MADE ME LOVE YOU, 1934, A
YOU MAY BE NEXT, 1936, A
YOU MUST BE JOKING?, 1965, A
YOU MUST GET MARRIED, 1936, A
YOU NEVER CAN TELL, 1920
YOU NEVER CAN TELL, 1951, A
YOU NEVER KNOW
YOU NEVER KNOW, 1922
YOU NEVER KNOW WOMEN, 1926
YOU NEVER KNOW YOUR LUCK, 1919
YOU NEVER SAID SUCH A GIRL, 1919
YOU ONLY LIVE ONCE, 1937, C
YOU ONLY LIVE ONCE, 1969, A
YOU ONLY LIVE TWICE, 1967, C
YOU PAY YOUR MONEY, 1957, A
YOU SAID A MOUTHFUL, 1932, A
YOU WERE MEANT FOR ME, 1948, A
YOU WERE NEVER LOVELIER, 1942, A
YOU WILL REMEMBER, 1941, A
YOU'D BE SURPRISED, 1926
YOU'D BE SURPRISED?, 1930, A
YOU'LL FIND OUT, 1940, A
YOU'LL LIKE MY MOTHER, 1972, C
YOU'LL NEVER GET RICH, 1941, A
YOU'RE A BIG BOY NOW, 1966, C
YOU'RE A LUCKY FELLOW, MR. SMITH, 1943, A
YOU'RE A SWEETHEART, 1937, A
YOU'RE DEAD RIGHT
YOU'RE FIRED, 1919
YOU'RE FIRED, 1925
YOU'RE IN THE ARMY NOW, 1937, A
YOU'RE IN THE ARMY NOW, 1941, A
YOU'RE IN THE NAVY NOW, 1951, A
YOU'RE MY EVERYTHING, 1949, A
YOU'RE NEVER TOO YOUNG, 1955, A
YOU'RE NOT SO TOUGH, 1940, A
YOU'RE ONLY YOUNG ONCE, 1938, A
YOU'RE ONLY YOUNG TWICE, 1952, A
YOU'RE OUT OF LUCK, 1941, A
YOU'RE TELLING ME, 1934, A
YOU'RE TELLING ME, 1942, A
YOU'RE THE DOCTOR, 1938, A
YOU'RE THE ONE, 1941, A
YOU'VE GOT TO BE SMART, 1967, A
YOU'VE GOT TO WALK IT LIKE YOU TALK IT OR
   YOU'LL LOSE THAT BEAT, 1971, O
YOUND AND WILD, 1958, A
YOUNG AMERICA, 1918
YOUNG AMERICA, 1932, AA
YOUNG AMERICA, 1942, AA
YOUNG AND BEAUTIFUL, 1934, A
YOUNG AND DANGEROUS, 1957, A
YOUNG AND EAGER
YOUNG AND EVIL, 1962, C
YOUNG AND IMMORAL, THE
YOUNG AND INNOCENT, 1938, A
YOUNG AND THE BRAVE, THE, 1963, A
YOUNG AND THE COOL, THE
YOUNG AND THE DAMNED, THE
YOUNG AND THE GUILTY, THE, 1958, A
YOUNG AND THE IMMORAL, THE
YOUNG AND THE PASSIONATE, THE
YOUNG AND WILD, 1975
YOUNG AND WILLING, 1943, A
YOUNG AND WILLING, 1964, C
YOUNG ANIMALS, THE
YOUNG APHRODITES, 1966, C
YOUNG APRIL, 1926
YOUNG AS YOU FEEL, 1931, AAA
YOUNG AS YOU FEEL, 1940, AAA
YOUNG AT HEART, 1955, A
YOUNG BESS, 1953, A
YOUNG BILL HICKOK, 1940, A

YOUNG BILLY YOUNG, 1969, A
YOUNG BLOOD, 1932, A
YOUNG BRIDE, 1932, C
YOUNG BUFFALO BILL, 1940, AAA
YOUNG CAPTIVES, THE, 1959, O
YOUNG CASSIDY, 1965, C
YOUNG CYCLE GIRLS, THE, 1979, O
YOUNG DANIEL BOONE, 1950, AAA
YOUNG DESIRE, 1930, C
YOUNG DETECTIVE, THE, 1964
YOUNG DIANA, THE, 1922
YOUNG DILLINGER, 1965, O
YOUNG DOCTORS IN LOVE, 1982, O
YOUNG DOCTORS, THE, 1961, A-C
YOUNG DON'T CRY, THE, 1957, C
YOUNG DONOVAN'S KID, 1931, A
YOUNG DR. KILDARE, 1938, A
YOUNG DRACULA
YOUNG DYNAMITE, 1937, A
YOUNG EAGLES, 1930, AA
YOUNG FRANKENSTEIN, 1974, C
YOUNG FUGITIVES, 1938, A
YOUNG FURY, 1965, C
YOUNG GIANTS, 1983, A
YOUNG GIRLS OF ROCHEFORT, THE, 1968, A
YOUNG GIRLS OF WILKO, THE, 1979, C
YOUNG GO WILD, THE, 1962, C
YOUNG GRADUATES, THE, 1971, O
YOUNG GUNS OF TEXAS, 1963, A
YOUNG GUNS, THE, 1956, A-C
YOUNG GUY GRADUATES, 1969, C
YOUNG GUY ON MT. COOK, 1969, A
YOUNG HELLIONS
YOUNG HUSBANDS, 1958, A
YOUNG IDEAS, 1924
YOUNG IDEAS, 1943, A
YOUNG IN HEART, THE, 1938, A
YOUNG INVADERS
YOUNG JACOBITES, 1959
YOUNG JESSE JAMES, 1960, C
YOUNG LAND, THE, 1959, A
YOUNG LIONS, THE, 1958, C-O
YOUNG LOCHINVAR, 1923
YOUNG LORD, THE, 1970, A
YOUNG LOVERS, THE, 1964, C-O
YOUNG LOVERS, THE, 1950
YOUNG LOVERS, THE, 1954
YOUNG MAN OF MANHATTAN, 1930, A
YOUNG MAN OF MUSIC
YOUNG MAN WITH A HORN, 1950, C
YOUNG MAN WITH IDEAS, 1952, A
YOUNG MAN'S BRIDE, THE, 1968
YOUNG MAN'S FANCY, 1943, A
YOUNG MISS, 1930
YOUNG MONK, THE, 1978, O
YOUNG MOTHER HUBBARD, 1917
YOUNG MR. LINCOLN, 1939, A
YOUNG MR. PITT, THE, 1942, A
YOUNG MRS. WINTHROP, 1920
YOUNG NOWHERES, 1929, A
YOUNG NURSES, THE, 1973, O
YOUNG ONE, THE, 1961, O
YOUNG ONES, THE
YOUNG PAUL BARONI
YOUNG PEOPLE, 1940, AAA
YOUNG PHILADELPHIANS, THE, 1959, C
YOUNG RACERS, THE, 1963, C
YOUNG RAHAH, THE, 1922
YOUNG REBEL, THE, 1969, C
YOUNG REBELS, THE
YOUNG ROMANCE, 1915
YOUNG RUNAWAYS, THE, 1968, O
YOUNG SAVAGES, THE, 1961, C
YOUNG SCARFACE
YOUNG SEDUCERS, THE, 1974
YOUNG SINNER, THE, 1965, C
YOUNG SINNERS, 1931, A
YOUNG STRANGER, THE, 1957, C
YOUNG SWINGERS, THE, 1963, AA
YOUNG SWORDSMAN, 1964, C
YOUNG TOM EDISON, 1940, AAA
YOUNG TORLESS, 1968, C
YOUNG WARRIORS, 1983, O
YOUNG WARRIORS, THE, 1967, C
YOUNG WHIRLWIND, 1928, A
YOUNG WIDOW, 1946, A
YOUNG WINSTON, 1972, A-C
YOUNG WIVES' TALE, 1954, A
YOUNG WOODLEY, 1929
YOUNG WOODLEY, 1930, C
YOUNG WORLD, A, 1966, C
YOUNG, THE EVIL AND THE SAVAGE, THE, 1968, O
YOUNG, WILLING AND EAGER, 1962, C
YOUNGBLOOD, 1978, O
YOUNGBLOOD HAWKE, 1964, O
YOUNGER BROTHERS, THE, 1949, A
YOUNGER GENERATION, 1929, A
YOUNGEST PROFESSION, THE, 1943, A
YOUNGEST SPY, THE
YOUR ACQUAINTANCE, 1927
YOUR BEST FRIEND, 1922
YOUR CHEATIN' HEART, 1964, A

YOUR FRIEND AND MINE, 1923
YOUR GIRL AND MINE, 1914
YOUR MONEY OR YOUR WIFE, 1965, A
YOUR NUMBER'S UP, 1931, C
YOUR OBEDIENT SERVANT, 1917
YOUR PAST IS SHOWING, 1958, A
YOUR SHADOW IS MINE, 1963, O
YOUR TEETH IN MY NECK
YOUR THREE MINUTES ARE UP, 1973, O
YOUR TURN, DARLING, 1963, C
YOUR UNCLE DUDLEY, 1935, A
YOUR WIFE AND MINE, 1919
YOUR WIFE AND MINE, 1927, O
YOUR WITNESS
YOURS FOR THE ASKING, 1936, A
YOURS TO COMMAND, 1927
YOURS, MINE AND OURS, 1968, AAA
YOUTH, 1917
YOUTH AFLAME, 1945, A
YOUTH AND ADVENTURE, 1925
YOUTH AND HIS AMULET, THE, 1963, C
YOUTH FOR SALE, 1924, A
YOUTH IN FURY, 1961, O
YOUTH MUST HAVE LOVE, 1922
YOUTH OF FORTUNE, A, 1916
YOUTH ON PARADE, 1943, AAA
YOUTH ON PAROLE, 1937, A
YOUTH ON TRIAL, 1945, A
YOUTH RUNS WILD, 1944, C
YOUTH TAKES A FLING, 1938, AA
YOUTH TAKES A HAND
YOUTH TO YOUTH, 1922, A
YOUTH WILL BE SERVED, 1940, A
YOUTH'S DESIRE, 1920
YOUTH'S ENDEARING CHARM, 1916
YOUTH'S GAMBLE, 1925
YOUTHFUL CHEATERS, 1923
YOUTHFUL FOLLY, 1920
YOUTHFUL FOLLY, 1934, A
YOYO
YR ALCOHOLIG LION, 1984, C
YUKIGUMI
YUKON FLIGHT, 1940, A
YUKON GOLD, 1952, A
YUKON MANHUNT, 1951, A
YUKON VENGEANCE, 1954, A
YUM-YUM GIRLS, 1976
YUSHA NOMI
YUSHU HEIYA
YVETTE, 1928
YVONNE FROM PARIS, 1919

-Z-

Z, 1969, C-O
Z.P.G., 1972, C
ZA DVUNMYA ZAYTSAMI
ZABRISKIE POINT, 1970, O
ZACHARIAH, 1971, C
ZAMBA, 1949, A
ZAMBA THE GORILLA
ZANDER THE GREAT, 1925, A
ZANDY'S BRIDE, 1974, A
ZANZIBAR, 1940, A
ZAPPA, 1984, O
ZAPPED, 1982, O
ZARAK, 1956, C
ZARDOZ, 1974, O
ZARTE HAUT IN SCHWARZER SEIDE
ZATO ICHI CHIKEMURI KAIDO
ZATO ICHI KENKATABI
ZATO ICHI TO YONJINBO
ZATOICHI, 1968, A
ZATOICHI CHALLENGED, 1970, A
ZATOICHI JOGKUTABI
ZATOICHI MEETS YOJIMBO, 1970, C
ZATOICHI'S CONSPIRACY, 1974, A
ZAZA, 1923
ZAZA, 1939, C
ZAZIE, 1961, A
ZAZIE DANS LE METRO
ZBEHOVIA A PUTNICI
ZEBRA FORCE, 1977
ZEBRA IN THE KITCHEN, 1965, AAA
ZEBRA KILLER, THE, 1974
ZEE & CO.
ZEEBRUGGE, 1924
ZELIG, 1983, A
ZEMLYA
ZENOBIA, 1939, A
ZEPPELIN, 1971, A
ZEPPELIN'S LAST RAID, THE, 1918
ZERO, 1928, C
ZERO HOUR, 1957, A
ZERO HOUR, THE, 1918
ZERO HOUR, THE, 1923
ZERO HOUR, THE, 1939, C
ZERO IN THE UNIVERSE, 1966, O
ZERO POPULATION GROWTH
ZERO TO SIXTY, 1978, C
ZETA ONE, 1969
ZHENITBA BALZAMINOVA
ZHILI-BYLI STARIK SO STARUKHOY

ZIEGFELD FOLLIES, 1945, AA
ZIEGFELD GIRL, 1941, A
ZIG-ZAG, 1975, O
ZIGZAG, 1970, C
ZIS BOOM BAH, 1941, A
ZISKA LA DANSEUSE ESPIONNE, 1922
ZITA, 1968, O
ZOKU MIYAMOTO MUSHASHI
ZOKU NINGEN NO JOKEN
ZOLLENSTEIN, 1917
ZOLTAN, HOUND OF DRACULA
ZOMBIE, 1980, O
ZOMBIE CREEPING FLESH, 1981, O
ZOMBIE ISLAND MASSACRE, 1984
ZOMBIE, 1971
ZOMBIES OF MORA TAU, 1957, O
ZOMBIES OF SUGAR HILL
ZOMBIES OF THE STRATOSPHERE
ZOMBIES ON BROADWAY, 1945, A
ZON, 1920
ZONGAR, 1918
ZONTAR, THE THING FROM VENUS, 1966, A
ZOO BABY, 1957, AAA
ZOO IN BUDAPEST, 1933, A
ZOOT SUIT, 1981, O
ZORBA THE GREEK, 1964, A
ZORRO CONTRO MACISTE
ZORRO, THE GAY BLADE, 1981, A-C
ZOTZ, 1962, A
ZULU, 1964, C
ZULU DAWN, 1980, C-O
ZVENIGORA, 1928
ZVEROLOVY
ZVONYAT, OTKROYTE DVER
ZVYODY I SOLDATY
ZWEI SARGE AUF BESTELLUNG

-1985 Films-

-A-

A ME MI PIACE, 1985, O
A MOURA ENCANTADA, 1985, A
A NOUS LES GARCONS, 1985, A
A REJTOZKODO, 1985, O
A TANITVANYOK, 1985, A
ABEL, 1985, O
ABIGEL, 1985, A
ACQUA E SAPONE, l985, C
ACTAS DE MARUSIA
ADIEU BLAIREAU, 1985, O
ADIEU, BONAPARTE, 1985, O
ADVENTURES OF HERCULES
ADVENTURES OF MARK TWAIN, THE, 1985, AAA
AFTER DARKNESS, 1985, O
AFTER HOURS, 1985, O
AGADA, 1985, O
AGNES OF GOD, 1985, C
AIDS—GEFAHR FUR DIE LIEBE, 1985, O
AKE AND HIS WORLD, 1985, O
AL LIMITE, CIOE, NON GLIELO DICO, 1985, C-O
ALAMO BAY, 1985, O
ALLONSANFAN, 1985, C
ALWAYS, 1985, O
AMATEUR HOUR, 1985, O
AMERICAN FLYERS, 1985, C
AMERICAN NINJA, 1985, O
AMICI MIEI ATTO III, 1985, C-O
AMONG THE CINDERS, 1985, O
ANA, 1985, C
ANNIE'S COMING OUT, 1985, C
ANNIHILATORS, THE, 1985, O
APPOINTMENT WITH FEAR, 1985, O
ASSAM GARDEN, THE, 1985, A-C
ASSISI UNDERGROUND, THE, 1985, C
ASTERIX VS. CESAR, 1985, AA
AT MIDDLE AGE, 1985, C
ATALIA, 1985, C
ATTENTION! UNE FEMME PEUT EN CACHER UNE
  AUTR
AURORA
AURORA ENCOUNTER, THE, 1985, C
AVENGING ANGEL, 1985, O
AVIATOR, THE, 1985, A-C
AZ ELVARAZSOLT DOLLAR, 1985, C

-B-

BABY: SECRET OF A LOST LEGEND, 1985, C
BACK TO THE FUTURE, 1985, C
BAD MEDICINE, 1985, C
BAR ESPERANZA, 1985, O
BARBARIAN QUEEN, 1985, O
BASIC TRAINING, 1985, O
BASTILLE, l985, C-O
BATON ROUGE, 1985, C
BAYAN KO, 1985, O
BEETHOVEN'S NEPHEW, 1985, O
BEFORE AND AFTER, 1985, C
BEKCI, 1985, C
BERLIN AFFAIR, THE, 1985, O
BETROGEN, l985, O
BETTER OFF DEAD, 1985, C
BEYOND THE WALLS, 1985, O

BILLY ZE KICK, 1985, C
BLACK CAULDRON, THE, 1985, A-C
BLANCHE ET MARIE, 1985, O
BLASTFIGHTER, 1985, O
BLESSURE, 1985, C
BLISS, 1985, O
BLUE HEAVEN, 1985, O
BLUES METROPOLITANO, 1985, O
BOGGY CREEK II, 1985, C
BOJ OM MOSKVU, 1985, A
BORDELLO, 1985, O
BOY MEETS GIRL, 1985, O
BOYS NEXT DOOR, THE, 1985, O
BRAS DE FER, 1985, C
BRAZIL, 1985, O
BREAKFAST CLUB, THE, 1985, O
BREAKING ALL THE RULES, 1985, O
BREWSTER'S MILLIONS, 1985, O
BRIDE, THE, 1985, O
BRIGADE DES MOEURS, 1985, O
BROKEN MIRRORS, 1985, O
BUDDIES, 1985, O
BURKE & WILLS, 1985, A-C
BURMESE HARP, THE, 1985, O

-C-

CA N'ARRIVE QU'A MOI, 1985, C
CAFFE ITALIA, 1985, C-O
CALAMARI UNION, 1985, C
CAME A HOT FRIDAY, 1985, C
CAMILA, 1985, O
CARABINIERI SI NASCE, 1985, C
CARE BEARS MOVIE, THE, 1985, AAA
CAROVNE DEDICTVI, 1985, AA
CARRE BLANC, 1985, C
CARRY ON DOCTORS AND NURSES, 1985, O
CASABLANCA CASABLANCA, 1985, C
CASAS VIEJAS, 1985, O
CASO CERRADO, 1985, C
CAT'S EYE, 1985, C
CAVE GIRL, 1985, O
CAVIAR ROUGE, 1985, C
CEASE FIRE, 1985, O
CEMENTERIO DEL TERROR, 1985, O
CENT FRANCS L'AMOUR, 1985, O
CERTAIN FURY, 1985, C
CHAIN GANG, 1985, O
CHAIN LETTERS, 1985, O
CHAIN, THE, 1985, C
CHAOS-KAOS
CHICK FOR CAIRO, A, 1985, AAA
CHILLY NIGHTS, 1985, A
CHORUS LINE, A, 1985, C
CHRONIC INNOCENCE, 1985, C
CIEN JUZ NIEDALEKO, 1985, A
CITY HERO, 1985, C
CITY LIMITS, 1985, C
CLIN D'OEIL, 1985, C
CLUE, 1985, C
COCA-COLA KID, THE, 1985, O
COCOON, 1985, C
CODE NAME: EMERALD, 1985, C
CODE OF SILENCE, 1985, O
CODENAME WILDGEESE, 1985, O
COLONEL REDL, 1985, O
COLOR PURPLE, THE, 1985, A-C
COLPI DI LUCE, 1985, O
COLPO DI FULMINE, 1985, C-O
COMMANDO, 1985, O
COMME LA NUIT, 1985, O
COMMITTED, 1985, O
COMPANY OF WOLVES, THE, 1985, O
COMPROMISING POSITIONS, 1985, C-O
COUNTDOWN, 1985, C
COURT OF THE PHARAOH, THE, 1985, C
CREATOR, 1985, O
CREATURE, 1985, O
CREEPERS, 1985, O
CRIMEWAVE, 1985, C
CROSSOVER DREAMS, 1985, C-O
CSAK EGY MOZI, 1985, C

-D-

D.A.R.Y.L., 1985, AA
DA CAPO, 1985, C
DANCE WITH A STRANGER, 1985, C-O
DANGEROUS MOVES, 1985, C
DARK OF THE NIGHT
DARSE CUENTA, 1985, C-O
DAWANDEH, 1985, A-C
DAY OF THE COBRA, THE, 1985, O
DAY OF THE DEAD, 1985, O
DAYS OF JUNE, THE, 1985, O
DE DEUR VAN HET HUIS, 1985, C
DE DROOM, 1985, C-O
DE L'AUTRE COTE DE L'IMAGE, 1985, C
DEADLY PASSION, 1985, O
DEATH OF AN ANGEL, 1985, C
DEATH OF MARIO RICCI, THE, 1985, C
DEATH WISH 3, 1985, O
DEF-CON 4, 1985, O
DEFENCE OF THE REALM, 1985, C-O

TERMINAL CHOICE, 1985, O
TEST OF LOVE
TEX E IL SIGNORE DEGLI ABISSI, 1985, A
THAT WAS THEN...THIS IS NOW, 1985, O
THAT'S MY BABY, 1985, O
THREE MEN AND A CRADLE, 1985, C
THUNDER ALLEY, 1985, O
TICHA RADOST, 1985, C
TIEMPO DE MORIR
TIGIPIO, 1985, O
TIME AFTER TIME, 1985, A-C
TIME TO DIE, A, 1985, C
TISNOVE VOLANI, 1985, A
TO AROMA TIS VIOLETTAS, 1985, C
TO KILL A STRANGER, 1985, O
TO KOLLIE, 1985, C
TO LIVE AND DIE IN L.A., 1985, O
TO THERMOKIPIO, 1985, O
TOMBOY, 1985, O
TOO SCARED TO SCREAM, 1985, O
TOPOS, 1985, C
TORNADO, 1985, C
TOXIC AVENGER, THE, 1985, O
TRANCERS, 1985, O
TRANSYLVANIA 6-5000, 1985, C
TREASURE OF THE AMAZON, THE, 1985, O
TREFFPUNKT LEIPZIG, 1985, O
TRETI SARKAN, 1985, A
TRIP TO BOUNTIFUL, THE, 1985, C
TRISTESSE ET BEAUTE, 1985, O
TROIS HOMMES ET UN COUFFIN
TROUBLE IN MIND, 1985, O
TRZY STOPY NAD ZIEMIA, 1985, O
TUFF TURF, 1985, O
TURK 182!, 1985, C
TURN OF THE SCREW, 1985, O
TURTLE DIARY, 1985, C
TUTTA COLPA DEL PARADISO, 1985, C
TVATTEN, 1985, AA
TWICE IN A LIFETIME, 1985, O

TWISTED PASSION, 1985, O
2020 TEXAS GLADIATORS, 1985, O
TWO LIVES OF MATTIA PASCAL, THE, 1985, O

-U-
UCCELLI D'ITALIA, 1985, O
UFORIA, 1985, C
UM ADEUS PORTUGUES, 1985, A
UNA NOVIA PARA DAVID, 1985, A
UNDERWORLD, 1985, C
UNE FEMME OU DEUX, 1985, C
UNFINISHED BUSINESS, 1985, O
UNSUITABLE JOB FOR A WOMAN, AN, 1985, C
UNWRITTEN LAW, THE, 1985, A
UP TO A CERTAIN POINT, 1985, C
URAMISTEN
URGENCE, 1985, O

-V-
VACANZE D'ESTATE, 1985, C
VAGABOND, 1985, O
VALS, THE, 1985, O
VARIETES, 1985, C
VAROSBUJOCSKA, 1985, C
VAUDEVILLE, 1985, C-O
VERGESST MOZART
VERONIKA, 1985, C
VERTIGES, 1985, C
VERY MORAL NIGHT, A, 1985, O
VIEW TO A KILL, A, 1985, C
VISION QUEST, 1985, O
VISSZASZAMLALAS
VOLUNTEERS, 1985, O
VYJIMECNA SITUALE, 1985, A

-W-
WALKING THE EDGE, 1985, O
WALL, THE, 1985, O
WALTER & CARLO: OP PA FARS HAT, 1985, C
WAR AND LOVE, 1985, O

WARNING SIGN, 1985, O
WATER, !985, C-O
WE THREE, 1985, C
WEIRD SCIENCE, 1985, O
WEST INDIES, 1985, A
WETHERBY, 1985, O
WHAT'S THE TIME, MR. CLOCK?, 1985, A
WHEN FATHER WAS AWAY ON BUSINESS, 1985, O
WHEN NATURE CALLS, 1985, O
WHEN THE RAVEN FLIES, 1985, O
WHERE THE GREEN ANTS DREAM, 1985, O
WHERE'S PICONE?, 1985, O
WHITE NIGHTS, 1985, C
WILD GEESE II, 1985, O
WILDROSE, 1985, C
WILDSCHUT, 1985, O
WILLS AND BURKE, 1985, C
WITNESS, 1985, C-O
WIVES—TEN YEARS AFTER, 1985, O
WIZARDS OF THE LOST KINGDOM, 1985, A
WORKING CLASS, 1985, O

-Y-
Y'A PAS LE FEU, 1985, C
YASHA, 1985, O
YEAR OF THE DRAGON, 1985, O
YOUNG SHERLOCK HOLMES, 1985, C
YUMECHIYO NITSUKI, 1985, O

-Z-
ZABICIE CIOTKI, 1985, C
ZABUDNITE NA MOZARTA
ZAHN UM ZAHN, 1985, C
ZASTIHLA ME NOC, 1985, A
ZATAH, 1985, C
ZED & TWO NOUGHTS, A, 1985, O
ZELENA LETA, 1985, A
ZINA, 1985, C
ZIVILE KNETE, 1985, A
ZOO GANG, THE, 1985, C

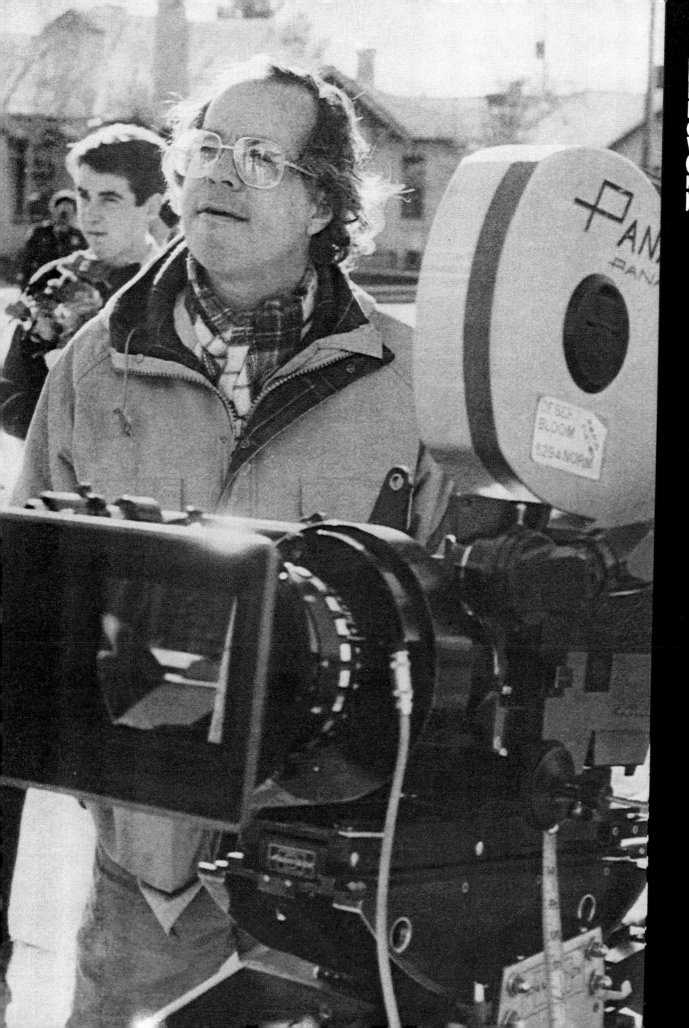

Films by Country of Origin

Below is a listing of all the films in the 1987 annual by the country which produced the film. Where more than one country is involved in a production, the film is listed under each of the producing countries, and a co-production notation (co:) included with the title. Foreign-language films listed under English titles are followed by the foreign title of the film if that information was available.

ALGERIA
LAST IMAGE, THE (LA DERNIERE IMAGE, co: Fr.)
RAI
TAHOUNET AL SAYED FABRE

ARGENTINA
ANOTHER LOVE STORY (OTRA HISTORIA DE AMOR)
AWAITING THE PALLBEARERS (ESPERANDO LA CARROZA)
BAD COMPANY (MALAYUNTA)
BAIROLETTO
CONTAR HASTA 10
DEBAJO DEL MUNDO (co: Czech.)
DIAPASON
EL HOMBRE QUE GANO LE RAZON (co: Neth.)
EL RIGOR DEL DESTINO
EL SOL EN BOTELLITAS
GERONIMA
INSOMNIACS (LOS INSOMNES)
KING AND HIS MOVIE, A (LA PELICULA DEL REY)
LA NOCHE DE LOS LAPICES
LES LONGS MANTEAUX (co: Fr.)
MAN FACING SOUTHEAST (HOMBRE MIRANDO AL SUDESTE)
MISS MARY
NIGHTMARE'S PASSENGERS (PASAJEROS DE UNA PESADILLA)
PERROS DE LA NOCHE
POBRE MARIPOSA
SERE CUALQUIER COSA PERO TE QUIERO
SOBREDOSIS
TE AMO

AUSTRALIA
AROUND THE WORLD IN EIGHTY WAYS
AUSTRALIAN DREAM
BACKLASH
BACKSTAGE
BIG HURT, THE
BULLSEYE
CACTUS
COOL CHANGE
CROCODILE DUNDEE
DARK AGE
DEAD END DRIVE-IN
DEATH OF A SOLDIER (THE LEONSKI INCIDENT)
DEPARTURE
DEVIL IN THE FLESH
DOGS IN SPACE
DOT AND KEETO
DOT AND THE WHALE
EMMA'S WAR
FAIR GAME
FOR LOVE ALONE
FREE ENTERPRISE
GOING SANE
GREAT EXPECTATIONS— THE AUSTRALIAN STORY
KANGAROO
MALCOLM
MORE THINGS CHANGE, THE
PLAYING BEATIE BOW
PROMISES TO KEEP
SHORT CHANGED
SKY PIRATES
SPIRITS OF THE AIR
STILL POINT, THE
TRAVELLING NORTH
TWELFTH NIGHT
TWO FRIENDS
WINDRIDER
WRONG WORLD
YOUNG EINSTEIN

AUSTRIA
DER SCHWARZE TANNER (co: Switz./Ger.)
DIE NACHTMEERFAHRT
DIE WALSCHE (co: Switz./Ger.)
ECHO PARK
ERDSEGEN (co: Ger.)
FRANZA
HEIDENLOCHER (co: Ger.)
KONZERT FUR ALICE (co: Ger./Switz.)
MULLERS BURO
SCHMUTZ
'38 (co: Ger.)
WELCOME IN VIENNA

BANGLADESH
DAHAN

BELGIUM
BABEL OPERA, OU LA REPETITION DE DON JUAN
CONGO EXPRESS
EXIT—EXILE (co: Fr.)
GENESIS (co: India/Fr./Switz.)
GOLDEN EIGHTIES (LES ANNEES 80, co: Fr./Switz.)
LA MOITIE D L'AMOUR
LA PURITAINE (co: Fr.)
MERCI MONSIEUR ROBERTSON
PANTHER SQUAD (co: Fr.)
SPRINGEN

BRAZIL
AS SETE VAMPIRAS
AVAETE, A SEMENTE DA VINGANCA
BRAS CUBAS
CHICO REI
CINEMA FALADO
COM LIENCA, EU VOU A LUTA
EU SEI QUE VOI TE AMAR
FILME DIMENCIA
FULANINHA
HAPPILY EVER AFTER (ALEM DA PAIXAO)
HOUR OF THE STAR (A HORA DA ESTRELA)
JOGO DURO
JUBIABA (co: Fr.)
MALANDRO (co: Fr.)
MARVADA CARNE
NEM TUDO E VERDADE
O HOMEM DA CAPA PRETA
PERDOA ME POR ME TRAIRES
QUILOMBO
REI DO RIO
SONHO SEM FIM

BULGARIA
DA EBICHASH NA INAT
ROMANTICHNA-ISTORIJA
SKUPA MOYA, SKUPI MOY
ZA KUDE PUTOVATE

BURKINA FASO
SARRAOUNIA

CANADA
ABDUCTED
ADVENTURE OF FAUSTUS BIDGOOD, THE
ANNE TRISTER
BLUE MAN
BOY IN BLUE, THE
BULLIES
BUSTED UP
CARE BEARS MOVIE II: A NEW GENERATION
CLOSE TO HOME
CONFIDENTIAL
CRAZY MOON
DANCING IN THE DARK
DECLINE OF THE AMERICAN EMPIRE (LE DECLIN DE L'EMPIRE AMERICAIN)
ELVIS GRETTON LE KING DES KINGS
EQUINOXE
EVIXION
FLYING
HENRI
INTIMATE POWER (POUVOIR INTIME)
JUDGEMENT IN STONE, A
LA GUEPE
LE MATOU
LOST
LOVE SONGS (co: Fr.)
LOYALTIES
NINETY DAYS
ONE NIGHT ONLY
OVERNIGHT
PINK CHIQUITAS, THE
QUI A TIRE SUR NOS HISTOIRES D'AMOUR
SAMUEL LOUNT
SAUVE-TOI, LOLA (co: Fr.)
SEPARATE VACATIONS
TIMING
TOBY MCTEAGUE
TRAMP AT THE DOOR
VISAGE PALE
WELCOME TO THE PARADE

CHILE
LOS HIJOS DE LA GUERRA FRIA (co: Fr.)
NEMESIO

CHINA
BEI AIQING YIWANG DI JIAOLUO
CAN YUE
IN THE WILD MOUNTAINS (YE SHAN)
JUE XIANG
LAST EMPEROR, THE (co: Hong Kong)
LIANGJIA FUNU
PIAOBO QIYU
QINGCHUN JI
REZHOU
XIANGNU XIAOXIAO
YELLOW EARTH (HUANG TUDI)

COLOMBIA
A LA SALIDA NOS VEMOS (co: Venezuela)
EL DIA QUE ME QUIRAS
EL TREN DE LOS PIONEROS
KAPAX DEL AMAZONS
LA BODA DEL ACORDEONISTA
LA MANSION DE ARAUCAIMA
PISINGANA
SAN ANTONITO
VISA U.S.A. (co: Cuba)

CUBA
AMIGOS
CAPABLANCA (co: USSR)
COME LA VIDA MISMA
EL CORAZON SOBRE LA TIERRA
JIBARO
LEJANIA
MALABRIGO (co: Brit./Ger./Peru)
PLACIDO
UN HOMBRE DE EXITO
VISA U.S.A. (co: Colombia)

CZECHOSLOVAKIA
ATOMOVA KATEDRALA
AZ DO KONCE
BLOUDENI ORIENTACNIHO BEZCE
BORIS GUDONOV (co: USSR)
DEBAJO DEL MUNDO (co: Arg.)
DOBRE SVETIO
FALOSNY PRINC
GALOSE STASTIA
HRY PRO MIRNE POKROCILE
JONAS, DEJME TOMU VE STREDU
JRI FALESNY HRAC
KAM DOSKACE RANNI PTACE
KDO SE BOJI, UTIKA
KOHUT NEZASPIEVA
KOUZELNIKUV NAVRAT
KRAJINA S NABYTKEM
KUKACKA V TEMNEM LESE (co: Pol.)
LEV S BILOU HRIVOU
MAHULIENA ZLATA PANNA
MLADE VINO
MUJ HRISNY MUZ
MUZ NA DRATE
NAVRAT JANA PETRU

NENI SIROTEK JAKO SIROTEK
O JE
O SLAVE A TRAVE
ODA NA RADOST
OLDRICH A BOZENA
OPERACE ME DCERY
OUTSIDER
PAPILIO
PASODOBLE PRE TROCH
PAVUCINA
PESTI VE TME
SIESTA VETA
SLADKE STAROSTI
SMICH SE LEPI NA PATY
SMRT KRASNYCH SRNCU
UTEKAME, UZ IDEI
VELKA FILMOVA LOUPEZ
VESELE VANOCE PREJI CHOBOTNICE
VLCI BOUDA
VYHRAVAT POTICHU
ZABY A INE RYBY
ZAKAZANE UVOLNEI
ZELENA LETA
ZKROCENI ZLEHO MUZE

DENMARK
BARNDOMMENS GADE
ET SKUD FRA HJERTET
FLAMBEREDE HJERTER
MANDEN I MAANEN
OFELIA KOMMER TIL BYEN
TAKE IT EASY
TWIST AND SHOUT (TRO HAB OG
  KARLIGHED)
VALHALLA
WOLF AT THE DOOR, THE (OVIRI, co: Fr.)
YES, DET ER FAR!

EAST GERMANY
AB HEUTE ERWACHSEN
DAS HAUS AM FLUSS
GRITTA VOM RATTENSCHLOSS
SPRING SYMPHONY
  (FRUHLINGSSINFONIE, co: Ger.)
UNTERMEHMEN GEIGENKASTEN

EGYPT
AL BEDAYA
AL DAHIYA
AL KETTAR
AWDAT MOWATIN
EL-GOOA
ELOGIO DELLA PAZZIA
EL-SADA EL RIGAL
EL-TOUK WA EL-ESSWERA
EL-YOM EL SADES
KAHIR ELZAMAN
LEL HAB KESSA AKHIRA
MESHWAR OMAR
SIKAT SAFAR

FINLAND
BORN AMERICAN (co: US)
FLIGHT NORTH (FLUCHT IN DEN
  NORDEN, co: Ger.)
HUOMENNA
KUNINGAS LAHTEE RANSKAAN
LINNA
MORENA
PIMEYS ODOTTA
RIISUMINEN
SININEN IMETAJA
SUURI ILLUSIONI
TUNTEMATON SOTILAS
VALKOINEN KAAPIO

FRANCE
ASTERIX CHEZ LES BRETONS
BEAU TEMPS, MAIS ORAGEUX EN FIN DE
  JOURNEE
BETTY BLUE (37:2 LE MATIN)
BLACK AND WHITE (NOIR ET BLANC)
BLACK MIC-MAC
BLEU COMME L'ENFER
CHARLOTTE FOR EVER
CONSEIL DE FAMILLE
CORPS ET BIEN
COURS PRIVE
DANS UN MIROIR
DE L'ARGENTINE (co: Brit.)
DERNIER CRI

DESCENTE AUX ENFERS
DESORDE
DOUBLE MESSIEURS
DOUCE FRANCE (co: Ger.)
ESTHER (co: Brit./Israel)
ETATS D'AME
EXIT—EXILE (co: Belg.)
FAUBOURG SAINT-MARTIN
FEAR (co: Italy)
FEMMES DE PERSONNE
FLAGRANT DESIR
FUTURE OF EMILY, THE (L'AVENIR
  D'EMILIE, co: Ger.)
GARDIEN DE LA NUIT
GENESIS (co: India/Belg./Switz.)
GINGER AND FRED (co: Ger./Italy)
GOLDEN EIGHTIES (co: Belg./Switz.)
GRANDEUR ET DECADENCE D'UN PETIT
  COMMERCE DE CINEMA
HIGH SPEED
HOTEL DU PARADIS (co: Brit.)
I LOVE YOU (co: Italy)
IL DIAVOLO IN CORPO (co: Italy)
INSPECTEUR LAVARDIN
JE HAIS LES ACTEURS
JEAN DE FLORETTE
JOUR ET NUIT (co: Switz.)
JUBIABA (co: Braz.)
KAMIKAZE
LA FEMME DE MA VIE
LA FEMME SECRETE
LA GALETTE DU ROI
LA GITANE
LA MACHINE A DECOUDRE
LA PURITAINE (co: Belg.)
L'AMANT MAGNIFIQUE
LAST IMAGE, THE (co: Alg.)
LAST SONG (co: Switz.)
L'AUBE (co: Israel)
LE BONHEUR A ENCORE FRAPPE
LE COMPLEXE DU KANGOUROU
LE DEBUTANT
LE MAL D'AIMER (co: Italy)
LE PALTOQUET
LE PASSAGE
LES CLOWNS DE DIEU
LES FRERES PETARD
LES FUGITIFS
LES LONGS MANTEAUX (co: Arg.)
L'ETAT DE GRACE
LET'S HOPE IT'S A GIRL (co: It.)
L'EXECUTRICE
LOS HIJOS DE LA GUERRA FRIA (co: Chile)
LOVE SONGS (PAROLES DE MUSIQUE,
  co: Can.)
L'UNIQUE
MAINE-OCEAN
MALANDRO (co: Braz.)
MAMMAME
MAN AND A WOMAN: 20 YEARS LATER, A
  (UN HOMME ET UNE FEMME: VINGT
  ANS DEJA)
MANON DES SOURCES
MAUVAIS SANG
MAX MON AMOUR
MELO
MEMOIRES D'UN JUIF TROPICAL
MENAGE (TENUE DE SOIREE)
MON BEAU-FRERE A TUE MA SOEUR
MON CAS (co: Port.)
MONSTER SHARK (co: Italy)
MORT UN DIMANCHE DE PLUIE (co: Switz.)
NANOU (co: Brit.)
NEXT SUMMER (L'ETE PROCHAIN)
NIGHTMARE WEEKEND (co: GB/US)
NTTURUDA (co: Guinea-Bissau)
NUIT D'IVRESSE
ON A VOLE CHARLIE SPENCER!
PANTHER SQUAD (co: Belg.)
PARENTAL CLAIM (LIEN DE PARENTE)
PARIS MINUIT
PAULETTE
PEAU D'ANGE
PEKIN CENTRAL
PIRATES (co: Tunisia)
POLICE
PRUNELLE BLUES
QUI TROP EMBRASSE
ROUND MIDNIGHT (co: US)
RUE DU DEPART
SCARIFICE, THE (OFFRET, co: Swed.)

SALOME (co-produced with Italy)
SAUVE-TOI, LOLA (co: Can.)
SCENE OF THE CRIME (LE LIEU DE CRIME)
SINCERELY CHARLOTTE
  (SIGNE CHARLOTTE)
SUIVEZ MON REGARD
SUMMER (LE RAYON VERT)
TAXI BOY
THERESE
TOP OF THE WHALE
TWIST AGAIN IN MOSCOU
WOLF AT THE DOOR (co: Den.)
WOMEN'S PRISON MASSACRE (co: Italy)
YIDDISH CONNECTION
ZONE ROUGE

GREAT BRITAIN
ABSOLUTE BEGINNERS
ARTHUR'S HALLOWED GROUND
BEST MAN, THE
BIGGLES
BLACK JOY
CAPTIVE
CAR TROUBLE
CARAVAGGIO
CASTAWAY
CLOCKWISE
COMING UP ROSES (RHOSYN A RHITH)
COMRADES
DEATH OF THE HEART, THE
DE L'ARGENTINE (co: Fr.)
DUET FOR ONE
ESTHER (co: Fr./Israel)
FATHERLAND (co: Ger.)
FOREIGN BODY
FRENCH LESSON (THE FROG PRINCE)
GIRL FROM MANI, THE (co: Gr.)
GOOD FATHER, THE
GOSPEL ACCORDING TO VIC
  (HEAVENLY PURSUITS)
HALF MOON STREET
HOTEL DU PARADIS (co: Fr.)
KIND OF ENGLISH, A
KNIGHTS AND EMERALDS
LETTER TO BREZHNEV
LINK
MALABRIGO (co: Cuba/Ger./Peru)
MILWYR BYCHAN
MISSION, THE
MISTER LOVE
MONA LISA
MY BEAUTIFUL LAUNDRETTE
NANOU (co: Fr.)
NIGHTMARE WEEKEND (co: US/Fr.)
NO SURRENDER
OUR EXPLOITS AT WEST POLEY
PASSION OF REMEMBRANCE, THE
PING PONG
PLAYING AWAY
ROCINANTE
ROOM WITH A VIEW, A
RUNNING OUT OF LUCK
SCHOOL FOR VANDALS
SCREAMTIME
SECOND VICTORY, THE
SHANGHAI SURPRISE
SID AND NANCY
SKY BANDITS (GUN BUS)
TERRY ON THE FENCE
WALKMAN BLUES (co: Ger.)
WHEN THE WIND BLOWS

GREECE
ALCESTES
ALLIGORIA
CARAVAN SARAI
DANILO TRELES, O FIMISMENOS
  ANDALOUISIANOS MOUSIKOS
ENAS ISICHOS THANATOS
GIRL FROM MANI, THE (co: Brit.)
I NICHTA ME TI SILENA
I PHOTOGRAPHIA
KALI PATRITHA SYNTROPHE
KNOCK OUT
O MELISSOKOMOS
SCHETIKA ME TON VASSILI
TO DENDRO POUU PLIGONAME

GUINEA-BISSAU
NTTURUDA (co: Fr.)

HONG KONG
ACES GO PLACES IV
ARMOUR OF GOD, THE
BETTER TOMORROW, A
CUODIAN YUANYANG
DARK NIGHT (co: Taiwan)
DREAM LOVERS (MENGZHONG REN)
FAMILY, THE
FEIFA YIMIN
1/2-DUAN QING
HAPPY DIN DON (HUANLE DINGDANG)
HUAJI SHIDAI
ISLE OF FANTASY
JUST LIKE THE WEATHER (AIQING
    QIANGFENG XUNHAO)
LAONIANG GOUSAO
LAST EMPEROR, THE (co: China)
LAST SONG IN PARIS
LUNATICS
MARTIAL ARTS OF SHAOLIN
MILLIONAIRE'S EXPRESS, THE
MISTER VAMPIRE
NUREN XIN
PASSION
PEKING OPERA BLUES
QINGCHUN NUCHAO
ROSE
ROYAL WARRIORS
SILENT LOVE (TINGBUDAODE SHUOHUA)
TONGS—A CHINATOWN STORY

HUNGARY
AKLI MIKLOS
AZ UTOLSO KEZIRAT
BANANHEJKERINGO
ELYSIUM
ERZEKENY BUCSU A FEJEDELEMTOL
GREAT GENERATION, THE (A NAGY
    GENERACIO)
HAJNALI HAZTETOK
KESERU IGAZSAG
KISMASZAT ES A GEZENGUZOK
KOJACK BUDAPESTEN
ORDOGI KISERTETEK
VAKVILAGBAN
VAROSBUJOCSKA

ICELAND
EINS OG SKEPNAN DEYR

INDIA
AGHAAT
AMMA ARIYAN
ANAADI ANANT
ANANTARAM
CHIDAMBARAM
CHOPPER
DEBSHISHU
GENESIS (co: Belg./Fr./Switz.)
GURU DAKSHINA
KAHAN KAHAN SE GUZAR GAYA
MASSEY SAHIB
MIRCH MASALA
MUKHAMUKHAM
NEW DELHI TIMES
ORIDATH
RAO SAHEB
SUSMAN
TABARANAKATHE
TRIKAL

INDONESIA
DOEA TANDA MATA
INTRUDER, THE
NO TIME TO DIE (co: Ger.)
SECANGKIR KOPI PAHIT
TITAN SERAMBUT DIBELAH

IRAN
BEYOND THE MIST
BOYCOTT
BUS, THE
CITY OF MICE, THE
CLOSED CIRCUIT
END, THE
FROSTY ROADS
GRANDFATHER
ILLUSION, THE
IN THE RAIN
MARE
MIRZA NOWROUZ' SHOES

MONSTER, THE
TELEPHONE CALLS, THE

IRAQ
AL ASHEKE
FLAMING BORDERS
HOB FEE BAGHDAD

IRELAND
EAT THE PEACH

ISRAEL
ALEX KHOLE AHAVA
AVANTI POPOLO
BAR 51
ESTHER (co: Brit./Fr.)
FLASH
HAKRAV AL HAVAAD
HAME'AHEV
HASHIGAON HAGADOL
KOL AHAVO-TAI
L'AUBE (co: Fr.)
MALKAT HAKITA
NADIA
SHTAY ETZBA'OT M'TZIDON
SMILE OF THE LAMB, THE (HIUCH HAGDI)

ITALY
AMORE INQUIETO DI MARIA
ANCHE LEI FUMAVA IL SIGARO
ANEMIA
ANGKOR—CAMBODIA EXPRESS
AURELIA
BLACK TUNNEL
BLADE IN THE DARK (LA CASA CON LA
    SCALA NEL BUIO)
CAMORRA (UN COMPLICATO INTRIGO DI
    DONNE, VICOLI E DELITTI)
CARNE CHE CRESCE
CASTIGHI
CATTIVI PIERROT
COBRA MISSION
CUT AND RUN (INFERNO IN DIRETTA)
DAYS OF HELL
DELITTI
DEMONS II - THE NIGHTMARE IS BACK
    (DEMONI II)
DESIDERANDO GIULIA
EHRENGARD
FEAR (co: Fr.)
FINAL EXECUTIONER, THE
FORMULA FOR MURDER
45 MO PARALLELO
FOTOROMANZO
FOXTRAP (co: US)
FRANCESCA E MIA
GINGER AND FRED (GINGER E FRED,
    co: Fr./Ger.)
GIOVANNI SENZA PENSIERI
GIURO CHE TI AMO
GRANDI MAGAZZINI
HANDS OF STEEL
I GIORNI DELL'INFERNO
I LOVE YOU (co: Fr.)
IL BI E IL BA
IL CAMMISSARIO LO GATTO
IL CAMORRISTA
IL CASO MORO
IL DIAVOLO IN CORPO (co: Fr.)
IL GIARDINO DEGLI INGANNI
IL MIELE DEL DIAVOLO
IL MOSTRO DE FIRENZE
IL RAGAZZO DEL PONY EXPRESS
IL TENENTE DEI CARABINIERI
ITALIAN FAST FOOD
JUNGLE RAIDERS (LA LEGENDA DEL
    RUBINO MALESE)
LA BALLATA DI EVA
LA BONNE
LA CASA DEL BUON RITORNO
LA CROCE DALLE 7 PIETRE
LA MONACA NEL PECCATO
LA RAGAZZA DEI LILLA
LA SECONDA NOTTE
LA SIGNORA DELLA NOTTE
LA SPOSA AMERICANA
LA SPOSA ERA BELLISSIMA
LA STORIA
LA VENEXIANA
LA VITA DI SCORTA
L'APACHE BIANCO (co: Spain)

LE MAL D'AIMER (co: Fr.)
LE MINIERE DEL KILIMANGIARO
LET'S HOPE IT'S A GIRL (SPERIAMO CHE
    SIA FEMMINA, co-prod with Fr.)
L'INCHIESTA
L'ISOLA
L'ULTIMA MAZURKA
L'ULTIMO GIORNO
LUSSURIA
MANHATTAN BABY
MANHUNT, THE
MEGLIO BACIARE UN COBRA
MIAMI GOLEM
MOMO (co: Ger.)
MONITORS
MONSTER SHARK (co: Fr.)
MORIRAI A MEZZANOTTE
NINI TERNOSECCO
OTELLO
RAGE (co: Spain)
REGALO DI NATALE
ROMANCE
SALOME (co: Fr.)
SAPORE DEL GRANO
SCALPS
SCUOLA DI LADRI
SEMBRA MORTO . . . MA E SOLO SVENUTO
SENSI
SENZA SCRUPOLI
SEPARATI IN CASA
7 KG. IN 7 GIORNI
SPOSERO SIMON LE BON
SQUADRA SELVAGGIA
STORIA D'AMORE
SUMMER NIGHT WITH GREEK PROFILE,
    ALMOND EYES, AND SCENT OF BASIL
    (NOTTE D'ESTATE CON PROFILO
    GRECO, OCCHI A MANDORLA E ODORE
    DI BASILICO)
THRONE OF FIRE, THE
THUNDER WARRIOR
TOMMASO BLU (co: Ger.)
TRE SUPERMAN A SANTO DOMINGO
TROPPO FORTE
UN RAGAZZO COME TANTI
UNA CASA IN BILICO
UNA DOMENICA SI
UNA DONNA SENZA NOME
UNA NOTTE DI PIOGGIA
UNA SPINA NEL CUORE
UNA STORIA AMBIGUA
UNA TENERA FOLLIA
VIOLENT BREED
VOGLIA DIGUARDARE
WHITE SLAVE (SCHIAVE BIANCHE,
    VIOLENZA IN AMAZZONIA)
WILD BEASTS
WOMEN'S PRISON MASSACRE (co: Fr.)
YUPPIES, I GIOVANI DI SUCCESSO

JAPAN
CABARET
COMIC MAGAZINE (KOMIKKU ZASSHI
    NANKA IRANI)
CRAZY FAMILY, THE
CYOEI NO MURE
GENKAI TSUREZURE BUSHI
GINGA-TETSUDO NO YORU
HANA ICHIMOMME
HARU NO KANE
HARUKOMA NO UTA
HITOHIRA NO YUKI
KATAKU NO HITO
KATAYOKU DAKE NO TENSHI
KIMI GA KAGAYAKU TOKI
KIMI WA HADASHI NO KAMI O MITAKA
KINEMA NO TENCHI
KONEKO MONOGATARI
LOST IN THE WILDERNESS (UEMURA
    NAOMI MONOGATARI)
LOVE LETTER (KOIBUMI)
MUTCHAN NO UTA
NEW MORNING OF BILLY THE KID, THE
NINGUEN NO YAKUSOKU
ORA TOKYO SA YUKUDA
OTOKO WA TSURAIYO, SHIBAMATA YORI
    AI O KOMETE
ROKUMEIKAN
SHIN YOROKOBIMO KANASHIMIMO
    IKUTOSHITSUKI
SHOKUTAKU NO NAI IE

SHUKUJI
SOREKARA
TAMPOPO
TO SLEEP SO AS TO DREAM (YUME
  MIRUYONI NEMURITAI)
TOKIMEDI NI SHISU
TYPHOON CLUB
USUGESHO
YAMASHITA SHONEN MONOGATARI
YARI NO GONZA

MADAGASCAR
DAHALO DAHALO

MALI
NYAMANTON

MEXICO
AMOR A LA VUELTA DE LA ESQUINA
ANGEL RIVER (co: US)
CALACAN
CONTACTO CHICANO
CRONICA DE FAMILIA
DONA HERLINDA AND HER SON
  (DONA HERLINDA Y SU HIJO)
EL BRONCO
EL DIA DE LOS ALBANILES II
EL EXTRANO HIJO DEL SHERIFF
EL IMPERIO DE LA FORTUNA
EL JUEGO DE LA MUERTE
EL MALEFICIO II
EL MERCADO DE HUMILDES
EL NARCO—DUELO ROJO
EL OMBLIGO DE LA LUNA
EL PUENTE
EL SECUESTRO DE CAMARENA
EL SEQUESTRO DE LOLA—LOLA LA
  TRAILERA II
EL VECINDARIO—LOS MEXICANOS
  CALIENTES
ES MI VIDA—EL NOA NOA 2
ESE LOCO LOCO HOSPITAL
ESQUADRON DE LA MUERTE
GAVILAN O PALOMA
HIJO DEL PALENQUE
IN 'N' OUT (GRINGO MOJADO, co: US)
LA ALACRANA
LA BANDA DE LOS PANCHITOS
LA MUERTE CRUZO EL RIO BRAVO
LA TERRA PROMETIDA
LAS NOCHES DEL CALIFAS
LOS ASES DE CONTRABANDO
MANANA DE COBRE
MATANZA EN MATAMOROS
NOCHE DE JUERGA
OBDULIA
PICARDIA MEXICANA NUMERO DOS
POR UN VESTIDO DE NOVIA
QUE ME MATEN DE UNA VEZ
RAFAGA DE PLOMO
REDONDO
SE SUFRA PERON SE GOZA
TERROR Y ENCAJES NEGROS
THANATOS
UN HOMBRE VIOLENTE
VENENO PARA LAS HADAS
YAKO—CAZADOR DE MALDITOS

MONGOLIA
BI CHAMD KHAYRTAY

MOROCCO
CHAMS
HADDA

THE NETHERLANDS
AFZIEN
ALMACITA DI DESOLATA
ASSAULT, THE (DE AANSLAG)
BALLERUP BOULEVARD
CHARLEY
DE VAL VAN PATRICIA HIGHSMITH
DE WISSELWACHTER
EL HOMBRE QUE GANO LE RAZON
  (co: Arg.)
FAILURE, THE (DE MISLUKKING)
FIELD OF HONOR
FLIGHT OF RAINBIRDS, A
FLODDER
MAMA IS MAD! (MAMA IS BOOS!)
MARIA

MORD I MORKET
OP HOOP VAN ZEGEN
PERVOLA: TRACKS IN THE SNOW
PPPERFORMER, THE
RIVERBED (co: US)
SHADOW OF VICTORY (IN DE SCHADUW
  VAN DE OVERWINNING)
THOMAS EN SENIOR OP HET SPOOR VAN
  BRUTE BAREND
WINDSCHADUW

NEW ZEALAND
ARRIVING TUESDAY
BRIDGE TO NOWHERE
DANGEROUS ORPHANS
FOOTROT FLATS
FRINGE DWELLERS, THE
QUEEN CITY ROCKER

NORTH KOREA
POMNALUI NUNSOGI

NORWAY
BIBBI, ELIN AND CHRISTINA
BLACKOUT
BRENNENDE BLOMSTER
DREAM OF NORTHERN LIGHTS
  (HAVLANDET)
DROMMESLOTTER
FAREWELL, ILLUSIONS
  (ADJO SOLIDARITET)
HARD ASFALT
HUD
MACARONI BLUES (MAKARONI BLUES)
NATTSEILERE
NOE HEIT ANNET
PLASTIKKPOSEN
X

PAKISTAN
ZANGIR

PERU
MALABRIGO (co: Cuba/Ger./Brit.)

THE PHILIPPINES
CRAZY BUNCH, THE
DIRTY GAMES
JAILBREAK . . . 1958
KILLING OF SATAN
NAKED VENGEANCE (co: US)
RAGING VENDETTA
REVENGE FOR JUSTICE
SILK
STONE BOY, THE

POLAND
CHREZSNISAK
DEATH SENTENCE (WYROK SMIERCI)
JEZIORO BODENSKIE
KRONICA WY PADKOW MYLO SINYCH
KUKACKA V TEMNEM LESE (co: Czech.)
OSOBISTY PAMIETNIK GRZESNIKA
  PRZEZ . . .
SCENY DZIECIECE Z ZYCIA PROWINCJI

PORTUGAL
A BALADA DA PRAIA DOS CAES
A FLOR DO MAR
MON CAS (co: Fr.)
O MEU CASO - REPETICOES
O VESTIDO COR DE FOGO
REPORTER X
UMA RAPARIGA NO VERAO

RUMANIA
DECLARATIE DE DRAGOSTE
DREPTATE IN LANTURI
LICEENII
NOI CEI DIN LINIA INTII
PASO DOBLE
SECVENTE
UN OASPETE LA CINA

SCOTLAND
BLOOD RED ROSES
SHOOT FOR THE SUN

SOUTH AFRICA
PLACE OF WEEPING

SOUTH KOREA
BBONG
ER WOO DONG (EO U-DONG)
GILSODOM (GILSODDEUM)
WAEBULLEO
YEOJAEUI BANRAN

SPAIN
A LA PALIDA LUZ DE LA LUNA
ADIOS PEQUENA
BANDERA NEGRA
CAGED GLASS (TRAS EL CRISTAL)
DRAGON RAPIDE
EL AMOR BRUJO
EL ANO DE LAS LUCES
EL CABALLERO DEL DRAGON
EL DISPUTADO VOTO DEL SR. CAYO
EL ESTRANGER—OH! DE LA CALLE CRUZ
  DEL SUR
EL HERMANO BASTARDO DE DIOS
EL RIO DE ORO (co: Switz.)
EN PENUMBRA
KILLING MACHINE
LA MITAD DEL CIELO
LA RADIO FOLLA
LA ROSSA DEL BAR
L'APACHE BIANCO (co: Italy)
LAST OF PHILIP BANTER, THE (co: Switz.)
LOLA
LOS PARAISOS PERDIDOS
LULU DE NOCHE
MAMBRU SE FEU A LA GUERRA
MATADOR
ME HACE FALTA UN BIGOTE
MES ENLLA DE LA PASSIO
PULSEBEAT
RAGE (co: Italy)
REQUIEM POR UN CAMPESINO ESPANOL
SEA SERPENT, THE
TEO EL PELIRROJO
TIEMPO DE SILENCIO
27 HORAS
VIAJE A NINGUNA PARTE
WERTHER

SRI LANKA
ARUNATA PERA

SWEDEN
ALLA VI BARN I BULLERBY
AMOROSA
BRODERNA MOZART
DEMONER
DEN FRUSNA LEOPARDEN
GRONA GUBBER FRAN Y.R.
I LAGENS NAMN
JONSSONLIGAN DYKER UPP IGEN
LOVE ME! (ALSKA MIG!)
MALACCA
MIN PAPA AR TARZAN
MOA
MORRHAR OCH ARTOR
ORMENS VAG PA HALLEBERGET
PA LIV OCH DOD
RATTIS
RAVEN
SACRIFICE, THE (OFFRET, co: Fr.)

SWITZERLAND
DER PENDLER
DER SCHWARZE TANNER (co: Aust./Ger.)
DIE WALSCHE (co: Aust./Switz.)
DUNKI-SCHOTT (co: Ger.)
EL RIO DE ORO (co: Spain)
EL SUIZO—UN AMOUR EN ESPAGNE
GENESIS (co: India/Belg./Fr.)
GHAME AFGHAN
GOLDEN EIGHTIES (co: Belg./Fr.)
INNOCENZA
JOUR ET NUIT (co: Fr.)
JOURNEY, THE (DIE REISE, co: Ger.)
KARMA
KONZERT FUR ALICE (co: Aust./Ger.)
LAST OF PHILIP BANTER, THE (co: Spain)
LAST SONG (co: Fr.)
LISI UND DER GENERAL
MORT UN DIMANCHE DE PLUIE (co: Fr.)
MOTTEN IM LICHT
NOAH UND DER COWBOY

SYRIA
SUN ON A HAZY DAY (SHAMS FI YUAM
  GHAIM)
WHAT HAPPENED NEXT YEAR

TAIWAN
DARK NIGHT (co: Hong Kong)
KUEI-MEI, A WOMAN (WO CHE-YANG
  KUO-LE YI-SHENG)
SUMMER AT GRANDPA'S
  (TUNG-TUNG-TE-CHIA-CH'I)
SUPER CITIZEN (CH'AO-CHI SHIH-MIN)
TIME TO LIVE AND A TIME TO DIE
  (TUNG-NIEN WANG-SHIH)
WO ERH HAN-SHENG
YU QING SAO

THAILAND
PEESUA LAE DOKMAI

TUNISIA
AL-KAS
MAN OF ASHES (L'HOMME DE CENDRES)
PIRATES (co: Fr.)

TURKEY
AAH . . . BELINDA
ADI VASFIYE
AMANSIZ UOL
ASILACAK KADIN
BIR AVUC CENNET
CIPLAK VATANDAS
14 NUMARA (ONDORT NUMARA)
GULSUSAN
GUNESE KOPRU
KIRPLANGIC FIRTINASI
KURBAGALAR
KURSUN ATA ATA BITER
KUYUCAKLI YUSUF
OLMEZ AGACI
PRENSES
SEN TURKULERINI SOYLE
SES
SEY SARSILIYOR
TEYZEM
UC HALKA YIRMIBES
UMUT SOKAGI
UMUTLU SAFAKLLAR
YILANLARIN
ZUGURT

UNITED STATES
ABOUT LAST NIGHT
ADVENTURES OF THE AMERICAN RABBIT
AGENT ON ICE
ALIENS
AMERICA
AMERICA 3000
AMERICAN ANTHEM
AMERICAN COMMANDOS
AMERICAN JUSTICE
AMERICAN TAIL, AN
ANGEL RIVER (co: Mex.)
APRIL FOOL'S DAY
ARMED AND DANGEROUS
ARMED RESPONSE
AT CLOSE RANGE
AVENGING FORCE
BACK TO SCHOOL
BAD GUYS
BALBOA
BAND OF THE HAND
BEER
BEGINNER'S LUCK
BELIZAIRE THE CAJUN
BEST OF TIMES, THE
BIG BET, THE
BIG TROUBLE
BIG TROUBLE IN LITTLE CHINA
BILLY GALVIN
BLACK MOON RISING
BLOODY BIRTHDAY
BLUE CITY
BLUE VELVET
BORN AMERICAN (co: Fin.)
BOSS' WIFE, THE
BOY WHO COULD FLY, THE
BREEDERS
BRIGHTON BEACH MEMOIRS
CARNAGE
CHECK IS IN THE MAIL, THE

CHILDREN OF A LESSER GOD
CHOKE CANYON
CHOPPING MALL
CLAN OF THE CAVE BEAR, THE
CLASS OF NUKE'EM HIGH
CLUB PARADISE
COBRA
COCAINE WARS
COLOR OF MONEY, THE
COMBAT SHOCK
COSMIC EYE, THE
CRAWLSPACE
CRIMES OF THE HEART
CRITTERS
CROSSROADS
CRY FROM THE MOUNTAIN
DANGEROUSLY CLOSE
DEAD END KIDS
DEADLY FRIEND
DEATHMASK
DELTA FORCE, THE
DESERT BLOOM
DESPERATE MOVES
DETECTIVE SCHOOL DROPOUTS
DEVASTATOR, THE
DIRT BIKE KID, THE
DOCTOR OTTO & THE RIDDLE OF THE
  GLOOM BEAM
DONNA ROSEBUD
DOWN AND OUT IN BEVERLY HILLS
DOWN BY LAW
DREAM LOVER
EAT AND RUN
8 MILLION WAYS TO DIE
ELIMINATORS
EVERY TIME WE SAY GOODBYE
EXTREMITIES
EYE OF THE TIGER
F/X
FAT GUY GOES NUTZOID
FERRIS BUELLER'S DAY OFF
52 PICK-UP
FINAL MISSION
FINE MESS, A
FIRE IN THE NIGHT
FIRE WITH FIRE
FIREWALKER
FLIGHT OF THE NAVIGATOR
FLIGHT OF THE SPRUCE GOOSE
FLOODSTAGE
FLY, THE
FOXTRAP (co: Italy)
FREE RIDE
FRIDAY THE 13TH PART VI: JASON LIVES
FROM BEYOND
GETTING EVEN
GIRLS SCHOOL SCREAMERS
GOBOTS: BATTLE OF THE ROCK LORDS
GOLDEN CHILD, THE
GOOD TO GO
GREAT MOUSE DETECTIVE, THE
GREAT WALL, A
GUNG HO
HAMBURGER—THE MOTION PICTURE
HANNAH AND HER SISTERS
HARDBODIES 2
HAUNTED HONEYMOON
HEAD OFFICE
HEARTBREAK RIDGE
HEARTBURN
HEATHCLIFF: THE MOVIE
HELL SQUAD
HELLFIRE
HIGHLANDER
HITCHER, THE
HOLLYWOOD VICE SQUAD
HOLLYWOOD ZAP
HOOSIERS
HOT CHILI
HOUSE
HOWARD THE DUCK
HYPER SAPIEN: PEOPLE FROM ANOTHER
  STAR
IMAGEMAKER, THE
IMPURE THOUGHTS
IN 'N' OUT (GRINGO MOJADO, co: Mex.)
IN THE SHADOW OF KILIMANJARO
INSIDE OUT
INSTANT JUSTICE
INVADERS FROM MARS
IRON EAGLE

JAKE SPEED
JO JO DANCER, YOUR LIFE IS CALLING
JUMPIN' JACK FLASH
JUST BETWEEN FRIENDS
KGB—THE SECRET WAR
KAMIKAZE HEARTS
KARATE KID PART II, THE
KILLER PARTY
KING KONG LIVES
KING OF THE STREETS
LABYRINTH
LADIES CLUB, THE
LADY JANE
LAND OF DOOM
LANDSCAPE SUICIDE
LAST RESORT
LEGAL EAGLES
LIGHTNING—THE WHITE STALLION
LIGHTSHIP, THE
LITTLE SHOP OF HORRORS
LONGSHOT, THE
LOW BLOW
LUCAS
MALA NOCHE
MANHATTAN PROJECT, THE
MANHUNTER
MAXIMUM OVERDRIVE
MEN'S CLUB, THE
MODERN GIRLS
MONEY PIT, THE
MONSTER DOG
MORNING AFTER, THE
MOSQUITO COAST, THE
MOUNTAINTOP MOTEL MASSACRE
MOVIE HOUSE MASSACRE
MURPHY'S LAW
MY CHAUFFEUR
MY LITTLE PONY
MY MAN ADAM
NAKED CAGE, THE
NAKED VENGEANCE (co: Phil.)
NAME OF THE ROSE, THE
NATIVE SON
NEON MANIACS
NEVER TOO YOUNG TO DIE
'NIGHT, MOTHER
NIGHT OF THE CREEPS
NIGHTMARE WEEKEND (co: GB/Fr.)
9 1/2 WEEKS
NINJA TURF
NO MERCY
NO RETREAT, NO SURRENDER
NOBODY'S FOOL
NOTHING IN COMMON
NUTCRACKER, THE: THE MOTION
  PICTURE
OCEAN DRIVE WEEKEND
ODD JOBS
OFF BEAT
ON VALENTINE'S DAY
ONE CRAZY SUMMER
ONE MORE SATURDAY NIGHT
OUT OF BOUNDS
OVER THE SUMMER
P.O.W. THE ESCAPE
PARTING GLANCES
PATRIOT, THE
PEGGY SUE GOT MARRIED
PERILS OF P.K., THE
PLATOON
PLAY DEAD
PLAYING FOR KEEPS
POLICE ACADEMY 3: BACK IN TRAINING
POLTERGEIST II
POPULATION: ONE
POSITIVE I.D.
POWER
PRAY FOR DEATH
PRETTY IN PINK
PSYCHO III
QUICKSILVER
QUIET COOL
RAD
RADIOCATIVE DREAMS
RATBOY
RAW DEAL
RAW TUNES
REBEL LOVE
RECRUITS
REFORM SCHOOL GIRLS
RETURN

REVENGE
REVENGE OF THE TEENAGE VIXENS FROM
    OUTER SPACE
RIVERBED (co: Neth.)
ROCKIN' ROAD TRIP
ROLLER BLADE
ROUND MIDNIGHT (co: Fr.)
RUNNING SCARED
RUTHLESS PEOPLE
RYDER, P.I.
SALVADOR
SAVING GRACE
SAY YES
SCORPION
SCREAMPLAY
SCREEN TEST
SEVEN MINUTES IN HEAVEN
SEX APPEAL
SEX O'CLOCK NEWS, THE
SHADOW PLAY
SHADOWS RUN BLACK
SHE'S GOTTA HAVE IT
SHORT CIRCUIT
SIZZLE BEACH, U.S.A.
SLEEPWALK (co: Ger.)
SLOANE
SMART ALEC
SWEET LIBERTY
TAI-PAN
TENEMENT
TERRORVISION
TEXAS CHAINSAW MASSACRE
    PART II, THE
THAT'S LIFE
THRASHIN'
THREE AMIGOS
3:15—THE MOMENT OF TRUTH
THUNDER RUN
TOMB, THE
TOP GUN
TORMENT
TOUCH AND GO
TOUGH GUYS
TRANSFORMERS, THE
TRICK OR TREAT
TROLL
TRUE STORIES
UNDER THE CHERRY MOON
UPHILL ALL THE WAY
VAMP
VASECTOMY: A DELICATE MATTER
VENDETTA
VERY CLOSE QUARTERS
VIOLATED
VIOLETS ARE BLUE
WAY IT IS?, THE
WEEKEND WARRIORS
WELCOME TO 18
WHAT COMES AROUND
WHAT WAITS BELOW
WHATEVER IT TAKES
WHERE ARE THE CHILDREN?
WHERE THE RIVER RUNS BLACK
WHOOPEE BOY, THE
WILD WIND, THE (co: USSR/Yugo.)
WILDCATS
WIRED TO KILL
WISDOM
WISE GUYS
WITCHFIRE
WORKING GIRLS
WRAITH, THE
YOUNGBLOOD
ZONE TROOPERS

USSR
BORIS GUDUNOV (co: Czech.)
CHICHERIN
CHTO U SENJKI BYIO
CHUZHAJA, BELAJA I RJABAJ
COME AND SEE (IDI I SMOTRI)
COPABLANCA (co: Cuba)
DEN GNEVA
DESCENDENT OF THE SNOW LEOPARD
    (POTOMOK BELOGO BARSA)
FOUETTE
GRANNY GENERAL
IDEAALMAASTIK
KAK MOLODY MY BYLI
KHOZIAIN
KHRANI MENIO, MOI TALISMAN

MOI DRUG IVAN LAPSHIN
MUZSKOE VOSPITANIE
NAERTA OMETI
NEBYVALSHINA
ODINOTCHNOYE PLAVANIYE
PISMA MERTVOGO CHELOVEKA
POTERYALSYA SLON
REIS 222
ROBINSONIADA ANU CHEMI INGLISELI
    PAPA
SAPIRHURIN
SUNUS PALAIDUNAS
SVESAS KAISLIBAS
TORPIDONOSTCI
VYITI ZAMUZH ZA KAPITANA
WILD WIND, THE (co: US/Yugo.)
YOUNG COMPOSER'S ODYSSEY, A
ZAKONNY BRAK
ZAZZENNYJ FONAR
ZIMNI VECHER V GAGRAKH

VENEZUELA
A LA SALIDA NOS VEMOS (co: Colombia)
MANON
PEQUENA REVANCHA

VIETNAM
LOI RE TRAI TREN DUONG MON

WEST GERMANY
AM NACHESTEN MORGAN KEHRTE DER
    MINISTER NICHT AN SEINEN
ARBEITSPLATZ ZURUCK
ANGRY HARVEST (BITTERE ARNTE)
AUF IMMER UND EWIG
BLIND DIRECTOR
CLASS RELATIONS
    (KLASSENVERHALTNISSE)
DAS SCHWEIGEN DES DICHTERS
DER POLENWEIHER
DER ROSENKONIG
DER SCHWARZE TANNER (co: Aust./Switz.)
DER SEXTE SINN
DER SOMMER DES SAMURAI
DER WILDE CLOWN
DIE LIEBESWUSTE
DIE WALSCHE (co: Aust./Switz.)
DIE ZWEI GEISCHTER DES JANUAR
DOUCE FRANCE (co: Fr.)
DUNKI-SCHOTT (co: Switz.)
EAST OF THE WALL (WESTLER)
EIN BLICK UNE DIE LIEBE BRICT AUS
EIN FLIEHENDES PFERD
ERDSEGEN (co: Aust.)
FATHERLAND (co: Brit.)
50/50
FLIGHT NORTH (FLUCHT IN DEN
    NORDEN, co: Fin.)
FOLLOWING THE FUHRER (DIE
    MITLAUFER)
40 SQUARE METERS OF GERMANY
    (40 M2 DEUTSCHLAND)
FUTURE OF EMILY, THE (FLUGEL UND
    FESSELN, co: Fr.)
GINGER AND FRED (co: Fr./Italy)
HEIDENLOCHER (co: Aust.)
HEILT HITLER
JOURNEY, THE (DIE REISE, co: Switz.)
KILLING CARS
KONZERT FUR ALICE (co: Aust./Switz.)
LAPUTA
MALABRIGO (co: Cuba/Brit./Peru)
MEIER
MOMO (co: Italy)
NO TIME TO DIE (co: Indonesia)
NOVEMBERKATZEN
PARADIES
ROSA LUXEMBURG
SCHLEUSE 17
SCHWARZ UND OHNE ZUCKER
SLEEPWALK (co: US)
SPRING SYMPHONY
    (FRUHLINGSSINFONIE, co: E. Ger.)
STAMMHEIM
TAGEDIEBE
TAROT
'38 (co: Aust.)
TOMMASO BLU (co: Italy)
VA BANQUE
VIRUS HAS NO MORALS, A (EIN VIRUS
    KENNT KEINE MORAL)

WALKMAN BLUES (co: Brit.)
WOHIN MIT WILLLFRIED
ZONING

YUGOSLAVIA
ADA
ANTICASANOVA
BAL NA VODI
BUTNSKALA
CHRISTOPHORUS
CRVENI I CRNI
DEBELI I MRSAVI
DO YOU REMEMBER DOLLY BELL?
    (SJECAS LI SE DOLLY BELL?)
DOBROVOLJCI
DOKTOR
DRZANJE ZA VAZDUH
HORVATOV IZBOR
I TO CE PROCI
JAZOL
KORMORAN
KRAJ RATA
LEPOTA POROKA
LIJEPE ZENE PROLAZE KROZ GRAD
LJUBAVNA
LJUBEZEN
NAS CLOVEK
NIJE LAKO S MUSKARCIMA
NJERIU PREJ DHEU
OBECANA ZEMLJA
OD PETKA DO PETKA
ORKESTAR JEDNE MLADOSTI
OVNI IN MAMUTI
PROKA
SAN O RUZI
SRECNA NOVA '49
VECERNJA ZVONA
WILD WIND, THE (co: US/USSR)
ZA SRECU JE POTREBNO TROJE
ZABRAVOTE TOZI SLOCHAI

Name Index

This index comprises a filmography of all the people listed in the acting and production credit sections of the movie reviews. It also gives reference to those names which appear in the Obituaries and People to Watch sections of this volume.

Unless otherwise noted, the credit given is for acting in the film listed. Technical credits are identified by abbreviations following film titles. The abbreviations stand for the following functions:

p: producer
w: writer (both screenplay and source)
m: musical score
ed: editor
art d: art director
cos: costumes
ch: choreography
anim: animation

d: director
ph: cinematographer
md: musical director
prod d: production designer
set d: set designer
spec eff: special effects
tech adv: technical adviser
m/l: music and lyrics

Unabbreviated functions are stunts and makeup. For those performing multiple functions on a film, the title is listed each time, with the function following.

Movie people are notorious name changers. This index lists names, aliases, and sobriquets of both players and technical staff has given in the credits for a particular picture. Thus, the same person may be listed more than once—as Robert, for example, then again as Bob.

Ackles, Kenneth V. [Kenneth Vincent Ackles]
Obituaries

Ackley, James
HOLLYWOOD ZAP!, m; HOLLYWOOD ZAP!, md

Acogny, George
PLAYING FOR KEEPS, m

Acosta, Ivan
AMIGOS, d&w

Acqlino, Mario
NTTURUDU

Acquisto, Sal
AMERICAN JUSTICE

Acremant, Germaine
Obituaries

Adair, Catherine
IMAGEMAKER, THE, cos

Adair, John
BEGINNER'S LUCK

Adam, Ken
CRIMES OF THE HEART, prod d

Adamek, Witold
JEZIORO BODENSKIE, ph

Adamira, Jiri
LEV S BILOU HRIVOU

Adamo, Sherry
AMERICAN JUSTICE

Adamovich, Ales
COME AND SEE, w

Adamovich, Les
COME AND SEE, w

Adams, Andrea
REVENGE

Adams, Brian
DEATH OF A SOLDIER

Adams, Eric Troy
TOUCH AND GO

Adams, Evan
TOBY MCTEAGUE

Adams, Gary
BIG HURT, THE

Adams, James
IMAGEMAKER, THE

Adams, John
VENDETTA, w

Adams, Lisa
3:15, THE MOMENT OF TRUTH

Adams, Mason
F/X

Adams, Michael
NOBODY'S FOOL, stunts

Adams, Phil
CHOKE CANYON, stunts

Adams, Ron
PATRIOT, THE

Adams, Tony
FINE MESS, A, p; THAT'S LIFE, p

Adcock, Christopher
HYPER SAPIEN: PEOPLE FROM ANOTHER STAR, w

Addario, Danny
PINK CHIQUITAS, THE, art d

Adderson, Wayne
BEST OF TIMES, THE

Addie, Brenda
MORE THINGS CHANGE, THE

Addison, Bernard
KING KONG LIVES

Addison, James
SMART ALEC, ed

Adducci, Franco
NAME OF THE ROSE, THE

Adefarasin, Remi
SHOOT FOR THE SUN, ph

Adelin, Jean-Claude
SCENE OF THE CRIME

Adelson, Gary
BOY WHO COULD FLY, THE, p

Adiba, Alain-Jacques
PRUNELLE BLUES

Adler, Charlie
MY LITTLE PONY

Adler, Matt
FLIGHT OF THE NAVIGATOR

Admovska, Zlata
LEV S BILOU HRIVOU

Adner, Jonas
RATTIS, anim

Adolfo, Antonio
SONHO SEM FIM, m

Adorf, Mario
CLASS RELATIONS; LA RAGAZZA DEI LILLA;
MOMO; SECOND VICTORY, THE

Adouani, Mustafa
MAN OF ASHES

Adriani, Patricia
LULU DE NOCHE; MES ENLLA DE LA PASSIO

Adrineda, Jovita
TAI-PAN

Adu, Sade
ABSOLUTE BEGINNERS, m/l

Aedma, Alar
BEER

Aerts, Elie
CONGO EXPRESS

Aeschlimann, Larry
GETTING EVEN, makeup

Affane, Mohamed
CHAMS, ph

Affolter, Therese
MOTTEN IM LICHT; STAMMHEIM

Afifi, Hussein
AL BEDAYA, ed

Afonso, Yves
MAINE-OCEAN

Agata, Morio
TO SLEEP SO AS TO DREAM; TO SLEEP SO AS TO
DREAM, m

Agbayani, Tetchie
MONEY PIT, THE

Ageli, Adam
SCORPION

Agenin, Beatrice
LA FEMME DE MA VIE

Agins, Robert
COLOR OF MONEY, THE

Agius, Jamie
SHORT CHANGED

Agoris, Takis
TO DENDRO POU PLIGONAME

Agostini, Claude
BLACK MIC-MAC, ph; PAULETTE, ph

Agostini, Diane
SWEET LIBERTY

Agostini, Didier
L'AMANT MAGNIFIQUE

Agostinucci, Giovanni
SENSI, art d; SEPARATI IN CASA, art d

Agouni, Sid-Ahmed
TAHOUNET AL SAYED FABRE

Agrasanchez, J. David
EL SECUESTRO DE CAMARENA, p

Agraz, Jose Luis Garcia
LAS NOCHES DEL CALIFAS, d

Agree, Donald
BEER

Agren, Janet
HANDS OF STEEL

Agresti, Alejandro
EL HOMBRE QUE GANO LA RAZON, p,d,w,ph&m

Aguanno, Dolores
CROSSROADS

Agudel, Pablo
EL TREN DE LOS PIONEROS

Agudelo, Marcela
VISA U.S.A.

Aguero, Ignacio
NEMESIO

Aguerre, Roberto
ELOGIO DELLA PAZZIA, d&w

Aguia, Bacheba
A LA SALIDA NOS VEMOS

Aguilar, Antonio
EL EXTRANO HIJO DEL SHERIFF

Aguilar, Chris
P.O.W. THE ESCAPE

Aguilar, Ernesto
EL TREN DE LOS PIONEROS

Aguilera, Alberto
ES MI VIDA—EL NOA NOA 2; ES MI VIDA—EL NOA
NOA 2, p

Aguirre, Hilda
RAFAGA DE PLOMO

Aguirresarobe, Javier
27 HORAS, ph; MANON, ph

Agulian, Daniel
WIRED TO KILL, ed

Ahlberg, Mac
ELIMINATORS, ph; FROM BEYOND, ph; HOUSE, ph;
ZONE TROOPERS, ph

Ahlstedt, Borje
AMOROSA

Ahmad, Hamdy
EL YOM EL SADES

Ahmad, Maher
ONE MORE SATURDAY NIGHT, art d; RAW DEAL, art
d; WHATEVER IT TAKES, prod d

Ahmadi, Morteza
BUS, THE

Ahmed, Buibul
DAHAN

Ahmed, Fouad
AL KETTAR

Ahmed, Hamdi
AL BEDAYA

Ahmed, Lalita
KIND OF ENGLISH, A

Ahmed, Mohsen
AL BEDAYA, ph

Ahrens, Paul
3:15, THE MOMENT OF TRUTH, prod d

Ahrle, Leif
PA LIV OCH DOD

Ahrne, Marianne
PA LIV OCH DOD, d; PA LIV OCH DOD, ed; PA LIV
OCH DOD, w

Ai, Hsiao
TIME TO LIVE AND A TIME TO DIE, A

Aichhorn, Hubsi
HEIDENLOCHER

Aichhorn, Maria
HEIDENLOCHER

Aichhorn, Matthias
HEIDENLOCHER

Aiello, Danny
DEATHMASK

Aiken, Joan
MORT UN DIMANCHE DE PLUIE, w

Aikens, Greg
WEEKEND WARRIORS

Aimee, Anouk
MAN AND A WOMAN: 20 YEARS LATER, A

Ain, Maxine
HARDBODIES 2

Aiszky, Gabor Kerny
AVENGING FORCE, makeup

Aitken, Laurie
ABSOLUTE BEGINNERS, m/l

Aitken, Maria
HALF MOON STREET

Aizawa, Akiko
TYPHOON CLUB

Aja, Philip
VAMP, art d

Ajvazjan, Agasi
ZAZZENNYJ FONAR, d&w

Akalaitis, JoAnne
DEAD END KIDS, d&w

Akan, Jean
TOUCH AND GO, set d

Akan, Tarik
BIR AVUO CENNET

Akay, Izzet
FORTY SQUARE METERS OF GERMANY, ph

Akendengue, Pierre
SARRAOUNIA, m

Akerman, Chantal
GOLDEN EIGHTIES, d; GOLDEN EIGHTIES, m/l;
GOLDEN EIGHTIES, w

Akers, Andra
JUST BETWEEN FRIENDS; ODD JOBS

Akers, George
CARAVAGGIO, ed

Akers, Karen
HEARTBURN

Akkemay
ASSAULT, THE

Akmatova, K.
DESCENDANT OF THE SNOW LEOPARD, THE

Ako
SLEEPWALK

Akutsu, Etsuo
UEMURA NAOMI MONOGATARI, ph

Al Choukrgi, Jawad
AL ASHEKE

Al Faucal, Hala
WHAT HAPPENED NEXT YEAR

Al Rakabi, Abdulkhalek
AL ASHEKE, w

Al Rawi, Abdul Hadi
HOB FEE BAGHDAD, d&w

Al Wadi, Helmi
AL ASHEKE, m

Alabisio, Daniele
SQUADRA SELVAGGIA, ed

Alabiso, Daniele
SENSI, ed

Alabiso, Eugenio
THUNDER WARRIOR, ed

Aladjem, Norman
FIREWALKER, w

Alaimo, Mark
AVENGING FORCE

Alan, Didi
BAD GUYS

Alarcon, Mario
PERROS DE LA NOCHE

Alarcon, Victor
EN PENUMBRA, set d

Alaverdjan, Genrich
ZAZZENNYJ FONAR

Alazraki, Robert
CONSEIL DE FAMILLE, ph; LA FEMME SECRETE, ph;
LOVE SONGS, ph; SAUVE-TOI, LOLA, ph

Alba, Guillermina
DONA HERLINDA AND HER SON

Alba, Maria Carolina
SEPARATI IN CASA

Albain, Richard
LONGSHOT, THE, spec eff

Albalos, Nestor C.
LOW BLOW

Albani, Romano
LA SPOSA AMERICANA, ph; TERRORVISION, ph;
TROLL, ph

Albano, Captain Lou
WISE GUYS

Albeniz, Raquel
PERROS DE LA NOCHE

Albert, Arthur
ODD JOBS, ph; STREETS OF GOLD, ph

Albert, Eddie
HEAD OFFICE

Albert, Edward
GETTING EVEN

Albert, Pierre
GOLDEN EIGHTIES, cos; L'AUBE, cos

Albert, Raoul
CHARLOTTE FOR EVER, art d

Albert, Ross
BLUE CITY, ed

Alberti, Guido
SAVING GRACE

Alberti, Willy
CHARLEY, m

Albertinazzi, Marta
MAN FACING SOUTHEAST, set d

Albertine, Charles
Obituaries

Albertini, Adalberto
TRE SUPERMEN A SANTO DOMINGO, w

Albertini, Pier Giorgio
TRE SUPERMEN A SANTO DOMINGO, ph

Albertson, Eric
KILLER PARTY, ed

Albiez, Peter
DEADLY FRIEND, spec eff

Albiston, Mark
COOL CHANGE

Albonico, Giulio
L'ULTIMA MAZURKA, ph; SENZA SCRUPOLI, ph

Albrecht-Lovell, Ute
ZONING, ed

Albulescu, Mircea
NOI, CEI DIN LINIA INTII

Alcaine, Jose Luis
EL CABALLERO DEL DRAGON, ph; LA MITAD DEL
CIELO, ph; LOS PARAISOS PERDIDOS, ph; MAMBRU
SE FUE A LA GUERRA, ph; VIAJE A NINGUNA
PARTE, ph

Alcala, Maria Luisa
LA ALACRANA

Alcalde, Jose
MANON, ed

Alcantara, Pedro
A LA SALIDA NOS VEMOS, art d

Alcarraf, Abdul Amtr
HOB FEE BAGHDAD, m

Alchin, Ray
GREAT EXPECTATIONS—THE AUSTRALIAN STORY,
p

Alcocer, Teresa
DRAGON RAPIDE, ed

Alcocer, Victor
POR UN VESTIDO DE NOVIA; UN HOMBRE
VIOLENTE

Alcoriza, Luis
TERROR Y ENCAJES NEGROS, d&w

Alda, Alan
SWEET LIBERTY; SWEET LIBERTY, d&w

Alda, Antony
SMART ALEC; SWEET LIBERTY

Alda, Elizabeth
NIGHT OF THE CREEPS

Alden, Norm
TRANSFORMERS: THE MOVIE, THE

Alderman, Jason
FERRIS BUELLER'S DAY OFF

Alderman, Jason Robert
LUCAS

Alders, Jose
AFZIEN, w

Alderskanz, Leif
GRONA GUBBAR FRAN Y.R.

Alderson, Brooke
FINE MESS, A

Alderson, Jude
SID AND NANCY

Alderson, Nancy
DR. OTTO AND THE RIDDLE OF THE GLOOM BEAM

Aldrich, John
WILD BEASTS

Aldrich, Kristen
BACK TO SCHOOL

Aldrich, Richard   [Richard Stoddard Aldrich]
Obituaries

Aldridge, Kitty
ROOM WITH A VIEW, A

Aldridge, Michael
CLOCKWISE; SHANGHAI SURPRISE

Aldridge, Shirley
SORORITY HOUSE MASSACRE

Alegre, Irma
P.O.W. THE ESCAPE

Alejandra, Mayra
MANON

Alekan, Henri
ESTHER, ph; TOP OF THE WHALE, ph

Aleksander, Grant
TOUGH GUYS

Aleman, Selva
CONTAR HASTA TEN

Aleman, Seva
INSOMNIACS

Alene, Fernanda
ROMANCE

Alessandrini, Toni
HELL SQUAD

Aletter, Frank
VASECTOMY: A DELICATE MATTER

Alexakis, Tassos
I NICHTA ME TI SILENA, ph

Alexander, Brigida
REDONDO

Alexander, Denyse
LADY JANE

Alexander, Dick
WRAITH, THE

Alexander, Frank
STAR CRYSTAL

Alexander, Gary
AVENGING FORCE; SEX O'CLOCK NEWS, THE

Alexander, Gerry
ABSOLUTE BEGINNERS

Alexander, Jason
BRIGHTON BEACH MEMOIRS; MOSQUITO COAST,
THE

Alexander, Louis
SCORPION

Alexander, Max
FAT GUY GOES NUTZOID!!

Alexander, Richard
NO SURRENDER

Alexander, Roland
ABSOLUTE BEGINNERS

Alexander, Shalin
ABSOLUTE BEGINNERS

Alexandre, Manuel
EL ANO DE LAS LUCES

Alexandre, Marcelo
SERE CUALQUIER COSA PERO TE QUIERO

Alexandridis, Helene
THERESE

Alexandropoulou, Electra
ENAS ISICHOS THANATOS

Alexandrov, Vadim
BORIS GODUNOV

Alexandru, George
NOI, CEI DIN LINIA INTII

Alexiev, Stoyan
ZA KUDE PUTOVATE

Alexis, Alvin
SWEET LIBERTY

Alfano, Albert
CARNAGE

Alfieri, Eric
MAMMAME

Alfred, Mark
FAT GUY GOES NUTZOID!!

Algora, Francisco
TIEMPO DE SILENCIO

Ali Fettar, Said
RAI, d&w

Ali, Jamal
BLACK JOY, w

Ali, Jamil
KIND OF ENGLISH, A

Ali, Jorge
UN HOMBRE DE EXITO

Ali, Nagat
AL BEDAYA

Ali, Nihad
FLAMING BORDERS, ph

Ali, Sheikh Niamat
DAHAN, d&w

Alianak, Hirant
HEAD OFFICE

Alianak, Hrant
ONE NIGHT ONLY

Alie, Makqsoom
TRIKAL

Aligholi, Mohammad Reza
CLOSED CIRCUIT, m; MONSTER, THE, m

Aligrudic, Slobodan
DO YOU REMEMBER DOLLY BELL?

Alim, Mamdouth Abdel
MESHWAR OMAR

Alimbajeva, Guinara
DESCENDANT OF THE SNOW LEOPARD, THE

Alimbau, Yolanda
EL RIO DE ORO, cos

Alisa, Nit
ANGKOR-CAMBODIA EXPRESS

Alkalay, Moscu
BAR 51—SISTER OF LOVE

Alkanov, N.
PISMA MERTVOGO CHELOVEKA

Allaire, Laurent
LAST SONG; LAST SONG, prod d

Allal, Rachid Ben
RAI, ed

Allan, Cameron
GOING SANE, m

Allan, Jack
AROUND THE WORLD IN EIGHTY WAYS

Allan, John
BIG HURT, THE

Allan, Lee Taylor
PULSEBEAT

Allan, Lewis   [Abel Meeropol]
Obituaries

Allaoui, Karim
PRUNELLE BLUES

Allard, Catherine
UNDER THE CHERRY MOON

Allard, Eric
SHORT CIRCUIT, spec eff

Allaz, Jean
UNDER THE CHERRY MOON

Alldredge, Michael
ABOUT LAST NIGHT

Allebust, Kine
NOE HEIT ANNET

Allen, A.K.
LADIES CLUB, THE, d

Amoros, Juan
DRAGON RAPIDE, ph; EL ANO DE LAS LUCES, ph;
LULU DE NOCHE, ph; TIEMPO DE SILENCIO, ph

Amoroso, Joe
SENZA SCRUPOLI, m

Amos, Beth
BULLIES

Amott, Sherry
LABYRINTH

Amphoux, Michel
PARENTAL CLAIM

Amrapurkar, Sadashiv
AGHAAT

Amshinskaya, Elena
PISMA MERTVOGO CHELOVEKA, art d

Amundsen, Steve
LOW BLOW, m

Amurri, Franco
IL RAGAZZO DEL PONY EXPRESS, d; IL RAGAZZO
DEL PONY EXPRESS, w

Amy, George J.
Obituaries

An, Le Dinh
LOI RE TRAI TREN DUONG MON, ph

An, Thuy
KARMA

An-shun, Yu
TIME TO LIVE AND A TIME TO DIE, A

Anaheed
HELL SQUAD

Anam, Saidul
DAHAN, ed

Anamar
REPORTER X

Anastasia, Alvin
COLOR OF MONEY, THE

Anastassiades, Stelios
DANILO TRELES, O FIMISMENOS ANDALOUSIANOS
MOUSIKOS

Anbar, Netaya
SMILE OF THE LAMB, THE, ed

Anchia, Juan Ruiz
AT CLOSE RANGE, ph; IN 'N' OUT, ph

Ancira, Carlos
LA ALACRANA

Anconina, Richard
LE MOME; LOVE SONGS; POLICE; ZONE ROUGE

Ander, Hedvig
MOA, cos

Anderle, David
ONE CRAZY SUMMER, md

Anders, Chris
NAKED CAGE, THE

Anders, Jamie
PRETTY IN PINK

Andersen, Claes
MORENA, m

Andersen, Knut
MACARONI BLUES

Andersen, Thyge
TWIST & SHOUT

Anderson, Adele
LADY JANE

Anderson, Andy
POSITIVE I.D., ed; POSITIVE I.D., p, d&w

Anderson, Bill
NEVER TOO YOUNG TO DIE, ed

Anderson, Bo   [Burt Anderson]
Obituaries

Anderson, Carol
NUTCRACKER: THE MOTION PICTURE

Anderson, Clyde
MONSTER DOG, d&w

Anderson, Dame Judith
IMPURE THOUGHTS

Anderson, Dave
GOSPEL ACCORDING TO VIC, THE

Anderson, Doug
AT CLOSE RANGE; BEER

Anderson, E. Erich
WELCOME TO 18

Anderson, Eric
SUNSET STRIP, ph

Anderson, Ernie
LONGSHOT, THE; THAT'S LIFE

Anderson, Gordon
RATBOY

Anderson, Hesper
CHILDREN OF A LESSER GOD, w

Anderson, Jane
HOOSIERS, cos

Anderson, Jean
SCREAMTIME

Anderson, Joey
DR. OTTO AND THE RIDDLE OF THE GLOOM BEAM

Anderson, John
MOSQUITO COAST, THE, set d; NEVER TOO YOUNG
TO DIE; SCORPION

Anderson, Kent
JONSSONLIGAN DYKER UPP IGEN

Anderson, Kevin
STILL POINT, THE, ph

Anderson, Laurie
SOMETHING WILD, m

Anderson, Louie
RATBOY

Anderson, Louis
FERRIS BUELLER'S DAY OFF; QUICKSILVER

Anderson, Max W.
BLACK MOON RISING, spec eff

Anderson, Melody
BOY IN BLUE, THE; FIREWALKER

Anderson, Michael
SEPARATE VACATIONS, d

Anderson, Miles
SKY BANDITS

Anderson, Mitchell
SPACECAMP

Anderson, Nelson
KING OF THE STREETS

Anderson, Pam
VIOLATED

Anderson, Richard Dean
ODD JOBS

Anderson, Selwyn
BRIDGE TO NOWHERE, spec eff

Anderson, Stanley
IMAGEMAKER, THE

Anderson-Gunter, Jeffrey
OFF BEAT

Andersson, Bibi
HUOMENNA; MATADOR; POBRE MARIPOSA

Andersson, Birgitta
JONSSONLIGAN DYKER UPP IGEN

Andersson, Claes
MORENA

Andersson, Gerd
BRODERNA MOZART

Andersson, Kent
MORRHAR OCH ARTOR

Andersson, Roger
BRODERNA MOZART

Andersson, Torbjorn
MIN PAPA AR TARZAN, ph

Anderzon, Kim
MIN PAPA AR TARZAN

Anderzon, Tin-Tin
PA LIV OCH DOD

Andes, John
NO RETREAT, NO SURRENDER

Andew, Chris
RADIOACTIVE DREAMS

Andolfi, Antonio
LA CROCE DALLE 7 PIETRE, d&w

Andorai, Peter
ERZEKENY BUCSU A FEJEDELEMTOL; GREAT
GENERATION, THE

Andras, Ferenc
GREAT GENERATION, THE, d; GREAT
GENERATION, THE, w

Andre, Alfonso
CRONICA DE FAMILIA

Andre, Camir
KILLER PARTY

Andre, Carole
VIOLENT BREED, THE

Andre, Dominique
COURS PRIVE, art d; FEMMES DE PERSONNE, art d;
LA GITANE, art d; LE DEBUTANT, art d

Andreacchio, Mario
FAIR GAME, d

Andreasson, Willie
RAVEN

Andrei, Frederic
PARIS MINUIT; PARIS MINUIT, d; PARIS MINUIT, w

Andreou, Lazaros
CARAVAN SARAI

Andreozzi, Jack
JO JO DANCER, YOUR LIFE IS CALLING

Andres, Gumersindo
ME HACE FALTA UN BIGOTE, set d; MONSTER DOG,
art d; TIEMPO DE SILENCIO, cos

Andreu, Simon
VIAJE A NINGUNA PARTE

Andrews, Ann
Obituaries

Andrews, Anthony
SECOND VICTORY, THE

Andrews, Barry
MANHUNTER, m/l

Andrews, Garfield
BUSTED UP

Andrews, Julie
DUET FOR ONE; THAT'S LIFE

Andrews, Real
BUSTED UP

Andrews, V.C.   [Virginia Cleo Andrews]
Obituaries

Andriessen, Jurriaan
ASSAULT, THE, m

Andrikos, Lefteris
HARDBODIES 2

Andry, Richard
PEAU D'ANGE, ph

Andzic-Ursulov, Bjanka
LIJEPE ZENE PROLAZE KROZ GRAD, cos

Anelli, Guido
LA MONACA NEL PECCATO, m; LUSSURI, m;
VOGLIA DI GUARDARE, m

Anemone
I LOVE YOU

Ange, Jerome
NEXT SUMMER

Angel, Jack
TRANSFORMERS: THE MOVIE, THE

Angel, Miguel
KAPAX DEL AMAZONAS, d&w

Angelakos, Christos
ENAS ISICHOS THANATOS, w

Angelakos, Kyriakos
ENAS ISICHOS THANATOS, w

Angelis, Michael
NO SURRENDER

Angelle, Gary
SNO-LINE

Angelopoulos, Theo
O MELISSOKOMOS, d; O MELISSOKOMOS, w

Anglade, Jean-Hugues
BETTY BLUE

Angrisano, Franco
CAMORRA

Ani, Youssef El
EL YOM EL SADES

Anka, Mustapha El
LAST IMAGE, THE

Ankito
BRAS CUBAS

Ann-Margret
52 PICK-UP

Ann-Morris, Tracey
TERRY ON THE FENCE

Annaud, Jean-Jacques
NAME OF THE ROSE, THE, d

Annaud, Monique
BLACK MIC-MAC, p; BLACK MIC-MAC, w

Anne, Mary
SORORITY HOUSE MASSACRE

Annear, Doug
RECRUITS

Annese, Frank
MURPHY'S LAW

Annesley, Imogen
PLAYING BEATIE BOW

Annett, Paul
GIRL FROM MANI, THE, d

Anni, Anna
OTELLO, cos

Annichiarico, Silvia
SETTE CHILI IN SETTE GIORNI

Annie-Belle
LA VENEXIANA

Annis, Francesca
EL RIO DE ORO; UNDER THE CHERRY MOON

Ansara, Michael
KGB—THE SECRET WAR

Ansel, Arlene
INSIDE OUT, cos

Anselmi, Renato
LISI UND DER GENERAL, m

Anselmo, Paul
ECHO PARK

Anselmo, Tony
GREAT MOUSE DETECTIVE, THE

Anshel, Eitan
ALEX KHOLE AHAVA

Anspaugh, David
HOOSIERS, d

Anstiss, Chic
ARTHUR'S HALLOWED GROUND, ph

Antaeus, Ayo
ABSOLUTE BEGINNERS

Anthony, Bob
Obituaries

Anthony, David   [William Dale Smith]
Obituaries

Anthony, Lee
HOWARD THE DUCK

Anthony, Michael
LEGAL EAGLES

Anthony, Wayne
FAIR GAME

Antico, Pete
STREETS OF GOLD

Antico, Peter
PLAYING FOR KEEPS

Antillano, Laura
PEQUENA REVANCHA, w

Antin, Robin
MY CHAUFFEUR

Antoine, Jean Michel
GINGER & FRED

Antona, Marc
LABYRINTH

Antonelli, Laura
GRANDI MAGAZZINI; LA VENEXIANA

Antonetti, Mickey
ONE MORE SATURDAY NIGHT, cos

Antoni, Thomas
WOLF AT THE DOOR, THE

Antonio, Estrella
P.O.W. THE ESCAPE

Antonio, Lauro
O VESTIDO COR DE FOGO, p, d&w

Antoniou, Theodore
GIRL FROM MANI, THE, m

Antonucci, Monica
GIRLS SCHOOL SCREAMERS

Anttila, Casper
BORN AMERICAN

Anwar, Dolly
DAHAN

Anz, Maria
AMERICAN ANTHEM

Anzaloni, John
PLAYING FOR KEEPS

Anzio
LONGSHOT, THE

Anzola, Alfredo J.
PEQUENA REVANCHA, p; PEQUENA REVANCHA, ph

Aparicio, Rafaela
EL ANO DE LAS LUCES

Aparicio, Yiran
ESE LOCO LOCO HOSPITAL

Aparijo, Martin
QUICKSILVER

Aplon, Boris
BACK TO SCHOOL

Apogee
VAMP, spec eff

Apone, Allan A.
NEON MANIACS, makeup

Apostolou, George
BUSTED UP

Appere, Caroline
LE BONHEUR A ENCORE FRAPPE

Appet, Leah
EVERY TIME WE SAY GOODBYE, w

Appignani, Luciano
FINAL EXECUTIONER, THE, p; JUNGLE RAIDERS, p

Applebaum, Lawrence
THUNDER RUN, p

Appleby, Bob
TAI-PAN

Applegate, Royce O.
ARMED AND DANGEROUS

Aprea, John
AMERICAN ANTHEM

April, Renee
CHILDREN OF A LESSER GOD, cos

Aptekman, Igor
LES FRERES PETARD, w

Aquilon, Raymond
LE BONHEUR A ENCORE FRAPPE; LES FRERES PETARD

Ar, Mujde
ADI VASFIYE

Aragon, Angelica
EL VECINDARIO—LOS MEXICANOS CALIENTES

Aragon, Jesse
3:15, THE MOMENT OF TRUTH; ECHO PARK

Aragon, Manuel Gutierrez
LA MITAD DEL CIELO, d; LA MITAD DEL CIELO, w

Aragon, Raul
SLOANE

Arai, Hiro
CAPTIVE

Araiza, Armando
LOS ASES DE CONTRABANDO

Araiza, Fabiola
OBDULIA

Araiza, Raul
EL MALEFICIO II, d&w

Arana, Miguel
RAFAGA DE PLOMO, ph

Aranda, Vicente
TIEMPO DE SILENCIO, d; TIEMPO DE SILENCIO, w

Aranyossy, Georges
THERESE

Araoz, Elida
EIN BLICK—UND DIE LIEBE BRICHT AUS

Arashtajev, A.
DESCENDANT OF THE SNOW LEOPARD, THE

Aratow, Paul
MY MAN ADAM, p

Arau, Alfonso
THREE AMIGOS

Araujo, Gabriela
THANATOS

Araujo, Guilherme
CINEMA FALADO, p

Aravindan, G.
CHIDAMBARAM, d&w; ORIDATH, d&w

Arbas, Derya
KUYUCAKLI YUSUF

Arbogast, Bob
ADVENTURES OF THE AMERICAN RABBIT, THE

Arbogast, Roy
THREE AMIGOS, spec eff

Arbogast, Thierry
GARDIEN DE LA NUIT, ph

Arbus, Allan
CROSSROADS

Arcand, Denys
DECLINE OF THE AMERICAN EMPIRE, THE, d&w

Arcand, Gabriel
DECLINE OF THE AMERICAN EMPIRE, THE

Arcand, Michel
ANNE TRISTER, ed; LA GUEPE, ed

Arcaraz, Luis
POR UN VESTIDO DE NOVIA, m

Arceo, Gil
PLATOON, stunts

Archer, Anne
CHECK IS IN THE MAIL, THE

Archer, Elizabeth
BIG HURT, THE

Archerd, Evan
AMERICAN ANTHEM, w; LAST RESORT, THE, m/l

Archibald, Dawn
BLOOD RED ROSES; MONA LISA; MY BEAUTIFUL LAUNDRETTE

Archie, John
FLIGHT OF THE NAVIGATOR

Arcure, Anthony
PLAYING FOR KEEPS

Arcuri, Francesco
JUNGLE RAIDERS

Ardant, Fanny
CONSEIL DE FAMILLE; LE PALTOQUET; MELO; NEXT SUMMER

Arden, Robert
LITTLE SHOP OF HORRORS

Ardenstam, Sten
PA LIV OCH DOD

Ardis, Judy
ROCKIN' ROAD TRIP

Ardisson, Giorgio
AMORE INQUIETO DI MARIA; CATTIVI PIERROT; LA CROCE DALLE 7 PIETRE

Arditi, Catherine
MELO

Arditi, Pierre
FEMMES DE PERSONNE; L'ETAT DE GRACE; MELO; SUIVEZ MON REGARD

Arditi, Ronnie
MALKAT HAKITA

Ardstrom, Mats
ALLA VI BARN I BULLERBY, ph; MOA, ph

Ardy, Jean
SINCERELY CHARLOTTE, p

Arellanos, Alberto
LA ALACRANA, ph

Areltanos, Alberto
MATANZA EN MATAMOROS, ph

Arena, Miguel
NOCHE DE JUERGA, ph

Arenin, Vladimir
BORIS GODUNOV, prod d

Arestrup, Niels
SINCERELY CHARLOTTE

Arevalo, Mario
SALVADOR

Arflot, Andreas
LOVE ME!, m

Arfman, Phil
RYDER, P.I., ph

Argall, Ray
WRONG WORLD, ed; WRONG WORLD, ph

Argento, Asia
DEMONI 2—L'INCUBO RITORNA

Argento, Dario
DEMONI 2—L'INCUBO RITORNA, p; DEMONI 2—L'INCUBO RITORNA, w

Argenziano, Carmen
DANGEROUSLY CLOSE; NAKED VENGEANCE

Argirov, Blagovest
SKUPA MOYA, SKUPI MOY

Argirov, Svetoslav
SKUPA MOYA, SKUPI MOY

Argo, Allison
CRY FROM THE MOUNTAIN

Argo, Victor
OFF BEAT; RAW DEAL

Argue, David
BACKLASH

Argyraki, Maria
SCHETIKA ME TON VASSILI

Arhancet, Juan Jose
GERONIMA, ed

Ari, Helio
BRAS CUBAS

Arias, Gersa
CLASS OF NUKE 'EM HIGH

Arias, Glaurys
CLASS OF NUKE 'EM HIGH

Arias, Imanol
BANDERA NEGRA; LULU DE NOCHE; TIEMPO DE SILENCIO

Arieli, Avigail
HAME'AHEV

Arimori, Narimi
KINEMA NO TENCHI

Arizono, Yoshiki
CRAZY FAMILY, THE

Arkin, Alan
BIG TROUBLE

Arkin, Eddie
HARDBODIES 2, m; HARDBODIES 2, m/l; MODERN GIRLS, m

Arlen, Elizabeth
WHOOPEE BOYS, THE

Arlen, Harold   [Hyman Arluck]
Obituaries

Arman, Aytac
ADI VASFIYE

Armanakova, Penka
SKUPA MOYA, SKUPI MOY

Armand, Debby
INTRUDER, THE, w

Armendariz, Montxo
27 HORAS, d; 27 HORAS, w

Armendariz, Olga
HOT CHILI

Armendariz, Pedro
MAINE-OCEAN

Armenta, Frank
AMERICAN JUSTICE

Armfield, Neil
TWELFTH NIGHT, d&w

Armiger, Martin
TWO FRIENDS

Armony, Daphne
EVERY TIME WE SAY GOODBYE

Armstrong, Bess
NOTHING IN COMMON

Armstrong, Curtis
CLAN OF THE CAVE BEAR, THE; ONE CRAZY
SUMMER

Armstrong, Herb
BIG TROUBLE

Armstrong, Jack
BAD GUYS

Armstrong, Michael
SCREAMTIME, w

Armstrong, Olwen
SHADOWS RUN BLACK

Armstrong, R.G.
BEST OF TIMES, THE

Armstrong, Richard
MIN PAPA AR TARZAN

Armstrong, Vic
TAI-PAN, stunts

Armus, Sidney
HEARTBURN

Armytage, Lisa
COOL CHANGE

Arnaud, J.
LES LONGS MANTEAUX, w; ZONE ROUGE, w

Arnaul, Eve Marie
LAST SONG, cos

Arndt, Adelheid
ROSA LUXEMBURG

Arndt, Jack
SOLDIER'S REVENGE

Arndt, Jacques
COCAINE WARS

Arndts, Angelica
KONZERT FUR ALICE

Arnemann, Dawn
ABOUT LAST NIGHT

Arneric, Neda
VECERNJA ZVONA

Arnett, M. James
MY MAN ADAM, stunts

Arney, Randall
COLOR OF MONEY, THE

Arnold, Chip
8 MILLION WAYS TO DIE

Arnold, Chris
BOY WHO COULD FLY, THE; NEON MANIACS, p

Arnold, Dickie
CLOCKWISE

Arnold, Henry
DR. OTTO AND THE RIDDLE OF THE GLOOM BEAM

Arnold, Monroe
AMERICA

Arnold, Nancy
SMART ALEC, art d

Arnold, Pamela Scott
DR. OTTO AND THE RIDDLE OF THE GLOOM BEAM,
ed; EAT AND RUN, ed

Arnold, Tichina
LITTLE SHOP OF HORRORS

Arnone, John
DEAD END KIDS, prod d

Arnone, Lee
THE KARATE KID PART II

Arnot, Matt
AMERICAN ANTHEM

Arntson, Bruce
DR. OTTO AND THE RIDDLE OF THE GLOOM BEAM,
m/l

Aroch, Jonathan
SMILE OF THE LAMB, THE, p

Aron, John
ABSOLUTE BEGINNERS; LABYRINTH

Aronin, Vladimir
BORIS GODUNOV, art d

Aronovich, Ricardo
LES LONGS MANTEAUX, ph

Aronovitch, Simon
TORPIDONOSTCI, d

Aronow, Maurice E.
INSTANT JUSTICE

Arquette, Alexis
DOWN AND OUT IN BEVERLY HILLS

Arquette, Lewis
CHECK IS IN THE MAIL, THE; JUST BETWEEN
FRIENDS; NOBODY'S FOOL

Arquette, Rosanna
8 MILLION WAYS TO DIE; NOBODY'S FOOL

Arraes, Augusto
QUILOMBO, p

Arrants, Bryant
MANHUNTER

Arrants, Christopher
MANHUNTER

Arrese-Igor, Silvia
27 HORAS

Arriagada, Jorge
LOS HIJOS DE LA GUERRA FRIA, m; TOP OF THE
WHALE, m

Arrieta, German
LA MANSION DE ARAUCAIMA, m

Arrington, Brad
ARMED RESPONSE; TOMB, THE

Arrington, Richard
AT CLOSE RANGE, makeup; EXTREMITIES, makeup

Arrojo, Ricardo Garcia
EL HERMANO BASTARDO DE DIOS, p

Arsan, Asuman
KIRLANGIC FIRTINASI

Arseni, Anastasia
CARAVAN SARAI, cos; DANILO TRELES, O
FIMISMENOS ANDALOUSIANOS MOUSIKOS, cos

Arslan, L.
WHAT HAPPENED NEXT YEAR, art d

Arsovski, Bogdan
ZA SRECU JE POTREBNO TROJE, m

Arsovski, Petar
SRECNA NOVA '49

Artesi, Benito
LA BONNE

Arthur, Rebecca
ABOUT LAST NIGHT

Arthur, Robert   [Robert Arthur Feder]
Obituaries

Arthuys, Phillippe
LAST IMAGE, THE, m

Artinano, Javier
EL CABALLERO DEL DRAGON, cos; EL HERMANO
BASTARDO DE DIOS, cos

Artioli, Odino
EHRENGARD

Artmane, Via
SVESAS KAISLIBAS

Artur, Jose
LAST IMAGE, THE

Arun, Ila
TRIKAL

Arvanitis, Giorgos
O MELISSOKOMOS, ph

Arvesen, Jon
NOE HEIT ANNET, prod d

Arvizu, Adelberto
RAFAGA DE PLOMO

Arya, Irshaan
KAHAN KAHAN SE GUZAR GAYA, ph

Arzoglou, Costas
KNOCK-OUT

Asada, Mae
SUNSET STRIP

Asam, Muhamad
GHAME AFGHAN

Asama, Yoshitaka
KINEMA NO TENCHI, w

Asbury, Anthony
LABYRINTH; LABYRINTH; LABYRINTH

Aschenbrenner, John
OCEAN DRIVE WEEKEND

Ascher, Oszkar
KESERU IGAZSAG

Asen, Gunvor
PERVOLA: TRACKS IN THE SNOW

Aserud, Bent
NATTSEILERE, m

Asgari-Nasab, Manoochehr
BEYOND THE MIST, d

Ash, Monty
TOUGH GUYS

Ashbrook, Daphne
QUIET COOL

Ashby, Hal
8 MILLION WAYS TO DIE, d

Ashcroft, Peggy
WHEN THE WIND BLOWS

Asher, Tova
BAR 51—SISTER OF LOVE, ed; HAME'AHEV, ed;
MALKAT HAKITA, ed

Ashiq, Mohammed
CLOCKWISE

Ashley, Bernard
TERRY ON THE FENCE, d&w

Ashley, Helmuth
NO TIME TO DIE, d; NO TIME TO DIE, w

Ashley, Rebecca
JAKE SPEED

Ashman, Howard
LITTLE SHOP OF HORRORS, m/l; LITTLE SHOP OF
HORRORS, w

Ashokan
MUKHAMUKHAM

Ashton, Al
ARTHUR'S HALLOWED GROUND

Ashton, John
KING KONG LIVES; LAST RESORT, THE

Ashton, Laura
AMERICA

Ashton-Griffiths, Roger
HAUNTED HONEYMOON; PIRATES

Ashworth, Elfrida
LABYRINTH

Ashworth, Tom
STEWARDESS SCHOOL

Askew, Reilly
NAKED VENGEANCE, w

Askin, Leon
ODD JOBS

Aslanian, Samson
TORMENT, p, d&w

Asmar, Rizal
DOEA TANDA MATA, ed

Asmawi
NO TIME TO DIE, ph

Asokan
ANANTARAM

Asou, Yumi
COMIC MAGAZINE

Asp, Anna
SACRIFICE, THE, art d

Asparagus, Fred
8 MILLION WAYS TO DIE; THREE AMIGOS

Aspin, Max
SKY PIRATES, stunts

Asquerino, Maria
MAMBRU SE FUE A LA GUERRA

Assante, Armand
BELIZAIRE THE CAJUN

Assayas, Olivier
DESORDRE, d&w; L'UNIQUE, w; SCENE OF THE
CRIME, w

Assonitis, Ovidio G.
CHOKE CANYON, p; CHOKE CANYON, w;
DESPERATE MOVES, p

Assoyan, Vacho
NINJA TURF

Ast, Pat
REFORM SCHOOL GIRLS

Asta, Mary
HELL SQUAD

Astaire, Flo
WOMEN'S PRISON MASSACRE

Astakhov, Sergei
REIS 222, ph

Astor, Thomas J.
WEEKEND WARRIORS

Astori, Gabrio
MONSTER DOG, ed

Astrom, Kim
MIN PAPA AR TARZAN, cos; MIN PAPA AR TARZAN,
makeup

Atherton, William
NO MERCY

Atkin, Feodor
SARRAOUNIA

Atkin, Harvey
SEPARATE VACATIONS

Atkine, Feodor
LOLA; SUIVEZ MON REGARD; WERTHER

Atkins, Dave
MR. LOVE

Atkins, Tom
NIGHT OF THE CREEPS

Atkinson, Adrian
SCREAMTIME, art d

Atkinson, Adrienne
MR. LOVE, art d

Atkinson, Linda
COSMIC EYE, THE

Atkinson, Mark
NOBODY'S FOOL

Atkinson, Martin
HIGHLANDER, art d; SCREAMTIME, art d

Atkinson, Michael
BACKLASH, m

Atojano, Levon
ZAZZENNYJ FONAR, ph

Atsumi, Kiyoshi
KINEMA NO TENCHI

Attewell, Warrick
DANGEROUS ORPHANS, ph

Attifi, Mohamed
MEGLIO BACIARE UN COBRA

Attille, Martina
PASSION OF REMEMBRANCE, THE, p

Atwater, Edith
Obituaries

Atwood, Colleen
MANHUNTER, cos

Atwood, Rhonda
MOUNTAINTOP MOTEL MASSACRE

Atzmon, Anat
EVERY TIME WE SAY GOODBYE

Au, Tony
DREAM LOVERS, d

Aubel, Joe
STAR TREK IV: THE VOYAGE HOME, art d

Auberjonois, Rene
3:15, THE MOMENT OF TRUTH

Audaz, Grupo
EL SECUESTRO DE LOLA-LOLA LA TRAILERA 2, m

Audran, Stephane
L'ISOLA; LA GITANE

Audray, Elvire
WHITE SLAVE

Audrey, Brigitte
EXIT-EXIL

Audsley, Mick
COMRADES, ed; MY BEAUTIFUL LAUNDRETTE, ed

Auel, Jean M.
CLAN OF THE CAVE BEAR, THE, w

Aufaure, Claude
BETTY BLUE

Auge, Jennifer
LAST SONG, ed

Augins, Charles
LABYRINTH; LABYRINTH, ch

August, Amadeus
ASSAULT, THE

August, Bille
TWIST & SHOUT, d; TWIST & SHOUT, w

Aulisi, Joseph G.
BRIGHTON BEACH MEMOIRS, cos; OFF BEAT, cos

Aumont, Jean-Pierre
ON A VOLE CHARLIE SPENCER!

Aumont, Michael
COURS PRIVE

Aumont, Michel
PRUNELLE BLUES

Aured, Carlos
MONSTER DOG, p

Aureli, Andrea
SQUADRA SELVAGGIA

Aust, Stefan
STAMMHEIM, w

Auster, Jo Ann
SCREEN TEST

Auster, Laura
SCREEN TEST, art d; SCREEN TEST, p; SCREEN TEST,
w

Auster, Sam
SCREEN TEST, d; SCREEN TEST, p; SCREEN TEST, w

Austin, Bud [Harold "Bud" Augenblick]
Obituaries

Austin, Ed
GREAT MOUSE DETECTIVE, THE, ph

Austin, Gary
WILDCATS

Austin, Karen
CLAN OF THE CAVE BEAR, THE; LADIES CLUB,
THE

Austin, Lauraine
CLASS OF NUKE 'EM HIGH

Austin, Ned
MAXIMUM OVERDRIVE

Austin, Pamela
NO SURRENDER

Austin, Paul
MANHATTAN PROJECT, THE

Austin, Robert
ABSOLUTE BEGINNERS

Austin, Shay
BILLY GALVIN, prod d

Austin, Tena
PATRIOT, THE, makeup

Austin, Teresa
VAMP, makeup

Auteuil, Daniel
JEAN DE FLORETTE; LE PALTOQUET; MANON DES
SOURCES

Auth, Vicki
HOLLYWOOD ZAP!, art d

Autio, Risto
LINNA

Autola, Aapo
BORN AMERICAN

Autry, Alan
AT CLOSE RANGE; HOUSE

Auvray, Dominique
CORPS ET BIENS, ed; L'AMANT MAGNIFIQUE, ed

Auwera, Fernand
SPRINGEN, w

Avakyan, G.
KHOZIAIN, ph

Avallon, Joe Mari
DEVASTATOR, THE, prod d

Avar, Istvan
ERZEKENY BUCSU A FEJEDELEMTOL

Avati, Antonio
REGALO DI NATALE, p

Avati, Pupi
REGALO DI NATALE, d; REGALO DI NATALE, w

Avdeliodis, Demos
TO DENDRO POU PLIGONAME; TO DENDRO POU
PLIGONAME, p, d&w

Avdeliodis, Maria
TO DENDRO POU PLIGONAME, cos

Avdeliodis, Yannis
TO DENDRO POU PLIGONAME

Avdhoot, Suresh
RAO SAHEB, ed

Avedekion, Serge
L'AUBE

Avedon, Loren Rains
NINJA TURF

Avelcana, J.M.
FINAL MISSION, w

Avellana, Joe Mari
SILK; SILK, prod d

Avellana, Jose Mari
KILLING OF SATAN, THE, w

Avery, James
8 MILLION WAYS TO DIE; EXTREMITIES;
STOOGEMANIA

Avery, John
BLOODY BIRTHDAY

Avery, Rick
ARMED AND DANGEROUS; NAKED CAGE, THE

Avery, Val
COBRA

Avila, Javier
CAPABLANCA

Avila, John
BACK TO SCHOOL

Avildsen, John G.
THE KARATE KID PART II, d; THE KARATE KID
PART II, ed

Avilez, Antonio
AS SETE VAMPIRAS, p

Avni, Moshe
HASHIGAON HAGADOL, ed

Avon, Rowen
DOT AND KEETO, anim

Avoth, Eddie
INSTANT JUSTICE

Avrahami, Doron
MALKAT HAKITA

Avron, Philippe
PAULETTE

Awazu, Kiyoshi
YARI NO GONZA, set d

Axelrad, Irving
COLOR OF MONEY, THE, p

Axelrod, Robert
BAD GUYS ; MURPHY'S LAW

Axelsson, Jean Frederic
LOVE ME!, m

Axelsson, Lars-Gunnar
BRODERNA MOZART

Axelsson, Stefan
RATTIS, m

Ayala, Fernando
LA NOCHE DE LOS LAPICES, p; NIGHTMARE'S
PASSENGERS, d; SOBREDOSIS, d

Ayala, Officer Renee
MANHUNTER

Ayari, Keyanoosh
MONSTER, THE, d, w&ph; MONSTER, THE, ed

Ayas, Frank
LOVE SONGS

Aylanc, Jale
KIRLANGIC FIRTINASI

Ayotte, Carolyn
SCREAMPLAY

Azarow, Martin
JO JO DANCER, YOUR LIFE IS CALLING

Azcona, Rafael
EL ANO DE LAS LUCES, w

Azema, Sabine
LA PURITAINE; MELO; ZONE ROUGE

Azevedo, Anna
L'AMANT MAGNIFIQUE

Azevedo, Gilberto
GOLDEN EIGHTIES, ph

Azmi, Shabana
GENESIS; SUSMAN

Azmi, Yahia
EL-TOUK WA EL-ESSWERA, w

Aznar, Monique
LAND OF DOOM, makeup

Aznar, Pedro
MAN FACING SOUTHEAST, m

Aznavour, Charles
MAUVAIS SANG, m/l; YIDDISH CONNECTION, w

Azoulai-Haspari, Hanna
NADIA

Azzeddine, Commandant
TAHOUNET AL SAYED FABRE, w

Baaf, Hassan Zand
BUS, THE, ed

Baal, Karin
FOLLOWING THE FUHRER; ROSA LUXEMBURG

Baas, Cas
ASSAULT, THE

Babanov, Aleksandr
REIS 222

Babar, Brendan
FERRIS BUELLER'S DAY OFF

Babbs, O.B.
STAND BY ME

Babchak, James
STREETS OF GOLD

Babchak, Jim
F/X

Babe, Fabienne
FATHERLAND; L'UNIQUE

Babic, Mira
BIG HURT, THE

Babita
DAHAN

Babur, Jawed
GHAME AFGHAN

Babushkin, Victor
ODINOTCHNOYE PLAVANIYE, m

Bac, Kung
LOI RE TRAI TREN DUONG MON

Bac, Le Cung
KARMA

Baca, Sam
LOW BLOW

Bacal, Joe
MY LITTLE PONY, p; TRANSFORMERS: THE MOVIE,
THE, p

Bacciucchi, Eros
SAVING GRACE, spec eff

Bach, Cristian
GAVILAN O PALOMA

Bach, Danilo
APRIL FOOL'S DAY, w

Bach, Johann Sebastian
A FLOR DO MAR, m; FLIGHT NORTH, m; LA MOITIE DE L'AMOUR, m; MELO, m; MONEY PIT, THE, m; SACRIFICE, THE, m

Bachan, Harold
PINK CHIQUITAS, THE

Bacharach, Burt
BEST OF TIMES, THE, m/l

Bachmann, Ingeborg
FRANZA, w

Bacich, Mike
BACK TO SCHOOL

Backe, John D.
BAD GUYS , p

Backer, Brian
MONEY PIT, THE

Backman, Edda
SCHWARZ UND OHNE ZUCKER

Backmann, Edda Heidrun
EINS OG SKEPNAN DEYR

Backstreet Girls
X

Backwood Film
HOUSE, spec eff

Bacon, James
LONGSHOT, THE

Bacon, Kevin
QUICKSILVER

Bacri, Jean-Pierre
ETATS D'AME; LA GALETTE DU ROI; MORT UN DIMANCHE DE PLUIE; RUE DU DEPART; SUIVEZ MON REGARD

Bacs, Ferenc
ELYSIUM

Badalamenti, Angelo
BLUE VELVET, m; BLUE VELVET, m/l; BLUE VELVET, md

Badale, Andy
BLUE VELVET

Badarou, Wally
MORNING AFTER, THE, m/l

Badendyck, Dag Richard
DROMMESLOTTER

Badger, Carin
NO RETREAT, NO SURRENDER

Badham, John
SHORT CIRCUIT, d

Badin, Jean
TOP OF THE WHALE

Badin, Whitney
VIOLATED

Badland, Annette
KNIGHTS AND EMERALDS

Badr, Salem Mohamed
SALOME

Badrakhan, Ali
EL-GOOA, d; EL-GOOA, w

Badral, N.
BI CHAMD KHAYRTAY

Baehr, Nicholas E.
Obituaries

Baer, Bill
BRIDGE TO NOWHERE, w; QUEEN CITY ROCKERS, w

Baer, Hanania
BAD GUYS , ph

Baer, Mark
CHOKE CANYON

Baer, Parley
PRAY FOR DEATH

Baes, Steve
LAST SONG

Baeza, Fernando
MONSTER DOG

Bafile, Marisa
PEQUENA REVANCHA, ed

Bagby, Milton
REBEL LOVE, d&w

Bagdonas, Vladas
COME AND SEE

Bages, Nuria
THANATOS

Bagge, Eva
ALLA VI BARN I BULLERBY, makeup

Baggerly, Glen
SHADOW PLAY

Baggot, King
TOUGH GUYS, ph

Baglivi, Christina
LUCAS

Bagneris, Vernel
DOWN BY LAW

Bagot, Jean-Pierre
ZONE ROUGE

Bahi, Ranbir
DOWN AND OUT IN BEVERLY HILLS

Bahler, Tom
RAW DEAL, m

Bahr, Michael
AMERICA

Bahr, Robert
PRUNELLE BLUES

Bahrami, Mahmood
CLOSED CIRCUIT

Bahs, Henning
MORD I MORKET, w; YES, DET ER FAR!, prod d; YES, DET ER FAR!, spec eff

Bai, Xue
YELLOW EARTH

Bail, Chuck
CHOKE CANYON, d

Bailey, Bill
HAUNTED HONEYMOON

Bailey, Frederick
NOBODY'S FOOL; SILK; SILK, w

Bailey, G.W.
SHORT CIRCUIT

Bailey, Janet
DANCING IN THE DARK

Bailey, Jef
OCEAN DRIVE WEEKEND

Bailey, Jerry
SILK

Bailey, John
BRIGHTON BEACH MEMOIRS, ph; CROSSROADS, ph

Bailey, Patrick
SPACECAMP, p

Bailey, Robert D.
WHAT WAITS BELOW, p; WHAT WAITS BELOW, spec eff

Bailey, Robin
SCREAMTIME

Bailey, Sandra K.
KGB—THE SECRET WAR, w

Bailey, Tom
DR. OTTO AND THE RIDDLE OF THE GLOOM BEAM; LUCAS, m/l

Baillie, Norman
ALIENS, spec eff

Baillot, Pierre
THERESE

Bailly, Pascale
PEKIN CENTRAL

Bainborough, Bob
BOY IN BLUE, THE

Baio, Jimmy
PLAYING FOR KEEPS

Baird, Nancy
ONE MORE SATURDAY NIGHT

Baird, Peter
HOWARD THE DUCK

Baird, S.L.
RATBOY

Baisho, Chieko
KINEMA NO TENCHI; UEMURA NAOMI MONOGATARI

Baisho, Mitsuko
CABARET; CRAZY FAMILY, THE; LOVE LETTER

Bajkschtite, Grazyan
DEN' GNEVA

Bajor, Piotr
OSOBISTY PAMIETNIK GRZESZNIKA PRZEZ NIEGO SAMEGO SPISANY

Bakaba, Sidiki
DESCENTE AUX ENFERS

Baker, Arthur
FERRIS BUELLER'S DAY OFF, m

Baker, Benny
LONGSHOT, THE

Baker, Blanche
RAW DEAL

Baker, Carroll
NATIVE SON

Baker, Carter
DR. OTTO AND THE RIDDLE OF THE GLOOM BEAM

Baker, Charles
DR. OTTO AND THE RIDDLE OF THE GLOOM BEAM

Baker, Chris
CARNAGE

Baker, Derek
3:15, THE MOMENT OF TRUTH

Baker, Gary D.
CRY FROM THE MOUNTAIN, ph

Baker, Henry
MONEY PIT, THE

Baker, Hoyle
ABSOLUTE BEGINNERS

Baker, Hylda
Obituaries

Baker, Jay
APRIL FOOL'S DAY

Baker, Joe Don
GETTING EVEN

Baker, Jud Henry
STREETS OF GOLD

Baker, Kai
ARMED RESPONSE

Baker, Kenny
LABYRINTH; MONA LISA

Baker, Leeanne
BREEDERS

Baker, Louise
HARDBODIES 2

Baker, Mark H.
FLIGHT OF THE NAVIGATOR, w

Baker, Martyn
MANHUNTER, m/l

Baker, Michael Conway
OVERNIGHT, m

Baker, Nancy
ON VALENTINE'S DAY, ed

Baker, Nicky
CLASS OF NUKE 'EM HIGH

Baker, Penny
MEN'S CLUB, THE

Baker, Richard
CLOSE TO HOME, m

Baker, Robbi
SEPARATE VACATIONS

Baker, Terry
AT CLOSE RANGE

Baker, Tim
NO RETREAT, NO SURRENDER

Baker-Bergen, Stuart   [Stuart Bergen, Jr.]
Obituaries

Bakir, Kamal
AWDAT MOWATIN, m

Bakke, Brenda
HARDBODIES 2; LAST RESORT, THE

Bakker, E.G.
NO TIME TO DIE, d

Bakocevic, Nebojsa
BAL NA VODI

Bakri, Mouhammad
ESTHER

Balaguer, Asuncion
EL HERMANO BASTARDO DE DIOS; LULU DE NOCHE

Balajan, Roman
KHRANI MENIO, MOI TALISMAN, d

Balamir, Hakan
FOURTEEN NUMARA

Balano, Charles
JUBIABA

Balasko, Josiane
LES FRERES PETARD; NUIT D'IVRESSE; NUIT D'IVRESSE, p; NUIT D'IVRESSE, w

Balasoiu, Dodu
UN OASPETE LA CINA, art d

Balazs, Ferenc
VAKVILAGBAN, m

Balbuena, Josu
27 HORAS

Balcazar, Jesus
IL MIELE DEL DIAVOLO, w

Balcerzak, Dusty
DESERT BLOOM

Balchev, Anatoly
FOUETTE, m

Bald, Alan
SOLDIER'S REVENGE, set d

Baldo, Maria
SAPORE DEL GRANO

Baldock, Chris
ABSOLUTE BEGINNERS

Baldridge, Bill
SILK

Baldridge, Sawnie R.
DIRT BIKE KID, THE, cos

Balducci, Armenia
IL CASO MORO, w

Baldwin, Adam
3:15, THE MOMENT OF TRUTH; BAD GUYS

Baldwin, Bob
NIGHTMARE WEEKEND, ph

Bales, Cynthia
JUST BETWEEN FRIENDS, cos

Balgobin, Jennifer
OUT OF BOUNDS

Balian, Haig
MAMA IS BOOS!, p

Balin, D.
VIOLATED

Balin, Ina
VASECTOMY: A DELICATE MATTER

Balin, Joey
MONEY PIT, THE

Balitzki, Jurgen
AB HEUTE ERWACHSEN, m

Baljinnyam, B.
BI CHAMD KHAYRTAY, p&d; BI CHAMD
KHAYRTAY, ph; BI CHAMD KHAYRTAY, w

Balkenhol, Thomas
FLIGHT NORTH, ed

Balkhirrat, Farid
RAI, m

Ball, Murray
FOOTROT FLATS, d&w

Ball, Nicholas
RUNNING OUT OF LUCK

Ball, Seamus
BEST MAN, THE

Ballan, Michael Henbury
LABYRINTH

Ballantine, Carl
BEST OF TIMES, THE

Ballantyne, Jane
CACTUS, p

Ballard, Carroll
NUTCRACKER: THE MOTION PICTURE, d

Ballard, Doug
SEX O'CLOCK NEWS, THE

Ballard, Jack
Obituaries

Ballard, Kaye
PERILS OF P.K., THE

Ballard, Ray
VAMP

Ballard, Terry
FIRE IN THE NIGHT

Ballette, Franca
GIOVANNI SENZAPENSIERI

Ballew, Jerry
CRY FROM THE MOUNTAIN

Ballhaus, Michael
COLOR OF MONEY, THE, ph; UNDER THE CHERRY
MOON, ph

Balling, Erik
MORD I MORKET, w

Ballo, Gabor
VAKVILAGBAN, set d

Balme, Cecile
LE PALTOQUET, cos

Balmer, Jean Francois
GOLDEN EIGHTIES; LAST IMAGE, THE

Balodis, Gunars
SVESAS KAISLIBAS, art d

Balos, Rowena
STEWARDESS SCHOOL

Balsam, Alan
ONE CRAZY SUMMER, ed

Balsam, Martin
DELTA FORCE, THE; WHATEVER IT TAKES

Balsam, Talia
CRAWLSPACE

Baltazar, H.
EL MERCADO DE HUMILDES, m

Balteano, Beba
UNA STORIA AMBIGUA

Balthaser, Harrison
PLAYING FOR KEEPS

Baltus, Gerd
ANGRY HARVEST

Balzaretti, Fernando
CRONICA DE FAMILIA; ES MI VIDA—EL NOA NOA
2; REDONDO

Bambang
DOEA TANDA MATA

Ban, Janos
ORDOGI KISERTETEK

Banah, Rin
ESTHER, m

Banai, Gavri
HAKRAV AL HAVA'AD

Banai, Meir
NADIA

Banai, Yuval
NADIA

Banas, Alexis
DANGEROUS ORPHANS

Banas, Bob
ODD JOBS, ch

Bancroft, Anne
'NIGHT, MOTHER

Bancroft, Bradford
3:15, THE MOMENT OF TRUTH; DANGEROUSLY
CLOSE

Bancroft, Cam
BOY WHO COULD FLY, THE

Band, Albert
TERRORVISION, p; TROLL; TROLL, p

Band, Charles
ELIMINATORS, p; TROLL

Band, Jacquelyn
TROLL

Band, Lockport High School
FERRIS BUELLER'S DAY OFF

Band, Richard
ELIMINATORS, m; FROM BEYOND, m;
TERRORVISION, m; TROLL, m; ZONE TROOPERS, m

Band, Rubber
TWIST & SHOUT

Banderas, Antonio
27 HORAS; MATADOR

Bandini, Armando
UNA CASA IN BILICO

Bandoni, Michael
AMERICAN JUSTICE

Banerjee, Victor
FOREIGN BODY

Banevitch, Sergei
REIS 222, m

Banfi, Lino
GRANDI MAGAZZINI; IL CAMMISSARIO LO GATTO;
SCUOLA DI LADRI

Banfi, Rosanna
CATTIVI PIERROT; GRANDI MAGAZZINI

Bang, Bernard
LOW BLOW

Banica, Stefan
LICEENI

Banjac, Mira
DO YOU REMEMBER DOLLY BELL?; LEPOTA
POROKA

Bank, Netta
REBEL LOVE, set d

Banks, Emily
CHECK IS IN THE MAIL, THE

Banks, Jonathan
ARMED AND DANGEROUS

Banks, Kathy
SHE'S GOTTA HAVE IT

Banks, Louis
NEW DELHI TIMES, m

Banks, Marcia
HOWARD THE DUCK

Banks, Peter
HIGHLANDER

Banks, Tony
QUICKSILVER, m

Bannerjee, Joy
CHOPPER

Banning, Jack
PLAYING FOR KEEPS

Bannister, Duke
DEATH OF A SOLDIER

Banov, Soultan
CHUZHAJA, BELAJA I RJABOJ

Banovich, Tamas
ERZEKENY BUCSU A FEJEDELEMTOL, prod d;
ORDOGI KISERTETEK, set d

Banshees, Siouxsie and the
OUT OF BOUNDS

Bansmer, Audrey
AVENGING FORCE, cos; P.O.W. THE ESCAPE, cos

Bantzer, Claus
DAS SCHWEIGEN DES DICHTERS, m; FORTY
SQUARE METERS OF GERMANY, m; PARADIES, m

Baquet, Maurice
LE DEBUTANT; PAULETTE

Bara, Fausto
ELIMINATORS

Baradach, Ann Louise
POLTERGEIST II

Baragli, Nino
GINGER & FRED, ed; LA STORIA, m, ed; TROPPO
FORTE, ed

Baraha, Kadicha
FAUBOURG SAINT-MARTIN, ed

Barahona, Edmundo
EL EXTRANO HIJO DEL SHERIFF

Barajas, Alfonso L.
PULSEBEAT, art d

Barak, Ari
SCORPION

Baraldi, Lorenzo
LE MAL D'AIMER, art d

Baran, Jack
BAND OF THE HAND, w

Baranski, Christine
9½ WEEKS; LEGAL EAGLES

Baratta, Massimo
MORIRAI A MEZZANOTTE

Barbalich, Elena
SAPORE DEL GRANO

Barbareschi, Luca
CUT AND RUN; ROMANCE

Barbeau, Adrienne
BACK TO SCHOOL

Barber, Billy
ROCKIN' ROAD TRIP

Barber, Edward
ABSOLUTE BEGINNERS, m/l

Barber, Ellen
VERY CLOSE QUARTERS

Barber, Frances
CASTAWAY

Barber, John
AVENGING FORCE

Barber, Samuel
PLATOON, m

Barberini, Urbano
LA VITA DI SCORTA; OTELLO

Barberis, Luis
GERONIMA, p

Barbero, Luis
EL SUIZO—UN AMOUR EN ESPAGNE

Barbey, Claude Inga
NOAH UND DER COWBOY

Barbier, Christian
SUIVEZ MON REGARD

Barbier, Gilette
PRUNELLE BLUES

Barbini, Elisabetta
SAPORE DEL GRANO

Barboo, Louis
INSTANT JUSTICE

Barbosa, Haroldo Marinho
FULANINHA, w

Barbosa, Luisa
O VESTIDO COR DE FOGO

Barbour, Malcolm
P.O.W. THE ESCAPE, w

Barbour, Thomas
LEGAL EAGLES; WHATEVER IT TAKES

Barclay, David
LABYRINTH; LABYRINTH

Barclay, Scott
AMERICAN ANTHEM

Barclay, William
POWER, art d

Bardach, Elinor
WRAITH, THE, cos

Bardeaux, Michelle
BOY WHO COULD FLY, THE

Bardet, Pascal
ETATS D'AME

Bardi, Emilio
PERROS DE LA NOCHE

Benedetti, Robert
LEGAL EAGLES

Benedetto, Bertino
JEAN DE FLORETTE

Benedict, Amy
ONE MORE SATURDAY NIGHT

Benedict, Max P.
Obituaries

Benedict, Nick
NAKED CAGE, THE

Benedict, Paul
DESPERATE MOVES

Benegal, Shyam
SUSMAN, d; TRIKAL, d&w

Benegas, Alberto
EL RIGOR DEL DESTINO

Benenson, Bill
LIGHTSHIP, THE, p

Benfield, Derek
ARTHUR'S HALLOWED GROUND

Bengali
BAD GUYS

Bengtsson, Christina
MANDEN I MAANEN

Bengtsson, Ralph
MIN PAPA AR TARZAN

Benguell, Norma
RUNNING OUT OF LUCK

Benguigui, Jean
LES FUGITIFS

Benhamou, Luc
GOLDEN EIGHTIES, ph

Benhardi, Benny
SECANGKIR KOPI PAHIT, art d

Benigni, Pierpaolo
STORIA D'AMORE

Benigni, Roberto
DOWN BY LAW; People to Watch

Benini, Cesare
IL GIARDINO DEGLI INGANNI

Benini, Fernando
FILME DEMENCIA

Benita
THREE AMIGOS

Benito, Eugenio
RAGE, w

Benjamin, Floella
BLACK JOY

Benjamin, Jeff
AMERICAN ANTHEM, w

Benjamin, Richard
MONEY PIT, THE, d

Bennato, Serena
SEPARATI IN CASA

Bennes, John
BEER; PLAYING FOR KEEPS

Bennett, Bill
BACKLASH, p, d&w; MORE THINGS CHANGE, THE

Bennett, Fran
MORNING AFTER, THE

Bennett, Harve
STAR TREK IV: THE VOYAGE HOME, p; STAR TREK
IV: THE VOYAGE HOME, w

Bennett, Jack
GETTING EVEN, spec eff; GETTING EVEN, spec eff

Bennett, Jill
LADY JANE

Bennett, John
TAI-PAN

Bennett, Laura
VIOLATED

Bennett, Laurence
MEN'S CLUB, THE, art d; MODERN GIRLS, prod d

Bennett, Mack
DR. OTTO AND THE RIDDLE OF THE GLOOM BEAM

Bennett, Marilyn
KNIGHTS AND EMERALDS

Bennett, Michael
PATRIOT, THE, p

Bennett, Reggie
VENDETTA

Bennett, Tracie
KNIGHTS AND EMERALDS

Benninghofen, Jeff
KING KONG LIVES

Bennys, Claud
MAN OF ASHES, art d

Benoit, Christine
JOUR ET NUIT, ed

Benoit, Susan
KILLER PARTY, makeup

Benoit-Fresco, Francoise
INSPECTEUR LAVARDIN, art d

Benotti, Alberto
LA SECONDA NOTTE, ed

Benrich, Robert
HYPER SAPIEN: PEOPLE FROM ANOTHER STAR, ed

Bensadoun, Daniel
UNDER THE CHERRY MOON

Benson, Arthur
BEST OF TIMES, THE, m/l

Benson, James
MR. LOVE

Benson, Paul
SEA SERPENT, THE

Benson, Perry
SID AND NANCY

Benson, Vickie
MY CHAUFFEUR; WRAITH, THE

Bentahar, Meaachou
POLICE

Benti, Galeazzo
IL CAMMISSARIO LO GATTO

Bentivoglio, Fabrizio
SALOME

Bentley, Christopher
INSTANT JUSTICE, d

Bentley, Robert
SHANGHAI SURPRISE, w

Bento, Joao
NTTURUDU

Benton, Jerome
UNDER THE CHERRY MOON

Benton, Robert
HEARTBREAK RIDGE, set d

Benton, Robert B.
TOP GUN, set d

Benton, Robert R.
ODD JOBS, prod d

Bentsvi, Yakov
KING OF THE STREETS, p

Benvenuti, Alessandro
IL RAGAZZO DEL PONY EXPRESS

Benvenuti, Leo
IL TENENTE DEI CARABINIERI, w; LET'S HOPE IT'S
A GIRL, w

Benvenuti, Leonardo
SETTE CHILI IN SETTE GIORNI, w; SETTE CHILI IN
SETTE GIORNI, w

Benvenuti, Nedo
L'ULTIMO GIORNO, m

Benyar, Lily
MURPHY'S LAW, makeup; NAKED CAGE, THE,
makeup

Benz, Donna Kei
PRAY FOR DEATH

Benzheng, Yu
PIAOBO QIYU, d; REZHOU, d

Beranger, Macha
SUIVEZ MON REGARD

Berardi, Mauro
IL CASO MORO, p

Berardini, Giuseppe
IL RAGAZZO DEL PONY EXPRESS, ph

Beraud, Luc
SINCERELY CHARLOTTE; SINCERELY CHARLOTTE,
w

Berbel, Jose Monje
LA NOCHE DE LOS LAPICES

Berci
KISMASZAT ES A GEZENGUZOK

Berckmans, Desire
MERCI MONSIEUR ROBERTSON, ph

Berckmans, Nicole
ON A VOLE CHARLIE SPENCER!, ed

Berco, Roxana
ANOTHER LOVE STORY; KING AND HIS MOVIE, A

Beremenyi, Geza
GREAT GENERATION, THE, w

Berenger, Tom
PLATOON

Berenguer, Elsa
INSOMNIACS

Berenson, Craig
THREE AMIGOS

Berenson, Marisa
FLAGRANT DESIR

Beresford, Al
SCREAMTIME, p&d

Beresford, Bruce
CRIMES OF THE HEART, d; FRINGE DWELLERS,
THE, d; FRINGE DWELLERS, THE, w

Beresford, Rhoisin
FRINGE DWELLERS, THE, w

Berg, Scott
TOUCH AND GO

Berg, Tony
WELCOME TO 18, m

Berg, Tracy
BEER

Bergamini, Gianni
RAGE, ph

Bergamo, Chantal
SAPORE DEL GRANO, p

Berge, John
DOT AND KEETO, anim

Bergema, Pieter
INSTANT JUSTICE, ed

Bergen, Frances
MORNING AFTER, THE

Bergendahl, Waldemar
ALLA VI BARN I BULLERBY, p; JONSSONLIGAN
DYKER UPP IGEN, p

Berger, Allan
DESPERATE MOVES, w

Berger, Anne
YIDDISH CONNECTION

Berger, Debra
DANGEROUSLY CLOSE; LIGHTNING—THE WHITE
STALLION

Berger, Gregg
TRANSFORMERS: THE MOVIE, THE

Berger, Gunter
ANGRY HARVEST

Berger, Howard
NIGHT OF THE CREEPS

Berger, Madeleine
OFF BEAT

Berger, Peter E.
FIRE WITH FIRE, ed; STAR TREK IV: THE VOYAGE
HOME, ed

Berger, Randall
DEATH OF A SOLDIER

Berger, Richard
STAR TREK IV: THE VOYAGE HOME, set d

Berger, Robert
PLAYING FOR KEEPS

Berger, Senta
KILLING CARS; L'ULTIMA MAZURKA

Berger, Stephen Myles
LADIES CLUB, THE, prod d

Berger, Steve
WILDCATS, art d

Berger, William
MONSTER SHARK; TAROT

Berggrreen, Tommy
LA SPOSA AMERICANA

Berglas, Ron
HIGHLANDER

Bergman, Britt
LA RAGAZZA DEI LILLA

Bergman, Mats
MOA

Bergman, Sandahl
STEWARDESS SCHOOL

Bergmark, Suzanne
DEMONER, makeup; DEN FRUSNA LEOPARDEN,
makeup

Bergqvist, Kjell
MALACCA

Bergstrom, Linda
ALLA VI BARN I BULLERBY

Beringer, Paul
LETTER TO BREZHNEV

Beristain, Gabriel
CARAVAGGIO, ph

Berke, Ed
'NIGHT, MOTHER

Berkeley, Michael
CAPTIVE, m; CAPTIVE, m

Berkeley, Xander
SID AND NANCY

Berkoff, Steven
ABSOLUTE BEGINNERS; UNDER THE CHERRY
MOON

Berlandson, Kristine
AMERICAN COMMANDOS

Blackman, Jack
MANHUNTER, art d

Blackner, Danny
LABYRINTH

Blackwell, Cheryl Beasley
8 MILLION WAYS TO DIE, cos

Blackwell, Douglas
LABYRINTH

Blackwood, Maureen
PASSION OF REMEMBRANCE, THE, d&w

Blackwood, Nina
RATBOY

Blackwood, Va
ARTHUR'S HALLOWED GROUND

Blagojevic, Ljiljana
DO YOU REMEMBER DOLLY BELL?

Blagojevic, Tatjana
VECERNJA ZVONA

Blaikie, Joanie
SCHOOL FOR VANDALS, p

Blain, Paul
L'AUBE

Blain, Roselia
LEJANIA

Blair, Betsy
DESCENTE AUX ENFERS

Blair, Jock
PLAYING BEATIE BOW, p

Blair, Lionel
ABSOLUTE BEGINNERS

Blair, Nicky
THAT'S LIFE

Blair, Richard
JUST BETWEEN FRIENDS, makeup

Blair, Vic
SOMETHING WILD

Blaisdel, Deborah
SCREEN TEST

Blake, Barry Edward
BOY IN BLUE, THE

Blake, Ellen
LAST RESORT, THE

Blake, Joel
PLAYING FOR KEEPS

Blake, Jon
COOL CHANGE

Blake, Josh
FAT GUY GOES NUTZOID!!

Blake, Julia
CACTUS; TRAVELLING NORTH

Blake, Patrick
IMAGEMAKER, THE

Blake, Richard
INVADERS FROM MARS, w

Blake, Stephanie
FERRIS BUELLER'S DAY OFF

Blakely, D.L.
BAND OF THE HAND

Blakely, Don
IN THE SHADOW OF KILIMANJARO; WIRED TO
KILL

Blakely, Jonathan
MOVIE HOUSE MASSACRE

Blanc, Anne-Marie
DER PENDLER; KONZERT FUR ALICE

Blanc, Barbara
SPOSERO SIMON LE BON

Blanc, Dominique
LA FEMME DE MA VIE

Blanc, Mel
HEATHCLIFF: THE MOVIE

Blanc, Michel
JE HAIS LES ACTEURS; LES FUGITIFS; MENAGE

Blanc, Yito
EL RIGOR DEL DESTINO, ph

Blancarte, Oscar
QUE ME MATEN DE UNA VEZ, d; QUE ME MATEN
DE UNA VEZ, w

Blancato, Ken
STEWARDESS SCHOOL, d&w

Blanchard, Vanessa
UPHILL ALL THE WAY

Blanche, Roland
LES FUGITIFS; PAULETTE; YIDDISH CONNECTION

Bland, Peter
DANGEROUS ORPHANS; QUEEN CITY ROCKERS

Blane, Sue
ABSOLUTE BEGINNERS, cos; LADY JANE, cos

Blaney, Tim
SHORT CIRCUIT

Blank, Boris
FERRIS BUELLER'S DAY OFF, m/l

Blank, Earl
ONE CRAZY SUMMER

Blank, Manfred
CLASS RELATIONS

Blank, Martin
COMBAT SHOCK

Blankenship, Linda
MOUNTAINTOP MOTEL MASSACRE

Blanks, Billy
LOW BLOW

Blas, Manuel de
DRAGON RAPIDE

Blas, Marvel De
INSTANT JUSTICE

Blasi, Alberto
CUT AND RUN, makeup

Blasi, Ernest
LOLA, ed; MES ENLLA DE LA PASSIO, ed

Blasi, Silverio
IL CASO MORO

Blass, Ben
SMART ALEC

Blatnik, Tommy
PRETTY IN PINK

Blau, Martin Maria
GINGER & FRED

Blaylock, Sylvester
WILDCATS

Blazek, Jiri
LEV S BILOU HRIVOU, w

Bleasdale, Alan
NO SURRENDER, w

Bleasing, Dagmar
WOHIN MIT WILLFRIED?, ed

Bledsoe, Anne Marie
SUNSET STRIP

Blee, Debra
HAMBURGER; SLOANE

Bleesz, Regina
FROM BEYOND

Blefari, Rosario
EIN BLICK—UND DIE LIEBE BRICHT AUS

Bleifer, John
INSIDE OUT

Bleont, Claudiu
DREPTATE IN LANTURI; PASO DOBLE

Blessing, Jack
HAMBURGER

Blewitt, David
PSYCHO III, ed

Blier, Bernard
JE HAIS LES ACTEURS; LET'S HOPE IT'S A GIRL;
TWIST AGAIN A MOSCOU

Blier, Bertrand
MENAGE, d&w

Blinco, Maggie
"CROCODILE" DUNDEE

Bliss, John
REVENGE

Blixen, Karen
EHRENGARD, w

Bljlani, Lalit M.
TRIKAL, p

Bloch, Bernard
FATHERLAND

Bloch, Debora
SONHO SEM FIM

Bloch, Jonas
O HOMEM DA CAPA PRETA

Bloch, Jones
AVAETE, A SEMENTE DA VINGANCA

Bloch, Robert
PSYCHO III, w

Block, Axel
FLIGHT NORTH, ph

Block, Becky
DIRT BIKE KID, THE, art d; REFORM SCHOOL GIRLS,
prod d

Block, Irving A.
Obituaries

Block, Lawrence
8 MILLION WAYS TO DIE, w

Blokker, Jan
MAMA IS BOOS!, art d

Blom, John
TOUCH AND GO

Blomqvist, Markku
BORN AMERICAN

Blood, John
ONE CRAZY SUMMER

Bloodworth, Bob
ROCKIN' ROAD TRIP

Bloom, Anne
DIRT BIKE KID, THE

Bloom, George Arthur
MY LITTLE PONY, w

Bloom, Leslie
WISE GUYS, set d

Bloom, Michael Allan
SCREEN TEST

Bloomfield, John
HAUNTED HONEYMOON; TAI-PAN, cos

Bloomfield, Phillip
SCREAMTIME

Blore, Cathianne
AMERICAN TAIL, AN

Blossier, Patrick
JOUR ET NUIT, ph

Blough, Noah
NAKED VENGEANCE, ed

Blount, Lisa
CUT AND RUN; RADIOACTIVE DREAMS; WHAT
WAITS BELOW

Blu, Susan
MY LITTLE PONY; TRANSFORMERS: THE MOVIE,
THE

Blue, Christopher
HYPER SAPIEN: PEOPLE FROM ANOTHER STAR, w

Blue, Michael
DOWN AND OUT IN BEVERLY HILLS

Blue, Michele
NUTCRACKER: THE MOTION PICTURE

Blue, Ruben
THRASHIN'

Blum, Betiana
AWAITING THE PALLBEARERS; INSOMNIACS; TE
AMO

Blum, Deborah
GUNG HO, p

Blum, Mark
JUST BETWEEN FRIENDS; "CROCODILE" DUNDEE

Blum, Richard
ARMED AND DANGEROUS

Blume, Ricardo
MALABRIGO

Blumenberg, Carroll
FORMULA FOR MURDER

Blumenberg, Hans Christof
DER SOMMER DES SAMURAI, d; DER SOMMER DES
SAMURAI, w

Blumenfeld, Alan
FRIDAY THE 13TH PART VI: JASON LIVES

Blumenfeld, Robert
BEER

Blumenthal, Andy
HARDBODIES 2, ed

Blumenthal, Herman Allen
Obituaries

Blundell, Graeme
AUSTRALIAN DREAM

Blunk, John
Obituaries

Bluth, Don
AMERICAN TAIL, AN, d; AMERICAN TAIL, AN, p

Blutman, Mark
RECRUITS

Bo, Fung Bo
FAMILY, THE

Bo-hee, Lee
ER WOO DONG

Board, John
OVERNIGHT, p

Board, Kevin
PRAY FOR DEATH, makeup

Board, Timothy
SPACECAMP, ed

Boardman, Chris
RAW DEAL, m

Boardman, Robert
ONE CRAZY SUMMER

Boassen, Oistein
BLACKOUT, m

Boatman, Ellis
ROCKIN' ROAD TRIP

Bobatoon, Star-Sheemah
FIRE WITH FIRE

Bobkowski, Dariusz
KRONIKA WYPADKOW MILOSNYCH

Bobst, Geanette
STAND BY ME

Bobulova, Brigita
SIESTA VETA

Boby, Earl
TOUCH AND GO

Bocci, Franca
PANTHER SQUAD

Boccoli, Birgitta
MANHATTAN BABY

Bock, Larry
CRITTERS, ed; OUT OF BOUNDS, ed

Bodard, Lucien
NAME OF THE ROSE, THE

Bode, Ralf
VIOLETS ARE BLUE, ph; WHOOPEE BOYS,
THE, ph

Bode, Susan
HEARTBURN, set d

Bodin-Jorgensen, Lars
NAME OF THE ROSE, THE

Bodkin, Richard
ABSOLUTE BEGINNERS; LABYRINTH

Bodrogi, Gyula
KISMASZAT ES A GEZENGUZOK

Boe, Heather
NUTCRACKER: THE MOTION PICTURE

Boe, Sigve
NOE HEIT ANNET

Boeke, Jim
IN THE SHADOW OF KILIMANJARO

Boel, Jeanne
TAKE IT EASY

Boen, Earl
STEWARDESS SCHOOL

Boerwald, David
ECHO PARK, m/l

Boes, Richard
DOWN BY LAW; SLEEPWALK

Boffety, Jean
MORT UN DIMANCHE DE PLUIE, ph

Boffety, Pierre
LES CLOWNS DE DIEU, ph

Bogardo, Florin
LICEENI, m

Bogart, Dan
SOLDIER'S REVENGE

Bogart, Jane
DOWN AND OUT IN BEVERLY HILLS, set d; VIOLETS
ARE BLUE, set d

Bogert, Bill
WHATEVER IT TAKES

Bogert, William
STEWARDESS SCHOOL

Bogle, Warren
BIG TROUBLE, w

Bogner, Ludvik
BUSTED UP, ph

Bohm, Berit
BRODERNA MOZART

Bohm, Katharina
TAROT

Bohmert, Axel
SCHMUTZ

Bohren, Geir
NATTSEILERE, m

Bohrer, Corinne
STEWARDESS SCHOOL

Bohringer, Richard
KAMIKAZE; LE PALTOQUET

Bohringer, Romane
KAMIKAZE

Boht, Jean
ARTHUR'S HALLOWED GROUND

Boiche, Marie-Therese
CAPTIVE, ed

Boigon, Gary
BUSTED UP

Boileau, Blanche-Danielle
HENRI, cos

Boissel, Anne
SINCERELY CHARLOTTE, ed

Boissery, Jean
LA VITA DI SCORTA

Boisset, Yves
BLEU COMME L'ENFER, d; BLEU COMME L'ENFER,
w

Boisson, Christine
L'AUBE; LE PASSAGE; RUE DU DEPART

Boisson, Noelle
JEAN DE FLORETTE, ed; LA FEMME DE MA VIE, ed;
LOVE SONGS, ed

Bok, An Su
POMNALUI NUNSOGI

Boke, Kevin
TOUCH AND GO

Bokel, Radost
MOMO

Bokma, Pierre
AFZIEN; ASSAULT, THE

Bokova, Jana
HOTEL DU PARADIS, d&w

Boland, Arnaud
MEMOIRES D'UN JUIF TROPICAL, ed

Boland, Melanie
MOSQUITO COAST, THE

Boland, Nora
BACK TO SCHOOL

Bolano, Tony
BAND OF THE HAND

Bolczak, Ted
LONGSHOT, THE

Boldi, Claudio
SCUOLA DI LADRI

Boldi, Massimo
GRANDI MAGAZZINI; IL TENENTE DEI
CARABINIERI; SCUOLA DI LADRI; YUPPIES, I
GIOVANI DI SUCCESSO

Boleau, Luc
TOUCH AND GO

Bolender, Charles
BEER

Boles, Steve
ROCKIN' ROAD TRIP; TRICK OR TREAT

Boles, Tom
ECHO PARK, m/l

Bolger, John
PARTING GLANCES

Bolger, Katy
SCREAMPLAY

Boll, Helen
POLTERGEIST II

Bolla, R.
DEATHMASK

Bolles, Emilio
LA SECONDA NOTTE, p; SEPARATI IN CASA, p

Bolles, Eric
EYE OF THE TIGER

Bolling, Angie
DIRT BIKE KID, THE

Bolling, Claude
LA GITANE, m

Bolling, Trevor
MANHATTAN PROJECT, THE

Bollinger, Alun
FOR LOVE ALONE, ph

Bollman, Horst
FOLLOWING THE FUHRER

Bollman, Susan
SORORITY HOUSE MASSACRE

Bolluyt, Fillip
ASSAULT, THE

Bologna, Ugo
WILD BEASTS; YUPPIES, I GIOVANI DI SUCCESSO

Bolognini, Mauro
LA VENEXIANA, d; LA VENEXIANA, w; LA
VENEXIANA, w

Bolshakova, Natalia
FOUETTE

Bolt, Faye
STAR CRYSTAL

Bolt, Robert
MISSION, THE, w

Boltnev, Andrei
MOI DRUG IVAN LAPSHIN

Bolton, Gregory
BAND OF THE HAND, prod d

Bolton, Heather
ARRIVING TUESDAY

Bolton, Joe [Joseph Reeves Bolton, Jr.]
Obituaries

Bolton, Marian
OCEAN DRIVE WEEKEND

Bolton, Michael
FIRE WITH FIRE, art d

Bolvary, Jean
ZONE ROUGE, p

Bom, Rim Chang
POMNALUI NUNSOGI, d

Boman, Iwa
BRODERNA MOZART; MORRHAR OCH ARTOR

Bomba, Raymond V.
Obituaries

Bombaci, Ross
SHORT CHANGED

Bombolo
GIURO CHE TI AMO

Bombyk, David
HITCHER, THE, p

Bonacelli, Paolo
CAMORRA; L'ISOLA; L'ULTIMA MAZURKA

Bonagura, Gianni
GRANDI MAGAZZINI

Bonanno, Louie
SEX APPEAL

Bonardi, Eugenio
NAME OF THE ROSE, THE

Bonardo, Augusto
POBRE MARIPOSA

Bonas, Mina Bern
TENEMENT

Bonczak, Jerzy
DEATH SENTENCE

Bond, Deanna
DOGS IN SPACE

Bond, Joy
SEX O'CLOCK NEWS, THE

Bond, Ruth
REVENGE OF THE TEENAGE VIXENS FROM OUTER
SPACE, THE

Bond, Timothy
ONE NIGHT ONLY, d

Bondarchuk, Elena
BORIS GODUNOV

Bondarchuk, Fjodr
BORIS GODUNOV

Bondarchuk, Sergei
BORIS GODUNOV; BORIS GODUNOV, d&w

Bondarenko, Boris
ODINOTCHNOYE PLAVANIYE, ph

Bonders, James
AVENGING FORCE

Bondo, Ulrikke Juul
TWIST & SHOUT

Bonezzi, Bernardo
MATADOR, m

Bonfim, Roberto
FULANINHA

Bonicelli, Vittori
L'INCHIESTA, w

Bonifacio, Antonio
LA MONACA NEL PECCATO, w

Bonifacio, Charles
CARE BEARS MOVIE II: A NEW GENERATION, anim d

Bonilla, Arturo
SALVADOR

Bonilla, Maria Teresa
A LA SALIDA NOS VEMOS, p

Bonilla, Socorro
POR UN VESTIDO DE NOVIA

Bonin, Arturo
ANOTHER LOVE STORY; CONTAR HASTA TEN

Bonin, Catherine
DERNIER CRI

Bonin, Claude
ANNE TRISTER, p; HENRI, p; INTIMATE POWER, p

Bonitzer, Pascal
GOLDEN EIGHTIES, w; SCENE OF THE CRIME, w

Bonivento, Claudio
IL RAGAZZO DEL PONY EXPRESS, p

Bonke, Peter
JOUR ET NUIT

Bonnafe, Jacques
LA FEMME SECRETE

Bonnaire, Jean-Paul
GARDIEN DE LA NUIT; LES FRERES PETARD

Bonnaire, Sandrine
LA PURITAINE; POLICE

Bonnard, Keith
SHANGHAI SURPRISE

Bonnay, Yvette
THERESE, cos

Bonnell, Lee
Obituaries

Bonner, Frank
LONGSHOT, THE

Bonnet, Isa
SUMMER

Bono, Cesar
ES MI VIDA—EL NOA NOA 2

Bono, Sonny
BALBOA; TROLL

Bonoff, Karla
ABOUT LAST NIGHT, m/l

Bontinas, Thomas
ALLIGORIA

Bonvoisin, Berangere
HOTEL DU PARADIS

Booher, Deanna
WELCOME TO 18

Booker, Jessica
SEPARATE VACATIONS

Bookman, Glenn
GIRLS SCHOOL SCREAMERS, art d

Boom, Peter
SAVING GRACE

Boone, Mark
WAY IT IS, THE

Boone, Walker
YOUNGBLOOD

Boorstin, Jon
DREAM LOVER, p; DREAM LOVER, w

Boorstin, Paul
FIRE WITH FIRE, w

Boorstin, Sharon
FIRE WITH FIRE, w

Booth, James
AVENGING FORCE; AVENGING FORCE, w; BAD
GUYS ; PRAY FOR DEATH; PRAY FOR DEATH, w

Booth, Tom
CRAZY MOON, makeup

Bor, Won Gam
SHANGHAI SURPRISE

Boratto, Caterina
EHRENGARD

Borbach, Arianne
DAS HAUS AM FLUSS

Borbijev, Nurtoy
DESCENDANT OF THE SNOW LEOPARD, THE, ph

Borchers, Donald P.
VAMP, p; VAMP, d&w

Borden, Lizzie
WORKING GIRLS, d; WORKING GIRLS, ed; WORKING
GIRLS, p; WORKING GIRLS, w

Borden, Ross
PATRIOT, THE

Bordeu, Fernando
TOP OF THE WHALE

Bordie, Bill
BEER, prod d

Bordie, Keith
LAND OF DOOM

Bordie, Thomas
LAND OF DOOM

Bordolini, Enrique
PERROS DE LA NOCHE, set d

Boren, Lamar
Obituaries

Boretz, Allen
Obituaries

Borg, Ole
TWIST & SHOUT

Borg, Sonia
DARK AGE, w

Borgeaud, Nelly
LOVE SONGS

Borges, Graciela
POBRE MARIPOSA

Borges, Mario
WHERE THE RIVER RUNS BLACK

Borges, Susana
REPORTER X

Borgese, Sal
SQUADRA SELVAGGIA; TRE SUPERMEN A SANTO
DOMINGO

Borghi, Renato
BRAS CUBAS

Borgli, Petter
FLIGHT OF THE NAVIGATOR, spec eff; PERVOLA:
TRACKS IN THE SNOW, spec eff

Borgnine, Ernest
MANHUNT, THE

Borjlind, Rolf
JONSSONLIGAN DYKER UPP IGEN, w; MORRHAR
OCH ARTOR, w

Borland, Jody
DOGS IN SPACE, art d

Borland, Skip
ABDUCTED

Borman, Moritz
LIGHTSHIP, THE, p

Bornazzini, Cesare
UNA DOMENICA SI, w

Bornstein, Charles
GETTING EVEN, ed

Bornstein, Deborah
SCREAMPLAY

Bornstein, Ken
LIGHTNING—THE WHITE STALLION, ed

Borodyansky, Aleksandr
ZIMNI VECHER V GAGRAKH, w

Boroumand, Zahra
MIRZA NOWROUZ' SHOES

Borowski, Henryk
JEZIORO BODENSKIE

Borresen, Geir
NOE HEIT ANNET

Borretzen, Odd
MACARONI BLUES; MACARONI BLUES, w

Borris, Clay
QUIET COOL, d; QUIET COOL, w

Borromeo, Christian
EHRENGARD

Borssen, Jarl
JONSSONLIGAN DYKER UPP IGEN

Bortnik, Aida
POBRE MARIPOSA, w

Borton, Steve
MANHATTAN PROJECT, THE

Borysse, Francois
SINCERELY CHARLOTTE

Bos, Henk
FIELD OF HONOR, w

Bosch, Lydia
EL DISPUTADO VOTO DEL SR. CAYO

Bosco, Philip
CHILDREN OF A LESSER GOD; MONEY PIT, THE

Boscoli, Tania
AS SETE VAMPIRAS; COM LICENCA, EU VOU A
LUTA

Bose, Miguel
EL CABALLERO DEL DRAGON; EN PENUMBRA

Bose, Nitin
Obituaries

Bose, Rajkumar
MASSEY SAHIB, ph

Bosic, Andrea
FORMULA FOR MURDER; MANHATTAN BABY

Bosmans, Christine
CONGO EXPRESS

Boss Film Corp.
DESERT BLOOM, spec eff; LEGAL EAGLES, spec eff

Bossidy, Tina
RUNNING OUT OF LUCK, cos

Bost, Bob
IMPURE THOUGHTS

Bost, Tim
ROCKIN' ROAD TRIP; ROCKIN' ROAD TRIP

Boston, Anne
FINE MESS, A, m/l

Bostwick, Jackson
WHAT WAITS BELOW

Boswell, Simon
DEMONI 2—L'INCUBO RITORNA, m

Botelli, Melina
CARAVAN SARAI

Botero, Jose Luis
A LA SALIDA NOS VEMOS

Botero, Yolanda
EL TREN DE LOS PIONEROS, set d

Both, Andrei
SECVENTE, art d

Bothur, Gunther
SCHMUTZ

Botkin, Perry
WEEKEND WARRIORS, m

Botosso, Claudio
GRANDI MAGAZZINI; IL DIAVOLO IN CORPO; IL
TENENTE DEI CARABINIERI

Botsford, Sara
JUMPIN' JACK FLASH; LEGAL EAGLES

Bott, Jochen
SPRING SYMPHONY

Botto, Juan Diego
EL RIO DE ORO; TEO EL PELIRROJO

Bottoms, Sam
IN 'N' OUT

Bottoms, Timothy
IN THE SHADOW OF KILIMANJARO; INVADERS
FROM MARS; SEA SERPENT, THE; WHAT WAITS
BELOW

Bottroff, Stephen M.
WEEKEND WARRIORS

Bouche, Claudine
RUE DU DEPART, ed

Bouchitey, Patrick
DOUCE FRANCE

Bouderba, Khadija
CHAMS

Boudov, Jeff
WISDOM

Bougaard, Corinne
KNIGHTS AND EMERALDS

Bougousslavsky, Axel
MON CAS

Bouhon, Jean-Jacques
BEAU TEMPS, MAIS ORAGEUX EN FIN DE
JOURNEE, ph

Bouise, Jean
LAST IMAGE, THE; ZONE ROUGE

Bouix, Evelyne
MAN AND A WOMAN: 20 YEARS LATER, A

Boujenah, Michel
LAST IMAGE, THE; PRUNELLE BLUES

Boujenah, Paul
YIDDISH CONNECTION, d

Boulanger, Guy
L'UNIQUE, m

Boulay, Muriel
MAMMAME

Boulee, Onno
ACES GO PLACES IV

Boulter, Peter
INSTANT JUSTICE

Bouman, Eva
DE VAL VAN PATRICIA HAGGERSMITH, m

Bouquet, Carole
DOUBLE MESSIEURS; LE MAL D'AIMER

Bouquin, Jacques
MAMMAME, ph

Bouquin, Martine
MAMMAME, ed

Bourbault, Jean-Claude
PRUNELLE BLUES

Bourboulon, Frederic
SINCERELY CHARLOTTE

Bourcier, Francois
GARDIEN DE LA NUIT

Bourgine, Elizabeth
COURS PRIVE

Bourgoin, Ingrid
FAUBOURG SAINT-MARTIN

Bourguiba, Ahmed
MAN OF ASHES, spec eff

Bourland, Kevin
ABOUT LAST NIGHT

Bourne, Lindsay
ABDUCTED, w

Bourne, Mel
F/X, prod d; MANHUNTER, prod d

Bourseiller, Christophe
LA GALETTE DU ROI

Boushel, Joy
FLY, THE

Bousquet, Jean
SCENE OF THE CRIME

Boustedt, Christer
Obituaries

Boutard, Herve
ON A VOLE CHARLIE SPENCER!, art d

Boutross, Tom
FREE RIDE, p

Boutsikaris, Dennis
VERY CLOSE QUARTERS

Bouvyer, Jacqueline
THERESE

Bouzid, Nouri
MAN OF ASHES, d&w

Bouzit, Mohamed
LAST IMAGE, THE, cos

Brauer, Charles
DIE ZWEI GESICHTER DES JANUAR

Brauer, Jurgen
GRITTA VOM RATTENSCHLOSS, d; GRITTA VOM RATTENSCHLOSS, ph

Brault, Michel
NO MERCY, ph

Braumann, Yvonne
BIG HURT, THE; BIG HURT, THE

Braumer, Fritz
FLIGHT OF THE NAVIGATOR

Braun, Charles
GIRLS SCHOOL SCREAMERS

Braun, Eddie
BORN AMERICAN, stunts

Braun, Herman
SINCERELY CHARLOTTE

Braun, Theodore
SCREAMPLAY; SCREAMPLAY, stunts

Braun, Zev
WHERE ARE THE CHILDREN?; WHERE ARE THE CHILDREN?, p

Braunstein, Jeff
ONE NIGHT ONLY

Brauren, Katharina
NOVEMBERKATZEN

Braverman, Bart
SCORPION

Braverman, Rosalyn
BEER

Bravo, Charley
MONSTER DOG

Bravo, Charlie
L'APACHE BIANCO; SCALPS

Bravo, Eva
KAPAX DEL AMAZONAS

Bravo, Richard
SCORPION

Bravo, Roberto
COME LA VIDA MISMA, ed; EL CORAZON SOBRE LA TIERRA, ed

Bravo, Tony
EL BRONCO

Bray, Catherine
YOUNGBLOOD

Braybrook, Johnny
YOUNGBLOOD

Brazzel, Greg
MOUNTAINTOP MOTEL MASSACRE

Brazzi, Rossano
FORMULA FOR MURDER

Bream, Reg
DUET FOR ONE, art d

Bredefeldt, Gosta
DEN FRUSNA LEOPARDEN

Bredin, Robert
PINK CHIQUITAS, THE

Breedlove, Jhoe
OFF BEAT

Breen, Danny
DIRT BIKE KID, THE

Brega, Mario
TROPPO FORTE

Bregman, Christopher
SWEET LIBERTY

Bregman, Martin
SWEET LIBERTY, p

Breillat, Catherine
POLICE, w

Breining, Michael
DIE WALSCHE, ed

Breit, Bert
FRANZA, m

Breit, Kevin
CRAZY MOON

Brell, Aldo San
INSTANT JUSTICE

Bremen, Lennie   [Leonard Bremen]
Obituaries

Bremer, Leslee
MY CHAUFFEUR

Brenguier, Dominique
BLEU COMME L'ENFER, ph

Brenguier, Laurence
GARDIEN DE LA NUIT, art d

Brennan, Patrick
BEST OF TIMES, THE

Brennan, Stephen
EAT THE PEACH

Brennan, Timothy
ABSOLUTE BEGINNERS

Brenner, Albert
MORNING AFTER, THE, prod d; RUNNING SCARED, prod d

Brenner, Eve
GREAT MOUSE DETECTIVE, THE; TORMENT

Brenner, Hans
HEILT HITLER!

Brenner, Jerome
SEX APPEAL

Brenner, Robert
SOLDIER'S REVENGE

Brent, Joy
BALBOA

Brentano, Amy
BREEDERS

Brenton, Gilbert
CLASS OF NUKE 'EM HIGH

Bresan, Ivo
OBECANA ZEMLJA, w

Brescia, Alfonso
CHOKE CANYON, w

Bresee, Bobbie
ARMED RESPONSE

Breslin, Kevin
OUT OF BOUNDS

Bressane, Julio
BRAS CUBAS, p&d; BRAS CUBAS, w; CINEMA FALADO

Brestoff, Richard
STOOGEMANIA

Bret, Anais
LES FUGITIFS

Brett, Jason
ABOUT LAST NIGHT, p

Bretzinger, Jurgen
HEIDENLOCHER

Breuer, Jaques
SECOND VICTORY, THE

Breuker, William
PPPERFORMER, THE, m

Brewer, Alan
PLAYING FOR KEEPS, md; PLAYING FOR KEEPS, p

Brewer, Charlie
MURPHY'S LAW

Brewer, Colin M.
FOREIGN BODY, p

Brewer, Gil
LA MACHINE A DECOUDRE, w

Brewer, Roy M.
GREAT MOUSE DETECTIVE, THE, ed

Brewer, Sharon
OCEAN DRIVE WEEKEND

Brezina, Polio
DIE NACHTMEERFAHRT, m

Brialy, Jean-Claude
INSPECTEUR LAVARDIN; LE DEBUTANT; SUIVEZ MON REGARD

Brian, Bent
TWIST & SHOUT

Bribiesca, Ricky
QUEEN CITY ROCKERS

Bricano, Carlos
PEQUENA REVANCHA, ph

Brickhardt, Craig
AT CLOSE RANGE, m/l

Brickman, June
NO RETREAT, NO SURRENDER, makeup

Brickman, Marshall
MANHATTAN PROJECT, THE, d; MANHATTAN PROJECT, THE, p; MANHATTAN PROJECT, THE, w

Bricmont, Wendy Greene
CLAN OF THE CAVE BEAR, THE, ed

Briden, Annelaine
SOLDIER'S REVENGE

Bridges, Ann
LOW BLOW

Bridges, Jeff
8 MILLION WAYS TO DIE; MORNING AFTER, THE

Bridges, Lloyd
WEEKEND WARRIORS

Bridges, Lynda
INSTANT JUSTICE

Bridges, Mellena
REBEL LOVE, ed

Bridges, Robert
MR. LOVE

Bridgewater, Ann
ISLE OF FANTASY

Brieger, Nicolas
WELCOME IN VIENNA

Briere, Daniel
DECLINE OF THE AMERICAN EMPIRE, THE

Brietner-Protat, Marie Angele
SEPARATE VACATIONS, makeup

Briganti, Elisa Livia
MANHATTAN BABY, w

Briggs, Jack
EAT AND RUN, p

Briggs, Joe Bob
TEXAS CHAINSAW MASSACRE PART 2, THE

Briggs, Mindy
DR. OTTO AND THE RIDDLE OF THE GLOOM BEAM

Briggs, Raymond
WHEN THE WIND BLOWS, w

Bright, Ho
ABSOLUTE BEGINNERS

Bright, John
ROOM WITH A VIEW, A, cos

Bright, Richard
BRIGHTON BEACH MEMOIRS; CUT AND RUN

Brigitte-Catillon
LAST IMAGE, THE

Briley, John
TAI-PAN, w

Brill, Aviva
ONE MORE SATURDAY NIGHT

Brilli, Nancy
DEMONI 2—L'INCUBO RITORNA

Brimley, Wilford
AMERICAN JUSTICE

Brine, Adrian
PERVOLA: TRACKS IN THE SNOW

Brine, Roland
ABSOLUTE BEGINNERS

Brink, Connie
MANHATTAN PROJECT, THE, spec eff

Brink, Rudolf
TWIST & SHOUT

Brinkers, Gert
DE WISSELWACHTER, art d

Brinton, Don
TRAMP AT THE DOOR, p

Brion, Francoise
FRENCH LESSON

Brisbin, David
DEAD END KIDS

Briscomb, Adam
DOGS IN SPACE

Brisebois, Eric
HENRI; INTIMATE POWER

Britneva, Maria
ROOM WITH A VIEW, A

Brittany, Tally
SEX APPEAL

Britten, Benjamin
MAUVAIS SANG, m

Britton, Aileen
Obituaries

Britton, Katherine
NIGHT OF THE CREEPS

Brizard, Philippe
LE DEBUTANT

Bro, Vigga
BARNDOMMENS GADE

Broadbent, Jim
GOOD FATHER, THE; RUNNING OUT OF LUCK

Broadley, Philip
GIRL FROM MANI, THE, w

Broberg, Curt
GRONA GUBBAR FRAN Y.R.

Broberg, Robert
MANDEN I MAANEN, m

Broccolino, Lidia
IL DIAVOLO IN CORPO

Brocer, Yves
L'AUBE, set d

Brochard, Martine
FEAR

Brochette, Eugene
NINJA TURF

Brock, Ed
NEVER TOO YOUNG TO DIE

Brock, George
COCAINE WARS, m

Brock, Major
MOUNTAINTOP MOTEL MASSACRE

Cagli, Leonardo Coen
DELTA FORCE, THE, set d

Cagney, James   [James Francis Cagney, Jr.]
Obituaries

Cahall, Robin
KING KONG LIVES

Cahn, Leo
MAMA IS BOOS!, spec eff

Caicedo, Franklin
LES LONGS MANTEAUX

Caillaud, Gerard
PAULETTE

Cain, Christopher
WHERE THE RIVER RUNS BLACK, d

Cain, John
BOY IN BLUE, THE

Cain, Marie
BEST OF TIMES, THE

Cain, Roger
LABYRINTH, art d

Cain, Tane
ARMED RESPONSE, m/l

Caine, Michael
HALF MOON STREET; HANNAH AND HER SISTERS;
MONA LISA; SWEET LIBERTY

Caine, Peter
THRONE OF FIRE, THE

Cakmakli, Serpil
FOURTEEN NUMARA

Cala, Jerry
IL RAGAZZO DEL PONY EXPRESS; IL RAGAZZO
DEL PONY EXPRESS, w; YUPPIES, I GIOVANI DI
SUCCESSO

Calabrese, Francesco
FOTOROMANZO, w; GIURO CHE TI AMO, w

Calabrese, Nick
YOUNGBLOOD

Calahelo, Billy
BUSTED UP

Calbino, Tony
AMIGOS

Calcagno, Eduardo
TE AMO, d

Calcumil, Luisa
GERONIMA

Calder, John F.
FINE MESS, A, m/l

Calderella, Anthony
PATRIOT, THE

Calderon, Alberto Cortes
AMOR A LA VUELTA DE LA ESQUINA, d&w

Calderon, Angela
SAN ANTONITO

Calderon, Paul
BAND OF THE HAND

Calderon, Ruben
QUE ME MATEN DE UNA VEZ

Caldron, Paul
TENEMENT

Caldwell, Don
Obituaries

Caldwell, Stephen
HELLFIRE

Cale, J.J.
50/50, m

Cale, John
SOMETHING WILD, m

Calero, Gerardo
VISA U.S.A.

Calfan, Nicole
MAX MON AMOUR

Calhoun, Jeff
WEEKEND WARRIORS

Calhoun, Scott
ARRIVING TUESDAY, m

Calimera, Francesco
DANILO TRELES, O FIMISMENOS ANDALOUSIANOS
MOUSIKOS

Calinescu, Ana-Maria
DREPTATE IN LANTURI

Call, R.D.
AT CLOSE RANGE

Callahan, Ed
SCREAMPLAY

Callahan, Gene
CHILDREN OF A LESSER GOD, prod d

Callahan, Jack
ONE MORE SATURDAY NIGHT

Callahan, Mushy   [Vincent Morris Scheer]
Obituaries

Callicot, Patti
ECHO PARK, cos

Callicott, Patti
SAY YES, cos

Callins, George
BLUE CITY, m/l

Callow, Simon
GOOD FATHER, THE; ROOM WITH A VIEW, A

Calmon, Antonio
HAPPILY EVER AFTER, p; HAPPILY EVER AFTER, w

Calonius, John
DEATHMASK

Caluten, Albhy
RAW DEAL, m

Calvert, Adams
AT CLOSE RANGE, spec eff

Calvert, Jim
HOUSE

Calvert, Phyllis
DEATH OF THE HEART, THE

Calvino, Tony
FLIGHT OF THE NAVIGATOR

Camacho, Alejandro
EL MALEFICIO II

Camacho, Angel
CONTACTO CHICANO, ed; EL EXTRANO HIJO DEL
SHERIFF, ed; ES MI VIDA—EL NOA NOA 2, ed

Camacho, Gonzalo J.
MANON

Camacho, Marcela
MATANZA EN MATAMOROS

Camacho, Miguel
AMOR A LA VUELTA DE LA ESQUINA, p

Camara, Mohamed
BLACK MIC-MAC

Camaya, Boyel
NAKED VENGEANCE, art d

Cambas, Jacqueline
MONEY PIT, THE, ed

Cambern, Donn
JO JO DANCER, YOUR LIFE IS CALLING, ed

Cameli, Claudio
CARNE CHE CRESCE

Camerano, Rafael
MISSION, THE

Cameron, Allan
HIGHLANDER, prod d; LADY JANE, prod d

Cameron, David
SALOME

Cameron, Heather
SCORPION; SCORPION, art d

Cameron, James
ALIENS, d; ALIENS, w

Cameron, Kirk
BEST OF TIMES, THE

Cameron, Steve
TOUCH AND GO

Camerum, David
'38

Camilleri, Joe
DOGS IN SPACE

Caminito, Augusto
LA SPOSA AMERICANA, p; LE MINIERE DEL
KILIMANGIARO, p; MEGLIO BACIARE UN COBRA, p;
TROPPO FORTE, p

Camino, Jaime
DRAGON RAPIDE, p&d; DRAGON RAPIDE, w

Camire, Nelson
ABDUCTED

Cammanrano, Salvatore
MONEY PIT, THE, m/l

Camorine, Marcelo
POBRE MARIPOSA, ph

Camorino, Marcelo
EIN BLICK—UND DIE LIEBE BRICHT AUS, ph

Camp, Joanne
MANHUNTER

Camp, Nelson
AVENGING FORCE

Camp, Wilson
ARMED AND DANGEROUS

Campagnoni, Wilf
FRINGE DWELLERS, THE

Campana, Enrico
KILLER PARTY, set d

Campanaro, Marino
INNOCENZA

Campanaro, Philip
SEX APPEAL

Campanella, Frank
FREE RIDE

Campanella, Pierfrancesco
CATTIVI PIERROT; CATTIVI PIERROT, w

Campanino, Franco
WHITE SLAVE, m

Campbell, Alan
WEEKEND WARRIORS

Campbell, Beck
POPULATION: ONE

Campbell, C. Jutson
STAR CRYSTAL

Campbell, Catherine
BALBOA

Campbell, Colin
MY BEAUTIFUL LAUNDRETTE

Campbell, Dick
WHITE SLAVE

Campbell, Don
YOUNGBLOOD

Campbell, Gerald
F/X

Campbell, Glen
UPHILL ALL THE WAY

Campbell, John
MALA NOCHE, ph

Campbell, Ken
LETTER TO BREZHNEV

Campbell, Malcolm
THREE AMIGOS, ed

Campbell, Martin
BLACK JOY, p

Campbell, Muriel   [Muriel Campbell Douglas]
Obituaries

Campbell, Patricia
SCREEN TEST

Campbell, Ron
MODERN GIRLS

Campbell, Sarah-Jane
KNIGHTS AND EMERALDS

Campbell, Stewart
APRIL FOOL'S DAY, art d

Campbell, Tisha
LITTLE SHOP OF HORRORS

Campion, Cris
PIRATES

Campion, Jane
TWO FRIENDS, d

Campo, Sabeline
CHARLOTTE FOR EVER

Campos, El Garcia
ANGEL RIVER, m

Campos, Lisa Marie
AMERICAN ANTHEM

Campos, Miguel A. Perez
MAMBRU SE FUE A LA GUERRA, p

Campos, Rosana
RUNNING OUT OF LUCK

Campos, Sergio Poves
EL HOMBRE QUE GANO LA RAZON

Camus, Mario
WERTHER, w

Canale, Sandra
SENZA SCRUPOLI

Canavan, Michael
RATBOY

Candelli, Stelio
RAGE

Candi, George
SOLDIER'S REVENGE

Candido, Candy
GREAT MOUSE DETECTIVE, THE

Candimir, Atilla
KIRLANGIC FIRTINASI, d

Candimir, Tulin
KIRLANGIC FIRTINASI, p

Candini, Case
CAGED GLASS, art d

Candy, John
ARMED AND DANGEROUS; LITTLE SHOP OF
HORRORS

Cane, Frank
SOLDIER'S REVENGE

Cane, Sharon
VIOLATED

Cann, David
KNIGHTS AND EMERALDS

Cannavacciolo, Angelo
CATTIVI PIERROT

Canning, Joanne
BIG HURT, THE

Canning, Victor
Obituaries

Cannistraro, Richard
VIOLATED; VIOLATED, p&d; VIOLATED, w

Cannom, Greg
RADIOACTIVE DREAMS, makeup; VAMP, spec eff

Cannon, Donna
MONA LISA

Cannon, Poppy
FIREWALKER, cos; FIREWALKER, set d

Canon, Jack
MAXIMUM OVERDRIVE

Canon, Mary
RAW DEAL

Cantarone, Elena
GINGER & FRED

Cantieni, Ursula
DER POLENWEIHER

Canto, Antonio
EN PENUMBRA

Canty, Marietta
Obituaries

Canutt, Yakima   [Enos Edward Canutt]
Obituaries

Capanga, Joe
COCAINE WARS

Caparas, Carlo J.
RAGING VENDETTA, w

Capell, Peter
Obituaries

Capello, Roger
UNDER THE CHERRY MOON

Capers, Virginia
FERRIS BUELLER'S DAY OFF; HOWARD THE DUCK;
JO JO DANCER, YOUR LIFE IS CALLING

Capetanos, Leon
DOWN AND OUT IN BEVERLY HILLS, w

Capetillo, Manuel
LAS NOCHES DEL CALIFAS

Capitanio, Fulvio
CARNE CHE CRESCE

Capitano, Francesco
IL CASO MORO

Capo, Armando
COCAINE WARS

Capolicchio, Lino
DIE WALSCHE

Capolupo, Vincent
SEVEN MINUTES IN HEAVEN

Caponbianco, Jorge
BAD COMPANY

Capone, Alberto
NAME OF THE ROSE, THE

Capone, Alessandro
LA BONNE, w

Capone, Clifford
KING KONG LIVES, cos; MAXIMUM OVERDRIVE, cos;
RAW DEAL, cos

Capone, Gino
LA SPOSA AMERICANA, w

Capone, Kim
SCORPION

Caporali, Aristide
NAME OF THE ROSE, THE

Cappello, Frank
DR. OTTO AND THE RIDDLE OF THE GLOOM BEAM,
spec eff

Cappiello, John E.
QUICKSILVER

Capraru, Jennifer
WALKMAN BLUES

Capri, Jezabel
SUIVEZ MON REGARD

Capshaw, Kate
POWER; SPACECAMP

Caputo, Michel
L'EXECUTRICE, p, d&w

Caquelin, Cynthia
FLIGHT OF THE NAVIGATOR

Cara, Irene
BUSTED UP; BUSTED UP, m/l

Cara, Jean Paul
LAST IMAGE, THE, m

Carabatsos, James
HEARTBREAK RIDGE, w

Carabatsos, Jim
NO MERCY, w

Caracchi, Patrizio
MACARONI BLUES

Carafotes, Paul
CLAN OF THE CAVE BEAR, THE; LADIES CLUB,
THE

Carameco, Robert
STAR CRYSTAL, ph

Caramitru, Ion
DECLARATIE DE DRAGOSTE; LICEENI

Carati, Lilli
LUSSURI; VOGLIA DI GUARDARE

Caravaggi, Anna
IL GIARDINO DEGLI INGANNI

Carax, Leos   [Alex Dupont]
MAUVAIS SANG, d&w; People to Watch

Carballeira, Enriqueta
LA MITAD DEL CIELO

Carballido, Emilio
MANON, w

Carben-Stotz, Christine
FOLLOWING THE FUHRER, p

Carboneau, Tracy
NUTCRACKER: THE MOTION PICTURE

Carcano, Alvaro
FIREWALKER

Carcassonne, Evy
THERESE

Carcelero, Ricart
CAGED GLASS

Cardak, Melih
KUYUCAKLI YUSUF

Cardan, Carlos
RAFAGA DE PLOMO

Carden, Gary
OVER THE SUMMER

Cardenas, Manolo
LOS ASES DE CONTRABANDO

Cardiff, Jack
TAI-PAN, ph

Cardinal, Ben
LOYALTIES

Cardinal, Tantoo
LOYALTIES

Cardinal, Yolanda
LOYALTIES

Cardinale, Claudia
LA STORIA; NEXT SUMMER

Cardona, Rene
EL MERCADO DE HUMILDES, d; SE SUFRE PERO SE
GOZA, w

Cardona, Richard
MANHATTAN PROJECT, THE

Cardos, John "Bud"
LAST RESORT, THE, stunts

Cardoso, Beny
SCALPS

Cardoso, Christian
INSOMNIACS

Cardoso, Ivan
AS SETE VAMPIRAS, d; AS SETE VAMPIRAS, p

Cardoso, Pedro
AS SETE VAMPIRAS

Cardoso, Yolanda
COM LICENCA, EU VOU A LUTA

Carducci, Mark Patrick
NEON MANIACS, w

Carduso, Benny
THRONE OF FIRE, THE

Carel, Roger
ASTERIX CHEZ LES BRETONS

Carella, Carlos
EL RIGOR DEL DESTINO

Carena, Fiammetta
LA CASA DEL BUON RITORNO

Caretti, Fabio
SAVING GRACE

Carew, Elaine
MY BEAUTIFUL LAUNDRETTE, makeup

Carew, Peter
BLUE VELVET; PLAYING FOR KEEPS

Carey, Denis
Obituaries

Carey, Earleen
PULSEBEAT

Carey, Geoffrey
LAST SONG

Carey, Harry
CROSSROADS

Carey, Michele
IN THE SHADOW OF KILIMANJARO

Carey, Peter
DEAD-END DRIVE-IN, w

Carey, Timothy
ECHO PARK

Carfagno, Edward
HEARTBREAK RIDGE, prod d; RATBOY, prod d

Carfora, Fabio
NAME OF THE ROSE, THE; SALOME

Carfora, Jessie
TROLL

Carhart, Timothy
MANHATTAN PROJECT, THE; PLAYING FOR KEEPS;
SWEET LIBERTY

Carides, Gia
BACKLASH

Caridi, Carmine
MONEY PIT, THE

Carina, Nadia
CLOCKWISE

Cariosia, Michael
SCREEN TEST

Carita
SUMMER

Carle, Gilles
EQUINOXE, w; LA GUEPE, d; LA GUEPE, w

Carlile, Robert
Obituaries

Carliner, Mark
CROSSROADS, p

Carlini, Carlo
LA RAGAZZA DEI LILLA, ph

Carlip, Hilary
VAMP

Carlos, Carissa
SLOANE

Carlos, Manuela
O VESTIDO COR DE FOGO

Carlotto, Alessandro
UNA NOTTE DI PIOGGIA, ph

Carlsen, Henning
WOLF AT THE DOOR, THE, p&d; WOLF AT THE
DOOR, THE, w

Carlson, Erica
SALVADOR

Carlson, Kimberlee
BACK TO SCHOOL

Carlson, Les
FLY, THE

Carlson, Steven L.
WILDCATS

Carlsson, Bengt CW
PA LIV OCH DOD

Carlsson, Bie
RATTIS, m

Carlsson, Ewa
YES, DET ER FAR!

Carlton, Margaret
DEVASTATOR, THE, ed

Carlton, Mark
ARMED AND DANGEROUS

Carmel, Roger C.
Obituaries; TRANSFORMERS: THE MOVIE, THE

Carmeli, Benny
HAKRAV AL HAVA'AD, ph

Carmen, Dawn
MANHUNTER

Carmen, Julie
BLUE CITY

Carmet, Jean
LE MATOU; LES FUGITIFS; MON BEAU-FRERE A
TUE MA SOEUR; SUIVEZ MON REGARD

Carmichael, Katherine J.
VAMP, set d

Carmine, Michael
BAND OF THE HAND

Carmita
RUNNING OUT OF LUCK

Carmody, Jaki
ONE NIGHT ONLY, ed

Carmona, Don
HOLLYWOOD ZAP!

Carnaghi, Roberto
INSOMNIACS

Carneiro, Mario
CHICO REI, ed; CHICO REI, ph

Carnelutti, Francesco
IL CASO MORO

Carnevale, Tony
ANCHE LEI FUMAVA IL SIGARO, m

Carnow, Stefan
GRITTA VOM RATTENSCHLOSS, m

Carocci, Patrick
UNDER THE CHERRY MOON

Carol, Linda
REFORM SCHOOL GIRLS

Carol, Madelaine
PLAYING FOR KEEPS

Caron, Michel
HENRI, ph; QUI A TIRE SUR NOS HISTOIRES
D'AMOUR?, ph

Carow, Evelyn
GRITTA VOM RATTENSCHLOSS, ed

Carpelan, Bo
VALKOINEN KAAPIO, d&w

Carpenter, David
CRIMES OF THE HEART

Carpenter, Ian
AGENT ON ICE, m

Carpenter, John
BIG TROUBLE IN LITTLE CHINA, d; BIG TROUBLE
IN LITTLE CHINA, m; BIG TROUBLE IN LITTLE
CHINA, m/l; BLACK MOON RISING, w; BOY WHO
COULD FLY, THE

Carpenter, Stephen
TORMENT, ph

Carpenter, Wanjun
SHORT CHANGED

Carpi, Fiorenzo
LA STORIA, m

Carpi, Jezabel
JE HAIS LES ACTEURS; L'UNIQUE

Carpi, Tito
DAYS OF HELL, w

Carpinteiro, Margarida
O VESTIDO COR DE FOGO

Carpio, Teresa
ISLE OF FANTASY

Carr, Frankie [Frank Carozza]
Obituaries

Carr, John
LETTER TO BREZHNEV

Carr, Terry
WELCOME TO 18, d; WELCOME TO 18, w

Carr, Warren
BOY WHO COULD FLY, THE

Carradine, David
ARMED RESPONSE; P.O.W. THE ESCAPE

Carradine, John
PEGGY SUE GOT MARRIED; REVENGE; TOMB, THE

Carradine, Keith
L'INCHIESTA

Carrafa, Michael
FAT GUY GOES NUTZOID!!

Carraro, Nicola
IL BI E IL BA, p

Carrasco, Queta
SALVADOR

Carre, Louise
QUI A TIRE SUR NOS HISTOIRES D'AMOUR?, d&w

Carreno, Meche
ES MI VIDA—EL NOA NOA 2

Carrera, Dorothea
NOVEMBERKATZEN

Carretti, Frank
PULSEBEAT, cos

Carrey, Jim
PEGGY SUE GOT MARRIED

Carrie
LINK

Carrie, Susana
SAN ANTONITO, cos

Carriere, Jean-Claude
L'UNIQUE, w; MAX MON AMOUR, w; WOLF AT THE
DOOR, THE, w

Carriere, Mathieu
FUTURE OF EMILY, THE

Carrillo, Elpedia
SALVADOR

Carrington, Debbie
HOWARD THE DUCK

Carrington, Scott
ODD JOBS

Carrion, Gustavo
HIJO DEL PALENQUE, m

Carrion, Rafael
EL EXTRANO HIJO DEL SHERIFF, m; LA TIERRA
PROMETIDA, m

Carrion, Ricardo
RAFAGA DE PLOMO, m

Carroll, Beeson
CRIMES OF THE HEART

Carroll, Gordon
BEST OF TIMES, THE, p

Carroll, Helena
BAD GUYS

Carroll, Peter
MORE THINGS CHANGE, THE

Carroll, Ronn
HOUSE

Carroll, Shelley
SEX O'CLOCK NEWS, THE

Carroll, Tyler Ann
ONE MORE SATURDAY NIGHT

Carroll, Willard
NUTCRACKER: THE MOTION PICTURE, p

Carrotes, Beal
NIGHT OF THE CREEPS

Carrotte
HANNAH AND HER SISTERS

Carruth, William
WHAT COMES AROUND, ed

Carson, Darwyn
JUST BETWEEN FRIENDS

Carson, Hunter
INVADERS FROM MARS

Carson, L.M. Kit
TEXAS CHAINSAW MASSACRE PART 2, THE, w

Carson, Mitch
NINJA TURF

Carsson, Ewa
ALLA VI BARN I BULLERBY

Carstensen, Margit
ANGRY HARVEST; LA MOITIE DE L'AMOUR

Cart, Susana
ANOTHER LOVE STORY

Cartaxo, Marcelia
HOUR OF THE STAR, THE

Carter, Anthony
MOSQUITO COAST, THE, m/l

Carter, Benny
COSMIC EYE, THE, m

Carter, Charles
BLUE MAN, THE, makeup

Carter, Deborah
KILLER PARTY, m/l

Carter, Frank
CHILDREN OF A LESSER GOD

Carter, Fred
KING KONG LIVES, art d; LADY JANE, art d

Carter, Gary
DIRT BIKE KID, THE

Carter, Helena Bonham
LADY JANE; ROOM WITH A VIEW, A; People to Watch

Carter, Jim
HAUNTED HONEYMOON

Carter, Kathy
HOT CHILI, m/l

Carter, Kelvin
ABSOLUTE BEGINNERS

Carter, Logan
HOLLYWOOD VICE SQUAD

Carter, Lynell
VENDETTA

Carter, Marsha
SORORITY HOUSE MASSACRE

Carter, Mitch
VAMP

Carter, Ric
AROUND THE WORLD IN EIGHTY WAYS

Carter, Ron
ROUND MIDNIGHT; ROUND MIDNIGHT

Carter, Ruth
COMING UP ROSES, w

Carter, Vincent
TOUCH AND GO

Cartocci, Fernando
SAVING GRACE

Cartwright, Nancy
MY LITTLE PONY

Cartwright, Veronica
FLIGHT OF THE NAVIGATOR; MY MAN ADAM;
WISDOM

Carucci, Silvana
GIURO CHE TI AMO

Caruso, David
BLUE CITY

Caruso, Fred
BLUE VELVET, p

Caruso, Kim
BUSTED UP

Caruso, Mauro
LA SECONDA NOTTE

Carvalho, Betty
THREE AMIGOS

Carvalho, Carlos Augusto
JOGO DURO

Carvalho, Danny
OVER THE SUMMER

Carvalho, Raimundo
WHERE THE RIVER RUNS BLACK

Carvalho, Simone
AS SETE VAMPIRAS

Carvalho, Walter
COM LICENCA, EU VOU A LUTA, ph

Carvana, Hugo
AVAETE, A SEMENTE DA VINGANCA

Carver, Joseph
NUTCRACKER: THE MOTION PICTURE

Carver, Randall
MURPHY'S LAW

Carvey, Dana
TOUGH GUYS

Cary, Christopher
KGB—THE SECRET WAR

Casacci, Massimiliano
IL GIARDINO DEGLI INGANNI, m

Casadei, Angelo
PIRATES

Casados, Eloy
BEST OF TIMES, THE; DOWN AND OUT IN BEVERLY
HILLS; HOLLYWOOD VICE SQUAD

Casale, Francesco
GINGER & FRED

Casals, Gregorio
LOS ASES DE CONTRABANDO; YAKO—CAZADOR DE
MALDITOS

Casanova, Fernando
EL SECUESTRO DE CAMARENA

Casanova, Michael
SOLDIER'S REVENGE

Casara, Mario
NINJA TURF

Casares, Francisco
DRAGON RAPIDE

Casares, Paco
EL DISPUTADO VOTO DEL SR. CAYO

Casati, Ferruccio
IL GIARDINO DEGLI INGANNI, d&w

Casaus, Victor
COME LA VIDA MISMA, d; COME LA VIDA MISMA,
w

Case, Regina
BRAS CUBAS; CINEMA FALADO

Caselnova, Richard
MANHATTAN PROJECT, THE

Casey, D. Ben
SPACECAMP

Casey, Frank
POWER

Casey, Harry W.
KILLER PARTY, m/l

Casey, Richard
LAND OF DOOM, ed

Cash, Jim
LEGAL EAGLES, w; TOP GUN, w; People to Watch

Cash, Johnny
BLUE CITY, m/l

Casillas, Graciela
FIRE IN THE NIGHT

Casin, Orlando
PLACIDO

Caso, Luis
QUE ME MATEN DE UNA VEZ

Caso, Maria Rebman
HAMBURGER, art d

Casperson, Debbie
FLIGHT OF THE NAVIGATOR

Cassady, John
HIGHLANDER

Cassandre, Agnes
PEAU D'ANGE

Cassavetes, John
BIG TROUBLE, d

Cassavetes, Nick
BLACK MOON RISING; QUIET COOL; WRAITH, THE

Cassavetti, Patrick
MONA LISA, p

Cassel, Jean Pierre
EHRENGARD

Cassel, Seymour
EYE OF THE TIGER

Cassell, Alan
BIG HURT, THE

Cassell, Tom
SCORPION

Cassidy, Joanna
CLUB PARADISE

Cassidy, Mike
CRITTERS, stunts

Cassidy, William J.
THE KARATE KID PART II, prod d

Cassinelli, Claudio
HANDS OF STEEL

Castagnola, Humberto
NEMESIO, ph

Castaldo, Robert J.
POSITIVE I.D., ed

Casteldi, Jean-Pierre
SARRAOUNIA

Castellano & Pipolo
GRANDI MAGAZZINI, d&w

Castellano, Franco
SCUOLA DI LADRI, w

Castellano, Rafael
BANDERA NEGRA, w

Castelli, Paulo
HAPPILY EVER AFTER

Castellito, Sergio
GIOVANNI SENZAPENSIERI; SEMBRA MORTO . . .
MA E SOLO SVENUTO; SEMBRA MORTO . . . MA E
SOLO SVENUTO, w

Castelo, Virgilio
UMA RAPARIGA NO VERAO

Castillejo, Chris
PLATOON

Castillo, Candy
THREE AMIGOS

Castillo, Carlos Ruiz
LULU DE NOCHE, art d

Castillo, Cecile
KILLING OF SATAN, THE

Castillo, Cecille
STONE BOY

Castillo, Eric del
EL EXTRANO HIJO DEL SHERIFF; EL EXTRANO
HIJO DEL SHERIFF, w

Castillon, Armando
EL VECINDARIO—LOS MEXICANOS CALIENTES, ph

Castle, Nick
BOY WHO COULD FLY, THE; BOY WHO COULD FLY,
THE, d&w; BOY WHO COULD FLY, THE, m/l

Castleberry, Farris
MANHUNT, THE

Caston, Hoite C.
DIRT BIKE KID, THE, d

Castrillion, Maria Lucia
VISA U.S.A.

Castro, Angela
RUNNING OUT OF LUCK

Castro, Krisnaiza
A LA SALIDA NOS VEMOS

Castro, Mar
QUE ME MATEN DE UNA VEZ

Castro, Marie
FLAGRANT DESIR, ed

Catalano-Carenza, Florence
DANCING IN THE DARK

Catanzano, Larry
SEX APPEAL

Catchlove, Don
TWELFTH NIGHT, p

Cathey, Dalton
WEEKEND WARRIORS

Catlett, Loyd
8 MILLION WAYS TO DIE

Catonne, Francois
LA FEMME DE MA VIE, ph; LA GALETTE DU ROI, ph

Cattan, Benjamin
FILME DEMENCIA

Cattand, Gabriel
PARIS MINUIT

Cattano, Ginny
COMBAT SHOCK

Cattrall, Kim
BIG TROUBLE IN LITTLE CHINA

Caula, Victor Hugo
NIGHTMARE'S PASSENGERS, ph

Causey, Matthew D.
MY CHAUFFEUR, md

Cauwenberghs, Chris
CONGO EXPRESS

Cavadini, Cathy
MY LITTLE PONY; VAMP

Cavalcanti, Claudia
CATTIVI PIERROT

Cavalcanti, Emmanoel
SONHO SEM FIM

Cavalier, Alain
THERESE, d; THERESE, w

Cavaliere, Marco
IL RAGAZZO DEL PONY EXPRESS, w

Cavaliere, Vincenzo
SENZA SCRUPOLI

Cavalini, Paul
YOUNGBLOOD

Cavalli, Valeria
BLADE IN THE DARK, A

Cavallo, Bob
UNDER THE CHERRY MOON, p

Cavallone, Giulio
CARNE CHE CRESCE, ph

Cavan, James
CRY FROM THE MOUNTAIN

Cavanaugh, Coleen
WHERE ARE THE CHILDREN?

Cavanaugh, Larry
CROSSROADS, spec eff; MOSQUITO COAST, THE, spec
eff

Cavanna, Francois
PAULETTE

Cavano, Thomas
SOMETHING WILD

Cavazza, Boris
KORMORAN; KORMORAN, w

Cavazza, Domitilla
SEPARATI IN CASA

Cavedon, Jane
WHERE ARE THE CHILDREN?, set d

Cavestani, Frank
DEADLY FRIEND

Cavestani, Laura
VENDETTA, w

Cavett, Morgan
SMART ALEC, m

Cavina, Gianni
REGALO DI NATALE

Caymmi, Dorival
CINEMA FALADO

Caziot, Jean-Jacques
LA FEMME DE MA VIE, art d; L'ETAT DE GRACE, art
d; MON BEAU-FRERE A TUE MA SOEUR, set d

Cazzaza, John
SCREEN TEST

Ceccarelli, Luigi
L'APACHE BIANCO, m; LE MINIERE DEL
KILIMANGIARO, m; SCALPS, m; WOMEN'S PRISON
MASSACRE, m

Ceccarelli, Pietro
NAME OF THE ROSE, THE

Cecchini, Mimi
EAT AND RUN; WISE GUYS

Cecco, Sergio De
SERE CUALQUIER COSA PERO TE QUIERO, w

Cecere, Tony
DEADLY FRIEND, stunts

Ceder, Elayne Barbara
HEAD OFFICE, prod d

Cederlund, Christian
NUTCRACKER: THE MOTION PICTURE

Cederlund, Erik
NUTCRACKER: THE MOTION PICTURE

Cekmez, Metin
KURBAGALAR

Cela, Violeta
EL ANO DE LAS LUCES

Celani, Isabella
ROOM WITH A VIEW, A

Celarie, Clementine
BETTY BLUE; LA FEMME SECRETE; LA GITANE; LE
COMPLEXE DU KANGOUROU

Celery, Alberto
NEMESIO, p

Celeste, Nino
GRANDI MAGAZZINI, ph; SEPARATI IN CASA, ph

Celi, Adolfo
Obituaries

Celik, Fatosh
LAND OF DOOM

Celik, Hikmet
KURBAGALAR

Celio, Teco
INNOCENZA

Celli, Davide
UNA DOMENICA SI

Cellier, Caroline
FEMMES DE PERSONNE

Cellier, Peter
CLOCKWISE; ROOM WITH A VIEW, A

Celulari, Edson
MALANDRO

Cem, Bixio
MEGLIO BACIARE UN COBRA, m

Cemcev, Laki
SRECNA NOVA '49, ed

Cenci, Athina
LET'S HOPE IT'S A GIRL

Cenet, Michel
JE HAIS LES ACTEURS, ph; SUIVEZ MON REGARD,
ph

Centazzo, Andrea
ROMANCE, m

Cerami, Vincenzo
FRANCESCA E MIA, w; LE MAL D'AIMER, w

Cerar, Mae
BREEDERS

Cerchio, Carlo
IL TENENTE DEI CARABINIERI, ph

Cerezales, Paco Rabal
EL HERMANO BASTARDO DE DIOS

Cerf, Michele
MENAGE, cos; MON BEAU-FRERE A TUE MA SOEUR,
cos

Cerise
PAULETTE

Cerjak, Slavko
DOKTOR

Cerqui, Anita
LOW BLOW

Cerra, Saturno
DRAGON RAPIDE

Cerrada, Carlos
LEGAL EAGLES, set d

Cerullo, Al
MANHATTAN PROJECT, THE

Cervantes, Marta Elena
RAFAGA DE PLOMO

Cervera, Jorge
LONGSHOT, THE; THREE AMIGOS

Cervinka, Milos
LEV S BILOU HRIVOU, art d

Cesena, Marcello
UNA DOMENICA SI

Cetera, Peter
THE KARATE KID PART II, m/l

Cetin, Sinan
FOURTEEN NUMARA, d&w

Cetinel, Nesrin
KURBAGALAR

Cetinkaya, Yavurer
AMANSIZ YOL

Cetinkaya, Yavuser
KURBAGALAR

Cetinkaya, Yavuzer
MANDEN I MAANEN

Cetta, Antonio
NAME OF THE ROSE, THE

Ceyrekbasi, Sema
KUYUCAKLI YUSUF

Ch'eng-ye, Luo
TIME TO LIVE AND A TIME TO DIE, A

Ch'i-yang, Wang
TIME TO LIVE AND A TIME TO DIE, A, ed

Ch'u-ch'u, Wu
TIME TO LIVE AND A TIME TO DIE, A, m

Chabrol, Claude
INSPECTEUR LAVARDIN, d; INSPECTEUR
LAVARDIN, w; JE HAIS LES ACTEURS; SUIVEZ MON
REGARD

Chabrol, Mathieu
INSPECTEUR LAVARDIN, m

Chacon, Thales Pan
EU SEI QUE VOU TE AMAR

Chadock, Rick
KILLER PARTY, m/l

Chadwick, Chad
DR. OTTO AND THE RIDDLE OF THE GLOOM BEAM

Chadwick, June
JUMPIN' JACK FLASH

Chagas, Luiz
FILME DEMENCIA, m

Chagoyan, Rosa Gloria
CONTACTO CHICANO; EL EXTRANO HIJO DEL
SHERIFF; EL SECUESTRO DE LOLA-LOLA LA
TRAILERA 2

Chahin, Mohamed
SUN ON A HAZY DAY, THE, d; SUN ON A HAZY
DAY, THE, w

Chahine, Youssef
EL YOM EL SADES, d&w

Chain, Angelica
EL DIA DE LOS ALBANILES II; EL VECINDARIO—
LOS MEXICANOS CALIENTES

Chakaya, Boris
YOUNG COMPOSER'S ODYSSEY, A, set d

Chakraborty, Goutam
CHOPPER

Chakraborty, Uptlendu
DEBSHISHU, d&w; DEBSHISHU, m

Chalaris, Christodoulos
I PHOTOGRAPHIA, m

Chalbaud, Roman
MANON, d; MANON, w

Chale, Eric
GOLDEN EIGHTIES

Chaliapin, Feodor
NAME OF THE ROSE, THE; SALOME

Chalk, Gary
FIRE WITH FIRE

Chalkias, Antonis
CARAVAN SARAI, set d

Chalkos, Panos
ALLIGORIA

Chalmemedov, Nury
MUZSKOE VOSPITANIE, m

Chalon, Ron
SEX APPEAL

Chalopin, Jean
HEATHCLIFF: THE MOVIE, p

Chamarande, Brigitte
FRENCH LESSON

Chamasmany, Afshin
OVER THE SUMMER, ed; OVER THE SUMMER, ph

Chamberlain, Chris
DR. OTTO AND THE RIDDLE OF THE GLOOM BEAM

Chamberlain, Dean
ECHO PARK, m/l

Chamberlain, Loren
HELL SQUAD

Chamberlin, Mya
SHADOW PLAY

Chambon, Bruno
LAND OF DOOM

Chammah, Ronald
SINCERELY CHARLOTTE

Champa, Jo
SALOME

Champel, Marcel
JEAN DE FLORETTE

Champenois, Denis
RUE DU DEPART, art d

Champetier, Caroline
GRANDEUR ET DECADENCE D'UN PETIT
COMMERCE DE CINEMA, ph

Champion, Marc
SAMUEL LOUNT, ph

Champion, Sandy-Alexander
SPIKER

Chan, Angie
HUAJIE SHIDAI, d

Chan, Anthony
MR. VAMPIRE

Chan, Charine
ISLE OF FANTASY

Chan, Danny
FAMILY, THE

Chan, David
HAPPY DIN DON, prod d

Chan, Dennis
LUNATICS, THE

Chan, Jackie
ARMOUR OF GOD, THE; ARMOUR OF GOD, THE, d

Chan, Kim
JUMPIN' JACK FLASH

Chan, Michael Paul
QUICKSILVER

Chan, Peter C. M.
TONGS—A CHINATOWN STORY, w

Chan, Philip
TONGS—A CHINATOWN STORY, d

Chanas, Francoise
MAMMAME, cos

Chance, Carlton
PASSION OF REMEMBRANCE, THE

Chance, Tiffany
FERRIS BUELLER'S DAY OFF

Chandavarkar, Bhaskar
RAO SAHEB, m

Chandler, Billy
AMERICAN JUSTICE

Chandler, David S.
STREETS OF GOLD

Chandler, Estee
WISDOM

Chandler, Michael
HOWARD THE DUCK, ed

Chandra, Samir
NEW DELHI TIMES, art d

Chang, Alex
NINJA TURF, ed

Chang, Emily Y.
DARK NIGHT

Chang, Gary
3:15, THE MOMENT OF TRUTH, m; 52 PICK-UP, m;
FIREWALKER, m

Chang, Lia
BIG TROUBLE IN LITTLE CHINA

Chang, Peter
DARK NIGHT, m

Chang, Silvia
PASSION; PASSION, d&w

Chang, William
DREAM LOVERS, art d; PASSION, art d

Chang-kwon, Choi
BBONG, m

Chaniolleau, Caroline
LE COMPLEXE DU KANGOUROU; YIDDISH
CONNECTION

Chankwetadse, Nineli
ROBINSONIADA ANU CHEMI INGLISELI PAPA

Channing, Stockard
HEARTBURN; MEN'S CLUB, THE

Chantre, Noele
THERESE

Chapin, Doug
AMERICAN ANTHEM, p

Chapin, Ken
MANHATTAN PROJECT, THE

Chapin, Miles
HOWARD THE DUCK

Chaplin, Charlie
MAUVAIS SANG, m

Chapman, Constance
CLOCKWISE

Chapman, Jan
TWO FRIENDS, p

Chapman, Joaquin Lopez
QUE ME MATEN DE UNA VEZ, m

Chapman, Lonny
52 PICK-UP

Chapman, Michael
CLAN OF THE CAVE BEAR, THE, d

Chapman, Mike
LEGAL EAGLES, m/l

Chapman, Richard
MAXIMUM OVERDRIVE

Chapman, Ted
Obituaries

Chappell, Anna
MOUNTAINTOP MOTEL MASSACRE

Chapuis, Dominique
ETATS D'AME, ph; L'ETAT DE GRACE, ph

Chara, Ricardo
LAST OF PHILIP BANTER, THE, ph

Charbonneau, Patricia
MANHUNTER

Chard, Taia
SCORPION

Chardeaux, Francois
DOUCE FRANCE, p&d; DOUCE FRANCE, w

Charlebois, Robert
LES LONGS MANTEAUX; SAUVE-TOI, LOLA

Charles, Aude
NAKED CAGE, THE

Charles, Gloria
JO JO DANCER, YOUR LIFE IS CALLING

Charles, Joseph
PASSION OF REMEMBRANCE, THE

Charles, Walter
FINE MESS, A

Charleson, Ian
CAR TROUBLE

Charleston, Mary
DEATH OF A SOLDIER

Charlone, Cesar
O HOMEM DA CAPA PRETA, ph

Charmetant, Christian
LE DEBUTANT

Charnay, Lynne
BILLY GALVIN

Charney, Suzanne
VASECTOMY: A DELICATE MATTER

Charnley, Diana
CLOCKWISE, art d

Charnota, Anthony
FREE RIDE

Chartoff, Melanie
STOOGEMANIA

Chartoff, Robert
BEER, p

Chartrand, Phillippe
AMERICAN ANTHEM

Chase, Candy
AMERICAN JUSTICE, m/l

Chase, Carl
LETTER TO BREZHNEV

Chase, Chevy
THREE AMIGOS

Chase, Gary
AMERICAN JUSTICE, m/l

Chase, James Hadley
GRANDEUR ET DECADENCE D'UN PETIT
COMMERCE DE CINEMA, d&w

Chase, Jennifer
BALBOA

Chase, Karen
VENDETTA

Chase, Ken
BIG TROUBLE IN LITTLE CHINA, makeup; GOLDEN
CHILD, THE, makeup

Chase, Thomas
PRAY FOR DEATH, m

Chase, Tom
ARMED RESPONSE, m

Chase, Tomas
ARMED RESPONSE, m/l

Chassapis, Stavros
CARAVAN SARAI, ph

Chateau, Corrine
TENEMENT

Chatham, Jack
ROCKIN' ROAD TRIP

Chatri, Sorapong
ANGKOR-CAMBODIA EXPRESS

Chatry, Bertrand
PARIS MINUIT, ph

Chattaway, Jay
VERY CLOSE QUARTERS, m

Chatterjee, Bidyut
CHOPPER

Chatterjee, Nabyendu
CHOPPER, d&w

Chatto, Daniel
DEATH OF THE HEART, THE

Chattopadhya, Mohit
GENESIS, w

Chattopadhyay, Nikhil
CHOPPER, m

Chau, Dung
SOMETHING WILD

Chaudhari, Aneel
RAO SAHEB, w

Chaun, Li Show
SUPER CITIZEN, m

Chautemps, Jean-Louis
FRENCH LESSON

Chauvet, Sylvie
LE BONHEUR A ENCORE FRAPPE, w

Chavaras, Gary
MANHUNTER

Chavarri, Jaime
EL RIO DE ORO, d&w

Chaves, Julio
KING AND HIS MOVIE, A

Chawki, Khalil
AL ASHEKE

Chawki, Wassila
MAN OF ASHES

Chayes, Sunny
SMART ALEC, cos

Chazel, Marie-Anne
LA GITANE

Chbib, Bachar
EVIXION, ed; EVIXION, p&d; EVIXION, w

Chcheidze, Otar
YOUNG COMPOSER'S ODYSSEY, A, w

Chebodejeva-Chaptykova, S.
DESCENDANT OF THE SNOW LEOPARD, THE

Chechick, Jeremiah
HEAD OFFICE

Chedid, Andree
EL YOM EL SADES, d&w

Chehardy, Darlene
ODD JOBS

Chelkoff, Noemie
LUSSURI

Chelo
UN HOMBRE VIOLENTE

Chemakhi, Amira
SUMMER

Cheminal, Mic
MAN AND A WOMAN: 20 YEARS LATER, A, cos

Chemouni, Charly
SUIVEZ MON REGARD

Chemouny, Charlie
YIDDISH CONNECTION

Chemouny, Charly
CONSEIL DE FAMILLE

Chen, Joan
TAI-PAN

Chen, Steven
SLEEPWALK

Chen-Chin-chen
TIME TO LIVE AND A TIME TO DIE, A

Cheng, Chang
TAI-PAN

Cheng, Mark
PEKING OPERA BLUES

Cheng, Olivia
MILLIONAIRE'S EXPRESS, THE

Cheng, Sylvia
ACES GO PLACES IV

Cheng-Hui, Yu
MARTIAL ARTS OF SHAOLIN

Cheng-lee, Shu
SUMMER AT GRANDPA'S, A

Chentini, Hermin
DOEA TANDA MATA

Cheong, Wong Ying
MARTIAL ARTS OF SHAOLIN, p

Cherif, Kamel
LE MOME

Cherney, Scott
LOW BLOW

Cherques, Jorge
BRAS CUBAS

Cherrington, Te Paki
ARRIVING TUESDAY

Cherry, J.R.
DR. OTTO AND THE RIDDLE OF THE GLOOM BEAM

Cherry, John
DR. OTTO AND THE RIDDLE OF THE GLOOM BEAM,
d; DR. OTTO AND THE RIDDLE OF THE GLOOM
BEAM, m/l; DR. OTTO AND THE RIDDLE OF THE
GLOOM BEAM, w

Cherry, John R.
DR. OTTO AND THE RIDDLE OF THE GLOOM BEAM

Cherry, Josh
DR. OTTO AND THE RIDDLE OF THE GLOOM BEAM

Cherry, Kathy
DR. OTTO AND THE RIDDLE OF THE GLOOM BEAM,
cos

Cherry, Najean
TORMENT

Chervigny, Emilie
LOYALTIES

Chesnais, Patrick
FEMMES DE PERSONNE

Chesney, Chris
VAMP, spec eff

Chesney, Diana
GREAT MOUSE DETECTIVE, THE

Chesney, Peter
VAMP, spec eff

Chesney, Tom
VAMP, spec eff

Chester, Colby
SALVADOR

Chestnut, Arthur
COCAINE WARS, stunts

Chetwyn, Derrick
COMRADES, art d

Cheung, George
BIG TROUBLE IN LITTLE CHINA

Cheung, Leslie
BETTER TOMORROW, A

Cheung, Maggie
ROSE

Cheung, Pang Yau
MR. VAMPIRE, stunts

Cheung, William
ARMOUR OF GOD, THE, art d

Chevalier, Ana
INSOMNIACS

Chevalier, Joe
SAVING GRACE; SAVING GRACE, set d

Chevrier, Arnaud
ROUND MIDNIGHT

Chew, Cheli
NOBODY'S FOOL

Chew, Edna
PLAYING FOR KEEPS

Chew, Richard
STREETS OF GOLD, ed; WHERE THE RIVER RUNS
BLACK, ed

Chi, Chao Li
BIG TROUBLE IN LITTLE CHINA

Chi, Joe
ACES GO PLACES IV, stunts

Chi-kwang, Wang
SUMMER AT GRANDPA'S, A

Chia-pao, Chiang
TIME TO LIVE AND A TIME TO DIE, A

Chiang, David
SILENT LOVE, d

Chiang-Chiapao
TIME TO LIVE AND A TIME TO DIE, A

Chiara, Maria
HANNAH AND HER SISTERS

Chiara, Piero
UNA SPINA NEL CUORE, w

Chiaravalle, Franco
FOTOROMANZO, m; GIURO CHE TI AMO, m

Chiari, Walter
ROMANCE

Chichinadze, Ira
SAPIRHURIN

Chicot, Etienne
DESORDRE; KAMIKAZE; MORT UN DIMANCHE DE
PLUIE

Chiesa, Francesco
INNOCENZA, w

Chiesa, Guila
CLAN OF THE CAVE BEAR, THE

Chievari, Sara
CARNE CHE CRESCE

Chihara, Paul
AMERICAN JUSTICE, m; AMERICAN JUSTICE, m/l;
MORNING AFTER, THE, m

Chikamatsu, Monzaemon
YARI NO GONZA, w

Chikos, Marianne
NUTCRACKER: THE MOTION PICTURE

Chilcot, Doris
LOYALTIES

Childers, Eddie
DR. OTTO AND THE RIDDLE OF THE GLOOM BEAM

Children's Film Unit
SCHOOL FOR VANDALS, w

Childress, Alvin
Obituaries

Childs, Raymond S.
DR. OTTO AND THE RIDDLE OF THE GLOOM BEAM

Chiles, Lois
SWEET LIBERTY

Chilton, Chip
DR. OTTO AND THE RIDDLE OF THE GLOOM BEAM

Chilvers, Simon
BIG HURT, THE; SKY PIRATES; WINDRIDER

Chin, Ansel
LOW BLOW

Chin, Deborah
SOLDIER'S REVENGE

Chin, Kara
NUTCRACKER: THE MOTION PICTURE

Chin, Wilbert
LOW BLOW

Chin, Winnie
HAPPY DIN DON

Chin-ch'en, Wang
WO ERH HAN-SHENG, ed

China
REVENGE OF THE TEENAGE VIXENS FROM OUTER
SPACE, THE

China, Nova
HOLLYWOOD VICE SQUAD

Chinai, Alisha
TRIKAL

Chinas, Fanis
KNOCK-OUT

Chinchilla, Jose Luis
ELIMINATORS, stunts

Ching, Tin
HAPPY DIN DON

Ching, Wong
HAPPY DIN DON

Ching-song, Liao
SUMMER AT GRANDPA'S, A, ed

Ching-wen, Chou
TIME TO LIVE AND A TIME TO DIE, A, cos

Chino, Shuichi
NEW MORNING OF BILLY THE KID, THE, m

Chiodo Brothers
CRITTERS, spec eff

Chiodo, Michael
CARNAGE

Chipman, Olwyn
DANCING IN THE DARK

Chiriac, Florin
DECLARATIE DE DRAGOSTE

Chiripua, Silvestre
MISSION, THE

Chisnall, Kevin
ACES GO PLACES IV, spec eff

Chisom, Linda
SCREAMPLAY

Chitnis, Sheila
MY BEAUTIFUL LAUNDRETTE

Chiu, Francisco
GAVILAN O PALOMA, ed; MATANZA EN
MATAMOROS, ed

Chivulescu, Sorin
NOI, CEI DIN LINIA INTII, ph

Chizam, Marcia
ARMOUR OF GOD, THE

Cho, Margarita
MOSQUITO COAST, THE

Cho, Rafael
MOSQUITO COAST, THE

Cho, Sofia
MOSQUITO COAST, THE

Chojnacki, Julian
DANCING IN THE DARK, makeup

Choksi, Charu Bala
MY BEAUTIFUL LAUNDRETTE

Chokubajev, A.
DESCENDANT OF THE SNOW LEOPARD, THE

Chola and Yeni
MATANZA EN MATAMOROS, m

Chong, Jun
NINJA TURF

Chong, Kim Tai
NO RETREAT, NO SURRENDER

Chong, Rae Dawn
RUNNING OUT OF LUCK; SOUL MAN

Chong, Wes
THE KARATE KID PART II

Chong-ku, Lee
ER WOO DONG, m

Chopel, Farid
SUIVEZ MON REGARD

Chopin, Frederic
DERNIER CRI, m

Chorney, Jo-Ann
AMERICAN ANTHEM, set d

Choudhury, Jenhangir
MIRCH MASALA, ph

Chouikar, Moheidine
EL YOM EL SADES

Choukou, Med
MAN OF ASHES, spec eff

Chouraqui, Elie
LOVE SONGS, d; LOVE SONGS, p

Chow, Michael
SHANGHAI SURPRISE

Chow, Tony
ACES GO PLACES IV, ed

Chowdhury
CHOPPER

Choy, Eugene
DOWN AND OUT IN BEVERLY HILLS

Chrigui, Tijani
HADDA, art d; HADDA, ed; HADDA, w

Christen-Giguet, Christine
UNDER THE CHERRY MOON

Christenfeld, Karen
FROM BEYOND

Christensen, Birte
WOLF AT THE DOOR, THE, makeup

Christensen, Bo
YES, DET ER FAR!, p

Christensen, Julie
RAW TUNES, m

Christian, Linda
AMORE INQUIETO DI MARIA

Christian, Michael
WILD WIND, THE

Christian, Natt
KING KONG LIVES

Christian, Russell
52 PICK-UP, art d

Christiansen, Harvey
DIRT BIKE KID, THE

Christiansen, Jorn
X

Christianson, Elizabeth
NUTCRACKER: THE MOTION PICTURE

Christie, Julie
MISS MARY; POWER

Christie, Louise
SHORT CHANGED

Christina, Dana
INTRUDER, THE

Christine, Angela
MOUNTAINTOP MOTEL MASSACRE

Christlein, Dr. Friedrich Gunther
SUMMER

Christlein, Paulette
SUMMER

Christoffersen, Nina
TWIST & SHOUT

Christonsen, Per
NOE HEIT ANNET

Christophe
I LOVE YOU

Christopher, David
Obituaries

Christopher, Dennis
FLIGHT OF THE SPRUCE GOOSE; JAKE SPEED

Christopher, Jordan
THAT'S LIFE

Christopher, Marc
SHADOWS RUN BLACK

Christopher, Nanci
CHECK IS IN THE MAIL, THE

Christopher, Sharon
GIRLS SCHOOL SCREAMERS

Christopoulos, Thanassis
HARDBODIES 2

Chron, Professor
PAULETTE

Chua-Kaa-Joo
ABSOLUTE BEGINNERS

Chubb, Paul
BULLSEYE

Chubiniswili, Dato
SAPIRHURIN, w

Chuck Brown and the Soul Searchers
GOOD TO GO, m

Chuen, Koo
SUMMER AT GRANDPA'S, A

Chukri, Nadia
AWDAT MOWATIN, ed

Chun, Lee Lai
FAMILY, THE

Chun, Lisa
LOW BLOW

Chun, Tang Kee
ISLE OF FANTASY

Chun-Hua, Ji
MARTIAL ARTS OF SHAOLIN

Chung, Chang Koon
HUAJIE SHIDAI, w

Chung, Cherie
PEKING OPERA BLUES

Chung, Cheung Yiu
ARMOUR OF GOD, THE, ed; HAPPY DIN DON, ed; MR. VAMPIRE, ed

Chung, Claudie
PEKING OPERA BLUES, p&d

Chung, David
OUT OF BOUNDS

Chung, George
LOW BLOW, ch

Chung, Leslie
LAST SONG IN PARIS

Chung, Michael Hui Cherie
HAPPY DIN DON

Chung-li, Kao
TIME TO LIVE AND A TIME TO DIE, A

Chung-wen, Lin
TIME TO LIVE AND A TIME TO DIE, A; TIME TO LIVE AND A TIME TO DIE, A, prod d

Chung-yi, Tuan
WO ERH HAN-SHENG

Churchill, Dennis
KILLER PARTY, m/l

Chuvalo, George
FLY, THE

Chvatal, Cynthia
MANHUNTER

Chyi, Lin Chih
SUPER CITIZEN

Ciabatti, Enrica
IL GIARDINO DEGLI INGANNI

Cianchetti, Fabio
ROMANCE, ph

Cianciolo, Chris
MANHUNTER

Ciannelli, Lewis E.
WILD BEASTS, d&w

Ciannelli, Lewis Eduard
SENSI

Ciavarro, Massimo
GRANDI MAGAZZINI

Ciccarese, Luigi
L'APACHE BIANCO, ph; MEGLIO BACIARE UN COBRA, ph; SCALPS, ph; UNA TENERA FOLLIA, ph

Cicero, Antonio
CINEMA FALADO; COM LICENCA, EU VOU A LUTA, m/l

Cicutto, Roberto
LA BALLATA DI EVA, p

Cid, Mario
EL MERCADO DE HUMILDES; EL NARCO—DUELO ROJO

Cielova, Hana
SIESTA VETA, w

Cilliers, Dianna
JAKE SPEED, cos

Cinco, Manuel "Fyke"
REVENGE FOR JUSTICE, d

Cini, Frank
YOUNGBLOOD

Cinieri, Francesco
DETECTIVE SCHOOL DROPOUTS

Cinini, Claudio
CUT AND RUN, art d

Cino, Beppe
LA CASA DEL BUON RITORNO, d&w

Cino, Eloisa
LA CASA DEL BUON RITORNO

Cinque, Luigi
LA SECONDA NOTTE, m

Cintra, Luis Miguel
MON CAS; O MEU CASO—REPETICOES

Ciotola, Gino
SEPARATI IN CASA

Ciotta, Stephen
LONGSHOT, THE

Cipot, Eddie
SEVEN MINUTES IN HEAVEN

Cipriani, Sergio
SQUADRA SELVAGGIA, m

Cipriani, Stelvio
ANGKOR-CAMBODIA EXPRESS, m; RAGE, m

Cirani, Flaminia
BLACK TUNNEL

Circe
STAMMHEIM

Cirillo, Claudio
IL MOSTRO DI FIRENZE, ph

Cirino, Chuck
CHOPPING MALL, m

Cisneros, Michael
DR. OTTO AND THE RIDDLE OF THE GLOOM BEAM

Cisneros, Roman
AMERICAN JUSTICE

Citti, Christine
PEKIN CENTRAL

Civera, Pedro
ME HACE FALTA UN BIGOTE

Civil, Fernando
EN PENUMBRA, m

Civilotti, Massimo
GRANDI MAGAZZINI

Civit, Jose Maria
LOLA, ph

Claire, Hermine
INSPECTEUR LAVARDIN

Claire, Jan
AMERICAN ANTHEM

Claitman, Gay
HEAD OFFICE

Clanelli, Lewis
HANDS OF STEEL, w

Clanton, Raymond W.
BEST OF TIMES, THE

Clapp, Howard
BIG TROUBLE

Clare, Imogen
ABSOLUTE BEGINNERS

Clare, Raymond
MOSQUITO COAST, THE

Clarens, Chris
VENDETTA, art d

Clarfield, Stuart
WELCOME TO THE PARADE, d&w; WELCOME TO THE PARADE, ed

Clark, Andrew B.
PLATOON

Clark, Brett
KING OF THE STREETS; LAST RESORT, THE

Clark, Bryan
SWEET LIBERTY

Clark, Candy
AT CLOSE RANGE

Clark, Capt. Melvin
MANHUNTER

Clark, Carey
SNO-LINE

Clark, Carol Higgins
WHERE ARE THE CHILDREN?

Clark, Clive
ABSOLUTE BEGINNERS

Clark, Curtis
EXTREMITIES, ph

Clark, Ian D.
BOY IN BLUE, THE

Clark, James
TOUGH GUYS

Clark, Janet
ODD JOBS

Clark, Jim
FRENCH LESSON, ed; MISSION, THE, ed

Clark, Kathie
TERRORVISION, cos

Clark, Kippy
NUTCRACKER: THE MOTION PICTURE

Clark, Mary Higgins
WHERE ARE THE CHILDREN?, w

Clark, Michael
COMRADES

Clark, Mike
ROCKIN' ROAD TRIP

Clark, Nancie
MURPHY'S LAW

Clark, Peter Kamealoha
SCORPION

Clark, Roy
UPHILL ALL THE WAY

Clark, Royce
DR. OTTO AND THE RIDDLE OF THE GLOOM BEAM

Clark, Rudy
LEGAL EAGLES, m/l

Clark, Russell
VAMP, ch

Clark, Toby
LABYRINTH

Clark-Hall, Steve
BLOOD RED ROSES, p

Clarke, Angela
LETTER TO BREZHNEV

Clarke, Frank
LETTER TO BREZHNEV; LETTER TO BREZHNEV, w

Clarke, Jamie
RAD

Clarke, Joe
NOBODY'S FOOL

Clarke, John
FOOTROT FLATS

Clarke, Margi
LETTER TO BREZHNEV

Clarke, Michael
MODERN GIRLS

Clarke, Vanessa
CAR TROUBLE, cos

Clarke, Zelah
LADY JANE

Clarson, Lisa
VENDETTA

Clasby, Bob
TOUCH AND GO

Clash, Kevin
LABYRINTH

Clason, Anders
BRODERNA MOZART

Clason, Charlotte
WOLF AT THE DOOR, THE, cos

Claudon, Paul
LE COMPLEXE DU KANGOUROU, p

Claus, Richard
PARADIES, p

Clausen, Erik
MANDEN I MAANEN, d&w

Clavel, Aurora
MOSQUITO COAST, THE

Clavell, James
TAI-PAN, w

Claver, Enriqueta
TIEMPO DE SILENCIO

Claver, Queta
VIAJE A NINGUNA PARTE

Clavier, Christian
LE MOME, w; TWIST AGAIN A MOSCOU; TWIST
AGAIN A MOSCOU, w

Clavijo, Uva
AMIGOS

Clay, Andrew "Dice"
PRETTY IN PINK

Clayburgh, Jill
WHERE ARE THE CHILDREN?

Clayton, Jill
FOR LOVE ALONE

Clayton, Kim
MOVIE HOUSE MASSACRE

Clayton, Miles
SUNSET STRIP

Clayton, R.G.
LUCAS

Clayton-Jones, Edward
DOGS IN SPACE

Cleary, Brigid
FLIGHT OF THE NAVIGATOR

Cleary, John F.
CHILDREN OF A LESSER GOD

Clee, Sara
SHOOT FOR THE SUN

Cleese, John
CLOCKWISE

Cleitman, Rene
MENAGE, p

Clelano, Allan
TOUCH AND GO

Clemenson, Christian
HANNAH AND HER SISTERS; HEARTBURN; LEGAL
EAGLES

Clement, Aurore
EL SUIZO—UN AMOUR EN ESPAGNE

Clement, Marc
KING KONG LIVES

Clemente, Jacques
CORPS ET BIENS, makeup

Clementelli, Anna Maria
L'INCHIESTA, p

Clementelli, Silvio
L'INCHIESTA, p

Clements, Carol
CHOPPING MALL, art d; VAMP, art d

Clements, Donna
ONE CRAZY SUMMER

Clements, Ron
GREAT MOUSE DETECTIVE, THE, d; GREAT MOUSE
DETECTIVE, THE, w

Clemons, Lorenzo
RAW DEAL

Clendinning, David
FRINGE DWELLERS, THE

Clennon, David
LEGAL EAGLES

Clerici, Gianfranco
COBRA MISSION, w; DESIDERANDO GIULIA, w;
MIAMI GOLEM, w; MONSTER SHARK, w; SENSI, w

Clermont, Nicolas
TOBY MCTEAGUE, p

Clery, Corinne
IL MIELE DEL DIAVOLO; YUPPIES, I GIOVANI DI
SUCCESSO

Cleveland, Carol
HALF MOON STREET

Cleveland, Patience
PSYCHO III

Cleven, Harry
KAMIKAZE

Cliff, Jimmy
CLUB PARADISE; CLUB PARADISE, m/l

Clifford, Michael
CLAN OF THE CAVE BEAR, THE, spec eff

Clifton, Keith
ODD JOBS

Clifton, Patti
ODD JOBS

Climo, Brett
DEAD-END DRIVE-IN

Cline, Georgia Ann
CHILDREN OF A LESSER GOD

Clinton, George
HOWARD THE DUCK, m/l

Clinton, George S.
AVENGING FORCE, m

Clipsham, Laura
LADY JANE

Clive, Teagan
ARMED AND DANGEROUS; JUMPIN' JACK FLASH

Cliver, Al
LUSSURI

Cloes, Peter
NAME OF THE ROSE, THE

Close, Del
FERRIS BUELLER'S DAY OFF; ONE MORE
SATURDAY NIGHT

Cloth, Sherry
SEX O'CLOCK NEWS, THE, w

Cloth, Sherwyn
SEX O'CLOCK NEWS, THE

Clothier, Lindsay
NUTCRACKER: THE MOTION PICTURE

Clotworthy, Robert
CHECK IS IN THE MAIL, THE

Cloud, Lisa
RATBOY

Cloudia
JO JO DANCER, YOUR LIFE IS CALLING, set d;
RATBOY, set d

Clough, Ina
NO SURRENDER

Clough, John Scott
3:15, THE MOMENT OF TRUTH

Cluff, Jennifer
BACKLASH

Clune, Liliane
TOBY MCTEAGUE

Clutesi, George
TOBY MCTEAGUE

Cluzet, Francois
ETATS D'AME; ROUND MIDNIGHT; RUE DU DEPART

Cmiral, Ilja
PA LIV OCH DOD, m

Coan, Sarah
NUTCRACKER: THE MOTION PICTURE

Coates, Anne V.
LADY JANE, ed; RAW DEAL, ed

Coates, Eric
ABSOLUTE BEGINNERS, m/l

Coates, John
WHEN THE WIND BLOWS, p

Coates, Kim
BOY IN BLUE, THE

Coates, Lewis
MONSTER SHARK, w

Cobb, Randall "Tex"
GOLDEN CHILD, THE

Cobbs, Bill
COLOR OF MONEY, THE; STREETS OF GOLD

Cobbs, Renata
SHE'S GOTTA HAVE IT

Coblenz, Walter
SPACECAMP, p

Coblifin, Dan
TOUCH AND GO

Cobo, Eva
MATADOR

Cobo, Roberto
TERROR Y ENCAJES NEGROS

Cobos, Jesus Lopez
EL AMOR BRUJO, md

Coburn, Arthur
EXTREMITIES, ed

Coburn, David
BORN AMERICAN

Coburn, James
DEATH OF A SOLDIER

Coburn, Mickey
BEGINNER'S LUCK

Coca, Richard
SUNSET STRIP

Cochran, David
LOW BLOW

Cochrell, Liza
SUNSET STRIP

Codareco, Daniela
DREPTATE IN LANTURI, cos

Codemann, Werner
DAS HAUS AM FLUSS

Codman, Paul
NO SURRENDER

Codner, Ron
SUNSET STRIP, m

Codrescu, Constantin
UN OASPETE LA CINA

Codron, Michael
CLOCKWISE, p

Cody, Deborah
SOLDIER'S REVENGE

Cody, Ellen
AMIGOS

Coe, George
HEAD OFFICE

Coe, Ronald O.
LAST RESORT, THE, spec eff

Coelho, Ariel
AS SETE VAMPIRAS; BRAS CUBAS; WHERE THE
RIVER RUNS BLACK

Coello, Gigi
SCORPION, ed

Coertzen, Kernels
PLACE OF WEEPING

Coesens, Anne
LA PURITAINE

Coffee, T. Scott
FERRIS BUELLER'S DAY OFF

Coffey, Anne S.
BEGINNER'S LUCK, ph

Coffey, T. Scott
SPACECAMP

Coffin, Frederick
FINE MESS, A; JO JO DANCER, YOUR LIFE IS
CALLING

Coffin, Sylvie
INSTANT JUSTICE

Coffin, Winnie
Obituaries

Coffing, Barry
8 MILLION WAYS TO DIE, m/l

Cofield, Carl
BAND OF THE HAND

Cogburn, Tammy
OVER THE SUMMER

Coggio, Roger
RUE DU DEPART

Coghill, Nikki
DARK AGE; PLAYING BEATIE BOW

Cohan, Theo
CLASS OF NUKE 'EM HIGH

Cohen, Adam
DOWN BY LAW

Cohen, Avi
HAKRAV AL HAVA'AD, d

Cohen, Barney
KILLER PARTY, w

Cohen, Bruce
BAND OF THE HAND, m/l

Cohen, Catherine
LA FEMME DE MA VIE, w

Cohen, Claude
TOUCH AND GO

Cohen, David
ESTHER; HOLLYWOOD ZAP!, d&w

Cohen, Denise
PEAU D'ANGE, art d

Cohen, Eli
SHTAY ETZBA'OT M'TZIDON, d; SHTAY ETZBA'OT
M'TZIDON, w

Cohen, Emma
MAMBRU SE FUE A LA GUERRA; VIAJE A NINGUNA
PARTE

Cohen, Howard
NINJA TURF

Cohen, Jeffrey Jay
FIRE WITH FIRE

Cohen, Lawrence
SCORPION

Cohen, Mark
SILK

Cohen, Marty
WEEKEND WARRIORS

Cohen, Sarah
ESTHER, m

Cohn, Mindy
BOY WHO COULD FLY, THE

Cokhale, Mohan
MIRCH MASALA

Cokliss, Harley
BLACK MOON RISING, d

Colbert, Jerry
ROCKIN' ROAD TRIP, art d

Colbert, Robert
SCORPION

Colbin, Marie
DIE WALSCHE; SPRING SYMPHONY

Colceri, Tim
NEVER TOO YOUNG TO DIE

Cole
AS SETE VAMPIRAS; BRAS CUBAS

Cole, Frank
CLASS OF NUKE 'EM HIGH

Cole, Gary
LUCAS

Cole, Gregory Uel
OFF BEAT

Cole, Harold J.
ABDUCTED, p

Cole, Jerry
NO RETREAT, NO SURRENDER

Cole, Jojo
DEATH OF THE HEART, THE

Cole, Kathy
OVER THE SUMMER

Cole, Ritta
OVER THE SUMMER

Cole, Stan
JUDGEMENT IN STONE, A, ed

Cole, Tom
STREETS OF GOLD, w

Coleby, Robert
GREAT EXPECTATIONS—THE AUSTRALIAN STORY

Colee, Cam
SCORPION

Coleman, Bryan
MONA LISA

Coleman, Cy
POWER, m

Coleman, Lisa
FIRE WITH FIRE, m/l

Coleman, Patrick
JUDGEMENT IN STONE, A, m

Coles, Barbara
ALIENS

Coles, Emma
TWO FRIENDS

Coles, John
EYE OF THE TIGER, spec eff

Coles, Martii
DOGS IN SPACE

Coles, Mary Ann
POLICE ACADEMY 3: BACK IN TRAINING

Coletti, Carlo
LA CROCE DALLE 7 PIETRE, ph

Coletti, Efisio
SAPORE DEL GRANO

Coley, Aisha
OFF BEAT

Colgan, Valerie
ALIENS

Colick, Lewis
DIRT BIKE KID, THE, w

Colin, Fernando
EL DIA DE LOS ALBANILES II, ph

Colin, Margaret
PRETTY IN PINK; SOMETHING WILD

Colin, Suzanne
PERVOLA: TRACKS IN THE SNOW

Coll, Ewin Mac
BEST OF TIMES, THE, m/l

Coll, Jose Luis
EL HERMANO BASTARDO DE DIOS; EL HERMANO
BASTARDO DE DIOS, w

Collas, Manuel
FRENCH LESSON

Collet, Christopher
MANHATTAN PROJECT, THE

Colli, Enrico
GIOVANNI SENZAPENSIERI, art d

Colli, Marco
GIOVANNI SENZAPENSIERI, d; GIOVANNI
SENZAPENSIERI, w

Colli, Tonino Delli
GINGER & FRED, ph; NAME OF THE ROSE, THE, ph

Collier, Christina
MR. LOVE

Collier, Drake
TOUCH AND GO

Collier, James F.
CRY FROM THE MOUNTAIN, d

Collier, Jensen
SAY YES

Collier, Ruth
SCREAMTIME, cos

Colligan, Sheila
LIGHTNING—THE WHITE STALLION

Collingwood, Lyn
DEAD-END DRIVE-IN

Collins, Alan
JUNGLE RAIDERS

Collins, Boon
ABDUCTED, d; ABDUCTED, w; ABDUCTED, w

Collins, Chet
JUST BETWEEN FRIENDS

Collins, Dan
THRONE OF FIRE, THE

Collins, Dana
ECHO PARK

Collins, George
BLUE CITY

Collins, Kim
DR. OTTO AND THE RIDDLE OF THE GLOOM BEAM;
VENDETTA

Collins, Olivia
TERROR Y ENCAJES NEGROS

Collins, Patrick
DIRT BIKE KID, THE

Collins, Rick
CLASS OF NUKE 'EM HIGH

Collins, Roberta
HARDBODIES 2; VENDETTA

Collins, Stephen
CHOKE CANYON; JUMPIN' JACK FLASH

Collins, Tommy
UPHILL ALL THE WAY

Collins, Wilkie
FRINGE DWELLERS, THE

Collins, Yukio G.
BIG TROUBLE; BIG TROUBLE IN LITTLE CHINA

Collinson, Jonathan
KIND OF ENGLISH, A, ph

Collis, Jack T.
CROSSROADS, prod d; STAR TREK IV: THE VOYAGE
HOME, prod d

Collison, Frank
WIRED TO KILL

Collister, Peter
EYE OF THE TIGER, ph; KGB—THE SECRET WAR, ph

Collister, Peter Lyons
GETTING EVEN, ph

Collomb, Emmanuelle
CONSEIL DE FAMILLE

Collomb, Florence
CONSEIL DE FAMILLE

Colls, Johnny
FIRE WITH FIRE, m/l

Colman, Ken
BAND OF THE HAND

Coloma, Milvia
UNA TENERA FOLLIA

Colombier, Michel
GOLDEN CHILD, THE, m; MONEY PIT, THE, m;
MONEY PIT, THE, m/l; MONEY PIT, THE, md;
RUTHLESS PEOPLE, m

Colombo, Francesca
YUPPIES, I GIOVANI DI SUCCESSO

Colombo, Julia Hiebaum
ROMANCE

Colombo, Paolo
TRE SUPERMEN A SANTO DOMINGO, m

Colomby, Harry
TOUCH AND GO, w

Colomer, Imma
CAGED GLASS

Colomo, Fernando
EL CABALLERO DEL DRAGON, p&d; EL CABALLERO
DEL DRAGON, w

Colosimo, Rosa
STILL POINT, THE, p; STILL POINT, THE, w

Colow, Josh
RIVERBED, THE, m

Colpin, Paul Yvon
FRENCH LESSON

Colquitt, Ken
MANHUNTER

Colt, Samuel [Samuel Barrymore Colt]
Obituaries

Colton, Chevi
LEGAL EAGLES

Colton, Jacque Lynn
QUICKSILVER; SAY YES; UPHILL ALL THE WAY

Coltrane, Robbie
ABSOLUTE BEGINNERS; CARAVAGGIO; MONA LISA

Coluche [Michel Colucci]
Obituaries

Colver, Clint
VAMP, anim

Colvig, Vance
MY CHAUFFEUR; ODD JOBS

Colwell, Chuck
THRASHIN', ph

Comanici, Sebastian
DREPTATE IN LANTURI

Comar, Richard
HEAD OFFICE

Comarlot, Joel
SUMMER

Comart, Jean-Paul
JE HAIS LES ACTEURS; PARIS MINUIT

Combes, Sylviane
LAST IMAGE, THE, cos

Combs, Jeffrey
FROM BEYOND

Comelas, Josine
PIRATES

Comellas, Josiane
SINCERELY CHARLOTTE

Comencini, Cristina
LA STORIA

Comencini, Luigi
LA STORIA, d; LA STORIA, w

Comencini, Paola
LA STORIA, art d

Cometa, Edizioni Musicali
CASTIGHI, m

Comets, Jacques
LA FEMME SECRETE, ed

Comi, Paul
HOWARD THE DUCK

Comisky, Chuck
STAR CRYSTAL, spec eff

Comka, Marcos
RUNNING OUT OF LUCK

Como, Rossella
Obituaries

Company, R. Beezts
ODD JOBS, spec eff

Compo, Lyle
LOW BLOW

Compton, Athol
SHORT CHANGED

Comtois, Guy
CLAN OF THE CAVE BEAR, THE, art d

Comyn, Charles
PLACE OF WEEPING

Conabere, Syd
BIG HURT, THE

Conaway, Jeff
PATRIOT, THE

Conaway-Parsloe, Linda
9½ WEEKS, art d

Concalves, Milton
REI DO RIO

Concari, Attilio
45MO PARALLELO, d; 45MO PARALLELO, w

Conchon, Georges
MON BEAU-FRERE A TUE MA SOEUR, w

Conde, Fernando
MONSTER DOG

Condeleo, Renato
ELOGIO DELLA PAZZIA

Conder, Robert
CHOKE CANYON

Condoluci, Rene
ROMANCE, ed

Condor, Chantal
CRAZY MOON

Condos, Melodye
SIZZLE BEACH, U.S.A., m

Confalone, Marina
SEMBRA MORTO . . . MA E SOLO SVENUTO;
SEPARATI IN CASA

Confortes, Claude
BETTY BLUE; PAULETTE, d&w

Congie, Terry
SHADOWS RUN BLACK; SIZZLE BEACH, U.S.A.

Coninx, Stijn
SPRINGEN, w

Conlan, Patrick
SCREAMPLAY

Conley, Darlene
TOUGH GUYS

Conley, Joe
IMPURE THOUGHTS

Conn, Jule
SALVADOR

Connell, Gerry
JUMPIN' JACK FLASH

Connell, Polly [Polly Mallitz Connell]
Obituaries

Connelly, Chris
FOXTRAP

Connelly, Christopher
COBRA MISSION; JUNGLE RAIDERS; LE MINIERE
DEL KILIMANGIARO; MANHATTAN BABY

Connelly, Jennifer
LABYRINTH; SEVEN MINUTES IN HEAVEN

Conner, Bart
RAD

Connery, Jason
LA VENEXIANA

Connery, Sean
HIGHLANDER; NAME OF THE ROSE, THE

Connolly, Jerry
BEER, m/l

Connor, Jim
SCREAMPLAY

Connor, Paul
NO SURRENDER

Connors, Chuck
BALBOA

Conrad, Janene
OVER THE SUMMER

Conrad, Jess
ABSOLUTE BEGINNERS

Conrad, Scott
WRAITH, THE, ed

Conrad, Sid
WISDOM

Conrad, William
KILLING CARS

Conradsen, Hannelore
WOHIN MIT WILLFRIED?, w

Constantin, Mihai
LICEENI

Constantine, Eddie
MACARONI BLUES

Constantine, Michael
PRAY FOR DEATH

Constantinescu, Mihai
UN OASPETE LA CINA, d

Constantinescu, Mircea
PASO DOBLE

Conte, D. Constantine
NO MERCY, p

Conte, Robert
ODD JOBS, w

Conti, Bill
BEER, m; BOSS' WIFE, THE, m; F/X, m; THE KARATE
KID PART II, m; THE KARATE KID PART II, m/l

Conti, Carlos
BETTY BLUE, art d

Conti, Daniela
IL BI E IL BA, w

Conti, Tom
GOSPEL ACCORDING TO VIC, THE; SAVING GRACE

Contreras, Luis
BIG TROUBLE; BLUE CITY

Contreras, Patricio
GERONIMA

Contreras, Roberto
BLUE CITY

Converse-Roberts, William
ON VALENTINE'S DAY

Conversi, Cleofe
LA BALLATA DI EVA, ed

Convertino, Michael
CHILDREN OF A LESSER GOD, m; HOLLYWOOD
VICE SQUAD, m

Conville, David
CLOCKWISE

Convy, Bert
WEEKEND WARRIORS, d

Conway, Jack
SCREEN TEST

Conway, Kelly
LONGSHOT, THE

Conway, Peter
TOMB, THE

Conway, Tim
LONGSHOT, THE; LONGSHOT, THE, m/l;
LONGSHOT, THE, w

Conwell, Beth
SNO-LINE, ed; VASECTOMY: A DELICATE MATTER,
ed

Cooder, Ry
BLUE CITY, m&m/l; CROSSROADS, m

Cooeyate, Doug
MALA NOCHE

Cook, Bonnie
KING KONG LIVES

Cook, Cathy
SID AND NANCY, art d, cos

Cook, Charlie
LOW BLOW

Cook, Dick
Obituaries

Cook, Edwin
EXTREMITIES, w

Cook, Graham Fletcher
SID AND NANCY

Cook, Roderick
9½ WEEKS

Cook, Sherry
KILLER PARTY

Cook, Steve
SILK

Cook, Steven
SOLDIER'S REVENGE

Cooke, Jennifer
FRIDAY THE 13TH PART VI: JASON LIVES

Cooke, Jim
ONE CRAZY SUMMER

Cooke, Malcolm
KING KONG LIVES, ed

Cooke, W.S.
DR. OTTO AND THE RIDDLE OF THE GLOOM BEAM

Cool J., L.L.
WILDCATS

Coolen, Kees
ASSAULT, THE

Cooley, Tamara
DESERT BLOOM

Coombes, Norman
PLACE OF WEEPING

Coonan, Sheila
PLAYING FOR KEEPS

Cooner, William
CARNAGE

Cooney, Jim
COMBAT SHOCK

Cooney, Robert
SLEEPWALK, art d

Cooper, Adrian
SONHO SEM FIM, prod d

Cooper, Alice
MONSTER DOG; MONSTER DOG, m/l

Cooper, Dee
ECHO PARK

Cooper, Garry
CARAVAGGIO; MY BEAUTIFUL LAUNDRETTE

Cooper, Glen
AMERICAN ANTHEM

Cooper, James M.
SHADOWS RUN BLACK

Cooper, John
SCHLEUSE 17; UNDER THE CHERRY MOON

Cooper, Lady Diana [Diana Olivia Winifred Maud
Manners]
Obituaries

Cooper, Louis R.
PSYCHO III, spec eff

Cooper, Marilyn
BRIGHTON BEACH MEMOIRS

Cooper, Merian C.
KING KONG LIVES, w

Cooper, Ray
SHOOT FOR THE SUN, m

Cooper, Steve
DUET FOR ONE, art d

Coote, Lissa
AROUND THE WORLD IN EIGHTY WAYS, prod d

Cope, Matt
PULSEBEAT, ed

Copeland, David
ARRIVING TUESDAY, w

Copeland, Stewart
OUT OF BOUNDS, m

Copeman, Michael
FLY, THE

Copleston, Geoffrey
SQUADRA SELVAGGIA

Copley, Alejandro
EL RIGOR DEL DESTINO

Copola, Claude
UNDER THE CHERRY MOON

Coppala, Scott
KILLER PARTY

Coppola, Andrew Louis
HANDS OF STEEL; WHITE SLAVE

Coppola, Francis
PEGGY SUE GOT MARRIED, d

Coppola, Gian Carlo
Obituaries

Coppola, Sofia
PEGGY SUE GOT MARRIED

Coquillon, John
CLOCKWISE, ph; HYPER SAPIEN: PEOPLE FROM
ANOTHER STAR, ph

Coranci, John
YOUNGBLOOD

Corazzari, Bruno
IL CASO MORO; LA VITA DI SCORTA

Corba, Milan
SIESTA VETA, cos

Corbi
DOEA TANDA MATA

Corbin, Barry
NOTHING IN COMMON; WHAT COMES AROUND

Corciova, Radu
NOI, CEI DIN LINIA INTII, art d

Corcoran, John
PLAYING FOR KEEPS

Corcos, Leon
WISDOM

Cordeiro, George
SCREAMPLAY; SCREAMPLAY, m

Cordell, Melinda
BLOODY BIRTHDAY

Cordero, Laurencio
POWER, spec eff

Cordero, Ralph
COMBAT SHOCK, makeup

Cordes, Jim
F/X

Cordic, Rege
TRANSFORMERS: THE MOVIE, THE

Corduner, Allan
VALHALLA

Cordwell, Harry
LADY JANE, set d

Corenblith, Michael
HOLLYWOOD VICE SQUAD, prod d

Corevi, Massimo
LA SECONDA NOTTE, art d

Corey, Phil
8 MILLION WAYS TO DIE, spec eff

Corey, Prof. Irwin
PERILS OF P.K., THE

Corfixen, Lizzie
ET SKUD FRA HJERTET

Corjos, Nicolae
DECLARATIE DE DRAGOSTE, d; LICEENI, d

Corman, Julie
CHOPPING MALL, p; DIRT BIKE KID, THE, p; LAST
RESORT, THE, p

Corman, Maddie
SEVEN MINUTES IN HEAVEN

Corman, Roger
COCAINE WARS, p

Cormio, Claudio
INNOCENZA, ed

Corneau, Alain
LE MOME, d; LE MOME, w

Cornell, John
"CROCODILE" DUNDEE, p; "CROCODILE" DUNDEE,
w

Cornfeld, Stuart
FLY, THE, p

Corona, Edgar Sosa
THANATOS, m

Corona, Nestor
LOS HIJOS DE LA GUERRA FRIA

Corone, Antonio
BAND OF THE HAND

Corr, Chris
DESERT BLOOM

Corr, Eugene
DESERT BLOOM, d&w; DESERT BLOOM, d&w

Corradi, Pio
DER PENDLER, ph

Corrado, Gus
WISDOM

Corrao, Angelo
OFF BEAT, ed

Correa, Raul Emilio
EL TREN DE LOS PIONEROS

Correa, Rubens W.
MAN FACING SOUTHEAST

Correard, Evelyne
ON A VOLE CHARLIE SPENCER!, cos

Corri, Nick
WILDCATS

Corridori, Giovanni
THUNDER WARRIOR, spec eff

Corrieri, Sergio
COME LA VIDA MISMA

Corriveau, Andre
HENRI, ed; INTIMATE POWER, ed

Corsini, Matteo
LE MINIERE DEL KILIMANGIARO

Corso, John W.
FERRIS BUELLER'S DAY OFF, prod d; PRETTY IN
PINK, prod d

Corson, Chester
ROCKIN' ROAD TRIP

Corson, Sadie
ROCKIN' ROAD TRIP

Cort, Bud
INVADERS FROM MARS

Cortazar, Ernesto
EL BRONCO, m; EL DIA DE LOS ALBANILES II, m;
EL VECINDARIO—LOS MEXICANOS CALIENTES, m;
UN HOMBRE VIOLENTE, m

Corti, Antonio C.
FEAR, w; TRE SUPERMEN A SANTO DOMINGO, w

Corti, Axel
WELCOME IN VIENNA, d; WELCOME IN VIENNA, w

Corti, Pia Ana
THANATOS, p

Cortijo, Basilio
EL AMOR BRUJO, spec eff

Cory, Christopher
BEST OF TIMES, THE

Cory, Phil
WRAITH, THE, spec eff

Coscas, Brigitte
LA PURITAINE

Coscia, Marcello
MOMO, w

Cosentino, Sergio
IL BI E IL BA

Cosgriff, William
PLAYING FOR KEEPS

Cosimano, Peter C.
GIRLS SCHOOL SCREAMERS

Cosma, Vladimir
ASTERIX CHEZ LES BRETONS, m/l; LA GALETTE DU
ROI, m; LES FUGITIFS, m; MORT UN DIMANCHE DE
PLUIE, m; MORT UN DIMANCHE DE PLUIE, m/l

Cosmatos, George P.
COBRA, d

Cosmo, James
HIGHLANDER

Cosse, Villanueva
KING AND HIS MOVIE, A

Cossi, Adele
L'ULTIMA MAZURKA

Cosson, Corinne
L'AMANT MAGNIFIQUE

Cosson, Gregory
L'AMANT MAGNIFIQUE

Costa e Silva, Manue
REPORTER X, ph

Costa, Diane
NOBODY'S FOOL

Costa, Francesco
LA CASA DEL BUON RITORNO

Costa, Marina
FINAL EXECUTIONER, THE; JUNGLE RAIDERS

Costa, Sara
STRIPPER

Costa-Gavras, Constantin
CONSEIL DE FAMILLE, d&w

Costantini, Fabrizio
GIOVANNI SENZAPENSIERI

Costantini, Romeo
UNA NOTTE DI PIOGGIA, d&w

Costanzo, Alessandra
IL BI E IL BA

Costanzo, Robert
BOSS' WIFE, THE; LIGHTSHIP, THE

Costea, Traian
NOI, CEI DIN LINIA INTII

Costello, Don
CLASS OF NUKE 'EM HIGH

Costello, Elvis
NO SURRENDER

Costello, George
HAMBURGER, prod d; NIGHT OF THE CREEPS, prod d

Costello, Joseph
LAND OF DOOM

Costello, Ward
BLOODY BIRTHDAY

Coster, Jeremy
SCHOOL FOR VANDALS

Costigan, Ken
HANNAH AND HER SISTERS

Costiniu, Geo
UN OASPETE LA CINA

Costner, Kevin
SHADOWS RUN BLACK; SIZZLE BEACH, U.S.A.

Cote, Louise
QUI A TIRE SUR NOS HISTOIRES D'AMOUR?, ed

Cotner, Carl
Obituaries

Cotney, Robert
QUICKSILVER

Cottencon, Fanny
FEMMES DE PERSONNE; GOLDEN EIGHTIES

Cotterill, Helen
MR. LOVE

Cotti, Carlo
SPOSERO SIMON LE BON, d

Cottone, John
DEATH OF A SOLDIER

Couch, Bill
RUNNING SCARED, stunts; STEWARDESS SCHOOL,
stunts; TOUCH AND GO, stunts

Coudari, Camille
LA GUEPE, w

Couet, Patrick
FAUBOURG SAINT-MARTIN

Coufos, Paul
BUSTED UP; CHOPPING MALL

Coughlin, Cari
DESERT BLOOM, ed

Coulais, Bruno
LA FEMME SECRETE, m; PARENTAL CLAIM, m; QUI
TROP EMBRASSE, m

Coulson, Bernie
BULLIES

Coulson, Gordon
KNIGHTS AND EMERALDS

Coulter, Elberta
ROCKIN' ROAD TRIP

Coulter, Michael
GOOD FATHER, THE, ph; GOSPEL ACCORDING TO
VIC, THE, ph

Coulter, Mick
NO SURRENDER, ph

Coulter, Terri
AT CLOSE RANGE

Council, Richard
MANHATTAN PROJECT, THE

Courbois, Kitty
OP HOOP VAN ZEGEN

Court, Alyson
CARE BEARS MOVIE II: A NEW GENERATION

Court, Ken
ALIENS, art d

Courtalon, Esteban
KING AND HIS MOVIE, A, ph

Courtenay, Margaret
DUET FOR ONE

Courtot, Marguerite
Obituaries

Courvoisier, Sibylle
MOTTEN IM LICHT

Cousson, Jean-Francois
BETTY BLUE, spec eff

Coutard, Raoul
MAX MON AMOUR, ph

Coutinho, Jorge
QUILOMBO; RUNNING OUT OF LUCK

Couto-Palos, Maria
SUMMER

Couture, Charlelie
SUIVEZ MON REGARD; SUIVEZ MON REGARD, m;
TAXI BOY, m

Covarrubias, Robert
AMERICAN JUSTICE

Covielleo, Franco
NAME OF THE ROSE, THE

Covington, Stephanie
SHE'S GOTTA HAVE IT

Covner, Henry
STREETS OF GOLD

Covner, Lillian
STREETS OF GOLD

Cowan, Grant
POLICE ACADEMY 3: BACK IN TRAINING

Cowan, Larry C.
GOBOTS: BATTLE OF THE ROCKLORDS, ed

Cowan, Marge
PERILS OF P.K., THE, p

Cowan, Phyllis
STEWARDESS SCHOOL

Cowan, Tom
EMMA'S WAR, ph

Cowl, Darry
SUIVEZ MON REGARD

Cowles, Matthew
MONEY PIT, THE; MONEY PIT, THE

Cowling, Bruce
Obituaries

Cox, Alex
SID AND NANCY, d; SID AND NANCY, w

Cox, Arthur
CASTAWAY

Cox, Betsy
QUICKSILVER, cos

Cox, Brian
MANHUNTER; SHOOT FOR THE SUN

Cox, David
LOW BLOW, set d

Cox, Doug
FINE MESS, A

Cox, E'lon
JO JO DANCER, YOUR LIFE IS CALLING

Cox, Edin
DANGEROUS ORPHANS

Cox, Elizabeth
NIGHT OF THE CREEPS; WRAITH, THE

Cox, Henry
OCEAN DRIVE WEEKEND

Cox, Joel
HEARTBREAK RIDGE, ed; RATBOY, ed

Cox, Kyra
CACTUS

Cox, Larry
HARDBODIES 2, m/l

Cox, Pat
FOOTROT FLATS, p

Cox, Paul
CACTUS, d; CACTUS, p; CACTUS, w

Cox, Ronny
HOLLYWOOD VICE SQUAD

Cox, Tony
HOLLYWOOD ZAP!

Cox, Walter
HELL SQUAD

Coy, Lee
HELL SQUAD

Coyle, Ann
ONE MORE SATURDAY NIGHT

Coyle, Brian
TERRY ON THE FENCE

Coyne, Kevin
VA BANQUE

Coyne, Maureen
HOWARD THE DUCK

Coyotte
MORT UN DIMANCHE DE PLUIE, spec eff

Cozzini, Nancy
VIOLATED

Cozzo, Gianni
CRAWLSPACE, art d

Crabe, James
THE KARATE KID PART II, ph

Craciun, Liviu
LICEENI

Craddock, Malcolm
PING PONG, p

Craft, Christine
COBRA

Craig, Diane
TRAVELLING NORTH

Craig, Helen
Obituaries

Craig, Laurie
MODERN GIRLS, w

Craig, Louis
FLY, THE, spec eff

Craig, Noble
BIG TROUBLE IN LITTLE CHINA; POLTERGEIST II

Craig, Paul
BOY IN BLUE, THE

Craig, Philip
BOY IN BLUE, THE

Craig, Stuart
MISSION, THE, prod d

Craig, Wendell
STOOGEMANIA

Cramarosa, Vito
YOUNGBLOOD

Cramer, Fred
PATRIOT, THE, spec eff

Cramer, Joey
CLAN OF THE CAVE BEAR, THE; FLIGHT OF THE
NAVIGATOR

Crampton, Barbara
CHOPPING MALL; FROM BEYOND

Crampton, Gerry
BIGGLES, stunts

Cranzano, Joe
POWER, makeup

Craven, Garth
BEST OF TIMES, THE, ed

Craven, Matt
AGENT ON ICE

Craven, Misty
OVER THE SUMMER

Craven, Tanya
OVER THE SUMMER

Craven, Wes
DEADLY FRIEND, d

Cravo, Mario
NEM TUDO E VERDADE

Crawford, Broderick   [William Broderick Crawford]
Obituaries

Crawford, Wayne
3:15, THE MOMENT OF TRUTH; JAKE SPEED; JAKE
SPEED, p; JAKE SPEED, w

Crayford, Jonathan
DANGEROUS ORPHANS, m

Creach, Everett
ONE CRAZY SUMMER, stunts

Creation Express
KAMIKAZE, cos

Creatore, Luigi
FINE MESS, A, m/l

Creber, William J.
FLIGHT OF THE NAVIGATOR, prod d

Creilier, Louis
KONZERT FUR ALICE, m

Cremades, Michel
CONSEIL DE FAMILLE

Cremer, Bruno
MENAGE

Crespo, J.C.
SOLDIER'S REVENGE, p

Cresta, Isolda
O HOMEM DA CAPA PRETA

Cretien, Renee
THERESE

Creton, Michel
MENAGE; PARIS MINUIT

Crevenna, Alfredo B.
EL SECUESTRO DE CAMARENA, d

Crew, A. Rosalind
MY CHAUFFEUR, set d

Crew, The
SOMETHING WILD

Crewe, Bob
FINE MESS, A, m/l

Crick, Ed
NAKED VENGEANCE

Crimmer, Celine
KILLER PARTY

Crimmins, Laura
OFF BEAT

Crippa, Maddalena
AURELIA

Crisanti, Andrea
IL DIAVOLO IN CORPO, art d

Criscuolo, Lou
EAT AND RUN; KING KONG LIVES

Crisman, Jerry
REVENGE OF THE TEENAGE VIXENS FROM OUTER
SPACE, THE

Crisp, Sandie
HOLLYWOOD VICE SQUAD

Cristadoro, Mary
COMBAT SHOCK

Cristante, Ivo
BAD GUYS , art d

Crivelli, Carlo
IL DIAVOLO IN CORPO, m

Crociani, Raimondo
IL RAGAZZO DEL PONY EXPRESS, ed; ITALIAN
FAST FOOD, ed; SPOSERO SIMON LE BON, ed;
YUPPIES, I GIOVANI DI SUCCESSO, ed

Crockett, Karlene
RETURN

Crockett, Tessa
LABYRINTH

Croft, Bill
BULLIES

Crombey, Bernard
JAKE SPEED

Crombie, Donald
PLAYING BEATIE BOW, d

Crombie, Jonathan
BULLIES; JUDGEMENT IN STONE, A

Cromwell, James
FINE MESS, A

Cron, Claudia
MEN'S CLUB, THE

Cronauer, Gail
POSITIVE I.D.

Crone, Bruce
AMERICAN JUSTICE, art d

Crone, Nina
TAKE IT EASY, p

Cronenberg, David
FLY, THE; FLY, THE, d; FLY, THE, w

Cronenberg, Denise
FLY, THE, cos

Cronenweth, Jordan
JUST BETWEEN FRIENDS, ph; PEGGY SUE GOT
MARRIED, ph

Cronin, Robert
AVENGING FORCE

Cronin, Sue
FERRIS BUELLER'S DAY OFF

Crook, Peter
INSTANT JUSTICE

Crooke, Leland
MY CHAUFFEUR

Crooks, Shauree
DR. OTTO AND THE RIDDLE OF THE GLOOM BEAM

Cropper, Linda
GOING SANE

Crosby, Denise
ELIMINATORS

Crosby, Lucinda
NAKED CAGE, THE; SMART ALEC

Cross, Bill
DOWN AND OUT IN BEVERLY HILLS

Cross, Donna
PANTHER SQUAD

Cross, Harley
WHERE ARE THE CHILDREN?

Cross, Ronnie
DEVASTATOR, THE, art d

Cross, Stephen
DARK AGE, w

Crossland, Harvey
CLOSE TO HOME, ed; CLOSE TO HOME, p; CLOSE TO
HOME, w

Crothers, Scatman
TRANSFORMERS: THE MOVIE, THE

Crovato, Luciano
ELOGIO DELLA PAZZIA

Crowder, Wally
WEEKEND WARRIORS, stunts

Crowley, David
BLUE CITY

Crowley, Edward
F/X

Crowley, Rory L.
CLAN OF THE CAVE BEAR, THE

Crowther, John
HANDS OF STEEL, w

Croydon, Nicky
LADY JANE

Crudo, Andrea
CASTIGHI

Cruickshank, Jim
TOUGH GUYS, w

Cruickshank, Su
PLAYING BEATIE BOW

Cruikshank, Sally
RUTHLESS PEOPLE, anim

Cruise, Tom
COLOR OF MONEY, THE; TOP GUN

Cruise, William
MURPHY'S LAW, prod d

Crumpacker, Amy
REVENGE OF THE TEENAGE VIXENS FROM OUTER
SPACE, THE

Crumrine, James
SILK

Crutchley, Roger
ANGKOR-CAMBODIA EXPRESS, w

Cruz, Carlos
UN HOMBRE DE EXITO

Cruz, Ernesto Gomez
CRONICA DE FAMILIA; EL IMPERIO DE LA
FORTUNA

Cruz, Javier
GAVILAN O PALOMA, ph

Cruz, Lito
LES LONGS MANTEAUX

Cruz, Miguel
8 MILLION WAYS TO DIE, m/l

Cruz, Rodel
PLATOON, art d

Cruz, Willie
SILK, m

D'Amore, Hallie
BACK TO SCHOOL, makeup

D'Angelo, Beverly
BIG TROUBLE

D'Angelo, Katia
FULANINHA

D'Angelo, Nino
FOTOROMANZO; FOTOROMANZO, m;
FOTOROMANZO, w; GIURO CHE TI AMO; GIURO
CHE TI AMO, d; GIURO CHE TI AMO, m; GIURO CHE
TI AMO, w; GIURO CHE TI AMO, w

D'Angiolillo, Cesar
MISS MARY, ed

D'Angiolillo, Luis Cesar
MAN FACING SOUTHEAST, ed

d'Anna, Claude
SALOME, d; SALOME, w

D'Annibale, Frank
QUICKSILVER

d'Arvor, Patrick Poivre
MAN AND A WOMAN: 20 YEARS LATER, A

D'Erama, Nicola
SALOME

D'Eva, Alessandro
SCUOLA DI LADRI, ph

D'Eva, Sandro
IL CAMMISSARIO LO GATTO, ph

d'Obici, Valeria
MORIRAI A MEZZANOTTE;
45MO PARALLELO; DESIDERANDO GIULIA
YUPPIES, I GIOVANI DI SUCCESSO

D'Offizi, Sergio
COBRA MISSION, ph

D'Orazio, Gena
PLAYING FOR KEEPS

D'Ottavi, Paolo
MIAMI GOLEM, ph

D'Salva, Ramon
SILK

D.A., Firman
TITAN SERAMBUT DIBELAH TUJUH

Da Campo, Gianni
SAPORE DEL GRANO, d&w

Da Costa, Jean Paul
BLACK AND WHITE, ph

Da Vinci, Sal
TROPPO FORTE

da Viola, Paulhino
FULANINHA, m/l

Da, Yu
QINGCHUN JI

Daalder, Bianca
POPULATION: ONE, ed; POPULATION: ONE, p

Daalder, Renee
POPULATION: ONE, d&w; POPULATION:
ONE, ed

Dabadie, Jean-Loup
DESCENTE AUX ENFERS, w

Dabner, Abbie
LITTLE SHOP OF HORRORS

Dabney, Augusta
VIOLETS ARE BLUE

Dacchille, Phillip
SAVING GRACE

Dachille, Phillip
FAT GUY GOES NUTZOID!!

Dacla, Corinne
CAPTIVE; DESORDRE; LA PURITAINE

Dacqmine, Jacques
INSPECTEUR LAVARDIN; MELO

Dada, Severino
NEM TUDO E VERDADE, ed

Dadi
CINEMA FALADO

Daevers, Madeleine
WALKMAN BLUES

Dafoe, Willem
PLATOON

Dafydd, Ifan Huw
COMING UP ROSES

Dagan, Ezra
AMERICA 3000

Dageby, Ulf
I LAGENS NAMN, m

Dahan, Alain
MAUVAIS SANG, p

Dahan, Yves
PRUNELLE BLUES, ph; YIDDISH CONNECTION, ph

Dahlen, Ciliane
AM NACHESTEN MORGEN KEHRTE DER MINISTER
NICHT AN SEINEN ARBEITSPLATZ

Dahlenborg, Asa
GRONA GUBBAR FRAN Y.R.

Dahlgren, David
DOWN BY LAW

Dahlin, Jacob
JONSSONLIGAN DYKER UPP IGEN

Daho, Etienne
DESORDRE

Dahr, Juni
BLACKOUT

Dailey, Arthur
IMAGEMAKER, THE

Dailey, Susanne
REVENGE OF THE TEENAGE VIXENS FROM OUTER
SPACE, THE

Daillie, Simon
SLEEPWALK

Dale, Cynthia
BOY IN BLUE, THE

Dale, Grover
QUICKSILVER, ch

Dale, Jennifer
SEPARATE VACATIONS

Daley, Kathryn
SCORPION

Dalhoff, Anja
BALLERUP BOULEVARD, ph

Dall, Peter
BRIDGE TO NOWHERE, stunts

Dalle, Beatrice
BETTY BLUE; ON A VOLE CHARLIE SPENCER!;
People to Watch

Dalmasso, Dominique
CORPS ET BIENS, art d

Dalton, Burt
AT CLOSE RANGE, spec eff

Dalton, Ken
VENDETTA, p

Dalunde, Carina
ALLA VI BARN I BULLERBY, cos

Dalvi, Jaywant
RAO SAHEB, w

Daly, Joe
MISSION, THE

Dalyan, Nathalie
BETTY BLUE

Dalzell, Mike
HOOSIERS

Damak, Mohamed
AL-KAS, d

Damamme, Rosalinde
LE PALTOQUET, p

Dambulugala, Joe
ARUNATA PERA; ARUNATA PERA, prod d

Damestoy, Irene
NUTCRACKER: THE MOTION PICTURE

Damiani, Alberto
L'ULTIMO GIORNO, w

Damiani, Alex
UNA TENERA FOLLIA

Damiani, Amasi
L'ULTIMO GIORNO, d

Damiani, Damiano
L'INCHIESTA, d; L'INCHIESTA, w

Damiani, Leo
Obituaries

Dammers, Jerry
ABSOLUTE BEGINNERS, m/l

Damon, Jace
HELL SQUAD

Dan, Alan
LA MACHINE A DECOUDRE

Dan, Fumi
KATAKU NO HITO

Danailov, Georgi
ZABRAVOTE TOZI SLOCHAI, w; ZA KUDE
PUTOVATE, w

Dance, Charles
ZABRAVOTE TOZI SLOCHAI, DGOLDEN CHILD, THE

Dane, Stephen
AMERICA 3000, art d

Dane, Terry
LABYRINTH

Danese, Shera
LADIES CLUB, THE

Danette, Leila
POWER

Dang, Hong
LOI RE TRAI TREN DUONG MON, m

Dangar, Henry
FOR LOVE ALONE, ed; TRAVELLING NORTH, ed

Danger, Craig
TOUCH AND GO

Dangerfield, Rodney
BACK TO SCHOOL; BACK TO SCHOOL, w

Dangler, Anita
STEWARDESS SCHOOL

Daniel, Jean-Louis
PEAU D'ANGE, d; PEAU D'ANGE, w

Daniel, William
AL ASHEKE, ph

Daniele, Graciela
HAUNTED HONEYMOON, ch

Danieli, Isa
CAMORRA

Daniels, Helen
KNIGHTS AND EMERALDS

Daniels, Jack
FINAL MISSION

Daniels, Jack S.
DEVASTATOR, THE

Daniels, Jeff
HEARTBURN; SOMETHING WILD

Daniels, Rudy
P.O.W. THE ESCAPE

Daniels, Terri
LOYALTIES

Danielsen, Dins
WISDOM, art d

Danielsson, Nadia
GRONA GUBBAR FRAN Y.R., cos

Danielsson, Ricky
GRONA GUBBAR FRAN Y.R.

Danika
VIOLENT BREED, THE

Danner, Blythe
BRIGHTON BEACH MEMOIRS

Danning, Sybil
PANTHER SQUAD; PANTHER SQUAD, p; REFORM
SCHOOL GIRLS; TOMB, THE

Dano, Royal
COCAINE WARS

Danon, Rami
SMILE OF THE LAMB, THE

Danping, Shen
BEI AIQING YIWANGDE JIAOLUO

Danson, Ted
FINE MESS, A; JUST BETWEEN FRIENDS

Dantas, Andreia
MALANDRO

Dantas, Nelson
FULANINHA

Danton, Dora
KILLER PARTY

Danton, Sylvie
POLICE, w

Danz, Cassandra
BEER

Danzelsen, Peter
STAMMHEIM

Danzig, Gad
FLASH, ph; HAKRAV AL HAVA'AD, ph; KOL AHAVO-
TAI, ph

Danziger, Kenneth
JUMPIN' JACK FLASH

Daou, Salim
AVANTI POPOLO

Daoudal, Gerard
LES FUGITIFS, art d; LOVE SONGS, art d

Dar, Ruth
HAKRAV AL HAVA'AD, cos

Darah, Marie-Christine
TAXI BOY

Darcus, Jack
OVERNIGHT, d&w; OVERNIGHT, p

Darcy, Lynne
MOVIE HOUSE MASSACRE

Darden, Severn
BACK TO SCHOOL

Dare, Beau
WISDOM

Dargin, Alan
FRINGE DWELLERS, THE

Darin, Richard
LES LONGS MANTEAUX

Dario, John
BUSTED UP

Dark, Vincent
SUNSET STRIP

Darling, Jeff
YOUNG EINSTEIN, ph

Darling, Joan
CHECK IS IN THE MAIL, THE, d

Darling, John
MONA LISA

Darling, Tim
AMERICAN ANTHEM

Darling, Todd
SORORITY HOUSE MASSACRE

Darlington, Bill
NINJA TURF

Darmois, Hugues
MAN AND A WOMAN: 20 YEARS LATER, A, ed

Darmon, Gerard
BETTY BLUE; RUE DU DEPART; SUIVEZ MON
REGARD

Darnell, Robert
SCORPION

Darrieux, Danielle
CORPS ET BIENS; SCENE OF THE CRIME

Darton, Roger
PANTHER SQUAD

Dartonne, Monique
HIGH SPEED, d; HIGH SPEED, ed; HIGH SPEED, w

Darussalam
TITAN SERAMBUT DIBELAH TUJUH

Das, Gautam
IN THE SHADOW OF KILIMANJARO, p

Das, Mohan
CHIDAMBARAM

Dash, Robert
3:15, THE MOMENT OF TRUTH

Daskalothanassis, Yannis
DANILO TRELES, O FIMISMENOS ANDALOUSIANOS
MOUSIKOS, ph

Dassault, Marcel
Obituaries

Dast, Ali Reza Zarin
CLOSED CIRCUIT, ph

Datz, Roy
BAND OF THE HAND

Daucus, Mindy
MOUNTAINTOP MOTEL MASSACRE, ed

Daugherty, Richard
JO JO DANCER, YOUR LIFE IS CALLING

Daughtrey, Ken
NINJA TURF

Daughtry, Reginald
GOOD TO GO

Daumerri, Danielle
AS SETE VAMPIRAS

Dauphin, Frieda
CONGO EXPRESS, cos

Dauphin, Jean-Claude
NUIT D'IVRESSE; YIDDISH CONNECTION

Davalos, Dominique
HOWARD THE DUCK

Davalos, Raul
SHADOWS RUN BLACK, ed

Davanzati, Roberto Forges
ANGKOR-CAMBODIA EXPRESS, ph

Davanzati, Stefano
FINAL EXECUTIONER, THE; LA VENEXIANA

Davao, Charlie
KILLING OF SATAN, THE; RAGING VENDETTA

Davenport, Nigel
CARAVAGGIO

Davey, Belinda
DEATH OF A SOLDIER

Davey, Bert
ALIENS, art d

Davey, John
FINE MESS, A

Davi, Robert
RAW DEAL

David Stripes Productions
NIGHT OF THE CREEPS, spec eff

David, Clifford
AGENT ON ICE

David, Hal
BEST OF TIMES, THE, m/l

David, Ingolf
FLAMBEREDE HJERTER

David, Keith
PLATOON

David, Kristina
WIRED TO KILL

David, Lolita
RECRUITS

Davide, Kristy
ABSOLUTE BEGINNERS

Davidovsky, Paul
STREETS OF GOLD

Davidson, Betsy
OVER THE SUMMER

Davidson, Boaz
ALEX KHOLE AHAVA, d; ALEX KHOLE AHAVA, w

Davidson, Bruria
ALEX KHOLE AHAVA, ed

Davidson, Clifford
ROLLER BLADE, stunts

Davidson, Diana
AROUND THE WORLD IN EIGHTY WAYS

Davies, E.R.
AT CLOSE RANGE

Davies, Freeman
CROSSROADS, ed

Davies, Glan
COMING UP ROSES

Davies, Janet
Obituaries

Davies, John
POSITIVE I.D.

Davies, Lane
IMPURE THOUGHTS

Davies, Lindy
MALCOLM

Davies, Melissa
DEAD-END DRIVE-IN

Davies, Rachel
KNIGHTS AND EMERALDS

Davies, Ralph
DANGEROUS ORPHANS, prod d

Davies, Ray
ABSOLUTE BEGINNERS; ABSOLUTE BEGINNERS, m/l

Davies, Sammi
MONA LISA

Davies, Stephen
WHOOPEE BOYS, THE

Davies, Tessa
LITTLE SHOP OF HORRORS, set d

Davila, Jacques
BEAU TEMPS, MAIS ORAGEUX EN FIN DE
JOURNEE, w; QUI TROP EMBRASSE, d; QUI TROP
EMBRASSE, w

Davion, Geoffrey
CLOCKWISE

Davis, Altovise
PERILS OF P.K., THE

Davis, B.J.
AVENGING FORCE; AVENGING FORCE, stunts

Davis, Becki
AVENGING FORCE

Davis, Bud
BLACK MOON RISING, stunts; MANHUNTER, stunts;
TRANSFORMERS: THE MOVIE, THE; WISDOM, stunts

Davis, Cathy Cheryl
BEST OF TIMES, THE

Davis, Charles
THUNDER RUN, w

Davis, Dane
NO RETREAT, NO SURRENDER, ed

Davis, Donald
SAMUEL LOUNT

Davis, Elliot
VAMP, ph

Davis, Elsa
CACTUS; CACTUS, m

Davis, Geena
FLY, THE

Davis, Gretchen
NAKED CAGE, THE

Davis, Hilary
BEST OF TIMES, THE

Davis, Janeen
VAMP

Davis, Jimmy Lynn
STEWARDESS SCHOOL, stunts

Davis, John Walter
QUICKSILVER

Davis, Joseph Lee
SOMETHING WILD

Davis, Judy
KANGAROO

Davis, Karen
LIGHTNING—THE WHITE STALLION

Davis, Ken
9½ WEEKS, prod d; MEN'S CLUB, THE, prod d

Davis, Kenny
FLIGHT OF THE NAVIGATOR

Davis, Lindsay W.
FAT GUY GOES NUTZOID!!, cos

Davis, Mary Bond
JO JO DANCER, YOUR LIFE IS CALLING

Davis, Melissa
SPIRITS OF THE AIR

Davis, Miles
ABSOLUTE BEGINNERS, m/l

Davis, Nathan
ONE MORE SATURDAY NIGHT; TOUGH GUYS

Davis, Patrice
VENDETTA

Davis, Patricia
COCAINE WARS

Davis, Paula
GOOD TO GO

Davis, Peter S.
HIGHLANDER, p

Davis, Philip
COMRADES; OVER THE SUMMER

Davis, Ricky
NINJA TURF; YOUNGBLOOD

Davis, Robin
SEA SERPENT, THE, m

Davis, Rod
KING KONG LIVES

Davis, Sammy
JAKE SPEED; PERILS OF P.K., THE

Davis, Shawni
VENDETTA

Davis, Sidney
AMERICA, w

Davis, Sonny Carl
TERRORVISION

Davis, Tom
ONE MORE SATURDAY NIGHT; ONE MORE
SATURDAY NIGHT, w

Davis, Tyrone
NINJA TURF

Davis, Warwick
LABYRINTH

Davis, William
HEAD OFFICE

Davison, Bruce
LADIES CLUB, THE

Davison, Noah
UPHILL ALL THE WAY

Davlos, Theodosis
HARDBODIES 2, art d

Davoli, Ninetto
MOMO

Dawkins, David
FLOODSTAGE; FLOODSTAGE, ed; FLOODSTAGE, p,
d&w

Dawn, Jefferson
BAD GUYS, makeup

Dawn, Vincent
L'APACHE BIANCO, d

Dawood, May
HOB FEE BAGHDAD, art d

Dawson, Anthony
PIRATES

Dawson, Anthony M.
JUNGLE RAIDERS, d

Day, David Van
SCREAMTIME

Day, Joe D.
TOUGH GUYS, spec eff

Day, Raymond
FATHERLAND, p; KNIGHTS AND EMERALDS, p

Dayan, Assaf
DELTA FORCE, THE

Dayan, Assi
HAKRAV AL HAVA'AD, w

Daye, Adam
ROCINANTE

Daye, Gabrielle
NO SURRENDER

Daye, Zouheir
WHAT HAPPENED NEXT YEAR, ed

de Roche, Everett
WINDRIDER, w

De Rolf, Paul
THE KARATE KID PART II, ch

de Rooy, Felix
ALMACITA DI DESOLATO, art d; ALMACITA DI
DESOLATO, d

de Rosa, Alberto Fernandez
INSOMNIACS

De Rose, Chris
MURPHY'S LAW

de Rozas, Maria Elena Sainz
ME HACE FALTA UN BIGOTE, ed

De Rubin, Yair
SALVADOR

De Sanctis, Dave
BOY IN BLUE, THE

De Santis, Gregory J.
CAR TROUBLE, p

De Sapio, Francesca
WITCHFIRE

De Sica, Christian
DETECTIVE SCHOOL DROPOUTS; GRANDI
MAGAZZINI; YUPPIES, I GIOVANI DI SUCCESSO

De Sica, Manuel
45MO PARALLELO, m; IL CAMMISSARIO LO GATTO,
m

De Silva, Daniela
IL CASO MORO

de Silva, Mike
NIGHTMARE WEEKEND, spec eff

De Silva, Pietro
IL BI E IL BA

de Sosa, Ruth
TOUGH GUYS

de Souza, Jackson
O HOMEM DA CAPA PRETA

De Souza, Marcia
RUNNING OUT OF LUCK

De Souza, Noel
WILDCATS

de Valle, Luis Manuel
EN PENUMBRA, ed; TEO EL PELIRROJO, ed

De Vega, Jose
THE KARATE KID PART II, ch

De Vernier, Hugo
HALF MOON STREET

De Vetta, Linda
HALF MOON STREET, makeup

de Vincentis, D.V.
TOUCH AND GO

De Vita, Pat
PLAYING FOR KEEPS

De Vivaise, Caroline
LOVE SONGS, cos

De Vivier, Moune
UNDER THE CHERRY MOON

De Vorges, Dominique
MELO, makeup

de Vos, Ingrid
SPRINGEN

de Vries, Edwin
SHADOW OF VICTORY; SHADOW OF VICTORY, w

De Winne, Kezia
CLOCKWISE, makeup

de Wit, Herman
DE VAL VAN PATRICIA HAGGERSMITH, m

de Witt, Caritas
DER ROSENKONIG, art d

De Wolf, Hans
DE WISSELWACHTER, w

De Young, Cliff
F/X; FLIGHT OF THE NAVIGATOR

de Zarate, Americo Ortiz
ANOTHER LOVE STORY, d; ANOTHER LOVE STORY,
w

Deacy, Ed
BRIGHTON BEACH MEMOIRS; OFF BEAT

Deaderick, John
WISDOM

Deadrick, Rock
PRETTY IN PINK

Deakin, Julia
MR. LOVE

Deakins, Lucy
BOY WHO COULD FLY, THE; People to Watch

Deakins, Roger
SID AND NANCY, ph

Dean, Larae
CLASS OF NUKE 'EM HIGH

Dean, Laura
MY LITTLE PONY

Dean, Richard
MANHATTAN PROJECT, THE, makeup; SOMETHING
WILD, makeup

Dean, Ron
COLOR OF MONEY, THE

Dean-Jones, Mercia
FOR LOVE ALONE

Deane, Alethea
SHORT CHANGED, set d

Dearberg, Bob
GIRL FROM MANI, THE, ed

Deas, Justin
DREAM LOVER

Debassige, Diane
LOYALTIES

Debaut, Denise
BABEL OPERA, OU LA REPETITION DE DON JUAN ,
w

DeBennedetti, Lisa
NOBODY'S FOOL

DeBenning, Burr
ARMED RESPONSE

Deblais, Jean-Claude
LE BONHEUR A ENCORE FRAPPE, m

DeBlanc, Bertrand
BELIZAIRE THE CAJUN

Debney, Louis
Obituaries

Debono, Vince
ABSOLUTE BEGINNERS

DeBont, Jan
RUTHLESS PEOPLE, ph

Debou, Dirk
MAMA IS BOOS!, art d

Dec, Ba Nam Sa
KARMA

DeCheser, Allan
HANNAH AND HER SISTERS; MANHATTAN
PROJECT, THE

DeCheser, Arthur
HANNAH AND HER SISTERS; MANHATTAN
PROJECT, THE

Deckert, Blue
GETTING EVEN; UPHILL ALL THE WAY

DeClue, Denise
ABOUT LAST NIGHT, w

DeCoste, Kim
ROCKIN' ROAD TRIP

DeCuir, Gabrielle
LEGAL EAGLES

DeCuir, John
JOJO DANCER, YOUR LIFE IS CALLING, prod d;
LEGAL EAGLES, prod d; TOP GUN, prod d

Dedet, Yann
POLICE, ed

Dedieu, Isabelle
THERESE, ed

Dedovich, Miguel
KING AND HIS MOVIE, A

Dee, John
BUSTED UP; KILLER PARTY

Dee, Konya
OCEAN DRIVE WEEKEND

Dee, Maurice
KNIGHTS AND EMERALDS

Dee, Robbie
LETTER TO BREZHNEV

Deegan, Dawn
SUNSET STRIP

Deering, Olive
Obituaries

Deeth, James
TOUGH GUYS

Deezen, Eddie
DESPERATE MOVES; LONGSHOT, THE; WHOOPEE
BOYS, THE

Defluiter, Stephen
HANNAH AND HER SISTERS

DeFrancesca, David
WISDOM

Dege, Hubert
MAINE-OCEAN, m

Degette, Andrea
SLEEPWALK, art d

Degi, Janos
VAKVILAGBAN

DeGovia, Jackson
NOBODY'S FOOL, prod d

deGuzman, Jossie
F/X

Degville, Martin
FERRIS BUELLER'S DAY OFF, m/l

DeHaven, Carter
HOOSIERS, p

DeHaven, Richard
NIGHT OF THE CREEPS

Dei, Gianni
AMORE INQUIETO DI MARIA

Deikman, Mark
FAT GUY GOES NUTZOID!!

Deisinger, Lutz
TAGEDIEBE

Dejert, Lars
JONSSONLIGAN DYKER UPP IGEN

Dekawa, Mitsuo
KINEMA NO TENCHI, art d

Dekker, Chris
NIGHT OF THE CREEPS

Dekker, Fred
HOUSE, w; NIGHT OF THE CREEPS, d&w

Dekko, Espen
BLACKOUT

DeKnight, Jimmy
THE KARATE KID PART II, m/l

del Amo, Pablo Gonzalez
EL RIO DE ORO, ed; MAMBRU SE FUE A LA
GUERRA, ed; VIAJE A NINGUNA PARTE, ed

del Bosque, Andres
NEMESIO

Del Brocco, Giancarlo
FROM BEYOND, makeup; SAVING GRACE, makeup

del Castillo, Michel
DOUCE FRANCE, w

Del Castillo, Siro
AMIGOS, art d

del Corral, Pedro D.
DRAGON RAPIDE

del Peon, Jose
DIAPASON, ed

del Real, Alfonso
MAMBRU SE FUE A LA GUERRA

del Rio, Pedro
DRAGON RAPIDE

Del Rosario, Xochitl
SALVADOR

Del Russo, Marie
BAND OF THE HAND, makeup

Del Ruth, Thomas
QUICKSILVER, ph; STAND BY ME, ph

del Sol, Laura
EL AMOR BRUJO; IL CAMORRISTA; VIAJE A
NINGUNA PARTE

Delachau, Christophe
MAMMAME

Delaez, Juan
LA ALACRANA

Delahoussaye, Marcus
BELIZAIRE THE CAJUN

Delan, Diane
RATBOY

Delaney, Cassandra
FAIR GAME

Delaney, Kim
DELTA FORCE, THE

Delaney, Rory
TWO FRIENDS

DeLange, David
BAD GUYS

Delano, Pilar
WILDCATS

Delany, Dana
WHERE THE RIVER RUNS BLACK

Delaporte, Jacques
LES FRERES PETARD, m; NUIT D'IVRESSE, m

DeLaunay, Andre
BELIZAIRE THE CAJUN

Delaune, Yvette
FEMMES DE PERSONNE

Delbourg, Veronique
PEAU D'ANGE

Deleanu, Cristina
DECLARATIE DE DRAGOSTE; LICEENI

Delerue, Georges
CONSEIL DE FAMILLE, m; CRIMES OF THE HEART,
m; DESCENTE AUX ENFERS, m; FEMMES DE
PERSONNE, m; PLATOON, md; SALVADOR, m

Deleu, Francoise
FLAGRANT DESIR, art d&cos

Delevingne, Philippe
SINCERELY CHARLOTTE

Delfosse, Raoul
FRENCH LESSON

Delgado, Arnulfo
CONTACTO CHICANO, p; ES MI VIDA—EL NOA NOA
2, p

Delgado, Guillermo Calle
VISA U.S.A., p

Delgado, Livio
EL CORAZON SOBRE LA TIERRA, ph; UN HOMBRE
DE EXITO, ph

Delgado, Manuel M.
NOCHE DE JUERGA, d

Delgado, Marcela
PICARDIA MEXICANA NUMERO DOS

Delgado, Nena
LOS ASES DE CONTRABANDO

Delibes, Miguel
EL DISPUTADO VOTO DEL SR. CAYO, w

Delivoria, Marina
TO DENDRO POU PLIGONAME

Delk, Denny
HOWARD THE DUCK

Dell'Acqua, Ottaviano
CUT AND RUN

Dell'Orco, Maurizio
STORIA D'AMORE, ph

Dell, Charlie
JO JO DANCER, YOUR LIFE IS CALLING; ODD JOBS

Dells, Dorothy
ECHO PARK

Delluc, Xavier
ETATS D'AME

Dellums, Erik
SHE'S GOTTA HAVE IT

Delmar, Mario
EL EXTRANO HIJO DEL SHERIFF

Delmare, Fred
GRITTA VOM RATTENSCHLOSS; UNTERMEHMEN
GEIGENKASTEN

DelNegro, Daniel
UMA RAPARIGA NO VERAO, ph

Delon, Alain
LE PASSAGE; LE PASSAGE, p

Delon, Anthony
UNA SPINA NEL CUORE

DeLongis, Anthony
DANGEROUSLY CLOSE

Delory, Al
WHAT COMES AROUND, m

Delory, Deni
RECRUITS, makeup

Delpy, Julie
MAUVAIS SANG

Delsaux, Chantal
FAUBOURG SAINT-MARTIN

Deluc, Xavier
BEAU TEMPS, MAIS ORAGEUX EN FIN DE
JOURNEE; CAPTIVE; COURS PRIVE

DeLuise, Dom
AMERICAN TAIL, AN; HAUNTED HONEYMOON

DeLuise, Peter
FREE RIDE; SOLARBABIES

Delvaux, Andre
BABEL OPERA, OU LA REPETITION DE DON JUAN,
d; BABEL OPERA, OU LA REPETITION DE DON
JUAN, w

Demare, Maria Jose
ANOTHER LOVE STORY

Demarle, Philippe
DESORDRE

Demchuk, Bob
WHATEVER IT TAKES, d; WHATEVER IT TAKES, ed;
WHATEVER IT TAKES, p; WHATEVER IT TAKES, w

Demenga, Frank
NOAH UND DER COWBOY

DeMeo, Paul
ELIMINATORS, w

Demers, Claude
TOBY MCTEAGUE, m

Demers, Nicole
PINK CHIQUITAS, THE, makeup

Demerus, Ellen
ALLA VI BARN I BULLERBY

Demetrau, Georges
MAN AND A WOMAN: 20 YEARS LATER, A, spec eff;
ZONE ROUGE, spec eff

Demetreau, Georges
BETTY BLUES, spec eff; KAMIKAZE, spec eff

Demian, Iarina
LICEENI

Demme, Dorothy
SOMETHING WILD

Demme, Jonathan
SOMETHING WILD, d; SOMETHING WILD, p

Demongeot, Mylene
MENAGE; PAULETTE

DeMora, Robert
BAND OF THE HAND, cos

Demorest, Daniel
P.O.W. THE ESCAPE

DeMorton, Reggie
KING OF THE STREETS

DeMoss, Darcy
FRIDAY THE 13TH PART VI: JASON LIVES; REFORM
SCHOOL GIRLS

Dempsey, Jerome
IMAGEMAKER, THE

Dempsey, Mike
SCREEN TEST

Dempsey, Susan
LETTER TO BREZHNEV

Dempster, Curt
MANHATTAN PROJECT, THE

DeMunn, Jeffrey
HITCHER, THE

Demy, John
TOUGH GUYS

Den Dooven, Leslie
CARNAGE

Denauneux, Patrick
L'AMANT MAGNIFIQUE, p

Dench, Judi
ROOM WITH A VIEW, A

Denegris, Tassos
SCHETIKA ME TON VASSILI

Deneuve, Catherine
LET'S HOPE IT'S A GIRL; LOVE SONGS; SCENE OF
THE CRIME

Dengel, Jake
AT CLOSE RANGE; BEST OF TIMES, THE

Denham, Maurice
MR. LOVE

DeNiro, Linda
POWER

Denisenko, Taras
KAK MOLODY MY BYLI

Deniz, Claire
HAUNTED HONEYMOON

Denkin, Marty
STREETS OF GOLD

Denly, Linda
ARMOUR OF GOD, THE

Denn, Marie
STEWARDESS SCHOOL

Dennehy, Brian
CHECK IS IN THE MAIL, THE; F/X; LEGAL EAGLES

Denner, Charles
GOLDEN EIGHTIES; L'UNIQUE

Denney, Charles
HEARTBURN

Denny, Jon S.
NOBODY'S FOOL, p

DeNove, Tom
BIG BET, THE, ph

DeNoyel, Veronique
UNDER THE CHERRY MOON

Dent, Frank
8 MILLION WAYS TO DIE

Dentici, Marco
STORIA D'AMORE, art d

Denton, Christa
8 MILLION WAYS TO DIE

Denton, Jack
Obituaries

Denton, Lisa
BACK TO SCHOOL

Denyck, Susan
POLICE ACADEMY 3: BACK IN TRAINING

Denysenko, Yuri
DEATHMASK, ph

Deodato, Ruggero
CUT AND RUN, d

DePalma, Brian
WISE GUYS, d

DePaolo, Theresa
RATBOY

Depardieu, Alain
TAXI BOY, p

Depardieu, Elisabeth
JEAN DE FLORETTE

Depardieu, Gerard
JEAN DE FLORETTE; LES FUGITIFS; MENAGE;
POLICE; RUE DU DEPART

Depardon, Raymond
PEKIN CENTRAL, ph

DePatis, Yvonne
THRASHIN', makeup

DePaula, Cynthia
BREEDERS, p

Depland, A. Michelle
BLUE VELVET

Depp, Johnny
PLATOON

Depusse, Jean
INSPECTEUR LAVARDIN

Derby, George
SUNSET STRIP

Dereck, Axel Van
WHERE ARE THE CHILDREN?

Derganc, Marko
OVNI IN MAMUTI

Derlick, Inger
BLACKOUT, cos

Dermer, Bonnie
'NIGHT, MOTHER, set d

Dern, Laura
BLUE VELVET

DeRoche, Everett
LINK, w

Deroski, Bonnie
SWEET LIBERTY

DeRossi, Gianetto
KING KONG LIVES, makeup

Derricks, Cleavant
OFF BEAT

DeRue, Carmen   [Carmen Faye DeRue]
Obituaries

Deruelle, Michel
JEAN DE FLORETTE, makeup; MENAGE, makeup

Deruelle, Michele
MANON DES SOURCES, makeup

Dervieu, Eric
FRENCH LESSON

DeSantis, Pasqualino
SALOME, ph

DeSantis, Patrick
STOOGEMANIA

Desanto, Susie
WEEKEND WARRIORS, cos

Desarthe, Gerard
PAULETTE

Desbois, Daniel
BLACK AND WHITE, ph

Descas, Alex
TAXI BOY

Deschamps, Sophie
PEKIN CENTRAL

Deschamps, Yves
EXIT-EXIL, ed; PRUNELLE BLUES, ed

Descouard, Marie-Chrisine
PAULETTE

Desfons, Delphine
I PHOTOGRAPHIA, ed; PARENTAL CLAIM, ed

Desha, Avraham
HAKRAV AL HAVA'AD, p

Desheng, Chen
BEI AIQING YIWANGDE JIAOLUO, art d

Desideri, Danilo
SETTE CHILI IN SETTE GIORNI, ph; TROPPO FORTE,
ph

Desideri, Giorgio
FEAR, cos; FEAR, set d; TAI-PAN, set d

Desideri, Osvaldo
IL CAMORRISTA, art d

DeSimone, Tom
REFORM SCHOOL GIRLS, d&w

DesJardins, Amoury
UNDER THE CHERRY MOON

Desjardins, Chris
RADIOACTIVE DREAMS

Desjonqueres, Ghislaine
LE DEBUTANT, ed; PAULETTE, ed

Deskin, Andrew
OVERNIGHT, art d

Didym, Michel
LAST SONG

Diego, Constante
EL CORAZON SOBRE LA TIERRA, d; EL CORAZON SOBRE LA TIERRA, w

Diego, Eliseo Alberto
CAPABLANCA, w; EL CORAZON SOBRE LA TIERRA, w

Diego, Gabino
VIAJE A NINGUNA PARTE

Diego, Juan
DRAGON RAPIDE; EL HERMANO BASTARDO DE DIOS; LOS PARAISOS PERDIDOS; VIAJE A NINGUNA PARTE

Diegues, Carlos
QUILOMBO, d&w

Diesing, Heinz
FATHERLAND

Dietl, Magdalena
JONAS, DEJME TOMU VE STREDU, w

Dietl, Robert
FATHERLAND

Dietmer, Knud
FLAMBEREDE HJERTER

Dietrich, Erwin C.
COBRA MISSION, w

Dieux, Richard
PIRATES

Diffring, Anton
DER SOMMER DES SAMURAI

DiGaetano II, Joseph
MANHUNTER, spec eff

DiGaetano III, Joe
MY MAN ADAM, spec eff

Dignam, Arthur
COMRADES

Diklic, Bogdan
I TO CE PROCI; ZA SRECU JE POTREBNO TROJE

Dikmen, Ugur
AMANSIZ YOL, m

DiLeo, Fernando
VIOLENT BREED, THE, d; VIOLENT BREED, THE, w

Dilge, Doug
GOOD TO GO, p

Dille, Flint
TRANSFORMERS: THE MOVIE, THE, w

Dilley, Leslie
INVADERS FROM MARS, prod d

Dillon, Denny
SEVEN MINUTES IN HEAVEN

Dillon, Emily
FAT GUY GOES NUTZOID!!, p

Dillon, Jeff
DR. OTTO AND THE RIDDLE OF THE GLOOM BEAM

Dillon, Kevin
PLATOON; People to Watch

Dillon, Matt
NATIVE SON

Dillon, Mia
MONEY PIT, THE

Dilulio, Ron
MOUNTAINTOP MOTEL MASSACRE, m

Dimaano, Charina
NUTCRACKER: THE MOTION PICTURE

Dimant, Grisha
MONEY PIT, THE

DiMarco, Anthony
NAKED CAGE, THE, ed

Dimensional Animation Effects
NIGHT OF THE CREEPS, spec eff

Dimitri, Nick
LONGSHOT, THE

Dimitrov, Olga
BEER, cos; SAMUEL LOUNT, cos

Dimitrova, Marianna
SKUPA MOYA, SKUPI MOY

Dimsey, Ross
KANGAROO, p

Din, Ayub Khan
MY BEAUTIFUL LAUNDRETTE

Dindo, Richard
EL SUIZO—UN AMOUR EN ESPAGNE, d; EL SUIZO—UN AMOUR EN ESPAGNE, w

Ding-A-Ling
SOMETHING WILD

Dingfeng, Ling
YU QING SAO

Dingo, Ernie
FRINGE DWELLERS, THE

Dingwall, Kelly
AROUND THE WORLD IN EIGHTY WAYS

Diniz, Vitor
NEM TUDO E VERDADE, ph

Dinner, Michael
OFF BEAT, d

Dinome, Jerry
DANGEROUSLY CLOSE

Dinos, Lou
QUICKSILVER

Dintenfass, Andrew
ABOUT LAST NIGHT, ph

Diogene, Franco
NAME OF THE ROSE, THE

Dion, Debra
TROLL

Dion, Dennis
QUICKSILVER, spec eff; THE KARATE KID PART II, spec eff

Dionisio, Silvia
FEAR

Diop, Wazis
NTTURUDU, m

Diot, Andre
LE PALTOQUET, ph; LE PASSAGE, ph

DiPasquale, James
ARMED AND DANGEROUS, m

DiPietro, David
HELLFIRE, spec eff

Diplan, Constantin
DECLARATIE DE DRAGOSTE

Diqing, Feng
JUE XIANG

Dirkson, Douglas
EYE OF THE TIGER

Dirtadian, Armen
DESERT BLOOM

DiRusso, Hollywood
SEVEN MINUTES IN HEAVEN, makeup

DiSanti, John
RUNNING SCARED

Dishy, Bob
BRIGHTON BEACH MEMOIRS

Ditlevsen, Tove
BARNDOMMENS GADE, w

Divkar, Bhanudas
TRIKAL, ed

Dixon, Boom Boom
VENDETTA

Dixon, David
DR. OTTO AND THE RIDDLE OF THE GLOOM BEAM

Dixon, Ernest
WHAT COMES AROUND

Dixon, Humphrey
ROOM WITH A VIEW, A, ed

Dixon, Malcolm
LABYRINTH

Dixon, Susan
SHADOW PLAY

Dizdarevic, Nenad
I TO CE PROCI, d

Djarot, Eros
SECANGKIR KOPI PAHIT, m

Djayam, Mostea
DER ROSENKONIG

Djian, Marpessa
ROUND MIDNIGHT

Djian, Philippe
BETTY BLUE, d&w; BLEU COMME L'ENFER, w

Djola, Badja
LIGHTSHIP, THE

Djorcev, Aco
SRECNA NOVA '49

Djosic, Slobodan
LIJEPE ZENE PROLAZE KROZ GRAD, art d

Djurkovic, George
CAPTIVE, art d

do Valle, Maurico
QUILOMBO

Doazan, Aurelle
GARDIEN DE LA NUIT

Dobbins, Bennie
FERRIS BUELLER'S DAY OFF, stunts

Dobbins, Bennie E.
JUMPIN' JACK FLASH, stunts

Dobbs, Frank Q.
UPHILL ALL THE WAY, d&w

Dobbyn, Dave
FOOTROT FLATS, m

Dobie, Laurence
Obituaries

Dobre, Geo
NOI, CEI DIN LINIA INTII

Dobrin, Lucille
MONEY PIT, THE

Dobrin-Besoiu, Emilia
SECVENTE

Dobrowolska, Gosia
AROUND THE WORLD IN EIGHTY WAYS

Dobs, Trea
CHARLEY, m

Dobtcheff, Vernon
NAME OF THE ROSE, THE

Docherty, James J.
HOLLYWOOD VICE SQUAD, w

Dodd, Steve
SHORT CHANGED

Dodet, Yann
DOUBLE MESSIEURS, ed

Dodson, Lisa
COLOR OF MONEY, THE

Doe, Barry
ONE CRAZY SUMMER

Doe, John
3:15, THE MOMENT OF TRUTH; SALVADOR

Doetz, Corinna
MEIER, ed

Dog, the
DIRT BIKE KID, THE

Doga, Evgenij
WILD WIND, THE, m

Doggett, Bill
BLUE VELVET, m/l

Doherty, Carol
OCEAN DRIVE WEEKEND

Dohlen, Lenny Von
BILLY GALVIN

Doillon, Jacques
LA PURITAINE, d; LA PURITAINE, w

Dok, Park Soon
GILSODOM, ed

Dolan, Clair
TOUCH AND GO

Dolata, Jan
JONSSONLIGAN DYKER UPP IGEN

Dolby, Thomas
HOWARD THE DUCK; HOWARD THE DUCK, m/l

Dolgy, Mike
RECRUITS

Dolgy, Sasha Mote
RECRUITS

Dolinsky, Alicia
KING AND HIS MOVIE, A

Doll, Birgit
SECOND VICTORY, THE

Dollar, William
Obituaries

Dolman, Martin
HANDS OF STEEL, d; HANDS OF STEEL, w; MONSTER SHARK, w

Dombasle, Arielle
BOSS' WIFE, THE; FLAGRANT DESIR

Domingo, Anni
PASSION OF REMEMBRANCE, THE

Domingo, Placido
OTELLO

Dominguez, Raul
EL MERCADO DE HUMILDES, ph; LA TIERRA PROMETIDA, ph; SE SUFRE PERO SE GOZA, ed

Dominic, Heather
MANHATTAN PROJECT, THE

Dominici, Germana
IL RAGAZZO DEL PONY EXPRESS

Domino, Antoine "Fats"
FINE MESS, A, m/l

Dommisch, Peter
GRITTA VOM RATTENSCHLOSS

Domnick, Olliver
ASSAULT, THE

Dompierre, Francois
DECLINE OF THE AMERICAN EMPIRE, THE, m

Donadoni, Maurizio
ANCHE LEI FUMAVA IL SIGARO; IL CASO MORO

Donaggio, Pino
CRAWLSPACE, m; IL CASO MORO, m; SETTE CHILI IN SETTE GIORNI, m

Donahue, Marc
MURPHY'S LAW, m

Donahue, Troy
LOW BLOW

Donaldson, Carron
NUTCRACKER: THE MOTION PICTURE

Donaldson, Tex
CROSSROADS; NIGHT OF THE CREEPS

Donaldson, W.
ABSOLUTE BEGINNERS, m/l

Donati, Danilo
GINGER & FRED, cos

Donati, Dario
LA MONACA NEL PECCATO, d

Donati, Kara
LA SECONDA NOTTE

Donati, Sergio
RAW DEAL, w

Donchev, Kiril
ZA KUDE PUTOVATE, m; ZABRAVOTE TOZI
SLOCHAI, m

Donen, Peter
FLIGHT OF THE NAVIGATOR, spec eff

Donev, Ivan
SKUPA MOYA, SKUPI MOY

Dong-choon, Hyung
ER WOO DONG, ed

Dongsheng, Er
CUODIAN YUANYANG

Donham, David
MY CHAUFFEUR

Donizetti, Gaetano
MONEY PIT, THE, m/l

Donlevy, Martin
YOUNGBLOOD

Donnadieu, Bernard-Pierre
FLAGRANT DESIR; MAX MON AMOUR

Donnati, Donatella
VOGLIA DI GUARDARE, w

Donnay, Christophe
LA MOITIE DE L'AMOUR

Donnelly, Janes
MILWR BYCHAN

Donnelly, Patrice
AMERICAN ANTHEM

Donnelly, Tom
QUICKSILVER, d&w

Donner, Jorn
RIISUMINEN, p

Donner, Otto
DIE WALSCHE; LINNA, m

Donner, Wolf
ANGRY HARVEST

Donnet, Christophe
PARIS MINUIT, m

Donno, Eddy
BAD GUYS , stunts

Donohoe, Amanda
CASTAWAY; FOREIGN BODY

Donohue, Walter
MY BEAUTIFUL LAUNDRETTE

Donovan, Kerry
MANHATTAN PROJECT, THE

Donovan, Tate
SPACECAMP

Donovan, Terence
EMMA'S WAR

Donovan, Terry
DEATH OF A SOLDIER

Donville, Teddy
BOY IN BLUE, THE

Doo-yong, Lee
BBONG, d

Doohan, James
STAR TREK IV: THE VOYAGE HOME

Dooley, Paul
BIG TROUBLE

Doolittle, John
CLAN OF THE CAVE BEAR, THE

Dop, Jan
WINDSCHADUW, ed

DoQui, Robert
GOOD TO GO

Doran, Ann
WILDCATS

Doran, Veronica
SCREAMTIME

Dore, Charlie
LUCAS, m/l

Dori, Eli
SHTAY ETZBA'OT M'TZIDON, p

Doria, Alejandro
AWAITING THE PALLBEARERS, d

Doria, Dexter
RAGING VENDETTA

Doria, Diogo
UMA RAPARIGA NO VERAO

Doria, Sergio
SALOME

Dorin, Jan Ivan
SPIKER

Doring, Arturo Rodriguez
SALVADOR

Doring, Jorg
WALKMAN BLUES

Dorn, Cyrilla
HEARTBURN

Dorn, Franchelle
IMAGEMAKER, THE

Dornacker, Jane
Obituaries

Dorner, Gyorgy
ORDOGI KISERTETEK; VAKVILAGBAN

Dornheim, Mike
REVENGE OF THE TEENAGE VIXENS FROM OUTER
SPACE, THE

Dornhelm, Robert
ECHO PARK, d

Dorning, Robert
MONA LISA; PIRATES

Doron, Rina
DAS SCHWEIGEN DES DICHTERS, cos; HASHIGAON
HAGADOL; SMILE OF THE LAMB, THE, cos

Dorrie, Doris
PARADIES, d&w

Dorsen, Gloria
HOOSIERS

Dorsey, Joe
STEWARDESS SCHOOL

Dorsey, Sandra
IMPURE THOUGHTS

Dorst, Christiane
SPRING SYMPHONY, cos

Dort, Tom Van
DE WISSELWACHTER

Dorual, Adrien
RECRUITS

Dorval, Adrien
BULLIES

dos Santos, Cosme
CHICO REI

dos Santos, Nelson Pereira
JUBIABA, d&w

Dosamantes, Susana
ESE LOCO LOCO HOSPITAL

Doskey, Janice
SEX APPEAL

Dossett, Don
SOLARBABIES, art d

Dossin, Kim
NIGHTMARE WEEKEND

Dostal, Martin
MEIER, art d

Dotan, Shimon
SMILE OF THE LAMB, THE, d; SMILE OF THE LAMB,
THE, w

Dotrice, Roy
ELIMINATORS

Doty, Kiysha
DESERT BLOOM

Doublin, Anthony
FROM BEYOND, spec eff

Doucet, Michael
BELIZAIRE THE CAJUN, m

Doucet, Mike
BELIZAIRE THE CAJUN

Doucette, Jeff
BEST OF TIMES, THE

Doud, Mike
POPULATION: ONE

Douet, Robin
MR. LOVE, p

Douglas, Bill
COMRADES, d&w

Douglas, Eric
FINE MESS, A, m/l

Douglas, James B.
BOY IN BLUE, THE

Douglas, Ken
FIRE WITH FIRE

Douglas, Kirk
TOUGH GUYS

Douglas, Mike
BEST OF TIMES, THE

Douglas, Morgan
CHOPPING MALL; LAST RESORT, THE

Douglas, Robbie
DR. OTTO AND THE RIDDLE OF THE GLOOM BEAM

Douglas, Sarah
SOLARBABIES

Douglass, Maureen
ROCINANTE

Doukoure, Cheik
BLACK MIC-MAC; BLACK MIC-MAC, w; LES FRERES
PETARD

Doumanian, John
F/X; HANNAH AND HER SISTERS; MANHATTAN
PROJECT, THE

Douridas, Chris
TEXAS CHAINSAW MASSACRE PART 2, THE

Dourif, Brad
BLUE VELVET; IMPURE THOUGHTS

Douyere, Olivier
HIGH SPEED, w

Dovletov, Ata
MUZSKOE VOSPITANIE

Dow, Ellen Albertini
TOUGH GUYS

Dowd, Kaye
VIOLATED

Dowd, M'eL
F/X

Dowdall, Jim
MY BEAUTIFUL LAUNDRETTE, stunts

Dowell, Raye
SHE'S GOTTA HAVE IT

Dowhen, Garrick
LAND OF DOOM

Downey, Brian
ADVENTURE OF FAUSTUS BIDGOOD, THE

Downey, Robert
AMERICA; AMERICA, d; AMERICA, w; BACK TO
SCHOOL

Downey, Roy L.
FINE MESS, A, spec eff

Downing, Ron
GOOD TO GO, art d

Downlearn, Richard
TRUE STORIES

Downs, Dermott
ODD JOBS

Doyen, Jacqueline
FRENCH LESSON

Doyhamboure, Yves
SUMMER

Doyle, Christophe
BLACK AND WHITE, ph

Doyle, Christopher
NAKED CAGE, THE

Doyle, Colin
CLAN OF THE CAVE BEAR, THE

Doyle, David
NO SURRENDER

Doyle, Kathleen
BRIGHTON BEACH MEMOIRS; VERY CLOSE
QUARTERS

Doyle, Keith
SHADOWS RUN BLACK

Doyle, Kelly
THRASHIN'

Doyle, Martin
CLAN OF THE CAVE BEAR, THE

Doyle, Richard
TRICK OR TREAT

Doyle, Susan
L'ULTIMO GIORNO

Doyle, Tony
EAT THE PEACH

Doyle-Murray, Brian
CLUB PARADISE; CLUB PARADISE, w; HEAD
OFFICE; LEGAL EAGLES

Drach, Michel
SAUVE-TOI, LOLA, d

Drach, Vanja
OBECANA ZEMLJA; ZA SRECU JE POTREBNO TROJE

Drago, Billy
VAMP

Dragotta, Jimi
LAST SONG

Edenfield, Eddie
BAND OF THE HAND

Edery, David
MAN FACING SOUTHEAST

Edfeldt, Catti
ALLA VI BARN I BULLERBY

Edfeldt, Tove
ALLA VI BARN I BULLERBY

Edgar, David
LADY JANE, w

Edgar, Ken
COCAINE WARS

Edgar, Wayne
RATBOY, spec eff

Edgcomb, James
JUMPIN' JACK FLASH

Edge, Johnny
ABSOLUTE BEGINNERS

Edge, The
CAPTIVE, m

Edgeworth, Patrick
COOL CHANGE, w

Edidin, Eric
FERRIS BUELLER'S DAY OFF

Edinberg, Ruth
WHERE ARE THE CHILDREN?

Edlund, Richard
BIG TROUBLE IN LITTLE CHINA, spec eff;
POLTERGEIST II, spec eff; SOLARBABIES, spec eff

Edmiston, Walker
GREAT MOUSE DETECTIVE, THE; TRANSFORMERS:
THE MOVIE, THE

Edmond, James
BOY IN BLUE, THE

Edmonds, Don
8 MILLION WAYS TO DIE

Edmundson, Bob
BELIZAIRE THE CAJUN

Edney, Beatie
HIGHLANDER

Edson, Richard
FERRIS BUELLER'S DAY OFF; HOWARD THE DUCK;
PLATOON

Eduardo
MISS MARY

Edwall, Allan
SACRIFICE, THE

Edwards, Anita
HALF MOON STREET

Edwards, Anthony
TOP GUN

Edwards, Ben
SWEET LIBERTY, prod d

Edwards, Blake
FINE MESS, A, d; THAT'S LIFE, d; THAT'S LIFE, w

Edwards, Bruce
YOUNGBLOOD

Edwards, Cassandra
SNO-LINE; VASECTOMY: A DELICATE MATTER

Edwards, Danny
OVER THE SUMMER

Edwards, Daryl
POWER

Edwards, Elizabeth
PINK CHIQUITAS, THE

Edwards, Fiona
KNIGHTS AND EMERALDS

Edwards, Geoffrey
RAD, w

Edwards, Guy
Obituaries

Edwards, Herman
BEST OF TIMES, THE

Edwards, Honey
THAT'S LIFE

Edwards, Jason
HOLLYWOOD ZAP!

Edwards, Jennifer
FINE MESS, A; THAT'S LIFE

Edwards, Joe
OVER THE SUMMER

Edwards, Louise
CLASS OF NUKE 'EM HIGH

Edwards, Lovette
NO SURRENDER

Edwards, Michael
AT CLOSE RANGE

Edwards, Paddi
BLUE CITY; STEWARDESS SCHOOL

Edwards, Percy
LABYRINTH; VALHALLA

Edwards, Ronnie Claire
NOBODY'S FOOL

Edwards, Scottie
OVER THE SUMMER

Edwards, Sheela
POPULATION: ONE

Edwards, Terry
OVER THE SUMMER

Edwards, Vaughan
SEVEN MINUTES IN HEAVEN, prod d

Edwards, Vince
SNO-LINE

Efroni, Yehuda
HASHIGAON HAGADOL

EFX Shop, The
NOBODY'S FOOL, spec eff

Egan, John
MORE THINGS CHANGE, THE

Egan, Maggie
SNO-LINE

Egan, Michael James
IN 'N' OUT, p

Egan, Rosemary
CARNAGE

Egelund, Nikolaj
TAKE IT EASY

Eger, Dennis
ONE CRAZY SUMMER, makeup

Egger, Urs
MOTTEN IM LICHT, d; MOTTEN IM LICHT, w

Eggert, Nicole
CLAN OF THE CAVE BEAR, THE

Eggleston, Colin
SKY PIRATES, d

Egizi, Mike
SUNSET STRIP, m

Egon
FRANZA, art d

Ehrenberg, Miguel
DONA HERLINDA AND HER SON, ph; SALVADOR

Ehrler, Anita
PLAYING FOR KEEPS

Ehrlich, Loy
NTTURUDU, m

Eiblmaier, Kerstin
TAROT

Eichhammer, Klaus
DIE WALSCHE, ph; MEIER, ph

Eichinger, Bernd
NAME OF THE ROSE, THE, p

Eichler, Kit
MORD I MORKET

Eiding, Paul
STEWARDESS SCHOOL; TRANSFORMERS: THE
MOVIE, THE

Eikenberry, Jill
MANHATTAN PROJECT, THE

Einarson, Odvar
X, d&w; X, p

Einhorn, Brad
PATRIOT, THE, art d

Eiseman, Jack
THE KARATE KID PART II

Eisenhardt, Bob
STRIPPER, ed

Eisenmann, Ike
GOBOTS: BATTLE OF THE ROCKLORDS

Eisman, Jack
BAD GUYS

Eisner, John
BEGINNER'S LUCK

Ejaz, Bushra
GHAME AFGHAN

Eje, Thomas
VALHALLA

Ejebrant, Lottie
BRODERNA MOZART; MIN PAPA AR TARZAN

Ejogo, Carmen
ABSOLUTE BEGINNERS

Ejve, Ingemar
JONSSONLIGAN DYKER UPP IGEN, p

Ek, Malin
BRODERNA MOZART

Ek, Niklas
BRODERNA MOZART

Ekblad, Stina
AMOROSA; ORMENS VAG PA HALLEBERGET; SUURI
ILLUSIONI

Ekborg, Anders
MOA

Ekborg, Dan
JONSSONLIGAN DYKER UPP IGEN; MOA

Ekinci, Cengiy
KURBAGALAR

Eklund, Nils
AMOROSA; MIN PAPA AR TARZAN

Ekman, Gosta
JONSSONLIGAN DYKER UPP IGEN; JONSSONLIGAN
DYKER UPP IGEN, w; MORRHAR OCH ARTOR;
MORRHAR OCH ARTOR, d; MORRHAR OCH ARTOR,
w

Ekman, Mikael
JONSSONLIGAN DYKER UPP IGEN, d;
JONSSONLIGAN DYKER UPP IGEN, w

Ekman, Sanna
MORRHAR OCH ARTOR

Ekmanner, Agneta
BRODERNA MOZART; DEN FRUSNA LEOPARDEN

Ekspres, Kurtalan
FOURTEEN NUMARA, m

El Alaily, Ezzat
EL-TOUK WA EL-ESSWERA

El Allaili, Ezzat
TAHOUNET AL SAYED FABRE

El Atrache, Naila
WHAT HAPPENED NEXT YEAR

El Charnaa, Jada
SUN ON A HAZY DAY, THE

El Cheik, Kamal
KAHIR ELZAMAN, d

El Cherii, Ammar
AL BEDAYA, m

El Deek, Bashir
AL DAHIYA, w; SIKAT SAFAR, d&w

El Fakharani, Yehia
AWDAT MOWATIN; AWDAT MOWATIN, p; LEL HAB
KESSA AKHIRA

El Feshaoui, Farouk
MESHWAR OMAR

El Ghazuli, Ali
AWDAT MOWATIN, ph

El Gindi, Nadia
AL DAHIYA

El Haj Slimane, Sabiha
AL-KAS, ed

El Hakim, Athar
KAHIR ELZAMAN

El Hakim, Hussain
AL BEDAYA

El Khamisi, Abdel Malik
SIKAT SAFAR, p

El Omari, Safiya
AL BEDAYA

El Ramli, Lenine
AL BEDAYA, w

El Wadi, Solhi
FLAMING BORDERS, m; SUN ON A HAZY DAY, THE,
m

Elazar, Irith
AVANTI POPOLO, makeup

Elcar, Dana
INSIDE OUT

Elcock, Dennis
ABSOLUTE BEGINNERS

Elders, Kevin
IRON EAGLE, w

Eleazari, Helen
AMERICA 3000

Elek, Katalin
SPACECAMP, makeup

Elfick, David
AROUND THE WORLD IN EIGHTY WAYS, p

Elfman, Danny
BACK TO SCHOOL; BACK TO SCHOOL, m; WISDOM,
m

Elfman, Howard
RAW DEAL

Elfving, Carl-Axel
MORRHAR OCH ARTOR

Elgar, Sir Edward
BEST OF TIMES, THE, m/l

Elgart, Sarah
FIRE WITH FIRE, ch; HOWARD THE DUCK, ch;
MODERN GIRLS, ch

Elias, Alix
TRUE STORIES

Elias, Christine
NUTCRACKER: THE MOTION PICTURE

Elias, Cyrus
LA BONNE

Elias, Hector
THREE AMIGOS

Elias, Jeannie
JUST BETWEEN FRIENDS

Elias, Jonathan
VAMP, m

Eliezer, Jose Roberto
FILME DEMENCIA, ph

Elig, Patricia
LE DEBUTANT

Elik, Terry
BEER

Eliopoulos, Yannis
DANILO TRELES, O FIMISMENOS ANDALOUSIANOS MOUSIKOS

Eliot, Michael
DEADLY FRIEND, ed

Eliot, Steve
DAYS OF HELL

Elizabeth
CLASS OF NUKE 'EM HIGH

Elizondo, Hector
NOTHING IN COMMON

Elizondo, Humberto
POR UN VESTIDO DE NOVIA; SALVADOR; UN HOMBRE VIOLENTE

Elizondo, Jesus
IN THE SHADOW OF KILIMANJARO, ph

Elizondo, Rafael
CONTACTO CHICANO, m

Elizondro, Rene
SUNSET STRIP

Elledge, Charles   [Charles Cowles Elledge]
Obituaries

Ellefsen, Tove
MIN PAPA AR TARZAN, d&w

Ellen, Cliff
WRONG WORLD

Ellen, Mary
LUCAS

Ellenstein, Robert
STAR TREK IV: THE VOYAGE HOME

Elley, Martin
TAKE IT EASY

Ellin, Stanley   [Stanley Bernard Ellin]
Obituaries

Elliot, Biff
THAT'S LIFE

Elliot, Chris
MANHUNTER

Elliot, Gizelle
FLIGHT OF THE NAVIGATOR

Elliot, Grant
OCEAN DRIVE WEEKEND

Elliot, Marianna
MEN'S CLUB, THE, cos

Elliot, Peter
KING KONG LIVES

Elliot, Shawn
OFF BEAT

Elliott, Chris
MY MAN ADAM

Elliott, David
POLICE ACADEMY 3: BACK IN TRAINING

Elliott, Denholm
ROOM WITH A VIEW, A; WHOOPEE BOYS, THE

Elliott, Don
AMERICAN ANTHEM, spec eff

Elliott, Jim
F/X

Elliott, John
THE KARATE KID PART II, makeup

Elliott, John R.
BLUE CITY, spec eff

Elliott, Lang
LONGSHOT, THE, p

Elliott, Mickey
LONGSHOT, THE

Elliott, Paul
ARMED RESPONSE, ph; TOMB, THE, ph

Elliott, Rick
STAND BY ME

Elliott, Ross
SCORPION

Elliott, Steve
AMERICAN ANTHEM

Elliott, Tom
AT CLOSE RANGE, m/l

Elliott, William
ABOUT LAST NIGHT, art d

Ellis, Amanda
KNIGHTS AND EMERALDS

Ellis, Bob
BULLSEYE, w; CACTUS, w

Ellis, Charles
REVENGE

Ellis, Earl
NIGHT OF THE CREEPS

Ellis, James
NO SURRENDER

Ellis, Mary
OVER THE SUMMER, cos; OVER THE SUMMER, makeup

Ellis, Sylvia
ABSOLUTE BEGINNERS

Ellis-Brown, Jeb
3:15, THE MOMENT OF TRUTH

Ellzey, David
PLAY DEAD

Elmendorf, Garry J.
BEST OF TIMES, THE, spec eff

Elmes, Frederick
BLUE VELVET, ph

Elmi, Maria Giovanna
IL BI E IL BA

Eloranta, Eeva
RIISUMINEN

Elorza, Jose
AMOR A LA VUELTA DE LA ESQUINA, m

Elphick, Michael
ARTHUR'S HALLOWED GROUND; PIRATES; VALHALLA

Elrod, Kay
SNO-LINE

Elsey, Robert
FINE MESS, A, m/l

Elswit, Robert
TRICK OR TREAT, ph

Elvegard, Charlie
GRONA GUBBAR FRAN Y.R.

Elvin, Louise
DEVIL IN THE FLESH

Elwes, Cary
LADY JANE

Elwyn, Michael
HALF MOON STREET

Elzondo, Humberto
YAKO—CAZADOR DE MALDITOS

Embden, Judi
RECRUITS

Embree, Colleen
SEPARATE VACATIONS

Emerson, Karrie
CHOPPING MALL

Emes, Ian
KNIGHTS AND EMERALDS, d&w

Emilfork, Daniel
PIRATES

Emiliano, Antonio
REPORTER X, m

Emilio
EL SECUESTRO DE LOLA-LOLA LA TRAILERA 2

Emlyn, Mari
COMING UP ROSES

Emmenegger, Pia
LISI UND DER GENERAL, m/l

Emshwiller, Susan
SORORITY HOUSE MASSACRE, art d

Enberg, Dick
LONGSHOT, THE

Ende, Michael
MOMO, w

Ender, Matthew
DEVASTATOR, THE, m

Endolf, Eddy
LA CROCE DALLE 7 PIETRE

Endoso, Ken
BIG TROUBLE IN LITTLE CHINA

Endoso, Kenny
BIG TROUBLE IN LITTLE CHINA, stunts

Enea, Carmen
DECLARATIE DE DRAGOSTE

Enescu, Adrian
DREPTATE IN LANTURI, m; NOI, CEI DIN LINIA INTII, m

Enescu, Cristina
DREPTATE IN LANTURI, ed

Engel, Andre
MAN AND A WOMAN: 20 YEARS LATER, A

Engel, Tobias
'38

Engelbach, David
AMERICA 3000, d&w

Engelbrecht, Nadja
MEIER

Engelen, Paul
LITTLE SHOP OF HORRORS, makeup

Engelhard, Katja
NOVEMBERKATZEN

Engelman, Leonard
THREE AMIGOS, makeup

Engelmann, Philipp
NOAH UND DER COWBOY

Engelson, George J.
SHADOWS RUN BLACK

Enger, Anders
BLACKOUT, p

Engin, Erdogan
KURBAGALAR, ph

Engin, Sema
WALKMAN BLUES

England, Jo
PLAYING BEATIE BOW

Engle, Harold
NO RETREAT, NO SURRENDER

Engle, Morris
Obituaries

Englefield, Nick
LETTER TO BREZHNEV, prod d

Engler, Lori-Nan
HEAD OFFICE

Engler, Rolf
DER SCHWARZE TANNER, art d

English, Ellia
WILDCATS

Englund, Bryan
Obituaries

Englund, Nina
ALLA VI BARN I BULLERBY

Englund, Robert
NEVER TOO YOUNG TO DIE

Engo, Tull
HUD, cos

Engster, Alan
SORORITY HOUSE MASSACRE

Engstrom, Ingemo
FLIGHT NORTH, d&w

Engstrom, Stig
MOA

Enli, Peng
PIAOBO QIYU, ph

Enoksen, Ivar
NATTSEILERE, w

Enrich, Teresa
CAGED GLASS, p

Enrico, Robert
ZONE ROUGE, d; ZONE ROUGE, w

Enriquez, Laarni
RAGING VENDETTA

Enriquez, Mercedes
AMIGOS

Ensign, Michael
HOUSE

Ensley, Susan
POPULATION: ONE

Eperjes, Karoly
GREAT GENERATION, THE

Ephraim, Lionel A.
INSTANT JUSTICE

Ephron, Nora
HEARTBURN, w; HEARTBURN, w

Eplin, Tom
SUNSET STRIP

Epper, Jeannie
EXTREMITIES, stunts

Epper, Tony
THRASHIN', stunts

Epps, Jack
LEGAL EAGLES, w; TOP GUN, w; People to Watch

Epps, Michael J.
SCORPION

Epstein, Temi
FRIDAY THE 13TH PART VI: JASON LIVES

Epstein, Yann
JE HAIS LES ACTEURS; LE MOME

Epting, Manfred
DER POLENWEIHER

Eran, Doron
FLASH, d; KOL AHAVO-TAI, p

Erbe, Micky
LOST!, m

Erdenbayer, D.
BI CHAMD KHAYRTAY

Erdman, Richard
STEWARDESS SCHOOL

Ergas, Debora
DELITTI

Ergun, Halil
KIRLANGIC FIRTINASI; KIRLANGIC FIRTINASI, w

Erhard, Bernard
GOBOTS: BATTLE OF THE ROCKLORDS

Eric, James
RAW DEAL; ROCKIN' ROAD TRIP; ROCKIN' ROAD
TRIP, prod d

Eric, Kai
WAY IT IS, THE

Erichsen, Bente
DREAM OF NORTHERN LIGHTS, p

Erickson, Leif   [William Wycliffe Anderson]
Obituaries

Erickson, Tina
NO RETREAT, NO SURRENDER

Ericson, Devon
SAY YES

Ericson, John
FINAL MISSION

Ericson, Karen
FINAL MISSION

Ericson, Rune
AMOROSA, ph

Eriksson, Dick
PA LIV OCH DOD

Eriksson, Elisabeth
BRODERNA MOZART

Eriksson, Sigfred
ALLA VI BARN I BULLERBY

Erkang, Zhao
CAN YUE

Erlandson, Leif
P.O.W. THE ESCAPE

Erlanger, Dominique
L'EXECUTRICE

Ernsberger, Duke
KING KONG LIVES; ROCKIN' ROAD TRIP

Ernst, Bob
JUMPIN' JACK FLASH

Ernst, Ole
BALLERUP BOULEVARD; MORD I MORKET; TAKE IT
EASY

Ernst, Robert
HELL SQUAD, ed

Eros, James
BAND OF THE HAND

Erquiaga, John
SOLDIER'S REVENGE

Errera, Nicolas
PAULETTE, m

Erskine, Chester
Obituaries

Erskine, Drummond
F/X

Ertmanis, Victor
OVERNIGHT

Ervin, Arthur
8 MILLION WAYS TO DIE

Erwin, William
STEWARDESS SCHOOL

Erwin, Yvonne
OFF BEAT

Escalada, Tito   [Roberto "Tito" Escalada]
Obituaries

Escamez, Elisa
PEQUENA REVANCHA

Escamilla, Teo
EL AMOR BRUJO, ph

Escandon, Jose
SEPARATE VACATIONS

Escardo, Vita
LA NOCHE DE LOS LAPICES

Escobar, Luis
TEO EL PELIRROJO

Escobedo, Richard
SHADOWS RUN BLACK

Escoffier, Jean-Yves
MAUVAIS SANG, ph

Escorel, Lauro
EU SEI QUE VOU TE AMAR, ph

Escovedo, Javier
BLUE CITY, m/l

Escriva, Eugenia
MONSTER DOG, cos

Esguerra, Donald
EL TREN DE LOS PIONEROS

Eshelman, Kevin
PLATOON

Eslami, Hadi
BUS, THE

Esmaeili, Habib
CLOSED CIRCUIT

Esparza, Moctesuma
RADIOACTIVE DREAMS, p

Espasande, Angel
UN HOMBRE DE EXITO

Espina, Luis
LA MANSION DE ARAUCAIMA, ed

Espinosa, Jose Angel
QUE ME MATEN DE UNA VEZ

Espinosa, Pedro
PERROS DE LA NOCHE, w

Espinoza, James
OUT OF BOUNDS

Espinoza, Salvatore
DOWN AND OUT IN BEVERLY HILLS

Esposito, Giancarlo
MAXIMUM OVERDRIVE

Esposito, Tony
CAMORRA, m; LA BALLATA DI EVA, m

Esposti, Piera Degli
LE MAL D'AIMER

Esprit, Patrick St.
FIRE IN THE NIGHT

Essex, Jon
Obituaries

Estanillo, Manuel
AMIGOS

Esteban, Julio
MAMBRU SE FUE A LA GUERRA, set d; VIAJE A
NINGUNA PARTE, set d&cos

Estelle, Laara
NUTCRACKER: THE MOTION PICTURE

Ester, Jenny
AMERICAN ANTHEM

Estevez, Emilio
MAXIMUM OVERDRIVE; WISDOM; WISDOM, d&w

Estrada Aguirre, Jose
Obituaries

Estrada, Anne Isabelle
BLACK AND WHITE, art d

Estregan, George
KILLING OF SATAN, THE; REVENGE FOR
JUSTICE

Estrin, Melvyn J.
STRIPPER, p

Estrin, Suellen
IMAGEMAKER, THE

Esztergalyos, Cecilia
KOJAK BUDAPESTEN; VAKVILAGBAN

Etaix, Pierre
MAX MON AMOUR

Etienne, Elisabeth
FEMMES DE PERSONNE

Etoh, Masaharu
ADVENTURES OF THE AMERICAN RABBIT, THE, p

Ettari, Anthony
FAT GUY GOES NUTZOID!!

Ettari, Thomas
FAT GUY GOES NUTZOID!!

Ettelson, Jack
SCORPION

Eubank, John
DR. OTTO AND THE RIDDLE OF THE GLOOM BEAM

Eugeni, Marina
TOMMASO BLU

Evans, Al
DIRT BIKE KID, THE

Evans, Aled
MILWR BYCHAN, ed

Evans, Angelo
SAVING GRACE

Evans, Art
JO JO DANCER, YOUR LIFE IS CALLING; NATIVE
SON; RUTHLESS PEOPLE

Evans, Bruce A.
STAND BY ME, p; STAND BY ME, w

Evans, Deborah K.
NEVER TOO YOUNG TO DIE, set d

Evans, Gil
ABSOLUTE BEGINNERS, m; ABSOLUTE BEGINNERS,
md

Evans, John H.
BLUE CITY

Evans, John Robert
POWER

Evans, Murray
YOUNGBLOOD

Evans, Ray
MONA LISA, m/l

Evans, Robin
FIRE IN THE NIGHT

Evans, Roger Pugh
MILWR BYCHAN, ph

Evans, Steve Jones
MORE THINGS CHANGE, THE, set d

Evans, Terry
BLUE CITY, m/l

Evans, Troy
MODERN GIRLS

Evanson, Ted
WHAT COMES AROUND, p

Evein, Bernard
THERESE, art d

Evensen, Caspar
X

Evenson, Kim
BIG BET, THE

Everett, Rupert
DUET FOR ONE

Everett, Tom
EXTREMITIES; HOLLYWOOD VICE SQUAD

Evers, Brian
BRIGHTON BEACH MEMOIRS; EAT AND RUN

Everson, Corinna
MORNING AFTER, THE

Evert, Ken
TEXAS CHAINSAW MASSACRE PART 2, THE

Evison, Pat
EMMA'S WAR

Evora, Cesar
CAPABLANCA; UN HOMBRE DE EXITO

Evrard, Clause
PAULETTE

Evro, Katerina
ZA KUDE PUTOVATE

Evstigneev, Evgeny
ZIMNI VECHER V GAGRAKH

Ewande, Lydia
BLACK MIC-MAC

Ewart, John
BIG HURT, THE

Ewen, Lesley
FIRE WITH FIRE

Ewer, Donald
BEER; JUDGEMENT IN STONE, A

Ewers, Mark
AMERICAN ANTHEM

Ewing, Michele
SNO-LINE

Excoffier, Stephane
BABEL OPERA, OU LA REPETITION DE DON JUAN ;
DE WISSELWACHTER

Eychenne, Jean-Pierre
JEAN DE FLORETTE, makeup; MANON DES SOURCES,
makeup

Eyk, Tonny
MARIA, m; THOMAS EN SENIOR OP HET SPOOR
VAN BRUTE BEREND, m

Eyzaguirre, Joaquin
NEMESIO

Ezralow, Daniel
CAMORRA; CAMORRA, ch

Ezzat, Abou Bak
AL KETTAR

Ezzidi, Saadia
FLAMING BORDERS

Faber, Peter
MAMA IS BOOS!

Fabian, Francoise
FAUBOURG SAINT-MARTIN

Fabien, Rachel
EVERY TIME WE SAY GOODBYE, w

Fabregas, Jimmy
REVENGE FOR JUSTICE, m

Fabrizi, Aldo
GIOVANNI SENZAPENSIERI

Fabrizi, Franco
GINGER & FRED; GIOVANNI SENZAPENSIERI

Facello, Abel
EL RIGOR DEL DESTINO, set d; MAN FACING
SOUTHEAST, art d

Fachini, Patrizia
ROMANCE

Fadel, Noutil
TAHOUNET AL SAYED FABRE, m

Faeth, William H.
DEADLY FRIEND

Faget, Hugette
FRENCH LESSON

Faget-Benard, George
NIGHTMARE WEEKEND, art d; NIGHTMARE
WEEKEND, w

Fagundes, Antonio
JOGO DURO

Fah, Beat
DER SCHWARZE TANNER

Fahey, Donald
DR. OTTO AND THE RIDDLE OF THE GLOOM BEAM

Fahey, Jeff
PSYCHO III

Fahey, Murray
DEAD-END DRIVE-IN

Fahey, Patrick
SORORITY HOUSE MASSACRE

Fahr, Hermann
BLIND DIRECTOR, THE, ph

Fahrmann, Tom
SCHWARZ UND OHNE ZUCKER, ph

Fai, Law Wing
DREAM LOVERS, m

Fails, J.W.
NO RETREAT, NO SURRENDER; VENDETTA

Faiman, Peter
"CROCODILE" DUNDEE, d

Fainello, Roberta
UNA CASA IN BILICO, p

Fairchild, Max
DEATH OF A SOLDIER

Fairfax, Kaarin
AROUND THE WORLD IN EIGHTY WAYS

Fairman, Blain
ALIENS

Fairminer, Paul
ABSOLUTE BEGINNERS

Faison, Frankie
MANHUNTER; MAXIMUM OVERDRIVE; MONEY PIT,
THE; MONEY PIT, THE

Faison, Matthew
FRIDAY THE 13TH PART VI: JASON LIVES; PRAY
FOR DEATH; TOUGH GUYS

Falardeau, Pierre
ELVIS GRATTON, LE KING DES KINGS, d

Falcao, Adriana
UNA NOTTE DI PIOGGIA

Falcao, Felipe
AS SETE VAMPIRAS

Falch, John
P.O.W. THE ESCAPE

Falch, Michael
MORD I MORKET

Falck, Michael
MORD I MORKET, m

Falck, Susanne
ALLA VI BARN I BULLERBY, cos; ORMENS VAG PA
HALLEBERGET, cos

Falco, Mirella
IL GIARDINO DEGLI INGANNI

Falcon, Andre
27 HORAS

Falcon, Yoleigret
PEQUENA REVANCHA

Falcone, Gary
NINJA TURF, m

Falconer, Sheila
LADY JANE, ch

Faldermeyer, Frank
PLAYING FOR KEEPS

Falenius, Yrsa
BRODERNA MOZART

Falk, Christian "Crillan"
DEN FRUSNA LEOPARDEN

Falk, Franz-Rudolf
LE PALTOQUET, d&w

Falk, Lauritz
AMOROSA

Falk, Lisanne
VIOLATED

Falk, Mek Pek
TAKE IT EASY

Falk, Peter
BIG TROUBLE

Falk, Suzy
MERCI MONSIEUR ROBERTSON

Falkenberg, Paul
Obituaries

Falkenhain, Patricia
HEARTBURN; SOMETHING WILD

Falkman, Loa
BRODERNA MOZART

Fall, Cheikh
ROUND MIDNIGHT

Fallender, Deborah
VAMP

Fallisi, Giuseppe
L'ULTIMA MAZURKA

Fallon, Edward
HELLFIRE

Fallquist, Doris
BRODERNA MOZART

Fallwell, Marshall
AT CLOSE RANGE

Falsini, Milly
IL GIARDINO DEGLI INGANNI

Faltermeyer, Harold
TOP GUN, m

Faltmeier, Harold
FIRE WITH FIRE, m/l

Falzoni, Giodano
NAME OF THE ROSE, THE

Fan, Fung Sui
LUNATICS, THE

Fanara, Shauna
CLAN OF THE CAVE BEAR, THE

Fanari, Mohamed Mournir
AL ASHEKE, d

Fanelli, Rita
SCREEN TEST

Fanetti, Pasquale
UNA STORIA AMBIGUA, ph

Fanfara, Stephan
RECRUITS, ed

Fang, Nei
TIME TO LIVE AND A TIME TO DIE, A

Fang, Wan
REZHOU, w

Fange, Eva
BRODERNA MOZART, makeup; LOVE ME!, makeup

Fann, Al
CROSSROADS

Fannon, Kathleen
VIOLETS ARE BLUE

Fansten, Jacques
ETATS D'AME, d&w

Fantasia, Franco
SQUADRA SELVAGGIA

Fantini, Michael
CARE BEARS MOVIE II: A NEW GENERATION

Farad, Chkili
HADDA, p

Farag, Samir
EL-SADA EL-RIGAL, ph

Faragher, Davey
BACK TO SCHOOL

Farago, Katinka
SACRIFICE, THE, p

Faraldo, Claude
FLAGRANT DESIR, d&w

Farc, Abrao
NEM TUDO E VERDADE

Farcy, Bernard
PARENTAL CLAIM

Fardon, Liz
SHORT CHANGED, makeup

Fardoulis, Monique
INSPECTEUR LAVARDIN, ed

Farelly, Edward
CUT AND RUN

Fares, Radid
LAST IMAGE, THE

Faress, Souad
MY BEAUTIFUL LAUNDRETTE

Farfen, Jorge
LOS ASES DE CONTRABANDO, spec eff

Fargey, Jillian
CLOSE TO HOME

Fargnoli, Steve
UNDER THE CHERRY MOON, p

Farhang, Daryoosh
BUS, THE, w; MIRZA NOWROUZ' SHOES, w

Faria, Betty
JUBIABA

Faria, Rosa Lobato
O VESTIDO COR DE FOGO

Farias, Lui
COM LICENCA, EU VOU A LUTA, d; COM LICENCA,
EU VOU A LUTA, w

Farias, Marise
BRAS CUBAS; COM LICENCA, EU VOU A LUTA

Farias, Reginaldo
COM LICENCA, EU VOU A LUTA

Farias, Roberto
COM LICENCA, EU VOU A LUTA, w

Farid, Aamir
GHAME AFGHAN

Farida, Jenny
INTRUDER, THE

Faridee, Humayun
DAHAN

Farina, Dennis
JO JO DANCER, YOUR LIFE IS CALLING;
MANHUNTER

Farina, Felice
SEMBRA MORTO . . . MA E SOLO SVENUTO, d;
SEMBRA MORTO . . . MA E SOLO SVENUTO, w

Fariselli, Patrizio
FOXTRAP, m

Farkas, Emil
VENDETTA, w

Farkas, Ferenc
KESERU IGAZSAG, m

Farkas, Pedro
CINEMA FALADO, ph

Farley, Albert
L'APACHE BIANCO

Farley, Jack L.
LOW BLOW

Farley, Oliver "Ollie"
8 MILLION WAYS TO DIE

Farley, Teresa
BREEDERS

Farmer, Loren
AVENGING FORCE

Farmer, Margaret
NUTCRACKER: THE MOTION PICTURE

Farmer, Mimsy
LA RAGAZZA DEI LILLA; SENSI

Farmer, Woody
LOW BLOW

Farnese, Tatiana
GIOVANNI SENZAPENSIERI

Faro, Caroline
SINCERELY CHARLOTTE

Farocki, Harun
CLASS RELATIONS

Farouge, Mohamed Mouri
SUN ON A HAZY DAY, THE, w

Farquhar, Anne
BOY IN BLUE, THE

Farr, Derek
Obituaries

Farr, Felicia
THAT'S LIFE

Farr, Gary
SALVADOR

Farr, Glenn
NOTHING IN COMMON, ed

Farr, Judi
FOR LOVE ALONE

Farrar, Bob
PLAY DEAD, m

Farre, Jean-Paul
PAULETTE

Farrel, Nicholas
PLAYING AWAY

Farrell, Jeff
REVENGE OF THE TEENAGE VIXENS FROM OUTER SPACE, THE, d; REVENGE OF THE TEENAGE VIXENS FROM OUTER SPACE, THE, p; REVENGE OF THE TEENAGE VIXENS FROM OUTER SPACE, THE, ph; REVENGE OF THE TEENAGE VIXENS FROM OUTER SPACE, THE, w

Farrell, Sondra
LAND OF DOOM

Farrell, Terry
BACK TO SCHOOL

Farren, Chris
LUCAS, m/l

Farris, Steve
FINE MESS, A, m/l

Farrow, Mia
HANNAH AND HER SISTERS

Farrow, Moses
HANNAH AND HER SISTERS

Fastabend, Tricia
FERRIS BUELLER'S DAY OFF

Fat, Chow Yun
BETTER TOMORROW, A; DREAM LOVERS; LUNATICS, THE

Fatiushin, Aleksandr
ODINOTCHNOYE PLAVANIYE

Fauchois, Rene
DOWN AND OUT IN BEVERLY HILLS, w

Faucon, Guy
THERESE

Fauntleroy, George
HOLLYWOOD VICE SQUAD

Fauron, Patricia
LE BONHEUR A ENCORE FRAPPE, p

Faussett, Peter
YOUNGBLOOD

Fava, Stefano
MANHUNTER, makeup

Favre, Francois
BLACK MIC-MAC, w

Fawcett, Farrah
EXTREMITIES

Fawdon, Michele
TRAVELLING NORTH

Fay, William
JAKE SPEED, p

Faybus, Mark
THREE AMIGOS, set d

Fayed, Dodi
F/X, p

Fecht, Ozay
FORTY SQUARE METERS OF GERMANY

Feder, David
SLOANE, p

Fedossov, Valeri
MOI DRUG IVAN LAPSHIN, ph; NEBYVALSHINA, ph

Feelies, The
SOMETHING WILD

Feeney, Donald A.
COLOR OF MONEY, THE

Feeney, Thomas
CLASS OF NUKE 'EM HIGH

Feferman, Linda
SEVEN MINUTES IN HEAVEN, d; SEVEN MINUTES IN HEAVEN, w

Fegan, Jorge
EL NARCO—DUELO ROJO; MATANZA EN MATAMOROS

Feger, John
DR. OTTO AND THE RIDDLE OF THE GLOOM BEAM

Feher, Anna
ORDOGI KISERTETEK

Fehr, Kaja
TOUGH GUYS, ed

Feijoo, Beda Docampo
DEBAJO DEL MUNDO, d; MISS MARY, w

Feik, Eberhard
DER POLENWEIHER

Feinberg, Nina
MANHATTAN PROJECT, THE, ed

Feirri, Bruna
FOTOROMANZO

Feist, Emil
NAME OF THE ROSE, THE

Feitosa, Tairone
O HOMEM DA CAPA PRETA, w

Felba, Drag
WILD WIND, THE

Feld, Lydia
MAINE-OCEAN; MAINE-OCEAN, w

Felder, Clarence
RUTHLESS PEOPLE

Feldman, Corey
STAND BY ME

Feldman, Dennis
GOLDEN CHILD, THE, w

Feldman, Edward S.
GOLDEN CHILD, THE, p; HAMBURGER, p

Feldman, Phil
STEWARDESS SCHOOL, p

Feldman, Shari
HAMBURGER, cos

Feldman, Stephen
HOT CHILI, m/l

Feldman, Tibor
FAT GUY GOES NUTZOID!!

Feldner, Sheldon
HOWARD THE DUCK

Felicijan, Irena
KORMORAN, cos

Felix, Maryse
PAULETTE, makeup

Felleghy, Tom
SAVING GRACE

Fellini, Federico
GINGER & FRED, d; GINGER & FRED, w

Fellman, Florence
PLAYING FOR KEEPS, set d

Fellner, Eric
SID AND NANCY, p

Fellows, Don
HAUNTED HONEYMOON

Felperlan, Marc
FLODDER, ph

Femenia, Paco
EL HERMANO BASTARDO DE DIOS, ph

Fendel, Rosemarie
MOMO, w

Feng, T'ien
TIME TO LIVE AND A TIME TO DIE, A

Fenger, Eva
BRODERNA MOZART, cos

Fengxu, Li
QINGCHUN JI

Fenn, Sherilyn
THRASHIN'; WRAITH, THE

Fenn, Suzanne
ANGEL RIVER, ed

Fenton, Betsy
NUTCRACKER: THE MOTION PICTURE

Fenton, George
CLOCKWISE, m

Fenwick, Perry
MONA LISA

Fenz, Silvia
STAMMHEIM

Ferari, Hahela
LIJEPE ZENE PROLAZE KROZ GRAD

Ferdag, Ferda
KUYUCAKLI YUSUF

Ferell, Conchata
WHERE THE RIVER RUNS BLACK

Ferguson, Denise
KILLER PARTY

Ferguson, Don
WELCOME TO 18, set d

Ferguson, J. Don
MAXIMUM OVERDRIVE

Ferguson, Jay
PATRIOT, THE, m; QUIET COOL, m

Ferguson, Larry
HIGHLANDER, w

Ferguson, Nancye
HOLLYWOOD ZAP!

Ferjac, Anouk
PARENTAL CLAIM

Ferlo, Laura
EL SECUESTRO DE LOLA-LOLA LA TRAILERA 2, ph

Fernan-Gomez, Fernando
MAMBRU SE FUE A LA GUERRA; MAMBRU SE FUE A LA GUERRA, d

Fernandes, Joao
HOLLYWOOD VICE SQUAD, ph

Fernandes, Remo
TRIKAL

Fernandez, Abel
QUICKSILVER

Fernandez, Angel Luis
MATADOR, ph

Fernandez, Benjamin
TAI-PAN, art d

Fernandez, Don
SUNSET STRIP, set d

Fernandez, Elios
VISA U.S.A.

Fernandez, Emilio
Obituaries; PIRATES

Fernandez, Javier
RAGE, set d

Fernandez, Juan
SALVADOR

Fernandez, Margarita
HOWARD THE DUCK

Fernandez, Raul
EL SECUESTRO DE LOLA-LOLA LA TRAILERA 2, d

Fernandez, Robert
THE KARATE KID PART II

Fernandez, Rolando
EL SECUESTRO DE LOLA-LOLA LA TRAILERA 2, w

Fernandez, Rudy
RAGING VENDETTA; REVENGE FOR JUSTICE

Fernandez, Vicente
PICARDIA MEXICANA NUMERO DOS; POR UN VESTIDO DE NOVIA, w

Fernando, Giancarlo
DETECTIVE SCHOOL DROPOUTS, ph

Ferran, Pascale
GARDIEN DE LA NUIT, w

Ferrando, Giancarlo
GIURO CHE TI AMO, ph; SQUADRA SELVAGGIA, ph

Ferrante, Emanuel
FAT GUY GOES NUTZOID!!

Ferrante, Russell
WIRED TO KILL, m

Ferrara, Carolina
LA STORIA, cos

Ferrara, Consuelo
IL CASO MORO

Ferrara, Frank
MANHATTAN PROJECT, THE; MANHATTAN PROJECT, THE, stunts; RAW DEAL; SWEET LIBERTY

Ferrara, Giuseppe
IL CASO MORO, d; IL CASO MORO, w

Ferrara, Juan
NOCHE DE JUERGA

Ferrara, Paolo
RAGE, p

Ferrara, Peter S.
SAY YES, d&w

Ferrara, Pino
IL CASO MORO

Ferrari, Ariel
DOT AND KEETO, anim

Ferrari, Isabella
IL RAGAZZO DEL PONY EXPRESS

Ferrario, Cesare
IL MOSTRO DI FIRENZE, d; IL MOSTRO DI FIRENZE, w

Ferrario, Davide
45MO PARALLELO, w

Ferraz, Helio Paula
EU SEI QUE VOU TE AMAR, p

Ferre, Francesca
LE MINIERE DEL KILIMANGIARO

Ferrell, Kristi
SPIKER

Ferren, Bran
LITTLE SHOP OF HORRORS, spec eff; MANHATTAN PROJECT, THE; MANHATTAN PROJECT, THE, spec eff

Ferreol, Andrea
DOUCE FRANCE; SUIVEZ MON REGARD

Ferrer, Filipe
REPORTER X

Ferrer, Jose
BLOODY BIRTHDAY

Ferrer, Lupita
BALBOA

Ferrer, Sean
GOOD TO GO, p

Ferrere, Jesus
MATADOR, w

Ferreri, Andrea
LA SECONDA NOTTE, w

Ferreri, Marco
I LOVE YOU, d; I LOVE YOU, w

Ferrero, Lorenzo
ANEMIA, m

Ferrero, Martin
MODERN GIRLS

Ferret, Eve
ABSOLUTE BEGINNERS; FOREIGN BODY; HAUNTED HONEYMOON

Ferreti, Diana
LOS ASES DE CONTRABANDO

Ferretti, Daniele
NAME OF THE ROSE, THE

Ferretti, Dante
GINGER & FRED, art d; NAME OF THE ROSE, THE, prod d

Ferretti, Diane
YAKO—CAZADOR DE MALDITOS

Ferri, Mark
ROCKIN' ROAD TRIP

Ferrier, Noel
GREAT EXPECTATIONS—THE AUSTRALIAN STORY

Ferriere, Catherine
MERCI MONSIEUR ROBERTSON

Ferriere, Martine
FRENCH LESSON

Ferrini, Franco
DEMONI 2—L'INCUBO RITORNA, w; UNA SPINA NEL CUORE, w

Ferrini, Maurizio
IL CAMMISSARIO LO GATTO

Ferro, Pablo
AMERICA

Ferry, April
BIG TROUBLE IN LITTLE CHINA, cos

Ferry, Bryan
FIRE WITH FIRE, m/l

Fersen, Allesandro
GIOVANNI SENZAPENSIERI

Fessler, Uli
WELCOME IN VIENNA, cos

Festa Campanile, Pasquale
Obituaries

Fiedel, Brad
DESERT BLOOM, m

Fiedler, Bea
HOT CHILI

Fiedlerova, Radka
PAVUCINA

Field, Chris
SCREEN TEST

Field, Elizabeth
ONE CRAZY SUMMER

Field, Hermann
ANGRY HARVEST, w

Field, Patrick
KNIGHTS AND EMERALDS

Field, Shirley Anne
MY BEAUTIFUL LAUNDRETTE

Field, Susan
CLOCKWISE

Fields, Adam
WHOOPEE BOYS, THE, p

Fields, Charlie
MANHATTAN PROJECT, THE

Fields, Edith
ARMED AND DANGEROUS; BIG TROUBLE

Fields, Freddie
CRIMES OF THE HEART, p

Fields, Greg
BACK TO SCHOOL, w

Fields, Maurie
CACTUS; DEATH OF A SOLDIER

Fields, Scott
DANGEROUSLY CLOSE, w

Fields, Tony
TRICK OR TREAT

Fieldsteel, Robert
POWER

Fierberg, Steven
SEVEN MINUTES IN HEAVEN, ph

Fierry, Patrick
JOUR ET NUIT

Fieschi, Jacques
POLICE, w

Figueiredo, Luciano
BRAS CUBAS, art d

Figueroa, Gabriel
EL MALEFICIO II, p

Figuerosa, Lisa
RATBOY

Figuly, Deborah
THAT'S LIFE; THAT'S LIFE, makeup

Figuly, Debra
LONGSHOT, THE, makeup

Figus, Lisa
ARMED AND DANGEROUS

Filac, Vilko
DO YOU REMEMBER DOLLY BELL?, ph

Filatov, Leonid
CHICHERIN

Filho, Daniel
QUILOMBO

Filho, Escorel
SONHO SEM FIM, w

Filho, Lauro Escorel
QUILOMBO, ph; SONHO SEM FIM, d

Filiault, Tom
MONEY PIT, THE

Filimonovi, Pavel
POTERYALSYA SLON, ph

Filipaswili, Archil
SAPIRHURIN, ph

Filipov, Valery
ZIMNI VECHER V GAGRAKH, art d

Filippini, Emidio Greco
EHRENGARD, w

Filippini, Enrico
EHRENGARD, w

Filippo, Luigi De
GIOVANNI SENZAPENSIERI

Filpi, Carmen
HOLLYWOOD ZAP!; MY CHAUFFEUR

Finan, Paul
PLAYING FOR KEEPS

Finazzo, Giselle
UNDER THE CHERRY MOON

Finbow, Colin
SCHOOL FOR VANDALS, d; SCHOOL FOR VANDALS, ed; SCHOOL FOR VANDALS, w

Finch, Brett
AMERICAN ANTHEM

Fincher, Ed
PRAY FOR DEATH, cos

Findlater, John
SOLDIER'S REVENGE

Findlay, Ian
TOBY MCTEAGUE

Findlay, Roberta
TENEMENT, d; TENEMENT, ph

Findley, Alistair
HIGHLANDER

Findley, Jim
PASSION OF REMEMBRANCE, THE

Fine, Larry
STOOGEMANIA

Finegan, James
GIRLS SCHOOL SCREAMERS

Finegan, James W.
GIRLS SCHOOL SCREAMERS, p

Finegan, John P.
GIRLS SCHOOL SCREAMERS, d&w; GIRLS SCHOOL SCREAMERS, p; GIRLS SCHOOL SCREAMERS, prod d

Finfer, David
INSIDE OUT, ed; SOUL MAN, ed

Fink, Charles
ONE MORE SATURDAY NIGHT

Fink, Eric
BOY IN BLUE, THE

Fink, Margaret
FOR LOVE ALONE, p

Finkel, Fyvush
BRIGHTON BEACH MEMOIRS; OFF BEAT

Finkelman, Wayne
GOLDEN CHILD, THE, cos

Finkelman, Wayne A.
WILDCATS, cos

Finkleman, Ken
HEAD OFFICE, d&w

Finkleman, Wayne
STEWARDESS SCHOOL, cos

Finland, Natalie
LABYRINTH

Finlay, Andrena
EMMA'S WAR, p

Finlayson, Bruce
COMRADES, cos

Finley, Greg
AMERICAN JUSTICE; DANGEROUSLY CLOSE; MURPHY'S LAW; VAMP; WILD WIND, THE

Finn, George
YOUNGBLOOD

Finn, Oscar Barney
CONTAR HASTA TEN, p&d

Finn-Chapman, Dianne
SEVEN MINUTES IN HEAVEN, cos

Finnegan, John
AMERICAN TAIL, AN; BIG TROUBLE

Finnegan, Tom
LONGSHOT, THE

Finnerty, James
INSTANT JUSTICE

Finney, Shirley Jo
ECHO PARK

Finstad, Liv
HARD ASFALT, d&w

Finzi, Linda
MY MAN ADAM

Fiola, Emily
NIGHT OF THE CREEPS

Fioramonti, Gloria
CHOKE CANYON

Fiore, John
ONE CRAZY SUMMER

Fiorentini, Enrico
LET'S HOPE IT'S A GIRL, art d

Fiorentini, Fiorenzo
LA STORIA

Fioretti, Dante
SQUADRA SELVAGGIA

Fiorino, Paolo
LA CROCE DALLE 7 PIETRE

Fiormonti, Glory
RADIOACTIVE DREAMS

Fioroni, Alexa
UNDER THE CHERRY MOON

Fioruni, Fred
YOUNGBLOOD

Firackiewicz, Piotr
HEIDENLOCHER

Fire House
KIND OF ENGLISH, A, m

Firestone, Ken
NO RETREAT, NO SURRENDER

Firpo, Florencia
BAD COMPANY

First, Hugo
ABSOLUTE BEGINNERS

Firstenberg, Sam
AVENGING FORCE, d

Firth, Julian
ABSOLUTE BEGINNERS

Firth, Peter
LETTER TO BREZHNEV

Fischbach, Erica
NUTCRACKER: THE MOTION PICTURE

Fischel, Matt
EAT AND RUN

Fischer, Gunther
DAS HAUS AM FLUSS, m

Fischer, Jens
ALLA VI BARN I BULLERBY, ph

Fischer, Joschka
VA BANQUE

Fischer, Kai
50/50

Fischer, Vera
QUILOMBO

Fischer, William
TENEMENT, m

Fischerova, Tatana
LEV S BILOU HRIVOU

Fischetti, Michael
F/X

Fiset, Nicole
NUTCRACKER: THE MOTION PICTURE

Fish, Nancy
HOWARD THE DUCK

Fishburne, Larry
BAND OF THE HAND; QUICKSILVER

Fisher, Al [Al Fichera]
Obituaries

Fisher, Carrie
HANNAH AND HER SISTERS; HOLLYWOOD VICE SQUAD

Fisher, George
MORNING AFTER, THE

Fisher, Gerry
HIGHLANDER, ph

Fisher, Gregor
BLOOD RED ROSES

Fisher, Jack
SUNSET STRIP

Fisher, Judith
AROUND THE WORLD IN EIGHTY WAYS

Fishgoit, Mikhail
VERY CLOSE QUARTERS, prod d

Fishman, Bill
MOVIE HOUSE MASSACRE, ph

Fishman, Hal
WISDOM

Fisk, Jack
VIOLETS ARE BLUE, d

Fisk, Martin
TERRY ON THE FENCE

Fiske, Michael
IMAGEMAKER, THE

Fitz-Gerald, Lewis
MORE THINGS CHANGE, THE

Fitzgerald, Brian
NOBODY'S FOOL

Fitzgerald, Dan
BAND OF THE HAND

Fitzgerald, Geraldine
POLTERGEIST II

Fitzgerald, Ron
MANHUNTER

Fitzhugh, Ellen
GREAT MOUSE DETECTIVE, THE; GREAT MOUSE
DETECTIVE, THE, m/l

Fitzsimmons, David
MANHUNTER

Fjeldmose, Grith
BRODERNA MOZART

Flack, Herbert
FLODDER; SPRINGEN

Flagherty, Jean
BEST MAN, THE

Flaherty, Dianna-Jean
CLASS OF NUKE 'EM HIGH

Flaherty, Joe
CLUB PARADISE; ONE CRAZY SUMMER

Flaiano, Ennio
L'INCHIESTA, w

Flaksman, Marcos
RUNNING OUT OF LUCK, prod d; STREETS OF GOLD,
prod d; WHERE THE RIVER RUNS BLACK, prod d

Flaksman, Paulo
WHERE THE RIVER RUNS BLACK, art d

Flamant, Jean-Claude
WOLF AT THE DOOR, THE

Flamini, Andrea
SALOME

Flanagan, Fionnula
YOUNGBLOOD

Flanagan, John
ARTHUR'S HALLOWED GROUND

Flanagan, Michael
MORNING AFTER, THE; SWEET LIBERTY

Flanagan, Neil
Obituaries; HOLLYWOOD ZAP!

Flather, Catherine
CLAN OF THE CAVE BEAR, THE

Flea
TOUGH GUYS

Fleck, John
HOWARD THE DUCK

Fleckenstein, John
MEN'S CLUB, THE, ph

Fleeks, Eric
BAD GUYS ; CHECK IS IN THE MAIL, THE

Fleeman, Gregory
F/X, w

Fleer, Alicia
KILLER PARTY

Fleetwood, Susan
SACRIFICE, THE

Fleischer, Charles
DEADLY FRIEND

Fleming, Bill
LOST!, art d

Fleming, Edie
PLAYING FOR KEEPS

Fleming, Edward
BALLERUP BOULEVARD

Fleming, John F.
EAT AND RUN

Fleming, Paul
REVENGE OF THE TEENAGE VIXENS FROM OUTER
SPACE, THE

Fleming, Roger
DR. OTTO AND THE RIDDLE OF THE GLOOM BEAM,
stunts

Fleming, William
BUSTED UP, set d

Flemming
YES, DET ER FAR!

Flesch, Gunther
STAMMHEIM

Fletcher, Dexter
CARAVAGGIO

Fletcher, Jack
OFF BEAT

Fletcher, Louise
INVADERS FROM MARS; NOBODY'S FOOL

Fletcher, Robert
STAR TREK IV: THE VOYAGE HOME, cos

Fletcher, Suzanne
SLEEPWALK

Fletcher-Cook, Graham
ABSOLUTE BEGINNERS

Fleury, Jean-Claude
CHARLOTTE FOR EVER, p; PAULETTE, p

Fleury, Pete
ODD JOBS

Flimm, Dieter
STAMMHEIM, set d

Flimm, Jurgen
STAMMHEIM, p

Flinck, Thorsten
MIN PAPA AR TARZAN

Flipo, Nicole
FUTURE OF EMILY, THE, p

Flippov, Roman
BORIS GODUNOV

Floersheim, Patrick
JE HAIS LES ACTEURS

Flora
X

Florance, Sheila
CACTUS

Florek, Dann
SWEET LIBERTY

Flores, Gabriela
NIGHTMARE'S PASSENGERS; PERROS DE LA
NOCHE

Flores, Marco
EL SECUESTRO DE CAMARENA, m

Flores, Rose
VENDETTA

Flores, Ursula
WOMEN'S PRISON MASSACRE

Floret, Alain
PRUNELLE BLUES; TAXI BOY

Floria, Emma
CLAN OF THE CAVE BEAR, THE

Florio, Francesca
SPOSERO SIMON LE BON

Flowers, Sher
NO RETREAT, NO SURRENDER, makeup

Floyd, Charles R.
P.O.W. THE ESCAPE

Fluegel, Darlanne
RUNNING SCARED; TOUGH GUYS

Fluker, Perry
BIG TROUBLE

Flumeri, Elisabetta
GINGER & FRED

Flye, Catherine
IMAGEMAKER, THE

Flygare, Claus
ET SKUD FRA HJERTET

Flynn, Brock
DR. OTTO AND THE RIDDLE OF THE GLOOM BEAM

Flynn, Daniel
BIGGLES

Flynn, Jeremy
COMRADES

Flynn, John
IMAGEMAKER, THE

Flynn, Michael
CHOKE CANYON

Flynn, Nick
POWER

Flynn, Owen
BREEDERS

Flyte, Ellis
LABYRINTH, cos

Foad, Hala
EL-SADA EL-RIGAL

Focas, Spiros
BLACK TUNNEL

Focine
EL TREN DE LOS PIONEROS, p

Foerch, Doug
AMERICAN ANTHEM

Fogarty, Gerry
NO SURRENDER

Fogle, Adeen
LITTLE SHOP OF HORRORS

Foglietti, Emanuele
UN RAGAZZO COME TANTI, ed

Folet, Lucien
THERESE

Foley, B.L.
PATRIOT, THE

Foley, Brian
FLYING, ph

Foley, Gary
DOGS IN SPACE

Foley, James
AT CLOSE RANGE; AT CLOSE RANGE, d

Foley, Joan
MEN'S CLUB, THE

Foley, Patty
IN THE SHADOW OF KILIMANJARO

Folguera, Juan
EL SUIZO—UN AMOUR EN ESPAGNE

Folk, Robert
ODD JOBS, m; POLICE ACADEMY 3: BACK IN
TRAINING, m; STEWARDESS SCHOOL, m

Folsey, George
THREE AMIGOS, p

Fonda, Jane
MORNING AFTER, THE

Fondacaro, Phil
TROLL

Foner, Naomi
VIOLETS ARE BLUE, w

Fong, Allen
JUST LIKE THE WEATHER; JUST LIKE THE
WEATHER, d

Fong, Brackie
ARMOUR OF GOD, THE

Fong, Leo
LOW BLOW; LOW BLOW, p; LOW BLOW, w

Fong, Lui
FAMILY, THE

Fong, Mei
SUMMER AT GRANDPA'S, A

Fong, Mona
HUAJIE SHIDAI, p

Fonora, Lindsey
MANHUNTER

Fonseca, Gregg
CRITTERS, prod d; HOUSE, prod d; SOUL MAN,
prod d

Font, Teresa
TIEMPO DE SILENCIO, ed

Fontaine, King Masher
ABSOLUTE BEGINNERS

Fontaine, Molly
DESERT BLOOM

Fontana, Cacho
POBRE MARIPOSA

Fontana, Fabrizio
NAME OF THE ROSE, THE

Fontayne, Denis
PIRATES

Fonteno, Masy
DAHALO DAHALO

Fontenot, Miriam Lafleur
BELIZAIRE THE CAJUN, ch

Fontoura, Denise
NEM TUDO E VERDADE, ed

Foo, Richard
TAI-PAN

Foody, Ralph
RAW DEAL

Foote, Hallie
ON VALENTINE'S DAY

Foote, Horton
ON VALENTINE'S DAY; ON VALENTINE'S DAY, w

Foote, Huger
SUMMER

Foote, Lillian V.
ON VALENTINE'S DAY, p

Forbes, Donna
AGENT ON ICE

Forch, Juan Enrique
LOS HIJOS DE LA GUERRA FRIA

Forchion, Raymond
FLIGHT OF THE NAVIGATOR

Ford, Buck
KING KONG LIVES; WHAT COMES AROUND

Ford, Corkey
PLATOON; TOUGH GUYS

Ford, David L.
UPHILL ALL THE WAY, p

Ford, Douglas M.
ECHO PARK

Ford, Harrison
MOSQUITO COAST, THE

Ford, Josephine
MORE THINGS CHANGE, THE, prod d

Ford, Peter
FAIR GAME

Ford, Rae
ABDUCTED

Ford, Timothy
VENDETTA, set d

Forde, Jessica
LA PURITAINE

Forder, Nick
KNIGHTS AND EMERALDS, makeup

Foree, Ken
FROM BEYOND; JO JO DANCER, YOUR LIFE IS
CALLING

Forella, Ronn
PLAYING FOR KEEPS, ch

Foreman, David
ABSOLUTE BEGINNERS

Foreman, Deborah
3:15, THE MOMENT OF TRUTH; APRIL FOOL'S DAY;
MY CHAUFFEUR

Foreman, Lorraine
YOUNGBLOOD

Foreman, Phillip
CRITTERS, art d; ELIMINATORS, prod d

Foreman, Ron
IN THE SHADOW OF KILIMANJARO, art d

Forese, Georgia
UNA DONNA SENZA NOME

Forest, Andy J.
MEGLIO BACIARE UN COBRA

Forest, Denis
HEAD OFFICE

Forest, Michael
KING KONG LIVES

Forest, Michele
HENRI, set d

Foresta, Carmine
OFF BEAT

Forestieri, Lou
CRAZY MOON, m

Foret, Merlyn
BELIZAIRE THE CAJUN

Forman, Milos
HEARTBURN

Forner, Lola
ARMOUR OF GOD, THE; L'APACHE BIANCO

Fornes, Rosita
PLACIDO

Fornstedt, Marianne
SCORPION

Foronjy, Richard
CHECK IS IN THE MAIL, THE; MORNING AFTER,
THE; ODD JOBS

Forque, Veronica
EL ANO DE LAS LUCES

Forrest, Frederic
RETURN; WHERE ARE THE CHILDREN?

Forrestal, Terry
MONA LISA, stunts

Forristal, Susan
HEARTBURN

Forsberg, Grant
MY MAN ADAM

Forsen, Mona Theresia
DEMONER, art d; DEN FRUSNA LEOPARDEN, art d

Forshaw, "Weasel"
DIRT BIKE KID, THE

Forslind, Karin
AMOROSA

Forster, E.M.
ROOME WITH A VIEW, A, w

Forster, Jill
DEVIL IN THE FLESH

Forster, Robert
DELTA FORCE, THE

Forstsch, Christel
DUNKI-SCHOTT

Forsythe, Drew
TRAVELLING NORTH

Forsythe, William
LIGHTSHIP, THE

Fortan, Thierry
ESTHER, cos

Forte, Maria Rosaria
SEPARATI IN CASA

Forte, Valentina
CUT AND RUN

Fortes, Maria do Carmo Cavalcanti
O HOMEM DA CAPA PRETA, w

Fortier, Monique
DECLINE OF THE AMERICAN EMPIRE, THE, ed

Fortin, Michel
L'AMANT MAGNIFIQUE; SINCERELY CHARLOTTE

Fortune, Howard L.W.
JO JO DANCER, YOUR LIFE IS CALLING

Fosbeim, Minken
NOE HEIT ANNET

Foschi, Massimo
OTELLO

Foss, Shirlene
IMPURE THOUGHTS

Foss, Wenche
FAREWELL ILLUSION

Fossey, Brigitte
FUTURE OF EMILY, THE

Fosso, Yvonne
DROMMESLOTTER

Foster, Bernadette
DEAD-END DRIVE-IN

Foster, David
RUNNING SCARED, p; SHORT CIRCUIT, p; THE
KARATE KID PART II, m/l

Foster, Frances
STREETS OF GOLD

Foster, Judy
ONE NIGHT ONLY

Foster, Kimberly
ONE CRAZY SUMMER

Foster, Phil
SNO-LINE

Foster, Robert
PANTHER SQUAD

Foster, Robin
THAT'S LIFE

Foster, Ron
LEGAL EAGLES; MONEY PIT, THE

Foster, Stan
MY CHAUFFEUR; WILDCATS

Fothergill, Mia
ROOM WITH A VIEW, A

Foti, Ursula
LUSSURI

Fotopoulos, Mimis
Obituaries

Fouad, Ahmed
AL KETTAR, d; AL KETTAR, w

Fougea, Berthelemy
DERNIER CRI, art d

Foulkrod, Howard
HELLFIRE, p

Foundas, Costas
TO DENDRO POU PLIGONAME, ed

Foundas, George
GIRL FROM MANI, THE

Fountain, John
CHOKE CANYON

Fouquier, Florence
SACRIFICE, THE, makeup

Fournier, Peter
BAND OF THE HAND

Foury, Pierre
KAMIKAZE, spec eff

Fowkes, Wayne
ABSOLUTE BEGINNERS

Fowler, Clement
PLAYING FOR KEEPS

Fowler, Maurice
TERRY ON THE FENCE, prod d

Fowler, Walt
KAMIKAZE HEARTS, m

Fox, Charles
LONGSHOT, THE, m; LONGSHOT, THE, m/l

Fox, David
SAMUEL LOUNT

Fox, J. Rae
BLOODY BIRTHDAY, art d; SID AND NANCY, art d

Fox, James
ABSOLUTE BEGINNERS; COMRADES

Fox, Jeanette
LADY JANE

Fox, Jerry
ARMED RESPONSE

Fox, Michael
QUICKSILVER

Fox, Peter
JAKE SPEED

Fox, Samantha
VIOLATED

Fox, Sara
BELIZAIRE THE CAJUN, cos

Fox, Stuart
SID AND NANCY

Foxxe, David
PIRATES

Foyer, Margaret
LABYRINTH

Fracassi, Alessandro
CUT AND RUN, p

Frade, Jose
PULSEBEAT, p; SEA SERPENT, THE, p

Fragasso, Claudio
WOMEN'S PRISON MASSACRE, w

Frair, Jason
MANHUNTER

Fraisse, Robert
COURS PRIVE, ph; LA GITANE, ph; LE DEBUTANT,
ph

Fraker, William
SPACECAMP, ph

Frakes, Randall
ROLLER BLADE, w

Frampton, Peter
ABSOLUTE BEGINNERS, makeup; LADY JANE,
makeup; SID AND NANCY, makeup

France, Marie
UNDER THE CHERRY MOON, cos

Francesca, Alba
HARDBODIES 2

Francezon, Ulises
GERONIMA, ed

Francia, Luisa
HEILT HITLER!

Franciosa, Massimo
LA VENEXIANA, w; LA VENEXIANA, w

Francis, Anne Lloyd
RETURN

Francis, Carol
CRAWLSPACE; VIOLATED

Francis, Dorothy
JUST BETWEEN FRIENDS

Francis, Edwin
OTELLO

Francis, Ivor
Obituaries

Francis, John
BLACK TUNNEL

Francis, Karl
MILWR BYCHAN, d&w; MILWR BYCHAN, p

Francis-Bruce, Richard
BULLSEYE, ed; SHORT CHANGED, ed

Francisco, Geraldo
NEM TUDO E VERDADE

Francisco, Martim
BRAS CUBAS

Francks, Cree Summer
CARE BEARS MOVIE II: A NEW GENERATION

Franco
PARTING GLANCES, makeup

Franco, Abel
THREE AMIGOS

Franco, Larry J.
BIG TROUBLE IN LITTLE CHINA, p

Franco, Ramon
HEARTBREAK RIDGE

Franco, Ricardo
IN 'N' OUT, d; IN 'N' OUT, w

Francois, Camille
Obituaries

Francois, Jacques
SAUVE-TOI, LOLA

Francos, Ania
SAUVE-TOI, LOLA, w

Frank, Anne Ray
Obituaries

Frank, Ben
HOLLYWOOD VICE SQUAD; HOLLYWOOD ZAP!;
HOLLYWOOD ZAP!, p

Frank, Bobbi
HOLLYWOOD ZAP!, p

Frank, Carol
SORORITY HOUSE MASSACRE, d&w

Frank, Christopher
COURS PRIVE, w; FEMMES DE PERSONNE, d&w

Frank, David
CHECK IS IN THE MAIL, THE, m

Frank, Gillian
SORORITY HOUSE MASSACRE

Frank, Gregory
FLOODSTAGE; FLOODSTAGE, art d

Frank, Johnny B.
RADIOACTIVE DREAMS

Frank, Phyllis
SORORITY HOUSE MASSACRE

Frank, Yvette
FEMMES DE PERSONNE, cos

Frankel, Jack
TOMB, THE

Franken, Al
ONE MORE SATURDAY NIGHT; ONE MORE
SATURDAY NIGHT, w

Frankenbauch, Larry
DR. OTTO AND THE RIDDLE OF THE GLOOM BEAM

Frankenheimer, John
52 PICK-UP, d

Frankhauser, Dick
DR. OTTO AND THE RIDDLE OF THE GLOOM BEAM

Franklin, Dave
WHAT COMES AROUND, w

Franklin, Diane
TERRORVISION

Franklin, Howard
NAME OF THE ROSE, THE, w

Franklin, Hugh
Obituaries

Franklin, Mark
Obituaries

Franklin, Richard
LINK, p&d

Frankoff, Kevin
PINK CHIQUITAS, THE

Frankola, Renato
ANGKOR-CAMBODIA EXPRESS, makeup

Fransen, Art
8 MILLION WAYS TO DIE

Franssens, Jean-Paul
DE WISSELWACHTER, w

Franz, Dennis
FINE MESS, A

Franzen, Filippa
SACRIFICE, THE

Franzetti, Carlos
KING AND HIS MOVIE, A, m

Franzoni, David H.
JUMPIN' JACK FLASH, w

Frappat, Francis
BLACK AND WHITE

Frappier, Roger
ANNE TRISTER, p; DECLINE OF THE AMERICAN
EMPIRE, THE, p

Frarassino, Alberto
L'ULTIMA MAZURKA, w

Fraschetti, Silvio
UN RAGAZZO COME TANTI, ph

Fraser, Bill
PIRATES

Fraser, Duncan
OVERNIGHT

Fraser, Ronald
ABSOLUTE BEGINNERS

Fraser, Tom
WIRED TO KILL, ph

Fraser, Tom Frisby
HOLLYWOOD ZAP!, ph

Frasier, George
DR. OTTO AND THE RIDDLE OF THE GLOOM BEAM

Frassica, Nino
IL BI E IL BA; IL BI E IL BA, w

Frayn, Michael
CLOCKWISE, w

Frazier, Roger
IMAGEMAKER, THE

Frazier, Ron
HEAD OFFICE

Frears, Stephen
MY BEAUTIFUL LAUNDRETTE, d

Freda, Bill
AGENT ON ICE, ed

Freda, Riccardo
FEAR, d; FEAR, w

Frederic, Anne
MAINE-OCEAN, m

Frederick, Sarah
NUTCRACKER: THE MOTION PICTURE

Frederick, Simon
ROCKIN' ROAD TRIP

Frederick, Vicki
STEWARDESS SCHOOL

Fredericks, Carole
PIRATES

Frederickson, Amanda
TWO FRIENDS

Frederique, Ariane
EQUINOXE

Fredrikson, Kristian
SHORT CHANGED, prod d; SKY PIRATES, prod d

Freeborn, Graham
SHANGHAI SURPRISE, makeup

Freeborn, Stuart
HAUNTED HONEYMOON, makeup

Freed, Reuben
JUDGEMENT IN STONE, A, art d; KILLER PARTY,
prod d

Freedland, George
PANTHER SQUAD, w

Freedman, Jerrold
NATIVE SON, d

Freedman, Steve
P.O.W. THE ESCAPE

Freedman, Winifred
CROSSROADS; MY MAN ADAM; RATBOY

Freeman, Alan
ABSOLUTE BEGINNERS

Freeman, Andy
BLOODY BIRTHDAY

Freeman, Damita Jo
MY CHAUFFEUR, ch; RATBOY

Freeman, J.E.
RUTHLESS PEOPLE

Freeman, Jeff
DIRT BIKE KID, THE, ed

Freeman, Jill
CHOKE CANYON

Freeman, Kathleen
BEST OF TIMES, THE

Freeman, Lon
CARNAGE

Freeman, Margaret
KING KONG LIVES

Freeman, Paul
SHANGHAI SURPRISE

Freeman, Tony
OCEAN DRIVE WEEKEND

Freeman-Fox, Lois
WELCOME TO 18, ed

Frees, Paul
Obituaries

Frei, Martha
PLAYING FOR KEEPS

Freilino, Brian
SEVEN MINUTES IN HEAVEN

Freire, Nonato
NEM TUDO E VERDADE

Freire, Vera
HAPPILY EVER AFTER, ed

Freiss, Stephane
LE COMPLEXE DU KANGOUROU

Freistadt, Peter
DAS SCHWEIGEN DES DICHTERS

Freitag, Hanna
SPRING SYMPHONY

Frejek, Pierre
ZONE ROUGE

Freley, Pat
ADVENTURES OF THE AMERICAN RABBIT, THE

French, Arthur
ROUND MIDNIGHT

French, Bruce
LEGAL EAGLES; WILDCATS

French, Ed
BREEDERS ; BREEDERS , spec eff

French, Edward
BLUE MAN, THE, makeup

French, Leigh
STOOGEMANIA

French, Susan
HOUSE

Frenkel, Art
CRITTERS

Frescas, Eddie
WILDCATS

Fresson, Josephine
BLACK AND WHITE

Fretin, Philippe
MAUVAIS SANG

Freudberg, Judy
AMERICAN TAIL, AN, w

Freuler, Albert
DER SCHWARZE TANNER

Frevert, Louise
TAKE IT EASY

Frey, Diana
AWAITING THE PALLBEARERS, p

Frey, Patrick
KONZERT FUR ALICE

Frey, Sami
L'ETAT DE GRACE; L'UNIQUE; LAPUTA; SAUVE-
TOI, LOLA

Freyd, Bernard
ZONE ROUGE

Freyse, Gunter
HEILT HITLER!; HEILT HITLER!, ph

Frezza, Giovanni
MANHATTAN BABY

Frias, Carmen
EL ANO DE LAS LUCES, ed

Friberg, Helene
AMOROSA

Fribo, Louise
BARNDOMMENS GADE

Fridley, Tom
FRIDAY THE 13TH PART VI: JASON LIVES

Frieb, Rainer
ZONING

Fried, Myra
HEAD OFFICE

Friedberg, Howard
GREAT WALL, A

Friederich, Zbigniew
STILL POINT, THE, ed

Friedman, Bernie
F/X

Friedman, Kinky
TEXAS CHAINSAW MASSACRE PART 2, THE

Friedman, Marvin
AMERICA 3000

Friedman, Max
THE KARATE KID PART II, m/l

Friedman, Richard
DEATHMASK, d; DEATHMASK, w

Friedman, Ron
TRANSFORMERS: THE MOVIE, THE, w

Friedman, Stephen
TOUCH AND GO, p

Friedman, Steve
AMERICAN ANTHEM

Friedrich, Gunter
UNTERMEHMEN GEIGENKASTEN, d

Friel, Eamon
BEST MAN, THE, m

Frielino, Brian
LA SPOSA AMERICANA, w

Friels, Colin
KANGAROO; MALCOLM; People to Watch

Fries, Charles
OUT OF BOUNDS, p

Frigeri, Francesco
IL CASO MORO, art d

Friis-Mikkelsen, Jarl
YES, DET ER FAR!; YES, DET ER FAR!, w

Frijda, Nelly
FLODDER

Frisch, Per
FAREWELL ILLUSION

Frischler, Brigitte
DIE NACHTMEERFAHRT, ed

Frishman, Daniel
NIGHT OF THE CREEPS

Frissung, Jean-Claude
GARDIEN DE LA NUIT

Frith, Rod
TOUCH AND GO

Fritz, Anton
NEVER TOO YOUNG TO DIE, w

Frizzi, Fabio
MANHATTAN BABY, m; SENSI, m

Froberg, Cindy
SCREEN TEST

Froboess, Cornelia
DER SOMMER DES SAMURAI

Froger, Henry
WOMEN'S PRISON MASSACRE, ph

Frogley, Louise
HALF MOON STREET, cos; MONA LISA, cos

Frohlich, Sig
JO JO DANCER, YOUR LIFE IS CALLING

Frolich, Josef
'38

Froling, Ewa
DEMONER; PA LIV OCH DOD

Fromholz, Steve
POSITIVE I.D.

Fromont, Raymond
MERCI MONSIEUR ROBERTSON, ph

Frost, Michael
MODERN GIRLS

Frot-Coutaz, Gerard
BEAU TEMPS, MAIS ORAGEUX EN FIN DE
JOURNEE, d; BEAU TEMPS, MAIS ORAGEUX EN FIN
DE JOURNEE, w

Froud, Brian
LABYRINTH, cos

Froud, Toby
LABYRINTH

Fruchtman, Lisa
CHILDREN OF A LESSER GOD, ed

Fruet, William
KILLER PARTY, d

Frugoni, Cesare
CUT AND RUN, w; IL RAGAZZO DEL PONY
EXPRESS, w; SPOSERO SIMON LE BON, w

Fruh, Giovanni
DER SCHWARZE TANNER

Frydman, Marta
DIAPASON

Frye, E. Max
SOMETHING WILD, w

Fryk, Tomas
LOVE ME!

Fuchizaki, Yuriko
TYPHOON CLUB

Fuchs, Matthias
DER SOMMER DES SAMURAI

Fucili, Rolando
NAME OF THE ROSE, THE

Fuentes, Fernando
CALACAN, p; CALACAN, ph

Fuentes, Larry
JO JO DANCER, YOUR LIFE IS CALLING, spec eff

Fuentes, Martin
SALVADOR

Fuentes, Miguel Angel
SEPARATE VACATIONS

Fuentes, Norberto
JIBARO, w

Fuentes, Toti
FIRE IN THE NIGHT, m

Fuentos, Angelica
PERROS DE LA NOCHE, cos

Fuhrer, Martin
KONZERT FUR ALICE, ph; NANOU, ph

Fuhrmann, Otto E.
DER WILDE CLOWN

Fujii, Hideo
KONEKO MONOGATARI, ph

Fujimine, Sadatoshi
SOREKARA, p

Fujimori, Yuni
LOVE SONGS

Fujimoto, Tak
FERRIS BUELLER'S DAY OFF, ph; PRETTY IN PINK,
ph; SOMETHING WILD, ph

Fujitani, Miwako
SOREKARA

Fukamizu, Fujiko
TO SLEEP SO AS TO DREAM

Fulci, Lucio
IL MIELE DEL DIAVOLO, d; MANHATTAN BABY;
MANHATTAN BABY, d

Fuli, Wan
REZHOU

Fulkerson, Lee
FREE RIDE, w

Fullarton, Alistair
LABYRINTH

Fulled, Sergio
PLACIDO, w

Fuller, Arthur
NINJA TURF

Fuller, Kathryn
EYE OF THE TIGER

Fuller, Rhiley
POLICE ACADEMY 3: BACK IN TRAINING, art d

Fullerton, Carl
F/X, makeup

Fullerton, Richard
MODERN GIRLS

Fulman, Richard
SCREEN TEST

Fulton, Lisa
ODD JOBS

Fumo, Nuccia
FOTOROMANZO

Fumo, Nunzia
LA BALLATA DI EVA

Fung, Chan
FAMILY, THE, ed

Fung, Lam
PING PONG

Fung, Raymond
FAMILY, THE, d

Funk, Trouble
GOOD TO GO, m

Funke-Stern, Monika
AM NACHSTEN MORGEN KEHRTE DER MINISTER
NICHT AN SEINEN ARBEITSPLATZ, p, d&w

Furey, Lewis
SAUVE-TOI, LOLA, m

Furie, Sidney J.
IRON EAGLE, d; IRON EAGLE, w

Furlan, Italo
SAVING GRACE

Furlan, Mira
LEPOTA POROKA; ZA SRECU JE POTREBNO TROJE

Furlong, John
ODD JOBS

Furness, Deborra-Lee
COOL CHANGE

Fursich, Julia
SQUADRA SELVAGGIA

Furst, Anton
FRENCH LESSON, prod d

Furtwaengler, David
NAME OF THE ROSE, THE

Furtwangler, Florian
TOMMASO BLU, d; TOMMASO BLU, w

Furuoya, Masato
UEMURA NAOMI MONOGATARI

Fusco, Anthony
HIGHLANDER

Fusco, John
CROSSROADS, w

Fuss, Hans
KAMIKAZE HEARTS, art d&set d

Fustukian, Bryan
LOYALTIES

Futang, Wang
REZHOU

Fuxing, Wu
FEIFA YIMIN

Gabel, Hans-Eberhard
SPRING SYMPHONY

Gabel, Michael
IMAGEMAKER, THE

Gabeli, Irakly
CHICHERIN, m

Gabin, Rosa
LOLA

Gabler, Milt
FERRIS BUELLER'S DAY OFF, m/l

Gabor, Miklos
KESERU IGAZSAG

Gabor, Pal
LA SPOSA ERA BELLISSIMA, d; LA SPOSA ERA
BELLISSIMA, w

Gabor, Zsa Zsa
SMART ALEC

Gabriel, Gilbert
FERRIS BUELLER'S DAY OFF, m/l

Gabriel, Tedra
REFORM SCHOOL GIRLS, m

Gabrielle, Monique
SCREEN TEST; WEEKEND WARRIORS

Gabrielsson, Lisbet
RATTIS, p

Gabrini, Stefano
LA CASA DEL BUON RITORNO

Gades, Antonio
EL AMOR BRUJO; EL AMOR BRUJO, ch; EL AMOR
BRUJO, w

Gadgil, Arvind
RAO SAHEB

Gadny, Courtney
RATBOY

Gaetani, Roffredo
CUT AND RUN

Gaffin, Melanie
ARMED AND DANGEROUS

Gaffney, Chris
MORE THINGS CHANGE, THE

Gage, Bob
ONE CRAZY SUMMER

Gage, Kevin
SPACECAMP

Gage, Rob
LIGHTNING—THE WHITE STALLION

Gagen, Annie
STOOGEMANIA

Gagnon, Claude
VISAGE PALE, d

Gagulachvili, Arkadi
MOI DRUG IVAN LAPSHIN, m

Gaiano, Fernando
GAVILAN O PALOMA, w

Gaigalas, Regina
FOR LOVE ALONE

Gail, Max
WHERE ARE THE CHILDREN?

Gail, Scanlon
TOUGH GUYS

Gaillard, Slim
ABSOLUTE BEGINNERS; ABSOLUTE BEGINNERS, m/l

Gaines, Boyd
HEARTBREAK RIDGE

Gaines, David
SHADOWS RUN BLACK

Gaines, George P.
RUNNING SCARED, set d

Gaines, James
P.O.W. THE ESCAPE

Gaines, Stephen
ECHO PARK

Gainey, M.C.
RATBOY

Gainsborg, Charlotte
CHARLOTTE FOR EVER; LOVE SONGS

Gainsbourg, Serge
CHARLOTTE FOR EVER; CHARLOTTE FOR EVER,
d&w; CHARLOTTE FOR EVER, m; MENAGE, m

Gair, Joann
VAMP, makeup

Gair, Teri
SEX O'CLOCK NEWS, THE

Gaitson, Bruce
HARDBODIES 2, m/l

Gal, Gyorgy
GREAT GENERATION, THE

Galabru, Michel
JE HAIS LES ACTEURS; KAMIKAZE; LES FRERES
PETARD; SUIVEZ MON REGARD

Galan, Garciela
MISS MARY, cos

Galan, Paul Keller
RADIOACTIVE DREAMS

Galarno, Bill
VIOLATED

Galarra, Pedro
YAKO—CAZADOR DE MALDITOS, m

Galasso, Michael
MY CHAUFFEUR, m/l

Galati, Eric
SAVING GRACE

Galdieri, Mico
LA BALLATA DI EVA

Gale, Bernadette
KILLER PARTY

Gale, Ed
HOWARD THE DUCK

Gale, Malcolm
KILLER PARTY

Galeano, Gia
OFF BEAT

Galen, Hetty
SEX O'CLOCK NEWS, THE

Galettini, Carlos
SERE CUALQUIER COSA PERO TE QUIERO, d; SERE
CUALQUIER COSA PERO TE QUIERO, w

Galhardo, Isabel
UMA RAPARIGA NO VERAO

Galiana, Fernando
EL MERCADO DE HUMILDES, w

Galiano, Cataldo
JUNGLE RAIDERS, spec eff; WILD BEASTS, spec eff

Galiano, Javier Garcia
REDONDO

Galiardo, Juan Luis
EL DISPUTADO VOTO DEL SR. CAYO

Galic, Joseph
SEA SERPENT, THE, art d

Galich, Steven
MAXIMUM OVERDRIVE, spec eff

Galiena, Anna
LA VITA DI SCORTA

Galik, Denise
EYE OF THE TIGER

Galimberti, Gil
VIOLENT BREED, THE, stunts

Galindo, Eduardo
RAFAGA DE PLOMO, p

Galindo, Michael
8 MILLION WAYS TO DIE

Galindo, Pedro
RAFAGA DE PLOMO, d; RAFAGA DE PLOMO, w

Galindo, Pete
8 MILLION WAYS TO DIE

Galindo, Raul
YAKO—CAZADOR DE MALDITOS, p

Galindo, Ruben
HIJO DEL PALENQUE, d&w; YAKO—CAZADOR DE
MALDITOS, d; YAKO—CAZADOR DE MALDITOS, w

Galisteo, Jose Garcia
MONSTER DOG, ph

Galiullin, Slava
POTERYALSYA SLON

Gallagher, Bernard
ARTHUR'S HALLOWED GROUND

Gallagher, Maurie
CHOPPING MALL

Gallagher, Vera
GIRLS SCHOOL SCREAMERS

Galland, Christophe
BLACK AND WHITE

Gallardo, Adrian
Obituaries

Gallardo, Juan
POR UN VESTIDO DE NOVIA; UN HOMBRE
VIOLENTE

Gallardo, Nuria
MAMBRU SE FUE A LA GUERRA; VIAJE A NINGUNA
PARTE

Gallarzo, Ricardo
POWER

Gallego, Leonel
EL TREN DE LOS PIONEROS, d&w

Gallego, Pepe
INSTANT JUSTICE

Gallegos, Gina
MEN'S CLUB, THE

Gallegos, Josh
THREE AMIGOS

Gallejos, Joshua
SALVADOR

Galler, Waltraud
HEILT HITLER!

Gallese, Simonetta
AMORE INQUIETO DI MARIA

Gallin, Tim
F/X

Gallina, Adriano
AMORE INQUIETO DI MARIA

Gallitti, Alberto
FRANCESCA E MIA, ed; IL CAMMISSARIO LO
GATTO, ed

Gallo, George
WISE GUYS, w

Gallo, Gianfranco
DELITTI

Gallo, Vincent
WAY IT IS, THE; WAY IT IS, THE, m

Gallon, Ana Maria
EL TREN DE LOS PIONEROS, cos

Gallota, Jean-Claude
MAMMAME; MAMMAME, ch

Gallouin, Jean-Claude
ZONE ROUGE, art d

Galloway, Carole
DANCING IN THE DARK

Gallup, Denise
STEWARDESS SCHOOL

Gallup, Dian
STEWARDESS SCHOOL

Galnakis, Mich.
ALLIGORIA

Galoyan, O.
KHOZIAIN

Galt, John William
DIRT BIKE KID, THE

Galvane, Candy
3:15, THE MOMENT OF TRUTH

Galvao, Flavio
HAPPILY EVER AFTER

Gam, Marta
INSOMNIACS

Gamboa, Jonee
SILK; SLOANE

Gamboa, Philip
REVENGE FOR JUSTICE

Gaminara, William
COMRADES

Gampu, Ken
JAKE SPEED

Gamulin, Lada
SAN O RUZI, cos

Ganapoler, Martin
HOWARD THE DUCK

Ganci, Giuseppa
ELOGIO DELLA PAZZIA, ph

Gandara, Eka
DOEA TANDA MATA

Gandia, Nestor
LOW BLOW

Gandus, Roberto
DESPERATE MOVES, w; UNA DOMENICA SI, w

Ganga, P.
MUKHAMUKHAM

Ganger, Theodore
PARTING GLANCES

Gann, Angela
BOY WHO COULD FLY, THE

Gannon, Ben
TRAVELLING NORTH, p

Ganoung, Richard
PARTING GLANCES

Ganru, Ge
GREAT WALL, A, m

Gant, Don
DELTA FORCE, THE, spec eff

Ganz, Bruno
DER PENDLER; EL RIO DE ORO

Ganz, Lowell
GUNG HO, w

Ganz, Tony
GUNG HO, p

Ganzino, Davide
SHADOWS RUN BLACK, ed

Gaon, Yehoram
HAME'AHEV

Garaciadiego, Paz Alicia
EL IMPERIO DE LA FORTUNA, w

Garas, Kaz
DEVASTATOR, THE; FINAL MISSION; NAKED
VENGEANCE

Garay, Jesus
MES ENLLA DE LA PASSIO, d&w

Garbarek, Jan
TEO EL PELIRROJO, m

Garbelli, Giancarlo
ROMANCE

Garber, Jay
LOW BLOW

Garber, John
SHORT CIRCUIT

Garbett, Nicola
KNIGHTS AND EMERALDS

Garcia, Andy
8 MILLION WAYS TO DIE

Garcia, Cesar
KING AND HIS MOVIE, A

Garcia, Consuleo
FRANZA, w

Garcia, Eduardo Emiro
PEQUENA REVANCHA

Garcia, Eleazar
RAFAGA DE PLOMO

Garcia, Elva
8 MILLION WAYS TO DIE

Garcia, Gloria
NAKED VENGEANCE, cos

Garcia, Guadalupe
VENENO PARA LAS HADAS, ph

Garcia, John
STREETS OF GOLD

Garcia, Jose Maria
EN PENUMBRA, cos

Garcia, Maria-Luisa
SUMMER, ed

Garcia, Martha
SHADOWS RUN BLACK

Garcia, Nicole
L'ETAT DE GRACE; MAN AND A WOMAN: 20 YEARS
LATER, A; MORT UN DIMANCHE DE PLUIE

Garcia, Rick
TOUGH GUYS

Garcia, Rodolfo "Boy"
REVENGE FOR JUSTICE

Garcia, Sigfrido
QUE ME MATEN DE UNA VEZ, ed

Garcia-Marruz, Sergio
AMIGOS, m

Garcin, Ginette
PARIS MINUIT

Garcin, Henri
FEAR

Garcia, Javier
RAFAGA DE PLOMO

Gardenia, Olga
GIURO CHE TI AMO

Gardenia, Vincent
LITTLE SHOP OF HORRORS

Gardner, Alex
NUTCRACKER: THE MOTION PICTURE

Gardner, Brooks
RAW DEAL

Gardner, Delynn
HELL SQUAD

Gardner, Gabrielle
NUTCRACKER: THE MOTION PICTURE

Gardner, Garth
WIRED TO KILL

Gardner, Micki
AROUND THE WORLD IN EIGHTY WAYS

Gardner, Pip
PLAYING AWAY, art d

Gardos, Eva
UNDER THE CHERRY MOON, ed

Gare, Nene
FRINGE DWELLERS, THE, w

Garen, Leo
BAND OF THE HAND, w

Garfath, Michael
CAR TROUBLE, ph

Garfield, Allen
DESERT BLOOM

Garfield, David
DESERT BLOOM, ed; THE KARATE KID PART II, ed

Garfield, Geoffrey
SHE'S GOTTA HAVE IT

Garfield, Joey
FERRIS BUELLER'S DAY OFF; ONE MORE
SATURDAY NIGHT

Garfinkle, Joanne
BUSTED UP

Garfunkel, Art
GOOD TO GO

Gargano, Giovanni
SQUADRA SELVAGGIA

Garia, Rick
HOLLYWOOD VICE SQUAD; MY CHAUFFEUR

Gariby, Ricardo
LA TIERRA PROMETIDA, w

Garisa, Antonio
EN PENUMBRA

Garitt, John
CARNAGE

Garko, Gianni
BLACK TUNNEL; MONSTER SHARK

Garlato, Paolo
SAPORE DEL GRANO

Garlington, Lee
COBRA; PSYCHO III

Garmache, Sergei
CHUZHAJA, BELAJA I RJABOJ

Garmany, Loyd
LOW BLOW

Garner, Helen
TWO FRIENDS, w

Garner, Katina
ROLLER BLADE

Garner, Nadine
STILL POINT, THE

Garner, Paul "Mousie"
STOOGEMANIA

Garner, Shay
BULLIES

Garnett, Gail
OVERNIGHT

Garnett, John E.
FINE MESS, A, m/l

Garnett, Richard
LINK

Garrel, Maurice
LA SECONDA NOTTE

Garret, Allyson
BAND OF THE HAND

Garret, Frank
LAND OF DOOM

Garrett, Donna
WILDCATS, stunts

Garrett, Hank
BAD GUYS

Garrett, Pat
LITTLE SHOP OF HORRORS, ch

Garrett, Robert
ROLLER BLADE, m

Garrett, Roy
WHITE SLAVE, d

Garrick, Hoyt
AT CLOSE RANGE, m/l

Garrison, Rob
THE KARATE KID PART II

Garrity, Joseph T.
FRIDAY THE 13TH PART VI: JASON LIVES, prod d

Garrone, Mirko
IL DIAVOLO IN CORPO, ed; UNA CASA IN BILICO, ed

Garth, John
DR. OTTO AND THE RIDDLE OF THE GLOOM BEAM

Gartz, Juhu
SININEN IMETTAJA, ed

Garvarentz, George
FINAL MISSION, m; YIDDISH CONNECTION, m

Garwood, Norman
LINK, prod d

Gary, Jerome
STRIPPER, d; STRIPPER, p

Gas, Gena
TRE SUPERMEN A SANTO DOMINGO

Gasalla, Antonio
AWAITING THE PALLBEARERS

Gasc, Christian
CORPS ET BIENS, cos

Gaskill, Jane
POPULATION: ONE

Gaspar, Chuck
SPACECAMP, spec eff; TOUGH GUYS, spec eff

Gasparelli, Andre
RUNNING OUT OF LUCK

Gasparini, Lodovico
ITALIAN FAST FOOD, d

Gasparri, Aldo
WHITE SLAVE, spec eff

Gasperini, Italo
SCALPS, w

Gassner, Dennis
WISDOM, prod d

Gastreghi, Gaia
ELOGIO DELLA PAZZIA

Gately, George
HEATHCLIFF: THE MOVIE, w

Gates, Dan
NIGHTMARE WEEKEND, spec eff

Gates, Dean
MAXIMUM OVERDRIVE, makeup; NIGHTMARE WEEKEND

Gates, Michael
CHOKE CANYON

Gates, Samantha
DEATH OF THE HEART, THE

Gatlif, Tony
RUE DU DEPART, d; RUE DU DEPART, w

Gatlin, Jerry
THREE AMIGOS, stunts

Gatsos, Nikos
GIRL FROM MANI, THE, w

Gatti, Manuela
FRANCESCA E MIA

Gatti, Marcello
NINI TERNO-SECCO, ph

Gaubert, Christian
MAN AND A WOMAN: 20 YEARS LATER, A, md

Gaudette, Claude
RAW DEAL, m

Gaudino, Lucio
LA SECONDA NOTTE, w

Gaudio, Bob
FINE MESS, A, m/l

Gauger, Kurt
EYE OF THE TIGER, set d

Gaukman-Sverdlov, Marxen
CHUZHAJA, BELAJA I RJABOJ, art d

Gausch, Josue
CAGED GLASS

Gauthier, Bob
AMERICAN ANTHEM

Gauthier, Claude
HENRI; LA GUEPE; QUI A TIRE SUR NOS HISTOIRES D'AMOUR?

Gauthier, Dave
LOYALTIES, spec eff

Gauthier, Jean-Yves
SAUVE-TOI, LOLA

Gauthier, Pierre
QUI A TIRE SUR NOS HISTOIRES D'AMOUR?, set d

Gauthier, Vianney
ANNE TRISTER, art d; QUI A TIRE SUR NOS HISTOIRES D'AMOUR?, set d

Gauthier, Vincent
SUMMER

Gautier, Anne
DERNIER CRI; GARDIEN DE LA NUIT

Gautier, Dick
GOBOTS: BATTLE OF THE ROCKLORDS

Gautier, Jean-Jacques
Obituaries

Gautier, Michel
QUI TROP EMBRASSE; QUI TROP EMBRASSE, w

Gautrelet, Sylvie
JEAN DE FLORETTE, cos; MANON DES SOURCES, cos

Gavala, Ula
HARDBODIES 2

Gavin, Craig
INTRUDER, THE

Gavin, Hellen
SOLDIER'S REVENGE

Gavor, Radu
MONEY PIT, THE

Gavrjusjov, Mischa
AMOROSA, ph

Gawad, Mokhtar Abdel
KAHIR ELZAMAN, art d

Gawler, Peter
PLAYING BEATIE BOW, w

Gaybis, Annie
HOLLYWOOD ZAP!

Gaye, Lucille
ABSOLUTE BEGINNERS

Gaylord, Mitch
AMERICAN ANTHEM

Gaynes, George
POLICE ACADEMY 3: BACK IN TRAINING

Gayo, Judith
BETTY BLUE, makeup; L'ETAT DE GRACE, makeup

Gazcon, Edgardo
EL BRONCO, p&d; EL BRONCO, w

Gazely, Jim
SCORPION

Gazzara, Ben
IL CAMORRISTA

Gazzola, Raul
RUNNING OUT OF LUCK

Gear, Tommy
POPULATION: ONE

Gearhardt, Pat
NOBODY'S FOOL, makeup

Gebhard, Fran
POLICE ACADEMY 3: BACK IN TRAINING

Gecks, Nicholas
TAI-PAN

Gedda, Bjorn
BRODERNA MOZART

Gedeon, Conroy
BIG TROUBLE

Gedeon, Ray
BAD GUYS

Gedis, Arie
8 MILLION WAYS TO DIE

Gedrick, Jason
IRON EAGLE

Geels, Laurens
FLODDER, p

Geer, Ellen
BLOODY BIRTHDAY

Geer, Lenny
BIG TROUBLE

Geerken, Anita
HEILT HITLER!

Geerken, Hartmut
HEILT HITLER!

Geerlings, Karen
UNDER THE CHERRY MOON

Geffen, David
LITTLE SHOP OF HORRORS, p

Geffen, Don
BREEDERS

Geffen, Eyal
HAKRAV AL HAVA'AD

Geffen, Rose
BREEDERS

Gehman, Martha
F/X

Gehman, Pleasant
THRASHIN'; VENDETTA

Gehrig, Ken
THAT'S LIFE

Gehring, Ted
OUT OF BOUNDS

Geick, Eberhard
LAPUTA, ph

Geier, Jamie
NUTCRACKER: THE MOTION PICTURE

Geier, Paul
COLOR OF MONEY, THE

Geisar, Tino
EL SECUESTRO DE LOLA-LOLA LA TRAILERA 2, m

Geisler, Mareile
SCHMUTZ

Geiss, Tony
AMERICAN TAIL, AN, w; AMERICAN TAIL, AN, w

Geissler, Margit
SPRING SYMPHONY

Geist, Gabi
HEILT HITLER!

Gelarza, Daniel
ANOTHER LOVE STORY

Gelber, Tuvia
AVANTI POPOLO

Geldary, Ed
UPHILL ALL THE WAY

Gelder, Charlotte Van
DANILO TRELES, O FIMISMENOS ANDALOUSIANOS MOUSIKOS, w

Geleng, A.M.
MONSTER SHARK, prod d

Geleng, Antonello
DETECTIVE SCHOOL DROPOUTS, prod d

Gelin, Daniel
KILLING CARS

Gellert, Andrea
KOJAK BUDAPESTEN, ed

Gellman, Judith R.
HEAD OFFICE, cos

Gellman, Larry
CHECK IS IN THE MAIL, THE

Gilbert, Ed
TRANSFORMERS: THE MOVIE, THE

Gilbert, Elizabeth A.
LABYRINTH

Gilbert, Elliot
ABSOLUTE BEGINNERS

Gilbert, Frank
BAND OF THE HAND

Gilbert, Gabrielle
RETURN, ed

Gilbert, Marcus
BIGGLES

Gilbert, Taylor
TORMENT

Gilbert, Yves
LE DEBUTANT, m

Gilberto, Joao
NEM TUDO E VERDADE, m

Gilch, Gerard
FAT GUY GOES NUTZOID!!

Gilda, Leslie
KIND OF ENGLISH, A, cos

Giler, David
ALIENS, w; MONEY PIT, THE, w

Giles, Nancy
OFF BEAT

Giles, Ron
CLASS OF NUKE 'EM HIGH

Giliay, Goert
AFZIEN, ph

Gilic, Vlatko
DOBROVOLJCI, w

Gill, Alan
LETTER TO BREZHNEV, m

Gill, Francois
EQUINOXE, ed

Gill, Inga
AMOROSA; MIN PAPA AR TARZAN

Gill, Jim
APRIL FOOL'S DAY, spec eff

Gill, John
PIRATES

Gill, Will
CHOPPING MALL

Gillert, Patrick
FATHERLAND

Gilles, Carol
ROCINANTE

Gillespie, Cynthia
KILLER PARTY

Gillespie, Dizzy
COSMIC EYE, THE; COSMIC EYE, THE, m

Gillespie, Emer
MILWR BYCHAN

Gillespie, James
CHECK IS IN THE MAIL, THE, makeup

Gilliam, Burton
UPHILL ALL THE WAY

Gillies, Andrew
SAMUEL LOUNT

Gillies, Carol
TAI-PAN

Gillin, Hugh
BEST OF TIMES, THE; PSYCHO III

Gillingham, Deborah
KNIGHTS AND EMERALDS, art d

Gilliom, Eric
HOOSIERS

Gillis, Joe
BAD GUYS , w

Gillmore, Margalo
Obituaries

Gilman, Albie
OVER THE SUMMER

Gilmore, Virginia   [Sherman Virginia Poole]
Obituaries

Gilot, Yolande
DIE ZWEI GESICHTER DES JANUAR

Gilou, Thomas
BLACK MIC-MAC, d; BLACK MIC-MAC, w

Gilpin, Jack
HEARTBURN; SOMETHING WILD

Gilreath, Paul
NO RETREAT, NO SURRENDER, m

Giltaij, Goert
DE WISSELWACHTER, ph

Gilvezan, Dan
TRANSFORMERS: THE MOVIE, THE

Gilyard, Clarence
THE KARATE KID PART II; TOP GUN

Gimenez, Claudia
MALANDRO

Gimenez-Rico, Antonio
EL DISPUTADO VOTO DEL SR. CAYO, d; EL
DISPUTADO VOTO DEL SR. CAYO, w

Gimenz, Ramon
BLACKOUT

Gimlinge, Finn
TWIST & SHOUT

Gingold, Tamar
HAKRAV AL HAVA'AD

Gingras, Jean-Claude
EVIXION

Gingras, Sylvain
EVIXION, ph

Ginsburg, Carol
3:15, THE MOMENT OF TRUTH

Ginsburg, Norine
3:15, THE MOMENT OF TRUTH

Ginza, Joey
WHATEVER IT TAKES

Giogelli, Gabriella
SQUADRA SELVAGGIA

Gioia, Anthony
TONGS—A CHINATOWN STORY

Giordana, Luca
FINAL EXECUTIONER, THE

Giordani, Rocky
THRASHIN'

Giordano, Gabriella
IL GIARDINO DEGLI INGANNI

Giordano, Jacky
LA MACHINE A DECOUDRE, m

Giordano, Martine
SCENE OF THE CRIME, ed

Giorgelli, Gabriella
STORIA D'AMORE

Giorgetti, Maria Isabel
JOGO DURO, art d

Giorgetti, Mauro
JOGO DURO, m

Giorgetti, Ugo
JOGO DURO, d&w

Giorgi, Eleonora
GIOVANNI SENZAPENSIERI

Giosa, Sue
AMERICA 3000

Giovana
EL AMOR BRUJO

Giovanni, Jim
BEST OF TIMES, THE

Giovannini, Bettina
IL MOSTRO DI FIRENZE

Giovannini, Giorgio
NAME OF THE ROSE, THE, art d

Giovannoni, Ferdinando
CRIMES OF THE HEART, art d

Giovinazzo, Buddy
COMBAT SHOCK, ed; COMBAT SHOCK, p, d&w

Giovinazzo, Carmine
COMBAT SHOCK

Giovinazzo, Ricky
COMBAT SHOCK; COMBAT SHOCK, m

Gipe, George
Obituaries

Giral, Sergio
PLACIDO, d; PLACIDO, w

Girard, Remy
DECLINE OF THE AMERICAN EMPIRE, THE

Girardi, Nicolae
NOI, CEI DIN LINIA INTII, ph

Girardot, Hippolyte
DESCENTE AUX ENFERS; L'AMANT MAGNIFIQUE;
MANON DES SOURCES; SUIVEZ MON REGARD

Giraud, Roland
LE COMPLEXE DU KANGOUROU; PAULETTE

Giraudeau, Bernard
LES LONGS MANTEAUX

Giraudi, Nicolas
SCENE OF THE CRIME

Girod, Francis
DESCENTE AUX ENFERS, d; DESCENTE AUX
ENFERS, w

Girodet, Marie-Dominique
ETATS D'AME, p

Girven, Ross
DANGEROUS ORPHANS

Gish, Annabeth
DESERT BLOOM

Gish, Bob
DESERT BLOOM

Gish, Judith
DESERT BLOOM

Gish, Lillian
SWEET LIBERTY

Gish, Sheila
HIGHLANDER

Gisladottir, Gudrun
SACRIFICE, THE

Gisler, Adi
EL RIO DE ORO, art d

Gisler, Marcel
TAGEDIEBE; TAGEDIEBE, d&w; TAGEDIEBE, m

Gismonti, Egberto
AVAETE, A SEMENTE DA VINGANCA, m

Gisotti, Michele
CHOKE CANYON, cos

Gist, Rod
JO JO DANCER, YOUR LIFE IS CALLING

Gitai, Amos
ESTHER, p&d; ESTHER, w; ESTHER, w

Gittelson, Celia
SAVING GRACE, w

Giudice, Carlo
L'ULTIMO GIORNO

Giuffre, Adriana
FORMULA FOR MURDER

Giuliani, Tito
MEGLIO BACIARE UN COBRA, w

Giuliano, Steven
RIVERBED, THE, ph

Giunta, Ana Maria
KING AND HIS MOVIE, A

Giurato, Blasco
IL CAMORRISTA, ph

Giusti, Viviana
TROLL

Gjokaj, Toma
NINJA TURF

Gladstone, Andi
WORKING GIRLS, p

Gladstone, Susan
NUTCRACKER: THE MOTION PICTURE

Gladys, Maria
BRAS CUBAS

Glaesner, Ole
WOLF AT THE DOOR, THE, cos

Glagoleva, Vera
VYITI ZAMUZH ZA KAPITANA

Glas-Drake, Amelia
ORMENS VAG PA HALLEBERGET

Glasberg, Jimmy
PARENTAL CLAIM, ph

Glasel, Jan
YES, DET ER FAR!, m

Glaser, Etienne
BRODERNA MOZART; BRODERNA MOZART, w

Glaser, Paul Michael
BAND OF THE HAND, d

Glass, Ann-Gisel
CONSEIL DE FAMILLE; DESORDRE; RUE DU
DEPART

Glass, Billy
OVER THE SUMMER

Glass, Philip
DEAD END KIDS, m

Glasser, Phillip
AMERICAN TAIL, AN

Glastein, Bert
CRAWLSPACE, ed

Glatzeder, Winfried
ROSA LUXEMBURG; VA BANQUE

Glaz, Liya
STREETS OF GOLD

Glazar, Tea
DOKTOR

Glazer, Ariel
AVANTI POPOLO, art d

Glazer, Eugene Robert
VENDETTA

Gleason, Jackie
NOTHING IN COMMON

Gleason, Joanna
HANNAH AND HER SISTERS; HEARTBURN

Gleizer, Michele
FRENCH LESSON

Glenn, Mary Francis
AMERICAN JUSTICE

Glenn, Warner
AMERICAN JUSTICE

Glennon, James
FLIGHT OF THE NAVIGATOR, ph; ONE MORE SATURDAY NIGHT, ph

Glick, Stacey
BRIGHTON BEACH MEMOIRS

Glickman, Paul
PERILS OF P.K., THE, ph

Globus, Yoram
52 PICK-UP, p; AMERICA 3000, p; AVENGING FORCE, p; CAMORRA, p; COBRA, p; DELTA FORCE, THE, p; DETECTIVE SCHOOL DROPOUTS, p; DUET FOR ONE, p; FIELD OF HONOR, p; FIREWALKER, p; HAME'AHEV, p; HASHIGAON HAGADOL, p; HOT CHILI, p; INVADERS FROM MARS, p; OTELLO, p; P.O.W. THE ESCAPE, p; TEXAS CHAINSAW MASSACRE PART 2, THE, p

Glomm, Lasse
DREAM OF NORTHERN LIGHTS, d; DREAM OF NORTHERN LIGHTS, w

Glover, Alberta
ONE CRAZY SUMMER

Glover, Cathy
MOUNTAINTOP MOTEL MASSACRE, makeup

Glover, Corey
PLATOON

Glover, J. Adam
PLATOON

Glover, John
52 PICK-UP

Glover, Karla
SALVADOR

Glowna, Vadim
EIN FLIEHENDES PFERD

Gluck, Christoph
EU SEI QUE VOU TE AMAR, m

Gluck, Dan
STAR TREK IV: THE VOYAGE HOME, set d

Gluck, Wolfgang
'38, d&w

Glutton, Francis
NO TIME TO DIE

Glynn, Deakin
SCHOOL FOR VANDALS

Glynn, Mike
CLOCKWISE

Go, Hiromi
COMIC MAGAZINE

Go, Jade
BIG TROUBLE IN LITTLE CHINA

Gobbi, Hilda
KOJAK BUDAPESTEN

Gober, Gary
AT CLOSE RANGE

Gobert, Boy [Boy Christian Klee Gobert]
Obituaries

Gobruegge, Les
BIG TROUBLE IN LITTLE CHINA, art d

Godard, Alain
NAME OF THE ROSE, THE, w

Godard, Jean-Luc
GRANDEUR ET DECADENCE D'UN PETIT COMMERCE DE CINEMA; GRANDEUR ET DECADENCE D'UN PETIT COMMERCE DE CINEMA, d&w

Godbout, Jacques
BLUE MAN, THE, spec eff

Goddard, Janet
LETTER TO BREZHNEV, p

Goddard, Jim
SHANGHAI SURPRISE, d

Goddard, Paul
BULLSEYE

Goddard, Richard C.
BLUE CITY, set d; SPACECAMP, set d

Godding, Kevin
BUSTED UP

Goded, Angel
EL IMPERIO DE LA FORTUNA, ph

Godfrey, Bruce
IMAGEMAKER, THE

Godfrey, Marian
DEAD END KIDS, p

Godfrey, Patrick
CLOCKWISE; ROOM WITH A VIEW, A

Godin, Jacques
EQUINOXE; HENRI; INTIMATE POWER

Godin, Michel
L'EXECUTRICE

Godina, Karpo
DOKTOR, ph; OVNI IN MAMUTI, ph

Godron, Ann
SCORPION

Godunov, Alexander
MONEY PIT, THE

Godwin, Frank
TERRY ON THE FENCE, d&w; TERRY ON THE FENCE, p

Godwin, John
OCEAN DRIVE WEEKEND, ed

Goelz, Dave
LABYRINTH

Goelz, Kristen
ONE CRAZY SUMMER

Goethe, Johann Wolfgang
WERTHER, w

Goethe, Johann Wolfgang von
TAROT, w

Goetz, Jindrich
LEV S BILOU HRIVOU, art d

Goetz, Peter Michael
BEER; JUMPIN' JACK FLASH; KING KONG LIVES

Goetze, Tina
DR. OTTO AND THE RIDDLE OF THE GLOOM BEAM

Goetzman, Gary
MODERN GIRLS; MODERN GIRLS, p; SOMETHING WILD

Goffin, Gerry
BEST OF TIMES, THE, m/l

Goforth, Fritz
ROCKIN' ROAD TRIP

Gogh, Theo van
CHARLEY, ed; CHARLEY, p, d&w

Gogin, Michael Lee
CRITTERS

Goglat, Michel
TWIST AGAIN A MOSCOU, m

Goh, Hiromi
YARI NO GONZA

Gokgol, Deir
FORTY SQUARE METERS OF GERMANY

Gokhale, Chandrakant
RAO SAHEB

Golan, Menahem
52 PICK-UP, p; AMERICA 3000, p; AVENGING FORCE, p; CAMORRA, p; COBRA, p; DELTA FORCE, THE, d; DELTA FORCE, THE, p; DELTA FORCE, THE, w; DETECTIVE SCHOOL DROPOUTS, p; DUET FOR ONE, p; FIELD OF HONOR, p; FIREWALKER, p; HAME'AHEV, p; HASHIGAON HAGADOL, p; HOT CHILI, p; INVADERS FROM MARS, p; OTELLO, p; P.O.W. THE ESCAPE, p; TEXAS CHAINSAW MASSACRE PART 2, THE, p

Golan, Menhem
HASHIGAON HAGADOL, w

Gold, Brandy
WILDCATS

Gold, Franie
FIRE WITH FIRE, m/l

Gold, Louise
LABYRINTH

Goldberg, Andy
EXTREMITIES, w

Goldberg, Barbara
LAND OF DOOM

Goldberg, Barry
THRASHIN', m

Goldberg, Dick
IMAGEMAKER, THE, w

Goldberg, Sheila
CHOKE CANYON, w

Goldberg, Whoopi
JUMPIN' JACK FLASH

Goldblatt, Mark
JUMPIN' JACK FLASH, ed

Goldblatt, Philip
FLIGHT OF THE NAVIGATOR, makeup

Goldblum, Jeff
FLY, THE

Golden, Bob
SCORPION

Golden, Bradley
LIGHTNING—THE WHITE STALLION

Golden, John
FAT GUY GOES NUTZOID!!, d; FAT GUY GOES NUTZOID!!, w

Golden, Natalie
NOBODY'S FOOL

Golden, Roger
FAT GUY GOES NUTZOID!!, w

Goldenberg, Carey
COLOR OF MONEY, THE

Goldenberg, Jeffrey
DEATHMASK, w

Goldenberg, Jorge
KING AND HIS MOVIE, A, w; MISS MARY, w; NIGHTMARE'S PASSENGERS, w

Goldie, Michael
LADY JANE

Goldin, Ricky Paull
HYPER SAPIEN: PEOPLE FROM ANOTHER STAR

Goldman, Charles
AMERICAN JUSTICE

Goldman, Danny
MY MAN ADAM

Goldman, Garry
BIG TROUBLE IN LITTLE CHINA, w

Goldman, Gary
AMERICAN TAIL, AN, p

Goldman, Joseph
HOT CHILI, w

Goldman, Martin F.
AMERICAN JUSTICE

Goldman, Sam
AMERICAN JUSTICE

Goldman, Sandy
LAND OF DOOM

Goldmark, Andy
FIRE WITH FIRE, m/l

Goldrich, Sam
FAT GUY GOES NUTZOID!!

Goldshmied, Gabriela
YAKO—CAZADOR DE MALDITOS

Goldsmith, Carlo
LAND OF DOOM

Goldsmith, Jerry
HOOSIERS, m; LINK, m; POLTERGEIST II, m

Goldstein, Jenette
ALIENS

Goldstein, Jerold
FAT GUY GOES NUTZOID!!

Goldstein, William
BAD GUYS , m; SAVING GRACE, m

Goldthwait, Bobcat
ONE CRAZY SUMMER; POLICE ACADEMY 3: BACK IN TRAINING

Goldwyn, Tony
FRIDAY THE 13TH PART VI: JASON LIVES

Golia, David
KAMIKAZE HEARTS, ph; NO RETREAT, NO SURRENDER, ph

Goliath
BAD GUYS

Golino, Valeria
DETECTIVE SCHOOL DROPOUTS; STORIA D'AMORE

Golonka, Arlene
FOXTRAP

Golubitski, Oleg
CHICHERIN

Golubovic, Predrag
DOBROVOLJCI, d; DOBROVOLJCI, w

Golusda, Christian
AM NACHESTEN MORGEN KEHRTE DER MINISTER NICHT AN SEINEN ARBEITSPLATZ

Golusda, Karl
ASSAULT, THE

Gombert, Julia
LAST RESORT, THE, cos

Gomes, F. Fernan
POBRE MARIPOSA

Gomes, Faustino
NTTURUDU

Gomes, Manuel Joao
REPORTER X, w

Gomez, Andres Vicente
EL ANO DE LAS LUCES, p

Gomez, Bya
NTTURUDU

Gomez, Fernando Fernan
LA MITAD DEL CIELO; VIAJE A NINGUNA PARTE; VIAJE A NINGUNA PARTE, d&w

Gomez, Jose Luis
LAST OF PHILIP BANTER, THE

Gomez, Mike
HEARTBREAK RIDGE; PATRIOT, THE

Gomez, Panchito
3:15, THE MOMENT OF TRUTH

Gomez, Ramiro
BANDERA NEGRA, set d

Gomez, Rosa-Maria
MAINE-OCEAN

Gompertz, Pierre
LA GALETTE DU ROI, art d

Gompf, Allison
CHILDREN OF A LESSER GOD

Goncalves, Enio
FILME DEMENCIA

Goncalves, Helder
BUSTED UP

Goncalves, Vitor
UMA RAPARIGA NO VERAO, d&w

Gondre, Jean-Francis
LE MOME, ph

Gonella, Franca
L'ULTIMO GIORNO

Gonshaw, Francesca
BIGGLES

Gonska, Masch
50/50

Gonsovski, Sever
DEN' GNEVA, w

Gonzales, Agustun
EL HERMANO BASTARDO DE DIOS

Gonzales, Lilian
CONTACTO CHICANO

Gonzalez, Agustin
MAMBRU SE FUE A LA GUERRA; VIAJE A NINGUNA
PARTE

Gonzalez, Angeles
REDONDO

Gonzalez, Arturo
Obituaries

Gonzalez, Carmelita
SE SUFRE PERO SE GOZA

Gonzalez, Cristian
THANATOS, d; THANATOS, p; THANATOS, w

Gonzalez, Dacia
ES MI VIDA—EL NOA NOA 2

Gonzalez, David
CALACAN

Gonzalez, Edith
EL MERCADO DE HUMILDES

Gonzalez, Federico
HOT CHILI

Gonzalez, Gabriel
INSOMNIACS; SAN ANTONITO, ed

Gonzalez, Leonel
EL NARCO—DUELO ROJO; EL NARCO—DUELO
ROJO, p

Gonzalez, Lilian
ES MI VIDA—EL NOA NOA 2

Gonzalez, Luis Carlos
MISSION, THE

Gonzalez, Luis Miguel
A LA SALIDA NOS VEMOS

Gonzalez, Maria
LOLA

Gonzalez, Miguel
LA MANSION DE ARAUCAIMA, art d

Gonzalez, Rafael
COME LA VIDA MISMA, w

Gonzalez, Tammy
EL NARCO—DUELO ROJO

Gonzalez-Gonzalez, Pedro
UPHILL ALL THE WAY

Good, Bobby
DOWN AND OUT IN BEVERLY HILLS

Good, Janet
BUSTED UP

Goodacre, Jill
ODD JOBS

Goodall, Caroline
EVERY TIME WE SAY GOODBYE

Goodbody, Sheila
SCREEN TEST

Goode, Ray
DEATH OF THE HEART, THE, ph

Gooden, Bob
MAXIMUM OVERDRIVE

Goodheart, Carol
ON VALENTINE'S DAY

Goodier, Harry
NO SURRENDER

Goodis, David
DESCENTE AUX ENFERS, w

Goodman, Andrew
KNIGHTS AND EMERALDS

Goodman, Benny [Benjamin David Goodman]
Obituaries

Goodman, Grant S.
RAD, set d

Goodman, Joel
MORNING AFTER, THE, ed

Goodman, John
TRUE STORIES

Goodman, Miles
ABOUT LAST NIGHT, m; LITTLE SHOP OF
HORRORS, m

Goodman, Robert
FLIGHT OF THE NAVIGATOR

Goodman, Tommy
MY LITTLE PONY, m/l

Goodnight, Irene
DESERT BLOOM

Goodrich, Deborah
APRIL FOOL'S DAY

Goodrow, Garry
LONGSHOT, THE; MY MAN ADAM

Goodson, Germaine
PLAYING FOR KEEPS

Goodstone, Tony
STOOGEMANIA

Goodwin, Amanda
WORKING GIRLS

Goodwin, Jeff
BLUE VELVET, makeup

Goodwin, Ron
VALHALLA, m

Goodyear, Morris
ANGKOR-CAMBODIA EXPRESS, ed

Goossens, Bob
CONGO EXPRESS, w; CONGO EXPRESS, w

Gopalakrishnan, Addor
MUKHAMUKHAM, d&w

Gopalakrishnan, Adoor
ANANTARAM, d&w

Gopi
AGHAAT; CHIDAMBARAM

Goraj, Maciej
CHRZESNISAK

Goranson, Linda
LOST!

Gorchinsky, Rodney
CRAZY MOON

Gord, Eva
RECRUITS, cos

Gordean, William
LEGAL EAGLES, ed

Gordon, Barbara
OVERNIGHT

Gordon, Barry
ADVENTURES OF THE AMERICAN RABBIT, THE

Gordon, Bert I.
BIG BET, THE, p, d&w

Gordon, Carl
VIOLATED

Gordon, Charles
NIGHT OF THE CREEPS, p

Gordon, Cindy
RAD, set d

Gordon, Dexter
ROUND MIDNIGHT

Gordon, Don
NAKED VENGEANCE; SILK

Gordon, George
Obituaries

Gordon, Hilary
MOSQUITO COAST, THE

Gordon, John
ABSOLUTE BEGINNERS

Gordon, Joyce
JUDGEMENT IN STONE, A

Gordon, Keith
BACK TO SCHOOL

Gordon, Lawrence
JUMPIN' JACK FLASH, p

Gordon, Michael
SCREAMTIME

Gordon, Pamela
POLTERGEIST II

Gordon, Philip
BRIDGE TO NOWHERE; THREE AMIGOS

Gordon, Rebecca
MOSQUITO COAST, THE

Gordon, Ruben
KING OF THE STREETS, w

Gordon, Stuart
FROM BEYOND, d; FROM BEYOND, w

Gordon-Clark, Susan
HANNAH AND HER SISTERS

Gordy, Denise
MY MAN ADAM; REFORM SCHOOL GIRLS

Gore, Michael
PRETTY IN PINK, m

Gorecki, Henryk Mikolaj
POLICE, m

Goren, Serif
KURBAGALAR, d

Gorg, Galyn
AMERICA 3000

Gorges, Ingolf
DER SEXTE SINN

Gori, Gabriele
LA MONACA NEL PECCATO; UNA STORIA
AMBIGUA

Gori, Kathy
DESPERATE MOVES, w

Gori, Mario Cecchi
GRANDI MAGAZZINI, p; ITALIAN FAST FOOD, p;
SCUOLA DI LADRI, p; SETTE CHILI IN SETTE
GIORNI, p

Gori, Vittorio Cecchi
GRANDI MAGAZZINI, p; ITALIAN FAST FOOD, p;
SCUOLA DI LADRI, p; SETTE CHILI IN SETTE
GIORNI, p

Goric, Vojo
MODERN GIRLS

Gorjestani, Syroos
MONSTER, THE

Gorji, Nemat
CLOSED CIRCUIT

Gorman, Pat
TAI-PAN

Gorman, Patrick
IN THE SHADOW OF KILIMANJARO

Gormley, Charles
GOSPEL ACCORDING TO VIC, THE, d&w

Goron, Joelle
SINCERELY CHARLOTTE, w

Gorr, Manfred
DAS HAUS AM FLUSS

Gorris, Arielle
SCORPION

Gorshin, Frank
HOLLYWOOD VICE SQUAD

Gorton, Adrian
PRAY FOR DEATH, art d

Gorton, Adrian H.
COBRA, art d

Goscinny, Rene
ASTERIX CHEZ LES BRETONS, w

Gosling, Paula
COBRA, w

Gosnell, Raja
SOLDIER'S REVENGE, ed; WEEKEND WARRIORS, ed

Gosnell, Robert
FIREWALKER, w

Gosney, Katherine
AMERICAN ANTHEM

Gosov, Maran
VIRUS HAS NO MORALS, A, m

Goss, David
ARMED RESPONSE

Gossar, J.R.
PANTHER SQUAD

Gossens, Anne
UNTERMEHMEN GEIGENKASTEN, w

Gossett, Lou
FIREWALKER

Gossett, Louis
IRON EAGLE

Gossom, Thom
REBEL LOVE

Gostischa, Teo
AUF IMMER UND EWIG

Gotell, Walter
KGB—THE SECRET WAR

Gothe, Micheal
AB HEUTE ERWACHSEN, ph

Gotlieb, Mark
NIGHTMARE WEEKEND

Gottfried, Howard
MEN'S CLUB, THE, p

Gottowac, Tom
LIJEPE ZENE PROLAZE KROZ GRAD

Goudinoux, Patricia
MAMMAME, cos

Goudsmit, Lex
THOMAS EN SENIOR OP HET SPOOR VAN BRUTE
BEREND

Goudsmith, Lex
OP HOOP VAN ZEGEN

Gough, Michael
CARAVAGGIO

Goulas, Charlie
BELIZAIRE THE CAJUN

Gould, Bob
WAY IT IS, THE, ed; WELCOME TO 18

Gould, Chris
P.O.W. THE ESCAPE

Gould, Elliott
INSIDE OUT

Gould, Harold
PLAYING FOR KEEPS

Gould, Heywood
STREETS OF GOLD, w

Gould, Jack
ON VALENTINE'S DAY

Goulian, Lisa
STAR CRYSTAL

Gounaris, Michalis
I NICHTA ME TI SILENA

Goursaud, Ann
JUST BETWEEN FRIENDS, ed

Goursaud, Anne
CRIMES OF THE HEART, ed

Gourson, Jeff
FLIGHT OF THE NAVIGATOR, ed

Gousias, Vangelis
ALLIGORIA, ed

Goussard, Francoise
JUBIABA

Governor, Mark
DEVASTATOR, THE, m; LAND OF DOOM, m

Gow, John
GOSPEL ACCORDING TO VIC, THE, ed

Gow, Michael
SHORT CHANGED

Gow, Richard
UNDER THE CHERRY MOON

Gowan
BUSTED UP

Gowan, Katherine
SWEET LIBERTY

Goyet, Jean-Francois
LA PURITAINE, w

Goyri, Sergio
LOS ASES DE CONTRABANDO; MATANZA EN
MATAMOROS

Gozlino, Paolo
CATTIVI PIERROT

Graber, Gary
NINJA TURF

Grabol, Sofie
BARNDOMMENS GADE; WOLF AT THE DOOR, THE

Grace, Wayne
ODD JOBS

Gradman, Eric
WRONG WORLD, m

Graef, Sue
WAY IT IS, THE, ed

Graf, Allan
BLUE CITY; CROSSROADS; OUT OF BOUNDS

Graf, Cera
DIE NACHTMEERFAHRT, cos

Graf, David
POLICE ACADEMY 3: BACK IN TRAINING

Graf, Roland
DAS HAUS AM FLUSS, d&w

Graft, Valentin
FOUETTE

Graham, C.J.
FRIDAY THE 13TH PART VI: JASON LIVES

Graham, David
COMRADES, m

Graham, Gerrit
CHOPPING MALL; LAST RESORT, THE; RATBOY;
TERRORVISION

Graham, Holter
MAXIMUM OVERDRIVE

Graham, Kathleen
BUSTED UP, makeup; YOUNGBLOOD, makeup

Graham, Richard
MY BEAUTIFUL LAUNDRETTE

Graham, Sam
GOSPEL ACCORDING TO VIC, THE

Graham, Steve
MONEY PIT, THE, art d

Graham, Virginia
PERILS OF P.K., THE

Graham, Winston
MY BEAUTIFUL LAUNDRETTE

Grall, Sebastien
LA FEMME SECRETE, d; LA FEMME SECRETE, w

Grall, Valerie
LA FEMME SECRETE, art d

Gran, Rojo
MATANZA EN MATAMOROS, m

Grana, Sam
90 DAYS

Granada, Jose Rodriguez
FIREWALKER, prod d

Granados, Daisy
UN HOMBRE DE EXITO

Granath, Bjorn
DEMONER; DEN FRUSNA LEOPARDEN; MIN PAPA
AR TARZAN

Granda, Juan
AMIGOS

Grandi, Serena
DESIDERANDO GIULIA; LA SIGNORA DELLA NOTTE

Grandinetti, Dario
LES LONGS MANTEAUX

Grandlund, Runa
DROMMESLOTTER

Granger, Farley
DEATHMASK; IMAGEMAKER, THE; VERY CLOSE
QUARTERS

Granger, Shanton
SEX O'CLOCK NEWS, THE

Granhagen, Lena
LOVE ME!

Granier, Patrick
LA MACHINE A DECOUDRE

Granier-Deferre, Pierre
COURS PRIVE, d; COURS PRIVE, w

Granlund, Maria
DEN FRUSNA LEOPARDEN

Grannelli, Steve
TOUCH AND GO

Granneman, Elizabeth
HUD

Grans, Marian
BRODERNA MOZART; PA LIV OCH DOD

Granstrom, Jonas
I LAGENS NAMN

Grant, Bill
CARNAGE

Grant, Cary [Alexander Archibald "Archie" Leach]
Obituaries

Grant, Dr. Toni
DOWN AND OUT IN BEVERLY HILLS

Grant, Helen
COCAINE WARS

Grant, James
BLOOD RED ROSES

Grant, Kirsty
STILL POINT, THE

Grant, Lee
ARRIVING TUESDAY

Grant, Leon W.
PLAYING FOR KEEPS

Grant, Moira
LABYRINTH

Grant, Paul
LABYRINTH

Grant, Ron
SAY YES, m

Granton, Alan
CLOCKWISE

Grantt, Leland
ROCKIN' ROAD TRIP

Granville, Eric
NO SURRENDER

Grasse, Gerd
UNTERMEHMEN GEIGENKASTEN

Grasshoff, Wolfgang
NO TIME TO DIE, ph

Grassia, Nini
UNA TENERA FOLLIA, d&w

Grasso, Aldo
L'ULTIMA MAZURKA, w

Grau, Louis
COURS PRIVE, p

Grau, Rojo
LA ALACRANA

Grauer, William
BACK TO SCHOOL

Gravat, Pascal
MAMMAME

Gravel, Robert
INTIMATE POWER

Graves, Carl
DR. OTTO AND THE RIDDLE OF THE GLOOM BEAM

Graves, Fred
REVENGE

Graves, Rupert
ROOM WITH A VIEW, A

Gray, Andy
FIRE WITH FIRE

Gray, Coleen
CRY FROM THE MOUNTAIN

Gray, George
ROCKIN' ROAD TRIP

Gray, Gretchen
WEEKEND WARRIORS

Gray, John
BILLY GALVIN, d&w

Gray, Lorna
ABSOLUTE BEGINNERS; KNIGHTS AND EMERALDS

Gray, Robert
ARMED AND DANGEROUS

Gray, Rolf
MISSION, THE

Gray, Spalding
SEVEN MINUTES IN HEAVEN; TRUE STORIES

Gray, William
BLACK MOON RISING, w

Graysmark, John
CLUB PARADISE, prod d; DUET FOR ONE, prod d

Grazer, Brian
ARMED AND DANGEROUS, p&w

Graziano, Antonio
UN RAGAZZO COME TANTI

Graziano, Kristin
FERRIS BUELLER'S DAY OFF

Graziosi, Stefania
UNA CASA IN BILICO

Grearson, Christopher
KNIGHTS AND EMERALDS

Great, Don
BREEDERS , m; SOLDIER'S REVENGE, m

Greatrex, Richard
KNIGHTS AND EMERALDS, ph

Greaves, John
ABSOLUTE BEGINNERS

Greco, Emidio
EHRENGARD, d

Greco, Joe
ABOUT LAST NIGHT

Greco, Lello
SUMMER NIGHT WITH GREEK PROFILE, ALMOND
EYES AND SCENT OF BASIL, m

Gredeby, Nils
BRODERNA MOZART

Green, Amy
AMERICAN TAIL, AN

Green, Bruce
APRIL FOOL'S DAY, ed; FRIDAY THE 13TH PART VI:
JASON LIVES, ed

Green, David
CAR TROUBLE, d

Green, Devonne L.
HEAD OFFICE

Green, Dick
BLUE VELVET

Green, Eitan
NADIA, w

Green, Gerald
SALVADOR, p

Green, Hilton A.
PSYCHO III, p

Green, Jack N.
HEARTBREAK RIDGE, ph

Green, Janet Laine
BULLIES

Green, Jay
TOUCH AND GO

Green, Joey
HOUSE

Green, Joseph
PERILS OF P.K., THE, d

Green, Katie
REVENGE OF THE TEENAGE VIXENS FROM OUTER SPACE, THE

Green, Kerri
LUCAS; People to Watch

Green, Lars
DEMONER

Green, Lisa
AMERICAN ANTHEM; AMERICAN ANTHEM, ch

Green, Patricia
BEER, makeup

Green, Pia
I LAGENS NAMN

Green, Tim
ON VALENTINE'S DAY

Green, Walon
SOLARBABIES, w

Greenberg, Adam
IRON EAGLE, ph; WISDOM, ph

Greenberg, Ed
SCREAMPLAY, w

Greenberg, Jerry
NO MERCY, ed; WISE GUYS, ed

Greenberg, Robert
CHOPPING MALL

Greenburg, Adam
LADIES CLUB, THE, ph

Greenbury, Christopher
HAUNTED HONEYMOON, ed

Greene, Amy
NUTCRACKER: THE MOTION PICTURE

Greene, Danford B.
HEAD OFFICE, ed

Greene, Daniel
HANDS OF STEEL; PULSEBEAT; WEEKEND WARRIORS

Greene, Ellen
LITTLE SHOP OF HORRORS

Greene, Joe
Obituaries

Greene, Jon
NEVER TOO YOUNG TO DIE

Greene, Lauren
BELIZAIRE THE CAJUN

Greene, Lorne
VASECTOMY: A DELICATE MATTER

Greene, Michael
DOWN AND OUT IN BEVERLY HILLS; WELCOME TO 18

Greene, Sergio Olhovich
ANGEL RIVER, d

Greene, Steve
HARDBODIES 2, w

Greenfield, Howard
Obituaries

Greenhill, Amy
HANNAH AND HER SISTERS

Greenhill, Geoffrey
CLOCKWISE

Greenhut, Robert
HANNAH AND HER SISTERS, p; HEARTBURN, p

Greenlee, David
IRON EAGLE

Greens, Gregory
SEA SERPENT, THE, d

Greenstein, Steven
TOUGH GUYS

Greenwood, Alan Gregory
CHOKE CANYON

Greenwood, Bobby
SILK

Greenwood, Carolyn
PLAY DEAD

Greenwood, Jane
SWEET LIBERTY, cos

Greer, Jane
JUST BETWEEN FRIENDS

Greese, Wolfgang
SPRING SYMPHONY

Gregg, Bradley
STAND BY ME

Gregg, John
TRAVELLING NORTH

Gregg, Stephanie
OUT OF BOUNDS

Gregg, Virginia
PSYCHO III

Greggio, Ezio
ITALIAN FAST FOOD, w; YUPPIES, I GIOVANI DI SUCCESSO

Gregoire, Richard
INTIMATE POWER, m

Gregorio, Angelo
INNOCENZA, w

Gregorio, Carlos
O HOMEM DA CAPA PRETA

Gregory, Andre
MOSQUITO COAST, THE

Gregory, Benji
JUMPIN' JACK FLASH

Gregory, Iola
COMING UP ROSES

Gregory, Jory
DR. OTTO AND THE RIDDLE OF THE GLOOM BEAM

Gregory, Mark
THUNDER WARRIOR

Gregory, Michael
BAND OF THE HAND

Greifova, Irena
LEV S BILOU HRIVOU, cos

Greisman, Alan
'NIGHT, MOTHER, p

Greist, Kim
MANHUNTER

Greley, Jack
POLICE ACADEMY 3: BACK IN TRAINING

Grenkowitz, Rainer
MEIER

Grennan, Larry
STEWARDESS SCHOOL

Grenville, George
IRON EAGLE, ed

Gresko, Richard
90 DAYS, m

Greta
PLAY DEAD

Grethe, P.J.
OCEAN DRIVE WEEKEND

Grewal, Jaquilline
MASSEY SAHIB

Grey, Bruce
CHECK IS IN THE MAIL, THE

Grey, Daphne
SHORT CHANGED

Grey, Ivan
COCAINE WARS

Grey, Jennifer
FERRIS BUELLER'S DAY OFF

Grey, Wilson
AS SETE VAMPIRAS; BRAS CUBAS; MALANDRO

Griakalova, N.
PISMA MERTVOGO CHELOVEKA

Gribble, Andy
YOUNGBLOOD

Griego, Mario
ROCKIN' ROAD TRIP

Griem, Helmut
SECOND VICTORY, THE

Grier, David Alan
BEER

Grier, Melissa
NOBODY'S FOOL

Grier, Raheim
BREEDERS

Gries, Jonathan
RUNNING SCARED; TERRORVISION

Grifasi, Joe
F/X

Griffeth, Simone
PATRIOT, THE

Griffin, Chris
ARTHUR'S HALLOWED GROUND, p

Griffin, Chuck
AMERICA

Griffin, Frank
THREE AMIGOS, makeup

Griffin, Julann
HAUNTED HONEYMOON

Griffin, Mary Alison
LEGAL EAGLES

Griffin, Peter
BAD GUYS ; PATRIOT, THE

Griffin, Tom
MY LITTLE PONY, p; TRANSFORMERS: THE MOVIE, THE, p

Griffith, Emile
STREETS OF GOLD, tech adv

Griffith, Melanie
SOMETHING WILD

Griffith, William
SCORPION

Griffiths, Linda
SAMUEL LOUNT

Griffiths, Mark
HARDBODIES 2, d; HARDBODIES 2, w

Griffiths, Richard
SHANGHAI SURPRISE

Griffiths, Rowan
COMING UP ROSES

Griffiths, Trevor
FATHERLAND, w

Griffo, Joseph S.
NIGHT OF THE CREEPS

Grigg, Gene
CLAN OF THE CAVE BEAR, THE, spec eff

Griggs, Bob
SHADOW PLAY

Grigoriu, Patricia
DREPTATE IN LANTURI

Grillo, Fernando
ELOGIO DELLA PAZZIA

Grillo, Gary
AMERICAN JUSTICE, d

Grimaldi, Alberto
GINGER & FRED, p

Grimaldi, Eva
LA MONACA NEL PECCATO

Grimau, Antonio
INSOMNIACS

Grimaud, Michel
SCENE OF THE CRIME

Grimblat, Pierre
GRANDEUR ET DECADENCE D'UN PETIT COMMERCE DE CINEMA, p

Grimes, Chester
BIG TROUBLE

Grimes, Ethne
LA GUEPE

Grimes, Scott
CRITTERS

Grimes, Tammy
AMERICA

Grimsby, Roger
POWER

Grimsey, Robert
ABSOLUTE BEGINNERS

Grimshaw, Jim
KING KONG LIVES

Grimward, Gordon
TERRY ON THE FENCE, ed

Grinberg, Anouk
LAST SONG

Grinnell, Danny
OCEAN DRIVE WEEKEND

Grippe, Ragnar
JONSSONLIGAN DYKER UPP IGEN, m; RETURN, m

Grisales, Amparo
REI DO RIO

Gritz, Hall
OCEAN DRIVE WEEKEND

Grlic, Rajko
ZA SRECU JE POTREBNO TROJE, d; ZA SRECU JE POTREBNO TROJE, w

Groddy, Gordon
BUSTED UP, m/l

Grodin, Charles
LAST RESORT, THE

Grondona, Payo
NEMESIO, m

Gronemeyer, Herbert
SPRING SYMPHONY

Groot, Hein
FIELD OF HONOR, ph

Gros, Berangere
SINCERELY CHARLOTTE

Grose, Robert
ABSOLUTE BEGINNERS

Gross, Arye
SOUL MAN

Gross, Guy
DOT AND KEETO, m; DOT AND THE WHALE, m

Gross, Holger
LIGHTSHIP, THE, art d

Gross, Larry
3:15, THE MOMENT OF TRUTH, d

Gross, Mary
CLUB PARADISE

Gross, Yoram
DOT AND KEETO, p&d; DOT AND THE WHALE, p&d

Grosser, Art
BOY IN BLUE, THE

Grossi, Jeffrey
CLASS OF NUKE 'EM HIGH

Grossman, Alice
SCREAMPLAY

Grossman, David
SMILE OF THE LAMB, THE, w

Grossman, Dr. Richard
JO JO DANCER, YOUR LIFE IS CALLING

Grossman, Karen
HAMBURGER, ph; MODERN GIRLS, ph

Grossman, Larry
GREAT MOUSE DETECTIVE, THE, m/l

Grossman, Marc
VAMP, ed

Grosz, Paul
Obituaries

Groth, Sylvester
DAS HAUS AM FLUSS

Grousset, Didier
KAMIKAZE, d; KAMIKAZE, w

Grove, Elaine
RIVERBED, THE

Grove-White, Will
SCHOOL FOR VANDALS, ph

Grover, John
LABYRINTH, ed

Groves, John
BIGGLES, w

Groza, Alexandru
LICEENI, ph

Grozdanov, Mite
SRECNA NOVA '49

Gruault, Jean
GOLDEN EIGHTIES, w

Gruber, Charles
PRAY FOR DEATH

Gruda, Jaroslaw
KRONIKA WYPADKOW MILOSNYCH

Grund, Bert
'38, m

Grundberg, Svante
PA LIV OCH DOD

Grunden, Per
JONSSONLIGAN DYKER UPP IGEN

Grunstein, Pierre
JEAN DE FLORETTE, p; MANON DES SOURCES, p

Grunwald, Morten
BALLERUP BOULEVARD;
MORD I MORKET; WOLF AT THE DOOR, THE

Grupo Issoco
ALMACITA DI DESOLATO, m

Grupp, Barbara
DER WILDE CLOWN, cos

Grusin, Dave
LUCAS, m

Grynbaum, Marc Andre
DERNIER CRI, p

Grythe, Hilde
DROMMESLOTTER

Gschwind, Karlheinz
DER WILDE CLOWN, ph

GSD'Arto
INTRUDER, THE, m

Gu, Lin Chun
POMNALUI NUNSOGI, w

Guadalcanal Diary
ROCKIN' ROAD TRIP

Guadalupe, Ignacio
OBDULIA

Guaita, Vittoria
SAVING GRACE, cos

Guanglan, Shen
GREAT WALL, A

Guanting, Lu
HALF-DUAN QING; HALF-DUAN QING, m

Guanying, Xu
HALF-DUAN QING

Guara
BRAS CUBAS

Guardia, Bob   [Albert H. Guardia]
Obituaries

Guardia, Maribel
EL BRONCO; LA ALACRANA; TERROR Y ENCAJES
NEGROS; UN HOMBRE VIOLENTE

Guariniello, Fernando
GERONIMA, ed

Guarnieri, Ennio
GINGER & FRED, ph; OTELLO, ph

Guastaferro, Joe
COLOR OF MONEY, THE

Guastaferro, Vincent
FRIDAY THE 13TH PART VI: JASON LIVES; LEGAL
EAGLES

Guastello, Michelle
BEST OF TIMES, THE

Gubbles, Luk
CONGO EXPRESS, d

Gubern, Roman
DRAGON RAPIDE, w

Gubser, Stefan
EL RIO DE ORO

Guce, Alejandro
LA TIERRA PROMETIDA

Gudjartson, Throstur
SCHWARZ UND OHNE ZUCKER

Gudmunds, Sigridur
SALVADOR

Gudnason, Torarinn
EINS OG SKEPNAN DEYR

Gudra
NEM TUDO E VERDADE

Guedes, Ann
ROCINANTE, d&w

Guedes, Eduardo
ROCINANTE, d&w; ROCINANTE, ed

Guedes, Paula
REPORTER X

Guegan, Philippe
LE MOME, stunts

Guenette, Richard
BUSTED UP

Guennoun, Bousalem
CHAMS

Guerin, Andre
WOLF AT THE DOOR, THE, art d

Guerin, Florence
LA BONNE

Guerin, Michel
ASTERIX CHEZ LES BRETONS, art d

Guerin, Paul-Andre
BLUE MAN, THE, cos

Guerman, Alexei
MOI DRUG IVAN LAPSHIN, d

Guernon, Christiane
QUI A TIRE SUR NOS HISTOIRES D'AMOUR?, ph

Guerra, Blanca
EL IMPERIO DE LA FORTUNA; EL JUEGO DE LA
MUERTE; SEPARATE VACATIONS

Guerra, Castulo
FINE MESS, A; JUST BETWEEN FRIENDS; WHERE
THE RIVER RUNS BLACK

Guerra, Jorge
MALABRIGO, w; RAFAGA DE PLOMO

Guerra, Robert
MANHATTAN PROJECT, THE, art d

Guerra, Ruy
MALANDRO, d; MALANDRO, p; MALANDRO, w

Guerra, Tonino
GINGER & FRED, w; O MELISSOKOMOS, w

Guerrero, Alvaro
EL TREN DE LOS PIONEROS; MISSION, THE

Guerrero, Angelica
OBDULIA

Guerrero, David
LA MANSION DE ARAUCAIMA

Guerrero, Francisco
EL ANO DE LAS LUCES, m

Guerrero, Franco
AMERICAN COMMANDOS

Guerrero, Mando
BAD GUYS

Guerri, Guy
PRUNELLE BLUES

Guerrieri, Romolo
FINAL EXECUTIONER, THE, d

Guerrini, Mino
LE MINIERE DEL KILIMANGIARO, d&w

Guerritore, Monica
LA VENEXIANA; SENSI

Guest, Christopher
LITTLE SHOP OF HORRORS

Guest, Don
AT CLOSE RANGE, p

Guest, Michael
PING PONG, p

Guevara, Nacha
MISS MARY

Guevara, Silvia
CALACAN

Guevara, Steve
PSYCHO III

Guffanti, Monica
LEJANIA

Guffroy, Pierre
MAX MON AMOUR, prod d; PIRATES, art d; TWIST
AGAIN A MOSCOU, art d

Guggenheim, Al
COCAINE WARS, set d

Guggenheim, Hermann
KONZERT FUR ALICE

Guglielmone, Aldo
ANOTHER LOVE STORY, prod d; ANOTHER LOVE
STORY, set d

Guidelli, Mirio
ROOM WITH A VIEW, A

Guido, Beatriz
INSOMNIACS, w

Guidotti, Isabella
SPOSERO SIMON LE BON

Guidotti, Laurentina
GINGER & FRED

Guiguet, Jean-Claude
FAUBOURG SAINT-MARTIN, d&w

Guilfoyle, Paul
BILLY GALVIN; HOWARD THE DUCK

Guilhe, Albane
ANNE TRISTER

Guilherme, Luiz
JOGO DURO

Guillaume, Isabelle
WINDSCHADUW

Guillermet, Robert
HALF MOON STREET

Guillermin, John
KING KONG LIVES, d

Guillon, Christian
L'UNIQUE, spec eff

Guimaraes, Alexandra
UMA RAPARIGA NO VERAO

Guimaraes, Ana Luisa
REPORTER X, ed; UMA RAPARIGA NO VERAO, ed

Guimaraes, Luiz Fernando
BRAS CUBAS

Guinee, Tim
TAI-PAN

Guinness, Matthew
LADY JANE

Guiol, Michele
BEER, set d

Guiomar, Julien
LE DEBUTANT

Guise, Roger
ARRIVING TUESDAY, prod d

Gukasyan, A.
KHOZIAIN

Gul, Anita
GHAME AFGHAN

Gulberlet, Karin
DIE WALSCHE, cos

Gullaksen, Yrsa
FLAMBEREDE HJERTER

Gullotta, Leo
IL BI E IL BA; IL CAMORRISTA

Gulpilil, David
DARK AGE; "CROCODILE" DUNDEE

Gulyamov, Najmidin
GRANNY GENERAL, ph

Gulzar
NEW DELHI TIMES, w

Gunasekara, Ananda
ARUNATA PERA, p

Gundareva, Natalya
ZIMNI VECHER V GAGRAKH

Gundersen, Svein
DROMMESLOTTER, m; FAREWELL ILLUSION, m

Gundert, Roger
LOW BLOW

Gunn, James
CORPS ET BIENS, d&w

Gunn, Moses
HEARTBREAK RIDGE

Gunnarsson, Togeir
EINS OG SKEPNAN DEYR; EINS OG SKEPNAN DEYR, art d; SCHWARZ UND OHNE ZUCKER

Gunnarsson, Trostur
EINS OG SKEPNAN DEYR

Gunnel, Kimm
VALKOINEN KAAPIO

Gunter, Bob
MAXIMUM OVERDRIVE

Gunther, Ernst
I LAGENS NAMN; LOVE ME!; ORMENS VAG PA HALLEBERGET

Gunther, Matthias
KONZERT FUR ALICE

Guoxi, Chen
HALF-DUAN QING, d

Gupinar, Mustapha
FORTY SQUARE METERS OF GERMANY

Gupta, Neena
SUSMAN; TRIKAL

Gupta, Sutanu
AGHAAT, ed

Gurfinkel, David
AMERICA 3000, ph; DELTA FORCE, THE, ph; HAME'AHEV, ph

Gurian, Paul R.
PEGGY SUE GOT MARRIED, p

Gurr, Michael
DEPARTURE, w; DEPARTURE, w

Gurrado, Lello
SPOSERO SIMON LE BON, w

Gurrado, lizia
SPOSERO SIMON LE BON, w

Gurrola, Alfredo
EL JUEGO DE LA MUERTE, d; GAVILAN O PALOMA, d

Gusberti, Sharon
YUPPIES, I GIOVANI DI SUCCESSO

Gusi, Carles
MES ENLLA DE LA PASSIO, ph

Gusman, Jeffrey G.
PANTHER SQUAD, m

Gusmao, Mario
CHICO REI

Guss, Louis
HIGHLANDER; SNO-LINE

Guss, Peter
REVENGE OF THE TEENAGE VIXENS FROM OUTER SPACE, THE

Guss, Reuben
CLASS OF NUKE 'EM HIGH

Gustafson, Bjorn
JONSSONLIGAN DYKER UPP IGEN

Gustafsson, Kjell
MOA, makeup

Gustafsson, Lennart
RATTIS, anim; RATTIS, d&w

Gustavson, Erik
BLACKOUT, d; BLACKOUT, w

Gustavsson, Kjell
I LAGENS NAMN, makeup; SACRIFICE, THE, makeup

Gutfried, Dieter
DER POLENWEIHER, m

Guthrie, Cedric
RAW DEAL; ROCKIN' ROAD TRIP

Gutierrez, Alfredo
EL EXTRANO HIJO DEL SHERIFF

Gutierrez, Angela
LOLA

Gutierrez, Armando
VISA U.S.A.

Gutierrez, Elisabeth
SEPARATI IN CASA

Gutierrez, Gary
TOP GUN, spec eff

Gutierrez, Miguel
PLACIDO

Gutierrez, Zaide Silvia
EL IMPERIO DE LA FORTUNA; FIREWALKER

Gutsev, Georgi
SKUPA MOYA, SKUPI MOY, set d

Guttenberg, Steve
POLICE ACADEMY 3: BACK IN TRAINING; SHORT CIRCUIT

Gutteridge, Martin
HIGHLANDER, spec eff; OP HOOP VAN ZEGEN, spec eff

Guttman, Amos
BAR 51—SISTER OF LOVE, d; BAR 51—SISTER OF LOVE, w

Gutty, J.L.
LOS HIJOS DE LA GUERRA FRIA

Guy, Lawrence
CHOPPING MALL

Guy, Louis
MEN'S CLUB, THE, m/l

Guyonnet, Marie
L'AMANT MAGNIFIQUE

Guyot, Raymonde
LE PALTOQUET, ed

Guzman, Claudia
LA ALACRANA; LA TIERRA PROMETIDA; TERROR Y ENCAJES NEGROS

Guzman, Luis
CALACAN, m

Guzman, Pato
DOWN AND OUT IN BEVERLY HILLS, prod d

Gwaltney, Robert
WHOOPEE BOYS, THE

Gwatkin, Ann-Marie
CLOCKWISE

Gwinn, Maggie
OUT OF BOUNDS

Gwynne, Fred
BOY WHO COULD FLY, THE; OFF BEAT

Gwynne, Michael C.
TAI-PAN

Gyarmathy, Livia
VAKVILAGBAN, d

Gyllenberg, Ben
FLIGHT NORTH, prod d

Ha, Pat
HUAJIE SHIDAI

Ha, Wong
MR. VAMPIRE

Haacke, Kathe
Obituaries

Haag, Catherine
SCREAMPLAY

Haake, James "Gypsy"
MORNING AFTER, THE

Haanstra, Rimko
DE WISSELWACHTER, ed

Haas, Amelia
EYE OF THE TIGER

Haas, Ludwig
ASSAULT, THE

Haas, Lukas
SOLARBABIES

Haavikko, Paavo
KUNINGAS LAHTEE RANSKAAN, w

Haavisto, Susanna
KUNINGAS LAHTEE RANSKAAN

Habault, Sylvie
THERESE

Habeck, Michael
NAME OF THE ROSE, THE

Haber, Alessandro
ANCHE LEI FUMAVA IL SIGARO; EHRENGARD; GRANDI MAGAZZINI; INNOCENZA; REGALO DI NATALE; TOMMASO BLU

Haber, Daniel
HANNAH AND HER SISTERS

Habercorn, Ray
EYE OF THE TIGER

Haberland, Magitta
AM NACHESTEN MORGEN KEHRTE DER MINISTER NICHT AN SEINEN ARBEITSPLATZ

Habets, Victorine
FIELD OF HONOR, ed; MARIA, ed

Hachuel, Herve
LAST OF PHILIP BANTER, THE, p&d; LAST OF PHILIP BANTER, THE, w

Hack, Shelley
TROLL

Hacker, Angelika
ZONING, w

Hackett, Sandy
HAMBURGER

Hackl, Karlheinz
WELCOME IN VIENNA

Hackman, Gene
HOOSIERS; POWER

Hacohen, Sharon
ALEX KHOLE AHAVA

Hadad, Suheil
AVANTI POPOLO

Hadar, Ronnie
TOMB, THE, p

Haddad, Sahib
FLAMING BORDERS, d

Haddoi, Fathi
AL-KAS

Haddon, Dayle
LOVE SONGS

Haddrick, Ron
SHORT CHANGED

Haddy, John
COOL CHANGE, ph

Hadej, Joanna
HEIDENLOCHER

Hadzinassios, George
KNOCK-OUT, m

Haesbrouck, Rosanne Van
MERCI MONSIEUR ROBERTSON, ed

Haeusermann, Ruedi
DUNKI-SCHOTT, m

Hafford, Teri
JO JO DANCER, YOUR LIFE IS CALLING

Hafner, Franz
HEIDENLOCHER

Hagan, Jennifer
FOR LOVE ALONE

Hagan, Kevin
LEGAL EAGLES; PLAYING FOR KEEPS; POWER

Hagen, Ross
ARMED RESPONSE

Hagerty, Michael
NOTHING IN COMMON; ONE MORE SATURDAY NIGHT

Haggerty, Dan
ABDUCTED

Haggerty, H.B.
HOLLYWOOD VICE SQUAD; RAD

Hagiwara, Kenichi
LOVE LETTER

Hagler, Nik
PRAY FOR DEATH

Hagstrand, Lisa
PA LIV OCH DOD, ph

Hagstrom, Lars
BRODERNA MOZART, ed; DEMONER, ed

Hagstrom, Lasse
Obituaries

Hahn, Archie
RADIOACTIVE DREAMS

Hahn, Donald
3:15, THE MOMENT OF TRUTH

Hahn, Eric
P.O.W. THE ESCAPE

Hahn, Jess
LA GALETTE DU ROI

Hahn-Peterson, John
BARNDOMMENS GADE

Hahne, Peter
ANGRY HARVEST, p

Hai, Yu
MARTIAL ARTS OF SHAOLIN

Haigh, Michael
DANGEROUS ORPHANS

Hailian, Yang
BEI AIQING YIWANGDE JIAOLUO

Haim, Carol
LUCAS

Haim, Corey
LUCAS

Haines, P.Y.
ONE NIGHT ONLY, w

Haines, Randa
CHILDREN OF A LESSER GOD, d

Haines, Richard W.
CLASS OF NUKE 'EM HIGH; CLASS OF NUKE 'EM HIGH, d

Haitkin, Jacques
IMAGEMAKER, THE, ph; QUIET COOL, ph

Hajdu, Alex
NAKED CAGE, THE, art d

Hakeem
WILDCATS

Haker, Gabrielle
ROUND MIDNIGHT

Hansen, Aase
TWIST & SHOUT

Hansen, Al
SUNSET STRIP

Hansen, Arne
MORD I MORKET; TWIST & SHOUT

Hansen, Benny
VALHALLA

Hansen, Danna
SALVADOR

Hansen, Litten
BARNDOMMENS GADE

Hanson, Annie
HALF MOON STREET

Hanson, Kathy
SPACECAMP

Hanson, Nigel
KNIGHTS AND EMERALDS

Hansson, Lars
BRODERNA MOZART

Hansson, Lena T.
BRODERNA MOZART

Haohuol, Herve
EL RIO DE ORO, p

Happ, Douglas
SCORPION

Haq, Badsha
KIND OF ENGLISH, A

Haque, Amanul
DAHAN, m

Harada, Kiwako
DAYS OF HELL

Harada, Mieko
KATAKU NO HITO

Harada, Yoshio
COMIC MAGAZINE

Harbor, Patty
DESERT BLOOM

Harbst, Rollie
REVENGE OF THE TEENAGE VIXENS FROM OUTER
SPACE, THE

Harbst, Sharon
REVENGE OF THE TEENAGE VIXENS FROM OUTER
SPACE, THE

Harclerode, Rebecca
SCREAMPLAY

Hardelin, Tobias
MOA

Harden, Elizabeth
RECRUITS

Harden, Marcia Gay
IMAGEMAKER, THE

Hardester, Crofton
DEVASTATOR, THE

Hardi, Marlia
TITAN SERAMBUT DIBELAH TUJUH

Hardie, Kate
MONA LISA

Hardin, Jerry
BIG TROUBLE IN LITTLE CHINA

Hardin, Melora
IRON EAGLE; SOUL MAN

Hardin, Tim
DR. OTTO AND THE RIDDLE OF THE GLOOM BEAM,
m/l

Harding, Axel
KING AND HIS MOVIE, A, p

Harding, Nicholas
DOT AND KEETO, anim

Hardwick, Katheryn
THRASHIN', prod d

Hardy, J.J.
NOBODY'S FOOL

Hardy, Jeremy
MONA LISA

Hardy, Jonathan
BACKSTAGE, d; BACKSTAGE, w

Hardy, Michel
PEKIN CENTRAL, m

Hardy, Robert
DEATH OF THE HEART, THE

Hare, Will
VENDETTA

Harel, Sharon
EVERY TIME WE SAY GOODBYE, p

Harfouch, Corinna
DAS HAUS AM FLUSS

Hargitay, Mariska
WELCOME TO 18

Hargreaves, John
COMRADES; MALCOLM; SKY PIRATES

Harington, Donald
RETURN, w

Hark, Tsui
BETTER TOMORROW, A, p

Harkonen, Anna-Leena
LINNA

Harlan, Robin
HOLLYWOOD VICE SQUAD

Harlan, Scott
POWER

Harley, Richard
THUNDER WARRIOR

Harlin, Renny
BORN AMERICAN, d; BORN AMERICAN, w

Harlow, Richard
SILK

Harman, Barry
MY LITTLE PONY, m/l

Harmon, Elizabeth
3:15, THE MOMENT OF TRUTH

Harmon, Robert
HITCHER, THE, d

Harmstorf, Raymund
MANHUNT, THE; THUNDER WARRIOR

Harnedy, Clare
COMBAT SHOCK

Harnois, Elisabeth
WHERE ARE THE CHILDREN?

Harper, David
3:15, THE MOMENT OF TRUTH

Harper, Jessica
IMAGEMAKER, THE

Harper, Sarah
CASTAWAY

Harper, Tess
CRIMES OF THE HEART

Harper, Virgil
WHAT WAITS BELOW, ph

Harrelson, Woody
WILDCATS

Harrigan, Donald
LUCAS

Harrington, Dennis
IMPURE THOUGHTS

Harrington, Laura
MAXIMUM OVERDRIVE

Harrington, Mark
BAND OF THE HAND, art d

Harris, Barbara
PEGGY SUE GOT MARRIED

Harris, Bonnie
WINDRIDER, w

Harris, David
FIRE WITH FIRE; HYPER SAPIEN: PEOPLE FROM
ANOTHER STAR, spec eff; QUICKSILVER

Harris, Dermot
Obituaries

Harris, Enid
FIRE WITH FIRE, cos

Harris, Fox
SID AND NANCY

Harris, Frank
LOW BLOW, d; LOW BLOW, ed; LOW BLOW, ph;
PATRIOT, THE, d; PATRIOT, THE, ph

Harris, Harold
THAT'S LIFE

Harris, Howard
Obituaries

Harris, Joan
MANHATTAN PROJECT, THE; MORE THINGS
CHANGE, THE

Harris, JoAnn
LAST RESORT, THE, ch

Harris, Joshua
JUST BETWEEN FRIENDS

Harris, Julius
MY CHAUFFEUR

Harris, Julius W.
HOLLYWOOD VICE SQUAD

Harris, June
NIGHT OF THE CREEPS

Harris, Leon
SPACECAMP, art d

Harris, Moira
ONE MORE SATURDAY NIGHT

Harris, Penny
ECHO PARK

Harris, Randy
DESERT BLOOM

Harris, Richard A.
GOLDEN CHILD, THE, ed; WILDCATS, ed

Harris, Ron
SPACECAMP

Harris, Tan'ya
WILDCATS

Harris, Tom
NO RETREAT, NO SURRENDER

Harris, Wynetta
ONE MORE SATURDAY NIGHT

Harris, Wynton
ONE MORE SATURDAY NIGHT

Harrison, Cathryn
DUET FOR ONE

Harrison, Cynthia
VENDETTA

Harrison, Eric
JUMPIN' JACK FLASH

Harrison, Evangeline
DUET FOR ONE, cos

Harrison, Frank Rollins
PLAYING FOR KEEPS

Harrison, George
SHANGHAI SURPRISE; SHANGHAI SURPRISE, m

Harrison, Harvey
CASTAWAY, ph

Harrison, Katherine
ROCKIN' ROAD TRIP

Harrison, Ken
ON VALENTINE'S DAY, d

Harrison, Noel
POWER

Harrison, Philip
52 PICK-UP, prod d

Harrison, Rachel
NUTCRACKER: THE MOTION PICTURE

Harrison, Richard
SCALPS, w

Harrison, Sebastian
L'APACHE BIANCO

Harrity, Colleen
GIRLS SCHOOL SCREAMERS

Harrold, Kathryn
RAW DEAL

Harry, Burton Lee
THUNDER RUN, ed

Harry, Deborah
MONEY PIT, THE, m/l

Harry, T. Michael
IN THE SHADOW OF KILIMANJARO, w

Harryson, John
JONSSONLIGAN DYKER UPP IGEN

Harsanyi, Gabor
KOJAK BUDAPESTEN

Hart, Christina
CHECK IS IN THE MAIL, THE

Hart, Christopher
EAT AND RUN, d; EAT AND RUN, w

Hart, David
LEGAL EAGLES

Hart, Ian
NO SURRENDER

Hart, Joe
WEEKEND WARRIORS

Hart, John
SLOANE, ph

Hart, Linda
BEST OF TIMES, THE

Hart, Maarten't
FLIGHT OF RAINBIRDS, A, w

Hart, Rod
NOBODY'S FOOL

Hart, Roxanne
HIGHLANDER

Hart, Stan
EAT AND RUN, w

Hart, Veronica
DEATHMASK; SEX APPEAL

Hartford, Glen
HELL SQUAD

Hartford, Ken
HELL SQUAD, p, d&w

Hartigan, John
JAKE SPEED, spec eff

Hartigan, John C.
THRASHIN', spec eff

Hartley, Derek
LABYRINTH

Hartley, Louise
HOLLYWOOD ZAP!

Hartley, Pat
ABSOLUTE BEGINNERS

Hartley, Richard
GOOD FATHER, THE, m

Hartline, Cynthia
MOVIE HOUSE MASSACRE

Hartline, Gene
THREE AMIGOS

Hartman, Billy
HIGHLANDER

Hartman, Dan
EYE OF THE TIGER, m/l

Hartman, Paul
AMERICAN ANTHEM

Hartman, Phil
LAST RESORT, THE

Hartmann, Phil E.
JUMPIN' JACK FLASH

Hartmann, Philip E.
THREE AMIGOS

Hartowicz, Hana
PARTING GLANCES

Hartowicz, Sylwia
PARTING GLANCES

Hartwig, Wolf C.
NO TIME TO DIE, p

Hartz, Jim
POWER

Harvest, Rainbow
STREETS OF GOLD

Harvey, Alicia Shonte
JO JO DANCER, YOUR LIFE IS CALLING

Harvey, Astley
ABSOLUTE BEGINNERS

Harvey, Jack
BLUE VELVET

Harvey, Richard
HALF MOON STREET, m; PING PONG, m

Harvey, Rolf
FLY, THE, art d

Harvey, Rupert
CRITTERS, p

Harvey, Terrence
SKY BANDITS

Harvey, Tracy
TWELFTH NIGHT

Harwell, Chris
DR. OTTO AND THE RIDDLE OF THE GLOOM BEAM

Harwell, Trey
DR. OTTO AND THE RIDDLE OF THE GLOOM BEAM

Harwood, Bo
ECHO PARK, m/l

Harwood, Linda
MURPHY'S LAW

Harwood, Stewart
LADY JANE

Has, Wojciech
OSOBISTY PAMIETNIK GRZESZNIKA PRZEZ NIEGO
SAMEGO SPISANY, d

Hasegawa, Kazuhiko
CRAZY FAMILY, THE, p

Hasenaecker, Maria
VIRUS HAS NO MORALS, A

Hashimoto, Natalie N.
THE KARATE KID PART II

Hassan, Mamoun
NO SURRENDER, p

Hassani, Hassan El
LAST IMAGE, THE

Hasselvall, Frida
BRODERNA MOZART

Hassim, Rina
SECANGKIR KOPI PAHIT

Hassler, Jurg
EL SUIZO—UN AMOUR EN ESPAGNE, ph

Hata, Masanori
KONEKO MONOGATARI, d; KONEKO MONOGATARI,
w

Hately, John
RAW DEAL

Hatfield, Hurd
CRIMES OF THE HEART

Hathaway, Noah
TROLL

Hathaway, Robert
TROLL

Hatley, T. Marvin   [Thomas Marvin Hatley]
Obituaries

Hatlo, Anders
DROMMESLOTTER

Hatoupi, Dimitra
CARAVAN SARAI

Hattangadi, Rohini
AGHAAT

Hattangady, Rohini
DEBSHISHU

Hatwig, Hans
GRONA GUBBAR FRAN Y.R., d; GRONA GUBBAR
FRAN Y.R., w

Hatzakis, Christos
SCHETIKA ME TON VASSILI

Hauberg, Annelise
MORD I MORKET, cos; WOLF AT THE DOOR, THE,
cos

Haudepin, Sabine
CORPS ET BIENS; MAX MON AMOUR

Hauer, Rutger
HITCHER, THE

Hauff, Alexander
MEIER

Hauff, Reinhard
STAMMHEIM, d

Haufrect, Alan
MY MAN ADAM

Hauft, Alexander
WOHIN MIT WILLFRIED?

Haug, Ole Fredrik
RAVEN, ph

Hauge, Torleif
BLACKOUT, ed

Haughey, Daniel
PARTING GLANCES; PARTING GLANCES, art d

Haugland, Aage
FLAMBEREDE HJERTER

Hausam, Edwin
JO JO DANCER, YOUR LIFE IS CALLING

Hauser, Fay
JO JO DANCER, YOUR LIFE IS CALLING

Hauser, Kim
PLAYING FOR KEEPS

Hauser, Nancy Locke
3:15, THE MOMENT OF TRUTH

Hauser, Wings
3:15, THE MOMENT OF TRUTH; JO JO DANCER,
YOUR LIFE IS CALLING

Hausman, Michael
DESERT BLOOM, p; FLIGHT OF THE SPRUCE
GOOSE, p

Hausserman, Mischa
MURPHY'S LAW

Havard, Sheyla
HELL SQUAD

Havas, Sari
BORN AMERICAN

Havens, Jenny
WILDCATS

Havers, Nigel
DEATH OF THE HEART, THE

Haverur, Kelly
MEN'S CLUB, THE

Haviland, Consuelo de
BETTY BLUE

Havilio, Harry
DIAPASON

Havukainen, Riita
PIMEYS ODOTTA

Havukainen, Riitta
KUNINGAS LAHTEE RANSKAAN

Hawk, Tony
THRASHIN'

Hawker, John
MURPHY'S LAW

Hawkes, Maureen
SORORITY HOUSE MASSACRE

Hawkes, Terri
KILLER PARTY

Hawkes, Terry
CRAZY MOON

Hawkins, Officer Stephen
MANHUNTER

Hawkins, Paul
SCREAMPLAY

Hawkins, Seth Oliver
CLASS OF NUKE 'EM HIGH

Hawksley, Brian
HALF MOON STREET

Hawn, Goldie
WILDCATS

Haworth, Ted
POLTERGEIST II, prod d

Hawthorne, Dave
RYDER, P.I.; RYDER, P.I., w

Hawtrey, Kay
CONFIDENTIAL

Hay, John
BOY IN BLUE, THE, cos

Hay, Rod
DOT AND KEETO, ed; DOT AND THE WHALE, ed

Hayard, Kevin
QUEEN CITY ROCKERS, ph

Hayashi, Kaizo
TO SLEEP SO AS TO DREAM, d&w; TO SLEEP SO AS
TO DREAM, ed; TO SLEEP SO AS TO DREAM, p

Hayashi, Marc
THE KARATE KID PART II

Hayashi, Michiko
ORA TOKYO SA YUKUDA

Hayden, Dennis
JO JO DANCER, YOUR LIFE IS CALLING; MURPHY'S
LAW

Hayden, Naura
PERILS OF P.K., THE; PERILS OF P.K., THE, ed;
PERILS OF P.K., THE, w

Hayden, Peter
ARRIVING TUESDAY; FOOTROT FLATS

Hayden, Sterling   [Sterling Relyea Walter]
Obituaries

Hayes, Allan
NEON MANIACS

Hayes, Billy
SCORPION

Hayes, Bruce
WIRED TO KILL, spec eff

Hayes, Carey
RAD

Hayes, Chad
RAD

Hayes, Elizabeth
KING KONG LIVES

Hayes, Holly
BACK TO SCHOOL

Hayes, Richard
F/X

Hayes, Roy
FINE MESS, A, m/l

Hayes, Steve
IMAGEMAKER, THE

Hayes, Vister
BEST OF TIMES, THE

Haygarth, Tony
CLOCKWISE

Hayman, Carole
LADY JANE

Hayman, Damaris
DEATH OF THE HEART, THE

Hayman, David
GOSPEL ACCORDING TO VIC, THE; MURPHY'S
LAW; SID AND NANCY

Haynes, Cal
MURPHY'S LAW

Haynes, Carol
IMPURE THOUGHTS

Haynes, Hilda
Obituaries

Haynes, Stacey
KNIGHTS AND EMERALDS

Haynes, Tiger
MOSQUITO COAST, THE; RATBOY

Haynie, Jim
PRETTY IN PINK

Hayward, Kevin
BRIDGE TO NOWHERE, ph

Hayward, Lisa
ARMED RESPONSE

Hayward, William
BLUE CITY, p

Haywood, Chris
DOGS IN SPACE; MALCOLM

Haywood, Steve
INSTANT JUSTICE

Hazell, C. Vaughn
AMERICA, ed

Hazelwood, John
FIREWALKER

Henning, Golden
WISDOM

Henning, Martin
MOTTEN IM LICHT, w

Henning-Jensen, Astrid
BARNDOMMENS GADE, d; BARNDOMMENS GADE, w

Hennings, Sam
JO JO DANCER, YOUR LIFE IS CALLING

Henricsson, Gudrun
BRODERNA MOZART

Henriksen, Lance
ALIENS; CHOKE CANYON

Henriksen, Sven
X

Henrikson, Mathias
I LAGENS NAMN

Henriksson, Krister
MOA

Henriques, Darryl
DOWN AND OUT IN BEVERLY HILLS; FINE MESS, A

Henriques, III, Edouard F.
BLUE CITY, makeup

Henritze, Bette
BRIGHTON BEACH MEMOIRS

Henry, Chuck
WISDOM

Henry, David Lee
8 MILLION WAYS TO DIE, w

Henry, Dolly
KNIGHTS AND EMERALDS

Henry, Gregg
LAST OF PHILIP BANTER, THE; LAST OF PHILIP BANTER, THE, m/l; PATRIOT, THE

Henry, Guy
LADY JANE

Henry, Jim
QUICKSILVER

Henry, Laura
SEPARATE VACATIONS

Henry, Martha
DANCING IN THE DARK

Henry, Pierre
AMERICA 3000

Hensel, Karen
PSYCHO III

Henson, Brian
LABYRINTH

Henson, Cheryl
LABYRINTH

Henson, Heather
LITTLE SHOP OF HORRORS

Henson, Jim
LABYRINTH, d; LABYRINTH, w

Henstell, Diana
DEADLY FRIEND, w

Henszelman, Stefan
BALLERUP BOULEVARD, ed

Henteloff, Alex
52 PICK-UP

Henze, Hans Werner
COMRADES, m

Henzel, Patrik
GRONA GUBBAR FRAN Y.R., m

Hepp, Hardy
DER SCHWARZE TANNER, m

Heppy, Marguerite
SHORT CIRCUIT

Herbert, John
AS SETE VAMPIRAS

Herbert, Martin
FORMULA FOR MURDER, d; FORMULA FOR MURDER, w

Herbert, Tim
Obituaries

Herce, Luis
LOLA, w

Herd, Andrew
LABYRINTH

Heredia, Lisa
SUMMER

Herek, Stephen
CRITTERS, d; CRITTERS, w

Herig, Jeff
SOMETHING WILD

Herland, Richard
SKY BANDITS, p

Herlihy, Ed
FINE MESS, A

Herlitzka, Roberto
SUMMER NIGHT WITH GREEK PROFILE, ALMOND EYES AND SCENT OF BASIL

Herman, Eugenia
SCENY DZIECIECE Z ZYCIA PROWINCJI

Herman, Jean
BLEU COMME L'ENFER, w

Herman, Paul
AT CLOSE RANGE; COLOR OF MONEY, THE; STREETS OF GOLD

Hermann, Betsy
SKY BANDITS, cos

Hermann, John
VIOLATED

Hermann, Villi
INNOCENZA, p&d; INNOCENZA, w

Hermary-Vielle, Catherine
LA GUEPE, w

Hermes, Hassen
AL-KAS

Hermida, Rodolfo
DIAPASON, art d

Hermitage, Doreen
LITTLE SHOP OF HORRORS

Hermosa, Sarai
TEO EL PELIRROJO

Hermosillo, Jaime Humberto
DONA HERLINDA AND HER SON, d&w

Herms, Gabriele
WALKMAN BLUES, ed

Hermus, Guus
ASSAULT, THE

Hernandez, Claudia
SALVADOR

Hernandez, Eduardo
KING AND HIS MOVIE, A

Hernandez, Fernando
GAVILAN O PALOMA

Hernandez, Humberto
LEJANIA, p; UN HOMBRE DE EXITO, p

Hernandez, John
BACK TO SCHOOL

Hernandez, Kathleen
SCORPION

Hernandez, Rene
SUMMER

Hernandez, Vicky
LA MANSION DE ARAUCAIMA; VISA U.S.A.

Hernandez, Wilfredo
8 MILLION WAYS TO DIE

Heron, Ken
NIGHT OF THE CREEPS

Herouet, Marc
GOLDEN EIGHTIES, m; GOLDEN EIGHTIES, m/l

Herran, Adriana
LA MANSION DE ARAUCAIMA

Herrecks, Peter
WHAT COMES AROUND, w

Herrera, Diego
LOS ASES DE CONTRABANDO, m

Herrera, Humberto
LOS ASES DE CONTRABANDO

Herrera, Lola
EN PENUMBRA

Herrera, Manuel
CAPABLANCA, d; CAPABLANCA, w

Herrera, Norma
NOCHE DE JUERGA

Herrera, Ricardo
KILLING OF SATAN, THE, ph

Herrera, Victor Manuel
YAKO—CAZADOR DE MALDITOS, ph

Herrero, George
PULSEBEAT, ph

Herring, Pem
LEGAL EAGLES, ed

Herrington, David
JUDGEMENT IN STONE, A, ph

Hershberger, Gary
FREE RIDE; MY MAN ADAM

Hershey, Barbara
HANNAH AND HER SISTERS; HOOSIERS

Hershkovitz, Zmira
MALKAT HAKITA, art d

Hertford, Chelsea
POLTERGEIST II

Hertford, Whitby
POLTERGEIST II

Hertz, Helle
BALLERUP BOULEVARD; TAKE IT EASY

Hertz-Hestranek, Miguel
'38

Hertzberg, Jordan
ARMED RESPONSE

Hertzberg, Lauren
ARMED RESPONSE

Hertzberg, Paul
ARMED RESPONSE, p&w

Hertzka, Vera
ELYSIUM, ed

Hertzog, Paul
HOLLYWOOD ZAP!, m; HOLLYWOOD ZAP!, md; MY CHAUFFEUR, m

Hervey, Jason
BACK TO SCHOOL

Herviale, Jeanne
FRENCH LESSON

Herz, Michael
CLASS OF NUKE 'EM HIGH, p

Herz, Sloane
CLASS OF NUKE 'EM HIGH

Herzfeld, John
COBRA

Herzner, Norbert
NO TIME TO DIE, ed

Herzog, John
CONFIDENTIAL, ph

Heschong, Albert
CROSSROADS, art d

Hesek, Miroslav
SIESTA VETA

Heshiki, Zenko
THE KARATE KID PART II, tech adv

Heslov, Grant
LEGAL EAGLES

Hess, David
ARMED AND DANGEROUS

Hess, Erika
SCORPION

Hess, Tom
SCORPION

Hess, Walter
DUNKI-SCHOTT

Hesse, Mark
SPIKER

Hesseman, Howard
FLIGHT OF THE NAVIGATOR; INSIDE OUT; MY CHAUFFEUR

Hesser, Michael
45MO PARALLELO, ed

Hessler, Gordon
PRAY FOR DEATH, d

Heufelder, Sylvio Michael
SPRING SYMPHONY

Heusch, Peter
TRANSITTRAUME

Heutschy, Eleanor C.
SHORT CIRCUIT

Hevenor, George
BUSTED UP

Hevilon, Bob
ARMED RESPONSE

Hewett, Christopher
RATBOY

Hewitt, Alan [Alan Everett Hewitt]
Obituaries

Hewitt, Jery
FAT GUY GOES NUTZOID!!, stunts; PLAYING FOR KEEPS; RAW DEAL

Hewitt, Martin
KILLER PARTY

Hewitt, Shawn
FLY, THE

Hewitt, Tessa
INSTANT JUSTICE

Hewitt, Virginia [Virginia Hewitt Meer]
Obituaries

Hewlett, Donald
SAVING GRACE

Hewson, David
SCHOOL FOR VANDALS, m

Hey, Jerry
RAW DEAL, m

Hey, Virginia
CASTAWAY

Heyer, Carol
THUNDER RUN, art d; THUNDER RUN, w

Heyman, Barton
BILLY GALVIN

Heyman, Edward
BLUE VELVET, m/l; MONA LISA, m/l

Heymann, Gotz
JOURNEY, THE, art d

Heynemann, Baptiste
SINCERELY CHARLOTTE

Heynemann, Justine
SINCERELY CHARLOTTE

Heywood, Anne
WHAT WAITS BELOW

Hi, Kim Bok
GILSODOM

Hibbard, Robert
PLAY DEAD

Hickey, Susan
ADVENTURE OF FAUSTUS BIDGOOD, THE, set d

Hickey, William
NAME OF THE ROSE, THE; ONE CRAZY SUMMER

Hickman, Bill
Obituaries

Hickman, Gail Morgan
MURPHY'S LAW, w

Hickman, Mike
REVENGE OF THE TEENAGE VIXENS FROM OUTER
SPACE, THE

Hickman, Rick
WEEKEND WARRIORS

Hicks, Caitlin
BEER

Hicks, Catherine
PEGGY SUE GOT MARRIED; STAR TREK IV: THE
VOYAGE HOME

Hicks, James
MORNING AFTER, THE, w

Hicks, John Alan
SWEET LIBERTY, set d

Hicks, Mark
NINJA TURF

Hicks, Marsha
NOBODY'S FOOL

Hicks, Peter
PLATOON

Hicks, Tommy Redmond
SHE'S GOTTA HAVE IT

Hickson, Joan
CLOCKWISE

Hidari, Tokie
LOVE LETTER

Hidaya, Rachmat
TITAN SERAMBUT DIBELAH TUJUH

Hiergesell, Geneva
OVER THE SUMMER

Hieronymus, Richard
BALBOA, m

Hietanen, Pedro
BRODERNA MOZART

Hieu, Joseph
QUICKSILVER

Hift, Gaby
MULLERS BURO

Higby, Mary Jane
Obituaries

Higgins, Anthony
MAX MON AMOUR

Higgins, Billy
ROUND MIDNIGHT

Higgins, Michael
ON VALENTINE'S DAY; SEVEN MINUTES IN
HEAVEN

Higginson, Tracey
FOR LOVE ALONE

Highsmith, Patricia
DIE ZWEI GESICHTER DES JANUAR, w

Hightower, Elaine
LOW BLOW

Higino, Raimundo
REI DO RIO, ed

Higuchi, Kanako
TOKIMEDI NI SHISU

Hikida, Soya
SHIN YOROKOBIMO KANASHIMIMO
IKUTOSHITSUKI, p

Hilal, Mohamed
LEL HAB KESSA AKHIRA, m

Hilario, Lusito
P.O.W. THE ESCAPE

Hilbard, John
YES, DET ER FAR!, d; YES, DET ER FAR!, w

Hilboldt, Lise
SWEET LIBERTY

Hildebrandt, Dieter
MEIER

Hilder, Kimble
FAIR GAME, art d

Hile, Joel
DEADLY FRIEND

Hiler, Katherine
MANHATTAN PROJECT, THE

Hilkamo, Pertti
KUNINGAS LAHTEE RANSKAAN, prod d

Hilkamo, Tuula
KUNINGAS LAHTEE RANSKAAN, prod d

Hill, Amy
MOUNTAINTOP MOTEL MASSACRE

Hill, Bernard
MILWR BYCHAN; NO SURRENDER

Hill, Charles
REBEL LOVE

Hill, Charlie
IMPURE THOUGHTS

Hill, Dean
ONE MORE SATURDAY NIGHT

Hill, Debra
HEAD OFFICE, p

Hill, Dennis M.
ODD JOBS, ed

Hill, Derek
GETTING EVEN, set d

Hill, George
BLUE VELVET, spec eff

Hill, Harry
CRAZY MOON

Hill, Michael
ARMED AND DANGEROUS, ed; GUNG HO, ed

Hill, Nicholas
PARTING GLANCES

Hill, Richard
DEVASTATOR, THE

Hill, Rodney
HEARTBREAK RIDGE; WILDCATS

Hill, Roland E.
Obituaries; NOTHING IN COMMON, set d

Hill, Steven
BRIGHTON BEACH MEMOIRS; HEARTBURN; LEGAL
EAGLES; ON VALENTINE'S DAY; RAW DEAL

Hill, Tricia
BACK TO SCHOOL

Hill, Walter
BLUE CITY, p; BLUE CITY, w; CROSSROADS, d

Hillebrandt, Stanley
DE WISSELWACHTER, p

Hillel, Ossi
NADIA; SHTAY ETZBA'OT M'TZIDON

Hiller, Colette
ALIENS

Hiller, Wendy
DEATH OF THE HEART, THE

Hilliard, Jay
DOWN BY LAW

Hilliard, Robert
SNO-LINE, w; VASECTOMY: A DELICATE MATTER, w

Hilliard, Ryan
HEARTBURN

Hills, Beverley
KNIGHTS AND EMERALDS

Hills, Joan
MORE THINGS CHANGE, THE, makeup

Hiltermann, Bob
CHILDREN OF A LESSER GOD

Himmelstein, David
POWER, w

Hinchman, Bert
STEWARDESS SCHOOL

Hindle, Art
SAY YES

Hinds, Marcia
AVENGING FORCE, prod d; DANGEROUSLY CLOSE,
prod d; P.O.W. THE ESCAPE, prod d

Hindy, Joseph
WHERE ARE THE CHILDREN?

Hines, Gregory
RUNNING SCARED

Hing, Kwan Pak
MILLIONAIRE'S EXPRESS, THE

Hing, Leung Chi
PEKING OPERA BLUES, art d

Hinger, Joel
LOW BLOW

Hingle, Pat
IN 'N' OUT; MAXIMUM OVERDRIVE

Hinkler, Dianne
SHADOWS RUN BLACK

Hino, Shohej
YARI NO GONZA

Hinojos, Deanna
AMERICAN JUSTICE

Hinojosa, Joaquin
TIEMPO DE SILENCIO

Hinojosa, Melo
SALVADOR, art d

Hinshaw, Robert
SCORPION

Hinton, Marcia
GIRLS SCHOOL SCREAMERS

Hinz, Joan
LOYALTIES

Hinz, Terry
SWEET LIBERTY

Hione, Sam
ARMED RESPONSE

Hippe, Laura
Obituaries

Hippolyte, Tony
ABSOLUTE BEGINNERS

Hirsch, Daniel
MY CHAUFFEUR

Hirsch, Lou
HAUNTED HONEYMOON

Hirsch, Paul
FERRIS BUELLER'S DAY OFF, ed

Hirschfeld, Gerald
HEAD OFFICE, ph

Hirschfeld, Leonard
CHECK IS IN THE MAIL, THE

Hirschler, Kurt
Obituaries

Hirschmeier, Alfred
DAS HAUS AM FLUSS, set d; GRITTA VOM
RATTENSCHLOSS, set d; SPRING SYMPHONY, art d;
SPRING SYMPHONY, set d

Hirsh, Michael
CARE BEARS MOVIE II: A NEW GENERATION, p;
SKY PIRATES, ed; SKY PIRATES, p

Hirshman, Cheryl
SCREAMPLAY; SCREAMPLAY, art d; SCREAMPLAY,
spec eff

Hirt, Christianne
BULLIES

Hirtle, Dale
BUSTED UP

Hirtz, Dagmar
ROSA LUXEMBURG, ed

Hisp, Shawn
SCREEN TEST

Hizkiyahu, Avner
EVERY TIME WE SAY GOODBYE

Hjelm, Asa
MOA, cos

Hjelm, Ingrid
MOA, cos

Hjelm, Keve
DEN FRUSNA LEOPARDEN; HUD

Hjulstrom, Lennart
I LAGENS NAMN; MOA

Hlavacova, Jana
LEV S BILOU HRIVOU

Ho, Chin Suit
MR. VAMPIRE

Ho, Michael
ABSOLUTE BEGINNERS

Hoag, Bill
SALVADOR

Hobbs, Christopher
CARAVAGGIO, prod d

Hobbs, Ron
LEGAL EAGLES, art d

Hobbs, Skip
BLUE MAN, THE, set d

Hobbs, William
PIRATES, ch

Hobson, Laura Z. [Laura Kean Zametkin]
Obituaries

Hobson, Verno O.
HANNAH AND HER SISTERS

Hochberg, Richard
MURPHY'S LAW

Hochle, Constanzia
SCHMUTZ

Hochmann, H.H.
SPRING SYMPHONY

Hodder, Kane
AVENGING FORCE; HOUSE, stunts

Hodge, Patricia
DEATH OF THE HEART, THE; HUD

Hodgeman, Edwin
PLAYING BEATIE BOW

Hodges, John
STAND BY ME

Hodges, Kenneth
STAND BY ME

Hodges, Thomas E.
LUCAS

Hodian, John
GIRLS SCHOOL SCREAMERS, m

Hodor, Darek
AMOROSA, ed

Hodson, Don
ELOGIO DELLA PAZZIA

Hoelcher, Philip
FLIGHT OF THE NAVIGATOR

Hoelscher, Devin
WIRED TO KILL

Hoeltz, Nikola
FOLLOWING THE FUHRER, cos

Hoenig, Dov
MANHUNTER, ed

Hoenig, Michael
9½ WEEKS, m; WRAITH, THE, m

Hoeree, Arthur
Obituaries

Hoesl, Tobias
LE MINIERE DEL KILIMANGIARO

Hof, Ursula
EIN BLICK—UND DIE LIEBE BRICHT AUS, ed

Hofer, Anita
ANGRY HARVEST

Hoffenberg, Mason
Obituaries

Hofferman, Jon
SORORITY HOUSE MASSACRE

Hoffman, .T.A.
NUTCRACKER: THE MOTION PICTURE, w

Hoffman, Beth Webb
Obituaries

Hoffman, Dee-Dee
MOVIE HOUSE MASSACRE

Hoffman, Iris
SMILE OF THE LAMB, THE

Hoffman, Monty
HOWARD THE DUCK

Hoffman, Sonia
EMMA'S WAR, ed

Hoffman, Thom
45MO PARALLELO; PERVOLA: TRACKS IN THE
SNOW

Hoffmann, Jutta
BLIND DIRECTOR, THE

Hoffmann, Nico
DER POLENWEIHER, d

Hoffmeyer, Stig
MANDEN I MAANEN; TAKE IT EASY

Hofstra, Jack
BAND OF THE HAND, ed; YOUNGBLOOD, ed

Hogan, Boscoe
SCREAMTIME

Hogan, Frankie
DEVIL IN THE FLESH, cos

Hogan, Katherine
SCREAMPLAY

Hogan, Michael
LOST!

Hogan, Paul
"CROCODILE" DUNDEE; "CROCODILE" DUNDEE,
w; People to Watch

Hogan, Steve
MANHUNTER

Hoger, Hannelore
DER SOMMER DES SAMURAI

Hogg, Ian
LADY JANE

Hogg, James
OSOBISTY PAMIETNIK GRZESZNIKA PRZEZ NIEGO
SAMEGO SPISANY, w

Hoglund, Lars
SACRIFICE, THE, spec eff

Hohler, Franz
DUNKI-SCHOTT; DUNKI-SCHOTT, w

Hohman, R.J.
RADIOACTIVE DREAMS, spec eff

Hohn, Gofi
PARADIES, set d

Hoier, John
ADVENTURES OF THE AMERICAN RABBIT, THE, m/l

Hoigard, Cecilie
HARD ASFALT, d&w

Hoimark, Peter
MORD I MORKET, prod d; MORD I MORKET, spec eff

Hojfeldt, Solbjorg
WOLF AT THE DOOR, THE

Hojmark, Pernille
FLAMBEREDE HJERTER

Holanda, Flavio
AS SETE VAMPIRAS, p

Holbrook, Brad
POWER

Holbrook, Ellen
SCREAMPLAY

Holby, Kristin
MANHUNTER

Holcomb, Kimberly
STRIPPER

Holcomb, Scott
SPACECAMP

Holden, Hal
PLAYING FOR KEEPS

Holden, Laurie
SEPARATE VACATIONS

Holder, Ram John
HALF MOON STREET; MY BEAUTIFUL
LAUNDRETTE; PASSION OF REMEMBRANCE, THE

Holdridge, Lee
MEN'S CLUB, THE, m; MEN'S CLUB, THE, m/l

Hole, Fred
ALIENS, art d

Holender, Adam
BOY WHO COULD FLY, THE, ph

Holewa, Thomas
LOVE ME!, ed

Holland, Agnieszka
ANGRY HARVEST, d; ANGRY HARVEST, w

Holland, Byrd
SAY YES, makeup

Holland, Rodney
NO SURRENDER, ed

Holland, Savage Steve
ONE CRAZY SUMMER, anim; ONE CRAZY SUMMER,
d; ONE CRAZY SUMMER, w

Hollander, Judith
MIN PAPA AR TARZAN, d&w

Hollar, Steve
HOOSIERS

Hollenbeck, Heather
NUTCRACKER: THE MOTION PICTURE

Hollergschwandtner, Fritz
WELCOME IN VIENNA, set d

Holliday, Charlie
WISDOM

Holliday, Elmo
ARUNATA PERA, ed

Hollie, Jeffrey
PRETTY IN PINK

Holliger, Peter
KONZERT FUR ALICE

Hollingsworth, Diane
BOY IN BLUE, THE

Hollingsworth, Hillary
SORORITY HOUSE MASSACRE

Hollis, John
VALHALLA

Holloman, Bridget
STOOGEMANIA

Holloway, Chris
ONE MORE SATURDAY NIGHT

Hollowell, Todd
TOUGH GUYS

Hollowood, Ann
KNIGHTS AND EMERALDS, cos; MR. LOVE, cos

Holly, Lauren
BAND OF THE HAND; SEVEN MINUTES IN HEAVEN

Hollywood, Peter
GOOD FATHER, THE, ed

Holm, Sven
I LAGENS NAMN

Holman, Billy J.
SNO-LINE

Holmberg, Henric
BRODERNA MOZART

Holmberg, Kaj
HUOMENNA, p

Holmebak, Torstein
DROMMESLOTTER

Holmes, Abbe
BIG HURT, THE

Holmes, Catherine
REVENGE OF THE TEENAGE VIXENS FROM OUTER
SPACE, THE

Holmes, Chris
FLAGRANT DESIR, ed

Holmes, Christopher
BAD GUYS , ed

Holmes, Ed
HOWARD THE DUCK; ON VALENTINE'S DAY

Holmes, Jesse
BEER

Holmes, Jim
MY CHAUFFEUR; ODD JOBS

Holmes, Leroy   [Alvin Holms]
Obituaries

Holmes, Paul
SILK

Holmes, Philip
CHILDREN OF A LESSER GOD

Holoubek, Gustaw
JEZIORO BODENSKIE

Holscher, Art
DR. OTTO AND THE RIDDLE OF THE GLOOM BEAM

Holst, Per
FLAMBEREDE HJERTER, p

Holt, Anders
RATTIS, ph

Holt, Bob
ADVENTURES OF THE AMERICAN RABBIT, THE

Holt, Jim
GOING SANE; SHORT CHANGED

Holt, Steve
RAW DEAL

Holte, Vera
NATTSEILERE

Holten, Bo
TWIST & SHOUT, m

Holtenau, Gert
SPRING SYMPHONY

Holtkamp, Hans
PERVOLA: TRACKS IN THE SNOW

Holton, Mark
MODERN GIRLS; MY CHAUFFEUR; STOOGEMANIA

Holtz, Gregory
STREETS OF GOLD

Holtz, Jurgen
ROSA LUXEMBURG

Hom, Jason
NINJA TURF

Hom, Jesper
TAKE IT EASY, d&w

Homans, Jennifer
NUTCRACKER: THE MOTION PICTURE

Hommais, Pascal
LA FEMME SECRETE, p

Homme, Carey
NUTCRACKER: THE MOTION PICTURE

Homolka, Marie
ERDSEGEN, ed

Homolkova, Maria
SCHMUTZ, ed

Homsey, Bonnie Oda
NOBODY'S FOOL; NOBODY'S FOOL, ch

Hon, Szeto Cheuk
MR. VAMPIRE, w

Hon-gung, Lee
ER WOO DONG, cos

Hondo, Med
SARRAOUNIA, p&d; SARRAOUNIA, w

Honess, Peter
HIGHLANDER, ed

Hong, James
BIG TROUBLE IN LITTLE CHINA; GOLDEN CHILD,
THE

Hong, Simon Blake
NINJA TURF, w

Hong, Yue
IN THE WILD MOUNTAINS

Hongyi, Zhang
YU QING SAO, m

Honorato, Marzio
SENZA SCRUPOLI

Honore, Patrick
LOLA

Honthaner, Ron
FREE RIDE, ed

Honzik, Zbynek
LEV S BILOU HRIVOU

Hoo, Walter Soo
BIG TROUBLE

Hood, Don
MORNING AFTER, THE

Hood, Ingram
KNIGHTS AND EMERALDS

Hoogenboom, Willem
CHARLEY, ed; CHARLEY, ph

Hoogendijk, Annemieke
MARIA

Hoogstra, Jaap
PERVOLA: TRACKS IN THE SNOW

Hooker, Buddy Joe
WRAITH, THE, stunts

Hooker, Hank
LONGSHOT, THE, stunts

Hooks, Jan
WILDCATS

Hooks, Regina
MY CHAUFFEUR

Hooper, Carin
INVADERS FROM MARS, cos; TEXAS CHAINSAW
MASSACRE PART 2, THE, cos

Hooper, Tobe
INVADERS FROM MARS, m&d; TEXAS CHAINSAW
MASSACRE PART 2, THE

Hoosein, Hatam
HOB FEE BAGHDAD, ph

Hooser, J. Michael
CRY FROM THE MOUNTAIN, ed; CRY FROM THE
MOUNTAIN, prod d

Hootkins, William
BIGGLES; HAUNTED HONEYMOON

Hoover, John
NOBODY'S FOOL

Hoover, Richard
WISDOM, set d

Hope, Dawn
BLACK JOY

Hope, Erica
BLOODY BIRTHDAY

Hope, Sharon
ONE CRAZY SUMMER

Hope, William
ALIENS

Hopf, Heinz
AMOROSA

Hopkins, Anthony
GOOD FATHER, THE

Hopkins, Bo
WHAT COMES AROUND

Hopkins, Chris
TORMENT, art d

Hopkins, John
TORMENT, p, d&w

Hopkins, Speed
F/X, art d

Hopkins, Virgil
OCEAN DRIVE WEEKEND

Hoppe, Eliana
MORIRAI A MEZZANOTTE

Hoppe, Rolf
DAS HAUS AM FLUSS; SPRING SYMPHONY

Hopper, Dennis
BLUE VELVET; HOOSIERS; RUNNING OUT OF LUCK;
TEXAS CHAINSAW MASSACRE PART 2, THE

Hopson, Lew
DOWN AND OUT IN BEVERLY HILLS; SUNSET STRIP

Horak, Edwin
LISI UND DER GENERAL, ph

Horan, Gerard
MY BEAUTIFUL LAUNDRETTE

Hordern, Michael
COMRADES; LADY JANE; LABYRINTH

Horino, Tad
ELIMINATORS

Horko, Antti
BORN AMERICAN

Hormann, Egbert
EAST OF THE WALL, w

Horn, Ellen
FAREWELL ILLUSION

Horn, Lew
ADVENTURES OF THE AMERICAN RABBIT, THE

Horne, Peter
NUTCRACKER: THE MOTION PICTURE, art d

Horner, James
ALIENS, m; AMERICAN TAIL, AN, m; AMERICAN
TAIL, AN, m/l; NAME OF THE ROSE, THE, m; OFF
BEAT, m; WHERE THE RIVER RUNS BLACK, m

Hornibrook, Timothy
SHORT CHANGED

Hornung, Matthieu
TAGEDIEBE

Hornyak, Paul
SCHLEUSE 17, m

Horowitz, Margherita
SAVING GRACE

Horrall, Craig
SEX APPEAL, w

Horrigan, Billy
TAI-PAN

Horse, Michael
CHECK IS IN THE MAIL, THE

Horsford, Anna Maria
HEARTBURN

Horst, Allen
PIRATES

Horton, Bobby
REBEL LOVE, m

Horton, Michael
DANGEROUS ORPHANS, ed; FOOTROT FLATS, ed

Horton, Peter
WHERE THE RIVER RUNS BLACK

Horton, Vaughn
DESERT BLOOM, m/l

Horvath, Andras
ORDOGI KISERTETEK, ed

Horvitch, Andrew
ELIMINATORS, ed; SLOANE, ed

Horwitz, Dominique
STAMMHEIM

Hosch, Karl
RYDER, P.I., d; RYDER, P.I., p; RYDER, P.I., w

Hosch, Kenneth
RYDER, P.I., art d

Hoshos, R.
WHAT HAPPENED NEXT YEAR, art d

Hoskins, Bob
MONA LISA; SWEET LIBERTY

Hoskins, Timothy
STEWARDESS SCHOOL

Hosni, Souad
EL-GOOA

Hosogoe, Seigo
TAMPOPO, p

Hosoi, Christian
THRASHIN'

Hosoishi, Terumi
CRAZY FAMILY, THE, art d

Hosokoshi, Shogo
TOKIMEDI NI SHISU, p

Hosono, Haruomi
NINGUEN NO YAKUSOKU, m

Hospowsky, Fred
STAMMHEIM

Hossain, Anwar
DAHAN, ph

Hossein, Robert
MAN AND A WOMAN: 20 YEARS LATER, A

Hossu, Emil
NOI, CEI DIN LINIA INTII

Hostalot, Luis
WERTHER

Hotch, Johnny
ABSOLUTE BEGINNERS

Hoth, George
TOMB, THE

Hott, Robert
HOT CHILI, m/l

Hou, So Chun
HUAJIE SHIDAI, m

Houck, Joy
DOWN BY LAW

Houdoy, Chantal
MAUVAIS SANG, makeup

Hough, John
BIGGLES, d

Houk, Benjamin
NUTCRACKER: THE MOTION PICTURE

Houlihan, Keri
MY LITTLE PONY

Houppin, Serge
MAMMAME, m

Houry, George
SUN ON A HAZY DAY, THE, ph

House, Ron
STOOGEMANIA

Houser, Patrick
SPIKER

Houssiau, Michel
LA MOITIE DE L'AMOUR, ph

Houston, Fitzhough
SORORITY HOUSE MASSACRE

Houston, Gary
RAW DEAL

Hove, Anders
FLAMBEREDE HJERTER

Hoversten, Bill
ONE CRAZY SUMMER

Hovik, Christopher
MAX MON AMOUR

Howar, Bader
PRETTY IN PINK

Howard, Adam Coleman
QUIET COOL

Howard, Arliss
LADIES CLUB, THE; LIGHTSHIP, THE

Howard, Clint
GUNG HO; WRAITH, THE

Howard, Curly
STOOGEMANIA

Howard, Duke
SHADOWS RUN BLACK, w

Howard, Frank
ONE MORE SATURDAY NIGHT

Howard, George
MORNING AFTER, THE

Howard, James Newton
8 MILLION WAYS TO DIE, m; HEAD OFFICE, m;
NOBODY'S FOOL, m; TOUGH GUYS, m; WILDCATS,
m

Howard, Jeff
BIG TROUBLE

Howard, Joe
MOVIE HOUSE MASSACRE

Howard, John
AROUND THE WORLD IN EIGHTY WAYS; OVER THE
SUMMER; YOUNG EINSTEIN

Howard, Ken
FOREIGN BODY, m

Howard, Moe
STOOGEMANIA

Howard, Rance
GUNG HO

Howard, Rick
CLASS OF NUKE 'EM HIGH

Howard, Ron
GUNG HO, d

Howard, Sandy
HOLLYWOOD VICE SQUAD, p; KGB—THE SECRET
WAR, p; WHAT WAITS BELOW, p

Howard, Shemp
STOOGEMANIA

Howard, Trevor
FOREIGN BODY

Howarth, Alan
BIG TROUBLE IN LITTLE CHINA, m

Howe, Nancy
BULLIES, makeup

Howe, Tracy
CRAZY MOON

Howell, C. Thomas
HITCHER, THE; SOUL MAN

Howell, Harry
REBEL LOVE

Howell, Hoke
VENDETTA

Howell, Prince
HIGHLANDER

Howell, Robert
OVER THE SUMMER

Howell, Teddy   [Edward Howell]
Obituaries

Howells, Viv
LETTER TO BREZHNEV, makeup

Howes, Douglas
LABYRINTH

Huppert, Caroline
SINCERELY CHARLOTTE, d; SINCERELY CHARLOTTE, w

Huppert, Isabelle
CACTUS; SINCERELY CHARLOTTE

Hurault, Bertrand
PA LIV OCH DOD, w

Hurd, Gale Anne
ALIENS, p

Hurd, James
SOMETHING WILD

Hurd, Malcolm
RAW TUNES

Hurdle, James
LEGAL EAGLES

Hurill, Isobel
ABSOLUTE BEGINNERS

Hurley, Jan
GOING SANE, cos

Hurley, Jay
ONE MORE SATURDAY NIGHT, cos

Hurst, Brian Desmond
Obituaries

Hurst, Michael
DANGEROUS ORPHANS

Hurst, Rick
AMERICAN JUSTICE; BLUE CITY

Hurt, John
JAKE SPEED; ROCINANTE

Hurwitz, Steven
PLAYING FOR KEEPS

Husak, Frantisek
PAVUCINA

Husebo, Nhut
FAREWELL ILLUSION

Huser, Fritz
DUNKI-SCHOTT, art d

Huskey, Happy
OCEAN DRIVE WEEKEND

Huster, Francis
ON A VOLE CHARLIE SPENCER!; ON A VOLE CHARLIE SPENCER!, d&w

Huston, Esther
DR. OTTO AND THE RIDDLE OF THE GLOOM BEAM

Huston, Jimmy
RUNNING SCARED, w

Huston, John
MOMO

Hutabarat, Sum
TITAN SERAMBUT DIBELAH TUJUH

Hutchence, Michael
DOGS IN SPACE

Hutchens, Robert
OVER THE SUMMER

Hutcherson, Bobby
ROUND MIDNIGHT

Hutcherson, Byron D.
SOMETHING WILD

Hutcherson, Eleana
SOMETHING WILD

Hutchings, Geoffrey
CLOCKWISE

Hutchinson, Jeff
ROLLER BLADE

Hutchinson, Peter
MISSION, THE, spec eff

Hutchinson, Ruby
KNIGHTS AND EMERALDS

Hutchinson, Tim
HIGHLANDER, art d

Hutchison, Fiona
BIGGLES

Hutman, Olivier
HIGH SPEED, m

Huttner, Peter
MORRHAR OCH ARTOR

Hutton, Christopher
LOST!, ed

Hutton, Lauren
FLAGRANT DESIR

Huun, Sigrid
X

Huxley, Craig
AMERICAN JUSTICE, m/l

Huyck, Willard
HOWARD THE DUCK, d; HOWARD THE DUCK, w

Huynh, Tran Ngoc
KARMA, ph

Hval, Ella
BLACKOUT

Hwa-kun, Chang
SUMMER AT GRANDPA'S, A, p

Hyams, Peter
RUNNING SCARED, d; RUNNING SCARED, ph

Hyatt, George
OVER THE SUMMER

Hyatt, Pam
CARE BEARS MOVIE II: A NEW GENERATION; POLICE ACADEMY 3: BACK IN TRAINING

Hyatt, Pat
KILLER PARTY

Hyde, Jonathan
DEATH OF THE HEART, THE

Hyde, Jonathon
CARAVAGGIO

Hyde, Michael
MONEY PIT, THE

Hyde-White, Alex
BIGGLES; GIRL FROM MANI, THE

Hyman, Myron A.
BAD GUYS , p

Hyon-hwa, Lee
ER WOO DONG, w

Hyttinen, Niilo
SININEN IMETTAJA; SININEN IMETTAJA, w

Hyunchae, Son
BBONG, ph

Hywel, Dafydd
COMING UP ROSES; MILWR BYCHAN

I, Young Pao
BETTER TOMORROW, A

Iamphungporn, Chareon
PEESUA LAE DOKMAI, p

Ianchevska, Zane
SVESAS KAISLIBAS

Ianmin, Zhang
PIAOBO QIYU, p

Iannicelli, Ray
F/X

Iannone, Bruno
MONEY PIT, THE

Ibanez, Joseph M.
SOLDIER'S REVENGE

Ibanez, Manuel
SE SUFRE PERO SE GOZA

Ibanez, Roger
NANOU

Ibarra, Mirta
PLACIDO

Ibolya, Fekete
KALI PATRITHA, SYNTROFE, w

Ibragimbekov, Roustam
KHRANI MENIO, MOI TALISMAN, w

Ichise, Takashige
TO SLEEP SO AS TO DREAM, p

Ickowicz, Irene
SERE CUALQUIER COSA PERO TE QUIERO, w

Idle, Eric
TRANSFORMERS: THE MOVIE, THE

Igar, Stanislaw
DEATH SENTENCE

Igawa, Togo
HALF MOON STREET

Igliozzi, Daniela
UNA CASA IN BILICO

Iglodi, Istvan
ORDOGI KISERTETEK

Ignez, Helena
NEM TUDO E VERDADE

Ignon, Sandy
DOWN AND OUT IN BEVERLY HILLS; LAST RESORT, THE

Iho, Arvo
IDEAALMAASTIK, ph; NAERATA OMETI, d; NAERATA OMETI, ph

III, Clarence Williams
52 PICK-UP

Ikebe, Ryo
UEMURA NAOMI MONOGATARI

Il-Song, Jong
GILSODOM, ph

Ilander, Kicki
ORMENS VAG PA HALLEBERGET, art d

Ildahl, Eirik
BLACKOUT, w

Iliopoulos, Dinos
O MELISSOKOMOS

Iliutschenko, Slava
CHUZHAJA, BELAJA I RJABOJ

Illarramedi, Angel
27 HORAS, m

Illes, Janos
KISMASZAT ES A GEZENGUZOK, ph

Ilyin, Vladimir
TORPIDONOSTCI, ph

Im, Gina S.
NINJA TURF

Imada, Brian
BIG TROUBLE IN LITTLE CHINA

Imada, Jeff
BIG TROUBLE IN LITTLE CHINA

Image Engineering
NEON MANIACS, spec eff; VAMP, spec eff; WHERE ARE THE CHILDREN?, spec eff

Imamura, Chikara
CABARET, art d

Imamura, Isutomu
SOREKARA, art d

Imberg, Silvian
AMERICA 3000

Imholte, Elisabeth
FOLLOWING THE FUHRER, ed

Imhoof, Markus
JOURNEY, THE, d; JOURNEY, THE, w

Imrie, Celia
HIGHLANDER

Imsland, Marty
SCORPION

Imus, Don
ODD JOBS

Inal, Engin
KUYUCAKLI YUSUF

Inanir, Kadir
AMANSIZ YOL

Inci, Kemal
KUYUCAKLI YUSUF

Inclan, Guillermo
EL EXTRANO HIJO DEL SHERIFF

Inclan, Rafael
EL MERCADO DE HUMILDES; EL VECINDARIO—LOS MEXICANOS CALIENTES; IN 'N' OUT; SE SUFRE PERO SE GOZA; UN HOMBRE VIOLENTE

Inda, Estela
EL SECUESTRO DE CAMARENA

Indares, D.
ALLIGORIA

Indoni, Fernanda
SAPORE DEL GRANO, ed

Industrial Light & Magic
GOLDEN CHILD, THE, spec eff

Inez, Frank
MEN'S CLUB, THE, spec eff

Infante, Pedro
HIJO DEL PALENQUE; POR UN VESTIDO DE NOVIA

Infanti, Angelo
L'INCHIESTA; UNA SPINA NEL CUORE

Infantino, A.
NINI TERNO-SECCO, m

Infascelli, Paolo
LA STORIA, p

Ingale, Vasant
RAO SAHEB

Ingelson, Katie
DR. OTTO AND THE RIDDLE OF THE GLOOM BEAM

Ingersoll, James
BACK TO SCHOOL; NAKED CAGE, THE

Ingersoll, Richard
ESTHER, prod d

Inget, Shirley
RAD, art d

Ingham, Barrie
GREAT MOUSE DETECTIVE, THE

Ingham, Keith
ASTERIX CHEZ LES BRETONS, anim d

Ingle, Doug
MANHUNTER, m/l

Ingle, John
TRUE STORIES

Ingledew, Rosalind
8 MILLION WAYS TO DIE

Inglehart, Barbara
EYE OF THE TIGER, cos

Ingleson, Amy
DR. OTTO AND THE RIDDLE OF THE GLOOM BEAM

Inglin, Meinrad
DER SCHWARZE TANNER, w

Jacoby, Bobby
IRON EAGLE

Jacoby, Corey
NO RETREAT, NO SURRENDER

Jacoby, Dale
NO RETREAT, NO SURRENDER

Jacoby, Laura
RAD

Jacques, Yves
DECLINE OF THE AMERICAN EMPIRE, THE

Jacquot, Benoit
CORPS ET BIENS, d&w

Jadali, Majid
SILK

Jaeckel, Richard
BLACK MOON RISING; KILLING MACHINE

Jaeger, Claude
MAX MON AMOUR

Jaeger, Denny
WHAT WAITS BELOW, m

Jaenicke, Hannes
ROSA LUXEMBURG

Jaenicke, Kathe
ANGRY HARVEST

Jaffe, Chapelle
CONFIDENTIAL

Jaffe, David
FLOODSTAGE

Jaffe, Gib
GOOD TO GO, ed

Jaffe, Jane Schwartz
TRICK OR TREAT, ed

Jaffe, Michael
ONE CRAZY SUMMER, p

Jaffrey, Saeed
MY BEAUTIFUL LAUNDRETTE

Jager, Okke
ASSAULT, THE

Jager, Siegrun
DAS SCHWEIGEN DES DICHTERS, ed

Jagger, Mick
AT CLOSE RANGE, m/l; RUNNING OUT OF LUCK; RUNNING OUT OF LUCK, w

Jago, June
DEPARTURE

Jahn, Hartmut
TRANSITTRAUME, d&w; TRANSITTRAUME, p

Jaime, Leo
AS SETE VAMPIRAS; AS SETE VAMPIRAS, m/l

Jakab, Anna
BIG HURT, THE, cos

Jake
BOY WHO COULD FLY, THE

Jakob, Jost
LE MAL D'AIMER, cos

Jakoby, Don
INVADERS FROM MARS, w

Jakovljev, Vadim
WILD WIND, THE, ph

Jakubowicz, Alain
AMERICA 3000, ed; DELTA FORCE, THE, ed; INVADERS FROM MARS, ed; TEXAS CHAINSAW MASSACRE PART 2, THE, ed

Jalan, Shyamalal
DEBSHISHU

Jalkanen, Pekka
SININEN IMETTAJA, m

Jalowyj, Nicolas
BETTY BLUE

Jamati, Luc
PIRATES

Jame, Michael
P.O.W. THE ESCAPE

James, Anthony
DEAD-END DRIVE-IN, cos

James, Billy T.
FOOTROT FLATS

James, Brion
ARMED AND DANGEROUS

James, Carole
PULSEBEAT; SEA SERPENT, THE

James, Claire
Obituaries

James, Clifton
WHERE ARE THE CHILDREN?

James, Doug
OVER THE SUMMER

James, Jesse
JOGO DURO

James, Jessica
POWER

James, Jimmy
SEX APPEAL, w

James, John
BACK TO SCHOOL

James, John Warren
LIGHTNING—THE WHITE STALLION

James, Ken
ONE NIGHT ONLY; YOUNGBLOOD

James, Linda
COMING UP ROSES, p

James, Lloyd
DEAD-END DRIVE-IN, makeup

James, Nick
NIGHTMARE WEEKEND

James, Oscar
BLACK JOY

James, Paul
WELCOME TO THE PARADE; WELCOME TO THE PARADE, m

James, Pepita
MONSTER DOG

James, Richard
GETTING EVEN, prod d

James, Ron
HEAD OFFICE

James, Steve
AVENGING FORCE; P.O.W. THE ESCAPE

James, Tarni
CACTUS

James, Tony
FERRIS BUELLER'S DAY OFF, m/l

Jameson, Nick
FINE MESS, A, m/l

Jameson, Susan
TERRY ON THE FENCE

Jamison, Peter
AT CLOSE RANGE, prod d; HOWARD THE DUCK, prod d; VIOLETS ARE BLUE, prod d

Janacek, Leos
LE PALTOQUET, m; LEV S BILOU HRIVOU, m

Jancso, Miklos
L'AUBE, d; L'AUBE, w

Janda, Krystyna
LAPUTA

Janett, Georg
EL SUIZO—UN AMOUR EN ESPAGNE, w; MOTTEN IM LICHT, ed

Jang-ho, Lee
ER WOO DONG, d

Janicijevic, Dusan
WILD WIND, THE

Janicki, Jerzy
CHRZESNISAK, w

Janko, Damian
PLAYING BEATIE BOW

Jankowski, Jan
SCENY DZIECIECE Z ZYCIA PROWINCJI

Jankura, Peter
ERZEKENY BUCSU A FEJEDELEMTOL, ph

Janneau, Daniel
LE DEBUTANT, d; LE DEBUTANT, w

Janner, Brigitte
PARADIES

Jannot, Veronique
LAST IMAGE, THE

Jano, Neil
STOOGEMANIA

Jansen, Janus Billeskov
TWIST & SHOUT, ed; WOLF AT THE DOOR, THE, ed

Jansen, Maaike
LE COMPLEXE DU KANGOUROU

Jansen, Nico
ASSAULT, THE

Jansen, Peter
OP HOOP VAN ZEGEN, set d

Jansky, Karel
LEV S BILOU HRIVOU

Janson, Horst
NO TIME TO DIE

Janssen, Per
HUD

Jansson, Claes
MORRHAR OCH ARTOR

Jansson, Kim
MANDEN I MAANEN

Jansson, Roland
GRONA GUBBAR FRAN Y.R.

Japan, Cary
MUZSKOE VOSPITANIE, w

Jaramillo, Carlos
SAN ANTONITO

Jarantau, Z.
BI CHAMD KHAYRTAY

Jarbyn, Siw
ORMENS VAG PA HALLEBERGET, makeup

Jarchow, Bruce
MANHATTAN PROJECT, THE

Jardim, Luis
RUNNING OUT OF LUCK, m

Jardine, Jules
YOUNGBLOOD

Jarin, Tim
TOUCH AND GO

Jarkov, Alexei
MOI DRUG IVAN LAPSHIN

Jarman, Derek
CARAVAGGIO, d&w

Jarmusch, Jim
DOWN BY LAW, d&w; SLEEPWALK, ph

Jaroslow, Ruth
EAT AND RUN

Jarratt, John
AUSTRALIAN DREAM; DARK AGE

Jarre, Maurice
MOSQUITO COAST, THE, m; SOLARBABIES, m; TAI-PAN, m; TAI-PAN, md

Jarret, Catherine
EHRENGARD

Jarrett, Hugh
WHAT COMES AROUND

Jarrott, Charles
BOY IN BLUE, THE, d

Jarvis, Graham
TOUGH GUYS; WEEKEND WARRIORS

Jarvis, Kathy Roshay
HOT CHILI, m/l

Jarvis, Mark
COLOR OF MONEY, THE

Jarvis, Ray
HOT CHILI, m/l

Jasaljar, Vasant
ANAADI ANANT

Jasmin
MON CAS, cos

Jaso, Susie
ARMED AND DANGEROUS

Jason
NIGHTMARE WEEKEND

Jason, Harvey
BAD GUYS

Jasso, Nicholas
SALVADOR

Jauchem, Esquire
NUTCRACKER: THE MOTION PICTURE, spec eff

Jaulmes, Hito
DOUCE FRANCE

Jaurequi, Emil
LOW BLOW

Javet, Francoise
LA GITANE, ed

Javicoli, Susanna
MONITORS

Javor, Zsofi
KISMASZAT ES A GEZENGUZOK

Jayatilaka, Amarnath
ARUNATA PERA, d; ARUNATA PERA, w

Jayatilaka, Madhuri Anjana
ARUNATA PERA

Jayatilaka, Ranjeewa Amarajit
ARUNATA PERA

Jayatilaka, Sundeep Sanjaya
ARUNATA PERA

Jean, Christiane
L'ISOLA

Jeanet, Valerie
FAUBOURG SAINT-MARTIN

Jeavons, Colin
ABSOLUTE BEGINNERS

Jebeli, Hamid
FROSTY ROADS

Jecko, Timothy
POWER

Jed
LINK

Jefferies, Annalee
VIOLETS ARE BLUE

Jeffre, Armand
JEAN DE FLORETTE

Jeffrey, Tom
GOING SANE, p

Jeger, Benedikt
DER PENDLER, m

Jegou, Daniel
L'AMANT MAGNIFIQUE

Jekan, Ali
MARE, THE, d&w

Jelks, Vaughan
HOLLYWOOD VICE SQUAD

Jelks, Vaughn Tyree
BLUE CITY

Jelliti, Belgacem
AL-KAS, ph

Jelmini, Tiziana
DER PENDLER

Jen, Wan
SUPER CITIZEN, d; SUPER CITIZEN, w

Jenesky, George
JUMPIN' JACK FLASH

Jeng, Chen Bor
SUPER CITIZEN

Jenkins, Eric
WHOOPEE BOYS, THE, ed

Jenkins, George
DREAM LOVER, prod d

Jenkins, Larry "Flash"
ARMED AND DANGEROUS; FERRIS BUELLER'S DAY
OFF

Jenkins, Mark
DESERT BLOOM

Jenkins, Richard
HANNAH AND HER SISTERS; MANHATTAN
PROJECT, THE; ON VALENTINE'S DAY

Jenkyns, Julian
SAVING GRACE

Jenn, Stephen
CASTAWAY

Jenney, Lucinda
PEGGY SUE GOT MARRIED; WHOOPEE BOYS, THE

Jennings, Candee
KILLER PARTY

Jennings, Gunther
EYE OF THE TIGER, spec eff

Jennings, Will
8 MILLION WAYS TO DIE, m/l

Jens, Salome
JUST BETWEEN FRIENDS

Jensen, Beate
KONZERT FUR ALICE

Jensen, Charles "Tatoo"
AT CLOSE RANGE

Jensen, Ejner
ET SKUD FRA HJERTET

Jensen, John R.
'NIGHT, MOTHER, art d; NOBODY'S FOOL, art d

Jensen, Lisa
SCORPION

Jensen, Soren
Obituaries

Jensen, Torben
BARNDOMMENS GADE; FLAMBEREDE HJERTER

Jeremic, Milenko
DOBROVOLJCI, art d; I TO CE PROCI, prod d;
OBECANA ZEMLJA, art d

Jergens, Earl
ABDUCTED

Jericevic, Dinka
ZA SRECU JE POTREBNO TROJE, art d

Jerome, Betty
IMAGEMAKER, THE

Jerome, Suzanne   [Susan Willis]
Obituaries

Jerry, Corinne
LA FEMME DE MA VIE, cos

Jesic, Jasminka
SRECNA NOVA '49, cos

Jessao, Clytie
EMMA'S WAR, d; EMMA'S WAR, p; EMMA'S WAR, w

Jessop, Sharon
DOGS IN SPACE

Jessup, Peter
ABSOLUTE BEGINNERS

Jeter, Michael
MONEY PIT, THE

Jett, Sue
BILLY GALVIN, p

Jewel, Jimmy
ARTHUR'S HALLOWED GROUND; ROCINANTE

Jewkes, Carl
KNIGHTS AND EMERALDS

Jezequel, Julie
SUIVEZ MON REGARD

Jha, Prakash
ANAADI ANANT, p, d&w

Jhabvala, Ruth Prawer
ROOM WITH A VIEW, A, w

Jhankal, Ravi
SUSMAN

Ji-Il, Han
GILSODOM

Ji-Yong, Kim
GILSODOM

Jian, Xiu
GREAT WALL, A

Jian, Zhang
LIANG JIA FUNU

Jian-Kiu, Sun
MARTIAL ARTS OF SHAOLIN

Jiang, Du
CAN YUE, m

Jiang-Qiang, Hu
MARTIAL ARTS OF SHAOLIN

Jianguo, Guo
QINGCHUN JI

Jianming, Lu
CUODIAN YUANYANG, d; CUODIAN YUANYANG, w

Jiaqing, Mi
IN THE WILD MOUNTAINS, ph

Jiaxin, Zhu
HALF-DUAN QING, p

Jie, Zhang
TAI-PAN

Jiesheng, He
CAN YUE, w

Jiesheng, Kung
JUE XIANG, d&w

Jillette, Penn
MY CHAUFFEUR; OFF BEAT

Jimenez, Armando
PICARDIA MEXICANA NUMERO DOS, d

Jimenez, Carol
27 HORAS, m

Jimenez, Juan Antonio
EL AMOR BRUJO

Jimenez, Luz
NEMESIO

Jimenez, Neal
WHERE THE RIVER RUNS BLACK, w

Jimenez, Roberto
8 MILLION WAYS TO DIE

Jiminez, Mary
LA MOITIE DE L'AMOUR, d&w

Jimmy Binkley Group
JO JO DANCER, YOUR LIFE IS CALLING

Jimmy, Top
ECHO PARK

Jinaki
LONGSHOT, THE

Jingwen, Zhang
JUE XIANG, prod d

Jingxin, Xu
REZHOU, m

Jinnett, Kathy
HELL SQUAD

Jiraskova, Jirina
SIESTA VETA

Jires, Jaromil
LEV S BILOU HRIVOU, d

Jirku, Christine
DIE NACHTMEERFAHRT

Jivaros, Les
I LOVE YOU, m

Joao, Adelaide
O VESTIDO COR DE FOGO

Joao, Los
EL SECUESTRO DE LOLA-LOLA LA TRAILERA 2, m

Job, Enrico
CAMORRA, prod d; SUMMER NIGHT WITH GREEK
PROFILE, ALMOND EYES AND SCENT OF BASIL, art
d

Jobert, Stephane
FAUBOURG SAINT-MARTIN

Joens, Michael
MY LITTLE PONY, d

Joffe, Carol
HANNAH AND HER SISTERS, set d

Joffe, Roland
MISSION, THE, d

Joffee, Kai
SEX APPEAL, m

Joffily, Jose
AVAETE, A SEMENTE DA VINGANCA, w; REI DO
RIO, w

Joffin, Jon
WELCOME TO THE PARADE, ph

Johannessen, Chip
LAST RESORT, THE

Johansson, Pelle
LOVE ME!, art d; ORMENS VAG PA HALLEBERGET,
art d

Johansson, Thomas
GRONA GUBBAR FRAN Y.R.

John, Alan
TRAVELLING NORTH, md

John, Allen
TWELFTH NIGHT, m

John, Barry
MASSEY SAHIB

John, Gottfried
FOLLOWING THE FUHRER; FRANZA

John, Heinz Werner
NO TIME TO DIE, w

John-Jules, Danny
LABYRINTH; LITTLE SHOP OF HORRORS

Johnene, Bob
NO RETREAT, NO SURRENDER

Johns, Capt. W.E.
BIGGLES, w

Johns, Stratford
CAR TROUBLE; FOREIGN BODY

Johns, Tracy Camila
SHE'S GOTTA HAVE IT

Johnson, Alan
SOLARBABIES, d

Johnson, Andrew
KIND OF ENGLISH, A

Johnson, Arch
DEATHMASK

Johnson, Arte
WHAT COMES AROUND

Johnson, Audre
PRETTY IN PINK

Johnson, Bill
TEXAS CHAINSAW MASSACRE PART 2, THE

Johnson, Bo
AVENGING FORCE, art d; DANGEROUSLY CLOSE, art
d; P.O.W. THE ESCAPE, art d

Johnson, Brett
THE KARATE KID PART II

Johnson, Brian
MAXIMUM OVERDRIVE, m/l

Johnson, Bruce
AVENGING FORCE; LES FRERES PETARD

Johnson, Carlton
Obituaries

Johnson, Cecilia
DR. OTTO AND THE RIDDLE OF THE GLOOM BEAM

Johnson, Christine
WRONG WORLD, prod d

Johnson, Christopher Michael
NOBODY'S FOOL

Johnson, Clark
BUSTED UP

Johnson, Clive
ABSOLUTE BEGINNERS

Johnson, Curtis
LOW BLOW

Johnson, Dave
LONGSHOT, THE

Johnson, Dave Alan
NIGHT OF THE CREEPS

Johnson, Eric Lison
I LAGENS NAMN, prod d

Johnson, Flip
SCREAMPLAY

Johnson, Franklin
FIRE WITH FIRE

Johnson, Garth
THE KARATE KID PART II

Johnson, Gary
MOSQUITO COAST, THE, m/l

Johnson, Geordie
BOY IN BLUE, THE

Joseph, Val
ABSOLUTE BEGINNERS

Josephsen, Rick H.
BAD GUYS , spec eff

Josephson, Erland
AMOROSA; L'ULTIMA MAZURKA; LE MAL
D'AIMER; SACRIFICE, THE; SAVING GRACE

Josephson, Jeffrey
RATBOY

Joshi, Pallavi
GURU DAKSHINA; SUSMAN

Joudrey, Rick
CRAZY MOON

Jourard, Jeff
SUNSET STRIP

Jourdan, Nicole
PLACE OF WEEPING

Jourdan, Raymond
TAXI BOY

Jovanovski, Meto
SRECNA NOVA '49

Jove, Angel
MES ENLLA DE LA PASSIO

Joy, Cindy
SEX APPEAL

Joy, Kara
SORORITY HOUSE MASSACRE

Joy, Robert
ADVENTURE OF FAUSTUS BIDGOOD, THE;
ADVENTURE OF FAUSTUS BIDGOOD, THE, m

Joya, Mario Garcia
LEJANIA, ph; MALABRIGO, ph

Joyce, Anna
Obituaries

Joyce, Elaine
TRICK OR TREAT; UPHILL ALL THE WAY

Joyce, John
MR. LOVE

Joyce, Tom
ONE MORE SATURDAY NIGHT

Joyner, David
FERRIS BUELLER'S DAY OFF, m/l

Jozani, Massood Jafari
FROSTY ROADS, d

Ju, Kim Ki
GILSODOM

Ju-yun, T'ang
TIME TO LIVE AND A TIME TO DIE, A

Juan, Fu
YU QING SAO

Juarez, Jose Miguel
EN PENUMBRA, p

Jubran, Duke
SCORPION

Judd, Robert
CROSSROADS

Judd, Ruth
PLAYING FOR KEEPS

Judd, Stephen
BRIDGE TO NOWHERE

Judges, Gordon
BUSTED UP

Jue, Jimmy
BIG TROUBLE IN LITTLE CHINA

Juerges, Juergen
50/50, ph

Juh, Boris
CHRISTOPHORUS

Juhlin, Benny
MORD I MORKET

Jukich, Doug
LOW BLOW

Julia, Raul
MORNING AFTER, THE

Julian, Janet
CHOKE CANYON

Julian, Yvan
PRUNELLE BLUES, m

Juliano, Lenny
CHOPPING MALL

Julien, Andre
BETTY BLUE

Julien, Issac
PASSION OF REMEMBRANCE, THE, d&w

Julien, Jean Marie
UNDER THE CHERRY MOON

Julienne, Remy
KILLING MACHINE, stunts; MAN AND A WOMAN: 20
YEARS LATER, A, stunts; TWIST AGAIN A MOSCOU,
stunts

Jullien, Alaric
SUMMER

Jullien, Claude
SUMMER

Julmiste, Erla
BAND OF THE HAND

July, Evelyne
L'AUBE, p

Jun, Peng
JUE XIANG, prod d

Junco, Tito
EL CORAZON SOBRE LA TIERRA; ES MI VIDA—EL
NOA NOA 2

Junco, Victor
EL JUEGO DE LA MUERTE; EL NARCO—DUELO
ROJO; NOCHE DE JUERGA

Jung, Calvin
IN THE SHADOW OF KILIMANJARO

Jung, Nathan
BIG TROUBLE IN LITTLE CHINA

Jung-Ha, Kim
BBONG

Jungwirth, Barbara
DOGS IN SPACE

Junkersdorf, Eberhard
ROSA LUXEMBURG, p; STAMMHEIM, p

Jupont, Catherine Poul
MANDEN I MAANEN

Jur, Jeff
SCREEN TEST, ph

Jur, Jeffrey
SOUL MAN, ph

Jurgensen, Randy
VIOLATED

Jurgenson, Albert
BABEL OPERA, OU LA REPETITION DE DON JUAN ,
ed; MELO, ed

Jurla, Mike
AMORE INQUIETO DI MARIA

Jury, Arnold
VIOLENT BREED, THE, ed

Jury, Chris
MR. LOVE

Jusid, Margarita
KING AND HIS MOVIE, A, art d&cos

Juso, Galliano
LA SIGNORA DELLA NOTTE, w

Just, Ellen
WELCOME IN VIENNA, makeup

Justiniano, Gonzalo
LOS HIJOS DE LA GUERRA FRIA, d&w

Jympson, John
KPM; LITTLE SHOP OF HORRORS, ed; SCREAMTIME,
m

Kaandorp, Brigitte
PERVOLA: TRACKS IN THE SNOW

Kaaniche, Nabil
AL-KAS

Kababajev, S.
DESCENDANT OF THE SNOW LEOPARD, THE

Kabakchiev, Lyubomir
ZABRAVOTE TOZI SLOCHAI

Kabiljo, Alfi
OBECANA ZEMLJA, m; SAN O RUZI, m

Kabiljo, Alfie
SKY BANDITS, m

Kabitzke, Siegfried
UNTERMEHMEN GEIGENKASTEN, p

Kaboli, Farzaneh
MONSTER, THE

Kacek, Frederic G.
DIE NACHTMEERFAHRT, ph

Kacic, Mila
KORMORAN

Kacmarek, Zdzislaw
SCENY DZIECIECE Z ZYCIA PROWINCJI, ph

Kaczenski, Chester
EXTREMITIES, prod d; RADIOACTIVE DREAMS, prod
d; WEEKEND WARRIORS, prod d

Kader, Jennifer
NUTCRACKER: THE MOTION PICTURE

Kadish, Lina
FLASH, ed

Kadish, Seth
CLASS OF NUKE 'EM HIGH

Kadiweu, Macsuara
AVAETE, A SEMENTE DA VINGANCA

Kadokawa, Haruki
CABARET, p&d

Kadyralijeva, G.
DESCENDANT OF THE SNOW LEOPARD, THE

Kafetzopoulos, Antonis
I NICHTA ME TI SILENA; I NICHTA ME TI SILENA,
w

Kafka, Franz
CLASS RELATIONS, w

Kafkaloff, Kim
SEX APPEAL

Kaga, Takeshi
CABARET

Kagan, Alex
MALKAT HAKITA, m

Kagan, Marilyn
LADIES CLUB, THE

Kagen, David
FRIDAY THE 13TH PART VI: JASON LIVES

Kageyama, Rodney
GUNG HO

Kahaloa, Vincent
SCORPION

Kahane, Maddie
DR. OTTO AND THE RIDDLE OF THE GLOOM BEAM

Kahfi, Rajul
TITAN SERAMBUT DIBELAH TUJUH, set d

Kahn, Buddha
BAD GUYS

Kahn, Cynthia
SCREEN TEST

Kahn, Hadassah
AFZIEN, art d

Kahn, Madeline
AMERICAN TAIL, AN; MY LITTLE PONY

Kahn, Michael
WISDOM, ed

Kahn, Rashon
JO JO DANCER, YOUR LIFE IS CALLING

Kahn, Sheldon
LEGAL EAGLES, ed

Kahra, Kalevi
KUNINGAS LAHTEE RANSKAAN

Kai, Ann Tse
MARTIAL ARTS OF SHAOLIN, p

Kai-Larsen, Jenny
LOVE ME!

Kaige, Chen
YELLOW EARTH, d

Kaija
HUOMENNA, cos

Kaikaka, Gary
KING KONG LIVES

Kail, Jim
THE KARATE KID PART II, makeup

Kailan
ANGKOR-CAMBODIA EXPRESS, w

Kaiser, Kevin
NUTCRACKER: THE MOTION PICTURE

Kaiser, Wolf
DER SCHWARZE TANNER

Kaitan, Elizabeth
VIOLATED

Kajander, Kristin
HARD ASFALT

Kakridas, Dimitris
KNOCK-OUT, set d

Kakutani, Masaru
KONEKO MONOGATARI, p

Kaleidjan, Lydia
NIGHTMARE WEEKEND, makeup

Kalem, Toni
BILLY GALVIN

Kalezic, Goran
RECRUITS

Kalinowski, Waldemar
PLAYING FOR KEEPS, prod d

Kaliuta, Vilene
KHRANI MENIO, MOI TALISMAN, ph

Kalla, Hussein
AL BEDAYA, p; EL-TOUK WA EL-ESSWERA, p

Kallai, Istvan
KOJAK BUDAPESTEN, w

Kalliala, Aake
HUOMENNA

Kallio, Ismo
BORN AMERICAN

Kallosh, Sandor
POTERYALSYA SLON, m

Kallstrom, Gunnar
JONSSONLIGAN DYKER UPP IGEN, ph

Kalman, Gyorgy
KESERU IGAZSAG

Kalo, Haruko
YARI NO GONZA

Kalogeras, Savas
CRAZY MOON, ph

Kalotzopoulou, Mirka
CARAVAN SARAI

Kaloyanchev, Georgi
ZA KUDE PUTOVATE

Kalpakoff, Gary
PATRIOT, THE

Kalte, Krister
MOA

Kaltsas, Maria
I NICHTA ME TI SILENA, set d

Kam, Siu
TAI-PAN

Kamarullah, Ed
SECANGKIR KOPI PAHIT, ed

Kamarullah, George
DOEA TANDA MATA, ph

Kamekona, Danny
THE KARATE KID PART II; THE KARATE KID PART II

Kamel, Abla
LEL HAB KESSA AKHIRA

Kamel, Hind
FLAMING BORDERS

Kamel, Madiha
MESHWAR OMAR

Kamen, Michael
HIGHLANDER, m; MONA LISA, m; SHANGHAI SURPRISE, m; SHOOT FOR THE SUN, m

Kamen, Robert Mark
THE KARATE KID PART II, w

Kaminka, Didier
I LOVE YOU, w; PARENTAL CLAIM, w; YIDDISH CONNECTION, w

Kaminska, Dorota
PROKA

Kammerer, Peter
TOMMASO BLU, w

Kampiert, Bert
FERRIS BUELLER'S DAY OFF, m/l

Kampmann, Steven
BACK TO SCHOOL, w; CLUB PARADISE

Kampvereen, Helene
DE VAL VAN PATRICIA HAGGERSMITH

Kamran, Farnouche
KGB—THE SECRET WAR, set d

Kamu, Ann Petren Okko
BRODERNA MOZART

Kamura, Moe
TO SLEEP SO AS TO DREAM; TO SLEEP SO AS TO DREAM, m

Kan, To Chee
SHANGHAI SURPRISE

Kanakes, David
WILDCATS

Kanaly, Steve
BALBOA

Kanazawa, Masatsugi
COMIC MAGAZINE, ed

Kancilia, Dirk
AMERICAN JUSTICE

Kane, Carol
JUMPIN' JACK FLASH

Kane, Irv
DR. OTTO AND THE RIDDLE OF THE GLOOM BEAM

Kane, Ivan
PLATOON

Kane, Jayson
HOUSE

Kane, Leila
QUICKSILVER

Kanellis, Elias
DANILO TRELES, O FIMISMENOS ANDALOUSIANOS MOUSIKOS

Kanew, Jeff
TOUGH GUYS, d

Kangqiao, Ho
HALF-DUAN QING, w

Kangzhen, Zheng
JUE XIANG, ph

Kania, Cynthia
FRIDAY THE 13TH PART VI: JASON LIVES

Kanig, Frank
CHOKE CANYON

Kanin, Wally
HEAD OFFICE

Kante, Alikaou
NYAMANTON

Kante, Macire
NYAMANTON

Kanter, Christoph
HEIDENLOCHER, set d

Kants, Ivar
TWELFTH NIGHT

Kantscheli, Gija
DEN' GNEVA, m

Kanwar, Anita
TRIKAL

Kapai, Orhan
LAND OF DOOM, ph

Kapelos, John
HEAD OFFICE; MY MAN ADAM; NOTHING IN COMMON; OFF BEAT

Kapic, Sulejman
VECERNJA ZVONA, p

Kaplan, Corey
CHOPPING MALL, set d

Kaplan, Isa
TORPIDONOSTCI, art d

Kaplan, Marvin
HOLLYWOOD VICE SQUAD

Kaplan, William
THREE AMIGOS

Kapoor, Anil
KAHAN KAHAN SE GUZAR GAYA

Kapoor, Pankaj
AGHAAT; KAHAN KAHAN SE GUZAR GAYA

Kapoor, Shashi
NEW DELHI TIMES

Kaprisky, Valerie
LA GITANE

Kapsouros, Vassilis
SCHETIKA ME TON VASSILI, ph

Kaptur, Michel
HIGH SPEED, d; HIGH SPEED, w

Kapur, Nisha
MY BEAUTIFUL LAUNDRETTE

Kapural, Vjenceslav
OBECANA ZEMLJA

Kar-Leung, Lau
MARTIAL ARTS OF SHAOLIN, d

Karadzic, Miodrag
LEPOTA POROKA

Karaindrou, Eleni
KALI PATRITHA, SYNTROFE, m

Karaindrou, Helen
O MELISSOKOMOS, m

Karakatsanis, Thimos
CARAVAN SARAI

Karakorpi, Titta
LINNA

Karamesinis, Vassili
HARDBODIES 2

Karan, Guilherme
O HOMEM DA CAPA PRETA

Karanovic, Mirjana
OBECANA ZEMLJA

Karapiet, Rashid
FOREIGN BODY

Karapiperis, Kes
GIRL FROM MANI, THE, art d

Karapiperis, Mikes [Mike]
DIE ZWEI GESICHTER DES JANUAR, set d; O MELISSOKOMOS, art d

Karas, Barry
ONE CRAZY SUMMER

Karatzas, Steve
SHADOW PLAY, art d

Karavaichuk, Oleg
FOUETTE, m

Karayannis, Spyros
I NICHTA ME TI SILENA, cos

Kardottir, Hanna Maria
SCHWARZ UND OHNE ZUCKER

Karen, James
HARDBODIES 2; INVADERS FROM MARS

Karen, Michael
ONE NIGHT ONLY, ed

Karimbeik, Hossein
HALF MOON STREET; MONA LISA

Karimi, Parto
REVENGE OF THE TEENAGE VIXENS FROM OUTER SPACE, THE

Karina, Anna
LAST SONG; LAST SONG, w

Karinen, Ingolf
NOE HEIT ANNET

Karioka, Tahia
LEL HAB KESSA AKHIRA

Karis, Vassili
SCALPS

Kark, Raymond
Obituaries

Kark, Tonu
IDEAALMAASTIK

Karlen, John
NATIVE SON

Karlin, Fred
VASECTOMY: A DELICATE MATTER, m

Karmann, Sam
UNDER THE CHERRY MOON

Karmelita, Svetlana
TORPIDONOSTCI, m

Karmento, Eva
VAKVILAGBAN, ed

Karmitz, Marin
INSPECTEUR LAVARDIN, p; MALANDRO, p; MELO, p

Karney, Colleen
RECRUITS

Karnowski, Thomas
RADIOACTIVE DREAMS, p

Karns, Fred
IMAGEMAKER, THE, m; IMAGEMAKER, THE, m/l

Karon, Marvin
HEAD OFFICE

Karoui, Franck
POLICE

Karp, Willis
CARNAGE

Karpick, Avi
P.O.W. THE ESCAPE

Karpik, Avi
MALKAT HAKITA, ph

Karr, Gary
PLAYING FOR KEEPS, ed

Karr, Marcia
SEX APPEAL

Karunaratna, Kumara
ARUNATA PERA, w

Karv, Monika
NAERATA OMETI

Karya, Teguh
DOEA TANDA MATA, d; DOEA TANDA MATA, w; SECANGKIR KOPI PAHIT, d&w

Karyo, Tcheky
BLEU COMME L'ENFER; ETATS D'AME; L'UNIQUE

Kasaemsri, M.L. Varapa
PEESUA LAE DOKMAI, ed

Kasai, Lester
THRASHIN'

Kasander, Kees
TOP OF THE WHALE, p

Kasaravalli, Girish
TABARANAKATHE, p, d&w

Kasarda, John
HEARTBURN, art d

Kasem, Casey
TRANSFORMERS: THE MOVIE, THE

Kaser, Peter
DIE WALSCHE, art d

Kash, Daniel
ALIENS

Kashefska, Evelyn
ONE MORE SATURDAY NIGHT

Kashiwabara, Yoshie
ORA TOKYO SA YUKUDA

Kasi, Zmarai
GHAME AFGHAN, d; GHAME AFGHAN, w

Kasow, Todd
MAXIMUM OVERDRIVE, md

Kasper, Gary F.
NEVER TOO YOUNG TO DIE

Kass, Ronald S.
Obituaries

Kassel, Dale
DIRT BIKE KID, THE

Kastner, Dafna
EVIXION, w

Kastner, Elliott
BLACK JOY, p

Kastning, Andreas
NOVEMBERKATZEN

Kasugi, Sho
PRAY FOR DEATH, ch

Kat
NOBODY'S FOOL

Katajisto, Heikki
KUNINGAS LAHTEE RANSKAAN, ph; KUNINGAS
LAHTEE RANSKAAN, w; KUNINGAS LAHTEE
RANSKAAN, w; MORENA, ph; PIMEYS ODOTTA, ph

Kataoka, Tsurutaro
COMIC MAGAZINE

Katch, Yuji
TYPHOON CLUB, w

Kato, Go
SHIN YOROKOBIMO KANASHIMIMO IKUTOSHITSUKI

Katramadas, Zafiris
CARAVAN SARAI

Katsaros, Doug
STAR CRYSTAL, m

Katt, William
HOUSE

Katuridis, George
GIRL FROM MANI, THE

Katz, David
SCREEN TEST

Katz, Erika
DEATHMASK

Katz, Gloria
HOWARD THE DUCK, p; HOWARD THE DUCK, w

Katz, Herbie
SHADOWS RUN BLACK

Katz, James C.
NOBODY'S FOOL, p

Katz, Joycee
LAST RESORT, THE

Katz, Robert
IL CASO MORO, w

Katz, Stephen
LAST RESORT, THE, ph

Katz, Steven M.
'NIGHT, MOTHER, ph

Kauders, Sylvia
ARMED AND DANGEROUS

Kauffman, Cristen
WELCOME TO 18

Kauffmann, Bettie
APRIL FOOL'S DAY, spec eff

Kaufhold, Nika
BUSTED UP

Kaufman, Alan
OCEAN DRIVE WEEKEND, m

Kaufman, Carlos
DIAPASON

Kaufman, Lily Hayes
CLASS OF NUKE 'EM HIGH

Kaufman, Lloyd
CLASS OF NUKE 'EM HIGH, p

Kaufman, Robert
CHECK IS IN THE MAIL, THE, p; CHECK IS IN THE
MAIL, THE, w; SEPARATE VACATIONS, w

Kaufman, Robin
CHECK IS IN THE MAIL, THE; VAMP

Kaufman, Seth
ARMED AND DANGEROUS; NAKED CAGE, THE;
TOUGH GUYS

Kaufmann, Judith
BLIND DIRECTOR, THE, ph

Kaulen, Victor
COCAINE WARS, ph

Kaupas, Natas
THRASHIN'

Kauranen, Anja
SUURI ILLUSIONI, w

Kausen, Norbert
RECRUITS

Kaushik, Satish
GURU DAKSHINA

Kautsky, Natasha
SMART ALEC

Kavanagh, Brian
DEPARTURE, d; DEPARTURE, p; GOING SANE, ed

Kavanagh, Patrick
HALF MOON STREET

Kavas, Aytan
KIRLANGIC FIRTINASI

Kavayias, Giorgos
ALLIGORIA, ph

Kavner, Julie
HANNAH AND HER SISTERS

Kavur, Omer
AMANSIZ YOL, d; AMANSIZ YOL, w

Kawachi, Masayuki
TRANSFORMERS: THE MOVIE, THE, spec eff

Kawahara, Takashi
EAT THE PEACH

Kawarazaki, Choichiro
NINGUEN NO YAKUSOKU

Kay, Beatrice [Hannah Beatrice Kuper]
Obituaries

Kay, Charles
SCHOOL FOR VANDALS

Kay, Hadley
CARE BEARS MOVIE II: A NEW GENERATION

Kay, John
LEGAL EAGLES, m/l

Kay, Sandra
WORKING GIRLS, w

Kayden, Tony
OUT OF BOUNDS; OUT OF BOUNDS, w

Kaye, Joey
LETTER TO BREZHNEV; NO SURRENDER

Kaye, Michael
QUICKSILVER

Kaye, Nancy
BUSTED UP, cos

Kaye, Norman
CACTUS; CACTUS, w

Kaygun, Sahin
ADI VASFIYE, art d

Kaylan, Howard
ADVENTURES OF THE AMERICAN RABBIT, THE, m/l

Kayser, Allan J.
HOT CHILI; NIGHT OF THE CREEPS

Kazan, Lainie
DELTA FORCE, THE

Kazan, Nicholas
AT CLOSE RANGE, w

Kazanecki, Waldemar
CHRZESNISAK, m

Kazazian, Georges
KAHIR ELZAMAN, m

Kazemirchuk, Jean
QUI A TIRE SUR NOS HISTOIRES D'AMOUR?, set d

Kazurinsky, Tim
ABOUT LAST NIGHT; ABOUT LAST NIGHT, w;
POLICE ACADEMY 3: BACK IN TRAINING

Kckholdt, Steven
ABOUT LAST NIGHT

Keach, James
ARMED AND DANGEROUS, p; ARMED AND
DANGEROUS, w; WILDCATS

Keach, Stacy
ARMED AND DANGEROUS

Kean, Betty [Betty Wynn Kean]
Obituaries

Kean, Carole
STEWARDESS SCHOOL

Kean, John
NANOU, m

Keane, Finn
BIG HURT, THE

Keane, Glen
GREAT MOUSE DETECTIVE, THE, anim

Keane, Laurence
SAMUEL LOUNT, d; SAMUEL LOUNT, w

Kearney, Michael
ADVENTURE OF FAUSTUS BIDGOOD, THE, set d

Keating, Daniel J.
GIRLS SCHOOL SCREAMERS

Keating, Katie
GIRLS SCHOOL SCREAMERS; GIRLS SCHOOL
SCREAMERS, cos; GIRLS SCHOOL SCREAMERS, d&w

Keating, Pierce J.
GIRLS SCHOOL SCREAMERS, p,d&w

Keaton, Diane
CRIMES OF THE HEART

Keaton, Michael
GUNG HO; TOUCH AND GO

Keaton, Trish
BOY WHO COULD FLY, THE, cos

Keaton, Will
HAUNTED HONEYMOON

Keays-Byrne, Hugh
FOR LOVE ALONE; KANGAROO

Kechavarz, Mohammad-Ali
MIRZA NOWROUZ' SHOES

Kedem, Daniel
DAS SCHWEIGEN DES DICHTERS

Kedziersky, Grzegorz
OSOBISTY PAMIETNIK GRZESZNIKA PRZEZ NIEGO
SAMEGO SPISANY, ph

Keen, Bonnie
DR. OTTO AND THE RIDDLE OF THE GLOOM BEAM

Keen, Pat
CLOCKWISE

Keenan, Paul
Obituaries

Keene, Tommy
OUT OF BOUNDS

Keener, Catherine
ABOUT LAST NIGHT

Keener, Elliott
DOWN BY LAW

Keenleyside, Eric
HEAD OFFICE

Kehlmann, Michael
'38

Kehoe, Pat
LONGSHOT, THE

Keillerman, Gina
KILLER PARTY, cos

Keim, John
STOOGEMANIA, spec eff

Keinar, Gad
ALEX KHOLE AHAVA

Keister, Aaron
DR. OTTO AND THE RIDDLE OF THE GLOOM BEAM,
m/l

Keister, Shane
DR. OTTO AND THE RIDDLE OF THE GLOOM BEAM,
m; DR. OTTO AND THE RIDDLE OF THE GLOOM
BEAM, m/l

Keita, Cheik Hamala
NYAMANTON, ph

Keita, Moriba
NYAMANTON, m

Keitel, Harvey
CAMORRA; EL CABALLERO DEL DRAGON;
L'INCHIESTA; LA SPOSA AMERICANA; MEN'S CLUB,
THE; OFF BEAT; WISE GUYS

Keith, Debora
VIOLENT BREED, THE

Keith, Sheila
CLOCKWISE

Keith, Warren
MANHATTAN PROJECT, THE

Kekoa, Sterling
NUTCRACKER: THE MOTION PICTURE

Kelber, Catherine
TWIST AGAIN A MOSCOU, ed

Kelleher, John
EAT THE PEACH, p; EAT THE PEACH, w

Keller, Marthe
FEMMES DE PERSONNE

Keller, Ricky
ROCKIN' ROAD TRIP, m

Keller, Tom
NINJA TURF

Kellerman, Sally
BACK TO SCHOOL; KGB—THE SECRET WAR;
THAT'S LIFE

Kelley, DeForest
STAR TREK IV: THE VOYAGE HOME

Kelley, Emily Rose
DIRT BIKE KID, THE

Kelley, Michael F.
TOUCH AND GO

Kellogg, Denise
TAI-PAN

Kellogg, John
VIOLETS ARE BLUE

Kelly, Ava
CLASS OF NUKE 'EM HIGH

Kelly, Brian
MANHUNTER

Kelly, Christian
9½ WEEKS, set d

Kelly, David
PIRATES

Kelly, Des
DANGEROUS ORPHANS

Kelly, Greg
MANHUNTER

Kelly, Kelita
VENDETTA

Kelly, Kevin
RYDER, P.I., m

Kelly, Luis
DONA HERLINDA AND HER SON, ed

Kelly, Lynn
VIOLATED

Kelly, Maureen
HELL SQUAD

Kelly, Michael
SAVING GRACE, ed

Kelly, Michael F.
TOUGH GUYS

Kelly, Oskar
ON VALENTINE'S DAY

Kelly, Patrick
BEER, d

Kelly, Paula
JO JO DANCER, YOUR LIFE IS CALLING

Kelly, Peter S.
LEGAL EAGLES, set d

Kelly, Sam
ARTHUR'S HALLOWED GROUND

Kelly, Stephen
TOUCH AND GO

Kelly, Trevor
ABSOLUTE BEGINNERS

Kelly, Vera
NO SURRENDER

Kelso, Sean
BOY WHO COULD FLY, THE

Kelter, Jerie
FRIDAY THE 13TH PART VI: JASON LIVES, set d

Kelty, Celeste
AMERICAN ANTHEM

Kemenes, Fanny
ELYSIUM, cos

Kemeny, John
BOY IN BLUE, THE, p; WRAITH, THE, p

Kemmer, Joachim
WELCOME IN VIENNA

Kemmer, Jochen
MEIER

Kemp, Brandis
WELCOME TO 18

Kemp, Tony
ABSOLUTE BEGINNERS

Kemper, Steven
3:15, THE MOMENT OF TRUTH, ed

Kempinski, Anja
BALLERUP BOULEVARD

Kempinski, Tom
DUET FOR ONE, w

Kempner, Brenda
SCREAMTIME

Kempner, Scott
ABOUT LAST NIGHT, m/l

Kempster, Victor
STREETS OF GOLD, set d

Kendal, Chrissie
ABSOLUTE BEGINNERS

Kendall, David
WHERE THE RIVER RUNS BLACK, w

Kendall, Joan
MANHATTAN PROJECT, THE

Kendall, Sarah
THE KARATE KID PART II

Kende, Janos
LA SPOSA ERA BELLISSIMA, ph

Kendrick, Elizabeth
POWER

Kenigsberg, Daniel
LES CLOWNS DE DIEU

Kenin, Alexa
PRETTY IN PINK

Kennedy, Barry
COOL CHANGE, art d

Kennedy, David
SHORT CHANGED

Kennedy, Eileen
NIGHT OF THE CREEPS, cos; YOUNGBLOOD, cos

Kennedy, George
DELTA FORCE, THE; RADIOACTIVE DREAMS

Kennedy, Graham
TRAVELLING NORTH

Kennedy, J.
ABSOLUTE BEGINNERS, m/l

Kennedy, Jihmi
GUNG HO

Kennedy, Jo
WRONG WORLD

Kennedy, Kathleen
MONEY PIT, THE, p

Kennedy, Kristy
NOBODY'S FOOL

Kennedy, Leon Isaac
HOLLYWOOD VICE SQUAD

Kennedy, Patricia
DEPARTURE

Kennedy, Patrick
BOY WHO COULD FLY, THE, ed

Kennedy, Tom
AMERICAN ANTHEM

Kennedy, Tracy
HANNAH AND HER SISTERS

Kenner, Robert
3:15, THE MOMENT OF TRUTH, p

Kenney, Bill
COBRA, prod d

Kenney, Johanna
SCREEN TEST

Kenny, George
SOLDIER'S REVENGE

Kenrick, Tony
SHANGHAI SURPRISE, w

Kensit, Patsy
ABSOLUTE BEGINNERS; ABSOLUTE BEGINNERS, m/l; People to Watch

Kent, Enid
EXTREMITIES

Kent, Faith
HALF MOON STREET

Kentner, Tommy
MORD I MORKET; TAKE IT EASY

Kenton, Linda
BALBOA

Kenworthy, Michael
'NIGHT, MOTHER

Keogh, Barbara
TAI-PAN

Kepekli, Abbas
DIE LIEBESWUSTE

Keppy, Don
HEAD OFFICE

Keramidas, Harry
ABOUT LAST NIGHT, ed

Kerber, Randy
RAW DEAL, m

Kerenyi, Zoltan
KESERU IGAZSAG, ed

Kerimova, Gulja
MUZSKOE VOSPITANIE

Kerman, David
AMERICA

Kerman, Robert
NIGHT OF THE CREEPS

Kern, Eliza
LADY JANE

Kern, Martin
TAROT

Kern, Peter
DER WILDE CLOWN

Kern, Pouel
ET SKUD FRA HJERTET

Kernochan, Sarah
9½ WEEKS, w

Kernot, Phil
NO SURRENDER

Kerns, Herb
CHECK IS IN THE MAIL, THE

Kernyaiszky, Gabor
NAKED CAGE, THE, makeup

Kerr, E. Katherine
CHILDREN OF A LESSER GOD; POWER

Kerr, Michael
NAKED CAGE, THE

Kersey, Yvonne Talton
OFF BEAT

Kershaw, Brian
HAUNTED HONEYMOON

Kershaw, Martin
NIGHTMARE WEEKEND, m

Kershaw, Whitney
QUICKSILVER

Kertesz, Csaba
ONE NIGHT ONLY, prod d; SEPARATE VACATIONS, prod d

Kertzner, Tzvika
SHTAY ETZBA'OT M'TZIDON, w

Kertzner, Zwika
HAME'AHEV, w

Kerwin, Brian
KING KONG LIVES

Keseman, Nadine
GOLDEN EIGHTIES, ed

Kesend, Eleen
IN 'N' OUT, w

Kessai, Mohamed
LAST IMAGE, THE, art d

Kessler, Quin
MODERN GIRLS

Kestelman, Sara
LADY JANE

Kesten, Christian
VIRUS HAS NO MORALS, A

Kester, Terry
ROCKIN' ROAD TRIP

Keszi, Imre
ELYSIUM, w

Ketilsson, Gudjon
SCHWARZ UND OHNE ZUCKER

Ketonen, Pekka
TUNTEMATON SOTILAS

Keurvorst, Derek
KILLER PARTY

Keus, Kika
MARIA

Key, John
LABYRINTH

Key, William
DR. OTTO AND THE RIDDLE OF THE GLOOM BEAM

Keyes, Thom
SKY BANDITS, w

Keyloun, Mark
SEPARATE VACATIONS

Keyne, Fiona
SOLDIER'S REVENGE

Keys, David
KNIGHTS AND EMERALDS

Keywan, Alicia
YOUNGBLOOD, art d

Kezer, Glenn
PLAY DEAD; POWER

Khaftan, Sami
FLAMING BORDERS

Khairat, Omar
EL YOM EL SADES, m

Khakdan, Valiollah
MIRZA NOWROUZ' SHOES, art d

Khalid, Rohia
LEL HAB KESSA AKHIRA

Khalili, Mansour
P.O.W. THE ESCAPE

Khan, Mohamed
AWDAT MOWATIN, d; MESHWAR OMAR, d; MESHWAR OMAR, w

Khan, Zar
GHAME AFGHAN

Kharbanda, Kulbhushan
NEW DELHI TIMES; SUSMAN; TRIKAL

Khatib, Awas
HAME'AHEV

Khen, Shyula
HAKRAV AL HAVA'AD

Kheng, Michelle
ROYAL WARRIORS

Kher, Anupam
GURU DAKSHINA; RAO SAHEB

Khorsand, Philippe
LA GALETTE DU ROI; LES FRERES PETARD; SAUVE-TOI, LOLA

Khouri, Makhram
SMILE OF THE LAMB, THE

Khrasatchev, Vadim
KHRANI MENIO, MOI TALISMAN, m

Khumalo, Siphiwe
PLACE OF WEEPING

Kibble, Perry L.
AT CLOSE RANGE, m/l

Kidd, Chris
CRY FROM THE MOUNTAIN

Kidd, Myrna
CRY FROM THE MOUNTAIN

Kidder, Margot
GOBOTS: BATTLE OF THE ROCKLORDS

Kidman, Nicole
WINDRIDER

Kiedis, Anthony
TOUGH GUYS

Kiefel, Russel
TWELFTH NIGHT

Kiel, Sue
DOWN AND OUT IN BEVERLY HILLS

Kiely, Chris
BIG HURT, THE, p

Kiely, Jeanne
CROSSROADS

Kier, Udo
AM NACHESTEN MORGEN KEHRTE DER MINISTER
NICHT AN SEINEN ARBEITSPLATZ

Kiesser, Jan
CHECK IS IN THE MAIL, THE, ph

Kiiski, Kaija
SININEN IMETTAJA

Kiiski, Seija
SININEN IMETTAJA, prod d

Kiklic, Bogdan
DOBROVOLJCI

Kikoine, Gilbert
WOMEN'S PRISON MASSACRE, ed

Kikuchi, Junichi
CRAZY FAMILY, THE, ed

Kikukawa, Yoshie
NINGUEN NO YAKUSOKU, art d

Kil-Han, Song
GILSODOM, w

Kilar, Wojciech
KRONIKA WYPADKOW MILOSNYCH, m

Kilbourne, Phil
BEGINNER'S LUCK

Kilchinsky, Semadar
BAR 51—SISTER OF LOVE

Kiley, Richard
HOWARD THE DUCK

Killum, Guy
CROSSROADS

Kilman, Buzz
SOMETHING WILD

Kilmer, Val
TOP GUN

Kim, David D.
NINJA TURF, ph

Kim, Dong Hyun
FIELD OF HONOR

Kim, Doo
COMBAT SHOCK

Kim, Evan
HOLLYWOOD VICE SQUAD

Kim, June
BIG TROUBLE IN LITTLE CHINA

Kim, Kathy
NINJA TURF

Kim, Robert
FERRIS BUELLER'S DAY OFF

Kimball, Jeffrey
TOP GUN, ph

Kimball, Kelly
CLAN OF THE CAVE BEAR, THE, cos

Kimber, Davin
YOUNGBLOOD

Kimbrough, Matthew
BEER

Kime, Jeffrey
PEAU D'ANGE

Kimoulis, Giorgos
KNOCK-OUT

Kimura, Takeo
TAMPOPO, art d

Kincaid, Tim
BREEDERS, d&w

Kindahl, Johan
AMOROSA, makeup

Kinderis, Diana
REVENGE OF THE TEENAGE VIXENS FROM OUTER
SPACE, THE

Kindler, Walter
SCHMUTZ, ph

Kinerk, John
AMERICAN JUSTICE

King, Betty R.
DIRT BIKE KID, THE

King, Carole
BEST OF TIMES, THE, m/l

King, Chuck
ROCKIN' ROAD TRIP

King, Deborah
BAND OF THE HAND

King, Dennis, Jr.
Obituaries

King, Diana
Obituaries

King, Don
HEAD OFFICE

King, Emory
MOSQUITO COAST, THE

King, Jan
SMART ALEC, m

King, Jill
MOUNTAINTOP MOTEL MASSACRE

King, John
MISSION, THE, art d

King, Nick
NINJA TURF

King, Nimrod
BUSTED UP

King, Robb Wilson
IRON EAGLE, prod d; WHERE ARE THE CHILDREN?,
prod d

King, Rosanna
NINJA TURF

King, Stephen
MAXIMUM OVERDRIVE, d&w; STAND BY ME, w

King, Zalman
9½ WEEKS, p&w

King-Phillips, Lawrence
ABDUCTED; BUSTED UP

Kingsley, Don
STAR CRYSTAL

Kingsley, Taylor
STAR CRYSTAL

Kingston, Lisa
THAT'S LIFE

Kinison, Sam
BACK TO SCHOOL

Kinnaman, Melinda
ORMENS VAG PA HALLEBERGET

Kinnear, Roy
PIRATES

Kinney, Kathy
PARTING GLANCES

Kinney, Terry
NO MERCY; SEVEN MINUTES IN HEAVEN

Kino, Kitty
DIE NACHTMEERFAHRT, d&w

Kino, Renee Jacque
VENDETTA

Kino, Robert
JUST BETWEEN FRIENDS; NIGHT OF THE CREEPS

Kinoshita, Chuji
SHIN YOROKOBIMO KANASHIMIMO
IKUTOSHITSUKI, m

Kinoshito, Keisuke
SHIN YOROKOBIMO KANASHIMIMO
IKUTOSHITSUKI, d&w

Kinsey, Jonathan
WISDOM, cos

Kinsey, Lance
POLICE ACADEMY 3: BACK IN TRAINING

Kinski, Klaus
CRAWLSPACE; EL CABALLERO DEL DRAGON

Kinski, Nastassja
SPRING SYMPHONY

Kinyon, Barry
TEXAS CHAINSAW MASSACRE PART 2, THE

Kipishidze, Zubar
YOUNG COMPOSER'S ODYSSEY, A

Kipp, Bill
NAKED VENGEANCE; P.O.W. THE ESCAPE; SILK

Kipp, Heide
GRITTA VOM RATTENSCHLOSS

Kirby, Bruce
ARMED AND DANGEROUS; STAND BY ME

Kirby, Sean
POLICE ACADEMY 3: BACK IN TRAINING, set d

Kirchenbauer, Bill
STOOGEMANIA

Kirchhoff, Corinna
JOURNEY, THE

Kirindongo, Yubi
ALMACITA DI DESOLATO

Kirkes, Shirley
THREE AMIGOS, ch

Kirkvaag, Trond
NOE HEIT ANNET

Kirouac, Roland
PINK CHIQUITAS, THE, ch

Kirschner, David
AMERICAN TAIL, AN, w

Kirsner, Jacques
L'ETAT DE GRACE, p; L'ETAT DE GRACE, w;
SAUVE-TOI, LOLA, w

Kirvaag, Trond
NOE HEIT ANNET, w

Kishibe, Ittoku
KINEMA NO TENCHI

Kiss, Mari
GREAT GENERATION, THE

Kisum, William
MORD I MORKET

Kitaen, Tawny
INSTANT JUSTICE

Kitamura, Michiko
SOREKARA, cos

Kitaro
MANHUNTER, m/l; SAMUEL LOUNT, m

Kitchen-Hurd, Joanna
SOMETHING WILD

Kitiparaporn, Lek
ANGKOR-CAMBODIA EXPRESS, d; ANGKOR-
CAMBODIA EXPRESS, p

Kitt, Eartha
PINK CHIQUITAS, THE

Kittler, Albert
DER SEXTE SINN, m

Kitzanuk, Andrew
90 DAYS, ph

Kiuru, Katja
HUOMENNA

Kiviola, Hannu
TUNTEMATON SOTILAS

Kivisto, Asko
I LAGENS NAMN

Kjeldsen, Leif Axel
MORD I MORKET, ed

Kjellman, Bjorn
BRODERNA MOZART

Kjellqvist, Tommy
SACRIFICE, THE

Kjellsby, Jorunn
FAREWELL ILLUSION

Kjelsby, Jorunn
DROMMESLOTTER

Klabin, Claudio
AS SETE VAMPIRAS, p

Klar, Gary
LEGAL EAGLES

Klassen, David
COBRA, set d

Klauss, Jurgen
MEIER

Klebanov, Igor
CAPABLANCA, ph

Kleber, Birgit
FUTURE OF EMILY, THE, w

Kleiber, Erich
DER WILDE CLOWN

Klein, Beverly
MODERN GIRLS, cos

Klein, Dennis
ONE MORE SATURDAY NIGHT, d

Klein, Irving
Obituaries

Klein, Jesper
VALHALLA

Klein, Mazie Murphy
FAT GUY GOES NUTZOID!!

Klein-Essink, Marc
MALACCA

Kleinberg, Alan
DOWN BY LAW; DOWN BY LAW, p

Kleinberger, Avi
P.O.W. THE ESCAPE, w

Kleiner, Towje
DAS SCHWEIGEN DES DICHTERS; KONZERT FUR
ALICE

Kleinman, Lou
BILLY GALVIN, ed

Kleinsma, Simone
FLIGHT OF RAINBIRDS, A

Kleiser, Randal
FLIGHT OF THE NAVIGATOR, d

Kleppan, Dagfinn
NOE HEIT ANNET, prod d

Kliban, Ken
LEGAL EAGLES

Klier, Kadja
GRITTA VOM RATTENSCHLOSS

Klier, Thomas V.
ZONING, art d

Klieverik, Gerrart
WINDSCHADUW

Klimenko, Youri
CHUZHAJA, BELAJA I RJABOJ, ph

Klimov, Elem
COME AND SEE, d; COME AND SEE, w

Klimovsky, Leon
SEA SERPENT, THE

Kline, Kevin
VIOLETS ARE BLUE

Kline, Phil
SLEEPWALK, m

Kline, Richard H.
HOWARD THE DUCK, ph; TOUCH AND GO, ph

Kling, Gustav
RAVEN

Kling, Howard
VIOLATED, art d

Klingberg, Dawn
CACTUS

Klingman, Lawrence L.
Obituaries

Klinkers, Frauke
WOHIN MIT WILLFRIED?, p

Klitgaard, Peter
TAKE IT EASY, ph

Klobassa, Elisabeth
DIE NACHTMEERFAHRT, set d

Klockar, Annakarin
LIGHTNING—THE WHITE STALLION, m

Klonis, John
A LA SALIDA NOS VEMOS

Kloomok, Darren
DEAD END KIDS, ed

Kloppel, Jutta
DER SEXTE SINN

Klosinski, Edward
KRONIKA WYPADKOW MILOSNYCH, ph

Klover, Micke
I LAGENS NAMN

Kluge, Alexander
BLIND DIRECTOR, THE, d&w

Kluger, Bruce
PLAYING FOR KEEPS

Klugman, Lynn
POWER

Kluttz, Jeff
ROCKIN' ROAD TRIP

Knapman, Steve
AROUND THE WORLD IN EIGHTY WAYS, p

Knapp, Charles
JO JO DANCER, YOUR LIFE IS CALLING

Knappe, Anna
BIG HURT, THE

Kneebone, Tom
JUDGEMENT IN STONE, A

Knef, Hildegarde
FUTURE OF EMILY, THE

Knepper, Jeff
AMERICAN ANTHEM

Knepper, Rob
THAT'S LIFE

Knezevic, Ruta
VECERNJA ZVONA, cos

Knieper, Jurgen
FUTURE OF EMILY, THE, m; ROCINANTE, m

Knight, Bobby
BLUE CITY, m/l

Knight, David
DEMONI 2—L'INCUBO RITORNA

Knight, Holly
LEGAL EAGLES, m/l

Knight, Peter
PANTHER SQUAD, d

Knight, Robert
KNIGHTS AND EMERALDS

Knight, Shirley
PANTHER SQUAD

Knight, Ted   [Tadeus Wladyslaw Konopka]
Obituaries

Knight, Tonga W.
MEN'S CLUB, THE, makeup

Knight, Wayne
SEX O'CLOCK NEWS, THE

Knoernschild, Rick
LOW BLOW

Knoop, John
KAMIKAZE HEARTS, ed

Knop, Patricia
9½ WEEKS, w

Knopfler, Mark
LUCAS, m/l

Knott, Doug
ECHO PARK

Knowland, Nic
PLAYING AWAY, ph

Knowland, Nick
PING PONG, ph

Knox, Ian
SHOOT FOR THE SUN, d

Knox, Mark
HELLFIRE, m

Knox, Terence
REBEL LOVE

Knox, Werner
SCALPS, d

Knudsen, Bitten
HOLLYWOOD VICE SQUAD

Knue, Michael N.
HOUSE, ed; NIGHT OF THE CREEPS, ed

Knus, David
SPIRITS OF THE AIR, ph

Knutzon, Kine
MORD I MORKET

Kobayashi, Kaoru
LOVE LETTER; SOREKARA

Kobayashi, Katsuya
CRAZY FAMILY, THE

Kobayashi, Kunyo
INSTANT JUSTICE

Kobayashi, Yoshinori
CRAZY FAMILY, THE, w

Kober, Jeff
OUT OF BOUNDS

Kober, Marta
RAD; VENDETTA

Koble, Michael
TOUCH AND GO

Kocarjan, Vladimir
ZAZZENNYJ FONAR

Koch, Eckehard
NAME OF THE ROSE, THE

Koch, Hans Georg
WELCOME IN VIENNA, m

Koch, Jan Pieter
ASSAULT, THE

Koch, Jason
LAND OF DOOM

Koch, Ken
DOWN AND OUT IN BEVERLY HILLS

Koch, Iona
PANTHER SQUAD, w

Koch, Peter
HEARTBREAK RIDGE

Kochian, John M.
BIG TROUBLE

Kocyigit, Hulya
KURBAGALAR

Kodisch, George
F/X

Koenekamp, Fred J.
STEWARDESS SCHOOL, ph

Koenig, Walter
STAR TREK IV: THE VOYAGE HOME

Koeppe, Sigrun
NOVEMBERKATZEN, p&d

Koerfer, Thomas
KONZERT FUR ALICE, d&w

Kofler, Karl
ECHO PARK, ph

Kofman, Teo
PERROS DE LA NOCHE, p&d; PERROS DE LA
NOCHE, w

Kogan, Milt
CHECK IS IN THE MAIL, THE

Kohl, Eric
REVENGE OF THE TEENAGE VIXENS FROM OUTER
SPACE, THE

Kohler, Bob
DEPARTURE, ph

Kohler, Jon
OCEAN DRIVE WEEKEND

Kohler, Mandus
WOHIN MIT WILLFRIED?, set d

Kohn, John
SHANGHAI SURPRISE, p; SHANGHAI SURPRISE, w

Kohnami, Fumio
CRAZY FAMILY, THE, w

Kohner, Frederick
Obituaries

Kohner, Pancho
MURPHY'S LAW, p

Kohrherr, Bob
PARTING GLANCES

Kohut-Svelko, Jean-Pierre
I LOVE YOU, art d; SCENE OF THE CRIME, art d;
TAXI BOY, art d

Koildehoff, Reinhardt
HIGH SPEED

Koivula, Pertti
TUNTEMATON SOTILAS

Koivuranta, Ulla
LINNA

Koja
LIJEPE ZENE PROLAZE KROZ GRAD, m

Kokshenkov, Mikhail
KAK MOLODY MY BYLI

Kokubo, Christina
JUST BETWEEN FRIENDS

Kolbert, Anita
DIE NACHTMEERFAHRT

Kolesnikov, Aleksander
REIS 222

Kolev, Vladimir
ROMANTICHNA-ISTORIJA

Kolgyessi, Gyorgy
VAKVILAGBAN

Koll, Don
SEVEN MINUTES IN HEAVEN

Koller, Ingrid
ECHO PARK, ed; MULLERS BURO, ed

Koller, Werner
WALKMAN BLUES

Koller, Xavier
DER SCHWARZE TANNER, d; DER SCHWARZE
TANNER, w

Kollmar, Erich
AGENT ON ICE, ph

Kolovos, Vassilis
CARAVAN SARAI

Kolpa, Peter
FAILURE, THE

Kolpa, Remy
LAST SONG

Kolstad, Morten
NOE HEIT ANNET, d&w

Kolstad, Nikolai
DROMMESLOTTER

Koltai, Robert
GREAT GENERATION, THE

Kolvig, Gitte
MANDEN I MAANEN, cos

Komang, Alex
DOEA TANDA MATA; DOEA TANDA MATA, w;
SECANGKIR KOPI PAHIT

Komar, Michal
OSOBISTY PAMIETNIK GRZESZNIKA PRZEZ NIEGO
SAMEGO SPISANY, w

Komar, Wladyslaw
PIRATES

Komarov, Sasha
POTERYALSYA SLON

Komarov, Shelley
MURPHY'S LAW, cos; NAKED CAGE, THE, cos

Komlosy, Olivia
ABSOLUTE BEGINNERS

Kon, Daniel
LA NOCHE DE LOS LAPICES, w

Konchalovsky, Andrei
DUET FOR ONE, d; DUET FOR ONE, w

Konda, Yoshihide
ORA TOKYO SA YUKUDA, p

Konermann, Lutz
SCHWARZ UND OHNE ZUCKER; SCHWARZ UND
OHNE ZUCKER, d&w

Konig, Tex
BUSTED UP; HEAD OFFICE

Konishi, Kuni
SHIN YOROKOBIMO KANASHIMIMO IKUTOSHITSUKI

Konno, Misako
SHIN YOROKOBIMO KANASHIMIMO IKUTOSHITSUKI

Konrad, Albrecht
VA BANQUE, set d

Konrad, Kazimierz
DEATH SENTENCE, ph

Konstantinov, Ljupco
SRECNA NOVA '49, m

Konwicki, Tadeusz
KRONIKA WYPADKOW MILOSNYCH; KRONIKA WYPADKOW MILOSNYCH, w

Koo, Johnny
ISLE OF FANTASY, ph

Koo, Joseph
BETTER TOMORROW, A, m

Kooiman, Dirk Ayelt
PERVOLA: TRACKS IN THE SNOW, w

Kooiman, Maria
CHARLEY

Koon, Rebecca
ROCKIN' ROAD TRIP

Koopman, Maarten
PERVOLA: TRACKS IN THE SNOW, m; PERVOLA: TRACKS IN THE SNOW, w

Kooris, Richard
TEXAS CHAINSAW MASSACRE PART 2, THE, ph

Kopelson, Arnold
PLATOON, p

Koper, Macit
ADI VASFIYE

Kopins, Karen
JAKE SPEED

Kopp, Bill
ONE CRAZY SUMMER, anim

Koppel, Pelle
BALLERUP BOULEVARD

Kopriva, Ota
JONAS, DEJME TOMU VE STREDU, ph

Korberg, Tommy
BLACKOUT

Koresh, Michael
AVANTI POPOLO

Korey, Martin
COCAINE WARS

Korijenac, Vojislav
NYAMANTON, ed

Korman, Harvey
LONGSHOT, THE

Korman, Maria
LONGSHOT, THE

Korner, Freddy
ROOM WITH A VIEW, A

Kornova, Yvetta
PAVUCINA

Korody, Ildiko
VAKVILAGBAN, w

Koroptsov, Mikhail
ZAKONNY BRAK, ph

Kortchmar, Danny
FIRE WITH FIRE, m/l

Kortes-Lynch, Kitty
LA PURITAINE

Korzynski, Andrzej
DEATH SENTENCE, m

Kosberg, Robert
ONE MORE SATURDAY NIGHT, p

Kosh, Yoav
AVANTI POPOLO, ph

Kosloff, Maurice
Obituaries

Kosmacheva, Yulia
CHTO U SENJKI BYLO

Koss, Dwight
BOY WHO COULD FLY, THE

Kosslyn, Jack
VENDETTA

Kossy, Al
NO SURRENDER

Koster, Dieter
WOHIN MIT WILLFRIED?, d; WOHIN MIT WILLFRIED?, w

Kostoglou, Yannis
DANILO TRELES, O FIMISMENOS ANDALOUSIANOS MOUSIKOS

Kostolevsky, Igor
ZAKONNY BRAK

Kostov, Krassimir
DA EBICHASH NA INAT, ph

Kostovski, Kusko
SRECNA NOVA '49

Kosugi, Kane
PRAY FOR DEATH

Kosugi, Shane
PRAY FOR DEATH

Kosugi, Sho
PRAY FOR DEATH

Kotandis, George
HARDBODIES 2

Kothari, Rajan
ANAADI ANANT, ph

Kotis, Peter
LAND OF DOOM, w

Kotman, Ines
LEPOTA POROKA

Kottke, Leo
FAT GUY GOES NUTZOID!!, m

Kotto, Maka
LE COMPLEXE DU KANGOUROU

Kotto, Yaphet
EYE OF THE TIGER

Kotzky, Jacob
EVERY TIME WE SAY GOODBYE, p

Kotzritzki, Michael
UNDER THE CHERRY MOON

Kouatili, Haithan
SUN ON A HAZY DAY, THE, ed

Kougianos, Vicky
HARDBODIES 2

Kouros, Nikos
O MELISSOKOMOS

Koutchoumow, Lisbeth
JOUR ET NUIT

Koutsaftis, Philippos
KNOCK-OUT, ph; TO DENDRO POU PLIGONAME, ph

Kouwenaar, Gerrit
WINDSCHADUW, w

Kovac, Kornelije
DOBROVOLJCI, m

Kovac, Mirko
VECERNJA ZVONA, w

Kovacevic, Emilija
WILD WIND, THE, cos

Kovacs, Attila
GREAT GENERATION, THE, set d

Kovacs, Gyorgy
GREAT GENERATION, THE, m

Kovacs, Kristof
BRODERNA MOZART

Kovacs, Laszlo
LEGAL EAGLES, ph

Kovacs, Maria
ORDOGI KISERTETEK

Kovanko, Lilga
VALKOINEN KAAPIO

Kove, Martin
THE KARATE KID PART II

Kovesi, Endre
KESERU IGAZSAG, w

Kovic, Janez
KORMORAN, art d

Kovnator, Shalom
STREETS OF GOLD

Kovner, Peter
WHERE ARE THE CHILDREN?

Kowal, Lionel
CACTUS

Kowanko, Peter
SOLARBABIES

Koytu, Margrethe
BARNDOMMENS GADE; FLAMBEREDE HJERTER

Kozak, Andras
ORDOGI KISERTETEK

Kozhinkova, Yulia
DA EBICHASH NA INAT

Kozik, Christa
GRITTA VOM RATTENSCHLOSS, w

Kozinc, Zeljko
CHRISTOPHORUS, w

Kozka, Stefan
SIESTA VETA

Kozlowski, Linda
"CROCODILE" DUNDEE

Kozlowski, Maciej
OSOBISTY PAMIETNIK GRZESZNIKA PRZEZ NIEGO SAMEGO SPISANY

Kraa, Gunter
SPRING SYMPHONY

Kraaykamp, John
ASSAULT, THE; DE WISSELWACHTER

Krabbe, Jeroen
FLIGHT OF RAINBIRDS, A; JUMPIN' JACK FLASH; NO MERCY; SHADOW OF VICTORY

Kracy, Danielle
KILLER PARTY

Kraft, Irene
WALKMAN BLUES, set d

Kraft, Robert
SEVEN MINUTES IN HEAVEN, m

Krag, James
LUCAS

Krahl, Hilde
FRANZA

Krakoff, Rocky
POLTERGEIST II; SPACECAMP

Krakowska, Emilia
CHRZESNISAK

Kramarov, Savely
ARMED AND DANGEROUS

Kramer, Bert
BLOODY BIRTHDAY

Kramer, Eric
LOYALTIES

Kramer, Jerry
MODERN GIRLS, d

Kramer, Joel
RAW DEAL

Kramer, Kim
REVENGE OF THE TEENAGE VIXENS FROM OUTER SPACE, THE

Kramer, Richard
SAVING GRACE, w

Kramreither, Anthony
CONFIDENTIAL, p; DANCING IN THE DARK, p

Kramreither, Tony
FLYING, p

Kraner, Doug
NO MERCY, art d

Kranhouse, Jon R.
FRIDAY THE 13TH PART VI: JASON LIVES, ph

Krantz, Gosta
AMOROSA

Krantz, Robert
SHORT CIRCUIT

Krapp, Helmut
DER WILDE CLOWN, p

Krassilschohikov, Arkadi
POTERYALSYA SLON, w

Kraus, Courtney
DIRT BIKE KID, THE

Kraus, Philip
PLAYING FOR KEEPS

Kraus-Rajteric, Vladimir
VECERNJA ZVONA, m

Krause, Robert
CHECK IS IN THE MAIL, THE, p

Krauss, Peter
DER SOMMER DES SAMURAI

Krauzer, Steven M.
COCAINE WARS, w

Kravchenko, Aleksei
COME AND SEE

Kravitz, Steve
HOWARD THE DUCK

Kravtshenko, Tatiana
KAK MOLODY MY BYLI

Krawczyk, Gerard
JE HAIS LES ACTEURS, d; JE HAIS LES ACTEURS, w; LE BONHEUR A ENCORE FRAPPE, w

Kray, Walter
WILD WIND, THE

Kreber, Vesna
SAN O RUZI, ed

Krebs, Susan
ODD JOBS

Kreer, Doris
HEIDENLOCHER

Kreigsman, Jan
DEMONER, stunts

Kremanova, Jana
PAVUCINA

Kremer, Gidon
SPRING SYMPHONY

Kremer, Hans
AUF IMMER UND EWIG; STAMMHEIM

Kremps-Ehrlich, Dorothee
WOHIN MIT WILLFRIED?

Krenkler, Ulrich
ZONING, d; ZONING, w

Kress, Carl
RAD, ed

Kreuners Group
CONGO EXPRESS, m

Kreuzer, Patrick
NAME OF THE ROSE, THE

Krevitt, Rosanne E.
LUCAS

Krevitz, Karen
GIRLS SCHOOL SCREAMERS

Krewson, Rollin
LABYRINTH

Krieger, Barbara
8 MILLION WAYS TO DIE, set d

Krieger, Martin-Theo
WALKMAN BLUES, ph

Kriener, Ulrike
PARADIES

Krik, Howard
SHORT CIRCUIT

Krikes, Peter
STAR TREK IV: THE VOYAGE HOME, w

Krimer, Jorge
SALOME; SAVING GRACE

Krishan, Mircea
PERVOLA: TRACKS IN THE SNOW

Krishen, Pradip
MASSEY SAHIB, d

Kriss, Katherine
HOT CHILI

Kristal-Andersson, Binnie
LOVE ME!, w

Kristel, Sylvia
BIG BET, THE

Kristiansen, Idar
DREAM OF NORTHERN LIGHTS, w

Kristiansen, Terje
HUD, ed; HUD, p; HUD, w

Kristiansen, Tonje Kamilla
HUD

Krivokapic, Miodrag
VECERNJA ZVONA

Krivoshieva, Irene
ROMANTICHNA-ISTORIJA

Kriwoluzky, Ilja
GRITTA VOM RATTENSCHLOSS

Kroeber, Carlos
CHICO REI

Kroeker, Allan
TRAMP AT THE DOOR, d&w

Krog, Frank
HARD ASFALT

Krogh, Frode
MACARONI BLUES, prod d

Krogtoft, Harald
MACARONI BLUES

Krohse, Matthias
UNTERMEHMEN GEIGENKASTEN

Kroll, Anatoly
ZIMNI VECHER V GAGRAKH, m

Kronenfeld, Ivan
HANNAH AND HER SISTERS

Krook, Margaretha
MORRHAR OCH ARTOR

Kroonenburg, Pieter
BLUE MAN, THE, p

Kropke, Stephanie
REVENGE

Krosche, Joan
NIGHTMARE WEEKEND

Krotochvil, Franz
QUICKSILVER

Krovel, Hans
DROMMESLOTTER

Krovel, Svein
NATTSEILERE, ph; X, ph

Krowka, Joe
ONE MORE SATURDAY NIGHT

Krsek, Vlasta
FERRIS BUELLER'S DAY OFF

Krueber, Carlos
RUNNING OUT OF LUCK

Krueger, Scott
MY CHAUFFEUR, m/l

Kruger, Caroline
MORENA

Kruger, Robert
POWER

Krum, Dorrie
HOLLYWOOD VICE SQUAD

Krupanszky, Judy
LOYALTIES, ed

Krupinski, Marzena
HEIDENLOCHER

Krusteva, Magda
SKUPA MOYA, SKUPI MOY, ed

Krutina, Eva
FATHERLAND

Ksouri, Khaled
MAN OF ASHES

Kuanding, Li
LIANG JIA FUNU, w

Kubitza, Ernst
DER POLENWEIHER, ph

Kuchar, George
SCREAMPLAY

Kudaba, Elena
BEER; DANCING IN THE DARK

Kudo, Yuki
CRAZY FAMILY, THE

Kudoh, Yuki
TYPHOON CLUB

Kuehn, Andrew J.
STEWARDESS SCHOOL

Kuen, Cheong Kwok
PASSION, ed

Kuervost, Derek
HEAD OFFICE

Kuhlman, Ron
SHADOW PLAY

Kuitka, Guillermo
EIN BLICK—UND DIE LIEBE BRICHT AUS, art d

Kukels, Hari
SVESAS KAISLIBAS, ph

Kukumagi, Arvo
IDEAALMAASTIK

Kulanbajev, A.
DESCENDANT OF THE SNOW LEOPARD, THE

Kulharni, Mangesh
RAO SAHEB

Kulic, Michal
PAVUCINA, ph

Kulichova, Eva
PAVUCINA

Kulik, Mark
TOBY MCTEAGUE

Kulish, Savra
FOUETTE, w

Kulkarni, Sudhir
MASSEY SAHIB

Kulzer, William
BAD GUYS

Kulzer, William J.
SHADOWS RUN BLACK; SHADOWS RUN BLACK, stunts

Kumagai, Yoko
TO SLEEP SO AS TO DREAM, m

Kumar, Krishna
MUKHAMUKHAM

Kumar, Milena
DOKTOR, cos

Kumar, Suman
ANAADI ANANT

Kumashiro, Tatsumi
LOVE LETTER, d; LOVE LETTER, w

Kumer, Jill
SEX APPEAL

Kun, Vilmos
ORDOGI KISERTETEK

Kunert, Christian
FATHERLAND, m

Kunev, Velko
DA EBICHASH NA INAT

Kunick, Boston
ROCKIN' ROAD TRIP

Kunstmann, Doris
DEATH SENTENCE

Kunze, Barbara
ANGRY HARVEST, ed

Kuo-Chu, Chang
DARK NIGHT

Kuo-pin, Liu
TIME TO LIVE AND A TIME TO DIE, A

Kupper, Yvonne
KONZERT FUR ALICE

Kurant, Willy
CHARLOTTE FOR EVER, ph; FLAGRANT DESIR, ph

Kurbandurdyev, Bengene
MUZSKOE VOSPITANIE

Kure, Henning
VALHALLA, w

Kurebayashi, Shigeru
TYPHOON CLUB

Kureishi, Hanif
MY BEAUTIFUL LAUNDRETTE, w; People to Watch

Kurent, Andrej
DOKTOR

Kurfirst, Gary
TRUE STORIES, p

Kuri, Rafael Villasenor
PICARDIA MEXICANA NUMERO DOS, d

Kurimoto, Kaoru
CABARET, w

Kuriyama, Tomio
ORA TOKYO SA YUKUDA, d

Kurland, Jeffrey
HANNAH AND HER SISTERS, cos; STREETS OF
GOLD, cos

Kurna, Wachtang
ROBINSONIADA ANU CHEMI INGLISELI PAPA, art d

Kurosawa, Mitsuru
SOREKARA, p

Kurson, Jane
THE KARATE KID PART II, ed

Kurtis, Jon
CLASS OF NUKE 'EM HIGH

Kurtis, Virginia
CLASS OF NUKE 'EM HIGH

Kurtiz, Tuncel
DEN FRUSNA LEOPARDEN; SMILE OF THE LAMB,
THE

Kurtz, David
INSTANT JUSTICE, m

Kurtz, Swoosie
TRUE STORIES; WILDCATS

Kurtz, Ted
HOWARD THE DUCK

Kurtzman, Robert
NIGHT OF THE CREEPS

Kurz, Anastasia
EIN FLIEHENDES PFERD, cos

Kurz, Eva
VIRUS HAS NO MORALS, A

Kusaba, Craig
SHADOWS RUN BLACK, w; SIZZLE BEACH, U.S.A., w

Kusabue, Mitsuko
SOREKARA

Kusajima, Kyoko
TO SLEEP SO AS TO DREAM

Kusatsu, Clyde
SHANGHAI SURPRISE

Kusdas, Ulf Dieter
'38

Kushner, Donald
NUTCRACKER: THE MOTION PICTURE, p

Kushnir, Avi
ALEX KHOLE AHAVA

Kuster, Diethard
VA BANQUE, d&w

Kusturica, Emir
DO YOU REMEMBER DOLLY BELL?, d

Kusuhara, Eiji
HALF MOON STREET

Kutman, Huseyin
KIRLANGIC FIRTINASI

Kutualgyi, Erzsebet
ELYSIUM

Kuveiller, Luigi
UNA SPINA NEL CUORE, ph; YUPPIES, I GIOVANI DI
SUCCESSO, ph

Kuwana, Masahiro
COMIC MAGAZINE

Kuzmanich, Dunav
SAN ANTONITO, w

Kuznetzov, Aleksandr
NEBYVALSHINA

Kuzyk, Kathy
ABDUCTED, makeup

Kverenchchiladze, Zinaida
YOUNG COMPOSER'S ODYSSEY, A

Kvilvidze, Rusudan
YOUNG COMPOSER'S ODYSSEY, A

Kwan, Danny
BIG TROUBLE IN LITTLE CHINA; UPHILL ALL THE
WAY

Kwan, Lam Ping
MARTIAL ARTS OF SHAOLIN, p

Kwan, Nancy
ANGKOR-CAMBODIA EXPRESS

Kwan, Pauline
FAMILY, THE

Kwan, Rosamund
ARMOUR OF GOD, THE

Kwen-hou, Chen
SUMMER AT GRANDPA'S, A, ph

Kwirikadze, Irakli
ROBINSONIADA ANU CHEMI INGLISELI PAPA, w

Kwon-Taek, Im
GILSODOM, d

Kwong, Chu
LAST SONG IN PARIS

Kwong, Li Yiu
FAMILY, THE, art d

Kwong, Peter
BIG TROUBLE IN LITTLE CHINA; GOLDEN CHILD,
THE; NEVER TOO YOUNG TO DIE

Kydralijev, Dokdurbek
DESCENDANT OF THE SNOW LEOPARD, THE

Kydryralijev, Aibek
DESCENDANT OF THE SNOW LEOPARD, THE

L.A. Effects Group, The
ALIENS, spec eff

La Courbiniere, Karl
MIN PAPA AR TARZAN

La Fleur, Art
COBRA; SAY YES; ZONE TROOPERS

La Freniere, Celine
FOREIGN BODY, w

La Greca, Paul
BIG TROUBLE

La Rosa, Vittorio
GIURO CHE TI AMO

La Saitta, Gabrie
IL RAGAZZO DEL PONY EXPRESS

La Salle, Eriq
WHERE ARE THE CHILDREN?

La Trouppe Theater Group
CALACAN

La Turner, Robert
NUTCRACKER: THE MOTION PICTURE

Labarthe, Francois-Renaud
DESORDRE, art d

Labonte, Francois
HENRI, d

Laborteaux, Matthew
DEADLY FRIEND

LaBounty, Bill
AT CLOSE RANGE, m/l

Labourier, Dominique
L'ETAT DE GRACE; SAUVE-TOI, LOLA

LaBove, Carl
JUMPIN' JACK FLASH

LaBry, Randall
BELIZAIRE THE CAJUN, prod d

Lacambre, Daniel
DIRT BIKE KID, THE, ph

Lacey, Ronald
ACES GO PLACES IV; SKY BANDITS

LaChance, Manette
MEN'S CLUB, THE

Lachman, Ed
STRIPPER, ph; TRUE STORIES, ph; People to Watch

Lacreta, Ide
HOUR OF THE STAR, THE, ed; MALANDRO, ed

Lacroix, Denis
VISAGE PALE

Lacy, Bertrand
LE DEBUTANT

Lafaurie, Nathalie
FEMMES DE PERSONNE, ed

Lafette, Jean
TOUCH AND GO

LaFong, Carl
THREE AMIGOS

Lafont, Bernadette
INSPECTEUR LAVARDIN

Lafont, Pauline
JE HAIS LES ACTEURS; LA GALETTE DU ROI

Laforet, Agustin Cerezales
EL HERMANO BASTARDO DE DIOS, w

Lafranchi, Damien
UNDER THE CHERRY MOON, art d

Lagerfelt, Caroline
IRON EAGLE

Lagrain, Jacqueline
THERESE

Lahaie, Brigitte
L'EXECUTRICE; SUIVEZ MON REGARD

Lahdenpera, Aino
SININEN IMETTAJA

Lahti, Christine
JUST BETWEEN FRIENDS

Lai, Francis
MAN AND A WOMAN: 20 YEARS LATER, A, m; MAN
AND A WOMAN: 20 YEARS LATER, A, m/l

Lai, Michael
HAPPY DIN DON; HAPPY DIN DON, m

Lai, Yon
COMBAT SHOCK

Laikin, Paul
SEX O'CLOCK NEWS, THE, w

Lain, Emilio
EN PENUMBRA

Laine, Karen
PRETTY IN PINK

Laine, Philippe
ASTERIX CHEZ LES BRETONS, ph

Laing, Celeste
NINJA TURF

Laing, John
DANGEROUS ORPHANS, d

Laing, Toby
DANGEROUS ORPHANS

Laird, Ian
KNIGHTS AND EMERALDS

Laird-Clowes, Nick
FERRIS BUELLER'S DAY OFF, m/l

Laiter, Tova
ONE MORE SATURDAY NIGHT, p

Laitinen, Aarno
RIISUMINEN

Laius, Leida
NAERATA OMETI, d

Lakanen, Anne
PIMEYS ODOTTA, ed

Lakatos, Ivan
KOJAK BUDAPESTEN, ph

Lake, Alan
DEAD-END DRIVE-IN, ed

Lake, Don
PINK CHIQUITAS, THE

Lake, Michael
SPIRITS OF THE AIR

Lake, Ollie
OUT OF BOUNDS

Lakhdar-Hamina, Malik
LAST IMAGE, THE

Lakhdar-Hamina, Merwan
LAST IMAGE, THE

Lakhdar-Hamina, Mohamed
LAST IMAGE, THE, d&w

Lakhoua, Lilia
MAN OF ASHES, cos

Laks, Bruce
FLIGHT OF THE NAVIGATOR

Lalama, Mark
WELCOME TO THE PARADE, m

Lalande, Guy
CRAZY MOON, art d

Lalanne, Francis
LE PASSAGE, p

Lalanne, Jean-Felix
LE PASSAGE, m

Lalinde, Rodrigo
LA MANSION DE ARAUCAIMA, ph

Lalitha
MUKHAMUKHAM

Lalo
PICARDIA MEXICANA NUMERO DOS

Laloux, Daniel
RUE DU DEPART

Lam
SILENT LOVE, m

Lam, Ardy
HAPPY DIN DON, ph

Lam, George
PASSION

Lam, Ringo
ACES GO PLACES IV, d; ACES GO PLACES IV, w

Lam, Sarah
SHANGHAI SURPRISE

Lamarque, Christian
LE COMPLEXE DU KANGOUROU, ph

Lamassone, Karen
LA MANSION DE ARAUCAIMA, ed

Lambach, Boguslaw
CHRZESNISAK, ph

Lambert, Christopher
HIGHLANDER; LOVE SONGS

Lambert, Dennis
FINE MESS, A, m/l

Lambert, Douglas
Obituaries

Lambert, Jerry
TEXAS CHAINSAW MASSACRE PART 2, THE, m

Lambert, Lothar
DER SEXTE SINN, d&w; DIE LIEBESWUSTE; DIE
LIEBESWUSTE, p, d, w, ph

Lambert, Paul
SOLDIER'S REVENGE

Lambert, Steven
BIG TROUBLE

Lambros, G.
ALLIGORIA

Lambrose, Gabrielle
FRINGE DWELLERS, THE

Lambton, Ann
SID AND NANCY

Lambton, Anne
HALF MOON STREET

Lamche, Gustav
ROCINANTE, p

Lamede, Jill
ROCINANTE

Lamielle, Pierre
CLAN OF THE CAVE BEAR, THE

Lamla, Norbert
ZONING

Lamm, Regina
EIN BLICK—UND DIE LIEBE BRICHT AUS

Lamond, John
SKY PIRATES, ed; SKY PIRATES, p; SKY PIRATES, w

Lamont, Michael
ALIENS, art d

Lamont, Peter
ALIENS, prod d

Lamor, Maria
EL CABALLERO DEL DRAGON

Lamothe, Arthur
EQUINOXE, d; EQUINOXE, w

Lamothe, Nicole
EQUINOXE, p

Lamotte, Martin
LA GITANE; TWIST AGAIN A MOSCOU; TWIST
AGAIN A MOSCOU, w

Lamour, Sophia
THREE AMIGOS

Lampert, Jeffrey
FINE MESS, A

Lampreave, Chus
EL ANO DE LAS LUCES; MATADOR

Lan, John
FINE MESS, A, m/l

Lan, Ke
YELLOW EARTH, w

Lan, Rosine
JE HAIS LES ACTEURS, cos

Lana, Gino
IL GIARDINO DEGLI INGANNI

Lanari, Ughetta
SEPARATI IN CASA

Lancaster, Burt
TOUGH GUYS

Lancaster, Pete
NAME OF THE ROSE, THE

Lanchester, Elsa [Elizabeth Sullivan]
Obituaries

Lanci, Beppe
LA VENEXIANA, ph

Lanci, Giuseppe
CAMORRA, ph; EHRENGARD, ph; EVERY TIME WE
SAY GOODBYE, ph; IL DIAVOLO IN CORPO, ph

Landa, Alfredo
BANDERA NEGRA; LOS PARAISOS PERDIDOS

Landa, Miguelangel
MANON

Landau, Michael
KILLING CARS, m

Landero, Federico
TERROR Y ENCAJES NEGROS, ed

Landero, Fernando
EL SECUESTRO DE CAMARENA, ed

Landers, Audrey
GETTING EVEN

Landers, Judy
ARMED AND DANGEROUS; STEWARDESS SCHOOL

Landers, Matt
JUMPIN' JACK FLASH

Landgre, Inga
BRODERNA MOZART

Landgree, Aina
AMOROSA

Landgree, Inga
AMOROSA

Landham, Sonny
FIREWALKER

Landis, Evan
CARE BEARS MOVIE II: A NEW GENERATION, ed

Landis, John
THREE AMIGOS, d

Landon, David
DR. OTTO AND THE RIDDLE OF THE GLOOM BEAM

Landon, Laurene
AMERICA 3000; ARMED RESPONSE

Landoulsi, Philippe
SCENE OF THE CRIME

Landre, Lou
FLODDER

Landry, Gerard
ANEMIA

Landry, Paul
BELIZAIRE THE CAJUN

Landry, Sophie
L'UNIQUE, makeup

Lands, Wendy
BUSTED UP; ONE NIGHT ONLY

Landsberg, David
DETECTIVE SCHOOL DROPOUTS; DETECTIVE SCHOOL DROPOUTS, w

Lane, Andrew
JAKE SPEED, d; JAKE SPEED, p; JAKE SPEED, w

Lane, Bill
OUT OF BOUNDS

Lane, Garrison
HEARTBURN

Lane, Jimmy Walker
WISDOM

Lane, Lauri Lupino
Obituaries

Lane, Mark Stuart
FIRE IN THE NIGHT

Lane, Niki
BIG HURT, THE

Lane, Paul
ONE CRAZY SUMMER

Lane, Rusty
Obituaries

Lane, Scott Edmund
OUT OF BOUNDS

Lanee, Jessica
DIE LIEBESWUSTE

Laneros, Federico
EL JUEGO DE LA MUERTE, ed

Lang, Andre
Obituaries

Lang, Caroline
SUIVEZ MON REGARD

Lang, Joel
MODERN GIRLS, prod d&art d

Lang, Li Dien
LAST EMPEROR, THE

Lang, Oliver
PARENTAL CLAIM, w

Lang, Philip J. [Philip Joseph Lang]
Obituaries

Lang, Stephen
BAND OF THE HAND; MANHUNTER

Lang, William
DESERT BLOOM

Langdon, Dick
ROCKIN' ROAD TRIP

Langdon, Richard
BLUE VELVET, stunts

Lange, Bruce
ABDUCTED, ed

Lange, Harold
HYPER SAPIEN: PEOPLE FROM ANOTHER STAR, prod d

Lange, Henry
SALOME, p

Lange, Hope
BLUE VELVET

Lange, Jessica
CRIMES OF THE HEART

Lange, Monique
MAN AND A WOMAN: 20 YEARS LATER, A, w

Langelaan, George
FLY, THE, w

Langella, Frank
MEN'S CLUB, THE

Langer, Clive
ABSOLUTE BEGINNERS, m/l

Langfeldt, Inge-Lise
DROMMESLOTTER, ed; FAREWELL ILLUSION, ed; X, ed

Langford, Barry
AVANTI POPOLO

Langhorne, Bruce
SMART ALEC, m

Langhorne, Ryan
MANHUNTER

Langlet, Daniel
ZONE ROUGE

Langley, John
P.O.W. THE ESCAPE, w

Langlois, Yves
TOBY MCTEAGUE, ed

Langmann, Arlette
JEAN DE FLORETTE, ed

Langsner, Jacobo
BAD COMPANY, w

Langston, Murray
LIGHTNING—THE WHITE STALLION

Laniel, Mark
YOUNGBLOOD

Lankford, T.L.
ARMED RESPONSE, w; ARMED RESPONSE, w; TOMB, THE, w

Lanni, Federico
FOTOROMANZO, ph

Lanoe, Henri
SAUVE-TOI, LOLA, ed

Lanoux, Victor
SCENE OF THE CRIME

Lanteri, Michael
STAR TREK IV: THE VOYAGE HOME, spec eff

Lantieri, Michael
BACK TO SCHOOL, spec eff

Lantos, Robert
ONE NIGHT ONLY, p; SEPARATE VACATIONS, p

Lanvin, Gerard
LES FRERES PETARD

Lanying, Song Shu
YU QING SAO, cos

Lanz, Juan
SAN ANTONITO, m

Lapadula, John
BUSTED UP

Lapid, Era
KOL AHAVO-TAI, ed

Laplace, Victor
EL RIGOR DEL DESTINO; LES LONGS MANTEAUX; POBRE MARIPOSA

Lapotaire, Jane
LADY JANE

Lapshin, Alexander
DEN' GNEVA, w

Lapshina, Tatyana
ODINOTCHNOYE PLAVANIYE, art d

Lara, Agustin
EL BRONCO, ph; EL EXTRANO HIJO DEL SHERIFF, ph; LOS ASES DE CONTRABANDO, ph; POR UN VESTIDO DE NOVIA, ph

Lara, Tina
SINCERELY CHARLOTTE

Larbi, Fatma
AL-KAS

Larder, Geoff
MONA LISA

Laretei, Kabi
FLIGHT NORTH

Larguier, Jean-Luc
MAMMAME, p

Larimer, Emmet
CHOKE CANYON

Larkin, Bob
FRIDAY THE 13TH PART VI: JASON LIVES

Larkin, Peter
POWER, prod d

Larkin, Sheena
CRAZY MOON

Laroche, Pierre
MERCI MONSIEUR ROBERTSON

Larochelle, Denis
HENRI, m

Larrain, Nene
LOS HIJOS DE LA GUERRA FRIA

Larrie, Sebastian
SOLDIER'S REVENGE

Larrieu, Jean-Claude
DOUCE FRANCE, ph

Larriva, Umberto "Tito"
TRUE STORIES

Larsen, Beth
DIRT BIKE KID, THE

Larsen, Henrik
WOLF AT THE DOOR, THE

Larsen, Lars Andreas
NOE HEIT ANNET

Larsen, Lars Oluf
ET SKUD FRA HJERTET

Larsen, Marina
KILLING CARS

Larson, Larry
REBEL LOVE

Larsson, Charlotta
MALACCA

Larsson, Henrik
ALLA VI BARN I BULLERBY

Lartigue, Jacques Henri
GINGER & FRED

Larzabal, Imanol
27 HORAS, m

Lasfargues, Alain
BLACK AND WHITE, ph; HIGH SPEED, ph

Lashly, James
HOWARD THE DUCK

Laskarin, Mari
SCREEN TEST

Laskus, Jacek
PARTING GLANCES, ph

Lasky, Kathy
HEAD OFFICE

Lasley, David
LAST RESORT, THE, m/l

Lasmezas, Anne
ON A VOLE CHARLIE SPENCER!

Lass, Barbara
DAS SCHWEIGEN DES DICHTERS; ROSA LUXEMBURG

Lassa, Henri
LES LONGS MANTEAUX, p; SINCERELY CHARLOTTE

Lassander, Dagmar
MONSTER SHARK

Lasser, Louise
PERILS OF P.K., THE

Lassick, Sydney
RATBOY

Lassoued, Mohamed
AL-KAS

Laster, Debbie
NIGHTMARE WEEKEND

Laszlo, Andrew
POLTERGEIST II, ph

Latham, Bernard
MILWR BYCHAN

Latham, Fiona
DOGS IN SPACE

Lathouris, Nicolas
WRONG WORLD

Lathrop, Philip
DEADLY FRIEND, ph

Latorraca, Ney
MALANDRO

Latta, Chris
TRANSFORMERS: THE MOVIE, THE

Lattanzi, Matt
THAT'S LIFE

Lattas, Danayota
DANILO TRELES, O FIMISMENOS ANDALOUSIANOS MOUSIKOS

Lattuada, Alberto
UNA SPINA NEL CUORE, d; UNA SPINA NEL CUORE, w

Lau, Billy
MR. VAMPIRE

Lau, Jim
BIG TROUBLE IN LITTLE CHINA; UPHILL ALL THE WAY

Laub, Marc
SEVEN MINUTES IN HEAVEN, ed

Lauber, Terry
LOVE SONGS

Lauda, Niki
SCHWARZ UND OHNE ZUCKER

Laudenbach, Philippe
BETTY BLUE

Lauersen, Linda
YES, DET ER FAR!

Laughlin, Lori
RAD

Laughride, Gloria
BLUE VELVET, cos

Launer, Dale
RUTHLESS PEOPLE, w; People to Watch

Laurain, Gilberte
THERESE

Laurant, Michael
WOMEN'S PRISON MASSACRE

Laure, Carole
SAUVE-TOI, LOLA

Lauren, Jeanne
HOWARD THE DUCK

Laurence, Mitchell
RAW TUNES

Laurent, Christine
DERNIER CRI; MORT UN DIMANCHE DE PLUIE

Laurent, Gilles
FRENCH LESSON

Laurent, Jean-Pierre
PRUNELLE BLUES

Laurenti, Mariano
FOTOROMANZO, d; FOTOROMANZO, w

Laurenzi, Anita
EHRENGARD; IL DIAVOLO IN CORPO

Laurenzi, Silvio
THRONE OF FIRE, THE, cos

Lauretta, Enzo
LA SPOSA ERA BELLISSIMA, w

Laurie, Jane
FOREIGN BODY

Laurie, Piper
CHILDREN OF A LESSER GOD

Laurier, Lucie
ANNE TRISTER; HENRI

Laurito, Marisa
IL TENENTE DEI CARABINIERI

Lausevic, Zarko
DOBROVOLJCI

Laustiola, Tomas
LOVE ME!

Lauten, Flora
COME LA VIDA MISMA; JIBARO

Lauter, Ed
3:15, THE MOMENT OF TRUTH; RAW DEAL;
YOUNGBLOOD

Lauterbach, Heiner
PARADIES

Lautsiavitchus, Lyubomiras
COME AND SEE

Lavanant, Dominique
JE HAIS LES ACTEURS; KAMIKAZE; LE DEBUTANT;
LES FRERES PETARD; LOVE SONGS; MORT UN
DIMANCHE DE PLUIE

Lavanon, Yeud
FLASH, p

Lavant, Denis
MAUVAIS SANG

Lavau, Joel
MENAGE, makeup; MORT UN DIMANCHE DE PLUIE,
makeup

Lavender, Dan
SCREAMPLAY

Lavery, Emmet   [Emmet Godfrey Lavery]
Obituaries

Lavi, Amos
FLASH

Lavia, Gabriele
SENSI; SENSI, d; SENSI, w

Lavie, Arik
HASHIGAON HAGADOL

Lavigne, Paula
CINEMA FALADO

Lavoie, Daniel
LES LONGS MANTEAUX, m/l

Lavoie, Reine
DEVIL IN THE FLESH

Lavric, Paul
UN OASPETE LA CINA

Lavsky, Richard
BEGINNER'S LUCK, m

Lavy, Pascal
TRANSITTRAUME

Law, Bonnie
ISLE OF FANTASY

Law, Christopher
AMERICAN JUSTICE

Law, Don
KING KONG LIVES

Law, John Phillip
AMERICAN COMMANDOS; NO TIME TO DIE

Law, May
FAMILY, THE

Law, Viv
ABSOLUTE BEGINNERS

Lawhon, Ben
DR. OTTO AND THE RIDDLE OF THE GLOOM BEAM

Lawn, Tony
MISSION, THE

Lawner, Mordecai
RAW DEAL

Lawrence, .H.
KANGAROO, w

Lawrence, Bruno
BRIDGE TO NOWHERE

Lawrence, Dorothy
BIG HURT, THE

Lawrence, Hap
BEST OF TIMES, THE

Lawrence, Jeremy
CRITTERS

Lawrence, Jody
Obituaries

Lawrence, Len
ONE CRAZY SUMMER

Lawrence, Madeleine
ABSOLUTE BEGINNERS

Lawrence, Patricia
ROOM WITH A VIEW, A

Lawrence, Richard
BLUE CITY, art d

Lawrence, Richard J.
SPACECAMP, art d

Lawrence, Robert
8 MILLION WAYS TO DIE, ed

Lawrence, Tom
SHORT CIRCUIT

Laws, Barry
SHADOW PLAY

Laws, Debra
CROSSROADS

Lawson, Tony
CASTAWAY, ed

Lawson, Veronica
DR. OTTO AND THE RIDDLE OF THE GLOOM BEAM

Lawther, Chas
POLICE ACADEMY 3: BACK IN TRAINING

Lawton, Jay
GREAT MOUSE DETECTIVE, THE, md

Layne, Randi
IMPURE THOUGHTS

Layng, Lissa
SAY YES

Layng, Rosemary Le Roy
SAY YES, p

Laynn, Ann
PANTHER SQUAD, cos

Lazar, Dorina
LICEENI

Lazare, Carol
FLY, THE

Lazareff, Serge
DEPARTURE

Lazarevski, Nikola
SRECNA NOVA '49, art d

Lazaridou, Olia
ALCESTES

Lazaro, Eusebio
EL DISPUTADO VOTO DEL SR. CAYO

Lazaro, Ronnie
REVENGE FOR JUSTICE

Lazarov, Jurij
BORIS GODUNOV

Lazarus, Jerry
HOT CHILI; MURPHY'S LAW

Lazenby, George
NEVER TOO YOUNG TO DIE

Lazier, Gil
SOMETHING WILD

Lazure, Gabrielle
LAST SONG

Lazzara, Lou
HOLLYWOOD ZAP!, makeup; STAR CRYSTAL, makeup

Lazzarini, Pedro Pablo
JOGO DURO, ph

Lazzaro, Claudio
LA BALLATA DI EVA, w

Le Beau, Edward
FERRIS BUELLER'S DAY OFF

Le Clezio, Odile
DEVIL IN THE FLESH; FOR LOVE ALONE; TWELFTH
NIGHT; YOUNG EINSTEIN

Le Cover, Lisa
BACK TO SCHOOL

Le Foulon, Etienne
JAKE SPEED

Le Francois, Joel
THERESE

Le Gassick, Steve
SAY YES, m

Le Gros, James
SOLARBABIES

Le Guellec, Guillaume
ETATS D'AME

Le Guernec, Anne
CHARLOTTE FOR EVER

Le Henry, Alain
LA FEMME DE MA VIE, w

Le Lann, Eric
ROUND MIDNIGHT

Le Marinel, Paul
SINCERELY CHARLOTTE, makeup

Le Mener, Jean-Yves
MAN AND A WOMAN: 20 YEARS LATER, A, ph

Le Page, Pierre
WOHIN MIT WILLFRIED?, p

Le Person, Paul
DOUCE FRANCE

Le Rigoleur, Dominique
L'AMANT MAGNIFIQUE, ph

Lea, Sharan
FINE MESS, A

Lea, Tracy
LETTER TO BREZHNEV

Leach, Doug
TORMENT

Leach, Rosemary
ROOM WITH A VIEW, A

Leach, Sarah
REVENGE OF THE TEENAGE VIXENS FROM OUTER
SPACE, THE

Leachman, Cloris
MY LITTLE PONY; SHADOW PLAY

Leadbitter, Bill
KNIGHTS AND EMERALDS; TAI-PAN

Leader, Bruce
KNIGHTS AND EMERALDS

Leadon, Paul
AROUND THE WORLD IN EIGHTY WAYS, w

Leaf, Fred
ECHO PARK

Leahy, Joe
QUICKSILVER

Leak, Jennifer
AGENT ON ICE

Leake, Damien
HIGHLANDER

Leal, Gina
ESE LOCO LOCO HOSPITAL

Leal, Nuno
REI DO RIO

Leal, Tomas
SALVADOR

Leamer, John
FROM BEYOND; TERRORVISION

Learned, Michael
POWER

Leassy, El
AL KETTAR, p

Leasure, Steven   [Steve]
DR. OTTO AND THE RIDDLE OF THE GLOOM BEAM;
DR. OTTO AND THE RIDDLE OF THE GLOOM BEAM,
w

Leath, Ron
FIRE IN THE NIGHT

Leatherbarrow, Penny
CLOCKWISE; NO SURRENDER

Leaud, Jean-Pierre
CORPS ET BIENS; GRANDEUR ET DECADENCE D'UN
PETIT COMMERCE DE CINEMA

Lembeck, Claus
ET SKUD FRA HJERTET

LeMen, Vinciane
LA PURITAINE

Lemesles, Annie
L'EXECUTRICE, ed

Lemmo, Joan
BAD GUYS ; STEWARDESS SCHOOL

Lemmon, Chris
THAT'S LIFE; WEEKEND WARRIORS

Lemmon, Jack
THAT'S LIFE

Lemnitz, Regina
FOLLOWING THE FUHRER; ROSA LUXEMBURG

Lemoine, Emmanuel
FAUBOURG SAINT-MARTIN

Lemoine, Joy
HALF MOON STREET

Lemos, Carlos
VIAJE A NINGUNA PARTE

Lemus, Jose Luis
PICARDIA MEXICANA NUMERO DOS, ph

Len, Jeannette
AMORE INQUIETO DI MARIA

Lena, Lorenzo
LA BONNE; SAPORE DEL GRANO

Lenard, John
BUSTED UP

Lenard, Mark
STAR TREK IV: THE VOYAGE HOME

Lenardi, Juan Carlos
AWAITING THE PALLBEARERS, ph; SERE
CUALQUIER COSA PERO TE QUIERO, ph

Lencina, Julio
PERROS DE LA NOCHE, ph

Lenehan, Nancy
STOOGEMANIA

Lenertz, James
REVENGE, ed

Lenk, Skischule
LISI UND DER GENERAL, stunts

Lenn, Gabriel
NIGHTMARE'S PASSENGERS; SOBREDOSIS

Lennartsson, Finn
MOA

Lennman, Ulla
I LAGENS NAMN, ed

Lennon, Jimmy
TOUGH GUYS

Lennox, Doug
BOY IN BLUE, THE; POLICE ACADEMY 3: BACK IN
TRAINING

Lenoir, Denis
DESORDRE, ph

Lenoire, Rosetta
WHATEVER IT TAKES

Lenorman, Maurice
UNDER THE CHERRY MOON

Lensky, Barry
PANTHER SQUAD, ed

Lensky, Leib
SOMETHING WILD

Lentini, Massimo
MANHATTAN BABY, cos; MANHATTAN BABY, prod
d; THUNDER WARRIOR, art d&cos

Lentz, Andy
PATRIOT, THE

Lentz, George
SCHLEUSE 17

Lentz, Sebastian
SCHLEUSE 17, d&w

Lenz, Kay
HOUSE

Lenz, Sigfried
LIGHTSHIP, THE, w

Lenzer, Norm
ADVENTURES OF THE AMERICAN RABBIT, THE;
ADVENTURES OF THE AMERICAN RABBIT, THE, w

Lenzi, Giovanni
DELITTI, w

Lenzi, Umberto
SQUADRA SELVAGGIA, d

Lenzini, Lia
ROMANCE

Leon, Annie
CAPTIVE

Leon, Carlos
CONTACTO CHICANO

Leon, Charles
SMILE OF THE LAMB, THE, set d

Leon, Charlie
DAS SCHWEIGEN DES DICHTERS, art d

Leon, Debbie
AMERICA 3000, cos; HASHIGAON HAGADOL, cos

Leon, Humberto
CALACAN

Leon, Israel
SALVADOR

Leon, Jean-Francois
LES LONGS MANTEAUX, m

Leonard, Elmore
52 PICK-UP, w

Leonard, Gloria
SEX APPEAL

Leonard, Jamie
MONA LISA, prod d

Leonard, Jonathan [Fudge]
SOUL MAN

Leonard, Patrick
AT CLOSE RANGE, m; AT CLOSE RANGE, m/l;
NOTHING IN COMMON, m

Leonard, Paul
ABSOLUTE BEGINNERS

Leonard, Robert
MANHATTAN PROJECT, THE

Leonard, Robin
SEX APPEAL

Leonard, Terry
COBRA, stunts; DEADLY FRIEND, stunts

Leonardi, Marco
LA SPOSA ERA BELLISSIMA

Leonardou, Sotiria
DANILO TRELES, O FIMISMENOS ANDALOUSIANOS
MOUSIKOS

Leoncini, Simonetta
LA SECONDA NOTTE, cos

Leone, Luigi
NAME OF THE ROSE, THE

Leonet, Louis
FRENCH LESSON

Leonetti, Matthew F.
JUMPIN' JACK FLASH, ph

Leong, Al
BIG TROUBLE IN LITTLE CHINA

Leong, Albert
BIG TROUBLE

Leong, Po-chih
PING PONG, d

Leoni, Mauro
NAME OF THE ROSE, THE

Leoni, Roberto
FINAL EXECUTIONER, THE, w; SQUADRA
SELVAGGIA, w

Leonidas, John
SWEET LIBERTY

Leonte, Aurora
PASO DOBLE

Leonti, Jerry
PLAYING FOR KEEPS

Leopold, Tom
CLUB PARADISE, w

Leotard, Philippe
EXIT-EXIL; FEMMES DE PERSONNE; L'AUBE;
L'ETAT DE GRACE; LE PALTOQUET

Lepetit, Jean-Francois
LA FEMME SECRETE, p

Lepiner, Michael
KILLER PARTY, p

LePrevost, Nicholas
CLOCKWISE

Leprince, Catherine
PAULETTE

Leproust, Thierry
LE PALTOQUET, art d

Lerios, Cory
ONE CRAZY SUMMER, m

Lerner, Alan Jay
Obituaries; HOWARD THE DUCK, m/l

Lerner, Ken
JAKE SPEED

Leroy, Gloria
SID AND NANCY; STEWARDESS SCHOOL

LeRoy, Zoaunne
8 MILLION WAYS TO DIE

Leroy-Beaulieu, Philippe
MAN AND A WOMAN: 20 YEARS LATER, A

Leschin, Luisa
8 MILLION WAYS TO DIE; SCORPION

Lescot, Jean
EXIT-EXIL

Lesmez, Alberto Rojas
KAPAX DEL AMAZONAS

Lesniak, Amelia
HOLLYWOOD VICE SQUAD

Lesnie, Andrew
AUSTRALIAN DREAM, ph; DARK AGE, ph; FAIR
GAME, ph

Lesoeur, Daniel
PANTHER SQUAD, p

Less, Dennis
LABYRINTH, w

Lesser, Robert
POLTERGEIST II

Lester, Dan
PSYCHO III, spec eff

Lester, Mark L.
ARMED AND DANGEROUS, d

Lester, Tom "Tiny"
ARMED AND DANGEROUS

Leszczylowski, Michal
SACRIFICE, THE, ed

Leterrier, Catherine
MELO, cos; TWIST AGAIN A MOSCOU, cos

Lethin, Lori
BLOODY BIRTHDAY

Letts, Don
FERRIS BUELLER'S DAY OFF, m/l

Leuken, Paul
SCREEN TEST

Leung, Andy
ROCKIN' ROAD TRIP

Leung, Tony
LAST EMPEROR, THE

Leussink, Phons
PERVOLA: TRACKS IN THE SNOW

Levanon, Yeud
KOL AHAVO-TAI, p

Levay, Sylvester
CHOKE CANYON, m; COBRA, m; MY MAN ADAM, m;
TOUCH AND GO, m; WHERE ARE THE CHILDREN?,
m

Leven, Boris
Obituaries; COLOR OF MONEY, THE, prod d;
WILDCATS, prod d

Leven, Jeremy
PLAYING FOR KEEPS, w

Levent, Alain
FAUBOURG SAINT-MARTIN, ph

Levert, Jim
BELIZAIRE THE CAJUN

Levey, William A.
LIGHTNING—THE WHITE STALLION; LIGHTNING—
THE WHITE STALLION, d

Levi-Bar, Anath
SMILE OF THE LAMB, THE, w

Levie, Pierre
MERCI MONSIEUR ROBERTSON, p, d&w

Levien, Philip
KGB—THE SECRET WAR

Levignac, Sylvain
UNDER THE CHERRY MOON

Levinas, Razi
FLASH, w

Levine, Anna
AT CLOSE RANGE; SOMETHING WILD

Levine, Harvey
ODD JOBS

Levine, Jeff
TOUGH GUYS

Levine, Jerry
IRON EAGLE; OUT OF BOUNDS

Levine, John
DOT AND KEETO, m

Levine, Keith
HOLLYWOOD VICE SQUAD, m

Levine, Peter A.
FAT GUY GOES NUTZOID!!

Levine, Stephen
ESTHER, w

Levine, Ted
ONE MORE SATURDAY NIGHT

Levinsky, Sheri
FRIDAY THE 13TH PART VI: JASON LIVES

Levinson, Anthony
TOBY MCTEAGUE

Levinson, Art
MONEY PIT, THE, p

Levinson, Barry
ARMED RESPONSE, m/l

Levinson, Carri Lyn
TOUCH AND GO

LeViseur, Tantar
KING KONG LIVES, set d

Levitan, Yacov
STREETS OF GOLD

Levitt, Steve
LAST RESORT, THE

Levring, Kristian
ET SKUD FRA HJERTET, d&w

Levtchenko, Alexei
KAK MOLODY MY BYLI, art d; KHRANI MENIO, MOI TALISMAN, art d

Levy, Ariel
HYPER SAPIEN: PEOPLE FROM ANOTHER STAR, p

Levy, Buz
SCORPION

Levy, Deena
BEER

Levy, Eugene
ARMED AND DANGEROUS; CLUB PARADISE

Levy, Eytan
HAME'AHEV, art d

Levy, Gary
RAW TUNES; RAW TUNES, ed; RAW TUNES, m; RAW TUNES, p, d&w

Levy, Jay
HARDBODIES 2, m; HARDBODIES 2, m/l; MODERN GIRLS, m; THUNDER RUN, m

Levy, John
AMERICAN ANTHEM

Levy, Ken
REVENGE OF THE TEENAGE VIXENS FROM OUTER SPACE, THE

Levy, Peter
SHORT CHANGED, ph

Levy, Robert L.
RAD, p

Levy, Shayke
HAKRAV AL HAVA'AD

Lew, Danny
BIG TROUBLE

Lew, James
BIG TROUBLE IN LITTLE CHINA; BIG TROUBLE IN LITTLE CHINA, ch; NINJA TURF

Lew, Joycelyne
TAI-PAN

Lewandowska-Cunio, Barbara
OSOBISTY PAMIETNIK GRZESZNIKA PRZEZ NIEGO SAMEGO SPISANY, ed

Lewgoy, Jose
LA MANSION DE ARAUCAIMA

Lewis, Aaron
ROCKIN' ROAD TRIP

Lewis, Bonnie
PLAYING FOR KEEPS

Lewis, Buddy
Obituaries

Lewis, C. James
FINE MESS, A

Lewis, Charlotte
GOLDEN CHILD, THE; PIRATES

Lewis, Christopher
REVENGE, d&w

Lewis, Daniel Day
MY BEAUTIFUL LAUNDRETTE; NANOU; ROOM WITH A VIEW, A; People to Watch

Lewis, Don
MONSTER SHARK, w

Lewis, Garrett
CRIMES OF THE HEART, set d; SHORT CIRCUIT, set d

Lewis, Greg
VAMP

Lewis, Henry
8 MILLION WAYS TO DIE

Lewis, Howard Lloyd
CLOCKWISE

Lewis, Huey
FIRE WITH FIRE, m/l

Lewis, Linda
REVENGE, p

Lewis, Lori
NIGHTMARE WEEKEND

Lewis, Mark
KNIGHTS AND EMERALDS

Lewis, Matthew
SEVEN MINUTES IN HEAVEN

Lewis, Nicki
BALBOA, cos; BALBOA, w

Lewis, Ray
LOW BLOW

Lewis, Robert Q.
MY CHAUFFEUR

Lewis, Robin
PATRIOT, THE, cos

Lewis, S.
ABSOLUTE BEGINNERS, m/l

Lewis, Tim
CACTUS, ed; DEVIL IN THE FLESH, ed

Lewis, Veronica
SCREAMPLAY

Lewis, Wes
AMERICAN ANTHEM

Lewitt, Elliott
AT CLOSE RANGE, p&w

Lewk, Dan
OUT OF BOUNDS; RAW TUNES; RAW TUNES, ed; RAW TUNES, m; RAW TUNES, p, d&w

Lewman, Lance
BREEDERS

Ley, Bruce
CONFIDENTIAL, m

Leycegui, Roberto
LA BANDA DE LOS PANCHITOS, p

Leyrado, Juan
INSOMNIACS

Leyro, Fred
3:15, THE MOMENT OF TRUTH

Leysen, Johan
DESIDERANDO GIULIA

Leza, Concha
LA MITAD DEL CIELO; TEO EL PELIRROJO

Lezcano, Mercedes
LA MITAD DEL CIELO

Lezzi, Inigo
LOVE SONGS

Lhermitte, Thierry
NUIT D'IVRESSE; NUIT D'IVRESSE, p; NUIT D'IVRESSE, w

Li, Christine
JUST LIKE THE WEATHER

Li, David
SHANGHAI SURPRISE

Li, Donald
BIG TROUBLE IN LITTLE CHINA; ONE CRAZY SUMMER

Li, Lap Kwan
KUEI-MEI, A WOMAN

Li, Pat
LONGSHOT, THE

Li-Eng, Sue
DARK NIGHT, d

Li-Hwa, Hsu
DARK NIGHT, p

Liampe, Grigori
CAPABLANCA

Liang, David
GREAT WALL, A, m

Liano, Carmen
EL SUIZO—UN AMOUR EN ESPAGNE

Liano, Chris
FAT GUY GOES NUTZOID!!

Liappa, Frieda
ENAS ISICHOS THANATOS, d; ENAS ISICHOS THANATOS, w

Libertini, Richard
BIG TROUBLE

Liberty, Richard
FLIGHT OF THE NAVIGATOR

Libman, Bob
WEEKEND WARRIORS

Libowwitzky, Herwig
'38, art d

Lichter, Curt
MANHUNTER, m/l

Lichter, Ellie
REVENGE OF THE TEENAGE VIXENS FROM OUTER SPACE, THE

Lichter, Michelle
REVENGE OF THE TEENAGE VIXENS FROM OUTER SPACE, THE, p,w,makeup&ed

Liddiard, Gary
LEGAL EAGLES, makeup; MORNING AFTER, THE, makeup

Liddle, George
PLAYING BEATIE BOW, prod d

Liddle, J. Michael
GETTING EVEN, p

Lidon, Christophe
NANOU

Lieber, Mimi
LAST RESORT, THE

Liebert, Judy
HALF MOON STREET

Liebman, Riton
KAMIKAZE; SUIVEZ MON REGARD

Liechti, Fee
DER SCHWARZE TANNER, ed; DUNKI-SCHOTT, ed; KONZERT FUR ALICE, ed

Liechti, Hans
DUNKI-SCHOTT, d; DUNKI-SCHOTT, ph; ERDSEGEN, ph; JOURNEY, THE, ph

Liechti, Manfred
LISI UND DER GENERAL

Liecier, Dulice
HALF MOON STREET

Liedtke, Christian
RECRUITS

Lifar, Serge
Obituaries

Ligenfelter, Tom
LOW BLOW

Liggett, Van W.
DR. OTTO AND THE RIDDLE OF THE GLOOM BEAM

Light, David
NAKED VENGEANCE; SILK

Lightfoot, Leonard
CHECK IS IN THE MAIL, THE

Lightfoot, Linda
VENDETTA

Lightstone, Marilyn
GOBOTS: BATTLE OF THE ROCKLORDS

Lightsy, Jack
NIGHT OF THE CREEPS; SCORPION

Liiski, Paavo
TUNTEMATON SOTILAS

Likon, Rado
CHRISTOPHORUS, ph

Lile, David
PLAYING FOR KEEPS

Lilienthal, Peter
DAS SCHWEIGEN DES DICHTERS, d&w

Lilja, Efva
AMOROSA

Lillian, Renee
HOUSE

Lillie, Ronald
LOYALTIES, p

Lillingston, Sandie
DEAD-END DRIVE-IN

Lilly, Anne
REVENGE OF THE TEENAGE VIXENS FROM OUTER SPACE, THE

Lim, Kay Tong
SHANGHAI SURPRISE

Lima, Marina
COM LICENCA, EU VOU A LUTA, m/l

Lima, Walter
CHICO REI, d&w; CHICO REI, ed; SONHO SEM FIM, w

Lime, Jean-Hugues
L'EXECUTRICE

Limnidis, John
CHILDREN OF A LESSER GOD

Limon, Hugo
HELL SQUAD

Limosin, Jean Pierre
GARDIEN DE LA NUIT, d; GARDIEN DE LA NUIT, w

Lin, Ma
LIANG JIA FUNU

Linar, Sonia
QUE ME MATEN DE UNA VEZ; QUE ME MATEN DE UNA VEZ, p

Linares, Aida
HEARTBURN

Linares, Annia
EL CORAZON SOBRE LA TIERRA

Linares, Marcelo Lopez
Obituaries

Linari, Peter
FAT GUY GOES NUTZOID!!

Lincoln, Erika
WISDOM

Lincoln, Scott
LADIES CLUB, THE

Lincoln, Warren
TORMENT

Lincovsky, Cipe
EL SOL EN BOTELLITAS; POBRE MARIPOSA

Lind, Jakov
DAS SCHWEIGEN DES DICHTERS

Linda, La Prieta
ES MI VIDA—EL NOA NOA 2

Lindahl, Tomas
LOVE ME!, m

Lindauer, Elisabeth
ELOGIO DELLA PAZZIA

Linday-Gray, Jayne
KING KONG LIVES

Lindbeck, Peter
BLACKOUT

Lindberg, Andy
STAND BY ME

Lindberg, Clas
RAVEN, d&w

Linden, Anna
LOVE ME!

Linden, Kenny
ABSOLUTE BEGINNERS

Linder, Emilio
MONSTER DOG

Lindgren, Astrid
ALLA VI BARN I BULLERBY, w

Lindgren, Bo
MIN PAPA AR TARZAN, art d

Lindgren, Gertie
AMOROSA, cos

Lindgren, Torgny
ORMENS VAG PA HALLEBERGET, w

Lindh, Bjorn Jison
BRODERNA MOZART, m

Lindley, John
KILLER PARTY, ph

Lindon, Vincent
BETTY BLUE; HALF MOON STREET; PRUNELLE
BLUES; SUIVEZ MON REGARD; YIDDISH
CONNECTION

Lindorff, Lone
TWIST & SHOUT

Lindquist, Antti
PIMEYS ODOTTA, w

Lindquist, Jans-Erick
I LAGENS NAMN

Lindqvist, Agneta
I LAGENS NAMN, makeup; MOA, makeup

Lindsay, Creighton
MALA NOCHE, m

Lindsay, Elijah
HEARTBURN

Lindsay, Helen
PLAYING AWAY

Lindsay, Ian
OVER THE SUMMER

Lindsay, Kevin D.
PRETTY IN PINK

Lindsay, Lance
STAR CRYSTAL, d&w

Lindsjoo, Christine
GRONA GUBBAR FRAN Y.R., w

Lindsley, Lisa
MOVIE HOUSE MASSACRE

Lindsoe, Carrie
DOWN BY LAW

Lindstedt, Carl Gustaf
MALACCA

Lindstrom, Goran
BRODERNA MOZART, p; LOVE ME!, p; ORMENS VAG
PA HALLEBERGET, p

Lindstrom, Rolf
ALLA VI BARN I BULLERBY, ph; ORMENS VAG PA
HALLEBERGET, ph

Lindtner, Lasse
DROMMESLOTTER

Line, Helga
PULSEBEAT

Lineback, Richard
STEWARDESS SCHOOL

Lineberger, Howard
ROCKIN' ROAD TRIP

Lineweaver, Steve
SOMETHING WILD, art d

Ling, Barbara
TRUE STORIES, prod d

Ling, Doug
WRONG WORLD, w

Ling, Ku Chia
HUAJIE SHIDAI

Ling, Li
BEI AIQING YIWANGDE JIAOLUO, ed

Ling, Ng Po
PEKING OPERA BLUES, cos

Ling, Wa
PIAOBO QIYU

Lingk, Wolf-Dieter
GRITTA VOM RATTENSCHLOSS

Linke, Paul
KGB—THE SECRET WAR

Linkesch, Herbert
SCHWARZ UND OHNE ZUCKER

Linley, Gary
SCREAMTIME

Linn, Joe
TENEMENT

Linn, Lawrence
COLOR OF MONEY, THE

Linn, Marcia
STAR CRYSTAL

Linn, Michael
HOT CHILI, m/l

Linn, Priscilla
STEWARDESS SCHOOL

Linna, Vaino
TUNTEMATON SOTILAS, w

Linnet, Ann
BARNDOMMENS GADE, m

Linnman, Susanne
ALLA VI BARN I BULLERBY, ed; MIN PAPA AR
TARZAN, ed

Linson, Donna
OUT OF BOUNDS, cos

Linthorst, Kees
ASSAULT, THE, ed

Linton, William
FINE MESS, A, m/l

Linza, Charles
STAR CRYSTAL

Lio
GOLDEN EIGHTIES

Lionello, Luca
SPOSERO SIMON LE BON

Liotta, Ray
SOMETHING WILD; People to Watch

Lipari, Joanna
JO JO DANCER, YOUR LIFE IS CALLING

Lipham, Kent
NO RETREAT, NO SURRENDER

Lipkind, David
BAR 51—SISTER OF LOVE, p; NADIA, p

Lipman, David
BEER; PLAYING FOR KEEPS

Lipp, Jeremy
DUET FOR ONE, w; P.O.W. THE ESCAPE, w

Lippe, Stewart
ROCKIN' ROAD TRIP

Lipscomb, Dennis
CROSSROADS

Lipsky, Oldrich
Obituaries

Lipuzic, Mirko
DOKTOR, art d

Lisenco, Michael
OFF BEAT

Lisi, Gaetano
BIG TROUBLE

Lisle, Mark
LABYRINTH

Lispector, Clarice
HOUR OF THE STAR, THE, w

List, Martina
MULLERS BURO, cos

List, Niki
MULLERS BURO, d&w

Lister, Tom
WIRED TO KILL

Lister, Tom "Tiny"
8 MILLION WAYS TO DIE

Lister, Tommy
BLUE CITY

Litchfield, Rodney
KNIGHTS AND EMERALDS

Lithgow, John
MANHATTAN PROJECT, THE

Litmanowitsch, Andreas
NOAH UND DER COWBOY, m

Litt, Richard
BEER

Little Richard
DOWN AND OUT IN BEVERLY HILLS

Little, Dwight
KGB—THE SECRET WAR, d&w

Little, Dwight H.
GETTING EVEN, d

Little, Helen
SAY YES, makeup

Little, Mark
SHORT CHANGED

Little, Michele
OUT OF BOUNDS; RADIOACTIVE DREAMS

Little, Rich
ONE CRAZY SUMMER

Littlejohn, Darryl
FINE MESS, A, m/l

Littlejohn, Gary
HOWARD THE DUCK; ONE CRAZY SUMMER

Littleton, Carol
BRIGHTON BEACH MEMOIRS, ed

Littman, Julian
LUCAS, m/l

Litton, Foster
MOUNTAINTOP MOTEL MASSACRE

Litwack, Sydney Z.
JUST BETWEEN FRIENDS, prod d

Litzitis, Arnis
ODINOTCHNOYE PLAVANIYE

Liu, Bernie
BETTER TOMORROW, A, art d

Liu, Jerry
PING PONG, w

Liuzzi, Carlos
AVAETE, A SEMENTE DA VINGANCA, art d

Livanov, Aristarkh
FOUETTE

Lively, Jason
NIGHT OF THE CREEPS

Lively, Robyn
BEST OF TIMES, THE; WILDCATS

Liverani, Eugenio
FINAL EXECUTIONER, THE, set d

Livingston, Charles D.
Obituaries

Livingston, Jo
PLAY DEAD

Livingstone, Jay
MONA LISA, m/l

Livni, Aspah
COMBAT SHOCK

Lizarraga, Jesse Hernandez
BAD GUYS

Liznev, Boris
VYITI ZAMUZH ZA KAPITANA, ph

Lizzani, Carlo
L'ISOLA, d; L'ISOLA, w

Ljungberg, Dick
GRONA GUBBAR FRAN Y.R., makeup

Ljunggren, Sten
MORRHAR OCH ARTOR

Llanes, Juan Antonio
MOSQUITO COAST, THE; QUE ME MATEN DE UNA
VEZ

Llaneza, Julio Ruiz
ESE LOCO LOCO HOSPITAL; ESE LOCO LOCO
HOSPITAL, d; SE SUFRE PERO SE GOZA, p&d

Llapur, Santiago
CAPABLANCA, p; JIBARO, p

Llaurado, Adolfo
CAPABLANCA; JIBARO

Llausas, Leonor
ES MI VIDA—EL NOA NOA 2

Llewellyn, David
KING AND HIS MOVIE, A

Llewellyn-Jones, Tony
CACTUS

Lloyd, David H.
ROCKIN' ROAD TRIP, ed

Lloyd, Frank
AROUND THE WORLD IN EIGHTY WAYS

Lloyd, John J.
BIG TROUBLE IN LITTLE CHINA, prod d

Lloyd, Ken
BLUE CITY

Lloyd, Kevin
LINK

Lloyd, Louisa
WILD BEASTS

Lloyd, Mickey
MANHUNTER

Lorit, Jean Pierre
JAKE SPEED

Lormer, Jon
Obituaries

Lorraine, Carrie
POLTERGEIST II

Los Cadetes de Linar
HIJO DEL PALENQUE; UN HOMBRE VIOLENTE

Los Invaciones de Nuero Leon
EL STECUESTRO DE CAMARENA

Losego, Giorgio
CASTIGHI; CASTIGHI, d

Losi, Allen
THRASHIN'

Losonci, Terez
ERZEKENY BUCSU A FEJEDELEMTOL, ed

Lotfi, Sharif
MARE, THE, m

Lothario, Salvadore
BAD GUYS

Lottman, Evan
MAXIMUM OVERDRIVE, ed

Loubert, Patrick
CARE BEARS MOVIE II: A NEW GENERATION, p

Loud, Grant
RATBOY

Lougaris, Betty
MORNING AFTER, THE

Louge, Wal
DOT AND KEETO, anim

Loughlin, Terry
ROCKIN' ROAD TRIP; TRICK OR TREAT

Louis, Jacqueline
LA MOITIE DE L'AMOUR, p

Louis-Dreyfus, Julia
HANNAH AND HER SISTERS; TROLL

Loukanov, Boris
ZABRAVOTE TOZI SLOCHAI

Lounsbery, Dan
WHERE ARE THE CHILDREN?

Lounsbury, Ruth
BREEDERS , set d

Lount, Elvira
SAMUEL LOUNT, p

Lourari, Hamid
RAI

Louret, Guy
INSPECTEUR LAVARDIN; ROUND MIDNIGHT

Lousek, Gilda
NIGHTMARE'S PASSENGERS

Louveau, Genevieve
MANON DES SOURCES, ed

Louw, Ot
PPPERFORMER, THE, ed

Louwriter, Wim
MAMA IS BOOS!, ed

Louzeiro, Jose
O HOMEM DA CAPA PRETA, w

Louzil, Eric
SHADOWS RUN BLACK, p; SIZZLE BEACH, U.S.A., p

Louzil, Eric Robert
SHADOWS RUN BLACK

Lovbom, Kjell
GRONA GUBBAR FRAN Y.R., m

Love, Courtney
SID AND NANCY

Love, Gary Lee
SNO-LINE

Love, Victor
NATIVE SON

Lovecraft, .P.
FROM BEYOND, w

Lovejoy, Ray
ALIENS, ed

Lovelett, James
F/X

Lovitz, Jon
JUMPIN' JACK FLASH; LAST RESORT, THE;
RATBOY; THREE AMIGOS

Low, Jurg
EL SUIZO—UN AMOUR EN ESPAGNE

Lowe, Edward
COCAINE WARS, ed

Lowe, Laura
COCAINE WARS, makeup

Lowe, Nick
ABSOLUTE BEGINNERS, m/l

Lowe, Rob
ABOUT LAST NIGHT; YOUNGBLOOD

Lowell, Carey
DANGEROUSLY CLOSE

Lowenstein, Richard
DOGS IN SPACE, d&w

Loy, Mino
MONSTER SHARK, p

Loza, Jose
EL SECUESTRO DE CAMARENA, w

Lozano, Alfonso Sanahuria
KAPAX DEL AMAZONAS

Lozano, Jose Luis
EN PENUMBRA, d; EN PENUMBRA, w

Lozano, Margarita
IL CASO MORO; JEAN DE FLORETTE; LA MITAD
DEL CIELO

Lozano, Rosario
SAN ANTONITO, cos

Lozinska, Stawromira
DEATH SENTENCE

Lu, Lisa
TAI-PAN

Lualdi, Antonella
UNA SPINA NEL CUORE

Luanu
RUNNING OUT OF LUCK

Luanxin, Zhang
QINGCHUN JI, d; QINGCHUN JI, w

Lubarsky, Anath
HAKRAV AL HAVA'AD, ed

Lubin, David
HOOSIERS, art d

Lubin, Janis
HOOSIERS, set d

Lubitsch, Fanny
HAME'AHEV

Lubosch, Mark
GRITTA VOM RATTENSCHLOSS

Lubtchansky, William
CLASS RELATIONS, ph; I LOVE YOU, ph; LA
PURITAINE, ph; NEXT SUMMER, ph

Lucarelli, Jack
AMERICAN JUSTICE; AMERICAN JUSTICE, p

Lucarelli, Spenser
AMERICAN JUSTICE

Lucas, Andi
EAST OF THE WALL

Lucas, Andy
HALF MOON STREET

Lucas, Arno
ODD JOBS

Lucas, Lisa
JAKE SPEED

Lucchetti, R.F.
AS SETE VAMPIRAS, w

Luce, Philippa
LADY JANE

Lucena, Carlos
BANDERA NEGRA

Luceno, Jack
DER WILDE CLOWN

Luchini, Fabrice
CONSEIL DE FAMILLE; HOTEL DU PARADIS; MAX
MON AMOUR

Luciani, Mario
GERONIMA; INSOMNIACS

Luciano, Felipe
TONGS—A CHINATOWN STORY, w

Lucidi, Alessandro
FINAL EXECUTIONER, THE, ed; LA VENEXIANA, ed;
THRONE OF FIRE, THE, ed

Lucio, Paco
TEO EL PELIRROJO, d&w

Lucisano, Fulvio
L'INCHIESTA, p

Luck, Susan
BAD GUYS

Lucot, Hubert
DERNIER CRI

Luczyc, Hugo
CAR TROUBLE, prod d

Ludlow, Graham
THUNDER RUN; WELCOME TO 18

Ludman, Larry
COBRA MISSION, d; MANHUNT, THE, p, d&w;
THUNDER WARRIOR, d; THUNDER WARRIOR, w

Ludwig, Daniel
LISI UND DER GENERAL

Ludwig, Heinz
DER WILDE CLOWN, spec eff

Ludwig, Pamela
UNDER THE CHERRY MOON

Ludwig, Salem
HEARTBURN

Ludwig, Ursula
FUTURE OF EMILY, THE, p

Lugo, Alejandro
CAPABLANCA

Luigi, Ghezzi Pier
SQUADRA SELVAGGIA

Luis, Martin
LAS NOCHES DEL CALIFAS, ed

Luisi, James
MURPHY'S LAW

Luiz, Luthero
MALANDRO

Lujan, Fernando
ESE LOCO LOCO HOSPITAL

Lukas, Karl
BIG TROUBLE

Lukather, Steve
RAW DEAL, m

Lukats, Andor
VAKVILAGBAN

Luke, Jorge
MATANZA EN MATAMOROS; SALVADOR

Luke, Keye
FINE MESS, A

Lukjaneko, Anatoli
KAK MOLODY MY BYLI

Lukomsky, Xavier
GOLDEN EIGHTIES

Luludis, Lidia
LICEENI, cos

Lum, Benjamin
CHECK IS IN THE MAIL, THE

Lum, Chua
ARMOUR OF GOD, THE, p

Luma
RUNNING OUT OF LUCK

Lumaldo, Miguel Angel
PERROS DE LA NOCHE, set d

Lumet, Sidney
MORNING AFTER, THE, d; POWER, d

Luna, Bigas
LOLA, d; LOLA, w

Luna, Mario
REDONDO, ph

Lunari, Luigi
L'ULTIMA MAZURKA, w

Lund, Heide
JUMPIN' JACK FLASH

Lund-Sorensen, Sune
MORD I MORKET, d; MORD I MORKET, w

Lundberg, Lasse
MIN PAPA AR TARZAN, p; RAVEN, ed; RAVEN, p

Lunden, Sven
MIN PAPA AR TARZAN, cos; MIN PAPA AR TARZAN,
makeup

Lundgren, Lars
ROCKIN' ROAD TRIP; ROCKIN' ROAD TRIP, stunts

Lundholm, Lars
DEN FRUSNA LEOPARDEN, w

Lundin, Justin
LIGHTNING—THE WHITE STALLION

Lundin, Rick
LIGHTNING—THE WHITE STALLION

Lundin, Roland
MIN PAPA AR TARZAN, ph

Lundquist, Peter
FLIGHT OF THE NAVIGATOR

Lung, Ti
BETTER TOMORROW, A

Lunghi, Cherie
MISSION, THE

Lunney, Leo
COMBAT SHOCK

Lunny, Donal
EAT THE PEACH, m

Lunson, Lian
BIG HURT, THE

Lunvad, Poul
TWIST & SHOUT

Luoma-Aho, Inkeri
BORN AMERICAN

Luond, Walo
LISI UND DER GENERAL

Luong, Min
BIG TROUBLE IN LITTLE CHINA

Luotto, Steve
CHOKE CANYON, w

Lupersio, Leticia
DONA HERLINDA AND HER SON

Lupi, Stefania
UN RAGAZZO COME TANTI

LuPone, Patti
WISE GUYS

Luppi, Federico
BAD COMPANY; COCAINE WARS; LES LONGS
MANTEAUX; NIGHTMARE'S PASSENGERS;
SOBREDOSIS

Luppi, Marcela
KING AND HIS MOVIE, A

Lupus, Peter
PULSEBEAT

Lurie, John
DOWN BY LAW; DOWN BY LAW, m

Lurie, Kim
RYDER, P.I.

Luring, Werner
BLIND DIRECTOR, THE, ph

Lurio, Antonio
GINGER & FRED

Lussier, Jacques
INTIMATE POWER

Lussier, Sheila
MY CHAUFFEUR

Lutkiewicz, Gustaw
CHRZESNISAK

Lutrell, Kent
STAND BY ME

Lutter, Claire
SHANGHAI SURPRISE

Lutz, Adelle
SOMETHING WILD

Lutz, Linda
STEWARDESS SCHOOL

Lutz, Luc
OP HOOP VAN ZEGEN

Lutz, Ton
SHADOW OF VICTORY

Luu, An
LE PALTOQUET

Luukas, Heikki
HUOMENNA

Luxford, Shelly
BRIDGE TO NOWHERE

Lyal, Bill
DEAD-END DRIVE-IN

Lybekk, Trond
X

Lycouressis, Tony
ALCESTES, p&d; ALCESTES, w

Lyle, Laurel
MORNING AFTER, THE

Lynas, Sid
YOUNGBLOOD

Lynch, Christopher
BALBOA, ph

Lynch, David
BLUE VELVET, d&w; BLUE VELVET, m/l

Lynch, Joe
EAT THE PEACH

Lynch, Paul
BULLIES, d; FLYING, d

Lynch, Richard
CUT AND RUN; MILWR BYCHAN

Lynch, Robyn
UNDER THE CHERRY MOON, makeup

Lynch, Terry
MANHUNT, THE

Lyndon, Michael
LIGHTSHIP, THE

Lyne, Adrian
9½ WEEKS, d

Lyngsoe, Birthe
WOLF AT THE DOOR, THE, makeup

Lynley, Carol
BALBOA

Lynn, Ann
SCREAMTIME

Lynn, Carol
THUNDER RUN, p&w

Lynn, Cheryl M.
THUNDER RUN

Lynn, Veronica
LEJANIA

Lyon, Lisa
VAMP

Lyons, Collette   [Collette Lyons Hearst]
Obituaries

Lyons, Larry
HELL SQUAD

Lyons, Marilynn
OFF BEAT

Lyons, Robert F.
MURPHY'S LAW

Lyons, Theresa
BACK TO SCHOOL

Lyons-Hansen, Mandi
NUTCRACKER: THE MOTION PICTURE

Lys, Lya   [Natalia Lyecht]
Obituaries

Lysak, Piotr
EVIXION

Lystad, Knut
NOE HEIT ANNET; NOE HEIT ANNET, d&w

Ma
PASSION, ph

Ma, Kam
BETTER TOMORROW, A, ed

Ma, Raymond
THE KARATE KID PART II

Ma, Season
SILENT LOVE

Ma, Tzi
MONEY PIT, THE

Ma, Wu
MR. VAMPIRE

Maalal, Imad
MAN OF ASHES

Maalismaa, Markku
HUOMENNA

Maar, Gyula
ORDOGI KISERTETEK, d&w

Maar, Pons
GOLDEN CHILD, THE

Maas, Dick
FLODDER, d&w; FLODDER, m; FLODDER, p

Maas, Ernest
Obituaries

Maas, Ikky
SALOME

Maasz, Ronald
TERRY ON THE FENCE, ph

Maazel, Lorin
OTELLO, md

Mabarak, Carlos Jimenez
VENENO PARA LAS HADAS, m

Macaluso, Lenny
LONGSHOT, THE, m/l

MacArthur, Dennis
HELL SQUAD

Macaully, Peter
ACES GO PLACES IV

MacCare, Bill
PIRATES

Maccari, Beppe
SPOSERO SIMON LE BON, ph

Macchi, Egisto
LE MAL D'AIMER, m; SALOME, m

Macchi, Lamberto
GIOVANNI SENZAPENSIERI, m; SEMBRA MORTO . . .
MA E SOLO SVENUTO, m

Macchio, Ralph
CROSSROADS; THE KARATE KID PART II

MacCready, Graham
BOY IN BLUE, THE

MacCullum, Paul
BUSTED UP

MacDevitt, John
SALVADOR

MacDonald, Bob
HOWARD THE DUCK, spec eff

MacDonald, Jim
CRAZY MOON

MacDonald, John D.   [John Dann MacDonald]
Obituaries

MacDonald, Mac
HALF MOON STREET

MacDonald, Peter
SOLARBABIES, ph

MacDonald, Richard
SPACECAMP, prod d

MacDonald, Ross
BLUE CITY, w

Macedo, Zeze
AS SETE VAMPIRAS

MacEwen, Walter
Obituaries

MacGregor, Brian
FREE RIDE; NIGHT OF THE CREEPS

MacGregor, Jeff
WELCOME TO 18

MacGregor, Robert
MORE THINGS CHANGE, THE

Macgregor-Scott, Peter
WHOOPEE BOYS, THE, p

Machacek, Miroslav
PAVUCINA

Machado, Djenane
MALANDRO

Machado, Pablo
LA NOCHE DE LOS LAPICES

Machaidze, S.
YOUNG COMPOSER'S ODYSSEY, A, ed

Machala, Bernadetta
KRONIKA WYPADKOW MILOSNYCH

Machmadov, M.
DESCENDANT OF THE SNOW LEOPARD, THE

Machtlinger, Otto
DER SCHWARZE TANNER

Macias, Carlos
POBRE MARIPOSA, ed

Maciel, Eliane
COM LICENCA, EU VOU A LUTA, w

Macina, Anne
CONSEIL DE FAMILLE

MacInnes, Angus
HALF MOON STREET

MacInnes, Colin
ABSOLUTE BEGINNERS, w

MacIntosh, Cathleen
STEWARDESS SCHOOL

Mack, Gene
BEER

Mack, Lonnie
8 MILLION WAYS TO DIE, m/l

Mack, Michael
VIOLETS ARE BLUE

Mackay, Angus
CLOCKWISE

MacKay, Denis
SHORT CHANGED

Mackay, Don
LOYALTIES

MacKay, Geoffrey
ONE NIGHT ONLY

Mackay, John
FAT GUY GOES NUTZOID!!

MacKenzie, Richard
STAND BY ME, set d

Mackerras, Charles
NUTCRACKER: THE MOTION PICTURE, md

Mackie, Tom
LUCAS

Mackintosh, Janis
LABYRINTH

MacKintosh, Woods
OFF BEAT, prod d

Mackler, Steven
NEON MANIACS, p

MacKrell, James
JUST BETWEEN FRIENDS

MacLachlan, Janet
BOY WHO COULD FLY, THE

MacLachlan, Kyle
BLUE VELVET

MacLachman, Janet
MURPHY'S LAW

Maclean, Stephen
AROUND THE WORLD IN EIGHTY WAYS, d;
AROUND THE WORLD IN EIGHTY WAYS, w

MacLennan, Elizabeth
BLOOD RED ROSES

MacManus, Matt
FLIGHT OF THE NAVIGATOR, w

MacMillian, Will
SALVADOR

MacNeill, Peter
JUDGEMENT IN STONE, A

MacNeill, Susan
LOYALTIES

MacPherson, Don
ABSOLUTE BEGINNERS, w

MacQuarrie, Don
BOY IN BLUE, THE

MacRae, Gordon
Obituaries

MacRae, Heather
PERILS OF P.K., THE

MacRae, Michael
WELCOME TO 18

MacRae, Sheila
PERILS OF P.K., THE; PERILS OF P.K., THE, p

Madarasz, Ivan
KISMASZAT ES A GEZENGUZOK, m

Madbouli, Abdelmoneim
TAHOUNET AL SAYED FABRE

Madda, Lucien
SCREEN TEST

Madda, Michelle
SCREEN TEST

Madden, Betty Pecha
ODD JOBS, cos; VAMP, cos

Madden, Tommy
BAD GUYS

Maddock, Brent
SHORT CIRCUIT, w

Madeiros, Jose
NEM TUDO E VERDADE, ph

Madia, Stefano
IL MIELE DEL DIAVOLO

Madlock, Shirley
LUCAS

Madonna
AT CLOSE RANGE, m/l; SHANGHAI SURPRISE

Madrid, Robb
8 MILLION WAYS TO DIE

Madrigal, Roberto
LA BANDA DE LOS PANCHITOS, w

Madrinan, Alejandro
A LA SALIDA NOS VEMOS

Madrinan, Santiago
A LA SALIDA NOS VEMOS

Madsen, Eva
BARNDOMMENS GADE

Madsen, Peter
VALHALLA, art d; VALHALLA, d; VALHALLA, w

Madsen, Virginia
FIRE WITH FIRE; MODERN GIRLS

Madureira, Marcelo
RUNNING OUT OF LUCK

Maeda, Yonezo
SOREKARA, ph; TOKIMEDI NI SHISU, ph

Maertens, Fred
STAMMHEIM

Mafdul, Deedee
DANILO TRELES, O FIMISMENOS ANDALOUSIANOS
MOUSIKOS; DANILO TRELES, O FIMISMENOS
ANDALOUSIANOS MOUSIKOS, m

Maffei, John
GIRLS SCHOOL SCREAMERS, makeup

Maforimbo, June
JAKE SPEED

Magadia, Raul
LOW BLOW

Magalhaes, Marcos
COM LICENCA, EU VOU A LUTA, prod d; COM
LICENCA, EU VOU A LUTA, w

Magalhaes, Vania
NEM TUDO E VERDADE

Magana, Jose
ESE LOCO LOCO HOSPITAL

Magee, Rusty
HANNAH AND HER SISTERS

Magidson, Herb
Obituaries

Maginnis, Molly
LUCAS, cos

Maglio, Mitch
COMBAT SHOCK

Magliulo, Giorgio
UNA CASA IN BILICO, d; UNA CASA IN BILICO, ph;
UNA CASA IN BILICO, w

Magnani, Umberto
HOUR OF THE STAR, THE

Magnet, Cecile
LE DEBUTANT

Magnolfi, Barbara
CUT AND RUN

Magnoli, Albert
AMERICAN ANTHEM, d

Magnotta, Vic
HIGHLANDER, stunts

Magnus, Imogen
SCREAMTIME, cos

Magnusdottir, Hulda
EINS OG SKEPNAN DEYR, cos

Magnuson, Ann
SLEEPWALK

Magnussem, Tony
THRASHIN'

Magnusson, Leif
ET SKUD FRA HJERTET, ed; ET SKUD FRA HJERTET,
w

Magnusson, Tivi
BARNDOMMENS GADE, p; ET SKUD FRA HJERTET, p

Maguioros, Constantinos
I NICHTA ME TI SILENA

Maguire, Jeff
TOBY MCTEAGUE, w

Maguire, Thomas F.
TOUGH GUYS

Magyar, Dezso
OFF BEAT, w; STREETS OF GOLD, w

Mah, Lawrence
BIG HURT, THE

Mahan, Lydia
SEX O'CLOCK NEWS, THE

Maharaj, Anthony
NAKED VENGEANCE, p&w

Maharavo, Justin Limby
DAHALO DAHALO, ph

Mahdi, Salah
MAN OF ASHES, m

Mahdi, Tamer
AL ASHEKE, w

Maher, Bill
RATBOY

Mahfoudh, Mohamed
AL-KAS, w

Mahfoudh, Slim
AL-KAS

Mahjoob, Hossein
MARE, THE

Mahlberg, George
SLOANE

Mahler, Bruce
POLICE ACADEMY 3: BACK IN TRAINING

Mahler, Gustav
DE L'ARGENTINE, m; LOVE ME!, m; YOUNG
COMPOSER'S ODYSSEY, A, m

Mahlich, Holger
DEATH SENTENCE; STAMMHEIM

Mahmoud, Fatma
LEL HAB KESSA AKHIRA

Mahmoud, Laila B.
MAN OF ASHES, cos

Mahnusson, Tivi
BALLERUP BOULEVARD, p

Mahon, Derek
DEATH OF THE HEART, THE, w

Mahon, Jackie
SEPARATE VACATIONS

Mahon, Joe
BEST MAN, THE, d&w

Mahon, Kevin
STREETS OF GOLD

Mahoney, John
MANHATTAN PROJECT, THE; STREETS OF GOLD

Mai, William
LIGHTSHIP, THE, w

Maia
REI DO RIO

Maia, Irenio
MALANDRO, md

Maia, Nuno Leal
AS SETE VAMPIRAS

Maia, Telmo
WHERE THE RIVER RUNS BLACK

Maiden, Sharon
CLOCKWISE

Maikai, Frederick A.C.
SCORPION

Mailhe, Juliette
DESORDRE

Maillie, D.M.
DR. OTTO AND THE RIDDLE OF THE GLOOM BEAM

Main, Laurie
GREAT MOUSE DETECTIVE, THE; MY CHAUFFEUR

Mainetti, Stefano
LA MONACA NEL PECCATO, m; LUSSURI, m;
VOGLIA DI GUARDARE, m

Mainiello, Neil P.
TONGS—A CHINATOWN STORY, w

Maintifneux, Emmanuel
LES CLOWNS DE DIEU, art d

Maintigneux, Pierre
THERESE

Maintigneux, Sophie
SUMMER, ph

Maiorova, V.
PISMA MERTVOGO CHELOVEKA

Mairesse, Valerie
LES FRERES PETARD; SACRIFICE, THE

Maisnik, Kathy
CHECK IS IN THE MAIL, THE

Maitland, Ian
DEATHMASK, ed

Maittret, Phuong
LAST IMAGE, THE, makeup

Majanlahti, Mikko
HUOMENNA

Majerowicz, Sandra
BLEU COMME L'ENFER, w

Majewski, Lech
FLIGHT OF THE SPRUCE GOOSE, d; FLIGHT OF THE
SPRUCE GOOSE, w

Majewski, Richard Paul
SALOME

Major, Boris
WAY IT IS, THE

Major, Mark
STOOGEMANIA

Major, Tamas
GREAT GENERATION, THE

Mak, Michael
ISLE OF FANTASY, d

Maka, Karl
ACES GO PLACES IV; ACES GO PLACES IV, w;
SUPER CITIZEN, p

Makari, Mohsen
MONSTER, THE

Makaro, J.J.
ABDUCTED, spec eff; ABDUCTED, stunts

Makela, Mika
TUNTEMATON SOTILAS

Makepeace, Chris
VAMP

Makhene, Ramolao
PLACE OF WEEPING

Makhiou, Abdel Aziz
LEL HAB KESSA AKHIRA

Makkar, Joseph
DOWN AND OUT IN BEVERLY HILLS

Makmudov, Mirhalil
GRANNY GENERAL, m

Mako
ARMED RESPONSE; P.O.W. THE ESCAPE

Makoun, Abdul-Aziz
EL-GOOA

Maksymiuk, Jerzy
OSOBISTY PAMIETNIK GRZESZNIKA PRZEZ NIEGO
SAMEGO SPISANY, m

Makuloluwa, W.B.
ARUNATA PERA, m

Malakova, Petra
OTELLO

Malallemo, Eduardo
ES MI VIDA—EL NOA NOA 2, m

Malallemo, Gabriel
ES MI VIDA—EL NOA NOA 2, m

Malamud, Allan
DOWN AND OUT IN BEVERLY HILLS

Malamud, Bernard
Obituaries

Malatesta, Andres
MALABRIGO, p

Malavoy, Christophe
LA FEMME DE MA VIE

Malbran, Nene
SERE CUALQUIER COSA PERO TE QUIERO

Malco, Paolo
MORIRAI A MEZZANOTTE; THUNDER WARRIOR

Malcolm, Christopher
HIGHLANDER; LABYRINTH

Malcolm, Doris
BOY IN BLUE, THE

Malden, Karl
BILLY GALVIN

Maldonado, Javier
LOS HIJOS DE LA GUERRA FRIA; NEMESIO

Maldonado, John
STOOGEMANIA, makeup

Maldonado, Paty
POR UN VESTIDO DE NOVIA

Maleczech, Ruth
DEAD END KIDS

Maleeva, Irina
LAST RESORT, THE

Malenec, Patrice
UNDER THE CHERRY MOON

Malepasso, Enzo
UNA TENERA FOLLIA, m

Malet, Laurent
LA PURITAINE

Malet, Leo
SUIVEZ MON REGARD

Malet, Pierre
FRANCESCA E MIA

Maley, Nick
SCREAMTIME, spec eff

Malfa, Aurelio
VA BANQUE

Malignon, Jean-Pierre
PARIS MINUIT; PARIS MINUIT, p

Malignon, Philippe
PARIS MINUIT; PARIS MINUIT, w

Malik, Pervaiz
ZANGIR, d

Malikyan, Kevork
HALF MOON STREET

Malin, Howard
CAR TROUBLE, p

Malin, Mary
THE KARATE KID PART II, cos

Malita, Maria
PASO DOBLE, cos

Malkames, Don
Obituaries

Malkin, Barry
PEGGY SUE GOT MARRIED, ed

Mall, Paul
FLIGHT OF THE NAVIGATOR

Mallacy, Tim
SHADOWS RUN BLACK

Mallak, Kasim Al
HOB FEE BAGHDAD

Mallarino, Victor
MANON

Mallinen, Sari
LINNA

Mallon, Johnny
NO SURRENDER

Mallorie, Jill
HOT CHILI

Malloy, Ed
VIOLATED

Malloy, John
RAW DEAL

Malloy, Michael J.
IMPURE THOUGHTS, p; IMPURE THOUGHTS, w

Malmuth, Bruce
THE KARATE KID PART II; WHERE ARE THE CHILDREN?; WHERE ARE THE CHILDREN?, d

Malmuth, Dan
WHERE ARE THE CHILDREN?

Malmuth, Evan
THE KARATE KID PART II; WHERE ARE THE CHILDREN?

Malo, Jean-Pierre
MORT UN DIMANCHE DE PLUIE

Malo, Rene
DECLINE OF THE AMERICAN EMPIRE, THE, p

Malone, Beni
ADVENTURE OF FAUSTUS BIDGOOD, THE

Malone, Greg
ADVENTURE OF FAUSTUS BIDGOOD, THE

Maloney, Jack
KING KONG LIVES

Maloney, Peter
MANHUNTER

Maloney, Stacy
AMERICAN ANTHEM

Malooly, Erin
VIOLETS ARE BLUE

Malooly, Megan
VIOLETS ARE BLUE

Malovic, Steve
AMERICA 3000

Malpas, George
MR. LOVE

Maltagliati, Evi
Obituaries

Maluenda, Luis
MONSTER DOG

Maly, Arturo
CONTAR HASTA TEN

Mamani, Abdoulaye
SARRAOUNIA, w

Mamberti, Claudio
AVAETE, A SEMENTE DA VINGANCA

Mamet, David
ABOUT LAST NIGHT, w

Mamilov, Sulambek
DEN' GNEVA, d

Mamootty
ANANTARAM

Man, Chung Chi
ROYAL WARRIORS, d&w; ROYAL WARRIORS, ph

Manadre, Mukhammad
AVANTI POPOLO

Manalili, Bernardo
PLATOON

Manan, Has
NO TIME TO DIE, d

Manard, Biff
ZONE TROOPERS

Manchester, Melissa
GREAT MOUSE DETECTIVE, THE, m/l

Mancinelli, Lidia
IL MOSTRO DI FIRENZE

Mancini, Henry
FINE MESS, A, m; FINE MESS, A, m/l; GREAT MOUSE DETECTIVE, THE, m; GREAT MOUSE DETECTIVE, THE, m/l; THAT'S LIFE, m

Mancini, Rico
HOLLYWOOD VICE SQUAD

Manco, Baris
FOURTEEN NUMARA, m

Mancori, Guglielmo
FINAL EXECUTIONER, THE, ph; JUNGLE RAIDERS, ph; MANHATTAN BABY, ph; THRONE OF FIRE, THE, ph; WILD BEASTS, ph

Mancori, Sandro
LE MINIERE DEL KILIMANGIARO, ph

Mancuso, Angel
INSTANT JUSTICE

Mancuso, Becky
QUICKSILVER, md

Mancuso, Frank
APRIL FOOL'S DAY, p

Mancuso, Maria
FRIDAY THE 13TH PART VI: JASON LIVES, cos

Mancuso, Nick
LOVE SONGS

Mandel, Babaloo
GUNG HO, w

Mandel, Howie
FINE MESS, A

Mandel, Robert
F/X, d; TOUCH AND GO, d

Mandel, Yoram
PARTING GLANCES, p

Mandell, Peter
LABYRINTH

Manderson, Tommie
FRENCH LESSON, makeup; MISSION, THE, makeup

Mandic, Miroslav
LIJEPE ZENE PROLAZE KROZ GRAD, w

Mandonca, Barbara
O HOMEM DA CAPA PRETA, set d

Mandozzi, Graziano
INNOCENZA, m

Mandruzzato, Angelo
MONITORS

Manel, Ze
NTTURUDU, m

Manes, Fritz
RATBOY, p

Manet, Eduardo
SINCERELY CHARLOTTE

Maneva, Tsvetana
ZABRAVOTE TOZI SLOCHAI

Manevitch, Bedia
VYITI ZAMUZH ZA KAPITANA, art d

Manfredi, Nino
GRANDI MAGAZZINI; IL TENENTE DEI CARABINIERI

Manfredini, Harry
FRIDAY THE 13TH PART VI: JASON LIVES, m; HOUSE, m

Mang, William
FINAL EXECUTIONER, THE

Mangine, Joseph
NEON MANIACS, d; NEON MANIACS, ph

Mangold, Lisi
FOLLOWING THE FUHRER

Mangrum, Brad
DR. OTTO AND THE RIDDLE OF THE GLOOM BEAM

Manguia, Jose J.
EL DIA DE LOS ALBANILES II, ed

Mani, M.
MUKHAMUKHAM, ed

Mani, Maya
BULLIES, cos

Manikin, Spanky
P.O.W. THE ESCAPE

Manino, Vincenzo
SENSI, w

Maniscalco, Carmelo
STOOGEMANIA

Maniscalco, Daneen
STOOGEMANIA

Manker, Paulus
SCHMUTZ, p, d&w

Mankey, Marlene
PRAY FOR DEATH

Mankiewicz, Christopher
ARMED AND DANGEROUS; BEST OF TIMES, THE

Mankofsky, Isidore
ONE CRAZY SUMMER; ONE CRAZY SUMMER, ph; SAY YES, ph

Manley, Danita
IMAGEMAKER, THE

Manley, Jerry
ABSOLUTE BEGINNERS

Manling, Zhang
QINGCHUN JI, w

Mann, Barry
AMERICAN TAIL, AN, m/l; BEST OF TIMES, THE, m/l

Mann, Dutch
BAD GUYS

Mann, Hubert
WELCOME IN VIENNA

Mann, Hummie
STOOGEMANIA, ph, m

Mann, Jo Ann
JO JO DANCER, YOUR LIFE IS CALLING

Mann, Joey-Lynn
NUTCRACKER: THE MOTION PICTURE

Mann, Klaus
FLIGHT NORTH, w

Mann, Leonard
CUT AND RUN; IL MOSTRO DI FIRENZE

Mann, Louis
FERRIS BUELLER'S DAY OFF, set d

Mann, Michael
MANHUNTER, d&w

Mann, Roderick
FOREIGN BODY, w

Mann, Sam
ROLLER BLADE

Mann, Stanley
TAI-PAN, w

Mann, Terrence
CRITTERS

Mannen, Lelijke
FAILURE, THE, m

Mannen, Monique
PLAYING FOR KEEPS

Manners, Harley
FAIR GAME, p

Mannetti, Franca
SCHWARZ UND OHNE ZUCKER

Manni, Carlo
AURELIA

Manni, Marco
UNA STORIA AMBIGUA

Manning, Michelle
BLUE CITY, d

Manning, Ned
DEAD-END DRIVE-IN

Manning, Ruth
STEWARDESS SCHOOL

Mannino, Anthony
HIGHLANDER

Mannino, Franco
FEAR, m

Mannino, incenzo
COBRA MISSION, w

Mannino, Vincenzo
COBRA MISSION, w; MIAMI GOLEM, w

Mannix, Peggy
ELIMINATORS

Manojlovic, Miki
ZA SRECU JE POTREBNO TROJE

Manoogian, Peter
ELIMINATORS, d

Manos, Melanie
PRETTY IN PINK

Manoslikakis, Andreas
GIRL FROM MANI, THE

Mans, Lorenzo
SLEEPWALK, w

Mansbridge, Mark W.
8 MILLION WAYS TO DIE, art d

Mansfield, David
CLUB PARADISE, m

Mansfield, Paul
FERRIS BUELLER'S DAY OFF, m/l

Mansfield, Todd
REVENGE OF THE TEENAGE VIXENS FROM OUTER
SPACE, THE

Mansier, Joseph
SORORITY HOUSE MASSACRE

Manso, Lenor
EL RIGOR DEL DESTINO

Mansoori, Tooraj
BEYOND THE MIST, ph

Mansson, Claes
MIN PAPA AR TARZAN

Mansurjan, Tigran
ZAZZENNYJ FONAR, m

Mansuryan, T.
KHOZIAIN, m

Manszky, Laura
I LOVE YOU

Mantegna, Joe
MONEY PIT, THE; OFF BEAT; THREE AMIGOS

Mantel, Bronwen
CRAZY MOON

Manteuffel, Felix von
FOLLOWING THE FUHRER

Manthey, Lawrence Blaine
AMERICAN JUSTICE

Manton, Marcus
P.O.W. THE ESCAPE, ed

Manttari, Anssi
KUNINGAS LAHTEE RANSKAAN, d; KUNINGAS
LAHTEE RANSKAAN, w; KUNINGAS LAHTEE
RANSKAAN, w; MORENA; MORENA, d&w

Manttari, Asko
MORENA, m

Manuel
EL MERCADO DE HUMILDES; LA TIERRA
PROMETIDA

Manz, Chantal
SILK

Manza, Ralph
BEER

Manzanero, Paul
FERRIS BUELLER'S DAY OFF

Manzano, Alberto
CAGED GLASS

Manzetti, Servando
MATANZA EN MATAMOROS

Manzi, Warren
MANHATTAN PROJECT, THE

Manzo, Tony
GIRLS SCHOOL SCREAMERS

Manzor, Rene
LE PASSAGE, anim; LE PASSAGE, d&w

Manzotti, Mabel
SERE CUALQUIER COSA PERO TE QUIERO

Maples, Marla

Maples, Tony
MARIA

Mar, Diana
THE KARATE KID PART II

Mar, Faye Fujisaki
OFF BEAT

Maraden, Frank
KING KONG LIVES; MONEY PIT, THE

Marais, Jean
PARENTAL CLAIM

Marando, Tony
THAT'S LIFE, set d

Marangoni, Elizabeth
ROOM WITH A VIEW, A

Marangoni, Giovanni
TWO FRIENDS

Marano, Ezio
GINGER & FRED; SPOSERO SIMON LE BON

Marceau, Marcel
ELOGIO DELLA PAZZIA

Marceau, Sophie
DESCENTE AUX ENFERS; POLICE

Marcelino, Mario
FREE RIDE

March, George
SOLDIER'S REVENGE, prod d

March, Marvin
PEGGY SUE GOT MARRIED, set d; QUICKSILVER, set
d

Marchand, Guy
CONSEIL DE FAMILLE; JE HAIS LES ACTEURS

Marchetti, Gianni
CATTIVI PIERROT, m

Marchi, Elio
EL HOMBRE QUE GANO LA RAZON

Marchini, Simona
SEPARATI IN CASA

Marciona, Anthony
PLAYING FOR KEEPS

Marco, Armand
L'AUBE, ph; LAST SONG, ph

Marcopoulos, Christos
DANILO TRELES, O FIMISMENOS ANDALOUSIANOS
MOUSIKOS

Marcos, Willy
COCAINE WARS

Marcotte, Pamela
HOWARD THE DUCK, set d

Marcucci, Luciano
DEVIL IN THE FLESH

Marculescu, Adela
DECLARATIE DE DRAGOSTE; UN OASPETE LA CINA

Marcus, Alan
AVENGING FORCE

Marcus, Richard
DEADLY FRIEND

Marcus, Stephen
MY BEAUTIFUL LAUNDRETTE

Marden, Richard
HALF MOON STREET, ed

Mardirosian, Tim
EAT AND RUN

Mardirosian, Tom
POWER

Marenych, Katrenna
NUTCRACKER: THE MOTION PICTURE

Mares, Teodora
DECLARATIE DE DRAGOSTE

Margolin, Stuart
FINE MESS, A

Margolis, Marshall
DANCING IN THE DARK

Margolyes, Miriam
GOOD FATHER, THE; LITTLE SHOP OF HORRORS

Margulies, David
9½ WEEKS; BRIGHTON BEACH MEMOIRS

Mari, Salah
EL-GOOA, art d

Maria, Elsa
VENENO PARA LAS HADAS

Maria, Guida
O VESTIDO COR DE FOGO

Maria, Patricia
HIJO DEL PALENQUE

Mariana, Michele
SHADOW PLAY

Mariano, Detto
GRANDI MAGAZZINI, m; IL BI E IL BA, m; ITALIAN
FAST FOOD, m; MIAMI GOLEM, m; YUPPIES, I
GIOVANI DI SUCCESSO, m

Mariano, John
TOUGH GUYS

Maribel
EL MERCADO DE HUMILDES

Marie, Lee Ann
FERRIS BUELLER'S DAY OFF

Marie, Lisa
ROLLER BLADE

Marielle, Jean-Pierre
MENAGE

Mariette, Mykle
ROCKIN' ROAD TRIP; ROCKIN' ROAD TRIP, spec eff

Marignac, Martine
GOLDEN EIGHTIES, p; LAST SONG, p

Marignano, Renzo
YUPPIES, I GIOVANI DI SUCCESSO

Marika, Banduk
CACTUS

Marin, Jerry
HOUSE

Marin, Richard
ECHO PARK

Marine, Jean
PAULETTE

Marine, Jeanne
I LOVE YOU

Marinelli, Lorenzo
VERY CLOSE QUARTERS, ed

Marinelli, Rudolph
VERY CLOSE QUARTERS, ed

Marineo, Ludovica
IL MIELE DEL DIAVOLO, w

Marinho, Jose
NEM TUDO E VERDADE

Marini, Giovanna Salviucci
STORIA D'AMORE, m

Marini, Raimund
DIE WALSCHE

Marino, Francesca
KNIGHTS AND EMERALDS

Marino, Franco
NAME OF THE ROSE, THE

Marino, Leo
MES ENLLA DE LA PASSIO, m

Marino, Nino
THRONE OF FIRE, THE, w; VIOLENT BREED, THE, w

Marinucci, Luciana
IL CAMORRISTA, cos

Marion, Estelle
GOLDEN EIGHTIES

Marion, John
LEGAL EAGLES

Maris, Peter
LAND OF DOOM, d; LAND OF DOOM, p

Mariscal, Lucila
ESE LOCO LOCO HOSPITAL

Marius, Robert
AMERICAN COMMANDOS

Marjanovic, Iva
SAN O RUZI

Mark, Ivan
ORDOGI KISERTETEK, ph

Mark, Tony
BILLY GALVIN, p

Markel, Gregory
MANHUNTER, m/l

Markert, Philip
BLUE VELVET

Markey, Jane
AROUND THE WORLD IN EIGHTY WAYS

Markham, Monte
JAKE SPEED

Markiewicz, Tim
ONE MORE SATURDAY NIGHT

Markland, Ted
EYE OF THE TIGER

Markle, Peter
YOUNGBLOOD, d&w

Markle, Stephen
MANHATTAN PROJECT, THE

Markopolous, Yannis
CACTUS, m

Markos, Miklos
KISMASZAT ES A GEZENGUZOK, d; KISMASZAT ES
A GEZENGUZOK, w

Markovic, Olivera
I TO CE PROCI

Markovic, Rade
LIJEPE ZENE PROLAZE KROZ GRAD

Markowitz, Michael
LAST RESORT, THE

Marks, Ada
ABOUT LAST NIGHT

Marks, Arthur D.
BREEDERS, ph

Marks, David
CARNAGE

Marks, Peter
PANTHER SQUAD, ed

Marks, Richard
PRETTY IN PINK, ed

Marks, Walter
MONEY PIT, THE, m/l

Marleau, Jeanne
MARIA

Marleau, Louise
ANNE TRISTER

Marley, Ben
BLOODY BIRTHDAY

Marloe, Michael
ECHO PARK

Marlon, Ged
ROUND MIDNIGHT

Marlowe, Linda
MR. LOVE

Marlowe, Raymond
BUSTED UP

Marmo, Joe
SHADOWS RUN BLACK

Marmolejo, Frank
NINJA TURF

Maron, Alfred
Obituaries; ABSOLUTE BEGINNERS

Maroney, Kelli
CHOPPING MALL

Maronka, Csilla
KISMASZAT ES A GEZENGUZOK

Marosi, Gyula
VAKVILAGBAN, w

Marott, Stine
ET SKUD FRA HJERTET, cos

Marquardt, Hans
DIE LIEBESWUSTE

Marquez, Pete
BAD GUYS

Marquez, William
8 MILLION WAYS TO DIE; BLACK MOON RISING

Marr, Erika
JO JO DANCER, YOUR LIFE IS CALLING

Marr, Johnny
FERRIS BUELLER'S DAY OFF, m/l

Marr, Leon
DANCING IN THE DARK, d; DANCING IN THE DARK, w

Marra, Armando
NAME OF THE ROSE, THE

Marrazzo, iuseppe
IL CAMORRISTA, w

Marrocco, Gino
BEER

Marrs, Johnny
SOMETHING WILD

Mars
ARMOUR OF GOD, THE; MY CHAUFFEUR, m/l

Mars, Ken
ADVENTURES OF THE AMERICAN RABBIT, THE

Mars, Kenneth
BEER

Marschall, Inge
SPRING SYMPHONY

Marschall, Marita
EIN FLIEHENDES PFERD; TRANSITTRAUME

Marsden, Megan
AMERICAN ANTHEM

Marsden, Penny
LABYRINTH

Marselos, Th.
ALLIGORIA

Marsh, Carl
MANHUNTER, m/l

Marsh, Dean
HELL SQUAD

Marsh, Michele
TOUGH GUYS

Marsh, Stephen
NATIVE SON, prod d; WHAT WAITS BELOW, art d

Marsh, Terence
HAUNTED HONEYMOON, prod d; HAUNTED HONEYMOON, w

Marsh-Edwards, Nadine
PASSION OF REMEMBRANCE, THE, ed

Marshall, Dick
WHITE SLAVE

Marshall, E.G.
MY CHAUFFEUR; POWER

Marshall, Frank
MONEY PIT, THE, p

Marshall, Garry
NOTHING IN COMMON, d

Marshall, Garry K.
JUMPIN' JACK FLASH

Marshall, John G.
ADVENTURES OF THE AMERICAN RABBIT, THE, p

Marshall, Kathy
HYPER SAPIEN: PEOPLE FROM ANOTHER STAR, cos

Marshall, Mike
JE HAIS LES ACTEURS; MAINE-OCEAN

Marshall, Penny
JUMPIN' JACK FLASH, d

Marshall, Phil
LAST OF PHILIP BANTER, THE, m; SLOANE, m

Marshall, Ray
Obituaries; CACTUS

Marshall, Sandy
SEX O'CLOCK NEWS, THE

Marshall, Steve
NIGHT OF THE CREEPS

Marshall, Tonie
BEAU TEMPS, MAIS ORAGEUX EN FIN DE JOURNEE; QUI TROP EMBRASSE

Marsillach, Blanca
IL MIELE DEL DIAVOLO

Marsillach, Cristina
EVERY TIME WE SAY GOODBYE

Marsina, Antonio
SENZA SCRUPOLI

Martano, Aldina
VOGLIA DI GUARDARE

Martel, Daria
MY CHAUFFEUR

Martel, K.C.
BLOODY BIRTHDAY

Martel, Wendy
SORORITY HOUSE MASSACRE

Martell, Jack
Obituaries

Martell, Paul
SEVEN MINUTES IN HEAVEN

Martevo, Pekka
SININEN IMETTAJA, ph

Martha, Istvan
ERZEKENY BUCSU A FEJEDELEMTOL, m

Marti, Maria Soley
EL SUIZO—UN AMOUR EN ESPAGNE

Marti, Pascal
DOUBLE MESSIEURS, ph; SCENE OF THE CRIME, ph

Martial, Jacques
BLACK AND WHITE

Martin, Alumo Jimenez
SCORPION

Martin, Andreu
EL CABALLERO DEL DRAGON, w

Martin, Charles Joseph
VENDETTA

Martin, David
SID AND NANCY, ed

Martin, Felix
SCORPION

Martin, Helen
MONA LISA

Martin, Herbert
MIAMI GOLEM, d&w

Martin, J. C.
THANATOS, ph

Martin, Jared
QUIET COOL; SEA SERPENT, THE

Martin, John
FIRE IN THE NIGHT; MY CHAUFFEUR

Martin, John Scott
LITTLE SHOP OF HORRORS

Martin, Juan Carlos
REDONDO, ph; THANATOS, w

Martin, Kellie
JUMPIN' JACK FLASH

Martin, Lucas
EL ANO DE LAS LUCES; EL HERMANO BASTARDO DE DIOS

Martin, Manuel
BANDERA NEGRA, makeup

Martin, Maribel
VIAJE A NINGUNA PARTE, p

Martin, Nieves
LULU DE NOCHE, ed

Martin, Pepper
BAD GUYS

Martin, Peyton
ABSOLUTE BEGINNERS

Martin, Remi
CONSEIL DE FAMILLE; DESORDRE

Martin, Richard
SAMUEL LOUNT, ed

Martin, Russ
DEADLY FRIEND

Martin, Sandy
EXTREMITIES; VENDETTA

Martin, Scott
SORORITY HOUSE MASSACRE

Martin, Steve
LITTLE SHOP OF HORRORS; THREE AMIGOS; THREE AMIGOS, w; TRE SUPERMEN A SANTO DOMINGO

Martin, Svante
PA LIV OCH DOD

Martin, Tania
PEAU D'ANGE, makeup

Martin, Vera
LOYALTIES

Martin, Vincent
CONSEIL DE FAMILLE

Martin, Whit
DR. OTTO AND THE RIDDLE OF THE GLOOM BEAM

Martineau, Tony
SCORPION

Martinelli, John A.
BOSS' WIFE, THE, ed

Martinenghi, Italo
TRE SUPERMEN A SANTO DOMINGO, d; TRE SUPERMEN A SANTO DOMINGO, w

Martinex, Jesse
THRASHIN'

Martinez, Arturo
EL NARCO—DUELO ROJO; POR UN VESTIDO DE NOVIA; POR UN VESTIDO DE NOVIA, d

Martinez, Claudio
DE L'ARGENTINE, ed; LOS HIJOS DE LA GUERRA FRIA, ed

Martinez, Cliff
TOUGH GUYS

Martinez, Dennis
THRASHIN'

Martinez, Julia
LA MITAD DEL CIELO

Martinez, Leo
SILK

Martinez, Mauricio
SALVADOR

Martinez, Nacho
LA MITAD DEL CIELO; MATADOR

Martinez, Oscar
CONTAR HASTA TEN; LES LONGS MANTEAUX

Martinez, Pablo
JIBARO, ph

Martinez, Patrice
THREE AMIGOS

Martinez, Ty
NO RETREAT, NO SURRENDER

Martinez-Lazaro, Emilio
LULU DE NOCHE, d&w

Martini, Annelie
AMOROSA

Martini, Ettore
SAVING GRACE

Martini, Roberto
LA SPOSA AMERICANA, ed

Martino, Lea
MORIRAI A MEZZANOTTE

Martins, Felipe
HAPPILY EVER AFTER

Martinus, John
MORD I MORKET

Martirosjan, Karpos
ZAZZENNYJ FONAR

Martirosyan, A.
KHOZIAIN

Martoriat, Massimiliano
STORIA D'AMORE

Marttila, Mattheus
VALKOINEN KAAPIO, art d

Martyn, John
MORNING AFTER, THE, m/l

Martyne, Robin
ABSOLUTE BEGINNERS

Marugon, Luis
SCORPION

Maruyama, Kenji
TOKIMEDI NI SHISU, w

Marvala, Persis
MY BEAUTIFUL LAUNDRETTE

Marvin, Eric
HOLLYWOOD ZAP!

Marvin, Lee
DELTA FORCE, THE

Marvin, Mike
HAMBURGER, d; WRAITH, THE, d&w

Marx, Alan
ROCKIN' ROAD TRIP

Marx, Brett
THRASHIN'

Marx, Christy
WHAT WAITS BELOW, w

Marx, Richard
FIREWALKER, ed; HARDBODIES 2, m/l

Marx, Rick
TENEMENT, w

Marziano, Gloria
NO RETREAT, NO SURRENDER

Marzio, Duilie
POBRE MARIPOSA

Marzo, Claudio
AVAETE, A SEMENTE DA VINGANCA; FULANINHA

Marzolff, Serge
GOLDEN EIGHTIES, art d

Marzouk, Ramses
KAHIR ELZAMAN, ph

Marzuk, Ramses
AL KETTAR, ph

Marzuk, Sayed Mohamed
AL KETTAR, w

Masche, Jacquelyn
FIRE IN THE NIGHT

Mascia, Giorgio
UN RAGAZZO COME TANTI

Mase, Marino
VOGLIA DI GUARDARE

Maselli, Francesco
NAME OF THE ROSE, THE; STORIA D'AMORE, d&w

Masin, Claudio
SAVING GRACE

Masina, Giulietta
GINGER & FRED

Mask, Ace
CHOPPING MALL

Maskell, Simon
VENDETTA, w

Maslansky, Paul
POLICE ACADEMY 3: BACK IN TRAINING, p

Maslarov, Plamen
SKUPA MOYA, SKUPI MOY, w

Masliah, Laurence
SINCERELY CHARLOTTE

Masmuoto, Nobutoshi
KINEMA NO TENCHI, p

Mason, George
NO RETREAT, NO SURRENDER

Mason, Geraldine
JO JO DANCER, YOUR LIFE IS CALLING

Mason, Hal
Obituaries

Mason, Jackie
PERILS OF P.K., THE

Mason, Madison
DANGEROUSLY CLOSE

Mason, Margery
TERRY ON THE FENCE

Mason, Marsha
HEARTBREAK RIDGE

Mason, Paul
LADIES CLUB, THE, p; LADIES CLUB, THE, w; TWO FRIENDS

Mason, Sharon
HELLFIRE

Mason, Tom
CRIMES OF THE HEART; WHATEVER IT TAKES

Mass, Jean
SENSI

Massaccesi, Aristide
LA MONACA NEL PECCATO, ph; LUSSURI, ph; VOGLIA DI GUARDARE, ph&w

Massara, Natale
IL CASO MORO, md

Massari, Esteban
NIGHTMARE'S PASSENGERS

Massaro, Francesco
SPOSERO SIMON LE BON, w

Massart, Clemence
THERESE

Massart, Sylvaine
THERESE

Massee, Kim
KAMIKAZE

Massenet, Jules
WERTHER, m

Massey, Alec
MANHATTAN PROJECT, THE; VIOLATED

Massey, Anna
FOREIGN BODY

Massey, Rupert
CLOCKWISE

Massey, Walter
BOY IN BLUE, THE

Massi, Ernesto
LA SECONDA NOTTE

Massieu, Patrick
ROUND MIDNIGHT

Massoni, Jean Paul
LA MACHINE A DECOUDRE

Masten, Gordon
BUSTED UP

Masten, J. Gordon
BOY IN BLUE, THE

Masten, Werner
DIE WALSCHE, d; DIE WALSCHE, w

Masters, Anthony
CLAN OF THE CAVE BEAR, THE, prod d

Masters, Ben
DREAM LOVER

Masters, Tony
TAI-PAN, prod d

Maston, Jerry
Obituaries

Mastramon, Boris
LOLA

Mastrantonio, Mary Elizabeth
COLOR OF MONEY, THE; People to Watch

Mastroianni, Marcello
GINGER & FRED; O MELISSOKOMOS

Mastroianni, Ruggero
ANCHE LEI FUMAVA IL SIGARO, ed; GINGER & FRED, m; I LOVE YOU, ed; LET'S HOPE IT'S A GIRL, ed; UNA SPINA NEL CUORE, ed

Mastroieni, Steven
DESERT BLOOM

Mastrosimone, William
EXTREMITIES, w

Masur, Richard
HEAD OFFICE; HEARTBURN

Masyulis, Algimantas
CHICHERIN

Mataix, Virginia
BANDERA NEGRA

Mataya, Jimmy
COLOR OF MONEY, THE

Mateos, Julian
VIAJE A NINGUNA PARTE, p

Matesanz, Jose Luis
WERTHER, ed

Matevosyan, Grant
KHOZIAIN, w

Mather, Matt
DR. OTTO AND THE RIDDLE OF THE GLOOM BEAM

Matheson, Linda
JUDGEMENT IN STONE, A, cos

Mathews, Grady
COLOR OF MONEY, THE

Mathews, Thom
DANGEROUSLY CLOSE; FRIDAY THE 13TH PART VI: JASON LIVES

Mathews, Walter
CHECK IS IN THE MAIL, THE

Mathias, Bunty
KNIGHTS AND EMERALDS

Mathias, Darian
MY CHAUFFEUR

Mathias, Harry
MY CHAUFFEUR, ph

Mathieu, Frank
BEAU TEMPS, MAIS ORAGEUX EN FIN DE JOURNEE, ed

Mathisen, Leo
TAKE IT EASY, m

Mathou, Jacques
BETTY BLUE

Matic, Peter
KILLING CARS

Matis, Barbara
CHILDREN OF A LESSER GOD, art d

Matji, Manuel
EL DISPUTADO VOTO DEL SR. CAYO, w

Matlin, Marlee
CHILDREN OF A LESSER GOD; People to Watch

Matos, Gustavo Adolfo
SQUADRA SELVAGGIA

Matos, Jose Richardo
WHERE THE RIVER RUNS BLACK

Matos, Suzana
AS SETE VAMPIRAS

Matscheck, David
BRODERNA MOZART

Matson, Audrey
EHRENGARD

Matsuda, Shunsui
TO SLEEP SO AS TO DREAM

Matsuda, Yusaku
SOREKARA

Matsumoto, Koshiro
KINEMA NO TENCHI

Matsunaga, Toshiyuki
TYPHOON CLUB

Matsuzaka, Keiko
KATAKU NO HITO; KINEMA NO TENCHI

Mattar, Mauricio
CINEMA FALADO

Matte, Luc
VISAGE PALE

Mattei, Bruno
SCALPS, w

Mattei, Danilo
IL CASO MORO; MEGLIO BACIARE UN COBRA

Matter, Franz
LISI UND DER GENERAL

Mattern, Kitty
SPRING SYMPHONY

Mattes, Eva
AUF IMMER UND EWIG

Matteson, Denver
TOUGH GUYS

Matteucci, Domenico
DESIDERANDO GIULIA, w

Matthau, Walter
PIRATES

Matthes, Jeff
COMBAT SHOCK, makeup; COMBAT SHOCK, spec eff

Matthew, Eric
SPIKER

Matthews III, Edward Talbot
SNO-LINE

Matthews, Al
ALIENS

Matthews, Geoffrey
VALHALLA

Matthews, Marlene
SPIKER, w

Matthews, Ross
SHORT CHANGED, p

Matthews, William F.
THE KARATE KID PART II, art d

Matthey, Peter
ANGEL RIVER

Matthiesen, Molly
HOLLYWOOD VICE SQUAD

Mattinson, Burny
GREAT MOUSE DETECTIVE, THE, d; GREAT MOUSE DETECTIVE, THE, p; GREAT MOUSE DETECTIVE, THE, w

Mattos, Paulo
JOGO DURO, ed

Mattson, Denver
CHOKE CANYON; RAW DEAL

Mattson, Steve
SCORPION

Mattsson, Majsan
MIN PAPA AR TARZAN

Matuszak, John
ONE CRAZY SUMMER

Matzievsky, I.
NEBYVALSHINA, m

Mauceri, Patricia
SAVING GRACE

Mauch, Thomas
BLIND DIRECTOR, THE, ph

Mauer, Annette
FAT GUY GOES NUTZOID!!

Mauer, Charlotte
ABOUT LAST NIGHT

Mauffroy, Olivier
KAMIKAZE, ed

Maughan, Monica
CACTUS

Maura, Carmen
MATADOR

Mauranen, Rea
SUURI ILLUSIONI

Maurel, Jean
JEAN DE FLORETTE

Maurer, Lisa
HOLLYWOOD VICE SQUAD

Maurer, Norman
Obituaries

Mauri, Maurizio
NAME OF THE ROSE, THE

Mauri, Paco
SEPARATE VACATIONS

Maurice, Jon
HELLFIRE

Maurstad, Mari
DROMMESLOTTER

Maury, Jacques
PIRATES

Maus, Rodger
FINE MESS, A, prod d

Maussion, Ivan
LES FRERES PETARD, art d; NUIT D'IVRESSE, art d

Mavroyanni, Magda
I NICHTA ME TI SILENA

Max the Dog
SOMETHING WILD

Max, Maria Bauza
KAPAX DEL AMAZONAS

Maximova, Ekaterina
FOUETTE

Maxine, Brian
PIRATES

Maxwell, Becky Bell
NOBODY'S FOOL

Maxwell, Bob
TOUGH GUYS

Maxwell, Jeff
ODD JOBS

Maxwell, Lyndsy
NINJA TURF

Maxwell, Norman
RAW DEAL

Maxwell, Paul
ALIENS

Maxwell, Roberta
PSYCHO III

May, Albert
SOLDIER'S REVENGE

May, Brian
SKY PIRATES, m

May, Daniel L.
MY MAN ADAM, set d

May, Debra
TWO FRIENDS

May, Floyd
SCREEN TEST

May, Jim
DR. OTTO AND THE RIDDLE OF THE GLOOM BEAM, ph

May, Lyn
EL MERCADO DE HUMILDES

May, Mariana
MAXIMUM OVERDRIVE, makeup

May, Michael
PLAYING FOR KEEPS

Mayall, Jason
ECHO PARK

Mayall, John
SUNSET STRIP

Maybank, Preston
NIGHTMARE WEEKEND

Mayer, Alexandre
O HOMEM DA CAPA PRETA, set d

Mayer, John
ADVENTURES OF THE AMERICAN RABBIT, THE

Mayer, Meg
VENDETTA, cos

Mayerberg, Paul
CAPTIVE, d&w

Mayers, Pauline
KNIGHTS AND EMERALDS

Mayes, Judith
CARNAGE

Maynard, Judy
HALF MOON STREET

Maynard, Ted
HIGHLANDER; SKY BANDITS

Mayne, Ferdy
HOT CHILI; PIRATES

Mayo, Alfredo
EL SUIZO—UN AMOUR EN ESPAGNE

Mayo, Karen
NIGHTMARE WEEKEND

Mayo-Chandler, Karen
HAMBURGER

Mayolo, Carlos
LA MANSION DE ARAUCAIMA; LA MANSION DE ARAUCAIMA, d

Mayron, Melanie
BOSS' WIFE, THE

Maza, Bob
FRINGE DWELLERS, THE

Mazia, Edna
BAR 51—SISTER OF LOVE, w

Mazibuko, Doreen
PLACE OF WEEPING

Mazini, Eder
FILME DEMENCIA, ed

Mazouza, Rachid
TAHOUNET AL SAYED FABRE, ed

Mazowics, Joseph
TOUCH AND GO

Mazumder, Sreela
CHOPPER

Mazur, Lara
TRAMP AT THE DOOR, ed

Mazurowna, Ernestine
JEAN DE FLORETTE

Mazursky, Betsy
DOWN AND OUT IN BEVERLY HILLS

Mazursky, Paul
DOWN AND OUT IN BEVERLY HILLS; DOWN AND OUT IN BEVERLY HILLS, p&d; DOWN AND OUT IN BEVERLY HILLS, w

Mazzarotto, Mario
UNA DOMENICA SI

Mazzoli, Dario
SENSI

Mazzucco, Massimo
ROMANCE, d; ROMANCE, w

McAdam, Jack
BULLIES, prod d

McAdam, Paul
DOT AND KEETO, anim

McAllister, Bill
BEER, art d

McAllister, Chip
HAMBURGER

McAllister, Jamie
YOUNGBLOOD

McAlpine, Andrew
SID AND NANCY, prod d

McAlpine, Donald
DOWN AND OUT IN BEVERLY HILLS, ph; FRINGE DWELLERS, THE, ph; MY MAN ADAM, ph

McAnally, Ray
MISSION, THE; NO SURRENDER

McArtney, Dave
QUEEN CITY ROCKERS, m

McAsh, Braun
BUSTED UP

McAteer, James
FLY, THE, set d

McAuley, Annie
HEAD OFFICE; RECRUITS

McBrayer, Mac
OVER THE SUMMER

McBride, Elizabeth
TRUE STORIES, cos

McBroom, Durga
VENDETTA

McBurnie, Peter
PINK CHIQUITAS, THE

McCabe, Ann
CLASS OF NUKE 'EM HIGH

McCabe, Leo
Obituaries

McCaddon, Wanda
HOWARD THE DUCK

McCain, Frances Lee
STAND BY ME

McCall, Mary C., Jr.
Obituaries

McCallister, Dea
SCORPION

McCallum, Nick
DEAD-END DRIVE-IN, art d

McCallum, Paul
MURPHY'S LAW; MURPHY'S LAW, m/l

McCallum, Rick
CASTAWAY, p; PATRIOT, THE

McCallum, Val
MURPHY'S LAW, m/l; MY CHAUFFEUR

McCallum, Valentine
MURPHY'S LAW, m

McCandless, Dee
TRUE STORIES, ch

McCann, Bryan
BULLIES, w

McCann, Chuck
HAMBURGER; THRASHIN'

McCann, Donal
MR. LOVE

McCann, James
SCREAMPLAY

McCann, Karen
SCREAMPLAY

McCann, Sean
CRAZY MOON; FLYING

McCarrol, Howie
YOUNGBLOOD

McCarter, Brooke
THRASHIN'

McCarthy, Andrew
PRETTY IN PINK

McCarthy, Bridget
FERRIS BUELLER'S DAY OFF

McCarthy, Bridget M.
ONE MORE SATURDAY NIGHT

McCarthy, Elizabeth
NUTCRACKER: THE MOTION PICTURE

McCarthy, Frank
Obituaries

McCarthy, Jeanne
ON VALENTINE'S DAY

McCarthy, Jeanny
SID AND NANCY

McCarthy, Jim
DESERT BLOOM

McCarthy, John F.
MURPHY'S LAW

McCarthy, Nobu
THE KARATE KID PART II

McCarthy, Peter
SID AND NANCY

McCarthy, Terry
FAIR GAME, m/l

McCarthy, Winnie
Obituaries

McCarty, Michael
DANGEROUSLY CLOSE, m

McCary, Rod
STEWARDESS SCHOOL

McCaughan, Charles
QUICKSILVER

McCaughry, Brigitte
BOY IN BLUE, THE, makeup

McCauley, Annie
BUSTED UP

McCauley, Matthew
THUNDER RUN, m

McCauley, Paul
MURPHY'S LAW

McCelland, Kay
OCEAN DRIVE WEEKEND

McCharen, David
VAMP

McClain, Jorli
HOWARD THE DUCK

McClarnon, Kevin
SWEET LIBERTY

McClellan, Lori
EYE OF THE TIGER, cos

McClenahan, Catherine
HEAD OFFICE

McClinton, Delbert
HOWARD THE DUCK, m/l

McClory, Sean
MY CHAUFFEUR

McCloskey, Leigh
HAMBURGER

McClure, Doug
52 PICK-UP

McClurg, Edie
BACK TO SCHOOL; FERRIS BUELLER'S DAY OFF;
LONGSHOT, THE

McColl, Billy
SHOOT FOR THE SUN

McCombs, George M.
SCORPION

McConnochie, Rhys
BULLSEYE; SHORT CHANGED

McCorkle, Kevin
OUT OF BOUNDS

McCormack, Doyle L.
TOUGH GUYS

McCormack, Pam
MOVIE HOUSE MASSACRE

McCormick, Marlene
NAKED CAGE, THE, set d

McCormick, Robert
BOY IN BLUE, THE

McCoy, Doc
NAKED VENGEANCE

McCoy, John
HELL SQUAD, ph

McCoy, Kathleen
VIOLATED, cos

McCoy, Kimberly
RECRUITS

McCoy, Matt
WEEKEND WARRIORS

McCoy, Peter
THRONE OF FIRE, THE

McCoy, William
HOWARD THE DUCK

McCracken, Darren
OVER THE SUMMER

McCracken, Devin
OVER THE SUMMER

McCraken, Gary
BUSTED UP

McCready, Keith
COLOR OF MONEY, THE

McCreery, Stuart
TWELFTH NIGHT

McCuaig, Malcolm
BUSTED UP

McCullough, Jarold J.
ABDUCTED

McCullough, Jim
MOUNTAINTOP MOTEL MASSACRE, p,d&w

McCune, Grant
AMERICAN JUSTICE, spec eff

McCurdy, Stephen
BRIDGE TO NOWHERE, m

McCurry, John
DEATHMASK; STREETS OF GOLD

McCurry, Natalie
DEAD-END DRIVE-IN

McDancer, Buck
ODD JOBS, stunts

McDaniels, Gene
LOVE SONGS, m/l

McDavid, Dee Ann
MANHATTAN PROJECT, THE

McDermott, Tom
JUMPIN' JACK FLASH; PLAYING FOR KEEPS

McDivitt, Bob
AT CLOSE RANGE

McDonald, Cona
SOLDIER'S REVENGE

McDonald, Frank
TOMB, THE

McDonald, Garry
PLAYING BEATIE BOW, m

McDonald, Gary
PASSION OF REMEMBRANCE, THE

McDonald, Mac
HAUNTED HONEYMOON

McDonald, Mike
RECRUITS

McDonald, Terry
BEST MAN, THE, ed; BEST MAN, THE, ph

McDonnel, Jo
SPIKER

McDonough, Ann
OFF BEAT

McDonough, Kit
LADIES CLUB, THE

McDonough, Mary
IMPURE THOUGHTS

McDougall, Lonny
SCREAMPLAY

McDougall, Peter
SHOOT FOR THE SUN, w

McDougall, Roxanne
KNIGHTS AND EMERALDS

McDowall, Roddy
GOBOTS: BATTLE OF THE ROCKLORDS

McElduff, Ellen
DEAD END KIDS; MAXIMUM OVERDRIVE; WORKING
GIRLS

McElheney, Carol
HOWARD THE DUCK

McEnroe, Annie
TRUE STORIES

McEvily, John
FAT GUY GOES NUTZOID!!

McEwan, Geraldine
FOREIGN BODY

McEwan, Hamish
TOBY MCTEAGUE

McFadden, Cheryl
LABYRINTH, ch

McFadden, Thom
SCORPION

McFee, Bruce
BOY IN BLUE, THE

McFerrand, John
HANDS OF STEEL, ph; MONSTER SHARK, ph

McGann, Joe
NO SURRENDER

McGann, Mark
NO SURRENDER

McGann, Marion
VAMP

McGarvin, Dick
AMERICAN ANTHEM

McGary, Kris
ROCKIN' ROAD TRIP

McGavin, Darren
RAW DEAL

McGee, Dwight
FIRE WITH FIRE

McGee, Gregg
WITCHFIRE, ed

McGee, Gwen
WILDCATS

McGee, Jerry
PLAYING FOR KEEPS

McGee, Katie
REVENGE OF THE TEENAGE VIXENS FROM OUTER
SPACE, THE

McGee, Mike
TOUCH AND GO

McGhee, Bill
ON VALENTINE'S DAY

McGill, Bruce
NO MERCY; WILDCATS

McGill, Everett
FIELD OF HONOR; HEARTBREAK RIDGE

McGill, Mike
THRASHIN'

McGillis, Kelly
TOP GUN

McGinley, John C.
PLATOON; SWEET LIBERTY

McGinnis, Charlotte
REFORM SCHOOL GIRLS

McGinnis, Scott
3:15, THE MOMENT OF TRUTH; ODD JOBS; SKY
BANDITS

McGinnis, Wayne
TOUCH AND GO

McGonagle, Richard
HOWARD THE DUCK

McGovern, Elizabeth
NATIVE SON

McGovern, Terry
RADIOACTIVE DREAMS

McGowan, Bennie Lee
REVENGE

McGowan, Bruce
LETTER TO BREZHNEV, ph

McGowan, Denis
BEST MAN, THE

McGowan, Mickey
BEST MAN, THE

McGrady, Michael
BACK TO SCHOOL

McGrath, Alethea
BIG HURT, THE

McGrath, Dick
TOBY MCTEAGUE

McGrath, George
RATBOY

McGrath, John
BLOOD RED ROSES, d&w

McGregor, Eduardo
DRAGON RAPIDE

McGregor, Kenneth
HELLFIRE

McGregor, Lisa
REVENGE OF THE TEENAGE VIXENS FROM OUTER
SPACE, THE

McGregor, Robbie
WRONG WORLD

McGregor-Stewart, Kate
VIOLETS ARE BLUE

McGroarty, Pat
ONE CRAZY SUMMER

McGuire, Bruce
FROM BEYOND

McGuire, Bryan
VAMP

McGuire, Eddie
BLOOD RED ROSES, m

McGuire, Saundra
SPACECAMP

McGurn, Rita
GOSPEL ACCORDING TO VIC, THE, prod d

McHale, Christopher
F/X

McHale, Rosemary
HALF MOON STREET

McHattie, Stephen
BELIZAIRE THE CAJUN

McHugh, David
ONE MORE SATURDAY NIGHT, m

McIlvain, James Terry
PLATOON

McIntire, Donald
MISS MARY

McIntire, Tim
Obituaries

McIntosh, Judy
ARRIVING TUESDAY

McIntosh, Todd
ABDUCTED, makeup

McIntosh, Valerie
JO JO DANCER, YOUR LIFE IS CALLING; NAKED
CAGE, THE; QUICKSILVER

McIntyre, Ghandi
DEAD-END DRIVE-IN

McIntyre, Hugh
BEST MAN, THE

McIntyre, Leanne
ROCKIN' ROAD TRIP, set d

McIntyre, Marvin
SHORT CIRCUIT

McKay, Craig
SOMETHING WILD, ed

McKay, Vince
SHADOWS RUN BLACK

McKean, Bruce
SHADOW PLAY, spec eff

McKean, Sue Ann
SALVADOR

McKee, Carlota
BUSTED UP, m/l

McKee, Elodie
KING OF THE STREETS

McKee, Lonette
ROUND MIDNIGHT

McKeen, Roger A.
BOY IN BLUE, THE

McKeever, John
GIRLS SCHOOL SCREAMERS

McKeever, Vicki
GIRLS SCHOOL SCREAMERS

McKegg, Dorothy
FOOTROT FLATS

McKeller, Melinda
MOUNTAINTOP MOTEL MASSACRE, cos

McKendrick, Eva Keating
GIRLS SCHOOL SCREAMERS

McKenna, James
HIGHLANDER

McKenna, Joe
ABSOLUTE BEGINNERS

McKenna, Scott L.
THAT'S LIFE

McKenna, Siobhan   [Siobhan Giollamhuire Nic Cionnaith
McKenna]
Obituaries

McKenzie, Mary Beth
SHADOWS RUN BLACK

McKern, Leo
TRAVELLING NORTH

McKibbon, Robert
FERRIS BUELLER'S DAY OFF

McKillip, Kimberly
RADIOACTIVE DREAMS

McKimmie, Jackie
AUSTRALIAN DREAM, d&w; AUSTRALIAN DREAM, p

McKinley, Philip
SEX O'CLOCK NEWS, THE

McKinley, Roz
NO RETREAT, NO SURRENDER

McKinley, Ruckins
NO RETREAT, NO SURRENDER

McKinney, Austin
ROCKIN' ROAD TRIP, ph

McKinney, Kurt
NO RETREAT, NO SURRENDER

McKinnon, Kate
WISDOM

McKlunn, Brian
SOLDIER'S REVENGE

McKnight, Annie
CRIMES OF THE HEART

McKnight, Bonnie
REVENGE OF THE TEENAGE VIXENS FROM OUTER
SPACE, THE

McLachlan, Robert
ABDUCTED, ph

McLarty, James
BOY WHO COULD FLY, THE

McLarty, Ron
HEARTBURN

McLaughlin, Bill
DEVASTATOR, THE; NAKED VENGEANCE; SILK

McLaughlin, John
ROUND MIDNIGHT

McLean, Bill
HOUSE

McLean, Donald
DESPERATE MOVES

McLean, Dwayne
FLY, THE, stunts

McLean, Garth
ROCKIN' ROAD TRIP

McLean, Larry
BULLIES, stunts

Mclean, Lisa
SHORT CIRCUIT

McLean, Nick
SHORT CIRCUIT, ph

McLean, Warren
PLATOON; SILK

McLellan, Diana
IMAGEMAKER, THE

McLellan, Liz
PLAYING FOR KEEPS

McLendon, Gordon
Obituaries

McLendon, Michael
KING KONG LIVES

McLennan, Dorothy
JO JO DANCER, YOUR LIFE IS CALLING

McLennan, Margo
MORE THINGS CHANGE, THE

McLeod, Debbie
KING KONG LIVES

McLeod, Sandy
SOMETHING WILD

McLeod, Shannon
LIGHTNING—THE WHITE STALLION

McLoughlin, Bronco
TAI-PAN

McLoughlin, John
F/X

McLoughlin, Nancy
FRIDAY THE 13TH PART VI: JASON LIVES

McLoughlin, Tom
FRIDAY THE 13TH PART VI: JASON LIVES, d&w

McMahan, Heather
CLASS OF NUKE 'EM HIGH

McManus, Bart
SCORPION

McManus, Don
HEAD OFFICE; KILLER PARTY

McManus, Mike
HEAD OFFICE

McMartin, John
DREAM LOVER; LEGAL EAGLES; NATIVE SON

McMillan, Kenneth
ARMED AND DANGEROUS

McMillan, Samantha
SCHOOL FOR VANDALS

McMillin, Robert
ROCKIN' ROAD TRIP

McMullen, Barbara
DANCING IN THE DARK

McMullen, Donna
THAT'S LIFE

McNabney, Ted
COCAINE WARS

McNally, Diz
RATBOY

McNally, Richard
TOUCH AND GO

McNamara, Brian
SHORT CIRCUIT

McNamara, Ed
Obituaries; TRAMP AT THE DOOR

McNamara, Richard
GIOVANNI SENZAPENSIERI

McNamee, Chris
CLASS OF NUKE 'EM HIGH

McNeely, Helen
NAKED VENGEANCE

McNeill, Elizabeth
9½ WEEKS, w

McNichol, Kristy
DREAM LOVER

McNicholl, Jack
TERRY ON THE FENCE

McPhail, Andrew
SPIRITS OF THE AIR, p

McPhaul, Sam
IMPURE THOUGHTS

McPherson, Wayne
BUSTED UP

McQuade, Kris
TWO FRIENDS

McQueen, Alan
DEAD-END DRIVE-IN; SHORT CHANGED

McQueen, Butterfly
MOSQUITO COAST, THE

McQueen, Chad
THE KARATE KID PART II

McQueen-Mason, Edward
KANGAROO, ed

McQuiggin, Kellie
RAD

McRae, Carmen
JO JO DANCER, YOUR LIFE IS CALLING

McRae, James
BIG HURT, THE

McRae, Michelle
NUTCRACKER: THE MOTION PICTURE

McRaney, Gerald
AMERICAN JUSTICE

McRobbie, Peter
MANHATTAN PROJECT, THE

McSherry, Rose Marie
CHILDREN OF A LESSER GOD, set d

McSweeney, Ellen Claire
STRIPPER

McTeer, Janet
HALF MOON STREET

McVey, Jeff
PLAY DEAD

McWatters, Nikki
DEAD-END DRIVE-IN

McWharters, Teddy
BUSTED UP

McWhirten, Jill
VIOLATED

McWilliams, John
ARRIVING TUESDAY, ed

McWilliams, Steve
REVENGE, ph

Meacock, Heather-Lynn
TIMING

Mead, Syd
SHORT CIRCUIT, spec eff

Meadows, Rebecca
OVER THE SUMMER

Meadows, Robert
Obituaries

Meagher, Ray
DARK AGE; SHORT CHANGED

Meanes, John
BEER

Meara, Anne
LONGSHOT, THE; PERILS OF P.K., THE

Meath, Joanne
CRAZY MOON

Meatloaf
CAR TROUBLE, m/l; OUT OF BOUNDS

Meaux, Ken
BELIZAIRE THE CAJUN

Meceni, Carlos
JOGO DURO

Mechaal, Mohamed
HADDA; HADDA, w

Mechanical & Makeup Imageries
TERRORVISION, spec eff; TROLL, spec eff

Mechoso, Julio
FLIGHT OF THE NAVIGATOR

Medaglia, Julio
AS SETE VAMPIRAS, m

Medak, Peter
MEN'S CLUB, THE, d

Medalis, Joseph G.
BIG TROUBLE

Medawar, Joseph
HARDBODIES 2, p

Medboe, Katja
NATTSEILERE

Medeiros, Jose
A LA SALIDA NOS VEMOS, ph; JUBIABA, ph

Medel, Marcela
NEMESIO

Medford, Paul
BLACK JOY

Medica, Leon
AT CLOSE RANGE, m/l

Medina, Antonio
BRAS CUBAS, w

Medina, Crispin
P.O.W. THE ESCAPE

Medina, Enrique
PERROS DE LA NOCHE, w

Medina, Hugo
NEMESIO

Medina, Oscar
LA BANDA DE LOS PANCHITOS

Medina, Reynaldo
AMIGOS

Medoff, Mark
CHILDREN OF A LESSER GOD, w; OFF BEAT; OFF
BEAT, w

Mee-sook, Lee
BBONG

Meeh, Gregory
NUTCRACKER: THE MOTION PICTURE, spec eff

Meekat, Ed
TOUCH AND GO

Meeker, Charles R.
HAMBURGER, p

Meeks, David
MANHUNTER

Meera
MUKHAMUKHAM, art d

Meerson, Steve
STAR TREK IV: THE VOYAGE HOME, w

Meffert, Wellington
NIGHTMARE WEEKEND

Megason, Eric
NINJA TURF

Megginson, Robert
SEX O'CLOCK NEWS, THE, ph

Megginson, Robert T.
F/X, w

Megino, Luis
LA MITAD DEL CIELO, p; LA MITAD DEL CIELO, w

Meharry, Brian
YOUNGBLOOD

Mehas, Marietta
ANCHE LEI FUMAVA IL SIGARO

Meher, Sadhu
DEBSHISHU

Mehner, Alexander
JOURNEY, THE

Mehrinia, Mehri
MONSTER, THE

Mehrten, Greg
DEAD END KIDS

Mehta, Ashok
SUSMAN, ph; TRIKAL, ph

Mehta, Ketan
MIRCH MASALA, d; MIRCH MASALA, w

Mehta, Vijaya
RAO SAHEB; RAO SAHEB, d; RAO SAHEB, w

Mehtonen, Tuula
RIISUMINEN, ed

Meier, Dieter
FERRIS BUELLER'S DAY OFF, m/l; ZONING

Meighen, John
BLUE MAN, THE, art d

Meigs, Warren
DR. OTTO AND THE RIDDLE OF THE GLOOM BEAM

Meillon, John
BULLSEYE; "CROCODILE" DUNDEE

Meininger, Frederique
ROUND MIDNIGHT

Meinke, Stefan
KILLING CARS

Meisner, Gunter
CAGED GLASS

Mejding, Bent
TWIST & SHOUT

Mejia, Ana Arango de
SAN ANTONITO

Mejia, Mauricio
EL TREN DE LOS PIONEROS, m

Mejinsky, Constantin
POLICE, art d

Mejo, Carlo De
MANHATTAN BABY; WOMEN'S PRISON MASSACRE

Mekin, Ahmet
KUYUCAKLI YUSUF

Melamed, Fred
HANNAH AND HER SISTERS; MANHATTAN
PROJECT, THE

Melancon, Andre
EQUINOXE

Melani, Daniele
SALOME

Melanton, Lotta
LOVE ME!, art d

Melato, Mariangela
SUMMER NIGHT WITH GREEK PROFILE, ALMOND
EYES AND SCENT OF BASIL

Mele, Peter
VIOLATED

Melendrez, Jimi
STONE BOY

Melennec, Patrice
PEAU D'ANGE

Meletopoulos, Nikos
I PHOTOGRAPHIA, set d&cos; L'UNIQUE, art d

Melevos, Dalma
NIGHTMARE'S PASSENGERS

Melfor, Eligio
ALMACITA DI DESOLATO

Melhuse, Peder
WRAITH, THE

Melilli, Lisa
ONE CRAZY SUMMER

Melinand, Monique
ON A VOLE CHARLIE SPENCER!

Melissis, Tom
RECRUITS

Melkonian, James
NO RETREAT, NO SURRENDER, ed

Melles, Sunnyi
'38; DER WILDE CLOWN; PARADIES

Melli, Elide
MOMO

Melling, Bob
NINJA TURF

Melliti, Adzine
VENDETTA

Melnick, Daniel
QUICKSILVER, p

Melnikov, Vitaly
VYITI ZAMUZH ZA KAPITANA, d

Melo, Anais de
EL VECINDARIO—LOS MEXICANOS CALIENTES

Melody, Tony
MR. LOVE

Meloni, Claudio
LA BALLATA DI EVA, ph

Melrose, Leigh
SCHOOL FOR VANDALS, ph

Melton, James
GREAT MOUSE DETECTIVE, THE, ed

Melton, Jerry
BAD GUYS

Melville, J.W.
JUMPIN' JACK FLASH, w

Melville, Pauline
MONA LISA

Melvoin, Wendy
FIRE WITH FIRE, m/l

Memel, Steven
TOUGH GUYS

Mena, Sonia
LOS HIJOS DE LA GUERRA FRIA

Menahem, David
DELTA FORCE, THE

Menapace, Jeff
GIRLS SCHOOL SCREAMERS

Menard, Claude
SINCERELY CHARLOTTE

Menche, Friederike
DIE LIEBESWUSTE

Menche, Stefan
DIE LIEBESWUSTE

Mencwel, Andrzej
SCENY DZIECIECE Z ZYCIA PROWINCJI, w

Mendenhall, David
TRANSFORMERS: THE MOVIE, THE; WITCHFIRE

Mendenhall, James
WITCHFIRE

Mendes, Antonio Luis
MALANDRO, ph

Mendes, Carlos
O VESTIDO COR DE FOGO, m

Mendes, Jose Manuel
UMA RAPARIGA NO VERAO

Mendez, Aaman
MATANZA EN MATAMOROS

Mendez, Abril
A LA SALIDA NOS VEMOS

Mendez, Francisco
Obituaries

Mendez, Guillermo
EL MALEFICIO II, m

Mendez, Kim
LABYRINTH

Mendez, Lucia
EL MALEFICIO II

Mendez, Nacho
NOCHE DE JUERGA, m

Mendo, Luis
27 HORAS, m

Mendola, Thomas
STREETS OF GOLD

Mendolicchio, Giuseppe
SENZA SCRUPOLI

Mendoza, Mauro
CALACAN; CALACAN, p

Mendoza, Miguel
EL CORAZON SOBRE LA TIERRA, p

Mendoza, Remia
NAKED VENGEANCE, cos

Mendoza, Rossy
EL VECINDARIO—LOS MEXICANOS CALIENTES

Mendoza, Ruben
SE SUFRE PERO SE GOZA, ph

Mendoza, William
NINJA TURF

Mendroch, Horst
STAMMHEIM

Menedez, Ramon
EL EXTRANO HIJO DEL SHERIFF

Menegoz, Margaret
SUMMER, p

Menendez, Ramon
SALVADOR

Meneses, Rogelio
CAPABLANCA

Menez, Bernard
MAINE-OCEAN

Menger, Gene
TRUE STORIES, ch

Menges, Chris
FATHERLAND, ph; MISSION, THE, ph

Menglet, Alex
MORE THINGS CHANGE, THE; SKY PIRATES; STILL
POINT, THE

Meniconi, Enzio
UNA NOTTE DI PIOGGIA, ed

Menken, Alan
LITTLE SHOP OF HORRORS, m; LITTLE SHOP OF
HORRORS, m/l

Menken, Robin
HEAD OFFICE

Mennett, Tigr
KAMIKAZE HEARTS; KAMIKAZE HEARTS, w

Menoud, Jean-Bernard
JOUR ET NUIT, d; JOUR ET NUIT, w

Menton, Loree
STRIPPER

Menville, Scott
MY LITTLE PONY

Menzano
TITAN SERAMBUT DIBELAH TUJUH

Menzel, Bernd
UNTERMEHMEN GEIGENKASTEN, m

Menzies, Bryce
WRONG WORLD, p

Menzies, Robert
CACTUS

Meo, Chuck
DOGS IN SPACE

Meo, Paul De
ZONE TROOPERS, p; ZONE TROOPERS, w

Mepham, Viv
FRINGE DWELLERS, THE, makeup

Meppiel, Armand
THERESE

Mer, Giuliano
BAR 51—SISTER OF LOVE; ESTHER

Merabtine, Rachid
TAHOUNET AL SAYED FABRE, ph

Mercader, Teresa
SILK, makeup

Mercedes, Teresa
NAKED VENGEANCE, makeup

Merchant, Ismail
ROOM WITH A VIEW, A, p

Merchet, Laurence
FRENCH LESSON

Mercier, Denise
ELVIS GRATTON, LE KING DES KINGS

Mercier, Jacques
LA FEMME DE MA VIE

Mercier, Laurence
SINCERELY CHARLOTTE

Mercier, Patrice
BLEU COMME L'ENFER, art d; SINCERELY
CHARLOTTE, prod d

Merck, Renate
FORTY SQUARE METERS OF GERMANY, ed

Merck, Wallace
FRIDAY THE 13TH PART VI: JASON LIVES; KING
KONG LIVES

Merckens, Marijke
FLIGHT OF RAINBIRDS, A

Mercure, Marthe
EQUINOXE

Mercure, Monique
QUI A TIRE SUR NOS HISTOIRES D'AMOUR?;
TRAMP AT THE DOOR

Mercurio, Joseph P.
BLUE CITY, spec eff; ONE CRAZY SUMMER, spec eff

Mercurio, Micole
BAD GUYS ; WELCOME TO 18

Mercury, Joseph
MANHUNT, THE, ph

Merea, Valerie
WOLF AT THE DOOR, THE

Meredith, Larry
LOW BLOW

Merengue, Son de
LAS NOCHES DEL CALIFAS, m

Meril, Macha
DUET FOR ONE; SUIVEZ MON REGARD

Merin, Jill D.
BACK TO SCHOOL

Merino, Francisco
LA MITAD DEL CIELO

Merkel, Una
Obituaries

Merkinson, Epatha
SHE'S GOTTA HAVE IT

Merlin, Claudine
MENAGE, ed

Merosi, Paolo
SAVING GRACE; UNA STORIA AMBIGUA

Merritt Jr., Robert
SHORT CHANGED

Merritt, Robert J.
SHORT CHANGED, w

Merritt, Ronald
SHORT CHANGED

Merryman, Terri
DR. OTTO AND THE RIDDLE OF THE GLOOM BEAM

Mertes, Raffaele
AURELIA, ph

Mertin, Anne
DIE NACHTMEERFAHRT

Mertz, Edward
TOUCH AND GO

Mery, Etienne
LA MACHINE A DECOUDRE, art d

Mes, Ruud
FAILURE, THE

Meschi, Dean
NINJA TURF

Meshelski, Tom
TERRORVISION, ed

Mesiatzev, Evgeny
ODINOTCHNOYE PLAVANIYE, w

Mesquita, Theresa
HOT CHILI

Messaggio, Susanna
ITALIAN FAST FOOD

Messer, David
OVER THE SUMMER

Messeri, Marco
IL BI E IL BA

Messick, Don
TRANSFORMERS: THE MOVIE, THE

Messina, Patricia
SAY YES, makeup

Messing, Carol
COLOR OF MONEY, THE; NOTHING IN COMMON

Messner, Anath
MALKAT HAKITA, cos

Messner, Claudia
WELCOME IN VIENNA

Mestheneos, Fotis
I NICHTA ME TI SILENA

Mestre, Marius des
WALKMAN BLUES, m

Mestriner, Marco
SAPORE DEL GRANO

Meszel, Paul
UPHILL ALL THE WAY

Meszlery, Judit
VAKVILAGBAN

Metas, Christopher
STOOGEMANIA

Metayer, Eric
PAULETTE

Metcalf, Mark
ONE CRAZY SUMMER

Metcalf, Ron
NO SURRENDER

Metcalfe, Ken
AMERICAN COMMANDOS; AMERICAN
COMMANDOS, w; P.O.W. THE ESCAPE

Metcalfe, Vince
DANCING IN THE DARK

Metheny, Russell
IMAGEMAKER, THE, art d

Metoyer, Julius
SHADOWS RUN BLACK

Metrano, Art
POLICE ACADEMY 3: BACK IN TRAINING

Metrov, Douglas Anthony
SOLARBABIES, w

Metter, Alan
BACK TO SCHOOL, d

Metz, Barrie
MOVIE HOUSE MASSACRE

Metz, Jason
ROCKIN' ROAD TRIP

Metzman, Irving
MONEY PIT, THE; OFF BEAT; "CROCODILE"
DUNDEE

Meuleman, Clemens
SCORPION

Meulen, Karst van der
THOMAS EN SENIOR OP HET SPOOR VAN BRUTE
BEREND, d; THOMAS EN SENIOR OP HET SPOOR
VAN BRUTE BEREND, ed

Meurisse, Jean-Paul
LES FRERES PETARD, tech adv

Meurisse, Theobald
MENAGE, set d

Meyer, Alejandra
LA TIERRA PROMETIDA

Meyer, Bess
ONE MORE SATURDAY NIGHT

Meyer, Dorothy
HOLLYWOOD VICE SQUAD

Meyer, Hans
MAUVAIS SANG

Meyer, Heidi
FERRIS BUELLER'S DAY OFF

Meyer, Jeff
WEEKEND WARRIORS

Meyer, Marc E.
BEST OF TIMES, THE, set d

Meyer, Matthis
LAPUTA, m

Meyer, Nicholas
STAR TREK IV: THE VOYAGE HOME, w

Meyers, Bill
ARMED AND DANGEROUS, m

Meyers, William
HELL SQUAD

Meyniel, Dagmar
SUIVEZ MON REGARD, p

Meyrow, Shifra
VIOLATED

Meza, Arturo
DONA HERLINDA AND HER SON

Mezzano, Carlo
UNA STORIA AMBIGUA, m

Mezzanotte, Luigi
LA SECONDA NOTTE

Mezzaros, Dave
YOUNGBLOOD

Mhlophe, Gcina
PLACE OF WEEPING

Mi, Kim Ji
GILSODOM

Miakar, Andrej
CHRISTOPHORUS, d

Mialkovszky, Erzsebet
ERZEKENY BUCSU A FEJEDELEMTOL, cos;
VAKVILAGBAN, cos

Miano, Robert
HOLLYWOOD VICE SQUAD

Miao, Cora
PASSION

Michael, Anthony
WOLF AT THE DOOR, THE

Michael, Olive
COMING UP ROSES

Michaelani
BIG TROUBLE

Michaels, Gregory
LAST RESORT, THE

Michaels, Hilly
FAT GUY GOES NUTZOID!!

Michaels, Joel B.
BLACK MOON RISING, p

Michaels, Johnny Lee
VALKOINEN KAAPIO, m

Michaels, Leonard
MEN'S CLUB, THE, w

Michaels, Lori
WHERE ARE THE CHILDREN?

Michaels, Lorne
THREE AMIGOS, p; THREE AMIGOS, w

Michaels, Mickey S.
PSYCHO III, set d

Michaels, Sherman
MANHUNTER

Michailov, V.
PISMA MERTVOGO CHELOVEKA

Michalak, Cathren
AROUND THE WORLD IN EIGHTY WAYS

Michalowski, Janusz
OSOBISTY PAMIETNIK GRZESZNIKA PRZEZ NIEGO
SAMEGO SPISANY

Michas, Jennifer
BOY WHO COULD FLY, THE

Michaud, Francois
MEMOIRES D'UN JUIF TROPICAL

Michaud, Francoise
CONSEIL DE FAMILLE; LA MACHINE A DECOUDRE

Michel, Albert
RATBOY; WILDCATS

Michel, Dominique
DECLINE OF THE AMERICAN EMPIRE, THE

Michel, Ernesto
BAD COMPANY; GERONIMA

Michel, Livia
CONTACTO CHICANO

Michel, Valerie
LE DEBUTANT

Micheli, Maurizio
IL CAMMISSARIO LO GATTO

Michelle, Shaun
ROLLER BLADE

Michelman, Ken
SPIKER

Michelot, Pierre
ROUND MIDNIGHT

Michels, Richard A.
8 MILLION WAYS TO DIE

Michelsen, Katrine
LA BONNE

Michener, Dave
GREAT MOUSE DETECTIVE, THE, d; GREAT MOUSE
DETECTIVE, THE, w

Michettoni, Ennio
ITALIAN FAST FOOD, art d

Michnevich, Anamarie
TAROT, art d

Michoacan, Conjunto
EL SECUESTRO DE LOLA-LOLA LA TRAILERA 2, m

Michotek, Jerzy
CHRZESNISAK

Michtom, Rose
Obituaries

Micula, Stasia
SEX APPEAL

Middleton, Bill
DR. OTTO AND THE RIDDLE OF THE GLOOM BEAM

Middleton, Candy
VIOLATED

Midkiff, Dale
NIGHTMARE WEEKEND

Midler, Bette
DOWN AND OUT IN BEVERLY HILLS; RUTHLESS
PEOPLE

Midnight, Charlie
EYE OF THE TIGER, m/l

Midon, Hugo
INSOMNIACS

Mielke, Sandy
BAND OF THE HAND

Mier, Hermanos
LOS ASES DE CONTRABANDO, m

Migdalek, Jack
ABSOLUTE BEGINNERS

Migliacci, Franco
ABSOLUTE BEGINNERS, m/l

Mignon, Jean-Pierre
CACTUS

Mignone, Toto
GINGER & FRED

Mignot, Heloise
MON CAS

Mignot, Pierre
ANNE TRISTER, ph; BOY IN BLUE, THE, ph

Mihailescu, Florin
SECVENTE; SECVENTE, ph

Mihailescu, Svetlana
SECVENTE, cos; UN OASPETE LA CINA, cos

Mihailovitch, Smilja
PIRATES

Mihalka, George
BLUE MAN, THE, d

Mihara, Junko
CABARET

Mihi, Rafaat El
EL-SADA EL-RIGAL, p, d&w; LEL HAB KESSA
AKHIRA, d&w

Mihic, Gordan
SRECNA NOVA '49, w

Mikaberidze, Ruslan
YOUNG COMPOSER'S ODYSSEY, A

Mikacevic, Svetolik
LIJEPE ZENE PROLAZE KROZ GRAD

Mikaelyan, Sergei
REIS 222, d&w

Mikami, Hiroshi
NEW MORNING OF BILLY THE KID, THE

Mikami, Yuichi
TYPHOON CLUB

Mike the Dog
DOWN AND OUT IN BEVERLY HILLS

Mikesch, Elfi
DER ROSENKONIG, ph; VIRUS HAS NO MORALS, A,
ph

Mikkelborg, Palle
ROUND MIDNIGHT

Mikkelsen, Laila
X, p

Miko
DER SOMMER DES SAMURAI

Mikuc, Hanna
ERZEKENY BUCSU A FEJEDELEMTOL

Mikuni, Rentaro
NINGUEN NO YAKUSOKU

Milaney, Ed
BULLIES

Milani, Marianne
DER PENDLER, art d

Milano, Tom
BREEDERS, m

Miled, Mika Ben
MAN OF ASHES, ed

Miles, Michele
FRINGE DWELLERS, THE

Miles, Sally
Obituaries

Miles, Terry
JO JO DANCER, YOUR LIFE IS CALLING, makeup

Mileti, Nick J.
LADIES CLUB, THE, p

Milford, John
SAY YES

Milford, Kim
WIRED TO KILL

Milhench, Ann
SLOANE

Milian, Tomas
SALOME

Milic, Nikola
LIJEPE ZENE PROLAZE KROZ GRAD

Milicevic, Djordje
TOBY MCTEAGUE, w

Milinaire, Gilles
SALVADOR

Milioto, Stefano
LA SPOSA ERA BELLISSIMA, w

Militka, Hana
LEV S BILOU HRIVOU

Milivojevic, Milivoje
DOBROVOLJCI, ph

Milladoiro
LA MITAD DEL CIELO, m

Millan, Paloma San
ME HACE FALTA UN BIGOTE

Milland, Ray   [Reginald Alfred John Truscott-Jones]
Obituaries; SEA SERPENT, THE

Millar, Henry
STAND BY ME, spec eff

Millenotti, Maurizio
OTELLO, cos

Miller, Alex
DOWN BY LAW

Miller, Andy
FROM BEYOND

Miller, Arlin
ODD JOBS

Miller, Barry
PEGGY SUE GOT MARRIED

Miller, Carlton
MY CHAUFFEUR

Miller, Chris
CLUB PARADISE, w

Miller, Court   [J. Courtlandt Miller]
Obituaries; PLAYING FOR KEEPS

Miller, Dan
TOUCH AND GO

Miller, Daniel
TEXAS CHAINSAW MASSACRE PART 2, THE, art d

Miller, David B.
NIGHT OF THE CREEPS; NIGHT OF THE CREEPS,
makeup

Miller, Dick
ARMED RESPONSE; CHOPPING MALL; NIGHT OF
THE CREEPS

Miller, Donita
DOWN BY LAW, makeup

Miller, Elizabeth
DONNA ROSEBUD

Miller, George
COOL CHANGE, d

Miller, Gorman
BOY IN BLUE, THE

Miller, Helen
HANNAH AND HER SISTERS

Miller, Ira
ARMED AND DANGEROUS

Miller, Josh
STOOGEMANIA

Miller, Julie
HELLFIRE

Miller, Karl G.
PSYCHO III, spec eff

Miller, Lara Jill
TOUCH AND GO

Miller, Lawrence
DESERT BLOOM, art d

Miller, Libby
CLASS OF NUKE 'EM HIGH; FAT GUY GOES
NUTZOID!!

Miller, Lydia
BACKLASH

Miller, Marvin
HELL SQUAD

Miller, Maxine
CARE BEARS MOVIE II: A NEW GENERATION; HEAD
OFFICE

Miller, Merle
Obituaries

Miller, Michael R.
VIOLATED, ed

Miller, Pat
MAXIMUM OVERDRIVE; RAW DEAL; ROCKIN'
ROAD TRIP

Miller, Rima
BEGINNER'S LUCK

Miller, Roger
MAXIMUM OVERDRIVE, m/l

Miller, Scott
INSTANT JUSTICE

Miller, Sherry
SEPARATE VACATIONS

Miller, Steve
PLAYING FOR KEEPS, art d

Miller, Steven E.
ABDUCTED

Miller, Willard
OVER THE SUMMER

Millet, Silvia
BAD COMPANY

Millette, Jean-Louis
INTIMATE POWER

Milli, Robert
PLAYING FOR KEEPS

Milligan, Andy
CARNAGE, d, w&ph

Milliken, Sue
FRINGE DWELLERS, THE, p

Millot, Charles
PARENTAL CLAIM

Mills, Alec
KING KONG LIVES, ph

Mills, Ann E.
BLOODY BIRTHDAY, ed; HAMBURGER, ed

Mills, Bob
DOWN AND OUT IN BEVERLY HILLS, makeup

Mills, John
WHEN THE WIND BLOWS

Mills, Rob
LABYRINTH

Mills, Robert
TOUCH AND GO, makeup

Millward, Wendy
LABYRINTH

Milne, Murray
ARRIVING TUESDAY, ph

Milner, Tony
KNIGHTS AND EMERALDS

Milo, Jean-Roger
LES CLOWNS DE DIEU; SARRAOUNIA

Milosavljevic, Vladica
SRECNA NOVA '49

Mina, Dimitra
SCORPION

Mina, Hana
SUN ON A HAZY DAY, THE, w

Minch, Genevieve
YIDDISH CONNECTION

Minchenberg, Richard
CHECK IS IN THE MAIL, THE; WISDOM

Minello, Gianni
UN RAGAZZO COME TANTI, d&w

Miner, Steve
HOUSE, d; SOUL MAN, d

Minervini, Gianni
LA SPOSA ERA BELLISSIMA, p; SUMMER NIGHT
WITH GREEK PROFILE, ALMOND EYES AND SCENT
OF BASIL, p

Ming, Chan Hou
FAMILY, THE, ph

Ming, Hsu
DARK NIGHT

Ming, Wang
BEI AIQING YIWANGDE JIAOLUO, m

Ming, Wong
ISLE OF FANTASY, ed

Ming, Xin
IN THE WILD MOUNTAINS

Ming-Ming, Sue
DARK NIGHT; SUPER CITIZEN

Mingace, Herb
ONE CRAZY SUMMER

Mingus, Charles
ABSOLUTE BEGINNERS, m/l

Minh, Ho Quang
KARMA, p&d; KARMA, w

Ministeri, George   [George Mirisola Ministeri]
Obituaries

Minkoff, Robert
GREAT MOUSE DETECTIVE, THE, anim

Minn, Haunani
CHECK IS IN THE MAIL, THE

Minnelli, Vincente
Obituaries

Minns, Cheri
AMERICAN ANTHEM, makeup; WILDCATS, makeup

Minooie, Mehrzad
MARE, THE, ed

Minoprio, Minnie
UNA STORIA AMBIGUA

Minor, Bob
MORNING AFTER, THE

Minou, Vana
ALLIGORIA

Minsky, Charles
APRIL FOOL'S DAY, ph; RADIOACTIVE DREAMS, ph;
WEEKEND WARRIORS, ph

Minton, Faith
NAKED CAGE, THE

Minty, David
SHANGHAI SURPRISE, art d

Mintz, Larry
HOLLYWOOD VICE SQUAD; PATRIOT, THE; TOUGH
GUYS

Minuci, Chieli
IN THE SHADOW OF KILIMANJARO, m/l

Minutolo, Antonio
LA CASA DEL BUON RITORNO, ph

Mioni, Sergio
NAME OF THE ROSE, THE, stunts

Mioni, Stefano
UN RAGAZZO COME TANTI

Mioteris, Nicos
TO DENDRO POU PLIGONAME

Miou-Miou
MENAGE

Miracco, Renato
FINAL EXECUTIONER, THE

Miracle, Irene
IN THE SHADOW OF KILIMANJARO; LAST OF
PHILIP BANTER, THE

Miraflor, Joeben
STONE BOY, w

Miramon, Inaki
EL DISPUTADO VOTO DEL SR. CAYO

Mirand, Evan
FIRE WITH FIRE

Miranda, D. Stanton
SOMETHING WILD

Miranda, John
NEVER TOO YOUNG TO DIE

Miranda, Regina
MALANDRO, ch

Miravalles, Reinaldo
EL CORAZON SOBRE LA TIERRA

Mireau, Bob
COMBAT SHOCK

Mireles, Ivar
NEVER TOO YOUNG TO DIE

Miric, Miodrag
LEPOTA POROKA, art d

Mirkin, Abraham
Obituaries

Mirkin, David
LAST RESORT, THE

Mirkovich, Steve
AMERICAN JUSTICE, ed; BIG TROUBLE IN LITTLE
CHINA, ed

Mirmont, Roger
RUE DU DEPART; SUIVEZ MON REGARD

Miro, Pilar
WERTHER, p&d; WERTHER, w

Mirojnick, Ellen
NOBODY'S FOOL, cos

Mirolo, Clary
GIOVANNI SENZAPENSIERI, cos

Mironov, Andrei
MOI DRUG IVAN LAPSHIN

Mironov, Valery
FOUETTE, ph

Mironova, Olga
COME AND SEE

Mirren, Helen
GOSPEL ACCORDING TO VIC, THE; MOSQUITO
COAST, THE

Mirua, Lautaro
POBRE MARIPOSA

Mirvis, Joe
FREE RIDE, set d

Mishkin, Lew
CARNAGE, p

Miskovsky, Gerrod
KGB—THE SECRET WAR

Missbach, Barbara Ann
CLASS OF NUKE 'EM HIGH

Missel, Renee
MY MAN ADAM, p; MY MAN ADAM, w

Missoni
CACTUS, cos

Mitchel, Will
MOUNTAINTOP MOTEL MASSACRE

Mitchell, Aleta
NO MERCY

Mitchell, Angella
JO JO DANCER, YOUR LIFE IS CALLING

Mitchell, Anne
PARTING GLANCES, set d

Mitchell, Cameron
LOW BLOW; TOMB, THE

Mitchell, Casey T.
SPACECAMP, w

Mitchell, Chuck "Porky"
HOLLYWOOD ZAP!

Mitchell, David
BUSTED UP; BUSTED UP, p

Mitchell, Eddy
I LOVE YOU; LA GALETTE DU ROI; ROUND
MIDNIGHT

Mitchell, Eric
DERNIER CRI; WAY IT IS, THE, d&w; WAY IT IS,
THE, p

Mitchell, Gavin
HEAD OFFICE, art d

Mitchell, Gordon
LA CROCE DALLE 7 PIETRE; LE MINIERE DEL
KILIMANGIARO

Mitchell, Heather
MALCOLM

Mitchell, Herb
SCORPION

Mitchell, James
RUNNING SCARED, ed

Mitchell, John
GOSPEL ACCORDING TO VIC, THE

Mitchell, John Cameron
BAND OF THE HAND; ONE MORE SATURDAY
NIGHT

Mitchell, Megan
SEX O'CLOCK NEWS, THE

Mitchell, Peter
MEN'S CLUB, THE, cos

Mitchell, Richard
BORN AMERICAN, m

Mitchell, Sharon
KAMIKAZE HEARTS

Mitchell, Sheila
PASSION OF REMEMBRANCE, THE

Mitchell, Steve
CHOPPING MALL, w

Mitchell, Warren
FOREIGN BODY; KNIGHTS AND EMERALDS

Mitchlll, Scoey
JO JO DANCER, YOUR LIFE IS CALLING

Mitchum, Christopher
AMERICAN COMMANDOS; NO TIME TO DIE

Miti, Michela
DELITTI

Mitler, Matt
BREEDERS

Mitra, Prasad
CHOPPER, art d

Mitra, Subrata
NEW DELHI TIMES, ph

Mitran, Doru
DECLARATIE DE DRAGOSTE, ph

Mitrofanov, Gennadij
BORIS GODUNOV

Mitrovitsa, Redjep
L'AUBE

Mitta, Aleksandr
MUZSKOE VOSPITANIE, art d

Mitterer, Felix
ERDSEGEN, w

Mittleman, Steve
BEER

Miu, Anita
LAST SONG IN PARIS

Miura, Kazuyoshi
COMIC MAGAZINE

Miura, Tomokazu
TYPHOON CLUB

Mixdorf, Gunther
HEIDENLOCHER

Mixon, Bret
TOMB, THE, spec eff

Miyagawa, Kazuo
YARI NO GONZA, ph

Miyamoto, Nobuko
TAMPOPO; THE KARATE KID PART II, ch

Miyashima, Joey
THE KARATE KID PART II

Miyashior, Masao
THRASHIN'

Miyauchi, Fukiko
NINGUEN NO YAKUSOKU, w

Mizerak, Steve
COLOR OF MONEY, THE

Mizrahi, Moshe
EVERY TIME WE SAY GOODBYE, d; EVERY TIME WE
SAY GOODBYE, w

Mizrahi, Shaul
SHTAY ETZBA'OT M'TZIDON

Mizushima, Kaori
YARI NO GONZA

Mjoen, Lars
NOE HEIT ANNET; NOE HEIT ANNET, w

Mkrtchyan, Albert
ZAKONNY BRAK, d

Mlynarska, Paulina
KRONIKA WYPADKOW MILOSNYCH

Mnich, Genevieve
LAST IMAGE, THE

Mnouchkine, Alexandre
JE HAIS LES ACTEURS

Mocky, Jean-Pierre
GRANDEUR ET DECADENCE D'UN PETIT
COMMERCE DE CINEMA; LA MACHINE A
DECOUDRE; LA MACHINE A DECOUDRE, p, d&w

Modena, Domenico
SAVING GRACE

Modo, Michel
L'EXECUTRICE

Modugno, Domenico
ABSOLUTE BEGINNERS, m/l

Modugno, Enrica Maria
IL CASO MORO; INNOCENZA

Moen, Catherine Mee
NUTCRACKER: THE MOTION PICTURE

Moffat, Donald
BEST OF TIMES, THE

Moffatt, George
QUICKSILVER

Mofidi, Roohollah
MONSTER, THE

Mogensen, Grethe
TWIST & SHOUT

Mogherini, Flavio
LA RAGAZZA DEI LILLA, d; LA RAGAZZA DEI
LILLA, w

Mogul, Philip
SPIKER

Mohamed, Abdel Salam
SIKAT SAFAR

Mohamed, Kacem
FLAMING BORDERS, w

Mohamed, Layla
AL ASHEKE

Mohammadi, Esmaiel
MONSTER, THE

Mohammadi, Esmail
FROSTY ROADS

Mohammadi, Firooz Behjat
MARE, THE

Mohammadi, Manijeh
CLOSED CIRCUIT

Mohar, Eli
HAKRAV AL HAVA'AD, m/l

Moharram, Mustapha
EL-GOOA, w

Mohr, Rick
COLOR OF MONEY, THE

Mohr, Rowena
DEATH OF A SOLDIER

Mohrmann, Al
ONE CRAZY SUMMER

Mohsen, Mahmoud
AL BEDAYA, art d

Moir, Richard
WRONG WORLD

Moize, Alain
L'UNIQUE, makeup

Mokrosinski, Peter
GRONA GUBBAR FRAN Y.R., ph; I LAGENS NAMN,
ph

Mol, Albert
OP HOOP VAN ZEGEN

Moland, Peter
TAROT

Molavcova, Jitka
JONAS, DEJME TOMU VE STREDU

Moldovan, Ovidiu Iuliu
DREPTATE IN LANTURI

Molen, Ina van der
ASSAULT, THE

Moletta, Carlos
FULANINHA, p

Molin, Bud
POLICE ACADEMY 3: BACK IN TRAINING, ed

Molina, Alfred
LETTER TO BREZHNEV

Molina, Angela
CAMORRA; EL RIO DE ORO; LA MITAD DEL CIELO;
LA SPOSA ERA BELLISSIMA; LOLA; STREETS OF
GOLD

Molina, Dan
AMERICAN TAIL, AN, ed

Molina, Juan Ramon
ELIMINATORS, spec eff

Molina, Kris
ODD JOBS

Molina, Miguel
DRAGON RAPIDE; EN PENUMBRA

Molina, Monica
LA MITAD DEL CIELO

Molina, Paola
IL MIELE DEL DIAVOLO

Molinero, Mari Paz
EL DISPUTADO VOTO DEL SR. CAYO

Molko, Daniele
PEAU D'ANGE, p

Moll, Richard
HOUSE

Mollberg, Rauni
TUNTEMATON SOTILAS, p&d; TUNTEMATON
SOTILAS, w

Moller, Carl Quist
BARNDOMMENS GADE

Moller-Jensen, Birger
FLAMBEREDE HJERTER, ed

Mollison, Clifford
Obituaries

Mollo, Andrew
NANOU, prod d; NO SURRENDER, prod d

Molloy, Mike
LINK, ph

Molnar, Stanko
BLADE IN THE DARK, A; LA SIGNORA DELLA
NOTTE

Molnar, Tibor
KESERU IGAZSAG

Molteni, Giorgio
AURELIA, d&w

Molvan, Cem
FOURTEEN NUMARA, ph

Molyneaux, Andree
SHOOT FOR THE SUN, p

Mompou, Federico
DEMONER, m

Mona, Ghislaine
THERESE

Monaghan, Phil
WINDRIDER, art d

Monard, Nicolas
UNDER THE CHERRY MOON

Monastrisky, Boris
STREETS OF GOLD

Moncalvo, Mario Buffa
ROMANCE

Mondale, Eleanor
ODD JOBS

Mondshein, Andrew
POWER, ed

Mondy, Pierre
ASTERIX CHEZ LES BRETONS

Moneagle, Kristin
PARTING GLANCES

Moneim, Sabri Abdel
AL BEDAYA

Moneir, Adel
EL-TOUK WA EL-ESSWERA, ed

Monero, Mark
SID AND NANCY

Monette, Richard
DANCING IN THE DARK

Money, Michael
OVER THE SUMMER

Money, "Zoot"
MONA LISA

Monge, Ray
MALA NOCHE

Monguia, Jose
EL VECINDARIO—LOS MEXICANOS CALIENTES, ed

Monheim, Luc
EXIT-EXIL, d&w

Moni, Stefano
MONITORS, m

Monicelli, Mario
LET'S HOPE IT'S A GIRL, d; LET'S HOPE IT'S A
GIRL, w

Monk, Meredith
TRUE STORIES, ch

Monn, Ursela
NOVEMBERKATZEN

Monni, Carlo
SAVING GRACE

Monnier, Valentine
MONSTER SHARK

Monroe, Bill
MONEY PIT, THE, m/l

Monsell, Antonio
EL MALEFICIO II

Montagna, Sandra
UNA CASA IN BILICO, cos

Montagnani, Nerina
IL RAGAZZO DEL PONY EXPRESS

Montagne, Guy
PAULETTE

Montague, Debra
FERRIS BUELLER'S DAY OFF

Montague, Lee
LADY JANE

Montaigu, Sandra
BLEU COMME L'ENFER

Montaldo, Giuliano
L'ISOLA, w

Montanari, Lidia
CASTIGHI; CASTIGHI, d; CASTIGHI, w&ph

Montanari, Sergio
LA BONNE, ed; SCUOLA DI LADRI, ed

Montanaro, Lucio
FOTOROMANZO

Montanaro, Tony
CLAN OF THE CAVE BEAR, THE

Montand, Yves
JEAN DE FLORETTE; MANON DES SOURCES

Montanio, Wayne
BEST OF TIMES, THE; HOLLYWOOD ZAP!;
SOLDIER'S REVENGE

Montano, Arlene
NINJA TURF

Monteforte, Corrado
SCUOLA DI LADRI

Monteiro, Joao Cesar
A FLOR DO MAR, d&w

Monteiro, Luis
MON CAS, art d

Monteiro, Mariana Rey
O VESTIDO COR DE FOGO

Monteiro, Mauro
MALANDRO, md

Montenegro, David
EL EXTRANO HIJO DEL SHERIFF

Montenegro, Fernanda
HOUR OF THE STAR, THE

Montenegro, Hugo
FERRIS BUELLER'S DAY OFF, m/l

Montenegro, Mario
RAGING VENDETTA

Montenegro, Sasha
EL SECUESTRO DE CAMARENA; LAS NOCHES DEL
CALIFAS

Montero, Tony
MURPHY'S LAW

Montes, Michael
SUNSET STRIP

Montes, Morau
LAS NOCHES DEL CALIFAS, p

Montes, Osvaldo
LA GUEPE, m

Montesano, Enrico
GRANDI MAGAZZINI; IL TENENTE DEI
CARABINIERI

Montezuma, Magdalena
DER ROSENKONIG; DER ROSENKONIG, w

Montgomery, George
WILD WIND, THE

Montgomery, John
SOMETHING WILD

Montgomery, Julia
STEWARDESS SCHOOL

Montgomery, Michael
EYE OF THE TIGER, w

Monti, Gerry
LOW BLOW

Monti, Pat
HANDS OF STEEL

Montiel, Roberto
YAKO—CAZADOR DE MALDITOS

Montillier, Georges
LE MOME; PIRATES

Montillor, Ovidi
TEO EL PELIRROJO

Monton, Vincent
WINDRIDER, d

Montoya, Luis Fernando
LA MANSION DE ARAUCAIMA

Montsalvatje, Xavier
DRAGON RAPIDE, m

Monty, Mike
JUNGLE RAIDERS; SILK

Moo-jung, Lee
BBONG

Moo-Song, Jon
GILSODOM

Moody, Che
CARNAGE

Mooney, Debra
AGENT ON ICE

Mooney, Paul
JO JO DANCER, YOUR LIFE IS CALLING, w

Mooney, William
BEER

Moor, Andrea
TRAVELLING NORTH

Moor, Dieter
DER SCHWARZE TANNER

Moorcroft, Judy
CLOCKWISE, cos; FRENCH LESSON, cos; SHANGHAI
SURPRISE, cos

Moore, Alice
PULSEBEAT

Moore, Bennie
OUT OF BOUNDS

Moore, Bill
MONA LISA

Moore, Bob
SORORITY HOUSE MASSACRE

Moore, Dan
CROSSROADS, cos

Moore, Demi
ABOUT LAST NIGHT; ONE CRAZY SUMMER;
WISDOM

Moore, Donald
BLUE VELVET

Moore, Donna
PLAYING FOR KEEPS

Moore, Edgar
COCAINE WARS

Moore, James C.
SCREEN TEST

Moore, John J.
DREAM LOVER, art d

Moore, Jonathan
MY BEAUTIFUL LAUNDRETTE

Moore, Mary Tyler
JUST BETWEEN FRIENDS

Moore, Mitchell
SCREEN TEST

Moore, Muriel
IMPURE THOUGHTS

Moore, Richard
LADY JANE

Moore, Robyn
DOT AND KEETO; DOT AND THE WHALE

Moore, Stephen
CLOCKWISE

Moore, Sue
STAND BY ME, cos

Moore, Tom
'NIGHT, MOTHER, d

Moores, Bill
NO SURRENDER

Mor, Avraham
ALEX KHOLE AHAVA

Mor, Rummel
BIG TROUBLE IN LITTLE CHINA

Mor, Tami
DELTA FORCE, THE, cos

Mora, Danny
STOOGEMANIA

Mora, Juan
CRONICA DE FAMILIA, ed; CRONICA DE FAMILIA, w

Mora, Philippe
DEATH OF A SOLDIER, d

Mora, Rosa Maria
KAPAX DEL AMAZONAS

Moraes, Mariana de
FULANINHA

Morahan, Christopher
CLOCKWISE, d

Morales, Eugenio
LOS HIJOS DE LA GUERRA FRIA

Morales, Felipe
LOS ASES DE CONTRABANDO, w

Morales, Hector
THREE AMIGOS

Morales, Mario de Jesus
LA BANDA DE LOS PANCHITOS

Morales, Santos
BACK TO SCHOOL; THREE AMIGOS; WISDOM

Moran, Dan
OCEAN DRIVE WEEKEND

Moran, Eugenia
DESERT BLOOM

Morandini Jr., Morando
MEGLIO BACIARE UN COBRA, w

Moranis, Rick
CLUB PARADISE; HEAD OFFICE; LITTLE SHOP OF
HORRORS

Morante, Elsa
LA STORIA, w

Morante, Laura
A FLOR DO MAR

Morawiecz, Barbara
DER SEXTE SINN

Morcillo, Gregorio Garcia
ME HACE FALTA UN BIGOTE

Morder, Joseph
MEMOIRES D'UN JUIF TROPICAL; MEMOIRES D'UN
JUIF TROPICAL, p, d&w

More, Carmen
SCORPION

Moreau, Jacqueline
ROUND MIDNIGHT, cos

Moreau, Jean-Luc
LE PASSAGE

Moreau, Jeanne
LE PALTOQUET; SAUVE-TOI, LOLA

Moreau, Philippe
ROUND MIDNIGHT

Moreira, Edgardo
BAD COMPANY; SOLDIER'S REVENGE

Morel, Jean Marc
JAKE SPEED

Morel, Olivier
NUIT D'IVRESSE, ed

Morell, Mihaly
GREAT GENERATION, THE, ed

Morelli, Charles
PLAYING FOR KEEPS

Morelli, Neomi
PERROS DE LA NOCHE

Morelli, Tony
BUSTED UP

Morena, Ita
RUNNING OUT OF LUCK

Moreno, Belita
NOBODY'S FOOL

Moreno, Carlos
SERE CUALQUIER COSA PERO TE QUIERO

Moreno, Eva
MANON

Moreno, Gary
ONE CRAZY SUMMER, set d

Moreno, Jaime
TERROR Y ENCAJES NEGROS

Morett, Gina
LA ALACRANA

Moretti, Mario
MANHATTAN BABY

Moreyra, Margot
DIAPASON

Morgan, Don
HAUNTED HONEYMOON

Morgan, Glen
TRICK OR TREAT

Morgan, Glenn
VENDETTA, ed

Morgan, Maitzi
ADVENTURES OF THE AMERICAN RABBIT, THE

Morgan, Michael
THE KARATE KID PART II

Morgan, Molly
SEX APPEAL

Morgan, Pamela
ADVENTURE OF FAUSTUS BIDGOOD, THE, m

Morgan, Read
JUST BETWEEN FRIENDS; LIGHTNING—THE WHITE
STALLION

Morgan, Riley
SUNSET STRIP, art d

Morgan, Roy
SNO-LINE

Morgan, Tania
PASSION OF REMEMBRANCE, THE

Morgan, Tom Junior
BLUE CITY; BLUE CITY, m/l

Morgan, Tracy
JO JO DANCER, YOUR LIFE IS CALLING

Morgan, Willard
FAT GUY GOES NUTZOID!!

Morgant, Lawrence
MONSTER SHARK

Morgensen, Per
TWIST & SHOUT

Morgenstern, Stephanie
TOBY MCTEAGUE

Mori, Jeanne
TOUGH GUYS

Moriani, Alberto
COBRA MISSION, ed; JUNGLE RAIDERS, ed

Moriarty, Michael
TROLL

Moriceau, Norma
SOMETHING WILD, prod d

Morina, Giovanni
AURELIA, p

Morini, Hector
ANOTHER LOVE STORY, ph

Morishige, Akira
NEW MORNING OF BILLY THE KID, THE, p

Morishita, Kozo
TRANSFORMERS: THE MOVIE, THE, d

Morita, Noriyuki "Pat"
THE KARATE KID PART II

Morita, Yoshimitsu
SOREKARA, d; TOKIMEDI NI SHISU, d&w

Moritz, Dorothea
DIE LIEBESWUSTE; VA BANQUE; WOHIN MIT
WILLFRIED?

Moritz, Louisa
HOT CHILI

Morley, Angela
ABSOLUTE BEGINNERS, m/l

Morley, Glenn
OVERNIGHT, m

Morley, Ruth
MONEY PIT, THE, cos

Moro, Federica
YUPPIES, I GIOVANI DI SUCCESSO

Moroder, Giorgio
MONEY PIT, THE, m/l

Morones, Bob
SALVADOR

Moroni, Breno
BRAS CUBAS

Morosan, Launa
QUICKSILVER

Morphett, Tony
DARK AGE, w

Morphew, Bill
VAMP

Morpurgo, Ponchi
BAD COMPANY, art d

Morra, Mario
CUT AND RUN, ed; IL CAMORRISTA, ed; WILD
BEASTS, ed

Morricone, Ennio
LA VENEXIANA, m; MISSION, THE, m

Morris, Anita
ABSOLUTE BEGINNERS; BLUE CITY; RUTHLESS
PEOPLE

Morris, Bruce M.
GREAT MOUSE DETECTIVE, THE, w

Morris, Gus
OVER THE SUMMER

Morris, John
DEVIL IN THE FLESH; HAUNTED HONEYMOON, m

Morris, Johnathon
SCREAMTIME

Morris, Jonathan
FATHERLAND, ed

Morris, Judy
GOING SANE; MORE THINGS CHANGE, THE

Morris, Lee
BLUE VELVET, m/l

Morris, Leslie
CROSSROADS

Morris, Michael
CLOCKWISE, makeup

Morris, Rolland   [Rolland "Rusty" Morris]
Obituaries

Morrison, Bill
TOUCH AND GO

Morrison, Bruce
QUEEN CITY ROCKERS, d

Morrison, Kathryn Greko
SALVADOR, cos

Morrison, Margaret
SAY YES, ed

Morrison, Wendi
RATBOY

Morriss, Frank
SHORT CIRCUIT, ed

Morrissey, Eamon
EAT THE PEACH

Morrissey, Steven
FERRIS BUELLER'S DAY OFF, m/l

Morse, Judith
LITTLE SHOP OF HORRORS

Morse, Karen
VIOLATED, prod d

Morse, Susan E.
HANNAH AND HER SISTERS, ed

Morsell, Fred
WHATEVER IT TAKES

Morsi, Medhat
AL BEDAYA

Mortensen, Marianne
MANDEN I MAANEN

Mortil, Janine
FIRE WITH FIRE

Mortil, Janne
CLAN OF THE CAVE BEAR, THE

Morton, Bruce
NIGHTMARE WEEKEND

Morton, Gregory
Obituaries

Morton, Joe
CROSSROADS

Morton, Rob
ABDUCTED

Mosaique
HADDA, cos

Moschen, Michael
LABYRINTH, ch

Moschin, Gastone
UNA SPINA NEL CUORE

Moschitta, John
TRANSFORMERS: THE MOVIE, THE

Moschopoulou, Marina
ALLIGORIA

Moschos, Giorgos
ENAS ISICHOS THANATOS

Moschos, Takis
ENAS ISICHOS THANATOS

Moseley, Bill
TEXAS CHAINSAW MASSACRE PART 2, THE

Moseley, Robin
MANHUNTER

Moseley, Ron
SID AND NANCY

Moseng, Eric
STAR CRYSTAL

Moser, Cactus
BACK TO SCHOOL

Moses, Mark
PLATOON

Moshanov, Moni
EVERY TIME WE SAY GOODBYE

Moshen, Dalida
EL YOM EL SADES

Moskoff, John
VASECTOMY: A DELICATE MATTER

Moskowitz, Stewart
ADVENTURES OF THE AMERICAN RABBIT, THE, w

Mosley, Irvin
HOLLYWOOD VICE SQUAD

Moss, Bob
ECHO PARK

Moss, Brent
BUSTED UP

Moss, Larry
PATRIOT, THE

Moss, Lloyd
COLOR OF MONEY, THE

Moss, Millie
HOLLYWOOD ZAP!

Moss, Russell
NIGHT OF THE CREEPS

Mossi, Carlo
AS SETE VAMPIRAS

Most, Donald
STEWARDESS SCHOOL

Mostad, Atle
X

Mostel, Josh
MONEY PIT, THE; STOOGEMANIA

Motevasselani, Mohammad
MIRZA NOWROUZ' SHOES, d

Mothle, Ernest
HAUNTED HONEYMOON

Motomochi, Tomiyuki
YARI NO GONZA, p

Mott, Nicholas
SCHOOL FOR VANDALS

Motta, Maria Cecilia
MALANDRO, cos

Motta, Zeze
JUBIABA; QUILOMBO

Mottrich, Sam
LOYALTIES

Mottura, Alba
SAPORE DEL GRANO

Mouchet, Catherine
THERESE; People to Watch

Mouissie, Alexander
MAMA IS BOOS!

Moukassei, Anatoli
CHICHERIN, ph

Moundroukas, Tony
EAT AND RUN

Mounir, Adel
EL-GOOA, ed; SIKAT SAFAR, ed

Mounir, Mohamad
EL-TOUK WA EL-ESSWERA; EL YOM EL SADES

Mounir, Sherif
AWDAT MOWATIN

Mour, Maher Abdel
LEL HAB KESSA AKHIRA, set d

Moura, Edgar
AVAETE, A SEMENTE DA VINGANCA, ph; HOUR OF
THE STAR, THE, ph

Moura, Gilson
FULANINHA

Mourgues, Ana Victoria
NEMESIO

Mourino, E.
SEVEN MINUTES IN HEAVEN, stunts

Mourino, Edgard
BRIGHTON BEACH MEMOIRS

Mouris, Caroline Ahfors
BEGINNER'S LUCK, p; BEGINNER'S LUCK, w

Mouris, Frank
BEGINNER'S LUCK, d; BEGINNER'S LUCK, w

Mourouzi, Nadia
O MELISSOKOMOS

Mouss
CONSEIL DE FAMILLE

Mousseau, Steve
BUSTED UP

Mowat, Douglas
LAST RESORT, THE, set d; TRICK OR TREAT, set d

Moxedano, Giovanni
SEPARATI IN CASA

Moy, William
SCORPION

Moy, Wood
HOWARD THE DUCK

Moya, Alejandrino
MISSION, THE

Moya, Bercelio
MISSION, THE

Moyer, Peggy
BEST OF TIMES, THE

Moyer, Ray
Obituaries

Moyer, Tawny
FINE MESS, A

Moynot, Bruno
PRUNELLE BLUES

Moyse, Sophie
LA MACHINE A DECOUDRE

Mozafari, Majid
MONSTER, THE

Mozart, Wolfgang Amadeus
BABEL OPERA, OU LA REPETITION DE DON JUAN ,
m; BRODERNA MOZART, m; EHRENGARD, m; EINS
OG SKEPNAN DEYR, m; ELOGIO DELLA PAZZIA, m;
ELYSIUM, m; UNA DONNA SENZA NOME, m

Moznett, Jeffery
LOW BLOW

Mtume, James
NATIVE SON, m

Mueck, Ron
LABYRINTH

Muel, Jean-Paul
PEAU D'ANGE

Mueller, Myke R.
AT CLOSE RANGE; DR. OTTO AND THE RIDDLE OF
THE GLOOM BEAM

Mueller, Peter E.
LISI UND DER GENERAL, m/l

Mueller-Stahl, Armin
ANGRY HARVEST; BLIND DIRECTOR, THE;
FOLLOWING THE FUHRER

Mues, Dietmar
EIN FLIEHENDES PFERD

Muggia, Dan
SMILE OF THE LAMB, THE

Muhamidjanov, Resivoi
GRANNY GENERAL, w

Muhammad, Eddie Mustafa
STREETS OF GOLD

Muhich, Donald F.
DOWN AND OUT IN BEVERLY HILLS

Muhlach, Nino
STONE BOY

Muhri, Renate
DER WILDE CLOWN

Mui, Anita
HAPPY DIN DON

Muir, Domonic
CRITTERS, w

Mujica, Barbara
BAD COMPANY

Mukama, Dorin
NINJA TURF

Mukdasnit, Euthana
PEESUA LAE DOKMAI, d; PEESUA LAE DOKMAI, w

Mukherjee, Pradip
CHOPPER

Mulcahy, Russell
HIGHLANDER, d

Mulconery, Walt
TOUCH AND GO, ed

Mulders, Michel
DE WISSELWACHTER, m

Muldoon, Mic
FAT GUY GOES NUTZOID!!

Mulhern, Matt
ONE CRAZY SUMMER

Mulholland, Mark
NO SURRENDER

Mulisch, Harry
ASSAULT, THE, w

Mulkey, Arthur
FORMULA FOR MURDER, stunts

Mulkey, Randy
MANHUNT, THE

Mull, Martin
BOSS' WIFE, THE

Mullally, Megan
ABOUT LAST NIGHT; LAST RESORT, THE

Mullan, Mairead
BEST MAN, THE

Mullavey, Greg
CHECK IS IN THE MAIL, THE

Muller, Brigitte
EYE OF THE TIGER

Muller, Eric
LES FRERES PETARD, makeup; ON A VOLE CHARLIE
SPENCER!, makeup

Muller, Eve
RADIOACTIVE DREAMS

Muller, Fiorenza
IL BI E IL BA, ed

Muller, Harrison
FINAL EXECUTIONER, THE; THRONE OF FIRE, THE;
VIOLENT BREED, THE

Muller, Marius
HARD ASFALT, m

Muller, Paul
SALOME

Muller, Robby
DOWN BY LAW, ph; LONGSHOT, THE, ph

Muller, Siegelinde
DIE WALSCHE

Muller, Torun
X, prod d

Muller, Uwe
SPRING SYMPHONY

Muller, Vera
VA BANQUE

Muller, Veronique
THERESE

Muller-Hirsch, Elisabeth
DUNKI-SCHOTT

Muller-Stahl, Armin
FRANZA; MOMO

Mulligan, Richard
FINE MESS, A

Mulligan, Terry D.
BOY WHO COULD FLY, THE

Mullins, Peter
SHANGHAI SURPRISE, prod d

Mullner, Charlotte
DIE NACHTMEERFAHRT, ed

Mulot, Claude
Obituaries

Mulrooney, John
RYDER, P.I.

Mulvehill, Charles
8 MILLION WAYS TO DIE, p

Muncke, Christopher
HAUNTED HONEYMOON

Mune, Ian
BRIDGE TO NOWHERE, d; BRIDGE TO NOWHERE, w;
DANGEROUS ORPHANS

Munich Factory
50/50, m

Munio, Celia De
AMIGOS

Munk, Danny de
OP HOOP VAN ZEGEN

Munk, Troels
TWIST & SHOUT

Munns, William
WHAT WAITS BELOW, makeup

Munos, Frank
THRASHIN', spec eff

Munoz, Amparo
EN PENUMBRA; LULU DE NOCHE

Munoz, Blanca Lidia
EL EXTRANO HIJO DEL SHERIFF

Munoz, Carlos
ANOTHER LOVE STORY

Munoz, Ernesto
LOS HIJOS DE LA GUERRA FRIA

Munoz, Eunice
REPORTER X

Munoz, Evita
SE SUFRE PERO SE GOZA

Munoz, Graciela
HOT CHILI, makeup

Munoz, Hektor
FAT GUY GOES NUTZOID!!

Munoz, Jose Martin
SCORPION

Munoz, Juan Carlos
EL MALEFICIO II, spec eff

Munoz, Margarita
EIN BLICK—UND DIE LIEBE BRICHT AUS

Munoz, Margarita Maria
SAN ANTONITO

Munoz, Sigfrido Garcia
QUE ME MATEN DE UNA VEZ, ed; THANATOS, ed

Munoz-Alonso, Angel
LULU DE NOCHE, m

Munro, Neil
CONFIDENTIAL; DANCING IN THE DARK

Munski, Mark
THRASHIN'

Munson, Brad
SUNSET STRIP, w

Munson, Warren
BIG TROUBLE

Munt, Jesus
EL SUIZO—UN AMOUR EN ESPAGNE

Munt, Silvia
EL SUIZO—UN AMOUR EN ESPAGNE

Munzar, Ludek
LEV S BILOU HRIVOU

Muoz, Rufino
GERONIMA

Mura, Hisako
ARMED RESPONSE

Mura, Roberto
WOMEN'S PRISON MASSACRE

Murai, Kunihiko
TAMPOPO, m

Murakami, James
LUCAS, art d

Murakami, Jimmy T.
WHEN THE WIND BLOWS, d

Murase, Sachiko
NINGUEN NO YAKUSOKU

Murcia, Felix
DRAGON RAPIDE, set d; EL CABALLERO DEL
DRAGON, art d; EL HERMANO BASTARDO DE DIOS,
art d

Murcott, Derek
EAT AND RUN

Murdaca, Domenico
IL GIARDINO DEGLI INGANNI, ph

Murdoch, George
SOLDIER'S REVENGE

Murdock, Jack
PSYCHO III

Murgia, Tiberio
IL RAGAZZO DEL PONY EXPRESS

Muriel, Darren
NINJA TURF

Murillo, Enrique
EL NARCO—DUELO ROJO, ed; LAS NOCHES DEL
CALIFAS, ph; YAKO—CAZADOR DE MALDITOS, ed

Murney, Christopher
MAXIMUM OVERDRIVE; WHERE ARE THE
CHILDREN?

Muroi, Shigeru
NEW MORNING OF BILLY THE KID, THE

Murphey, Michael S.
TRICK OR TREAT, p; TRICK OR TREAT, w

Murphy, E. Danny
FINAL MISSION

Murphy, Eddie
GOLDEN CHILD, THE

Murphy, Edward D.
MANHATTAN PROJECT, THE

Murphy, Fred
HOOSIERS, ph

Murphy, Harry
RETURN

Murphy, Joan
BAND OF THE HAND

Murphy, John
DEATH OF A SOLDIER; DEVIL IN THE FLESH

Murphy, Larry
JO JO DANCER, YOUR LIFE IS CALLING

Murphy, Maezie
CLASS OF NUKE 'EM HIGH

Murphy, Martha
LUCAS

Murphy, Michael
SALVADOR

Murphy, Mike
PERILS OF P.K., THE

Murphy, Paul
DEAD-END DRIVE-IN, ph

Murphy, Renee
FLYING

Murphy, Rob E.
SCREAMPLAY

Murphy, Robert
JUDGEMENT IN STONE, A, m

Murphy, Roberta
SCREAMPLAY, set d

Murphy, Thomas
BREEDERS, ph

Murphy, Walter
PULSEBEAT, m

Murray, Bill
LITTLE SHOP OF HORRORS

Murray, Don
PEGGY SUE GOT MARRIED; RADIOACTIVE
DREAMS; SCORPION

Murray, Felipe
CINEMA FALADO

Murray, Forrest
AMERICA

Murray, Graeme
BOY WHO COULD FLY, THE, art d

Murray, Guillermo
ES MI VIDA—EL NOA NOA 2

Murray, Joel
ONE CRAZY SUMMER

Murray, John B.
DEVIL IN THE FLESH, p

Murray, Juleen
SHADOW PLAY

Murray, Linda
AMERICAN JUSTICE

Murray, Lolo
PA LIV OCH DOD, makeup

Murray, Michael
AMERICAN JUSTICE

Murray, Patricia
SCORPION

Murray, Patty
AMERICAN JUSTICE

Murray, Peter
AMERICAN JUSTICE

Murray, Ryan
FLIGHT OF THE NAVIGATOR

Murray, Scott
DEVIL IN THE FLESH, d&w

Murray, Sean
SCORPION, m

Murray, William
HELLFIRE, d&w

Murray-Leach, Roger
CLOCKWISE, prod d

Murrey, John B.
DR. OTTO AND THE RIDDLE OF THE GLOOM BEAM

Murrillo, Enrique
LOS ASES DE CONTRABANDO, ed

Murry, James
SOLDIER'S REVENGE

Murtinho, Rita
O HOMEM DA CAPA PRETA, art d; O HOMEM DA
CAPA PRETA, cos; SONHO SEM FIM, cos

Murton, Peter
KING KONG LIVES, prod d

Muscat, Mike
CLAN OF THE CAVE BEAR, THE; MODERN GIRLS;
PATRIOT, THE

Musch, Jan
PERVOLA: TRACKS IN THE SNOW, p

Muse, Joseph
DR. OTTO AND THE RIDDLE OF THE GLOOM BEAM

Musgos, Los
LA BANDA DE LOS PANCHITOS

Music, Lorenzo
ADVENTURES OF THE AMERICAN RABBIT, THE

Musick, Pat
AMERICAN TAIL, AN

Musker, John
GREAT MOUSE DETECTIVE, THE, d; GREAT MOUSE
DETECTIVE, THE, w

Muskus, Ana
ALMACITA DI DESOLATO

Musser, Larry
LOYALTIES

Musson, Bernard
PIRATES

Mustafic, Mustafa
I TO CE PROCI, ph

Mustapha, Hasam
SIKAT SAFAR

Mustapha, Niazi
Obituaries

Mustin, Thomas R.
SORORITY HOUSE MASSACRE

Musumarra, Romano
LA FEMME DE MA VIE, m

Musy, Alain
LE PASSAGE

Mutanen, Pertti
VALKOINEN KAAPIO, ph

Muti, Ornella
GRANDI MAGAZZINI

Mutierrez, Alfredo
MATANZA EN MATAMOROS

Mutis, Ivaro
LA MANSION DE ARAUCAIMA, w

Mutti, Luis
EL RIGOR DEL DESTINO, ed

Muu, Tran Dinh
KARMA, ph

Muzio, Francesca
IL MOSTRO DI FIRENZE

Mwendwa, Estrild
KNIGHTS AND EMERALDS

Myagkov, Aleksandr
ODINOTCHNOYE PLAVANIYE, art d

Myers, Ruth
HAUNTED HONEYMOON, cos

Myers, Stanley
CASTAWAY, m; LIGHTSHIP, THE, m; SECOND
VICTORY, THE, m

Myhrdal, Pia
YES, DET ER FAR!, cos

Mylett, Jeffrey
MY MAN ADAM

Mylonas, Alexandros
ALCESTES

Mylones, Alexi
HARDBODIES 2

N'Guyen, Thi Loan
POLICE, makeup

Naaim, Ikbal
HOB FEE BAGHDAD

Nabonsal, Jedd
MY MAN ADAM

Nacaracci, Duse
COM LICENCA, EU VOU A LUTA

Nada
PARTING GLANCES

Nadarevic, Mustafa
DOBROVOLJCI; VECERNJA ZVONA

Nadasy, Laszlo
KESERU IGAZSAG, w

Nadler, Rudolf
TAGEDIEBE

Nadon, Claire
EVIXION; EVIXION, w

Nadoolman, Deborah
THREE AMIGOS, cos

Nadotti, Nelson
SONHO SEM FIM, w

Naeslund, Mikael
MOA

Naff, Lycia
CLAN OF THE CAVE BEAR, THE

Nag, Bidyut
CHOPPER

Nag, Pantu
CHOPPER, ph

Naganuma, Mitsuo
CYOEI NO MURE, ph

Nagari, Benny
SHTAY ETZBA'OT M'TZIDON, m

Nagata, Yuichi
TO SLEEP SO AS TO DREAM, ed; TO SLEEP SO AS TO
DREAM, ph

Nagayama, Ken
NINJA TURF

Nagle, William
DEATH OF A SOLDIER, p; DEATH OF A SOLDIER, w

Nagy, Christina
FORMULA FOR MURDER

Nagy, Zoltan
ELYSIUM

Naha, Ed
TROLL, w

Nahan, Mark
TOUCH AND GO

Naidu, Ajay
TOUCH AND GO; WHERE THE RIVER RUNS BLACK

Naidu, Leela
TRIKAL

Nail, Jimmy
SHOOT FOR THE SUN

Nair, B.K.
ANANTARAM; MUKHAMUKHAM

Nair, Chandran
ORIDATH

Najem
AL ASHEKE, art d

Nakai, Kiichi
KINEMA NO TENCHI; SHIN YOROKOBIMO
KANASHIMIMO IKUTOSHITSUKI

Nakamoto, Tatsuo
TO SLEEP SO AS TO DREAM

Nakamoto, Tsuneo
TO SLEEP SO AS TO DREAM

Nakamura, Katsuo
SOREKARA

Nakano, Desmond
BLACK MOON RISING, w

Nakaya, Noburo
LOVE LETTER

Nakazawa, Katsumi
TOKIMEDI NI SHISU, prod d

Nakhapietov, Rodion
TORPIDONOSTCI

Nakkara-Hadad, Salwa
NADIA

Nalleck, Daniel
MURPHY'S LAW

Name, Hernando
HOT CHILI, stunts

Namiki, Hiroyuki
UEMURA NAOMI MONOGATARI, ph

Namson, Jamie
WISDOM

Nan, Kuan Yi
HUAJIE SHIDAI

Nana
HARDBODIES 2

Nance, Jack
BLUE VELVET

Nancy
WHAT COMES AROUND

Nangle, Bruce
MOVIE HOUSE MASSACRE

Nanni, Pedro
O HOMEM DA CAPA PRETA, set d

Nannini, Gianna
DEMONER, m

Nannuzzi, Armando
MAXIMUM OVERDRIVE, ph

Nantel, Linda
RECRUITS

Nanty, Isabelle
ON A VOLE CHARLIE SPENCER!

Napier, Carla
CRAZY MOON

Napier, Charles
INSTANT JUSTICE; SOMETHING WILD

Napier, Eve
CRAZY MOON

Napier, Marshall
FOOTROT FLATS

Naples, Toni
CHOPPING MALL

Napoli, Anna
SEPARATI IN CASA, ed

Napoli, Manna Di
AMORE INQUIETO DI MARIA, m

Napoli, William J.
QUICKSILVER

Napolitano, Silvia
IL BI E IL BA, w

Naranjo, Jorge
PEQUENA REVANCHA, ph

Narayama
HELL SQUAD

Nardino, Gary
FIRE WITH FIRE, p

Nardo, Donna
CLASS OF NUKE 'EM HIGH

Nardone, Sebastiano
CAMORRA

Narita, Hiro
FIRE WITH FIRE, ph

Narros, Miguel
LOS PARAISOS PERDIDOS

Narusawa, Mamoru
ORA TOKYO SA YUKUDA, art d

Nascimento, Jose
REPORTER X, ed; REPORTER X, p&d; REPORTER X,
w

Naseri, Fereydoon
BEYOND THE MIST, m

Nash, Chris
MODERN GIRLS; WRAITH, THE

Nash, Michael
COLOR OF MONEY, THE

Nasr, Moshen
AL DAHIYA, ph; EL YOM EL SADES, ph

Nasr, Soad
AL BEDAYA

Nasrallah, Nahed
EL YOM EL SADES, cos

Nass, Halvor
NOE HEIT ANNET, ph

Nasseri, Freydoun
MIRZA NOWROUZ' SHOES, m

Nassi, Joe
SORORITY HOUSE MASSACRE

Nassiri, Majid
FROSTY ROADS

Nassirian, Ali
FROSTY ROADS; MIRZA NOWROUZ' SHOES

Nasta, Nick
COMBAT SHOCK

Nastasi, Frank
EAT AND RUN

Naszinski, Lara
BLADE IN THE DARK, A

Natali, Germano
MONSTER SHARK, spec eff

Natalucci, Giovanni
CRAWLSPACE, prod d; FROM BEYOND, prod d;
SAVING GRACE, prod d

Natalucci, Judy
SAVING GRACE

Natan, Mischa
DAS SCHWEIGEN DES DICHTERS

Natelli, Jay
FAT GUY GOES NUTZOID!!

Natera, Jose
ESE LOCO LOCO HOSPITAL

Nathan, Adam
PARTING GLANCES; STREETS OF GOLD

Nathan, Adele   [Adele Gutman Nathan]
Obituaries

Nathenson, Zoe
MONA LISA

Natili, Claudio
IL MIELE DEL DIAVOLO, m

Nations, Mike
ROCKIN' ROAD TRIP

Natividad, Kitten
TOMB, THE

Natsume, Masako
CYOEI NO MURE

Natsume, Soseki
SOREKARA, w

Natwick, Myron
HEAD OFFICE

Naudon, Jean-Francois
LE COMPLEXE DU KANGOUROU, ed

Nauer, Bernard
NUIT D'IVRESSE, d

Nauffts, Geoffrey
MANHATTAN PROJECT, THE

Naughton, David
BOY IN BLUE, THE; SEPARATE VACATIONS

Naulin, John
FROM BEYOND, spec eff

Naval, Deepti
MIRCH MASALA

Navaretto, Javier
CAGED GLASS, m

Navarro, Guillermo
AMOR A LA VUELTA DE LA ESQUINA, ph

Navarro, Miguel
UN HOMBRE DE EXITO

Navas, Erika
SCHMUTZ, cos

Navoa, J. Erastheo
STONE BOY, d

Nay, Igor
GOING SANE, prod d

Nay, Louise Le
MORE THINGS CHANGE, THE

Naylor, Jason
STAND BY ME

Nazare, Ecaterina
PASO DOBLE

Nazarro, Ray   [Raymond Nazarro]
Obituaries

Nazli, Nilgun
KUYUCAKLI YUSUF

Nazzareno, Natale
SAVING GRACE

Ne'eman, Yehiel
P.O.W. THE ESCAPE, ph; SHTAY ETZBA'OT
M'TZIDON, ph

Neagle, Anna   [Florence Marjorie Robertson]
Obituaries

Neal, Billie
DOWN BY LAW

Neal, Chris
AROUND THE WORLD IN EIGHTY WAYS, m;
BULLSEYE, m; SHORT CHANGED, m

Neal, Rome
OFF BEAT

Nealy, Ron
AMERICA

Neam, Jack
HEARTBURN

Neame, Ronald
FOREIGN BODY, d

Nebb, Andrej
X, m

Nebbia, Litto
BAD COMPANY, m

Nebe, Chris D.
NAKED CAGE, THE, p

Nebolini, Renato
NAME OF THE ROSE, THE

Nebout, Claire
LA FEMME SECRETE; SCENE OF THE CRIME

Nedd, Priscilla
LUCAS, ed

Nedelcu, Ion
DECLARATIE DE DRAGOSTE, art d; LICEENI, art d

Nedia
8 MILLION WAYS TO DIE, makeup

Needham, Hal
RAD, d

Needham, Peter
CLOCKWISE

Needles, Nique
DOGS IN SPACE

Neely, Alistair
COOL CHANGE

Neely, Mark
STEWARDESS SCHOOL

Neeson, Liam
DUET FOR ONE; MISSION, THE

Negby, Barak
AMERICA 3000

Negolli, Faruk
PROKA

Negri, Gino
L'ULTIMA MAZURKA, m

Negri, Nanda Pucci
GINGER & FRED

Negron, Alberto
HOT CHILI, prod d

Negron, Taylor
ONE CRAZY SUMMER; WHOOPEE BOYS, THE

Nehm, Kristina
FRINGE DWELLERS, THE

Neiches, Robert
ABOUT LAST NIGHT

Neidorf, David
HOOSIERS; PLATOON

Neil, Alex
MANHUNTER

Neill, Sam
FOR LOVE ALONE

Neill, Ve
RADIOACTIVE DREAMS, makeup

Neilson, Bill
GREAT WALL, A

Neilson, David
KNIGHTS AND EMERALDS

Neilson, Philip
BOY IN BLUE, THE

Neitzel, Edith
TRANSITTRAUME

Nejedly, Milan
BORIS GODUNOV, prod d

Nelka, Rose-Marie
RUE DU DEPART, cos

Nell, Nathalie
ETATS D'AME

Nelska, Liliana
WELCOME IN VIENNA

Nelson, Anders
MR. VAMPIRE, m

Nelson, Andrew
FOREIGN BODY, ed

Nelson, Bob
RYDER, P.I.; RYDER, P.I., w; YAKO—CAZADOR DE
MALDITOS

Nelson, Byron
SCORPION

Nelson, Colleen
SCORPION

Nelson, Craig T.
POLTERGEIST II

Nelson, Ed
POLICE ACADEMY 3: BACK IN TRAINING

Nelson, Elizabeth
SCORPION

Nelson, Felix
BLUE CITY; STEWARDESS SCHOOL

Nelson, Fred A.
BEST OF TIMES, THE

Nelson, George R. "Bob"
BIG TROUBLE IN LITTLE CHINA, set d

Nelson, Greg
RATBOY, makeup

Nelson, James D.
TRICK OR TREAT

Nelson, John J.
FIRE WITH FIRE, m/l

Nikitaidis, Christos
ENAS ISICHOS THANATOS

Nikkenin, Amanda
SHORT CHANGED

Nikkonen, Harri
KUNINGAS LAHTEE RANSKAAN

Niklas, Jan
FRANZA

Nikolic, Dragan
OBECANA ZEMLJA

Nikolic, Zivko
LEPOTA POROKA, d&w

Nikolov, Miaden
ROMANTICHNA-ISTORIJA, d

Nikonenko, Sergei
ZIMNI VECHER V GAGRAKH

Nilsen, Marianne
HARD ASFALT

Nilsson, Goran
DEMONER, ph; DEN FRUSNA LEOPARDEN, ph

Nilsson, Stefan
MORRHAR OCH ARTOR, m; ORMENS VAG PA
HALLEBERGET, m

Nimchareonpong, Panya
PEESUA LAE DOKMAI, ph

Nimoy, Leonard
STAR TREK IV: THE VOYAGE HOME; STAR TREK IV:
THE VOYAGE HOME, d; TRANSFORMERS: THE
MOVIE, THE

Nina, Ilva
MALANDRO

Nineteen, Johnny
SEX APPEAL

Ning, Chang
TIME TO LIVE AND A TIME TO DIE, A

Nini, Diane
THE KARATE KID PART II, m/l

Ninidze, Mirab
SAPIRHURIN

Nino, Miguel A.
COLOR OF MONEY, THE

Nirenberg, Les
POLICE ACADEMY 3: BACK IN TRAINING

Nirvana, Yana
ECHO PARK

Nishida, Toshiyuki
UEMURA NAOMI MONOGATARI

Nishizawa, Nobutaka
ADVENTURES OF THE AMERICAN RABBIT, THE, d

Niskanen, Tuija-Maija
SUURI ILLUSIONI, d

Nissen, Claus
BARNDOMMENS GADE

Nissen, Richard Egede
DROMMESLOTTER

Nissl, Toni
VA BANQUE, m

Nitsch, Regina
ROMANCE

Nitzsche, Jack
9½ WEEKS, m; STAND BY ME, m; STREETS OF
GOLD, m; STRIPPER, m; WHOOPEE BOYS, THE, m

Niva, Tero
TUNTEMATON SOTILAS

Nix, Tom
DR. OTTO AND THE RIDDLE OF THE GLOOM BEAM

Nixon, Cynthia
MANHATTAN PROJECT, THE

Nobecourt, Jerome
PARIS MINUIT

Nobercourt, Agnes
SAVING GRACE

Noble, Ray
MONA LISA, m/l

Noble, Roger
SILK

Noble, Thom
MOSQUITO COAST, THE, ed; POLTERGEIST II, ed

Noble, Tom
BLACK JOY, ed

Noci, Cristina
LA VENEXIANA

Noel, Magali
EXIT-EXIL

Nofal, Emil
Obituaries

Nogisto, Jaanus
IDEAALMAASTIK, m

Nogueira, Joao
QUILOMBO

Nogueras, Luis Rogelio
COME LA VIDA MISMA, w

Noguschi, Donna L.
BIG TROUBLE IN LITTLE CHINA

Noiret, Philippe
LA FEMME SECRETE; LET'S HOPE IT'S A GIRL;
NEXT SUMMER; ROUND MIDNIGHT; TWIST AGAIN
A MOSCOU

Nojgard, Anne
MANDEN I MAANEN

Nola, Ante
SAN O RUZI, art d

Nolan, Barry
KING KONG LIVES, spec eff

Nolan, Lloyd
HANNAH AND HER SISTERS

Nolan, Robin
MY CHAUFFEUR

Nolden, Gunther
AM NACHESTEN MORGEN KEHRTE DER MINISTER
NICHT AN SEINEN ARBEITSPLATZ

Nolfo, Andy
COLOR OF MONEY, THE

Nollas, Demetris
ALCESTES, w

Nollas, Dimitris
O MELISSOKOMOS, w

Nolot, Jacques
DOUCE FRANCE; SCENE OF THE CRIME; ZONE
ROUGE

Nolte, Nick
DOWN AND OUT IN BEVERLY HILLS

Nomad, Michael
FRIDAY THE 13TH PART VI: JASON LIVES

Nomad, Mike
APRIL FOOL'S DAY

Nomura, Hironobu
CABARET

Nomura, Yoshitaro
KINEMA NO TENCHI, p

Nonno, Carlo De
FINAL EXECUTIONER, THE, m

Nono, Clare
TRICK OR TREAT

Nono, Luigi
UN HOMBRE DE EXITO, m

Noonan, Gregory
RAW DEAL

Noonan, Kerry
FRIDAY THE 13TH PART VI: JASON LIVES

Noonan, Polly
FERRIS BUELLER'S DAY OFF

Noonan, Polly Augusta
LUCAS

Noonan, Tom
F/X; MANHUNTER

Noor, Soekarno M.
TITAN SERAMBUT DIBELAH TUJUH

Noori, Ali Reza Shoja
BEYOND THE MIST

Noort, Sanne van der
MAMA IS BOOS!

Norby, Ghita
WOLF AT THE DOOR, THE

Norden, Peter Van
BEST OF TIMES, THE

Nordheim, Arne
HUD, m

Nordike, Mark
ODD JOBS

Nordkvist, Elisabeth
ALLA VI BARN I BULLERBY

Nordlund, Solveig
MOA, ed

Nordone, Terri
SCREAMPLAY

Nordstrom, Christer
GRONA GUBBAR FRAN Y.R.

Nordstrom, Roger
GRONA GUBBAR FRAN Y.R.

Noren, Lars
DEMONER, w

Norena, Anel
GAVILAN O PALOMA

Norena, Manolo
GAVILAN O PALOMA

Noriega, Ricardo
RAFAGA DE PLOMO

Noris, Bruno
IL MOSTRO DI FIRENZE, p

Norman, Marsha
'NIGHT, MOTHER, w

Norman, Nicole
INSIDE OUT

Norman, Wayne
OVER THE SUMMER

Norman, Zack
AMERICA

Normandine, Guylaine
QUI A TIRE SUR NOS HISTOIRES D'AMOUR?

Norris, Buckley
HIGHLANDER; LONGSHOT, THE

Norris, Carolina
EL RIO DE ORO

Norris, Chuck
DELTA FORCE, THE; FIREWALKER

Norris, Guy
DEAD-END DRIVE-IN, stunts

Norris, Jane
EMMA'S WAR, art d

Norris, Mike
BORN AMERICAN

Norris, Patricia
BEST OF TIMES, THE, cos; BLUE VELVET, prod d;
FINE MESS, A, cos; SPACECAMP, cos; WHOOPEE
BOYS, THE, cos

North, Alan
BILLY GALVIN; HIGHLANDER

North, Anna
FOR LOVE ALONE

North, Jay
WILD WIND, THE

Northcott, William
LIGHTNING—THE WHITE STALLION, set d

Norton, Alex
COMRADES

Norton, Charles
DR. OTTO AND THE RIDDLE OF THE GLOOM BEAM

Norton, Escott O.
STOOGEMANIA, spec eff

Norton, Rosanna
NOTHING IN COMMON, cos; RUTHLESS PEOPLE, cos

Norup, Lise-Lotte
MORD I MORKET

Norway, Hot Club of
MACARONI BLUES

Nosibov, Sergei
ODINOTCHNOYE PLAVANIYE

Nossik, Vladimir
CHTO U SENJKI BYLO

Noterman, Mitchelle
LA MOITIE DE L'AMOUR, art d

Noth, Christopher
OFF BEAT

Noth, Dana Lee
SCREEN TEST

Nottingham, Lisa
HELL SQUAD

Nougaro, Pierre
JEAN DE FLORETTE

Nouny, Alain
LEPOTA POROKA

Noura
SIKAT SAFAR

Nourafchan, Tori
PATRIOT, THE, set d

Noureddine, Mouna
MAN OF ASHES

Nouri, Michael
GOBOTS: BATTLE OF THE ROCKLORDS;
IMAGEMAKER, THE

Nourollahi, Houchang
MIRZA NOWROUZ' SHOES, p

Nova, Eliska
BORIS GODUNOV, cos

Novak, Blaine
GOOD TO GO, d&w

Novak, Jasna
OBECANA ZEMLJA, cos

Novak, John
BLUE MAN, THE

Novaro, Augusto
CONTACTO CHICANO, w

Novarro, Pablo
LA NOCHE DE LOS LAPICES

Novat, Patricia
ON A VOLE CHARLIE SPENCER!, p

Novat, Pierre
ON A VOLE CHARLIE SPENCER!, p

Novecento, Nik
UNA DOMENICA SI

Novell, Rosa
MES ENLLA DE LA PASSIO

Novello, Don
HEAD OFFICE

Novembre, Tom
SUIVEZ MON REGARD; SUIVEZ MON REGARD, m

Novotny, Michael
FLIGHT OF THE NAVIGATOR, art d

Nowak, Christopher
SWEET LIBERTY, art d

Nowark, Vera
UNTERMEHMEN GEIGENKASTEN, ed

Nowell, Justin
FRIDAY THE 13TH PART VI: JASON LIVES

Nowell, Tommy
FRIDAY THE 13TH PART VI: JASON LIVES

Nowland, Ray
DOT AND KEETO, anim

Noyan, Engin
KIRLANGIC FIRTINASI, m

Noyes-Kyriazis
GIRL FROM MANI, THE, p

Nozhkin, Mikhail
ODINOTCHNOYE PLAVANIYE

Ntshinga, Thoko
PLACE OF WEEPING

Nubile, Carl
SHADOWS RUN BLACK

Nugent, John
SCORPION

Numminen, N.A.
BRODERNA MOZART

Nunes, Bene
AS SETE VAMPIRAS

Nunes, Bia
BRAS CUBAS

Nunez, Miguel
DANGEROUSLY CLOSE

Nunez, Miguel A.
JUMPIN' JACK FLASH

Nunn, Alice
TRICK OR TREAT

Nunn, Trevor
LADY JANE, d

Nunn, William
ABDUCTED; BULLIES

Nunnery, Hope
KING KONG LIVES

Nunzio, Marc De
CHOKE CANYON

Nuora, Annika
GRONA GUBBAR FRAN Y.R.

Nuryadi
NO TIME TO DIE, spec eff

Nussbaum, Karl Erich
SCREAMPLAY

Nussbaumer, Sally
ROCKIN' ROAD TRIP

Nuti, Al
PERILS OF P.K., THE

Nutt, John
NUTCRACKER: THE MOTION PICTURE, ed

Nutu, Dan
STREETS OF GOLD

Nuyen, Robin
DEADLY FRIEND

Nuys, Ed Van
POWER

Nuytten, Bruno
JEAN DE FLORETTE, ph; MANON DES SOURCES, ph

Nyamgwaaa, N.
BI CHAMD KHAYRTAY, w

Nyberg, Borje
MORRHAR OCH ARTOR

Nyberget, Hissa
NOE HEIT ANNET, m

Nye, Ben
ARMED AND DANGEROUS, makeup; DESERT BLOOM, makeup

Nye, Ben, Sr.
Obituaries

Nyholm, Torsti
BORN AMERICAN, set d

Nykvist, Sven
DREAM LOVER, ph; SACRIFICE, THE, ph

Nyman, Lena
MORRHAR OCH ARTOR

Nyoohansiang
SECANGKIR KOPI PAHIT, p

Nype, Russell
BALBOA

Nyquist, Arild
MACARONI BLUES

Nyroos, Gunilla
MOA

O'Banion, Brie
ABOUT LAST NIGHT

O'Bannon, Dan
ALIENS, w; INVADERS FROM MARS, w

O'Brian, Donal
NAME OF THE ROSE, THE

O'Brian, Kerry
VENDETTA

O'Brian, Peter
INTRUDER, THE

O'Brien, Bernadette
HOUSE, cos; THRASHIN', cos

O'Brien, Doc
NO SURRENDER

O'Brien, Donald
HANDS OF STEEL; PANTHER SQUAD

O'Brien, Joseph J.
PLAYING FOR KEEPS

O'Brien, Lauri
ADVENTURES OF THE AMERICAN RABBIT, THE

O'Brien, Niall
HALF MOON STREET

O'Brien, Paul
WHERE ARE THE CHILDREN?

O'Brien, Skip
ECHO PARK

O'Brien, Ted
WHERE ARE THE CHILDREN?

O'Callaghan, Matthew
GREAT MOUSE DETECTIVE, THE, w

O'Connell, Eddie
ABSOLUTE BEGINNERS

O'Connell, Jerry
STAND BY ME

O'Connell, Natalie
BREEDERS

O'Connell, Patricia
SEVEN MINUTES IN HEAVEN

O'Connell, Taaffe
HOT CHILI

O'Connell, William
STEWARDESS SCHOOL

O'Connor, Christopher
TONGS—A CHINATOWN STORY

O'Connor, Dennis
DANGEROUSLY CLOSE, ed; RADIOACTIVE DREAMS, ed

O'Connor, Gary
BUSTED UP

O'Connor, Hazel
CAR TROUBLE

O'Connor, Justin Sean
SCREAMPLAY

O'Connor, Kevin J.
ONE MORE SATURDAY NIGHT; PEGGY SUE GOT MARRIED

O'Connor, Marilyn
THUNDER RUN

O'Connor, Ray
BEER

O'Connor, Steve
NO SURRENDER

O'Dell, Tony
CHOPPING MALL; THE KARATE KID PART II

O'Donnell, Tara
CRAZY MOON

O'Donnell, Tim
TOUCH AND GO

O'Donoghue, Anne
CLOSE TO HOME, art d

O'Donoghue, Michael
HEAD OFFICE

O'Dougherty, Brian
BACK TO SCHOOL

O'Farrell, Marc
QUI A TIRE SUR NOS HISTOIRES D'AMOUR?, m

O'Guinne, Michael
HOOSIERS

O'Haco, Danny
AMERICAN JUSTICE

O'Haco, Jeff
THREE AMIGOS

O'Haco, Kathleen
STEWARDESS SCHOOL

O'Hanlon, George
THE KARATE KID PART II

O'Har, Turas
FRIDAY THE 13TH PART VI: JASON LIVES

O'Hara, Catherine
HEARTBURN

O'Hara, Corky
FLIGHT OF THE SPRUCE GOOSE, ed

O'Hara, Dave
ARMED RESPONSE

O'Hara, David
LINK

O'Hara, Karen
ONE MORE SATURDAY NIGHT, set d

O'Hara, Karen A.
COLOR OF MONEY, THE, set d

O'Hara, Terence
DEVASTATOR, THE; NAKED VENGEANCE

O'Herlihy, Dan
WHOOPEE BOYS, THE

O'Keefe, Karla
BIG HURT, THE, makeup

O'Keefe, Michael
WHOOPEE BOYS, THE

O'Laughlin, Gerald S.
QUICKSILVER

O'Leary, Jack
FINE MESS, A

O'Leary, John
MY CHAUFFEUR; STEWARDESS SCHOOL

O'Malley, Beth
GIRLS SCHOOL SCREAMERS

O'Mara, Mollie
GIRLS SCHOOL SCREAMERS

O'Meara, C. Timothy
HOOSIERS, ed

O'Neal, Cynthia
HEARTBURN

O'Neal, Griffin
APRIL FOOL'S DAY; WRAITH, THE

O'Neans, Douglas F.
INSTANT JUSTICE, ph

O'Neil, David Michael
TOUGH GUYS

O'Neil, Norris
SEX APPEAL

O'Neil, Robert Vincent
WHAT WAITS BELOW, w

O'Neill, Angela
SORORITY HOUSE MASSACRE

O'Neill, Dick
MOSQUITO COAST, THE

O'Neill, Maggie
MONA LISA

O'Neons, Douglas F.
SNO-LINE, d

O'Quinn, Terry
SPACECAMP

O'Ree, Robert
BUSTED UP

O'Reilly, Cyril
BLOODY BIRTHDAY

O'Reilly, Terry
DEAD END KIDS

O'Ross, Ed
SEVEN MINUTES IN HEAVEN

O'Rourke, Heather
POLTERGEIST II

O'Rourke, Michael
QUICKSILVER

O'Shea, Dan
FLIGHT OF THE SPRUCE GOOSE; STREETS OF GOLD

O'Steen, Sam
HEARTBURN, ed

O'Sullivan, Maureen
HANNAH AND HER SISTERS; PEGGY SUE GOT MARRIED

O'Sullivan, Moya
PLAYING BEATIE BOW

O'Sullivan, Thaddeus
ROCINANTE, ph

O'Toole, Donald
CLASS OF NUKE 'EM HIGH

O'Toole, Katy
ROCKIN' ROAD TRIP

O'Toole, Peter
CLUB PARADISE

Oakley, Kenneth
ASSAULT, THE

Oates, John
ABOUT LAST NIGHT, m/l

Oates, Mark
AMERICAN ANTHEM

Obaha, Zohra
HADDA

Ober, Arlon
BLOODY BIRTHDAY, m; HOT CHILI, m/l; IN THE
SHADOW OF KILIMANJARO, m

Oberoi, Suresh
MIRCH MASALA

Obolensky, Leonid
SVESAS KAISLIBAS

Obon, Ramon
ESE LOCO LOCO HOSPITAL, w

Obregon, Ana
KILLING MACHINE

Obst, David
WHOOPEE BOYS, THE, w

Ocal, Tarik
BIR AVUO CENNET, m

Ocampo, Oscar Cardozo
NIGHTMARE'S PASSENGERS, m

Occhipinti, Andrea
BLADE IN THE DARK, A

Ochoa, Ana Maria
EL TREN DE LOS PIONEROS

Ochoa, Antonio Jose
MONSTER DOG, ed

Oczion, Milena
HEIDENLOCHER

Oczlon, Walter
HEIDENLOCHER

Oda, Akira
CYOEI NO MURE, p

Oddsson, Hilmar
EINS OG SKEPNAN DEYR; EINS OG SKEPNAN DEYR,
d&w; EINS OG SKEPNAN DEYR, ed; EINS OG
SKEPNAN DEYR, m

Odjig, Allison
VISAGE PALE

Oeby, Kalle
BLACKOUT; NATTSEILERE

Oegard, Philip
DROMMESLOTTER, ph

Oehlke, Thomas
FATHERLAND

Oestergaard, Soren
FLAMBEREDE HJERTER

Oestermann, Gregoire
MON CAS

Offrein, Frederich
JONSSONLIGAN DYKER UPP IGEN

Ofir, Uri
AVANTI POPOLO, m

Ogaard, Philip
FAREWELL ILLUSION, ph

Oganesyan, Bagrat
KHOZIAIN, d

Oganyan, N.
KHOZIAIN, ed

Ogata, Ken
CYOEI NO MURE; KATAKU NO HITO

Ogata, Satoru
KONEKO MONOGATARI, p

Ogden, Jennifer
MANHATTAN PROJECT, THE, p

Ogier, Bulle
MON CAS

Ogilvie, George
SHORT CHANGED, d

Ogles, Beverlee
DR. OTTO AND THE RIDDLE OF THE GLOOM BEAM

Oguz, Orhan
ADI VASFIYE, ph; AMANSIZ YOL, ph

Ohana, Claudia
LES LONGS MANTEAUX; MALANDRO

Ohanneson, Jill
ELIMINATORS, cos; HOLLYWOOD VICE SQUAD, cos;
TROLL, cos

Ohara, Reiko
SHIN YOROKOBIMO KANASHIMIMO IKUTOSHITSUKI

Ohman, Kip
HITCHER, THE, p

Ohnishi, Yuka
TYPHOON CLUB

Ohrt, Christoph M.
WOHIN MIT WILLFRIED?

Ohtani, Nobuyoshi
SHIN YOROKOBIMO KANASHIMIMO
IKUTOSHITSUKI, p

Ohye, Tsuruko
THE KARATE KID PART II

Oizumi, Akira
TO SLEEP SO AS TO DREAM

Ojeda, Manuel
EL MALEFICIO II

Okac, Oldrich
BORIS GODUNOV, prod d

Okada, Hiroshi
TOKIMEDI NI SHISU, p

Okada, Yutaka
COMIC MAGAZINE, p

Okai, Zorak
HAUNTED HONEYMOON

Okamoto, Hayao
SHIN YOROKOBIMO KANASHIMIMO IKUTOSHITSUKI

Okamura, Gerald
BIG TROUBLE IN LITTLE CHINA

Okay, Yaman
FORTY SQUARE METERS OF GERMANY;
KURBAGALAR

Okazaki, Kozo
SHIN YOROKOBIMO KANASHIMIMO
IKUTOSHITSUKI, ph

Oken, Stuart
ABOUT LAST NIGHT, p

Okeyev, Tolomush
DESCENDANT OF THE SNOW LEOPARD, THE, d&w

Oksanen, Leila
FLIGHT NORTH, cos

Okugawa, Daria
SALVADOR

Okumoto, Yjui
CHECK IS IN THE MAIL, THE

Okumoto, Yuji
THE KARATE KID PART II

Olaciregui, Julio
LA MANSION DE ARAUCAIMA, w

Olafsson, Jon
EINS OG SKEPNAN DEYR, p

Olandt, Ken
APRIL FOOL'S DAY

Olavanetta, Ramon
AVENGING FORCE

Olbrychski, Daniel
ROSA LUXEMBURG

Olcay, Zuhal
AMANSIZ YOL

Old, John
MONSTER SHARK, d; MORIRAI A MEZZANOTTE, d;
MORIRAI A MEZZANOTTE, ed; MORIRAI A
MEZZANOTTE, w

Oldman, Gary
SID AND NANCY; People to Watch

Oldoini, Enrico
UNA SPINA NEL CUORE, w

Oldoni, Enrico
I LOVE YOU, w

Olea, Pedro
BANDERA NEGRA, d; BANDERA NEGRA, w

Olech, Adam
HEILT HITLER!, ph

Oleska
BILLY GALVIN, cos

Olfson, Ken
CHECK IS IN THE MAIL, THE; FREE RIDE; ODD
JOBS

Olga, Elga
TWIST & SHOUT

Olgeirsson, Fridgeir
EINS OG SKEPNAN DEYR

Olha, Matus
SIESTA VETA

Olin, Lena
FLIGHT NORTH; PA LIV OCH DOD

Oliney, Ron
JO JO DANCER, YOUR LIFE IS CALLING, stunts

Olivas, Max
PLAYING FOR KEEPS

Oliveira, Paulo Sergio
WHERE THE RIVER RUNS BLACK

Oliver, Christoph
TAROT, m

Oliver, David
NIGHT OF THE CREEPS

Oliver, Deanna
JUMPIN' JACK FLASH

Oliver, James
AMERICAN ANTHEM, ed

Oliver, Jason
STAND BY ME

Oliver, Mike
DR. OTTO AND THE RIDDLE OF THE GLOOM BEAM

Oliver, Pom
BIGGLES, p

Oliver, Robin Martin
LADY JANE

Oliver, Rochelle
ON VALENTINE'S DAY

Oliver, Stephen
LADY JANE, m

Olivera, Hector
COCAINE WARS, d&w; LA NOCHE DE LOS LAPICES,
d; LA NOCHE DE LOS LAPICES, w

Oliverio, James
IMPURE THOUGHTS, m

Olivieri, Roberta
GIURO CHE TI AMO

Oljelund, Ivan
MOA

Ollie the Fish
LONGSHOT, THE

Olmi, Boy
INSOMNIACS

Olmos, Edward James
SAVING GRACE

Olofsson-Carmback, Helena
ALLA VI BARN I BULLERBY, makeup

Olschewski, Gerhard
50/50; DER POLENWEIHER

Olsen, Allen
BALLERUP BOULEVARD

Olsen, Carla
BLUE CITY

Olsen, Eirin
DROMMESLOTTER, cos

Olsen, Gary
RAW DEAL

Olsen, Kristin
SOMETHING WILD

Olsen, Leila Hee
BAD GUYS ; VAMP

Olsen, Martin Spang
MORD I MORKET

Olsen, Merritt
DEADLY FRIEND

Olsen, Ollie
DOGS IN SPACE, md

Olsen, William
ROCKIN' ROAD TRIP, d; ROCKIN' ROAD TRIP, p;
ROCKIN' ROAD TRIP, w

Olson, Gerald T.
BLOODY BIRTHDAY, p; QUIET COOL, p

Olson, Reid
NUTCRACKER: THE MOTION PICTURE

Olson, Steve
THRASHIN'

Olsonoski, Steve
BAD GUYS

Olsson, Claes
SUURI ILLUSIONI, p

Olsson, Evelyn
TAKE IT EASY, cos

Olsson, Gunilla
MALACCA

Olsson, Ola
LOVE ME!, w

Omartian, Michael
BUSTED UP, m/l; THE KARATE KID
PART II, m/l

Omilami, Afemo
MONEY PIT, THE; MONEY PIT, THE

Omori, Shin
TOKIMEDI NI SHISU, p

Ondricek, Miroslav
F/X, ph

Onesa, Anda
NOI, CEI DIN LINIA INTII; PASO DOBLE

Onishi, Whitney
NUTCRACKER: THE MOTION PICTURE

Ono, Katsuo
COMIC MAGAZINE, m

Onofre, Waldir
RUNNING OUT OF LUCK

Ontiveros, Asuncion
MISSION, THE

Ooms, Amanda
BRODERNA MOZART

Ophir, Shai K.
AMERICA 3000

Opoku, Michael
MOSQUITO COAST, THE

Opolski, Nicholas
FOR LOVE ALONE

Oppenheim, Rich
FAT GUY GOES NUTZOID!!

Opper, Don
BLACK MOON RISING; CRITTERS

Oqvist, Jan
AMOROSA, art d

Orachelashvili, Ketevan
YOUNG COMPOSER'S ODYSSEY, A

Oraev, Dyrdymamet
MUZSKOE VOSPITANIE

Oramas, Nelson
BAND OF THE HAND

Oran, Bulent
KUYUCAKLI YUSUF

Oranen, Raija
RIISUMINEN, w

Orava Family
BORN AMERICAN

Orbach, Jerry
F/X; IMAGEMAKER, THE

Orban, Gyorgy
ORDOGI KISERTETEK, m

Orbison, Roy
BLUE VELVET, m/l

Orbit, William
YOUNGBLOOD, m

Orchid, Ellen
CARNAGE

Ordish, Mary
KNIGHTS AND EMERALDS

Ordonez, Victor
SLOANE

Oresta, Gordon
OCEAN DRIVE WEEKEND

Orfei, Lara
DELITTI

Orfini, Mario
SEPARATI IN CASA, p

Orgambide, Carlos
INSOMNIACS, d; INSOMNIACS, w

Orgolini, Arnold
HOLLYWOOD VICE SQUAD, p

Orgolini, Lisa
TRICK OR TREAT

Orieux, Ron
SHADOW PLAY, ph; TRAMP AT THE DOOR, ph

Orlandi, Ferdinando
UNA DOMENICA SI

Orlando, Antonio
DER ROSENKONIG

Orlov, Dal
CAPABLANCA, w

Orlovki, Dimitri
CAPABLANCA

Orman, Rick
BUSTED UP

Orman, Roscoe
F/X

Ormeny, Tom
AGENT ON ICE

Ormieres, Jean-Luc
HIGH SPEED, p

Ormrod, Peter
EAT THE PEACH, d; EAT THE PEACH, w

Ormsby, Alan
TOUCH AND GO, w

Oropesa, Elizabeth
KILLING OF SATAN, THE

Oroz, Alfredo
HOUR OF THE STAR, THE, w

Orr, Bill
TOBY MCTEAGUE, spec eff

Orr, James
TOUGH GUYS, w

Orr, James R.
WITCHFIRE, p; WITCHFIRE, w

Orr, Lindsey
WILDCATS

Orrison, Brad
PLAYING FOR KEEPS

Orry, Marie-Christine
LE BONHEUR A ENCORE FRAPPE

Orso, Anna
IL DIAVOLO IN CORPO; IL MOSTRO DI FIRENZE; LA VITA DI SCORTA

Ort-Snep, Josef
ANGRY HARVEST, ph

Ortacio, Clarisa
PLATOON

Ortamo, Heikki
KUNINGAS LAHTEE RANSKAAN

Ortega, Anna
SCORPION

Ortega, Enrique
EL AMOR BRUJO

Ortega, Gonzalo Martinez
ES MI VIDA—EL NOA NOA 2, d&w

Ortega, Kenny
FERRIS BUELLER'S DAY OFF, ch; PRETTY IN PINK, ch

Ortegon, Angela Maria
A LA SALIDA NOS VEMOS

Orthel, Rolf
AFZIEN, p

Orthwaite, Mark
JAKE SPEED

Ortin, Polo
ESE LOCO LOCO HOSPITAL

Ortiz, Humberto
THREE AMIGOS

Ortiz, Martha
TERROR Y ENCAJES NEGROS

Ortiz, Miguel
EN PENUMBRA

Ortiz, Susan
CARNAGE

Ortolani, Riz
L'INCHIESTA, m; LA BONNE, m; REGALO DI NATALE, m; UNA DOMENICA SI, m

Orton, Harold
TERRY ON THE FENCE, p

Orwig, Bob
PLATOON

Orzabal, Roland
THE KARATE KID PART II, m/l

Orzechowski, Witold
DEATH SENTENCE, d&w

Osada, Chizuko
KONEKO MONOGATARI, ed

Osborn, Sally
HAUNTED HONEYMOON

Osborne, Glenys
DOGS IN SPACE

Osborne, Smith
PATRIOT, THE

Osbourne, Ozzy
TRICK OR TREAT

Osburn, Gordon A.
SEA SERPENT, THE, w

Oscarsson, Per
HUD; NATTSEILERE

Oscarsson, Pia
DEMONER

Oses, Fernando
SE SUFRE PERO SE GOZA, w

Oshima, Nagisa
MAX MON AMOUR, d; MAX MON AMOUR, w

Oskamp, Helmut
SPRING SYMPHONY

Oskarsdottir, Valdis
EINS OG SKEPNAN DEYR, ed

Oskarsson, Larus
DEN FRUSNA LEOPARDEN, d; DEN FRUSNA LEOPARDEN, ed

Osmon, Rebecca
NUTCRACKER: THE MOTION PICTURE

Osmond, Steve
RECRUITS

Osorio, Javier Cruz
EL JUEGO DE LA MUERTE, ph

Ospina, Luis
LA MANSION DE ARAUCAIMA

Ossard, Claudie
BETTY BLUE, p; CHARLOTTE FOR EVER, p

Ossenfort, Kurt
WORKING GIRLS, prod d

Ossenkopp, Barbara
AUF IMMER UND EWIG

Osswold, Wolfhard
WOHIN MIT WILLFRIED?, ph

Ostalot, Luis
BANDERA NEGRA

Ostashenko, Yevgeni
POTERYALSYA SLON, d; POTERYALSYA SLON, w

Osten, Suzanne
BRODERNA MOZART, d; BRODERNA MOZART, w

Ostergren, Pernilla W.
ORMENS VAG PA HALLEBERGET

Osterhage, Jeff
SKY BANDITS

Osterrieth, Marie Pascale
GENESIS, p

Ostojic, Dubravka
ZA SRECU JE POTREBNO TROJE

Ostry, Samantha
CLAN OF THE CAVE BEAR, THE

Otake, Koji
TO SLEEP SO AS TO DREAM

Otaki, Shuji
TAMPOPO

Otelo, Grande
JUBIABA; NEM TUDO E VERDADE; QUILOMBO; RUNNING OUT OF LUCK

Otero, Isabelle
L'AMANT MAGNIFIQUE

Otmezguine, Jacques
PRUNELLE BLUES, d&w; PRUNELLE BLUES, d&w, w

Ottavis, Irene
JE HAIS LES ACTEURS, makeup

Ottesen, Anne Marie
MACARONI BLUES

Otto, Barry
MORE THINGS CHANGE, THE

Otto, Miranda
EMMA'S WAR

Ottoni, Filippo
DETECTIVE SCHOOL DROPOUTS, d

Oudry, Pierre
L'EXECUTRICE

Oulton, Bawnie
ADVENTURE OF FAUSTUS BIDGOOD, THE, set d

Ourabi, Jamila
AL-KAS

Outinen, Kati
KUNINGAS LAHTEE RANSKAAN

Ovcharov, Sergei
NEBYVALSHINA, d&w

Ovchinnikov, Vyacheslav
BORIS GODUNOV, m

Ove, Horace
PLAYING AWAY, d

Oven, Margot von
FOLLOWING THE FUHRER, ed

Overgaard, Peter Hesse
FLAMBEREDE HJERTER

Overton, Bill
BEST OF TIMES, THE

Overton, Rick
FINE MESS, A; GUNG HO; MODERN GIRLS; ODD JOBS

Owen, Donna
FOXTRAP

Owen, Jennifer
NUTCRACKER: THE MOTION PICTURE

Owen, Lyla Kay
AVENGING FORCE

Owen, Sion Tudor
HIGHLANDER

Owens, Charlie
STAND BY ME

Owens, Dennis
IMAGEMAKER, THE

Owens, Harry
Obituaries

Owens, Rusty
ROCKIN' ROAD TRIP

Oz, Frank
LABYRINTH; LITTLE SHOP OF HORRORS, d

Ozawa, Kazunari
TO SLEEP SO AS TO DREAM

Ozdemiroglu, Atilla
ADI VASFIYE, m; KURBAGALAR, m

Ozdogru, Nuvit
ANNE TRISTER

Oze, Lajos
KOJAK BUDAPESTEN; ORDOGI KISERTETEK

Ozer, Muammer
BIR AVUO CENNET, p, d

Ozog, Freedom
NUTCRACKER: THE MOTION PICTURE

Ozolinia, Vizme
SVESAS KAISLIBAS

Ozsahin, Huseyin
BIR AVUO CENNET, ph

Ozsda, Erika
SIESTA VETA

Paataschwili, Lewan
ROBINSONIADA ANU CHEMI INGLISELI PAPA, ph

Paatashvili, Levan
YOUNG COMPOSER'S ODYSSEY, A, ph

Paavilainen, Heikki
KUNINGAS LAHTEE RANSKAAN

Pacadis, Alain
LES FRERES PETARD

Pace, Arnaldo di
GERONIMA, m

Pace, Ron
TOUCH AND GO

Pacelli, Joseph
OUT OF BOUNDS, set d

Pacey, Ann
DANGEROUS ORPHANS

Pacheco, Antonio
AS SETE VAMPIRAS, makeup; AS SETE VAMPIRAS, spec eff

Pacheco, Arlette
EL DIA DE LOS ALBANILES II; EL SECUESTRO DE CAMARENA

Pacheco, Marc
NIGHTMARE WEEKEND

Pachorek, Richard
KGB—THE SECRET WAR; TRICK OR TREAT

Pacifici, Federico
IL MOSTRO DI FIRENZE

Packard, Jake
VIOLATED

Paddle, Heidi
COCAINE WARS

Padilla, Raul
ESE LOCO LOCO HOSPITAL

Padovani, Lea
EHRENGARD

Padovano, Nina
3:15, THE MOMENT OF TRUTH, cos

Padron, Carmencita
PEQUENA REVANCHA

Paduraru, Adrian
DECLARATIE DE DRAGOSTE

Paerchs, Henrik
BORN AMERICAN, ph

Paez, Jorge Lopez
DONA HERLINDA AND HER SON, d&w

Pagan, Jose Manuel
LOLA, m

Page, Barbara
RAW DEAL, makeup

Page, Bradley
Obituaries

Page, Geraldine
NATIVE SON

Page, Grant
JAKE SPEED, stunts

Page, Laurel
MY LITTLE PONY

Page, Marnie
HYPER SAPIEN: PEOPLE FROM ANOTHER STAR, w

Page, Richard
FINE MESS, A, m/l

Page, Stephen
KNIGHTS AND EMERALDS

Pagni, Riccardo
ELOGIO DELLA PAZZIA

Pagnol, Marcel
JEAN DE FLORETTE, w; MANON DES SOURCES, w

Pagnoni, Paolo
45MO PARALLELO, p; ROMANCE, p

Pahernik, Albin
ABSOLUTE BEGINNERS

Pahl, Ulrike
WELCOME IN VIENNA, ed

Pai, Suzee
BIG TROUBLE IN LITTLE CHINA

Paige, Alain
TAXI BOY, d&w

Paige, Sheila
NOBODY'S FOOL

Pain, Keith
LINK, art d

Painchaud, Brian   [Brian Roger Painchaud]
Obituaries

Paine, Aime
GERONIMA, m

Pais, Joao
MON CAS, m

Paiva, Manoel
FILME DEMENCIA, m

Paiva, Onezio
FULANINHA, w

Pajala, Turo
PIMEYS ODOTTA

Pajic, Ksenija
ZA SRECU JE POTREBNO TROJE

Pak, Christine
90 DAYS

Pak, Master Ho Sik
3:15, THE MOMENT OF TRUTH

Pakkasvirta, Jaakko
LINNA, d&w; LINNA, d&w; VALKOINEN KAAPIO

Pakula, Alan J.
DREAM LOVER, d; DREAM LOVER, p

Pakulnis, Maria
JEZIORO BODENSKIE

Palacio, Luis
MOSQUITO COAST, THE

Palacios, German
NIGHTMARE'S PASSENGERS

Palacios, Ricardo
MONSTER DOG

Paladino, Tommaso
GIURO CHE TI AMO

Palaez, Juan
ESE LOCO LOCO HOSPITAL

Palaizidis, Tassos
CARAVAN SARAI

Palance, Holly
BEST OF TIMES, THE

Palanci, Hulta
LAND OF DOOM

Palau, Carlos
A LA SALIDA NOS VEMOS, d; A LA SALIDA NOS VEMOS, w

Palau, Esperanza
A LA SALIDA NOS VEMOS, p

Paley, Ron
SHE'S GOTTA HAVE IT, art d

Palillo, Ron
FRIDAY THE 13TH PART VI: JASON LIVES

Pallenberg, Barbara
LEGAL EAGLES

Pallete, Leonie
LABYRINTH

Palmateer, Jeff
YOUNGBLOOD

Palme, Beatrice
FOXTRAP

Palmeira, Marcos
FULANINHA

Palmer, Debbie
KNIGHTS AND EMERALDS

Palmer, Elizabeth
SOLDIER'S REVENGE

Palmer, Gary
LITTLE SHOP OF HORRORS

Palmer, Geoffrey
CLOCKWISE

Palmer, Gretchen
CROSSROADS

Palmer, Janet
PASSION OF REMEMBRANCE, THE

Palmer, John
DOT AND KEETO, m; DOT AND KEETO, w; DOT AND THE WHALE, w

Palmer, Norman
Obituaries

Palmer, Patrick
CHILDREN OF A LESSER GOD, p

Palmer, R.
ABSOLUTE BEGINNERS, m/l

Palmer, Robert
MORNING AFTER, THE, m/l

Palmero, Rafael
EL DISPUTADO VOTO DEL SR. CAYO, set d

Palmieri, Marie
PARENTAL CLAIM

Palmisano, Conrad E.
BUSTED UP; BUSTED UP, d; TOUGH GUYS, stunts

Palmqvist, Lars
SACRIFICE, THE, spec eff

Palo, Elisabet
LOVE ME!

Palo, Jukka-Pekka
FLIGHT NORTH; HUOMENNA

Palok, Sandor
KISMASZAT ES A GEZENGUZOK

Palomino, Juan
LES LONGS MANTEAUX

Palotai, Eva
VAKVILAGBAN, ed

Palsdottir, Kristin
EINS OG SKEPNAN DEYR, ed

Palsikar, Suhas
GURU DAKSHINA

Palsson, Sigudur Sverrir
EINS OG SKEPNAN DEYR, ph

Palsson, Sigurdur
EINS OG SKEPNAN DEYR

Paluch, Beata
SCENY DZIECIECE Z ZYCIA PROWINCJI

Palud, Herve
LES FRERES PETARD, d; LES FRERES PETARD, w

Palumir, Raul
HOT CHILI, spec eff

Pan, Kwang
TAI-PAN

Panagopoulou, Vassia
O MELISSOKOMOS

Panahi, Farid
NO RETREAT, NO SURRENDER

Panajotovic, Ika
WILD WIND, THE, p

Panarella, Angelo
SAVING GRACE

Panassenkova, Vera
POTERYALSYA SLON

Panayotatos, Demetris
I NICHTA ME TI SILENA, p&d; I NICHTA ME TI SILENA, w

Panchitos, Los
LA BANDA DE LOS PANCHITOS

Panelli, Paolo
GRANDI MAGAZZINI

Pang, May
HEARTBURN

Pani, Corrado
FRANCESCA E MIA

Pani, Nada
DO YOU REMEMBER DOLLY BELL?

Panicali, Francesca
CUT AND RUN, set d&cos

Panieri, Livio
STORIA D'AMORE

Pankau, Justus
DAS SCHWEIGEN DES DICHTERS, ph

Pankin, Stuart
DIRT BIKE KID, THE

Pankratov-Chyorny, Aleksandr
ZIMNI VECHER V GAGRAKH

Pannach, Gerulf
FATHERLAND; FATHERLAND, m

Pannequin, Guy
GARDIEN DE LA NUIT

Pantazica, Elena
DECLARATIE DE DRAGOSTE, ed

Pantoja, Diego
EL AMOR BRUJO

Pantoliano, Joe
RUNNING SCARED

Panza, Piero
MONITORS; MONITORS, d&w

Panzer, William N.
HIGHLANDER, p

Paola, Carlos
GERONIMA, w

Paolercio, Domenico
AMORE INQUIETO DI MARIA, ph; DELITTI, ph

Paoli, Dennis
FROM BEYOND, w

Paoli, Gino
LA SPOSA AMERICANA, m

Paoli, Marco
ELOGIO DELLA PAZZIA

Penguin Cafe Orchestra, The
MALCOLM, m/l

Penhollow, Emily
NUTCRACKER: THE MOTION PICTURE

Peniche, Alejandra
ESE LOCO LOCO HOSPITAL

Penido, Antonio
FULANINHA, ph

Penn, Christopher
AT CLOSE RANGE

Penn, Matthew
DREAM LOVER; PLAYING FOR KEEPS

Penn, Sean
AT CLOSE RANGE; SHANGHAI SURPRISE

Penney, Allan
AROUND THE WORLD IN EIGHTY WAYS

Penney, John
TORMENT, ed

Penney, Julian
TWO FRIENDS, ph

Pennington, Donald
WHERE THE RIVER RUNS BLACK, spec eff

Penny, Joe
BLOODY BIRTHDAY

Penny, Julian
TRAVELLING NORTH, ph

Penny, Sydney
HYPER SAPIEN: PEOPLE FROM ANOTHER STAR

Pensa, Rita
UN RAGAZZO COME TANTI

Penso, Rina
ALMACITA DI DESOLATO

Pentti, Pauli
PIMEYS ODOTTA, p&d; PIMEYS ODOTTA, w

Penttila, Matti
SUURI ILLUSIONI, p

Penzer, Jean
MENAGE, ph

Pepin, Pierre-Yves
EQUINOXE, w

Pepiot, Ken
BAND OF THE HAND, spec eff

Pepitone, Ed
COMBAT SHOCK

Pera, Edgar
REPORTER X, w

Peracaula, Jaume
CAGED GLASS, ph

Peradze, Giya
YOUNG COMPOSER'S ODYSSEY, A

Perathoner, Serge
LE COMPLEXE DU KANGOUROU, m

Percival, Edward
TAI-PAN, cos

Percy, Lee
FROM BEYOND, ed; TROLL, ed

Perdigon, Leticia
EL MERCADO DE HUMILDES

Pereda, Lucy
AMIGOS

Perego, Didi
CATTIVI PIERROT

Pereio, Paolo Cesare
UNA NOTTE DI PIOGGIA

Pereio, Paulo Cesar
RUNNING OUT OF LUCK

Pereira, Christin
ZONE ROUGE

Pereira, Cristina
BRAS CUBAS

Pereira, Hamilton Vaz
CINEMA FALADO

Pereira, Jun
AMERICAN COMMANDOS, ph

Pereira, Tonico
O HOMEM DA CAPA PRETA; RUNNING OUT OF LUCK

Pereira, Zeni
RUNNING OUT OF LUCK

Peretti, Huge
FINE MESS, A, m/l

Peretz, Susan
POLTERGEIST II

Perevra, Rene
SALVADOR

Perez, Fernando
ME HACE FALTA UN BIGOTE, makeup

Perez, Inez
AMERICAN JUSTICE

Perez, Jose R.
COME LA VIDA MISMA, p

Perez, Michel
ROUND MIDNIGHT

Perez, Patrick
L'AMANT MAGNIFIQUE

Perez, Tim
LOW BLOW

Perez, Vincent
GARDIEN DE LA NUIT

Pergament, Robert
FINE MESS, A, ed

Pergola, James
WHAT COMES AROUND, ph

Pergolese, Giovanni
CACTUS, m

Pericolo, Elizabeth
HARDBODIES 2

Perini, Franco
LA RAGAZZA DEI LILLA, m

Perisic, Zoran
SKY BANDITS, d

Perkins, Anthony
PSYCHO III; PSYCHO III, d

Perkins, Elizabeth
ABOUT LAST NIGHT

Perkins, Jo
UPHILL ALL THE WAY

Perkins, Kent
BREEDERS

Perkins, Millie
AT CLOSE RANGE; JAKE SPEED

Perkins, Rob
MALCOLM, prod d

Perkins, Wayne
THE KARATE KID PART II, m/l

Perlich, Max
FERRIS BUELLER'S DAY OFF

Perlini, Meme
LA RAGAZZA DEI LILLA

Perlman, Rhea
MY LITTLE PONY

Perlman, Ron
NAME OF THE ROSE, THE

Perlmuter, Marshall
BUSTED UP

Permanent, Bobbi
ECHO PARK, m/l

Peron, Denise
LE BONHEUR A ENCORE FRAPPE

Perpignani, Robert
SALOME, ed

Perpignani, Roberto
IL CASO MORO, ed

Perr, Harvey
SLEEPWALK

Perrer, Rosita
TEO EL PELIRROJO, m

Perret, Pierre
L'ETAT DE GRACE, m/l

Perri, Paul
MANHUNTER

Perrie, William
ABSOLUTE BEGINNERS

Perrier, Jean-Francois
PAULETTE; YIDDISH CONNECTION

Perrier, Mireille
GARDIEN DE LA NUIT; HIGH SPEED; JOUR ET NUIT; MAUVAIS SANG

Perrier, Olivier
GARDIENDE LA NUIT

Perrin, Francis
LE DEBUTANT; LE DEBUTANT, w

Perrin, Jacques
LOVE SONGS

Perron, Michel
BOY IN BLUE, THE

Perrot, Francoise
LE DEBUTANT; WOMEN'S PRISON MASSACRE

Perrot, Yves
MORT UN DIMANCHE DE PLUIE, p

Perrotti, Riccardo
SEPARATI IN CASA

Perry, Anthony
HUAJIE SHIDAI

Perry, Cathy
VIOLATED

Perry, David
ABSOLUTE BEGINNERS, cos; LADY JANE, cos

Perry, Don
JAKE SPEED, md

Perry, Ernest
COLOR OF MONEY, THE

Perry, Felton
DOWN AND OUT IN BEVERLY HILLS

Perry, Joao
UMA RAPARIGA NO VERAO

Perry, John Carroll
PLAY DEAD

Perry, Lou
TEXAS CHAINSAW MASSACRE PART 2, THE

Perry, Simon
HOTEL DU PARADIS, p; NANOU, p

Perryman, Jill
WINDRIDER

Persaud, Stephen
MONA LISA

Persico, Benito
CAMORRA, cos

Persky, Lisa Jane
PEGGY SUE GOT MARRIED

Persoff, Nehemiah
AMERICAN TAIL, AN

Personne, Fred
MON CAS

Persons, Fern
HOOSIERS

Persson, Bo Anders
RAVEN, m

Persson, Jan
MORRHAR OCH ARTOR, ed

Persson, Jorgen
ORMENS VAG PA HALLEBERGET, ph

Persson, Leif G.W.
I LAGENS NAMN, w

Persy, Nicole
LA PURITAINE

Peruyero, Lupito
HOT CHILI

Pervanje, Jure
KORMORAN, ph

Pescarolo, Leo
IL DIAVOLO IN CORPO, p

Pescia, Lisa
TOUGH GUYS

Pescow, Donna
JAKE SPEED

Pescucci, Gabriella
NAME OF THE ROSE, THE, cos

Pescucci, Gastone
GIOVANNI SENZAPENSIERI

Pestana, Rosa Maria
FILME DEMENCIA

Petach, Glenn
DR. OTTO AND THE RIDDLE OF THE GLOOM BEAM, prod d; DR. OTTO AND THE RIDDLE OF THE GLOOM BEAM, w

Petach, Laura
DR. OTTO AND THE RIDDLE OF THE GLOOM BEAM

Petangelo, Joseph
F/X

Petech, Glenn
DR. OTTO AND THE RIDDLE OF THE GLOOM BEAM

Petellius, Pirkka-Pekka
LINNA; TUNTEMATON SOTILAS

Peterick, Jim
EYE OF THE TIGER, m/l

Peterkin, Leslie
TAI-PAN

Peterman, Don
GUNG HO, ph; STAR TREK IV: THE VOYAGE HOME, ph

Peterman, Steve
RAW TUNES

Peters, Adam
FERRIS BUELLER'S DAY OFF, m/l

Peters, Bengt
JONSSONLIGAN DYKER UPP IGEN, prod d

Peters, Beth
BACK TO SCHOOL

Peters, Brock
STAR TREK IV: THE VOYAGE HOME

Peters, Chris
COOL CHANGE, stunts

Peters, Clarke
MONA LISA

Peters, Dennis
HELLFIRE, ph

Peters, Janne
WORKING GIRLS

Peters, Kelly Jean
POLTERGEIST II

Peters, Laurent
CONSEIL DE FAMILLE

Peters, Matthew
SCREAMTIME

Peters, Phil
8 MILLION WAYS TO DIE

Peters, Randolph
TRAMP AT THE DOOR, m

Peters, Timothy
HALF MOON STREET

Peters, Virginia
RATBOY

Peters, Wilfred
MOSQUITO COAST, THE

Petersen, Antje
FATHERLAND, cos

Petersen, Else
FLAMBEREDE HJERTER

Petersen, Gudjon
SCHWARZ UND OHNE ZUCKER

Petersen, Leif Sylvester
MANDEN I MAANEN, prod d

Petersen, Ted
CHOKE CANYON

Petersen, Wenche
NOE HEIT ANNET, cos

Petersen, William
MANHUNTER

Peterson, Beau
THRASHIN', set d

Peterson, Cassandra
BALBOA; ECHO PARK

Peterson, David
EYE OF THE TIGER, spec eff

Peterson, Eric
TRAMP AT THE DOOR

Peterson, Jenifer
NUTCRACKER: THE MOTION PICTURE

Peterson, John
KGB—THE SECRET WAR, ed

Peterson, Robyn
FLIGHT OF THE NAVIGATOR

Peterson, Shelley
JUDGEMENT IN STONE, A

Petillo, Vanessa
LA BALLATA DI EVA

Petiniot, Jean Marie
MERCI MONSIEUR ROBERTSON

Petit, Alan
THUNDER WARRIOR, stunts

Petit, Jean-Claude
JEAN DE FLORETTE, m; MANON DES SOURCES, ph

Petit, Lenard
FLOODSTAGE

Petitjean, Dave
DOWN BY LAW

Petito, Al
DESERT BLOOM

Petko, Alex
WILD WIND, THE, d

Petraglia, Jorge
BAD COMPANY

Petraglia, Mario
FULANINHA

Petrali, Tony
LOW BLOW; LOW BLOW

Petrashevich, Victor
ANGEL RIVER, ed

Petren, Anne
I LAGENS NAMN

Petrenko, Alexei
DEN' GNEVA

Petrescu, Petre
UN OASPETE LA CINA, ph

Petri, Paula
ASSAULT, THE

Petrica, Nicolae
DREPTATE IN LANTURI

Petrie, Anne
CLOSE TO HOME

Petrie, Doris
CONFIDENTIAL

Petritsch, Barbara
ERDSEGEN

Petro, Mark
ROCKIN' ROAD TRIP

Petrov, Alexander
POTERYALSYA SLON, set d

Petrovic, Nemanja
WILD WIND, THE, art d

Petrullo, Joe
BAND OF THE HAND

Petrut, Tudor
LICEENI

Pettersson, Allan
LOVE ME!, m

Pettersson, Margareta
MORRHAR OCH ARTOR

Pettersson, Soren
ALLA VI BARN I BULLERBY

Pettersson, Tord
DEN FRUSNA LEOPARDEN

Pettifer, Brian
GOSPEL ACCORDING TO VIC, THE

Pettit, Suzanne
'NIGHT, MOTHER, ed

Petty, Jack
IN THE SHADOW OF KILIMANJARO, makeup

Petty, Ross
JUDGEMENT IN STONE, A

Petuffo, Ana Luisa
POR UN VESTIDO DE NOVIA

Peuliche, Kirsten
FLAMBEREDE HJERTER

Pewsnar, Lara
REVENGE OF THE TEENAGE VIXENS FROM OUTER
SPACE, THE

Peyer, Johannes
DER SCHWARZE TANNER

Peynard, Iris
MONSTER SHARK

Peyser, Michael
RUTHLESS PEOPLE, p

Peza, Maria
I NICHTA ME TI SILENA

Pezas, Alexis
I NICHTA ME TI SILENA

Pezzutto, Marcello
SUMMER

Pfeifer, Chuck
ODD JOBS

Pfeiffer, Dedee
DANGEROUSLY CLOSE; VAMP

Pfeiffer, Klaus-Jurgen
WALKMAN BLUES, set d

Pfeiffer, Michelle
SWEET LIBERTY

Pfenning, Wesley A.
ODD JOBS

Pflaum, Lujan
MAN FACING SOUTHEAST, p

Phelps, Peter
PLAYING BEATIE BOW

Phenicle, Michael
DESPERATE MOVES

Philbin, Bill
SCORPION, ph

Philippe, Andre
DOWN AND OUT IN BEVERLY HILLS

Philippi, Rainer
STAMMHEIM

Philips, Martin
LA MONACA NEL PECCATO; LUSSURI

Phillips, Alex
FIREWALKER, ph; MURPHY'S LAW, ph

Phillips, Anna
FOR LOVE ALONE

Phillips, Betty
BOY WHO COULD FLY, THE

Phillips, Beverly
MALCOLM

Phillips, Bill
FIRE WITH FIRE, w; SPACECAMP

Phillips, Caryl
PLAYING AWAY, w

Phillips, Erica
TOUGH GUYS, cos

Phillips, Ethan
CRITTERS

Phillips, Helen
DOGS IN SPACE

Phillips, Jacqy
TWELFTH NIGHT

Phillips, Julianne
ODD JOBS

Phillips, Mary
CARAVAGGIO, m

Phillips, Meredith
SKY PIRATES

Phillips, Michelle
AMERICAN ANTHEM

Phillips, Mike
JAKE SPEED, set d

Phillips, Mouche
PLAYING BEATIE BOW

Phillips, Peter
DEATH OF THE HEART, THE, art d

Phillips, Rick
ARMED RESPONSE, m/l

Phillips, Tim
LIGHTSHIP, THE

Phillips, W.J.
COMING UP ROSES

Philpot, Toby
LABYRINTH

Phipps, Max
DARK AGE; SKY PIRATES

Phipps, Sam
BACK TO SCHOOL

Phoenix, Leaf
SPACECAMP

Phoenix, Pat
Obituaries

Phoenix, River
MOSQUITO COAST, THE; STAND BY ME; People to
Watch

Pholyiem, Vasana
PEESUA LAE DOKMAI

Phongvilai, Suchow
PEESUA LAE DOKMAI

Phue, Jeanne Van
P.O.W. THE ESCAPE, makeup; PLAYING FOR KEEPS,
makeup

Phule, Nilu
RAO SAHEB

Phung, Dennis
BIG TROUBLE

Phuoc, Ngo Huu
KARMA, art d

Piacentini, Franco
ELOGIO DELLA PAZZIA

Piaf, Edith
MEN'S CLUB, THE, m/l

Pialat, Maurice
POLICE, d; POLICE, w

Piana, Dennis M.
SCREAMPLAY; SCREAMPLAY, p; SCREAMPLAY, ph

Piana, Max
SCREAMPLAY

Piane, Carlo Delle
REGALO DI NATALE

Piani, Lorenzo
SALOME

Piazzoli, Roberto D'Ettore
DESPERATE MOVES, ph

Pibarot, Jacques
PEKIN CENTRAL

Picardo, Robert
BACK TO SCHOOL

Picchio, Ana Maria
EL RIGOR DEL DESTINO; EL SOL EN BOTELLITAS

Picciano, Anthony
SEX O'CLOCK NEWS, THE

Piccio, Ana Maria
POBRE MARIPOSA

Piccioni, Fabio
FEAR, w

Piccoli, Michel
LA PURITAINE; LE PALTOQUET; MAUVAIS SANG;
MON BEAU-FRERE A TUE MA SOEUR

Picerni, Charles
BAD GUYS ; PLAYING FOR KEEPS

Pickard, Sorrells
HARDBODIES 2; HARDBODIES 2, m/l

Pickens, James
F/X

Pickering, Donald
HALF MOON STREET

Pickering, Joe
WINDRIDER, ph

Pickett, Cindy
FERRIS BUELLER'S DAY OFF; MEN'S CLUB, THE

Pickett, Justin
KNIGHTS AND EMERALDS

Pickler, Fred
BLUE VELVET

Pickup, Ronald
MISSION, THE

Pickwoad, Michael
COMRADES, prod d

Pieczka, Franciszek
CHRZESNIAK; OSOBISTY PAMIETNIK GRZESZNIKA PRZEZ NIEGO SAMEGO SPISANY

Pieczynska, Malgorzata
JEZIORO BODENSKIE

Pieczynski, Krzysztof
JEZIORO BODENSKIE

Piedra, Emiliano
EL AMOR BRUJO, p

Piel, Yannick
ASTERIX CHEZ LES BRETONS, p

Pieplu, Claude
BEAU TEMPS, MAIS ORAGEUX EN FIN DE JOURNEE; LA GALETTE DU ROI; LE PALTOQUET

Pieranunzi, Enrico
UN RAGAZZO COME TANTI, m

Pierce, Denny
TRICK OR TREAT

Pierce, Fred
HOLLYWOOD VICE SQUAD; ODD JOBS

Pierce, Hayden
MILWR BYCHAN, p; MILWR BYCHAN, prod d

Pierce, Mark
NO RETREAT, NO SURRENDER, ed

Pierce, Patience
FLOODSTAGE

Pierce, Stack
LOW BLOW; PATRIOT, THE

Pierce, Tony
P.O.W. THE ESCAPE

Pierce, Wendell
MONEY PIT, THE

Pierfederici, Antonio
OTELLO

Pierre, Pierre
STILL POINT, THE, m

Piersanti, Franco
SAPORE DEL GRANO, m; UNA CASA IN BILICO, m

Pieters, Guido
OP HOOP VAN ZEGEN, d

Pietropinto, Angela
HEARTBURN

Pieuchot, Jean
THERESE

Pigg, Alexandra
LETTER TO BREZHNEV

Pigott, Colin
PING PONG, prod d

Pike, Don
DELTA FORCE, THE, stunts

Pike, Hy
VAMP

Pilgrim, Wolfgang
VA BANQUE, ph

Pilisi, Mark
QUEEN CITY ROCKERS

Piller, Jerry
COLOR OF MONEY, THE

Pilloud, Rod
GETTING EVEN

Pilo, Eli
AMERICA 3000

Pilon, Donald
LA GUEPE

Pin, Chui Dai An
DREAM LOVERS, w

Pinelli, Tullio
GINGER & FRED, w; LET'S HOPE IT'S A GIRL, w

Pinero, Ray
COMBAT SHOCK

Pineyro, Gloria
AMIGOS, ed

Ping'ao, Jia
IN THE WILD MOUNTAINS, w

Ping, Li Shih
HUAJIE SHIDAI

Ping, Sze Yeung
MARTIAL ARTS OF SHAOLIN, w

Ping-pin, Li
TIME TO LIVE AND A TIME TO DIE, A, ph

Pini, Tiziana
SETTE CHILI IN SETTE GIORNI

Pink, Steve
ONE MORE SATURDAY NIGHT

Pinkard, Fred
CHECK IS IN THE MAIL, THE

Pinkovitz, Ronnie
SHTAY ETZBA'OT M'TZIDON

Pinkus, Jaime
INSOMNIACS, p

Pinnell, Ron
DEATH OF A SOLDIER

Pinner, Steven
LINK

Pinnow, Horst
WOHIN MIT WILLFRIED?

Pinnt, Paul E.
NOBODY'S FOOL

Pino, Ilva
COM LICENCA, EU VOU A LUTA

Pinoli, Mattia
SAPORE DEL GRANO

Pinon, Dominique
SUIVEZ MON REGARD

Pinon, Efren C.
KILLING OF SATAN, THE, d; RAGING VENDETTA, d

Pinsent, Leah King
APRIL FOOL'S DAY

Pinson, Martha
POWER

Pint, Steve
TOUCH AND GO

Pinter, Herbert
FRINGE DWELLERS, THE, prod d

Pinter, Tomislav
BAL NA VODI, ph

Pintos, Alejo Garcia
LA NOCHE DE LOS LAPICES

Piovani, Nicola
GINGER & FRED, m; IL CAMORRISTA, m; LA SPOSA ERA BELLISSIMA, m

Pipart, Arlette
SAUVE-TOI, LOLA, makeup

Piper, Geseke
WOHIN MIT WILLFRIED?

Piper, Jacki
MR. LOVE

Pipolo
SCUOLA DI LADRI, w; SCUOLA DI LADRI, w

Pippin, Donald
EAT AND RUN, m

Pirchalawa, Guram
ROBINSONIADA ANU CHEMI INGLISELI PAPA

Pircher, Anni
DIE WALSCHE

Pircher, Florian
HEIDENLOCHER

Pirhasan, Baris
ADI VASFIYE, w; AMANSIZ YOL, w

Pirie, Bruce
POLICE ACADEMY 3: BACK IN TRAINING

Pirkle, Mac
DR. OTTO AND THE RIDDLE OF THE GLOOM BEAM; KING KONG LIVES

Pirnat, Helmut
ERDSEGEN, ph

Pirri, Massimo
MEGLIO BACIARE UN COBRA, d; MEGLIO BACIARE UN COBRA, w; MEGLIO BACIARE UN COBRA, w

Pirrie, Bruce
PINK CHIQUITAS, THE

Pirrotta, Giuseppe
REGALO DI NATALE, art d

Pisanti, Achille
ANEMIA, d; ANEMIA, w

Pischiutta, Andriano
NAME OF THE ROSE, THE, spec eff; SAVING GRACE, spec eff

Piscitello, Clelia
IL BI E IL BA

Piscopo, Joe
WISE GUYS

Piskonen, Paavo
KUNINGAS LAHTEE RANSKAAN

Pislaru, Dragos
SECVENTE

Pisoni, Edward
IMAGEMAKER, THE, prod d; WISE GUYS, prod d

Pistarino, Carlo
ITALIAN FAST FOOD

Pistilli, Luigi
UNA CASA IN BILICO

Pistoia, Nicola
AURELIA

Pistola, Loukia
SCHETIKA ME TON VASSILI

Pistone, Kimberly
ABOUT LAST NIGHT

Pistor, Ludger
NAME OF THE ROSE, THE

Pita, Dan
DREPTATE IN LANTURI, d; DREPTATE IN LANTURI, w; PASO DOBLE, d; PASO DOBLE, w

Pitaluga, Ana Maria
INSOMNIACS

Pitanga, Antonio
CHICO REI; QUILOMBO

Pithart, Aura
BOY WHO COULD FLY, THE

Pitkin, Randolph L.
ARMED AND DANGEROUS

Pitman, Phillip
OVER THE SUMMER

Pitofsky, Peter
HOUSE

Pitre, Glen
BELIZAIRE THE CAJUN, p; BELIZAIRE THE CAJUN, d&w

Pitre, Loulan
BELIZAIRE THE CAJUN

Pitt, Charles
LIGHTNING—THE WHITE STALLION

Pitt, Chris
ABSOLUTE BEGINNERS; MY BEAUTIFUL LAUNDRETTE

Pittman, Bruce
CONFIDENTIAL, d&w; CONFIDENTIAL, ed

Pitufos, Los
LA BANDA DE LOS PANCHITOS

Pitzalis, Federico
IL DIAVOLO IN CORPO

Pivcevic, Andrija
VECERNJA ZVONA, ph

Piven, Jeremy
LUCAS; ONE CRAZY SUMMER

Pizer, Larry
WHERE ARE THE CHILDREN?, ph

Pizzo, Angelo
HOOSIERS, p; HOOSIERS, w

Placencia, Pedro
TERROR Y ENCAJES NEGROS, m

Placido, Michele
GRANDI MAGAZZINI; SUMMER NIGHT WITH GREEK PROFILE, ALMOND EYES AND SCENT OF BASIL

Plackinger, Tina
ARMED AND DANGEROUS

Plain, Andrew
DOT AND KEETO, ed

Plana, Tony
BEST OF TIMES, THE; SALVADOR; THREE AMIGOS

Platt, Josefine
SCHMUTZ

Platt, Victoria Gabrielle
ROUND MIDNIGHT

Platts, Diana
PINK CHIQUITAS, THE

Plavin, Doug
MONEY PIT, THE

Player, Shawn
SCORPION

Playten, Alice
MY LITTLE PONY

Pleasence, Donald
COBRA MISSION

Pleitgen, Ulrich
STAMMHEIM

Plemiannikov, Helen
MAX MON AMOUR, ed

Plenizio, Gianfranco
UNA NOTTE DI PIOGGIA, m

Plenzdorf, Ulrich
EIN FLIEHENDES PFERD, w

Pleuka, Jonathan
SHADOWS RUN BLACK

Plimpton, Martha
MOSQUITO COAST, THE

Plough, Greg
ROCKIN' ROAD TRIP

Plourde, Jeffrey
NUTCRACKER: THE MOTION PICTURE

Plowden, Piers
DANGEROUSLY CLOSE, set d

Plummer, Christopher
AMERICAN TAIL, AN; BOSS' WIFE, THE; BOY IN BLUE, THE

Pnevmatikakis, Iraklis
ALLIGORIA

Po-Wen, Chen
DARK NIGHT, ed

Pochat, Marie-Sophie
MAN AND A WOMAN: 20 YEARS LATER, A

Pochat, Werner
RAGE

Pochath, Werner
DAYS OF HELL; SQUADRA SELVAGGIA

Pochna, John
ECHO PARK

Pochon, Caroline
CONSEIL DE FAMILLE

Podell, Art
HOLLYWOOD ZAP!, m; HOLLYWOOD ZAP!, md

Podell, Rick
NOTHING IN COMMON, w

Poderosi, Augusto
GINGER & FRED

Podrasky, Jimmer
PRETTY IN PINK

Poe, Harlan Cary
MANHATTAN PROJECT, THE

Pogany, Cristiano
FEAR, ph; IL BI E IL BA, ph

Poggi, Jack
CARNAGE

Pogodin, Radi
CHTO U SENJKI BYLO, w

Pogue, Charles Edward
FLY, THE, w; PSYCHO III, w

Pogue, Ken
CRAZY MOON

Pogues, The
SID AND NANCY, m

Pohl, Jim
HOWARD THE DUCK, set d

Pohland, Britta
DER POLENWEIHER; FLIGHT NORTH

Pohnel, Ron
NO RETREAT, NO SURRENDER

Pointer, Priscilla
BLUE VELVET

Poiret, Jean
INSPECTEUR LAVARDIN; JE HAIS LES ACTEURS

Poiroux, Claude-Eric
DESORDRE, p

Poitrenaud, Jacques
ROUND MIDNIGHT

Poivre, Annette
SUIVEZ MON REGARD

Pol, Jorge
SALVADOR

Polac, Roberto
DAS SCHWEIGEN DES DICHTERS

Polaca, La
EL AMOR BRUJO

Polacco, Cesare
Obituaries

Polaco, Jorge
DIAPASON, d&w

Polak, Hanus
DIE NACHTMEERFAHRT, ph

Polakof, James
BALBOA, p&d; BALBOA, w

Polakof, Michael
BALBOA

Polanski, Darius
HEIDENLOCHER

Polanski, Roman
PIRATES, d; PIRATES, w

Polck, Johnny
PANTHER SQUAD, stunts

Poledouris, Basil
IRON EAGLE, m

Polen, Rosemary
IMAGEMAKER, THE

Poletti, Carlo
CATTIVI PIERROT, ph

Poletti, Victor
ANCHE LEI FUMAVA IL SIGARO

Polhammer, Sigfrid
LOS HIJOS DE LA GUERRA FRIA

Poli, Gina
NAME OF THE ROSE, THE

Poliakoff, Israel
HAKRAV AL HAVA'AD

Poliakov, Valentin
ZAKONNY BRAK, prod d

Polic, Radko
CHRISTOPHORUS; DOBROVOLJCI

Polich, Julie
SCREEN TEST

Poliscuk, Ljuba
WILD WIND, THE

Polito, Jon
FIRE WITH FIRE; HIGHLANDER

Polizos, Vic
FINE MESS, A; NIGHT OF THE CREEPS

Poll, Lee
MORNING AFTER, THE, set d; THE KARATE KID PART II, set d

Pollack, Bernie
TOUCH AND GO, cos

Pollak, Kay
LOVE ME!, d; LOVE ME!, w

Pollak, Mimi
AMOROSA

Pollak, Roberto
HAME'AHEV

Pollanah, Rui
RUNNING OUT OF LUCK

Pollard, Korey Scott
STAND BY ME

Pollard, Michael J.
AMERICA; PATRIOT, THE

Pollatschek, Susanne
GREAT MOUSE DETECTIVE, THE

Pollitt, Clyde
COMING UP ROSES; LADY JANE

Pollitt, Erin
BREEDERS, makeup

Pollock, Bill
STREETS OF GOLD, art d

Pololanik, Zdenek
LEV S BILOU HRIVOU, m

Polonsky, Alan
ALIENS; BIGGLES

Polop, Paco Lara
ME HACE FALTA UN BIGOTE

Polson, Colin
JAKE SPEED, makeup

Polson, John
FOR LOVE ALONE

Polyakova, Larisa
REIS 222

Pomeroy, John
AMERICAN TAIL, AN, p

Pompei, Elena
LE MINIERE DEL KILIMANGIARO

Pompeo, Antonio
QUILOMBO

Ponazecki, Joe
MONEY PIT, THE

Ponce, Manuel Barbachano
DONA HERLINDA AND HER SON, p

Poncela, Eusebio
MATADOR; WERTHER

Pongratz, Karl
ERDSEGEN

Pongwilai, Suchao
ANGKOR-CAMBODIA EXPRESS

Ponnamma
MUKHAMUKHAM

Ponte, Maria Luisa
EL HERMANO BASTARDO DE DIOS; MAMBRU SE FUE A LA GUERRA; VIAJE A NINGUNA PARTE

Ponterotto, Donna
JUMPIN' JACK FLASH

Ponton, Yvan
HENRI; INTIMATE POWER

Pontonutti, Dario
JUNGLE RAIDERS

Pontrelli, Lisa
SCORPION

Ponzi, Maurizio
IL TENENTE DEI CARABINIERI, d; IL TENENTE DEI CARABINIERI, w

Pool, Lea
ANNE TRISTER, d; ANNE TRISTER, w

Poole, Kent
HOOSIERS

Poole, Roy
Obituaries

Poomala, Anuchart
ANGKOR-CAMBODIA EXPRESS, set d

Poon, Alan
NO RETREAT, NO SURRENDER, ed

Poon, Dickson
DREAM LOVERS, p; FAMILY, THE, p; SILENT LOVE, p

Pooy, Moji Long Danesh
MARE, THE

Pop, Iggy
COLOR OF MONEY, THE

Popa, Temistocle
UN OASPETE LA CINA, m

Popaj, Hila
NINJA TURF

Popaud, Melvil
DANS UN MIROIR

Pope, Caroline
LABYRINTH

Pope, Dick
COMING UP ROSES, ph

Pope, Jeff
PLAYING FOR KEEPS

Popescu, Valentin
PASO DOBLE

Popeye
AMERICAN ANTHEM; OUT OF BOUNDS; STAND BY ME

Popolizio, Massimo
UN RAGAZZO COME TANTI

Popov, Stole
SRECNA NOVA '49, d

Popovici, Titus
NOI, CEI DIN LINIA INTII, w

Popowitz, Michael
CLASS OF NUKE 'EM HIGH

Poppel, Ann
HEILT HITLER!, cos&makeup

Popper, Michael
SALOME

Poppiti, Ciro
LUCAS

Pops
VAMP

Poranen, Pauli
TUNTEMATON SOTILAS

Porath, Gideon
AVENGING FORCE, ph

Porcelli, Enzo
SAPORE DEL GRANO, p

Porfido, Antonella
TOMMASO BLU

Porras, Elza Cristina
KAPAX DEL AMAZONAS

Porro, Joseph
NEON MANIACS, cos; STOOGEMANIA, cos

Porta, Annamaria
UN RAGAZZO COME TANTI

Porta, Elvio
CAMORRA; CAMORRA, d, w

Portal, Louise
DECLINE OF THE AMERICAN EMPIRE, THE

Portal, Michel
MAX MON AMOUR, m

Porte, Pierre
BLEU COMME L'ENFER, m

Porteous, Emma
ALIENS, cos; NO SURRENDER, cos

Porteous, Peter
SOLDIER'S REVENGE

Porter, Carol
VENDETTA

Porter, Connie
HELL SQUAD

Porter, Jennifer
NUTCRACKER: THE MOTION PICTURE

Porter, Nelson
ADVENTURE OF FAUSTUS BIDGOOD, THE

Porter, Shea
SHADOWS RUN BLACK

Porter, Will
BACK TO SCHOOL, w

Portillo, Alfonso Torres
EL MERCADO DE HUMILDES, w

Portillo, Enrique Puente
LA TIERRA PROMETIDA, ed

Porto, Paulo
COM LICENCA, EU VOU A LUTA

Portugues, Gladys
MORNING AFTER, THE

Porzio, Yari
UNA TENERA FOLLIA

Poschl, Hanno
SCHMUTZ

Posey, John
MANHUNTER

Posey, Matthew
TRUE STORIES

Posey, Stephen L.
BLOODY BIRTHDAY, ph; WELCOME TO 18, ph

Poshek, Suzen
SEX O'CLOCK NEWS, THE, makeup

Posnick, Susan
PLAY DEAD, makeup

Possi, Jose
RUNNING OUT OF LUCK, ch

Post, Saskia
DOGS IN SPACE

Postelnicu, Cesonia
LICEENI

Poster, Steven
BLUE CITY, ph; BOY WHO COULD FLY, THE, ph

Postiglione, Giorgio
MAXIMUM OVERDRIVE, prod d; RAW DEAL, prod d

Postiglione, Mimmo
UNA TENERA FOLLIA

Postrel, Leo
HANNAH AND HER SISTERS

Pothier, Marcel
HENRI, md

Potter, Gregg
LUCAS

Potter, Leslie
DR. OTTO AND THE RIDDLE OF THE GLOOM BEAM

Potts, Alex
SCORPION

Potts, Anita Marie
SCORPION

Potts, Annie
JUMPIN' JACK FLASH; PRETTY IN PINK

Pou, Jose Maria
EL CABALLERO DEL DRAGON

Pouch, Rusty
FLIGHT OF THE NAVIGATOR

Pougatch, Yuri
MOI DRUG IVAN LAPSHIN, art d

Pouille, Hubert
CONGO EXPRESS, art d; FLODDER, art d

Poulain, Brigitte
SUMMER

Poulain, Patricia
UNDER THE CHERRY MOON

Poulikakos, Dimitris
O MELISSOKOMOS

Poulin, Julien
ELVIS GRATTON, LE KING DES KINGS; HENRI

Pouliot, Carlos
LA ALACRANA

Poulsen, Benny
BARNDOMMENS GADE

Poure, Alain
TWIST AGAIN A MOSCOU, p

Poure, Jean-Marie
TWIST AGAIN A MOSCOU, d; TWIST AGAIN A MOSCOU, w

Poveda, Jean-Louis
ETATS D'AME, art d

Povich, Maury
IMAGEMAKER, THE

Powell, Amanda Jane
ABSOLUTE BEGINNERS

Powell, Anthony
PIRATES, cos

Powell, Bu
ROUND MIDNIGHT, w

Powell, David
HOT CHILI, m/l

Powell, Joe
HALF MOON STREET, stunts

Powell, Josef
ODD JOBS

Powell, Marykay
VIOLETS ARE BLUE, p

Powell, Nosher
MY BEAUTIFUL LAUNDRETTE, stunts

Powell, Robert
WHAT WAITS BELOW

Powell, Sandy
CARAVAGGIO, cos

Power, Sharon
LETTER TO BREZHNEV

Power, Steve
DESPERATE MOVES, m

Power, Taryn
SEA SERPENT, THE

Powers, Terry
SEX APPEAL

Poyser, Brian
LADY JANE

Poysti, Lasse
KUNINGAS LAHTEE RANSKAAN

Poysti, Tom
FLIGHT NORTH

Pozzato, Pierangelo
UNA DONNA SENZA NOME; WOMEN'S PRISON MASSACRE

Pozzetto, Renato
GRANDI MAGAZZINI; SETTE CHILI IN SETTE GIORNI

Pradal, Bruno
RUE DU DEPART

Prado, Lilia
EL MERCADO DE HUMILDES; LA TIERRA PROMETIDA

Prado, Monica
POR UN VESTIDO DE NOVIA

Prahakar, Sharon
KAHAN KAHAN SE GUZAR GAYA

Prakash, Sushma
TRIKAL

Prange, Greg
EYE OF THE TIGER, ed

Prange, Gregory
ARMED AND DANGEROUS, ed; ONE MORE SATURDAY NIGHT, ed

Prange, Laurie
SAY YES

Pratt, Anthony
SOLARBABIES, prod d

Pratt, Dennis A.
AMERICAN JUSTICE; AMERICAN JUSTICE, w

Pratt, Hugo
MAUVAIS SANG

Pratt, Roger
MONA LISA, ph

Pray for Rain
SID AND NANCY, m

Prechtel, Volker
DER SCHWARZE TANNER; NAME OF THE ROSE, THE

Predin, Zoran
KORMORAN, m

Preen, Gero
JOURNEY, THE

Preiss, Wolfgang
SECOND VICTORY, THE

Preissel, Miriam L.
ARMED RESPONSE, ed; TOMB, THE, ed

Preistley, Tom
NANOU, ed

Prell, Karen
LABYRINTH

Preminger, Michael
NOTHING IN COMMON, w

Prentice, Ernie
BULLIES

Prentice, Jordan
HOWARD THE DUCK

Presle, Micheline
BEAU TEMPS, MAIS ORAGEUX EN FIN DE JOURNEE

Presnell, Robert, Jr.
Obituaries

Press, Bill
OUT OF BOUNDS

Press, Laura
HEAD OFFICE

Pressfield, Steven
KING KONG LIVES, w

Presson, Ron
TOUCH AND GO; WISDOM

Prestes, Analu
COM LICENCA, EU VOU A LUTA

Prestia, Shirley
HOLLYWOOD ZAP!

Preston, Christopher
LABYRINTH

Preston, Kay
NUTCRACKER: THE MOTION PICTURE

Preston, Kelly
52 PICK-UP; SPACECAMP

Preston, Ward
AMERICAN ANTHEM, prod d

Prestopino, Rosario
DEMONI 2—L'INCUBO RITORNA, makeup

Preu, Dana
SOMETHING WILD

Preur, Mustapha
LAST IMAGE, THE

Preussler, Anja-Christine
SPRING SYMPHONY

Prevette, Cyndy
ROCKIN' ROAD TRIP

Previn, Daisy
HANNAH AND HER SISTERS

Previn, Fletcher
HANNAH AND HER SISTERS

Price, Doug
TOBY MCTEAGUE

Price, Hannah
VIOLATED

Price, Johnny
A LA SALIDA NOS VEMOS

Price, Marc
TRICK OR TREAT

Price, Maria
COMING UP ROSES, cos

Price, Michael
FINE MESS, A, m/l

Price, Peter
NO SURRENDER

Price, Richard
AMERICA, ph; COLOR OF MONEY, THE; COLOR OF MONEY, THE, w; STREETS OF GOLD, w

Price, Vincent
GREAT MOUSE DETECTIVE, THE

Prichard, Robert
CLASS OF NUKE 'EM HIGH

Prichard, Ted
KING KONG LIVES

Priestley, Robert
Obituaries

Priestly, Jason
BOY WHO COULD FLY, THE

Prieto, Aurore
THERESE

Prieto, Carlos
RUNNING OUT OF LUCK, makeup

Prim, Monique
BETTY BLUE, ed

Prima, Barry
NO TIME TO DIE

Primes, Robert
GREAT WALL, A, ph

Primus, Barry
DOWN AND OUT IN BEVERLY HILLS; JAKE SPEED; SPACECAMP

Prince
BAND OF THE HAND, m/l; FIRE WITH FIRE, m/l; UNDER THE CHERRY MOON; UNDER THE CHERRY MOON, d

Prince & The Revolution
UNDER THE CHERRY MOON, m

Prince, George
AMIGOS

Prince, Michael
JO JO DANCER, YOUR LIFE IS CALLING; MORNING AFTER, THE

Prince, Peter
GOOD FATHER, THE, w

Prine, Andrew
ELIMINATORS

Pringle, Bryan
HAUNTED HONEYMOON

Pringle, Ian
WRONG WORLD, d; WRONG WORLD, w

Prinzi, Franz
SLEEPWALK, ph

Prior, Penny
HELL SQUAD

Pritchard, Sara
NUTCRACKER: THE MOTION PICTURE

Pritchard, Terry
BIGGLES, prod d

Privitera, Vincent J.
WITCHFIRE, d; WITCHFIRE, w

Priwieziencew, Eugeniusz
PIRATES

Proach, Henry
Obituaries; WISDOM

Proano, Raul
NINJA TURF

Probst, Gisela
WOHIN MIT WILLFRIED?

Prochazka, Borik
LEV S BILOU HRIVOU

Prochnow, Jurgen
KILLING CARS

Procter, Laura
RUNNING OUT OF LUCK

Proctor, John
RUNNING OUT OF LUCK

Proctor, Philip
STOOGEMANIA

Proctor, Scott
NIGHTMARE WEEKEND

Proft, Pat
POLICE ACADEMY 3: BACK IN TRAINING, w

Progrin, Yves
NOAH UND DER COWBOY

Prokofiev, Serge
MAUVAIS SANG, m

Prokopcev, Nikolai
PISMA MERTVOGO CHELOVEKA, ph

Prokopetz, Joesi
DIE NACHTMEERFAHRT

Prono, Nelly
ANOTHER LOVE STORY; NIGHTMARE'S
PASSENGERS

Props, Babette
FREE RIDE

Proskourine, Viktor
VYITI ZAMUZH ZA KAPITANA

Proskurin, Victor
WILD WIND, THE

Prosperi, Federico
WILD BEASTS, p

Prosperi, Franco
L'APACHE BIANCO, w; THRONE OF FIRE, THE, d;
WHITE SLAVE, w

Prosperi, Franco E.
WILD BEASTS, d&w

Prosperi, Mario
SEMBRA MORTO . . . MA E SOLO SVENUTO

Prossler, irjam
NOVEMBERKATZEN, w

Protat, Francois
SEPARATE VACATIONS, ph

Protho, Carl
LAND OF DOOM, m/l

Proulx, Luc
EQUINOXE

Proulx, Michel
INTIMATE POWER, art d

Provenza, Paul
ODD JOBS

Provenzano, Mariano
LA BALLATA DI EVA

Provis, Spyros
DANILO TRELES, O FIMISMENOS ANDALOUSIANOS
MOUSIKOS, ed

Prowse, A.J.
FAIR GAME, ed; PLAYING BEATIE BOW, ed

Proyas, Alexander
SPIRITS OF THE AIR, d; SPIRITS OF THE AIR, w

Prugal-Ketling, Halina
JEZIORO BODENSKIE, ed

Prugar-Ketling, Halina
KRONIKA WYPADKOW MILOSNYCH, ed

Pruvost, Pierre-Yves
LE DEBUTANT

Pryce, Jonathan
HAUNTED HONEYMOON; JUMPIN' JACK FLASH

Pryor, Donnie
SHORT CHANGED

Pryor, Nicholas
CHOKE CANYON

Pryor, Richard
JO JO DANCER, YOUR LIFE IS CALLING; JO JO
DANCER, YOUR LIFE IS CALLING, p&d; JO JO
DANCER, YOUR LIFE IS CALLING, w

Pryts, Ingvall
PERVOLA: TRACKS IN THE SNOW

Przedworski, Andrzej
OSOBISTY PAMIETNIK GRZESZNIKA PRZEZ NIEGO
SAMEGO SPISANY, prod d

Psarras, Tassos
CARAVAN SARAI, d&w

Psenny, Armand
ROUND MIDNIGHT, ed

Pszioniak, Wojciech
ANGRY HARVEST

Pszoniak, Vojtek
JE HAIS LES ACTEURS

Publishing, Artem
MEGLIO BACIARE UN COBRA, m

Pucciariello, Benito
SAVING GRACE

Puccini, Giacomo
DEMONER, m; O VESTIDO COR DE FOGO, m

Puchan, Dave
WITCHFIRE, m

Pudney, Alan
SCREAMTIME, ph

Puente, Tito
ARMED AND DANGEROUS

Pugh, Mickey
MANHUNTER

Pugh, Willard E.
BLUE CITY; NATIVE SON

Puglisi, Andrea
45MO PARALLELO

Puhony, Vladimir
BRODERNA MOZART

Pui, Chun
LUNATICS, THE

Pui, Tung
HAPPY DIN DON

Puigcorbe, Junajo
MES ENLLA DE LA PASSIO

Pujol, Dahlia
RATBOY

Pulci, Antonio
MANHATTAN BABY

Pulido, Maria Luisa Medina
THANATOS, p

Pulkkinen, Helmi Paula
SININEN IMETTAJA, w

Pullara, Bruno
YOUNGBLOOD

Pullman, Bill
RUTHLESS PEOPLE

Punarwan, Haryoko
DOEA TANDA MATA, p

Punjabi, Dhamoo
INTRUDER, THE, p

Punjabi, Raam
INTRUDER, THE, p

Punt, Shane
CLAN OF THE CAVE BEAR, THE

Puotila, Jukka
HUOMENNA

Purcell, Evelyn
NOBODY'S FOOL, d

Purcell, James
WHERE ARE THE CHILDREN?

Purcell, Jim
RAW TUNES

Purcell, Julie
MODERN GIRLS, makeup; ODD JOBS, makeup

Purcell, William O.
AVENGING FORCE, spec eff

Purdy-Gordon, Carolyn
FROM BEYOND

Purevmaa, D.
BI CHAMD KHAYRTAY

Puri, Amrish
AGHAAT

Puri, Om
AGHAAT; DEBSHISHU; GENESIS; MIRCH MASALA;
NEW DELHI TIMES; SUSMAN

Purvis, Jack
LABYRINTH

Purvis, Katie
LABYRINTH

Pushkin, Alexander
BORIS GODUNOV, d&w

Pusich, Marilyn
CHECK IS IN THE MAIL, THE, cos

Pustil, Jeff
KILLER PARTY

Putch, John
IMPURE THOUGHTS; WELCOME TO 18

Putnam, Ashley
BABEL OPERA, OU LA REPETITION DE DON JUAN

Putnam, Gary
MANHUNTER, m/l

Putt, Robert
LADY JANE

Puttnam, David
MISSION, THE, p

Puzic, Milan
WILD WIND, THE

Puzzi, Nicole
AS SETE VAMPIRAS

Pyles, Officer Keith
MANHUNTER

Pyun, Albert
DANGEROUSLY CLOSE, d; RADIOACTIVE DREAMS,
d&w

Pzoniak, Wojciech
DER SOMMER DES SAMURAI

Qi, Zhang
BEI AIQING YIWANGDE JIAOLUO, d

Qiang, Liu
YELLOW EARTH

Qihua, Zhao
QINGCHUN JI, ed

Qing, Lu
PIAOBO QIYU

Qorra, Xhevat
PROKA

Qosja, Isa
PROKA, d

Quadflieg, Will
JOURNEY, THE

Quaid, Randy
WRAITH, THE

Qualtinger, Helmut
NAME OF THE ROSE, THE

Quan, Stuart
BIG TROUBLE IN LITTLE CHINA

Quang, Tran
KARMA

Quaranta, Gianni
OTELLO, prod d; ROOM WITH A VIEW, A, prod d

Quarshie, Jugh
HIGHLANDER

Quarto, Charles John
AT CLOSE RANGE, m/l

Quast, Philip
AROUND THE WORLD IN EIGHTY WAYS

Quattro, Van
3:15, THE MOMENT OF TRUTH

Queen
HIGHLANDER, m; HIGHLANDER, m/l

Queen, Jeffrey
OVER THE SUMMER

Queen, Sam L.
OVER THE SUMMER

Queen, Sara Margaret "Buffy"
OVER THE SUMMER; OVER THE SUMMER, p

Quellet, Rene
DUNKI-SCHOTT

Quenelle, John
REBEL LOVE, p

Quentin
THERESE

Quere, Gerard
SUMMER

Querejeta, Elias
27 HORAS, p; 27 HORAS, w

Quester, Hugues
ANNE TRISTER; RUE DU DEPART

Quettier, Nelly
MAUVAIS SANG, ed

Qui-Yan, Huang
MARTIAL ARTS OF SHAOLIN

Quibell, Linda
CLAN OF THE CAVE BEAR, THE

Quick, David L.
CRY FROM THE MOUNTAIN, w

Quick, Dennis
MANHUNTER

Quick, Diana
MAX MON AMOUR

Quigley, Monica
UNDER THE CHERRY MOON

Quilley, Denis
FOREIGN BODY

Quindere, Paulo
WHERE THE RIVER RUNS BLACK

Quinn, Aidan
MISSION, THE

Quinn, Brian
CLASS OF NUKE 'EM HIGH

Quinn, Chance
STAND BY ME

Quinn, Christopher
NO SURRENDER

Quinn, Daniele
BAND OF THE HAND

Quinn, David
MANHATTAN PROJECT, THE

Quinn, Francesco
PLATOON

Quinn, Frank P.
Obituaries

Quinn, J.C.
AT CLOSE RANGE; MAXIMUM OVERDRIVE;
VIOLATED

Quinn, Thomas
ODD JOBS

Quinnell, Ken
SHORT CHANGED, w

Quinqin, Li
GREAT WALL, A

Quintall, Graziana
LA VITA DI SCORTA, ed

Quintana, Lei
REDONDO

Quintanilla, Luis
CONTACTO CHICANO, d

Quintano, Gene
POLICE ACADEMY 3: BACK IN TRAINING, w

Quinteros, Lorenzo
LA NOCHE DE LOS LAPICES; MAN FACING
SOUTHEAST

Quinton, Everett
LEGAL EAGLES

Quiro, Luo
FEIFA YIMIN, w

Quiroz, Gerardo
SALVADOR

Quiroz, Luis Mario
EL EXTRANO HIJO DEL SHERIFF

Quistgaard, Berthe
MANDEN I MAANEN

Raab, Kurt
ANGRY HARVEST; MOTTEN IM LICHT;
TRANSITTRAUME

Raaen, John
BIG HURT, THE

Raawi, Raad
MONA LISA

Rabaeus, Johan
MIN PAPA AR TARZAN

Rabago, Alejandro
THANATOS

Rabal, Benito
EL HERMANO BASTARDO DE DIOS, d; EL
HERMANO BASTARDO DE DIOS, w

Rabal, Francisco
CAMORRA; EL DISPUTADO VOTO DEL SR. CAYO;
EL HERMANO BASTARDO DE DIOS; LA STORIA; LOS
PARAISOS PERDIDOS; TIEMPO DE SILENCIO

Rabasa, Ruben
AMIGOS

Rabau, Erika
DIE LIEBESWUSTE

Rabb, Roger
FLOODSTAGE

Rabelo, Alessandro
WHERE THE RIVER RUNS BLACK

Rabelo, Marcelo
WHERE THE RIVER RUNS BLACK

Raben, Peer
FLAMBEREDE HJERTER, m; INSIDE OUT, m;
TOMMASO BLU, m

Rabeus, Johan
AMOROSA

Rabier, Jean
INSPECTEUR LAVARDIN, ph

Rabin, Peer
50/50, m

Rabinat, Antonio
TIEMPO DE SILENCIO, w

Rabinowitz, Harry
F/X, md

Rabson, Jan
VAMP

Rachedi, Ahmed
TAHOUNET AL SAYED FABRE, d; TAHOUNET AL
SAYED FABRE, w

Rachini, Pasquale
REGALO DI NATALE, ph; UNA DOMENICA SI, ph

Rachins, Alan
THUNDER RUN

Rachline, Nicole
SAUVE-TOI, LOLA, art d

Rachman, Jenny
DOEA TANDA MATA

Rachman, Sigurd
EAST OF THE WALL

Rachmil, Michael
QUICKSILVER, p

Racimo, Victoria
CHOKE CANYON

Rack, Tom
TOBY MCTEAGUE

Rackevei, Anna
ELYSIUM

Racki, Branco
KILLER PARTY

Racki, Branko
BUSTED UP

Rackman, Steve
"CROCODILE" DUNDEE

Racz, Valerie
SALOME

Radakovic, Goran
BAL NA VODI

Radclyffe, Sarah
CARAVAGGIO, p; MY BEAUTIFUL LAUNDRETTE, p

Radell, Daniel
LAND OF DOOM

Rademakers, Fons
ASSAULT, THE, p&d

Rader, Chuck
RYDER, P.I.

Radermacher, Jochen
FOLLOWING THE FUHRER, ph

Radeva, Tatiana
SIESTA VETA

Radichev, Anton
SKUPA MOYA, SKUPI MOY

Radiguet, Raymond
DEVIL IN THE FLESH, d&w; IL DIAVOLO IN CORPO,
w

Radjaian, Mehdi
MIRZA NOWROUZ' SHOES, ed

Radley, Ken
SHORT CHANGED

Radner, Gilda
HAUNTED HONEYMOON

Radner, Mike
STREETS OF GOLD

Radstrom, Niklas
BRODERNA MOZART, w

Radszuhn, Peter
WALKMAN BLUES, m

Rae, Claude
BOY IN BLUE, THE

Rae, Laura
JO JO DANCER, YOUR LIFE IS CALLING

Rae, Taija
SEX APPEAL

Rae, Tannis
BOY WHO COULD FLY, THE

Rae, Ted
NIGHT OF THE CREEPS; NIGHT OF THE CREEPS,
spec eff

Raeder, Louise
ALLA VI BARN I BULLERBY

Raen, Franki
TITAN SERAMBUT DIBELAH TUJUH, m

Rafeld, Jon Scott
TOUCH AND GO

Rafelson, Peter
LUCAS, m/l

Raff, Gary
VASECTOMY: A DELICATE MATTER

Ragalyi, Elemer
DER SCHWARZE TANNER, ph; GREAT GENERATION,
THE, ph

Raganelli, Caterina
UNA DOMENICA SI

Ragland, Mark
AT CLOSE RANGE, set d

Ragland, Patrick
PARTING GLANCES

Ragland, Robert
HOT CHILI, m/l

Rago, Juan
INSOMNIACS

Ragsdale, Michael
ODD JOBS

Rahbani, Ziad
WHAT HAPPENED NEXT YEAR, m

Rahlmann, Reed Kirk
HOWARD THE DUCK

Rahman, Sanaa Abdul
HOB FEE BAGHDAD

Rahmani, Ahmed
MORD I MORKET

Rahn, Fred
SEPARATE VACATIONS

Raho, Umberto
IL CASO MORO

Rai, Michael
ARMOUR OF GOD, THE, m

Railsback, Steve
ARMED AND DANGEROUS

Raina, K.K.
AGHAAT; GURU DAKSHINA; TRIKAL

Raina, M.K.
AGHAAT; GENESIS

Raines, Frances
BREEDERS ; RYDER, P.I.

Raines, Kennon
EVIXION

Rais, Mohsen
MAN OF ASHES, art d

Raisi, Youtine
TITAN SERAMBUT DIBELAH TUJUH

Raison, Kater
GOING SANE

Raitman, Bernardo
INSOMNIACS, w

Rajot, Pierre-Loup
LA GALETTE DU ROI

Rak, Rita
GRONA GUBBAR FRAN Y.R., makeup

Raketa, Jim
FATHERLAND

Rakotoyao, Thomas
DAHALO DAHALO

Raley, Alice
MOVIE HOUSE MASSACRE; MOVIE HOUSE
MASSACRE, p, d&w

Ralston, Glenn
WRAITH, THE, cos

Ram, Buck
DANCING IN THE DARK, m/l

Ramalho, Elba
MALANDRO

Ramampy, Benoit
DAHALO DAHALO, d

Rambaldi, Carlo
KING KONG LIVES, spec eff

Ramberg, Orjan
LOVE ME!

Ramberg, Sterling
REVENGE OF THE TEENAGE VIXENS FROM OUTER
SPACE, THE

Ramdane, Babeth Si
CHARLOTTE FOR EVER, ed

Rameau, Willy
PARENTAL CLAIM, d; PARENTAL CLAIM, w

Ramel, Jacqueline
DEN FRUSNA LEOPARDEN

Ramirez, Amando
LAS NOCHES DEL CALIFAS, w

Ramirez, Carlos   [Carlos Julio Ramirez]
Obituaries

Ramirez, Claudia
CRONICA DE FAMILIA

Ramirez, Juan
COLOR OF MONEY, THE

Ramirez, Luis Kelly
CALACAN, d&w; CALACAN, p

Ramis, Harold
ARMED AND DANGEROUS, w; ARMED AND
DANGEROUS, w; BACK TO SCHOOL, w; CLUB
PARADISE, d; CLUB PARADISE, w

Ramme, Margrit
DOWN AND OUT IN BEVERLY HILLS

Ramomoorthy
TABARANAKATHE

Ramos, Jaime
REDONDO

Ramos, Jose Ortiz
EL MALEFICIO II, ph

Ramos, Loyda
HOLLYWOOD VICE SQUAD; THREE AMIGOS

Ramos, Oscar
AS SETE VAMPIRAS, art d; HAPPILY EVER AFTER, set d

Ramos, Rudy
QUICKSILVER

Ramos, Santiago
DRAGON RAPIDE; EL ANO DE LAS LUCES; LA MITAD DEL CIELO

Ramos, Sergio
ESE LOCO LOCO HOSPITAL; LAS NOCHES DEL CALIFAS

Rampelli, Fabrizio
CATTIVI PIERROT, d

Rampling, Charlotte
MAX MON AMOUR

Ramras, Len
DAS SCHWEIGEN DES DICHTERS

Ramsay, Severs
MANHUNTER, m/l

Ramsay, Todd
BLACK MOON RISING, ed

Ramsey, Anne
DEADLY FRIEND; SAY YES

Ramsey, Chuck
BEST OF TIMES, THE

Ramsey, Logan
SAY YES

Ramsey, Marion
POLICE ACADEMY 3: BACK IN TRAINING

Ramsey, Nicola
HIGHLANDER

Ramsey, Nina
MANHATTAN PROJECT, THE, set d

Ramsey, Van Broughton
ON VALENTINE'S DAY, cos

Ramus, Theda De
SID AND NANCY, art d, cos

Ranama, Silvia
NAERATA OMETI, w

Rancke-Madsen, Hans
VALHALLA, w

Rand, Ande
DANCING IN THE DARK, m/l

Rand, Craig
LAND OF DOOM, w

Randall, Glenn
MAXIMUM OVERDRIVE, stunts

Randall, Richard
ANGKOR-CAMBODIA EXPRESS, p

Randall, Tony
MY LITTLE PONY

Randolph, Chase
FLIGHT OF THE NAVIGATOR

Randolph, Virginia
GOLDEN CHILD, THE, set d

Random, Ida
ABOUT LAST NIGHT, prod d

Randrianarison, Eugene
DAHALO DAHALO

Rankin, David Logan
UPHILL ALL THE WAY

Ranni, Rodolfo
COCAINE WARS

Ranody, P.
ZONING, art d

Ransom, Kenny
TOUGH GUYS

Rantos, Spiros
CACTUS, md

Rao, C.R. Sinha Vishwanath
TABARANAKATHE

Rapado, Norbert
PERROS DE LA NOCHE, ed

Rapin, Martine
LES FRERES PETARD, cos

Rasca, Jun
RAGING VENDETTA, ph

Rasch, Steve
SCREAMPLAY

Rasche, David
COBRA; COBRA; NATIVE SON

Rascoe, Stephanie
POSITIVE I.D.

Rasho, Nafa
BIG TROUBLE

Rasika, Chandi
ARUNATA PERA

Raski, Jaana
VALKOINEN KAAPIO

Rasmussen, Frode
NATTSEILERE

Rasmussen, Jesper Bruun
WOLF AT THE DOOR, THE

Rasmussen, Laura
DESERT BLOOM

Rasmussen, Manon
BARNDOMMENS GADE, cos; TWIST & SHOUT, cos

Raspe, Gioia
TAROT, cos

Rassimov, Ivan
SQUADRA SELVAGGIA

Rastegar, Morteza
BUS, THE, ph

Rasulala, Thalmus
BORN AMERICAN; BOSS' WIFE, THE

Rasumny, Jay
LIGHTNING—THE WHITE STALLION

Ratap, Gamil
KAHIR ELZAMAN

Rateb, Ahmed
LEL HAB KESSA AKHIRA

Rath, Franz
ROSA LUXEMBURG, ph

Rath, Lutz
MONEY PIT, THE

Rathbone, Basil
GREAT MOUSE DETECTIVE, THE

Rather, Bjarne
TWIST & SHOUT, w; TWIST & SHOUT, w

Rathery, Isabelle
PEAU D'ANGE, ed

Ratib, Gamil
AL BEDAYA

Ratliff, Garette
RADIOACTIVE DREAMS

Ratray, Devin
WHERE ARE THE CHILDREN?

Rattan, Aubrey K.
FOXTRAP, w; SLOANE, w

Ratti, Robert
MORE THINGS CHANGE, THE

Rattray, Eric
LABYRINTH, p

Raub, Jan
PPPERFORMER, THE

Rauch, Michael
BAND OF THE HAND, p

Raulamo, Jaako
SININEN IMETTAJA

Rauseo, Mike
BAD GUYS

Ravan, Kambiz Roshan
FROSTY ROADS, m

Ravasz, Akos
ELYSIUM, p

Ravel, Jean
COURS PRIVE, ed

Ravel, Maurice
EU SEI QUE VOU TE AMAR, m

Ravenstein, Appolonia van
FLODDER

Ravi
MUKHAMUKHAM, p

Ravin, Linda
OFF BEAT

Ravix, Julie
LOVE SONGS

Ravn, Kurt
TWIST & SHOUT

Rawi, Al
HOB FEE BAGHDAD, ed

Rawi, Ousama
JUDGEMENT IN STONE, A, d

Rawlings, Terry
F/X, ed

Rawlins, David
BACK TO SCHOOL, ed

Ray, Celest
STAND BY ME, md

Ray, Chris Douglas-Olen
ROLLER BLADE

Ray, Fred Olen
ARMED RESPONSE; ARMED RESPONSE, d; ARMED RESPONSE, w; TOMB, THE, d; TOMB, THE, p

Ray, Johnny
THRASHIN'

Ray, Michele
CONSEIL DE FAMILLE, p

Rayfiel, David
ROUND MIDNIGHT, w; ROUND MIDNIGHT, w

Rayhall, Tom
HOWARD THE DUCK

Rayle, Geoffrey
ROCKIN' ROAD TRIP, set d

Rayle, Hal
TRANSFORMERS: THE MOVIE, THE

Raymond, Butch
FLIGHT OF THE NAVIGATOR

Raymond, Camille
FUTURE OF EMILY, THE

Raymond, Richard
DAYS OF HELL

Raymond, Stephen
SEX APPEAL

Raynal, Jackie
FEMMES DE PERSONNE, makeup

Razdan, Soni
TRIKAL

Rea, Chris
AUF IMMER UND EWIG, m; AUF IMMER UND EWIG, m/l

Read, Bobbie
9½ WEEKS, cos

Read, Cheryl
REVENGE OF THE TEENAGE VIXENS FROM OUTER SPACE, THE

Read, Joe
BLUE CITY; BLUE CITY, m/l

Read, Nicholas
LABYRINTH

Reading, Beatrice
ABSOLUTE BEGINNERS, m/l; LITTLE SHOP OF HORRORS

Reading, Tony
CLUB PARADISE, art d; KING KONG LIVES, art d

Ready, Lynn
BIG TROUBLE

Realle, Tony
P.O.W. THE ESCAPE

Reamer, Keith L.
HELLFIRE, ed

Reardon, Paddy
BIG HURT, THE, art d; DEPARTURE, art d; DEVIL IN THE FLESH, art d; STILL POINT, THE, art d

Reate, J.L.
GOLDEN CHILD, THE

Reategui, Eddie
THRASHIN'

Reaves-Phillips, Sandra
ROUND MIDNIGHT

Rebengiuc, Victor
DREPTATE IN LANTURI

Rebhorn, James
WHATEVER IT TAKES

Rechter, Yoni
NADIA, m

Reckley, Mary
SHORT CIRCUIT

Red, Anthony
SEA SERPENT, THE, ed

Red, Eric
HITCHER, THE, w

Red, Simply
UNA DOMENICA SI

Reddick, Cecil
Obituaries

Redding, Otis
LE MOME, m/l

Reddington, Ian
HIGHLANDER

Redds and the Boys
GOOD TO GO, m

Reder, Gigi
UNA DONNA SENZA NOME

Redford, J.A.C.
CRY FROM THE MOUNTAIN, m; EXTREMITIES, m

Redford, Robert
LEGAL EAGLES

Redglare, Rockets
DOWN BY LAW; WAY IT IS, THE

Redgrave, Vanessa
COMRADES

Redies, Frank
EAST OF THE WALL

Reding, Nic
CAPTIVE

Redinger, Gay
WIRED TO KILL, art d

Redmond, Charles
OCEAN DRIVE WEEKEND; OCEAN DRIVE WEEKEND, w

Redmond, Siobhan
HALF MOON STREET

Redmond, Will
OCEAN DRIVE WEEKEND

Reds, The
BAND OF THE HAND, m/l; MANHUNTER, m

Redshaw, Marie
COOL CHANGE

Reece, Christy
OVER THE SUMMER

Reece, David
DEATH OF THE HEART, THE, ed

Reed, Dean
Obituaries

Reed, Jerry
WHAT COMES AROUND; WHAT COMES AROUND, d

Reed, Kelly
WEEKEND WARRIORS

Reed, Oliver
CAPTIVE; CASTAWAY

Reed, Pamela
BEST OF TIMES, THE; CLAN OF THE CAVE BEAR, THE

Reed, Rondi
ONE MORE SATURDAY NIGHT

Reed, Tracy
RUNNING SCARED

Reedall, Mark
PSYCHO III, makeup; THREE AMIGOS, makeup

Reefer, John Michael
SHE'S GOTTA HAVE IT, cos

Reehuis, Jerome
THOMAS EN SENIOR OP HET SPOOR VAN BRUTE BEREND

Reekie, Rita
SHOOT FOR THE SUN, cos

Reel SFX
APRIL FOOL'S DAY, spec eff

Reenberg, Jorgen
WOLF AT THE DOOR, THE

Reents, Claus-Dieter
HEIDENLOCHER; VA BANQUE

Reeve, Geoffrey
HALF MOON STREET, p

Reeves, Keanu
FLYING; YOUNGBLOOD

Refn, Anders
TAKE IT EASY, ed

Regalbuto, Joe
RAW DEAL

Regan, Christian
CLOCKWISE

Regan, Michael
HEARTBURN

Regent, Benoit
BLACK AND WHITE; ROUND MIDNIGHT

Reggiani, Serge
MAUVAIS SANG; MAUVAIS SANG, m/l; O MELISSOKOMOS

Regio, Jose
MON CAS, d&w; O MEU CASO—REPETICOES, w

Regnier, Inez
DIE ZWEI GESICHTER DES JANUAR, ed

Regnoli, Piero
FOTOROMANZO, w; GIURO CHE TI AMO, w; UNA STORIA AMBIGUA, w

Rego, Luis
MAINE-OCEAN; PAULETTE

Reguli, Chris
DR. OTTO AND THE RIDDLE OF THE GLOOM BEAM

Rehak, Frantisek
LEV S BILOU HRIVOU

Rehberg, Hans Michael
SCHMUTZ; STAMMHEIM

Rehberg, Michael
BLIND DIRECTOR, THE

Rehfeldt, Lothar
STAMMHEIM

Reich, Gunther
BLIND DIRECTOR, THE

Reich, Nadia Klovedal
TAKE IT EASY

Reichel, Achim
VA BANQUE; VA BANQUE, m

Reichel, Horst
ASSAULT, THE

Reichenbach, Carlos
FILME DEMENCIA, d&w

Reichman, Rachel
RIVERBED, THE, ed; RIVERBED, THE, p, d

Reichmann, Wolfgang
SECOND VICTORY, THE

Reid, David
BEER, spec eff

Reid, Elizabeth A.
TOMB, THE, cos

Reid, Kate
FIRE WITH FIRE

Reid, Katie
BLUE VELVET

Reid, Mary
CLAN OF THE CAVE BEAR, THE

Reid, Michael
BACK TO SCHOOL

Reid, Philip
COOL CHANGE, ed

Reijen, Jan Wouter van
AFZIEN, ed

Reineke, Dieter
NOVEMBERKATZEN, set d

Reiner, Rob
STAND BY ME, d

Reiner, Tracey
JUMPIN' JACK FLASH

Reinhard, Carol
BIG TROUBLE

Reinhart, George
JOURNEY, THE, p

Reinhart, John
HOUSE, art d

Reinhold, Judge
HEAD OFFICE; OFF BEAT; RUTHLESS PEOPLE

Reins, Marsky
VENDETTA

Reis, Imara
FILME DEMENCIA; SONHO SEM FIM

Reis, Joanna
AMERICA 3000

Reiser, Paul
ALIENS; ODD JOBS

Reiser, Rio
VA BANQUE

Reiss, Stuart A.
FINE MESS, A, set d

Reitman, Ivan
LEGAL EAGLES, p,d&w

Reitter, Barbara
HEIDENLOCHER

Reitz, Edgar
DAS SCHWEIGEN DES DICHTERS, p

Reizes, Stephen
EVIXION, w

Reizner, Lou
BLACK JOY, m

Rekert, Winston
BLUE MAN, THE; TOBY MCTEAGUE

Rekhviascwili, Alexander
SAPIRHURIN, d; SAPIRHURIN, ed; SAPIRHURIN, w

Rellan, Miguel
VIAJE A NINGUNA PARTE

Rellan, Miguel Angel
EL ANO DE LAS LUCES; EL HERMANO BASTARDO DE DIOS

Relle, Federico
IL GIARDINO DEGLI INGANNI

Rellstab, Felix
NOAH UND DER COWBOY

Relph, Michael
GOSPEL ACCORDING TO VIC, THE, p

Relph, Simon
COMRADES, p

Remacle, Donald
JUMPIN' JACK FLASH, set d

Remal, Gary
HOT CHILI, m/l

Remar, James
BAND OF THE HAND; CLAN OF THE CAVE BEAR, THE; QUIET COOL

Remen, Maximilian
SIESTA VETA, ed

Remias, Norma
NAKED VENGEANCE, makeup; SILK, makeup

Remias, Ricardo
FINAL MISSION, ph; NAKED VENGEANCE, ph; SILK, ph

Remick, Lee
EMMA'S WAR

Remington, Richard
DEVASTATOR, THE, ph

Remotti, Michele Remo
DIE WALSCHE

Remotti, Remo
OTELLO

Remsen, Bert
EYE OF THE TIGER; TAI-PAN; TERRORVISION

Remsen, Guy
CHECK IS IN THE MAIL, THE

Remsen, Kerry
SMART ALEC

Remy, Danica
DESERT BLOOM

Remy, Linda
DESERT BLOOM, w

Remy, Tony
PASSION OF REMEMBRANCE, THE, m

Rendell, Ruth
JUDGEMENT IN STONE, A, w

Renderer, Scott
LAST SONG

Renfield, Robert
ANGEL RIVER, p; ANGEL RIVER, w

Renhard, Ann
NUTCRACKER: THE MOTION PICTURE

Renier, Yves
PEKIN CENTRAL

Renjo, Mikihiko
LOVE LETTER, w

Rennard, Deborah
LAND OF DOOM

Rennes, Juliette
CONSEIL DE FAMILLE

Reno, Jean
I LOVE YOU; ZONE ROUGE

Renom, Gabriel
EL DISPUTADO VOTO DEL SR. CAYO

Rens, Peter Jan
MARIA; MARIA, d&w

Renteria, Pedro
COME LA VIDA MISMA

Renterio, Mauricio
LEJANIA

Renucci, Robin
ETATS D'AME; L'AMANT MAGNIFIQUE; LE MAL D'AIMER; PEAU D'ANGE; SUIVEZ MON REGARD

Repas, Eric
TOUCH AND GO

Repete, Pete
MORD I MORKET, m

Requeraz, Jean Pierre
MAN FACING SOUTHEAST

Rescher, Dee Dee
FERRIS BUELLER'S DAY OFF

Reshovsky, Marc
SORORITY HOUSE MASSACRE, ph

Resines, Antonio
LULU DE NOCHE

Resnais, Alain
MELO, d&w

Resnick, Arthur
LEGAL EAGLES, m/l

Resnik, Alejandro
INSOMNIACS

Resnik, Robert
SLOANE

Ress, Gunter
NOVEMBERKATZEN, m

Reston, Telma
BRAS CUBAS; RUNNING OUT OF LUCK

Restrepo, Manuel
EL TREN DE LOS PIONEROS

Retes, Rene
EL BRONCO, w

Retsek, John
SAY YES, set d

Riedel, Georg
ALLA VI BARN I BULLERBY, m; MIN PAPA AR
TARZAN, m

Rieder, Leslie Ann
JUST BETWEEN FRIENDS

Rieneck, Claudia
WELCOME IN VIENNA, ed

Riera, Emilio Garcia
REDONDO

Riesel, Robert
HOT CHILI

Rieta, Vernon
BIG TROUBLE IN LITTLE CHINA

Rif, Vladimir
VERY CLOSE QUARTERS, d; VERY CLOSE
QUARTERS, w

Rifbjerg, Synne
BALLERUP BOULEVARD, w

Rigacci, Emanuela
ELOGIO DELLA PAZZIA

Rihr, Sue
8 MILLION WAYS TO DIE

Riis, Sharon
LOYALTIES, w

Rijnders, Gerardjan
AFZIEN

Riklin, Shimon
SMILE OF THE LAMB, THE, w

Riley, Doug
WHERE ARE THE CHILDREN?

Riley, Gary
JUST BETWEEN FRIENDS; RATBOY; STAND BY ME

Riley, Steve
BEST OF TIMES, THE

Rillie, Maisie
ADVENTURE OF FAUSTUS BIDGOOD, THE

Rim, Ko Hak
POMNALUI NUNSOGI, d

Rimas, Markunas
SUNUS PALAIDUNAS

Rimbaud, Robert
LE COMPLEXE DU KANGOUROU

Rimmer, Meredith
LOYALTIES

Rin, Kim Ryong
POMNALUI NUNSOGI

Rinaldi, Gerard
DESCENTE AUX ENFERS

Rinaldi, Giuditta
UNA CASA IN BILICO, w

Rinaldi, Joy
SCORPION

Rincon, Miguel Angel
KAPAX DEL AMAZONAS, m

Rincon, Rodney
PRAY FOR DEATH

Rinehardt, Heidi
ROCKIN' ROAD TRIP

Rinell, Susan
JUST BETWEEN FRIENDS

Ring, Borge
VALHALLA, anim

Ringwald, Molly
PRETTY IN PINK

Ringwood, Bob
SOLARBABIES, cos

Rio, Nicole
SORORITY HOUSE MASSACRE

Rios, Fabio
EL TREN DE LOS PIONEROS

Rioux, Genevieve
DECLINE OF THE AMERICAN EMPIRE, THE

Rioux, Jeffery R.
SOMETHING WILD

Riparetti, Tony
SAY YES, m

Ripoll, Maria Teresa
MISSION, THE

Ripoll, Silvia
AWAITING THE PALLBEARERS, ed

Ripper, Michael
NO SURRENDER

Rippon, Todd
CASTAWAY

Rippy, Leon
KING KONG LIVES; MAXIMUM OVERDRIVE; RAW
DEAL; ROCKIN' ROAD TRIP

Ripstein, Arturo
EL IMPERIO DE LA FORTUNA, d

Risch, Maurice
PAULETTE

Risdale, Chris
ARTHUR'S HALLOWED GROUND, ed

Riser, Chris
AMERICAN ANTHEM

Risi, Dino
IL CAMMISSARIO LO GATTO, d; IL CAMMISSARIO
LO GATTO, w

Risley, Ann
DESERT BLOOM

Rissi, Mark M.
GHAME AFGHAN, d; GHAME AFGHAN, m; GHAME
AFGHAN, p; LISI UND DER GENERAL, p&d

Rist, Gary
SOLDIER'S REVENGE, m

Rist, Robbie
IRON EAGLE

Ristic, Biljana
DOBROVOLJCI

Ristic, Ljubisa
LIJEPE ZENE PROLAZE KROZ GRAD

Rita, Massimo De
IL CAMORRISTA, w; LA RAGAZZA DEI LILLA, w

Ritchie
RUNNING OUT OF LUCK

Ritchie, John
BUSTED UP

Ritchie, Michael
GOLDEN CHILD, THE, d; WILDCATS, d

Ritter, Amy
NUTCRACKER: THE MOTION PICTURE

Ritter, Angele
PSYCHO III

Ritz, Harry [Herschel Joachim]
Obituaries

Ritz, Madelynn Von
RADIOACTIVE DREAMS

Riva, J. Michael
GOLDEN CHILD, THE, prod d

Rivaler, Aston Reymers
LOVE ME!, m

Rivas, Andy
VAMP

Rivas, Guillermo
ESE LOCO LOCO HOSPITAL; SE SUFRE PERO SE
GOZA

Rivas, Isabel
STONE BOY

Rivas, Maria Teresa
EL MALEFICIO II

Rivelin, Michel
THERESE

Rivera, Jorge
EL SECUESTRO DE LOLA-LOLA LA TRAILERA 2, ed

Rivera, Maria Elena
EIN BLICK—UND DIE LIEBE BRICHT AUS

Rivera, Matilde
LOS ASES DE CONTRABANDO, w

Rivera, Patricia
MATANZA EN MATAMOROS

Rivera, Rene
STREETS OF GOLD

Rivera, Roberto G.
LA TIERRA PROMETIDA, p&d

Rivera, Victor
BAD GUYS

Rivero, George "Jorge"
KILLING MACHINE

Rivers, Victor
8 MILLION WAYS TO DIE; LAST RESORT, THE

Rivet, Rene
LUSSURI, w

Riviera, Gloria
NUTCRACKER: THE MOTION PICTURE

Rivieras, Smitty Flynn and The
OCEAN DRIVE WEEKEND

Riviere, Dominique
SUMMER

Riviere, Isabelle
SUMMER

Riviere, Jean-Marie
PAULETTE

Riviere, Laetitia
SUMMER

Riviere, Marie
SUMMER

Rivkin, Stephen E.
YOUNGBLOOD, ed

Rivlin, Seffi
HASHIGAON HAGADOL

Rizell, Eva
BRODERNA MOZART, makeup; LOVE ME!, makeup

Rizzo, Gianni
NAME OF THE ROSE, THE

Rizzo, Jeffrey
SCORPION

Rizzo, Raul
LES LONGS MANTEAUX

Rizzolino, Pat
BREEDERS

Rjachovsky, Roman
SIESTA VETA, art d

Roach, Daryl
SPACECAMP

Roach, David
YOUNG EINSTEIN, p; YOUNG EINSTEIN, w

Roache, Linus
NO SURRENDER

Roads, Craig
DR. OTTO AND THE RIDDLE OF THE GLOOM BEAM,
m/l

Roanne, Robert
MERCI MONSIEUR ROBERTSON

Robar-Dorin, Filip
OVNI IN MAMUTI, d&w

Robb, Jill
MORE THINGS CHANGE, THE, p

Robb-King, Peter
ALIENS, makeup

Robbins, Carol
'NIGHT, MOTHER

Robbins, Richard
ROOM WITH A VIEW, A, m

Robbins, Tim
HOWARD THE DUCK; TOP GUN

Roberson, Clement
FAT GUY GOES NUTZOID!!

Robert Pusilo Studio
SEX APPEAL, cos

Robert, Marie
LA PURITAINE, ed

Robert, Nathan
BLOODY BIRTHDAY

Roberti, Francesca
SAVING GRACE

Roberts, Arthur
CHOPPING MALL

Roberts, Axel
SORORITY HOUSE MASSACRE

Roberts, Bruce
KILLER PARTY, m/l

Roberts, Colwyn
MORE THINGS CHANGE, THE

Roberts, Conrad
MOSQUITO COAST, THE

Roberts, Doug
VIOLETS ARE BLUE

Roberts, Edy
JO JO DANCER, YOUR LIFE IS CALLING

Roberts, Eric
NOBODY'S FOOL

Roberts, Janine
MR. LOVE

Roberts, Jean-Marc
COURS PRIVE, w

Roberts, Michael D.
MANHUNTER

Roberts, Morgan
Obituaries

Roberts, Richard
SACRIFICE, THE, spec eff

Roberts, Teresa
GREAT WALL, A

Robertson, B.A.
GOSPEL ACCORDING TO VIC, THE, m

Robertson, George R.
POLICE ACADEMY 3: BACK IN TRAINING

Robertson, Heilan
SHORT CHANGED

Robertson, James
SHORT CHANGED

Robertson, Malcolm
MORE THINGS CHANGE, THE

Robertson, Michael
GOING SANE, d

Robertson, Robbie
COLOR OF MONEY, THE, m

Robertson, Tim
GOING SANE; KANGAROO

Robey
MONEY PIT, THE; RAW DEAL

Robie, John
FERRIS BUELLER'S DAY OFF, m

Robillard, Brian
P.O.W. THE ESCAPE

Robillard, Glen Robert
PLAYING FOR KEEPS

Robin, Bernard
BETTY BLUE

Robin, Diane
CROSSROADS; HEAD OFFICE

Robin, Jean-Francois
BETTY BLUE, ph; KAMIKAZE, ph; L'UNIQUE, ph

Robins, Barry
Obituaries

Robins, Oliver
POLTERGEIST II

Robins, Pietra
CACTUS, makeup

Robinson, Andrea
CRAZY MOON

Robinson, Andrew
COBRA

Robinson, Bartlett [Bart Robinson]
Obituaries

Robinson, Cardew
PIRATES

Robinson, Dar [Dar Allen Robinson]
Obituaries; SCORPION, stunts; VAMP; VAMP, stunts

Robinson, Dave
NO RETREAT, NO SURRENDER

Robinson, Elizabeth
JO JO DANCER, YOUR LIFE IS CALLING

Robinson, Hank
SHADOWS RUN BLACK

Robinson, Harry
TERRY ON THE FENCE, m

Robinson, Holly
HOWARD THE DUCK

Robinson, J. Peter
WRAITH, THE, m

Robinson, Kevin
YOUNGBLOOD

Robinson, Kim
GIRLS SCHOOL SCREAMERS

Robinson, Leon
BAND OF THE HAND

Robinson, M. Lynda
SCREAMPLAY

Robinson, Matt
WISDOM

Robinson, McKinlay
PINK CHIQUITAS, THE

Robinson, Pete
RADIOACTIVE DREAMS, m

Robinson, Sharon
ODD JOBS

Robinson, Terrie M.
STOOGEMANIA

Robinson, Tim
WRONG WORLD

Robles, Walter
CHOKE CANYON

Robling, Laura
HOOSIERS

Robotham, John
SOMETHING WILD, stunts

Roboto, Ed
CLUB PARADISE, w

Robsahm, Thomas
FAREWELL ILLUSION

Robson, Wayne
BULLIES

Robutti, Enzo
45MO PARALLELO

Roca-Rey, Bals
STORIA D'AMORE

Rocard, Pascale
POLICE

Rocca, Emilia Della
GIRL FROM MANI, THE

Rocha, Raul
JOGO DURO, p

Roche, France
NUIT D'IVRESSE

Roche, Jim
SOMETHING WILD

Roche, Mabel
UN HOMBRE DE EXITO

Rochefort, Jean
LA GALETTE DU ROI

Rocheman, Lionel
JE HAIS LES ACTEURS; LOVE SONGS

Rochon, Lela
FOXTRAP; STEWARDESS SCHOOL

Rock-Savage, Steven
SHADOW PLAY

Rocklin, Gary
WRAITH, THE, ed

Rocky
DIRT BIKE KID, THE

Rodarte, Cecilia
BILLY GALVIN, art d

Rodas, Rodolfo
MAN FACING SOUTHEAST

Roddenberry, Gene
STAR TREK IV: THE VOYAGE HOME, w

Roddy, James D.
Obituaries

Rode, Hester
YUPPIES, I GIOVANI DI SUCCESSO

Rode, Thierry
L'UNIQUE; ZONE ROUGE

Rodensky, Shmuel
ALEX KHOLE AHAVA

Roderer, Daniela
DER PENDLER, ed

Roderick, B.K.
RECRUITS, w

Roderick, Steve
NAKED VENGEANCE

Roderick-Jones, Alan
VAMP, prod d

Rodes, Marian
LOLA

Rodgers, Alito
BANDERA NEGRA

Rodgers, Scott
NINJA TURF

Rodionov, Alexi
COME AND SEE, ph

Rodrigues, Marcia
BRAS CUBAS

Rodrigues, Milton
AVAETE, A SEMENTE DA VINGANCA

Rodrigues, Ylmara
JUBIABA

Rodriguez, Diane
PSYCHO III

Rodriguez, Elisabeth
ON A VOLE CHARLIE SPENCER!

Rodriguez, Flor Marina
KAPAX DEL AMAZONAS

Rodriguez, Manuel
EL AMOR BRUJO

Rodriguez, Marina
LA MITAD DEL CIELO, cos

Rodriguez, Miguel
MISS MARY, ph

Rodriguez, Nacho
EL RIO DE ORO

Rodriguez, Nelson
PLACIDO, ed; UN HOMBRE DE EXITO, ed; VISA
U.S.A., ed

Rodriguez, Paul
QUICKSILVER; WHOOPEE BOYS, THE

Rodriguez, Ramon
STREETS OF GOLD

Rodriguez, Raul
COME LA VIDA MISMA, ph; PLACIDO, ph

Rodriguez, Roberto
EL JUEGO DE LA MUERTE, w; LA ALACRANA, p&w;
MATANZA EN MATAMOROS, p

Rodriguez, Silvio
COME LA VIDA MISMA, m

Rodriguez, Susan
MATANZA EN MATAMOROS, m

Rodriguez, Susy
LA ALACRANA

Rodriguez, Suzy
EL JUEGO DE LA MUERTE, m

Rodway, Norman
TAI-PAN

Rodzianko, Alexandra
STEWARDESS SCHOOL

Roediger, Rolf
Obituaries

Roedl, Josef
DER WILDE CLOWN, d&w

Roeg, Nicolas
CASTAWAY, d

Roeg, Waldo
HIGHLANDER

Roel, Gabriela
AMOR A LA VUELTA DE LA ESQUINA

Roelfs, Jan
SHADOW OF VICTORY, art d

Roessel, Skip
VIOLATED, ph

Roestad, Paul
HUD, ph

Rofeh, Jamal
STRIPPER

Rogers, B.J.
DR. OTTO AND THE RIDDLE OF THE GLOOM BEAM

Rogers, Cletus
SOLDIER'S REVENGE

Rogers, Frank
IMAGEMAKER, THE, spec eff

Rogers, Jeffrey
THE KARATE KID PART II

Rogers, Ken
BOY IN BLUE, THE

Rogers, Keri
FLIGHT OF THE NAVIGATOR

Rogers, Lisa
TWO FRIENDS

Rogers, Michael
MOSQUITO COAST, THE

Rogers, Michele
HOLLYWOOD VICE SQUAD

Rogers, Mimi
GUNG HO

Rogers, Rita
SUNSET STRIP

Rogers, Steve
DEVASTATOR, THE; NINJA TURF; SILK

Rogers, Stuart
VAMP

Rogers, Than
PLATOON

Rogerson, Majda
KILLER PARTY

Roggisch, Peter
BLIND DIRECTOR, THE

Rognvaldsson, Hjalti
DEN FRUSNA LEOPARDEN

Rogosin, Roy M.
WEEKEND WARRIORS, w

Rogowski, Gator
THRASHIN'

Rogucci, Leandro
INSOMNIACS, set d

Rohmer, Eric
SUMMER, d&w

Rohner, Clayton
APRIL FOOL'S DAY; MODERN GIRLS

Rohr, Tony
NO SURRENDER; ROCINANTE

Rohrbough, Richard
FERRIS BUELLER'S DAY OFF

Rohrig, H.G.
SPRING SYMPHONY

Roival, Olivia
CONTACTO CHICANO

Rojan, Valerie
LA GITANE; LE DEBUTANT

Rojas, Alberto
EL BRONCO

Rojo, Ana Patricia
VENENO PARA LAS HADAS

Rojo, Helena
NOCHE DE JUERGA

Rojo, Jose
KAPAX DEL AMAZONAS, ed

Roland, George
AMERICAN JUSTICE

Roland, Marie-Rose
GOLDEN EIGHTIES

Rolapp, Thomas
RETURN

Roldan, Juan Manuel
EL AMOR BRUJO

Rolf, Tom
9½ WEEKS, ed; QUICKSILVER, ed

Rolffes, Kirsten
YES, DET ER FAR!

Roli, Mino
SENZA SCRUPOLI, w

Rolike, Hank
LONGSHOT, THE

Roll, Gernot
EIN FLIEHENDES PFERD, ph; WELCOME IN VIENNA,
ph

Rolle, Marian
ALMACITA DI DESOLATO

Rolle, Roxanne
BAD GUYS ; JO JO DANCER, YOUR LIFE IS CALLING

Rollerson, Thomas
CHECK IS IN THE MAIL, THE

Rolston, Mark
ALIENS

Romachine, Anatoli
BORIS GODUNOV

Roman, Candy
EL AMOR BRUJO

Roman, Joseph Spallina
MURPHY'S LAW

Roman, Pedro
TEO EL PELIRROJO, p

Roman, Raul
CAGED GLASS, ed

Romancik, Elo
SIESTA VETA

Romancik, Ivan
SIESTA VETA

Romand, Beatrice
SUMMER

Romand, Gina
GAVILAN O PALOMA

Romano, Frank
HELL SQUAD

Romano, Jimmy
QUICKSILVER

Romano, Kim
BEST OF TIMES, THE

Romano, Manuela
YUPPIES, I GIOVANI DI SUCCESSO

Romano, Maria
FINAL EXECUTIONER, THE; WOMEN'S PRISON
MASSACRE

Romano, Norma
DIAPASON, set d&cos

Romanus, Richard
MURPHY'S LAW

Romberg, Carolyn
SCREAMPLAY

Romero, Constantino
LOLA

Romero, David
OVER THE SUMMER

Romero, Joanelle Nadine
VENDETTA

Romero, Sandro
A LA SALIDA NOS VEMOS, w

Romeuf, Ivan
PARENTAL CLAIM

Romiti, Loredana
MORIRAI A MEZZANOTTE

Romm, Harry A.
Obituaries

Romor, Laurent
CONSEIL DE FAMILLE

Ron-Feder, Galila
NADIA, w

Ronard, Jason
JAKE SPEED

Ronaszegi, Miklos
KISMASZAT ES A GEZENGUZOK, w

Rondinella, Clelia
LA VENEXIANA

Rondinella, Thomas R.
GIRLS SCHOOL SCREAMERS, ed

Rong, Hong
CAN YUE

Ronglu, Deng
CUODIAN YUANYANG, w

Roodt, Darrell
PLACE OF WEEPING, d; PLACE OF WEEPING, w

Rooney, Mickey
LIGHTNING—THE WHITE STALLION

Roos, Fred
SEVEN MINUTES IN HEAVEN, p

Roosen, Adelheid
MAMA IS BOOS!

Roosendahl, Jennifer
'NIGHT, MOTHER

Roosje, Gwendomar
ALMACITA DI DESOLATO

Roper, Cindy
ROCKIN' ROAD TRIP

Roperto, Andrew
DEADLY FRIEND

Roque, Elso
O VESTIDO COR DE FOGO, ph

Ros, Tarrago
PERROS DE LA NOCHE, m

Rosa, Geraldo
RUNNING OUT OF LUCK

Rosal, Maia
NUTCRACKER: THE MOTION PICTURE

Rosales, Thomas
RAW DEAL

Rosales, Tom
EYE OF THE TIGER

Rosas, John
NINJA TURF

Rosato, Tony
BUSTED UP; SEPARATE VACATIONS

Rose, Alan
DANCING IN THE DARK

Rose, Alexandra
NOTHING IN COMMON, p

Rose, Cristine
FATHERLAND

Rose, Gorilla
POPULATION: ONE

Rose, Jamie
REBEL LOVE

Rose, Mark
ROCKIN' ROAD TRIP

Rose, Robin Pearson
LAST RESORT, THE

Rose, Roger
FRIDAY THE 13TH PART VI: JASON LIVES

Rose, Sandy
HOLLYWOOD ZAP!

Rose, Sherman A.
Obituaries

Rose, Stuart
ABSOLUTE BEGINNERS, art d

Rose, Tim
HOWARD THE DUCK

Rosegger, Peter
ERDSEGEN, w

Rosell, Josep
EL ANO DE LAS LUCES, set d; TIEMPO DE SILENCIO,
set d

Rosella
SE SUFRE PERO SE GOZA

Rosemarin, Hilton
MAXIMUM OVERDRIVE, set d; RAW DEAL, set d

Rosen, Brian
BULLSEYE, p

Rosen, Charles
NOTHING IN COMMON, prod d; QUICKSILVER, prod
d; TOUCH AND GO, prod d; WHOOPEE BOYS, THE,
prod d

Rosen, Daniel
WAY IT IS, THE

Rosen, Nestor
SOLDIER'S REVENGE

Rosenbaum, David
IMAGEMAKER, THE

Rosenbaum, J.D.
PLAYING FOR KEEPS

Rosenbaum, Jeffrey M.
FIREWALKER, w

Rosenbaum, Joel
BILLY GALVIN, m; RAW DEAL, m

Rosenberg, Alan
STEWARDESS SCHOOL

Rosenberg, Ilan
HASHIGAON HAGADOL, ph; NADIA, ph

Rosenberg, Louis
HASHIGAON HAGADOL

Rosenberg, Philip
MANHATTAN PROJECT, THE, prod d

Rosenblat, Barbara
HAUNTED HONEYMOON; LITTLE SHOP OF
HORRORS

Rosenblatt, Gary
CLASS OF NUKE 'EM HIGH

Rosenblatt, Mark
VENDETTA

Rosenfeld, Hilary
AT CLOSE RANGE, cos; DESERT BLOOM, cos; NO
MERCY, cos

Rosenfeld, Mike
OUT OF BOUNDS, p

Rosenfeld, Ree
NADIA

Rosenfeld, Ri
KOL AHAVO-TAI

Rosengren, Bertil
RAVEN, ph

Rosenman, Leonard
STAR TREK IV: THE VOYAGE HOME, m

Rosensweig, Scott
NOBODY'S FOOL

Rosenthal, Daniel
SLOANE, d; SLOANE, p

Rosenthal, Leslie
CHOPPING MALL, ed

Rosette
SUMMER

Roshko, Ariel
BAR 51—SISTER OF LOVE, art d

Rosma, Juha
HUOMENNA, d&w

Rosner, Dean
SCREEN TEST

Ross, Alex
COLOR OF MONEY, THE; TOUCH AND GO

Ross, Andy
HAUNTED HONEYMOON

Ross, Arnie
FLIGHT OF THE NAVIGATOR

Ross, Brian Lee
SMART ALEC, ed

Ross, Charlotte
TOUCH AND GO

Ross, Chelcie
HOOSIERS; ONE MORE SATURDAY NIGHT

Ross, Donald
HAMBURGER, w

Ross, Eddie
LETTER TO BREZHNEV; SCREEN TEST

Ross, Gene
8 MILLION WAYS TO DIE; WISDOM

Ross, George
FAT GUY GOES NUTZOID!!

Ross, Howard
DAYS OF HELL

Ross, J. Christopher
JUMPIN' JACK FLASH

Ross, Jason
FINAL MISSION

Ross, Jo
HAUNTED HONEYMOON

Ross, Lola
CARNAGE

Ross, Martin
MY CHAUFFEUR, m/l

Ross, Marty
DANGEROUSLY CLOSE, w; MY CHAUFFEUR

Ross, Monty
SHE'S GOTTA HAVE IT

Ross, Neil
AMERICAN TAIL, AN; TRANSFORMERS: THE
MOVIE, THE

Ross, Pamela
SORORITY HOUSE MASSACRE

Ross, Ricco
ALIENS

Ross, Ron
STEWARDESS SCHOOL

Ross, Ronnie
THRASHIN', stunts

Ross, Sharyn
PLAYING FOR KEEPS, ed

Ross, Stan
HOLLYWOOD ZAP!

Ross, Stanley Ralph
BOSS' WIFE, THE

Ross, Ted
FLY, THE, spec eff

Ross, Valeria
THUNDER WARRIOR

Rossall, Kerry
NO TIME TO DIE, stunts

Rosselli, Bernard
FRENCH LESSON

Rossellini, Isabella
BLUE VELVET

Rosser, Jimmy
REBEL LOVE

Rossi, Giannetto De
TAI-PAN, makeup

Rossi, Lucca
ROOM WITH A VIEW, A

Rossi, Ugo De
GINGER & FRED, m

Rossiello, Philip
FAT GUY GOES NUTZOID!!, set d

Rossip, Marty
FLOODSTAGE

Rossman, Erna
SEVEN MINUTES IN HEAVEN

Rosso, Enrica
IL CASO MORO

Rossovich, Rick
MORNING AFTER, THE; TOP GUN

Rostaing, Hubert
PRUNELLE BLUES, m

Rostock, Gert
TAKE IT EASY

Roswell, Maggie
PRETTY IN PINK

Rota, Nino
BLUE CITY, m/l

Rotblatt, Janet
MURPHY'S LAW; WISDOM

Roth, Ann
HEARTBURN, cos; MORNING AFTER, THE, cos

Roth, Danny
AVANTI POPOLO

Roth, Dena
CHECK IS IN THE MAIL, THE, set d

Roth, Hana
ALEX KHOLE AHAVA

Roth, Ivan E.
3:15, THE MOMENT OF TRUTH; HOLLYWOOD ZAP!;
NIGHT OF THE CREEPS

Roth, Joe
OFF BEAT, p; STREETS OF GOLD, d; STREETS OF
GOLD, p; WHERE THE RIVER RUNS BLACK, p

Roth, Jorge
LOS HIJOS DE LA GUERRA FRIA, ph

Roth, Richard
MANHUNTER, p

Roth, Roberto
NEMESIO

Roth, Stephen J.
ONE NIGHT ONLY, p; SEPARATE VACATIONS, p

Roth, Steve
8 MILLION WAYS TO DIE, p

Rothman, John
HEARTBURN

Rothman, Marion
CLUB PARADISE, ed

Rothman, Shirley
BALBOA

Rothschild, Michael
ROCKIN' ROAD TRIP, p

Rothstein, Debbie
ODD JOBS

Rothwell, Robert
JUST BETWEEN FRIENDS

Rottier, Caroline
CONGO EXPRESS

Rotundo, Ernie
FLYING, ed

Rotundo, Nick
BLUE MAN, THE, ed; BULLIES, ed; PINK CHIQUITAS,
THE, w

Rouden, Thierry
LE BONHEUR A ENCORE FRAPPE, ed

Rouffio, Jacques
L'ETAT DE GRACE, d; L'ETAT DE GRACE, w; MON
BEAU-FRERE A TUE MA SOEUR, d; MON BEAU-
FRERE A TUE MA SOEUR, w

Roughley, Lill
MR. LOVE

Roulet, Dominique
INSPECTEUR LAVARDIN, w

Rounds, John
PANTHER SQUAD

Rounsavelle, Rick
SCORPION

Rourke, Mickey
9½ WEEKS

Rouslsnova, Nina
MOI DRUG IVAN LAPSHIN

Roussakov, Konstantin
DA EBICHASH NA INAT, art d

Roussea, Jenny
O MELISSOKOMOS

Rousseau, Marie Christine
FAUBOURG SAINT-MARTIN

Roussel, Anne
FLAGRANT DESIR

Roussel, Gilbert
WOMEN'S PRISON MASSACRE, d

Roussel, Myriem
BLEU COMME L'ENFER

Rousselot, Philippe
THERESE, ph

Roussillon, Jean-Paul
LES CLOWNS DE DIEU

Roussilon, Jean-Paul
ETATS D'AME

Roussimoff, Ari M.
HEARTBURN

Routledge, Alison
BRIDGE TO NOWHERE

Routt, Denise
ODD JOBS

Rouvel, Catherine
JUBIABA

Rovere, Liliane
ROUND MIDNIGHT

Rovere, Lucrezia Lante Della
LET'S HOPE IT'S A GIRL

Rowe, Glenys
DOGS IN SPACE, p

Rowe, John
CLOCKWISE

Rowe, Lindel
SHORT CHANGED

Rowe, Lyndel
PLAYING BEATIE BOW

Rowe, Peter
LOST!, p, d&w

Rowell, Shannon
KING KONG LIVES

Rowen, Mark
JUMPIN' JACK FLASH

Rowland, Bruce
COOL CHANGE, m

Rowles, Polly
POWER; SWEET LIBERTY

Rowley, Peter
FOOTROT FLATS

Roxane
SCHLEUSE 17

Roxie
BREEDERS

Roy, Arundhati
MASSEY SAHIB

Roy, Dominique
PARIS MINUIT, ed

Roy, Eddie
CRAZY MOON

Roy, Gabrielle
TRAMP AT THE DOOR, w

Roy, Niranjan
CHOPPER

Roy, Nitish
AGHAAT, art d; GENESIS, prod d; NEW DELHI TIMES,
art d

Roy, Soumendu
DEBSHISHU, ph

Royalle, Candida
SEX APPEAL

Royce, Roselyn
SIZZLE BEACH, U.S.A.

Roysden, Thomas Lee
MEN'S CLUB, THE, set d

Rozbaruch, Neil
NO RETREAT, NO SURRENDER

Rozier, Jacques
MAINE-OCEAN, d; MAINE-OCEAN, ed; MAINE-
OCEAN, w

Rubbo, Joe
HOT CHILI

Rubell, Maria
SALVADOR

Ruben, Andy
PATRIOT, THE, w

Ruben, Katt Shea
PATRIOT, THE, w; PSYCHO III

Rubens, Giovanni
ANCHE LEI FUMAVA IL SIGARO

Rubenstein, Arthur B.
HYPER SAPIEN: PEOPLE FROM ANOTHER STAR, m

Rubenstein, Michael
AMERICA

Rubenstein, Phil
BACK TO SCHOOL; HOLLYWOOD VICE SQUAD

Rubeo, Bruno
PLATOON, prod d; SALVADOR; SALVADOR, prod d

Rubiales, Marcela
ES MI VIDA—EL NOA NOA 2

Rubin, Benny
Obituaries

Rubin, Bruce Joel
DEADLY FRIEND, w

Rubin, Dada
AMERICA 3000

Rubinek, Saul
SWEET LIBERTY

Rubini, Michael
BAND OF THE HAND, m

Rubini, Michel
ABDUCTED, m; MANHUNTER, m; MANHUNTER, m/l;
WHAT WAITS BELOW, m

Rubini, Sergio
IL CASO MORO

Rubinoff, David
Obituaries

Rubinstein, Amnon
NADIA, d; NADIA, w

Rubinstein, Arthur B.
BEST OF TIMES, THE, m

Rubinstein, Keith
KGB—THE SECRET WAR, p

Rubinstein, Keith Fox
ODD JOBS, p

Rubinstein, Zelda
POLTERGEIST II

Rubio, Martxelo
27 HORAS

Ruccolo, Jimi
BAND OF THE HAND

Ruch, Walter
EL SUIZO—UN AMOUR EN ESPAGNE

Ruchpaul, Shanti
ABSOLUTE BEGINNERS

Ruck, Alan
FERRIS BUELLER'S DAY OFF

Rucker, Luther
HEARTBURN; STREETS OF GOLD

Rucker, Steve
ARMED RESPONSE, m; ARMED RESPONSE, m/l;
PRAY FOR DEATH, m

Rudel, Marie-Helene
RUE DU DEPART; RUE DU DEPART, w

Rudich, Erich
BAR 51—SISTER OF LOVE, m; HAKRAV AL
HAVA'AD, m; HAKRAV AL HAVA'AD, m/l

Rudine, Francine C.
PLAY DEAD, p

Rudnick, Regina
VIRUS HAS NO MORALS, A

Rudnik, Barbara
DOUCE FRANCE; MULLERS BURO

Rudolf, Rainer
CHICO REI

Rudolph, Claude Oliver
JOURNEY, THE

Rudolph, Hans Christian
STAMMHEIM

Rudy, Reed
FREE RIDE

Ruehil, Mercedes
HEARTBURN

Ruethlein, Maximilian
VA BANQUE

Ruff, Billy
THRASHIN'

Ruffalo, Joe
UNDER THE CHERRY MOON, p

Sabbatini, Enrico
MISSION, THE, cos

Sabella, Ernie
TOUGH GUYS

Sabella, Paul
GOBOTS: BATTLE OF THE ROCKLORDS, anim

Sabelli, Stefano
IL RAGAZZO DEL PONY EXPRESS

Sabine, Thierry
MAN AND A WOMAN: 20 YEARS LATER, A

Sabinin, A.
PISMA MERTVOGO CHELOVEKA

Sablone, Lidia
VALHALLA, ed

Sabourin, Michel
EQUINOXE

Sacchetti, Dardano
CUT AND RUN, w; DEMONI 2—L'INCUBO RITORNA,
w; MANHATTAN BABY, w; MORIRAI A
MEZZANOTTE, w; SENSI, w

Sacha, J.J.
IMPURE THOUGHTS

Sache, Bernadette Le
DOUCE FRANCE

Sachs, Alain
PARIS MINUIT

Sachs, William
HOT CHILI, d; HOT CHILI, m/l; HOT CHILI, w

Sacks, Alan
THRASHIN', p; THRASHIN', w

Sacks, Ezra
WILDCATS, w

Sacks, Quinny
KNIGHTS AND EMERALDS, ch

Sacripanti, Mauro
SAVING GRACE

Sacristan, Jose
VIAJE A NINGUNA PARTE

Sade
ABSOLUTE BEGINNERS

Sader, Alan
KING KONG LIVES

Sadler, Bill
OFF BEAT

Sadler, Brian
DIRT BIKE KID, THE

Sadrieva, Zainob
GRANNY GENERAL

Sae, Shuichi
NINGUEN NO YAKUSOKU, w

Saegusa, S.
CYOEI NO MURE, m

Saeki, Masahisa
ADVENTURES OF THE AMERICAN RABBIT, THE, p

Saez, Fernando
WERTHER, art d

Safkouni, Najah
WHAT HAPPENED NEXT YEAR

Sagal, Liz
HOWARD THE DUCK

Sagliani, Ric
THREE AMIGOS, makeup

Sagodi, Bence
KISMASZAT ES A GEZENGUZOK

Sahd, Jihad
SUN ON A HAZY DAY, THE

Sahetapy, Ray
SECANGKIR KOPI PAHIT

Sahi, Deepa
AGHAAT

Sahin, Osman
KURBAGALAR, w

Sahlin, Anna
ALLA VI BARN I BULLERBY

Sahn, Doug
ECHO PARK, m/l

Sahraoui, Youcef
LAST IMAGE, THE, ph

Saieb, Azouz
UNDER THE CHERRY MOON

Saiet, Eric
FERRIS BUELLER'S DAY OFF; ONE MORE
SATURDAY NIGHT

Saiia, Armand
SCREAMPLAY

Saijonmaa, Arja
DREAM OF NORTHERN LIGHTS

Saiko, Natalia
CHICHERIN

Sailer, Sherry
CHOKE CANYON

Saint Jean, Antoine
GINGER & FRED

Saint, Eva Marie
NOTHING IN COMMON

Saint, George
DEVASTATOR, THE, ed

Saint, Jan
BEER

Saint-Macary, Xavier
LE DEBUTANT

Sainte-Marie, Buffy
STRIPPER, m

Sainte-Marie, Chloe
LA GUEPE

Saire, Warren
LADY JANE

Saito, Shinri
COMBAT SHOCK

Sakamoto, Ryuichi
KONEKO MONOGATARI, m

Sakata, Gerald
LOW BLOW

Saks, Gene
BRIGHTON BEACH MEMOIRS, d

Sakura, Kinzo
TAMPOPO

Sala, Henry
NIGHTMARE WEEKEND, d

Saladin, Soultan
TITAN SERAMBUT DIBELAH TUJUH

Salah, Mafi
AMERICA 3000

Salam, Malek
GHAME AFGHAN, m

Salama, Gamal
AL DAHIYA, m

Salcedo, Jose
BANDERA NEGRA, ed; LA MITAD DEL CIELO, ed;
MATADOR, ed

Salcido, Oscar Torrero
QUE ME MATEN DE UNA VEZ, ph

Saldutti, Peter V.
PSYCHO III, cos

Saleb, Suheer
GRITTA VOM RATTENSCHLOSS

Salem, Pamela
SALOME

Salerno, Enrico Maria
SCUOLA DI LADRI

Salerno, Sabrina
GRANDI MAGAZZINI

Sales, Daniel
WAY IT IS, THE, p

Sales, Robin
SHOOT FOR THE SUN, ed

Salfa, Amedeo
ELOGIO DELLA PAZZIA, ed; REGALO DI NATALE,
ed; UNA DOMENICA SI, ed

Salguero, Aldolpho
MOSQUITO COAST, THE

Salim, Atif
AL DAHIYA, d

Salim, Yusuf
REVENGE FOR JUSTICE

Salima
RAI

Salinas, Julio
ANCHE LEI FUMAVA IL SIGARO, w

Salinger, Diane
MORNING AFTER, THE

Salinger, Matt
POWER

Salisbury, Anne
DEATH OF THE HEART, THE, cos

Salkin, Pascale
GOLDEN EIGHTIES; LA PURITAINE

Salles, Geraldo
WHERE THE RIVER RUNS BLACK

Salles, Maria Helena
EU SEI QUE VOU TE AMAR, art d

Sallet, Emmanuelle
UNDER THE CHERRY MOON

Sallinen, Aulis
KUNINGAS LAHTEE RANSKAAN, m

Sallis, Crispian
ALIENS, set d

Sallows, Ken
DEPARTURE, ed; MALCOLM, ed

Salmela, Irma
SUURI ILLUSIONI, ed

Salmela, Keijo
GRONA GUBBAR FRAN Y.R.

Salmela, Sari
SUURI ILLUSIONI, cos

Salmi, Albert
BORN AMERICAN

Salminen, Esko
VALKOINEN KAAPIO

Salminen, Saara
BRODERNA MOZART

Salmon, Andres
LOLA

Salmon, Peter
LABYRINTH

Salmon, Tim
YOUNGBLOOD

Salome, Tony
WILDCATS

Salomon, Amnon
ALEX KHOLE AHAVA, ph

Salomon, Emilio
MALABRIGO, p

Salomon, Mikael
BARNDOMMENS GADE, ph; WOLF AT THE DOOR,
THE, ph

Salomon, Ron
ALEX KHOLE AHAVA, cos

Salonia, Adriana
LA NOCHE DE LOS LAPICES

Salovic, Dennis
BUSTED UP

Salter, Greg
YOUNGBLOOD

Salter, Henry
PLAYING BEATIE BOW

Salter, Phoebe
PLAYING BEATIE BOW

Salter, Stephen
FAT GUY GOES NUTZOID!!

Saluja, Rene
NEW DELHI TIMES, ed

Salvador, Augusto
REVENGE FOR JUSTICE, ed

Salvadori, Roger
DESPERATE MOVES, prod d

Salvas, Claude
BUSTED UP

Salvati, Sergio
CRAWLSPACE, ph; THUNDER WARRIOR, ph

Salvati, Valentino
SEMBRA MORTO . . . MA E SOLO SVENUTO, art d

Salviani, Vincenzo
IL MIELE DEL DIAVOLO, w

Sam the Dog
SCREAMPLAY

Sam, Kwak Chol
POMNALUI NUNSOGI, ph

Sam-yook, Yoon
BBONG, w

Samadi, Yadollah
BUS, THE, d

Samardzic, Ljubisa
DOBROVOLJCI

Sambrell, Aldo
KAPAX DEL AMAZONAS

Samdar, Dodik
AMERICA 3000

Samec, Milan
ZA SRECU JE POTREBNO TROJE, p

Sameii, Mahmoud Abdel
LEL HAB KESSA AKHIRA, ph

Samioths, Yannis
HARDBODIES 2, spec eff

Samobor, Igor
KORMORAN

Samoilovski, Miso
SRECNA NOVA '49, ph

Samoljiov, Jevgenij
BORIS GODUNOV

Sampaio, Antonio Luis
LA MANSION DE ARAUCAIMA

Samperi, Salvatore
LA BONNE, d; LA BONNE, w

Sampier, Archie
DOWN BY LAW

Sampietro, Mercedes
WERTHER

Sampson, Will
FIREWALKER; POLTERGEIST II

Sams, Coke
DR. OTTO AND THE RIDDLE OF THE GLOOM BEAM,
m/l; DR. OTTO AND THE RIDDLE OF THE GLOOM
BEAM, p; DR. OTTO AND THE RIDDLE OF THE
GLOOM BEAM, w

Sams, Mark
ROCKIN' ROAD TRIP

Samtani, Gope T.
NO TIME TO DIE, p

Samuel, Fiona
FOOTROT FLATS

Samuel, Stephan
FATHERLAND

Samuels, Ron
IRON EAGLE, p

Samuelsson, Bo
BRODERNA MOZART

San Jose, Maria Luisa
TEO EL PELIRROJO

San Mateo, Juan I.
27 HORAS, ed

San Sebastian, Jon
27 HORAS

Sanchez, Anna
EL IMPERIO DE LA FORTUNA, art d

Sanchez, Carlos
EL TREN DE LOS PIONEROS, ph; PEQUENA
REVANCHA; SAN ANTONITO, ph

Sanchez, Claudia
LA BANDA DE LOS PANCHITOS

Sanchez, Cristeta
ANGKOR-CAMBODIA EXPRESS, makeup

Sanchez, Hector
EL NARCO—DUELO ROJO, m

Sanchez, Jaime
BIG TROUBLE

Sanchez, Ma. Del Carmen
SALVADOR

Sanchez, Marcelino
Obituaries

Sanchez, Max
PICARDIA MEXICANA NUMERO DOS, ed

Sanchez, Pacifico
NAKED VENGEANCE, ed; SILK, ed

Sanchez, Paul
PLATOON

Sanchez, Pepe
SAN ANTONITO, d; SAN ANTONITO, w

Sanchez, Salvador
ANGEL RIVER; SALVADOR

Sand, Bob
TOUCH AND GO, w

Sand, Elizabeth
BLACKOUT

Sand, Hans-Jacob
BLACKOUT

Sand, John
GRONA GUBBAR FRAN Y.R.

Sanda, Dominique
CORPS ET BIENS

Sandberg, Francine
GOLDEN EIGHTIES, ed

Sander, Casey
RATBOY; STEWARDESS SCHOOL

Sander, Kuli
AMERICA 3000, art d

Sander, Otto
ROSA LUXEMBURG

Sanderovitch, Anath
MALKAT HAKITA

Sanders, Andrew
CASTAWAY, prod d

Sanders, Beverly
JUST BETWEEN FRIENDS

Sanders, Fred
SWEET LIBERTY

Sanders, Jack Frost
SOLARBABIES, p

Sanders, Mark
NOBODY'S FOOL

Sanders, Ronald
FLY, THE, ed

Sanders, Suzanne
BORN AMERICAN, makeup

Sanders-Brahms, Helma
FUTURE OF EMILY, THE, d; LAPUTA, d&w

Sanderson, William
BLACK MOON RISING

Sandford, David
FAIR GAME

Sandford, John
GOING SANE, w; NIGHTMARE WEEKEND

Sandoval, Douglas
EL NARCO—DUELO ROJO

Sandoval, Lupita
EL DIA DE LOS ALBANILES II; EL MERCADO DE
HUMILDES

Sandoval, Michael
HOWARD THE DUCK

Sandre, Didier
LA FEMME DE MA VIE

Sandrelli, Amanda
LA CASA DEL BUON RITORNO

Sandrelli, Stefania
LA SPOSA AMERICANA; LA SPOSA ERA
BELLISSIMA; LET'S HOPE IT'S A GIRL

Sandrie, Stefano
IL RAGAZZO DEL PONY EXPRESS, w

Sands, Julian
ROOM WITH A VIEW, A

Sandstrom, Bobby
FINE MESS, A, m/l

Sandy, Bill
FRINGE DWELLERS, THE

Sandy, Gary
TROLL

Sanford, Chris
FIRE WITH FIRE, m/l

Sanford, Isabel
DESPERATE MOVES

Sang-A, Lee
GILSODOM

Sanger, Jonathan
FLIGHT OF THE NAVIGATOR

Sanguineti, Tatti
L'ULTIMA MAZURKA, w

Sani, Asrul
TITAN SERAMBUT DIBELAH TUJUH, w

Sano, Shiro
TO SLEEP SO AS TO DREAM

Sanogo, Diarrah
NYAMANTON

Santacroce, Mary Nell
IMPURE THOUGHTS

Santamaria, Jose
PIRATES

Santamaria, M.A.
EL CABALLERO DEL DRAGON, ed

Santana, Jose
JUMPIN' JACK FLASH; MORNING AFTER, THE

Santana, Luiz
JUBIABA

Santanelli, Manlio
LA BALLATA DI EVA, w

Santeiro, Gilberto
AS SETE VAMPIRAS, ed; AVAETE, A SEMENTE DA
VINGANCA, ed; SONHO SEM FIM, ed

Santella, Maria Luisa
LA BALLATA DI EVA

Santi, Laura
HOT CHILI, cos

Santiago, Cirio H.
DEVASTATOR, THE, p&d; FINAL MISSION, p&d;
NAKED VENGEANCE, d; NAKED VENGEANCE, p;
SILK, p&d; SILK, w

Santiso, Jose
BAD COMPANY, d; BAD COMPANY, w

Santoni, Joel
MORT UN DIMANCHE DE PLUIE, d; MORT UN
DIMANCHE DE PLUIE, w; SUIVEZ MON REGARD

Santoni, Reni
COBRA; RADIOACTIVE DREAMS

Santos, Bass
FINAL MISSION, ed

Santos, Butch
AMERICAN COMMANDOS, prod d

Santos, Edson
NEM TUDO E VERDADE, ph

Santos, Elvira
NAKED VENGEANCE, cos

Santos, Hermo
STONE BOY, ph

Santos, Isabel
LEJANIA

Santos, Lucelia
AS SETE VAMPIRAS

Santos, Luis Martin
TIEMPO DE SILENCIO, w

Sanudo, Paco
ESE LOCO LOCO HOSPITAL

Sanurio, Carlos
MONSTER DOG

Sanyal, Sushanta
DEBSHISHU

Sanz, Jorge
EL ANO DE LAS LUCES; MAMBRU SE FUE A LA
GUERRA

Sanz, Margarita
EL IMPERIO DE LA FORTUNA

Sanz, Nestor
EL HOMBRE QUE GANO LA RAZON, ph

Saparov, Usman
MUZSKOE VOSPITANIE, d; MUZSKOE VOSPITANIE,
w

Sapiensze, Rod
YOUNGBLOOD

Sapoff, Robert
SEX O'CLOCK NEWS, THE

Saponaro, Nicola
MONITORS

Sapunor, Tim
WISDOM

Sara, Mia
FERRIS BUELLER'S DAY OFF

Saraceni, Sergio G.
FULANINHA, m

Sarafian, Richard
EYE OF THE TIGER, d

Sarafinchan, Lillian
DANCING IN THE DARK, art d

Sarara, Tarak
AL KETTAR, m

Sarasuk, Bung
ANGKOR-CAMBODIA EXPRESS, spec eff

Sarcey, Martine
ETATS D'AME

Sarchielli, Massimo
SALOME; SAVING GRACE

Sarda, Yves
BLACK AND WHITE, ed

Sardanis, Steve
LEGAL EAGLES, set d; STAR CRYSTAL, prod d

Sarde, Alain
NEXT SUMMER, p; PRUNELLE BLUES, p; ROUND
MIDNIGHT; YIDDISH CONNECTION

Sarde, Philippe
COURS PRIVE, m; DEVIL IN THE FLESH, m; EVERY
TIME WE SAY GOODBYE, m; L'ETAT DE GRACE, m;
L'ETAT DE GRACE, m/l; LA PURITAINE, m;
MANHATTAN PROJECT, THE, m; MON BEAU-FRERE
A TUE MA SOEUR, m; PIRATES, m; SCENE OF THE
CRIME, m; SINCERELY CHARLOTTE, m

Sarde, Phillipe
NEXT SUMMER, m

Sardi, Idris
DOEA TANDA MATA, m

Sarelle, Leilani
NEON MANIACS

Sargent, Brian
FOOTROT FLATS

Sargis, Brian
VIOLETS ARE BLUE

Sargis, Keith
VIOLETS ARE BLUE

Sarin, Vic
DANCING IN THE DARK, ph; LOYALTIES, ph

Sarkisian, Daryl
BUSTED UP

Sarkisov, Leonid
ZAZZENNYJ FONAR

Sarlui, Eduard
SOLDIER'S REVENGE, w

Sarmiento, Valeria
TOP OF THE WHALE, ed

Sarner, Arlene
PEGGY SUE GOT MARRIED, w

Sarno, Janet
POWER

Sarolapova, Nina
KAK MOLODY MY BYLI

Sarot, Luc
ROUND MIDNIGHT

Sarrazin, Ibertine
AMOR A LA VUELTA DE LA ESQUINA, d&w

Sarri, Inga
BRODERNA MOZART

Schell, Ronnie
CHECK IS IN THE MAIL, THE

Schellenberg, August
CONFIDENTIAL; QUI A TIRE SUR NOS HISTOIRES
D'AMOUR?; TRAMP AT THE DOOR

Schellenberg, Joanna
TRAMP AT THE DOOR

Schembri, Julian
REVENGE OF THE TEENAGE VIXENS FROM OUTER
SPACE, THE

Schenck, Bob
CLASS OF NUKE 'EM HIGH

Schenck, Holly
DIRT BIKE KID, THE

Schenck, Wade
HOOSIERS

Schener, Patricia
COCAINE WARS

Schenkel, Hansueli
NOAH UND DER COWBOY, ph

Schenkkan, Robert
MANHATTAN PROJECT, THE; SWEET LIBERTY

Scherbakov, Pyotr
ZIMNI VECHER V GAGRAKH

Scherer, Theres
DER PENDLER, p

Scherick, Gregory
LAST RESORT, THE, ed

Scherr, Walter J.
WHATEVER IT TAKES, p

Scheutz, Wilfried
DIE NACHTMEERFAHRT

Schewe, Elisabeth
SPRING SYMPHONY, cos

Schiavi, Antonio Degli
LA STORIA

Schiavo, Francesca Lo
NAME OF THE ROSE, THE, set d

Schiavone, Roberto
GIOVANNI SENZAPENSIERI, ed; SEMBRA MORTO . . .
MA E SOLO SVENUTO, ed

Schidor, Dieter
DIE LIEBESWUSTE

Schier, Irwin
QUICKSILVER

Schiffer, Robert J.
TOUGH GUYS, makeup

Schifrin, Lalo
BLACK MOON RISING, m; LADIES CLUB, THE, m;
LADIES CLUB, THE, md

Schildkraut, Eric
STAMMHEIM

Schildt, Deborah
BELIZAIRE THE CAJUN, art d

Schildt, Henrik
AMOROSA

Schildt, Johan
AMOROSA

Schildt, Peter
AMOROSA

Schillaci, Charles
HOT CHILI

Schillemans, Dick
OP HOOP VAN ZEGEN, art d

Schiller, DonnaSu
ON VALENTINE'S DAY, set d

Schilling, William
BEST OF TIMES, THE; FIRE WITH FIRE

Schilling, William G.
RUTHLESS PEOPLE

Schindler, Monika
DAS HAUS AM FLUSS, ed

Schiopu, Nicolae
SECVENTE, art d

Schisgal, Reene
POWER, p

Schivazappa, Piero
LA SIGNORA DELLA NOTTE, d&w

Schlanger, Andras
KISMASZAT ES A GEZENGUZOK

Schlarth, Sharon
EAT AND RUN

Schlensag, Eva
LAPUTA, ed

Schlesinger, Peter
HIGH SPEED; WOHIN MIT WILLFRIED?

Schliessler, Tobias
CLOSE TO HOME, ph

Schlifke, Adam
SCREEN TEST

Schlifke, Michelle
SCREEN TEST

Schlitt, Marnie Ross
REBEL LOVE, makeup

Schlom, Marla Denise
PSYCHO III, cos

Schlumberger, Emmanuel
POLICE, p

Schmid, Monika
DUNKI-SCHOTT, cos; KONZERT FUR ALICE, cos

Schmidt, Arthur
RUTHLESS PEOPLE, ed

Schmidt, Benno
HANNAH AND HER SISTERS

Schmidt, Christian
MULLERS BURO

Schmidt, Dolly
LES CLOWNS DE DIEU, p

Schmidt, Hartwig
EIN FLIEHENDES PFERD, p

Schmidt, Jean
LES CLOWNS DE DIEU, d&w

Schmidt, Kendall
NEON MANIACS, m

Schmidt, Nathalie
LES CLOWNS DE DIEU

Schmidt, Ole
WOLF AT THE DOOR, THE, m

Schmidt, Stephen F.
WEEKEND WARRIORS

Schmidtke, Ned
MANHATTAN PROJECT, THE

Schmitt, Charles
MAUVAIS SANG

Schmitt, Lyn
AMERICAN ANTHEM

Schmitt, Sophie
TAXI BOY, ed

Schmitt-Klink, Liesgret
EIN FLIEHENDES PFERD, ed

Schmock, Jonathan
FERRIS BUELLER'S DAY OFF; RATBOY

Schmoeller, David
CRAWLSPACE, d&w

Schneider, Dawn
FREE RIDE

Schneider, De
ECHO PARK

Schneider, Dr. Charles
THAT'S LIFE

Schneider, Gary
CLASS OF NUKE 'EM HIGH

Schneider, John
COCAINE WARS

Schneider, Kurt
BIG HURT, THE

Schneider, Peter
LISI UND DER GENERAL

Schneider, Rick
FAT GUY GOES NUTZOID!!

Schneider, Vicky
RUNNING OUT OF LUCK

Schneider, Werner
GHAME AFGHAN, ph

Schneiderman, Leon
BACK TO SCHOOL

Schneiderman, Wally
LABYRINTH, makeup

Schnell, Curt
TRICK OR TREAT, prod d

Schnell, Curtis A.
LAST RESORT, THE, prod d

Schnell, Reinald
CLASS RELATIONS

Schneuer, Danny
SMILE OF THE LAMB, THE, ph

Schnmidt, Ken
KILLER PARTY

Schock, Rudolf
Obituaries

Schoedel, Hans
NAME OF THE ROSE, THE

Schoeffling, Michael
BELIZAIRE THE CAJUN

Schoeller, Valerie
LE BONHEUR A ENCORE FRAPPE

Schoenberg, Steven
HAMBURGER, ed

Schoener, Eberhard
DER WILDE CLOWN, m; DIE ZWEI GESICHTER DES
JANUAR, m

Schofield, Drew
SID AND NANCY

Schofield, Katharine
HALF MOON STREET

Schofield, Nell
AROUND THE WORLD IN EIGHTY WAYS

Schoklender, Pablo
NIGHTMARE'S PASSENGERS, w

Scholz, Gunther
AB HEUTE ERWACHSEN, d; AB HEUTE
ERWACHSEN, w

Schonborn, Michael
STAMMHEIM

Schonbrodt, Lothar
NAME OF THE ROSE, THE

Schonecker, Sabine
NOVEMBERKATZEN, ed

Schonfeld, Swetlana
UNTERMEHMEN GEIGENKASTEN

Schonherr, Dietmar
DER SCHWARZE TANNER

School, Ray Anne
BEGINNER'S LUCK, ed

Schoonmaker, Thelma
COLOR OF MONEY, THE, ed

Schoppe, James
GUNG HO, prod d

Schorgmeyer, Henriette
SPRING SYMPHONY, makeup

Schott, Bob
VAMP

Schott, Dale
CARE BEARS MOVIE II: A NEW GENERATION, d

Schoukine, Serge
DOUCE FRANCE, w

Schoyen, Hege
X

Schrader, Mathis
DAS HAUS AM FLUSS

Schrader, Paul
MOSQUITO COAST, THE, w

Schreffler, Marilyn
VAMP

Schreiber, Klaus
STAMMHEIM

Schreier, Gerd Hartmut
UNTERMEHMEN GEIGENKASTEN

Schreiner, Dirk
PPPERFORMER, THE, p

Schreurs, Eric
CHARLEY

Schroder, Dawn
NIGHT OF THE CREEPS

Schroder, Peter
BARNDOMMENS GADE; MORD I MORKET

Schroder, Susan
FIRE IN THE NIGHT

Schroeder, Camile
MY CHAUFFEUR, cos

Schroeder, Noelle
NUTCRACKER: THE MOTION PICTURE

Schroeder, Peter Henry
FIRE IN THE NIGHT

Schroeppel, Pat
REVENGE OF THE TEENAGE VIXENS FROM OUTER
SPACE, THE

Schroeter, Werner
DE L'ARGENTINE, p, d&w; DE L'ARGENTINE, ph;
DER ROSENKONIG, d; DER ROSENKONIG, p; DER
ROSENKONIG, w

Schrotter, Heike
FATHERLAND

Schrum, Peter
ELIMINATORS

Schtorev, Mitko
SKUPA MOYA, SKUPI MOY, m

Schubach, Miriam E.
8 MILLION WAYS TO DIE

Schuberg, Carol
PLAYING FOR KEEPS

Schubert, Franz
WELCOME IN VIENNA, m

Schubert, Helga
AB HEUTE ERWACHSEN, w

Schubert, Karin
PANTHER SQUAD

Seear, Andrew
HALF MOON STREET

Seely, Joe
ARMED AND DANGEROUS; TOUGH GUYS

Sefrioui, Abdou
CHAMS

Sefrioui, Aicha
CHAMS

Sefrioui, Najib
CHAMS, d&w; CHAMS, ed

Segal, Jaime
SEPARATE VACATIONS

Segal, Jeff
GOBOTS: BATTLE OF THE ROCKLORDS, w

Segal, Marion
LADIES CLUB, THE, ed

Segal, Misha
KGB—THE SECRET WAR, m

Segal, Nick
CHOPPING MALL

Segarini, Bob
RECRUITS

Seger, Bob
ABOUT LAST NIGHT, m/l

Segerstrom, Mikael
MOA

Segev, Danny
AVANTI POPOLO

Sehkurpelo, Jelena
KAK MOLODY MY BYLI

Seidakmatova, Sh.
DESCENDANT OF THE SNOW LEOPARD, THE

Seidel, Jodoc
DUNKI-SCHOTT

Seif, Salah Abou
AL BEDAYA, d; AL BEDAYA, w

Seigler, Dah've
ARMED RESPONSE

Seigner, Emmanuelle
COURS PRIVE

Seiler, Chrigi
DUNKI-SCHOTT, art d

Seiler, Elisabeth
DER PENDLER; DER SCHWARZE TANNER

Seip, Mattijn
DE VAL VAN PATRICIA HAGGERSMITH, d&w

Seippel, Edda
SPRING SYMPHONY

Seirton, Michael
HAUNTED HONEYMOON, set d

Seiter, Robert
Obituaries

Seitov, R.
DESCENDANT OF THE SNOW LEOPARD, THE

Seitz, Jane
AUF IMMER UND EWIG, ed; BLIND DIRECTOR, THE,
ed; NAME OF THE ROSE, THE, ed

Sekine, Toshio
ORA TOKYO SA YUKUDA, w

Sela, Zohar
AVANTI POPOLO, ed

Selby, Hubert
JOUR ET NUIT, w

Selby, Rodrick
COLOR OF MONEY, THE

Selcuk, Timur
KUYUCAKLI YUSUF, m

Selemon, Mark
EAT AND RUN, art d

Selesnow, Joan
RADIOACTIVE DREAMS

Selesnow, Rhonda
SHADOWS RUN BLACK

Selfe, Jim
PARTING GLANCES

Selikovsky, Hans
MULLERS BURO, ph

Selin, Markus
BORN AMERICAN, p; BORN AMERICAN, w

Selin, Riitta
VALKOINEN KAAPIO

Sellars, Gary
ABSOLUTE BEGINNERS

Sellars, Randy
RAW TUNES, ph

Selle, Lorraine de
WILD BEASTS; WOMEN'S PRISON MASSACRE

Seltzer, David
LUCAS, d&w

Seltzer, Dov
HAME'AHEV, m

Seltzer, Emily
LUCAS

Selzer, Milton
SID AND NANCY

Semenovich, Wesley
LOYALTIES

Semenovicz, Danka
L'AMANT MAGNIFIQUE, art d

Semionova, L.
MOI DRUG IVAN LAPSHIN, ed

Semler, Anne
GOING SANE

Semler, Dean
BULLSEYE, ph; GOING SANE, ph

Semler, Peter
LA MACHINE A DECOUDRE

Semmler, Lyn
STILL POINT, THE

Semple, Lorenzo
NEVER TOO YOUNG TO DIE, w

Sen, Bachoo
NIGHTMARE WEEKEND, p

Sen, Mrinal
GENESIS, d; GENESIS, w

Sen, Sova
CHOPPER

Sendak, Maurice
NUTCRACKER: THE MOTION PICTURE, cos;
NUTCRACKER: THE MOTION PICTURE, prod d;
NUTCRACKER: THE MOTION PICTURE, w

Seneca, Joe
CROSSROADS

Senese, James
SENZA SCRUPOLI, m

Seng, Poon Hung
PEKING OPERA BLUES, ph

Senia, Jean-Marie
ETATS D'AME, m

Senini, M. Phil
GETTING EVEN, w

Senmoto, Seizo
CABARET, ph

Senna, Ayrton
SCHWARZ UND OHNE ZUCKER

Senna, Orlando
MALANDRO, w

Sentier, Jean-Pierre
EXIT-EXIL; RUE DU DEPART; SARRAOUNIA

Senyal, Jorge
HOT CHILI, ph

Sepulveda, Winzlia
NEMESIO

Serato, Massimo
SAVING GRACE

Seray, Bernard
IL MIELE DEL DIAVOLO

Serbedzija, Rade
SAN O RUZI; VECERNJA ZVONA

Serdena, Gene
SORORITY HOUSE MASSACRE, set d

Serena, Franco
INNOCENZA

Seriano, Pepe
POBRE MARIPOSA

Serious, Yahoo
YOUNG EINSTEIN; YOUNG EINSTEIN, d; YOUNG
EINSTEIN, p; YOUNG EINSTEIN, w

Serna, Assumpta
LOLA; LULU DE NOCHE; MATADOR

Serna, Pepe
OUT OF BOUNDS

Seroka, Henri
FLIGHT OF THE SPRUCE GOOSE, m

Serra, Alex
SALOME; SQUADRA SELVAGGIA

Serra, Eric
KAMIKAZE, m

Serra, Luis Maria
CONTAR HASTA TEN, m; INSOMNIACS, m; MISS
MARY, m

Serra, Norberto
EIN BLICK—UND DIE LIEBE BRICHT AUS

Serra, Noun
LES CLOWNS DE DIEU, ed

Serrano, Julieta
EL CABALLERO DEL DRAGON; MATADOR

Serrano, Nestor
MONEY PIT, THE; MONEY PIT, THE

Serrano, Tina
LA NOCHE DE LOS LAPICES

Serrano, Tom
SCORPION

Serrault, Michel
MON BEAU-FRERE A TUE MA SOEUR

Serry, Viviane
MAMMAME

Servain, Philippe
PEAU D'ANGE, m

Sessa, Alex
COCAINE WARS, p

Sessions, Bob
LITTLE SHOP OF HORRORS

Sessions, John
CASTAWAY

Setbon, Philippe
MORT UN DIMANCHE DE PLUIE, w; PEAU D'ANGE,
w

Seth, Roshan
MY BEAUTIFUL LAUNDRETTE

Sethi, Nitin
KAHAN KAHAN SE GUZAR GAYA

Setta, Ivan
FULANINHA; HAPPILY EVER AFTER

Sette, Mauricio
COM LICENCA, EU VOU A LUTA, set d

Setwater, Brady W.
BAD GUYS , w

Seubert, Ernie
MULLERS BURO, m

Seunke, Orlow
PERVOLA: TRACKS IN THE SNOW, d; PERVOLA:
TRACKS IN THE SNOW, ed; PERVOLA: TRACKS IN
THE SNOW, p; PERVOLA: TRACKS IN THE SNOW, w

Severino, Joe
CLASS OF NUKE 'EM HIGH

Severino, Jose
O VESTIDO COR DE FOGO

Severo, Marieta
COM LICENCA, EU VOU A LUTA; COM LICENCA, EU
VOU A LUTA, w; O HOMEM DA CAPA PRETA;
SONHO SEM FIM

Severson, Jeff
BEST OF TIMES, THE

Sevieri, Kristina
REGALO DI NATALE

Sevilla, Alfredo
REDONDO

Sevilla, Manolo
EL AMOR BRUJO

Sevilla, Romy
PLATOON

Seville, Aaron
THE KARATE KID PART II

Seward, Mabel
NO SURRENDER

Sewell, James
CRY FROM THE MOUNTAIN, set d

Seweryn, Andrzej
LA FEMME DE MA VIE; LE MAL D'AIMER; QUI
TROP EMBRASSE

Sexton, Tommy
ADVENTURE OF FAUSTUS BIDGOOD, THE

Seydor, Paul
NEVER TOO YOUNG TO DIE, ed

Seye, Khoudia
BLACK MIC-MAC

Seyfried, Robert
MAMMAME

Seymour, Jane
HEAD OFFICE

Seymour, John D.   [John Russell Davenport Seymour]
Obituaries

Seymour, Phil
BLUE CITY

Seymour, Ralph
KILLER PARTY

Seynes, Catherine de
AMOROSA

Seyrig, Delphine
GOLDEN EIGHTIES

Sfetsas, Kyriacos
I NICHTA ME TI SILENA, m

Sfika, Anna
ALLIGORIA, p

Sfikas, Costas
ALLIGORIA, d&w

Sganzerla, Rogerio
NEM TUDO E VERDADE, p, d&w

Simtaine, Felix
MERCI MONSIEUR ROBERTSON

Sinanos, Andreas
KALI PATRITHA, SYNTROFE, ph

Sinclair, John
HALF MOON STREET

Sinclair, Karey
HELL SQUAD

Sinclair, Madge
STAR TREK IV: THE VOYAGE HOME

Sinclair, Patrick
BOY IN BLUE, THE

Sinclair, Peter
GOOD TO GO, ph

Sinclair, Ron
DEAD-END DRIVE-IN

Sinde, Miguel Gonzalez
EL DISPUTADO VOTO DEL SR. CAYO, ed

Sing, Ho Kim
PEKING OPERA BLUES, art d

Sing, Yee Tung
LUNATICS, THE, d&w

Singer, Jonathan
ONE MORE SATURDAY NIGHT

Singer, Maria
'38

Singh, Anant
PLACE OF WEEPING, p

Singh, Manohar
NEW DELHI TIMES

Singleton, Cheryl
SHE'S GOTTA HAVE IT

Sinkovits, Imre
KESERU IGAZSAG

Sinniger, Christian
PAULETTE

Sinoway, Mitchell
MODERN GIRLS, ed

Sio, Giuliana De
LET'S HOPE IT'S A GIRL

Siqueira, Sandro
BRAS CUBAS

Sir, Kati
VAKVILAGBAN

Sira, Gurdial
MY BEAUTIFUL LAUNDRETTE

Sirakov, Plamen
SKUPA MOYA, SKUPI MOY

Sirbu, Oana
LICEENI

Sire, Antoine
MAN AND A WOMAN: 20 YEARS LATER, A

Sirigzda, Algimantas
SUNUS PALAIDUNAS, art d

Sirisombat, U-Rai
ANGKOR-CAMBODIA EXPRESS, art d

Sirvimoskas, Jusras
SUNUS PALAIDUNAS, m

Sis, Vladimir
JONAS, DEJME TOMU VE STREDU, d

Sisak, David
RECRUITS

Siskind, Leda
JUST BETWEEN FRIENDS

Sisowath, Monirak
MISSION, THE

Sissoko, Cheik Omar
NYAMANTON, d&w

Sisson, Lim
LOW BLOW

Sitar, Peter
LEV S BILOU HRIVOU, ed

Sitou, Mustapha
HADDA, ph

Sivan
MUKHAMUKHAM, prod d

Sivers, Alexandre Von
LA MOITIE DE L'AMOUR

Sjoblom, Robert
MORRHAR OCH ARTOR

Sjogren, Olof
ALLA VI BARN I BULLERBY

Sjollema, Liesbeth
MARIA

Sjoman, Licka
RAVEN

Sjoman, Vilgot
MALACCA, p&d

Sjostrom, Carl
MOA

Skaaren, Warren
FIRE WITH FIRE, w

Skagen, Solve
HARD ASFALT, d&w

Skagestad, Bjorn
FAREWELL ILLUSION

Skaggs, Calvin
ON VALENTINE'S DAY, p

Skarsgard, Stellan
ORMENS VAG PA HALLEBERGET

Skeaping, Colin
HAUNTED HONEYMOON, stunts

Skeen, Charlie
AVENGING FORCE

Skell, Marina
EL HOMBRE QUE GANO LA RAZON

Skerritt, Tom
SPACECAMP; TOP GUN; WISDOM

Skinner, Margo
SEVEN MINUTES IN HEAVEN

Skinner, William L.
COBRA, art d; NOTHING IN COMMON, set d

Skjelfjord, Tone
DROMMESLOTTER, prod d

Skjonberg, Pal
BLACKOUT

Sklerov, Gloria
LONGSHOT, THE, m/l

Skobcevova, Irina
BORIS GODUNOV

Skobline, Irene
SUMMER

Skoglund, Rolf
I LAGENS NAMN

Skolimowski, Jerzy
LIGHTSHIP, THE, d

Skoller, Eddie
TAKE IT EASY

Skoog, Helge
BRODERNA MOZART

Skopek, Jozef
SIESTA VETA, makeup

Skorsky, Nicolas
DOUCE FRANCE, m; DOUCE FRANCE, m/l

Skousen, Niels
ET SKUD FRA HJERTET

Sky
ONE CRAZY SUMMER

Skyers, Michael
KNIGHTS AND EMERALDS

Skylight
AS SETE VAMPIRAS, p

Slack, Ben
MY CHAUFFEUR

Slade, Demian
RADIOACTIVE DREAMS

Slaff, Jonathan
BEER

Slama, Mark
3:15, THE MOMENT OF TRUTH

Slane, Rod
REVENGE, m

Slater, Christian
NAME OF THE ROSE, THE

Slater, Helen
RUTHLESS PEOPLE

Slater, Suzee
CHOPPING MALL

Slatinaru, Maria
BLIND DIRECTOR, THE

Slaughter, Sergeant
BAD GUYS

Slavi, Delia
SHADOW PLAY

Sleap, Steve
HOWARD THE DUCK

Sleete, Gena
DIRT BIKE KID, THE

Slingsby, David
BULLSEYE; SHORT CHANGED

Sloan, Jesse
DESERT BLOOM

Sloan, Lisa
8 MILLION WAYS TO DIE

Sloane, Lance
BIG BET, THE

Slocombe, Douglas
LADY JANE, ph

Slot, Pie
FAILURE, THE

Slovak, Hillel
TOUGH GUYS

Slovik, Sam
MY MAN ADAM

Slue, Errol
BUSTED UP

Slyde, Jimmy
ROUND MIDNIGHT

Slyter, Fred
SHORT CIRCUIT

Smaila, Umberto
IL RAGAZZO DEL PONY EXPRESS, m

Smal, Ewa
CHRZESNISAK, ed

Small, Bob
PULSEBEAT

Small, Michael
BRIGHTON BEACH MEMOIRS, m;
DREAM LOVER, m

Small, Ralph
HEAD OFFICE

Small, Robert
FLIGHT OF THE NAVIGATOR

Small, Wylie
NOBODY'S FOOL

Smalley, Peter
DEAD-END DRIVE-IN, w; EMMA'S WAR, w; SPIRITS
OF THE AIR, w

Smallwood, Allan
IN THE SHADOW OF KILIMANJARO, m/l

Smaragdis, Nikos
ENAS ISICHOS THANATOS, ph

Smart, Jean
FIRE WITH FIRE

Smathers, Nicole
OVER THE SUMMER

Smeaton, Bruce
DEPARTURE, m

Smidt, Burr
UPHILL ALL THE WAY, p

Smidt, Christopher
NUTCRACKER: THE MOTION PICTURE

Smirnoff, Alexia
BAD GUYS

Smirnoff, Yakov
HEARTBURN; MONEY PIT, THE

Smirnova, S.
PISMA MERTVOGO CHELOVEKA

Smit, Robbert
FOOTROT FLATS, anim

Smith Boucher, Savannah
ODD JOBS

Smith, Adrian
GOOD FATHER, THE, prod d

Smith, Alexis
TOUGH GUYS

Smith, Amanda
DANCING IN THE DARK

Smith, Andrew
QUICKSILVER

Smith, Anne
BACKLASH

Smith, Billy
BIG HURT, THE

Smith, Brendan
HOOSIERS, set d

Smith, Bubba
BLACK MOON RISING; POLICE ACADEMY 3: BACK
IN TRAINING

Smith, Cedric
SAMUEL LOUNT

Smith, Chad
ONE MORE SATURDAY NIGHT

Smith, Charles Martin
TRICK OR TREAT; TRICK OR TREAT, d

Smith, Christina
QUICKSILVER, makeup; STEWARDESS SCHOOL,
makeup

Smith, Clive A.
CARE BEARS MOVIE II: A NEW GENERATION, p

Smith, Curt
COLOR OF MONEY, THE, spec eff

Smith, Darryl B.
BEST OF TIMES, THE

Smith, Dawn
HELL SQUAD

Smith, Desiree
DEAD-END DRIVE-IN

Smith, Don
BACKLASH

Smith, Eddie
THE KARATE KID PART II

Smith, Eddie Roe
MY MAN ADAM

Smith, Eve
ODD JOBS

Smith, Evelyne
NIGHT OF THE CREEPS

Smith, Fred C.
DESERT BLOOM

Smith, Fred G.
MANHATTAN PROJECT, THE

Smith, Gary
WHAT COMES AROUND, w

Smith, Georgina
NO SURRENDER

Smith, Gordon J.
KILLER PARTY, spec eff; PLATOON, makeup

Smith, Graham
ROCKIN' ROAD TRIP; TRICK OR TREAT

Smith, H. Paul
SCREAMPLAY

Smith, Hal
ADVENTURES OF THE AMERICAN RABBIT, THE;
AMERICAN TAIL, AN

Smith, Heather
PINK CHIQUITAS, THE

Smith, Herb
SHORT CIRCUIT

Smith, Howard
AT CLOSE RANGE, ed

Smith, Iain
FRENCH LESSON, p

Smith, J. Grey
DIRT BIKE KID, THE, set d

Smith, J.W.
CROSSROADS

Smith, Jace
ARMED RESPONSE, m/l

Smith, Jeffrey
LOYALTIES; OUT OF BOUNDS

Smith, Jennifer
BALBOA

Smith, Jim
ECHO PARK

Smith, John
STAR CRYSTAL; SUNSET STRIP

Smith, Justin
Obituaries

Smith, Kate   [Kathryn Elizabeth Smith]
Obituaries

Smith, Keith
DEVIL IN THE FLESH

Smith, Kevin
DANGEROUS ORPHANS, w; SCREAMTIME

Smith, Lane
NATIVE SON

Smith, Lee
DEAD-END DRIVE-IN, ed

Smith, Leslie
ODD JOBS

Smith, Louise
WORKING GIRLS

Smith, Lydia
KING KONG LIVES

Smith, Maggie
ROOM WITH A VIEW, A

Smith, Marilee K.
SOMETHING WILD

Smith, Maurice
RECRUITS, p

Smith, Megan
HEAD OFFICE

Smith, Merva
KNIGHTS AND EMERALDS

Smith, Nicholas
THRASHIN', ed

Smith, Paul
SNO-LINE

Smith, Paul L.
HAUNTED HONEYMOON

Smith, Paul Martin
BORN AMERICAN, ed

Smith, Penny
CLAN OF THE CAVE BEAR, THE

Smith, Pete
STAR TREK IV: THE VOYAGE HOME, art d

Smith, Peter
LAST SONG; NO SURRENDER, d

Smith, Philip
MANHATTAN PROJECT, THE, set d

Smith, Roland
EVIXION

Smith, Ronnie
3:15, THE MOMENT OF TRUTH

Smith, Selden
BLUE VELVET

Smith, Sheenika
ABOUT LAST NIGHT

Smith, Simon
KNIGHTS AND EMERALDS

Smith, Slim
THUNDER WARRIOR

Smith, Smitty
FIRE WITH FIRE

Smith, Terry
LINK, cos

Smith, Walter Edward
WISDOM

Smith, Wendell
LOYALTIES

Smith, Will
IMAGEMAKER, THE

Smith, William
EYE OF THE TIGER

Smith, William Craig
Obituaries

Smith, Willy
COCAINE WARS, spec eff

Smith, Yeardley
MAXIMUM OVERDRIVE

Smith-Kee, Sydney Ann
ODD JOBS, set d

Smith-Simmons, Hallie
JUST BETWEEN FRIENDS, makeup

Smitrovitch, Bill
BAND OF THE HAND; MANHUNTER

Smits, Jimmy
RUNNING SCARED

Smolanoff, Bruce
MANHATTAN PROJECT, THE

Smoot, Reed
WRAITH, THE, ph

Smrz, Brett
Obituaries

Smudla, Ilja
DER SCHWARZE TANNER

Smuin, Paula Tracy
WILDCATS, ch

Smythe, Karen A.
WHOOPEE BOYS, THE

Sneddon, Graeme
LABYRINTH

Snee, Dennis
BACK TO SCHOOL, w

Sneed, Alice
MOSQUITO COAST, THE

Snell, Jerry
EQUINOXE

Snell, Peter
LADY JANE, p

Snell, Richard
NUTCRACKER: THE MOTION PICTURE, makeup

Snell, Timothy
NEON MANIACS, ed

Sneller, Jeffrey M.
IN THE SHADOW OF KILIMANJARO, p; IN THE
SHADOW OF KILIMANJARO, w

Snipes, Jon Jon
BLUE VELVET

Snipes, Wesley
WILDCATS

Snipp, Al
REVENGE OF THE TEENAGE VIXENS FROM OUTER
SPACE, THE

Snodgrass, Ken
DEAD-END DRIVE-IN

Snodgress, Carrie
MURPHY'S LAW

Snow, Daniel T.
MANHUNTER

Snow, Mark
JAKE SPEED, m

Snow, Norman
MANHUNTER

Snow, Tom
ABOUT LAST NIGHT, m/l

Snowden, Jane
FRENCH LESSON

Snyder, Arlen Dean
HEARTBREAK RIDGE

Snyder, David L.
ARMED AND DANGEROUS, prod d; BACK TO
SCHOOL, prod d

Snyder, Jared
AMERICAN JUSTICE

Snyder, John
SID AND NANCY

Snyder, Suzanne
NIGHT OF THE CREEPS

Soans, Robin
COMRADES

Soares, Elza
CINEMA FALADO

Soares, Jofre
QUILOMBO

Soavi, Michele
BLADE IN THE DARK, A

Sobbhana
ANANTARAM

Sobel, Harold
DANGEROUSLY CLOSE, p; VERY CLOSE QUARTERS,
p

Sobocinski, Witold
PIRATES, ph

Sobrevals, Cesar
SALVADOR

Socas, Maria
SOLDIER'S REVENGE

Sodann, Peter
GRITTA VOM RATTENSCHLOSS

Soderberg, Roland
BRODERNA MOZART, prod d

Soderstrom, Gunilla
BRODERNA MOZART

Sodikin
INTRUDER, THE, ph

Soeberg, Camilla
TWIST & SHOUT

Soet, John Steven
FIRE IN THE NIGHT, d&w

Soeteman, Gerard
ASSAULT, THE, w

Sofron, Cristian
NOI, CEI DIN LINIA INTII

Sohlberg, Kari
SUURI ILLUSIONI, ph

Soileau, Craig
BELIZAIRE THE CAJUN

Soinio, Olli
TUNTEMATON SOTILAS, ed

Soisson, Joel
TRICK OR TREAT, p; TRICK OR TREAT, w

Sojcher, Jacques
BABEL OPERA, OU LA REPETITION DE DON JUAN ;
BABEL OPERA, OU LA REPETITION DE DON JUAN ,
w

Sok, Kim Jong
GILSODOM

Sokol, Erin
NUTCRACKER: THE MOTION PICTURE

Sokol, Yuri
CACTUS, ph

Sola, Jose G. Blanco
EL DISPUTADO VOTO DEL SR.
CAYO, p

Sola, Miguel Angel
BAD COMPANY

Solano, Rosalio
ANGEL RIVER, ph

Solans, Jose
EL SUIZO—UN AMOUR EN ESPAGNE

Solares, Adolfo Martinez
EL DIA DE LOS ALBANILES II, p; EL DIA DE LOS
ALBANILES II, w

Solares, Alfonso Martinez
EL VECINDARIO—LOS MEXICANOS CALIENTES, p;
EL VECINDARIO—LOS MEXICANOS CALIENTES, w

Solares, Gilberto Martinez
EL DIA DE LOS ALBANILES II, d; EL DIA DE LOS
ALBANILES II, p; EL DIA DE LOS ALBANILES II, w;
EL VECINDARIO—LOS MEXICANOS CALIENTES, d;
EL VECINDARIO—LOS MEXICANOS CALIENTES, w

Solari, John
ARMED AND DANGEROUS

Solari, Suzanne
ROLLER BLADE

Solas, Humberto
UN HOMBRE DE EXITO, d&w

Soldati, Giovanni
LA SPOSA AMERICANA, d; LA SPOSA AMERICANA, w

Soldati, Mario
LA SPOSA AMERICANA, w

Soleimani, Said Amir
MIRZA NOWROUZ' SHOES

Solera, Antonio
EL AMOR BRUJO

Solis, Leonard
SOLDIER'S REVENGE, ph

Solis, Leonardo Rodriguez
LA NOCHE DE LOS LAPICES, ph

Sollenberger, Dick
FERRIS BUELLER'S DAY OFF

Solomon, Bruce
NIGHT OF THE CREEPS

Solomon, Elliott
SUNSET STRIP, m

Solomon, Ken
HARDBODIES 2, p; VENDETTA; VENDETTA, p

Solomon, Maribeth
LOST!, m

Solony, William
SHADOWS RUN BLACK

Soloviev, Alexander
BORIS GODUNOV

Soloviev, Sergei
CHUZHAJA, BELAJA I RJABOJ, d&w

Solow, Herbert F.
SAVING GRACE, p

Soltani, Barbara Lee
OUT OF BOUNDS

Solum, Ola
X; X, p

Solviatt, Sandro
RUNNING OUT OF LUCK

Somai, Shinji
CYOEI NO MURE, d; TYPHOON CLUB, d

Somersaulter, J.P.
DONNA ROSEBUD, d

Somma, Sebastiano
VOGLIA DI GUARDARE

Sommer, Andrew
P.O.W. THE ESCAPE

Sommer, Robert
SAVING GRACE

Sondag, Alan J.
QUICKSILVER

Sonego, Rodolfo
TROPPO FORTE, w

Song, Liao Cheng
SUPER CITIZEN, ed; SUPER CITIZEN, w

Song, Liu Hui
POMNALUI NUNSOGI, ph

Song, Patti
MORNING AFTER, THE

Song-Il, Sin
GILSODOM

Sood, Veena
LOYALTIES

Soorya
ORIDATH

Soose, William
PLAYING FOR KEEPS

Sop, So Gyong
POMNALUI NUNSOGI

Sopkiw, Michael
MONSTER SHARK

Soral, Agnes
BLEU COMME L'ENFER; I LOVE YOU; KILLING CARS; TWIST AGAIN A MOSCOU

Sordi, Alberto
TROPPO FORTE; TROPPO FORTE, w

Sorel, Ted
FROM BEYOND

Sorensen, Soren Krag
BARNDOMMENS GADE, prod d; TAKE IT EASY, prod d

Sorensen, Soren Kragh
TWIST & SHOUT, prod d

Sorenson, Iwa
BRODERNA MOZART

Soriano, Pepe
TE AMO

Sorin, Carlos
KING AND HIS MOVIE, A, d; KING AND HIS MOVIE, A, w

Sorkin, Arleen
ODD JOBS

Sorko-Ram, Ari
AMERICA 3000

Sorman, Marie
GRONA GUBBAR FRAN Y.R., cos

Sorrah, Renata
AVAETE, A SEMENTE DA VINGANCA

Sorvali, Ritva
PIMEYS ODOTTA

Sorvino, Paul
FINE MESS, A; VASECTOMY: A DELICATE MATTER; VERY CLOSE QUARTERS

Sosa, Argelio
EL CORAZON SOBRE LA TIERRA

Sosa, Roberto
SALVADOR

Sosa, Victor Manuel
CONTACTO CHICANO

Sosnowski, Janusz
HUOMENNA, art d

Soto, Frank
AMERICAN JUSTICE

Soto, Hugo
MAN FACING SOUTHEAST

Soto, Sergio
EL BRONCO, ed; EL MERCADO DE HUMILDES, ed; UN HOMBRE VIOLENTE, ed

Soubeil, Rafik El
SUN ON A HAZY DAY, THE

Souder, Larry
KING KONG LIVES

Soukouli, Rasme
ENAS ISICHOS THANATOS

Soutendijk, Renee
MOTTEN IM LICHT; OP HOOP VAN ZEGEN; SECOND VICTORY, THE

South Shore Drill Team
FERRIS BUELLER'S DAY OFF

South, Nicky
UNDER THE CHERRY MOON

Souther, J.D.
ABOUT LAST NIGHT, m/l; FIRE WITH FIRE, m/l

Southern, Mike
CAPTIVE, ph

Souto, Paulo Henrique
RUNNING OUT OF LUCK

Sovagovic, Anja
SAN O RUZI

Sovagovic, Fabijan
I TO CE PROCI; SAN O RUZI

Soviatt, Sandro
WHERE THE RIVER RUNS BLACK

Sovu, George
DECLARATIE DE DRAGOSTE, w; LICEENI, w

Sowinetz, Kurt
WELCOME IN VIENNA

Sowton, Ronald
CLOCKWISE

Soygazi, Hale
BIR AVUO CENNET

Sozen, Joyce
FAT GUY GOES NUTZOID!!

Spaangard, Helle
TWIST & SHOUT

Spacek, Sissy
'NIGHT, MOTHER; CRIMES OF THE HEART; VIOLETS ARE BLUE

Spacey, Kevin
HEARTBURN

Spack, Caroline
LETTER TO BREZHNEV, p

Spada, Andrea
LA STORIA

Spadaro, Adriana
SALOME, cos

Spadaro, Claudio
GIOVANNI SENZAPENSIERI; SEMBRA MORTO . . . MA E SOLO SVENUTO

Spader, James
PRETTY IN PINK

Spadoni, Lucisano
DELTA FORCE, THE, prod d

Spagnini, Egidio
IL RAGAZZO DEL PONY EXPRESS, art d

Spagnoli, Alberto
CUT AND RUN, ph

Spagnuolo, Ettore
THRONE OF FIRE, THE, p; VIOLENT BREED, THE, p

Spalding, Harriet
MORE THINGS CHANGE, THE

Spaltro, Enzo
MONITORS

Sparber, Hershel
KING KONG LIVES

Sparks, Adrian
MANHATTAN PROJECT, THE; VIOLETS ARE BLUE

Sparks, Charlie
NO RETREAT, NO SURRENDER

Sparks, Dana
THAT'S LIFE

Sparks, Don
RATBOY

Sparks, Jill Renee
OVER THE SUMMER

Sparks, Teresa
OVER THE SUMMER, d&w; OVER THE SUMMER, ed

Sparks, Tom
DR. OTTO AND THE RIDDLE OF THE GLOOM BEAM

Sparrflo, Cia
MOA, makeup

Sparv, Camilla
AMERICA 3000

Spashu, Arim
PROKA, ph

Spassov, Krassimir
ZABRAVOTE TOZI SLOCHAI, d; ZABRAVOTE TOZI SLOCHAI, w

Spassov, Radoslav
ZA KUDE PUTOVATE, ph; ZABRAVOTE TOZI SLOCHAI, ph

Spassova, Ruth
ZABRAVOTE TOZI SLOCHAI

Spatola, Michael
NEVER TOO YOUNG TO DIE, makeup; VENDETTA, makeup

Spatzek, Christian
ERDSEGEN

Spaziani, Monique
LE MATOU

Speck, Jan
SHORT CIRCUIT

Speck, Wieland
EAST OF THE WALL, d; EAST OF THE WALL, w

Spector, Ronnie
HOUSE, makeup

Spedding, Chris
HOLLYWOOD VICE SQUAD, m; HOLLYWOOD VICE SQUAD, m/l

Speed, Ken
DOWN AND OUT IN BEVERLY HILLS, spec eff; VIOLETS ARE BLUE, spec eff

Speights, Leslie
GOBOTS: BATTLE OF THE ROCKLORDS

Spelling, Aaron
'NIGHT, MOTHER, p

Spelvin, Georgina
POLICE ACADEMY 3: BACK IN TRAINING

Spence, Bruce
BULLSEYE

Spence, Michael
REFORM SCHOOL GIRLS, ed

Spence, Peter
CRAZY MOON

Spence, Stephen
LITTLE SHOP OF HORRORS, art d

Spencer, Alan
ABSOLUTE BEGINNERS

Spencer, Erastus
JO JO DANCER, YOUR LIFE IS CALLING

Spendlove, Rob
TAI-PAN

Spera, Mike
SCREAMTIME, ph

Sperber, Wendie Jo
STEWARDESS SCHOOL

Sperdouklis, Denis
DECLINE OF THE AMERICAN EMPIRE, THE, cos

Spezi, Mario
IL MOSTRO DI FIRENZE, w

Spheeris, Penelope
HOLLYWOOD VICE SQUAD, d

Spicer, Michael
BACKLASH, m

Spiegel, Harry
YOUNGBLOOD

Spiegel, Howard
FAT GUY GOES NUTZOID!!

Spiegler-Jacobs, Shirley
ONE MORE SATURDAY NIGHT

Spielvogel, Laurent
MAX MON AMOUR

Spier, Carol
FLY, THE, prod d

Spiers, David
PING PONG, ed

Spiesser, Jacques
ON A VOLE CHARLIE SPENCER!

Spijker, Monique
ASSAULT, THE

Spila, Otello
MEGLIO BACIARE UN COBRA, ph

Spillane, Jean
PLAYING FOR KEEPS

Spiller, Miriam
GIRLS SCHOOL SCREAMERS

Spiller, Ray
GIRLS SCHOOL SCREAMERS

Spillman, Harry
SEX O'CLOCK NEWS, THE

Spinak, Larry
VAMP

Spindale, Frederick
DER SOMMER DES SAMURAI, w

Spinell, Joe
WHOOPEE BOYS, THE

Spinelli, Maurizio
CASTIGHI, p

Spinelli, Philip
A FLOR DO MAR

Spinetti, Victor
UNDER THE CHERRY MOON

Spink, Flo
SCREEN TEST

Spinka, Ray
SORORITY HOUSE MASSACRE

Spinotti, Dante
CHOKE CANYON, ph; CRIMES OF THE HEART, ph;
MANHUNTER, ph

Spirov, Yordan
DA EBICHASH NA INAT

Spivak, Alice
HOLLYWOOD VICE SQUAD

Spoerri, Peter
DER SCHWARZE TANNER, p

Spoletini, Antonio
PIRATES

Sponsoli, Valeria
GIOVANNI SENZAPENSIERI, cos

Spoor, Berto
SILK

Sporcic, Ivica
VECERNJA ZVONA, art d

Sportel, Hemmo
MARIA, art d

Sportolaro, Tina
SINCERELY CHARLOTTE

Spottiswoode, Roger
BEST OF TIMES, THE, d

Sprang, John
SIZZLE BEACH, U.S.A., ph

Sprankle, Cyndi
REVENGE OF THE TEENAGE VIXENS FROM OUTER
SPACE, THE

Spratley, Tom
DEADLY FRIEND; FERRIS BUELLER'S DAY OFF

Sprattling, Rene
WISDOM

Spreckley, Arthur
NO SURRENDER

Sprenger, Wolf-Dietrich
DER POLENWEIHER

Spriggs, Gred
IMAGEMAKER, THE

Spriggs, Linda
LABYRINTH

Springfield, Wayne
EYE OF THE TIGER, art d

Springsteen, Pamela
MODERN GIRLS

Sprinkle, Larry
KING KONG LIVES; TRICK OR TREAT

Sprogoe, Ove
MORD I MORKET

Sprung, John
SHADOWS RUN BLACK, ph

Sprungalla, Walter
AM NACHESTEN MORGEN KEHRTE DER MINISTER
NICHT AN SEINEN ARBEITSPLATZ

Spudeas, Louis
BREEDERS

Spurling, Daria Jo
AMERICAN JUSTICE

Spurlock, Carl
REBEL LOVE

Squillante, Vittorio
CAMORRA

Squillo, Fred
COLOR OF MONEY, THE

Squire, Bonnie Kristian
SEPARATE VACATIONS

Sreenivasan
CHIDAMBARAM

Srinivasan, M.B.
MUKHAMUKHAM, m

Srp, Fred
KILLING CARS, ed

St. Croix, Dominique
RECRUITS

St. George, Clement
KGB—THE SECRET WAR

St. Germaine, Lizette
LOST!, set d

St. Hill, Krister
BRODERNA MOZART

St. James, Kim
ABSOLUTE BEGINNERS

St. Julian, Tracette
VENDETTA

Staab, Kevin
THRASHIN'

Stabulnieks, Uldis
SVESAS KAISLIBAS, m

Stace, Jennifer
JO JO DANCER, YOUR LIFE IS CALLING, ch

Stacey, Bill
COOL CHANGE, stunts

Stack, Patrick
F/X

Stack, Robert
BIG TROUBLE; TRANSFORMERS: THE MOVIE, THE

Stack, Rosemarie
BIG TROUBLE

Stack, Timothy
BACK TO SCHOOL

Stackpole, Mary Ann
BILLY GALVIN

Stacy, Emerald
NUTCRACKER: THE MOTION PICTURE

Stadlinger, Horst
ORMENS VAG PA HALLEBERGET, makeup

Stadwijk, Gerald
DE VAL VAN PATRICIA HAGGERSMITH

Stafford, Fred
JAKE SPEED, ed

Stafford, Theresa
FRINGE DWELLERS, THE

Stagnaro, Carola
UNA SPINA NEL CUORE

Stagnaro, Juan Bautista
DEBAJO DEL MUNDO, d; MISS MARY, w

Stahl, Kimberly
NIGHTMARE WEEKEND

Stahl, Lasse
ALLA VI BARN I BULLERBY

Stahl, Steven
SWEET LIBERTY

Stahl, Susanne
DER SEXTE SINN

Stall, Barbara
UNDER THE CHERRY MOON

Stallone, Frank
PINK CHIQUITAS, THE

Stallone, Sylvester
COBRA; COBRA, w

Stamatiou, G.
ALLIGORIA

Stamey, Betty
OVER THE SUMMER

Stamm, Barbara
WISDOM

Stamm, Raimund
BOY WHO COULD FLY, THE

Stamos, John
NEVER TOO YOUNG TO DIE

Stamp, Terence
HUD; LEGAL EAGLES; LINK

Stamps, Donna
HOLLYWOOD VICE SQUAD, set d

Stanciu, Marin
PASO DOBLE, ph

Stancu, Stelian
NOI, CEI DIN LINIA INTII

Stanculescu, Silviu
LICEENI

Stanczak, Wadeck
DESORDRE; SCENE OF THE CRIME

Standal, Rana
NUTCRACKER: THE MOTION PICTURE

Stander, Lionel
TRANSFORMERS: THE MOVIE, THE

Standiford, Jim
VIOLETS ARE BLUE

Standish, David
CLUB PARADISE, w

Stanger, Hugh
BEST OF TIMES, THE

Stanger, Hugo
TOUGH GUYS

Stanger, Hugo L.
PSYCHO III

Stanislas
BIGGLES, m

Stankowna, Hanna
OSOBISTY PAMIETNIK GRZESZNIKA PRZEZ NIEGO
SAMEGO SPISANY

Stanley, Catherine
ROMANTICHNA-ISTORIJA, ed

Stanley, Chris
MURPHY'S LAW

Stanley, Ian
THE KARATE KID PART II, m/l

Stannard, Roy
FOREIGN BODY, prod d

Stanoevici, Bogdan
NOI, CEI DIN LINIA INTII

Stantic, Lita
MISS MARY, p

Stanton, Harry Dean
PRETTY IN PINK

Stanton, John
GREAT EXPECTATIONS—THE AUSTRALIAN STORY;
TAI-PAN

Stanton, Penny
SHORT CIRCUIT

Stany, Jacques
WOMEN'S PRISON MASSACRE

Stapel, Huub
FLODDER; MARIA; OP HOOP VAN ZEGEN

Staphanou, Helen
DANILO TRELES, O FIMISMENOS ANDALOUSIANOS
MOUSIKOS

Staples, Paul
AVENGING FORCE

Staples, Roebuck "Pops"
TRUE STORIES

Stapleton, Maureen
COSMIC EYE, THE; HEARTBURN; MONEY PIT, THE

Stapleton, Oliver
ABSOLUTE BEGINNERS, ph; MY BEAUTIFUL
LAUNDRETTE, ph; RUNNING OUT OF LUCK, ph

Starbuck, Michele
AVENGING FORCE, set d; WRAITH, THE, set d

Starbuck, Michelle
NEVER TOO YOUNG TO DIE, art d

Stark, Col. Richard S.   [Richard Salisbury Stark]
Obituaries

Stark, Hilda
VERY CLOSE QUARTERS, art d

Stark, Jim
SLEEPWALK

Stark, Ray
BRIGHTON BEACH MEMOIRS, p

Stark, Suzanne
EVIXION

Starke, Mike
NO SURRENDER

Starkey, Alan
MR. LOVE

Starkmeth, Nikolaus
ZONING, ph

Stewart, John
TOMB, THE, stunts

Stewart, Lynne Marie
JUMPIN' JACK FLASH

Stewart, Patrick
LADY JANE

Stewart, Paul [Paul Sternberg]
Obituaries

Stewart, Rick
DR. OTTO AND THE RIDDLE OF THE GLOOM BEAM

Stewart-Richardson, Alison
GOOD FATHER, THE, art d; NO SURRENDER, set d

Steyn, Jacques
KILLING CARS, ph

Stice, David
REVENGE; REVENGE, stunts

Sticky, Captain
SEX O'CLOCK NEWS, THE

Stidham, Cary
NUTCRACKER: THE MOTION PICTURE

Stiglitz, Hugo
EL DIA DE LOS ALBANILES II; KILLING MACHINE

Stiliadis, Nicolas
PINK CHIQUITAS, THE, p; PINK CHIQUITAS, THE, ph

Stillman, Winslow
DR. OTTO AND THE RIDDLE OF THE GLOOM BEAM

Stillwagon, Arick
NIGHT OF THE CREEPS

Stilwell, Diane
BOSS' WIFE, THE; JUST BETWEEN FRIENDS

Stimac, Slavko
DO YOU REMEMBER DOLLY BELL?; OVNI IN MAMUTI

Stimpson, Viola Kates
STEWARDESS SCHOOL

Stines, Mike
WHERE ARE THE CHILDREN?

Stinson and Mars
MY CHAUFFEUR, m/l

Stirber, John
STEWARDESS SCHOOL, spec eff

Stivaleti, Sergio
DEMONI 2—L'INCUBO RITORNA, spec eff

Stiven, David
"CROCODILE" DUNDEE, ed

Stjepanovic, Boro
DO YOU REMEMBER DOLLY BELL?

Stocker, Emily
TWO FRIENDS

Stocker, Walter
HOLLYWOOD ZAP!

Stocker, Werner
AUF IMMER UND EWIG

Stockle, Wendy
JAKE SPEED

Stockwell, Dean
BLUE VELVET

Stockwell, John
DANGEROUSLY CLOSE; DANGEROUSLY CLOSE, w; RADIOACTIVE DREAMS; TOP GUN

Stockwell, Lisa-Jane
FRINGE DWELLERS, THE

Stoddart, John
FOR LOVE ALONE, prod d; MOSQUITO COAST, THE, prod d

Stoev, Stoyan
SKUPA MOYA, SKUPI MOY

Stofer, Dawn
ABDUCTED, stunts

Stoian, Mihai
DREPTATE IN LANTURI, w

Stojanova, Milica
SRECNA NOVA '49

Stokes, Demitri
DR. OTTO AND THE RIDDLE OF THE GLOOM BEAM

Stokes, George
SHADOW PLAY

Stokes, Ron
TOUCH AND GO

Stokey, Susan
ARMED RESPONSE; TOMB, THE

Stokke, Linn
NOE HEIT ANNET

Stoklosa, Carolyn
NUTCRACKER: THE MOTION PICTURE

Stolzy, Lisa
NUTCRACKER: THE MOTION PICTURE

Stone, Charles
SOLDIER'S REVENGE, set d

Stone, Chris
NINJA TURF, m

Stone, Clay
WELCOME TO 18

Stone, Cliffie
BACK TO SCHOOL

Stone, Curtis
BACK TO SCHOOL; LUCAS, m/l

Stone, Danton
BAND OF THE HAND

Stone, Dee Wallace
CRITTERS; SHADOW PLAY

Stone, Douglas
FAT GUY GOES NUTZOID!!

Stone, Joseph G.
SCORPION

Stone, Laurie
PLAYING BEATIE BOW, m

Stone, Oliver
8 MILLION WAYS TO DIE, w; PLATOON; PLATOON, d&w; SALVADOR, d; SALVADOR, p; SALVADOR, w; People to Watch

Stone, Sam
POLICE ACADEMY 3: BACK IN TRAINING

Stone, Sean
SALVADOR

Stoner, Sherri
REFORM SCHOOL GIRLS

Stonham, Kay
MR. LOVE

Stoppi, Franca
WOMEN'S PRISON MASSACRE

Storch, Larry
FINE MESS, A; PERILS OF P.K., THE

Storch, Norma
PERILS OF P.K., THE

Storch, Wolfgang
DIE ZWEI GESICHTER DES JANUAR, d; DIE ZWEI GESICHTER DES JANUAR, w

Storey, Howard
FIRE WITH FIRE

Storey, Michael
COMING UP ROSES, m

Stori, Bruno
MOMO

Storick, Robert
SCORPION

Stork, Veronica
COMBAT SHOCK

Storm, Esben
WRONG WORLD

Storm, Howard
CHECK IS IN THE MAIL, THE

Stormare, Peter
DEN FRUSNA LEOPARDEN

Storozik, Valerij
BORIS GODUNOV

Storrs, David
P.O.W. THE ESCAPE, m; SUNSET STRIP, m

Storstein, Are
X

Story, Mark
ODD JOBS, d

Storz, Oliver
FOLLOWING THE FUHRER, w

Stoutz, Sylvia de
DER SCHWARZE TANNER, cos; INNOCENZA, cos

Stovitz, Ken
BLUE VELVET

Stowell, Kent
NUTCRACKER: THE MOTION PICTURE, ch; NUTCRACKER: THE MOTION PICTURE, w

Straat, Hans
LOVE ME!

Stradling, Harry
FINE MESS, A, ph

Straetz, Ursula
DER WILDE CLOWN

Straight, Beatrice
POWER

Strandberg, Jytte
TWIST & SHOUT

Strandberg, Keith W.
NO RETREAT, NO SURRENDER, w

Strange, Keith
NO RETREAT, NO SURRENDER

Strange, Richard
MONA LISA

Strangio, Frank
DEAD-END DRIVE-IN, m

Strano, Michael
FLIGHT OF THE NAVIGATOR

Strapko, Dave
RECRUITS

Strapko, Mike
RECRUITS

Strasberg, Susan
BLOODY BIRTHDAY; DELTA FORCE, THE

Strassburger, Jorg
ANGRY HARVEST, m

Strasser, Ralph
BIG HURT, THE, ed

Stratford, Judith
MALCOLM

Stratford, Willie
ROCKIN' ROAD TRIP

Strathairn, David
AT CLOSE RANGE

Straub, Jean-Marie
CLASS RELATIONS, d&w

Strauch, Joseph, Jr.
Obituaries

Straus, Vivien
SEVEN MINUTES IN HEAVEN

Stravinsky, Igor
EL HOMBRE QUE GANO LA RAZON, m

Strawa, Isabelle
LA MACHINE A DECOUDRE

Strawn, C.J.
AMERICA, art d; MY CHAUFFEUR, prod d

Stray, Anne
NOE HEIT ANNET

Strazalkowski, Henry
P.O.W. THE ESCAPE

Strazzer, Carlos Augusto
COM LICENCA, EU VOU A LUTA

Streater, Billy
GETTING EVEN

Streatfield, Noel
Obituaries

Strecker, Rainer
EAST OF THE WALL

Strecter, Tim
MALA NOCHE

Streddo, Dominic
SCREEN TEST

Streep, Dana
HEARTBURN

Streep, Mary
HEARTBURN

Streep, Meryl
HEARTBURN

Streitch, Ianas
SVESAS KAISLIBAS, d&w; SVESAS KAISLIBAS, ed

Stremien, Jaroslav
STREETS OF GOLD

Streng, Keith
MY CHAUFFEUR, m/l

Strickland, Bob
FLIGHT OF THE NAVIGATOR

Stricklin, Debra
LEGAL EAGLES

Strietzel, Oliver
SCHLEUSE 17

Striglos, William
SHORT CIRCUIT

Strindberg, Anita
FEAR

Stringer, D.C.
GOOD TO GO, ed

Strittmater, Thomas
DER POLENWEIHER, d; DER POLENWEIHER, w

Strljic, Milan
BAL NA VODI

Strobel, Al
SHADOW PLAY; SHADOW PLAY

Strode, Woody
ANGKOR-CAMBODIA EXPRESS; FINAL EXECUTIONER, THE; VIOLENT BREED, THE

Stromdal, Terje
BLACKOUT

Strome, Harold
LOW BLOW

Stromstedt, Lars
MOA

Strong, Brenda
WEEKEND WARRIORS

Strong, Dennis
BUSTED UP

Strongbow, Chief Jay
BAD GUYS

Stroppa, Daniele
LA MONACA NEL PECCATO, w

Stroppiana, Steve
AMERICA 3000

Stroud, Don
ARMED AND DANGEROUS

Stroupe, Gary R.
LOW BLOW

Strozer, Scott
SNO-LINE

Strozier, Henry
IMAGEMAKER, THE

Strugacki, Boris
PISMA MERTVOGO CHELOVEKA, w

Strummer, Joe
SID AND NANCY, m

Strup, Lori
NIGHTMARE WEEKEND

Struycken, Carel
POPULATION: ONE, ed

Stryker, Jack
MY CHAUFFEUR

Strzalkowski, Henry
NAKED VENGEANCE; SILK

Stuart, Alan
TERRY ON THE FENCE, stunts

Stuart, Gloria
WILDCATS

Stuart, Kim Rossi
NAME OF THE ROSE, THE

Stubbs, Imogen
NANOU

Stubbs, Levi
LITTLE SHOP OF HORRORS

Stubing, Solvi
DELITTI

Stucker, Stephen
Obituaries

Studstill, Pat
LONGSHOT, THE

Stull, Lee
SOLDIER'S REVENGE, w

Stuntgruppen, Svenska
SACRIFICE, THE, spec eff

Stur, Svetozar
SIESTA VETA, m

Sturgeon, Mark
OVER THE SUMMER

Sturgis, William
HANNAH AND HER SISTERS

Sturz, Lisa
HOWARD THE DUCK

Stutchbury, Jessica
WAY IT IS, THE

Stutzmann, Sabine
LISI UND DER GENERAL

Styler, Trudie
LA SPOSA AMERICANA

Styles, John
SCREAMTIME

Su-ying, Wu
TIME TO LIVE AND A TIME TO DIE, A

Suares, Carlos
EL RIO DE ORO, ph

Suarez
AMERICAN COMMANDOS, ed

Suarez, Bobby A.
AMERICAN COMMANDOS, d&w

Suarez, Carlos
BANDERA NEGRA, ph

Suarez, Edgardo
EL SOL EN BOTELLITAS; INSOMNIACS

Suarez, Hector
LAS NOCHES DEL CALIFAS; PICARDIA MEXICANA
NUMERO DOS

Suarez, Lisa
STRIPPER

Suba, Vicky
SILK

Subiela, Eliseo
MAN FACING SOUTHEAST, d&w; People to Watch

Such, Michel
JE HAIS LES ACTEURS

Sucher, Elion
LANDSCAPE SUICIDE

Suchet, David
IRON EAGLE

Suchy, Jiri
JONAS, DEJME TOMU VE STREDU; JONAS, DEJME
TOMU VE STREDU, w

Sudell, Marjorie
NO SURRENDER

Sudrow, Penelope
FIRE WITH FIRE

Sudzin, Jeffrey
WRAITH, THE

Sugarman, Burt
CHILDREN OF A LESSER GOD, p; EXTREMITIES, p

Sugarman, Joseph
DEVASTATOR, THE, w

Sugarman, Sara
SID AND NANCY

Suggs, Hollye Rebecca
SPACECAMP

Sugihara, Yoshi
SHIN YOROKOBIMO KANASHIMIMO
IKUTOSHITSUKI, ed

Sugimoto, Tetsuta
NINGUEN NO YAKUSOKU

Sugisaki, Shigemi
KINEMA NO TENCHI, p

Sugiura, Naoki
TOKIMEDI NI SHISU

Suhonen, Alpo
RIISUMINEN

Suhrstedt, Tim
CRITTERS, ph

Suikkari, Anitta
DREAM OF NORTHERN LIGHTS

Suissa, Meir
NADIA

Sukowa, Barbara
ROSA LUXEMBURG

Suli, Christine
DEPARTURE, p

Sullivan, Chris
ABSOLUTE BEGINNERS

Sullivan, Freddie
EYE OF THE TIGER, m/l

Sullivan, James
FAT GUY GOES NUTZOID!!

Sullivan, Katharine
SCREEN TEST

Sullivan, Liam
WHAT WAITS BELOW; WISDOM

Sullivan, Rob
SMART ALEC, w

Sullivan, Sean
BOY IN BLUE, THE

Sultan, Arne
Obituaries

Sum, Ko Chi
FAMILY, THE, w

Sum, Lydia
MILLIONAIRE'S EXPRESS, THE

Suma, Kei
KINEMA NO TENCHI

Sumera, Lepo
NAERATA OMETI, m

Sumiljanik, Bosidale
ARMOUR OF GOD, THE

Summer, Donna
BUSTED UP, m/l

Summer, Robert
SOLDIER'S REVENGE, art d

Summers, Andy
BAND OF THE HAND, m/l; DOWN AND OUT IN
BEVERLY HILLS, ph, m

Summers, Bunny
FROM BEYOND

Summers, David
ME HACE FALTA UN BIGOTE, m

Summers, Manuel
ME HACE FALTA UN BIGOTE; ME HACE FALTA UN
BIGOTE, d&w

Summers, Ray
52 PICK-UP, cos

Summers, Scott
HOOSIERS

Summey, Chip
OVER THE SUMMER

Sumner, Graham
SOLARBABIES, set d

Sumner, Murray
SEPARATE VACATIONS, set d

Sun, Cho Ji
POMNALUI NUNSOGI

Sun, Leland
BIG TROUBLE; DOWN AND OUT IN BEVERLY HILLS

Sun, Shirley
GREAT WALL, A, p; GREAT WALL, A, w

Sun, Yung
DOWN AND OUT IN BEVERLY HILLS

Sundberg, Bert
MIN PAPA AR TARZAN, p; RAVEN, p

Sunderland, Janet
ANGEL RIVER

Sunderland, Per
FAREWELL ILLUSION

Sundquist, Bjorn
DREAM OF NORTHERN LIGHTS

Sundvall, Kjell
I LAGENS NAMN, d

Sung, Richard Lee
ARMED RESPONSE

Sung-bae, Park
ER WOO DONG, ph

Sung-ghi, Ahn
ER WOO DONG

Sunina, Brian
COLOR OF MONEY, THE

Sunn, Ron
NINJA TURF

Suola, Liu
QINGCHUN JI, m

Suominen, Ensio
TUNTEMATON SOTILAS, prod d

Suominen, Tapio
VALKOINEN KAAPIO, ed

Supernaw, W.M.
BEER

Suppan, Martin
ECHO PARK

Surchadijev, Yossif
ZA KUDE PUTOVATE

Surgere, Helene
ZONE ROUGE

Surjik, Stephen
BUSTED UP, art d

Surtees, Bruce
OUT OF BOUNDS, ph; PSYCHO III, ph; RATBOY, ph

Suryadi, Tantra
SECANGKIR KOPI PAHIT, ph

Suslov, Mikhail
NOBODY'S FOOL, ph; VERY CLOSE QUARTERS, ph

Suslov, Misha
3:15, THE MOMENT OF TRUTH, ph; BLACK MOON
RISING, ph

Susskind, Steve
HOUSE

Sust, David
CAGED GLASS

Sutherland, Donald
WOLF AT THE DOOR, THE

Sutherland, Esther
Obituaries

Sutherland, Kiefer
AT CLOSE RANGE; CRAZY MOON; STAND BY ME;
People to Watch

Sutherland, Kristine
LEGAL EAGLES

Suttles, Wesley
LOW BLOW

Sutton, Charlie
OVER THE SUMMER

Sutton, David
PRETTY IN PINK

Sutton, Dennis
OVER THE SUMMER

Sutton, John
LUCAS, set d

Sutton, Mary Ann
OVER THE SUMMER

Suurballe, Morten
ET SKUD FRA HJERTET; FLAMBEREDE HJERTER

Suzuki, Akira
NINGUEN NO YAKUSOKU, ed; SOREKARA, ed;
TAMPOPO, ed

Suzuki, Kan
NEW MORNING OF BILLY THE KID, THE, ed

Sveholm, Pertti
HUOMENNA; KUNINGAS LAHTEE RANSKAAN

Svendsen, Brigitte Victoria
DROMMESLOTTER

Svenneby, Tage
HUD

Svenson, Bo
CHOKE CANYON; DELTA FORCE, THE;
HEARTBREAK RIDGE; MANHUNT, THE; THUNDER
WARRIOR

Svenson, Virginia
PANTHER SQUAD

Svensson, Allan
RAVEN

Svensson, Ingwar
ALLA VI BARN I BULLERBY

Sviridovski, Alexander
KAK MOLODY MY BYLI

Svobodova, Milena
PAVUCINA

Swaby, Paul
LITTLE SHOP OF HORRORS

Swados, Elizabeth
COSMIC EYE, THE, m

Swafford, Mary
KING KONG LIVES

Swailes, Gary
VAMP

Swaim, Bob
HALF MOON STREET, d; HALF MOON STREET, w

Swain, Jonathan
LETTER TO BREZHNEV, prod d

Swan, Robert
HOOSIERS

Swansen, Larry
PLAYING FOR KEEPS

Swanson, Gary
WITCHFIRE

Swanson, Greg
BOY IN BLUE, THE

Swanson, Kristy
DEADLY FRIEND; FERRIS BUELLER'S DAY OFF;
PRETTY IN PINK

Swanson, Laura
DOGS IN SPACE

Swanson, Stephen
REVENGE OF THE TEENAGE VIXENS FROM OUTER
SPACE, THE

Swatik, Barry
YOUNGBLOOD

Swayze, Alan
HEATHCLIFF: THE MOVIE, w

Swayze, Patrick
YOUNGBLOOD

Sweeney, Chip
CLOCKWISE

Sweeney, D.B.
FIRE WITH FIRE; POWER

Sweeney, Mark
PARTING GLANCES, art d

Sweeney, Richard
KNIGHTS AND EMERALDS

Sweeney, Steve
BACK TO SCHOOL; BILLY GALVIN

Sweet, Leroy
TRICK OR TREAT

Sweigart, Charles
TOUGH GUYS

Swerdlow, Tommy
HOWARD THE DUCK

Swift, Brenton
BOSS' WIFE, THE, prod d

Swift, Chris
FRIDAY THE 13TH PART VI: JASON LIVES, makeup

Swift, Christopher
APRIL FOOL'S DAY, spec eff

Swift, David
ARTHUR'S HALLOWED GROUND

Swift, Francine
VAMP

Swift, Jeremy
MR. LOVE

Swift, Madeleine
STAND BY ME

Swift, Sally
HELL SQUAD

Swinson, Howard
HAUNTED HONEYMOON

Swinton, Tilda
CARAVAGGIO

Swit, Loretta
BEER

Switkes, Willy
PLAYING FOR KEEPS

Sykora, Kathleen
DONNA ROSEBUD

Sylbert, Anthea
WILDCATS, p

Sylbert, Richard
UNDER THE CHERRY MOON, prod d

Sylvester, Julian
HELL SQUAD

Symons, James
COBRA, ed

Syms, Sylvia
ABSOLUTE BEGINNERS

Synkova, Katarina
LEV S BILOU HRIVOU

Syron, Brian
BACKLASH

Syrovy, Jan
'38, p

Szabo, Gabor Madj
KESERU IGAZSAG

Szabo, Lajos
VAKVILAGBAN

Szabo, Lazslo
LOVE SONGS

Szalkai, Sandor
KOJAK BUDAPESTEN, d; KOJAK BUDAPESTEN, w

Szanto, Erika
ELYSIUM, d; ELYSIUM, w

Szarabajka, Keith
BILLY GALVIN

Szczepkowska, Joanna
JEZIORO BODENSKIE

Szczepkowski, Andrzej
JEZIORO BODENSKIE

Sze, Wong Waan
HAPPY DIN DON

Szemenyei, Andrew
DOT AND KEETO, anim

Szemere, Vera
KESERU IGAZSAG

Szepesy, Andrew
DREAM OF NORTHERN LIGHTS, w

Szeps, Henri
TRAVELLING NORTH

Szilagyi, Tibor
ELYSIUM

Szirtes, Adam
KOJAK BUDAPESTEN

Szomolanyi, Stanislav
SIESTA VETA, ph

Szuchmacher, Ruben
KING AND HIS MOVIE, A

T., Maggie
SOMETHING WILD

Tabori, George
TAROT

Tabuchi, Eric
GARDIEN DE LA NUIT, m

Tacchella, Patrick
INNOCENZA

Tadei, Alvamar
AS SETE VAMPIRAS

Tadesse, Myriam
UNDER THE CHERRY MOON

Tadeu, Jose
BRAS CUBAS, ph

Tadic, Ljuba
DOBROVOLJCI

Tadic, Zoran
SAN O RUZI, d

Tadjer, Abdelkader
RAI

Tadzic, Ljuba
LIJEPE ZENE PROLAZE KROZ GRAD

Tae-gun, Lee
BBONG

Tae-won, Lee
BBONG, p; ER WOO DONG, p

Tafuri, Renato
45MO PARALLELO, ph; SEMBRA MORTO . . . MA E
SOLO SVENUTO, ph

Tagawa, Cary
ARMED RESPONSE

Taghipoor, Seyamak
FROSTY ROADS, w

Tagliaferro, Pat
AMERICA 3000, set d; FRIDAY THE 13TH PART VI:
JASON LIVES, art d

Tagliavia, Adriano
LA RAGAZZA DEI LILLA, ed

Tagore, Sharmila
NEW DELHI TIMES

Taguet, Francoise
PEKIN CENTRAL

Tahil, Dalip
TRIKAL

Tahmasb, Iraj
BEYOND THE MIST

Tai, Chan Koon
TAI-PAN

Taibo, Paco Ignacio
REDONDO, p, d&w

Taicher, Robert
INSIDE OUT, d; INSIDE OUT, w

Taina, Irma
KUNINGAS LAHTEE RANSKAAN, ed

Tait, Melissa
COMBAT SHOCK

Tait, Stacy
COMBAT SHOCK

Takaba, Tetsuo
KINEMA NO TENCHI, ph

Takacs, Lisa
ASSAULT, THE

Takada, Jun
LOVE LETTER, w

Takagi, Isao
COMIC MAGAZINE, w

Takahashi, Genichiro
NEW MORNING OF BILLY THE KID, THE, w

Takahashi, Haruyuki
UEMURA NAOMI MONOGATARI, p

Takahashi, Keiko
LOVE LETTER

Takahashi, Masakuni
ORA TOKYO SA YUKUDA, w

Takama, Kenji
NEW MORNING OF BILLY THE KID, THE, ph

Takamaki, Jouni
BORN AMERICAN

Takamaru, Jason
NUTCRACKER: THE MOTION PICTURE

Takayama, Hiroshi
UEMURA NAOMI MONOGATARI, p

Takeda, Kumiko
NINGUEN NO YAKUSOKU

Takei, George
STAR TREK IV: THE VOYAGE HOME

Takemitsu, Toru
YARI NO GONZA, m

Takeshi, Beat
COMIC MAGAZINE

Takewaki, Muga
UEMURA NAOMI MONOGATARI

Takita, Yojiro
COMIC MAGAZINE, d

Takushi, Yasukazu
THE KARATE KID PART II, tech adv

Tal, Ada Valeria
BAR 51—SISTER OF LOVE

Talalaeff, Nicholas
MERCI MONSIEUR ROBERTSON

Talbert, Tom
REFORM SCHOOL GIRLS, set d; STOOGEMANIA, set d

Talbot, Alan
MONA LISA

Talbot, Brud   [Joseph Talbot]
Obituaries

Talbot, Kate
BEGINNER'S LUCK

Talbot, Nita
CHECK IS IN THE MAIL, THE

Talbott, Michael
MANHUNTER

Talking Heads, The
TRUE STORIES, m

Tallermaa, Touri
NAERATA OMETI

Talvio, Raija
MORENA, ed

Tam, Alan
ARMOUR OF GOD, THE

Tamanes, Tita
POBRE MARIPOSA, cos

Tamaoki, Yasushi
TAMPOPO, p

Tamara, Rosita
PPPERFORMER, THE

Tedesco, Dino
SPOSERO SIMON LE BON, w

Tedford, Vivian
ROCKIN' ROAD TRIP

Teegarden, Jim
BOY WHO COULD FLY, THE, set d

Teegarden, William
RUTHLESS PEOPLE, set d

Teets, Edward
JUST BETWEEN FRIENDS, p

Tegelaar, Monica
TOP OF THE WHALE, p

Teichmann, Edith
FOLLOWING THE FUHRER

Teiger, Benedicte
LA MACHINE A DECOUDRE, ed

Teijido, Veronica
JOGO DURO

Teitel, Carol   [Carolyn Sally Kahn]
Obituaries

Telegen, Rachel C.
ONE CRAZY SUMMER

Telesco, Michael
MANHATTAN PROJECT, THE

Telford, Paul
ABSOLUTE BEGINNERS

Telio, Ana
IL BI E IL BA

Tellefsen, Tom
HARD ASFALT

Teller
MY CHAUFFEUR

Telles, Antonio Cunha
L'AMANT MAGNIFIQUE, p

Telletxea, Fernando
LAST OF PHILIP BANTER, THE

Tellez, Hector
SALVADOR

Tello, Lucy Martinez
VISA U.S.A.

Telmisani, Tarak El
SIKAT SAFAR, ph

Telmissany, Tarek El
EL-TOUK WA EL-ESSWERA, ph

Temeles, Sam
HARDBODIES 2

Temessy, Hedy
VAKVILAGBAN

Temperton, Rod
RUNNING SCARED, m

Temple, Julien
ABSOLUTE BEGINNERS, d; ABSOLUTE BEGINNERS,
m/l; RUNNING OUT OF LUCK, d; RUNNING OUT OF
LUCK, w; People to Watch

Temple, Renny
CHECK IS IN THE MAIL, THE

Templeman, Conny
NANOU, d&w

Templeton, Claudia
HOLLYWOOD VICE SQUAD; TRICK OR TREAT

Tempos, Antonis
KALI PATRITHA, SYNTROFE, ed

ten Bruggecate, Cathrien
AFZIEN

Tendoh, Ryuko
TYPHOON CLUB

Tendulkar, Nijay
AGHAAT, w

Tenenbaum, Irwin
HANNAH AND HER SISTERS

Tennyson, Owen
CRAZY MOON

Tenorio
O HOMEM DA CAPA PRETA, w

Tenoudji, Edmond
Obituaries

Tenser, Marilyn J.
MY CHAUFFEUR, p

Tepoztle, Feberon
ES MI VIDA—EL NOA NOA 2, ph

Tepper, Leonard
CLASS OF NUKE 'EM HIGH

Terada, Kyoko
NUTCRACKER: THE MOTION PICTURE

Teran, Carlos
MATANZA EN MATAMOROS

Teran, Los Liricos de
LOS ASES DE CONTRABANDO, m

Terceiro, Otavio
NEM TUDO E VERDADE

Terlesky, John
CHOPPING MALL; NAKED CAGE, THE

Termine, Egidio
SAPORE DEL GRANO

Termini, Charles
Obituaries

Terrell, John Canada
RECRUITS; SHE'S GOTTA HAVE IT

Terry, Nigel
CARAVAGGIO

Terry, Sonny   [Saunders Terrill]
Obituaries

Terzian, Alain
FEMMES DE PERSONNE, p; LA GITANE, p; LE
DEBUTANT, p; SCENE OF THE CRIME, p

Terzieff, Laurent
LA RAGAZZA DEI LILLA

Teschner, Peter
MONSTER DOG, ed

Tesoriero, Brendan
COMBAT SHOCK

Tessalone, Kathy
STAR CRYSTAL, makeup

Tessari, Fiorenza
UNA DOMENICA SI

Testa, Giacomo
DAYS OF HELL, ph

Testa, Nicholas
EYE OF THE TIGER

Tevis, Walter
COLOR OF MONEY, THE, w

Tewari, P.K.
NEW DELHI TIMES, p

Tews, Bobby J.
MY CHAUFFEUR

Texas Kid, The
SOMETHING WILD

Texier, Isabelle
PARIS MINUIT

Thacker, Tab
WILDCATS

Thalbach, Katharina
FLIGHT NORTH; PARADIES

Thalheimer, Norman
ODD JOBS

Thames, Byron
SEVEN MINUTES IN HEAVEN

Thames, R.S.
HEARTBURN

Thampi, Vembayam
ANANTARAM

Thamwong, Kusarin
ANGKOR-CAMBODIA EXPRESS, set d

Thanh, Huy
LOI RE TRAI TREN DUONG MON, d

Thanh, Kim
LOI RE TRAI TREN DUONG MON

Thanheiser, Johannes
DIE WALSCHE

Thao, Li Mai
PLATOON

Thastrom, Joakim
DEN FRUSNA LEOPARDEN

Thau, Pierre
BABEL OPERA, OU LA REPETITION DE DON JUAN

Thauvette, Guy
ANNE TRISTER

The Group's Power
SPOSERO SIMON LE BON, m

Theater Group of Escambray, The
COME LA VIDA MISMA

Thelen, Tom
EYE OF THE TIGER, spec eff

Theodoracopoulos, Antonis
ALCESTES

Theodorakis, Mikis
LES CLOWNS DE DIEU, m

Theroux, Paul
HALF MOON STREET, w; MOSQUITO COAST, THE, w

Therrian, Al
RECRUITS

Thi, Kim
LOI RE TRAI TREN DUONG MON

Thiago, Flavio Sao
FULANINHA; HAPPILY EVER AFTER

Thiago, Paulo
FULANINHA, p; FULANINHA, w

Thibodeau, Rick
SUNSET STRIP, m

Thiede, Erich
DEATH SENTENCE

Thiedot, Jacqueline
BLACK MIC-MAC, ed; SINCERELY CHARLOTTE, ed

Thiel, Peter
MANDEN I MAANEN

Thielbar, Jan
SCORPION, makeup

Thiele, Acacia
O VESTIDO COR DE FOGO

Thieltges, Gary
SNO-LINE, ph; VASECTOMY: A DELICATE MATTER,
ph

Thieltges, Gary P.
BOSS' WIFE, THE, ph

Thigpen, Lynne
SWEET LIBERTY

Thijm, Francois
WHERE THE RIVER RUNS BLACK

Thijs, Ger
AFZIEN

Thijssen, Willum
EXIT-EXIL, p

Thilakan, Karamana
MUKHAMUKHAM

Thilo, Jesper
TAKE IT EASY

Thinius, Ole
BUSTED UP

Thiocary, Ada
NYAMANTON

Thom, Ian
LABYRINTH

Thoma, Gesa
SPRING SYMPHONY

Thomas, Allan
SCORPION

Thomas, Antonia
PASSION OF REMEMBRANCE, THE

Thomas, Brad
TRICK OR TREAT

Thomas, Carmen
IMPURE THOUGHTS

Thomas, Damien
PIRATES

Thomas, Dave
MY MAN ADAM

Thomas, David C.
WELCOME TO 18, p

Thomas, Dudley
MY BEAUTIFUL LAUNDRETTE

Thomas, Gerald
SECOND VICTORY, THE, p&d

Thomas, Gerard
SHADOWS RUN BLACK

Thomas, Gillian Elisa
COMING UP ROSES

Thomas, Gloria
SCORPION

Thomas, Guy
LOVE SONGS

Thomas, Jay
LEGAL EAGLES

Thomas, Jennifer Anne
NAKED CAGE, THE

Thomas, John
BOY WHO COULD FLY, THE, spec eff; FIRE WITH
FIRE, spec eff

Thomas, Kelly
BEST OF TIMES, THE

Thomas, Leslie
SALOME

Thomas, R. Christopher
POLICE ACADEMY 3: BACK IN TRAINING

Thomas, Robin
ABOUT LAST NIGHT

Thomas, Ron
BIG BET, THE; THE KARATE KID PART II

Thomas, Scott
COMING UP ROSES, ed

Thomas, Stan
TRAMP AT THE DOOR, p

Thomas, Steve
YOUNGBLOOD

Thomas, Trevor
BLACK JOY

Thomas, Vincent P.
FORMULA FOR MURDER, ed

Thomas, Wynn
SHE'S GOTTA HAVE IT, prod d

Thomashefsky, Howard
AMERICA

Thome, Rudolph
TAROT, d

Thomerson, Tim
IRON EAGLE; ZONE TROOPERS

Thompson, Andrea
NIGHTMARE WEEKEND

Thompson, Bill
IMAGEMAKER, THE

Thompson, Brian
COBRA; THREE AMIGOS

Thompson, Christopher
JUMPIN' JACK FLASH, w

Thompson, Donald
TOUGH GUYS

Thompson, Frank G.
RECRUITS; RECRUITS

Thompson, J. Lee
FIREWALKER, d; MURPHY'S LAW, d

Thompson, Jack
SHORT CIRCUIT

Thompson, Jo
ROCINANTE, cos

Thompson, John Robert
HOOSIERS

Thompson, Kevin
NIGHT OF THE CREEPS

Thompson, Kim
SCREAMTIME

Thompson, Lea
HOWARD THE DUCK; SPACECAMP

Thompson, Mary
ECHO PARK

Thompson, Michael
SHORT CHANGED

Thompson, Mitchell Scott
CHOKE CANYON

Thompson, Peter Lee
MURPHY'S LAW, ed

Thompson, Richard L.
STAND BY ME, spec eff

Thompson, Rob
RATBOY, w

Thompson, Shelley
LABYRINTH

Thompson, Sophie
DEATH OF THE HEART, THE

Thompson, Steve
REVENGE OF THE TEENAGE VIXENS FROM OUTER
SPACE, THE

Thompson, Terry
FRINGE DWELLERS, THE

Thompson, Thomas
LOST!, p, d&w

Thomson, Alex
DUET FOR ONE, ph; LABYRINTH, ph; RAW DEAL, ph

Thomson, Barry
HEAD OFFICE

Thomson, Beatrix
Obituaries

Thomson, Margaret
HEARTBURN

Thomson, R.H.
SAMUEL LOUNT

Thomson, Scott
POLICE ACADEMY 3: BACK IN TRAINING

Thomson, Shawn
HEAD OFFICE

Thong, Huangjian
LIANG JIA FUNU, d

Thoolen, Gerard
PERVOLA: TRACKS IN THE SNOW; PERVOLA:
TRACKS IN THE SNOW, w

Thor, Cameron
MODERN GIRLS

Thor, Jerome
MURPHY'S LAW

Thor, John Mikl
RECRUITS

Thorarinsson, Leifur
DEN FRUSNA LEOPARDEN, m

Thorin, Donald E.
AMERICAN ANTHEM, ph; GOLDEN CHILD, THE, ph;
WILDCATS, ph

Thorne, Brian
BOY IN BLUE, THE

Thorne, Edwina
SEX APPEAL

Thorne, Michelle
ABSOLUTE BEGINNERS

Thorne, Raymond
PLAYING FOR KEEPS

Thorne, Stephen
VALHALLA

Thorne-Smith, Courtney
LUCAS; WELCOME TO 18

Thornton, Artist
ON VALENTINE'S DAY

Thornton, Christina
ABSOLUTE BEGINNERS

Thornton, Sigrid
GREAT EXPECTATIONS—THE AUSTRALIAN STORY

Thorpe, Susan
STAND BY ME

Thorson, Linda
SWEET LIBERTY

Thorup, Kirsten
BALLERUP BOULEVARD, w

Thourayah
HADDA

Threlkeld, Budge
NOBODY'S FOOL

Throne, Malachi
EAT AND RUN

Thronsen, Mari
VIOLATED

Thunberg, Olof
AMOROSA

Thurman, Annette
FERRIS BUELLER'S DAY OFF

Thurman, Bill
MOUNTAINTOP MOTEL MASSACRE

Thurman, Bruce
HIGH SPEED

Thurmann, Erling
HARD ASFALT, ph

Thurmann-Andersen, Erling
DREAM OF NORTHERN LIGHTS, ph

Thygesen, Erik
BARNDOMMENS GADE, w

Thyren, Peo
GRONA GUBBAR FRAN Y.R., m

Tiano, Lou
WEEKEND WARRIORS

Tiberghien, Jerome
BUSTED UP; TOBY MCTEAGUE, stunts

Tichy, Gerard
SEA SERPENT, THE

Tickner, Clive
FRENCH LESSON, ph; MR. LOVE, ph

Tickner, Shane
SHORT CHANGED

Tidemanson, Laurie
MOVIE HOUSE MASSACRE

Tidy, Frank
SWEET LIBERTY, ph

Tielinen, Marja-Liisa
FLIGHT NORTH, cos

Tien-wen, Chou
TIME TO LIVE AND A TIME TO DIE, A, w; SUMMER
AT GRANDPA'S, A, w

Tierney, Lawrence
MURPHY'S LAW

Tierno, Mike
COMBAT SHOCK

Tieu, Le Troung
KARMA, art d

Tifo, Marie
INTIMATE POWER

Tiger, Stephen
BAND OF THE HAND, m/l

Tigerman, Gary
STOOGEMANIA, ph, m

Tijssen, Willem
CONGO EXPRESS, p

Tikkanen, Aino-Maija
SININEN IMETTAJA

Tilakan
ORIDATH

Tillack, Elfie
SPRING SYMPHONY, ed

Tillegren, Lillian
FLAMBEREDE HJERTER

Tillen, Jodie
AMERICAN ANTHEM, cos

Tiller, Nadja
DER SOMMER DES SAMURAI

Tillet, Doug
IMAGEMAKER, THE

Tilli, Andrea
NAME OF THE ROSE, THE

Tillis, Mel
UPHILL ALL THE WAY

Tillstrom, Jenny
BRODERNA MOZART

Tilly, Grant
DANGEROUS ORPHANS

Tilly, Jennifer
INSIDE OUT

Tilly, Meg
OFF BEAT

Tilly, Miles
DANGEROUS ORPHANS

Tilson, Wanda H.
WEEKEND WARRIORS

Tilton, Debbie
ODD JOBS

Tilton, Roger
SPIKER, p&d, w

Tilvern, Alan
LITTLE SHOP OF HORRORS

Timbes, Graham
MURPHY'S LAW

Timm, Peter
MEIER, d&w

Timmler, Thomas
DER POLENWEIHER, m

Timmons, J. Paul
TOUCH AND GO

Timothea
DOWN BY LAW

Tinbergen, Tijs
PERVOLA: TRACKS IN THE SNOW, p

Ting, Betty
HUAJIE SHIDAI

Tinguely, Miriam
KAMIKAZE HEARTS, art d&set d

Tingwell, Charles
MALCOLM; WINDRIDER

Tinti, Gabriele
CUT AND RUN; GIURO CHE TI AMO; IL MOSTRO DI
FIRENZE; WOMEN'S PRISON MASSACRE

Tipping, A.J.
CAR TROUBLE, w

Tipping, Tip
ALIENS

Tippo, Patricia
ECHO PARK

Tirl, George
ON VALENTINE'S DAY, ph

Tisch, Steve
SOUL MAN, p

Tison, Pascale
LA PURITAINE

Tisseraud, Pascale
FAUBOURG SAINT-MARTIN, makeup

Tissi, Felix
NOAH UND DER COWBOY, p, d&w

Tissue, Su
SOMETHING WILD

Titta, George De
MONEY PIT, THE, set d

Tittel, Volker
NOVEMBERKATZEN, ph

Titus, Eve
GREAT MOUSE DETECTIVE, THE, w

Titus, Libby
HEARTBURN

Titus, Marshall
MORT UN DIMANCHE DE PLUIE

Tiven, Jon
ONE MORE SATURDAY NIGHT

Tiven, Sally
ONE MORE SATURDAY NIGHT

Toake, Yukiyo
CYOEI NO MURE

Tober, Beate
WOHIN MIT WILLFRIED?

Tobias, Marice
PULSEBEAT, d

Tobias, Oliver
COBRA MISSION

Tobias, Ruben
INSTANT JUSTICE

Tobiason, Julie
NUTCRACKER: THE MOTION PICTURE

Tobni, Youcef
LAST IMAGE, THE, ed

Toboada, Carlos Enrique
VENENO PARA LAS HADAS, d&w

Tobolowsky, Stephen
NOBODY'S FOOL; TRUE STORIES, w

Tocci, James
CROSSROADS, set d

Tochi, Brian
POLICE ACADEMY 3: BACK IN TRAINING

Todd, Beth
SUIVEZ MON REGARD

Todd, Beverly
LADIES CLUB, THE

Todd, Brenda
'NIGHT, MOTHER, makeup; VIOLETS ARE BLUE,
makeup

Todd, Cecilia
PEQUENA REVANCHA

Todd, Hallie
CHECK IS IN THE MAIL, THE

Todd, Richard
BUSTED UP

Todd, Russell
CHOPPING MALL

Todd, Tony
PLATOON; SLEEPWALK

Todorov, Andrei
SKUPA MOYA, SKUPI MOY

Todorov, Georgi
ZA KUDE PUTOVATE, art d; ZABRAVOTE TOZI
SLOCHAI, prod d

Todorova, Katya
SKUPA MOYA, SKUPI MOY

Todorovic, Marko
BAL NA VODI

Todorovic, Srdan
BAL NA VODI

Todorovski, Goce
SRECNA NOVA '49

Toei Animation Co.
TRANSFORMERS: THE MOVIE, THE, anim

Toelle, Jacki Easton
ECHO PARK

Tofflemire, Anne
HOWARD THE DUCK

Toft, Anja
BALLERUP BOULEVARD

Tognazzi, Gianmarco
SPOSERO SIMON LE BON

Tognazzi, Ugo
YIDDISH CONNECTION

Tognini, Steve
LOW BLOW; LOW BLOW

Toguchi, Traci
THE KARATE KID PART II

Toguri, David
ABSOLUTE BEGINNERS, ch

Toi, Lam
LOI RE TRAI TREN DUONG MON

Toibin, Niall
EAT THE PEACH

Toikka, Markku
KUNINGAS LAHTEE RANSKAAN; SUURI
ILLUSIONI

Toikka, Timo
KUNINGAS LAHTEE RANSKAAN

Toit, Michelle Du
PLACE OF WEEPING

Tokos, Lubor
LEV S BILOU HRIVOU

Tol, Henriette
FLIGHT OF RAINBIRDS, A

Toledano, Vincent
MEMOIRES D'UN JUIF TROPICAL

Toledo, Fabiola
BLADE IN THE DARK, A

Tolkan, James
ARMED AND DANGEROUS; TOP GUN

Tolkin, Wendy
SHADOWS RUN BLACK

Tolley, Jim
DR. OTTO AND THE RIDDLE OF THE GLOOM BEAM

Tolnay, Klari
KOJAK BUDAPESTEN

Tolsky, Susan
LONGSHOT, THE

Toma, Svetlana
WILD WIND, THE

Tomasevicius, Jonas
SUNUS PALAIDUNAS, ph

Tomasic, Anton
KORMORAN, d

Tomassi, Serge
FAUBOURG SAINT-MARTIN, m

Tomassi, Vincenzo
DAYS OF HELL, ed; IL MIELE DEL DIAVOLO, ed;
MANHATTAN BABY, ed; RAGE, ed

Tomazani, Despina
I PHOTOGRAPHIA

Tomei, Marisa
PLAYING FOR KEEPS

Tomioka, Taeko
YARI NO GONZA, w

Tomita, Isao
TYPHOON CLUB, ed

Tomita, Shinji
KONEKO MONOGATARI, ph

Tomita, Tamlyn
THE KARATE KID PART II

Tomkins, Alan
HAUNTED HONEYMOON, art d

Tomlinson, Charles D.
BALBOA, prod d; STOOGEMANIA, art d

Tomov, Aleksander
ROMANTICHNA-ISTORIJA, w; ROMANTICHNA-
ISTORIJA, w; SKUPA MOYA, SKUPI MOY, w

Tompkins, Angel
DANGEROUSLY CLOSE; MURPHY'S LAW; NAKED
CAGE, THE

Tompkins, Joe
HOWARD THE DUCK, cos

Tompkins, Joe I.
VIOLETS ARE BLUE, cos

Tompson, Bob
ARMOUR OF GOD, THE, ph

Tomter, Tore
NOE HEIT ANNET, ed

Tonalis, Ludus
MY BEAUTIFUL LAUNDRETTE, m

Tonery, Thomas C.
POWER, set d

Tong, Ye
HALF-DUAN QING

Tong-fei, Lin
TIME TO LIVE AND A TIME TO DIE, A, p

Tonioli, Bruno
ABSOLUTE BEGINNERS

Tonke, Klaus
MORENA

Tonkovicova, Irena
SIESTA VETA, cos

Tonnerfors, Emma
ORMENS VAG PA HALLEBERGET

Tonnerfors, Lisa
ORMENS VAG PA HALLEBERGET

Tonnerre, Jerome
MAN AND A WOMAN: 20 YEARS LATER, A, w

Tonoyama, Taiji
COMIC MAGAZINE

Tonsberg, Adam
TWIST & SHOUT

Tony, George
NINJA TURF

Toomayan, Alan
LONGSHOT, THE, ed

Toompers, Hendrik
NAERATA OMETI

Toop, Carl
ALIENS

Topaz
VENDETTA

Topham, Rhet
TRICK OR TREAT, w

Topi, Francesca
LA SIGNORA DELLA NOTTE

Topor, Roland
LA GALETTE DU ROI, w

Torberg, Friedrich
'38, d&w

Torchsong
YOUNGBLOOD, m

Tordi, Pietro
FOTOROMANZO

Toreg, Edith
NATTSEILERE, ed

Toreg, Svein H.
NATTSEILERE, p

Torell, Robin
JO JO DANCER, YOUR LIFE IS CALLING

Toren, Johan
SACRIFICE, THE, spec eff

Torhonen, Lauri
RIISUMINEN, d; RIISUMINEN, w

Torkos, Steve
YOUNGBLOOD

Torlaschi, Carlos
DIAPASON, ph; GERONIMA, ph

Torleifsson, Reine
HUD

Torn, Rip
BEER

Tornade, Pierre
ASTERIX CHEZ LES BRETONS

Tornado, Toni
QUILOMBO

Tornado, Tony
RUNNING OUT OF LUCK

Tornatore, Giuseppe
IL CAMORRISTA, d; IL CAMORRISTA, w

Tornatore, Joe
FREE RIDE

Tornes, Stavros
DANILO TRELES, O FIMISMENOS ANDALOUSIANOS
MOUSIKOS, p&d; DANILO TRELES, O FIMISMENOS
ANDALOUSIANOS MOUSIKOS, w

Torno, Randall
LADIES CLUB, THE, ed

Toro, Federico Alvarez del
LA BANDA DE LOS PANCHITOS, m

Toro, Guadalupe Del
DONA HERLINDA AND HER SON

Torokvei, Peter
ARMED AND DANGEROUS, w; BACK TO
SCHOOL, w

Torosjan, Grigor
ZAZZENNYJ FONAR, art d

Torossian, Angela
LE DEBUTANT

Torque, Henry
MAMMAME, m

Torre, Guillermo de la
SERE CUALQUIER COSA PERO TE QUIERO, set d

Torre, Luis Arino
EN PENUMBRA, w

Torre, Raul de la
POBRE MARIPOSA, d; POBRE MARIPOSA, w

Torreblanca, Pachi
LOS HIJOS DE LA GUERRA FRIA

Torrebruna, Riccardo de
IL DIAVOLO IN CORPO;
MACARONI BLUES

Torrens, Pip
LADY JANE

Torrent, Ana
LOS PARAISOS PERDIDOS

Torrente, Eduardo
ANGKOR-CAMBODIA EXPRESS, spec eff

Torrente, Fabiana
SALOME

Torrero, Oscar
QUE ME MATEN DE UNA VEZ, w

Torres, Caio
COM LICENCA, EU VOU A LUTA

Torres, Carlos
ESE LOCO LOCO HOSPITAL, m

Torres, Daniel Diaz
JIBARO, d; JIBARO, w

Torres, Dr. Donald R.
Obituaries

Torres, Fernanda
COM LICENCA, EU VOU A LUTA; COM LICENCA, EU
VOU A LUTA, w; EU SEI QUE VOU TE AMAR;
SONHO SEM FIM

Torres, Liz
AMERICA

Torres, Michelle
FRINGE DWELLERS, THE

Torres, Omar
POWER

Torri, Manuela
LA VITA DI SCORTA

Torstad, Tor M.
NATTSEILERE, d

Torstensson, Stig
LOVE ME!

Toschi, Valter
UN RAGAZZO COME TANTI

Tosello, Garance
UNDER THE CHERRY MOON

Tosso, Raul
GERONIMA, d; GERONIMA, w

Toten, Stacey
BACK TO SCHOOL

Touati, Kamel
AL-KAS

Toumarkine, Francois
LA MACHINE A DECOUDRE

Tourangeau, Dale
BUSTED UP

Touret, Giselle
PARENTAL CLAIM

Tournier, Jean
FEMMES DE PERSONNE, ph

Tova, Theresa
HEAD OFFICE

Tovar, Juan
CRONICA DE FAMILIA, w

Tovoli, Luciano
LES FUGITIFS, ph; POLICE, ph

Towels, The Beach
SIZZLE BEACH, U.S.A., m

Towers, Harry Alan
LIGHTNING—THE WHITE STALLION, p

Towers, Robert
STEWARDESS SCHOOL

Towery, Julie Kay
BAD GUYS , set d

Townes, Harry
CHECK IS IN THE MAIL, THE

Towns, Colin
KNIGHTS AND EMERALDS, m

Townsend, Grace
STOOGEMANIA

Townsend, Jim
NIGHT OF THE CREEPS

Townsend, John
AT CLOSE RANGE, m/l

Townsend, Robert
ODD JOBS; RATBOY

Townsend, Robin
CROSSROADS

Toy, Gary
BIG TROUBLE IN LITTLE CHINA

Toy, Holy
X; X, m

Toy, Noel
BIG TROUBLE IN LITTLE CHINA

Toy, Patty
TAI-PAN

Tozzi, Gabriele
SPOSERO SIMON LE BON

Trabaud, Pierre
ROUND MIDNIGHT

Tracey, Ian
FIRE WITH FIRE

Tracey, Kevin G.
MY CHAUFFEUR

Tracy, Steve
Obituaries; DESPERATE MOVES

Tracy, Tony
FLIGHT OF THE NAVIGATOR

Tramm, Peter
AMERICAN ANTHEM

Tranelli, Deborah
NAKED VENGEANCE

Trani, Maurizio
CUT AND RUN, makeup; MANHATTAN BABY, makeup;
WILD BEASTS, makeup

Tranquilli, Silvano
L'ULTIMO GIORNO

Trapp, Robin
MANHUNTER; OVER THE SUMMER

Trauner, Alexandre
ROUND MIDNIGHT, prod d

Travena, David
ROCINANTE

Travers, Sean
TWO FRIENDS

Travis, Gregory
CRIMES OF THE HEART

Travis, Tony
RECRUITS

Travolta, Joey
HOLLYWOOD VICE SQUAD

Trbovich, Tom
FREE RIDE, d

Trbuljak, Goran
OBECANA ZEMLJA, ph; SAN O RUZI, ph

Trearty, Steve
YOUNGBLOOD

Trebicka, Jirina
PAVUCINA

Trebor, Robert
52 PICK-UP; SEX O'CLOCK NEWS, THE

Trei, Cammy
ODD JOBS

Trei, Julie
ODD JOBS

Trejo, Paul
BELIZAIRE THE CAJUN, ed

Trejos, Ruben Dario
EL TREN DE LOS PIONEROS

Trela, Jerzy
SCENY DZIECIECE Z ZYCIA PROWINCJI

Tremblay, Jean Charles
QUI A TIRE SUR NOS HISTOIRES D'AMOUR?, ph

Tremblay, Tony
ROLLER BLADE, spec eff

Trenas, Tote
EN PENUMBRA, ph; KAPAX DEL AMAZONAS, ph; ME
HACE FALTA UN BIGOTE, ph

Trenchard-Smith, Brian
DEAD-END DRIVE-IN, d

Trent, John
BOY IN BLUE, THE, w

Trepanier, Micheline
DECLINE OF THE AMERICAN EMPIRE, THE, makeup

Trettre, I
ITALIAN FAST FOOD

Treu, Wolfgang
DIE ZWEI GESICHTER DES JANUAR, ph

Treusch, Hermann
FUTURE OF EMILY, THE

Treves, Giorgio
LE MAL D'AIMER, d

Treviglio, Leonardo
MORIRAI A MEZZANOTTE; UNA SPINA NEL CUORE

Trevino, Marco Antonio
DONA HERLINDA AND HER SON

Trevino, Oscar
EL NARCO—DUELO ROJO

Trevisi, Franco
IL CASO MORO

Trevor, Richard
BIGGLES, ed

Trevors, Carl
ABSOLUTE BEGINNERS

Trew, Grafton
STREETS OF GOLD

Tri, El
LA BANDA DE LOS PANCHITOS, m

Triantafillou, Giorgos
ALCESTES, ed

Tribiger, Alexander
LOYALTIES

Tribiger, Jonathan
LOYALTIES

Tricottet, Fabienne
FRENCH LESSON

Trieste, Leopoldo
MOMO; NAME OF THE ROSE, THE

Trifonov, Filip
ZABRAVOTE TOZI SLOCHAI

Trifonov, Stefan
SKUPA MOYA, SKUPI MOY, ph

Trillat, Georges
PIRATES

Trimble, Toni
ODD JOBS, makeup

Trinchot, Jorge
LEJANIA; UN HOMBRE DE EXITO

Trineer, Neil
YOUNGBLOOD

Trinidad, Arsenio "Sonny"
THE KARATE KID PART II

Trinkler, Ranier
EL SUIZO—UN AMOUR EN ESPAGNE, ed; EL
SUIZO—UN AMOUR EN ESPAGNE, ph

Trintignant, Jean-Louis
FEMMES DE PERSONNE; LA FEMME DE MA VIE;
MAN AND A WOMAN: 20 YEARS LATER, A; NEXT
SUMMER

Trintignant, Marie
NEXT SUMMER

Trintignant, Nadine
NEXT SUMMER, d&w

Tripi, Alicia
LIGHTNING—THE WHITE STALLION, makeup

Trissenaar, Elisabeth
ANGRY HARVEST; FRANZA

Tristan, Dorothy
DOWN AND OUT IN BEVERLY HILLS

Tristancho, Carlos
EL CABALLERO DEL DRAGON

Trivette, Alpha
ROCKIN' ROAD TRIP

Trixner, Heinz
'38; WELCOME IN VIENNA

Troch, Ludo
SPRINGEN, ed

Troisi, Lino
IL CAMORRISTA; LA BALLATA DI EVA; NINI
TERNO-SECCO

Trojanovsky, Daniela
EIN BLICK—UND DIE LIEBE BRICHT AUS

Trokan, Peter
KALI PATRITHA, SYNTROFE

Troller, Georg Stefan
WELCOME IN VIENNA, w

Trolley, Leonard
IN THE SHADOW OF KILIMANJARO

Tromp, Winfried
FATHERLAND

Tronc, Nicolas
GOLDEN EIGHTIES

Trop, Barry
ARMED RESPONSE, m/l

Tropp, Stan
THREE AMIGOS, set d

Trosper, Elizabeth
SHADOWS RUN BLACK

Trotha, Thilo von
VIRUS HAS NO MORALS, A

Trotignon, Jean-Luc
LE BONHEUR A ENCORE FRAPPE, d; LE BONHEUR
A ENCORE FRAPPE, w

Trotman, George
MORE THINGS CHANGE, THE

Trotta, Margarethe von
ROSA LUXEMBURG, d&w

Trotter, Laura
MIAMI GOLEM

Troup, The Antonio Gades Dance
EL AMOR BRUJO

Troutman, Larry
FERRIS BUELLER'S DAY OFF, m/l

Troutman, Zapp
FERRIS BUELLER'S DAY OFF, m/l

Trovaioli, Armando
L'ISOLA, m; UNA SPINA NEL CUORE, m

Trowe, Jose Chavez
SALVADOR

Troxclair, Cory
LOW BLOW

Trueba, Fernando
EL ANO DE LAS LUCES, d; EL ANO DE LAS LUCES,
w

Trueman, Paula
SAY YES

Trujillo, Gilberto
EL VECINDARIO—LOS MEXICANOS CALIENTES; UN
HOMBRE VIOLENTE

Trujillo, Valentin
EL BRONCO; EL JUEGO DE LA MUERTE; HIJO DEL
PALENQUE; UN HOMBRE VIOLENTE; UN HOMBRE
VIOLENTE, d

Trumbull, Brad
LONGSHOT, THE

Trummer, Gudrun
ERDSEGEN

Trummer, Sepp
ERDSEGEN

Trumpower, Max
ECHO PARK; WELCOME TO 18

Truschkovski, Vassili
KAK MOLODY MY BYLI, ph

Trussell, Hal
NAKED CAGE, THE, ph

Truxa, Erik
MANDEN I MAANEN

Tsang, Barry Wong
ARMOUR OF GOD, THE, w

Tsangaris, Giorgos
CARAVAN SARAI, m

Tsangas, Christos
I PHOTOGRAPHIA

Tsao, Samuel
SHANGHAI SURPRISE

Tschechowa, Vera
TAROT

Tschetter, Dean
NEVER TOO YOUNG TO DIE, art d; WRAITH, THE, art d

Tse-chung, Luo
TIME TO LIVE AND A TIME TO DIE, A

Tseren, G.
BI CHAMD KHAYRTAY, ph

Tsioli, Katerina
SCHETIKA ME TON VASSILI

Tsiolis, Stavros
SCHETIKA ME TON VASSILI, p&d; SCHETIKA ME TON VASSILI, w

Tsitsopoulos, Yannis
I NICHTA ME TI SILENA, ed; KNOCK-OUT, ed

Tsu, Irene
DOWN AND OUT IN BEVERLY HILLS

Tsumura, Takashi
YARI NO GONZA

Tsuruta, Masuichi
ORA TOKYO SA YUKUDA, ed

Tsutsui, Tomomi
SOREKARA, w

Tuan, Nguyen Manh
LOI RE TRAI TREN DUONG MON, w

Tubb, Barry
TOP GUN

Tubens, Joe
Obituaries

Tucci, Maria
TOUCH AND GO

Tuchmann, Sonja
SPRING SYMPHONY

Tucker, Forrest   [Forrest Meredith Tucker]
Obituaries; THUNDER RUN

Tucker, Lorenzo
Obituaries

Tucker, Martin
MAXIMUM OVERDRIVE

Tucker, Marty
ROCKIN' ROAD TRIP

Tucker, Tom
ONE MORE SATURDAY NIGHT

Tuckett, Rita
POLICE ACADEMY 3: BACK IN TRAINING

Tucy, Kyle
WISDOM, makeup

Tudor, Christine L.
FINAL MISSION

Tudor, Tenpole
ABSOLUTE BEGINNERS; SID AND NANCY

Tudor-Phillips, Graham
LABYRINTH

Tudorpole, Edward
ABSOLUTE BEGINNERS, m/l

Tufano, Dennis
VAMP

Tufelli, Nicole
MEMOIRES D'UN JUIF TROPICAL

Tufty, Christopher
STOOGEMANIA, ph

Tuggle, Richard
OUT OF BOUNDS, d

Tukur, Ulrich
STAMMHEIM

Tull, Patrick
PARTING GLANCES

Tulleners, Tonny
SCORPION

Tumanishvili, Mikhail
ODINOTCHNOYE PLAVANIYE, d

Tumar, Sikumar
ESTHER, m

Tuna, Feyzi
KUYUCAKLI YUSUF, d&w; KUYUCAKLI YUSUF, d&w, w

Tunca, Cetin
KUYUCAKLI YUSUF, ph

Tung-hung, Chou
TIME TO LIVE AND A TIME TO DIE, A

Tunis, Roxanne
BLUE CITY

Tuo, Tan
YELLOW EARTH

Tuorila, Risto
TUNTEMATON SOTILAS

Tupinamba, Mario
FULANINHA

Tur, David
NADIA, ed

Tura, Consol
LOLA, cos

Turchi, Lionel
UNDER THE CHERRY MOON

Turchin, Scott
MONEY PIT, THE

Turell, Chili
WOLF AT THE DOOR, THE

Turell, Dan
MORD I MORKET, w

Turenne, Louis
EAT AND RUN

Turgeman, Dan
AVANTI POPOLO

Turgeon, Dianne
RECRUITS

Turgeon, Marthe
HENRI

Turine, Jean Marc
MERCI MONSIEUR ROBERTSON

Turlure, Philippe
ROUND MIDNIGHT, set d

Turman, Glynn
OUT OF BOUNDS

Turman, Lawrence
RUNNING SCARED, p; SHORT CIRCUIT, p

Turner, Dale
BACK TO SCHOOL

Turner, David
LABYRINTH

Turner, Janine
TAI-PAN

Turner, Joan
NO SURRENDER

Turner, John
GIRLS SCHOOL SCREAMERS

Turner, Kathleen
PEGGY SUE GOT MARRIED

Turner, Marcus
SHE'S GOTTA HAVE IT

Turner, Simon Fisher
CARAVAGGIO, m

Turnier, Dona
L'UNIQUE, cos

Turp, Gilbert
LA GUEPE

Turrell, Robert
HAUNTED HONEYMOON

Turturro, John
COLOR OF MONEY, THE; GUNG HO; HANNAH AND HER SISTERS; OFF BEAT

Tushingham, Aisha
JUDGEMENT IN STONE, A

Tushingham, Rita
FLYING; JUDGEMENT IN STONE, A

Tuttle, Chris
MONEY PIT, THE

Tuttle, Guy
IMPURE THOUGHTS, prod d

Tuttle, Lurene
Obituaries

Tuur, Erkki-Sven
IDEAALMAASTIK, m

Tuura, Kristiina
FLIGHT NORTH, prod d

Tuzii, Carlo
STORIA D'AMORE, p

Tweedle, Caroline
RECRUITS

Twiggy
CLUB PARADISE

Twomey, Anne
DEADLY FRIEND; IMAGEMAKER, THE

Tygel, David
O HOMEM DA CAPA PRETA, m

Tylar, Anne
SEX APPEAL

Tyler, Ian
HIGHLANDER

Tynan, Alexandra
DEATH OF A SOLDIER, cos

Tynan, Tracy
THAT'S LIFE, cos

Tyner, Charles
HAMBURGER

Tyson, Cathy
MONA LISA; People to Watch

Tyzack, Margaret
MR. LOVE

Tzifos, George
HARDBODIES 2

Tzinin, I.
ODINOTCHNOYE PLAVANIYE, ed

Tzoumas, Constantine
SCHETIKA ME TON VASSILI, w

Tzoumas, Constantinos
SCHETIKA ME TON VASSILI

U'Kset, Umban
DESCENTE AUX ENFERS; NTTURUDU, d; NTTURUDU, w

Ubarry, Hechter
STREETS OF GOLD

Ubell, Marc
SEX APPEAL, ed

Ubrette, Serge
PARENTAL CLAIM

Uchelen, Marc van
ASSAULT, THE

Uchida, Yuya
COMIC MAGAZINE; COMIC MAGAZINE, w

Udell, Robert
TOUCH AND GO

Uden, Marianne
KNIGHTS AND EMERALDS

Udenio, Fabiana
HARDBODIES 2

Uderzo, Alberto
ASTERIX CHEZ LES BRETONS, w

Udvaros, Dorottya
GREAT GENERATION, THE

Udy, Claudia
PINK CHIQUITAS, THE

Udy, Helene
ONE NIGHT ONLY

Ueki, Hitoshi
CRAZY FAMILY, THE; ORA TOKYO SA YUKUDA; SHIN YOROKOBIMO KANASHIMIMO IKUTOSHITSUKI

Uemura, Naomi
UEMURA NAOMI MONOGATARI, w

Ufland, Harry
OFF BEAT, p; STREETS OF GOLD, p; WHERE THE RIVER RUNS BLACK, p

Ugle, Robert
FRINGE DWELLERS, THE

Ugresic, Dubravka
ZA SRECU JE POTREBNO TROJE, w

Uher, Stefan
SIESTA VETA, d; SIESTA VETA, w

Uhlig, Gerald
TRANSITTRAUME

Uhrmacher, Adolf
WELCOME IN VIENNA, makeup

Ulfsson, Birgitta
ORMENS VAG PA HALLEBERGET

Ullett, Nick
DOWN AND OUT IN BEVERLY HILLS

Ullman, Tracey
JUMPIN' JACK FLASH

Ullmann, Liv
LET'S HOPE IT'S A GIRL

Ullner, Ingelise
TWIST & SHOUT

Ulloa, Alejandro
EL DISPUTADO VOTO DEL SR. CAYO, ph

Ulloa, Alessandro
IL MIELE DEL DIAVOLO, ph

Ulloa, Alexander
KILLING MACHINE, ph

Ullrich, Ulli
ASSAULT, THE, makeup

Ulsen, Henk van
THOMAS EN SENIOR OP HET SPOOR VAN BRUTE BEREND

Ulusoy, Keriman
FOURTEEN NUMARA

Ulvesson, Johan
I LAGENS NAMN

Uman, Chaerul
TITAN SERAMBUT DIBELAH TUJUH, d; TITAN SERAMBUT DIBELAH TUJUH, w

Umbers, Margaret
BRIDGE TO NOWHERE

Ummar, Hadja Sitti Aiza
REVENGE FOR JUSTICE, p

Umnhoyoshi, Shigaru
SOREKARA, m

Umphlett, James
THAT'S LIFE

Underwood, Jay D.
BOY WHO COULD FLY, THE; DESERT BLOOM

Underwood, Rebecca
THREE AMIGOS

Underwood, William
OVER THE SUMMER

Ungar, Jill
MODERN GIRLS, set d

Ungaro, Emanuel
MAN AND A WOMAN: 20 YEARS LATER, A, cos

Unger, Abe
MANHATTAN PROJECT, THE

Unsain, Jose Maria Fernandez
NOCHE DE JUERGA, w

Unterkrainer, Hans-Jorg
HEIDENLOCHER

Uppoor, Pradeep
AGHAAT, p

Urann, Martha Jane
ODD JOBS

Urayama, Hidehiko
TO SLEEP SO AS TO DREAM, m

Urbisci, Rocco
JO JO DANCER, YOUR LIFE IS CALLING; JO JO
DANCER, YOUR LIFE IS CALLING, w

Urdimulas, Pedro
PICARDIA MEXICANA NUMERO DOS, d

Ureta, Raul Perez
VISA U.S.A., ph

Uribe, Alejandro Blanco
A LA SALIDA NOS VEMOS, m

Urioste, Frank J.
HITCHER, THE, ed

Uris, Albert
SOLDIER'S REVENGE

Uritescu, Valentin
NOI, CEI DIN LINIA INTII

Urlina, Elizaveta
REIS 222, art d

Urlina, Yelizaveta
FOUETTE, art d

Urlreger, Rene
FRENCH LESSON

Urquhart, Robert
PLAYING AWAY

Urquieta, Jose Luis
LA ALACRANA, d; MATANZA EN MATAMOROS, d

Urquisa, Juliana
SALVADOR

Urquiza, Ma. De Los Angeles
SALVADOR

Urruzola, Taida
RAGE

Urso, Giula
LA BALLATA DI EVA

Urup, Edda
YES, DET ER FAR!, ed

Utay, William
SCORPION

Utt, Kenneth
SOMETHING WILD; SOMETHING WILD, p

Uysallar, Semra
DIE LIEBESWUSTE

Uytterhoeven, Pierre
MAN AND A WOMAN: 20 YEARS LATER, A, w

Uyuer, Phil
PANTHER SQUAD, ph

Uzan, Serge
FRENCH LESSON

Uzzaman, Badi
MY BEAUTIFUL LAUNDRETTE

Uzzo, Gigi
LA BALLATA DI EVA

Uzzo, Luigi
SEPARATI IN CASA

Vacalopoulos, Christos
SCHETIKA ME TON VASSILI; SCHETIKA ME TON
VASSILI, w

Vacano, Jost
52 PICK-UP, ph

Vaccari, Laura
IL CASO MORO, cos

Vaccaro, Karen
SCREEN TEST

Vacek, Karel
ROSA LUXEMBURG, set d

Vacher, Philippe
ZONE ROUGE

Vackova, Zuzana
SIESTA VETA

Vadas, Ed
MONEY PIT, THE

Vadmand, Per
VALHALLA, w

Vaghen, Zoltan
LEPOTA POROKA, ed

Vagsas, Dag
NOE HEIT ANNET

Vaher, Priit
IDEAALMAASTIK, art d

Vai, Steve
CROSSROADS

Vail, Beverly
FAT GUY GOES NUTZOID!!

Vail, Eddie
THAT'S LIFE

Vail, Lorin
PATRIOT, THE

Vaillant, Lisl
NUTCRACKER: THE MOTION PICTURE

Vails, Nelson
QUICKSILVER

Vaissaire, Daniel
PARENTAL CLAIM, p

Vaissi, Tupuna
KUNINGAS LAHTEE RANSKAAN

Vajda, Laszlo
ERZEKENY BUCSU A FEJEDELEMTOL

Valainis, Maris
HOOSIERS

Valandrey, Charlotte
TAXI BOY

Valavaara, Pipsa
LINNA, ed

Valavanidis, Christos
I PHOTOGRAPHIA

Valdemar, Carlos
EL SECUESTRO DE LOLA-LOLA LA TRAILERA 2, w;
LOS ASES DE CONTRABANDO, w; RAFAGA DE
PLOMO, w; YAKO—CAZADOR DE MALDITOS, w

Valderrama, Luis
BAND OF THE HAND

Valdes, Beatriz
CAPABLANCA; LEJANIA

Valdes, Omar
UN HOMBRE DE EXITO

Valdez, Beatriz
COME LA VIDA MISMA

Vale, Jorge
O VESTIDO COR DE FOGO

Vale, Peter
ABOUT LAST NIGHT, m/l

Vale, Suzanne
SEX APPEAL

Valencia, Vance
8 MILLION WAYS TO DIE

Valencia-Blanco
BAD COMPANY, ed

Valens, Ritchie
MONEY PIT, THE, m/l

Valente, Jobby
UNDER THE CHERRY MOON

Valentin, Gorm
MORD I MORKET

Valentin, Juan
LOS ASES DE CONTRABANDO

Valentine, Cindy
PINK CHIQUITAS, THE

Valentino
SUMMER NIGHT WITH GREEK PROFILE, ALMOND
EYES AND SCENT OF BASIL, cos

Valentino, Charly
ESE LOCO LOCO HOSPITAL

Valenzuela, Jorge
NEMESIO, ed

Valenzuela, Leticia
SALVADOR

Valera, Marie
GRANDEUR ET DECADENCE D'UN PETIT
COMMERCE DE CINEMA

Valerianus, Imelda
ALMACITA DI DESOLATO

Valerii, Tonino
SENZA SCRUPOLI, d; SENZA SCRUPOLI, w

Valero, Antonio V.
LA MITAD DEL CIELO

Valero, Armando
A LA SALIDA NOS VEMOS, ed

Valero, Jean-Louis
SUMMER, m

Valio, Dare
DOKTOR

Valiquette, Rick
CLAN OF THE CAVE BEAR, THE

Valkeasuo, Pentti
LINNA, prod d

Valkeejarvi, Pekka
PIMEYS ODOTTA; SUURI ILLUSIONI

Valladares, Edmund
EL SOL EN BOTELLITAS, d

Valle, Gaetano
UNA NOTTE DI PIOGGIA, ph

Vallee, Rudy   [Hubert Pryor Vallee]
Obituaries

Vallejo, Gerardo
EL RIGOR DEL DESTINO, p, d&w

Vallely, James
RATBOY

Valler, Jorge
KOL AHAVO-TAI, d&w

Valles, Luis
TEO EL PELIRROJO, prod d

Valley, Jafar
CLOSED CIRCUIT

Vallin, Katherine
NEON MANIACS, art d

Vallone, Saverio
DELITTI; UNA TENERA FOLLIA

Valobra, Franco
NAME OF THE ROSE, THE

Valota, Patrice
SUIVEZ MON REGARD

Valusiak, Jozef
LEV S BILOU HRIVOU, ed

Valve, Marjo
KUNINGAS LAHTEE RANSKAAN, ed

Valverde, Juan Jesus
BANDERA NEGRA; EL DISPUTADO VOTO DEL SR.
CAYO

Valverde, Rafael
O HOMEM DA CAPA PRETA, ed

Van Ammelrooy, Willeke
FLIGHT OF RAINBIRDS, A; OP HOOP VAN ZEGEN;
TOP OF THE WHALE

Van Atta, Don
PRAY FOR DEATH, p

van Beers, Anna
PERVOLA: TRACKS IN THE SNOW

van Beverwijk, Anne-Marie
ASSAULT, THE, cos

Van Cleef, Lee
ARMED RESPONSE; JUNGLE RAIDERS; KILLING
MACHINE

Van Dalsem, Dutch
SUNSET STRIP

Van Dam, Jose
BABEL OPERA, OU LA REPETITION DE DON JUAN

van Damme, Charlie
BABEL OPERA, OU LA REPETITION DE DON JUAN ,
ph; DESCENTE AUX ENFERS, ph; MELO, ph

Van Damme, Jean-Claude
NO RETREAT, NO SURRENDER

van de Sande Bakhuijzen, Willem
ASSAULT, THE

van de Sande, Theo
ASSAULT, THE, ph; DE WISSELWACHTER, ph;
MAMA IS BOOS!, ph

van de Staak, Frans
DE VAL VAN PATRICIA HAGGERSMITH, p;
WINDSCHADUW, ed; WINDSCHADUW, p&d;
WINDSCHADUW, w

Van Den Berge, Jugo Van
PPPERFORMER, THE

Van Den Bos, Paul
DE WISSELWACHTER, ph; FLIGHT OF RAINBIRDS,
A, ph

van den Broccke, Maja
SPRINGEN

van den Dop, Tamar
OP HOOP VAN ZEGEN

van den Ende, Walter
BABEL OPERA, OU LA REPETITION DE DON JUAN ,
ph

van der Enden, Eddy
SHADOW OF VICTORY, ph

van der Hoff, Eric
ASSAULT, THE

van der Linden, Dorus
ASSAULT, THE, art d; MAMA IS BOOS!, art d

van der Linden, Hiske
ASSAULT, THE

Van der Linden, Paul
BLUE MAN, THE, ph

van der Lubbe, Huub
ASSAULT, THE

Van Der Made, Guus
FIELD OF HONOR

van der Pol, Marieke
SHADOW OF VICTORY

van der Ronk, Eric
ASSAULT, THE

Van Der Velde, Nadine
CRITTERS

van der Vlugt, Bram
PERVOLA: TRACKS IN THE SNOW

Van Der Woude, Jim
DE WISSELWACHTER

Van DeVere, Trish
HOLLYWOOD VICE SQUAD; UPHILL ALL THE WAY

van Dongen, Hans
FLODDER, ed

Van Doren, Mamie
FREE RIDE

van Dreelen, John
MONEY PIT, THE

van Dyck, Linda
SHADOW OF VICTORY

Van Dyke, Willard   [Willard Ames Van Dyke]
Obituaries

van Eeghem, Mark
CONGO EXPRESS; FIELD OF HONOR

Van Elk, Johnny
PPPERFORMER, THE

van Elst, Gerrit
AFZIEN, w

van Essen, Melle
PERVOLA: TRACKS IN THE SNOW

van Grieken, Irene
ALMACITA DI DESOLATO

Van Haren Noman, Eric
PLAYING FOR KEEPS, ph

van Heijst, Eric
ASSAULT, THE

van Hemert, Ruud
MAMA IS BOOS!, d&w; MAMA IS BOOS!, m

van Hensbergen, Mat
WINDSCHADUW, ph

Van Heyningen, Mattijs
FLIGHT OF RAINBIRDS, A, p

Van Horn, Wayne
RATBOY, stunts

van Husen, Dan
MORENA

van Laer, Michel
SPRINGEN, ph

Van Lamsweerde, Pino
ASTERIX CHEZ LES BRETONS, d

van Loon, Puck
FAILURE, THE

van Luchene, Filip
CONGO EXPRESS

van Os, Ben
SHADOW OF VICTORY, art d

Van Ostade, Ben
BABEL OPERA, OU LA REPETITION DE DON JUAN

van Oterloo, Rogier
ASSAULT, THE, md

van Otterloo, Rogier
OP HOOP VAN ZEGEN, m

Van Patten, Joyce
BILLY GALVIN

Van Patten, Timothy
ZONE TROOPERS

Van Peebles, Mario
3:15, THE MOMENT OF TRUTH; HEARTBREAK
RIDGE; LAST RESORT, THE

Van Peebles, Melvin
AMERICA

van Ransum, Willem
ASSAULT, THE

van Rooij, Michel
ASSAULT, THE

Van Runkle, Theadora
PEGGY SUE GOT MARRIED, cos

Van Sant, Gus
MALA NOCHE, ed; MALA NOCHE, p, d&w

van Tieghem, David
WORKING GIRLS, m

van't Hof, Rene
FLODDER

Van, Li Thi
PLATOON

Vance, Joe
NO RETREAT, NO SURRENDER

Vance, Marilyn
FERRIS BUELLER'S DAY OFF, cos; JO JO DANCER,
YOUR LIFE IS CALLING, cos

Vandegrift, Lynn
ARMED AND DANGEROUS

Vandenberg, Gerard
'38, ph; FOLLOWING THE FUHRER, ph; SPRING
SYMPHONY, ph

Vanderbes, Romano
SEX O'CLOCK NEWS, THE, p&d; SEX O'CLOCK
NEWS, THE, w

VanDerKloot, William
IMPURE THOUGHTS, ed; IMPURE THOUGHTS, p;
IMPURE THOUGHTS, ph

Vandernoot, Alexandra
BABEL OPERA, OU LA REPETITION DE DON JUAN

Vanderwalt, Lesley
FOR LOVE ALONE, makeup

Vaner, Maria
INSOMNIACS

Vanessa
RUNNING OUT OF LUCK

Vanetta, Dennis
SHADOWS RUN BLACK

Vanicola, Joanne
TOBY MCTEAGUE

Vanity
52 PICK-UP; NEVER TOO YOUNG TO DIE

Vannier, Jean-Claude
DERNIER CRI

Vanorio, Frank
CHOKE CANYON, prod d

Vansittart, Rupert
HALF MOON STREET

Vanzina, Carlo
ITALIAN FAST FOOD, w; YUPPIES, I GIOVANI DI
SUCCESSO, d; YUPPIES, I GIOVANI DI SUCCESSO, w

Vanzina, Enrico
IL CAMMISSARIO LO GATTO, w; ITALIAN FAST
FOOD, w; YUPPIES, I GIOVANI DI SUCCESSO, w

Varda, Rosalie
BLEU COMME L'ENFER, cos

Varga, Count Billy
BAD GUYS; STEWARDESS SCHOOL

Vargas, Angel
SALVADOR

Vargas, Henry
AMIGOS, ph

Vargas, Jacob
LAST RESORT, THE

Vargas, John
WILDCATS

Vargas, Jorge
EL SECUESTRO DE CAMARENA

Vargas, Juan Manuel
AMOR A LA VUELTA DE LA ESQUINA, ed;
REDONDO, ed

Vargas, Pepe Lozano
KAPAX DEL AMAZONAS

Vargas, Valentina
NAME OF THE ROSE, THE

Variava, Freni M.
TRIKAL, p

Varini, Carlo
GENESIS, ph; NUIT D'IVRESSE, ph

Variot, Frederic
EXIT-EXIL, ph

Varkonyi, Zoltan
KESERU IGAZSAG, d; KESERU IGAZSAG, w

Varma, Ravi
ANANTARAM, ph; MUKHAMUKHAM, ph

Varman, Ajit
AGHAAT, m

Varney, Jim
DR. OTTO AND THE RIDDLE OF THE GLOOM BEAM;
DR. OTTO AND THE RIDDLE OF THE GLOOM BEAM,
w

Vartenian, Zare
ESTHER

Varuolo, Ed
COMBAT SHOCK, spec eff

Varveris, Stella
COMBAT SHOCK, ph

Vasallo, Carlos
ESE LOCO LOCO HOSPITAL, p; KILLING MACHINE,
p

Vasary, Melinda
KESERU IGAZSAG, prod d

Vasaryova, Magda
LEV S BILOU HRIVOU

Vasegard, Lene
BARNDOMMENS GADE

Vasiliev, Vladimir
FOUETTE

Vasilovich, Guy
GREAT MOUSE DETECTIVE, THE, art d

Vasilovik, Claudia
AVENGING FORCE

Vasilyev, Vladimir
FOUETTE, d

Vassdal, Kjell
BLACKOUT, ph

Vassilevsky, Radomir
CHTO U SENJKI BYLO, d

Vassilicos, Vassilis
I NICHTA ME TI SILENA, w

Vassiliev, Anatoli
BORIS GODUNOV

Vassilieva, Vera
VYITI ZAMUZH ZA KAPITANA

Vassilyeva, Yekaterina
CHTO U SENJKI BYLO

Vastano, Sergio
ITALIAN FAST FOOD; YUPPIES, I GIOVANI DI
SUCCESSO

Vatsula, Anthony
SCORPION

Vauban, Jean-Paul
L'AUBE, ed

Vauge, Celine
MORT UN DIMANCHE DE PLUIE

Vaugeois, Gerard
QUI TROP EMBRASSE, p

Vaughan, Peter
HAUNTED HONEYMOON

Vaughan, Vanessa
CRAZY MOON

Vaughn, Robert
BLACK MOON RISING; DELTA FORCE, THE

Vaughter, Marcus
SORORITY HOUSE MASSACRE

Vaury, Genevieve
LES LONGS MANTEAUX, ed

Vayer, Tamas
ELYSIUM, art d

Vaz, Adalgiza
NTTURUDU

Vazdiks, Petras
SUNUS PALAIDUNAS

Vazquez, Luis
INSTANT JUSTICE, art d&set d

Veber, Francis
LES FUGITIFS, d&w

Vecchiali, Paul
BEAU TEMPS, MAIS ORAGEUX EN FIN DE
JOURNEE, ed; QUI TROP EMBRASSE, ed

Veeder, Deeann
CARNAGE

Vega, Gonzalo
TERROR Y ENCAJES NEGROS

Vega, Isela
EL SECUESTRO DE LOLA-LOLA LA TRAILERA 2; IN
'N' OUT

Vega, Justo
CAPABLANCA, ed; JIBARO, ed; LEJANIA, ed;
MALABRIGO, ed

Vega, Tony
MOSQUITO COAST, THE

Veileborg, Steen
ET SKUD FRA HJERTET, ph

Velasco, Manuel
NEMESIO

Velasquez, Oscar
LA BANDA DE LOS PANCHITOS

Velazco, Arturo
LA BANDA DE LOS PANCHITOS, d; LA BANDA DE
LOS PANCHITOS, w

Velchi, Franco
TROPPO FORTE, art d

Velez, Eddie
EXTREMITIES

Velis, Pedro
SCORPION

Velko, Ivan
DA EBICHASH NA INAT

Vella, Marlow
PINK CHIQUITAS, THE

Velmiski, Nicolai
CAPABLANCA, p

Veloso, Caetano
CINEMA FALADO, d&w; CINEMA FALADO, md;
CINEMA FALADO, p

Veloso, Dede
BRAS CUBAS; CINEMA FALADO

Veloso, Dona Cano
CINEMA FALADO

Veloz, Ramon
CAPABLANCA

Veloz, Ramoncito
PLACIDO

Veltheim, Verkehrs-Sicherheitszentrum
LISI UND DER GENERAL, stunts

Velthuis, Hennie
PERVOLA: TRACKS IN THE SNOW

Veluzet, Andre
ODD JOBS

Vembayan
MUKHAMUKHAM

Ven, Monique van de
ASSAULT, THE

Venasky, Victor
TOUCH AND GO

Venczel, Vera
CHICHERIN

Venditti, Antonello
TROPPO FORTE, m

Vendroux, Laurence
LE BONHEUR A ENCORE FRAPPE, art d

Vennerod, Petter
DROMMESLOTTER; DROMMESLOTTER, p, d&w;
FAREWELL ILLUSION, p, d&w

Venora, Diane
F/X

Ventilla, Melanie Jane
GREAT GENERATION, THE

Ventola, Anthony
CLASS OF NUKE 'EM HIGH

Ventura, Enric
EL CABALLERO DEL DRAGON, prod d

Ventura, Jose Antonio
CHICO REI, ph

Ventura, Michael
ECHO PARK, w

Ventura, Ray
P.O.W. THE ESCAPE

Ventura, Stefania
GIURO CHE TI AMO

Venturoli, Giorgio
FOXTRAP, ed

Venu
AMMA ARIYAN, ph; ORIDATH

Venu, Nedumudi
CHIDAMBARAM

Venzky, Gert B.
DER WILDE CLOWN, prod d

Vera, Ana Maria
HOT CHILI, art d

Vera, Gararardo
EL AMOR BRUJO, set d&cos

Vera, Gerardo
LA MITAD DEL CIELO, set d

Vera, Sonia
SCORPION

Vera, Victoria
MONSTER DOG

Verastegui, Charo
MALABRIGO

Verbiest, Chris
CONGO EXPRESS, ed

Verbit, Helen
HOLLYWOOD ZAP!

Verbrugge, Casper
PPPERFORMER, THE, d; PPPERFORMER, THE, w

Vercellino, Susan
QUIET COOL, w

Vercheval, Paul
MERCI MONSIEUR ROBERTSON, ph

Verdecchi, Alessandro
SEMBRA MORTO . . . MA E SOLO SVENUTO, p

Verdegiglio, Diego
SQUADRA SELVAGGIA

Verdi, Giuseppe
DEMONER, m; EU SEI QUE VOU TE AMAR, m;
FAUBOURG SAINT-MARTIN, m

Verdinelli, Francesco
LA VITA DI SCORTA, m

Verdone, Carlo
SETTE CHILI IN SETTE GIORNI; SETTE CHILI IN
SETTE GIORNI, w; TROPPO FORTE; TROPPO FORTE,
d; TROPPO FORTE, w

Verdone, Luca
SETTE CHILI IN SETTE GIORNI, d; SETTE CHILI IN
SETTE GIORNI, w

Verdu, Maribel
27 HORAS; EL ANO DE LAS LUCES

Verduzco, Martha
CRONICA DE FAMILIA

Vere-Jones, Peter
DANGEROUS ORPHANS

Verhage, Gerrard
AFZIEN, d; AFZIEN, w

Verhavert, Roland
SPRINGEN, p

Verhoeven, Anna
PERVOLA: TRACKS IN THE SNOW, cos

Verhoeven, Michael
KILLING CARS, p, d&w

Verita, Raffaele
CAMORRA

Verley, Bernard
PEKIN CENTRAL, p

Verman, Ajit
GURU DAKSHINA, m

Vermeiren, Misjel
PERVOLA: TRACKS IN THE SNOW, art d

Vermig, Tom
LAND OF DOOM

Vernengo, Ines
MAN FACING SOUTHEAST

Vernier, Pierre
FRENCH LESSON

Vernon, Alma
WHITE SLAVE

Vernon, Gabor
LADY JANE

Vernon, Harvey
STOOGEMANIA

Vernon, Howard
FAUBOURG SAINT-MARTIN

Vernon, James Nugent
CLASS OF NUKE 'EM HIGH

Vernon, Kate
LAST OF PHILIP BANTER, THE; PRETTY IN PINK

Vernon, Richard
LADY JANE

Verrell, Cec
HOLLYWOOD VICE SQUAD; SILK

Verstaete, Mark
SPRINGEN

Verstraete, Mark
CONGO EXPRESS

Verzier, Rene
BULLIES, ph; ONE NIGHT ONLY, ph; TOBY
MCTEAGUE, ph

Vesala, Edward
HUOMENNA, m

Vesper, Bernward
JOURNEY, THE, w

Vesperini, Edith
PAULETTE, cos

Vesselov, Alyshoa
CHTO U SENJKI BYLO

Vest, Oya
LAND OF DOOM, cos

Vest, Sunny
LAND OF DOOM, p

Vetrano, Frank
DESPERATE MOVES, set d

Vettorazzo, Giovanni
THUNDER WARRIOR

Vezat, Bernard
JEAN DE FLORETTE, prod d; MANON DES SOURCES,
prod d

Viafale, Pevise
QUEEN CITY ROCKERS

Viale, Jean Pierre
BLUE VELVET

Viana, Afonso
NEM TUDO E VERDADE, ph

Viana, Mis
RUNNING OUT OF LUCK

Viana, Zelito
AVAETE, A SEMENTE DA VINGANCA, d; AVAETE, A
SEMENTE DA VINGANCA, w

Vicario, Elvira
INSOMNIACS

Vice, Lisa
MURPHY'S LAW

Vichi, Gerald
BEER

Viciano, Enrique
LOLA, w

Vickery, Courtney
FRIDAY THE 13TH PART VI: JASON LIVES

Vickery, John
OUT OF BOUNDS

Victor, Dania
AMIGOS

Victor, Paula
BAD GUYS

Victor, Renaud
FAUBOURG SAINT-MARTIN; GARDIEN DE LA NUIT,
p

Victor-Smith, John
KNIGHTS AND EMERALDS, ed

Victoria, Jorge
MATANZA EN MATAMOROS; SEPARATE
VACATIONS

Vida, Piero
IL CASO MORO; LA VITA DI SCORTA; LA VITA DI
SCORTA, d&w

Vidakovic, Branko
I TO CE PROCI

Vidal, Alexandra
CONSEIL DE FAMILLE

Vidal, Francisco
MAMBRU SE FUE A LA GUERRA

Vidal, Stephanie
CONSEIL DE FAMILLE

Videnovic, Ahdrijana
PROKA

Videnovic, Gala
BAL NA VODI

Vieges, Mario
REPORTER X

Viera, Joey
FERRIS BUELLER'S DAY OFF

Vierikko, Vesa
BORN AMERICAN; LINNA

Vierny, Sacha
FUTURE OF EMILY, THE, ph

Vierthaler, Heidi
NUTCRACKER: THE MOTION PICTURE

Viezzi, Adolphe
LES LONGS MANTEAUX, p; SINCERELY
CHARLOTTE; SINCERELY CHARLOTTE, p

Vignal, Pascale
ROUND MIDNIGHT

Vignet, Dominique
BLEU COMME L'ENFER, p

Vigoda, Abe
VASECTOMY: A DELICATE MATTER

Vigran, Herbert
Obituaries

Vikberg, Jukka
FLIGHT NORTH, prod d

Vila, Camilo
AMIGOS, p

Vilaboim, Paschoal
BRAS CUBAS

Vilaboim, Pascoal
FULANINHA

Vilaca, Paulo
FULANINHA; O HOMEM DA CAPA PRETA

Vilanch, Bruce
MORNING AFTER, THE

Vilar, Stephane
LAST SONG, m

Vilardebo, Arnau
MES ENLLA DE LA PASSIO

Vilcu, Ion
SECVENTE

Villa, Donna
REVENGE FOR JUSTICE

Villa, Federico
CONTACTO CHICANO; ES MI VIDA—EL NOA NOA 2

Villa, Gabriele
FOTOROMANZO; IL CASO MORO

Villa, Jose M.
LEJANIA, set d&cos

Villa, Monica
AWAITING THE PALLBEARERS

Villaggio, Paolo
GRANDI MAGAZZINI; SCUOLA DI LADRI

Villagra, Nelson
EL CORAZON SOBRE LA TIERRA

Villalobos, Juan
UNDER THE CHERRY MOON

Villalobos, Reynaldo
BAND OF THE HAND, ph; DESERT BLOOM; DESERT
BLOOM, ph; LUCAS, ph; SAVING GRACE, ph

Villalon, Jorge
PLACIDO

Villanuevo, Phil
3:15, THE MOMENT OF TRUTH

Villara, Tom
ONE CRAZY SUMMER

Villard, Dimitri
FLIGHT OF THE NAVIGATOR, p

Villard, Tom
HEARTBREAK RIDGE; WEEKEND WARRIORS

Villaronga, Agustin
CAGED GLASS, d&w

Villeaux, Robert
NO RETREAT, NO SURRENDER

Villela, Luciola
SONHO SEM FIM, p

Villeret, Jacques
BLACK MIC-MAC; LA GALETTE DU ROI; LES
FRERES PETARD

Villers, Claude
HALF MOON STREET

Villiers, James
RUNNING OUT OF LUCK

Villiers, Muriel
HALF MOON STREET

Villon, Henri
ZONE ROUGE

Vilozhni, Shmuel
HASHIGAON HAGADOL

Vina, Ana
JIBARO

Vinas, David
COCAINE WARS, w

Vince, Barry
LIGHTSHIP, THE, ed

Vincent, Chuck
SEX APPEAL, p&d; SEX APPEAL, w

Vincent, Claude
VIOLATED

Vincent, Ernie
BELIZAIRE THE CAJUN

Vincent, Frank
NO SURRENDER

Vincent, Roland
BEAU TEMPS, MAIS ORAGEUX EN FIN DE
JOURNEE, m; JE HAIS LES ACTEURS, m

Vincent, Stan
BEST OF TIMES, THE, m/l

Vincent, Virginia
LONGSHOT, THE

Vincenz, Iulia
SECVENTE, ed

Vincenzoni, Luciano
RAW DEAL, w

Vincze, Ernest
BIGGLES, ph; SHANGHAI SURPRISE, ph

Vinding, Mads
ROUND MIDNIGHT; ROUND MIDNIGHT

Vinegar, Theresa
NINJA TURF

Viner, Fanny
GOOD FATHER, THE

Ving, Lee
BLACK MOON RISING

Vinicius, Marcus
HOUR OF THE STAR, THE, m

Vinitzki, David
CHICHERIN, art d

Vinken, Dorith
PERVOLA: TRACKS IN THE SNOW, ed

Vinnik, Yuri
KAK MOLODY MY BYLI, m

Vint, Colin
LOYALTIES

Vinton, Will
SHADOW PLAY, p

Viola, Gail
KGB—THE SECRET WAR, cos

Violla, J.C.
MALANDRO

Viovanni, Nicola
LET'S HOPE IT'S A GIRL, m

Virkler, Dennis
NOBODY'S FOOL, ed

Virlojeux, Henri
LA GITANE

Virly, Joan
PANTHER SQUAD

Virtanen, Arno
PIMEYS ODOTTA

Virtanen, Pauli
BORN AMERICAN

Virtzberg, Ilan
SMILE OF THE LAMB, THE, m

Viruboff, Sofia
MISS MARY

Virve, Tonu
NAERATA OMETI, art d

Visan, Dorel
DECLARATIE DE DRAGOSTE

Vischkof, Katia
PRUNELLE BLUES, art d

Visconti, Piero
BLIND DIRECTOR, THE

Viscuso, Sal
JAKE SPEED

Vishwanathan
MUKHAMUKHAM

Viskocil, Joseph
VAMP, spec eff

Visone, Antonio
IL CAMORRISTA, art d

Vitagliano, Joseph
CARNAGE

Vitale, Antonella
GRANDI MAGAZZINI

Vitale, Lito
DIAPASON, m

Vitali, Cirillo
JUNGLE RAIDERS

Vitaly, John
COCAINE WARS

Vitasek, Andreas
MULLERS BURO

Vitella, Sel
PLAYING FOR KEEPS

Vitezy, Laszlo
ERZEKENY BUCSU A FEJEDELEMTOL, d

Vitier, Jose Marie
EL CORAZON SOBRE LA TIERRA, m

Vitier, Sergio
CAPABLANCA, m

Viton, Abel
EL DISPUTADO VOTO DEL SR. CAYO

Vitti, Monica
FRANCESCA E MIA; FRANCESCA E MIA, w

Vittier, Sergio
PLACIDO, m

Vitug, Officer Micheal
MANHUNTER

Vivaldi, Antonio
KONZERT FUR ALICE, m; UNA DONNA SENZA
NOME, m

Vivaldi, Piero
LA CROCE DALLE 7 PIETRE

Vivanco, Fernando
LULU DE NOCHE

Vivas, Marc
SUMMER

Viveiros, Anthony
ONE CRAZY SUMMER

Viviani, Sonia
UNA TENERA FOLLIA

Vivo, Jose
EL CABALLERO DEL DRAGON

Vivo, Marco
DEMONI 2—L'INCUBO RITORNA; GIURO CHE TI
AMO

Vizziello, Carlos
ME HACE FALTA UN BIGOTE, m

Vladic, Radoslav
LEPOTA POROKA, ph

Vlady, Marina
L'ISOLA; SAPORE DEL GRANO; TWIST AGAIN A
MOSCOU; UNA CASA IN BILICO

Vlahakou, Eva
I NICHTA ME TI SILENA; SCHETIKA ME TON
VASSILI

Vocca, Ginella
IL CASO MORO

Voetman, Hans Henrik
MORD I MORKET

Vogel, Claes
GRONA GUBBAR FRAN Y.R., w

Vogel, Daniel
ON A VOLE CHARLIE SPENCER!, ph

Vogel, Helmut
HEIDENLOCHER

Vogel, Jurgen
NOVEMBERKATZEN

Vogel, Matt
BREEDERS , spec eff

Vogler, Rudiger
TAROT

Vohrer, Alfred
Obituaries

Voight, Jon
DESERT BLOOM

Voiss, Peter
DIE WALSCHE, p

Voldmester, Susanne
ET SKUD FRA HJERTET

Voldstedlund, Merete
WOLF AT THE DOOR, THE

Voletti, Michael
DOWN AND OUT IN BEVERLY HILLS

Volev, Nikolai
DA EBICHASH NA INAT, d; DA EBICHASH NA INAT,
w

Volker, Francine
HEAD OFFICE

Vollmer, Britta
EIN BLICK—UND DIE LIEBE BRICHT AUS, cos

Vollmer, Marion
EIN BLICK—UND DIE LIEBE BRICHT AUS, cos

Volman, Mark
ADVENTURES OF THE AMERICAN RABBIT, THE, m/l

Volodaraki, Edouard
MOI DRUG IVAN LAPSHIN, w

Volonte, Gian Maria
IL CASO MORO

Volpe, Les
PLACE OF WEEPING, w

Voltan, Gionni
ELOGIO DELLA PAZZIA

Volz, Dorte
TAROT, ed

von Arnim, Bettina
GRITTA VOM RATTENSCHLOSS, w

von Arnim, Gisela
GRITTA VOM RATTENSCHLOSS, w

von Brandenstein, Patrizia
MONEY PIT, THE, prod d; NO MERCY, prod d

von Bromssen, Tomas
ORMENS VAG PA HALLEBERGET

von Buuren, Marc
AROUND THE WORLD IN EIGHTY WAYS, ed

von Grolman, Julia
CONTAR HASTA TEN

von Hanno, Eva
AMOROSA

von Hartenstein, Gloria
SOLDIER'S REVENGE, cos

von Hassel, Karl-Heinz
DER SOMMER DES SAMURAI

von Helmolt, Bonnie
TRAMP AT THE DOOR, art d

Von Hugo, Hasso
NAME OF THE ROSE, THE, makeup

von Kieseritsky, Georg
AUF IMMER UND EWIG, art d

Von Kugelgen, Karl
BORN AMERICAN, spec eff

Von Ledenburg, Frederick
GINGER & FRED

Wallis, Gary
ARMED RESPONSE, m/l

Wallis, Hal B.   [Harold Brent Wallis]
Obituaries

Wallis, Rit
BOY IN BLUE, THE, ed

Wallis, Roger
AMOROSA, m

Wallis, Shani
GREAT MOUSE DETECTIVE, THE

Wallner, Jack
INSIDE OUT, ph

Waln, Rick
REBEL LOVE

Walser, Martin
EIN FLIEHENDES PFERD, w

Walsh, Brock
ABOUT LAST NIGHT, m/l

Walsh, David
SOLDIER'S REVENGE

Walsh, Edward
CROSSROADS

Walsh, Eileen
NO SURRENDER

Walsh, J.T.
HANNAH AND HER SISTERS; POWER

Walsh, M. Emmet
BACK TO SCHOOL; BEST OF TIMES, THE; CRITTERS;
WILDCATS

Walsh, Mandy
LETTER TO BREZHNEV

Walsh, Mary
ADVENTURE OF FAUSTUS BIDGOOD, THE

Walsh, Peter
DOGS IN SPACE

Walsh, Richard
ARMED AND DANGEROUS

Walsh, Rob
MY LITTLE PONY, m

Walsh, Thomas A.
SEVEN MINUTES IN HEAVEN, art d

Walston, Ray
RAD

Waltari, Mika
SUURI ILLUSIONI, w

Walter, Harriet
GOOD FATHER, THE

Walter, Mike
EYE OF THE TIGER

Walter, Richard
BIG TROUBLE

Walter, Rita
CRY FROM THE MOUNTAIN

Walter, Tracey
AT CLOSE RANGE; SOMETHING WILD

Walters, Julie
CAR TROUBLE

Walthall, Wade
NUTCRACKER: THE MOTION PICTURE

Walther, Jurg Victor
POPULATION: ONE, ph

Waltman, Alan
CLAN OF THE CAVE BEAR, THE

Walton, Cedar
ROUND MIDNIGHT

Walton, Chutney
THAT'S LIFE

Walton, Emma
FINE MESS, A; THAT'S LIFE

Walton, Fred
APRIL FOOL'S DAY, d

Walton, Jeff
BAD GUYS

Walton, John
KANGAROO

Walton, Lee-Max
BOY IN BLUE, THE; SEPARATE VACATIONS

Walton, Mark
ECHO PARK, m/l

Walton, Tony
HEARTBURN, prod d

Walton, Willie J.
WILDCATS

Waltz, Lisa
BRIGHTON BEACH MEMOIRS

Walwin, Ken
BIGGLES, p; BIGGLES, w

Walzer, Irene
SOLARBABIES, p

Wam, Svend
DROMMESLOTTER, p, d&w; FAREWELL ILLUSION, p,
d&w

Wambe, Oke
ABSOLUTE BEGINNERS; KNIGHTS AND EMERALDS

Wan, Carman
HAPPY DIN DON, art d

Wan, Lau Ching
SILENT LOVE

Wanamaker, Sam
RAW DEAL

Wanchun, Shi
LIANG JIA FUNU, m

Wandachristine
COLOR OF MONEY, THE

Wandruszka, Marina
STAMMHEIM

Wang, Cilli
ERDSEGEN

Wang, Donald Z.
FREE RIDE, w

Wang, Peter
GREAT WALL, A; GREAT WALL, A, d; GREAT
WALL, A, w

Wang, Ronald Z.
FREE RIDE, w

Wanting, Zhang
FEIFA YIMIN, d

Wapler, Eric
ON A VOLE CHARLIE SPENCER!

Wapshott, Garry
SKY PIRATES, ph

War, Abdul
SARRAOUNIA, w

Warakagoda, Wijertna
ARUNATA PERA

Warbeck, David
FORMULA FOR MURDER; MIAMI GOLEM

Warburg, Bent
MORD I MORKET

Ward, Burt
FIRE IN THE NIGHT

Ward, Charles
Obituaries

Ward, Christopher
HEAD OFFICE

Ward, David S.
SAVING GRACE, w

Ward, Jeff
STREETS OF GOLD; TERRY ON THE FENCE

Ward, Jonathan
VIOLATED

Ward, Justin
HAUNTED HONEYMOON

Ward, Lyman
FERRIS BUELLER'S DAY OFF

Ward, Mary B.
PLAYING FOR KEEPS

Ward, Merrill
ECHO PARK

Ward, Olivia
LEGAL EAGLES

Ward, Sela
NOTHING IN COMMON

Ward, Tom
MORNING AFTER, THE, spec eff

Ward, Wally
THUNDER RUN

Ward, Wayne
SCORPION

Ward-Lealand, Jennifer
DANGEROUS ORPHANS

Warde, Hanna
WHAT HAPPENED NEXT YEAR, ph

Warden, Steve
DR. OTTO AND THE RIDDLE OF THE GLOOM BEAM

Wardlow, John
APRIL FOOL'S DAY, stunts; CLAN OF THE CAVE
BEAR, THE; CLAN OF THE CAVE BEAR, THE, stunts

Wardlow, Keith
CLAN OF THE CAVE BEAR, THE

Warfield, Marlene
JO JO DANCER, YOUR LIFE IS CALLING

Warfield, Marsha
WHOOPEE BOYS, THE

Wargnier, Regis
LA FEMME DE MA VIE, d; LA FEMME DE MA VIE, w

Warhit, Doug
PLAYING FOR KEEPS

Warlock, Richard
QUICKSILVER

Warnecke, Gordon
MY BEAUTIFUL LAUNDRETTE

Warner, Chet
UPHILL ALL THE WAY

Warner, Mark
BIG TROUBLE IN LITTLE CHINA, ed

Warner, Martin Charles
ARMED AND DANGEROUS; LIGHTNING—THE
WHITE STALLION

Warner, Solveig
BRODERNA MOZART, ph

Warners, Robert
Obituaries

Warokka, Lia
INTRUDER, THE

Warr, Daniel
SOLDIER'S REVENGE

Warr, James
NINJA TURF

Warren, Jason
KILLER PARTY; YOUNGBLOOD

Warren, Kim
OVER THE SUMMER

Warren, Linda
ONE CRAZY SUMMER

Warren, Marcia
MR. LOVE

Warrick, Ruth
DEATHMASK

Warschilka, Edward
BIG TROUBLE IN LITTLE CHINA, ed; VIOLETS ARE
BLUE, ed

Wasef, Mouna
SUN ON A HAZY DAY, THE

Washington, Dennis
STAND BY ME, prod d

Washington, Denzel
POWER

Washington, Eddy
LOYALTIES

Washington, Ludie C.
JO JO DANCER, YOUR LIFE IS CALLING

Wasley, Charlie
YOUNGBLOOD

Wass, Ted
LONGSHOT, THE

Wasserman, Irving
STOOGEMANIA

Wasserman, Yael
ALEX KHOLE AHAVA

Wasson, Craig
MEN'S CLUB, THE

Watanabe, Gedde
GUNG HO; VAMP

Watanabe, Kazuo
SHIN YOROKOBIMO KANASHIMIMO
IKUTOSHITSUKI, p

Watanabe, Ken
TAMPOPO

Waterbury, Laura
ONE CRAZY SUMMER

Waters, Andre
LOW BLOW

Waters, Chris
COOL CHANGE

Waters, Chuck
AMERICAN ANTHEM, stunts; AT CLOSE RANGE,
stunts

Waters, John
GOING SANE; SOMETHING WILD

Waters, Nick
BIG HURT, THE

Waters, Roger
WHEN THE WIND BLOWS, m

Waterston, Sam
FLAGRANT DESIR; JUST BETWEEN FRIENDS

Watkin, David
SKY BANDITS, ph

Watkins, Ben
FERRIS BUELLER'S DAY OFF, m/l

Watkins, David
SHANGHAI SURPRISE, spec eff

Watkins, Johnny L.
DESERT BLOOM

Watkins, Leonard
BLUE VELVET

Watkins, Marcia
POLICE ACADEMY 3: BACK IN TRAINING

Watkins, Toney Davis
Obituaries

Watkins, Wade
IMPURE THOUGHTS, ed

Watkinson, Doreen
COMRADES, cos

Watrinet, Hubert
PEKIN CENTRAL

Watson, Christopher
LAND OF DOOM, set d

Watson, Donald
ONE CRAZY SUMMER

Watson, Douglass
MONEY PIT, THE

Watson, Maureen
FRINGE DWELLERS, THE

Watson, Neville
TERRY ON THE FENCE

Watson, Rob
YOUNGBLOOD

Watson, Waldon O.
Obituaries

Watson, Woody
PRAY FOR DEATH

Wattal, K.K.
GURU DAKSHINA, p

Watters, Mark
IN THE SHADOW OF KILIMANJARO

Watts, Jane
PARENTAL CLAIM

Watts, Lynn
SARRAOUNIA

Watts, Naomi
FOR LOVE ALONE

Watts, Roy
WHERE ARE THE CHILDREN?, ed

Waumans, Veronique
CONGO EXPRESS

Wawzynczak, Piotr
KRONIKA WYPADKOW MILOSNYCH

Wax, Nathan
FOR LOVE ALONE, m

Waxman, Anath
HASHIGAON HAGADOL

Way, Ann
CLOCKWISE; HAUNTED HONEYMOON

Way, Stewart
FRINGE DWELLERS, THE, art d

Wayne, Bernie
BLUE VELVET, m/l

Wayne, Ethan
COBRA MISSION

Wayne, Jill
MY LITTLE PONY

Wayne, John Ethan
MANHUNT, THE

Wayne, Ken
DEATH OF A SOLDIER

Wayne, Patrick
REVENGE

Wdiantono, Sylvia
DOEA TANDA MATA

Weagle, Cynthia
BEGINNER'S LUCK

Weagle, Stephen
BEGINNER'S LUCK

Weary, A.C.
WHAT WAITS BELOW

Weatherhead, Chris
WHATEVER IT TAKES; WHATEVER IT TAKES, w

Weatherly, Shawn
POLICE ACADEMY 3: BACK IN TRAINING

Weaver, Courtland
NUTCRACKER: THE MOTION PICTURE

Weaver, Fritz
POWER

Weaver, Kenneth
P.O.W. THE ESCAPE

Weaver, Kent
AMERICAN ANTHEM

Weaver, Lee
WILDCATS

Weaver, Michelle
AMERICAN JUSTICE

Weaver, Sigourney
ALIENS; HALF MOON STREET

Weaving, Hugo
FOR LOVE ALONE

Webb, Chloe
SID AND NANCY; People to Watch

Webb, Damon
RADIOACTIVE DREAMS

Webb, Monica
SUNSET STRIP, p

Webb, Roger
BOY IN BLUE, THE, m

Webb, Simon
PLAYING AWAY, m

Webb, William
SUNSET STRIP, d; SUNSET STRIP, p; SUNSET STRIP, w

Webber, Arthur
FORMULA FOR MURDER

Webber, Deborah
WILDCATS

Webber, Timothy
TOBY MCTEAGUE

Weber, Billy
TOP GUN, ed

Weber, Jacques
MAN AND A WOMAN: 20 YEARS LATER, A; SUIVEZ MON REGARD

Weber, Pedro
EL MERCADO DE HUMILDES; LA TIERRA PROMETIDA; LAS NOCHES DEL CALIFAS; PICARDIA MEXICANA NUMERO DOS; YAKO—CAZADOR DE MALDITOS

Weber, Tim
BOY IN BLUE, THE

Webster, Daniel
FREE RIDE, art d

Webster, Harry
NO SURRENDER

Webster, Hugh
Obituaries

Webster, Paul
RECRUITS

Wedderburn, Clive
KNIGHTS AND EMERALDS

Weddington, Maurice
TAKE IT EASY

Weddle, Vernon
SHORT CIRCUIT

Wedeles, Rodolfo
DANS UN MIROIR, ed; LOS HIJOS DE LA GUERRA FRIA, ed

Wedgeworth, Ann
MEN'S CLUB, THE

Weeks, Alan
BRIGHTON BEACH MEMOIRS

Weeks, Becki
ODD JOBS

Weeks, Christopher
UPHILL ALL THE WAY

Weeks, Doug
LOW BLOW

Weeks, Jimmie Ray
KING KONG LIVES

Weeks, Jimmy Ray
MANHATTAN PROJECT, THE

Weeks, Michelle
LITTLE SHOP OF HORRORS

Weerasingha, Suminda
ARUNATA PERA, ph

Wehrmann, Mike
TOUCH AND GO

Wei, Deng
QINGCHUN JI, ph

Wei, Li
PIAOBO QIYU

Wei-Han, Yang
DARK NIGHT, ph; KUEI-MEI, A WOMAN, ph; WO ERH HAN-SHENG, ph

Wei-Yen, Yu
DARK NIGHT, art d; DARK NIGHT, cos

Weichenhanh, Gudrun
DAS SCHWEIGEN DES DICHTERS

Weigl, Vladimir
DAS SCHWEIGEN DES DICHTERS

Weil, Cynthia
8 MILLION WAYS TO DIE, m/l; ABOUT LAST NIGHT, m/l; AMERICAN TAIL, AN, m/l; BEST OF TIMES, THE, m/l

Weil, Dan
BLACK MIC-MAC, art d; KAMIKAZE, art d

Weil, Samuel
CLASS OF NUKE 'EM HIGH, d

Weiler, Clay
RAD, set d

Weill, Avigdor
SHTAY ETZBA'OT M'TZIDON, ed

Weiman, Kate
SEX O'CLOCK NEWS, THE

Wein, Dean
JO JO DANCER, YOUR LIFE IS CALLING

Wein, Yossi
BAR 51—SISTER OF LOVE, ph

Weinbren, Graham
GREAT WALL, A, ed

Weincke, Jan
TWIST & SHOUT, ph

Weindler, Helge
PARADIES, ph

Weiner, Hal
IMAGEMAKER, THE, d; IMAGEMAKER, THE, p; IMAGEMAKER, THE, w

Weiner, Howie
HOLLYWOOD VICE SQUAD

Weiner, Marilyn
IMAGEMAKER, THE, p

Weiner, Robert
MY MAN ADAM, cos

Weinstein, Bob
PLAYING FOR KEEPS, d; PLAYING FOR KEEPS, p; PLAYING FOR KEEPS, w

Weinstein, David Z.
BIG TROUBLE IN LITTLE CHINA, w

Weinstein, Harvey
PLAYING FOR KEEPS, d; PLAYING FOR KEEPS, p; PLAYING FOR KEEPS, w

Weinstein, Vickie
PLAYING FOR KEEPS

Weinthal, Eric
TIMING; TIMING, p, d

Weintraub, Bruce
JUST BETWEEN FRIENDS, set d

Weintraub, Carl
MODERN GIRLS

Weintraub, Jerry
THE KARATE KID PART II, p

Weir, Arabella
FRENCH LESSON

Weir, Peter
MOSQUITO COAST, THE, d

Weisbecker, Allan
BEER, w

Weiser, Shari
LABYRINTH

Weisgerber, Eleonore
ZONING

Weisinger, Allen
BRIGHTON BEACH MEMOIRS, makeup

Weisman, Orit
EVERY TIME WE SAY GOODBYE

Weismeir, Lynda
TOUCH AND GO

Weiss, George
FINE MESS, A, m/l

Weiss, Jamie Sue
LUCAS, makeup; SCREEN TEST, makeup

Weiss, Joel
QUICKSILVER

Weiss, Julie
F/X, cos

Weiss, Roberta
ABDUCTED

Weiss, Rudiger
TAGEDIEBE, ph

Weisse, Nikola
DER SCHWARZE TANNER

Weisser, Norbert
RADIOACTIVE DREAMS; THREE AMIGOS

Weist, Dwight
9½ WEEKS; NAME OF THE ROSE, THE

Weivers, Margreth
AMOROSA; MOA

Weivers-Norstrom, Margreth
I LAGENS NAMN

Weixen, Zhang
LIANG JIA FUNU

Welbeck, Peter
LIGHTNING—THE WHITE STALLION, w

Welch, Bo
VIOLETS ARE BLUE, art d

Welch, Eric
VAMP

Welch, Jackie
DR. OTTO AND THE RIDDLE OF THE GLOOM BEAM

Welch, James
RADIOACTIVE DREAMS

Welch, Lynetta
NO RETREAT, NO SURRENDER

Welin, Hans
BRODERNA MOZART, ph; PA LIV OCH DOD, ph

Welinder, Per
THRASHIN'

Welker, Frank
MY LITTLE PONY; SPACECAMP; TRANSFORMERS: THE MOVIE, THE

Well, Karin
LA MONACA NEL PECCATO

Wellburn, Tim
FRINGE DWELLERS, THE, ed

Weller, Elly
ASSAULT, THE

Weller, Paul
ABSOLUTE BEGINNERS, m/l

Welles, Gwen
MEN'S CLUB, THE; NOBODY'S FOOL

Welles, Laurence
MANHATTAN BABY

Welles, Mel
CHOPPING MALL

Welles, Orson
TRANSFORMERS: THE MOVIE, THE

Welles, Paola Mori [Countess di Girafalco]
Obituaries

Welles, T.G.
FAT GUY GOES NUTZOID!!

Welling, Vinay
RAO SAHEB, p

Wellingkar, Tatoba
RAO SAHEB

Wellington, Anthony
ABSOLUTE BEGINNERS

Wellington, David
EVIXION, ph

Wells, Adrian
SPACECAMP

Wells, Cheri
JO JO DANCER, YOUR LIFE IS CALLING

Wells, Hubert
HELL SQUAD

Wells, Mary
HOWARD THE DUCK

Wells, Orlando
SCHOOL FOR VANDALS, ph

Wells, Patrick
YOUNGBLOOD, p

Wells, Tiny
AMERICAN ANTHEM

Wellurtz, George
SOLDIER'S REVENGE

Welsh, John
ABDUCTED

Welsh, Kenneth
HEARTBURN; LOST!; LOYALTIES

Welsh, Robert
BUSTED UP

Welsome, Pat
TEXAS CHAINSAW MASSACRE PART 2, THE, set d

Weltman, Stu
TOMB, THE

Welz, Peter
NAME OF THE ROSE, THE

Wendel, Lara
MORIRAI A MEZZANOTTE

Wendel, Linda
BALLERUP BOULEVARD, d; BALLERUP BOULEVARD, w

Wendenius, Crispin Dickson
ALLA VI BARN I BULLERBY

Wendon, Elizabeth
ABSOLUTE BEGINNERS

Wendt, George
GUNG HO; HOUSE

Wenger, Allan
JE HAIS LES ACTEURS

Wenger, Cliff
WILDCATS, spec eff

Wenger, Clifford
THUNDER RUN, spec eff; THUNDER RUN, w

Wengler, Marcel
STAMMHEIM, m

Wenk, Richard
VAMP, d&w; VAMP, d&w

Wenn, Odd
NOE HEIT ANNET, p

Wensierski, Peter
TRANSITTRAUME, d&w

Wentworth, Nicholas
KILLING MACHINE, ed

Wenyao, Yun
LIANG JIA FUNU, ph

Wer, Hisham
HELL SQUAD

Werba, Amy
HANDS OF STEEL

Werkmuster, Brita
AMOROSA, p

Werle, Keith
NIGHT OF THE CREEPS

Wermus, Alain
LA FEMME DE MA VIE, w

Wertmuller, Lina
CAMORRA, d; CAMORRA, d, w; SUMMER NIGHT WITH GREEK PROFILE, ALMOND EYES AND SCENT OF BASIL, d&w; SUMMER NIGHT WITH GREEK PROFILE, ALMOND EYES AND SCENT OF BASIL, m

Wertmuller, Massimo
SUMMER NIGHT WITH GREEK PROFILE, ALMOND EYES AND SCENT OF BASIL

Wescott, Anne
NUTCRACKER: THE MOTION PICTURE

Wesenlund, Mette
DROMMESLOTTER

Wesley, Billy
LIGHTNING—THE WHITE STALLION

Wesley, Richard
NATIVE SON, w

Weslow, William
MANHATTAN PROJECT, THE

Wessel, Hanne-Lore
ANGRY HARVEST, cos

Wesslau, Jennifer
GRONA GUBBAR FRAN Y.R.

West, Brian
NOBODY'S FOOL

West, Johnson
OVER THE SUMMER

West, Kit
TAI-PAN, spec eff

West, Leslie
MONEY PIT, THE

West, Morris
SECOND VICTORY, THE, w

West, Paul
DREAM LOVER

West, Ursula
FUTURE OF EMILY, THE, ed; JOURNEY, THE, ed

West, Wendy
SCORPION

Westbrock, Darrin
LOW BLOW

Westcott, Carol
NEVER TOO YOUNG TO DIE, set d

Westerberg
MY CHAUFFEUR, m/l

Westerdale, Donald J.
ODD JOBS

Westergren, Meg
MIN PAPA AR TARZAN

Westfall, Mathew
PLATOON

Westfeldt, Lasse
MOA, art d

Westfelt, Lasse
ALLA VI BARN I BULLERBY, prod d

Westlund, Chris
AMERICAN ANTHEM, set d

Westlund, R. Chris
AT CLOSE RANGE, set d

Westmore, Joy
MORE THINGS CHANGE, THE

Westmore, Michael
PSYCHO III, makeup

Westmore, Michael G.
CLAN OF THE CAVE BEAR, THE, makeup

Westmore, Monty
COLOR OF MONEY, THE, makeup; STAND BY ME, makeup

Westmore, Pamela S.
VAMP, makeup

Weston, Bill
MY BEAUTIFUL LAUNDRETTE, stunts

Weston, Garry
DEAD-END DRIVE-IN

Weston, Jack
LONGSHOT, THE; RAD

Weston, Paul
ALIENS, stunts

Weston, Stan
TORMENT

Westover, Richard E.
MY CHAUFFEUR, ed; PATRIOT, THE, ed

Westover, Rick
HOLLYWOOD ZAP!, ed

Wetherwax, Michael
SORORITY HOUSE MASSACRE, m

Wexler, Howard
REFORM SCHOOL GIRLS, ph

Wexler, Milton
THAT'S LIFE, w

Wexler, Norman
RAW DEAL, w

Wey, Sandra
SENZA SCRUPOLI

Weyers, Kelcey
MEN'S CLUB, THE, makeup

Weyrauch, Miguel
INSOMNIACS, p

Whaley, James
CAR TROUBLE, w

Whalley, Joanne
GOOD FATHER, THE; NO SURRENDER

Wharton, Wally
LAST RESORT, THE

Wheat, Belle Maria
CLASS OF NUKE 'EM HIGH

Wheater, Mac
TAI-PAN

Wheatley, Ken
ABSOLUTE BEGINNERS, art d

Wheaton, Wil
STAND BY ME

Wheeler, Anne
LOYALTIES, d,p&w

Wheeler, Bob
MONSTER SHARK, ed

Wheeler, Charles F.
BEST OF TIMES, THE, ph

Wheeler, Ira
HANNAH AND HER SISTERS

Wheeler, John W.
SPACECAMP, ed

Wheeler, Karen
SCREEN TEST

Wheeler, W. Brooke
MURPHY'S LAW, set d

Whigham, Joseph A.
REBEL LOVE, ph

Whinnery, Barbara
CRAWLSPACE; HAMBURGER; STEWARDESS SCHOOL

Whipp, Joseph
SCORPION

Whipple, Kay H.
WILDCATS, stunts

Whipple, Sam
BLUE CITY

Whitaker, Albie
FLIGHT OF THE NAVIGATOR

Whitaker, Christina
NAKED CAGE, THE

Whitaker, Forest
COLOR OF MONEY, THE; PLATOON; People to Watch

Whitaker, Harvey
SCORPION

Whitchurch, Philip
HALF MOON STREET

White Lion
MONEY PIT, THE; MONEY PIT, THE, m/l

White, Al
BIG TROUBLE

White, Andrew M.
AMERICAN ANTHEM

White, April Daisy
VIOLATED

White, Betty
ROCKIN' ROAD TRIP

White, Bob
SCREAMPLAY

White, Carole Ita
NAKED CAGE, THE

White, Cary
TEXAS CHAINSAW MASSACRE PART 2, THE, prod d

White, Diz
STOOGEMANIA

White, Douglas J.
NEON MANIACS, makeup

White, Erik
SCORPION

White, Gery
NO SURRENDER

White, Ian
OVERNIGHT

White, Jack
TOUCH AND GO

White, Joniruth
FAT GUY GOES NUTZOID!!

White, Joseph
HELLFIRE

White, Karla
FAT GUY GOES NUTZOID!!

White, Kerryann
MY BEAUTIFUL LAUNDRETTE

White, King
MANHUNTER

White, Michael
GOOD TO GO; LABYRINTH, art d

White, Nick
RECRUITS, set d

White, Sharon
LABYRINTH

White, Ted
FIRE IN THE NIGHT, ch; OVER THE SUMMER

White, Terry
SPACECAMP

White, Theodore H. [Theodore Harold White]
Obituaries

Whitecloud, John P.
POLTERGEIST II

Whited, William
IMAGEMAKER, THE, makeup

Whitehead, Paxton
BACK TO SCHOOL; JUMPIN' JACK FLASH

Whitehouse, Max
52 PICK-UP, set d

Whitford, Peter
DEAD-END DRIVE-IN

Whiting, Richard
SWEET LIBERTY

Whitlock, Graham
PLAYING AWAY, ed

Whitlow, Jill
NIGHT OF THE CREEPS; THUNDER RUN

Whitman, Everett
OVER THE SUMMER

Whitman, Peter
LITTLE SHOP OF HORRORS

Whitmire, Steve
LABYRINTH; LABYRINTH; LABYRINTH

Whitmore, John
YOUNGBLOOD, w

Whitmore, Neil
FERRIS BUELLER'S DAY OFF, m/l

Whitney, Paul
LOYALTIES

Whitrow, Benjamin
CLOCKWISE

Whittaker, Ian
HIGHLANDER, set d; UNDER THE CHERRY MOON,
set d

Whittaker, Steve
THRASHIN'

Whittle, Miranda
FERRIS BUELLER'S DAY OFF

Whitton, Margaret
9½ WEEKS; BEST OF TIMES, THE

Whitworth, Dean
KING KONG LIVES

Who, Garry
FAIR GAME

Whyhowski, Hugo Luczyc
MY BEAUTIFUL LAUNDRETTE, prod d

Whyle, James
PLACE OF WEEPING

Wiart, Marie
CORPS ET BIENS

Wiazemsky, Anne
QUI TROP EMBRASSE

Wibe, Gert
MORRHAR OCH ARTOR, art d

Wickenburg, Kim
REVENGE OF THE TEENAGE VIXENS FROM OUTER
SPACE, THE

Wicket, W. W.
SPACECAMP, w

Wickham, Jeffry
CLOCKWISE

Wicki, Bernhard
KILLING CARS

Wicking, Christopher
ABSOLUTE BEGINNERS, w

Wickliff, Vivian
ARMOUR OF GOD, THE

Wide, Wilbur
DEAD-END DRIVE-IN

Widen, Gregory
HIGHLANDER, w

Widerberg, Bo
ORMENS VAG PA HALLEBERGET, d&w; ORMENS
VAG PA HALLEBERGET, ed

Widerberg, Johan
ORMENS VAG PA HALLEBERGET

Widiantono, Sylvia
SECANGKIR KOPI PAHIT

Widitomo, Bambang
SECANGKIR KOPI PAHIT, p

Widlowski, Jim
COLOR OF MONEY, THE

Widmer, Marion
NOAH UND DER COWBOY

Wiebel, Martin
JOURNEY, THE, w; ROSA LUXEMBURG, p

Wieck, Dorothea
Obituaries

Wieder, Hanne
PARADIES

Wiedlin, Jane
STAR TREK IV: THE VOYAGE HOME

Wiegmans, Rene
EL HOMBRE QUE GANO LA RAZON, ed

Wieme, Dries
CONGO EXPRESS

Wiener, Charles
RECRUITS; RECRUITS, w

Wiener, Jack
F/X, p

Wiertz, Lex
ASSAULT, THE

Wiesel, Elie
L'AUBE, w

Wiesenhaan, Harry
ASSAULT, THE, spec eff

Wiessenhaan, Harry
MAMA IS BOOS!, spec eff

Wiest, Dianne
HANNAH AND HER SISTERS; People to Watch

Wiggins, Jimmy
KING KONG LIVES

Wiik, Lars
BRODERNA MOZART

Wiik, Oystein
FRENCH LESSON

Wijn, Piet de
ASSAULT, THE

Wiklander, Iwar
BRODERNA MOZART

Wikramanayake, "Lucky"
SHORT CHANGED

Wikstrom, Markus
RATTIS, m

Wilbur, George
RAW DEAL

Wilcots, Joe
MOUNTAINTOP MOTEL MASSACRE, ph

Wilcox, Richard
CLAN OF THE CAVE BEAR, THE, art d

Wilcox, Shannon
LEGAL EAGLES

Wild, Christopher
KNIGHTS AND EMERALDS

Wild, Susan
AUSTRALIAN DREAM, p

Wilde, Oscar
SALOME, w

Wilde, Wilbur
COOL CHANGE

Wildenauer, Ingold
DER SCHWARZE TANNER

Wilder, Bradley
BEST OF TIMES, THE, makeup

Wilder, Don
LOST!, ph

Wilder, Gene
HAUNTED HONEYMOON; HAUNTED HONEYMOON,
d; HAUNTED HONEYMOON, w

Wilder, John
UNA DONNA SENZA NOME, ph

Wildgruber, Ulrich
AUF IMMER UND EWIG

Wildman, Valerie
FINE MESS, A; SALVADOR

Wildsmith, Dawn
ARMED RESPONSE; TOMB, THE

Wiley, Ed
LITTLE SHOP OF HORRORS

Wiley, Edward
HAUNTED HONEYMOON; HIGHLANDER

Wiley, Ethan
HOUSE, w

Wilhite, Thomas L.
NUTCRACKER: THE MOTION PICTURE, p

Wilhoite, Benji
IMPURE THOUGHTS

Wilhoite, Kathleen
MORNING AFTER, THE; MURPHY'S LAW;
MURPHY'S LAW, m/l; RATBOY

Wilker, Jose
O HOMEM DA CAPA PRETA

Wilkes, Elaine
FINE MESS, A; KILLER PARTY; MY CHAUFFEUR

Wilkes, Jack
STREETS OF GOLD

Wilkey, Lloyd C.
ODD JOBS

Wilkins, Eric
SHE'S GOTTA HAVE IT

Wilkinson, Albert
LABYRINTH

Wilkinson, Barrie J.
ABSOLUTE BEGINNERS; LABYRINTH

Wilkinson, Elizabeth
LOW BLOW

Wilkinson, Glen
ABSOLUTE BEGINNERS

Wilkinson, June
SNO-LINE

Wilkinson, Linden
FOR LOVE ALONE

Wilkinson, Robert
CLOCKWISE

Wilkus, Patti
LUCAS

Will
WHITE SLAVE

Will Vinton Productions
SHADOW PLAY, spec eff

Will-Ellis, Thomas
WISDOM

Willaidom, Gerald
CLASS OF NUKE 'EM HIGH

Willard, Jean
CRIMES OF THE HEART

Willer, Isabelle
PARIS MINUIT

Willer, Lisa
EL NARCO—DUELO ROJO

Willet, John
ABSOLUTE BEGINNERS

Willette, Jo Ann
WELCOME TO 18

Willetts, Shelly
KNIGHTS AND EMERALDS

William, Thomas
STAR CRYSTAL

Williams, Allen
SCORPION

Williams, Andrew
DEAD-END DRIVE-IN, p

Williams, Barbara
JO JO DANCER, YOUR LIFE IS CALLING

Williams, Bernard
WISDOM, p

Williams, Bert
COBRA; MURPHY'S LAW

Williams, Bill
PULSEBEAT, ch

Williams, Billy
MANHATTAN PROJECT, THE, ph

Williams, Caroline
GETTING EVEN; TEXAS CHAINSAW MASSACRE PART 2, THE

Williams, Catherine
OVER THE SUMMER; ROCKIN' ROAD TRIP

Williams, Chino Fats
JUMPIN' JACK FLASH; WILDCATS

Williams, Curtis
THE KARATE KID PART II, m/l

Williams, Danny
SUNSET STRIP

Williams, Dean
NO SURRENDER

Williams, Denise
ROCKIN' ROAD TRIP

Williams, Diana
WIRED TO KILL, art d

Williams, Dootsie
THE KARATE KID PART II, m/l

Williams, Doris Sherman
PLATOON, art d

Williams, Ed
RATBOY

Williams, Elaine
DIRT BIKE KID, THE

Williams, Emery
8 MILLION WAYS TO DIE, m/l

Williams, Grace
WHITE SLAVE

Williams, Graham
MILWR BYCHAN, m

Williams, Huw
FOR LOVE ALONE

Williams, Ian Patrick
TERRORVISION

Williams, Jason
DOWN AND OUT IN BEVERLY HILLS

Williams, Jimmy
ARMED RESPONSE

Williams, JoBeth
DESERT BLOOM; POLTERGEIST II

Williams, John
EMMA'S WAR, m; FERRIS BUELLER'S DAY OFF, m/l; SPACECAMP, m

Williams, Kevin
PRETTY IN PINK

Williams, Larry
FINE MESS, A, m/l

Williams, Larry B.
SPACECAMP, w

Williams, Matt
STAND BY ME

Williams, Michael
JO JO DANCER, YOUR LIFE IS CALLING

Williams, Officer Pat
MANHUNTER

Williams, Patrick
JUST BETWEEN FRIENDS, m; JUST BETWEEN FRIENDS, md; VIOLETS ARE BLUE, m

Williams, Peter
HALF MOON STREET, art d

Williams, R.J.
AMERICAN ANTHEM

Williams, Robin
BEST OF TIMES, THE; CLUB PARADISE

Williams, Sabra
ABSOLUTE BEGINNERS; KNIGHTS AND EMERALDS

Williams, Steven
HOUSE

Williams, Susan
AMERICAN ANTHEM, w

Williams, Tony
P.O.W. THE ESCAPE; ROUND MIDNIGHT; ROUND MIDNIGHT; SILK

Williams, Treat
MEN'S CLUB, THE

Williams, Trevor
POLICE ACADEMY 3: BACK IN TRAINING, prod d

Williams, Trudel
VAMP

Williams, Wally
P.O.W. THE ESCAPE

Williams, Wendy O.
REFORM SCHOOL GIRLS

Williams, Willie
AMERICAN COMMANDOS

Williams, Willy
SILK

Williamson, David
TRAVELLING NORTH, w; TRAVELLING NORTH, w

Williamson, Fred
FOXTRAP; FOXTRAP, p&d; FOXTRAP, w

Williamson, Mykel T.
WILDCATS

Willie, Dap "Sugar"
WILDCATS

Willier, Dale
LOYALTIES

Willis, Allee
HOWARD THE DUCK, m/l

Willis, Austin
BOY IN BLUE, THE

Willis, Donald
HOUSE

Willis, Gordon
MONEY PIT, THE, ph

Willis, James
ONE MORE SATURDAY NIGHT

Willis, Robert Earl
BELIZAIRE THE CAJUN

Willis-Burch, Sherry
KILLER PARTY

Willman, Tom E.
WILDCATS

Willmann, Marlene
UNTERMEHMEN GEIGENKASTEN, set d

Willoughby, Kim
QUEEN CITY ROCKERS

Willrich, Rudy
LEGAL EAGLES

Wills, Lou
VASECTOMY: A DELICATE MATTER, p

Willschrei, Karl Heinz
DIE ZWEI GESICHTER DES JANUAR, w

Willumsen, Gail
BALBOA, w

Wilmot, Curt
HOUSE

Wilmot, Curtis Scott
HARDBODIES 2; HARDBODIES 2, w

Wilmot, John
AVENGING FORCE

Wilshire, Leslie
STOOGEMANIA; STOOGEMANIA, cos

Wilshire, Richard
SHADOW PLAY

Wilson, Alan
ABDUCTED, set d

Wilson, Alec
COOL CHANGE

Wilson, Andrew
NUTCRACKER: THE MOTION PICTURE

Wilson, Barry
3:15, THE MOMENT OF TRUTH

Wilson, Bob
SCREAMPLAY

Wilson, Brad
SCORPION

Wilson, Carlos
AS SETE VAMPIRAS, ch; COM LICENCA, EU VOU A LUTA

Wilson, Clara
NUTCRACKER: THE MOTION PICTURE

Wilson, David
90 DAYS, ed; 90 DAYS, p; 90 DAYS, w; EAT THE PEACH, prod d

Wilson, David Patrick
BAR 51—SISTER OF LOVE

Wilson, Elizabeth
WHERE ARE THE CHILDREN?

Wilson, Frank
GOING SANE

Wilson, Jeannie
AMERICAN JUSTICE

Wilson, Jim
SMART ALEC, p&d; SMART ALEC, w

Wilson, John
ECHO PARK, m/l

Wilson, Johnny
REVENGE FOR JUSTICE

Wilson, Julian
FORMULA FOR MURDER, art d

Wilson, Kara
GOSPEL ACCORDING TO VIC, THE

Wilson, Kevin
DANGEROUS ORPHANS

Wilson, Lambert
BLEU COMME L'ENFER; CORPS ET BIENS; LA STORIA

Wilson, Lester
MEN'S CLUB, THE, ch

Wilson, Lisle
JUST BETWEEN FRIENDS

Wilson, Mak
LITTLE SHOP OF HORRORS

Wilson, Mary Louise
MONEY PIT, THE

Wilson, Nancy
BUSTED UP

Wilson, Pete Lee
SID AND NANCY

Wilson, Peter
NO SURRENDER

Wilson, S.S.
SHORT CIRCUIT, w

Wilson, Scott
BLUE CITY

Wilson, Susan
MANHUNT, THE

Wilson, T-Bone
KNIGHTS AND EMERALDS

Wilson, Teddy
Obituaries

Wilson, Terry
PRETTY IN PINK

Wilson, Theodore
BIG TROUBLE; FINE MESS, A; STEWARDESS SCHOOL; THAT'S LIFE

Wilson, Thick
BULLIES

Wilson, Thomas F.
APRIL FOOL'S DAY

Wilson, Tom
NINJA TURF

Wilson, Tony
BACKLASH, ph

Wilson, Trey
F/X

Wilson, Woody
POPULATION: ONE, ed

Wilson, "Iron Jaws"
BEST OF TIMES, THE

Wilton, Garth
FINE MESS, A

Wilton, Penelope
CLOCKWISE

Wiltsie, Melissa
LITTLE SHOP OF HORRORS

Winch, Mandy
MONA LISA

Wincott, Jeff
BOY IN BLUE, THE

Winding, Genevieve
DESCENTE AUX ENFERS, ed; LA GALETTE DU ROI, ed

Winding, Kasper
TAKE IT EASY; TAKE IT EASY, md

Wineinger, Bruce
DESERT BLOOM

Winer, Harry
SPACECAMP, d

Winerdal, Max
MIN PAPA AR TARZAN

Winfield, Paul
BLUE CITY

Winfrey, Oprah
NATIVE SON

Wing, John
RECRUITS

Winger, Debra
LEGAL EAGLES

Winger, Michael
YOUNGBLOOD

Wingrove, Ian
SKY BANDITS, spec eff

Wingrove, John
FOR LOVE ALONE, art d; MOSQUITO COAST, THE, art d

Winitsky, Mark
9½ WEEKS, ed

Winkler, Dallas
BACK TO SCHOOL

Winkler, Irwin
ROUND MIDNIGHT, p

Winkler, K.C.
ARMED AND DANGEROUS

Winkler, Mel
OFF BEAT

Winley, Robert
JAKE SPEED

Winningham, Mare
NOBODY'S FOOL

Wino, Jean-Claude
DANS UN MIROIR

Winsett, Jerry
ONE CRAZY SUMMER; SEX O'CLOCK NEWS, THE

Winslow, Alex Bond
PLAY DEAD

Winslow, Michael
POLICE ACADEMY 3: BACK IN TRAINING

Winstanley, Michele
SID AND NANCY

Winston, David
FLOODSTAGE

Winston, Hattie
GOOD TO GO

Winston, Helene
JUST BETWEEN FRIENDS

Winston, Leslie
FLOODSTAGE

Winston, Mary Ellen
WHERE ARE THE CHILDREN?, cos

Winston, Stan
ALIENS, spec eff

Winter, Catherine
FLAGRANT DESIR, p

Winter, Clive
COMRADES, set d

Winters, David
THRASHIN', d

Winters, Jonathan
LONGSHOT, THE; SAY YES

Winters, Lisa
MANHUNTER

Winters, Shelley
DELTA FORCE, THE; VERY CLOSE QUARTERS;
WITCHFIRE

Wipperlich, Beatrix
DIE NACHTMEERFAHRT

Wirth, Billy
SEVEN MINUTES IN HEAVEN

Wise, Addington
HOLLYWOOD ZAP!

Wise, Alfie
RAD

Wise, Peter
OFF BEAT

Wishengra, Jeff
SORORITY HOUSE MASSACRE, ed

Wishner, Suzanne
JUST BETWEEN FRIENDS

Wisman, Ron
SEPARATE VACATIONS, ed

Wisniewska, Eva
OSOBISTY PAMIETNIK GRZESZNIKA PRZEZ NIEGO
SAMEGO SPISANY

Wisniewska, Ewa
SCENY DZIECIECE Z ZYCIA PROWINCJI

Witherspoon, John
RATBOY

Withrow, Glenn
ARMED AND DANGEROUS; PATRIOT, THE

Withrow, Stephen F.
PINK CHIQUITAS, THE, ed

Witker, Kristi
POWER

Witt, Kathryn
COCAINE WARS

Witt, Randall
LOW BLOW

Witt, William
TORMENT

Witta, Jacques
BLEU COMME L'ENFER, ed

Witte, Paul
PLACE OF WEEPING, ph

Witter, Karen
DANGEROUSLY CLOSE; RATBOY

Wittman, Peter
PLAY DEAD, d

Wittwer, Stephane
MOTTEN IM LICHT, m

Wixted, Kevin Gerard
LUCAS

Wizan, Joe
IRON EAGLE, p; TOUGH GUYS, p

Woan-Ho, Lee
GILSODOM, p

Wockner, Leo
FRINGE DWELLERS, THE

Wodoslawsky, Stefan
90 DAYS; CRAZY MOON, p; CRAZY MOON, w

Woessner, Hank
BLUE CITY

Wohl, David
ARMED AND DANGEROUS; BEER

Wohl, Ray
ABOUT LAST NIGHT

Woinski, Mark
COCAINE WARS

Wolberg, Robert
BEER

Wolf, Fred
ADVENTURES OF THE AMERICAN RABBIT, THE;
ADVENTURES OF THE AMERICAN RABBIT, THE, d

Wolf, Friedrich
DAS HAUS AM FLUSS, d&w

Wolf, Gregory
LONGSHOT, THE

Wolf, Jeffrey
FAT GUY GOES NUTZOID!!, ed

Wolf, Kelly
MY MAN ADAM; PLAYING FOR KEEPS

Wolf, Marilyn
CHECK IS IN THE MAIL, THE

Wolf, Richard
THE KARATE KID PART II, m/l

Wolf, Rita
MY BEAUTIFUL LAUNDRETTE

Wolf, Shmuel
ESTHER

Wolfe, Theresa
SCREEN TEST

Wolff, Vernika
ZONING

Wolfing, Silke
AUF IMMER UND EWIG

Wolgamott, Nicole
NUTCRACKER: THE MOTION PICTURE

Wolin, Judith Sherman
WELCOME TO 18, w

Wolinski, Hawk
WILDCATS, m

Wolinsky, Sidney
HOWARD THE DUCK, ed

Wollet, Michael
WIRED TO KILL

Wollter, Sven
DREAM OF NORTHERN LIGHTS; I LAGENS NAMN;
SACRIFICE, THE

Wolniec, Roman
SCENY DZIECIECE Z ZYCIA PROWINCJI, set d

Wolsky, Albert
CRIMES OF THE HEART, cos; DOWN AND OUT IN
BEVERLY HILLS, cos; LEGAL EAGLES, cos

Wong, Bill
DREAM LOVERS, ph

Wong, Bradd
THE KARATE KID PART II

Wong, Carter
BIG TROUBLE IN LITTLE CHINA

Wong, Daniel
BIG TROUBLE IN LITTLE CHINA

Wong, Danny
SUNSET STRIP

Wong, James
PEKING OPERA BLUES, m

Wong, James J.S.
MARTIAL ARTS OF SHAOLIN, m

Wong, Lynda
LOW BLOW

Wong, Mandred
DREAM LOVERS

Wong, Michael
ROYAL WARRIORS

Wong, Pauline
MR. VAMPIRE

Wong, Raymond
ACES GO PLACES IV, p; ISLE OF FANTASY; ISLE OF
FANTASY, w; SUPER CITIZEN, p

Wong, Russell
TAI-PAN

Wong, Victor
BIG TROUBLE IN LITTLE CHINA; GOLDEN CHILD,
THE; SHANGHAI SURPRISE

Wong, Vincent
LITTLE SHOP OF HORRORS

Wong, Willie
BIG TROUBLE IN LITTLE CHINA

Woo, James Wing
SUNSET STRIP

Woo, John
BETTER TOMORROW, A, d&w

Wood, Carol
DOWN BY LAW, cos

Wood, Durinda
BACK TO SCHOOL, cos

Wood, Gene
WEEKEND WARRIORS

Wood, Jane
BLOOD RED ROSES, ed

Wood, Janet
VASECTOMY: A DELICATE MATTER

Wood, Jennifer
DR. OTTO AND THE RIDDLE OF THE GLOOM BEAM

Wood, John
BULLSEYE; HEARTBURN; JUMPIN' JACK FLASH;
KING KONG LIVES, art d; LADY JANE; TWELFTH
NIGHT

Wood, Karen
RECRUITS; SCALPS

Wood, Michael
MONEY PIT, THE, spec eff

Wood, Mike
ARMED AND DANGEROUS, spec eff

Wood, Moya
MORE THINGS CHANGE, THE, w

Wood, Noanie
FRINGE DWELLERS, THE

Wood, Oliver
NEON MANIACS, ph; SEX O'CLOCK NEWS, THE, ph

Wood, Robin
BELIZAIRE THE CAJUN

Wood, Salvador
JIBARO

Wood, Ted
LETTER TO BREZHNEV

Woodard, Alfre
EXTREMITIES

Woodard, Don
RATBOY

Woodcroft, Jay
SEPARATE VACATIONS

Woodgate, Alison
LADY JANE

Woodrich, Abel
MOSQUITO COAST, THE

Woodruff, Donald
RUTHLESS PEOPLE, art d

Woodruff, Kurt
CHOKE CANYON

Woods, Bill
KING OF THE STREETS

Woods, Bob
RYDER, P.I.

Woods, Charles
TAI-PAN

Woods, James
SALVADOR

Woods, Jimmy
ECHO PARK, m/l

Woods, Kipp
THRASHIN'

Woods, Nan
ONE MORE SATURDAY NIGHT

Woods, Ren
BEER; JUMPIN' JACK FLASH

Woods, Stephen
SCORPION

Woods, Tryon
NUTCRACKER: THE MOTION PICTURE

Woodward, Lenore
STEWARDESS SCHOOL

Woodward, Meredith B.
BOY WHO COULD FLY, THE

Woodward, Tim
SALOME

Wool, Abbe
SID AND NANCY, w

Wooldridge, Susan
LOYALTIES

Yamazaki, Tsutomu
TAMPOPO

Yamazaki, Yoshihiro
LOVE LETTER, ph; NINGUEN NO YAKUSOKU, ph

Yampolsky, Alexander
STREETS OF GOLD

Yan, Liang
LIANG JIA FUNU

Yan-fat, Chow
ROSE

Yaname, Toyoji
CRAZY FAMILY, THE, p

Yanez, Eduardo
EL MALEFICIO II; YAKO—CAZADOR DE MALDITOS

Yanez, Ernesto
EL IMPERIO DE LA FORTUNA

Yang, Edward
SUMMER AT GRANDPA'S, A, m

Yang, Loretta
KUEI-MEI, A WOMAN

Yang, Pamela
SHANGHAI SURPRISE

Yanjin, Wang
QINGCHUN JI, art d

Yankovski, Oleg
KHRANI MENIO, MOI TALISMAN

Yanne, Jean
LE PALTOQUET; WOLF AT THE DOOR, THE

Yannopoulos, Takis
ENAS ISICHOS THANATOS, ed; O MELISSOKOMOS, ed

Yanovitch, Peter
SCORPION

Yaovasang, Suriya
PEESUA LAE DOKMAI

Yarbaugh, Officer Charles
MANHUNTER

Yared, Gabriel
BETTY BLUE, m; DESORDRE, m; FLAGRANT DESIR, m; ZONE ROUGE, m

Yarnall, Bob
REVENGE OF THE TEENAGE VIXENS FROM OUTER SPACE, THE

Yaroshevskaya, Kim
HENRI

Yashi, Isi
ESTHER, m

Yasuda, Kosuke
ORA TOKYO SA YUKUDA, ph

Yasuoka, Rikiya
COMIC MAGAZINE; TAMPOPO

Yatis, Jack
MY MAN ADAM

Yeager, Biff
ECHO PARK; SID AND NANCY

Yee, Helen
LOW BLOW

Yee, Karen
LOW BLOW

Yee, Kelvin Han
GREAT WALL, A

Yee, Lam Mun
FAMILY, THE, m

Yee, Wayne
NO RETREAT, NO SURRENDER

Yefrimov, Vadim
CHTO U SENJKI BYLO, ph

Yeh, Sally
ACES GO PLACES IV; PEKING OPERA BLUES

Yehoshua, B.
HAME'AHEV, w

Yergin, Irving
Obituaries

Yerkes, Bob
PSYCHO III, stunts; RATBOY

Yerles, Bernard
BABEL OPERA, OU LA REPETITION DE DON JUAN

Yermolayev, Boris
FOUETTE, d; FOUETTE, w

Yeshida, Calvin
3:15, THE MOMENT OF TRUTH

Yeshurun, Itzhak   [Zeppel]
MALKAT HAKITA, p, d&w

Yeu, Wang
SUPER CITIZEN

Yeung, Cher
DREAM LOVERS

Yi, Chang
KUEI-MEI, A WOMAN, d; KUEI-MEI, A WOMAN, w; WO ERH HAN-SHENG, d; WO ERH HAN-SHENG, w

Yi, Paul
3:15, THE MOMENT OF TRUTH

Yi, Tao
CAN YUE, p

Yi, Zhang
YU QING SAO, d

Yiasomi, George
KING KONG LIVES

Yigit, Atilla
KUYUCAKLI YUSUF

Yildiz, Seda
KUYUCAKLI YUSUF

Yilmaz, Atif
ADI VASFIYE, d

Yilmaz, Levent
ADI VASFIYE

Yim, Sing
AMERICAN COMMANDOS, ed

Yimou, Zhang
YELLOW EARTH, ph

Ying, Lam Ching
MR. VAMPIRE; MR. VAMPIRE, ch

Ying, Wong
MR. VAMPIRE, w

Ying, Wong Joe
LAST SONG IN PARIS

Yip, Cecilia
LAST SONG IN PARIS

Yip, David
PING PONG

Yip, Deanie
HUAJIE SHIDAI; LUNATICS, THE; LUNATICS, THE, m

Yohn, Erica
AMERICAN TAIL, AN

Yohoshua, Abraham B.
DAS SCHWEIGEN DES DICHTERS, d&w

Yollo
SCHMUTZ, m

Yonfan, Manshi
ROSE, p&d

Yong, Daisey
TONGS—A CHINATOWN STORY

Yongde, Zhu
REZHOU, ph

Yongxin, Li
QINGCHUN JI, art d

Yongzhuo, Jing
FEIFA YIMIN

Yontan, Gurel
KUYUCAKLI YUSUF, set d

Yoo, Min
FIELD OF HONOR

Yoosefian, Davood
BEYOND THE MIST, ed

Yordanoff, Wladimir
LA FEMME SECRETE

York, Jay
BAD GUYS

York, John J.
NIGHT OF THE CREEPS

York, Kristin Collins
TOUCH AND GO

York, Michael
L'AUBE

York, Mike
LOW BLOW

Yosefian, Davood
FROSTY ROADS, ed

Yoseliani, Lili
YOUNG COMPOSER'S ODYSSEY, A

Yosh
PRAY FOR DEATH

Yoshi, Ikuzo
ORA TOKYO SA YUKUDA

Yoshida, Yoshio
TO SLEEP SO AS TO DREAM

Yoshida, Yoshishige
NINGUEN NO YAKUSOKU, d; NINGUEN NO YAKUSOKU, w

Yoshimura, kira
CYOEI NO MURE, w

Yosra
EL-GOOA

Youfu, Xu
IN THE WILD MOUNTAINS, m

Yound, Victor
BLUE VELVET, m/l

Younes, Sanaa
EL YOM EL SADES

Young, Alan
GREAT MOUSE DETECTIVE, THE

Young, Angus
MAXIMUM OVERDRIVE, m/l

Young, Barrie
ABSOLUTE BEGINNERS

Young, Bruce A.
COLOR OF MONEY, THE

Young, Buck
LAST RESORT, THE

Young, Burt
BACK TO SCHOOL

Young, Carmel
FAIR GAME

Young, Christopher
GETTING EVEN, m; INVADERS FROM MARS, m; TORMENT, m; TRICK OR TREAT, m

Young, Cletus
WELCOME TO 18

Young, Crawford
FAT GUY GOES NUTZOID!!

Young, David
BALBOA

Young, David Morgan
ABSOLUTE BEGINNERS

Young, Eric
HEAD OFFICE

Young, Freddie
ARTHUR'S HALLOWED GROUND, d

Young, Greta
3:15, THE MOMENT OF TRUTH

Young, J.
ABSOLUTE BEGINNERS, m/l

Young, Jennifer
LIGHTNING—THE WHITE STALLION

Young, John
BACK TO SCHOOL; HAMBURGER; HOUSE

Young, Karen
9½ WEEKS

Young, Malcolm
MAXIMUM OVERDRIVE, m/l

Young. Onna
DESERT BLOOM

Young, Paul
BIG HURT, THE

Young, Paul M.
KAMIKAZE HEARTS, m

Young, Pete
GREAT MOUSE DETECTIVE, THE, w

Young, Peter
CLUB PARADISE, set d; DUET FOR ONE, set d; HALF MOON STREET, set d

Young, Richard
FINAL MISSION

Young, Robert M.
EXTREMITIES, d; SAVING GRACE, d

Young, Sallee
DESPERATE MOVES

Young, Victor
MONA LISA, m/l

Young, William Allen
WISDOM

Younger, Jack
8 MILLION WAYS TO DIE

Youngs, Gail
BELIZAIRE THE CAJUN

Youngs, Jim
NOBODY'S FOOL; YOUNGBLOOD

Yousra
AL BEDAYA

Yousri, Ibrahim
EL-SADA EL-RIGAL

Youssef, Mamdo
EL-GOOA, p

Youssef, Youssef Ben
MAN OF ASHES, ph

Youth, Rational
CRAZY MOON

Yoyotte, Marie Josef
HADDA, ed; JE HAIS LES ACTEURS, ed; LE MOME, ed; NEXT SUMMER, ed

Yu, Angela
HUAJIE SHIDAI

Yu, Cao
REZHOU, w

Yu, David
3:15, THE MOMENT OF TRUTH

Yu, Li Shin
SLEEPWALK, ed

Yu, Wang
MILLIONAIRE'S EXPRESS, THE

Yuan, Du
IN THE WILD MOUNTAINS

Yuanzheng, Feng
QINGCHUN JI

Yuejiu, Li
AMERICAN ANTHEM

Yuen, Chor
LAST SONG IN PARIS, d

Yuen, Corey
NO RETREAT, NO SURRENDER, d; NO RETREAT, NO
SURRENDER, w

Yuen, Fennie
ISLE OF FANTASY

Yuen, Liu Yet
MARTIAL ARTS OF SHAOLIN, p

Yuen, Ng See
NO RETREAT, NO SURRENDER, p&w

Yuesuf, Muhamad
GHAME AFGHAN

Yuk, Sin Lam
ACES GO PLACES IV

Yule, Ian
JAKE SPEED

Yulin, Harris
GOOD TO GO

Yuo
PIAOBO QIYU

Yurdatap, Kadri
KUYUCAKLI YUSUF, p

Yusov, Vadim
BORIS GODUNOV, ph

Yust, Larry
SAY YES, d&w; SAY YES, p

Yuzhen, Qiu
IN THE WILD MOUNTAINS

Yuzna, Brian
FROM BEYOND, p; FROM BEYOND, w

Yxner, Marvin
I LAGENS NAMN

Z.R.
LA BANDA DE LOS PANCHITOS

Zabat, Fiel
FINAL MISSION, art d

Zabka, William
BACK TO SCHOOL; THE KARATE KID PART II

Zabou
ETATS D'AME; LE COMPLEXE DU KANGOUROU;
SUIVEZ MON REGARD

Zach, Marusia
WORKING GIRLS

Zacharaios, Mark
NO RETREAT, NO SURRENDER

Zacharias, Steve
LAST RESORT, THE, w; WHOOPEE BOYS, THE, w

Zachary
THRASHIN'

Zachary, Charity Ann
SNO-LINE

Zacher, Rolf
HEIDENLOCHER; VA BANQUE

Zachor, Anat
AMERICA 3000

Zackparias, John
AMOROSA

Zadeh, Firooz Malek
MARE, THE, ph

Zadori, Ferenc
ELYSIUM, ph

Zafer, Yilmaz
ADI VASFIYE

Zafiraki, Maria
ALCESTES

Zafranovic, Andrija
KORMORAN, ed; VECERNJA ZVONA, ed

Zafranovic, Lordan
VECERNJA ZVONA, d

Zagaria, Anita
SEMBRA MORTO . . . MA E SOLO SVENUTO

Zahajsky, Jiri
PAVUCINA

Zahar, Micky
EVERY TIME WE SAY GOODBYE, art d

Zahariev, Eduard
SKUPA MOYA, SKUPI MOY, d; SKUPA MOYA, SKUPI
MOY, w

Zahniser, Jack
POWER

Zakhi, Magda
AWDAT MOWATIN

Zaki, Ahmed
AL BEDAYA

Zaki, Khalid
KAHIR ELZAMAN

Zalar, Zivko
ZA SRECU JE POTREBNO TROJE, ph

Zaldeh, Yoosef Samad
BUS, THE

Zale, Dan
BOY WHO COULD FLY, THE

Zalewski, Krzysztof
JEZIORO BODENSKIE

Zamani, Asghar
BUS, THE

Zambelli, Zaira
FULANINHA

Zamberlan, Anne
CHARLOTTE FOR EVER

Zamborain, Rosa
POBRE MARIPOSA, cos

Zambrini, Bruno
IL TENENTE DEI CARABINIERI, m; SCUOLA DI
LADRI, m

Zamperla, Neno
DAYS OF HELL, stunts

Zamperla, Roland
RAGE, stunts

Zand, Michael
MORNING AFTER, THE

Zanden, Philip
AMOROSA; BRODERNA MOZART

Zandt, Walt
NOBODY'S FOOL

Zane, Billy
CRITTERS

Zanetti, Christian
ON A VOLE CHARLIE SPENCER!

Zanin, Bruno
IL CASO MORO

Zann, Lenore
ONE NIGHT ONLY; RETURN

Zano, Muni
FIRE IN THE NIGHT

Zano, Simeon Muni
FIRE IN THE NIGHT, p

Zaoral, Zdenek
PAVUCINA, d&w

Zaorski, Janusz
JEZIORO BODENSKIE, d

Zappa, Dweezil
PRETTY IN PINK

Zar, John La
SCORPION

Zarem, Robert
SWEET LIBERTY

Zaremba, Peter
MY CHAUFFEUR, m/l

Zarfati, Vittorio
NAME OF THE ROSE, THE

Zarkhi, Alexander
CHICHERIN, d; CHICHERIN, w

Zarpa, Zozo
I PHOTOGRAPHIA

Zarzo, Manolo
EL HERMANO BASTARDO DE DIOS

Zaslow, Michael
SEVEN MINUTES IN HEAVEN

Zatt, Erika
CLASS OF NUKE 'EM HIGH

Zavod, Alan
BIG HURT, THE, m; DEATH OF A SOLDIER, m

Zavradinos, Yannis
O MELISSOKOMOS

Zawada, Nancy
COMBAT SHOCK

Zawadska, Valerie
LEV S BILOU HRIVOU

Zawslak, Steve
TOUCH AND GO

Zayani, George Kaza
EL-GOOA, m

Zayas, Alfonso
EL DIA DE LOS ALBANILES II; EL VECINDARIO—
LOS MEXICANOS CALIENTES

Zayed, Maali
LEL HAB KESSA AKHIRA

Zayed, Mali
EL-SADA EL-RIGAL

Zaza, Paul
BULLIES, m; BULLIES, m/l

Zaza, Paul J.
PINK CHIQUITAS, THE, m

Zbrouev, Alexandre
KHRANI MENIO, MOI TALISMAN

Zdar, Robert
HOT CHILI

Zea, Kristi
DEAD END KIDS, cos

Zecevic, George
BAL NA VODI, p

Zecevic, Ljubo
SAN O RUZI

Zech, Mark von
VENDETTA

Zech, Rosel
BLIND DIRECTOR, THE; EIN FLIEHENDES PFERD

Zee, Eleanor
TOUGH GUYS

Zeeman, George E.
BOY IN BLUE, THE

Zeffirelli, Franco
OTELLO, d; OTELLO, w

Zegveld, Peter
DE VAL VAN PATRICIA HAGGERSMITH

Zei, Lucia
ROMANCE, w

Zeier, Robert
HELLFIRE, art d

Zeitoun, Ariel
DESCENTE AUX ENFERS, p; LA GALETTE DU ROI, p

Zelniker, Michael
TOUCH AND GO

Zeming, Zhang
JUE XIANG, d&w

Zenaide
MALANDRO

Zepeda, Gerardo
EL DIA DE LOS ALBANILES II

Zepeda, Jorge
MOSQUITO COAST, THE

Zepeda, "Chiquilin"
SALVADOR

Zerbe, Anthony
OFF BEAT

Zerbib, Sylvia
COURS PRIVE

Zermeno, Alvaro
CONTACTO CHICANO

Zertuche, Braulio
EL NARCO—DUELO ROJO

Zervoulakis, Takis
GIRL FROM MANI, THE, ph

Zetterling, Mai
AMOROSA, d&w; AMOROSA, ed

Zetterstrom, Rune
BRODERNA MOZART

Zettler, Steve
MANHATTAN PROJECT, THE

Zezel, Peter
YOUNGBLOOD

Zezima, Michael
BREEDERS ; LOW BLOW

Zgraggen, John
LOW BLOW

Zharkov, Alexei
TORPIDONOSTCI

Zheng, Cao
CAN YUE, d

Zhenyao, Zheng
CAN YUE

Zhijuan, Ran
GREAT WALL, A

Zhiliang, Zou
YU QING SAO, prod d

Zhurbin, Alexander
PISMA MERTVOGO CHELOVEKA, m

Zi, Zhu
IN THE WILD MOUNTAINS, w

Ziakas, Giorgos
O MELISSOKOMOS, cos

Zianzhu, Kung
JUE XIANG

Ziegler, Regina
JOURNEY, THE, p

Zielinski, Jerzy
FLIGHT OF THE SPRUCE GOOSE, ph

Zielinski, Jerzy Karol
CHRZESNISAK, set d

Zielinski, Juan Pablo Munoz
EL HERMANO BASTARDO DE DIOS, m

Zielinski, Rafal
RECRUITS, d

Ziembicki, Bob
RADIOACTIVE DREAMS, set d

Zien, Chip
HOWARD THE DUCK

Ziherle, Toni
DOKTOR, ed

Zihlmann, Hans
TAROT, w

Ziker, Dick
BACK TO SCHOOL, stunts; OUT OF BOUNDS

Zikora, Vitaly
ODINOTCHNOYE PLAVANIYE

Zikra, Samir
WHAT HAPPENED NEXT YEAR, d&w

Ziliang, Zhang
YELLOW EARTH, d, w

Zilliox, Bob
DESERT BLOOM, set d

Zillkova, Veronika
LEV S BILOU HRIVOU

Zilnik, Zelmir
LIJEPE ZENE PROLAZE KROZ GRAD, d; LIJEPE
ZENE PROLAZE KROZ GRAD, w

Zimet, Victor
SEX O'CLOCK NEWS, THE, ed; SEX O'CLOCK NEWS,
THE, w

Zimmerling, Robert
NOVEMBERKATZEN

Zimmerman, Barry
INSTANT JUSTICE

Zimmerman, Don
COBRA, ed; MY MAN ADAM, ed

Zimmerman, Herman
ONE CRAZY SUMMER, prod d

Zimmerman, Matt
HAUNTED HONEYMOON

Zimmerman, Peter
DAS HAUS AM FLUSS

Zimmerschied, Sigi
DER WILDE CLOWN

Zinner, Peter
SAVING GRACE, ed

Zinny, Karl
FINAL EXECUTIONER, THE

Zirner, August
AUF IMMER UND EWIG

Zirong, Lin
YU QING SAO, ph

Zischler, Hanns
ANEMIA; DOUCE FRANCE; TAROT

Zisswiller, Maurice
UNDER THE CHERRY MOON, spec eff

Zita, Jose Bogalheiro e
UMA RAPARIGA NO VERAO, p

Zito, Pasquale
GIOVANNI SENZAPENSIERI

Zitta, Luigi
CAMORRA, ed; SUMMER NIGHT WITH GREEK
PROFILE, ALMOND EYES AND SCENT OF BASIL, ed

Zitzermann, Bernard
RUE DU DEPART, ph

Zivojinovic, Bata
OBECANA ZEMLJA

Zivojinovic, Velimir Bata
DOBROVOLJCI; I TO CE PROCI

Zlaty, Eddy
MORE THINGS CHANGE, THE

Zlotnitzky, Eva
AUF IMMER UND EWIG

Zlotoff, Lee
LINK, w

Zoccheddu, Zaira
LA CROCE DALLE 7 PIETRE

Zochow, Michael
MOTTEN IM LICHT, w

Zoderer, Joseph
DIE WALSCHE, w

Zoe
COLOR OF MONEY, THE

Zoffoli, Marta
SAVING GRACE

Zolotukhin, Valeri
CHICHERIN

Zoltan
SPACECAMP, makeup

Zonis, Joanne
FLOODSTAGE

Zora, Eva
YIDDISH CONNECTION, ed

Zorich, Louis
WHERE ARE THE CHILDREN?

Zorilla, China
AWAITING THE PALLBEARERS

Zorrilla, China
CONTAR HASTA TEN; POBRE MARIPOSA

Zouni, Pemy
ENAS ISICHOS THANATOS

Zsombolyai, Janos
RETURN, ph

Zuanelli, Umberto
NAME OF THE ROSE, THE

Zubarry, Olga
CONTAR HASTA TEN

Zubeck, Gary
BUSTED UP, ed

Zuber, Karol
FEMMES DE PERSONNE

Zubiaga, Antonio
MATANZA EN MATAMOROS

Zubiena, Jim
BAND OF THE HAND; MANHUNTER

Zucca, Jerome
CORPS ET BIENS; MAUVAIS SANG

Zuccero, Joseph
NAKED VENGEANCE

Zucchero, Joe
SILK

Zucchero, Joseph
FINAL MISSION, w

Zucker, Charles
MODERN GIRLS

Zucker, David
RUTHLESS PEOPLE, d

Zucker, Jerry
RUTHLESS PEOPLE, d

Zucker, Marcos
INSOMNIACS

Zujing, Wu
BEI AIQING YIWANGDE JIAOLUO, art d

Zulaikha, John
DOT AND KEETO, m

Zunbiaga, Antonio
EL NARCO—DUELO ROJO

Zuniga, Daphne
MODERN GIRLS

Zuniga, Rogelio
LA ALACRANA, ed

Zuniga, Rosario
SALVADOR

Zupancic, Milena
CHRISTOPHORUS; KORMORAN

Zurkow, Marina
BREEDERS , art d

Zutaut, Brad
BACK TO SCHOOL; HARDBODIES 2

Zvoleff, Marianne
HELL SQUAD

Zvoleff, Mayann
ARMED RESPONSE

Zwick, Edward
ABOUT LAST NIGHT, d

Zygaldo, Tomasz
SCENY DZIECIECE Z ZYCIA PROWINCJI, d; SCENY
DZIECIECE Z ZYCIA PROWINCJI, w

PHOTO CREDITS

ALIVE FILMS: Betty Blue 2.

AMBLIN: American Tail, An 1; Money Pit, The 3.

ATLANTIC: Echo Park 1; Extremities 2; Men's Club, The 1; Modern Girls 1; Nutcracker: The Motion Picture 2.

BLACKBEARD PRODS.: 'Night Mother 2.

CANNON: Assault, The 2; Delta Force, The 2; Duet for One 2; Firewalker 1; Invaders from Mars 2; Link 2; Otello 2.

CASTLE HILL PRODS.: Imagemaker, The 1; Lightship, The 2.

CHROMA: Hardbodies 2 1.

CINEMA GROUP VENTURE: Born American 2; Hollywood Vice Squad 2.

CINEPHILE: Pervola: Tracks in the Snow 1.

CINEPLEX ODEON FILMS: Decline of the American Empire, The 2.

CINEQUONON/FILM DALLAS: Man Facing Southeast 1.

CINETEL FILMS: Armed Response 2; Screen Test 1.

CIRCLE FILMS: Letter to Brezhnev 1.

COLUMBIA: Armed and Dangerous 1; Big Trouble 2; Crossroads 2; Desert Bloom 2; Fine Mess, A 1; Jo Jo Dancer, Your Life Is Calling 2; Karate Kid Part II, The 3; Out of Bounds 1; Quicksilver 2; Stand by Me 3; That's Life 2; Violets Are Blue 1; Where Are the Children? 1.

CONCORDE CINEMA GROUP: Cocaine Wars 1; Last Resort 2.

CROWN INTERNATIONAL: Low Blow 1; My Chauffeur 2; Patriot, The 2; Scorpion 1.

DEG: Blue Velvet 4; Crimes of the Heart 2; King Kong Lives 2; Man and a Woman: 20 Years Later, A 1; Manhunter 2; Maximum Overdrive 2; Raw Deal 2; Tai-Pan 2; Trick or Treat 2.

DISNEY/SILVER SCREEN PARTNERS: Great Mouse Detective, The 1.

EMBASSY PICTURES: Saving Grace 1.

EMPIRE PICTURES: Eliminators 1; From Beyond 2; Troll 2; Terrorvision 1.

FRIES ENTERTAINMENT, INC.: Thrashin' 2.

GEFFEN FILM CO.: Little Shop of Horrors 3.

GLADDON ENTERTAINMENT-FOX: Manhattan Project, The 2.

GREEK FILM CENTER: Alcestes 1; Alligoria 1; Enas Isichos 1; Thanatos 1; Kali Patritha, Syntrofe 1; Knock-Out 1.

GREENTREE/ZDF-DEFA: Spring Symphony 1.

HEMDALE: Salvador 2.

INTERNATIONAL SPECTRAFILM: Cactus 1; Love Songs 2; Nineteen Nineteen 1; Toby McTeague 2.

ISLAND PICTURES: Down by Law 2; Mona Lisa 2; Nobody's Fool 2; She's Gotta Have It 3.

ISLAND VISUAL ARTS: Good to Go 1.

LORIMAR: American Anthem 2; Boy Who Could Fly, The 2; Morning After, The 2; Power 2.

MAGPIE-GREATER UNION: Short Changed 1.

MEDIA HOME ENTERTAINMENT: Avenging Force 1; Choke Canyon 2; 52 Pick-Up 2; Lightning—The White Stallion 1; Murphy's Law 1; P.O.W. The Escape 1; Texas Chainsaw Massacre Part 2, The 2.

MGM: Dream Lover 2; Killer Party 1; 9 1/2 Weeks 2; Poltergeist II 2; Running Scared 2; Solarbabies 2; Where the River Runs Black 2; Wise Guys 2.

MGM/UA: Ginger and Fred 2.

MIRAMAX FILMS: Twist & Shout 1.

MOVIE STORE, INC., THE: American Justice 1.

NETHERLANDS FOX FILM: Boy in Blue, The 1.

NEW CENTURY PRODS. LTD.: Wraith, The 2.

NEW LINE CINEMA: Critters 2; Quiet Cool 1; Sincerely Charlotte 2.

NEW STAR ENTERTAINMENT: Flight of the Navigator 2.

NEW WORLD PICTURES: House 1; Jake Speed 2; Shadow Play 1.

NEW WORLD VIDEO: Black Moon Rising 1; No Retreat, No Surrender 1; Reform School Girls 2; Soul Man 1; Torment 1; Uphill All the Way 1; Vamp 2.

ORION: Absolute Beginners; At Close Range 2; Longshot, The 1; Back to School 2; FX 2; Hannah and Her Sisters 3; Haunted Honeymoon 2; Hoosiers 4; Just Between Friends 2; My Beautiful Laundrette 2; Platoon 4; Sacrifice, The 1; Something Wild 3; Three Amigos 2.

PARAMOUNT: April Fool's Day 1; Blue City 2; Children of a Lesser God 2; Ferris Bueller's Day Off 2; Friday the 13th Part VI: Jason Lives 1; Golden Child, The 2; Lady Jane 2; Pretty in Pink 3; Star Trek IV: The Voyage Home 2; Top Gun 2.

RIMFIRE FILMS, LTD.: Crocodile Dundee 2.

SAMUEL GOLDWYN CO.: Sid and Nancy 2.

SHAPIRO ENTERTAINMENT: Agent on Ice 1; Busted Up 1; King of the Streets 1; Over the Summer 1; Witchfire 1.

SIMCON/UNIV.: Bullies 2.

SKOURAS: Belizaire the Cajun 1.

SPRINGVALE/NEW SOUTH WALES: Dead-End Drive-In 1.

SUATU/SCOTTI BROS.: Death of a Soldier 1; Eye of the Tiger 2.

SUNBOW PRODUCTIONS, INC.: My Little Pony 1; Transformers: The Movie, The 1.

THALIA: Welcome in Vienna 2.

TOUCHSTONE PICTURES: Color of Money, The 3; Down and Out in Beverly Hills 2; Off Beat 2; Ruthless People 2; Tough Guys 2.

TRI-STAR: About Last Night 2; Band of the Hand 2; 8 Million Ways to Die 2; Head Office 1; Hitcher, The 1; Iron Eagle 1; Labyrinth 2; No Mercy 1; Nothing in Common 2; Peggy Sue Got Married 2; Rad 1; Short Circuit 1.

TROMA: Class of Nuke 'Em High 1; Combat Shock 1; Fat Guy Goes Nutzoid 1; Girls School Screamers 1; Nightmare Weekend 1; Rebel Love 1; Rockin' Road Trip 1; Screamplay 1; Sizzle Beach, U.S.A. 1.

TWENTIETH CENTURY FOX: Aliens 2; Big Trouble in Little China 3; Fly, The 3; Highlander 2; Jumpin' Jack Flash 1; Lucas 3; Name of the Rose, The 2; Spacecamp 2; Streets of Gold 2; Wisdom 2.

UNITED ARTISTS CORP.: Youngblood 2.

UNIVERSAL: Best of Times, The 2; Brighton Beach Memoirs 1; Clockwise 2; Howard the Duck 2; Legal Eagles 2; Playing for Keeps 1; Psycho III 3; Sweet Liberty 2.

VIRGIN FILMS: Fringe Dwellers, The 1; Malcolm 1.

WARNER BROS.: Clan of the Cave Bear, The 2; Club Paradise 2; Cobra 2; Deadly Friend 1; Heartbreak Ridge 2; Knights and Emeralds 1; Mission, The 3; Mosquito Coast, The 2; One Crazy Summer 2; Police Academy 3: Back in Training 2; Ratboy 1; Round Midnight 4; Seven Minutes in Heaven 1; True Stories 2; Under the Cherry Moon 2; Wildcats 2.

AN AMERICAN TAIL

SOUL MAN

¡THREE AMIGOS!

LUCAS

Nobody's Fo

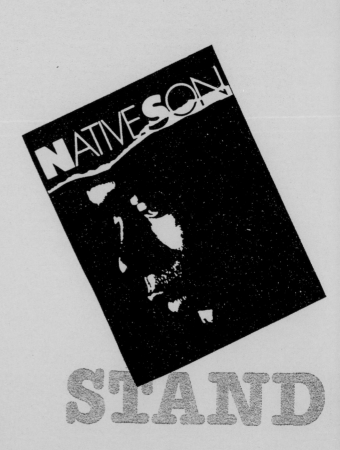

NATIVE SON

STAND